Why You Need This New Edition?

If you are wondering why you should add this new edition of *An Introduction to Literature* to your personal library, here are ten good reasons:

1 This book contains **works of literature from the ancient Greeks up to the present,** which is to say that it contains powerful explorations of what it means to be a human being.

2 New Chapter 1, **"College Readiness: How to Respond to Stories, Poems, and Plays"** provides a brief guide to help you respond thoughtfully to what you have read. Among its features are examples of student annotations and checklists for responding to each genre.

3 **A wealth of new stories** have been added including Annie Proulx's tall tale called "The Blood Bay," Ron Wallace's "Worry," Tobias Wolff's "Hunters in the Snow" and "Bullet in the Brain," and Jesse Lee Kercheval's "Carpathia."

4 You'll find expanded coverage of the elements of fiction, **with new separate chapters on plot, character, setting, and theme.**

5 **A new chapter on graphic fiction** includes four selections and gives guidance as to how to understand the art of pictorial story-telling.

6 **Twenty-four poems are new to this edition** including such classics as Elizabeth Barrett Browning's "How do I love thee?" and Dylan Thomas's "Fern Hill," and also some very recent poems, such as Kay Ryan's "Turtle."

7 **A new one-act play, Samuel Beckett's *Krapp's Last Tape,*** introduces you to the work of a great contemporary dramatist.

8 **A new casebook on Arthur Miller's *Death of a Salesman*** gives you stimulating outside sources that you can draw on if you are required to write a research paper.

9 **A new appendix on plagiarism provides a quiz—with answers—**so that you can test yourself and immediately (and entertainingly) see the degree to which you understand your academic responsibilities.

10 **The appendix on documentation** reflects all of the latest MLA guidelines to ensure your documentation is up to date.

Manuscript for Robert Frost's "Stopping by Woods on a Snowy Evening." The first page of the manuscript is lost. (Manuscript for Robert Frost's "Stopping by Woods on a Snowy Evening." By permission of the Jones Library, Inc., Amherst, Massachusetts.)

We print all that survives of the draft—the first stanza of the draft is lost—of Robert Frost's most famous poem, "Stopping by Woods on a Snowy Evening." (The published version appears on page 755.) And on pages 759 to 761 we print some comments by Frost about the ways poems get written. Here is a sample:

[A poem] begins in delight, it inclines to the impulse, it assumes direction with the first line laid down, it runs a course of lucky events, and ends in a clarification of life....

Take the assertion that a poem "assumes direction with the first line laid down." The first stanza of the published version runs "Whose woods these are I think I know. / His house is in the village though; / He will not see me stopping here / To watch his woods fill up with snow." Frost always used rhyme, so as soon as he wrote his first line the poem began to take direction: Almost surely he would have to come up with a line that rhymed with "know." Three of the four lines rhyme, and Frost decided to take the *un*rhymed word of his first stanza ("here," at the end of the third line) and use it to establish the rhyme of the next stanza: "queer," "near," "lake," "year." (The third line is unrhymed, as in the first stanza, because, again, a poem "assumes direction with the first line.") Frost wrote "The steaming horses think it queer" (revised into "The horse begins to think it queer" and then into "The little horse must think it queer"); then, "To stop without a farmhouse near / Between a forest and a lake / The darkest evening of the year." He revised "a forest and a lake" into "the woods and frozen lake" but he preserved the rhyme scheme. Almost surely the *next* stanza will take the unrhymed word ("lake") and use it for the three rhyming lines, and indeed that is what we find: "shake," "mistake," "sweep," "flake." (In this stanza he then changed the sex of the horse, and changed "falling flake" to "downy flake.") But if the poet continued thus, the third line of the final stanza would not rhyme with anything, and this lack of rhyme will give some sense of incompleteness. Frost wrote, for the third line of his final stanza "That bid me give the reins a shake," thus tying the line back to the rhymes of the previous stanza, but he found the result uncomfortable, so he revised, and wrote—if we read his writing correctly—"that bid me on but there are miles," but this too he found unsatisfactory. And then he hit on the perfect solution, the rhyme scheme that leaves nothing unsettled, nothing incomplete: He rhymed all four words in the final stanza.

What do you make of some of the other changes in the draft—for instance from "The steaming horses" to "My little horse," from "a forest and a lake" to "the woods and frozen lake," and from "falling flake" to "downy flake"?

SIXTEENTH EDITION

An Introduction to Literature

Fiction, Poetry, and Drama

Sylvan Barnet
Tufts University

William Burto
University of Massachusetts at Lowell

William E. Cain
Wellesley College

Longman
Boston   Columbus   Indianapolis   New York   San Francisco   Upper Saddle River
Amsterdam   Cape Town   Dubai   London   Madrid   Milan   Munich   Paris   Montreal   Toronto
Delhi   Mexico City   Sao Paulo   Sydney   Hong Kong   Seoul   Singapore   Taipei   Tokyo

Editor-in-Chief: Joseph Terry
Senior Development Editor: Katharine Glynn
Senior Supplements Editor: Donna Campion
Senior Media Producer: Stefanie Liebman
Executive Marketing Manager: Joyce Nilsen
Production Manager: Eric Jorgensen
Project Coordination, Text Design, and Electronic Page Makeup: Nesbitt Graphics, Inc.
Cover Design Manager: John Callahan
Cover Image: ©2010 C. Herscovici, London/Artists Rights Society (ARS), New York
Visual Researcher: Rona Tuccillo
Senior Manufacturing Buyer: Dennis J. Para
Printer and Binder: Quebecor World/Taunton
Cover Printer: Lehigh Phoenix

For permission to use copyrighted material, grateful acknowledgment is made to the copyright holders on pp. 1479–1492, which are hereby made part of this copyright page.

Library of Congress Cataloging-in-Publication Data

An introduction to literature : fiction, poetry, and drama / [edited by]
Sylvan Barnet, William Burto, William E. Cain. — 16th ed.
    p. cm.
Includes bibliographical references and index.
  ISBN 978-0-205-63309-8
  1. Literature—Collections. I. Barnet, Sylvan. II. Burto, William. III. Cain, William E., 1952- IV. Title.
PN6014.I57 2010
  808—dc22

                                                                          2010018274

1 2 3 4 5 6 7 8 9 10—QWT—13 12 11 10

Longman
is an imprint of

PEARSON

www.pearsonhighered.com

ISBN-13: 978-0-205-63309-8
ISBN-10: 0-205-63309-9

CONTENTS

PART I

Reading, Thinking, and Writing Critically About Literature   1

3   The Pleasures of Reading—and of Writing Arguments About Literature   46

4   More About Writing About Literature: From Idea to Essay   65

PART II

Fiction   97

15   A Collection of Short Fiction   363

PART III

Poetry 539

20 Figurative Language: Simile, Metaphor, Personification, Apostrophe   618

21 Imagery and Symbolism   632

28 A Collection of Poems   774

PART IV

Drama   837

29   How to Read a Play   839

30   Tragedy   905

A Guide to MyLiteratureLab

Visit *MyLiteratureLab.com* to access a wealth of online writing and research aids. There is an abundant array of multimedia resources in MyLiteratureLab that brings literature to life by enriching the authors and selections you will study.

Fiction

James Baldwin   About the Author, Bibliography, Critical Archive
Sonny's Blues: Longman Lecture

Toni Cade Bambara   About the Author
The Lesson: Longman Lecture

Ambrose Bierce   About the Author
An Occurrence at Owl Creek Bridge: Video Essay, Critical Essay

T. Coraghessan Boyle   About the Author
Greasy Lake: Critical Essay

Raymond Carver   About the Author, Bibliography, Critical Essay
Cathedral: Longman Lecture

Willa Cather   About the Author/Photos, Bibliography, Critical Archive
Paul's Case: Video, Audio, Critical Essay

Anton Chekhov   About the Author, Bibliography, Critical Archive

Kate Chopin   About the Author, Bibliography, Critical Archive
Désirée's Baby: Longman Lecture
The Storm: Longman Lecture, Interactive Reading, Student Paper, Critical Essay

The Story of an Hour: Longman Lecture

Joseph Conrad   About the Author
Heart of Darkness: Longman Lecture

William Faulkner   About the Author/Photos, Bibliography, Critical Archive
Barn Burning: Video (2), Audio (2), Critical Essay (2)
A Rose for Emily: Critical Essay

F. Scott Fitzgerald   About the Author

Charlotte Perkins Gilman   About the Author, Bibliography, Critical Archive
The Yellow Wallpaper: Critical Essay

Nathaniel Hawthorne   About the Author, Bibliography, Critical Archive
Young Goodman Brown: Longman Lecture

Ernest Hemingway   About the Author, Bibliography, Critical Archive
A Clean Well-Lighted Place: Critical Essay

Zora Neale Hurston
Sweat: Longman Lecture, Interactive Reading

Shirley Jackson   About the Author
The Lottery: Interactive Reading, Critical Essay

Poetry

Writers on Writing

Kim Addonizio

Aliki Barnstone

Jay Boyer

Andrea Hollander Budy

Janet Burroway

Ron Carlson

Rita Dove

Stephen Dunn

Bart Edelman

Albert Garcia

John Hershman

Jeff Knorr

Ruth Ellen Kocher

Craig Lesley

Valerie Miner

Stephen Minot

Todd Pierce

Alberto Ríos

Tim Schell

Virgil Suarez

Diane Thiel

C.K. Williams

Richard Yañez

Interactive Timeline

Timeline Part 1: 20,000 B.C. to 1600 A.D

Timeline Part 2: 1601 A.D. to 1775 A.D.

Timeline Part 3: 1776 A.D. to 1860 A.D.

Timeline Part 4: 1861 A.D. to 1919 A.D.

Timeline Part 5: 1920 A.D. to 1959 A.D.

Timeline Part 6: 1960 A.D. to 2008 A.D.

Literature eAnthology

Two hundred additional selections are available with this interactive eAnthology, which is organized by genre and alphabetized within each genre. In addition to providing more selections, the eAnthology is an excellent study aid: students can search, highlight, and take notes.

An Introduction to Literature, Sixteenth Edition, begins with four introductory chapters concerned with writing, reading, and thinking. The book then offers an anthology arranged by genre (stories, poems, plays). This genre anthology, like the introductory chapters, includes abundant material to help students to become active readers and careful, engaged writers.

New to This Edition

- **New Chapter 1, "College Readiness: How to Respond to Stories, Poems, and Plays,"** offers a brief but thorough guide to help students respond to what they have read. Among its features are examples of student annotations and checklists for responding to each genre.
- The revised second chapter emphasizes not only **literature as a performance** in words, but also **literature as a journey** (a walk in the writer's shoes).
- **A wealth of new stories have been added** including Annie Proulx's tall tale called "The Blood Bay," Ron Wallace's "Worry," and Jesse Lee Kercheval's "Carpathia."
- In addition to Flannery O'Connor, **Tobias Wolff** is now presented in depth (four stories, and a selection of his remarks about fiction).
- The fiction section offers expanded coverage of the elements with new separate chapters on plot, character, setting, and theme.
- **A new chapter on graphic fiction** helps students to understand the art of pictorial story telling.
- **Twenty-four new poems.** We have added such favorites as Elizabeth Barrett Browning's "How do I love thee?" and Dylan Thomas's "Fern Hill," and also some very recent poems, such as Kay Ryan's "Turtle." We have also added a few older poems (for instance Stephen Duck's "On Mites") that may well be unfamiliar even to many experienced instructors.
- **A new one-act play, Samuel Beckett's *Krapp's Last Tape,*** now increases the number of short plays—plays that can be fully discussed and perhaps even performed within a single meeting— to five. The eight full-length plays continue to offer instructors a wide range of choices.

- **A new casebook on Arthur Miller's *Death of a Salesman*** includes not only Miller's well-known essay on tragedy but also a generous selection from his later remarks, as well as reviews of early and recent productions.
- **A new appendix on plagiarism provides a quiz—with answers**—so that students can test themselves and immediately (and entertainingly) see the degree to which they understand their academic responsibilities.
- **The appendix on documentation has been revised in accordance with the newest MLA guidelines.**

About the Literature

- **Canonical works.** The book contains 70 stories, including four pieces of graphic fiction, 255 poems, and 14 plays. About a third of the selections are canonical works that for many decades—in some cases even centuries—have given readers great pleasure. Writers such as Sophocles, Shakespeare, Walt Whitman, and Emily Dickinson have stood the test of time, including the test of today's students enrolled in introductory courses in literature and composition. No editor and no instructor need apologize for asking students to read, think, and write about these authors. In "Tradition and the Individual Talent," T. S. Eliot makes the point well: "Someone said, 'The dead writers are remote from us because we know so much more than they did.' Precisely, and they are that which we know."
- **A new canon.** The remaining two-thirds of the selections are contemporary material, some of it by writers who established their reputations several decades ago (for instance, John Updike and Alice Walker), but much of it by writers who are still young (for instance, Amy Tan and Lorrie Moore). We have tried to read widely in today's writing, and we think we have found important new stories, poems, and plays worth the time of busy students and busy instructors. Again, no editor and no instructor need apologize for asking students to study and take pleasure in these authors and to see how they often return us to the authors of the past, the authors whose place in the canon is established and secure.
- **In-depth representation and critical perspectives.** We represent three fiction writers in depth—Flannery O'Connor (two stories and several of her important comments about fiction), Kate Chopin (four stories), and Tobias Wolff (four stories and important comments about fiction). Among the poets, we represent in depth Emily Dickinson (poems and letters), Robert Frost (poems and comments on poetry), and Langston Hughes (poems and comments on poetry). Of the dramatists, we give two plays by Sophocles and two by Shakespeare; we also include relevant comments by playwrights on their work—for instance, Arthur Miller

on tragedy. We think these features of the book are especially valuable and that the kinds of writing assignments we have developed—assignments that have emerged from our experiences in the classroom—will interest students and be productive for them.

- **Plays in contexts.** Several of the plays are accompanied by stimulating comments by their authors, giving students a look behind the scenes.

Writing About Literature

Instructors know that one of the best ways to become an active reader is to read with a pencil in hand—that is, to annotate a text, to make jottings in a journal, and ultimately to draft and revise essays. We think that students, too, will find themselves saying of their experiences with literature what the philosopher Arthur C. Danto said about his experience with works of art:

> I get a lot more out of art, now that I am writing about it, than I ever did before. I think what is true of me must be true of everyone, that until one tries to write about it, the work of art remains a sort of aesthetic blur. . . . I think in a way everyone might benefit from becoming a critic in his or her own right. After seeing the work, write about it. You cannot be satisfied for very long in simply putting down what you felt. You have to go further.
>
> —*EMBODIED MEANINGS* (1994)

To this end, we have included the following:

- **Samples of annotated pages, entries in journals, and 26 essays by students.** To prompt students to respond to the works of literature in this book and then to think and write critically about their responses, we include not only a chapter devoted to the concepts of getting ideas and revising them by means of writing (Chapter 3), but also examples of annotated pages, entries in journals, and twenty-six essays by students (some with the student's preliminary journal entries, some with our marginal comments, some with our analytic comments appended to the essays, and some with questions that ask the reader to evaluate the strengths or weaknesses of the essays).
- **Critical thinking questions.** About a third of the selections in the book are equipped with questions intended to help draw attention to matters that deserve careful thinking. Most of these questions are in effect invitations to write argumentative essays, not mere paragraphs or descriptions.
- **Material about argument.** In addition to furnishing "Your Turn" questions that raise issues for argument, our apparatus emphasizes that students, in their essays, must advance a thesis and support it

with evidence, rather than merely provide reports of their responses.

- **Critical perspectives.** A chapter on "Critical Approaches," sketching such approaches as reader-response criticism and the New Historicism, will help students develop a repertoire of points of view.
- **Glossary.** Literary terms, defined and discussed throughout the text, are concisely defined in a convenient glossary at the end of the book, with page references to fuller discussions.
- **Manuscript form.** An appendix includes pages on the format of an essay—for example, margins, capitalization in a title, and so on.
- **Research and Internet resources.** An Appendix gives information about manuscript form and documenting sources in MLA style.

A complete list of available student and instructor resources begins on the following page.

Resources for Students and Instructors

MYLITERATURELAB

MyLiteratureLab is a dynamic and comprehensive Web site that engages students as it helps to foster an understanding of literature and literary writing and research skills. The Resource area contains instructional material, multimedia tutorials, and exercises for a wide array of literature, writing, grammar, and research topics. Some of the more popular features include:

- **Longman Lectures**
  Featuring our renowned authors, including Sylvan Barnet, these engaging, illustrated audio lectures provide students with suggestions on how to read, analyze, and write about literature. Each lecture includes a reading of an influential or illustrative work, cultural/historical context for interpreting the featured author's work, and insights for writing. All the lectures are illustrated with evocative photos, pictures, and images.

- **eAnthology**
  - Two hundred additional selections are available with this Interactive eAnthology, which is organized by genre and alphabetized within each genre.
  - In addition to providing more selections, the eAnthology is an excellent study aid: students can search, highlight, and take notes.

- **Full-length films**
  - Feature-length films from Films for the Humanities and Sciences help students stay engaged with their course material.

- **Interactive Readings**
  - Interactive readings provide students with annotated readings and questions to guide analysis.

- **Gradebook**
  - You can assign pre- and post-diagnostics to help students pinpoint their needs and track their progress.
  - Export MyLiteratureLab grades to a gradebook you already use or include any that you've created in a course management system.

PRINT SUPPLEMENTS

Screening Shakespeare: Understanding The Plays Through Film, Second Edition, by Michael Greer and Toby Widdicombe (Student / 0-205-63950-X)
This brief guide is an accessible introduction to Shakespeare's most popular plays on film. It provides analytical tools and suggestions for responding to films, with discussion questions and writing prompts that move from formal analysis to considerations of historical and cultural contexts.

Evaluating a Performance, by Michael Greenwald (Student/ 0-321-09541-3)
Designed to look like a Playbill, this is the perfect tool for the student assigned to review a local theater production. This supplement offers students a convenient place to record their evaluation of the staging, acting, costuming, set design, etc. Useful tips and suggestions of things to consider when evaluating a production are included.

Responding to Literature: A Writer's Journal, by Daniel Kline (Student/ 0-321-09542-1)
This spiral-bound journal provides students with their own personal space for recording their reactions to the literature they read. Guided writing prompts, suggested writing assignments, and overviews of literary terms provide students with the tools—and ideas—they need for responding to fiction, poetry, and drama.

Analyzing Literature, Second Edition, by Sharon James McGee (Student/ 0-321-09338-0)
This brief supplement provides critical reading strategies, writing advice, and sample student papers to help students interpret and discuss literary works in a variety of genres. Suggestions for collaborative activities and online research on literary topics are also featured, as well as numerous exercises and writing assignments.

Glossary of Literary and Critical Terms, by Heidi L. M. Jacobs (Student/ 0-321-12691-2)
The Glossary of Literary and Critical Terms is a quick, reliable and portable resource for students of Literature and Creative Writing. This easy-to-use glossary includes definitions, explanations, and examples for over 100 literary and critical terms which students commonly encounter in their reading or hear in their lectures and class discussions. In addition to basic terms related to form and genre, the glossary also includes terms and explanations related to literary history, criticism, and theory.

Literature Timeline, by Heidi L. M. Jacobs (Student / 0-321-14315-9)
This laminated four-page timeline provides students with a chronological overview of the major literary works throughout history. In addition, the

timeline also lists major sociocultural and political events to provide students with historical and contextual insights into the impact historical events have had on writers and their works and vice versa.

What Every Student Should Know About . . . Series
A collection of guide books designed to help students with specific topics that are important in a number of different college courses. Instructors can package any one of these booklets with their Pearson textbook for no additional charge, or the booklets can be purchased separately.

- Avoiding Plagiarism (ISBN 0-321-44689-5)
- Citing Sources with MLA Documentation: Update Edtion (ISBN 0-205-71511-7)
- Creating Portfolios (ISBN 0-205-57250-2)
- Procrastination (ISBN 0-205-58211-7)
- Researching Online (ISBN 0-321-44531-7)
- Practicing Peer Review (ISBN 0-321-44848-0)
- Preparing Effective Oral Presentations (ISBN 0-205-50545-7)
- Study Skills (ISBN 0-321-44736-0)

A Student's Guide to Getting Published, by Susan Swartwout and Jim Elledge (Student/0-321-11779-4)
This clear and concise "how-to" guide takes writers of all genres through the process of publishing their work—including the considerations of submission and contracts, how to research markets, the processes of self-editing and being edited, how to produce a "well-wrought manuscript," among other useful and practical information. The manual addresses first-submission concerns as well as addressing the entire publishing process and includes practical advice from editors and publishers on what industry professionals expect from a writer.

Journal for Creative Writing, by Sibyl Johnston (Student/ 0-321-09540-5)
This spiral-bound journal provides students with plenty of space for writing. Helpful writing prompts and strategies are included as well as guidelines for participating in a workshop.

A Workshop Guide for Creative Writing, by Sibyl Johnston (Student/ 0-321-09539-1)

This laminated reference offers suggestions/tips for students to keep in mind in a workshop situation—both as a participant and presenter. Blank space is provided for students to record additional guidelines provided by their instructor.

DICTIONARIES AND OTHER REFERENCES

Merriam-Webster's Reader's Handbook:Your Complete Guide to Literary Terms (Student/ 0-321-10541-9)

Includes nearly 2,000 entries including Greek and Latin terminology, descriptions for every major genre, style, and era of writing and assured authority from the combined resources of Merriam-Webster and Encyclopedia Britannica.

The New American Webster Handy College Dictionary (Student/ 0-451-18166-2)
This superior paperback reference text contains more than 100,000 entries, including clear and concise definitions, selected etymologies, current phrases, slang, abbreviations, and scientific terms.

Merriam-Webster Collegiate Dictionary with CD-ROM (ISBN 0-877-79809-5)
This new edition of America's best-selling hardcover dictionary sets the standard with: a fully revised print edition featuring more than 225,000 definitions; more than 10,000 new words and meanings; Win/Mac CD-ROM for local electronic access; free one-year subscription to Collegiate Web site: www.Merriam-WebsterCollegiate.com.

The Oxford American Desk Dictionary and Thesaurus, Second Edition (ISBN 0-425-18068-9)
From the Oxford University Press and Berkley Publishing Group comes this one-of-a-kind reference book that combines both of the essential language tools—dictionary and thesaurus—in a single, integrated A-to-Z volume. The 1,024 page book offers more than 150,000 entries, definitions, and synonyms so you can find the right word every time, as well as appendices of valuable quick-reference information including: signs and symbols, weights and measures, presidents of the U. S., U. S. states and capitals, and more.

The Oxford Essential Thesaurus (ISBN 0-425-16421-7)
From Oxford University Press, renowned for quality educational and reference works, comes this concise, easy-to-use thesaurus—the essential tool for finding just the right word for every occasion. The 528-page book includes 175,000 synonyms in a simple A-to-Z format, more than 10,000 entries, extensive word choices, example sentences and phrases, and guidance on usage, punctuation, and more in exclusive "Writers Toolkit."

PENGUIN DISCOUNT NOVEL PROGRAM

In cooperation with Penguin Group U. S. A., Longman is proud to offer a variety of Penguin paperbacks at a significant discount when packaged with any Longman title. Excellent additions to any literature course, Penguin titles give students the opportunity to explore contemporary and classical fiction and drama. The available titles include works by authors as diverse as Toni Morrison, Julia Alvarez, Mary Shelley, and Shakespeare.

To review the complete list of titles available, visit the Longman-Penguin Web site: http://www.pearsonhighered.com/penguin.

VIDEO PROGRAM

For qualified adopters, an impressive selection of videotapes is available to enrich students' experience of literature. One video per 100 students per semester with a limit of three per semester. Contact your Pearson Longman sales consultant for more information.

INSTRUCTOR SUPPLEMENTS

Instructor's Manual for Barnet, An Introduction to Literature, Sixteenth Edition (0-205-77967-0)
An instructor's manual with detailed comments and suggestions for teaching each selection is available. This important resource, prepared by the authors of this volume, also contains references to critical articles and books.

The Longman Test Bank for Literature, by Heidi L. M. Jacobs (Instructor / 0-321-14312-4)
This test bank features various objective questions on the major works of fiction, short fiction, poetry, and drama. A versatile and handy resource, this test bank can be used for all quizzing and testing needs.

ACKNOWLEDGMENTS

We wish to thank the people who have helped us to write this book. For preparation of the sixteenth edition we are deeply indebted to Joe Terry, Katharine Glynn, Eric Jorgensen, and John Callahan at Longman; and to Lois Lombardo, Cathy Harlem, Stephanie Magean, Chuck Gandy, and the design team at Nesbitt Graphics, Inc. For assistance in obtaining permission to reprint copyrighted works, we have relied on Virginia Creeden.

Because their queries have caused us to think second and third thoughts, we know from our own experience the soundness of the advice we give when we tell students that they should submit their drafts to their peers and should pay serious attention to suggested changes. We hope that every author receives the kind of help that we have received.

We are grateful to reviewers of this edition and previous editions: Olga Abella, Eastern Illinois University; Michael Anzelone, Nassau Community College; Dr. Karen Aubrey, Augusta State University; Lillie Bailey, Virginia State University; Arnold J. Bradford, Northern Virginia Community College; Bob Brien, Madison Area Technical College; Carol Ann Britt, San Antonio College; Mark Brosamer, Ohlone College; Mark J. Bruhn, Regis University; Sandra Bryzek, Moraine Valley Community College; Christine Caver, The University of Texas at San Antonio; Vilma Chemers, California State University, Long Beach; Mickie Christensen, San Francisco State University; Anne Cipri, Carlow University; Philip Collington, Niagara University; Nancy Cox, Arkansas Tech University; Tracey Cummings, Lock Haven University of Pennsylvania; Corla Dawson, Missouri Western State College; Michael de Benedictis, Miami-Dade Community College; April M. Dolata, Northwestern CT Community College; Bill Dynes, University of Indianapolis; Gabriel Fagan, La Salle University; Mindy Faines, Gateway Community College; Bart Friedberg, Nassau Community College; Margaret Gardineer, Felician College; Wendy Greenstein, Long Beach City College; George V. Griffith, Chadron State College; Styron Harris, East Tennessee State University; Ruth Harrison, Arkansas Tech University; Mary Hickerson, Southwest State University; Susan Hines, LaSalle University; Kristen Isabelle, Columbia-Greene Community College; Jennifer Jett, Bakersfield College; Susan E. Jones, Palm Beach Atlantic University; Andrea Kaston Tange, Eastern Michigan University; Donald Kummings, University of Wisconsin–Parkside; Lois Leveen, University of California at Los Angeles; Elaine Lomber, Community College of the Finger Lakes; Beverly A. McCabe, John A. Logan College; Linda J. McPherson, Indiana University of

Pennsylvania; Walter S. Minot, Spring Hill College; Lyle W. Morgan, Pittsburg State University; Stacy Mulder, Davenport University; Carlene Murphy, University of Toledo; Lee Newton, Bradley University; Philip F. O'-Mara, Bridgewater College; Leland S. Person, University of Alabama at Birmingham; Trey Philpotts, Arkansas Tech University; Caroline Poor, Wharton County Junior College; Tony Procell, El Paso Community College; Elaine Razzano, Lyndon State College; Christie Rubio, American River College; Patricia Sheehy Colella, Bunker Hill Community College; Kathleen Shumate, Grossmant College; Andrew Silver, Mercer University; Diane Sims, Carlow University; Carolyn Smith Geyer, Augustana College; Barbara L. Stafford, City College of San Francisco; JoAnna Stephens Mink, Minnesota State University; Darlene Sybert, University of Missouri-Columbia; Marcia E. Tannebaum, Nichols College; David Thomson, Henderson State University; Catherine G. Thwing, Pima Community College; William Wilson, San Jose State University; Ann Woodlief, Virginia Commonwealth University; and Xiao-Ming Yang, Ocean County College; and Sue Ziefler, DeAnza College.

Our debt to those whom we have named is deep, but we are still not done with acknowledging our indebtedness. We owe much to the instructors and friends who advised us when we were preparing earlier editions: Judith Leet, Janet Frick, Ken Anderson, Floyd College; Alfred Arteaga, University of California, Berkeley; Rance Baker, San Antonio College; Lois Birky, Illinois Central College; Carol Boyd, Black Hawk College; Lois Bragg, Galludet University; Conrad Carroll, Northern Kentucky University; Robert Coltrane, Lock Haven University; Charles Darling, Greater Hartford Community College; Richard Dietrich, University of South Florida; Gail Duffy, Dean Junior College; Marilyn Edelstein, Santa Clara University; Toni Empringham, El Camino College; Craig Etchison, Glenville State College; Robert Farrell, Housatonic Community College; Elaine Fitzpatrick, Massasoit College; James E. Ford, University of Nebraska–Lincoln; Donna Galati, University of South Dakota; Marvin P. Garrett, University of Cincinnati; Francis B. Hanify, Luzerne County Community College; Blair Hemstock, Keyano College (Canada); Paul Hester, Indian Hills Community College; James L. Johnson, California State University, Fresno; Edwina Jordan, Illinois Central College; Kate Kiefer, Colorado State University; Sandra Lakey, Pennsylvania College of Technology; Wayne P. Lindquist, University of Wisconsin–Eau Claire; Cecilia G. Martyn, Montclair State College; Paul McVeign, Northern Virginia Community College, Elizabeth Metzger, University of South Florida; William S. Nicholson, Eastern Shore Community College; Stephen O'Neill, Bucks County Community College; Richard Pepp, Massasoit Community College; Betty Jo Hicks Peters, Morehead State University; Frank Perkins, Quincy College; Barbara Pokdowka, Commonwealth College; John C. Presley, Central Virginia Community College; Patricia R. Rochester, University of Southwestern Louisiana; Betty Rhodes, Faulkner State College; Martha Saunders, West Georgia College; Allison Shumsky, Northwestern Michigan College; Isabel B. Stanley, East Tennessee State University; LaVonne Swanson, National

College; Beverly Taylor, University of North Carolina, Chapel Hill; Merle Thompson, North Virginia Community College; Cyrilla Vessey, North Virginia Community College; Mildred White, Oholone College; Margaret Whitt, University of Denver; Betty J. Williams, East Tennessee State University; Donald R. Williams, North Shore Community College; and Donnie Yeilding, Central Texas College.

Our thanks also to the many users of the earlier editions who gave us advice on how and where to make improvements: Linda Bamber, David Cavitch, Robert Cyr, Arthur Friedman, Nancy Grayson, Martha Hicks-Courant, Billie Ingram, Martha Lappen, Judy Maas, Deirdre McDonald, Patricia Meier, Ronald E. Pepin, William Roberts, Claire Seng-Niemoeller, Virginia Shine, and Charles L. Walker.

We are especially grateful for the comments and suggestions offered by the following scholars: Priscilla B. Bellair, Carroll Britch, Don Brunn, Malcolm B. Clark, William C. Clayton (a veteran of over 40 years of teaching at Nassau Community College), Terence A. Dalrymple, Franz Douskey, Gerald Duchovnay, Peter Dumanis, Estelle Easterly, Adam Fischer, Martha Flint, Robert H. Fossum, Gerald Hasham, Richard Henze, Catherine M. Hoff, Grace S. Kehrer, Nancy E. Kensicki, Linda Kraus, Juanita Laing, Vincent J. Liesenfeld, Martha McGowan, John H. Meagher III, Stuart Millner, Edward Anthony Nagel, Peter L. Neff, Robert F. Panara, Ronald E. Pepin, Jane Pierce, Robert M. Post, Kris Rapp, Mark Reynolds, John Richardson, Donald H. Sanborn, Marlene Sebeck, Frank E. Sexton, Peggy Skaggs, David Stuchler, James E. Tamer, Carol Teaff, C. Uejio, Hugh Witemeyer, Manfred Wolf, and Joseph Zaitchik.

Finally, we are also grateful for valuable suggestions made by Barbara Harman, X. J. Kennedy, Carolyn Potts, Marcia Stubbs, Helen Vendler, and Ann Chalmers Watts.

SYLVAN BARNET
WILLIAM BURTO
WILLIAM E. CAIN

We hope that you already enjoy reading literature and that *An Introduction to Literature* will help you enjoy it even more. But as you begin your course this semester with our book, we want to say a little more about why we wrote it, how we believe it can help you, and in what ways we think it can deepen and enrich your pleasure in studying literature.

Throughout the process of writing and rewriting *An Introduction to Literature* we saw ourselves as teachers, offering the kinds of suggestions and strategies that, over many years, we have offered to our students.

As you can tell from a glance at the Table of Contents, *An Introduction to Literature* includes practical advice about reading and responding to literature and writing analytical papers, advice that comes directly from our experience not only as readers and writers but also as teachers. This experience derives from classrooms, from conferences with students, and from assignments we have given, read, responded to, and graded. We have learned from our experiences and have done our best to give you the tools that will help you make yourself a more perceptive reader and a more careful, cogent writer.

Speaking of making and remaking, we are reminded of a short poem by William Butler Yeats, who was a persistent reviser of his work. (You can find three versions of his poem "Leda and the Swan" on pages 724 and 725.)

> The friends that have it I do wrong
> Whenever I remake a song,
> Should know what issue is at stake:
> It is myself that I remake.

Like Yeats, you will develop throughout your life: you will find you have new things to say, and you may even come to find that the tools you acquired in college—and that suited you for a while—are not fully adequate to the new self that you have become. We cannot claim to equip you for the rest of your life—though some of these works of literature surely will remain in your mind for years—but we do claim that, with your instructor, we are helping you develop skills that are important for your mental progress. We have in mind skills useful not merely in the course in which you are now enrolled, or other literature courses, or even courses in the humanities in general that you may take. We go further. We think that these skills in reading and writing are important for your development as an educated adult. Becoming an alert reader and an effective writer should be among the central goals of your education, and they are goals that *An Introduction to Literature* is designed to help you reach.

The skills we stress in *An Introduction to Literature* will enable you to gain confidence as a reader of literary works so that you will increase your understanding of what literature offers. You need not enjoy all authors equally. You will have your favorites—and also some authors whom you do not like much at all. There's nothing wrong with that; reading literature is very much a personal encounter. But, at the same time, the skills we highlight in *An Introduction to Literature* can help you know and explain why one author means much to you and another does not. In this respect, reading and studying literature is more than personal; as we share our responses and try to express them effectively in writing, the work that we perform becomes cooperative and communal, a type of cultural conversation among fellow students, teachers, and friends.

As you proceed through *An Introduction to Literature* and gain further experience as a reader and writer, you will start to see features of poems, stories, and plays that you had not noticed before, or that you had noticed but not really understood, or that you had understood but not, so to speak, fully experienced. You may even find yourself enjoying an author you thought you disliked and would never be able to understand. The study of literature calls for concentration, commitment, and discipline. It is work—sometimes hard, challenging work. But it is rewarding work, and we believe that it will lead you to find literature more engaging and more pleasurable.

We hope that *An Introduction to Literature* will have this effect for you. Feel free to contact us with your comments and suggestions. We are eager to know what in this book has served you well, and what we might do better. You can write to us in care of Literature Editor, Longman Publishers, 51 Madison Ave, New York, NY 10010.

SYLVAN BARNET
WILLIAM BURTO
WILLIAM E. CAIN

An Introduction
to Literature

I

Reading, Thinking, and Writing
Critically About Literature

Writers of literature (as opposed to other writers, such as journalists, authors of do-it-yourself manuals, and authors of textbooks) specialize in recording their responses to life and in imagining the responses of others. They tell us how it feels to live the life they live, or the lives they know about or imagine, and by some sort of magic they set forth their responses so effectively that our own lives are expanded. Their reports, for at least a moment, become ours and cause our own pulses to beat faster. As Ezra Pound put it, "Literature is news that stays news." In Chapter 2 of this book you will read a very short story (The Parable of the Prodigal Son) that is almost two thousand years old as well as half a dozen works—stories and poems—that were written in the last fifty or so years, some by men, some by women. One of the stories in a later chapter is by Ernest Hemingway, here shown revising his work.

Good writers are good readers, careful readers: they know that they must read and reread their own drafts at least as carefully as they read published writing. They know that not until they put words down can they know what they think—and then they usually see that the thoughts are not quite good enough, that the words they put down need to be revised, and revised again. Hemingway, in an interview, commented on this business of writing and revising a couple of more times:

> I always rewrite each day up to the point where I stopped. When it is all finished, naturally you go over it. You get another chance to correct and rewrite when someone else types it, and you see it in clean type. The last chance is in the proofs. You're grateful for these different chances. (*Writers at Work*, Second Series, 222)

There is a lesson here for all of us, even though our own writing probably is of a humbler sort.

What are the aims of the writers of literature? Well, one of our authors, Jamaica Kincaid, in various interviews mentions her "insistence on truth," even if—especially if—the truth is painful. It is not unusual for writers to insist that in their fictions they present truths, they tell it as it is, they wake us up, they seek to make us take off our rose-colored glasses, and to make us see and feel reality. Joseph Conrad, for example, said: "My task . . . is by the power of the written word to make you hear, to make you feel—it is, before all, to make you see."

The truth that a writer makes us see is the "news that stays news" that Ezra Pound spoke of. Here is Hemingway talking about the writer's work:

> All good books are alike in that they are truer than if they had really happened and after you are finished reading one you will feel that all that happened to you and afterwards it all belongs to you; the good and the bad, the ecstasy, the remorse, and sorrow, the people and the places and how the weather was. (*Esquire* [December 1934], 68)

The Hemingway story that we reprint, "Cat in the Rain" (page 99), deals with a young woman and a young man. It's our hunch that you will find the story true: you will believe the characters and "how the weather was," and you will also find the story highly entertaining—two qualities we hope you find in all of the works in this book.

1

College Readiness:
How to Respond to Stories,
Poems, and Plays

My task ... is by the power of the written word to make you hear, to make you feel—it is, before all, to make you see.

—Joseph Conrad

A book must be the ax that breaks the frozen sea within us.

—Franz Kafka

The best of all ways to make one's reading valuable is to write about it.

—Ralph Waldo Emerson

Full Disclosure

First, we must admit that the title of our book, *An Introduction to Literature,* is misleading, even false. You were introduced to one kind of literature, poetry, long ago, when you heard your first lullaby.

> Rock-a-bye baby, in the treetop
> When the wind blows, the cradle will rock
> When the bough breaks, the cradle will fall
> And down will come baby, cradle and all.

Probably this or maybe another lullaby put you to sleep, as it was supposed to do, but most literature seeks to keep you awake, to deepen or heighten your experience of life. And, again years ago, you were further introduced to poetry when you heard—and soon recited—nursery rhymes and counting-out rhymes. A little later you heard and sang songs, perhaps "The Star Spangled Banner," "Swing Low, Sweet Chariot," and Robert Burns's "Auld Lang Syne" or perhaps Burns's "Coming through the Rye." (Maybe you first encountered "Coming through the Rye" in J. D. Salinger's *The Catcher in the Rye;* if so, that is yet another work that you were introduced to, a work that deepened your acquaintance with literature.)

When you heard your first fairy tales, maybe "Cinderella," "Hansel and Gretel," or "Snow White and the Seven Dwarfs," you were introduced to short stories—another form of literature—and somewhere along the line you were further introduced to short stories when you heard about the Parable of the Prodigal Son, or the Good Samaritan, or when you heard someone tell an Aesop fable, or even when you heard a joke. And then perhaps you graduated to telling an occasional joke, thereby becoming an interpreter or performer of one kind of popular literature.

Such was (probably) your introduction to two kinds of literature, poetry and fiction. You were introduced to a third kind, *dramatic* literature (stories presented by actors), when you first looked at television, or first went to the movies or saw a live theatrical production. Perhaps you have even performed in high school, maybe in Thornton Wilder's play, *Our Town.*

Analyzing Literature

If our book does not in fact *introduce* you to literature, what *does* it do? We hope that it will do at least two things:

- introduce you to a *wider range* of literature than you are already familiar with, and
- introduce you to the process of *analyzing* literature.

You may perhaps regard this as Good News and Bad News—Good that you will encounter new literature, not so good (maybe even Bad) that we will be encouraging you to read analytically, critically, thoughtfully, and to write essays in the same spirit.

Why not leave well-enough alone, and just let people read in their own way, for fun? Why this business about analysis? Because some works of literature are deep, and they deserve to be read attentively, seriously, analytically. When you think about it for a moment, you will recall that *thinking* can heighten your daily experience, can increase your enjoyment. Take, for instance, attendance at spectator sports. The person who knows something about baseball surely enjoys the game more than the person who knows almost nothing and who attends the game chiefly to be in the fresh air and to eat a couple of hot dogs. Experienced viewers, for instance, find themselves thinking, "He'll probably bunt," or "Now is the time for the hit and run." Knowing the records of the players and thinking about the players in a specific context heightens—perhaps we can even say "deepens"—one's interest and one's enjoyment in the game.

Somewhat similarly, experienced readers of, say, novels by Toni Morrison, get more out of a new book by Morrison than readers who have read very few novels and who now pick up their first Morrison. Yes, of course inexperienced readers can enjoy the book, but, again, experienced readers will see more, hear more, *enjoy* more, because they know what to look for, know (so to speak) *how* to read.

A good way to learn to read analytically is to annotate a text—our next topic.

Annotating a Text as a Way of Thinking

If you glance back to the beginning of this chapter, you will see that we quote the nineteenth-century American poet and essayist, Ralph Waldo Emerson:

> The best of all ways to make one's reading valuable is to write about it.

You probably have had the experience—whether in e-mailing a friend or in writing a paper for a course—of putting down words, and then finding, *in the act of writing,* and *only* in the act of writing, that, well,

- No, you do *not* really think what you just wrote down is quite right. A better way to put it would be to say. . . . Or you may feel, Yes, that's a step in the right direction, but
- Now that I see what I've said, I would go even further, and would add. . . .

Some of your earliest annotations of a literary text are likely to be even briefer than the jottings we have indicated. They are likely to be things like these:

- ???
- ugh
- X
- great!

Or you may find yourself putting down such things as

- this character seems to be behaving inconsistently,

or

- this setting--a forest--seems to symbolize darkness, and maybe even moral confusion,

or

- Why these terribly long sentences??? And do we need all those technical words!

Remarks such as these, the product of **close reading,** may turn out to be wrong-headed, but they are the product of a mind that is *responding* to the text, not just an eye that is mindlessly running over some print.

And of course thoughtful reading may occasionally take the form of

- underlining
- highlighting
- marking a passage with a vertical line
- circling some words, perhaps even connecting circled words with a line, thereby indicating that they have some sort of relationship

Caution: If you highlight whole pages you may *not* be thinking; you probably are just expending pigment, just kidding yourself into believing that you are thinking.

What advice can we give you about annotating, beyond cautioning against mindless highlighting? The best advice we can give is this: Begin by indicating

- what you especially like—thinking about what pleases you is a pretty good first step—and also by indicating
- what you are especially puzzled by. If you don't know the meaning of a word, put a question mark in the margin, and then look up the meaning in a dictionary

A First Assignment: Annotating Robert Frost's "Come In"

But here is yet another way to begin thinking about a work of literature, especially a short poem. To get our students started, we gave them as their first homework assignment a poem by Robert Frost, "Come In," accompanied by the following prose quotation drawn from a preface that Frost wrote for his short play, *A Way Out:*

> Everything written is as good as it is dramatic. . . . [A poem is] heard as sung or spoken by a person in a scene—in character, in a setting. By whom, where and when is the question. By the dreamer of a better world out in a storm in Autumn; by a lover under a window at night.

Frost says that writing is "dramatic." Presumably "dramatic" implies

- *a situation that is suspenseful,* perhaps especially because we sense
- *a conflict* (the conflict may be between two people, or between one person and his or her surroundings, or even within a single person—for instance, concerning a decision).

So we told our students that in annotating "Come In" they might want to begin by thinking about the "dramatic" situation in the poem:

- Who is speaking?
- Where?
- What conflict, if any, is implied?
- If there is a conflict, how is it resolved?

But beyond responses to these questions, the students were to jot down whatever puzzled them or interested them. Here is Frost's poem, followed by the responses of one student. Read the poem, preferably aloud, and then look at the student's annotations.

Come In   [1942]

As I came to the edge of the woods,
Thrush music—hark!
Now if it was dusk outside,
Inside it was dark.   4

Too dark in the woods for a bird
By sleight of wing
To better its perch for the night,
Though it still could sing.   8

The last of the light of the sun
That had died in the west
Still lived for one song more
In a thrush's breast.   12

Far in the pillared dark
Thrush music went—
Almost like a call to come in
To the dark and lament.   16

But no, I was out for stars:
I would not come in.
I meant not even if asked,
And I hadn't been.   20

Please note:

- We suggested that students read the poem (aloud at least once) and then jot down in the margins whatever responses they wished to record—their likes, dislikes, uncertainties, whatever they thought might be helpful in finding their way into the poem associations.
- We also suggested that *after* they had read the poem several times and jotted down some responses in the margins, they might at the top or bottom of the page respond to Frost's prose comment, and indicate (1) who is speaking in this poem, in what specific context, and (2) what is "dramatic" about the situation.

Come In   *Sounds like a friendly invitation*

As I came to the edge of the woods,
Thrush music—hark!   *Unusual word--old fashioned.*
Now if it was dusk outside,
Inside it was dark.   4

Too dark in the woods for a bird
By sleight of wing
To better its perch for the night,
Though it still could sing.   8

The last of the light of the sun   *light dying, but also still living in bird's song*
That had died in the west
Still lived for one song more
In a thrush's breast.   12

Far in the pillared dark   *Trees like pillars in a Greek temple or in a cathedral*
Thrush music went—   *Religious?*
Almost like a call to come in   *"Dark" is associated with sorrow ("lament")*
To the dark and lament.   16
Very strong, emphatic!
But no, I was out for stars: *light, not darkness.*
I would not come in.
I meant not even if asked,
And I hadn't been.   20

Sort of a joke. He realizes he had not been invited to "Come in," a sort of rejection of his own title. So--the "drama" is that he realizes his mistake. Nature did not invite him to "come in" or to "lament."

Thinking Critically About Responses to Literature: Arguing with Yourself

Ordinarily you will begin with a noticeable response to your reading—perhaps interest, boredom, bafflement, annoyance, shock, or pleasure. But if you are going to think critically about what you have read, you will go on to *examine* your response by checking it against the work. Revisiting the reading in the context of your response to it can help you deepen or change your response.

How can you change an instinctive emotional response? **Critical thinking** involves seeing an issue from all sides, to as great a degree as possible. As you know, in ordinary language "to criticize" usually means to find fault, but in literary studies the term does not have a negative connotation. Rather, it means "to examine carefully." (The word "criticism" comes from a Greek verb meaning "to distinguish," "to decide," "to judge.") In one respect, however, the term "critical thinking" does approach the usual meaning of "criticism," since critical thinking requires you to take a skeptical view of *your own* response. You will, so to speak, argue with yourself or seek to find fault with your initial view. That is, in an effort to improve your position you try to raise questions that a skeptical reader might raise.

Critical thinking, in short, involves examining or exploring one's own responses by questioning and testing them. Critical thinking is not so much a skill (though it does require the ability to understand a text) as it is a habit of mind, or, rather, several habits, including

- open-mindedness,
- intellectual curiosity, and
- a willingness to work.

A Very Short Story: Fyodor Dostoevsky's "The Onion"

"The Onion" is a story within a story, almost a fable or a fairy tale told by a character within a nineteenth-century novel. (What do the words "fable" and "tale" suggest to you?)

FYODOR DOSTOEVSKY

A novelist of Russia's Golden Age, Fyodor Dostoevsky (1821–1881)—pronounced approximately like DAHS-tuh-yef-skee—wrote five major works: Notes from Underground *(1864),* Crime and Punishment *(1866),* The Idiot *(1869),* The Possessed *(1871), and* The Brothers Karamazov *(1880).*

Within The Brothers Karamazov *(in Book 7, Chapter 3), one of the characters, Grushenka, says, rather puzzlingly, "Although I'm bad, I did give away an onion." She goes on to explain what she means: She says that when she was a child she heard a story from her cook, and she then tells the story. We give the story as she retells it.*

The Onion

The story goes like this. Once upon a time there was a woman, and a very wicked woman she was. When she died, no one could think of a single good deed she had done. The devils caught her and pushed her into a lake of fire, but her Guardian Angel thought hard, and he remembered that she once pulled up an onion from her garden and gave it to a beggar. The angel told this to God, and God said to the angel, "Take that very same onion and hold it out to her, and let her take hold of it, and you pull, and if she gets out of the lake she can come to Paradise, but if the onion breaks, she must stay where she is."

The angel hurried to the woman, and he held out the onion. "Take hold of it and I'll pull you out." And he began pulling, and she began to get out, and when she was nearly out, other sinners in the lake saw her, and they tried to hold on to her so that they would be pulled out with her, but the woman was a wicked woman and she began to kick them away, saying "It's my onion, not yours!"

As soon as she spoke those words, the onion broke, and she fell back into the lake, and she is still there, burning to this very day. And the angel wept, and went away.

We once gave copies of this story to students at the first meeting of a course and asked them to read it and then to annotate it as a way of helping them to read it carefully. These are the annotations that one student produced.

The Onion

The story goes like this. Once upon a time there was a woman, and a very wicked woman she was. When she died, no one could think of a single good deed she had done. The devils caught her and pushed her into a lake of fire, but her Guardian Angel thought hard, and he remembered that she once pulled up an onion from her garden and gave it to a beggar. The angel told this to God, and God said to the angel, "Take that very same onion and hold it out to her, and let her take hold of it, and you pull, and if she gets out of the lake she can come to Paradise, but if the onion breaks, she must stay where she is."

The angel hurried to the woman, and he held out the onion. "Take hold of it and I'll pull you out." And he began pulling, and she began to get out, and when she was nearly out, other sinners in the lake saw her, and they tried to hold on to her so that they would be pulled out with her, but the woman was a wicked woman and she began to kick them away, saying "It's my onion, not yours!"

As soon as she spoke those words, the onion broke, and she fell back into the lake, and she is still there, burning to this very day. And the angel wept, and went away.

language of a fairy tale

again, the world of fairy tales

almost child-like in the way the story is told

again, simple style--of a fairy tale

again the language of a fairy tale

a sort of evil version of "and they lived happily ever after."

Would the story be better without this sentence?

YOUR TURN

1. Suppose the last sentence of the story, about the angel weeping and departing, were omitted. Would the story be better? Better in what way? More interesting? Truer? (Does it make any sense to talk about the "truth" of a story that is obviously fictional rather than historical?)
2. Suppose the onion did not break, and the story ended thus:

> Even though she spoke these unkind words, the onion did not break, and she was rescued from the lake of fire.

Do you think the revision is a better—more interesting, more effective— story than the original? Please explain.
3. Do you think that a nonbeliever can find this story of much interest? Please explain.

Prompts that Stimulate Responses to Stories, Poems, and Plays: Three Checklists

We think you may find the following checklists (reprinted in expanded form later in the book) helpful as ways of getting ideas about the literature that you read, and especially helpful if you are writing about literature.

✔ Responding to Stories

PLOT

☐ Does the plot grow out of the characters, or does it depend on chance or coincidence?

☐ Does surprise play an important role, or does fore-shadowing?

☐ What conflicts does the story include?

☐ Are certain episodes narrated out of chronological order?

CHARACTER

☐ Which character chiefly engages your interest?

☐ What purposes do minor characters serve?

☐ How does the author reveal character?

☐ Is the behavior plausible—that is, are the characters well motivated?

☐ If a character changes, why and how does he or she change?

☐ Are the characters round or flat?

☐ How has the author caused you to sympathize with certain characters?

POINT OF VIEW	☐ Who tells the story? ☐ How does the point of view help shape the theme? ☐ Does the narrator's language help you to construct a picture of the narrator's character, class, attitude, strengths, and limitations?
SETTING	☐ Do you have a strong sense of time and place? ☐ What is the relation of the setting to the plot and characters?
SYMBOLISM	☐ Do certain characters seem to you to stand for something in addition to themselves? ☐ If you do believe that the story has symbolic elements, do you think they are adequately integrated within the story, or do they strike you as being too obviously stuck in?
STYLE	☐ How would you characterize the style? ☐ How has the point of view shaped or determined the style? ☐ Do you think the style is consistent? ☐ Is the title informative?
THEME	☐ Is the title informative? ☐ Do certain passages—dialogue or description—seem to you to point especially toward the theme? ☐ Is the meaning of the story embodied in the whole story, or does it seem conveyed chiefly by certain passages of editorializing? ☐ Suppose someone asked you to state the point—the theme—of the story. Could you?

✔ Responding to Poems

FIRST RESPONSE	☐ What was your response to the poem on first reading?
SPEAKER AND TONE	☐ Who is the speaker?
	☐ Do you think the speaker is fully aware of what he or she is saying, or does the speaker unconsciously reveal his or her personality and values?
	☐ Is the speaker narrating on an earlier experience or attitude?
AUDIENCE	☐ To whom is the speaker speaking?
STRUCTURE AND FORM	☐ Does the poem proceed in a straightforward way, or at some point or points does the speaker reverse course, altering his or her tone or perception?
	☐ Is the poem organized into sections?
	☐ What is the effect on you of the form—say quatrains (stanzas of four lines) or blank verse (unrhymed lines of ten syllables of iambic pentameter)?
CENTER OF INTEREST AND THEME	☐ What is the poem about?
	☐ Is the theme stated explicitly (directly) or implicitly?
DICTION	☐ How would you characterize the language?
	☐ Do certain words have rich and relevant associations that relate to other words and help to define the speaker or the theme or both?
	☐ What is the role of figurative language, if any?
	☐ What do you think is to be taken figuratively or symbolically, and what literally?
SOUND EFFECTS	☐ What is the role of sound effects, including repetitions of sound (for instance, alliteration) and of entire words, and shifts in versification?
	☐ If there are off-rhymes (for instance, dizzy and easy, or home and come), what effect do they have on you?
	☐ If there are unexpected stresses or pauses, what do they communicate about the speaker's experience?

✔ Responding to Plays

PLOT AND CONFLICT

☐ Does the exposition introduce elements that will be ironically fulfilled? During the exposition do you perceive things differently from the way the characters perceive them?

☐ Are certain happenings or situations recurrent? If so, what significance do you attach to them?

☐ If there is more than one plot, do the plots seem to you to be related? Is one plot clearly the main plot and another plot a sort of subplot, a minor variation on the theme?

☐ Do any scenes strike you as irrelevant?

☐ Are certain scenes so strongly foreshadowed that you anticipated them? If so, did the happenings in these scenes merely fulfill your expectations, or did they also surprise you?

☐ What kinds of conflict are there? One character against another, one group against another, one part of a personality against another part in the same person?

☐ How is the conflict resolved? By an unambiguous triumph of one side or by a triumph that is also in some degree a loss for the triumphant side? Do you find the resolution satisfying, or unsettling, or what? Why?

CHARACTER

☐ A dramatic character is not likely to be thoroughly realistic, a copy of someone we might know. Still, we can ask if the character is consistent and coherent. We can also ask if the character is complex or is, on the other hand, a rather simple representative of some human type.

☐ How is the character defined? Consider what the character says and does and what others say about him or her and do to him or her. Also consider other characters who more or less resemble the character in question, because the similarities—and the differences—may be significant.

☐ How trustworthy are the characters when they characterize themselves? When they characterize others?

CHARACTER *(continued)*	☐ Do characters change as the play goes on, or do we simply know them better at the end?
	☐ What do you make of the minor characters? Are they merely necessary to the plot, or are they foils to other characters? Or do they serve some other functions?
	☐ If a character is tragic, does the tragedy seem to you to proceed from a moral flaw, from an intellectual error, from the malice of others, from sheer chance, or from some combination of these?
	☐ What are the character's goals? To what degree do you sympathize with them? If a character is comic, do you laugh with or at the character?
	☐ Do you think the characters are adequately motivated?
	☐ Is a given character so meditative that you feel he or she is engaged less in a dialogue with others than in a dialogue with the self? If so, do you feel that this character is in large degree a spokesperson for the author, commenting not only on the world of the play but also on the outside world?
NONVERBAL LANGUAGE	☐ If the playwright does not provide full stage directions, try to imagine for at least one scene what gestures and tones might accompany each speech. (The first scene is usually a good one to try your hand at.)
	☐ What do you make of the setting? Does it help to reveal character? Do changes of scene strike you as symbolic? If so, symbolic of what?

Converting Responses into Readable Writing

When you write about your responses, you are not just knocking off an assignment. You are writing an essay, engaging in a process that, first, will teach you, and second, will ultimately engage the interest of your readers.

After you have written your first draft, consult the following checklist. (And consult the list again, after each later draft.)

✔ Checklist: Readable Writing

☐ Is my title engaging?

☐ Does my introduction provide essential information (writer, work, topic, approach of essay)?

☐ Does my paper have a point, a thesis?

☐ Do I support my argument (thesis) with sufficient persuasive detail, for instance with brief quotations from the text? That is, will a reader clearly see *why* I respond as I do?

☐ Have I kept the needs of my readers in mind—for instance, have I defined unfamiliar terms? (If you keep the needs of your readers in mind, you find that you have a collaborator at your shoulder, someone who prompts you to clarify certain points.)

☐ Is the paper organized and is the organization clear to the readers?

☐ Have I set forth my views effectively and yet not talked too much about myself?

☐ Does my essay fulfill the assignment (length, scope)?

A Story for Analysis: Kate Chopin, "The Storm"

Here is a second story for you to read critically. Notice how the student's annotations help deepen her appreciation of the story.

KATE CHOPIN

For a complete biographical note, see page 67. Although Kate Chopin was from St. Louis, she married a man of French descent from Louisiana and lived there for many years. Some of the characters in her stories speak a mixture of French and English, and she draws heavily on the French culture that was prevalent in coastal Louisiana at the turn of the twentieth century.

The Storm   [1898]

I

The leaves were so still that even Bibi thought it was going to rain. Bobinôt, who was accustomed to converse on terms of perfect equality with his little son, called the child's attention

What does this detail tell us about Bobinôt?

to certain somber clouds that were rolling with sinister intention from the west, accompanied by a sullen, threatening roar.
They were at Friedheimer's store and decided to remain there
till the storm had passed. They sat within the door on two
empty kegs. Bibi was four years old and looked very wise.

"Mama'll be 'fraid, yes," he suggested with blinking eyes.

"She'll shut the house. Maybe she got Sylvie helpin' her
this evenin'," Bobinôt responded reassuringly.

"No; she ent got Sylvie. Sylvie was helpin' her yistiday,"
piped Bibi.

5   Bobinôt arose and going across to the counter purchased a can of shrimps, of which Calixta was very fond.
Then he returned to his perch on the keg and sat stolidly
holding the can of shrimps while the storm burst. It shook
the wooden store and seemed to be ripping great furrows in
the distant field. Bibi laid his little hand on his father's knee
and was not afraid.

II

Calixta, at home, felt no uneasiness for their safety. She sat at a
side window sewing furiously on a sewing machine. She was
greatly occupied and did not notice the approaching storm.
But she felt very warm and often stopped to mop her face on
which the perspiration gathered in beads. She unfastened her
white sacque at the throat. It began to grow dark, and suddenly
realizing the situation she got up hurriedly and went about
closing windows and doors.

Why does the narrator point out that Calixta has not seen Alcée alone since her marriage? Does this statement set up any expectations about what may happen?

Out on the small front gallery[1] she had hung Bobinôt's Sunday clothes to air and she hastened out to gather them before the
rain fell. As she stepped outside Alcée Laballière rode in at the
gate. She had not seen him very often since her marriage, and
never alone. She stood there with Bobinôt's coat in her hands,
and the big rain drops began to fall. Alcée rode his horse under
the shelter of a side projection where the chickens had huddled
and there were plows and a harrow piled up in the corner.

"May I come and wait in your gallery till the storm is over
Calixta?" he asked.

"Come 'long in, M'sieur Alcée."

10   His voice and her own startled her as if from a trance, and
she seized Bobinôt's vest. Alcée, mounting to the porch,
grabbed the trousers and snatched Bibi's braided jacket that
was about to be carried away by a sudden gust of wind. He expressed an intention to remain outside, but it was soon apparent that he might as well have been out in the open: the water
beat in upon the boards in driving sheets, and he went inside,
closing the door after him. It was even necessary to put something beneath the door to keep the water out.

Later Alcée will, so to speak, wear Bobinôt's pants.

---

[1]**gallery** porch or passageway along a wall, open to the air but protected
by a roof supported by columns.

"My! What a rain! It's a good two years sence it rain like that," exclaimed Calixta as she rolled up a piece of bagging and Alcée helped her to thrust it beneath the crack.

She was a little fuller of figure than five years before when she married; but she had lost nothing of her vivacity. Her blue eyes still retained their melting quality; and her yellow hair, disheveled by wind and rain, kinked more stubbornly than ever about her ears and temples.

The rain beat upon the low, shingled roof with a force and clatter that threatened to break an entrance and deluge them there. They were in the dining room—the sitting room—the general utility room. Adjoining was her bed room, with Bibi's couch along side her own. The door stood open, and the room with its white, monumental bed, its closed shutters, looked dim and mysterious.

Alcée flung himself in a rocker and Calixta nervously began to gather up from the floor the lengths of a cotton sheet which she had been sewing.

15   "If this keeps up, *Dieu sait*[2] if the levees going to stan' it!" she exclaimed.

"What have you got to do with the levees?"

"I got enough to do! An' there's Bobinôt with Bibi out in that storm—if he only didn't left Friedheimer's!"

"Let us hope, Calixta, that Bobinôt got sense enough to come in out of a cyclone."

She went and stood at the window with a greatly disturbed look on her face. She wiped the frame that was clouded with moisture. It was stiflingly hot. Alcée got up and joined her at the window, looking over her shoulder. The rain was coming down in sheets obscuring the view of far-off cabins and enveloping the distant wood in a gray mist. The playing of the lightning was incessant. A bolt struck a tall chinaberry tree at the edge of the field. It filled all visible space with a blinding glare and the crash seemed to invade the very boards they stood upon.

20   Calixta put her hands to her eyes, and with a cry, staggered backward. Alcée's arm encircled her, and for an instant he drew her close and spasmodically to him.

"*Bonté!*"[3] she cried, releasing herself from his encircling arm and retreating from the window, "the house'll go next! If I only knew w'ere Bibi was!" She would not compose herself; she would not be seated. Alcée clasped her shoulders and looked into her face. The contact of her warm palpitating body when he had unthinkingly drawn her into his arms, had aroused all the old-time infatuation and desire for her flesh.

"Calixta," he said, "don't be frightened. Nothing can happen. The house is too low to be struck, with so many tall trees standing about. There! aren't you going to be quiet? say, aren't you?" He pushed her hair back from her face that was warm and steaming. Her lips were as red and moist as pomegranate seed.

---

[2]**Dieu sait** God only knows.   [3]**Bonté!** Heavens!

Who is making this observation? The narrator? Alcée? As you continue reading this scene, think about who is relating the events, and how they are presented.

Consider how the storm outside mirrors the growing storm inside the house. How does Chopin use the setting to reflect the feelings of her characters?

Her white neck and a glimpse of her full, firm bosom disturbed him powerfully. As she glanced up at him the fear in her liquid blue eyes had given place to a drowsy gleam that unconsciously betrayed a sensuous desire. He looked down into her eyes and there was nothing for him to do but gather her lips in a kiss. It reminded him of Assumption.[4]

"Do you remember—in Assumption, Calixta?" he asked in a low voice broken with passion. Oh! she remembered; for in Assumption he had kissed her and kissed and kissed her; until his senses would well nigh fail, and to save her he would resort to a desperate flight. If she was not an immaculate dove in those days, she was still inviolate; a passionate creature whose very defenselessness had made her defense, against which his honor forbade him to prevail. Now—well, now—her lips seemed in a manner free to be tasted, as well as her round, white throat and her whiter breasts.

They did not heed the crashing torrents, and the roar of the elements made her laugh as she lay in his arms. She was a revelation in that dim, mysterious chamber; as white as the couch she lay upon. Her firm, elastic flesh that was knowing for the first time its birthright, was like a creamy lily that the sun invites to contribute its breath and perfume to the undying life of the world.

25 The generous abundance of her passion, without guile or trickery, was like a white flame which penetrated and found response in depths of his own sensuous nature that had never yet been reached.

When he touched her breasts they gave themselves up in quivering ecstasy, inviting his lips. Her mouth was a fountain of delight. And when he possessed her, they seemed to swoon together at the very borderland of life's mystery.

He stayed cushioned upon her, breathless, dazed, enervated, with his heart beating like a hammer upon her. With one hand she clasped his head, her lips lightly touching his forehead. The other hand stroked with a soothing rhythm his muscular shoulders.

The growl of the thunder was distant and passing away. The rain beat softly upon the shingles, inviting them to drowsiness and sleep. But they dared not yield.

The rain was over; and the sun was turning the glistening green world into a palace of gems. Calixta, on the gallery, watched Alcée ride away. He turned and smiled at her with a beaming face; she lifted her pretty chin in the air and laughed aloud.

III

Bobinôt and Bibi, trudging home, stopped without at the cistern to make themselves presentable.

30 "My! Bibi, w'at will yo' mama say! You ought to be ashame'. You oughtn' put on those good pants. Look at' em! An'

---

[4]**Assumption** a parish (i.e., county) west of New Orleans.

Margin notes (handwritten):

The fact that Alcée and Calixta dare not yield to their drowsiness indicates that they realize they must not be caught. But do they feel they have done something wrong?

Instead of feeling guilty or nervous about what has just happened, Calixta laughs "aloud." Chopin does not give any signals to the reader that we should disapprove of Calixta's infidelity.

that mud on yo' collar! How you got that mud on yo' collar, Bibi? I never saw such a boy!" Bibi was a picture of pathetic resignation. Bobinôt was the embodiment of serious solicitude as he strove to remove from his own person and his son's the signs of their tramp over heavy roads and through wet fields. He scraped the mud off Bibi's bare legs and feet with a stick and carefully removed all traces from his heavy brogans. Then, prepared for the worst—the meeting with an overscrupulous housewife, they entered cautiously at the back door.

Calixta was preparing supper. She had set the table and was dripping coffee at the hearth. She sprang up as they came in.

"Oh, Bobinôt! You back! My! but I was uneasy. W'ere you been during the rain? An' Bibi? he ain't wet? he ain't hurt?" She had clasped Bibi and was kissing him effusively. Bobinôt's explanations and apologies which he had been composing all along the way, died on his lips as Calixta felt him to see if he were dry, and seemed to express nothing but satisfaction at their safe return.

"I bought you some shrimps, Calixta," offered Bobinôt, hauling the can from his ample side pocket and laying it on the table.

35   "Shrimps! Oh, Bobinôt! you too good fo' anything!" and she gave him a smacking kiss on the cheek that resounded. "*J'vous résponds*,[5] we'll have a feas' tonight! umph-umph!"

Bobinôt and Bibi began to relax and enjoy themselves, and when the three seated themselves at table they laughed much and so loud that anyone might have heard them as far away as LaBallière's.

IV

Alcée LaBallière wrote to his wife, Clarisse, that night. It was a loving letter, full of tender solicitude. He told her not to hurry back, but if she and the babies liked it at Biloxi, to stay a month longer. He was getting on nicely; and though he missed them, he was willing to bear the separation a while longer—realizing that their health and pleasure were the first things to be considered.

V

As for Clarisse, she was charmed upon receiving her husband's letter. She and the babies were doing well. The society was agreeable; many of her old friends and acquaintances were at the bay. And the first free breath since her marriage seemed to restore the pleasant liberty of her maiden days. Devoted as she was to her husband, their conjugal life was something which she was more than willing to forgo for a while.

So the storm passed and everyone was happy.

---

[5] **J'vous résponds** Take my word; let me tell you.

[margin note:] Bobinôt had prepared himself for another "storm"--that of Calixta's reprimands. When she happily greets her husband and child, without chiding them, they relax and have a wonderful evening. It appears that the storm--the one that occurred inside the house--has cleared the air.

[margin note:] Why does Chopin end the story this way? What sort of moral judgment, if any, does she make on the actions of Calixta and Alcée?

YOUR TURN

1. How would you characterize the narrator?
2. How would you characterize Calixta?
3. In Part III, do you think Calixta is insincere in her expressions of solicitation for Bobinôt? Why or why not?
4. Do you take Part IV to imply that Alcée and Calixta will continue their affair for another month? Support your answer.
5. Why does Chopin bother, in Part V, to tell us about Clarisse? And exactly what do you make of the last line of the story?
6. Is it fair to say that the story is cynical? Explain.
7. Do you think the story is immoral and, if so, ought not to be assigned in a course in literature? Explain.

Last Words

You are in college, so you must know something, and you must have already developed methods of getting your work done, and getting it done well. Keep at it, keep thinking, keep responding—perhaps in new ways—to new experiences. Do not rely simply on the knowledge and the methods that you already have. New experiences require new responses. Remember the words of A. E. Housman, the twentieth-century poet and professor of classics:

> Knowledge is good, method is good, but one thing beyond all others is necessary; and that is to have a head, not a pumpkin on your shoulders, and brains, not pudding, in your head.

2

Reading and Responding to Literature

What Is Literature?

Large books have been written on this subject, and large books will continue to be written on it. But we can offer a few brief generalizations that may be useful.

First, the word "literature" can be used to refer to anything written. The Department of Agriculture will, upon request, send a correspondent "literature on canning tomatoes." People who ask for such material expect it to be clear and informative, but they do not expect it to be interesting in itself. They do not read it for the experience of reading it; they read it only if they are thinking about canning tomatoes.

There is, however, a sort of literature that people *do* read without expecting a practical payoff. They read the sort of writing that is in *An Introduction to Literature* because they expect it to hold their interest and to provide pleasure. They may vaguely feel that it will be good for them, but they don't read it *because* it will be good for them, any more than they dance because dancing provides healthful exercise. Dancing may indeed be healthful, but that's not why people dance. They dance because dancing affords a special kind of pleasure. For similar reasons people watch athletic contests and go to concerts or to the theater. We participate in activities such as these not because we expect some sort of later reward but because we know that the experience of participating is in itself rewarding. Perhaps the best explanation is that the experiences are absorbing—which is to say they take us out of ourselves for a while—and that (especially in the case of concerts, dance performances, and athletic contests) they allow us to appreciate excellence, to admire achievement. Most of us can swim or toss a ball and maybe even hit a ball, but when we go to a swimming meet or to a ball game we see a level of performance that evokes our admiration.

Literature as Performance

Let's begin, then, by thinking of literature as (to quote Robert Frost) "a performance in words." Here's a very short poem by Frost (1874-1963), probably America's most famous poet.

21

ROBERT FROST

The Span of Life [1936]

The old dog barks backward without getting up.
I can remember when he was a pup.

Read the poem aloud once or twice, physically experiencing Frost's "performance in words." The most immediately obvious part of the performance is that Frost has written lines that rhyme. No two readers will read the lines in exactly the same way, but it is safe to say that in reading the first line most readers will put a fairly heavy stress on as many as seven or even eight syllables, whereas in reading the second line they probably will stress only three or four:

The óld dóg bárks báckward withoút gétting úp.
Í can remémber when hé was a púp.

Notice that the first line is harder to say than the second line, which more or less rolls off the tongue. Why? Because in the first line we must pause between "old" and "dog," between "backward" and "without," and between "without" and "getting"—and in fact between "back" and "ward."

And so we can say that the form (a relatively effortful hard-to-speak line followed by an easy bouncy line) is part of the content: first, a description with pauses and relatively heavy stresses of a dog that no longer has the energy or the strength to leap up, and second, a line that in a rather jingling way reports a memory of the dog as a puppy. The language, then, is highly patterned. Take a moment to read the lines again, and to enjoy the rhyme; rhyme—the repetition of a sound—is also a pattern. We can easily see what Frost meant when he said that a poem is a performance in words. The thing looks easy enough, but we know that it takes skill to make words behave properly—that is, to get the right words into the right places. Frost went into the lions' cage, did his act, and came out unharmed.

Significance

We've been talking about Frost's skill in handling words, but we have said only a little about *what* Frost is saying. One of the things that literature does is to make us see—hear, feel, love—what the author thinks is a valuable part of the experience of living. A thousand years ago a Japanese writer, Lady Murasaki, made this point when she had one of the characters in her book talk about what motivates an author:

Again and again something in one's own life or in that around one will seem so important that one cannot bear to let it pass into oblivion. There must never come a time, the writer feels, when people do not know about this.

We can probably agree with Lady Murasaki that writers of literature try to get at something important in their experiences, emotions, or visions, and try to make the reader experience the importance. And so a writer shows us what the span of life is like, or (for instance) what it is like to be in love (plenty of room for comedy as well as tragedy here), or what it is like to be an immigrant worrying whether his or her baby will be accepted as an American. (Later in this chapter we will see Pat Mora's poem on this last topic.)

Thinking further about Frost's poem, we notice something else about the form. The first line is about a dog, but the second line is about a dog *and* a human being ("I can remember"). The speaker must be getting on, too. And although nothing is said about the dog as a symbol of human life, surely the reader, prompted by the title of the poem, makes a connection between the lifespan of a dog and that of a human being. Part of what makes the poem effective is that this point is not stated explicitly, not belabored. Readers have the pleasure of making the connection for themselves—under Frost's careful guidance.

Everyone knows that puppies are frisky and that old dogs are not—though perhaps not until we encountered this poem did we think twice about the fact that "the old dog barks backward without getting up." Or let's put it this way:

- Many people may have noticed this behavior, but
- perhaps only Frost thought (to use Lady Murasaki's words) "There must never come a time ... when people do not know about this." And
- fortunately for all of us, Frost had the ability to put his perception into memorable words.

Part of what makes Frost's performance in words especially memorable is the relationship between the two lines. Neither line in itself is anything very special, but because of the counterpoint the whole is more than the sum of the parts. Skill in handling language, obviously, is indispensable if the writer is to produce literature. A person may know a great deal about dogs and may be a great lover of dogs, but knowledge and love are not enough equipment to write even a two-line poem about a dog (or the span of life, or both). Poems, like other kinds of literature, are produced by people who know how to delight us with verbal performances.

We can easily see that Robert Frost's "The Span of Life" is a work of literature rather than mere versification if we contrast it with another short work in rhyme:

Thirty days hath September,
April, June, and November;
All the rest have thirty-one
Excepting February alone,
Which has twenty-eight in fine,
Till leap year gives it twenty-nine.

This information is important, but it is only information. The lines rhyme, giving the work some form, but there is nothing very interesting about it, nothing insightful. (Perhaps you will want to take issue with this opinion.) The verse is true and therefore useful; it is valuable but it is not of compelling interest, probably because it only tells us facts rather than presents human experience. We all remember "Thirty days" but the lines offer neither the pleasure of an insight nor the pleasure of an interesting tune.

Two Poems About Immigrants

Let's now think a little more about what it means to read and respond to literature. Once again we'll start with a poem by Robert Frost, but this one, titled "Immigrants," takes a little more time and effort to figure out. Frost wrote these lines for a pageant at Plymouth, Massachusetts, celebrating the three-hundredth anniversary of the arrival of the *Mayflower* from England. The *Mayflower*, a ship about 100 feet long and 25 feet wide, had a crew of about 25 and 102 passengers. The journey took 66 days.

ROBERT FROST

Immigrants [1920]

No ship of all that under sail or steam
Have gathered people to us more and more
But Pilgrim-manned the *Mayflower* in a dream
Has been her anxious convoy in to shore.

To find this poem—this performance in words—of any interest, a reader probably has to know that the *Mayflower* brought the Pilgrims to America. Second, a reader has to grasp a slightly unfamiliar construction: "No ship . . . but . . . has . . ." which means, in effect, "every ship has." (Compare: "No human being but is born of woman," which means "Every human being is born of woman.")

If, then, we **paraphrase** the poem—translate it into other words in the same language—we get something roughly along these lines:

> All of the ships (whether sailing vessels or steamships) that have collected people in increasing numbers and brought them to this country have had the *Mayflower,* with its Pilgrims, as its eager (or worried?) escort to the coast.

We have tried to make this paraphrase as accurate and as concise as possible, but for reasons that we'll explain in a moment, we have omitted giving an equivalent for Frost's "in a dream." Why, one might ask, is our paraphrase so much less interesting than the original?

We come back to Frost's idea that a work of literature is a "performance in words." The lines are metrical (stresses recur more or less regularly) and they rhyme (*steam/dream, more/shore*), which is to say Frost, like a figure-skater, has created patterns. Probably, too, the repetition, of *s* in "sail or steam" catches the ear. The words "sail" and "steam" are somewhat alike in that they are both monosyllables, they both begin with the same sound, and they both evoke images of ships. Compare "sail or steam" with "sail or oil" or "sail or engine" and you will probably agree that the original is more pleasing and more interesting.

We can't be certain about what Frost really thought of the Pilgrims and of the *Mayflower,* but we do have the poem, and that's what we are concerned with. It celebrates the anniversary, of course, but it also celebrates at least two other things: the continuing arrival of new immigrants and the close connection between the early and the later immigrants.

Persons whose ancestors came over on the *Mayflower* have a reputation for being rather sniffy about later arrivals, but Frost reminds his Yankee audience that their ancestors, the *Mayflower* passengers, were themselves immigrants. However greatly the histories and the experiences of the early immigrants differed from those of later immigrants, the experience of emigration and the hopes for a better life link the *Mayflower* passengers with more recent arrivals.

The poem says, if our paraphrase is roughly accurate, that the *Mayflower* and its passengers accompany all later immigrants. Now, what does this mean? Literally, of course, it is nonsense. The *Mayflower* and its passengers disappeared centuries ago.

YOUR TURN

1. In our paraphrase, in an effort to avoid complexities, we did not give any equivalent for "in a dream" (line 3). The time has now come to face this

puzzle: "But Pilgrim-manned the *Mayflower* in a dream." Some readers take Frost to be saying that the long-deceased passengers of the
Mayflower still dream of others following them. Other readers, however, interpret the line as saying that later immigrants dream of the
Mayflower. Now, this paraphrase, even if accurate, makes an assertion
that is not strictly true, since many later immigrants probably had
never even heard of the *Mayflower*. But in a larger sense the statement
is true. Most later immigrants, with the terrible exception of involuntary immigrants from Africa who were brought here in chains,
dreamed of a better life, just as the *Mayflower* passengers did. Some
hoped for religious freedom, some hoped to escape political oppression or starvation, but again, all were seeking a better life. What do
you make of line 3?

2. In our paraphrase we mentioned that "anxious" might be paraphrased
   either as "eager" or as "worried." (Contrast, for instance, "She was anxious to serve the community" and "She was anxious about the exam.")
   Is Frost's "anxious convoy" *eagerly* accompanying the ships with immigrants, or is it *nervously* accompanying them, perhaps worried
   that these new arrivals may not be the right sort of people, or worried
   that the new arrivals may not be able to get on in the new country? Or
   does the word "anxious," which seems to modify "convoy" (here,
   Mayflower), really refer to the new immigrants, who are worried that
   they may not succeed? Or perhaps they are worried that America may
   not in fact correspond to their hopes.

   Read the poem aloud two or three times, and then think about
   which of these meanings—or some other meanings that you come up
   with—you find most rewarding. You might consider, too, whether more
   than one meaning can be present. Frost himself in a letter wrote that he
   liked to puzzle his readers a bit—to baffle them and yet (or thereby)
   propel them forward:

   > My poems—I should suppose everybody's poems—are all set to
   > trip the reader head foremost into the boundless. Ever since in-
   > fancy I have had the habit of leaving my blocks carts chairs and
   > such like ordinaries where people would be pretty sure to fall
   > forward over them in the dark. Forward, you understand, *and* in
   > the dark.

   What we have been saying is this: A reader of a work of literature finds
   meanings in the work, but also (even when the meaning is uncertain)
   takes delight in the details, takes delight in the way that the work has
   been constructed, takes delight in (again) the performance. When we
   have got at what we think may be the "meaning" of a work, we do not
   value or hold on to the meaning only and turn away from the work
   itself; rather, we value even more the craftsmanship that the work
   displays. And we come to see that the meaning is inseparable from all
   of the details that go to make up the work.

3. "Pilgrim-manned" may disturb some readers. Conscious of sexist language, today we try to avoid saying things like "This shows the greatness of man" or "Man is a rational animal" when we are speaking not
   about males but about all people. Does Frost's "Pilgrim-manned" strike
   you as slighting women? If not, why not?

4. We have already mentioned that Frost's poem cannot possibly be thought to describe involuntary immigrants. Is this a weakness in the poem? If so, how serious a weakness?

5. Frost's poem celebrates immigration and does not consider its effect on the American Indian population. The poem does not, so to speak, tell the whole truth; but no statement, however long, could tell the "whole truth" about such a complex topic. Do you agree that if the poem doesn't give us the whole truth, perhaps we get enough if it reminds us of a truth?

PAT MORA

Pat Mora, born in El Paso, Texas, in 1942, after graduating from Texas Western College earned a master's degree at the University of Texas at El Paso. She is best known for her poems, but she has also published books and essays on Chicano culture and is the author of many award-winning books for children. She lives in Sante Fe, New Mexico.

Immigrants

[1986]

wrap their babies in the American flag,
feed them mashed hot dogs and apple pie,
name them Bill and Daisy,
buy them blonde dolls that blink blue
eyes or a football and tiny cleats   5
before the baby can even walk
speak to them in thick English, hallo, babee, hallo,
whisper in Spanish or Polish,
when the babies sleep, whisper
in a dark parent bed, that dark   10
parent fear, "Will they like
our boy, our girl, our fine american
boy, our fine american girl?"

Pat Mora's experience—that of a Mexican American woman in the United States—obviously must be very different from that of Frost, an Anglo-Saxon male and almost the official poet of the country. Further, Mora is writing in our own time, not almost a century ago. A reader expects, and finds, a very different sort of poem. We won't discuss this poem at length, but we will say that in our view she too gets at something important. Among the many things in this verbal performance that give us pleasure are these:

- The wit of making the title part of the first sentence. A reader expects the title to be relevant to the poem but does not expect it to be grammatically the first word of the poem. We like the fresh way in which the title is used.

- The aptness with which Mora has caught the immigrants' eager yet worried attempt to make their children "100% American."
- The mimicry of the immigrants talking to their children: "hallo, babee, hallo." If this mimicry came from an outsider it would be condescending and offensive, but since it is written by someone known for her concern with Mexican American culture, it probably is not offensive. It is almost affectionate.

YOUR TURN

1. The last comment may be right, so far as it goes, but isn't it too simple? Reread the poem—preferably aloud—and then try to decide exactly what Mora's attitude is toward the immigrants. Do you think that she fully approves of their hopes? On what do you base your answer?
2. What does it mean to say that someone—a politician, for instance— "wraps himself in the American flag"? What does Mora mean when she says that immigrants "wrap their babies in the American flag"? How would you paraphrase the line?
3. After reading the poem aloud two or three times, what elements of "verbal performance"—we might say of skillful play—do you notice? Mora does not use rhyme, but she does engage in some verbal play. What examples can you point to?
4. What is your own attitude toward the efforts of some immigrants to assimilate themselves to an Anglo-American model? How does your attitude affect your reading of the poem?

Literature as a Performance, and Literature as a Journey

You have already heard Robert Frost say that a poem is a performance in words, and we hope that our commentary on Frost's "The Span of Life" made his point clear. We showed Frost performing his act, juggling words and taming sentences. And in Pat Mora's "Immigrants" you heard performances within the performance, speeches within the overall speech of the poem. When Mora lets us hear a recent immigrant say "hallo, babee, hallo," we hear this inner performance, and when we read it, even if we read silently, in some degree we are engaging in our own performance or re-creation of the poem. And, of course, if the work is a play, it is intended to be read aloud. In short, writers expect us to walk in their shoes, to reenact their performances in words. You and millions of others at least since the seventeenth century probably performed literature in the most obvious way when, as children, you recited such a nursery rhyme as

> Pat-a-cake, pat-a-cake, baker's man.
> Bake me a cake as fast as you can,

where the spoken words are accompanied by hand-clapping. But even as adults, in silently reading a work of literature, we sometimes experience a degree of muscular response to the actions that the words describe.

In a moment we will return to this idea of reenacting the writer's performance, but for the moment let's turn to a related topic, literature as a journey.

When we read a particularly engrossing work, or when we see a movie, we may say to a friend that we were "carried away." Or we may speak of certain kinds of writing as "escape literature," again suggesting that the writing takes us out of our ordinary world. The following short poem by Emily Dickinson (1830–1886) uses the idea that literature carries us away. Dickinson first compares a book to a swift square-rigged ship ("frigate" in line 1), then in line 3 to swift horses ("coursers") and finally, in the next-to-last line, to a chariot, normally the vehicle of kings and warriors but also of angels (cf. "Swing low, sweet chariot,/Coming for to carry me home"). One other word in the poem may require comment: "traverse" (line 5) is a route or a journey—again a word associated with being "carried away."

EMILY DICKINSON

There is no frigate like a book   [c. 1873]

There is no frigate like a book
To take us lands away,
Nor any coursers like a page
Of prancing poetry.
This traverse may the poorest take   5
Without oppress of toll;
How frugal is the chariot
That bears a human soul!

For Dickinson, none of these swift means of transportation can carry us—we might say "transport" us—as effectively as a book can. And a book is a lot cheaper (note "frugal" in line 7) than, say, taking a cruise on a frigate.

Let's now put these two points together: (1) literature as a performance not only by the writer but also by the spectator, and (2) literature as a journey. Robert Frost put the following poem at the beginning of his collected poems. Each of the two stanzas announces that the speaker, the poet, is going to the pasture, and each stanza ends with the words "You come too." Clearly the reader is invited to journey along with the writer—that is, to enter into the writer's world.

ROBERT FROST

The Pasture   [1915]

I'm going out to clean the pasture spring;
I'll only stop to rake the leaves away
(And wait to watch the water clear, I may):
I sha'n't be gone long. You come too.   4

I'm going out to fetch the little calf
That's standing by the mother. It's so young,
It totters when she licks it with her tongue.
I sha'n't be gone long. You come too.   8

Even in this very short poem there is a variety of tones of voice. The first line is probably spoken matter-of-factly:

I'm going out to clean the pasture spring,

but the parenthesis in the third line,

(And wait to watch the water clear, I may)

especially because of "I may" at the end of the line, introduces an engaging tentative note. And in the last line of the first stanza ("I sha'n't be gone long. You come too") we probably hear *two* tones: "I sha'n't be gone long" is, again, matter-of-fact, but in "You come too" we hear a warm, engaging invitation, we hear affection. Frost has, so to speak, performed the role of a particular person (someone who has a chore to do) speaking in a particular situation (that is, speaking to someone whom he cherishes).

Read the poem *aloud* two or three times, and listen to the tones that you find yourself uttering during your performance. We think that when, for instance, you read about the calf being licked by its mother—

It's so young,
It totters when she licks it with her tongue—

you may hear yourself reading in a tone of amused affection, maybe tinged with wonder.

If we are right in our conjectures about the tones you will hear, we think we are also right in saying that when readers read, they are *performing* literary works. As we have already said, readers walk in the author's shoes. And in this walk—in this journey they are performing—they acquire an experience.

A Story About a Journey

EUDORA WELTY

Eudora Welty (1909–2001) was born in Jackson, Mississippi. Although she earned a bachelor's degree at the University of Wisconsin and spent a year studying advertising in New York City at the Columbia University Graduate School of Business, she lived almost all of her life in Jackson.

In the preface to her Collected Stories *she says:*

> *I have been told, both in approval and in accusation, that I seem to love all my characters. What I do in writing of any character is to try to enter into the mind, heart and skin of a human being who is not myself. Whether this happens to be a man or a woman, old or young, with skin black or white, the primary challenge lies in making the jump itself. It is the act of a writer's imagination that I set most high.*

In addition to writing stories and novels, Welty wrote a book about fiction, The Eye of the Story *(1977), and a memoir,* One Writer's Beginnings *(1984).*

A Worn Path

[1941]

It was December—a bright frozen day in the early morning. Far out in the country there was an old Negro woman with her head tied in a red rag, coming along a path through the pinewoods. Her name was Phoenix Jackson. She was very old and small and she walked slowly in the dark pine shadows, moving a little from side to side in her steps, with the balanced heaviness and lightness of a pendulum in a grandfather clock. She carried a thin, small cane made from an umbrella, and with this she kept tapping the frozen earth in front of her. This made a grave and persistent noise in the still air, that seemed meditative like the chirping of a solitary little bird.

She wore a dark striped dress reaching down to her shoe tops, and an equally long apron of bleached sugar sacks, with a full pocket: all neat and tidy, but every time she took a step she might have fallen over her shoelaces, which dragged from her unlaced shoes. She looked straight ahead. Her eyes were blue with age. Her skin had a pattern all its own of numberless branching wrinkles and as though a whole little tree stood in the middle of her forehead, but a golden color ran underneath, and the two knobs of her cheeks were illuminated by a yellow burning under the dark. Under the red rag her hair came down on her neck in the frailest of ringlets, still black, and with an odor like copper.

Now and then there was a quivering in the thicket. Old Phoenix said, "Out of my way, all you foxes, owls, beetles, jack rabbits, coons and wild animals! . . . Keep out from under these feet, little bob-whites. . . . Keep the big wild hogs out of my path. Don't let none of those come running my direction. I got a long way." Under her small black-freckled hand her cane, limber as a buggy whip, would switch at the brush as if to rouse up any hiding things.

On she went. The woods were deep and still. The sun made the pine needles almost too bright to look at, up where the wind rocked. The cones dropped as light as feathers. Down in the hollow was the mourning dove— it was not too late for him.

5   The path ran up a hill. "Seem like there is chains about my feet, time I get this far," she said, in the voice of argument old people keep to use with themselves. "Something always take a hold of me on this hill—pleads I should stay."

After she got to the top she turned and gave a full, severe look behind her where she had come. "Up through pines," she said at length. "Now down through oaks."

Her eyes opened their widest, and she started down gently. But before she got to the bottom of the hill a bush caught her dress.

Her fingers were busy and intent, but her skirts were full and long, so that before she could pull them free in one place they were caught in another. It was not possible to allow the dress to tear. "I in the thorny bush," she said. "Thorns, you doing your appointed work. Never want to let folks pass, no sir. Old eyes thought you was a pretty little *green* bush."

Finally, trembling all over, she stood free, and after a moment dared to stoop for her cane.

10   "Sun so high!" she cried, leaning back and looking, while the thick tears went over her eyes. "The time getting all gone here."

At the foot of this hill was a place where a log was laid across the creek. "Now comes the trial," said Phoenix.

Putting her right foot out, she mounted the log and shut her eyes. Lifting her skirt, levelling her cane fiercely before her, like a festival figure in some parade, she began to march across. Then she opened her eyes and she was safe on the other side.

"I wasn't as old as I thought," she said.

15   But she sat down to rest. She spread her skirts on the bank around her and folded her hands over her knees. Up above her was a tree in a pearly cloud of mistletoe. She did not dare to close her eyes, and when a little boy brought her a plate with a slice of marble-cake on it she spoke to him. "That would be acceptable," she said. But when she went to take it there was just her own hand in the air.

So she left that tree, and had to go through a barbed-wire fence. There she had to creep and crawl, spreading her knees and stretching her fingers like a baby trying to climb the steps. But she talked loudly to herself: she could not let her dress be torn now, so late in the day, and she could not pay for having her arm or leg sawed off if she got caught fast where she was.

At last she was safe through the fence and risen up out in the clearing. Big dead trees, like black men with one arm, were standing in the purple stalks of the withered cotton field. There sat a buzzard.

"Who you watching?"

In the furrow she made her way along.

20   "Glad this not the season for bulls," she said, looking sideways, "and the good Lord made his snakes to curl up and sleep in the winter. A pleasure I don't see no two-headed snake coming around that tree, where it come once. It took a while to get by him, back in the summer."

She passed through the old cotton and went into a field of dead corn. It whispered and shook and was taller than her head. "Through the maze now," she said, for there was no path.

Then there was something tall, black, and skinny there, moving before her.

At first she took it for a man. It could have been a man dancing in the field. But she stood still and listened, and it did not make a sound. It was as silent as a ghost.

"Ghost," she said sharply, "who be you the ghost of? For I have heard of nary death close by."

25   But there was no answer—only the ragged dancing in the wind.

She shut her eyes, reached out her hand, and touched a sleeve. She found a coat and inside that an emptiness, cold as ice.

"You scarecrow," she said. Her face lighted. "I ought to be shut up for good," she said with laughter. "My senses is gone. I too old. I the oldest people I ever know. Dance, old scarecrow," she said, "while I dancing with you."

She kicked her foot over the furrow, and with mouth drawn down, shook her head once or twice in a little strutting way. Some husks blew down and whirled in streamers about her skirts.

Then she went on, parting her way from side to side with the cane, through the whispering field. At last she came to the end, to a wagon track where the silver grass blew between the red ruts. The quail were walking around like pullets, seeming all dainty and unseen.

30   "Walk pretty," she said. "This the easy place. This the easy going."

She followed the track, swaying through the quiet bare fields, through the little strings of trees silver in their dead leaves, past cabins silver from weather, with the doors and windows boarded shut, all like old women under a spell sitting there. "I walking in their sleep," she said, nodding her head vigorously.

In a ravine she went where a spring was silently flowing through a hollow log. Old Phoenix bent and drank. "Sweet-gum makes the water sweet," she said, and drank more. "Nobody know who made this well, for it was here when I was born."

The track crossed a swampy part where the moss hung as white as lace from every limb. "Sleep on, alligators, and blow your bubbles." Then the track went into the road.

Deep, deep the road went down between the high green-colored banks. Overhead the live-oaks met, and it was as dark as a cave.

35   A black dog with a lolling tongue came up out of the weeds by the ditch. She was meditating, and not ready, and when he came at her she only hit him a little with her cane. Over she went in the ditch, like a little puff of milk-weed.

Down there, her senses drifted away. A dream visited her, and she reached her hand up, but nothing reached down and gave her a pull. So she lay there and presently went to talking. "Old woman," she said to herself, "that black dog come up out of the weeds to stall you off, and now there he sitting on his fine tail, smiling at you."

A white man finally came along and found her—a hunter, a young man, with his dog on a chain.

"Well, Granny!" he laughed. "What are you doing there?"

"Lying on my back like a June-bug waiting to be turned over, mister," she said, reaching up her hand.

40   He lifted her up, gave her a swing in the air, and set her down. "Anything broken, Granny?"

"No sir, them old dead weeds is springy enough," said Phoenix, when she had got her breath. "I thank you for your trouble."

"Where do you live, Granny?" he asked, while the two dogs were growling at each other.

"Away back yonder, sir, behind the ridge. You can't even see it from here."

"On your way home?"

45   "No, sir, I going to town."

"Why, that's too far! That's as far as I walk when I come out myself, and I get something for my trouble." He patted the stuffed bag he carried, and there hung down a little closed claw. It was one of the bob-whites, with its beak hooked bitterly to show it was dead. "Now you go on home, Granny!"

"I bound to go to town, mister," said Phoenix. "The time come around."

He gave another laugh, filling the whole landscape. "I know you old colored people! Wouldn't miss going to town to see Santa Claus!"

But something held old Phoenix very still. The deep lines in her face went into a fierce and different radiation. Without warning, she had seen with her own eyes a flashing nickel fall out of the man's pocket onto the ground.

50   "How old are you, Granny?" he was saying.

"There is no telling, mister," she said, "no telling."

Then she gave a little cry and clapped her hands and said, "Git on away from here, dog! Look! Look at that dog!" She laughed as if in admiration. "He ain't scared of nobody. He a big black dog." She whispered, "Sic him!"

"Watch me get rid of that cur," said the man. "Sic him, Pete! Sic him!"

Phoenix heard the dogs fighting, and heard the man running and throwing sticks. She even heard a gunshot. But she was slowly bending forward by that time, further and further forward, the lids stretched down over her eyes, as if she were doing this in her sleep. Her chin was lowered almost to her knees. The yellow palm of her hand came out from the fold of her apron. Her fingers slid down and along the ground under the piece of money with the grace and care they would have in lifting an egg from under a sitting hen. Then she slowly straightened up, she stood erect, and the nickel was in her apron pocket. A bird flew by. Her lips moved. "God watching me the whole time. I come to stealing."

55   The man came back, and his own dog panted about them. "Well, I scared him off that time," he said, and then he laughed and lifted his gun and pointed it at Phoenix.

She stood straight and faced him.

"Doesn't the gun scare you?" he said, still pointing it.

"No, sir, I seen plenty go off closer by, in my day, and for less than what I done," she said, holding utterly still.

He smiled, and shouldered the gun. "Well, Granny," he said, "you must be a hundred years old, and scared of nothing. I'd give you a dime if I had any money with me. But you take my advice and stay home, and nothing will happen to you."

60   "I bound to go on my way, mister," said Phoenix. She inclined her head in the red rag. Then they went in different directions, but she could hear the gun shooting again and again over the hill.

She walked on. The shadows hung from the oak trees to the road like curtains. Then she smelled wood-smoke, and smelled the river, and she saw a steeple and the cabins on their steep steps. Dozens of little black children whirled around her. There ahead was Natchez shining. Bells were ringing. She walked on.

In the paved city it was Christmas time. There were red and green electric lights strung and crisscrossed everywhere, and all turned on in the daytime. Old Phoenix would have been lost if she had not distrusted her eyesight and depended on her feet to know where to take her.

She paused quietly on the sidewalk where people were passing by. A lady came along in the crowd, carrying an armful of red-, green-, and silver-wrapped presents; she gave off perfume like the red roses in hot summer, and Phoenix stopped her.

"Please, missy, will you lace up my shoe?" She held up her foot.

65   "What do you want, Grandma?"

"See my shoe," said Phoenix. "Do all right for out in the country, but wouldn't look right to go in a big building."

"Stand still then, Grandma," said the lady. She put her packages down on the sidewalk beside her and laced and tied both shoes tightly.

"Can't lace 'em with a cane," said Phoenix. "Thank you, missy. I doesn't mind asking a nice lady to tie up my shoe, when I gets out on the street."

Moving slowly and from side to side, she went into the big building and into a tower of steps, where she walked up and around and around until her feet knew to stop.

70   She entered a door, and there she saw nailed up on the wall the document that had been stamped with the gold seal and framed in the gold frame, which matched the dream that was hung up in her head.

"Here I be," she said. There was a fixed and ceremonial stiffness over her body.

"A charity case, I suppose," said an attendant who sat at the desk before her.

But Phoenix only looked above her head. There was sweat on her face, the wrinkles in her skin shone like a bright net.

"Speak up, Grandma," the woman said. "What's your name? We must have your history, you know. Have you been here before? What seems to be the trouble with you?"

75   Old Phoenix only gave a twitch to her face as if a fly were bothering her.

"Are you deaf?" cried the attendant.

But then the nurse came in.

"Oh, that's just old Aunt Phoenix," she said. "She doesn't come for herself—she has a little grandson. She makes these trips just as regular as clockwork. She lives away back off the Old Natchez Trace." She bent down. "Well, Aunt Phoenix, why don't you just take a seat? We won't keep you standing after your long trip." She pointed.

The old woman sat down, bolt upright in the chair.

80   "Now, how is the boy?" asked the nurse.

Old Phoenix did not speak.

"I said, how is the boy?"

But Phoenix only waited and stared straight ahead, her face very solemn and withdrawn into rigidity.

"Is his throat any better?" asked the nurse. "Aunt Phoenix, don't you hear me? Is your grandson's throat any better since the last time you came for the medicine?"

85   With her hands on her knees, the old woman waited, silent, erect and motionless, just as if she were in armor.

"You mustn't take up our time this way, Aunt Phoenix," the nurse said. "Tell us quickly about your grandson, and get it over. He isn't dead, is he?"

At last there came a flicker and then a flame of comprehension across her face, and she spoke.

"My grandson. It was my memory had left me. There I sat and forgot why I made my long trip."

"Forgot?" The nurse frowned. "After you came so far?"

90   Then Phoenix was like an old woman begging a dignified forgiveness for waking up frightened in the night. "I never did go to school, I was too old at the Surrender," she said in a soft voice. "I'm an old woman without an education. It was my memory fail me. My little grandson, he is just the same, and I forgot it in the coming."

"Throat never heals, does it?" said the nurse, speaking in a loud, sure voice to old Phoenix. By now she had a card with something written on it, a little list. "Yes. Swallowed lye. When was it—January—two-three years ago—"

Phoenix spoke unasked now. "No, missy, he not dead, he just the same. Every little while his throat begin to close up again, and he not able to swallow. He not get his breath. He not able to help himself. So the time come around, and I go on another trip for the soothing medicine."

"All right. The doctor said as long as you came to get it, you could have it," said the nurse. "But it's an obstinate case."

"My little grandson, he sit up there in the house all wrapped up, waiting by himself," Phoenix went on. "We is the only two left in the world. He suffer and it don't seem to put him back at all. He got a sweet look. He going to last. He wear a little patch quilt and peep out holding his mouth open like a little bird. I remembers so plain now. I not going to forget him again, no, the whole enduring time. I could tell him from all the others in creation."

95   "All right." The nurse was trying to hush her now. She brought her a bottle of medicine. "Charity," she said, making a check mark in a book.

Old Phoenix held the bottle close to her eyes and then carefully put it into her pocket.

"I thank you," she said.

"It's Christmas time, Grandma," said the attendant. "Could I give you a few pennies out of my purse?"

"Five pennies is a nickel," said Phoenix stiffly.

100   "Here's a nickel," said the attendant.

Phoenix rose carefully and held out her hand. She received the nickel and then fished the other nickel out of her pocket and laid it beside the new one. She stared at her palm closely, with her head on one side.

Then she gave a tap with her cane on the floor.

"This is what come to me to do," she said. "I going to the store and buy my child a little windmill they sells, made out of paper. He going to find it hard to believe there such a thing in the world. I'll march myself back where he waiting, holding it straight up in his hand."

She lifted her free hand, gave a little nod, turned round, and walked out of the doctor's office. Then her slow step began on the stairs, going down.

YOUR TURN

1. If you do not know the legend of the Phoenix, look it up in a dictionary or, even better, in an encyclopedia. Then carefully reread "A Worn Path" to learn whether the story in any way connects with the legend.
2. What do you think of the hunter?
3. What would be lost if the episode (with all of its dialogue) of Phoenix falling into the ditch and being helped out of it by the hunter were omitted?
4. Is Christmas a particularly appropriate time in which to set the story? Why or why not?
5. What do you make of the title?
6. "A Worn Path" treats race relations as one of its themes. Is this theme primary, or would you say instead that it is secondary? How would the story be different in its effect if everything stayed the same except for Phoenix's race?
7. Have you ever made a difficult trip by foot? Was there a point when you were tempted to turn back? What kept you going? Do you think that your experience could be made the basis for a short story? How would you structure such a story—its beginning, middle, and end?

Two Very Short Contemporary Short Stories

LYDIA DAVIS

Lydia Davis, born in 1947 in Northampton, Massachusetts, grew up in New York City and then lived for several years in France and Ireland. A professor of creative writing at the State University of New York (Albany), Davis has translated French literature and has written several books of stories; The Collected Stories of Lydia Davis, *published in 2009, contains all of her stories to date. Among her awards is a MacArthur Fellowship.*

Childcare
[2007]

It's his turn to take care of the baby. He is cross.
    He says, "I never get enough done."
    The baby is in a bad mood, too.
    He gives the baby a bottle of juice and sits him well back in a big armchair.
    He sits himself down in another chair and turns on the television.
    Together they watch *The Odd Couple*.

In Davis's *Varieties of Disturbance* (2007), the book from which we reprint "Childcare," the story appears in the middle of a page that is otherwise blank. The very appearance on the page is part of the performance, and it is also part of—dare we say?—the meaning. We see a largely blank page, a bare world, not much to look at, not much to make life rich. What do we know about the inhabitants of this world?

- The unnamed man (he is merely "he") is "cross," and the unnamed baby "is in a bad mood, too."
- The next thing we learn about the man is what we deduce from his statement, "I never get enough done." Ah, he is someone who wants to accomplish something. That sounds admirable.
- But he thinks the temporary job ("it's his turn") of caring for the baby interferes with his unspecified aspirations. That sounds not so nice, and we may wonder, "What sort of a guy is this who resents caring for his infant?"

The next things we learn dispose us favorably toward the man:

- "He gives the baby a bottle of juice and sits him well back in a big armchair." This business of sitting the child "well back in a big armchair" suggests that the man takes some care to make sure that the child is secure, is safely placed. We like that, we are reassured.
- The man then sits down in another chair and "turns on the television." Television? We might have thought that this man who can "never get enough done" would balance his checkbook, or read the newspaper, or answer a letter, but no, he watches television. That's not a crime, but for

a guy who complains that he "can never get enough done," it does seem a bit much.

- The final sentence is, "Together they watch *The Odd Couple*." Surely the thought crosses a reader's mind that these two are themselves an odd couple, and the reader may reasonably conclude that in some ways the man—cross, claiming that he can't get anything done—is as infantile as the baby.

It's a story told very simply, chiefly in simple sentences, "He says," "The baby is," "He gives," etc. Only twice does the author use compound sentences (simple sentences joined by a conjunction, in this case the most child-like of all conjunctions, "and," the language found in Dick and Jane children's books). Not much happens in this very simply told story, but it tells us all that we need to know about the unnamed man. And perhaps it tells us something about life, even about our own lives, for instance about the disparity between our own grand view of ourselves and the simple reality.

Now for a second very short story by Lydia Davis.

City People   [2001]

They have moved to the country. The country is nice enough: there are quail sitting in the bushes and frogs peeping in the swamps. But they are uneasy. They quarrel more often. They cry, or she cries and he bows his head. He is pale all the time now. She wakes in a panic at night, hearing him sniffle. She wakes in a panic again, hearing a car go up the driveway. In the morning there is sunlight on their faces but mice are chattering in the walls. He hates the mice. The pump breaks. They replace the pump. They poison the mice. Their neighbor's dog barks. It barks and barks. She could poison the dog.

"We're city people," he says, "and there aren't any nice cities to live in."

YOUR TURN

1. What elements of "performance"—perhaps we can say Davis's "craftsmanship"—do you see in this tiny narrative?
2. We are not told *why* these people have moved from the city to the country. Is it reasonable to offer a guess? If you think a reader can plausibly guess why they moved, what, in your view, is the reason for the move?
3. Does the story give at least a tiny glimpse of some aspect of life? Please explain.

Thinking About a Classic Story

This story, told by Jesus, is reported in the fifteenth chapter of the Gospel According to Luke. Jesus here recounts a **parable,** a short story from which a lesson is to be drawn. Luke reports that just before Jesus told the story, the Pharisees and scribes—persons whom the Gospels depict as opposed to Jesus because he sometimes found their traditions and teachings inadequate—complained that

Jesus was a man of loose morals, one who "receives sinners and eats with them." According to Luke, Jesus responded thus:

The Parable of the Prodigal Son

And he said, "A certain man had two sons: and the younger of them said to his father, 'Father, give me the portion of goods that falleth to me.' And he divided unto them his living. And not many days after, the younger son gathered all together, and took his journey into a far country, and there wasted his substance with riotous living.

And when he had spent all, there arose a mighty famine in that land, and he began to be in want. And he went and joined himself to a citizen of that country, and he sent him into his fields to feed swine. And he would fain have filled his belly with the husks that the swine did eat: and no man gave unto him.

And when he came to himself he said, 'How many hired servants of my father's have bread enough and to spare, and I perish with hunger? I will arise and go to my father, and will say unto him, "Father, I have sinned against heaven, and before thee. And am no more worthy to be called thy son: make me as one of thy hired servants."'

And he arose, and came to his father. But when he was yet a great way off, his father saw him, and had compassion, and ran, and fell on his neck, and kissed him. And the son said unto him, 'Father, I have sinned against heaven, and in thy sight, and am no more worthy to be called thy son.' But the father said to his servants, 'Bring forth the best robe, and put it on him, and put a ring on his hand, and shoes on his feet. And bring hither the fatted calf and kill it, and let us eat, and be merry. For this my son was dead, and is alive again; he was lost, and is found.' And they began to be merry.

Now his elder son was in the field, and as he came and drew nigh to the house, he heard music and dancing. And he called one of the servants, and asked what these things meant. And he said unto him, 'Thy brother is come, and thy father hath killed the fatted calf, because he hath received him safe and sound.' And he was angry, and would not go in: therefore came his father out, and entreated him. And he answering said to his father, 'Lo, these many years do I serve thee, neither transgressed I at any time thy commandment, and yet thou never gavest me a kid, that I might make merry with my friends: but as soon as this thy son was come, which hath devoured thy living with harlots, thou has killed for him the fatted calf.' And he said unto him, 'Son, thou art ever with me, and all that I have is thine. It was meet that we should make merry, and be glad: for this thy brother was dead, and is alive again: and was lost, and is found.' " (Luke 15. 11–32, King James Version)

Now, to begin with a small point, it is not likely that any but strictly observant Jews, or Muslims (who, like these Jews, do not eat pork), can feel the disgust that Jesus's audience must have felt at the thought that the son was reduced to feeding swine and that he even envied the food that swine ate. Further, some of us may be vegetarians; if so, we are not at all delighted at the thought that the father kills the fatted calf (probably the wretched beast has been force-fed) in order to celebrate the son's return.

And some readers do not believe in God, and hence are not prepared to take the story, as many people take it, as a story whose message is that we, like God (the father in this parable is usually taken to stand for God), ought to rejoice in the restoration of the sinner. Probably, then, for all sorts of obvious reasons none of us can put ourselves back into the first century CE and hear the story exactly as Jesus's audience heard it.

Still, most of us can probably agree on what we take to be the gist of the story, and we can enjoy the skillful way in which it is told. This skill will become apparent, however, only after several readings. What are some examples of superb storytelling here, and what can a reader gain from a thoughtful reading? We begin by noting a few points:

- Although the story is customarily called "The Parable of the Prodigal Son" or "The Parable of the Lost Son," it tells of two sons, not of one. When we reread the story, we increasingly see that these brothers are compared and contrasted: the prodigal leaves his father's house for a different way of life—he thus seems lost to the father—but then he repents and returns to the father, whereas the older son, who physically remains with the father, is spiritually remote from the father, or is lost in a different way. By virtue of his self-centeredness the older son is remote from the father in feeling or spirit.
- Again, reading and rereading reveal small but telling details. For instance, when the prodigal plans to return home, he thinks of what he will say to his father. He has come to his senses and repudiated his folly, but he still does not understand his father, for we will see in a moment that the prodigal has no need of this speech. Jesus tells us that as soon as the father saw the prodigal returning, he "had compassion, and ran, and fell on his neck, and kissed him." And (another very human touch) the prodigal— although already forgiven—nevertheless cannot refrain from uttering his heartfelt but, under the circumstances, unnecessary speech of repentance.
- The elder son, learning that the merrymaking is for the returning prodigal, "was angry, and would not go in." This character is sketched only briefly, but a reader immediately recognizes the type: self-centered, unforgiving, and petulant. The older son does not realize it, but he is as distant from his father as the younger son had been. What is the father's response to this son, who is so different from the forgiving father?

    Therefore came his father out, and entreated him.

The father goes out to the dutiful son, just as he had *gone out* to the prodigal son. (What the father *does* is as important as what he *says*.) Notice, too, speaking of sons, that the older son, talking to his father, somewhat distances himself from his brother, disdainfully referring to the prodigal as "this thy son." And what is the father's response? To the elder son's "this thy son," the father replies, "this thy brother."

YOUR TURN

This story is traditionally called the Parable of the Prodigal Son. Can a case be made for the view that it ought to be called the Parable of the Prodigal Father? Forget, if you can, the traditional title, and ask yourself if the story tells of a father who is prodigal with his property and who at the end is prodigal with his love. Explain why you accept or reject this interpretation.

Stories True and False

The word story comes from history—the stories that historians, biographers, and journalists narrate are supposed to be true accounts of what happened. The stories of novelists and short-story writers, however, are admittedly untrue; they are fiction, things made up, imagined, manufactured. As readers, we come to a supposedly true story with expectations different from those we bring to fiction.

Consider the difference between reading a narrative in a newspaper and one in a book of short stories. If, while reading a newspaper, we come across a story of, say, a subway accident, we assume that the account is true, and we read it for the information about a relatively unusual event. Anyone hurt? What sort of people? In our neighborhood? Whose fault? When we read a book of fiction, however, we do not expect to encounter literal truths; we read novels and short stories not for facts but for pleasure and for some insight or for a sense of what an aspect of life means to the writer. Consider the following short story by Grace Paley.

GRACE PALEY

 *Grace Paley (1922–2007) was born in New York City, where she attended Hunter College and New York University, but left without a degree. While raising two children she wrote poetry and then, in the 1950s, turned to writing fiction. Paley's books include two collections of short stories,* The Little Disturbances of Man *(1959) and* Enormous Changes at the Last Minute *(1974).*

Paley's chief subject is the life of little people struggling in the Big City. Of life she has said, "How daily life is lived is a mystery to me. You write about what's mysterious to you. What is it like? Why do people do this?" Of the short story she has said, "It can be just telling a little tale, or writing a complicated philosophical story. It can be a song, almost."

Samuel

[1968]

Some boys are very tough. They're afraid of nothing. They are the ones who climb a wall and take a bow at the top. Not only are they brave on the roof, but they make a lot of noise in the darkest part of the cellar where even the super hates to go. They also jiggle and hop on the platform between the locked doors of the subway cars.

Four boys are jiggling on the swaying platform. Their names are Alfred, Calvin, Samuel, and Tom. The men and the women in the cars on either side watch them. They don't like them to jiggle or jump but don't want to interfere. Of course some of the men in the cars were once brave boys like these. One of them had ridden the tail of a speeding truck from New York to Rockaway Beach without getting off, without his sore fingers losing hold. Nothing happened to him then or later. He had made a compact with other boys who preferred to watch: Starting at Eighth Avenue and Fifteenth Street, he would get to some specified place, maybe Twenty-third and the river, by hopping the tops of the moving trucks. This was hard to do when one truck turned a corner in the wrong direction and the nearest truck was a couple of feet too high. He made three or four starts before succeeding. He had gotten his idea from a film at school called *The Romance of Logging.* He had finished high school, married a good friend, was in a responsible job and going to night school.

These two men and others looked at the four boys jumping and jiggling on the platform and thought, It must be fun to ride that way, especially now the weather is nice and we're out of the tunnel and way high over the Bronx. Then they thought, These kids do seem to be acting sort of stupid. They *are* little. Then they thought of some of the brave things they had done when they were boys and jiggling didn't seem so risky.

The ladies in the car became very angry when they looked at the four boys. Most of them brought their brows together and hoped the boys could see their extreme disapproval. One of the ladies wanted to get up and say, Be careful you dumb kids, get off that platform or I'll call a cop. But three of the boys were Negroes and the fourth was something else she couldn't tell for sure. She was afraid they'd be fresh and laugh at her and embarrass her. She wasn't afraid they'd hit her, but she was afraid of embarrassment. Another lady thought, Their mothers never know where they are. It wasn't true in this particular case. Their mothers all knew that they had gone to see the missile exhibit on Fourteenth Street.

5   Out on the platform, whenever the train accelerated, the boys would raise their hands and point them up to the sky to act like rockets going off, then they rat-tat-tatted the shatterproof glass pane like machine guns, although no machine guns had been exhibited.

For some reason known only to the motorman, the train began a sudden slowdown. The lady who was afraid of embarrassment saw the boys jerk forward and backward and grab the swinging guard chains. She had her own boy at home. She stood up with determination and went to the door. She slid it open and said, "You boys will be hurt. You'll be killed. I'm going to call the conductor if you don't just go into the next car and sit down and be quiet."

Two of the boys said, "Yes'm," and acted as though they were about to go. Two of them blinked their eyes a couple of times and pressed their lips together. The train resumed its speed. The door slid shut, parting the lady and the boys. She leaned against the side door because she had to get off at the next stop.

The boys opened their eyes wide at each other and laughed. The lady blushed. The boys looked at her and laughed harder. They began to pound each other's back. Samuel laughed the hardest and pounded Alfred's back until Alfred coughed and the tears came. Alfred held tight to the chain hook. Samuel pounded him even harder when he saw the tears. He said, "Why you bawling? You a baby, huh?" and laughed. One of the men whose boyhood had been more watchful than brave became angry. He stood up straight and looked at the boys for a couple of seconds. Then he walked in a citizenly way to the end of the car, where he pulled the emergency cord. Almost at once, with a terrible hiss, the pressure of air abandoned the brakes and the wheels were caught and held.

People standing in the most secure places fell forward, then backward. Samuel had let go of his hold on the chain so he could pound Tom as well as Alfred. All the passengers in the cars whipped back and forth, but he pitched only forward and fell head first to be crushed and killed between the cars.

10   The train had stopped hard, halfway into the station, and the conductor called at once for the trainmen who knew about this kind of death and how to take the body from the wheels and brakes. There was silence except for passengers from other cars who asked, What happened! What happened! The ladies waited around wondering if he might be an only child. The men recalled other afternoons with very bad endings. The little boys stayed close to each other, leaning and touching shoulders and arms and legs.

When the policeman knocked at the door and told her about it, Samuel's mother began to scream. She screamed all day and moaned all night, though the doctors tried to quiet her with pills.

Oh, oh, she hopelessly cried. She did not know how she could ever find another boy like that one. However, she was a young woman and she became pregnant. Then for a few months she was hopeful. The child born to her was a boy. They brought him to be seen and nursed. She smiled. But immediately she saw that this baby wasn't Samuel. She and her husband together have had other children, but never again will a boy exactly like Samuel be known.

You might think about the ways in which "Samuel" differs from a newspaper story of an accident in a subway. (You might even want to write a newspaper version of the happening.) In some ways, Paley's story faintly resembles an account that might appear in a newspaper. Journalists are taught to give information about Who, What, When, Where, and Why, and Paley does provide this. Thus, the *characters* (Samuel and others) are the journalist's Who; the *plot* (the boys were jiggling on the platform, and when a man pulled the emergency cord one of them was killed) is the What; the *setting* (the subway, presumably in modern times) is the When and the Where; the *motivation* (the irritation of the man who pulls the emergency cord) is the Why.

Ask yourself questions about each of these elements, and think about how they work in Paley's story. You might also think about responses to the following questions. Your responses will teach you a good deal about what literature is and about some of the ways in which it works.

YOUR TURN

1. Paley wrote the story, but an unspecified person *tells* it. Describe the voice of this narrator in the first paragraph. Is the voice neutral and objective, or do you hear some sort of attitude, a point of view? If you do hear an attitude, what words or phrases in the story indicate it?

2. What do you know about the setting of "Samuel"? What can you infer about the neighborhood?

3. In the fourth paragraph we are told that "three of the boys were Negroes and the fourth was something else." Is race important in this story? Is Samuel "Negro" or "something else"? Does it matter?

4. Exactly *why* did a man walk "in a citizenly way to the end of the car, where he pulled the emergency cord"? Do you think the author blames him? What evidence can you offer to support your view? Do *you* blame him? Or do you blame the boys? Or anyone? Explain.

5. The story is called "Samuel," and it is, surely, about him. But what happens after Samuel dies? (You might want to list the events.) What else is the story about? (You might want to comment on why you believe the items in your list are important.)

6. Can you generalize about what the men think of the jigglers and about what the women think? Is Paley saying something about the sexes? About the attitudes of onlookers in a big city?

What's Past Is Prologue

The poems and stories that you have just read cannot, of course, stand for all works of literature. For one thing, although Mora's "Immigrants" and the prose stories include some dialogue, none of these works is in dramatic form, designed for presentation on a stage. Still, these examples, as well as works of literature that you are already familiar with, will provide something of a background against which you can read the other works in this book. For instance, if you read a story that, like the parable of the prodigal son, seems strongly to imply a moral, think about how the moral is controlled by what the characters *do* as well as by what they *say*, and how one character is defined by being set against another. If you read a poem that, like Mora's "Immigrants," seems to play one tone of voice against another (for instance, the voice of the speaker of the poem against a voice quoted within the poem), think about how the voices relate to each other and how they perhaps harmonize to create a complex vision.

In short, a work of literature is not a nut to be cracked open so that a kernel of meaning can be extracted and devoured, and the rest thrown away; the whole—a performance in words—is something to be experienced and enjoyed.

We end this chapter with two short stories.

JAMAICA KINCAID

Jamaica Kincaid (b. 1949) was born in St. John's, Antigua, in the West Indies. She was educated at the Princess Margaret School in Antigua, and, briefly, at Westchester Community College and Franconia College. Since 1974 she has been a contributor to the New Yorker.

Kincaid is the author of many works of fiction and nonfiction, including At the Bottom of the River *(1983, a collection of short pieces, including "Girl"),* Annie John *(1985, a second book recording a girl's growth, including "Columbus in Chains"),* A Small Place *(1988, a passionate essay about the destructive effects of colonialism), and* Lucy *(1990, a short novel about a young black woman who comes to the United States from the West Indies).*

Girl

[1978]

Wash the white clothes on Monday and put them on the stone heap; wash the color clothes on Tuesday and put them on the clothesline to dry; don't walk barehead in the hot sun; cook pumpkin fritters in very hot sweet oil; soak your little clothes right after you take them off; when buying cotton to make yourself a nice blouse, be sure that it doesn't have gum on it, because that way it won't hold up well after a wash; soak salt fish overnight before you cook it; is it true that you sing benna[1] in Sunday School? always eat your food in such a way that it won't turn someone else's stomach; on Sundays try to walk like a lady and not like the slut you are so bent on becoming; don't sing benna in Sunday School; you mustn't speak to wharf-rat boys, not even to give directions; don't eat fruits on the street—flies will follow you; *but I don't sing benna on Sundays at all and never in Sunday school;* this is how to sew on a button; this is how to make a buttonhole for the button you have just sewed on; this is how to hem a dress when you see the hem coming down and so to prevent yourself from looking like the slut I know you are so bent on becoming; this is how you iron your father's khaki pants so that they don't have a crease; this is how you grow okra—far from the house, because okra tree harbors red ants; when you are growing dasheen, make sure it gets plenty of water or else it makes your throat itch when you are eating it; this is how you sweep a corner; this is how you sweep a whole house; this is how you sweep a yard; this is how you smile to someone you don't like too much; this is how you set a table for dinner with an important guest; this is how you smile to someone you don't like at all; this is how you smile to someone you like completely; this is how you set a table for tea; this is how you set a table for dinner; this is how you set a table for lunch; this is how you set a table for breakfast; this is how to behave in the presence of men who don't know you very well, and this way they won't recognize immediately the slut I have warned you against becoming; be sure to wash every day, even if it is with your own spit; don't squat down to play marbles—you are not a boy, you know; don't pick people's flowers—you might catch something; don't throw stones at blackbirds, because it might not be a blackbird at all; this is how to make a bread pudding; this is how to make duokona;[2] this is how to make a pepper pot; this is how to make a good medicine for a cold; this is how to make a good medicine to throw away a child before it even becomes a child; this is how to catch a fish; this is how to throw back a fish you don't like, and that way something bad won't fall on you; this is how to bully a man; this is how a man bullies you; this is how to love a man, and if this doesn't work there are other ways, and if they don't work don't feel too bad about giving up; this is how to spit up in the air if you feel like it, and this is how to move quick so that it doesn't fall on you; this is how to make ends meet; always squeeze bread to make sure it's fresh; *but what if the baker won't let me feel the bread?;* you mean to say that after all you are really going to be the kind of woman who the baker won't let near the bread?

---

[1]**benna** Calypso music.   [2]**duokona** a spicy pudding made of plantains.

YOUR TURN

1. In a paragraph, identify the two characters whose voices we hear in this story. Explain what we know about them (their circumstances and their relationship). Cite specific evidence from the text. For example, what is the effect of the frequent repetition of "this is how"? Are there other words or phrases frequently repeated?
2. Try reading a section of "Girl" aloud in a rhythmical pattern, giving the principal and the second voices. Then reread the story, trying to incorporate this rhythm mentally into your reading. How does this rhythm contribute to the overall effect of the story? How does it compare to or contrast with speech rhythms that are familiar to you?

3

The Pleasures of Reading— and of Writing Arguments About Literature

"The pleasures of reading," a student may say, are obvious, "but when it comes to talking about the 'pleasures' of writing, surely you must be kidding." Students who make this reply have on their side the authority of a good many distinguished writers. To cite only three: Edna Ferber said that writing "is a combination of ditch-digging, mountain-climbing, treadmill, and childbirth"; Ernest Hemingway is reported to have said, "There is nothing to writing. All you do is sit down at a typewriter and bleed"; and in our own day the novelist William Styron said, "Let's face it, writing is hell."

Every student and every professor understands what these writers are talking about. The bad news is that they are talking about the difficult job of getting on to paper some coherent thoughts that they think are good enough to share with a reader. But there is good news too: All writers know that the very act of writing will stimulate *better* thoughts than those that they begin with. Writers— professionals as well as students—put words on paper with the understanding that the process of writing is a way of getting better ideas, a way of improving the nearly incoherent stuff that at first drifts through our minds.

- *A Common Misapprehension:* Students often think they are writing "for the teacher." Such an assumption leads to (1) miserable attempts to guess about what this mysterious figure has in mind, and (2) writing that ultimately satisfies neither the student nor the instructor.
- *The Facts:* You are, first of all, *writing for yourself;* you are trying to clarify something. The instructor may have set the problem—let's say (to take a famous example), "Is Hamlet mad or only pretending to be?"—or the problem may be one of your own choosing, possibly even so broad and so basic as "Why don't I care for this work?" In any event, you start looking again at the text, thinking, jotting down brief notes that come to mind, then perhaps commenting on these notes, perhaps amplifying them, perhaps almost immediately seeing that even though you wrote them only a few seconds ago you no longer agree with them. Again, you are writing in order, ultimately, to explain something *to yourself.*

• *The Results:* Finally, of course, you will revise your thoughts and offer them to the instructor and perhaps to your classmates, *in an effort to help readers to see things your way.* You have listened to yourself, quarreled with yourself, taught yourself something, arrived at a place where you think you at last have some clear and coherent ideas, and now you want to teach your readers.

The Open Secret of Good Writing

We have just said that in drafting your essay you have "quarreled with yourself." One of the great open secrets of decent writing is this: Good writers are good critics *of their own writing.* In words attributed to Truman Capote, "Writing is rewriting." When writers reread their own writing, they read in a skeptical spirit, arguing with themselves

• "Have I adequately supported this point?"
• "Have I considered all of the possible counter-evidence?"
• "Do I really want to say . . . ? Ought I to have said . . . ?"
• "Come to think of it, there aren't two reasons but three reasons why I think such-and-such,"

and so forth.

Your pleasure in writing will come chiefly from your awareness that you are *improving* your writing, getting better ideas than those that you had at the beginning. You will feel pleasure, too, in knowing that you are using words well—a pleasure of the sort we all experience when we read any work that we enjoy and admire, a work by an author who uses words skillfully. By the time you finish— although there is much to the saying that a writer doesn't finish a work, but rather just finally abandons it—you mentally say of your material, "Not at all bad." If, for instance, you are writing an analysis of a story, by the time that you abandon your essay you ought to think that you now have some neat ideas that were only half-formulated (at best) when you sat down to write your first draft.

After revising and revising again, you can reasonably feel that you have thought about an issue—for instance, about characterization in a short story— and, having argued with yourself in the process of revising your drafts, you now have come to some conclusions that you are willing to share with readers.

Let's look at a very short story, a contemporary version of a traditional Chinese story.

EMILY WU

The Lesson of the Master   [2005]

In fourteenth-century China a Buddhist monk named Tung-ming, who was also a painter, was fortunate in having a merchant who supported him by buying his ink-paintings. Tung-ming excelled in his art, a very difficult art because an Asian ink painting, unlike a Western oil painting, cannot be changed as the artist works on it. Once the brush touches the paper, the ink makes its mark, and it cannot be removed. The brushstroke cannot even be widened or lengthened because a knowledgeable observer will easily detect the change, the places where the first stroke was widened or extended or whatever; the painting's lack of grace and spontaneity will be evident. Part of the beauty of ink painting is that the viewer understands the difficulty, and appreciates the skill that is evident in each line.

Tung-ming excelled in paintings of plum branches, but one day the merchant, who was a wholesaler of fish, asked him if he would paint a carp. The monk assured the merchant that he would paint the picture, and he then departed. A week passed. Then two weeks. Then three weeks, and still there was no painting. It was not that the merchant and the monk did not meet. No, they met every few days because the merchant often invited the monk to dinner. And in the past the monk sometimes invited the merchant to have a cup of tea at the temple and to discuss matters of Buddhism, but he had not invited the merchant since the conversation about the carp.

After the second week the merchant began to fret: "Have I offended Tung-ming?" he wondered. "Might he think that I don't sufficiently appreciate his paintings of plum blossoms?" And: "Is it possible that he thinks it is vulgar of me to ask for a picture of a fish because I am a fish merchant?" And: "Could it be that he thinks, because I am a specialist in fish, I will notice that in fact his picture of a carp is not very good, that he can't catch the essence of its fishiness?" Day after day, week after week, month after month the merchant tormented himself with such thoughts.

Now that months had gone by, the merchant summoned up the courage to ask Tung-ming if they might not, for a change, meet at the temple and have a cup of tea. Tung-ming agreed.

On the appointed day they met in the monk's quarters, drank tea, talked about Buddhist matters and other things, and then the merchant—having noticed that brush, ink-cake, and paper were in view—nervously broached the subject of the picture of the carp. Tung-ming ground some fresh ink from an ink-cake, dipped the brush in the ink, stood over the paper, paused for five seconds (but the pause seemed like eternity to the merchant) and then, in another five seconds, with five strokes brushed a marvelous silvery-gray carp and handed the sheet to the merchant.

The merchant was beside himself with joy. When he recovered his composure, he hesitantly asked Tung-ming why, since the task was apparently so easy, he had not produced a picture months earlier. Tung-ming walked across the room, opened the door of a cabinet, and hundreds of sheets of paper—each with a picture of a carp—streamed to the floor.

Getting Ready to Write

We hope that this brief story gave you at least a little pleasure. When you come to write about a work of literature, it's not a bad idea to begin by thinking about *why* the work pleased you—or did not please you. In this instance, for example, you may have enjoyed the fact that

- the story has a moral (something along the lines of "Practice makes perfect"), and
- the moral is *not* stated explicitly.

Could it be that

- readers sometimes take pleasure in reading a work that offers a satisfying moral, but
- readers sometimes also take pleasure in *not* having a moral hammered home?

(We hasten to add that not all works of literature have morals; we will discuss this issue in a later chapter.)

You might have found, too, if you had been asked to write an analysis of Emily Wu's "The Lesson of the Master," that you would want to consider the following topics:

- *The title:* Although the title of a story may be the last thing the author writes, it is the first thing that the reader encounters, and it is therefore highly important. The story called "The Lesson of the Master" *might* have been called "A Very Short Story," or "Tung-ming's Fish" or "A Fishy Story" or "The Patron and the Painter" or "The Painter and the Patron" or "Easy When You Know How" or. . . . Consider the original title and the six alternate titles. Which do you think is the best? Why? Can you think of a title that is better than the original and the proposed alternatives? If so, state it and explain why you think it is better.
- *The plot:* It is probably fair to say that the ending of this small story comes as a surprise. But it is probably also fair to say that, as soon as the reader absorbs the surprise, he or she thinks, "Yes, this ending makes perfect sense. That's the way it ought to be." Some authors—notably O. Henry—are famous for their surprise endings, many of which are ingenious but seem arbitrary, unlikely, unconvincing—but on the whole serious literature does not give much weight to such surprises. This is not to say that surprise has no place in serious literature. The novelist E. M. Forster, in *Aspects of the Novel* (1927), has a shrewd comment on the importance of both fulfilling expectation and offering a slight surprise:

  > Shock, followed by the feeling, "oh, that's all right," is a sign that all is well with the plot: characters, to be real, ought to run smoothly, but a plot ought to cause surprise.

  The important point Forster is making is the "oh, that's all right." The plot causes a surprise, but upon reflection we realize that it makes sense, it is coherent, not tricky.
- *The characterization:* Suppose you were asked to characterize each of the two figures. Given this assignment, you would reread the story in preparation for jotting down (or keyboarding) some characteristics of each figure. On rereading, you might notice that although the author on several occasions takes her readers into the mind of the merchant (for example, "the merchant began to fret," "the merchant summoned up the courage to ask Tung-ming," "The merchant was beside himself with joy") but she never takes her readers into the mind of the painter. What do you make of this fact? Do you feel that you know the merchant but not the painter? Do you think the author should have told us more about the painter—for instance, more about his appearance or his mental processes?

A Student Writes: From Jottings to a Final Draft

Here, in fact, is what one reader made out of this third topic. The assignment was to analyze, in about 250 words, the characterization in the story. We begin with the student's jottings, including his later revisions of the jottings.

> Artist (Tung-ming)
>
> ~~historical figure? Does it matter???~~ Yes and no.
>
> specialist (plum pictures)—but can (with practice) paint other things
>
> says nothing; rude?? maybe just not talkative
>
> strong silent type?
>
> age? appearance? attitude toward merchant?
>
> Merchant (not named)
>
> rich (supports painter); ~~generous? may be for prestige?~~
> ~~nothing in story about family. Maybe lonely???~~
>
> Very worried about his request for picture. Insecure? Is the idea that
> the merchant is of lower class than the artist? But they socialize
> Equals?
>
> We keep hearing the merchant worrying, but we don't hear about the
> artist
>
> In fact, we don't really know anything about the artist, except
> that he is a great artist. Should we be told his thoughts?
> Would it spoil the story if we knew he needed time to
> practice?

The student's drafts are not available to us, but here is the final short essay, used with the student's permission.

Berger 1

Will Berger

Professor Cass

English 101A

30 June 2010

Less Is More: Characterization in

"The Lesson of the Master"

     There are two characters in Emily Wu's short story called "The Lesson of the Master," but only one of the two does any speaking or, so far as a reader is at first concerned, any thinking. The one who does the speaking and thinking is the merchant, who is not given a name. The fact that he is not given a name is itself a part of his characterization.

Berger 2

He talks and he worries, but so far as the writer goes he is a nobody. On the other hand the painter is given the dignity of having a name and thus (or at least by the end of the story) the reader understands that the painter is the more important person, the person with, so to speak, a powerful identity, a powerful individuality.

We are told that "the merchant began to fret," and that he wondered if the painter thought he (the merchant) was coarse. A little later we are told that "the merchant summoned up the courage" to ask the painter if they could meet, and when the painter finally paints the picture we are told that "The merchant was beside himself with joy." In short, we understand that the merchant is a person with ordinary feelings, feelings just like our own. Meanwhile, we have heard nothing at all about the painter's thoughts or emotions or words. The painter thus remains a mystery.

What the story gives to us is not the painter's ideas or emotions but his actions, and (as usual) actions speak louder than words, or, to use another cliche, one picture is worth a thousand words. When we have finished reading the story, we understand that the painter doesn't have to talk, and readers do not have to hear about his mental processes. Wu could have written something like "The painter realized that he would have to practice for a long time," but we get no such sentences. In fact, much of the strength of the story, a reader realizes when rereading the story, is in the fact that we know so little about the painter. By the end of the story we realize that if we are to characterize him, it will be as a person who keeps his thoughts to himself and whose actions are what counts. Of course he *does* have a personality, a character. We can say he is quiet, he apparently does not express his emotions, and so forth. But when we think about him, we chiefly think of his accomplishment.

Much of the pleasure of the story undoubtedly results from the surprise ending, but unlike most stories with surprise endings, this ending is not inconsistent with what has happened earlier in the story. That is, it makes perfect sense for the painter to be able to produce a great painting of a fish—after he has had time to practice. And we are just as glad that he didn't bother to tell the merchant that he was practicing. He is a somewhat mysterious figure and perhaps that's what most great artists are. Wu tells us less about the artist than she tells us about the merchant, but in the end we see that the artist is the more interesting figure.

The Student's Analysis Analyzed

Let's look, very briefly, at this short essay.

- **The title** is not simply "An Analysis of a Story." Rather, it is interesting ("Less Is More") and it is focused: It lets the readers know where they will be going ("Characterization"). When you write an essay, try to give it an interesting title and try to indicate the focus.
- **The opening paragraph** names the author whose work is discussed (i.e., the opening provides necessary information) and it makes an interesting assertion (the difference in the treatment of the two characters) at the very beginning. In short, it is interesting, not mere throat-clearing.
- **The second paragraph** deals with one character, the third paragraph with the other character. Conceivably the two characters could both have been discussed in one paragraph, but the division here is reasonable.
- **The final paragraph** generalizes a bit, asserting that although the artist is scarcely described he turns out to be the more interesting character. Note two other things about this final paragraph: (1) although it introduces a new point (the ending is surprising but not inconsistent), this point is closely connected to what has been said, so the paragraph does not leave the reader wondering where the writer is going, and (2) in the final sentence, the word "more" connects neatly with the title, thus helping to round off the essay. In short, the concluding paragraph is satisfying rather than boring (as a mere summary would be) or puzzling (as the introduction of a new issue might be).
- **The essay makes a point, has a thesis;** it is not a mere summary of the plot, and it is not a mere presentation of what other people have said.

Three Poems

Probably most people would agree that one of the pleasures of literature—stories, poems, plays—is that a work of literature reveals a new world to the reader. This new world may be as strange as the world offered by a work of science fiction, or it may seem as familiar—and yet still as fresh—as the world that Robert Frost offers in "Stopping by Woods on a Snowy Evening," which ends thus:

> The woods are lovely, dark and deep,
> But I have promises to keep,
> And miles to go before I sleep,
> And miles to go before I sleep.

(If you are not already familiar with this poem, please turn to pages 755–56 and read it.)

Consider, for instance, this poem in which the writer lets us hear the thoughts of a woman who lifts weights.

DIANE ACKERMAN

Poet, essayist, and naturalist, Diane Ackerman was born in Washington, Illinois, in 1948. The author of many works of nonfiction and poetry, she is perhaps best known for A Natural History of the Senses *(1990), an exploration in prose of the nature and meaning of the five senses.*

Pumping Iron [1985]

She doesn't want
the bunchy look
of male lifters:
torso an unyielding love-knot,
arms hard at mid-boil.   5
Doesn't want
the dancing bicepses
of pros.
Just to run her flesh
up the flagpole   10
of her body,
to pull her roaming flab
into tighter cascades,
machete a waist
through the jungle   15
of her hips,
a trim waist
two hands might grip
as a bouquet.

Doubtless most people who pump iron do so in order to improve their appearance, but each person has his or her own individual thoughts. Ackerman gets us into a very specific—and interesting—mind. She gives us the feel, so to speak, of the thoughts of her speaker. That's what most poems do. In Robert Frost's words, a poem embodies "the *act* of having an idea and how it feels to have an idea."

THEODORE ROETHKE

Theodore Roethke (1908–1963) was born in Saginaw, Michigan, and educated at the University of Michigan and Harvard. From 1947 until his death he taught at the University of Washington in Seattle, where he exerted considerable influence on the next generation of poets. Many of Roethke's best poems are lyrical memories of his childhood.

My Papa's Waltz [1948]

The whiskey on your breath
Could make a small boy dizzy;
but I hung on like death:
Such waltzing was not easy.   4

We romped until the pans
Slid from the kitchen shelf;
My mother's countenance
Could not unfrown itself.   8

The hand that held my wrist
Was battered on one knuckle;
At every step you missed
My right ear scraped a buckle.   12

You beat time on my head
With a palm caked hard by dirt,
Then waltzed me off to bed
Still clinging to your shirt.   16

YOUR TURN

1. Do the syntactical pauses vary much from stanza to stanza? Be specific. Would you say that the rhythm suggests lightness? Why?
2. Does the rhythm parallel or ironically contrast with the episode described? Was the dance a graceful waltz? Explain.
3. What would you say is the function of the stresses in lines 13–14?

WILLIAM BUTLER YEATS

William Butler Yeats (1865–1939) was born in Dublin, Ireland. The early Yeats was much interested in highly lyrical, romantic poetry, often drawing on Irish mythology. The later poems, from about 1910 (and especially after Yeats met Ezra Pound in 1911), are often more colloquial. Although these later poems often employ mythological references, too, one feels that the poems are more down-to-earth. He was awarded the Nobel Prize in Literature in 1923.

Yeats was 65 when he wrote this poem for Anne Gregory, the 19-year-old granddaughter of Lady Augusta Gregory, a woman whom Yeats had admired.

For Anne Gregory   [1930]

"Never shall a young man,
Thrown into despair
By those great honey-coloured
Ramparts at your ear
Love you for yourself alone   5
And not your yellow hair."

"But I can get a hair-dye
And set such colour there,
Brown, or black, or carrot,
That young men in despair   10
May love me for myself alone
And not my yellow hair."

"I heard an old religious man
But yesternight declare
That he had found a text to prove   15
That only God, my dear,
Could love you for yourself alone
And not your yellow hair."

YOUR TURN

1. What can you imagine Anne saying that provoked the poem?
2. In the first stanza Anne's hair is described both as "great honey-coloured ramparts" and as "yellow." Why does the speaker use these two rather different descriptions? Judging from the second stanza, how would Anne describe her hair?
3. If you did not know that Yeats was 65 when he wrote the poem, would you be able to deduce from the poem itself that the speaker of the first and third stanzas is considerably older than Anne?
4. Anne says that she wants to be loved "for myself alone." Exactly what do you think this expression means?
5. Why would "an old religious man" search until he found a text that would prove that only God could love her for herself alone? Do you think Yeats shares this view?
6. In a sentence or two characterize Yeats as he reveals himself in this poem and then characterize Anne.

Two Stories

KATHERINE MANSFIELD

Katherine Mansfield (1888-1923), née Kathleen Mansfield Beauchamp, was born in New Zealand. In 1902 she went to London for schooling; in 1906 she returned to New Zealand, but dissatisfied with its provincialism, she returned to London in 1908 to become a writer. After a disastrous marriage and a love affair, she went to Germany, where she wrote stories; in 1910 she returned to London, published a book of stories in 1911, and in 1912 met and began living with the writer John Middleton Murry. In 1918, after her first husband at last divorced her, she married Murry. She died of tuberculosis in 1923, a few months after her thirty-fourth birthday.

Mansfield published about seventy stories, and left some others unpublished. An early admirer of Chekhov, she read his works in German translations before they were translated into English.

Miss Brill   [1920]

Although it was so brilliantly fine—the blue sky powdered with gold and great spots of light like white wine splashed over the Jardins Publiques[1]—

---

[1]**Jardins Publiques** Public Gardens (French).

Miss Brill was glad that she had decided on her fur. The air was motionless, but when you opened your mouth there was just a faint chill, like a chill from a glass of iced water before you sip, and now and again a leaf came drifting—from nowhere, from the sky. Miss Brill put up her hand and touched her fur. Dear little thing! It was nice to feel it again. She had taken it out of its box that afternoon, shaken out the moth-powder, given it a good brush, and rubbed the life back into the dim little eyes. "What has been happening to me?" said the sad little eyes. Oh, how sweet it was to see them snap at her again from the red eiderdown! . . . But the nose, which was of some black composition, wasn't at all firm. It must have had a knock, somehow. Never mind—a little dab of black sealing-wax when the time came— when it was absolutely necessary. . . . Little rogue! Yes, she really felt like that about it. Little rogue biting its tail just by her left ear. She could have taken it off and laid it on her lap and stroked it. She felt a tingling in her hands and arms, but that came from walking, she supposed. And when she breathed, something light and sad—no, not sad, exactly—something gentle seemed to move in her bosom.

There were a number of people out this afternoon, far more than last Sunday. And the band sounded louder and gayer. That was because the Season had begun. For although the band played all year round on Sundays, out of season it was never the same. It was like some one playing with only the family to listen; it didn't care how it played if there weren't any strangers present. Wasn't the conductor wearing a new coat, too? She was sure it was new. He scraped with his foot and flapped his arms like a rooster about to crow, and the bandsmen sitting in the green rotunda blew out their cheeks and glared at the music. Now there came a little "flutey" bit—very pretty!—a little chain of bright drops. She was sure it would be repeated. It was; she lifted her head and smiled.

Only two people shared her "special" seat: a fine old man in a velvet coat, his hands clasped over a huge carved walking-stick, and a big old woman, sitting upright, with a roll of knitting on her embroidered apron. They did not speak. This was disappointing, for Miss Brill always looked forward to the conversation. She had become really quite expert, she thought, at listening as though she didn't listen, at sitting in other people's lives just for a minute while they talked round her.

She glanced, sideways, at the old couple. Perhaps they would go soon. Last Sunday, too, hadn't been as interesting as usual. An Englishman and his wife, he wearing a dreadful Panama hat and she button boots. And she'd gone on the whole time about how she ought to wear spectacles; she knew she needed them; but that it was no good getting any; they'd be sure to break and they'd never keep on. And he'd been so patient. He'd suggested everything—gold rims, the kind that curved round your ears, little pads inside the bridge. No, nothing would please her. "They'll always be sliding down my nose!" Miss Brill had wanted to shake her.

5   The old people sat on the bench, still as statues. Never mind, there was always the crowd to watch. To and fro, in front of the flower-beds and the band rotunda, the couples and groups paraded, stopped to talk, to greet, to buy a handful of flowers from the old beggar who had his tray fixed to the railings. Little children ran among them, swooping and laughing; little boys with big white silk bows under their chins, little girls, little French dolls, dressed up in velvet and lace. And sometimes a tiny staggerer came suddenly

rocking into the open from under the trees, stopped, stared, as suddenly sat down "flop," until its small high-stepping mother, like a young hen, rushed scolding to its rescue. Other people sat on the benches and green chairs, but they were nearly always the same, Sunday after Sunday, and—Miss Brill had often noticed—there was something funny about nearly all of them. They were odd, silent, nearly all old, and from the way they stared they looked as though they'd just come from dark little rooms or even—even cupboards!

Behind the rotunda the slender trees with yellow leaves down drooping, and through them just a line of sea, and beyond the blue sky with gold-veined clouds.

Tum-tum-tum tiddle-um! tiddle-um! tum tiddley-um tum ta! blew the band.

Two young girls in red came by and two young soldiers in blue met them, and they laughed and paired and went off arm-in-arm. Two peasant women with funny straw hats passed, gravely, leading beautiful smoke-colored donkeys. A cold, pale nun hurried by. A beautiful woman came along and dropped her bunch of violets, and a little boy ran after to hand them to her, and she took them and threw them away as if they'd been poisoned. Dear me! Miss Brill didn't know whether to admire that or not! And now an ermine toque[2] and a gentleman in grey met just in front of her. He was tall, stiff, dignified, and she was wearing the ermine toque she'd bought when her hair was yellow. Now everything, her hair, her face, even her eyes, was the same color as the shabby ermine, and her hand, in its cleaned glove, lifted to dab her lips, was a tiny yellowish paw. Oh, she was so pleased to see him—delighted! She rather thought they were going to meet that afternoon. She described where she'd been—everywhere, here, there, along by the sea. The day was so charming—didn't he agree? And wouldn't he, perhaps? . . . But he shook his head, lighted a cigarette, slowly breathed a great deep puff into her face, and, even while she was still talking and laughing, flicked the match away and walked on. The ermine toque was alone; she smiled more brightly than ever. But even the band seemed to know what she was feeling and played more softly, played tenderly, and the drum beat, "The Brute! The Brute!" over and over. What would she do? What was going to happen now? But as Miss Brill wondered, the ermine toque turned, raised her hand as though she'd seen some one else, much nicer, just over there, and pattered away. And the band changed again and played more quickly, more gaily than ever, and the old couple on Miss Brill's seat got up and marched away, and such a funny old man with long whiskers hobbled along in time to the music and was nearly knocked over by four girls walking abreast.

Oh, how fascinating it was! How she enjoyed it! How she loved sitting here, watching it all! It was like a play. It was exactly like a play. Who could believe the sky at the back wasn't painted? But it wasn't till a little brown dog trotted on solemn and then slowly trotted off, like a little "theatre" dog, a little dog that had been drugged, that Miss Brill discovered what it was that made it so exciting. They were all on the stage. They weren't only the audience, not only looking on; they were acting. Even she had a part and came every Sunday. No doubt somebody would have noticed if she hadn't been there; she was part of the performance after all. How strange she'd never thought of it like that before! And yet it explained why she made such a

---

[2] **toque** a brimless, close-fitting woman's hat.

point of starting from home at just the same time each week—so as not to be late for the performance—and it also explained why she had quite a queer, shy feeling at telling her English pupils how she spent her Sunday afternoons. No wonder! Miss Brill nearly laughed out loud. She was on the stage. She thought of the old invalid gentleman to whom she read the newspaper four afternoons a week while he slept in the garden. She had got quite used to the frail head on the cotton pillow, the hollowed eyes, the open mouth and the high pinched nose. If he'd been dead she mightn't have noticed for weeks; she wouldn't have minded. But suddenly he knew he was having the paper read to him by an actress! "An actress!" The old head lifted; two points of light quivered in the old eyes. "An actress—are ye?" And Miss Brill smoothed the newspaper as though it were the manuscript of her part and said gently: "Yes, I have been an actress for a long time."

10   The band had been having a rest. Now they started again. And what they played was warm, sunny, yet there was just a faint chill—a something, what was it?—not sadness—no, not sadness—a something that made you want to sing. The tune lifted, lifted, the light shone; and it seemed to Miss Brill that in another moment all of them, all the whole company, would begin singing. The young ones, the laughing ones who were moving together, they would begin, and the men's voices, very resolute and brave, would join them. And then she too, she too, and the others on the benches—they would come in with a kind of accompaniment—something low, that scarcely rose or fell, something so beautiful—moving. . . . And Miss Brill's eyes filled with tears and she looked smiling at all the other members of the company. Yes, we understand, we understand, she thought—though what they understood she didn't know.

Just at that moment a boy and a girl came and sat down where the old couple had been. They were beautifully dressed; they were in love. The hero and heroine, of course, just arrived from his father's yacht. And still soundlessly singing, still with that trembling smile, Miss Brill prepared to listen.

"No, not now," said the girl. "Not here, I can't."

"But why? Because of that stupid old thing at the end there?" asked the boy. "Why does she come here at all—who wants her? Why doesn't she keep her silly old mug at home?"

"It's her fu-fur which is so funny," giggled the girl. "It's exactly like a fried whiting."[3]

15   "Ah, be off with you!" said the boy in an angry whisper. Then: "Tell me, my petite chère[4]—"

"No, not here," said the girl. "Not *yet*."

On her way home she usually bought a slice of honey-cake at the baker's. It was her Sunday treat. Sometimes there was an almond in her slice, sometimes not. It made a great difference. If there was an almond it was like carrying home a tiny present—a surprise—something that might very well not have been there. She hurried on the almond Sundays and struck the match for the kettle in quite a dashing way.

But today she passed the baker's by, climbed the stairs, went into the little dark room—her room like a cupboard—and sat down on the red eiderdown. She sat there for a long time. The box that the fur came out of was on

---

[3]**whiting** a kind of fish.   [4]**petite chère** darling.

the bed. She unclasped the necklet quickly; quickly, without looking, laid it inside. But when she put the lid on she thought she heard something crying.

YOUR TURN

1. Why do you think Mansfield did not give Miss Brill a first name?
2. What would be lost (or gained?) if the first paragraph were omitted?
3. Suppose someone said that the story is about a woman who is justly punished for her pride. What might be your response?

TONI CADE BAMBARA

Toni Cade Bambara (1939–1995), an African American writer, was born in New York City and grew up in black districts of the city. After studying at the University of Florence and at City College in New York, where she received a master's degree, she worked for a while as a case investigator for the New York State Welfare Department. Later she directed a recreation program for hospital patients. Once her literary reputation was established, she spent most of her time writing, though she also served as writer in residence at Spelman College in Atlanta. Perhaps the best of Bambara's books are Gorilla, My Love *(1972), a collection of stories, and* The Salt Eaters *(1980), a novel.*

The Lesson   [1972]

Back in the days when everyone was old and stupid or young and foolish and me and Sugar were the only ones just right, this lady moved on our block with nappy hair and proper speech and no makeup. And quite naturally we laughed at her, laughed the way we did at the junk man who went about his business like he was some big-time president and his sorry-ass horse his secretary. And we kinda hated her too, hated the way we did the winos who cluttered up our parks and pissed on our handball walls and stank up our hallways and stairs so you couldn't halfway play hide-and-seek without a goddam gas mask. Miss Moore was her name. The only woman on the block with no first name. And she was black as hell, cept for her feet, which were fish-white and spooky. And she was always planning these boring-ass things for us to do, us being my cousin, mostly, who lived on the block cause we all moved North the same time and to the same apartment then spread out gradual to breathe. And our parents would yank our heads into some kinda shape and crisp up our clothes so we'd be presentable for travel with Miss Moore, who always looked like she was going to church, though she never did. Which is just one of the things the grownups talked about when they talked behind her back like a dog. But when she came calling with some sachet she'd sewed up or some gingerbread she'd made or some book, why then they'd all be too embarrassed to turn her down and we'd get handed over all spruced up. She'd been to college and said it was only right that she should take responsibility for the young ones' education, and she not even related by marriage or blood. So they'd go for it. Specially Aunt Gretchen. She was the main gofer in the family. You got some old dumb shit foolishness you want somebody to go for, you send for Aunt Gretchen. She been screwed into the go-along for so long, it's a blood-deep natural thing with her. Which is how she got saddled with me and Sugar and Junior in the first place while our mothers were in la-de-da apartment up the block having a good ole time.

So this one day Miss Moore rounds us all up at the mailbox and it's puredee hot and she's knockin herself out about arithmetic. And school suppose to let up in summer I heard, but she don't never let up. And the starch in my pinafore scratching the shit outta me and I'm really hating this nappy-head bitch and her goddam college degree. I'd much rather go to the pool or to the show where it's cool. So me and Sugar leaning on the mailbox being surly, which is a Miss Moore word. And Flyboy checking out what everybody brought for lunch. And Fat Butt already wasting his peanut-butter-and-jelly sandwich like the pig he is. And Junebug punchin on Q.T.'s arm for potato chips. And Rosie Giraffe shifting from one hip to the other wait-ing for somebody to step on her foot or ask her if she from Georgia so she can kick ass, preferably Mercedes'. And Miss Moore asking us do we know what money is, like we a bunch of retards. I mean real money, she say, like it's only poker chips or monopoly papers we lay on the grocer. So right away I'm tired of this and say so. And would much rather snatch Sugar and go to the Sunset and terrorize the West Indian kids and take their hair ribbons and their money too. And Miss Moore files that remark away for next week's les-son on brotherhood, I can tell. And finally I say we oughta get to the subway cause it's cooler and besides we might meet some cute boys. Sugar done swiped her mama's lipstick, so we ready.

So we heading down the street and she's boring us silly about what things cost and what our parents make and how much goes for rent and how money ain't divided up right in this country. And then she gets to the part about we all poor and live in the slums, which I don't feature. And I'm ready to speak on that, but she steps out in the street and hails two cabs just like that. Then she hustles half the crew in with her and hands me a five-dollar bill and tells me to calculate 10 percent tip for the driver. And we're off. Me and Sugar and Junebug and Flyboy hangin out the window and hollering to everybody, putting lipstick on each other cause Flyboy a faggot anyway, and making farts with our sweaty armpits. But I'm mostly trying to figure how to spend this money. But they all fascinated with the meter ticking and Junebug starts laying bets as to how much it'll read when Flyboy can't hold his breath no more. Then Sugar lays bets as to how much it'll be when we get there. So I'm stuck. Don't nobody want to go for my plan, which is to jump out at the next light and run off to the first bar-b-que we can find. Then the driver tells us to get the hell out cause we there already. And the meter reads eighty-five cents. And I'm stalling to figure out the tip and Sugar say give him a dime. And I decide he don't need it bad as I do, so later for him. But then he tries to take off with Junebug foot still in the door so we talk about his mama something ferocious. Then we check out that we on Fifth Avenue and everybody dressed up in stockings. One lady in a fur coat, hot as it is. White folks crazy.

"This is the place," Miss Moore say, presenting it to us in the voice she uses at the museum. "Let's look in the windows before we go in."

5   "Can we steal?" Sugar asks very serious like she's getting the ground rules squared away before she plays. "I beg your pardon," say Miss Moore, and

we fall out. So she leads us around the windows of the toy store and me and Sugar screamin, "This is mine, that's mine. I gotta have that, that was made for me. I was born for that," till Big Butt drowns us out.

"Hey, I'm going to buy that there."

"That there? You don't even know what it is, stupid."

"I do so," he say punchin on Rosie Giraffe. "It's a microscope."

"Whatcha gonna do with a microscope, fool?"

10   "Look at things."

"Like what, Ronald?" ask Miss Moore. And Big Butt ain't got the first notion. So here go Miss Moore gabbing about the thousands of bacteria in a drop of water and the somethinorother in a speck of blood and the million and one living things in the air around us is invisible to the naked eye. And what she say that for? Junebug go to town on that "naked" and we rolling. Then Miss Moore ask what it cost. So we all jam into the window smudgin it up and the price tag say $300. So then she ask how long'd take for Big Butt and Junebug to save up their allowances. "Too long," I say. "Yeh," adds Sugar, "outgrown it by that time." And Miss Moore say no, you never outgrow learning instruments. "Why, even medical students and interns and," blah, blah, blah. And we ready to choke Big Butt for bringing it up in the first damn place.

"This here cost four hundred eighty dollars," say Rosie Giraffe. So we pile up all over her to see what she pointin out. My eyes tell me it's a chunk of glass cracked with something heavy, and different-color inks dripped into the spits, then the whole thing put into a oven or something. But for $480 it don't make sense.

"That's a paperweight made of semi-precious stones fused together under tremendous pressure," she explains slowly, with her hands doing the mining and all the factory work.

"So what's a paperweight?" asks Rosie Giraffe.

15   "To weight paper with, dumbbell," say Flyboy, the wise man from the East.

"Not exactly," say Miss Moore, which is what she say when you warm or way off too. "It's to weigh paper down so it won't scatter and make your desk untidy." So right away me and Sugar curtsy to each other and then to Mercedes who is more the tidy type.

"We don't keep paper on top of the desk in my class," say Junebug, figuring Miss Moore crazy or lyin one.

"At home, then," she say. "Don't you have a calendar and a pencil case and a blotter and a letter-opener on your desk at home where you do your homework?" And she know damn well what our homes look like cause she nosys around in them every chance she gets.

"I don't even have a desk," say Junebug. "Do we?"

20   "No. And I don't get no homework neither," says Big Butt.

"And I don't even have a home," say Flyboy, like he do at school to keep the white folks off his back and sorry for him. Send this poor kid to camp posters, is his specialty.

"I do," says Mercedes. "I have a box of stationery on my desk and a picture of my cat. My godmother bought the stationery and the desk. There's a big rose on each sheet and the envelopes smell like roses."

"Who wants to know about your smelly-ass stationery," say Rosie Giraffe fore I can get my two cents in.

"It's important to have a work area all your own so that . . . ."

25   "Will you look at this sailboat, please," say Flyboy, cuttin her off and pointin to the thing like it was his. So once again we tumble all over each other to gaze at this magnificent thing in the toy store which is just big enough to maybe sail two kittens across the pond if you strap them to the posts tight. We all start reciting the price tag like we in assembly. "Handcrafted sailboat of fiberglass at one thousand one hundred ninety-five dollars."

"Unbelievable," I hear myself say and am really stunned. I read it again for myself just in case the group recitation put me in a trance. Same thing. For some reason this pisses me off. We look at Miss Moore and she lookin at us, waiting for I dunno what.

"Who'd pay all that when you can buy a sailboat set for a quarter at Pop's, a tube of glue for a dime, and a ball of string for eight cents? It must have a motor and a whole lot else besides," I say. "My sailboat cost me about fifty cents."

"But will it take water?" say Mercedes with her smart ass.

"Took mine to Alley Pond Park once," say Flyboy. "String broke. Lost it. Pity."

30   "Sailed mine in Central Park and it keeled over and sank. Had to ask my father for another dollar."

"And you got the strap," laugh Big Butt. "The jerk didn't even have a string on it. My old man wailed on his behind."

Little Q.T. was staring hard at the sailboat and you could see he wanted it bad. But he too little and somebody'd just take it from him. So what the hell. "This boat for kids, Miss Moore?"

"Parents silly to buy something like that just to get all broke up," say Rosie Giraffe.

"That much money it should last forever," I figure.

35   "My father'd buy it for me if I wanted it."

"Your father, my ass," say Rosie Giraffe getting a chance to finally push Mercedes.

"Must be rich people shop here," say Q.T.

"You are a very bright boy," say Flyboy. "What was your first clue?" And he rap him on the head with the back of his knuckles, since Q.T. the only one he could get away with. Though Q.T. liable to come up behind you years later and get his licks in when you half expect it.

"What I want to know is," I says to Miss Moore though I never talk to her, I wouldn't give the bitch that satisfaction, "is how much a real boat costs? I figure a thousand'd get you a yacht any day."

40   "Why don't you check that out," she says, "and report back to the group?" Which really pains my ass. If you gonna mess up a perfectly good swim day least you could do is have some answers. "Let's go in," she say like she got something up her sleeve. Only she don't lead the way. So me and Sugar turn the corner to where the entrance is, but when we get there I kinda hang back. Not that I'm scared, what's there to be afraid of, just a toy store. But I feel funny, shame. But what I got to be shamed about? Got as much right to go in as anybody. But somehow I can't seem to get hold of the door, so I step away for Sugar to lead. But she hangs back too. And I look at her and she looks at me and this is ridiculous. I mean, damn, I have never ever been shy about doing nothing or going nowhere. But then Mercedes steps up and then Rosie Giraffe and Big Butt crowd in behind and shove, and next thing we all stuffed into the doorway with only Mercedes squeezing past us, smoothing

out her jumper and walking right down the aisle. Then the rest of us tumble in like a glued-together jigsaw done all wrong. And people lookin at us. And it's like the time me and Sugar crashed into the Catholic church on a dare. But once we got in there and everything so hushed and holy and the candles and the bowin and the handkerchiefs on all the drooping heads, I just couldn't go through with the plan. Which was for me to run up to the altar and do a tap dance while Sugar played the nose flute and messed around in the holy water. And Sugar kept giving me the elbow. Then later teased me so bad I tied her up in the shower and turned it on and locked her in. And she'd be there till this day if Aunt Gretchen hadn't finally figured I was lying about the boarder takin a shower.

Same thing in the store. We all walkin on tiptoe and hardly touchin the games and puzzles and things. And I watched Miss Moore who is steady watchin us like she waiting for a sign. Like Mama Drewery watches the sky and sniffs the air and takes note of just how much slant is in the bird forma-tion. Then me and Sugar bump smack into each other, so busy gazing at the toys, 'specially the sailboat. But we don't laugh and go into our fat-lady bump-stomach routine. We just stare at that price tag. Then Sugar run a fin-ger over the whole boat. And I'm jealous and want to hit her. Maybe not her, but I sure want to punch somebody in the mouth.

"Watcha bring us here for, Miss Moore?"

"You sound angry, Sylvia. Are you mad about something?" Givin me one of them grins like she tellin a grown-up joke that never turns out to be funny. And she's looking very closely at me like maybe she plannin to do my portrait from memory. I'm mad, but I won't give her the satisfaction. So I slouch around the store being very bored and say, "Let's go."

Me and Sugar at the back of the train watchin the tracks whizzin by large then small then gettin gobbled up in the dark. I'm thinkin about this tricky toy I saw in the store. A clown that somersaults on a bar then does chin-ups just cause you yank lightly at his leg. Cost $35. I could see me askin my mother for a $35 birthday clown. "You wanna who that costs what?" she'd say, cocking her head to the side to get a better view of the hole in my head. Thirty-five dollars could buy new bunk beds for Junior and Gretchen's boy. Thirty-five dollars and the whole household could go visit Granddaddy Nelson in the country. Thirty-five dollars would pay for the rent and the piano bill too. Who are these people that spend that much for performing clowns and $1000 for toy sailboats? What kinda work they do and how they live and how come we ain't in on it? Where we are is who we are, Miss Moore always pointin out. But it don't necessarily have to be that way, she always adds then waits for somebody to say that poor people have to wake up and demand their share of the pie and don't none of us know what kind of pie she talkin about in the first damn place. But she ain't so smart cause I still got her four dollars from the taxi and she sure ain't getting it. Messin up my day with this shit. Sugar nudges me in my pocket and winks.

45   Miss Moore lines us up in front of the mailbox where we started from, seem like years ago, and I got a headache for thinkin so hard. And we lean all over each other so we can hold up under the draggy-ass lecture she always finishes off with at the end before we thank her for borin us to tears. But she just looks at us like she readin tea leaves. Finally she say, "Well, what did you think of F.A.O. Schwarz?"

Rosie Giraffe mumbles, "White folks crazy."

"I'd like to go there again when I get my birthday money," says Mercedes, and we shove her out the pack so she has to lean on the mailbox by herself.

"I'd like a shower. Tiring day," say Flyboy.

Then Sugar surprises me by saying, "You know, Miss Moore, I don't think all of us here put together eat in a year what that sailboat costs." And Miss Moore lights up like somebody goosed her. "And?" she say, urging Sugar on. Only I'm standin on her foot so she don't continue.

50   "Imagine for a minute what kind of society it is in which some people can spend on a toy what it would cost to feed a family of six or seven. What do you think?"

"I think," say Sugar pushing me off her feet like she never done before, cause I whip her ass in a minute, "that this is not much of a democracy if you ask me. Equal chance to pursue happiness means an equal crack at the dough, don't it?" Miss Moore is beside herself and I am disgusted with Sugar's treachery. So I stand on her foot one more time to see if she'll shove me. She shuts up, and Miss Moore looks at me, sorrowfully I'm thinkin. And somethin weird is goin on, I can feel it in my chest.

"Anybody else learn anything today?" lookin dead at me. I walk away and Sugar has to run to catch up and don't even seem to notice when I shrug her arm off my shoulder.

"Well, we got four dollars anyway," she says.

"Uh hunh."

55   "We could go to Hascombs and get half a chocolate layer and then go to the Sunset and still have plenty of money for potato chips and ice cream sodas."

"Un hunh."

"Race you to Hascombs," she say.

We start down the block and she gets ahead which is O.K. by me cause I'm going to the West End and then over to the Drive to think this day through. She can run if she want to and even run faster. But ain't nobody gonna beat me at nuthin.

YOUR TURN

1. What is "the lesson" that Miss Moore is trying to teach the children? How much, if any, of this lesson does Sylvia learn? Point to specific passages to support your answers.
2. Since Miss Moore intends the lesson for the children's own good, why is Sylvia so resistant to it, so impatient and exasperated?
3. Toward the end of the story, Sylvia says that she is "disgusted with Sugar's treachery." Describe their relationship. What would be missing from the story if Bambara had not included Sugar among its characters?

4

More About Writing About Literature: From Idea to Essay

Why Write Arguments About Literature?

If you have ever put exclamation points or questions marks or brief annotations ("this is ridiculous," or "great!") in the margins of your books, you are aware of the *pleasure* one gets from putting responses into writing. But people also write about literature—not only in margins of books but, let's say, in notebooks or journals and ultimately in essays—in order to clarify and account for their responses to works that interest or excite or frustrate them.

In putting words on paper you will have to take a second and a third look at what is in front of you and what is within you. Writing, then, is not only a way of expressing pleasure but also a way of *learning*. The last word about complex thoughts and feelings is never said, but when we write we hope to make at least a little progress in the difficult but rewarding job of talking about our responses. We learn, and then we hope to interest our readers because we are communicating to them our responses to something that for one reason or another is worth talking about.

This communication is, in effect, teaching. You may think that you are writing for the teacher, but that is a misconception; when you write, *you* are the teacher, offering an argument. An essay on literature is an attempt to help someone see the work as you see it. If this chapter had to be boiled down to a single sentence, that sentence would be: Because you are teaching, your essay should embody those qualities that you value in teachers—intelligence, open-mindedness, effort, a desire to offer what help one can.

Getting Ideas: Prewriting

"All there is to writing," Robert Frost said, "is having ideas. To learn to write is to learn to have ideas." But how does one "learn to have ideas"? What can one do *before* writing? Among the activities are these: reading with a pen or pencil in hand, so that you can annotate the text; keeping a journal, in which you jot down reflections about your reading; talking with others (including your instructor) about the reading. Let's look at the first of these, annotating.

Annotating a Text

When reading a book that you own, don't hesitate to mark it up, indicating (by highlighting or underlining or by making marginal notes) what puzzles you, what pleases or interests you, and what displeases or bores you. Later, of course, you'll want to think further about these responses, asking yourself, on reread- ing, if you still feel that way, and if not, why not, but these first responses will get you started.

One kind of annotation is a question mark in the margin, jotted down in order to indicate your uncertainty about the meaning of a word. It's a good idea to keep a *dictionary* nearby while you are reading. Of course you won't look up every word that you are unsure about—this might spoil the fun of reading—but sometimes you will sense that you need to know the precise meanings and im- plications of the writer's words in order to feel and appreciate the effects he or she is trying to create. And the more you become aware of how richly meaning- ful the words can be in a literary text, the more sensitive and self-aware you will be about the words you use in your own prose.

We have already looked at Pat Mora's short poem "Immigrants" (page 26), but here it is again, with a student's first annotations.

unusual to use title as first word?

Immigrants

wrap their babies in the American flag,   *so what's wrong with hot dogs*
feed them mashed hot dogs and apple pie, *— and apple pie?*
name them Bill and Daisy,
buy them (blonde) dolls that blink (blue)   *Anglo types—not*
eyes or a football and tiny cleats   *Asian American*   5
before the baby can even walk,   *or Latino types*
speak to them in thick English, (hallo, babee, hallo,)
whisper in Spanish or Polish

do only immigrants show a "parent fear"? Don't all parents fear for their children?

when the babies sleep, whisper   *Is Mora*
in a dark parent bed, that dark   *making fun of* 10
(parent fear,) "Will they like   *immigrants?*
our boy, our girl, our fine (a)merican
boy, our fine (a)merican girl?"   *why not a capital letter?*

Notice that most of these annotations are questions that the student is asking herself. Asking questions is an excellent way to get yourself thinking. We will re- turn to this method shortly.

Brainstorming to Get Ideas for Writing

Unlike annotating, which consists of making brief notes and small marks on the printed page, "brainstorming"—the free jotting down of ideas—asks that you jot down at length whatever comes to mind, without inhibition. But before we talk further about brainstorming, read the following short story.

KATE CHOPIN

Kate Chopin (1851-1904)—the name is pronounced in the French way, somewhat like "show pan"—was born in St. Louis, with the name Katherine O'Flaherty. Her father was an immigrant from Ireland, and her mother was descended from an old Creole family. (In the United States, a Creole is a person descended from the original French settlers in Louisiana or the original Spanish settlers in the Gulf States.) At the age of nineteen she married Oscar Chopin, a cotton broker in New Orleans. They had six children, and though Kate Chopin had contemplated a literary career, she did not turn seriously to writing until after her husband's death in 1883. Most of her fiction concerns the lives of the descendants of the French who had settled in Louisiana.

The Story of an Hour

[1894]

Knowing that Mrs. Mallard was afflicted with a heart trouble, great care was taken to break to her as gently as possible the news of her husband's death.

It was her sister Josephine who told her, in broken sentences, veiled hints that revealed in half concealing. Her husband's friend Richards was there, too, near her. It was he who had been in the newspaper office when intelligence of the railroad disaster was received, with Brently Mallard's name leading the list of "killed." He had only taken the time to assure himself of its truth by a second telegram, and had hastened to forestall any less careful, less tender friend in bearing the sad message.

She did not hear the story as many women have heard the same, with a paralyzed inability to accept its significance. She wept at once, with sudden, wild abandonment, in her sister's arms. When the storm of grief had spent itself she went away to her room alone. She would have no one follow her.

There stood, facing the open window, a comfortable, roomy armchair. Into this she sank, pressed down by a physical exhaustion that haunted her body and seemed to reach into her soul.

5   She could see in the open square before her house the tops of trees that were all aquiver with the new spring life. The delicious breath of rain was in the air. In the street below a peddler was crying his wares. The notes of a distant song which some one was singing reached her faintly, and countless sparrows were twittering in the eaves.

There were patches of blue sky showing here and there through the clouds that had met and piled one above the other in the west facing her window. She sat with her head thrown back upon the cushion of the chair quite motionless, except when a sob came up into her throat and shook her, as a child who has cried itself to sleep continues to sob in its dreams.

She was young, with a fair, calm face, whose lines bespoke repression and even a certain strength. But now there was a dull stare in her eyes, whose gaze was fixed away off yonder on one of those patches of blue sky. It was not a glance of reflection, but rather indicated a suspension of intelligent thought.

There was something coming to her and she was waiting for it, fearfully. What was it? She did not know; it was too subtle and elusive to name. But she felt it, creeping out of the sky, reaching toward her through the sounds, the scents, the color that filled the air.

Now her bosom rose and fell tumultuously. She was beginning to recognize this thing that was approaching to possess her, and she was striving to beat it back with her will—as powerless as her two white slender hands would have been.

10   When she abandoned herself a little whispered word escaped her slightly parted lips. She said it over and over under her breath: "Free, free, free!" The vacant stare and the look of terror that had followed it went from her eyes. They stayed keen and bright. Her pulses beat fast, and the coursing blood warmed and relaxed every inch of her body.

She did not stop to ask if it were not a monstrous joy that held her. A clear and exalted perception enabled her to dismiss the suggestion as trivial.

She knew that she would weep again when she saw the kind, tender hands folded in death; the face that had never looked save with love upon her, fixed and gray and dead. But she saw beyond that bitter moment a long procession of years to come that would belong to her absolutely. And she opened and spread her arms out to them in welcome.

There would be no one to live for her during those coming years; she would live for herself. There would be no powerful will bending her in that blind persistence with which men and women believe they have a right to impose a private will upon a fellow creature. A kind intention or a cruel intention made the act seem no less a crime as she looked upon it in that brief moment of illumination.

And yet she had loved him—sometimes. Often she had not. What did it matter! What could love, the unsolved mystery, count for in face of this possession of self-assertion which she suddenly recognized as the strongest impulse of her being.

15   "Free! Body and soul free!" she kept whispering.

Josephine was kneeling before the closed door with her lips to the keyhole, imploring for admission. "Louise, open the door! I beg; open the door— you will make yourself ill. What are you doing, Louise? For heaven's sake open the door."

"Go away. I am not making myself ill." No; she was drinking in a very elixir of life through that open window.

Her fancy was running riot along those days ahead of her. Spring days, and summer days, and all sorts of days that would be her own. She breathed a quick prayer that life might be long. It was only yesterday she had thought with a shudder that life might be long.

She arose at length and opened the door to her sister's importunities. There was a feverish triumph in her eyes, and she carried herself unwittingly like a goddess of Victory. She clasped her sister's waist, and together they descended the stairs. Richards stood waiting for them at the bottom.

20   Some one was opening the front door with a latchkey. It was Brently Mallard who entered, a little travel-stained, composedly carrying his gripsack and umbrella. He had been far from the scene of accident, and did not even know there had been one. He stood amazed at Josephine's piercing cry; at Richards' quick motion to screen him from the view of his wife.

But Richards was too late.

When the doctors came they said she had died of heart disease—of joy that kills.

When brainstorming, don't worry about spelling, about writing complete sentences, or about unifying your thoughts; just let one thought lead to another. Later you can review your jottings, deleting some, connecting with arrows others that are related, expanding still others, but for now you want to get going, and so there is no reason to look back. Thus you might jot down something about the title.

> Title speaks of an hour, and story covers an hour, but maybe takes five minutes to read

And then, perhaps prompted by "an hour," you might happen to add something to this effect:

> Doubt that a woman who got news of the death of her husband could move from grief to joy within an hour

Your next jotting might have little or nothing to do with this issue; it might simply say:

> Enjoyed "Hour" especially because "Hour" is so shocking

And then you might ask yourself:

> By shocking, do I mean "improbable," or what? Come to think of it, maybe it's not so improbable. A lot depends on what the marriage was like.

Focused Freewriting

Focused, or directed, freewriting is a method related to brainstorming that some writers use to uncover ideas they may want to write about. Concentrating on one issue—for instance, a question that strikes them as worth puzzling over (What kind of person is Mrs. Mallard?)—they write at length, nonstop, for perhaps 5 or 10 minutes.

Writers who find freewriting helpful put down everything they can think of that has bearing on the one issue or question they are examining. They do not stop at this stage to evaluate the results, and they do not worry about niceties of sentence structure or of spelling. They just pour out their ideas in a steady stream of writing, drawing on whatever associations come to mind. If they pause in their writing, it is only to refer to the text, to search for more detail—perhaps a quotation—that will help them answer their question.

After the freewriting session, these writers usually go back and reread what they have written, highlighting or underlining what seems to be of value. Of course they find much that is of little or no use, but they also usually find that some strong ideas have surfaced and have received some development. At this point the writers are often able to make a scratch outline and then begin a draft.

Here is an example of one student's focused freewriting, again on Chopin's "The Story of an Hour."

> What do I know about Mrs. Mallard? Let me put everything down here I know about her or can figure out from what Kate Chopin tells me. When she finds herself alone after the death of her husband, she says, "Free! Body and

soul free!" and before that she said, "Free, free, free!" Three times. So she has suddenly perceived that she has not been free: she has been under the influence of a "powerful will." In this case it has been her husband, but she says no one, man nor woman, should impose their will on anyone else. So it's not a feminist issue—it's a power issue. No one should push anyone else around is what I guess Chopin means, force someone to do what the other person wants. I used to have a friend that did that to me all the time; he had to run everything. They say that fathers—before the women's movement—used to run things, with the father in charge of all the decisions, so maybe this is an honest reaction to having been pushed around by a husband. I think Mrs. Mallard is a believable character, even if the plot is not all that believable—all those things happening in such quick succession.

Listing and Clustering

In your preliminary thinking you may find it useful to make lists or to jot down clusters of your ideas, insights, comments, questions. For "The Story of an Hour" you might list Mrs. Mallard's traits, or you might list the stages of her development. (Such a list is not the same as a summary of a plot. Lists help writers to see the sequence of psychological changes, helping them to offer a coherent argument about what happens.)

> weeps (when she gets the news)
> goes to room, alone
> "pressed down by a physical exhaustion"
> "dull stare"
> "something coming to her"
> strives to beat back "this thing"
> "Free, free, free!" The "vacant stare went from her eyes"
> "A clear and exalted perception"
> rejects Josephine
> "she was drinking in a very elixir of life"
> gets up, opens door, "a feverish triumph in her eyes"
> sees B, and dies

Unlike brainstorming and annotating, which let you go in all directions, listing requires that you first make a decision about what you will be listing—traits of character, images, puns, or whatever. Once you make the decision, you can then construct the list, and, with a list in front of you, you will probably see patterns that you were not fully conscious of earlier.

On the other hand, don't be unduly concerned if something does not seem to fit into a list or cluster. You can return to it, and give it more thought—maybe it will come to fit later. But you might also realize that this point needs to be placed to the side. As far as you can tell, it doesn't appear to belong in one of your lists or to link well to other points you have begun to make, and in this way you may come to realize that it is not relevant to your development of possible topics for your essay.

Developing an Awareness of the Writer's Use of Language

In the first line of the story, Chopin notes that "Mrs. Mallard was afflicted with a heart trouble." You might want to look up "afflicted" in your dictionary. Why do you think that Chopin chose this word, as opposed to other words she might have chosen? How would the effect of the opening line be different if, for example, Chopin had written "Mrs. Mallard had a heart problem" or "Mrs. Mallard's heart was weak"?

Earlier we recommended that you keep a dictionary at hand when you read. It will help you, especially if you get into the habit of asking questions about the writer's choice of language. And this brings us to our next point.

Asking Questions

If you feel stuck, ask yourself questions. We suggest questions for fiction on pages 265-68, for poetry on pages 690-93, and for drama on pages 1172-75. If, for instance, you are thinking about a work of fiction, you might ask yourself questions about the plot and the characters—are they believable, are they interesting, and what does it all add up to? What does the story mean *to you?* One student found it helpful to jot down the following questions:

Plot

   Ending false? unconvincing? or prepared for?

Character?

   Mrs. M. unfeeling? Immoral?

   Mrs. M. unbelievable character?

      What might her marriage have been like? Many gaps. (Can we tell what her
         husband was like?) "And yet she loved him—sometimes." Fickle?
         Realistic?

   What is "this thing that was approaching to possess her"?

Symbolism

   Set on spring day = symbolic of new life?

But, again, you don't have to be as tidy as this student was. You can begin by jotting down notes and queries about what you like or dislike and about what puzzles or amuses you. Here are the jottings of another student. They are, obviously, in no particular order—the student is brainstorming, putting down whatever occurs to her—though it is equally obvious that one note sometimes led to the next:

   Title nothing special. What might be better title?

   Could a woman who loved her husband be so heartless?

   Is she heartless? *Did* she love him?

   What are (were) Louise's feelings about her husband?

   Did she want too much? *What* did she want?

   Could this story happen today? Feminist interpretation?

   Sister (Josephine)—a busybody?

Tricky ending—but maybe it could be true

"And yet she loved him—sometimes. Often she had not."

Why does one love someone "sometimes"?

Irony: plot has reversal. Are characters ironic too?

These jottings will help the reader-writer to think about the story, to find a special point of interest and to develop a thoughtful argument about it.

Keeping a Journal

A journal is not a diary, a record of what the writer did each day ("today I read Chopin's 'Hour'"); rather, a journal is a place to store some of the thoughts that you may have inscribed on a scrap of paper or in the margin of the text—for instance, your initial response to the title of a work or to the ending. It's also a place to jot down some further reflections. These reflections may include thoughts about what the work means to you or what was said in the classroom about writing in general or about specific works. You may, for instance, want to reflect on why your opinion is so different from that of another student, or you may want to apply a concept such as "character" or "irony" or "plausibility" to a story that later you may write an essay about.

You might even make an entry in the form of a letter to the author or in the form of a letter from one character to another. Similarly, you might write a dialogue between characters in two works or between two authors, or you might record an experience of your own that is comparable to something in the work.

A student who wrote about "The Story of an Hour" began with the following entry in his journal. In reading this entry, notice that one idea stimulates another. The student was, quite rightly, concerned with getting and exploring ideas, not with writing a unified paragraph.

> Apparently a "well-made" story, but seems clever rather than moving or real. Doesn't seem plausible. Mrs. M's change comes out of the blue—maybe *some* women might respond like this, but probably not most.
>
> Does literature deal with unusual people, or with usual (typical?) people? Shouldn't it deal with typical? Maybe not. (Anyway, how can I know?) Is "typical" same as "plausible"? Come to think of it, prob. not.
>
> Anyway, whether Mrs. M. is typical or not, is her change plausible, believable?
>
> Why did she change? Her husband dominated her life and controlled her action; he did "impose a private will upon a fellow creature." She calls this a crime. Why? Why not?

Arguing a Thesis

Having raised some questions, a reader goes back to the story, hoping to read it now with increased awareness. Some of the jottings will be dead ends, but some will lead to further ideas that can be arranged in lists. What the **thesis** of the essay will be—the idea that will be asserted and supported—is still in doubt, but there is no doubt about one thing: A good essay will have a thesis, a point, an argument. You ought to be able to state your point in a **thesis sentence.**

Consider these candidates as possible thesis sentences, as assertions that can be supported in an argument:

1. Mrs. Mallard dies soon after hearing that her husband had died.

True, but scarcely a point that can be argued, or even developed. About the most the essayist can do with this sentence is to amplify it by summarizing the plot of the story, a task not worth doing. An analysis may include a sentence or two of summary, to give readers their bearings, but a summary is not an essay.

2. The story is a libel on women.

In contrast to the first statement, this one can be developed into an argument. Probably the writer will try to demonstrate that Mrs. Mallard's behavior is despicable. Whether this point can be convincingly argued is another matter; the thesis may be untenable, but it is a thesis. A second problem, however, is this: Even if the writer demonstrates that Mrs. Mallard's behavior is despicable, he or she will have to go on to demonstrate that the presentation of one despicable woman constitutes a libel on women in general. That's a pretty big order.

3. The story is clever but superficial because it is based on an unreal character.

Here, too, is a thesis, a point of view that can be argued. Whether or not this thesis is true is another matter. The writer's job will be to support it by presenting evidence. Probably the writer will have no difficulty in finding evidence that the story is "clever"; the difficulty probably will be in establishing a case that the characterization of Mrs. Mallard is "unreal." The writer will have to set forth some ideas about what makes a character real and then will have to show that Mrs. Mallard is an "unreal" (unbelievable) figure.

4. The irony of the ending is believable partly because it is consistent with earlier ironies in the story.

It happens that the student who wrote the essay printed on page 78 began by drafting an essay based on the third of these thesis topics, but as she worked on a draft she found that she couldn't support her assertion that the character was unconvincing. In fact, she came to believe that although Mrs. Mallard's joy was the reverse of what a reader might expect, several early reversals in the story helped to make Mrs. Mallard's shift from grief to joy acceptable.

Writing a Draft

After jotting down notes and then adding more notes stimulated by rereading and further thinking, you'll probably be able to formulate a tentative thesis. At this point most writers find it useful to clear the air by glancing over their preliminary notes and by jotting down the thesis and a few especially promising notes—brief statements of what they think their key points may be. These notes may include some brief key quotations that the writer thinks will help to support the thesis.

Here are the notes (not the original brainstorming notes, but a later selection from them, with additions) and a draft (following) that makes use of them. The final version of the essay—the product produced by the process—is given on page 78.

title: Ironies in an Hour (?) An Hour of Irony (?) Kate Chopin's Irony (?)

thesis: irony at the end is prepared for by earlier ironies

chief irony: Mrs. M. dies just as she is beginning to enjoy life

smaller ironies: 1. "sad message" brings her joy

                2. Richards is "too late" at end

                3. Richards is too early at start

Sample Draft of an Essay on Kate Chopin's "The Story of an Hour"

Now for the student's draft—not the first version, but a revised draft with some of the irrelevancies of the first draft omitted and some evidence added.

The digits within the parentheses refer to the page numbers from which the quotations are drawn, though with so short a work as "The Story of an Hour," page references are hardly necessary. Unless instructed otherwise, always provide page numbers for your quotations. This will enable your readers to quickly locate the passages to which you refer. (Detailed information about how to document a paper is given on pages 1456–67.)

Crowe 1

Lynn Crowe

Professor O'Brian

English 102

1 June 2010

Ironies in an Hour

After we know how the story turns out, if we reread it we find irony at the very start, as is true of many other stories. Mrs. Mallard's friends assume, mistakenly, that Mrs. Mallard was deeply in love with her husband, Brently Mallard. They take great care to tell her gently of his death. The friends mean well, and in fact they *do* well. They bring her an hour of life, an hour of freedom. They think their news is sad. Mrs. Mallard at first expresses grief when she hears the news, but soon she finds joy in it. So Richards's "sad message" (67), though sad in Richards's eyes, is in fact a happy message.

Among the ironic details is the statement that when Mallard entered the house, Richards tried to conceal him from Mrs. Mallard, but "Richards was too late" (68). This is ironic because earlier Richards

---

Crowe 2

"hastened" (67) to bring his sad message; if he had at the start been "too late" (68), Brently Mallard would have arrived at home first, and Mrs. Mallard's life would not have ended an hour later but would simply have gone on as it had before. Yet another irony at the end of the story is the diagnosis of the doctors. The doctors say she died of "heart disease—of joy that kills" (68). In one sense the doctors are right: Mrs. Mallard has experienced a great joy. But of course the doctors totally misunderstood the joy that kills her.

The central irony resides not in the well-intentioned but ironic actions of Richards, nor in the unconsciously ironic words of the doctors, but in her own life. In a way she has been dead. She "sometimes" (68) loved her husband, but in a way she has been dead. Now, his apparent death brings her new life. This new life comes to her at the season of the year when "the tops of trees . . . were all aquiver with the new spring life" (67). But, ironically, her new life will last only an hour. She looks forward to "summer days" (68) but she will not see even the end of this spring day. Her years of marriage were ironic. They brought her a sort of living death instead of joy. Her new life is ironic too. It grows out of her moment of grief for her supposedly dead husband, and her vision of a new life is cut short.

Crowe 3

Work Cited

Chopin, Kate. "The Story of an Hour." *An Introduction to Literature.*
    Ed. Sylvan Barnet, William Burto, and William E. Cain. 16th ed.
    New York: Longman, 2011. 67–68. Print.

Revising a Draft

The draft, although thoughtful and clear, is not yet a finished essay. The student went on to improve it in many small but important ways.

First, the draft needs a good introductory paragraph, a paragraph that will let readers know where the writer will be taking them. Doubtless you know from your own experience as a reader that readers can follow an argument more easily—and with more pleasure—if early in the discussion the writer alerts them to the gist of the argument. (The title, too, can strongly suggest the thesis.) Second, some of the paragraphs could be clearer.

In revising paragraphs—or, for that matter, in revising an entire draft—writers unify, organize, clarify, and polish. Let's look at the nouns implicit in these verbs.

1. **Unity** is achieved partly by eliminating irrelevancies. Notice that in the final version, printed on pages 78–79, the writer has deleted "as is true of many other stories" from the first sentence of the draft.
2. **Organization** is largely a matter of arranging material into a sequence that will assist the reader to grasp the point.
3. **Clarity** is achieved largely by providing concrete details and quotations to support generalizations and by providing helpful transitions ("for instance," "furthermore," "on the other hand," "however").
4. **Polishing** is small-scale revision. For instance, a writer may delete unnecessary repetitions. In the second paragraph of the draft, the phrase "the doctors" appears three times, but it appears only once in the final version of the paragraph. Similarly, in polishing, a writer combines choppy sentences into longer sentences, and breaks overly long sentences into shorter ones.

Later, after producing a draft that seems close to a finished essay, writers engage in yet another activity.

5. **Editing** concerns such things as checking the accuracy of quotations by comparing them with the original, checking a dictionary for the spelling of doubtful words, checking a handbook for doubtful punctuation—for instance, whether a comma or a semicolon is needed in a particular sentence.

Peer Review

Your instructor may encourage (or even require) you to discuss your draft with another student or with a small group of students. That is, you may be asked to get a review from your peers. Such a procedure is helpful in several ways. First, it gives the writer a real audience, readers who can point to what pleases or puzzles them, who make suggestions, who may often disagree (with the writer or with each other), and who frequently, though not intentionally, *misread*. Though writers don't necessarily like everything they hear (they seldom hear "This is perfect. Don't change a word!"), reading and discussing their work with others almost always gives them a fresh perspective on their work, and a fresh perspective may stimulate thoughtful revision. (Having your intentions *misread* because your writing isn't clear enough can be particularly stimulating.)

The writer whose work is being reviewed is not the sole beneficiary. When students regularly serve as readers for each other, they become better readers of their own work and consequently better revisers.

When you produce a draft of your paper for peer review, it will not be in final form; the draft is an important step toward shaping the paper and bringing it to final form. But aim to do the best job possible on your draft; let your classmates respond to the best work you can do at this stage of the process.

You will have more work to do on this paper—you know that. But you don't want your classmates to be pointing out mistakes that you know are in the draft and that you could have fixed yourself.

If peer review is a part of the writing process in your course, the instructor may distribute a sheet with some suggestions and questions. An example of such a sheet is shown here.

QUESTIONS FOR PEER REVIEW   ENGLISH 125A

Read each draft once, quickly. Then read it again, with the following questions in mind.

1. What is the essay's topic? Is it one of the assigned topics, or a variation from it? Does the draft show promise of fulfilling the assignment?

2. Look at the essay as a whole. What thesis (main idea) is stated or implied? If implied, try to state it in your own words.

3. Is the thesis plausible? How might the argument be strengthened?

4. Look at each paragraph separately:

   a. What is the basic point? (If it isn't clear to you, ask for clarification.)

   b. How does the paragraph relate to the essay's main idea or to the previous paragraph?

   c. Should some paragraphs be deleted? Be divided into two or more paragraphs? Be combined? Be put elsewhere? (If you outline the essay by jotting down the gist of each paragraph, you will get help in answering these questions.)

   d. Is each sentence clearly related to the sentence that precedes and to the sentence that follows?

   e. Is each paragraph adequately developed?

   f. Are there sufficient details, perhaps brief supporting quotations from the text?

5. What are the paper's chief strengths?

6. Make at least two specific suggestions that you think will assist the author to improve the paper.

The Final Version

Here is the final version of the student's essay. The essay that was submitted to her instructor had been retyped, but here, so that you can easily see how the draft has been revised, we print the draft with the final changes written in by hand.

Crowe 1

Lynn Crowe

Professor O'Brian

English 102

1 June 2010

Ironies of Life in Kate Chopin's "The Story of an Hour"
~~Ironies in an Hour~~

Despite its title, Kate Chopin's "The Story of an Hour" ironically takes only a few minutes to read. In addition, the story turns out to have an ironic ending, but on rereading it one sees that the irony is not concentrated only in the outcome of the plot—Mrs. Mallard dies just when she is beginning to live—but is also present in many details.

After we know how the story turns out, if were read it we find irony at the very start. ~~as is true of many other stories.~~ Because Mrs. Mallard's friends and her sister assume, mistakenly, that ~~Mrs. Mallard~~ she was deeply in love with her husband, Brently Mallard. They take great care to tell her gently of his death. ~~The friends~~ They mean well, and in fact they do well. ~~They bring~~ bringing her an hour of life, an hour of joyous freedom. They think their news is sad. but it is ironic that True, Mrs. Mallard at first expresses grief when she hears the news, but soon (unknown to her friends) she finds joy in it. So Richards's "sad message" (67), though sad in Richards's eyes, is in fact a happy message.

Among the small but significant ironic details is the statement near the end of the story that when Mallard entered the house, Richards tried to conceal him from Mrs. Mallard, but "Richards was too late" (68). This is ironic because almost at the start of the story, in the second paragraph, ~~earlier~~ Richards "hastened" (67) to bring his sad message; if he had at the start been "too late" (68), Brently Mallard would have arrived at home first, and Mrs. Mallard's life would not have ended an hour later but would simply have gone on as it had before. Yet another irony at the end of the story is the diagnosis of the doctors. ~~The doctors~~ They say she died of "heart disease—

Crowe 2

life would not have ended an hour later but would simply have gone on

as it had before. Yet another irony at the end of the story is the

diagnosis of the doctors. ~~The doctors~~ *They* say she died of "heart disease—

of joy that kills" (68). In one sense ~~the doctors~~ *they* are right: Mrs. Mallard *for the last hour*

experienced a great joy. But of course the doctors totally misunder-

stand the joy that kills her. *It is not joy at seeing her husband alive, but*

her realization that the great joy she experienced during the last hour is over.

All of these ironic details add richness to the story, but

The central irony resides not in the well-intentioned but ironic

actions of Richards, nor in the unconsciously ironic words of the

Mrs. Mallard's

doctors, but in ~~her~~ own life. ~~In a way she has been dead.~~ She "some-

a body subjected to her husband's will

times" (68) loved her husband, but in a way she has been dead. Now,

his apparent death brings her new life. This new life comes to her at

the season of the year when "the tops of trees . . . were all aquiver with

the new spring life" (67). But, ironically, her new life will last only an

She is "free, free, free"—but only until her husband walks through the doorway.

hour. She looks forward to "summer days" (68) but she will not see

If

even the end of this spring day. Her years of marriage were ironic.

bringing

~~They brought~~ her a sort of living death instead of joy. Her new life is

not only because

ironic too. It grows out of her moment of grief for her supposedly dead

but also because her vision of "a long progression of years"

husband, and her vision of a new life is cut short.

within an hour on a spring day.

Crowe 3

Work Cited

Chopin, Kate. "The Story of an Hour." *An Introduction to Literature.*

   Ed. Sylvan Barnet, William Burto, and William E. Cain. 16th ed.

   New York: Longman, 2011. 67–68. Print.

A Brief Overview of the Final Version

Finally, as a quick review, let's look at several principles illustrated by this essay.

1. The **title of the essay** is not merely the title of the work discussed; rather, it gives the readers a clue, a small idea of the essayist's topic.
2. The **opening** or **introductory paragraph** does not begin by saying "In this story . . ." Rather, by naming the author and the title, it lets the reader know exactly what story is being discussed. It also develops the writer's thesis so readers know where they will be going.
3. The **organization** is effective. The smaller ironies are discussed in the second and third paragraphs, the central (chief) irony in the last paragraph. That is, the essay does not dwindle or become anticlimactic; rather, it builds up from the least important to the most important point.
4. Some **brief quotations** are used, both to provide evidence and to let the reader hear—even if only fleetingly—Kate Chopin's writing.
5. The essay is chiefly devoted to **analysis** (how the parts relate to each other), not to summary (a brief restatement of the happenings). The writer, properly assuming that the reader has read the work, does not tell the plot in great detail. But, aware that the reader has not memorized the story, the writer gives helpful reminders.
6. The **present tense** is used in narrating the action: "Mrs. Mallard dies"; "Mrs. Mallard's friends and her sister assume."
7. Although a **concluding paragraph** is often useful—if it does more than merely summarize what has already been clearly said—it is not essential in a short analysis. In this essay, the last sentence explains the chief irony and therefore makes an acceptable ending.

Explication

A line-by-line commentary on what is going on in a text is an **explication** (literally, unfolding, or spreading out). Although your explication will for the most part move steadily from the beginning to the end of the selection, try to avoid writing along these lines (or, one might say, along this one line): "In line one. . . . In the second line. . . . In the third line. . . ." That is, don't hesitate to write such things as

> The poem begins. . . . In the next line. . . . The speaker immediately adds. . . . He then introduces. . . . The next stanza begins by saying. . . .

And of course you can discuss the second line before the first if that seems the best way of handling the passage.

An explication is not concerned with the writer's life or times, and it is not a paraphrase (a rewording)—though it may include paraphrase if a passage in the original seems unclear, perhaps because of an unusual word or an unfamiliar expression. On the whole, however, an explication goes beyond paraphrase, seeking to make explicit what the reader perceives as implicit in the work. To this end it calls attention, as it proceeds, to the implications of words (for instance, to their **tone**), the function of rhymes (for instance, how they may connect ideas, as

in "throne" and "alone"), the development of contrasts, and any other contributions to the meaning.

Obviously you will have ideas about the merit and the meaning of a poem,
and your paper will implicitly have a *thesis*—an argument, for instance this
poem is very difficult, or this poem begins effectively but quickly goes downhill,
or this poem is excessively sentimental. Your essay, however, is largely devoted
not to making assertions of this sort but to explaining how the details make the
meaning.

A good way to stimulate responses to the poem is to ask some of the questions given on pages 690–93.

Many students find that by copying the poem (by hand, or on a computer)
they gain an understanding of the uses of language in a literary work. Don't photocopy the poem; the act of writing or typing it will help you to get into the
piece, word by word, comma by comma. Double-space, so that you have ample
room for annotations.

If you write on the computer, you can highlight key words, lines, stanzas.
You can also rearrange lines and stanzas, and perhaps substitute different words
for the words that the poet has selected. Some students like to make multiple
printouts for contrast and comparison—the poem as the poet wrote it,
the poem as the student has marked it up by using the highlighting feature of
the computer program, the poem as it stands after the student has somewhat
rearranged it.

A computer cannot interpret a poem or story for you. But you can employ it
as a tool to deepen your own sense of how a poem is structured—why this or
that word or image is crucial at this juncture, why this or that stanza or passage
belongs here and could not be placed elsewhere, and so on. Your goal is to gain
insight into how writers of literary texts use their artistic medium, and often a
computer can be a good complement to the dictionary that you always keep
nearby.

A Sample Explication

Read this short poem (published in 1917) by the Irish poet William Butler Yeats
(1865–1939). The "balloon" in the poem is a dirigible, a blimp.

WILLIAM BUTLER YEATS

The Balloon of the Mind   [1917]

Hands, do what you're bid:
Bring the balloon of the mind
That bellies and drags in the wind
Into its narrow shed.

A student began thinking about the poem by copying it, double-spaced.
Then she jotted down her first thoughts.

sounds abrupt

Hands, do what you're bid:

—balloon imagined by the mind? Or a mind like a balloon?

Bring the balloon of the mind

That bellies and drags in the wind

no real rhymes?

Into its narrow shed.

line seems to drag— it's so long!

Later she wrote some notes in a journal.

I'm still puzzled about the meaning of the words, "The balloon of the mind." Does "balloon of the mind" mean a balloon that belongs to the mind, sort of like "a disease of the heart"? If so, it means a balloon that the mind *has,* a balloon that the mind possesses, I guess by imagining it. Or does it mean that the mind is *like* a balloon, as when you say "he's a pig of a man," meaning he is like a pig, he is a pig? Can it mean both? What's a balloon that the mind imagines? Something like dreams of fame, wealth? Castles in Spain.

Is Yeats saying that the "hands" have to work hard to make dreams a reality? Maybe. But maybe the idea really is that the mind is *like* a balloon—hard to keep under control, floating around. Very hard to keep the mind on the job. If the mind is like a balloon, it's hard to get it into the hangar (shed).

"Bellies." Is there such a verb? In this poem it seems to mean something like "puffs out" or "flops around in the wind." Just checked *The American Heritage Dictionary,* and it says "belly" can be a verb, "to swell out," "to bulge." Well, you learn something every day.

A later entry:

OK; I think the poem is about a writer trying to keep his balloon-like mind from floating around, trying to keep the mind under control, trying to keep it working at the job of writing something, maybe writing something with the "clarity, unity, and coherence" I keep hearing about in this course.

Here is the student's final version of the explication.

Yeats's "Balloon of the Mind" is about writing poetry, specifically about the difficulty of getting one's floating thoughts down in lines on the page. The first line, a short, stern, heavily stressed command to the speaker's hands, perhaps implies by its severe or impatient tone that these hands will be disobedient or inept or careless if not watched closely: the poor bumbling body so often fails to achieve the goals of the mind. The bluntness of the command in the first line is emphasized by the fact that all the subsequent lines have more syllables. Furthermore, the first line is a grammatically complete sentence, whereas the thought of line 2 spills over into the next lines, implying the difficulty of fitting ideas into confining spaces, that is, of getting one's thoughts into order, especially into a coherent poem.

Lines 2 and 3 amplify the metaphor already stated in the title (the product of the mind is an airy but unwieldy balloon), and they also contain a second command, "Bring." Alliteration ties this command, "Bring," to the earlier "bid"; it also ties both of these verbs to their object, "balloon," and to the verb that most effectively describes the balloon, "bellies." In comparison with the abrupt first line of the poem, lines 2 and 3 themselves seem almost swollen, bellying and dragging, an effect aided by using adjacent unstressed syllables ("of the," "[bell]ies and," "in the") and by using an eye rhyme ("mind" and "wind") rather than an exact rhyme. And then comes the short last line: almost before we could expect it, the cumbersome balloon—here, the idea that is to be packed into the stanza—is successfully lodged in its "narrow shed."

Aside from the relatively colorless "into," the only words of more than one syllable in the poem are "balloon," "bellies," and "narrow," and all three emphasize the difficulty of the task. But after "narrow"—the word itself almost looks long and narrow, in this context like a hangar—we get the simplicity of the monosyllable "shed." The difficult job is done, the thought is safely packed away, the poem is completed—but again with an off rhyme ("bid" and "shed"), for neatness can go only so far when hands and mind and a balloon are involved.

Note: The reader of an explication needs to see the text, and because the explicated text is usually short, it is advisable to quote it all. (Remember, your imagined audience probably consists of your classmates; even if they have already read the work you are explicating, they have not memorized it, and so you helpfully remind them of the work by quoting it.) You can quote the entire text at the outset, or you can quote the first unit (for example, a stanza), then explicate that unit, and then quote the next unit, and so on. And if the poem or passage of prose is longer than, say, six lines, it is advisable to number every fifth line at the right for easy reference, or every fourth line if the poem is written in four-line stanzas.

Explication as Argument

An explication unfolds or interprets a work; it is partly an exposition but it is also an *argument*, offering assertions that are supported by *reasons*. Reread the explication of "The Balloon of the Mind," and notice that the first sentence makes a claim—the poem is "about" such-and-such—and notice, too, that the subsequent assertions are supported by evidence. For instance, when the writer says that lines 2 and 3 seem to drag, she goes on to support the claim by calling attention to "adjacent unstressed syllables." She does not merely assert; she argues.

Comparison and Contrast: A Way of Arguing

Something should be said about an essay organized around a comparison or a contrast, say, of the settings in two short stories, of two characters in a novel, or of the symbolism in two poems. (A comparison emphasizes resemblances whereas a contrast emphasizes differences, but we can use the word "comparison" to cover both kinds of writing.) Probably the student's first thought, after making some jottings, is to discuss one-half of the comparison and then go on to the second half. Instructors and textbooks (though not this one) usually condemn such an organization, arguing that the essay breaks into two parts and that the second part involves a good deal of repetition of categories set up in the first part. Usually they recommend that students organize their thoughts differently, making point-by-point comparisons. For example, in comparing *Adventures of Huckleberry Finn* with *The Catcher in the Rye,* you might organize the material like this:

1. First similarity: the narrator and his quest
   a. Huck
   b. Holden
2. Second similarity: the corrupt world surrounding the narrator
   a. society in *Huckleberry Finn*
   b. society in *Catcher*
3. First difference: degree to which the narrator fulfills his quest and escapes from society
   a. Huck's plan to "light out" to the frontier
   b. Holden's breakdown

Here is another way of organizing a comparison and contrast:

1. First point: the narrator and his quest
   a. similarities between Huck and Holden
   b. differences between Huck and Holden
2. Second point: the corrupt world
   a. similarities between the worlds in *Huck* and *Catcher*
   b. differences between the worlds in *Huck* and *Catcher*
3. Third point: degree of success
   a. similarities between Huck and Holden
   b. differences between Huck and Holden

But a comparison need not employ either of these structures. There is even the danger that an essay employing either of them may not come into focus until the essayist stands back from the seven-layer cake and announces, in the concluding paragraph, that the odd layers taste better. In your preparatory thinking, you may want to make comparisons in pairs, but you must come to some conclusions about what these add up to before writing the final version. This final version should not duplicate the thought processes; rather, it should be organized to make the point clearly and effectively. You are making a list; you are arguing a case.

The point of the essay presumably is not to list pairs of similarities or differences, but to illuminate a work or works by making thoughtful comparisons. Although in a long essay the writer cannot postpone until page 30 a discussion of the second half of the comparison, in an essay of, say, fewer than ten pages nothing is wrong with setting forth one-half of the comparison and then, in light of it, the second half. The essay will break into two unrelated parts if the second half makes no use of the first or if it fails to modify the first half, but not if the second half looks back to the first half and calls attention to differences that the new material reveals. Learning how to write an essay with interwoven comparisons is worthwhile, but be aware that there is another, simpler and clearer way to write a comparison.

Review: How to Write an Effective Essay

Every writer must work out his or her own writing procedures and rituals. (Hemingway liked to sharpen pencils; Robert Frost liked to do farm work before writing.) The following suggestions may provide some help.

1. **Read the work carefully.**
2. **Choose a worthwhile subject,** something that interests you and is not so big that your handling of it must be superficial. As you work, shape and narrow your topic—for example, from "The Character of Hester Prynne" to "The Effects of Alienation on Hester Prynne."
3. **Reread the work, jotting down notes of all relevant matters.** As you read, reflect on your reading and record your reflections. If you have a feeling or an idea, jot it down; don't assume that you will remember it when you get around to writing your essay. The margins of the book are a good place for initial jottings, but many people find that in the long run it is easiest to transfer these notes to 3×5 cards, writing on one side only, or to a file on your computer.
4. **Arrange and organize your thoughts into reasonable divisions,** and reject those irrelevant to your topic. If you are writing an explication, the order probably is essentially the order of the lines or of the episodes, but if you are writing an analysis you almost surely will want to rearrange your notes. If you took notes on your computer, it is best to print them out and do one of two things. (1) Either add notes on the printout (such as "put this with X" or "put this at the end of file; probably not useful") so that you can, by moving blocks of type, rearrange the sequence in your file and have something fairly well-organized to look at and think about on-screen; or (2) Cut the notes apart, reorganize them as you would index cards, and after they are in good order, go back to your file and rearrange them there.
   Whichever method you use, get the notes into order. For instance, you may wish to organize your essay from the lesser material to the greater (to avoid anticlimax) or from the simple to the complex (to ensure intelligibility). If, for instance, you are discussing the roles of three characters in a story, it may be best to build up to the one of the three that you think the most important. If you are comparing two characters it may be best to move from the most obvious contrasts to the least obvious. When you have arranged your notes into a meaningful sequence of packets, you have approximately divided your material into paragraphs, though of course two or three notes may be combined into one paragraph, or one packed note may turn into two or more paragraphs.
5. **Prepare an outline.** Most essayists find it useful to jot down some sort of outline, indicating the main idea of each paragraph and, under each main idea, supporting details that give it substance. An outline—not necessarily

anything highly formal with capital and lowercase letters and roman and arabic numerals, but merely key phrases in some sort of order—will help you to overcome the paralysis called "writer's block" that commonly afflicts professionals as well as students. A page of paper with ideas in some sort of sequence, however rough, ought to encourage you to realize that you do have something to say. And so, despite the temptation to sharpen another pencil or put a new ink cartridge into your printer or check your e-mail, the best thing to do at this point is to sit down and start writing.

If you don't feel that you can work from note cards and a rough outline, try another method: get something down on paper (or on a disk) by writing freely, sloppily, automatically, or whatever, but allowing your ideas about what the work means to you and how it conveys its meaning—rough as your ideas may be—to begin to take visible form. If you are like most people, you can't do much precise thinking until you have committed to paper at least a rough sketch of your initial ideas. Later you can push and polish your ideas into shape, perhaps even deleting all of them and starting over, but it is a lot easier to improve your ideas once you see them in front of you than it is to do the job in your head. On paper or on the screen of a computer one word leads to another; in your head one word often blocks another.

Just keep going; you may realize, as you near the end of a sentence, that you no longer believe it. OK, be glad that your first idea led you to a better one, and pick up your better one and keep going with it. What you are doing is, in a sense, by trial and error pushing your way not only toward clear expression but also toward sharper ideas and richer responses.

6. If there is time, **reread the work,** looking for additional material that strengthens or weakens your main point; take account of it in your outline or draft.

7. As soon as **your thesis (your argument) is clear to you, give your essay an informative title**—*not* simply the title of the story, poem, or play, but something that lets your reader know where you will be going.

    With a thesis and title clearly in mind, **improve your draft,** checking your notes for fuller details, such as supporting quotations. If, as you work, you find that some of the points in your earlier jottings are no longer relevant, eliminate them, but make sure that the argument flows from one point to the next. As you write, your ideas will doubtless become clearer; some may prove to be poor ideas. (We rarely know exactly what our ideas are until we have them set down on paper. As the little girl said, replying to the suggestion that she should think before she spoke, "How do I know what I think until I say it?") Not until you have written a draft do you really have a strong sense of what your ideas are and how good your essay may be.

8. After a suitable interval, preferably a few days, **read the draft with a view toward revising it,** not with a view toward congratulating yourself. A revision, after all, is a re-vision, a second (and presumably sharper) view. When you revise, you will be in the company of Picasso, who said that in painting he advanced by a series of destructions. A revision—say, the substitution of a precise word for an imprecise one—is not a matter of prettifying but of thinking. As you read, correct things that disturb you (for example, awkward repetitions that bore, inflated utterances that grate), add supporting detail where the argument is undeveloped (a paragraph of only one or two sentences is usually an undeveloped paragraph), and ruthlessly delete irrelevancies however well written they may be.

But remember that a deletion probably requires some adjustment in the preceding and subsequent material.

Use transitions to make sure that the argument runs smoothly. The details should be relevant, the organization reasonable, the argument clear. **Check all quotations for accuracy.** Quotations are evidence, usually intended to support your assertions, and it is not nice to alter the evidence, even unintentionally. If there is time (there almost never is), put the revision aside, reread it in a day or two, and revise it again, especially with a view toward deleting wordiness and, on the other hand, supporting generalizations with evidence.

9. **Type, write, or print a clean copy,** following the principles concerning margins, pagination, footnotes, and so on set forth on pages 1452–56. If you have borrowed any ideas, be sure to give credit, usually in footnotes, to your sources. Remember that plagiarism is not limited to the unacknowledged borrowing of words; a borrowed idea, even when put into your own words, requires acknowledgment.

10. **Proofread and make corrections** as explained on page 1453. Remember that writing is a form of self-representation. Fairly or unfairly, readers will make judgments about you based on how you present yourself to them in your writing. With this in mind, proofread your work carefully, making sure that there are no misspellings, misquotations, and the like. The trick, of course, is not to feel so good about the paper that you find yourself skimming and congratulating yourself on your ideas, rather than reading word by word, with an eye for small errors.

Additional Readings

KATE CHOPIN

For a biographical note, see page 67.

Ripe Figs   [1893]

Maman-Nainaine said that when the figs were ripe Babette might go to visit her cousins down on the Bayou-Lafourche[1] where the sugar cane grows. Not that the ripening of figs had the least thing to do with it, but that is the way Maman-Nainaine was.

It seemed to Babette a very long time to wait; for the leaves upon the trees were tender yet, and the figs were like little hard, green marbles.

But warm rains came along and plenty of strong sunshine, and though Maman-Nainaine was as patient as the statue of la Madone,[2] and Babette as restless as a humming-bird, the first thing they both knew it was hot summertime. Every day Babette danced out to where the fig-trees were in a long line against the fence. She walked slowly beneath them, carefully peering

---

[1]**Bayou-Lafourche** a bayou in southeastern Louisiana that flows into the Gulf of Mexico.
[2]**la Madone** the Madonna.

between the gnarled, spreading branches. But each time she came disconsolate away again. What she saw there finally was something that made her
sing and dance the whole long day.

When Maman-Nainaine sat down in her stately way to breakfast, the following morning, her muslin cap standing like an aureole about her white,
placid face, Babette approached. She bore a dainty porcelain platter, which
she set down before her godmother. It contained a dozen purple figs,
fringed around with their rich, green leaves.

5   "Ah," said Maman-Nainaine arching her eyebrows, "how early the figs
have ripened this year!"

"Oh," said Babette. "I think they have ripened very late."

"Babette," continued Maman-Nainaine, as she peeled the very plumpest
figs with her pointed silver fruit-knife, "you will carry my love to them all
down on Bayou-Lafourche. And tell your Tante[3] Frosine I shall look for her at
Toussaint[4]—when the chrysanthemums are in bloom."

YOUR TURN

1. Compare and contrast Maman-Nainaine and Babette.
2. Two questions here: What, if anything, "happens" in "Ripe Figs"? And
   what, in your opinion, is the story about?
3. What, if anything, would be lost if the last line were omitted? (If you
   can think of a better final line, write it, and explain why your version is
   preferable.)

WILLIAM STAFFORD

*William Stafford (1914–1993) was born in Hutchinson, Kansas, and was edu-
cated at the University of Kansas and the State University of Iowa. A conscientious objector during World War II, he worked for the Brethren Service and the
Church World Service. After the war he taught at several universities and then
settled at Lewis and Clark College in Portland, Oregon. In addition to writing
several books of poems, Stafford is the author of many books of poetry and
prose, including* Down in My Heart *(1947), an account of his experiences as a
conscientious objector.*

Traveling Through the Dark   [1960]

Traveling through the dark I found a deer
dead on the edge of the Wilson River road.
It is usually best to roll them into the canyon:
the road is narrow; to swerve might make more dead.   4

By glow of the tail-light I stumbled back of the car
and stood by the heap, a doe, a recent killing;
she had stiffened already, almost cold.
I dragged her off; she was large in the belly.   8

---

[3]**Tante** aunt.   [4]**Toussaint** a bayou town in Louisiana. "La Toussaint" is the Cajun-French
name for All Saints' Day, a day of religious festival and celebration.

My fingers touching her side brought me the reason—
her side was warm; her fawn lay there waiting,
alive, still, never to be born.
Beside that mountain road I hesitated.   12

The car aimed ahead its lowered parking lights;
under the hood purred the steady engine.
I stood in the glare of the warm exhaust turning red;
around our group I could hear the wilderness listen.   16

I thought hard for us all—my only swerving—
Then pushed her over the edge into the river.

YOUR TURN

1. Look at the first sentence (the first two lines) and try to recall what your impression of the speaker was, based only on these two lines, or pretend that you have not read the entire poem, and characterize him merely on these two lines. Then take the entire poem into consideration and characterize him.
2. What do you make of the title? Do you think it is a good title for this poem? Explain.

LINDA PASTAN

Linda Pastan was born in New York City in 1932 and educated at Radcliffe College, Simmons College, and Brandeis University. The author of many books of poems, she has won numerous prizes and has received a grant from the National Endowment for the Arts.

Ethics   [1980]

In ethics class so many years ago
our teacher asked this question every fall:
if there were a fire in a museum
which would you save, a Rembrandt painting
or an old woman who hadn't many   5
years left anyhow? Restless on hard chairs
caring little for pictures or old age
we'd opt one year for life, the next for art
and always half-heartedly. Sometimes
the woman borrowed my grandmother's face   10
leaving her usual kitchen to wander
some drafty, half-imagined museum.
One year, feeling clever, I replied
Why not let the woman decide herself?
Linda, the teacher would report, eschews   15
the burdens of responsibility.

This fall in a real museum I stand
before a real Rembrandt, old woman,
or nearly so, myself. The colors
Within this frame are darker than autumn,   20
darker even than winter—the browns of earth,
though earth's most radiant elements burn
through the canvas. I know now that woman
and painting and season are almost one
and all beyond saving by children.   25

YOUR TURN

1. What, if anything, do we know about the teacher in the poem? Do you
   think you would like to take a course with this teacher? Why?
2. Lines 3-6 report a question that a teacher asked. Does the rest of the
   poem answer the question? If so, what is the answer? If not, what does
   the rest of the poem do?
3. Do you assume that, for this poem, the responses of younger readers
   (say, ages 17–22) as a group would differ from those of older readers? If
   so, why?

LORNA DEE CERVANTES

*Lorna Dee Cervantes, born in San Francisco in 1954, founded a press and a
poetry magazine,* Mango, *chiefly devoted to Chicano literature. In 1978 she received a fellowship from the National Endowment for the Arts, and in 1981
she published her first book of poems. "Refugee Ship," originally written in
1974, was revised for the book. We print the revised version. Cervantes is currently a professor at the University of Colorado at Boulder.*

Refugee Ship   [1981]

Like wet cornstarch, I slide
past my grandmother's eyes. Bible
at her side, she removes her glasses.
The pudding thickens.

Mama raised me without language.   5
I'm orphaned from my Spanish name.
The words are foreign, stumbling
on my tongue. I see in the mirror
my reflection: bronzed skin, black hair.

I feel I am a captive   10
aboard the refugee ship.
The ship that will never dock.
El barco que nunca atraca.°

---

13 El barco que nunca atraca   The ship that never docks.

YOUR TURN

1. What do you think the speaker means by the comparison with "wet cornstarch" in line 1? And what do you take her to mean in line 6 when she says, "I'm orphaned from my Spanish name"?
2. Judging from the poem as a whole, why does the speaker feel she is "a captive / aboard the refugee ship"? How would you characterize such feelings?
3. In an earlier version of the poem, instead of "my grandmother's eyes" Cervantes wrote "*mi abuelita's* eyes"; that is, she used the Spanish words for "my grandmother." In line 5 instead of "Mama" she wrote "*mamá*" (again, the Spanish equivalent), and in line 9 she wrote "brown skin" instead of "bronzed skin." The final line of her original version was not in Spanish but in English, a repetition of the preceding line, which ran thus: "The ship that will never dock." How does each of these changes strike you?

JOSÉ ARMAS

Born in 1944, José Armas has been a teacher (at the University of New Mexico and at the University of Albuquerque), publisher, critic, and community organizer. His interest in community affairs won him a fellowship, which in 1974-1975 brought him into association with the Urban Planning Department at the Massachusetts Institute of Technology. In 1980 he was awarded a writing fellowship by the National Endowment for the Arts, and he now writes a column on Hispanic affairs for De Colores.

El Tonto del Barrio *

Romero Estrado was called "El Cotorro"[1] because he was always whistling and singing. He made nice music even though his songs were spontaneous compositions made up of words with sounds that he liked but which seldom made any sense. But that didn't seem to bother either Romero or anyone else in the Golden Heights Centro where he lived. Not even the kids made fun of him. It just was not permitted.

Romero had a ritual that he followed almost every day. After breakfast he would get his broom and go up and down the main street of the Golden Heights Centro whistling and singing and sweeping the sidewalks for all the businesses. He would sweep in front of the Tortillería America,[2] the XXX Liquor Store, the Tres Milpas[3] bar run by Tino Gabaldon, Barelas' Barber Shop, the used furniture store owned by Goldstein, El Centro Market of the Avila family, the Model Cities Office, and Lourdes Printing Store. Then, in the

---

***El Tonto del Barrio** the barrio dummy (in the United States, a *barrio* is a Spanish-speaking community). All notes are by the editors.   [1]**El Cotorro** The Parrot.   [2]**Tortillería America** America Tortilla Factory.   [3]**Tres Milpas** Three Cornfields.

afternoons, he would come back and sit in Barelas' Barber Shop and spend the day looking at magazines and watching and waving to the passing people as he sang and composed his songs without a care in the world.

When business was slow, Barelas would let him sit in the barber's chair. Romero loved it. It was a routine that Romero kept every day except Sundays and Mondays when Barelas' Barber Shop was closed. After a period of years, people in the barrio got used to seeing Romero do his little task of sweeping the sidewalks and sitting in Barelas' Barber Shop. If he didn't show up one day someone assumed the responsibility to go to his house to see if he was ill. People would stop to say hello to Romero on the street and although he never initiated a conversation while he was sober, he always smiled and responded cheerfully to everyone. People passing the barber shop in the afternoons made it a point to wave even though they couldn't see him; they knew he was in there and was expecting some salutation.

When he was feeling real good, Romero would sweep in front of the houses on both sides of the block also. He took his job seriously and took great care to sweep cleanly, between the cracks and even between the sides of buildings. The dirt and small scraps went into the gutter. The bottles and bigger pieces of litter were put carefully in cardboard boxes, ready for the garbage man.

5   If he did it the way he wanted, the work took him the whole morning. And always cheerful—always with some song.

Only once did someone call attention to his work. Frank Avila told him in jest that Romero had forgotten to pick up an empty bottle of wine from his door. Romero was so offended and made such a commotion that it got around very quickly that no one should criticize his work. There was, in fact, no reason to.

Although it had been long acknowledged that Romero was a little "touched," he fit very well into the community. He was a respected citizen.

He could be found at the Tres Milpas Bar drinking his occasional beer in the evenings. Romero had a rivalry going with the Ranchera songs on the jukebox. He would try to outsing the songs using the same melody but inserting his own selection of random words. Sometimes, like all people, he would "bust out" and get drunk.

One could always tell when Romero was getting drunk because he would begin telling everyone that he loved them.

10   "I looov youuu," he would sing to someone and offer to compose them a song.

"Ta bueno, Romero. Ta bueno, ya bete,"[4] they would tell him.

Sometimes when he got too drunk he would crap in his pants and then Tino would make him go home.

Romero received some money from Social Security but it wasn't much. None of the merchants gave him any credit because he would always forget to pay his bills. He didn't do it on purpose, he just forgot and spent his money on something else. So instead, the businessmen preferred to do little things for him occasionally. Barelas would trim his hair when things were slow. The Tortillería America would give him menudo[5] and fresh-made tortillas at noon when he was finished with his sweeping. El Centro Market would give him the overripe fruit and broken boxes of food that no one else would buy. Although

---

[4]**Ta bueno, ya bete** OK, now go away.   [5]**menudo** tripe soup.

it was unspoken and unwritten, there was an agreement that existed between Romero and the Golden Heights Centro. Romero kept the sidewalks clean and the barrio looked after him. It was a contract that worked well for a long time.

Then, when Seferino, Barelas' oldest son, graduated from high school he went to work in the barber shop for the summer. Seferino was a conscientious and sensitive young man and it wasn't long before he took notice of Romero and came to feel sorry for him.

15   One day when Romero was in the shop Seferino decided to act.

"Mira, Romero. Yo te doy 50 centavos por cada día que me barres la banqueta. Fifty cents for every day you sweep the sidewalk for us. Qué te parece?"[6]

Romero thought about it carefully.

"Hecho! Done!" he exclaimed. He started for home right away to get his broom.

"Why did you do that for, m'ijo?"[7] asked Barelas.

20   "It don't seem right, Dad. The man works and no one pays him for his work. Everyone should get paid for what they do."

"He don't need no pay. Romero has everything he needs."

"It's not the same, Dad. How would you like to do what he does and be treated the same way? It's degrading the way he has to go around getting scraps and handouts."

"I'm not Romero. Besides you don't know about these things, m'ijo. Romero would be unhappy if his schedule was upset. Right now everyone likes him and takes care of him. He sweeps the sidewalks because he wants something to do, not because he wants money."

"I'll pay him out of my money, don't worry about it then."

25   "The money is not the point. The point is that money will not help Romero. Don't you understand that?"

"Look, Dad. Just put yourself in his place. Would you do it? Would you cut hair for nothing?"

Barelas just knew his son was putting something over on him but he didn't know how to answer. It seemed to make sense the way Seferino explained it. But it still went against his "instinct." On the other hand, Seferino had gone and finished high school. He must know something. There were few kids who had finished high school in the barrio, and fewer who had gone to college. Barelas knew them all. He noted (with some pride) that Seferino was going to be enrolled at Harvard University this year. That must count for something, he thought. Barelas himself had never gone to school. So maybe his son had something there. On the other hand . . . it upset Barelas that he wasn't able to get Seferino to see the issue. How can we be so far apart on something so simple, he thought. But he decided not to say anything else about it.

Romero came back right away and swept the front of Barelas' shop again and put what little dirt he found into the curb. He swept up the gutter, put the trash in a shoe box and threw it in a garbage can.

Seferino watched with pride as Romero went about his job and when he was finished he went outside and shook Romero's hand. Seferino told him he had done a good job. Romero beamed.

30   Manolo was coming into the shop to get his hair cut as Seferino was giving Romero his wages. He noticed Romero with his broom.

---

[6]**Qué te parece?** How does that strike you?   [7]**m'ijo** (mi hijo) my son

"What's going on?" he asked. Barelas shrugged his shoulders. "Qué tiene Romero?[8] Is he sick or something?"

"No, he's not sick," explained Seferino, who had now come inside. He told Manolo the story.

"We're going to make Romero a businessman," said Seferino. "Do you re-alize how much money Romero would make if everyone paid him just fifty cents a day? Like my dad says, 'Everyone should be able to keep his dignity, no matter how poor.' And he does a job, you know."

"Well, it makes sense," said Manolo.

35   "Hey, maybe I'll ask people to do that," said Seferino. "That way the poor old man could make a decent wage. Do you want to help, Manolo? You can go with me to ask people to pay him."

"Well," said Manolo as he glanced at Barelas, "I'm not too good at asking people for money."

This did not discourage Seferino. He went out and contacted all the businesses on his own, but no one else wanted to contribute. This didn't dis-courage Seferino either. He went on giving Romero fifty cents a day.

After a while, Seferino heard that Romero had asked for credit at the grocery store. "See, Dad. What did I tell you? Things are getting better for him already. He's becoming his own man. And look. It's only been a couple of weeks." Barelas did not reply.

But then the next week Romero did not show up to sweep any side-walks. He was around but he didn't do any work for anybody the entire week. He walked around Golden Heights Centro in his best gray work pants and his slouch hat, looking important and making it a point to walk right past the barber shop every little while.

40   Of course, the people in the Golden Heights Centro noticed the change immediately, and since they saw Romero in the street, they knew he wasn't ill. But the change was clearly disturbing the community. They dis-cussed him in the Tortillería America where people got together for coffee, and at the Tres Milpas Bar. Everywhere the topic of conversation was the great change that had come over Romero. Only Barelas did not talk about it.

The following week Romero came into the barber shop and asked to talk with Seferino in private. Barelas knew immediately something was wrong. Romero never initiated a conversation unless he was drunk.

They went into the back room where Barelas could not hear and then Romero informed Seferino, "I want a raise."

"What? What do you mean, a raise? You haven't been around for a week. You only worked a few weeks and now you want a raise?" Seferino was clearly angry but Romero was calm and insistent.

Romero correctly pointed out that he had been sweeping the sidewalks for a long time. Even before Seferino finished high school.

45   "I deserve a raise," he repeated after an eloquent presentation.

Seferino looked coldly at Romero. It was clearly a stand-off.

Then Seferino said, "Look, maybe we should forget the whole thing. I was just trying to help you out and look at what you do."

Romero held his ground. "I helped you out too. No one told me to do it and I did it anyway. I helped you many years."

---

[8]**Qué tiene Romero?** What's with Romero?

"Well, let's forget about the whole thing then," said Seferino.

50   "I quit then," said Romero.

"Quit?" exclaimed Seferino as he laughed at Romero.

"Quit! I quit!" said Romero as he walked out the front of the shop past Barelas, who was cutting a customer's hair.

Seferino came out shaking his head and laughing.

"Can you imagine that old guy?"

55   Barelas did not seem too amused. He felt he could have predicted that something bad like this would happen.

Romero began sweeping the sidewalks again the next day with the exception that when he came to the barber shop he would go around it and continue sweeping the rest of the sidewalks. He did this for the rest of the week. And the following Tuesday he began sweeping the sidewalk all the way up to the shop and then pushing the trash to the sidewalk in front of the barber shop. Romero then stopped coming to the barber shop in the afternoon.

The barrio buzzed with fact and rumor about Romero. Tino commented that Romero was not singing anymore. Even if someone offered to buy him a beer he wouldn't sing. Frank Avila said the neighbors were complaining because he was leaving his TV on loud the whole day and night. He still greeted people but seldom smiled. He had run up a big bill at the liquor store and when the manager stopped his credit, he caught Romero stealing bottles of whiskey. He was also getting careless about his dress. He didn't shave and clean like he used to. Women complained that he walked around in soiled pants, that he smelled bad. Even one of the little kids complained that Romero had kicked his puppy, but that seemed hard to believe.

Barelas felt terrible. He felt responsible. But he couldn't convince Seferino that what he had done was wrong. Barelas himself stopped going to the Tres Milpas Bar after work to avoid hearing about Romero. Once he came across Romero on the street and Barelas said hello but with a sense of guilt. Romero responded, avoiding Barelas' eyes and moving past him awkwardly and quickly. Romero's behavior continued to get erratic and some people started talking about having Romero committed.

"You can't do that," said Barelas when he was presented with a petition.

60   "He's flipped," said Tino, who made up part of the delegation circulating the petition. "No one likes Romero more than I do, you know that Barelas."

"But he's really crazy," said Frank Avila.

"He was crazy before. No one noticed," pleaded Barelas.

"But it was a crazy we could depend on. Now he just wants to sit on the curb and pull up the women's skirts. It's terrible. The women are going crazy. He's also running into the street stopping the traffic. You see how he is. What choice do we have?"

"It's for his own good," put in one of the workers from the Model Cities Office. Barelas dismissed them as outsiders. Seferino was there and wanted to say something but a look from Barelas stopped him.

65   "We just can't do that," insisted Barelas. "Let's wait. Maybe he's just going through a cycle. Look. We've had a full moon recently, qué no?[9] That must be it. You know how the moon affects people in his condition."

---

[9]**qué no?** right?

"I don't know," said Tino. "What if he hurts. . . ."

"He's not going to hurt anyone," cut in Barelas.

"No, Barelas. I was going to say, what if he hurts himself. He has no one at home. I'd say, let him come home with me for a while but you know how stubborn he is. You can't even talk to him any more."

"He gives everyone the finger when they try to pull him out of the traffic," said Frank Avila. "The cops have missed him, but it won't be long before they see him doing some of his antics and arrest him. Then what? Then the poor guy is in real trouble."

70   "Well, look," said Barelas. "How many names you got on the list?"

Tino responded slowly, "Well, we sort of wanted you to start off the list."

"Let's wait a while longer," said Barelas. "I just know that Romero will come around. Let's wait just a while, okay?"

No one had the heart to fight the issue and so they postponed the petition.

There was no dramatic change in Romero even though the full moon had completed its cycle. Still, no one initiated the petition again and then in the middle of August Seferino left for Cambridge to look for housing and to register early for school. Suddenly everything began to change again. One day Romero began sweeping the entire sidewalk again. His spirits began to pick up and his strange antics began to disappear.

75   At the Tortillería America the original committee met for coffee and the talk turned to Romero.

"He's going to be all right now," said a jubilant Barelas. "I guarantee it."

"Well, don't hold your breath yet," said Tino. "The full moon is coming up again."

"Yeah," said Frank Avila dejectedly.

When the next full moon was in force the group was together again drinking coffee and Tino asked, "Well, how's Romero doing?"

80   Barelas smiled and said, "Well. Singing songs like crazy."

YOUR TURN

1. What sort of man do you think Barelas is? In your response take account of the fact that the townspeople sort of want [Barelas] "to start off the list" of petitioners seeking to commit Romero.
2. The narrator, introducing the reader to Seferino, tells us that "Seferino was a conscientious and sensitive young man." Do you agree? Why, or why not?
3. What do you make of the last line of the story?
4. Do you think this story could take place in almost any community? If you did not grow up in a barrio, could it take place in your community?

II

Fiction

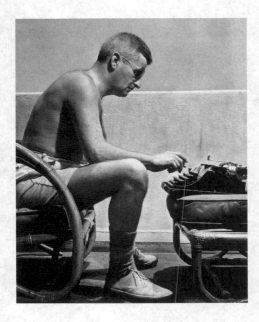

For many readers, William Faulkner, here shown half-naked and pecking away at a type-writer, is the greatest American writer of fiction in the twentieth century. But let's begin our discussion of fiction not with this twentieth-century writer but with Lady Murasaki, a Japanese writer of the eleventh century, who in her novel, *The Tale of Genji,* has a character comment on *why* fiction-writers write. We quote the passage elsewhere in our book, but it is worth repeating:

> Again and again something in one's own life or in that around one will seem so important that one cannot bear to let it pass into oblivion. There must never come a time, the writer feels, when people do not know about this.

When Faulkner was asked how much of his writing was based on personal experience, he replied:

> I can't say. I never counted up. Because "how much" is not important. A writer needs three things, experience, observation, and imagination, any two of which, at times any one of which, can supply the lack of the others. With me, a story usually begins with a single idea or memory or mental picture. The writing of the story is simply a matter of working up to that moment, to explain why it happened or what it caused to follow. A writer is trying to create believable peo-ple in credible moving situations in the most moving way he can. Obviously he must use as one of his tools the environment which he knows. (*Writers at Work,* ed. Malcolm Cowley [1958], 133.)

All good writers draw on the life around them as well as on their own inner lives, and all good writers develop a distinctive style and vision. No one else can write a good Faulkner story, just as no one else can write a good Chekhov story, or Chopin story, or Flannery O'Connor story. The writers whom we value, the writers whose work we want to read and reread, draw on the worlds around them, telling us of their responses to highly local conditions. (Much of Faulkner's work concerns an invented Mississippi county, Yoknapatawpha.) Yet these writers make their readers value what might be thought to be remote experiences. We care about their reports of their worlds, and they help us to see our own worlds (and especially ourselves) freshly.

Approaching Fiction: Responding in Writing

The next six chapters will look at specific elements, one by one, in fiction—plot, character, setting, and so on—but first let's read a brief story by Ernest Hemingway and then talk about it (and see how one student talked about it) with little or no technical language.

ERNEST HEMINGWAY

Ernest Hemingway (1899-1961) was born in Oak Park, Illinois. After graduating from high school in 1917 he worked on the Kansas City Star *but left to serve as a volunteer ambulance driver in Italy, where he was wounded in action. He returned home, married, and then served as European correspondent for the* Toronto Star, *but he soon gave up journalism for fiction. In 1922 he settled in Paris, where he moved in a circle of American expatriates that included Ezra Pound, Gertrude Stein, and F. Scott Fitzgerald. It was in Paris that he wrote stories and novels about what Gertrude Stein called a "lost generation" of rootless Americans in Europe. (For Hemingway's reminiscences of the Paris years, see his posthumously published* A Moveable Feast.) *He served as a journalist during the Spanish Civil War and during World War II, but he was also something of a private soldier during World War II.*

After World War II his reputation sank, though he was still active as a writer (for instance, he wrote The Old Man and the Sea *in 1952). In 1954 Hemingway was awarded the Nobel Prize in Literature, but in 1961, depressed by a sense of failing power, he took his own life.*

Cat in the Rain [1925]

There were only two Americans stopping at the hotel. They did not know any of the people they passed on the stairs on their way to and from their room. Their room was on the second floor facing the sea. It also faced the

99

public garden and the war monument. There were big palms and green benches in the public garden. In the good weather there was always an artist with his easel. Artists liked the way the palms grew and the bright colors of the hotels facing the gardens and the sea. Italians came from a long way off to look up at the war monument. It was made of bronze and glistened in the rain. It was raining. The rain dripped from the palm trees. Water stood in pools on the gravel paths. The sea broke in a long line in the rain and slipped back down the beach to come up and break again in a long line in the rain. The motor cars were gone from the square by the war monument. Across the square in the doorway of the café a waiter stood looking out at the empty square.

The American wife stood at the window looking out. Outside right under their window a cat was crouched under one of the dripping green tables. The cat was trying to make herself so compact that she would not be dripped on.

"I'm going down and get that kitty," the American wife said.

"I'll do it," her husband offered from the bed.

5   "No, I'll get it. The poor kitty out trying to keep dry under a table."

The husband went on reading, lying propped up with the two pillows at the foot of the bed.

"Don't get wet," he said.

The wife went downstairs and the hotel owner stood up and bowed to her as she passed the office. His desk was at the far end of the office. He was an old man and very tall.

"Il piove,"[1] the wife said. She liked the hotel-keeper.

10   "Si, si, Signora, brutto tempo. It's very bad weather."

He stood behind his desk in the far end of the dim room. The wife liked him. She liked the deadly serious way he received any complaints. She liked his dignity. She liked the way he wanted to serve her. She liked the way he felt about being a hotel-keeper. She liked his old, heavy face and big hands.

Liking him she opened the door and looked out. It was raining harder. A man in a rubber cape was crossing the empty square to the café. The cat would be around to the right. Perhaps she could go along under the eaves. As she stood in the doorway an umbrella opened behind her. It was the maid who looked after their room.

"You must not get wet," she smiled, speaking Italian. Of course, the hotel-keeper had sent her.

With the maid holding the umbrella over her, she walked along the gravel path until she was under their window. The table was there, washed bright green in the rain, but the cat was gone. She was suddenly disappointed. The maid looked up at her.

15   "Ha perduto qualque cosa, Signora?"[2]

"There was a cat," said the American girl.

"A cat?"

"Si, il gatto."

"A cat?" the maid laughed. "A cat in the rain?"

20   "Yes," she said, "under the table." Then, "Oh, I wanted it so much. I wanted a kitty."

---

[1]**Il piove** It's raining (Italian).   [2]**Ha . . . Signora** Have you lost something, Madam?

When she talked English the maid's face tightened.

"Come, Signora," she said. "We must get back inside. You will be wet."

"I suppose so," said the American girl.

They went back along the gravel path and passed in the door. The maid stayed outside to close the umbrella. As the American girl passed the office, the padrone bowed from his desk. Something felt very small and tight inside the girl. The padrone made her feel very small and at the same time really important. She had a momentary feeling of being of supreme importance. She went on up the stairs. She opened the door of the room. George was on the bed, reading.

25   "Did you get the cat?" he asked, putting the book down.

"It was gone."

"Wonder where it went to," he said, resting his eyes from reading.

She sat down on the bed.

"I wanted it so much," she said. "I don't know why I wanted it so much. I wanted that poor kitty. It isn't any fun to be a poor kitty out in the rain."

30   George was reading again.

She went over and sat in front of the mirror of the dressing table looking at herself with the hand glass. She studied her profile, first one side and then the other. Then she studied the back of her head and her neck.

"Don't you think it would be a good idea if I let my hair grow out?" she asked, looking at her profile again.

George looked up and saw the back of her neck, clipped close like a boy's.

"I like it the way it is."

35   "I get so tired of it," she said. "I get so tired of looking like a boy."

George shifted his position in the bed. He hadn't looked away from her since she started to speak.

"You look pretty darn nice," he said.

She laid the mirror down on the dresser and went over to the window and looked out. It was getting dark.

"I want to pull my hair back tight and smooth and make a big knot at the back that I can feel," she said. "I want to have a kitty to sit on my lap and purr when I stroke her."

40   "Yeah?" George said from the bed.

"And I want to eat at a table with my own silver and I want candles. And I want it to be spring and I want to brush my hair out in front of a mirror and I want a kitty and I want some new clothes."

"Oh, shut up and get something to read," George said. He was reading again.

His wife was looking out of the window. It was quite dark now and still raining in the palm trees.

"Anyway, I want a cat," she said, "I want a cat. I want a cat now. If I can't have long hair or any fun, I can have a cat."

45   George was not listening. He was reading his book. His wife looked out of the window where the light had come on in the square.

Someone knocked at the door.

"Avanti,"[3] George said. He looked up from his book.

---

[3]**Avanti** Come in.

In the doorway stood the maid. She held a big tortoise-shell cat pressed tight against her and swung down against her body.

"Excuse me," she said, "the padrone asked me to bring this for the Signora."

Responses: Annotations and Journal Entries

When you read a story—or, perhaps more accurately, when you reread a story before discussing it or writing about it—you'll find it helpful to jot an occasional note (for instance, a brief response or a question) in the margins and to underline or highlight passages that strike you as especially interesting. Here is part of the story, with a student's annotations.

The cat was trying to make herself so compact that she would not be dripped on.

"I'm going down and get that kitty," the American wife said.

"I'll do it," her husband offered from the bed. — *He doesn't make a move*

"No, I'll get it. The poor kitty out trying to keep dry under a table."

The husband went on reading, lying propped up with the two pillows at the foot of the bed. — *still doesn't move!*

"Don't get wet," he said. ← *Is he making a joke? Or maybe he just isn't even thinking about what he is saying?*

contrast with the husband — The wife went downstairs and the hotel owner stood up and bowed to her as she passed the office. His desk was at the far end of the office. He was an old man and very tall.

"Il piove," the wife said. She liked the hotel-keeper.

"Si, si, Signora, brutto tempo. It's very bad weather."

He stood behind his desk in the far end of the dim room. The wife liked him. She liked the deadly serious way he received any complaints. She liked his dignity. *She respects him and she is pleased by the attention he shows* She liked the way he wanted to serve her. She liked the way he felt about being a hotel-keeper. She liked his old, heavy face and big hands.

to emphasize the bad weather?? Liking him she opened the door and looked out. It was raining harder. A man in a rubber cape was crossing the empty square to the café. The cat would be around to the right.

Everything in a story presumably is important, but having read the story once, you are probably especially interested (or puzzled) by something, such as the relationship between two people, or the way the end of the story is connected to the beginning. On rereading, then, pen in hand, you'll find yourself noticing things that you missed or didn't find especially significant on your first reading. Now that you know the end of the story, you will read the beginning in a different way.

And of course if your instructor asks you to think about certain questions, you'll keep them in mind while you reread, and you will find ideas coming to you. In "Cat in the Rain," suppose you are asked (or you ask yourself) if the story might just as well be about a dog in the rain. Would anything be lost?

Here are a few questions that you can ask of almost any story. After scanning the questions, you will want to reread the story, pen in hand, and then jot down your responses on a sheet of paper. As you write, doubtless you will go back and reread the story or at least parts of it.

- *What happens?* In two or three sentences—say, 25 to 50 words—summarize the gist of what happens in the story.
- *What sorts of people are the chief characters?* In "Cat in the Rain" the chief characters are George, George's wife, and the innkeeper (the padrone). Jot down the traits that each seems to possess, and next to each trait briefly give some supporting evidence.
- *What especially pleased or displeased you in the story?* Devote at least a sentence or two to the end of the story. Do you find the end satisfying? Why or why not? What evidence can you offer to support an argument with someone whose response differs from yours?
- *Have you any thoughts about the title?* If so, what are they? If the story did not have a title, what would you call it?

After you have made your own jottings, compare them with these responses by a student. No two readers will respond in exactly the same way, but all readers can examine their responses and try to account for them, at least in part. If your responses are substantially different, how do you account for the differences?

1. *A summary.* A young wife, stopping with her husband at an Italian hotel, from her room sees a cat in the rain. She goes to get it, but it is gone, and so she returns empty-handed. A moment later the maid knocks at the door, holding a tortoise-shell cat.

2. *The characters: The woman.*

   kind-hearted (pities cat in rain)

   appreciates innkeeper's courtesy ("liked the way he wanted to serve her") and admires him ("She liked his dignity")

   unhappy (wants a cat, wants to change her hair, wants to eat at a table with her own silver)

   The husband, George.

   not willing to put himself out (says he'll go to garden to get cat but doesn't move)

   doesn't seem very interested in wife (hardly talks to her—he's reading; tells her to "shut up")

   but he does say he finds her attractive ("You look pretty darn nice")

   The innkeeper.

   serious, dignified ("She liked the deadly serious way he received any complaints. She liked his dignity")

   courteous, helpful (sends maid with umbrella; at end sends maid with cat)

3. *Dislikes and likes*. "Dislikes" is too strong, but I was disappointed that more
   didn't happen at the end. What is the husband's reaction to the cat? Or his
   final reaction to his wife? I mean, what does he think about his wife when
   the maid brings the cat? And, for that matter, what is the wife's reaction? Is
   she satisfied? Or does she realize that the cat can't really make her happy?
   Now for the *likes*. (1) I guess I did like the way it turned out; it's sort of a
   happy ending, I think, since she wants the cat and gets it. (2) I also
   especially like the innkeeper. Maybe I like him partly because the wife likes
   him, and if she likes him he must be nice. And he *is* nice—very helpful. And I
   also like the way Hemingway shows the husband. I don't mean that I like the
   man himself, but I like the way Hemingway shows he is such a bastard—not
   getting off the bed to get the cat, telling his wife to shut up and read.

   Another thing about him is that the one time he says something nice
   about her, it's about her hair, and she isn't keen on the way her hair is. She
   says it makes her look "like a boy," and she is "tired" of looking like a boy.
   There's something wrong with this marriage. George hardly pays attention to
   his wife, but he wants her to look like a boy. Maybe the idea is that this
   macho guy wants to keep her looking like an inferior (immature) version
   of himself. Anyway, he certainly doesn't seem interested in letting her fulfill
   herself as a woman.

   I think my feelings add up to this: I like the way Hemingway shows us the
   relation between the husband and wife (even though the relation is pretty
   bad), and I like the innkeeper. Even if the relation with the couple ends
   unhappily, the story has a sort of happy ending, so far as it goes, since the
   innkeeper does what he can to please his guest: he sends the maid, with the
   cat. There's really nothing more that he can do.

   More about the ending. The more I think about it, the more I feel that the
   ending is as happy as it can be. George is awful. When his wife says "I want a
   cat and I want a cat now," Hemingway tells us "George was not listening."
   And then, a moment later, almost like a good fairy the maid appears and
   grants the wife's wish.

4. *The title*. I don't suppose that I would have called it "Cat in the Rain," but I
   don't know what I would have called it. Maybe "An American Couple in Italy."
   Or maybe "The Innkeeper." I really do think that the innkeeper is very
   important, even though he only has a few lines. He's very impressive—not
   only to the girl, but to me (and maybe to all readers), since at the end of the
   story we see how caring the innkeeper is.

   But the more I think about Hemingway's title, the more I think that
   maybe it also refers to the girl. Like the "poor kitty" in the rain, the wife is in

a pretty bad situation. "It isn't any fun to be a poor kitty out in the rain." Of course, the woman is indoors, but her husband generates lots of unpleasant weather. She may as well be out in the rain. She says "I want to have a kitty to sit on my lap and purr when I stroke her." This shows that she wants to be affectionate and that she also wants to have someone respond to her affection. She *is* like a cat in the rain.

Oh, I just noticed that the wife at first calls the cat "her" rather than "it." ("The cat was trying to make herself compact. . . .") Later she says "it," but at first she thinks of the cat as female—because (I think) she identifies with the cat.

The responses of this student probably include statements that you want to take issue with. Or perhaps you feel that the student did not even mention some things that you think are important. You may want to jot down some notes and raise some questions in class.

A Sample Essay by a Student

The responses that we have quoted were written by Bill Yanagi, who later wrote an essay developing one of them. Here is the essay.

Yanagi 1

Bill Yanagi

Professor Lange

English 10B

20 June 2010

Hemingway's American Wife

My title alludes not to any of the four women to whom Hemingway was married, but to "the American wife" who is twice called by this term in his short story "Cat in the Rain." We first meet her in the first sentence of the story ("There were only two Americans stopping at the hotel"), and the next time she is mentioned (apart from a reference to the wife and her husband as "they") it is as "the American wife," at the beginning of the second paragraph of the story. The term is used again at the end of the third paragraph.

Yanagi 2

She is, then, at least in the early part of this story, just an American or an American wife—someone identified only by her nationality and her marital status, but not at all by her personality, her individuality, her inner self. She first becomes something of an individual when she separates herself from her husband by leaving the hotel room and going to look for a cat that she has seen in the garden, in the rain. This act of separation, however, has not the slightest effect on her husband, who "went on reading" (100).

When she returns, without the cat, he puts down his book and speaks to her, but it is obvious that he has no interest in her, beyond as a physical object ("You look pretty darn nice"). This comment is produced when she says she is thinking of letting her hair grow out because she is "so tired of looking like a boy" (101). Why, a reader wonders, does her husband, who has paid almost no attention to her up to now, assure her that she looks "pretty darn nice"? I think it is reasonable to conclude that he *wants* her to look like someone who is not truly a woman, in particular someone who is immature. That she does not feel she has much identity is evident when she continues to talk about letting her hair grow, and she says "I want to pull my hair back tight and smooth and make a big knot at the back that I can feel" (101). Long hair is, or at least was, the traditional sign of a woman; she wants long hair, and at the same time she wants to keep it under her control by tying it in a "big knot," a knot that she can feel, a knot whose presence reminds her, because she can feel it, of her feminine nature.

She goes on to say that she wants to brush her hair "in front of a mirror." That is, she wants to *see* and to feel her femininity, since her husband apparently—so far as we can see in the story, at least—scarcely recognizes it or her. Perhaps her desire for the cat ("I want a cat") is a veiled way of saying that she wants to express her animal nature and not be simply a neglected woman who is made by her husband to look like a boy. Hemingway tells us, however, that when she looked for the cat in the garden she could not find it, a sign, I think, of her failure to break from the man. At the end of the story the maid brings her the cat, but a woman cannot just be handed a new nature and accept it, just like that. She has to find it herself, and in herself, so I think the story ends with "the American wife" still nothing more than an American wife.

Yanagi 3

Work Cited

Hemingway, Ernest. "Cat in the Rain." *An Introduction to Literature.*
Ed. Sylvan Barnet, William Burto, and William E. Cain. 16th ed.
New York: Longman, 2011. 99–102. Print.

A few comments and questions may be useful.

- Do you find the essay interesting? Explain your response.
- Do you find the essay well written? Explain.
- Do you find the essay convincing? Can you suggest ways of strengthening it, or do you think its argument is mistaken? Carefully reread "Cat in the Rain," taking note of passages that give further support to this student's argument, or that seem to challenge or qualify it.
- We often say that a good critical essay sends us back to the literary work with a fresh point of view. Our rereading differs from our earlier reading. Does this essay change your reading of Hemingway's story?

YOUR TURN

1. Can we be certain that the cat at the end of the story is the cat that the woman saw in the rain? (When we first hear about the cat in the rain we are not told anything about its color, and at end of the story we are not told that the tortoiseshell cat is wet.) Does it matter if there are two cats?
2. One student argued that the cat represents the child that the girl wants to have. Do you think there is something to this idea? How might you support or refute it?
3. Consider the following passage:

    > As the American girl passed the office, the padrone bowed from his desk. Something felt very small and tight inside the girl. The padrone made her feel very small and at the same time really important. She had a momentary feeling of being of supreme importance.

    Do you think there is anything sexual here? And if so, that the passage tells us something about her relations with her husband? Support your view.
4. What do you suppose Hemingway's attitude is toward each of the three chief characters? How might you support your hunch?
5. Hemingway wrote the story in Italy, when his wife Hadley was pregnant. In a letter to F. Scott Fitzgerald he said,

    > Cat in the Rain wasn't about Hadley. . . . When I wrote that we were at Rapallo but Hadley was 4 months pregnant with Bumby. The Inn Keeper was the one at Cortina D'Ampezzo. . . . Hadley

never made a speech in her life about wanting a baby because she had been told various things by her doctor and I'd—no use going into all that. (*Letters*, p 180)

According to some biographers, the story shows that Hemingway knew his marriage was in trouble (Hemingway and Hadley divorced). Does knowing that Hemingway's marriage turned out unhappily help you to understand the story? Does it make the story more interesting? And do you think that the story tells a biographer something about Hemingway's life?

6. It is sometimes said that a good short story does two things at once: It provides a believable picture of the surface of life, and it also illuminates some moral or psychological complexity that we feel is part of the essence of human life. This dual claim may not be true, but for the moment accept it. Do you think that Hemingway's story fulfills either or both of these specifications? Support your view.

Later chapters will offer some technical vocabulary and will examine specific elements of fiction, but familiarity with technical vocabulary will not itself ensure that you will understand and enjoy fiction. There is no substitute for reading carefully, thinking about your responses, and (pen in hand) rereading the text, looking for evidence that accounts for your responses or that will lead you to different and perhaps richer responses. The essays that you will submit to your instructor are, finally, rooted in the annotations that you make in your text and the notes in which you record and explore your responses.

6

Plot

Often we use the terms **story** and **plot** as if they mean the same thing, but in literary interpretation their meanings are different. "Story" comes from the same Latin word that gives us "history." What is history? Even the soberest historians have sometimes felt that, in the memorable words of a member of the profession, "History is one damned thing after another." That is, history—and a story—is just a bunch of things that happened (or that we pretend happened, as in "Once upon a time . . .") one after the other ("and they lived happily ever after"). But when an author writes a short story, he or she designs a *structure* for it, an *organization* of events.

- This is the plot—the arrangement of episodes or doings or incidents or actions or happenings or whatever we wish to call them. The plot, again, is the cunning contrivance that is an organized whole.
- If you think of another sense of "plot," a secret plan or a scheme, you are close to the literary use of the term.

Thus, in the plot of a good story, everything hangs together, just as in a good criminal plot everything is well-coordinated: The getaway car is in place, a decoy distracts the bank guard at a crucial moment, and so forth, and the whole thing coheres. (The painter Edgar Degas had something of this sort in mind when he said that it takes as much cunning to paint a picture as to commit a crime.) Or, to return to the law-abiding world, we can recall a comparison suggested by the twentieth-century English writer Ivy Compton-Burnett: "A plot is like the bones of a person. . . the support of the whole."

Perhaps the best point of departure for understanding plot is the British novelist and short-story writer E. M. Forster's definition in *Aspects of the Novel* (1927). He states that in a good plot the episodes are connected by causality:

> We have defined a story as a narrative of events arranged in their time-sequence. A plot is also a narrative of events, the emphasis falling on causality. "The king died and then the queen died" is a story. "The king died and then the queen died of grief" is a plot. The time-sequence is preserved, but the sense of causality overshadows it.

Notice how Forster goes on to develop and complicate his insight:

> Or again: "The queen died, no one knew why, until it was discovered that it was through grief at the death of the king." This is a plot with a

mystery in it, a form capable of high development. It suspends the time-sequence, it moves as far away from the story as its limitations will allow. Consider the death of the queen. If it is in a story we say: "And then?" If it is in a plot we ask: "Why?" That is the fundamental difference between these two aspects of the novel.

Thus, if "The king died, and a week later the queen was killed by a drunk driver who was driving the wrong way down a one-way street," we would have one thing after another, a story but not a plot.

Most of the time, the plot of a short story proceeds chronologically, as Forster indicates: this happened first, and this happened next, and so on to the end. There may be **foreshadowing** along the way, where the author hints at or implies a turn or twist that the story will take. We also may encounter a **flashback,** which occurs when the author returns us to an incident or episode that preceded the events being recounted in the story. For this reason it often can be useful to set out the plot on a timeline so that we can perceive its structure visually. Such a visual aid can help us to see what happens and prompt us to analyze why it happens as it does—the motives, the causes that move the plot from here to there.

Sometimes, though, an author will choose not to present the plot of a story in chronological order. We might start in the middle (*in medias res* is the Latin phrase), with, say, the death of the king, then move backward to the marriage of the king and queen, and then move forward to the death of the queen. Or the plot might begin in the middle, move backward, forward, then backward again, and so on. The novelist Joseph Conrad, author of *Heart of Darkness* (1899), has a good term for this—he calls it "sifting," moving the plot back and forth like a miner prospecting by a stream, back and forth, back and forth, sifting as the gold comes into view.

In the *Poetics* (c. 330 BCE), the Greek philosopher Aristotle examines the plot of tragic drama, not of prose fiction, but his observations also highlight plot as a structure, as a principle for the organization of a literary work. He emphasizes that the beginning, middle, and end should be unified: "The whole, the structural union of the parts [must be] such that, if any one of them is displaced or removed, the whole will be disjointed and disturbed." If the end of the plot is in some ways implicit in the beginning, and the narrative is, so to speak, the unfolding of the plot, does this mean that the reader can guess the end even at the beginning? Almost never. We can again quote E. M. Forster, who says that the incidents, the episodes, are "unexpected. This shock, followed by the feeling, 'Oh, that's all right,' is a sign that all is well with the plot: characters, to be real, ought to run smoothly, but a plot ought to cause surprise." We don't think this point can be overstated: A good plot surprises—but *not* because the author is free to write anything and everything. The plot must not only surprise but must also evoke the sense, "Oh, that's all right."

Some authors favor simple plots, whereas others prefer complex plots that require us to do careful work to figure out what happened. Even at the end, we might not be certain that we know. We then might be tempted to say that the story is confusing, and we might go so far as to say that it is badly written. But authors have their reasons for what they decide to do. The purpose of an intricate plot might be to show us that it sometimes is difficult to know what happened in a situation and why it did. The meaning and significance of this situation might be ambiguous, or indeterminate.

A short story is short: usually it focuses on a single plot. In this respect it differs from a play like Shakespeare's *King Lear,* which weaves together for comparison and contrast the main plot and the subplot—sometimes termed the primary and the secondary plots. Charles Dickens, Leo Tolstoy, and other novelists work on a wide-ranging, panoramic scale. In their books, we find multiple plots, a half-dozen or more. In Dickens's *Bleak House* (1852–1853) and in Tolstoy's *War and Peace* (1869) the authors present a number of intersecting plots. They design an elaborate structure that the author of a short story, whose space is limited, does not. A short story is perhaps closer to a lyric poem than to a novel: It usually aims at a single effect.

Authors enjoy telling stories; they take pleasure in leading us through a plot. The Canadian novelist and critic Robertson Davies (1913–1995) explains it this way:

> If you're a writer, a real writer, you're a descendant of those medieval storytellers who used to go into the square of a town and spread a little mat on the ground and sit on it and beat on a bowl and say, "if you give me a copper coin I will tell you a golden tale."

Here is a very short story told by a writer who often said he worked in the tradition of the old storyteller, sitting on a mat, that Robertson Davies speaks of.

W. SOMERSET MAUGHAM

W(illiam) Somerset Maugham (1874–1965), born in Paris but of English origin, grew up in England, where he was trained as a physician but never practiced medicine. Rather, he preferred to make his living as a novelist, playwright, and writer of short stories. The following story is in fact a speech uttered by a character, Death, in one of Maugham's plays, Sheppey *(1933).*

The Appointment in Samarra

[1933]

Death speaks: There was a merchant in Baghdad who sent his servant to market to buy provisions and in a little while the servant came back, white and trembling, and said, Master, just now when I was in the marketplace I was jostled by a woman in the crowd and when I turned I saw it was Death that jostled me. She looked at me and made a threatening gesture; now, lend me your horse, and I will ride away from the city and avoid my fate. I will go to Samarra and there Death will not find me. The merchant lent him his horse, and the servant mounted it, and he dug his spurs in its flanks and as fast as the horse could gallop he went. Then the merchant went down to the marketplace and he saw me standing in the crowd and he came to me and said, Why did you make a threatening gesture to my servant when you saw him this morning? That was not a threatening gesture, I said, it was only a start of surprise. I was astonished to see him in Baghdad, for I had an appointment with him tonight in Samarra.

The plot here is everything. Neither the merchant nor the servant has any "character" in the sense of a distinctive personality. We don't know if they are young or old, stupid or wise, easily angered, oversexed, or whatever. Our interest is not in a clash of personalities shaped by differences in race or in economic class, nor is our interest in a profound relationship that goes beyond the bounds of economic class. All we know is that the servant acts reasonably, and his master is generous enough to lend the servant a horse. Our interest is not in what sort of people are these but rather in what happens next. And when we get to the end of the story, we are surprised but we don't feel that the author has tricked us by pulling an ace out of his sleeve, and we do not say the ending is improbable. On the contrary, we feel that despite the nonsense of Death speaking, it all makes sense. The end of the story is, so to speak, implicit in the beginning. The moral—the author's thesis, we might say—is not stated explicitly, and perhaps we might quibble a little about whether there really is any moral here, and, if there is, how we might state it, but the gist surely is clear: Human beings cannot elude death; it comes to us at an appointed time, whether appointed by God, or by fate, or by biology or by chance. The first thing for you, as a reader, to do when you read a short story is to enjoy it. You are not obliged to like each and every story in this chapter or in this book as a whole—all of us have our favorites—but if you approach each story with an open mind, and with some curiosity, you will find yourself engaged by and interested in most of them. You will be "caught up in the plot."

A good plot captivates and intrigues us—which, again, reminds us that the word "plot" also evokes sly maneuvering and conspiracy. When we read a story, we are something like a detective: We notice details, we wonder about their significance, we form expectations about what is going to happen next, we interpret the meaning of words and actions and the motives of the characters, and so on. Then on a second reading, or in an analytical essay, we might do even more rigorous and thorough analytical thinking about how the author crafted this plot: What is its structure? How do the pieces fit together?

Thinking About Plot

Here are a few questions to think about:

- **The beginning:** What is the first thing that happens in the story, and in what time-period and setting?
- **The middle:** What happens next, and next, and after that? Be as specific as you can.
- What does the author do to create **suspense?**
- Does anything in the plot **surprise** you?
- Does the author present a **conflict, crisis,** or **climax** in the plot? What is the conflict? Where in the plot is the crisis? What is the climax of the plot—and its consequences? What is the **dénouement** (literally, the "un-knotting") of the plot?
- Does the main **character** change a lot, or a little, or not at all as the plot unfolds?
- **The ending:** what happens as the author brings the story to its close? Is everything, or are at least some things, resolved and settled? Or not?

MARGARET ATWOOD

Born in 1939 in Ottawa, Canada, the poet, critic, novelist, and short-story writer Margaret Atwood now lives in Toronto. Her novels include The Edible Woman *(1969),* Surfacing *(1972), and* The Handmaid's Tale *(1985), and more recently,* The Penelopiad *(2005) and* The Year of the Flood *(2009).*

Happy Endings

[1983]

John and Mary meet.
What happens next?
If you want a happy ending, try A.

A

John and Mary fall in love and get married. They both have worthwhile and remunerative jobs which they find stimulating and challenging. They buy a charming house. Real estate values go up. Eventually, when they can afford live-in help, they have two children, to whom they are devoted. The children turn out well. John and Mary have a stimulating and challenging sex life and worthwhile friends. They go on fun vacations together. They retire. They both have hobbies which they find stimulating and challenging. Eventually they die. This is the end of the story.

B

Mary falls in love with John but John doesn't fall in love with Mary. He merely uses her body for selfish pleasure and ego gratification of a tepid kind. He comes to her apartment twice a week and she cooks him dinner, you'll notice that he doesn't even consider her worth the price of a dinner out, and after he's eaten the dinner he fucks her and after that he falls asleep, while she does the dishes so he won't think she's untidy, having all those dirty dishes lying around, and puts on fresh lipstick so she'll look good when he wakes up, but when he wakes up he doesn't even notice, he puts on his socks and his shorts and his pants and his shirt and his tie and his shoes, the reverse order from the one in which he took them off. He doesn't take off Mary's clothes, she takes them off herself, she acts as if she's dying for it every time, not because she likes sex exactly, she doesn't, but she wants John to think she does because if they do it often enough surely he'll get used to her, he'll come to depend on her and they will get married, but John goes out the door with hardly so much as a good-night and three days later he turns up at six o'clock and they do the whole thing over again.

Mary gets run-down. Crying is bad for your face, everyone knows that and so does Mary but she can't stop. People at work notice. Her friends tell her John is a rat, a pig, a dog, he isn't good enough for her, but she can't believe it. Inside John, she thinks, is another John who is much nicer. This other John will emerge like a butterfly from a cocoon, a Jack from a box, a pit from a prune, if the first John is only squeezed enough.

5   One evening John complains about the food. He has never complained about the food before. Mary is hurt.

Her friends tell her they've seen him in a restaurant with another woman, whose name is Madge. It's not even Madge that finally gets to Mary; it's the restaurant. John has never taken Mary to a restaurant. Mary collects all the sleeping pills and aspirins she can find, and takes them and half a bottle of sherry. You can see what kind of a woman she is by the fact that it's not even whiskey. She leaves a note for John. She hopes he'll discover her and get her to the hospital in time and repent and then they can get married, but this fails to happen and she dies.

John marries Madge and everything continues as in A.

C

John, who is an older man, falls in love with Mary, and Mary, who is only twenty-two, feels sorry for him because he's worried about his hair falling out. She sleeps with him even though she's not in love with him. She met him at work. She's in love with someone called James, who is twenty-two also and not yet ready to settle down.

John on the contrary settled down long ago: this is what is bothering him. John has a steady, respectable job and is getting ahead in his field, but Mary isn't impressed by him, she's impressed by James, who has a motorcycle and a fabulous record collection. But James is often away on his motorcycle, being free. Freedom isn't the same for girls, so in the meantime Mary spends Thursday evenings with John. Thursdays are the only days John can get away.

John is married to a woman called Madge and they have two children, a charming house which they bought just before the real estate values went up, and hobbies which they find stimulating and challenging, when they have the time. John tells Mary how important she is to him, but of course he can't leave his wife because a commitment is a commitment. He goes on about this more than is necessary and Mary finds it boring, but older men can keep it up longer so on the whole she has a fairly good time.

One day James breezes in on his motorcycle with some top-grade California hybrid and James and Mary get higher than you'd believe possible and they climb into bed. Everything becomes very underwater, but along comes John, who has a key to Mary's apartment. He finds them stoned and entwined. He's hardly in any position to be jealous, considering Madge, but nevertheless he's overcome with despair. Finally he's middle-aged, in two years he'll be bald as an egg and he can't stand it. He purchases a handgun, saying he needs it for target practice—this is the thin part of the plot, but it can be dealt with later—and shoots the two of them and himself.

Madge, after a suitable period of mourning, marries an understanding man called Fred and everything continues as in A, but under different names.

D

Fred and Madge have no problems. They get along exceptionally well and are good at working out any little difficulties that may arise. But their charming house is by the seashore and one day a giant tidal wave approaches. Real estate values go down. The rest of the story is about what caused the tidal wave and how they escape from it. They do, though thousands drown, but Fred and Madge are virtuous and lucky. Finally on high ground they clasp each other, wet and dripping and grateful, and continue as in A.

E

Yes, but Fred has a bad heart. The rest of the story is about how kind and understanding they both are until Fred dies. Then Madge devotes herself to charity work until the end of A. If you like, it can be "Madge," "cancer," "guilty and confused," and "bird watching."

F

15   If you think this is all too bourgeois, make John a revolutionary and Mary a counterespionage agent and see how far that gets you. Remember, this is Canada. You'll still end up with A, though in between you may get a lustful brawling saga of passionate involvement, a chronicle of our times, sort of.

You'll have to face it, the endings are the same however you slice it. Don't be deluded by any other endings, they're all fake, either deliberately fake, with malicious intent to deceive, or just motivated by excessive optimism if not by downright sentimentality.

The only authentic ending is the one provided here:

John and Mary die. John and Mary die. John and Mary die.

So much for endings. Beginnings are almost more fun. True connoisseurs, however, are known to favor the stretch in between, since it's the hardest to do anything with.

20   That's about all that can be said for plots, which anyway are just one thing after another, a what and a what and a what.

Now try How and Why.

> **YOUR TURN**

1. Did the form of Atwood's story surprise you?
2. Does this story have a plot? Does it present and develop characters?
3. Describe your response to the final paragraphs, which focus on endings and beginnings. Which, in your view, is harder for a short-story writer, the beginning or the ending?
4. Some short stories are extremely short, while others are quite long. What do you think is the right length for a short story? Why do you say that? What kinds of arguments can you use to support your claim?
5. Please compose a part G for "Happy Endings."

KATE CHOPIN

For a biographical note, see page 67.

Désirée's Baby   [1892]

As the day was pleasant, Madame Valmondé drove over to L'Abri to see Désirée and the baby.

It made her laugh to think of Désirée with a baby. Why, it seemed but yesterday that Désirée was little more than a baby herself; when Monsieur in riding through the gateway of Valmondé had found her lying asleep in the shadow of the big stone pillar.

The little one awoke in his arms and began to cry for "Dada." That was as much as she could do or say. Some people thought she might have strayed there of her own accord, for she was of the toddling age. The prevailing belief was that she had been purposely left by a party of Texans, whose canvas-covered wagon, late in the day, had crossed the ferry that Coton Maïs kept, just below the plantation. In time Madame Valmondé abandoned every speculation but the one that Désirée had been sent to her by a beneficent Providence to be the child of her affection, seeing that she was without child of the flesh. For the girl grew to be beautiful and gentle, affectionate and sincere,—the idol of Valmondé.

It was no wonder, when she stood one day against the stone pillar in whose shadow she had lain asleep, eighteen years before, that Armand Aubigny riding by and seeing her there, had fallen in love with her. That was the way all the Aubignys fell in love, as if struck by a pistol shot. The wonder was that he had not loved her before; for he had known her since his father brought him home from Paris, a boy of eight, after his mother died there. The passion that awoke in him that day, when he saw her at the gate, swept along like an avalanche, or like a prairie fire, or like anything that drives headlong over all obstacles.

5   Monsieur Valmondé grew practical and wanted things well considered: that is, the girl's obscure origin. Armand looked into her eyes and did not care. He was reminded that she was nameless. What did it matter about a name when he could give her one of the oldest and proudest in Louisiana? He ordered the *corbeille*[1] from Paris, and contained himself with what patience he could until it arrived; then they were married.

Madame Valmondé had not seen Désirée and the baby for four weeks. When she reached L'Abri she shuddered at the first sight of it, as she always did. It was a sad looking place, which for many years had not known the gentle presence of a mistress, old Monsieur Aubigny having married and buried his wife in France, and she having loved her own land too well ever to leave it. The roof came down steep and black like a cowl, reaching out beyond the wide galleries that encircled the yellow stuccoed house. Big, solemn oaks grew close to it, and their thick-leaved, far-reaching branches shadowed it like a pall. Young Aubigny's rule was a strict one, too, and under it his negroes had forgotten how to be gay, as they had been during the old master's easy-going and indulgent lifetime.

The young mother was recovering slowly, and lay full length, in her soft white muslins and laces, upon a couch. The baby was beside her, upon her arm, where he had fallen asleep, at her breast. The yellow nurse woman sat beside a window fanning herself.

Madame Valmondé bent her portly figure over Désirée and kissed her, holding her an instant tenderly in her arms. Then she turned to the child.

"This is not the baby!" she exclaimed, in startled tones. French was the language spoken at Valmondé in those days.

10   "I knew you would be astonished," laughed Désirée, "at the way he has grown. The little *cochon de lait!*[2] Look at his legs, mamma, and his hands

---

[1]**corbeille** wedding gifts from the groom to the bride.   [2]**cochon de lait** suckling pig (French).

and finger-nails,—real finger-nails. Zandrine had to cut them this morning. Isn't it true, Zandrine?"

The woman bowed her turbaned head majestically, "*Mais si,*[3] Madame."

"And the way he cries," went on Désirée, "is deafening. Armand heard him the other day as far away as La Blanche's cabin."

Madame Valmondé had never removed her eyes from the child. She lifted it and walked with it over to the window that was lightest. She scanned the baby narrowly, then looked as searchingly at Zandrine, whose face was turned to gaze across the fields.

"Yes, the child has grown, has changed;" said Madame Valmondé, slowly, as she replaced it beside its mother. "What does Armand say?"

15   Désirée's face became suffused with a glow that was happiness itself.

"Oh, Armand is the proudest father in the parish, I believe, chiefly because it is a boy, to bear his name; though he says not,—that he would have loved a girl as well. But I know it isn't true. I know he says that to please me. And mamma," she added, drawing Madame Valmondé's head down to her, and speaking in a whisper, "he hasn't punished one of them—not one of them—since baby is born. Even Négrillon, who pretended to have burnt his leg that he might rest from work—he only laughed, and said Négrillon was a great scamp. Oh, mamma, I'm so happy; it frightens me."

What Désirée said was true. Marriage, and later the birth of his son, had softened Armand Aubigny's imperious and exacting nature greatly. This was what made the gentle Désirée so happy, for she loved him desperately. When he frowned she trembled, but loved him. When he smiled, she asked no greater blessing of God. But Armand's dark, handsome face had not often been disfigured by frowns since the day he fell in love with her.

When the baby was about three months old, Désirée awoke one day to the conviction that there was something in the air menacing her peace. It was at first too subtle to grasp. It had only been a disquieting suggestion; an air of mystery among the blacks; unexpected visits from far-off neighbors who could hardly account for their coming. Then a strange, an awful change in her husband's manner, which she dared not ask him to explain. When he spoke to her, it was with averted eyes, from which the old love-light seemed to have gone out. He absented himself from home; and when there, avoided her presence and that of her child, without excuse. And the very spirit of Satan seemed suddenly to take hold of him in his dealings with the slaves. Désirée was miserable enough to die.

She sat in her room, one hot afternoon, in her *peignoir;*[4] listlessly drawing through her fingers the strands of her long, silky brown hair that hung about her shoulders. The baby, half naked, lay asleep upon her own great mahogany bed, that was like a sumptuous throne, with its satin-lined half-canopy. One of La Blanche's little quadroon boys—half naked too—stood fanning the child slowly with a fan of peacock feathers. Désirée's eyes had been fixed absently and sadly upon the baby, while she was striving to penetrate the threatening mist that she felt closing about her. She looked from her child to the boy who stood beside him, and back again; over and over. "Ah!" It was a cry that she could not help; which she was not conscious of having uttered. The blood turned like ice in her veins, and a clammy moisture gathered upon her face.

---

[3]**Mais si** Certainly (French).   [4]**peignoir** long outer garment (French).

20   She tried to speak to the little quadroon boy; but no sound would come, at first. When he heard his name uttered, he looked up, and his mistress was pointing to the door. He laid aside the great, soft fan, and obediently stole away, over the polished floor, on his bare tiptoes.

She stayed motionless, with gaze riveted upon her child, and her face the picture of fright.

Presently her husband entered the room, and without noticing her, went to a table and began to search among some papers which covered it.

"Armand," she called to him, in a voice which must have stabbed him, if he was human. But he did not notice. "Armand," she said again. Then she rose and tottered towards him. "Armand," she panted once more, clutching his arm, "look at our child. What does it mean? Tell me."

He coldly but gently loosened her fingers from about his arm and thrust the hand away from him. "Tell me what it means!" she cried despairingly.

25   "It means," he answered lightly, "that the child is not white; it means that you are not white."

A quick conception of all that this accusation meant for her nerved her with unwonted courage to deny it. "It is a lie; it is not true, I am white! Look at my hair, it is brown; and my eyes are gray, Armand, you know they are gray. And my skin is fair," seizing his wrist. "Look at my hand; whiter than yours, Armand," she laughed hysterically.

"As white as La Blanche's," he returned cruelly; and went away leaving her alone with their child.

When she could hold a pen in her hand, she sent a despairing letter to Madame Valmondé.

"My mother, they tell me I am not white. Armand has told me I am not white. For God's sake tell them it is not true. You must know it is not true. I shall die. I must die. I cannot be so unhappy, and live."

30   The answer that came was as brief:

"My own Désirée: Come home to Valmondé; back to your mother who loves you. Come with your child."

When the letter reached Désirée she went with it to her husband's study, and laid it open upon the desk before which he sat. She was like a stone image: silent, white, motionless after she placed it there.

In silence he ran his cold eyes over the written words. He said nothing. "Shall I go, Armand?" she asked in tones sharp with agonized suspense.

"Yes, go."

35   "Do you want me to go?"

"Yes, I want you to go."

He thought Almighty God had dealt cruelly and unjustly with him; and felt, somehow, that he was paying Him back in kind when he stabbed thus into his wife's soul. Moreover he no longer loved her, because of the unconscious injury she had brought upon his home and his name.

She turned away like one stunned by a blow, and walked slowly towards the door, hoping he would call her back.

"Good-by, Armand," she moaned.

40   He did not answer her. That was his last blow at fate.

Désirée went in search of her child. Zandrine was pacing the sombre gallery with it. She took the little one from the nurse's arms with no word of explanation, and descending the steps, walked away, under the live-oak branches.

It was an October afternoon; the sun was just sinking. Out in the still fields the negroes were picking cotton.

Désirée had not changed the thin white garment nor the slippers which she wore. Her hair was uncovered and the sun's rays brought a golden gleam from its brown meshes. She did not take the broad, beaten road which led to the far-off plantation of Valmondé. She walked across a deserted field, where the stubble bruised her tender feet, so delicately shod, and tore her thin gown to shreds.

She disappeared among the reeds and willows that grew thick along the banks of the deep, sluggish bayou; and she did not come back again.

45   Some weeks later there was a curious scene enacted at L'Abri. In the centre of the smoothly swept back yard was a great bonfire. Armand Aubigny sat in the wide hallway that commanded a view of the spectacle; and it was he who dealt out to a half dozen negroes the material which kept this fire ablaze.

A graceful cradle of willow, with all its dainty furbishings, was laid upon the pyre, which had already been fed with the richness of a priceless *layette*.[5] Then there were silk gowns, and velvet and satin ones added to these; laces, too, and embroideries; bonnets and gloves; for the *corbeille* had been of rare quality.

The last thing to go was a tiny bundle of letters; innocent little scribblings that Désirée had sent to him during the days of their espousal. There was the remnant of one back in the drawer from which he took them. But it was not Désirée's; it was part of an old letter from his mother to his father. He read it. She was thanking God for the blessing of her husband's love:—

"But, above all," she wrote, "night and day, I thank the good God for having so arranged our lives that our dear Armand will never know that his mother, who adores him, belongs to the race that is cursed with the brand of slavery."

YOUR TURN

1. Let's start with the ending. Readers find the ending powerful, but they differ in their interpretations of it. Do you think that when Armand reads the letter he learns something he had never suspected or, instead, something that he had sensed about himself all along? Find evidence in the text to support your view.
2. Describe Désirée's feelings toward Armand. Do you agree with the student who told us, "She makes him into a God"?
3. Chopin writes economically: each word counts, each phrase and sentence is significant. What is she revealing about Armand (and perhaps about the discovery he has made) when she writes, "And the very spirit of Satan seemed suddenly to take hold of him in his dealings with the slaves"?
4. Is this story primarily a character study, or is Chopin seeking to make larger points in it about race, slavery, and gender?

---

[5]**layette** collection of clothing for a newborn child.

ALICE WALKER

Alice Walker was born in 1944 in Eatonton, Georgia, where her parents eked out a living as sharecroppers and dairy farmers; her mother also worked as a domestic. (In a collection of essays, In Search of Our Mothers' Gardens *[1984], Walker celebrates women who, like her mother, passed on a "respect for the possibilities [of life]—and the will to grasp them.") Walker attended Spelman College in Atlanta, and in 1965 she finished her undergraduate work at Sarah Lawrence College near New York City. She then became active in the welfare rights movement in New York and in the voter registration movement in Georgia. Later she taught writing and literature in Mississippi, at Jackson State College and Tougaloo College, and at Wellesley College, the University of Massachusetts, and Yale University.*

Walker has written essays, poetry, and fiction. Her best-known novel, The Color Purple *(1982), won a Pulitzer Prize and the National Book Award. She has said that her chief concern is "exploring the oppressions, the insanities, the loyalties, and the triumphs of black women."*

Everyday Use   [1973]

for your grandmama

I will wait for her in the yard that Maggie and I made so clean and wavy yesterday afternoon. A yard like this is more comfortable than most people know. It is not just a yard. It is like an extended living room. When the hard clay is swept clean as a floor and the fine sand around the edges lined with tiny, irregular grooves, anyone can come and sit and look up into the elm tree and wait for the breezes that never come inside the house.

Maggie will be nervous until after her sister goes: she will stand hopelessly in corners, homely and ashamed of the burn scars down her arms and legs, eying her sister with a mixture of envy and awe. She thinks her sister has held life always in the palm of one hand, that "no" is a word the world never learned to say to her.

You've no doubt seen those TV shows where the child who has "made it" is confronted, as a surprise, by her own mother and father, tottering in weakly from backstage. (A pleasant surprise, of course: What would they do if parent and child came on the show only to curse out and insult each other?) On TV mother and child embrace and smile into each other's faces. Sometimes the mother and father weep, the child wraps them in her arms and leans across the table to tell how she would not have made it without their help. I have seen these programs.

Sometimes I dream a dream in which Dee and I are suddenly brought together on a TV program of this sort. Out of a dark and soft-seated limousine I am ushered into a bright room filled with many people. There I meet a smiling, gray, sporty man like Johnny Carson[1] who shakes my hand

---

[1]**Johnny Carson** a popular TV comedian, best known as host of the long-running *The Tonight Show Starring Johnny Carson* (1962–1992).

and tells me what a fine girl I have. Then we are on the stage and Dee is embracing me with tears in her eyes. She pins on my dress a large or-chid, even though she has told me once that she thinks orchids are tacky flowers.

5   In real life I am a large, big-boned woman with rough, man-working hands. In the winter I wear flannel nightgowns to bed and overalls during the day. I can kill and clean a hog as mercilessly as a man. My fat keeps me hot in zero weather. I can work outside all day, breaking ice to get water for washing; I can eat pork liver cooked over the open fire minutes after it comes steaming from the hog. One winter I knocked a bull calf straight in the brain between the eyes with a sledge hammer and had the meat hung up to chill before nightfall. But of course all this does not show on televi-sion. I am the way my daughter would want me to be: a hundred pounds lighter, my skin like an uncooked barley pancake. My hair glistens in the hot bright lights. Johnny Carson has much to do to keep up with my quick and witty tongue.

But that is a mistake. I know even before I wake up. Who ever knew a Johnson with a quick tongue? Who can even imagine me looking a strange white man in the eye? It seems to me I have talked to them always with one foot raised in flight, with my head turned in whichever way is farthest from them. Dee, though. She would always look anyone in the eye. Hesitation was no part of her nature.

"How do I look, Mama?" Maggie says, showing just enough of her thin body enveloped in pink skirt and red blouse for me to know she's there, almost hidden by the door.

"Come out into the yard," I say.

Have you ever seen a lame animal, perhaps a dog run over by some careless person rich enough to own a car, sidle up to someone who is igno-rant enough to be kind to him? That is the way my Maggie walks. She has been like this, chin on chest, eyes on ground, feet in shuffle, ever since the fire that burned the other house to the ground.

10   Dee is lighter than Maggie, with nicer hair and a fuller figure. She's a woman now, though sometimes I forget. How long ago was it that the other house burned? Ten, twelve years? Sometimes I can still hear the flames and feel Maggie's arms sticking to me, her hair smoking and her dress falling off her in little black papery flakes. Her eyes seemed stretched open, blazed open by the flames reflected in them. And Dee. I see her standing off under the sweet gum tree she used to dig gum out of; a look of concentration on her face as she watched the last dingy gray board of the house fall in toward the red-hot brick chimney. Why don't you do a dance around the ashes? I'd wanted to ask her. She had hated the house that much.

I used to think she hated Maggie, too. But that was before we raised the money, the church and me, to send her to Augusta to school. She used to read to us without pity; forcing words, lies, other folks' habits, whole lives upon us two, sitting trapped and ignorant underneath her voice. She washed us in a river of make-believe, burned us with a lot of knowledge we didn't necessarily need to know. Pressed us to her with the serious way she read, to shove us away at just the moment, like dimwits, we seemed about to understand.

Dee wanted nice things. A yellow organdy dress to wear to her gradua-tion from high school; black pumps to match a green suit she'd made from an old suit somebody gave me. She was determined to stare down any disaster in her efforts. Her eyelids would not flicker for minutes at a time. Often I fought off the temptation to shake her. At sixteen she had a style of her own: and knew what style was.

I never had an education myself. After second grade the school was closed down. Don't ask me why: in 1927 colored asked fewer questions than they do now. Sometimes Maggie reads to me. She stumbles along good-naturedly but can't see well. She knows she is not bright. Like good looks and money, quickness passed her by. She will marry John Thomas (who has mossy teeth in an earnest face) and then I'll be free to sit here and I guess just sing church songs to myself. Although I never was a good singer. Never could carry a tune. I was always better at a man's job. I used to love to milk till I was hooked in the side in '49. Cows are soothing and slow and don't bother you, unless you try to milk them the wrong way.

I have deliberately turned my back on the house. It is three rooms, just like the one that burned, except the roof is tin; they don't make shingle roofs any more. There are no real windows, just some holes cut in the sides, like the portholes in a ship, but not round and not square, with rawhide holding the shutters up on the outside. This house is in a pasture, too, like the other one. No doubt when Dee sees it she will want to tear it down. She wrote me once that no matter where we "choose" to live, she will manage to come see us. But she will never bring her friends. Maggie and I thought about this and Maggie asked me, "Mama, when did Dee ever *have* any friends?"

15   She had a few. Furtive boys in pink shirts hanging about on washday after school. Nervous girls who never laughed. Impressed with her they worshiped the well-turned phrase, the cute shape, the scalding humor that erupted like bubbles in lye. She read to them.

When she was courting Jimmy T she didn't have much time to pay to us, but turned all her faultfinding power on him. He *flew* to marry a cheap city girl from a family of ignorant flashy people. She hardly had time to re-compose herself.

When she comes I will meet—but there they are!

Maggie attempts to make a dash for the house, in her shuffling way, but I stay her with my hand. "Come back here," I say. And she stops and tries to dig a well in the sand with her toe.

It is hard to see them clearly through the strong sun. But even the first glimpse of leg out of the car tells me it is Dee. Her feet were always neat-looking, as if God himself had shaped them with a certain style. From the other side of the car comes a short, stocky man. Hair is all over his head a foot long and hanging from his chin like a kinky mule tail. I hear Maggie suck in her breath. "Uhnnnh," is what it sounds like. Like when you see the wriggling end of a snake just in front of your foot on the road. "Uhnnnh."

20   Dee next. A dress down to the ground, in this hot weather. A dress so loud it hurts my eyes. There are yellows and oranges enough to throw back the light of the sun. I feel my whole face warming from the heat waves it throws out. Earrings gold, too, and hanging down to her shoulders. Bracelets dangling and making noises when she moves her arm up to shake the folds of the dress out of her armpits. The dress is loose and flows, and as she walks closer, I like it. I hear Maggie go "Uhnnnh" again. It is her sister's hair. It

stands straight up like the wool on a sheep. It is black as night and around the edges are two long pigtails that rope about like small lizards disappearing behind her ears.

"Wa-su-zo-Tean-o!" she says, coming on in that gliding way the dress makes her move. The short stocky fellow with the hair to his navel is all grinning and he follows up with "Asalamalakim, my mother and sister!" He moves to hug Maggie but she falls back, right up against the back of my chair. I feel her trembling there and when I look up I see the perspiration falling off her chin.

"Don't get up," says Dee. Since I am stout it takes something of a push. You can see me trying to move a second or two before I make it. She turns, showing white heels through her sandals, and goes back to the car. Out she peeks next with a Polaroid. She stoops down quickly and lines up picture after picture of me sitting there in front of the house with Maggie cowering behind me. She never takes a shot without making sure the house is included. When a cow comes nibbling around the edge of the yard she snaps it and me and Maggie *and* the house. Then she puts the Polaroid in the back seat of the car, and comes up and kisses me on the forehead.

Meanwhile Asalamalakim is going through the motions with Maggie's hand. Maggie's hand is as limp as a fish, and probably as cold, despite the sweat, and she keeps trying to pull it back. It looks like Asalamalakim wants to shake hands but wants to do it fancy. Or maybe he don't know how people shake hands. Anyhow, he soon gives up on Maggie.

"Well," I say. "Dee."

25   "No, Mama," she says. "Not 'Dee,' Wangero Leewanika Kemanjo!"

"What happened to 'Dee'?" I wanted to know.

"She's dead," Wangero said. "I couldn't bear it any longer, being named after the people who oppress me."

"You know as well as me you was named after your aunt Dicie," I said. Dicie is my sister. She named Dee. We called her "Big Dee" after Dee was born.

"But who was *she* named after?" asked Wangero.

30   "I guess after Grandma Dee," I said.

"And who was she named after?" asked Wangero.

"Her mother," I said, and saw Wangero was getting tired. "That's about as far back as I can trace it," I said. Though, in fact, I probably could have carried it back beyond the Civil War through the branches.

"Well," said Asalamalakim, "there you are."

"Uhnnnh," I heard Maggie say.

35   "There I was not," I said, "before 'Dicie' cropped up in our family, so why should I try to trace it that far back?"

He just stood there grinning, looking down on me like somebody inspecting a Model A car. Every once in a while he and Wangero sent eye signals over my head.

"How do you pronounce this name?" I asked.

"You don't have to call me by it if you don't want to," said Wangero.

"Why shouldn't I?" I asked. "If that's what you want us to call you, we'll call you."

40   "I know it might sound awkward at first," said Wangero.

"I'll get used to it," I said. "Ream it out again."

Well, soon we got the name out of the way. Asalamalakim had a name twice as long and three times as hard. After I tripped over it two or three times he told me to just call him Hakim-a-barber. I wanted to ask him was he a barber, but I didn't really think he was, so I didn't ask.

"You must belong to those beef-cattle peoples down the road," I said. They said "Asalamalakim" when they met you, too, but they didn't shake hands. Always too busy: feeding the cattle, fixing the fences, putting up salt-lick shelters, throwing down hay. When the white folks poisoned some of the herd the men stayed up all night with rifles in their hands. I walked a mile and a half just to see the sight.

Hakim-a-barber said, "I accept some of their doctrines, but farming and raising cattle is not my style." (They didn't tell me, and I didn't ask, whether Wangero (Dee) had really gone and married him.)

45   We sat down to eat and right away he said he didn't eat collards and pork was unclean. Wangero, though, went on through the chitlins and corn bread, the greens and everything else. She talked a blue streak over the sweet potatoes. Everything delighted her. Even the fact that we still used the benches her daddy made for the table when we couldn't afford to buy chairs.

"Oh, Mama!" she cried. Then turned to Hakim-a-barber. "I never knew how lovely these benches are. You can feel the rump prints," she said, running her hands underneath her and along the bench. Then she gave a sigh and her hand closed over Grandma Dee's butter dish. "That's it!" she said. "I knew there was something I wanted to ask you if I could have." She jumped up from the table and went over in the corner where the churn stood, the milk in it clabber by now. She looked at the churn and looked at it.

"This churn top is what I need," she said. "Didn't Uncle Buddy whittle it out of a tree you all used to have?"

"Yes," I said.

"Uh huh," she said happily. "And I want the dasher, too."

50   "Uncle Buddy whittle that, too?" asked the barber.

Dee (Wangero) looked up at me.

"Aunt Dee's first husband whittled the dash," said Maggie so low you almost couldn't hear her. "His name was Henry, but they called him Stash."

"Maggie's brain is like an elephant's," Wangero said, laughing. "I can use the churn top as a centerpiece for the alcove table," she said, sliding a plate over the churn, "and I'll think of something artistic to do with the dasher."

When she finished wrapping the dasher the handle stuck out. I took it for a moment in my hands. You didn't even have to look close to see where hands pushing the dasher up and down to make butter had left a kind of sink in the wood. In fact, there were a lot of small sinks; you could see where thumbs and fingers had sunk into the wood. It was beautiful light yellow wood, from a tree that grew in the yard where Big Dee and Stash had lived.

55   After dinner Dee (Wangero) went to the trunk at the foot of my bed and started rifling through it. Maggie hung back in the kitchen over the dishpan. Out came Wangero with two quilts. They had been pieced by Grandma Dee and then Big Dee and me had hung them on the quilt frames on the front porch and quilted them. One was in the Lone Star pattern. The other was Walk Around the Mountain. In both of them were scraps of dresses Grandma Dee had worn fifty and more years ago. Bits and pieces of Grandpa Jarrell's Paisley shirts. And one teeny faded blue piece, about the size of a penny matchbox, that was from Great Grandpa Ezra's uniform that he wore in the Civil War.

Quilt made by a slave in Mississippi about 1855–1858. (Courtesy of Michigan State University Museum.)

The crafting of a family heirloom.

"Mama," Wangero said sweet as a bird. "Can I have these old quilts?"

I heard something fall in the kitchen, and a minute later the kitchen door slammed.

"Why don't you take one or two of the others?" I asked. "These old things was just done by me and Big Dee from some tops your grandma pieced before she died."

"No," said Wangero. "I don't want those. They are stitched around the borders by machine."

60   "That'll make them last better," I said.

"That's not the point," said Wangero. "These are all pieces of dresses Grandma used to wear. She did all this stitching by hand. Imagine!" She held the quilts securely in her arms, stroking them.

"Some of the pieces, like those lavender ones, come from old clothes her mother handed down to her," I said, moving up to touch the quilts. Dee (Wangero) moved back just enough so that I couldn't reach the quilts. They already belonged to her.

"Imagine!" she breathed again, clutching them closely to her bosom.

"The truth is," I said, "I promised to give them quilts to Maggie, for when she marries John Thomas."

65   She gasped like a bee had stung her.

"Maggie can't appreciate these quilts!" she said. "She'd probably be backward enough to put them to everyday use."

"I reckon she would," I said. "God knows I been saving 'em for long enough with nobody using 'em. I hope she will!" I didn't want to bring up how I had offered Dee (Wangero) a quilt when she went away to college. Then she had told me they were old-fashioned, out of style.

"But they're *priceless!*" she was saying now, furiously; for she has a temper. "Maggie would put them on the bed and in five years they'd be in rags. Less than that!"

"She can always make some more," I said. "Maggie knows how to quilt."

70   Dee (Wangero) looked at me with hatred. "You just will not understand. The point is these quilts, *these* quilts!"

"Well," I said, stumped. "What would *you* do with them?"

"Hang them," she said. As if that was the only thing you *could* do with quilts.

Maggie by now was standing in the door. I could almost hear the sound her feet made as they scraped over each other.

"She can have them, Mama," she said, like somebody used to never winning anything, or having anything reserved for her. "I can 'member Grandma Dee without the quilts."

75   I looked at her hard. She had filled her bottom lip with checkerberry snuff and it gave her face a kind of dopey, hangdog look. It was Grandma Dee and Big Dee who taught her how to quilt herself. She stood there with her scarred hands hidden in the folds of her skirt. She looked at her sister with something like fear but she wasn't mad at her. This was Maggie's portion. This was the way she knew God to work.

When I looked at her like that something hit me in the top of my head and ran down to the soles of my feet. Just like when I'm in church and the spirit of God touches me and I get happy and shout. I did something I never had done before: hugged Maggie to me, then dragged her on into the room, snatched the quilts out of Miss Wangero's hands and dumped them into Maggie's lap. Maggie just sat there on my bed with her mouth open.

"Take one or two of the others," I said to Dee.

But she turned without a word and went out to Hakim-a-barber.

"You just don't understand," she said, as Maggie and I came out to the car.

80   "What don't I understand?" I wanted to know.

"Your heritage," she said. And then she turned to Maggie, kissed her, and said, "You ought to try to make something of yourself, too, Maggie. It's really a new day for us. But from the way you and Mama still live you'd never know it."

She put on some sunglasses that hid everything above the tip of her nose and her chin.

Maggie smiled; maybe at the sunglasses. But a real smile, not scared. After we watched the car dust settle I asked Maggie to bring me a dip of snuff. And then the two of us sat there just enjoying, until it was time to go in the house and go to bed.

YOUR TURN

1. Alice Walker wrote the story, but the story is narrated by one of the characters, Mama. How would you characterize Mama?
2. At the end of the story, Dee tells Maggie, "It's really a new day for us. But from the way you and Mama still live you'd never know it." What does Dee mean? And how do Maggie and Mama respond?"
3. In paragraph 76 the narrator says, speaking of Maggie, "When I looked at her like that something hit me in the top of my head and ran down to the soles of my feet." What "hit" Mama? That is, what does she understand at this moment that she had not understood before?
4. In "Everyday Use" why does the family conflict focus on who will possess the quilts? Why are the quilts important? What do they symbolize?

CHAPTER

7

Character

It is a bit misleading to devote separate chapters to plot and character. The novelist Henry James often stressed that the two are interdependent; a good novel or short story, he said, is an "organism," which possesses vitality and hence is lifelike because its parts form a coherent, unified whole. Using the word "incident" for almost any sort of action, large or small, James said,

> What is character but the determination of incident? What is incident but the illustration of character?

In fact, James was very clear that an "incident" need not be of the magnitude of a train wreck or even a slap in the face:

> It is an incident for a woman to stand up with her hand resting on a table and look out at you in a certain way.

That is, what we are—our personalities, our characters—are what we *do,* are the "incidents" we participate in. And "incidents" are the demonstrations of what we are, what our characters (personalities) are.

Still, just as some stories are mostly plot—the whodunit is a good example, where the reader's interest is almost entirely in what happens next rather than in the personalities—some stories are mostly character, mostly revelations of personalities.

Among the most ancient stories in Western literature are the fables of Aesop, some of which go back to the seventh century BCE. These stories also teach lessons by recounting brief incidents from which homely morals may easily be drawn, even though the stories are utterly fanciful. Among famous examples are the stories of the hare and the tortoise, the boy who cried "Wolf," the ant and the grasshopper, and a good many others that stick in the mind because of the sharply contrasted characters in sharply imagined situations. The fables just mentioned take only four or five sentences apiece, but brief as they are, Aesop told some briefer ones. Here is the briefest of all, about a female fox and a lioness.

AESOP

Aesop, a semi-legendary Greek storyteller, was said to have lived in the sixth century BCE, but some of the stories he told are found in Egypt, in texts that are hundreds of years older.

The Vixen and the Lioness

A vixen sneered at a lioness because she never bore more than one cub. "Only one," the lioness replied, "but a lion."

Just that: Nothing much happens, in the sense of a plot with comings and goings. Just a confrontation between two strongly opposed kinds of creatures: The mere confrontation of a fox and a lion brings together the ignoble and the noble. There is no setting (we are not told that "one day in June a vixen, walking down a dusty road in Nairobi, met a lioness"), but none is needed here. What there is—however briefly set forth—is characterization. The fox's baseness is effectively communicated through the verb "sneered" and through her taunt, and the lioness's nobility is even more effectively communicated through the brevity and decisiveness of her reply. This reply at first seems to agree with the fox ("Only one") and then, after a suspenseful delay provided by the words "the lioness replied," the reply is tersely and powerfully completed ("but a lion"), placing the matter firmly in a new light. Granted that the story is not much of a story, still, it is finely told, and more potent—more memorable, more lively, we might even say more real, despite its talking animals—than the mere moral: "Small-minded people confuse quantity with quality."

The fable is frankly imaginative, made-up; no one believes that foxes and lions discuss their offspring, or, for that matter, that tortoises and hares engage in races. Here is another of Aesop's animal fables, again with a striking contrast of personalities.

The Ant and the Grasshopper

One cold winter day an ant was dragging out a grain which he had buried during the winter. A hungry grasshopper asked for a bit of the grain.
"What did you do all summer?" asked the ant.
"I was busy all summer long, singing," replied the grasshopper.
"Well," said the ant, "since you sang all summer, now dance all winter."

YOUR TURN

1. Let's rewrite the ant's final remark, thus: "Well, since you spent the whole summer singing, I guess you'll dance now in the winter." We assume you agree that the original version is more effective. Exactly what makes the original better?
2. Grasshoppers make great leaps, whereas ants are earthbound. Write a fable in which the grasshopper represents the imaginative thinker and the ant represents the unimaginative plodder.
3. Do you think we can draw lessons from nature about how we should behave? Is a significant part of the argument (so to speak) of an Aesop

fable that it is "natural," that it shows us "nature's way"? Think of some other fables, such as "The City Mouse and the Country Mouse" and "The Fox and the Grapes," that draw upon the nonhuman world. (The gist of "The Fox and the Grapes" is this: A starving fox, seeing bunches of grapes hanging from a vine, but out of reach, went away saying, "Those grapes aren't ripe, they're sour.")

What do such fables gain by being set in the nonhuman world? Why not just say, "A starving man, seeing bunches of grapes that were out of reach, said 'Those grapes aren't ripe, they're sour'"? Again, what, if anything, is gained by using talking animals? Is the moral enforced by nature?

Let's return to this matter of plot and character: Plot is character in action, and character is the motivation for plot. This is the view that James and many other writers have expressed. There are stories in which plot is more prominent than character, and vice versa, but it is hard for us to imagine one without the other. We focus both on the events of the story and on the person or persons involved in the action, the characters that are in the midst of it. A comment by Tobias Wolff, a contemporary writer who is represented in this book with stories and observations in fiction (pages 338–362) is relevant:

> Stories are about problems, and not the kind of problems that result from a safe falling out of a window, but from somebody having a choice and having a problem with that choice, and then the series of consequences that follow from making that choice.

Wolff clearly is very much in agreement with Henry James and E. M. Forster that plot is the result of character in action, the result of (in Wolff's word) "choice."

One of the reasons we turn to novels and stories is for the pleasure we experience in the company of interesting characters. We know that they are not real persons, we know that authors use their skills to imagine and invent the characters we meet in fiction. But in a good work of fiction, we often feel nonetheless that we are coming to know and understand a character as if he or she were a person—someone whom we might meet in real life. This character's words and actions, thoughts and feelings, lead us to become interested in them. We enjoy being in their company, and this even is the case when we are reading about a character whose actions we deplore. Why is this character like that? What would it be like to be such a character? Characters need not be sympathetic, but they must be *interesting*. Consider the following very short story, a story about two, no, three characters.

RON WALLACE

Ron Wallace, born in 1945, is the author of numerous books of poems and stories. He is a professor of English and the codirector of the creative writing program at the University of Wisconsin–Madison.

Worry   [1996]

She worried about people; he worried about things. And between them, that about covered it.

"What would you think of our daughter sleeping around?" she said.

"The porch steps are rotting," he replied. "Someone's going to fall through."

They were lying in bed together, talking. They had been lying in bed together talking these twenty-five years: first, about whether to have children—she wanted to (although there was Down's Syndrome, leukemia, microcephaly, mumps); he didn't (the siding was warped; the roof was going fast)—and then, after their daughter was born, a healthy seven pounds eleven ounces ("She's not eating enough;" "The furnace is failing"), about family matters, mostly ("Her friends are hoodlums, her room is a disaster," "The brakes are squealing, the water heater's rusting out.").

5   Worry grew between them like a son, with his own small insistencies and then more pressing demands. They stroked and coddled him; they set a place for him at the table; they sent him to kindergarten, private school, and college. Because he failed at nearly everything and always returned home, they loved him. After all, he was their son.

"I've been reading her diary. She does drugs. She sleeps around."

"I just don't think I can fix them myself. Where will we find a carpenter?"

And so it went. Their daughter married her high school sweetheart, had a family, and started a health food store in a distant town. Although she recalled her childhood as fondly as anyone—how good her parents had been and how they worried for her, how old and infirm they must be growing, their house going to ruin—she rarely called or visited. She had worries of her own.

YOUR TURN

In our discussion of plot, in the previous chapter, we quoted E. M. Forster on plot and surprise. The episodes in a plot, Forster said, ought to be "unexpected. This shock, followed by the feeling, 'Oh, that's all right,' is a sign that all is well with the plot: characters, to be real, ought to run smoothly, but a plot ought to cause surprise." Were you surprised to hear, at the end of Wallace's story, that the daughter married her high school sweetheart, started a health food store, and recalled her childhood fondly? And were you surprised to learn that although she worried about them, "she rarely called or visited" because "she had worries of her own"? Did you experience a slight surprise as well as a sense of "Oh, that's all right"?

Kinds of Characters

Soon in this chapter you will be making the acquaintance of characters in longer stories. Each of these stories offers its own special reward, with a vivid set of characters; each will become all the more rewarding for you when you complete your reading of this chapter and consider the stories as a group, comparing and contrasting one to the others. But before we turn to these stories, we should do some further thinking about character in general—what it is and how we might approach it as readers, interpreters, and writers of analytical essays.

In simplest terms, a character is the representation of a person in a literary work. In this chapter we are focusing on short stories, but there are characters in poems and, of course, in plays as well. The author presents a character to us through

- what the character says (dialogue),
- what the character does (actions),

- what the author explicitly tells us about the character (authorial comment), and
- what the author tells us about where the character lives (setting)—but that is a topic treated in the next chapter.

Through these techniques, the author makes a character come to life, and to many authors their characters are "alive" indeed. The English short-story writer and novelist Graham Greene noted, "I have to watch my characters crossing the room . . . . I have to see everything they do, even if I don't write it down." Deborah Moggach, a contemporary British novelist, screen writer, and author of many short stories, says this:

> Once a character has gelled it's an unmistakable sensation, like an engine starting up within one's body. From then onwards one is driven by this other person, seeing things through their eyes, shuffling round the shops as a 57-year-old man and practically feeling one has grown a beard.

In *Aspects of the Novel,* from which we have already quoted, E. M. Forster makes a distinction between **flat characters** and **round characters.** "Flat" implies a person who is two-dimensional, fairly simple, and probably unchanging: the character who we encounter at the outset is more or less the same from first appearance to last. Clearly Aesop's characters are flat: The vixen is mean-spirited, the lioness is noble, the grasshopper is imprudent, and the ant is a workaholic. "Round" characters, on the other hand, are three-dimensional, with depth and complexity. A round character is subject to change and indeed during the course of the story might change significantly. We take a special interest in round characters; we want to get to know them, and we give close attention to their words and actions—which sometimes, as in real life, can surprise us. Such characters, we could say, are dynamic, growing and progressing, moving to a new level of insight and understanding. The chief interest in such a story may be in the character's change—for instance, in the loss of innocence.

Some mention should be made of the so-called **stock character.** This term is not quite just another name for a flat character. True, stock character are highly typical or stereotypical, characters whom we recognize because we have seen others like them in other literary works, TV shows, or films. There is the damsel in distress, for example, and the absent-minded professor, the tough-as-nails army sergeant, the prostitute with a heart of gold, and so on. But good authors can give an individuality to a stock character that a flat character cannot have. We can enjoy seeing this or that variation on a stock character, especially if it is a kind of character whom we like. To say that we like the character is not to say that we need to admire him or her. (In *Seinfeld,* George Costanza is a blowhard and a loser, but there is something engaging about him. You just don't want him to be your roommate, or even to work at the desk next to yours.) It can also be interesting to observe how an author may begin with stock characters and develop and deepen them, making them more complex, giving them a distinctive personality.

When you turn to the stories that follow, and to others that are in this book, you might find it useful to keep these tips and questions in mind:

1. **Protagonist:** Is there a main character in the story, one who is the center of our interest? Note: "protagonist" derives from a Greek word for "first actor" or "first contender," from *protos* (= first) and *agonistes* (= contender).

Do not confuse *protos* with the Latin *pro,* meaning "for." Avoid using the word (not only in your essays in English classes but in your daily speech) in the sense of an advocate, as in "He was a protagonist for vegetarianism."

2. **Antagonist:** Is there a character who is in conflict with the main character? What is the nature of this conflict? How does it reveal itself in the story? *Note:* Here, the Greek word means "against the contender."

3. **Foil:** Is there a foil or are there foils in the story? That is, are there characters who bring out the qualities of the protagonist, as a sheet of gold or silver foil sets off a gem? (In *Hamlet,* Laertes and Fortinbras are foils to Hamlet: each has lost a father, and each behaves differently.)

4. **Appearance:** What does the character look like?

5. **Action:** What does each character do in the story?

6. **Dialogue:** What does each character say, and with whom (and in what ways) does the character speak? Dialogue is—though this at first sounds odd—a kind of action. As the novelist Elizabeth Bowen said, "Dialogue is what characters *do* to each other."

7. **Thoughts and feelings:** What do we learn about how the character thinks and feels—about himself or herself, other people, work, politics, and other things? That is, what is the character's inner life?

8. **Setting:** Does the locale (place and time)—nineteenth-century New England or contemporary South, for instance—help to shape the character?

9. **Point of view:** Does the author *show* or does the author *tell*—that is, does the author let us see and hear the characters in action, thereby allowing us to draw our own conclusions, or does the author tell us about them, giving us explicit guidance, perhaps even offering an explicit judgment of the character? Showing (rather than telling) is frequently termed the **objective** or the **dramatic method** of characterization.

10. **Making connections:** How is *this* character in *this* story you are studying similar to and different from the characters in other literary works you have read in this book, or have encountered in reading you have done on your own?

WILLIAM CARLOS WILLIAMS

William Carlos Williams (1883-1963) was the son of an English traveling salesman and a Basque-Jewish woman. The couple met in Puerto Rico and settled in Rutherford, New Jersey, where Williams was born. He spent his life there, practicing as a pediatrician and writing poems in the moments between seeing patients. In addition to many books of poetry and literary and cultural criticism, Williams also published fifty-two short stories, many of them, such as "The Use of Force," reflecting his experiences as a practicing physician.

The Use of Force [1938]

They were new patients to me, all I had was the name, Olson. Please come down as soon as you can, my daughter is very sick.

When I arrived I was met by the mother, a big startled looking woman, very clean and apologetic who merely said, Is this the doctor? and let me in.

In the back, she added. You must excuse us, doctor, we have her in the kitchen where it is warm. It is very damp here sometimes.

The child was fully dressed and sitting on her father's lap near the kitchen table. He tried to get up, but I motioned for him not to bother, took off my overcoat and started to look things over. I could see that they were all very nervous, eyeing me up and down distrustfully. As often, in such cases, they weren't telling me more than they had to, it was up to me to tell them; that's why they were spending three dollars on me.

The child was fairly eating me up with her cold, steady eyes, and no expression to her face whatever. She did not move and seemed, inwardly, quiet; an unusually attractive little thing, and as strong as a heifer in appearance. But her face was flushed, she was breathing rapidly, and I realized that she had a high fever. She had magnificent blond hair, in profusion. One of those picture children often reproduced in advertising leaflets and the photogravure sections of the Sunday papers.

5   She's had a fever for three days, began the father and we don't know what it comes from. My wife has given her things, you know, like people do, but it don't do no good. And there's been a lot of sickness around. So we tho't you'd better look her over and tell us what is the matter.

As doctors often do I took a trial shot at it as a point of departure. Has she had a sore throat?

Both parents answered me together, No . . . No, she says her throat don't hurt her.

Does your throat hurt you? added the mother to the child. But the little girl's expression didn't change nor did she move her eyes from my face.

Have you looked?

10   I tried to, said the mother, but I couldn't see.

As it happens we had been having a number of cases of diphtheria in the school to which this child went during that month and we were all, quite apparently, thinking of that, though no one had as yet spoken of the thing.

Well, I said, suppose we take a look at the throat first. I smiled in my best professional manner and asking for the child's first name I said, come on, Mathilda, open your mouth and let's take a look at your throat.

Nothing doing.

Aw, come on, I coaxed, just open your mouth wide and let me take a look. Look, I said opening both hands wide, I haven't anything in my hands. Just open up and let me see.

15   Such a nice man, put in the mother. Look how kind he is to you. Come on, do what he tells you to, he won't hurt you.

At that I ground my teeth in disgust. If only they wouldn't use the word "hurt" I might be able to get somewhere. But I did not allow myself to be hurried or disturbed but speaking quietly and slowly I approached the child again.

As I moved my chair a little nearer suddenly with one catlike movement both her hands clawed instinctively for my eyes and she almost reached them too. In fact she knocked my glasses flying and they fell, though unbroken, several feet away from me on the kitchen floor.

Both the mother and father almost turned themselves inside out in embarrassment and apology. You bad girl, said the mother, taking her and shaking her by one arm. Look what you've done. The nice man . . .

For heaven's sake, I broke in. Don't call me a nice man to her. I'm here to look at her throat on the chance that she might have diphtheria and possibly die of it. But that's nothing to her. Look here, I said to the child, we're going to look at your throat. You're old enough to understand what I'm saying. Will you open it now by yourself or shall we have to open it for you?

20   Not a move. Even her expression hadn't changed. Her breaths however were coming faster and faster. Then the battle began. I had to do it. I had to have a throat culture for her own protection. But first I told the parents that it was entirely up to them. I explained the danger but said that I would not insist on a throat examination so long as they would take the responsibility.

If you don't do what the doctor says you'll have to go to the hospital, the mother admonished her severely.

Oh yeah? I had to smile to myself. After all, I had already fallen in love with the savage brat, the parents were contemptible to me. In the ensuing struggle they grew more and more abject, crushed, exhausted while she surely rose to magnificent heights of insane fury of effort bred of her terror of me.

The father tried his best, and he was a big man but the fact that she was his daughter, his shame at her behavior and his dread of hurting her made him release her just at the critical moment several times when I had almost achieved success, till I wanted to kill him. But his dread also that she might have diphtheria made him tell me to go on, go on though he himself was almost fainting, while the mother moved back and forth behind us raising and lowering her hands in an agony of apprehension.

Put her in front of you on your lap, I ordered, and hold both her wrists.

25   But as soon as he did the child let out a scream. Don't, you're hurting me. Let go of my hands. Let them go I tell you. Then she shrieked terrifyingly, hysterically. Stop it! Stop it! You're killing me!

Do you think she can stand it, doctor! said the mother.

You get out, said the husband to his wife. Do you want her to die of diphtheria?

Come on now, hold her, I said.

Then I grasped the child's head with my left hand and tried to get the wooden tongue depressor between her teeth. She fought, with clenched teeth, desperately! But now I also had grown furious—at a child. I tried to hold myself down but I couldn't. I know how to expose a throat for inspection. And I did my best. When finally I got the wooden spatula behind the last teeth and just the point of it into the mouth cavity, she opened up for an instant but before I could see anything she came down again and gripping the wooden blade between her molars she reduced it to splinters before I could get it out again.

30   Aren't you ashamed, the mother yelled at her. Aren't you ashamed to act like that in front of the doctor?

Get me a smooth-handled spoon of some sort, I told the mother. We're going through with this. The child's mouth was already bleeding. Her tongue was cut and she was screaming in wild hysterical shrieks. Perhaps I should have desisted and come back in an hour or more. No doubt it would have been better. But I have seen at least two children lying dead in bed of neglect in such cases, and feeling that I must get a diagnosis now or never I went at it again. But the worst of it was that I too had got beyond reason. I could have torn the child apart in my own fury and enjoyed it. It was a pleasure to attack her. My face was burning with it.

The damned little brat must be protected against her own idiocy, one says to one's self at such times. Others must be protected against her. It is social necessity. And all these things are true. But a blind fury, a feeling of adult shame, bred of a longing for muscular release are the operatives. One goes on to the end.

In a final unreasoning assault I overpowered the child's neck and jaws. I forced the heavy silver spoon back of her teeth and down her throat till she gagged. And there it was—both tonsils covered with membrane. She had fought valiantly to keep me from knowing her secret. She had been hiding that sore throat for three days at least and lying to her parents in order to escape just such an outcome as this.

Now truly she *was* furious. She had been on the defensive before but now she attacked. Tried to get off her father's lap and fly at me while tears of defeat blinded her eyes.

YOUR TURN

In paragraph 16, the doctor grinds his teeth "in disgust" after the mother has called him "a nice man," and in paragraph 18 he specifically tells the mother not to call him a nice man. How would you characterize him? Keep in mind, of course, the basic situation in which he must act.

JAMES JOYCE

James Joyce (1882–1941) was born into a middle-class family in Dublin, Ireland. His father drank, became increasingly irresponsible and unemployable, and the family sank in the social order. Still, Joyce received a strong classical education at excellent Jesuit schools and at University College, Dublin, where he studied modern languages. In 1902, at the age of twenty, he left Ireland so that he might spend the rest of his life writing about life in Ireland. ("The shortest way to Tara," he said, "is via Holyhead," i.e., the shortest way to the heart of Ireland is to take a ship away.) In Trieste, Zurich, and Paris he supported his family in a variety of ways, sometimes teaching English in a Berlitz language school. His fifteen stories, collected under the title of Dubliners, *were written between 1904 and 1907, but he could not get them published until 1914. Next came a highly autobiographical novel,* A Portrait of the Artist as a Young Man *(1916).* Ulysses *(1922), a long and complex novel covering eighteen hours in Dublin, was for some years banned by the United States Post Office, though few if any readers today find it offensive. Joyce spent most of his remaining years working on* Finnegans Wake *(1939).*

Nine years before he succeeded in getting Dubliners *published, Joyce described the manuscript in these terms:*

> *My intention was to write a chapter of the moral history of my country and I chose Dublin for the scene because that city seemed to me the centre of paralysis. . . . I have written it for the most part in a style of scrupulous meanness and with the conviction that he is a very*

*bold man who dares to alter in the presentment, still more to
deform, whatever he has seen and heard.*

Araby   [1905]

North Richmond Street, being blind,[1] was a quiet street except at the hour
when the Christian Brothers' School set the boys free. An uninhabited house
of two stories stood at the blind end, detached from its neighbors in a
square ground. The other houses of the street, conscious of decent lives
within them, gazed at one another with brown imperturbable faces.

The former tenant of our house, a priest, had died in the back drawing-
room. Air, musty from having long been enclosed, hung in all the rooms,
and the waste room behind the kitchen was littered with old useless papers. Among these I found a few paper-covered books, the pages of which
were curled and damp: *The Abbot,* by Walter Scott, *The Devout Communicant* and *The Memoirs of Vidocq.*[2] I liked the last best because its leaves
were yellow. The wild garden behind the house contained a central apple-
tree and a few straggling bushes under one of which I found the late tenant's rusty bicycle-pump. He had been a very charitable priest; in his will
he had left all his money to institutions and the furniture of his house to
his sister.

When the short days of winter came dusk fell before we had well eaten
our dinners. When we met in the street the houses had grown somber. The
space of sky above us was the color of ever-changing violet and towards it
the lamps of the street lifted their feeble lanterns. The cold air stung us and
we played till our bodies glowed. Our shouts echoed in the silent street. The
career of our play brought us through the dark muddy lanes behind the
houses where we ran the gauntlet of the rough tribes from the cottages, to
the back doors of the dark dripping gardens where odors arose from the ashpits, to the dark odorous stables where a coachman smoothed and combed
the horse or shook music from the buckled harness. When we returned to
the street light from the kitchen windows had filled the area. If my uncle was
seen turning the corner we hid in the shadow until we had seen him safely
housed. Or if Mangan's sister came out on the doorstep to call her brother in
to his tea we watched her from our shadow peer up and down the street. We
waited to see whether she would remain or go in and, if she remained, we
left our shadow and walked up to Mangan's steps resignedly. She was waiting
for us, her figure defined by the light from the half-opened door. Her brother
always teased her before he obeyed and I stood by the railings looking at her.
Her dress swung as she moved her body and the soft rope of her hair tossed
from side to side.

Every morning I lay on the floor in the front parlor watching her door.
The blind was pulled down to within an inch of the sash so that I could not
be seen. When she came out on the doorstep my heart leaped. I ran to the
hall, seized my books and followed her. I kept her brown figure always in my

[1]**blind** a dead-end street.   [2]**The Abbot** was one of Scott's popular historical romances;
The Devout Communicant was a Catholic religious manual; **The Memoirs of Vidocq**
were the memoirs of the chief of the French detective force.

eye and, when we came near the point at which our ways diverged, I quickened my pace and passed her. This happened morning after morning. I had
never spoken to her, except for a few casual words, and yet her name was
like a summons to all my foolish blood.

5   Her image accompanied me even in places the most hostile to romance. On Saturday evenings when my aunt went marketing I had to go to
carry some of the parcels. We walked through the flaring streets, jostled by
drunken men and bargaining women, amid the curses of laborers, the shrill
litanies of shop-boys who stood on guard by the barrels of pigs' cheeks, the
nasal chanting of street-singers, who sang a *come-all-you* about O'Donovan
Rossa,[3] or a ballad about the troubles in our native land. These noises con-
verged in a single sensation of life for me: I imagined that I bore my chalice safely through a throng of foes. Her name sprang to my lips at moments in strange prayers and praises which I myself did not understand.
My eyes were often full of tears (I could not tell why) and at times a flood
from my heart seemed to pour itself out into my bosom. I thought little of
the future. I did not know whether I would ever speak to her or not or, if
I spoke to her, how I could tell her of my confused adoration. But my
body was like a harp and her words and gestures were like fingers running upon the wires.

One evening I went into the back drawing-room in which the priest
had died. It was a dark rainy evening and there was no sound in the house.
Through one of the broken panes I heard the rain impinge upon the earth,
the fine incessant needles of water playing in the sodden beds. Some distant
lamp or lighted window gleamed below me. I was thankful that I could see
so little. All my senses seemed to desire to veil themselves and, feeling that I
was about to slip from them, I pressed the palms of my hands together until
they trembled, murmuring: *O love! O love!* many times.

At last she spoke to me. When she addressed the first words to me I was
so confused that I did not know what to answer. She asked me was I going
to *Araby*. I forget whether I answered yes or no. It would be a splendid
bazaar, she said; she would love to go.

—And why can't you? I asked.

While she spoke she turned a silver bracelet round and round her wrist.
She could not go, she said, because there would be a retreat that week in her
convent. Her brother and two other boys were fighting for their caps and I
was alone at the railings. She held one of the spikes, bowing her head towards me. The light from the lamp opposite our door caught the white curve
of her neck, lit up her hair that rested there and, falling, lit up the hand upon
the railing. It fell over one side of her dress and caught the white border of a
petticoat, just visible as she stood at ease.

10   —It's well for you, she said.

—If I go, I said, I will bring you something.

What innumerable follies laid waste my waking and sleeping thoughts
after that evening! I wished to annihilate the tedious intervening days. I
chafed against the work of school. At night in my bedroom and by day in the

---

[3]**come-all-you about O'Donovan Rossa** A "come-all-you" was a topical song that began
"Come all you gallant Irishmen." In this case, the song is about Jeremiah O'Donovan Rossa
(1831–1915), a popular Irish leader in the struggle for Irish independence from England.

classroom her image came between me and the page I strove to read. The syllables of the word *Araby* were called to me through the silence in which my soul luxuriated and cast an Eastern enchantment over me. I asked for leave to go to the bazaar on Saturday night. My aunt was surprised and hoped it was not some Freemason[4] affair. I answered few questions in class. I watched my master's face pass from amiability to sternness; he hoped I was not beginning to idle. I could not call my wandering thoughts together. I had hardly any patience with the serious work of life which, now that it stood between me and my desire, seemed to me child's play, ugly monotonous child's play.

On Saturday morning I reminded my uncle that I wished to go to the bazaar in the evening. He was fussing at the hallstand, looking for the hat-brush, and answered me curtly:

—Yes, boy, I know.

15   As he was in the hall I could not go into the front parlor and lie at the window. I left the house in bad humor and walked slowly towards the school. The air was pitilessly raw and already my heart misgave me.

When I came home to dinner my uncle had not yet been home. Still it was early. I sat staring at the clock for some time and, when its ticking began to irritate me, I left the room. I mounted the staircase and gained the upper part of the house. The high cold empty gloomy rooms liberated me and I went from room to room singing. From the front window I saw my companions playing below in the street. Their cries reached me weakened and indistinct and, leaning my forehead against the cool glass, I looked over at the dark house where she lived. I may have stood there for an hour, seeing nothing but the brown-clad figure cast by my imagination, touched discreetly by the lamplight at the curved neck, at the hand upon the railings and at the border below the dress.

When I came downstairs again I found Mrs. Mercer sitting at the fire. She was an old garrulous woman, a pawnbroker's widow, who collected used stamps for some pious purpose. I had to endure the gossip of the tea-table. The meal was prolonged beyond an hour and still my uncle did not come. Mrs. Mercer stood up to go: she was sorry she couldn't wait any longer, but it was after eight o'clock and she did not like to be out late, as the night air was bad for her. When she had gone I began to walk up and down the room, clenching my fists. My aunt said:

—I'm afraid you may put off your bazaar for this night of Our Lord.

At nine o'clock I heard my uncle's latchkey in the halldoor. I heard him talking to himself and heard the hallstand rocking when it had received the weight of his overcoat. I could interpret these signs. When he was midway through his dinner I asked him to give me the money to go to the bazaar. He had forgotten.

20   —The people are in bed and after their first sleep now, he said.

I did not smile. My aunt said to him energetically:

—Can't you give him the money and let him go? You've kept him late enough as it is.

My uncle said he was very sorry he had forgotten. He said he believed in the old saying: *All work and no play makes Jack a dull boy.* He asked me

---

[4]**Freemason** A Freemason was a member of the Free and Accepted Masons, a fraternal organization viewed with suspicion by Irish Catholics.

where I was going and, when I had told him a second time he asked me did I know *The Arab's Farewell to His Steed.*[5] When I left the kitchen he was about to recite the opening lines of the piece to my aunt.

I held a florin tightly in my hand as I strode down Buckingham Street towards the station. The sight of the streets thronged with buyers and glaring with gas recalled to me the purpose of my journey. I took my seat in a third-class carriage of a deserted train. After an intolerable delay the train moved out of the station slowly. It crept onward among ruinous houses and over the twinkling river. At Westland Row Station a crowd of people pressed to the carriage doors; but the porters moved them back, saying that it was a special train for the bazaar. I remained alone in the bare carriage. In a few minutes the train drew up beside an improvised wooden platform. I passed out on to the road and saw by the lighted dial of a clock that it was ten minutes to ten. In front of me was a large building which displayed the magical name.

25   I could not find any sixpenny entrance and, fearing that the bazaar would be closed, I passed in quickly through a turnstile, handing a shilling to a weary-looking man. I found myself in a big hall girdled at half its height by a gallery. Nearly all the stalls were closed and the greater part of the hall was in darkness. I recognised a silence like that which pervades a church after a service. I walked into the center of the bazaar timidly. A few people were gathered about the stalls which were still open. Before a curtain, over which the words *Café Chantant* were written in colored lamps, two men were counting money on a salver. I listened to the fall of the coins.

Remembering with difficulty why I had come I went over to one of the stalls and examined porcelain vases and flowered tea-sets. At the door of the stall a young lady was talking and laughing with two young gentlemen. I remarked their English accents and listened vaguely to their conversation.

—O, I never said such a thing!

—O, but you did!

—O, but I didn't!

30   —Didn't she say that?

—Yes! I heard her.

—O, there's a … fib!

Observing me the young lady came over and asked me did I wish to buy anything. The tone of her voice was not encouraging; she seemed to have spoken to me out of a sense of duty. I looked humbly at the great jars that stood like eastern guards at either side of the dark entrance to the stall and murmured:

—No, thank you.

35   The young lady changed the position of one of the vases and went back to the two young men. They began to talk of the same subject. Once or twice the young lady glanced at me over her shoulder.

I lingered before her stall, though I knew my stay was useless, to make my interest in her wares seem the more real. Then I turned away slowly

---

[5]**The Arab's Farewell to His Steed** Joyce is referring to "The Arab to His Favorite Steed," a popular sentimental poem by Caroline Norton (1808–1877).

and walked down the middle of the bazaar. I allowed the two pennies to fall against the sixpence in my pocket. I heard a voice call from one end of the gallery that the light was out. The upper part of the hall was now completely dark.

Gazing up into the darkness I saw myself as a creature driven and derided by vanity; and my eyes burned with anguish and anger.

YOUR TURN

1. *Setting* in fiction—the time and place where the story occurs, the environment in which the characters move—will be discussed in the next chapter, but here we can make the obvious point that setting often has an influence on the characters: For instance, it may shape them or they may respond to it. What does the second paragraph of "Araby" tell us about the boy's nature?

2. Reread the story, underlining or highlighting religious images. What is the point of these images?

3. If you had to summarize the *plot* briefly, what would you say? If you briefly had to describe the personality—the character—of the protagonist, what would you say?

RAYMOND CARVER

Raymond Carver (1938–1988) was born in Clatskanie, a logging town in Oregon. In 1963 he graduated from Humboldt State College in northern California and then did further study at the University of Iowa.

His early years were not easy—he married while still in college, divorced a little later, and sometimes suffered from alcoholism. In his last years he found both personal happiness and literary success, but he died of cancer at the age of fifty.

As a young man he wrote poetry while working at odd jobs (janitor, deliveryman, etc.); later he turned to fiction, though he continued to write poetry. Most of his fiction is of a sort called "minimalist," narrating in a spare, understated style stories about bewildered and sometimes exhausted men and women.

Cathedral

[1983]

This blind man, an old friend of my wife's, he was on his way to spend the night. His wife had died. So he was visiting the dead wife's relatives in Connecticut. He called my wife from his in-laws'. Arrangements were made. He would come by train, a five-hour trip, and my wife would meet him at the station. She hadn't seen him since she worked for him one summer in Seattle ten years ago. But she and the blind man had kept in touch. They made tapes and mailed them back and forth. I wasn't enthusiastic about his visit. He was no one I knew. And his being blind bothered me. My idea of blindness came from the movies. In the movies, the blind moved slowly and never laughed. Sometimes they were led by seeing-eye dogs. A blind man in my house was not something I looked forward to.

That summer in Seattle she had needed a job. She didn't have any money. The man she was going to marry at the end of the summer was in officers' training school. He didn't have any money, either. But she was in love with the guy, and he was in love with her, etc. She'd seen something in the paper: HELP WANTED—*Reading to Blind Man,* and a telephone number. She phoned and went over, was hired on the spot. She'd worked with this blind man all summer. She read stuff to him, case studies, reports, that sort of thing. She helped him organize his little office in the county social-service department. They'd become good friends, my wife and the blind man. How do I know these things? She told me. And she told me something else. On her last day in the office, the blind man asked if he could touch her face. She agreed to this. She told me he touched his fingers to every part of her face, her nose—even her neck! She never forgot it. She even tried to write a poem about it. She was always trying to write a poem. She wrote a poem or two every year, usually after something really important had happened to her.

When we first started going out together, she showed me the poem. In the poem, she recalled his fingers and the way they had moved around over her face. In the poem, she talked about what she had felt at the time, about what went through her mind when the blind man touched her nose and lips. I can remember I didn't think much of the poem. Of course, I didn't tell her that. Maybe I just don't understand poetry. I admit it's not the first thing I reach for when I pick up something to read.

Anyway, this man who'd first enjoyed her favors, the officer-to-be, he'd been her childhood sweetheart. So okay. I'm saying that at the end of the summer she let the blind man run his hands over her face, said goodbye to him, married her childhood etc., who was now a commissioned officer, and she moved away from Seattle. But they'd kept in touch, she and the blind man. She made the first contact after a year or so. She called him up one night from an Air Force base in Alabama. She wanted to talk. They talked. He asked her to send a tape and tell him about her life. She did this. She sent the tape. On the tape, she told the blind man about her husband and about their life together in the military. She told the blind man she loved her husband but she didn't like it where they lived and she didn't like it that he was part of the military-industrial thing. She told the blind man she'd written a poem and he was in it. She told him that she was writing a poem about what it was like to be an Air Force officer's wife. The poem wasn't finished yet. She was still writing it. The blind man made a tape. He sent her the tape. She made a tape. This went on for years. My wife's officer was posted to one base and then another. She sent tapes from Moody AFB, McGuire, McConnell, and finally Travis, near Sacramento, where one night she got to feeling lonely and cut off from people she kept losing in that moving-around life. She got to feeling she couldn't go it another step. She went in and swallowed all the pills and capsules in the medicine chest and washed them down with a bottle of gin. Then she got into a hot bath and passed out.

5   But instead of dying, she got sick. She threw up. Her officer—why should he have a name? he was the childhood sweetheart, and what more does he want?—came home from somewhere, found her, and called the

ambulance. In time, she put it all on a tape and sent the tape to the blind man. Over the years, she put all kinds of stuff on tapes and sent the tapes off lickety-split. Next to writing a poem every year, I think it was her chief means of recreation. On one tape, she told the blind man she'd decided to live away from her officer for a time. On another tape, she told him about her divorce. She and I began going out, and of course she told her blind man about it. She told him everything, or so it seemed to me. Once she asked me if I'd like to hear the latest tape from the blind man. This was a year ago. I was on the tape, she said. So I said okay, I'd listen to it. I got us drinks and we settled down in the living room. We made ready to listen. First she inserted the tape into the player and adjusted a couple of dials. Then she pushed a lever. The tape squeaked and someone began to talk in this loud voice. She lowered the volume. After a few minutes of harmless chitchat, I heard my own name in the mouth of this stranger, this blind man I didn't even know! And then this: "From all you've said about him, I can only conclude—" But we were interrupted, a knock at the door, something, and we didn't ever get back to the tape. Maybe it was just as well. I'd heard all I wanted to.

Now this same blind man was coming to sleep in my house.

"Maybe I could take him bowling," I said to my wife. She was at the draining board doing scalloped potatoes. She put down the knife she was using and turned around.

"If you love me," she said, "you can do this for me. If you don't love me, okay. But if you had a friend, any friend, and the friend came to visit, I'd make him feel comfortable." She wiped her hands with the dish towel.

"I don't have any blind friends," I said.

10   "You don't have *any* friends," she said. "Period. Besides," she said, "goddamn it, his wife's just died! Don't you understand that? The man's lost his wife!"

I didn't answer. She'd told me a little about the blind man's wife. Her name was Beulah. Beulah! That's a name for a colored woman.

"Was his wife a Negro?" I asked.

"Are you crazy?" my wife said. "Have you just flipped or something?" She picked up a potato. I saw it hit the floor, then roll under the stove. "What's wrong with you?" she said. "Are you drunk?"

"I'm just asking," I said.

15   Right then my wife filled me in with more detail than I cared to know. I made a drink and sat at the kitchen table to listen. Pieces of the story began to fall into place.

Beulah had gone to work for the blind man the summer after my wife had stopped working for him. Pretty soon Beulah and the blind man had themselves a church wedding. It was a little wedding—who'd want to go to such a wedding in the first place?—just the two of them, plus the minister and the minister's wife. But it was a church wedding just the same. It was what Beulah had wanted, he'd said. But even then Beulah must have been carrying the cancer in her glands. After they had been inseparable for eight years—my wife's word, *inseparable*—Beulah's health went into a rapid decline. She died in a Seattle hospital room, the blind man sitting beside the bed and holding on to her hand. They'd married, lived and worked together, slept together—had sex, sure—and then the blind man had to bury her. All this without his having ever seen what the goddamned woman looked like. It was beyond my understanding. Hearing this, I felt sorry for the blind man for a little bit. And then I found myself thinking what a pitiful life this woman must have led. Imagine a woman who could never see herself as she was seen in the eyes of her loved one. A woman who could go on day after day and never receive the smallest compliment from her beloved. A woman whose husband could never read the expression on her face, be it misery or something better. Someone who could wear makeup or not— what difference to him? She could, if she wanted, wear green eye-shadow around one eye, a straight pin in her nostril, yellow slacks, and purple shoes, no matter. And then to slip off into death, the blind man's hand on her hand, his blind eyes streaming tears—I'm imagining now—her last thought maybe this: that he never even knew what she looked like, and she on an express to the grave. Robert was left with a small insurance policy and a half of a twenty-peso Mexican coin. The other half of the coin went into the box with her. Pathetic.

So when the time rolled around, my wife went to the depot to pick him up. With nothing to do but wait—sure, I blamed him for that—I was having a drink and watching the TV when I heard the car pull into the drive. I got up from the sofa with my drink and went to the window to have a look.

I saw my wife laughing as she parked the car. I saw her get out of the car and shut the door. She was still wearing a smile. Just amazing. She went around to the other side of the car to where the blind man was already start-ing to get out. This blind man, feature this, he was wearing a full beard! A beard on a blind man! Too much, I say. The blind man reached into the back seat and dragged out a suitcase. My wife took his arm, shut the car door, and, talking all the way, moved him down the drive and then up the steps to the front porch. I turned off the TV. I finished my drink, rinsed the glass, dried my hands. Then I went to the door.

My wife said, "I want you to meet Robert. Robert, this is my husband. I've told you all about him." She was beaming. She had this blind man by his coat sleeve.

20   The blind man let go of his suitcase and up came his hand.

I took it. He squeezed hard, held my hand, and then he let it go.

"I feel like we've already met," he boomed.

"Likewise," I said. I didn't know what else to say. Then I said, "Wel-come. I've heard a lot about you." We began to move then, a little group, from the porch into the living room, my wife guiding him by the arm. The blind man was carrying his suitcase in his other hand. My wife said things like, "To your left here, Robert. That's right. Now watch it, there's a chair. That's it. Sit down right here. This is the sofa. We just bought this sofa two weeks ago."

I started to say something about the old sofa. I'd liked that old sofa. But I didn't say anything. Then I wanted to say something else, small-talk, about the scenic ride along the Hudson. How going *to* New York, you should sit on the right-hand side of the train, and coming *from* New York, the left-hand side.

25   "Did you have a good train ride?" I said. "Which side of the train did you sit on, by the way?"

"What a question, which side!" my wife said. "What's it matter which side?" she said.

"I just asked," I said.

"Right side," the blind man said. "I hadn't been on a train in nearly forty years. Not since I was a kid. With my folks. That's been a long time. I'd nearly forgotten the sensation. I have winter in my beard now," he said. "So I've been told, anyway. Do I look distinguished, my dear?" the blind man said to my wife.

"You look distinguished, Robert," she said. "Robert," she said. "Robert, it's just so good to see you."

30   My wife finally took her eyes off the blind man and looked at me. I had the feeling she didn't like what she saw. I shrugged.

I've never met, or personally known, anyone who was blind. This blind man was late forties, a heavy-set, balding man with stooped shoulders, as if he carried a great weight there. He wore brown slacks, brown shoes, a light-brown shirt, a tie, a sports coat. Spiffy. He also had this full beard. But he didn't use a cane and he didn't wear dark glasses. I'd always thought dark glasses were a must for the blind. Fact was, I wished he had a pair. At first glance, his eyes looked like anyone else's eyes. But if you looked close, there was something different about them. Too much white in the iris, for one thing, and the pupils seemed to move around in the sockets without his knowing it or being able to stop it. Creepy. As I stared at his face, I saw the left pupil turn in toward his nose while the other made an effort to keep in one place. But it was only an effort, for that eye was on the roam without his knowing it or wanting it to be.

I said, "Let me get you a drink. What's your pleasure? We have a little of everything. It's one of our pastimes."

"Bub, I'm a Scotch man myself," he said fast enough in this big voice.

"Right," I said. Bub! "Sure you are. I knew it."

35   He let his fingers touch his suitcase, which was sitting alongside the sofa. He was taking his bearings. I didn't blame him for that.

"I'll move that up to your room," my wife said.

"No, that's fine," the blind man said loudly. "It can go up when I go up."

"A little water with the Scotch?" I said.

"Very little," he said.

40   "I knew it," I said.

He said, "Just a tad. The Irish actor, Barry Fitzgerald? I'm like that fellow. When I drink water, Fitzgerald said, I drink water. When I drink whiskey, I drink whiskey." My wife laughed. The blind man brought his hand up under his beard. He lifted his beard slowly and let it drop.

I did the drinks, three big glasses of Scotch with a splash of water in each. Then we made ourselves comfortable and talked about Robert's travels. First the long flight from the West Coast to Connecticut, we covered that. Then from Connecticut up here by train. We had another drink concerning that leg of the trip.

I remembered having read somewhere that the blind didn't smoke because, as speculation had it, they couldn't see the smoke they exhaled. I thought I knew that much and that much only about blind people. But this blind man smoked his cigarette down to the nubbin and then lit another one. This blind man filled his ashtray and my wife emptied it.

When we sat down at the table for dinner, we had another drink. My wife heaped Robert's plate with cube steak, scalloped potatoes, green beans. I buttered him up two slices of bread. I said, "Here's bread and butter for you." I swallowed some of my drink. "Now let us pray," I said, and the blind man lowered his head. My wife looked at me, her mouth agape. "Pray the phone won't ring and the food doesn't get cold," I said.

45   We dug in. We ate everything there was to eat on the table. We ate like there was no tomorrow. We didn't talk. We ate. We scarfed. We grazed that table. We were into serious eating. The blind man had right away located his foods, he knew just where everything was on his plate. I watched with admiration as he used his knife and fork on the meat. He'd cut two pieces of meat, fork the meat into his mouth, and then go all out for the scalloped potatoes, the beans next, and then he'd tear off a hunk of buttered bread and eat that. He'd follow this up with a big drink of milk. It didn't seem to bother him to use his fingers once in a while, either.

          We finished everything, including half a strawberry pie. For a few moments, we sat as if stunned. Sweat beaded on our faces. Finally, we got up from the table and left the dirty plates. We didn't look back. We took ourselves into the living room and sank into our places again. Robert and my wife sat on the sofa. I took the big chair. We had us two or three more drinks while they talked about the major things that had come to pass for them in the past ten years. For the most part, I just listened. Now and then I joined in. I didn't want him to think I'd left the room, and I didn't want her to think I was feeling left out. They talked of things that had happened to them—to them!—these past ten years. I waited in vain to hear my name on my wife's sweet lips: "And then my dear husband came into my life"—something like that. But I heard nothing of the sort. More talk of Robert. Robert had done a little of everything, it seemed, a regular blind jack-of-all-trades. But most recently he and his wife had had an Amway distributorship, from which, I gathered, they'd earned their living, such as it was. The blind man was also a ham radio operator. He talked in his loud voice about conversations he'd had with fellow operators in Guam, in the Philippines, in Alaska, and even in Tahiti. He said he'd have a lot of friends there if he ever wanted to go visit those places. From time to time, he'd turn his blind face toward me, put his hand under his beard, ask me something. How long had I been in my present position? (Three years.) Did I like my work? (I didn't.) Was I going to stay with it? (What were the options?) Finally, when I thought he was beginning to run down, I got up and turned on the TV.

          My wife looked at me with irritation. She was heading toward a boil. Then she looked at the blind man and said, "Robert, do you have a TV?"

          The blind man said, "My dear, I have two TVs. I have a color set and a black-and-white thing, an old relic. It's funny, but if I turn the TV on, and I'm always turning it on, I turn on the color set. It's funny, don't you think?"

          I didn't know what to say to that. I had absolutely nothing to say to that. No opinion. So I watched the news program and tried to listen to what the announcer was saying.

50   "This is a color TV," the blind man said. "Don't ask me how, but I can tell."

          "We traded up a while ago," I said.

          The blind man had another taste of his drink. He lifted his beard, sniffed it, and let it fall. He leaned forward on the sofa. He positioned his ashtray on the coffee table, then put the lighter to his cigarette. He leaned back on the sofa and crossed his legs at the ankles.

My wife covered her mouth, and then she yawned. She stretched. She said, "I think I'll go upstairs and put on my robe. I think I'll change into something else. Robert, you make yourself comfortable," she said.

"I'm comfortable," the blind man said.

55   "I want you to feel comfortable in this house," she said.

"I am comfortable," the blind man said.

After she'd left the room, he and I listened to the weather report and then to the sports roundup. By that time, she'd been gone so long I didn't know if she was going to come back. I thought she might have gone to bed. I wished she'd come back downstairs. I didn't want to be left alone with a blind man. I asked him if he wanted another drink, and he said sure. Then I asked if he wanted to smoke some dope with me. I said I'd just rolled a number. I hadn't, but I planned to do so in about two shakes.

"I'll try some with you," he said.

"Damn right," I said. "That's the stuff."

60   I got our drinks and sat down on the sofa with him. Then I rolled us two fat numbers. I lit one and passed it. I brought it to his fingers. He took it and inhaled.

"Hold it as long as you can," I said. I could tell he didn't know the first thing.

My wife came back downstairs wearing her pink robe and her pink slippers.

"What do I smell?" she said.

"We thought we'd have us some cannabis," I said.

65   My wife gave me a savage look. Then she looked at the blind man and said, "Robert, I didn't know you smoked."

He said, "I do now, my dear. There's a first time for everything. But I don't feel anything yet."

"This stuff is pretty mellow," I said. "This stuff is mild. It's dope you can reason with," I said. "It doesn't mess you up."

"Not much it doesn't, bub," he said, and laughed.

My wife sat on the sofa between the blind man and me. I passed her the number. She took it and toked and then passed it back to me. "Which way is this going?" she said. Then she said, "I shouldn't be smoking this. I can hardly keep my eyes open as it is. That dinner did me in. I shouldn't have eaten so much."

70   "It was the strawberry pie," the blind man said. "That's what did it," he said, and he laughed his big laugh. Then he shook his head.

"There's more strawberry pie," I said.

"Do you want some more, Robert?" my wife said.

"Maybe in a little while," he said.

We gave our attention to the TV. My wife yawned again. She said, "Your bed is made up when you feel like going to bed, Robert. I know you must have had a long day. When you're ready to go to bed, say so." She pulled his arm. "Robert?"

75   He came to and said, "I've had a real nice time. This beats tapes, doesn't it?"

I said, "Coming at you," and I put the number between his fingers. He inhaled, held the smoke, and then let it go. It was like he'd been doing it since he was nine years old.

"Thanks, bub," he said. "But I think this is all for me. I think I'm beginning to feel it," he said. He held the burning roach out for my wife.

"Same here," she said. "Ditto. Me, too." She took the roach and passed it
to me. "I may just sit here for a while between you two guys with my eyes
closed. But don't let me bother you, okay? Either one of you. If it bothers
you, say so. Otherwise, I may just sit here with my eyes closed until you're
ready to go to bed," she said. "Your bed's made up, Robert, when you're
ready. It's right next to our room at the top of the stairs. We'll show you up
when you're ready. You wake me up now, you guys, if I fall asleep." She said
that and then she closed her eyes and went to sleep.

The news program ended. I got up and changed the channel. I sat back
down on the sofa. I wished my wife hadn't pooped out. Her head lay across
the back of the sofa, her mouth open. She'd turned so that her robe slipped
away from her legs, exposing a juicy thigh. I reached to draw her robe back
over her, and it was then that I glanced at the blind man. What the hell! I
flipped the robe open again.

80   "You say when you want some strawberry pie," I said.

"I will," he said.

I said, "Are you tired? Do you want me to take you up to your bed? Are
you ready to hit the hay?"

"Not yet," he said. "No, I'll stay up with you, bub. If that's all right. I'll
stay up until you're ready to turn in. We haven't had a chance to talk.
Know what I mean? I feel like me and her monopolized the evening." He
lifted his beard and he let it fall. He picked up his cigarettes and his
lighter.

"That's all right," I said. Then I said, "I'm glad for the company."

85   And I guess I was. Every night I smoked dope and stayed up as long as I
could before I fell asleep. My wife and I hardly ever went to bed at the same
time. When I did go to sleep, I had these dreams. Sometimes I'd wake up
from one of them, my heart going crazy.

Something about the church and the Middle Ages was on the TV. Not
your run-of-the-mill TV fare. I wanted to watch something else. I turned to
the other channels. But there was nothing on them, either. So I turned back
to the first channel and apologized.

"Bub, it's all right," the blind man said. "It's fine with me. Whatever you
want to watch is okay. I'm always learning something. Learning never ends.
It won't hurt me to learn something tonight. I got ears," he said.

We didn't say anything for a time. He was leaning forward with his head
turned at me, his right ear aimed in the direction of the set. Very disconcert-
ing. Now and then his eyelids drooped and then they snapped open again.
Now and then he put his fingers into his beard and tugged, like he was
thinking about something he was hearing on the television.

On the screen, a group of men wearing cowls was being set upon and
tormented by men dressed in skeleton costumes and men dressed as devils.
The men dressed as devils wore devil masks, horns, and long tails. This
pageant was part of a procession. The Englishman who was narrating the
thing said it took place in Spain once a year. I tried to explain to the blind
man what was happening.

90   "Skeletons," he said. "I know about skeletons," he said, and he nodded.

The TV showed this one cathedral. Then there was a long, slow look at another one. Finally, the picture switched to the famous one in Paris, with its flying buttresses and its spires reaching up to the clouds. The camera pulled away to show the whole of the cathedral rising above the skyline.

There were times when the Englishman who was telling the thing would shut up, would simply let the camera move around the cathedrals. Or else the camera would tour the countryside, men in fields walking behind oxen. I waited as long as I could. Then I felt I had to say something. I said, "They're showing the outside of this cathedral now. Gargoyles. Little statues carved to look like monsters. Now I guess they're in Italy. Yeah, they're in Italy. There's paintings on the walls of this one church."

"Are those fresco paintings, bub?" he asked, and he sipped from his drink.

I reached for my glass. But it was empty. I tried to remember what I could remember. "You're asking me are those frescoes?" I said. "That's a good question. I don't know."

95   The camera moved to a cathedral outside Lisbon. The differences in the Portuguese cathedral compared with the French and Italian were not that great. But they were there. Mostly the interior stuff. Then something occurred to me, and I said, "Something has occurred to me. Do you have any idea what a cathedral is? What they look like, that is? Do you follow me? If somebody says cathedral to you, do you have any notion what they're talking about? Do you know the difference between that and a Baptist church, say?"

He let the smoke dribble from his mouth. "I know they took hundreds of workers fifty or a hundred years to build," he said. "I just heard the man say that, of course. I know generations of the same families worked on a cathedral. I heard him say that, too. The men who began their life's work on them, they never lived to see the completion of their work. In that wise, bub, they're no different from the rest of us, right?" He laughed. Then his eyelids drooped again. His head nodded. He seemed to be snoozing. Maybe he was imagining himself in Portugal. The TV was showing another cathedral now. This one was in Germany. The Englishman's voice droned on. "Cathedrals," the blind man said. He sat up and rolled his head back and forth. "If you want the truth, bub, that's about all I know. What I just said. What I heard him say. But maybe you could describe one to me? I wish you'd do it. I'd like that. If you want to know, I really don't have a good idea."

I stared hard at the shot of the cathedral on the TV. How could I even begin to describe it? But say my life depended on it. Say my life was being threatened by an insane guy who said I had to do it or else.

I stared some more at the cathedral before the picture flipped off into the countryside. There was no use. I turned to the blind man and said, "To begin with, they're very tall." I was looking around the room for clues. "They reach way up. Up and up. Toward the sky. They're so big, some of them, they have to have these supports. To help hold them up, so to speak. These supports are called buttresses. They remind me of viaducts, for some reason. But maybe you don't know viaducts, either? Sometimes the cathedrals have devils and such carved into the front. Sometimes lords and ladies. Don't ask me why this is," I said.

He was nodding. The whole upper part of his body seemed to be moving back and forth.

100   "I'm not doing so good, am I?" I said.

He stopped nodding and leaned forward on the edge of the sofa. As he listened to me, he was running his fingers through his beard. I wasn't getting through to him, I could see that. But he waited for me to go on just the same. He nodded, like he was trying to encourage me. I tried to think what else to say. "They're really big," I said. "They're massive. They're built of stone. Marble, too, sometimes. In those olden days, when they built cathedrals, men wanted to be close to God. In those olden days, God was an important part of everyone's life. You could tell this from their cathedral-building. I'm sorry," I said, "but it looks like that's the best I can do for you. I'm just no good at it."

"That's all right, bub," the blind man said. "Hey, listen. I hope you don't mind my asking you. Can I ask you something? Let me ask you a simple question, yes or no. I'm just curious and there's no offense. You're my host. But let me ask if you are in any way religious? You don't mind my asking?"

I shook my head. He couldn't see that, though. A wink is the same as a nod to a blind man. "I guess I don't believe in it. In anything. Sometimes it's hard. You know what I'm saying?"

"Sure, I do," he said.

105   "Right," I said.

The Englishman was still holding forth. My wife sighed in her sleep. She drew a long breath and went on with her sleeping.

"You'll have to forgive me," I said. "But I can't tell you what a cathedral looks like. It just isn't in me to do it. I can't do any more than I've done."

The blind man sat very still, his head down, as he listened to me.

I said, "The truth is, cathedrals don't mean anything special to me. Nothing. Cathedrals. They're something to look at on late-night TV. That's all they are."

110   It was then that the blind man cleared his throat. He brought something up. He took a handkerchief from his back pocket. Then he said, "I get it, bub. It's okay. It happens. Don't worry about it," he said. "Hey, listen to me. Will you do me a favor? I got an idea. Why don't you find us some heavy paper? And a pen. We'll do something. We'll draw one together. Get us a pen and some heavy paper. Go on, bub, get the stuff," he said.

So I went upstairs. My legs felt like they didn't have any strength in them. They felt like they did after I'd done some running. In my wife's room, I looked around. I found some ballpoints in a little basket on her table. And then I tried to think where to look for the kind of paper he was talking about.

Downstairs, in the kitchen, I found a shopping bag with onion skins in the bottom of the bag. I emptied the bag and shook it. I brought it into the living room and sat down with it near his legs. I moved some things, smoothed the wrinkles from the bag, spread it out on the coffee table.

The blind man got down from the sofa and sat next to me on the carpet.

He ran his fingers over the paper. He went up and down the sides of the paper. The edges, even the edges. He fingered the corners.

115   "All right," he said. "All right, let's do her."

He found my hand, the hand with the pen. He closed his hand over my hand. "Go ahead, bub, draw," he said. "Draw. You'll see. I'll follow along with you. It'll be okay. Just begin now like I'm telling you. You'll see. Draw," the blind man said.

So I began. First I drew a box that looked like a house. It could have been the house I lived in. Then I put a roof on it. At either end of the roof, I drew spires. Crazy.

"Swell," he said. "Terrific. You're doing fine," he said. "Never thought anything like this could happen in your lifetime, did you, bub? Well, it's a strange life, we all know that. Go on now. Keep it up."

I put in windows with arches. I drew flying buttresses. I hung great doors. I couldn't stop. The TV station went off the air. I put down the pen and closed and opened my fingers. The blind man felt around over the paper. He moved the tips of his fingers over the paper, all over what I had drawn, and he nodded.

120   "Doing fine," the blind man said.

I took up the pen again, and he found my hand. I kept at it. I'm no artist. But I kept drawing just the same.

My wife opened up her eyes and gazed at us. She sat up on the sofa, her robe hanging open. She said, "What are you doing? Tell me, I want to know."

I didn't answer her.

The blind man said, "We're drawing a cathedral. Me and him are working on it. Press hard," he said to me. "That's right. That's good," he said. "Sure. You got it, bub, I can tell. You didn't think you could. But you can, can't you? You're cooking with gas now. You know what I'm saying? We're going to really have us something here in a minute. How's the old arm?" he said. "Put some people in there now. What's a cathedral without people?"

125   My wife said, "What's going on? Robert, what are you doing? What's going on?"

"It's all right," he said to her. "Close your eyes now," the blind man said to me.

I did it. I closed them just like he said.

"Are they closed?" he said. "Don't fudge."

"They're closed," I said.

130   "Keep them that way," he said. He said, "Don't stop now. Draw."

So we kept on with it. His fingers rode my fingers as my hand went over the paper. It was like nothing else in my life up to now.

Then he said, "I think that's it. I think you got it," he said. "Take a look. What do you think?"

But I had my eyes closed. I thought I'd keep them that way for a little longer. I thought it was something I ought to do.

"Well?" he said. "Are you looking?"

135   My eyes were still closed. I was in my house. I knew that. But I didn't feel like I was inside anything.

"It's really something," I said.

YOUR TURN

1. What was your impression of the narrator after reading the first five paragraphs?
2. Why does the narrator feel threatened by the blind man? Has he any reason to feel threatened?

3. What attitude does the narrator reveal in the following passage:

> She'd turned so that her robe had slipped away from her legs, expos-
> ing a juicy thigh. I reached to draw her robe back over her, and it
> was then that I glanced at the blind man. What the hell! I flipped the
> robe open again.

4. Why does the narrator not open his eyes at the end of the story?
5. The television program happens to be about cathedrals, but if the point
   is to get the narrator to draw something while the blind man's hand
   rests on the narrator's, the program could have been about some other
   topic, for example, about skyscrapers or about the Statue of Liberty. Do
   you think that a cathedral is a better choice, for Carver's purposes, than
   these other subjects? Why?
6. In what ways does Carver prepare us for the narrator's final state of
   mind?

8

Setting

Aesop's fable of the vixen and the lioness (page 129) could take place anywhere—in a jungle or at the town dump. The particular place is of no importance; all that matters is the meeting of the two beasts. But in some stories the setting—the place and the time—plays so large a role that it is almost a character. Indeed, some writers have said that their ideas for stories came from particular settings, particular places, and particular times. Note that the setting consists not only of the locale—for instance, Texas—but also the time—for instance, during the Great Depression. If we take a moment or two to brainstorm examples—this is a favorite exercise in creative writing courses—each of us can begin to imagine all sorts of interesting settings for stories: a working-class neighborhood in a city in the Midwest in the 1950s; a small town in Jamaica at the turn of the century; a village in the English countryside two hundred years ago; a town on the Texas-Mexico border in the year 2010. The settings for novels and stories are innumerable, emerging from the experiences and memories of authors, or from the curious imaginations of authors who look forward to exploring times and places unlike any they have known themselves.

Authors of short stories usually keep the focus on a single setting—they do not have the space to do much more than that. But not always: The action may shift from one setting to another, as the authors use this second setting in counterpoint to the first. They might begin in one time and place, but end up in a time and place that are significantly different.

Through the careful use of details in the setting or settings, the author also implies the historical and political contexts, the customs and conventions and values of the community, and the dominant issues and conflicts of the society as a whole. Novelists, working on a bigger canvas, can do even more, but it is an ambition, a goal, for authors of short stories too. The setting is there for the character and the plot, but the character and plot are there for the setting as well—for giving us knowledge about and insight into specific times and places, thereby enriching and deepening our human understanding. We move outside our own experience, perceiving the diverse and complex ways of life that people have lived or are living now.

The setting may strike us as real and recognizable. On the other hand, it may not: We may find ourselves in the midst of a time and a place far distant and different from any with which we are familiar. It may feel to us strange, exotic, alien, even otherworldly, as we know from the settings of ghost stories and works of science fiction—and in the settings for much popular fiction, such as the Middle

Earth where J. R. R. Tolkien locates *The Lord of the Rings* trilogy. Again, what we have known and experienced is extended and complicated: We travel to new and unusual times and strange (sometimes very strange) places. We see ourselves from a new perspective.

In this chapter, we present three short stories, Nathaniel Hawthorne's "Young Goodman Brown," which is set in Puritan New England; Charlotte Perkins Gilman's "The Yellow Wallpaper," which is set in a country estate in the late nineteenth century, where a woman is undergoing treatment for depression; and Ralph's Ellison's "Battle Royal," which is set in a rural area somewhere in the segregated American South in the late 1920s. Here are questions to keep in mind about the settings for these stories and for others in this book that you will be reading and studying:

1. What is the setting when the story begins?
2. Does the action remain in this setting throughout, or does the author move from one setting to another or others? How are these settings similar to and different from one another?
3. What does the author show us in action and tell us in description about the setting?
4. How much detail about the setting does the author give us? What kinds of details does the author draw our attention to?
5. Does the setting take on a special significance as the story progresses, perhaps becoming symbolic in its own right? Consider, for example, how an author might present New York City or London or some other great urban center—as a place of excitement, opportunity, and freedom, or as a place of anonymity, loneliness, and widespread poverty and degradation.
6. How is the main character affected, shaped, or influenced by the setting? Does the main character, in turn, cause the setting—his or her time and place—to change in any way?

NATHANIEL HAWTHORNE

Nathaniel Hawthorne (1804–1864) was born in Salem, Massachusetts, the son of a sea captain. Two of his ancestors were judges; one had persecuted Quakers, and another had served at the Salem witch trials. In his stories and novels Hawthorne keeps returning to the Puritan past, studying guilt, sin, and isolation.

Young Goodman Brown   [1835]

Young Goodman[1] Brown came forth, at sunset, into the street at Salem village; but put his head back, after crossing the threshold, to exchange a parting kiss with his young wife. And Faith, as the wife was aptly named, thrust her own pretty head into the street, letting the wind play with the pink ribbons of her cap while she called to Goodman Brown.

"Dearest heart," whispered she, softly and rather sadly, when her lips were close to his ear, "prithee put off your journey until sunrise and sleep in

---

[1]**Goodman** polite term of address for a man of humble standing.

your own bed to-night. A lone woman is troubled with such dreams and such thoughts that she's afeared of herself sometimes. Pray tarry with me this night, dear husband, of all nights in the year."

"My love and my Faith," replied young Goodman Brown, "of all nights in the year, this one night must I tarry away from thee. My journey, as thou callest it, forth and back again, must needs be done 'twixt now and sunrise. What, my sweet, pretty wife, dost thou doubt me already, and we but three months married?"

"Then God bless you!" said Faith, with the pink ribbons; "and may you find all well when you come back."

5   "Amen!" cried Goodman Brown. "Say thy prayers, dear Faith, and go to bed at dusk, and no harm will come to thee."

So they parted; and the young man pursued his way until, being about to turn the corner by the meeting-house, he looked back and saw the head of Faith still peeping after him with a melancholy air, in spite of her pink ribbons.

"Poor little Faith!" thought he, for his heart smote him. "What a wretch am I to leave her on such an errand! She talks of dreams, too. Methought as she spoke there was trouble in her face, as if a dream had warned her what work is to be done to-night. But no, no; 'twould kill her to think it. Well, she's a blessed angel on earth; and after this one night, I'll cling to her skirts and follow her to heaven."

With this excellent resolve for the future, Goodman Brown felt himself justified in making more haste on his present evil purpose. He had taken a dreary road, darkened by all the gloomiest trees of the forest, which barely stood aside to let the narrow path creep through, and closed immediately behind. It was all as lonely as could be; and there is this peculiarity in such a solitude, that the traveler knows not who may be concealed by the innumerable trunks and the thick boughs overhead; so that with lonely footsteps he may yet be passing through an unseen multitude.

"There may be a devilish Indian behind every tree," said Goodman Brown, to himself and he glanced fearfully behind him as he added, "What if the devil himself should be at my very elbow!"

10   His head being turned back, he passed a crook of the road, and, looking forward again, beheld the figure of a man, in grave and decent attire, seated at the foot of an old tree. He arose at Goodman Brown's approach and walked onward side by side with him.

"You are late, Goodman Brown," said he. "The clock of the Old South was striking as I came through Boston, and that is full fifteen minutes agone."

"Faith kept me back a while," replied the young man, with a tremor in his voice, caused by the sudden appearance of his companion, though not wholly unexpected.

It was now deep dusk in the forest, and deepest in that part of it where these two were journeying. As nearly as could be discerned, the second traveler was about fifty years old, apparently in the same rank of life as Goodman Brown, and bearing a considerable resemblance to him, though perhaps more in expression than features. Still they might have been taken for father and son. And yet, though the elder person was as simply clad as the younger, and as simple in manner too, he had an indescribable air of one who knew the world, and who would not have felt abashed at the governor's dinner table or in King William's court, were it possible that his affairs should call

him thither. But the only thing about him that could be fixed upon as remarkable was his staff, which bore the likeness of a great black snake, so curiously wrought that it might almost be seen to twist and wriggle itself like a
living serpent. This, of course, must have been an ocular deception, assisted
by the uncertain light.

"Come, Goodman Brown," cried his fellow-traveler, "this is a dull pace
for the beginning of a journey. Take my staff, if you are so soon weary."

15   "Friend," said the other, exchanging his slow pace for a full stop, "having
kept covenant by meeting thee here, it is my purpose now to return whence
I came. I have scruples touching the matter thou wot'st[2] of."

"Sayest thou so?" replied he of the serpent, smiling apart. "Let us walk
on, nevertheless, reasoning as we go; and if I convince thee not thou shalt
turn back. We are but a little way in the forest yet."

"Too far! too far!" exclaimed the goodman, unconsciously resuming his
walk. "My father never went into the woods on such an errand, nor his father before him. We have been a race of honest men and good Christians
since the days of the martyrs; and shall I be the first of the name of Brown
that ever took this path and kept—"

"Such company, thou wouldst say," observed the elder person, interpreting his pause. "Well said, Goodman Brown! I have been as well acquainted
with your family as with ever a one among the Puritans; and that's no trifle
to say. I helped your grandfather, the constable, when he lashed the Quaker
woman so smartly through the streets of Salem; and it was I that brought
your father a pitch-pine knot, kindled at my own hearth, to set fire to an
Indian village, in King Philip's war.[3] They were my good friends, both; and
many a pleasant walk have we had along this path, and returned merrily
after midnight. I would fain be friends with you for their sake."

"If it be as thou sayest," replied Goodman Brown, "I marvel they never
spoke of these matters; or, verily, I marvel not, seeing that the least rumor of
the sort would have driven them from New England. We are a people of
prayer, and good works to boot, and abide no such wickedness."

20   "Wickedness or not," said the traveler with the twisted staff, "I have a
very general acquaintance here in New England. The deacons of many a
church have drunk the communion wine with me; the selectmen of divers
towns make me their chairman; and a majority of the Great and General
Court are firm supporters of my interest. The governor and I, too—But these
are state secrets."

"Can this be so?" cried Goodman Brown, with a stare of amazement at
his undisturbed companion. "Howbeit, I have nothing to do with the governor and council; they have their own ways, and are no rule for a simple husbandman[4] like me. But, were I to go on with thee, how should I meet the eye
of that good old man, our minister, at Salem village? Oh, his voice would
make me tremble both Sabbath day and lecture day."

Thus far the elder traveler had listened with due gravity; but now burst
into a fit of irrepressible mirth, shaking himself so violently that his snake-
like staff actually seemed to wriggle in sympathy.

---

[2]**wot'st** knowest.   [3]**King Philip's war** war waged in 1675–76 by the English colonists
against the Wampanoag Indian leader Metcom, known as "King Philip."   [4]**husbandman**
farmer, or, more generally, any man of humble standing.

"Ha! ha! ha!" shouted he again and again; then composing himself, "Well, go on, Goodman Brown, go on; but, prithee, don't kill me with laughing."

"Well, then, to end the matter at once," said Goodman Brown, considerably nettled, "there is my wife, Faith. It would break her dear little heart; and I'd rather break my own."

25   "Nay, if that be the case," answered the other, "e'en go thy ways, Goodman Brown. I would not for twenty old women like the one hobbling before us that Faith should come to any harm."

As he spoke he pointed his staff at a female figure on the path, in whom Goodman Brown recognized a very pious and exemplary dame, who had taught him his catechism in youth, and was still his moral and spiritual adviser, jointly with the minister and Deacon Gookin.

"A marvel, truly, that Goody[5] Cloyse should be so far in the wilderness at nightfall," said he. "But with your leave, friend, I shall take a cut through the woods until we have left this Christian woman behind. Being a stranger to you, she might ask whom I was consorting with and whither I was going."

"Be it so," said his fellow-traveler. "Betake you the woods, and let me keep the path."

Accordingly the young man turned aside, but took care to watch his companion, who advanced softly along the road until he had come within a staff's length of the old dame. She, meanwhile, was making the best of her way, with singular speed for so aged a woman, and mumbling some indistinct words—a prayer, doubtless—as she went. The traveler put forth his staff and touched her withered neck with what seemed the serpent's tail.

30   "The devil!" screamed the pious old lady.

"Then Goody Cloyse knows her old friend?" observed the traveler, confronting her and leaning on his writhing stick.

"Ah, forsooth, and is it your worship indeed?" cried the good dame. "Yea, truly is it, and in the very image of my old gossip, Goodman Brown, the grandfather of the silly fellow that now is. But—would your worship believe it?—my broomstick hath strangely disappeared, stolen, as I suspect, by that unhanged witch, Goody Cory, and that, too, when I was all anointed with the juice of smallage and cinquefoil, and wolf's bane—"

"Mingled with fine wheat and the fat of a new-born babe," said the shape of old Goodman Brown.

"Ah, your worship knows the recipe," cried the old lady, cackling aloud. "So, as I was saying, being all ready for the meeting, and no horse to ride on, I made up my mind to foot it; for they tell me there is a nice young man to be taken into communion to-night. But now your good worship will lend me your arm, and we shall be there in a twinkling."

35   "That can hardly be," answered her friend. "I may not spare you my arm, Goody Cloyse; but here is my staff, if you will."

So saying, he threw it down at her feet, where, perhaps, it assumed life, being one of the rods which its owner had formerly lent to the Egyptian magi. Of this fact, however, Goodman Brown could not take cognizance. He had cast up his eyes in astonishment, and, looking down again, beheld neither Goody

---

[5]**Goody** contraction of Goodwife, a polite term of address for a married woman of humble standing.

Cloyse nor the serpentine staff but his fellow-traveler alone, who waited for him as calmly as if nothing had happened.

"That old woman taught me my catechism," said the young man; and there was a world of meaning in this simple comment.

They continued to walk onward, while the elder traveler exhorted his companion to make good speed and persevere in the path, discoursing so aptly that his arguments seemed rather to spring up in the bosom of his auditor than to be suggested by himself. As they went, he plucked a branch of maple to serve for a walking stick, and began to strip it of the twigs and little boughs, which were wet with evening dew. The moment his fingers touched them they became strangely withered and dried up as with a week's sunshine. Thus the pair proceeded, at a good free pace, until suddenly, in a gloomy hollow of the road, Goodman Brown sat himself down on the stump of a tree and refused to go any farther.

"Friend," said he, stubbornly, "my mind is made up. Not another step will I budge on this errand. What if a wretched old woman do choose to go to the devil when I thought she was going to heaven: is that any reason why I should quit my dear Faith and go after her?"

40   "You will think better of this by and by," said his acquaintance, composedly. "Sit here and rest yourself a while; and when you feel like moving again, there is my staff to help you along."

Without more words, he threw his companion the maple stick, and was as speedily out of sight as if he had vanished into the deepening gloom. The young man sat a few moments by the roadside, applauding himself greatly, and thinking with how clear a conscience he should meet the minister in his morning walk, nor shrink from the eye of good old Deacon Gookin. And what calm sleep would be his that very night, which was to have been spent so wickedly, but so purely and sweetly now, in the arms of Faith! Amidst these pleasant and praiseworthy meditations, Goodman Brown heard the tramp of horses along the road, and deemed it advisable to conceal himself within the verge of the forest, conscious of the guilty purpose that had brought him thither, though now so happily turned from it.

On came the hoof-tramps and the voices of the riders, two grave old voices, conversing soberly as they drew near. These mingled sounds appeared to pass along the road, within a few yards of the young man's hiding-place; but, owing doubtless to the depth of the gloom at that particular spot, neither the travelers nor their steeds were visible. Though their figures brushed the small boughs by the wayside, it could not be seen that they intercepted, even for a moment, the faint gleam from the strip of bright sky athwart which they must have passed. Goodman Brown alternately crouched and stood on tiptoe, pulling aside the branches and thrusting forth his head as far as he durst without discerning so much as a shadow. It vexed him the more, because he could have sworn, were such a thing possible, that he recognized the voices of the minister and Deacon Gookin, jogging along quietly, as they were wont to do, when bound to some ordination or ecclesiastical council. While yet within hearing, one of the riders stopped to pluck a switch.

"Of the two, reverend sir," said the voice like the deacon's, "I had rather miss an ordination dinner than to-night's meeting. They tell me that some of our community are to be here from Falmouth and beyond, and others from Connecticut and Rhode Island, besides several of the Indian powwows, who, after their fashion, know almost as much deviltry as the best of us. Moreover, there is a goodly young woman to be taken into communion."

"Mighty well, Deacon Gookin!" replied the solemn old tones of the minister. "Spur up, or we shall be late. Nothing can be done, you know, until I get on the ground."

45   The hoofs clattered again; and the voices, talking so strangely in the empty air, passed on through the forest, where no church had ever been gathered or solitary Christian prayed. Whither, then, could these holy men be journeying so deep into the heathen wilderness? Young Goodman Brown caught hold of a tree for support, being ready to sink down on the ground, faint and overburdened with the heavy sickness of his heart. He looked up to the sky, doubting whether there really was a heaven above him. Yet there was the blue arch, and the stars brightening in it.

"With heaven above and Faith below, I will yet stand firm against the devil!" cried Goodman Brown.

While he still gazed upward into the deep arch of the firmament and had lifted his hands to pray, a cloud, though no wind was stirring, hurried across the zenith and hid the brightening stars. The blue sky was still visible, except directly overhead, where this black mass of cloud was sweeping swiftly northward. Aloft in the air, as if from the depths of the cloud, came a confused and doubtful sound of voices. Once the listener fancied that he could distinguish the accents of towns-people of his own, men and women, both pious and ungodly, many of whom he had met at the communion table, and had seen others rioting at the tavern. The next moment, so indistinct were the sounds, he doubted whether he had heard aught but the murmur of the old forest, whispering without a wind. Then came a stronger swell of those familiar tones, heard daily in the sunshine at Salem village, but never until now from a cloud of night. There was one voice, of a young woman, uttering lamentations, yet with an uncertain sorrow, and entreating for some favor, which, perhaps, it would grieve her to obtain; and all the unseen multitude, both saints and sinners, seemed to encourage her onward.

"Faith!" shouted Goodman Brown, in a voice of agony and desperation; and the echoes of the forest mocked him, crying, "Faith! Faith!" as if bewildered wretches were seeking her all through the wilderness.

The cry of grief, rage, and terror was yet piercing the night, when the unhappy husband held his breath for a response. There was a scream, drowned immediately in a louder murmur of voices, fading into far-off laughter, as the dark cloud swept away, leaving the clear and silent sky above Goodman Brown. But something fluttered lightly down through the air and caught on the branch of a tree. The young man seized it, and beheld a pink ribbon.

50   "My Faith is gone!" cried he, after one stupefied moment. "There is no good on earth; and sin is but a name. Come, devil; for to thee is this world given."

And, maddened with despair, so that he laughed loud and long, did Goodman Brown grasp his staff and set forth again, at such a rate that he seemed to fly along the forest path rather than to walk or run. The road grew wilder and drearier and more faintly traced, and vanished at length, leaving him in the heart of the dark wilderness, still rushing onward with the instinct that guides mortal man to evil. The whole forest was peopled with frightful sounds—the creaking of the trees, the howling of wild beasts, and the yell of Indians; while sometimes the wind tolled like a distant church bell, and sometimes gave a broad roar around the traveler, as if all Nature were laughing him to scorn. But he was himself the chief horror of the scene, and shrank not from its other horrors.

"Ha! ha! ha!" roared Goodman Brown when the wind laughed at him. "Let us hear which will laugh loudest. Think not to frighten me with your deviltry. Come witch, come lizard, come Indian powwow, come devil himself, and here comes Goodman Brown. You may as well fear him as he fear you!"

In truth, all through the haunted forest there could be nothing more frightful than the figure of Goodman Brown. On he flew among the black pines, brandishing his staff with frenzied gestures, now giving vent to an inspiration of horrid blasphemy, and now shouting forth such laughter as set all the echoes of the forest laughing like demons around him. The fiend in his own shape is less hideous than when he rages in the breast of man. Thus sped the demoniac on his course, until, quivering among the trees, he saw a red light before him, as when the felled trunks and branches of a clearing have been set on fire, and throw up their lurid blaze against the sky, at the hour of midnight. He paused, in a lull of the tempest that had driven him onward, and heard the swell of what seemed a hymn, rolling solemnly from a distance with the weight of many voices. He knew the tune; it was a familiar one in the choir of the village meeting-house. The verse died heavily away, and was lengthened by a chorus, not of human voices, but of all the sounds of the benighted wilderness pealing in awful harmony together. Goodman Brown cried out; and his cry was lost to his own ear by its unison with the cry of the desert.

In the interval of silence he stole forward until the light glared full upon his eyes. At one extremity of an open space, hemmed in by the dark wall of the forest, arose a rock, bearing some rude, natural resemblance either to an altar or a pulpit, and surrounded by four blazing pines, their tops aflame, their stems untouched, like candles at an evening meeting. The mass of foliage that had overgrown the summit of the rock was all on fire, blazing high into the night and fitfully illuminating the whole field. Each pendent twig and leafy festoon was in a blaze. As the red light arose and fell, a numerous congregation alternately shone forth, then disappeared in shadow, and again grew, as it were, out of the darkness, peopling the heart of the solitary woods at once.

55   "A grave and dark-clad company," quoth Goodman Brown.

In truth they were such. Among them, quivering to-and-fro between gloom and splendor, appeared faces that would be seen next day at the council board of the province, and others which, Sabbath after Sabbath, looked devoutly heavenward, and benignantly over the crowded pews, from the holiest pulpits in the land. Some affirm that the lady of the governor was there. At least three were high dames well known to her, and wives of honored husbands, and widows, a great multitude, and ancient maidens, all of excellent repute, and fair young girls, who trembled lest their mothers should espy them. Either the sudden gleams of light flashing over the obscure field bedazzled Goodman Brown, or he recognized a score of the church-members of Salem village famous for their especial sanctity. Good old Deacon Gookin had arrived, and waited at the skirts of that venerable saint, his revered pastor. But, irreverently consorting with these grave, reputable, and pious people, these elders of the church, these chaste dames and dewy virgins, there were men of dissolute lives and women of spotted fame, wretches given over to all mean and filthy vice, and suspected even of horrid crimes. It was strange to see that the good shrank not from the wicked, nor were the sinners abashed by the saints. Scattered also among their pale-faced enemies were the Indian priests, or powwows, who had often scared their native forest with more hideous incantations than any known to English witchcraft.

"But, where is Faith?" thought Goodman Brown; and, as hope came into his heart, he trembled.

Another verse of the hymn arose, a slow and mournful strain, such as the pious love, but joined to words which expressed all that our nature can conceive of sin, and darkly hinted at far more. Unfathomable to mere mortals is the lore of fiends. Verse after verse was sung; and still the chorus of the desert swelled between, like the deepest tone of a mighty organ; and with the final peal of that dreadful anthem there came a sound, as if the roaring wind, the rushing streams, the howling beasts, and every other voice of the unconcerted wilderness were mingling and according with the voice of guilty man in homage to the prince of all. The four blazing pines threw up a loftier flame, and obscurely discovered shapes and visages of horror on the smoke wreaths above the impious assembly. At the same moment the fire on the rock shot redly forth and formed a glowing arch above its base, where now appeared a figure. With reverence be it spoken, the figure bore no slight similitude, both in garb and manner, to some grave divine of the New England churches.

"Bring forth the converts!" cried a voice that echoed through the field and rolled into the forest.

60   At the word, Goodman Brown stepped forth from the shadow of the trees and approached the congregation, with whom he felt a loathful brotherhood by the sympathy of all that was wicked in his heart. He could have wellnigh sworn that the shape of his own dead father beckoned him to advance, looking downward from a smoke wreath, while a woman, with dim features of despair, threw out her hand to warn him back. Was it his mother? But he had no power to retreat one step, nor to resist, even in thought, when the minister and good old Deacon Gookin seized his arms and led him to the blazing rock. Thither came also the slender form of a veiled female, led between Goody Cloyse, that pious teacher of the catechism, and Martha Carrier, who had received the devil's promise to be queen of hell. A rampant hag was she. And there stood the proselytes beneath the canopy of fire.

"Welcome, my children," said the dark figure, "to the communion of your race. Ye have found thus young your nature and your destiny. My children, look behind you!"

They turned; and flashing forth, as it were, in a sheet of flame, the fiend worshippers were seen; the smile of welcome gleamed darkly on every visage.

"There," resumed the sable form, "are all whom ye have reverenced from youth. Ye deemed them holier than yourselves, and shrank from your own sin, contrasting it with their lives of righteousness and prayerful aspirations heavenward. Yet here are they all in my worshipping assembly. This night it shall be granted you to know their secret deeds: how hoary-bearded elders of the church have whispered wanton words to the young maids of their households; how many a woman, eager for widows' weeds, has given her

husband a drink at bedtime and let him sleep his last sleep in her bosom;
how beardless youths have made haste to inherit their fathers' wealth;
and how fair damsels—blush not, sweet ones—have dug little graves in the
garden, and bidden me, the sole guest, to an infant's funeral. By the sympathy
of your human hearts for sin ye shall scent out all the places—whether in
church, bedchamber, street, field, or forest—where crime has been committed, and shall exult to behold the whole earth one stain of guilt, one mighty
blood spot. Far more than this. It shall be yours to penetrate, in every bosom,
the deep mystery of sin, the fountain of all wicked arts, and which inex-
haustibly supplies more evil impulses than human power—than my power
at its utmost—can make manifest in deeds. And now, my children, look upon
each other."

They did so; and, by the blaze of the hell-kindled torches, the wretched
man beheld his Faith, and the wife her husband, trembling before that unhallowed altar.

65   "Lo, there ye stand, my children," said the figure, in a deep and solemn
tone, almost sad with its despairing awfulness, as if his once angelic nature
could yet mourn for our miserable race. "Depending upon one another's
hearts, ye had still hoped that virtue were not all a dream. Now are ye undeceived. Evil is the nature of mankind. Evil must be your only happiness. Welcome, again, my children, to the communion of your race."

"Welcome," repeated the fiend worshippers, in one cry of despair and
triumph.

And there they stood, the only pair, as it seemed, who were yet hesitating on the verge of wickedness in this dark world. A basin was hollowed,
naturally, in the rock. Did it contain water, reddened by the lurid light? or
was it blood? or, perchance, a liquid flame? Herein did the shape of evil dip
his hand and prepare to lay the mark of baptism upon their foreheads, that
they might be partakers of the mystery of sin, more conscious of the secret
guilt of others, both in deed and thought, than they could now be of their
own. The husband cast one look at his pale wife, and Faith at him. What pol-
luted wretches would the next glance show them to each other, shuddering
alike at what they disclosed and what they saw!

"Faith! Faith!" cried the husband, "look up to heaven, and resist the
wicked one."

Whether Faith obeyed he knew not. Hardly had he spoken when he
found himself amid calm night and solitude, listening to a roar of the wind
which died heavily away through the forest. He staggered against the rock,
and felt it chill and damp; while a hanging twig, that had been all on fire, be-
sprinkled his cheek with the coldest dew.

70   The next morning young Goodman Brown came slowly into the street
of Salem village, staring around him like a bewildered man. The good old
minister was taking a walk along the graveyard to get an appetite for breakfast and meditate his sermon, and bestowed a blessing, as he passed, on
Goodman Brown. He shrank from the venerable saint as if to avoid an anath-
ema. Old Deacon Gookin was at domestic worship, and the holy words of
his prayer were heard through the open window. "What God doth the wizard
pray to?" quoth Goodman Brown. Goody Cloyse, that excellent old Christian,
stood in the early sunshine at her own lattice, catechizing a little girl who
had brought her a pint of morning's milk. Goodman Brown snatched away
the child as from the grasp of the fiend himself. Turning the corner by the

meeting-house, he spied the head of Faith, with the pink ribbons, gazing anxiously forth, and bursting into such joy at sight of him that she skipped along the street and almost kissed her husband before the whole village. But Goodman Brown looked sternly and sadly into her face, and passed on without a greeting.

Had Goodman Brown fallen asleep in the forest and only dreamed a wild dream of a witch-meeting?

Be it so, if you will; but alas! it was a dream of evil omen for young Goodman Brown. A stern, a sad, a darkly meditative, a distrustful, if not a desperate man did he become from the night of that fearful dream. On the Sabbath day, when the congregation were singing a holy psalm, he could not listen because an anthem of sin rushed loudly upon his ear and drowned all the blessed strain. When the minister spoke from the pulpit with power and fervid eloquence, and, with his hand on the open Bible, of the sacred truths of our religion, and of saint-like lives and triumphant deaths, and of future bliss or misery unutterable, then did Goodman Brown turn pale, dreading lest the roof should thunder down upon the gray blasphemer and his hearers. Often, awaking suddenly at midnight, he shrank from the bosom of Faith; and at morning or eventide, when the family knelt down at prayer, he scowled and muttered to himself, and gazed sternly at his wife, and turned away. And when he had lived long, and was borne to his grave a hoary[6] corpse, followed by Faith, an aged woman, and children and grandchildren, a goodly procession, besides neighbors not a few, they carved no hopeful verse upon his tombstone, for his dying hour was gloom.

YOUR TURN

1. Do you take Faith to stand only for religious faith, or can she here also stand for one's faith in one's fellow human beings? Explain.
2. Hawthorne describes the second traveler as "about fifty years old, apparently in the same rank as Goodman Brown, and bearing a considerable resemblance to him." Further, "they might have been taken for father and son." What do you think Hawthorne is getting at here?
3. In the forest Brown sees (or thinks he sees) Goody Cloyse, the minister, Deacon Gookin, and others. Does he in fact meet them, or does he dream of them? Or does he encounter "figures" and "forms" (rather than real people) whom the devil conjures up in order to deceive Brown?
4. Evaluate the view that when Brown enters the dark forest he is really entering his own evil mind.
5. A Hawthorne scholar we know says that he finds this story "terrifying." Do you agree? Or would you characterize your response to it differently? Explain, making reference to passages in the text.
6. Does a person have to be a Christian in order to understand "Young Goodman Brown"? Would a Christian reader find this story reassuring or disturbing? Can a non-Christian reader understand and appreciate the story? What might he or she learn from reading it?
7. Having read and studied "Young Goodman Brown," do you find you want to read more of Hawthorne's stories? Are you very eager, a little eager, or not really? Please explain.

---

[6]**hoary** gray or white with age; very old, ancient.

8. "Young Goodman Brown" is often included in anthologies of American literature and in collections of short stories. In your view, why is this the case? Do you agree with this decision, or does it puzzle you?

CHARLOTTE PERKINS GILMAN

Charlotte Perkins Gilman (1860–1935), née Charlotte Perkins, was born in Hartford, Connecticut. Her father deserted the family soon after Charlotte's birth; she was brought up by her mother, who found it difficult to make ends meet. For a while Charlotte worked as an artist and teacher of art, and in 1884, when she was twenty-four, she married an artist. In 1885 she had a daughter, but soon after the birth of the girl Charlotte had a nervous breakdown. At her husband's urging she spent a month in the sanitarium of Dr. S. Weir Mitchell, a physician who specialized in treating women with nervous disorders. (Mitchell is specifically named in "The Yellow Wallpaper.") Because the treatment—isolation and total rest—nearly drove her to insanity, she fled Mitchell and her husband. In California she began a career as a lecturer and writer on feminist topics. (She also supported herself by teaching school and by keeping a boardinghouse.) Among her books are Women and Economics *(1899) and* The Man-Made World *(1911), which were revived by the feminist movement in the 1960s and 1970s. In 1900 she married a cousin, George Gilman. From all available evidence, the marriage was successful. Certainly it did not restrict her activities as a feminist. In 1935, suffering from inoperable cancer, she took her own life.*

"The Yellow Wallpaper," written in 1892—that is, written after she had been treated by S. Weir Mitchell for her nervous breakdown—was at first interpreted either as a ghost story or as a Poe-like study of insanity. Only in recent years has it been seen as a feminist story. One might ask oneself if these interpretations are mutually exclusive.

The Yellow Wallpaper   [1892]

It is very seldom that mere ordinary people like John and myself secure ancestral halls for the summer.

A colonial mansion, a hereditary estate. I would say a haunted house, and reach the height of romantic felicity—but that would be asking too much of fate!

Still I will proudly declare that there is something queer about it.

Else, why should it be let so cheaply? And why have stood so long untenanted?

5   John laughs at me, of course, but one expects that in marriage.

John is practical in the extreme. He has no patience with faith, an intense horror of superstition, and he scoffs openly at any talk of things not to be felt and seen and put down in figures.

John is a physician, and *perhaps*—(I would not say it to a living soul, of course, but this is dead paper and a great relief to my mind)—*perhaps* that is one reason I do not get well faster.

You see he does not believe I am sick!

And what can one do?

10   If a physician of high standing, and one's own husband, assures friends and relatives that there is really nothing the matter with one but temporary nervous depression—a slight hysterical tendency—what is one to do?

My brother is also a physician, and also of high standing, and he says the same thing.

So I take phosphates or phosphites—whichever it is, and tonics, and journeys, and air, and exercise, and am absolutely forbidden to "work" until I am well again.

Personally, I disagree with their ideas.

Personally, I believe that congenial work, with excitement and change, would do me good.

15   But what is one to do?

I did write for a while in spite of them; but it *does* exhaust me a good deal—having to be so sly about it, or else meet with heavy opposition.

I sometimes fancy that in my condition if I had less opposition and more society and stimulus—but John says the very worst thing I can do is to think about my condition, and I confess it always makes me feel bad.

So I will let it alone and talk about the house.

The most beautiful place! It is quite alone, standing well back from the road, quite three miles from the village. It makes me think of English places that you read about, for there are hedges and walls and gates that lock, and lots of separate little houses for the gardeners and people.

20   There is a *delicious* garden! I never saw such a garden—large and shady, full of box-bordered paths, and lined with long grape-covered arbors with seats under them.

There were greenhouses, too, but they are all broken now.

There was some legal trouble, I believe, something about the heirs and coheirs; anyhow, the place has been empty for years.

That spoils my ghostliness, I am afraid, but I don't care—there is something strange about the house—I can feel it.

I even said so to John one moonlight evening, but he said what I felt was a *draught*, and shut the window.

25   I get unreasonably angry with John sometimes. I'm sure I never used to be so sensitive. I think it is due to this nervous condition.

But John says if I feel so, I shall neglect proper self-control; so I take pains to control myself—before him, at least, and that makes me very tired.

I don't like our room a bit. I wanted one downstairs that opened on the piazza and had roses all over the window, and such pretty old-fashioned chintz hangings! But John would not hear of it.

He said there was only one window and not room for two beds, and no near room for him if he took another.

He is very careful and loving, and hardly lets me stir without special direction.

30   I have a schedule prescription for each hour in the day; he takes all care from me, and so I feel basely ungrateful not to value it more.

He said we came here solely on my account, that I was to have perfect rest and all the air I could get. "Your exercise depends on your strength, my dear," said he, "and your food somewhat on your appetite; but air you can absorb all the time." So we took the nursery at the top of the house.

It is a big, airy room, the whole floor nearly, with windows that look all ways, and air and sunshine galore. It was nursery first and then playroom and gymnasium, I should judge; for the windows are barred for little children, and there are rings and things in the walls.

The paint and paper look as if a boys' school had used it. It is stripped off—the paper—in great patches all around the head of my bed, about as far as I can reach, and in a great place on the other side of the room low down. I never saw a worse paper in my life.

One of those sprawling flamboyant patterns committing every artistic sin.

35   It is dull enough to confuse the eye in following, pronounced enough to constantly irritate and provoke study, and when you follow the lame uncertain curves for a little distance they suddenly commit suicide—plunge off at outrageous angles, destroy themselves in unheard of contradictions.

The color is repellent, almost revolting; a smouldering unclean yellow, strangely faded by the slow-turning sunlight.

It is a dull yet lurid orange in some places, a sickly sulphur tint in others.

No wonder the children hated it! I should hate it myself if I had to live in this room long.

There comes John, and I must put this away,—he hates to have me write a word.

40   We have been here two weeks, and I haven't felt like writing before, since that first day.

I am sitting by the window now, up in this atrocious nursery, and there is nothing to hinder my writing as much as I please, save lack of strength.

John is away all day, and even some nights when his cases are serious.

I am glad my case is not serious!

But these nervous troubles are dreadfully depressing.

45   John does not know how much I really suffer. He knows there is no *reason* to suffer, and that satisfies him.

Of course it is only nervousness. It does weigh on me so not to do my duty in any way!

I meant to be such a help to John, such a real rest and comfort, and here I am a comparative burden already!

Nobody would believe what an effort it is to do what little I am able,—to dress and entertain, and order things.

It is fortunate Mary is so good with the baby. Such a dear baby!

50   And yet I *cannot* be with him, it makes me so nervous.

I suppose John never was nervous in his life. He laughs at me so about this wallpaper!

At first he meant to repaper the room, but afterwards he said that I was letting it get the better of me, and that nothing was worse for a nervous patient than to give way to such fancies.

He said that after the wallpaper was changed it would be the heavy bedstead, and then the barred windows, and then that gate at the head of the stairs, and so on.

"You know the place is doing you good," he said, "and really, dear, I don't care to renovate the house just for a three months' rental."

55   "Then do let us go downstairs," I said, "there are such pretty rooms there."

Then he took me in his arms and called me a blessed little goose, and said he would go down to the cellar, if I wished, and have it whitewashed into the bargain.

But he is right enough about the beds and windows and things.

It is an airy and comfortable room as any one need wish, and, of course, I would not be so silly as to make him uncomfortable just for a whim.

I'm really getting quite fond of the big room, all but that horrid paper.

60   Out of one window I can see the garden, those mysterious deep-shaded arbors, the riotous old-fashioned flowers, and bushes and gnarly trees.

Out of another I get a lovely view of the bay and a little private wharf belonging to the estate. There is a beautiful shaded lane that runs down there from the house. I always fancy I see people walking in these numerous paths and arbors, but John has cautioned me not to give way to fancy in the least. He says that with my imaginative power and habit of story-making, a nervous weakness like mine is sure to lead to all manner of excited fancies, and that I ought to use my will and good sense to check the tendency. So I try.

I think sometimes that if I were only well enough to write a little it would relieve the press of ideas and rest me.

But I find I get pretty tired when I try.

It is so discouraging not to have any advice and companionship about my work. When I get really well, John says we will ask Cousin Henry and Julia down for a long visit; but he says he would as soon put fireworks in my pillow-case as to let me have those stimulating people about now.

65   I wish I could get well faster.

But I must not think about that. This paper looks to me as if it *knew* what a vicious influence it had!

There is a recurrent spot where the pattern lolls like a broken neck and two bulbous eyes stare at you upside down.

I get positively angry with the impertinence of it and the everlastingness. Up and down and sideways they crawl, and those absurd, unblinking eyes are everywhere. There is one place where two breadths didn't match, and the eyes go all up and down the line, one a little higher than the other.

I never saw so much expression in an inanimate thing before, and we all know how much expression they have! I used to lie awake as a child and get more entertainment and terror out of blank walls and plain furniture than most children could find in a toystore.

70   I remember what a kindly wink the knobs of our big, old bureau used to have, and there was one chair that always seemed like a strong friend.

I used to feel that if any of the other things looked too fierce I could always hop into that chair and be safe.

The furniture in this room is no worse than inharmonious, however, for we had to bring it all from downstairs. I suppose when this was used as a playroom they had to take the nursery things out, and no wonder! I never saw such ravages as the children have made here.

The wallpaper, as I said before, is torn off in spots, and it sticketh closer than a brother—they must have had perseverance as well as hatred.

Then the floor is scratched and gouged and splintered, the plaster itself is dug out here and there, and this great heavy bed which is all we found in the room, looks as if it had been through the wars.

75   But I don't mind it a bit—only the paper.

There comes John's sister. Such a dear girl as she is, and so careful of me! I must not let her find me writing.

She is a perfect and enthusiastic housekeeper, and hopes for no better profession. I verily believe she thinks it is the writing which made me sick!

But I can write when she is out, and see her a long way off from these windows.

There is one that commands the road, a lovely shaded winding road, and one that just looks off over the country. A lovely country, too, full of great elms and velvet meadows.

80 This wallpaper has a kind of sub-pattern in a different shade, a particularly irritating one, for you can only see it in certain lights, and not clearly then.

But in the places where it isn't faded and where the sun is just so—I can see a strange, provoking, formless sort of figure, that seems to skulk about behind that silly and conspicuous front design.

There's sister on the stairs!

Well, the Fourth of July is over! The people are all gone and I am tired out. John thought it might do me good to see a little company, so we just had mother and Nellie and the children down for a week.

Of course I didn't do a thing. Jennie sees to everything now.

85 But it tired me all the same.

John says if I don't pick up faster he shall send me to Weir Mitchell in the fall.

But I don't want to go there at all. I had a friend who was in his hands once, and she says he is just like John and my brother, only more so!

Besides, it is such an undertaking to go so far.

I don't feel as if it was worth while to turn my hand over for anything, and I'm getting dreadfully fretful and querulous.

90 I cry at nothing, and cry most of the time.

Of course I don't when John is here, or anybody else, but when I am alone.

And I am alone a good deal just now. John is kept in town very often by serious cases, and Jennie is good and lets me alone when I want her to.

So I walk a little in the garden or down that lovely lane, sit on the porch under the roses, and lie down up here a good deal.

I'm getting really fond of the room in spite of the wallpaper. Perhaps *because* of the wallpaper.

95 It dwells in my mind so!

I lie here on this great immovable bed—it is nailed down, I believe— and follow that pattern about by the hour. It is as good as gymnastics, I assure you. I start, we'll say, at the bottom, down in the corner over there where it has not been touched, and I determine for the thousandth time that I *will* follow that pointless pattern to some sort of a conclusion.

I know a little of the principle of design, and I know this thing was not arranged on any laws of radiation, or alternation, or repetition, or symmetry, or anything else that I ever heard of.

It is repeated, of course, by the breadths, but not otherwise.

Looked at in one way each breadth stands alone, the bloated curves and flourishes—a kind of "debased Romanesque"[1] with *delirium tremens*—go waddling up and down in isolated columns of fatuity.

100 But, on the other hand, they connect diagonally, and the sprawling outlines run off in great slanting waves of optic horror, like a lot of wallowing seaweeds in full chase.

---

[1]**Romanesque** a style of architecture developed in Italy and western Europe 1000–1200, between the Roman and the Gothic styles, characterized by the use of the round arch.

The whole thing goes horizontally, too, at least it seems so, and I exhaust myself in trying to distinguish the order of its going in that direction.

They have used a horizontal breadth for a frieze, and that adds wonderfully to the confusion.

There is one end of the room where it is almost intact, and there, when the crosslights fade and the low sun shines directly upon it, I can almost fancy radiation after all,—the interminable grotesques seem to form around a common center and rush off in headlong plunges of equal distraction.

It makes me tired to follow it. I will take a nap I guess.

105   I don't know why I should write this.

I don't want to.

I don't feel able.

And I know John would think it absurd. But I *must* say what I feel and think in some way—it is such a relief.

But the effort is getting to be greater than the relief!

110   Half the time now I am awfully lazy, and lie down ever so much.

John says I mustn't lose my strength, and has me take cod liver oil and lots of tonics and things, to say nothing of ale and wine and rare meat.

Dear John! He loves me very dearly, and hates to have me sick. I tried to have a real earnest reasonable talk with him the other day, and tell him how I wish he would let me go and make a visit to Cousin Henry and Julia.

But he said I wasn't able to go, nor able to stand it after I got there; and I did not make out a very good case for myself, for I was crying before I had finished.

It is getting to be a great effort for me to think straight. Just this nervous weakness I suppose.

115   And dear John gathered me up in his arms, and just carried me upstairs and laid me on the bed, and sat by me and read to me till it tired my head.

He said I was his darling and his comfort and all he had, and that I must take care of myself for his sake, and keep well.

He says no one but myself can help me out of it, that I must use my will and self-control and not let any silly fancies run away with me.

There's one comfort, the baby is well and happy, and does not have to occupy this nursery with the horrid wallpaper.

If we had not used it, that blessed child would have! What a fortunate escape! Why, I wouldn't have a child of mine, an impressionable little thing, live in such a room for worlds.

120   I never thought of it before, but it is lucky that John kept me here after all; I can stand it so much easier than a baby, you see.

Of course I never mention it to them any more—I am too wise,—but I keep watch of it all the same.

There are things in that paper that nobody knows but me, or ever will.

Behind that outside pattern the dim shapes get clearer every day.

It is always the same shape, only very numerous.

125   And it is like a woman stooping down and creeping about behind that pattern. I don't like it a bit. I wonder—I begin to think—I wish John would take me away from here!

* * *

It is so hard to talk to John about my case, because he is so wise, and because he loves me so.

But I tried last night.

It was moonlight. The moon shines in all around just as the sun does.

I hate to see it sometimes, it creeps so slowly, and always comes in by one window or another.

130   John was asleep and I hated to waken him, so I kept still and watched the moonlight on that undulating wallpaper till I felt creepy.

The faint figure behind seemed to shake the pattern, just as if she wanted to get out.

I got up softly and went to feel and see if the paper *did* move, and when I came back John was awake.

"What is it, little girl?" he said. "Don't go walking about like that—you'll get cold."

I thought it was a good time to talk, so I told him that I really was not gaining here, and that I wished he would take me away.

135   "Why darling!" said he, "our lease will be up in three weeks, and I can't see how to leave before.

"The repairs are not done at home, and I cannot possibly leave town just now. Of course if you were in any danger, I could and would, but you really are better, dear, whether you can see it or not. I am a doctor, dear, and I know. You are gaining flesh and color, your appetite is better, I feel really much easier about you."

"I don't weigh a bit more," said I, "nor as much; and my appetite may be better in the evening when you are here, but it is worse in the morning when you are away!"

"Bless her little heart!" said he with a big hug, "she shall be as sick as she pleases! But now let's improve the shining hours by going to sleep, and talk about it in the morning!"

"And you won't go away?" I asked gloomily.

140   "Why, how can I, dear? It is only three weeks more and then we will take a nice little trip of a few days while Jennie is getting the house ready. Really dear you are better!"

"Better in body perhaps—" I began, and stopped short, for he sat up straight and looked at me with such a stern, reproachful look that I could not say another word.

"My darling," said he, "I beg of you, for my sake and for our child's sake, as well as for your own, that you will never for one instant let that idea enter your mind! There is nothing so dangerous, so fascinating, to a temperament like yours. It is a false and foolish fancy. Can you trust me as a physician when I tell you so?"

So of course I said no more on that score, and we went to sleep before long. He thought I was asleep first, but I wasn't and lay there for hours trying to decide whether that front pattern and the back pattern really did move together or separately.

On a pattern like this, by daylight, there is a lack of sequence, a defiance of law, that is a constant irritant to a normal mind.

145   The color is hideous enough, and unreliable enough, and infuriating enough, but the pattern is torturing.

You think you have mastered it, but just as you get well underway in following, it turns a back-somersault and there you are. It slaps you in the face, knocks you down, and tramples upon you. It is like a bad dream.

The outside pattern is a florid arabesque, reminding one of a fungus. If you can imagine a toadstool in joints, an interminable string of toadstools, budding and sprouting in endless convolutions—why, that is something like it.

That is, sometimes!

There is one marked peculiarity about this paper, a thing nobody seems to notice but myself, and that is that it changes as the light changes.

150   When the sun shoots in through the east window—I always watch for that first long, straight ray—it changes so quickly that I never can quite believe it.

That is why I watch it always.

By moonlight—the moon shines in all night when there is a moon—I wouldn't know it was the same paper.

At night in any kind of light, in twilight, candlelight, lamplight, and worst of all by moonlight, it becomes bars! The outside pattern I mean, and the woman behind it is as plain as can be.

I didn't realize for a long time what the thing was that showed behind, that dim sub-pattern, but now I am quite sure it is a woman.

155   By daylight she is subdued, quiet. I fancy it is the pattern that keeps her so still. It is so puzzling. It keeps me quiet by the hour.

I lie down ever so much now. John says it is good for me, and to sleep all I can.

Indeed he started the habit by making me lie down for an hour after each meal.

It is a very bad habit I am convinced, for you see I don't sleep.

And that cultivates deceit, for I don't tell them I'm awake—O no!

160   The fact is I am getting a little afraid of John.

He seems very queer sometimes, and even Jennie has an inexplicable look.

It strikes me occasionally, just as a scientific hypothesis,—that perhaps it is the paper!

I have watched John when he did not know I was looking, and come into the room suddenly on the most innocent excuses, and I've caught him several times *looking at the paper!* And Jennie too. I caught Jennie with her hand on it once.

She didn't know I was in the room, and when I asked her in a quiet, a very quiet voice, with the most restrained manner possible, what she was doing with the paper—she turned around as if she had been caught stealing, and looked quite angry—asked me why I should frighten her so!

165   Then she said that the paper stained everything it touched, that she had found yellow smooches on all my clothes and John's, and she wished we would be more careful!

Did not that sound innocent? But I know she was studying that pattern, and I am determined that nobody shall find it out but myself!

Life is very much more exciting now than it used to be. You see I have something more to expect, to look forward to, to watch. I really do eat better, and am more quiet than I was.

John is so pleased to see me improve! He laughed a little the other day, and said I seemed to be flourishing in spite of my wallpaper.

I turned it off with a laugh. I had no intention of telling him it was *because* of the wallpaper—he would make fun of me. He might even want to take me away.

170   I don't want to leave now until I have found it out. There is a week more, and I think that will be enough.

I'm feeling ever so much better! I don't sleep much at night, for it is so interesting to watch developments; but I sleep a good deal in the daytime.

In the daytime it is tiresome and perplexing.

There are always new shoots on the fungus, and new shades of yellow all over it. I cannot keep count of them, though I have tried conscientiously.

It is the strangest yellow, that wallpaper! It makes me think of all the yellow things I ever saw—not beautiful ones like buttercups, but old foul, bad yellow things.

175   But there is something else about that paper—the smell! I noticed it the moment we came into the room, but with so much air and sun it was not bad. Now we have had a week of fog and rain, and whether the windows are open or not, the smell is here.

It creeps all over the house.

I find it hovering in the dining-room, skulking in the parlor, hiding in the hall, lying in wait for me on the stairs.

It gets into my hair.

Even when I go to ride, if I turn my head suddenly and surprise it— there is that smell!

180   Such a peculiar odor, too! I have spent hours in trying to analyze it, to find what it smelled like.

It is not bad—at first, and very gentle, but quite the subtlest, most enduring odor I ever met.

In this damp weather it is awful, I wake up in the night and find it hanging over me.

It used to disturb me at first. I thought seriously of burning the house— to reach the smell.

But now I am used to it. The only thing I can think of that it is like is the *color* of the paper! A yellow smell.

185   There is a very funny mark on this wall, low down, near the mopboard. A streak that runs round the room. It goes behind every piece of furniture, except the bed, a long, straight, even *smooch,* as if it had been rubbed over and over.

I wonder how it was done and who did it, and what they did it for. Round and round and round—round and round and round—it makes me dizzy!

I really have discovered something at last.

Through watching so much at night, when it changes so, I have finally found out.

The front pattern *does* move—and no wonder! The woman behind shakes it!

190   Sometimes I think there are a great many women behind, and sometimes only one, and she crawls around fast, and her crawling shakes it all over.

Then in the very bright spots she keeps still, and in the very shady spots she just takes hold of the bars and shakes them hard.

And she is all the time trying to climb through. But nobody could climb through that pattern—it strangles so; I think that is why it has so many heads.

They get through, and then the pattern strangles them off and turns them upside down, and makes their eyes white!

If those heads were covered or taken off it would not be half so bad.

195   I think that woman gets out in the daytime!

And I'll tell you why—privately—I've seen her!

I can see her out of every one of my windows!

It is the same woman, I know, for she is always creeping, and most women do not creep by daylight.

I see her in that long shaded lane, creeping up and down. I see her in those dark grape arbors, creeping all around the garden.

200   I see her on that long road under the trees, creeping along, and when a carriage comes she hides under the blackberry vines.

I don't blame her a bit. It must be very humiliating to be caught creeping by daylight!

I always lock the door when I creep by daylight. I can't do it at night, for I know John would suspect something at once.

And John is so queer now, that I don't want to irritate him. I wish he would take another room! Besides, I don't want anybody to get that woman out at night but myself.

I often wonder if I could see her out of all the windows at once.

205   But, turn as fast as I can, I can only see out of one at one time.

And though I always see her, she *may* be able to creep faster than I can turn!

I have watched her sometimes away off in the open country, creeping as fast as a cloud shadow in a high wind.

If only that top pattern could be gotten off from the under one! I mean to try it, little by little.

I have found out another funny thing, but I shan't tell it this time! It does not do to trust people too much.

210   There are only two more days to get this paper off, and I believe John is beginning to notice. I don't like the look in his eyes.

And I heard him ask Jennie a lot of professional questions about me. She had a very good report to give.

She said I slept a good deal in the daytime.

John knows I don't sleep very well at night, for all I'm so quiet!

He asked me all sorts of questions, too, and pretended to be very loving and kind.

215   As if I couldn't see through him!

Still, I don't wonder he acts so, sleeping under this paper for three months.

It only interests me, but I feel sure John and Jennie are secretly affected by it.

Hurrah! This is the last day, but it is enough. John is to stay in town over night, and won't be out until this evening.

Jennie wanted to sleep with me—the sly thing! But I told her I should undoubtedly rest better for a night all alone.

220   That was clever, for really I wasn't alone a bit! As soon as it was moonlight and that poor thing began to crawl and shake the pattern, I got up and ran to help her.

I pulled and she shook, I shook and she pulled, and before morning we had peeled off yards of that paper.

A strip about as high as my head and half around the room.

And then when the sun came and that awful pattern began to laugh at me, I declared I would finish it to-day!

We go away to-morrow, and they are moving all the furniture down again to leave things as they were before.

225   Jennie looked at the wall in amazement, but I told her merrily that I did it out of pure spite at the vicious thing.

She laughed and said she wouldn't mind doing it herself, but I must not get tired.

How she betrayed herself that time!

But I am here, and no person touches this paper but me—not *alive!*

She tried to get me out of the room—it was too patent! But I said it was so quiet and empty and clean now that I believed I would lie down again and sleep all I could, and not to wake me even for dinner—I would call when I woke.

230   So now she is gone, and the servants are gone, and the things are gone, and there is nothing left but that great bedstead nailed down, with the canvas mattress we found on it.

We shall sleep downstairs to-night, and take the boat home to-morrow.

I quite enjoy the room, now it is bare again.

How those children did tear about here!

This bedstead is fairly gnawed!

235   But I must get to work.

I have locked the door and thrown the key down into the front path.

I don't want to go out, and I don't want to have anybody come in, till John comes.

I want to astonish him.

I've got a rope up here that even Jennie did not find. If that woman does get out, and tries to get away, I can tie her!

240   But I forgot I could not reach far without anything to stand on!

This bed will *not* move!

I tried to lift and push it until I was lame, and then I got so angry I bit off a little piece at one corner—but it hurt my teeth.

Then I peeled off all the paper I could reach standing on the floor. It sticks horribly and the pattern just enjoys it! All those strangled heads and bulbous eyes and waddling fungus growths just shriek with derision!

I am getting angry enough to do something desperate. To jump out of the window would be admirable exercise, but the bars are too strong even to try.

245   Besides I wouldn't do it. Of course not. I know well enough that a step like that is improper and might be misconstrued.

I don't like to *look* out of the windows even—there are so many of those creeping women, and they creep so fast.

I wonder if they all come out of that wallpaper as I did?

But I am securely fastened now by my well-hidden rope—you don't get *me* out in the road there!

I suppose I shall have to get back behind the pattern when it comes night, and that is hard!

250 It is so pleasant to be out in this great room and creep around as I please!

I don't want to go outside. I won't, even if Jennie asks me to.

For outside you have to creep on the ground, and everything is green instead of yellow.

But here I can creep smoothly on the floor, and my shoulder just fits in that long smooch around the wall, so I cannot lose my way.

Why there's John at the door!

255 It is no use, young man, you can't open it!

How he does call and pound!

Now he's crying for an axe.

It would be a shame to break down that beautiful door!

"John dear!" said I in the gentlest voice, "the key is down by the front steps, under a plantain leaf!"

260 That silenced him for a few moments.

Then he said—very quietly indeed, "Open the door, my darling!"

"I can't," said I. "The key is down by the front door under a plantain leaf!"

And then I said it again, several times, very gently and slowly, and said it so often that he had to go and see, and he got it of course, and came in. He stopped short by the door.

"What is the matter?" he cried. "For God's sake, what are you doing!"

265 I kept on creeping just the same, but I looked at him over my shoulder.

"I've got out at last," said I, "in spite of you and Jane. And I've pulled off most of the paper, so you can't put me back!"

Now why should that man have fainted? But he did, and right across my path by the wall, so that I had to creep over him every time!

YOUR TURN

1. At the beginning of the story, Gilman's narrator tells us where she is. What is the setting? What do we learn about the setting as the story unfolds?
2. One scholar has said that Gilman presents a "setting within a setting"? What do you think he is referring to? Please explain.
3. How would you describe the narrator's state of mind at the start of the story? Would you agree that by the end it has changed? A lot? A little? Explain as carefully as you can, citing evidence from the text.
4. How are men presented in this story? What is your response to how they are presented?
5. Gilman's story is often included in American history courses. What does this story reveal to us about the lives of American women in the 1890s?
6. Compose a letter, written by the narrator's husband, to her parents (that is, his in-laws), in which he describes what has happened to the narrator.

RALPH ELLISON

Ralph Ellison (1914–1994) was born in Oklahoma City. His father died when Ellison was three, and his mother supported herself and her child by working as a domestic. A trumpeter since boyhood, after graduating from high school Ellison went to study music at Tuskegee Institute, a black college in Alabama founded by Booker T. Washington. In 1936 he dropped out of Tuskegee and went to Harlem to study music composition and the visual arts; there he met Langston Hughes and Richard Wright, who encouraged him to turn to fiction. Ellison published stories and essays, and in 1942 became the managing editor of Negro Quarterly. *During World War II he served in the Merchant Marines. After the war he returned to writing. Acclaimed for his fiction and literary and cultural criticism, Ellison lectured and taught at various American colleges and universities, including Bard, Columbia, Rutgers, Yale, Chicago, and New York University, where he was Albert Schweitzer professor in the Humanities.*

"Battle Royal" was first published in 1947 and slightly revised (a transitional paragraph was added at the end of the story) for the opening chapter of Ellison's novel, Invisible Man *(1952), a book cited by* Book-Week *as "the most significant work of fiction written by an American" in the years between 1945 and 1965. In addition to publishing stories and one novel, Ellison published critical essays, which are brought together in* The Collected Essays of Ralph Ellison *(1995).*

Battle Royal   [1947]

It goes a long way back, some twenty years. All my life I had been looking for something, and everywhere I turned someone tried to tell me what it was. I accepted their answers too, though they were often in contradiction and even self-contradictory. I was naïve. I was looking for myself and asking everyone except myself questions which I, and only I, could answer. It took me a long time and much painful boomeranging of my expectations to achieve a realization everyone else appears to have been born with: That I am nobody but myself. But first I had to discover that I am an invisible man!

And yet I am no freak of nature, nor of history. I was in the cards, other things having been equal (or unequal) eighty-five years ago. I am not ashamed of my grandparents for having been slaves. I am only ashamed of myself for having at one time been ashamed. About eighty-five years ago they were told that they were free, united with others of our country in everything pertaining to the common good, and, in everything social, separate like the fingers of the hand. And they believed it. They exulted in it. They stayed in their place, worked hard, and brought up my father to do the same. But my grandfather is the one. He was an odd old guy, my grandfather, and I am told I take after him. It was he who caused the trouble. On his deathbed he called my father to him and said, "Son, after I'm gone I want you to keep up the good fight. I never told you, but our life is a war and I have been a traitor all my born days, a spy in the enemy's country ever since I give up my gun back in the Reconstruction. Live with your head in the lion's mouth. I want you to overcome 'em with yeses, undermine 'em with grins, agree 'em to death and destruction, let 'em swoller you till they vomit or bust wide open." They thought the old man had gone out of his mind. He

Gordon Parks (1912–2006), *Ralph Ellison*. Parks, an African American photographer with an international reputation, published many books of photographs, including *Camera Portraits: The Techniques and Principles of Documentary Portraiture* (1948), where this picture appears.

had been the meekest of men. The younger children were rushed from the room, the shades drawn and the flame of the lamp turned so low that it sputtered on the wick like the old man's breathing. "Learn it to the young-uns," he whispered fiercely; then he died.

But my folks were more alarmed over his last words than over his dying. It was as though he had not died at all, his words caused so much anxiety. I was warned emphatically to forget what he had said and, indeed, this is the first time it has been mentioned outside the family circle. It had a tremendous effect upon me, however. I could never be sure of what he meant. Grandfather had been a quiet old man who never made any trouble, yet on his deathbed he had called himself a traitor and a spy, and he had spoken of his meekness as a dangerous activity. It became a constant puzzle which lay unanswered in the back of my mind. And whenever things went well for me I remembered my grandfather and felt guilty and uncomfortable. It was as though I was carrying out his advice in spite of myself. And to make it worse, everyone loved me for it. I was praised by the most lily-white men of the town. I was considered an example of desirable conduct—just as my grandfather had been. And what puzzled me was that the old man had defined it as *treachery*. When I was praised for my conduct I felt a guilt that in some way I was doing something that was really against the wishes of the white folks, that if they had understood they would have desired me to act just the opposite, that I should have been sulky and mean, and that that really would have been what they wanted, even though they were fooled and thought they wanted me to act as I did. It made me afraid that some day they would look upon me as a traitor and I would be lost. Still I was more afraid to act any other way because they didn't like that at all. The old man's words were like a curse. On my graduation day I delivered an oration in which I showed that humility was the secret, indeed, the very essence of progress.

(Not that I believed this—how could I, remembering my grandfather?—I only believed that it worked.) It was a great success. Everyone praised me and I was invited to give the speech at a gathering of the town's leading white citizens. It was a triumph for our whole community.

It was in the main ballroom of the leading hotel. When I got there I discovered that it was on the occasion of a smoker, and I was told that since I was to be there anyway I might as well take part in the battle royal to be fought by some of my schoolmates as part of the entertainment. The battle royal came first.

All of the town's big shots were there in their tuxedoes, wolfing down the buffet foods, drinking beer and whiskey and smoking black cigars. It was a large room with a high ceiling. Chairs were arranged in neat rows around three sides of a portable boxing ring. The fourth side was clear, revealing a gleaming space of polished floor. I had some misgivings over the battle royal, by the way. Not from a distaste for fighting, but because I didn't care too much for the other fellows who were to take part. They were tough guys who seemed to have no grandfather's curse worrying their minds. No one could mistake their toughness. And besides, I suspected that fighting a battle royal might detract from the dignity of my speech. In those pre-invisible days I visualized myself as a potential Booker T. Washington. But the other fellows didn't care too much for me either, and there were nine of them. I felt superior to them in my way, and I didn't like the manner in which we were all crowded together into the servants' elevator. Nor did they like my being there. In fact, as the warmly lighted floors flashed past the elevator we had words over the fact that I, by taking part in the fight, had knocked one of their friends out of a night's work.

We were led out of the elevator through a rococo hall into an anteroom and told to get into our fighting togs. Each of us was issued a pair of boxing gloves and ushered out into the big mirrored hall, which we entered looking cautiously about us and whispering, lest we might accidentally be heard above the noise of the room. It was foggy with cigar smoke. And already the whiskey was taking effect. I was shocked to see some of the most important men of the town quite tipsy. They were all there—bankers, lawyers, judges, doctors, fire chiefs, teachers, merchants. Even one of the more fashionable pastors. Something we could not see was going on up front. A clarinet was vibrating sensuously and the men were standing up and moving eagerly forward. We were a small tight group, clustered together, our bare upper bodies touching and shining with anticipatory sweat; while up front the big shots were becoming increasingly excited over something we still could not see. Suddenly I heard the school superintendent, who had told me to come, yell. "Bring up the shines,[1] gentlemen! Bring up the little shines!"

We were rushed up to the front of the ballroom, where it smelled even more strongly of tobacco and whiskey. Then we were pushed into place. I almost wet my pants. A set of faces, some hostile, some amused, ringed around us, and in the center, facing us, stood a magnificent blond—stark naked. There was dead silence. I felt a blast of cold air chill me. I tried to back away, but they were behind me and around me. Some of the boys stood with lowered heads, trembling. I felt a wave of irrational guilt and fear. My teeth chattered, my skin turned to goose flesh, my knees knocked. Yet I was strongly attracted and looked in spite of myself. Had the price of looking

---

[1]**shines** a racist term applied to African Americans; implying high gloss of skin color.

been blindness, I would have looked. The hair was yellow like that of a circus kewpie doll, the face heavily powdered and rouged, as though to form an abstract mask, the eyes hollow and smeared a cool blue, the color of a baboon's butt. I felt a desire to spit upon her as my eyes brushed slowly over her body. Her breasts were firm and round as the domes of East Indian temples, and I stood so close as to see the fine skin texture and beads of pearly perspiration glistening like dew around the pink and erected buds of her nipples. I wanted at one and the same time to run from the room, to sink through the floor, or go to her and cover her from my eyes and the eyes of the others with my body; to feel the soft thighs, to caress her and destroy her, to love her and murder her, to hide from her, and yet to stroke where below the small American flag tattooed upon her belly her thighs formed a capital V. I had a notion that of all in the room she saw only me with her impersonal eyes.

And then she began to dance, a slow sensuous movement; the smoke of a hundred cigars clinging to her like the thinnest of veils. She seemed like a fair bird-girl girdled in veils calling to me from the angry surface of some gray and threatening sea. I was transported. Then I became aware of the clarinet playing and the big shots yelling at us. Some threatened us if we looked and others if we did not. On my right I saw one boy faint. And now a man grabbed a silver pitcher from a table and stepped close as he dashed ice water upon him and stood him up and forced two of us to support him as his head hung and moans issued from his thick bluish lips. Another boy began to plead to go home. He was the largest of the group, wearing dark red fighting trunks much too small to conceal the erection which projected from him as though in answer to the insinuating low-registered moaning of the clarinet. He tried to hide himself with his boxing gloves.

And all the while the blonde continued dancing, smiling faintly at the big shots who watched her with fascination, and faintly smiling at our fear. I noticed a certain merchant who followed her hungrily, his lips loose and drooling. He was a large man who wore diamond studs in a shirtfront which swelled with the ample paunch underneath, and each time the blonde swayed her undulating hips he ran his hand through the thin hair of his bald head and, with his arms upheld, his posture clumsy like that of an intoxicated panda, wound his belly in a slow and obscene grind. This creature was completely hypnotized. The music had quickened. As the dancer flung herself about with a detached expression on her face, the men began reaching out to touch her. I could see their beefy fingers sink into her soft flesh. Some of the others tried to stop them and she began to move around the floor in graceful circles, as they gave chase, slipping and sliding over the polished floor. It was mad. Chairs went crashing, drinks were spilt, as they ran laughing and howling after her. They caught her just as she reached a door, raised her from the floor, and tossed her as college boys are tossed at a hazing, and above her red, fixed-smiling lips I saw the terror and disgust in her eyes, almost like my own terror and that which I saw in some of the other boys. As I watched, they tossed her twice and her soft breasts seemed to flatten against the air and her legs flung wildly as she spun. Some of the more sober ones helped her to escape. And I started off the floor, heading for the anteroom with the rest of the boys.

10   Some were still crying and in hysteria. But as we tried to leave we were stopped and ordered to get into the ring. There was nothing to do but what we were told. All ten of us climbed under the ropes and allowed ourselves

to be blindfolded with broad bands of white cloth. One of the men seemed to feel a bit sympathetic and tried to cheer us up as we stood with our backs against the ropes. Some of us tried to grin. "See that boy over there?" one of the men said. "I want you to run across at the bell and give it to him right in the belly. If you don't get him, I'm going to get you. I don't like his looks." Each of us was told the same. The blindfolds were put on. Yet even then I had been going over my speech. In my mind each word was as bright as flame. I felt the cloth pressed into place, and frowned so that it would be loosened when I relaxed.

But now I felt a sudden fit of blind terror. I was unused to darkness. It was as though I had suddenly found myself in a dark room filled with poisonous cottonmouths. I could hear the bleary voices yelling insistently for the battle royal to begin.

"Get going in there!"

"Let me at that big nigger!"

I strained to pick up the school superintendent's voice, as though to squeeze some security out of that slightly more familiar sound.

15   "Let me at those black sonsabitches!" someone yelled.

"No, Jackson, no!" another voice yelled. "Here, somebody, help me hold Jack."

"I want to get at that ginger-colored nigger. Tear him limb from limb," the first voice yelled.

I stood against the ropes trembling. For in those days I was what they called ginger-colored, and he sounded as though he might crunch me between his teeth like a crisp ginger cookie.

Quite a struggle was going on. Chairs were being kicked about and I could hear voices grunting as with a terrific effort. I wanted to see, to see more desperately than ever before. But the blindfold was as tight as a thick skin-puckering scab and when I raised my gloved hands to push the layers of white aside a voice yelled, "Oh, no, you don't, black bastard! Leave that alone!"

20   "Ring the bell before Jackson kills him a coon!" someone boomed in the sudden silence. And I heard the bell clang and the sound of the feet scuffling forward.

A glove smacked against my head. I pivoted, striking out stiffly as someone went past, and felt the jar ripple along the length of my arm to my shoulder. Then it seemed as though all nine of the boys had turned upon me at once. Blows pounded me from all sides while I struck out as best I could. So many blows landed upon me that I wondered if I were not the only blindfolded fighter in the ring, or if the man called Jackson hadn't succeeded in getting me after all.

Blindfolded, I could no longer control my motions. I had no dignity. I stumbled about like a baby or a drunken man. The smoke had become thicker and with each new blow it seemed to sear and further restrict my lungs. My saliva became like hot bitter glue. A glove connected with my head, filling my mouth with warm blood. It was everywhere. I could not tell if the moisture I felt upon my body was sweat or blood. A blow landed hard against the nape of my neck. I felt myself going over, my head hitting the floor. Streaks of blue light filled the black world behind the blindfold. I lay prone, pretending that I was knocked out, but felt myself seized by hands and yanked to my feet. "Get going, black boy! Mix it up!" My arms were like lead, my head smarting from blows. I managed to feel my way to the ropes and held on, trying to catch my breath. A glove landed in my mid-section and I went over again, feeling as though the smoke had become a knife jabbed into my guts. Pushed this way and that by the legs milling around me, I finally pulled erect and discovered that I could see the black, sweat-washed forms weaving in the smoky-blue atmosphere like drunken dancers weaving to the rapid drum-like thuds of blows.

Everyone fought hysterically. It was complete anarchy. Everybody fought everybody else. No group fought together for long. Two, three, four, fought one, then turned to fight each other, were themselves attacked. Blows landed below the belt and in the kidney, with the gloves open as well as closed, and with my eye partly opened now there was not so much terror. I moved carefully, avoiding blows, although not too many to attract attention, fighting from group to group. The boys groped about like blind, cautious crabs crouching to protect their mid-sections, their heads pulled in short against their shoulders, their arms stretched nervously before them, with their fists testing the smoke-filled air like the knobbed feelers of hypersensitive snails. In one corner I glimpsed a boy violently punching the air and heard him scream in pain as he smashed his hand against a ring post. For a second I saw him bent over holding his hand, then going down as a blow caught his unprotected head. I played one group against the other, slipping and throwing a punch then stepping out of range while pushing the others into the melee to take the blows blindly aimed at me. The smoke was agonizing and there were no rounds, no bells at three-minute intervals to relieve our exhaustion. The room spun round me, a swirl of lights, smoke, sweating bodies surrounded by tense white faces. I bled from both nose and mouth, the blood spattering upon my chest.

The men kept yelling, "Slug him, black boy! Knock his guts out!"

25   "Uppercut him! Kill him! Kill that big boy!"

Taking a fake fall, I saw a boy going down heavily beside me as though we were felled by a single blow, saw a sneaker-clad foot shoot into his groin as the two who had knocked him down stumbled upon him. I rolled out of range, feeling a twinge of nausea.

The harder we fought the more threatening the men became. And yet, I had begun to worry about my speech again. How would it go? Would they recognize my ability? What would they give me?

I was fighting automatically when suddenly I noticed that one after another of the boys was leaving the ring. I was surprised, filled with panic, as though I had been left alone with an unknown danger. Then I understood. The boys had arranged it among themselves. It was the custom for the two men left in the ring to slug it out for the winner's prize. I discovered this too late. When the bell sounded two men in tuxedoes leaped into the ring and removed the blindfold. I found myself facing Tatlock, the biggest of the gang. I felt sick at my stomach. Hardly had the bell stopped ringing in my ears than it clanged again and I saw him moving swiftly toward me. Thinking of nothing else to do I hit him smash on the nose. He kept coming, bringing the rank, sharp violence of stale sweat. His face was a black blank of a face, only his eyes alive—with hate of me and aglow with a feverish terror from what had happened to us all. I became anxious. I wanted to deliver my speech and he came at me as though he meant to beat it out of me. I smashed him again and again, taking his blows as they came. Then on a sudden impulse I struck him lightly and as we clinched, I whispered, "Fake like I knocked you out, you can have the prize."

"I'll break your behind," he whispered hoarsely.

30   "For *them?*"

"For *me,* sonofabitch!"

They were yelling for us to break it up and Tatlock spun me half around with a blow, and as a joggled camera sweeps in a reeling scene, I saw the howling red faces crouching tense beneath the cloud of blue-gray smoke. For a moment the world wavered, unraveled, flowed, then my head cleared and Tatlock bounced before me. That fluttering shadow before my eyes was his jabbing left hand. Then falling forward, my head against his damp shoulder, I whispered,

"I'll make it five dollars more."

"Go to hell!"

35   But his muscles relaxed a trifle beneath my pressure and I breathed, "Seven!"

"Give it to your ma," he said, ripping me beneath the heart.

And while I still held him I butted him and moved away. I felt myself bombarded with punches. I fought back with hopeless desperation. I wanted to deliver my speech more than anything else in the world, because I felt that only these men could judge truly my ability, and now this stupid clown was ruining my chances. I began fighting carefully now, moving in to punch him and out again with my greater speed. A lucky blow to his chin and I had him going too—until I heard a loud voice yell, "I got my money on the big boy."

Hearing this, I almost dropped my guard. I was confused: Should I try to win against the voice out there? Would not this go against my speech, and was not this a moment for humility, for nonresistance? A blow to my head as I danced about sent my right eye popping like a jack-in-the-box and settled my dilemma. The room went red as I fell. It was a dream fall, my body languid and fastidious as to where to land, until the floor became impatient and smashed up to meet me. A moment later I came to. An hypnotic voice said FIVE emphatically. And I lay there, hazily watching a dark red spot of my own blood shaping itself into a butterfly, glistening and soaking into the soiled gray world of the canvas.

When the voice drawled TEN I was lifted up and dragged to a chair. I sat dazed. My eye pained and swelled with each throb of my pounding heart and I wondered if now I would be allowed to speak. I was wringing wet, my mouth still bleeding. We were grouped along the wall now. The other boys ignored me as they congratulated Tatlock and speculated as to how much they would be paid. One boy whimpered over his smashed hand. Looking up front, I saw attendants in white jackets rolling the portable ring away and placing a small square rug in the vacant space surrounded by chairs. Perhaps, I thought, I will stand on the rug to deliver my speech.

40   Then the M.C. called to us, "Come on up here boys and get your money."

We ran forward to where the men laughed and talked in their chairs, waiting. Everyone seemed friendly now.

"There it is on the rug," the man said. I saw the rug covered with coins of all dimensions and a few crumpled bills. But what excited me, scattered here and there, were the gold pieces.

"Boys, it's all yours," the man said. "You get all you grab."

"That's right, Sambo,"[2] a blond man said, winking at me confidentially.

45   I trembled with excitement, forgetting my pain. I would get the gold and the bills, I thought. I would use both hands. I would throw my body against the boys nearest me to block them from the gold.

---

[2]**Sambo** a racist slur, deriving from Zambo, a Spanish term used to identify individuals in the Americas who are of mixed African and Amerindian ancestry.

"Get down around the rug now," the man commanded, "and don't any-one touch it until I give the signal."

"This ought to be good," I heard.

As told, we got around the square rug on our knees. Slowly the man raised his freckled hand as we followed it upward with our eyes.

I heard, "These niggers look like they're about to pray!"

50   Then, "Ready," the man said. "Go!"

I lunged for a yellow coin lying on the blue design of the carpet, touch-ing it and sending a surprised shriek to join those rising around me. I tried frantically to remove my hand but could not let go. A hot, violent force tore through my body, shaking me like a wet rat. The rug was electrified. The hair bristled up on my head as I shook myself free. My muscles jumped, my nerves jangled, writhed. But I saw that this was not stopping the other boys. Laughing in fear and embarrassment, some were holding back and scooping up the coins knocked off by the painful contortions of the others. The men roared above us as we struggled.

"Pick it up, goddamnit, pick it up!" someone called like a bass-voiced parrot. "Go on, get it!"

I crawled rapidly around the floor, picking up the coins, trying to avoid the coppers and to get greenbacks and the gold. Ignoring the shock by laughing, as I brushed the coins off quickly, I discovered that I could contain the electricity—a contradiction, but it works. Then the men began to push us onto the rug. Laughing embarrassedly, we struggled out of their hands and kept after the coins. We were all wet and slippery and hard to hold. Suddenly I saw a boy lifted into the air, glistening with sweat like a circus seal, and dropped, his wet back landing flush upon the charged rug, heard him yell and saw him literally dance upon his back, his elbows beating a frenzied tattoo upon the floor, his muscles twitching like the flesh of a horse stung by many flies. When he finally rolled off, his face was gray and no one stopped him when he ran from the floor amid booming laughter.

"Get the money," the M.C. called. "That's good hard American cash!"

55   And we snatched and grabbed, snatched and grabbed. I was careful not to come too close to the rug now, and when I felt the hot whiskey breath descend upon me like a cloud of foul air I reached out and grabbed the leg of a chair. It was occupied and I held on desperately.

"Leggo, nigger! Leggo!"

The huge face wavered down to mine as he tried to push me free. But my body was slippery and he was too drunk. It was Mr. Colcord, who owned a chain of movie houses and "entertainment palaces." Each time he grabbed me I slipped out of his hands. It became a real struggle. I feared the rug more than I did the drunk, so I held on, surprising myself for a moment by trying to topple *him* upon the rug. It was such an enormous idea that I found my-self actually carrying it out. I tried not to be obvious, yet when I grabbed his leg, trying to tumble him out of the chair, he raised up roaring with laughter, and, looking at me with soberness dead in the eye, kicked me viciously in the chest. The chair leg flew out of my hand. I felt myself going and rolled. It was as though I had rolled through a bed of hot coals. It seemed a whole century would pass before I would roll free, a century in which I was seared through the deepest levels of my body to the fearful breath within me and the breath seared and heated to the point of explosion. It'll all be over in a flash, I thought as I rolled clear. It'll all be over in a flash.

But not yet, the men on the other side were waiting, red faces swollen as though from apoplexy as they bent forward in their chairs. Seeing their fingers coming toward me I rolled away as a fumbled football rolls off the receiver's fingertips, back into the coals. That time I luckily sent the rug sliding out of place and heard the coins ringing against the floor and the boys scuffling to pick them up and the M.C. calling, "All right, boys, that's all. Go get dressed and get your money."

I was limp as a dish rag. My back felt as though it had been beaten with wires.

60   When we had dressed the M.C. came in and gave us each five dollars, except Tatlock, who got ten for being the last in the ring. Then he told us to leave. I was not to get a chance to deliver my speech, I thought. I was going out into the dim alley in despair when I was stopped and told to go back. I returned to the ballroom, where the men were pushing back their chairs and gathering in groups to talk.

The M.C. knocked on a table for quiet. "Gentlemen," he said, "we almost forgot an important part of the program. A most serious part, gentlemen. This boy was brought here to deliver a speech which he made at his graduation yesterday. . . ."

"Bravo!"

"I'm told that he is the smartest boy we've got out there in Greenwood. I'm told that he knows more big words than a pocket-sized dictionary."

Much applause and laughter.

65   "So now, gentlemen, I want you to give him your attention."

There was still laughter as I faced them, my mouth dry, my eye throbbing. I began slowly, but evidently my throat was tense, because they began shouting, "Louder! Louder!"

"We of the younger generation extol the wisdom of that great leader and educator," I shouted, "who first spoke these flaming words of wisdom: 'A ship lost at sea for many days suddenly sighted a friendly vessel. From the mast of the unfortunate vessel was seen a signal: "Water, water; we die of thirst!" The answer from the friendly vessel came back: "Cast down your bucket where you are." The captain of the distressed vessel, at last heeding the injunction, cast down his bucket, and it came up full of fresh sparkling water from the mouth of the Amazon River.' And like him I say, and in his words, 'To those of my race who depend upon bettering their condition in a foreign land, or who underestimate the importance of cultivating friendly relations with the Southern white man, who is his next-door neighbor, I would say: "Cast down your bucket where you are"—cast it down in making friends in every manly way of the people of all races by whom we are surrounded. . . .'"[3]

I spoke automatically and with such fervor that I did not realize that the men were still talking and laughing until my dry mouth, filling up with blood from the cut, almost strangled me. I coughed, wanting to stop and go to one of the tall brass, sand-filled spittoons to relieve myself, but a few of the men, especially the superintendent, were listening and I was afraid. So I gulped it down, blood, saliva and all, and continued. (What powers of endurance I had during those days! What enthusiasm! What a belief in the

---

[3]The narrator here is quoting from an important speech by the African American educator Booker T. Washington, delivered at the Atlanta Exposition in 1895, in which he expressed his willingness to accept segregation in exchange for economic advancement.

rightness of things!) I spoke even louder in spite of the pain. But still they talked and still they laughed, as though deaf with cotton in dirty ears. So I spoke with greater emotional emphasis. I closed my ears and swallowed blood until I was nauseated. The speech seemed a hundred times as long as before, but I could not leave out a single word. All had to be said, each memorized nuance considered, rendered. Nor was that all. Whenever I uttered a word of three or more syllables a group of voices would yell for me to repeat it. I used the phrase "social responsibility" and they yelled:

"What's the word you say, boy?"

70 "Social responsibility," I said.

"What?"

"Social . . ."

"Louder."

". . . responsibility."

75 "More!"

"Respon—"

"Repeat!"

"—sibility."

The room filled with the uproar of laughter until, no doubt, distracted by having to gulp down my blood, I made a mistake and yelled a phrase I had often seen denounced in newspaper editorials, heard debated in private.

80 "Social . . ."

"What?" they yelled.

". . . equality—"

The laughter hung smokelike in the sudden stillness. I opened my eyes, puzzled. Sounds of displeasure filled the room. The M.C. rushed forward. They shouted hostile phrases at me. But I did not understand.

A small dry mustached man in the front row blared out, "Say that slowly, son!"

85 "What, sir?"

"What you just said!"

"Social responsibility, sir," I said.

"You weren't being smart, were you, boy?" he said, not unkindly.

"No, sir!"

90 "You sure that about 'equality' was a mistake?"

"Oh, yes, sir," I said. "I was swallowing blood."

"Well, you had better speak more slowly so we can understand. We mean to do right by you, but you've got to know your place at all times. All right now, go on with your speech."

I was afraid. I wanted to leave but I wanted also to speak and I was afraid they'd snatch me down.

"Thank you, sir," I said, beginning where I had left off, and having them ignore me as before.

95 Yet when I finished there was a thunderous applause. I was surprised to see the superintendent come forth with a package wrapped in white tissue paper and, gesturing for quiet, address the men.

"Gentlemen, you see that I did not overpraise this boy. He makes a good speech and some day he'll lead his people in the proper paths. And I don't have to tell you that that is important in these days and times. This is a good, smart boy, and so to encourage him in the right direction, in the name of the Board of Education I wish to present him a prize in the form of this . . ."

He paused, removing the tissue paper and revealing a gleaming calfskin brief case.

"... in the form of this first-class article from Shad Whitmore's shop."

"Boy," he said, addressing me, "take this prize and keep it well. Consider it a badge of office. Prize it. Keep developing as you are and some day it will be filled with important papers that will help shape the destiny of your people."

100   I was so moved that I could hardly express my thanks. A rope of bloody saliva forming a shape like an undiscovered continent drooled upon the leather and I wiped it quickly away. I felt an importance that I had never dreamed.

"Open it and see what's inside," I was told.

My fingers a-tremble, I complied, smelling the fresh leather and finding an official-looking document inside. It was a scholarship to the state college for Negroes. My eyes filled with tears and I ran awkwardly off the floor.

I was overjoyed; I did not even mind when I discovered that the gold pieces I had scrambled for were brass pocket tokens advertising a certain make of automobile.

When I reached home everyone was excited. Next day the neighbors came to congratulate me. I even felt safe from grandfather, whose deathbed curse usually spoiled my triumphs. I stood beneath his photograph with my brief case in hand and smiled triumphantly into his stolid black peasant's face. It was a face that fascinated me. The eyes seemed to follow everywhere I went.

105   That night I dreamed I was at a circus with him and that he refused to laugh at the clowns no matter what they did. Then later he told me to open my brief case and read what was inside and I did, finding an official envelope stamped with the state seal; and inside the envelope I found another and another, endlessly, and I thought I would fall of weariness. "Them's years," he said. "Now open that one." And I did and in it I found an engraved document containing a short message in letters of gold. "Read it," my grandfather said. "Out loud."

"To Whom It May Concern," I intoned, "Keep This Nigger-Boy Running."

I awoke with the old man's laughter ringing in my ears.

(It was a dream I was to remember and dream again for many years after. But at the time I had no insight into its meaning. First I had to attend college.)

YOUR TURN

1. Ellison's narrator says that this incident in his life took place "in the main ballroom of the leading hotel." How does he describe this setting? What are the features of it that he emphasizes?
2. Much of the action takes place within the boxing ring. How is it described? Why do you think that Ellison chose this setting for the main action?
3. Note the scene of the naked blonde woman. Why is it in the story?
4. How would you respond to someone who said, "This is a powerful story, but something like this could not happen in real life"?
5. How are white people presented in "Battle Royal"? What is your response to the way in which they are presented?
6. What is your response to the narrator overall? What kind of person is he?

9

Narrative Point of View

Every story is told by someone. Mark Twain wrote *Adventures of Huckleberry Finn,* but he does not tell the story; Huck tells the story, and he begins thus:

> You don't know about me without you have read a book by the name of *The Adventures of Tom Sawyer,* but that ain't no matter. That book was made by Mr. Mark Twain, and he told the truth, mainly. There was things which he stretched, but mainly he told the truth.

Similarly, Edgar Allan Poe wrote "The Cask of Amontillado" (page 509), but the story is told by a man whose name, we learn later, is Montresor. Here is the opening:

> The thousand injuries of Fortunato I had borne as I best could, but when he ventured upon insult, I vowed revenge.

Each of these passages gives a reader a very strong sense of the narrator, that is, of the invented person who tells the story, and it turns out that the works are chiefly about the speakers. Compare those opening passages, however, with two others, which sound far more objective. The first comes from Chekhov's "Misery" (page 403):

> The twilight of evening. Big flakes of wet snow are whirling lazily about the street lamps, which have just been lighted, and lying in a thin soft layer on roofs, horses' backs, shoulders, caps. Iona Potapov, the sledge-driver, is all white like a ghost. He sits on the box without stirring, bent as double as the living body can be bent.

And another example, this one from Hawthorne's "Young Goodman Brown" (page 154):

> Young Goodman Brown came forth, at sunset, into the street at Salem village; but put his head back, after crossing the threshold, to exchange a parting kiss with his young wife. And Faith, as the wife was aptly named, thrust her own pretty head into the street, letting the wind play with the pink ribbons of her cap while she called to Goodman Brown.

In each of these two passages, a reader is scarcely aware of the personality of the narrator; our interest is almost entirely in the scene that each speaker reveals, not in the speaker's response to the scene.

The narrators of *Huckleberry Finn* and of "The Cask of Amontillado" immediately impress us with their distinctive personalities. We realize that whatever happenings they report will be colored by the special ways in which such personalities see things. But what can we say about the narrators of "Misery" and of "Young Goodman Brown"? A reader hardly notices them, at least in comparison with Huck and Montresor. We look, so to speak, not *at* these narrators, but at others (the cabman and Goodman Brown and Faith).

Of course, it is true that as we read "Misery" and "Young Goodman Brown" we are looking through the eyes of the narrators, but these narrators seem (unlike Huck and Montresor) to have 20/20 vision. This is not to say, however, that these apparently colorless narrators really are colorless or invisible. The narrator of "Misery" seems, at least if we judge from the opening sentences, to want to evoke an atmosphere. He describes the setting in some detail, whereas the narrator of "Young Goodman Brown" seems chiefly concerned with reporting the actions of people whom he sees. Moreover, if we listen carefully to Hawthorne's narrator, perhaps we can say that when he mentions that Faith was "aptly" named, he makes a judgment. Still, it is clear that the narrative voices we hear in "Misery" and "Young Goodman Brown" are relatively impartial and inconspicuous; when we hear them, we feel, for the most part, that they are talking about something objective, about something "out there." These narrative voices will produce stories very different from the narrative voices used by Twain and Poe. The voice that the writer chooses, then, will in large measure shape the story; different voices, different stories.

The narrative point of view of *Huckleberry Finn* and of "The Cask of Amontillado" (and of any other story in which a character in the story tells the story) is a **participant** (or **first-person**) point of view. The point of view of "Young Goodman Brown" (and of any other story in which a nearly invisible outsider tells the story) is a **nonparticipant** (or **third-person**) point of view.

Participant (or First-Person) Point of View

In John Updike's "A & P" (page 191) the narrator is, like Mark Twain's Huck and Poe's Montresor, a major character. Updike has invented an adolescent boy who undergoes certain experiences and who has certain perceptions. Since the story is narrated by one of its characters, we can say that the author uses a first-person (or participant) point of view.

It happens that in Updike's "A & P" the narrator is the central character, the character whose actions—whose life, we might say—most interests the reader. But sometimes a first-person narrator tells a story that focuses on another character; the narrator still says "I" (thus the point of view is first person), but the reader feels that the story is not chiefly about this "I" but is about some other figure. For instance, the narrator may be a witness to a story about Jones, and our interest is in what happens to Jones, though we get the story of Jones filtered through, say, the eyes of Jones's friend, or brother, or cat.

When any of us tells a story (for instance, why we quit a job), our hearers may do well to take what we say with a grain of salt. After all, we are giving *our* side, our version of what happened. And so it is with first-person narrators of fiction. They may be reliable, in which case the reader can pretty much accept what they say, or they may be **unreliable narrators,** perhaps because they have an ax to grind, perhaps because they are not perceptive enough to grasp the full implications of what they report, or perhaps because they are mentally impaired, even insane. Poe's Montresor, in "The Cask of Amontillado," is so obsessed that we cannot be certain that Fortunato really did inflict a "thousand injuries" on him.

One special kind of unreliable first-person narrator (whether major or minor) is the **innocent eye:** the narrator is naive (usually a child, or a not-too-bright adult), telling what he or she sees and feels; the contrast between what the narrator perceives and what the reader understands produces an ironic effect. Such a story, in which the reader understands more than the teller himself does, is Ring Lardner's "Haircut" (1925), a story told by a garrulous barber who does not perceive that the "accident" he is describing is in fact a murder.

Nonparticipant (or Third-Person) Points of View

In a story told from a nonparticipant (third-person) point of view, the teller of the tale is not a character in the tale. The narrator has receded from the story. If the point of view is **omniscient,** the narrator relates what he or she wishes about the thoughts as well as the deeds of the characters. The omniscient teller can at any time enter the mind of any or all of the characters; whereas the first-person narrator can only say "I was angry" or "Jones seemed angry to me," the omniscient narrator can say, "Jones was inwardly angry but gave no sign; Smith continued chatting, but he sensed Jones's anger."

Furthermore, a distinction can be made between **neutral omniscience** (the narrator recounts deeds and thoughts, but does not judge) and **editorial omniscience** (the narrator not only recounts, but also judges). The narrator in Hawthorne's "Young Goodman Brown" knows what goes on in the mind of Brown, and he comments approvingly or disapprovingly: "With this excellent resolve for the future, Goodman Brown felt himself justified in making more haste on his present evil purpose."

Because a short story can scarcely hope to effectively develop a picture of several minds, an author may prefer to limit his or her omniscience to the minds of only a few of the characters, or even to that of one of the characters; that is, the author may use **selective omniscience** as the point of view. Selective omniscience provides a focus, especially if it is limited to a single character. When thus limited, the author hovers over the shoulder of one character, seeing him or her from outside and from inside and seeing other characters only from the outside and from the impact they make on the mind of this selected receptor. In "Young Goodman Brown" the reader sees things mostly as they make their impact on the protagonist's mind.

> He could have well nigh sworn that the shape of his own dead father beckoned him to advance, looking downward from a smoke wreath, while a woman, with dim features of despair, threw out her hand to warn him back. Was it his mother? But he had no power to retreat one step, nor to resist, even in thought, when the minister and good old Deacon Gookin seized his arms and led him to the blazing rock.

When selective omniscience attempts to record mental activity ranging from consciousness to the unconscious, from clear perceptions to confused longings, point of view is sometimes labeled **stream of consciousness.** In an effort to reproduce the unending activity of the mind, some authors who use the stream-of-consciousness point of view dispense with conventional word order, punctuation, and logical transitions. The last forty-six pages in James Joyce's *Ulysses* are an unpunctuated flow of one character's thoughts.

Finally, sometimes a third-person narrator does not enter even a single mind, but records only what crosses a dispassionate eye and ear. Such a point of view is **objective** (sometimes called **the camera** or **fly-on-the-wall narrator**). The absence of editorializing and of dissection of the mind often produces the effect of a play; we see and hear the characters in action. Much of Hemingway's "Cat in the Rain" (page 99) is objective, consisting of bits of dialogue that make the story look like a play:

> "I'm going down and get that kitty," the American wife said.
> "I'll do it," her husband offered from the bed.
> "No, I'll get it. The poor kitty out trying to keep dry under a table."
> The husband went on reading, lying propped up with the two pil-
> lows at the foot of the bed.
> "Don't get wet," he said. (100)

The absence of comment on the happenings forces readers to make their own evaluations of the happenings. In the passage just quoted, when Hemingway writes "'Don't get wet,' he said," readers are probably forced to think (and to sense that Hemingway is guiding them to think) that the husband is indifferent to his wife. After all, how can she go out into the rain and not get wet? A writer can use an objective point of view, then, and still control the feelings of the reader.

The Point of a Point of View

Generalizations about the effect of a point of view are risky, but two have already been made: that the innocent eye can achieve an ironic effect otherwise unattainable, and that an objective point of view (because we hear dialogue but get little or no comment about it) is dramatic. Three other generalizations are often made:

- that a first-person point of view lends a sense of immediacy or reality,
- that an omniscient point of view suggests human littleness, and
- that the point of view must be consistent.

To take the first of these: it is true that when Poe begins a story "The thousand injuries of Fortunato I had borne as I best could, but when he ventured upon insult, I vowed revenge," we feel that the author has gripped us by the lapels; but, on the other hand, we know that we are only reading a piece of fiction, and we do not really believe in the existence of the "I" or of Fortunato; and furthermore, when we pick up a story that begins with *any* point of view, we agree (by picking up the book) to pretend to believe the fictions we are being told. That is, all fiction—whether in the first person or not—is known to be literally false but is read with the pretense that it is true (probably because we hope to get some sort of insight, or truth). The writer must hold our attention and make us feel that the fiction is meaningful, but the use of the first-person pronoun does not of itself confer reality.

The second generalization, that an omniscient point of view can make puppets of its characters, is equally misleading; this point of view can also reveal in them a depth and complexity quite foreign to the idea of human littleness.

The third generalization, that the narrator's point of view must be consistent lest the illusion of reality be shattered, has been much preached by the followers of Henry James. But E. M. Forster has suggested, in *Aspects of the Novel,* that what is important is not consistency but "the power of the writer to bounce the reader into accepting what he says." Forster notes that in *Bleak House* Dickens uses in Chapter 1 an omniscient point of view, in Chapter 2 a selective omniscient point of view, and in Chapter 3 a first-person point of view. "Logically," Forster says, "*Bleak House* is all to pieces, but Dickens bounces us, so that we do not mind the shiftings of the viewpoint."

Perhaps the only sound generalizations possible are these:

1. Because point of view is one of the things that give form to a story, a good author chooses the point (or points) of view that he or she feels is best for the particular story.
2. The use of any other point or points of view would turn the story into a different story.

JOHN UPDIKE

John Updike (1932–2009) grew up in Shillington, Pennsylvania, where his father was a teacher and his mother a writer. After receiving a B.A. degree in 1954 from Harvard, where he edited the Harvard Lampoon (for which he both wrote and drew), he studied drawing at Oxford for a year, but an offer from the New Yorker *brought him back to the United States. He was hired as a reporter for the magazine but soon began contributing poetry, essays, and fiction. In 1957 he left the* New Yorker *in order to write independently full time, though his stories and book reviews appeared regularly in it until his death.*

In 1959 Updike published his first book of stories, The Same Door *as well as his first novel,* The Poorhouse Fair; *the next year he published* Rabbit, Run, *a highly successful novel whose protagonist, "Rabbit" Angstrom, reappears in three later novels,* Rabbit Redux *(1971),* Rabbit Is Rich *(1981), and* Rabbit at Rest *(1990). The first and the last Rabbit books each won a Pulitzer Prize.*

A & P   [1962]

In walks these three girls in nothing but bathing suits. I'm in the third checkout slot, with my back to the door, so I don't see them until they're over by the bread. The one that caught my eye first was the one in the plaid green two-piece. She was a chunky kid, with a good tan and a sweet broad soft-looking can with those two crescents of white just under it, where the sun never seems to hit, at the top of the backs of her legs. I stood there with my hand on a box of HiHo crackers trying to remember if I rang it up or not. I ring it up again and the customer starts giving me hell. She's one of these cash-register-watchers, a witch about fifty with rouge on her cheekbones and no eyebrows, and I know it made her day to trip me up. She'd been watching cash registers for fifty years and probably never seen a mistake before.

By the time I got her feathers smoothed and her goodies into a bag— she gives me a little snort in passing, if she'd been born at the right time they would have burned her over in Salem[1]—by the time I get her on her way the girls had circled around the bread and were coming back, without a pushcart, back my way along the counters, in the aisle between the check-outs and the Special bins. They didn't even have shoes on. There was this chunky one, with the two-piece—it was bright green and the seams on the bra were still sharp and her belly was still pretty pale so I guessed she just got it (the suit)—there was this one, with one of those chubby berry-faces, the lips all bunched together under her nose, this one, and a tall one, with black hair that hadn't quite frizzed right, and one of these sunburns right across under the eyes, and a chin that was too long—you know, the kind of girl other girls think is very "striking" and "attractive" but never quite makes it, as they very well know, which is why they like her so much—and then the third one, that wasn't quite so tall. She was the queen. She kind of led them, the other two peeking around and making their shoulders round. She didn't look around, not this queen, she just walked straight on slowly, on these long white prima-donna legs. She came down a little hard on her heels, as if she didn't walk in her bare feet that much, putting down her heels and then letting the weight move along to her toes as if she was testing the floor with every step, putting a little deliberate extra action into it. You never know for sure how girls' minds work (do you really think it's a mind in there or just a little buzz like a bee in a glass jar?) but you got the idea she had talked the other two into coming in here with her, and now she was showing them how to do it, walk slow and hold yourself straight.

She had on a kind of dirty-pink—beige maybe, I don't know—bathing suit with a little nubble all over it and, what got me, the straps were down. They were off her shoulders looped loose around the cool tops of her arms, and I guess as a result the suit had slipped a little on her, so all around the top of the cloth there was this shining rim. If it hadn't been there you wouldn't have known there could have been anything whiter than those shoulders. With the straps pushed off, there was nothing between the top of the suit and the top of her head except just *her*, this clean bare plane of the top of her chest down from the shoulder bones like a dented sheet of metal tilted in the light. I mean, it was more than pretty.

She had sort of oaky hair that the sun and salt had bleached, done up in a bun that was unravelling, and a kind of prim face. Walking into the A & P with your straps down, I suppose it's the only kind of face you *can* have. She held her head so high her neck, coming up out of those white shoulders, looked kind of stretched, but I didn't mind. The longer her neck was, the more of her there was.

5   She must have felt in the corner of her eye me and over my shoulder Stokesie in the second slot watching, but she didn't tip. Not this queen. She kept her eyes moving across the racks, and stopped, and turned so slow it

---

[1]**Salem** town in Massachusetts, where the witch trials of the 1690s occurred. Many women and men were hanged for their supposed sins and crimes; no one was burned at the stake.

made my stomach rub the inside of my apron, and buzzed to the other two, who kind of huddled against her for relief, and then they all three of them went up the cat-and-dog-food-breakfast-cereal-macaroni-rice-raisins-seasonings-spreads-spaghetti-soft-drinks-crackers-and-cookies aisle. From the third slot I look straight up this aisle to the meat counter, and I watched them all the way. The fat one with the tan sort of fumbled with the cookies, but on second thought she put the package back. The sheep pushing their carts down the aisle—the girls were walking against the usual traffic (not that we have one-way signs or anything)—were pretty hilarious. You could see them, when Queenie's white shoulders dawned on them, kind of jerk, or hop, or hiccup, but their eyes snapped back to their own baskets and on they pushed. I bet you could set off dynamite in an A & P and the people would by and large keep reaching and checking oatmeal off their lists and muttering "Let me see, there was a third thing, began with A, asparagus, no, ah, yes, applesauce!" or whatever it is they do mutter. But there was no doubt, this jiggled them. A few houseslaves in pin curlers even look around after pushing their carts past to make sure what they had seen was correct.

You know, it's one thing to have a girl in a bathing suit down on the beach, where what with the glare nobody can look at each other much anyway, and another thing in the cool of the A & P, under the fluorescent lights, against all those stacked packages, with her feet paddling along naked over our checkerboard green-and-cream rubber-tile floor.

"Oh, Daddy," Stokesie said beside me. "I feel so faint."

"Darling," I said. "Hold me tight." Stokesie's married, with two babies chalked up on his fuselage already, but as far as I can tell that's the only difference. He's twenty-two, and I was nineteen this April.

"Is it done?" he asks, the responsible married man finding his voice. I forgot to say he thinks he's going to be a manager some sunny day, maybe in 1990 when it's called the Great Alexandrov and Petrooshki Tea Company or something.

10   What he meant was, our town is five miles from a beach, with a big summer colony out on the Point, but we're right in the middle of town, and the women generally put on a shirt or shorts or something before they get out of the car into the street. And anyway these are usually women with six children and varicose veins mapping their legs and nobody, including them, could care less. As I say, we're right in the middle of town, and if you stand at our front doors you can see two banks and the Congregational church and the newspaper store and three real estate offices and about twenty-seven old freeloaders tearing up Central Street because the sewer broke again. It's not as if we're on the Cape;[2] we're north of Boston and there's people in this town haven't seen the ocean for twenty years.

The girls had reached the meat counter and were asking McMahon something. He pointed, they pointed, and they shuffled out of sight behind a pyramid of Diet Delight peaches. All that was left for us to see was old McMahon patting his mouth and looking after them sizing up their joints. Poor kids, I began to feel sorry for them, they couldn't help it.

Now here comes the sad part of the story, at least my family says it's sad, but I don't think it's so sad myself. The store's pretty empty, it being Thursday

---

[2]**Cape** Cape Cod, a peninsula in easternmost Massachusetts.

afternoon, so there was nothing much to do except lean on the register and wait for the girls to show up again. The whole store was like a pinball machine and I didn't know which tunnel they'd come out of. After a while they come around out of the far aisle, around the light bulbs, records at discount of the Caribbean Six or Tony Martin Sings or some such gunk you wonder they waste the wax on, six-packs of candy bars, and plastic toys done up in cellophane that fall apart when a kid looks at them anyway. Around they come, Queenie still leading the way, and holding a little gray jar in her hand. Slots Three through Seven are unmanned and I could see her wondering between Stokes and me, but Stokesie with his usual luck draws an old party in baggy gray pants who stumbles up with four giant cans of pineapple juice (what do these bums *do* with all that pineapple juice? I've often asked myself) so the girls come to me. Queenie puts down the jar and I take it into my fingers icy cold. Kingfish Fancy Herring Snacks in Pure Sour Cream: 49¢. Now her hands are empty, not a ring or a bracelet, bare as God made them, and I wonder where the money's coming from. Still with that prim look she lifts a folded dollar bill out of the hollow at the center of her nubbled pink top. The jar went heavy in my hand. Really, I thought that was so cute.

Then everybody's luck begins to run out. Lengel comes in from haggling with a truck full of cabbages on the lot and is about to scuttle into the door marked MANAGER behind which he hides all day when the girls touch his eye. Lengel's pretty dreary, teaches Sunday school and the rest, but he doesn't miss that much. He comes over and says, "Girls, this isn't the beach."

Queenie blushes, though maybe it's just a brush of sunburn I was noticing for the first time, now that she was so close. "My mother asked me to pick up a jar of herring snacks." Her voice kind of startled me, the way voices do when you see the people first, coming out so flat and dumb yet kind of tony, too, the way it ticked over "pick up" and "snacks." All of a sudden I slid right down her voice into her living room. Her father and the other men were standing around in ice-cream coats and bow ties and the women were in sandals picking up herring snacks on toothpicks off a big glass plate and they were all holding drinks the color of water with olives and sprigs of mint in them. When my parents have somebody over they get lemonade and if it's a real racy affair Schlitz in tall glasses with "They'll Do It Every Time" cartoons stencilled on.

15   "That's all right," Lengel said. "But this isn't the beach." His repeating this struck me as funny, as if it had just occurred to him, and he had been thinking all these years the A & P was a great big dune and he was the head lifeguard. He didn't like my smiling—as I say he doesn't miss much—but he concentrates on giving the girls that sad Sunday-school-superintendent stare.

Queenie's blush is no sunburn now, and the plump one in plaid, that I liked better from the back—a really sweet can—pipes up, "We weren't doing any shopping. We just came in for the one thing."

"That makes no difference," Lengel tells her, and I could see from the way his eyes went that he hadn't noticed she was wearing a two-piece before. "We want you decently dressed when you come in here."

"We *are* decent," Queenie says suddenly, her lower lip pushing, getting sore now that she remembers her place, a place from which the crowd that runs the A & P must look pretty crummy. Fancy Herring Snacks flashed in her very blue eyes.

"Girls, I don't want to argue with you. After this come in here with your shoulders covered. It's our policy." He turns his back. That's policy for you. Policy is what the kingpins want. What the others want is juvenile delinquency.

20   All this while, the customers had been showing up with their carts but, you know, sheep, seeing a scene, they had all bunched up on Stokesie, who shook open a paper bag as gently as peeling a peach, not wanting to miss a word. I could feel in the silence everybody getting nervous, most of all Lengel, who asks me, "Sammy, have you rung up this purchase?"

I thought and said "No" but it wasn't about that I was thinking. I go through the punches, 4, 9, GROC, TOT—it's more complicated than you think, and after you do it often enough, it begins to make a little song, that you hear words to, in my case "Hello (*bing*) there, you (*gung*) hap-py *pee*pul (*splat*)!"—the *splat* being the drawer flying out. I uncrease the bill, tenderly as you may imagine, it just having come from between the two smoothest scoops of vanilla I had ever known were there, and pass a half and a penny into her narrow pink palm, and nestle the herrings in a bag and twist its neck and hand it over, all the time thinking.

The girls, and who'd blame them, are in a hurry to get out, so I say "I quit" to Lengel quick enough for them to hear, hoping they'll stop and watch me, their unsuspected hero. They keep right on going, into the electric eye; the door flies open and they flicker across the lot to their car, Queenie and Plaid and Big Tall Goony-Goony (not that as raw material she was so bad), leaving me with Lengel and a kink in his eyebrow.

"Did you say something, Sammy?"

"I said I quit."

25   "I thought you did."

"You didn't have to embarrass them."

"It was they who were embarrassing us."

I started to say something that came out "Fiddle-de-doo." It's a saying of my grandmother's, and I know she would have been pleased.

"I don't think you know what you're saying," Lengel said.

30   "I know you don't," I said. "But I do." I pull the bow at the back of my apron and start shrugging it off my shoulders. A couple customers that had been heading for my slot begin to knock against each other, like scared pigs in a chute.

Lengel sighs and begins to look very patient and old and gray. He's been a friend of my parents for years. "Sammy, you don't want to do this to your Mom and Dad," he tells me. It's true, I don't. But it seems to me that once you begin a gesture it's fatal not to go through with it. I fold the apron, "Sammy" stitched in red on the pocket, and put it on the counter, and drop the bow tie on top of it. The bow tie is theirs, if you've ever wondered. "You'll feel this for the rest of your life," Lengel says, and I know that's true, too, but remembering how he made that pretty girl blush makes me so scrunchy inside I punch the No Sale tab and the machine whirs "pee-pul" and the drawer splats out. One advantage to this scene taking place in summer, I can follow this up with a clean exit, there's no fumbling around getting your coat and galoshes, I just saunter into the electric eye in my white shirt that my mother ironed the night before, and the door heaves itself open, and outside the sunshine is skating around on the asphalt.

I look around for my girls, but they're gone, of course. There wasn't anybody but some young married screaming with her children about some candy they didn't get by the door of a powder-blue Falcon station wagon. Looking back in the big windows, over the bags of peat moss and aluminum lawn furniture stacked on the pavement, I could see Lengel in my place in the slot, checking the sheep through. His face was dark gray and his back stiff, as if he'd just had an injection of iron, and my stomach kind of fell as I felt how hard the world was going to be to me hereafter.

YOUR TURN

1. In what sort of community is this A & P located? To what extent does this community resemble yours?
2. Do you think Sammy is a male chauvinist pig? Why, or why not? And if you think he is, do you find the story offensive? Again, why or why not?
3. In the last line of the story Sammy says, "I felt how hard the world was going to be to me hereafter." Do you think the world is going to be hard to Sammy? Why, or why not? And if it is hard to him, is this because of a virtue or a weakness in Sammy?
4. Write Lengel's version of the story (500–1000 words) as he might narrate it to his wife during dinner. Or write the story from Queenie's point of view.
5. In speaking of contemporary fiction Updike said:

> I want stories to startle and engage me within the first few sentences, and in their middle to widen or deepen or sharpen my knowledge of human activity, and to end by giving me a sensation of completed statement.

   Let's assume that you share Updike's view of what a story should do. To what extent do you think "A & P" fulfills these demands? (You may want to put your response in the form of a letter to Updike.)
6. During the course of an interview published in the *Southern Review* (Spring 2002), Updike said that the original ending of "A & P" differed from the present ending. In the original, after Sammy resigns he "goes down to the beach to try to see these three girls on whose behalf he's made this sacrifice of respectability, on whose behalf he's broken with the bourgeois norm and let his parents down and Mr. Lengel down. And he doesn't see the girls, and the story ended somewhere there." Updike's editor at the *New Yorker* persuaded him that the story "ended with the resignation." Your view?

ANONYMOUS

The following story about King Solomon, customarily called "The Judgment of Solomon," appears in the Hebrew Bible, in the latter part of the third chapter of the book called 1 Kings or First Kings, probably written in the mid-sixth century BCE. *The translation is from the King James Version of the Bible (1611). Two expressions in the story need clarification: (1) The woman who "overlaid" her child in her sleep rolled over on the child and suffocated it; and (2) it is said of a woman that her "bowels yearned upon her son"—that is, her heart longed for her son. (In Hebrew psychology, the bowels were thought to be the seat of emotion.)*

The Judgment of Solomon

Then came there two women, that were harlots, unto the king, and stood before him. And the one woman said, "O my lord, I and this woman dwell in one house, and I was delivered of a child with her in the house. And it came to pass the third day after that I was delivered, that this woman was delivered also: and we were together; there was no stranger in the house, save we two in the house. And this woman's child died in the night; because she overlaid it. And she arose at midnight, and took my son from beside me, while thine handmaid slept, and laid it in her bosom, and laid her dead child in my bosom. And when I rose in the morning to give my child suck, behold, it was dead: but when I considered it in the morning, behold, it was not my son, which I did bear."

And the other woman said, "Nay; but the living is my son, and the dead is thy son." And this said, "No; but the dead is thy son, and the living is my son." Thus they spake before the king.

Then said the king, "The one saith, 'This is my son that liveth, and thy son is dead': and the other saith, 'Nay; but thy son is the dead, and my son is the living.'" And the king said, "Bring me a sword." And they brought a sword before the king. And the king said, "Divide the living child in two, and give half to the one, and half to the other."

Then spake the woman whose the living child was unto the king, for her bowels yearned upon her son, and she said, "O my lord, give her the living child, and in no wise slay it." But the other said, "Let it be neither mine nor thine, but divide it."

5   Then the king answered and said, "Give her the living child, and in no wise slay it: she is the mother thereof."

And all Israel heard of the judgment which the king had judged; and they feared the king, for they saw that the wisdom of God was in him to do judgment.

> **YOUR TURN**
>
> 1. In what ways is this story like a detective story?
> 2. Solomon was known for his wisdom. How would you characterize his wisdom?

KATHERINE ANNE PORTER

Katherine Anne Porter (1890–1980) had the curious habit of inventing details in her life, but it is true that she was born in a log cabin in Indian Creek, Texas, that she was originally named Callie Russell Porter, that her mother died when she was two years old, and that Callie was brought up by her maternal grandmother in Kyle, Texas. Apparently the family was conscious of former wealth and position in Louisiana and Kentucky. She was sent to convent schools, where, in her words, she received "a strangely useless and ornamental education." At sixteen she left school, married (and soon divorced), and worked as a reporter, first in Texas and later in Denver and Chicago. She moved around a good deal, both within the United States and abroad; she lived in Mexico, Belgium, Switzerland, France, and Germany.

Even as a child Porter was interested in writing, but she did not publish her first story until she was thirty-three. She wrote essays and one novel (Ship of Fools, 1962), *but she is best known for her stories. Porter's* Collected Stories *won the Pulitzer Prize and the National Book Award in 1965.*

The Jilting of Granny Weatherall   [1929]

She flicked her wrist neatly out of Doctor Harry's pudgy careful fingers and pulled the sheet up to her chin. The brat ought to be in knee breeches. Doctoring around the country with spectacles on his nose! "Get along now, take your schoolbooks and go. There's nothing wrong with me."

Doctor Harry spread a warm paw like a cushion on her forehead where the forked green vein danced and made her eyelids twitch. "Now, now, be a good girl, and we'll have you up in no time."

"That's no way to speak to a woman nearly eighty years old just because she's down. I'd have you respect your elders, young man."

"Well, Missy, excuse me." Doctor Harry patted her cheek. "But I've got to warn you, haven't I? You're a marvel, but you must be careful or you're going to be good and sorry."

5   "Don't tell me what I'm going to be. I'm on my feet now, morally speaking. It's Cornelia. I had to go to bed to get rid of her."

Her bones felt loose, and floated around in her skin, and Doctor Harry floated like a balloon around the foot of the bed. He floated and pulled down his waistcoat and swung his glasses on a cord. "Well, stay where you are, it certainly can't hurt you."

"Get along and doctor your sick," said Granny Weatherall. "Leave a well woman alone. I'll call for you when I want you. . . . Where were you forty years ago when I pulled through milk-leg and double pneumonia? You weren't even born. Don't let Cornelia lead you on," she shouted, because Doctor Harry appeared to float up to the ceiling and out. "I pay my own bills, and I don't throw my money away on nonsense!"

She meant to wave good-by, but it was too much trouble. Her eyes closed of themselves, it was like a dark curtain drawn around the bed. The pillow rose and floated under her, pleasant as a hammock in a light wind. She listened to the leaves rustling outside the window. No, somebody was swishing newspapers: no, Cornelia and Doctor Harry were whispering together. She leaped broad awake, thinking they whispered in her ear.

"She was never like this, *never* like this!" "Well, what can we expect?" "Yes, eighty years old. . . ."

10   Well, and what if she was? She still had ears. It was like Cornelia to whisper around doors. She always kept things secret in such a public way. She was always being tactful and kind. Cornelia was dutiful; that was the trouble with her. Dutiful and good: "So good and dutiful," said Granny, "that I'd like to spank her." She saw herself spanking Cornelia and making a fine job of it.

"What'd you say, Mother?"

Granny felt her face tying up in hard knots.

"Can't a body think, I'd like to know?"

"I thought you might want something."

15   "I do. I want a lot of things. First off, go away and don't whisper."

She lay and drowsed, hoping in her sleep that the children would keep out and let her rest a minute. It had been a long day. Not that she was tired. It was always pleasant to snatch a minute now and then. There was always so much to be done, let me see: tomorrow.

Tomorrow was far away and there was nothing to trouble about. Things were finished somehow when the time came; thank God there was always a little margin over for peace: then a person could spread out the plan of life and tuck in the edges orderly. It was good to have everything clean and folded away, with the hair brushes and tonic bottles sitting straight on the white embroidered linen: the day started without fuss and the pantry shelves laid out with rows of jelly glasses and brown jugs and white stone-china jars with blue whirligigs and words painted on them: coffee, tea, sugar, ginger, cinnamon, allspice: and the bronze clock with the lion on top nicely dusted off. The dust that lion could collect in twenty-four hours! The box in the attic with all those letters tied up, well, she'd have to go through that tomorrow. All those letters—George's letters and John's letters and her letters to them both—lying around for the children to find afterwards made her uneasy. Yes, that would be tomorrow's business. No use to let them know how silly she had been once.

While she was rummaging around she found death in her mind and it felt clammy and unfamiliar. She had spent so much time preparing for death there was no need for bringing it up again. Let it take care of itself now. When she was sixty she had felt very old, finished, and went around making farewell trips to see her children and grandchildren, with a secret in her mind: This is the very last of your mother, children! Then she made her will and came down with a long fever. That was all just a notion like a lot of other things, but it was lucky too, for she had once for all got over the idea of dying for a long time. Now she couldn't be worried. She hoped she had better sense now. Her father had lived to be one hundred and two years old and had drunk a noggin of strong hot toddy on his last birthday. He told the reporters it was his daily habit, and he owed his long life to that. He had made quite a scandal and was very pleased about it. She believed she'd just plague Cornelia a little.

"Cornelia! Cornelia!" No footsteps, but a sudden hand on her cheek. "Bless you, where have you been?"

20   "Here, Mother."

"Well, Cornelia, I want a noggin of hot toddy."

"Are you cold, darling?"

"I'm chilly, Cornelia. Lying in bed stops the circulation. I must have told you that a thousand times."

Well, she could just hear Cornelia tell her husband that Mother was getting a little childish and they'd have to humor her. The thing that most annoyed her was that Cornelia thought she was deaf, dumb, and blind. Little hasty glances and tiny gestures tossed around her and over her head saying, "Don't cross her, let her have her way, she's eighty years old," and she sitting there as if she lived in a thin glass cage. Sometimes Granny almost made up her mind to pack up and move back to her own house where nobody could remind her every minute that she was old. Wait, wait, Cornelia, till your own children whisper behind your back!

25   In her day she had kept a better house and had got more work done. She wasn't too old yet for Lydia to be driving eighty miles for advice when one of the children jumped the track, and Jimmy still dropped in and talked things over: "Now, Mammy, you've a good business head, I want to know what you think of this? . . ." Old. Cornelia couldn't change the furniture around without asking. Little things, little things! They had been so sweet when they were little. Granny wished the old days were back again with the children young and everything to be done over. It had been a hard pull, but not too much for her. When she thought of all the food she had cooked, and all the clothes she had cut and sewed, and all the gardens she had made— well, the children showed it. There they were, made out of her, and they couldn't get away from that. Sometimes she wanted to see John again and point to them and say, Well, I didn't do so badly, did I? But that would have to wait. That was for tomorrow. She used to think of him as a man, but now all the children were older than their father, and he would be a child beside her if she saw him now. It seemed strange and there was something wrong in the idea. Why, he couldn't possibly recognize her. She had fenced in a hundred acres once, digging the post holes herself and clamping the wires with just a negro boy to help. That changed a woman. John would be looking for a young woman with the peaked Spanish comb in her hair and the painted fan. Digging post holes changed a woman. Riding country roads in the winter when women had their babies was another thing: sitting up nights with sick horses and sick negroes and sick children and hardly ever losing one. John, I hardly ever lost one of them! John would see that in a minute, that would be something he could understand, she wouldn't have to explain anything!

It made her feel like rolling up her sleeves and putting the whole place to rights again. No matter if Cornelia was determined to be everywhere at once, there were a great many things left undone on this place. She would start tomorrow and do them. It was good to be strong enough for everything, even if all you made melted and changed and slipped under your hands, so that by the time you finished you almost forgot what you were working for. What was it I set out to do? she asked herself intently, but she could not remember. A fog rose over the valley, she saw it marching across the creek swallowing the trees and moving up the hill like an army of ghosts. Soon it would be at the near edge of the orchard, and then it was time to go in and light the lamps. Come in, children, don't stay out in the night air.

Lighting the lamps had been beautiful. The children huddled up to her and breathed like little calves waiting at the bars in the twilight. Their eyes followed the match and watched the flame rise and settle in a blue curve, then they moved away from her. The lamp was lit, they didn't have to be scared and hang on to mother any more. Never, never, never more. God, for all my life I thank Thee. Without Thee, my God, I could never have done it. Hail, Mary, full of grace.

I want you to pick all the fruit this year and see that nothing is wasted. There's always someone who can use it. Don't let good things rot for want of using. You waste life when you waste good food. Don't let things get lost. It's bitter to lose things. Now, don't let me get to thinking, not when I am tired and taking a little nap before supper. . . .

The pillow rose about her shoulders and pressed against her heart and the memory was being squeezed out of it: oh, push down the pillow, somebody: it would smother her if she tried to hold it. Such a fresh breeze blowing and such a green day with no threats in it. But he had not come, just the same. What does a woman do when she has put on the white veil and set out the white cake for a man and he doesn't come? She tried to remember. No, I swear he never harmed me but in that. He never harmed me but in that . . . and what if he did? There was the day, the day, but a whirl of dark smoke rose and covered it, crept up and over into the bright field where everything was planted so carefully in orderly rows. That was hell, she knew hell when she saw it. For sixty years she had prayed against remembering him and against losing her soul in the deep pit of hell, and now the two things were mingled in one and the thought of him was a smoky cloud from hell that moved and crept in her head when she had just got rid of Doctor Harry and was trying to rest a minute. Wounded vanity, Ellen, said a sharp voice in the top of her mind. Don't let your wounded vanity get the upper hand of you. Plenty of girls get jilted. You were jilted, weren't you? Then stand up to it. Her eyelids wavered and let in streamers of blue-gray light like tissue paper over her eyes. She must get up and pull the shades down or she'd never sleep. She was in bed again and the shades were not down. How could that happen? Better turn over, hide from the light, sleeping in the light gave you nightmares. "Mother, how do you feel now?" and a stinging wetness on her forehead. But I don't like having my face washed in cold water!

30   Hapsy? George? Lydia? Jimmy? No, Cornelia, and her features were swollen and full of little puddles. "They're coming, darling, they'll all be here soon." Go wash your face, child, you look funny.

Instead of obeying, Cornelia knelt down and put her head on the pillow. She seemed to be talking but there was no sound. "Well, are you tongue-tied? Whose birthday is it? Are you going to give a party?"

Cornelia's mouth moved urgently in strange shapes. "Don't do that, you bother me, daughter."

"Oh, no, Mother. Oh, no. . . ."

Nonsense. It was strange about children. They disputed your every word. "No what, Cornelia?"

35   "Here's Doctor Harry."

"I won't see that boy again. He just left five minutes ago."

"That was this morning, Mother. It's night now. Here's the nurse."

"This is Doctor Harry, Mrs. Weatherall. I never saw you look so young and happy!"

"Ah, I'll never be young again—but I'd be happy if they'd let me lie in peace and get rested."

40   She thought she spoke up loudly, but no one answered. A warm weight on her forehead, a warm bracelet on her wrist, and a breeze went on whispering, trying to tell her something. A shuffle of leaves in the everlasting hand of God. He blew on them and they danced and rattled. "Mother, don't mind, we're going to give you a little hypodermic." "Look here, daughter, how do ants get in this bed? I saw sugar ants yesterday." Did you send for Hapsy too?

It was Hapsy she really wanted. She had to go a long way back through a great many rooms to find Hapsy standing with a baby on her arm. She seemed to herself to be Hapsy also, and the baby on Hapsy's arm was Hapsy and himself and herself, all at once, and there was no surprise in the meeting. Then Hapsy melted from within and turned flimsy as gray gauze and the baby was a gauzy shadow, and Hapsy came up close and said, "I thought you'd never come," and looked at her very searchingly and said, "You haven't changed a bit!" They leaned forward to kiss, when Cornelia began whispering from a long way off, "Oh, is there anything you want to tell me? Is there anything I can do for you?"

Yes, she had changed her mind after sixty years and she would like to see George. I want you to find George. Find him and be sure to tell him I forgot him. I want him to know I had my husband just the same and my children and my house like any other woman. A good house too and a good husband that I loved and fine children out of him. Better than I hoped for even. Tell him I was given back everything he took away and more. Oh, no, oh, God, no, there was something else besides the house and the man and the children. Oh, surely they were not all? What was it? Something not given back. . . . Her breath crowded down under her ribs and grew into a monstrous frightening shape with cutting edges; it bored up into her head, and the agony was unbelievable: Yes, John, get the doctor now, no more talk, my time has come.

When this one was born it should be the last. The last. It should have been born first, for it was the one she had truly wanted. Everything came in good time. Nothing left out, left over. She was strong, in three days she would be as well as ever. Better. A woman needed milk in her to have her full health.

"Mother, do you hear me?"

45   "I've been telling you—"

"Mother, Father Connolly's here."

"I went to Holy Communion only last week. Tell him I'm not so sinful as all that."

"Father just wants to speak to you."

He could speak as much as he pleased. It was like him to drop in and inquire about her soul as if it were a teething baby, and then stay on for a cup of tea and a round of cards and gossip. He always had a funny story of some sort, usually about an Irishman who made his little mistakes and confessed them, and the point lay in some absurd thing he would blurt out in the confessional showing his struggles between native piety and original sin. Granny felt easy about her soul. Cornelia, where are your manners? Give Father Connolly a chair. She had her secret comfortable understanding with a few favorite saints who cleared a straight road to God for her. All as surely signed and sealed as the papers for the new Forty Acres. Forever . . . heirs and assigns forever. Since the day the wedding cake was not cut, but thrown out and wasted. The whole bottom dropped out of the world, and there she was blind and sweating with nothing under her feet and the walls falling away. His hand had caught her under the breast, she had not fallen, there was the freshly polished floor with the green rug on it, just as before. He had cursed like a sailor's parrot and said, "I'll kill him for you." Don't lay a hand on him, for my sake leave something to God. "Now, Ellen, you must believe what I tell you. . . ."

50   So there was nothing, nothing to worry about any more, except sometimes in the night one of the children screamed in a nightmare, and they

both hustled out shaking and hunting for the matches and calling, "There, wait a minute, here we are!" John, get the doctor now, Hapsy's time has come. But there was Hapsy standing by the bed in a white cap. "Cornelia, tell Hapsy to take off her cap. I can't see her plain."

Her eyes opened very wide and the room stood out like a picture she had seem somewhere. Dark colors with the shadows rising towards the ceiling in long angles. The tall black dresser gleamed with nothing on it but John's picture, enlarged from a little one, with John's eyes very black when they should have been blue. You never saw him, so how do you know how he looked? But the man insisted the copy was perfect, it was very rich and handsome. For a picture, yes, but it's not my husband. The table by the bed had a linen cover and a candle and a crucifix. The light was blue from Cornelia's silk lampshades. No sort of light at all, just frippery. You had to live forty years with kerosene lamps to appreciate honest electricity. She felt very strong and she saw Doctor Harry with a rosy nimbus around him.

"You look like a saint, Doctor Harry, and I vow that's as near as you'll ever come to it."

"She's saying something."

"I heard you, Cornelia. What's all this carrying on?"

55   "Father Connolly's saying—"

Cornelia's voice staggered and bumped like a cart in a bad road. It rounded corners and turned back again and arrived nowhere. Granny stepped up in the cart very lightly and reached for the reins, but a man sat beside her and she knew him by his hands, driving the cart. She did not look in his face, for she knew without seeing, but looked instead down the road where the trees leaned over and bowed to each other and a thousand birds were singing a Mass. She felt like singing too, but she put her hand in the bosom of her dress and pulled out a rosary, and Father Connolly murmured Latin in a very solemn voice and tickled her feet. My God, will you stop that nonsense? I'm a married woman. What if he did run away and leave me to face the priest by myself? I found another a whole world better. I wouldn't have exchanged my husband for anybody except St. Michael himself, and you may tell him that for me with a thank you in the bargain.

Light flashed on her closed eyelids, and a deep roaring shook her. Cornelia, is that lightning? I hear thunder. There's going to be a storm. Close all the windows. Call all the children in. . . . "Mother, here we are, all of us." "Is that you, Hapsy?" "Oh, no, I'm Lydia. We drove as fast as we could." Their faces drifted above her, drifted away. The rosary fell out of her hands and Lydia put it back. Jimmy tried to help, their hands fumbled together, and Granny closed two fingers around Jimmy's thumb. Beads wouldn't do, it must be something alive. She was so amazed her thoughts ran round and round. So, my dear Lord, this is my death and I wasn't even thinking about it. My children have come to see me die. But I can't, it's not time. Oh, I always hated surprises. I wanted to give Cornelia the amethyst set—Cornelia, you're to have the amethyst set, but Hapsy's to wear it when she wants, and, Doctor Harry, do shut up. Nobody sent for you. Oh, my dear Lord, do wait a minute. I meant to do something about the Forty Acres, Jimmy doesn't need it and Lydia will later on, with that worthless husband of hers. I meant to finish the altar cloth and send six bottles of wine to Sister Borgia for her dyspepsia. I want to send six bottles of wine to Sister Borgia, Father Connolly, now don't let me forget.

Cornelia's voice made short turns and tilted over and crashed. "Oh, Mother, oh, Mother, oh, Mother. . . ."

"I'm not going, Cornelia. I'm taken by surprise. I can't go."

60   You'll see Hapsy again. What about her? "I thought you'd never come." Granny made a long journey outward, looking for Hapsy. What if I don't find her? What then? Her heart sank down and down, there was no bottom to death, she couldn't come to the end of it. The blue light from Cornelia's lampshade drew into a tiny point in the center of her brain, it flickered and winked like an eye, quietly it fluttered and dwindled. Granny lay curled down within herself, amazed and watchful, staring at the point of light that was herself; her body was now only a deeper mass of shadow in an endless darkness and this darkness would curl around the light and swallow it up. God, give a sign!

For the second time there was no sign. Again no bridegroom and the priest in the house. She could not remember any other sorrow because this grief wiped them all away. Oh, no, there's nothing more cruel than this—I'll never forgive it. She stretched herself with a deep breath and blew out the light.

YOUR TURN

1. How would you describe Granny Weatherall? In what ways does her name suit her?
2. The final paragraph begins: "For the second time there was no sign." What happened the first time? What is happening now? How are the two events linked? (The paragraph alludes to Christ's parable of the bridegroom, in Matthew 25.1–13. If you are unfamiliar with the parable, read it in the Gospel According to Matthew.)
3. What do you think happens in the last line of the story?

ANNIE PROULX

Annie Proulx (pronounced proo) *was born in Norwich, Connecticut, in 1935, but her family moved frequently, not only within New England but also to North Carolina. She studied at Colby College briefly, received a bachelor's degree from the University of Vermont, and did graduate work in history at Concordia University in Quebec but abandoned the doctoral program and set out as a freelance journalist. After writing several "how to" books (such as* Sweet and Hard Cider: Making It, Using It, and Enjoying It *[1980]) and bringing up three sons, she began writing short fiction, some of it for a men's magazine. In 1988 she published her first book, a collection of nine stories,* Heart Songs and Other Stories. *Since then she has published additional novels and two collections of stories,* Close Range: Wyoming Stories *(2000)—she had moved to Wyoming in 1995—and* Bad Dirt *(2004). We reprint a story from* Close Range, *the collection that includes "Brokeback Mountain," a story that in 2005 was made into a movie.*

The Blood Bay

[2000]

For Buzzy Malli[1]

The winter of 1886–87 was terrible. Every goddamn history of the high plains says so. There were great stocks of cattle on overgrazed land during the droughty summer. Early wet snow froze hard so the cattle could not break through the crust to the grass. Blizzards and freeze-eye cold followed, the gaunt bodies of cattle piling up in draws and coulees.

A young Montana cowboy, somewhat vain, had skimped on coat and mittens and put all his wages into a fine pair of handmade boots. He crossed into Wyoming Territory thinking it would be warmer, for it was south of where he was. That night he froze to death on Powder River's bitter west bank, that stream of famous dimensions and direction—an inch deep, a mile wide, and she flows uphill from Texas.

The next afternoon three cowpunchers from the Box Spring outfit near Suggs rode past his corpse, blue as a whetstone and half-buried in snow. They were savvy and salty. They wore blanket coats, woolly chaps, grease-wool scarves tied over their hats and under their bristled chins, sheepskin mitts, and two of them were fortunate enough to park their feet in good boots and heavy socks. The third, Dirt Sheets, a cross-eyed drinker of hair-oil, was all right on top but his luck was running muddy near the bottom, no socks and curl-toe boots cracked and holed.

"That can a corn beef's wearin my size boots," Sheets said and got off his horse for the first time that day. He pulled at the Montana cowboy's left boot but it was frozen on. The right one didn't come off any easier.

5   "Son of a sick steer in a snowbank," he said, "I'll cut em off and thaw em after supper." Sheets pulled out a Bowie knife and sawed through Montana's shins just above the boot tops, put the booted feet in his saddlebags, admiring the tooled leather and topstitched hearts and clubs. They rode on down the river looking for strays, found a dozen bogged in deep drifts and lost most of the daylight getting them out.

"Too late to try for the bunkhouse. Old man Grice's shack is somewheres up along. He's bound a have dried prunes or other dainties or at least a hot stove." The temperature was dropping, so cold that spit crackled in the air and a man didn't dare to piss for fear he'd be rooted fast until spring. They agreed it must be forty below and more, the wind scything up a nice Wyoming howler.

They found the shack four miles north. Old man Grice opened the door a crack.

"Come on in, puncher or rustler, I don't care."

"We'll put our horses up. Where's the barn?"

10   "Barn. Never had one. There's a lean-to out there behind the woodpile should keep em from blowin away or maybe freezin. I got my two horses in here beside the dish cupboard. I pamper them babies somethin terrible. Sleep where you can find a space, but I'm tellin you don't bother that blood

---

[1]**Buzzy Malli** the proprietor of a bar in Arvada, Wyoming.

bay none, he will mull you up and spit you out. He's a spirited steed. Pull up a chair and have some a this son-of-a-bitch stew. And I got plenty conversation juice a wash it down. Hot biscuits just comin out a the oven."

It was a fine evening, eating, drinking, and playing cards, swapping lies, the stove kicking out heat, old man Grice's spoiled horses sighing in comfort. The only disagreeable tone to the evening from the waddies[2] point of view was the fact that their host cleaned them out, took them for three dollars and four bits. Around midnight Grice blew out the lamp and got in his bunk and the three punchers stretched out on the floor. Sheets set his trophies behind the stove, laid his head on his saddle, and went to sleep.

He woke half an hour before daylight, recalled it was his mother's birthday and if he wanted to telegraph a filial sentiment to her he would have to ride faster than chain lightning with the links snapped, for the Overland office closed at noon. He checked his grisly trophies, found them thawed and pulled the boots and socks off the originals, drew them onto his own pedal extremities. He threw the bare Montana feet and his old boots in the corner near the dish cupboard, slipped out like a falling feather, saddled his horse, and rode away. The wind was low and the fine cold air refreshed him.

Old man Grice was up with the sun grinding coffee beans and frying bacon. He glanced down at his rolled-up guests and said, "Coffee's ready." The blood bay stamped and kicked at something that looked like a man's foot. Old man Grice took a closer look.

"There's a bad start to the day," he said, "it is a man's foot and there's the other." He counted the sleeping guests. There were only two of them.

15   "Wake up, survivors, for god's sake wake up and get up."

The two punchers rolled out, stared wild-eyed at the old man who was fairly frothing, pointing at the feet on the floor behind the blood bay.

"He's ate Sheets. Ah, I knew he was a hard horse, but to eat a man whole. You savage bugger," he screamed at the blood bay and drove him out into the scorching cold. "You'll never eat human meat again. You'll sleep out with the blizzards and wolves, you hell-bound fiend." Secretly he was pleased to own a horse with the sand to eat a raw cowboy.

The leftover Box Spring riders were up and drinking coffee. They squinted at old man Grice, hitched at their gun belts.

"Ah, boys, for god's sake, it was a terrible accident. I didn't know what a brute of a animal was that blood bay. Let's keep this to ourselves. Sheets was no prize and I've got forty gold dollars says so and the three and four bits I took off a you last night. Eat your bacon, don't make no trouble. There's enough trouble in the world without no more."

20   No, they wouldn't make trouble and they put the heavy money in their saddlebags, drank a last cup of hot coffee, saddled up, and rode out into the grinning morning.

When they saw Sheets that night at the bunkhouse they nodded, congratulated him on his mother's birthday but said nothing about blood bays or forty-three dollars and four bits. The arithmetic stood comfortable.

---

[2]**Waddies** cowboys.

YOUR TURN

1. At what point did you first realize that you were reading a tall tale, a yarn, not a realistic short story?
2. What sorts of special pleasure—that is, pleasures different from those of the conventional short story—does the tall tale offer?
3. What, if anything, would be lost if the final paragraph of this yarn were omitted?

CHAPTER
10
Allegory and Symbolism

In Chapter 7 we looked at a fable, a short fiction that was meant to teach us: the characters clearly stood for principles of behavior, and the fictions as a whole evidently taught lessons. If you think of a fable such as "The Ant and the Grasshopper" (the ant wisely collects food during the summer in order to provide for the winter, whereas the grasshopper foolishly sings all summer and goes hungry in the winter), you can easily see that the characters may stand for something other than themselves. The ant, let's say, is the careful, foresighted person, and the grasshopper is the person who lives for the moment. Similarly, in the fable of the tortoise and the hare, the tortoise represents the person who is slow but steady, the rabbit the person who is talented but overly confident and, in the end, foolish.

A story in which each character is understood to have an equivalent is an **allegory.** Further, in an allegory, not only characters but also things (roads, forests, houses) have fairly clear equivalents. Thus, in John Bunyan's *The Pilgrim's Progress* (1678) we meet a character named Christian, who, on the road to the Celestial City, meets Giant Despair, Mr. Worldly Wiseman, and Faithful, and passes through the City of Destruction and Vanity Fair. What all of these are equivalent to is clear from their names. It is also clear that Christian's journey stands for the trials of the soul in this world. There is, so to speak, a one-to-one relationship: A = B =, and so on. If, for example, we are asked what the road represents in *The Pilgrim's Progress,* we can confidently say that it stands for the journey of life. Thus, *The Pilgrim's Progress* tells two stories, the surface story of a man making a trip, during which he meets various figures and visits various places, and a second story, understood through the first, of the trials that afflict the soul during its quest for salvation.

Modern short stories rarely have the allegory's clear system of equivalents, but we may nevertheless feel that certain characters and certain things in the story stand for more than themselves, or hint at larger meanings. We feel, that is, that they are **symbolic.** But here we must be careful. How does one know that this or that figure or place is symbolic? In Hemingway's "Cat in the Rain" (page 99), is the cat symbolic? Is the innkeeper? Is the rain? Reasonable people may differ in their answers. Again, in Chopin's "The Story of an Hour" (page 67), is the railroad accident a symbol? Is Josephine a symbol? Is the season (springtime) a symbol? And again, reasonable people may differ in their responses.

Let's assume for the moment, however, that if writers use symbols, they want readers to perceive—at least faintly—that certain characters or places or seasons or happenings have rich implications, stand for something more than what they are on the surface. How do writers help us to perceive these things? By emphasizing them—for instance, by describing them at some length, or by introducing them at times when they might not seem strictly necessary, or by calling attention to them repeatedly.

Consider, for example, Chopin's treatment of the season in which "The Story of an Hour" takes place. The story has to take place at *some* time, but Chopin does not simply say, "On a spring day," or an autumn day, and let things go at that. Rather, she tells us about the sky, the trees, the rain, the twittering sparrows—and all of this in an extremely short story where we might think there is no time for talk about the setting. After all, none of this material is strictly necessary to a story about a woman who has heard that her husband was killed in an accident, who grieves, then recovers, and then dies when he suddenly reappears.

Why, then, does Chopin give such emphasis to the season? Because, we think, she is using the season symbolically. In this story, the spring is not just a bit of detail added for realism. It is rich with suggestions of renewal, of the new life that Louise achieves for a moment. But here, a caution. We think that the spring in this story is symbolic, but this is not to say that whenever spring appears in a story, it always stands for renewal, any more than whenever winter appears it always symbolizes death. Nor does it mean that since spring recurs, Louise will be reborn. In short, in *this* story Chopin uses the season to convey specific implications.

Is the railroad accident also a symbol? Our answer is no—though we don't expect all readers to agree with us. We think that the railroad accident in "The Story of an Hour" is just a railroad accident. It's our sense that Chopin is *not* using this event to say something about (for instance) modern travel, or about industrialism. The steam-propelled railroad train could of course be used, symbolically, to say something about industrialism displacing an agrarian economy, but does Chopin give her train any such suggestion? We don't think so. Had she wished to do so, she would probably have talked about the enormous power of the train, the shriek of its whistle, the smoke pouring out of the smokestack, the intense fire burning in the engine, its indifference as it charged through the countryside, and so forth. Had she done so, the story would be a different story. Or she might have made the train a symbol of fate overriding human desires. But, again in our opinion, Chopin does not endow her train with such suggestions. She gives virtually no emphasis to the train, and so we believe it has virtually no significance for the reader.

What of Chopin's "Ripe Figs" (page 87)? Maman-Nainaine tells Babette that when the figs are ripe Babette can visit her cousins. Maman may merely be setting an arbitrary date, but as we read the story we probably feel—because of the emphasis on the *ripening* of the figs, which occurs in the spring or early summer—that the ripening of the figs in some way suggests the maturing of Babette. If we do get such ideas, we will in effect be saying that the story is not simply an anecdote about an old woman whose behavior is odd. True, the narrator of the story, after telling us of Maman-Nainaine's promise, adds, "Not that the ripening of figs had the least thing to do with it, but that is the way Maman-Nainaine was." The narrator sees nothing special—merely Maman-Nainaine's eccentricity—in the connection between the ripening of the figs and Babette's visit to her cousins. Readers, however, may see more than the narrator sees or says. They may see in Babette a young girl maturing; they may see in Maman-Nainaine an older woman who, almost collaborating with nature, helps Babette to mature.

Symbolism and Theme

And here, as we talk about symbolism we are getting into the theme of the story. An apparently inconsequential and even puzzling action, such as is set forth in "Ripe Figs," may cast a long shadow. As Robert Frost once said,

> There is no story written that has any value at all, however straightforward it looks and free from doubleness, double entendre, that you'd value at all if it didn't have intimations of something more than itself.

The stranger, the more mysterious the story, the more likely we are to suspect some sort of significance, but even realistic stories such as Chopin's "The Storm" and "The Story of an Hour" may be rich in suggestions. This is not to say, however, that the suggestions (rather than the details of the surface) are what count. A reader does not discard the richly detailed, highly specific narrative (Mrs. Mallard learned that her husband was dead and reacted in such-and-such a way) in favor of some supposedly universal message or theme that it implies. We do not throw away the specific narrative—the memorable characters, or the interesting things that happen in the story—and move on to some "higher truth." Robert Frost went on to say, "The anecdote, the parable, the surface meaning has got to be good and got to be sufficient in itself."

Between these two extremes—on the one hand, writing that is almost all a richly detailed surface and, on the other hand, writing that has a surface so thin that we are immediately taken up with the implications or meanings—are stories in which we strongly feel both the surface happenings and their implications. In *Place in Fiction,* Eudora Welty uses an image of a china lamp to explain literature that presents an interesting surface texture filled with rich significance. When unlit, the lamp showed London; when lit, it showed the Great Fire of London. Like a painted porcelain lamp that, when illuminated, reveals an inner picture shining through the outer, the physical details in a work are illuminated from within by the author's imaginative vision. The outer painting (the literal details) presents "a continuous, shapely, pleasing, and finished surface to the eye," but this surface is not the whole. Welty happens to be talking about the novel, but her words apply equally to the short story:

> The lamp alight is the combination of internal and external, glowing at the imagination as one; and so is the good novel. . . . The good novel should be steadily alight, revealing.

Details that glow, that are themselves and are also something more than themselves, are symbols. Readers may disagree about whether in any particular story something is or is not symbolic—let's say the figs and chrysanthemums in Chopin's "Ripe Figs," or the season in "The Story of an Hour." And an ingenious reader may overcomplicate or overemphasize the symbolism of a work or may distort it by omitting some of the details and by unduly focusing on others. In many works the details glow, but the glow is so gentle and subtle that even to talk about the details is to overstate them and to understate other equally important aspects of the work.

Yet if it is false to overstate the significance of a detail, it is also false to understate a significant detail. The let's-have-no-nonsense literal reader who holds that "the figure of a man" whom Brown meets in the forest in Hawthorne's "Young Goodman Brown" is simply a man—rather than the Devil—impoverishes the story by neglecting the rich implications just as much as the symbol-hunter impoverishes "The Story of an Hour" by losing sight of Mrs. Mallard in an interpretation of the story as a symbolic comment on industrialism. To take only a single piece of evidence: the man whom Brown encounters holds a staff, "which bore the likeness of a great black snake, so curiously wrought that it might almost be seen to twist and wriggle itself like a living serpent." If we are familiar with the story of Adam and Eve, in which Satan took the form of a serpent, it is hard not to think that Hawthorne is here implying that Brown's new acquaintance is Satan. And, to speak more broadly, when reading the story we can hardly not set up opposing meanings (or at least suggestions) for the village (from which Brown sets out) and the forest (into which he enters). The village is associated with daylight, faith, and goodness; the forest with darkness, loss of faith, and evil. This is not to say that the story sets up neat categories. If you read the story, you will find that Hawthorne is careful to be ambiguous. Even in the passage quoted, about the serpent-staff, you'll notice that he does not say it twisted and wriggled, but that it "might almost be seen to twist and wriggle."

JOHN STEINBECK

John Steinbeck (1902–1968) was born in Salinas, California, and much of his fiction concerns this landscape and its people. As a young man he worked on ranches, farms, and road gangs, and sometimes attended Stanford University— he never graduated—but he wrote whenever he could find the time. His early efforts at writing, however, were rejected by publishers. Even when he did break into print, he did not achieve much notice for several years: a novel in 1929, a book of stories in 1932, and another novel in 1933 attracted little attention. But the publication of Tortilla Flat *(1935), a novel about Mexican-Americans, changed all that. It was followed by other successful novels—In* Dubious Battle *(1936) and* Of Mice and Men *(1937)—and by* The Long Valley *(1938), a collection of stories that included "The Chrysanthemums." His next book,* The Grapes of Wrath *(1939), about dispossessed sharecropper migrants from the Oklahoma dustbowl, was also immensely popular and won a Pulitzer Prize. During World War II Steinbeck sent reports from battlefields in Italy and Africa. In 1962 he was awarded the Nobel Prize in Literature.*

The Chrysanthemums   [1937]

The high grey-flannel fog of winter closed off the Salinas Valley[1] from the sky and from all the rest of the world. On every side it sat like a lid on the mountains and made of the great valley a closed pot. On the broad, level land floor the gang plows bit deep and left the black earth shining like metal where the shares had cut. On the foothill ranches across the Salinas River, the yellow stubble fields seemed to be bathed in pale cold sunshine, but there was no sunshine in the valley now in December. The thick willow scrub along the river flamed with sharp and positive yellow leaves.

---

[1]**the Salinas Valley** a fertile area in central California.

It was a time of quiet and of waiting. The air was cold and tender. A light wind blew up from the southwest so that the farmers were mildly hopeful of a good rain before long; but fog and rain do not go together.

Across the river, on Henry Allen's foothill ranch there was little work to be done, for the hay was cut and stored and the orchards were plowed up to receive the rain deeply when it should come. The cattle on the higher slopes were becoming shaggy and rough-coated.

Elisa Allen, working in her flower garden, looked down across the yard and saw Henry, her husband, talking to two men in business suits. The three of them stood by the tractor shed, each man with one foot on the side of the little Fordson.[2] They smoked cigarettes and studied the machine as they talked.

5   Elisa watched them for a moment and then went back to her work. She was thirty-five. Her face was lean and strong and her eyes were as clear as water. Her figure looked blocked and heavy in her gardening costume, a man's black hat pulled low down over her eyes, clod-hopper shoes, a figured print dress almost completely covered by a big corduroy apron with four big pockets to hold the snips, the trowel and scratcher, the seeds and the knife she worked with. She wore heavy leather gloves to protect her hands while she worked.

She was cutting down the old year's chrysanthemum stalks with a pair of short and powerful scissors. She looked down toward the men by the tractor shed now and then. Her face was eager and mature and handsome; even her work with the scissors was over-eager, over-powerful. The chrysanthemum stems seemed too small and easy for her energy.

She brushed a cloud of hair out of her eyes with the back of her glove, and left a smudge of earth on her cheek in doing it. Behind her stood the neat white farm house with red geraniums close-banked around it as high as the windows. It was a hard-swept looking little house with hard-polished windows, and a clean mud-mat on the front steps.

Elisa cast another glance toward the tractor shed. The strangers were getting into their Ford coupe. She took off a glove and put her strong fingers down into the forest of new green chrysanthemum sprouts that were growing around the old roots. She spread the leaves and looked down among the close-growing stems. No aphids were there, no sowbugs or snails or cutworms. Her terrier fingers destroyed such pests before they could get started.

Elisa started at the sound of her husband's voice. He had come near quietly, and he leaned over the wire fence that protected her flower garden from the cattle and dogs and chickens.

10   "At it again," he said. "You've got a strong new crop coming."

Elisa straightened her back and pulled on the gardening glove again. "Yes, they'll be strong this coming year." In her tone and on her face there was a little smugness.

"You've got a gift with things," Henry observed. "Some of those yellow chrysanthemums you had this year were ten inches across. I wish you'd work out in the orchard and raise some apples that big."

---

[2]**Fordson** a two-door Ford car.

Her eyes sharpened. "Maybe I could do it, too. I've a gift with things, all right. My mother had it. She could stick anything in the ground and make it grow. She said it was having planters' hands that knew how to do it."

"Well, it sure works with flowers," he said.

15   "Henry, who were those men you were talking to?"

"Why, sure, that's what I came to tell you. They were from the Western Meat Company. I sold those thirty head of three-year-old steers. Got nearly my own price, too."

"Good," she said. "Good for you."

"And I thought," he continued, "I thought how it's Saturday afternoon, and we might go into Salinas for dinner at a restaurant, and then to a picture show—to celebrate, you see."

"Good," she repeated. "Oh, yes. That will be good."

20   Henry put on his joking tone. "There's fights tonight. How'd you like to go to the fights?"

"Oh, no," she said breathlessly. "No, I wouldn't like the fights."

"Just fooling, Elisa. We'll go to a movie. Let's see. It's two now. I'm going to take Scotty and bring down those steers from the hill. It'll take us maybe two hours. We'll go in town about five and have dinner at the Cominos Hotel. Like that?"

"Of course I'll like it. It's good to eat away from home."

"All right, then. I'll go get up a couple of horses."

25   She said, "I'll have plenty of time to transplant some of these sets, I guess."

She heard her husband calling Scotty down by the barn. And a little later she saw the two men ride up the pale yellow hillside in search of the steers.

There was a little square sandy bed kept for rooting the chrysanthemums. With her trowel she turned the soil over and over, and smoothed it and patted it firm. Then she dug ten parallel trenches to receive the sets. Back at the chrysanthemum bed she pulled out the little crisp shoots, trimmed off the leaves of each one with her scissors and laid it on a small orderly pile.

A squeak of wheels and plod of hoofs came from the road. Elisa looked up. The country road ran along the dense bank of willows and cottonwoods that bordered the river, and up this road came a curious vehicle, curiously drawn. It was an old springwagon, with a round canvas top on it like the cover of a prairie schooner. It was drawn by an old bay horse and a little grey-and-white burro. A big stubble-bearded man sat between the cover flaps and drove the crawling team. Underneath the wagon, between the hind wheels, a lean and rangy mongrel dog walked sedately. Words were painted on the canvas, in clumsy, crooked letters. "Pots, pans, knives, sisors, lawn mores, Fixed." Two rows of articles, and the triumphantly definitive "Fixed" below. The black paint had run down in little sharp points beneath each letter.

Elisa, squatting on the ground, watched to see the crazy, loose-jointed wagon pass by. But it didn't pass. It turned into the farm road in front of her house, crooked old wheels skirling and squeaking. The rangy dog darted from between the wheels and ran ahead. Instantly the two ranch shepherds flew out at him. Then all three stopped, and with stiff and quivering tails, with taut straight legs, with ambassadorial dignity, they slowly circled, sniffing daintily. The caravan pulled up to Elisa's wire fence and stopped. Now the newcomer dog, feeling out-numbered, lowered his tail and retired under the wagon with raised hackles and bared teeth.

30   The man on the wagon called out, "That's a bad dog in a fight when he gets started."

Elisa laughed. "I see he is. How soon does he generally get started?"

The man caught up her laughter and echoed it heartily. "Sometimes not for weeks and weeks," he said. He climbed stiffly down, over the wheel. The horse and donkey drooped like unwatered flowers.

Elisa saw that he was a very big man. Although his hair and beard were greying, he did not look old. His worn black suit was wrinkled and spotted with grease. The laughter had disappeared from his face and eyes the moment his laughing voice ceased. His eyes were dark, and they were full of the brooding that gets in the eyes of teamsters and of sailors. The calloused hands he rested on the wire fence were cracked, and every crack was a black line. He took off his battered hat.

"I'm off my general road, ma'am," he said. "Does this dirt road cut over across the river to the Los Angeles highway?"

35   Elisa stood up and shoved the thick scissors in her apron pocket. "Well, yes, it does, but it winds around and then fords the river. I don't think your team could pull it through the sand."

He replied with some asperity. "It might surprise you what them beasts can pull through."

"When they get started?" she asked.

He smiled for a second. "Yes. When they get started."

"Well," said Elisa, "I think you'll save time if you go back to the Salinas road and pick up the highway there."

40   He drew a big finger around the chicken wire and made it sing. "I ain't in any hurry, ma'am. I go from Seattle to San Diego and back every year. Takes all my time. About six months each way. I aim to follow nice weather."

Elisa took off her gloves and stuffed them in the apron pocket with the scissors. She touched under the edge of her man's hat, searching for fugitive hairs. "That sounds like a nice kind of a way to live," she said.

He leaned confidentially over the fence. "Maybe you noticed the writing on my wagon. I mend pots and sharpen knives and scissors. You got any of them things to do?"

"Oh, no," she said quickly. "Nothing like that." Her eyes hardened with resistance.

"Scissors is the worst thing," he explained. "Most people just ruin scissors trying to sharpen 'em, but I know how. I got a special tool. It's a little bobbit kind of thing, and patented. But it sure does the trick."

45   "No. My scissors are all sharp."

"All right, then. Take a pot," he continued earnestly, "a bent pot, or a pot with a hole. I can make it like new so you don't have to buy no new ones. That's a saving for you."

"No." she said shortly. "I tell you I have nothing like that for you to do."

His face fell to an exaggerated sadness. His voice took on a whining undertone. "I ain't had a thing to do today. Maybe I won't have no supper tonight. You see I'm off my regular road. I know folks on the highway clear from Seattle to San Diego. They save their things for me to sharpen up because they know I do it so good and save them money."

"I'm sorry," Elisa said irritably. "I haven't anything for you to do."

50   His eyes left her face and fell to searching the ground. They roamed about until they came to the chrysanthemum bed where she had been working. "What's them plants, ma'am?"

The irritation and resistance melted from Elisa's face. "Oh, those are chrysanthemums, giant whites and yellows. I raise them every year, bigger than anybody around here."

"Kind of a long-stemmed flower? Looks like a quick puff of colored smoke?" he asked.

"That's it. What a nice way to describe them."

"They smell kind of nasty till you get used to them," he said.

55   "It's a good bitter smell," she retorted, "not nasty at all."

He changed his tone quickly. "I like the smell myself."

"I had ten-inch blooms this year," she said.

The man leaned farther over the fence. "Look. I know a lady down the road a piece, has got the nicest garden you ever seen. Got nearly every kind of flower but no chrysanthemums. Last time I was mending a copper-bottom washtub for her (that's a hard job but I do it good), she said to me, 'If you ever run acrost some nice chrysanthemums I wish you'd try to get me a few seeds.' That's what she told me."

Elisa's eyes grew alert and eager. "She couldn't have known much about chrysanthemums. You *can* raise them from seed, but it's much easier to root the little sprouts you see here."

60   "Oh," he said. "I s'pose I can't take none to her then."

"Why yes you can," Elisa cried. "I can put some in damp sand, and you can carry them right along with you. They'll take root in the pot if you keep them damp. And then transplant them."

"She'd sure like to have some, ma'am. You say they're nice ones?"

"Beautiful," she said. "Oh, beautiful." Her eyes shone. She tore off the battered hat and shook out her dark pretty hair. "I'll put them in a flower pot, and you can take them right with you. Come into the yard."

While the man came through the picket gate Elisa ran excitedly along the geranium-bordered path to the back of the house. And she returned carrying a big red flower pot. The gloves were forgotten now. She kneeled on the ground by the starting bed and dug up the sandy soil with her fingers and scooped it into the bright new flower pot. Then she picked up the little pile of shoots she had just prepared. With her strong fingers she pressed them into the sand and tamped around them with her knuckles. The man stood over her. "I'll tell you what to do," she said. "You remember so you can tell the lady."

65   "Yes, I'll try to remember."

"Well, look. These will take root in about a month. Then she must set them out, about a foot apart in good rich earth like this, see?" She lifted a handful of dark soil for him to look at. "They'll grow fast and tall. Now remember this: In July tell her to cut them down, about eight inches from the ground."

"Before they bloom?" he asked.

"Yes, before they bloom." Her face was tight with eagerness. "They'll grow right up again. About the last of September the buds will start."

She stopped and seemed perplexed. "It's the budding that takes the most care," she said hesitantly. "I don't know how to tell you." She looked deep into his eyes, searchingly. Her mouth opened a little, and she seemed to be listening. "I'll try to tell you," she said. "Did you ever hear of planting hands?"

70   "Can't say I have, ma'am."

"Well, I can only tell you what it feels like. It's when you're picking off the buds you don't want. Everything goes right down into your fingertips. You watch your fingers work. They do it themselves. You can feel how it is. They pick and pick the buds. They never make a mistake. They're with the plant. Do you see? Your fingers and the plant. You can feel that, right up your arm. They know. They never make a mistake. You can feel it. When you're like that you can't do anything wrong. Do you see that? Can you understand that?"

She was kneeling on the ground looking up at him. Her breast swelled passionately.

The man's eyes narrowed. He looked away self-consciously. "Maybe I know," he said. "Sometimes in the night in the wagon there—"

Elisa's voice grew husky. She broke in on him, "I've never lived as you do, but I know what you mean. When the night is dark—why, the stars are sharp-pointed, and there's quiet. Why, you rise up and up! Every pointed star gets driven into your body. It's like that. Hot and sharp and—lovely."

75   Kneeling there, her hand went out toward his legs in the greasy black trousers. Her hesitant fingers almost touched the cloth. Then her hand dropped to the ground. She crouched low like a fawning dog.

He said, "It's nice, just like you say. Only when you don't have no dinner, it ain't."

She stood up then, very straight, and her face was ashamed. She held the flower pot out to him and placed it gently in his arms. "Here. Put it in your wagon, on the seat, where you can watch it. Maybe I can find something for you to do."

At the back of the house she dug in the can pile and found two old and battered aluminum saucepans. She carried them back and gave them to him. "Here, maybe you can fix these."

His manner changed. He became professional. "Good as new I can fix them." At the back of his wagon he set a little anvil, and out of an oily tool box dug a small machine hammer. Elisa came through the gate to watch him while he pounded out the dents in the kettles. His mouth grew sure and knowing. At a difficult part of the work he sucked his under-lip.

80   "You sleep right in the wagon?" Elisa asked.

"Right in the wagon, ma'am. Rain or shine I'm dry as a cow in there."

"It must be nice," she said. "It must be very nice. I wish women could do such things."

"It ain't the right kind of life for a woman."

Her upper lip raised a little, showing her teeth. "How do you know? How can you tell?" she said.

85   "I don't know, ma'am," he protested. "Of course I don't know. Now here's your kettles done. You don't have to buy no new ones."

"How much?"

"Oh, fifty cents'll do. I keep my prices down and my work good. That's why I have all them satisfied customers up and down the highway."

Elisa brought him a fifty-cent piece from the house and dropped it in his hand. "You might be surprised to have a rival some time. I can sharpen scissors, too. And I can beat the dents out of little pots. I could show you what a woman might do."

He put his hammer back in the oily box and shoved the little anvil out of sight. "It would be a lonely life for a woman, ma'am, and a scarey life, too, with animals creeping under the wagon all night." He climbed over the sin-gletree, steadying himself with a hand on the burro's white rump. He settled himself in the seat, picked up the lines. "Thank you kindly, ma'am," he said. "I'll do like you told me; I'll go back and catch the Salinas road."

90   "Mind," she called, "if you're long in getting there, keep the sand damp."

"Sand, ma'am? . . . Sand? Oh, sure. You mean around the chrysanthe-mums. Sure I will." He clucked his tongue. The beasts leaned luxuriously into their collars. The mongrel dog took his place between the back wheels. The wagon turned and crawled out the entrance road and back the way it had come, along the river.

Elisa stood in front of her wire fence watching the slow progress of the caravan. Her shoulders were straight, and her head thrown back, her eyes half-closed, so that the scene came vaguely into them. Her lips moved silently, forming the words "Good-bye—good-bye." Then she whispered, "That's a bright direction. There's a glowing there." The sound of her whis-per startled her. She shook herself free and looked about to see whether anyone had been listening. Only the dogs had heard. They lifted their heads toward her from their sleeping in the dust, and then stretched out their chins and settled asleep again. Elisa turned and ran hurriedly into the house.

In the kitchen she reached behind the stove and felt the water tank. It was full of hot water from the noonday cooking. In the bathroom she tore off her soiled clothes and flung them into the corner. And then she scrubbed herself with a little block of pumice, legs and thighs, loins and chest and arms, until her skin was scratched and red. When she had dried herself she stood in front of a mirror in her bedroom and looked at her body. She tightened her stomach and threw out her chest. She turned and looked over her shoulder at her back.

After a while she began to dress, slowly. She put on her newest under-clothing and her nicest stockings and the dress which was the symbol of her prettiness. She worked carefully on her hair, penciled her eyebrows and rouged her lips.

95   Before she was finished she heard the little thunder of hoofs and the shouts of Henry and his helper as they drove the red steers into the corral. She heard the gate bang shut and set herself for Henry's arrival.

His step sounded on the porch. He entered the house calling, "Elisa, where are you?"

"In my room, dressing. I'm not ready. There's hot water for your bath. Hurry up. It's getting late."

When she heard him splashing in the tub, Elisa laid his dark suit on the bed, and shirt and socks and tie beside it. She stood his polished shoes on the floor beside the bed. Then she went to the porch and sat primly and stiffly down. She looked toward the river road where the willow-line was still yellow with frosted leaves so that under the high grey fog they seemed a thin band of sunshine. This was the only color in the grey afternoon. She sat unmoving for a long time. Her eyes blinked rarely.

Henry came banging out of the door, shoving his tie inside his vest as he came. Elisa stiffened and her face grew tight. Henry stopped short and looked at her. "Why—why, Elisa. You look so nice!"

100   "Nice? You think I look nice? What do you mean by 'nice'?"

Henry blundered on. "I don't know. I mean you look different, strong and happy."

"I am strong? Yes, strong. What do you mean by 'strong'?"

He looked bewildered. "You're playing some kind of a game," he said helplessly. "It's a kind of a play. You look strong enough to break a calf over your knee, happy enough to eat it like a watermelon."

For a second she lost her rigidity. "Henry! Don't talk like that. You didn't know what you said." She grew complete again. "I'm strong," she boasted. "I never knew before how strong."

105   Henry looked down toward the tractor shed, and when he brought his eyes back to her, they were his own again. "I'll get out the car. You can put on your coat while I'm starting."

Elisa went into the house. She heard him drive to the gate and idle down his motor, and then she took a long time to put on her hat. She pulled it here and pressed it there. When Henry turned the motor off she slipped into her coat and went out.

The little roadster bounced along on the dirt road by the river, raising the birds and driving the rabbits into the brush. Two cranes flapped heavily over the willow-line and dropped into the river-bed.

Far ahead on the road Elisa saw a dark speck. She knew.

She tried not to look as they passed it, but her eyes would not obey. She whispered to herself sadly, "He might have thrown them off the road. That wouldn't have been much trouble, not very much. But he kept the pot," she explained. "He had to keep the pot. That's why he couldn't get them off the road."

110   The roadster turned a bend and she saw the caravan ahead. She swung full around toward her husband so she could not see the little covered wagon and the mismatched team as the car passed them.

In a moment it was over. The thing was done. She did not look back.

She said loudly, to be heard above the motor, "It will be good, tonight, a good dinner."

"Now you're changed again," Henry complained. He took one hand from the wheel and patted her knee. "I ought to take you in to dinner oftener. It would be good for both of us. We get so heavy out on the ranch."

"Henry," she asked, "could we have wine at dinner?"

115   "Sure we could. Say! That will be fine."

She was silent for a while; then she said, "Henry, at those prize fights, do the men hurt each other very much?"

"Sometimes a little, not often. Why?"

"Well, I've read how they break noses, and blood runs down their chests. I've read how the fighting gloves get heavy and soggy with blood."

He looked around at her. "What's the matter, Elisa? I didn't know you read things like that." He brought the car to a stop, then turned to the right over the Salinas River bridge.

120   "Do any women ever go to the fights?" she asked.

"Oh, sure, some. What's the matter, Elisa? Do you want to go? I don't think you'd like it, but I'll take you if you really want to go."

She relaxed limply in the seat. "Oh, no. No. I don't want to go. I'm sure I don't." Her face was turned away from him. "It will be enough if we can have wine. It will be plenty." She turned up her coat collar so he could not see that she was crying weakly—like an old woman.

YOUR TURN

1. In the first paragraph of the story, the valley, shut off by fog, is said to be "a closed pot." Is this setting significant? Would any other setting do equally well? Why, or why not?
2. What does Elisa's clothing tell us about her? By the way, do you believe that all clothing says something about the wearers? Please explain.
3. Should we make anything special out of Elisa's interest in gardening? If so, what?
4. Describe Elisa's and Henry's marriage.
5. Evaluate the view that Elisa is responsible for her troubles.

GABRIEL GARCÍA MÁRQUEZ

Gabriel García Márquez (b. 1928) was born in Aracataca, a small village in Colombia. After being educated in Bogota, where he studied journalism and law, he worked as a journalist in Latin America, Europe, and the United States. He began writing fiction when he was in Paris, and at twenty-seven he published his first novel, La hojarasca (Leaf Storm, 1955). *During most of the 1960s he lived in Mexico, where he wrote film scripts and the novel that made him famous:* Cien años de soledad *(1967, translated in 1970 as* One Hundred Years of Solitude). *In 1982 García Márquez was awarded the Nobel Prize in Literature.*

Márquez's novels include The Autumn of the Patriarch *(1975);* Love in the Time of Cholera *(1985);* The General in his Labyrinth *(1989); and* Of Love and Demons *(1994).*

A Very Old Man with Enormous Wings   [1968]

A Tale for Children

Translated by Gregory Rabassa

On the third day of rain they had killed so many crabs inside the house that Pelayo had to cross his drenched courtyard and throw them into the sea, because the newborn child had a temperature all night and they thought it was due to the stench. The world had been sad since Tuesday. Sea and sky were a single ash-gray thing and the sands of the beach, which on March nights glimmered like powdered light, had become a stew of mud and rotten shellfish. The light was so weak at noon that when Pelayo was coming back to the house after throwing away the crabs, it was hard for him to see what it was that was moving and groaning in the rear of the courtyard. He had to go very close to see that it was an old man, a very old man, lying face down in the mud, who, in spite of his tremendous efforts, couldn't get up, impeded by his enormous wings.

Frightened by that nightmare, Pelayo ran to get Elisenda, his wife, who was putting compresses on the sick child, and he took her to the rear of the courtyard. They both looked at the fallen body with mute stupor. He was dressed like a rag-picker. There were only a few faded hairs left on his bald skull and very few teeth in his mouth, and his pitiful condition of a drenched great-grandfather had taken away any sense of grandeur he might have had. His huge buzzard wings, dirty and half-plucked, were forever entangled in the mud. They looked at him so long and so closely that Pelayo and Elisenda very soon overcame their surprise and in the end found him familiar. Then they dared speak to him, and he answered in an incomprehensible dialect with a strong sailor's voice. That was how they skipped over the inconvenience of the wings and quite intelligently concluded that he was a lonely castaway from some foreign ship wrecked by the storm. And yet, they called in a neighbor woman who knew everything about life and death to see him, and all she needed was one look to show them their mistake.

"He's an angel," she told them. "He must have been coming for the child, but the poor fellow is so old that the rain knocked him down."

On the following day everyone knew that a flesh-and-blood angel was held captive in Pelayo's house. Against the judgment of the wise neighbor woman, for whom angels in those times were the fugitive survivors of a celestial conspiracy, they did not have the heart to club him to death. Pelayo watched over him all afternoon from the kitchen, armed with his bailiff's club, and before going to bed he dragged him out of the mud and locked him up with the hens in the wire chicken coop. In the middle of the night, when the rain stopped, Pelayo and Elisenda were still killing crabs. A short time afterward the child woke up without a fever and with a desire to eat. Then they felt magnanimous and decided to put the angel on a raft with fresh water and provisions for three days and leave him to his fate on the high seas. But when they went out into the courtyard with the first light of dawn, they found the whole neighborhood in front of the chicken coop having fun with the angel, without the slightest reverence, tossing him things to eat through the openings in the wire as if he weren't a supernatural creature but a circus animal.

5   Father Gonzaga arrived before seven o'clock, alarmed at the strange news. By that time onlookers less frivolous than those at dawn had already arrived and they were making all kinds of conjectures concerning the captive's future. The simplest among them thought that he should be named mayor of the world. Others of sterner mind felt that he should be promoted to the rank of five-star general in order to win all wars. Some visionaries hoped that he could be put to stud in order to implant on earth a race of winged wise men who could take charge of the universe. But Father Gonzaga, before becoming a priest, had been a robust woodcutter. Standing by the wire, he reviewed his catechism in an instant and asked them to open the door so that he could take a close look at that pitiful man who looked more like a huge decrepit hen among the fascinated chickens. He was lying in a corner drying his open wings in the sunlight among the fruit peels and breakfast leftovers that the early risers had thrown him. Alien to the impertinences of the world, he only lifted his antiquarian eyes and murmured

something in his dialect when Father Gonzaga went into the chicken coop and said good morning to him in Latin. The parish priest had his first suspicion of an impostor when he saw that he did not understand the language of God or know how to greet His ministers. Then he noticed that seen close up he was much too human: he had an unbearable smell of the outdoors, the back side of his wings were strewn with parasites and his main feathers had been mistreated by terrestrial winds, and nothing about him measured up to the proud dignity of angels. Then he came out of the chicken coop and in a brief sermon warned the curious against the risks of being ingenuous. He reminded them that the devil had the bad habit of making use of carnival tricks in order to confuse the unwary. He argued that if wings were not the essential element in determining the difference between a hawk and an airplane, they were even less so in the recognition of angels. Nevertheless, he promised to write a letter to his bishop so that the latter would write to his primate so that the latter would write to the Supreme Pontiff in order to get the final verdict from the highest courts.

His prudence fell on sterile hearts. The news of the captive angel spread with such rapidity that after a few hours the courtyard had the bustle of a marketplace and they had to call in troops with fixed bayonets to disperse the mob that was about to knock the house down. Elisenda, her spine all twisted from sweeping up so much marketplace trash, then got the idea of fencing in the yard and charging five cents admission to see the angel.

The curious came from far away. A traveling carnival arrived with a flying acrobat who buzzed over the crowd several times, but no one paid any attention to him because his wings were not those of an angel but, rather, those of a sidereal bat. The most unfortunate invalids on earth came in search of health: a poor woman who since childhood had been counting her heartbeats and had run out of numbers; a Portuguese man who couldn't sleep because the noise of the stars disturbed him; a sleepwalker who got up at night to undo the things he had done while awake; and many others with less serious ailments. In the midst of that shipwreck disorder that made the earth tremble, Pelayo and Elisenda were happy with fatigue, for in less than a week they had crammed their rooms with money and the line of pilgrims waiting their turn to enter still reached beyond the horizon.

The angel was the only one who took no part in his own act. He spent his time trying to get comfortable in his borrowed nest, befuddled by the hellish heat of the oil lamps and sacramental candles that had been placed along the wire. At first they tried to make him eat some mothballs, which, according to the wisdom of the wise neighbor woman, were the food prescribed for angels. But he turned them down, just as he turned down the papal lunches that the penitents brought him, and they never found out whether it was because he was an angel or because he was an old man that in the end ate nothing but eggplant mush. His only supernatural virtue seemed to be patience. Especially during the first days, when the hens pecked at him, searching for the stellar parasites that proliferated in his wings, and the cripples pulled out feathers to touch their defective parts with, and even the most merciful threw stones at him, trying to get him to rise so they could see him standing. The only time they succeeded in arousing him was when they burned his side with an iron for branding steers, for he had been motionless for so many hours that they thought he was dead.

He awoke with a start, ranting in his hermetic language and with tears in his eyes, and he flapped his wings a couple of times, which brought on a whirl-wind of chicken dung and lunar dust and a gale of panic that did not seem to be of this world. Although many thought that his reaction had been one not of rage but of pain, from then on they were careful not to annoy him, because the majority understood that his passivity was not that of a hero taking his ease but that of a cataclysm in repose.

Father Gonzaga held back the crowd's frivolity with formulas of maid-servant inspiration while awaiting the arrival of a final judgment on the nature of the captive. But the mail from Rome showed no sense of urgency. They spent their time finding out if the prisoner had a navel, if his dialect had any connection with Aramaic, how many times he could fit on the head of a pin, or whether he wasn't just a Norwegian with wings. Those meager letters might have come and gone until the end of time if a providential event had not put an end to the priest's tribulations.

10   It so happened that during those days, among so many other carnival at-tractions, there arrived in town the traveling show of the woman who had been changed into a spider for having disobeyed her parents. The admission to see her was not only less than the admission to see the angel, but people were permitted to ask her all manner of questions about her absurd state and to examine her up and down so that no one would ever doubt the truth of her horror. She was a frightful tarantula the size of a ram and with the head of a sad maiden. What was most heart-rending, however, was not her outlandish shape but the sincere affliction with which she recounted the details of her misfortune. While still practically a child she had sneaked out of her parents' house to go to a dance, and while she was coming back through the woods after having danced all night without permission, a fear-ful thunderclap rent the sky in two and through the crack came the light-ning bolt of brimstone that changed her into a spider. Her only nourishment came from the meatballs that charitable souls chose to toss into her mouth. A spectacle like that, full of so much human truth and with such a fearful les-son, was bound to defeat without even trying that of a haughty angel who scarcely deigned to look at mortals. Besides, the few miracles attributed to the angel showed a certain mental disorder, like the blind man who didn't recover his sight but grew three new teeth, or the paralytic who didn't get to walk but almost won the lottery, and the leper whose sores sprouted sun-flowers. Those consolation miracles, which were more like mocking fun, had already ruined the angel's reputation when the woman who had been changed into a spider finally crushed him completely. That was how Father Gonzaga was cured forever of his insomnia and Pelayo's courtyard went back to being as empty as during the time it had rained for three days and crabs walked through the bedrooms.

The owners of the house had no reason to lament. With the money they saved they built a two-story mansion with balconies and gardens and high netting so that crabs wouldn't get in during the winter, and with iron bars on the windows so that angels couldn't get in. Pelayo also set up a rabbit warren close to town and gave up his job as bailiff for good, and Elisenda bought some satin pumps with high heels and many dresses of iridescent silk, the kind worn on Sunday by the most desirable women in those times. The chicken coop was the only thing that didn't receive any attention. If they washed it down with creolin and burned tears of myrrh inside it every so often, it was not in homage to the angel but to drive away the dungheap stench that still hung everywhere like a ghost and was turning the new house into an old one. At first, when the child learned to walk, they were careful that he not get too close to the chicken coop. But then they began to lose their fears and got used to the smell, and before the child got his second teeth he'd gone inside the chicken coop to play, where the wires were falling apart. The angel was no less stand-offish with him than with other mortals, but he tolerated the most ingenious infamies with the patience of a dog who had no illusions. They both came down with chicken pox at the same time. The doctor who took care of the child couldn't resist the temptation to listen to the angel's heart, and he found so much whistling in the heart and so many sounds in his kidneys that it seemed impossible for him to be alive. What surprised him most, however, was the logic of his wings. They seemed so natural on that completely human organism that he couldn't understand why other men didn't have them too.

When the child began school it had been some time since the sun and rain had caused the collapse of the chicken coop. The angel went dragging himself about here and there like a stray dying man. They would drive him out of the bedroom with a broom and a moment later find him in the kitchen. He seemed to be in so many places at the same time that they grew to think that he'd been duplicated, that he was reproducing himself all through the house, and the exasperated and unhinged Elisenda shouted that it was awful living in that hell full of angels. He could scarcely eat and his antiquarian eyes had also become so foggy that he went about bumping into posts. All he had left were the bare cannulae of his last feathers. Pelayo threw a blanket over him and extended him the charity of letting him sleep in the shed, and only then did they notice that he had a temperature at night, and was delirious with the tongue twisters of an old Norwegian. That was one of the few times they became alarmed, for they thought he was going to die and not even the wise neighbor woman had been able to tell them what to do with dead angels.

And yet he not only survived his worst winter, but seemed improved with the first sunny days. He remained motionless for several days in the farthest corner of the courtyard, where no one would see him, and at the beginning of December some large, stiff feathers began to grow on his wings, the feathers of a scarecrow, which looked more like another misfortune of decrepitude. But he must have known the reason for those changes, for he was quite careful that no one should notice them, that no one should hear the sea chanteys that he sometimes sang under the stars. One morning Elisenda was cutting some bunches of onions for lunch when a wind that seemed to come from the high seas blew into the kitchen. Then she went to the window and caught the angel in his first attempts at flight. They were so clumsy that his fingernails opened a furrow in the vegetable patch and he was on the point of knocking the shed down with the ungainly flapping that slipped on the light and couldn't get a grip on the air. But he did manage to gain altitude. Elisenda let out a sigh of relief, for herself and for him, when she saw him pass over the last houses, holding himself up in some way with the risky flapping of a senile vulture. She kept watching him even when she was through cutting the onions and she kept on watching until it was no longer possible for her to see him, because then he was no longer an annoyance in her life but an imaginary dot on the horizon of the sea.

YOUR TURN

1. The subtitle is "A Tale for Children." Do you think that the story is more suited to children than to adults? What in the story do you think children would especially like, or dislike?
2. Is the story chiefly about the inability of adults to perceive and respect the miraculous world?
3. Characterize the narrator of the story.
4. Characterize Pelayo, Elisenda, their son, and the man with wings.
5. What does it mean to say that a story is "realistic"? Could a story deal with magical events and supernatural experiences and still, somehow, be realistic? Please explain.
6. Do you enjoy stories that include elements of fantasy and magic? Are there examples that come to mind? Or do you prefer stories that are based only on the possible? Again, please give examples and reasons.

11

Theme

Theme is an essential term for literary study and interpretation, but it can be confusing because we tend to use it in different, if related, senses. Sometimes "theme" may refer to the subject of a literary work, as when we note that a story treats the theme of good and evil, or has as its theme the relationship between parents and children. But sometimes "theme" may suggest the point of view—the attitude—that an author has taken toward his or her subject. It is not just that the author is dealing with the nature of good and evil, but that he or she *has something special to say about it*, a perspective on it that makes this story different from others on this same subject. Probably it is best *not* to use "theme" in this second sense but instead to use **thesis**, especially for works by authors who seem to be arguing, even preaching. An Aesop fable pretty clearly offers a thesis, but most contemporary short stories do not.

Consider the following anonymous short Japanese narrative. It is said to be literally true, but whether it really occurred or not is scarcely of any importance. It is the story, not the history, that counts.

ANONYMOUS

Muddy Road

Two monks, Tanzan and Ekido, were once traveling together down a muddy road. A heavy rain was still falling.

Coming around a bend, they met a lovely girl in a silk kimono and sash, unable to cross the intersection.

"Come on, girl," said Tanzan at once. Lifting her in his arms, he carried her over the mud.

Ekido did not speak again until that night when they reached a lodging temple. Then he no longer could restrain himself. "We monks don't go near females," he told Tanzan, "especially not young and lovely ones. It is dangerous. Why did you do that?"

5   "I left the girl there," said Tanzan. "Are you still carrying her?"

Do we want to say that this story *argues* that priests should not lust for women? Surely not. But we can say, reasonably, that the theme is about proper and improper responses to a potentially sexual situation. And we can admire the skill with which the story is told. After the introduction of the two characters and the setting, we quickly get the complication, the encounter with the girl. Still there is apparently no conflict, though in "Ekido did not speak again until that night" we sense an unspoken conflict, an action (or, in this case, an inaction) that must be explained, an imbalance that must be righted before we are finished. At last Ekido, no longer able to contain his thoughts, lets his indignation burst out: "We monks don't go near females . . . especially not young and lovely ones. It is dangerous. Why did you do that?" His statement and his question reveal not only his moral principles, but also his insecurity and the anger that grows from it. And now, when the conflict is out in the open, comes the brief reply that reveals Tanzan's very different character as clearly as the outburst revealed Ekido's. This reply—though we could not have predicted it—strikes us as exactly right, bringing the story to a perfect end, that is to a point at which there is no more to be said. It provides the dénouement (literally, the "unknotting"), or resolution. But, again, although we can say that the theme deals with lust, we hardly want to say that the author is arguing a thesis.

Most literary works do not offer arguments to us—not exactly at any rate. A short story is not a legal document or a case in court. But readers may sense that an author has an attitude toward his or her characters. Interviewing Tobias Wolff, a writer of novels and short stories (see page 359), Julie Orringer asked if Wolff sometimes was too "hard on the protagonists" of his stories. Wolff replied:

> It isn't so much matter of wishing to be hard on people as wishing to be truthful. If there is a moral quality to my work, I suppose it has to do with will and the exercise of choice within one's will. The choices we make tend to narrow down a myriad of opportunities to just a few, and those choices tend to reinforce themselves in whatever direction we've started to go, including the wrong direction. . . . Well, maybe it's not such a good idea to stay the course if you're headed toward the rocks. There's something to be said for changing course if you're about to drive your ship onto the shoals.

Putting aside the issue of whether writers judge their characters and thereby offer arguments, it is obviously true that good literary works often *provoke* arguments—debate and discussion about what the work means, what its theme is. In a general sense all of us might agree that the theme of Shakespeare's play *The Taming of the Shrew* is the relationship between men and women, "the battle of the sexes." But what in more precise terms is this play's theme? What is the insight into or the understanding of the relationship between men and women that Shakespeare gives us in *The Taming of the Shrew,* or that D. H. Lawrence or John Updike in a story, or John Donne or Andrew Marvell in a poem, present?

It might be best, then, to agree to use two separate terms, **subject** and **theme.** What is the subject of Ozick's story "The Shawl"? We could say that it is the unspeakable pain that the protagonist Rosa experiences when her child Magda is brutally killed in the concentration camp. What is its theme? We might propose that the theme is twofold: the extreme evil of the Holocaust and the bond—horrifically assaulted but not wholly annihilated—between mother and daughter. Ozick's writing from beginning to end gives to her treatment of the subject, and to her presentation of the theme, emotional power and depth.

Perhaps your key task as an interpreter and writer of analytical essays is for you to be as specific as you can when you describe your response to the poem, play, or novel before you. What is the theme of *this* literary work? Not another one or others, but *this* one? Fate and free will: many literary works have this theme in common, but what counts, and what makes reading and interpretation rewarding, is to perceive the distinctive way in which a given author develops this theme in a given story.

Several literary scholars have in effect said that the theme of a short story is "everything in it." What they are getting at is that in order for us to perceive the theme, we need to pay close attention to the plot, character, setting, point of view, style—all of the elements of the story as they function together. When you write an essay about the theme of a literary work, consider each of these elements and the role that it performs by itself and in relationship to the others.

Here are some additional points and questions to consider:

1. **The title:** Sometimes the title offers an insight into the story's theme.
2. **The first paragraph:** How does the story begin?
3. **The final paragraph:** How does the story end, and what is the connection between where we end and where we began in our experience of this story?
4. **Significant details:** We know that details matter: What are the most significant details in the story? Do you see a pattern or patterns among them?
5. **Conflict:** What is the major conflict presented in the story? Is there more than one?
6. **Choices:** In the beginning, middle, or conclusion of a story, the main character might make an important choice. He does something, or he says something, or else decides not to do or say something. Does this choice and its consequences help us to understand the story's theme?
7. **Change:** When the story concludes, what has changed, if anything, from the way it was at the outset? Has the main character, or other characters, changed?
8. **Responding to theme:** What have you learned from your reading and study of this story? Has it changed your thinking in any way?

Sometimes you will be asked in an assignment to do some outside reading, and in such cases you might find in an author's letters, memoirs, diary entries, interviews, and other sources a clue or two about the theme that he or she explores.

In his Preface to *The House of the Seven Gables* (1851), for example, Nathaniel Hawthorne says: "The author has provided himself with a moral—the truth, namely, that the wrongdoing of one generation lives into the successive ones." Thomas Hardy, author of *Tess of the d'Urbervilles* (1891) and *Jude the Obscure* (1895), jotted in his notebook (April 19, 1885): "The business of the poet and novelist is to show the sorriness underlying the grandest things, and the grandeur underlying the sorriest things." With these examples we can reasonably talk about the authors' *thesis* as well as about *theme* and *subject*. Flannery O'Connor, whose work we feature in this book, states in "Catholic Novelists and Their Readers" (1964): "The main concern of the fiction writer is with mystery as it is incarnated in real life."

Much of the time, though, what we are doing first is reading a story in its own terms, responding to it, thinking about it, deciding how much or little we have enjoyed and learned from it. There are points we look for, questions we ask. We then can make comparisons with other literary works in our experience inside and outside the classroom. This is how we build up and develop our literary experience and understanding.

In the pages that follow, you will find three stories: "Carpathia," "The Shawl," and "Who's Irish?" Read each one of them carefully, and ask yourself why each one is special, and also how each compares and contrasts with the other two.

JESSE LEE KERCHEVAL

Jesse Lee Kercheval was born in France but received her bachelor's degree from Florida State University and her master's degree (in creative writing) from the University of Iowa. The author of several books of poetry and of fiction, as well as a book about how to write fiction (Building Fiction [1997]), Kercheval has received numerous awards. She teaches at the University of Wisconsin–Madison. The story we include here was written in response to a challenge to write a short story consisting of no more than 300 words.

As this story indicates, Carpathia *was the ship that in 1912 picked up survivors from the* Titanic, *after the* Titanic *struck an iceberg and sank.*

Carpathia

It happened on my parents' honeymoon. The fourth morning out from New York, Mother woke to find the *Carpathia* still, engines silent. She woke Father; they rushed to the deck in their nightgowns. The first thing they saw was the white of an ocean filled with ice, then they saw white boats, in groups of two or three, pulling slowly toward the *Carpathia.* My father read the name written in red across their bows—*Titanic.* The sun was shining. Here and there a deck chair floated on the calm sea. There was nothing else.

The survivors came on board in small groups. Women and children. Two sailors for each boat. The women of the *Carpathia* went to the women of the *Titanic,* wrapping them in their long warm furs. My mother left my father's side to go to them. The women went down on their knees on the deck and prayed, holding each other's children. My father stood looking at the icy water where, if he had been on the other ship, he would be.

When the *Carpathia* dropped off the survivors in New York, my parents too got off and took the train home, not talking much, the honeymoon anything but a success. At the welcome-home party, my father got drunk. When someone asked about the *Titanic,* he said, "They should have put the men in the lifeboats. Men can marry-again, have new families. What's the use of all those widows and orphans?" My mother, who was standing next to him, turned her face away. She was pregnant, eighteen. She was the one drowning. But there was no one there to rescue her.

YOUR TURN

1. In the second paragraph, the second and third sentences have no verbs. Do you suppose verbs have been omitted simply because the author was limited to 300 words, or are these two sentences more effective than they would be if they were equipped with verbs? Explain.
2. The speaker's father offers an argument—that is, he advances a thesis. Is the story about the issue that he raises—in effect, that the traditional doctrine of "women and children first" is misguided—or is it about something else. If something else, what is it about?
3. What is the narrator's attitude toward her father? Toward her mother?
4. Please complete the following sentence: "The lesson that this story teaches is. . . ." What is your evidence for this?
5. A teacher of creative writing, commenting on this story, says, "its ending is exactly right." Do you agree? Please explain.

CYNTHIA OZICK

Cynthia Ozick, born in 1928 in New York of Russian Jewish parentage, graduated from New York University in 1949 with a bachelor's degree in English. In 1950 she earned a master's degree at Ohio State University, writing a thesis on "Parable in the Later Novels of Henry James." In an essay in Art and Ardor *(1983) she says that her early worship of James caused her to worship art and to try to "live unsoiled by what we mean when we say 'Life'—relationship, family mess, distraction, exhaustion, anxiety, above all disappointment." Later, she says, she learned that the true "Lesson of the Master" was "to seek to be young while young, primitive while primitive, ungainly when ungainly—to look for crudeness and rudeness, to husband one's own stupidity or ungenius."*

Ozick's many books include the novels The Messiah of Stockholm *(1987),* The Puttermesser Papers *(1997), and* Heir to the Glimmering World *(2004), and* Collected Stories *(2007).*

The Shawl

[1980]

Stella, cold, cold the coldness of hell. How they walked on the roads together, Rosa with Magda curled up between sore breasts, Magda wound up in the shawl. Sometimes Stella carried Magda. But she was jealous of Magda. A thin girl of fourteen, too small, with thin breasts of her own, Stella wanted to be wrapped in a shawl, hidden away, asleep, rocked by the march, a baby, a round infant in arms. Magda took Rosa's nipple, and Rosa never stopped walking, a walking cradle. There was not enough milk; sometimes Magda sucked air; then she screamed. Stella was ravenous. Her knees were tumors on sticks, her elbows chicken bones.

Rosa did not feel hunger; she felt light, not like someone walking but like someone in a faint, in trance, arrested in a fit, someone who is already a floating angel, alert and seeing everything, but in the air, not there, not touching the road. As if teetering on the tips of her fingernails. She looked into Magda's face through a gap in the shawl: a squirrel in a nest, safe, no one could reach her inside the little house of the shawl's windings. The face, very round, a pocket mirror of a face: but it was not Rosa's bleak complexion, dark like cholera, it was another kind of face altogether, eyes blue as air, smooth feathers of hair nearly as yellow as the Star sewn into Rosa's coat. You could think she was one of *their* babies.

Rosa, floating, dreamed of giving Magda away in one of the villages. She could leave the line for a minute and push Magda into the hands of any woman on the side of the road. But if she moved out of line they might shoot. And even if she fled the line for half a second and pushed the shawl-bundle at a stranger, would the woman take it? She might be surprised, or afraid; she might drop the shawl, and Magda would fall out and strike her head and die. The little round head. Such a good child, she gave up scream-ing, and sucked now only for the taste of the drying nipple itself. The neat grip of the tiny gums. One mite of a tooth tip sticking up in the bottom gum, how shining, an elfin tombstone of white marble gleaming there. Without complaining, Magda relinquished Rosa's teats, first the left, then the right; both were cracked, not a sniff of milk. The duct-crevice extinct, a dead vol-cano, blind eye, chill hole, so Magda took the corner of the shawl and milked it instead. She sucked and sucked, flooding the threads with wetness. The shawl's good flavor, milk of linen.

It was a magic shawl, it could nourish an infant for three days and three nights. Magda did not die, she stayed alive, although very quiet. A peculiar smell, of cinnamon and almonds, lifted out of her mouth. She held her eyes open every moment, forgetting how to blink or nap, and Rosa and some-times Stella studied their blueness. On the road they raised one burden of a leg after another and studied Magda's face. "Aryan,"[1] Stella said, in a voice grown as thin as a string; and Rosa thought how Stella gazed at Magda like a young cannibal. And the time that Stella said "Aryan," it sounded to Rosa as if Stella had really said "Let us devour her."

5   But Magda lived to walk. She lived that long, but she did not walk very well, partly because she was only fifteen months old, and partly because the spindles of her legs could not hold up her fat belly. It was fat with air, full and round. Rosa gave almost all her food to Magda, Stella gave nothing; Stella was ravenous, a growing child herself, but not growing much. Stella did not menstruate. Rosa did not menstruate. Rosa was ravenous, but also not; she learned from Magda how to drink the taste of a finger in one's mouth. They were in a place without pity, all pity was annihilated in Rosa, she looked at Stella's bones without pity. She was sure that Stella was waiting for Magda to die so she could put her teeth into the little thighs.

Rosa knew Magda was going to die very soon; she should have been dead already, but she had been buried away deep inside the magic shawl, mistaken there for the shivering mound of Rosa's breasts; Rosa clung to the shawl as if it covered only herself. No one took it away from her. Magda was mute. She never cried. Rosa hid her in the barracks, under the shawl, but she knew that one day someone would inform; or one day someone, not even Stella, would steal Magda to eat her. When Magda began to walk Rosa knew

---

[1]**Aryan** According to *The American Heritage Dictionary of the English Language,* "Aryan, a word nowadays referring to the blond-haired, blue-eyed physical ideal of Nazi Germany, originally referred to a people who looked vastly different. Its history starts with the ancient Indo-Iranians, peoples who inhabited parts of what are now Iran, Afghanistan, Pakistan and India."

that Magda was going to die very soon, something would happen. She was afraid to fall asleep; she slept with the weight of her thigh on Magda's body; she was afraid she would smother Magda under her thigh. The weight of Rosa was becoming less and less; Rosa and Stella were slowly turning into air.

Magda was quiet, but her eyes were horribly alive, like blue tigers. She watched. Sometimes she laughed—it seemed a laugh, but how could it be? Magda had never seen anyone laugh. Still, Magda laughed at her shawl when the wind blew its corners, the bad wind with pieces of black in it, that made Stella's and Rosa's eyes tear. Magda's eyes were always clear and tearless. She watched like a tiger. She guarded her shawl. No one could touch it; only Rosa could touch it. Stella was not allowed. The shawl was Magda's own baby, her pet, her little sister. She tangled herself up in it and sucked on one of the corners when she wanted to be very still.

Then Stella took the shawl away and made Magda die.

Afterward Stella said: "I was cold."

And afterward she was always cold, always. The cold went into her heart: Rosa saw that Stella's heart was cold. Magda flopped onward with her little pencil legs scribbling this way and that, in search of the shawl; the pencils faltered at the barracks opening, where the light began. Rosa saw and pursued. But already Magda was in the square outside the barracks, in the jolly light. It was the roll-call arena. Every morning Rosa had to conceal Magda under the shawl against a wall of the barracks and go out and stand in the arena with Stella and hundreds of others, sometimes for hours, and Magda, deserted, was quiet under the shawl, sucking on her corner. Every day Magda was silent, and so she did not die. Rosa saw that today Magda was going to die, and at the same time a fearful joy ran in Rosa's two palms, her fingers were on fire, she was astonished, febrile: Magda, in the sunlight, swaying on her pencil legs, was howling. Ever since the drying up of Rosa's nipples, ever since Magda's last scream on the road, Magda had been devoid of any syllable; Magda was a mute. Rosa believed that something had gone wrong with her vocal cords, with her windpipe, with the cave of her larynx; Magda was defective, without a voice; perhaps she was deaf; there might be something amiss with her intelligence; Magda was dumb. Even the laugh that came when the ash-stippled wind made a clown out of Magda's shawl was only the air-blown showing of her teeth. Even when the lice, head lice and body lice, crazed her so that she became as wild as one of the big rats that plundered the barracks at daybreak looking for carrion, she rubbed and scratched and kicked and bit and rolled without a whimper. But now Magda's mouth was spilling a long viscous rope of clamor.

"Maaaa—"

It was the first noise Magda had ever sent out from her throat since the drying up of Rosa's nipples.

"Maaaa . . . aaa!"

Again! Magda was wavering in the perilous sunlight of the arena, scribbling on such pitiful little bent shins. Rosa saw. She saw that Magda was grieving for the loss of her shawl, she saw that Magda was going to die. A tide of commands hammered in Rosa's nipples: Fetch, get, bring! But she did not know which to go after first, Magda or the shawl. If she jumped out into the arena to snatch Magda up, the howling would not stop, because Magda would still not have the shawl; but if she ran back into the barracks to find the shawl, and if she found it, and if she came after Magda holding it and shaking it, then she would get Magda back, Magda would put the shawl in her mouth and turn dumb again.

15   Rosa entered the dark. It was easy to discover the shawl. Stella was heaped under it, asleep in her thin bones. Rosa tore the shawl free and flew—she could fly, she was only air—into the arena. The sunheat murmured of another life, of butterflies in summer. The light was placid, mellow. On the other side of the steel fence, far away, there were green meadows speckled with dandelions and deep-colored violets; beyond them, even farther, innocent tiger lilies, tall, lifting their orange bonnets. In the barracks they spoke of "flowers," of "rain": excrement, thick turd-braids, and the slow stinking maroon waterfall that slunk down from the upper bunks, the stink mixed with a bitter fatty floating smoke that greased Rosa's skin. She stood for an instant at the margin of the arena. Sometimes the electricity inside the fence would seem to hum; even Stella said it was only an imagining, but Rosa heard real sounds in the wire: grainy sad voices. The farther she was from the fence, the more clearly the voices crowded at her. The lamenting voices strummed so convincingly, so passionately, it was impossible to suspect them of being phantoms. The voices told her to hold up the shawl, high; the voices told her to shake it, to whip with it, to unfurl it like a flag. Rosa lifted, shook, whipped, unfurled. Far off, very far, Magda leaned across her airfed belly, reaching out with the rods of her arms. She was high up, elevated, riding someone's shoulder. But the shoulder that carried Magda was not coming toward Rosa and the shawl, it was drifting away, the speck of Magda was moving more and more into the smoky distance. Above the shoulder a helmet glinted. The light tapped the helmet and sparkled it into a goblet. Below the helmet a black body like a domino and a pair of black boots hurled themselves in the direction of the electrified fence. The electric voices began to chatter wildly. "Maamaa, maaamaaa," they all hummed together. How far Magda was from Rosa now, across the whole square, past a dozen barracks, all the way on the other side! She was no bigger than a moth.

All at once Magda was swimming through the air. The whole of Magda traveled through loftiness. She looked like a butterfly touching a silver vine. And the moment Magda's feathered round head and her pencil legs and balloonish belly and zigzag arms splashed against the fence, the steel voices went mad in their growling, urging Rosa to run and run to the spot where Magda had fallen from her flight against the electrified fence; but of course Rosa did not obey them. She only stood, because if she ran they would shoot, and if she tried to pick up the sticks of Magda's body they would shoot, and if she let the wolf's screech ascending now through the ladder of her skeleton break out, they would shoot; so she took Magda's shawl and filled her own mouth with it, stuffed it in and stuffed it in, until she was swallowing up the wolf's screech and tasting the cinnamon and almond depth of Magda's saliva; and Rosa drank Magda's shawl until it dried.

YOUR TURN

1. The fourth paragraph begins, "It was a magic shawl." Why does the narrator say this? Now notice the last clause in the story: "Rosa drank Magda's shawl until it dried." Does this mean that the magic stopped working? Or that, for some reason, there was no longer a need for a magic shawl? Or what?

2. The story combines an apparently simple, matter-of-fact, realistic style with a highly figurative style. What is the effect of this combination?
3. There is very little dialogue in the story. What is the effect of the relative absence of dialogue?

GISH JEN

Gish Jen was born in 1955 in Yonkers, New York. The daughter of Chinese immigrants, she was named Lillian Jen by her parents. She disliked the name Lillian, and her school friends created a new name for her, derived from the name of a famous actress of the silent screen—Lillian Gish. Jen graduated from Harvard and then, in accordance with her parents' wishes, went to Stanford Business School (MBA, 1980). Jen's books include the novels Typical American *(1991) and* Mona in the Promised Land *(1996) and a collection of stories,* Who's Irish? *(1999).*

Who's Irish?

[1998]

In China, people say mixed children are supposed to be smart, and definitely my granddaughter Sophie is smart. But Sophie is wild, Sophie is not like my daughter Natalie, or like me. I am work hard my whole life, and fierce besides. My husband always used to say he is afraid of me, and in our restaurant, busboys and cooks all afraid of me too. Even the gang members come for protection money, they try to talk to my husband. When I am there, they stay away. If they come by mistake, they pretend they are come to eat. They hide behind the menu, they order a lot of food. They talk about their mothers. Oh, my mother have some arthritis, need to take herbal medicine, they say. Oh, my mother getting old, her hair all white now.

I say, Your mother's hair used to be white, but since she dye it, it become black again. Why don't you go home once in a while and take a look? I tell them, Confucius[1] say a filial son knows what color his mother's hair is.

My daughter is fierce too, she is vice president in the bank now. Her new house is big enough for everybody to have their own room, including me. But Sophie take after Natalie's husband's family, their name is Shea. Irish. I always thought Irish people are like Chinese people, work so hard on the railroad, but now I know why the Chinese beat the Irish. Of course, not all Irish are like the Shea family, of course not. My daughter tell me I should not say Irish this, Irish that.

How do you like it when people say the Chinese this, the Chinese that, she say.

5   You know, the British call the Irish heathen, just like they call the Chinese, she say.

You think the Opium War[2] was bad, how would you like to live right next door to the British, she say.

---

[1]**Confucius** Chinese religious leader and philosopher (551–479 BCE).   [2]**Opium War** conflicts, 1839–1842 and 1856–1860, between China and Great Britain involving the opium trade.

And that is that. My daughter have a funny habit when she win an argument, she take a sip of something and look away, so the other person is not embarrassed. So I am not embarrassed. I do not call anybody anything either. I just happen to mention about the Shea family, an interesting fact: four brothers in the family, and not one of them work. The mother, Bess, have a job before she got sick, she was executive secretary in a big company. She is handle everything for a big shot, you would be surprised how complicated her job is, not just type this, type that. Now she is a nice woman with a clean house. But her boys, every one of them is on welfare, or so-called severance pay, or so-called disability pay. Something. They say they cannot find work, this is not the economy of the fifties, but I say, Even the black people doing better these days, some of them live so fancy, you'd be surprised. Why the Shea family have so much trouble? They are white people, they speak English. When I come to this country, I have no money and do not speak English. But my husband and I own our restaurant before he die. Free and clear, no mortgage. Of course, I understand I am just lucky, come from a country where the food is popular all over the world. I understand it is not the Shea family's fault they come from a country where everything is boiled. Still, I say.

She's right, we should broaden our horizons, say one brother, Jim, at Thanksgiving. Forget about the car business. Think about egg rolls.

Pad thai, say another brother, Mike. I'm going to make my fortune in pad thai. It's going to be the new pizza.

10   I say, You people too picky about what you sell. Selling egg rolls not good enough for you, but at least my husband and I can say, We made it. What can you say? Tell me. What can you say?

Everybody chew their tough turkey.

I especially cannot understand my daughter's husband John, who has no job but cannot take care of Sophie either. Because he is a man, he say, and that's the end of the sentence.

Plain boiled food, plain boiled thinking. Even his name is plain boiled: John. Maybe because I grew up with black bean sauce and hoisin sauce and garlic sauce, I always feel something is missing when my son-in-law talk.

But, okay: so my son-in-law can be man, I am baby-sitter. Six hours a day, same as the old sitter, crazy Amy, who quit. This is not so easy, now that I am sixty-eight, Chinese age almost seventy. Still, I try. In China, daughter take care of mother. Here it is the other way around. Mother help daughter, mother ask, Anything else I can do? Otherwise daughter complain mother is not supportive. I tell daughter, We do not have this word in Chinese, *supportive*. But my daughter too busy to listen, she has to go to meeting, she has to write memo while her husband go to the gym to be a man. My daughter say otherwise he will be depressed. Seems like all his life he has this trouble, depression.

15   No one wants to hire someone who is depressed, she say. It is important for him to keep his spirits up.

Beautiful wife, beautiful daughter, beautiful house, oven can clean itself automatically. No money left over, because only one income, but lucky enough, got the baby-sitter for free. If John lived in China, he would be very happy. But he is not happy. Even at the gym things go wrong. One day, he pull a muscle. Another day, weight room too crowded. Always something.

Until finally, hooray, he has a job. Then he feel pressure.

I need to concentrate, he say. I need to focus.

He is going to work for insurance company. Salesman job. A paycheck, he say, and at least he will wear clothes instead of gym shorts. My daughter

buy him some special candy bars from the health-food store. They say
THINK! on them, and are supposed to help John think.

20   John is a good-looking boy, you have to say that, especially now that he
shave so you can see his face.

I am an old man in a young man's game, say John.

I will need a new suit, say John.

This time I am not going to shoot myself in the foot, say John.

Good, I say.

25   She means to be supportive, my daughter say. Don't start the send her
back to China thing, because we can't.

Sophie is three years old American age, but already I see her nice Chinese side swallowed up by her wild Shea side. She looks like mostly Chinese.
Beautiful black hair, beautiful black eyes. Nose perfect size, not so flat looks
like something fell down, not so large looks like some big deal got stuck in
wrong face. Everything just right, only her skin is a brown surprise to John's
family. So brown, they say. Even John say it. She never goes in the sun, still
she is that color, he say. Brown. They say, Nothing the matter with brown.
They are just surprised. So brown. Nattie is not that brown, they say. They
say, It seems like Sophie should be a color in between Nattie and John.
Seems funny, a girl named Sophie Shea be brown. But she is brown, maybe
her name should be Sophie Brown. She never go in the sun, still she is that
color, they say. Nothing the matter with brown. They are just surprised.

The Shea family talk is like this sometimes, going around and around
like a Christmas-tree train.

Maybe John is not her father, I say one day, to stop the train. And sure
enough, train wreck. None of the brothers ever say the word *brown* to me
again.

Instead, John's mother, Bess, say, I hope you are not offended.

30   She say, I did my best on those boys. But raising four boys with no father
is no picnic.

You have a beautiful family, I say.

I'm getting old, she say.

You deserve a rest, I say. Too many boys make you old.

I never had a daughter, she say. You have a daughter.

35   I have a daughter, I say. Chinese people don't think a daughter is so
great, but you're right. I have a daughter.

I was never against the marriage, you know, she say. I never thought
John was marrying down. I always thought Nattie was just as good as white.

I was never against the marriage either, I say. I just wonder if they look
at the whole problem.

Of course you pointed out the problem, you are a mother, she say. And
now we both have a granddaughter. A little brown granddaughter, she is so
precious to me.

I laugh. A little brown granddaughter, I say. To tell you the truth, I don't
know how she came out so brown.

40   We laugh some more. These days Bess need a walker to walk. She take
so many pills, she need two glasses of water to get them all down. Her favorite TV show is about bloopers, and she love her bird feeder. All day long,
she can watch that bird feeder, like a cat.

I can't wait for her to grow up, Bess say. I could use some female company.

Too many boys, I say.

Boys are fine, she say. But they do surround you after a while.

You should take a break, come live with us, I say. Lots of girls at our house.

45   Be careful what you offer, say Bess with a wink. Where I come from, people mean for you to move in when they say a thing like that.

Nothing the matter with Sophie's outside, that's the truth. It is inside that she is like not any Chinese girl I ever see. We go to the park, and this is what she does. She stand up in the stroller. She take off all her clothes and throw them in the fountain.

Sophie! I say. Stop!

But she just laugh like a crazy person. Before I take over as baby-sitter, Sophie has that crazy-person sitter, Amy the guitar player. My daughter thought this Amy very creative—another word we do not talk about in China. In China, we talk about whether we have difficulty or no difficulty. We talk about whether life is bitter or not bitter. In America, all day long, people talk about creative. Never mind that I cannot even look at this Amy, with her shirt so short that her belly button showing. This Amy think Sophie should love her body. So when Sophie take off her diaper, Amy laugh. When Sophie run around naked, Amy say she wouldn't want to wear a diaper either. When Sophie go *shu-shu* in her lap, Amy laugh and say there are no germs in pee. When Sophie take off her shoes, Amy say bare feet is best, even the pediatrician say so. That is why Sophie now walk around with no shoes like a beggar child. Also why Sophie love to take off her clothes.

Turn around! say the boys in the park. Let's see that ass!

50   Of course, Sophie does not understand. Sophie clap her hands, I am the only one to say, No! This is not a game.

It has nothing to do with John's family, my daughter say. Amy was too permissive, that's all.

But I think if Sophie was not wild inside, she would not take off her shoes and clothes to begin with.

You never take off your clothes when you were little, I say. All my Chinese friends had babies, I never saw one of them act wild like that.

Look, my daughter say. I have a big presentation tomorrow.

55   John and my daughter agree Sophie is a problem, but they don't know what to do.

You spank her, she'll stop, I say another day.

But they say, Oh no.

In America, parents not supposed to spank the child.

It gives them low self-esteem, my daughter say. And that leads to problems later, as I happen to know.

60   My daughter never have big presentation the next day when the subject of spanking come up.

I don't want you to touch Sophie, she say. No spanking, period.

Don't tell me what to do, I say.

I'm not telling you what to do, say my daughter. I'm telling you how I feel.

I am not your servant, I say. Don't you dare talk to me like that.

65   My daughter have another funny habit when she lose an argument. She spread out all her fingers and look at them, as if she like to make sure they are still there.

My daughter is fierce like me, but she and John think it is better to explain to Sophie that clothes are a good idea. This is not so hard in the cold weather. In the warm weather, it is very hard.

Use your words, my daughter say. That's what we tell Sophie. How about if you set a good example.

As if good example mean anything to Sophie. I am so fierce, the gang members who used to come to the restaurant all afraid of me, but Sophie is not afraid.

I say, Sophie, if you take off your clothes, no snack.

70   I say, Sophie, if you take off your clothes, no lunch.

I say, Sophie, if you take off your clothes, no park.

Pretty soon we are stay home all day, and by the end of six hours she still did not have one thing to eat. You never saw a child stubborn like that.

I'm hungry! she cry when my daughter come home.

What's the matter, doesn't your grandmother feed you? My daughter laugh.

75   No! Sophie say. She doesn't feed me anything!

My daughter laugh again. Here you go, she say.

She say to John, Sophie must be growing.

Growing like a weed, I say.

Still Sophie take off her clothes, until one day I spank her. Not too hard, but she cry and cry, and when I tell her if she doesn't put her clothes back on I'll spank her again, she put her clothes back on. Then I tell her she is good girl, and give her some food to eat. The next day we go to the park and, like a nice Chinese girl, she does not take off her clothes.

80   She stop taking off her clothes, I report. Finally!

How did you do it? my daughter ask.

After twenty-eight years experience with you, I guess I learn something, I say.

It must have been a phase, John say, and his voice is suddenly like an expert.

His voice is like an expert about everything these days, now that he carry a leather briefcase, and wear shiny shoes, and can go shopping for a new car. On the company, he say. The company will pay for it, but he will be able to drive it whenever he want.

85   A free car, he say. How do you like that.

It's good to see you in the saddle again, my daughter say. Some of your family patterns are scary.

At least I don't drink, he say. He say, And I'm not the only one with scary family patterns.

That's for sure, say my daughter.

Everyone is happy. Even I am happy, because there is more trouble with Sophie, but now I think I can help her Chinese side fight against her wild side. I teach her to eat food with fork or spoon or chopsticks, she cannot just grab into the middle of a bowl of noodles. I teach her not to play with garbage cans. Sometimes I spank her, but not too often, and not too hard.

90   Still, there are problems. Sophie like to climb everything. If there is a railing, she is never next to it. Always she is on top of it. Also, Sophie like to hit the mommies of her friends. She learn this from her playground best friend, Sinbad, who is four. Sinbad wear army clothes every day and like to ambush his mommy. He is the one who dug a big hole under the play structure, a foxhole he call it, all by himself. Very hardworking. Now he wait in the foxhole with a shovel full of wet sand. When his mommy come, he throw it right at her.

Oh, it's all right, his mommy say. You can't get rid of war games, it's part of their imaginative play. All the boys go through it.

Also, he like to kick his mommy, and one day he tell Sophie to kick his mommy too.

I wish this story is not true.

Kick her, kick her! Sinbad say.

95   Sophie kick her. A little kick, as if she just so happened was swinging her little leg and didn't realize that big mommy leg was in the way. Still I spank Sophie and make Sophie say sorry, and what does the mommy say?

Really, it's all right, she say. It didn't hurt.

After that, Sophie learn she can attack mommies in the playground, and some will say, Stop, but others will say, Oh, she didn't mean it, especially if they realize Sophie will be punished.

This is how, one day, bigger trouble come. The bigger trouble start when Sophie hide in the foxhole with that shovel full of sand. She wait, and when I come look for her, she throw it at me. All over my nice clean clothes.

Did you ever see a Chinese girl act this way?

100   Sophie! I say. Come out of there, say you're sorry.

But she does not come out. Instead, she laugh. Naaah, naah-na, naaa-naaa, she say.

I am not exaggerate: millions of children in China, not one act like this.

Sophie! I say. Now! Come out now!

But she know she is in big trouble. She know if she come out, what will happen next. So she does not come out. I am sixty-eight, Chinese age almost seventy, how can I crawl under there to catch her? Impossible. So I yell, yell, yell, and what happen? Nothing. A Chinese mother would help, but American mothers, they look at you, they shake their head, they go home. And, of course, a Chinese child would give up, but not Sophie.

105   I hate you! she yell. I hate you, Meanie!

Meanie is my new name these days.

Long time this goes on, long long time. The foxhole is deep, you cannot see too much, you don't know where is the bottom. You cannot hear too much either. If she does not yell, you cannot even know she is still there or not. After a while, getting cold out, getting dark out. No one left in the playground, only us.

Sophie, I say. How did you become stubborn like this? I am go home without you now.

I try to use a stick, chase her out of there, and once or twice I hit her, but still she does not come out. So finally I leave. I go outside the gate.

110   Bye-bye! I say. I'm go home now.

But still she does not come out and does not come out. Now it is dinnertime, the sky is black. I think I should maybe go get help, but how can I leave a little girl by herself in the playground? A bad man could come. A rat could come. I go back in to see what is happen to Sophie. What if she have a shovel and is making a tunnel to escape?

Sophie! I say.

No answer.

Sophie!

115   I don't know if she is alive. I don't know if she is fall asleep down there. If she is crying, I cannot hear her.

So I take the stick and poke.

Sophie! I say. I promise I no hit you. If you come out, I give you a lol-lipop.

No answer. By now I worried. What to do, what to do, what to do? I poke some more, even harder, so that I am poking and poking when my daughter and John suddenly appear.

What are you doing? What is going on? say my daughter.

120   Put down that stick! say my daughter.

You are crazy! say my daughter.

John wiggle under the structure, into the foxhole, to rescue Sophie.

She fell asleep, say John the expert. She's okay. That is one big hole.

Now Sophie is crying and crying.

125   Sophie, my daughter say, hugging her. Are you okay, peanut? Are you okay?

She's just scared, say John.

Are you okay? I say too. I don't know what happen, I say.

She's okay, say John. He is not like my daughter, full of questions. He is full of answers until we get home and can see by the lamplight.

Will you look at her? he yell then. What the hell happened?

130   Bruises all over her brown skin, and a swollen-up eye.

You are crazy! say my daughter. Look at what you did! You are crazy!

I try very hard, I say.

How could you use a stick? I told you to use your words!

She is hard to handle, I say.

135   She's three years old! You cannot use a stick! say my daughter.

She is not like any Chinese girl I ever saw, I say.

I brush some sand off my clothes. Sophie's clothes are dirty too, but at least she has her clothes on.

Has she done this before? ask my daughter. Has she hit you before?

She hits me all the time, Sophie say, eating ice cream.

140   Your family, say John.

Believe me, say my daughter.

A daughter I have, a beautiful daughter. I took care of her when she could not hold her head up. I took care of her before she could argue with me, when she was a little girl with two pigtails, one of them always crooked. I took care of her when we have to escape from China, I took care of her when suddenly we live in a country with cars everywhere, if you are not careful your little girl get run over. When my husband die, I promise him I will keep the family together, even though it was just two of us, hardly a family at all.

But now my daughter take me around to look at apartments. After all, I can cook, I can clean, there's no reason I cannot live by myself, all I need is a telephone. Of course, she is sorry. Sometimes she cry, I am the one to say everything will be okay. She say she have no choice, she doesn't want to end up divorced. I say divorce is terrible, I don't know who invented this terrible idea. Instead of live with a telephone, though, surprise, I come to live with Bess. Imagine that. Bess make an offer and, sure enough, where she come from, people mean for you to move in when they say things like that. A crazy idea, go to live with someone else's family, but she like to have some female company, not like my daughter, who does not believe in company. These days when my daughter visit, she does not bring Sophie. Bess say we should give Nattie time, we will see Sophie again soon. But seems like my daughter have more presentation than ever before, every time she come she have to leave.

I have a family to support, she say, and her voice is heavy, as if soaking wet. I have a young daughter and a depressed husband and no one to turn to.

145   When she say no one to turn to, she mean me.

These days my beautiful daughter is so tired she can just sit there in a chair and fall asleep. John lost his job again, already, but still they rather hire a baby-sitter than ask me to help, even they can't afford it. Of course, the new baby-sitter is much younger, can run around. I don't know if Sophie these days is wild or not wild. She call me Meanie, but she like to kiss me too, sometimes. I remember that every time I see a child on TV. Sophie like to grab my hair, a fistful in each hand, and then kiss me smack on the nose. I never see any other child kiss that way.

The satellite TV has so many channels, more channels than I can count, including a Chinese channel from the Mainland and a Chinese channel from Taiwan, but most of the time I watch bloopers with Bess. Also, I watch the bird feeder—so many, many kinds of birds come. The Shea sons hang around all the time, asking when will I go home, but Bess tell them, Get lost.

She's a permanent resident, say Bess. She isn't going anywhere.

Then she wink at me, and switch the channel with the remote control.

150   Of course, I shouldn't say Irish this, Irish that, especially now I am become honorary Irish myself, according to Bess. Me! Who's Irish? I say, and she laugh. All the same, if I could mention one thing about some of the Irish, not all of them of course, I like to mention this: Their talk just stick. I don't know how Bess Shea learn to use her words, but sometimes I hear what she say a long time later. *Permanent resident. Not going anywhere.* Over and over I hear it, the voice of Bess.

YOUR TURN

1. When you began this story, what was your response to the title? Did your response to it change by the time you reached the conclusion?
2. How is the title connected to the main theme of the story? What is the main theme? Please explain what it is, with reference to a key passage or passages in the text.
3. A critic has said that the voice that Gish Jen chose for her narrator is connected to the theme of the story as a whole. Do you agree? Please explain why or why not.
4. Another critic has said that this story focuses on "the war between generations." Do you agree? Does "war" strike you as the right term, or not?
5. In an interview, Gish Jen said that as a writer she finds she is keenly interested in the "different realities" of her characters. Does this apply to "Who's Irish"? Please point to evidence in the text to explain what these different realities are.
6. Did anything in this story surprise you?

12

Graphic Fiction

Letters and Pictures

Literature is, literally speaking, made out of letters ("literature," "literally," "literate," and "letters" all come from a Latin word, *littera,* "letter"). A person who can read letters is literate. Yet today we hear a good deal about "visual literacy," which means the ability to understand visual things. In short, in this usage, "literacy" is metaphoric. You cannot literally (again that word!) read a picture; you can look at it and either understand it or not understand it. For the next few minutes, in order to help prepare you to read a story that is partly told by means of pictures, we will be talking about achieving visual literacy—that is, achieving the ability to understand pictures, to "read" pictures, specifically pictures that are used as part of a way of telling stories.

The good news is that if you have spent any time at all looking at comic strips you already know a great deal about how to "read" pictures that tell stories.

- You know, for instance, that you should read the pictures and the words from left to right (if you were brought up in China or Japan, you would begin at the right and read the first column downward, then the next column, again reading downward, unless the book were a Western-style book).
- You also know that in the usual comic strip a box represents a particular scene; the next box may show the same characters, but at a later moment in time.
- You know that human actions can be conveyed by showing figures in certain postures (walking, eating, etc.) making certain gestures (pointing, making a fist).
- You know that emotions can be conveyed by facial expressions (think Smiley Face, where two dots and a curve say it all).
- You know that the setting can easily be established (a tree indicates the outdoors, the Capitol indicates Washington, D.C.).
- You know that if a heavy object is shown on the ground with the word "bang" in large thick letters next to it, a character has just dropped the object.

- You know that words that are enclosed in a circle over the character's head indicate words that the character is speaking.
- You know that a character is cursing or using dirty language when words are represented not by letters but by symbols such as @ and # and !
- You know that if the line that encloses words is scalloped, or looks something like a cloud, the words represent *thoughts* rather than utterances.

In short, you know the conventions that enable you to understand what the cartoonist/storyteller is doing, is saying, so that you can follow the story, the narrative conveyed by words and pictures. All of which says that you are already visually literate.

Nevertheless, because you may not have developed the habit of reading images closely, of taking in all the subtleties that they may offer, we will talk a bit about reading pictures.

The first thing we want to say is that although in some contexts a picture is worth a thousand words, pictures are not very good at telling *stories.* Think of any familiar story—let's say the story of Cain and Abel, or of Cinderella, or (to take an example in our text) the story of King Solomon and the two women who disputed about who was the mother of an infant. Solomon ordered a servant to bring the sword, and to divide the living child so that each woman could have half. A sword was brought, and (here we give the translated text in the Revised Standard Version of the Bible)

> then the woman whose son was alive said to the king, because her heart yearned for her son, "Oh, no my lord, give her [i.e., the other woman] the living child, and by no means slay it." But the other said, "It shall be neither mine nor yours: divide it." Then the king answered and said, "Give the living child to the first woman, and by no means slay it; she is its mother." (I Kings 3.26-27)

Striking images come to mind when reading this story—for instance, an image of two women quarreling over an infant, an image of a servant entering with a massive sword, and an image of the infant being handed over to one woman. But we think it would be impossible by images alone to tell the story, which essentially causes the reader to draw two conclusions:

- A loving mother will give up a child rather than let it die, and
- Solomon was a wise judge.

Tradition says that in the Middle Ages, when most people were illiterate, pictures such as those in stained glass windows were "the Bible of the people," and these windows did tell stories—but the stories could be understood only if the viewers were already familiar with verbal tellings. Similarly, such narratives as those told on Trajan's Column (built 113 CE), adorned with images of the Roman emperor's victories, or the Bayeux Tapestry (late eleventh century, showing the French invasion of England) show us lots of energetic figures, but to *understand* what is going on, we must already know the story.

Still, pictures can communicate meanings, and so let's now look at a picture that is accompanied by words.

Reading an Image: A Short Story Told in One Panel

TONY CARRILLO

Tony Carrillo was born and raised in Tempe, Arizona. He conceived F Minus *when he was a sophomore at Arizona State University. The strip is currently syndicated in more than a hundred newspapers.*

F Minus

Tony Carrillo: "F Minus" © United Feature Syndicate, Inc.

For the moment, let's pretend that the picture didn't exist, and we were given only some text:

> One day, in a quiet office building somewhere, a small calculator suddenly became self-aware.
> In eight seconds, it plotted the extinction of all mankind.
> Then the battery died.
> Two weeks later, it was thrown away.

We don't want to make extravagant claims, but we think this is pretty good as a mini-sci-fi story. We hear much about the possibility that some day there may be machines that "think," and we hear even more about technology getting out of control and possibly destroying its creators. In the words of Elias Canetti,[1] "The planet's survival has become so uncertain that any effort, any thought that presupposes an assured future amounts to a mad gamble." So the graphic story begins with something fantastic yet something that we hear about and that we can imagine may become real:

> One day, in a quiet office building somewhere, a small calculator suddenly became self-aware.
> In eight seconds, it plotted the extinction of all mankind.

There is an engaging combination of vagueness ("One day," "somewhere") and of the highly specific ("In eight seconds"); that is, things in a leisurely

---

[1]**Elias Canetti** Bulgarian novelist (1905–1994) who won the Nobel Prize in literature in 1981.

once-upon-a-time land suddenly get down to a matter of seconds. The vague fairy-tale world of "one day" has been transformed into real time, and the "small calculator" is now a big threat. Like all good fiction, each sentence of this tiny story stimulates the reader to wonder, "What happens next?"

What does happen after the calculator "plotted the extinction of all mankind"? "Then the battery died." Well, that makes sense. We hadn't anticipated this happening, but, again, the happening that is narrated to us is plausible, and we are relieved, satisfied. In a sense the story is over—the battery is dead, so what more can be said?—but we see additional words:

> Two weeks later, it was thrown away.

We think this ending is masterful. E. M. Forster's comment about a good plot, already quoted on page 110, comes to mind:

> Shock, followed by the feeling, "Oh, that's all right," is a sign that all is well with plot: characters, to be real, ought to run smoothly, but a plot ought to cause surprise.

It is as if we heard a joke, laughed, and therefore thought we heard the end of the matter and then the narrator went on to top the joke, giving us an unexpected joke that builds on the first joke, a line that, after we have heard it, seems inevitable. The calculator, once an enormous menace, fails to be of even the slightest significance because—as is entirely natural, if we can speak of naturalness in connection with a mechanical device—the battery dies. The story seems to be over, there is nothing more to say. But there *is* more to say. The battery-dead calculator for two weeks is not even noticed, and then, when presumably it somehow comes to some unspecified person's attention, it is unceremoniously discarded, "thrown away." The way of all flesh.

What is convincing is not simply that A is followed by B and B is followed by C, but that there is a *logic* to the sequence, even (may we say?) a *truth* to the sequence. Notice, too, that the artist-writer does not moralize; rather, it is the reader-viewer who draws conclusions.

The theme is a great one, the humbling of the ambitious. Shakespeare, of course, often treated it—for instance, in *Richard II,* where the king meditates on his "state" (i.e., high status, exalted rank) and sees death as an "antic" (buffoon, jester) mocking even a king:

> Within the hollow crown
> That rounds the mortal temples of a king
> Keeps Death his court and there the antic sits,
> Scoffing his state and grinning at his pomp,
> Allowing him a breath, a little scene,
> To monarchize, be feared and kill with looks,
> Infusing him with self and vain conceit,
> As if this flesh which walls about our life,
> Were brass impregnable, and humored thus
> Comes at the last and with a little pin
> Bores through his castle wall, and farewell king!
>   (3.2.160-70)

Or consider some lines by Shakespeare's later contemporary, James Shirley:

The glories of our blood and state
Are shadows, not substantial things;
There is no armor against fate;
Death lays his icy hand on kings:
Scepter and crown
Must tumble down,
And in the dust be equal made
With the poor crooked scythe and spade.

We are not claiming that the story about the calculator is in the same league, but we do find it memorable. We have indicated that we think the *text* of this graphic story makes a pretty good short-short story, even without the picture. Now let's examine the accompanying picture.

First of all, we think it is clever, sort of cute. The cartoonist might simply have drawn a calculator, but he cleverly—is it too much to say brilliantly?—put two eyes into the liquid crystal display, and thus animated the whole thing. The calculator *does* seem to be a person, doesn't it? So, in our view, the story becomes enriched by the image. We can call this sort of thing "graphic fiction," but, to go back to our earlier point, the truth is that the picture doesn't tell the story. It merely enriches a story that is told in words.

But our last sentence is, we admit, unfair. The image doesn't "merely" enrich the words. The picture is literally (that word again!) central to the story. If the story consisted only of text, or if all of the text were written above or below the story, the story would not be as effective. We admit it: The image is integral.

And that's our point: The best graphic fiction does not merely illustrate the verbal story; rather, the images are inseparable from the words. The story is text-and-image, not just text-adorned-with-image.

A Second Example of Reading Images: A Story Told in Sequential Panels

Let's look now at a somewhat more complex work of graphic fiction, this one consisting of eight panels. The artist-author is Art Spiegelman. See below for a brief biography, and see page 246 for Spiegelman's work, "Nature vs. Nurture."

ART SPIEGELMAN

Born in Sweden in 1948, Art Spiegelman was raised in New York City. His two-part graphic story (part novel, part memoir), Maus *(1986,1991), based on his Polish-Jewish parents' experiences during the Holocaust, was awarded a Pulitzer Prize in 1992. A highly inventive fellow, Spiegelman not only cofounded several outlets for comic books but he also created Garbage Candy (edible candy in the shape of garbage, packaged in miniature garbage cans). In 2005* Time *magazine included Spiegelman in its list of the top 100 most influential people.*

If you were explaining the page to critters from outer space you might point out the following conventions, going panel by panel:

- Spiegelman sets the scene, in the extreme upper left, i.e. at the very beginning of the first panel, with some text in a small box. This text-box, providing the reader-viewer with background rather than with dialogue, is appropriately distinct in shape from the speech balloons.
- The little girl in the first panel is obviously happy. Her happiness is conveyed not only by the text's expressions of motherly love but also by the expression on her face. The father is also smiling.
- In the second panel the well-intentioned, politically correct father takes the doll from the girl. The girl is puzzled (the balloon says "uk" and the smile is gone from her face).
- In the third panel, the father is full of enthusiasm—his mouth is open, with a big smile—and the text conveys his enthusiasm. Additional text, "Skreeee," in different lettering (to indicate it is not human speech) comes out of the fire truck. The father has presumably pushed a button or flicked a switch so that the truck emits a sound. The girl's face and posture show puzzlement.
- The enthusiastic father (still with a big smile) seeks to show the girl how to play. His talk is (how shall we put it?) male talk, loud and aggressive ("Clang! Clang! Clang! Everybody get outa the way!").
- In the fifth panel the father, still teaching his daughter but evidently having a great time, is verging on the maniacal with his toothy grin and his "Vroom! Vroom." A viewer-reader probably thinks, "Hmmm, boys will be boys"—and may also think, seeing this father's childish enthusiasm, "You can't take the boy out of the man."
- The next panel shows the smiling—and complacent—father handing the truck to the girl, whose face conveys uncertainty.
- The bottom row begins with more uncertainty, indicated by a big question mark over the girl's head. She says nothing—there is no speech balloon—but we know that she is puzzled.
- The final panel show that the girl has covered half of the fire truck with a blanket—instead of thrusting it crazily around and making loud noises—and the father is reduced to silence. His posture—hands thrust into pockets, head slightly turned down—shows that he has given up, his attempt (the "nurture" of the title) to stifle the expression of motherly feelings (the "nature" of the title) and a balloon indicates that he is heaving a sigh of resignation. The sigh is conveyed by enclosing the word "sigh" within elongated dots, indicating he is sighing rather than *saying* "sigh."

If we were to think about the story in terms of the elements of fiction, what might we say? Well, so far as **character** (personality) goes, each of the two figures is relatively simple: The girl is just a girl—at her young age we hardly expect her to be a richly complex figure—and the father is essentially a well-meaning dad who wants his daughter to grow up free from gender stereotypes. Surely that is an admirable ambition. The **plot**—the sequence of happenings—shows his attempt to free her by offering her an alternative, a fire truck instead of a doll. He apparently is rather pleased with his efforts (the seventh panel shows him smiling when his little daughter touches the truck)—but with the final panel, reality breaks in. The girl does not career around the room shouting "Vroom," as the father did; rather, her maternal instinct manifests itself even toward the fire truck.

But this is not quite the end of the story: At the extreme right side we see the father heaving a sigh, shoulders slumped and hands in pocket: He has been forced to accept reality. Not always a bad thing, really, when you think about it. If we are asked what the **theme** of the story is—i.e., "What does the story *add up* to?" (which is very different from the plot, which is "What *happens* in the story?")—we can say that the theme concerns (as the title of the story indicates) the conflict between Nature and Nurture, or, to put it a bit differently, biology versus socialization. We most emphatically do not wish to say anything like "Spiegelman shows that human nature is unchangeable." For one thing, Spiegelman doesn't "show" us (in the sense of prove or demonstrate) anything. He just drew some pictures and wrote some words; he didn't offer anything that can be called evidence. Even if the pictures represent something that actually happened in his own family, his graphic report of his experience would not prove that other fathers will have the same experience with their daughters. Spiegelman is entertaining us, not arguing, not even preaching. Still, one feels that Spiegelman's story—the happenings that he illustrates, the doings of two figures—are plausible. One thing follows from another:

- The father sees his daughter playing with dolls, and
- being a good father, he wishes to free his daughter from stereotypical limited behavior, so
- he gives his daughter a toy that is usually associated with boys, but
- nature will have its way, and the girl turns the fire truck into an object that allows her to express her maternal instinct.
- Heaving a sigh, the father appears to recognize that his efforts have failed.

You have now instructed your Martian visitor in the language of graphic fiction. Yes, you knew it all along, and maybe the Martian did also.

WILL EISNER

Born in Brooklyn, New York, Will Eisner (1917–2005) drew cartoons for his high school newspaper, and after graduation studied for a year at the Art Students League of New York. He was soon publishing cartoons and comic strips, and he became an important figure in establishing the graphic novel ("sequential art") as a form of fiction. He taught at the School of Visual Arts in New York, and he published two highly informative books derived from his lectures, Comics and Sequential Art *(1985) and* Graphic Storytelling and Visual Narrative *(1996). In* Comics and Sequential Art *Eisner includes a chapter titled "Expressive Anatomy." Among the illustrations in this chapter is "Hamlet on a Rooftop," first published in June 1981. Eisner prefaces the* Hamlet *drawings with the following remark, and then offers a running commentary on the pictures.*

Hamlet on a Rooftop

The Body and the Face

The employment of body posture and facial expression (both having equal attention) is a major undertaking and an area of frequent failure. Properly and skillfully done, it can carry the narrative without resorting to unnecessary props or scenery. The use of expressive anatomy in the absence of words is less demanding because the latitude for the art is wider. Where the words have a depth of meaning and nuance, the task is more difficult.

This represents an example of a classic situation — that of author vs. artist. The artist must decide at the outset what his 'input' shall be; to slavishly make visual that which is in the author's mind or to embark on the raft of the author's words onto a visual sea of his own charting.

HAMLET ON A ROOFTOP

HIS FATHER IS DEAD, MYSTERIOUSLY! HIS MOTHER, WITHIN BUT A MONTH, MARRIES HIS UNCLE! SO SOON?, SO SOON? CAN THERE BE ANYTHING OTHER THAN **SOMETHING ROTTEN** HERE? CAN IT BE ANYTHING BUT MURDER!? WELL, THEN, IF MURDER IT BE ALL HE VALUES, INDEED, HIS MANHOOD CRIES OUT FOR RETRIBUTION ....VENGEANCE .. TO HONOR THE FILIAL DUTY HIS FATHER'S VOICE DEMANDS IN THE HOT CAULDRON OF HIS MIND! AYE, TO PUNISH THEM, TO **MURDER HIS MOTHER AND UNCLE**... AS THEY LAY IN VIOLATION OF HIS CODE!!! ...OR PERHAPS SOMETHING MORE UNSPEAKABLE WITHIN HIM.

YET... CAN HE FIND IN HIMSELF THE CAPACITY TO COMMIT SO UNNATURAL AN ACT AND IN DOING IT FORFEIT THE LOVE OF OPHELIA, HIS BETROTHED? WAIT... HOLD STILL FOR A MOMENT, CLING BRIEFLY TO A PASSING RAFT OF REASON BEFORE IT LEAVES THE BRAIN, BEFORE SURRENDERING TO THE SWIFT RIVER OF HIS PASSION, AND SO TO BE CARRIED OUT INTO THE TURGID SEA OF VIOLENCE FROM WHICH THERE IS NO RETURN.

In this experiment, Shakespeare's words are intact. The soliloquy is broken up into balloons at the artist's discretion. The intent here is to permit a meaningful fusing of word, imagery and timing. The result should provide the reader with necessary pauses.

The artist here functions as actor and in the process gives his own meaning to the lines.

A gesture signifying contemplation.

Furniture employed in intimate involvement with the actor gives the 'background' story value because it is part of the action.

Submission . . . to a ''heavy'' thought.

Here, the postures are more than a classical portrayal of emotions. This man is not the Danish Prince Hamlet! His gestures and postures are derivative of his special background. The question of how he would deliver the standard gesture for self-doubt and internal agony is the artist's real challenge!

WHETHER 'TIS NOBLER IN THE MIND TO SUFFER THE SLINGS AND ARROWS OF OUTRAGEOUS FORTUNE...

OR...

TO TAKE ARMS AGAINST A SEA OF TROUBLES, AND BY OPPOSING *END* THEM!

Bravado . . . he envisions himself as challenging the forces of troubles.

Exhaustion — beaten by the enormity of his problems

Seeking comfort he lets his body slide down along the wall

Retreat . . . into his refuge . . . sleep

The language of posture is universal and inter-changeable — the application is not.

Withdraw-ing into sleep or oblivion, he assumes an almost fetal posture.

Wishing with all his might.

Terror . . . in the realization of his options

Awake
again to the
thoughts
that will not
leave him!

Candor . . .
addressing
the unseen
manipulator
of his fate

Anger . . . now he builds his resolution

Arguing
. . . he
begins to
make a
case to but-
tress grow-
ing resolve.

Debating . . . the postures of a courtroom advocate

The use of a long-shot, here is meant to reinforce realism — and in that way try to deal with the problem of putting Shakespeare's language in the mouth of such a man.

Hesitation . . . a recurrence of doubt

This wedding of Shakespearean language with a modern denizen of the ghetto may not be appropriate but the exercise serves to demonstrate the potential of the medium because the emotional content is so universal.

Thus far we have looked at three graphic works: A one-panel original story with a picture (Carrillo's piece, page 243, about the malevolent calculator that died and two weeks later was discarded), an eight-panel original story (Spiegelman's "Nature vs. Nurture, page 246"), and twenty-six panels, spread over ten pages (pages 249–58, devoted to a soliloquy from *Hamlet*). Now let's examine a contemporary graphic treatment of an early twentieth-century short story, Franz Kafka's "A Hunger Artist." In one obvious way the job of the illustrator of a classic text is easier than the job of the creator of an entirely original work, but in another way it is also more difficult, because the artist who illustrates a classic is in some sense putting himself or herself up against a classic writer: Reader/viewers will inevitably expect the artist to contribute something to the work, to do more than ride piggy-back on the original author.

R. CRUMB AND DAVID ZANE MAIROWITZ

Robert Dennis Crumb, born in Philadelphia in 1943, worked for a while in Cleveland as a designer of greeting cards, and then began drawing for underground newspapers. In 1967 he moved to San Francisco, but he now lives in France. Some of his work is strongly sexual and highly satiric, but he has also drawn R. Crumb's Kafka *(1993), with a text by David Zane Mairowitz, illustrating several works of fiction by the writer Franz Kafka (1883–1924).*

David Zane Mairowitz, born in New York City in 1943, emigrated in 1968 to England, where he works as a freelance writer.

We include here the Crumb and Mairowitz version of Kafka's "A Hunger Artist," a short story found on page 438.

In June 1924, his "phantoms" saw to it — with their usual irony — that while dying of *starvation*, he would be correcting the galley-proofs of an astonishing masterwork called…

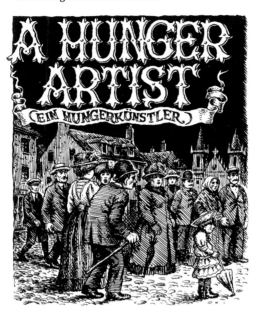

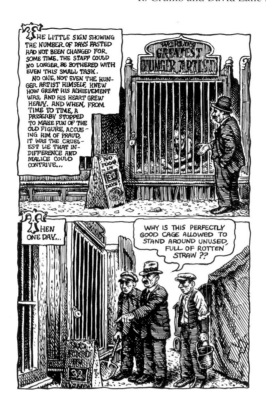

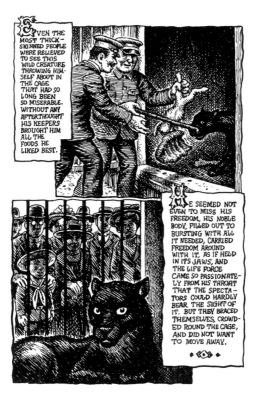

13

Students Writing About Stories in Print and on the Screen

Prompts for Writing About Fiction

The questions that follow below will help to stimulate ideas about stories. Not every question will be relevant to every story, but if after reading a story and thinking about it, you then run your eye over these pages, you will find some questions that will help you to think further about the story—in short, that will help you to get ideas, to develop a thesis that can effectively be supported with evidence.

It's best to do your thinking with a pen or pencil in hand. If some of the following questions seem to you to be especially relevant to the story you will be writing about, jot down—freely, without worrying about spelling—your initial responses, interrupting your writing only to glance again at the story when you feel the need to check the evidence you are offering in support of your thesis.

Plot

1. Does the plot grow out of the characters, or does it depend on chance or coincidence? Did something at first strike you as irrelevant that later you perceived as relevant? Do some parts continue to strike you as irrelevant?
2. Does surprise play an important role, or does foreshadowing? If surprise is very important, can the story be read a second time with any interest? If so, what gives it this further interest?
3. What conflicts does the story include? Conflicts of one character against another? Of one character against the setting, or against society? Conflicts within a single character?
4. Are certain episodes narrated out of chronological order? If so, were you puzzled? Annoyed? On reflection, does the arrangement of episodes seem effective? Why or why not? Are certain situations repeated? If so, what do you make out of the repetitions?

Character

1. Which character chiefly engages your interest? Why?
2. What purposes do minor characters serve? Do you find some who by their similarities and differences help to define each other or help to define the

major character? How else is a particular character defined—by his or her words, actions (including thoughts and emotions), dress, setting, narrative point of view? Do certain characters act differently in the same, or in a similar, situation?

3. How does the author reveal character? By explicit authorial (editorial) comment, for instance, or, on the other hand, by revelation through dialogue? Through depicted action? Through the actions of other characters? How are the author's methods especially suited to the whole of the story?

4. Is the behavior plausible—that is, are the characters well motivated?

5. If a character changes, why and how does he or she change? (You may want to jot down each event that influences a change.) Or did you change your attitude toward a character not because the character changes but because you came to know the character better?

6. Are the characters round or flat? Are they complex or, on the other hand, highly typical (for instance, one-dimensional representatives of a social class or age)? Are you chiefly interested in a character's psychology, or does the character strike you as standing for something, such as honesty or the arrogance of power?

7. How has the author caused you to sympathize with certain characters? How does your response—your sympathy or lack of sympathy—contribute to your judgment of the conflict?

Point of View

1. Who tells the story? How much does the narrator know? Does the narrator strike you as reliable? What effect is gained by using this narrator?

2. How does the point of view help shape the theme? After all, the basic story of "Little Red Riding Hood"—what happens—remains unchanged whether told from the wolf's point of view or the girl's, but if we hear the story from the wolf's point of view we may feel that the story is about terrifying yet pathetic compulsive behavior; if from the girl's point of view, about terrified innocence and male violence.

3. Does the narrator's language help you to construct a picture of the narrator's character, class, attitude, strengths, and limitations? (Jot down some evidence, such as colloquial or—on the other hand—formal expressions, ironic comments, figures of speech.) How far can you trust the narrator? Why?

Setting

1. Do you have a strong sense of the time and place? Is the story very much about, say, New England Puritanism, or race relations in the South in the late nineteenth century, or midwestern urban versus small-town life? If time and place are important, how and at what points in the story has the author conveyed this sense? If you do not strongly feel the setting, do you think the author should have made it more evident?

2. What is the relation of the setting to the plot and the characters? (For instance, do houses or rooms or their furnishings say something about their

residents?) Would anything be lost if the descriptions of the setting were deleted from the story or if the setting were changed?

Symbolism

1. Do certain characters seem to you to stand for something in addition to themselves? Does the setting—whether a house, a farm, a landscape, a town, a period—have an extra dimension?
2. If you do believe that the story has symbolic elements, do you think they are adequately integrated within the story, or do they strike you as being too obviously stuck in?

Style

Style may be defined as *how* the writer says what he or she says. It is the writer's manner of expression. The writer's choice of words, of sentence structure, and of sentence length are all aspects of style. Example: "Shut the door" and "Would you mind closing the door, please" differ substantially in style. Another example: Lincoln begins the Gettysburg Address by speaking of "Four score and seven years ago"—that is, by using language that has a biblical overtone. If he had said "Eighty-seven years ago," his style would have been different.

1. How would you characterize the style? Simple? Understated? Figurative?
2. How has the point of view shaped or determined the style?
3. Do you think that the style is consistent? If it isn't—for instance, if there are shifts from simple sentences to highly complex ones—what do you make of the shifts?

Theme

1. Is the title informative? What does it mean or suggest? Does the meaning change after you have read the story? Does the title help you to formulate a theme? If you had written the story, what title would you use?
2. Do certain passages—dialogue or description—seem to you to point especially toward the theme? Do you find certain repetitions of words or pairs of incidents highly suggestive and helpful in directing your thoughts toward stating a theme? Flannery O'Connor, in *Mystery and Manners* (1969), says, "In good fiction, certain of the details will tend to accumulate meaning from the action of the story itself, and when that happens, they become symbolic in the way they work." Does this story work that way?
3. Is the meaning of the story embodied in the whole story, or does it seem stuck in, for example in certain passages of editorializing?
4. Suppose someone asked you to state the point—the theme—of the story. Could you? And if you could, would you say that the theme of a particular story reinforces values you hold, or does it to some degree challenge them? (It is sometimes said that the best writers are subversive, forcing readers to see something that they do not want to see.)

Fiction into Film

Because many stories have been filmed, here we offer some comments about the nature of film, some definitions of indispensable technical terms, a few suggestions about topics, and a list of questions to consider as you begin to think about writing on a film derived from a story.

Film as a Medium

Your first thought may be that a film (excluding cartoons, documentaries, newsreels, and so on) is rather like a play: A story is presented by means of actors. There are, however, crucial distinctions between film and drama. First, though drama uses such visual matters as gestures, tableaux effects, and scenery, the plays that we value most highly are *literature:* The word dominates, the visual component is subordinate. You need not be a film fanatic who believes that the invention of the sound track was an impediment to film in order to realize that a film is more a matter of pictures than of words. The camera usually roves, giving us crowded streets, empty skies, rainy nights, or close-ups of filled ashtrays and chipped coffee cups. A critic has aptly said that in Ingmar Bergman's *Smiles of a Summer Night* (1955) "the almost unbearably ornate crystal goblets, by their aspect and their positioning in the image, convey the oppressive luxuriousness of the diners' lives in purely and uniquely filmic terms."

In short, the speaker in a film does not usually dominate. In a play the speaker normally holds the spectator's attention, but in a film when a character speaks, the camera often gives us a **reaction shot,** focusing not on the speaker but on the face or gestures of a character who is affected by the speech, thus giving the spectator a visual interpretation of the words. In François Truffaut's *400 Blows* (1959), for example, we hear a reform school official verbally assault a boy, but we see the uncomfortable boy, not the official. Even when the camera does focus on the speaker, it is likely to offer an interpretation. An extreme example is a scene from David Lean's *Brief Encounter* (1945): A gossip is talking, and the camera gives us a close-up of her jabbering mouth, which monstrously fills the screen.

The difference between film and drama can be put another way: A film is more like a short story or a novel than it is like a play, the action being presented not directly by actors but by a narrator, in this case the camera. The camera, like a narrator telling a story from a particular point of view, *comments* on the story while telling it. Thus, a filmmaker may use out-of-focus shots or slow-motion shots to communicate the strangeness of an experience. At the end of Arthur Penn's *Bonnie and Clyde* (1968), when Clyde is riddled with bullets, because his collapse is shot in slow motion he seems endowed not only with unusual grace but also with almost superhuman powers of endurance.

Even the choice of film stock is part of the comment. A highly sensitive or "fast" film needs less light to catch an image than a "slow" film does, but it is usually grainier. Perhaps because black-and-white newsreels often used fast film, a grainy quality may suggest authenticity or realism. Robert Enrico's 1962 film of Ambrose Bierce's short story "An Occurrence at Owl Creek Bridge," a story about the hanging of a civilian farmer who is a Southern sympathizer during the Civil

War, begins with low-contrast stock that gives a rich gradation of tones from white to black, reminiscent of Civil War photographs. The director John Huston similarly chose to use black and white for his film version (1951) of Stephen Crane's *The Red Badge of Courage,* a novel about cowardice and courage in the Civil War. Different film stocks may be used within a single motion picture. In Bergman's *Wild Strawberries* (1957), for instance, Bergman uses high-contrast stock for the nightmare sequence, though elsewhere in the film the contrasts are subtle. Color film has its own methods of tone and texture control.

The medium, as everyone knows, is part of the message; Laurence Olivier made Shakespeare's *Henry V* (1944) in color but *Hamlet* (1948) in black and white because these media say different things. Similarly, although by 1971 most fiction films were being made in color, Peter Bogdanovich made *The Last Picture Show* (1971) in black and white, partly to convey a sense of the unexciting life of a small town in America in the 1950s and partly to evoke the films of the fifties.

When a film is made in color, however, the colors may be symbolic (or at least suggestive) as well as realistic. In Stanley Kubrick's *A Clockwork Orange* (1971), for example, which is based on a novel of the same title by Anthony Burgess (1962), hot colors (oranges and reds) conveying vitality and aggressiveness in the first half of the film are displaced in the second half by cool colors (blues and greens) when the emphasis turns to "clockwork"—to mechanization.

The kind of lens used also helps determine what the viewer sees. In Mike Nichols's *The Graduate* (1967), Benjamin runs toward the camera (he is trying to reach a church before his girl marries another man), but he seems to make no progress because a **telephoto lens** was used and thus his size does not increase as it normally would. The lens, that is, helps communicate Benjamin's desperate sense of frustration. Similarly, in *An Occurrence at Owl Creek Bridge*, Peyton Farquhar runs toward his wife in the foreground, but the telephoto lens makes it seem that he is making no progress. Conversely, a **wide-angle lens** makes a character approach the camera with menacing rapidity; she or he quickly looms into the foreground.

But of course filmmakers, though resembling fiction writers in offering a pervasive indirect comment, are not fiction writers any more than they are playwrights or directors of plays. The medium has its own techniques, and a filmmaker works with these techniques, not with those of a playwright or of a short-story writer.

Perhaps the most obvious way that a film may comment (as a story-writer may) on the events and characters is through the use of **voice-over:** The voice of the narrator or of an off-camera person speaks, while the visuals and other sounds (music, birds twittering, whatever) continue. Discussing the film version (1993) of a novel by Edith Wharton, *The Age of Innocence* (1920), Martin Scorsese said that he found the narrator's voice enjoyable for its satiric observations about New York society and important for an understanding of the characters, and thus he chose to present some phases of the film with a voice-over that sets the background for and interprets the action. Some reviewers criticized this decision, saying that the voice-over was imposed and artificial, as though Scorsese did not think he could trust the characters on screen to communicate their thoughts and feelings. The implication of their criticism was that Scorsese had not found visual equivalents for a fiction-writer's verbal techniques.

For the film version (1987) of James Joyce's story "The Dead" (1914), John Huston made a related, though somewhat different and perhaps more successful, choice. At the close of the story, Gabriel Conroy discovers that his wife, Gretta, has for many years harbored a deep affection for a young man who died a tragic early death. The narrator concludes by describing Gabriel's mournful feelings as he reflects on his wife, his family and friends, the past, and the approach of death (e.g., "The time had come for him to set out on his journey westward."). Huston adapted the narrator's words and gave them to Gabriel, who speaks them in a voice-over as the camera moves from one shot to the next, from inside to outside the hotel room where he and Gretta are staying. Perhaps in this way Huston avoids the distancing effect that reviewers complained about in Scorsese's film; in the case of *The Dead,* the voice speaking is that of a central character.

Film Techniques

At this point it may be well to suspend generalizations temporarily and to look more methodically at some techniques of filmmaking. What follows is a brief grammar and dictionary of film, naming and explaining the cinematic devices that help filmmakers embody their vision in a work of art. An essay on film will discuss some of these devices, but there is no merit in mechanically trotting them all out.

Shots

A **shot** is what is recorded between the time a camera starts and the time it stops, that is, between the director's call for "action" and the call to "cut." Perhaps the average shot is about 10 seconds (very rarely a fraction of a second, and usually not more than 15 or so seconds). The average film is about an hour and a half, with about 600 shots, but Alfred Hitchcock's *The Birds* (1963) uses 1,360 shots. Three common shots are (1) a **long shot** or **establishing shot,** showing the main object at a considerable distance from the camera and thus presenting it in relation to its general surroundings (for example, captured soldiers, seen across a prison yard, entering the yard); (2) a **medium shot,** showing the object in relation to its immediate surroundings (a couple of soldiers, from the knees up, with the yard's wall behind them); and (3) a **close-up,** showing only the main object, or, more often, only a part of it (a soldier's face or his bleeding feet).

In the outside world we can narrow our vision to the detail that interests us by moving our head and by focusing our eyes, ignoring what is not of immediate interest. The close-up is the movie director's chief way of directing our vision and of emphasizing a detail. (Another way is to focus sharply on the significant image, leaving the rest of the image in soft focus.) The close-up, a way of getting emphasis, has been heavily used in recent years, not always successfully. As the American essayist and film critic Dwight Macdonald said of John Schlesinger's *Midnight Cowboy* (1969) and *Getting Straight* (1970):

> [A] movie told in close-ups is like a comic book, or like a novel composed in punchy one-sentence paragraphs and set throughout in large caps. How refreshing is a long or middle shot, a glimpse of the real world, so lovely and so *far away,* in the midst of those interminable processions of [a] hairy ogre face.

Two excellent film versions of Shakespeare's *Henry V* nicely show the different effects that long shots and close-ups can produce. Laurence Olivier's version (1944) uses abundant long shots and, on the whole, conveys a highly pictorial, sweeping epic version of the war in which Henry was engaged. The film was made during World War II as a patriotic effort to inspire the English by showing the heroism of combat. On the other hand, Kenneth Branagh's version, made in 1989, uses lots of close-ups of soldiers with mud-splattered faces, emphasizing the grittiness of war. Olivier brought out the splendor and romance, Branagh the labor and pain, of war.

While taking a shot, the camera can move: It can swing to the right or left while its base remains fixed (a **pan shot**), up or down while fixed on its axis (a **tilt shot**), forward or backward (a **traveling shot**), or in and out and up and down fastened to a crane (a **crane shot**). The **zoom lens,** introduced in the 1950s and widespread by the middle 1960s, enables the camera to change its focus fluidly so that it can approach a detail—as a traveling shot does—while remaining fixed in place. Much will depend on the angle (high or low) from which the shots are made. If the camera is high (a **high-angle shot**), looking down on figures, it will usually dwarf them, perhaps even reduce them to crawling insects, making them vulnerable, pitiful, or contemptible. The higher the angle, the more likely it is to suggest a God's-eye view of entrapped people. If the camera is low (a **low-angle shot**), close to the ground and looking up, thereby showing figures against the sky, it will probably give them added dignity.

In F. W. Murnau's *Last Laugh* (1924), we first get low-angle shots of the self-confident doorman, communicating his grand view of himself; later, when he loses his strength and is reduced to working as a lavatory attendant, we see him from above, and he seems dwarfed. But these are not inevitable principles. A shot in Enrico's film version of Bierce's "An Occurrence at Owl Creek Bridge" shows the hangman from below, making him seem threatening. And a shot in Orson Welles's *Citizen Kane* (1941) shows Kane from above, but it does not dwarf him; rather, it shows him dominating his wife and then in effect obliterating her by casting a shadow over her. Similarly, a low-angle shot does not always add dignity: films in which children play important parts often have lots of low-angle shots showing adults as menacing giants.

In short, by its distance from the subject, its height from the ground, and its angle of elevation, the camera comments on or interprets what happens. It seems to record reality, but it offers its own version. It is only a slight exaggeration to say that the camera always lies, that is, gives a personal vision of reality.

Slow motion and **fast motion** also offer comments. In Kenneth Branagh's *Henry V* (1989), as in Orson Welles's *Falstaff* (1966; also titled *Chimes at Midnight*), part of the battle is filmed in slow motion; thus, the weariness of the soldiers is emphasized. In Enrico's *An Occurrence at Owl Creek Bridge,* Peyton Farquhar, imagining that he has escaped from his executioners, sees them in slow motion.

Sequences

A group of related scenes—such as the three scenes of soldiers mentioned earlier—is a **sequence,** though a sequence is more likely to have thirty scenes than three. A sequence corresponds roughly to a chapter in a novel, the shots being sentences and the scenes being paragraphs. Within a sequence may be an **intercut,** a switch to another action that, for example, provides an ironic comment on the main action of the sequence. If intercuts are so abundant in a sequence that, in effect, two or more sequences are going at once (for example, shots of the villain about to ravish the heroine, alternating with shots of the hero riding to her rescue), we have **parallel editing** (also called a **crosscut**). In the example just given, probably the tempo would increase, the shots being progressively shorter as we get to the rescue.

Within a sequence, the **transitions** are normally made by **straight cuts**—a strip of film is spliced to another, and the result is an instantaneous transfer from one shot to the next. Usually, an audience is scarcely (if at all) conscious of transitions from, say, a long shot of a character to a medium shot of her or him, or from a close-up of a speaker to a close-up of her or his auditor. But sometimes the director wants the audience to be fully aware of the change, as an author may emphasize a change by beginning a new paragraph or, even more sharply, by beginning a new chapter. Two older, and now rather unfashionable, relatively conspicuous transitions are sometimes still used, usually between sequences rather than within a sequence. These are the **dissolve** (the shot dissolves while a new shot appears to emerge from beneath it, there being a moment when we get a superimposition of both scenes), and the **fade** (in the **fade-out** the screen grows darker until black; in the **fade-in** the screen grows lighter until the new scene is fully visible).

In effect the camera is saying, "Let us now leave X and turn to Y" or "Two weeks later." Two older methods, even less in favor today than the dissolve and the fade but used in many excellent old films and in some modern films that seek an archaic effect, are the **wipe** (a sort of windshield wiper crosses the screen, wiping off the first scene and revealing the next) and the **iris** (in an **iris-in,** the new scene first appears in the center of the previous scene and then this circle expands until it fills the screen; an **iris-out** shows the new scene first appearing around the perimeter and then the circle closes in on the previous scene). Charles Chaplin more than once ended a scene with an iris-out of the tramp walking jauntily toward the horizon. François Truffaut used iris shots in *The Wild Child* (1970), suggesting by the encircling darkness the boy's isolation from most of the world surrounding him as he concentrated on a single object before him.

Editing

All of the transitions just discussed are examples of editing techniques. A film, no less than a poem or a play or a picture or a palace, is something made, and it is not made by simply exposing some film footage. Shots—often taken at widely separated times and places—must be appropriately joined. For example, we see a man look off to the right, and then we get a shot of what he is looking at and then a shot of his reaction. Until the shots are assembled, we don't have a film—we merely have the footage. The Russian director V. I. Pudovkin put it this way: "The film is not *shot,* but built, built up from the separate strips of celluloid that are its raw material." This building-up is the process of **editing.**

More than a story can be told, of course; something of the appropriate emotion can be communicated by juxtaposing, say, a medium-long shot of a group of impassively advancing soldiers against a close-up of a single terrified victim. Similarly, emotion can be communicated by the duration of the shots (quick shots suggest haste; prolonged shots suggest slowness) and by the lighting (progressively darker shots can suggest melancholy; progressively lighter shots can suggest hope or joy). An extremely obvious but effective example occurs in Charlie Chaplin's *Modern Times* (1936), a satire on industrialism. We see a mass of workers hurrying to their jobs, and a moment later we see a herd of sheep on the move, this shot providing a bitter comic comment on the previous shot.

The Russian theorists of film called this process of building by quick cuts **montage.** The theory held that shots, when placed together, add up to more than the sum of the parts. Montage, for them, was what made a film a work of art and not a mere replica of reality. American writers commonly use the term merely to denote quick cutting, and French writers use it merely in the sense of cutting.

All this talk about ingenious shots and their arrangement, then, assumes that the camera is a sort of pen, carefully setting forth images and thus at every point guiding the perceiver. The director (through the actors, camera technicians, cutters, and a host of others) makes an artifact, rather as a novelist makes a book or a sculptor makes a statue, and this artifact is an elaborate contraption that manipulates the spectators by telling them at every second exactly how they ought to feel.

But since the 1950s, a reaction has occurred against such artistry, a feeling that although the elaborate editing of Sergei Eisenstein and the other Russians is an aesthetic triumph, it is also a moral failure because by its insistent tricky commentary it seems to deny the inherent worth of the event in itself as it happens. Moreover, just as the nineteenth-century narrator in the novel, who continually guided the reader ("Do not fear, gentle reader, for even at this moment plans were being laid . . ."), was in the twentieth-century novel sloughed off, forcing the readers in large measure to deduce the story for themselves, so, too, some contemporary filmmakers emphasize improvisation, fully aware that the film thus made will not at every point guide or dominate the viewer.

Film affects us through sound as well as sight, and a good film usually succeeds in integrating the action with well-handled and carefully paced dialogue and keen choices of music. The long opening sequence of Francis Ford Coppola's *Apocalypse Now* (1979)—a film loosely based on Joseph Conrad's *Heart of Darkness*—unfolds to the music of the late 1960s/early 1970s rock group The Doors, as lead singer Jim Morrison sings the haunting song "The End." Later, an astonishingly vivid, breathtaking helicopter assault on a Vietnamese village takes place to the accompaniment of the German composer Richard Wagner's stirring "Ride of the Valkyries," which blasts from a speaker mounted on one of the attacking helicopters.

Theme in Film

It is time now to point out that mastery of technique, though necessary to good filmmaking, will not in itself make a good film. A good film is not a bag of cinematic devices but the embodiment, through cinematic devices, of a vision, an underlying theme. What is this theme or vision? It is a filmmaker's perception of some aspect of existence that he or she thinks is worthy of our interest. Normally, this perception involves characters and a plot. Recent American films, relying heavily on color, rock music in surround sound, quick cutting, and the wide screen, have tended to emphasize the emotional experience and deemphasize narrative. Still, most of the best cinema—and virtually every film based on a short story—is concerned with what people do, that is, with character and plot. Character is what people are, plot is what happens, but the line between character and plot fades, for what people are is in large measure what they do, and what is done is in large measure the result of what people are.

Comparing Filmed and Printed Stories

After seeing a film based on a novel or short story that we know, most of us are drawn to compare the two and make judgments about which one is better. If the film is not conspicuously faithful to the story, we may complain about the loss of this character or that episode; but when it is highly faithful we may find ourselves complaining, "What a disappointment! It was just like the book but it seemed so dead!" This second response is not surprising; as indicated earlier, good films use the camera creatively, and a film that is content merely to record a narrative is likely to be a dull film.

Most of the time we will conclude that the printed fiction is superior to what is shown on the screen. Yet we might do well on occasion not to emphasize which is better but, rather, to observe how entertainingly, interestingly, each works on its own. It's true that the use of voice-over may feel a bit wrong or jarring in *The Age of Innocence,* but the film is so stunning visually that the voice-over seems only a minor element in it—a distraction perhaps, but hardly a serious flaw. A similar argument could be raised about the choices made in the film versions of E. M. Forster's novel *Maurice* (published posthumously in 1971; film version 1987) and Henry James's *The Wings of the Dove* (1902; film version 1997). The frontal nudity and explicit lovemaking depicted in these films seems very far removed from the restraint and indirection of the novels themselves, in which sexual desire and activity are implied rather than shown, frequently touched on but never in graphic detail. But we could claim nonetheless that the films are in a sense true to the meanings of the novels—dramatizing encounters and themes that Forster and James, writing many decades ago, simply could not render with the fully detailed candor that is now possible.

These films, then, are not literally faithful to the novel—on the subject of sexuality, they show more, much more, than the novels do. But the changes in the films may be for the better, or at least they may strike us as understandable and defensible on the ground that they are in keeping with the expectations of a contemporary audience. The novels become revitalized—made to feel contemporary—because of the films' greater openness about daring illicit behavior.

Getting Ready to Write

Mastery of terminology does not make anyone a perceptive film critic, but it helps writers communicate their perceptions to their readers. Probably an essay on a film will not be primarily about the use of establishing shots or of wipes or of any such matters; rather, it will be about the reasons why a particular film pleases or displeases, succeeds or fails, seems significant or insignificant, and in discussing these large matters it is sometimes necessary (or at least economical) to use the commonest technical terms. Large matters are often determined in part by such seemingly small matters as the distance of the camera from its subject or how transitions are made, and the writer may as well use the conventional terms. But it is also true that a filmmaker's technique and technology alone cannot make a first-rate film. An idea, a personal vision, a theme must be embodied in all that is flashed on the screen.

Writing an essay about a new film—one only shown in the movie theaters and not yet available for personal viewing at home—presents difficulties not encountered in writing about printed stories. If we experience film in a darkened room, we cannot easily take notes, and because the film may be shown only once, we cannot always take another look at passages that puzzle us. But

- You can take some brief notes even in the dark; it is best to amplify them as soon as light is available, while you still know what the scrawls mean.
- If you can see the film more than once, do so, and of course if the script has been published, study it.
- Draft your paper as soon as possible after your first viewing, and then see the film again, if possible.
- If you can, check hazy memories of certain scenes and techniques with fellow viewers.

Drafting an Essay About a Film

First—but you may not discover this until you have written a draft or two—you need to have a *point*, a *thesis*. Your essay must do more than say that the film of a story is faithful to the original in points A, B, C, and D, and departs from the original in points E, F, G, and H. Your readers doubtless can see these things for themselves. Probably in your preliminary notes you will indeed want to list such things, but you will then want to go on to think about the significance of the resemblances and the differences. What do you make of them? Given the fact that film is a visual medium, is it possible that too much fidelity to a story—for instance, failure to give us interesting pictures—has turned a memorable short story into a boring movie? You will want to think about the resemblances and the differences between the story and the film, and you will want to account for them, first to yourself (probably you will have to write and revise at least one draft before you can do this). Then in your essay you will explain to your reader why you respond the way you do.

Early in the essay it is desirable to sketch enough of the plot to give readers an idea of what happens. Do not try to recount everything that happens; it can't be done, and the attempt will frustrate you and bore your readers. Once you introduce the main characters and devote a few sentences to the plot, thus giving the readers a comfortable seat, get down to the job of convincing them that you have something interesting to say about the film—that the plot is trivial, or that the hero is not really cool but cruel, or that the plot and the characters are fine achievements but the camera work is sometimes needlessly tricky, or that all is well.

Incidentally, a convenient way to give an actor's name in your essay is to put it in parentheses after the character's name or role, thus: "The detective

(Humphrey Bogart) finds a clue. . . ." Then, as you go on to talk about the film, use the names of the characters or the roles, not the names of the actors, except of course when you are talking about the actors themselves, as in "Bogart is exactly right for the part."

✔ CHECKLIST: *Getting Ideas for Writing Arguments About Film*

These questions may help to bring impressions out into the open and may with some reworking provide topics for essays.

Preliminaries

❑ Is the title significant? If the film's title differs from that of the published story, account for and evaluate the change.

Literary Adaptations

❑ Does the film slavishly follow its original and neglect the potentialities of the camera? Or does it so revel in cinematic devices that it distorts the original work? (Of course, an adaptation need not go to either extreme. Enrico's *An Occurrence at Owl Creek Bridge* is a close adaptation of Ambrose Bierce's story, and yet it is visually interesting.)

❑ Does the film do violence to the theme of the original? Is the film better than its source? Are the additions or omissions due to the medium or to a crude or faulty interpretation of the original?

Plot and Character

❑ How faithful is the film to the story in plot and in character? Evaluate the changes, if any.

❑ In the film version (1984) of Henry James's novel *The Bostonians* (1886), one of the protagonists, an impassioned feminist reformer, delivers a speech to an unruly crowd in a theater, which significantly changes the effect of the novel itself, where the speech is not given. What is the impact of a decision like this one (which is so at odds with the plot as the author shaped it), and what is your assessment of it? Is the film to be faulted for such a change, or does the change make good sense for the film's development of character and theme, however unfaithful it might be to the author's story?

❑ Can film deal as effectively with inner action—mental processes—as with external, physical action? In a given film, how is the inner action conveyed? By voice-over? Or by visual equivalents?

Setting

❑ How effectively does the film convey the setting or settings that the author chose for his or her story? Do the film's settings somehow fall short of the expressive power that they possess in the story itself?

Editing

❑ Does the editing—for instance, frequent sharp juxtapositions or slow panoramic shots—convey qualities that the story writer conveyed by means of sentence length or sentence structure?

❑ Are shots and sequences adequately developed, or do they seem jerky? (A shot may be jerky by being extremely brief or at an odd angle; a sequence may be jerky by using discontinuous images or fast cuts. Sometimes, of course, jerkiness may be desirable.) If such cinematic techniques as wipes, dissolves, and slow motion are used, are they meaningful and effective?

❑ Are the actors appropriately cast? Was it a mistake to cast Robert Redford as Gatsby in Jack Clayton's film version (1974) of *The Great Gatsby* (1925)? John Huston, in his film (1951) of Stephen Crane's *The Red Badge of Courage* (1894) used Audie Murphy, one of the most highly decorated and best-known heroes of World War II, as Henry Fleming, the young soldier who flees from battle but later gets a second chance to fight bravely. What is the effect of this casting?

Symbolism

❑ If in the story certain objects acquire symbolic meanings, are these same objects similarly used in the film? Or does the film introduce new symbols?

❑ Is the lighting in the film realistic, symbolic, or both?

Soundtrack

❑ Does the soundtrack offer more than realistic dialogue? Is the music appropriate and functional? (Music may, among other things, imitate natural sounds, give a sense of locale or of ethnic group, suggest states of mind, provide ironic commentary, or—by repeated melodies—help establish connections.) Are volume, tempo, and pitch—whether of music or of such sounds as the wind blowing or cars moving—used to stimulate emotions?

Thinking About Filming Fiction

When you read a story and consider its possibilities as a film, you may want to begin thinking along these lines:

- Which story included in this book is your favorite? Do you think that this story could be made into a good film? Are there features of the story—its setting, for example—that, in your view, would work very well in a film version? Are there also features of this story that would be hard to convey in a film?

- There have been film versions (in some instances, more than one) of a number of well-known novels by English and American authors, including Jane Austen, Emily and Charlotte Brontë, Charles Dickens, Thomas Hardy, Edith Wharton, E. M. Forster, and Ernest Hemingway, to name just a few. Have you seen a film version of a novel by one of these authors, or by another author whom you admire? What was your response to the film? (*Note:* If you'd like to check on whether a novel or story has been made into a film, you can search for the title on the Web site "The Internet Movie Database" at <http://www.us.imdb.com>.)

- What does it feel like to read a really absorbing story or novel? Do you have the same feeling, or a different one, when you watch an absorbing film? Which experience appeals to you more, reading literature or seeing films?

Seven Students Write About Short Stories

One Student's Thoughts About Character in Poe's "The Cask of Amontillado"

If your instructor assigns a topic in advance—such as "Irony in 'The Cask of Amontillado'" or "Is Montresor Insane?"—even on your first reading of the story you will be thinking in a specific direction, looking for relevant evidence. But if a topic is not assigned, it will be up to you to find something that you think is worth talking about to your classmates. (All writers must imagine a fairly specific audience, such as the readers of *Ms.* or the readers of *Playboy*—these audiences are quite different—or the readers of the high school newspaper, or the readers of a highly technical professional journal, and so on. It's a good idea to imagine your classmates as your audience.)

You may want to begin by asking yourself (and responding in your journal) what you like or dislike in the story; or you may want to think about some of the questions mentioned, at the beginning of this chapter, on plot, character, point of view, setting, symbolism, style, and theme. Or you may have annotated some passage that puzzled you, and, on rereading, you may feel that *this* passage is what you want to talk about. In any case, after several readings of the story you will settle not only on a *topic* (for instance, symbolism) but also on a *thesis,* an argument, a point (for instance, the symbolism is for the most part effective but in two places is annoyingly obscure).

It happens that the student (Ann Geraghty) whose essay we reprint decided to write about the narrator in Poe's story, which appears on pages 509–514. The following notes are not her earliest jottings but the jottings she recorded after she had tentatively chosen her topic.

Two characters: narrator (Montresor) and his enemy,
     Fortunato
1st person narrator, so we know Fort. only through
     what M. tells us
Fortunato
     has wronged Montresor ("thousand injuries"; but
        is M. telling the truth?)
     drinks a lot ("he had been drinking much")

vain (Fort. insists he knows much more than
    Luchesi)
courteous (in the vaults, drinks to M's buried
    relatives)
foolish (?? Hard to be sure about this)
Montresor
    first parag. tells us he seeks vengeance ("I vowed revenge") for "the
        thousand injuries" he suffered from Fort. ("I would be avenged")
    of high birth
       1) he comes from a family with a motto: *Nemo me impune lacessit*
          (no one dare attack me with impunity)
       2) has coat of arms (human foot crushing serpent whose fangs are
          in heel). But what's the connection? Is the idea that he and his
          noble family are like the *foot* crushing a serpent that has bitten
          them, or on the other hand is the idea that he and family are
          like the *serpent*—if stepped on (attacked, insulted), they will
          fight back? Maybe we are supposed to think that he thinks
          he is like the human foot, but *we* see that he is like the
          serpent
highly educated? At least he uses hard words
    ("unredressed," "the thought of his immolation").
    (Check *"immolation"*)   Dictionary says
                                         it is a sacrifice,
cunning: knows how to work on Fortunato   a ritual killing
    (implies that Luchesi is more highly
    regarded than F)
rich: lives in a "palazzo," and has servants
crazy:
       1) murders for vengeance
       2) enjoys hearing the sound of Fort. shaking
          chains ("that I might hearken to it with
          the more satisfaction, I ceased my labors")
       3) when he hears the screams of F., *he* screams ("I surpassed them in
          volume and in strength")
    Can we possibly sympathize with him? Can he possibly
be acting fairly? Do we judge him? Do we judge (condemn)
ourselves for liking the story? Why do I find the story interesting
instead of repulsive? Because (thesis here) his motive is good, he
thinks he is upholding family honor (in his eyes the killing is a
family duty, a sacrifice; "immolation")

The Final Version of the Student Essay

Ann Geraghty
Professor Duff
English 102
1 March 2010

Revenge, Noble and Ignoble

Because Edgar Allan Poe's "The Cask of Amontillado" is told by a first person narrator, a man named Montresor, we cannot be sure that what the narrator tells us is true. There are some things in the story, however, that we can scarcely believe. For instance, we can accept the fact that there is a character (even though we never see him) named Luchesi, because the narrator mentions him and the other character in the story—Fortunato—also talks about him. But how sure can we be that Fortunato is the sort of man that the narrator says Fortunato is?

In the first paragraph, Montresor says that Fortunato has done him a "thousand injuries" (510). He is never specific about these, and Fortunato never says anything that we can interpret as evidence that he has injured Montresor. Further, Fortunato is courteous when he meets Montresor, which seems to suggest that he is not aware that he has injured Montresor. It seems fair to conclude, then, that Fortunato has not really injured Montresor, and that Montresor has insanely imagined that Fortunato has injured him.

What evidence is there that Montresor is insane? First, we should notice the intensity with which Montresor speaks, especially in the first paragraph. He tells us that he "vowed revenge" and that he "would be avenged" and that he would "punish with impunity" (510). He also tells us, all in the first paragraph, that he himself must not get punished for his act of vengeance ("A wrong is unredressed when retribution overtakes its redresser") and that "It is equally unredressed when the avenger fails to make himself felt as such to him who has done the wrong." There is a common saying, "Don't get mad, get even," but Montresor is going way beyond getting even, and anyway it's not certain that he was injured in the first place. He *is* getting "mad," not in the sense of "angry" but in the sense of "crazy."

If we agree that Montresor is insane, we can ask ourselves two questions about this story. First, is "The Cask of Amontillado" just a story about a mysterious madman, a story that begins and ends with a madman and does not even try to explain his madness? Second, why have people read this story for almost a hundred and fifty years? If we can answer the first question negatively, we may be able to answer the second.

I think that Montresor is insane, but his insanity is understandable, and it is even based on a concept of honor. He comes from a noble family, a family with a coat of arms (a foot is crushing a serpent that is biting the heel) and a motto (*Nemo me impune lacessit*, which means "No one dare attack me with impunity").

Fortunato may not have really injured him, but for some reason Montresor thinks he has been injured. As a nobleman who must uphold the honor of his family, Montresor acts with a degree of energy that is understandable for someone in his high position. That is, he must live up to his coat of arms, which shows a gold foot (symbolizing a nobleman) crushing a serpent. The motto in effect means that Montresor *must* take vengeance if he is to uphold his family honor. In fact, the unusual word "immolation" (510) in the second paragraph tells us a good deal about Montresor's action. To "immolate" is to "sacrifice," to perform a ritual killing. Since Montresor says his vengeance will be the "immolation" of Fortunato, we can assume that Montresor thinks that he has a duty, imposed by his noble family, to kill Fortunato. He sees himself as a priest performing a solemn sacrifice.

Interestingly, however, the *reader* can interpret the motto in a different way. The reader may see Montresor as the serpent, viciously stinging an enemy, and Fortunato as an almost innocent victim who has somehow accidentally offended (stepped on) Montresor. In reading the story we take pleasure in hearing, and seeing, a passionate nobleman performing what he thinks is a duty imposed on him by his rank. We also take pleasure in judging him accurately, that is, in seeing that his action is not really noble but is serpent-like, or base. We can thus eat our cake and have it too; we see a wicked action, a clever murder (and we enjoy seeing it), and, on the other hand, we can sit back and judge it as wicked (we see Montresor as a serpent), and therefore we can feel that we are highly moral.

Geraghty 3

Work Cited

Poe, Edgar Allan. "The Cask of Amontillado." *An Introduction to Literature*. Ed. Sylvan Barnet, William Burto, and William E. Cain. 16th ed. New York: Longman, 2011. 509–514. Print.

YOUR TURN

In reading this essay, you may wish to ask yourself the following questions (with an eye toward applying them also to your own writing):

1. Is the title appropriate and at least moderately interesting?
2. Does the essay have a thesis? If so, what is it?
3. Is the thesis (if there is one) adequately supported by evidence?
4. Is the organization satisfactory? Does one paragraph lead easily into the next, and is the argument presented in reasonable sequence?

Gender Criticism: A Response to "The Judgment of Solomon"

An analytic essay might go beyond the structure of the individual work, to the relation of the work to some larger whole. For instance, we might approach "The Judgment of Solomon" (page 196) from the point of view of gender criticism (discussed in Chapter 35), which often concentrates on the ways in which women are represented. In this story, we might argue, wisdom is an attribute only of a male; women are either deceitful or emotional. Here is an essay that is an example of gender criticism. It was written by Alice McCauley, a first-year college student who tried to look at the story without preconceptions, with fresh eyes, forgetting all that she had heard about the wisdom of Solomon, or, rather, remembering it but questioning it.

Sample Student Essay: "How Wise Was Solomon?"

McCauley 1

Alice McCauley
Professor O'Brien
English 10lb
20 June 2010

How Wise Was Solomon?

The point of the story of Solomon, told in 1 Kings 3.16–28, is apparently to show that "the wisdom of God" was in Solomon. But if it shows something about Solomon's nature, it also shows the nature of two women. What does it show them to be? First, that neither woman is wise; wisdom is reserved for Solomon. One woman, in the obvious interpretation of the story, is a loving mother, willing to sacrifice her own happiness for the good of her child. The other woman, again in the traditional interpretation of the story, is cruel, spiteful, willing to kill the baby rather than to allow her rival to have it. Given the depiction of these two women, what is a reader to conclude about women? Women are emotional; women act on impulses—in one case, the maternal instinct and in the other case a selfish instinct ("If-I-can't-have-it-nobody-will-have-it").

That is, in this world run by men, men have all of the wisdom and women have all of the emotion. Some of this emotion is good (maternal love) and some of it is nasty (selfishness or spitefulness), but in any case women cannot (the story seems to show us) be trusted to be fair or to be wise.

And what of Solomon's justice? Solomon, by threatening to do violence with a sword, evokes the two responses from the women. It is interesting to see that his proposal evokes no exclamations of horror from members of his court. Presumably the king can do whatever he wishes. It happens that Solomon does not proceed to divide the child because the responses of the women convince him that he knows who is the true mother. But what would he have done if the women had not responded as they did? We don't know, but the fact that both women assume he really will divide the child gives us a clear sense that the women live in a world in which men rule by violence, a world in which indeed the judge might have solved the problem with the sword, just as he threatened to do.

In such a world, the woman who told Solomon to divide the child might have been daring him to act in accordance with his speech. That is, although the usual interpretation is that she is acting spitefully—this is the way her act is perceived in a world with patriarchal views—she might have been acting from a very different motive. If we look at the story through eyes opened by the Women's Movement, maybe we can see an unconventional woman who was in effect saying, "Violence is at the heart of your way of life, and you make all of the rules here. Go ahead, divide the child, if you dare; see if you can live with your decision." That is, if we free ourselves from the traditional view that Solomon is

McCauley 3

wise, we see that she bravely (and intelligently) challenges Solomon and in effect reveals the violence on which his "justice" and his "wisdom" rest. The fact that she is a harlot—a woman whose whole life is spent in subordination to men—makes her bold defiance of the powerful king especially impressive.

McCauley 4

Work Cited

Anonymous. "The Judgment of Solomon." *An Introduction to Literature.* Ed. Sylvan Barnet, William Burto, and William E. Cain. 16th ed. New York: Longman, 2011. 196–97. Print.

YOUR TURN

Do you find the essay convincing? Why? If you do not find it convincing, do you nevertheless find it interesting? Why?

A Feminist Reading of James Thurber's "The Secret Life of Walter Mitty"

Working Toward a Thesis: Journal Entries

Before reading the following entries about "The Secret Life of Walter Mitty" (pages 530–33), write some of your own. You may want to think about what (if anything) you found amusing in the story, or about whether the story is dated, or about some aspect of Mitty's character or of his wife's. But the choice is yours.

A student, Susan Levy, wrote the following entry in her journal after the story was discussed in class.

March 21. Funny, I guess, especially the business about him as a doctor performing an operation. And that "pocketa-pocketa," but I don't think that it's as hysterical as everyone else seems to think it is. And how could anyone stand being married to a man like that? In fact, it's a good thing he has her to look after him. He ought to be locked up, driving into the "Exit Only" lane, talking to himself in the street, and having those crazy daydreams. No wonder the woman in the street laughs at him.

March 24. He's certainly a case, and she's not nearly as bad as everyone was saying. So she tells him to put his overshoes on; well, he ought to put them on, since Thurber says there is slush in the street, and he's no kid any more. About the worst I can say of her is that she seems a little unreasonable in always wanting him to wait for her, rather than sometimes the other way around, but probably she's really telling him not to wander off, because if he ever drifts away there'll be no finding him. The joke, I guess, is that he's supposed to have these daydreams because he's henpecked, and henpecked men are supposed to be funny. Would people find the story just as funny if she had the daydreams, and he bullied her?

Developing the Thesis: List Notes

In preparation for writing a draft, Levy reread the story and jotted down some tentative notes based on her journal and on material that she had highlighted in the text. (At this point you may want to make your own list, based on your notes.)

> Mitty helpless: he needs her
> chains on tires
> enters Exit Only
> ~~Waterbury~~
> cop tells him to get going
> fantasies
> wife a nag? →causes his daydreams? Evidence?
> Makes him get to hotel first
> overshoes
> backseat driver?
>
> "Does it ever occur to you that I am sometimes thinking?" Is he thinking, or just having dreams?
> M. confuses Richthoven with someone called Richtman.
> Funny--or anti-woman? Would it be funny if he nagged her, and she had daydreams?

Next, Levy wrote a draft; then she revised the draft and submitted the revision (printed here) to some classmates for peer review.

Sample Draft: "Walter Mitty Is No Joke"

Susan Levy

Professor Markus

English 102

5 April 2010

Walter Mitty Is No Joke

James Thurber's "The Secret Life of Walter Mitty" seems to be highly regarded as a comic story about a man who is so dominated by his wife that he has to escape through fantasies. In my high school course in English, everyone found Mitty's dreams and his wife's bullying funny, and everyone seems to find them funny in college, too. Everyone except me.

If we look closely at the story, we see that Mitty is a pitiful man who needs to be told what to do. The slightest glimpse of reality sets him off on a daydream, as when he passes a hospital and immediately begins to imagine that he is a famous surgeon, or when he hears a newsboy shouting a headline about a crime and he imagines himself in a courtroom. The point seems to be that his wife nags him, so he escapes into daydreams. But the fact is that she needs to keep after him because he needs someone to tell him what to do. It depends on what one considers nagging. She tells him he is driving too fast, and (given the date of the story, 1939) he probably is, since he is going 55 on a slushy or snowy road. She tells him to wear overshoes, and he probably ought to, since the weather is bad. He resents all of these orders, but he clearly is incompetent, since he delays when the traffic light turns from red to green, and he enters an "Exit Only" lane in a parking lot. We are also told that he can't put chains on tires.

In fact, he can't do anything right. All he can do is daydream, and the dreams, though they are funny, are proof of his inability to live in the real world. When his wife asks him why he didn't put the overshoes on in the store, instead of carrying them in a box, he says, "Does it ever occur to you that I am sometimes thinking?" (533). But he doesn't "think," he just daydreams. Furthermore, he can't even get things straight in his daydreams. He gets everything mixed up, confusing Richthoven with Richtman, for example.

Is "The Secret Life of Walter Mitty" really a funny story about a man who daydreams because he is henpecked? Probably it is supposed,

Levy 2

to be so, but it's also a story about a man who is lucky to have a wife who can put up with him and keep him from getting killed on the road or lost in town.

Levy 3

Work Cited

Thurber, James. "The Secret Life of Walter Mitty." *An Introduction to Literature*. Ed. Sylvan Barnet, William Burto, and William E. Cain. 16th ed. New York: Longman, 2011. 530–33. Print.

Writing About Setting as Symbolic: Notes and an Essay on Kate Chopin's "The Story of an Hour"

The following essay is about Kate Chopin's "The Story of an Hour" (pages 67–68). If you have not yet read the story, take a moment now to do so.

Amy Jones, a first-year student, has kindly provided her last notes, an outline that guided her while she wrote her first draft. Not all of the notes ended up in the final version, but they were a great help in shaping the essay.

thesis: setting here not place but time–springtime title?
    Chopin and Spring
    Chopin's Spring
    Mrs. M's Spring
    Mrs. M's Symbolic Spring
    Spring in "The Story of an Hour"
    Spring Comes to Mrs. M
    Setting as Symbol
    Setting as Symbol: Spring in...
setting in "Hour"
Define Setting??? Place and time
    Chopin doesn't give date (or city); but in a house
spring: "the tops of the trees . . . were all aquiver with the new
    spring" (parag. 5)
    "sparrows were twittering in the eaves" (parag. 5)

"There were patches of blue sky showing here and there
    through the clouds" (parag. 6)
    why clouds? brightness pushing through darkness, like
joyous new life pushing aside grief???
    ~~"spring days and summer days" special significance of~~
        ~~summer??. Or just means "lots of days"?~~
        ~~etc way of life~~
        ~~"Louise, open the door! I beg, open the door"~~
elixir (near end) medicine???
doctors say died of heart disease
End with a quotation? Or with something about life turning to death?

Jones 1

Amy Jones

Professor Lucas

English 222

9 March 2010

Spring Comes to Mrs. Mallard

Title implies thesis. Opening paragraph identifies author and story; topic (setting) is introduced.

In reading Kate Chopin's "The Story of an Hour" a reader is hardly aware of where the story is set. We are not told the country or the city, or the period, and so (if we think about it at all) we probably assume the story is set during Chopin's own lifetime, perhaps even during the year in which she wrote it, in Chopin's own territory, although there really is nothing very specific about Louisiana in this story. Nor do we learn, at the very beginning of the story, whether the action is taking place indoors or outdoors. However, since the story begins by telling us that Mrs. Mallard's sister, Josephine, gently breaks the news of the death of Mr. Mallard, we probably assume it is taking place at Mrs. Mallard's house. This assumption is confirmed a little later, when we hear that Mrs. Mallard, once she has heard the terrible news, "went away to her room alone" (67).

Transition ("But") leads to next point (that the season is emphasized).

But if Kate Chopin doesn't tell us anything about the society in which the figures in the story live, she tells us quite a bit about the time of the year during which the story takes place. The story is very short—only about two and a half pages—but Chopin finds space in which to tell us not only that the time is spring, but also that from a window in her room Mrs. Mallard could see the tops of trees that were

Jones 2

all aquiver with the new spring life. The delicious breath of
rain was in the air. In the street below a peddler was crying
his wares. The notes of distant song which someone was
singing finally reached her faintly, and countless sparrows
were twittering in the eaves. (67)

This is the fullest description of the time of year in the story, but
there are other shorter references, so we can say that the springtime is
given considerable emphasis, considering how short the story is. For
instance, the quoted paragraph is followed by a shorter paragraph that
mentions "patches of blue sky" (67), and in fact "blue sky" is mentioned
again, two paragraphs later. There is nothing especially remarkable
about the sky's being blue, and so one might wonder why Chopin
bothers to tell us that the sky is blue when she doesn't even tell us
where her story is set. And then, in the next paragraph, she tells us
more about the sky: "There was something coming to her. . . . What was
it? She did not know. . . . But she felt it, creeping out of the sky,
reaching toward her through the sounds, the scents, the color that filled
the air" (67).

Given this emphasis on the spring air, we can now see that Chopin
is contrasting two aspects of setting, the season versus the place,
springtime versus the closed room. The spring air is invading the room in
which Mrs. Mallard has locked herself. At first Mrs. Mallard resists the
mysterious invasion: "She was beginning to recognize this thing that
was approaching to possess her, and she was striving to beat it back"
(68), but, the reader comes to understand, "this thing" is the spirit of
"the new spring life" which, we learned earlier in the story, set the tops
of the trees aquiver. The trees, the swallows, and the blue sky are signs
of the spring, and the spring symbolizes life. The locked room, where
Mrs. Mallard goes to grieve, is a place of mourning, of death, but Mrs.
Mallard is a living creature, and though she sincerely grieves she cannot
shut out life.

Now it is clear why Chopin did not bother to tell us in what city,
or even in what kind of house, the action takes place. It doesn't
matter. What does matter is the feeling of new life that Mrs. Mallard
feels, and this can best be shown by relating it to springtime, a time
of new life.

*Quotation
introduced as
supporting
evidence (set
off because it
is longer than
four lines).*

*Brief
quotations
used as
additional
evidence.*

*Thesis is
further
clarified.*

*Thesis is
hammered
home.*

Jones 3

Concluding   Even though she has confined herself to her room, through the
paragraph   window Mrs. Mallard drinks the spring air. In Chopin's words, "She was
furthers the   drinking in the very elixir of life through that open window" (68). An
argument   elixir, according to *The American Heritage Dictionary*, Fourth Edition, is
(passage about
"elixir") and   "a substance believed to maintain life indefinitely." This word is an
also, in its   effective word to describe the way Mrs. Mallard feels, as the sights and
final sentences, sounds of spring press upon her and give her a new sense of life. But of
wraps up   course although spring renews life indefinitely, each year bringing new
essay.   vegetation, people do not live indefinitely. In fact Mrs. Mallard will live

for less than an hour. Chopin does not make it clear to a reader whether

Mrs. Mallard dies because she really has "heart trouble," as we are told in

the first paragraph, or because she has lived an intense spring moment as

an individual and so she cannot stand the thought of a lifetime with her

husband. But what is perfectly clear is that one aspect of the setting—

springtime, a season full of new life—is essential to convey to the reader

a sense of Mrs. Mallard's new (and tragically brief) feelings.

Jones 4

Work Cited

Documentation Chopin, Kate. "The Story of an Hour." *An Introduction to Literature.*
Ed. Sylvan Barnet, William Burto, and William E. Cain. 16th ed.
New York: Longman, 2011. 67–68. Print.

Two Students Interpret Shirley Jackson's "The Lottery": Notes and Essays

Here are the preliminary notes and the final essays of two students who chose to
write about the theme of Shirley Jackson's "The Lottery," which appears on pages
431–38.

Nat Komor, the first student, after reading and rereading the story jotted
down the following notes as a sort of preliminary outline. Some of the notes
were based on passages he had underlined. Notice that the jottings include some
material specifically on the story and other material—references to the outside
world—that is relevant to what the writer takes to be the theme of the story.
When he reviewed his notes before starting on a first draft, Komor deleted some

of them, having decided that they were not especially useful for his essay. Still, they were worth jotting down; only in retrospect can a writer clearly see which notes are useful.

> Is Jackson saying that human nature is evil? Prob. no; here, people just follow a tradition, and don't examine it. Mr. Warner defends lottery, saying "There's *always* been a lottery." No real argument in defense of it.
>
> We are least conscious of the things we take for granted; ~~I recall someone's saying "a fish is not aware of water until it is out of it."~~
>
> examples of blindly following society's customs
>
> > ~~Compulsory schooling (how many people ever even remotely *think* of schooling their children at home?)~~
> >
> > ~~school is 5 days a week, why not 4 or 6? Bachelor's degree is 4 years, why not 3 or 5?~~
> >
> > segregation (until 1960s)
> >
> > ~~women not permitted to drive in Saudi Arabia~~
> >
> > ~~women must wear veil in Saudi Arabia~~
> >
> > eating of meat; might a vegetarian society not look with horror at our habit of eating meat?
> >
> > slavery (thought to be "natural" by almost all societies until nineteenth century)
>
> thoughtless following of custom in "The Lottery"
>
> > ~~exact words of ritual lost, but still necessary to address "each person approaching"~~
> >
> > ~~original box gone, but present box said to be made of parts of previous box~~
> >
> > lottery an established ritual: "The lottery was conducted—as were the square dances, the teenage club, the Halloween program—by Mr. Summers, who had time and energy to devote to civic activities." *Important*: the lottery is a civic activity, a social action, a *summer* (pun?) ritual.
>
> Evil? Certainly yes, since killing an innocent, but no one in the story says it's evil.
>
> > BUT Adams does say that in the north village "they're talking of giving up the lottery," and his wife says "Some places have already quit lotteries."
> >
> > Also: a girl whispers, "I hope it's not Nancy," so at least one person feels uneasy about the whole thing
>
> Are these people evil? No, they seem pretty decent. They just don't much question what they are doing, and they do something terrible

the box
  black = death?
  made out of pieces of old box
  "faded," "splintered badly": does this
    symbolize a need for a new tradition?
the papers
  earlier, wood chips. At end, wind blows away
    slips of paper? Symbolic of life fluttering
    away? (Prob. not)
the three-legged stool
  symbolic? If so, of what?
Possible title
    The Violent Lottery
    The Irrational Lottery
    We All Participate in "The Lottery"
    The Meaning of the Lottery

A lot of the material here is good, though some of it would be more suited for an essay on symbolism, and it is chiefly this material that the writer wisely deleted in preparing to draft an essay on the theme of Jackson's story. After writing a draft and then revising it, Komor submitted the revision to a group for peer review. Ultimately, he turned in the following essay.

Komor 1

Nat Komor

Professor Lee

English 101B

7 March 2010

We All Participate in "The Lottery"

The townsfolk in Shirley Jackson's "The Lottery" engage in a horrible ritual. They stone an innocent person to death. It would be horrible enough if the person they stoned were guilty of some crime, and stoning was a form of capital punishment that the society practiced, but in the case of "The Lottery" the person is not guilty of any crime. Tessie Hutchinson simply has the bad luck to pick the wrong slip of paper from a box, a paper marked with a black spot.

The people in this unnamed town every year hold a lottery to find a victim. On the whole, they seem to believe that the lottery is necessary, or is natural; at least they hardly question it. True, Mr. Adams says that in the north village "they're talking of giving up the lottery," (435) and his wife says that "Some places have already quit lotteries," (435) but that's about as much as one hears of anybody questioning this institution of society. Probably most of the people in the village would agree with Old Man Warner, who says that people who talk about giving up the lottery are a "pack of crazy fools." He adds, "There's *always* been a lottery," (435) and that seems to be about the best answer that anyone can give. Of course the people don't take any special pleasure in the lottery, and there is at least one expression of sympathy, when a girl says, "I hope it's not Nancy." (437) On the whole, however, the people seem to believe that the lottery must be held, and someone has to die.

It's important to notice that the lottery is one of the "civic activities," that is, it is part of the regular life of these people, part (so to speak) of the air they breathe. For the most part they don't question the lottery any more than we question compulsory education, the length of the school year, or the eating of meat. When one thinks about it, one might ask why the government should have the power to compel parents to send children to school, or, for that matter, why a child shouldn't have the right to leave school whenever he or she feels like it. Why should children have almost no rights? People simply don't bother to think about this issue, or about *many* others. For instance, I can imagine that a member of a vegetarian society—say a Hindu Brahmin society—must be horrified by the way almost all Americans think nothing of raising animals (bringing life into the world) for the sole purpose of eating them. We just accept these things, without thinking, but from the view of another culture they may be horrible customs.

What Jackson seems to be saying to her readers is this: "Unthinkingly you follow certain conventions. These conventions seem to you to be natural, and for the most part they are harmless, but some of them are barbaric and destructive." That is, Jackson is telling us to examine our lives, and to stop assuming that all of our customs are right. Some of the beliefs we share today may, in time, come to be seen to be as evil as slavery or murder.

Komor 3

Work Cited

Jackson, Shirley. "The Lottery." *An Introduction to Literature.*
Ed. Sylvan Barnet, William Burto, and William E. Cain. 16th ed.
New York: Longman, 2011. 431–38. Print.

Now for the notes and the essay by a second student, Anne Hearn. This writer came to a very different conclusion about the theme of "The Lottery." After reading Hearn's notes and her essay, you may want to compare the two essays. Do you find one essay more interesting than the other? More persuasive? If so, why? You may feel that even though the writers come to different conclusions, the two essays are equally interesting and equally valid.

surprise *and* shock
  Shock
    violence (at end)
    esp. shocking because violence comes from people
      who seem normal and decent
    (only a few expressions of hesitation; Mr. and Mrs. Adams)
    Jackson claimed violence was normal *(quote passage)*
  (talk of giving up lotteries)
    surprise
    we don't know, until late, what's going on;
    on rereading, we see lots of clues about what
      will happen
      Example: references to stones
Meanings?
  lottery = the draft in wartime?
  lottery = community violence? Example: War (??)
  lottery = violent U.S. society??
  " "   *any* violent custom; bad tradition?
  human nature corrupt? sinful? (Note name of Adams,
    also Graves) (other significant names: Summers,
    Warner);
    human tendency to look for a scapegoat. Is it
      true?
Jackson quoted on her meaning: "violence and
  general inhumanity" but do we have to believe
  her?

Maybe just a horror story, without "meaning" *Example*
                                        of such a story?

Are normal people willing to kill without great provocation?

Possible titles

  Shirley Jackson on Human Nature

  Do We All Participate in "The Lottery"?

  How Fair is Shirley Jackson's Lottery?

  Is "The Lottery" Fair?

When you read Hearn's essay, you'll notice that for a title the author settled on the last of her four tentative titles. The first title, "Shirley Jackson on Human Nature," is too broad since the essay is not on all of Jackson's work but on only one story. The second tentative title, "Do We All Participate in 'The Lottery'?" is acceptable, but it sounds a bit clumsy, so the choice apparently came down to the last two titles or to some entirely new title that the writer might discover during the process of revising her drafts.

Notice also that some points mentioned in the preliminary notes—for instance, the reference to Mr. Summers and to Mr. Warner—are omitted from the essay. And some points scarcely mentioned in the outline are emphasized in the essay. In drafting and revising the essay, the writer found that certain things weren't relevant to her point, so she dropped them and found that others required considerable amplification.

Hearn 1

Anne Hearn

Professor Martinez

English 101B

9 April 2010

Is "The Lottery" Fair?

Probably all readers are surprised by the ending of Shirley Jackson's "The Lottery." But the story does more than offer a surprise. It shocks, because it seems to say that people who are perfectly ordinary, just like ourselves, are capable of killing an innocent neighbor for apparently no reason at all. On rereading the story, we can see that Jackson has carefully prepared for the ending, and we can admire her skill. For instance, the second paragraph tells us that "Bobby Martin had already stuffed his pockets full of stones, and other boys soon followed his example, selecting the smoothest and roundest stones" (432). We almost feel, when we reread the story, that we should not have been surprised. But even after we see that the ending has been foreshadowed, we remain shocked by the violence, and by what the story says about human beings. But exactly what *does* it say about them? And does it say anything that strikes us as true?

If we assume that the story *does* say something about life, and is not simply a meaningless shocker, we may come up with several possible interpretations. Is Jackson saying that Americans seem peaceful and neighborly but really are quite willing to engage in violence? (Although she does not clearly set the story in an identifiable region, she clearly sets it in a small town in the United States.) Certainly newspapers every day tell us of violent acts, but the violent acts are usually of an individual (a mad killer, or a rapist) or are of nature (an earthquake, a tornado).

Of course someone might conceivably argue that this story, which is about a community, is a sort of allegory about the United States as a whole. It was written in 1948, only three years after the end of World War II, and someone might claim that it is about American willingness to use violence, that is, to go to war. Or one might even say that it is about the wartime draft, which was a sort of lottery that chose certain people whose lives were risked.

But to see the story as a reference to World War II seems very strained. Nothing in the story suggests a conscious conflict between groups, as, for instance, Jackson could have suggested if members of this town were allied against another town. And though the story certainly is set in the United States, nothing in the story calls attention to a particularly *American violence*.

Another way of thinking about "The Lottery" is to see it as a story about all human beings—not just Americans—who unthinkingly submit to destructive traditions. This interpretation can be better supported than the first interpretation. For instance, at least two people in the story briefly question the tradition of the lottery. Steve Adams says, "Over in the north village they're talking of giving up the lottery," and a moment later his wife adds, "Some places have already quit lotteries" (435). But of course the story tells us that this community does not give up the lottery; in fact, we are particularly shocked to learn, near the end, that Steve Adams is "in the front of the crowd of villagers" when they attack Tessie Hutchinson (438).

Hearn 3

It's obvious that the story is about a terrible tradition that is accepted with relatively little objection, but we can still ask what connection the story has with our own lives. What traditions do we engage in that are so deadly? The wartime draft has already been mentioned, but even pacifists would probably grant that most of the people who engage in war are aware that war is terrible, and thus they are unlike Jackson's villagers. The story may be about the deadliness of certain traditions, but a reader is left wondering which of our traditions are represented in Jackson's lottery. Racism and sexism have had terrible effects, but it is hard to relate the lottery, which picks a victim at random, to discrimination against people of a certain color or a certain sex.

A third view, and one that I think is somewhat sounder than the first two views, is that the story is about human nature. Although most people are decent, they are also capable of terrible irrational violence. In Christian terms this is explained by original sin, a sinfulness that we have inherited from Adam. Jackson certainly allows for the possibility of some sort of Biblical interpretation, since, as we have seen, Mr. Adams is one of the leaders of the assault, and he is accompanied by Mr. Graves. The original sin of the first Adam led to death, and thus to the grave.

Shirley Jackson herself from time to time offered comments on the story. According to Judy Oppenheimer, in *Private Demons: The Life of Shirley Jackson*, when the fiction editor of the *New Yorker* asked her if "there was anything special she was trying to convey," she said, "Not really." When the editor pressed her, and asked if the story "made its point by an ironic juxtaposition of ancient superstition and modern setting," Jackson said, "Sure, that would be fine," since she didn't like to discuss her work (128). Her fullest comment, according to Oppenheimer, was given to a columnist who was writing for the *San Francisco Chronicle*:

> I suppose I hoped, by setting a particularly brutal rite in the present and in my own village, to shock the readers with a graphic demonstration of the pointless violence and general inhumanity of their own lives. (qtd. in Oppenheimer 131)

There are obvious problems with accepting this comment. First of all, as has been mentioned, Jackson offered contradictory comments on the meaning of the story. She seems not to have worried about being consistent. Second, the words she used by way of introducing her intention—"I suppose I hoped"—indicate that she herself was not entirely clear about what she had intended. Third, even if she did correctly state her intention, she may not have fulfilled it adequately.

Certainly the story shows people who seem quite decent but who with only a little hesitation participate in a barbaric ritual. Perhaps Jackson did intend to say in her story that this is what we are also like. And since the story is related to ancient rituals in which societies purify themselves by finding a scapegoat, Jackson seems to be saying that all people, no matter how normal or decent they seem, engage in violence that they think purifies them or is at least in some way necessary for their own well-being. But just because Jackson *said* something like this, and said it in a gripping story, it isn't necessarily true. Despite all of the realistic detail—for instance, Mrs. Hutchinson's desperate charge that "It isn't fair"—the final picture of life that "The Lottery" gives does not seem to me to be at all realistic, and therefore I don't think the story says anything about life. The story surprises and it shocks, like Poe's "The Fall of the House of Usher." Maybe it even shows "the pointless violence and general inhumanity" in the lives of Jackson's neighbors, but does it reflect the lives of her readers? Do apparently normal, decent people routinely engage in barbaric behavior? I'm not like these people, and I doubt that Jackson and her neighbors were like them either. "The Lottery" is a cleverly plotted story, but the more you look at it, and the more you admire the skillful foreshadowing, the more it seems to be a clever trick, and the less it seems to be related to life.

Works Cited

Jackson, Shirley. "The Lottery." *An Introduction to Literature.*
    Ed. Sylvan Barnet, William Burto, and William E. Cain. 16th ed.
    New York: Longman, 2011. 431–38. Print.
Oppenheimer, Judy. *Private Demons: The Life of Shirley Jackson.*
    New York: Putnam's, 1988. Print.

Sample Essay with Documentation

Jean Lee

Professor McCabe

English 102

18 June 2010

Do the Pink Ribbons in Hawthorne's

"Young Goodman Brown" Have a Meaning?

In the first six paragraphs of "Young Goodman Brown," Nathaniel Hawthorne mentions three times that Faith, Brown's wife, wears a cap with pink ribbons (154). The pink ribbons are mentioned twice more in the story. The first of these later references occurs when Brown is in the forest. Having recognized Faith's voice, Brown gazes heavenward, calls to her, sees something fluttering down, seizes it, and finds that it is a "pink ribbon" (159). "My Faith is gone!" he immediately calls out. "There is no good on earth; and sin is but a name. Come devil! for to thee the world is given" (159). The next (and final) reference to the pink ribbons occurs near the end of the story. When he enters Salem village on "the next morning," Brown "spied the head of Faith, with the pink ribbons" (161), not surprising since he now sees the townspeople in their usual dress and activities.

No one can doubt that Brown's wife, named Faith, symbolizes Brown's religious faith, but many scholars have expressed some doubt about the meaning of her pink ribbons. More precisely, scholars have usually expressed doubt about someone else's interpretation of the ribbons, and then confidently offered their own. One of the first persons to comment on the pink ribbons suggested that Hawthorne himself made a mistake in giving them so much emphasis in the scene in the forest. In 1941 F. O. Matthiessen, in *American Renaissance*, quoted approximately a full page of the story, beginning with the paragraph that starts "Aloft in the air" and ending with the paragraph that begins "'My Faith is gone!' cried he, after one stupefied moment." Matthiessen praised the scene but offered one objection:

> As long as what Brown saw is left wholly in the realm of
> hallucination, Hawthorne's created illusion is compelling.
> . . . Only the literal insistence on that damaging pink

ribbon obtrudes the labels of a confining allegory and short-
circuits the range of association. (284)

Matthiessen does not explain why he finds the ribbon more
"literal" than, say, the "blue arch [of the sky] and the stars brightening
in it" or the cloud that "hurried across the zenith and hid the
brightening stars" (159). After all, Brown does not emerge from the
forest carrying this ribbon, and the next morning compare it with the
ribbons in Faith's cap. If he did, we could, like Matthiessen, complain
about the author's "literal insistence on that damaging pink ribbon," but
as Edward Wagenknecht has pointed out, the ribbon that flutters from
the sky is no more real than anything else that Brown sees in the forest
(61). If the devil can conjure up images of Brown's townspeople, surely
he can also conjure up an image of a ribbon.

A few years after Matthiessen expressed reservations about the
ribbon, Mark Van Doren quoted the passage about Brown's seizing
the ribbon after it catches on the branch of a tree, and then
commented:

> Few things in fiction are more startling, or more important,
> than this pink ribbon. Is it there, or is it only dreamed? If
> it is there, what explanation can there be save the one
> young Brown accepts? The Devil exists, and Faith has
> become one of his converts. All three answers come at once,
> in a texture of fact and implication which Hawthorne has
> woven as closely as life is woven. The ribbon may not be
> there, but in that case this is no ordinary dream, no
> nightmare. . . . which will be gone tomorrow. For Brown is
> changed. He thinks there is no good on earth, "and sin is
> but a name." (78)

What is especially interesting is Van Doren's clear implication that
it doesn't matter whether Brown seizes a real ribbon or, on the other
hand, only dreams that he does. What matters is that for Brown it is
evidence that his wife is unholy. Probably all readers will agree with Van
Doren that the encounter in the forest, real or dreamed or conjured by
the devil, changes Brown.

There is no such agreement, however, about the significance of
the color of the ribbon. According to E. Arthur Robinson, "Faith's pink
ribbons symbolize passion" (223). Robinson compares the pink ribbon to

"crimson or purple" symbols of "woman's physical nature" in other stories by Hawthorne, particularly Georgiana's flaw in "The Birthmark" and Beatrice's poisonous plant in "Rappaccini's Daughter" (224). But the connection with Goodman Brown's faith is unclear. A pink ribbon worn by Faith, if clarified by other details in the story, might serve to tell a reader what to make out of this woman—for instance, that she *really* is highly sexual, or that this faith *really* is "faith in the flesh," or some such thing—but Robinson does not offer these arguments, and the text does nothing to support them with additional details. Robinson's conclusion is that Brown comes to realize that "his father was a man like himself and his mother a woman like Faith" and that Brown glumly accepts sensuality in his wife's nature as well as in his own (222).

Robinson was not the first to argue that the pink ribbon implied passion. In 1957, six years before Robinson published his essay, Roy R. Male saw the pink ribbons as one element in "a fiery orgy of lust" (77). But given that pink suggests, if anything, innocent little baby girls, why conclude that here it suggests "lust" or even "passion"? If one wants to argue that Faith pretends to be sweet and innocent but is not, one would argue that she is hypocritical, and might even argue that the ribbons symbolize hypocrisy disguised as innocence, but there is no evidence that the ribbons symbolize sexual passion. Further, if they do symbolize Brown's wife's sexual passion, what is their connection with Brown? What do they tell us about Brown's religious faith? In the forest, he takes the pink ribbon as evidence that his wife is of the devil's party, and he therefore announces that he has lost his faith, but if the pink color is to suggest passion, Brown's loss of faith would be a loss of belief in passion—an interpretation that makes no sense in the story.

Another school of thought argues that the pink symbolizes not lust but youthful femininity, and by extension, the weakness, superficiality, or frivolity of Brown's religious beliefs. Thomas E. Connolly argues that "the ribbons seem to be symbolic of [Brown's] initial illusion . . . that his faith will lead him to heaven. The pink ribbons on a Puritan lady's cap, signs of youth, joy, and happiness, are actually entirely out of keeping with the severity of the rest of her dress . . ." (374). James W. Mathews offers a roughly similar view, arguing that "the insubstantiality of Brown's religious faith manifests itself in the pink ribbons of his wife's cap; their texture is aery and their color the pastel of infancy" (74).

Paul J. Hurley, though without commenting explicitly on the color of the ribbons, belongs to the same school:

> Goodman Brown . . . intends to get to heaven by clinging to Faith's skirts. . . . The ribbons, with their suggestions of the frivolous and ornamental, represent the ritualistic trappings of religious observance. Goodman Brown, it seems, has placed his faith and his hopes of salvation in the formal observances of religious worship rather than in the purity of his own heart and soul. (416)

Not all recent critics, of course, accept the view that the ribbons are a sign of the superficiality of Brown's faith. Edward Wagenknecht suggests that the arguments of Mathews and Hurley would be more convincing if Brown, rather than his wife, wore a ribbon (62). Against Wagenknecht's view, however, one might argue that allegory works in a different way. If in this allegory Faith stands for Brown's religious faith, then what is said about Faith—for instance what is said about her clothing—is understood to be said about Brown himself.

It seems to be a mistake to insist that the color of the ribbons is symbolic of lust, feminine passion, or insubstantial faith. None of these interpretations is traditional and therefore immediately plausible even without additional supporting detail. And no such additional detail is offered in the story to make them plausible. For instance, none of Faith's pious (or apparently pious) neighbors object to the ribbons, nor does Brown find the ribbons out of keeping with Puritan dress. Similarly, the alleged association of pink with superficiality is not traditional, and Hawthorne does not establish it by giving related details.

What, then, can we make of the ribbons? Looking at the unconvincing allegorical interpretations, perhaps the first thing to say is that we should not try to make too much of these ribbons. Perhaps the second thing to say is that the early references to the ribbons do not serve to characterize Faith as lustful, superficial, or whatever (and certainly not to characterize Brown's religious faith as marked by any of these traits) but do serve to identify Faith as a specific person—the woman who wears pink ribbons in her cap. In the forest, then, when the ribbon drifts down, Brown cannot doubt that his wife is present, is a participant in the wicked assembly. (Of course Brown may be deceived; perhaps he has dreamed the episode, or perhaps he has been duped by a show conjured up by the devil, but that's another issue.) Convinced that even Faith is a worshipper of evil, Brown loses his faith not so much in God as in his fellow creatures. "Young Goodman Brown" of course has allegorical elements, but there is no reason to insist that every detail, down to the color of the ribbons, is allegorical. Nothing is gained by insisting that the pink ribbons "mean" something. Their function is to convince Brown that his wife is in the forest, and that is enough for some ribbons to do.

On the other hand, we know that Hawthorne was a careful writer, and that in his novels and stories he is aware of the significance of details of appearance and clothing. Perhaps in "Young Goodman Brown" it is not that the pink ribbons mean one thing in particular, but, instead, that Hawthorne intends their meaning to be ambiguous. As James C. Keil has noted, the first description of Faith, with "the pink ribbons of her cap" playing in the wind, can suggest that she is either "modest or immodest," and this ambiguity, he adds, recurs "throughout the story" (37–38). If we accept Keil's interpretation, we may better understand the nature of Brown's anguish and sorrow. He becomes unsure of who Faith is—and whether she is faithful to God and to him or not. Thus the ambiguity of the pink ribbons is connected to the uncertainty that perplexes and agonizes Brown and drives him to madness. The pink ribbons do not have a single meaning, but they are nonetheless meaningful.

Lee 6

Works Cited

Connolly, Thomas E. "Hawthorne's 'Young Goodman Brown': An Attack on Puritanic Calvinism." *American Literature* 28 (1956): 370–75. Print.

Hawthorne, Nathaniel. "Young Goodman Brown." *An Introduction to Literature.* Ed. Sylvan Barnet, William Burto, and William E. Cain. 16th ed. New York: Longman, 2011. 154–63. Print.

Hurley, Paul J. "Young Goodman Brown's 'Heart of Darkness.'" *American Literature* 37 (1966): 410–19. Print.

Keil, James C. "Hawthorne's 'Young Goodman Brown': Early Nineteenth-Century and Puritan Constructions of Gender." *New England Quarterly* 69:1 (March 1996): 33–55. Print.

Male, Roy R. *Hawthorne's Tragic Vision.* Austin: U of Texas P, 1957. Print.

Mathews, James W. "Antinomianism in 'Young Goodman Brown.'" *Studies in Short Fiction* 3 (1965): 73–75. Print.

Matthiessen, F. O. *American Renaissance: Art and Expression in the Age of Emerson and Whitman.* New York: Oxford UP, 1941. Print.

Robinson, E. Arthur. "The Vision of Goodman Brown: A Source and Interpretation." *American Literature* 35 (1963): 218–25. Print.

Van Doren, Mark. *Nathaniel Hawthorne.* New York: William Sloane, 1948. Print.

Wagenknecht, Edward. *Nathaniel Hawthorne: The Man, His Tales and Romances.* New York: Continuum, 1989. Print.

14

Two Fiction Writers in Depth: Flannery O'Connor and Tobias Wolff

We read stories by authors we are unfamiliar with, just as we try new foods or play new games or listen to the music of new groups, because we want to extend our experience. But we also sometimes stay with the familiar—for pretty much the same reason, oddly. We want, so to speak, to taste more fully, to experience not something utterly unfamiliar but a variation on a favorite theme. Having read, say, one story by Poe or by Alice Walker, we want to read another, and another, because we like the sort of thing that this author does, and we find that with each succeeding story we get deeper into an interesting mind describing experiences that interest us.

We believe you'll find that each story by Flannery O'Connor and by Tobias Wolff takes on a richer significance when thought of alongside other stories and comments by the same writer.

Flannery O'Connor: Two Stories and Comments About Writing

Flannery O'Connor (1925-1964)—her first name was Mary but she did not use it—was born in Savannah, Georgia, but spent most of her life in Milledgeville, Georgia, where her family moved when she was twelve. She was educated in parochial schools and at the local college and then went to the Iowa Writers' Workshop, where she earned an MFA in 1946. For a few months she lived at a writers' colony in Saratoga Springs, New York, and then for a few weeks she lived in New York City, but most of her life was spent back in Milledgeville, where she wrote stories, novels, essays (posthumously published as Mystery and Manners *in 1969), and letters (posthumously published under the title* The Habit of Being *in 1979).*

In 1951, when she was 25, Flannery O'Connor discovered that she was a victim of lupus erythematosus, an incurable autoimmune disease that had crippled and then killed her father ten years before. She died at the age of thirty-nine. O'Connor faced her illness with stoic courage, Christian fortitude—and tough humor. Here is a glimpse, from one of her letters, of how she dealt with those who pitied her:

> *An old lady got on the elevator behind me and as soon as I turned around she fixed me with a moist gleaming eye and said in a loud voice, "Bless you, darling!" I felt exactly like The Misfit [in "A Good Man Is Hard to Find"] and I gave her a weakly lethal look, whereupon greatly encouraged she grabbed my arm and whispered (very loud) in my ear, "Remember what they said to John at the gate, darling!" It was not my floor but I got off and I suppose the old lady was astounded at how quick I could get away on crutches. I have a one-legged friend and I asked her what they said to John at the gate. She said she reckoned they said, "The lame shall enter first." This may be because the lame will be able to knock everybody else aside with their crutches.*

A devout Catholic, O'Connor forthrightly summarized the relation between her belief and her writing:

> *I see from the standpoint of Christian orthodoxy. This means that for me the meaning of life is centered in our Redemption by Christ and what I see in the world I see in its relation to that.*

A Good Man Is Hard to Find [1953]

The grandmother didn't want to go to Florida. She wanted to visit some of her connections in east Tennessee and she was seizing at every chance to change Bailey's mind. Bailey was the son she lived with, her only boy. He was sitting on the edge of his chair at the table, bent over the orange sports section of the *Journal.* "Now look here, Bailey," she said, "see here, read this," and she stood with one hand on her thin hip and the other rattling the newspaper at his bald head. "Here this fellow that calls himself The Misfit is aloose from the Federal Pen and headed toward Florida and you read here what it says he did to these people. Just you read it. I wouldn't take my children in any direction with a criminal like that aloose in it. I couldn't answer to my conscience if I did."

Bailey didn't look up from his reading so she wheeled around then and faced the children's mother, a young woman in slacks, whose face was as broad and innocent as a cabbage and was tied around with a green headkerchief that had two points on the top like rabbit's ears. She was sitting on the sofa, feeding the baby his apricots out of a jar. "The children have been to Florida before," the old lady said. "You all ought to take them somewhere else for a change so they would see different parts of the world and be broad. They never have been to east Tennessee."

The children's mother didn't seem to hear her but the eight-year-old boy, John Wesley, a stocky child with glasses, said, "If you don't want to go to Florida, why dontcha stay at home?" He and the little girl, June Star, were reading the funny papers on the floor.

"She wouldn't stay at home to be queen for a day," June Star said without raising her yellow head.

5   "Yes and what would you do if this fellow, The Misfit, caught you?" the grandmother asked.

"I'd smack his face," John Wesley said.

"She wouldn't stay at home for a million bucks," June Star said. "Afraid she'd miss something. She has to go everywhere we go."

"All right, Miss," the grandmother said. "Just remember that the next time you want me to curl your hair."

June Star said her hair was naturally curly.

10   The next morning the grandmother was the first one in the car, ready to go. She had her big black valise that looked like the head of a hippopotamus in one corner, and underneath it she was hiding a basket with Pitty Sing, the cat, in it. She didn't intend for the cat to be left alone in the house for three days because he would miss her too much and she was afraid he might brush against one of the gas burners and accidentally asphyxiate himself. Her son, Bailey, didn't like to arrive at a motel with a cat.

She sat in the middle of the back seat with John Wesley and June Star on either side of her. Bailey and the children's mother and the baby sat in front and they left Atlanta at eight forty-five with the mileage on the car at 55890. The grandmother wrote this down because she thought it would be interesting to say how many miles they had been when they got back. It took them twenty minutes to reach the outskirts of the city.

The old lady settled herself comfortably, removing her white cotton gloves and putting them up with her purse on the shelf in front of the back window. The children's mother still had on slacks and still had her head tied up in a green kerchief, but the grandmother had on a navy blue straw sailor hat with a bunch of white violets on the brim and a navy blue dress with a small white dot in the print. Her collars and cuffs were white organdy trimmed with lace and at her neckline she had pinned a purple spray of cloth violets containing a sachet. In case of an accident, anyone seeing her dead on the highway would know at once that she was a lady.

She said she thought it was going to be a good day for driving, neither too hot nor too cold, and she cautioned Bailey that the speed limit was fifty-five miles an hour and that the patrolmen hid themselves behind bill-boards and small clumps of trees and sped out after you before you had a chance to slow down. She pointed out interesting details of the scenery: Stone Mountain; the blue granite that in some places came up to both sides of the highway; the brilliant red clay banks slightly streaked with purple; and the various crops that made rows of green lace-work on the ground. The trees were full of silver-white sunlight and the meanest of them sparkled. The children were reading comic magazines and their mother had gone back to sleep.

"Let's go through Georgia fast so we won't have to look at it much," John Wesley said.

15   "If I were a little boy," said the grandmother, "I wouldn't talk about my native state that way. Tennessee has the mountains and Georgia has the hills."

"Tennessee is just a hillbilly dumping ground," John Wesley said, "and Georgia is a lousy state too."

"You said it," June Star said.

2

the grandmother

~~Of course she~~ was the first one ready to load up the next morning at six o'clock. She had Baby Brother's bucking bronco ~~that~~ and ~~hxxxxxixx~~ what she called her "*grip*" and Pitty Sing, the cat, ~~xx xxx~~ packed in the car before Boatwrite had a chance to ~~gxtxanxthingxzxxexinx~~ *get the* ~~come out of the door with the~~ rest of the luggage. out of the hall. They got off at seven-thirty, Boatwrite and ~~Baby~~ the children's mother in the front and Granny, John Wesley, Baby Brother, Little Sister Mary Ann, Pitty Sing, and the bucking bronco in the back.

"Why the hell did you bring that goddam rocking horse?" Boatwrite asked because as soon as ~~the car began to move~~, *they were out of the city on the smooth highway*, Baby Brother began to squall to get on the bucking bronco. "He can't get on that thing in this car and that's final," his father who was a stern man said.

"Can we open the lunch now?" Little Sister ~~Maxyxxxx~~ asked. "It'll shut Baby Brother up. Mamma, can we open up the lunch?"

"No," their grandmother said. *It's only eight-thirty*

Their mother was ~~xxixx~~ reading SCREEN MOTHERS AND THEIR CHILDREN. "Yeah, sure," she said. without looking up. She was all dressed up today. She had on a purple silk dress and a hat and ~~gxxxxxxxxxx~~ a choker of pink beads and a new *harried* pocket book, and high heel pumps.

"Let's go through Georgia quick so we won't have to look at it much," John Wesley said. ~~"I seen enough of it by now."~~

"You should see Tennessee," his grandmother said. "Now there is a *beautiful* state."

"Like hell," John Wesley said. "That's just a hillbilly dumping ground."

"He," his mother said, *now*, and nudged Boatwrite. "Didjer hear that?" ~~She was~~ *from Arkansas,*

They ate their lunch and got along fine ~~after that~~ for a while until Pitty Sing who had been asleep jumped into the front of the car and caused Boatwrite to swerve to the right into a ditch. Pitty Sing was a large grey-striped cat with a yellow hind leg and a ~~x~~ *big* ~~large~~ soiled white face. Granny thought that she *the truth was* was the only person in the world that he really loved but he had never ~~really~~ looked ~~axzfaxzapxzxzxxxzxxx~~ ~~xxx~~ farther *up* than her middle and he didn't even like other cats. He jumped snarling into the front seat and Boatwrite's shoulders

Draft page from Flannery O'Connor's "A Good Man Is Hard to Find."

"In my time," said the grandmother, folding her thin veined fingers, "children were more respectful of their native states and their parents and everything else. People did right then. Oh look at the cute little pickaninny!" she said and pointed to a Negro child standing in the door of a shack. "Wouldn't that make a picture, now?" she asked and they all turned and looked at the little Negro out of the back window. He waved.

"He didn't have any britches on," June Star said.

20 "He probably didn't have any," the grandmother explained. "Little niggers in the country don't have things like we do. If I could paint, I'd paint that picture," she said.

The children exchanged comic books.

The grandmother offered to hold the baby and the children's mother passed him over the front seat to her. She set him on her knee and bounced him and told him about the things they were passing. She rolled her eyes and screwed up her mouth and stuck her leathery thin face into his smooth bland one. Occasionally he gave her a faraway smile. They passed a large cotton field with five or six graves fenced in the middle of it, like a small island. "Look at the graveyard!" the grandmother said, pointing it out. "That was the old family burying ground. That belonged to the plantation."

"Where's the plantation?" John Wesley asked.

"Gone With the Wind," said the grandmother. "Ha. Ha."

25   When the children finished all the comic books they had brought, they opened the lunch and ate it. The grandmother ate a peanut butter sandwich and an olive and would not let the children throw the box and the paper napkins out the window. When there was nothing else to do they played a game by choosing a cloud and making the other two guess what shape it suggested. John Wesley took one the shape of a cow and June Star guessed a cow and John Wesley said, no, an automobile, and June Star said he didn't play fair, and they began to slap each other over the grandmother.

The grandmother said she would tell them a story if they would keep quiet. When she told a story, she rolled her eyes and waved her head and was very dramatic. She said once when she was a maiden lady she had been courted by a Mr. Edgar Atkins Teagarden from Jasper, Georgia. She said he was a very good-looking man and a gentleman and that he brought her a watermelon every Saturday afternoon with his initials cut in it, E. A. T. Well, one Saturday, she said, Mr. Teagarden brought the watermelon and there was nobody at home and he left it on the front porch and returned in his buggy to Jasper, but she never got the watermelon, she said, because a nigger boy ate it when he saw the initials, E. A. T.! This story tickled John Wesley's funny bone and he giggled and giggled but June Star didn't think it was any good. She said she wouldn't marry a man that just brought her a watermelon on Saturday. The grandmother said she would have done well to marry Mr. Teagarden because he was a gentleman and had bought Coca-Cola stock when it first came out and that he had died only a few years ago, a very wealthy man.

They stopped at The Tower for barbecued sandwiches. The Tower was a part stucco and part wood filling station and dance hall set in a clearing outside of Timothy. A fat man named Red Sammy Butts ran it and there were signs stuck here and there on the building and for miles up and down the highway saying, TRY RED SAMMY'S FAMOUS BARBECUE. NONE LIKE FAMOUS RED SAMMY'S! RED SAM! THE FAT BOY WITH THE HAPPY LAUGH. A VETERAN! RED SAMMY'S YOUR MAN!

Red Sammy was lying on the bare ground outside The Tower with his head under a truck while a gray monkey about a foot high, chained to a small chinaberry tree, chattered nearby. The monkey sprang back into the tree and got on the highest limb as soon as he saw the children jump out of the car and run toward him.

Inside, The Tower was a long dark room with a counter at one end and tables at the other and dancing space in the middle. They all sat down at a board table next to the nickelodeon and Red Sam's wife, a tall burnt-brown woman with hair and eyes lighter than her skin, came and took their order. The children's mother put a dime in the machine and played "The Tennessee

Waltz," and the grandmother said that tune always made her want to dance. She asked Bailey if he would like to dance but he only glared at her. He didn't have a naturally sunny disposition like she did and trips made him nervous. The grandmother's brown eyes were very bright. She swayed her head from side to side and pretended she was dancing in her chair. June Star said play something she could tap to so the children's mother put in another dime and played a fast number and June Star stepped out onto the dance floor and did her tap routine.

30   "Ain't she cute?" Red Sam's wife said, leaning over the counter. "Would you like to come be my little girl?"

"No, I certainly wouldn't," June Star said. "I wouldn't live in a broken-down place like this for a million bucks!" and she ran back to the table.

"Ain't she cute?" the woman repeated, stretching her mouth politely.

"Arn't you ashamed?" hissed the grandmother.

Red Sam came in and told his wife to quit lounging on the counter and hurry with these people's order. His khaki trousers reached just to his hip bones and his stomach hung over them like a sack of meal swaying under his shirt. He came over and sat down at a table nearby and let out a combination sigh and yodel. "You can't win," he said. "You can't win," and he wiped his sweating red face off with a gray handkerchief. "These days you don't know who to trust," he said. "Ain't that the truth?"

35   "People are certainly not nice like they used to be," said the grandmother.

"Two fellers come in here last week," Red Sammy said, "driving a Chrysler. It was a old beat-up car but it was a good one and these boys looked all right to me. Said they worked at the mill and you know I let them fellers charge the gas they bought? Now why did I do that?"

"Because you're a good man!" the grandmother said at once.

"Yes'm, I suppose so," Red Sam said as if he were struck with this answer.

His wife brought the orders, carrying the five plates all at once without a tray, two in each hand and one balanced on her arm. "It isn't a soul in this green world of God's that you can trust," she said. "And I don't count nobody out of that, not nobody," she repeated, looking at Red Sammy.

40   "Did you read about that criminal, The Misfit, that's escaped?" asked the grandmother.

"I wouldn't be a bit surprised if he didn't attact this place right here," said the woman. "If he hears about it being here, I wouldn't be none surprised to see him. If he hears it's two cent in the cash register, I wouldn't be a tall surprised if he . . ."

"That'll do," Red Sam said. "Go bring these people their Co'-Colas," and the woman went off to get the rest of the order.

"A good man is hard to find," Red Sammy said. "Everything is getting terrible. I remember the day you could go off and leave your screen door unlatched. Not no more."

He and the grandmother discussed better times. The old lady said that in her opinion Europe was entirely to blame for the way things were now. She said the way Europe acted you would think we were made of money and Red Sam said it was no use talking about it, she was exactly right. The children ran outside into the white sunlight and looked at the monkey in the lacy chinaberry tree. He was busy catching fleas on himself and biting each one carefully between his teeth as if it were a delicacy.

45   They drove off again into the hot afternoon. The grandmother took cat naps and woke up every few minutes with her own snoring. Outside of Toombsboro she woke up and recalled an old plantation that she had visited in this neighborhood once when she was a young lady. She said the house had six white columns across the front and that there was an avenue of oaks leading up to it and two little wooden trellis arbors on either side in front where you sat down with your suitor after a stroll in the garden. She recalled exactly which road to turn off to get to it. She knew that Bailey would not be willing to lose any time looking at an old house, but the more she talked about it, the more she wanted to see it once again and find out if the little twin arbors were still standing. "There was a secret panel in this house," she said craftily, not telling the truth but wishing that she were, "and the story went that all the family silver was hidden in it when Sherman came through but it was never found . . ."

"Hey!" John Wesley said. "Let's go see it! We'll find it! We'll poke all the woodwork and find it! Who lives there? Where do you turn off at? Hey Pop, can't we turn off there?"

"We never have seen a house with a secret panel!" June Star shrieked. "Let's go to the house with the secret panel! Hey Pop, can't we go see the house with the secret panel!"

"It's not far from here, I know," the grandmother said. "It wouldn't take over twenty minutes."

Bailey was looking straight ahead. His jaw was as rigid as a horseshoe. "No," he said.

50   The children began to yell and scream that they wanted to see the house with the secret panel. John Wesley kicked the back of the front seat and June Star hung over her mother's shoulder and whined desperately into her ear that they never had any fun even on their vacation, that they could never do what THEY wanted to do. The baby began to scream and John Wesley kicked the back of the seat so hard that his father could feel the blows in his kidney.

"All right!" he shouted and drew the car to a stop at the side of the road. "Will you all shut up? Will you all just shut up for one second? If you don't shut up, we won't go anywhere."

"It would be very educational for them," the grandmother murmured.

"All right," Bailey said, "but get this: this is the only time we're going to stop for anything like this: this is the one and only time."

"The dirt road that you have to turn down is about a mile back," the grandmother directed. "I marked it when we passed."

55   "A dirt road," Bailey groaned.

After they had turned around and were headed toward the dirt road, the grandmother recalled other points about the house, the beautiful glass over the front doorway and the candle-lamp in the hall. John Wesley said that the secret panel was probably in the fireplace.

"You can't go inside this house," Bailey said. "You don't know who lives there."

"While you all talk to the people in front, I'll run around behind and get in a window," John Wesley suggested.

"We'll all stay in the car," his mother said.

60   They turned onto the dirt road and the car raced roughly along in a swirl of pink dust. The grandmother recalled the times when there were no paved roads and thirty miles was a day's journey. The dirt road was hilly and

there were sudden washes in it and sharp curves on dangerous embankments. All at once they would be on a hill, looking down over the blue tops of trees for miles around, then the next minute, they would be in a red depression with the dust-coated trees looking down on them.

"This place had better turn up in a minute," Bailey said, "or I'm going to turn around."

The road looked as if no one had traveled on it in months.

"It's not much farther," the grandmother said and just as she said it, a horrible thought came to her. The thought was so embarrassing that she turned red in the face and her eyes dilated and her feet jumped up, upsetting her valise in the corner. The instant the valise moved, the newspaper top she had over the basket under it rose with a snarl and Pitty Sing, the cat, sprang onto Bailey's shoulder.

The children were thrown to the floor and their mother, clutching the baby, was thrown out the door onto the ground; the old lady was thrown into the front seat. The car turned over once and landed right-side-up in a gulch off the side of the road. Bailey remained in the driver's seat with the cat—gray-striped with a broad white face and an orange nose—clinging to his neck like a caterpillar.

65   As soon as the children saw they could move their arms and legs, they scrambled out of the car, shouting, "We've had an ACCIDENT!" The grandmother was curled up under the dashboard, hoping she was injured so that Bailey's wrath would not come down on her all at once. The horrible thought she had had before the accident was that the house she had remembered so vividly was not in Georgia but in Tennessee.

Bailey removed the cat from his neck with both hands and flung it out the window against the side of a pine tree. Then he got out of the car and started looking for the children's mother. She was sitting against the side of the red gutted ditch, holding the screaming baby, but she only had a cut down her face and a broken shoulder. "We've had an ACCIDENT!" the children screamed in a frenzy of delight.

"But nobody's killed," June Star said with disappointment as the grandmother limped out of the car, her hat still pinned to her head but the broken front brim standing up at a jaunty angle and the violet spray hanging off the side. They all sat down in the ditch, except the children, to recover from the shock. They were all shaking.

"Maybe a car will come along," said the children's mother hoarsely.

"I believe I have injured an organ," said the grandmother, pressing her side, but no one answered her. Bailey's teeth were clattering. He had on a yellow sport shirt with bright blue parrots designed in it and his face was as yellow as the shirt. The grandmother decided that she would not mention that the house was in Tennessee.

70   The road was about ten feet above and they could see only the tops of the trees on the other side of it. Behind the ditch they were sitting in there were more woods, tall and dark and deep. In a few minutes they saw a car some distance away on top of a hill, coming slowly as if the occupants were watching them. The grandmother stood up and waved both arms dramatically to attract their attention. The car continued to come on slowly, disappeared around a bend and appeared again, moving even slower, on top of the hill they had gone over. It was a big black battered hearse-like automobile. There were three men in it.

It came to a stop just over them and for some minutes, the driver looked down with a steady expressionless gaze to where they were sitting, and didn't speak. Then he turned his head and muttered something to the other two and they got out. One was a fat boy in black trousers and a red sweat shirt with a silver stallion embossed on the front of it. He moved around on the right side of them and stood staring, his mouth partly open in a kind of loose grin. The other had on khaki pants and a blue striped coat and a gray hat pulled down very low, hiding most of his face. He came around slowly on the left side. Neither spoke.

The driver got out of the car and stood by the side of it, looking down at them. He was an older man than the other two. His hair was just beginning to gray and he wore silver-rimmed spectacles that gave him a scholarly look. He had a long creased face and didn't have on any shirt or undershirt. He had on blue jeans that were too tight for him and was holding a black hat and a gun. The two boys also had guns.

"We've had an ACCIDENT!" the children screamed.

The grandmother had the peculiar feeling that the bespectacled man was someone she knew. His face was as familiar to her as if she had known him all her life but she could not recall who he was. He moved away from the car and began to come down the embankment, placing his feet carefully so that he wouldn't slip. He had on tan and white shoes and no socks, and his ankles were red and thin. "Good afternoon," he said. "I see you all had you a little spill."

75 "We turned over twice!" said the grandmother.

"Oncet," he corrected. "We seen it happen. Try their car and see will it run, Hiram," he said quietly to the boy with the gray hat.

"What you got that gun for?" John Wesley asked. "Whatcha gonna do with that gun?"

"Lady," the man said to the children's mother, "would you mind calling them children to sit down by you? Children make me nervous. I want all you all to sit down right together there where you're at."

"What are you telling US what to do for?" June Star asked.

80 Behind them the line of woods gaped like a dark open mouth. "Come here," said their mother.

"Look here now," Bailey began suddenly, "we're in a predicament! We're in . . ."

The grandmother shrieked. She scrambled to her feet and stood staring. "You're The Misfit!" she said. "I recognized you at once!"

"Yes'm," the man said, smiling slightly as if he were pleased in spite of himself to be known, "but it would have been better for all of you, lady, if you hadn't of reckernized me."

Bailey turned his head sharply and said something to his mother that shocked even the children. The old lady began to cry and The Misfit reddened.

85 "Lady," he said, "don't you get upset. Sometimes a man says things he don't mean. I don't reckon he meant to talk to you thataway."

"You wouldn't shoot a lady, would you?" the grandmother said and removed a clean handkerchief from her cuff and began to slap at her eyes with it.

The Misfit pointed the toe of his shoe into the ground and made a little hole and then covered it up again. "I would hate to have to," he said.

"Listen," the grandmother almost screamed, "I know you're a good man. You don't look a bit like you have common blood. I know you must come from nice people!"

"Yes mam," he said, "finest people in the world." When he smiled he showed a row of strong white teeth. "God never made a finer woman than my mother and my daddy's heart was pure gold," he said. The boy with the red sweat shirt had come around behind them and was standing with his gun at his hip. The Misfit squatted down on the ground. "Watch them children, Bobby Lee," he said. "You know they make me nervous." He looked at the six of them huddled together in front of him and he seemed to be embarrassed as if he couldn't think of anything to say. "Ain't a cloud in the sky," he remarked, looking up at it. "Don't see no sun but don't see no cloud neither."

90   "Yes, it's a beautiful day," said the grandmother. "Listen," she said, "you shouldn't call yourself The Misfit because I know you're a good man at heart. I can just look at you and tell."

"Hush!" Bailey yelled. "Hush! Everybody shut up and let me handle this!" He was squatting in the position of a runner about to sprint forward but he didn't move.

"I pre-chate that, lady," The Misfit said and drew a little circle in the ground with the butt of his gun.

"It'll take a half a hour to fix this here car," Hiram called, looking over the raised hood of it.

"Well, first you and Bobby Lee get him and that little boy to step over yonder with you," The Misfit said, pointing to Bailey and John Wesley. "The boys want to ast you something," he said to Bailey. "Would you mind stepping back in them woods there with them?"

95   "Listen," Bailey began, "we're in a terrible predicament! Nobody realizes what this is," and his voice cracked. His eyes were as blue and intense as the parrots in his shirt and he remained perfectly still.

The grandmother reached up to adjust her hat brim as if she were going to the woods with him but it came off in her hand. She stood staring at it and after a second she let it fall on the ground. Hiram pulled Bailey up by the arm as if he were assisting an old man. John Wesley caught hold of his father's hand and Bobby Lee followed. They went off toward the woods and just as they reached the dark edge, Bailey turned and supporting himself against a gray naked pine trunk, he shouted, "I'll be back in a minute, Mamma, wait on me!"

"Come back this instant!" his mother shrilled but they all disappeared into the woods.

"Bailey Boy!" the grandmother called in a tragic voice but she found she was looking at The Misfit squatting on the ground in front of her. "I just know you're a good man," she said desperately. "You're not a bit common!"

"Nome, I ain't a good man," The Misfit said after a second as if he had considered her statement carefully, "but I ain't the worst in the world neither. My daddy said I was a different breed of dog from my brothers and sisters. 'You know,' Daddy said, 'It's some that can live their whole life out without asking about it and it's others has to know why it is, and this boy is one of the latters. He's going to be into everything!'" He put on his black hat and looked up suddenly and then away deep into the woods as if he were embarrassed again. "I'm sorry I don't have on a shirt before you ladies," he said, hunching his shoulders slightly. "We buried our clothes that we had on when we escaped and we're just making do until we can get better. We borrowed these from some folks we met," he explained.

100   "That's perfectly all right," the grandmother said. "Maybe Bailey has an extra shirt in his suitcase."

"I'll look and see terrectly," The Misfit said.

"Where are they taking him?" the children's mother screamed.

"Daddy was a card himself," The Misfit said. "You couldn't put anything over on him. He never got in trouble with the Authorities though. Just had the knack of handling them."

"You could be honest too if you'd only try," said the grandmother. "Think how wonderful it would be to settle down and live a comfortable life and not have to think about somebody chasing you all the time."

105   The Misfit kept scratching in the ground with the butt of his gun as if he were thinking about it. "Yes'm, somebody is always after you," he murmured.

The grandmother noticed how thin his shoulder blades were just behind his hat because she was standing up looking down on him. "Do you ever pray?" she asked.

He shook his head. All she saw was the black hat wiggle between his shoulder blades. "Nome," he said.

There was a pistol shot from the woods, followed closely by another. Then silence. The old lady's head jerked around. She could hear the wind move through the tree tops like a long satisfied insuck of breath. "Bailey Boy!" she called.

"I was a gospel singer for a while," The Misfit said. "I been most everything. Been in the arm service, both land and sea, at home and abroad, been twict married, been an undertaker, been with the railroads, plowed Mother Earth, been in a tornado, seen a man burnt alive oncet," and he looked up at the children's mother and the little girl who were sitting close together, their faces white and their eyes glassy; "I even seen a woman flogged," he said.

110   "Pray, pray," the grandmother began, "pray, pray . . ."

"I never was a bad boy that I remember of," The Misfit said in an almost dreamy voice, "but somewheres along the line I done something wrong and got sent to the penitentiary. I was buried alive," and he looked up and held her attention to him by a steady stare.

"That's when you should have started to pray," she said. "What did you do to get sent up to the penitentiary that first time?"

"Turn to the right, it was a wall," The Misfit said, looking up again at the cloudless sky. "Turn to the left, it was a wall. Look up it was a ceiling, look down it was a floor. I forget what I done, lady. I set there and set there, trying to remember what it was I done and I ain't recalled it to this day. Oncet in a while, I would think it was coming to me, but it never come."

"Maybe they put you in by mistake," the old lady said vaguely.

115   "Nome," he said. "It wasn't no mistake. They had the papers on me."

"You must have stolen something," she said.

The Misfit sneered slightly. "Nobody had nothing I wanted," he said. "It was a head-doctor at the penitentiary said what I had done was kill my daddy but I known that for a lie. My daddy died in nineteen ought nineteen of the epidemic flu and I never had a thing to do with it. He was buried in the Mount Hopewell Baptist churchyard and you can go there and see for yourself."

"If you would pray," the old lady said, "Jesus would help you."

"That's right," The Misfit said.

120   "Well then, why don't you pray?" she asked trembling with delight suddenly.

"I don't want no hep," he said. "I'm doing all right by myself."

Bobby Lee and Hiram came ambling back from the woods. Bobby Lee was dragging a yellow shirt with bright blue parrots in it.

"Thow me that shirt, Bobby Lee," The Misfit said. The shirt came flying at him and landed on his shoulder and he put it on. The grandmother couldn't name what the shirt reminded her of. "No, lady," The Misfit said while he was buttoning it up, "I found out the crime don't matter. You can do one thing or you can do another, kill a man or take a tire off his car, because sooner or later you're going to forget what it was you done and just be punished for it."

The children's mother had begun to make heaving noises as if she couldn't get her breath. "Lady," he asked, "would you and that little girl like to step off yonder with Bobby Lee and Hiram and join your husband?"

125   "Yes, thank you," the mother said faintly. Her left arm dangled helplessly and she was holding the baby, who had gone to sleep, in the other. "Hep that lady up, Hiram," The Misfit said as she struggled to climb out of the ditch, "and Bobby Lee, you hold onto that little girl's hand."

"I don't want to hold hands with him," June Star said. "He reminds me of a pig."

The fat boy blushed and laughed and caught her by the arm and pulled her off into the woods after Hiram and her mother.

Alone with The Misfit, the grandmother found that she had lost her voice. There was not a cloud in the sky nor any sun. There was nothing around her but woods. She wanted to tell him that he must pray. She opened and closed her mouth several times before anything came out. Finally she found herself saying, "Jesus. Jesus," meaning, Jesus will help you, but the way she was saying it, it sounded as if she might be cursing.

"Yes'm," The Misfit said as if he agreed. "Jesus thown everything off balance. It was the same case with Him as with me except He hadn't committed any crime and they could prove I had committed one because they had the papers on me. Of course," he said, "they never shown me my papers. That's why I sign myself now. I said long ago, you get you a signature and sign everything you do and keep a copy of it. Then you'll know what you done and you can hold up the crime to the punishment and see do they match and in the end you'll have something to prove you ain't been treated right. I call myself The Misfit," he said, "because I can't make what all I done wrong fit what all I gone through in punishment."

130   There was a piercing scream from the woods, followed closely by a pistol report. "Does it seem right to you, lady, that one is punished a heap and another ain't punished at all?"

"Jesus!" the old lady cried. "You've got good blood! I know you wouldn't shoot a lady! I know you come from nice people! Pray! Jesus, you ought not to shoot a lady. I'll give you all the money I've got!"

"Lady," The Misfit said, looking beyond her far into the woods, "there never was a body that give the undertaker a tip."

There were two more pistol reports and the grandmother raised her head like a parched old turkey hen crying for water and called, "Bailey Boy, Bailey Boy!" as if her heart would break.

"Jesus was the only One that ever raised the dead," The Misfit continued, "and He shouldn't have done it. He thown everything off balance. If He did what He said, then it's nothing for you to do but thow away everything and follow Him, and if He didn't, then it's nothing for you to do but enjoy the few minutes you got left the best way you can—by killing somebody or burning down his house or doing some other meanness to him. No pleasure but meanness," he said and his voice had become almost a snarl.

135 "Maybe He didn't raise the dead," the old lady mumbled, not knowing what she was saying and feeling so dizzy that she sank down in the ditch with her legs twisted under her.

"I wasn't there so I can't say He didn't," The Misfit said. "I wisht I had of been there," he said, hitting the ground with his fist. "It ain't right I wasn't there because if I had of been there I would of known. Listen lady," he said in a high voice, "if I had of been there I would of known and I wouldn't be like I am now." His voice seemed about to crack and the grandmother's head cleared for an instant. She saw the man's face twisted close to her own as if he were going to cry and she murmured, "Why you're one of my babies. You're one of my own children!" She reached out and touched him on the shoulder. The Misfit sprang back as if a snake had bitten him and shot her three times through the chest. Then he put his gun down on the ground and took off his glasses and began to clean them.

Hiram and Bobby Lee returned from the woods and stood over the ditch, looking down at the grandmother who half sat and half lay in a puddle of blood with her legs crossed under her like a child's and her face smiling up at the cloudless sky.

Without his glasses, The Misfit's eyes were red-rimmed and pale and defenseless-looking. "Take her off and thow her where you thown the others," he said, picking up the cat that was rubbing itself against his leg.

"She was a talker, wasn't she?" Bobby Lee said, sliding down the ditch with a yodel.

140 "She would of been a good woman," The Misfit said, "if it had been somebody there to shoot her every minute of her life."

"Some fun!" Bobby Lee said.

"Shut up, Bobby Lee," The Misfit said. "It's no real pleasure in life."

YOUR TURN

1. Explain the significance of the title.
2. Interpret and evaluate The Misfit's comment on the grandmother: "She would of been a good woman if it had been somebody there to shoot her every minute of her life."
3. O'Connor reported that once, when she read aloud "A Good Man Is Hard to Find," a member of the audience said that "it was a shame someone with so much talent should look upon life as a horror show." Two questions: What evidence of O'Connor's "talent" do you see in the story, and does the story suggest that O'Connor looked on life as a horror show?
4. What are the values of the members of the family?

5. As we noted earlier, Flannery O'Connor, a Roman Catholic, said, "I see from the standpoint of Christian orthodoxy. This means that for me the meaning of life is centered in our Redemption by Christ and what I see in the world I see in relation to that." In the light of this statement, and drawing on "A Good Man Is Hard to Find," explain what O'Connor saw in the world.

Revelation [1964]

The doctor's waiting room, which was very small, was almost full when the Turpins entered and Mrs. Turpin, who was very large, made it look even smaller by her presence. She stood looming at the head of the magazine table set in the center of it, a living demonstration that the room was inadequate and ridiculous. Her little bright black eyes took in all the patients as she sized up the seating situation. There was one vacant chair and a place on the sofa occupied by a blond child in a dirty blue romper who should have been told to move over and make room for the lady. He was five or six, but Mrs. Turpin saw at once that no one was going to tell him to move over. He was slumped down in the seat, his arms idle at his sides and his eyes idle in his head; his nose ran unchecked.

Mrs. Turpin put a firm hand on Claud's shoulder and said in a voice that included anyone who wanted to listen, "Claud, you sit in that chair there," and gave him a push down into the vacant one. Claud was florid and bald and sturdy, somewhat shorter than Mrs. Turpin, but he sat down as if he were accustomed to doing what she told him to.

Mrs. Turpin remained standing. The only man in the room besides Claud was a lean stringy old fellow with a rusty hand spread out on each knee, whose eyes were closed as if he were asleep or dead or pretending to be so as not to get up and offer her his seat. Her gaze settled agreeably on a well-dressed grey-haired lady whose eyes met hers and whose expression said: if that child belonged to me, he would have some manners and move over—there's plenty of room there for you and him too.

Claud looked up with a sigh and made as if to rise.

5   "Sit down," Mrs. Turpin said. "You know you're not supposed to stand on that leg. He has an ulcer on his leg," she explained.

Claud lifted his foot onto the magazine table and rolled his trouser leg up to reveal a purple swelling on a plump marble-white calf.

"My!" the pleasant lady said. "How did you do that?"

"A cow kicked him," Mrs. Turpin said.

"Goodness!" said the lady.

10   Claud rolled his trouser leg down.

"Maybe the little boy would move over," the lady suggested, but the child did not stir.

"Somebody will be leaving in a minute," Mrs. Turpin said. She could not understand why a doctor—with as much money as they made charging five dollars a day to just stick their head in the hospital door and look at you—couldn't afford a decent-sized waiting room. This one was hardly bigger than a garage. The table was cluttered with limp-looking magazines and at one end of it there was a big green glass ash tray full of cigaret butts and cotton wads with little blood spots on them. If she had had anything to do with the running of the place, that would have been emptied every so often. There were no chairs against the wall at the head of the room. It had a rectangular-shaped panel in it that permitted a view of the office where the nurse came and went and the secretary listened to the radio. A plastic fern in a gold pot sat in the opening and trailed its fronds down almost to the floor. The radio was softly playing gospel music.

Just then the inner door opened and a nurse with the highest stack of yellow hair Mrs. Turpin had ever seen put her face in the crack and called for the next patient. The woman sitting beside Claud grasped the two arms of her chair and hoisted herself up; she pulled her dress free from her legs and lumbered through the door where the nurse had disappeared.

Mrs. Turpin eased into the vacant chair, which held her tight as a corset. "I wish I could reduce," she said, and rolled her eyes and gave a comic sigh.

15   "Oh, *you* aren't fat," the stylish lady said.

"Ooooo I am too," Mrs. Turpin said. "Claud he eats all he wants to and never weighs over one hundred and seventy-five pounds, but me I just look at something good to eat and I gain some weight," and her stomach and shoulders shook with laughter. "You can eat all you want to, can't you, Claud?" she asked, turning to him.

Claud only grinned.

"Well, as long as you have such a good disposition," the stylish lady said, "I don't think it makes a bit of difference what size you are. You just can't beat a good disposition."

Next to her was a fat girl of eighteen or nineteen, scowling into a thick blue book which Mrs. Turpin saw was entitled *Human Development.* The girl raised her head and directed her scowl at Mrs. Turpin as if she did not like her looks. She appeared annoyed that anyone should speak while she tried to read. The poor girl's face was blue with acne and Mrs. Turpin thought how pitiful it was to have a face like that at that age. She gave the girl a friendly smile but the girl only scowled the harder. Mrs. Turpin herself was fat but she had always had good skin, and, though she was forty-seven years old, there was not a wrinkle in her face except around her eyes from laughing too much.

20   Next to the ugly girl was the child, still in exactly the same position, and next to him was a thin leathery old woman in a cotton print dress. She and Claud had three sacks of chicken feed in their pump house that was in the same print. She had seen from the first that the child belonged with the old woman. She could tell by the way they sat—kind of vacant and white-trashy, as if they would sit there until Doomsday if nobody called and told them to get up. And at right angles but next to the well-dressed pleasant lady was a lank-faced woman who was certainly the child's mother. She had on a yellow sweat shirt and wine-colored slacks, both gritty-looking, and the rims of her lips were stained with snuff. Her dirty yellow hair was tied behind with a little piece of red paper ribbon. Worse than niggers any day, Mrs. Turpin thought.

The gospel hymn playing was, "When I looked up and He looked down," and Mrs. Turpin, who knew it, supplied the last line mentally, "And wona these days I know I'll we-eara crown."

Without appearing to, Mrs. Turpin always noticed people's feet. The well-dressed lady had on red and grey suede shoes to match her dress. Mrs. Turpin had on her good black patent leather pumps. The ugly girl had on

Girl Scout shoes and heavy socks. The old woman had on tennis shoes and the white-trashy mother had on what appeared to be bedroom slippers, black straw with gold braid threaded through them—exactly what you would have expected her to have on.

Sometimes at night when she couldn't go to sleep, Mrs. Turpin would occupy herself with the question of who she would have chosen to be if she couldn't have been herself. If Jesus had said to her before he made her, "There's only two places available for you. You can either be a nigger or white-trash," what would she have said? "Please, Jesus, please," she would have said, "just let me wait until there's another place available," and he would have said, "No, you have to go right now and I have only those two places so make up your mind." She would have wiggled and squirmed and begged and pleaded but it would have been no use and finally she would have said, "All right, make me a nigger then—but that don't mean a trashy one." And he would have made her a neat clean respectable Negro woman, herself but black.

Next to the child's mother was a red-headed youngish woman, reading one of the magazines and working a piece of chewing gum, hell for leather, as Claud would say. Mrs. Turpin could not see the woman's feet. She was not white-trash, just common. Sometimes Mrs. Turpin occupied herself at night naming the classes of people. On the bottom of the heap were most colored people, not the kind she would have been if she had been one, but most of them; then next to them—not above, just away from—were the white-trash; then above them were the homeowners, and above them the home-and-land owners, to which she and Claud belonged. Above she and Claud were people with a lot of money and much bigger houses and much more land. But here the complexity of it would begin to bear in on her, for some of the people with a lot of money were common and ought to be below she and Claud and some of the people who had good blood had lost their money and had to rent and then there were colored people who owned their homes and land as well. There was a colored dentist in town who had two red Lincolns and a swimming pool and a farm with registered white-face cattle on it. Usually by the time she had fallen asleep all the classes of people were moiling and roiling around in her head, and she would dream they were all crammed in together in a box car, being ridden off to be put in a gas oven.

25   "That's a beautiful clock," she said and nodded to her right. It was a big wall clock, the face encased in a brass sunburst.

"Yes, it's very pretty," the stylish lady said agreeably. "And right on the dot too," she added, glancing at her watch.

The ugly girl beside her cast an eye upward at the clock, smirked, then looked directly at Mrs. Turpin and smirked again. Then she returned her eyes to her book. She was obviously the lady's daughter because, although they didn't look anything alike as to disposition, they both had the same shape of face and the same blue eyes. On the lady they sparkled pleasantly but in the girl's seared face they appeared alternately to smolder and to blaze.

What if Jesus had said, "All right, you can be white-trash or a nigger or ugly"!

Mrs. Turpin felt an awful pity for the girl, though she thought it was one thing to be ugly and another to act ugly.

30   The woman with the snuff-stained lips turned around in her chair and looked up at the clock. Then she turned back and appeared to look a little to

the side of Mrs. Turpin. There was a cast in one of her eyes. "You want to know wher you can get you one of themther clocks?" she asked in a loud voice.

"No, I already have a nice clock," Mrs. Turpin said. Once somebody like her got a leg in the conversation, she would be all over it.

"You can get you one with green stamps," the woman said. "That's most likely wher he got hisn. Save you up enough, you can get you most anythang. I got me some joo'ry."

Ought to have got you a wash rag and some soap, Mrs. Turpin thought.

"I get contour sheets with mine," the pleasant lady said.

35   The daughter slammed her book shut. She looked straight in front of her, directly through Mrs. Turpin and on through the yellow curtain and the plate glass window which made the wall behind her. The girl's eyes seemed lit all of a sudden with a peculiar light, an unnatural light like night road signs give. Mrs. Turpin turned her head to see if there was anything going on outside that she should see, but she could not see anything. Figures passing cast only a pale shadow through the curtain. There was no reason the girl should single her out for her ugly looks.

"Miss Finley," the nurse said, cracking the door. The gum-chewing woman got up and passed in front of her and Claud and went into the office. She had on red high-heeled shoes.

Directly across the table, the ugly girl's eyes were fixed on Mrs. Turpin as if she had some very special reason for disliking her.

"This is wonderful weather, isn't it?" the girl's mother said.

"It's good weather for cotton if you can get the niggers to pick it," Mrs. Turpin said, "but niggers don't want to pick cotton any more. You can't get the white folks to pick it and now you can't get the niggers—because they got to be right up there with the white folks."

40   "They gonna *try* anyways," the white-trash woman said, leaning forward.

"Do you have one of those cotton-picking machines?" the pleasant lady asked.

"No," Mrs. Turpin said, "they leave half the cotton in the field. We don't have much cotton anyway. If you want to make it farming now, you have to have a little of everything. We got a couple of acres of cotton and a few hogs and chickens and just enough white-face that Claud can look after them himself."

"One thang I don't want," the white-trash woman said, wiping her mouth with the back of her hand. "Hogs. Nasty stinking things, a-gruntin and a-rootin all over the place."

Mrs. Turpin gave her the merest edge of her attention. "Our hogs are not dirty and they don't stink," she said. "They're cleaner than some children I've seen. Their feet never touch the ground. We have a pig-parlor— that's where you raise them on concrete," she explained to the pleasant lady, "and Claud scoots them down with the hose every afternoon and washes off the floor." Cleaner by far than that child right there, she thought. Poor nasty little thing. He had not moved except to put the thumb of his dirty hand into his mouth.

45   The woman turned her face away from Mrs. Turpin. "I know I wouldn't scoot down no hog with no hose," she said to the wall.

You wouldn't have no hog to scoot down, Mrs. Turpin said to herself.

"A-gruntin and a-rootin and a-groanin," the woman muttered.

"We got a little of everything," Mrs. Turpin said to the pleasant lady. "It's no use in having more than you can handle yourself with help like it is. We found enough niggers to pick our cotton this year but Claud he has to go after them and take them home again in the evening. They can't walk that half a mile. No they can't. I tell you," she said and laughed merrily, "I sure am tired of buttering up niggers, but you got to love em if you want em to work for you. When they come in the morning, I run out and I say, 'Hi yawl this morning?' and when Claud drives them off to the field I just wave to beat the band and they just wave back." And she waved her hand rapidly to illustrate.

"Like you read out of the same book," the lady said, showing she understood perfectly.

50   "Child, yes," Mrs. Turpin said. "And when they come in from the field, I run out with a bucket of icewater. That's the way it's going to be from now on," she said. "You may as well face it."

"One thang I know," the white-trash woman said. "Two thangs I ain't going to do: love no niggers or scoot down no hog with no hose." And she let out a bark of contempt.

The look that Mrs. Turpin and the pleasant lady exchanged indicated they both understood that you had to *have* certain things before you could *know* certain things. But every time Mrs. Turpin exchanged a look with the lady, she was aware that the ugly girl's peculiar eyes were still on her, and she had trouble bringing her attention back to the conversation.

"When you got something," she said, "you got to look after it." And when you ain't got a thing but breath and britches, she added to herself, you can afford to come to town every morning and just sit on the Court House coping and spit.

A grotesque revolving shadow passed across the curtain behind her and was thrown palely on the opposite wall. Then a bicycle clattered down against the outside of the building. The door opened and a colored boy glided in with a tray from the drug store. It had two large red and white paper cups on it with tops on them. He was a tall, very black boy in discolored white pants and a green nylon shirt. He was chewing gum slowly, as if to music. He set the tray down in the office opening next to the fern and stuck his head through to look for the secretary. She was not in there. He rested his arms on the ledge and waited, his narrow bottom stuck out, swaying slowly to the left and right. He raised a hand over his head and scratched the base of his skull.

55   "You see that button there, boy?" Mrs. Turpin said. "You can punch that and she'll come. She's probably in the back somewhere."

"Is that right?" the boy said agreeably, as if he had never seen the button before. He leaned to the right and put his finger on it. "She sometime out," he said and twisted around to face his audience, his elbows behind him on the counter. The nurse appeared and he twisted back again. She handed him a dollar and he rooted in his pocket and made the change and counted it out to her. She gave him fifteen cents for a tip and he went out with the empty tray. The heavy door swung to slowly and closed at length with the sound of suction. For a moment no one spoke.

"They ought to send all them niggers back to Africa," the white-trash woman said. "That's wher they come from in the first place."

"Oh, I couldn't do without my good colored friends," the pleasant lady said.

"There's a heap of things worse than a nigger," Mrs. Turpin agreed. "It's all kinds of them just like it's all kinds of us."

60   "Yes, and it takes all kinds to make the world go round," the lady said in her musical voice.

As she said it, the raw-complexioned girl snapped her teeth together. Her lower lip turned downwards and inside out, revealing the pale pink inside of her mouth. After a second it rolled back up. It was the ugliest face Mrs. Turpin had ever seen anyone make and for a moment she was certain that the girl had made it at her. She was looking at her as if she had known and disliked her all her life—all of Mrs. Turpin's life, it seemed too, not just all the girl's life. Why, girl, I don't even know you, Mrs. Turpin said silently.

She forced her attention back to the discussion. "It wouldn't be practical to send them back to Africa," she said. "They wouldn't want to go. They got it too good here."

"Wouldn't be what they wanted—if I had anythang to do with it," the woman said.

"It wouldn't be a way in the world you could get all the niggers back over there," Mrs. Turpin said. "They'd be hiding out and lying down and turning sick on you and wailing and hollering and raring and pitching. It wouldn't be a way in the world to get them over there."

65   "They got over here," the trashy woman said. "Get back like they got over."

"It wasn't so many of them then," Mrs. Turpin explained.

The woman looked at Mrs. Turpin as if here was an idiot indeed but Mrs. Turpin was not bothered by the look, considering where it came from.

"Nooo," she said, "they're going to stay here where they can go to New York and marry white folks and improve their color. That's what they all want to do, every one of them, improve their color."

"You know what comes of that, don't you?" Claud asked.

70   "No, Claud, what?" Mrs. Turpin said.

Claud's eyes twinkled. "White-faced niggers," he said with never a smile. Everybody in the office laughed except the white-trash and the ugly girl. The girl gripped the book in her lap with white fingers. The trashy woman looked around her from face to face as if she thought they were all idiots. The old woman in the feed sack dress continued to gaze expressionless across the floor at the high-top shoes of the man opposite her, the one who had been pretending to be asleep when the Turpins came in. He was laughing heartily, his hands still spread out on his knees. The child had fallen to the side and was lying now almost face down in the old woman's lap.

While they recovered from their laughter, the nasal chorus on the radio kept the room from silence.

"You go to blank blank
And I'll go to mine
But we'll all blank along
To-geth-ther,
And all along the blank
We'll hep eachother out
Smile-ling in any kind of
Weath-ther!"

Mrs. Turpin didn't catch every word but she caught enough to agree with the spirit of the song and it turned her thoughts sober. To help anybody out that needed it was her philosophy of life. She never spared herself when she found somebody in need, whether they were white or black, trash or decent. And of all she had to be thankful for, she was most thankful that this was so. If Jesus had said, "You can be high society and have all the money you want and be thin and svelte-like, but you can't be a good woman with it," she would have had to say, "Well don't make me that then. Make me a good woman and it don't matter what else, how fat or how ugly or how poor!" Her heart rose. He had not made her a nigger or white-trash or ugly! He had made her herself and given her a little of everything. Jesus, thank you! she said. Thank you thank you thank you! Whenever she counted her blessings she felt as buoyant as if she weighed one hundred and twenty-five pounds instead of one hundred and eighty.

75   "What's wrong with your little boy?" the pleasant lady asked the white-trashy woman.

"He has a ulcer," the woman said proudly. "He ain't give me a minute's peace since he was born. Him and her are just alike," she said, nodding at the old woman, who was running her leathery fingers through the child's pale hair. "Look like I can't get nothing down them two but Co' Cola and candy."

That's all you try to get down em, Mrs. Turpin said to herself. Too lazy to light the fire. There was nothing you could tell her about people like them that she didn't know already. And it was not just that they didn't have anything. Because if you gave them everything, in two weeks it would all be broken or filthy or they would have chopped it up for lightwood. She knew all this from her own experience. Help them you must, but help them you couldn't.

All at once the ugly girl turned her lips inside out again. Her eyes were fixed like two drills on Mrs. Turpin. This time there was no mistaking that there was something urgent behind them.

Girl, Mrs. Turpin exclaimed silently, I haven't done a thing to you! The girl might be confusing her with somebody else. There was no need to sit by and let herself be intimidated. "You must be in college," she said boldly, looking directly at the girl. "I see you reading a book there."

80   The girl continued to stare and pointedly did not answer.

Her mother blushed at this rudeness. "The lady asked you a question, Mary Grace," she said under her breath.

"I have ears," Mary Grace said.

The poor mother blushed again. "Mary Grace goes to Wellesley College,"[1] she explained. She twisted one of the buttons on her dress. "In Massachusetts," she added with a grimace. "And in the summer she just keeps right on studying. Just reads all the time, a real book worm. She's done real well at Wellesley; she's taking English and Math and History and Psychology and Social Studies," she rattled on, "and I think it's too much. I think she ought to get out and have fun."

The girl looked as if she would like to hurl them all through the plate glass window.

85   "Way up north," Mrs. Turpin murmured and thought, well, it hasn't done much for her manners.

---

[1]**Wellesley College** a distinguished women's college.

"I'd almost rather to have him sick," the white-trash woman said, wrenching the attention back to herself. "He's so mean when he ain't. Look like some children just take natural to meanness. It's some gets bad when they get sick but he was the opposite. Took sick and turned good. He don't give me no trouble now. It's me waitin to see the doctor," she said.

If I was going to send anybody back to Africa, Mrs. Turpin thought, it would be your kind, woman. "Yes, indeed," she said aloud, but looking up at the ceiling, "it's a heap of things worse than a nigger." And dirtier than a hog, she added to herself.

"I think people with bad dispositions are more to be pitied than anyone on earth," the pleasant lady said in a voice that was decidedly thin.

"I thank the Lord he has blessed me with a good one," Mrs. Turpin said. "The day has never dawned that I couldn't find something to laugh at."

90   "Not since she married me anyways," Claud said with a comical straight face.

Everybody laughed except the girl and the white-trash.

Mrs. Turpin's stomach shook. "He's such a caution," she said, "that I can't help but laugh at him."

The girl made a loud ugly noise through her teeth.

Her mother's mouth grew thin and tight. "I think the worst thing in the world," she said, "is an ungrateful person. To have everything and not appreciate it. I know a girl," she said, "who has parents who would give her anything, a little brother who loves her dearly, who is getting a good education, who wears the best clothes, but who can never say a kind word to anyone, who never smiles, who just criticizes and complains all day long."

95   "Is she too old to paddle?" Claud asked.

The girl's face was almost purple.

"Yes," the lady said. "I'm afraid there's nothing to do but leave her to her folly. Some day she'll wake up and it'll be too late."

"It never hurt anyone to smile," Mrs. Turpin said. "It just makes you feel better all over."

"Of course," the lady said sadly, "but there are just some people you can't tell anything to. They can't take criticism."

100   "If it's one thing I am," Mrs. Turpin said with feeling, "it's grateful. When I think who all I could have been besides myself and what all I got, a little of everything, and a good disposition besides, I just feel like shouting, 'Thank you, Jesus, for making everything the way it is!' It could have been different!" For one thing, somebody else could have got Claud. At the thought of this, she was flooded with gratitude and a terrible pang of joy ran through her. "Oh thank you, Jesus, Jesus, thank you!" she cried aloud.

The book struck her directly over her left eye. It struck almost at the same instant that she realized the girl was about to hurl it. Before she could utter a sound, the raw face came crashing across the table toward her, howling. The girl's fingers sank like clamps into the soft flesh of her neck. She heard the mother cry out and Claud shout, "Whoa!" There was an instant when she was certain that she was about to be in an earthquake.

All at once her vision narrowed and she saw everything as if it were happening in a small room far away, or as if she were looking at it through the wrong end of a telescope. Claud's face crumpled and fell out of sight. The nurse ran in, then out, then in again. Then the gangling figure of the doctor rushed out of the inner door. Magazines flew this way and that as the table turned over. The girl fell with a thud and Mrs. Turpin's vision suddenly reversed itself and she saw everything large instead of small. The eyes of the white-trashy woman were staring hugely at the floor. There the girl, held down on one side by the nurse and on the other by her mother, was wrenching and turning in their grasp. The doctor was kneeling astride her, trying to hold her arm down. He managed after a second to sink a long needle into it.

Mrs. Turpin felt entirely hollow except for her heart which swung from side to side as if it were agitated in a great empty drum of flesh.

"Somebody that's not busy call for the ambulance," the doctor said in the off-hand voice young doctors adopt for terrible occasions.

105   Mrs. Turpin could not have moved a finger. The old man who had been sitting next to her skipped nimbly into the office and made the call, for the secretary still seemed to be gone.

"Claud!" Mrs. Turpin called.

He was not in his chair. She knew she must jump up and find him but she felt like some one trying to catch a train in a dream, when everything moves in slow motion and the faster you try to run the slower you go.

"Here I am," a suffocated voice, very unlike Claud's, said.

He was doubled up in the corner on the floor, pale as paper, holding his leg. She wanted to get up and go to him but she could not move. Instead, her gaze was drawn slowly downward to the churning face on the floor, which she could see over the doctor's shoulder.

110   The girl's eyes stopped rolling and focused on her. They seemed a much lighter blue than before, as if a door that had been tightly closed behind them was now open to admit light and air.

Mrs. Turpin's head cleared and her power of motion returned. She leaned forward until she was looking directly into the fierce brilliant eyes. There was no doubt in her mind that the girl did know her, knew her in some intense and personal way, beyond time and place and condition. "What you got to say to me?" she asked hoarsely and held her breath, waiting, as for a revelation.

The girl raised her head. Her gaze locked with Mrs. Turpin's. "Go back to hell where you came from, you old wart hog," she whispered. Her voice was low but clear. Her eyes burned for a moment as if she saw with pleasure that her message had struck its target.

Mrs. Turpin sank back in her chair.

After a moment the girl's eyes closed and she turned her head wearily to the side.

115   The doctor rose and handed the nurse the empty syringe. He leaned over and put both hands for a moment on the mother's shoulders, which were shaking. She was sitting on the floor, her lips pressed together, holding Mary Grace's hand in her lap. The girl's fingers were gripped like a baby's around her thumb. "Go on to the hospital," he said. "I'll call and make the arrangements."

"Now let's see that neck," he said in a jovial voice to Mrs. Turpin. He began to inspect her neck with his first two fingers. Two little moon-shaped lines like pink fish bones were indented over her windpipe. There was the beginning of an angry red swelling above her eye. His fingers passed over this also.

"Lea' me be," she said thickly and shook him off. "See about Claud. She kicked him."

"I'll see about him in a minute," he said and felt her pulse. He was a thin gray-haired man, given to pleasantries. "Go home and have yourself a vacation the rest of the day," he said and patted her on the shoulder.

Quit your pattin me, Mrs. Turpin growled to herself.

120   "And put an ice pack over that eye," he said. Then he went and squatted down beside Claud and looked at his leg. After a moment he pulled him up and Claud limped after him into the office.

Until the ambulance came, the only sounds in the room were the tremulous moans of the girl's mother, who continued to sit on the floor. The white-trash woman did not take her eyes off the girl. Mrs. Turpin looked straight ahead at nothing. Presently the ambulance drew up, a long dark shadow, behind the curtain. The attendants came in and set the stretcher down beside the girl and lifted her expertly onto it and carried her out. The nurse helped the mother gather up her things. The shadow of the ambulance moved silently away and the nurse came back in the office.

"That there girl is going to be a lunatic, ain't she?" the white-trash woman asked the nurse, but the nurse kept on to the back and never answered her.

"Yes, she's going to be a lunatic," the white-trash woman said to the rest of them.

"Po' critter," the old woman murmured. The child's face was still in her lap. His eyes looked idly out over her knees. He had not moved during the disturbance except to draw one leg up under him.

125   "I thank Gawd," the white-trash woman said fervently, "I ain't a lunatic."

Claud came limping out and the Turpins went home.

As their pick-up truck turned into their own dirt road and made the crest of the hill, Mrs. Turpin gripped the window ledge and looked out suspiciously. The land sloped gracefully down through a field dotted with lavender weeds and at the start of the rise their small yellow frame house, with its little flower beds spread out around it like a fancy apron, sat primly in its accustomed place between two giant hickory trees. She would not have been startled to see a burnt wound between two blackened chimneys.

Neither of them felt like eating so they put on their house clothes and lowered the shade in the bedroom and lay down, Claud with his leg on a pillow and herself with a damp washcloth over her eye. The instant she was flat on her back, the image of a razor-backed hog with warts on its face and horns coming out behind its ears snorted into her head. She moaned, a low quiet moan.

"I am not," she said tearfully, "a wart hog. From hell." But the denial had no force. The girl's eyes and her words, even the tone of her voice, low but clear, directed only to her, brooked no repudiation. She had been singled out for the message, though there was trash in the room to whom it might justly have been applied. The full force of this fact struck her only now. There was a woman there who was neglecting her own child but she had been overlooked. The message had been given to Ruby Turpin, a respectable, hardworking, church-going woman. The tears dried. Her eyes began to burn instead with wrath.

130   She rose on her elbow and the washcloth fell into her hand. Claud was lying on his back, snoring. She wanted to tell him what the girl had said. At

the same time she did not wish to put the image of herself as a wart hog from hell into his mind.

"Hey, Claud," she muttered and pushed his shoulder.

Claud opened one pale baby blue eye.

She looked into it warily. He did not think about anything. He just went his way.

"Wha, whasit?" he said and closed his eye again.

135 "Nothing," she said. "Does your leg pain you?"

"Hurts like hell," Claud said.

"It'll quit terreckly," she said and lay back down. In a moment Claud was snoring again. For the rest of the afternoon they lay there. Claud slept. She scowled at the ceiling. Occasionally she raised her fist and made a small stabbing motion over her chest as if she was defending her innocence to invisible guests who were the comforters of Job, reasonable-seeming but wrong.

About five-thirty Claud stirred. "Got to go after those niggers," he sighed, not moving.

She was looking straight up as if there were unintelligible handwriting on the ceiling. The protuberance over her eye had turned a greenish-blue. "Listen here," she said.

140 "What?"

"Kiss me."

Claud leaned over and kissed her loudly on the mouth. He pinched her side and their hands interlocked. Her expression of ferocious concentration did not change. Claud got up, groaning and growling, and limped off. She continued to study the ceiling.

She did not get up until she heard the pick-up truck coming back with the Negroes. Then she rose and thrust her feet in her brown oxfords, which she did not bother to lace, and stumped out onto the back porch and got her red plastic bucket. She emptied a tray of ice cubes into it and filled it half full of water and went out into the back yard. Every afternoon after Claud brought the hands in, one of the boys helped him put out hay and the rest waited in the back of the truck until he was ready to take them home. The truck was parked in the shade under one of the hickory trees.

"Hi yawl this evening?" Mrs. Turpin asked grimly, appearing with the bucket and the dipper. There were three women and a boy in the truck.

145 "Us doin nicely," the oldest woman said. "Hi you doin?" and her gaze stuck immediately on the dark lump on Mrs. Turpin's forehead. "You done fell down, ain't you?" she asked in a solicitous voice. The old woman was dark and almost toothless. She had on an old felt hat of Claud's set back on her head. The other two women were younger and lighter and they both had new bright green sun hats. One of them had hers on her head; the other had taken hers off and the boy was grinning beneath it.

Mrs. Turpin set the bucket down on the floor of the truck. "Yawl hep yourselves," she said. She looked around to make sure Claud had gone. "No. I didn't fall down," she said, folding her arms. "It was something worse than that."

"Ain't nothing bad happen to you!" the old woman said. She said it as if they all knew Mrs. Turpin was protected in some special way by Divine Providence. "You just had you a little fall."

"We were in town at the doctor's office for where the cow kicked Mr. Turpin," Mrs. Turpin said in a flat tone that indicated they could leave off their foolishness. "And there was this girl there. A big fat girl with her face all broke out. I could look at that girl and tell she was peculiar but I couldn't tell how. And me and her mama were just talking and going along and all of a sudden WHAM! She throws this big book she reading at me and . . ."

"Naw!" the old woman cried out.

150 "And then she jumps over the table and commences to choke me."

"Naw!" they all exclaimed, "naw!"

"Hi come she do that?" the old woman asked. "What ail her?"

Mrs. Turpin only glared in front of her.

"Somethin ail her," the old woman said.

155 "They carried her off in an ambulance," Mrs. Turpin continued, "but before she went she was rolling on the floor and they were trying to hold her down to give her a shot and she said something to me." She paused. "You know what she said to me?"

"What she say?" they asked.

"She said," Mrs. Turpin began, and stopped, her face very dark and heavy. The sun was getting whiter and whiter, blanching the sky overhead so that the leaves of the hickory tree were black in the face of it. She could not bring forth the words. "Something real ugly," she muttered.

"She sho shouldn't said nothin ugly to you," the old woman said. "You so sweet. You the sweetest lady I know."

"She pretty too," the one with the hat on said.

160 "And stout," the other one said. "I never knowed no sweeter white lady."

"That's the truth befo' Jesus," the old woman said. "Amen! You des as sweet and pretty as you can be."

Mrs. Turpin knew just exactly how much Negro flattery was worth and it added to her rage. "She said," she began again and finished this time with a fierce rush of breath, "that I was an old wart hog from hell."

There was an astounded silence.

"Where she at?" the youngest woman cried in a piercing voice.

165 "Lemme see her. I'll kill her!"

"I'll kill her with you!" the other one cried.

"She b'long in the sylum," the old woman said emphatically. "You the sweetest white lady I know."

"She pretty too," the other two said. "Stout as she can be and sweet. Jesus satisfied with her!"

"Deed he is," the old woman declared.

170 Idiots! Mrs. Turpin growled to herself. You could never say anything intelligent to a nigger. You could talk at them but not with them. "Yawl ain't drunk your water," she said shortly. "Leave the bucket in the truck when you're finished with it. I got more to do than just stand around and pass the time of day," and she moved off and into the house.

She stood for a moment in the middle of the kitchen. The dark protuberance over her eye looked like a miniature tornado cloud which might any moment sweep across the horizon of her brow. Her lower lip protruded dangerously. She squared her massive shoulders. Then she marched into the front of the house and out the side door and started down the road to the pig parlor. She had the look of a woman going single-handed, weaponless, into battle.

The sun was a deep yellow now like a harvest moon and was riding westward very fast over the far tree line as if it meant to reach the hogs before she did. The road was rutted and she kicked several good-sized stones out of her path as she strode along. The pig parlor was on a little knoll at the end of a lane that ran off from the side of the barn. It was a square of concrete as large as a small room, with a board fence about four feet high around it. The concrete floor sloped slightly so that the hog wash could drain off into a trench where it was carried to the field for fertilizer. Claud was standing on the outside, on the edge of the concrete, hanging onto the top board, hosing down the floor inside. The hose was connected to the faucet of a water trough nearby.

Mrs. Turpin climbed up beside him and glowered down at the hogs inside. There were seven long-snouted bristly shoats in it—tan with liver-colored spots—and an old sow a few weeks off from farrowing. She was lying on her side grunting. The shoats were running about shaking themselves like idiot children, their little slit pig eyes searching the floor for anything left. She had read that pigs were the most intelligent animal. She doubted it. They were supposed to be smarter than dogs. There had even been a pig astronaut. He had performed his assignment perfectly but died of a heart attack afterwards because they left him in his electric suit, sitting upright throughout his examination when naturally a hog should be on all fours.

A-gruntin and a-rootin and a-groanin.

175   "Gimme that hose," she said, yanking it away from Claud. "Go on and carry them niggers home and then get off that leg."

"You look like you might have swallowed a mad dog," Claud observed, but he got down and limped off. He paid no attention to her humors.

Until he was out of earshot, Mrs. Turpin stood on the side of the pen, holding the hose and pointing the stream of water at the hind quarter of any shoat that looked as if it might try to lie down. When he had had time to get over the hill, she turned her head slightly and her wrathful eyes scanned the path. He was nowhere in sight. She turned back again and seemed to gather herself up. Her shoulders rose and she drew in her breath.

"What do you send me a message like that for?" she said in a low fierce voice, barely above a whisper but with the force of a shout in its concentrated fury. "How am I a hog and me both? How am I saved and from hell too?" Her free fist was knotted and with the other she gripped the hose, blindly pointing the stream of water in and out of the eye of the old sow whose outraged squeal she did not hear.

The pig parlor commanded a view of the back pasture where their twenty beef cows were gathered around the hay-bales Claud and the boy had put out. The freshly cut pasture sloped down to the highway. Across it was their cotton field and beyond that a dark green dusty wood which they owned as well. The sun was behind the wood, very red, looking over the paling of trees like a farmer inspecting his own hogs.

180   "Why me?" she rumbled. "It's no trash around here, black or white, that I haven't given to. And break my back to the bone every day working. And do for the church."

She appeared to be the right size woman to command the arena before her. "How am I a hog?" she demanded. "Exactly how am I like them?" and she jabbed the stream of water at the shoats. "There was plenty of trash there. It didn't have to be me."

"If you like trash better, go get yourself some trash then," she railed. "You could have made me trash. Or a nigger. If trash is what you wanted why didn't you make me trash?" She shook her fist with the hose in it and a watery snake appeared momentarily in the air. "I could quit working and take it easy and be filthy," she growled. "Lounge about the sidewalks all day drinking root beer. Dip snuff and spit in every puddle and have it all over my face. I could be nasty.

"Or you could have made me a nigger. It's too late for me to be a nigger," she said with deep sarcasm, "but I could act like one. Lay down in the middle of the road and stop traffic. Roll on the ground."

In the deepening light everything was taking on a mysterious hue. The pasture was growing a peculiar glassy green and the streak of highway had turned lavender. She braced herself for a final assault and this time her voice rolled out over the pasture. "Go on," she yelled, "call me a hog! Call me a hog again. From hell. Call me a wart hog from hell. Put that bottom rail on top. There'll still be a top and bottom!"

185   A garbled echo returned to her.

A final surge of fury shook her and she roared, "Who do you think you are?"

The color of everything, field and crimson sky, burned for a moment with a transparent intensity. The question carried over the pasture and across the highway and the cotton field and returned to her clearly like an answer from beyond the wood.

She opened her mouth but no sound came out of it.

A tiny truck, Claud's, appeared on the highway, heading rapidly out of sight. Its gears scraped thinly. It looked like a child's toy. At any moment a bigger truck might smash into it and scatter Claud's and the niggers' brains all over the road.

190   Mrs. Turpin stood there, her gaze fixed on the highway, all her muscles rigid, until in five or six minutes the truck reappeared, returning. She waited until it had had time to turn into their own road. Then like a monumental statue coming to life, she bent her head slowly and gazed, as if through the very heart of mystery, down into the pig parlor at the hogs. They had settled all in one corner around the old sow who was grunting softly. A red glow suffused them. They appeared to pant with a secret life.

Until the sun slipped finally behind the tree line, Mrs. Turpin remained there with her gaze bent to them as if she were absorbing some abysmal life-giving knowledge. At last she lifted her head. There was only a purple streak in the sky, cutting through a field of crimson and leading, like an extension of the highway, into the descending dusk. She raised her hands from the side of the pen in a gesture hieratic and profound. A visionary light settled in her eyes. She saw the streak as a vast swinging bridge extending upward from the earth through a field of living fire. Upon it a vast horde of souls were rumbling toward heaven. There were whole companies of white-trash, clean for the first time in their lives, and bands of black niggers in white robes, and battalions of freaks and lunatics shouting and clapping and leaping like frogs. And bringing up the end of the procession was a tribe of people whom she recognized at once as those who, like herself and Claud, had always had a little of everything and the God-given wit to use it right. She leaned forward to observe them closer. They were marching behind the others with great dignity, accountable as they had always been for good order and common sense and respectable behavior. They alone were on key. Yet she could see by their shocked and altered faces that even their virtues were being burned away. She lowered her hands and gripped the rail of the hog pen, her eyes small but fixed unblinkingly on what lay ahead. In a moment the vision faded but she remained where she was, immobile.

At length she got down and turned off the faucet and made her slow way on the darkening path to the house. In the woods around her the invisible cricket choruses had struck up, but what she heard were the voices of the souls climbing upward into the starry field and shouting hallelujah.

YOUR TURN

1. Why does Mary Grace attack Mrs. Turpin?
2. Characterize Mrs. Turpin before her revelation. Did your attitude toward her change at the end of the story?
3. The two chief settings are a doctor's waiting room and a "pig parlor." Can these settings reasonably be called "symbolic"? If so, symbolic of what?
4. When Mrs. Turpin goes toward the pig parlor, she has "the look of a woman going single-handed, weaponless, into battle." Once there, she dismisses Claud, uses the hose as a weapon against the pigs, and talks to herself "in a low fierce voice." What is she battling, besides the pigs?

On Fiction: Remarks from O'Connor's Essays and Letters

From "The Fiction Writer and His Country"   [1957]

In the greatest fiction, the writer's moral sense coincides with his dramatic sense, and I see no way for it to do this unless his moral judgment is part of the very act of seeing, and he is free to use it. I have heard it said that belief in Christian dogma is a hindrance to the writer, but I myself have found nothing further from the truth. Actually, it frees the storyteller to observe. It is not a set of rules which fixes what he sees in the world. It affects his writing primarily by guaranteeing his respect for mystery. . . .

When I look at stories I have written I find that they are, for the most part, about people who are poor, who are afflicted in both mind and body, who have little—or at best a distorted—sense of spiritual purpose, and whose actions do not apparently give the reader a great assurance of the joy of life.

Yet how is this? For I am no disbeliever in spiritual purpose and no vague believer. I see from the standpoint of Christian orthodoxy. This means that for me the meaning of life is centered in our Redemption by Christ and that what I see in the world I see in its relation to that. . . .

The novelist with Christian concerns will find in modern life distortions which are repugnant to him, and his problem will be to make these appear as distortions to an audience which is used to seeing them as natural; and he may well be forced to take ever more violent means to get his vision across to this hostile audience. When you can assume that your audience holds the same beliefs you do, you can relax a little and use more normal ways of talking to it;

when you have to assume that it does not, then you have to make your vision apparent by shock—to the hard of hearing you shout, and for the almost blind you draw large and startling figures.

From "Some Aspects of the Grotesque in Southern Fiction"   [1960]

If the writer believes that our life is and will remain essentially mysterious, if he looks upon us as beings existing in a created order to whose laws we freely respond, then what he sees on the surface will be of interest to him only as he can go through it into an experience of mystery itself. His kind of fiction will always be pushing its own limits outward toward the limits of mystery, because for this kind of writer, the meaning of a story does not begin except at a depth where the adequate motivation and the adequate psychology and the various determinations have been exhausted. Such a writer will be interested in what we don't understand rather than in what we do. He will be interested in possibility rather than in probability. He will be interested in characters who are forced out to meet evil and grace and who act on a trust beyond themselves—whether they know very clearly what it is they act upon or not. To the modern mind, this kind of character, and his creator, are typical Don Quixotes, tilting at what is not there.

From "The Nature and Aim of Fiction"   [Date Unknown]

The novel works by a slower accumulation of detail than the short story does. The short story requires more drastic procedures than the novel because more has to be accomplished in less space. The details have to carry more immediate weight. In good fiction, certain of the details will tend to accumulate meaning from the story itself, and when this happens, they become symbolic in their action.

   Now the word *symbol* scares a good many people off, just as the word *art* does. They seem to feel that a symbol is some mysterious thing put in arbitrarily by the writer to frighten the common reader—sort of a literary Masonic grip that is only for the initiated. They seem to think that it is a way of saying something that you aren't actually saying, and so if they can be got to read a reputedly symbolic work at all, they approach it as if it were a problem in algebra. Find x. And when they do find or think they find this abstraction, x, then they go off with an elaborate sense of satisfaction and the notion that they have "understood" the story. Many students confuse the *process* of understanding a thing with understanding it.

   I think that for the fiction writer himself, symbols are something he uses simply as a matter of course. You might say that these are details that, while having their essential place in the literal level of the story, operate in depth as well as on the surface, increasing the story in every direction. . . .

   People have a habit of saying, "What is the theme of your story?" and they expect you to give them a statement: "The theme of my story is the economic pressure of the machine on the middle class"—or some such absurdity. And when they've got a statement like that, they go off happy and feel it is no longer necessary to read the story.

Some people have the notion that you read the story and then climb out of it into the meaning, but for the fiction writer himself the whole story is the meaning, because it is an experience, not an abstraction.

From "Writing Short Stories"

[Date Unknown]

Being short does not mean being slight. A short story should be long in depth and should give us an experience of meaning. . . .

Meaning is what keeps the short story from being short. I prefer to talk about the meaning in a story rather than the theme of a story. People talk about the theme of a story as if the theme were like the string that a sack of chicken feed is tied with. They think that if you can pick out the theme, the way you pick the right thread in the chicken-feed sack, you can rip the story open and feed the chickens. But this is not the way meaning works in fiction.

When you can state the theme of a story, when you can separate it from the story itself, then you can be sure the story is not a very good one. The meaning of a story has to be embodied in it, has to be made concrete in it. A story is a way to say something that can't be said any other way, and it takes every word in the story to say what the meaning is. You tell a story because a statement would be inadequate. When anybody asks what a story is about, the only proper thing is to tell him to read the story. The meaning of fiction is not abstract meaning but experienced meaning, and the purpose of making statements about the meaning of a story is only to help you to experience that meaning more fully.

"A Reasonable Use of the Unreasonable"

[1957]

Last fall I received a letter from a student who said she would be "graciously appreciative" if I would tell her "just what enlightenment" I expected her to get from each of my stories. I suspect she had a paper to write. I wrote her back to forget about the enlightenment and just try to enjoy them. I knew that was the most unsatisfactory answer I could have given because, of course, she didn't want to enjoy them, she just wanted to figure them out.

In most English classes the short story has become a kind of literary specimen to be dissected. Every time a story of mine appears in a Freshman anthology, I have a vision of it, with its little organs laid open, like a frog in a bottle.

I realize that a certain amount of this what-is-the-significance has to go on, but I think something has gone wrong in the process when, for so many students, the story becomes simply a problem to be solved, something which you evaporate to get Instant Enlightenment.

A story really isn't any good unless it successfully resists paraphrase, unless it hangs on and expands in the mind. Properly, you analyze to enjoy, but it's equally true that to analyze with any discrimination, you have to have enjoyed already, and I think that the best reason to hear a story read is that it should stimulate that primary enjoyment.

I don't have any pretensions to being an Aeschylus or Sophocles and providing you in this story with a cathartic experience out of your mythic background, though this story I'm going to read certainly calls up a good deal of the South's mythic background, and it should elicit from you a degree of pity and terror, even though its way of being serious is a comic one. I do think, though, that like the Greeks you should know what is going to happen in this story so that any element of suspense in it will be transferred from its surface to its interior.

I would be most happy if you had already read it, happier still if you knew it well, but since experience has taught me to keep my expectations along these lines modest, I'll tell you that this is the story of a family of six which, on its way driving to Florida, gets wiped out by an escaped convict who calls himself The Misfit. The family is made up of the Grandmother and her son, Bailey, and his children, John Wesley and June Star and the baby, and there is also the cat and the children's mother. The cat is named Pitty Sing, and the Grandmother is taking him with them, hidden in a basket.

Now I think it behooves me to try to establish with you the basis on which reason operates in this story. Much of my fiction takes its character from a reasonable use of the unreasonable, though the reasonableness of my use of it may not always be apparent. The assumptions that underlie this use of it, however, are those of the central Christian mysteries. These are assumptions to which a large part of the modern audience takes exception. About this I can only say that there are perhaps other ways than my own in which this story could be read, but none other by which it could have been written. Belief, in my own case anyway, is the engine that makes perception operate.

The heroine of this story, the Grandmother, is in the most significant position life offers the Christian. She is facing death. And to all appearances she, like the rest of us, is not too well prepared for it. She would like to see the event postponed. Indefinitely.

I've talked to a number of teachers who use this story in class and who tell their students that the Grandmother is evil, that in fact, she's a witch, even down to the cat. One of these teachers told me that his students, and particularly his Southern students, resisted this interpretation with a certain bemused vigor, and he didn't understand why. I had to tell him that they resisted it because they all had grandmothers or great-aunts just like her at home, and they knew, from personal experience, that the old lady lacked comprehension, but that she had a good heart. The Southerner is usually tolerant of those weaknesses that proceed from innocence, and he knows that a taste for self-preservation can be readily combined with the missionary spirit.

This same teacher was telling his students that morally The Misfit was several cuts above the Grandmother. He had a really sentimental attachment to The Misfit. But then a prophet gone wrong is almost always more interesting than your grandmother, and you have to let people take their pleasures where they find them.

It is true that the old lady is a hypocritical old soul; her wits are no match for The Misfit's, nor is her capacity for grace equal to his; yet I think the unprejudiced reader will feel that the Grandmother has a special kind of triumph in this story which instinctively we do not allow to someone altogether bad.

I often ask myself what makes a story work, and what makes it hold up as a story, and I have decided that it is probably some action, some gesture of a character that is unlike any other in the story, one which indicates where the real heart of the story lies. This would have to be an action or a gesture which was both totally right and totally unexpected; it would have to be one that was both in character and beyond character; it would have to suggest both the world and eternity. The action or gesture I'm talking about would have to be on the anagogical level, that is, the level which has to do with the Divine life and our participation in it. It would be a gesture that transcended any neat allegory that might have been intended or any pat moral categories a reader could make. It would be a gesture which somehow made contact with mystery.

There is a point in this story where such a gesture occurs. The Grandmother is at last alone, facing The Misfit. Her head clears for an instant and she realizes, even in her limited way, that she is responsible for the man before her and joined to him by ties of kinship which have their roots deep in the mystery she has been merely prattling about so far. And at this point, she does the right thing, she makes the right gesture.

I find that students are often puzzled by what she says and does here, but I think myself that if I took out this gesture and what she says with it, I would have no story. What was left would not be worth your attention. Our age not only does not have a very sharp eye for the almost imperceptible intrusions of grace, it no longer has much feeling for the nature of the violences which precede and follow them. The devil's greatest wile, Baudelaire has said, is to convince us that he does not exist.

I suppose the reasons for the use of so much violence in modern fiction will differ with each writer who uses it, but in my own stories I have found that violence is strangely capable of returning my characters to reality and preparing them to accept their moment of grace. Their heads are so hard that almost nothing else will do the work. This idea, that reality is something to which we must be returned at considerable cost, is one which is seldom understood by the casual reader, but it is one which is implicit in the Christian view of the world.

I don't want to equate The Misfit with the devil. I prefer to think that, however unlikely this may seem, the old lady's gesture, like the mustard-seed, will grow to be a great crow-filled tree in The Misfit's heart, and will be enough of a pain to him there to turn him into the prophet he was meant to become. But that's another story.

This story has been called grotesque, but I prefer to call it literal. A good story is literal in the same sense that a child's drawing is literal. When a child draws, he doesn't intend to distort but to set down exactly what he sees, and as his gaze is direct, he sees the lines that create motion. Now the lines of motion that interest the writer are usually invisible. They are lines of spiritual motion. And in this story you should be on the lookout for such things as the action of grace in the Grandmother's soul, and not for the dead bodies.

We hear many complaints about the prevalence of violence in modern fiction, and it is always assumed that this violence is a bad thing and meant to be an end in itself. With the serious writer, violence is never an end in itself. It is the extreme situation that best reveals what we are essentially, and I believe these are times when writers are more interested in what we are essentially than in the tenor of our daily lives. Violence is a force which can be used for good or evil, and among other things taken by it is the kingdom of heaven. But regardless of what can be taken by it, the man in the violent situation reveals those qualities least dispensable in his personality, those qualities which are all he will have to take into eternity with him; and since the characters in this story are all on the verge of eternity, it is appropriate to think of what they take with them. In any case, I hope that if you consider these points in connection with the story, you will come to see it as something more than an account of a family murdered on the way to Florida.

On Interpreting "A Good Man is Hard to Find"

A professor of English had sent O'Connor the following letter:

"I am writing as spokesman for three members of our department and some ninety university students in three classes who for a week now have been discussing your story 'A Good Man Is Hard to Find.' We have debated at length several possible interpretations, none of which fully satisfies us. In general we believe that the appearance of The Misfit is not 'real' in the same sense that the incidents of the first half of the story are real. Bailey, we believe, imagines the appearance of The Misfit, whose activities have been called to his attention on the night before the trip and again during the stopover at the roadside restaurant. Bailey, we further believe, identifies himself with The Misfit and so plays two roles in the imaginary last half of the story. But we cannot, after great effort, determine the point at which reality fades into illusion or reverie. Does the accident literally occur, or is it a part of Bailey's dream? Please believe me when I say we are not seeking an easy way out of our difficulty. We admire your story and have examined it with great care, but we are convinced that we are missing something important which you intended for us to grasp. We will all be very grateful if you comment on the interpretation which I have outlined above and if you will give us further comments about your intention in writing 'A Good Man Is Hard to Find.'"

She replied:

28 March 61

(To a Professor of English)

The interpretation of your ninety students and three teachers is fantastic and about as far from my intentions as it could get to be. If it were a legitimate interpretation, the story would be little more than a trick and its interest would be simply for abnormal psychology. I am not interested in abnormal psychology.

There is a change of tension from the first part of the story to the second where The Misfit enters, but this is no lessening of reality. This story is, of course, not meant to be realistic in the sense that it portrays the everyday doings of people in Georgia. It is stylized and its conventions are comic even though its meaning is serious.

Bailey's only importance is as the Grandmother's boy and the driver of the car. It is the Grandmother who first recognizes The Misfit and who is most concerned with him throughout. The story is a duel of sorts between the Grandmother and her superficial beliefs and The Misfit's more profoundly felt involvement with Christ's action which set the world off balance for him.

The meaning of a story should go on expanding for the reader the more he thinks about it, but meaning cannot be captured in an interpretation. If teachers are in the habit of approaching a story as if it were a research problem for which any answer is believable so long as it is not obvious, then I think students will never learn to enjoy fiction. Too much interpretation is certainly worse than too little, and where feeling for a story is absent, theory will not supply it.

My tone is not meant to be obnoxious. I am in a state of shock.

Tobias Wolff: Four Stories, Comments About Writing, and an Essay by a Student

 *Tobias Wolff was born in Birmingham, Alabama, in 1945, but he was raised in the state of Washington. He served in the army between 1964 and 1968, including a tour of duty in Vietnam. He graduated from Oxford University in 1972 and then studied creative writing at Stanford. Wolff's first two books were* In the Garden of North American Martyrs *(1981) and* Back in the World *(1985), collections of short stories that both received good reviews. He achieved greater success and acclaim with the publication of* The Boy's Life *(1989), a memoir of his teenage years. He also has written a memoir of his military service,* In Pharaoh's Army *(1994). The author of many short stories and two novels, his recent publications include* Our Story Begins: New and Selected Stories *(2008). From 1980 to 1997, Wolff taught courses in English and in creative writing at Syracuse University, and, since then, he has taught at Stanford, where he is the Ward W. and Priscilla B. Woods Professor in the School of Humanities and Sciences.*

In an essay in the London Review of Books, *on Wolff's work, the critic Wyatt Mason comments: "Typically, his protagonists face an acute moral dilemma, unable to reconcile what they know to be true with what they feel to be true. Duplicity is their great failing, and Wolff's main theme." The novelist and essayist Robert Stone, focusing on Wolff's achievement as a writer of short stories, states:*

> *The work of Tobias Wolff provides a blend of satisfactions not always available in combination. Wolff is both subtle and passionate. He often appears as a wry but sympathetic observer of the disappointments and petty strategies that define obscure unexamined lives. Yet, his true subject is nothing less than the world, how it goes. (*Times Literary Supplement, *15 November 1996)*

Hunters in the Snow

[1982]

Tub had been waiting for an hour in the falling snow. He paced the sidewalk to keep warm and stuck his head out over the curb whenever he saw lights approaching. The fall of snow thickened. Tub stood below the overhang of a building. Across the road the clouds whitened just above the rooftops, and the whiteness seeped up through the sky. He shifted the rifle strap to his other shoulder.

A truck slid around the corner, horn blaring, rear end sashaying. Tub moved to the sidewalk and held up his hand. The truck jumped the curb and kept coming, half on the street and half on the sidewalk. It wasn't slowing down at all. Tub stood for a moment, still holding up his hand, then jumped back. His rifle slipped off his shoulder, clattering on the ice, and a sandwich fell out of his pocket. The truck went careening past him and stopped at the end of the block.

Tub picked up his sandwich and slung the rifle and walked down to the truck. The driver was bent against the steering wheel, slapping his knees and drumming his feet on the floorboards. He looked like a cartoon of a person laughing. "Tub, you ought to see yourself," he said. "You look just like a beach ball with a hat on. Doesn't he, Frank?"

The man beside him smiled and looked off.

5   "You almost ran me down," Tub said. "You could've killed me."

"Come on, Tub," said the man beside the driver. "Be mellow. Kenny was just messing around." He opened the door and slid over to the middle of the seat.

Tub took the bolt out of his rifle and climbed in beside him. "My feet are frozen," he said. "If you meant ten o'clock, why didn't you *say* ten o'clock?"

"Tub, you haven't done anything but complain since we got here," said the man in the middle. "If you want to piss and moan all day you might as well go home and bitch at your kids. Take your pick." When Tub didn't say anything, he turned to the driver. "Okay, Kenny, let's hit the road."

Some juvenile delinquents had heaved a brick through the windshield on the driver's side, so the cold and snow funneled right into the cab. The heater didn't work. They covered themselves with a couple of blankets Kenny had brought along and pulled down the flaps on their caps. Tub tried to keep his hands warm by rubbing them under the blanket, but Frank made him stop.

10   They left Spokane and drove deep into the country, running along black lines of fences. The snow let up, but still there was no edge to the land where it met the sky. Nothing moved in the chalky fields. The cold bleached their faces and made the stubble stand out on their cheeks and along their upper lips. They stopped twice for coffee before they got to the woods where Kenny wanted to hunt.

Tub was for trying someplace different; two years in a row they'd been up and down this land and hadn't seen a thing. Frank didn't care one way or the other, he just wanted to get out of the goddamned truck. "Feel that," he said, slamming the door. He spread his feet and closed his eyes and leaned his head back and breathed deeply. "Tune in on that energy."

"Another thing," Kenny said. "This is open land. Most of the land around here is posted."

"I'm cold," Tub said.

Frank breathed out. "Stop bitching, Tub. Get centered."

"I wasn't bitching."

15   "Centered," Kenny said. "Next thing you'll be wearing a nightgown, Frank. Selling flowers out at the airport."

"Kenny," Frank said, "you talk too much."

"Okay," Kenny said. "I won't say a word. Like I won't say anything about a certain babysitter."

"What babysitter?" Tub asked.

20   "That's between us," Frank said, looking at Kenny.

Kenny laughed.

"You're asking for it," Frank said.

"Asking for what? "

"Hey," Tub said, "are we hunting or what?"

25   They started off across the field. Tub had trouble getting through the fences. Frank and Kenny could have helped him; they could've lifted up the top wire and stepped on the bottom wire, but they didn't. They stood and watched him. There were a lot of fences, and Tub was puffing when they reached the woods.

They hunted for two hours and saw no deer, no tracks, no sign. Finally they stopped by the creek to eat. Kenny had several slices of pizza and a couple of candy bars; Frank had a sandwich, an apple, two carrots, and a square of chocolate; Tub ate one hard-boiled egg and a stick of celery.

"You ask me how I want to die today," Kenny said, "I'll tell you burn me at the stake." He turned to Tub. "You still on that diet?" He winked at Frank.

"What do you think? You think I like hard-boiled eggs?"

"All I can say is, it's the first diet I ever heard of where you gained weight from it."

30   "Who said I gained weight?"

"Oh, pardon me. I take it back. You're just wasting away before my very eyes. Isn't he, Frank?"

Frank had his fingers fanned out on the stump where he'd laid his food. His knuckles were hairy. He wore a heavy wedding band and on his right pinkie another gold ring with a flat face and an "F" in what looked like diamonds. "Tub," he said, "you haven't seen your own balls in ten years."

Kenny doubled over laughing. He took off his hat and slapped his leg with it.

"What am I supposed to do?" Tub said. "It's my glands."

35   They left the woods and hunted along the creek. Frank and Kenny worked one bank and Tub worked the other, moving upstream. The snow was light but the drifts were deep and hard to move through. Wherever Tub looked the surface was smooth, undisturbed, and after a time he lost interest. He stopped looking for tracks and just tried to keep up with Frank and Kenny on the other side. A moment came when he realized he hadn't seen them in a long time. The breeze was moving from him to them; when it stilled he could sometimes hear Kenny laughing—nothing more. He quickened his pace, breasting the drifts, fighting away the snow. He heard his heart and felt the flush on his face but never once stopped.

Tub caught up with Frank and Kenny at a bend of the creek. They were standing on a log that stretched from their bank to his. Ice had backed up behind the log. Frozen reeds stuck out.

"See anything?" Frank asked.

Tub shook his head.

There wasn't much daylight left and they decided to head back toward the road. Frank and Kenny crossed the log and they all started downstream,

using the trail Tub had broken. Before they'd gone very far Kenny stopped.
"Look at that," he said, and pointed to some tracks going from the creek back
into the woods. Tub's footprints crossed right over them. There on the bank,
plain as day, were several mounds of deer shit. "What do you think that is,
Tub?" Kenny kicked at it. "Walnuts on vanilla icing?"

"I guess I didn't notice."

Kenny looked at Frank.

"I was lost."

"You were lost. Big deal."

40   They followed the tracks into the woods. The deer had gone over a
fence half buried in drifting snow. A no-hunting sign was nailed to the top of
one of the posts. Kenny wanted to go after him but Frank said no way, the
people out here didn't mess around. He thought maybe the farmer who
owned the land would let them use it if they asked. Kenny wasn't so sure.
Anyway, he figured that by the time they walked to the truck and drove up
the road and doubled back it would be almost dark.

"Relax," Frank said. "You can't hurry nature. If we're meant to get that
deer, we'll get it. If we're not, we won't."

They started back toward the truck. This part of the woods was mainly
pine. The snow was shaded and had a glaze on it. It held up Kenny and Frank
but Tub kept falling through. As he kicked forward, the edge of the crust
bruised his shins. Kenny and Frank pulled ahead of him, to where he couldn't
even hear their voices anymore. He sat down on a stump and wiped his
face. He ate both his sandwiches and half the cookies, taking his own sweet
time. It was dead quiet.

When Tub crossed the last fence into the road the truck started moving. He had to run for it and just managed to grab hold of the tailgate and
hoist himself into the bed. He lay there, panting. Kenny looked out the rear
window and grinned. Tub crawled into the lee of the cab to get out of the
freezing wind. He pulled his earflaps low and pushed his chin into the
collar of his coat. Someone rapped on the window but Tub wouldn't turn
around.

He and Frank waited outside while Kenny went into the farmhouse to
ask permission. The house was old and paint was curling off the sides. The
smoke streamed westward off the top of the chimney, fanning away into a
thin gray plume. Above the ridge of the hills another ridge of blue clouds
was rising.

45   "You've got a short memory," Tub said.

"What?" Frank said. He had been staring off.

"I used to stick up for you."

"Okay, so you used to stick up for me. What's eating you?"

"You shouldn't have just left me back there like that."

50   "You're a grown-up, Tub. You can take care of yourself. Anyway, if you
think you're the only person with problems I can tell you that you're not."

"Is something bothering you, Frank?"

Frank kicked at a branch poking out of the snow. "Never mind," he said.

"What did Kenny mean about the babysitter?"

"Kenny talks too much," Frank said.

55   Kenny came out of the farmhouse and gave the thumbs-up and they began walking back toward the woods. As they passed the barn a large black
hound with a grizzled snout ran out and barked at them. Every time he

barked he slid backward a bit, like a cannon recoiling. Kenny got down on all fours and snarled and barked back at him, and the dog slunk away into the barn, looking over his shoulder and peeing a little as he went.

"That's an old-timer," Frank said. "A real graybeard. Fifteen years if he's a day."

"Too old," Kenny said.

Past the barn they cut off through the fields. The land was unfenced and the crust was freezing up thick, so they made good time. They kept to the edge of the field until they picked up the tracks again and followed them into the woods, farther and farther back toward the hills. The trees started to blur with the shadows, and the wind rose and needled their faces with the crystals it swept off the glaze. Finally they lost the tracks.

Kenny swore and threw down his hat. "This is the worst day of hunting I ever had, bar none." He picked up his hat and brushed off the snow. "This will be the first season since I was fifteen I haven't got my deer."

60   "It isn't the deer," Frank said. "It's the hunting. There are all these forces out here and you just have to go with them."

"You go with them," Kenny said. "I came out here to get me a deer, not listen to a bunch of hippie bullshit. And if it hadn't been for Dimples here I would have too."

"That's enough," Frank said.

"And you—you're so busy thinking about that little jailbait of yours you wouldn't know a deer if you saw one."

"Drop dead," Frank said, and turned away.

65   Kenny and Tub followed him back across the fields. When they were coming up to the barn Kenny stopped and pointed. "I hate that post," he said. He raised his rifle and fired. It sounded like a dry branch cracking. The post splintered along its right side, up toward the top. "There," Kenny said. "It's dead."

"Knock it off," Frank said, walking ahead.

Kenny looked at Tub. He smiled. "I hate that tree," he said, and fired again. Tub hurried to catch up with Frank. He started to speak but just then the dog ran out of the barn and barked at them. "Easy, boy," Frank said.

"I hate that dog." Kenny was behind them.

"That's enough," Frank said. "You put that gun down."

70   Kenny fired. The bullet went in between the dog's eyes. He sank right down into the snow, his legs splayed out on each side, his yellow eyes open and staring. Except for the blood he looked like a small bearskin rug. The blood ran down the dog's muzzle into the snow.

They all looked at the dog lying there.

"What did he ever do to you?" Tub asked. "He was just barking."

Kenny turned to Tub. "I hate you."

Tub shot from the waist. Kenny jerked backward against the fence and buckled to his knees. He knelt there with his hands pressed across his stomach. "Look," he said. His hands were covered with blood. In the dusk his blood was more blue than red. It seemed to belong to the shadows. It didn't seem out of place. Kenny eased himself onto his back. He sighed several times, deeply. "You shot me," he said.

75   "I had to," Tub said. He knelt beside Kenny. "Oh God," he said. "Frank. Frank."

Frank hadn't moved since Kenny killed the dog.

"Frank!" Tub shouted.

"I was just kidding around," Kenny said. "It was a joke. Oh!" he said, and arched his back suddenly. "Oh!" he said again, and dug his heels into the snow and pushed himself along on his head. Then he stopped and lay there, rocking back and forth on his heels and head like a wrestler doing warm-up exercises.

"Kenny," Frank said. He bent down and put his gloved hand on Kenny's brow. "You shot him," he said to Tub.

80   "He made me," Tub said.

"No, no, no," Kenny said.

Tub was weeping from the eyes and nostrils. His whole face was wet. Frank closed his eyes, then looked down at Kenny again. "Where does it hurt?"

"Everywhere," Kenny said, "just everywhere."

"Oh God," Tub said.

85   "I mean, where did it go in?" Frank said.

"Here." Kenny pointed at the wound in his stomach. It was welling slowly with blood.

"You're lucky," Frank said. "It's on the left side. It missed your appendix. If it had hit your appendix you'd really be in the soup." He turned and threw up onto the snow, holding his sides as if to keep warm.

"Are you all right?" Tub said.

"There's some aspirin in the truck," Kenny said.

90   "I'm all right," Frank said.

"For me," Kenny said.

"We'd better call an ambulance," Tub said.

"Jesus," Frank said. "What are we going to say?"

"Exactly what happened," Tub said. "He was going to shoot me but I shot him first."

95   "No sir!" Kenny said. "I wasn't either!"

Frank patted Kenny on the arm. "Easy does it, partner." He stood. "Let's go."

Tub picked up Kenny's rifle as they walked down toward the farm-house. "No sense leaving this around," he said. "Kenny might get ideas."

"I can tell you one thing," Frank said. "You've really done it this time. This definitely takes the cake."

They had to knock on the door twice before it was opened by a thin man with lank hair. The room behind him was filled with smoke. He squinted at them. "You get anything?" he asked.

100   "No," Frank said.

"I knew you wouldn't. That's what I told the other fellow."

"We've had an accident."

The man looked past Frank and Tub into the gloom. "Shoot your friend, did you?"

Frank nodded.

105   "I did," Tub said.

"I suppose you want to use the phone."

"If it's okay."

The man in the doorway looked behind him, then stepped back. Frank and Tub followed him into the house. There was a woman sitting by the stove in the middle of the room. The stove was smoking badly. She looked up and then down again at the child asleep in her lap. Her face was white and damp; strands of hair were pasted across her forehead. Tub warmed his hands over the stove while Frank went into the kitchen to call. The man who'd let them in stood at the window, his hands in his pockets.

"My friend shot your dog," Tub said.

110   The man nodded without turning around. "I should have done it myself. I just couldn't."

"He loved that dog so much," the woman said. The child squirmed and she rocked it.

"You asked him to?" Tub said. "You asked him to shoot your dog?"

"He was old and sick. Couldn't chew his food anymore. I should have done it myself."

"You couldn't have," the woman said. "Never in a million years."

115   The man shrugged.

Frank came out of the kitchen. "We'll have to take him ourselves. The nearest hospital is fifty miles from here and all their ambulances are out already."

The woman knew a shortcut but the directions were complicated and Tub had to write them down. The man told them where they could find some boards to carry Kenny on. He didn't have a flashlight but said he'd turn the porch light on.

It was dark outside. The clouds were low and heavy and the wind blew in shrill gusts. There was a screen loose on the house and it banged slowly and then quickly as the wind rose again. Frank went for the boards while Tub looked for Kenny, who was not where they had left him. Tub found him farther up the drive, lying on his stomach. "You okay?" Tub said.

"It hurts."

120   "Frank says it missed your appendix."

"I already had my appendix out."

"All right," Frank said, coming up to them. "We'll have you in a nice warm bed before you can say Jack Robinson." He put the two boards on Kenny's right side.

"Just as long as I don't have one of those male nurses," Kenny said.

"Ha ha," Frank said. "That's the spirit. Ready, set, *over you go,*" and he rolled Kenny onto the boards. Kenny screamed and kicked his legs in the air. When he quieted down Frank and Tub lifted the boards and carried him down the drive. Tub had the back end, and with the snow blowing into his face he had trouble with his footing. Also he was tired and the man inside had forgotten to turn the porch light on. Just past the house Tub slipped and threw out his hands to catch himself. The boards fell and Kenny tumbled out and rolled to the bottom of the drive, yelling the whole way down. He came to rest against the right front wheel of the truck.

125   "You fat moron," Frank said. "You aren't good for diddly."

Tub grabbed Frank by the collar and backed him hard up against the fence. Frank tried to pull his hands away but Tub shook him and snapped his head back and forth and finally Frank gave up.

"What do you know about fat," Tub said. "What do you know about glands." As he spoke he kept shaking Frank. "What do you know about me."

"All right," Frank said.

"No more," Tub said.

130   "All right."
       "No more talking to me like that. No more watching. No more laughing."
       "Okay, Tub. I promise."
       Tub let go of Frank and turned away. His arms hung straight at his sides.
       "I'm sorry, Tub." Frank touched him on the shoulder. "I'll be down at the
       truck."
135   Tub stood by the fence for a while and then got the rifles off the porch.
       Frank had rolled Kenny back onto the boards and they lifted him into the
       bed of the truck. Frank spread the seat blankets over him. "Warm enough?"
       he asked.
       Kenny nodded.
       "Okay. Now how does reverse work on this thing?"
       "All the way to the left and up." Kenny sat up as Frank started forward to
       the cab. "Frank!"
       "What?"
140   "If it sticks don't force it."
       The truck started right away. "One thing," Frank said, "you've got to hand
       it to the Japanese. A very ancient, very spiritual culture and they can still
       make a hell of a truck." He glanced over at Tub. "Look, I'm sorry. I didn't
       know you felt like that, honest to God I didn't. You should've said some-
       thing."
       "I did."
       "When? Name one time."
       "A couple hours ago."
145   "I guess I wasn't paying attention."
       "That's true, Frank," Tub said. "You don't pay attention very much."
       "Tub," Frank said, "what happened back there, I should've been more
       sympathetic. I realize that. You were going through a lot. I just want you to
       know it wasn't your fault. He was asking for it."
       "You think so?"
       "Absolutely. It was him or you. I would've done the same thing in your
       shoes, no question."
150   The wind was blowing into their faces. The snow was a moving white
       wall in front of their lights; it swirled into the cab through the hole in the
       windshield and settled on them. Tub clapped his hands and shifted around
       to stay warm, but it didn't work.
       "I'm going to have to stop," Frank said. "I can't feel my fingers."
       Up ahead they saw some lights off the road. It was a tavern. In the parking
       lot there were several jeeps and trucks. A couple of them had deer strapped
       across their hoods. Frank parked and they went back to Kenny. "How you
       doing, partner?" Frank said.
       "I'm cold."
       "Well, don't feel like the Lone Ranger. It's worse inside, take my word for
       it. You should get that windshield fixed."
155   "Look," Tub said, "he threw the blankets off." They were lying in a heap
       against the tailgate.
       "Now look, Kenny," Frank said, "it's no use whining about being cold if
       you're not going to try and keep warm. You've got to do your share." He
       spread the blankets over Kenny and tucked them in at the corners.
       "They blew off."

"Hold on to 'em, then."

"Why are we stopping, Frank?"

160   "Because if me and Tub don't get warmed up we're going to freeze solid and then where will you be?" He punched Kenny lightly in the arm. "So just hold your horses."

The bar was full of men in colored jackets, mostly orange. The waitress brought coffee. "Just what the doctor ordered," Frank said, cradling the steaming cup in his hand. "Tub, I've been thinking. What you said about me not paying attention, that's true."

"It's okay."

"No. I really had that coming. I guess I've just been a little too interested in old number one. I've had a lot on my mind. Not that that's any excuse."

"Forget it, Frank. I sort of lost my temper back there. I guess we're both a little on edge."

165   Frank shook his head. "It isn't just that."

"You want to talk about it?"

"Just between us, Tub?"

"Sure, Frank. Just between us."

"Tub, I think I'm going to be leaving Nancy."

170   "Oh, Frank. Oh, Frank." Tub sat back and shook his head.

Frank reached out and laid his hand on Tub's arm. "Tub, have you ever been really in love?"

"Well—"

"I mean *really* in love." He squeezed Tub's wrist. "With your whole being."

"I don't know. When you put it like that, I don't know."

175   "Then you haven't. Nothing against you, but you'd know it if you had." Frank let go of Tub's arm. "This isn't just some bit of fluff I'm talking about."

"Who is she, Frank?"

Frank paused. He looked into his empty cup. "Roxanne Brewer."

"Cliff Brewer's kid? The babysitter?"

"You can't just put people into categories like that, Tub. That's why the whole system is wrong. And that's why this country's going to hell in a row-boat."

180   Tub shook his head. "But she can't be more than—"

"Sixteen. She'll be seventeen in May." Frank smiled. "May fourth, three twenty-seven p.m. Hell, Tub, a hundred years ago she'd have been an old maid by that age. Juliet was only thirteen."

"Juliet? Juliet Miller? Jesus, Frank, she doesn't even have breasts. She's still collecting frogs."

"Not Juliet Miller. The *real* Juliet. Tub, don't you see how you're dividing people up into categories? He's an executive, she's a secretary, he's a truck driver, she's sixteen years old. Tub, this so-called babysitter, this so-called sixteen-year-old, has more in her little finger than most of us have in our entire bodies. I can tell you this little lady is something special."

"I know the kids like her."

185   "She's opened up whole worlds to me that I never knew were there."

"What does Nancy think about all this?"

"She doesn't know."

"You haven't told her?"

"Not yet. It's not so easy. She's been damned good to me all these years. Then there's the kids to consider." The brightness in Frank's eyes trembled and he wiped quickly at them with the back of his hand. "I guess you think I'm a complete bastard."

190   "No, Frank. I don't think that."

"Well, you *ought* to."

"Frank, when you've got a friend it means you've always got someone on your side, no matter what. That's how I feel about it, anyway."

"You mean that, Tub?"

"Sure I do."

195   "You don't know how good it feels to hear you say that."

Kenny had tried to get out of the truck. He was jackknifed over the tailgate, his head hanging above the bumper. They lifted him back into the bed and covered him again. He was sweating and his teeth chattered. "It hurts, Frank."

"It wouldn't hurt so much if you just stayed put. Now we're going to the hospital. Got that? Say it—'I'm going to the hospital.'"

"I'm going to the hospital."

"Again."

200   "I'm going to the hospital."

"Now just keep saying that to yourself and before you know it we'll be there."

After they had gone a few miles Tub turned to Frank. "I just pulled a real boner," he said.

"What's that?"

"I left the directions on the table back there."

205   "That's okay. I remember them pretty well."

The snowfall lightened and the clouds began to roll back off the fields, but it was no warmer, and after a time both Frank and Tub were bitten through and shaking. Frank almost didn't make it around a curve, and they decided to stop at the next roadhouse.

There was an automatic hand dryer in the bathroom and they took turns standing in front of it, opening their jackets and shirts and letting the jet of hot air blow across their faces and chests.

"You know," Tub said, "what you told me back there, I appreciate it. Trusting me."

Frank opened and closed his fingers in front of the nozzle. "The way I look at it, Tub, no man is an island. You've got to trust someone."

210   "Frank?"

Frank waited.

"When I said that about my glands, that wasn't true. The truth is I just shovel it in. Day and night. In the shower. On the freeway." He turned and let the air play over his back. "I've even got stuff in the paper-towel machine at work."

"There's nothing wrong with your glands at all?" Frank had taken his boots and socks off. He held first his right foot, then his left, up to the nozzle.

"No. There never was."

215   "Does Alice know?" The machine went off and Frank started lacing up his boots.

"Nobody knows. That's the worst of it, Frank. Not the being fat—I never got any big kick out of being thin—but the lying. Having to lead a double life like a spy or a hit man. I understand those guys, I know what they go through. Always having to think about what you say and do. Always feeling like people are watching you, trying to catch you at something. Never able to just be yourself. Like when I make a big deal about only having an orange for breakfast and then scarf all the way to work. Oreos, Mars bars, Twinkies. Sugar Babies. Snickers." Tub glanced at Frank and looked quickly away. "Pretty disgusting, isn't it?"

"Tub. Tub." Frank shook his head. "Come on." He took Tub's arm and led him into the restaurant half of the bar. "My friend is hungry," he told the waitress. "Bring four orders of pancakes, plenty of butter and syrup."

"Frank—"

"Sit down."

220   When the dishes came Frank carved out slabs of butter and just laid them on the pancakes. Then he emptied the bottle of syrup, moving it back and forth over the plates. He leaned forward on his elbows and rested his chin in one hand. "Go on, Tub."

Tub ate several mouthfuls, then started to wipe his lips. Frank took the napkin away from him. "No wiping," he said. Tub kept at it. The syrup covered his chin; it dripped to a point like a goatee. "Weigh in, Tub," Frank said, pushing another fork across the table. "Get down to business." Tub took the fork in his left hand and lowered his head and started really chowing down. "Clean your plate," Frank said when the pancakes were gone, and Tub lifted each of the four plates and licked it clean. He sat back, trying to catch his breath.

"Beautiful," Frank said. "Are you full?"

"I'm full," Tub said. "I've never been so full."

Kenny's blankets were bunched up against the tailgate again.

225   "They must've blown off," Tub said.

"They're not doing him any good," Frank said. "We might as well get some use out of them."

Kenny mumbled. Tub bent over him. "What? Speak up."

"I'm going to the hospital," Kenny said.

"Attaboy," Frank said.

230   The blankets helped. The wind still got their faces and Frank's hands, but it was much better. The fresh snow on the road and the trees sparkled under the beam of the headlight. Squares of light from farmhouse windows fell onto the blue snow in the fields.

"Frank," Tub said after a time, "you know that farmer? He told Kenny to kill his dog."

"You're kidding!" Frank leaned forward, considering. "That Kenny. What a card." He laughed, and so did Tub.

Tub smiled out the back window. Kenny lay with his arms folded over his stomach, moving his lips at the stars. Right overhead was the Big Dipper, and behind, hanging between Kenny's feet in the direction of the hospital, was the North Star, polestar, Help to Sailors. As the truck twisted through the gentle hills the star went back and forth between Kenny's boots, staying always in his sight. "I'm going to the hospital," Kenny said. But he was wrong. They had taken a different turn a long way back.

Say Yes

[1985]

They were doing the dishes, his wife washing while he dried. He'd washed the night before. Unlike most men he knew, he really pitched in on the housework. A few months earlier he'd overheard a friend of his wife's congratulate her on having such a considerate husband, and he thought, *I try.* Helping out with the dishes was one way of showing how considerate he was.

They talked about different things and somehow got on the subject of whether white people should marry black people. He said that all things considered, he thought it was a bad idea.

"Why?" she asked.

Sometimes his wife got this look where she pinched her brows together and bit her lower lip and stared down at something. When he saw her like this he knew he should keep his mouth shut, but he never did. Actually it made him talk more. She had that look now.

5   "Why?" she asked again, and stood there with her hand inside a bowl, not washing it but just holding it above the water.

"Listen," he said, "I went to school with blacks and I've worked with blacks and lived on the same street with blacks and we've always gotten along just fine. I don't need you coming along now and implying that I'm a racist."

"I didn't imply anything," she said, and began washing the bowl again, turning it around in her hand as though she were shaping it. "I just don't see what's wrong with a white person marrying a black person, that's all."

"They don't come from the same culture as we do. Listen to them sometime—they even have their own language. That's okay with me, I *like* hearing them talk"—he did; for some reason it always lifted his mood—"but it's different. A person from their culture and a person from our culture could never really *know* each other."

"Like you know me?" his wife asked.

10   "Yes. Like I know you."

"But if they love each other," she said. She was washing faster now, not looking at him.

Oh boy, he thought. He said, "Don't take my word for it. Look at the statistics. Most of those marriages break up."

"Statistics." She was piling dishes on the drainboard at a terrific rate, just swiping at them with the cloth. Many of them were greasy, and he could see flecks of food between the tines of the forks. "All right," she said, "what about foreigners? I suppose you think the same thing about two foreigners getting married."

"Yes," he said, "as a matter of fact I do. How can you understand someone who comes from a completely different background?"

15   "Different," said his wife. "Not the same, like us."

"Yes, different," he snapped, angry with her for resorting to this trick of repeating his words so they sounded crass, or hypocritical. "These are dirty," he said, and dumped all the silverware back into the sink.

The water had gone flat and gray. She stared down at it, her lips pressed tight together, then plunged her hands under the surface. "Oh!" she cried, and jumped back. She took her right hand by the wrist and held it up. Her thumb was bleeding.

"Ann, don't move," he said. "Stay right there." He ran upstairs to the bathroom and rummaged in the medicine chest for alcohol, cotton, and a Band-Aid. When he came back down she was leaning against the refrigerator with her eyes closed, still holding her hand by the wrist. He took the hand and dabbed at her thumb with the cotton. The bleeding had stopped. He squeezed it to see how deep the wound was and a single drop of blood welled up, trembling and bright, and fell to the floor. Over the thumb she stared at him accusingly. "It's shallow," he said. "Tomorrow you won't even know it's there." He hoped that she appreciated how quickly he'd come to her aid. He had acted out of concern for her, with no thought of getting anything in return, but now the thought occurred to him that it would be a nice gesture on her part not to start up that conversation again, as he was tired of it. "I'll finish up here," he said. "You go and relax."

"That's okay," she said. "I'll dry."

20   He began to wash the silverware again, giving a lot of attention to the forks.

"So," she said, "you wouldn't have married me if I'd been black."

"For Christ's sake, Ann!"

"Well, that's what you said, didn't you?"

"No, I did not. The whole question is ridiculous. If you had been black we probably wouldn't even have met. You would've had your friends and I would've had mine. The only black girl I ever really knew was my partner in the debating club, and I was already going out with you by then."

25   "But if we had met, and I'd been black?"

"Then you probably would have been going out with a black guy." He picked up the rinsing nozzle and sprayed the silverware. The water was so hot that the metal darkened to pale blue, then turned silver again.

"Let's say I wasn't," she said. "Let's say I'm black and unattached and we meet and fall in love."

He glanced over at her. She was watching him, and her eyes were bright. "Look," he said, taking a reasonable tone, "this is stupid. If you were black you wouldn't be you." As he said this he realized it was absolutely true. There was no possible argument against the fact that she would not be herself if she were black. So he said it again: "If you were black you wouldn't be you."

"I know," she said, "but let's just say."

30   He took a deep breath. He had won the argument but still felt cornered. "Say what?" he asked.

"That I'm black, but still me, and we fall in love. Will you marry me?"

He thought about it.

"Well?" she said, and stepped close to him. Her eyes were even brighter. "Will you marry me?"

"I'm thinking," he said.

35   "You won't, I can tell. You're going to say no."

"Let's not move too fast on this," he said. "There are lots of things to consider. We don't want to do something we might regret for the rest of our lives."

"No more considering. Yes or no."

"Since you put it that way—"

"Yes or no."

40   "Jesus, Ann. All right—no."

"Thank you," she said, and walked from the kitchen into the living room. A moment later he heard her turning the pages of a magazine. He knew she was too angry to be actually reading it, but she wasn't snapping through the pages like he would've done; she turned them slowly, as if she were studying every word. She was demonstrating her indifference to him, and it had the effect he knew she'd intended. It hurt him.

He had no choice but to demonstrate his indifference to her. Quietly, thoroughly, he washed the rest of the dishes. Then he dried them and put them away. He wiped the counters and the stove and scoured the linoleum where the drop of blood had fallen. While he was at it, he decided, he might as well mop the whole floor. When he was done the kitchen looked new, just as it had when they were first shown the house, before they had ever lived here.

He picked up the garbage pail and went outside. The night was clear and he could see a few stars to the west, where the lights of the town didn't blur them out. On El Camino the traffic was steady and light, peaceful as a river. He felt ashamed that he'd let his wife get him into a fight. In another thirty years or so they both would be dead. What would all that stuff matter then? He thought of the years they had spent together and how close they were and how well they knew each other, and his throat tightened so that he could hardly breathe. His face and neck began to tingle. Warmth flooded his chest. He stood there for a while, enjoying these sensations, then picked up the pail and went out the back gate.

The two mutts from down the street had pulled over the garbage can again. One of them was rolling around on his back and the other had something in its mouth. When they saw him coming they trotted away with short, mincing steps. Normally he would've tossed a rock or two after them, but this time he let them go.

45   The house was dark when he came back inside. She was in the bathroom. He stood outside the door and called her name. He heard bottles clinking, but she didn't answer him. "Ann, I'm really sorry," he said. "I'll make it up to you, I promise."

"How?" she asked.

He wasn't expecting this. But from a sound in her voice, a level and definite note that was strange to him, he knew he had to come up with the right answer. He leaned against the door. "I'll marry you," he whispered.

"We'll see," she said. "Go on to bed. I'll be out in a minute."

He undressed and got under the covers. Finally he heard the bathroom door open and close.

50   "Turn off the light," she said from the hallway.

"What?"

"Turn off the light."

He reached over and pulled the chain on the bedside lamp. The room went dark. "All right," he said. He lay there, but nothing happened. "All right," he said again. Then he heard a movement across the room. He sat up but couldn't see a thing. The room was silent. His heart pounded as it had on their first night together, as it still did when he woke at a noise in the darkness and waited to hear it again—the sound of someone moving through the house, a stranger.

Powder

[1992]

Just before Christmas my father took me skiing at Mount Baker. He'd had to fight for the privilege of my company, because my mother was still angry with him for sneaking me into a nightclub during his last visit, to see Thelonius Monk.

He wouldn't give up. He promised, hand on heart, to take good care of me and have me home for dinner on Christmas Eve, and she relented. But as we were checking out of the lodge that morning it began to snow, and in this snow he observed some quality that made it necessary for us to get in one last run. We got in several last runs. He was indifferent to my fretting. Snow whirled around us in bitter, blinding squalls, hissing like sand, and still we skied. As the lift bore us to the peak yet again, my father looked at his watch and said: "Criminey. This'll have to be a fast one."

By now I couldn't see the trail. There was no point in trying. I stuck to him like white on rice and did what he did and somehow made it to the bottom without sailing off a cliff. We returned our skis and my father put chains on the Austin-Healy while I swayed from foot to foot, clapping my mittens and wishing I were home. I could see everything. The green tablecloth, the plates with the holly pattern, the red candles waiting to be lit.

We passed a diner on our way out. "You want some soup?" my father asked. I shook my head. "Buck up," he said. "I'll get you there. Right, doctor?"

5   I was supposed to say, "Right, doctor," but I didn't say anything.

A state trooper waved us down outside the resort. A pair of sawhorses were blocking the road. The trooper came up to our car and bent down to my father's window. His face was bleached by the cold. Snowflakes clung to his eyebrows and to the fur trim of his jacket and cap.

"Don't tell me," my father said.

The trooper told him. The road was closed. It might get cleared, it might not. Storm took everyone by surprise. So much, so fast. Hard to get people moving. Christmas Eve. What can you do?

My father said: "Look. We're talking about four, five inches. I've taken this car through worse than that."

10   The trooper straightened up, boots creaking. His face was out of sight but I could hear him. "The road is closed."

My father sat with both hands on the wheel, rubbing the wood with his thumbs. He looked at the barricade for a long time. He seemed to be trying to master the idea of it. Then he thanked the trooper, and with a weird, old-maidy show of caution turned the car around. "Your mother will never forgive me for this," he said.

"We should have left before," I said. "Doctor."

He didn't speak to me again until we were both in a booth at the diner, waiting for our burgers. "She won't forgive me," he said. "Do you understand? Never."

"I guess," I said, but no guesswork was required; she wouldn't forgive him.

15   "I can't let that happen." He bent toward me. "I'll tell you what I want. I want us to be all together again. Is that what you want?"

"Yes, sir."

He bumped my chin with his knuckles. "That's all I needed to hear."

When we finished eating he went to the pay phone in the back of the diner, then joined me in the booth again. I figured he'd called my mother, but he didn't give a report. He sipped at his coffee and stared out the window at the empty road. "Come on, come on," he said. A little while later he said, "Come on!" When the trooper's car went past, lights flashing, he got up and dropped some money on the check. "O.K. Vámonos."

The wind had died. The snow was falling straight down, less of it now; lighter. We drove away from the resort, right up to the barricade. "Move it," my father told me. When I looked at him he said, "What are you waiting for?" I got out and dragged one of the sawhorses aside, then put it back after he drove through. He pushed the door open for me. "Now you're an accomplice," he said. "We go down together." He put the car into gear and gave me a look. "Joke, doctor."

20   "Funny, doctor."

Down the first long stretch I watched the road behind us, to see if the trooper was on our tail. The barricade vanished. Then there was nothing but snow: snow on the road, snow kicking up from the chains, snow on the trees, snow in the sky; and our trail in the snow. I faced around and had a shock. The lie of the road behind us had been marked by our own tracks, but there were no tracks ahead of us. My father was breaking virgin snow between a line of tall trees. He was humming "Stars Fell on Alabama." I felt snow brush along the floorboards under my feet. To keep my hands from shaking, I clamped them between my knees.

My father grunted in a thoughtful way and said, "Don't ever try this yourself."

"I won't."

"That's what you say now, but someday you'll get your license and then you'll think you can do anything. Only you won't be able to do this. You need, I don't know—a certain instinct."

25   "Maybe I have it."

"You don't. You have your strong points, but not . . . this. I only mention it, because I don't want you to get the idea this is something just anybody can do. I'm a great driver. That's not a virtue, O.K.? It's just a fact, and one you should be aware of. Of course you have to give the old heap some credit, too—there aren't many cars I'd try this with. Listen!"

I listened. I heard the slap of the chains, the stiff, jerky rasps of the wipers, the purr of the engine. It really did purr. The car was almost new. My father couldn't afford it, and kept promising to sell it, but here it was.

I said, "Where do you think that policeman went to?"

"Are you warm enough?" He reached over and cranked up the blower. Then he turned off the wipers. We didn't need them. The clouds had brightened. A few sparse, feathery flakes drifted into our slipstream and were swept away. We left the trees and entered a broad field of snow that ran level for a while and then tilted sharply downward. Orange stakes had been planted at intervals in two parallel lines and my father steered a course between them, though they were far enough apart to leave considerable doubt in my mind as to where exactly the road lay. He was humming again, doing little scat riffs around the melody.

30   "O.K. then. What are my strong points?"

"Don't get me started," he said. "It'd take all day."

"Oh, right. Name one."

"Easy. You always think ahead."

True. I always thought ahead. I was a boy who kept his clothes on numbered hangers to insure proper rotation. I bothered my teachers for homework assignments far ahead of their due dates so I could make up schedules.

I thought ahead, and that was why I knew that there would be other troopers waiting for us at the end of our ride, if we got there. What I did not know was that my father would wheedle and plead his way past them—he didn't sing "O Tannenbaum" but just about—and get me home for dinner, buying a little more time before my mother decided to make the split final. I knew we'd get caught; I was resigned to it. And maybe for this reason I stopped moping and began to enjoy myself.

35   Why not? This was one for the books. Like being in a speedboat, but better. You can't go downhill in a boat. And it was all ours. And it kept coming, the laden trees, the unbroken surface of snow, the sudden white vistas. Here and there I saw hints of the road, ditches, fences, stakes, but not so many that I could have found my way. But then I didn't have to. My father was driving. My father in his 48th year, rumpled, kind, bankrupt of honor, flushed with certainty. He was a great driver. All persuasion, no coercion. Such subtlety at the wheel, such tactful pedalwork. I actually trusted him. And the best was yet to come—the switchbacks and hairpins. Impossible to describe. Except maybe to say this: If you haven't driven fresh powder, you haven't driven.

Bullet in the Brain   [1995]

Anders couldn't get to the bank until just before it closed, so of course the line was endless and he got stuck behind two women whose loud, stupid conversation put him in a murderous temper. He was never in the best of tempers anyway, Anders—a book critic known for the weary, elegant savagery with which he dispatched almost everything he reviewed.

With the line still doubled around the rope, one of the tellers stuck a POSITION CLOSED sign in her window and walked to the back of the bank, where she leaned against a desk and began to pass the time with a man shuffling papers. The women in front of Anders broke off their conversation and watched the teller with hatred. "Oh, that's nice," one of them said. She turned to Anders and added, confident of his accord, "One of those little human touches that keep us coming back for more."

Anders had conceived his own towering hatred of the teller, but he immediately turned it on the presumptuous crybaby in front of him. "Damned unfair," he said. "Tragic, really. If they're not chopping off the wrong leg or bombing your ancestral village, they're closing their positions."

She stood her ground. "I didn't say it was tragic," she said. "I just think it's a pretty lousy way to treat your customers."

5   "Unforgivable," Anders said. "Heaven will take note."

She sucked in her cheeks but stared past him and said nothing. Anders saw that her friend was looking in the same direction. And then the tellers stopped what they were doing, the other customers slowly turned, and silence came over the bank. Two men wearing black ski masks and blue business suits were standing to the side of the door. One of them had a pistol pressed against the guard's neck. The guard's eyes were closed, and his lips were moving. The other man had a sawed-off shotgun. "Keep your big mouth shut!" the man with the pistol said, though no one had spoken a word. "One of you tellers hits the alarm, you're all dead meat."

"Oh, bravo," Anders said. "'*Dead meat.*'" He turned to the woman in front of him. "Great script, eh? The stern, brass-knuckled poetry of the dangerous classes."

She looked at him with drowning eyes.

The man with the shotgun pushed the guard to his knees. He handed the shotgun to his partner and yanked the guard's wrists up behind his back and locked them together with a pair of handcuffs. He toppled him onto the floor with a kick between the shoulder blades, then took his shotgun back and went over to the security gate at the end of the counter. He was short and heavy and moved with peculiar slowness. "Buzz him in," his partner said. The man with the shotgun opened the gate and sauntered along the line of tellers; handing each of them a plastic bag. When he came to the empty position he looked over at the man with the pistol, who said, "Whose slot is that?"

10   Anders watched the teller. She put her hand to her throat and turned to the man she'd been talking to. He nodded. "Mine," she said.

"Then get your ugly ass in gear and fill that bag."

"There you go," Anders said to the woman in-front of him. "Justice is done."

"Hey! Bright boy! Did I tell you to talk?"

"No," Anders said.

15   "Then shut your trap."

"Did you hear that?" Anders said, " 'Bright boy.' Right out of *The Killers*."[1]

"Please, be quiet," the woman said.

"Hey, you deaf or what?" The man with the pistol walked over to Anders and poked the weapon into his gut. "You think I'm playing games?"

"No," Anders said, but the barrel tickled like a stiff finger and he had to fight back the titters. He did this by making himself stare into the man's eyes, which were clearly visible behind the holes in the mask: pale blue and rawly red-rimmed. The man's left eyelid kept twitching. He breathed out a piercing, ammoniac smell that shocked Anders more than anything that had happened, and he was beginning to develop a sense of unease when the man prodded him again with the pistol.

20   "You like me, bright boy?" he said. "You want to suck my dick?"

"No," Anders said.

"Then stop looking at me."

Anders fixed his gaze on the man's shiny wing-tip shoes.

"Not down there. Up there." He stuck the pistol under Anders's chin and pushed it upward until he was looking at the ceiling.

25   Anders had never paid much attention to that part of the bank, a pompous old building with marble floors and counters and gilt scroll-work over the tellers' cages. The domed ceiling had been decorated with mythological figures whose fleshy, toga-draped ugliness Anders had taken in at a glance many years earlier and afterward declined to notice. Now he had no choice but to scrutinize the painter's work. It was even worse than he remembered, and all of it executed with the utmost gravity. The artist had a few tricks up his sleeve and used them again and again—a certain rosy blush on the underside of the clouds, a coy backward glance on the faces of the cupids and fauns. The ceiling was crowded with various dramas, but the one that caught Anders's eye was Zeus and Europa— portrayed, in this rendition, as a bull ogling a cow from behind a haystack. To make the cow sexy, the painter had canted her hips suggestively and

---

[1]**Bright boy . . . The killers** a gunman in Ernest Hemingway's short story "The Killers" (1927) uses this term.

given her long, droopy eyelashes through which she gazed back at the bull with sultry welcome. The bull wore a smirk and his eyebrows were arched. If there'd been a caption bubbling out of his mouth, it would have said HUBBA HUBBA.

"What's so funny, bright boy?"

"Nothing."

30   "You think I'm comical? You think I'm some kind of clown?"

"No."

"You think you can fuck with me?"

"No."

"Fuck with me again, you're history. *Capiche?*"[2]

Anders burst out laughing. He covered his mouth with both hands and said, "I'm sorry, I'm sorry," then snorted helplessly through his fingers and said, "*Capiche*—oh, God, *capiche*," and at that the man with the pistol raised the pistol and shot Anders right in the head.

The bullet smashed Anders's skull and plowed through his brain and exited behind his right ear, scattering shards of bone into the cerebral cortex, the corpus callosum, back toward the basal ganglia, and down into the thalamus. But before all this occurred, the first appearance of the bullet in the cerebrum set off a crackling chain of ion transports and neurotransmissions. Because of their peculiar origin these traced a peculiar pattern, flukishly calling to life a summer afternoon some forty years past, and long since lost to memory. After striking the cranium, the bullet was moving at nine hundred feet per second, a pathetically sluggish, glacial pace compared with the synaptic lightning that flashed around it. Once in the brain, that is, the bullet came under the mediation of brain time, which gave Anders plenty of leisure to contemplate the scene that, in a phrase he would have abhorred, "passed before his eyes."

35   It is worth noting what Anders did not remember, given what he did recall. He did not remember his first lover, Sherry, or what he had most madly loved about her, before it came to irritate him—her unembarrassed carnality, and especially the cordial way she had with his unit, which she called Mr. Mole, as in *Uh-oh, looks like Mr. Mole wants to play.* Anders did not remember his wife, whom he had also loved before she exhausted him with her predictability, or his daughter, now a sullen professor of economics at Dartmouth. He did not remember standing just outside his daughter's door as she lectured her bear about his naughtiness and described the appalling punishments Paws would receive unless he changed his ways. He did not remember a single line of the hundreds of poems he had committed to memory in his youth so he could give himself the shivers at will—not "Silent, upon a peak in Darien," or "My God, I heard this day," or "All my pretty ones? Did you say all? O hell-kite! All?"[3] None of these did he remember; not one. Anders did not remember his dying mother saying of his father. "I should have stabbed him in his sleep."

---

[2]**Capiche?** Get it? (from the Italian verb, capire, "to understand").   [3]**He did not remember . . . O hell-kite! All?"** The first quotation ("Silent . . . Darien") is from John Keats's "On First Looking into Chapman's Homer" (see page 622); the second ("My God") is from George Herbert's poem called "Man" (early seventeenth century); the third quotation ("All. . .All?") is from Shakespeare's *Macbeth*, 4.3.217, when Macduff learns that Macbeth has killed Macduff's children.

He did not remember Professor Josephs telling his class how Athenian prisoners in Sicily had been released if they could recite Aeschylus,[4] and then reciting Aeschylus himself, right there, in the Greek. Anders did not remember how his eyes had burned at those sounds. He did not remember the surprise of seeing a college classmate's name on the dust jacket of a novel not long after they graduated, or the respect he had felt after reading the book. He did not remember the pleasure of giving respect.

Nor did Anders remember seeing a woman leap to her death from the building opposite his own just days after his daughter was born. He did not remember shouting, "Lord have mercy!" He did not remember deliberately crashing his father's car into a tree, or having his ribs kicked in by three policemen at an antiwar rally, or waking himself up with laughter. He did not remember when he began to regard the heap of books on his desk with boredom and dread, or when he grew angry at writers for writing them. He did not remember when everything began to remind him of something else.

This is what he remembered. Heat. A baseball field. Yellow grass, the whir of insects, himself leaning against a tree as the boys of the neighborhood gather for a pickup game. He looks on as the others argue the relative genius of Mantle and Mays. They have been worrying this subject all summer, and it has become tedious to Anders: an oppression, like the heat.

Then the last two boys arrive, Coyle and a cousin of his from Mississippi. Anders has never met Coyle's cousin before and will never see him again. He says hi with the rest but takes no further notice of him until they've chosen sides and someone asks the cousin what position he wants to play. "Shortstop," the boy says. "Short's the best position they is." Anders turns and looks at him. He wants to hear Coyle's cousin repeat what he's just said, though he knows better than to ask. The others will think he's being a jerk, ragging the kid for his grammar. But that isn't it, not at all—it's that Anders is strangely roused, elated, by those final two words, their pure unexpectedness and their music. He takes the field in a trance, repeating them to himself.

40   The bullet is already in the brain; it won't be outrun forever, or charmed to a halt. In the end it will do its work and leave the troubled skull behind, dragging its comet's tail of memory and hope and talent and love into the marble hall of commerce. That can't be helped. But for now Anders can still make time. Time for the shadows to lengthen on the grass, time for the tethered dog to bark at the flying ball, time for the boy in right field to smack his sweat-blackened mitt and softly chant, *They is, they is, they is.*

---

[4]**Aeschylus** Wolff seems to have made a mistake: Tradition says that some Athenian prisoners in Sicily earned a reprieve by reciting verses from the Greek dramatist Euripides (not, as Wolff says, Aeschylus).

YOUR TURN

1. How would you characterize the Anders whom we see in the first part of "Bullet in the Brain" (i.e., up to the place where Wolff indicates a break)? How would you characterize the youthful Anders, the Anders whom we see in the second part of the story?

2. The second part itself can be thought of as having two parts—first, What Anders *did not* remember and second, What Anders *did* remember.

Suppose these two parts (of the second part) had been reversed. What would the story gain or lose?

3. Suppose Wolff showed you the manuscript and said he had not yet chosen a title but he was thinking of the following possibilities, given here in alphabetic order: "Anders," "The Bank Robbery," "Brain Works," "Bullet in the Brain," "Memories, " "Shortstop," "They Is." In an argumentative essay of about 500 words, set forth your choice. You may want to devote approximately equal space to your examination of each candidate, or you may want to (for instance) quickly dispose of the two or three that you think are obviously poor choices—but you will have to explain, briefly why you think they are obviously poor choices—and then spend more time on the remaining (serious) candidates. In any case, please remember that you are writing an argument. *Optional variation:* In your essay you may want to reject all of these candidates and offer a title of your own invention.

Tobias Wolff on Novels and Short Stories

On Stories and Poems

INTERVIEWER: Your stories remind me of poems, actually.

WOLFF: Good. I believe that the short story is as different a form from the novel as poetry is, and the best stories seem to me to be perhaps closer in spirit to poetry than to novels. They have to be; there just can't be any kind of relaxation of the narrative. Everything has to be pulling weight in a short story for it to be really of the first order. And you can't do that with a novel. A novel invites digression and a little relaxation of the grip because a reader can't endure being held that tightly in hand for so long a time.

—From interview, *Salon*, December 1996. Web. 22 Jan, 2010. www.salon.com.

On Stories and Novels

INTERVIEWER: How do the processes of working on a short story or novel or memoir differ from one another, for you? Is there any difference once you've actually sat down and begun to work?

WOLFF: In the process itself, no, not really. The great thing about writing a short story is that you know the damn thing's going to end—no time soon, perhaps, but you can see the horizon. But then you're also thinking, Oh no, when I get there I'm going to have to call another world into existence. The beauty of working in a longer form is that, though you can't always see the horizon, and usually don't, you are returning to the same world day after day, enriching it and deepening it. But there's always the anxiety—My God, I haven't finished anything in years. Will I ever do this or will lightning strike me dead before I finish, and will all this time and work be wasted? I have great admiration for people who spend ten, fifteen, twenty years on a single piece of work, the courage and fortitude it takes to do that.

—From "The Art of Fiction," Interview by Jack Livings. *Paris Review* 171. 183 (Fall 2004). Print.

On Judging Characters

ORRINGER: Do you think that the tendency to be hard on yourself in your memoirs translates to the tendency to be hard on the protagonists of your fictional narratives?

WOLFF: I hope not. I do write, as indeed most writers do, about things that have gone wrong. There's not much of a story if things have gone right. Stories are about problems, and not the kinds of problems that result from a safe falling out of a window, but from somebody having a choice and having a problem with that choice, and then the series of consequences that follow from making that choice. To portray that honestly is to show the way people parse out their choices, and self-interest naturally comes into play. It isn't so much a matter of wishing to be hard on people as wishing to be truthful. If there's a moral quality to my work, I suppose it has to do with will and the exercise of choice within one's will. The choices we make tend to narrow down a myriad of opportunities to just a few, and those choices tend to reinforce themselves in whatever direction we've started to go, including the wrong direction. Our present government[1] likes to lecture us on the virtue of *staying the course*. Well, maybe it's not such a good idea to stay the course if you're headed toward the rocks. There's something to be said for changing course if you're about to drive your ship onto the shoals.

—From interview by Julie Orringer, *Believer Magazine,* June 2004. Web. 22 Jan. 2010. www.believermag.com.

On Ambiguity

Wolff discussed the importance of leaving some ambiguity in each story he writes, in response to an audience member/teacher who asked about the details Wolff used, and their symbolism. "Otherwise,'" he said, "it would just be another Op-Ed piece."

—From Adam Daum, "Tobias Wolff Speaks About Perfection and His New Collection of Short Stories," *Bay Area Intellect,* 30 April 2008. Web. 22 Jan. 2010. www.bayareaintellect.com.

On Economy in Writing

INTERVIEWER: More important than irony to you seems to be economy. You strategically parse out details to create mood and character, such as a character pouring "a long stream of sugar into her coffee." Are you ever nervous that you've pared it too much?

WOLFF: If I repeat something, it'll spoil the effect I'm after. When I finish a story and it feels starved or I find I've cut too much into the bone, I can always go back and add flesh afterwards.

INTERVIEWER: You have a lot of faith in your readers to pay attention, don't you?

WOLFF: Short story readers tend to be a self-screening group, but, yes, I've been pretty lucky in my readers. The best writing is writing that trusts the reader.

—From "In Conversation with Tobias Wolff," Interview by Daniel Asa Rose. *Washington Post,* 13 April, 2008. Print.

---

[1]**present government** the administration of George W. Bush, with reference to the war in Iraq.

On the Elements of a Good Story

TAVIS: What for you, since you teach this and since you write rather well yourself, what are the elements? I'm not looking so much for an example, although I'm happy to take it. I'm not looking so much for an example as I am for the elements of what you think makes for a good or a great short story.

WOLFF: Well, that's a good question. I suppose the first thing is that it be of compelling interest to the reader in some way, that the reader should feel that even though the character may come from a different country, different ethnicity, different faith, that what is at stake for the character in a short story is somehow at stake for you too, that that shared humanity is somehow made—that the reader is made to feel that with the character.

So what is consequential to the people in the story is consequential for you as the reader. That, I think, is what you're after in the novel as well as the short story. From then on, I think, you know, all bets are off. How you do that is up to each writer, but that's the essential.

TAVIS: That's a good answer. I like that. That said, how would you describe the new and selected stories in this text?

WOLFF: Well, I hope that, in some way or other, they all, each in its own way, advance that sense of particular humanity and the various moral and spiritual crises that all of us undergo, that somehow they're tracked in these stories. Our tendency to duplicity, to self-interest, to putting conditions on our love, to posing, all those sorts of things that we, in ways large and small, find ourselves doing.

The short story, I think, is a very good form for that. It kind of catches those moments beautifully. In a novel, in a more sustained narrative, you need more colors, you know, more facets, but a short story is very good at catching that thing, you know, seen almost out of the corner of the eye in your own nature. So I find dramatic form for these things and that's how these stories took their shape.

—From interview by Tavis Smiley, "A Conversation with Tobias Wolff."
2 May 2008. Web. 22 Jan. 2010. www.pbs.org.

Student Essay About Gender Conflict in "Say Yes"

A student, Bob Williams, was assigned in a literature course to write a short essay about "gender conflict" in Tobias Wolff's story "Say Yes." After reading the story carefully, he noted some impressions in his journal:

> I'm not sure how I am supposed to feel about the husband. Sometimes he seems to be basically a good guy who loves his wife even though they are having problems. But then sometimes he seems to be the problem himself, in this scene just itching for a fight. But she's no prize either.
>
> I can't figure out why Wolff has included the conversation about interracial marriages. Why did he pick this subject for the couple to fight about?

Here is the final version of the essay that Bob wrote about "Say Yes." Notice how he keyed it to the opening paragraph of the story.

Bob Williams
Professor Jacobs
Literature 100
1 June 2010

He's the Problem: The Husband in "Say Yes"

Tobias Wolff's insights into "gender conflict" are evident in the first paragraph of his story. He starts by showing the couple doing something together—"they were washing the dishes"—but then in the next phrase he indicates that they performed separate tasks—"his wife washing while he dried." It seems like a small point, but in its own way I think this sentence is already revealing the emotional divide between the husband and the wife, and is foreshadowing the angry argument to come.

The next sentences seem to portray the husband in a positive light. He helped with the dishes the night before, and that time *he* washed, so it seems that this couple shares the domestic chores each night. Wolff appears, then, to be bringing them back together a bit after separating them, through their different activities, in the first sentence of the story. This husband is a good, sensitive person who doesn't expect his wife to handle all of the messy chores in the kitchen.

But maybe Wolff wants us to realize that the husband is taken with himself—that not only does he help his wife with the chores, but also likes to compliment himself, as though he were doing her a favor. He likes to think of himself as better than other husbands; when Wolff writes how the husband "pitches in," I can hear the husband saying these words to himself as evidence of what a decent, down-to-earth guy he is. I notice that the husband also enjoys hearing other people compliment him: "he'd overheard a friend of his wife's congratulate her on having such a considerate husband." Is Wolff's main point that the husband *is* considerate, or that he is a little too proud of himself?

When Wolff writes in the final sentence of this paragraph that "helping out with the dishes was a way he had of showing how considerate he was," he makes clear how we are to respond to the husband. What matters to the husband is not what he feels toward his wife, but, instead, *showing* what he feels. He wants to prove to the world that unlike other men, he treats his wife as an equal; he won't take advantage of her or insist that because she is the wife, she ought

Williams 2

to do the household duties. From one point of view, this sounds appealing. But Wolff's aim is to make the reader understand the difference between doing something for its own sake and doing something for the purpose of self-approval. For this husband, washing the dishes is just another opportunity for feeling pleased with himself.

Williams 3

Work Cited

Wolff, Tobias, "Say Yes." *An Introduction to Literature*. Sylvan Barnet, William Burto, and William E. Cain. 16th ed. Ed. New York: Longman, 2011. 349–51. Print.

The Analysis Briefly Analyzed

- The student pays close attention to Wolff's language in the opening paragraph. Do you agree with his interpretations—for example, his explanation of the meaning of "showing how considerate he was"?
- Do you think it is effective to focus the entire paper on this single opening paragraph? Should the student have included references to later passages, or does his point not require them?
- The student several times uses italics to give extra emphasis to a word. Is this a good idea?
- In his journal, the student said that he didn't know how to make sense of the subject of interracial marriages that takes up so much of the story, and this no doubt explains why his essay makes no mention of it. Is this a wise or a risky strategy? Explain.
- Notice, too, that the student wrote in his journal that the wife's "no prize either." Should he have addressed this issue in his essay? Can you find evidence in the text that might support such a claim?

A Collection of Short Fiction

The stories of Cain and Abel, Ruth, Samson, and Joseph in the Hebrew Bible and the parables of Jesus in the New Testament are sufficient evidence that brief narratives existed in ancient times. The short tales in Boccaccio's *Decameron* and Chaucer's *Canterbury Tales* (the latter an amazing variety of narrative poems ranging from bawdy stories to legends of saints) are medieval examples of the ancient form. But, speaking generally, short narratives before the nineteenth century were either didactic pieces, with the narrative existing for the sake of a moral point, or they were "curious and striking" tales (to use Somerset Maugham's words for his favorite kind of story) recounted in order to entertain.

The contemporary short story is rather different from both of these genres, which can be called the **parable** and the **anecdote.** Like the parable, the contemporary short story has a point, a meaning; but, unlike the parable, it has a richness of surface as well as depth, so that it is interesting whether or not the reader goes on to ponder "the meaning." Like the anecdote, the short story relates a happening, but whereas the happening in the anecdote is curious and is the center of interest, the happening in the contemporary story often is less interesting in itself than as a manifestation of a character's state of mind. A good short story usually has a psychological interest that an anecdote lacks.

The anecdotal story is what "story" means for most readers. It is an interesting happening or series of happenings, usually with a somewhat surprising ending. The anecdotal story, however, is quite different from most of the contemporary short stories in this book. The anecdote is good entertainment, and good entertainment should not be lightly dismissed. But it has two elements within it that prevent it (unless it is something in addition to an anecdote) from taking a high place among the world's literature. First, it cannot be reread with increasing or even continued pleasure. Even when it is well told, once we know the happening we may lose patience with the telling. Second, effective anecdotes are often highly implausible. Now, implausible anecdotes alleged to be true have a special impact by virtue of their alleged truth: They make us say to ourselves, "Truth is stranger than fiction." But the invented anecdote lacks this power; its unlikely coincidence, its unconvincing ironic situation, its surprise ending, are both untrue and unbelievable. It is entertaining but it is usually not especially meaningful.

The short story of the last hundred and fifty years is not an anecdote and is not an abbreviated novel. If it were the latter, *Reader's Digest* condensations of novels would be short stories. But they are not; they are only eviscerated novels. Novelists usually cover a long period of time, presenting not only a few individuals but also something of a society. They often tell of the development of several many-sided figures. In contrast, short-story writers, having only a few pages, usually focus on a single figure in a single episode, revealing a character rather than recording its development.

Whereas the novel is narrative, the contemporary short story often seems less narrative than lyric or dramatic: In the short story we have a sense of a present mood or personality revealed, rather than the sense of a history reported. The revelation in a story is presented through incidents, of course, but the interest commonly resides in the character revealed through the incidents, rather than in the incidents themselves. Little "happens," in the sense that there is little rushing from place to place. What does "happen" is usually a mental reaction to an experience, and the mental reaction, rather than the external experience, is the heart of the story. In older narratives the plot usually involves a conflict that is resolved, bringing about a change in the protagonist's condition; in contemporary stories the plot usually is designed to reveal a protagonist's state of mind. This de-emphasis of overt actions results in a kinship with the lyric and the drama.

One way of looking at the matter is to distinguish between literature of *resolution* and literature of *revelation*—that is, between

1. literature that resolves a plot (literature that stimulates us to ask, "And what happened next?" and that finally leaves us with a settled state of affairs), and
2. literature that reveals a condition (literature that causes us to say, "Ah, now I understand how these people feel").

Two great writers of the later nineteenth century can be taken as representatives of the two kinds: Guy de Maupassant (1850–1893), who usually put the emphasis on resolution, and Anton Chekhov (1860–1904), who usually focused on revelation. Maupassant's tightly plotted stories move to a decisive end, ordinarily marked by a great change in fortune (usually to the characters' disadvantage). Chekhov's stories, on the other hand, seem loosely plotted and may end with the characters pretty much in the condition they were in at the start, but *we* see them more clearly, even if *they* have not achieved any self-knowledge.

A slightly different way of putting the matter is this: Much of the best short fiction from Chekhov onward is less concerned with *what happens* than it is with how a character (often the narrator) *feels* about the happenings. Thus the emphasis is not on external action but on inner action, feeling. Perhaps one can say that the reader is left with a mood rather than with an awareness of a decisive happening.

The distinction between a story of resolution and a story of revelation will probably be clear enough if you are familiar with stories by Maupassant and Chekhov, but of course the distinction should not be overemphasized. These are poles; most stories exist somewhere in between, closer to one pole or the other, but not utterly apart from the more remote pole. Consider again "The Parable of the Prodigal Son," in Chapter 2. Insofar as the story stimulates responses such as "The son left, *and then what happened? Did he prosper?*" it is a story of resolution. Insofar as it makes increasingly evident the unchanging love of the father, it is a story of revelation.

The de-emphasis on narrative in the contemporary short story is not an invention of the twentieth-century mind. It goes back at least to three important American writers of the early nineteenth century—Washington Irving, Nathaniel Hawthorne, and Edgar Allan Poe. In 1824 Irving wrote:

> I fancy much of what I value myself upon in writing, escapes the observation of the great mass of my readers: who are intent more upon the story than the way in which it is told. For my part I consider a story merely as a frame on which to stretch my materials. It is the play of thought, and sentiments and language; the weaving in of characters, lightly yet expressively delineated; the familiar and faithful exhibition of scenes in common life; and the half-concealed vein of humor that is often playing through the whole—these are among what I aim at, and upon which I felicitate myself in proportion as I think I succeed.

Hawthorne and Poe may seem stranger than Irving as forebears of the contemporary short story: Both are known for their fantastic narratives (and, in addition, Poe is known as the inventor of the detective story, a genre in which there is strong interest in curious happenings). But because Hawthorne's fantastic narratives are, as he said, highly allegorical, the reader's interest is pushed beyond the narrative to the moral significance. Poe's "arabesques," as he called his fanciful tales (in distinction from his detective tales of "ratiocination"), are aimed at revealing and arousing unusual mental states. The weird happenings and personages are symbolic representations of the mind or soul. In "The Cask of Amontillado," for instance, perhaps the chief interest is not in what happens but rather in the representation of an almost universal fear of being buried alive. But, it must be noted, in both Hawthorne and Poe we usually get what is commonly called the tale rather than the short story: We get short prose fiction dealing with the strange rather than the usual.

A paragraph from Poe's review (1842) of Hawthorne's *Twice-Told Tales,* though more useful in revealing Poe's theory of fiction than Hawthorne's, illuminates something of the kinship between the contemporary short story and the best short fictions of the earlier nineteenth century. In the review Poe has been explaining that because "unity of effect or impression" is essential, a tale (Poe doubtless uses "tale" to mean short fiction in general, rather than the special type just discussed) that can be read at a single sitting has an advantage over the novel.

> A skillful artist has constructed a tale. He has not fashioned his thoughts to accommodate his incidents, but having deliberately conceived a certain single effect to be wrought, he then invents such incidents, he then combines such events, and discusses them in such tone as may best serve him in establishing this preconceived effect. If his very first sentence tends not to be outbringing of this effect, then in his very first step has he committed a blunder. In the whole composition there should be no word written of which the tendency, direct or indirect, is not to the one pre-established design. And by such means, with such care and skill a picture is at length painted which leaves in the mind of him who contemplates it with a kindred art, a sense of the fullest satisfaction. The idea of the tale, its thesis, has been presented unblemished, because undisturbed—an end absolutely demanded, yet, in the novel, altogether unattainable.

Nothing that we have said should be construed as suggesting that short fiction from the mid-nineteenth century to the present is necessarily better than older short narratives. The object of these comments has been less to evaluate than to call attention to the characteristics dominating short fiction of the last century and a half. Not that all of this fiction is of a piece; the stories in this book demonstrate something of its variety. Readers who do not like one story need not despair; they need only (in the words of an early writer of great short fiction) "turne over the leef and chese another tale."

JAMES BALDWIN

A prolific essayist, playwright, novelist, and lecturer, James Baldwin (1924-1987) is one of the foremost African American authors of the twentieth century. He was born in Harlem, the son of an unwed mother. After graduation from high school, Baldwin worked briefly in New York City and New Jersey. In 1944 he moved to Greenwich Village, where he wrote his first essays and book reviews, and began to work on the writing of fiction.

From the 1940s to the end of his life Baldwin traveled widely, spending long periods in France, Switzerland, and Turkey. His novels include Go Tell It on the Mountain *(1953) and* Giovanni's Room *(1956), but many find his nonfiction, especially* Notes of a Native Son *(1955),* Nobody Knows My Name *(1961), and* The Fire Next Time *(1963), even more compelling. His story "Sonny's Blues" was first published in 1957 and later was included in the collection* Going to Meet the Man *(1965).*

Sonny's Blues   [1948]

I read about it in the paper, in the subway, on my way to work. I read it, and I couldn't believe it, and I read it again. Then perhaps I just stared at it, at the newsprint spelling out his name, spelling out the story. I stared at it in the swinging lights of the subway car, and in the faces and bodies of the people, and in my own face, trapped in the darkness which roared outside.

It was not to be believed and I kept telling myself that, as I walked from the subway station to the high school. And at the same time I couldn't doubt it. I was scared, scared for Sonny. He became real to me again. A great block of ice got settled in my belly and kept melting there slowly all day long, while I taught my classes algebra. It was a special kind of ice. It kept melting, sending trickles of ice water all up and down my veins, but it never got less. Sometimes it hardened and seemed to expand until I felt my guts were going to come spilling out or that I was going to choke or scream. This would always be at a moment when I was remembering some specific thing Sonny had once said or done.

When he was about as old as the boys in my classes his face had been bright and open, there was a lot of copper in it; and he'd had wonderfully direct brown eyes, and great gentleness and privacy. I wondered what he looked like now. He had been picked up, the evening before, in a raid on an apartment downtown, for peddling and using heroin.

I couldn't believe it: but what I mean by that is that I couldn't find any room for it anywhere inside me. I had kept it outside me for a long time. I hadn't wanted to know. I had had suspicions, but I didn't name them, I kept putting them away. I told myself that Sonny was wild, but he wasn't crazy. And he'd always been a good boy, he hadn't ever turned hard or evil or disrespectful, the way kids can, so quick, so quick, especially in Harlem. I didn't want to believe that I'd ever see my brother going down, coming to nothing, all that light in his face gone out, in the condition I'd already seen so many others. Yet it had happened and here I was, talking about algebra to a lot of boys who might, every one of them for all I knew, be popping off needles every time they went to the head.[1] Maybe it did more for them than algebra could.

5   I was sure that the first time Sonny had ever had horse,[2] he couldn't have been much older than these boys were now. These boys, now, were living as we'd been living then, they were growing up with a rush and their heads bumped abruptly against the low ceiling of their actual possibilities. They were filled with rage. All they really knew were two darknesses, the darkness of their lives, which was now closing in on them, and the darkness of the movies, which had blinded them to that other darkness, and in which they now, vindictively, dreamed, at once more together than they were at any other time, and more alone.

When the last bell rang, the last class ended, I let out my breath. It seemed I'd been holding it for all that time. My clothes were wet—I may have looked as though I'd been sitting in a steam bath, all dressed up, all afternoon. I sat alone in the classroom a long time. I listened to the boys outside, downstairs, shouting and cursing and laughing. Their laughter struck me for perhaps the first time. It was not the joyous laughter which—God knows why—one associates with children. It was mocking and insular, its intent was to denigrate. It was disenchanted, and in this, also, lay the authority of their curses. Perhaps I was listening to them because I was thinking about my brother and in them I heard my brother. And myself.

One boy was whistling a tune, at once very complicated and very simple, it seemed to be pouring out of him as though he were a bird, and it sounded very cool and moving through all that harsh, bright air, only just holding its own through all those other sounds.

I stood up and walked over to the window and looked down into the courtyard. It was the beginning of the spring and the sap was rising in the boys. A teacher passed through them every now and again, quickly, as though he or she couldn't wait to get out of that courtyard, to get those boys out of their sight and off their minds. I started collecting my stuff. I thought I'd better get home and talk to Isabel.

The courtyard was almost deserted by the time I got downstairs. I saw this boy standing in the shadow of a doorway, looking just like Sonny. I almost called his name. Then I saw that it wasn't Sonny, but somebody we used to know, a boy from around our block. He'd been Sonny's friend. He'd never been mine, having been too young for me, and, anyway, I'd never liked him. And now, even though he was a grown-up man, he still hung around that block, still spent hours on the street corners, was always high and raggy.

---

[1]**head** toilet.   [2]**horse** heroin.

I used to run into him from time to time and he'd often work around to asking me for a quarter or fifty cents. He always had some real good excuse,
too, and I always gave it to him. I don't know why.

10   But now, abruptly, I hated him. I couldn't stand the way he looked at
me, partly like a dog, partly like a cunning child. I wanted to ask him what
the hell he was doing in the school courtyard.

He sort of shuffled over to me, and he said, "I see you got the papers. So
you already know about it."

"You mean about Sonny? Yes, I already know about it. How come they
didn't get you?"

He grinned. It made him repulsive and it also brought to mind what
he'd looked like as a kid. "I wasn't there. I stay away from them people."

"Good for you." I offered him a cigarette and I watched him through the
smoke. "You come all the way down here just to tell me about Sonny?"

15   "That's right." He was sort of shaking his head and his eyes looked
strange, as though they were about to cross. The bright sun deadened his
damp dark brown skin and it made his eyes look yellow and showed up
the dirt in his kinked hair. He smelled funky.[3] I moved a little away from
him and I said, "Well, thanks. But I already know about it and I got to get
home."

"I'll walk you a little ways," he said. We started walking. There were a
couple of kids still loitering in the courtyard and one of them said goodnight
to me and looked strangely at the boy beside me.

"What're you going to do?" he asked me. "I mean, about Sonny?"

"Look. I haven't seen Sonny for over a year, I'm not sure I'm going to do
anything. Anyway, what the hell *can* I do?"

"That's right," he said quickly, "ain't nothing you can do. Can't much
help old Sonny no more, I guess."

20   It was what I was thinking and so it seemed to me he had no right to
say it.

"I'm surprised at Sonny, though," he went on—he had a funny way of
talking, he looked straight ahead as though he were talking to himself—
"I thought Sonny was a smart boy, I thought he was too smart to get hung."

"I guess he thought so too," I said sharply, "and that's how he got hung.
And how about you? You're pretty goddamn smart, I bet."

Then he looked directly at me, just for a minute. "I ain't smart," he said.
"If I was smart, I'd have reached for a pistol a long time ago."

"Look. Don't tell *me* your sad story, if it was up to me, I'd give you one."
Then I felt guilty—guilty, probably, for never having supposed that the poor
bastard *had* a story of his own, much less a sad one, and I asked, quickly,
"What's going to happen to him now?"

25   He didn't answer this. He was off by himself some place.

"Funny thing," he said, and from his tone we might have been discussing
the quickest way to get to Brooklyn, "when I saw the papers this morning,
the first thing I asked myself was if I had anything to do with it. I felt sort of
responsible."

I began to listen more carefully. The subway station was on the corner,
just before us, and I stopped. He stopped, too. We were in front of a bar and

---

[3]**funky** smelly.

he ducked slightly, peering in, but whoever he was looking for didn't seem to be there. The juke box was blasting away with something black and bouncy and I half watched the barmaid as she danced her way from the juke box to her place behind the bar. And I watched her face as she laughingly responded to something someone said to her, still keeping time to the music. When she smiled one saw the little girl, one sensed the doomed, still-struggling woman beneath the battered face of the semi-whore.

"I never *give* Sonny nothing," the boy said finally, "but a long time ago I come to school high and Sonny asked me how it felt." He paused, I couldn't bear to watch him, I watched the barmaid, and I listened to the music which seemed to be causing the pavement to shake. "I told him it felt great." The music stopped, the barmaid paused and watched the juke box until the music began again. "It did."

All this was carrying me some place I didn't want to go. I certainly didn't want to know how it felt. It filled everything, the people, the houses, the music, the dark, quicksilver barmaid, with menace; and this menace was their reality.

30   "What's going to happen to him now?" I asked again.

"They'll send him away some place and they'll try to cure him." He shook his head. "Maybe he'll even think he's kicked the habit. Then they'll let him loose"—he gestured, throwing his cigarette into the gutter. "That's all."

"What do you mean, that's *all?*"

But I knew what he meant.

"I *mean,* that's *all.*" He turned his head and looked at me, pulling down the corners of his mouth. "Don't you know what I mean?" he asked, softly.

35   "How the hell *would* I know what you mean?" I almost whispered it, I don't know why.

"That's right," he said to the air, "how would *he* know what I mean?" He turned toward me again, patient and calm, and yet I somehow felt him shaking, shaking as though he were going to fall apart. I felt that ice in my guts again, the dread I'd felt all afternoon; and again I watched the barmaid, moving about the bar, washing glasses, and singing. "Listen. They'll let him out and then it'll just start all over again. That's what I mean."

"You mean—they'll let him out. And then he'll just start working his way back in again. You mean he'll never kick the habit. Is that what you mean?"

"That's right," he said, cheerfully. "*You* see what I mean."

"Tell me," I said at last, "why does he want to die? He must want to die, he's killing himself, why does he want to die?"

40   He looked at me in surprise. He licked his lips. "He don't want to die. He wants to live. Don't nobody want to die, ever."

Then I wanted to ask him—too many things. He could not have answered, or if he had, I could not have borne the answers. I started walking. "Well, I guess it's none of my business."

"It's going to be rough on old Sonny," he said. We reached the subway station. "This is your station?" he asked. I nodded. I took one step down. "Damn!" he said, suddenly. I looked up at him. He grinned again. "Damn it if I didn't leave all my money home. You ain't got a dollar on you, have you? Just for a couple of days, is all."

All at once something inside gave and threatened to come pouring out of me. I didn't hate him any more. I felt that in another moment I'd start crying like a child.

"Sure," I said. "Don't sweat." I looked in my wallet and didn't have a dollar, I only had a five. "Here," I said. "That hold you?"

45   He didn't look at it—he didn't want to look at it. A terrible, closed look came over his face, as though he were keeping the number on the bill a secret from him and me. "Thanks," he said, and now he was dying to see me go. "Don't worry about Sonny. Maybe I'll write him or something."

"Sure," I said. "You do that. So long."

"Be seeing you," he said. I went on down the steps.

And I didn't write Sonny or send him anything for a long time. When I finally did, it was just after my little girl died, and he wrote me back a letter which made me feel like a bastard.

Here's what he said:

Dear brother,

You don't know how much I needed to hear from you. I wanted to write you many a time but I dug how much I must have hurt you and so I didn't write. But now I feel like a man who's been trying to climb up out of some deep, real deep and funky hole and just saw the sun up there, outside. I got to get outside.

I can't tell you much about how I got here. I mean I don't know how to tell you. I guess I was afraid of something or I was trying to escape from something and you know I have never been very strong in the head (smile). I'm glad Mama and Daddy are dead and can't see what's happened to their son and I swear if I'd known what I was doing I would never have hurt you so, you and a lot of other fine people who were nice to me and who believed in me.

I don't want you to think it had anything to do with me being a musician. It's more than that. Or maybe less than that. I can't get anything straight in my head down here and I try not to think about what's going to happen to me when I get outside again. Sometime I think I'm going to flip and *never* get outside and sometime I think I'll come straight back. I tell you one thing, though, I'd rather blow my brains out than go through this again. But that's what they all say, so they tell me. If I tell you when I'm coming to New York and if you could meet me, I sure would appreciate it. Give my love to Isabel and the kids and I was sure sorry to hear about little Grace. I wish I could be like Mama and say the Lord's will be done, but I don't know it seems to me that trouble is the one thing that never does get stopped and I don't know what good it does to blame it on the Lord. But maybe it does some good if you believe it.

Your brother,
Sonny

50   Then I kept in constant touch with him and I sent him whatever I could and I went to meet him when he came back to New York. When I saw him many things I thought I had forgotten came flooding back to me. This was because I had begun, finally, to wonder about Sonny, about the life that Sonny lived inside. This life, whatever it was, had made him older and thinner and it had deepened the distant stillness in which he had always moved. He looked very unlike my baby brother. Yet, when he smiled, when we shook hands, the baby brother I'd never known looked out from the depths of his private life, like an animal waiting to be coaxed into the light.

"How you been keeping?" he asked me.

"All right. And you?"

"Just fine." He was smiling all over his face. "It's good to see you again."

"It's good to see you."

55   The seven years' difference in our ages lay between us like a chasm: I wondered if these years would ever operate between us as a bridge. I was remembering, and it made it hard to catch my breath, that I had been there when he was born; and I had heard the first words he had ever spoken. When he started to walk, he walked from our mother straight to me. I caught him just before he fell when he took the first steps he ever took in this world.

"How's Isabel?"

"Just fine. She's dying to see you."

"And the boys?"

"They're fine, too. They're anxious to see their uncle."

60   "Oh, come on. You know they don't remember me."

"Are you kidding? Of course they remember you."

He grinned again. We got into a taxi. We had a lot to say to each other, far too much to know how to begin.

As the taxi began to move, I asked, "You still want to go to India?"

He laughed. "You still remember that. Hell, no. This place is Indian enough for me."

65   "It used to belong to them," I said.

And he laughed again. "They damn sure knew what they were doing when they got rid of it."

Years ago, when he was around fourteen, he'd been all hipped on the idea of going to India. He read books about people sitting on rocks, naked, in all kinds of weather, but mostly bad, naturally, and walking barefoot through hot coals and arriving at wisdom. I used to say that it sounded to me as though they were getting away from wisdom as fast as they could. I think he sort of looked down on me for that.

"Do you mind," he asked, "if we have the driver drive alongside the park? On the west side—I haven't seen the city in so long."

"Of course not," I said. I was afraid that I might sound as though I were humoring him, but I hoped he wouldn't take it that way.

70   So we drove along, between the green of the park and the stony, lifeless elegance of hotels and apartment buildings, toward the vivid, killing streets of our childhood. These streets hadn't changed, though housing projects jutted up out of them now like rocks in the middle of a boiling sea. Most of the houses in which we had grown up had vanished, as had the stores from which we had stolen, the basements in which we had first tried sex, the rooftops from which we had hurled tin cans and bricks. But houses exactly like the houses of our past yet dominated the landscape, boys exactly like the boys we once had been found themselves smothering in these houses, came down into the streets for light and air and found themselves encircled by disaster. Some escaped the trap, most didn't. Those who got out always left something of themselves behind, as some animals amputate a leg and leave it in the trap. It might be said, perhaps, that I had escaped, after all, I was a school teacher; or that Sonny had, he hadn't lived in Harlem for years. Yet, as the cab moved uptown through streets which seemed, with a rush, to darken with dark people, and as I covertly studied Sonny's face, it came to

me that what we both were seeking through our separate cab windows was that part of ourselves which had been left behind. It's always at the hour of trouble and confrontation that the missing member aches.

We hit 110th Street and started rolling up Lenox Avenue. And I'd known this avenue all my life, but it seemed to me again, as it had seemed on the day I'd first heard about Sonny's trouble, filled with a hidden menace which was its very breath of life.

"We almost there," said Sonny.

"Almost." We were both too nervous to say anything more.

We live in a housing project. It hasn't been up long. A few days after it was up it seemed uninhabitably new, now, of course, it's already rundown. It looks like a parody of the good, clean, faceless life—God knows the people who live in it do their best to make it a parody. The beat-looking grass lying around isn't enough to make their lives green, the hedges will never hold out the streets, and they know it. The big windows fool no one, they aren't big enough to make space out of no space. They don't bother with the windows, they watch the TV screen instead. The playground is most popular with the children who don't play at jacks, or skip rope, or roller skate, or swing, and they can be found in it after dark. We moved in partly because it's not too far from where I teach, and partly for the kids; but it's really just like the houses in which Sonny and I grew up. The same things happen, they'll have the same things to remember. The moment Sonny and I started into the house I had the feeling that I was simply bringing him back into the danger he had almost died trying to escape.

75   Sonny has never been talkative. So I don't know why I was sure he'd be dying to talk to me when supper was over the first night. Everything went fine, the oldest boy remembered him, and the youngest boy liked him, and Sonny had remembered to bring something for each of them; and Isabel, who is really much nicer than I am, more open and giving, had gone to a lot of trouble about dinner and was genuinely glad to see him. And she's always been able to tease Sonny in a way that I haven't. It was nice to see her face so vivid again and to hear her laugh and watch her make Sonny laugh. She wasn't, or, anyway, she didn't seem to be, at all uneasy or embarrassed. She chatted as though there were no subject which had to be avoided and she got Sonny past his first, faint stiffness. And thank God she was there, for I was filled with that icy dread again. Everything I did seemed awkward to me, and everything I said sounded freighted with hidden meaning. I was trying to remember everything I'd heard about dope addiction and I couldn't help watching Sonny for signs. I wasn't doing it out of malice. I was trying to find out something about my brother. I was dying to hear him tell me he was safe.

"Safe!" my father grunted, whenever Mama suggested trying to move to a neighborhood which might be safer for children. "Safe, hell! Ain't no place safe for kids, nor nobody."

He always went on like this, but he wasn't, ever, really as bad as he sounded, not even on weekends, when he got drunk. As a matter of fact, he was always on the lookout for "something a little better," but he died before he found it. He died suddenly, during a drunken weekend in the middle of the war, when Sonny was fifteen. He and Sonny hadn't ever got on too well. And this was partly because Sonny was the apple of his father's eye. It was because he loved Sonny so much and was frightened for him, that he was always fighting with him. It doesn't do any good to fight with Sonny. Sonny

just moves back, inside himself, where he can't be reached. But the principal reason that they never hit it off is that they were so much alike. Daddy
was big and rough and loud-talking, just the opposite of Sonny, but they
both had—that same privacy.

Mama tried to tell me something about this, just after Daddy died. I was
home on leave from the army.

This was the last time I ever saw my mother alive. Just the same, this
picture gets all mixed up in my mind with pictures I had of her when she
was younger. The way I always see her is the way she used to be on a Sunday afternoon, say, when the old folks were talking after the big Sunday
dinner. I always see her wearing pale blue. She'd be sitting on the sofa. And
my father would be sitting in the easy chair, not far from her. And the living
room would be full of church folks and relatives. There they sit, in chairs all
around the living room, and the night is creeping up outside, but nobody
knows it yet. You can see the darkness growing against the windowpanes
and you hear the street noises every now and again, or maybe the jangling
beat of a tambourine from one of the churches close by, but it's real quiet in
the room. For a moment nobody's talking, but every face looks darkening,
like the sky outside. And my mother rocks a little from the waist, and my
father's eyes are closed. Everyone is looking at something a child can't see.
For a minute they've forgotten the children. Maybe a kid is lying on the rug,
half asleep. Maybe somebody's got a kid in his lap and is absent-mindedly
stroking the kid's head. Maybe there's a kid, quiet and big-eyed, curled up in
a big chair in the corner. The silence, the darkness coming, and the darkness
in the faces frighten the child obscurely. He hopes that the hand which
strokes his forehead will never stop—will never die. He hopes that there
will never come a time when the old folks won't be sitting around the living
room, talking about where they've come from, and what they've seen, and
what's happened to them and their kinfolk.

80   But something deep and watchful in the child knows that this is bound
to end, is already ending. In a moment someone will get up and turn on the
light. Then the old folks will remember the children and they won't talk any
more that day. And when light fills the room, the child is filled with darkness. He knows that every time this happens he's moved just a little closer
to that darkness outside. The darkness outside is what the old folks have
been talking about. It's what they've come from. It's what they endure. The
child knows that they won't talk any more because if he knows too much
about what's happened to *them*, he'll know too much too soon, about
what's going to happen to *him*.

The last time I talked to my mother, I remember I was restless. I wanted
to get out and see Isabel. We weren't married then and we had a lot to
straighten out between us.

There Mama sat, in black, by the window. She was humming an old
church song, *Lord, you brought me from a long ways off.* Sonny was out
somewhere. Mama kept watching the streets.

"I don't know," she said, "if I'll ever see you again, after you go off from
here. But I hope you'll remember the things I tried to teach you."

"Don't talk like that," I said, and smiled. "You'll be here a long time yet."

85   She smiled, too, but she said nothing. She was quiet for a long time. And
I said, "Mama, don't you worry about nothing. I'll be writing all the time, and
you be getting the checks. . . ."

"I want to talk to you about your brother," she said, suddenly. "If any-thing happens to me he ain't going to have nobody to look out for him."

"Mama," I said, "ain't nothing going to happen to you *or* Sonny. Sonny's all right. He's a good boy and he's got good sense."

"It ain't a question of his being a good boy," Mama said, "nor of his hav-ing good sense. It ain't only the bad ones, nor yet the dumb ones that gets sucked under." She stopped, looking at me. "Your Daddy once had a brother," she said, and she smiled in a way that made me feel she was in pain. "You didn't never know that, did you?"

"No," I said, "I never knew that," and I watched her face.

90   "Oh, yes," she said, "your Daddy had a brother." She looked out of the window again. "I know you never saw your Daddy cry. But *I* did—many a time, through all these years."

I asked her, "What happened to his brother? How come nobody's ever talked about him?"

This was the first time I ever saw my mother look old.

"His brother got killed," she said, "when he was just a little younger than you are now. I knew him. He was a fine boy. He was maybe a little full of the devil, but he didn't mean nobody no harm."

Then she stopped and the room was silent, exactly as it had sometimes been on those Sunday afternoons. Mama kept looking out into the streets.

95   "He used to have a job in the mill," she said, "and, like all young folks, he just liked to perform on Saturday nights. Saturday nights, him and your father would drift around to different places, go to dances and things like that, or just sit around with people they knew, and your father's brother would sing, he had a fine voice, and play along with himself on his guitar. Well, this par-ticular Saturday night, him and your father was coming home from some place, and they were both a little drunk and there was a moon that night, it was bright like day. Your father's brother was feeling kind of good, and he was whistling to himself, and he had his guitar slung over his shoulder. They was coming down a hill and beneath them was a road that turned off from the highway. Well, your father's brother, being always kind of frisky, decided to run down this hill, and he did, with that guitar banging and clang-ing behind him, and he ran across the road, and he was making water be-hind a tree. And your father was sort of amused at him and he was still com-ing down the hill, kind of slow. Then he heard a car motor and that same minute his brother stepped from behind the tree, into the road, in the moon-light. And he started to cross the road. And your father started to run down the hill, he says he don't know why. This car was full of white men. They was all drunk, and when they seen your father's brother they let out a great whoop and holler and they aimed the car straight at him. They was having fun, they just wanted to scare him, the way they do sometimes, you know. But they was drunk. And I guess the boy, being drunk, too, and scared, kind of lost his head. By the time he jumped it was too late. Your father says he heard his brother scream when the car rolled over him, and he heard the wood of that guitar when it give, and he heard them strings go flying, and he heard them white men shouting, and the car kept on a-going and it ain't stopped till this day. And, time your father got down the hill, his brother weren't nothing but blood and pulp."

Tears were gleaming on my mother's face. There wasn't anything I could say.

"He never mentioned it," she said, "because I never let him mention it before you children. Your Daddy was like a crazy man that night and for many a night thereafter. He says he never in his life seen anything as dark as that road after the lights of that car had gone away. Weren't nothing, weren't nobody on that road, just your Daddy and his brother and that busted guitar. Oh, yes. Your Daddy never did really get right again. Till the day he died he weren't sure but that every white man he saw was the man that killed his brother."

She stopped and took out her handkerchief and dried her eyes and looked at me.

"I ain't telling you all this," she said, "to make you scared or bitter or to make you hate nobody. I'm telling you this because you got a brother. And the world ain't changed."

100   I guess I didn't want to believe this. I guess she saw this in my face. She turned away from me, toward the window again, searching those streets.

"But I praise my Redeemer," she said at last, "that He called your Daddy home before me. I ain't saying it to throw no flowers at myself, but, I declare, it keeps me from feeling too cast down to know I helped your father get safely through this world. Your father always acted like he was the roughest, strongest man on earth. And everybody took him to be like that. But if he hadn't had me there—to see his tears!"

She was crying again. Still, I couldn't move. I said, "Lord, Lord, Mama, I didn't know it was like that."

"Oh, honey," she said, "there's a lot that you don't know. But you are going to find out." She stood up from the window and came over to me. "You got to hold on to your brother," she said, "and don't let him fall, no matter what it looks like is happening to him and no matter how evil you gets with him. You going to be evil with him many a time. But don't you forget what I told you, you hear?"

"I won't forget," I said. "Don't you worry, I won't forget. I won't let nothing happen to Sonny."

105   My mother smiled as though she were amused at something she saw in my face. Then, "You may not be able to stop nothing from happening. But you got to let him know you's *there*."

Two days later I was married, and then I was gone. And I had a lot of things on my mind and I pretty well forgot my promise to Mama until I got shipped home on a special furlough for her funeral.

And, after the funeral, with just Sonny and me alone in the empty kitchen, I tried to find out something about him.

"What do you want to do?" I asked him.

"I'm going to be a musician," he said.

110   For he had graduated, in the time I had been away, from dancing to the juke box to finding out who was playing what, and what they were doing with it, and he had bought himself a set of drums.

"You mean, you want to be a drummer?" I somehow had the feeling that being a drummer might be all right for other people but not for my brother Sonny.

"I don't think," he said, looking at me very gravely, "that I'll ever be a good drummer. But I think I can play a piano."

I frowned. I'd never played the role of the older brother quite so seriously before, had scarcely ever, in fact, *asked* Sonny a damn thing. I sensed myself in the presence of something I didn't really know how to handle, didn't understand. So I made my frown a little deeper as I asked: "What kind of musician do you want to be?"

He grinned. "How many kinds do you think there are?"

115   "Be *serious*," I said.

He laughed, throwing his head back, and then looked at me. "I *am* serious."

"Well, then, for Christ's sake, stop kidding around and answer a serious question. I mean, do you want to be a concert pianist, you want to play classical music and all that; or—or what?" Long before I finished he was laughing again. "For Christ's *sake*, Sonny!"

He sobered, but with difficulty. "I'm sorry. But you sound so—*scared!*" and he was off again.

"Well, you may think it's funny now, baby, but it's not going to be so funny when you have to make your living at it, let me tell you *that*." I was furious because I knew he was laughing at me and I didn't know why.

120   "*No*," he said, very sober now, and afraid, perhaps, that he'd hurt me, "I don't want to be a classical pianist. That isn't what interests me. I mean"— he paused, looking hard at me, as though his eyes would help me to understand, and then gestured helplessly, as though perhaps his hand would help—"I mean, I'll have a lot of studying to do, and I'll have to study *everything*, but, I mean, I want to play *with*—jazz musicians." He stopped. "I want to play jazz," he said.

Well, the word had never before sounded as heavy, as real, as it sounded that afternoon in Sonny's mouth. I just looked at him and I was probably frowning a real frown by this time. I simply couldn't see why on earth he'd want to spend his time hanging around nightclubs, clowning around on bandstands, while people pushed each other around a dance floor. It seemed—beneath him, somehow. I had never thought about it before, had never been forced to, but I suppose I had always put jazz musicians in a class with what Daddy called "good-time people."

"Are you *serious?*"

"Hell, *yes*, I'm serious."

He looked more helpless than ever, and annoyed, and deeply hurt.

125   I suggested, helpfully: "You mean—like Louis Armstrong?"

His face closed as though I'd struck him. "No. I'm not talking about none of that old-time, down home crap."

"Well, look, Sonny, I'm sorry, don't get mad. I just don't altogether get it, that's all. Name somebody—you know, a jazz musician you admire."

"Bird."[4]

"Who?"

130   "Bird! Charlie Parker! Don't they teach you nothing in the goddamn army?"

I lit a cigarette. I was surprised and then a little amused to discover that I was trembling. "I've been out of touch," I said. "You'll have to be patient with me. Now. Who's this Parker character?"

"He's just one of the greatest jazz musicians alive," said Sonny, sullenly, his hands in his pockets, his back to me. "Maybe *the* greatest," he added, bitterly, "that's probably why *you* never heard of him."

---

[4]**Bird** Charlie "Bird" Parker (1920–1955), saxophonist and jazz innovator for whom the Birdland ballroom in New York City is named.

"All right," I said, "I'm ignorant. I'm sorry. I'll go out and buy all the cat's records right away, all right?"

"It don't," said Sonny, with dignity, "make any difference to me. I don't care what you listen to. Don't do me no favors."

135   I was beginning to realize that I'd never seen him so upset before. With another part of my mind I was thinking that this would probably turn out to be one of those things kids go through and that I shouldn't make it seem important by pushing it too hard. Still, I didn't think it would do any harm to ask: "Doesn't all this take a lot of time? Can you make a living at it?"

He turned back to me and half leaned, half sat, on the kitchen table. "Everything takes time," he said, "and—well, yes, sure, I can make a living at it. But what I don't seem to be able to make you understand is that it's the only thing I want to do."

"Well, Sonny," I said, gently, "you know people can't always do exactly what they *want* to do—"

"*No,* I don't know that," said Sonny, surprising me. "I think people *ought* to do what they want to do, what else are they alive for?"

"You getting to be a big boy," I said desperately, "it's time you started thinking about your future."

140   "I'm thinking about my future," said Sonny, grimly. "I think about it all the time."

I gave up. I decided, if he didn't change his mind, that we could always talk about it later. "In the meantime," I said, "you got to finish school." We had already decided that he'd have to move in with Isabel and her folks. I knew this wasn't the ideal arrangement because Isabel's folks are inclined to be dicty[5] and they hadn't especially wanted Isabel to marry me. But I didn't know what else to do. "And we have to get you fixed up at Isabel's."

There was a long silence. He moved from the kitchen table to the window. "That's a terrible idea. You know it yourself."

"Do you have a *better* idea?"

He just walked up and down the kitchen for a minute. He was as tall as I was. He had started to shave. I suddenly had the feeling that I didn't know him at all.

145   He stopped at the kitchen table and picked up my cigarettes. Looking at me with a kind of mocking, amused defiance, he put one between his lips. "You mind?"

"You smoking already?"

He lit the cigarette and nodded, watching me through the smoke. "I just wanted to see if I'd have the courage to smoke in front of you." He grinned and blew a great cloud of smoke to the ceiling. "It was easy." He looked at my face. "Come on, now. I bet you was smoking at my age, tell the truth."

I didn't say anything but the truth was on my face, and he laughed. But now there was something very strained in his laugh. "Sure. And I bet that ain't all you was doing."

He was frightening me a little. "Cut the crap," I said. "We already decided that you was going to go and live at Isabel's. Now what's got into you all of a sudden?"

---

[5]**dicty** dictatorial, bossy, and snobbish.

150   "*You* decided it," he pointed out. "I didn't decide nothing." He stopped
in front of me, leaning against the stove, arms loosely folded. "Look, brother.
I don't want to stay in Harlem no more, I really don't." He was very earnest. He
looked at me, then over toward the kitchen window. There was something in
his eyes I'd never seen before, some thoughtfulness, some worry all his own.
He rubbed the muscle of one arm. "It's time I was getting out of here."

"Where do you want to *go,* Sonny?"

"I want to join the army. Or the navy, I don't care. If I say I'm old
enough, they'll believe me."

Then I got mad. It was because I was so scared. "You must be crazy. You
goddamn fool, what the hell do you want to go and join the *army* for?"

"I just told you. To get out of Harlem."

155   "Sonny, you haven't even finished *school.* And if you really want to be a
musician, how do you expect to study if you're in the *army?*"

He looked at me, trapped, and in anguish. "There's ways. I might be able to
work out some kind of deal. Anyway, I'll have the G.I. Bill when I come out."

"*If* you come out." We stared at each other. "Sonny, please. Be reasonable.
I know the setup is far from perfect. But we got to do the best we can."

"I ain't learning nothing in school," he said. "Even when I go." He turned
away from me and opened the window and threw his cigarette out into the
narrow alley. I watched his back. "At least, I ain't learning nothing you'd want
me to learn." He slammed the window so hard I thought the glass would fly
out, and turned back to me. "And I'm sick of the stink of these garbage cans!"

"Sonny," I said, "I know how you feel. But if you don't finish school
now, you're going to be sorry later that you didn't." I grabbed him by the
shoulders. "And you only got another year. It ain't so bad. And I'll come back
and I swear I'll help you do *whatever* you want to do. Just try to put up with
it till I come back. Will you please do that? For me?"

160   He didn't answer and he wouldn't look at me.

"Sonny. You hear me?"

He pulled away. "I hear you. But you never hear anything *I* say."

I didn't know what to say to that. He looked out of the window and
then back at me. "OK," he said, and sighed. "I'll try."

Then I said, trying to cheer him up a little, "They got a piano at Isabel's.
You can practice on it."

165   And as a matter of fact, it did cheer him up for a minute. "That's right,"
he said to himself. "I forgot that." His face relaxed a little. But the worry, the
thoughtfulness, played on it still, the way shadows play on a face which is
staring into the fire.

But I thought I'd never hear the end of that piano. At first, Isabel would
write me, saying how nice it was that Sonny was so serious about his music
and how, as soon as he came in from school, or wherever he had been when
he was supposed to be at school, he went straight to that piano and stayed
there until suppertime. And, after supper, he went back to that piano and
stayed there until everybody went to bed. He was at the piano all day Saturday and all day Sunday. Then he bought a record player and started playing
records. He'd play one record over and over again, all day long sometimes,
and he'd improvise along with it on the piano. Or he'd play one section of
the record, one chord, one change, one progression, then he'd do it on the
piano. Then back to the record. Then back to the piano.

Well, I really don't know how they stood it. Isabel finally confessed that it wasn't like living with a person at all, it was like living with sound. And the sound didn't make any sense to her, didn't make any sense to any of them—naturally. They began, in a way, to be afflicted by this presence that was living in their home. It was as though Sonny were some sort of god, or monster. He moved in an atmosphere which wasn't like theirs at all. They fed him and he ate, he washed himself, he walked in and out of their door; he certainly wasn't nasty or unpleasant or rude, Sonny isn't any of those things; but it was as though he were all wrapped up in some cloud, some fire, some vision all his own; and there wasn't any way to reach him.

At the same time, he wasn't really a man yet, he was still a child, and they had to watch out for him in all kinds of ways. They certainly couldn't throw him out. Neither did they dare to make a great scene about that piano because even they dimly sensed, as I sensed, from so many thousands of miles away, that Sonny was at that piano playing for his life.

But he hadn't been going to school. One day a letter came from the school board and Isabel's mother got it—there had, apparently, been other letters but Sonny had torn them up. This day, when Sonny came in, Isabel's mother showed him the letter and asked where he'd been spending his time. And she finally got it out of him that he'd been down in Greenwich Village, with musicians and other characters, in a white girl's apartment. And this scared her and she started to scream at him and what came up, once she began—though she denies it to this day—was what sacrifices they were making to give Sonny a decent home and how little he appreciated it.

170 Sonny didn't play the piano that day. By evening, Isabel's mother had calmed down but then there was the old man to deal with, and Isabel herself. Isabel says she did her best to be calm but she broke down and started crying. She says she just watched Sonny's face. She could tell, by watching him, what was happening with him. And what was happening was that they penetrated his cloud, they had reached him. Even if their fingers had been a thousand times more gentle than human fingers ever are, he could hardly help feeling that they had stripped him naked and were spitting on that nakedness. For he also had to see that his presence, that music, which was life or death to him, had been torture for them and that they had endured it, not at all for his sake, but only for mine. And Sonny couldn't take that. He can take it a little better today than he could then but he's still not very good at it and, frankly, I don't know anybody who is.

The silence of the next few days must have been louder than the sound of all the music ever played since time began. One morning, before she went to work, Isabel was in his room for something and she suddenly realized that all of his records were gone. And she knew for certain that he was gone. And he was. He went as far as the navy would carry him. He finally sent me a postcard from some place in Greece and that was the first I knew that Sonny was still alive. I didn't see him any more until we were both back in New York and the war had long been over.

He was a man by then, of course, but I wasn't willing to see it. He came by the house from time to time, but we fought almost every time we met. I didn't like the way he carried himself, loose and dreamlike all the time, and I didn't like his friends, and his music seemed to be merely an excuse for the life he led. It sounded just that weird and disordered.

Then we had a fight, a pretty awful fight, and I didn't see him for months. By and by I looked him up, where he was living, in a furnished room in the Village, and I tried to make it up. But there were lots of other people in the room and Sonny just lay on his bed, and he wouldn't come downstairs with me, and he treated these other people as though they were his family and I weren't. So I got mad and then he got mad, and then I told him that he might just as well be dead as live the way he was living. Then he stood up and he told me not to worry about him any more in life, that he *was* dead as far as I was concerned. Then he pushed me to the door and the other people looked on as though nothing were happening, and he slammed the door behind me. I stood in the hallway, staring at the door. I heard somebody laugh in the room and then the tears came to my eyes. I started down the steps, whistling to keep from crying, I kept whistling to myself, *You going to need me, baby, one of these cold, rainy days.*

I read about Sonny's trouble in the spring. Little Grace died in the fall. She was a beautiful little girl. But she only lived a little over two years. She died of polio and she suffered. She had a slight fever for a couple of days, but it didn't seem like anything and we just kept her in bed. And we would certainly have called the doctor, but the fever dropped, she seemed to be all right. So we thought it had just been a cold. Then, one day, she was up, playing, Isabel was in the kitchen fixing lunch for the two boys when they'd come in from school, and she heard Grace fall down in the living room. When you have a lot of children you don't always start running when one of them falls, unless they start screaming or something. And, this time, Gracie was quiet. Yet, Isabel says that when she heard that *thump* and then that silence, something happened to her to make her afraid. And she ran to the living room and there was little Grace on the floor, all twisted up, and the reason she hadn't screamed was that she couldn't get her breath. And when she did scream, it was the worst sound, Isabel says, that she'd ever heard in all her life, and she still hears it sometimes in her dreams. Isabel will sometimes wake me up with a low, moaning, strangling sound and I have to be quick to awaken her and hold her to me and where Isabel is weeping against me seems a mortal wound.

175   I think I may have written Sonny the very day that little Grace was buried. I was sitting in the living room in the dark, by myself, and I suddenly thought of Sonny. My trouble made his real.

One Saturday afternoon, when Sonny had been living with us, or anyway, been in our house, for nearly two weeks, I found myself wandering aimlessly about the living room, drinking from a can of beer, and trying to work up courage to search Sonny's room. He was out, he was usually out whenever I was home, and Isabel had taken the children to see their grandparents. Suddenly I was standing still in front of the living room window, watching Seventh Avenue. The idea of searching Sonny's room made me still. I scarcely dared to admit to myself what I'd be searching for. I didn't know what I'd do if I found it. Or if I didn't.

On the sidewalk across from me, near the entrance to a barbecue joint, some people were holding an old-fashioned revival meeting. The barbecue cook, wearing a dirty white apron, his conked[6] hair reddish and metallic in the

---

[6]**conked** straightened and greased

pale sun, and a cigarette between his lips, stood in the doorway, watching them. Kids and older people paused in their errands and stood there, along with some older men and a couple of very tough-looking women who watched everything that happened on the avenue, as though they owned it, or were maybe owned by it. Well, they were watching this, too. The revival was being carried on by three sisters in black, and a brother. All they had were their voices and their Bibles and a tambourine. The brother was testifying and while he testified two of the sisters stood together, seeming to say, amen, and the third sister walked around with the tambourine outstretched and a couple of people dropped coins into it. Then the brother's testimony ended and the sister who had been taking up the collection dumped the coins into her palm and transferred them to the pocket of her long black robe. Then she raised both hands, striking the tambourine against the air, and then against one hand, and she started to sing. And the two other sisters and the brother joined in.

It was strange, suddenly, to watch, though I had been seeing these meetings all my life. So, of course, had everybody else down there. Yet, they paused and watched and listened and I stood still at the window. *"'Tis the old ship of Zion,"* they sang, and the sister with the tambourine kept a steady, jangling beat, *"it has rescued many a thousand!"* Not a soul under the sound of their voices was hearing this song for the first time, not one of them had been rescued. Nor had they seen much in the way of rescue work being done around them. Neither did they especially believe in the holiness of the three sisters and the brother, they knew too much about them, knew where they lived, and how. The woman with the tambourine, whose voice dominated the air, whose face was bright with joy, was divided by very little from the woman who stood watching her, a cigarette between her heavy, chapped lips, her hair a cuckoo's nest, her face scarred and swollen from many beatings, and her black eyes glittering like coal. Perhaps they both knew this, which was why, when, as rarely, they addressed each other, they addressed each other as Sister. As the singing filled the air the watching, listening faces underwent a change, the eyes focusing on something within; the music seemed to soothe a poison out of them; and time seemed, nearly, to fall away from the sullen, belligerent, battered faces, as though they were fleeing back to their first condition, while dreaming of their last. The barbecue cook half shook his head and smiled, and dropped his cigarette and disappeared into his joint. A man fumbled in his pockets for change and stood holding it in his hand impatiently, as though he had just remembered a pressing appointment further up the avenue. He looked furious. Then I saw Sonny, standing on the edge of the crowd. He was carrying a wide, flat notebook with a green cover, and it made him look, from where I was standing, almost like a schoolboy. The coppery sun brought out the copper in his skin, he was very faintly smiling, standing very still. Then the singing stopped, the tambourine turned into a collection plate again. The furious man dropped in his coins and vanished, so did a couple of the women, and Sonny dropped some change in the plate, looking directly at the woman with a little smile. He started across the avenue, toward the house. He has a slow, loping walk, something like the way Harlem hipsters walk, only he's imposed on this his own half-beat. I had never really noticed it before.

I stayed at the window, both relieved and apprehensive. As Sonny disappeared from my sight, they began singing again. And they were still singing when his key turned in the lock.

180   "Hey," he said.

"Hey, yourself. You want some beer?"

"No. Well, maybe." But he came up to the window and stood beside me, looking out. "What a warm voice," he said.

They were singing *If I could only hear my mother pray again!*

"Yes," I said, "and she can sure beat that tambourine."

185   "But what a terrible song," he said, and laughed. He dropped his notebook on the sofa and disappeared into the kitchen. "Where's Isabel and the kids?"

"I think they went to see their grandparents. You hungry?"

"No." He came back into the living room with his can of beer. "You want to come some place with me tonight?"

I sensed, I don't know how, that I couldn't possibly say no. "Sure. Where?"

He sat down on the sofa and picked up his notebook and started leafing through it. "I'm going to sit in with some fellows in a joint in the Village."

190   "You mean, you're going to play, tonight?"

"That's right." He took a swallow of his beer and moved back to the window. He gave me a sidelong look. "If you can stand it."

"I'll try," I said.

He smiled to himself and we both watched as the meeting across the way broke up. The three sisters and the brother, heads bowed, were singing *God be with you till we meet again.* The faces around them were very quiet. Then the song ended. The small crowd dispersed. We watched the three women and the lone man walk slowly up the avenue.

"When she was singing before," said Sonny, abruptly, "her voice reminded me for a minute of what heroin feels like sometimes—when it's in your veins. It makes you feel sort of warm and cool at the same time. And distant. And—and sure." He sipped his beer, very deliberately not looking at me. I watched his face. "It makes you feel—in control. Sometimes you've got to have that feeling."

195   "Do you?" I sat down slowly in the easy chair.

"Sometimes." He went to the sofa and picked up his notebook again. "Some people do."

"In order," I asked, "to play?" And my voice was very ugly, full of contempt and anger.

"Well"—he looked at me with great, troubled eyes, as though, in fact, he hoped his eyes would tell me things he could never otherwise say—"they *think* so. And *if* they think so—!"

"And what do *you* think?" I asked.

200   He sat on the sofa and put his can of beer on the floor. "I don't know," he said, and I couldn't be sure if he were answering my question or pursuing his thoughts. His face didn't tell me. "It's not so much to *play.* It's to *stand* it, to be able to make it at all. On any level." He frowned and smiled: "In order to keep from shaking to pieces."

"But these friends of yours," I said, "they seem to shake themselves to pieces pretty goddamn fast."

"Maybe." He played with the notebook. And something told me that I should curb my tongue, that Sonny was doing his best to talk, that I should listen. "But of course you only know the ones that've gone to pieces. Some don't—or at least they haven't *yet* and that's just about all *any* of us can say."

He paused. "And then there are some who just live, really, in hell, and they know it and they see what's happening and they go right on. I don't know." He sighed, dropped the notebook, folded his arms. "Some guys, you can tell from the way they play, they on something *all* the time. And you can see that, well, it makes something real for them. But of course," he picked up his beer from the floor and sipped it and put the can down again, "they *want* to, too, you've got to see that. Even some of them that say they don't—*some, not all.*"

"And what about you?" I asked—I couldn't help it. "What about you? Do *you* want to?"

He stood up and walked to the window and I remained silent for a long time. Then he sighed. "Me," he said. Then: "While I was downstairs before, on my way here, listening to that woman sing, it struck me all of a sudden how much suffering she must have had to go through—to sing like that. It's *repulsive* to think you have to suffer that much."

205   I said: "But there's no way not to suffer—is there, Sonny?"

"I believe not," he said and smiled, "but that's never stopped anyone from trying." He looked at me. "Has it?" I realized, with this mocking look, that there stood between us, forever, beyond the power of time or forgiveness, the fact that I had held silence—so long!—when he had needed human speech to help him. He turned back to the window. "No, there's no way not to suffer. But you try all kinds of ways to keep from drowning in it, to keep on top of it, and to make it seem—well, like *you*. Like you did something, all right, and now you're suffering for it. You know?" I said nothing. "Well you know," he said, impatiently, "why *do* people suffer? Maybe it's better to do something to give it a reason, *any* reason."

"But we just agreed," I said, "that there's no way not to suffer. Isn't it better, then, just to—take it?"

"But nobody just takes it," Sonny cried, "that's what I'm telling you! *Everybody* tries not to. You're just hung up on the *way* some people try—it's not *your* way!"

The hair on my face began to itch, my face felt wet. "That's not true," I said, "that's not true. I don't give a damn what other people do, I don't even care how they suffer. I just care how *you* suffer." And he looked at me. "Please believe me," I said, "I don't want to see you—die—trying not to suffer."

210   "I won't," he said flatly, "die trying not to suffer. At least, not any faster than anybody else."

"But there's no need," I said, trying to laugh, "is there? in killing yourself."

I wanted to say more, but I couldn't. I wanted to talk about will power and how life could be—well, beautiful. I wanted to say that it was all within; but was it? or, rather, wasn't that exactly the trouble? And I wanted to promise that I would never fail him again. But it would all have sounded—empty words and lies.

So I made the promise to myself and prayed that I would keep it.

"It's terrible sometimes, inside," he said, "that's what's the trouble. You walk these streets, black and funky and cold, and there's not really a living ass to talk to, and there's nothing shaking, and there's no way of getting it out—that storm inside. You can't talk it and you can't make love with it, and when you finally try to get with it and play it, you realize *nobody's* listening. So *you've* got to listen. You got to find a way to listen."

215   And then he walked away from the window and sat on the sofa again, as though all the wind had suddenly been knocked out of him. "Sometimes you'll do *anything* to play, even cut your mother's throat." He laughed and looked at me. "Or your brother's." Then he sobered. "Or your own." Then: "Don't worry. I'm all right now and I think I'll *be* all right. But I can't forget—where I've been. I don't mean just the physical place I've been, I mean where I've *been*. And *what* I've been."

"What have you been, Sonny?" I asked.

He smiled—but sat sideways on the sofa, his elbow resting on the back, his fingers playing with his mouth and chin, not looking at me. "I've been something I didn't recognize, didn't know I could be. Didn't know anybody could be." He stopped, looking inward, looking helplessly young, looking old. "I'm not talking about it now because I feel *guilty* or anything like that—maybe it would be better if I did, I don't know. Anyway, I can't really talk about it. Not to you, not to anybody," and now he turned and faced me. "Sometimes, you know, and it was actually when I was most *out* of the world, I felt that I was in it, that I was *with* it, really, and I could play or I didn't really have to *play*, it just came out of me, it was there. And I don't know how I played, thinking about it now, but I know I did awful things, those times, sometimes, to people. Or it wasn't that I *did* anything to them—it was that they weren't real." He picked up the beer can; it was empty; he rolled it between his palms: "And other times—well, I needed a fix, I needed to find a place to lean, I needed to clear a space to *listen*—and I couldn't find it, and I—went crazy, I did terrible things to *me*, I was terrible *for* me." He began pressing the beer can between his hands, I watched the metal begin to give. It glittered, as he played with it like a knife, and I was afraid he would cut himself, but I said nothing. "Oh well. I can never tell you. I was all by myself at the bottom of something, stinking and sweating and crying and shaking, and I smelled it, you know? *my* stink, and I thought I'd die if I couldn't get away from it and yet, all the same, I knew that everything I was doing was just locking me in with it. And I didn't know," he paused, still flattening the beer can, "I didn't know, I still *don't* know, something kept telling me that maybe it was good to smell your own stink, but I didn't think that *that* was what I'd been trying to do—and—who can stand it?" and he abruptly dropped the ruined beer can, looking at me with a small, still smile, and then rose, walking to the window as though it were the lodestone rock. I watched his face, he watched the avenue. "I couldn't tell you when Mama died—but the reason I wanted to leave Harlem so bad was to get away from drugs. And then, when I ran away, that's what I was running from—really. When I came back, nothing had changed, *I* hadn't changed, I was just—older." And he stopped, drumming with his fingers on the windowpane. The sun had vanished, soon darkness would fall. I watched his face. "It can come again," he said, almost as though speaking to himself. Then he turned to me. "It can come again," he repeated. "I just want you to know that."

"All right," I said, at last. "So it can come again. All right."

He smiled, but the smile was sorrowful. "I had to try to tell you," he said.

220   "Yes," I said. "I understand that."

"You're my brother," he said, looking straight at me, and not smiling at all.

"Yes," I repeated, "yes. I understand that."

He turned back to the window, looking out. "All that hatred down there," he said, "all that hatred and misery and love. It's a wonder it doesn't blow the avenue apart."

We went to the only nightclub on a short, dark street, downtown. We squeezed through the narrow, chattering, jampacked bar to the entrance of the big room, where the bandstand was. And we stood there for a moment, for the lights were very dim in this room and we couldn't see. Then, "Hello, boy," said the voice and an enormous black man, much older than Sonny or myself, erupted out of all that atmospheric lighting and put an arm around Sonny's shoulder. "I been sitting right here," he said, "waiting for you."

225   He had a big voice, too, and heads in the darkness turned toward us.

Sonny grinned and pulled a little away, and said, "Creole, this is my brother. I told you about him."

Creole shook my hand. "I'm glad to meet you, son," he said, and it was clear that he was glad to meet me *there,* for Sonny's sake. And he smiled, "You got a real musician in *your* family," and he took his arm from Sonny's shoulder and slapped him, lightly, affectionately, with the back of his hand.

"Well. Now I've heard it all," said a voice behind us. This was another musician, and a friend of Sonny's, a coal-black, cheerful-looking man, built close to the ground. He immediately began confiding to me, at the top of his lungs, the most terrible things about Sonny, his teeth gleaming like a lighthouse and his laugh coming up out of him like the beginning of an earthquake. And it turned out that everyone at the bar knew Sonny, or almost everyone; some were musicians, working there, or nearby, or not working, some were simply hangers-on, and some were there to hear Sonny play. I was introduced to all of them and they were all very polite to me. Yet, it was clear that, for them, I was only Sonny's brother. Here, I was in Sonny's world. Or, rather: his kingdom. Here, it was not even a question that his veins bore royal blood.

They were going to play soon and Creole installed me, by myself, at a table in a dark corner. Then I watched them, Creole, and the little black man, and Sonny, and the others, while they horsed around, standing just below the bandstand. The light from the bandstand spilled just a little short of them and, watching them laughing and gesturing and moving about, I had the feeling that they, nevertheless, were being most careful not to step into that circle of light too suddenly: that if they moved into the light too suddenly, without thinking, they would perish in flame. Then, while I watched, one of them, the small black man, moved into the light and crossed the bandstand and started fooling around with his drums. Then—being funny and being, also, extremely ceremonious—Creole took Sonny by the arm and led him to the piano. A woman's voice called Sonny's name and a few hands started clapping. And Sonny, also being funny and being ceremonious, and so touched, I think, that he could have cried, but neither hiding it nor showing it, riding it like a man, grinned, and put both hands to his heart and bowed from the waist.

230   Creole then went to the bass fiddle and a lean, very bright-skinned brown man jumped up on the bandstand and picked up his horn. So there they were, and the atmosphere on the bandstand and in the room began to change and tighten. Someone stepped up to the microphone and announced them. Then there were all kinds of murmurs. Some people at the bar shushed

others. The waitress ran around, frantically getting in the last orders, guys and chicks got closer to each other, and the lights on the bandstand, on the quartet, turned to a kind of indigo. Then they all looked different there. Creole looked about him for the last time, as though he were making certain that all his chickens were in the coop, and then he—jumped and struck the fiddle. And there they were.

All I know about music is that not many people ever really hear it. And even then, on the rare occasions when something opens within, and the music enters, what we mainly hear, or hear corroborated, are personal, private, vanishing evocations. But the man who creates the music is hearing something else, is dealing with the roar rising from the void and imposing order on it as it hits the air. What is evoked in him, then, is of another order, more terrible because it has no words, and triumphant, too, for that same reason. And his triumph, when he triumphs, is ours. I just watched Sonny's face. His face was troubled, he was working hard, but he wasn't with it. And I had the feeling that, in a way, everyone on the bandstand was waiting for him, both waiting for him and pushing him along. But as I began to watch Creole, I realized that it was Creole who held them all back. He had them on a short rein. Up there, keeping the beat with his whole body, wailing on the fiddle, with his eyes half closed, he was listening to everything, but he was listening to Sonny. He was having a dialogue with Sonny. He wanted Sonny to leave the shoreline and strike out for the deep water. He was Sonny's witness that deep water and drowning were not the same thing— he had been there, and he knew. And he wanted Sonny to know. He was waiting for Sonny to do the things on the keys which would let Creole know that Sonny was in the water.

And, while Creole listened, Sonny moved, deep within, exactly like someone in torment. I had never before thought of how awful the relationship must be between the musician and his instrument. He has to fill it, this instrument, with the breath of life, his own. He has to make it do what he wants it to do. And a piano is just a piano. It's made out of so much wood and wires and little hammers and big ones, and ivory. While there's only so much you can do with it, the only way to find this out is to try; and try and make it do everything.

And Sonny hadn't been near a piano for over a year. And he wasn't on much better terms with his life, not the life that stretched before him. He and the piano stammered, started one way, got scared, stopped; started another way, panicked, marked time, started again; then seemed to have found a direction, panicked again, got stuck. And the face I saw on Sonny I'd never seen before. Everything had been burned out of it, and, at the same time, things usually hidden were being burned in, by the fire and fury of the battle which was occurring in him up there.

Yet, watching Creole's face as they neared the end of the first set, I had the feeling that something had happened, something I hadn't heard. Then they finished, there was scattered applause, and then, without an instant's warning, Creole started into something else, it was almost sardonic, it was *Am I Blue*. And, as though he commanded, Sonny began to play. Something began to happen. And Creole let out the reins. The dry, low, black man said something awful on the drums, Creole answered, and the drums talked back. Then the horn insisted, sweet and high, slightly detached perhaps, and Creole listened, commenting now and then, dry, and driving, beautiful and calm and old. Then they all came together again, and Sonny was part of the family again. I could tell this from his face. He seemed to have found, right there beneath his fingers, a damn brand-new piano. It seemed that he couldn't get over it. Then, for a while, just being happy with Sonny, they seemed to be agreeing with him that brand-new pianos certainly were a gas.

235   Then Creole stepped forward to remind them that what they were playing was the blues. He hit something in all of them, he hit something in me, myself, and the music tightened and deepened, apprehension began to beat the air. Creole began to tell us what the blues were all about. They were not about anything very new. He and his boys up there were keeping it new, at the risk of ruin, destruction, madness, and death, in order to find new ways to make us listen. For, while the tale of how we suffer, and how we are delighted, and how we may triumph is never new, it always must be heard. There isn't any other tale to tell, it's the only light we've got in all this darkness.

And this tale, according to that face, that body, those strong hands on those strings, has another aspect in every country, and a new depth in every generation. Listen, Creole seemed to be saying, listen. Now these are Sonny's blues. He made the little black man on the drums know it, and the bright, brown man on the horn. Creole wasn't trying any longer to get Sonny in the water. He was wishing him Godspeed. Then he stepped back, very slowly, filling the air with the immense suggestion that Sonny speak for himself.

Then they all gathered around Sonny and Sonny played. Every now and again one of them seemed to say, amen. Sonny's fingers filled the air with life, his life. But that life contained so many others. And Sonny went all the way back, he really began with the spare, flat statement of the opening phrase of the song. Then he began to make it his. It was very beautiful because it wasn't hurried and it was no longer a lament. I seemed to hear with what burning he had made it his, with what burning we had yet to make it ours, how we could cease lamenting. Freedom lurked around us and I understood, at last, that he could help us to be free if we would listen, that he would never be free until we did. Yet, there was no battle in his face now, I heard what he had gone through, and would continue to go through until he came to rest in earth. He had made it his: that long line, of which we knew only Mama and Daddy. And he was giving it back, as everything must be given back, so that, passing through death, it can live forever. I saw my mother's face again, and felt, for the first time, how the stones of the road she had walked on must have bruised her feet. I saw the moonlit road where my father's brother died. And it brought something else back to me, and carried me past it. I saw my little girl again and felt Isabel's tears again, and I felt my own tears begin to rise. And I was yet aware that this was only a moment, that the world waited outside, as hungry as a tiger, and that trouble stretched above us, longer than the sky.

Then it was over. Creole and Sonny let out their breath, both soaking wet, and grinning. There was a lot of applause and some of it was real. In the dark, the girl came by and I asked her to take drinks to the bandstand. There was a long pause, while they talked up there in the indigo light and after awhile I saw the girl put a Scotch and milk on top of the piano for Sonny. He didn't seem to notice it, but just before they started playing again, he sipped from it and looked toward me, and nodded. Then he put it back on top of the piano. For me, then, as they began to play again, it glowed and shook above my brother's head like the very cup of trembling.[7]

---

[7]**cup of trembling** an allusion to Isaiah 51.22: "Thus saith thy Lord the Lord, and thy God that pleadeth the cause of his people, Behold, I have taken out of thine hand the cup of trembling, even the dregs of the cup of my fury; thou shalt no more drink it again."

JORGE LUIS BORGES

Jorge Luis Borges (1899–1986), one of the first writers in Spanish to achieve an international reputation, was born in Buenos Aires. His paternal grandfather was English, and Borges learned English before he learned Spanish. When his family went to Geneva before World War I, he became fluent in German and French. After the war the family spent two years in Spain, in 1921 Borges returned to Argentina, and in 1925 he published his first book, a collection of poems. In 1938 he accepted a post as a municipal librarian in Buenos Aires, but in 1946—by which time Borges's fiction had won him an international reputation—the dictator Juan Perón removed him from the post. In 1955, after Perón was deposed, Borges—already blind from a congenital disease— was made the director of the National Library of Buenos Aires, and in 1956 he was appointed Professor of English at the University of Buenos Aires.

Borges, widely regarded as the greatest contemporary writer in Spanish, is known for his poetry, literary criticism, and especially his highly innovative and immensely influential short fiction. For him, stories are not representations of the surface of life but are re-creations of the cultural myths that human beings have devised.

The Gospel According to Mark   [1970]

These events took place at La Colorada ranch, in the southern part of the township of Junín, during the last days of March, 1928. The protagonist was a medical student named Baltasar Espinosa. We may describe him, for now, as one of the common run of young men from Buenos Aires, with nothing more noteworthy about him than an almost unlimited kindness and a capacity for public speaking that had earned him several prizes at the English school in Ramos Mejía. He did not like arguing, and preferred having his listener rather than himself in the right. Although he was fascinated by the probabilities of chance in any game he played, he was a bad player because it gave him no pleasure to win. His wide intelligence was undirected; at the age of thirty-three, he still lacked credit for graduation, by one course—the course to which he was most drawn. His father, who was a freethinker (like all the gentlemen of his day), had introduced him to the lessons of Herbert Spencer,[1] but his mother, before his leaving on a trip for Montevideo, once asked him to say the Lord's Prayer[2] and make the sign of the cross every night. Through the years, he had never gone back on that promise.

---

[1]**Herbert Spencer** British philosopher and sociologist (1820–1903).   [2]**the Lord's Prayer** the prayer Jesus taught to his disciples (Matthew 6.9–13).

Espinosa was not lacking in spirit; one day, with more indifference than anger, he had exchanged two or three punches with a group of fellow-students who were trying to force him to take part in a university demonstration. Owing to an acquiescent nature, he was full of opinions, or habits of mind, that were questionable: Argentina mattered less to him than a fear that in other parts of the world people might think of us as Indians; he worshiped France but despised the French; he thought little of Americans but approved the fact that there were tall buildings, like theirs, in Buenos Aires; he believed the gauchos of the plains to be better riders than those of hill or mountain country. When his cousin Daniel invited him to spend the summer months out at La Colorada, he said yes at once—not because he was really fond of the country, but more out of his natural complacency and also because it was easier to say yes than to dream up reasons for saying no.

The ranch's main house was big and slightly run-down; the quarters of the foreman, whose name was Gutre, were close by. The Gutres were three: the father, an unusually uncouth son, and a daughter of uncertain paternity. They were tall, strong, and bony, and had hair that was on the reddish side and faces that showed traces of Indian blood. They were barely articulate. The foreman's wife had died years before.

There in the country, Espinosa began learning things he never knew, or even suspected—for example, that you do not gallop a horse when approaching settlements, and that you never go out riding except for some special purpose. In time, he was to come to tell the birds apart by their calls.

5   After a few days, Daniel had to leave for Buenos Aires to close a deal on some cattle. At most, this bit of business might take him a week. Espinosa, who was already somewhat weary of hearing about his cousin's incessant luck with women and his tireless interest in the minute details of men's fashion, preferred staying on at the ranch with his textbooks. But the heat was unbearable, and even the night brought no relief. One morning at daybreak, thunder woke him. Outside, the wind was rocking the Australian pines. Listening to the first heavy drops of rain, Espinosa thanked God. All at once, cold air rolled in. That afternoon, the Salado overflowed its banks.

The next day, looking out over the flooded fields from the gallery of the main house, Baltasar Espinosa thought that the stock metaphor comparing the pampas to the sea was not altogether false—at least, not that morning—though W. H. Hudson[3] had remarked that the sea seems wider because we view it from a ship's deck and not from a horse or from eye level.

The rain did not let up. The Gutres, helped or hindered by Espinosa, the town dweller, rescued a good part of the livestock, but many animals were drowned. There were four roads leading to La Colorada; all of them were under water. On the third day, when a leak threatened the foreman's house, Espinosa gave the Gutres a room near the tool shed, at the back of the main house. This drew them all closer; they ate together in the big dining room. Conversation turned out to be difficult. The Gutres, who knew so much about country things, were hard put to it to explain them.

---

[3]**W. H. Hudson** William Henry Hudson (1841–1922), born of American parents in Argentina, went to England in 1869 and spent most of the rest of his life there. Several of his books are about Argentina.

One night, Espinosa asked them if people still remembered the Indian raids from back when the frontier command was located there in Junín. They told him yes, but they would have given the same answer to a question about the beheading of Charles I. Espinosa recalled his father's saying that almost every case of longevity that was cited in the country was really a case of bad memory or of a dim notion of dates. Gauchos are apt to be ignorant of the year of their birth or of the name of the man who begot them.

In the whole house, there was apparently no other reading matter than a set of the *Farm Journal*, a handbook of veterinary medicine, a deluxe edition of the Uruguayan epic *Tabaré*, a *History of Shorthorn Cattle in Argentina*, a number of erotic or detective stories, and a recent novel called *Don Segundo Sombra*. Espinosa, trying in some way to bridge the inevitable after-dinner gap, read a couple of chapters of this novel to the Gutres, none of whom could read or write. Unfortunately, the foreman had been a cattle drover, and the doings of the hero, another cattle drover, failed to whet his interest. He said that the work was light, that drovers always traveled with a pack horse that carried everything they needed, and that, had he not been a drover, he would never have seen such far-flung places as the Laguna de Gómez, the town of Bragado, and the spread of the Núñez family in Chacabuco. There was a guitar in the kitchen; the ranch hands, before the time of the events I am describing, used to sit around in a circle. Someone would tune the instrument without ever getting around to playing it. This was known as a guitarfest.

10 Espinosa, who had grown a beard, began dallying in front of the mirror to study his new face, and he smiled to think how, back in Buenos Aires, he would bore his friends by telling them the story of the Salado flood. Strangely enough, he missed places he never frequented and never would: a corner of Cabrera Street on which there was a mailbox; one of the cement lions of a gateway on Jujuy Street, a few blocks from the Plaza del Once; an old bar-room with a tiled floor, whose exact whereabouts he was unsure of. As for his brothers and his father, they would already have learned from Daniel that he was isolated—etymologically, the word was perfect—by the floodwaters.

Exploring the house, still hemmed in by the watery waste, Espinosa came across an English Bible. Among the blank pages at the end, the Guthries—such was their original name—had left a handwritten record of their lineage. They were natives of Inverness;[4] had reached the New World, no doubt as common laborers, in the early part of the nineteenth century; and had intermarried with Indians. The chronicle broke off sometime during the eighteen-seventies, when they no longer knew how to write. After a few generations, they had forgotten English; their Spanish, at the time Espinosa knew them, gave them trouble. They lacked any religious faith, but there survived in their blood, like faint tracks, the rigid fanaticism of the Calvinists and the superstitions of the pampas Indians. Espinosa later told them of his find, but they barely took notice.

Leafing through the volume, his fingers opened it at the beginning of the Gospel according to St. Mark. As an exercise in translation, and maybe to find out whether the Gutres understood any of it, Espinosa decided to begin reading them that text after their evening meal. It surprised him that they listened attentively, absorbed. Maybe the gold letters on the cover lent the

---

[4]**Inverness** a county in northwest Scotland.

book authority. It's still there in their blood, Espinosa thought. It also occurred to him that the generations of men, throughout recorded time, have always told and retold two stories—that of a lost ship which searches the Mediterranean seas for a dearly loved island, and that of a god who is crucified on Golgotha.[5] Remembering his lessons in elocution from his schooldays in Ramos Mejía, Espinosa got to his feet when he came to the parables.

The Gutres took to bolting their barbecued meat and their canned sardines so as not to delay the Gospel. A pet lamb that the girl adorned with a small blue ribbon had injured itself on a strand of barbed wire. To stop the bleeding, the three had wanted to apply a cobweb to the wound, but Espinosa treated the animal with some pills. The gratitude that this treatment awakened in them took him aback. (Not trusting the Gutres at first, he'd hidden away in one of his books the two hundred and forty pesos he had brought with him.) Now, with the owner of the place away, Espinosa took over and gave timid orders, which were immediately obeyed. The Gutres, as if lost without him, liked following him from room to room and along the gallery that ran around the house. While he read to them, he noticed that they were secretly stealing the crumbs he had dropped on the table. One evening, he caught them unawares, talking about him respectfully, in very few words.

Having finished the Gospel according to St. Mark, he wanted to read another of the three Gospels that remained, but the father asked him to repeat the one he had just read, so that they could understand it better. Espinosa felt that they were like children, to whom repetition is more pleasing than variations or novelty. That night—this is not to be wondered at—he dreamed of the Flood; the hammer blows of the building of the Ark woke him up, and he thought that perhaps they were thunder. In fact, the rain, which had let up, started again. The cold was bitter. The Gutres had told him that the storm had damaged the roof of the tool shed, and that they would show it to him after the beams were fixed. No longer a stranger now, he was treated by them with special attention, almost to the point of spoiling him. None of them liked coffee, but for him there was always a small cup into which they heaped sugar.

15   The second storm had broken out on a Tuesday. Thursday night, Espinosa was awakened by a soft knock at his door, which—just in case—he always kept locked. He got out of bed and opened it; there was the girl. In the dark he could hardly make her out, but by her footsteps he could tell she was barefoot, and moments later, in bed, that she must have come all the way from the other end of the house naked. She did not embrace him or speak a single word; she lay beside him, trembling. It was the first time she had known a man. When she left, she did not kiss him; Espinosa realized that he didn't even know her name. For some reason that he did not want to pry into, he made up his mind that upon returning to Buenos Aires he would tell no one about what had taken place.

The next day began like the previous ones, except that the father spoke to Espinosa and asked him if Christ had let Himself be killed so as to save all

---

[5]**two stories . . . Golgotha** the first story is Homer's *Odyssey,* in which Homer tells of the wanderings of Odysseus; the second story is of Jesus's crucifixion at Golgotha, "Place of the Skull" (the Semitic name for Calvary).

other men on earth. Espinosa, who was a freethinker but who felt committed to what he had read to the Gutres, answered, "Yes, to save everyone from Hell."

Gutre then asked, "What's Hell?"

"A place under the ground where souls burn and burn."

"And the Roman soldiers who hammered in the nails—were they saved, too?"

20   "Yes," said Espinosa, whose theology was rather dim.

All along, he was afraid that the foreman might ask him about what had gone on the night before with his daughter. After lunch, they asked him to read the last chapters over again.

Espinosa slept a long nap that afternoon. It was a light sleep, disturbed by persistent hammering and by vague premonitions. Toward evening, he got up and went out onto the gallery. He said, as if thinking aloud, "The waters have dropped. It won't be long now."

"It won't be long now," Gutre repeated, like an echo.

The three had been following him. Bowing their knees to the stone pavement, they asked his blessing. Then they mocked at him, spat on him, and shoved him toward the back part of the house. The girl wept. Espinosa understood what awaited him on the other side of the door. When they opened it, he saw a patch of sky. A bird sang out. A goldfinch,[6] he thought. The shed was without a roof; they had pulled down the beams to make the cross.

---

[6]**goldfinch** in art the infant Jesus is often shown holding a goldfinch. Legend says that at Calvary a goldfinch drew a thorn from Christ's brow.

OSCAR CASARES

Oscar Casares, born (1964) and raised in Brownsville, Texas, is a graduate of the Iowa Writers' Workshop. Casares, who teaches creative writing at the University of Texas in Austin, has published widely and received numerous prizes, including the James Michener Award. We reprint a story from his collection, Brownsville Stories *(2003).*

Yolanda
[2003]

When I can't sleep at night I think of Yolanda Castro. She was a woman who lived next door to us one summer when I was growing up. I've never told Maggie about her because it's not something she'd appreciate knowing. Trust me. Tonight, like most nights, she fell asleep before I was even done brushing my teeth. And now all I can hear are little snores. Sometimes she even talks to herself, shouts out other people's names, and then in the morning says she can't remember any of it. Either way, I let her go on sleeping. She's over on her side of the bed. It's right where she ought to be. This thing with Yolanda doesn't really concern her.

I was only twelve years old when Frank and Yolanda Castro moved into the beige house with green trim. Frank pulled up on our street in a U-Haul he'd driven all the way from California to Texas. I remember it being a different neighborhood back then. Everybody knew everybody, and people left their doors unlocked at night. You didn't worry about people stealing shit you didn't lock up. I'm talking about more than twenty years ago now. I'm talking about before some drunk spent all afternoon in one of the cantinas on Fourteenth Street, then drove his car straight into the Rivas front yard and ran over the Baby Jesus that was still lying in the manger because Lonny Rivas was too flojo[1] to put it away a month after Christmas, and then the guy tried to run, but fell down, asleep, in our yard, and when the cops were handcuffing him all he could say was *ma-ri-juan-a,* which even then, at the age of fifteen, I knew wasn't a good thing to say when you were being arrested. This was before Pete Zuniga was riding his brand-new ten-speed from Western Auto and, next to the Friendship Garden, saw a white dude who'd been knifed a couple of dozen times and was floating in the green water of the resaca.[2] Before some crazy woman hired a curandera[3] to put a spell on her daughter's ex-boyfriend, which really meant hiring a couple of hit men from Matamoros to do a drive-by. Before the cops ever had to show up at El Disco de Oro Tortillería. Like holding up a 7-Eleven was getting old, right? You know, when you could sit at the Brownsville Coffee Shop #1 and not worry about getting it in the back while you ate your menudo.[4] When you didn't have to put an alarm *and* the Club on your car so it wouldn't end up in Reynosa. Before my father had to put iron bars on the windows and doors because some future convict from the junior high was always breaking into the house. And before my father had to put a fence in the front because, in his words, I'm sick and tired of all those damn dogs making poo in my yard. I guess what I'm trying to say is, things were different back then.

Frank Castro was an older man, in his fifties by that point, and Yolanda couldn't have been more than thirty, if that. My mother got along with Yolanda okay and even helped her get a job at the HEB store where she had worked since before I was born. You could say that was where the problems started, because Frank Castro didn't want his wife working at HEB, or any other place for that matter. You have no business being in that grocery store, I heard him yell one night when I was trying to fall asleep. I could hear almost everything Frank yelled that summer. Our houses were only a few yards apart, and my window was the closest to the action. My father's bougainvilleas were the dividing line between the two properties. I heard Yolanda beg Frank to please let her take the job. I heard Frank yell something in Spanish about how no woman in his family had ever worked behind a cosmetics counter, selling lipstick. I heard her promise she'd only work part-time, and she'd quit if they ever scheduled her on nights or weekends. I heard her tell him how much she loved him and how she'd never take a job that would keep them apart. Francisco, tú eres mi vida,[5] she said to him. I heard him get real quiet. Then I heard Frank and Yolanda Castro making love. I didn't know what making love sounded like back then, but I can tell you now that's what it was.

If you saw what Yolanda looked like, you might not have blamed Frank for not wanting her to leave the house. It also wouldn't have been a big mystery to you how she went into the store applying for a job in the meat department and ended up getting one in cosmetics. The only girl I'd ever seen that even

---

[1]**flojo** weak-willed.   [2]**resaca** dry streambed.   [3]**curandera** midwife.   [4]**menudo** tripe soup.   [5]**tú . . . vida** you are my life.

came close to being as beautiful as Yolanda was in a *Playboy* I found under my parents' bed the summer before. The girl in the magazine had the same long black hair, light brown skin, and green eyes that Yolanda did, only she was sitting bareback on an Appaloosa.

5   The thing I remember most about Frank was his huge forearms. They were like Popeye's, except with a lot more black and gray hair mixed in. But the hair on his arms was just the beginning. There wasn't a time I saw the guy that he didn't look like he could've used a good shave. And it didn't help that his thick eyebrows were connected into one long eyebrow that stretched across the bottom of his forehead like a piece of electrical tape. He was average size, but he looked short and squatty when he stood next to Yolanda. Frank was a mechanic at the airport and, according to my father, probably made good money. I was with my father the first time he met Frank. He always made it a point to meet any new neighbors and then come back to the house and give a full report to my mother, who would later meet the neighbors herself and say he was exaggerating about how shifty so-and-so's eyes were or how rich he thought another neighbor might be because he had one of those new foreign cars in the driveway, un carro extranjero,[6] a Toyota or a Honda. Frank was beginning to mow his front yard when we walked up. My father introduced me as his boy, and I shook our neighbor's sweaty hand. I've lived thirty-six years on this earth and never shaken hands with a bear, but I have a good idea that it wouldn't be much different from shaking Frank Castro's hand. Even his fingers needed a haircut. Frank stood there answering a couple of my father's questions about whether he liked the neighborhood (he liked it) and how long he had lived in California before moving back to Texas (ten years—he held up both hands to show us exactly how many). Suddenly, my father nodded and said we had to go. He turned around and walked off, then looked over his shoulder and yelled at me to hurry up. This whole time, Frank had not shut off his mower. My father was forced to stand there and shout over the sound of the engine. The report on Frank wasn't pretty when we got back to the house. From that point on, my father would only refer to him as El Burro.

It wasn't just my father. Nobody liked Frank. He had this thing about his yard where he didn't want anybody getting near it. We found this out one day when Lonny and I were throwing the football around in the street. Lonny was showing off and he threw the ball over my head, way over, and it landed in Frank's yard. When I was getting the ball, Frank opened the front door and yelled something about it being private property. Then he went over, turned on the hose, and started watering his yard and half the street in front of his yard. He did this every afternoon from that day on. The hose with a spray gun in his right hand, and a Schlitz tallboy in his left. Lonny thought we should steal the hose when Frank wasn't home, or maybe poke a few holes in it, just to teach the fucker a lesson. One Saturday morning we even saw him turn the hose on some Jehovahs who were walking up the street towards his house. A skinny man wearing a tie and short-sleeve shirt kept trying to give him a pamphlet, but Frank wasn't listening.

My mother gave Yolanda a ride to work every day. In the afternoons, Yolanda got off work early enough to be waiting for Frank to pull up in his

---

[6]**carro extranjero** foreign car.

car and drive her back to the house. My mother told us at home that Yolanda had asked Frank to teach her how to drive when they first got married but that Frank had said she was his princesa now and any place she needed to go, he'd take her. One morning, when both my mother and Yolanda had the day off, my mother asked her if she wanted to learn how to drive. They drove out by the port, and my mother pulled over so Yolanda could take the wheel. I was hanging out at the Jiffy-Mart, down the street, when I saw Yolanda driving my mother's car. Yolanda honked the horn, and they both waved at me as they turned the corner.

That night—like a lot of nights that summer—I listened to Frank and Yolanda Castro. What they said went something like this:

"I can show you."

10   "I don't wanna see."

"Why not?"

"Because you have *no* business driving a car around town."

"But this way you don't have to pick me up every day. You can come straight home, and I'll be here already, waiting."

"I don't care. I'm talking about you learning to drive."

15   "Frank, it's nothing."

"You don't even have a car. What do you want with a license?"

"I can buy one."

"With what?"

"I've been getting bonuses. The companies gives us a little extra if we sell more of their makeup."

20   "Is that right?"

"It isn't that much, Frank."

"And then?"

"Well, maybe I can buy a used one."

"It's because of that store."

25   "What's wrong with the store?"

"It's putting ideas in your head."

"Frank, what ideas?"

"Ideas! Is there some place I haven't taken you?"

"No."

30   "Well, then?"

"Francisco."

"Don't 'Francisco' me."

"Baby . . ."

"¡Qué no!"[7]

35   They were beginning to remind me of one of my mother's novellas, which she was probably watching in the living room at that very moment. Things like that usually made me want to laugh—and I did a little, into my pillow, but it was only because I couldn't believe I was actually hearing it, and I could see Frank Castro pounding me into the ground with his big fore-arms if he ever found out.

"No! I said."

"I'm not Trini."

"I never said . . ."

---

[7]**¡Qué no!** Why not?

"Then stop treating me like her. ¿No sabes qué tanto te quiero, Francisco?"[8]

40   It got quiet for a while after that. Then there was the sound of something hitting the floor, the sound of two bodies dropping on a bed with springs that had seen better days (and nights), the sound of Yolanda saying, *Ay, Diosito,*[9] over and over and over again—just like my tía[10] Hilda did the day her son, my cousin Rudy, almost drowned in the swimming pool at the Civic Center—then the sound of the bed springs making their own crazy music, and the sound of what I imagine a bear is like when he's trying to make little bears.

Yolanda kept getting a ride to work with my mother, and Frank kept bringing her home in the afternoons. My mother had offered to drive Yolanda to the DPS office and let her borrow our car for the driving part of the test, but Yolanda said she'd changed her mind and didn't want to talk about it. I heard my mother telling my father what she'd said, and they agreed it probably had something to do with Frank. El Burro, my father let out when they didn't have anything else to say.

It was the Fourth of July when I got sick that summer. I remember my mother wouldn't let me go outside with Lonny. He kept yelling at me from the street that night to stop being a baby and come out of the house so I could pop some firecrackers. We'd been talking all week about shooting some bottle rockets in the direction of Frank's house. It didn't feel like anything at first, just a fever, but the next morning we knew it was the chicken pox. My mother had to miss a few days of work, staying home with me until I got over the worst part. After that, Yolanda volunteered to come look in on me when she wasn't working. But I told my mother I didn't want her coming over when I still looked like those dead people in that *Night of the Living Dead* movie. My mother said Yolanda would understand I was sick, and if she didn't, that's what I'd get for watching those kinds of movies. So for about a week she came over in the mornings and we watched *The Price Is Right* together. Yolanda was great at guessing the prices of things, and she said it was from working in a grocery store and having a good memory. I told her I thought she should go on the show. She laughed and said she probably wouldn't win anything, since she'd be too nervous. What I meant to say was that she should go on the show and be one of the girls who stands next to the car, smiling. She was prettier than any of them, but I never told her that, because I got embarrassed whenever I thought about saying it.

If Yolanda came over in the afternoon, we'd watch *General Hospital* together. She said she'd been watching it for years. There wasn't anything else on at that hour, so I didn't really care. Once, she brought over some lime sherbert, and we played Chinese checkers in my room until she had to get home to Frank Castro. Each time she left she'd reach down and give me a little kiss on the cheek, and each time her hair smelled like a different fruit. Sometimes like a pear, sometimes like a strawberry, sometimes like an apple. The strawberry was my favorite.

---

[8]**¿No . . . Francisco?** Don't you know how much I love you, Francisco?   [9]***Ay, Diosito*** Oh, God.   [10]**tía** aunt.

* * *

This was about the time when Frank said that from now on, he would take Yolanda to work in the morning—no matter how out of the way it was for him, or the fact that he and my mother were always pulling out of the driveway at the same time. A week or two went by, and then my mother told my father that Frank had started showing up at the store in the middle of the day, usually during his lunch hour, but sometimes also at two or three in the afternoon. He wouldn't talk to Yolanda, but instead just hung out by the magazine rack, pretending to read a wrestling magazine. Yolanda tried to ignore him. My mother said she had talked to her in the break room, but Yolanda kept saying it was nothing, that Frank's hours had changed at the airport.

45   There was one Saturday when he was off from work, and as usual, he spent it in his front yard, sitting in a green lawn chair, drinking tallboys. He had turned on the sprinkler and was watching his grass and half the street get a good watering. Lonny and I were throwing the football around. Frank sat in that stupid chair all afternoon. He only went in to grab another beer and, I guess, take a piss. Each time he got up and turned around, we shot him the finger.

That night, I heard Frank's voice loud and clear. He wanted answers. Something about a phone number. Something about a customer he'd seen Yolanda talking to a couple of days earlier. Did she think he was blind? What the hell was so funny when the two of them were talking? How many times? he wanted to know. ¡Desgraciado![11] Where? Goddammit! he wanted to know. What game show? ¡El sanavabiche! Something shattered against the wall and then a few seconds later Yolanda screamed. I sat up. I didn't know if I could form words if I had to. What the hell were you doing listening anyway? they would ask me. There was another scream and then the sound of the back door slamming. I looked out my window and saw Frank Castro chase Yolanda into their backyard. She was wearing a nightgown that came down to her knees. Frank had on the same khakis and muscle shirt he'd worn that afternoon. He only ran a few feet down from the back steps before his head hit the clothesline, and he fell to the ground, hard. Yolanda didn't turn to look back and ran around the right side of their house. I thought she'd gone back inside to call the police. Then I heard footsteps and a tapping on my window. It was Yolanda whispering, Open it, open it.

I didn't say anything for a long time. Yolanda had climbed in and let down the blinds. We were lying on the bed, facing the window. She was behind me, holding me tight. I finally asked her if she wanted a glass of water or some Kool-Aid. I made it myself, I told her. It's the orange kind, I said. I didn't know what else to talk about. She said no, and then she told me to be quiet. I kept thinking, This has to be a dream and any minute now my mother's going to walk in and tell me the barbacoa[12] is sitting on the table and to come eat because we're going to eleven o'clock mass and don't even think about putting on those blue jeans with the patches in the knees ¿me entiendes?[13] But that wasn't happening, and something told me then that no matter what happened after tonight, this was something I'd never forget. There would always be a time *before* Yolanda crawled into my bed and a

---

[11]**Desgraciado** disgraceful.   [12]**barbacoa** baked lamb or goat.   [13]**me entiendes** do you understand me?

time *after*. As she held me, I could feel her heart beating. Then I felt her chiches[14] pressed against my back. And even though I couldn't see them, I knew they were perfect like the rest of her. I knew that they'd fit right in the palms of my hands, if only I had enough guts to turn around. Just turn around, that's all I had to do. I thought back to when she was tapping on the window, and I was sure she wasn't wearing a bra. I was sure there was nothing but Yolanda underneath her nightgown. I could have sworn I'd seen even more. I'd been close to a woman's body before. But this wasn't like when my tía Gloria came into town and couldn't believe how much I'd grown, and then she squeezed me so hard my head got lost in her huge and heavily perfumed chiches. And it wasn't anything like the Sears catalog where the girls had a tiny rose at the top of their panties. No, this was Yolanda and she was in my bed, pressed up against my back, like it was the only place in the world for us to be.

I could go on and tell you the rest of the details—how I never turned around and always regretted it, how we stayed there and listened to Frank crying in his backyard, how Lonny's dad finally called the cops on his ass, how Yolanda had a cousin pick her up the next morning, how she ended up leaving Frank for a man who worked for one of the shampoo companies, how it didn't matter because she'd also been seeing an assistant manager and would be having his baby soon enough, and how it really didn't matter because the assistant manager was already married and wasn't about to leave his wife and kids, and how, actually, none of it mattered because she'd been taking money out of the register and was about to be caught—but that's not the part of the story I like to remember.

In that bed of mine, the one with the Dallas Cowboy pillows and covers, Yolanda and I were safe. We were safe from Frank Castro and safe from anybody else that might try to hurt us. And it was safe for me to fall asleep in Yolanda's arms, with her warm, beautiful body pressed against mine, and dream that we were riding off to some faraway place on an Appaloosa.

---

[14]**chiches** breasts.

DIANA CHANG

Diana Chang (1934–2009), the author of several novels and books of poems, taught creative writing at Barnard College. Chang identified herself as an American writer whose background was mostly Chinese.

The Oriental Contingent   [1989]

Connie couldn't remember whose party it was, whose house. She had an impression of kerosene lamps on brown wicker tables, of shapes talking in doorways. It was summer, almost the only time Connie has run into her since, too, and someone was saying, "You must know Lisa Mallory."

"I don't think so."

"She's here. You must know her."

Later in the evening, it was someone else who introduced her to a figure perched on the balustrade of the steps leading to the lawn where more shapes milled. In stretching out a hand to shake Connie's, the figure almost fell off sideways. Connie had pushed her back upright onto her perch and, peering, took in the fact that Lisa Mallory had a Chinese face. For a long instant, she felt nonplussed, and was rendered speechless.

5   But Lisa Mallory was filling the silence. "Well, now, Connie Sung," she said, not enthusiastically but with a kind of sophisticated interest, "I'm not in music myself, but Paul Wu's my cousin. Guilt by association!" She laughed. "No-tone music, I call his. He studied with John Cage, Varese, and so forth."

Surprised that Lisa knew she was a violinist, Connie murmured something friendly, wondering if she should simply ask outright, "I'm sure I should know, but what do you do?" but she hesitated, taking in her appearance instead, while Lisa went on with, "It's world class composing. Nothing's wrong with the level. But it's hard going for the layman, believe me."

Lisa Mallory wore a one-of-a-kind kimono dress, but it didn't make her look Japanese at all, and her hair was drawn back tightly in a braid which stood out from close to the top of her head horizontally. You could probably lift her off her feet by grasping it, like the handle of a pot.

"You should give a concert here, Connie," she said, using her first name right away, Connie noticed, like any American. "Lots of culturati around." Even when she wasn't actually speaking, she pursued her own line of thought actively and seemed to find herself mildly amusing.

"I'm new to the area," Connie said, deprecatingly. "I've just been a weekend guest, actually, till a month ago."

10   "It's easy to be part of it. Nothing to it. I should know. You'll see."

"I wish it weren't so dark," Connie found herself saying, waving her hand in front of her eyes as if the night were a veil to brush aside. She recognized in herself that intense need to see, to see into fellow Orientals, to fathom them. So far, Lisa Mallory had not given her enough clues, and the darkness itself seemed to be interfering.

Lisa dropped off her perch. "It's important to be true to oneself," she said. "Keep the modern stuff out of your repertory. Be romantic. Don't look like that! You're best at the romantics. Anyhow, take it from me. I know. And *I* like what I like."

Released by her outspokenness, Connie laughed and asked, "I'm sure I should know, but what is it that you do?" She was certain Lisa would say something like, "I'm with a public relations firm." "I'm in city services."

But she replied, "What do all Chinese excel at?" Not as if she'd asked a rhetorical question, she waited, then answered herself. "Well, aren't we all physicists, musicians, architects, or in software?"

15   At that point a voice broke in, followed by a large body which put his arms around both women, "The Oriental contingent! I've got to break this up."

Turning, Lisa kissed him roundly, and said over her shoulder to Connie, "I'll take him away before he tells us we look alike!"

They melted into the steps below, and Connie, feeling put off balance and somehow slow-witted, was left to think over her new acquaintance.

"Hello, Lisa Mallory," Connie Sung always said on the infrequent occasions when they ran into one another. She always said "Hello, Lisa Mallory," with a shyness she did not understand in herself. It was strange, but they had no mutual friends except for Paul Wu, and Connie had not seen him in ages.

Connie had no one of whom to ask her questions. But sometime soon, she'd be told Lisa's maiden name. Sometime she'd simply call her Lisa. Sometime what Lisa did with her life would be answered.

Three, four years passed, with their running into one another at receptions and openings, and still Lisa Mallory remained an enigma. Mildly amused herself, Connie wondered if other people, as well, found her inscrutable. But none of her American friends (though, of course, Lisa and she were Americans, too, she had to remind herself), none of the Caucasian friends seemed curious about backgrounds. In their accepting way, they did not wonder about Lisa's background, or about Connie's or Paul Wu's. Perhaps they assumed they were all cut from the same cloth. But to Connie, the Orientals she met were unread books, books she never had the right occasion or time to fully pursue.

20   She didn't even see the humor in her situation—it was such an issue with her. The fact was she felt less, much less, sure of herself when she was with real Chinese.

As she was realizing this, the truth suddenly dawned on her. Lisa Mallory never referred to her own background because it was more Chinese than Connie's, and therefore a higher order. She was tact incarnate. All along, she had been going out of her way not to embarrass Connie. Yes, yes. Her assurance was definitely uppercrust (perhaps her father had been in the diplomatic service), and her offhand didacticness, her lack of self-doubt, was indeed characteristically Chinese-Chinese. Connie was not only impressed by these traits, but also put on the defensive because of them.

Connie let out a sigh—a sigh that follows the solution to a nagging problem . . . Lisa's mysteriousness. But now Connie knew only too clearly that her own background made her decidedly inferior. Her father was a second-generation gynecologist who spoke hardly any Chinese. Yes, inferior and totally without recourse.

Of course, at one of the gatherings, Connie met Bill Mallory, too. He was simply American, maybe Catholic, possibly lapsed. She was not put off balance by him at all. But most of the time he was away on business, and Lisa cropped up at functions as single as Connie.

Then one day, Lisa had a man in tow—wiry and tall, he looked Chinese from the Shantung area, or perhaps from Beijing, and his styled hair made him appear vaguely artistic.

25   "Connie, I'd like you to meet Eric Li. He got out at the beginning of the *détente,* went to Berkeley, and is assimilating a mile-a-minute," Lisa said, with her usual irony. "Bill found him and is grooming him, though he came with his own charisma."

Eric waved her remark aside. "Lisa has missed her calling. She was born to be in PR," he said, with an accent.

"Is that what she does?" Connie put in at once, looking only at him. "Is that her profession?"

"You don't know?" he asked, with surprise.

Though she was greeting someone else, Lisa turned and answered, "I'm a fabrics tycoon, I think I can say without immodesty." She moved away and continued her conversation with the other friend.

30   Behind his hand, he said, playfully, as though letting Connie in on a secret, "Factories in Hongkong and Taipei, and now he's—Bill, that is—is exploring them on the mainland."

"With her fabulous contacts over there!" Connie exclaimed, now seeing it all. "Of course, what a wonderful business combination they must make."

Eric was about to utter something, but stopped, and said flatly, "I have all the mainland contacts, even though I was only twenty when I left, but my parents . . ."

"How interesting," Connie murmured lamely. "I see," preoccupied as she was with trying to put two and two together.

Lisa was back and said without an introduction, continuing her line of thought, "You two look good together, if I have to say so myself. Why don't you ask him to one of your concerts? And you, Eric, you're in America now, so don't stand on ceremony, or you'll be out in left field." She walked away with someone for another drink.

35   Looking uncomfortable, but recovering himself with a smile, Eric said, "Lisa makes me feel more Chinese than I am becoming—it is her directness, I suspect. In China, we'd say she is too much like a man."

At which Connie found herself saying, "She makes me feel *less* Chinese."

"Less!"

"Less Chinese than she is."

"That is not possible," Eric said, with a shade of contempt—for whom? Lisa or Connie? He barely suppressed a laugh, cold as Chinese laughter could be.

40   Connie blurted out, "I'm a failed Chinese. Yes, and it's to you that I need to say it." She paused and repeated emphatically, "I am a failed Chinese." Her heart was beating quicker, but she was glad to have got that out, a confession and a definition that might begin to free her. "Do you know you make me feel that, too? You've been here only about ten years, right?"

"Right, and I'm thirty-one."

"You know what I think? I think it's harder for a Chinese to do two things."

At that moment, an American moved in closer, looking pleased somehow to be with them.

She continued, "It's harder for us to become American than, say, for a German, and it's also harder not to remain residually Chinese, even if you are third generation."

45   Eric said blandly, "Don't take yourself so seriously. You can't help being an American product."

Trying to be comforting, the American interjected with, "The young lady is not a product, an object. She is a human being, and there is no difference among peoples that I can see."

"I judge myself both as a Chinese and as an American," Connie said.

"You worry too much," Eric said, impatiently. Then he looked around and though she wasn't in sight, he lowered his voice. "She is what she is. I know what she is. But she avoids going to Hong Kong. She avoids it."

Connie felt turned around. "Avoids it?"

50   "Bill's in Beijing right now. She's here. How come?"

"I don't know," Connie replied, as though an answer had been required of her.

"She makes up many excuses, reasons. Ask her. Ask her yourself," he said, pointedly.

"Oh, I couldn't do that. By the way, I'm going on a concert tour next year in three cities—Shanghai, Beijing, and Nanking," Connie said. "It'll be my first time in China."

"Really! You must be very talented to be touring at your age," he said, genuinely interested for the first time. Because she was going to China, or because she now came across as an over-achiever, even though Chinese American?

55   "I'm just about your age," she said, realizing then that maybe Lisa Mallory had left them alone purposely.

"You could both pass as teenagers!" the American exclaimed.

Two months later, she ran into Lisa again. As usual, Lisa began in the middle of her own thought. "Did he call?"

"Who? Oh. No, no."

"Well, it's true he's been in China the last three weeks with Bill. They'll be back this weekend."

60   Connie saw her opportunity. "Are you planning to go to China yourself?"

For the first time, Lisa seemed at a loss for words. She raised her shoulders, then let them drop. Too airily, she said, "You know, there's always Paris. I can't bear not to go to Paris, if I'm to take a trip."

"But you're Chinese. You *have* been to China, you came from China originally, didn't you?"

"I could go to Paris twice a year, I love it so," Lisa said. "And then there's London, Florence, Venice."

"But—but your business contacts?"

65   "*My* contacts? Bill, he's the businessman who makes the contacts. Always has. I take care of the New York office, which is a considerable job. We have a staff of eighty-five."

Connie said, "I told Eric I'll be giving a tour in China. I'm taking Chinese lessons right now."

Lisa Mallory laughed, "Save your time. They'll still be disdainful over there. See, *they* don't care," and she waved her hand at the crowd. "Some of them have been born in Buffalo, too! It's the Chinese you can't fool. They know you're not the genuine article—you and I."

Her face was suddenly heightened in color, and she was breathing as if ready to flee from something. "Yes, you heard right. I was born in Buffalo."

"You were!" Connie exclaimed before she could control her amazement.

70   "Well, what about you?" Lisa retorted. She was actually shaking and trying to hide it by making sudden gestures.

"Westchester."

"But your parents at least were Chinese."

"Well, so were, so are, yours!"

"I was adopted by Americans. My full name is Lisa Warren Mallory."

75   Incredulous, Connie said, "I'm more Chinese than you!"

"Who isn't?" She laughed, unhappily. "Having Chinese parents makes all the difference. We're worlds apart."

"And all the time I thought . . . never mind what I thought."

"You have it over me. It's written all over you. I could tell even in the dark that night."

"Oh, Lisa," Connie said to comfort her, "none of this matters to anybody except us. Really and truly. They're too busy with their own problems."

80   "The only time I feel Chinese is when I'm embarrassed I'm not more Chinese—which is a totally Chinese reflex I'd give anything to be rid of!"

"I know what you mean."

"And as for Eric looking down his nose at me, he's knocking himself out to be so American, *but as a secure Chinese!* What's so genuine about that article?"

Both of them struck their heads laughing, but their eyes were not merry.

"Say it again," Connie asked of her, "say it again that my being more Chinese is written all over me."

85   "Consider it said," Lisa said. "My natural mother happened to be there at the time—I can't help being born in Buffalo."

"I know, I know," Connie said with feeling. "If only you had had some say in the matter."

"It's only Orientals who haunt me!" Lisa stamped her foot. "Only them!"

"I'm so sorry," Connie Sung said, for all of them. "It's all so turned around."

"So I'm made in America, so there!" Lisa Mallory declared, making a sniffing sound, and seemed to be recovering her *sangfroid.*

90   Connie felt tired—as if she'd traveled—but a lot had been settled on the way.

ANTON CHEKHOV

Anton Chekhov (1860–1904) was born in Russia, the son of a shopkeeper. While a medical student at Moscow University, Chekhov wrote stories, sketches, and reviews to help support his family and to finance his education. In 1884 he received his medical degree, began to practice medicine, published his first book of stories, and suffered the first of a series of hemorrhages from tuberculosis. In his remaining twenty years, in addition to writing several hundred stories, he wrote plays, half a dozen of which have established themselves as classics. He died from tuberculosis at the age of forty-four.

Misery   [1886]

Translated by Constance Garnett

"To Whom Shall I Tell My Grief?"

The twilight of evening. Big flakes of wet snow are whirling lazily about the street lamps, which have just been lighted, and lying in a thin soft layer on roofs, horses' backs, shoulders, caps. Iona Potapov, the sledgedriver, is all white like a ghost. He sits on the box without stirring, bent as double as the living body can be bent. If a regular snowdrift fell on him it seems as though even then he would not think it necessary to shake it off. . . . His little mare is white and motionless too. Her stillness, the angularity of her lines, and the stick-like straightness of her legs make her look like a halfpenny gingerbread horse. She is probably lost in thought. Anyone who has been torn away from the plough, from the familiar gray landscapes, and cast into this slough, full of monstrous lights, of unceasing uproar and hurrying people, is bound to think.

It is a long time since Iona and his nag have budged. They came out of
the yard before dinner-time and not a single fare yet. But now the shades of
evening are falling on the town. The pale light of the street lamps changes to
a vivid color, and the bustle of the street grows noisier.

"Sledge to Vyborgskaya!" Iona hears. "Sledge!"

Iona starts, and through his snow-plastered eyelashes sees an officer in
a military overcoat with a hood over his head.

5   "To Vyborgskaya," repeats the officer. "Are you asleep? To Vyborgskaya!"

In token of assent Iona gives a tug at the reins which sends cakes of
snow flying from the horse's back and shoulders. The officer gets into the
sledge. The sledge-driver clicks to the horse, cranes his neck like a swan,
rises in his seat, and more from habit than necessity brandishes his whip.
The mare cranes her neck, too, crooks her stick-like legs, and hesitatingly
sets off. . . .

"Where are you shoving, you devil?" Iona immediately hears shouts
from the dark mass shifting to and fro before him. "Where the devil are you
going? Keep to the r-right!"

"You don't know how to drive! Keep to the right," says the officer angrily.

A coachman driving a carriage swears at him; a pedestrian crossing the
road and brushing the horse's nose with his shoulder looks at him angrily
and shakes the snow off his sleeve. Iona fidgets on the box as though he
were sitting on thorns, jerks his elbows, and turns his eyes about like one
possessed, as though he did not know where he was or why he was there.

10   "What rascals they all are!" says the officer jocosely. "They are simply doing their best to run up against you or fall under the horse's feet. They must
be doing it on purpose."

Iona looks at his fare and moves his lips. . . . Apparently he means to say
something, but nothing comes out but a sniff.

"What?" inquires the officer.

Iona gives a wry smile, and straining his throat, brings out huskily: "My
son . . . , er . . . my son died this week, sir."

"H'm! What did he die of?"

15   Iona turns his whole body round to his fare, and says:

"Who can tell! It must have been from fever. . . . He lay three days in the
hospital and then he died. . . . God's will."

"Turn round, you devil!" comes out of the darkness. "Have you gone
cracked, you old dog? Look where you are going!"

"Drive on! drive on! . . ." says the officer. "We shan't get there till tomorrow going on like this. Hurry up!"

The sledge-driver cranes his neck again, rises in his seat, and with heavy
grace swings his whip. Several times he looks round at the officer, but the
latter keeps his eyes shut and is apparently disinclined to listen. Putting his
fare down at Vyborgskaya, Iona stops by a restaurant, and again sits huddled
up on the box. . . . Again the wet snow paints him and his horse white. One
hour passes, and then another. . . .

20   Three young men, two tall and thin, one short and hunchbacked, come
up, railing at each other and loudly stamping on the pavement with their galoshes.

"Cabby, to the Police Bridge!" the hunchback cries in a cracked voice.
"The three of us, . . . twenty kopecks!"

Iona tugs at the reins and clicks to his horse. Twenty kopecks is not a fair price, but he has no thoughts for that. Whether it is a rouble or whether it is five kopecks does not matter to him now so long as he has a fare. . . . The three young men, shoving each other and using bad language, go up to the sledge, and all three try to sit down at once. The question remains to be settled: Which are to sit down and which one is to stand? After a long altercation, ill-temper, and abuse, they come to the conclusion that the hunchback must stand because he is the shortest.

"Well, drive on," says the hunchback in his cracked voice, settling himself and breathing down Iona's neck. "Cut along! What a cap you've got, my friend! You wouldn't find a worse one in all Petersburg. . . ."

"He-he! . . . he-he! . . ." laughs Iona. "It's nothing to boast of!"

25 "Well, then, nothing to boast of, drive on! Are you going to drive like this all the way? Eh? Shall I give you one in the neck?"

"My head aches," says one of the tall ones. "At the Dukmasovs' yesterday Vaska and I drank four bottles of brandy between us."

"I can't make out why you talk such stuff," says the other tall one angrily. "You lie like a brute."

"Strike me dead, it's the truth! . . ."

"It's about as true as that a louse coughs."

30 "He-he!" grins Iona. "Me-er-ry gentlemen!"

"Tfoo! the devil take you!" cries the hunchback indignantly. "Will you get on, you old plague, or won't you? Is that the way to drive? Give her one with the whip. Hang it all, give it her well."

Iona feels behind his back the jolting person and quivering voice of the hunchback. He hears abuse addressed to him, he sees people, and the feeling of loneliness begins little by little to be less heavy on his heart. The hunchback swears at him, till he chokes over some elaborately whimsical string of epithets and is overpowered by his cough. His tall companions begin talking of a certain Nadyezhda Petrovna. Iona looks round at them. Waiting till there is a brief pause, he looks round once more and says:

"This week. . . er . . . my . . . er . . . son died!"

"We shall all die, . . ." says the hunchback with a sigh, wiping his lips after coughing. "Come, drive on! drive on! My friends, I simply cannot stand crawling like this! When will he get us there?"

35 "Well, you give him a little encouragement . . . one in the neck!"

"Do you hear, you old plague? I'll make you smart. If one stands on ceremony with fellows like you one may as well walk. Do you hear, you old dragon? Or don't you care a hang what we say?"

And Iona hears rather than feels a slap on the back of his neck.

"He-he! . . ." he laughs. "Merry gentlemen . . . God give you health!"

"Cabman, are you married?" asks one of the tall ones.

40 "I? He-he! Me-er-ry gentlemen. The only wife for me now is the damp earth. . . . He-ho-ho! . . . The grave that is! . . . Here my son's dead and I am alive. . . . It's a strange thing, death has come in at the wrong door. . . . Instead of coming for me it went for my son. . . ."

And Iona turns round to tell them how his son died, but at that point the hunchback gives a faint sigh and announces that, thank God! they have arrived at last. After taking his twenty kopecks, Iona gazes for a long while after the revelers, who disappear into a dark entry. Again he is alone and again there is silence for him. . . . The misery which has been for a brief space eased comes back again and tears his heart more cruelly than ever. With a look of anxiety and suffering Iona's eyes stray restlessly among the crowds moving to and fro on both sides of the street: can he not find among those thousands someone who will listen to him? But the crowds flit by heedless of him and his misery. . . . His misery is immense, beyond all bounds. If Iona's heart were to burst and his misery to flow out, it would flood the whole world, it seems, but yet it is not seen. It has found a hiding-place in such an insignificant shell that one would not have found it with a candle by daylight. . . .

Iona sees a house-porter with a parcel and makes up his mind to address him.

"What time will it be, friend?" he asks.

"Going on for ten. . . . Why have you stopped here? Drive on!"

45   Iona drives a few paces away, bends himself double, and gives himself up to his misery. He feels it is no good to appeal to people. But before five minutes have passed he draws himself up, shakes his head as though he feels a sharp pain, and tugs at the reins. . . . He can bear it no longer.

"Back to the yard!" he thinks. "To the yard!"

And his little mare, as though she knew his thoughts, falls to trotting. An hour and a half later Iona is sitting by a big dirty stove. On the stove, on the floor, and on the benches are people snoring. The air is full of smells and stuffiness. Iona looks at the sleeping figures, scratches himself, and regrets that he has come home so early. . . .

"I have not earned enough to pay for the oats, even," he thinks. "That's why I am so miserable. A man who knows how to do his work, . . . who has had enough to eat, and whose horse has had enough to eat, is always at ease. . . ."

In one of the corners a young cabman gets up, clears his throat sleepily, and makes for the waterbucket.

50   "Want a drink?" Iona asks him.

"Seems so."

"May it do you good. . . . But my son is dead, mate. . . . Do you hear? This week in the hospital. . . . It's queer business. . . ."

Iona looks to see the effect produced by his words, but he sees nothing. The young man has covered his head over and is already asleep. The old man sighs and scratches himself. . . . Just as the young man had been thirsty for water, he thirsts for speech. His son will soon have been dead a week, and he has not really talked to anybody yet. . . . He wants to talk of it properly, with deliberation. . . . He wants to tell how his son was taken ill, how he suffered, what he said before he died, how he died. . . . He wants to describe the funeral, and how he went to the hospital to get his son's clothes. He still has his daughter Anisya in the country. . . . And he wants to talk about her too. . . . Yes, he has plenty to talk about now. His listener ought to sigh and exclaim and lament. . . . It would be even better to talk to women. Though they are silly creatures, they blubber at the first word.

"Let's go out and have a look at the mare," Iona thinks. "There is always time for sleep. . . . You'll have sleep enough, no fear. . . ."

55   He puts on his coat and goes into the stables where his mare is standing. He thinks about oats, about hay, about the weather. . . . He cannot think about his son when he is alone. . . . To talk about him with someone is possible, but to think of him and picture him is insufferable anguish. . . .

"Are you munching?" Iona asks his mare, seeing her shining eyes. "There, munch away, munch away. . . . Since we have not earned enough for oats, we will eat hay. . . . Yes, . . . I have grown too old to drive. . . . My son ought to be driving, not I. . . . He was a real coachman. . . . He ought to have lived. . . ."

Iona is silent for a while, and then he goes on:

"That's how it is, old girl. . . . Kuzma Ionitch is gone. . . . He said good-by to me. . . . He went and died for no reason. . . . Now, suppose you had a little colt, and you were mother to that little colt. . . . And all at once that same little colt went and died. . . . You'd be sorry, wouldn't you?. . . ."

The little mare munches, listens, and breathes on her master's hands. Iona is carried away and tells her all about it.

WILLIAM FAULKNER

William Faulkner (1897-1962) was brought up in Oxford, Mississippi. His great-grandfather had been a Civil War hero, and his father was treasurer of the University of Mississippi in Oxford; the family was no longer rich, but it was still respected. In 1918 he enrolled in the Royal Canadian Air Force, though he never saw overseas service. After the war he returned to Mississippi and went to the university for two years. He then moved to New Orleans, where he became friendly with Sherwood Anderson, who was already an established writer. Faulkner's major novels include The Sound and the Fury *(1929),* As I Lay Dying *(1930), and* Light in August *(1932). Even after he had established himself as a major novelist with* The Sound and the Fury *(1929), he had to do some work in Hollywood in order to make ends meet. In 1950 he was awarded the Nobel Prize in Literature*

Barn Burning

[1939]

The store in which the Justice of the Peace's court was sitting smelled of cheese. The boy, crouched on his nail keg at the back of the crowded room, knew he smelled cheese, and more: from where he sat he could see the ranked shelves close-packed with the solid, squat, dynamic shapes of tin cans whose labels his stomach read, not from the lettering which mean nothing to his mind but from the scarlet devils and the silver curve of fish— this, the cheese which he knew he smelled and the hermetic meat which his intestines believed he smelled coming in intermittent gusts momentary and brief between the other constant one, the smell and sense just a little of fear because mostly of despair and grief, the old fierce pull of blood. He could not see the table where the Justice sat and before which his father and his father's enemy (*our enemy* he thought in that despair; *ourn! mine and hisn both! He's my father!*) stood, but he could hear them, the two of them, that is, because his father had said no word yet:

"But what proof have you, Mr. Harris?"

"I told you. The hog got into my corn. I caught it up and sent it back to him. He had no fence that would hold it. I told him so, warned him. The next time I put the hog in my pen. When he came to get it I gave him enough wire to patch up his pen. The next time I put the hog up and kept it. I rode down to his house and saw the wire I gave him still rolled on to the spool in his yard. I told him he could have the hog when he paid me a dollar pound fee. That evening a nigger came with the dollar and got the hog. He was a strange nigger. He said, 'He say to tell you wood and hay kin burn.' I said, 'What?' 'That whut he say to tell you,' the nigger said. 'Wood and hay kin burn.' That night my barn burned. I got the stock out but I lost the barn."

"Where is the nigger? Have you got him?"

5   "He was a strange nigger, I tell you. I don't know what became of him."

"But that's not proof. Don't you see that's not proof?"

"Get that boy up here. He knows." For a moment the boy thought too that the man meant his older brother until Harris said, "Not him. The little one. The boy," and, crouching, small for his age, small and wiry like his father, in patched and faded jeans even too small for him, with straight, uncombed, brown hair and eyes gray and wild as storm scud, he saw the men between himself and the table part and become a lane of grim faces, at the end of which he saw the Justice, a shabby, collarless, graying man in spectacles, beckoning him. He felt no floor under his bare feet; he seemed to walk beneath the palpable weight of the grim turning faces. His father, stiff in his black Sunday coat donned not for the trial but for the moving, did not even look at him. *He aims for me to lie,* he thought, again with that frantic grief and despair. *And I will have to do hit.*

"What's your name, boy?" the Justice said.

"Colonel Sartoris Snopes," the boy whispered.

10   "Hey?" the Justice said. "Talk louder. Colonel Sartoris? I reckon anybody named for Colonel Sartoris in this country can't help but tell the truth, can they?" The boy said nothing. *Enemy! Enemy!* he thought; for a moment he could not even see, could not see that the Justice's face was kindly nor discern that his voice was troubled when he spoke to the man named Harris: "Do you want me to question this boy?" But he could hear, and during those subsequent long seconds while there was absolutely no sound in the crowded little room save that of quiet and intent breathing it was as if he had swung outward at the end of a grape vine, over a ravine, and at the top of the swing had been caught in a prolonged instant of mesmerized gravity, weightless in time.

"No!" Harris said violently, explosively. "Damnation! Send him out of here!" Now time, the fluid world, rushed beneath him again, the voices coming to him again through the smell of cheese and sealed meat, the fear and despair and the old grief of blood:

"This case is closed. I can't find against you, Snopes, but I can give you advice. Leave this country and don't come back to it."

His father spoke for the first time, his voice cold and harsh, level, without emphasis: "I aim to. I don't figure to stay in a country among people who . . ." he said something unprintable and vile, addressed to no one.

"That'll do," the Justice said. "Take your wagon and get out of this country before dark. Case dismissed."

15   His father turned, and he followed the stiff black coat, the wiry figure walking a little stiffly from where a Confederate provost's man's musket ball had taken him in the heel on a stolen horse thirty years ago, followed the two backs now, since his older brother had appeared from somewhere in

the crowd, no taller than the father but thicker, chewing tobacco steadily, between the two lines of grim-faced men and out of the store and across the worn gallery and down the sagging steps and among the dogs and half-grown boys in the mild May dust, where as he passed a voice hissed:

"Barn burner!"

Again he could not see, whirling; there was a face in a red haze, moonlike, bigger than the full moon, the owner of it half again his size, he leaping in the red haze toward the face, feeling no blow, feeling no shock when his head struck the earth, scrabbling up and leaping again, feeling no blow this time either and tasting no blood, scrabbling up to see the other boy in full flight and himself already leaping into pursuit as his father's hand jerked him back, the harsh, cold voice speaking above him: "Go get in the wagon."

It stood in a grove of locusts and mulberries across the road. His two hulking sisters in their Sunday dresses and his mother and her sister in calico and sunbonnets were already in it, sitting on and among the sorry residue of the dozen and more movings which even the boy could remember—the battered stove, the broken beds and chairs, the clock inlaid with mother-of-pearl, which would not run, stopped at some fourteen minutes past two o'clock of a dead and forgotten day and time, which had been his mother's dowry. She was crying, though when she saw him she drew her sleeve across her face and began to descend from the wagon. "Get back," the father said.

"He's hurt. I got to get some water and wash his . . ."

20 "Get back in the wagon," his father said. He got in too, over the tail-gate. His father mounted to the seat where the older brother already sat and struck the gaunt mules two savage blows with the peeled willow, but without heat. It was not even sadistic; it was exactly that same quality which in later years would cause his descendants to over-run the engine before putting a motor car into motion, striking and reining back in the same movement. The wagon went on, the store with its quiet crowd of grimly watching men dropped behind; a curve in the road hid it. *Forever* he thought. *Maybe he's done satisfied now, now that he has . . .* stopping himself, not to say it aloud even to himself. His mother's hand touched his shoulder.

"Does hit hurt?" she said.

"Naw," he said. "Hit don't hurt. Lemme be."

"Can't you wipe some of the blood off before hit dries?"

"I'll wash to-night," he said. "Lemme be, I tell you."

25 The wagon went on. He did not know where they were going. None of them ever did or ever asked, because it was always somewhere, always a house of sorts waiting for them a day or two days or even three days away. Likely his father had already arranged to make a crop on another farm before he . . . Again he had to stop himself. He (the father) always did. There was something about his wolflike independence and even courage when the advantage was at least neutral which impressed strangers, as if they got from his latent ravening ferocity not so much a sense of dependability as a feeling that his ferocious conviction in the rightness of his own actions would be of advantage to all whose interest lay with his.

That night they camped, in a grove of oaks and beeches where a spring ran. The nights were still cool and they had a fire against it, of a rail lifted from a nearby fence and cut into lengths—a small fire, neat, niggard almost, a shrewd fire; such fires were his father's habit and custom always, even in freezing weather. Older, the boy might have remarked this and wondered why not a big one; why should not a man who had not only seen the waste and extravagance of war, but who had in his blood an inherent voracious prodigality with material not his own, have burned everything in sight? Then he might have gone a step farther and thought that that was the reason: that niggard blaze was the living fruit of nights passed during those four years in the woods hiding from all men, blue or gray, with his strings of horses (captured horses, he called them). And older still, he might have divined the true reason: that the element of fire spoke to some deep mainspring of his father's being, as the element of steel or of powder spoke to other men, as the one weapon for the preservation of integrity, else breath were not worth the breathing, and hence to be regarded with respect and used with discretion.

But he did not think this now and he had seen those same niggard blazes all his life. He merely ate his supper beside it and was already half asleep over his iron plate when his father called him, and once more he followed the stiff back, the stiff and ruthless limp, up the slope and on to the starlit road where, turning, he could see his father against the stars but without face or depth—a shape black, flat, and bloodless as though cut from tin in the iron folds of the frockcoat which had not been made for him, the voice harsh like tin and without heat like tin:

"You were fixing to tell them. You would have told him." He didn't answer. His father struck him with the flat of his hand on the side of the head, hard but without heat, exactly as he had struck the two mules at the store, exactly as he would strike either of them with any stick in order to kill a horse fly, his voice still without heat or anger: "You're getting to be a man. You got to learn. You got to learn to stick to your own blood or you ain't going to have any blood to stick to you. Do you think either of them, any man there this morning, would? Don't you know all they wanted was a chance to get at me because they knew I had them beat? Eh?" Later, twenty years later, he was to tell himself, "If I had said they wanted only truth, justice, he would have hit me again." But now he said nothing. He was not crying. He just stood there. "Answer me," his father said.

"Yes," he whispered. His father turned.

30   "Get on to bed. We'll be there to-morrow."

Tomorrow they were there. In the early afternoon the wagon stopped before a paintless two-room house identical almost with the dozen others it had stopped before even in the boy's ten years, and again, as on the other dozen occasions, his mother and aunt got down and began to unload the wagon, although his two sisters and his father and brother had not moved.

"Likely hit ain't fitten for hawgs," one of the sisters said.

"Nevertheless, fit it will and you'll hog it and like it," his father said. "Get out of them chairs and help your Ma unload."

The two sisters got down, big, bovine, in a flutter of cheap ribbons; one of them drew from the jumbled wagon bed a battered lantern, the other a worn broom. His father handed the reins to the older son and began to climb stiffly over the wheel. "When they get unloaded, take the team to the barn and feed them." Then he said, and at first the boy thought he was still speaking to his brother: "Come with me."

35   "Me?" he said.

"Yes," his father said. "You."

"Abner," his mother said. His father paused and looked back—the harsh level stare beneath the shaggy, graying, irascible brows.

"I reckon I'll have a word with the man that aims to begin tomorrow owning me body and soul for the next eight months."

They went back up the road. A week ago—or before last night, that is—he would have asked where they were going, but not now. His father had struck him before last night but never before had he paused afterward to explain why; it was as if the blow and the following calm, outrageous voice still rang, repercussed, divulging nothing to him save the terrible handicap of being young, the light weight of his few years, just heavy enough to prevent his soaring free of the world as it seemed to be ordered but not heavy enough to keep him footed solid in it, to resist it and try to change the course of its events.

40   Presently he could see the grove of oaks and cedars and the other flowering trees and shrubs where the house would be, though not the house yet. They walked beside a fence massed with honeysuckle and Cherokee roses and came to a gate swinging open between two brick pillars, and now, beyond a sweep of drive, he saw the house for the first time and at that instant he forgot his father and the terror and despair both, and even when he remembered his father again (who had not stopped) the terror and despair did not return. Because, for all the twelve movings, they had sojourned until now in a poor country, a land of small farms and fields and houses, and he had never seen a house like this before. *Hit's big as a courthouse* he thought quietly, with a surge of peace and joy whose reason he could not have thought into words, being too young for that: *They are safe from him. People whose lives are a part of this peace and dignity are beyond his touch, he no more to them than a buzzing wasp: capable of stinging for a little moment but that's all; the spell of this peace and dignity rendering even the barns and stable and cribs which belong to it impervious to the puny flames he might contrive* . . . . this, the peace and joy, ebbing for an instant as he looked again at the stiff black back, the stiff and implacable limp of the figure which was not dwarfed by the house, for the reason that it had never looked big anywhere and which now, against the serene columned backdrop, had more than ever that impervious quality of something cut ruthlessly from tin, depthless, as though, sidewise to the sun, it would cast no shadow. Watching him, the boy remarked the absolutely undeviating course which his father held and saw the stiff foot come squarely down in a pile of fresh droppings where a horse had stood in the drive and which his father could have avoided by a simple change of stride. But it ebbed only for a moment, though he could not have thought this into words either, walking on in the spell of the house, which he could even want but without envy, without sorrow, certainly never with that ravening and jealous rage which unknown to him walked in the ironlike black coat before him: *Maybe he will feel it too. Maybe it will even change him now from what maybe he couldn't help but be.*

They crossed the portico. Now he could hear his father's stiff foot as it came down on the boards with clocklike finality, a sound out of all proportion to the displacement of the body it bore and which was not dwarfed either by the white door before it, as though it had attained to a sort of vicious and ravening minimum not to be dwarfed by anything—the flat, wide, black hat, the formal coat of broadcloth which had once been black but which had now that friction-glazed greenish cast of the bodies of old house flies, the lifted sleeve which was too large, the lifted hand like a curled claw. The door opened so promptly that the boy knew the Negro must have been watching them all the time, an old man with neat grizzled hair, in a linen jacket, who stood barring the door with his body, saying, "Wipe yo foots, white man, fo you come in here. Major ain't home nohow."

"Get out of my way, nigger," his father said, without heat too, flinging the door back and the Negro also and entering, his hat still on his head. And now the boy saw the prints of the stiff foot on the doorjamb and saw them appear on the pale rug behind the machinelike deliberation of the foot which seemed to bear (or transmit) twice the weight which the body compassed. The Negro was shouting "Miss Lula! Miss Lula!" somewhere behind them, then the boy, deluged as though by a warm wave by a suave turn of carpeted stair and a pendant glitter of chandeliers and a mute gleam of gold frames, heard the swift feet and saw her too, a lady—perhaps he had never seen her like before either—in a gray, smooth gown with lace at the throat and an apron tied at the waist and the sleeves turned back, wiping cake or biscuit dough from her hands with a towel as she came up the hall, looking not at his father at all but at the tracks on the blond rug with an expression of incredulous amazement.

"I tried," the Negro cried. "I tole him to . . ."

"Will you please go away?" she said in a shaking voice. "Major de Spain is not at home. Will you please go away?"

45   His father had not spoken again. He did not speak again. He did not even look at her. He just stood stiff in the center of the rug, in his hat, the shaggy iron-gray brows twitching slightly above the pebble-colored eyes as he appeared to examine the house with brief deliberation. Then with the same deliberation he turned; the boy watched him pivot on the good leg and saw the stiff foot drag round the arc of the turning, leaving a final long and fading smear. His father never looked at it, he never once looked down at the rug. The Negro held the door. It closed behind them, upon the hysteric and indistinguishable woman-wail. His father stopped at the top of the steps and scraped his boot clean on the edge of it. At the gate he stopped again. He stood for a moment, planted stiffly on the stiff foot, looking back at the house. "Pretty and white, ain't it?" he said. "That's sweat. Nigger sweat. Maybe it ain't white enough yet to suit him. Maybe he wants to mix some white sweat with it."

Two hours later the boy was chopping wood behind the house within which his mother and aunt and the two sisters (the mother and aunt, not the two girls, he knew that; even at this distance and muffled by walls the flat loud voices of the two girls emanated an incorrigible idle inertia) were setting up the stove to prepare a meal, when he heard the hooves and saw the linen-clad man on a fine sorrel mare, whom he recognized even before he saw the rolled rug in front of the Negro youth following on a fat bay carriage horse—a suffused, angry face vanishing, still at full gallop, behind the corner of the house where his father and brother were sitting in the two tilted chairs; and a moment later, almost before he could have put the axe down, he heard the hooves again and watched the sorrel mare go back out of the yard, already galloping again. Then his father began to shout one of the sisters' names, who presently emerged backward from the kitchen door dragging the rolled rug along the ground by one end while the other sister walked behind it.

"If you ain't going to tote, go on and set up the wash pot," the first said.

"You, Sarty!" the second shouted. "Set up the wash pot!" His father appeared at the door, framed against that shabbiness, as he had been against that other bland perfection, impervious to either, the mother's anxious face at his shoulder.

"Go on," the father said. "Pick it up." The two sisters stooped, broad, lethargic; stooping, they presented an incredible expanse of pale cloth and a flutter of tawdry ribbons.

50   "If I thought enough of a rug to have to git hit all the way from France I wouldn't keep hit where folks coming in would have to tromp on hit," the first said. They raised the rug.

"Abner," the mother said. "Let me do it."

"You go back and git dinner," his father said. "I'll tend to this."

From the woodpile through the rest of the afternoon the boy watched them, the rug spread flat in the dust beside the bubbling washpot, the two sisters stooping over it with that profound and lethargic reluctance, while the father stood over them in turn, implacable and grim, driving them though never raising his voice again. He could smell the harsh homemade lye they were using; he saw his mother come to the door once and look toward them with an expression not anxious now but very like despair; he saw his father turn, and he fell to with the axe and saw from the corner of his eye his father raise from the ground a flattish fragment of field stone and examine it and return to the pot, and this time his mother actually spoke: "Abner. Abner. Please don't. Please, Abner."

Then he was done too. It was dusk; the whippoorwills had already begun. He could smell coffee from the room where they would presently eat the cold food remaining from the mid-afternoon meal, though when he entered the house he realized they were having coffee again probably because there was a fire on the hearth, before which the rug now lay spread over the backs of the two chairs. The tracks of his father's foot were gone. Where they had been were now long, water-cloudy scoriations resembling the sporadic course of a Liliputian mowing machine.

55   It still hung there while they ate the cold food and then went to bed, scattered without order or claim up and down the two rooms, his mother in one bed, where his father would later lie, the older brother in the other, himself, the aunt, and the two sisters on pallets on the floor. But his father was not in bed yet. The last thing the boy remembered was the depthless, harsh silhouette of the hat and coat bending over the rug and it seemed to him that he had not even closed his eyes when the silhouette was standing over him, the fire almost dead behind it, the stiff foot prodding him awake. "Catch up the mule," his father said.

When he returned with the mule his father was standing in the back door, the rolled rug over his shoulder. "Ain't you going to ride?" he said.

"No. Give me your foot."

He bent his knee into his father's hand, the wiry, surprising power flowed smoothly, rising, he rising with it, on to the mule's bare back (they had owned a saddle once; the boy could remember it though not when or where) and with the same effortlessness his father swung the rug up in front of him. Now in the starlight they retraced the afternoon's path, up the dusty road rife with honeysuckle, through the gate and up the black tunnel of the drive to the lightless house, where he sat on the mule and felt the rough warp of the rug drag across his thighs and vanish.

"Don't you want me to help?" he whispered. His father did not answer and now he heard again that stiff foot striking the hollow portico with that wooden and clocklike deliberation, that outrageous overstatement of the weight it carried. The rug, hunched, not flung (the boy could tell that even in the darkness) from his father's shoulder struck the angle of wall and floor with a sound unbelievably loud, thunderous, then the foot again, unhurried and enormous; a light came on in the house and the boy sat, tense, breathing steadily and quietly and just a little fast, though the foot itself did not increase its beat at all, descending the steps now; now the boy could see him.

60   "Don't you want to ride now?" he whispered. "We kin both ride now," the light within the house altering now, flaring up and sinking. *He's coming down the stairs now,* he thought. He had already ridden the mule up beside the horse block; presently his father was up behind him and he doubled the reins over and slashed the mule across the neck, but before the animal could begin to trot the hard, thin arm came round him, the hard, knotted hand jerking the mule back to a walk.

In the first red rays of the sun they were in the lot, putting plow gear on the mules. This time the sorrel mare was in the lot before he heard it at all, the rider collarless and even bareheaded, trembling, speaking in a shaking voice as the woman in the house had done, his father merely looking up once before stooping again to the hame he was buckling, so that the man on the mare spoke to his stooping back:

"You must realize you have ruined that rug. Wasn't there anybody here, any of your women . . ." he ceased, shaking, the boy watching him, the older brother leaning now in the stable door, chewing, blinking slowly and steadily at nothing apparently. "It cost a hundred dollars. But you never had a hundred dollars. You never will. So I'm going to charge you twenty bushels of corn against your crop. I'll add it in your contract and when you come to the commissary you can sign it. That won't keep Mrs. de Spain quiet but maybe it will teach you to wipe your feet off before you enter her house again."

Then he was gone. The boy looked at his father, who still had not spoken or even looked up again, who was now adjusting the logger-head in the hame.

"Pap," he said. His father looked at him—the inscrutable face, the shaggy brows beneath which the gray eyes glinted coldly. Suddenly the boy went toward him, fast, stopping as suddenly. "You done the best you could!" he cried. "If he wanted hit done different why didn't he wait and tell you how? He won't git no twenty bushels! He won't git none! We'll gether hit and hide hit! I kin watch . . ."

65   "Did you put the cutter back in that straight stock like I told you?"

"No, sir," he said.

"Then go do it."

That was Wednesday. During the rest of that week he worked steadily, at what was within his scope and some which was beyond it, with an industry that did not need to be driven nor even commanded twice; he had this from his mother, with the difference that some at least of what he did he liked to do, such as splitting wood with the half-size axe which his mother and aunt had earned, or saved money somehow, to present him with at Christmas. In company with the two older women (and on one afternoon, even one of the sisters), he built pens for the shoat and the cow which were a part of his father's contract with the landlord, and one afternoon, his father being absent, gone somewhere on one of the mules, he went to the field.

They were running a middle buster now, his brother holding the plow straight while he handled the reins, and walking beside the straining mule, the rich black soil shearing cool and damp against his bare ankles, he thought *Maybe this is the end of it. Maybe even that twenty bushels that seems hard to have to pay for just a rug will be a cheap price for him to stop forever and always from being what he used to be;* thinking, dreaming now, so that his brother had to speak sharply to him to mind the mule: *Maybe he even won't collect the twenty bushels. Maybe it will all add up and balance and vanish—corn, rug, fire; the terror and grief, the being pulled two ways like between two teams of horses—gone, done with for ever and ever.*

70   Then it was Saturday; he looked up from beneath the mule he was harnessing and saw his father in the black coat and hat. "Not that," his father said. "The wagon gear." And then, two hours later, sitting in the wagon bed behind his father and brother on the seat, the wagon accomplished a final curve, and he saw the weathered paintless store with its tattered tobacco- and patent-medicine posters and the tethered wagons and saddle animals below the gallery. He mounted the gnawed steps behind his father and brother, and there again was the lane of quiet, watching faces for the three of them to walk through. He saw the man in spectacles sitting at the plank table and he did not need to be told this was a Justice of the Peace; he sent one glare of fierce, exultant, partisan defiance at the man in collar and cravat now, whom he had seen but twice before in his life, and that on a galloping horse, who now wore on his face an expression not of rage but of amazed unbelief which the boy could not have known was at the incredible circumstance of being sued by one of his own tenants, and came and stood against his father and cried at the Justice: "He ain't done it! He ain't burnt . . ."

"Go back to the wagon," his father said.

"Burnt?" the Justice said. "Do I understand this rug was burned too?"

"Does anybody here claim it was?" his father said. "Go back to the wagon." But he did not, he merely retreated to the rear of the room, crowded as that other had been, but not to sit down this time, instead, to stand pressing among the motionless bodies, listening to the voices:

"And you claim twenty bushels of corn is too high for the damage you did to the rug?"

75   "He brought the rug to me and said he wanted the tracks washed out of it. I washed the tracks out and took the rug back to him."

"But you didn't carry the rug back to him in the same condition it was in before you made the tracks on it."

His father did not answer, and now for perhaps half a minute there was no sound at all save that of breathing, the faint, steady suspiration of complete and intent listening.

"You decline to answer that, Mr. Snopes?" Again his father did not answer. "I'm going to find against you, Mr. Snopes. I'm going to find that you were responsible for the injury to Major de Spain's rug and hold you liable for it. But twenty bushels of corn seems a little high for a man in your circumstances to have to pay. Major de Spain claims it costs a hundred dollars. October corn will be worth about fifty cents. I figure that if Major de Spain can stand a ninety-five-dollar loss on something he paid cash for, you can stand a five-dollar loss you haven't earned yet. I hold you in damages to Major de Spain to the amount of ten bushels of corn over and above your contract with him, to be paid to him out of your crop at gathering time. Court adjourned."

It had taken no time hardly, the morning was but half begun. He thought they would return home and perhaps back to the field, since they were late, far behind all other farmers. But instead his father passed on behind the wagon, merely indicating with his hand for the older brother to follow with it, and crossed the road toward the blacksmith shop opposite, pressing on after his father, overtaking him, speaking, whispering up at the harsh, calm face beneath the weathered hat: "He won't git no ten bushels neither. He won't git one. We'll . . ." until his father glanced for an instant down at him, the face absolutely calm, the grizzled eyebrows tangled above the cold eyes, the voice almost pleasant, almost gentle:

80   "You think so? Well, we'll wait till October anyway."

The matter of the wagon—the setting of a spoke or two and the tightening of the tires—did not take long either, the business of the tires accomplished by driving the wagon into the spring branch behind the shop and letting it stand there, the mules nuzzling into the water from time to time, and the boy on the seat with the idle reins, looking up the slope and through the sooty tunnel of the shed where the slow hammer rang and where his father sat on an upended cypress bolt, easily, either talking or listening, still sitting there when the boy brought the dripping wagon up out of the branch and halted it before the door.

"Take them on to the shade and hitch," his father said. He did so and returned. His father and the smith and a third man squatting on his heels inside the door were talking, about crops and animals; the boy, squatting too in the ammoniac dust and hoof-parings and scales of rust, heard his father tell a long and unhurried story out of the time before the birth of the older brother even when he had been a professional horsetrader. And then his father came up beside him where he stood before a tattered last year's circus poster on the other side of the store, gazing rapt and quiet at the scarlet horses, the incredible poisings and convolutions of tulle and tights and the painted leers of comedians, and said, "It's time to eat."

But not at home. Squatting beside his brother against the front wall, he watched his father emerge from the store and produce from a paper sack a segment of cheese and divide it carefully and deliberately into three with his pocket knife and produce crackers from the same sack. They all three squatted on the gallery and ate, slowly, without talking; then in the store again, they drank from a tin dipper tepid water smelling of the cedar bucket and of living beech trees. And still they did not go home. It was a horse lot this time, a tall rail fence upon and along which men stood and sat and out of which one by one horses were led, to be walked and trotted and then cantered back and forth along the road while the slow swapping and buying went on and the sun began to slant westward, they—the three of them— watching and listening, the older brother with his muddy eyes and his steady, inevitable tobacco, the father commenting now and then on certain of the animals, to no one in particular.

It was after sundown when they reached home. They ate supper by lamplight, then, sitting on the doorstep, the boy watched the night fully accomplish, listening to the whippoorwills and the frogs, when he heard his mother's voice: "Abner! No! No! Oh, God. Oh, God. Abner!" and he rose, whirled, and saw the altered light through the door where a candle stub now burned in a bottle neck on the table and his father, still in the hat and coat, at once formal and burlesque as though dressed carefully for some shabby and ceremonial violence, emptying the reservoir of the lamp back into the five-gallon kerosene can from which it had been filled, while the mother tugged at his arm until he shifted the lamp to the other hand and flung her back, not savagely or viciously, just hard, into the wall, her hands flung out against the wall for balance, her mouth open and in her face the same quality of hopeless despair as had been in her voice. Then his father saw him standing in the door.

85   "Go to the barn and get that can of oil we were oiling the wagon with," he said. The boy did not move. Then he could speak.

"What . . ." he cried. "What are you . . ."

"Go get that oil," his father said. "Go."

Then he was moving, running, outside the house, toward the stable: this the old habit, the old blood which he had not been permitted to choose for himself, which had been bequeathed him willy nilly and which had run for so long (and who knew where, battening on what of outrage and savagery and lust) before it came to him. *I could keep on,* he thought. *I could run on and on and never look back, never need to see his face again. Only I can't. I can't,* the rusted can in his hand now, the liquid sploshing in it as he ran back to the house and into it, into the sound of his mother's weeping in the next room, and handed the can to his father.

"Ain't you going to even send a nigger?" he cried. "At least you sent a nigger before!"

90   This time his father didn't strike him. The hand came even faster than the blow had, the same hand which had set the can on the table with almost excruciating care flashing from the can toward him too quick for him to follow it, gripping him by the back of his shirt and on to tiptoe before he had seen it quit the can, the face stooping at him in breathless and frozen ferocity, the cold, dead voice speaking over him to the older brother who leaned against the table, chewing with that steady, curious, sidewise motion of cows: "Empty the can into the big one and go on. I'll catch up with you."

"Better tie him up to the bedpost," the brother said.

"Do like I told you," the father said. Then the boy was moving, his bunched shirt and the hard, bony hand between his shoulderblades, his toes just touching the floor, across the room and into the other one, past the sisters sitting with spread heavy thighs in the two chairs over the cold hearth, and to where his mother and aunt sat side by side on the bed, the aunt's arms about his mother's shoulders.

"Hold him," the father said. The aunt made a startled movement. "Not you," the father said. "Lennie. Take hold of him. I want to see you do it." His mother took him by the wrist. "You'll hold him better than that. If he gets loose don't you know what he is going to do? He will go up yonder." He jerked his head toward the road. "Maybe I'd better tie him."

95   "I'll hold him," his mother whispered.

"See you do then." Then his father was gone, the stiff foot heavy and measured upon the boards, ceasing at last.

Then he began to struggle. His mother caught him in both arms, he jerking and wrenching at them. He would be stronger in the end, he knew that. But he had no time to wait for it. "Lemme go!" he cried. "I don't want to have to hit you!"

"Let him go!" the aunt said. "If he don't go, before God, I am going up there myself!"

"Don't you see I can't?" his mother cried. "Sarty! Sarty! No! No! Help me, Lizzie!"

100   Then he was free. His aunt grasped at him but it was too late. He whirled, running, his mother stumbled forward on to her knees behind him, crying to the nearer sister: "Catch him, Net! Catch him!" But that was too late too, the sister (the sisters were twins, born at the same time, yet either of them now gave the impression of being, encompassing as much living meat and volume and weight as any other two of the family) not yet having begun to rise from the chair, her head, face, alone merely turned, presenting to him in the flying instant an astonishing expanse of young female features untroubled by any surprise even, wearing only an expression of bovine interest. Then he was out of the room, out of the house, in the mild dust of the starlit road and the heavy rifeness of honeysuckle, the pale ribbon unspooling with terrific slowness under his running feet, reaching the gate at last and turning in, running, his heart and lungs drumming, on up the drive toward the lighted house, the lighted door. He did not knock, he burst in, sobbing for breath, incapable for the moment of speech; he saw the astonished face of the Negro in the linen jacket without knowing when the Negro had appeared.

"De Spain!" he cried, panted. "Where's . . ." then he saw the white man too emerging from a white door down the hall. "Barn!" he cried. "Barn!"

"What?" the white man said. "Barn?"

"Yes!" the boy cried. "Barn!"

"Catch him!" the white man shouted.

105   But it was too late this time too. The Negro grasped his shirt, but the entire sleeve, rotten with washing, carried away, and he was out that door too and in the drive again, and had actually never ceased to run even while he was screaming into the white man's face.

Behind him the white man was shouting, "My horse! Fetch my horse!" and he thought for an instant of cutting across the park and climbing the fence into the road, but he did not know the park nor how high the vine-massed fence might be and he dared not risk it. So he ran on down the drive, blood and breath roaring; presently he was in the road again though he could not see it. He could not hear either: the galloping mare was almost upon him before he heard her, and even then he held his course, as if the very urgency of his wild grief and need must in a moment more find him wings, waiting until the ultimate instant to hurl himself aside and into the weed-choked roadside ditch as the horse thundered past and on, for an instant in furious silhouette against the stars, the tranquil early summer night sky which, even before the shape of the horse and rider vanished, strained abruptly and violently upward: a long, swirling roar incredible and soundless, blotting the stars, and he springing up and into the road again, running again, knowing it was too late yet still running even after he heard the shot and, an instant later, two shots, pausing now without knowing he had ceased to run, crying "Pap! Pap!," running again before he knew he had begun to run, stumbling, tripping over something and scrabbling up again without ceasing to run, looking backward over his shoulder at the glare as he got up, running on among the invisible trees, panting, sobbing, "Father! Father!"

At midnight he was sitting on the crest of a hill. He did not know it was midnight and he did not know how far he had come. But there was no glare behind him now and he sat now, his back toward what he had called home for four days anyhow, his face toward the dark woods which he would enter when breath was strong again, small, shaking steadily in the chill darkness, hugging himself into the remainder of his thin, rotten shirt, the grief and despair now no longer terror and fear but just grief and despair. *Father. My father,* he thought. "He was brave!" He cried suddenly, aloud but not loud, no more than a whisper: "He was! He was in the war! He was in Colonel Sartoris' cav'ry!" not knowing that his father had gone to that war a private in the fine old European sense, wearing no uniform, admitting the authority of and giving fidelity to no man or army or flag, going to war as Malbrouck himself did: for booty—it meant nothing and less than nothing to him if it were enemy booty or his own.

The slow constellations wheeled on. It would be dawn and then sun-up after a while and he would be hungry. But that would be tomorrow and now he was only cold, and walking would cure that. His breathing was easier now and he decided to get up and go on, and then he found that he had been asleep because he knew it was almost dawn, the night almost over. He could tell that from the whippoorwills. They were everywhere now among the dark trees below him, constant and inflectioned and ceaseless, so that, as the instant for giving over to the day birds drew nearer and nearer, there was no interval at all between them. He got up. He was a little stiff, but walking would cure that too as it would the cold, and soon there would be the sun. He went on down the hill, toward the dark woods within which the liquid silver voices of the birds called unceasing—the rapid and urgent beating of the urgent and quiring heart of the late spring night. He did not look back.

WILLIAM FAULKNER

For a biographical note, see page 407.
The illustrations, by Weldon Barley (1905–1945) were published when the story was first printed in a magazine called Forum *in 1930.*

A Rose for Emily

I

When Miss Emily Grierson died, our whole town went to her funeral: the men through a sort of respectful affection for a fallen monument, the

women mostly out of curiosity to see the inside of her house, which no one save an old Negro manservant—a combined gardener and cook—had seen in at least ten years.

It was a big, squarish, frame house that had once been white, decorated with cupolas and spires and scrolled balconies in the heavily lightsome style of the seventies, set on what had once been our most select street. But garages and cotton gins had encroached and obliterated even the august names of that neighborhood; only Miss Emily's house was left, lifting its stubborn and coquettish decay above the cotton wagons and the gasoline pumps—an eyesore among eyesores. And now Miss Emily had gone to join the representatives of those august names where they lay in the cedar-bemused cemetery among the ranked and anonymous graves of Union and Confederate soldiers who fell at the battle of Jefferson.

Alive, Miss Emily had been a tradition, a duty, and a care; a sort of hereditary obligation upon the town, dating from that day in 1894 when Colonel Sartoris, the mayor—he who fathered the edict that no Negro woman should appear on the streets without an apron—remitted her taxes, the dispensation dating from the death of her father on into perpetuity. Not that Miss Emily would have accepted charity. Colonel Sartoris invented an involved tale to the effect that Miss Emily's father had loaned money to the town, which the town, as a matter of business, preferred this way of repaying. Only a man of Colonel Sartoris' generation and thought could have invented it, and only a woman could have believed it.

When the next generation, with its more modern ideas, became mayors and aldermen, this arrangement created some little dissatisfaction. On the first of the year they mailed her a tax notice. February came, and there was no reply. They wrote her a formal letter, asking her to call at the sheriff's office at her convenience. A week later the mayor wrote her himself, offering to call or to send his car for her, and received in reply a note on paper of an archaic shape, in a thin, flowing calligraphy in faded ink, to the effect that she no longer went out at all. The tax notice was also enclosed, without comment.

5   They called a special meeting of the Board of Aldermen. A deputation waited upon her, knocked at the door through which no visitor had passed since she ceased giving china-painting lessons eight or ten years earlier. They were admitted by the old Negro into a dim hall from which a stairway mounted into still more shadow. It smelled of dust and disuse—a close, dank smell. The Negro led them into the parlor. It was furnished in heavy, leather-covered furniture. When the Negro opened the blinds of one window, they could see that the leather was cracked; and when they sat down, a faint dust rose sluggishly about their thighs, spinning with slow motes in the single sun-ray. On a tarnished gilt easel before the fireplace stood a crayon portrait of Miss Emily's father.

They rose when she entered—a small, fat woman in black, with a thin gold chain descending to her waist and vanishing into her belt, leaning on an ebony cane with a tarnished gold head. Her skeleton was small and spare; perhaps that was why what would have been merely plumpness in another was obesity in her. She looked bloated, like a body long submerged in motionless water, and of that pallid hue. Her eyes, lost in the fatty ridges of her face, looked like two small pieces of coal pressed into a lump of dough as they moved from one face to another while the visitors stated their errand.

She did not ask them to sit. She just stood in the door and listened quietly until the spokesman came to a stumbling halt. Then they could hear the invisible watch ticking at the end of the gold chain.

Her voice was dry and cold. "I have no taxes in Jefferson. Colonel Sartoris explained it to me. Perhaps one of you can gain access to the city records and satisfy yourselves."

"But we have. We are the city authorities, Miss Emily. Didn't you get a notice from the sheriff, signed by him?"

10   "I received a paper, yes," Miss Emily said. "Perhaps he considers himself the sheriff. . . . I have no taxes in Jefferson."

"But there is nothing on the books to show that, you see. We must go by the—"

"See Colonel Sartoris. I have no taxes in Jefferson."

"But, Miss Emily—"

"See Colonel Sartoris." (Colonel Sartoris had been dead almost ten years.) "I have no taxes in Jefferson. Tobe!" The Negro appeared. "Show these gentlemen out."

II

15   So she vanquished them, horse and foot, just as she had vanquished their fathers thirty years before about the smell. That was two years after her father's death and a short time after her sweetheart—the one we believed would marry her—had deserted her. After her father's death she went out very little; after her sweetheart went away, people hardly saw her at all. A few of the ladies had the temerity to call, but were not received, and the only sign of life about the place was the Negro man—a young man then—going in and out with a market basket.

"Just as if a man—any man—could keep a kitchen properly," the ladies said; so they were not surprised when the smell developed. It was another link between the gross, teeming world and the high and mighty Griersons.

A neighbor, a woman, complained to the mayor, Judge Stevens, eighty years old.

"But what will you have me do about it, madam?" he said.

"Why, send her word to stop it," the woman said. "Isn't there a law?"

20   "I'm sure that won't be necessary," Judge Stevens said. "It's probably just a snake or a rat that nigger of hers killed in the yard. I'll speak to him about it."

The next day he received two more complaints, one from a man who came in diffident deprecation. "We really must do something about it, Judge. I'd be the last one in the world to bother Miss Emily, but we've got to do something." That night the Board of Aldermen met—three graybeards and one younger man, a member of the rising generation.

"It's simple enough," he said. "Send her word to have her place cleaned up. Give her a certain time to do it in, and if she don't . . ."

"Dammit, sir," Judge Stevens said, "will you accuse a lady to her face of smelling bad?"

So the next night, after midnight, four men crossed Miss Emily's lawn and slunk about the house like burglars, sniffing along the base of the brick-work and at the cellar openings while one of them performed a regular sowing motion with his hand out of a sack slung from his shoulder. They broke open the cellar door and sprinkled lime there, and in all the out-buildings. As they recrossed the lawn, a window that had been dark was lighted and Miss Emily sat in it, the light behind her, and her upright torso motionlesss as that of an idol. They crept quietly across the lawn and into the shadow of the locusts that lined the street. After a week or two the smell went away.

25   That was when people had begun to feel really sorry for her. People in our town, remembering how old lady Wyatt, her great-aunt, had gone com-pletely crazy at last, believed that the Griersons held themselves a little too high for what they really were. None of the young men were quite good enough for Miss Emily and such. We had long thought of them as a tableau, Miss Emily a slender figure in white in the background, her father a sprad-dled silhouette in the foreground, his back to her and clutching a horse-whip, the two of them framed by the back-flung front door. So when she got to be thirty and was still single, we were not pleased exactly, but vindicated; even with insanity in the family she wouldn't have turned down all of her chances if they had really materialized.

When her father died, it got about that the house was all that was left to her; and in a way, people were glad. At last they could pity Miss Emily. Being left alone, and a pauper, she had become humanized. Now she too would know the old thrill and the old despair of a penny more or less.

The day after his death all the ladies prepared to call at the house and offer condolence and aid, as is our custom. Miss Emily met them at the door, dressed as usual and with no trace of grief on her face. She told them that her father was not dead. She did that for three days, with the ministers call-ing on her, and the doctors, trying to persuade her to let them dispose of the body. Just as they were about to resort to law and force, she broke down, and they buried her father quickly.

We did not say she was crazy then. We believed she had to do that. We remembered all the young men her father had driven away, and we knew that with nothing left, she would have to cling to that which had robbed her, as people will.

III

She was sick for a long time. When we saw her again, her hair was cut short, making her look like a girl, with a vague resemblance to those angels in colored church windows—sort of tragic and serene.

30   The town had just let the contracts for paving the sidewalks, and in the summer after her father's death they began the work. The construction company came with niggers and mules and machinery, and a foreman named Homer Barron, a Yankee—a big, dark, ready man, with a big voice and eyes lighter than his face. The little boys would follow in groups to hear him cuss the niggers, and the niggers singing in time to the rise and fall of picks. Pretty soon he knew everybody in town. Whenever you heard a lot of laughing anywhere about the square, Homer Barron would be in the center of the group. Presently we began to see him and Miss Emily on Sunday afternoons driving in the yellow-wheeled buggy and the matched team of bays from the livery stable.

At first we were glad that Miss Emily would have an interest, because the ladies all said, "Of course a Grierson would not think seriously of a Northerner, a day laborer." But there were still others, older people, who said that even grief could not cause a real lady to forget *noblesse oblige*—without calling it *noblesse oblige*. They just said, "Poor Emily. Her kinfolks should come to her." She had some kin in Alabama; but years ago her father had fallen out with them over the estate of old lady Wyatt, the crazy woman, and there was no communication between the two families. They had not even been represented at the funeral.

And as soon as the old people said, "Poor Emily," the whispering began. "Do you suppose it's really so?" they said to one another. "Of course it is. What else could . . ." This behind their hands; rustling of craned silk and satin behind jalousies closed upon the sun of Sunday afternoon as the thin, swift clop-clop-clop of the matched team passed: "Poor Emily."

She carried her head high enough—even when we believed that she was fallen. It was as if she demanded more than ever the recognition of her dignity as the last Grierson; as if it had wanted that touch of earthiness to reaffirm her imperviousness. Like when she bought the rat poison, the arsenic. That was over a year after they had begun to say "Poor Emily," and while the two female cousins were visiting her.

"I want some poison," she said to the druggist. She was over thirty then, still a slight woman, though thinner than usual, with cold, haughty black eyes in a face the flesh of which was strained across the temples and about the eye-sockets as you imagine a lighthouse-keeper's face ought to look. "I want some poison," she said.

35   "Yes, Miss Emily. What kind? For rats and such? I'd recom—"

"I want the best you have. I don't care what kind."

The druggist named several. "They'll kill anything up to an elephant. But what you want is—"

"Arsenic," Miss Emily said. "Is that a good one?"

"Is . . . arsenic? Yes, ma'am. But what you want—"

40   "I want arsenic."

The druggist looked down at her. She looked back at him, erect, her face like a strained flag. "Why, of course," the druggist said. "If that's what you want. But the law requires you to tell what you are going to use it for."

Miss Emily just stared at him, her head tilted back in order to look him eye to eye, until he looked away and went and got the arsenic and wrapped it up. The Negro delivery boy brought her the package; the druggist didn't come back. When she opened the package at home there was written on the box, under the skull and bones: "For rats."

IV

So the next day we all said, "She will kill herself"; and we said it would be the best thing. When she had first begun to be seen with Homer Barron, we had said, "She will marry him." Then we said, "She will persuade him yet," because Homer himself had remarked—he liked men, and it was known that he drank with the younger men in the Elks' Club—that he was not a marrying man. Later we said, "Poor Emily" behind the jalousies as they passed on Sunday afternoon in the glittering buggy, Miss Emily with her head high and Homer Barron with his hat cocked and a cigar in his teeth, reins and whip in a yellow glove.

Then some of the ladies began to say that it was a disgrace to the town and a bad example to the young people. The men did not want to interfere, but at last the ladies forced the Baptist minister—Miss Emily's people were Episcopal—to call upon her. He would never divulge what happened during that interview, but he refused to go back again. The next Sunday they again drove about the streets, and the following day the minister's wife wrote to Miss Emily's relations in Alabama.

45   So she had blood-kin under her roof again and we sat back to watch developments. At first nothing happened. Then we were sure that they were to be married. We learned that Miss Emily had been to the jeweler's and ordered a man's toilet set in silver, with the letters H. B. on each piece. Two days later we learned that she had bought a complete outfit of men's clothing, including a nightshirt, and we said, "They are married." We were really glad. We were glad because the two female cousins were even more Grierson than Miss Emily had ever been.

So we were not surprised when Homer Barron—the streets had been finished some time since—was gone. We were a little disappointed that there was not a public blowing-off, but we believed that he had gone on to prepare for Miss Emily's coming, or to give her a chance to get rid of the cousins. (By that time it was a cabal, and we were all Miss Emily's allies to help circumvent the cousins.) Sure enough, after another week they departed. And, as we had expected all along, within three days Homer Barron was back in town. A neighbor saw the Negro man admit him at the kitchen door at dusk one evening.

And that was the last we saw of Homer Barron. And of Miss Emily for some time. The Negro man went in and out with the market basket, but the front door remained closed. Now and then we would see her at a window for a moment, as the men did that night when they sprinkled the lime, but for almost six months she did not appear on the streets. Then we knew that this was to be expected too; as if that quality of her father which had thwarted her woman's life so many times had been too virulent and too furious to die.

When we next saw Miss Emily, she had grown fat and her hair was turning gray. During the next few years it grew grayer and grayer until it attained an even pepper-and-salt iron gray, when it ceased turning. Up to the day of her death at seventy-four it was still that vigorous iron-gray, like the hair of an active man.

From that time on her front door remained closed, save for a period of six or seven years, when she was about forty, during which she gave lessons in china-painting. She fitted up a studio in one of the downstairs rooms, where the daughters and grand-daughters of Colonel Sartoris' contemporaries were sent to her with the same regularity and in the same spirit that they were sent to church on Sundays with a twenty-five cent piece for the collection plate. Meanwhile her taxes had been remitted.

50 Then the newer generation became the backbone and the spirit of the town, and the painting pupils grew up and fell away and did not send their children to her with boxes of color and tedious brushes and pictures cut from the ladies' magazines. The front door closed upon the last one and remained closed for good. When the town got free postal delivery, Miss Emily alone refused to let them fasten the metal numbers above her door and attach a mailbox to it. She would not listen to them.

Daily, monthly, yearly we watched the Negro grow grayer and more stooped, going in and out with the market basket. Each December we sent her a tax notice, which would be returned by the post office a week later, unclaimed. Now and then we would see her in one of the downstairs windows—she had evidently shut up the top floor of the house—like the carven torso of an idol in a niche, looking or not looking at us, we could never tell which. Thus she passed from generation to generation—dear, inescapable, impervious, tranquil, and perverse.

And so she died. Fell ill in the house filled with dust and shadows, with only a doddering Negro man to wait on her. We did not even know she was sick; we had long since given up trying to get any information from the Negro. He talked to no one, probably not even to her, for his voice had grown harsh and rusty, as if from disuse.

She died in one of the downstairs rooms, in a heavy walnut bed with a curtain, her gray head propped on a pillow yellow and moldy with age and lack of sunlight.

V

The Negro met the first of the ladies at the front door and let them in, with their hushed, sibilant voices and their quick, curious glances, and then he disappeared. He walked right through the house and out the back and was not seen again.

55   The two female cousins came at once. They held the funeral on the second day, with the town coming to look at Miss Emily beneath a mass of bought flowers, with the crayon face of her father musing profoundly above the bier and the ladies sibilant and macabre; and the very old men—some in their brushed Confederate uniforms—on the porch and the lawn, talking of Miss Emily as if she had been a contemporary of theirs, believing that they had danced with her and courted her perhaps, confusing time with its mathematical progression, as the old do, to whom all the past is not a diminishing road but, instead, a huge meadow which no winter ever quite touches, divided from the now by the narrow bottle-neck of the most recent decade of years.

Already we knew that there was one room in that region above stairs which no one had seen in forty years, and which would have to be forced. They waited until Miss Emily was decently in the ground before they opened it.

The violence of breaking down the door seemed to fill this room with pervading dust. A thin, acrid pall as of the tomb seemed to lie everywhere upon this room decked and furnished as for a bridal: upon the valance curtains of faded rose color, upon the rose-shaded lights, upon the dressing table, upon the delicate array of crystal and the man's toilet things backed with tarnished silver, silver so tarnished that the monogram was obscured. Among them lay a collar and tie, as if they had just been removed, which, lifted, left upon the surface a pale crescent in the dust. Upon a chair hung the suit, carefully folded; beneath it the two mute shoes and the discarded socks.

The man himself lay in the bed.

For a long while we just stood there, looking down at the profound and fleshless grin. The body had apparently once lain in the attitude of an embrace, but now the long sleep that outlasts love, that conquers even the grimace of love, had cuckolded him. What was left of him, rotted beneath what was left of the nightshirt, had become inextricable from the bed in which he lay; and upon him and upon the pillow beside him lay that even coating of the patient and biding dust.

60   Then we noticed that in the second pillow was the indentation of a head. One of us lifted something from it, and leaning forward, that faint and invisible dust dry and acrid in the nostrils, we saw a long strand of iron-gray hair.

AMY HEMPEL

Born in Chicago in 1951, Amy Hempel published her first collection of stories in 1985. The New York Times *called her* Collected Stories *(2006) one of the ten best books of the year. The winner of numerous awards for writing, Hempel, currently teaching fiction at Harvard University, has taught at Brooklyn College, the New School, Bennington College, and Princeton University.*

Today Will Be a Quiet Day   [1986]

"I think it's the other way around," the boy said. "I think if the quake hit now the *bridge* would collapse and the *ramps* would be left."

He looked at his sister with satisfaction.

"You are just trying to scare your sister," the father said. "You know that is not true."

"No, really," the boy insisted, "and I heard birds in the middle of the night. Isn't that a warning?"

5   The girl gave her brother a toxic look and ate a handful of Raisinets. The three of them were stalled in traffic on the Golden Gate Bridge.

That morning, before waking his children, the father had canceled their music lessons and decided to make a day of it. He wanted to know how they were, is all. Just—how were they. He thought his kids were as self-contained as one of those dogs you sometimes see carrying home its own leash. But you could read things wrong.

Could you ever.

The boy had a friend who jumped from a floor of Langley Porter. The friend had been there for two weeks, mostly playing Ping-Pong. All the friend said the day the boy visited and lost every game was never play Ping-Pong with a mental patient because it's all we do and we'll kill you. That night the friend had cut the red belt he wore in two and left the other half on his bed. That was this time last year when the boy was twelve years old.

You think you're safe, the father thought, but it's thinking you're invisible because you closed your eyes.

10   This day they were headed for Petaluma—the chicken, egg, and arm-wrestling capital of the nation—for lunch. The father had offered to take them to the men's arm-wrestling semifinals. But it was said that arm wrestling wasn't so interesting since the new safety precautions, that hardly anyone broke an arm or a wrist anymore. The best anyone could hope to see would be dislocation, so they said they would rather go to Pete's. Pete's was a gas station turned into a place to eat. The hamburgers there were named after cars, and the gas pumps in front still pumped gas.

"Can I have one?" the boy asked, meaning the Raisinets.

"No," his sister said.

"Can I have two?"

"Neither of you should be eating candy before lunch," the father said. He said it with the good sport of a father who enjoys his kids and gets a kick out of saying Dad things.

15   "You mean dinner," said the girl. "It will be dinner before we get to Pete's."

Only the northbound lanes were stopped. Southbound traffic flashed past at the normal speed.

"Check it out," the boy said from the back seat. "Did you see the bumper sticker on that Porsche? 'If you don't like the way I drive, stay off the sidewalk.'"

He spoke directly to his sister. "I've just solved my Christmas shopping."

"I got the highest score in my class in Driver's Ed," she said.

20   "I thought I would let your sister drive home today," the father said.

From the back seat came sirens, screams for help, and then a dirge.

The girl spoke to her father in a voice rich with complicity. "Don't people make you want to give up?"

"Don't the two of you know any jokes? I haven't laughed all day," the father said.

"Did I tell you the guillotine joke?" the girl said.

25   "He hasn't laughed all day, so you must've," her brother said.

The girl gave her brother a look you could iron clothes with. Then her gaze dropped down. "Oh-oh," she said, "Johnny's out of jail."

Her brother zipped his pants back up. He said, "Tell the joke."

"Two Frenchmen and a Belgian were about to be beheaded," the girl began. "The first Frenchman was led to the block and blindfolded. The executioner let the blade go. But it stopped a quarter inch above the Frenchman's neck. So he was allowed to go free, and ran off shouting, 'C'est un miracle! C'est un miracle!'"

"It's a miracle," the father said.

30 "Then the second Frenchman was led to the block, and same thing—the blade stopped just before cutting off his head. So *he* got to go free, and ran off shouting, 'C'est un miracle!'

"Finally the Belgian was led to the block. But before they could blind-fold him, he looked up, pointed to the top of the guillotine, and cried, 'Voilà la difficulté!'"

She doubled over.

"Maybe I would be wetting *my* pants if I knew what that meant," the boy said.

"You can't explain after the punch line," the girl said, "and have it still be funny."

35 "There's the problem," said the father.

The waitress handed out menus to the party of three seated in the corner booth of what used to be the lube bay. She told them the specialty of the day was Moroccan chicken.

"That's what I want," the boy said. "Morerotten chicken."

But he changed his order to a Studeburger and fries after his father and sister had ordered.

"So," the father said, "who misses music lessons?"

40 "I'm serious about what I asked you last week," the girl said. "About switching to piano? My teacher says a real flutist only breathes with the stomach, and I can't."

"The real reason she wants to change," said the boy, "is her waist will get two inches bigger when she learns to stomach-breathe. That's what *else* her teacher said."

The boy buttered a piece of sourdough bread and flipped a chunk of cold butter onto his sister's sleeve.

"Jeezo-beezo," the girl said, "why don't they skip the knife and fork and just set his place with a slingshot!"

"Who will ever adopt you if you don't mind your manners?" the father said. "Maybe we could try a little quiet today."

45 "You sound like your tombstone," the girl said. "Remember what you wanted it to say?"

Her brother joined in with his mouth full: "Today will be a quiet day."

"Because it never is with us around," the boy said.

"You guys," said the father.

The waitress brought plates. The father passed sugar to the boy and salt to the girl without being asked. He watched the girl shake out salt onto the fries.

50 "If I had a sore throat, I would gargle with those," he said.

"Looks like she's trying to melt a driveway," the boy offered.

The father watched his children eat. They ate fast. They called it Hoover-ing. He finished while they sucked at straws in empty drinks.

"Funny," he said thoughtfully, "I'm not hungry anymore."

Every meal ended this way. It was his benediction, one of the Dad things they expected him to say.

55 "That reminds me," the girl said. "Did you feed Rocky before we left?"

"Uh-uh," her brother said. "I fed him yesterday."

"*I* fed him yesterday!" the girl said.

"Okay, we'll compromise," the boy said."We won't feed the cat today."

"I'd say you are out of bounds on that one," the father said.

60   He meant you could not tease her about animals. Once, during dinner, that cat ran into the dining room shot from guns. He ran around the table at top speed, then spun out on the parquet floor into a leg of the table. He fell over onto his side and made short coughing sounds."Isn't he smart?" the girl had crooned, kneeling beside him."He knows he's hurt."

For years, her father had to say that the animals seen on shoulders of roads were napping.

"He never would have not fed Homer," she said to her father.

"Homer was a dog," the boy said."If I forgot to feed him, he could just go into the hills and bite a deer."

"Or a Campfire Girl selling mints at the front door," their father reminded them.

65   "Homer," the girl sighed."I hope he likes chasing sheep on that ranch in the mountains."

The boy looked at her, incredulous.

"You *believed* that? You actually *believed* that?"

In her head, a clumsy magician yanked the cloth and the dishes all crashed to the floor. She took air into her lungs until they filled, and then she filled her stomach, too.

"I thought she knew," the boy said.

70   The dog was five years ago.

"The girl's parents insisted," the father said."It's the law in California."

"Then I hate California," she said."I hate its guts."

The boy said he would wait for them in the car, and left the table.

"What would help?" the father asked.

75   "For Homer to be alive," she said.

"What would help?"

"Nothing."

"Help."

She pinched a trail of salt on her plate.

80   "A ride," she said."I'll drive."

The girl started the car and screamed,"Goddammit."

With the power off, the boy had tuned in the Spanish station. Mariachis exploded on ignition.

"Dammit isn't God's last name," the boy said, quoting another bumper sticker.

"Don't people make you want to give up?" the father said.

85   "No talking," the girl said to the rearview mirror, and put the car in gear.

She drove for hours. Through groves of eucalyptus with their damp peeling bark, past acacia bushes with yellow flowers pulsing off their stems. She cut over to the coast route and the stony gray-green tones of Inverness.

"What you'd call scenic," the boy tried.

Otherwise they were quiet.

No one said anything else until the sky started to close, and then it was the boy again, asking shouldn't they be going home.

90   "No, no," the father said, and made a show of looking out the window, up at the sky and back at his watch. "No," he said, "keep driving—it's getting earlier."

But the sky spilled rain, and the girl headed south toward the bridge. She turned on the headlights and the dashboard lit up green. She read off the odometer on the way home: "Twenty-six thousand, three hundred eighty three and eight-tenths miles."

"Today?" the boy said.

The boy got to Rocky first. "Let's play the cat," he said, and carried the Siamese to the upright piano. He sat on the bench holding the cat in his lap and pressed its paws to the keys. Rocky played "Born Free." He tried to twist away.

"Come on, Rocky, ten more minutes and we'll break."

95   "Give him to me," the girl said.

She puckered up and gave the cat a five-lipper.

"Bring the Rock upstairs," the father called. "Bring sleeping bags, too."

Pretty soon three sleeping bags formed a triangle in the master bedroom. The father was the hypotenuse. The girl asked him to brush out her hair, which he did while the boy ate a tangerine, peeling it up close to his face, inhaling the mist. Then he held each segment to the light to find seeds. In his lap, cat paws fluttered like dreaming eyes.

"What are you thinking?" the father asked.

100   "Me?" the girl said. "Fifty-seven T-bird, white with red interior, convertible. I drive it to Texas and wear skirts with rick-rack. I'm changing my name to Ruby," she said, "or else Easy."

The father considered her dream of a checkered future.

"Early ripe, early rot," he warned.

A wet wind slammed the window in its warped sash, and the boy jumped.

"I hate rain," he said. "I hate its guts."

105   The father got up and closed the window tighter against the storm. "It's a real frog-choker," he said.

In darkness, lying still, it was no less camp-like than if they had been under the stars, singing to a stone-ringed fire burned down to embers.

They had already said good-night some minutes earlier when the boy and girl heard their father's voice in the dark.

"Kids, I just remembered—I have some good news and some bad news. Which do you want first?"

It was his daughter who spoke. "Let's get it over with," she said. "Let's get the bad news over with."

110   The father smiled. They are all right, he decided. My kids are as right as this rain. He smiled at the exact spots he knew their heads were turned to his, and doubted he would ever feel—not better, but *more* than he did now.

"I lied," he said. "There is no bad news."

SHIRLEY JACKSON

Shirley Jackson (1919–1965) was born in San Francisco and went to college in New York, first at the University of Rochester and then at Syracuse University. Although one of her stories was published in The Best American Short

Stories 1944, *she did not receive national attention until 1948 when the* New Yorker *published "The Lottery." The magazine later reported that none of its earlier publications had produced so strong a response.*

In 1962 she experienced a breakdown and was unable to write, but she recovered and worked on a new novel. Before completing the book, however, she died of cardiac arrest at the age of forty-six. The book was published posthumously under the title Come Along with Me.

Two of her books, Life Among the Savages *(1953) and* Raising Demons *(1957), are engaging self-portraits of a harried mother in a house full of children. But what seems amusing also has its dark underside. After her breakdown Jackson said, "I think all my books laid end to end would be one long documentary of anxiety."*

Her husband, Stanley Edgar Hyman (her college classmate and later a professor of English), said of Jackson, "If she used the resources of supernatural terror, it was to provide metaphors for the all-too-real terrors of the natural."

The Lottery   [1948]

The morning of June 27th was clear and sunny, with the fresh warmth of a full-summer day; the flowers were blossoming profusely and the grass was richly green. The people of the village began to gather in the square, between the post office and the bank, around ten o'clock; in some towns there were so many people that the lottery took two days and had to be started on June 26th, but in this village, where there were only about three hundred people, the whole lottery took less than two hours, so it could begin at ten o'clock in the morning and still be through in time to allow the villagers to get home for noon dinner.

The children assembled first, of course. School was recently over for the summer, and the feeling of liberty sat uneasily on most of them; they tended to gather together quietly for a while before they broke into boisterous play, and their talk was still of the classroom and the teacher, of books and reprimands. Bobby Martin had already stuffed his pockets full of stones, and the other boys soon followed his example, selecting the smoothest and roundest stones; Bobby and Harry Jones and Dickie Delacroix—the villagers pronounced this name "Dellacroy"—eventually made a great pile of stones in one corner of the square and guarded it against the raids of the other boys. The girls stood aside, talking among themselves, looking over their shoulders at the boys, and the very small children rolled in the dust or clung to the hands of their older brothers or sisters.

Soon the men began to gather, surveying their own children, speaking of planting and rain, tractors and taxes. They stood together, away from the pile of stones in the corner, and their jokes were quiet and they smiled rather than laughed. The women, wearing faded house dresses and sweaters, came shortly after their menfolk. They greeted one another and exchanged bits of gossip as they went to join their husbands. Soon the women, standing by their husbands, began to call to their children, and the children came reluctantly, having to be called four or five times. Bobby Martin ducked under his mother's grasping hand and ran, laughing, back to the pile of stones. His father spoke up sharply, and Bobby came quickly, and took his place between his father and his oldest brother.

The lottery was conducted—as were the square dances, the teenage club, the Halloween program—by Mr. Summers, who had time and energy to devote to civic activities. He was a roundfaced, jovial man and he ran the coal business, and people were sorry for him, because he had no children and his wife was a scold. When he arrived in the square, carrying the black wooden box, there was a murmur of conversation among the villagers and he waved and called, "Little late today, folks." The postmaster, Mr. Graves, followed him, carrying a three-legged stool, and the stool was put in the center of the square and Mr. Summers set the black box down on it. The villagers kept their distance, leaving a space between themselves and the stool, and when Mr. Summers said, "Some of you fellows want to give me a hand?" there was a hesitation before two men, Mr. Martin and his oldest son, Baxter, came forward to hold the box steady on the stool while Mr. Summers stirred up the papers inside it.

5   The original paraphernalia for the lottery had been lost long ago, and the black box now resting on the stool had been put into use even before Old Man Warner, the oldest man in town, was born. Mr. Summers spoke frequently to the villagers about making a new box, but no one liked to upset even as much tradition as was represented by the black box. There was a story that the present box had been made with some pieces of the box that had preceded it, the one that had been constructed when the first people settled down to make a village here. Every year, after the lottery, Mr. Summers began talking again about a new box, but every year the subject was allowed to fade off without anything's being done. The black box grew shabbier each year; by now it was no longer completely black but splintered badly along one side to show the original wood color, and in some places faded or stained.

Mr. Martin and his oldest son, Baxter, held the black box securely on the stool until Mr. Summers had stirred the papers thoroughly with his hand. Because so much of the ritual had been forgotten or discarded, Mr. Summers had been successful in having slips of paper substituted for the chips of wood that had been used for generations. Chips of wood, Mr. Summers had argued, had been all very well when the village was tiny, but now that the population was more than three hundred and likely to keep on growing, it was necessary to use something that would fit more easily into the black box. The night before the lottery, Mr. Summers and Mr. Graves made up the slips of paper and put them in the box, and it was then taken to the safe of Mr. Summers's coal company and locked up until Mr. Summers was ready to take it to the square next morning. The rest of the year, the box was put away, sometimes one place, sometimes another; it had spent one year in Mr. Graves's barn and another year underfoot in the post office, and sometimes it was set on a shelf in the Martin grocery and left there.

There was a great deal of fussing to be done before Mr. Summers declared the lottery open. There were lists to make up—of heads of families, heads of households in each family, members of each household in each family. There was the proper swearing-in of Mr. Summers by the postmaster, as the official of the lottery; at one time, some people remembered, there had been a recital of some sort, performed by the official of the lottery, a perfunctory, tuneless chant that had been rattled off duly each year; some people believed that the official of the lottery used to stand just so when he said or sang it, others believed that he was supposed to walk among the people, but years and years ago this part of the ritual had been allowed to lapse. There had been, also, a ritual salute, which the official of the lottery had had to use in addressing each person who came up to draw from the box, but this also had changed with time, until now it was felt necessary only for the official to speak to each person approaching. Mr. Summers was very good at all this; in his clean white shirt and blue jeans, with one hand resting carelessly on the black box, he seemed very proper and important as he talked interminably to Mr. Graves and the Martins.

Just as Mr. Summers left off talking and turned to the assembled villagers, Mrs. Hutchinson came hurriedly along the path to the square, her sweater thrown over her shoulders, and slid into place in the back of the crowd. "Clean forgot what day it was," she said to Mrs. Delacroix, who stood next to her, and they both laughed softly. "Thought my old man was out back stacking wood," Mrs. Hutchinson went on, "and then I looked out the window and the kids were gone, and then I remembered it was the twenty-seventh and came a-running." She dried her hands on her apron, and Mrs. Delacroix said, "You're in time, though. They're still talking away up there."

Mrs. Hutchinson craned her neck to see through the crowd and found her husband and children standing near the front. She tapped Mrs. Delacroix on the arm as a farewell and began to make her way through the crowd. The people separated good-humoredly to let her through; two or three people said, in voices just loud enough to be heard across the crowd, "Here comes your Missus, Hutchinson," and "Bill, she made it after all." Mrs. Hutchinson reached her husband, and Mr. Summers, who had been waiting, said cheerfully, "Thought we were going to have to get on without you, Tessie." Mrs. Hutchinson said, grinning, "Wouldn't have me leave m'dishes in the sink, now would you, Joe?," and soft laughter ran through the crowd as the people stirred back into position after Mrs. Hutchinson's arrival.

10   "Well, now," Mr. Summers said soberly, "guess we better get started, get this over with, so's we can go back to work. Anybody ain't here?"

"Dunbar," several people said. "Dunbar, Dunbar."

Mr. Summers consulted his list. "Clyde Dunbar," he said. "That's right. He's broke his leg, hasn't he? Who's drawing for him?"

"Me, I guess," a woman said, and Mr. Summers turned to look at her. "Wife draws for her husband," Mr. Summers said. "Don't you have a grown boy to do it for you, Janey?" Although Mr. Summers and everyone else in the village knew the answer perfectly well, it was the business of the official of the lottery to ask such questions formally. Mr. Summers waited with an expression of polite interest while Mrs. Dunbar answered.

"Horace's not but sixteen yet," Mrs. Dunbar said regretfully. "Guess I gotta fill in for the old man this year."

15   "Right," Mr. Summers said. He made a note on the list he was holding. Then he asked, "Watson boy drawing this year?"

A tall boy in the crowd raised his hand. "Here," he said. "I'm drawing for m'mother and me." He blinked his eyes nervously and ducked his head as several voices in the crowd said things like "Good fellow, Jack," and "Glad to see your mother's got a man to do it."

"Well," Mr. Summers said, "guess that's everyone. Old Man Warner make it?"

"Here," a voice said, and Mr. Summers nodded.

A sudden hush fell on the crowd as Mr. Summers cleared his throat and looked at the list. "All ready?" he called. "Now, I'll read the names—heads of families first—and the men come up and take a paper out of the box. Keep the paper folded in your hand without looking at it until everyone has had a turn. Everything clear?"

20   The people had done it so many times that they only half listened to the directions; most of them were quiet, wetting their lips, not looking around. Then Mr. Summers raised one hand high and said, "Adams." A man disengaged himself from the crowd and came forward. "Hi, Steve," Mr. Summers said, and Mr. Adams said, "Hi, Joe." They grinned at one another humorlessly and nervously. Then Mr. Adams reached into the black box and took out a folded paper. He held it firmly by one corner as he turned and went hastily back to his place in the crowd, where he stood a little apart from his family, not looking down at his hand.

"Allen," Mr. Summers said. "Anderson. . . . Bentham."

"Seems like there's no time at all between lotteries any more," Mrs. Delacroix said to Mrs. Graves in the back row. "Seems like we got through with the last one only last week."

"Time sure goes fast," Mrs. Graves said.

"Clark. . . . Delacroix."

25   "There goes my old man," Mrs. Delacroix said. She held her breath while her husband went forward.

"Dunbar," Mr. Summers said, and Mrs. Dunbar went steadily to the box while one of the women said, "Go on, Janey," and another said, "There she goes."

"We're next," Mrs. Graves said. She watched while Mr. Graves came around from the side of the box, greeted Mr. Summers gravely, and selected a slip of paper from the box. By now, all through the crowd there were men holding the small folded papers in their large hands, turning them over and over nervously. Mrs. Dunbar and her two sons stood together, Mrs. Dunbar holding the slip of paper.

"Harburt. . . . Hutchinson."

"Get up there, Bill," Mrs. Hutchinson said, and the people near her laughed.

30   "Jones."

"They do say," Mr. Adams said to Old Man Warner, who stood next to him, "that over in the north village they're talking of giving up the lottery."

Old Man Warner snorted. "Pack of crazy fools," he said. "Listening to the young folks, nothing's good enough for *them.* Next thing you know, they'll be wanting to go back to living in caves, nobody work any more, live *that* way for a while. Used to be a saying about 'Lottery in June, corn be heavy soon.' First thing you know, we'd all be eating stewed chickweed and acorns. There's *always* been a lottery," he added petulantly. "Bad enough to see young Joe Summers up there joking with everybody."

"Some places have already quit lotteries," Mrs. Adams said.

"Nothing but trouble in *that,*" Old Man Warner said stoutly. "Pack of young fools."

35   "Martin." And Bobby Martin watched his father go forward. "Overdyke. . . . Percy."

"I wish they'd hurry," Mrs. Dunbar said to her older son. "I wish they'd hurry."

"They're almost through," her son said.

"You get ready to run tell Dad," Mrs. Dunbar said.

Mr. Summers called his own name and then stepped forward precisely and selected a slip from the box. Then he called, "Warner."

40   "Seventy-seventh year I been in the lottery," Old Man Warner said as he went through the crowd. "Seventy-seventh time."

"Watson." The tall boy came awkwardly through the crowd. Someone said, "Don't be nervous, Jack," and Mr. Summers said, "Take your time, son."

"Zanini."

After that, there was a long pause, a breathless pause, until Mr. Summers, holding his slip of paper in the air, said, "All right, fellows." For a minute, no one moved, and then all of the slips of paper were opened. Suddenly, all women began to speak at once, saying, "Who is it?" "Who's got it?" "Is it the Dunbars?" "Is it the Watsons?" Then the voices began to say, "It's Hutchinson. It's Bill." "Bill Hutchinson's got it."

"Go tell your father," Mrs. Dunbar said to her older son.

45   People began to look around to see the Hutchinsons. Bill Hutchinson was standing quiet, staring down at the paper in his hand. Suddenly, Tessie Hutchinson shouted to Mr. Summers, "You didn't give him time enough to take any paper he wanted. I saw you. It wasn't fair!"

"Be a good sport, Tessie," Mrs. Delacroix called, and Mrs. Graves said, "All of us took the same chance."

"Shut up, Tessie," Bill Hutchinson said.

"Well, everyone," Mr. Summers said, "That was done pretty fast, and now we've got to be hurrying a little more to get done in time." He consulted his next list. "Bill," he said, "you draw for the Hutchinson family. You got any other households in the Hutchinsons?"

"There's Don and Eva," Mrs. Hutchinson yelled. "Make *them* take their chance!"

50   "Daughters draw with their husbands' families, Tessie," Mr. Summers said gently. "You know that as well as anyone else."

"It wasn't fair," Tessie said.

"I guess not, Joe," Bill Hutchinson said regretfully. "My daughter draws with her husband's family, that's only fair. And I've got no other family except the kids."

"Then, as far as drawing for families is concerned, it's you," Mr. Summers said in explanation, "and as far as drawing for households is concerned, that's you, too. Right?"

"Right," Bill Hutchinson said.

55   "How many kids, Bill?" Mr. Summers asked formally.

"Three," Bill Hutchinson said. "There's Bill, Jr., and Nancy, and little Dave. And Tessie and me."

"All right, then," Mr. Summers said. "Harry, you got their tickets back?"

Mr. Graves nodded and held up the slips of paper. "Put them in the box, then," Mr. Summers directed. "Take Bill's and put it in."

"I think we ought to start over," Mrs. Hutchinson said, as quietly as she could. "I tell you it wasn't *fair*. You didn't give him time enough to choose. *Everybody* saw that."

60   Mr. Graves had selected the five slips and put them in the box, and he dropped all the papers but those onto the ground, where the breeze caught them and lifted them off.

"Listen, everybody," Mrs. Hutchinson was saying to the people around her.

"Ready, Bill?" Mr. Summers asked, and Bill Hutchinson, with one quick glance around at his wife and children, nodded.

"Remember," Mr. Summers said, "take the slips and keep them folded until each person has taken one. Harry, you help little Dave." Mr. Graves took the hand of the little boy, who came willingly with him up to the box. "Take a paper out of the box, Davy," Mr. Summers said. Davy put his hand into the box and laughed. "Take just *one* paper," Mr. Summers said. "Harry, you hold it for him." Mr. Graves took the child's hand and removed the folded paper from the tight fist and held it while little Dave stood next to him and looked up at him wonderingly.

"Nancy next," Mr. Summers said. Nancy was twelve, and her school friends breathed heavily as she went forward, switching her skirt, and took a slip daintily from the box. "Bill, Jr.," Mr. Summers said, and Billy, his face red and his feet overlarge, nearly knocked the box over as he got a paper out. "Tessie," Mr. Summers said. She hesitated for a minute, looking around defiantly, and then set her lips and went up to the box. She snatched a paper out and held it behind her.

65   "Bill," Mr. Summers said, and Bill Hutchinson reached into the box and felt around, bringing his hand out at last with the slip of paper in it.

The crowd was quiet. A girl whispered, "I hope it's not Nancy," and the sound of the whisper reached the edges of the crowd.

"It's not the way it used to be," Old Man Warner said clearly. "People ain't the way they used to be."

"All right," Mr. Summers said. "Open the papers. Harry, you open little Dave's."

Mr. Graves opened the slip of paper and there was a general sigh through the crowd as he held it up and everyone could see that it was blank. Nancy and Bill, Jr., opened theirs at the same time, and both beamed and laughed, turning around to the crowd and holding their slips of paper above their heads.

70   "Tessie," Mr. Summers said. There was a pause, and then Mr. Summers looked at Bill Hutchinson, and Bill unfolded his paper and showed it. It was blank.

"It's Tessie," Mr. Summers said, and his voice was hushed. "Show us her paper, Bill."

Bill Hutchinson went over to his wife and forced the slip of paper out of her hand. It had a black spot on it, the black spot Mr. Summers had made the night before with the heavy pencil in the coal-company office. Bill Hutchinson held it up, and there was a stir in the crowd.

"All right, folks," Mr. Summers said, "let's finish quickly."

Although the villagers had forgotten the ritual and lost the original black box, they still remembered to use stones. The pile of stones the boys had made earlier was ready; there were stones on the ground with the blowing scraps of paper that had come out of the box. Mrs. Delacroix selected a stone so large she had to pick it up with both hands and turned to Mrs. Dunbar. "Come on," she said. "Hurry up."

75   Mrs. Dunbar had small stones in both hands, and she said, gasping for breath, "I can't run at all. You'll have to go ahead and I'll catch up with you."

The children had stones already, and someone gave little Davy Hutchinson a few pebbles.

Tessie Hutchinson was in the center of a cleared space by now, and she held her hands out desperately as the villagers moved in on her. "It isn't fair," she said. A stone hit her on the side of the head.

Old Man Warner was saying, "Come on, come on, everyone." Steve Adams was in the front of the crowd of villagers, with Mrs. Graves beside him.

"It isn't fair, it isn't right," Mrs. Hutchinson screamed, and then they were upon her.

FRANZ KAFKA

Franz Kafka (1883–1924) was born in Prague, Austria-Hungary, the son of German-speaking middle-class Jewish parents. Trained in law, he worked from 1907 to 1922 in an insurance company sponsored by the government. In 1923 he moved to Berlin to concentrate on becoming a writer, but he suffered from poor health and during his brief literary career he published only a few stories, including "A Hunger Artist" (1914).

Through the agency of his friend Max Brod, a number of works by Kafka were published posthumously, including The Trial *(1925, trans. 1937),* The Castle *(1926, trans. 1937), and* Amerika *(1927, trans. 1938). Among twentieth-century authors, Kafka's accounts of alienation and anxiety, of bewildered, isolated individuals trapped by law and bureaucracy, are unparalleled in their power and pain. In the words of the poet-critic W. H. Auden, writing in the late 1950s, "Had one to name the author who comes nearest to bearing the same kind of relation to our age as Dante, Shakespeare, and Goethe bore to theirs, Kafka is the first one would think of."*

See the graphic story version of "A Hunger Artist" by R. Crumb and David Zane Mairowitz in Chapter 12, page 259.

A Hunger Artist   [1924]

Translated by Edwin and Willa Muir

During these last decades the interest in professional fasting has markedly diminished. It used to pay very well to stage such great performances under one's own management, but today that is quite impossible. We live in a different world now. At one time the whole town took a lively interest in the hunger artist; from day to day of his fast the excitement mounted; everybody wanted to see him at least once a day; there were people who bought season tickets for the last few days and sat from morning till night in front of his small barred cage; even in the nighttime there were visiting hours, when the whole effect was heightened by torch flares; on fine days the cage was set out in the open air, and then it was the children's special treat to see the hunger artist; for their elders he was often just a joke that happened to be in fashion, but the children stood open-mouthed, holding each other's hands for greater security, marveling at him as he sat there pallid in black tights, with his ribs sticking out so prominently, not even on a seat but down among straw on the ground, sometimes giving a courteous nod, answering questions with a constrained smile, or perhaps stretching an arm through the bars so that one might feel how thin it was, and then again withdrawing deep into himself, paying no attention to anyone or anything, not even to the all-important striking of the clock that was the only piece of furniture in his cage, but merely staring into vacancy with half-shut eyes, now and then taking a sip from a tiny glass of water to moisten his lips.

Besides casual onlookers there were also relays of permanent watchers selected by the public, usually butchers, strangely enough, and it was their task to watch the hunger artist day and night, three of them at a time, in case he should have some secret recourse to nourishment. This was nothing but a formality, instituted to reassure the masses, for the initiates knew well enough that during his fast the artist would never in any circumstances, not even under forcible compulsion, swallow the smallest morsel of food; the honor of his profession forbade it. Not every watcher, of course, was capable of understanding this, there were often groups of night watchers who were very lax in carrying out their duties and deliberately huddled together in a retired corner to play cards with great absorption, obviously intending to give the hunger artist the chance of a little refreshment, which they supposed he could draw from some private hoard. Nothing annoyed the artist more than such watchers; they made him miserable; they made his fast seem unendurable; sometimes he mastered his feebleness sufficiently to sing during their watch for as long as he could keep going, to show them how unjust their suspicions were. But that was of little use; they only wondered at his cleverness in being able to fill his mouth even while singing. Much more to his taste were the watchers who sat close up to the bars, who were not content with the dim night lighting of the hall but focused him in the full glare of the electric pocket torch given them by the impresario. The harsh light did not trouble him at all, in any case he could never sleep properly, and he could always drowse a little, whatever the light, at any hour, even when the hall was thronged with noisy onlookers. He was quite happy at the prospect of spending a sleepless night with such watchers; he was ready to exchange jokes with them, to tell them stories out of his nomadic life, anything at all to keep them awake and demonstrate to them again that he had no eatables in his cage and that he was fasting as not one of them could fast. But his happiest moment was when the morning came and an enormous breakfast was brought them, at his expense, on which they flung themselves with the keen appetite of healthy men after a weary night of wakefulness. Of course there were people who argued that this breakfast was an unfair attempt to bribe the watchers, but that was going rather too far, and when they were invited to take on a night's vigil without a breakfast, merely for the sake of the cause, they made themselves scarce, although they stuck stubbornly to their suspicions.

Such suspicions, anyhow, were a necessary accompaniment to the profession of fasting. No one could possibly watch the hunger artist continuously, day and night, and so no one could produce first-hand evidence that the fast had really been rigorous and continuous; only the artist himself could know that, he was therefore bound to be the sole completely satisfied spectator of his own fast. Yet for other reasons he was never satisfied; it was not perhaps mere fasting that had brought him to such skeleton thinness that many people had regretfully to keep away from his exhibitions, because the sight of him was too much for them, perhaps it was dissatisfaction with himself that had worn him down. For he alone knew, what no other initiate knew, how easy it was to fast. It was the easiest thing in the world. He made no secret of this, yet people did not believe him; at the best they set him down as modest; most of them, however, thought he was out for publicity or else was some kind of cheat who found it easy to fast because he had discovered a way of making it easy, and then had the impudence to admit the fact, more or less. He had to put up with all that, and in the course of time had got used to it, but his inner dissatisfaction always rankled, and never yet, after any term of fasting—this must be granted to his credit—had he left the cage of his own free will. The longest period of fasting was fixed by his impresario at forty days, beyond that term he was not allowed to go, not even in great cities, and there was good reason for it, too. Experience had proved that for about forty days the interest of the public could be stimulated by a steadily increasing pressure of advertisement, but after that the town began to lose interest, sympathetic support began notably to fall off; there were of course local variations as between one town and another or one country and another, but as a general rule forty days marked the limit. So on the fortieth day the flower-bedecked cage was opened, enthusiastic spectators filled the hall, a military band played, two doctors entered the cage to measure the results of the fast, which were announced through a megaphone, and finally two young ladies appeared, blissful at having been selected for the honor, to help the hunger artist down the few steps leading to a small table on which was spread a carefully chosen invalid repast. And at this very moment the artist always turned stubborn. True, he would entrust his bony arms to the outstretched helping hands of the ladies bending over him, but stand up he would not. Why stop fasting at this particular moment, after forty days of it? He had held out for a long time, an illimitably long time; why stop now, when he was in his best fasting form, or rather, not yet quite in his best fasting form? Why should he be cheated of the fame he would get for fasting longer, for being not only the record hunger artist of all time, which presumably he was already, but for beating his own record by a performance beyond human imagination, since he felt that there were no limits to his capacity for fasting? His public pretended to admire him so much, why should it have so little patience with him; if he could endure fasting longer, why shouldn't the public endure it? Besides, he was tired, he was comfortable sitting in the straw, and now he was supposed to lift himself to his full height and go down to a meal the very thought of which gave him a nausea that only the presence of the ladies kept him from betraying, and even that with an effort. And he looked up into the eyes of the ladies who were apparently so friendly and in reality so cruel, and shook his head, which felt too heavy on its strengthless neck. But then there happened yet again what always happened. The impresario came forward, without a word—for the band made speech impossible—lifted his arms in the air above the artist, as if inviting Heaven to look down upon its creature here in the straw, this suffering martyr, which indeed he was, although in quite another sense; grasped him around the emaciated waist, with exaggerated caution, so that the frail condition he was in might be appreciated; and committed him to the care of the blenching ladies, not without secretly giving him a shaking so that his legs and body tottered and swayed. The artist now submitted completely; his head lolled on his breast as if it had landed there by chance; his body was hollowed out; his legs in a spasm of self-preservation clung close to each other at the knees, yet scraped on the ground as if it were not really solid ground, as if they were only trying to find solid ground; and the whole weight of his body, a featherweight after all, relapsed onto one of the ladies, who, looking around for help and panting a little—this post of honor was not at all what she had expected it to be—first stretched her neck as far as she could to keep her face at least free from contact with the artist, then finding this impossible, and her more fortunate companion not coming to her aid but merely holding extended in her own trembling hand the little bunch of knucklebones that was the artist's, to the great delight of the spectators burst into tears and had to be replaced by an attendant who had long been stationed in readiness. Then came the food, a little of which the impresario managed to get between the artist's lips, while he sat in a kind of half-fainting trance, to the accompaniment of cheerful patter designed to distract the public's attention from the artist's condition; after that, a toast was drunk to the public, supposedly prompted by a whisper from the artist in the impresario's ear; the band confirmed it with a mighty flourish, the spectators melted away, and no one had any cause to be dissatisfied with the proceedings, no one except the hunger artist himself, he only, as always.

So he lived for many years, with small regular intervals of recuperation, in visible glory, honored by the world, yet in spite of that troubled in spirit, and all the more troubled because no one would take his trouble seriously. What comfort could he possibly need? What more could he possibly wish for? And if some good-natured person, feeling sorry for him, tried to console him by pointing out that his melancholy was probably caused by fasting, it could happen, especially when he had been fasting for some time, that he reacted with an outburst of fury and to the general alarm began to shake the bars of his cage like a wild animal. Yet the impresario had a way of punishing these outbreaks which he rather enjoyed putting into operation. He would apologize publicly for the artist's behavior, which was only to be excused, he admitted, because of the irritability caused by fasting; a condition hardly to be understood by well-fed people; then by natural transition he went on to mention the artist's equally incomprehensible boast that he could fast for much longer than he was doing; he praised the high ambition, the good will, the great self-denial undoubtedly implicit in such a statement; and then quite simply countered it by bringing out photographs, which were also on sale to the public, showing the artist on the fortieth day of a fast lying in bed almost dead from exhaustion. This perversion of the truth, familiar to the artist though it was, always unnerved him afresh and proved too much for him. What was a consequence of the premature ending of his fast was here presented as the cause of it! To fight against this lack of understanding, against a whole world of non-understanding, was impossible. Time and again in good faith he stood by the bars listening to the impresario, but as soon as the photographs appeared he always let go and sank with a groan back onto his straw, and the reassured public could once more come close and gaze at him.

5   A few years later when the witnesses of such scenes called them to mind, they often failed to understand themselves at all. For meanwhile the aforementioned change in public interest had set in; it seemed to happen almost overnight; there may have been profound causes for it, but who was going to bother about that; at any rate the pampered hunger artist suddenly found himself deserted one fine day by the amusement seekers, who went streaming past him to other more favored attractions. For the last time the impresario hurried him over half Europe to discover whether the old interest might still survive here and there; all in vain; everywhere, as if by secret agreement, a positive revulsion from professional fasting was in evidence. Of course it could not really have sprung up so suddenly as all that, and many premonitory symptoms which had not been sufficiently remarked or suppressed during the rush and glitter of success now came retrospectively to

mind, but it was now too late to take any countermeasures. Fasting would surely come into fashion again at some future date, yet that was no comfort for those living in the present. What, then, was the hunger artist to do? He had been applauded by thousands in his time and could hardly come down to showing himself in a street booth at village fairs, and as for adopting another profession, he was not only too old for that but too fanatically devoted to fasting. So he took leave of the impresario, his partner in an unparalleled career, and hired himself to a large circus; in order to spare his own feelings he avoided reading the conditions of his contract.

A large circus with its enormous traffic in replacing and recruiting men, animals and apparatus can always find a use for people at any time, even for a hunger artist, provided of course that he does not ask too much, and in this particular case anyhow it was not only the artist who was taken on but his famous and long-known name as well; indeed considering the peculiar nature of his performance, which was not impaired by advancing age, it could not be objected that here was an artist past his prime, no longer at the height of his professional skill, seeking a refuge in some quiet corner of a circus; on the contrary, the hunger artist averred that he could fast as well as ever, which was entirely credible; he even alleged that if he were allowed to fast as he liked, and this was at once promised him without more ado, he could astound the world by establishing a record never yet achieved, a statement which certainly provoked a smile among the other professionals, since it left out of account the change in public opinion, which the hunger artist in his zeal conveniently forgot.

He had not, however, actually lost his sense of the real situation and took it as a matter of course that he and his cage should be stationed, not in the middle of the ring as a main attraction, but outside, near the animal cages, on a site that was after all easily accessible. Large and gaily painted placards made a frame for the cage and announced what was to be seen inside it. When the public came thronging out in the intervals to see the animals, they could hardly avoid passing the hunger artist's cage and stopping there for a moment, perhaps they might even have stayed longer had not those pressing behind them in the narrow gangway, who did not understand why they should be held up on their way toward the excitements of the menagerie, made it impossible for anyone to stand gazing quietly for any length of time. And that was the reason why the hunger artist, who had of course been looking forward to these visiting hours as the main achievement of his life, began instead to shrink from them. At first he could hardly wait for the intervals; it was exhilarating to watch the crowds come streaming his way, until only too soon—not even the most obstinate self-deception, clung to almost consciously, could hold out against the fact—the conviction was borne in upon him that these people, most of them, to judge from their actions, again and again, without exception, were all on their way to the menagerie. And the first sight of them from the distance remained the best. For when they reached his cage he was at once deafened by the storm of shouting and abuse that arose from the two contending factions, which renewed themselves continuously, of those who wanted to stop and stare at him—he soon began to dislike them more than the others—not out of real interest but only out of obstinate self-assertiveness, and those who wanted to go straight on to the animals. When the first great rush was past, the stragglers came along, and these, whom nothing could have prevented from stopping to look at him as long as they had breath, raced past with long strides, hardly even glancing at him, in their haste to get to the menagerie in time. And all too rarely did it happen that he had a stroke of luck, when some father of a family fetched up before him with his children, pointed a finger at the hunger artist, and explained at length what the phenomenon meant, telling stories of earlier years when he himself had watched similar but much more thrilling performances, and the children, still rather uncomprehending, since neither inside nor outside school had they been sufficiently prepared for this lesson—what did they care about fasting?—yet showed by the brightness of their intent eyes that new and better times might be coming. Perhaps, said the hunger artist to himself many a time, things would be a little better if his cage were set not quite so near the menagerie. That made it too easy for people to make their choice, to say nothing of what he suffered from the stench of the menagerie, the animals' restlessness by night, the carrying past of raw lumps of flesh for the beasts of prey, the roaring at feeding times, which depressed him continually. But he did not dare to lodge a complaint with the management; after all, he had the animals to thank for the troops of people who passed his cage, among whom there might always be one here and there to take an interest in him, and who could tell where they might seclude him if he called attention to his existence and thereby to the fact that, strictly speaking, he was only an impediment on the way to the menagerie.

A small impediment, to be sure, one that grew steadily less. People grew familiar with the strange idea that they could be expected, in times like these, to take an interest in a hunger artist, and with this familiarity the verdict went out against him. He might fast as much as he could, and he did so; but nothing could save him now, people passed him by. Just try to explain to anyone the art of fasting! Anyone who has no feeling for it cannot be made to understand it. The fine placards grew dirty and illegible, they were torn down; the little notice board telling the number of fast days achieved, which at first was changed carefully every day, had long stayed at the same figure, for after the first few weeks even this small task seemed pointless to the staff; and so the artist simply fasted on and on, as he had once dreamed of doing, and it was no trouble to him, just as he had always foretold, but no one counted the days, no one, not even the artist himself, knew what records he was already breaking, and his heart grew heavy. And when once in a while some leisurely passer-by stopped, made merry over the old figure on the board, and spoke of swindling, that was in its way the stupidest lie ever invented by indifference and inborn malice, since it was not the hunger artist who was cheating, he was working honestly, but the world was cheating him of his reward.

Many more days went by, however, and that too came to an end. An overseer's eye fell on the cage one day and he asked the attendants why this perfectly good cage should be left standing there unused with dirty straw inside it; nobody knew, until one man, helped out by the notice board, remembered about the hunger artist. They poked into the straw with sticks and found him in it. "Are you still fasting?" asked the overseer, "when on earth do you mean to stop?" "Forgive me, everybody," whispered the hunger artist; only the overseer, who had his ear to the bars, understood him. "Of course," said the overseer, and tapped his forehead with a finger to let the attendants know what state the man was in, "we forgive you." "I always wanted you to admire my fasting," said the hunger artist. "We do admire it," said the overseer, affably. "But you shouldn't admire it," said the hunger artist. "Well then we don't admire it," said the overseer, "but why shouldn't we admire it?" "Because I have to fast, I can't help it," said the hunger artist. "What a fellow you are," said the overseer, "and why can't you help it?" "Because," said the hunger artist, lifting his head a little and speaking, with his lips pursed, as if for a kiss, right into the overseer's ear, so that no syllable might be lost, "because I couldn't find the food I liked. If I had found it, believe me, I should have made no fuss and stuffed myself like you or anyone else." These were his last words, but in his dimming eyes remained the firm though no longer proud persuasion that he was still continuing to fast.

10   "Well, clear this out now!" said the overseer, and they buried the hunger artist, straw and all. Into the cage they put a young panther. Even the most insensitive felt it refreshing to see this wild creature leaping around the cage that had so long been dreary. The panther was all right. The food he liked was brought him without hesitation by the attendants; he seemed not even to miss his freedom; his noble body, furnished almost to the bursting point with all that it needed, seemed to carry freedom around with it too; somewhere in his jaws it seemed to lurk; and the joy of life streamed with such ardent passion from his throat that for the onlookers it was not easy to stand the shock of it. But they braced themselves, crowded around the cage, and did not want ever to move away.

BOBBIE ANN MASON

Bobbie Ann Mason, born in 1940 in rural western Kentucky is a graduate of the University of Kentucky, where she is writer in residence. She received a master's degree from the State University of New York at Binghamton, and a PhD from the University of Connecticut, writing a dissertation on a novel by Vladimir Nabokov. Between graduate degrees she worked for various magazines, including T.V. Star Parade. *In 1974 she published her first book—the dissertation on Nabokov—and in 1975 she published her second,* The Girl Sleuth: A Guide to the Bobbsey Twins, Nancy Drew and Their Sisters. *She is, however, most widely known for her fiction, which usually deals with blue-collar people in rural Kentucky.*

> *I write [she says in an interview published in* Boca Raton News, *January 9, 1983] about people trapped in circumstances. . . . I identify with people who are ambivalent about their situation. And I guess in my stories, I'm in a way imagining myself as I would have felt if I had not gotten away and gotten a different perspective on things—if, for example, I had gotten pregnant in high school and had to marry a truck driver as the woman did in my story "Shiloh."*

Shiloh [1982]

Leroy Moffitt's wife, Norma Jean, is working on her pectorals. She lifts three-pound dumbbells to warm up, then progresses to a twenty-pound barbell. Standing with her legs apart, she reminds Leroy of Wonder Woman.

"I'd give anything if I could just get these muscles to where they're real hard," says Norma Jean. "Feel this arm. It's not as hard as the other one."

"That's cause you're right-handed," says Leroy, dodging as she swings the barbell in an arc.

"Do you think so?"

5   "Sure."

Leroy is a truckdriver. He injured his leg in a highway accident four months ago, and his physical therapy, which involves weights and a pulley, prompted Norma Jean to try building herself up. Now she is attending a body-building class. Leroy has been collecting temporary disability since his tractor-trailer jackknifed in Missouri, badly twisting his left leg in its socket. He has a steel pin in his hip. He will probably not be able to drive his rig again. It sits in the backyard, like a gigantic bird that has flown home to roost. Leroy has been home in Kentucky for three months, and his leg is almost healed, but the accident frightened him and he does not want to drive any more long hauls. He is not sure what to do next. In the meantime, he makes things from craft kits. He started by building a miniature log cabin from notched Popsicle sticks. He varnished it and placed it on the TV set, where it remains. It reminds him of a rustic Nativity scene. Then he tried string art (sailing ships on black velvet), a macramé owl kit, a snap-together B-17 Flying Fortress, and a lamp made out of a model truck, with a light fixture screwed in the top of the cab. At first the kits were diversions, something to kill time, but now he is thinking about building a full-scale log house from a kit. It would be considerably cheaper than building a regular house, and besides, Leroy has grown to appreciate how things are put together. He has begun to realize that in all the years he was on the road he never took time to examine anything. He was always flying past scenery.

"They won't let you build a log cabin in any of the new subdivisions," Norma Jean tells him.

"They will if I tell them it's for you," he says, teasing her. Ever since they were married, he has promised Norma Jean he would build her a new home one day. They have always rented, and the house they live in is small and nondescript. It does not even feel like a home, Leroy realizes now.

Norma Jean works at the Rexall drugstore, and she has acquired an amazing amount of information about cosmetics. When she explains to Leroy the three stages of complexion care, involving creams, toners, and moisturizers, he thinks happily of other petroleum products—axle grease, diesel fuel. This is a connection between him and Norma Jean. Since he has been home, he has felt unusually tender about his wife and guilty over his long absences. But he can't tell what she feels about him. Norma Jean has never complained about his traveling; she has never made hurt remarks, like calling his truck a "widow-maker." He is reasonably certain she has been faithful to him, but he wishes she would celebrate his permanent home-coming more happily. Norma Jean is often startled to find Leroy at home, and he thinks she seems a little disappointed about it. Perhaps he reminds her too much of the early days of their marriage, before he went on the road. They had a child who died as an infant, years ago. They never speak about their memories of Randy, which have almost faded, but now that Leroy is home all the time, they sometimes feel awkward around each other, and Leroy wonders if one of them should mention the child. He has the feeling that they are waking up out of a

dream together—that they must create a new marriage, start afresh. They are
lucky they are still married. Leroy has read that for most people losing a child
destroys the marriage—or else he heard this on *Donahue*.[1] He can't always
remember where he learns things anymore.

10   At Christmas, Leroy bought an electric organ for Norma Jean. She used
to play the piano when she was in high school. "It don't leave you," she told
him once. "It's like riding a bicycle."

The new instrument had so many keys and buttons that she was bewildered by it at first. She touched the keys tentatively, pushed some buttons,
then pecked out "Chopsticks." It came out in an amplified fox-trot rhythm,
with marimba sounds.

"It's an orchestra!" she cried.

The organ had a pecan-look finish and eighteen preset chords, with optional flute, violin, trumpet, clarinet, and banjo accompaniments. Norma Jean
mastered the organ almost immediately. At first she played Christmas songs.
Then she bought *The Sixties Songbook* and learned every tune in it, adding
variations to each with the rows of brightly colored buttons.

"I didn't like these old songs back then," she said. "But I have this crazy
feeling I missed something."

15   "You didn't miss a thing," said Leroy.

Leroy likes to lie on the couch and smoke a joint and listen to Norma
Jean play "Can't Take My Eyes Off You" and "I'll Be Back." He is back again.
After fifteen years on the road, he is finally settling down with the woman
he loves. She is still pretty. Her skin is flawless. Her frosted curls resemble
pencil trimmings.

Now that Leroy has come home to stay, he notices how much the town
has changed. Subdivisions are spreading across western Kentucky like an oil
slick. The sign at the edge of town says "Pop: 11,500"—only seven hundred
more than it said twenty years before. Leroy can't figure out who is living in
all the new houses. The farmers who used to gather around the courthouse
square on Saturday afternoons to play checkers and spit tobacco juice have
gone. It has been years since Leroy has thought about the farmers, and they
have disappeared without his noticing.

Leroy meets a kid named Stevie Hamilton in the parking lot at the new
shopping center. While they pretend to be strangers meeting over a stalled
car, Stevie tosses an ounce of marijuana under the front seat of Leroy's car.
Stevie is wearing orange jogging shoes and a T-shirt that says CHATTAHOOCHEE
SUPER-RAT. His father is a prominent doctor who lives in one of the expensive
subdivisions in a new white-columned brick house that looks like a funeral
parlor. In the phone book under his name there is a separate number, with
the listing "Teenagers."

"Where do you get this stuff?" asks Leroy. "From your pappy?"

20   "That's for me to know and you to find out," Stevie says. He is slit-eyed
and skinny.

"What else you got?"

"What you interested in?"

"Nothing special. Just wondered."

---

[1]**Donahue** The Phil Donahue Show, a popular television program, 1972–1991.

Leroy used to take speed on the road. Now he has to go slowly. He needs to be mellow. He leans back against the car and says, "I'm aiming to build me a log house, soon as I get time. My wife, though, I don't think she likes the idea."

25   "Well, let me know when you want me again," Stevie says. He has a cigarette in his cupped palm, as though sheltering it from the wind. He takes a long drag, then stomps it on the asphalt and slouches away.

Stevie's father was two years ahead of Leroy in high school. Leroy is thirty-four. He married Norma Jean when they were both eighteen, and their child Randy was born a few months later, but he died at the age of four months and three days. He would be about Stevie's age now. Norma Jean and Leroy were at the drive-in, watching a double feature (*Dr. Strangelove* and *Lover Come Back*), and the baby was sleeping in the back seat. When the first movie ended, the baby was dead. It was the sudden infant death syndrome. Leroy remembers handing Randy to a nurse at the emergency room, as though he were offering her a large doll as a present. A dead baby feels like a sack of flour. "It just happens sometimes," said the doctor, in what Leroy always recalls as a nonchalant tone. Leroy can hardly remember the child anymore, but he still sees vividly a scene from *Dr. Strangelove* in which the President of the United States was talking in a folksy voice on the hot line to the Soviet premier about the bomber accidentally headed toward Russia. He was in the War Room, and the world map was lit up. Leroy remembers Norma Jean standing catatonically beside him in the hospital and himself thinking: Who is this strange girl? He had forgotten who she was. Now scientists are saying that crib death is caused by a virus. Nobody knows anything, Leroy thinks. The answers are always changing.

When Leroy gets home from the shopping center, Norma Jean's mother, Mabel Beasley, is there. Until this year, Leroy has not realized how much time she spends with Norma Jean. When she visits, she inspects the closets and then the plants, informing Norma Jean when a plant is droopy or yellow. Mabel calls the plants "flowers," although there are never any blooms. She also notices if Norma Jean's laundry is piling up. Mabel is a short, overweight woman whose tight, brown-dyed curls look more like a wig than the actual wig she sometimes wears. Today she has brought Norma Jean an off-white dust ruffle she made for the bed; Mabel works in a custom-upholstery shop.

"This is the tenth one I made this year," Mabel says. "I got started and couldn't stop."

"It's real pretty," says Norma Jean.

30   "Now we can hide things under the bed," says Leroy, who gets along with his mother-in-law primarily by joking with her. Mabel has never really forgiven him for disgracing her by getting Norma Jean pregnant. When the baby died, she said that fate was mocking her.

"What's that thing?" Mabel says to Leroy in a loud voice, pointing to a tangle of yarn on a piece of canvas.

Leroy holds it up for Mabel to see. "It's my needlepoint," he explains. "This is a *Star Trek* pillow cover."

"That's what a woman would do," says Mabel. "Great day in the morning!"

"All the big football players on TV do it," he says.

35   "Why, Leroy, you're always trying to fool me. I don't believe you for one minute. You don't know what to do with yourself—that's the whole trouble. Sewing!"

"I'm aiming to build us a log house," says Leroy. "Soon as my plans come."

"Like *heck* you are," says Norma Jean. She takes Leroy's needlepoint and shoves it into a drawer. "You have to find a job first. Nobody can afford to build now anyway."

Mabel straightens her girdle and says. "I still think before you get tied down y'all ought to take a little run to Shiloh."

"One of these days, Mama," Norma Jean says impatiently.

40   Mabel is talking about Shiloh, Tennessee. For the past few years, she has been urging Leroy and Norma Jean to visit the Civil War battleground there. Mabel went there on her honeymoon—the only real trip she ever took. Her husband died of a perforated ulcer when Norma Jean was ten, but Mabel, who was accepted into the United Daughters of the Confederacy in 1975, is still preoccupied with going back to Shiloh.

"I've been to kingdom come and back in that truck out yonder," Leroy says to Mabel, "but we never yet set foot in that battleground. Ain't that something? How did I miss it?"

"It's not even that far," Mabel says.

After Mabel leaves, Norma Jean reads to Leroy from a list she has made. "Things you could do," she announces. "You could get a job as a guard at Union Carbide, where they'd let you set on a stool. You could get on at the lumberyard. You could do a little carpenter work, if you want to build so bad. You could—"

"I can't do something where I'd have to stand up all day."

45   "You ought to try standing up all day behind a cosmetics counter. It's amazing that I have strong feet, coming from two parents that never had strong feet at all." At the moment Norma Jean is holding on to the kitchen counter, raising her knees one at a time as she talks. She is wearing two-pound ankle weights.

"Don't worry," says Leroy. "I'll do something."

"You could truck calves to slaughter for somebody. You wouldn't have to drive any big old truck for that."

"I'm going to build you this house," says Leroy. "I want to make you a real home."

"I don't want to live in any log cabin."

50   "It's not a cabin. It's a house."

"I don't care. It looks like a cabin."

"You and me together could lift those logs. It's just like lifting weights."

Norma Jean doesn't answer. Under her breath, she is counting. Now she is marching through the kitchen. She is doing goose steps.

Before his accident, when Leroy came home he used to stay in the house with Norma Jean, watching TV in bed and playing cards. She would cook fried chicken, picnic ham, chocolate pie—all his favorites. Now he is home alone much of the time. In the mornings, Norma Jean disappears, leaving a cooling place in the bed. She eats a cereal called Body Buddies, and she leaves the bowl on the table, with the soggy tan balls floating in a milk puddle. He sees things about Norma Jean that he never realized before. When she chops onions, she stares off into a corner, as if she can't bear to look. She puts on her house slippers almost precisely at nine o'clock every evening and nudges her jogging shoes under the couch. She saves bread heels for the birds. Leroy watches the birds at the feeder. He notices the peculiar way goldfinches fly past the window. They close their wings, then fall, then spread their wings to catch and lift themselves. He wonders if they close their eyes when they fall. Norma Jean closes her eyes when they are in bed. She wants the lights turned out. Even then, he is sure she closes her eyes.

55   He goes for long drives around town. He tends to drive a car rather carelessly. Power steering and an automatic shift make a car feel so small and inconsequential that his body is hardly involved in the driving process. His injured leg stretches out comfortably. Once or twice he has almost hit something, but even the prospect of an accident seems minor in a car. He cruises the new subdivisions, feeling like a criminal rehearsing for a robbery. Norma Jean is probably right about a log house being inappropriate here in the new subdivision. All the houses look grand and complicated. They depress him.

One day when Leroy comes home from a drive he finds Norma Jean in tears. She is in the kitchen making a potato and mushroom-soup casserole, with grated cheese topping. She is crying because her mother caught her smoking.

"I didn't hear her coming. I was standing here puffing away pretty as you please," Norma Jean says, wiping her eyes.

"I knew it would happen sooner or later," says Leroy, putting his arm around her.

"She don't know the meaning of the word 'knock,'" says Norma Jean. "It's a wonder she hadn't caught me years ago."

60   "Think of it this way," Leroy says. "What if she caught me with a joint?"

"You better not let her!" Norma Jean shrieks. "I'm warning you, Leroy Moffitt!"

"I'm just kidding. Here, play me a tune. That'll help you relax."

Norma Jean puts the casserole in the oven and sets the timer. Then she plays a ragtime tune, with horns and banjo, as Leroy lights up a joint and lies on the couch, laughing to himself about Mabel's catching him at it. He thinks of Stevie Hamilton—a doctor's son pushing grass. Everything is funny. The whole town seems crazy and small. He is reminded of Virgil Mathis, a boastful policeman Leroy used to shoot pool with. Virgil recently led a drug bust in a back room at a bowling alley, where he seized ten thousand dollars' worth of marijuana. The newspaper had a picture of him holding up the bags of grass and grinning widely. Right now, Leroy can imagine Virgil breaking down the door and arresting him with a lungful of smoke. Virgil would probably have been alerted to the scene because of all the racket Norma Jean is making. Now she sounds like a hard-rock band. Norma Jean is terrific. When she switches to a Latin-rhythm version of "Sunshine Superman," Leroy hums along. Norma Jean's foot goes up and down, up and down.

"Well, what do you think?" Leroy says, when Norma Jean pauses to search through her music.

65   "What do I think about what?"

His mind has gone blank. Then he says, "I'll sell my rig and build us a house." That wasn't what he wanted to say. He wanted to know what she thought—what she *really* thought—about them.

"Don't start in on that again," says Norma Jean. She begins playing "Who'll Be the Next in Line?"

Leroy used to tell hitchhikers his whole life story—about his travels, his hometown, the baby. He would end with a question: "Well, what do you think?" It was just a rhetorical question. In time, he had the feeling that he'd been telling the same story over and over to the same hitchhikers. He quit talking to hitchhikers when he realized how his voice sounded—whining and self-pitying, like some teenage-tragedy song. Now Leroy has the sudden impulse to tell Norma Jean about himself, as if he had just met her. They have known each other so long they have forgotten a lot about each other. They could become reacquainted. But when the oven timer goes off and she runs to the kitchen, he forgets why he wants to do this.

The next day, Mabel drops by. It is Saturday and Norma Jean is cleaning. Leroy is studying the plans of his log house, which have finally come in the mail. He has them spread out on the table—big sheets of stiff blue paper, with diagrams and numbers printed in white. While Norma Jean runs the vacuum, Mabel drinks coffee. She sets her coffee cup on a blueprint.

70   "I'm just waiting for time to pass," she says to Leroy, drumming her fingers on the table.

As soon as Norma Jean switches off the vacuum, Mabel says in a loud voice, "Did you hear about the datsun dog that killed the baby?"

Norma Jean says, "The word is 'dachshund.'"

"They put the dog on trial. It chewed the baby's legs off. The mother was in the next room all the time." She raises her voice. "They thought it was neglect."

Norma Jean is holding her ears. Leroy manages to open the refrigerator and get some Diet Pepsi to offer Mabel. Mabel still has some coffee and she waves away the Pepsi.

75   "Datsuns are like that," Mabel says. "They're jealous dogs. They'll tear a place to pieces if you don't keep an eye on them."

"You better watch out what you're saying, Mabel," says Leroy.

"Well, facts is facts."

Leroy looks out the window at his rig. It is like a huge piece of furniture gathering dust in the backyard. Pretty soon it will be an antique. He hears the vacuum cleaner. Norma Jean seems to be cleaning the living room rug again.

Later, she says to Leroy, "She just said that about the baby because she caught me smoking. She's trying to pay me back."

80   "What are you talking about?" Leroy says, nervously shuffling blueprints.

"You know good and well," Norma Jean says. She is sitting in a kitchen chair with her feet up and her arms wrapped around her knees. She looks small and helpless. She says, "The very idea, her bringing up a subject like that! Saying it was neglect."

"She didn't mean that," Leroy says.

"She might not have *thought* she meant it. She always says things like that. You don't know how she goes on."

"But she didn't really mean it. She was just talking."

85   Leroy opens a king-sized bottle of beer and pours it into two glasses dividing it carefully. He hands a glass to Norma Jean and she takes it from him mechanically. For a long time, they sit by the kitchen window watching the birds at the feeder.

Something is happening. Norma Jean is going to night school. She has graduated from her six-week body-building course and now she is taking an adult-education course in composition at Paducah Community College. She spends her evenings outlining paragraphs.

"First, you have a topic sentence," she explains to Leroy. "Then you divide it up. Your secondary topic has to be connected to your primary topic."

To Leroy, this sounds intimidating. "I never was any good in English," he says.

"It makes a lot of sense."

90   "What are you doing this for, anyhow?"

She shrugs. "It's something to do." She stands up and lifts her dumbbells a few times.

"Driving a rig, nobody cared about my English."

"I'm not criticizing your English."

Norma Jean used to say, "If I lose ten minutes' sleep, I just drag all day." Now she stays up late, writing compositions. She got a B on her first paper— a how-to theme on soup-based casseroles. Recently Norma Jean has been cooking unusual foods—tacos, lasagna, Bombay chicken. She doesn't play the organ anymore, though her second paper was called "Why Music Is Important to Me." She sits at the kitchen table, concentrating on her outlines, while Leroy plays with his log house plans, practicing with a set of Lincoln Logs. The thought of getting a truckload of notched, numbered logs scares him, and he wants to be prepared. As he and Norma Jean work together at the kitchen table, Leroy has the hopeful thought that they are sharing something, but he knows he is a fool to think this. Norma Jean is miles away. He knows he is going to lose her. Like Mabel, he is just waiting for time to pass.

95   One day, Mabel is there before Norma Jean gets home from work, and Leroy finds himself confiding in her. Mabel, he realizes, must know Norma Jean better than he does.

"I don't know what's got into that girl," Mabel says. "She used to go to bed with the chickens. Now you say she's up all hours. Plus her a-smoking. I like to died."

"I want to make her this beautiful home," Leroy says, indicating the Lincoln Logs. "I don't think she even wants it. Maybe she was happier with me gone."

"She don't know what to make of you, coming home like this."

"Is that it?"

100   Mabel takes the roof off his Lincoln Log cabin. "You couldn't get *me* in a log cabin," she says. "I was raised in one. It's no picnic, let me tell you."

"They're different now," says Leroy.

"I tell you what," Mabel says, smiling oddly at Leroy.

"What?"

"Take her on down to Shiloh. Y'all need to get out together, stir a little. Her brain's all balled up over them books."

105   Leroy can see traces of Norma Jean's features in her mother's face. Mabel's worn face has the texture of crinkled cotton, but suddenly she looks pretty. It occurs to Leroy that Mabel has been hinting all along that she wants them to take her with them to Shiloh.

"Let's all go to Shiloh," he says. "You and me and her. Come Sunday."

Mabel throws up her hand in protest. "Oh, no, not me. Young folks want to be by theirselves."

When Norma Jean comes in with groceries, Leroy says excitedly. "Your mama here's been dying to go to Shiloh for thirty-five years. It's about time we went, don't you think?"

"I'm not going to butt in on anybody's second honeymoon," Mabel says.

110   "Who's going on a honeymoon, for Christ's sake?" Norma Jean says loudly.

"I never raised no daughter of mine to talk that-a-way," Mabel says.

"You ain't seen nothing yet," says Norma Jean. She starts putting away boxes and cans, slamming cabinet doors.

"There's a log cabin at Shiloh," Mabel says. "It was there during the battle. There's bullet holes in it."

"When are you going to *shut up* about Shiloh, Mama?" asks Norma Jean.

115   "I always thought Shiloh was the prettiest place, so full of history," Mabel goes on. "I just hoped y'all could see it once before I die, so you could tell me about it." Later, she whispers to Leroy. "You do what I said. A little change is what she needs."

"Your name means 'the king,'" Norma Jean says to Leroy that evening. He is trying to get her to go to Shiloh, and she is reading a book about another century.

"Well, I reckon I ought to be right proud."

"I guess so."

"Am I still king around here?"

120   Norma Jean flexes her biceps and feels them for hardness. "I'm not fooling around with anybody, if that's what you mean," she says.

"Would you tell me if you were?"

"I don't know."

"What does *your* name mean?"

"It was Marilyn Monroe's real name."

125   "No kidding!"

"Norma comes from the Normans. They were invaders," she says. She closes her book and looks hard at Leroy. "I'll go to Shiloh with you if you'll stop staring at me."

On Sunday, Norma Jean packs a picnic and they go to Shiloh. To Leroy's relief Mabel says she does not want to come with them. Norma Jean drives, and Leroy, sitting beside her, feels like some boring hitchhiker she has picked up. He tries some conversation, but she answers him in monosyllables. At Shiloh, she drives aimlessly through the park, past bluffs and trails and steep ravines. Shiloh is an immense place, and Leroy cannot see it as a battleground. It is not what he expected. He thought it would look like a golf course. Monuments are everywhere, showing through the thick clusters of trees. Norma Jean passes the log cabin Mabel mentioned. It is surrounded by tourists looking for bullet holes.

"That's not the kind of log house I've got in mind," says Leroy apologetically.

"I know *that*."

130   "This is a pretty place. Your mama was right."

"It's O.K.," says Norma Jean. "Well, we've seen it. I hope she's satisfied."

They burst out laughing together.

At the park museum, a movie on Shiloh is shown every half hour, but they decide that they don't want to see it. They buy a souvenir Confederate flag for Mabel, and then they find a picnic spot near the cemetery. Norma Jean has brought a picnic cooler, with pimento sandwiches, soft drinks, and

Yodels. Leroy eats a sandwich and then smokes a joint, hiding it behind the picnic cooler. Norma Jean has quit smoking altogether. She is picking cake crumbs from the cellophane wrapper, like a fussy bird.

Leroy says, "So the boys in gray ended up in Corinth. The Union soldiers zapped 'em finally. April 7, 1862."

135   They both know that he doesn't know any history. He is just talking about some of the historical plaques they have read. He feels awkward, like a boy on a date with an older girl. They are still just making conversation.

"Corinth is where Mama eloped to," says Norma Jean.

They sit in silence and stare at the cemetery for the Union dead and, beyond, at a tall cluster of trees. Campers are parked nearby, bumper to bumper, and small children in bright clothing are cavorting and squealing. Norma Jean wads up the cake wrapper and squeezes it tightly in her hand. Without looking at Leroy, she says, "I want to leave you."

Leroy takes a bottle of Coke out of the cooler and flips off the cap. He holds the bottle poised near his mouth but cannot remember to take a drink. Finally he says, "No, you don't."

"Yes, I do."

140   "I won't let you."

"You can't stop me."

"Don't do me that way."

Leroy knows Norma Jean will have her own way. "Didn't I promise to be home from now on?" he says.

"In some ways, a woman prefers a man who wanders," says Norma Jean. "That sounds crazy, I know."

145   "You're not crazy." Leroy remembers to drink from his Coke. Then he says, "Yes, you *are* crazy. You and me could start all over again. Right back at the beginning."

"We *have* started all over again," says Norma Jean. "And this is how it turned out."

"What did I do wrong?"

"Nothing."

"Is this one of those women's lib things?" Leroy asks.

150   "Don't be funny."

The cemetery, a green slope dotted with white markers, looks like a subdivision site. Leroy is trying to comprehend that his marriage is breaking up, but for some reason he is wondering about white slabs in a graveyard.

"Everything was fine till Mama caught me smoking," says Norma Jean, standing up. "That set something off."

"What are you talking about?"

"She won't leave me alone—*you* won't leave me alone." Norma Jean seems to be crying, but she is looking away from him. "I feel eighteen again. I can't face that all over again." She starts walking away. "No, it *wasn't* fine. I don't know what I'm saying. Forget it."

155   Leroy takes a lungful of smoke and closes his eyes as Norma Jean's words sink in. He tries to focus on the fact that thirty-five hundred soldiers died on the grounds around him. He can only think of that war as a board game with plastic soldiers. Leroy almost smiles, as he compares the Confederates' daring attack on the Union camps and Virgil Mathis's raid on the bowling alley. General Grant, drunk and furious, shoved the Southerners back to Corinth, where Mabel and Jet Beasley were married years later,

when Mabel was still thin and good-looking. The next day, Mabel and Jet visited the battleground, and then Norma Jean was born, and then she married Leroy and they had a baby, which they lost, and now Leroy and Norma Jean are here at the same battleground. Leroy knows he is leaving out a lot. He is leaving out the insides of history. History was always just names and dates to him. It occurs to him that building a house of logs is similarly empty—too simple. And the real inner workings of a marriage, like most of history, have escaped him. Now he sees that building a log house is the dumbest idea he could have had. It was clumsy of him to think Norma Jean would want a log house. It was a crazy idea. He'll have to think of something else, quickly. He will wad the blueprints into tight balls and fling them into the lake. Then he'll get moving again. He opens his eyes. Norma Jean has moved away and is walking through the cemetery, following a serpentine brick path.

Leroy gets up to follow his wife, but his good leg is asleep and his bad leg still hurts him. Norma Jean is far away, walking rapidly toward the bluff by the river, and he tries to hobble toward her. Some children run past him, screaming noisily. Norma Jean has reached the bluff, and she is looking out over the Tennessee River. Now she turns toward Leroy and waves her arms. Is she beckoning to him? She seems to be doing an exercise for her chest muscles. The sky is unusually pale—the color of the dust ruffle Mabel made for their bed.

GUY DE MAUPASSANT

Guy de Maupassant (1850–1893) was born in Dieppe, France. (When referring to him by his last name only, the name is Maupassant, not de Maupassant.) He studied law briefly, served in the Franco-Prussian War (1870–1871), and then lived in Paris, where he met such distinguished writers as Émile Zola and Gustave Flaubert. Maupassant for a time worked as a civil servant, but he resigned his job in 1880 when he published (in an anthology edited by Zola) the first of his two hundred or so stories. He had meanwhile contracted syphilis, which in later years affected his mind. He attempted suicide in 1891 and was confined to an asylum, where he died two years later.

The Necklace   [1885]

Translated by Marjorie Laurie

She was one of those pretty and charming girls who are sometimes, as if by a mistake of destiny, born in a family of clerks. She had no dowry, no expectations, no means of being known, understood, loved, wedded by any rich and distinguished man; and she let herself be married to a little clerk at the Ministry of Public Instruction.

She dressed plainly because she could not dress well, but she was as unhappy as though she had really fallen from her proper station, since with women there is neither caste nor rank: and beauty, grace and charm act instead of family and birth. Natural fineness, instinct for what is elegant, suppleness of wit, are the sole hierarchy, and make from women of the people the equals of the very greatest ladies.

She suffered ceaselessly, feeling herself born for all the delicacies and all the luxuries. She suffered from the poverty of her dwelling, from the wretched look of the walls, from the worn-out chairs, from the ugliness of the curtains. All those things, of which another woman of her rank would never even have been conscious, tortured her and made her angry. The sight of the little Breton peasant who did her humble housework aroused in her regrets which were despairing, and distracted dreams. She thought of the silent antechambers hung with Oriental tapestry, lit by tall bronze candelabra, and of the two great footmen in knee breeches who sleep in the big armchairs, made drowsy by the heavy warmth of the hot-air stove. She thought of the long *salons*[1] fitted up with ancient silk, of the delicate furniture carrying priceless curiosities, and of the coquettish perfumed boudoirs made for talks at five o'clock with intimate friends, with men famous and sought after, whom all women envy and whose attention they all desire.

When she sat down to dinner, before the round table covered with a table-cloth three days old, opposite her husband, who uncovered the soup tureen and declared with an enchanted air, "Ah, the good *pot-au-feu!*[2] I don't know anything better than that," she thought of dainty dinners, of shining silverware, of tapestry which peopled the walls with ancient personages and with strange birds flying in the midst of a fairy forest; and she thought of delicious dishes served on marvelous plates, and of the whispered gallantries which you listen to with a sphinxlike smile, while you are eating the pink flesh of a trout or the wings of a quail.

5   She had no dresses, no jewels, nothing. And she loved nothing but that; she felt made for that. She would so have liked to please, to be envied, to be charming, to be sought after.

She had a friend, a former schoolmate at the convent, who was rich, and whom she did not like to go and see any more, because she suffered so much when she came back.

But one evening, her husband returned home with a triumphant air, and holding a large envelope in his hand.

"There," said he. "Here is something for you."

She tore the paper sharply, and drew out a printed card which bore these words:

10   "The Minister of Public Instruction and Mme. Georges Ramponneau
request the honor of M. and Mme. Loisel's company at the palace of
the Ministry on Monday evening, January eighteenth."

Instead of being delighted, as her husband hoped, she threw the invitation on the table with disdain, murmuring:

"What do you want me to do with that?"

"But, my dear, I thought you would be glad. You never go out, and this is such a fine opportunity. I had awful trouble to get it. Everyone wants to go; it is very select, and they are not giving many invitations to clerks. The whole official world will be there."

She looked at him with an irritated glance, and said, impatiently:

15   "And what do you want me to put on my back?"

---

[1]**salons** drawing rooms.   [2]**pot-au-feu** stew.

He had not thought of that; he stammered:

"Why, the dress you go to the theater in. It looks very well, to me."

He stopped, distracted, seeing his wife was crying. Two great tears descended slowly from the corners of her eyes toward the corners of her mouth. He stuttered:

"What's the matter? What's the matter?"

20   But, by violent effort, she had conquered her grief, and she replied, with a calm voice, while she wiped her wet cheeks:

"Nothing. Only I have no dress and therefore I can't go to this ball. Give your card to some colleague whose wife is better equipped than I."

He was in despair. He resumed:

"Come, let us see, Mathilde. How much would it cost, a suitable dress, which you could use on other occasions, something very simple?"

She reflected several seconds, making her calculations and wondering also what sum she could ask without drawing on herself an immediate refusal and a frightened exclamation from the economical clerk.

25   Finally, she replied, hesitatingly:

"I don't know exactly, but I think I could manage it with four hundred francs."

He had grown a little pale, because he was laying aside just that amount to buy a gun and treat himself to a little shooting next summer on the plain of Nanterre, with several friends who went to shoot larks down there, of a Sunday.

But he said:

"All right. I will give you four hundred francs. And try to have a pretty dress."

30   The day of the ball drew near, and Mme. Loisel seemed sad, uneasy, anxious. Her dress was ready, however. Her husband said to her one evening:

"What is the matter? Come, you've been so queer these last three days."

And she answered:

"It annoys me not to have a single jewel, not a single stone, nothing to put on. I shall look like distress. I should almost rather not go at all."

He resumed:

35   "You might wear natural flowers. It's very stylish at this time of the year. For ten francs you can get two or three magnificent roses."

She was not convinced.

"No; there's nothing more humiliating than to look poor among other women who are rich."

But her husband cried:

"How stupid you are! Go look up your friend Mme. Forestier, and ask her to lend you some jewels. You're quite thick enough with her to do that."

40   She uttered a cry of joy:

"It's true. I never thought of it."

The next day she went to her friend and told of her distress.

Mme. Forestier went to a wardrobe with a glass door, took out a large jewel-box, brought it back, opened it, and said to Mme. Loisel:

"Choose, my dear."

45   She saw first of all some bracelets, then a pearl necklace, then a Venetian cross, gold and precious stones of admirable workmanship. She tried on the ornaments before the glass, hesitated, could not make up her mind to part with them, to give them back. She kept asking:

"Haven't you any more?"

"Why, yes. Look. I don't know what you like."

All of a sudden she discovered, in a black satin box, a superb necklace of diamonds, and her heart began to beat with an immoderate desire. Her hands trembled as she took it. She fastened it around her throat, outside her high-necked dress, and remained lost in ecstasy at the sight of herself.

Then she asked, hesitating, filled with anguish:

50   "Can you lend me that, only that?"

"Why, yes, certainly."

She sprang upon the neck of her friend, kissed her passionately, then fled with her treasure.

The day of the ball arrived. Mme. Loisel made a great success. She was prettier than them all, elegant, gracious, smiling, and crazy with joy. All the men looked at her, asked her name, endeavored to be introduced. All the attachés of the Cabinet wanted to waltz with her. She was remarked by the minister himself.

She danced with intoxication, with passion, made drunk by pleasure, forgetting all, in the triumph of her beauty, in the glory of her success, in a sort of cloud of happiness composed of all this homage, of all this admiration, of all these awakened desires, and of that sense of complete victory which is so sweet to a woman's heart.

55   She went away about four o'clock in the morning. Her husband had been sleeping since midnight, in a little deserted anteroom, with three other gentlemen whose wives were having a very good time. He threw over her shoulders the wraps which he had brought, modest wraps of common life, whose poverty contrasted with the elegance of the ball dress. She felt this, and wanted to escape so as not to be remarked by the other women, who were enveloping themselves in costly furs.

Loisel held her back.

"Wait a bit. You will catch cold outside. I will go and call a cab."

But she did not listen to him, and rapidly descended the stairs. When they were in the street they did not find a carriage; and they began to look for one, shouting after the cabmen whom they saw passing by at a distance.

They went down toward the Seine, in despair, shivering with cold. At last they found on the quay one of those ancient noctambulant coupés which, exactly as if they were ashamed to show their misery during the day, are never seen round Paris until after nightfall.

60   It took them to their door in the Rue des Martyrs, and once more, sadly, they climbed up homeward. All was ended, for her. And as to him, he reflected that he must be at the Ministry at ten o'clock.

She removed the wraps which covered her shoulders, before the glass, so as once more to see herself in all her glory. But suddenly she uttered a cry. She no longer had the necklace around her neck!

Her husband, already half undressed, demanded:

"What is the matter with you?"

She turned madly toward him:

65   "I have—I have—I've lost Mme. Forestier's necklace."

He stood up, distracted.

"What!—how?—impossible!"

And they looked in the folds of her dress, in the folds of her cloak, in her pockets, everywhere. They did not find it.

He asked:

70   "You're sure you had it on when you left the ball?"

"Yes, I felt it in the vestibule of the palace."

"But if you had lost it in the street we should have heard it fall. It must be in the cab."

"Yes. Probably. Did you take his number?"

"No. And you, didn't you notice it?"

75   "No."

They looked, thunderstruck, at one another. At last Loisel put on his clothes.

"I shall go back on foot," said he, "over the whole route which we have taken to see if I can find it."

And he went out. She sat waiting on a chair in her ball dress, without strength to go to bed, overwhelmed, without fire, without a thought.

Her husband came back about seven o'clock. He had found nothing.

80   He went to Police Headquarters, to the newspaper offices, to offer a reward: he went to the cab companies—everywhere, in fact, whither he was urged by the least suspicion of hope.

She waited all day, in the same condition of mad fear before this terrible calamity.

Loisel returned at night with a hollow, pale face; he had discovered nothing.

"You must write to your friend," said he, "that you have broken the clasp of her necklace and that you are having it mended. That will give us time to turn round."

She wrote at his dictation.

85   At the end of a week they had lost all hope.

And Loisel, who had aged five years, declared:

"We must consider how to replace that ornament."

The next day they took the box which had contained it, and they went to the jeweler whose name was found within. He consulted his books.

"It was not I, madame, who sold that necklace; I must simply have furnished the case."

90   Then they went from jeweler to jeweler, searching for a necklace like the other, consulting their memories, sick both of them with chagrin and anguish.

They found, in a shop at the Palais Royal, a string of diamonds which seemed to them exactly like the one they looked for. It was worth forty thousand francs. They could have it for thirty-six.

So they begged the jeweler not to sell it for three days yet. And they made a bargain that he should buy it back for thirty-four thousand francs, in case they found the other one before the end of February.

Loisel possessed eighteen thousand francs which his father had left him. He would borrow the rest.

He did borrow, asking a thousand francs of one, five hundred of another, five louis[3] here, three louis there. He gave notes, took up ruinous obligations, dealt with usurers and all the race of lenders. He compromised all the rest of his life, risked his signature without even knowing if he could

_____

[3]**louis** a gold coin worth 20 francs.

meet it; and, frightened by the pains yet to come, by the black misery which was about to fall upon him, by the prospect of all the physical privation and of all the moral tortures which he was to suffer, he went to get the new necklace, putting down upon the merchant's counter thirty-six thousand francs.

95   When Mme. Loisel took back the necklace, Mme. Forestier said to her, with a chilly manner:

"You should have returned it sooner; I might have needed it."

She did not open the case, as her friend had so much feared. If she had detected the substitution, what would she have thought, what would she have said? Would she not have taken Mme. Loisel for a thief?

Mme. Loisel now knew the horrible existence of the needy. She took her part, moreover, all of a sudden, with heroism. That dreadful debt must be paid. She would pay it. They dismissed their servant; they changed their lodgings; they rented a garret under the roof.

She came to know what heavy housework meant and the odious cares of the kitchen. She washed the dishes, using her rosy nails on the greasy pots and pans. She washed the dirty linen, the shirts, and the dishcloths, which she dried upon a line; she carried the slops down to the street every morning, and carried up the water, stopping for breath at every landing. And, dressed like a woman of the people, she went to the fruiterer, the grocer, the butcher, her basket on her arm, bargaining, insulted, defending her miserable money sou by sou.

100   Each month they had to meet some notes, renew others, obtain more time.

Her husband worked in the evening making a fair copy of some tradesman's accounts, and late at night he often copied manuscript for five sous a page.

And this life lasted for ten years.

At the end of ten years, they had paid everything, everything, with the rates of usury, and the accumulations of the compound interest.

Mme. Loisel looked old now. She had become the woman of impoverished households—strong and hard and rough. With frowsy hair, skirts askew, and red hands, she talked loud while washing the floor with great swishes of water. But sometimes, when her husband was at the office, she sat down near the window, and she thought of that gay evening of long ago, of the ball where she had been so beautiful and so fêted.

105   What would have happened if she had not lost that necklace? Who knows? Who knows? How life is strange and changeful! How little a thing is needed for us to be lost or to be saved!

But, one Sunday, having gone to take a walk in the Champs Elysées to refresh herself from the labor of the week, she suddenly perceived a woman who was leading a child. It was Mme. Forestier, still young, still beautiful, still charming.

Mme. Loisel felt moved. Was she going to speak to her? Yes, certainly. And now that she had paid, she was going to tell her all about it. Why not?

She went up.

"Good day, Jeanne."

110   The other, astonished to be familiarly addressed by this plain goodwife, did not recognize her at all, and stammered:

"But—madam!—I do not know—You must be mistaken."

"No. I am Mathilde Loisel."

Her friend uttered a cry.

"Oh, my poor Mathilde! How you are changed!"

115   "Yes, I have had days hard enough, since I have seen you, days wretched enough—and that because of you!"

"Of me! How so?"

"Do you remember that diamond necklace which you lent me to wear at the ministerial ball?"

"Yes. Well?"

"Well, I lost it."

120   "What do you mean? You brought it back."

"I brought you back another just like it. And for this we have been ten years paying. You can understand that it was not easy for us, us who had nothing. At last it is ended, and I am very glad."

Mme. Forestier had stopped.

"You say that you bought a necklace of diamonds to replace mine?"

"Yes. You never noticed it, then! They were very like."

125   And she smiled with a joy which was proud and naïve at once.

Mme. Forestier, strongly moved, took her two hands.

"Oh, my poor Mathilde! Why, my necklace was paste. It was worth at most five hundred francs!"

LORRIE MOORE

Lorrie Moore, born Marie Lorena Moore in 1957 in Glen Falls, New York, did her undergraduate work at St. Lawrence University and received an MFA, from Cornell University. While still an undergraduate she won first prize in the nationwide Seventeen *magazine short story contest (1976), and she has won numerous prizes in recent years. She is the author of stories, novels, and essays. Recent books include* The Collected Stories *(2008) and the novel* A Gate at the Stairs *(2009). We reprint a story from her first collection,* Self-Help *(1985). This story, like most of the stories in* Self-Help, *is written in what Moore in an interview (in* Contemporary Authors: New Revision Series, *No. 39, 1992) called "The second person, mock-imperative narrative." She went on to explain:*

Let's see what happens when one eliminates the subject, leaves the verb shivering at the start of a clause; what happens when one appropriates the "how-to" form for a fiction, for an irony, for a "how-not-to." I was interested in whatever tensions resulted when a writer foisted fictional experience off of the "I" of the first person and onto the more generalized "you" of the second—the vernacular "one."

The second person stories begin, ostensibly, to tell the generic tale, give the categorical advice, but become so entrenched in their own individuated details that they succeed in telling only their own specific story, suggesting that although life is certainly not jokeless, it probably is remediless.

How to Become a Writer

[1985]

First, try to be something, anything, else. A movie star/astronaut. A movie star/missionary. A movie star/kindergarten teacher. President of the World. Fail miserably. It is best if you fail at an early age—say, fourteen. Early, critical disillusionment is necessary so that at fifteen you can write long haiku sequences about thwarted desire. It is a pond, a cherry blossom, a wind brushing against sparrow wing leaving for mountain. Count the syllables. Show it to your mom. She is tough and practical. She has a son in Vietnam and a husband who may be having an affair. She believes in wearing brown because it hides spots. She'll look briefly at your writing, then back up at you with a face blank as a donut. She'll say: "How about emptying the dishwasher?" Look away. Shove the forks in the fork drawer. Accidentally break one of the freebie gas station glasses. This is the required pain and suffering. This is only for starters.

In your high school English class look at Mr. Killian's face. Decide faces are important. Write a villanelle about pores. Struggle. Write a sonnet. Count the syllables: nine, ten, eleven, thirteen. Decide to experiment with fiction. Here you don't have to count syllables. Write a short story about an elderly man and woman who accidentally shoot each other in the head, the result of an inexplicable malfunction of a shotgun which appears mysteriously in their living room one night. Give it to Mr. Killian as your final project. When you get it back, he has written on it: "Some of your images are quite nice, but you have no sense of plot." When you are home, in the privacy of your own room, faintly scrawl in pencil beneath his black-inked comments: "Plots are for dead people, pore-face."

Take all the babysitting jobs you can get. You are great with kids. They love you. You tell them stories about old people who die idiot deaths. You sing them songs like "Blue Bells of Scotland," which is their favorite. And when they are in their pajamas and have finally stopped pinching each other, when they are fast asleep, you read every sex manual in the house, and wonder how on earth anyone could ever do those things with someone they truly loved. Fall asleep in a chair reading Mr. McMurphy's *Playboy.* When the McMurphys come home, they will tap you on the shoulder, look at the magazine in your lap, and grin. You will want to die. They will ask you if Tracey took her medicine all right. Explain, yes, she did, that you promised her a story if she would take it like a big girl and that seemed to work out just fine. "Oh, marvelous," they will exclaim.

Try to smile proudly.

5   Apply to college as a child psychology major.

As a child psychology major, you have some electives. You've always liked birds. Sign up for something called "The Ornithological Field Trip." It meets Tuesdays and Thursdays at two. When you arrive at Room 134 on the first day of class, everyone is sitting around a seminar table talking about metaphors. You've heard of these. After a short, excruciating while, raise your hand and say diffidently, "Excuse me, isn't this Birdwatching One-oh-one?" The class stops and turns to look at you. They seem to all have one face—giant and blank as a vandalized clock. Someone with a beard booms out, "No, this is Creative Writing." Say: "Oh—right," as if perhaps you knew all along. Look down at your schedule. Wonder how the hell you ended up here. The computer, apparently, has made an error. You start to get up to leave and then don't. The lines at the registrar this week are huge. Perhaps you should stick with this mistake. Perhaps your creative writing isn't all that bad. Perhaps it is fate. Perhaps this is what your dad meant when he said, "It's the age of computers, Francie, it's the age of computers."

Decide that you like college life. In your dorm, you meet many nice people. Some are smarter than you. And some, you notice, are dumber than you. You will continue, unfortunately, to view the world in exactly these terms for the rest of your life.

The assignment this week in creative writing is to narrate a violent happening. Turn in a story about driving with your Uncle Gordon and another one about two old people who are accidentally electrocuted when they go to turn on a badly wired desk lamp. The teacher will hand them back to you with comments: "Much of your writing is smooth and energetic. You have, however, a ludicrous notion of plot." Write another story about a man and a woman who, in the very first paragraph, have their lower torsos accidentally blitzed away by dynamite. In the second paragraph, with the insurance money, they buy a frozen yogurt stand together. There are six more paragraphs. You read the whole thing out loud in class. No one likes it. They say your sense of plot is outrageous and incompetent. After class someone asks you if you are crazy.

Decide that perhaps you should stick to comedies. Start dating someone who is funny, someone who has what in high school you called a "really great sense of humor" and what now your creative writing class calls "self-contempt giving rise to comic form." Write down all of his jokes, but don't tell him you are doing this. Make up anagrams of his old girlfriend's name and name all of your socially handicapped characters with them. Tell him his old girlfriend is in all of your stories and then watch how funny he can be, see what a really great sense of humor he can have.

10   Your child psychology advisor tells you you are neglecting courses in your major. What you spend the most time on should be what you're majoring in. Say yes, you understand.

In creative writing seminars over the next two years, everyone continues to smoke cigarettes and ask the same things: "But does it work?" "Why should we care about this character?" "Have you earned this cliché?" These seem like important questions.

On days when it is your turn, you look at the class hopefully as they scour your mimeographs for a plot. They look back up at you, drag deeply, and then smile in a sweet sort of way.

You spend too much time slouched and demoralized. Your boyfriend suggests bicycling. Your roommate suggests a new boyfriend. You are said to be self-mutilating and losing weight, but you continue writing. The only happiness you have is writing something new, in the middle of the night, armpits damp, heart pounding, something no one has yet seen. You have only those brief, fragile, untested moments of exhilaration when you know:

you are a genius. Understand what you must do. Switch majors. The kids in your nursery project will be disappointed, but you have a calling, an urge, a delusion, an unfortunate habit. You have, as your mother would say, fallen in with a bad crowd.

Why write? Where does writing come from? These are questions to ask yourself. They are like: Where does dust come from? Or: Why is there war? Or: If there's a God, then why is my brother now a cripple?

15   These are questions that you keep in your wallet, like calling cards. These are questions, your creative writing teacher says, that are good to address in your journals but rarely in your fiction.

The writing professor this fall is stressing the Power of the Imagination. Which means he doesn't want long descriptive stories about your camping trip last July. He wants you to start in a realistic context but then to alter it. Like recombinant DNA. He wants you to let your imagination sail, to let it grow big-bellied in the wind. This is a quote from Shakespeare.

Tell your roommate your great idea, your great exercise of imaginative power: a transformation of Melville to contemporary life. It will be about mono-mania and the fish-eat-fish world of life insurance in Rochester, New York. The first line will be "Call me Fishmeal," and it will feature a menopausal suburban husband named Richard, who because he is so depressed all the time is called "Mopey Dick" by his witty wife Elaine. Say to your roommate: "Mopey Dick, get it?" Your roommate looks at you, her face blank as a large Kleenex. She comes up to you, like a buddy, and puts an arm around your burdened shoulders. "Listen, Francie," she says, slow as speech therapy. "Let's go out and get a big beer."

The seminar doesn't like this one either. You suspect they are beginning to feel sorry for you. They say: "You have to think about what is happening. Where is the story here?"

The next semester the writing professor is obsessed with writing from personal experience. You must write from what you know, from what has happened to you. He wants deaths, he wants camping trips. Think about what has happened to you. In three years there have been three things: you lost your virginity; your parents got divorced; and your brother came home from a forest ten miles from the Cambodian border with only half a thigh, a permanent smirk nestled into one corner of his mouth.

20   About the first you write: "It created a new space, which hurt and cried in a voice that wasn't mine, 'I'm not the same anymore, but I'll be okay.'"

About the second you write an elaborate story of an old married couple who stumble upon an unknown land mine in their kitchen and accidentally blow themselves up. You call it: "For Better or for Liverwurst."

About the last you write nothing. There are no words for this. Your typewriter hums. You can find no words.

At undergraduate cocktail parties, people say, "Oh, you write? What do you write about?" Your roommate, who has consumed too much wine, too little cheese, and no crackers at all, blurts: "Oh, my god, she always writes about her dumb boyfriend."

Later on in life you will learn that writers are merely open, helpless texts with no real understanding of what they have written and therefore must half-believe anything and everything that is said of them. You, however, have not yet reached this stage of literary criticism. You stiffen and say, "I do not," the same way you said it when someone in the fourth grade accused you of really liking oboe lessons and your parents really weren't just making you take them.

25   Insist you are not very interested in any one subject at all, that you are interested in the music of language, that you are interested in—in—syllables, because they are the atoms of poetry, the cells of the mind, the breath of the soul. Begin to feel woozy. Stare into your plastic wine cup.

"Syllables?" you will hear someone ask, voice trailing off, as they glide slowly toward the reassuring white of the dip.

Begin to wonder what you do write about. Or if you have anything to say. Or if there even is such a thing as a thing to say. Limit these thoughts to no more than ten minutes a day; like sit-ups, they can make you thin.

You will read somewhere that all writing has to do with one's genitals. Don't dwell on this. It will make you nervous.

Your mother will come visit you. She will look at the circles under your eyes and hand you a brown book with a brown briefcase on the cover. It is entitled: *How to Become a Business Executive.* She has also brought the *Names for Baby* encyclopedia you asked for; one of your characters, the aging clown-school teacher, needs a new name. Your mother will shake her head and say: "Francie, Francie, remember when you were going to be a child psychology major?"

30   Say: "Mom, I like to write."

She'll say: "Sure you like to write. Of course. Sure you like to write."

Write a story about a confused music student and title it: "Schubert Was the One with the Glasses, Right?" It's not a big hit, although your roommate likes the part where the two violinists accidentally blow themselves up in a recital room. "I went out with a violinist once," she says, snapping her gum.

Thank god you are taking other courses. You can find sanctuary in nineteenth-century ontological snags and invertebrate courting rituals. Certain globular mollusks have what is called "Sex by the Arm." The male octopus, for instance, loses the end of one arm when placing it inside the female body during intercourse. Marine biologists call it "Seven Heaven." Be glad you know these things. Be glad you are not just a writer. Apply to law school.

From here on in, many things can happen. But the main one will be this: you decide not to go to law school after all, and, instead, you spend a good, big chunk of your adult life telling people how you decided not to go to law school after all. Somehow you end up writing again. Perhaps you go to graduate school. Perhaps you work odd jobs and take writing courses at night. Perhaps you are working on a novel and writing down all the clever remarks and intimate personal confessions you hear during the day. Perhaps you are losing your pals, your acquaintances, your balance.

35   You have broken up with your boyfriend. You now go out with men who, instead of whispering "I love you," shout: "Do it to me, baby." This is good for your writing.

Sooner or later you have a finished manuscript more or less. People look at it in a vaguely troubled sort of way and say, "I'll bet becoming a writer was always a fantasy of yours, wasn't it?" Your lips dry to salt. Say that of all the fantasies possible in the world, you can't imagine being a writer even making the top twenty. Tell them you were going to be a child psychology major. "I bet," they always sigh, "you'd be great with kids." Scowl fiercely. Tell them you're a walking blade.

Quit classes. Quit jobs. Cash in old savings bonds. Now you have time like warts on your hands. Slowly copy all of your friends' addresses into a new address book.

Vacuum. Chew cough drops. Keep a folder full of fragments.

An eyelid darkening sideways.
40   *World as conspiracy.*
Possible plot? A woman gets on a bus.
Suppose you threw a love affair and nobody came.

At home drink a lot of coffee. At Howard Johnson's order the cole slaw. Consider how it looks like the soggy confetti of a map: where you've been, where you're going—"You Are Here," says the red star on the back of the menu.

Occasionally a date with a face blank as a sheet of paper asks you whether writers often become discouraged. Say that sometimes they do and sometimes they do. Say it's a lot like having polio.

45   "Interesting," smiles your date, and then he looks down at his arm hairs and starts to smooth them, all, always, in the same direction.

ALICE MUNRO

Alice Munro was born in 1931 in Wingham, Ontario, a relatively rural community and the sort of place in which she sets much of her fiction. She began publishing stories when she was an undergraduate at the University of Western Ontario. She left Western after two years, worked in a library and in a bookstore, then married, moved to Victoria, British Columbia, and founded a bookstore there. She continued to write while raising three children. She divorced and remarried; much of her fiction concerns marriage or divorce, which is to say it concerns shifting relationships in a baffling world. Munro's recent books include two collections of short stories, The View from Castle Rock *(2006) and* Too Much Happiness *(2009).*

Boys and Girls   [1968]

My father was a fox farmer. That is, he raised silver foxes, in pens; and in the fall and early winter, when their fur was prime, he killed them and skinned them and sold their pelts to the Hudson's Bay Company or the Montreal Fur Traders. These companies supplied us with heroic calendars to hang, one on each side of the kitchen door. Against a background of cold blue sky and black pine forests and treacherous northern rivers, plumed adventurers planted the flags of England or of France; magnificent savages bent their backs to the portage.

For several weeks before Christmas, my father worked after supper in the cellar of our house. The cellar was whitewashed, and lit by a hundred-watt bulb over the worktable. My brother Laird and I sat on the top step and watched. My father removed the pelt inside-out from the body of the fox, which looked surprisingly small, mean and rat-like, deprived of its arrogant weight of fur. The naked, slippery bodies were collected in a sack and buried at the dump. One time the hired man, Henry Bailey, had taken a swipe at me with this sack, saying, "Christmas present!" My mother thought that was not funny. In fact she disliked the whole pelting operation—that was what the killing, skinning, and preparation of the furs was called—and wished it did not have to take place in the house. There was the smell. After the pelt had been stretched inside-out on a long board my father scraped away delicately, removing the little clotted webs of blood vessels, the bubbles of fat; the smell of blood and animal fat, with the strong primitive odour of the fox itself, penetrated all parts of the house. I found it reassuringly seasonal, like the smell of oranges and pine needles.

Henry Bailey suffered from bronchial troubles. He would cough and cough until his narrow face turned scarlet, and his light blue, derisive eyes filled up with tears; then he took the lid off the stove, and, standing well back, shot out a great clot of phlegm—hsss—straight into the heart of the flames. We admired him for this performance and for his ability to make his stomach growl at will, and for his laughter, which was full of high whistlings and gurglings and involved the whole faulty machinery of his chest. It was sometimes hard to tell what he was laughing at, and always possible that it might be us.

After we had been sent to bed we could still smell fox and still hear Henry's laugh, but these things, reminders of the warm, safe, brightly lit downstairs world, seemed lost and diminished, floating on the stale cold air upstairs. We were afraid at night in the winter. We were not afraid of *outside* though this was the time of year when snowdrifts curled around our house like sleeping whales and the wind harassed us all night, coming up from the buried fields, the frozen swamp, with its old bugbear chorus of threats and misery. We were afraid of *inside,* the room where we slept. At this time the upstairs of our house was not finished. A brick chimney went up one wall. In the middle of the floor was a square hole, with a wooden railing around it; that was where the stairs came up. On the other side of the stairwell were the things that nobody had any use for anymore—a soldiery roll of linoleum, standing on end, a wicker baby carriage, a fern basket, china jugs and basins with cracks in them, a picture of the Battle of Balaclava,[1] very sad to look at. I had told Laird, as soon as he was old enough to understand such things, that bats and skeletons lived over there; whenever a man escaped from the county jail, twenty miles away, I imagined that he had somehow let himself in the window and was hiding behind the linoleum. But we had rules to

---

[1]**Battle of Balaclava** A major battle, fought in October 1854, during the Crimean War. It culminated in the tragic Charge of the Light Brigade.

keep us safe. When the light was on, we were safe as long as we did not step off the square of worn carpet which defined our bedroom-space; when the light was off no place was safe but the beds themselves. I had to turn out the light kneeling on the end of my bed, and stretching as far as I could to reach the cord.

5   In the dark we lay on our beds, our narrow life rafts, and fixed our eyes on the faint light coming up the stairwell, and sang songs. Laird sang "Jingle Bells," which he would sing any time, whether it was Christmas or not, and I sang "Danny Boy." I loved the sound of my own voice, frail and supplicating, rising in the dark. We could make out the tall frosted shapes of the windows now, gloomy and white. When I came to the part, *When I am dead, as dead I well may be*—a fit of shivering caused not by the cold sheets but by plea-surable emotion almost silenced me. *You'll kneel and say, an Ave there above me*—What was an Ave? Every day I forgot to find out.

Laird went straight from singing to sleep. I could hear his long, satisfied, bubbly breaths. Now for the time that remained to me, the most perfectly private and perhaps the best time of the whole day, I arranged myself tightly under the covers and went on with one of the stories I was telling myself from night to night. These stories were about myself, when I had grown a lit-tle older; they took place in a world that was recognizably mine, yet one that presented opportunities for courage, boldness and self-sacrifice, as mine never did. I rescued people from a bombed building (it discouraged me that the real war had gone on so far away from Jubilee). I shot two rabid wolves who were menacing the schoolyard (the teachers cowered terrified at my back). I rode a fine horse spiritedly down the main street of Jubilee, ac-knowledging the townspeople's gratitude for some yet-to-be-worked-out piece of heroism (nobody ever rode a horse there, except King Billy in the Orangemen's Day[2] parade). There was always riding and shooting in these stories, though I had only been on a horse twice—bareback because we did not own a saddle—and the second time I had slid right around and dropped under the horse's feet; it had stepped placidly over me. I really was learning to shoot, but I could not hit anything yet, not even tin cans on fence posts.

Alive, the foxes inhabited a world my father made for them. It was sur-rounded by a high guard fence, like a medieval town, with a gate that was padlocked at night. Along the streets of this town were ranged large, sturdy pens. Each of them had a real door that a man could go through, a wooden ramp along the wire, for the foxes to run up and down on, and a kennel—something like a clothes chest with airholes—where they slept and stayed in winter and had their young. There were feeding and watering dishes at-tached to the wire in such a way that they could be emptied and cleaned from the outside. The dishes were made of old tin cans, and the ramps and kennels of odds and ends of old lumber. Everything was tidy and ingenious; my father was tirelessly inventive and his favourite book in the world was *Robinson Crusoe*. He had fitted a tin drum on a wheelbarrow, for bringing water down to the pens. This was my job in summer, when the foxes had to

---

[2]**Orangemen's Day** The Orange Society is named for William of Orange, who, as King William III of England, defeated James II of England at the Battle of the Boyne on 12 July 1690. It sponsors an annual procession on 12 July.

have water twice a day. Between nine and ten o'clock in the morning, and again after supper, I filled the drum at the pump and trundled it down through the barnyard to the pens, where I parked it, and filled my watering can and went along the streets. Laird came too, with his little cream and green gardening can, filled too full and knocking against his legs and slopping water on his canvas shoes. I had the real watering can, my father's, though I could only carry it three-quarters full.

The foxes all had names, which were printed on a tin plate and hung beside their doors. They were not named when they were born, but when they survived the first year's pelting and were added to the breeding stock. Those my father had named were called names like Prince, Bob, Wally and Betty. Those I had named were called Star or Turk, or Maureen or Diana. Laird named one Maud after a hired girl we had when he was little, one Harold after a boy at school, and one Mexico, he did not say why.

Naming them did not make pets out of them, or anything like it. Nobody but my father ever went into the pens, and he had twice had blood-poisoning from bites. When I was bringing them their water they prowled up and down on the paths they had made inside their pens, barking seldom—they saved that for nighttime, when they might get up a chorus of community frenzy—but always watching me, their eyes burning, clear gold, in their pointed, malevolent faces. They were beautiful for their delicate legs and heavy, aristocratic tails and the bright fur sprinkled on dark down their backs—which gave them their name—but especially for their faces, drawn exquisitely sharp in pure hostility, and their golden eyes.

10   Besides carrying water I helped my father when he cut the long grass, and the lamb's quarter and flowering money-musk, that grew between the pens. He cut with the scythe and I raked into piles. Then he took a pitchfork and threw fresh-cut grass all over the top of the pens, to keep the foxes cooler and shade their coats, which were browned by too much sun. My father did not talk to me unless it was about the job we were doing. In this he was quite different from my mother, who, if she was feeling cheerful, would tell me all sorts of things—the name of a dog she had had when she was a little girl, the names of boys she had gone out with later on when she was grown up, and what certain dresses of hers had looked like—she could not imagine now what had become of them. Whatever thoughts and stories my father had were private, and I was shy of him and would never ask him questions. Nevertheless I worked willingly under his eyes, and with a feeling of pride. One time a feed salesman came down into the pens to talk to him and my father said, "Like to have you meet my new hired man." I turned away and raked furiously, red in the face with pleasure.

"Could of fooled me," said the salesman. "I thought it was only a girl."

After the grass was cut, it seemed suddenly much later in the year. I walked on stubble in the earlier evening, aware of the reddening skies, the entering silences, of fall. When I wheeled the tank out of the gate and put the padlock on, it was almost dark. One night at this time I saw my mother and father standing on the little rise of ground we called the gangway, in front of the barn. My father had just come from the meathouse; he had his stiff bloody apron on, and a pail of cut-up meat in his hand.

It was an odd thing to see my mother down at the barn. She did not often come out of the house unless it was to do something—hang out the wash or dig potatoes in the garden. She looked out of place, with her bare lumpy legs, not touched by the sun, her apron still on and damp across the stomach from the supper dishes. Her hair was tied up in a kerchief, wisps of it falling out. She would tie her hair up like this in the morning, saying she did not have time to do it properly, and it would stay tied up all day. It was true, too; she really did not have time. These days our back porch was piled with baskets of peaches and grapes and pears, bought in town, and onions and tomatoes and cucumbers grown at home, all waiting to be made into jelly and jam and preserves, pickles and chili sauce. In the kitchen there was a fire in the stove all day, jars clinked in boiling water, sometimes a cheese-cloth bag was strung on a pole between two chairs straining blue-black grape pulp for jelly. I was given jobs to do and I would sit at the table peel-ing peaches that had been soaked in the hot water, or cutting up onions, my eyes smarting and streaming. As soon as I was done I ran out of the house, trying to get out of earshot before my mother thought of what she wanted me to do next. I hated the hot dark kitchen in summer, the green blinds and the flypapers, the same old oilcloth table and wavy mirror and bumpy linoleum. My mother was too tired and preoccupied to talk to me, she had no heart to tell about the Normal School Graduation Dance; sweat trickled over her face and she was always counting under her breath, pointing at jars, dumping cups of sugar. It seemed to me that work in the house was endless, dreary and peculiarly depressing; work done out of doors, and in my father's service, was ritualistically important.

I wheeled the tank up to the barn, where it was kept, and I heard my mother saying, "Wait till Laird gets a little bigger, then you'll have a real help."

15   What my father said I did not hear. I was pleased by the way he stood listening, politely as he would to a salesman or a stranger, but with an air of wanting to get on with his real work. I felt my mother had no business down here and I wanted him to feel the same way. What did she mean about Laird? He was no help to anybody. Where was he now? Swinging himself sick on the swing, going around in circles, or trying to catch caterpillars. He never once stayed with me till I was finished.

"And then I can use her more in the house," I heard my mother say. She had a dead-quiet, regretful way of talking about me that always made me un-easy. "I just get my back turned and she runs off. It's not like I had a girl in the family at all."

I went and sat on a feed bag in the corner of the barn, not wanting to appear when this conversation was going on. My mother, I felt, was not to be trusted. She was kinder than my father and more easily fooled, but you could not depend on her, and the real reasons for the things she said and did were not to be known. She loved me, and she sat up late at night making a dress of the difficult style I wanted, for me to wear when school started, but she was also my enemy. She was always plotting. She was plotting now to get me to stay in the house more, although she knew I hated it (*because* she knew I hated it) and keep me from working for my father. It seemed to me she would do this simply out of perversity, and to try her power. It did not occur to me that she could be lonely, or jealous. No grown-up could be; they were too fortunate. I sat and kicked my heels monotonously against a feedbag, raising dust, and did not come out till she was gone.

At any rate, I did not expect my father to pay any attention to what she said. Who could imagine Laird doing my work—Laird remembering the pad-lock and cleaning out the watering-dishes with a leaf on the end of a stick, or even wheeling the tank without it tumbling over? It showed how little my mother knew about the way things really were.

I have forgotten to say what the foxes were fed. My father's bloody apron reminded me. They were fed horsemeat. At this time most farmers still kept horses, and when a horse got too old to work, or broke a leg or got down and would not get up, as they sometimes did, the owner would call my father, and he and Henry went out to the farm in the truck. Usually they shot and butchered the horse there, paying the farmer from five to twelve dollars. If they had already too much meat on hand, they would bring the horse back alive, and keep it for a few days or weeks in our stable, until the meat was needed. After the war the farmers were buying tractors and gradually getting rid of horses altogether, so it sometimes happened that we got a good healthy horse, that there was just no use for any more. If this happened in the winter we might keep the horse in our stable till spring, for we had plenty of hay and if there was a lot of snow—and the plow did not always get our road cleared—it was convenient to be able to go to town with a horse and cutter.[3]

20   The winter I was eleven years old we had two horses in the stable. We did not know what names they had had before, so we called them Mack and Flora. Mack was an old black workhorse, sooty and indifferent. Flora was a sorrel mare, a driver. We took them both out in the cutter. Mack was slow and easy to handle. Flora was given to fits of violent alarm, veering at cars and even at other horses, but we loved her speed and high-stepping, her general air of gallantry and abandon. On Saturdays we went down to the stable and as soon as we opened the door on its cosy, animal-smelling darkness Flora threw up her head, rolled her eyes, whinnied despairingly and pulled herself through a crisis of nerves on the spot. It was not safe to go into her stall; she would kick.

This winter also I began to hear a great deal more on the theme my mother had sounded when she had been talking in front of the barn. I no longer felt safe. It seemed that in the minds of the people around me there was a steady undercurrent of thought, not to be deflected, on this one subject. The word *girl* had formerly seemed to me innocent and unburdened, like the word *child;* now it appeared that it was no such thing. A girl was not, as I had supposed, simply what I was; it was what I had to become. It was a definition, always touched with emphasis, with reproach and disappointment. Also it was a joke on me. Once Laird and I were fighting, and for the first time ever I had to use all my strength against him; even so, he caught and pinned my arm for a moment, really hurting me. Henry saw this, and laughed, saying, "Oh, that there Laird's gonna show you, one of these days!" Laird was getting a lot bigger. But I was getting bigger too.

My grandmother came to stay with us for a few weeks and I heard other things. "Girls don't slam doors like that." "Girls keep their knees together when they sit down." And worse still, when I asked some questions, "That's none of girls' business." I continued to slam the doors and sit as awkwardly as possible, thinking by such measures I kept myself free.

---

[3]**cutter** a small sleigh.

When spring came, the horses were let out in the barnyard. Mack stood against the barn wall trying to scratch his neck and haunches, but Flora trotted up and down and reared at the fences, clattering her hooves against the rails. Snow drifts dwindled quickly, revealing the hard gray and brown earth, the familiar rise and fall of the ground, plain and bare after the fantastic landscape of winter. There was a great feeling of opening-out, of release. We just wore rubbers now, over our shoes; our feet felt ridiculously light. One Saturday we went out to the stable and found all the doors open, letting in the unaccustomed sunlight and fresh air. Henry was there, just idling around looking at his collection of calendars which were tacked up behind the stalls in a part of the stable my mother had probably never seen.

"Come to say goodbye to your old friend Mack?" Henry said. "Here, you give him a taste of oats." He poured some oats in Laird's cupped hands and Laird went to feed Mack. Mack's teeth were in bad shape. He ate very slowly, patiently shifting the oats around in his mouth, trying to find a stump of a molar to grind it on. "Poor old Mack," said Henry mournfully. "When a horse's teeth's gone, he's gone. That's about the way."

25   "Are you going to shoot him today?" I said. Mack and Flora had been in the stable so long I had almost forgotten they were going to be shot.

Henry didn't answer me. Instead he started to sing in a high, trembly, mocking-sorrowful voice. *Oh, there's no more work, for poor Uncle Ned, he's gone where the good darkies go.* Mack's thick, blackish tongue worked diligently at Laird's hand. I went out before the song was ended and sat down on the gangway.

I had never seen them shoot a horse, but I knew where it was done. Last summer Laird and I had come upon a horse's entrails before they were buried. We had thought it was a big black snake, coiled up in the sun. That was around in the field that ran up beside the barn. I thought that if we went inside the barn, and found a wide crack or a knothole to look through, we would be able to see them do it. It was not something I wanted to see; just the same, if a thing really happened, it was better to see it, and know.

My father came down from the house, carrying the gun.

"What are you doing here?" he said.

30   "Nothing."

"Go on up and play around the house."

He sent Laird out of the stable. I said to Laird, "Do you want to see them shoot Mack?" and without waiting for an answer led him around to the front door of the barn, opened it carefully, and went in. "Be quiet or they'll hear us," I said. We could hear Henry and my father talking in the stable, then the heavy, shuffling steps of Mack being backed out of his stall.

In the loft it was cold and dark. Thin, crisscrossed beams of sunlight fell through the cracks. The hay was low. It was a rolling country, hills and hollows, slipping under our feet. About four feet up was a beam going around the walls. We piled hay up in one corner and I boosted Laird up and hoisted myself. The beam was not very wide; we crept along it with our hands flat on the barn walls. There were plenty of knotholes, and I found one that gave me the view I wanted—a corner of the barnyard, the gate, part of the field. Laird did not have a knothole and began to complain.

I showed him a widened crack between two boards. "Be quiet and wait. If they hear you you'll get us in trouble."

35   My father came in sight carrying the gun. Henry was leading Mack by the halter. He dropped it and took out his cigarette papers and tobacco; he rolled cigarettes for my father and himself. While this was going on Mack nosed around in the old, dead grass along the fence. Then my father opened the gate and they took Mack through. Henry led Mack away from the path to a patch of ground and they talked together, not loud enough for us to hear. Mack again began searching for a mouthful of fresh grass, which was not to be found. My father walked away in a straight line, and stopped short at a distance which seemed to suit him. Henry was walking away from Mack too, but sideways, still negligently holding on to the halter. My father raised the gun and Mack looked up as if he had noticed something and my father shot him.

Mack did not collapse at once but swayed, lurched sideways and fell, first on his side; then he rolled over on his back and, amazingly, kicked his legs for a few seconds in the air. At this Henry laughed, as if Mack had done a trick for him. Laird, who had drawn a long, groaning breath of surprise when the shot was fired, said out loud, "He's not dead." And it seemed to me it might be true. But his legs stopped, he rolled on his side again, his muscles quivered and sank. The two men walked over and looked at him in a businesslike way; they bent down and examined his forehead where the bullet had gone in, and now I saw his blood on the brown grass.

"Now they just skin him and cut him up," I said. "Let's go." My legs were a little shaky and I jumped gratefully down into the hay. "Now you've seen how they shoot a horse," I said in a congratulatory way, as if I had seen it many times before. "Let's see if any barn cats had kittens in the hay." Laird jumped. He seemed young and obedient again. Suddenly I remembered how, when he was little, I had brought him into the barn and told him to climb the ladder to the top beam. That was in the spring, too, when the hay was low. I had done it out of a need for excitement, a desire for something to happen so that I could tell about it. He was wearing a little bulky brown and white checked coat, made down from one of mine. He went all the way up just as I told him, and sat down on the top beam with the hay far below him on one side, and the barn floor and some old machinery on the other. Then I ran screaming to my father. "Laird's up on the top beam!" My father came, my mother came, my father went up the ladder talking very quietly and brought Laird down under his arm, at which my mother leaned against the ladder and began to cry. They said to me, "Why weren't you watching him?" but nobody ever knew the truth. Laird did not know enough to tell. But whenever I saw the brown and white checked coat hanging in the closet, or at the bottom of the rag bag, which was where it ended up, I felt a weight in my stomach, the sadness of unexorcised guilt.

I looked at Laird who did not even remember this, and I did not like the look on his thin, winter-paled face. His expression was not frightened or upset, but remote, concentrating. "Listen," I said, in an unusually bright and friendly voice, "you aren't going to tell, are you?"

"No," he said absently.

40   "Promise."

"Promise," he said. I grabbed the hand behind his back to make sure he was not crossing his fingers. Even so, he might have a nightmare; it might come out that way. I decided I had better work hard to get all thoughts of what he had seen out of his mind—which, it seemed to me, could not hold very many things at a time. I got some money I had saved and that afternoon we went into Jubilee and saw a show, with Judy Canova,[4] at which we both laughed a great deal. After that I thought it would be all right.

Two weeks later I knew they were going to shoot Flora. I knew from the night before, when I heard my mother ask if the hay was holding out all right, and my father said, "Well, after to-morrow there'll just be the cow, and we should be able to put her out to grass in another week." So I knew it was Flora's turn in the morning.

This time I didn't think of watching it. That was something to see just one time. I had not thought about it very often since, but sometimes when I was busy, working at school, or standing in front of the mirror combing my hair and wondering if I would be pretty when I grew up, the whole scene would flash into my mind: I would see the easy, practised way my father raised the gun, and hear Henry laughing when Mack kicked his legs in the air. I did not have any great feeling of horror and opposition, such as a city child might have had; I was too used to seeing the death of animals as a necessity by which we lived. Yet I felt a little ashamed, and there was a new wariness, a sense of holding-off, in my attitude to my father and his work.

It was a fine day, and we were going around the yard picking up tree branches that had been torn off in winter storms. This was something we had been told to do, and also we wanted to use them to make a teepee. We heard Flora whinny, and then my father's voice and Henry's shouting, and we ran down to the barnyard to see what was going on.

45   The stable door was open. Henry had just brought Flora out, and she had broken away from him. She was running free in the barnyard, from one end to the other. We climbed up on the fence. It was exciting to see her running, whinnying, going up on her hind legs, prancing and threatening like a horse in a Western movie, an unbroken ranch horse, though she was just an old driver, an old sorrel mare. My father and Henry ran after her and tried to grab the dangling halter. They tried to work her into a corner, and they had almost succeeded when she made a run between them, wild-eyed, and disappeared around the corner of the barn. We heard the rails clatter down as she got over the fence, and Henry yelled, "She's into the field now!"

That meant she was in the long L-shaped field that ran up by the house. If she got around the center, heading towards the lane, the gate was open; the truck had been driven into the field this morning. My father shouted to me, because I was on the other side of the fence, nearest the lane, "Go shut the gate!"

I could run very fast. I ran across the garden, past the tree where our swing was hung, and jumped across a ditch into the lane. There was the open gate. She had not got out, I could not see her up the road; she must have run to the other end of the field. The gate was heavy. I lifted it out of the gravel and carried it across the roadway. I had it half-way across when she came in sight, galloping straight towards me. There was just time to get the chain on. Laird came scrambling through the ditch to help me.

Instead of shutting the gate, I opened it as wide as I could. I did not make any decision to do this, it was just what I did. Flora never slowed down; she galloped straight past me, and Laird jumped up and down,

---

[4]**Judy Canova** American comedian, popular in films in the 1940s.

yelling, "Shut it, shut it!" even after it was too late. My father and Henry appeared in the field a moment too late to see what I had done. They only saw Flora heading for the township road. They would think I had not got there in time.

They did not waste any time asking about it. They went back to the barn and got the gun and the knives they used, and put these in the truck; then they turned the truck around and came bouncing up the field towards us. Laird called to them, "Let me go too, let me go too!" and Henry stopped the truck and they took him in. I shut the gate after they were all gone.

50   I supposed Laird would tell. I wondered what would happen to me. I had never disobeyed my father before, and I could not understand why I had done it. Flora would not really get away. They would catch up with her in the truck. Or if they did not catch her this morning somebody would see her and telephone us this afternoon or tomorrow. There was no wild country here for her to run to, only farms. What was more, my father had paid for her, we needed the meat to feed the foxes, we needed the foxes to make our living. All I had done was make more work for my father who worked hard enough already. And when my father found out about it he was not going to trust me any more; he would know that I was not entirely on his side. I was on Flora's side, and that made me no use to anybody, not even to her. Just the same, I did not regret it; when she came running at me and I held the gate open, that was the only thing I could do.

I went back to the house, and my mother said, "What's all the commotion?" I told her that Flora had kicked down the fence and got away. "Your poor father," she said, "now he'll have to go chasing over the countryside. Well, there isn't any use planning dinner before one." She put up the ironing board. I wanted to tell her, but thought better of it and went upstairs and sat on my bed.

Lately I had been trying to make my part of the room fancy, spreading the bed with old lace curtains, and fixing myself a dressing-table with some leftovers of cretonne for a skirt. I planned to put up some kind of barricade between my bed and Laird's, to keep my section separate from his. In the sunlight, the lace curtains were just dusty rags. We did not sing at night any more. One night when I was singing Laird said, "You sound silly," and I went right on but the next night I did not start. There was not so much need to anyway, we were no longer afraid. We knew it was just old furniture over there, old jumble and confusion. We did not keep to the rules. I still stayed awake after Laird was asleep and told myself stories, but even in these stories something different was happening, mysterious alterations took place. A story might start off in the old way, with a spectacular danger, a fire or wild animals, and for a while I might rescue people; then things would change around, and instead, somebody would be rescuing me. It might be a boy from our class at school, or even Mr. Campbell, our teacher, who tickled girls under the arms. And at this point the story concerned itself at great length with what I looked like—how long my hair was, and what kind of dress I had on; by the time I had these details worked out the real excitement of the story was lost.

It was later than one o'clock when the truck came back. The tarpaulin was over the back, which meant there was meat in it. My mother had to heat dinner up all over again. Henry and my father had changed from their bloody overalls into ordinary working overalls in the barn, and they washed their arms and necks and faces at the sink, and splashed water on their hair and combed it. Laird lifted his arm to show off a streak of blood. "We shot old Flora," he said, "and cut her up in fifty pieces."

"Well I don't want to hear about it," my mother said. "And don't come to my table like that."

55   My father made him go and wash the blood off.

We sat down and my father said grace and Henry pasted his chewing-gum on the end of his fork, the way he always did; when he took it off he would have us admire the pattern. We began to pass the bowls of steaming, overcooked vegetables. Laird looked across the table at me and said proudly, distinctly, "Anyway it was her fault Flora got away."

"What?" my father said.

"She could of shut the gate and she didn't. She just open' it up and Flora run out."

"Is that right?" my father said.

60   Everybody at the table was looking at me. I nodded, swallowing food with great difficulty. To my shame, tears flooded my eyes.

My father made a curt sound of disgust. "What did you do that for?"

I did not answer. I put down my fork and waited to be sent from the table, still not looking up.

But this did not happen. For some time nobody said anything, then Laird said matter-of-factly, "She's crying."

"Never mind," my father said. He spoke with resignation, even good humour, the words which absolved and dismissed me for good. "She's only a girl," he said.

65   I didn't protest that, even in my heart. Maybe it was true.

GLORIA NAYLOR

Gloria Naylor (b. 1950), a native of New York City, holds a bachelor's degree from Brooklyn College and a master's degree in Afro-American studies from Yale University. "The Two" comes from The Women of Brewster Place *(1982), a "novel in seven stories" that won the American Book Award for First Fiction. Naylor's books include the novels* Linden Hills *(1985) and* Mama Days *(1988).*

The Two   [1982]

At first they seemed like such nice girls. No one could remember exactly when they had moved into Brewster. It was earlier in the year before Ben[1] was killed—of course, it had to be before Ben's death. But no one remembered if it was in the winter or spring of that year that the two had come. People often came and went on Brewster Place like a restless night's dream, moving in and out in the dark to avoid eviction notices or neighborhood bulletins about the dilapidated condition of their furnishings. So it wasn't until the two were clocked leaving in the mornings and returning in the evenings at regular intervals that it was quietly absorbed that they now

---

[1]**Ben** the custodian of Brewster Place.

claimed Brewster as home. And Brewster waited, cautiously prepared to claim them, because you never knew about young women, and obviously single at that. But when no wild music or drunken friends careened out of the corner building on weekends, and especially, when no slightly eager husbands were encouraged to linger around that first-floor apartment and run errands for them, a suspended sigh of relief floated around the two when they dumped their garbage, did their shopping, and headed for the morning bus.

The women of Brewster had readily accepted the lighter, skinny one. There wasn't much threat in her timid mincing walk and the slightly pro-truding teeth she seemed so eager to show everyone in her bell-like good mornings and evenings. Breaths were held a little longer in the direction of the short dark one—too pretty, and too much behind. And she insisted on wearing those thin Qiana dresses that the summer breeze molded against the maddening rhythm of the twenty pounds of rounded flesh that she swung steadily down the street. Through slitted eyes, the women watched their men watching her pass, knowing the bastards were praying for a wind. But since she seemed oblivious to whether these supplications went an-swered, their sighs settled around her shoulders too. Nice girls.

And so no one even cared to remember exactly when they had moved into Brewster Place, until the rumor started. It had first spread through the block like a sour odor that's only faintly perceptible and easily ignored until it starts growing in strength from the dozen mouths it had been lying in, among clammy gums and scum-coated teeth. And then it was everywhere—lining the mouths and whitening the lips of everyone as they wrinkled up their noses at its pervading smell, unable to pinpoint the source or time of its initial arrival. Sophie could—she had been there.

It wasn't that the rumor had actually begun with Sophie. A rumor needs no true parent. It only needs a willing carrier, and it found one in Sophie. She had been there—on one of those August evenings when the sun's absence is a mockery because the heat leaves the air so heavy it presses the naked skin down on your body, to the point that a sheet becomes unbearable and sleep impossible. So most of Brewster was outside that night when the two had come in together, probably from one of those air-conditioned movies down-town, and had greeted the ones who were loitering around their building. And they had started up the steps when the skinny one tripped over a child's ball and the darker one had grabbed her by the arm and around the waist to break her fall. "Careful, don't wanna lose you now." And the two of them had laughed into each other's eyes and went into the building.

5   The smell had begun there. It outlined the image of the stumbling woman and the one who had broken her fall. Sophie and a few other women sniffed at the spot and then, perplexed, silently looked at each other. Where had they seen that before? They had often laughed and touched each other—held each other in joy or its dark twin—but where had they seen *that* before? It came to them as the scent drifted down the steps and entered their nostrils on the way to their inner mouths. They had seen that—done that—with their men. That shared moment of invisible commu-nion reserved for two and hidden from the rest of the world behind laugh-ter or tears or a touch. In the days before babies, miscarriages, and other broken dreams, after stolen caresses in barn stalls and cotton houses, after intimate walks from church and secret kisses with boys who were now long

forgotten or permanently fixed in their lives—that was where. They could almost feel the odor moving about in their mouths, and they slowly knitted themselves together and let it out into the air like a yellow mist that began to cling to the bricks on Brewster.

So it got around that the two in 312 were *that* way. And they had seemed like such nice girls. Their regular exits and entrances to the block were viewed with a jaundiced eye. The quiet that rested around their door on the weekends hinted of all sorts of secret rituals, and their friendly indifference to the men on the street was an insult to the women as a brazen flaunting of unnatural ways.

Since Sophie's apartment windows faced theirs from across the air shaft, she became the official watchman for the block, and her opinions were deferred to whenever the two came up in conversation. Sophie took her position seriously and was constantly alert for any telltale signs that might creep out around their drawn shades, across from which she kept a religious vigil. An entire week of drawn shades was evidence enough to send her flying around with reports that as soon as it got dark they pulled their shades down and put on the lights. Heads nodded in knowing unison—a definite sign. If doubt was voiced with a "But I pull my shades down at night too," a whispered "Yeah, but you're not *that* way" was argument enough to win them over.

Sophie watched the lighter one dumping their garbage, and she went outside and opened the lid. Her eyes darted over the crushed tin cans, vegetable peelings, and empty chocolate chip cookie boxes. What do they do with all them chocolate chip cookies? It was surely a sign, but it would take some time to figure that one out. She saw Ben go into their apartment, and she waited and blocked his path as he came out, carrying his toolbox.

"What ya see?" She grabbed his arm and whispered wetly in his face.

10   Ben stared at her squinted eyes and drooping lips and shook his head slowly. "Uh, uh, uh, it was terrible."

"Yeah?" She moved in a little closer.

"Worst busted faucet I seen in my whole life." He shook her hand off his arm and left her standing in the middle of the block.

"You old sop bucket," she muttered, as she went back up on her stoop. A broken faucet, huh? Why did they need to use so much water?

Sophie had plenty to report that day. Ben had said it was terrible in there. No, she didn't know exactly what he had seen, but you can imagine—and they did. Confronted with the difference that had been thrust into their predictable world, they reached into their imaginations and, using an ancient pattern, weaved themselves a reason for its existence. Out of necessity they stitched all of their secret fears and lingering childhood nightmares into this existence, because even though it was deceptive enough to try and look as they looked, talk as they talked, and do as they did, it had to have some hidden stain to invalidate it—it was impossible for them both to be right. So they leaned back, supported by the sheer weight of their numbers and comforted by the woven barrier that kept them protected from the yellow mist that enshrouded the two as they came and went on Brewster Place.

15   Lorraine was the first to notice the change in the people on Brewster Place. She was a shy but naturally friendly woman who got up early, and had

read the morning paper and done fifty sit-ups before it was time to leave for work. She came out of her apartment eager to start her day by greeting any of her neighbors who were outside. But she noticed that some of the people who had spoken to her before made a point of having something else to do with their eyes when she passed, although she could almost feel them staring at her back as she moved on. The ones who still spoke only did so after an uncomfortable pause, in which they seemed to be peering through her before they begrudged her a good morning or evening. She wondered if it was all in her mind and she thought about mentioning it to Theresa, but she didn't want to be accused of being too sensitive again. And how would Tee even notice anything like that anyway? She had a lousy attitude and hardly ever spoke to people. She stayed in that bed until the last moment and rushed out of the house fogged-up and grumpy, and she was used to being stared at—by men at least—because of her body.

Lorraine thought about these things as she came up the block from work, carrying a large paper bag. The group of women on her stoop parted silently and let her pass.

"Good evening," she said, as she climbed the steps.

Sophie was standing on the top step and tried to peek into the bag. "You been shopping, huh? What ya buy?" It was almost an accusation.

"Groceries." Lorraine shielded the top of the bag from view and squeezed past her with a confused frown. She saw Sophie throw a knowing glance to the others at the bottom of the stoop. What was wrong with this old woman? Was she crazy or something?

20   Lorraine went into her apartment. Theresa was sitting by the window, reading a copy of *Mademoiselle*. She glanced up from her magazine. "Did you get my chocolate chip cookies?"

"Why good evening to you, too, Tee. And how was my day? Just wonderful." She sat the bag down on the couch. "The little Baxter boy brought in a puppy for show-and-tell, and the damn thing pissed all over the floor and then proceeded to chew the heel off my shoe, but, yes, I managed to hobble to the store and bring you your chocolate chip cookies."

Oh, Jesus, Theresa thought, she's got a bug up her ass tonight.

"Well, you should speak to Mrs. Baxter. She ought to train her kid better than that." She didn't wait for Lorraine to stop laughing before she tried to stretch her good mood. "Here, I'll put those things away. Want me to make dinner so you can rest? I only worked half a day, and the most tragic thing that went down was a broken fingernail and that got caught in my typewriter."

Lorraine followed Theresa into the kitchen. "No, I'm not really tired, and fair's fair, you cooked last night. I didn't mean to tick off like that; it's just that . . . . well, Tee, have you noticed that people aren't as nice as they used to be?"

25   Theresa stiffened. Oh, God, here she goes again. "What people, Lorraine? Nice in what way?"

"Well, the people in this building and on the street. No one hardly speaks anymore. I mean, I'll come in and say good evening—and just silence. It wasn't like that when we first moved in. I don't know, it just makes you wonder; that's all. What are they thinking?"

"I personally don't give a shit what they're thinking. And their good evenings don't put any bread on my table."

"Yeah, but you didn't see the way that woman looked at me out there. They must feel something or know something. They probably—"

"They, they, they!" Theresa exploded. "You know, I'm not starting up with this again, Lorraine. Who in the hell are they? And where in the hell are we? Living in some dump of a building in this God-forsaken part of town around a bunch of ignorant niggers with the cotton still under their finger-nails because of you and your theys. They knew something in Linden Hills, so I gave up an apartment for you that I'd been in for the last four years. And then they knew in Park Heights, and you made me so miserable there we had to leave. Now these mysterious theys are on Brewster Place. Well, look out that window, kid. There's a big wall down that block, and this is the end of the line for me. I'm not moving anymore, so if that's what you're working yourself up to—save it!"

30   When Theresa became angry she was like a lump of smoldering coal, and her fierce bursts of temper always unsettled Lorraine.

"You see, that's why I didn't want to mention it." Lorraine began to pull at her fingers nervously. "You're always flying up and jumping to con-clusions—no one said anything about moving. And I didn't know your life has been so miserable since you met me. I'm sorry about that," she fin-ished tearfully.

Theresa looked at Lorraine, standing in the kitchen door like a wilted leaf, and she wanted to throw something at her. Why didn't she ever fight back? The very softness that had first attracted her to Lorraine was now a frequent cause for irritation. Smoked honey. That's what Lorraine had re-minded her of, sitting in her office clutching that application. Dry autumn days in Georgia woods, thick bloated smoke under a beehive, and the first glimpse of amber honey just faintly darkened about the edges by the burning twigs. She had flowed just that heavily into Theresa's mind and had stuck there with a persistent sweetness.

But Theresa hadn't known then that this softness filled Lorraine up to the very middle and that she would bend at the slightest pressure, would be constantly seeking to surround herself with the comfort of everyone's good-will, and would shrivel up at the least touch of disapproval. It was becoming a drain to be continually called upon for this nurturing and support that she just didn't understand. She had supplied it at first out of love for Lorraine, hoping that she would harden eventually, even as honey does when ex-posed to the cold. Theresa was growing tired of being clung to—of being the one who was leaned on. She didn't want a child—she wanted someone who could stand toe to toe with her and be willing to slug it out at times. If they practiced that way with each other, then they could turn back to back and beat the hell out of the world for trying to invade their territory. But she had found no such sparring partner in Lorraine, and the strain of fighting alone was beginning to show on her.

"Well, if it was that miserable, I would have been gone a long time ago," she said, watching her words refresh Lorraine like a gentle shower.

35   "I guess you think I'm some sort of a sick paranoid, but I can't afford to have people calling my job or writing letters to my principal. You know I've al-ready lost a position like that in Detroit. And teaching is my whole life, Tee."

"I know," she sighed, not really knowing at all. There was no danger of that ever happening on Brewster Place. Lorraine taught too far from this neighborhood for anyone here to recognize her in that school. No, it wasn't her job she feared losing this time, but their approval. She wanted to stand out there and chat and trade makeup secrets and cake recipes. She wanted to be secretary of their block association and be asked to mind their kids while they ran to the store. And none of that was going to happen if they couldn't even bring themselves to accept her good evenings.

Theresa silently finished unpacking the groceries. "Why did you buy cottage cheese? Who eats that stuff?"

"Well, I thought we should go on a diet."

"If *we* go on a diet, then you'll disappear. You've got nothing to lose but your hair."

40   "Oh, I don't know. I thought that we might want to try and reduce our hips or something." Lorraine shrugged playfully.

"No, thank you. We are very happy with our hips the way they are," Theresa said, as she shoved the cottage cheese to the back of the refrigerator. "And even when I lose weight, it never comes off there. My chest and arms just get smaller, and I start looking like a bottle of salad dressing."

The two women laughed, and Theresa sat down to watch Lorraine fix dinner. "You know, this behind has always been my downfall. When I was coming up in Georgia with my grandmother, the boys used to promise me penny candy if I would let them pat my behind. And I used to love those jawbreakers—you know, the kind that lasted all day and kept changing colors in your mouth. So I was glad to oblige them, because in one afternoon I could collect a whole week's worth of jawbreakers."

"Really. That's funny to you? Having some boy feeling all over you."

Theresa sucked her teeth. "We were only kids, Lorraine. You know, you remind me of my grandmother. That was one straight-laced old lady. She had a fit when my brother told her what I was doing. She called me into the smokehouse and told me in this real scary whisper that I could get pregnant from letting little boys pat my butt and that I'd end up like my cousin Willa. But Willa and I had been thick as fleas, and she had already given me a step-by-step summary of how she'd gotten into her predicament. But I sneaked around to her house that night just to double-check her story, since that old lady had seemed so earnest. 'Willa, are you sure?' I whispered through her bedroom window. 'I'm tellin' ya, Tee,' she said. 'Just keep both feet on the ground and you home free.' Much later I learned that advice wasn't too biologically sound, but it worked in Georgia because those country boys didn't have much imagination."

45   Theresa's laughter bounced off of Lorraine's silent, rigid back and died in her throat. She angrily tore open a pack of the chocolate chip cookies. "Yeah," she said, staring at Lorraine's back and biting down hard into the cookie, "it wasn't until I came up north to college that I found out there's a whole lot of things that a dude with a little imagination can do to you even with both feet on the ground. You see, Willa forgot to tell me not to bend over or squat or—"

"Must you!" Lorraine turned around from the stove with her teeth clenched tightly together.

"Must I what, Lorraine? Must I talk about things that are as much a part of life as eating or breathing or growing old? Why are you always so uptight about sex or men?"

"I'm not uptight about anything. I just think it's disgusting when you go on and on about—"

"There's nothing disgusting about it, Lorraine. You've never been with a man, but I've been with quite a few—some better than others. There were a couple who I still hope to this day will die a slow, painful death, but then there were some who were good to me—in and out of bed."

50   "If they were so great, then why are you with me?" Lorraine's lips were trembling.

"Because—" Theresa looked steadily into her eyes and then down at the cookie she was twirling on the table. "Because," she continued slowly, "you can take a chocolate chip cookie and put holes in it and attach it to your ears and call it an earring, or hang it around your neck on a silver chain and pretend it's a necklace—but it's still a cookie. See—you can toss it in the air and call it a Frisbee or even a flying saucer, if the mood hits you, and it's still just a cookie. Send it spinning on a table—like this—until it's a wonderful blur of amber and brown light that you can imagine to be a topaz or rusted gold or old crystal, but the law of gravity has got to come into play, sometime, and it's got to come to rest—sometime. Then all the spinning and pretending and hoopla is over with. And you know what you got?"

"A chocolate chip cookie," Lorraine said.

"Uh-uh." Theresa put the cookie in her mouth and winked. "A lesbian." She got up from the table. "Call me when dinner's ready, I'm going back to read." She stopped at the kitchen door. "Now, why are you putting gravy on that chicken, Lorraine? You know it's fattening."

JOYCE CAROL OATES

Joyce Carol Oates was born in 1938 in Millerport, New York. She won a scholarship to Syracuse University, from which she graduated (Phi Beta Kappa and valedictorian) in 1960. She then did graduate work in English, first at the University of Wisconsin and then at Rice University, but she withdrew from Rice to devote more time to writing. Her first collection of stories, By the North Gate, *was published in 1963; since then she has published many stories, poems, essays, and novels. She has received many awards, has been elected to the American Academy and Institute of Arts and Letters, and now teaches creative writing at Princeton University.*

Where Are You Going, Where Have You Been?   [1966]

To Bob Dylan

Her name was Connie. She was fifteen and she had a quick nervous giggling habit of craning her neck to glance into mirrors or checking other people's faces to make sure her own was all right. Her mother, who noticed everything and knew everything and who hadn't much reason any longer to look at her own face, always scolded Connie about it. "Stop gawking at yourself, who are you? You think you're so pretty?" she would say. Connie would raise her eyebrows at these familiar complaints and look right through her mother, into a shadowy vision of herself as she was right at that moment: she knew she was pretty and that was everything. Her mother had been pretty once too, if you could believe those old snapshots in the album, but now her looks were gone and that was why she was always after Connie.

"Why don't you keep your room clean like your sister? How've you got your hair fixed—what the hell stinks? Hair spray? You don't see your sister using that junk."

Her sister June was twenty-four and still lived at home. She was a secretary in the high school Connie attended, and if that wasn't bad enough—with her in the same building—she was so plain and chunky and steady that Connie had to hear her praised all the time by her mother and her mother's sisters. June did this, June did that, she saved money and helped clean the house and cooked and Connie couldn't do a thing, her mind was all filled with trashy daydreams. Their father was away at work most of the time and when he came home he wanted supper and he read the newspaper at supper and after supper he went to bed. He didn't bother talking much to them, but around his bent head Connie's mother kept picking at her until Connie wished her mother was dead and she herself was dead and it was all over. "She makes me want to throw up sometimes," she complained to her friends. She had a high, breathless, amused voice which made everything she said sound a little forced, whether it was sincere or not.

There was one good thing: June went places with girl friends of hers, girls who were just as plain and steady as she, and so when Connie wanted to do that her mother had no objections. The father of Connie's best girl friend drove the girls the three miles to town and left them off at a shopping plaza, so that they could walk through the stores or go to a movie, and when he came to pick them up again at eleven he never bothered to ask what they had done.

5   They must have been familiar sights, walking around that shopping plaza in their shorts and flat ballerina slippers that always scuffed the sidewalk, with charm bracelets jingling on their thin wrists; they would lean together to whisper and laugh secretly if someone passed by who amused or interested them. Connie had long dark blond hair that drew anyone's eye to it, and she wore part of it pulled up on her head and puffed out and the rest of it she let fall down her back. She wore a pull-over jersey blouse that looked one way when she was at home and another way when she was away from home. Everything about her had two sides to it, one for home and one for anywhere that was not home: her walk that could be childlike and bobbing, or languid enough to make anyone think she was hearing music in her head, her mouth which was pale and smirking most of the time, but bright and pink on these evenings out, her laugh which was cynical and drawling at home—"Ha, ha, very funny"—but high-pitched and nervous anywhere else, like the jingling of the charms on her bracelet.

Sometimes they did go shopping or to a movie, but sometimes they went across the highway, ducking fast across the busy road, to a drive-in restaurant where older kids hung out. The restaurant was shaped like a big bottle, though squatter than a real bottle, and on its cap was a revolving figure of a grinning boy who held a hamburger aloft. One night in midsummer they ran across, breathless with daring, and right away someone leaned out a car window and invited them over, but it was just a boy from high school they didn't like. It made them feel good to be able to ignore him. They went up through the maze of parked and cruising cars to the bright-lit, fly-infested restaurant, their faces pleased and expectant as if they were entering a sacred building that loomed out of the night to give them what haven and what blessing they yearned for. They sat at the counter and crossed their legs at the ankles, their thin shoulders rigid with excitement, and listened to the music that made everything so good: the music was always in the background like music at a church service, it was something to depend upon.

A boy named Eddie came in to talk with them. He sat backward on his stool, turning himself jerkily around in semicircles and then stopping and turning again, and after a while he asked Connie if she would like something to eat. She said she did and so she tapped her friend's arm on her way out— her friend pulled her face up into a brave droll look—and Connie said she would meet her at eleven, across the way. "I just hate to leave her like that," Connie said earnestly, but the boy said that she wouldn't be alone for long. So they went out to his car and on the way Connie couldn't help but let her eyes wander over the windshields and faces all around her, her face gleaming with a joy that had nothing to do with Eddie or even this place; it might have been the music. She drew her shoulders up and sucked in her breath with the pure pleasure of being alive, and just at that moment she happened to glance at a face just a few feet from hers. It was a boy with shaggy black hair, in a convertible jalopy painted gold. He stared at her and then his lips widened into a grin. Connie slit her eyes at him and turned away, but she couldn't help glancing back and there he was still watching her. He wagged a finger and laughed and said, "Gonna get you, baby," and Connie turned away again without Eddie noticing anything.

She spent three hours with him, at the restaurant where they ate hamburgers and drank Cokes in wax cups that were always sweating, and then down an alley a mile or so away, and when he left her off at five to eleven only the movie house was still open at the plaza. Her girl friend was there, talking with a boy. When Connie came up the two girls smiled at each other and Connie said, "How was the movie?" and the girl said, "*You* should know." They rode off with the girl's father, sleepy and pleased, and Connie couldn't help but look at the darkened shopping plaza with its big empty parking lot and its signs that were faded and ghostly now, and over at the drive-in restaurant where cars were still circling tirelessly. She couldn't hear the music at this distance.

Next morning June asked her how the movie was and Connie said, "So-so."

10   She and that girl and occasionally another girl went out several times a week that way, and the rest of the time Connie spent around the house—it was summer vacation—getting in her mother's way and thinking, dreaming, about the boys she met. But all the boys fell back and dissolved into a single face that was not even a face, but an idea, a feeling, mixed up with the urgent insistent pounding of the music and the humid night air of July. Connie's mother kept dragging her back to the daylight by finding things for her to do or saying, suddenly, "What's this about the Pettinger girl?"

And Connie would say nervously, "Oh, her. That dope." She always drew thick clear lines between herself and such girls, and her mother was simple and kindly enough to believe her. Her mother was so simple, Connie thought, that it was maybe cruel to fool her so much. Her mother went scuffling around the house in old bedroom slippers and complained over the telephone to one sister about the other, then the other called up and the two of them complained about the third one. If June's name was mentioned her mother's tone was approving, and if Connie's name was mentioned it was disapproving. This did not really mean she disliked Connie and actually Connie thought that her mother preferred her to June because she was prettier, but the two of them kept up a pretense of exasperation, a sense that they were tugging and struggling over something of little value to either of them. Sometimes, over coffee, they were almost friends, but something would come up—some vexation that was like a fly buzzing suddenly around their heads—and their faces went hard with contempt.

One Sunday Connie got up at eleven—none of them bothered with church—and washed her hair so that it could dry all day long, in the sun. Her parents and sister were going to a barbecue at an aunt's house and Connie said no, she wasn't interested, rolling her eyes to let her mother know just what she thought of it. "Stay home alone then," her mother said sharply. Connie sat out back in a lawn chair and watched them drive away, her father quiet and bald, hunched around so that he could back the car out, her mother with a look that was still angry and not at all softened through the windshield, and in the back seat poor old June all dressed up as if she didn't know what a barbecue was, with all the running yelling kids and the flies. Connie sat with her eyes closed in the sun, dreaming and dazed with the warmth about her as if this were a kind of love, the caresses of love, and her mind slipped over onto thoughts of the boy she had been with the night before and how nice he had been, how sweet it always was, not the way someone like June would suppose but sweet, gentle, the way it was in movies and promised in songs; and when she opened her eyes she hardly knew where she was, the back yard ran off into weeds and a fence line of trees and behind it the sky was perfectly blue and still. The asbestos "ranch house" that was now three years old startled her—it looked small. She shook her head as if to get awake.

It was too hot. She went inside the house and turned on the radio to drown out the quiet. She sat on the edge of her bed, barefoot, and listened for an hour and a half to a program called XYZ Sunday Jamboree, record after record of hard, fast, shrieking songs she sang along with, interspersed by exclamations from "Bobby King": "An' look here you girls at Napoleon's—Son and Charley want you to pay real close attention to this song coming up!"

And Connie paid close attention herself, bathed in a glow of slow-pulsed joy that seemed to rise mysteriously out of the music itself and lay languidly about the airless little room, breathed in and breathed out with each gentle rise and fall of her chest.

15   After a while she heard a car coming up the drive. She sat up at once, startled, because it couldn't be her father so soon. The gravel kept crunching all the way in from the road—the driveway was long—and Connie ran to the window. It was a car she didn't know. It was an open jalopy, painted a bright gold that caught the sunlight opaquely. Her heart began to pound and her fingers snatched at her hair, checking it, and she whispered "Christ, Christ," wondering how bad she looked. The car came to a stop at the side door and the horn sounded four short taps as if this were a signal Connie knew.

She went into the kitchen and approached the door slowly, then hung out the screen door, her bare toes curling down off the step. There were two boys in the car and now she recognized the driver: he had shaggy, shabby black hair that looked crazy as a wig and he was grinning at her.

"I ain't late, am I?" he said.

"Who the hell do you think you are?" Connie said.

"Toldja I'd be out, didn't I?"

20   "I don't even know who you are."

She spoke sullenly, careful to show no interest or pleasure, and he spoke in a fast bright monotone. Connie looked past him to the other boy, taking her time. He had fair brown hair, with a lock that fell onto his forehead. His sideburns gave him a fierce, embarrassed look, but so far he hadn't even bothered to glance at her. Both boys wore sunglasses. The driver's glasses were metallic and mirrored everything in miniature.

"You wanta come for a ride?" he said.

Connie smirked and let her hair fall loose over one shoulder.

"Don'tcha like my car? New paint job," he said. "Hey."

25   "What?"

"You're cute."

She pretended to fidget, chasing flies away from the door.

"Don'tcha believe me, or what?" he said.

"Look, I don't even know who you are," Connie said in disgust.

30   "Hey, Ellie's got a radio, see. Mine's broke down." He lifted his friend's arm and showed her the little transistor the boy was holding, and now Connie began to hear the music. It was the same program that was playing inside the house.

"Bobby King?" she said.

"I listen to him all the time. I think he's great."

"He's kind of great," Connie said reluctantly.

"Listen, that guy's *great*. He knows where the action is."

35   Connie blushed a little, because the glasses made it impossible for her to see just what this boy was looking at. She couldn't decide if she liked him or if he was just a jerk, and so she dawdled in the doorway and wouldn't come down or go back inside. She said, "What's all that stuff painted on your car?"

"Can'tcha read it?" He opened the door very carefully, as if he was afraid it might fall off. He slid out just as carefully, planting his feet firmly on the ground, the tiny metallic world in his glasses slowing down like gelatine hardening and in the midst of it Connie's bright green blouse. "This here is my name, to begin with," he said. ARNOLD FRIEND was written in tarlike black letters on the side, with a drawing of a round grinning face that reminded Connie of a pumpkin, except it wore sunglasses. "I wanta introduce myself, I'm Arnold Friend and that's my real name and I'm gonna be your friend, honey, and inside the car's Ellie Oscar, he's kinda shy." Ellie brought his transistor radio up to his shoulder and balanced it there. "Now these numbers are a secret code, honey," Arnold Friend explained. He read off the numbers 33, 19, 17 and raised his eyebrows at her to see what she thought of that, but she didn't think much of it. The left rear fender had been smashed and around it was written, on the gleaming gold background: DONE BY CRAZY WOMAN DRIVER. Connie had to laugh at that. Arnold Friend was pleased at her laughter and looked up at her. "Around the other side's a lot more—you wanta come and see them?"

"No."

"Why not?"

"Why should I?"

40   "Don'tcha wanta see what's on the car? Don'tcha wanta go for a ride?"

"I don't know."

"Why not?"

"I got things to do."

"Like what?"

45   "Things."

He laughed as if she had said something funny. He slapped his thighs. He was standing in a strange way, leaning back against the car as if he were balancing himself. He wasn't tall, only an inch or so taller than she would be if she came down to him. Connie liked the way he was dressed, which was the way all of them dressed: tight faded jeans stuffed into black, scuffed boots, a belt that pulled his waist in and showed how lean he was, and a white pullover shirt that was a little soiled and showed the hard small muscles of his arms and shoulders. He looked as if he probably did hard work, lifting and carrying things. Even his neck looked muscular. And his face was a familiar face, somehow: the jaw and chin and cheeks slightly darkened, because he hadn't shaved for a day or two, and the nose long and hawklike, sniffing as if she were a treat he was going to gobble up and it was all a joke.

"Connie, you ain't telling the truth. This is your day set aside for a ride with me and you know it," he said, still laughing. The way he straightened and recovered from his fit of laughing showed that it had been all fake.

"How do you know what my name is?" she said suspiciously.

"It's Connie."

50   "Maybe and maybe not."

"I know my Connie," he said, wagging his finger. Now she remembered him even better, back at the restaurant, and her cheeks warmed at the thought of how she sucked in her breath just at the moment she passed him—how she must have looked to him. And he had remembered her. "Ellie and I come out here especially for you," he said. "Ellie can sit in back. How about it?"

"Where?"

"Where what?"

"Where're we going?"

55   He looked at her. He took off the sunglasses and she saw how pale the skin around his eyes was, like holes that were not in shadow but instead in light. His eyes were like chips of broken glass that catch the light in an amiable way. He smiled. It was as if the idea of going for a ride somewhere, to some place, was a new idea to him.

"Just for a ride, Connie sweetheart."

"I never said my name was Connie," she said.

"But I know what it is. I know your name and all about you, lots of things," Arnold Friend said. He had not moved yet but stood still leaning back against the side of his jalopy. "I took a special interest in you, such a pretty girl, and found out all about you like I know your parents and sister are gone somewheres and I know where and how long they're going to be gone, and I know who you were with last night, and your best girl friend's name is Betty. Right?"

He spoke in a simple lilting voice, exactly as if he were reciting the words to a song. His smile assured her that everything was fine. In the car Ellie turned up the volume on his radio and did not bother to look around at them.

60   "Ellie can sit in the back seat," Arnold Friend said. He indicated his friend
with a casual jerk of his chin, as if Ellie did not count and she should not
bother with him.

"How'd you find out all that stuff?" Connie said.

"Listen: Betty Schultz and Tony Fitch and Jimmy Pettinger and Nancy
Pettinger," he said, in a chant. "Raymond Stanley and Bob Hutter—"

"Do you know all those kids?"

"I know everybody."

65   "Look, you're kidding. You're not from around here."

"Sure."

"But—how come we never saw you before?"

"Sure you saw me before," he said. He looked down at his boots, as if he
were a little offended. "You just don't remember."

"I guess I'd remember you," Connie said.

70   "Yeah?" He looked up at this, beaming. He was pleased. He began to mark
time with the music from Ellie's radio, tapping his fists lightly together. Connie looked away from his smile to the car, which was painted so bright it almost hurt her eyes to look at it. She looked at that name, ARNOLD FRIEND.
And up at the front fender was an expression that was familiar—MAN THE
FLYING SAUCERS. It was an expression kids had used the year before, but
didn't use this year. She looked at it for a while as if the words meant something to her that she did not yet know.

"What're you thinking about? Huh?" Arnold Friend demanded. "Not worried about your hair blowing around in the car, are you?"

"No."

"Think I maybe can't drive good?"

"How do I know?"

75   "You're a hard girl to handle. How come?" he said. "Don't you know I'm
your friend? Didn't you see me put my sign in the air when you walked by?"

"What sign?"

"My sign." And he drew an X in the air, leaning out toward her. They
were maybe ten feet apart. After his hand fell back to his side the X was still
in the air, almost visible. Connie let the screen door close and stood perfectly still inside it, listening to the music from her radio and the boy's blend
together. She stared at Arnold Friend. He stood there so stiffly relaxed, pretending to be relaxed, with one hand idly on the door handle as if he were
keeping himself up that way and had no intention of ever moving again. She
recognized most things about him, the tight jeans that showed his thighs
and buttocks and the greasy leather boots and the tight shirt, and even that
slippery friendly smile of his, that sleepy dreamy smile that all the boys used
to get across ideas they didn't want to put into words. She recognized all
this and also the singsong way he talked, slightly mocking, kidding, but serious and a little melancholy, and she recognized the way he tapped one fist
against the other in homage to the perpetual music behind him. But all these
things did not come together.

She said suddenly, "Hey, how old are you?"

His smile faded. She could see then that he wasn't a kid, he was much
older—thirty, maybe more. At this knowledge her heart began to pound
faster.

80   "That's a crazy thing to ask. Can'tcha see I'm your own age?"

"Like hell you are."

"Or maybe a coupla years older, I'm eighteen."

"Eighteen?" she said doubtfully.

He grinned to reassure her and lines appeared at the corners of his mouth. His teeth were big and white. He grinned so broadly his eyes became slits and she saw how thick the lashes were, thick and black as if painted with a black tarlike material. Then he seemed to become embarrassed, abruptly, and looked over his shoulder at Ellie. "*Him,* he's crazy," he said. "Ain't he a riot, he's a nut, a real character." Ellie was still listening to the music. His sunglasses told nothing about what he was thinking. He wore a bright orange shirt unbuttoned halfway to show his chest, which was a pale, bluish chest and not muscular like Arnold Friend's. His shirt collar was turned up all around and the very tips of the collar pointed out past his chin as if they were protecting him. He was pressing the transistor radio up against his ear and sat there in a kind of daze, right in the sun.

85   "He's kinda strange," Connie said.

"Hey, she says you're kinda strange! Kinda strange!" Arnold Friend cried. He pounded on the car to get Ellie's attention. Ellie turned for the first time and Connie saw with shock that he wasn't a kid either—he had a fair, hairless face, cheeks reddened slightly as if the veins grew too close to the surface of his skin, the face of a forty-year-old baby. Connie felt a wave of dizziness rise in her at this sight and she stared at him as if waiting for something to change the shock of the moment, make it all right again. Ellie's lips kept shaping words, mumbling along, with the words blasting in his ear.

"Maybe you two better go away," Connie said faintly.

"What? How come?" Arnold Friend cried. "We come out here to take you for a ride. It's Sunday." He had the voice of the man on the radio now. It was the same voice, Connie thought. "Don'tcha know it's Sunday all day and honey, no matter who you were with last night today you're with Arnold Friend and don't you forget it!—Maybe you better step out here," he said, and this last was in a different voice. It was a little flatter, as if the heat was finally getting to him.

"No. I got things to do."

90   "Hey."

"You two better leave."

"We ain't leaving until you come with us."

"Like hell I am—"

"Connie, don't fool around with me. I mean, I mean, don't fool *around,*" he said, shaking his head. He laughed incredulously. He placed his sunglasses on top of his head, carefully, as if he were indeed wearing a wig, and brought the stems down behind his ears. Connie stared at him, another wave of dizziness and fear rising in her so that for a moment he wasn't even in focus but was just a blur, standing there against his gold car, and she had the idea that he had driven up the driveway all right but had come from nowhere before that and belonged nowhere and that everything about him and even about the music that was so familiar to her was only half real.

95   "If my father comes and sees you—"

"He ain't coming. He's at a barbecue."

"How do you know that?"

"Aunt Tillie's. Right now they're—uh—they're drinking. Sitting around," he said vaguely, squinting as if he were staring all the way to town and over to Aunt Tillie's backyard. Then the vision seemed to get clear and he nodded energetically. "Yeah. Sitting around. There's your sister in a blue dress, huh? And high heels, the poor sad bitch—nothing like you, sweetheart! And your mother's helping some fat woman with the corn, they're cleaning the corn—husking the corn—"

"What fat woman?" Connie cried.

100   "How do I know what fat woman. I don't know every goddam fat woman in the world!" Arnold Friend laughed.

"Oh, that's Mrs. Hornby. . . . Who invited her?" Connie said. She felt a little light-headed. Her breath was coming quickly.

"She's too fat. I don't like them fat. I like them the way you are, honey," he said, smiling sleepily at her. They stared at each other for a while, through the screen door. He said softly, "Now what you're going to do is this: you're going to come out that door. You're going to sit up front with me and Ellie's going to sit in the back, the hell with Ellie, right? This isn't Ellie's date. You're my date. I'm your lover, honey."

"What? You're crazy—"

"Yes, I'm your lover. You don't know what that is but you will," he said. "I know that too. I know all about you. But look: it's real nice and you couldn't ask for nobody better than me, or more polite. I always keep my word. I'll tell you how it is, I'm always nice at first, the first time. I'll hold you so tight you won't think you have to try to get away or pretend anything because you'll know you can't. And I'll come inside you where it's all secret and you'll give in to me and you'll love me—"

105   "Shut up! You're crazy!" Connie said. She backed away from the door. She put her hands against her ears as if she'd heard something terrible, something not meant for her. "People don't talk like that, you're crazy," she muttered. Her heart was almost too big now for her chest and its pumping made sweat break out all over her. She looked out to see Arnold Friend pause and then take a step toward the porch lurching. He almost fell. But, like a clever drunken man, he managed to catch his balance. He wobbled in his high boots and grabbed hold of one of the porch posts.

"Honey?" he said. "You still listening?"

"Get the hell out of here!"

"Be nice, honey. Listen."

"I'm going to call the police—"

110   He wobbled again and out of the side of his mouth came a fast spat curse, an aside not meant for her to hear. But even this "Christ!" sounded forced. Then he began to smile again. She watched this smile come, awkward as if he were smiling from inside a mask. His whole face was a mask, she thought wildly, tanned down onto his throat but then running out as if he had plastered makeup on his face but had forgotten about his throat.

"Honey—? Listen, here's how it is. I always tell the truth and I promise you this: I ain't coming in that house after you."

"You better not! I'm going to call the police if you—if you don't—"

"Honey," he said, talking right through her voice, "honey, I'm not coming in there but you are coming out here. You know why?"

She was panting. The kitchen looked like a place she had never seen before, some room she had run inside but which wasn't good enough, wasn't going to help her. The kitchen window had never had a curtain, after three years, and there were dishes in the sink for her to do—probably—and if you ran your hand across the table you'd probably feel something sticky there.

115   "You listening, honey? Hey?"
            "—going to call the police—"
            "Soon as you touch the phone I don't need to keep my promise and can
       come inside. You won't want that."
            She rushed forward and tried to lock the door. Her fingers were shak-
       ing. "But why lock it," Arnold Friend said gently, talking right into her face.
       "It's just a screen door. It's just nothing." One of his boots was at a strange
       angle, as if his foot wasn't in it. It pointed out to the left, bent at the ankle.
       "I mean, anybody can break through a screen door and glass and wood and
       iron or anything else if he needs to, anybody at all and specially Arnold
       Friend. If the place got lit up with a fire honey you'd come runnin' out into
       my arms, right into my arms an' safe at home—like you knew I was your
       lover and'd stopped fooling around. I don't mind a nice shy girl but I don't
       like no fooling around." Part of those words were spoken with a slight
       rhythmic lilt, and Connie somehow recognized them—the echo of a song
       from last year, about a girl rushing into her boyfriend's arms and coming
       home again—
            Connie stood barefoot on the linoleum floor, staring at him. "What do
       you want?" she whispered.
120   "I want you," he said.
            "What?"
            "Seen you that night and thought, that's the one, yes sir. I never needed
       to look any more."
            "But my father's coming back. He's coming to get me. I had to wash
       my hair first—" She spoke in a dry, rapid voice, hardly raising it for him to
       hear.
            "No, your Daddy is not coming and yes, you had to wash your hair and
       you washed it for me. It's nice and shining and all for me, I thank you,
       sweetheart," he said, with a mock bow, but again he almost lost his balance.
       He had to bend and adjust his boots. Evidently his feet did not go all
       the way down; the boots must have been stuffed with something so that he
       would seem taller. Connie stared out at him and behind him Ellie in the car,
       who seemed to be looking off toward Connie's right, into nothing. This Ellie
       said, pulling the words out of the air one after another as if he were just dis-
       covering them, "You want me to pull out the phone?"
125   "Shut your mouth and keep it shut," Arnold Friend said, his face red from
       bending over or maybe from embarrassment because Connie had seen his
       boots. "This ain't none of your business."
            "What—what are you doing? What do you want?" Connie said. "If I call
       the police they'll get you, they'll arrest you—"
            "Promise was not to come in unless you touch that phone, and I'll keep
       that promise," he said. He resumed his erect position and tried to force his
       shoulders back. He sounded like a hero in a movie, declaring something
       important. He spoke too loudly and it was as if he were speaking to some-
       one behind Connie. "I ain't made plans for coming in that house where
       I don't belong but just for you to come out to me, the way you should. Don't
       you know who I am?"
            "You're crazy," she whispered. She backed away from the door but did
       not want to go into another part of the house, as if this would give him per-
       mission to come through the door. "What do you . . . You're crazy, you . . . ."
            "Huh? What're you saying, honey?"

130   Her eyes darted everywhere in the kitchen. She could not remember what it was, this room.

"This is how it is, honey: you come out and we'll drive away, have a nice ride. But if you don't come out we're gonna wait till your people come home and then they're all going to get it."

"You want that telephone pulled out?" Ellie said. He held the radio away from his ear and grimaced, as if without the radio the air was too much for him.

"I toldja shut up, Ellie," Arnold Friend said, "you're deaf, get a hearing aid, right? Fix yourself up. This little girl's no trouble and's gonna be nice to me, so Ellie keep to yourself, this ain't your date—right? Don't hem in on me. Don't hog. Don't crush. Don't bird dog. Don't trail me," he said in a rapid meaningless voice, as if he were running through all the expressions he'd learned but was no longer sure which one of them was in style, then rushing on to new ones, making them up with his eyes closed, "Don't crawl under my fence, don't squeeze in my chipmunk hole, don't sniff my glue, suck my popsicle, keep your own greasy fingers on yourself!" He shaded his eyes and peered in at Connie, who was backed against the kitchen table. "Don't mind him honey he's just a creep. He's a dope. Right? I'm the boy for you and like I said you come out here nice like a lady and give me your hand, and nobody else gets hurt, I mean, your nice old bald-headed daddy and your mummy and your sister in her high heels. Because listen: why bring them in this?"

"Leave me alone," Connie whispered.

135   "Hey, you know that old woman down the road, the one with the chickens and stuff—you know her?"

"She's dead!"

"Dead? What? You know her?" Arnold Friend said.

"She's dead—"

"Don't you like her?"

140   "She's dead—she's—she isn't here any more—"

"But don't you like her, I mean, you got something against her? Some grudge or something?" Then his voice dipped as if he were conscious of a rudeness. He touched the sunglasses perched on top of his head as if to make sure they were still there. "Now you be a good girl."

"What are you going to do?"

"Just two things, or maybe three," Arnold Friend said. "But I promise it won't last long and you'll like me the way you get to like people you're close to. You will. It's all over for you here, so come on out. You don't want your people in any trouble, do you?"

She turned and bumped against a chair or something, hurting her leg, but she ran into the back room and picked up the telephone. Something roared in her ear, a tiny roaring, and she was so sick with fear that she could do nothing but listen to it—the telephone was clammy and very heavy and her fingers groped down to the dial but were too weak to touch it. She began to scream into the phone, into the roaring. She cried out, she cried for her mother, she felt her breath start jerking back and forth in her lungs as if it were something Arnold Friend were stabbing her with again and again with no tenderness. A noisy sorrowful wailing rose all about her and she was locked inside it the way she was locked inside the house.

145   After a while she could hear again. She was sitting on the floor with her wet back against the wall.

Arnold Friend was saying from the door, "That's a good girl. Put the phone back."

She kicked the phone away from her.

"No, honey. Pick it up. Put it back right."

She picked it up and put it back. The dial tone stopped.

150   "That's a good girl. Now come outside."

She was hollow with what had been fear, but what was now just an emptiness. All that screaming had blasted it out of her. She sat, one leg cramped under her, and deep inside her brain was something like a pinpoint of light that kept going and would not let her relax. She thought, I'm not going to see my mother again. She thought, I'm not going to sleep in my bed again. Her bright green blouse was all wet.

Arnold Friend said, in a gentle-loud voice that was like a stage voice, "The place where you came from ain't there any more, and where you had in mind to go is canceled out. This place you are now—inside your daddy's house—is nothing but a cardboard box I can knock down any time. You know that and always did know it. You hear me?"

She thought, I have got to think. I have to know what to do.

"We'll go out to a nice field, out in the country here where it smells so nice and it's sunny," Arnold Friend said. "I'll have my arms tight around you so you won't need to try to get away and I'll show you what love is like, what it does. The hell with this house! It looks solid all right," he said. He ran a fingernail down the screen and the noise did not make Connie shiver, as it would have the day before. "Now put your hand on your heart, honey. Feel that? That feels solid too but we know better, be nice to me, be sweet like you can because what else is there for a girl like you but to be sweet and pretty and give in?—and get away before her people come back?"

155   She felt her pounding heart. Her hand seemed to enclose it. She thought for the first time in her life that it was nothing that was hers, that belonged to her, but just a pounding, living thing inside this body that wasn't really hers either.

"You don't want them to get hurt," Arnold Friend went on. "Now get up, honey. Get up all by yourself."

She stood up.

"Now turn this way. That's right. Come over here to me—Ellie, put that away, didn't I tell you? You dope. You miserable creepy dope," Arnold Friend said. His words were not angry but only part of an incantation. The incantation was kindly. "Now come out through the kitchen to me honey, and let's see a smile, try it, you're a brave sweet little girl and now they're eating corn and hot dogs cooked to bursting over an outdoor fire, and they don't know one thing about you and never did and honey you're better than them because not a one of them would have done this for you."

Connie felt the linoleum under her feet; it was cool. She brushed her hair back out of her eyes. Arnold Friend let go of the post tentatively and opened his arms for her, his elbows pointing in toward each other and his wrists limp, to show that this was an embarrassed embrace and a little mocking, he didn't want to make her self-conscious.

160   She put out her hand against the screen. She watched herself push the door slowly open as if she were safe back somewhere in the other doorway, watching this body and this head of long hair moving out into the sunlight where Arnold Friend waited.

"My sweet little blue-eyed girl," he said, in a half-sung sigh that had nothing to do with her brown eyes but was taken up just the same by the vast sunlit reaches of the land behind him and on all sides of him, so much land that Connie had never seen before and did not recognize except to know that she was going to it.

TIM O'BRIEN

Tim O'Brien, born in 1947 in Austin, Minnesota, was drafted into the army in 1968 and served as an infantryman in Vietnam. Drawing on this experience he wrote a memoir, If I Die in a Combat Zone *(1973), in which he explains that he did not believe in the Vietnam War, considered dodging the draft, but, lacking the courage to do so, he served, largely out of fear and embarrassment. A later book, a novel titled* Going after Cacciato, *won the National Book Award in 1979. O'Brien's recent books include the novels* Tomcat in Love *(1998) and* July, July *(2002).*

"The Things They Carried," first published in 1986, in 1990 was republished as one of a series of interlocking stories in a book titled The Things They Carried. *In one of the stories, "How To Tell a True War Story," O'Brien writes,*

> *A true war story is never moral. It does not instruct, nor encourage virtue, nor suggest models of proper human behavior. . . . If a story seems moral, do not believe it. If at the end of a war story you feel uplifted, or if you feel that some small bit of rectitude has been salvaged from the larger waste, then you have been made the victim of a very old and terrible lie. There is no rectitude whatsoever. There is no virtue. As a first rule of thumb, therefore, you can tell a true war story by its absolute and uncompromising allegiance to obscenity and evil.*

The Things They Carried   [1986]

First Lieutenant Jimmy Cross carried letters from a girl named Martha, a junior at Mount Sebastian College in New Jersey. They were not love letters, but Lieutenant Cross was hoping, so he kept them folded in plastic at the bottom of his rucksack. In the late afternoon, after a day's march, he would dig his foxhole, wash his hands under a canteen, unwrap the letters, hold them with the tips of his fingers, and spend the last hour of light pretending. He would imagine romantic camping trips into the White Mountains in New Hampshire. He would sometimes taste the envelope flaps, knowing her tongue had been there. More than anything, he wanted Martha to love him as he loved her, but the letters were mostly chatty, elusive on the matter of love. She was a virgin, he was almost sure. She was an English major at Mount Sebastian, and she wrote beautifully about her professors and roommates and midterm exams, about her respect for Chaucer and her great affection for Virginia Woolf. She often quoted lines of poetry; she never mentioned the war, except to say, Jimmy, take care of yourself. The letters weighed 10 ounces. They were signed Love, Martha, but Lieutenant Cross understood that Love was only a way of signing and did not mean what he sometimes pretended it meant. At dusk, he would carefully return the letters to his rucksack. Slowly, a bit distracted, he would get up and move among his men, checking the perimeter, then at full dark he would return to his hole and watch the night and wonder if Martha was a virgin.

The things they carried were largely determined by necessity. Among the necessities or near-necessities were P-38 can openers, pocket knives, heat tabs, wrist watches, dog tags, mosquito repellent, chewing gum, candy, cigarettes, salt tablets, packets of Kool-Aid, lighters, matches, sewing kits, Military Payment Certificates, C rations, and two or three canteens of water. Together, these items weighed between 15 and 20 pounds, depending upon a man's habits or rate of metabolism. Henry Dobbins, who was a big man, carried extra rations; he was especially fond of canned peaches in heavy syrup over pound cake. Dave Jensen, who practiced field hygiene, carried a toothbrush, dental floss, and several hotel-sized bars of soap he'd stolen on R&R[1] in Sydney, Australia. Ted Lavender, who was scared, carried tranquilizers until he was shot in the head outside the village of Than Khe in mid-April. By necessity, and because it was SOP,[2] they all carried steel helmets that weighed 5 pounds including the liner and camouflage cover. They carried the standard fatigue jackets and trousers. Very few carried underwear. On their feet they carried jungle boots—2.1 pounds—and Dave Jensen carried three pairs of socks and a can of Dr. Scholl's foot powder as a precaution against trench foot. Until he was shot, Ted Lavender carried 6 or 7 ounces of premium dope, which for him was a necessity. Mitchell Sanders, the RTO,[3] carried condoms. Norman Bowker carried a diary. Rat Kiley carried comic books. Kiowa, a devout Baptist, carried an illustrated New Testament that had been presented to him by his father, who taught Sunday school in Oklahoma City, Oklahoma. As a hedge against bad times, however, Kiowa also carried his grandmother's distrust of the white man, his grandfather's old hunting hatchet. Necessity dictated. Because the land was mined and booby-trapped, it was SOP for each man to carry a steel-centered, nylon-covered flak jacket, which weighed 6.7 pounds, but which on hot days seemed much heavier. Because you could die so quickly, each man carried at least one large compress bandage, usually in the helmet band for easy access. Because the nights were cold, and because the monsoons were wet, each carried a green plastic poncho that could be used as a raincoat or groundsheet or makeshift tent. With its quilted liner, the poncho weighed almost 2 pounds, but it was worth every ounce. In April, for instance, when Ted Lavender was shot, they used his poncho to wrap him up, then to carry him across the paddy, then to lift him into the chopper that took him away.

They were called legs or grunts.

To carry something was to hump it, as when Lieutenant Jimmy Cross humped his love for Martha up the hills and through the swamps. In its intransitive form, to hump meant to walk, or to march, but it implied burdens far beyond the intransitive.

5   Almost everyone humped photographs. In his wallet, Lieutenant Cross carried two photographs of Martha. The first was a Kodacolor snapshot

---

[1]**R&R** rest and recreation leave.   [2]**SOP** standard operating procedure.   [3]**RTO** radio and telephone operator.

signed Love, though he knew better. She stood against a brick wall. Her eyes were gray and neutral, her lips slightly open as she stared straight-on at the camera. At night, sometimes, Lieutenant Cross wondered who had taken the picture, because he knew she had boyfriends, because he loved her so much, and because he could see the shadow of the picture taker spreading out against the brick wall. The second photograph had been clipped from the 1968 Mount Sebastian yearbook. It was an action shot—women's volleyball—and Martha was bent horizontal to the floor, reaching, the palms of her hands in sharp focus, the tongue taut, the expression frank and competitive. There was no visible sweat. She wore white gym shorts. Her legs, he thought, were almost certainly the legs of a virgin, dry and without hair, the left knee cocked and carrying her entire weight, which was just over 100 pounds. Lieutenant Cross remembered touching that left knee. A dark theater, he remembered, and the movie was *Bonnie and Clyde,* and Martha wore a tweed skirt, and during the final scene, when he touched her knee, she turned and looked at him in a sad, sober way that made him pull his hand back, but he would always remember the feel of the tweed skirt and the knee beneath it and the sound of the gunfire that killed Bonnie and Clyde, how embarrassing it was, how slow and oppressive. He remembered kissing her goodnight at the dorm door. Right then, he thought, he should've done something brave. He should've carried her up the stairs to her room and tied her to the bed and touched that left knee all night long. He should've risked it. Whenever he looked at the photographs, he thought of new things he should've done.

What they carried was partly a function of rank, partly of field specialty.

As a first lieutenant and platoon leader, Jimmy Cross carried a compass, maps, code books, binoculars, and a .45-caliber pistol that weighed 2.9 pounds fully loaded. He carried a strobe light and the responsibility for the lives of his men.

As an RTO, Mitchell Sanders carried the PRC-25 radio, a killer, 26 pounds with its battery.

As a medic, Rat Kiley carried a canvas satchel filled with morphine and plasma and malaria tablets and surgical tape and comic books and all the things a medic must carry, including M&M's[4] for especially bad wounds, for a total weight of nearly 20 pounds.

10   As a big man, therefore a machine gunner, Henry Dobbins carried the M-60, which weighed 23 pounds unloaded, but which was almost always loaded. In addition, Dobbins carried between 10 and 15 pounds of ammunition draped in belts across his chest and shoulders.

As PFCs or Spec 4s, most of them were common grunts and carried the standard M-16 gas-operated assault rifle. The weapon weighed 7.5 pounds unloaded, 8.2 pounds with its full 20-round magazine. Depending on numerous factors, such as topography and psychology, the riflemen carried anywhere from 12 to 20 magazines, usually in cloth bandoliers, adding on another 8.4 pounds at minimum, 14 pounds at maximum. When it was available, they also carried M-16 maintenance gear—rods and steel brushes and swabs and tubes of LSA oil—all of which weighed about a pound.

---

[4]**M&M** joking term for medical supplies.

Among the grunts, some carried the M-79 grenade launcher, 5.9 pounds unloaded, a reasonably light weapon except for the ammunition, which was
heavy. A single round weighed 10 ounces. The typical load was 25 rounds.
But Ted Lavender, who was scared, carried 34 rounds when he was shot and
killed outside Than Khe, and he went down under an exceptional burden,
more than 20 pounds of ammunition, plus the flak jacket and helmet and rations and water and toilet paper and tranquilizers and all the rest, plus the
unweighed fear. He was dead weight. There was no twitching or flopping.
Kiowa, who saw it happen, said it was like watching a rock fall, or a big sand-
bag or something—just boom, then down—not like the movies where the
dead guy rolls around and does fancy spins and goes ass over teakettle—not
like that, Kiowa said, the poor bastard just flat-fuck fell. Boom. Down. Nothing else. It was a bright morning in mid-April. Lieutenant Cross felt the pain.
He blamed himself. They stripped off Lavender's canteens and ammo, all the
heavy things, and Rat Kiley said the obvious, the guy's dead, and Mitchell
Sanders used his radio to report one U.S. KIA[5] and to request a chopper.
Then they wrapped Lavender in his poncho. They carried him out to a dry
paddy, established security, and sat smoking the dead man's dope until the
chopper came. Lieutenant Cross kept to himself. He pictured Martha's
smooth young face, thinking he loved her more than anything, more than his
men, and now Ted Lavender was dead because he loved her so much and
could not stop thinking about her. When the dustoff arrived, they carried
Lavender aboard. Afterward they burned Than Khe. They marched until
dusk, then dug their holes, and that night Kiowa kept explaining how you
had to be there, how fast it was, how the poor guy just dropped like so
much concrete. Boom-down, he said. Like cement.

In addition to the three standard weapons—the M-60, M-16, and M-79—
they carried whatever presented itself, or whatever seemed appropriate as a
means of killing or staying alive. They carried catch-as-catch-can. At various
times, in various situations, they carried M-14s and CAR-15s and Swedish Ks
and grease guns and captured AK-47s and Chi-Coms and RPGs and Simonov
carbines and black market Uzis and .38-caliber Smith & Wesson handguns
and 66 mm LAWs and shotguns and silencers and blackjacks and bayonets
and C-4 plastic explosives. Lee Strunk carried a slingshot; a weapon of last
resort, he called it. Mitchell Sanders carried brass knuckles. Kiowa carried
his grandfather's feathered hatchet. Every third or fourth man carried a Clay-
more antipersonnel mine—3.5 pounds with its firing device. They all carried fragmentation grenades—14 ounces each. They all carried at least one
M-18 colored smoke grenade—24 ounces. Some carried CS or tear gas
grenades. Some carried white phosphorus grenades. They carried all they
could bear, and then some, including a silent awe for the terrible power of
the things they carried.

In the first week of April, before Lavender died, Lieutenant Jimmy Cross
received a good-luck charm from Martha. It was a simple pebble, an ounce at
most. Smooth to the touch, it was a milky white color with flecks of orange
and violet, oval-shaped, like a miniature egg. In the accompanying letter,

---

[5]**KIA** killed in action.

Martha wrote that she had found the pebble on the Jersey shoreline, precisely where the land touched water at high tide, where things came together but also separated. It was this separate-but-together quality, she
wrote, that had inspired her to pick up the pebble and to carry it in her
breast pocket for several days, where it seemed weightless, and then to send
it through the mail, by air, as a token of her truest feelings for him. Lieutenant Cross found this romantic. But he wondered what her truest feelings
were, exactly, and what she meant by separate-but-together. He wondered
how the tides and waves had come into play on that afternoon along the Jersey shoreline when Martha saw the pebble and bent down to rescue it from
geology. He imagined bare feet. Martha was a poet, with the poet's sensibilities, and her feet would be brown and bare, the toenails unpainted, the eyes
chilly and somber like the ocean in March, and though it was painful, he
wondered who had been with her that afternoon. He imagined a pair of
shadows moving along the strip of sand where things came together but
also separated. It was phantom jealousy, he knew, but he couldn't help himself. He loved her so much. On the march, through the hot days of early
April, he carried the pebble in his mouth, turning it with his tongue, tasting
sea salt and moisture. His mind wandered. He had difficulty keeping his attention on the war. On occasion he would yell at his men to spread out the
column, to keep their eyes open, but then he would slip away into daydreams, just pretending, walking barefoot along the Jersey shore, with
Martha, carrying nothing. He would feel himself rising. Sun and waves and
gentle winds, all love and lightness.

What they carried varied by mission.

15   When a mission took them to the mountains, they carried mosquito netting, machetes, canvas tarps, and extra bug juice.

If a mission seemed especially hazardous, or if it involved a place they
knew to be bad, they carried everything they could. In certain heavily mined
AOs,[6] where the land was dense with Toe Poppers and Bouncing Betties,
they took turns humping a 28-pound mine detector. With its headphones
and big sensing plate, the equipment was a stress on the lower back and
shoulders, awkward to handle, often useless because of the shrapnel in the
earth, but they carried it anyway, partly for safety, partly for the illusion of
safety.

On ambush, or other night missions, they carried peculiar little odds
and ends. Kiowa always took along his New Testament and a pair of moccasins for silence. Dave Jensen carried night-sight vitamins high in carotene.
Lee Strunk carried his slingshot; ammo, he claimed, would never be a problem. Rat Kiley carried brandy and M&M's candy. Until he was shot, Ted
Lavender carried the starlight scope, which weighed 6.3 pounds with its aluminum carrying case. Henry Dobbins carried his girlfriend's pantyhose
wrapped around his neck as a comforter. They all carried ghosts. When dark
came, they would move out single file across the meadows and paddies to
their ambush coordinates, where they would quietly set up the Claymores
and lie down and spend the night waiting.

---

[6]**AOs** areas of operation.

Other missions were more complicated and required special equipment. In mid-April, it was their mission to search out and destroy the elaborate tunnel complexes in the Than Khe area south of Chu Lai. To blow the tunnels, they carried one-pound blocks of pentrite high explosives, four blocks to a man, 68 pounds in all. They carried wiring, detonators, and battery-powdered clackers. Dave Jensen carried earplugs. Most often, before blowing the tunnels, they were ordered by higher command to search them, which was considered bad news, but by and large they just shrugged and carried out orders. Because he was a big man, Henry Dobbins was excused from tunnel duty. The others would draw numbers. Before Lavender died there were 17 men in the platoon, and whoever drew the number 17 would strip off his gear and crawl in headfirst with a flashlight and Lieutenant Cross's .45-caliber pistol. The rest of them would fan out as security. They would sit down or kneel, not facing the hole, listening to the ground beneath them, imagining cobwebs and ghosts, whatever was down there—the tunnel walls squeezing in—how the flashlight seemed impossibly heavy in the hand and how it was tunnel vision in the very strictest sense, compression in all ways, even time, and how you had to wiggle in—ass and elbows—a swallowed-up feeling—and how you found yourself worrying about odd things: Will your flashlight go dead? Do rats carry rabies? If you screamed, how far would the sound carry? Would your buddies hear it? Would they have the courage to drag you out? In some respects, though not many, the waiting was worse than the tunnel itself. Imagination was a killer.

On April 16, when Lee Strunk drew the number 17, he laughed and muttered something and went down quickly. The morning was hot and very still. Not good, Kiowa said. He looked at the tunnel opening, then out across a dry paddy toward the village of Than Khe. Nothing moved. No clouds or birds or people. As they waited, the men smoked and drank Kool-Aid, not talking much, feeling sympathy for Lee Strunk but also feeling the luck of the draw. You win some, you lose some, said Mitchell Sanders, and sometimes you settle for a rain check. It was a tired line and no one laughed.

20   Henry Dobbins ate a tropical chocolate bar. Ted Lavender popped a tranquilizer and went off to pee.

After five minutes, Lieutenant Jimmy Cross moved to the tunnel, leaned down, and examined the darkness. Trouble, he thought—a cave-in maybe. And then suddenly, without willing it, he was thinking about Martha. The stresses and fractures, the quick collapse, the two of them buried alive under all that weight. Dense, crushing love. Kneeling, watching the hole, he tried to concentrate on Lee Strunk and the war, all the dangers, but his love was too much for him, he felt paralyzed, he wanted to sleep inside her lungs and breathe her blood and be smothered. He wanted her to be a virgin and not a virgin, all at once. He wanted to know her. Intimate secrets: Why poetry? Why so sad? Why that grayness in her eyes? Why so alone? Not lonely, just alone—riding her bike across campus or sitting off by herself in the cafeteria—even dancing, she danced alone—and it was the aloneness that filled him with love. He remembered telling her that one evening. How she nodded and looked away. And how, later, when he kissed her, she received the kiss without returning it, her eyes wide open, not afraid, not a virgin's eyes, just flat and uninvolved.

Lieutenant Cross gazed at the tunnel. But he was not there. He was buried with Martha under the white sand at the Jersey shore. They were pressed together, and the pebble in his mouth was her tongue. He was smiling. Vaguely, he was aware of how quiet the day was, the sullen paddies, yet he could not bring himself to worry about matters of security. He was beyond that. He was just a kid at war, in love. He was twenty-four years old. He couldn't help it.

A few moments later Lee Strunk crawled out of the tunnel. He came up grinning, filthy but alive. Lieutenant Cross nodded and closed his eyes while the others clapped Strunk on the back and made jokes about rising from the dead.

Worms, Rat Kiley said. Right out of the grave. Fuckin' zombie.

25   The men laughed. They all felt great relief.

Spook city, said Mitchell Sanders.

Lee Strunk made a funny ghost sound, a kind of moaning, yet very happy, and right then, when Strunk made that high happy moaning sound, when he went *Ahhooooo,* right then Ted Lavender was shot in the head on his way back from peeing. He lay with his mouth open. The teeth were broken. There was a swollen black bruise under his left eye. The cheekbone was gone. Oh shit, Rat Kiley said, the guy's dead. The guy's dead, he kept saying, which seemed profound—the guy's dead. I mean really.

The things they carried were determined to some extent by superstition. Lieutenant Cross carried his good-luck pebble. Dave Jensen carried a rabbit's foot. Norman Bowker, otherwise a very gentle person, carried a thumb that had been presented to him as a gift by Mitchell Sanders. The thumb was dark brown, rubbery to the touch, and weighed 4 ounces at most. It had been cut from a VC corpse, a boy of fifteen or sixteen. They'd found him at the bottom of an irrigation ditch, badly burned, flies in his mouth and eyes. The boy wore black shorts and sandals. At the time of his death he had been carrying a pouch of rice, a rifle, and three magazines of ammunition.

You want my opinion, Mitchell Sanders said, there's a definite moral here.

30   He put his hand on the dead boy's wrist. He was quiet for a time, as if counting a pulse, then he patted the stomach, almost affectionately, and used Kiowa's hunting hatchet to remove the thumb.

Henry Dobbins asked what the moral was.

Moral?

You know. *Moral.*

Sanders wrapped the thumb in toilet paper and handed it across to Norman Bowker. There was no blood. Smiling, he kicked the boy's head, watched the flies scatter, and said, It's like with that old TV show—Paladin. Have gun, will travel.

35   Henry Dobbins thought about it.

Yeah, well, he finally said. I don't see no moral.

There it *is,* man.

Fuck off.

They carried USO stationery and pencils and pens. They carried Sterno, safety pins, trip flares, signal flares, spools of wire, razor blades, chewing tobacco, liberated joss sticks and statuettes of the smiling Buddha, candles, grease pencils, *The Stars and Stripes,* fingernail clippers, Psy Ops leaflets, bush hats, bolos, and much more. Twice a week, when the resupply choppers came in, they carried hot chow in green Mermite cans and large canvas bags filled with iced beer and soda pop. They carried plastic water containers, each with a 2-gallon capacity. Mitchell Sanders carried a set of starched tiger fatigues for special occasions. Henry Dobbins carried Black Flag insecticide. Dave Jensen carried empty sandbags that could be filled at night for added protection. Lee Strunk carried tanning lotion. Some things they carried in common. Taking turns, they carried the big PRC-77 scrambler radio, which weighed 30 pounds with its battery. They shared the weight of memory. They took up what others could no longer bear. Often, they carried each other, the wounded or weak. They carried infections. They carried chess sets, basketballs, Vietnamese-English dictionaries, insignia of rank, Bronze Stars and Purple Hearts, plastic cards imprinted with the Code of Conduct. They carried diseases, among them malaria and dysentery. They carried lice and ringworm and leeches and paddy algae and various rots and molds. They carried the land itself—Vietnam, the place, the soil—a powdery orange-red dust that covered their boots and fatigues and faces. They carried the sky. The whole atmosphere, they carried it, the humidity, the monsoons, the stink of fungus and decay, all of it, they carried gravity. They moved like mules. By daylight they took sniper fire, at night they were mortared, but it was not battle, it was just the endless march, village to village, without purpose, nothing won or lost. They marched for the sake of the march. They plodded along slowly, dumbly, leaning forward against the heat, unthinking, all blood and bone, simple grunts, soldiering with their legs, toiling up the hills and down into the paddies and across the rivers and up again and down, just humping, one step and then the next and then another, but no volition, no will, because it was automatic, it was anatomy, and the war was entirely a matter of posture and carriage, the hump was everything, a kind of inertia, a kind of emptiness, a dullness of desire and intellect and conscience and hope and human sensibility. Their principles were in their feet. Their calculations were biological. They had no sense of strategy or mission. They searched the villages without knowing what to look for, nor caring, kicking over jars of rice, frisking children and old men, blowing tunnels, sometimes setting fires and sometimes not, then forming up and moving on to the next village, then other villages, where it would always be the same. They carried their own lives. The pressures were enormous. In the heat of early afternoon, they would remove their helmets and flak jackets, walking bare, which was dangerous but which helped ease the strain. They would often discard things along the route of march. Purely for comfort, they would throw away rations, blow their Claymores and grenades, no matter, because by nightfall the resupply choppers would arrive with more of the same, then a day or two later still more, fresh watermelons and crates of ammunition and sunglasses and woolen sweaters—the resources were stunning—sparklers for the Fourth of July, colored eggs for Easter—it was the great American war chest—the fruits of science, the smoke stacks, the canneries, the arsenals at Hartford, the Minnesota forests, the machine shops, the vast fields of corn and wheat—they carried like freight trains; they carried it on their backs and shoulders—and for all the ambiguities of Vietnam, all the mysteries and unknowns, there was at least the single abiding certainty that they would never be at a loss for things to carry.

* * *

40   After the chopper took Lavender away, Lieutenant Jimmy Cross led his men into the village of Than Khe. They burned everything. They shot chickens and dogs, they trashed the village well, they called in artillery and watched the wreckage, then they marched for several hours through the hot afternoon, and then at dusk, while Kiowa explained how Lavender died, Lieutenant Cross found himself trembling.

He tried not to cry. With his entrenching tool, which weighed 5 pounds, he began digging a hole in the earth.

He felt shame. He hated himself. He had loved Martha more than his men, and as a consequence Lavender was now dead, and this was something he would have to carry like a stone in his stomach for the rest of the war.

All he could do was dig. He used his entrenching tool like an ax, slashing, feeling both love and hate, and then later, when it was full dark, he sat at the bottom of his foxhole and wept. It went on for a long while. In part, he was grieving for Ted Lavender, but mostly it was for Martha, and for himself, because she belonged to another world, which was not quite real, and because she was a junior at Mount Sebastian College in New Jersey, a poet and a virgin and uninvolved, and because he realized she did not love him and never would.

Like cement, Kiowa whispered in the dark. I swear to God—boom, down. Not a word.

45   I've heard this, said Norman Bowker.

A pisser, you know? Still zipping himself up. Zapped while zipping.

All right, fine. That's enough.

Yeah, but you had to see it, the guy just—

I *heard*, man. Cement. So why not shut the fuck *up?*

50   Kiowa shook his head sadly and glanced over at the hole where Lieutenant Jimmy Cross sat watching the night. The air was thick and wet. A warm dense fog had settled over the paddies and there was the stillness that precedes rain.

After a time Kiowa sighed.

One thing for sure, he said. The lieutenant's in some deep hurt. I mean that crying jag—the way he was carrying on—it wasn't fake or anything, it was real heavy-duty hurt. The man cares.

Sure, Norman Bowker said.

Say what you want, the man does care.

55   We all got problems.

Not Lavender.

No, I guess not, Bowker said. Do me a favor, though.

Shut up?

That's a smart Indian. Shut up.

60   Shrugging, Kiowa pulled off his boots. He wanted to say more, just to lighten up his sleep, but instead he opened his New Testament and arranged it beneath his head as a pillow. The fog made things seem hollow and unattached. He tried not to think about Ted Lavender, but then he was thinking how fast it was, no drama, down and dead, and how it was hard to feel anything except surprise. It seemed unchristian. He wished he could find some great sadness, or even anger, but the emotion wasn't there and he couldn't make it happen. Mostly he felt pleased to be alive. He liked the smell of the

New Testament under his cheek, the leather and ink and paper and glue, whatever the chemicals were. He liked hearing the sounds of night. Even his fatigue, it felt fine, the stiff muscles and the prickly awareness of his own body, a floating feeling. He enjoyed not being dead. Lying there, Kiowa admired Lieutenant Jimmy Cross's capacity for grief. He wanted to share the man's pain, he wanted to care as Jimmy Cross cared. And yet when he closed his eyes, all he could think was Boom-down, and all he could feel was the pleasure of having his boots off and the fog curling in around him and the damp soil and the Bible smells and the plush comfort of night.

After a moment Norman Bowker sat up in the dark.

What the hell, he said. You want to talk, *talk*. Tell it to me.

Forget it.

No, man, go on. One thing I hate, it's a silent Indian.

65   For the most part they carried themselves with poise, a kind of dignity. Now and then, however, there were times of panic, when they squealed or wanted to squeal but couldn't, when they twitched and made moaning sounds and covered their heads and said Dear Jesus and flopped around on the earth and fired their weapons blindly and cringed and sobbed and begged for the noise to stop and went wild and made stupid promises to themselves and to God and to their mothers and fathers, hoping not to die. In different ways, it happened to all of them. Afterward, when the firing ended, they would blink and peek up. They would touch their bodies, feeling shame, then quickly hiding it. They would force themselves to stand. As if in slow motion, frame by frame, the world would take on the old logic—absolute silence, then the wind, then sunlight, then voices. It was the burden of being alive. Awkwardly, the men would reassemble themselves, first in private, then in groups, becoming soldiers again. They would repair the leaks in their eyes. They would check for casualties, call in dustoffs, light cigarettes, try to smile, clear their throats and spit and begin cleaning their weapons. After a time someone would shake his head and say, No lie, I almost shit my pants, and someone else would laugh, which meant it was bad, yes, but the guy had obviously not shit his pants, it wasn't that bad, and in any case nobody would ever do such a thing and then go ahead and talk about it. They would squint into the dense, oppressive sunlight. For a few moments, perhaps, they would fall silent, lighting a joint and tracking its passage from man to man, inhaling, holding in the humiliation. Scary stuff, one of them might say. But then someone else would grin or flick his eyebrows and say, Roger-dodger, almost cut me a new asshole, *almost*.

There were numerous such poses. Some carried themselves with a sort of wistful resignation, others with pride or stiff soldierly discipline or good humor or macho zeal. They were afraid of dying but they were even more afraid to show it.

They found jokes to tell.

They used a hard vocabulary to contain the terrible softness. *Greased*, they'd say. *Offed, lit up, zapped while zipping*. It wasn't cruelty, just stage presence. They were actors. When someone died, it wasn't quite dying, because in a curious way it seemed scripted, and because they had their lines mostly memorized, irony mixed with tragedy, and because they called it by other names, as if to encyst and destroy the reality of death itself. They kicked

corpses. They cut off thumbs. They talked grunt lingo. They told stories about
Ted Lavender's supply of tranquilizers, how the poor guy didn't feel a thing,
how incredibly tranquil he was.

There's a moral here, said Mitchell Sanders.

70   They were waiting for Lavender's chopper, smoking the dead man's dope.

The moral's pretty obvious, Sanders said, and winked. Stay away from
drugs. No joke, they'll ruin your day every time.

Cute, said Henry Dobbins.

Mind-blower, get it? Talk about wiggy. Nothing left, just blood and brains.

They made themselves laugh.

75   There it is, they'd say. Over and over—there it is, my friend, there it is—
as if the repetition itself were an act of poise, a balance between crazy and
almost crazy, knowing without going, there it is, which meant be cool, let it
ride, because Oh yeah, man, you can't change what can't be changed, there
it is, there it absolutely and positively and fucking well *is*.

They were tough.

They carried all the emotional baggage of men who might die. Grief, terror, love, longing—these were intangibles, but the intangibles had their own
mass and specific gravity, they had tangible weight. They carried shameful
memories. They carried the common secret of cowardice barely restrained,
the instinct to run or freeze or hide, and in many respects this was the heav-
iest burden of all, for it could never be put down, it required perfect balance
and perfect posture. They carried their reputations. They carried the
soldier's greatest fear, which was the fear of blushing. Men killed, and died,
because they were embarrassed not to. It was what had brought them to the
war in the first place, nothing positive, no dreams of glory or honor, just to
avoid the blush of dishonor. They died so as not to die of embarrassment.
They crawled into tunnels and walked point and advanced under fire. Each
morning, despite the unknowns, they made their legs move. They endured.
They kept humping. They did not submit to the obvious alternative, which
was simply to close the eyes and fall. So easy, really. Go limp and tumble to
the ground and let the muscles unwind and not speak and not budge until
your buddies picked you up and lifted you into the chopper that would roar
and dip its nose and carry you off to the world. A mere matter of falling, yet
no one ever fell. It was not courage, exactly; the object was not valor. Rather,
they were too frightened to be cowards.

By and large they carried these things inside, maintaining the masks of
composure. They sneered at sick call. They spoke bitterly about guys who
had found release by shooting off their own toes or fingers. Pussies, they'd
say. Candy-asses. It was fierce, mocking talk, with only a trace of envy or awe,
but even so the image played itself out behind their eyes.

They imagined the muzzle against flesh. So easy: squeeze the trigger
and blow away a toe. They imagined it. They imagined the quick, sweet pain,
then the evacuation to Japan, then a hospital with warm beds and cute
geisha nurses.

80   And they dreamed of freedom birds.

At night, on guard, staring into the dark, they were carried away by
jumbo jets. They felt the rush of takeoff. *Gone!* they yelled. And then
velocity—wings and engines—a smiling stewardess—but it was more
than a plane, it was a real bird, a big sleek silver bird with feathers and
talons and high screeching. They were flying. The weights fell off; there

He was realistic about it. There was that new hardness in his stomach. He loved her but he hated her.

No more fantasies, he told himself.

Henceforth, when he thought about Martha, it would be only to think that she belonged elsewhere. He would shut down the daydreams. This was not Mount Sebastian, it was another world, where there were no pretty poems or midterm exams, a place where men died because of carelessness and gross stupidity. Kiowa was right. Boom-down, and you were dead, never partly dead.

95   Briefly, in the rain, Lieutenant Cross saw Martha's gray eyes gazing back at him.

He understood.

It was very sad, he thought. The things men carried inside. The things men did or felt they had to do.

He almost nodded at her, but didn't.

Instead he went back to his maps. He was now determined to perform his duties firmly and without negligence. It wouldn't help Lavender, he knew that, but from this point on he would comport himself as an officer. He would dispose of his good-luck pebble. Swallow it, maybe, or use Lee Strunk's slingshot, or just drop it along the trail. On the march he would impose strict field discipline. He would be careful to send out flank security, to prevent straggling or bunching up, to keep his troops moving at the proper pace and at the proper interval. He would insist on clean weapons. He would confiscate the remainder of Lavender's dope. Later in the day, perhaps, he would call the men together and speak to them plainly. He would accept the blame for what had happened to Ted Lavender. He would be a man about it. He would look them in the eyes, keeping his chin level, and he would issue the new SOPs in a calm, impersonal tone of voice, a lieutenant's voice, leaving no room for argument or discussion. Commencing immediately, he'd tell them, they would no longer abandon equipment along the route of march. They would police up their acts. They would get their shit together, and keep it together, and maintain it neatly and in good working order.

100   He would not tolerate laxity. He would show strength, distancing himself.

Among the men there would be grumbling, of course, and maybe worse, because their days would seem longer and their loads heavier, but Lieutenant Jimmy Cross reminded himself that his obligation was not to be loved but to lead. He would dispense with love; it was not now a factor. And if anyone quarreled or complained, he would simply tighten his lips and arrange his shoulders in the correct command posture. He might give a curt little nod. Or he might not. He might just shrug and say, Carry on, then they would saddle up and form into a column and move out toward the villages west of Than Khe.

DANIEL OROZCO

Daniel Orozco, born in San Francisco in 1957, is chiefly known for his short stories. A professor of creative writing at the University of Idaho, Orozco has received several important awards, including a grant from the National Endowment for the Arts.

Orientation

[1994]

Those are the offices and these are the cubicles. That's my cubicle there, and this is your cubicle. This is your phone. Never answer your phone. Let the Voicemail System answer it. This is your Voicemail System Manual. There are no personal phone calls allowed. We do, however, allow for emergencies. If you must make an emergency phone call, ask your supervisor first. If you can't find your supervisor, ask Phillip Spiers, who sits over there. He'll check with Clarissa Nicks, who sits over there. If you make an emergency phone call without asking, you may be let go.

These are your IN and OUT boxes. All the forms in your IN box must be logged in by the date shown in the upper left-hand corner, initialed by you in the upper right-hand corner, and distributed to the Processing Analyst whose name is numerically coded in the lower left-hand corner. The lower right-hand corner is left blank. Here's your Processing Analyst Numerical Code Index. And here's your Forms Processing Procedures Manual.

You must pace your work. What do I mean? I'm glad you asked that. We pace our work according to the eight-hour workday. If you have twelve hours of work in your IN box, for example, you must compress that work into the eight-hour day. If you have one hour of work in your IN box, you must expand that work to fill the eight-hour day. That was a good question. Feel free to ask questions. Ask too many questions, however, and you may be let go.

That is our receptionist. She is a temp. We go through receptionists here. They quit with alarming frequency. Be polite and civil to the temps. Learn their names, and invite them to lunch occasionally. But don't get close to them, as it only makes it more difficult when they leave. And they always leave. You can be sure of that.

5   The men's room is over there. The women's room is over there. John LaFountaine, who sits over there, uses the women's room occasionally. He says it is accidental. We know better, but we let it pass. John LaFountaine is harmless, his forays into the forbidden territory of the women's room simply a benign thrill, a faint blip on the dull flat line of his life.

Russell Nash, who sits in the cubicle to your left, is in love with Amanda Pierce, who sits in the cubicle to your right. They ride the same bus together after work. For Amanda Pierce, it is just a tedious bus ride made less tedious by the idle nattering of Russell Nash. But for Russell Nash, it is the highlight of his day. It is the highlight of his life. Russell Nash has put on forty pounds; and grows fatter with each passing month, nibbling on chips and cookies while peeking glumly over the partitions at Amanda Pierce, and gorging himself at home on cold pizza and ice cream while watching adult videos on TV.

Amanda Pierce, in the cubicle to your right, has a six-year-old son named Jamie, who is autistic. Her cubicle is plastered from top to bottom with the boy's crayon artwork—sheet after sheet of precisely drawn concentric circles and ellipses, in black and yellow. She rotates them every other Friday. Be sure to comment on them. Amanda Pierce also has a husband, who is a lawyer. He subjects her to an escalating array of painful and humiliating sex games, to which Amanda Pierce reluctantly submits. She comes to work exhausted and freshly wounded each morning, wincing from the abrasions on her breasts, or the bruises on her abdomen, or the second-degree burns on the backs of her thighs.

But we're not supposed to know any of this. Do not let on. If you let on, you may be let go.

Amanda Pierce, who tolerates Russell Nash, is in love with Albert Bosch, whose office is over there. Albert Bosch, who only dimly registers Amanda Pierce's existence, has eyes only for Ellie Tapper, who sits over there. Ellie Tapper, who hates Albert Bosch, would walk through fire for Curtis Lance. But Curtis Lance hates Ellie Tapper. Isn't the world a funny place? Not in the ha-ha sense, of course.

10   Anika Bloom sits in that cubicle. Last year, while reviewing quarterly reports in a meeting with Barry Hacker, Anika Bloom's left palm began to bleed. She fell into a trance, stared into her hand, and told Barry Hacker when and how his wife would die. We laughed it off. She was, after all, a new employee. But Barry Hacker's wife is dead. So unless you want to know exactly when and how you'll die, never talk to Anika Bloom.

Colin Heavey sits in that cubicle over there. He was new once, just like you. We warned him about Anika Bloom. But at last year's Christmas Potluck, he felt sorry for her when he saw that no one was talking to her. Colin Heavey brought her a drink. He hasn't been himself since. Colin Heavey is doomed. There's nothing he can do about it, and we are powerless to help him. Stay away from Colin Heavey. Never give any of your work to him. If he asks to do something, tell him you have to check with me. If he asks again, tell him I haven't gotten back to you.

This is the Fire Exit. There are several on this floor, and they are marked accordingly. We have a Floor Evacuation Review every three months, and an Escape Route Quiz once a month. We have our Biannual Fire Drill twice a year, and our Annual Earthquake Drill once a year. These are precautions only. These things never happen.

For your information, we have a comprehensive health plan. Any catastrophic illness, any unforeseen tragedy is completely covered. All dependents are completely covered. Larry Bagdikian, who sits over there, has six daughters. If anything were to happen to any of his girls, or to all of them, if all six were to simultaneously fall victim to illness or injury—stricken with a hideous degenerative muscle disease or some rare toxic blood disorder, sprayed with semiautomatic gunfire while on a class field trip, or attacked in their bunk beds by some prowling nocturnal lunatic—if any of this were to pass, Larry's girls would all be taken care of. Larry Bagdikian would not have to pay one dime. He would have nothing to worry about.

We also have a generous vacation and sick leave policy. We have an excellent disability insurance plan. We have a stable and profitable pension fund. We get group discounts for the symphony, and block seating at the ballpark. We get commuter ticket books for the bridge. We have Direct Deposit. We are all members of Costco.

15   This is our kitchenette. And this, this is our Mr. Coffee. We have a coffee pool, into which we each pay two dollars a week for coffee, filters, sugar, and CoffeeMate. If you prefer Cremora or half-and-half to CoffeeMate, there is a special pool for three dollars a week. If you prefer Sweet 'n Low to sugar, there is a special pool for two-fifty a week. We do not do decaf. You are allowed to join the coffee pool of your choice, but you are not allowed to touch the Mr. Coffee.

This is the microwave oven. You are allowed to *heat* food in the microwave oven. You are not, however, allowed to *cook* food in the microwave oven.

We get one hour for lunch. We also get one fifteen-minute break in the morning, and one fifteen-minute break in the afternoon. Always take your breaks. If you skip a break, it is gone forever. For your information, your break is a privilege, not a right. If you abuse the break policy, we are authorized to rescind your breaks. Lunch, however, is a right, not a privilege. If you abuse the lunch policy, our hands will be tied, and we will be forced to look the other way. We will not enjoy that.

This is the refrigerator. You may put your lunch in it. Barry Hacker, who sits over there, steals food from this refrigerator. His petty theft is an outlet for his grief. Last New Year's Eve, while kissing his wife, a blood-vessel burst in her brain. Barry Hacker's wife was two months pregnant at the time, and lingered in a coma for half a year before dying. It was a tragic loss for Barry Hacker. He hasn't been himself since. Barry Hacker's wife was a beautiful woman. She was also completely covered. Barry Hacker did not have to pay one dime. But his dead wife haunts him. She haunts all of us. We have seen her, reflected in the monitors of our computers, moving past our cubicles. We have seen the dim shadow of her face in our photocopies. She pencils herself in in the receptionist's appointment book, with the notation: To see Barry Hacker. She has left messages in the receptionist's Voicemail box, messages garbled by the electronic chirrups and buzzes in the phone line, her voice echoing from an immense distance within the ambient hum. But the voice is hers. And beneath her voice, beneath the tidal *whoosh* of static and hiss, the gurgling and crying of a baby can be heard.

In any case, if you bring a lunch, put a little something extra in the bag for Barry Hacker. We have four Barrys in this office. Isn't that a coincidence?

20   This is Matthew Payne's office. He is our Unit Manager, and his door is always closed. We have never seen him, and you will never see him. But he is here. You can be sure of that. He is all around us.

This is the Custodian's Closet. You have no business in the Custodian's Closet.

And this, this is our Supplies Cabinet. If you need supplies, see Curtis Lance. He will log you in on the Supplies Cabinet Authorization Log, then give you a Supplies Authorization Slip. Present your pink copy of the Supplies Authorization Slip to Ellie Tapper. She will log you in on the Supplies Cabinet Key Log, then give you the key. Because the Supplies Cabinet is located outside the Unit Manager's office, you must be very quiet. Gather your supplies quietly. The Supplies Cabinet is divided into four sections. Section One contains letterhead stationary, blank paper and envelopes, memo and note pads, and so on. Section Two contains pens and pencils and typewriter and printer ribbons, and the like. In Section Three we have erasers, correction fluids, transparent tapes, glue sticks, et cetera. And in Section Four we have paper clips and push pins and scissors and razor blades. And here are the spare blades for the shredder. Do not touch the shredder, which is located over there. The shredder is of no concern to you.

Gwendolyn Stich sits in that office there. She is crazy about penguins, and collects penguin knickknacks: penguin posters and coffee mugs and stationery, penguin stuffed animals, penguin jewelry, penguin sweaters and T-shirts and socks. She has a pair of penguin fuzzy slippers she wears when working late at the office. She has a tape cassette of penguin sounds which she listens to for relaxation. Her favorite colors are black and white. She has personalized license plates that read PEN GWEN. Every morning, she passes through all the cubicles to wish each of us a *good* morning. She brings Danish on Wednesdays for Hump Day morning break, and doughnuts on Fridays for TGIF afternoon break. She organizes the Annual Christmas Potluck, and is in charge of the Birthday List. Gwendolyn Stich's door is always open to all of us. She will always lend an ear, and put in a good word for you; she will always give you a hand, or the shirt off her back, or a shoulder to cry on. Because her door is always open, she hides and cries in a stall in the women's room. And John LaFountaine—who, enthralled when a woman enters, sits quietly in his stall with his knees to his chest—John LaFountaine has heard her vomiting in there. We have come upon Gwendolyn Stich huddled in the stairwell, shivering in the updraft, sipping a Diet Mr. Pibb and hugging her knees. She does not let any of this interfere with her work. If it interfered with her work, she might have to be let go.

Kevin Howard sits in that cubicle over there. He is a serial killer, the one they call the Carpet Cutter, responsible for the mutilations across town. We're not supposed to know that, so do not let on. Don't worry. His compulsion inflicts itself on strangers only, and the routine established is elaborate and unwavering. The victim must be a white male, a young adult no older than thirty, heavyset, with dark hair and eyes, and the like. The victim must be chosen at random, before sunset, from a public place; the victim is followed home, and must put up a struggle, et cetera. The carnage inflicted is precise: the angle and direction of the incisions; the layering of skin and muscle tissue; the rearrangement of the visceral organs, and so on. Kevin Howard does not let any of this interfere with his work. He is, in fact, our fastest typist. He types as if he were on fire. He has a secret crush on Gwendolyn Stich, and leaves a red-foil-wrapped Hershey's Kiss on her desk every afternoon. But he hates Anika Bloom, and keeps well away from her. In his presence, she has uncontrollable fits of shaking and trembling. Her left palm does not stop bleeding.

25   In any case, when Kevin Howard gets caught, act surprised. Say that he seemed like a nice person, a bit of a loner, perhaps, but always quiet and polite.

This is the photocopier room. And this, this is our view. It faces southwest. West is down there, toward the water. North is back there. Because we are on the seventeenth floor, we are afforded a magnificent view. Isn't it beautiful? It overlooks the park, where the tops of those trees are. You can see a segment of the bay between those two buildings there. You can see the sun set in the gap between those two buildings over there. You can see this building reflected in the glass panels of that building across the way. There. See? That's you, waving. And look there. There's Anika Bloom in the kitchenette, waving back.

Enjoy this view while photocopying. If you have problems with the photocopier, see Russell Nash. If you have any questions, ask your supervisor. If you can't find your supervisor, ask Phillip Spiers. He sits over there. He'll check with Clarissa Nicks. She sits over there. If you can't find them, feel free to ask me. That's my cubicle. I sit in there.

EDGAR ALLAN POE

Edgar Allan Poe (1809–1849) born in Boston, was the son of traveling actors. His father abandoned the family almost immediately after Poe was born, and his mother died when he was two. The child was adopted—though never legally—by a prosperous merchant and his wife in Richmond, Virginia. The tensions were great, aggravated by Poe's drinking and heavy gambling, and in 1827 Poe left Richmond for Boston. He wrote, served briefly in the army, attended West Point but left within a year, and became an editor for the remaining eighteen years of his life. It was during these years, too, that he wrote the poems, essays, and fiction—especially detective stories and horror stories—that have made him famous.

The Cask of Amontillado   [1846]

The thousand injuries of Fortunato I had borne as I best could; but when he ventured upon insult, I vowed revenge. You, who so well know the nature of my soul, will not suppose, however, that I gave utterance to a threat. *At length* I would be avenged; this was a point definitely settled—but the very definitiveness with which it was resolved, precluded the idea of risk. I must not only punish, but punish with impunity. A wrong is unredressed when retribution overtakes its redresser. It is equally unredressed when the avenger fails to make himself felt as such to him who has done the wrong.

It must be understood, that neither by word nor deed had I given Fortunato cause to doubt my good will. I continued, as was my wont, to smile in his face, and he did not perceive that my smile *now* was at the thought of his immolation.

He had a weak point—this Fortunato—although in other regards he was a man to be respected and even feared. He prided himself on his connoisseurship in wine. Few Italians have the true virtuoso spirit. For the most part their enthusiasm is adopted to suit the time and opportunity—to practise imposture upon the British and Austrian *millionaires.* In painting and gemmary Fortunato, like his countrymen, was a quack—but in the matter of old wines he was sincere. In this respect I did not differ from him materially: I was skilful in the Italian vintages myself, and bought largely whenever I could.

It was about dusk, one evening during the supreme madness of the carnival season, that I encountered my friend. He accosted me with excessive warmth, for he had been drinking much. The man wore motley. He had on a tight-fitting parti-striped dress, and his head was surmounted by the conical cap and bells. I was so pleased to see him, that I thought I should never have done wringing his hand.

5   I said to him—"My dear Fortunato, you are luckily met. How remarkably well you are looking to-day! But I have received a pipe[1] of what passes for Amontillado, and I have my doubts."

"How?" said he. "Amontillado? A pipe? Impossible! And in the middle of the carnival?"

"I have my doubts," I replied; "and I was silly enough to pay the full Amontillado price without consulting you in the matter. You were not to be found, and I was fearful of losing a bargain."

"Amontillado!"

"I have my doubts."

10   "Amontillado!"

---

[1] **pipe** wine cask.

"And I must satisfy them."

"Amontillado!"

"As you are engaged, I am on my way to Luchesi. If any one has a critical turn, it is he. He will tell me——"

"Luchesi cannot tell Amontillado from Sherry."

15 "And yet some fools will have it that his taste is a match for your own."

"Come, let us go."

"Whither?"

"To your vaults."

"My friend, no; I will not impose upon your good nature. I perceive you have an engagement. Luchesi——"

20 "I have no engagement;—come."

"My friend, no. It is not the engagement, but the severe cold with which I perceive you are afflicted. The vaults are insufferably damp. They are encrusted with nitre."

"Let us go, nevertheless. The cold is merely nothing. Amontillado! You have been imposed upon. And as for Luchesi, he cannot distinguish Sherry from Amontillado."

Thus speaking, Fortunato possessed himself of my arm. Putting on a mask of black silk, and drawing a *roquelaire*[2] closely about my person, I suffered him to hurry me to my palazzo.

There were no attendants at home; they had absconded to make merry in honor of the time. I had told them that I should not return until the morning, and had given them explicit orders not to stir from the house. These orders were sufficient, I well knew, to insure their immediate disappearance, one and all, as soon as my back was turned.

25 I took from their sconces two flambeaux, and giving one to Fortunato, bowed him through several suites of rooms to the archway that led into the vaults. I passed down a long and winding staircase, requesting him to be cautious as he followed. We came at length to the foot of the descent, and stood together on the damp ground of the catacombs of the Montresors.

The gait of my friend was unsteady, and the bells upon his cap jingled as he strode.

"The pipe," said he.

"It is farther on," said I; "but observe the white web-work which gleams from these cavern walls."

He turned towards me, and looked into my eyes with two filmy orbs that distilled the rheum of intoxication.

30 "Nitre?" he asked, at length.

"Nitre." I replied. "How long have you had that cough?"

"Ugh! ugh! ugh!—ugh! ugh! ugh!—ugh! ugh! ugh!—ugh! ugh! ugh!—ugh! ugh! ugh!"

My poor friend found it impossible to reply for many minutes.

"It is nothing," he said, at last.

35 "Come," I said, with decision, "we will go back; your health is precious. You are rich, respected, admired, beloved; you are happy, as once I was. You are a man to be missed. For me it is no matter. We will go back; you will be ill, and I cannot be responsible. Besides, there is Luchesi——"

---

[2]**roquelaire** short cloak.

"Enough," he said; "the cough is a mere nothing; it will not kill me. I shall not die of a cough."

"True—true," I replied; "and, indeed, I had no intention of alarming you unnecessarily—but you should use all proper caution. A draught of this Medoc will defend us from the damps."

Here I knocked off the neck of a bottle which I drew from a long row of its fellows that lay upon the mould.

"Drink," I said, presenting him the wine.

40   He raised it to his lips with a leer. He paused and nodded to me familiarly, while his bells jingled.

"I drink," he said, "to the buried that repose around us."

"And I to your long life."

He again took my arm, and we proceeded.

"These vaults," he said, "are extensive."

45   "The Montresors," I replied, "were a great and numerous family."

"I forget your arms."

"A huge human foot d'or, in a field azure; the foot crushes a serpent rampant whose fangs are imbedded in the heel."

"And the motto?"

"*Nemo me impune lacessit.*"[3]

50   "Good!" he said.

The wine sparkled in his eyes and the bells jingled. My own fancy grew warm with the Medoc. We had passed through walls of piled bones, with casks and puncheons intermingling, into the inmost recesses of the catacombs. I paused again, and this time I made bold to seize Fortunato by an arm above the elbow.

"The nitre!" I said; "see, it increases. It hangs like moss upon the vaults. We are below the river's bed. The drops of moisture trickle among the bones. Come, we will go back ere it is too late. Your cough——"

"It is nothing," he said; "let us go on. But first, another draught of the Medoc."

I broke and reached him a flaçon of De Grâve. He emptied it at a breath. His eyes flashed with a fierce light. He laughed and threw the bottle upwards with a gesticulation I did not understand.

55   I looked at him in surprise. He repeated the movement—a grotesque one.

"You do not comprehend?" he said.

"Not I," I replied.

"Then you are not of the brotherhood."

"How?"

60   "You are not of the masons."

"Yes, yes," I said, "yes, yes."

"You? Impossible! A mason?"

"A mason," I replied.

"A sign," he said.

65   "It is this," I answered, producing a trowel from beneath the folds of my *roquelaire.*

---

[3]**Nemo me impune lacessit.** No one dare attack me with impunity (the motto of Scotland).

"You jest," he exclaimed, recoiling a few paces. "But let us proceed to the Amontillado."

"Be it so," I said, replacing the tool beneath the cloak, and again offering him my arm. He leaned upon it heavily. We continued our route in search of the Amontillado. We passed through a range of low arches, descended, passed on, and descending again, arrived at a deep crypt, in which the foulness of the air caused our flambeaux rather to glow than flame.

At the most remote end of the crypt there appeared another less spacious. Its walls had been lined with human remains, piled to the vault overhead, in the fashion of the great catacombs of Paris. Three sides of this interior crypt were still ornamented in this manner. From the fourth the bones had been thrown down, and lay promiscuously upon the earth, forming at one point a mound of some size. Within the wall thus exposed by the displacing of the bones, we perceived a still interior recess, in depth about four feet, in width three, in height six or seven. It seemed to have been constructed for no especial use within itself, but formed merely the interval between two of the colossal supports of the roof of the catacombs, and was backed by one of their circumscribing walls of solid granite.

It was in vain that Fortunato, uplifting his dull torch, endeavored to pry into the depth of the recess. Its termination the feeble light did not enable us to see.

70   "Proceed," I said; "herein is the Amontillado. As for Luchesi——"

"He is an ignoramus," interrupted my friend, as he stepped unsteadily forward, while I followed immediately at his heels. In an instant he had reached the extremity of the niche, and finding his progress arrested by the rock, stood stupidly bewildered. A moment more and I had fettered him to the granite. In its surface were two iron staples, distant from each other about two feet, horizontally. From one of these depended a short chain, from the other a padlock. Throwing the links about his waist, it was but the work of a few seconds to secure it. He was too much astounded to resist. Withdrawing the key I stepped back from the recess.

"Pass your hand," I said, "over the wall; you cannot help feeling the nitre. Indeed it is *very* damp. Once more let me *implore* you to return. No? Then I must positively leave you. But I must first render you all the little attentions in my power."

"The Amontillado!" ejaculated my friend, not yet recovered from his astonishment.

"True," I replied; "the Amontillado."

75   As I said these words I busied myself among the pile of bones of which I have before spoken. Throwing them aside, I soon uncovered a quantity of building stone and mortar. With these materials and with the aid of my trowel, I began vigorously to wall up the entrance of the niche.

I had scarcely laid the first tier of the masonry when I discovered that the intoxication of Fortunato had in a great measure worn off. The earliest indication I had of this was a low moaning cry from the depth of the recess. It was *not* the cry of a drunken man. There was then a long and obstinate silence. I laid the second tier, and the third, and the fourth; and then I heard the furious vibrations of the chain. The noise lasted for several minutes, during which, that I might hearken to it with the more satisfaction, I ceased my labors and sat down upon the bones. When at last the clanking subsided, I resumed the trowel, and finished without interruption the fifth, the sixth, and the seventh tier. The wall was now nearly upon a level with my breast. I again paused, and holding the flambeaux over the mason-work, threw a few feeble rays upon the figure within.

A succession of loud and shrill screams, bursting suddenly from the throat of the chained form, seemed to thrust me violently back. For a brief moment I hesitated—I trembled. Unsheathing my rapier, I began to grope with it about the recess: but the thought of an instant reassured me. I placed my hand upon the solid fabric of the catacombs, and felt satisfied. I reapproached the wall. I replied to the yells of him who clamored. I re-echoed—I aided—I surpassed them in volume and in strength. I did this, and the clamorer grew still.

It was now midnight, and my task was drawing to a close. I had completed the eighth, the ninth, and the tenth tier. I had finished a portion of the last and the eleventh; there remained but a single stone to be fitted and plastered in. I struggled with its weight; I placed it partially in its destined position. But now there came from out the niche a low laugh that erected the hairs upon my head. It was succeeded by a sad voice, which I had difficulty in recognising as that of the noble Fortunato. The voice said—

"Ha! ha! ha!—he! he!—a very good joke indeed—an excellent jest. We will have many a rich laugh about it at the palazzo—he! he! he!—over our wine—he! he! he!"

80   "The Amontillado!" I said.

"He! he! he!—he! he! he!—yes, the Amontillado. But is it not getting late? Will not they be awaiting us at the palazzo, the Lady Fortunato and the rest? Let us be gone."

"Yes," I said, "let us be gone."

"For the love of God, Montresor!"

"Yes," I said, "for the love of God!"

85   But to these words I hearkened in vain for a reply. I grew impatient. I called aloud—

"Fortunato!"

No answer. I called again—

"Fortunato!"

No answer still. I thrust a torch through the remaining aperture and let it fall within. There came forth in return only a jingling of the bells. My heart grew sick—on account of the dampness of the catacombs. I hastened to make an end of my labor. I forced the last stone into its position; I plastered it up. Against the new masonry I re-erected the old rampart of bones. For the half of a century no mortal has disturbed them. *In pace requiescat!*[4]

---

[4]**In pace requiescat!** May he rest in peace!

MICHELE SERROS

Michele Serros, born in Oxnard, California, in 1966, published her first book of poems and stories, Chicana Falsa and Other Stories of Death, Identity and Oxnard, *while she was still a student at Santa Monica City College. We reprint a story from her second book,* How to Be a Chicana Role Model *(2000), which achieved national attention.*

Senior Picture Day   [2000]

Sometimes I put two different earrings in the same ear. And that's on a day I'm feeling preppy, not really new wave or anything. One time, during a track meet over at Camarillo High, I discovered way too late that I'd forgot to put on deodorant and that was the worst 'cause everyone knows how snooty those girls at Camarillo can be. Hmmm. Actually the worst thing I've ever forgotten to do was take my pill. That happened three mornings in a row and you can bet I was praying for weeks after that.

So many things to remember when you're seventeen years old and your days start at six a.m. and sometimes don't end until five in the afternoon. But today of all days there's one thing I have to remember to do and that's to squeeze my nose. I've been doing it since the seventh grade. Every morning with my thumb and forefinger I squeeze the sides of it, firmly pressing my nostrils as close as they possibly can get near the base. Sometimes while I'm waiting for the tortilla to heat up, or just when I'm brushing my teeth, I squeeze. Nobody ever notices. Nobody ever asks. With all the other shit seniors in high school go through, squeezing my nose is nothing. It's just like some regular early-morning routine, like yawning or wiping the egg from my eyes. Okay, so you might think it's just a total waste of time, but to tell you the truth, I do see the difference. Just last week I lined up all my class pictures and could definitely see the progress. My nose has actually become smaller, narrower. It looks less Indian. *I* look less Indian and you can bet that's the main goal here. Today, when I take my graduation pictures, my nose will look just like Terri's and then I'll have the best picture in the yearbook. I think about this as Mrs. Milne's Duster comes honking in the driveway to take me to school.

Terri was my best friend in seventh grade. She came from Washington to Rio Del Valle Junior High halfway through October. She was the first girl I knew who had contact lenses and *four* pairs of Chemin de Fers. Can you believe that? She told everyone that her daddy was gonna build 'em a swimming pool for the summer. She told me that I could go over to swim anytime I wanted. But until then, she told me, I could go over and we could play on her dad's CB.[1]

"Your dad's really got a CB?" I asked her.

5   "Oh, yeah," she answered, jiggling her locker door. "You can come over and we can make up handles for ourselves and meet lots of guys. Cute ones."

"Whaddaya mean, handles?" I asked.

"Like names, little nicknames. I never use my real name. I'm 'G.G.' when I get on. That stands for Golden Girl. Oh, and you gotta make sure you end every sentence with 'over.' You're like a total nerd if you don't finish with 'over.' I never talk to anyone who doesn't say 'over.' They're the worst."

Nobody's really into citizen band radios anymore. I now see 'em all lined up in pawnshops over on Oxnard Boulevard. But back in the seventh grade, everyone was getting them. They were way better than using a phone 'cause, first of all, there was no phone bill to bust you for talking to boys who lived

---

[1]**CB** Citizens Band (a radio frequency used by the general public to talk to one another over a short distance).

past The Grade and second, you didn't have your stupid sister yelling at you for tying up the phone line. Most people had CBs in their cars, but Terri's dad had his in the den.

When I showed up at Terri's to check out the CB, her mama was in the front yard planting some purple flowers.

10   "Go on in already." She waved me in. "She's in her father's den."

I found Terri just like her mama said. She was already on the CB, looking flustered and sorta excited.

"Hey," I called out to her, and plopped my tote bag on her dad's desk.

She didn't answer but rather motioned to me with her hands to hurry up. Her mouth formed an exaggerated, "Oh, *my* God!" She held out a glass bowl of Pringles and pointed to a glass of Dr Pepper on the desk.

It turned out Terri had found a boy on the CB. An older *interested* one. He was fifteen, a skateboarder, and his handle was Lightning Bolt.

15   "Lightning Bolt," he bragged to Terri. "Like, you know, powerful and fast. That's the way I skate. So," he continued, "where you guys live? Over."

"We live near Malibu," Terri answered. "Between Malibu and Santa Barbara. Over."

"Oh, excuse me, fan-ceee. Over."

"That's right." Terri giggled. "Over."

We actually lived in Oxnard. Really, in El Rio, a flat patch of houses, churches, and schools surrounded by lots of strawberry fields and some new snooty stucco homes surrounded by chainlink. But man, did Terri have this way of making things sound better. I mean, it *was* the truth, geographically, and besides it sounded way more glamorous.

20   I took some Pringles from the bowl and thought we were gonna have this wonderful afternoon of talking and flirting with Lightning Bolt until Terri's dad happened to come home early and found us gabbing in his den.

"What the . . . !" he yelled as soon as he walked in and saw us hunched over his CB. "What do you think this is? Party Central? Get off that thing!" He grabbed the receiver from Terri's hand. "This isn't a toy! It's a tool. A tool for communication, you don't use it just to meet boys!"

"Damn, Dad," Terri complained as she slid off her father's desk. "Don't have a cow." She took my hand and led me to her room. "Come on, let's pick you out a handle."

When we were in her room, I told her I had decided on Cali Girl as my handle.

"You mean, like California?" she asked.

25   "Yeah, sorta."

"But you're Mexican."

"So?"

"So, you look like you're more from Mexico than California."

"What do you mean?"

30   "I mean, California is like, blond girls, you know."

"Yeah, but I *am* Californian. I mean, real Californian. Even my great-grandma was born here."

"It's just that you don't look like you're from California."

"And you're not exactly golden," I snapped.

* * *

We decided to talk to Lightning Bolt the next day, Friday, right after school. Terri's dad always came home real late on Fridays, sometimes even early the next Saturday morning. It would be perfect. When I got to her house the garage door was wide open and I went in through the side door. I almost bumped into Terri's mama. She was spraying the house with Pine Scent and offered me some Hi-C.

35   "Help yourself to a Pudding Pop, too," she said before heading into the living room through a mist of aerosol. "They're in the freezer."

Man, Terri's mama made their whole life like an afternoon commercial. Hi-C, Pringles in a bowl, the whole house smelling like a pine forest. Was Terri lucky or what? I grabbed a Pudding Pop out of the freezer and was about to join her when I picked up on her laugh. She was already talking to Lightning Bolt. Dang, she didn't waste time!

"Well, maybe we don't ever want to meet you," I heard Terri flirt with Lightning Bolt. "How do you know we don't already have boyfriends? Over."

"Well, you both sound like foxes. So, uh, what *do* you look like? Over."

"I'm about five-four and have green eyes and ginger-colored hair. Over."

40   Green? Ginger? I always took Terri for having brown eyes and brown hair.

"What about your friend? Over."

"What about her? Over."

Oh, this was about me! I *had* to hear this. Terri knew how to pump up things good.

"I mean, what does she look like?" Lightning Bolt asked. "She sounds cute. Over."

45   "Well . . ." I overheard Terri hesitate. "Well, she's real skinny and, uh . . ."

"I like skinny girls!"

"You didn't let me finish!" Terri interrupted. "And you didn't say 'over.' Over."

"Sorry," Lightning Bolt said. "Go ahead and finish. Over."

I tore the wrapper off the Pudding Pop and continued to listen.

50   "Well," Terri continued. "She's also sorta flat-chested, I guess. Over."

What? How could Terri say that?

"Flat-chested? Oh yeah? Over." Lightning Bolt answered.

"Yeah. Over."

Terri paused uncomfortably. It was as if she knew what she was saying was wrong and bad and she should've stopped but couldn't. She was saying things about a friend, things a real friend shouldn't be saying about another friend, but now there was a boy involved and he was interested in that other friend, in me, and her side was losing momentum. She would have to continue to stay ahead.

55   "Yeah, and she also has this, this nose, a nose like . . . like an *Indian*. Over."

"An, Indian?" Lightning Bolt asked. "What do ya mean an Indian? Over."

"You know, *Indian*. Like powwow Indian."

"Really?" Lightning Bolt laughed on the other end. "Like Woo-Woo-Woo Indian?" He clapped his palm over his mouth and wailed. A sound I knew all too well.

"Yeah, just like that!" Terri laughed. "In fact, I think she's gonna pick 'Li'l Squaw' as her handle!"

60   I shut the refrigerator door quietly. I touched the ridge of my nose. I felt the bump my mother had promised me would be less noticeable once my face "filled out." The base of my nose was far from feminine and was broad, like, well, like Uncle Rudy's nose, Grandpa Rudy's nose, and yeah, a little bit of Uncle Vincente's nose, too. Men in my family who looked like Indians and here their Indian noses were lumped together on me, on my face. My nose made me look like I didn't belong, made me look less Californian than my blond counterparts. After hearing Terri and Lightning Bolt laugh, more than anything I hated the men in my family who had given me such a hideous nose.

I grabbed my tote bag and started to leave out through the garage door when Terri's mama called out from the living room. "You're leaving already?" she asked. "I know Terri would love to have you for dinner. Her daddy's working late again."

I didn't answer and I didn't turn around. I just walked out and went home.

And so that's how the squeezing began. I eventually stopped hanging out with Terri and never got a chance to use my handle on her dad's CB. I know it's been almost four years since she said all that stuff about me, about my nose, but man, it still stings.

During freshman year I heard that Terri's dad met some lady on the CB and left her mama for this other woman. Can you believe that? Who'd wanna leave a house that smelled like a pine forest and always had Pudding Pops in the freezer?

65   As Mrs. Milne honks from the driveway impatiently, I grab my books and run down the driveway, squeezing my nose just a little bit more. I do it because today is Senior Picture Day and because I do notice the difference. I might be too skinny. My chest might be too flat. But God forbid I look too Indian.

LESLIE MARMON SILKO

Leslie Marmon Silko was born in 1948 in Albuquerque, New Mexico, and grew up on the Laguna Pueblo Reservation some fifty miles to the west. Of her family she says,

> *We are mixed blood—Laguna, Mexican, white. . . . All those languages, all those ways of living are combined, and we live somewhere on the fringes of all three. But I don't apologize for this any more—not to whites, not to full bloods—our origin is unlike any other. My poetry, my storytelling rise out of this source.*

After graduating from the University of New Mexico in 1969, Silko entered law school but soon left to become a writer. She taught for two years at Navajo Community College at Many Farms, Arizona, and then went to Alaska for two years where she studied Eskimo-Aleut culture and worked on a novel, Ceremony. *After returning to the Southwest, she taught at the University of Arizona and then at the University of New Mexico. Silko's recent books include the novels* Almanac of the Dead *(1991) and* Gardens in the Dunes *(2000).*

In addition to writing stories, a novel, and poems, Silko has written the screenplay for Marlon Brando's film, Black Elk. *In 1981 she was awarded one of the so-called genius grants from the MacArthur Foundation, which supports "exceptionally talented individuals."*

The Man to Send Rain Clouds

[1969]

They found him under a big cottonwood tree. His Levi jacket and pants were faded light blue so that he had been easy to find. The big cottonwood tree stood apart from a small grove of winterbare cottonwoods which grew in the wide, sandy arroyo. He had been dead for a day or more, and the sheep had wandered and scattered up and down the arroyo. Leon and his brother-in-law, Ken, gathered the sheep and left them in the pen at the sheep camp before they returned to the cottonwood tree. Leon waited under the tree while Ken drove the truck through the deep sand to the edge of the arroyo. He squinted up at the sun and unzipped his jacket—it sure was hot for this time of year. But high and northwest the blue mountains were still in snow. Ken came sliding down the low, crumbling bank about fifty yards down, and he was bringing the red blanket.

Before they wrapped the old man, Leon took a piece of string out of his pocket and tied a small gray feather in the old man's long white hair. Ken gave him the paint. Across the brown wrinkled forehead he drew a streak of white and along the high cheekbones he drew a strip of blue paint. He paused and watched Ken throw pinches of corn meal and pollen into the wind that fluttered the small gray feather. Then Leon painted with yellow under the old man's broad nose, and finally, when he had painted green across the chin, he smiled.

"Send us rain clouds, Grandfather." They laid the bundle in the back of the pickup and covered it with a heavy tarp before they started back to the pueblo.

They turned off the highway onto the sandy pueblo road. Not long after they passed the store and post office they saw Father Paul's car coming toward them. When he recognized their faces he slowed his car and waved for them to stop. The young priest rolled down the car window.

5   "Did you find old Teofilo?" he asked loudly.

Leon stopped the truck. "Good morning, Father. We were just out to the sheep camp. Everything is O.K. now."

"Thank God for that. Teofilo is a very old man. You really shouldn't allow him to stay at the sheep camp alone."

"No, he won't do that any more now."

"Well, I'm glad you understand. I hope I'll be seeing you at Mass this week—we missed you last Sunday. See if you can get old Teofilo to come with you." The priest smiled and waved at them as they drove away.

10   Louise and Teresa were waiting. The table was set for lunch, and the coffee was boiling on the black iron stove. Leon looked at Louise and then at Teresa.

"We found him under a cottonwood tree in the big arroyo near sheep camp. I guess he sat down to rest in the shade and never got up again." Leon walked toward the old man's bed. The red plaid shawl had been shaken and spread carefully over the bed, and a new brown flannel shirt and pair of stiff new Levi's were arranged neatly beside the pillow. Louise held the screen door open while Leon and Ken carried in the red blanket. He looked small and shriveled, and after they dressed him in the new shirt and pants he seemed more shrunken.

It was noontime now because the church bells rang the Angelus.[1] They ate the beans with hot bread, and nobody said anything until after Teresa poured the coffee.

Ken stood up and put on his jacket. "I'll see about the gravediggers. Only the top layer of soil is frozen. I think it can be ready before dark."

Leon nodded his head and finished his coffee. After Ken had been gone for a while, the neighbors and clanspeople came quietly to embrace Teofilo's family and to leave food on the table because the gravediggers would come to eat when they were finished.

15   The sky in the west was full of pale yellow light. Louise stood outside with her hands in the pockets of Leon's green army jacket that was too big for her. The funeral was over, and the old men had taken their candles and medicine bags and were gone. She waited until the body was laid into the pickup before she said anything to Leon. She touched his arm, and he noticed that her hands were still dusty from the corn meal that she had sprinkled around the old man. When she spoke, Leon could not hear her.

"What did you say? I didn't hear you."

"I said that I had been thinking about something."

"About what?"

"About the priest sprinkling holy water for Grandpa. So he won't be thirsty."

20   Leon stared at the new moccasins that Teofilo had made for the ceremonial dances in the summer. They were nearly hidden by the red blanket. It was getting colder, and the wind pushed gray dust down the narrow pueblo road. The sun was approaching the long mesa where it disappeared during the winter. Louise stood there shivering and watching his face. Then he zipped up his jacket and opened the truck door. "I'll see if he's there."

Ken stopped the pickup at the church, and Leon got out; and then Ken drove down the hill to the graveyard where people were waiting. Leon knocked at the old carved door with its symbols of the Lamb. While he waited he looked up at the twin bells from the king of Spain with the last sunlight pouring around them in their tower.

The priest opened the door and smiled when he saw who it was. "Come in! What brings you here this evening?"

The priest walked toward the kitchen, and Leon stood with his cap in his hand, playing with the earflaps and examining the living room—the brown sofa, the green armchair, and the brass lamp that hung down from the ceiling by links of chain. The priest dragged a chair out of the kitchen and offered it to Leon.

"No thank you, Father. I only came to ask you if you would bring your holy water to the graveyard."

---

[1]**Angelus** a devotional prayer commemorating the Annunciation (the angel Gabriel's announcement of the Incarnation of God in the human form of Jesus).

25   The priest turned away from Leon and looked out the window at the patio full of shadows and the dining-room windows of the nuns' cloister across the patio. The curtains were heavy, and the light from within faintly penetrated; it was impossible to see the nuns inside eating supper. "Why didn't you tell me he was dead? I could have brought the Last Rites anyway."

Leon smiled. "It wasn't necessary, Father."

The priest stared down at his scuffed brown loafers and the worn hem of his cassock. "For a Christian burial it was necessary."

His voice was distant, and Leon thought that his blue eyes looked tired.

"It's O.K., Father, we just want him to have plenty of water."

30   The priest sank down into the green chair and picked up a glossy missionary magazine. He turned the colored pages full of lepers and pagans without looking at them.

"You know I can't do that, Leon. There should have been the Last Rites and a funeral Mass at the very least."

Leon put on his green cap and pulled the flaps down over his ears. "It's getting late, Father. I've got to go."

When Leon opened the door Father Paul stood up and said, "Wait." He left the room and came back wearing a long brown overcoat. He followed Leon out the door and across the dim churchyard to the adobe steps in front of the church. They both stooped to fit through the low adobe entrance. And when they started down the hill to the graveyard only half of the sun was visible above the mesa.

The priest approached the grave slowly, wondering how they had managed to dig into the frozen ground; and then he remembered that this was New Mexico, and saw the pile of cold loose sand beside the hole. The people stood close to each other with little clouds of steam puffing from their faces. The priest looked at them and saw a pile of jackets, gloves, and scarves in the yellow, dry tumbleweeds that grew in the graveyard. He looked at the red blanket, not sure that Teofilo was so small, wondering if it wasn't some perverse Indian trick—something they did in March to ensure a good harvest— wondering if maybe old Teofilo was actually at sheep camp corraling the sheep for the night. But there he was, facing into a cold dry wind and squinting at the last sunlight, ready to bury a red wool blanket while the faces of his parishioners were in shadow with the last warmth of the sun on their backs.

35   His fingers were stiff, and it took him a long time to twist the lid off the holy water. Drops of water fell on the red blanket and soaked into dark icy spots. He sprinkled the grave and the water disappeared almost before it touched the dim, cold sand; it reminded him of something—he tried to remember what it was, because he thought if he could remember he might understand this. He sprinkled more water; he shook the container until it was empty, and the water fell through the light from sundown like August rain that fell while the sun was still shining, almost evaporating before it touched the wilted squash flowers.

The wind pulled at the priest's brown Franciscan robe and swirled away the corn meal and pollen that had been sprinkled on the blanket. They lowered the bundle into the ground, and they didn't bother to untie the stiff pieces of new rope that were tied around the ends of the blanket. The sun was gone, and over on the highway the eastbound lane was full of headlights. The priest walked away slowly. Leon watched him climb the hill, and when he had disappeared within the tall, thick walls, Leon turned to look up at the high blue mountains in the deep snow that reflected a faint red light from the west. He felt good because it was finished, and he was happy about the sprinkling of the holy water; now the old man could send them big thunderclouds for sure.

AMY TAN

Amy Tan was born in 1952 in Oakland, California, two and a half years after her parents had emigrated from China. She entered Linfield College in Oregon but then followed a boyfriend to California State University at San Jose, where she shifted her major from premedical studies to English. After earning a master's degree in linguistics from San Jose, Tan worked as a language consultant and then, under the name of May Brown, as a freelance business writer.

In 1985, having decided to try her hand at fiction, she joined the Squaw Valley Community of Writers, a fiction workshop. In 1987 she visited China with her mother; on her return to the United States she learned that her agent had sold her first book, The Joy Luck Club, *a collection of 16 interwoven stories (including "Two Kinds") about four Chinese mothers and their four American daughters. She is also author of* The Kitchen God's Wife *(1991),* The Hundred Secret Senses *(1995), and* The Bonesetter's Daughter *(2001).*

Two Kinds

[1989]

My mother believed you could be anything you wanted to be in America. You could open a restaurant. You could work for the government and get good retirement. You could buy a house with almost no money down. You could become rich. You could become instantly famous.

"Of course you can be prodigy, too," my mother told me when I was nine. "You can be best anything. What does Auntie Lindo know? Her daughter, she is only best tricky."

America was where all my mother's hopes lay. She had come here in 1949 after losing everything in China: her mother and father, her family home, her first husband, and two daughters, twin baby girls. But she never looked back with regret. There were so many ways for things to get better.

We didn't immediately pick the right kind of prodigy. At first my mother thought I could be a Chinese Shirley Temple. We'd watch Shirley's old movies on TV as though they were training films. My mother would poke my arm and say, "*Ni kan*"—You watch. And I would see Shirley tapping her feet, or singing a sailor song, or pursing her lips into a very round O while saying, "Oh my goodness."

5   "*Ni kan*," said my mother as Shirley's eyes flooded with tears. "You already know how. Don't need talent for crying!"

Soon after my mother got this idea about Shirley Temple, she took me to a beauty training school in the Mission district and put me in the hands of a student who could barely hold the scissors without shaking. Instead of getting big fat curls, I emerged with an uneven mass of crinkly black fuzz. My mother dragged me off to the bathroom and tried to wet down my hair.

"You look like Negro Chinese," she lamented, as if I had done this on purpose.

The instructor of the beauty training school had to lop off these soggy clumps to make my hair even again. "Peter Pan is very popular these days," the instructor assured my mother. I now had hair the length of a boy's, with straight-across bangs that hung at a slant two inches above my eyebrows. I liked the haircut and it made me actually look forward to my future fame.

In fact, in the beginning, I was just as excited as my mother, maybe even more so. I pictured this prodigy part of me as many different images, trying each one on for size. I was a dainty ballerina girl standing by the curtains, waiting to hear the right music that would send me floating on my tiptoes. I was like the Christ child lifted out of the straw manger, crying with holy indignity. I was Cinderella stepping from her pumpkin carriage with sparkly cartoon music filling the air.

10   In all of my imaginings, I was filled with a sense that I would soon become *perfect*. My mother and father would adore me. I would be beyond reproach. I would never feel the need to sulk for anything.

But sometimes the prodigy in me became impatient. "If you don't hurry up and get me out of here, I'm disappearing for good," it warned. "And then you'll always be nothing."

Every night after dinner, my mother and I would sit at the Formica kitchen table. She would present new tests, taking her examples from stories of amazing children she had read in *Ripley's Believe It or Not*, or *Good Housekeeping, Reader's Digest*, and a dozen other magazines she kept in a pile in our bathroom. My mother got these magazines from people whose houses she cleaned. And since she cleaned many houses each week, we had a great assortment. She would look through them all, searching for stories about remarkable children.

The first night she brought out a story about a three-year-old boy who knew the capitals of all the states and even most of the European countries. A teacher was quoted as saying the little boy could also pronounce the names of the foreign cities correctly.

"What's the capital of Finland?" my mother asked me, looking at the magazine story.

15   All I knew was the capital of California, because Sacramento was the name of the street we lived on in Chinatown. "Nairobi!" I guessed, saying the most foreign word I could think of. She checked to see if that was possibly one way to pronounce "Helsinki" before showing me the answer.

The tests got harder—multiplying numbers in my head, finding the queen of hearts in a deck of cards, trying to stand on my head without using my hands, predicting the daily temperatures in Los Angeles, New York, and London.

One night I had to look at a page from the Bible for three minutes and then report everything I could remember. "Now Jehoshaphat had riches and honor in abundance and . . . that's all I remember, Ma," I said.

And after seeing my mother's disappointed face once again, something inside of me began to die. I hated the tests, the raised hopes and failed expectations. Before going to bed that night, I looked in the mirror above the bathroom sink and when I saw only my face staring back—and that it would always be this ordinary face—I began to cry. Such a sad, ugly girl! I made high-pitched noises like a crazed animal, trying to scratch out the face in the mirror.

And then I saw what seemed to be the prodigy side of me—because I had never seen that face before. I looked at my reflection, blinking so I could see more clearly. The girl staring back at me was angry, powerful. This girl and I were the same. I had new thoughts, willful thoughts, or rather thoughts filled with lots of won'ts. I won't let her change me, I promised myself. I won't be what I'm not.

20   So now on nights when my mother presented her tests, I performed listlessly, my head propped on one arm. I pretended to be bored. And I was. I got so bored I started counting the bellows of the foghorns out on the bay while my mother drilled me in other areas. The sound was comforting and reminded me of the cow jumping over the moon. And the next day, I played a game with myself, seeing if my mother would give up on me before eight bellows. After a while I usually counted only one, maybe two bellows at most. At last she was beginning to give up hope.

Two or three months had gone by without any mention of my being a prodigy again. And then one day my mother was watching *The Ed Sullivan Show* on TV. The TV was old and the sound kept shorting out. Every time my mother got halfway up from the sofa to adjust the set, the sound would go back on and Ed would be talking. As soon as she sat down, Ed would go silent again. She got up, the TV broke into loud piano music. She sat down. Silence. Up and down, back and forth, quiet and loud. It was like a stiff embraceless dance between her and the TV set. Finally she stood by the set with her hand on the sound dial.

She seemed entranced by the music, a little frenzied piano piece with this mesmerizing quality, quick sort of passages and then teasing lilting ones before it returned to the quick playful parts.

"*Ni kan,*" my mother said, calling me over with hurried hand gestures, "Look here."

I could see why my mother was fascinated by the music. It was being pounded out by a little Chinese girl, about nine years old, with a Peter Pan haircut. The girl had the sauciness of a Shirley Temple. She was proudly modest like a proper Chinese child. And she also did this fancy sweep of a curtsy, so that the fluffy skirt of her white dress cascaded slowly to the floor like the petals of a large carnation.

25   In spite of these warning signs, I wasn't worried. Our family had no piano and we couldn't afford to buy one, let alone reams of sheet music and piano lessons. So I could be generous in my comments when my mother bad-mouthed the little girl on TV.

"Play note right, but doesn't sound good! No singing sound," complained my mother.

"What are you picking on her for?" I said carelessly. "She's pretty good. Maybe she's not the best, but she's trying hard." I knew almost immediately I would be sorry I said that.

"Just like you," she said. "Not the best. Because you not trying." She gave a little huff as she let go of the sound dial and sat down on the sofa.

The little Chinese girl sat down also to play an encore of "Anitra's Dance" by Grieg.[1] I remember the song, because later on I had to learn how to play it.

---

[1]**"Anitra's Dance"** a section from the incidental music that Edvard Grieg (1843–1907) wrote for *Peer Gynt,* a play by Henrik Ibsen.

30   Three days after watching *The Ed Sullivan Show,* my mother told me what my schedule would be for piano lessons and piano practice. She had talked to Mr. Chong, who lived on the first floor of our apartment building. Mr. Chong was a retired piano teacher and my mother had traded house-cleaning services for weekly lessons and a piano for me to practice on every day, two hours a day, from four until six.

When my mother told me this, I felt as though I had been sent to hell. I whined and then kicked my foot a little when I couldn't stand it anymore.

"Why don't you like me the way I am? I'm not a genius! I can't play the piano. And even if I could, I wouldn't go on TV if you paid me a million dollars!" I cried.

My mother slapped me. "Who ask you be genius?" she shouted. "Only ask you be your best. For you sake. You think I want you be genius? Hnnh! What for! Who ask you!"

"So ungrateful," I heard her mutter in Chinese. "If she had as much talent as she has temper, she would be famous now."

35   Mr. Chong, whom I secretly nicknamed Old Chong, was very strange, always tapping his fingers to the silent music of an invisible orchestra. He looked ancient in my eyes. He had lost most of the hair on top of his head and he wore thick glasses and had eyes that always looked tired and sleepy. But he must have been younger than I thought, since he lived with his mother and was not yet married.

I met Old Lady Chong once and that was enough. She had this peculiar smell like a baby that had done something in its pants. And her fingers felt like a dead person's, like an old peach I once found in the back of the refrigerator; the skin just slid off the meat when I picked it up.

I soon found out why Old Chong had retired from teaching piano. He was deaf. "Like Beethoven!" he shouted to me. "We're both listening only in our head!" And he would start to conduct his frantic silent sonatas.

Our lessons went like this. He would open the book and point to different things, explaining their purpose: "Key! Treble! Bass! No sharps or flats! So this is C major! Listen now and play after me!"

And then he would play the C scale a few times, a simple chord, and then, as if inspired by an old, unreachable itch, he gradually added more notes and running trills and a pounding bass until the music was really something quite grand.

40   I would play after him, the simple scale, the simple chord, and then I just played some nonsense that sounded like a cat running up and down on top of garbage cans. Old Chong smiled and applauded and then said, "Very good! But now you must learn to keep time!"

So that's how I discovered that Old Chong's eyes were too slow to keep up with the wrong notes I was playing. He went through the motions in half-time. To help me keep rhythm, he stood behind me, pushing down on my right shoulder for every beat. He balanced pennies on top of my wrists so I would keep them still as I slowly played scales and arpeggios. He had me curve my hand around an apple and keep that shape when playing chords. He marched stiffly to show me how to make each finger dance up and down, staccato like an obedient little soldier.

He taught me all these things, and that was how I also learned I could be lazy and get away with mistakes, lots of mistakes. If I hit the wrong notes because I hadn't practiced enough, I never corrected myself. I just kept playing in rhythm. And Old Chong kept conducting his own private reverie.

So maybe I never really gave myself a fair chance. I did pick up the basics pretty quickly, and I might have become a good pianist at that young age. But I was so determined not to try, not to be anybody different that I learned to play only the most ear-splitting preludes, the most discordant hymns.

Over the next year, I practiced like this, dutifully in my own way. And then one day I heard my mother and her friend Lindo Jong both talking in a loud bragging tone of voice so others could hear. It was after church, and I was leaning against the brick wall wearing a dress with stiff white petticoats. Auntie Lindo's daughter, Waverly, who was about my age, was standing farther down the wall about five feet away. We had grown up together and shared all the closeness of two sisters squabbling over crayons and dolls. In other words, for the most part, we hated each other. I thought she was snotty. Waverly Jong had gained a certain amount of fame as "Chinatown's Littlest Chinese Chess Champion."

45   "She bring home too many trophy," Auntie Lindo lamented that Sunday. "All day she play chess. All day I have no time do nothing but dust off her winnings." She threw a scolding look at Waverly, who pretended not to see her.

"You lucky you don't have this problem," said Auntie Lindo with a sigh to my mother.

And my mother squared her shoulders and bragged: "Our problem worser than yours. If we ask Jing-mei wash dish, she hear nothing but music. It's like you can't stop this natural talent."

And right then, I was determined to put a stop to her foolish pride.

A few weeks later, Old Chong and my mother conspired to have me play in a talent show which would be held in the church hall. By then, my parents had saved up enough to buy me a secondhand piano, a black Wurlitzer spinet with a scarred bench. It was the showpiece of our living room.

50   For the talent show, I was to play a piece called "Pleading Child" from Schumann's *Scenes from Childhood*.[2] It was a simple, moody piece that sounded more difficult than it was. I was supposed to memorize the whole thing, playing the repeat parts twice to make the piece sound longer. But I dawdled over it, playing a few bars and then cheating, looking up to see what notes followed. I never really listened to what I was playing. I daydreamed about being somewhere else, about being someone else.

The part I liked to practice best was the fancy curtsy: right foot out, touch the rose on the carpet with a pointed foot, sweep to the side, left leg bends, look up and smile.

My parents invited all the couples from the Joy Luck Club to witness my debut. Auntie Lindo and Uncle Tin were there. Waverly and her two older brothers had also come. The first two rows were filled with children both younger and older than I was. The littlest ones got to go first. They recited simple nursery rhymes, squawked out tunes on miniature violins, twirled Hula Hoops, pranced in pink ballet tutus, and when they bowed or curtsied, the audience would sigh in unison, "Awww," and then clap enthusiastically.

---

[2]**Scenes from Childhood** a piano work by Robert Schumann (1810–1856) with twelve titled sections and an epilogue.

When my turn came, I was very confident. I remember my childish excitement. It was as if I knew, without a doubt, that the prodigy side of me really did exist. I had no fear whatsoever, no nervousness. I remember thinking to myself, This is it! This is it! I looked out over the audience, at my mother's blank face, my father's yawn, Auntie Lindo's stiff-lipped smile, Waverly's sulky expression. I had on a white dress layered with sheets of lace, and a pink bow in my Peter Pan haircut. As I sat down I envisioned people jumping to their feet and Ed Sullivan rushing up to introduce me to everyone on TV.

And I started to play. It was so beautiful. I was so caught up in how lovely I looked that at first I didn't worry how I would sound. So it was a surprise to me when I hit the first wrong note and I realized something didn't sound quite right. And then I hit another and another followed that. A chill started at the top of my head and began to trickle down. Yet I couldn't stop playing, as though my hands were bewitched. I kept thinking my fingers would adjust themselves back, like a train switching to the right track. I played this strange jumble through two repeats, the sour notes staying with me all the way to the end.

55   When I stood up, I discovered my legs were shaking. Maybe I had just been nervous and the audience, like Old Chong, had seen me go through the right motions and had not heard anything wrong at all. I swept my right foot out, went down on my knee, looked up and smiled. The room was quiet, except for Old Chong, who was beaming and shouting, "Bravo! Bravo! Well done!" But then I saw my mother's face, her stricken face. The audience clapped weakly, and as I walked back to my chair, with my whole face quivering as I tried not to cry, I heard a little boy whisper loudly to his mother, "That was awful," and the mother whispered back, "Well, she certainly tried."

And now I realized how many people were in the audience, the whole world it seemed. I was aware of eyes burning into my back. I felt the shame of my mother and father as they sat stiffly throughout the rest of the show.

We could have escaped during intermission. Pride and some strange sense of honor must have anchored my parents to their chairs. And so we watched it all: the eighteen-year-old boy with a fake mustache who did a magic show and juggled flaming hoops while riding a unicycle. The breasted girl with white makeup who sang from *Madama Butterfly* and got honorable mention. And the eleven-year-old boy who won first prize playing a tricky violin song that sounded like a busy bee.

After the show, the Hsus, the Jongs, and the St. Clairs from the Joy Luck Club came up to my mother and father.

"Lots of talented kids," Auntie Lindo said vaguely, smiling broadly.

60   "That was somethin' else," said my father, and I wondered if he was referring to me in a humorous way, or whether he even remembered what I had done.

Waverly looked at me and shrugged her shoulders. "You aren't a genius like me," she said matter-of-factly. And if I hadn't felt so bad, I would have pulled her braids and punched her stomach.

But my mother's expression was what devastated me: a quiet, blank look that said she had lost everything. I felt the same way, and it seemed as if everybody were now coming up, like gawkers at the scene of an accident, to see what parts were actually missing. When we got on the bus to go home, my father was humming the busy-bee tune and my mother was silent. I kept thinking she wanted to wait until we got home before shouting at me. But when my father unlocked the door to our apartment, my mother walked in and then went to the back, into the bedroom. No accusations. No blame. And in a way, I felt disappointed. I had been waiting for her to start shouting, so I could shout back and cry and blame her for all my misery.

I assumed my talent-show fiasco meant I never had to play the piano again. But two days later, after school, my mother came out of the kitchen and saw me watching TV.

"Four clock," she reminded me as if it were any other day. I was stunned, as though she were asking me to go through the talent-show torture again. I wedged myself more tightly in front of the TV.

65   "Turn off TV," she called from the kitchen five minutes later.

I didn't budge. And then I decided. I didn't have to do what my mother said anymore. I wasn't her slave. This wasn't China. I had listened to her before and look what happened. She was the stupid one.

She came out from the kitchen and stood in the arched entryway of the living room. "Four clock," she said once again, louder.

"I'm not going to play anymore," I said nonchalantly. "Why should I? I'm not a genius."

She walked over and stood in front of the TV. I saw her chest was heaving up and down in an angry way.

70   "No!" I said, and I now felt stronger, as if my true self had finally emerged. So this was what had been inside me all along.

"No! I won't!" I screamed.

She yanked me by the arm, pulled me off the floor, snapped off the TV. She was frighteningly strong, half pulling, half carrying me toward the piano as I kicked the throw rugs under my feet. She lifted me up and onto the hard bench. I was sobbing by now, looking at her bitterly. Her chest was heaving even more and her mouth was open, smiling crazily as if she were pleased I was crying.

"You want me to be someone that I'm not!" I sobbed. "I'll never be the kind of daughter you want me to be!"

"Only two kinds of daughters," she shouted in Chinese. "Those who are obedient and those who follow their own mind! Only one kind of daughter can live in this house. Obedient daughter!"

75   "Then I wish I wasn't your daughter. I wish you weren't my mother," I shouted. As I said these things I got scared. I felt like worms and toads and slimy things were crawling out of my chest, but it also felt good, as if this awful side of me had surfaced, at last.

"Too late change this," said my mother shrilly.

And I could sense her anger rising to its breaking point. I wanted to see it spill over. And that's when I remembered the babies she had lost in China, the ones we never talked about. "Then I wish I'd never been born!" I shouted. "I wish I were dead! Like them."

It was as if I had said the magic words. Alakazam!—and her face went blank, her mouth closed, her arms went slack, and she backed out of the room, stunned, as if she were blowing away like a small brown leaf, thin, brittle, lifeless.

It was not the only disappointment my mother felt in me. In the years that followed, I failed her so many times, each time asserting my own will, my right to fall short of expectations. I didn't get straight As. I didn't become class president. I didn't get into Stanford. I dropped out of college.

80   For unlike my mother, I did not believe I could be anything I wanted to be. I could only be me.

And for all those years, we never talked about the disaster at the recital or my terrible accusations afterward at the piano bench. All that remained unchecked, like a betrayal that was now unspeakable. So I never found a way to ask her why she had hoped for something so large that failure was inevitable.

And even worse, I never asked her what frightened me the most: Why had she given up hope?

For after our struggle at the piano, she never mentioned my playing again. The lessons stopped. The lid to the piano was closed, shutting out the dust, my misery, and her dreams.

So she surprised me. A few years ago, she offered to give me the piano, for my thirtieth birthday. I had not played in all those years. I saw the offer as a sign of forgiveness, a tremendous burden removed.

85   "Are you sure?" I asked shyly. "I mean, won't you and Dad miss it?"

"No, this your piano," she said firmly. "Always your piano. You only one can play."

"Well, I probably can't play anymore," I said. "It's been years."

"You pick up fast," said my mother, as if she knew this was certain. "You have natural talent. You could been genius if you want to."

"No I couldn't."

90   "You just not trying," said my mother. And she was neither angry nor sad. She said it as if to announce a fact that could never be disproved. "Take it," she said.

But I didn't at first. It was enough that she had offered it to me. And after that, every time I saw it in my parents' living room, standing in front of the bay windows, it made me feel proud, as if it were a shiny trophy I had won back.

Last week I sent a tuner over to my parents' apartment and had the piano reconditioned, for purely sentimental reasons. My mother had died a few months before and I had been getting things in order for my father, a little bit at a time. I put the jewelry in special silk pouches. The sweaters she had knitted in yellow, pink, bright orange—all the colors I hated—I put those in moth-proof boxes. I found some old Chinese silk dresses, the kind with little slits up the sides. I rubbed the old silk against my skin, then wrapped them in tissue and decided to take them home with me.

After I had the piano tuned, I opened the lid and touched the keys. It sounded even richer than I remembered. Really, it was a very good piano. Inside the bench were the same exercise notes with handwritten scales, the same secondhand music books with their covers held together with yellow tape.

I opened up the Schumann book to the dark little piece I had played at the recital. It was on the left-hand page, "Pleading Child." It looked more difficult than I remembered. I played a few bars, surprised at how easily the notes came back to me.

95   And for the first time, or so it seemed, I noticed the piece on the right-hand side. It was called "Perfectly Contented." I tried to play this one as well.

It had a lighter melody but the same flowing rhythm and turned out to be quite easy. "Pleading Child" was shorter but slower; "Perfectly Contented" was longer but faster. And after I played them both a few times, I realized they were two halves of the same song.

JAMES THURBER

James Thurber (1894–1961) was born in Columbus, Ohio. He attended Ohio State University, where he edited the college humor magazine, but he left without a degree. During World War I, ineligible for military service because of an eye injury, he worked for the State Department in Washington and in Paris. He then returned to Columbus, where he worked as a reporter for the Columbus Dispatch *and began writing and directing musical comedies for a theatrical group at Ohio State University. Thurber then went to New York as a journalist; in 1927 he accepted Harold Ross's invitation to join the staff of the* New Yorker—*an association that lasted for thirty years and is remembered in Thurber's book,* The Years with Ross.

Thurber wrote, or drew (he was a cartoonist as well as a writer), more than twenty books of essays, stories, autobiographical sketches, and memoirs. T. S. Eliot said of Thurber's work:

> *It is a form of humour which is also a way of saying something serious. Unlike so much humour it is not merely a criticism of manners—that is, of the superficial aspects of society at a given moment—but something more profound. His writing and also his illustrations are capable of surviving the immediate environment and time out of which they spring. To some extent they will be a document of the age they belong to.*
>
> *When asked to define humour, Thurber quoted someone whose name he had forgotten: He said that "the English treat the commonplace as if it were remarkable and the Americans treat the remarkable as if it were commonplace. . . . In 'The Secret Life of Walter Mitty' I tried to treat the remarkable as commonplace."*

The Secret Life of Walter Mitty   [1939]

"We're going through!" The Commander's voice was like thin ice breaking. He wore his full-dress uniform, with the heavily braided white cap pulled down rakishly over one cold gray eye. "We can't make it, sir. It's spoiling for a hurricane, if you ask me." "I'm not asking you, Lieutenant Berg," said the Commander. "Throw on the power lights! Rev her up to 8,500! We're going through!" The pounding of the cylinders increased: ta-pocketa-pocketa-pocketa-*pocketa-pocketa*. The Commander stared at the ice forming on the pilot window. He walked over and twisted a row of complicated dials. "Switch on No. 8 auxiliary!" he shouted. "Switch on No. 8 auxiliary!" repeated Lieutenant Berg. "Full strength in No. 3 turret!" shouted the Commander. "Full strength in No. 3 turret!" The crew, bending to their various tasks in the huge, hurtling eight-engined Navy hydroplane, looked at each other and grinned. "The Old Man'll get us through," they said to one another. "The Old Man ain't afraid of Hell!" . . .

"Not so fast! You're driving too fast!" said Mrs. Mitty. "What are you driving so fast for?"

"Hmm?" said Walter Mitty. He looked at his wife, in the seat beside him, with shocked astonishment. She seemed grossly unfamiliar, like a strange woman who had yelled at him in a crowd. "You were up to fifty-five," she said. "You know I don't like to go more than forty. You were up to fifty-five." Walter Mitty drove on toward Waterbury in silence, the roaring of the SN202 through the worst storm in twenty years of Navy flying fading in the remote, intimate airways of his mind. "You're tensed up again," said Mrs. Mitty. "It's one of your days. I wish you'd let Dr. Renshaw look you over."

Walter Mitty stopped the car in front of the building where his wife went to have her hair done. "Remember to get those overshoes while I'm having my hair done," she said. "I don't need overshoes," said Mitty. She put her mirror back into her bag. "We've been all through that," she said, getting out of the car. "You're not a young man any longer." He raced the engine a little. "Why don't you wear your gloves? Have you lost your gloves?" Walter Mitty reached in a pocket and brought out the gloves. He put them on, but after she had turned and gone into the building and he had driven on to a red light, he took them off again. "Pick it up, brother!" snapped a cop as the light changed, and Mitty hastily pulled on his gloves and lurched ahead. He drove around the streets aimlessly for a time, and then he drove past the hospital on his way to the parking lot.

5   . . . "It's the millionaire banker, Wellington McMillan," said the pretty nurse. "Yes?" said Walter Mitty, removing his gloves slowly. "Who has the case?" "Dr. Renshaw and Mr. Benbow, but there are two specialists here, Dr. Remington from New York and Mr. Pritchard-Mitford from London. He flew over." A door opened down a long, cool corridor and Dr. Renshaw came out. He looked distraught and haggard. "Hello, Mitty," he said. "We're having the devil's own time with McMillan, the millionaire banker and close personal friend of Roosevelt. Obstreosis of the ductal tract. Tertiary. Wish you'd take a look at him." "Glad to," said Mitty.

In the operating room there were whispered introductions: "Dr. Remington, Dr. Mitty. Mr. Pritchard-Mitford, Dr. Mitty." "I've read your book on streptothricosis," said Pritchard-Mitford, shaking hands. "A brilliant performance, sir." "Thank you," said Walter Mitty. "Didn't know you were in the States, Mitty," grumbled Remington. "Coals to Newcastle, bringing Mitford and me up here for a tertiary." "You are very kind," said Mitty. A huge, complicated machine, connected to the operating table, with many tubes and wires, began at this moment to go pocketa-pocketa-pocketa. "The new anesthetizer is giving way!" shouted an interne. "There is no one in the East who knows how to fix it!" "Quiet, man!" said Mitty, in a low, cool voice. He sprang to the machine, which was now going pocketa-pocketa-queep-pocketa-queep. He began fingering delicately a row of glistening dials. "Give me a fountain pen!" he snapped. Someone handed him a fountain pen. He pulled a faulty piston out of the machine and inserted the pen in its place. "That will hold for ten minutes," he said. "Get on with the operation." A nurse hurried over and whispered to Renshaw, and Mitty saw the man turn pale. "Coreopsis has set in," said Renshaw nervously. "If you would take over, Mitty?" Mitty looked at him and at the craven figure of Benbow, who drank, and at the grave, uncertain faces of the two great specialists. "If you wish," he said. They slipped a white gown on him; he adjusted a mask and drew on thin gloves; nurses handed him shining . . .

"Back it up, Mac! Look out for that Buick!" Walter Mitty jammed on the brakes. "Wrong lane, Mac," said the parking-lot attendant, looking at Mitty closely. "Gee. Yeh," muttered Mitty. He began cautiously to back out of the lane marked "Exit Only." "Leave her sit there," said the attendant. "I'll put her away." Mitty got out of the car. "Hey, better leave the key." "Oh," said Mitty, handing the man the ignition key. The attendant vaulted into the car, backed it up with insolent skill, and put it where it belonged.

They're so damn cocky, thought Walter Mitty, walking along Main Street; they think they know everything. Once he had tried to take his chains off, outside New Milford, and he had got them wound around the axles. A man had had to come out in a wrecking car and unwind them, a young, grinning garageman. Since then Mrs. Mitty always made him drive to a garage to have the chains taken off. The next time, he thought, I'll wear my right arm in a sling; they won't grin at me then. I'll have my right arm in a sling and they'll see I couldn't possibly take the chains off myself. He kicked at the slush on the sidewalk. "Overshoes," he said to himself, and he began looking for a shoe store.

When he came out into the street again, with the overshoes in a box under his arm, Walter Mitty began to wonder what the other thing was his wife had told him to get. She had told him, twice, before they set out from their house for Waterbury. In a way he hated these weekly trips to town—he was always getting something wrong. Kleenex, he thought, Squibb's, razor blades? No. Toothpaste, toothbrush, bicarbonate, carborundum, initiative and referendum? He gave it up. But she would remember it. "Where's the what's-its-name?" she would ask. "Don't tell me you forgot the what's-its-name." A newsboy went by shouting something about the Waterbury trial.

10   . . . "Perhaps this will refresh your memory." The District Attorney suddenly thrust a heavy automatic at the quiet figure on the witness stand. "Have you ever seen this before?" Walter Mitty took the gun and examined it expertly. "This is my Webley-Vickers 50.80," he said calmly. An excited buzz ran around the courtroom. The Judge rapped for order. "You are a crack shot with any sort of firearms, I believe?" said the District Attorney, insinuatingly. "Objection!" shouted Mitty's attorney. "We have shown that the defendant could not have fired the shot. We have shown that he wore his right arm in a sling on the night of the fourteenth of July." Walter Mitty raised his hand briefly and the bickering attorneys were stilled. "With any known make of gun," he said evenly, "I could have killed Gregory Fitzhurst at three hundred feet *with my left hand*." Pandemonium broke loose in the courtroom. A woman's scream rose above the bedlam and suddenly a lovely, dark-haired girl was in Walter Mitty's arms. The District Attorney struck at her savagely. Without rising from his chair, Mitty let the man have it on the point of the chin. "You miserable cur!" . . .

"Puppy biscuit," said Walter Mitty. He stopped walking and the buildings of Waterbury rose up out of the misty courtroom and surrounded him again. A woman who was passing laughed. "He said 'Puppy biscuit,'" she said to her companion. "That man said 'Puppy biscuit' to himself." Walter Mitty hurried on. He went into an A. & P., not the first one he came to but a smaller one farther up the street. "I want some biscuit for small, young dogs," he said to the clerk. "Any special brand, sir?" The greatest pistol shot in the world thought a moment. "It says 'Puppies Bark for It' on the box," said Walter Mitty.

His wife would be through at the hairdresser's in fifteen minutes, Mitty saw in looking at his watch, unless they had trouble drying it; sometimes they had trouble drying it. She didn't like to get to the hotel first; she would want him to be there waiting for her as usual. He found a big leather chair in the lobby, facing a window, and he put the overshoes and the puppy biscuit on the floor beside it. He picked up an old copy of *Liberty* and sank down into the chair. "Can Germany Conquer the World Through the Air?" Walter Mitty looked at the pictures of bombing planes and of ruined streets.

. . . "The cannonading has got the wind up in young Raleigh, sir," said the sergeant. Captain Mitty looked up at him through tousled hair. "Get him to bed," he said wearily. "With the others. I'll fly alone." "But you can't, sir," said the sergeant anxiously. "It takes two men to handle that bomber and the Archies are pounding hell out of the air. Von Richtman's circus is between here and Saulier." "Somebody's got to get that ammunition dump," said Mitty. "I'm going over. Spot of brandy?" He poured a drink for the sergeant and one for himself. War thundered and whined around the dugout and battered at the door. There was a rending of wood and splinters flew through the room. "A bit of a near thing," said Captain Mitty carelessly. "The box barrage is closing in," said the sergeant. "We only live once, Sergeant," said Mitty, with his faint, fleeting smile. "Or do we?" He poured another brandy and tossed it off. "I never see a man could hold his brandy like you, sir," said the sergeant. "Begging your pardon, sir." Captain Mitty stood up and strapped on his huge Webley-Vickers automatic. "It's forty kilometers through hell, sir," said the sergeant. Mitty finished one last brandy. "After all," he said softly, "what isn't?" The pounding of the cannon increased; there was the rat-tat-tatting of machine guns, and from somewhere came the menacing pocket-pocketa-pocketa of the new flame-throwers. Walter Mitty walked to the door of the dugout humming "Auprès de Ma Blonde." He turned and waved to the sergeant. "Cheerio!" he said. . . .

Something struck his shoulder. "I've been looking all over this hotel for you," said Mrs. Mitty. "Why do you have to hide in this old chair? How did you expect me to find you?" "Things close in," said Walter Mitty vaguely. "What?" Mrs. Mitty said. "Did you get the what's-its-name? The puppy biscuit? What's in that box?" "Overshoes," said Mitty. "Couldn't you have put them on in the store?" "I was thinking," said Walter Mitty. "Does it ever occur to you that I am sometimes thinking?" She looked at him. "I'm going to take your temperature when I get you home," she said.

15   They went out through the revolving doors that made a faintly derisive whistling sound when you pushed them. It was two blocks to the parking lot. At the drugstore on the corner she said, "Wait here for me. I forgot something. I won't be a minute." She was more than a minute. Walter Mitty lighted a cigarette. It began to rain, rain with sleet in it. He stood up against the wall of the drugstore, smoking. . . . He put his shoulders back and his heels together. "To hell with the handkerchief," said Walter Mitty scornfully. He took one last drag on his cigarette and snapped it away. Then, with that faint, fleeting smile playing about his lips, he faced the firing squad; erect and motionless, proud and disdainful, Walter Mitty the Undefeated, inscrutable to the last.

HELENA MARIA VIRAMONTES

Helena Maria Viramontes was born in East Los Angeles in 1954. After completing her undergraduate studies at Immaculate Heart College, she did graduate work at California State University, Los Angeles, and further work between 1979 and 1981 in the MFA Creative Writing Program at the University of California, Irvine. Viramontes has won first prize in several fiction contests, including the Irvine Chicano Literary Contest. In 1989, the year in which she was awarded a Creative Writing Fellowship from the National Endowment for the Arts, she participated in a "Storytelling for Film" workshop at the Sundance Film Institute.

Viramontes writes chiefly about women whose lives are circumscribed by a patriarchal Latino society. Eight of her stories have been collected in "The Moths" and Other Stories (1985).

The Moths   [1982]

I was fourteen years old when Abuelita[1] requested my help. And it seemed only fair. Abuelita had pulled me through the rages of scarlet fever by placing, removing and replacing potato slices on the temples of my forehead; she had seen me through several whippings, an arm broken by a dare jump off Tío Enrique's toolshed, puberty, and my first lie. Really, I told Amá, it was only fair.

Not that I was her favorite granddaughter or anything special. I wasn't even pretty or nice like my older sisters and I just couldn't do the girl things they could do. My hands were too big to handle the fineries of crocheting or embroidery and I always pricked my fingers or knotted my colored threads time and time again while my sisters laughed and called me bull hands with their cute waterlike voices. So I began keeping a piece of jagged brick in my sock to bash my sisters or anyone who called me bull hands. Once, while we all sat in the bedroom, I hit Teresa on the forehead, right above her eyebrow and she ran to Amá with her mouth open, her hand over her eye while blood seeped between her fingers. I was used to the whippings by then.

I wasn't respectful either. I even went so far as to doubt the power of Abuelita's slices, the slices she said absorbed my fever. "You're still alive, aren't you?" Abuelita snapped back, her pasty gray eye beaming at me and burning holes in my suspicions. Regretful that I had let secret questions drop out of my mouth, I couldn't look into her eyes. My hands began to fan out, grow like a liar's nose until they hung by my side like low weights. Abuelita made a balm out of dried moth wings and Vicks and rubbed my hands, shaped them back to size and it was the strangest feeling. Like bones melting. Like sun shining through the darkness of your eyelids. I didn't mind helping Abuelita after that, so Amá would always send me over to her.

In the early afternoon Amá would push her hair back, hand me my sweater and shoes, and tell me to go to Mama Luna's. This was to avoid another fight and another whipping, I knew. I would deliver one last direct shot on Marisela's arm and jump out of our house, the slam of the screen door burying her cries of anger, and I'd gladly go help Abuelita plant her wild lilies or jasmine or heliotrope or cilantro or hierbabuena in red Hills

---

[1]**Abuelita** Grandma (Spanish); other Spanish words for relatives mentioned in the story are *Tío,* Uncle, *Amá,* Mother, and *Apá,* Dad.

Brothers coffee cans. Abuelita would wait for me at the top step of her porch holding a hammer and nail and empty coffee cans. And although we hardly spoke, hardly looked at each other as we worked over root transplants, I always felt her gray eye on me. It made me feel, in a strange sort of way, safe and guarded and not alone. Like God was supposed to make you feel.

5   On Abuelita's porch, I would puncture holes in the bottom of the coffee cans with a nail and a precise hit of a hammer. This completed, my job was to fill them with red clay mud from beneath her rose bushes, packing it softly, then making a perfect hole, four fingers round, to nest a sprouting avocado pit, or the spidery sweet potatoes that Abuelita rooted in mayonnaise jars with toothpicks and daily water, or prickly chayotes[2] that produced vines that twisted and wound all over her porch pillars, crawling to the roof, up and over the roof, and down the other side, making her small brick house look like it was cradled within the vines that grew pear-shaped squashes ready for the pick, ready to be steamed with onions and cheese and butter. The roots would burst out of the rusted coffee cans and search for a place to connect. I would then feed the seedlings with water.

But this was a different kind of help, Amá said, because Abuelita was dying. Looking into her gray eye, then into her brown one, the doctor said it was just a matter of days. And so it seemed only fair that these hands she had melted and formed found use in rubbing her caving body with alcohol and marihuana, rubbing her arms and legs, turning her face to the window so that she could watch the Bird of Paradise blooming or smell the scent of clove in the air. I toweled her face frequently and held her hand for hours. Her gray wiry hair hung over the mattress. Since I could remember, she'd kept her long hair in braids. Her mouth was vacant and when she slept, her eyelids never closed all the way. Up close, you could see her gray eye beaming out the window, staring hard as if to remember everything. I never kissed her. I left the window open when I went to the market.

Across the street from Jay's Market there was a chapel. I never knew its denomination, but 1 went in just the same to search for candles. I sat down on one of the pews because there were none. After I cleaned my fingernails, I looked up at the high ceiling. I had forgotten the vastness of these places, the coolness of the marble pillars and the frozen statues with blank eyes. I was alone. I knew why I had never returned.

That was one of Apá's biggest complaints. He would pound his hands on the table, rocking the sugar dish or spilling a cup of coffee and scream that if I didn't go to mass every Sunday to save my goddamn sinning soul, then I had no reason to go out of the house, period. Punto final.[3] He would grab my arm and dig his nails into me to make sure I understood the importance of catechism. Did he make himself clear? Then he strategically directed his anger at Amá for her lousy ways of bringing up daughters, being disrespectful and unbelieving, and my older sisters would pull me aside and tell me if I didn't get to mass right this minute, they were all going to kick the holy shit out of me. Why am I so selfish? Can't you see what it's

---

[2]**chayotes** squashlike fruit.   [3]**Punto final** period.

doing to Amá, you idiot? So I would wash my feet and stuff them in my black Easter shoes that shone with Vaseline, grab a missal and veil, and wave good-bye to Amá.

I would walk slowly down Lorena to First to Evergreen, counting the cracks on the cement. On Evergreen I would turn left and walk to Abuelita's. I liked her porch because it was shielded by the vines of the chayotes and I could get a good look at the people and car traffic on Evergreen without them knowing. I would jump up the porch steps, knock on the screen door as I wiped my feet and call Abuelita? mi Abuelita? As I opened the door and stuck my head in, I would catch the gagging scent of toasting chile on the placa.[4] When I entered the sala,[5] she would greet me from the kitchen, wringing her hands in her apron. I'd sit at the corner of the table to keep from being in her way. The chiles made my eyes water. Am I crying? No, Mama Luna, I'm sure not crying. I don't like going to mass, but my eyes watered anyway, the tears dropping on the tablecloth like candle wax. Abuelita lifted the burnt chiles from the fire and sprinkled water on them until the skins began to separate. Placing them in front of me, she turned to check the menudo.[6] I peeled the skins off and put the flimsy, limp looking green and yellow chiles in the molcajete[7] and began to crush and crush and twist and crush the heart out of the tomato, the clove of garlic, the stupid chiles that made me cry, crushed them until they turned into liquid under my bull hand. With a wooden spoon, I scraped hard to destroy the guilt, and my tears were gone. I put the bowl of chile next to a vase filled with freshly cut roses. Abuelita touched my hand and pointed to the bowl of menudo that steamed in front of me. I spooned some chile into the menudo and rolled a corn tortilla thin with the palms of my hands. As I ate, a fine Sunday breeze entered the kitchen and a rose petal calmly feathered down to the table.

10   I left the chapel without blessing myself and walked to Jay's. Most of the time Jay didn't have much of anything. The tomatoes were always soft and the cans of Campbell soups had rusted spots on them. There was dust on the tops of cereal boxes. I picked up what I needed: rubbing alcohol, five cans of chicken broth, a big bottle of Pine Sol. At first Jay got mad because I thought I had forgotten the money. But it was there all the time, in my back pocket.

When I returned from the market, I heard Amá crying in Abuelita's kitchen. She looked up at me with puffy eyes. I placed the bags of groceries on the table and began putting the cans of soup away. Amá sobbed quietly. I never kissed her. After a while, I patted her on the back for comfort. Finally: "¿Y mi Amá?"[8] she asked in a whisper, then choked again and cried into her apron.

Abuelita fell off the bed twice yesterday, I said, knowing that I shouldn't have said it and wondering why I wanted to say it because it only made Amá cry harder. I guess I became angry and just so tired of the quarrels and beatings and unanswered prayers and my hands just there hanging helplessly by my side. Amá looked at me again, confused, angry, and her

---

[4]**placa** round cast-iron griddle.   [5]**sala** living room.   [6]**menudo** tripe soup.
[7]**molcajete** mixing vessel, mortar.   [8]**¿Y mi Amá?** And my Mother?

eyes were filled with sorrow. I went outside and sat on the porch swing and watched the people pass. I sat there until she left. I dozed off repeating the words to myself like rosary prayers: when do you stop giving when do you start giving when do you . . . and when my hands fell from my lap, I awoke to catch them. The sun was setting, an orange glow, and I knew Abuelita was hungry.

There comes a time when the sun is defiant. Just about the time when moods change, inevitable seasons of a day, transitions from one color to another, that hour or minute or second when the sun is finally defeated, finally sinks into the realization that it cannot with all its power to heal or burn, exist forever, there comes an illumination where the sun and earth meet, a final burst of burning red orange fury reminding us that although endings are inevitable, they are necessary for rebirths, and when that time came, just when I switched on the light in the kitchen to open Abuelita's can of soup, it was probably then that she died.

The room smelled of Pine Sol and vomit and Abuelita had defecated the remains of her cancerous stomach. She had turned to the window and tried to speak, but her mouth remained open and speechless. I heard you, Abuelita, I said, stroking her cheek, I heard you. I opened the windows of the house and let the soup simmer and overboil on the stove. I turned the stove off and poured the soup down the sink. From the cabinet I got a tin basin, filled it with lukewarm water and carried it carefully to the room. I went to the linen closet and took out some modest bleached white towels. With the sacredness of a priest preparing his vestments, I unfolded the towels one by one on my shoulders. I removed the sheets and blankets from her bed and peeled off her thick flannel nightgown. I toweled her puzzled face, stretching out the wrinkles, removing the coils of her neck, toweled her shoulders and breasts. Then I changed the water. I returned to towel the creases of her stretch-marked stomach, her sporadic vaginal hairs, and her sagging thighs. I removed the lint from between her toes and noticed a mapped birthmark on the fold of her buttock. The scars on her back which were as thin as the life lines on the palms of her hands made me realize how little I really knew of Abuelita. I covered her with a thin blanket and went into the bathroom. I washed my hands, and turned on the tub faucets and watched the water pour into the tub with vitality and steam. When it was full, I turned off the water and undressed. Then, I went to get Abuelita.

15   She was not as heavy as I thought and when I carried her in my arms, her body fell into a V, and yet my legs were tired, shaky, and I felt as if the distance between the bedroom and bathroom was miles and years away. Amá, where are you?

I stepped into the bathtub one leg first, then the other. I bent my knees slowly to descend into the water slowly so I wouldn't scald her skin. There, there, Abuelita, I said, cradling her, smoothing her as we descended, I heard you. Her hair fell back and spread across the water like eagle's wings. The water in the tub overflowed and poured onto the tile of the floor. Then the moths came. Small, gray ones that came from her soul and out through her mouth fluttering to light, circling the single dull light bulb of the bathroom. Dying is lonely and I wanted to go to where the moths were, stay with her and plant chayotes whose vines would crawl up her fingers and into the clouds; I wanted to rest my head on her chest with her stroking my hair, telling me about the moths that lay within the soul and slowly eat the spirit up; I wanted to return to the waters of the womb with her so that we would never be alone again. I wanted. I wanted my Amá. I removed a few strands of hair from Abuelita's face and held her small light head within the hollow of my neck. The bathroom was filled with moths, and for the first time in a long time I cried, rocking us, crying for her, for me, for Amá, the sobs emerging from the depths of anguish, the misery of feeling half born, sobbing until finally the sobs rippled into circles and circles of sadness and relief. There, there, I said to Abuelita, rocking us gently, there, there.

III

Poetry

The original caption for this photograph of poet Gwendolyn Brooks, taken in 1950, ran as follows:

> A 32-year-old housewife and part-time secretary has won the Pulitzer Prize in poetry for *Annie Allen,* a ballad of Chicago Negro life. The first woman to capture one of the famed awards, she is the mother of a 9-year-old boy and the wife of Henry Blakely, partner in an auto repair shop.

These sentences are informative and accurate, and perhaps that is enough to ask of them, but we can't help remarking that if you want to know what poetry is *not*, you have only to read those sentences again. Despite the metaphor in "capture," the language is unexciting, even trite ("famed awards"). We are not talking about the lack of rhyme or of meter, qualities that of course are not found in prose (though they are not essential to poetry either). We might compare the caption with the prose that begins Brooks's most famous poem, "We Real Cool" (page 594), which starts thus: "The Pool Players. / Seven at the Golden Shovel." "Seven" has a mystical hint (it is widely regarded as a lucky number, there are seven days in the week, Seven Deadly Sins, Seven Wonders of the World, Seven Seas, and a host of other sevens) and "Golden Shovel"—presumably the name of a pool parlor—has an interesting paradoxical quality: "Golden" suggests great wealth, "Shovel" suggests the humble soil, and in the context of the poem it suggests death.

As you will see when you come to read Brooks's poems (and the poems of others in this section of the book), poets do not use language the way journalists (including the writer of the caption for the photograph) use language. It is not, we hasten to add, that poets do not write about life. They certainly do: Brooks herself said "Poetry is life distilled," and "I wrote about what I saw and heard on the street." But for poets, words are sensuous materials, like colors for a painter or stones for a sculptor, and when words are combined they make not only good sense but also an almost physical thing that the reader feels as he or she recites the poem aloud or silently. We urge you to turn to page 594 and to read Brooks's "We Real Cool."

16

Approaching Poetry: Responding in Writing

The title of this chapter is a bit misleading, since we have already spent a few pages discussing poems in Chapter 2, "Reading and Responding to Literature." But here we will begin again, taking a different approach.

First, some brief advice about how to approach a poem:

1. Read the poem aloud; or, if you can't bring yourself to read aloud, at least sound the poem in your mind's ear. Try to catch the speaker's tone of voice.
2. Pay attention not only to the black marks on the white paper but also to the white spaces between groups of lines. If a space follows some lines, pause briefly, and take the preceding lines as a unit of thought.
3. Read the poem a second and a third time. Now that you know how it ends, you'll be able to see the connections between the beginning and what follows.

LANGSTON HUGHES

Langston Hughes (1902–1967), an African American writer born in Joplin, Missouri, lived part of his youth in Mexico, spent a year at Columbia University, served as a merchant seaman, and worked in a Paris nightclub. There, he showed some of his poems to Alain Locke, an African American patron of the arts and a strong advocate of African American literature. Encouraged by Locke, Hughes continued to write when he returned to the United States, publishing fiction, plays, essays, and biographies; he also founded theaters and gave public readings. The poem that we reprint, "Harlem" (1951), provided Lorraine Hansberry with the title of her well-known play A Raisin in the Sun *(1958). For a generous selection of poems by Langston Hughes, see Chapter 27.*

Harlem   [1951]

What happens to a dream deferred?

   Does it dry up
   like a raisin in the sun?

Or fester like a sore—
And then run?   5
Does it stink like rotten meat?
Or crust and sugar over—
like a syrupy sweet?

Maybe it just sags
like a heavy load.   10

Or does it explode?

Read the poem at least twice, and then think about its effect on you.

1. Do you find the poem interesting? Why or why not?
2. Do some things in it interest you more than others? If so, why?
3. Does anything in it puzzle you? If so, what?

Before reading any further, you might jot down your responses to some of these questions. And, whatever your responses, can you point to features of the poem to account for them?

Of course, different readers will respond at least somewhat differently to any work. On the other hand, since writers want to communicate, they try to control their readers' responses, and they count on their readers to understand the meanings of words as the writers understand them. Thus, Hughes assumed his readers knew that Harlem was the site of a large African American community in New York City.

Let's assume that the reader understands Hughes is talking about Harlem, New York, and, further, that the reader understands the "dream deferred" to refer to the unfulfilled hopes of African Americans who live in a society dominated by whites. But Hughes does not say "hopes," he says "dream," and he does not say "unfulfilled," he says "deferred." You might ask yourself exactly what differences there are between these words. Next, when you have read the poem several times, you might think about which expression is better in the context, "unfulfilled hopes" or "dream deferred," and why.

Thinking About "Harlem"

Let's turn to an analysis of the poem, an examination of how the parts fit. As you look at the poem, think about the parts, and jot down whatever notes come to mind. After you have written your own notes, consider the annotations of one student.

These annotations chiefly get at the structure of the poem, the relationship of the parts. The student notices that the poem begins with a line set off by itself and ends with a line set off by itself, and he also notices that each of these lines is a question. Further, he indicates that each of these two lines is emphasized in other ways. The first begins further to the left than any of the other lines—as though the other lines are subheadings or are in some way subordinate—and the last is italicized. In short, he comments on the structure of the poem.

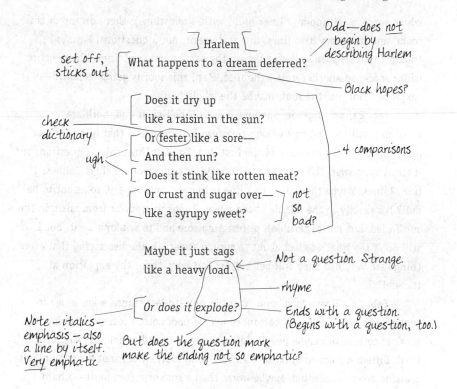

The annotations read:

Odd—does *not* begin by describing Harlem

set off, sticks out] Harlem [
What happens to a *dream* deferred?

Black hopes?

[Does it dry up
check dictionary — like a raisin in the sun?
Or (fester) like a sore—
ugh < And then run?
4 comparisons

[Does it stink like rotten meat?
Or crust and sugar over— ⌝ not
like a syrupy sweet? ⌟ so bad?

Maybe it just sags
like a heavy/load. ← Not a question. Strange.

— rhyme

[Or does it (explode?) — Ends with a question. (Begins with a question, too.)

Note—italics—emphasis—also a line by itself. Very emphatic

But does the question mark make the ending *not* so emphatic?

Some Journal Entries

The student who made these annotations later wrote an entry in his journal:

Feb. 18. Since the title is "Harlem," it's obvious that the "dream" is by African American people. Also, obvious that Hughes thinks that if the "dream" doesn't become real there may be riots ("explode"). I like "raisin in the sun" (maybe because I like the play), and I like the business about "a syrupy sweet"—much more pleasant than the festering sore and the rotten meat. But if the dream becomes "sweet," what's wrong with that? Why should something "sweet" explode?

Feb. 21. Prof. Stahl said to think of structure or form of a poem as a sort of architecture, a building with a foundation, floors, etc., topped by a roof—but since we read a poem from top to bottom, it's like a building upside down. Title or first line is foundation (even though it's at top); last line is roof, capping the whole. As you read, you add layers. Foundation of "Harlem" is a question (first line). Then, set back a bit from foundation, or built on it by white space, a tall room (7 lines high, with 4 questions); then, on top of this room, another room (two lines, one statement, not a question). Funny; I thought that in poems all stanzas are the same number of lines. Then—more white space, so another unit—the roof. Man, this roof is going to fall in— "explode." Not just the roof, maybe the whole house.

Feb. 21, pm. I get it; one line at start, one line at end; both are questions, but the last sort of says (because it is in italics) that it is the *most likely* answer to the question of the first line. The last line is also a question, but it's still an answer. The big stanza (7 lines) has 4 questions: 2 lines, 2 lines, 1 line, 2 lines. Maybe the switch to 1 line is to give some variety, so as not to be dull? It's exactly in the middle of the poem. I get the progress from raisin in the sun (dried, but not so terrible), to festering sore and to stinking meat, but I still don't see what's so bad about "a syrupy sweet." Is Hughes saying that after things are very bad they will get better? But why, then, the explosion at the end?

Feb. 23. "Heavy load" and "sags" in next-to-last stanza seem to me to suggest slaves with bales of cotton, or maybe poor cotton pickers dragging big sacks of cotton. Or maybe people doing heavy labor in Harlem. Anyway, very tired. Different from running sore and stinking meat earlier; not disgusting, but pressing down, deadening. Maybe *worse* than a sore or rotten meat—a hard, hopeless life. And then the last line. Just one line, no fancy (and disgusting) simile. Boom! Not just pressed down and tired, like maybe some racist whites think (hope?) blacks will be? Bang! Will there be survivors?

Drawing chiefly on these notes, the student jotted down some key ideas to guide him through a draft of an analysis of the poem. (The organization of the draft posed no problem; the student simply followed the organization of the poem.)

```
11 lines; short, but powerful; explosive
Question (first line)
Answers (set off by space & also indented)
"raisin in the sun": shrinking
"sore"                          } disgusting
"rotten meat"
"syrupy sweet": relief from disgusting comparisons
final question (last line): explosion?
    explosive (powerful) because:
        short, condensed, packed
        in italics
        stands by itself—like first line
        no fancy comparison; very direct
```

Here is the student's final draft of his essay.

Michael Locke
Professor Stahl
English 2B
10 June 2010

Langston Hughes's "Harlem"

"Harlem" is a poem that is only eleven lines long, but it is charged with power. It explodes. Hughes sets the stage, so to speak, by telling us in the title that he is talking about Harlem, and then he begins by asking, "What happens to a dream deferred?" The rest of the poem is set off by being indented, as though it is the answer to his question. This answer is in three parts (three stanzas, of different lengths).

In a way, it's wrong to speak of the answer, since the rest of the poem consists of questions, but I think Hughes means that each question (for instance, does a "deferred" hope "dry up / like a raisin in the sun?") really is an answer, something that really has happened and that will happen again. The first question, "Does it dry up / like a raisin in the sun?," is a famous line. To compare hope to a raisin dried in the sun is to suggest a terrible shrinking. The next two comparisons are to a "sore" and to "rotten meat." These comparisons are less clever, but they are very effective because they are disgusting. Then, maybe because of the disgusting comparisons, he gives a comparison that is not at all disgusting. In this comparison he says that maybe the "dream deferred" will "crust and sugar over— / like a syrupy sweet."

The seven lines with four comparisons are followed by a stanza of two lines with just one comparison:

Maybe it just sags
like a heavy load.

So if we thought that this postponed dream might finally turn into something "sweet," we were kidding ourselves. Hughes comes down to earth, in a short stanza, with an image of a heavy load, which probably also calls to mind images of people bent under heavy loads, maybe of cotton, or maybe just any sort of heavy load carried by African Americans in Harlem and elsewhere.

Locke 2

The opening question ("What happens to a dream deferred?") was followed by four questions in seven lines, but now, with "Maybe it just sags / like a heavy load," we get a statement, as though the poet at last has found an answer. But at the end we get one more question, set off by itself and in italics: *Or does it explode?* This line itself is explosive for three reasons: it is short, it is italicized, and it is a stanza in itself. It's also interesting that this line, unlike the earlier lines, does *not* use a simile. It's almost as though Hughes is saying, "OK, we've had enough fancy ways of talking about this terrible situation; here it is, straight."

Locke 3

Work Cited

Hughes, Langston. "Harlem." *An Introduction to Literature*. Ed. Sylvan Barnet, William Burto, and William E. Cain. 16th ed. New York: Longman, 2011. 541–42. Print.

YOUR TURN

1. The student's analysis suggests that the comparison with "a syrupy sweet" is a deliberately misleading happy ending that serves to make the real ending even more powerful. In class another student suggested that Hughes may be referring to African Americans who play the Uncle Tom, people who adopt a smiling manner in order to cope with an oppressive society. Which explanation do you prefer, and why? What do you think of combining the two? Or can you offer a different explanation?

2. Do you suppose that virtually all African Americans respond to this poem in a way that is substantially different from the way virtually all Caucasians or Asian Americans respond? Explain your position.

3. When Hughes reprinted this poem in 1959, he retitled it "Dream Deferred." Your response?

Let's now look at another poem, and at the responses of another student. Here is a seventeenth-century poem—actually a song—that makes use of the idea that the eyes of the beloved woman can dart fire, and that she can kill (or at least severely wound) the sighing, helpless male lover. The male speaker describes the appearance of Cupid, the tyrannic god of love, who (he claims) is equipped with darts and death-dealing fire taken from the eyes of the proud, cruel woman whom the speaker loves.

APHRA BEHN

Aphra Behn (1640-1689) is regarded as the first English woman to have made a living by writing. Not much is known of her life, but she seems to have married a London merchant of Dutch descent, and after his death to have served as a spy in the Dutch Wars (1665-1667). After her return to England she took up playwriting, and she gained fame with The Rover *(1677). Behn also wrote novels, the most important of which is* Oroonoko, or The Royal Slave *(1688), which is among the first works in English to express sympathy for enslaved Africans.*

In the following poem, Cupid represents love. The poem was written by a woman but the imagined speaker is a male, who laments that the woman whom he loves is indifferent to him.

Song: Love Armed [1676]

Love in fantastic triumph sate,
    Whilst bleeding hearts around him flowed,
For whom fresh pains he did create,
    And strange tyrannic power he showed:
From thy bright eyes he took his fire,   5
    Which round about in sport he hurled;
But 'twas from mine he took desire,
    Enough to undo the amorous world.

From me he took his sighs and tears:
    From thee, his pride and cruelty;   10
From me, his languishments and fears;
    And every killing dart from thee.
Thus thou and I the god have armed
    And set him up a deity;
But my poor heart alone is harmed,   15
    Whilst thine the victor is, and free.

YOUR TURN

1. The speaker talks of the suffering he is undergoing (Behn is using the poetic convention of the passionate man who addresses a disdainful woman). Can we nevertheless feel that he enjoys his plight? *Why*, by the way, do we (as readers, singers, or listeners) often enjoy songs of unhappy love?
2. The woman ("thee") is said to exhibit "pride and cruelty" (line 10). Is the poem sexist? Is it therefore offensive?
3. Do you suppose that men can enjoy the poem more than women? Explain.

Some Journal Entries

The subject is Aphra Behn's "Song." We begin with two entries in a journal, kept by a first-year student, Geoffrey Sullivan, and we follow these entries with Sullivan's completed essay.

October 10. The title "Love Armed" puzzled me at first; funny, I somehow was thinking of the expression "strong-armed" and at first I didn't understand that "Love" in this poem is a human—no, not a human, but the god Cupid, who has a human form—and that he is shown as armed, with darts and so forth.

October 13. This god of "Love" is Cupid, and so he is something like what is on a valentine card—Cupid with his bow and arrow. But valentine cards just show cute little Cupids, and in this poem Cupid is a real menace. He causes lots of pain ("bleeding hearts," "tears," "killing dart," etc.). So what is Aphra Behn telling us about the god of love, or love? That love hurts? And she is *singing* about it! But we *do* sing songs about how hard life is. But do we sing them when we are really hurting, or only when we are pretty well off and just thinking about being hurt?

When you love someone and they don't return your love, it hurts, but even when love isn't returned it still gives some intense pleasure. Strange, but I think true. I wouldn't say that love always has this two-sided nature, but I do see the idea that love *can* have two sides, pleasure and pain. And love takes two kinds of people, male and female. Well, for most people, anyway. Maybe there's also something to the idea that "opposites attract." Anyway, Aphra Behn seems to be talking about men vs. women, pain vs. pleasure, power vs. weakness, etc. Pairs, opposites. And in two stanzas (a pair of stanzas?).

The final essay makes use of some, but not all, of the preliminary jottings. It includes much that Sullivan did not think of until he reread his jottings, reread the poem, and began drafting the essay.

Sullivan 1

Geoffrey Sullivan

Professor Diaz

English 2G

15 June 2010

The Double Nature of Love

Aphra Behn's "Love Armed" is in two stanzas, and it is about two people, "me" and "thee"—that is, you and I, the lover and the woman he loves. I think the speaker is a man, since according to the usual code men are supposed to be the active lovers and women are the (relatively) passive people who are loved. In this poem, the beloved—the woman, I think—has "bright eyes" (line 5) that provide the God of Love with fire, and she also provides the god with "pride and cruelty" (10). This of course is the way the man sees it if a woman doesn't respond to him; if she doesn't love him in return, she is (he thinks) arrogant and cruel.

What does the man give to Love? He provides "desire" (7), "sighs and tears" (9), "languishments and fears" (11). None of this sounds very manly, but the joke is that the God of Love—which means love—can turn a strong man into a crybaby when a woman does not respond to him.

Although both stanzas are clever *descriptions* of the God of Love, the poem is not just a description. Of course there is not a plot in the way that a short story has a plot, but there is a sort of a switch at the end, giving the poem something of a plot. The poem is, say, ninety percent expression of feeling and description of love, but during the course of expressing feelings and describing love something happens, so there is a tiny *story*. The first stanza sets the scene ("Love in fantastic triumph sate" [1]) and tells of some of the things that the speaker and the woman contributed to the God of Love. The woman's eyes provided Love with fire, and the man's feelings provided Love with "desire" (7). The second stanza goes on to mention other things that Love got from the speaker ("sighs and tears," etc. [9]), and other things that Love got from the beloved ("pride and cruelty," etc. [10]), and in line 13 the poet says, "Thus thou and I the god have armed," so the two humans share something. They have both given Love his weapons. But—and this is the story I spoke of—the poem ends by emphasizing their difference: Only the man is "harmed," and the woman is the "victor" because her heart is not captured, as the man's heart is. In the battle that Love presides over, the woman is the winner; the man's heart has fallen for the woman, but, according to the last line, the woman's heart remains "free."

We have all seen the God of Love on valentine cards, a cute little Cupid armed with a bow and arrow. But despite the bow and arrow that the Valentine's Day Cupid carries, I think that until I read Aphra Behn's "Love Armed" I had never really thought about Cupid as *powerful* and as capable of causing real pain. On valentine cards, he is just cute, but when I think about it, I realize the truth of Aphra Behn's concept of love. Love *is* (or can be) two-sided, whereas the valentine cards show only the sweet side.

I think it is interesting to notice that although the poem is about the destructive power of love, it is fun to read. I am not bothered by the fact that the lover is miserable. Why? I think I enjoy the poem, rather than am bothered by it, because *he is enjoying his misery.* After all, he is singing about it, sort of singing in the rain, telling anyone who will listen about how miserable he is, and he is having a very good time doing it.

Sullivan 3

Work Cited

Behn, Aphra. "Love Armed." *An Introduction to Literature.* Ed. Sylvan
Barnet, William Burto, and William E. Cain. 16th ed. New York:
Longman, 2011. 547. Print.

DAVID MURA

David Mura (b. 1952) is a sansei, *a third-generation Japanese American.
Mura's publications include novels, books of poetry, and two memoirs. He has
received several awards, including a US/Japan Creative Artist Fellowship, and
an NEA Literature Fellowship.*

An Argument: On 1942   [1989]

For my mother

Near Rose's Chop Suey and Jinosuke's grocery,
the temple where incense hovered and inspired
dense evening chants (prayers for Buddha's mercy,
colorless and deep), that day he was fired . . .   4

—No, no, no, she tells me. Why bring it back?
The camps are over. (Also overly dramatic.)
Forget *shoyu*-stained *furoshiki*,° *mochi*° on a stick:
You're like a terrier, David, gnawing a bone, an old, old trick . . .   8

Mostly we were bored. Women cooked and sewed,
men played blackjack, dug gardens, a *benjo*.°
Who noticed barbed wire, guards in the towers?
We were children, hunting stones, birds, wild flowers.   12

Yes, Mother hid tins of *tsukemono*° and eel
beneath the bed. And when the last was peeled,
clamped tight her lips, growing thinner and thinner.
But cancer not the camps made her throat blacker   16

. . . And she didn't die then . . . after the war, in St. Paul,
you weren't even born. Oh I know, I know, it's all
part of your job, your way, but why can't you glean
how far we've come, how much I can't recall—   20

David, it was so long ago—how useless it seems . . .

---

7 shoyu-stained furoshiki a soy-sauce-stained scarf that is used to carry things.
mochi rice cakes.   **10 benjo** toilet.   **13 tsukemono** Japanese pickles [Author's notes].

ELIZABETH BARRETT BROWNING

Elizabeth Barrett (1806–1861) was the eldest of twelve children. Largely self-edu-cated, and often suffering from poor health, she became an avid reader of poetry in English and in foreign languages. While living in London, under the sway of her domineering father, she began a correspondence with the poet Robert Browning, and, after a meeting, they eventually became secretly engaged. In 1846, Elizabeth and Robert eloped and left for Italy. Highly regarded for both her poems and her translations, she died in her husband's arms in 1861.

"How Do I Love Thee" is the next-to-last in a series of 44 sonnets that Elizabeth wrote in secret about the intense love she felt for her husband-to-be. She called the series Sonnets from the Portuguese, *a reference to the pet name that Robert had given to her, "my little Portugee," which itself was a reference to a poem that Elizabeth had written about a Portugese woman's devotion to her poet-lover.*

How Do I Love Thee?

How do I love thee? Let me count the ways.
I love thee to the depth and breadth and height
My soul can reach, when feeling out of sight
For the ends of Being and ideal Grace.   4
I love thee to the level of everyday's
Most quiet need, by sun and candle-light.
I love thee freely, as men strive for Right;
I love thee purely, as they turn from Praise.   8
I love thee with a passion put to use
In my old griefs, and with my childhood's faith.
I love thee with a love I seemed to lose
With my lost saints,—I love thee with the breath,   12
Smiles, tears, of all my life!—and, if God choose,
I shall but love thee better after death.

YOUR TURN

1. One scholar has said, "In truth this is a religious poem, not a love poem." Do you agree? Please explain.
2. This poem, a sonnet, begins with a question and proceeds to give an-swers to it. How many "ways" are there? Please count and comment on each of them one by one. For discussion of the sonnet form, see page 674–75.
3. If this poem were addressed to you, what would be your response to it?
4. Consider this response: "In this poem, Browning presents herself as willing to be a slave to the man she loves." What evidence (if any) in the text can you point to that supports this view?

ROBERT HAYDEN

Robert Hayden (1913-1980) was born in Detroit, Michigan. His parents divorced when he was a child, and he was brought up by a neighboring family, whose name he adopted. In 1942, at the age of twenty-nine, he graduated from Detroit City College (now Wayne State University), and he received a master's degree from the University of Michigan. He taught at Fisk University from 1946 to 1969 and after that, for the remainder of his life, at the University of Michigan. In 1979 he was appointed Consultant in Poetry to the Library of Congress, the first African American to hold the post. Hayden's books include his Collected Poems *(1985).*

Frederick Douglass*   [1947]

When it is finally ours, this freedom, this liberty, this beautiful
and terrible thing, needful to man as air,
usable as earth; when it belongs at last to all,
when it is truly instinct, brain matter, diastole, systole,
reflex action; when it is finally won; when it is more   5
than the gaudy mumbo jumbo of politicians:
this man, this Douglass, this former slave, this Negro
beaten to his knees, exiled, visioning a world
where none is lonely, none hunted, alien,
this man, superb in love and logic, this man   10
shall be remembered. Oh, not with statues' rhetoric,
not with legends and poems and wreaths of bronze alone,
but with the lives grown out of his life, the lives
fleshing his dream of the beautiful, needful thing.

*****Frederick Douglass** Born a slave, Frederick Douglass (1818-1895) escaped and became an important spokesman for the abolitionist movement and later for civil rights for African Americans.

YOUR TURN

1. When, according to Hayden, will Douglass "be remembered"? And *how* will he be remembered?
2. "Frederick Douglass" consists of two sentences (or one sentence and a fragment). In what line do you find the subject of the first sentence? What is the main verb (the predicate) and where do you find it? How would you describe the effect of the long delaying of the subject? And of the predicate?
3. Does Hayden assume or seem to predict that there *will* come a time when freedom "is finally ours" (line 1), and "belongs at last to all" (line 3)?
4. Hayden wrote "Frederick Douglass" in 1947. In your opinion are we closer now to Hayden's vision or farther away? (You may find that we are closer in some ways and farther in others.) In your answer—perhaps an essay of 500 words—try to be as specific as possible.
5. "Frederick Douglass" consists of fourteen lines. Is it a sonnet?

Narrative Poetry

The Limerick, the Popular Ballad, and Other Narrative Poems

Most of us are so used to reading stories—whether factual in history books or fictional in novels—that we normally associate storytelling with prose, not with poetry. But in fact some of the world's great stories have been told in poetry—from the Greek epics the *Iliad* (about the Trojan War) and the *Odyssey* (about Odysseus' ten years of wandering), and the medieval tales of King Arthur to the Sanskrit epic *The Mahabharata* (about a war in ancient India) and African and American Indian tales of the creation of the world and of the sublime deeds of heroes. And, to descend to the ridiculous, countless narratives are still being told in the form of the limerick:

There Was a Young Fellow of Riga

There was a young fellow of Riga,
Who smiled as he rode on a tiger.
   They returned from the ride,
    With the fellow inside,
And the smile on the face of the tiger.

In short, although we are accustomed to thinking of a story as prose in a book, until a few hundred years ago stories were commonly poetry that was sung or recited. In nonliterate societies people got their stories from storytellers who relied on memory rather than on the written word; the memorized stories were often poems, partly because (in the words of Shakespeare's early contemporary, Sir Philip Sidney), "Verse far exceedeth prose in the knitting up of the memory." Even in literate societies, few people could read or write until the invention of the printing press in the middle of the fifteenth century. Although the printing press did not immediately destroy oral verse narratives, as the centuries passed, an increasingly large reading public developed that preferred prose narratives.

Among the great verse narratives are the English and Scottish **popular ballads,** some of the best of which are attributed to the fifteenth century, though they were not recorded until much later. These anonymous stories in song acquired their distinctive flavor by being passed down orally from generation to generation, each singer consciously or unconsciously modifying his or her inheritance. It is not known who created the popular ballads; often they were made up partly out of earlier ballads by singers as bold as Kipling's cockney:

> When 'Omer smote 'is blooming lyre,
> He'd 'eard men sing by land an' sea;
> An' what he thought 'e might require,
> 'E went an' took—the same as me!

Most ballad singers probably were composers only by accident; they intended to transmit what they had heard, but their memories were sometimes faulty and their imaginations active. The modifications effected by oral transmission generally give a ballad three noticeable qualities:

1. It is impersonal; even if there is an "I" who sings the tale, he or she is usually characterless.
2. The ballad—like other oral literature such as the nursery rhyme and the counting-out rhyme ("one potato, two potato")—is filled with repetition, sometimes of lines, sometimes of words. Consider, for example, "Go saddle me the black, the black, / Go saddle me the brown," or "O wha is this has done this deid, / This ill deid don to me?" Sometimes in fact, the story is told by repeating lines with only a few significant variations. Oddly, these clichés do not bore us but by their impersonality often lend a simplicity that effectively contrasts with the frequent violence of the tales.
3. Because ballads are transmitted orally, residing in the memory rather than on the printed page, weak stanzas have often been dropped, leaving a series of sharp scenes, frequently with dialogue:

> The king sits in Dumferling toune,
>   Drinking the blude-reid wine:
> "O whar will I get guid sailor,
>   To sail this schip of mine?"

Because ballads were sung rather than printed, and because singers made alterations, no one version of a ballad is the "correct" one. The versions printed here have become such favorites that they are almost regarded as definitive, but the reader should consult a collection of ballads to get some idea of the wide variety.*

Popular ballads have been much imitated by professional poets, especially since the late eighteenth century. Two such literary ballads are Keats's "La Belle Dame sans Merci" (page 560) and Coleridge's "The Rime of the Ancient Mariner." In a literary ballad the story is often infused with multiple meanings, with the insistent symbolic implications. Ambiguity is often found in the popular ballad also, but it is of a rather different sort. Perhaps because stanzas are lost, or perhaps because the singer was unconcerned with some elements of the story, the ambiguity of the popular ballad commonly lies in the story itself (who did what?) rather than in the significance of the story (what does it all add up to, what does it mean?).

---

*See Albert B. Friedman, ed., *The Penguin Book of Folk Ballads of the English-Speaking World* (1977); and Frederick Woods, ed., *The Oxford Book of English Traditional Verse* (1983).

Finally, a word about some of the most popular professional folksingers today. They have aptly been called "folksongers" because unlike illiterate or scarcely literate folksingers—who intend only to sing the traditional songs in the traditional way for themselves or their neighbors—these professionals are vocal artists who make commercial and political use (not bad things in themselves) of traditional folk songs, deliberately adapting old songs and inventing new songs that only loosely resemble the old ones. These contemporary ballads tend to be more personal than traditional ballads and they tend to have a social consciousness that is alien to traditional balladry. Many of the songs of Pete Seeger and Bob Dylan, for instance, are conspicuous examples of art in the service of morality or politics; they call attention to injustice and they seek to move the hearers to action. That traditional ballads have assisted in this task is not the least of their value; the influence of a work of art is never finished, and the old ballads can rightly claim to share in the lives of their modern descendants.

We print a popular traditional English ballad here ("Sir Patrick Spence"), followed (page 560) by a poem that is indebted to traditional ballads (John Keats's "La Belle Dame sans Merci"). We also present several short narrative poems—poems that tell a story—that are *not* in the ballad tradition. (For additional ballads, see "The Three Ravens," "The Twa Corbies," and "John Henry" in Chapter 28; for a literary ballad by an African American author, see Langston Hughes's "Ballad of the Landlord," page 765.)

ANONYMOUS BRITISH BALLAD

Sir Patrick Spence

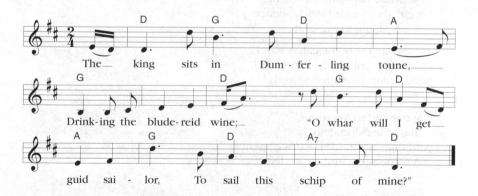

The king sits in Dumferling toune,
   Drinking the blude-reid wine:
"O whar will I get guid sailor,
   To sail this schip of mine?"   4

Up and spak an eldern knicht,
   Sat at the kings richt kne:
"Sir Patrick Spence is the best sailor,
   That sails upon the se."   8

The king has written a braid° Letter,
   And signed it wi' his hand,
And sent it to Sir Patrick Spence,
   Was walking on the sand.   12

The first line that Sir Patrick red,
   A loud lauch° lauched he;
The next line that Sir Patrick red,
   The tier blinded his ee.   16

"O wha is this has done this deid,
   This ill deid don to me,
To send me out this time o' the yeir,
   To sail upon the se?   20

"Mak hast, mak hast, my mirry men all,
   Our guid schip sails the morne":
"O say na sae, my master deir,
   For I feir a deadlie storme."   24

"Late late yestreen I saw the new moone,
   Wi' the auld moone in hir arme,
And I feir, I feir, my deir master,
   That we will cum to harme."   28

O our Scots nobles wer richt laith°
   To weet their cork-heild schoone;°
Bot lang owre° a' the play wer playd,
   Thair hats they swam aboone,°   32

O lang, lang may their ladies sit,
   Wi' thair fans into their hand,
Or eir° they se Sir Patrick Spence
   Cum sailing to the land.   36

O lang, lang may the ladies stand,
   Wi' thair gold kems in their hair,
Waiting for their ain deir lords,
   For they'll se thame na mair.   40

Have owre° to Aberdour,
   It's fiftie fadon deip,
And thair lies guid Sir Patrick Spence,
   Wi' the Scots lords at his feit.   44

YOUR TURN

1. The shipwreck occurs between lines 29 and 32, but it is not described.
   Does the omission stimulate the reader to imagine the details of the
   wreck? Or does the omission suggest that the poem is not so much

---

9 braid broad, open.   **14 lauch** laugh.   **29 laith** loath.   **30 cork-heild schoone** cork-
heeled shoes.   **31 owre** ere.   **32 aboone** above.   **35 eir** evere.   **41 Have owre** Half
over.

about a shipwreck as it is about kinds of behavior? Explain. What do lines 33–40 contribute?

2. Might lines 17–18 warrant the inference that the "eldern knicht" (line 5) is Sir Patrick's enemy?
3. Explain lines 13–16.
4. In place of lines 37–40, another version of this ballad has the following stanza:

The ladies crack't their fingers white,
    The maidens tore their hair,
A' for the sake o' their true loves,
    For them they ne'er saw mair.

Why is one more effective than the other?

5. In the other version, the stanza that is here the final one (lines 41–44) precedes the stanzas about the ladies (lines 33–40). Which stanza makes a better conclusion? Why?
6. Is Sir Patrick heroic? Please explain.
7. Is Sir Patrick's decision to obey the king's command right or wrong? Is he responsible for the deaths of his "mirry men"?
8. What do you imagine was the response of the first readers to this poem, many centuries ago? What is your own response to it? How do you explain the continuities, or the differences, between these past and present responses?

GARY SNYDER

Gary Snyder, born in 1930, grew up on a farm north of Seattle and then in Portland, Oregon. He then went to Reed College, working during the summers with the U.S. Forest Service and in logging camps. After studying linguistics and American Indian culture at the University of Indiana, he moved to San Francisco, where he studied Japanese and became part of the "Beat" movement. (He is the hero of Jack Kerouac's novel, The Dharma Bums, *1958.) In 1956 he went to Japan, where he lived for ten years. He then returned and settled with his family in the foothills of the northern Sierra Nevada. His publications include* The Gary Snyder Reader: Prose, Poetry, and Translations *(1999).*

Hay for the Horses   [1959]

He had driven half the night
From far down San Joaquin
Through Mariposa, up the
Dangerous mountain roads,
And pulled in at eight a.m.   5
With his big truckload of hay
        behind the barn.
With winch and ropes and hooks
We stacked the bales up clean
To splintery redwood rafters   10
High in the dark, flecks of alfalfa
Whirling through shingle-cracks of light,

Itch of haydust in the
      sweaty shirt and shoes.
At lunchtime under Black oak   15
Out in the hot corral,
—The old mare nosing lunchpails,
Grasshoppers crackling in the weeds—
"I'm sixty-eight" he said,
"I first bucked hay when I was seventeen.   20
I thought, that day I started,
I sure would hate to do this all my life.
And dammit, that's just what
I've gone and done."

YOUR TURN

1. The speaker does not explicitly offer his opinion of the man who "had
   driven half the night" but do the first two sentences (lines 1–14) communicate at least a hint of an attitude?
2. The old man who speaks lines 19–24 sums up his life. He seems to regard it as wasted, but as we hear his words do we hear bitterness? Self-
   pity? What is our attitude toward him, and how does it compare with
   that of the speaker of the poem?

PHILLIS WHEATLEY

*Kidnapped in Africa when she was a child of about age seven, and brought to
Boston on the schooner* Phillis, *Phillis Wheatley (1753–1784) owed her first
name to the ship and her second to the family name of the merchant who
bought her to attend on his wife. She was educated in English, Latin, history,
and geography, and especially in the Bible, and within a few years she was
writing poetry in the approved manner—that is, the manner of eighteenth-
century England. In 1773, the year she was granted freedom, she published a
book of her poems in England.*

    *Despite her education and the style of writing that she adopted, Wheatley
of course did not move freely in the white world. But neither did she move
freely in the black world, since her educators kept her away from other persons of African origin. Perhaps the best single sentence ever written about
Phillis Wheatley is Richard Wright's: "Before the webs of slavery had so tightened as to snare nearly all Negroes in our land, one was freed by accident to
give in clear, bell-like limpid cadence the hope of freedom in the New World."
One other sentence about Wheatley, by another African American writer,
should also be quoted here. Alice Walker, commenting on Wheatley's much criticized assumption of white values, says, in an address to Wheatley, "It is not so
much what you sang, as that you kept alive, in so many of our ancestors, the
notion of song."*

    *"On Being Brought from Africa to America" alludes to the story of Cain
and Abel (Genesis 4.15), which reports that Cain killed Abel, and that "the
Lord set a mark upon Cain." The biblical text explicitly says that the mark was
to protect Cain from someone who might take vengeance on him, but it does*

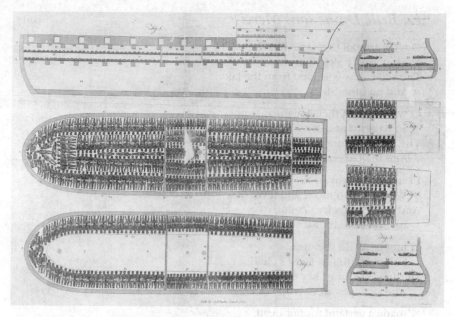

Phillis Wheatley was probably brought to America on a slave ship such as this one showing how the slaves were packed. The English abolitionist Thomas Clarkson (1760–1846)
distributed this drawing with his *Essay on the Slavery and Commerce of the Human Species*
(1786; rpt. 1804).

*not say what the mark was. Nevertheless, some Christians developed the idea
that the color of Africans was the mark of Cain.*

On Being Brought from Africa to America   [1772]

'Twas mercy brought me from my pagan land,
Taught my benighted soul to understand
That there's a God, that there's a Savior too:
Once I redemption neither sought nor knew.
Some view our sable race with scornful eye,   5
"Their color is a diabolic dye."
Remember, Christians; Negroes, black as Cain,
May be refined, and join the angelic train.

JOHN KEATS

*John Keats (1795–1821), son of a London stable keeper, was taken out of
school at age fifteen and apprenticed to a surgeon and apothecary. In 1816 he
was licensed to practice as an apothecary-surgeon, but he almost immediately
abandoned medicine and decided to make a career as a poet. His progress
was amazing; he published books of poems—to mixed reviews—in 1817,
1818, and 1820, before dying of tuberculosis at the age of twenty-five. Today
he is esteemed as one of England's greatest poets.*

Additional poems by Keats appear on pages 587, 622, and 810.

*La Belle Dame sans Merci**   [1819]

O what can ail thee, knight-at-arms,
    Alone and palely loitering?
The sedge has withered from the lake,
    And no birds sing.   4

O what can ail thee, knight-at-arms,
    So haggard and so woe-begone?
The squirrel's granary is full,
    And the harvest's done.   8

I see a lily on thy brow,
    With anguish moist and fever dew,
And on thy cheeks a fading rose
    Fast withereth too.   12

"I met a lady in the meads,
    Full beautiful—a faery's child,
Her hair was long, her foot was light,
    And her eyes were wild.   16

"I made a garland for her head,
    And bracelets too, and fragrant zone;°
She looked at me as she did love,
    And made sweet moan.   20

"I set her on my pacing steed,
    And nothing else saw all day long,
For sidelong would she bend and sing
    A faery's song.   24

"She found me roots of relish sweet,
    And honey wild, and manna dew,
And sure in language strange she said
    'I love thee true.'   28

"She took me to her elfin grot,
    And there she wept and sighed full sore,
And there I shut her wild wild eyes
    With kisses four.   32

"And there she lullèd me asleep,
    And there I dreamed—Ah! woe betide!
The latest dream I ever dreamed
    On the cold hill side.   36

"I saw pale kings and princes too,
    Pale warriors, death-pale were they all;
They cried, 'La Belle Dame sans Merci
    Hath thee in thrall!'   40

La Belle Dame sans Merci* the beautiful lady without pity.   **18 fragrant zone belt of flowers.

"I saw their starved lips in the gloam
  With horrid warning gapèd wide,
And I awoke, and found me here,
  On the cold hill's side.   44

"And this is why I sojourn here,
  Alone and palely loitering,
Though the sedge has withered from the lake,
  And no birds sing."   48

> **YOUR TURN**

1. In the first three stanzas the speaker describes the knight as pale, haggard, and so forth. In the rest of the poem the knight recounts his experience. In a few sentences summarize the knight's experience, and indicate why it has caused him to appear as he now does.
2. The *femme fatale*—the dangerously seductive woman—appears often in literature. If you are familiar with one such work, compare it with Keats's poem.
3. What characteristics of the popular ballad (see page 554) do you find in this poem? What characteristic does it *not* share with popular ballads? Set forth your response in an essay of 500 words.
4. Is this poem about love, or death, or both? Please explain, making references to details in the text.
5. What is your response to this poem? Do you feel a connection to the characters? What kind of connection?
6. Keats said that "La Belle Dame sans Merci" was not one of his best or most serious poems, yet later generations of readers have valued it highly. How do you explain this discrepancy? Are poets reliable judges of the merits of their own poems?

SIEGFRIED SASSOON

Siegfried Sassoon (1886–1967), a wealthy Englishman, served with such distinction in World War I—in 1915 under heavy fire he helped a wounded soldier to safety—that he was awarded the Military Cross. Later, wounded by a bullet in the chest, he was sent from France back to England, where, upon reflection, he concluded that the war was not a war of defense but of aggression. Military officials shrewdly chose not to dispute him, but merely asserted that he was shell-shocked. When Sassoon recovered from the bullet wound, he was again sent into combat, and was again wounded and hospitalized.

   Sassoon expressed his views in Memoirs of a Fox-Hunting Man *(1928) and* Memoirs of an Infantry Officer *(1930), as well as in* Collected Poems, 1908–1956 *(1961).*

The General   [1917]

"Good-morning, good-morning!" the General said
When we met him last week on our way to the line.
Now the soldiers he smiled at are most of 'em dead,

And we're cursing his staff for incompetent swine.
"He's a cheery old card," grunted Harry to Jack
As they slogged up to Arras with rifle and pack.

But he did for them both by his plan of attack.

YOUR TURN

1. Who is the storyteller, and what is the story he tells?
2. Why do you suppose Sassoon put an extra space between the next-to-last line and the last line? Speaking of the last line, notice that it rhymes with the two preceding lines—i.e., the last three lines end with identical sounds, whereas in the preceding four lines, no two adjacent lines rhyme. Why do you suppose Sassoon changed the rhyme-scheme for the final lines?
3. How would you characterize the General? How would you characterize Harry? How would you characterize the storyteller?

COUNTEE CULLEN

Countee Cullen (1903–1946) was born Countee Porter in New York City, raised by his grandmother, and then adopted by the Reverend Frederick A. Cullen, a Methodist minister in Harlem. Cullen received a bachelor's degree from New York University (Phi Beta Kappa) and a master's degree from Harvard. He earned his living as a high school teacher of French, but his literary gifts were recognized in his own day, and he went on to become a leading African American poet of the modern period.

Incident   [1925]

(For Eric Walrond)

Once riding in old Baltimore,
   Heart-filled, head-filled with glee,
I saw a Baltimorean
   Keep looking straight at me.   4

Now I was eight and very small,
   And he was no whit bigger,
And so I smiled, but he poked out
   His tongue, and called me, "Nigger."   8

I saw the whole of Baltimore
   From May until December;
Of all the things that happened there
   That's all that I remember.   12

YOUR TURN

1. How would you define an "incident"? A serious occurrence? A minor occurrence, or what? Think about the word, and then think about Cullen's use of it as a title for the event recorded in this poem. Test out

one or two other possible titles as a way of helping yourself to see the strengths or weaknesses of Cullen's title.

2. The dedicatee, Eric Walrond (1898–1966) was an African American essayist and writer of fiction, who in an essay, "On Being Black," had described his experiences of racial prejudice. How does the presence of the dedication bear on our response to Cullen's account of the "incident"?

3. What is the tone of the poem? Indifferent? Angry? Or what? What do you think is the speaker's attitude toward the "incident"? What is your attitude?

4. Ezra Pound, poet and critic, once defined literature as "news that *stays* news." What do you think he meant by this? Do you think that the definition fits Cullen's poem?

EDWIN ARLINGTON ROBINSON

Edwin Arlington Robinson (1869–1935) grew up in Gardiner, Maine, spent two years at Harvard, and then returned to Maine, where he published his first book of poetry in 1896. Though he received encouragement from neighbors, his finances were precarious, even after President Theodore Roosevelt, having been made aware of the book, secured for him an appointment as customs inspector in New York from 1905 to 1909. Additional books won fame for Robinson, and in 1922 he was awarded the first of the three Pulitzer Prizes for poetry that he would win.

Richard Cory [1897]

Whenever Richard Cory went down town,
We people on the pavement looked at him:
He was a gentleman from sole to crown,
Clean favored, and imperially slim.   4

And he was always quietly arrayed,
And he was always human when he talked;
But still he fluttered pulses when he said,
"Good-morning," and he glittered when he walked.   8

And he was rich—yes, richer than a king—
And admirably schooled in every grace:
In fine,° we thought that he was everything
To make us wish that we were in his place.   12

So on we worked, and waited for the light,
And went without the meat, and cursed the bread;
And Richard Cory, one calm summer night,
Went home and put a bullet through his head.   16

---

11 In fine in short.

YOUR TURN

1. Consult the entry on **irony** in the glossary (page 1473). Then read the pages referred to in the entry. Finally, write an essay of 500 words on irony in "Richard Cory."

2. What do you think were Richard Cory's thoughts shortly before he "put a bullet through his head"? In 500 words, set forth his thoughts and actions (what he sees and does). If you wish, you can write in the first person, from Cory's point of view. Further, if you wish, your essay can be in the form of a suicide note.

3. Write a sketch (250–350 words) setting forth your early impression or understanding of someone whose later actions revealed you had not understood the person.

EMILY DICKINSON

Emily Dickinson (1830–1886), born into a proper New England family in Amherst, Massachusetts, was brought up as a Protestant. Much of her poetry concerns death and heaven, but it is far from being conventionally Christian.

For a more complete biographical note and a selection of Dickinson's poems and letters, see Chapter 27.

Because I could not stop for Death   [1890]

Because I could not stop for Death—
He kindly stopped for me—
The Carriage held but just Ourselves—
And Immortality.   4

We slowly drove—He knew no haste
And I had put away
My labor and my leisure too,
For His Civility—   8

We passed the School, where Children strove
At Recess—in the Ring—
We passed the Fields of Gazing Grain—
We passed the Setting Sun—   12

Or rather—He passed Us—
The Dews drew quivering and chill—
For only Gossamer, my Gown—
My Tippet—only Tulle—   16

We paused before a House that seemed
A Swelling of the Ground—
The Roof was scarcely visible—
The Cornice—in the Ground—   20

Since then—'tis Centuries—and yet
Feels shorter than the Day
I first surmised the Horses' Heads
Were toward Eternity—   24

YOUR TURN

1. Characterize death as it appears in lines 1–8.
2. What is the significance of the details and their arrangement in the third stanza? Why "strove" rather than "played" (line 9)? What meaning does "Ring" (line 10) have? Is "Gazing Grain" better than "Golden Grain"?
3. The "House" in the fifth stanza is a sort of riddle. What is the answer? Does this stanza introduce an aspect of death not present—or present only very faintly—in the rest of the poem? Explain.
4. Evaluate this statement about the poem (from Yvor Winters's *In Defense of Reason*): "In so far as it concentrates on the life that is being left behind, it is wholly successful; in so far as it attempts to experience the death to come, it is fraudulent, however exquisitely."

WALTER DE LA MARE

Walter de la Mare (1873–1956), was born in Kent, in England. He worked for many years as an accountant for the London office of Standard Oil until a legacy enabled him to devote his life to writing lyric poetry and fiction.

The Listeners

[1912]

"Is there anybody there?" said the Traveler,
   Knocking on the moonlit door;
And his horse in the silence champed the grasses
   Of the forest's ferny floor.
And a bird flew up out of the turret,   5
   Above the Traveler's head:
And he smote upon the door again a second time;
   "Is there anybody there?" he said.
But no one descended to the Traveler;
   No head from the leaf-fringed sill   10
Leaned over and looked into his gray eyes,
   Where he stood perplexed and still.
But only a host of phantom listeners
   That dwelt in the lone house then
Stood listening in the quiet of the moonlight   15
   To that voice from the world of men:
Stood thronging the faint moonbeams on the dark stair
   That goes down to the empty hall,
Hearkening in an air stirred and shaken
   By the lonely Traveler's call.   20
And he felt in his heart their strangeness,
   Their stillness answering his cry,
While his horse moved, cropping the dark turf,
   'Neath the starred and leafy sky;
For he suddenly smote on the door, even   25
   Louder, and lifted his head: —

"Tell them I came, and no one answered,
   That I kept my word," he said.
Never the least stir made the listeners,
   Though every word he spake   30
Fell echoing through the shadowiness of the still house
   From the one man left awake:
Aye, they heard his foot upon the stirrup,
   And the sound of iron on stone,
And how the silence surged softly backward,   35
   When the plunging hoofs were gone.

YOUR TURN

1. Walter de la Mare is reported to have said that the Traveler is a ghost. He is also reported to have said on another occasion that the poem records a class reunion at which he found himself the only one present. Is either of these explanations convincing? Is there anything in the poem to refute the first explanation?

2. Is the poem a narrative of a man who fulfilled a promise, though the ones to whom the promise was made are dead? Is it a narrative of a man who fulfilled a promise in the face of evil forces? Of a frustrated, heroic search for the meaning of life? Of our mysterious separation from the dead? In 100 to 150 words, evaluate one of these interpretations.

3. Why are the actions of the horse described (lines 3, 23)?

4. Why did de la Mare call the poem "The Listeners" rather than "The Traveler"?

JOHN LENNON AND PAUL McCARTNEY

John Lennon (1940–1980) and Paul McCartney (b. 1942) were original members of the Beatles.

Eleanor Rigby   [1966]

Ah, look at all the lonely people!
Ah, look at all the lonely people!

Eleanor Rigby
Picks up the rice in the church where a wedding has been,
Lives in a dream.   5
Waits at the window
Wearing the face that she keeps in a jar by the door.
Who is it for?

All the lonely people,
Where do they all come from?   10
All the lonely people,
Where do they all belong?

Father McKenzie,
Writing the words of a sermon that no one will hear,
No one comes near.   15
Look at him working,
Darning his socks in the night when there's nobody there.
What does he care?

All the lonely people,
Where do they all come from?   20
All the lonely people,
Where do they all belong?

Ah, look at all the lonely people!
Ah, look at all the lonely people!
Eleanor Rigby   25
Died in the church and was buried along with her name,
Nobody came.
Father McKenzie,
Wiping the dirt from his hands as he walks from the grave,
No one was saved.   30

All the lonely people,
Where do they all come from?
All the lonely people,
Where do they all belong?

Ah, look at all the lonely people!   35
Ah, look at all the lonely people!

YOUR TURN

Is the poem chiefly about Eleanor Rigby? What is Father McKenzie doing
in the poem?

E. E. CUMMINGS

*e. e. cummings was the pen name of Edward Estlin Cummings (1894–1962),
who grew up in Cambridge, Massachusetts, and graduated from Harvard,
where he became interested in modern literature and art, especially in the
movements called cubism and futurism. His father, a conservative clergyman
and a professor at Harvard, seems to have been baffled by the youth's interests, but cummings's mother encouraged his artistic activities, including his
use of unconventional punctuation and capitalization.*

*Politically liberal in his youth, cummings became more conservative after
a visit to Russia in 1931, but early and late his work emphasizes individuality and freedom of expression.*

anyone lived in a pretty how town   [1940]

anyone lived in a pretty how town
(with up so floating many bells down)
spring summer autumn winter
he sang his didn't he danced his did.   4

Women and men(both little and small)
cared for anyone not at all
they sowed their isn't they reaped their same
sun moon stars rain   8

children guessed(but only a few
and down they forgot as up they grew
autumn winter spring summer)
that noone loved him more by more   12

when by now and tree by leaf
she laughed his joy she cried his grief
bird by snow and stir by still
anyone's any was all to her   16

someones married their everyones
laughed their cryings and did their dance
(sleep wake hope and then)they
said their nevers they slept their dream   20

stars rain sun moon
(and only the snow can begin to explain
how children are apt to forget to remember
with up so floating many bells down)   24

one day anyone died i guess
(and noone stooped to kiss his face)
busy folk buried them side by side
little by little and was by was   28

all by all and deep by deep
and more by more they dream their sleep
noone and anyone earth by april
wish by spirit and if by yes.   32

Women and men(both dong and ding)
summer autumn winter spring
reaped their sowing and went their came
sun moon stars rain   36

YOUR TURN

1. Put into normal order (as far as possible) the words of the first two stanzas, and then compare your version with cummings's. What does cummings gain—or lose?
2. Characterize the "anyone" who "sang his didn't" and "danced his did."
   In your opinion, how does he differ from the people who "sowed their
   isn't they reaped their same"?
3. Some readers interpret "anyone died" (line 25) to mean that the child
   matured and became as dead as the other adults. How might you support or refute this interpretation?

18

Lyric Poetry

For the ancient Greeks, a **lyric** was a song accompanied by a lyre. It was short, and it usually expressed a single emotion, such as joy or sorrow. The word is now used more broadly, referring to a poem that, neither narrative (telling a story) nor strictly dramatic (performed by actors), is an emotional or reflective soliloquy. Still, it is rarely very far from a singing voice. In *A Portrait of the Artist as a Young Man* (1916), James Joyce describes the lyric as the "verbal vesture of an instant of emotion, a rhythmical cry such as ages ago cheered on the man who pulled at the oar." Such lyrics, too, were sung more recently than "ages ago." Here is a song that American slaves sang when rowing heavy loads.

ANONYMOUS

Michael Row the Boat Ashore

Michael row the boat ashore, Hallelujah!
Michael's boat's a freedom boat, Hallelujah!
Sister, help to trim the sail, Hallelujah!
Jordan stream is wide and deep, Hallelujah!
Freedom stands on the other side, Hallelujah!   5

We might pause for a moment to comment on why people sing at work. There are at least three reasons: (1) work done rhythmically goes more efficiently; (2) the songs relieve the boredom of the work; and (3) the songs—whether narrative or lyrical—provide something of an outlet for the workers' frustrations.

Speaking roughly, we can say that whereas a narrative (whether in prose or poetry) is set in the past, telling what happened, a lyric is set in the present, catching a speaker in a moment of expression. But a lyric can, of course, glance backward or forward, as in this folk song, usually called "Careless Love."

ANONYMOUS

Careless Love

Love, O love, O careless love,
You see what careless love can do.

When I wore my apron low,
Couldn't keep you from my do,°
   Fare you well, fare you well.   5
Now I wear my apron high,
Scarce see you passin' by,
   Fare you well, fare you well.

---

4 do door.

Notice, too, that a lyric, like a narrative, can have a plot: "Michael" moves toward the idea of freedom, and "Careless Love" implies a story of desertion—something has happened between the time that the singer could not keep the man from her door and now, when she "scarce" sees him passing by—but, again, the emphasis is on a present state of mind.

Lyrics are sometimes differentiated among themselves. For example, if a lyric is melancholy or mournfully contemplative, especially if it laments a death, it may be called an **elegy.** If a lyric is rather long, elaborate, and on a lofty theme such as immortality or a hero's victory, it may be called an **ode** or a **hymn.** Distinctions among lyrics are often vague, and one person's ode may be another's elegy. Still, when writers use one of these words in their titles, they are inviting the reader to recall the tradition in which they are working. Of the poet's link to tradition T. S. Eliot said:

> No poet, no artist of any art, has his complete meaning alone. His significance, his appreciation is the appreciation of his relation to the dead poets and artists. You cannot value him alone; you must set him, for contrast and comparison, among the dead.

Although the lyric is often ostensibly addressed to someone (the "you" in "Careless Love"), the reader usually feels that the speaker is really talking to himself or herself. In "Careless Love," the speaker need not be in the presence of her man; rather, her heart is overflowing (the reader senses) and she pretends to address him.

A comment by the nineteenth-century english philosopher John Stuart Mill on poetry is especially true of the lyric:

> Eloquence is *heard,* poetry is *over*heard. Eloquence supposes an audience; the peculiarity of poetry appears to us to lie in the poet's utter unconsciousness of a listener. Poetry is feeling confessing itself to itself, in moments of solitude.

This is particularly true in work songs such as "Michael Row the Boat Ashore," where there is no audience: the singers sing for themselves, participating rather than performing. As one prisoner in Texas said: "They really be singing about the way they feel inside. Since they can't say it to nobody, they sing a song about it." The sense of "feeling confessing itself to itself, in moments of solitude" or of "singing about the way they feel inside" is strong and clear in this short cowboy song.

ANONYMOUS

The Colorado Trail

Eyes like the morning star,
Cheeks like a rose,
Laura was a pretty girl
God Almighty knows.   4

Weep all ye little rains,
Wail winds wail,
All along, along, along
The Colorado trail.   8

When we read a lyric poem, no matter who the speaker is, for a moment—while we recite or hear the words—we become the speaker. That is, we get into the speaker's mind, or, perhaps more accurately, the speaker takes charge of our mind, and we undergo (comfortably seated in a chair or sprawled on a bed) the mental experience that is embodied in the words.

Next, another anonymous poem, this one written in England, probably in the early sixteenth century. Aside from modern reprintings, it survives in only one manuscript, a song book, the relevant portion of which we reproduce here. But first, here is the poem in modern typography.

ANONYMOUS

Western Wind

Westron wind, when will thou blow?
The small rain down can rain.
Christ, that my love were in my arms,
And I in my bed again.

Westron wynde when wilt thou blow. Musical setting in a tenor part-book; early sixteenth century. (Reproduced by permission of the British Library Royal Appendix 58 f.5. © British Library Board. All rights reserved.)

The angular handwriting is in a style quite different from modern writing, but when you are told that the first three words are "Westron [i.e., western] wynde when," you can probably see some connections. And you can probably make out the last handwritten word on the second line ("And"), and all of the third line: "I yn my bed A gayne" ("I in my bed again").

Incidentally—we hope we are not boring you with trifles—some controversy surrounds the transcription of one of the words—the fifth word in the second line of writing, the word that looks like a *y* followed by an *f* (just after "Chryst" and just before "my"). The issue is this: Is the letter a *y*, in which case the word is "if," or is it a letter we no longer have, a letter called *thorn*, which was pronounced "th," as in either "thin" or "this"? If indeed it is a thorn, the next letter is a *t*, not an *f*, and the word therefore is not "if" but "that." (Incidentally, signs that say "Ye Olde Antique Shoppe" make no sense; "Ye" was never used as a definite article. What these signs are reproducing is a thorn, and the word really is "The," not "Ye.")

YOUR TURN

1. In "Western Wind," what do you think is the tone of the speaker's voice in the first two lines? Angry? Impatient? Supplicating? Be as precise as possible. What is the tone in the next two lines?
2. In England the west wind, warmed by the Gulf Stream, rises in the spring. What associations link the wind and rain of lines 1 and 2 with lines 3 and 4?
3. Should we have been told why the lovers are separated? Explain.

Love poems are by no means all the same—to take an obvious point, some are happy and some are sad—but those that are about the loss of a beloved or about the pains of love seem to be especially popular.

JULIA WARD HOWE

Julia Ward Howe (1819–1910) was born in New York City. A social reformer, her work for the emancipation of African Americans and the right of women to vote is notable. She was the first woman to be elected to the American Academy of Arts and Letters. Howe is the author of many poems, including "The Battle Hymn of the Republic," set to already-existing music composed by William Steffe. The poem was first published in The Atlantic Monthly *in 1862. It soon became one of the most popular songs of the Union during the Civil War.*

Battle Hymn of the Republic

[1861]

Mine eyes have seen the glory of the coming of the Lord:
He is trampling out the vintage where the grapes of wrath are stored;
He hath loosed the fateful lightning of his terrible swift sword;
    His truth is marching on.   4

Chorus
    Glory! glory! Hallelujah!
    Glory! glory! Hallelujah!
    Glory! glory! Hallelujah!
        His truth is marching on!   8

I have seen him in the watch-fires of a hundred circling camps;
They have builded him an altar in the evening dews and damps;
I can read his righteous sentence by the dim and flaring lamps;
   His day is marching on.   12

I have read a fiery gospel, writ in burnished rows of steel:
"As ye deal with my contemners, so with you my grace shall deal;
Let the Hero, born of woman, crush the serpent with his heel,
   Since God is marching on."   16

He has sounded forth the trumpet that shall never call retreat;
He is sifting out the hearts of men before his judgment seat;
Oh, be swift, my soul, to answer him! be jubilant, my feet!
   Our God is marching on.   20

In the beauty of the lilies Christ was born across the sea,
With a glory in his bosom that transfigures you and me:
As he died to make men holy, let us die to make men free,
   While God is marching on.   24

YOUR TURN

1. This poem of the Civil War, draws some of its militant imagery from the Bible, especially from Isaiah 63.1–6 and Revelation 19.11–15. Do you think the lines about Christ are inappropriate here? Explain.
2. If you know the tune to which "Battle Hymn of the Republic" is sung, think about the interplay between the music and the words. Do you think people have a different response to Howe's words when they read her text as a poem, rather than experience it as a song?

WILLIAM SHAKESPEARE

William Shakespeare (1564–1616) is best known as the writer of sonnets and of plays, but he also wrote lyrics for songs in some of the plays. The following two lyrics are sung at the end of an early comedy, Love's Labor's Lost. *Conflict is essential in drama, and in these two poems we get a sort of melodious conflict, a song in praise of spring, juxtaposed against a song in praise of winter. But notice that within each song there are elements of conflict. For other works by Shakespeare* (Hamlet, a Midsummer Night's Dream, *and several sonnets), consult the index.*

Spring   [c. 1595]

When daisies pied and violets blue
   And lady-smocks° all silver-white
And cuckoo-buds° of yellow hue
   Do paint the meadows with delight,
The cuckoo then, on every tree,   5
Mocks married men; for thus sings he,
                "Cuckoo,
Cuckoo, cuckoo!" O word of fear,

---

2 lady-smocks also called cuckooflowers.   **3 cuckoo-buds** buttercups.

Unpleasing to a married ear!
When shepherds pipe on oaten straws,°   10
   And merry larks are ploughmen's clocks,
When turtles tread,° and rooks, and daws,
   And maidens bleach their summer smocks,
The cuckoo then, on every tree,
Mocks married men; for thus sings he,   15
                        "Cuckoo,
Cuckoo, cuckoo!" O word of fear,
Unpleasing to a married ear!

---

10 oaten straws musical instruments.   **12 turtles tread** turtledoves mate.

Winter   [c. 1595]

When icicles hang by the wall,
   And Dick the shepherd blows his nail,°
And Tom bears logs into the hall,
   And milk comes frozen home in pail,
When blood is nipped, and ways° be foul,   5
Then nightly sings the staring owl,
                        "Tu-whit, tu-who!"
A merry note,
While greasy Joan doth keel° the pot.
When all aloud the wind doth blow,   10
   And coughing drowns the parson's saw,°
And birds sit brooding in the snow,
   And Marian's nose looks red and raw,
When roasted crabs° hiss in the bowl,
Then nightly sings the staring owl,   15
                        "Tu-whit, tu-who!"
A merry note,
While greasy Joan doth keel the pot.

---

2 blows his nail breathes on his fingernails to warm them.   **5 ways** roads.   **9 keel** cool, by skimming.   **11 coughing . . . saw** wise saying.   **14 crabs** crab apples.

> ### YOUR TURN
>
> 1. Why is the cuckoo appropriate to spring? The owl to winter?
> 2. Did you expect a poem on spring to bring in infidelity? Is the poem bitter? Explain. (If in doubt, check the word "cuckold" in a dictionary.)
> 3. Does "Winter" describe only the hardships of the season, or does it communicate also the joys?

Here is another song from one of Shakespeare's plays, a comedy called *Much Ado about Nothing* (1598–99). The song (2.3.62–79) is about male infidelity, and it seems to be addressed to women ("Sigh no more, ladies, sigh no more") but in fact it is sung by a male singer and, in the play, his listeners are all males.

Sigh no more, ladies, sigh no more

Sigh no more, ladies, sigh no more;
   Men were deceivers ever;
One foot in sea and one on shore,
   To one thing constant never;
     Then sigh not so,   5
     But let them go,
   And be you blithe and bonny;°
Converting all your sounds of woe
   Into Hey nonny, nonny.

Sing no more ditties, sing no mo,°   10
   Of dumps° so dull and heavy;
The fraud of men was ever so,
   Since summer first was leavy.°
     Then sigh not so,
     But let them go,   15
   And be you blithe and bonny,
Converting all your sounds of woe
   Into Hey, nonny, nonny.

---

7 bonny carefree.   **10 mo** more.   **11 dumps** mournful songs.   **13 leavy** leafy.

> **YOUR TURN**
>
> 1. Is the song offensive? Trivial? Engaging? Probably true in its assertion about males?
> 2. Given that the subject of this lyric is "the fraud of men," and the advice to women is "sigh not so / But let them go, / And be you blithe and bonny," do you think that the female response to the lyric is very different from the male response? Please explain.
> 3. The two stanzas are pretty similar—in fact, each stanza ends with the same four lines—but do you agree that there is, in a very quiet way, a sort of plot, or narrative? Our thought is that although the first stanza says that "Men were deceivers ever," in the next stanza the word "fraud" goes a step further, thereby justifying the advice to "let them go." Do you agree that if the stanzas were reversed, the poem would not be equally satisfactory?

In a later chapter you will find an even shorter poem on this topic, Dorothy Parker's "General Review of the Sex Situation." (Skipping ahead is permissible; the poem appears on page 651. You may want to compare the *tone*—the attitude of each speaker as you detect it from the printed words.)

W. H. AUDEN

Wystan Hugh Auden (1907–1973) was born in York, England, and educated at Oxford. In the 1930s his left-wing poetry earned him wide acclaim as the leading poet of his generation. In 1939 Auden came to the United States, and in 1946 he became an American citizen, though he spent his last years in

England. In addition to being a prolific poet, Auden also wrote many essays on literature and other subjects.

Funeral Blues   [1936]

Stop all the clocks, cut off the telephone,
Prevent the dog from barking with a juicy bone,
Silence the pianos and with muffled drum
Bring out the coffin, let the mourners come.   4

Let aeroplanes circle moaning overhead
Scribbling on the sky the message He Is Dead,
Put crêpe bows round the white necks of the public doves,
Let the traffic policemen wear black cotton gloves.   8

He was my North, my South, my East and West,
My working week and my Sunday rest,
My noon, my midnight, my talk, my song;
I thought that love would last for ever: I was wrong.   12

The stars are not wanted now: put out every one;
Pack up the moon and dismantle the sun;
Pour away the ocean and sweep up the wood.
For nothing now can ever come to any good.   16

YOUR TURN

1. Let's assume that poems are rooted in real-life situations—that is, they take their origin from responses to experience, whether the experience is falling in love or losing a loved one, or praising God or losing one's faith, or celebrating a war (as in "Battle Hymn of the Republic") or lamenting the tragic destruction of war. But of course the poet then shapes the experience into a memorable statement and somehow makes a distinctive work on a traditional theme. Cite some phrases in Auden's poem that you would *not* expect to find in a poem on the death of the beloved. (For example, would you expect to find a reference to a dog eating "a juicy bone" in a poem on this theme?) Do you think these passages are effective, or do you think they are just silly? Explain.
2. Perhaps another way of getting at the question we have just asked is this: Can you imagine reading this at the funeral of someone you love? Or would you want a lover to read it at your funeral? Why?
3. The words of the last line of the poem are simple, almost a cliché. Yet we find them very powerful, and we wonder if you agree. What is the relationship of this line to the preceding lines of the stanza, with its images of mighty actions and cosmic gestures, and to the poem as a whole?

EMILY BRONTË

Emily Brontë (1818–1848) spent most of her short life (she died of tuberculosis) in an English village on the Yorkshire moors. The sister of Charlotte Brontë (author of Jane Eyre, *1847) and of Anne Brontë (author of* Agnes Grey, *1847), Emily is best known for her novel* Wuthering Heights *(1847), but she was a considerable poet, and her first significant publication (1846) was in a volume of poems by the three sisters.*

Spellbound

The night is darkening round me,
The wild winds coldly blow;
But a tyrant spell has bound me
And I cannot, cannot go.   4

The giant trees are bending
Their bare boughs weighed with snow.
And the storm is fast descending,
And yet I cannot go.   8

Clouds beyond clouds above me,
Wastes beyond wastes below;
But nothing drear can move me;
I will not, cannot go.   12

YOUR TURN

1. What exactly is a "spell," and what does it mean to be "spellbound"?
2. What difference, if any, would it make if the first line said "has darkened" instead of "is darkening"?
3. What difference would it make, if any, if lines 4 and 12 were switched?
4. What does "drear" (line 11) mean? Is this word too unusual? Should the poet have used a more familiar word?
5. Describe the speaker's state of mind. Have you ever experienced anything like this yourself? What was the situation and how did you move beyond it?

Spirituals, or Sorrow Songs

We have already mentioned that the lyric can range from expressions of emotion focused on personal matters to expressions of emotion focused on public matters, and the latter are sometimes characterized as odes or hymns. Among the most memorable hymns produced in the United States are the spirituals, or Sorrow Songs, created by black slaves in the United States, chiefly in the first half of the nineteenth century. The origins of the spirituals are still a matter of some dispute, but most specialists agree that the songs represent a distinctive fusion of African rhythms with European hymns.

Many of the texts derive ultimately from biblical sources: One of the chief themes, the desire for release, is sometimes presented with imagery drawn from ancient Israel. Examples include references to crossing the river Jordan (which runs from north of the Sea of Galilee to the Dead Sea), the release of the Israelites from slavery in Egypt (Exodus), Jonah's release from the whale (Book of Jonah), and Daniel's deliverance from a fiery furnace and from the lions' den (Book of Daniel, chapters 3 and 6).

Texts were collected and published during the 1860s in such books as *Slave Songs of the United States* (1867).

ANONYMOUS AFRICAN AMERICAN SPIRITUAL

Go Down, Moses

Two pages from *Jubilee Songs* (1872), an early printed collection of spirituals.

(continued)

5.
0, 'twas a dark and dismal night,
    Let my people go;
When Moses led the Israelites,
    Let my people go.

6.
'Twas good old Moses and Aaron, too,
    Let my people go;
'Twas they that led the armies through,
    Let my people go.

7.
The Lord told Moses what to do,
    Let my people go;
To lead the children of Israel through,
    Let my people go.

8.
0 come along Moses, you'll not get lost,
    Let my people go;
Stretch out your rod and come across,
    Let my people go.

9.
As Israel stood by the water side,
    Let my people go;
At the command of God it did divide,
    Let my people go.

10.
When they had reached the other shore,
    Let my people go;
They sang a song of triumph o'er,
    Let my people go.

11.
Pharaoh said he would go across,
    Let my people go;
But Pharaoh and his host were lost,
    Let my people go.

12.
0 Moses the cloud shall cleave the way,
    Let my people go;
A fire by night, a shade by day,
    Let my people go.

13.
You'll not get lost in the wilderness,
    Let my people go;
With a lighted candle in your breast,
    Let my people go.

14.
Jordan shall stand up like a wall,
    Let my people go;
And the walls of Jericho shall fall
    Let my people go.

15.
Your foes shall not before you stand,
    Let my people go;
And you'll possess fair Canaan's land,
    Let my people go.

16.
'Twas just about in harvest time,
    Let my people go;
When Joshua led his host divine,
    Let my people go.

17.
0 let us all from bondage flee,
    Let my people go;
And let us all in Christ be free,
    Let my people go

18.
We need not always weep and moan,
    Let my people go;
And wear these slavery chains forlorn,
    Let my people go.

19.
This world's a wilderness of woe,
    Let my people go ;
0, let us on to Canaan go,
    Let my people go.

20.
What a beautiful morning that will be,
    Let my people go ;
When time breaks up in eternity,
    Let my people go.

21.
The Devil he thought he had me fast,
    Let my people go;
But I thought I'd break his chains at
    Let my people go.   [last,

22.
0 take yer shoes from off yer feet,
    Let my people go;
And walk into the golden street,
    Let my people go.

23.
I'll tell you what I likes de best,
    Let my people go ;
It is the shouting Methodist,
    Let my people go.

24.
I do believe without a doubt,
    Let my people go;
That a Christian has the right to shout,
    Let my people go.

ANONYMOUS

Swing Low, Sweet Chariot

We reprint here a song from J. B. T. March's The Story of the Jubilee Singers *(1881).*

126

From J. B. T. March, *The Story of the Jubilee Singers,* 1881.

"Swing Low, Sweet Chariot" derives its basic images from the geography of ancient Israel (the Jordan River flows north from the Sea of Galilee to the

Dead Sea) and from a book in the Hebrew Bible (2 Kings 2.11 reports that Elijah and his friend Elisha were walking by the Jordan, when "there appeared a chariot of fire, and horses of fire, and parted them both asunder, and Elijah went up by a whirlwind into heaven"). There may also be some influence of the New Testament, Luke 16.22, which reports that a rich man named Dives and a poor man were "carried by the angels into Abraham's bosom." Further, the line "I'm sometimes up and sometimes down," from a secular song, "Nobody Knows the Trouble I've Seen," often found its way into "Swing Low," as in this version, where the fourth verse goes:

> *I'm sometimes up and sometimes down.*
> *But still my soul feels heavenly bound.*

LANGSTON HUGHES

For a biographical note, see page 761.

Evenin' Air Blues   [1942]

Folks, I come up North
Cause they told me de North was fine.
I come up North
Cause they told me de North was fine.
Been up here six months—   5
I'm about to lose my mind.

This mornin' for breakfast
I chawed de mornin' air.
This mornin' for breakfast
Chawed de mornin' air.   10
But this evenin' for supper,
I got evenin' air to spare.

Believe I'll do a little dancin'
Just to drive my blues away—
A little dancin'   15
To drive my blues away,
Cause when I'm dancin'
De blues forgets to stay.

But if you was to ask me
How de blues they come to be,   20
Says if you was to ask me
How de blues they come to be—
You wouldn't need to ask me:
Just look at me and see!

YOUR TURN

In what ways (subject, language) does this poem resemble blues you may have heard? Does it differ in any way? If so, how?

LI-YOUNG LEE

Li-Young Lee was born in 1957 in Jakarta, Indonesia, of Chinese parents. In 1964 his family brought him to the United States. He was educated at the University of Pittsburgh, the University of Arizona, and the State University of New York, Brockport. He now lives in Chicago. Lee's books of poetry include Book of My Nights *(2001) and* Behind My Eyes *(2008).*

I Ask My Mother to Sing [1986]

She begins, and my grandmother joins her.
Mother and daughter sing like young girls.
If my father were alive, he would play
his accordion and sway like a boat.   4

I've never been in Peking, or the Summer Palace,
nor stood on the great Stone Boat to watch
the rain begin on Kuen Ming Lake, the picnickers
running away in the grass.   8

But I love to hear it sung;
how the waterlilies fill with rain until
they overturn, spilling water into water,
then rock back, and fill with more.   12

Both women have begun to cry.
But neither stops her song.

> **YOUR TURN**

1. Why might the speaker ask the women to sing?
2. Why do the women cry? Why do they continue to sing?

EDNA ST. VINCENT MILLAY

Edna St. Vincent Millay (1892–1950) was born in Rockland, Maine. Even as a child she wrote poetry, and by the time she graduated from Vassar College (1917) she had achieved some notice as a poet. Millay settled for a while in Greenwich Village, a center of Bohemian activity in New York City, where she wrote, performed in plays, and engaged in feminist causes. In 1923, the year she married, she became the first woman to win the Pulitzer Prize for Poetry. Numerous other awards followed. Though she is best known as a lyric poet— especially as a writer of sonnets—she also wrote memorable political poetry and nature poetry as well as short stories, plays, and a libretto for an opera.

The Spring and the Fall [1923]

In the spring of the year, in the spring of the year,
I walked the road beside my dear.
The trees were black where the bark was wet.
I see them yet, in the spring of the year.
He broke me a bough of the blossoming peach   5
That was out of the way and hard to reach.

In the fall of the year, in the fall of the year,
I walked the road beside my dear.
The rooks went up with a raucous trill.
I hear them still, in the fall of the year.   10
He laughed at all I dared to praise,
And broke my heart, in little ways.

Year be springing or year be falling,
The bark will drip and the birds be calling.
There's much that's fine to see and hear   15
In the spring of a year, in the fall of a year.
'Tis not love's going hurts my days,
But that it went in little ways.

YOUR TURN

1. The first stanza describes the generally happy beginning of a love story.
   Where do you find the first hint of an unhappy ending?
2. Describe the rhyme scheme of the first stanza, including internal
   rhymes. Do the second and third stanzas repeat the pattern, or are there
   some variations? What repetition of sounds other than rhyme do you
   note?
3. Put the last two lines into your own words. How do you react to them;
   that is, do you find the conclusion surprising, satisfying, recognizable
   from your own experience, anticlimactic, or what?
4. In two or three paragraphs, explain how the imagery of the poem
   (drawn from the seasons of the year) contributes to its meaning.

WILFRED OWEN

*Wilfred Owen (1893–1918) was born in Shropshire, in England, and studied at
London University. He enlisted in the army at the outbreak of World War I and
fought in the Battle of the Somme in July–December 1916, in which 1.5 million
men were killed or wounded, until he was hospitalized with shell shock. After
his recuperation in England, he returned to the front, only to be killed in
action one week before the end of the war. His collected poems were published
posthumously.*

For another poem by Owen, see page 606.

Anthem for Doomed Youth   [1920]

What passing-bells for these who die as cattle?
Only the monstrous anger of the guns.
Only the stuttering rifles' rapid rattle
Can patter out their hasty orisons.
No mockeries for them from prayers or bells,   5
Nor any voice of mourning save the choirs—
The shrill, demented choirs of wailing shells;
And bugles calling for them from sad shires.

What candles may be held to speed° them all?
Not in the hands of boys, but in their eyes   10
Shall shine the holy glimmers of good-byes.
The pallor of girls' brows shall be their pall;
Their flowers the tenderness of patient minds,
And each slow dusk a drawing-down of blinds.

---

9 speed aid.

> **YOUR TURN**
>
> 1. What is an anthem? What are some of the words or phrases in this poem that might be found in a traditional anthem? What are some of the words or phrases that you would not expect in an anthem?
> 2. How would you characterize the speaker's state of mind? (Your response probably will require more than one word.)

WALT WHITMAN

Walt Whitman (1819–1892) was born on Long Island, the son of a farmer. The young Whitman taught school and worked as a carpenter, a printer, a newspaper editor, and, during the Civil War, as a volunteer nurse on the Union side. In Whitman's own day his poetry was highly controversial because of its unusual form (formlessness, many people said) and (though not in the following poem) its abundant erotic implications. Whitman's important book Leaves of Grass, *was first published in 1855 and then revised and greatly expanded it in a number of editions until his death.*

Other poems by Whitman appear on pages 633, 687, 721, and 828.

A Noiseless Patient Spider   [1862–1863]

A noiseless patient spider,
I mark'd where on a little promontory it stood isolated,
Mark'd how to explore the vacant vast surrounding,
It launch'd forth filament, filament, filament, out of itself,
Ever unreeling them, ever tirelessly speeding them.   5

And you O my soul where you stand,
Surrounded, detached, in measureless oceans of space,
Ceaselessly musing, venturing, throwing, seeking the spheres to
    connect them,
Till the bridge you will need be form'd, till the ductile anchor hold,
Till the gossamer thread you fling catch somewhere, O my soul.   10

> **YOUR TURN**
>
> 1. How are the suggestions in "launch'd" (line 4) and "unreeling" (line 5) continued in the second stanza?
> 2. How are the varying lengths of lines 1, 4, and 8 relevant to their ideas?
> 3. The second stanza is not a complete sentence. Why? The poem is unrhymed. What effect does the near-rhyme (*hold: soul*) in the last two lines have on you?

DYLAN THOMAS

Dylan Thomas (1914-1953) was born and grew up in Swansea, in Wales. His first volume of poetry, published in 1934, immediately made him famous. Endowed with a highly melodious voice, on three tours of the United States he was immensely successful as a reader of both his own and other poets' work. He died in New York City.

Fern Hill

[1946]

Now as I was young and easy under the apple boughs
About the lilting house and happy as the grass was green,
    The night above the dingle starry,
        Time let me hail and climb
     Golden in the heydays of his eyes,   5
And honored among wagons I was prince of the apple towns
And once below a time I lordly had the trees and leaves
     Trail with daisies and barley
    Down the rivers of the windfall light.

And as I was green and carefree, famous among the barns   10
About the happy yard and singing as the farm was home,
    In the sun that is young once only,
        Time let me play and be
     Golden in the mercy of his means,
And green and golden I was huntsman and herdsman,
    the calves   15
Sang to my horn, the foxes on the hills barked clear and cold,
       And the sabbath rang slowly
    In the pebbles of the holy streams.

All the sun long it was running, it was lovely, the hay
Fields high as the house, the tunes from the chimneys,
      it was air   20
        And playing, lovely and watery
          And fire green as grass.
And nightly under the simple stars
As I rode to sleep the owls were bearing the farm away,
All the moon long I heard, blessed among stables, the night-
    jars   25
      Flying with the ricks, and the horses
        Flashing into the dark.
And then to awake, and the farm, like a wanderer white
With the dew, come back, the cock on his shoulder: it was all
      Shining, it was Adam and maiden,   30
        The sky gathered again
        And the sun grew round that very day.
So it must have been after the birth of the simple light
In the first, spinning place, the spellbound horses walking warm
      Out of the whinnying green stable   35
        On to the fields of praise.

And honored among foxes and pheasants by the gay house
Under the new made clouds and happy as the heart was long,
    In the sun born over and over,
        I ran my heedless ways,   40
    My wishes raced through the house high hay
And nothing I cared, at my sky blue trades, that time allows
In all his tuneful turning so few and such morning songs
    Before the children green and golden
        Follow him out of grace,   45

Nothing I cared, in the lamb white days, that time would take me
Up to the swallow thronged loft by the shadow of my hand,
    In the moon that is always rising,
        Nor that riding to sleep
    I should hear him fly with the high fields   50
And wake to the farm forever fled from the childless land.
Oh as I was young and easy in the mercy of his means,
        Time held me green and dying
    Though I sang in my chains like the sea.

> **YOUR TURN**

Evaluate the thesis that Thomas's poem is about nature deceiving the
speaker by furnishing him with an unrealistic attitude toward reality.

JOHN KEATS

For a biographical note, see page 559.

Ode on a Grecian Urn   [1820]

I

Thou still unravished bride of quietness,
    Thou foster-child of silence and slow time,
Sylvan historian, who canst thus express
    A flowery tale more sweetly than our rhyme:
What leaf-fringed legend haunts about thy shape   5
    Of deities or mortals, or of both,
        In Tempe or the dales of Arcady?
    What men or gods are these? What maidens loth?
What mad pursuit? What struggle to escape?
        What pipes and timbrels? What wild ecstasy?   10

II

Heard melodies are sweet, but those unheard
    Are sweeter; therefore, ye soft pipes, play on;
Not to the sensual° ear, but, more endeared,

---

13 **sensual** sensuous.

Pipe to the spirit ditties of no tone:
Fair youth, beneath the trees, thou canst not leave   15
    Thy song, nor ever can those trees be bare;
        Bold Lover, never, never canst thou kiss,
Though winning near the goal—yet, do not grieve;
        She cannot fade, though thou hast not thy bliss,
    For ever wilt thou love, and she be fair!   20

III

Ah, happy, happy boughs! that cannot shed
    Your leaves, nor ever bid the Spring adieu;
And, happy melodist, unwearied,
    For ever piping songs for ever new;
More happy love! more happy, happy love!   25
    For ever warm and still to be enjoyed,
        For ever panting, and for ever young;
All breathing human passion far above,
    That leaves a heart high-sorrowful and cloyed,
        A burning forehead, and a parching tongue.   30

IV

Who are these coming to the sacrifice?
    To what green altar, O mysterious priest,
Lead'st thou that heifer lowing at the skies,
    And all her silken flanks with garlands drest?
What little town by river or sea shore,   35
    Or mountain-built with peaceful citadel,
        Is emptied of this folk, this pious morn?
And, little town, thy streets for evermore
    Will silent be; and not a soul to tell
        Why thou art desolate, can e'er return.   40

V

O Attic shape! Fair attitude! with brede°
    Of marble men and maidens overwrought,
With forest branches and the trodden weed;
    Thou, silent form, dost tease us out of thought
As doth eternity: Cold Pastoral!   45
    When old age shall this generation waste,
        Thou shalt remain, in midst of other woe
Than ours, a friend to man, to whom thou say'st,
"Beauty is truth, truth beauty,"—that is all
    Ye know on earth, and all ye need to know.   50

---

41 brede design.

YOUR TURN

1. If you do not know the meaning of "sylvan," check a dictionary. Why does Keats call the urn a "sylvan" historian (line 3)? As the poem continues, what evidence is there that the urn cannot "express" (line 3) a tale so sweetly as the speaker said?
2. What do you make of lines 11–14?
3. What do you think the urn may stand for in the first three stanzas? In the third stanza, is the speaker caught up in the urn's world or is he sharply aware of his own?
4. Do you take "tease us out of thought" (line 44) to mean "draw us into a realm of imaginative experience superior to that of reason" or to mean "draw us into futile and frustrating questions"? Or both? Or neither? What suggestions do you find in "Cold Pastoral" (line 45)?
5. Do lines 49–50 perhaps mean that imagination, stimulated by the urn, achieves a realm richer than the daily world? Or perhaps that art, the highest earthly wisdom, suggests there is a realm wherein earthly troubles are resolved?

LINDA PASTAN

Linda Pastan was born in New York City in 1932 and educated at Radcliffe College, Simmons College, and Brandeis University. The author of many books of poems, she has won numerous prizes and has received grants from the National Endowment for the Arts. In the following poem she wittily plays with repetitions and with pauses.

Jump Cabling   [1984]

When our cars	touched
When you lifted the hood	of mine
To see the intimate workings	underneath,
When we were bound	together
By a pulse of pure	energy, 5
When my car like the	princess
In the tale woke with a	start,

I thought why not ride the rest of the way together?

YOUR TURN

1. Suppose someone argued that this is merely prose broken up into arbitrary units. Would you agree? Explain.
2. As you read the poem aloud, think about the spacing that Pastan designed for it. What is the effect of the space between the first and second parts of the first seven lines? Why does she do something different for the final line?

BILLY COLLINS

"Billy Collins writes lovely poems," the novelist, critic, and poet John Updike has said: "Limpid, gently and consistently startling, more serious than they

seem, they describe all the worlds that are and were and some others besides."
The recipient of many honors and awards, and a former poet laureate of the
United States, Collins was born in New York City in 1941. He has taught at
both the City University of New York and Sarah Lawrence College.

    Collins wrote the following poem on the first anniversary of the attack on
the United States that took place on September 11, 2001, when al-Qaeda ter-
rorists hijacked four commercial passenger jet airliners, crashing two of them
into the Twin Towers of the World Trade Center in New York City. (For another
poem by Collins, see page 680.)

The Names [2002]

Yesterday, I lay awake in the palm of the night.
A soft rain stole in, unhelped by any breeze,
And when I saw the silver glaze on the windows,
I started with A, with Ackerman, as it happened,
Then Baxter and Calabro,   5
Davis and Eberling, names falling into place
As droplets fell through the dark.

Names printed on the ceiling of the night.
Names slipping around a watery bend.
Twenty-six willows on the banks of a stream.   10

In the morning, I walked out barefoot
Among thousands of flowers
Heavy with dew like the eyes of tears,
And each had a name—
Fiori inscribed on a yellow petal   15
Then Gonzalez and Han, Ishikawa and Jenkins.

Names written in the air
And stitched into the cloth of the day.
A name under a photograph taped to a mailbox.
Monogram on a torn shirt,   20
I see you spelled out on storefront windows
And on the bright unfurled awnings of this city.
I say the syllables as I turn a corner—
Kelly and Lee,
Medina, Nardella, and O'Connor.   25

When I peer into the woods,
I see a thick tangle where letters are hidden
As in a puzzle concocted for children.
Parker and Quigley in the twigs of an ash,
Rizzo, Schubert, Torres, and Upton,   30
Secrets in the boughs of an ancient maple.

Names written in the pale sky.
Names rising in the updraft amid buildings.
Names silent in stone
Or cried out behind a door.   35
Names blown over the earth and out to sea.

In the evening—weakening light, the last swallows.
A boy on a lake lifts his oars.
A woman by a window puts a match to a candle,
And the names are outlined on the rose clouds—   40
Vanacore and Wallace,
(let X stand, if it can, for the ones unfound)
Then Young and Ziminsky, the final jolt of Z.

Names etched on the head of a pin.
One name spanning a bridge, another undergoing a tunnel.   45
A blue name needled into the skin.
Names of citizens, workers, mothers and fathers,
The bright-eyed daughter, the quick son.
Alphabet of names in a green field.
Names in the small tracks of birds.   50
Names lifted from a hat
Or balanced on the tip of the tongue.
Names wheeled into the dim warehouse of memory.
So many names, there is barely room on the walls of the heart.

YOUR TURN

1. In an interview that appeared several years before "The Names" was published, Collins says of his intention as a poet: "By the end of the poem, the reader should be in a different place from where he started." When you finished reading "The Names," did you find yourself in a "different place"? How would you describe this place?

2. Collins has also observed, again in an interview before he wrote "The Names": "Poetry is clearly very serious for me, but without heaviness or a glib sense of spirituality." Do you perceive a "spiritual" dimension to this poem—one that is not "glib"? What does it mean to say that a poem is "spiritual," that it creates a spiritual effect? Is this the same thing as saying that a poem is "religious," or is it something different?

3. Many readers have expressed their high regard for "The Names," referring to it as a "great poem." Do you agree? What defines a great poem? Do you think a poet does or does not face a special challenge in trying to write a poem, great or simply good, about the tragedy of September 11, 2001? Please explain.

4. One critic, who otherwise admires Collins's work, has objected to "The Names" for being "too sentimental." How would you define "sentimentality"? (Clarify your definition with an example.) Can you locate evidence in the text that might support the judgment that Collins's poem is sentimental? Are there other passages you could cite and analyze in order to argue against it? And what's the matter with sentimentality? Is sentimentality something that poets should always avoid?

5. How do you feel about your own name? Is it something you give much thought to? Any thought? Why is that? Now that you have read Collins's poem, has your relationship to your own name changed in any way?

19

The Speaking Tone of Voice

> Everything is as good as it is dramatic. . . . [A poem is] heard as sung or spoken by a person in a scene—in character, in a setting. By whom, where and when is the question. By the dreamer of a better world out in a storm in Autumn; by a lover under a window at night.
>
> —Robert Frost, Preface, *A Way Out*

If we fall into the habit of saying, "Julia Ward Howe says that her 'eyes have seen the glory of the coming of the Lord,'" or "Robert Frost says that he thinks he knows 'Whose woods these are,'" we neglect the important truth in Frost's comment about poetry as drama: A poem is written by an author (Howe, Frost), but it is spoken by an invented speaker. The author counterfeits the speech of a person in a particular situation.

The anonymous author of "Western Wind" (page 571), for instance, invents the speech of an unhappy lover who longs for the spring ("Westron wind, when will thou blow?"); Julia Ward Howe invents the speech of someone who has seen God working in this world; Robert Frost, in "Stopping by Woods on a Snowy Evening" (page 755), invents a speaker who, sitting in a horse-drawn sleigh, watches the woods fill up with snow.

The speaker's voice often has the ring of the author's own voice—certainly Robert Frost did a great deal to cultivate the idea that he was a farmer-poet—but even when the resemblance seems close, we should recall that in the poem we get a particular speaker in a particular situation. That is, we get, for instance, not the whole of Frost (the father, the competitive poet, the public lecturer, and so on), but only a man in a horse-drawn sleigh watching the woods fill up with snow. It is customary, then, in writing about the voice one hears in a poem, to write not about the author but about the **speaker,** or **voice,** or **mask,** or **persona** (Latin for "mask") that speaks the poem.

In reading a poem, the first and most important question to ask yourself is this: *Who is speaking?* If an audience and a setting are suggested, keep them in mind, too. Consider, for example, the following poem.

EMILY DICKINSON

Emily Dickinson (1830–1886) was born into a proper New England family in Amherst, Massachusetts. Because she never married, and because in her last twenty years she may never have left her house, she has sometimes been pitied. But as the critic Allen Tate said, "All pity for Miss Dickinson's 'starved life' is misdirected. Her life was one of the richest and deepest ever lived on this continent." Her brother was probably right in saying that, having seen something of the rest of the world, "she could not resist the feeling that it was painfully hollow. It was to her so thin and unsatisfying in the face of the Great Realities of Life." For a more complete biographical account, and for a selection of Dickinson's poems and letters, see Chapter 27.

I'm Nobody! Who are you?   [1861?]

I'm Nobody! Who are you?
Are you—Nobody—too?
Then there's a pair of us!
Don't tell! they'd banish us—you know!   4

How dreary—to be—Somebody!
How public—like a Frog—
To tell your name—the livelong June—
To an admiring Bog!   8

Let's consider the sort of person we hear in "I'm Nobody! Who are you?" (Read it aloud, to see if you agree. In fact, you should test each of our assertions by reading the poem aloud.) The voice in line 1 is rather like that of a child playing a game with a friend. In lines 2 and 3 the speaker sees the reader as a fellow spirit ("Are you—Nobody—too?") and invites the reader to join her ("Then there's a pair of us!") in forming a sort of conspiracy of silence against outsiders ("Don't tell!"). In "they'd banish us," however, we hear a word that a child would not be likely to use, and we probably feel that the speaker is a shy but (with the right companion) playful adult, who here is speaking to an intimate friend. And since we hear this voice—we are reading the poem—we are or we become the friend. Because "banish" is a word that brings to mind images of a king's court, the speaker almost comically inflates and thereby makes fun of the "they" who are opposed to "us."

In the second stanza, or we might better say in the space between the two stanzas, the speaker puts aside the childlike manner. In "How dreary," the first words of the second stanza, we hear a sophisticated voice, one might even say a world-weary voice, or a voice with perhaps more than a touch of condescension. But since by now we are paired with the speaker in a conspiracy against outsiders, we enjoy the contrast that the speaker makes between the Nobodies and the Somebodies. Who are these Somebodies, these people who would imperiously "banish" the speaker and the friend? What are the Somebodies like?

How dreary—to be—Somebody!
How public—like a Frog—
To tell your name—the livelong June—
To an admiring Bog!

The last two lines do at least two things: They amusingly explain to the speaker's new friend (the reader) in what way a Somebody is public (it proclaims its presence all day). They also indicate the absurdity of the Somebody-Frog's behavior (the audience is "an admiring Bog"). By the end of the poem we are quite convinced that it is better to be a Nobody (like Dickinson's speaker, and the reader?) than a Somebody (a loudmouth, like a croaking frog).

Often we tend to think of reading as something we do in private, and silently. But it is important to remember that writers, especially poets, care greatly about how their words *sound*. Poets pay attention not only to how the poem is arranged on the page—the length of the lines, for example—but also to how the poem sounds when actually read aloud, or, at least, when heard within the reader's mind.

One of the pleasures of reading literature, in fact, is the pleasure of listening to the sound of a voice, with its special rhythms, tones, accents, and emphases. Getting to know a poem, and becoming engaged by a poet's style, is very much a matter of getting to know a voice, acquiring a feeling for its familiar intonations, yet also being surprised, puzzled, even startled by it on occasion.

If you have done a little acting, you know from this experience how crucial it is to discover the way a character's lines in a play should sound. Directors and actors spend a great deal of time reading the lines, trying them in a variety of ways to catch their truest pace and verbal shape. And so do poets. We aren't making this up; in a letter, Robert Frost talks about "the sound of sense," a sort of abstraction in which an emotion or attitude comes through, even if the words are not clearly heard. He writes:

> The best place to get the abstract sound of sense is from voices behind
> a door that cuts off the words. Ask yourself how these sentences would
> sound without the words in which they are embodied:

> You mean to tell me you can't read?
> I said no such thing.
> Well read then.
> You're not my teacher.

In another letter, continuing the discussion of the topic, after giving some additional examples (for instance, "Unless I'm greatly mistaken," "No fool like an old fool"), Frost says, "It is so and not otherwise that we get the variety that makes it fun to write and read. *The ear does it.* The ear is the only true writer and the only true reader." (For a group of poems by Frost, see Chapter 27.)

In reading, then, your goal is to achieve a deeper sense of character—what this voice sounds like, what kind of person speaks like this. Read aloud; imagine how the writer might have meant his or her words to sound; read aloud again; and listen carefully all the while to the echoes and resonances of the words.

Consider the dramatic situation and the voice in each of the following poems.

GWENDOLYN BROOKS

Gwendolyn Brooks (1917–2000) was born in Topeka, Kansas, but was raised on Chicago's South Side, where she spent most of her life. In 1950, when she won the Pulitzer Prize for Poetry, she became the first African American writer to win a Pulitzer Prize.

We Real Cool   [1960]

The Pool Players.
Seven at the Golden Shovel.

We real cool. We
Left school. We

Lurk late. We
Strike straight. We

Sing sin. We   5
Thin gin. We

Jazz June. We
Die soon.

YOUR TURN

1. Exactly why do you identify the speaker as you do?
2. The stanzas could have been written thus:

> We real cool.
> We left school.
>
> We lurk late.
> We strike straight.

And so forth. Why do you think Brooks wrote them, or arranged the
words, the way she did?

Here is another poem by the same poet, speaking in a different voice.

The Mother   [1945]

Abortions will not let you forget.
You remember the children you got that you did not get,
The damp small pulps with a little or with no hair,
The singers and workers that never handled the air.
You will never neglect or beat   5
Them, or silence or buy with a sweet.
You will never wind up the sucking-thumb
Or scuttle off ghosts that come.
You will never leave them, controlling your luscious sigh,
Return for a snack of them, with gobbling mother-eye.   10

I have heard in the voices of the wind the voices of my
    dim killed children.
I have contracted. I have eased
My dim dears at the breasts they could never suck.
I have said, Sweets, if I sinned, if I seized
Your luck   15
And your lives from your unfinished reach,
If I stole your births and your names,
Your straight baby tears and your games,
Your stilted or lovely loves, your tumults, your marriages,
    aches, and your deaths,
If I poisoned the beginnings of your breaths,   20
Believe that even in my deliberateness I was not deliberate.

Though why should I whine,
Whine that the crime was other than mine?—
Since anyhow you are dead.
Or rather, or instead,   25
You were never made.
But that too, I am afraid,
Is faulty: oh, what shall I say, how is the truth to be said?
You were born, you had body, you died.
It is just that you never giggled or planned or cried.   30

Believe me, I loved you all.
Believe me, I knew you, though faintly, and I loved, I loved you
All.

YOUR TURN

1. Who is being addressed?
2. The first ten lines sound like a chant. What gives them that quality?
   What makes them nonetheless serious?
3. In lines 20–23 the mother attempts to deny the "crime" but cannot.
   What is her reasoning here?
4. Do you find the last lines convincing? Explain.
5. The poem was first published in 1945. Do you think that the abundant
   debate about abortion in recent years has somehow made the poem
   seem dated, or more timely than ever? Explain.

LINDA PASTAN

For a biographical note, see page 589.

Marks   [1978]

My husband gives me an A
for last night's supper,
an incomplete for my ironing,

a B plus in bed.
My son says I am average,
an average mother, but if   5
I put my mind to it
I could improve.

My daughter believes
in Pass/Fail and tells me
I pass. Wait 'til they learn   10
I'm dropping out.

YOUR TURN

1. In addition to the A and B that are mentioned, where else in the poem
   does Pastan use the language of the world of the school? The speaker of
   the poem receives grades, but does she also give a grade, or imply one?
2. What would be gained or lost if Pastan's first sentence came last?

The Reader as the Speaker

We have been arguing that the speaker of the poem usually is not the author but a dramatized form of the author, and that we overhear this speaker in some situation. But with poems of the sort that we have been looking at, we can also say that *the reader* is the speaker. That is, as we read the poem, at least to some degree *we* utter the thoughts, and *we* experience the sensations or emotions that the writer sets forth. Probably this is what Robert Frost was getting at, in a remark we quoted in Chapter 2, when he said that a poem "is the *act* of having an idea and how it feels to have an idea." Thus, when we read "Stopping by Woods on a Snowy Evening" (page 755), *we* are acting, *we* are having the ideas presented in the poem.

Similarly, when we read Emily Dickinson's "I'm Nobody! Who are you?" (page 593) we set forth feelings about what it is to be Nobody in a world where others are Somebody (and Dickinson has also helped us to say that the Somebody is a noisy frog); with Gwendolyn Brooks (page 594) we hear or overhear thoughts and feelings that perhaps strike us as more relevant and more profound and more moving than most of what we hear on television or read in the newspapers about urban violence.

In the following poem you will hear at least three voices—the voice of the person who begins the poem by telling us about a dead man ("Nobody heard him, the dead man"), the voice of the dead man ("I was much further out than you thought / And not waving but drowning"), and the collective voice of the dead man's friends ("Poor chap, he always loved larking"). But see if you don't find that all of the voices together say things that you have said (or almost said).

STEVIE SMITH

Stevie Smith (1902–1971), christened Florence Margaret Smith, was born in England, in Hull. In addition to writing poems, (see her Collected Poems, *1983) she wrote stories, essays, and three novels. She is the subject of* Stevie *(1978), a film in which the acclaimed English actress Glenda Jackson plays Smith.*

Not Waving but Drowning   [1957]

Nobody heard him, the dead man,
But still he lay moaning:
I was much further out than you thought
And not waving but drowning.   4

Poor chap, he always loved larking
And now he's dead
It must have been too cold for him his heart gave way,
They said.   8

Oh, no no no, it was too cold always
(Still the dead one lay moaning)
I was much too far out all my life
And not waving but drowning.   12

1. Identify the speaker of each line.
2. What sort of man did the friends of the dead man think he was? What type of man do you think he was?
3. The first line, "Nobody heard him, the dead man," is literally true. Dead men do not speak. In what other ways is it true?

WISLAWA SZYMBORSKA

Born in 1923, Wislawa Szymborska (pronounced "Vislawa Zimborska"), a native of Poland, is a renowned poet, essayist and translater. In 1996 she received the Nobel Prize for her poetry.

The Terrorist, He Watches [1981]

Translated by Robert A. Maguire and Magnus Jan Krynski

The bomb will go off in the bar at one twenty p.m.
Now it's only one sixteen p.m.
Some will still have time to get in,
some to get out.

The terrorist has already crossed to the other side of the street.   5
The distance protects him from any danger,
and what a sight for sore eyes:

A woman in a yellow jacket, she goes in.
A man in dark glasses, he comes out.

Guys in jeans, they are talking.   10
One seventeen and four seconds.
That shorter guy's really got it made, and gets on a scooter,
and that taller one, he goes in.

One seventeen and forty seconds.
That girl there, she's got a green ribbon in her hair.   15
Too bad that bus just cut her off.
One eighteen p.m.
The girl's not there any more.
Was she dumb enough to go in, or wasn't she?
That we'll see when they carry them out.   20

One nineteen p.m.
No one seems to be going in.
Instead a fat baldy's coming out.
Like he's looking for something in his pockets and
at one nineteen and fifty seconds   25
he goes back for those lousy gloves of his.

It's one twenty p.m.
The time, how it drags.
Should be any moment now.
Not yet.   30
Yes, this is it.
The bomb, it goes off.

1. Who speaks the poem? The terrorist? Or someone watching the terrorist? Or a sort of combination? Or what?
2. Characterize the speaker.

JOHN UPDIKE

*John Updike (1932-2009) was best known as a writer of fiction—short sto-
ries and novels—but throughout his professional career he also wrote essays
and poems. (For a more complete biographical note, see page 191.)*

Icarus   [2001]

O.K., you are sitting in an airplane and
the person in the seat next to you is a sweaty, swarthy gentleman of
   Middle Eastern origin
whose carry-on luggage consists of a bulky black briefcase he
   stashes,
in compliance with airline regulations,
underneath the seat ahead.   5
He keeps looking at his watch and closing his eyes in prayer,
resting his profusely dank forehead against the seatback ahead of him
just above the black briefcase,
which if you listen through the droning of the engines seems to be
   ticking, ticking
softly, softer than your heartbeat in your ears.   10

Who wants to have all their careful packing—the travellers' checks,
   the folded underwear—
end as floating sea-wrack five miles below,
drifting in a rainbow scum of jet fuel,
and their docile hopes of a plastic-wrapped meal
dashed in a concussion whiter than the sun?   15

I say to my companion, "Smooth flight so far."
"So far."
"That's quite a briefcase you've got there."
He shrugs and says, "It contains my life's work."
"And what is it, exactly, that you do?"   20
"You could say I am a lobbyist."

He does not want to talk.
He wants to keep praying.
His hands, with their silky beige backs and their nails cut close like
    a technician's,
tremble and jump in handling the plastic glass of Sprite when it
    comes with its exploding bubbles.   25

Ah, but one gets swept up
in the airport throng, all those workaday faces,
faintly pampered and spoiled in the boomer style,
and those elders dressed like children for flying
in hi-tech sneakers and polychrome catsuits,   30
and those gum-chewing attendants taking tickets
while keeping up a running flirtation with a uniformed bystander,
    a stoic blond pilot—
all so normal, who could resist
this vault into the impossible?

Your sweat has slowly dried. Your praying neighbor   35
has fallen asleep, emitting an odor of cardamom.
His briefcase seems to have deflated.
Perhaps not this time, then.
But the possibility of impossibility will keep drawing us back
to this scrape against the numbed sky,   40
to this sleek sheathed tangle of color-coded wires, these million rivets,
    this wing
like a frozen lake at your elbow.

YOUR TURN

1. Take a moment to look up the Icarus myth in a classical dictionary or encyclopedia. Do you see connections between the myth and the story that Updike tells in this poem?
2. Who is the "you" in the first line?
3. What kinds of assumptions does the poem make about the "gentleman of Middle Eastern origin"? Are these assumptions challenged? Point to specific details in the language to explain your responses.
4. What kind of conclusion does the poem reach?
5. Does "Icarus" disturb you? If so, why?
6. Which poem do you think is more effective: Updike's "Icarus" or Syzmborska's "The Terrorist"? What, more generally, does it mean to say that one poem is more effective than another?

AURORA LEVINS MORALES

Aurora Levins Morales, born in Puerto Rico in 1954, came to the United States with her family in 1967. She has lived in Chicago and New Hampshire and now lives in the San Francisco Bay area. A member of the Latina Feminist Group, Levins Morales has published stories, essays, prose poems, and poems.

Child of the Americas

[1986]

I am a child of the Americas,
a light-skinned mestiza of the Caribbean,
a child of many diaspora,° born into this continent at a crossroads.

I am a U.S. Puerto Rican Jew,
a product of the ghettos of New York I have never known.   5
An immigrant and the daughter and granddaughter of immigrants.
I speak English with passion: it's the tongue of my consciousness,
a flashing knife blade of crystal, my tool, my craft.

I am Caribeña,° island grown. Spanish is in my flesh,
ripples from my tongue, lodges in my hips: 10
the language of garlic and mangoes,
the singing in my poetry, the flying gestures of my hands.

I am of Latinoamerica, rooted in the history of my continent:
I speak from that body.

I am not african. Africa is in me, but I cannot return.   15
I am not taína.° Taíno is in me, but there is no way back.
I am not european. Europe lives in me, but I have no home there.

I am new. History made me. My first language was spanglish.°
I was born at the crossroads
and I am whole.   20

---

3 diaspora literally, "scattering"; the term is used especially to refer to the dispersion of the Jews outside of Israel from the sixth century BCE, when they were exiled to Babylonia, to the present time.   **9 Caribeña** Caribbean woman.   **16 taína** the Taínos were the Indian tribe native to Puerto Rico.   **18 spanglish** a mixture of Spanish and English.

JOSEPH BRUCHAC III

Joseph Bruchac III (the name is pronounced "Brew-shack") was born in Saratoga Springs, New York, in 1942, and educated at Cornell University, Syracuse University, and Union Graduate School. Like many other Americans, he has a multicultural ethnic heritage, and he includes Native Americans as well as Slovaks among his ancestors. Bruchac is a widely published writer, editor, teacher, and storyteller. He lives in Greenfield Center, New York, in the Adirondack mountain region.

"Much of my writing and my life," Bruchac says, "relates to the problem of being an American. . . . While in college I was active in Civil Rights work and in the antiwar movement. . . . I went to Africa to teach—but more than that to be taught. It showed me many things. How much we have as Americans and take for granted. How much our eyes refuse to see because they are blinded to everything in a man's face except his color."

Ellis Island   [1978]

Beyond the red brick of Ellis Island
where the two Slovak children
who became my grandparents
waited the long days of quarantine,
after leaving the sickness,   5
the old Empires of Europe,
a Circle Line ship slips easily
on its way to the island
of the tall woman, green
as dreams of forests and meadows   10
waiting for those who'd worked
a thousand years
yet never owned their own.

Like millions of others,
I too come to this island,   15
nine decades the answerer
of dreams.

Yet only one part of my blood loves that memory.
Another voice speaks
of native lands   20
within this nation.
Lands invaded
when the earth became owned.
Lands of those who followed
the changing Moon,   25
knowledge of the seasons
in their veins.

The Dramatic Monologue

We have said at some length that in most poems the speaker is not quite the author (say, Robert Frost) but is a dramatized version (a man sitting in a sleigh,
watching the "woods fill up with snow"). We have also said that in most poems
the reader can imagine himself or herself as the speaker; as we read Dickinson or
even Brooks and Pastan, we say to ourselves that the poet is expressing thoughts
and emotions that might be our own. But in some poems the poet creates so distinct a speaker that the character clearly is not us but is something Other. Such a
poem is called a **dramatic monologue.** In it, a highly specific character speaks, in
a clearly specified situation. The most famous example is Robert Browning's "My
Last Duchess," where a Renaissance duke is addressing an emissary from a count.

ROBERT BROWNING

*Born in a suburb of London into a middle-class family, Robert Browning
(1812-1889) was educated primarily at home, where he read widely. For a
while he wrote for the English stage, but after marrying Elizabeth Barrett in
1846—she too was a poet—he lived with her in Italy until her death in 1861.
He then returned to England and settled in London with their son. Regarded*

as one of the most distinguished poets of the Victorian period, he is buried in Westminster Abbey.

My Last Duchess

[1844]

Ferrara*

That's my last Duchess painted on the wall,
Looking as if she were alive. I call
That piece a wonder, now; Frà Pandolf's° hands
Worked busily a day, and there she stands.
Will't please you sit and look at her? I said   5
"Frà Pandolf" by design, for never read
Strangers like you that pictured countenance,
The depth and passion of its earnest glance,
But to myself they turned (since none puts by
The curtain I have drawn for you, but I)   10
And seemed as they would ask me, if they durst,
How such a glance came there; so, not the first
Are you to turn and ask thus. Sir, 'twas not
Her husband's presence only, called that spot
Of joy into the Duchess' cheek; perhaps   15
Frà Pandolf chanced to say "Her mantle laps
Over my Lady's wrist too much," or, "Paint
Must never hope to reproduce the faint
Half-flush that dies along her throat." Such stuff
Was courtesy, she thought, and cause enough   20
For calling up that spot of joy. She had
A heart—how shall I say?—too soon made glad,
Too easily impressed; she liked whate'er
She looked on, and her looks went everywhere.
Sir, 'twas all one! My favor at her breast,   25
The dropping of the daylight in the west,
The bough of cherries some officious fool
Broke in the orchard for her, the white mule
She rode with round the terrace—all and each
Would draw from her alike the approving speech,   30
Or blush, at least. She thanked men—good! but thanked
Somehow—I know not how—as if she ranked
My gift of a nine-hundred-years-old name
With anybody's gift. Who'd stoop to blame
This sort of trifling? Even had you skill   35
In speech—(which I have not)—to make your will
Quite clear to such an one, and say, "Just this
Or that in you disgusts me; here you miss,
Or there exceed the mark"—and if she let
Herself be lessoned so, nor plainly set   40
Her wits to yours, forsooth, and made excuse,
—E'en then would be some stooping; and I choose

*Ferrara a town in Italy.   3 Frà Pandolf a fictitious painter.

Never to stoop. Oh, Sir, she smiled, no doubt,
Whene'er I passed her; but who passed without
Much the same smile? This grew; I gave commands;   45
Then all smiles stopped together. There she stands
As if alive. Will't please you rise? We'll meet
The company below, then. I repeat,
The Count your master's known munificence
Is ample warrant that no just pretense   50
Of mine for dowry will be disallowed;
Though his fair daughter's self, as I avowed
At starting, is my object. Nay, we'll go
Together down, Sir. Notice Neptune, though,
Taming a sea-horse, thought a rarity,   55
Which Claus of Innsbruck° cast in bronze for me!

---

56 Claus of Innsbruck a fictitious sculptor.

> **YOUR TURN**
>
> 1. What is the occasion for the meeting?
> 2. What words or lines do you think especially convey the speaker's arro-
>   gance? What is your attitude toward the speaker? Loathing? Fascina-
>   tion? Respect? Explain.
> 3. The time and place are Renaissance Italy; how do they affect your atti-
>   tude toward the duke? What would be the effect if the poem were set
>   in the early twenty-first century?
> 4. Years after writing this poem, Browning explained that the duke's "com-
>   mands" (line 45) were "that she should be put to death, or he might
>   have had her shut up in a convent." Do you think the poem should have
>   been more explicit? Does Browning's later uncertainty indicate that the
>   poem is badly thought out? Suppose we did not have Browning's com-
>   ment on line 45. Do you think the line then could mean only that he
>   commanded her to stop smiling and that she obeyed? Explain.

Diction and Tone

From the whole of language, one consciously or unconsciously selects certain
words and grammatical constructions; this selection constitutes one's **diction**. It
is partly by the diction that we come to know the speaker of a poem. Stevie
Smith's speaker (page 597) used words such as "chap" and "larking," which are
scarcely imaginable in the mouth of Browning's Renaissance duke. But of course
some words are used in both poems: "I," "you," "thought," "the," and so on. The fact
remains, however, that although a large part of language is shared by all speakers,
certain parts of language are used only by certain speakers.

Like some words, some grammatical constructions are used only by certain
kinds of speakers. Consider these two passages:

In Adam's fall
We sinned all.

—Anonymous, *The New England Primer*

Of Man's first disobedience, and the fruit
Of that forbidden tree whose mortal taste
Brought death into the World, and all our woe,
With loss of Eden, till one greater Man
Restore us, and regain the blissful seat,
Sing, Heavenly Muse, that, on the secret top
Of Oreb, or of Sinai, didst inspire
That shepherd who first taught the chosen seed
In the beginning how the heavens and earth
Rose out of Chaos. . . .

—John Milton, *Paradise Lost*

There is an enormous difference in the diction of these two passages. Milton, speaking as an inspired poet, appropriately uses words and grammatical constructions somewhat removed from common life. Hence, while the anonymous author of the primer speaks directly of "Adam's fall," Milton speaks allusively of the fall, calling it "Man's first disobedience." Milton's sentence is nothing that any Englishman ever said in conversation; its genitive beginning ("Of Man's first disobedience"), its length (the sentence continues for six lines beyond the quoted passage), and its postponement of the main verb ("Sing") until the sixth line mark it as the utterance of a poet working in the tradition of Latin poetry. The primer's statement, by its choice of words as well as by its brevity, suggests a far less sophisticated speaker.

Speakers have attitudes toward themselves, their subjects, and their audiences, and (consciously or unconsciously) they choose their words, pitch, and modulation accordingly; all these add up to the **tone.** In written literature, tone must be detected without the aid of the ear; the reader must understand by the selection and sequence of words the way in which they are meant to be heard (that is, playfully, angrily, confidentially, sarcastically, etc.). The reader must catch what Frost calls "the speaking tone of voice somehow entangled in the words and fastened to the page of the ear of the imagination."

Finally, we should mention that although this discussion concentrates on the speaker's tone, we can also talk of the author's tone—that is, of the author's attitude toward the invented speaker. The speaker's tone might, for example, be angry, but the author's tone (as detected by the reader) might be humorous.

ROBERT HERRICK

Robert Herrick (1591–1674) was born in London, the son of a goldsmith. After taking an MA at Cambridge, he was ordained in the Church of England. Later, he was sent to the country parish of Dean Prior in Devonshire, where he wrote most of his poetry. A loyal supporter of the king, in 1647 he was expelled from his parish by the Puritans, though in 1662 he was restored to Dean Prior.

To the Virgins, to Make Much of Time   [1648]

Gather ye rosebuds while ye may,
    Old Time is still a-flying;
And this same flower that smiles today,
    Tomorrow will be dying.   4

The glorious lamp of heaven, the sun,
   The higher he's a-getting,
The sooner will his race be run,
   And nearer he's to setting.   8

That age is best which is the first,
   When youth and blood are warmer;
But being spent, the worse, and worst
   Times still succeed the former.   12

Then be not coy, but use your time;
   And while ye may, go marry:
For having lost but once your prime,
   You may for ever tarry.   16

Carpe diem (Latin:"seize the day") is the theme. But if we want to get the full force of the poem, we must understand who is talking to whom. Look, for example, at "Old Time" in line 2. Time is "old" in the sense of having been around a long while, but doesn't "old" in this context suggest also that the speaker regards Time with easy familiarity, almost affection? We visit the old school, and our friend is old George. Time is destructive, yes, and the speaker urges the young maidens to make the most of their spring. But the speaker is neither bitter nor importunate; rather, he seems to be the wise old man, the counselor, the man who has made his peace with Time and is giving advice to the young. Time moves rapidly in the poem (the rosebud of line 1 is already a flower in line 3), but the speaker is unhurried; in line 5 he has leisure to explain that the glorious lamp of heaven is the sun.

In "To the Virgins," the pauses, indicated by punctuation at the ends of the lines (except in line 11, where we tumble without stopping from "worst" to "Times"), slow the reader down. But even if there is no punctuation at the end of a line of poetry, the reader probably pauses slightly or gives the final word an additional bit of emphasis. Similarly, the space between stanzas slows a reader down, increasing the emphasis on the last word of one stanza and the first word of the next.

WILFRED OWEN

For a biographical note, see page 584.

Dulce et Decorum Est*   [1917]

Bent double, like old beggars under sacks,
Knock-kneed, coughing like hags, we cursed through sludge,
Till on the haunting flares we turned our backs
And towards our distant rest began to trudge.
Men marched asleep. Many had lost their boots   5
But limped on, blood-shod. All went lame; all blind;
Drunk with fatigue; deaf even to the hoots
Of tired, outstripped Five-Nines° that dropped behind.

*****Dulce et Decorum Est** From the Latin poet Horace's *Odes* (3:2.13): *Dulce et decorum est pro patria mori*—"It is sweet and honorable to die for your country." **8 Five-Nines** shells containing poison gas.

Gas! Gas! Quick, boys!—An ecstasy of fumbling,
Fitting the clumsy helmets just in time;   10
But someone still was yelling out and stumbling
And flound'ring like a man in fire or lime . . .
Dim, through the misty panes and thick green light,
As under a green sea, I saw him drowning.

In all my dreams, before my helpless sight,   15
He plunges at me, guttering, choking, drowning.
If in some smothering dreams you too could pace
Behind the wagon that we flung him in,
And watch the white eyes writhing in his face,
His hanging face, like a devil's sick of sin;   20
If you could hear, at every jolt, the blood
Come gargling from the froth-corrupted lungs,
Obscene as cancer, bitter as the cud
Of vile, incurable sores on innocent tongues,—
My friend,° you would not tell with such high zest   25
To children ardent for some desperate glory,
The old Lie: Dulce et decorum est
Pro patria mori.

---

25 My friend Early drafts of "Dulce et Decorum Est" are dedicated to Jessie Pope, author
of children's books and conventional patriotic verse.

YOUR TURN

1. Owen uses two similes in the first two lines. Please explain the meaning of each one.
2. Describe in your own words what is happening in the second stanza.
3. Please focus on the word "guttering" in line 16. In one of the drafts of
   this poem, Owen first wrote "gargling" here but then he crossed it out
   and wrote "gurgling" instead. He crossed out that word too and wrote
   "goggling," which he also crossed out, before finally settling on "guttering." Do you think he made the right choice, or do you prefer one of
   the other three words?
4. What might have led Owen to decide to present the poem in a first-
   person voice? What is a relationship of this speaker to the reader?
5. One scholar has highly praised Owen's poem but also has said of it,
   "The poem is almost too disturbing." Do you agree? Provide evidence
   from the text to explain and support your response.

THOMAS HARDY

*Thomas Hardy (1840–1928) was born in Dorset, England, the son of a stone-
mason. Despite great obstacles he studied the classics and architecture, and in
1862 he moved to London to study and practice as an architect. Ill health
forced him to return to Dorset, where he continued to work as an architect
and to write. Best known for his novels, Hardy ceased writing fiction after the*

hostile reception of Jude the Obscure *in 1896—it was attacked as indecent—*
and turned to writing lyric poetry.

The Man He Killed   [1902]

"Had he and I but met
By some old ancient inn,
We should have sat us down to wet
    Right many a nipperkin!°   4

"But ranged as infantry,
And staring face to face,
I shot at him as he at me,
    And killed him in his place.   8

"I shot him dead because—
Because he was my foe,
Just so: my foe of course he was;
    That's clear enough; although   12

"He thought he'd 'list, perhaps,
Off-hand like—just as I—
Was out of work—had sold his traps°—
    No other reason why.   16

"Yes; quaint and curious war is!
You shoot a fellow down
You'd treat if met where any bar is,
    Or help to half-a-crown."   20

---

4 nipperkin cup.   **15 traps** personal belongings.

YOUR TURN

1. What do we learn about the speaker's life before he enlisted in the infantry? How does his diction characterize him?
2. What is the effect of the series of monosyllables in lines 7 and 8?
3. Consider the punctuation of the third and fourth stanzas. Why are the heavy, frequent pauses appropriate? What question is the speaker trying to answer?
4. In the last stanza, what attitudes toward war does the speaker express? What, from the evidence of this poem, would you infer Hardy's attitude toward war to be?

The Ruined Maid   [1902]

"O 'Melia, my dear, this does everything crown!°
Who could have supposed I should meet you in Town?
And whence such fair garments, such prosperi-ty?"—
"O didn't you know I'd been ruined?" said she.   4

---

1 O 'Melia . . . crown O Amelia, this crowns (i.e., tops) everything.

—"You left us in tatters, without shoes or socks,
Tired of digging potatoes, and spudding up docks;°
And now you've gay bracelets and bright feathers three!"—
"Yes: that's how we dress when we're ruined," said she.   8

—"At home in the barton° you said 'thee' and 'thou,'
And 'thik oon,' and 'theäs oon,' and 't'other';° but now
Your talking quite fits ee° for high compa-ny!"—
"Some polish is gained with one's ruin," said she.   12

—"Your hands were like paws then, your face blue and bleak
But now I'm bewitched by your delicate cheek,
And your little gloves fit as on any la-dy!"—
"We never do work when we're ruined," said she.   16

—"You used to call home-life a hag-ridden dream,
And you'd sigh, and you'd sock;° but at present you seem
To know not of megrims° or melancho-ly!"—
"True. One's pretty lively when ruined," said she.   20

—"I wish I had feathers, a fine sweeping gown,
And a delicate face, and could strut about Town!"—
"My dear—a raw country girl, such as you be,
Cannot quite expect that. You ain't ruined," said she.   24

---

6 spudding up docks digging up weeds.   **9 in the barton** on the farm.   **9–10 thee . . . t' other** rural words for "you," "that one," "this one," and "the other."   **11 'ee** rural word for "you."   **18 sock** groan.   **19 megrims** migraine headaches.

> **YOUR TURN**
>
> 1. Thomas Hardy wrote the poem more than a hundred years ago. What did it mean for a woman to be "ruined"? Who are the two speakers? What is the attitude of each speaker toward the other?
> 2. Amelia's clothing and her citified speech (she no longer uses "thee" and "thou," and so forth) imply sophistication. What does the final line of the poem tell us about the degree of her sophistication? What do you suppose the author's attitude is toward Amelia?

COUNTEE CULLEN

For a biographical note, see page 562.

For a Lady I Know   [1925]

She even thinks that up in heaven
   Her class lies late and snores,
While poor black cherubs rise at seven
   To do celestial chores.

> **YOUR TURN**
>
> 1. What is the gist of what Cullen is saying?
> 2. How would you characterize the tone? Furious? Indifferent?

ANNE BRADSTREET

Anne Bradstreet (1612–1678) was born in Northampton, England; her father was Thomas Dudley, who later served several terms as governor of the Massachusetts Bay Colony. She married at age sixteen, and two years later she and her husband, Simon Bradstreet, along with her father, made the long, arduous voyage to Massachusetts. She settled in North Andover, and she lived there until her death. Bradstreet was a devoted wife, the mother of eight children, and a gifted poet.

To My Dear and Loving Husband   [1678]

If ever two were one, then surely we.
If ever man were lov'd by wife, then thee;
If ever wife was happy in a man,
Compare with me ye women if you can.
I prize thy love more than whole Mines of gold,   5
Or all the riches that the East doth hold.
My love is such that Rivers cannot quench,
Nor ought but love from thee, give recompence.
Thy love is such I can no way repay,
The heavens reward thee manifold I pray.   10
Then while we live, in love let's so persever,
That when we live no more, we may live ever.

> **YOUR TURN**

1. Each of the first three lines begins with "if." What is the effect of this repetition on your response as a reader?
2. The title suggests that Bradstreet is addressing her husband. But if this is the case, how do we explain line 4?
3. Please explain the comparison between love and wealth that Bradstreet gives in lines 5 and 6.
4. What does the word "quench" in line 7 imply? What are the implications of the references to reward and repayment in lines 8–10?
5. Please explain the paradox that Bradstreet describes in the final two lines. *Note:* Each line in the poem has ten syllables, except for these final two lines, which have an extra syllable. Also, the word "persevere" should be pronounced to rhyme with "ever," as in the word "sever."
6. What is your response to this poem as a whole? Do you find it simple, or complicated?
7. Could you try your hand at a poem written in reply to this one? Imagine that you are Bradstreet's husband, and that your poem is titled "My Dear and Loving Wife."

LYN LIFSHIN

Born in Burlington, Vermont, in 1944 and educated at Syracuse University and the University of Vermont, Lyn Lifshin has written many books of poetry on a range of topics, from Shaker communities of early America to Eskimo culture in the Arctic. Much of her work shows a strong feminist concern.

My Mother and the Bed   [1999]

No, not that way she'd
say when I was 7, pulling
the bottom sheet smooth,
you've got to   saying
hospital corners   5

I wet the bed much later
than I should, until
just writing this I
hadn't thought of
the connection   10

My mother would never
sleep on sheets someone
else had   I never
saw any stains on hers
tho her bedroom was   15

a maze of powder   hair
pins   black dresses
Sometimes she brings her
own sheets to my house,
carries toilet seat covers   20

Did anybody sleep
in my   she always asks
Her sheets   her hair
she says the rooms here
smell funny   25

We drive at 3 am
slowly into Boston and
strip what looks like
two clean beds as the
sky gets light   I   30

smooth on the form
fitted flower bottom,
she redoes it

She thinks of my life
as a bed only she   35
can make right

YOUR TURN

1. What do you make of the extra spaces—for instance, the space between "to" and "saying" in line 4? In reading the poem aloud, how do
   you "read" the spaces?
2. Would you agree that the poem is humorous and, on the whole, genial? Or do you think that bitterness overshadows the humor? Explain.
3. One student made the suggestion that the final stanza, perhaps because it seems to "explain" the poem to the reader, is the least

effective part of the poem. Do you agree? If you do, write a new final
stanza.

MITSUYE YAMADA

*Mitsuye Yamada, the daughter of Japanese immigrants to the United States,
was born in Japan in 1923, during her mother's return visit to her native
land. Yamada was raised in Seattle, but in 1942 she and her family were incarcerated and then relocated in a camp in Idaho, when Executive Order
9066 gave military authorities the right to remove any and all persons from
"military areas." In 1954 she became an American citizen.*

To the Lady   [1976]

The one in San Francisco who asked:
Why did the Japanese Americans let
the government put them in
those camps without protest?

Come to think of it I   5
   should've run off to Canada
   should've hijacked a plane to Algeria
   should've pulled myself up from my
   bra straps
   and kicked'm in the groin   10
   should've bombed a bank
   should've tried self-immolation
   should've holed myself up in a
   woodframe house
   and let you watch me   15
   burn up on the six o'clock news
   should've run howling down the street
   naked and assaulted you at breakfast
   by AP wirephoto
   should've screamed bloody murder   20
   like Kitty Genovese°

Then
YOU would've
   come to my aid in shining armor
   laid yourself across the railroad track   25
   marched on Washington
   tatooed a Star of David on your arm
   written six million enraged
   letters to Congress

   But we didn't draw the line   30

---

21 Kitty Genovese In 1964 Kitty Genovese of Kew Gardens, New York, was stabbed to
death when she left her car and walked toward her home. Thirty-eight persons heard her
screams, but no one came to her assistance.

anywhere
law and order Executive Order 9066°
social order moral order internal order

YOU let'm
I let'm   35
All are punished.

---

32 **Executive Order 9066** an authorization, signed in 1941 by President Franklin D.
Roosevelt, allowing military authorities to relocate Japanese and Japanese-Americans who
resided on the Pacific Coast of the United States.

> **YOUR TURN**
>
> 1. Has the lady's question (lines 2–4) ever crossed your mind? If so, what
>   answers did you think of?
> 2. What, in effect, is the speaker really saying in lines 5–21? And in lines
>   24–29?
> 3. Explain the last line.

The Voice of the Satirist

The writer of **satire,** in one way or another, ridicules an aspect or several aspects of human behavior, seeking to arouse in the reader some degree of amused
contempt for the object. However urbane in tone, the satirist is always critical. By
cleverly holding up foibles or vices for the world's derision, satire (Alexander
Pope claimed) "heals with morals what it hurts with wit." The laughter of comedy is an end in itself; the laughter of satire is a weapon against the world: "The
intellectual dagger," Frank O'Connor called satire, "opposing the real dagger."
Jonathan Swift, of whom O'Connor is speaking, insisted that his satires were not
malice but medicine:

> His satire points at no defect
> But what all mortals may correct. . . .
> He spared a hump or crooked nose,
> Whose owners set not up for beaux.

But Swift, although he claimed that satire is therapeutic, also saw its futility:
"Satire is a sort of glass [i.e., mirror] wherein beholders do generally discover
everybody's face but their own."

Sometimes the satirist speaks out directly as defender of public morals, abu-
sively but wittily chopping off heads. Byron, for example, wrote:

> Prepare for rhyme—I'll publish, right or wrong:
> Fools are my theme, let Satire be my song.

But sometimes the satirist chooses to invent a speaker far removed from himself
or herself, just as Browning chose to invent a Renaissance duke. The satirist may
invent a callous brigadier general or a pompous judge who unconsciously annihi-
lates himself. Consider this satirical poem by e. e. cummings.

E. E. CUMMINGS

For a biographical note, see page 567.

next to of course god america i
[1926]

"next to of course god america i
love you land of the pilgrims' and so forth oh
say can you see by the dawn's early my
country 'tis of centuries come and go
and are no more what of it we should worry   5
in every language even deaf and dumb
thy sons acclaim your glorious name by gorry
by jingo by gee by gosh by gum
why talk of beauty what could be more beautiful than these heroic happy dead   10
who rushed like lions to the roaring slaughter
they did not stop to think they died instead
then shall the voice of liberty be mute?"

He spoke. And drank rapidly a glass of water

Cummings might have written, in the voice of a solid citizen or a good poet, a direct attack on chauvinistic windbags; instead, he chose to invent a windbag whose
rhetoric punctures itself. Yet the last line tells that we are really hearing someone
who is recounting what the windbag said; that is, the speaker of all the lines but
the last is a combination of the chauvinist *and* the satiric observer of the chauvinist. (When cummings himself recited these lines, there was mockery in his voice.)

Only in the final line of the poem does the author seem to speak entirely on
his own, and even here he adopts a matter-of-fact pose that is far more potent
than **invective** (direct abuse) would be. Yet the last line is not totally free of explicit hostility.

MARGE PIERCY

*Marge Piercy, born in Detroit in 1936, was the first member of her family to at-
tend college. After earning a bachelor's degree from the University of Michigan in
1957 and a master's degree from Northwestern University in 1958, she moved
to Chicago. There she worked at odd jobs while writing novels (unpublished)
and engaging in action on behalf of women and blacks and against the war in
Vietnam. In 1970 she moved to Wellfleet, Massachusetts, where she still lives. She
is the author of many novels as well as short stories, poems, and essays.*

Barbie Doll
[1969]

This girlchild was born as usual
and presented dolls that did pee-pee
and miniature GE stoves and irons
and wee lipsticks the color of cherry candy.
Then in the magic of puberty, a classmate said: 5
You have a great big nose and fat legs.

She was healthy, tested intelligent,
possessed strong arms and back,
abundant sexual drive and manual dexterity.
She went to and fro apologizing.   10
Everyone saw a fat nose on thick legs.

She was advised to play coy,
exhorted to come on hearty,
exercise, diet, smile and wheedle.
Her good nature wore out   15
like a fan belt.
So she cut off her nose and her legs
and offered them up.

In the casket displayed on satin she lay
with the undertaker's cosmetics painted on,   20
a turned-up putty nose,
dressed in a pink and white nightie.
Doesn't she look pretty? everyone said.
Consummation at last.
To every woman a happy ending.   25

YOUR TURN

1. Why is the poem called "Barbie Doll"?
2. What voice do you hear in lines 1–4? Line 6 is, we are told, the voice of "a classmate." How do these voices differ? What voice do you hear in the first three lines of the second stanza?
3. Explain in your own words what Piercy is saying about women in this poem. Does her view seem to you fair, slightly exaggerated, or greatly exaggerated?

LOUISE ERDRICH

Louise Erdrich, born in 1954 in Little Falls, Minnesota, grew up in North Dakota, a member of the Turtle Mountain Band of Chippewa. Her father had been born in Germany; her mother was a Chippewa; both parents taught at the Bureau of Indian Affairs School. After graduating from Dartmouth College (major in anthropology) in 1976, Erdrich returned briefly to North Dakota to teach in the Poetry in the Schools Program, and went to Johns Hopkins University, where she earned a master's degree in creative writing.

Erdrich has published several collections of poems and many novels, one of which, Love Medicine *(1986), won the National Book Critics Circle Award.*

Dear John Wayne   [1984]

August and the drive-in picture is packed.
We lounge on the hood of the Pontiac
surrounded by the slow-burning spirals they sell
at the window, to vanquish the hordes of mosquitoes.
Nothing works. They break through the smoke screen for blood.   5

Always the lookout spots the Indians first,
spread north to south, barring progress.
The Sioux or some other Plains bunch
in spectacular columns, ICBM missiles,
feathers bristling in the meaningful sunset.   10
The drum breaks. There will be no parlance.
Only the arrows whining, a death-cloud of nerves
swarming down on the settlers
who die beautifully, tumbling like dust weeds
into the history that brought us all here   15
together: this wide screen beneath the sign of the bear.

The sky fills, acres of blue squint and eye
that the crowd cheers. His face moves over us,
a thick cloud of vengeance, pitted
like the land that was once flesh. Each rut,   20
each scar makes a promise: *It is
not over, this fight, not as long as you resist.*
Everything we see belongs to us.

A few laughing Indians fall over the hood
slipping in the hot spilled butter.   25
The eye sees a lot, John, but the heart is so blind.
Death makes us owners of nothing.
He smiles, a horizon of teeth
the credits reel over, and then the white fields
again blowing in the true-to-life dark.   30
The dark films over everything.
We get into the car
scratching our mosquito bites, speechless and small
as people are when the movie is done.
We are back in our skins.   35
How can we help but keep hearing his voice,
the flip side of the sound track, still playing:
Come on, boys, we got them
where we want them, drunk, running.
They'll give us what we want, what we need.   40

Even his disease was the idea of taking everything.
Those cells, burning, doubling, splitting out of their skins.

YOUR TURN

1. Who is the speaker of most of the poem? Who speaks the italicized lines?
2. There are curious shifts in the diction, for instance from "some other Plains bunch" (line 8) to "parlance" (line 11). Whose voice do we hear in "some. . . bunch"? Consider, too, the diction in "to vanquish the hordes of mosquitoes" (line 4). If you were talking about mosquitoes, you probably would not use the word "vanquish." What do you think Erdrich is up to?
3. What do you make of lines 24–25, talking of Indians "slipping in the hot spilled butter"? What connection do these lines have with what presumably is going on in the film?

STEPHEN DUCK

Stephen Duck (1705?–1756), born in rural England of impoverished parents, left school at thirteen and became a farm laborer. He later wrote about such work, but he also wrote on other topics, as in the satiric piece that we reprint here.

Note: *Pronunciation in eighteenth-century England was not identical with pronunciation today, and in any case Duck's pronunciation would not have been identical with the pronunciation of an educated Londoner. In line 2, "cheese" rhymes with "gaze" in line 1; in line 4, "live" rhymes with "perceive" in line 3; and in line 9 "cream" was probably pronounced "crem," rhyming with "them."*

On Mites   [1736]

To a Lady

"Tis but by way of Simile."

　　　　　　　—Prior°

Dear Madam, did you never gaze,
Through optic-glass,° on rotten Cheese?
There, Madam, did you ne'er perceive
A crowd of dwarfish creatures live?
The little things, elate with pride,   5
Strut to and fro, from side to side:
In tiny pomp, and pertly vain,
Lords of their pleasing orb they reign;
And, filled with hardened curds and cream,
Think the whole dairy made for them.   10
So men, conceited lords of all,
Walk proudly o'er this pendent° Ball,
Fond of their little spot below,
Nor greater beings care to know;
But think those worlds which deck the skies,   15
Were only formed to please their eyes.

Prior Matthew Prior (1664–1721), important English diplomat and minor poet. **2 optic glass** microscope. **12 pendent** floating in space.

> **YOUR TURN**
>
> Duck is pretty straightforward in his attack on human pride. Is he merely abusive, or does he also display some wit? To put the matter bluntly: Is there anything enjoyable about the poem? Or think about the poem from this angle: In Chapter 2 we discuss Robert Frost's opinion that literature is "a performance in words." Obviously Duck is giving a performance when he rhymes certain words, but are there other aspects to his performance?

20

Figurative Language: Simile, Metaphor, Personification, Apostrophe

HIPPOLYTA. 'Tis strange, my Theseus, that these lovers speak of.
THESEUS.   More strange than true. I never may believe
    These antique fables, nor these fairy toys.
    Lovers and madmen have such seething brains,
    Such shaping fantasies, that apprehend
    More than cool reason ever comprehends.
    The lunatic, the lover, and the poet
    Are of imagination all compact.
    One sees more devils than vast hell can hold,
    That is the madman. The lover, all as frantic,
    Sees Helen's beauty in a brow of Egypt.
    The poet's eye, in a fine frenzy rolling,
    Doth glance from heaven to earth, from earth to heaven;
    And as imagination bodies forth
    The forms of things unknown, the poet's pen
    Turns them to shapes, and gives to airy nothing
    A local habitation and a name.
               —Shakespeare, *A Midsummer Night's Dream,* 5.1-17

Theseus was neither the first nor the last to suggest that poets, like lunatics and lovers, freely employ their imaginations. Terms such as *poetic license* and *poetic justice* imply that poets are free to depict a never-never land. One has only to leaf through any anthology of poetry to encounter numerous statements that are, from a logical point of view, lunacies. Here are two quotations:

    Look like th' innocent flower,
    But be the serpent under 't.

                    —Shakespeare

    Each outcry from the hunted hare
    A fiber from the brain does tear.

                    —William Blake

The first of these is spoken by Lady Macbeth, when she urges her husband to murder King Duncan. How can a human being "Look like th' innocent flower," and how can a human being "be the serpent"? But Macbeth knows, and we know, exactly what she means. We see and we feel her point, in a way that we would not if she had said, "Put on an innocent-looking face, but in fact kill the king."

And in the quotation from Blake, when we read that the hunted hare's plaintive cry serves to "tear" a "fiber" from our brain, we almost wince, even though we know that the statement is literally untrue.

On a literal level, then, such assertions are nonsense (so, too, is Theseus's notion that reason is cool). But of course they are not to be taken literally; rather, they employ **figures of speech**—departures from logical usage that are aimed at gaining special effects. Consider the lunacies that Robert Burns heaps up here.

ROBERT BURNS

Robert Burns (1759-1796) was born in Ayrshire in southwestern Scotland. Many of his best poems and songs were written in the Scots dialect, though he also wrote English as the English spoke it.

A Red, Red Rose   [1796]

O, my luve is like a red, red rose,
   That's newly sprung in June.
O, my luve is like the melodie,
   That's sweetly played in tune.   4

As fair art thou, my bonnie lass,
   So deep in luve am I,
And I will luve thee still, my dear,
   Till a'° the seas gang° dry.   8

Till a' the seas gang dry, my dear,
   And the rocks melt wi' the sun!
And I will luve thee still, my dear,
   While the sands o' life shall run.   12

And fare thee weel, my only luve,
   And fare thee weel awhile!
And I will come again, my luve,
   Though it were ten thousand mile!   16

---

8 a' all. **gang** go.

To the charge that these lines are lunacies or untruths, at least two replies can be made. First, it might be said that the speaker is not really making assertions about a woman; he is saying he feels a certain way. His words, it can be argued, are not assertions about external reality but expressions of his state of mind, just as a tune one whistles asserts nothing about external reality but expresses the whistler's state of mind. In this view, the nonlogical language of poetry (like a groan of pain or an exclamation of joy) is an expression of emotion; its further aim, if it has one, is to induce in the hearer an emotion.

Second, and more to the point here, it can be said that nonlogical language does indeed make assertions about external reality, and even gives the reader an insight into this reality that logical language cannot. The opening comparison in Burns's poem ("my luve is like a red, red rose") brings before our eyes the lady's beauty in a way that the reasonable assertion "She is beautiful" does not. By comparing the woman to a rose, the poet invites us to see the woman through a special sort of lens: she is fragrant; her lips (and perhaps her cheeks) are like a rose in texture and color; she will not keep her beauty long. Also, "my love is like a red, red rose" says something different from "like a red, red beet," or "a red, red cabbage."

The poet, then, has not only communicated a state of mind but also discovered, through the lens of imagination, some things (both in the beloved and in the lover's own feelings) that interest us. The discovery is not world-shaking; it is less important than the discovery of America or the discovery that the meek are blessed, but it *is* a discovery and it leaves the reader with the feeling, "Yes, that's right. I hadn't quite thought of it that way, but that's right."

A poem, Robert Frost said, "assumes direction with the first line laid down, . . . runs a course of lucky events, and ends in a clarification of life—not necessarily a great clarification, such as sects and cults are founded on, but in a momentary stay against confusion." What is clarified? In another sentence Frost gives an answer: "For me the initial delight is in the surprise of remembering something I didn't know I knew." John Keats made a similar statement: "Poetry . . . should strike the Reader as a wording of his own highest thoughts, and appear almost a Remembrance."

Some figures of speech are, in effect, riddling ways of speech. To call fishermen "farmers of the sea"—a metaphor—is to give a sort of veiled description of fishermen, bringing out, when the term is properly understood, certain aspects of a fisherman's activities. And a riddle, after all, is a veiled description—though intentionally obscure or deceptive—calling attention to characteristics, especially similarities, not usually noticed. (*Riddle,* like *read,* is from Old English *redan,* "to guess," "to interpret," and thus its solution provides knowledge.) "Two sisters upstairs, often looking but never seeing each other" is (after the riddle is explained) a way of calling attention to the curious fact that the eye, the instrument of vision, never sees its mate.

SYLVIA PLATH

Sylvia Plath (1932–1963) was born in Boston, the daughter of German immigrants. While still an undergraduate at Smith College, she published in Seventeen *and* Mademoiselle; *but her years at college, like her later years, were marked by manic-depressive periods. After graduating from college, she went to England to study at Cambridge University, where she met the English poet Ted Hughes, whom she married in 1956. The marriage was unsuccessful, and they separated. One day she committed suicide by turning on the kitchen gas.*

Metaphors   [1960]

I'm a riddle in nine syllables,
An elephant, a ponderous house,
A melon strolling on two tendrils.

O red fruit, ivory, fine timbers!
This loaf's big with its yeasty rising.   5
Money's new-minted in this fat purse.
I'm a means, a stage, a cow in calf.
I've eaten a bag of green apples,
Boarded the train there's no getting off.

> **YOUR TURN**

The riddling speaker says that she is, among other things, "a ponderous house" and "a cow in calf." What is she?

Simile

In a **simile,** items from different classes are explicitly compared by a connective such as *like, as,* or *than* or by a verb such as *appears* or *seems.* (If the objects compared are from the same class—for example, "New York is like Chicago"—no simile is present.)

Sometimes I feel like a motherless child.

—Anonymous

It is a beauteous evening, calm and free.
The holy time is quiet as a Nun,
Breathless with adoration.

—Wordsworth

How sharper than a serpent's tooth it is
To have a thankless child.

—Shakespeare

Seems he a dove? His feathers are but borrowed.

—Shakespeare

Again, although the comparison is explicit (*like, as*) there is something uncanny in it, in a way that there is not in, say, "John's hair is like Jane's."

Metaphor

A **metaphor** asserts the identity, without a connective such as *like* or a verb such as *appears,* of terms that are literally incompatible.

She is the rose, the glory of the day.

—Spenser

O western orb sailing the heaven.

—Whitman

Notice how in the second example only one of the terms ("orb") is stated; the other ("ship") is implied in "sailing."

JOHN KEATS

For a biographical note, see page 559.

*On First Looking into Chapman's Homer**   [1816]

Much have I traveled in the realms of gold,
   And many goodly states and kingdoms seen;
   Round many western islands have I been
Which bards in fealty to Apollo° hold.
Oft of one wide expanse had I been told   5
   That deep-browed Homer ruled as his demesne;°
   Yet did I never breathe its pure serene°
Till I heard Chapman speak out loud and bold:
Then felt I like some watcher of the skies
   When a new planet swims into his ken;   10
Or like stout Cortez when with eagle eyes
   He stared at the Pacific—and all his men
Looked at each other with a wild surmise—
   Silent, upon a peak in Darien.

---

*George Chapman (1559–1634?), Shakespeare's contemporary, is chiefly known for his translations (from the Greek) of Homer's *Odyssey* and *Iliad.* In lines 11–14 Keats mistakenly says that Cortés was the first European to see the Pacific, from the heights of Darien, in Panama. In fact, Balboa was the first.   **4 Apollo** god of poetry.   **6 demesne** domain.
7 serene open space.

> **YOUR TURN**

1. In line 1, what do you think "realms of gold" stands for? Chapman lived during the late sixteenth and the early seventeenth centuries; how does this fact add relevance to the metaphor in the first line?
2. Does line 9 introduce a totally new idea, or can you somehow connect it to the opening metaphor?

Two types of metaphor deserve special mention. In **metonymy,** something is named that replaces something closely related to it; "City Hall," for example, sometimes is used to stand for municipal authority. In the following passage James Shirley names certain objects (scepter and crown; scythe and spade), using them to replace social classes (royalty; agricultural labor) to which they are related:

> Scepter and crown must tumble down
> And in the dust be equal made
> With the poor crooked scythe and spade.

In **synecdoche,** the whole is replaced by the part, or the part by the whole. For example, *bread* in "Give us this day our daily bread" replaces the whole class of edibles. Similarly, an automobile can be "wheels," and workers are "hands." Robert Frost was fond of calling himself "a Synecdochist" because he believed that it is the nature of poetry to "have intimations of something more than itself. It almost always comes under the head of synecdoche, a part, a hem of the garment for the whole garment."

Sometimes a poet will describe and explore the nature of a person, place, or thing through a metaphor, or, as in this poem, through a series of metaphors.

KAY RYAN

Kay Ryan, born in San Jose, California, in 1945, holds a bachelor's and a master's degree in English from the University of California, Los Angeles. She has published a number of books of poetry, and in 2009 she was appointed the sixteenth Poet Laureate Consultant in Poetry to the Library of Congress.

Turtle   [1994]

Who would be a turtle who could help it?
A barely mobile hard roll, a four-oared helmet,
She can ill afford the chances she must take
In rowing toward the grasses that she eats.
Her track is graceless, like dragging   5
A packing-case places, and almost any slope
Defeats her modest hopes. Even being practical,
She's often stuck up to the axle on her way
To something edible. With everything optimal,
She skirts the ditch which would convert   10
Her shell into a serving dish. She lives
Below luck-level, never imagining some lottery
Will change her load of pottery to wings.
Her only levity is patience,
The sport of truly chastened things.   15

Notice that Ryan begins with a question, and her poem might be understood as an answer, or set of answers, to this question, unfolding through witty, vivid, playful metaphors. The turtle is a "roll"—and a hard one at that. Then, it is a helmet, but a curious kind of helmet that also has four oars (the turtle's four feet), a metaphor that Ryan extends by saying that the turtle rows toward the grass that it eats. But then, in line 6, she depicts the turtle as a heavy packing case that is hard to move. And so on, to the ending—an ending that implies the way in which the turtle is itself a metaphor, suggesting the important lesson of patience for all of us.

Perhaps the turtle, then, for all of its limitations that Ryan illustrates through engaging metaphors, possesses a virtue that many of us do not. Turtles and human beings might (or could) have something in common after all—something we come to see and think about through the metaphors that Ryan presents in her poem.

Incidentally, although metaphor is essential to "Turtle," and metaphor is our chief topic here, we cannot resist pointing out that Ryan is also exploiting other aspects of the poet's craft, notably rhyme. Notice that some rhymes occur at the ends of lines—"wings" in 13 and "things" in 15—but some rhymes, or near-rhymes (also called "off-rhymes"), occur within lines: "oared" in line 2 and "afford" in line 3; "graceless" in 5, "packing-case places" in 6; "practical" in 7 and "axle" in 8; "slope" in 6, "hopes" in 7; "ditch" and "which" in 10; "lottery" in 12 and "pottery" in 13. The effect, we think, is to communicate something of the lumbering quality of this beast whose patience Ryan is celebrating largely through metaphors.

MARGE PIERCY

For a biographical note, see page 614.

A Work of Artifice   [1973]

The bonsai tree
in the attractive pot
could have grown eighty feet tall
on the side of a mountain
till split by lightning.   5
But a gardener
carefully pruned it.
It is nine inches high.
Every day as he
whittles back the branches   10
the gardener croons,
It is your nature
to be small and cozy,
domestic and weak;
how lucky, little tree,   15
to have a pot to grow in.
With living creatures
one must begin very early
to dwarf their growth:
the bound feet,   20
the crippled brain,
the hair in curlers,
the hands you
love to touch.

YOUR TURN

1. Piercy uses a bonsai tree as a metaphor—but a metaphor for what? (If
   you have never seen a bonsai tree, try to visit a florist or a nursery to
   take a close look at one. You can find a picture of a bonsai by looking
   online.)
2. The gardener "croons" (line 11) a song to the bonsai tree. If the tree
   could respond, what might it say?
3. Explain lines 17–24 to someone who doesn't get the point. In your response, explain how these lines are connected with "hair in curlers."
   Explain, too, what "the hands you / love to touch" has to do with the
   rest of the poem. What tone of voice do you hear in "the hands you /
   love to touch"?
4. How does the form of the poem suggest its subject?

Personification

The attribution of human feelings or characteristics to abstractions or to inanimate objects is called **personification.**

> But Time did beckon to the flowers, and they
> By noon most cunningly did steal away.
>
> —Herbert

Herbert attributes a human gesture to Time and shrewdness to flowers. Of all figures, personification most surely gives to airy nothings a local habitation and a name:

> There's Wrath who has learnt every trick of guerrilla warfare,
> The shamming dead, the night-raid, the feinted retreat.
>
> —Auden

> Hope, thou bold taster of delight.
>
> —Crashaw

> The alarm clock meddling in somebody's sleep.
>
> —Brooks

> . . . neon script leering from the shuddering asphalt.
>
> —Dove

In the next poem, the speaker, addressing a former mistress ("come let us kiss and part"), seems to grant that their love is over—is dying—and he personifies this love, this passion, as a person on his deathbed ("Now at last gasp of Love's latest breath"). Further, he surrounds the dying Love with two mourners, Faith, who is kneeling by Love's bed, and Innocence, who is closing Love's eyes. But notice that the poem takes a sudden twist at the end where, it seems, Love may not have to die.

MICHAEL DRAYTON

Michael Drayton (1563–1631) was born in Warwickshire in England a year before Shakespeare, and like Shakespeare he wrote sonnets. Among his other works is a long poem, Poly-Olbion *(1612/13, 1622), on the geography and local lore of England.*

Since There's No Help

[1619]

Since there's no help, come let us kiss and part;
Nay, I have done, you get no more of me,
And I am glad, yea glad with all my heart
That thus so cleanly I myself can free;
Shake hands for ever, cancel all our vows,   5
And when we meet at any time again,
Be it not seen in either of our brows
That we one jot of former love retain.
Now at the last gasp of Love's latest breath,
When, his pulse failing, Passion speechless lies,   10
When Faith is kneeling by his bed of death,
And Innocence is closing up his eyes,
    Now if thou wouldst, when all have given him over,
    From death to life you mightst him yet recover.

YOUR TURN

1. What do you think is the tone of lines 1–8? What words especially establish this tone? What do you think is the tone of lines 9–14?

2. Some readers find the personifications in lines 9–14 a sign that the speaker is not deeply moved, and perhaps is putting on an act. Do you agree or not? Please explain.

Apostrophe

Crashaw's personification, "Hope, thou bold taster of delight," quoted a moment ago, is also an example of the figure of speech called **apostrophe,** an address to a person or thing not literally listening. Wordsworth begins a sonnet by apostrophizing John Milton:

> Milton, thou shouldst be living at this hour,

And Shelley begins an ode by apostrophizing a skylark:

> Hail to thee, blithe Spirit!

The following poem is largely built on apostrophe.

EDMUND WALLER

Edmund Waller (1606–1687), born into a wealthy country family in Buckinghamshire in England, attended Eton and Cambridge before spending most of his life as a member of Parliament. When the Puritans came to power, he was imprisoned and eventually banished to France, although he was soon allowed to return to England. When the monarchy was restored to the throne, he returned to Parliament.

Esteemed for his poetry and wit, Waller circulated many of his poems in manuscript before eventually publishing them in books. John Dryden, Alexander Pope, and other writers greatly admired Waller, especially for his skillful use of the heroic couplet (pairs of rhyming lines of iambic pentameter).

Song   [1645]

Go, lovely rose,
Tell her that wastes her time and me,
  That now she knows,
When I resemble her to thee,
  How sweet and fair she seems to be.   5

  Tell her that's young,
And shuns to have her graces spied,
  That hadst thou sprung
In deserts where no men abide,
  Thou must have uncommended died.   10

  Small is the worth
Of beauty from the light retired:
  Bid her come forth,
Suffer her self to be desired,
  And not blush so to be admired.   15

Then die, that she
The common fate of all things rare
    May read in thee,
How small a part of time they share,
    That are so wondrous sweet and fair.   20

What conclusions, then, can we draw about **figurative language?** First, such language, with its literally incompatible terms, forces the reader to attend to the **connotations** (suggestions, associations) rather than to the **denotations** (dictionary definitions) of a term.

Second, although figurative language is said to differ from ordinary discourse, it is found in ordinary discourse as well as in literature. "It rained cats and dogs," "War is hell," "Don't be a pig," and other tired figures are part of our daily utterances. But through repeated use, these (and most of the figures we use) have lost whatever impact they once had and are only a shade removed from expressions that, though once figurative, have become literal: the *eye* of a needle, a *branch* office, the *face* of a clock.

Third, good figurative language is usually

1. concrete,
2. condensed, and
3. interesting.

The concreteness lends precision and vividness; when Keats writes that he felt

like some watcher of the skies / When a new planet swims into his ken,

he more sharply characterizes his feelings than if he had said, "I felt excited." His simile isolates for us a precise kind of excitement, and the metaphoric "swims" vividly brings up the oceanic aspect of the sky. The second of these three qualities, condensation, can be seen by attempting to paraphrase some of the figures. A paraphrase or rewording will commonly use more words than the original and will have less impact—as the gradual coming of night usually has less impact on us than a sudden darkening of the sky, or as a prolonged push has less impact than a sudden blow. The third quality, interest, largely depends on the previous two: the successful figure often makes us open our eyes wider and take notice. Keats's "deep-browed Homer" arouses our interest in Homer as "thoughtful Homer" or "meditative Homer" does not. Similarly, when W. B. Yeats says (page 834):

An aged man is but a paltry thing,
A tattered coat upon a stick, unless
Soul clap its hands and sing, and louder sing
For every tatter in its mortal dress,

the metaphoric identification of an old man with a scarecrow jolts us out of all our usual unthinking attitudes about old men as kind, happy folk content to have passed from youth to senior citizenship.

Finally, the point must be made that although figurative language is one of the poet's chief tools, a poem does not have to contain figures. Here is a poem by William Carlos Williams. Does it contain any figures of speech?

WILLIAM CARLOS WILLIAMS

William Carlos Williams (1883-1963) was the son of an English traveling salesman and a Basque-Jewish woman. The couple met in Puerto Rico and settled in Rutherford, New Jersey, where Williams was born. He spent his life there, practicing as a pediatrician and writing poems in the moments between seeing patients who were visiting his office.

The Red Wheelbarrow [1923]

so much depends
upon

a red wheel
barrow

glazed with rain   5
water

beside the white
chickens

The poems that follow rely heavily on figures of speech.

ALFRED, LORD TENNYSON

Alfred, Lord Tennyson (1809-1892), the son of an English clergyman, was born in Lincolnshire, where he began writing verse at age five. Educated at Cambridge, he had to leave without a degree when his father died and Alfred had to accept responsibility for bringing up his brothers and sisters. In fact, the family had inherited ample funds, but for some years the money was tied up by litigation. In 1850 following Wordsworth's death, Tennyson was made poet laureate. With his government pension he moved with his family to the Isle of Wight, where he lived in comfort until his death.

The Eagle [1851]

A Fragment

He clasps the crag with crooked hands;
Close to the sun in lonely lands,
Ringed with the azure world, he stands.

The wrinkled sea beneath him crawls:
He watches from his mountain walls,   5
And like a thunderbolt he falls.

YOUR TURN

1. What figure is used in line 1? In line 4? In line 6? Can it be argued that the figures give us a sense of the eagle that is not to be found in a literal description?

2. In line 2 we get overstatement, or hyperbole, for the eagle is not really close to the sun. Suppose instead of "Close to the sun" Tennyson had written "Waiting on high"? Do you think the poem would be improved or worsened?

SEAMUS HEANEY

Seamus Heaney was born in Belfast, Northern Ireland, in 1939. He grew up on a farm, and then went to Queens University in Belfast. "Digging," the first poem in his first book, reveals his concern with getting to the bottom of things. Heaney, who now lives in Dublin, has lectured widely in Ireland, England, and the United States. In addition to writing poetry, he has written essays about poetry, many of which are collected in Finders Keepers: Selected Prose 1971–2001 *(2002). In 1995 he was awarded the Nobel Prize in Literature.*

Digging
[1966]

Between my finger and my thumb
The squat pen rests; snug as a gun.

Under my window, a clean rasping sound
When the spade sinks into gravelly ground:
My father, digging, I look down   5

Till his straining rump among the flowerbeds
Bends low, comes up twenty years away
Stooping in rhythm through potato drills
Where he was digging.

The coarse boot nestled on the lug, the shaft   10
Against the inside knee was levered firmly.
He rooted out tall tops, buried the bright edge deep
To scatter new potatoes that we picked
Loving their cool hardness in our hands.

By God, the old man could handle a spade.   15
Just like his old man.

My grandfather cut more turf in a day
Than any other man on Toner's bog.
Once I carried him milk in a bottle
Corked sloppily with paper. He straightened up   20
To drink it, then fell to right away
Nicking and slicing neatly, heaving sods
Over his shoulder, going down and down
For the good turf. Digging.

The cold smell of potato mould, the squelch and slap   25
Of soggy peat, the curt cuts of an edge
Through living roots awaken in my head.
But I've no spade to follow men like them.

Between my finger and my thumb
The squat pen rests.   30
I'll dig with it.

> **YOUR TURN**
>
> 1. The poem ends with the speaker saying that he will "dig" with his pen. Given all the preceding lines, what will he dig?
> 2. The first lines compare the pen with a gun. What implications are suggested by this comparison?

LINDA PASTAN

For a biographical note, see page 589.

Baseball   [1995]

When you tried to tell me
baseball was a metaphor

for life: the long, dusty travail
around the bases, for instance,

to try to go home again;   5
the Sacrifice for which you win

approval but not applause;
the way the light closes down

in the last days of the season—
I didn't believe you.   10

It's just a way of passing
the time, I said.

And you said: that's it.
Yes.

> **YOUR TURN**
>
> 1. What does it mean to say that baseball is "a metaphor for life"? Does the speaker agree? She seems not to at first, but perhaps by the end she changes her mind. Or is that a misreading of the poem?
> 2. Take a step back: What is the story that this poem is telling? How does it begin? What takes place in the middle? How does it conclude?
> 3. Do you understand this poem? How would you explain its meaning to someone who found it perplexing?
> 4. Why is the word "Sacrifice" capitalized?
> 5. "Baseball" consists of seven short two-line stanzas. Why did Pastan structure it this way? Would her poem have been more effective if she had presented it as a single stanza?

WILLIAM SHAKESPEARE

You will encounter Shakespeare (1564–1616) several times in this book—for instance, as the author of songs (Chapter 18), sonnets (Chapter 23), a tragedy (Chapter 30), and a comedy (Chapter 31).

Here we give one of his sonnets (probably written in the mid-1590s), in which he playfully rejects similes and other figures of speech. His contemporaries often compared a woman's hair to fine-spun gold, her lips to coral or to cherries, her cheeks to roses, her white breast to snow; when such a woman walked, she seemed to walk on air (the grass did not bend beneath her), and when she spoke, her voice was music. Shakespeare himself uses such figures in some of his poems and plays, but in this sonnet he praises his beloved by saying she does not need such figures.

Sonnet 130

My mistress' eyes are nothing like the sun;
Coral is far more red than her lips' red;
If snow be white, why then her breasts are dun;
If hairs be wires, black wires grow on her head.
I have seen roses damasked, red and white,   5
But no such roses see I in her cheeks;
And in some perfumes is there more delight
Than in the breath that from my mistress reeks.
I love to hear her speak, yet well I know
That music hath a far more pleasing sound;   10
I grant I never saw a goddess go;°
My mistress, when she walks, treads on the ground.
   And yet, by heaven, I think my love as rare°
   As any she belied° with false compare.

---

11 **go** walk.   13 **rare** exceptional.   14 **any she belied** any woman misrepresented.

Imagery and Symbolism

When we read the word "rose"—or, for that matter, "finger" or "thumb"—we may more or less call to mind a picture, an image. The term **imagery** is used to refer to whatever in a poem appeals to any of our sensations, including sensations of pressure and heat as well as of sight, smell, taste, touch, and sound.

Consider the opening lines of Seamus Heaney's "Digging" (page 629):

Between my finger and my thumb
The squat pen rests; snug as a gun.

We may in our mind's eye see a finger, thumb, and pen; and perhaps, stimulated by "squat," we may almost feel the pen. Notice, too, that in Heaney's line the pen is compared to a gun, so there is yet another image in the line. In short, images are the sensory content of the work, whether literal (the finger, thumb, and pen) or figurative (the gun, to which the pen is compared). Edmund Waller's rose in "Go, lovely rose" (page 626) is an image that happens to be compared in the first stanza to a woman ("I resemble her to thee"); later in the poem this image comes to stand for "all things rare." Yet we never forget that the rose is a rose, and that the poem is chiefly a revelation of the poet's attitude toward his beloved.

If a poet says "my rose" and is speaking about a rose, we have an image, even though we do not have a figure of speech. If a poet says "my rose" and, we gather, is speaking not really or chiefly about a rose but about something else—let's say the transience of beauty—we can say that the poet is using the rose as a symbol.

Some symbols are **natural symbols,** recognized as standing for something in particular even by people from different cultures. Rain, for instance, usually stands for fertility or the renewal of life. A forest often stands for mental darkness or chaos, a mountain for stability, a valley for a place of security, and so on. There are many exceptions, but by and large these meanings prevail.

Other symbols, however, are **conventional symbols,** which people have agreed to accept as standing for something other than themselves: A poem about the cross would probably be about Christianity. Similarly, the rose has long been a symbol for love. In Virginia Woolf's novel *Mrs. Dalloway* (1925), the husband communicates his love by proffering this conventional symbol: "He was holding out flowers—roses, red and white roses. (But he could not bring himself to say he loved her; not in so many words.)" Objects that are not conventional symbols, however, also may give rise to rich, multiple, indefinable associations. The following poem uses the symbol of the rose, but uses it in a nontraditional way.

WILLIAM BLAKE

A biography of Blake, followed by five additional poems, appears on page 784.

The Sick Rose
[1794]

O rose, thou are sick!
The invisible worm
That flies in the night
In the howling storm   4

Has found out thy bed
Of crimson joy,
And his dark secret love
Does thy life destroy.   8

One might argue that the worm is "invisible" (line 2) merely because it is hidden within the rose, but an "invisible worm / That flies in the night" is more than a long, slender, soft-bodied creeping animal; and a rose that has, or is, a "bed/ Of crimson joy" is more than a gardener's rose.

Blake's worm and rose suggest things beyond themselves—a stranger, more vibrant world than the world we are usually aware of. Many readers find themselves half-thinking, for example, that the worm is male, the rose female, and that the poem is about the violation of virginity. Or that the poem is about the destruction of beauty: woman's beauty, rooted in joy, is destroyed by a power that feeds on her. But these interpretations are not fully satisfying: the poem presents a worm and a rose, and yet it is not merely about a worm and a rose. These objects resonate, stimulating our thoughts toward something else, but the something else is elusive, whereas it is not elusive in Burns's "A Red, Red Rose" (page 619).

A **symbol,** then, is an image so loaded with significance that it is not simply literal, and it does not simply stand for something else; it is both itself *and* something else that it richly suggests, a manifestation of something too complex or too elusive to be otherwise revealed. Blake's poem is about a blighted rose and at the same time about much more. In a symbol, as Thomas Carlyle wrote in *Sartor Resartus* (1836), "the Infinite is made to blend with the Finite, to stand visible, and as it were, attainable there." Probably it is not fanciful to say that the American slaves who sang "Joshua fought the battle of Jericho, / And the walls came tumbling down" were singing both about an ancient occurrence *and* about a new embodiment of the ancient, the imminent collapse of slavery in the nineteenth century. Not one or the other, but both: the present partook of the past, and the past partook of the present.

WALT WHITMAN

Walt Whitman (1819-1892) was born in a farmhouse in rural Long Island, New York, but was brought up in Brooklyn, then an independent city in New York. He attended public school for a few years (1825-1830), apprenticed as a printer in the 1830s, and then worked as a typesetter, journalist, and newspaper editor. In 1855 he published the first edition of a collection of his poems,

II

I saw in Louisiana a
live-oak growing,
All alone stood it, and the
moss hung down from the
branches,
Without any companion it grew
there, glistening out with
joyous leaves of dark green,
And its look, rude, unbending,
lusty, made me think of
myself;
But I wondered how it could
utter joyous leaves, standing
alone there without its friend,
its lover — For I knew I could
not;
And I plucked a twig with
a certain number of leaves
upon it, and twined around
it a little moss, and brought
it away — And I have placed
it in sight in my room,

2

Walt Whitman, "I Saw in Louisiana a Live-Oak Growing," manuscript of 1860. On the first leaf, in line 3 Whitman deleted "with." On the second leaf (see page 635), in the third line (line 8 of the printed text) he added, with a caret, "lately." In the sixth line on this leaf he deleted "I write these pieces, and name them after it," replacing the deletion with "it makes me think of manly love." In the next line he deleted "tree" and inserted "live oak." When he reprinted the poem in the 1867 version of *Leaves of Grass*, he made further changes, as you will see if you compare the printed text with this manuscript version. (Manuscript of Walt Whitman's "I Saw in Louisiana a Live-Oak Growing" in *Leaves of Grass*, MSS 3829, Clifton Waller Barrett Library of American Literature, Special Collections, University of Virginia Library. Used by permission.)

It is not needed to remind
me as of my friends, (for I
believe *lately* think of little
else than of them,)
Yet it remains to me a
curious token — it *makes*
~~me~~ *me thik of many love,*
~~those faces and name
them after it~~ ;
For all that, and though the
live oak
~~tree~~ glistens there in Louisiana, solitary in a wide
flat space, uttering joyous
leaves all its life, without
a friend, a lover, near — I
know very well I could
not.

Whitman's manuscript, *continued*.

Leaves of Grass, *a book that he revised and published in one edition after another throughout the remainder of his life. During the Civil War, he served as a
volunteer nurse for the Union army.*

In the third edition of *Leaves of Grass* (1860), Whitman added two groups
of poems, one called "Children of Adam" and the other (named for an aromatic
grass that grows near ponds and swamps) called "Calamus." "Children of Adam"
celebrates heterosexual relations, whereas "Calamus" celebrates what Whitman
called "manly love." Although many of the "Calamus" poems seem clearly homosexual, perhaps the very fact that Whitman published them made them seem relatively innocent; in any case, those nineteenth-century critics who condemned
Whitman for the sexuality of his writing concentrated on the poems in "Children
of Adam."

"I Saw in Louisiana" is from the "Calamus" section. It was originally published
in the third edition of *Leaves of Grass* and was revised into its final form in the
1867 edition. The poem on page 636 is from the 1867 version. We also include
here the manuscript, showing it in its earliest extant version.

I Saw in Louisiana a Live-Oak Growing   [1867]

I saw in Louisiana a live-oak growing,
All alone stood it and the moss hung down from the branches,
Without any companion it grew there uttering joyous leaves
    of dark green,
And its look, rude, unbending, lusty, made me think of myself,
But I wonder'd how it could utter joyous leaves standing alone there
    without its friend near, for I knew I could not,   5
And I broke off a twig with a certain number of leaves upon it,
    and twined around it a little moss,
And brought it away, and I have placed it in sight in my room,
It is not needed to remind me as of my own dear friends,
(For I believe lately I think of little else than of them,)
Yet it remains to me a curious token, it makes me think of manly love;   10
For all that, and though the live-oak glistens there in Louisiana solitary
    in a wide flat space,
Uttering joyous leaves all its life without a friend a lover near,
I know very well I could not.

YOUR TURN

Compare the final version (1867) of the poem with the manuscript version
of 1860. Which version do you prefer? Why?

SAMUEL TAYLOR COLERIDGE

*Samuel Taylor Coleridge (1772–1834) was born in Devonshire in England, the
son of a clergyman. He attended Christ's Hospital school in London and Cambridge University, which he left without receiving a degree. With his friend
William Wordsworth he published anonymously in 1798 a volume of poetry,*
Lyrical Ballads, *which became the manifesto of the Romantic movement.*

Kubla Khan   [1798]

Or, A Vision in a Dream. A Fragment.

In Xanadu did Kubla Khan
A stately pleasure-dome decree:
Where Alph, the sacred river, ran
Through caverns measureless to man
    Down to a sunless sea.   5
So twice five miles of fertile ground
With walls and towers were girdled round:
And here were gardens bright with sinuous rills,
Where blossomed many an incense-bearing tree;
And here were forests ancient as the hills,   10
Enfolding sunny spots of greenery.

But oh! that deep romantic chasm which slanted
Down the green hill athwart a cedarn cover!

A savage place! as holy and enchanted
As e'er beneath a waning moon was haunted   15
By woman wailing for her demon-lover!
And from this chasm, with ceaseless turmoil seething,
As if this earth in fast thick pants were breathing
A mighty fountain momently was forced;
Amid whose swift half-intermitted burst   20
Huge fragments vaulted like rebounding hail,
Or chaffy grain beneath the thresher's flail:
And 'mid these dancing rocks at once and ever
It flung up momently the sacred river.
Five miles meandering with a mazy motion   25
Through wood and dale the sacred river ran,
Then reached the caverns measureless to man,
And sank in tumult to a lifeless ocean:
And 'mid this tumult Kubla heard from far
Ancestral voices prophesying war!   30
   The shadow of the dome of pleasure
   Floated midway on the waves;
   Where was heard the mingled measure
   From the fountain and the caves.
It was a miracle of rare device,   35
A sunny pleasure-dome with caves of ice!

   A damsel with a dulcimer
   In a vision once I saw:
   It was an Abyssinian° maid,
   And on her dulcimer she played,   40
   Singing of Mount Abora.
   Could I revive within me
   Her symphony and song,
   To such a deep delight 'twould win me,
That with music loud and long,   45
I would build that dome in air,
That sunny dome! those caves of ice!
And all who heard should see them there,
And all should cry, Beware! Beware!
His flashing eyes, his floating hair!   50
Weave a circle round him thrice,
And close your eyes with holy dread,
For he on honey-dew hath fed,
And drunk the milk of Paradise.

When Coleridge published "Kubla Khan" in 1816, he prefaced it with this explanatory note:

The following fragment is here published at the request of a poet of
great and deserved celebrity, and, as far as the author's own opinions are
concerned, rather as a psychological curiosity, than on the ground of
any supposed *poetic* merits.

---

39 Abyssinian Abyssinia was the Ethiopian Empire, in East Africa.

In the summer of the year 1797, the author, then in ill health, had retired to a lonely farmhouse between Porlock and Linton, on the Exmoor confines of Somerset and Devonshire. In consequence of a slight indisposition, an anodyne had been prescribed, from the effects of which he fell asleep in his chair at the moment that he was reading the following sentence, or words of the same substance, in *Purchas' Pilgrimage*: "Here the Khan Kubla commanded a palace to be built, and a stately garden thereunto. And thus ten miles of fertile ground were inclosed with a wall." The author continued for about three hours in a profound sleep, at least of the external senses, during which time he has the most vivid confidence that he could not have composed less than from two to three hundred lines; if that indeed can be called composition in which all the images rose up before him as *things*, with a parallel production of the correspondent expressions, without any sensation or consciousness of effort. On awaking he appeared to himself to have a distinct recollection of the whole, and taking his pen, ink, and paper, instantly and eagerly wrote down the lines that are here preserved. At this moment he was unfortunately called out by a person on business from Porlock, and detained by him above an hour, and on his return to his room, found, to his no small surprise and mortification, that though he still retained some vague and dim recollection of the general purport of the vision, yet, with the exception of some eight or ten scattered lines and images, all the rest had passed away like the images on the surface of a stream into which a stone has been cast, but, alas! without the after restoration of the latter!

> Then all the charm
> Is broken—all that phantom world so fair
> Vanishes, and a thousand circlets spread,
> And each misshape[s] the other. Stay awhile,
> Poor youth! who scarcely dar'st lift up thine eyes—
> The stream will soon renew its smoothness, soon
> The visions will return! And lo, he stays,
> And soon the fragments dim of lovely forms
> Come trembling back, unite, and now once more
> The pool becomes a mirror.
>   —Coleridge, *The Picture; or, the Lover's Resolution,* lines 91–100

Yet from the still surviving recollections in his mind, the author has frequently purposed to finish for himself what had been originally, as it were, given to him. Σαμερου αδιου ασω [today I shall sing more sweetly]: "But the tomorrow is yet to come."

YOUR TURN

1. Coleridge changed the "palace" of his source into a "dome" (line 2). What do you think are the relevant associations of "dome"?
2. What pairs of contrasts (e.g., underground river, fountain) do you find? What do you think they contribute to the poem?
3. If Coleridge had not said that the poem is a fragment, might you take it as a complete poem, the first thirty-six lines describing the creative imagination, and the remainder lamenting the loss of poetic power?

EMMA LAZARUS

Emma Lazarus (1849–1887) was of German-Jewish descent on her mother's side, and of Sephardic descent on her father's side. (Sephardic Jews trace their ancestry back to Spain under Moslem rule, before the Jews were expelled by the Christians in 1492.)

In 1883 a committee was formed to raise funds for a pedestal for the largest statue in the world, Liberty Enlightening the People, *to be installed on a small island in New York Harbor. Authors were asked to donate manuscripts which then were auctioned to raise money. Emma Lazarus, keenly aware of ancient persecutions and of contemporary Jewish refugees fleeing Russian persecutions, contributed the following poem. It was read when the statue was unveiled in 1886, and the words of Liberty, spoken in the last five lines, were embossed on a plaque inside the pedestal.*

For the ancients, a colossus was a statue larger than life. "The brazen giant of Greek fame," mentioned in Lazarus's first line, was a statue of the sun god, erected in the harbor of the Greek island of Rhodes, celebrating the island's success in resisting the Macedonians in 305–304 BCE. More than 100 feet tall, it stood in the harbor until it toppled during an earthquake in 225 BCE. In later years its size became mythical; it was said to have straddled the harbor (Lazarus speaks of "limbs astride from land to land"), so that ships supposedly entered the harbor by sailing between its legs.

In Lazarus's poem, the "imprisoned lightning" (line 5) in the torch is electricity. The harbor is said to be "air-bridged" because in 1883, the year of the poem, the Brooklyn Bridge was completed, connecting Brooklyn with New York. (These are the "twin cities" of the poem.)

The New Colossus   [1883]

Not like the brazen giant of Greek fame,
With conquering limbs astride from land to land;
Here at our sea-washed, sunset gates shall stand
A mighty woman with a torch, whose flame
Is the imprisoned lightning, and her name   5
Mother of Exiles. From her beacon-hand
Glows world-wide welcome; her mild eyes command
The air-bridged harbor that twin cities frame.
"Keep, ancient lands, your storied pomp!" cries she
With silent lips. "Give me your tired, your poor,   10
Your huddled masses yearning to breathe free,
The wretched refuse of your teeming shore.
Send these, the homeless, tempest-tost to me,
I lift my lamp beside the golden door!"

YOUR TURN

Why should a woman be a symbol of liberty? and why should she hold a torch? Why "golden door"?

NILA NORTHSUN

Nila northSun was born in 1951 in Schurz, Nevada, of Shoshone-Chippewa stock. She studied at the California State University campuses at Hayward and Humboldt and the University of Montana at Missoula, beginning as a psychology major but switching to art history, specializing in American Indian art. She is a photographer, a teacher, and the author of a number of books of poetry.

Moving Camp Too Far   [1977]

i can't speak of
   many moons
   moving camp on travois°
i can't tell of
   the last great battle   5
   counting coup° or
   taking scalp
i don't know what it
   was to hunt buffalo
   or do the ghost dance   10

---

3 travois a frame slung between trailing poles that are pulled by a horse. Plains Indians used the device to transport their goods.   **6 counting coup** recounting one's exploits in battle

Blackfoot travois. (Photograph by Edward S. Curtis. Vol. 18, No. 637, *The North American Indian*. Courtesy of Laboratory of Anthropology/Museum of Indian Arts & Culture)

but
i can see an eagle
    almost extinct
    on slurpee plastic cups
i can travel to powwows   15
    in campers & winnebagos
i can eat buffalo meat
    at the tourist burger stand
i can dance to indian music
    rock-n-roll hey-a-hey-o   20
i can
    & unfortunately
    i do

ADRIENNE RICH

Adrienne Rich's most recent books of poetry are Telephone Ringing in the Labyrinth: Poems 2004–2006 *and* The School Among the Ruins: 2000–2004. *A selection of her essays,* Arts of the Possible: Essays and Conversations, *appeared in 2003. She edited Muriel Rukeyser's* Selected Poems *for the Library of America.* A Human Eye: Essays on Art in Society, *appeared in April 2009. She is a recipient of the National Book Foundation's 2006 Medal for Distinguished Contribution to American Letters, among other honors. She lives in California.*

Aunt Jennifer's Tigers   [1951]

Aunt Jennifer's tigers prance across a screen,
Bright topaz denizens of a world of green.
They do not fear the men beneath the tree;
They pace in sleek chivalric certainty.   4

Aunt Jennifer's fingers fluttering through her wool
Find even the ivory needle hard to pull.
The massive weight of Uncle's wedding band
Sits heavily upon Aunt Jennifer's hand.   8

When Aunt is dead, her terrified hands will lie
Still ringed with ordeals she was mastered by.
The tigers in the panel that she made
Will go on prancing, proud and unafraid.   12

Diving into the Wreck   [1973]

First having read the book of myths,
and loaded the camera,
and checked the edge of the knife-blade,
I put on
the body-armor of black rubber   5

the absurd flippers
the grave and awkward mask.
I am having to do this
not like Cousteau° with his
assiduous team   10
aboard the sun-flooded schooner
but here alone.

There is a ladder.
The ladder is always there
hanging innocently   15
close to the side of the schooner.
We know what it is for,
we who have used it.
Otherwise
it's a piece of maritime floss   20
some sundry equipment.

I go down.
Rung after rung and still
the oxygen immerses me
the blue light   25
the clear atoms
of our human air.
I go down.
My flippers cripple me,
I crawl like an insect down the ladder   30
and there is no one
to tell me when the ocean
will begin.

First the air is blue and then
it is bluer and then green and then   35
black I am blacking out and yet
my mask is powerful
it pumps my blood with power
the sea is another story
the sea is not a question of power   40
I have to learn alone
to turn my body without force
in the deep element.

And now: it is easy to forget
what I came for   45
among so many who have always
lived here
swaying their crenellated fans
between the reefs
and besides   50
you breathe differently down here.

---

9 **Cousteau** Jacques Cousteau (1910–1997), French underwater explorer.

* * *

I came to explore the wreck.
The words are purposes.
The words are maps.
I came to see the damage that was done   55
and the treasures that prevail.
I stroke the beam of my lamp
slowly along the flank
of something more permanent
than fish or weed   60

the thing I came for:
the wreck and not the story of the wreck
the thing itself and not the myth
the drowned face always staring
toward the sun   65
the evidence of damage
worn by salt and sway into this threadbare beauty
the ribs of the disaster
curving their assertion
among the tentative haunters.   70

This is the place.
And I am here, the mermaid whose dark hair
streams black, the merman in his armored body
We circle silently
about the wreck   75
we dive into the hold.
I am she: I am he

whose drowned face sleeps with open eyes
whose breasts still bear the stress
whose silver, copper, vermeil cargo lies   80
obscurely inside barrels
half-wedged and left to rot
we are the half-destroyed instruments
that once held to a course
the water-eaten log   85
the fouled compass

We are, I am, you are
by cowardice or courage
the one who find our way
back to this scene   90
carrying a knife, a camera
a book of myths
in which
our names do not appear.

CHRISTINA ROSSETTI

*Christina Rossetti (1830–1894) was the daughter of an exiled Italian patriot
who lived in London and the sister of the poet and painter Dante Gabriel
Rossetti. After her father became an invalid, she led an extremely ascetic life,*

devoting most of her life to doing charitable work. Her first and best-known volume of poetry, Goblin Market and Other Poems, *was published in 1862.*

Uphill   [1858]

Does the road wind uphill all the way?
  Yes, to the very end.
Will the day's journey take the whole long day?
  From morn to night, my friend.   4

But is there for the night a resting-place?
  A roof for when the slow dark hours begin.
May not the darkness hide it from my face?
  You cannot miss that inn.   8

Shall I meet other wayfarers at night?
  Those who have gone before.
Then must I knock, or call when just in sight?
  They will not keep you standing at that door.   12

Shall I find comfort, travel-sore and weak?
  Of labor you shall find the sum.
Will there be beds for me and all who seek?
  Yea, beds for all who come.   16

YOUR TURN

1. Suppose that someone told you this poem is about a person preparing to go on a hike. The person is supposedly making inquiries about the road and the possible hotel arrangements. What would you reply?
2. Who is the questioner? A woman? A man? All human beings collectively? "Uphill" does not use quotation marks to distinguish between two speakers. Can one say that in "Uphill" the questioner and the answerer are the same person?
3. Are the answers unambiguously comforting? Or can it, for instance, be argued that the "roof" is (perhaps among other things) the lid of a coffin—hence the questioner will certainly not be kept "standing at that door"? If the poem can be read along these lines, is it chilling rather than comforting?

WALLACE STEVENS

Wallace Stevens (1879-1955), educated at Harvard and at New York Law School, earned his living as a lawyer and an insurance executive; at his death he was a vice president of the Hartford Accident and Indemnity Company. While pursuing this career, however, he also achieved distinction as a poet, and today he is widely regarded as among the most important American poets of the twentieth century.

The Emperor of Ice-Cream   [1923]

Call the roller of big cigars,
The muscular one, and bid him whip

In kitchen cups concupiscent curds.
Let the wenches dawdle in such dress
As they are used to wear, and let the boys   5
Bring flowers in last month's newspapers.
Let be be finale of seem.
The only emperor is the emperor of ice-cream.

Take from the dresser of deal,°
Lacking the three glass knobs, that sheet   10
On which she embroidered fantails once
And spread it so as to cover her face.
If her horny feet protrude, they come
To show how cold she is, and dumb.
Let the lamp affix its beam.   15
The only emperor is the emperor of ice-cream.

---

9 **deal** fir or pine wood.

YOUR TURN

What associations does the word "emperor" have for you? The word "ice-cream"? What, then, do you make of "the emperor of ice-cream"? The poem describes the preparations for a wake, and in line 15 ("Let the lamp affix its beam") it insists on facing the reality of death. In this context, then, what do you make of the last line of each stanza?

EDGAR ALLAN POE

For a biographical note, see page 509.

*To Helen**   [1831–1843]

Helen, thy beauty is to me
  Like those Nicean° barks of yore,
That gently, o'er a perfumed sea,
  The weary, way-worn wanderer bore
    To his own native shore.   5

On desperate seas long wont to roam,
  Thy hyacinth hair,° thy classic face
Thy Naiad° airs have brought me home
  To the glory that was Greece
And the grandeur that was Rome.   10

*****Helen** Helen of Troy, considered the most beautiful woman of ancient times.   **2 Nicean** perhaps referring to Nicea, an ancient city associated with the god Dionysus, or perhaps meaning "victorious," from Nike, Greek goddess of Victory.   **7 hyacinth hair** naturally curling hair, like that of Hyacinthus, beautiful Greek youth beloved by Apollo.   **8 Naiad** a nymph associated with lakes and streams.

Lo! in yon brilliant window-niche
    How statue-like I see thee stand,
    The agate lamp within thy hand!
Ah, Psyche,° from the regions which
    Are Holy-Land!°   15

---

14 Psyche Greek for "soul."   **15 Holy-Land** ancient Rome or Athens, i.e., a sacred realm
of art.

> **YOUR TURN**

1. In the first stanza, to what is Helen's beauty compared? To whom does
   the speaker apparently compare himself? What does "way-worn" in
   line 4 suggest to you? To what in the speaker's experience might the
   "native shore" in line 5 correspond?
2. What do you take "desperate seas" to mean in line 6, and who has
   been traveling them? To what are they contrasted in line 8? How does
   "home" seem to be defined in this stanza (stanza 2)?
3. What further light is shed on the speaker's home or destination in
   stanza 3?
4. Do you think that "To Helen" can be a love poem and also a poem
   about spiritual beauty or about the love of art? Why or why not?

A Note on Haiku

One form of poetry that puts a great emphasis on sharp images is the **haiku,** a
Japanese poem of seventeen syllables, arranged in three lines of five, seven, and
five syllables. Japanese poetry is unrhymed, but English versions sometimes
rhyme the first and third lines. The subject matter can be high or low—the
Milky Way or the screech of automobile brakes—but usually it is connected
with the seasons, and it is described objectively and sharply. Most haiku set
forth a sense of *where, what,* and *when*—but the when may be implicit, as in
the first haiku.

MORITAKE (1452–1540)

Fallen petals rise

Translated by Harold G. Henderson

Fallen petals rise
back to the branch—I watch
oh . . . butterflies!

Concentrating his attention on the phenomenon (butterflies moving upward),
the poet nevertheless conveys an emotion through the images (wonder, and then
the recognition of the familiar), stirring the reader's imagination to supply the
emotion that completes the experience.

SÔKAN (1465–1553)

If only we could

Translated by Kenneth Yasuda

If only we could
Add a handle to the moon
It would make a good fan.

SHIKI (1867–1902)

River in summer

River in summer
there is a bridge, but my horse
walks through the water.

Writing a Haiku

Although the haiku originated in Japan, it is now written throughout the world.

To start writing your own haiku, you may want to take some ordinary experience—tying your shoelaces, seeing a cat at the foot of the stairs, glancing out of a window and seeing unexpected snowflakes, hearing the alarm clock—and present it interestingly. One way to make it interesting is to construct the poem in two parts—the first line balanced against the next two lines, or the first two lines balanced against the last line. If you construct a poem on this principle, the two sections should be related to each other, but they should also in some degree make a contrast with each other. For instance, in the following poem by Taigi, there is a contrast between pleasant sociability (the first two lines) and loneliness (the last line).

TAIGI (1723–1776)

Look, O look, there go

Translated by Kenneth Yasuda

"Look, O look, there go
Fireflies," I would like to say—
But I am alone.

Basho said, "He who creates three to five haiku during a lifetime is a haiku poet. He who attains to ten is a master."

Cyber-Haiku

It has come to our attention that students have enjoyed composing haiku as substitutes for Microsoft's error messages. Here are four examples:

> First snow, then silence.
> This thousand-dollar screen dies
> So beautifully.

> A crash reduces
> Your expensive computer
> To a simple stone.

> A file that big?
> It might be very useful
> But now it is gone.

> You step in the stream,
> But the water has moved on.
> This page is not here.

Why not try your hand at something on this topic?

CHAPTER

22

Irony

There is a kind of discourse which, though nonliteral, need not use similes, metaphors, apostrophes, personification, or symbols. Without using these figures, speakers may say things that are not to be taken literally. They may, in short, employ **irony.**

In Greek comedy, the *eiron* was the sly underdog who, by dissembling inferiority, outwitted his opponent. As Aristotle puts it, irony (employed by the *eiron*) is a "pretense tending toward the underside" of truth. Later, Cicero somewhat altered the meaning of the word: He defined it as saying one thing and meaning another, and he held that Socrates, who feigned ignorance and let his opponents entrap themselves in their own arguments, was the perfect example of an ironist.

In **verbal irony,** as the term is now used, what is *stated* is in some degree negated by what is *suggested*. A classic example is Lady Macbeth's order to get ready for King Duncan's visit: "He that's coming / Must be provided for." The words seem to say that she and Macbeth must busy themselves with household preparations so that the king may be received in appropriate style, but this suggestion of hospitality is undercut by an opposite meaning: preparations must be made for the murder of the king. Two other examples of verbal irony are Melville's comment

> What like a bullet can undeceive!

and the lover's assertion (in Marvell's "To His Coy Mistress") that

> The grave's a fine and private place,
> But none, I think, do there embrace.

Under Marvell's cautious words ("I think") we detect a wryness; the **understatement** masks yet reveals a deep-felt awareness of mortality and the barrenness of the grave. The self-mockery in this understatement proclaims modesty, but suggests assurance. The speaker here, like most ironists, is both playful and serious at once. Irony packs a great deal into a few words.* What we call

---

*A word of caution: We have been talking about verbal irony, not **irony of situation.** Like ironic words, ironic situations have in them an element of contrast. A clown whose heart is breaking must make his audience laugh; an author's worst book is her only financial success; a fool solves a problem that vexes the wise.

irony here, it should be mentioned, is often called **sarcasm,** but a distinction can be made: sarcasm is notably contemptuous and crude or heavy-handed ("You're a great guy, a real friend," said to a friend who won't lend you ten dollars). Sarcasm is only one kind of irony, and a kind almost never found in literature.

Overstatement (hyperbole), like understatement, is ironic when it contains a contradictory suggestion:

> For Brutus is an honorable man;
> So are they all, all honorable men.
>
> —Shakespeare

The sense of contradiction that is inherent in verbal irony is also inherent in a paradox. **Paradox** has several meanings for philosophers, but we need only be concerned with its meaning of an apparent contradiction. Examples of paradox follow:

> The child is father of the man;
>
> —Wordsworth

and (on the soldiers who died to preserve the British Empire)

> The saviors come not home tonight;
> Themselves they could not save;
>
> —Housman

and

> One short sleep past, we wake eternally,
> And Death shall be no more; Death, thou shalt die.
>
> —Donne

Donne's lines are a reminder that paradox is not only an instrument of the poet. Christianity embodies several paradoxes: God became a human being; through the death on the cross, human beings can obtain eternal life; human beings do not live fully until they die.

Some critics have put a high premium on ironic and paradoxical poetry. Briefly, their argument runs that great poetry recognizes the complexity of experience, and that irony and paradox are ways of doing justice to this complexity. I. A. Richards uses "irony" to denote "The bringing in of the opposite, the complementary impulses," and suggests in *The Principles of Literary Criticism* (1924/25) that irony in this sense is a characteristic of poetry of "the highest order." It is dubious that all poets must always bring in the opposite, but it is certain that much poetry is ironic and paradoxical.

DOROTHY PARKER

Dorothy Parker (1893–1967), born in West End, New Jersey, but brought up in New York City, from 1917 to 1920 served as drama critic for the magazine Vanity Fair, *where her witty, satiric reviews gained her the reputation of being hard to please. She distinguished between wit and wisecracking: "Wit has truth in it; wisecracking is simply calisthenics with words." In addition to writing essays and stories, Parker also wrote light verse, especially about love.*

General Review of the Sex Situation [1926]

Woman wants monogamy;
Man delights in novelty.
Love is woman's moon and sun;
Man has other forms of fun.   4

Woman lives but in her lord;
Count to ten, and man is bored.
With this the gist and sum of it,
What earthly good can come of it?   8

YOUR TURN

1. How would you characterize Parker's message? (For instance, is it sad, happy, pitiful, or what?) How would you characterize her tone—her attitude, as you perceive it?
2. Take note of and describe Parker's use of language—for example, the contrast she makes between "monogamy" and "novelty," and the image she gives in line 3, "Love is woman's moon and sun." Where else in this short poem do you see evidence of careful handling of language?
3. How much truth do you think there is in Parker's lines? (Remember: No poem, or, for that matter, no novel—however long—can tell the whole truth about life.) As for truth, how would you compare it with the following passage, from Barbara Dafoe Whitehead's review (*The Times Literary Supplement*, 9 June 1995) of two sociological studies, *The Social Organization of Sexuality: Sexual Practice in the U.S.* and *Sex in America?*

   > Men and women have different sexual interests, stakes and appetites, with men more oriented to the sex act and women more interested in sex as an expression of affiliative and romantic love.

4. Compare the tone of Parker's poem with the tone of Shakespeare's "Sigh no more, ladies" (page 576).

PERCY BYSSHE SHELLEY

Percy Bysshe Shelley (1792–1822) was born in Sussex in England, the son of a prosperous country squire. Educated at Eton, he went on to Oxford but was expelled for having written a pamphlet supporting a belief in atheism. Like John Keats he was a member of the second generation of English Romantic poets. (The first generation included Wordsworth and Coleridge.) And like Keats, Shelley died young; he was drowned during a violent storm off the coast of Italy while sailing with a friend.

Ozymandias* [1817]

I met a traveler from an antique land
Who said: Two vast and trunkless legs of stone

---

*Ozymandias is another name for Ramesses the Great, Pharaoh of the nineteenth dynasty of ancient Egypt. He is believed to have taken the throne in his early twenties and to have ruled Egypt from 1279 BCE to 1213 BCE.

Stand in the desert . . . Near them, on the sand,
Half sunk, a shattered visage lies, whose frown,
And wrinkled lip, and sneer of cold command,   5
Tell that its sculptor well those passions read
Which yet survive, stamped on these lifeless things,
The hand that mocked them, and the heart that fed:
And on the pedestal these words appear:
"My name is Ozymandias, king of kings: 10
Look on my works, ye Mighty, and despair!"
Nothing beside remains. Round the decay
Of that colossal wreck, boundless and bare
The lone and level sands stretch far away.

Lines 4–8 are somewhat obscure, but the gist is that the passions—still evident in the "shattered visage"—survive the sculptor's hand that "mocked"—that is, (1) imitated or copied, (2) derided—them, and the passions also survive the king's heart that had nourished them.

YOUR TURN

There is an irony of plot here: Ozymandias believed that he created enduring works, but his intentions came to nothing. However, another irony is also present: How are his words, in a way he did not intend, true?

ANDREW MARVELL

Born near Hull in England, Andrew Marvell (1621–1678) attended Trinity College, Cambridge, and graduated in 1638. During the English Civil War, he was tutor to the daughter of Sir Thomas Fairfax in Yorkshire at Nun Appleton House, where most of his best-known poems were written. In 1657 he was appointed assistant to John Milton, the Latin Secretary for the Commonwealth. After the Restoration of the monarchy in 1660, Marvell represented Hull as a member of Parliament until his death. Most of his poems were not published until after his death.

To His Coy Mistress   [1681]

Had we but world enough, and time,
This coyness, lady, were no crime.
We would sit down, and think which way
To walk, and pass our long love's day.
Thou by the Indian Ganges° side   5
Should'st rubies find: I by the tide
Of Humber° would complain.° I would
Love you ten years before the Flood,
And you should, if you please, refuse

---

5 Indian Ganges the Ganges is the major river of India, running for 1,560 miles from the Himalayas to the Bay of Bengal.   **7 Humber** the Humber is a large tidal estuary on the east coast of Northern England.   **complain** write love poems.

Till the conversion of the Jews.   10
My vegetable° love should grow
Vaster than empires, and more slow.
An hundred years should go to praise
Thine eyes, and on thy forehead gaze:
Two hundred to adore each breast: 15
But thirty thousand to the rest.
An age at least to every part,
And the last age should show your heart.
For, lady, you deserve this state,
Nor would I love at lower rate.   20
      But at my back I always hear
Time's wing'ed chariot hurrying near;
And yonder all before us lie
Deserts of vast eternity.
Thy beauty shall no more be found,   25
Nor in thy marble vault shall sound
My echoing song; then worms shall try
That long preserved virginity,
And your quaint honor turn to dust,
And into ashes all my lust.   30
The grave's a fine and private place,
But none, I think, do there embrace.
      Now therefore, while the youthful hue
Sits on thy skin like morning dew,
And while thy willing soul transpires   35
At every pore with instant fires,
Now let us sport us while we may;
And now, like am'rous birds of prey,
Rather at once our time devour,
Than languish in his slow-chapt° power,   40
Let us roll all our strength, and all
Our sweetness, up into one ball;
And tear our pleasures with rough strife
Thorough° the iron gates of life.
Thus, though we cannot make our sun   45
Stand still, yet we will make him run.

---

11 vegetable i.e., unconsciously growing.   **40 slow-chapt** slowly devouring.
44 Thorough through.

YOUR TURN

1. Do you find the assertions in lines 1–20 so inflated that you detect behind them a playfully ironic tone? Explain. Why does the speaker say,
   in line 8, that he would love "ten years before the Flood," rather than
   merely "since the Flood"?
2. Explain lines 21–24. Why is time behind the speaker, and eternity in
   front of him? Is this "eternity" the same as the period discussed in lines
   1–20? What do you make of the change in the speaker's tone after
   line 20?

3. Do you agree with the comment on page 649 about the understatement in lines 31–32? What more can you say about these lines, in context?
4. Why "am'rous birds of prey" (line 38) rather than the conventional doves? Is the idea of preying continued in the poem?
5. Try to explain the last two lines, and characterize the speaker's tone. Do you find these lines anticlimactic?
6. The poem is organized in the form of an argument. Trace the steps.

JOHN DONNE

John Donne (1572–1631) was born into a Roman Catholic family in England, but in the 1590s he abandoned that faith. In 1615 he became an Anglican priest and soon was known as a great preacher. Of his sermons, 160 survive, including one with the famous line, "No man is an island, entire of itself; every man is a piece of the continent, a part of the main; if a clod be washed away by the sea, Europe is the less . . . ; and therefore never send to know for whom the bell tolls; it tolls for thee." From 1621 until his death, Donne was dean of St. Paul's Cathedral in London. His love poems (often bawdy and cynical) are said to be his early work, and his "Holy Sonnets" (among the greatest religious poems written in English) his later work.

Holy Sonnet 14   [1633]

Batter my heart, three-personed God; for you
As yet but knock, breathe, shine, and seek to mend;
That I may rise and stand, o'erthrow me, and bend
Your force, to break, blow, burn, and make me new.
I, like an usurped town, to another due,   5
Labor to admit you, but oh, to no end,
Reason, your viceroy in me, me should defend,
But is captived, and proves weak or untrue.
Yet dearly I love you, and would be loved fain,
But am betrothed unto your enemy: 10
Divorce me, untie, or break that knot again,
Take me to you, imprison me, for I
Except you enthrall me, never shall be free,
Nor ever chaste, except you ravish me.

YOUR TURN

1. Explain the paradoxes in lines 1, 3, 13, and 14. Explain the double meanings of "enthrall" (line 13) and "ravish" (line 14).
2. In lines 1–4, what is God implicitly compared to (considering especially lines 2 and 4)? How does this comparison lead into the comparison that dominates lines 5–8? What words in lines 9–12 are especially related to the earlier lines?

3. What do you think is gained by piling up verbs in lines 2–4?
4. Do you find sexual references irreverent in a religious poem? (As already mentioned, Donne was an Anglican priest.)

LANGSTON HUGHES

A biographical note and other poems by Langston Hughes appear on pages 761–768 in Chapter 27.

Dream Boogie   [1951]

Good morning, daddy!
Ain't you heard
The boogie-woogie rumble
Of a dream deferred?

Listen closely: 5
You'll hear their feet
Beating out and beating out a—

   You think
   It's a happy beat?

Listen to it closely: 10
Ain't you heard
something underneath
like a—

   What did I say?

Sure,   15
I'm happy!
Take it away!

   Hey, pop!
   Re-bop!
   Mop!   20

   Y-e-a-h!

YOUR TURN

1. What is boogie, or boogie-woogie?
2. Why did many whites assume that boogie was "a happy beat" (line 9)? In fact, what was boogie chiefly an expression of?

MARTÍN ESPADA

Martín Espada was born in Brooklyn in 1957. He received a bachelor's degree from the University of Wisconsin and a law degree from Northeastern University. A poet who publishes regularly, Espada teaches creative writing at the University of Massachusetts-Amherst.

Tony Went to the Bodega*
but He Didn't Buy Anything   [1987]

para Angel Guadalupe

Tony's father left the family
and the Long Island city projects,
leaving a mongrel-skinny puertorriqueño boy
nine years old
who had to find work.   5

Makengo the Cuban
let him work at the bodega.
In grocery aisles
he learned the steps of the dry-mop mambo,
banging the cash register   10
like piano percussion
in the spotlight of Machito's orchestra,
polite with the abuelas° who bought on credit,
practicing the grin on customers
he'd seen Makengo grin   15
with his bad yellow teeth.

Tony left the projects too,
with a scholarship for law school.
But he cursed the cold primavera°
in Boston;   20
the cooking of his neighbors
left no smell in the hallway
and no one spoke Spanish
(not even the radio).

So Tony walked without a map   25
through the city,
a landscape of hostile condominiums
and the darkness of white faces,
sidewalk-searcher lost
till he discovered the projects.   30

Tony went to the bodega
but he didn't buy anything:
he sat by the doorway satisfied
to watch la gente° (people
island-brown as him)   35
crowd in and out,
hablando español,°
thought: this is beautiful,
and grinned
his bodega grin.   40

*****Bodega** grocery and liquor store; in the dedication, after the title, *para* means "for."
13 abuelas grandmothers.   **19 primavera** spring season.   **34 la gente** the people.
37 hablando español speaking Spanish.

This is a rice and beans
success story:
today Tony lives on Tremont Street,
above the bodega.

YOUR TURN

1. Why do you suppose Espada included the information about Tony's father? The information about young Tony "practicing" a grin?
2. Why does Tony leave?
3. How would you characterize Tony?

EDNA ST. VINCENT MILLAY

For a biographical note, see page 583.

Love Is Not All: It Is Not Meat nor Drink   [1931]

Love is not all: it is not meat nor drink
Nor slumber nor a roof against the rain;
Nor yet a floating spar to men that sink
And rise and sink and rise and sink again;
Love can not fill the thickened lung with breath,   5
Nor clean the blood, nor set the fractured bone;
Yet many a man is making friends with death
Even as I speak, for lack of love alone.
It well may be that in a difficult hour,
Pinned down by pain and moaning for release,   10
Or nagged by want past resolution's power,
I might be driven to sell your love for peace,
Or trade the memory of this night for food.
It well may be. I do not think I would.

YOUR TURN

1. "Love Is Not All" is a sonnet. Using your own words, briefly summarize the argument of the octet (the first 8 lines). Next, paraphrase the sestet (the six lines from line 9 through line 14), line by line. On the whole, does the sestet repeat the idea of the octet, or does it add a new idea? Whom did you imagine to be speaking the octet? What does the sestet add to your knowledge of the speaker and the occasion? (And how did you paraphrase line 11?)
2. The first and last lines of the poem consist of words of one syllable, and both lines have a distinct pause in the middle. Do you imagine the lines to be spoken in the same tone of voice? If not, can you describe the difference and account for it?
3. Lines 7 and 8 appear to mean that the absence of love can be a cause of death. To what degree do you believe that to be true?
4. Would you call "Love Is Not All" a love poem? Why or why not? Describe the kind of person who might include the poem in a love letter or valentine, or who would be happy to receive it. (One of our friends recited it at her wedding. What do you think of that idea?)

SHERMAN ALEXIE

The short-story writer, essayist, poet, and film director Sherman J. Alexie Jr. was born in October 1966 and was raised on the Spokane Indian Reservation in Wellpinit, Washington, located fifty miles northwest of Spokane. He went to high school off reservation in the small town of Reardan, Washington, where he was an excellent student and played on the basketball team. He attended Gonzaga University in Spokane for two years and then transferred to Washington State University in Pullman. There, he began writing poetry, graduating with a degree in American Studies. His books include The Business of Fancydancing: Stories and Poems *(1992),* The Lone Ranger and Tonto Fistfight in Heaven *(1994), and* Reservation Blues *(1995).*

For another poem by Alexie, see page 777.

Evolution   [1992]

Buffalo Bill opens a pawn shop on the reservation
right across the border from the liquor store
and he stays open 24 hours a day, 7 days a week

and the Indians come running in with jewelry
television sets, a VCR, a full-length beaded buckskin outfit   5
it took Inez Muse 12 years to finish. Buffalo Bill

takes everything the Indians have to offer, keeps it
all catalogued and filed in a storage room. The Indians
pawn their hands, saving the thumbs for last, they pawn

their skeletons, falling endlessly from the skin   10
and when the last Indian has pawned everything
but his heart, Buffalo Bill takes that for twenty bucks

closes up the pawn shop, paints a new sign over the old
calls his venture THE MUSEUM OF NATIVE AMERICAN CULTURES
charges the Indians five bucks a head to enter.   15

HENRY REED

Born in Birmingham, England, Henry Reed (1914–1986) served in the British army during World War II. Later, in civilian life he had a distinguished career as a journalist, a translator of French and Italian literature, a writer of radio plays, and a poet. "Naming of Parts" draws on his experience as a military recruit.

Naming of Parts   [1946]

Today we have naming of parts. Yesterday,
We had daily cleaning. And tomorrow morning,
We shall have what to do after firing. But today,
Today we have naming of parts. Japonica°
Glistens like coral in all of the neighboring gardens,   5
                And today we have naming of parts.

---

4 Japonica shrub with glossy green leaves and showy fragrant rose-like flowers.

This is the lower sling swivel. And this
Is the upper sling swivel, whose use you will see,
When you are given your slings. And this is the piling swivel,
Which in your case you have not got. The branches   10
Hold in the gardens their silent, eloquent gestures,
                    Which in our case we have not got.

This is the safety-catch, which is always released
With an easy flick of the thumb. And please do not let me
See anyone using his finger. You can do it quite easy   15
If you have any strength in your thumb. The blossoms
Are fragile and motionless, never letting anyone see
                    Any of them using their finger.

And this you can see is the bolt. The purpose of this
Is to open the breech, as you see. We can slide it   20
Rapidly backwards and forwards: we call this
Easing the spring. And rapidly backwards and forwards
The early bees are assaulting and fumbling the flowers:
                    They call it easing the Spring.

They call it easing the Spring: it is perfectly easy   25
If you have any strength in your thumb: like the bolt,
And the breech, and the cocking-piece, and the point of balance,
Which in our case we have not got; and the almond-blossom
Silent in all of the gardens and the bees going backwards and forwards,
                    For today we have naming of parts.   30

> ### YOUR TURN

1. How many speakers do you hear in the poem? How would you characterize each of them?
2. Why do we include this poem in a chapter on "irony"?

23

Rhythm and Versification

Up and down the City Road,
In and out the Eagle;
That's the way the money goes,
Pop goes the weasel.

Probably very few of the countless children—and adults—who sometimes find themselves singing this ditty have the faintest idea of what it is about. It endures because it is catchy—a strong, easily remembered rhythm. Even if you just read it aloud without singing it, we think you will agree.

If you try to specify exactly what the rhythm is—for instance, by putting an **accent** mark on each syllable that you stress heavily—you may run into difficulties. You may become unsure of whether you stress *up* and *down* equally; maybe you will decide that *up* is hardly stressed more than *and,* at least compared with the heavy stress that you put on *down.* Different readers (really, singers) will recite it differently. Does this mean that anything goes? Of course not. No one will emphasize *and* or *the,* just as no one will emphasize the second syllable in *city* or the second syllable in *money.* There may be some variations from reader to reader, but there will also be a good deal that all readers will agree on. And surely all readers agree that it is memorable.

Does this song have a meaning? Well, historians say that the Eagle was a tavern and music hall in the City Road, in Victorian London. People went there to eat, drink, and sing, with the result that they sometimes spent too much money and then had to pawn (or "pop") the "weasel"—though no one is sure what the weasel is. It doesn't really matter; the song lives by its rhythm.

Now consider this poem by Ezra Pound (1885-1972). Pound's early work is highly rhythmical; later he became sympathetic to Fascism and he grew increasingly anti-Semitic, with the result that for many readers his later work is much less interesting—just a lot of nasty ideas, rather than memorable expressions. Pound ought to have remembered his own definition of literature: "Literature is news that *stays* news." One way of staying is to use unforgettable rhythms.

EZRA POUND

An Immorality   [1912]

Sing we for love and idleness,
Naught else is worth the having.

Though I have been in many a land,
There is naught else in living.

And I would rather have my sweet,   5
Though rose-leaves die of grieving,

Than do high deeds in Hungary
To pass all men's believing.

A good poem. To begin with, it sings; as Pound said, "Poetry withers and dries out when it leaves music, or at least imagined music, too far behind it. Poets who are not interested in music are, or become, bad poets." Hymns and ballads, it must be remembered, are songs, and other poetry, too, is sung, especially by children. Children reciting a counting-out rhyme, or singing on their way home from school, are enjoying poetry:

Pease-porridge hot,
    Pease-porridge cold,
Pease-porridge in the pot
    Nine days old.

Nothing very important is being said, but for generations children have enjoyed the music of these lines, and adults, too, have recalled them with pleasure—though few people know what pease-porridge is.

The "music"—the catchiness of certain sounds—should not be underestimated. Here are lines chanted by the witches in *Macbeth:*

Double, double, toil and trouble;
Fire burn and cauldron bubble.

This is rather far from words that mean approximately the same thing: "Twice, twice, work and care; / Fire ignite, and pot boil." The difference is more in the sounds than in the instructions. What is lost in the paraphrase is the magic, the incantation, which resides in elaborate repetitions of sounds and stresses.

Rhythm (most simply, in English poetry, stresses at regular intervals) has a power of its own. A good march, said John Philip Sousa (the composer of "Stars and Stripes Forever"), "should make even someone with a wooden leg step out." A highly pronounced rhythm is common in such forms of poetry as charms, college yells, and lullabies; all of them (like the witches' speech) are aimed at inducing a special effect magically. It is not surprising that *carmen,* the Latin word for "poem" or "song," is also the Latin word for *charm,* and the word from which "charm" is derived.

Rain, rain, go away;
Come again another day.

Block that kick! Block that kick! Block that kick!

Rock-a-bye baby, on the tree top,
When the wind blows, the cradle will rock.

In much poetry, rhythm is only half-heard, but its omnipresence is suggested by the fact that when poetry is printed it is customary to begin each line with a capital letter. Prose (from Latin *prorsus,* "forward," "straight on") keeps running across the paper until the right-hand margin is reached, and then, merely because the paper has given out, the writer or printer starts again at the left, with a small letter. But verse (Latin *versus,* "a turning") often ends well short of the right-hand margin, and the next line begins at the left—usually with a capital—not because paper has run out but because the rhythmic pattern begins again. Lines of poetry are continually reminding us that they have a pattern.

Before turning to some other highly rhythmical pieces, a word of caution: a mechanical, unvarying rhythm may be good to put the baby to sleep, but it can be deadly to readers who wish to keep awake. Poets vary their rhythm according to their purpose; a poet ought not to be so regular that he or she is (in W. H. Auden's words) an "accentual pest." In competent hands, rhythm contributes to meaning; it says something. The rhythm in the lines from *Macbeth,* for example, helps suggest the strong binding power of magic. Again Ezra Pound has a relevant comment: "Rhythm *must* have meaning. It can't be merely a careless dash off, with no grip and no real hold to the words and sense, a tumty tum tumty tum tum ta." Some examples will be useful.

Consider this description of Hell from John Milton's *Paradise Lost* (the relatively unstressed syllables are marked by a symbol called *breve,* whereas heavier stresses are marked by ´, an acute accent, thus):

Rócks, caves, lakes, fens, bogs, dens, and shádes of death.

Such a succession of stresses is highly unusual. Elsewhere in the poem Milton chiefly uses iambic feet—alternating unstressed and stressed syllables—but here he immediately follows one heavy stress with another, thereby helping to communicate the "meaning"—the impressive monotony of Hell. As a second example, consider the function of the rhythm in two lines by Alexander Pope:

Whĕn Ájax strives sŏme rock's vast weight tŏ throw,
Thĕ line toó lábŏrs, ănd thĕ words móve slów.

The heavier stresses (again, marked by ´) do not merely alternate with the lighter ones (marked ˘); rather, the great weight of the rock is suggested by three consecutive stressed words, "rock's vast weight," and the great effort involved in moving it is suggested by another three consecutive stresses, "line too labors," and by yet another three, "words move slow." Note, also, the abundant pauses within the lines. In the first line, unless one's speech is slovenly, one must pause at least slightly after "Ajax," "strives," "rock's," "vast," "weight," and "throw." The grating sounds in "Ajax" and "rock's" do their work, too, and so do the explosive *t*'s. When—in the second line, below—Pope wishes to suggest lightness, he reverses his procedure and he groups *un*stressed syllables:

Not so, when swift Camilla scours the plain,
Fliés o'ĕr th'uñbéndĭng córn, ănd skíms ălŏng thĕ máin.

This last line has twelve syllables and is thus longer than the line about Ajax, but the addition of "along" helps to communicate lightness and swiftness because in this line (it can be argued) neither syllable of "along" is strongly stressed. If "along" is omitted, the line still makes grammatical sense and becomes more "regular," but it also becomes less imitative of lightness.

The very regularity of a line may be meaningful too. Shakespeare begins a sonnet thus:

Whĕn Í dŏ cóunt thĕ clóck thăt télls thĕ tíme.

This line about a mechanism runs with appropriate regularity. (It is worth noting, too, that "count the clock" and "tells the time" emphasize the regularity by the repetition of sounds and syntax.) But notice what Shakespeare does in the middle of the next line:

Aňd sée thĕ bráve dáy suňk iň hídeŏus níght.

What has he done? And what is the effect?

Here is another poem that refers to a clock. In England, until capital punishment was abolished, executions regularly took place at 8:00 AM.

A. E. HOUSMAN

A. E. Housman (1859–1936) was one of the most distinguished classical scholars of his time. Though he left Oxford without a degree (having failed his examinations), through hard work, discipline, and rigorous study he earned an appointment in 1892 as professor of Latin at University College, London, and in 1911 as professor of Latin at Cambridge and fellow of Trinity College. Only two volumes of Housman's poems appeared during his lifetime: A Shropshire Lad *(1896) and* Last Poems *(1922).*

Eight O'Clock   [1922]

He stood, and heard the steeple
  Sprinkle the quarters on the morning town.
One, two, three, four, to market-place and people
  It tossed them down.   4

Strapped, noosed, nighing his hour,
  He stood and counted them and cursed his luck;
And then the clock collected in the tower
  Its strength, and struck.   8

The chief (but not unvarying) pattern is iambic; that is, the odd syllables are less emphatic than the even ones, as in

Hĕ stóod, aňd heárd thĕ stéeplĕ

Try to mark the syllables, stressed and unstressed, in the rest of the poem. Be guided by your ear, not by a mechanical principle, and don't worry too much about difficult or uncertain parts; different readers may reasonably come up with different results.

YOUR TURN

1. Where do you find two or more consecutive stresses? What explanations (related to meaning) can be offered?
2. What do you think is the effect of the short line at the end of each stanza? And what significance can you attach to the fact that these lines (unlike the first and third lines in each stanza) end with a stress?

Following are some poems in which the strongly felt pulsations are highly important.

WILLIAM CARLOS WILLIAMS

A poem by William Carlos Williams (1883–1963), along with a brief biography, appears on page 628. The Breughel (also spelled Brueghel) painting described in "The Dance" is shown below.

The Dance   [1944]

In Breughel's great picture,The Kermess,°
the dancers go round, they go round and
around, the squeal and the blare and the
tweedle of bagpipes, a bugle and fiddles
tipping their bellies (round as the thick-   5
sided glasses whose wash they impound)
their hips and their bellies off balance
to turn them. Kicking and rolling about
the Fair Grounds, swinging their butts, those
shanks must be sound to bear up under such   10
rollicking measures, prance as they dance
in Breughel's great picture,The Kermess.

---

1 Kermess in the Netherlands, Belgium, etc., an outdoor fair or carnival, originally the feast day of the local patron saint, hence a fair or carnival held on that day.

Pieter Breughel the Eider. *Peasant Dance*, c 1568, oil on wood, 114 × 164 cm. (Kunsthistorisches Museum, Vienna.)

YOUR TURN

1. Read Williams's poem aloud several times, and decide where the heavy stresses fall. Mark the heavily stressed syllables ´, the lightly stressed ones ^, and the unstressed ones ˘. Are all the lines identical? What effect is thus gained, especially when the poem is read aloud? What does the parenthetical statement (lines 5–6) do to the rhythm? Does a final syllable often receive a heavy stress here? Are there noticeable pauses at the ends of the lines? What is the consequence? Are the dancers waltzing?

2. What syllables rhyme or are repeated (e.g., "round" in lines 2 and 5, and "–pound" in line 6; "–ing" in lines 5, 8, 9, and 11)? What effect do they have?

3. What do you think the absence at the beginning of each line of the customary capital contributes to the meaning? Why is the last line the same as the first?

Versification: A Glossary for Reference

The technical vocabulary of **prosody** (the study of the principles of verse structure, including meter, rhyme, and other sound effects, and stanzaic patterns) is large. An understanding of these terms will not turn anyone into a poet, but it will enable one to discuss some aspects of poetry more efficiently. A knowledge of them, like a knowledge of most other technical terms (e.g., "misplaced modifier," "woofer," "automatic transmission"), allows for quick and accurate communication. The following are the chief terms of prosody.

Meter

Most English poetry has a pattern of **stressed (accented)** sounds, and this pattern is the **meter** (from the Greek word for "measure"). Although in Old English poetry (poetry written in England before the Norman-French Conquest in 1066) a line may have any number of unstressed syllables in addition to four stressed syllables, most poetry written in England since the Conquest not only has a fixed number of stresses in a line but also has a fixed number of unstressed syllables before or after each stressed one. (One really ought not to talk of "unstressed" or "unaccented" syllables, since to utter a syllable—however lightly—is to give it some stress. It is really a matter of *relative* stress, but the fact is that "unstressed" and "unaccented" are parts of the established terminology of versification.)

In a line of poetry, the **foot** is the basic unit of measurement. On rare occasions it is a single stressed syllable, but generally a foot consists of two or three syllables, one of which is stressed. (Stress is indicated by the acute symbol ´, lack of stress by the breve symbol ˘.) The repetition of feet, then, produces a pattern of stresses throughout the poem.

Two cautions:

1. A poem will seldom contain only one kind of foot throughout; significant variations usually occur, but one kind of foot is dominant.

2. In reading a poem pay attention to the sense as well as to the metrical pattern. By paying attention to the sense, you will often find that the stress falls on a word that according to the metrical pattern would be unstressed. Or a word that according to the pattern would be stressed may be seen to be unstressed. Furthermore, by reading for sense, you will find that not all stresses are equally heavy; some are almost as light as unstressed syllables, and sometimes there is a **hovering stress;** that is, the stress is equally distributed over two adjacent syllables. To repeat: *read for sense,* allowing the meaning to help indicate the stresses.

Metrical Feet

The most common feet in English poetry are the following six:

1. **Iamb** (adjective: **iambic**): one unstressed syllable followed by one stressed syllable. The iamb, said to be the most common pattern in English speech, is surely the most common in English poetry. The following example has four iambic feet:

    Mў héart ĭs líke ă síngĭng bírd.

    —Christina Rossetti

2. **Trochee (trochaic):** one stressed syllable followed by one unstressed.

    Wé wĕřy véřy tírĕd, wé wĕre véřy mérřy

    —Edna St. Vincent Millay

3. **Anapest (anapestic):** two unstressed syllables followed by one stressed.

    Thĕre ăre mánў whŏ sáy thăt ă dóg hăs hís dáy

    —Dylan Thomas

4. **Dactyl (dactylic):** one stressed syllable followed by two unstressed. This trisyllabic foot, like the anapest, is common in light verse or verse suggesting joy, but its use is not limited to such material, as Longfellow's *Evangeline* shows. Thomas Hood's sentimental "The Bridge of Sighs" begins:

    Tăke hĕr ŭp téndĕrlў.

5. **Spondee (spondaic):** two stressed syllables; most often used as a substitute for an iamb or trochee.

    Smárt lád, tŏ slíp bĕtímes ăwáy.

    —A. E. Housman

6. **Pyrrhic:** two unstressed syllables; it is often not considered a legitimate foot in English.

Metrical Lines

A metrical line consists of one or more feet and is named for the number of feet in it. The following names are used:

monometer: one foot	**pentameter:** five feet
dimeter: two feet	**hexameter:** six feet
trimeter: three feet	**heptameter:** seven feet
tetrameter: four feet	**octameter:** eight feet

A line is scanned for the kind and number of feet in it, and the **scansion** tells you if it is, say, anapestic trimeter (three anapests):

Ăs Ĭ cáme tŏ the édge ŏf the wóods.

—Robert Frost

Or, in another example, iambic pentameter:

The súmmĕr thúndĕr, likĕ ă wóodĕn béll

—Louise Bogan

A line ending with a stress has a **masculine ending;** a line ending with an extra unstressed syllable has a **feminine ending.** The **caesura** (usually indicated by the symbol //) is a slight pause within the line. It need not be indicated by punctuation (notice the fourth and fifth lines in the following quotation), and it does not affect the metrical count:

Awake, my St. John! // leave all meaner things
To low ambition, // and the pride of kings.
Let us // (since life can little more supply
Than just to look about us // and to die)
Expatiate free // o'er all this scene of Man;
A mighty maze! // but not without a plan;
A wild, // where weeds and flowers promiscuous shoot;
Or garden, // tempting with forbidden fruit.

—Alexander Pope

The varying position of the caesura helps to give Pope's lines an informality that plays against the formality of the pairs of rhyming lines.

An **end-stopped line** concludes with a distinct syntactical pause, but a **run-on line** has its sense carried over into the next line without syntactical pause. (The running on of a line is called **enjambment.**) In the following passage, only the first is a run-on line:

Yet if we look more closely we shall find
Most have the seeds of judgment in their mind:
Nature affords at least a glimmering light;
The lines, though touched but faintly, are drawn right.

—Alexander Pope

Meter produces **rhythm,** recurrences at equal intervals; but rhythm (from a Greek word meaning "flow") is usually applied to larger units than feet. Often it depends most obviously on pauses. Thus, a poem with run-on lines will have a different rhythm from a poem with end-stopped lines, even though both are in the same meter. And prose, though it is unmetrical, can have rhythm, too.

In addition to being affected by syntactical pauses, rhythm is affected by pauses attributable to consonant clusters and to the length of words. Words of several syllables establish a different rhythm from words of one syllable, even in metrically identical lines. One can say, then, that rhythm is altered by shifts in meter, syntax, and the length and ease of pronunciation. But even with no such shift, even if a line is repeated word for word, a reader may sense a change in rhythm. The rhythm of the final line of a poem, for example, may well differ from that of the line before, even though in all other respects the lines are identical, as in Frost's "Stopping by Woods on a Snowy Evening" (page 755), which concludes by repeating "And miles to go before I sleep." One may simply sense that the final line ought to be spoken, say, more slowly and with more stress on "miles."

Patterns of Sound

Though rhythm is basic to poetry, **rhyme**—the repetition of the identical or similar stressed sound or sounds—is not. Rhyme is, presumably, pleasant in itself; it suggests order; and it may also be related to meaning, for it brings two words sharply together, often implying a relationship, as in the now trite *dove* and *love,* or in the more imaginative *throne* and *alone.*

Perfect, or exact, rhyme: Differing consonant sounds are followed by identical stressed vowel sounds, and the following sounds, if any, are identical *(foe—toe; meet—fleet; buffer—rougher)*. Notice that perfect rhyme involves identity of sound, not of spelling. *Fix* and *sticks,* like *buffer* and *rougher,* are perfect rhymes.

Half-rhyme (or **off-rhyme**): Only the final consonant sounds of the words are identical; the stressed vowel sounds as well as the initial consonant sounds, if any, differ *(soul—oil; mirth—forth; trolley—bully)*.

Eye-rhyme: The sounds do not in fact rhyme, but the words look as though they would rhyme *(cough—bough)*.

Masculine rhyme: The final syllables are stressed and, after their differing initial consonant sounds, are identical in sound *(stark—mark; support—retort)*.

Feminine rhyme (or **double rhyme**): Stressed rhyming syllables are followed by identical unstressed syllables *(revival—arrival; flatter—batter)*.

Triple rhyme is a kind of feminine rhyme in which identical stressed vowel sounds are followed by two identical unstressed syllables *(machinery—scenery; tenderly—slenderly)*.

End rhyme (or **terminal rhyme**): The rhyming words occur at the ends of the lines.

Internal rhyme: At least one of the rhyming words occurs within the line (Oscar Wilde's "Each narrow *cell* in which we *dwell*").

Other patterns of sound are:

Alliteration: Sometimes defined as the repetition of initial sounds ("*A*ll the *a*wful *a*uguries," or "*B*ring me my *b*ow of *b*urning gold"), and sometimes as the prominent repetition of a consonant ("a*f*ter li*f*e's *f*it*f*ul *f*ever").

Assonance: The repetition, in words of proximity, of identical vowel sounds preceded and followed by differing consonant sounds. Whereas *tide* and *hide* are rhymes, *tide* and *mine* are assonantal.

Consonance: The repetition of identical consonant sounds and differing vowel sounds in words in proximity *(fail—feel; rough—roof; pitter—patter)*. Sometimes consonance is more loosely defined merely as the repetition of a consonant *(fail—peel)*.

Onomatopoeia: The use of words that imitate sounds, such as *hiss* and *buzz.* There is a mistaken tendency to see onomatopoeia everywhere—for example in *thunder* and *horror.* Many words sometimes thought to be onomatopoeic are not clearly imitative of the thing they refer to; they merely contain some sounds that, when we know what the word means, seem to have some resemblance to the thing they denote. Tennyson's lines from "Come down, O maid" are usually cited as an example of onomatopoeia:

> The moan of doves in immemorial elms
> And murmuring of innumerable bees.

If you have read the preceding—and, admittedly, not entirely engaging—paragraphs, you may have found yourself mentally repeating some catchy sounds, let's say our example of internal rhyme ("Each narrow cell in which we dwell") or our example of alliteration ("Bring me my bow of burning gold"). As the creators of advertising slogans know, all of us—not just poets—can be hooked by the sounds of words, but probably poets are especially fond of savoring words. Consider the following poem.

GALWAY KINNELL

Born in 1927 in Providence, Rhode Island, Galway Kinnell was educated at Princeton and the University of Rochester. He is the author of many books of poems, a novel, and translations of French and German literature. Among Kinnell's many awards are the Pulitzer Prize for Poetry and the National Book Award for Selected Poems *(1980).*

Blackberry Eating

[1980]

I love to go out in late September
among the fat, overripe, icy, black blackberries
to eat blackberries for breakfast,
the stalks very prickly, a penalty
they earn for knowing the black art   5
of blackberry-making: and as I stand among them
lifting the stalks to my mouth, the ripest berries
fall almost unbidden to my tongue,
as words sometimes do, certain peculiar words
like *strengths* or *squinched,*   10
many-lettered, one-syllabled lumps,
which I squeeze, squinch open, and splurge well
in the silent, startled, icy, black language
of blackberry-eating in late September.

Kinnell does not use rhyme, but he uses other kinds of aural repetition. For instance, in the first line we get "*l*ove" and "*l*ate," and the *l* sound (already present in the title of the poem) is picked up in the second line, in "black blackberries." The *k* sound is then continued in the next line, in "stalks" and the *l* and *k* in "prickly," and "prickly" contains not only the *k* and the *l* of "blackberry" but also the *r.*

In lines 7–9 Kinnell compares eating blackberries—an action involving the tongue and the lips, and the mind also, if one is savoring the berries—to speaking "certain peculiar words." There is no need for us to point out additional connections between words in the poem, but we do want to mention that the last line ends with the same three words as the first, providing closure, which is one of the things rhyme normally does.

> **YOUR TURN**
>
> 1. Specify three words that you like to "squinch," and explain why.
> 2. Specify one poem, other than a poem in this chapter (the poem need not be in this book), in which you think the repetitions of sounds are especially important, and explain why you hold this view.

WILLIAM CARLOS WILLIAMS

For a biographical note, see page 628.

The Artist   [1954]

Mr. T.
          bareheaded
                    in a soiled undershirt
his hair standing out
          on all sides   5
                    stood on his toes
heels together
          arms gracefully
                    for the moment
curled above his head.   10
          Then he whirled about
                    bounded
into the air
          and with an *entrechat*°
                    perfectly achieved   15
completed the figure.
          My mother
                    taken by surprise
where she sat
          in her invalid's chair   20
                    was left speechless.
Bravo! she cried at last
          and clapped her hands.
                    The man's wife
came from the kitchen: 25
          What goes on here? she said.
                    But the show was over.

---

14 entrechat a leap, in ballet.

YOUR TURN

1. Why does Williams tell us that Mr. T.'s hair was untidy and that he wore "a soiled undershirt"?
2. Suppose the poem ended with line 23, "and clapped her hands." Would it be just as good, better, or less good? Why?

LAWRENCE FERLINGHETTI

Lawrence Ferlinghetti (b. 1919) has been much concerned with bringing poetry to the people. To this end he has not only written poetry but has also been the editor and publisher of City Lights Books in San Francisco and (since 1953) has operated a bookstore, the City Lights Bookshop, the first all-paperback bookstore in the United States. In 1956 Ferlinghetti achieved national fame when, as the publisher of Allen Ginsberg's Howl, *he was arrested (and later acquitted) on an obscenity charge.*

Constantly Risking Absurdity   [1958]

Constantly risking absurdity
                    and death
        whenever he performs
                above the heads
                            of his audience   5
    the poet like an acrobat
                climbs on rime
                to a high wire of his own making
    and balancing on eyebeams
                            above a sea of faces   10
                paces his way
                    to the other side of day
    performing entrechats°
                    and sleight-of-foot tricks
    and other high theatrics   15
                and all without mistaking
        any thing
            for what it may not be

For he's the super realist
                who must perforce perceive   20
            taut truth
                    before the taking of each stance or step
    in his supposed advance
                    toward that still higher perch
    where Beauty stands and waits   25
                    with gravity
                    to start her death-defying leap

---

13 entrechats a leap in ballet.

And he
> a little charleychaplin man
>> who may or may not catch   30
her fair eternal form
> spreadeagled in the empty air
of existence

YOUR TURN

1. In this poem, which compares a poet to an acrobat, is Ferlinghetti "constantly risking absurdity"?
2. What examples of wordplay do you find, in addition to "above the heads / of his audience"?

A Note About Poetic Forms

"Art is nothing without form," the French author Gustave Flaubert maintained, and it is true that works of art have a carefully designed shape. Most obviously, for instance, a good story has an ending that satisfies the reader or hearer. In real life, things keep going, but when a good story ends, the audience feels that there is nothing more to say, at least nothing more of interest to say.

With poems that rhyme, the rhyme-scheme provides a pattern, a shape, a structure that seems inseparable from the content. If you recite a limerick, you will immediately see how the shape is inseparable from the content:

There was a young fellow from Lynn
Who was so exceedingly thin
> That when he essayed
> To drink lemonade
He slipped through the straw and fell in.

If you put the words in a different order, and you ignore meter and rhyme—that is, if you destroy the form and turn the passage into something like "A young man, so thin that he fell through a straw into a glass of lemonade, lived in Lynn"—you can instantly see the importance of form.

Let's briefly look again at a more serious example—Housman's "Eight O'Clock" (page 663), a poem whose title corresponds to the hour at which executions used to take place in England.

He stood, and heard the steeple
> Sprinkle the quarters on the morning town.
One, two, three, four, to market-place and people
> It tossed them down.

Strapped, noosed, nighing his hour,
> He stood and counted them and cursed his luck;
And then the clock collected in the tower
> Its strength, and struck.

The rhyme of "struck" with "luck" (in this instance, bad luck) is conclusive. We don't ask if the body was removed from the gallows and buried, or if the condemned man's wife (if he had one) grieved, or if his children (if he had any) turned out well or badly. None of these things is of any relevance. There is nothing more to say. The form and the content perfectly go together. In this example, the lines, each of which rhymes with another line—we might say that each line is tied to another line—seem especially appropriate for a man who is "strapped" and "noosed."

But why do poets use forms established by rhyme? In an essay called "The Constant Symbol," Robert Frost says that a poet regards rhymes as "stepping stones. . . .The way will be zigzag, but it will be a straight crookedness like the walking stick he cuts in the bushes for an emblem." Housman's stepping stones in the second stanza took Housman (and take the reader) from *hour* to *luck,* then to *tower* and then with great finality to the end of the walk, *struck*.We think this stanza is inspired, and we imagine that Housman's inspiration was mightily helped by his need for rhymes—his need to get "stepping stones" that would allow him to continue the "straight crookedness" of his walk with this condemned man. His walk-with-words, or rather his walk with words-that-set-forth-ideas, produced "luck" and "struck," and enabled him to give to his readers the memorable image of the clock as a machine that executes the man.

When you read Housman's or Frost's actual lines—or better, when you read them aloud and hear and feel the effect of these rhymes—you can understand why Frost more than once said he would as soon write unrhymed poetry as he would "play tennis with the net down." The rules governing the game of tennis or the game of writing do not interfere with the game; rather, the rules allow the players to play the game. The rules allow poets to write poems; the rules—the restraints—provide the structure that allows poets to accomplish something.

Poets are somewhat like Houdini, who accepted shackles so that he could triumph over them. Without the handcuffs and other restraints, he could accomplish nothing. Or consider the string on a kite; far from impeding the kite's flight, the string allows the kite to fly. Speaking in less high-flying terms, we can quote from a talk that Frost gave to college students in 1937, "The Poet's Next of Kin in College." He told them—and he was speaking not only to young poets but to all students—that in their endeavors, of whatever sort, they "must have form—performance. The thing itself is indescribable, but it is felt like athletic form. To have form, feel form in sports—and by analogy feel form in verse."

Poets have testified that they use rhyme partly because, far from impeding them, it helps them to say interesting things in a memorable way. True, some rhymes have been used so often that although they were once rich in meaning—for instance—"love" and "dove" or "moon" and "June"—they have become clichés, their use indicating not an imaginative leap but a reliance on what has been said too often. But other rhymes—let's say "earth" and "birth" or "law" and "flaw"—can lead poets to say interesting things that they might otherwise not have thought of.

In his "Letter of Advice to a Young Poet," Jonathan Swift (whom you may know as the author of *Gulliver's Travels,* 1726), said: "Verse without rhyme is a body without a soul." A striking, and indeed surprising, comment: Swift dares to propose that the soul of a poem depends not on the content but, rather, on a crucial element of its form, the presence of rhyme. In part he is reminding us here of the importance of craft in the writing of a poem, of the sheer skill and deliberation that make the literary work feel exactly right, as though it *had* to be this way.

Stanzaic Patterns

Lines of poetry are commonly arranged in a rhythmical unit called a **stanza** (from an Italian word meaning "room" or "stopping-place"). Usually all the stanzas in a poem have the same rhyme pattern. A stanza is sometimes called a **verse,** though *verse* may also mean a single line of poetry. (In discussing stanzas, rhymes are indicated by identical letters. Thus, *abab* indicates that the first and third lines rhyme with each other, while the second and fourth lines are linked by a different rhyme. An unrhymed line is denoted by *x*.) Common stanzaic forms in English poetry are the following:

1. **Couplet**: a stanza of two lines, usually but not necessarily with end rhymes. *Couplet* is also used for a pair of rhyming lines. The **octosyllabic couplet** is iambic or trochaic tetrameter:

    > Had we but world enough and time,
    > This coyness, lady, were no crime.
    >
    > —Andrew Marvell

2. **Heroic couplet**: a rhyming couplet of iambic pentameter, often "closed—" that is, containing a complete thought, with a fairly heavy pause at the end of the first line and a still heavier one at the end of the second. Commonly, there is a parallel or an *antithesis* (contrast) within a line or between the two lines. It is called heroic because in England, especially in the eighteenth century, it was much used for heroic (epic) poems.

    > Some foreign writers, some our own despise;
    > The ancients only, or the moderns, prize.
    >
    > —Alexander Pope

3. **Triplet** (or **tercet**): a three-line stanza, usually with one rhyme.

    > Whenas in silks my Julia goes
    > Then, then (methinks) how sweetly flows
    > That liquefaction of her clothes.
    >
    > —Robert Herrick

4. **Quatrain**: a four-line stanza, rhymed or unrhymed. The **heroic** (or **elegiac) quatrain** is iambic pentameter, rhyming *abab*. That is, the first and third lines rhyme (so they are designated *a*), and the second and fourth lines rhyme (so they are designated *b*).

Three Complex Forms: The Sonnet, the Villanelle, and the Sestina

The Sonnet

A sonnet is a fourteen-line poem, predominantly in iambic pentameter. The rhyme is usually according to one of two schemes. The **Italian** or **Petrarchan sonnet,** named for the Italian poet Petrarch (1304–1374), has two divisions: The first eight lines (rhyming *abba abba*) are the octave, and the last six (rhyming *cd cd cd,* or a variant) are the **sestet.** Gerard Manley Hopkins's "God's Grandeur" (page 807) is an Italian sonnet. The second kind of sonnet, the **English** or **Shakespearean sonnet,** is usually arranged into three quatrains and a couplet, rhyming *abab cdcd efef gg.* (For examples see the next two poems.)

In many sonnets there is a marked correspondence between the rhyme scheme and the development of the thought. Thus an Italian sonnet may state a generalization in the octave and a specific example in the sestet. Or an English sonnet may give three examples—one in each quatrain—and draw a conclusion in the couplet.

Why poets choose to imprison themselves in fourteen tightly rhymed lines is something of a mystery. Tradition has a great deal to do with it: the form, having been handled successfully by major poets, stands as a challenge. In writing a sonnet a poet gains a little of the authority of Petrarch, Shakespeare, Milton, Wordsworth, and other masters who showed that the sonnet is not merely a trick. A second reason perhaps resides in the very tightness of the rhymes, which can help as well as hinder. Many poets have felt, along with Richard Wilbur (in *Mid-Century American Poets,* ed. John Ciardi), that the need for a rhyme has suggested

> . . . arbitrary connections of which the mind may take advantage if it likes. For example, if one has to rhyme with *tide,* a great number of rhyme-words at once come to mind (ride, bide, shied, confide, Akenside, etc.). Most of these, in combination with *tide,* will probably suggest nothing apropos, but one of them may reveal precisely what one wanted to say. If none of them does, *tide* must be dispensed with. Rhyme, austerely used, may be a stimulus to discovery and a stretcher of the attention.

WILLIAM SHAKESPEARE

William Shakespeare (1564–1616), born in Stratford-upon-Avon in England, is chiefly known as a dramatic poet, but he also wrote nondramatic poetry. In 1609 a volume of 154 of his sonnets was published, apparently without his permission. Probably he chose to keep his sonnets unpublished not because he thought that they were of little value, but because it was more prestigious to be an amateur (unpublished) poet than a professional (published) one. Although the sonnets were published in 1609, they were probably written in the mid-1590s, when there was a vogue for sonneteering. A contemporary writer in 1598 said that Shakespeare's "sugred Sonnets [circulate] among his private friends."

Other sonnets by Shakespeare are on pages 822–23.

Sonnet 73

That time of year thou mayst in me behold
When yellow leaves, or none, or few, do hang
Upon those boughs which shake against the cold,
Bare ruined choirs° where late the sweet birds sang.
In me thou see'st the twilight of such day   5
As after sunset fadeth in the west,

---

4 choir the part of the church where services were sung.

Which by-and-by black night doth take away,
Death's second self that seals up all in rest.
In me thou see'st the glowing of such fire
That on the ashes of his youth doth lie,   10
As the deathbed whereon it must expire,
Consumed with that which it was nourished by.
   This thou perceiv'st, which makes thy love more strong,
   To love that well which thou must leave ere long.

YOUR TURN

1. In the first quatrain (the first four lines) to what "time of year" does Shakespeare compare himself? In the second quatrain (lines 5–8) to what does he compare himself? In the third? If the sequence of the three quatrains were reversed, what would be gained or lost?
2. In line 8, what is "Death's second self"? What implications do you perceive in "seals up all in rest," as opposed, for instance, to "brings most welcome rest"?
3. In line 13, exactly what is "This"?
4. In line 14, suppose in place of "To love that well which thou must leave ere long," Shakespeare had written "To love me well whom thou must leave ere long." What, if anything, would have been gained or lost?
5. What is your personal response to this sonnet? Do you feel that its lessons apply to you? Please explain.
6. Did you find this sonnet hard to understand when you read it for the first time? After you reread and studied it, did it become more difficult, or less so? Do you like to read difficult poems?

Sonnet 146

Poor soul, the center of my sinful earth,
My sinful earth° these rebel pow'rs that thee array,
Why doest thou pine within and suffer dearth,
Painting thy outward walls so costly gay?
Why so large cost,° having so short a lease,   5
Dost thou upon thy fading mansion spend?
Shall worms, inheritors of this excess,
Eat up thy charge? Is this thy body's end?
Then, soul, live thou upon thy servant's loss,
And let that pine to aggravate thy store;   10
Buy terms divine° in selling hours of dross;
Within be fed, without be rich no more.
   So shalt thou feed on Death, that feeds on men,
   And death once dead, there's no more dying then.

---

2 My sinful earth see the comment beneath the facsimile on page 677.   **5 cost** expense.   **11 Buy terms divine** buy ages of immortality.

POore foule the center of my finfull earth,
  My finfull earth thefe rebbell powres that thee array
Why doft thou pine within and fuffer dearth?
Painting thy outward walls fo coftlie gay?
Why fo large coft hauing fo fhort a leafe,
Doft thou vpon thy fading manfion fpend?
Shall wormes inheritors of this exceffe,
Eate vp thy charge? is this thy bodies end?
Then foule liue thou vpon thy feruants loffe,
And let that pine to aggrauat thy ftore;
Buy tearmes diuine in felling houres of droffe:
Within be fed, without be rich no more,
  So fhalt thou feed on death, that feeds on men,
  And death once dead, ther's no more dying then.

Sonnet 146 as it appears in the first publication of Shakespeare's sonnets, 1609. Notice that the first line ends with the words "my sinful earth," and the second line begins with the same words. Virtually all readers agree that the printer mistakenly repeated the words. First of all, the line makes almost no sense; secondly, it has 12 syllables ("powres" is monosyllabic) where 10 syllables are normal. Among attractive suggested emendations— usually two syllables instead of the four of "My sinful earth"—are those that pick up imagery of conflict explicit in "rebbell powres," such as "Prey to," "Thrall to," "Foiled by," and "Vexed by," and emendations that pick up imagery of hunger explicit in "Eate" and "fed," such as "Feeding" and "Starved by." But there are plenty of other candidates, such as "Fooled by," "Rebuke these," and "Leagued with."

YOUR TURN

1. As we indicate in our comment on the facsimile of this poem, the first three words of the second line probably should be replaced with other words. What words would you suggest? (We give some of the most widely accepted suggestions, but feel free to offer your own.)

2. In what tone of voice would you speak the first line? The last line? Trace the speaker's shifts in emotion throughout the poem.

3. What is your personal response to this poem? Do you feel that its lessons apply to you? Do you find this sonnet more meaningful, or less meaningful, to you than Sonnet 73 (page 675)? Please explain.

4. Did you find this poem hard to understand when you read it for the first time? After you reread and studied it, did the poem become more difficult, or less so? Is this sonnet more difficult than Sonnet 73? What is the difference between a poem that is challenging, a poem that is difficult, and a poem that is obscure?

JOHN MILTON

John Milton (1608–1674) was born into a well-to-do family in London, where from childhood he was a student of languages, mastering at an early age Latin, Greek, Hebrew, and a number of modern languages. Instead of becoming a minister in the Anglican Church, he resolved to become a poet and spent five years at his family's country home, reading. His attacks against the monarchy secured him a position in Oliver Cromwell's Puritan government as Latin secretary for foreign affairs. He became totally blind, but he continued his work through secretaries, one of whom was Andrew Marvell, author of "To His Coy Mistress" (page 652). With the restoration of the monarchy in 1660, Milton was for a time confined but was later pardoned in the general amnesty. Until his death he continued to work on many subjects, including his greatest poem, the epic Paradise Lost.

When I Consider How My Light Is Spent   [1655]

When I consider how my light is spent
  Ere half my days, in this dark world and wide,
  And that one talent which is death to hide°
  Lodged with me useless,° though my soul more bent
To serve therewith my Maker, and present   5
  My true account, lest he returning chide;
  "Doth God exact day-labor, light denied?"
  I fondly° ask; but Patience to prevent°
That murmur, soon replies, "God doth not need
  Either man's work or his own gifts; who best   10
  Bear his mild yoke, they serve him best. His state
Is kingly. Thousands at his bidding speed
  And post o'er land and ocean without rest:
  They also serve who only stand and wait."

---

3 There is a pun in *talent,* relating Milton's literary talent to Christ's Parable of the Talents (Matthew 25.14 ff.), in which a servant is rebuked for not putting his talent (a unit of money) to use.   **4 useless** a pun on *use,* i.e., usury, interest.   **8 fondly** foolishly. **prevent** forestall.

YOUR TURN

1. This sonnet is sometimes called "On His Blindness," though Milton never gave it a title. Do you think this title gets toward the heart of the poem? Explain. If you were to give it a title, what would the title be?
2. Read the parable in Matthew 25.14–30, and then consider how close the parable is to Milton's life as Milton describes it in this poem.
3. Where is the turn? What characteristics are attributed to God after the turn?
4. Compare the tone of the first and the last sentences. How does the length of each of these sentences contribute to the tone?
5. Could you imagine someone saying, "This poem changed my life"? What kind of change in a person's life might this sonnet produce?

6. What is your own experience of blindness? Have you ever lost your eyesight? For a long or a short period? Do you know a blind person? What is the nature of your interaction with him or her?

X. J. KENNEDY

X. J. Kennedy was born in New Jersey in 1929. He has taught at Tufts University and is the author of many books of poems, books for children, and college textbooks.

Kennedy alludes (line 4) to Milton's Paradise Lost, *VII, 205–207: "Heaven opened wide / Her ever-during gates, harmonious sound / On golden hinges moving. . . ." For an account of the slaughter of the innocents (line 5), see Matthew 2.16. The Venerable Bede (675–735), in line 6, was an English theologian and historian.*

Nothing in Heaven Functions as It Ought   [1965]

Nothing in Heaven functions as it ought:
Peter's bifocals, blindly sat on, crack;
His gates lurch wide with the cackle of a cock,
Not turn with a hush of gold as Milton had thought;
Gangs of the slaughtered innocents keep huffing   5
The nimbus off the Venerable Bede
Like that of an old dandelion gone to seed;
And the beatific choir keep breaking up, coughing.

But Hell, sleek Hell hath no freewheeling part:
None takes his own sweet time, none quickens pace.   10
Ask anyone, How come you here, poor heart?—
And he will slot a quarter through his face,
You'll hear an instant click, a tear will start
Imprinted with an abstract of his case.

YOUR TURN

In the octave Kennedy uses off-rhymes *(crack, cock; huffing, coughing)*, but in the sestet all the rhymes are exact. How do the rhymes help to convey the meaning? (Notice, too, that lines, 3, 4, 5, 7, and 8 all have more than the usual ten syllables. Again, why?)

BILLY COLLINS

For a bibliographical note, see page 589.

The following sonnet uses the Petrarchan form of an octave and a sestet (see page 674). Petrarch is additionally present in the poem by the allusion in line 3 to "a little ship on love's storm-tossed seas," because Petrarch compared the hapless lover, denied the favor of his mistress, to a ship in a storm: The lover cannot guide his ship because the North Star is hidden (Petrarch's beloved Laura averts her eyes), and the sails of the ship are agitated by the lover's pitiful sighs. As you will see, Petrarch and Laura explicitly enter the poem in the last three lines.

In line 8 Collins refers to the stations of the cross. In Roman Catholicism, one of the devotions consists of prayers and meditations before each of fourteen crosses or images set up along a path that commemorates the fourteen places at which Jesus halted when, just before the Crucifixion, he was making his way in Jerusalem to Golgotha.

Sonnet   [2001]

All we need is fourteen lines, well, thirteen now,
and after this next one just a dozen
to launch a little ship on love's storm-tossed seas,
then only ten more left like rows of beans.
How easily it goes unless you get Elizabethan   5
and insist the iambic bongos must be played
and rhymes positioned at the ends of lines,
one for every station of the cross.
But hang on here while we make the turn
into the final six where all will be resolved,   10
where longing and heartache will find an end,
where Laura will tell Petrarch to put down his pen,
take off those crazy medieval tights,
blow out the lights, and come at last to bed.

YOUR TURN

1. The headnote explains the stations of the cross (line 8), but what is the point of introducing this image into a sonnet?
2. Normally the "turn" (*volta*) in an Italian sonnet occurs at the beginning of the ninth line; the first eight lines (the octave) establish some sort of problem, and the final six lines (the sestet) respond, for instance by answering a question, or by introducing a contrasting emotion. In your view, how satisfactorily does Collins handle this form?
3. Does this sonnet interest you? Do you find it clever? Is that a good thing or a bad thing?
4. Do you think that you could have written this sonnet? Could you have written Shakespeare's sonnets 73 and 146 (pages 675–76)? What do your responses to these questions suggest to you about the writing of poetry?

The Villanelle

The name comes from an Italian words, *villanella*, meaning "country song" or "peasant song," and originally, in the sixteenth century, the subject was the supposedly simple life of the shepherd, but in France in the seventeenth century elaborate rules were developed. Variations occur, but usually a **villanelle** has the following characteristics:

• Five stanzas with three lines each (tercets), rhyming *aba,* and a final stanza with four lines (a quatrain).

- The first line of the first stanza is repeated as the last line of the second stanza and the last line of the fourth stanza.
- The third line of the first stanza is repeated as the last line of the third stanza and the last line of the fifth stanza.
- The quatrain that concludes the villanelle rhymes *abaa,* using the first and third lines of the first stanza as the next-to-last and the last lines of the final stanza—i.e., the poem ends with a couplet.

Because the villanelle repeats one sound thirteen times (in the first and last line of each tercet, and in the first, third, and fourth lines of the quatrain), it strongly conveys a sense of return, a sense of not going forward, even a sense of dwelling on the past. We give four examples of the form.

If you are going to write a villanelle, here are two tips:

- Begin by writing a couplet (a pair of rhyming lines); in fact, write several couplets on different topics, and then decide which couplet you think is most promising. Next, insert between these two lines a line that makes sense in the context but that does *not* rhyme with them.
- Each line need not end with a pause, and in fact some run-on lines probably will help to prevent the poem from becoming too sing-songy.

DYLAN THOMAS

For a biographical note, see page 586.

Do Not Go Gentle into That Good Night   [1952]

Do not go gentle into that good night,
Old age should burn and rave at close of day;
Rage, rage against the dying of the light.

Though wise men at their end know dark is right,
Because their words had forked no lightning they   5
Do not go gentle into that good night.

Good men, the last wave by, crying how bright
Their frail deeds might have danced in a green bay,
Rage, rage against the dying of the light.

Wild men who caught and sang the sun in flight,   10
And learn, too late, they grieved it on its way,
Do not go gentle into that good night.

Grave men, near death, who see with blinding sight
Blind eyes could blaze like meteors and be gay,
Rage, rage against the dying of the light.   15

And you, my father, there on the sad height,
Curse, bless, me now with your fierce tears, I pray.
Do not go gentle into that good night.
Rage, rage against the dying of the light.

YOUR TURN

1. The intricate form of the villanelle might seem too fussy for a serious poem about dying. Do you find it too fussy? Or does the form here somehow succeed?
2. How would you describe the speaker's tone? Is it accurate or misleading to say that "Do Not Go Gentle into That Good Night" is an angry poem?
3. What is the speaker's attitude toward death? Do you share this attitude or not? Please explain.
4. This is a famous poem. Why do you think that is the case?

ELIZABETH BISHOP

Elizabeth Bishop (1911–1979) was born in Worcester, Massachusetts. Because her father died when she was eight months old and her mother was confined to a sanitarium four years later, Bishop was raised by relatives in New England and Nova Scotia. After graduation from Vassar College in 1934, where she was co-editor of the student literary magazine, she lived (on a small private income) for a while in Key West, France, and Mexico, and then for much of her adult life in Brazil, before returning to the United States to teach at Harvard. A one-volume collection of Bishop's work, Poems, Prose, and Letters, has been published by the Library of America (2008).

One Art   [1976]

The art of losing isn't hard to master;
so many things seem filled with the intent
to be lost that their loss is no disaster.

Lose something every day. Accept the fluster
of lost door keys, the hour badly spent.   5
The art of losing isn't hard to master.

Then practice losing farther, losing faster:
places, and names, and where it was you meant
to travel. None of these will bring disaster.

I lost my mother's watch. And look! my last, or   10
next-to-last, of three loved houses went.
The art of losing isn't hard to master.

I lost two cities, lovely ones. And, vaster,
some realms I owned, two rivers, a continent.
I miss them, but it wasn't a disaster.   15

—Even losing you (the joking voice, a gesture
I love) I shan't have lied. It's evident
the art of losing's not too hard to master
though it may look like (*Write* it!) like disaster.

YOUR TURN

1. What was your response to the title when you first read it? Did your response change after you read the poem and studied it further?
2. Is the form connected to the poem's theme? If so, in what way?
3. Linger over line 1: Why is "losing" an "art"? And why does Bishop echo the phrasing of the first line in lines later in the poem? Does the echo make the poem feel repetitive?
4. Follow Bishop's uses of the words "lose," "losing," and "loss" from one to the next. Do you find her reliance on these very closely related words to be important for the poem's meaning, or does it strike you as a lot or a little confusing? Can a poem be a lot or a little confusing and yet still be a good poem?
5. Can we tell what kind of loss Bishop is exploring? If we can, where does this kind of loss become clear?
6. Whom is Bishop addressing when she says (note the exclamation point) "*Write* it!"? Why is this command in the poem, and why is it in parentheses?
7. Has this poem helped you to understand a loss or losses that you have experienced yourself? Something, perhaps, that you did not understand before about what "losing" someone or something important means? Do you have an insight of your own into losing and loss that Bishop has not considered, at least not in this poem? Is this an insight that you would want to share with others—in a poem, for example—or keep to yourself?

The Sestina

This fiendishly elaborate form developed in twelfth-century Europe, especially in southern France, among the troubadours, court poets who sang for nobles. (The name comes from the Italian *sesto*, "sixth," because there are six stanzas of six lines each—but then, to complicate matters, there is a seventh stanza, a three-line "envoy" or "envoi," a summing up that uses key words of the first six stanzas.)

More precisely—this is mind-boggling—the six words that end the six lines of the first stanza are used at the ends of all the following lines but in a different though fixed order in each stanza. (Rhyme is *not* used in this form.) This fixed order has been characterized as a sort of bottoms-up pattern, a term that will become clear as we describe the stanzas. In the second stanza the *first* line ends with the *last* word of the *last* line (the bottom) of the first stanza; the second line of the second stanza ends with the first line of the first; the third line ends with the last word of the fifth line of the first stanza—i.e., with the next-to-bottom line of the first stanza. The fourth line of the second stanza ends with the second line of the first, the fifth with the fourth line of the first, and the sixth with the third line of the first.

Thus, if we designate the final words of the first stanza, line by line, as 1, 2, 3, 4, 5, 6,

the final words of the second stanza are 6, 1, 5, 2, 4, 3;
the third stanza: 3, 6, 4, 1, 2, 5
the fourth stanza: 5, 3, 2, 6, 1, 4
the fifth stanza: 4, 5, 1, 3, 6, 2
the sixth stanza: 2, 4, 6, 5, 3, 1

The envoy of three lines must use these six words, but there are various possible patterns—for instance, 5, 3, 1 at the ends of the three lines, and 2, 4, 6 in the middle of the lines.

If you are going to write a sestina, two tips:

- Once you have settled on your topic—let's say "loss" or "a restless spirit of adventure"—jot down six words that you think are relevant, and get going.
- You need not end each line with a pause, and in fact most good sestinas use considerable enjambment—i.e., the sense of the line runs over into the next line.

ELIZABETH BISHOP

For a biographical note, see page 682.

Sestina   [1965]

September rain falls on the house.
In the failing light, the old grandmother
sits in the kitchen with the child
beside the Little Marvel Stove,
reading the jokes from the almanac,   5
laughing and talking to hide her tears.

She thinks that her equinoctial tears
and the rain that beats on the roof of the house
were both foretold by the almanac,
but only known to a grandmother.   10
The iron kettle sings on the stove.
She cuts some bread and says to the child,

It's time for tea now; but the child
is watching the teakettle's small hard tears
dance like mad on the hot black stove,   15
the way the rain must dance on the house.
Tidying up, the old grandmother
hangs up the clever almanac

on its string. Birdlike, the almanac
hovers half open above the child,   20
hovers above the old grandmother
and her teacup full of dark brown tears.
She shivers and says she thinks the house
feels chilly, and puts more wood in the stove.

It was to be, says the Marvel° Stove.   25
I know what I know, says the almanac.
With crayons the child draws a rigid house
and a winding pathway. Then the child
puts in a man with buttons like tears
and shows it proudly to the grandmother.   30

---

25 Marvel a brand of stoves and appliances.

But secretly, while the grandmother
busies herself about the stove,
the little moons fall down like tears
from between the pages of the almanac
into the flower bed the child   35
has carefully placed in the front of the house.

Time to plant tears, says the almanac.
The grandmother sings to the marvelous stove
and the child draws another inscrutable house.

YOUR TURN

1. Does Bishop's choice of title seem strange to you? Why would she use
   the name of the poetic form for her title? Do you think that a different
   title might be more effective? Please give examples, and explain why
   they would or would not be better.
2. As carefully as you can, describe the effect of line 1.
3. In the first stanza, why is the grandmother crying? How are her tears in
   lines 6 and 7 related to the "small hard tears" of the teakettle in line 14?
   Note, too, the later references to tears. Please comment on these as
   well.
4. Several of the lines in this poem are italicized. Do the italics make the
   lines more forceful? Should Bishop have made the force of the lines
   clear without changing the "look" of the lines on the page?
5. What is an almanac? Have you ever seen one? Why would someone
   want an almanac? What is the significance of the almanac in this
   poem?
6. What is your response to the fact that this poem is a sestina? Do you
   think you could write a poem in this form? What would be the benefit
   to you of such an assignment?

Shaped Poetry or Pattern Poetry

We have been talking about shapes or patterns determined by rhymes, but some
poems—admittedly few—take their shape from the length of the lines, which
form a simple image, such as a sphere, an egg, a vase, or a wing.

Here is a famous example of shaped poetry, a pair of wings. We print it
sideways, as it was printed in the earliest edition, in 1633, though in that edition the first stanza was printed on the left-hand page, the second on the right-
hand page.

GEORGE HERBERT

*George Herbert (1593–1633), born into a distinguished Welsh family, studied
at the University of Cambridge (England) and became a clergyman. By all accounts he lived an admirable life and was deservedly known in his community as "Holy Mr. Herbert."*

Note: *In line 1,* store *means "abundance," "plenty." In line 10, the* fall *refers to the loss of innocence that resulted when Adam ate the forbidden fruit in the garden of Eden. In the next-to-last line,* imp, *a term from falconry, means "to graft, to insert feathers into a wing."*
We print the poem in the way that it was originally printed.

Easter-Wings   [1633]

Lord, who createdst man in wealth and store,
　Though foolishly he lost the same,
　　Decaying more and more,
　　　Till he became
　　　　Most poor:
　　　　With thee
　　　O let me rise
　　As larks, harmoniously,
　And sing this day thy victories:
Then shall the fall further the flight in me.   5 / 10

My tender age in sorrow did begin:
　And still with sicknesses and shame
　　Thou didst so punish sin,
　　　That I became
　　　　Most thin.
　　　　With thee
　　　Let me combine,
　　And feel this day thy victory:
　For, if I imp my wing on thine,
Affliction shall advance the flight in me.   15 / 20

> **YOUR TURN**

1. Why are wings especially relevant to a poem about Easter?
2. We don't think one can argue that the length of every line is exactly suited to the meaning of the line, but we do think that some of the lengths are parallel or reinforce some of the ideas within those lines. For instance, the first line, speaking of a man's original "wealth and store," is a long line. Why is this length more appropriate to the meaning than it would be to, say, "Lord, who created a man who soon would fall"? And note especially the fifth and sixth lines of each stanza: Would you agree that their length suits their meaning?
3. Do you think this poem is a mere novelty, or do you think it deserves close attention and indeed is memorable? Please explain.

Blank Verse and Free Verse

A good deal of English poetry is unrhymed, much of it in **blank verse**—that is, unrhymed iambic pentameter. Introduced into English poetry by Henry Howard, the Earl of Surrey, in the middle of the sixteenth century, late in the century it became the standard medium (especially in the hands of Marlowe and Shakespeare) of English drama. In the seventeenth century, Milton used it for *Paradise Lost,* and it has continued to be used in both dramatic and nondramatic literature. For an example see the first scene of *Hamlet* (page 1001). A passage of blank verse that has a rhetorical unity is sometimes called a **verse paragraph.**

The second kind of unrhymed poetry fairly common in English, especially in the twentieth century, is **free verse** (or **vers libre**): rhythmical lines varying in length, adhering to no fixed metrical pattern and usually unrhymed. Such poetry may seem formless; Robert Frost, who strongly preferred regular meter and rhyme, said that he would not consider writing free verse any more than he would consider playing tennis without a net. But free verse does have a form or pattern, often largely based on repetition and parallel grammatical structure. Whitman's "A Noiseless Patient Spider" (page 585) is an example; Arnold's "Dover Beach" (page 778) is another example, though less typical because it uses rhyme. Thoroughly typical is Whitman's "When I Heard the Learn'd Astronomer."

WALT WHITMAN

For a biographical note, see page 633.

When I Heard the Learn'd Astronomer   [1865]

When I heard the learn'd astronomer,
When the proofs, the figures, were ranged in columns before me,
When I was shown the charts and diagrams, to add, divide, and measure
    them,
When I sitting heard the astronomer where he lectured with much
    applause in the lecture-room,
How soon unaccountable I became tired and sick,   5
Till rising and gliding out I wander'd off by myself,
In the mystical moist night-air, and from time to time,
Look'd up in perfect silence at the stars.

What can be said about the rhythmic structure of this poem? Rhymes are absent, and the lines vary greatly in the number of syllables, ranging from 9 (the first line) to 23 (the fourth line), but when we read the poem we sense a rhythmic structure. The first four lines obviously hang together, each beginning with "When"; indeed, three of these four lines begin "When I." We may notice, too, that each of these four lines has more syllables than its predecessor (the numbers are 9, 14, 18, and 23); this increase in length, like the initial repetition, is a kind of pattern. But then, with the fifth line, which speaks of fatigue and surfeit, there is a shrinkage to 14 syllables, offering an enormous relief from the previous swollen line with its 23 syllables. The second half of the poem—the pattern established by "When" in the first four lines is dropped, and in effect we get a new stanza, also of four lines—does not relentlessly diminish the number of syllables in each succeeding line, but it *almost* does so: 14, 14, 13, 10.

The second half of the poem thus has a pattern too, and this pattern is more or less the reverse of the first half of the poem. We may notice too that the last line (in which the poet, now released from the oppressive lecture hall, is in communion with nature) is very close to an iambic pentameter line; that is, the poem concludes with a metrical form said to be the most natural in English. The effect of naturalness or ease in this final line, moreover, is increased by the absence of repetitions (e.g., not only of "When I," but even of such syntactic repetitions as "charts and diagrams," "tired and sick," "rising and gliding") that characterize most of the previous lines. This final effect of naturalness is part of a carefully constructed pattern in which rhythmic structure is part of meaning. Though at first glance free verse may appear unrestrained, as T. S. Eliot (a practitioner) said, "No *vers* is *libre* for the man who wants to do a good job"—or for the woman who wants to do a good job.

The Prose Poem

The term *prose poem* is sometimes applied to a short work that looks like prose but that is highly rhythmical or rich in images, or both. Here is a modern example.

CAROLYN FORCHÉ

Carolyn Forché was born in Detroit in 1950. After earning a bachelor's degree from Michigan State University and a master's degree from Bowling Green State University, she traveled widely in the Southwest, living among Pueblo Indians. Between 1978 and 1986 she made several visits to El Salvador, documenting human rights violations for Amnesty International. Her first book of poems, Gathering the Tribes, *won the Yale Younger Poets award in 1975. Forché is the Director of the Lannan Center for Poetry and Poetics and holds the Lannan Chair in Poetry at Georgetown University in Washington D.C.*

The Colonel   [1978, publ. 1981]

What you have heard is true. I was in his house. His wife carried a tray of coffee and sugar. His daughter filed her nails, his son went out for the night. There were daily papers, pet dogs, a pistol on the cushion beside him. The moon swung bare on its black cord over the house. On the television was a cop show. It was in English. Broken bottles were embedded in the walls around the house to scoop the kneecaps from a man's legs or cut his hands to lace. On the windows there were gratings like those in liquor stores. We had dinner, rack of lamb, good wine, a gold bell was on the table for calling the maid. The maid brought green mangoes, salt, a type of bread. I was asked how I enjoyed the country. There was a brief commercial in Spanish. His wife took everything away. There was some talk then of how difficult it had become to govern. The parrot said hello on the terrace. The colonel told it to shut up, and pushed himself from the table. My friend said to me with his eyes: say nothing. The colonel returned with a sack used to bring groceries home. He spilled many human ears on the table. They were like dried peach halves. There is no other way to say this. He took one of them in his hands, shook it in our faces, dropped it into a water glass. It came alive there. I am tired of fooling around he said. As for the rights of anyone, tell your people they can go fuck themselves. He swept the ears to the floor with his arm and held the last of his wine in the air. Something for your poetry, no? he said. Some of the ears on the floor caught this scrap of his voice. Some of the ears on the floor were pressed to the ground.

May 1978

YOUR TURN

1. How would you characterize the colonel in a few sentences?
2. We are told that the colonel spoke of "how difficult it had become to govern." What do you suppose the colonel assumes is the purpose of government? What do you assume its purpose is?
3. How much do we know about the narrator? Can we guess the narrator's purpose in visiting the colonel? How would you characterize the narrator's tone? Do you believe the narrator?
4. What is your response to the last sentence?
5. What, if anything, is gained by calling this work a "prose poem" rather than a short story?

24

Students Writing About Poems

If you are going to write about a fairly short poem (say, under 30 lines), it's not a bad idea to copy out the poem, writing or typing it double-spaced. By writing it out you will be forced to notice details, down to the punctuation. After you have copied the poem, proofread it carefully against the original. Catching an error— even the addition or omission of a comma—may help you to notice a detail in the original that you might otherwise have overlooked. And now that you have the poem with ample space between the lines, you have a worksheet with room for jottings.

A good essay is based on a genuine response to a poem; a response may be stimulated in part by first reading the poem aloud and then considering the questions that follow in the sections below.

Remember, even an explication—an unfolding of the implications of the poem—is an argument. In the example on page 545, the student begins by asserting a thesis, a claim: "'Harlem' is only eleven lines long, but it is charged with power." The thesis, the arguable claim, of course is not that "the poem is only eleven lines long" but that "it is charged with power," and the rest of the explication is devoted to supporting this claim, to pointing out almost word by word the sources of the power,

First Response

1. What was your response to the poem on first reading?
2. Did some parts of the poem especially please or displease you, or puzzle you?
3. After some study—perhaps checking the meanings of some of the words in a dictionary and reading the poem several times—did you modify your initial response to the parts and to the whole?

Speaker and Tone

1. Who is the speaker? (Consider age, sex, personality, frame of mind, and tone of voice.) Is the speaker defined fairly precisely (for instance, an older woman speaking to a child), or is the speaker simply a voice meditating? (Jot down your first impressions, then reread the poem and make further jottings, if necessary.)

2. Do you think the speaker is fully aware of what he or she is saying, or does the speaker unconsciously reveal his or her personality and values? What is your attitude toward this speaker?
3. Is the speaker narrating or reflecting on an earlier experience or attitude? If so, does he or she convey a sense of new awareness, such as regret for innocence lost?

Audience

1. To whom is the speaker speaking?
2. What is the situation (including time and place)? In some poems a listener is strongly implied, but in others, especially those in which the speaker is meditating, there may be no audience other than the reader, who "overhears" the speaker.

Structure and Form

1. Does the poem proceed in a straightforward way, or at some point or points does the speaker reverse course, altering his or her tone or perception? If there is a shift, what do you make of it?
2. Is the poem organized into sections? If so, what are these sections—stanzas, for instance—and how does each section (characterized, perhaps, by a certain tone of voice, or a group of rhymes) grow out of what precedes it?
3. What is the effect on you of the form—say, quatrains (stanzas of four lines) or blank verse (unrhymed lines of ten syllables of iambic pentameter)? If the sense overflows the form, running without pause from (for example) one quatrain into the next, what effect is created?

Center of Interest and Theme

1. What is the poem about? Is the interest chiefly in a distinctive character, or is it in meditation? That is, is the poem chiefly psychological or chiefly philosophical?
2. Is the theme stated explicitly (directly) or implicitly? How might you state the theme in a sentence? What is lost by reducing the poem to a statement of a theme?

Diction

1. How would you characterize the language? Colloquial, elevated, or what?
2. Do certain words have rich and relevant associations that relate to other words and help to define the speaker or the theme or both?
3. What is the role of figurative language, if any? Does it help to define the speaker or the theme?
4. What do you think is to be taken figuratively or symbolically, and what literally?

Sound Effects

1. What is the role of sound effects, including repetitions of sound (for instance, alliteration) and of entire words, and shifts in versification?
2. If there are off-rhymes (for instance, *dizzy* and *easy*, or *home* and *come*), what effect do they have on you? Do they, for instance, add a note of tentativeness or uncertainty?
3. If there are unexpected stresses or pauses, what do they communicate about the speaker's experience? How do they affect you?

A Note on Explication

On pages 80–81 we discuss the form known as *explication,* a line-by-line commentary seeking to make explicit or to explain the meaning that is implicit or hidden within the words. (*Explication* comes from the Latin *explicare,* meaning "to unfold," from *ex* = out + *plicare* = to fold.) The implication of such an activity is that writers "fold" a meaning into their words, and the reader perceives or unfolds the message. (*Implication,* also from the Latin word for "fold," means something entangled or involved in something else.)

Think about someone who says, "Shut the door" rather than "Would you mind shutting the door, please?" Obviously, the message in "Shut the door" is *not* exactly the same as the message in "Would you mind shutting the door, please?" An explication would point out that the first sentence contains an authoritative tone that is not found in the second. In effect, the first sentence "says" (in addition to the point about the door) that the speaker may give orders to the hearer; or, to put it the other way around, folded into the second sentence (but not the first) is the speaker's awareness that the person receiving the words is the speaker's social equal.

A slightly more complicated and much more interesting example is Julius Caesar's "I came, I saw, I conquered" (Latin: *veni, vidi, vici*). An explication would point out that in addition to the explicit meaning there are implicit meanings, for example that a man like Caesar does not waste words, that he is highly disciplined (the pattern of words suggests that he is a master of language), and that he is the sort of person who, on seeing something, immediately gets it under control by taking the appropriate action.

Because explication is chiefly concerned with making explicit what is implicit in a text, it is not concerned with such matters as the poet's place in history or the poet's biography, nor is it concerned with the reader's response to the poem—except to the degree that the reader's explication really may *not* be an objective decoding of the poem but may depend in large part on the reader's private associations. (Some literary critics would argue that the underlying premise of explication—that a writer puts a specific meaning into a work and that a reader can objectively recover that meaning—is based on the mistaken belief that readers can be objective.) If you look at the sample explication on page 82, you can decide for yourself whether the student unfolded implicit meanings that the author (William Butler Yeats) had tucked into the words of his poem or whether the explication really is a personal response to the poem.

Seven Students Write About Poems

The first student essay in this chapter is not only an explication but also, first, a more personal response to a poem by Louise Glück. Like an explication, it is concerned with the author's meaning; but unlike an explication, it does not hesitate to go beyond the poem and into "the real world" that the writer of the paper lives in. The essay is not so personal that the poem disappears (as it might in an essay that says something like "This poem reminds me of the time that I . . ."), but it does not claim merely to unfold meanings that Glück has embodied or entangled in her words.

First read the following biographical note and the poem.

LOUISE GLÜCK

One of the leading contemporary poets, Louise Glück (pronounced "glick") was born in New York City in 1943, grew up on Long Island, and attended Sarah Lawrence College and Columbia University. She has taught at a number of colleges and universities, including the University of Iowa and Williams College. Firstborn, *her first book of poems, was published in 1968. Her later books include* The House on Marshland *(1975), from which the following poem is taken;* The Triumph of Achilles *(1985);* The Wild Iris *(1992);* Vita Nova *(1999) and* Averno *(2006). Glück's poetry has been widely anthologized and translated.* Proofs and Theories: Essays on Poetry *(1995) is a collection of her literary criticism on Stanley Kunitz, T. S. Eliot, and other authors.*

Gretel in Darkness   [1975]

This is the world we wanted.
All who would have seen us dead
are dead. I hear the witch's cry
break in the moonlight through a sheet
of sugar: God rewards.   5
Her tongue shrivels into gas . . . .

Now, far from women's arms
and memory of women, in our father's hut
we sleep, are never hungry.
Why do I not forget?   10
My father bars the door, bars harm
from this house, and it is years.

No one remembers. Even you, my brother,
summer afternoons you look at me as though
you meant to leave,   15
as though it never happened.
But I killed for you. I see armed firs,
the spires of that gleaming kiln—

Nights I turn to you to hold me
but you are not there.
Am I alone? Spies   20
hiss in the stillness, Hansel,
we are there still and it is real, real,
that black forest and the fire in earnest.

Jennifer Anderson was assigned to write about this poem in an introduction to literature course. Anderson started her work by copying the poem on a sheet of paper and annotating it.

Speaker?????   (Gretel) in Darkness   — *Gretel and her brother*

This is the world (we) wanted.

All who would have seen us (dead) are (dead,)

I hear the witch's cry break in the moonlight

through a sheet of sugar: <u>God</u> rewards.   *Christian theme?*

Her tongue shrivels into gas. . . .

Why this space?   Now, far from women's arms   — *Women (mother) vs.*

and memory of women, in our father's hut

we sleep, are never hungry.   — *Father*

Why do I not forget? ——— *the Key Question*

My father (bars) the door, (bars) harm

from this house, and it is years.

The speaker does   <u>No one remembers.</u> Even you, my brother,

summer afternoons <u>you look at me as though</u>

<u>you meant to leave,</u> as though it never happened.

intense, direct word choice   But I <u>killed</u> for you. I see armed firs,   *oven, furnace*

the spires of that gleaming (kiln—)

Nights I turn to you to hold me   *Hansel's separation / distance from Gretel*

<u>but you are not there.</u>

"S" sounds   Am I alone? Spies   *compare with opening lines— everything's not dead*

hiss in the stillness, Hansel,

(we are there) still and it is (real,) (real,)

that black forest and the fire in <u>earnest.</u>   *serious + intense*

To follow up on these annotations and develop them, Anderson turned next to her writing journal. She jotted down responses and ideas and her questions about aspects of the poem and details of the language that intrigued and puzzled her.

Here are the pages from Anderson's journal:

Great poem! Haunting, eerie. My favorite so far in the course.

Story of Hansel and Gretel—Look this up. Should I summarize the story in the paper?

Speaker—Gretel. Why *her*, and not Hansel? Not both of them as speakers? "in darkness"—really in darkness, or is darkness a metaphor?

Repetition in the poem: dead/dead, bar/bar, real/real.

The tone of the opening stanza—scary, ominous. Darkness, dead.

The reference to the witch. "Shrivels into gas"—creepy detail.

But the witch has been defeated. Through the power of God? *Why is God mentioned* in this line?—not mentioned elsewhere.

Women (not mothers) seem the enemy in stanza two. (Odd that the second stanza is indented.) The *father* provides safety. But safety is not enough. Gretel cannot forget the past: the real enemy is not the witch or the mothers, but her memory.

She has to talk about her memory, her experiences. "No one remembers," but she *does*.

I think that this is a poem about Memory: "Why do I not forget?"

Gretel doesn't want her brother to forget. She reminds him.

"Killed"—such a strong word, very direct. *Gretel is angry with her brother;* she feels him pulling away from her.

Something disturbed, unnatural about the poem?—the detail about Gretel looking for her brother to hold her. But he is absent. Where is he?

Who are the "Spies"? Lots of "s" sounds in these lines—spies, hiss, stillness, Hansel, still.

She addresses him *by name*.

She cannot escape, maybe she doesn't want to escape. Note that Gretel is *describing her memories of what happened*—not a poem that *tells the story* of Hansel and Gretel. Glück is interested in how Gretel *remembers,* how she feels about remembering.

Anderson knew the main features of the Hansel and Gretel story—the brother and sister, their abandonment, their capture by a witch, and their escape. But she wanted to remind herself about the details, as her note to herself in her journal indicates.

As an experiment, Anderson went to Google and searched for "hansel and gretel." A number of the results looked promising, and she linked to this one:

Grimm's Fairy Tales—Hansel and Gretel
http://www.mordent.com/folktales/grimms/hng/hng.html

Anderson had not reread "Hansel and Gretel" since she was a child. Reread-ing it now was very helpful, for it clarified a number of important details in Glück's poem. It explained, for example, "the witch's cry" in the first stanza, which alludes to the witch's "horrible howl" when Gretel pushes her into the oven. It also fills out the reference to the "women" in the second stanza, who in the story include the children's cruel stepmother as well as the evil witch. Anderson could have prepared and written her paper without taking the time to check on the story, but it was better that she did.

Here is the essay that Jennifer Anderson wrote.

Anderson 1

Jennifer Anderson
Professor Washington
English 102
12 June 2010

A Memory Poem:
Louise Glück's "Gretel in Darkness"

Everyone knows the story of Hansel and Gretel, one of the best-known of Grimm's fairy tales. In her poem "Gretel in Darkness," Louise Glück takes for granted that we know the story—the brother and sister who are mistreated by their father and, especially, by their stepmother; their abandonment in a forest; their capture by a witch who lives in a house made of cakes and candy; the witch's plan to fatten them up (Hansel first) and then eat them; Gretel's killing of the witch by pushing her into an oven; and, finally, the children's discovery of the witch's jewels that makes them and their father (the stepmother has died) rich and happy at last. Glück's subject is not the story itself but, instead, Gretel's memories. "Gretel in Darkness" is a haunting poem about horrors that Gretel, Glück's speaker, cannot forget.

The poem takes place after the witch has been killed and Hansel and Gretel have returned to the safety of their father's cottage. Everything now should be fine, Gretel says: "This is the world we wanted." "God rewards": God has heard their prayers and saved them. But as if it were still present, Gretel hears "the witch's cry," the witch whom Gretel killed. And the image about the witch's death that she uses is graphic and disturbing: "Her tongue shrivels into gas. . . ." The witch was horrible, but this image is horrifying; it sticks in Gretel's mind, and the reader's too, like a shocking detail from a nightmare.

In a way the entire poem reports on a nightmare that Gretel is doomed to live in forever. "Why do I not forget?"—the key line in the poem, I think—really means that she knows she will always remember what happened to her and her brother. For Gretel this fairy tale does not have a happy ending.

Yet it does for her brother, or so it seems to Gretel. She resents Hansel's failure to remember as she does, and, with a vivid, direct choice of verb, she reminds him: "I killed for you." The nightmarish quality of Gretel's thoughts and feelings is shown again in the next lines, which once more make clear how much her past dominates the present:

> . . . I see armed firs,
>
> the spires of that gleaming kiln—

Gretel is safe but threatened, sheltered at home but still in danger. She is caught by a terrifying and terrible past she cannot break free from. The repetitions—dead/dead, bars/bar, real/real—imply that she is trapped, not able to re-enter the present and look forward to the future. She turns to her brother for help, yet without finding the support she seeks:

> Nights I turn to you to hold me
>
> but you are not there.

Hansel (who is only named once) is not there for Gretel, and at first I felt her hurt. But Glück is not meaning to criticize Hansel for his distance, his separation from his sister. Or if Glück is, she is balancing that against Gretel's absorption in the terror of her experiences. She feels that she and her brother are still in the middle of them.

As I thought further about this poem, I wondered: Strange as it sounds, maybe Gretel prefers the past to the present because the past was so real. Life is all too safe and comfortable now, while *then* everything, like the fire in the oven, was so earnest, that is, so serious and intense. It was not the world she wanted—who would want to be in that house of horrors! Even now her life is menaced, as those snaky "s" sounds in the middle of the final stanza suggest. But perhaps the frightful feelings, in their intensity, were (and still are) keener and deeper than anything that Gretel knew before, or knows now, in the secure world she lives in with her father and brother. She and her brother then were so absolutely close, as they are not now. Gretel cannot let go of her past, and she does not want to.

Anderson 3

Work Cited

Glück, Louise. "Gretel in Darkness." *An Introduction to Literature*. Ed.
Sylvan Barnet, William Burto, and William E. Cain. 16th ed.
New York: Longman, 2011. 693. Print.

YOUR TURN

1. Jennifer Anderson's instructor told the class that the essay should be "about 500 words." Anderson's paper is more than that—about 650 words. Do you think that she uses her space well? Could she have shortened the essay to bring it closer to the assigned length? If you had to suggest cuts, where would you propose to make them?
2. Does Anderson omit important details in the poem that you think she should have included in the paper? Explain why these elements should be part of her response.
3. Give Anderson's paper a grade, and in a paragraph written to her, highlight the strengths and limitations of this paper. Provide her, too, with one or two specific suggestions for improving her writing in the next paper.

Annotation and Essay on Adrienne Rich's "Aunt Jennifer's Tigers"

Maria Fuentes, a first-year student, produced the following jottings, annotations, and essay concerning a poem that we print on page 641.

odd–arouses interest

Aunt Jennifer's Tigers

Aunt Jennifer's tigers prance across a screen, Bright

topaz denizens of a world of green. They do not fear the men

beneath the tree; They pace in sleek chivalric certainty.??

her work embroidery?

Aunt Jennifer's fingers fluttering through her wool Find

even the ivory needle hard to pull. The massive weight of Uncle's

wedding band Sits heavily upon Aunt Jennifer's hand.

he tyrannized over her

When Aunt is dead, her terrified hands will

lie Still ringed with ordeals she was mastered by.

The tigers in the panel that she made

will go on prancing, proud and unafraid. *uncle?*

contrast to the prancing tigers she created

we are told only that she was oppressed & that she created a lively work of art That's about all we know of her.

in contrast to "terrified"
Aunt J. BUT She created these "proud and unafraid" tigers.
Her vision of a better life?

Maria Fuentes
Professor Johnston
English 1202
8 April 2010

Aunt Jennifer's Screen and Adrienne Rich's Poem

What especially pleases me in Adrienne Rich's "Aunt Jennifer's Tigers" is the combination of neat, tight, highly disciplined stanzas of four rhyming lines (like marching squadrons) with the explosive rebellious content of the poem. Somehow the message seems especially powerful *because* it is so tightly packed, because the form is so restrained.

The poem is, on the surface at least, about what the title says it is about, "Aunt Jennifer's Tigers." Aunt Jennifer has made a screen, in embroidery or needlepoint, showing tigers that "prance." Presumably Aunt Jennifer was a sweet old lady, but she has created a picture of enormous energy, expressing, through her work of art, her own repressed energy.

We learn in the second stanza that she was repressed by the man she was married to:

> The massive weight of Uncle's wedding band
> Sits heavily upon Aunt Jennifer's hand.

The wedding band for her, as for many women in the present as well as in the past, is like a heavy chain. Rich tells us that Aunt Jennifer was "terrified" and was "mastered," obviously by Uncle. Rich makes a pun on the word "ringed," but the joke is very bitter:

> When Aunt is dead, her terrified hands will lie
> Still ringed with ordeals she was mastered by.

And yet, Rich points out, this "terrified" woman created something beautiful, a picture of tigers who "go on prancing, proud and unafraid." Apparently Aunt Jennifer was able, despite being oppressed by Uncle, to make something that gives pleasure to a later generation—just as the poet, however unhappy she may be, produces a work of art that gives pleasure to those who later read it.

Aunt Jennifer's work of art shows, in the prancing tigers, an energy that she apparently felt and understood, but because of her husband and perhaps because of the period in which she lived, she could express herself only in a "ladylike" activity such as embroidering. Aunt Jennifer was "mastered" (line 10), but she had nevertheless "made" (line 11) something depicting creatures who are "proud and unafraid." She was "terrified" (line 9), as many women were terrified by the patriarchal society in which they lived (and still live), but in her art she created an image of energy. Adrienne Rich, too, makes a work of art—a highly patterned poem consisting of three rhymed quatrains—that is as elegantly crafted as a work of embroidery. Rich speaks matter-of-factly and in a disciplined way in her quatrains about Aunt Jennifer and her tigers, but in this elegant poem she conveys energy and outrage on behalf of her terrified aunt who could not openly protest against the role that society had assigned to her.

Work Cited

Rich, Adrienne. "Aunt Jennifer's Tigers." *An Introduction to Literature.* Ed. Sylvan Barnet, William Burto, and William E. Cain. 16th ed. New York: Longman, 2011. 641. Print.

An Essay on a Theme in Several Poems by One Poet

For a collection of poems by Emily Dickinson including the ones discussed in the following essay, see pages 736–47.

Peter Gottsegen

Professor Laurey

English 150G

12 April 2010

Religion and Religious Imagery in Emily Dickinson

Emily Dickinson was not a preacher but a poet, so if we read her poetry about God we should not be surprised if we do not find a simple, consistent view or even a clear development from one view—for instance, belief—to another—for instance, loss of faith. Rather, judging from some examples of her poetry, she explored various views, and we should not try to convert this variety into unity.

We can begin by looking at extreme views, first two poems of faith, and then a poem of doubt. One of the poems of faith, "Papa above!" (737), begins with a childlike or almost playful version of the Lord's Prayer. (In Matthew 6.9 Jesus begins a prayer by saying, "Our father who art in heaven.") I think this poem says that God will see to it that even a mouse or rat will get into heaven and will remain there for eternity. But Dickinson's God is not always concerned for all of the creatures of the world. In another poem that expresses belief in the existence of God, "Apparently with no surprise" (744), Dickinson describes the frost as beheading a flower—that is, beauty perishes—and she goes on to make the point that this occurs under the eyes of "an Approving God." Here she seems to be saying that evil takes place, and God approves of it. It is important to realize that in this poem Dickinson still says that God exists, even if he is indifferent to suffering.

In another poem, "Those—dying, then" (743), Dickinson expresses doubt that God exists. In olden days, she says, people mistakenly thought that God would protect them, but now, she says, "God cannot be found." She uses a particularly terrifying image to convey the loss of God. In the past, Dickinson says, the faithful went to "God's Right Hand," but, she goes on to say, "The Hand is amputated now. . . ." The faith in God that earlier people had was an illusion, but it was something, and it was "better" than the nothingness we now experience. This nothingness, or something not much more than nothingness, is the subject of "I heard a Fly buzz—when I died" (739). In this poem, the speaker expects "the King" (God) to appear to her as she dies, but all she sees is a fly, and then she hears its buzz. God ("the King") never appears.

Even these few poems show that Dickinson held a variety of views about God and religion, and it is difficult or perhaps impossible for us to say exactly what her religious beliefs were. But what is certain is that religious ideas were so important to her, so much a part of her mind, that even when she was not explicitly writing about the existence of a benevolent God or the absence of God, she used religious imagery—for instance, to describe impressive things in the natural world around her.

Gottsegen 3

In "These are the days when Birds come back" (736), she talks about what we call Indian summer, fall days that are like summer days. But the poem is filled with religious words: "belief," "Sacrament," "Communion," "consecrated bread," "immoral wine." The fifth stanza goes like this:

> Oh Sacrament of summer days,
>
> Oh Last Communion in the Haze—
>
> Permit a child to join.

I don't think Dickinson is really talking about traditional religion here. Instead, she is using religious imagery to talk about a particular precious moment in the seasons. As a second example of her use of religious imagery in a poem that is about nature and not about God, we might look at "There's a certain Slant of light" (737). In this poem she says that on "Winter Afternoons" this particular light has "the Heft / Of Cathedral Tunes." That is, the wintry light has the solidity, the feel, the "heft" of religious music. When we see this light, Dickinson says, we are moved in a way that we are moved by music in church. She is not saying anything here about whether God is benevolent or not, or whether he exists or not. Rather, she is drawing on experiences in church—probably experiences shared by many people even today—to help us to see nature more effectively.

Speaking as someone who was brought up with traditional religious beliefs but who does not go to church now, I can say that Dickinson effectively represents the ideas of a believer and also of a non-believer. But what I think is especially impressive is that she sees that someone who no longer is a believer can't help but still think in religious terms when he or she sees something exceptionally beautiful, for instance on a winter day "a certain Slant of light."

Gottsegen 4

Works Cited

Barnet, Sylvan, William Burto, and William E. Cain, eds. *An Introduction to Literature*. 16th ed. New York: Longman, 2011. Print.

Dickinson, Emily. "Apparently with no surprise." Barnet, Burto, and Cain 744.

Gottsegen 5

---. "I heard a Fly buzz—when I died." Barnet, Burto, and Cain 739.

---. "Papa above!" Barnet, Burto, and Cain 737.

---. "There's a certain Slant of light." Barnet, Burto, and Cain 737.

---. "These are the days when Birds come back." Barnet, Burto, and Cain
    736.

---. "Those—dying, then." Barnet, Burto, and Cain 743.

YOUR TURN

1. In this essay Gottsegen comments on the poems "Papa above!," "Apparently with no surprise," "Those—dying, then," "I heard a Fly buzz—when I died," "These are the days when Birds come back," and "There's a certain Slant of light." Read or reread each of these poems to see if you agree with Gottsegen's interpretations.
2. Are there other poems by Dickinson that you think Gottsegen could have used with better effect than poems he did use? Explain.
3. Reread the concluding paragraph. Do you think it is effective? Explain.

An Essay on the Structure of a Poem

The arrangement of its parts, the organization of an entire poem, is its **structure.** Sometimes a poem is divided into blocks of, say, four lines each, but even when the poem is printed as a solid block, it probably has some principle of organization—for example, from sorrow in the first two lines to joy in the next two, or from a question in the first three lines to an answer in the last line.

Consider this short poem by an English poet of the seventeenth century.

ROBERT HERRICK

For a biographical note, see page 605.

Upon Julia's Clothes

Whenas in silks my Julia goes,
Then, then, methinks, how sweetly flows
That liquefaction of her clothes.

Next, when I cast mine eyes, and see
That brave° vibration, each way free,   5
O how that glittering taketh me!

David Thurston, a student, began thinking about this poem by copying it, double-spaced, and by making the following notes on his copy.

---

5 Brave splendid.

Upon Julia's Clothes

Whenas in silks (my Julia) goes, ———————————— *cool tone?*

3 Then, the*n, methinks,* how sweetly flows

That liquefaction of her clothes. ————————————— *"Then, then"—more*
excited? almost at
a loss for words?

Next, when I cast mine eyes, and see

3 That brave vibration, each way free, ———————————— *free to do what?*
free from what?

O how that glittering taketh me!

emotional?

Thurston got further ideas by thinking about several of the questions that we have given earlier in this chapter, such as:

> Does the poem proceed in a straightforward way, or at some point or points does the speaker reverse course, altering his or her tone or perception?

With various questions in mind, Thurston was stimulated to see if Herrick's poem has a reversal or change and, if so, how it is related to the structure. After rereading the poem several times, thinking about it in the light of these questions and perhaps others, he produced the following notes:

> Two stanzas, each of three lines, with the same structure
> Basic structure of 1st stanza: When X (one line), then Y (Two lines)
> Basic structure of second stanza: Next (one line), then Z (two lines)

When he marked the text after reading the poem a few times, he noticed that the last line—an exclamation of delight ("O, how that glittering taketh me")—is much more personal than the rest of the poem. A little further thought enabled him to refine this last perception:

> Although the pattern of stanzas is repeated, the somewhat analytic, detached tone of the beginning ("Whenas," "Then," "Next") changes to an open, enthusiastic confession of delight in what the poet sees.

Further thinking led to this:

> Although the title is "Upon Julia's Clothes," and the first five lines describe Julia's silken dress, the poem finally is not only about Julia's clothing but about the effect of Julia (moving in silk that liquefies or seems to become a liquid) on the poet.

This is a nice observation, but when Thurston looked again at the poem the next day and started to write about it, he found that he was able to refine his observation.

Even at the beginning, the speaker is not entirely detached, for he speaks of "*my* Julia."

In writing about Herrick's "Upon Julia's Clothes," Thurston reported, the thoughts did not come quickly or neatly. After two or three thoughts, he started to write. Only after drafting a paragraph and rereading the poem did he notice that the personal element appears not only in the last line ("taketh *me*") but even in the first line ("*my* Julia"). In short, for almost all of us, the only way to get to a good final essay is to read, to think, to jot down ideas, to write a draft, and to revise and revise again. Having gone through such processes, David Thurston came up with the following excellent essay.

By the way, Thurston did not hit on the final version of his title until shortly before he typed his final version. His preliminary title was

Structure and Personality in

Herrick's "Upon Julia's Clothes"

That's a bit heavy-handed, but at least it is focused, as opposed to such an uninformative title as "On a poem." He soon revised his tentative title to

Julia, Julia's Clothing, and Julia's Poet

That's a good title: It is neat, and it is appropriate; it moves (as the poem and the essay do) from Julia and her clothing to the poet. It doesn't tell the reader exactly what the essay will be about, and three uses of Julia may be one too many, but it does stimulate the reader's interest. The essayist's final title, however, is even better:

Herrick's Julia, Julia's Herrick

Again, it is neat (the balanced structure, and structure is part of the essay's topic), less repetitive, and it moves (as the poem itself moves) from Julia to the poet.

Thurston 1

David Thurston

Professor James

English 102

31 May 2010

Herrick's Julia, Julia's Herrick

Robert Herrick's "Upon Julia's Clothes" begins as a description of Julia's clothing and ends as an expression of the poet's response not just to Julia's clothing but to Julia herself. Despite the apparently objective or detached tone of the first stanza and the first two lines of the second stanza, the poem finally conveys a strong sense of the speaker's excitement.

The first stanza seems to say, "Whenas" X (one line), "Then" Y (two lines). The second stanza repeats this basic structure of one line of assertion and two lines describing the consequence: "Next" (one line), "then" (two lines). But the logic or coolness of "Whenas," "Then," and "Next," and of such rather scientific language as *liquefaction* (a more technical-sounding word than "melting") and *vibration* is undercut by the breathlessness or excitement of "Then, then" (that is very different from a simple "Then"). It is also worth mentioning that although there is a personal rather than a fully detached note even in the first line, in "*my* Julia," this expression scarcely reveals much feeling. In fact, it reveals a touch of male chauvinism, a suggestion that the woman is a possession of the speaker's. Not until the last line does the speaker reveal that, far from Julia's being his possession, he is possessed by Julia: "O how that glittering taketh me!" If he begins coolly, objectively, and somewhat complacently and uses a structure that suggests a somewhat detached mind, in the exclamatory "O" he nevertheless at last confesses (to our delight) that he is enraptured by Julia.

Work Cited

Herrick, Robert. "Upon Julia's Clothes." *An Introduction to Literature*. Ed. Sylvan Barnet, William Burto, and William E. Cain. 16th ed. New York: Longman, 2011. 703. Print.

Other things might be said about this poem. For instance, the writer says nothing about the changes in the meter and their possible value in the poem. Nor does he say anything about the sounds of any of the words (he might have commented on the long vowels in "sweetly flows" and shown how the effect would have been different if instead of "sweetly flows" Herrick had written "swiftly flits"). But such topics might be material for another essay. Furthermore, another reader might have found the poem less charming—even offensive in its exclusive concern with Julia's appearance and its utter neglect of her mind. Still, this essay is, in itself, an interesting and perceptive discussion of the way the poet used a repeated structure to set forth a miniature drama in which observation is, at the end, replaced by emotion.

An Essay on Metrics

Here is an excellent analysis by a student, Julia Jeffords, of a poem by A. E. Housman that appears on page 663. Notice that she quotes the poem and indicates the metrical pattern and that she proceeds chiefly by explaining the effect of the variations or departures from the norm in the order in which they occur.

Notice, too, that although it is a good idea to announce your thesis early— that is, in the first paragraph—this writer does *not* say, "This paper will show that Housman effectively uses rhythm to support his ideas" or some such thing. It's sufficient that the writer announces her topic in the title and again, in slightly different words, in the first sentence (the paper will "analyze the effects of sounds and rhythms in Housman's 'Eight O'Clock'"). We know where we will be going, and we read even with a bit of suspense, looking to see what the analysis will produce.

Jeffords 1

Julia Jeffords
Professor Rozan
English 2
15 March 2010

Sound and Sense in A. E. Housman's "Eight O'Clock"

Before trying to analyze the effects of sounds and rhythms in A. E. Housman's "Eight O'Clock" (1922) it will be useful to quote the poem and to indicate which syllables are stressed and which are unstressed. It must be understood, however, that the following scansion is relatively crude, because it falsely suggests that all stressed syllables (marked /) are equally stressed, but of course they are not: In reading the poem aloud, one would stress some of them relatively heavily, and one would stress others only a trifle more than the unstressed syllables. It should be understood, too, that in the discussion that follows the poem some other possible scansions will be proposed.

He stood, | and heard | the steeple
Sprinkle | the quar | ters on | the mor | ning town.
One, two, | three, four, | to mar | ket-place | and people
It tossed | them down.
Strapped, noosed, | nighing | his hour.

He stood|and coun|ted them|and cursed|his luck;
And then|the clock|collec|ted in|the tower
Its strength,|and struck.

As the first line of the second stanza makes especially clear, the poem is about a hanging at eight o'clock, according to the title. Housman could have written about the man's thoughts on the justice or injustice of his fate, or about the reasons for the execution, but he did not. Except for the second line of the second stanza—"He stood and counted them and cursed his luck"—he seems to tell us little about the man's thoughts. But the poem is not merely a narrative of an event; the sound effects in the poem help to convey an idea as well as a story.

The first line establishes an iambic pattern. The second line begins with a trochee ("Sprinkle"), not an iamb, and later in the line possibly "on" should not be stressed even though I marked it with a stress and made it part of an iambic foot, but still the line is mainly iambic. The poem so far is a fairly jingling description of someone's hearing the church clock chiming at each quarter of the hour. Certainly, even though the second line begins with a stress, there is nothing threatening in "Sprinkle," a word in which we almost hear a tinkle.

But the second half of the first stanza surprises us and maybe even jolts us. In "One, two, three, four" we get four consecutive heavy stresses. These stresses are especially emphatic because there is a pause, indicated by a comma, after each of them. Time is not just passing to the chimes of a clock: This is a countdown, and we sense that it may lead to something significant. Moreover, the third line, which is longer than the two previous lines, does not end with a pause. This long line (eleven syllables) runs on into the next line, almost as though once the countdown has begun there is no stopping it. But then we do stop suddenly, because the last line of the stanza has only four syllables—far fewer than we would have expected. In other words, this line stops unexpectedly because it has only two feet. The first line had three feet, and the second and third lines had five feet. Furthermore, this short, final line of the stanza ends with a heavy stress in contrast to the previous line, which ends with an unstressed syllable, "people." As we will see, the sudden stopping at the end is a sort of preview of a life cut short. Perhaps it is also a preview of a man dropping through a trapdoor and then suddenly stopping when the slack in the hangman's rope has been taken up.

In the first line of the second stanza the situation is made clear, and it is also made emphatic by three consecutive stresses: "Strápped, noósed, níghĭňg his hoŭŕ." The pauses before the first three stresses make the words especially emphatic. And though I have marked the first two words of the next line "Hĕ stoód," possibly "He" should be stressed too. In any case even if "He" is not heavily stressed, it is certainly stressed more than the other unstressed syllables, "and," "-ed" (in "counted"), and "his." Similarly in the third line of the stanza an effective reading might even stress the first word as well as the second, thus: "Aňd thén." And although normal speech would stress only the second syllable in "collécteď," in this poem the word appears after "clock," and so one must pause after the *k* sound in "clock" (one simply can't say "clock collected" without pausing briefly between the two words), and the effect is to put more than usual stress on the first syllable, almost turning it into "cóllécteď." And so this line can reasonably be scanned like this:

Aňd thén thĕ clocḱ colĺécteď iň thĕ tóweř

And again the third line of the stanza runs over into the fourth, propelling us onward. The final line surely begins with a stress, even though "Its" is not a word usually stressed, and so in the final line we begin with two strong stresses, "Itś stréngth." This line, like the last line of the first stanza, is unusually short, and it, too, ends with a heavy stress. The total effect, then, of the last two lines of this stanza is of a clock striking, not just sprinkling music but forcefully and emphatically and decisively striking. The pause after "strength" is almost like the suspenseful pause of a man's collecting his strength before he strikes a blow, and that is what the clock does:

Aňd thén thĕ clóck colĺécteď iň thĕ tóweř
Itś streňgth aňd strúck.

If "clock collected" has in its *k* sounds a sort of ticktock effect, the clock at the end shows its force, for when it strikes the hour, the man dies.

I said near the beginning of this essay that Housman did not write about the man's thoughts about the justice or injustice of the sentence, and I think this is more or less true, but if we take into account the sound effects in the poem we can see that in part the poem is about the man's thoughts: He sees himself as the victim not only of his "luck" but of this machine, this ticking, unstoppable contraption that strikes not only the hours but a man's life.

Work Cited

Housman, A. E. "Eight O'Clock." *An Introduction to Literature*. Ed. Sylvan Barnet, William Burto, and William E. Cain. 16th ed. New York: Longman, 2011. 663. Print.

A Brief Overview of the Essay

- The *title* suggests the writer's topic, and the first sentence of the *opening paragraph* establishes it without doubt: "the effects of sounds and rhythms" in a particular poem. This paragraph also includes some sentences whereby the author quite reasonably indicates her awareness that not everyone will scan the poem exactly as she does. Willingness to concede differences of opinion is a good argumentative strategy; it establishes the reader as a person who is open-minded.

- Jeffords provides the reader with the *text of the poem*, marked with her sense of the stresses. Don't expect your reader to read your paper and also to be thumbing through a book to find the poem.

- The *organization* is simple but adequate. Jeffords begins at the beginning and moves through the poem to its end.

- In her *final paragraph* Jeffords interestingly modifies an assertion she made earlier, that Housman "did not write about the man's thoughts about the justice or injustice of the sentence." She now shows that, in a way, the metrical effects—her chief topic—do tell us something about the victim's thoughts. This modification is not a contradiction. If indeed she now sees that Housman did write about these topics, she of course should have revised the earlier passage. But the earlier passage remains true, at least in a broad sense. Housman did not write about the victim's thoughts about justice. What Jeffords is saying, at the end of her essay, is that the metrical effects *do* in some degree get us into the mind of the victim, helping us to see him as someone struck down by an implacable machine.

Two Essays, for Evaluation, on Robert Frost's "Stopping by Woods on a Snowy Evening"

Here are the annotations that a student, Darrel MacDonald, jotted down, followed by the final version of the essay that he developed from the annotations.

Whose woods these are I think I know.
His house is in the village, though;

afraid of being seen? Why? Because on private property? Or because not going about his business?

He will not see me stopping here
To watch his woods fill up with snow.

My little horse must think it queer 〔 *odd? gay?*
To stop without a farmhouse near
Between the woods and frozen lake
The darkest evening of the year.

He gives his harness bells a shake 　*What is the*
To ask if there is some mistake. 　*mistake? Is it a*
The only other sound's the sweep 　*mistake to enjoy*
Of easy wind and downy flake. 　*nature?*

The woods are lovely dark and deep, 　*a women's*
But I have promises to keep, 　*word? But isn't the*

Why twice? Is he emphatically telling himself to get moving?

And miles to go before I sleep, 　*speaker a man? May*
And miles to go before I sleep. 　*be a woman?*

apparently he does not stay to see the "woods fill up with snow."

Now for the essay that MacDonald developed out of these annotations.

MacDonald 1

Darrel MacDonald
Professor Lui
English 102
5 May 2010

Stopping by Woods—and Going On

Robert Frost's "Stopping by Woods on a Snowy Evening" is about
what the title says it is. It is also about something more than the title
says.

When I say it is about what the title says, I mean that the poem
really does give us the thoughts of a person who pauses (that is, a person
who is "stopping") by woods on a snowy evening. (This person probably is
a man, since Robert Frost wrote the poem and nothing in the poem clearly
indicates that the speaker is not a. But, and this point will be
important, the speaker perhaps feels that he is not a very masculine man.
As we will see, the word "queer" appears in the poem, and, also, the
speaker uses the word "lovely," which sounds more like the word a woman
would use than a man.) In line 3 the speaker says he is "stopping here,"
and it is clear that "here" is by woods, since "woods" is mentioned not
only in the title but also in the first line of the poem, and again in the
second stanza, and still again in the last stanza. It is equally clear that, as
the title says, there is snow, and that the time is evening. The speaker
mentions "snow" and "downy flake," and he says this is "The darkest
evening of the year."

But in what sense is the poem about *more* than the title? The title
does not tell us anything about the man who is "stopping by woods,"
but the poem—the man's meditation—tells us a lot about him. In the
first stanza he reveals that he is uneasy at the thought that the owner
of the woods may see him stopping by the woods. Maybe he is uneasy
because he is trespassing, but the poem does not actually say that he
has illegally entered someone else's property. More likely, he feels
uneasy, almost ashamed, of watching the "woods fill up with snow."
That is, he would not want anyone to see that he is enjoying a beautiful
aspect of nature and is not hurrying about whatever his real business is
in thrifty Yankee style.

The second stanza gives more evidence that he feels guilty about
enjoying beauty. He feels so guilty that he even thinks the horse thinks
there is something odd about him. In fact, he says that the horse thinks

MacDonald 2

he is "queer," which of course may just mean odd, but also (as is shown by *The American Heritage Dictionary*) it can mean "gay," "homosexual." A real man, he sort of suggests, wouldn't spend time looking at snow in the woods.

So far, then, the speaker in two ways has indicated that he feels insecure, though perhaps he does not realize that he has given himself away. First, he expresses uneasiness that someone might see him watching the woods fill up with snow. Second, he expresses uneasiness when he suggests that even the horse thinks he is strange, maybe even "queer" or unmanly, or at least unbusinesslike. And so in the last stanza, even though he finds the woods beautiful, he decides *not* to stop and to see the woods fill up with snow. And his description of the woods as "lovely"—a woman's word—sounds as though he may be something less than a he-man. He seems to feel ashamed of himself for enjoying the sight of the snowy woods and for seeing them as "lovely," and so he tells himself that he has spent enough time looking at the woods and that he must go on about his business. In fact, he tells himself *twice* that he has business to attend to. Why? Perhaps he is insisting too much. Just as we saw that he was excessively nervous in the first stanza, afraid that someone might see him trespassing and enjoying the beautiful spectacle, now at the end he is again afraid that someone might see him loitering, and so he very firmly, using repetition as a form of emphasis, tries to reassure himself that he is not too much attracted by beauty and is a man of business who keeps his promises.

Frost gives us, then, a man who indeed is seen "stopping by woods on a snowy evening," but a man who, afraid of what society will think of him, is also afraid to "stop" long enough to fully enjoy the sight that attracts him because he is driven by a sense that he may be seen to be trespassing and also may be thought to be unmanly. So after only a brief stop in the woods he forces himself to go on, a victim (though he probably doesn't know it) of the work ethic and of an over-simple idea of manliness.

MacDonald 3

Work Cited

Frost, Robert. "Stopping by Woods on a Snowy Evening." *An Introduction to Literature*. Ed. Sylvan Barnet, William Burto, and William E. Cain. 16th ed. New York: Longman, 2011. 755. Print.

YOUR TURN

1. In a sentence or two state the thesis of the essay.
2. Is the thesis adequately supported? Explain, pointing out strengths, if any, and weaknesses, if any.
3. Do you find the organization satisfactory? Why, or why not?
4. Do you find the title and the opening paragraph of interest? If not, how might you improve them?
5. Given the thesis and the development of it, is the final paragraph satisfactory? Why, or why not?
6. If you think that, on the whole, the essay is effectively written, take two or three sentences and explain what their strengths are. If you think that, on the whole, the writing could be more effective, take two or three sentences and revise them into more effective sentences. (It's not a matter of agreeing or of disagreeing with the argument; we are talking chiefly about style.)

The second student, Sara Fong, kept a journal. We give an entry from her journal concerning Frost's poem and then the final version of her essay.

I think that when the class talked about "the death wish" in "Stopping by Woods," they were on to something, but they went too far. It's not really a "death wish." The poet wants to lose himself, so to speak, by merging himself with the woods ("the woods are lovely, dark and deep"), or maybe with the soft white snow ("downy flake"), but that's not really the same as saying he wishes for death. Still, the beauty of the woods—we might say the world of peaceful solitude—is set against the world of the living, the world of "promises" to other humans.

We have already studied short stories this term, and I think it is a good idea to see this poem as a very short short story. As I see it, the plot has three stages: (1) the character (the poet) has fairly ordinary thoughts as he looks at the wood (he thinks of the person who owns it and of the owner's house in the village), but soon he begins to feel that there is something special, something odd ("queer") in looking at the woods on what is, in fact, a special day ("The darkest evening of the year"). Then (2) he seems to get almost fully caught up with (or drawn in by) the beauty of the scene ("easy wind and downy flake," "The woods are lovely, dark and deep"), and then, finally, (3) he shakes off the pull of nature, the appeal of nature that has almost made him forget everything else.

I'm not so sure, come to think of it, that at the very end he does completely reject the impulse to give himself up to nature. He repeats the last line ("And miles to go before I sleep, / And miles to go before I sleep"), and it seems to me that maybe this repetition is sort of hypnotic, almost as though he is drowsing off. I *feel* this, and when I read the lines aloud I can make them sound almost as though the speaker is drowsing off, but I'm not really sure that I'm right. After all, I can also read them aloud so they sound sort of perky or chipper, with a sense of "Well, I've put that behind me." I wonder if there is any way of deciding exactly how the last two lines should be read.

Now for Sara Fong's essay. You'll notice that it draws heavily on her journal, but it differs in two important ways. First, whereas in the journal she saw the story as having three stages, in the final essay she sees four stages. (What in the journal is said to be the first stage of the poem, in the essay becomes two stages.) Second, you'll notice that the point made in the last paragraph of the journal is not included in the essay. Why? Here are three possibilities: (1) Fong came to feel that the point was not sound; (2) she came to feel that the point was sound but not worth making; (3) she came to feel that the point, though interesting and sound and worth making, required more space than was available. It was, so to speak, the material for a different paper. Doubtless you can think of other reasons why Fong omitted the point in the final paper.

Fong 1

Sara Fong
Professor Nagle
English 1204
5 April 2010

"Stopping by Woods on a Snowy Evening"
as a Short Story

Robert Frost's "Stopping by Woods on a Snowy Evening" can be read as a poem about a man who pauses to observe the beauty of nature, and it can also be read as a poem about a man with a death wish, a man who seems to long to give himself up completely to nature and thus escape his responsibilities as a citizen. Much depends, apparently, on what a reader wants to emphasize. For instance, a reader can emphasize especially appealing lines about the beauty of nature: "The only other sound's the sweep / Of easy wind and downy flake," and "The woods are lovely, dark and deep." On the other hand, a reader can emphasize lines that show the speaker is fully aware of the responsibilities that most of us agree we have. For instance, at the very start of the poem he recognizes that the woods are not his but are owned by someone else, and at the end of the poem he recognizes that he has "promises to keep" and that before he sleeps (dies?) he must accomplish many things (go for "miles").

Does a reader have to choose between these two interpretations? I don't think so; to the contrary, I think it makes sense to read the poem as a kind of very short story, with a character whose developing thoughts make up a plot with four stages. In the first stage, the central figure is an ordinary person with rather ordinary thoughts. His very first thought is of the owner of the woods. He knows who the owner is, and since the owner lives in the village, the poet feels safe in trespassing, or at least in watching the woods "fill up with snow." Then, very subtly, the poet begins to tell us that although this seems to be an ordinary person thinking ordinary thoughts, he is a somewhat special person in a special situation. First, the horse thinks something is strange. He shakes his bells, wondering why the driver doesn't keep moving, as presumably ordinary drivers would. Second, we are told that this is "The darkest evening of the year." Frost could simply have said that the evening is dark, but he goes out of his way to make the evening a special evening.

We are now through with the first ten lines, and only six lines remain, yet in these six lines the story goes through two additional phases. The first three of these lines ("The only other sound's the sweep/ Of easy wind and downy flake" and "The woods are lovely, dark and deep") are probably the most beautiful lines, in the sense that they are the ones that make us say, "I wish I were there," or "I'd love to experience this." We feel that the poet has moved from the ordinary thoughts of the first stanza, about such business-like things as who owns the woods and where the owner's house is, to less materialistic thoughts, thoughts about the beauty of the non-human world of nature. And now, with the three final lines, we get the fourth stage of the story, the return to the ordinary world of people, the world of "promises." But this world that we get at the end is not exactly the same as the world we got at the beginning. The world at the beginning of the poem is a world of property (who owns the woods, and where the house is), but the world at the end of the poem is a world of unspecified and rather mysterious responsibilities ("promises to keep," "miles to go before I sleep"). It is almost as though the poet's experience of the beauty of nature—a beauty that for a moment made him forget the world of property—has in fact served to sharpen his sense that human beings have responsibilities. He clearly sees that "The woods are lovely, dark and deep," and then he says (I add the italics) "*But* I have promises to keep." The "but" would be logical if after saying that the woods are lovely, dark and deep, he had said something like "But in the daylight they look different," or "But one can freeze to death in them." The logic of what Frost says, however, is not at all clear: "The woods are lovely, dark and deep, / But I have promises to keep." What is the logical connection? We have to supply one, something like "but, *because we are human beings we have responsibilities;* we can refresh ourselves by perceiving the beauties of nature, and we can even for a moment get so caught up that we seem to enter an enchanted forest ('the woods are lovely, dark and deep'), but we cannot forget our responsibilities."

My point is not that Frost ends with an important moral, and it is also not that we have to choose between saying it is a poem about nature or a poem about a man with a death wish. Rather, my point is that the poem takes us through several stages and that, although the poem begins and ends with the speaker in the woods, the speaker has undergone mental experiences—has, we might say, gone through a plot with a conflict (the appeal of the snowy woods versus the call to return to the human world). It's not a matter of good versus evil and of one side's winning. Frost in no way suggests that it is wrong to feel the beauty of nature—even to the momentary exclusion of all other thoughts. But the poem is certainly not simply a praise of the beauty of nature. Frost shows us, in this mini-story or mini-drama, one character who sees the woods as property, then sees them as a place of almost overwhelming beauty, and then (maybe refreshed by this experience) rejoins the world of chores and responsibilities.

Fong 4

Work Cited

Frost, Robert. "Stopping by Woods on a Snowy Evening." *An Introduction to Literature*. Ed. Sylvan Barnet, William Burto, and William E. Cain. 16th ed. New York: Longman, 2011. 755. Print.

YOUR TURN

We can ask of this essay the same questions we asked of the previous essay.

1. In a sentence or two state the thesis of the essay.
2. Is the thesis adequately supported? Explain, pointing out strengths, if any, and weaknesses, if any.
3. Do you find the organization satisfactory? Why, or why not?
4. Do you find the title and the opening paragraph of interest? If not, how might you improve them?
5. Given the thesis and the development of it, is the final paragraph satisfactory? Why, or why not?

25

Poets at Work

When we read a poem aloud, whether an anonymous nursery rhyme such as "Jack and Jill went up the hill" or a work by one of the great names, the words seem so right, so inevitable, that it is hard to believe they did not flow easily. Reading, say, Keats's "On First Looking into Chapman's Homer" (page 622), we may think that he must have sat down and simply let the words stream from his pen. And certainly Keats himself emphasized spontaneity: In a letter he says, "If poetry comes not as naturally as leaves to a tree it had better not come at all." Yet Keats's manuscripts indicated that he revised his work heavily, so heavily that some of the manuscripts are almost indecipherable. Probably William Butler Yeats was speaking for all poets when he said (in a poem called "Adam's Curse") that a poem must seem spontaneous but is the result of hard work:

> A line will take us hours maybe;
> Yet if it does not seem a moment's thought,
> Our stitching and unstitching has been naught.

In this chapter we give the following material:

1. Two versions of a poem by Walt Whitman.
2. Two versions of a poem by Cathy Song, introduced by her comments.
3. Three versions of a poem by Yeats.

WALT WHITMAN

For a biographical note, see page 633.

In the third edition of *Leaves of Grass* (1860) Whitman added two groups of poems, one called "Children of Adam" and the other (named for an aromatic grass that grows near ponds and swamps) called "Calamus." "Children of Adam" celebrates heterosexual relations, whereas "Calamus" celebrates what Whitman called "manly love." Although many of the "Calamus" poems seem clearly homosexual, perhaps the very fact that Whitman published them made them seem relatively innocent; in any case, those nineteenth-century critics who condemned Whitman for the sexuality of his writing concentrated on the poems in "Children of Adam."

Manuscript of Walt Whitman's "Once I Passed Through a Populous City" in *Leaves of Grass,*
Walt Whitman, MSS 3829, Clifton Waller Barrett Library of American Literature, Special Collections, University of Virginia Library. Used by permission.

We give here the 1860 manuscript of the poem "Once I Passed Through a
Populous City," included in the "Enfans d'Adam" (Children of Adam) section of
Leaves of Grass (1860 ed.). The extensive markings on this page, some of them
in dark ink and others in light pencil, show that Whitman revised this poem carefully. Notice, for example, that Whitman wrote and crossed out both "great" and
"populous" and then seemed to settle on the word "celebrated," only to write
(barely visible in the upper right corner) "populous" again, which became his
final choice for the phrase "a populous city." Note, too, the changes in gender

from "only a man" and "that youth" (crossed out) and "one rude and ignorant man" to—in the published poem—"that woman" and "she holds me."

Enfans d'Adam, number 9   [1860]

[*Leaves of Grass*, 1860 edition]

Once, I passed through a populous city, imprinting my brain, for
    future use, with its shows, architecture, customs, and traditions;
Yet now, of all that city, I remember only a woman I casually met
    there, who detained me for love of me,
Day by day and night by night we were together,—
    All else has long been forgotten by me,
I remember, I say only that woman who passionately clung to me,
Again we wander—we love—we separate again,
Again she holds me by the hand—I must not go!
I see her close beside me, with silent lips, sad and tremulous.

CATHY SONG

Cathy Song, born in Honolulu in 1955 of a Chinese-American mother and a Korean-American father, holds a bachelor's degree from Wellesley College and a master's degree in creative writing from Boston University. The author of three books of poems, she won the Yale Series of Younger Poets award for Picture Bride *(1983), her first book. She has also won the Hawaii Award for Literature and the Shelley Memorial Award from the Poetry Society of America. Song's recent books include* The Land of Bliss *(2001) and* Cloud Moving Hands *(2007).*

Here we print a draft of an untitled poem and the final version, now titled "Out of Our Hands." Ms. Song's comment on the origins of the poem follow:

"Out of Our Hands" was written for the poet Wing Tek Lum. Long before Wing Tek and I became friends, I had already encountered his work. The poem is informed by our friendship; my abiding respect for the poet is deepened by my affection for the man. Knowing the reality of his warm humanity allowed me to imagine the poem in a larger context—what I had felt in his poems was present and true—and in a sense, when I first encountered his work, I was ready to receive the "seeds of a language / I needed to know." I was ready for this poet who had something to teach me.

The sense of magic and transformation is alive and well in the poem because his poems, his presence allowed that to happen with me. The images of birds and flight, children and language have everything to do with the way gifts are given and received—serendipitous and yet, there are no coincidences. When a poem is written there is someone out there waiting to read it, to have the gift descend, touch you like a leaf, a feather, a letter written just for you.

Out of a hat
on a piece of paper
someone gave me your name.
Your name flew
out of my hand,
the black letters dismantling in the air
above the lake.
I watched the letters
become the bird seeds of a language
I needed to know
the a language I borrowed from the children
my students it borrowed coats
who scattered outside the school —
red-bricked and torn on the edge of Chinatown —
undisciplined like starlings, they the children I taught disappeared
in the broken shoes of the wind.
One day your name
came back in a poem
you were writing
on the edge of another city,
a poem you were determined
to write for the rest of your life.
The poem a subversive act.
The poem about being Chinese,
skin the glorious color of chicken fat.

Cathy Song's draft for "Out of Our Hands." ("Out of Our Hands" by Cathy Song. Draft is reprinted with permission of the author.)

Out of Our Hands [1994]

—*for Wing Tek Lum*

Out of a hat
on a piece of paper
someone once gave me your name.

Your name flew
out of my hand,   5
the black letters
dismantling the air
above the school.
I watched the letters

form the bird   10
seeds of a language
I needed to know,

a language borrowed
from the children I taught
who shivered in borrowed coats.   15

Toward evening they scattered
outside the school,
red-bricked and torn

on the edge of Chinatown.
I watched them disappear   20
into their lives,

undisciplined like starlings,
they disappeared
in the broken shoes of the wind.

One day your name   25
came back
in a poem you were

writing in another city,
a poem you were determined
to write for the rest of your life.   30

The poem a subversive act.
The poem about being Chinese,
skin the glorious color of chicken fat.

WILLIAM BUTLER YEATS

"Leda and the Swan" (Three Versions)

William Butler Yeats (1865–1939) was born in Dublin, Ireland. The young Yeats was much interested in highly lyrical, romantic poetry, often drawing on Irish mythology. The later poems, from about 1910 (and especially after Yeats met Ezra Pound in 1911), are often more colloquial. Although these later poems often employ mythological references, too, they seem more down-to-earth. Yeats was awarded the Nobel Prize in Literature in 1923.

According to Greek mythology, Zeus fell in love with Leda, disguised himself as a swan, and ravished her. Among the offspring of this union were Helen and Clytemnestra. Paris abducted Helen, causing the Greeks to raze Troy; Clytemnestra, wife of Agamemnon, murdered her husband on his triumphant return to Greece. Yeats saw political significance in the myth of beauty and war engendered by a god; but, as he tells us, when he was composing "Leda and the Swan" the political significance evaporated:

> After the individualistic, demagogic movements, founded by Hobbes and popularized by the Encyclopaedists and the French Revolution, we have a soil so exhausted that it cannot grow that crop again for centuries. Then I thought "Nothing is now possible but some movement, or birth from above, preceded by some violent annunciation." My fancy began to play with "Leda and the Swan" for metaphor, and I began this

poem, but as I wrote, bird and lady took such possession of the scene that all politics went out of it.

The first version of the poem, titled "Annunciation," is from a manuscript dated 18 September 1923—"annunciation" is the act of announcing or of being announced, and, more specifically, it refers to the angel Gabriel's announcement of the Incarnation to the Virgin Mary, in Luke 1.26-38; the second version was printed in a magazine in June 1924; the third version, first published in his *Collected Poems* of 1933, is Yeats's final one. But this third version had been almost fully achieved by 1925; the 1933 version differs from the 1925 version only in two punctuation marks: The question marks at the ends of lines 6 and 8 in the latest version were, in 1925, respectively, a comma and a semicolon.

Annunciation   [1923]

Now can the swooping Godhead have his will
Yet hovers, though her helpless thighs are pressed
By the webbed toes; and that all powerful bill
Has suddenly bowed her face upon his breast,
How can those terrified vague fingers push   5
The feathered glory from her loosening thighs?

William Butler Yeats's first drafts of "Leda and the Swan," 1923.

All the stretched body's laid on that white rush
And feels the strange heart beating where it lies
A shudder in the loins engenders there
The broken wall, the burning roof and tower   10
And Agamemnon dead . . .
                              Being so caught up
Did nothing pass before her in the air?
Did she put on his knowledge with his power
Before the indifferent beak could let her drop.   15

Leda and the Swan   [1924]

A rush, a sudden wheel, and hovering still
The bird descends, and her frail thighs are pressed
By the webbed toes, and that all-powerful bill
Has laid her helpless face upon his breast.
How can those terrified vague fingers push   5
The feathered glory from her loosening thighs!
All the stretched body's laid on the white rush
And feels the strange heart beating where it lies;
A shudder in the loins engenders there
The broken wall, the burning roof and tower   10
And Agamemnon dead.
                              Being so caught up,
So mastered by the brute blood of the air,
Did she put on his knowledge with his power
Before the indifferent beak could let her drop?   15

Leda and the Swan   [1933]

A sudden blow: the great wings beating still
Above the staggering girl, her thighs caressed
By the dark webs, her nape caught in his bill,
He holds her helpless breast upon his breast.

How can those terrified vague fingers push   5
The feathered glory from her loosening thighs?
And how can body, laid in that white rush,
But feel the strange heart beating where it lies?

A shudder in the loins engenders there
The broken wall, the burning roof and tower   10
And Agamemnon dead.
                              Being so caught up,
So mastered by the brute blood of the air,
Did she put on his knowledge with his power
Before the indifferent beak could let her drop?   15

26

Variations on Themes: Poems and Paintings

Writing About Poems and Paintings

Are there, one may ask, significant correspondences among the arts? If we talk about *rhythm* in a painting, are we talking about a quality similar to *rhythm* in a poem? Are the painter's colors comparable to the poet's images? Does it make sense to say, as the German writer Johann Wolfgang von Goethe (1749–1832) said, that architecture is frozen music? Or to call architecture "music in space"? Many artists of one sort have felt that their abilities *ought* to enable them to move into a "sister art," and they have tried their hand at something outside their specialty, usually with no great success. (William Blake, represented in this book by several poems, is often said to be the only figure in English arts who is significant both as a poet and as a painter.) For instance, the painter Edgar Degas (1834–1917) tried to write sonnets, but could not satisfy even himself. When he complained to his friend, the poet Stéphane Mallarmé, that he couldn't write poems even though he had plenty of ideas, Mallarmé replied, "You don't write poems with ideas; you write them with words."

Painters have been moved, for many centuries, to illustrate texts. More than two thousand years ago the painters of Greek vases illustrated the Greek myths, and from the Middle Ages onward artists have illustrated the Bible. Conversely, poets have been moved to write about paintings or sculptures. In this chapter we reprint three poems about paintings by Brueghel, van Gogh, and Demuth.

Despite Mallarmé's witty remark that poems are made not with ideas but with words (and despite Archibald MacLeish's assertion, on page 814, that "A poem should not mean / But be"), poems use ideas, and they have meanings. When you read the poems that we include here along with paintings, you might think about some of the following questions:

• What is your own first response to the painting? (Using Google, find the images online.) In interpreting the painting, consider the subject matter, the composition (for instance, balanced masses, as opposed to an apparent lack of equilibrium), the technique (for instance, vigorous brushstrokes of thick

Vincent van Gogh, *The Starry Night,* 1889, oil on canvas, 29 × 36 1/4 in. [73.7 × 92.1 cm.]. (Museum of Modern Art, New York. Acquired through the Lillie P. Bliss Request/Art Resource.)

paint, as opposed to thinly applied strokes that leave no trace of the artist's hand), the color, and the title.

- Now that you have read the poem, do you see the painting in a somewhat different way?
- To what extent does the poem illustrate the painting, and to what extent does it depart from the painting and make a very different statement?
- Beyond the subject matter, what (if anything) do the two works have in common?

ANNE SEXTON

Anne Sexton (1928–1974) was born in Newton, Massachusetts. She attended Garland Junior College, married at twenty, and began a life as a housewife. After a mental breakdown at the age of twenty-eight she took up writing poetry at the suggestion of a therapist. She published many books of poetry, the third of which, Live or Die *(1966), won a Pulitzer Prize, as well as a number of children's books (co-authored with the poet Maxine Kumin). Despite her literary success, her life was deeply troubled. She committed suicide in 1974.*

Another poem by Anne Sexton appears on page 821.

The Starry Night   [1961]

That does not keep me from having a terrible need of—shall I say the
word—religion. Then I go out at night to paint the stars.
                                —Vincent van Gogh in a letter to his brother

The town does not exist
except where one black-haired tree slips
up like a drowned woman into the hot sky.
The town is silent. The night boils with eleven stars.
Oh starry starry night! This is how   5
I want to die.

It moves. They are all alive.
Even the moon bulges in its orange irons
to push children, like a god, from its eye.
The old unseen serpent swallows up the stars.   10
Oh starry starry night! This is how
I want to die:

into that rushing beast of the night,
sucked up by that great dragon, to split
from my life with no flag,   15
no belly,
no cry.

> **YOUR TURN**

Sexton calls her poem "The Starry Night" and uses an epigraph from van
Gogh (1853–1890). In what ways does her poem *not* describe or evoke
van Gogh's painting? In what ways *does* it describe the painting?

Washington 1

Tina Washington
Professor Serno
English 10G
12 June 2010

Two Ways of Looking at a Starry Night

About a hundred years ago Vincent van Gogh looked up into the
sky at night and painted what he saw, or what he felt. We know that
he was a very religious man, but even if we had not heard this in an
art course or read it in a book we would know it from his painting

The Starry Night, which shows a glorious heaven, with stars so bright that they all have halos. Furthermore, almost in the lower center of the picture is a church, with its steeple rising above the hills and pointing to the heavens.

Anne Sexton's poem is about this painting, and also (we know from the line she quotes above the poem) about van Gogh's religious vision of the stars. But her poem is not about the heavenly comfort that the starry night offered van Gogh. It is a poem about her wish to die. As I understand the poem, she wants to die in a blaze of light, and to become extinct. She says, in the last line of the poem, that she wants to disappear with "no cry" (728), but this seems to me to be very different from anything van Gogh is saying. His picture is about the glorious heavens, not about himself. Or if it is about himself, it is about how wonderful he feels when he sees God's marvelous creation. Van Gogh is concerned with praising God as God expresses himself in nature; Anne Sexton is concerned with expressing her anguish and with her hope that she can find extinction. Sexton's world is not ruled by a benevolent God but is ruled by an "old unseen serpent." The night is a "rushing beast," presided over by a "great dragon."

Sexton has responded to the painting in a highly unique way. She is not trying to put van Gogh's picture into words that he might approve of. Rather, she has boldly used the picture as a point of departure for her own word-picture.

Work Cited

Sexton, Anne. "The Starry Night." *An Introduction to Literature.* Ed. Sylvan Barnet, William Burto, and William E. Cain. 16th ed. New York: Longman, 2011. 728. Print.

YOUR TURN

1. Do you agree with this student's analysis, especially her point about Sexton's poem?
2. Has the student cited and examined passages from the poem in a convincing way?
3. A general question: Do you think poets are obliged to be faithful to the paintings that they write about, or do poets enjoy the freedom—a kind of poetic license—to interpret a painting just as they choose, doing with it whatever the purpose of the poem requires?

W. H. AUDEN

For a biographical note, see page 576.

In the following poem, Auden offers a meditation triggered by a painting in the Museum of Fine Arts in Brussels. The painting, by Pieter Brueghel (c. 1525-1569), is based on the legend of Icarus, told by the Roman poet Ovid (43 BCE-17 CE) in his *Metamorphoses*. The story goes thus: Daedalus, father of Icarus, was confined with his son on the island of Crete. In order to escape, Daedalus made wings for himself and for Icarus by fastening feathers together with wax, but Icarus flew too near the sun, the wax melted, and Icarus fell into the sea. According to Ovid, the event—a boy falling through the sky— was witnessed with amazement by a ploughman, a shepherd, and an angler. In the painting, however, these figures seem to pay no attention to Icarus, who is

Pieter Brueghel the Elder, *Landscape with the Fall of Icarus*, c. 1558. (Musées Royaux des Beaux-Arts, Brussels.)

represented not falling through the sky but already in the water (in the lower-right corner, near the ship), with only his lower legs still visible.

Musée des Beaux Arts   [1940]

About suffering they were never wrong,
The Old Masters: how well they understood
Its human position; how it takes place
While someone else is eating or opening a window or just
    walking dully along;
How, when the aged are reverently, passionately waiting   5
For the miraculous birth, there always must be
Children who did not specially want it to happen, skating
On a pond at the edge of the wood:
They never forgot
That even the dreadful martyrdom must run its course   10
Anyhow in a corner, some untidy spot
Where the dogs go on with their doggy life and the torturer's horse
Scratches its innocent behind on a tree.

In Brueghel's *Icarus,* for instance: how everything turns away
Quite leisurely from the disaster; the plowman may   15
Have heard the splash, the forsaken cry,
But for him it was not an important failure; the sun shone
As it had to on the white legs disappearing into the green
Water; and the expensive delicate ship that must have seen
Something amazing, a boy falling out of the sky,   20
Had somewhere to get to and sailed calmly on.

YOUR TURN

1. In your own words sum up what, according to the speaker (in lines 1–13), the Old Masters understood about human suffering. (The Old Masters were the great European painters who worked from about 1500 to about 1750.)
2. Suppose the first lines read:

   The Old Masters were never wrong about suffering.
   They understood its human position well.

   What (beside the particular rhymes) would change or be lost?
3. Reread the poem (preferably over the course of several days) a number of times, jotting down your chief responses after each reading. Then, in connection with a final reading, study your notes, and write an essay of 500 words setting forth the history of your final response to the poem. For example, you may want to report that certain difficulties soon were clarified and that your enjoyment increased. Or, conversely, you may want to report that the poem became less interesting (for reasons you will set forth) the more you studied it. Probably your history will be somewhat more complicated than these simple examples. Try to find a chief pattern in your experience, and shape it into a thesis.

4. Consider a picture, either in a local museum or reproduced in a book, and write a 500-word reflection on it. If the picture is not well known, include a reproduction (a postcard from the museum, a photocopy of a page of a book or from an online site via Google).

Charles Demuth. *I Saw the Figure 5 in Gold.* 1928. (Oil on composition board, 36 × 29 3/4 in. Metropolitan Museum of Art, New York. Alfred Stieglitz Collection, 1949)

WILLIAM CARLOS WILLIAMS

For a biographical note, see page 628.

In his autobiography Williams gives an account of the origin of this poem. He was walking in New York City, on his way to visit a friend:

> As I approached his number I heard a great clatter of bells and the roar of a fire engine passing the end of the street down Ninth Avenue. I turned just in time to see a golden 5 on a red background flash by. The impression was so sudden and forceful that I took a piece of paper out of my pocket and wrote a short poem about it.

Several years later his friend Charles Demuth (1883–1939), an American painter who has been called a cubist-realist, painted this picture, inspired by the poem. The picture is one of a series of paintings about Demuth's friends.

The Great Figure   [1920]

Among the rain
and lights
I saw the figure 5
in gold
on a red   5
firetruck
moving
tense
unheeded
to gong clangs   10
siren howls
and wheels rumbling
through the dark city.

YOUR TURN

Williams's draft for the poem runs thus:

> Among the rain
> and lights
> I saw the figure 5
> gold on red
> moving
> to gong clangs
> siren howls
> and wheels rumbling
> tense
> unheeded
> through the dark city

Do you think the final version is better in all respects, some respects, or no respects? Explain.

27

Three Poets in Depth: Emily Dickinson, Robert Frost, and Langston Hughes

On Reading Authors Represented in Depth

If you have read several works by an author, whether tragedies by Shakespeare or detective stories about Sherlock Holmes by Arthur Conan Doyle, you know that authors return again and again to certain themes (tragedy for Shakespeare, crime for Conan Doyle), yet each treatment is different. *Hamlet, Macbeth,* and *Romeo and Juliet* are all tragedies, and they all share certain qualities that we think of as Shakespearean, yet each is highly distinctive.

When we read several works by an author, we find ourselves thinking about resemblances and differences. We enjoy seeing the author return to some theme (for instance, God, or nature, or love) or to some literary form (for instance, the sonnet, or blank verse, or pairs of rhyming lines); and we may find, to our delight, that the author has handled things differently and that we are getting a sense of the writer's variety and perhaps even of the writer's development. Indeed, we sometimes speak of the *shape* or *design* of the author's career, meaning that our careful study of the writings has led us to an understanding of the story—with its beginning, middle, and end—that the writings tell across a period of time. Often, once we read one poem by an author and find it intriguing or compelling, we want to read more: Are there other poems like this one? What kinds of poems were written before or after this one? Our enjoyment and understanding of one poem help us to enjoy and understand others, and make us curious about the place that each one occupies in a larger structure, the shape of the author's career.

We can go further and say that the reading of a second author can help us—perhaps by way of contrast—to understand the first. In the preface to one of his volumes of poetry, Robert Frost put it this way:

A poem is best read in the light of all the other poems ever written. We read A the better to read B (we have to start somewhere; we may get very little out of A). We read B the better to read C, C the better to read D, D the better to go back and get something more out of A.

Progress is not the aim, but circulation. The thing is to get among the poems where they hold each other apart in their places as the stars do.

In an introduction to literature course, although you'll often be asked to write analytical papers about a single poem, story, or play, sometimes you'll be assigned a paper that requires a comparison and contrast of, for example, two poems by different authors. Less frequent perhaps, but equally important, is the paper that examines a central theme or idea as it is expressed and explored in three or more works.

At first this might seem a daunting task, but there are helpful ways of getting in control of the assignment. One of the best is to begin with a single work and then to move outward from it, making connections to works that show interesting similarities to, or differences from, it.

One of our students, Mark Bradley, was asked to write on a theme (which he had to define himself) in a selection of poems by Langston Hughes. Mark started by closely studying a poem by Hughes that had caught his attention when he made his way through the group of poems for the first time. In one of his journal entries, Mark wrote:

> The poem "The South" surprised me. It wasn't what I expected. I thought Hughes would attack the South for being so racist—he wrote the poem in the 1920s, when segregation was everywhere in the South. He says some tough stuff about the South, that's for sure: "Beast strong, / Idiot-brained." But he also says that the South is attractive in some ways, and I'm not convinced that when he brings in the North at the end, he really believes that the North is superior.

Intrigued by this poem, Mark made it his point of departure for the thematic paper he was assigned. He judged that if he worked intensively on this poem and came to know it well, he could review other Hughes poems and see how they were both like and unlike the poem with which he began.

When you write an essay on several works, keep two points especially in mind: the length of the assignment, and the choice of examples. You want to treat the right number of examples for the space you are given, and, furthermore, to provide sufficient detail in your analysis of each of them. You might call this the principle of proportion.

Preparing an outline can be valuable. It will lead you to think carefully about which examples you have selected for your argument and the main idea about each one that you will present. You might begin by examining one poem in depth, and then proceed to relate it to key passages in other poems. Or maybe you'll find one passage in a poem so significant that it—rather than the poem in its entirety—can serve as a good beginning. Whichever strategy you choose, when you review the rough draft, use a highlighter to mark off the amount of space that you have devoted to each example. Ask yourself:

- Is this example clearly connected to my argument in the paper as a whole?
- Have I not only referred to the example but also provided adequate quotation from it?

- Have I made certain to comment on the passage? (Remember that passages do not interpret themselves. You have to explicate and explain them.)
- Has each example received its due?

There is no easy rule of thumb for knowing how much space each example should be given. Some passages are more complicated than others; some demand more intensive scrutiny. But you'll be well on the way toward handling this aspect of the paper effectively if you are self-aware about your choices, alert to the principle of proportion.

EMILY DICKINSON

Emily Dickinson (1830–1886) was born into a proper New England family in Amherst, Massachusetts. Although she spent her seventeenth year a few miles away, at Mount Holyoke Seminary (now Mount Holyoke College), in the next twenty years she left Amherst only five or six times, and in her last twenty years she may never have left her house. Her brother was probably right when he said that having seen something of the rest of the world— she had visited Washington with her father, when he was a member of Congress—"she could not resist the feeling that it was painfully hollow. It was to her so thin and un-satisfying in the face of the Great Realities of Life."

Dickinson lived with her parents (a somewhat reclusive mother and an austere, remote father) and a younger sister; a married brother lived in the house next door. She formed some passionate attachments, to women as well as men, but there is no evidence that they found physical expression.

By the age of twelve Dickinson was writing witty letters, but she apparently did not write more than an occasional poem before her late twenties. At her death—she died in the house where she was born—she left nearly 1800 poems, only seven of which had been published (anonymously) during her lifetime.

We begin this section with sixteen poems by Dickinson. Next, we present a seventeenth poem, "I felt a Funeral, in my Brain," in multiple versions: the poem as we know it today; the poem in manuscript; and the poem in its first published version. Two more poems follow, which are similar in phrasing to one another and show an affinity to "I Felt a Funeral, in my Brain." We conclude with three of Dickinson's letters about poetry.

These are the days when Birds come back   [1859]

These are the days when Birds come back—
A very few—a Bird or two—
To take a backward look.

These are days when skies resume
The old—old sophistries° of June—   5
A blue and gold mistake.

---

5 sophistries deceptively subtle arguments.

O fraud that cannot cheat the Bee—
Almost thy plausibility
Induces my belief.

Till ranks of seeds their witness bear—   10
And softly thro' the altered air
Hurries a timid leaf.

Oh Sacrament of summer days,
Oh Last Communion in the Haze—
Permit a child to join.   15

Thy sacred emblems to partake—
Thy consecrated bread to take
And thine immortal wine!

Papa above!   [c. 1859]

Papa above!
Regard a Mouse
O'erpowered by the Cat!
Reserve within thy kingdom
A "Mansion" for the Rat!   5

Snug in seraphic Cupboards
To nibble all the day,
While unsuspecting Cycles°
Wheel solemnly away!

---

8 **Cycles** long periods, eons.

Wild Nights—Wild Nights!   [1861]

Wild Nights—Wild Nights!
Were I with thee
Wild Nights should be
Our luxury!   4

Futile—the Winds—
To a Heart in port—
Done with the Compass—
Done with the Chart!   8

Rowing in Eden—
Ah, the Sea!
Might I but moor—Tonight—
In Thee!   12

There's a certain Slant of light   [c. 1861]

There's a certain Slant of light,
Winter Afternoons—

That oppresses, like the Heft°
Of Cathedral Tunes—   4

Heavenly Hurt, it gives us—
We can find no scar,
But internal difference,
Where the Meanings, are—   8

None may teach it—Any—
'Tis the Seal Despair—
An imperial affliction
Sent us of the Air—   12

When it comes, the Landscape listens—
Shadows—hold their breath—
When it goes, 'tis like the Distance
On the look of Death—   16

---

3 Heft weight.

I got so I could hear his name   [1861]

I got so I could hear his name—
Without—Tremendous gain—
That Stop-sensation—on my Soul—
And Thunder—in the Room—   4

I got so I could walk across
That Angle in the floor,
Where he turned so, and I turned—how—
And all our Sinew tore—   8

I got so I could stir the Box—
In which his letters grew
Without that forcing, in my breath—
As Staples—driven through—   12

Could dimly recollect a Grace—
I think, they call it "God"—
Renowned to ease Extremity—
When Formula, had failed—   16

And shape my Hands—
Petition's way,
Tho' ignorant of a word
That Ordination°—utters—   20
My Business, with the Cloud,
If any Power behind it, be,
Not subject to Despair—
It care, in some remoter way,   24

---

20 Ordination the ministry.

For so minute affair
As Misery—
Itself, too great, for interrupting—more—

The Soul selects her own Society   [1862]

The Soul selects her own Society—
Then—shuts the Door—
To her divine Majority—
Present no more—   4

Unmoved—she notes the Chariots—pausing—
At her low Gate—
Unmoved—an Emperor be kneeling
Upon her Mat—   8

I've known her—from an ample nation—
Choose One—
Then—close the Valves° of her attention—
Like Stone—   12

---

11 Valves the two halves of a hinged door such as is now found on old telephone
booths. Possibly also an allusion to a bivalve, such as an oyster or a clam, having a shell
consisting of two hinged parts.

This was a Poet—It is That   [1862]

This was a Poet—It is That
Distills amazing sense
From ordinary Meanings—
And Attar° so immense   4

From the familiar species
That perished by the Door—
We wonder it was not Ourselves
Arrested it—before—   8

Of Pictures, the Discloser—
The Poet—it is He—
Entitles Us—by Contrast—
To ceaseless Poverty—   12

Of Portion—so unconscious—
The Robbing—could not harm—
Himself—to Him—a Fortune—
Exterior—to Time—   16

---

4 Attar a fragrant oil or perfume.

Manuscript for Emily Dickinson's "I heard a Fly buzz—when I died." (Manuscript of Emily Dickinson's "I heard a fly buzz—when I died." Amherst College Archives and Special Collections. By permission of the Trustees of Amherst College.)

I heard a Fly buzz—when I died   [1862]

I heard a Fly buzz—when I died—
The Stillness in the Room
Was like the Stillness in the Air—
Between the Heaves of Storm—

The Eyes around—had wrung them dry—
And Breaths were gathering firm

4

For the last Onset—when the King
Be witnessed—in the Room—   8

I willed my Keepsakes—Signed away
What portion of me be
Assignable—and then it was
There interposed a Fly—   12

With Blue—uncertain stumbling Buzz—
Between the light—and me—
And then the Windows failed—and then
I could not see to see—   16

This World is not Conclusion   [c. 1862]

This World is not Conclusion.
A Species stands beyond—
Invisible, as Music—
But positive, as Sound—
It beckons, and it baffles—   5
Philosophy—don't know—
And through a Riddle, at the last—
Sagacity, must go—
To guess it, puzzles scholars—
To gain it, Men have borne   10
Contempt of Generations
And Crucifixion, shown—
Faith slips—and laughs, and rallies—
Blushes, if any see—
Plucks at a twig of Evidence—   15
And asks a Vane, the way—
Much Gesture, from the Pulpit—
Strong Hallelujahs roll—
Narcotics cannot still the Tooth
That nibbles at the soul—   20

I like to see it lap the Miles   [1862]

I like to see it lap the Miles—
And lick the Valleys up—
And stop to feed itself at Tanks—
And then—prodigious step   4

Around a Pile of Mountains—
And supercilious peer
In Shanties—by the sides of Roads—
And then a Quarry pare   8

To fit its Ribs
And crawl between
Complaining all the while
In horrid—hooting stanza—   12
Then chase itself down Hill—

And neigh like Boanerges°
Then—punctual as a Star
Stop—docile and omnipotent   16
At its own stable door—

---

14 **Boanerges** a name said (in Mark 3.17) to mean "Sons of Thunder."

A narrow Fellow in the Grass   [c. 1865]

A narrow Fellow in the Grass
Occasionally rides—
You may have met Him—did you not
His notice sudden is—   4

The Grass divides as with a Comb—
A spotted shaft is seen—
And then it closes at your feet
And opens further on—   8

He likes a Boggy Acre
A Floor too cool for Corn—
Yet when a Boy, and Barefoot—
I more than once at Noon   12
Have passed, I thought, a Whip lash
Unbraiding in the Sun
When stopping to secure it
It wrinkled, and was gone—   16

Several of Nature's People
I know, and they know me—
I feel for them a transport
Of cordiality—   20

But never met this Fellow
Attended, or alone
Without a tighter breathing
And Zero at the Bone—   24

Further in Summer than the Birds   [1866]

Further in Summer than the Birds
Pathetic from the Grass
A minor Nation celebrates
Its unobtrusive Mass.   4

No Ordinance° be seen
So gradual the Grace
A pensive Custom it becomes
Enlarging Loneliness.   8

---

5 **Ordinance** religious rite of Holy Communion.

Antiquest felt at Noon
When August burning low
Arise this spectral Canticle°
Repose to typify   12

Remit as yet no Grace
No Furrow on the Glow
Yet a Druidic° Difference
Enhances Nature now   16

---

11 Canticle hymn.   **15 Druidic** pertaining to pre-Christian Celtic priests.

Tell all the Truth but tell it slant   [c. 1868]

Tell all the Truth but tell it slant—
Success in Circuit lies
Too bright for our infirm Delight
The Truth's superb surprise   4

As Lightning to the Children eased
With explanation kind
The Truth must dazzle gradually
Or every man be blind—   8

*A Route of Evanescence**   [c. 1879]

A Route of Evanescence
With a revolving Wheel—
A Resonance of Emerald—
A Rush of Cochineal°
And every Blossom on the Bush   5
Adjusts its tumbled Head—
The mail from Tunis,° probably,
An easy Morning's Ride—

***A Route of Evanescence** In letters to friends Dickinson said the poem referred to a
hummingbird.   **4 Cochineal** bright red.   **7 Tunis** City in North Africa.

Those—dying, then   [1882]

Those—dying then,
Knew where they went
They went to God's Right Hand—
The Hand is amputated now
And God cannot be found—   5

The abdication of Belief
Makes the Behavior small—
Better an ignis fatuus°
Than no illume at all—

---

8 ignis fatuus a phosphorescent light that hovers over swampy ground, hence something deceptive.

Apparently with no surprise   [c. 1884]

Apparently with no surprise
To any happy Flower
The Frost beheads it at its play—
In accidental power—
The blonde Assassin passes on—   5
The Sun proceeds unmoved
To measure off another Day
For an Approving God.

We reprint here and on the next page Dickinson's manuscript for "I felt a Funeral, in my Brain," and we follow it with the version of the poem as we know it today, where it is #280 in *The Complete Poems of Emily Dickinson*, ed. Thomas H. Johnson (Boston: Little, Brown, 1957). This edition follows the text that Johnson presented in his three-volume scholarly edition, *The Poems of*

Manuscript for "I felt a Funeral, in my Brain." (Manuscript of Emily Dickinson's "I felt a Funeral, in my Brain." By permission of The Houghton Library, Harvard University, MS Am 1118.3 (53c) © The President and Fellows of Harvard College.)

Manuscript for "I felt a Funeral in my Brain" (*continued*).

Emily Dickinson (Cambridge: Harvard UP, 1955). Johnson proposes a date of sometime in 1861 for this poem, but the editor of a new scholarly edition, *The Poems of Emily Dickinson:* Variorum Edition, 3 vols. (Cambridge: Harvard UP, 1998), R. W. Franklin, while agreeing with Johnson's version of the poem, suggests a date of summer 1862.

I felt a Funeral, in my Brain   [1861 or 1862]

I felt a Funeral, in my Brain,
And Mourners to and fro
Kept treading—treading—till it seemed
That Sense was breaking through—

And when they all were seated,
A Service, like a Drum—
Kept beating—beating—till I thought

4

My Mind was going numb—   8

And then I heard them lift a Box
And creak across my Soul
With those same Boots of Lead, again,
Then Space—began to toll,   12

As all the Heavens were a Bell,
And Being, but an Ear,
And I, and Silence, some strange Race
Wrecked, solitary, here—   16

And then a Plank in Reason, broke,
And I dropped down, and down—
And hit a World, at every plunge,
And Finished knowing—then—   20

Pages 744-45 reproduce the poem as it appears in Dickinson's own hand. Our copy is taken from *The Manuscript Books of Emily Dickinson,* edited by R.W. Franklin and published in 1981. Like nearly all of Dickinson's poems, this one was not published in her lifetime. She wrote her poems on sheets of letter paper, which she then bound together with string into packets. Perhaps these personal manuscript books or "fascicles" (that is, a small bundle, or the divisions of a book published in parts) represented for Dickinson a form of publication—though a very private one.

Notice that in line 10, Dickinson wrote "Brain," but then crossed it out and selected the word "Soul" instead. Notice also that in manuscript, the poem concludes with a line not in the poem, but that seems to give alternatives for words in lines 19 and 20. Refer to the poem as shown above to see how Thomas Johnson has worked from the manuscript to make his choices about how the poem should read.

In her will Dickinson stipulated that upon her death, her papers and letters should be burned. Her sister, Lavinia, however, who discovered the poems, decided that her sister's request did not include them, and she soon became determined to see the poems published. This task was taken up by Mabel Loomis Todd (1856-1932), who was a friend of Dickinson's—and the lover of Austin Dickinson, Emily's older (and already married) brother. With help from the critic and man of letters Thomas Wentworth Higginson (1823-1911), Todd edited two series of Dickinson's poems (1890, 1891), and then edited a third series (1896) and the *Letters of Emily Dickinson* (2 vols., 1894) herself. Both Todd and Higginson removed many of the boldly original features of the poems' language, structure, and punctuation. They sought to make Dickinson more conventional, more like other poets of the age. This, in their view, was the best way to make her less difficult and hence more accessible to readers. But the result was that they eliminated the daring, brilliant innovations that make Dickinson extraordinary. This first published version of "I felt a Funeral, in my Brain" is taken from *Poems by Emily Dickinson,* third series (Boston: Little, Brown, 1896).

I felt a funeral in my brain,
And mourners, to and fro,
Kept treading, treading, till it seemed
That sense was breaking through.   4

And when they all were seated,
A service like a drum

Kept beating, beating, till I thought
My mind was going numb.   8

And then I heard them lift a box,
And creak across my soul
With those same boots of lead, again.
Then space began to toll   12

As all the heavens were a bell,
And Being but an ear,
And I and silence some strange race,
Wrecked, solitary, here.   16

Here are two more poems, similar to one another and somewhat similar to "I felt a Funeral, in my Brain." Thomas Johnson dates the first one as having been written in 1864, and the second in the following year. The second, Johnson explains, is not so much a separate poem as a variant on the first, a variant that Dickinson probably sent to her sister-in-law Susan Gilbert Dickinson, who was married to Dickinson's brother, Austin. In his more recent edition, R. W. Franklin says more firmly that the first poem was written in early 1864 and that, without address or signature, Dickinson sent a version of its second stanza to Susan.

I felt a Cleaving in my Mind   [1864]

I felt a Cleaving in my Mind—
As if my Brain had split—
I tried to match it—Seam by Seam—
But could not make them fit.   4

The thought behind, I strove to join
Unto the thought before—
But Sequence ravelled out of Sound
Like Balls—upon a Floor.   8

The Dust behind I strove to join   [1865]

The Dust behind I strove to join
Unto the Disk before—
But Sequence ravelled out of Sound
Like Balls upon a Floor—   4

Letters About Poetry

We include three of Dickinson's letters, the first of which is addressed to Susan Gilbert, probably her dearest friend and the wife of Dickinson's brother, Austin. The two other letters are addressed to Thomas Wentworth Higginson (1823-1911), a writer and leading abolitionist. After reading in *Atlantic Monthly* (April 1862) Higginson's article offering advice to young authors, Dickinson (thirty-one at the time) sent Higginson some of her poems along with a letter, and a correspondence ensued, lasting until Dickinson's death.

To Susan Gilbert (Dickinson)

So sweet and still, and Thee, Oh Susie, what need I more, to make my heaven whole?

Sweet Hour, blessed Hour, to carry me to you, and to bring you back to me, long enough to snatch one kiss, and whisper Good bye, again.

I have thought of it all day, Susie, and I fear of but little else, and when I was gone to meeting it filled my mind so full, I could not find a *chink* to put the worthy pastor; when he said "Our Heavenly Father," I said "Oh Darling Sue"; when he read the 100th Psalm, I kept saying your precious letter all over to myself, and Susie, when they sang—it would have made you laugh to hear one little voice, piping to the departed. I made up words and kept singing how I loved you, and you had gone, while all the rest of the choir were singing Hallelujahs. I presume nobody heard me, because I sang *so small,* but it was a kind of a comfort to think I might put them out, singing of you. I a'nt there this afternoon, tho', because I am here, writing a little letter to my dear Sue, and I am very happy. I think of ten weeks—Dear One, and I think of love, and you, and my heart grows full and warm, and my breath stands still. The sun does'nt shine at all, but I can feel a sunshine stealing into my soul and making it all summer, and every thorn, a *rose.* And I pray that such summer's sun shine on my Absent One, and cause her bird to sing!

You have been happy, Susie, and now are sad—and the whole world seems lone; but it wont be so always, "some days *must* be dark and dreary"! You wont cry any more, will you, Susie, for my father will be your father, and my home will be your home, and where you go, I will go, and we will lie side by side in the kirkyard.

I have parents on earth, dear Susie, but your's are in the skies, and I have an earthly fireside, but you have one above, and you have a "Father in Heaven," where I have *none*—and *sister* in heaven, and I know they love you dearly, and think of you every day.

Oh I wish I had half so many dear friends as you in heaven—I couldn't spare them now—but to know they had got there safely, and should suffer nevermore—Dear Susie! . . .

Emilie—

To Thomas Wentworth Higginson

Mr Higginson,
Your kindness claimed earlier gratitude—but I was ill—and write today, from my pillow.

Thank you for the surgery[1]—it was not so painful as I supposed. I bring you others—as you ask—though they might not differ—

While my thought is undressed—I can make the distinction, but when I put them in the Gown—they look alike, and numb.

You asked how old I was? I made no verse—but one or two—until this winter—Sir—

---

[1]**surgery** probably cuts that Higginson suggested be made in her poems.

I had a terror—since September—I could tell to none—and so I sing, as the Boy does by the Burying Ground—because I am afraid—You inquire my Books—For Poets—I have Keats—and Mr and Mrs Browning. For Prose—Mr Ruskin—Sir Thomas Browne—and the Revelations.[2] I went to school—but in your manner of the phrase—had no education. When a little Girl, I had a friend, who taught me Immortality—but venturing too near, himself—he never returned—Soon after, my Tutor, died—and for several years, my Lexicon—was my only companion—Then I found one more—but he was not contented I be his scholar—so he left the Land.

You ask of my Companions Hills—Sir—and the Sundown—and a Dog—large as myself, that my Father bought me—They are better than Beings—because they know—but do not tell—and the noise in the Pool, at Noon—excels my Piano. I have a Brother and Sister—My Mother does not care for thought—and Father, too busy with his Briefs[3]—to notice what we do—He buys me many Books—but begs me not to read them—because he fears they joggle the Mind. They are religious—except me—and address an Eclipse, every morning—whom they call their "Father." But I fear my story fatigues you—I would like to learn—Could you tell me how to grow—or is it unconveyed—like Melody—or Witchcraft?

You speak of Mr Whitman—I never read his Book[4]—but was told that he was disgraceful—

I read Miss Prescott's "Circumstance,"[5] but it followed me, in the Dark—so I avoided her—

Two Editors of Journals came to my Father's House, this winter—and asked me for my Mind—and when I asked them "Why," they said I was penurious—and they, would use it for the World—

I could not weigh myself—Myself—

My size felt small—to me—I read your Chapters in the Atlantic—and experienced honor for you—I was sure you would not reject a confiding question—

Is this—Sir—what you asked me to tell you?

Your friend,
E—Dickinson.

---

[2]**Keats . . . Revelations** John Keats, Robert Browning, and Elizabeth Barrett Browning were nineteenth-century English poets; Thomas Browne was a seventeenth-century English writer of prose; John Ruskin was a nineteenth-century English art critic and social critic; Revelation, which Dickinson calls Revelations, is the last book of the New Testament.   [3]**Briefs** legal documents (Dickinson's father was a lawyer).   [4]**Mr Whitman . . . Book** Walt Whitman's *Leaves of Grass* was first published in 1855. Its unconventional punctuation and its celebration of Whitman's passions shocked many readers.
[5]**Miss Prescott's "Circumstance"** Harriet Prescott Spofford's story, published in *Atlantic Monthly* in May 1860. It tells of a woman who, returning from a visit to a sick friend, is held hostage by a beast who is calmed only when she sings to him. Her husband eventually rescues her, but when they arrive home they find that their house has been burned down.

To Thomas Wentworth Higginson   [1876]

Nature is a Haunted House—but Art—a House that tries to be haunted.

ROBERT FROST

Robert Frost (1874–1963) was born in California. After his father's death in 1885, Frost's mother brought the family to New England, where she taught in high schools in Massachusetts and New Hampshire. Frost studied for part of one term at Dartmouth College in New Hampshire, then did odd jobs (including teaching), and from 1897 to 1899 was enrolled as a special student at Harvard. He then farmed in New Hampshire, published a few poems in local newspapers, left the farm and taught again, and in 1912 left for England, where he hoped to achieve more popular success as a writer. By 1915 he had won a considerable reputation, and he returned to the United States, settling on a farm in New Hampshire and cultivating the image of the country-wise farmer-poet. In fact he was well read in the classics, the Bible, and English and American literature.

Among Frost's many comments about literature, here are three: "Writing is unboring to the extent that it is dramatic"; "Every poem is . . . a figure of the will braving alien entanglements"; and, finally, a poem "begins in delight and ends in wisdom. . . . It runs a course of lucky events, and ends in a clarification of life—not necessarily a great clarification, such as sects and cults are founded on, but in a momentary stay against confusion."
And for good measure, here is Frost, in a letter, writing about his own work.

You get more credit for thinking if you restate formulae or cite cases that fall in easily under formulae, but all the fun is outside[,] saying things that suggest formulae that won't formulate—that almost but don't quite formulate. I should like to be so subtle at this game as to seem to the casual person altogether obvious. The casual person would assume I meant nothing or else I came near enough meaning something he was familiar with to mean it for all practical purposes. Well, well, well.

We give fifteen of Frost's poems, arranged in chronological order, and we follow these poems with some of Frost's comments about poetry. The first poem, "The Pasture," is one that Frost customarily put at the beginning of his collected poems. The last words of each stanza, "You come too," are an invitation to the reader to join him.

The Pasture   [1913]

I'm going out to clean the pasture spring;
I'll only stop to rake the leaves away
(And wait to watch the water clear, I may):
I shan't be gone long.—You come too.   4

I'm going out to fetch the little calf
That's standing by the mother. It's so young,
It totters when she licks it with her tongue.
I shan't be gone long.—You come too.   8

Mending Wall   [1914]

Something there is that doesn't love a wall,
That sends the frozen-ground-swell under it,
And spills the upper boulder in the sun;
And makes gaps even two can pass abreast.
The work of hunters is another thing: 5
I have come after them and made repair
Where they have left not one stone on a stone,
But they would have the rabbit out of hiding,
To please the yelping dogs. The gaps I mean,
No one has seen them made or heard them made,   10
But at spring mending-time we find them there.
I let my neighbor know beyond the hill;
And on a day we meet to walk the line
And set the wall between us once again.
We keep the wall between us as we go.   15
To each the boulders that have fallen to each.
And some are loaves and some so nearly balls
We have to use a spell to make them balance:
"Stay where you are until our backs are turned!"
We wear our fingers rough with handling them.   20
Oh, just another kind of outdoor game,
One on a side. It comes to little more:
There where it is we do not need the wall:
He is all pine and I am apple orchard.
My apple trees will never get across   25
And eat the cones under his pines, I tell him.
He only says, "Good fences make good neighbors."
Spring is the mischief in me, and I wonder
If I could put a notion in his head:
"*Why* do they make good neighbors? Isn't it   30
Where there are cows? But here there are no cows.
Before I built a wall I'd ask to know
What I was walling in or walling out,
And to whom I was like to give offense.
Something there is that doesn't love a wall,   35
That wants it down." I could say "Elves" to him,
But it's not elves exactly, and I'd rather
He said it for himself. I see him there
Bringing a stone grasped firmly by the top
In each hand, like an old-stone savage armed.   40
He moves in darkness as it seems to me,
Not of woods only and the shade of trees.
He will not go behind his father's saying,
And he likes having thought of it so well
He says again, "Good fences make good neighbors."   45

The Wood-Pile   [1914]

Out walking in the frozen swamp one gray day,
I paused and said, "I will turn back from here.
No, I will go on farther—and we shall see."
The hard snow held me, save where now and then
One foot went through. The view was all in lines   5
Straight up and down of tall slim trees
Too much alike to mark or name a place by
So as to say for certain I was here
Or somewhere else: I was just far from home.
A small bird flew before me. He was careful   10
To put a tree between us when he lighted,
And say no word to tell me who he was
Who was so foolish as to think what *he* thought.
He thought that I was after him for a feather—
The white one in his tail; like one who takes   15
Everything said as personal to himself.
One flight out sideways would have undeceived him.
And then there was a pile of wood for which
I forgot him and let his little fear
Carry him off the way I might have gone,   20
Without so much as wishing him good-night.
He went behind it to make his last stand.
It was a cord of maple, cut and split
And piled—and measured, four by four by eight.
And not another like it could I see.   25
No runner tracks in this year's snow looped near it.
And it was older sure than this year's cutting,
Or even last year's or the year's before.
The wood was gray and the bark warping off it
And the pile somewhat sunken. Clematis   30
Had wound strings round and round it like a bundle.
What held it though on one side was a tree
Still growing, and on one a stake and prop,
These latter about to fall. I thought that only
Someone who lived in turning to fresh tasks   35
Could so forget his handiwork on which
He spent himself, the labor of his axe,
And leave it there far from a useful fireplace
To warm the frozen swamp as best it could
With the slow smokeless burning of decay.   40

The Road Not Taken   [1916]

Two roads diverged in a yellow wood,
And sorry I could not travel both
And be one traveler, long I stood
And looked down one as far as I could
To where it bent in the undergrowth;   5

Then took the other, as just as fair,
And having perhaps the better claim,
Because it was grassy and wanted wear;
Though as for that the passing there
Had worn them really about the same,   10

And both that morning equally lay
In leaves no step had trodden black.
Oh, I kept the first for another day!
Yet knowing how way leads on to way,
I doubted if I should ever come back.   15

I shall be telling this with a sigh
Somewhere ages and ages hence:
Two roads diverged in a wood, and I—
I took the one less traveled by,
And that has made all the difference.   20

The Telephone   [1916]

"When I was just as far as I could walk
From here today
There was an hour
All still
When leaning with my head against a flower   5
I heard you talk.
Don't say I didn't, for I heard you say—
You spoke from that flower on the window sill—
Do you remember what it was you said?"

"First tell me what it was you thought you heard."   10

"Having found the flower and driven a bee away,
I leaned my head,
And holding by the stalk,
I listened and I thought I caught the word—
What was it? Did you call me by my name?   15
Or did you say—
Someone said 'Come'—I heard it as I bowed."

"I may have thought as much, but not aloud."

"Well, so I came."

The Oven Bird   [1916]

There is a singer everyone has heard,
Loud, a mid-summer and a mid-wood bird,
Who makes the solid tree trunks sound again.
He says that leaves are old and that for flowers
Mid-summer is to spring as one to ten.   5
He says the early petal-fall is past

When pear and cherry bloom went down in showers
On sunny days a moment overcast;
And comes that other fall we name the fall.
He says the highway dust is over all.   10
The bird would cease and be as other birds
But that he knows in singing not to sing.
The question that he frames in all but words
Is what to make of a diminished thing.

The Aim Was Song   [1923]

Before man came to blow it right
    The wind once blew itself untaught,
And did its loudest day and night
    In any rough place where it caught.   4

Man came to tell it what was wrong:
    It hadn't found the place to blow;
It blew too hard—the aim was song.
    And listen—how it ought to go!   8

He took a little in his mouth,
    And held it long enough for north
To be converted into south,
    And then by measure blew it forth.   12

By measure. It was word and note,
    The wind the wind had meant to be—
A little through the lips and throat.
    The aim was song—the wind could see.   16

The Need of Being Versed in Country Things   [1923]

The house had gone to bring again
To the midnight sky a sunset glow.
Now the chimney was all of the house that stood,
Like a pistil after the petals go.   4

The barn opposed across the way,
That would have joined the house in flame
Had it been the will of the wind, was left
To bear forsaken the place's name.   8

No more it opened with all one end
For teams that came by the stony road
To drum on the floor with scurrying hoofs
And brush the mow with the summer load.   12

The birds that came to it through the air
At broken windows flew out and in,
Their murmur more like the sigh we sigh
From too much dwelling on what has been.   16

Yet for them the lilac renewed its leaf,
And the aged elm, though touched with fire;
And the dry pump flung up an awkward arm;
And the fence post carried a strand of wire.   20

For them there was really nothing sad.
But though they rejoiced in the nest they kept,
One had to be versed in country things
Not to believe the phoebes[1] wept.   24

---

[1]Small birds native to eastern North America.

Stopping by Woods on a Snowy Evening   [1923]

Whose woods these are I think I know.
His house is in the village though;

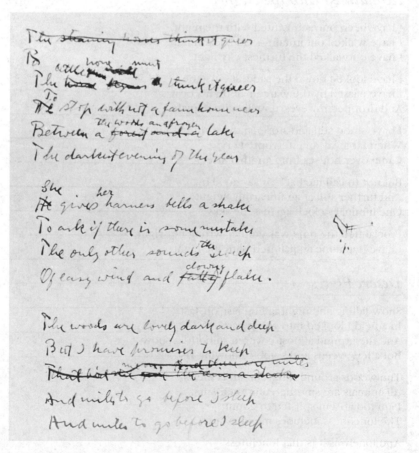

Manuscript for Robert Frost's "Stopping by Woods on a Snowy Evening." The first page of the manuscript is lost. (Manuscript for Robert Frost's "Stopping by Woods on a Snowy Evening." By permission of the Jones Library, Inc., Amherst, Massachusetts.)

He will not see me stopping here
To watch his woods fill up with snow.   4

My little horse must think it queer
To stop without a farmhouse near
Between the woods and frozen lake
The darkest evening of the year.   8

He gives his harness bells a shake
To ask if there is some mistake.
The only other sound's the sweep
Of easy wind and downy flake.   12

The woods are lovely, dark and deep,
But I have promises to keep,
And miles to go before I sleep,
And miles to go before I sleep.   16

Acquainted with the Night   [1928]

I have been one acquainted with the night.
I have walked out in rain—and back in rain.
I have outwalked the furthest city light.

I have looked down the saddest city lane.
I have passed by the watchman on his beat   5
And dropped my eyes, unwilling to explain.

I have stood still and stopped the sound of feet
When far away an interrupted cry
Came over houses from another street,

But not to call me back or say good-by;   10
And further still at an unearthly height,
One luminary clock against the sky

Proclaimed the time was neither wrong nor right.
I have been one acquainted with the night.

Desert Places   [1936]

Snow falling and night falling fast, oh, fast
In a field I looked into going past,
And the ground almost covered smooth in snow,
But a few weeds and stubble showing last.   4

The woods around it have it—it is theirs.
All animals are smothered in their lairs.
I am too absent-spirited to count;
The loneliness includes me unawares.   8

And lonely as it is that loneliness
Will be more lonely ere it will be less—
A blanker whiteness of benighted snow

With no expression, nothing to express.   12

They cannot scare me with their empty spaces
Between stars—on stars where no human race is.
I have it in me so much nearer home
To scare myself with my own desert places.   16

Design   [1936]

I found a dimpled spider, fat and white,
On a white heal-all, holding up a moth
Like a white piece of rigid satin cloth—
Assorted characters of death and blight
Mixed ready to begin the morning right,   5
Like the ingredients of a witches' broth—
A snow-drop spider, a flower like froth,
And dead wings carried like a paper kite.

What had that flower to do with being white,
The wayside blue and innocent heal-all?   10
What brought the kindred spider to that height,
Then steered the white moth thither in the night?
What but design of darkness to appall?—
If design govern in a thing so small.

Come In   [1942]

As I came to the edge of the woods,
Thrush music—hark!
Now if it was dusk outside,
Inside it was dark.   4

Too dark in the woods for a bird
By sleight of wing
To better its perch for the night,
Though it still could sing.   8

The last of the light of the sun
That had died in the west
Still lived for one song more
In a thrush's breast.   12

Far in the pillared dark
Thrush music went—
Almost like a call to come in
To the dark and lament.   16

But no, I was out for stars:
I would not come in.
I meant not even if asked,
And I hadn't been.   20

A page from Robert Frost's notebooks, showing "The Silken Tent."

The Silken Tent   [1942]

She is as in a field a silken tent
At midday when a sunny summer breeze
Has dried the dew and all its ropes relent,
So that in guys it gently sways at ease,
And its supporting central cedar pole,   5
That is its pinnacle to heavenward
And signifies the sureness of the soul,
Seems to owe naught to any single cord,
But strictly held by none, is loosely bound
By countless silken ties of love and thought   10
To everything on earth the compass round,
And only by one's going slightly taut
In the capriciousness of summer air
Is of the slightest bondage made aware.

The Most of It   [1942]

He thought he kept the universe alone;
For all the voice in answer he could wake
Was but the mocking echo of his own
From some tree-hidden cliff across the lake.
Some morning from the boulder-broken beach   5
He would cry out on life, that what it wants
Is not its own love back in copy speech,
But counter-love, original response.
And nothing ever came of what he cried
Unless it was the embodiment that crashed   10
In the cliff's talus on the other side,
And then in the far distant water splashed,
But after a time allowed for it to swim,
Instead of proving human when it neared
And someone else additional to him,   15
As a great buck it powerfully appeared,
Pushing the crumpled water up ahead,
And landed pouring like a waterfall,
And stumbled through the rocks with horny tread,
And forced the underbrush—and that was all.   20

Robert Frost on Poetry

The Figure a Poem Makes   [1939]

Abstraction is an old story with the philosophers, but it has been like a new
toy in the hands of the artists of our day. Why can't we have any one quality
of poetry we choose by itself? We can have in thought. Then it will go hard if
we can't in practice. Our lives for it.

   Granted no one but a humanist much cares how sound a poem is if it
is only *a* sound. The sound is the gold in the ore. Then we will have the
sound out alone and dispense with the inessential. We do till we make the
discovery that the object in writing poetry is to make all poems sound as
different as possible from each other, and the resources for that of vowels,
consonants, punctuation, syntax, words, sentences, meter are not enough.
We need the help of context—meaning—subject matter. That is the greatest help towards variety. All that can be done with words is soon told. So
also with meters—particularly in our language where there are virtually
but two, strict iambic and loose iambic. The ancients with many were still
poor if they depended on meters for all tune. It is painful to watch our
sprung-rhythmists straining at the point of omitting one short from a foot
for relief from monotony. The possibilities for tune from the dramatic
tones of meaning struck across the rigidity of a limited meter are endless.
And we are back in poetry as merely one more art of having something to
say, sound or unsound. Probably better if sound, because deeper and from
wider experience.

Then there is this wildness whereof it is spoken. Granted again that it has an equal claim with sound to being a poem's better half. If it is a wild tune, it is a poem. Our problem then is, as modern abstractionists, to have the wildness pure; to be wild with nothing to be wild about. We bring up as aberrationists, giving way to undirected associations and kicking ourselves from one chance suggestion to another in all directions as of a hot afternoon in the life of a grasshopper. Theme alone can steady us down. Just as the first mystery was how a poem could have a tune in such a straightness as meter, so the second mystery is how a poem can have wildness and at the same time a subject that shall be fulfilled.

It should be of the pleasure of a poem itself to tell how it can. The figure a poem makes. It begins in delight and ends in wisdom. The figure is the same as for love. No one can really hold that the ecstasy should be static and stand still in one place. It begins in delight, it inclines to the impulse, it assumes direction with the first line laid down, it runs a course of lucky events, and ends in a clarification of life—not necessarily a great clarification, such as sects and cults are founded on, but in a momentary stay against confusion. It has denouement. It has an outcome that though unforeseen was predestined from the first image of the original mood—and indeed from the very mood. It is but a trick poem and no poem at all if the best of it was thought of first and saved for the last. It finds its own name as it goes and discovers the best waiting for it in some final phrase at once wise and sad—the happy-sad blend of the drinking song.

No tears in the writer, no tears in the reader. No surprise for the writer, no surprise for the reader. For me the initial delight is in the surprise of remembering something I didn't know I knew. I am in a place, in a situation, as if I had materialized from cloud or risen out of the ground. There is a glad recognition of the long lost and the rest follows. Step by step the wonder of unexpected supply keeps growing. The impressions most useful to my purpose seem always those I was unaware of and so made no note of at the time when taken, and the conclusion is come to that like giants we are always hurling experience ahead of us to pave the future with against the day when we may want to strike a line of purpose across it for somewhere. The line will have the more charm for not being mechanically straight. We enjoy the straight crookedness of a good walking stick. Modern instruments of precision are being used to make things crooked as if by eye and hand in the old days.

I tell how there may be a better wildness of logic than of inconsequence. But the logic is backward, in retrospect, after the act. It must be more felt than seen ahead like prophecy. It must be a revelation, or a series of revelations, as much for the poet as for the reader. For it to be that there must have been the greatest freedom of the material to move about in it and to establish relations in it regardless of time and space, previous relation, and everything but affinity. We prate of freedom. We call our schools free because we are not free to stay away from them till we are sixteen years of age. I have given up my democratic prejudices and now willingly set the lower classes free to be completely taken care of by the upper classes. Political freedom is nothing to me. I bestow it right and left. All I would keep for myself is the freedom of my material—the condition of body and mind now and then to summons aptly from the vast chaos of all I have lived through.

Scholars and artists thrown together are often annoyed at the puzzle of where they differ. Both work from knowledge; but I suspect they differ most importantly in the way their knowledge is come by. Scholars get theirs with conscientious thoroughness along projected lines of logic; poets theirs cavalierly and as it happens in and out of books. They stick to nothing deliberately, but let what will stick to them like burrs where they walk in the fields. No acquirement is on assignment, or even self-assignment. Knowledge of the second kind is much more available in the wild free ways of wit and art. A school boy may be defined as one who can tell you what he knows in the order in which he learned it. The artist must value himself as he snatches a thing from some previous order in time and space into a new order with not so much as a ligature clinging to it of the old place where it was organic.

More than once I should have lost my soul to radicalism if it had been the originality it was mistaken for by young converts. Originality and initiative are what I ask for my country. For myself the originality need be no more than the freshness of a poem run in the way I have described: from delight to wisdom. The figure is the same as for love. Like a piece of ice on a hot stove the poem must ride on its own melting. A poem may be worked over once it is in being, but may not be worried into being. Its most precious quality will remain its having run itself and carried away the poet with it. Read it a hundred times: it will forever keep its freshness as a metal keeps its fragrance. It can never lose its sense of a meaning that once unfolded by surprise as it went.

From "The Constant Symbol"   [1946]

[T]here are many other things I have found myself saying about poetry, but the chieftest of these is that it is metaphor, saying one thing and meaning another, saying one thing in terms of another, the pleasure of ulteriority. Poetry is simply made of metaphor. So also is philosophy—and science, too, for that matter, if it will take the soft impeachment from a friend. Every poem is a new metaphor inside or it is nothing. And there is a sense in which all poems are the same old metaphor always.

Every single poem written regular is a symbol small or great of the way the will has to pitch into commitments deeper and deeper to a rounded conclusion and then be judged for whether any original intention it had has been strongly spent or weakly lost; be it in art, politics, school, church, business, love, or marriage—in a piece of work or in a career. Strongly spent is synonymous with kept.

LANGSTON HUGHES

Langston Hughes (1902–1967) was an accomplished poet, short-story writer, dramatist, essayist, and editor. He was born in Joplin, Missouri; he grew up in Lawrence, Kansas, and Cleveland, Ohio; and he spent a year living in Mexico before entering Columbia University in 1921. He left Columbia the following year and traveled extensively in Europe, returning to the United States in the mid-1920s. During these years, Hughes pursued his academic studies at Lincoln University in Pennsylvania (graduating in 1929) and published his first two books of verse, The Weary Blues *(1926) and* Fine Clothes to the Jew *(1927). His many*

achievements in literature, drawing upon spirituals, blues, jazz, and folk expression, and his rich, productive career have led his biographer, Arnold Rampersad, to describe him as "perhaps the most representative black American writer."

Here we provide a selection of Hughes's poetry that shows the range of his themes and the variety of his speaking voices. We begin with one of his best-known works, "The Negro Speaks of Rivers," a poem first published in the June 1921 issue of *The Crisis,* the official magazine of the NAACP. We give eleven of Hughes's poems here (and we have already given some of his poems in earlier chapters), and two selections from his prose.

The Negro Speaks of Rivers
[1921]

I've known rivers:
I've known rivers ancient as the world and older than the flow of
    human blood in human veins.

My soul has grown deep like the rivers.

I bathed in the Euphrates when dawns were young.
I built my hut near the Congo and it lulled me to sleep.   5
I looked upon the Nile and raised the pyramids above it.
I heard the singing of the Mississippi when Abe Lincoln went
    down to New Orleans, and I've seen its muddy bosom turn all
    golden in the sunset.

I've known rivers:
Ancient, dusky rivers.

My soul has grown deep like the rivers.   10

Mother to Son
[1922]

Well, son, I'll tell you:
Life for me ain't been no crystal stair.
It's had tacks in it,
And splinters,
And boards torn up,   5
And places with no carpet on the floor—
Bare.
But all the time
I'se been a-climbin' on,
And reachin' landin's,   10
And turnin' corners,
And sometimes goin' in the dark
Where there ain't been no light.
So boy, don't you turn back.
Don't you set down on the steps   15
'Cause you finds it's kinder hard.
Don't you fall now—
For I'se still goin', honey,
I'se still climbin',
And life for me ain't been no crystal stair.   20

The Weary Blues

[1925]

Droning a drowsy syncopated tune,
Rocking back and forth to a mellow croon,
    I heard a Negro play.
Down on Lenox Avenue° the other night
By the pale dull pallor of an old gas light   5
    He did a lazy sway . . . .
    He did a lazy sway . . . .
To the tune o' those Weary Blues.
With his ebony hands on each ivory key
He made that poor piano moan with melody.   10
    O Blues!
Swaying to and fro on his rickety stool
He played that sad raggy tune like a musical fool.
    Sweet Blues!
Coming from a black man's soul.   15
    O Blues!
In a deep song voice with a melancholy tone
I heard that Negro sing, that old piano moan—
    "Ain't got nobody in all this world,
    Ain't got nobody but ma self.   20
    I's gwine to quit ma frownin'
    And put ma troubles on the shelf."
Thump, thump, thump, went his foot on the floor.
He played a few chords then he sang some more—
    "I got the Weary Blues   25
    And I can't be satisfied.
    Got the Weary Blues
    And can't be satisfied—
    I ain't happy no mo'
    And I wish that I had died."   30
And far into the night he crooned that tune.
The stars went out and so did the moon.
The singer stopped playing and went to bed
While the Weary Blues echoed through his head.
He slept like a rock or a man that's dead.   35

---

4 **Lenox Avenue** Lenox Avenue is a main street in Harlem, in New York City.

The South

[1922]

The lazy, laughing South
With blood on its mouth.
The sunny-faced South,
    Beast-strong,
    Idiot-brained.   5
The child-minded South
Scratching in the dead fire's ashes
For a Negro's bones.
    Cotton and the moon,

Warmth, earth, warmth,   10
   The sky, the sun, the stars,
   The magnolia-scented South.
Beautiful, like a woman,
Seductive as a dark-eyed whore,
   Passionate, cruel,   15
   Honey-lipped, syphilitic—
   That is the South.
And I, who am black, would love her
But she spits in my face.
And I, who am black,   20
Would give her many rare gifts
But she turns her back upon me.
   So now I seek the North—
   The cold-faced North,
   For she, they say,   25
   Is a kinder mistress,
And in her house my children
May escape the spell of the South.

Ruby Brown   [1926]

She was young and beautiful
And golden like the sunshine
That warmed her body.
And because she was colored
Mayville had no place to offer her,   5
Nor fuel for the clean flame of joy
That tried to burn within her soul.

One day,
Sitting on old Mrs. Latham's back porch
Polishing the silver,   10
She asked herself two questions
And they ran something like this:
What can a colored girl do
On the money from a white woman's kitchen?
And ain't there any joy in this town?   15

Now the streets down by the river
Know more about this pretty Ruby Brown,
And the sinister shuttered houses of the bottoms
Hold a yellow girl
Seeking an answer to her questions.   20
The good church folk do not mention
Her name any more.

But the white men,
Habitués of the high shuttered houses,
Pay more money to her now   25
Than they ever did before,
When she worked in their kitchens.

Poet to Patron

[1939]

What right has anyone to say
That I
Must throw out pieces of my heart
For pay?   4

For bread that helps to make
My heart beat true,
I must sell myself
To you?   8

A factory shift's better,
A week's meagre pay,
Than a perfumed note asking:
What poems today?   12

Ballad of the Landlord

[1940]

Landlord, landlord,
My roof has sprung a leak.
Don't you member I told you about it
Way last week?   4

Landlord, landlord,
These steps is broken down.
When you come up yourself
It's a wonder you don't fall down.   8

Ten Bucks you say I owe you?
Ten Bucks you say is due?
Well, that's Ten Bucks more'n I'll pay you
Till you fix this house up new.   12

What? You gonna get eviction orders?
You gonna cut off my heat?
You gonna take my furniture and
Throw it in the street?   16

Um-huh! You talking high and mighty.
Talk on—till you get through.
You ain't gonna be able to say a word
If I land my fist on you.   20

Police! Police!
Come and get this man!
He's trying to ruin the government
And overturn the land!   24

Copper's whistle!
Patrol bell!
Arrest.

Precinct Station.   28
Iron cell.

Headlines in press:

MAN THREATENS LANDLORD
∴
TENANT HELD NO BAIL   32
∴
JUDGE GIVES NEGRO 90 DAYS IN COUNTY JAIL.

Too Blue   [1943]

I got those sad old weary blues.
I don't know where to turn.
I don't know where to go.
Nobody cares about you
When you sink so low.   5

What shall I do?
What shall I say?
Shall I take a gun
And put myself away?

I wonder if   10
One bullet would do?
As hard as my head is,
It would probably take two.

But I ain't got
Neither bullet nor gun—   15
And I'm too blue
To look for one.

Harlem [1]   [1949]

Here on the edge of hell
Stands Harlem—
Remembering the old lies,
The old kicks in the back,
The old "Be patient"   5
They told us before.

Sure, we remember.
Now when the man at the corner store
Says sugar's gone up another two cents,
And bread one,   10
And there's a new tax on cigarettes—
We remember the job we never had,
Never could get,
And can't have now
Because we're colored.   15

So we stand here
On the edge of hell
In Harlem

And look out on the world
And wonder   20
What we're gonna do
In the face of what
We remember.

Theme for English B   [1949]

The instructor said,

> *Go home and write*
> *a page tonight.*
> *And let that page come out of you—*
> *Then, it will be true.*   5

I wonder if it's that simple?
I am twenty-two, colored, born in Winston-Salem.
I went to school there, then Durham, then here
to this college on the hill above Harlem.
I am the only colored student in my class.   10
The steps from the hill lead down into Harlem,
through a park, then I cross St. Nicholas,
Eighth Avenue, Seventh, and I come to the Y,
the Harlem Branch Y, where I take the elevator
up to my room, sit down, and write this page: 15

It's not easy to know what is true for you or me
at twenty-two, my age. But I guess I'm what
I feel and see and hear, Harlem, I hear you:
hear you, hear me—we two—you, me, talk on this page.
(I hear New York, too.) Me—who?   20
Well, I like to eat, sleep, drink, and be in love.
I like to work, read, learn, and understand life.
I like a pipe for a Christmas present,
or records—Bessie,° bop,° or Bach.°
I guess being colored doesn't make me *not* like   25
the same things other folks like who are other races.
So will my page be colored that I write?
Being me, it will not be white.
But it will be
a part of you, instructor.   30
You are white—
yet a part of me, as I am a part of you.
That's American.
Sometimes perhaps you don't want to be a part of me.
Nor do I often want to be a part of you.   35
But we are, that's true!

---

24 Bessie Bessie Smith (1894–1937), American blues singer.   **bop** Bop, a style of fast-
tempo jazz, popular in the 1940s and 1950s.   **Bach** Johann Sebastian Bach (1685–1750),
German composer of the Baroque period.

As I learn from you,
I guess you learn from me—
although you're older—and white—
and somewhat more free.   40

This is my page for English B.

Poet to Bigot   [1953]

I have done so little
For you,
And you have done so little
For me,
That we have good reason   5
Never to agree.

I, however,
Have such meagre
Power,
Clutching at a   10
Moment,
While you control
An hour.

But your hour is
A stone.   15

My moment is
A flower.

Langston Hughes on Poetry

The Negro Artist and the Racial Mountain   [1926]

*Hughes often examined the challenges he faced in writing both as an
American and an African American, as in this provocative essay published in 1926.*

One of the most promising of the young Negro poets said to me once, "I want
to be a poet—not a Negro poet," meaning, I believe, "I want to write like a
white poet"; meaning subconsciously, "I would like to be a white poet";
meaning behind that, "I would like to be white." And I was sorry the young
man said that, for no great poet has ever been afraid of being himself. And I
doubted then that, with his desire to run away spiritually from his race, this
boy would ever be a great poet. But this is the mountain standing in the way
of any true Negro art in America—this urge within the race toward whiteness, the desire to pour racial individuality into the mold of American stan-
dardization, and to be as little Negro and as much American as possible.

But let us look at the immediate background of this young poet. His
family is of what I suppose one would call the Negro middle class: people

who are by no means rich yet never uncomfortable nor hungry—smug, contented, respectable folk, members of the Baptist church. The father goes to work every morning. He is a chief steward at a large white club. The mother sometimes does fancy sewing or supervises parties for the rich families of the town. The children go to a mixed school. In the home they read white papers and magazines. And the mother often says "Don't be like niggers" when the children are bad. A frequent phrase from the father is, "Look how well a white man does things." And so the word white comes to be unconsciously a symbol of all the virtues. It holds for the children beauty, morality, and money. The whisper of "I want to be white" runs silently through their minds. This young poet's home is, I believe, a fairly typical home of the colored middle class. One sees immediately how difficult it would be for an artist born in such a home to interest himself in interpreting the beauty of his own people. He is never taught to see that beauty. He is taught rather not to see it, or if he does, to be ashamed of it when it is not according to Caucasian patterns.

For racial culture the home of a self-styled "high-class" Negro has nothing better to offer. Instead there will perhaps be more aping of things white than in a less cultured or less wealthy home. The father is perhaps a doctor, lawyer, landowner, or politician. The mother may be a social worker, or a teacher, or she may do nothing and have a maid. Father is often dark but he has usually married the lightest woman he could find. The family attend a fashionable church where few really colored faces are to be found. And they themselves draw a color line. In the North they go to white theaters and white movies. And in the South they have at least two cars and a house "like white folks." Nordic manners, Nordic faces, Nordic hair, Nordic art (if any), and an Episcopal heaven. A very high mountain indeed for the would-be racial artist to climb in order to discover himself and his people.

But then there are the low-down folks, the so-called common element, and they are the majority—may the Lord be praised! The people who have their nip of gin on Saturday nights and are not too important to themselves or the community, or too well fed, or too learned to watch the lazy world go round. They live on Seventh Street in Washington or State Street in Chicago and they do not particularly care whether they are like white folks or anybody else. Their joy runs, bang! into ecstasy. Their religion soars to a shout. Work maybe a little today, rest a little tomorrow. Play awhile. Sing awhile. O, let's dance! These common people are not afraid of spirituals, as for a long time their more intellectual brethren were, and jazz is their child. They furnish a wealth of colorful, distinctive material for any artist because they still hold their own individuality in the face of American standardizations. And perhaps these common people will give to the world its truly great Negro artist, the one who is not afraid to be himself. Whereas the better-class Negro would tell the artist what to do, the people at least let him alone when he does appear. And they are not ashamed of him—if they know he exists at all. And they accept what beauty is their own without question.

5   Certainly there is, for the American Negro artist who can escape the restrictions the more advanced among his own group would put upon him, a great field of unused material ready for his art. Without going outside his race and even among the better classes with their "white" culture and conscious American manners, but still Negro enough to be different, there is sufficient matter to furnish a black artist with a lifetime of creative work. And

when he chooses to touch on the relations between Negroes and whites in this country with their innumerable overtones and undertones, surely, and especially for literature and the drama, there is an inexhaustible supply of themes at hand. To these the Negro artist can give his racial individuality, his heritage of rhythm and warmth, and his incongruous humor that so often, as in the Blues, becomes ironic laughter mixed with tears. But let us look again at the mountain.

A prominent Negro clubwoman in Philadelphia paid eleven dollars to hear Raquel Meller[1] sing Andalusian[2] popular songs. But she told me a few weeks before she would not think of going to hear "that woman," Clara Smith, a great black artist, sing Negro folksongs. And many an upper-class Negro church, even now, would not dream of employing a spiritual in its services. The drab melodies in white folks' hymnbooks are much to be preferred. "We want to worship the Lord correctly and quietly. We don't believe in 'shouting.' Let's be dull like the Nordics," they say, in effect.

The road for the serious black artist, then, who would produce a racial art is most certainly rocky and the mountain is high. Until recently he received almost no encouragement for his work from either white or colored people. The fine novels of Chesnutt[3] go out of print with neither race noticing their passing. The quaint charm and humor of Dunbar's[4] dialect verse brought to him, in his day, largely the same kind of encouragement one would give a sideshow freak (A colored man writing poetry! How odd!) or a clown (How amusing!).

The present vogue in things Negro, although it may do as much harm as good for the budding colored artist, has at least done this: it has brought him forcibly to the attention of his own people among whom for so long, unless the other race had noticed him beforehand, he was a prophet with little honor. I understand that Charles Gilpin[5] acted for years in Negro theaters without any special acclaim from his own, but when Broadway gave him eight curtain calls, Negroes, too, began to beat a tin pan in his honor. I know a young colored writer, a manual worker by day, who had been writing well for the colored magazines for some years, but it was not until he recently broke into the white publications and his first book was accepted by a prominent New York publisher that the "best" Negroes in his city took the trouble to discover that he lived there. Then almost immediately they decided to give a grand dinner for him. But the society ladies were careful to whisper to his mother that perhaps she'd better not come. They were not sure she would have an evening gown.

The Negro artist works against an undertow of sharp criticism and misunderstanding from his own group and unintentional bribes from the whites. "O, be respectable, write about nice people, show how good we are," say the Negroes. "Be stereotyped, don't go too far, don't shatter our illusions about you, don't amuse us too seriously. We will pay you," say the whites. Both would have told Jean Toomer[6] not to write "Cane." The colored

---

[1]**Raquel Meller** (1888–1962), a popular Spanish singer and actress.   [2]**Andalusian** a community in southern Spain   [3]**Chesnutt** Charles Chesnutt (1858–1932), African American novelist.   [4]**Dunbar** Paul Laurence Dunbar (1872–1906), African American poet.   [5]**Charles Gilpin** (1878–1930), renowned African American actor   [6]**Jean Toomer** (1894–1967), African American poet and novelist and author of *Cane* (1923).

people did not praise it. The white people did not buy it. Most of the colored people who did read "Cane" hate it. They are afraid of it. Although the
critics gave it good reviews the public remained indifferent. Yet (excepting
the work of Du Bois[7]) "Cane" contains the finest prose written by a Negro
in America. And like the singing of Robeson,[8] it is truly racial.

10   But in spite of the Nordicized Negro intelligentsia and the desires of
some white editors we have an honest American Negro literature already with
us. Now I await the rise of the Negro theater. Our folk music, having achieved
world-wide fame, offers itself to the genius of the great individual American
Negro composer who is to come. And within the next decade I expect to
see the work of a growing school of colored artists who paint and model the
beauty of dark faces and create with new technique the expressions of their
own soul-world. And the Negro dancers who will dance like flame and the
singers who will continue to carry our songs to all who listen—they will be
with us in even greater numbers tomorrow.

Most of my own poems are racial in theme and treatment, derived from
the life I know. In many of them I try to grasp and hold some of the meanings and rhythms of jazz. I am as sincere as I know how to be in these poems
and yet after every reading I answer questions like these from my own people:
Do you think Negroes should always write about Negroes? I wish you
wouldn't read some of your poems to white folks. How do you find anything
interesting in a place like a cabaret? Why do you write about black people?
You aren't black. What makes you do so many jazz poems?

But jazz to me is one of the inherent expressions of Negro life in America:
the eternal tom-tom beating in the Negro soul—the tom-tom of revolt
against weariness in a white world, a world of subway trains, and work,
work, work; the tom-tom of joy and laughter, and pain swallowed in a smile.
Yet the Philadelphia clubwoman is ashamed to say that her race created it
and she does not like me to write about it. The old subconscious "white is
best" runs through her mind. Years of study under white teachers, a lifetime
of white books, pictures, and papers, and white manners, morals, and Puritan
standards made her dislike the spirituals. And now she turns up her nose at
jazz and all its manifestations—likewise almost everything else distinctly
racial. She doesn't care for the Winold Reiss[9] portraits of Negroes because
they are "too Negro." She does not want a true picture of herself from anybody. She wants the artist to flatter her, to make the white world believe that
all Negroes are as smug and as near white in soul as she wants to be. But, to
my mind, it is the duty of the younger Negro artist, if he accepts any duties at
all from outsiders, to change through the force of his art that old whispering
"I want to be white," hidden in the aspirations of his people, to "Why should
I want to be white? I am a Negro—and beautiful!"

So I am ashamed for the black poet who says, "I want to be a poet, not a
Negro poet," as though his own racial world were not as interesting as any
other world. I am ashamed, too, for the colored artist who runs from the
painting of Negro faces to the painting of sunsets after the manner of the
academicians because he fears the strange un-whiteness of his own features.

---

[7]**Du Bois** William Edward Burghardt Du Bois (1868–1963), African American historian,
sociologist, writer.   [8]**Robeson** Paul Robeson (1898–1976), African American singer
and actor.   [9]**Winold Reiss** (1886–1953), German immigrant artist and designer.

An artist must be free to choose what he does, certainly, but he must also never be afraid to do what he might choose.

Let the blare of Negro jazz bands and the bellowing voice of Bessie Smith singing Blues penetrate the closed ears of the colored near-intellectuals until they listen and perhaps understand. Let Paul Robeson singing "Water Boy," and Rudolph Fisher[10] writing about the streets of Harlem, and Jean Toomer holding the heart of Georgia in his hands, and Aaron Douglas[11] drawing strange black fantasies cause the smug Negro middle class to turn from their white, respectable, ordinary books and papers to catch a glimmer of their own beauty. We younger Negro artists who create now intend to express our individual dark-skinned selves without fear or shame. If white people are pleased we are glad. If they are not, it doesn't matter. We know we are beautiful. And ugly too. The tom-tom cries and the tom-tom laughs. If colored people are pleased we are glad. If they are not, their displeasure doesn't matter either. We build our temples for tomorrow, strong as we know how, and we stand on top of the mountain, free within ourselves.

On the Cultural Achievements of African Americans   [1960]

Without them, on my part, there would have been no poems; without their hopes and fears and dreams, no stories; without their struggles, no dramas; without their music, no songs.

Had I not heard as a child in the little churches of Kansas and Missouri, "Deep river, my home is over Jordan," or "My Lord, what a morning when the stars begin to fall," I might not have come to realize the lyric beauty of *living* poetry. . . .

There is so much richness in Negro humor, so much beauty in black dreams, so much dignity in our struggle, and so much universality in our problems, in *us*—in each living human being of color—that I do not understand the tendency today that some American Negro artists have of seeking to run away from themselves, of running away from *us,* of being afraid to sing our own songs, paint our pictures, write about ourselves—when it is our music that has given America its greatest music, our humor that has enriched its entertainment media for the past 100 years, our rhythm that has guided its dancing feet from plantation days to the Charleston. . . . Yet there are some of us who say, "Why write about Negroes? Why not be *just a writer?*" And why not—if one wants to be "just a writer?" Negroes in a free world should be whatever each wants to be—even if it means being "just a writer. . . ."

There is nothing to be ashamed of in the strength and dignity and laughter of the Negro people. And there is nothing to be afraid of in the use of their material.

Could you be possibly afraid that the rest of the world will not accept it? Our spirituals are sung and loved in the great concert halls of the whole

---

[10]**Rudolph Fisher** (1897–1934), African American writer.   [11]**Aaron Douglas** (1899–1979), an African American painter and a leading figure in the Harlem Renaissance.

world. Our blues are played from Topeka to Tokyo. Harlem's jive talk delights
Hong Kong and Paris. Those of our writers who have *most* concerned themselves with our very special problems are translated and read around the
world. The local, the regional can—and does—become universal. Sean
O'Casey's[12] Irishmen are an example. So I would say to young Negro writers, do not be afraid of yourself. *You* are the world. . . .

---

[12]**Sean O'Casey** (1880–1964), important Irish playwright.

A Collection of Poems

The first four selections in this chapter are folk ballads (also called "popular ballads"). For a discussion of this kind of literature, see pages 553–555.

ANONYMOUS BRITISH BALLAD

The Three Ravens

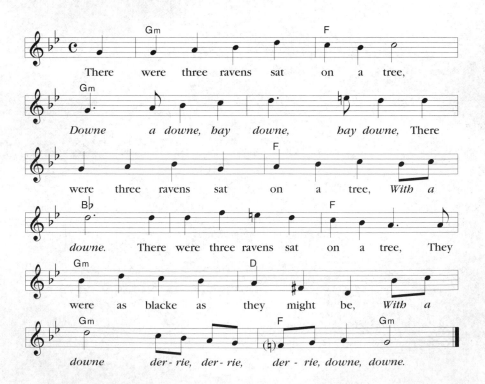

There were three ravens sat on a tree,
Downe a downe, hay downe, hay downe, There
were three ravens sat on a tree, With a
downe. There were three ravens sat on a tree, They
were as blacke as they might be, With a
downe der-rie, der-rie, der-rie, downe, downe.

There were three ravens sat on a tree,
Downe a downe, hay downe, hay downe

There were three ravens sat on a tree,
With a downe
There were three ravens sat on a tree,   5
They were as blacke as they might be,
With a downe derrie, derrie, derrie, downe, downe.

The one of them said to his mate,
"Where shall we our breakfast take?"

"Down in yonder greene field,   10
There lies a knight slain under his shield.

His hounds they lie downe at his feete,
So well they can their master keepe.

His haukes they flie so eagerly,
There's no fowle dare him come nie."   15

Downe there comes a fallow° doe,°
As great with yong as she might goe.

She lift up his bloudy hed,
And kist his wounds that were so red.

She got him up upon her backe,   20
And carried him to earthen lake.°

She buried him before the prime,°
She was dead herselfe ere even-song time.

God send every gentleman
Such haukes, such hounds, and such a leman.°   25

---

16 fallow brown.   **doe** The "doe," often taken as a suggestive description of the knight's beloved, is probably a vestige of the folk belief that an animal may be an enchanted human being.   **21 lake** pit.   **22 prime** about 9 AM.   **25 leman** sweetheart.

ANONYMOUS BRITISH BALLAD

The Twa Corbies

As I was walking all alane,
I heard twa corbies° making a mane;°
The tane° unto the t' other say,
"Where sall we gang° and dine to-day?"   4
"In behint yon auld fail dyke,°
I wot° there lies a new-slain knight;

---

2 twa corbies two ravens.   **mane** lament.   **3 tane** one.   **4 sall we gang** shall we go.
5 auld fail dyke old turf wall.   **6 wot** know.

And naebody kens° that he lies there,
But his hawk, his hound, and lady fair.   8

"His hound is to the hunting gane,
His hawk, to fetch the wild-fowl hame,
His lady's ta'en another mate,
So we may mak our dinner sweet.   12

"Ye'll sit on his white hause-bane,°
And I'll pike out his bonny blue een.°
Wi' ae° lock o' his gowden° hair
We'll theek° our nest when it grows bare.   16

"Mony a one for him makes mane,
But nane sall ken whare he is gane;
O'er his white banes, when they are bare,
The wind sall blaw for evermair."   20

-----

7 kens knows.   **13 hause-bane** neck bone.   **14 een** eyes.   **15 Wi' ae** With one.
gowden golden.   **16 theek** thatch.

ANONYMOUS AFRICAN AMERICAN BALLAD

*John Henry**

John Henry was a very small boy,
Sitting on his mammy's knee;
He picked up a hammer and a little piece of steel,
Saying,"A hammer'll be the death of me, O Lord,
A hammer'll be the death of me."   5

John Henry went up on the mountain
And he came down on the side.
The mountain was so tall and John Henry was so small
That he laid down his hammer and he cried,"O Lord,"
He laid down his hammer and he cried.   10

John Henry was a man just six feet in height,
Nearly two feet and a half across the breast.
He'd take a nine-pound hammer and hammer all day long
And never get tired and want to rest, O Lord,
And never get tired and want to rest.   15

John Henry was a steel-driving man, O Lord,
He drove all over the world.
He come to Big Bend Tunnel on the C. & O. Road

-----

*__John Henry,__ a black steel driver from West Virginia, worked on the Chesapeake &
Ohio's Big Bend Tunnel around 1870. The steel driver hammered a drill (held by his assistant, the "shaker") into rocks so that explosives could then be poured in. In the 1870s, mechanical steel drills were introduced, displacing the steel driver.

Where he beat the steam drill down, O Lord,
Where he beat the steam drill down.   20

John Henry said to the captain,
"Captain, you go to town,
Bring me back a twelve-pound hammer
And I'll beat that steam drill down, O Lord,
And I'll beat that steam drill down."   25

They placed John Henry on the right-hand side,
The steam drill on the left;
He said, "Before I let that steam drill beat me down
I'll die with my hammer in my hand, O Lord,
And send my soul to rest."   30

The white folks all got scared,
Thought Big Bend was a-fallin' in;
John Henry hollered out with a very loud shout,
"It's my hammer a-fallin' in the wind, O Lord,
It's my hammer a-fallin' in the wind."   35

John Henry said to his shaker,
"Shaker, you better pray,
For if I miss that little piece of steel
Tomorrow'll be your buryin' day, O Lord,
Tomorrow'll be your buryin' day."   40

The man that invented that steam drill
He thought he was mighty fine.
John Henry sunk the steel fourteen feet
While the steam drill only made nine, O Lord,
While the steam drill only made nine.   45

John Henry said to his loving little wife,
"I'm sick and want to go to bed.
Fix me a place to lay down, Child;
There's a roarin' in my head, O Lord,
There's a roarin' in my head."   50

SHERMAN ALEXIE

For a biographical note, see page 658.

On the Amtrak from Boston to New York City   [1993]

The white woman across the aisle from me says, "Look,
look at all the history, that house
on the hill there is over two hundred years old,"
as she points out the window past me   4

into what she has been taught. I have learned
little more about American history during my few days
back East than what I expected and far less
of what we should all know of the tribal stories   8

whose architecture is 15,000 years older
than the corners of the house that sits
museumed on the hill. "Walden Pond,"°
the woman on the train asks, "Did you see Walden Pond?"   12

and I don't have a cruel enough heart to break
her own by telling her there are five Walden Ponds
on my little reservation out West
and at least a hundred more surrounding Spokane,   16

the city I pretend to call my home. "Listen,"
I could have told her. "I don't give a shit
about Walden. I know the Indians were living stories
around that pond before Walden's grandparents were born   20

and before his grandparents' grandparents were born.
I'm tired of hearing about Don-fucking-Henley° saving it, too,
because that's redundant. If Don Henley's brothers and sisters
and mothers and fathers hadn't come here in the first place   24

then nothing would need to be saved."
But I didn't say a word to the woman about Walden
Pond because she smiled so much and seemed delighted
that I thought to bring her an orange juice   28

back from the food car. I respect elders
of every color. All I really did was eat
my tasteless sandwich, drink my Diet Pepsi
and nod my head whenever the woman pointed out   32

another little piece of her country's history
while I, as all Indians have done
since this war began, made plans
for what I would do and say the next time   36

somebody from the enemy thought I was one of their own.

---

11 **Walden Pond** site in Massachusetts where Henry David Thoreau (1817–1862) lived
from 4 July 1845 to 6 September 1847, and about which he wrote in his most famous book,
Walden (1854).   22 **Don Henley** American singer and songwriter (b. 1947), who was active in preserving Walden Pond.

MATTHEW ARNOLD

*Matthew Arnold (1822–1888) was the son of a famous educator, Dr. Thomas
Arnold, the headmaster of Rugby School. After graduating from Oxford,
Matthew Arnold became an inspector of schools, a post he held until two years
before his death. Besides writing poetry, Arnold wrote literary criticism and
was appointed professor of poetry at Oxford from 1857 to 1867. He traveled
widely on the Continent and lectured in the United States.*

Dover Beach   [c. 1851]

The sea is calm to-night.
The tide is full, the moon lies fair
Upon the straits;—on the French coast the light

Gleams and is gone; the cliffs of England stand,
Glimmering and vast, out in the tranquil bay.   5
Come to the window, sweet is the night-air!
Only, from the long line of spray
Where the sea meets the moon-blanch'd land,
Listen! you hear the grating roar
Of pebbles which the waves draw back, and fling,   10
At their return, up the high strand,
Begin, and cease, and then again begin,
With tremulous cadence slow, and bring
The eternal note of sadness in.

Sophocles long ago   15
Heard it on the Ægean, and it brought
Into his mind the turbid ebb and flow
Of human misery; we
Find also in the sound a thought,
Hearing it by this distant northern sea.   20

The Sea of Faith
Was once, too, at the full, and round earth's shore
Lay like the folds of a bright girdle furl'd.
But now I only hear
Its melancholy, long, withdrawing roar,   25
Retreating, to the breath
Of the night-wind, down the vast edges drear
And naked shingles° of the world.

Ah, love, let us be true
To one another! for the world, which seems   30
To lie before us like a land of dreams,
So various, so beautiful, so new,
Hath really neither joy, nor love, nor light,
Nor certitude, nor peace, nor help for pain;
And we are here as on a darkling plain   35
Swept with confused alarms of struggle and flight,
Where ignorant armies clash by night.

---

28 **shingles** pebbled beaches.

W. H. AUDEN

For a biographical note, see page 576.

The Unknown Citizen   [1940]

(To JS/07/M378
This Marble Monument Is Erected by the State)

He was found by the Bureau of Statistics to be
One against whom there was no official complaint,
And all the reports on his conduct agree
That, in the modern sense of an old-fashioned word, he was a saint,

For in everything he did he served the Greater Community.   5
Except for the War till the day he retired
He worked in a factory and never got fired,
But satisfied his employers, Fudge Motors Inc.
Yet he wasn't a scab or odd in his views,
For his Union reports that he paid his dues,   10
(Our report on his Union shows it was sound)
And our Social Psychology workers found
That he was popular with his mates and liked a drink.
The Press are convinced that he bought a paper every day
And that his reactions to advertisements were normal in every way.   15
Policies taken out in his name prove that he was fully insured,
And his Health-card shows he was once in hospital but left it cured.
Both Producers Research and High-Grade Living declare
He was fully sensible to the advantages of the Installment Plan
And had everything necessary to the Modern Man,   20
A phonograph, a radio, a car and a frigidaire.
Our researchers into Public Opinion are content
That he held the proper opinions for the time of year;
When there was peace, he was for peace; when there was war, he went.
He was married and added five children to the population,   25
Which our Eugenist° says was the right number for a parent of his
    generation,
And our teachers report that he never interfered with their education.
Was he free? Was he happy? The question is absurd:
Had anything been wrong, we should certainly have heard.

---

26 Eugenist Eugenics is the study and practice of selective breeding applied to humans, with the aim of improving the species.

JIMMY SANTIAGO BACA

Jimmy Santiago Baca, of Chicano and Apache descent, was born in 1952. When he was two his parents divorced, and a grandparent brought him up until he was five, when he was placed in an orphanage in New Mexico. He ran away when he was eleven, lived on the streets, took drugs, and at the age of twenty was convicted of drug possession. In prison he taught himself to read and write, and he began to compose poetry. A fellow inmate urged him to send some poems to Mother Jones *magazine, and the work was accepted. In 1979 Louisiana State University Press published a book of his poems,* Immigrants in Our Own Land. *He has since published several other books. Baca is the author of a number of books of poems, stories, and essays, and of a memoir,* A Place to Stand *(2001).*

So Mexicans Are Taking Jobs from Americans   [1979]

O Yes? Do they come on horses
with rifles, and say,
        Ese gringo,° gimmee your job?

---

3 Ese gringo Hey, whitey.

And do you, gringo, take off your ring,
drop your wallet into a blanket   5
spread over the ground, and walk away?

I hear Mexicans are taking your jobs away.
Do they sneak into town at night,
and as you're walking home with a whore,
do they mug you, a knife at your throat,   10
saying, I want your job?

Even on TV, an asthmatic leader
crawls turtle heavy, leaning on an assistant,
and from a nest of wrinkles on his face,
a tongue paddles through flashing waves   15
of lightbulbs, of cameramen, rasping
"They're taking our jobs away."

Well, I've gone about trying to find them,
asking just where the hell are these fighters.

The rifles I hear sound in the night   20
are white farmers shooting blacks and browns
whose ribs I see jutting out
and starving children,
I see the poor marching for a little work,
I see small white farmers selling out   25
to clean-suited farmers living in New York,
who've never been on a farm,
don't know the look of a hoof or the smell
of a woman's body bending all day long in fields.

I see this, and I hear only a few people   30
got all the money in this world, the rest
count their pennies to buy bread and butter.

Below that cool green sea of money,
millions and millions of people fight to live,
search for pearls in the darkest depths   35
of their dreams, hold their breath for years
trying to cross poverty to just having something.

The children are dead already. We are killing them,
that is what America should be saying;
on TV, in the streets, in offices, should be saying,   40
    "We aren't giving the children a chance to live."

    Mexicans are taking our jobs, they say instead.
    What they really say is, let them die,
    and the children too.

AMIRI BARAKA

*Amiri Baraka (b. 1934) in his early years was Everett LeRoi (or LeRoy) Jones,
but with an increasing awareness of his African heritage he altered his name,
first to Imamu ("spiritual leader") Ameer ("blessed") Baraka ("prince") and*

then to Amiri Baraka. Baraka was educated at Howard University, Columbia University, and the New School for Social Research.

After serving in the U.S. Air Force, he settled in Greenwich Village, in New York City, and became part of the (chiefly white) literary scene; he and his wife published a journal that included works by Jack Kerouac, Allen Ginsberg, and others. The assassination of Malcolm X in 1965 had a profound effect on Baraka, and in this year he left his white wife and the artistic life of Greenwich Village and moved to Harlem, where he established the Black Arts Repertory Theater/School. In 1966 he returned to Newark, where he founded a similar school and, perhaps because of his heightened socialism, dropped Imamu from his name. The author of many plays and books of poetry, he is an emeritus professor at the State University of New York, Stony Brook.

Malcolm X (1925–1965), the subject of the following poem, was a militant black leader who rose to prominence in the Black Muslims. When in 1963 Elijah Muhammad suspended him, Malcolm formed his own organization, the Muslim Mosque. In 1964 he converted to orthodox Islam, and he proclaimed the brotherhood of blacks and whites, although he continued to support black nationalism. In February 1965 he was shot to death by an unidentified assassin.

A Poem for Black Hearts   [1965]

For Malcolm's eyes, when they broke
the face of some dumb white man, For
Malcolm's hands raised to bless us
all black and strong in his image
of ourselves, For Malcolm's words   5
fire darts, the victor's tireless
thrusts, words hung above the world
change as it may, he said it, and
for this he was killed, for saying,
and feeling, and being / change, all   10
collected hot in his heart, For Malcolm's
heart, raising us above our filthy cities,
for his stride, and his beat, and his address
to the gray monsters of the world, For Malcolm's
pleas for your dignity, black men, for your life,   15
black man, for the filling of your minds
with righteousness, For all of him dead and
gone and vanished from us, and all of him which
clings to our speech black god of our time.
For all of him, and all of yourself, look up,   20
black man, quit stuttering and shuffling, look up,
black man, quit whining and stooping, for all of him,
For Great Malcolm a prince of the earth, let nothing in us rest
until we avenge ourselves for his death, stupid animals
that killed him, let us never breathe a pure breath if   25
we fail, and white men call us faggots till the end of
the earth.

ELIZABETH BISHOP

For a biographical note, see page 682.

The Fish   [1946]

I caught a tremendous fish
and held him beside the boat
half out of water, with my hook
fast in a corner of his mouth.
He didn't fight.   5
He hadn't fought at all.
He hung a grunting weight,
battered and venerable
and homely. Here and there
his brown skin hung in strips   10
like ancient wallpaper,
and its pattern of darker brown
was like wallpaper:
shapes like full-blown roses
stained and lost through age.   15
He was speckled with barnacles,
fine rosettes of lime,
and infested
with tiny white sea-lice,
and underneath two or three   20
rags of green weed hung down.
While his gills were breathing in
the terrible oxygen
—the frightening gills,
fresh and crisp with blood,   25
that can cut so badly—
I thought of the coarse white flesh
packed in like feathers,
the big bones and the little bones,
the dramatic reds and blacks   30
of his shiny entrails,
and the pink swim-bladder
like a big peony.
I looked into his eyes
which were far larger than mine   35
but shallower, and yellowed,
the irises backed and packed
with tarnished tinfoil
seen through the lenses
of old scratched isinglass.°   40

---

40 isinglass isinglass is mica (a type of mineral) in thin, transparent sheets.

They shifted a little, but not
to return my stare.
—It was more like the tipping
of an object toward the light.
I admired his sullen face,   45
the mechanism of his jaw,
and then I saw
that from his lower lip
—if you could call it a lip—
grim, wet, and weaponlike,   50
hung five old pieces of fish-line,
or four and a wire leader
with the swivel still attached,
with all their five big hooks
grown firmly in his mouth.   55
A green line, frayed at the end
where he broke it, two heavier lines,
and a fine black thread
still crimped from the strain and snap
when it broke and he got away.   60
Like medals with their ribbons
frayed and wavering,
a five-haired beard of wisdom
trailing from his aching jaw.
I stared and stared   65
and victory filled up
the little rented boat,
from the pool of bilge
where oil had spread a rainbow
around the rusted engine   70
to the bailer rusted orange,
the sun-cracked thwarts,
the oarlocks on their strings,
the gunnels—until everything
was rainbow, rainbow, rainbow!   75
And I let the fish go.

WILLIAM BLAKE

William Blake (1757–1827) was born in London and at fourteen was ap-
prenticed for seven years to an engraver. A Christian visionary poet, he made
his living by giving drawing lessons and by illustrating books, including his
own Songs of Innocence *(1789) and* Songs of Experience *(1794). These two*
books represent, he said, "two contrary states of the human soul." ("Infant Joy"
comes from Innocence, *"Infant Sorrow" from* Experience.*) In 1809 Blake ex-*
hibited his art, but the show was a failure. Not until he was in his sixties,
when he stopped writing poetry, did he achieve any public recognition—and
then it was as a painter.

"The Lamb," like "Infant Joy," comes from Songs of Innocence; *"The Tyger"*
and "London," like "Infant Sorrow," come from Songs of Experience.

Infant Joy

[1789]

"I have no name,
I am but two days old."
What shall I call thee?
"I happy am,
Joy is my name." 5
Sweet joy befall thee!

Pretty joy!
Sweet joy but two days old,
Sweet joy I call thee:
Thou dost smile, 10
I sing the while—
Sweet joy befall thee.

Infant Sorrow

[1794]

My mother groaned! my father wept.
Into the dangerous world I leapt,
Helpless, naked, piping loud;
Like a fiend hid in a cloud. 4

Struggling in my father's hands,
Striving against my swadling bands;
Bound and weary I thought best
To sulk upon my mother's breast. 8

The Lamb

[1789]

Little Lamb, who made thee?
Dost thou know who made thee?
Gave thee life, and bid thee feed
By the stream and o'er the mead;
Gave thee clothing of delight, 5
Softest clothing, wooly, bright;
Gave thee such a tender voice,
Making all the vales rejoice?
Little Lamb, who made thee?
Dost thou know who made thee? 10

Little Lamb, I'll tell thee,
Little Lamb, I'll tell thee:
He is calléd by thy name,
For he calls himself a Lamb.
He is meek, and he is mild; 15
He became a little child.
I a child, and thou a lamb,
We are calléd by his name.
Little Lamb, God bless thee!
Little Lamb, God bless thee! 20

The Tyger

[1794]

Tyger! Tyger! burning bright
In the forests of the night,
What immortal hand or eye
Could frame thy fearful symmetry?   4

In what distant deeps or skies
Burnt the fire of thine eyes?
On what wings dare he aspire?
What the hand dare seize the fire?   8

And what shoulder, and what art,
Could twist the sinews of thy heart?
And, when thy heart began to beat,
What dread hand? and what dread feet?   12

What the hammer? what the chain?
In what furnace was thy brain?
What the anvil? what dread grasp
Dare its deadly terrors clasp?   16

When the stars threw down their spears,
And water'd heaven with their tears,
Did he smile his work to see?
Did he who made the lamb make thee?   20

Tyger! Tyger! burning bright
In the forests of the night,
What immortal hand or eye,
Dare frame thy fearful symmetry?   24

London

[1794]

I wander thro' each charter'd street,
Near where the charter'd Thames does flow,
And mark in every face I meet
Marks of weakness, marks of woe.   4

In every cry of every Man,
In every Infant's cry of fear,
In every voice, in every ban,
The mind-forg'd manacles I hear.   8

How the Chimney-sweeper's cry
Every black'ning Church appalls;
And the hapless Soldier's sigh
Runs in blood down Palace walls.   12

But most thro' midnight streets I hear
How the youthful Harlot's curse
Blasts the new-born Infant's tear,
And blights with plagues the Marriage hearse.   16

ROBERT BLY

Robert Bly, born in 1926 in Madison, Minnesota, is one of the few poets who have been able to support themselves by writing and by giving readings, rather than by teaching. In 1990 his Iron John, *a set of reflections on his own life and on male identity, became a bestseller. Bly is the author of many books of poetry and prose, and is also a widely published translator and an editor of a number of collections and anthologies, including* The Soul is Here for Its Own Joy: Sacred Poems from Many Cultures *(1995).*

Driving to Town Late to Mail a Letter   [1962]

It is a cold and snowy night. The main street is deserted.
The only things moving are swirls of snow.
As I lift the mailbox door, I feel its cold iron.
There is a privacy I love in this snowy night.
Driving around, I will waste more time.   5

GWENDOLYN BROOKS

For a biographical note, see page 594.

The subject of Brooks's poem, the civil rights leader Martin Luther King Jr. (1929–1968), was assassinated at the height of his career.

Martin Luther King Jr.   [1970]

A man went forth with gifts.

He was a prose poem.
He was a tragic grace.
He was a warm music.

He tried to heal the vivid volcanoes.   5
His ashes are
   reading the world.
His Dream still wishes to anoint
   the barricades of faith and of control.

His word still burns the center of the sun,   10
   above the thousands and the
   hundred thousands.

The word was Justice. It was spoken.

So it shall be spoken.
So it shall be done.   15

The Bean Eaters   [1960]

They eat beans mostly, this old yellow pair.
Dinner is a casual affair.

Funeral march for Martin Luther King Jr., held in Atlanta, Georgia, 1968.

Plain chipware on a plain and creaking wood,
Tin flatware.   4

Two who are Mostly Good.
Two who have lived their day,
But keep on putting on their clothes
And putting things away.   8

And remembering . . .
Remembering, with twinklings and twinges,
As they lean over the beans in their rented back room that is full of
    beads and receipts and dolls and cloths, tobacco crumbs, vases and
    fringes.

ROBERT BROWNING

For a biographical note, see page 602.

Porphyria's Lover   [1834]

The rain set early in tonight,
    The sullen wind was soon awake,

It tore the elm-tops down for spite,
    And did its worst to vex the lake:
    I listened with heart fit to break.   5
When glided in Porphyria; straight
    She shut the cold out and the storm,
And kneeled and made the cheerless grate
    Blaze up, and all the cottage warm;
    Which done, she rose, and from her form   10
Withdrew the dripping cloak and shawl,
    And laid her soiled gloves by, untied
Her hat and let the damp hair fall,
    And, last, she sat down by my side
    And called me. When no voice replied,   15
She put my arm around her waist,
    And made her smooth white shoulder bare,
And all her yellow hair displaced,
    And stooping, made my cheek lie there,
    And spread, o'er all, her yellow hair   20
Murmuring how she loved me—she
    Too weak, for all her heart's endeavor,
To set its struggling passion free
    From pride, and vainer ties dissever,
    And give herself to me forever.   25
But passion sometimes would prevail,
    Nor could tonight's gay feast restrain
A sudden thought of one so pale
    For love of her, and all in vain:
    So, she was come through wind and rain.   30
Be sure I looked up at her eyes
    Happy and proud; at last I knew
Porphyria worshipped me; surprise
    Made my heart swell, and still it grew
    While I debated what to do.   35
That moment she was mine, mine, fair,
    Perfectly pure and good: I found
A thing to do, and all her hair
    In one long yellow string I wound
    Three times her little throat around,   40
And strangled her. No pain felt she;
    I am quite sure she felt no pain.
As a shut bud that holds a bee,
    I warily oped her lids: again
    Laughed the blue eyes without a stain.   45
And I untightened next the tress
    About her neck; her cheek once more
Blushed bright beneath my burning kiss:
    I propped her head up as before,
    Only, this time my shoulder bore   50
Her head, which droops upon it still:
    The smiling rosy little head,

So glad it has its utmost will,
    That all it scorned at once is fled,
    And I, its love, am gained instead!   55
Porphyria's love: she guessed not how
    Her darling one wish would be heard.
And thus we sit together now,
    And all night long we have not stirred,
    And yet God has not said a word!   60

GEORGE GORDON, LORD BYRON

George Gordon Byron (1788-1824), the sixth Baron Byron, was an English romantic poet of approximately the same generation as John Keats. Byron wrote not only lyrical poems—we reprint one of his lyrics here—but also satiric verse.

"She Walks in Beauty" is from a volume entitled Hebrew Melodies *(1815), written to be set to adaptations of traditional Hebrew tunes. Byron wrote the poem the day after seeing at a party a beautiful young woman, the wife of his first cousin, who wore a black mourning gown with spangles.*

She Walks in Beauty   [1814]

1

She walks in beauty, like the night
    Of cloudless climes and starry skies;
And all that's best of dark and bright
    Meet in her aspect and her eyes:
Thus mellow'd to that tender light   5
    Which heaven to gaudy day denies.

2

One shade the more, one ray the less,
    Had half impair'd the nameless grace
Which waves in every raven tress,
    Or softly lightens o'er her face;   10
Where thoughts serenely sweet express
    How pure, how dear their dwelling place.

3

And on that cheek, and o'er that brow,
    So soft, so calm, yet eloquent,
The smiles that win, the tints that glow,   15
    But tell of days in goodness spent,
A mind at peace with all below,
    A heart whose love is innocent!

LUCILLE CLIFTON

Lucille Clifton (1936–2010) was born in Depew, New York, and was educated at Howard University and Fredonia State Teachers College. In addition to being a prolific poet, she is the author of many children's books. Clifton has received numerous awards, including a grant from the National Endowment for the Arts. She served as poet laureate of Maryland from 1979 to 1982. Clifton's volume, Blessing the Boats: New and Collected Poems, 1988–2000, *won the National Book Award for Poetry in 2000.*

in the inner city

[1969]

in the inner city
or
like we call it
home
we think a lot about uptown   5
and the silent nights
and the houses straight as
dead men
and the pastel lights
and we hang on to our no place   10
happy to be alive
and in the inner city
or
like we call it
home   15

JUDITH ORTIZ COFER

Born in Puerto Rico in 1952 of a Puerto Rican mother and an American father who served in the Navy, Judith Ortiz Cofer was educated both in Puerto Rico and on the mainland. After earning a bachelor's and a master's degree in English, she did further graduate work at Oxford and then taught English in Florida. Her publications include books of poetry, a novel, and collections of stories and essays. Cofer is a professor of English and creative writing at the University of Georgia.

My Father in the Navy

[1987]

A Childhood Memory

Stiff and immaculate
in the white cloth of his uniform
and a round cap on his head like a halo,
he was an apparition on leave from a shadow-world
and only flesh and blood when he rose from below   5
the waterline where he kept watch over the engines
and dials making sure the ship parted the waters

on a straight course.
Mother, brother and I kept vigil
on the nights and dawns of his arrivals,   10
watching the corner beyond the neon sign of a quasar
for the flash of white our father like an angel
heralding a new day.
His homecomings were the verses
we composed over the years making up   15
the siren's song that kept him coming back
from the bellies of iron whales
and into our nights
like the evening prayer.

JOHN DONNE

For a biographical note, see page 654.

A Valediction: Forbidding Mourning   [1633]

As virtuous men pass mildly away;
   And whisper to their souls, to go,
Whilst some of their sad friends do say,
   "The breath goes now," and some say, "No":   4

So let us melt, and make no noise.
   No tear-floods, nor sigh-tempests move.
Twere profanation of our joys
   To tell the laity our love.   8

Moving of the earth° brings harms and fears,
   Men reckon what it did and meant;
But trepidation of the spheres,
   Though greater far, is innocent.°   12

Dull sublunary° lovers' love
   (Whose soul is sense) cannot admit
Absence, because it doth remove
   Those things which elemented it.   16

But we, by a love so much refined
   That our selves know not what it is,
Inter-assuréd of the mind,
   Care less, eyes, lips, and hands to miss.   20

Our two souls therefore, which are one,
   Though I must go, endure not yet
A breach, but an expansion,
   Like gold to airy thinness beat.   24

---

9 Moving of the earth an earthquake.   **11–12 But . . . innocent** But the movement
of the heavenly spheres (in Ptolemaic astronomy), though far greater, is harmless.
13 sublunary under the moon (i.e., earthly).

If they be two, they are two so
   As stiff twin compasses° are two:
Thy soul, the fixed foot, makes no show
   To move, but doth, if the other do.   28

And though it in the center sit,
   Yet when the other far doth roam,
It leans, and hearkens after it,
   And grows erect, as that comes home.   32

Such wilt thou be to me, who must
   Like the other foot, obliquely run:
Thy firmness makes my circle just,
   And makes me end where I begun.   36

---

26 twin compasses a carpenter's compass, used for making circles.

The Flea   [1633]

Mark but this flea, and mark in this,
How little that which thou deny'st me is;
Me it sucked first, and now sucks thee,
And in this flea our two bloods mingled be;
Thou know'st that this cannot be said   5
A sin, no shame, no loss of maidenhead;
   Yet this enjoys before it woo,
   And pampered swells with one blood made of two,
   And this, alas, is more than we would do.

Oh stay, three lives in one flea spare,   10
Where we almost, nay, more than married are.
This flea is you and I, and this
Our marriage bed and marriage temple is;
Though parents grudge, and you, we are met
And cloistered in these living walls of jet.   15
   Though use° make you apt to kill me,
   Let not to that, self-murder added be,
   And sacrilege, three sins in killing three.

Cruel and sudden, has thou since
Purpled thy nail in blood of innocence?   20
Wherein could this flea guilty be,
Except in that drop which it sucked from thee?
Yet thou triumph'st, and say'st that thou
Find'st not thy self nor me the weaker now.
   'Tis true; Then learn how false fears be: 25
   Just so much honor, when thou yield'st to me,
   Will waste, as this flea's death took life from thee.

---

16 use custom.

Death, Be Not Proud   [1633]

Death, be not proud, though some have callèd thee
Mighty and dreadful, for thou art not so;
For those whom thou think'st thou dost overthrow
Die not, poor Death, not yet canst thou kill me.
From rest and sleep, which but thy pictures be,   5
Much pleasure; then from thee much more must flow,
And soonest our best men with thee do go,
Rest of their bones, and soul's delivery.
Thou art slave to fate, chance, kings, and desperate men,
And dost with poison, war, and sickness dwell,   10
And poppy°, or charms can make us sleep as well
And better than thy stroke; why swell'st thou then?
One short sleep past, we wake eternally
And death shall be no more: Death, thou shalt die.

---

11 poppy opium.

RITA DOVE

Rita Dove was born in 1952 in Akron, Ohio. After graduating summa cum laude and Phi Beta Kappa from Miami University (Ohio), Dove earned an MFA at the Iowa Writers' Workshop. She has received numerous awards, including fellowships from the Guggenheim Foundation and the National Endowment for the Arts, and a Pulitzer Prize for Poetry. In 1993–1995 she served as Poet Laureate of the United States and as Consultant to the Library of Congress, in 1996 she was awarded the National Humanities Medal, and in 2001 she was awarded the Duke Ellington Lifetime Achievement Award. Dove is the author of a number of books of poetry, a book of short stories, a novel, a book of her laureate lectures, and a book of assays. She is Commonwealth Professor of English at the University of Virginia in Charlottesville.

Daystar   [1986]

She wanted a little room for thinking:
but she saw diapers steaming on the line,
a doll slumped behind the door.

So she lugged a chair behind the garage
to sit out the children's naps.   5

Sometimes there were things to watch—
the pinched armor of a vanished cricket,
a floating maple leaf. Other days
she stared until she was assured
when she closed her eyes   10
she'd see only her own vivid blood.

She had an hour, at best, before Liza appeared
pouting from the top of the stairs.

And just *what* was mother doing
out back with the field mice? Why,   15

building a palace. Later
that night when Thomas rolled over and
lurched into her, she would open her eyes
and think of the place that was hers
for an hour—where   20
she was nothing,
pure nothing, in the middle of the day.

BOB DYLAN

*Bob Dylan, born Robert Zimmerman in 1941 in Duluth, Minnesota, played
the guitar as a child and learned the harmonica when he was fifteen.
Among his chief models were Huddie Lead Belly (better known as Lead
Belly), an African American folk singer and guitarist, and Woody Guthrie, a
white folk singer, guitarist, and harmonica player. Dylan's music ranges
from folk to folk-rock to country blues, but perhaps his most influential
songs were those of social protest, such as "Blowin' in the Wind" and "The
Times They Are A-Changin'."*

The Times They Are A-Changin'   [1963]

Come gather 'round people
Wherever you roam
And admit that the waters
Around you have grown
And accept it that soon   5
You'll be drenched to the bone.
If your time to you
Is worth savin'
Then you better start swimmin'
Or you'll sink like a stone   10
For the times they are a-changin'.

Come writers and critics
Who prophesize with your pen
And keep your eyes wide
The chance won't come again   15
And don't speak too soon
For the wheel's still in spin
And there's no tellin' who
That it's namin'.
For the loser now   20
Will be later to win
For the times they are a-changin'.

Come senators, congressmen
Please heed the call
Don't stand in the doorway   25

Don't block up the hall
For he that gets hurt
Will be he who has stalled
There's a battle outside
And it is ragin'.   30
It'll soon shake your windows
And rattle your walls
For the times they are a-changin'.

Come mothers and fathers
Throughout the land   35
And don't criticize
What you can't understand
Your sons and your daughters
Are beyond your command
Your old road is   40
Rapidly agin'.
Please get out of the new one
If you can't lend your hand
For the times they are a-changin'.

The line it is drawn   45
The curse it is cast
The slow one now
Will later be fast
As the present now
Will later be past   50
The order is
Rapidly fadin'.
And the first one now
Will later be last
For the times they are a-changin'.   55

T. S. ELIOT

Thomas Stearns Eliot (1888–1965) was born into a New England family that had moved to St. Louis. He attended a preparatory school in Massachusetts, then graduated from Harvard and did further study in literature and philosophy in France, Germany, and England. In 1914 he began working for Lloyds Bank in London, and three years later he published his first book of poems (it included "The Love Song of J. Alfred Prufrock"). In 1925 he joined a publishing firm, and in 1927 he became a British citizen and a member of the Church of England. Much of his later poetry is highly religious. In 1948 Eliot received the Nobel Prize in Literature.

The Love Song of J. Alfred Prufrock   [1917]

S'io credesse che mia risposta fosse
A persona che mai tornasse al mondo,
Questa fiamma staria senza più scosse.
Ma perciocchè giammai di questo fondo

Non torno vivo alcun, s' i' odo il vero,
Senza tema d'infamia ti rispondo.*

Let us go then, you and I,
When the evening is spread out against the sky
Like a patient etherised upon a table;
Let us go, through certain half-deserted streets,
The muttering retreats   5
Of restless nights in one-night cheap hotels
And sawdust restaurants with oyster-shells;
Streets that follow like a tedious argument
Of insidious intent
To lead you to an overwhelming question . . .   10
Oh, do not ask, "What is it?"
Let us go and make our visit.

In the room the women come and go
Talking of Michelangelo.

The yellow fog that rubs its back upon the window-panes,   15
The yellow smoke that rubs its muzzle on the window-panes
Licked its tongue into the corners of the evening,
Lingered upon the pools that stand in drains,
Let fall upon its back the soot that falls from chimneys,
Slipped by the terrace, made a sudden leap,   20
And seeing that it was a soft October night,
Curled once about the house, and fell asleep.

And indeed there will be time
For the yellow smoke that slides along the street,
Rubbing its back upon the window-panes;   25
There will be time, there will be time
To prepare a face to meet the faces that you meet;
There will be time to murder and create,
And time for all the works and days of hands
That lift and drop a question on your plate;   30
Time for you and time for me,
And time yet for a hundred indecisions,
And for a hundred visions and revisions,
Before the taking of a toast and tea.

---

*In Dante's *Inferno* XXVII: 61–66, a damned soul who had sought absolution before committing a crime addresses Dante, thinking that his words will never reach the earth: "If I
believed that my answer were to a person who could ever return to the world, this flame
would no longer quiver. But because no one ever returned from this depth, if what I hear
is true, without fear of infamy, I answer you."
    Explanations of allusions in the poem may be helpful. "Works and days" (line 29) is the
title of a poem on farm life by Hesiod (eighth century BCE); "dying fall" (line 52) echoes
Twelfth Night 1.1.4; lines 81–83 allude to John the Baptist (see Matthew 14.1–11); line 92
echoes lines 41–42 of Marvell's "To His Coy Mistress" (see page 652); for "Lazarus" (line
94) see Luke 16 and John 11; lines 112–117 allude to Polonius and perhaps to other figures in *Hamlet;* "full of high sentence" (line 117) comes from Chaucer's description of
the Clerk of Oxford in the *Canterbury Tales.*

In the room the women come and go   35
Talking of Michelangelo.

And indeed there will be time
To wonder, "Do I dare?" and, "Do I dare?"—
Time to turn back and descend the stair,
With a bald spot in the middle of my hair—   40
[They will say: "How his hair is growing thin!"]
My morning coat, my collar mounting firmly to the chin,
My necktie rich and modest, but asserted by a simple pin—
[They will say: "But how his arms and legs are thin!"]
Do I dare   45
Disturb the universe?
In a minute there is time
For decisions and revisions which a minute will reverse.

For I have known them all already, known them all:—
Have known the evenings, mornings, afternoons,   50
I have measured out my life with coffee spoons;
I know the voices dying with a dying fall
Beneath the music from a farther room.
      So how should I presume?

And I have known the eyes already, known them all—   55
The eyes that fix you in a formulated phrase,
And when I am formulated, sprawling on a pin,
When I am pinned and wriggling on the wall,
Then how should I begin
To spit out all the butt-ends of my days and ways?   60
      And how should I presume?

And I have known the arms already, known them all—
Arms that are braceleted and white and bare
[But in the lamplight, downed with light brown hair!]
Is it perfume from a dress   65
That makes me so digress?
Arms that lie along a table, or wrap about a shawl.
      And should I then presume?
      And how should I begin?

                 . . .

Shall I say, I have gone at dusk through narrow streets   70
And watched the smoke that rises from the pipes
Of lonely men in shirt-sleeves, leaning out of windows? . . .

I should have been a pair of ragged claws
Scuttling across the floors of silent seas.

                 . . .

And the afternoon, the evening, sleeps so peacefully!   75
Smoothed by long fingers,
Asleep . . . tired . . . or it malingers,
Stretched on the floor, here beside you and me.
Should I, after tea and cakes and ices,

Have the strength to force the moment to its crisis?   80
But though I have wept and fasted, wept and prayed,
Though I have seen my head [grown slightly bald]
    brought in upon a platter,
I am no prophet—and here's no great matter;
I have seen the moment of my greatness flicker,
And I have seen the eternal Footman hold my coat, and snicker,   85
And in short, I was afraid.

And would it have been worth it, after all,
After the cups, the marmalade, the tea,
Among the porcelain, among some talk of you and me,
Would it have been worth while,   90
To have bitten off the matter with a smile,
To have squeezed the universe into a ball
To roll it toward some overwhelming question,
To say: "I am Lazarus, come from the dead,
Come back to tell you all, I shall tell you all"—   95
If one, settling a pillow by her head,
    Should say: "That is not what I meant at all.
    That is not it, at all."

And would it have been worth it, after all,
Would it have been worth while,   100
After the sunsets and the dooryards and the sprinkled streets,
After the novels, after the teacups, after the skirts that trail
    along the floor—
And this, and so much more?—
It is impossible to say just what I mean!
But as if a magic lantern threw the nerves in patterns on a
    screen: 105
Would it have been worth while
If one, settling a pillow or throwing off a shawl,
And turning toward the window, should say:
    "That is not it at all,
    That is not what I meant, at all."   110

       . . .

No! I am not Prince Hamlet, nor was meant to be;
Am an attendant lord, one that will do
To swell a progress, start a scene or two,
Advise the prince; no doubt, an easy tool,
Deferential, glad to be of use,   115
Politic, cautious, and meticulous;
Full of high sentence, but a bit obtuse;
At times, indeed, almost ridiculous—
Almost, at times, the Fool.

I grow old . . . I grow old . . .   120
I shall wear the bottoms of my trousers rolled.

Shall I part my hair behind? Do I dare to eat a peach?
I shall wear white flannel trousers, and walk upon the beach.

I have heard the mermaids singing, each to each.

I do not think that they will sing to me.   125

I have seen them riding seaward on the waves
Combing the white hair of the waves blown back
When the wind blows the water white and black.

We have lingered in the chambers of the sea
By sea-girls wreathed with seaweed red and brown   130
Till human voices wake us, and we drown.

MARTÍN ESPADA

For a biographical note, see page 655.

Bully   [1990]

Boston, Massachusetts, 1987

In the school auditorium,
the Theodore Roosevelt statue
is nostalgic
for the Spanish-American War,
each fist lonely for a saber   5
or the reins of anguish-eyed horses,
or a podium to clatter with speeches
glorying in the malaria of conquest.

But now the Roosevelt school
is pronounced Hernández.   10
Puerto Rico has invaded Roosevelt
with its army of Spanish-singing children
in the hallways,
brown children devouring

the stockpiles of the cafeteria,   15
children painting Taíno ancestors
that leap naked across murals.

Roosevelt is surrounded
by all the faces
he ever shoved in eugenic spite   20
and cursed as mongrels, skin of one race,
hair and cheekbones of another.

Once Marines tramped
from the newsreel of his imagination;
now children plot to spray graffiti   25
in parrot-brilliant colors
across the Victorian mustache
and monocle.

ALLEN GINSBERG

Allen Ginsberg (1926–1997) was born in Newark, New Jersey, and graduated from Columbia University in 1948. After eight months in Columbia Psychiatric Institute—Ginsberg had pleaded insanity to avoid prosecution when the police discovered that a friend stored stolen goods in Ginsberg's apartment—he worked at odd jobs and finally left the nine-to-five world for a freer life in San Francisco. In the 1950s he established a reputation as an uninhibited declamatory poet whose chief theme was a celebration of those who were alienated from a repressive America. Among Ginsberg's many books is the posthumous Collected Poems, 1947–1997 *(2006).*

A Supermarket in California

[1956]

What thoughts I have of you tonight, Walt Whitman, for I walked down the sidestreets under the trees with a headache self-conscious looking at the full moon.

In my hungry fatigue, and shopping for images, I went into the neon fruit supermarket, dreaming of your enumerations!

What peaches and what penumbras! Whole families shopping at night! Aisles full of husbands! Wives in the avocados, babies in the tomatoes!—and you, García Lorca,° what were you doing down by the watermelons?

I saw you, Walt Whitman, childless, lonely old grubber, poking among the meats in the refrigerator and eyeing the grocery boys.

I heard you asking questions of each: Who killed the pork chops?   5
What price bananas? Are you my Angel?

I wandered in and out of the brilliant stacks of cans following you, and followed in my imagination by the store detective.

We strode down the open corridors together in our solitary fancy tasting artichokes, possessing every frozen delicacy, and never passing the cashier.

Where are we going, Walt Whitman? The doors close in an hour. Which way does your beard point tonight?

(I touch your book and dream of our odyssey in the supermarket and feel absurd.)

Will we walk all night through solitary streets? The trees add shade   10
to shade, lights out in the houses, we'll both be lonely.

Will we stroll dreaming of the lost America of love past blue automobiles in driveways, home to our silent cottage?

Ah, dear father, graybeard, lonely old courage-teacher, what America did you have when Charon quit poling his ferry and you got out on a smoking bank and stood watching the boat disappear on the black waters of Lethe?°

---

3 García Lorca Federico García Lorca (1899–1936), Spanish poet (and, like Whitman and Ginsberg, a homosexual).   **12 Lethe** In classical mythology, Charon ferried the souls of the dead across the river Styx, to Hades, where, after drinking from the river Lethe, they forgot the life they had lived.

NIKKI GIOVANNI

Nikki Giovanni was born in Knoxville, Tennessee, in 1943 and educated at Fisk University, the University of Pennsylvania School of Social Work, and Columbia University. She has taught at Queens College, Rutgers University, and Ohio State University, and she is University Distinguished Professor at Virginia Tech. Giovanni has published many books of poems, an autobiography (Gemini: An Extended Autobiographical Statement on My First Twenty-Five Years of Being a Black Poet), *a book of essays, and a book consisting of a conversation with James Baldwin.*

Master Charge Blues   [1970]

its wednesday night baby
and i'm all alone
wednesday night baby
and i'm all alone
sitting with myself   5
waiting for the telephone

wanted you baby
but you said you had to go
wanted you yeah
but you said you had to go   10
called your best friend
but he can't come 'cross no more

did you ever go to bed
at the end of a busy day
look over and see the smooth   15
where your hump usta lay
feminine odor and no reason why
i said feminine odor and no reason why
asked the lord to help me
he shook his head "not i"   20
but i'm a modern woman baby
ain't gonna let this get me down
i'm a modern woman
ain't gonna let this get me down
gonna take my master charge   25
and get everything in town

LOUISE GLÜCK

For a biographical note, see page 693.

The School Children   [1975]

The children go forward with their little satchels.
And all morning the mothers have labored

to gather the late apples, red and gold,
like words of another language.

And on the other shore   5
are those who wait behind great desks
to receive these offerings.

How orderly they are—the nails
on which the children hang
their overcoats of blue or yellow wool.   10

And the teachers shall instruct them in silence
and the mothers shall scour the orchards for a way out,
drawing to themselves the gray limbs of the fruit trees
bearing so little ammunition.

H. D.

*H. D. was the pen name of Hilda Doolittle (1886–1961). Born in Bethlehem,
Pennsylvania, of a socially prominent family, Doolittle met Ezra Pound when
she was fifteen and he was sixteen. Their relationship was complicated—
Doolittle was sexually attracted to women as well as to men—and met with
opposition from her family. She further distressed her family when she
dropped out of Bryn Mawr College. In 1911 H. D. and a female friend who
had once loved Doolittle and now loved Pound followed Pound to England,
where Doolittle was active in various literary movements.*

*We print a poem about a Greek mythological figure, Helen, wife of
Menelaus, king of the Greek city-state of Sparta. Paris, a Trojan prince, abducted her and thereby initiated the Trojan War. Poets—ever since the days of
ancient Greece—have been interested in this story, but H. D. had an especially
strong interest in classical Greece and in psychoanalytic and feminist interpretations of mythology.*

Helen   [1924]

All Greece hates
the still eyes in the white face,
the lustre as of olives
where she stands,
and the white hands.   5

All Greece reviles
the wan face when she smiles,
hating it deeper still
when it grows wan and white,
remembering past enchantments   10
and past ills.

Greece sees, unmoved,
God's daughter, born of love,
the beauty of cool feet
and slenderest knees,   15

could love indeed the maid,
only if she were laid,
white ash amid funereal cypresses.

THOMAS HARDY

For a biographical note, see page 607.

Ah, Are You Digging on My Grave?   [1916]

"Ah, are you digging on my grave,
   My loved one?—planting rue?"
—"No: yesterday he went to wed
One of the brightest wealth has bred.
'It cannot hurt her now,' he said,   5
   'That I should not be true.'"

"Then who is digging on my grave?
   My nearest dearest kin?"
—"Ah, no: they sit and think, 'What use!
What good will planting flowers produce?   10
No tendance of her mound can loose
   Her spirit from Death's gin.'"°

"But some one digs upon my grave?
   My enemy?—prodding sly?"
—"Nay: when she heard you had passed the Gate   15
That shuts on all flesh soon or late,
She thought you no more worth her hate,
   And cares not where you lie."

"Then, who is digging on my grave?
   Say—since I have not guessed!"   20
—"O it is I, my mistress dear,
Your little dog, who still lives near,
And much I hope my movements here
   Have not disturbed your rest?"

"Ah, yes! *You* dig upon my grave . . .   25
   Why flashed it not on me
That one true heart was left behind!
What feeling do we ever find
To equal among human kind
   A dog's fidelity!"   30

"Mistress, I dug upon your grave
   To bury a bone, in case
I should be hungry near this spot
When passing on my daily trot.
I am sorry, but I quite forgot   35
   It was your resting-place."

---

12 gin snare.

JOY HARJO

Joy Harjo, a Creek Indian, was born in Tulsa, Oklahoma, in 1951. She was educated at the Institute of American Indian Arts in Sante Fe, New Mexico, and at the University of Iowa Writers' Workshop. She lives in Albuquerque, New Mexico. Harjo's books include How We Became Human: New and Selected Poems *(2002).*

Vision   [1983]

The rainbow touched down
"somewhere in the Rio Grande,"
we said. And saw the light of it
from your mother's house in Isleta.°
How it curved down between earth   5
and the deepest sky to give us horses
of color
            horses that were within us all of this time
but we didn't see them because
we wait for the easiest vision   10
                        to save us.
In Isleta the rainbow was a crack
in the universe. We saw the barest
of all life that is possible.
Bright horses rolled over   15
and over the dusking sky.
I heard the thunder of their beating
hearts. Their lungs hit air
and sang. All the colors of horses
formed the rainbow,   20
                        and formed us
watching them.

---

4 **Isleta** a pueblo in New Mexico.

ROBERT HAYDEN

For a biographical note, see page 551.

Those Winter Sundays   [1962]

Sundays too my father got up early
and put his clothes on in the blueblack cold,
then with cracked hands that ached
from labor in the weekday weather made
banked fires blaze. No one ever thanked him.   5

I'd wake and hear the cold splintering, breaking.
When the rooms were warm, he'd call,

and slowly I would rise and dress,
fearing the chronic angers of that house,

Speaking indifferently to him,   10
who had driven out the cold
and polished my good shoes as well.
What did I know, what did I know
of love's austere and lonely offices?

ANTHONY HECHT

*Anthony Hecht (1923-2004), born in New York City, was educated at Bard
College and Columbia University. He taught at several institutions (notably at
The University of Rochester), and he served as poetry consultant to the Library
of Congress. Hecht's many books of poetry and prose include* Collected Earlier
Poems *(1990),* Collected Later Poems *(2003), and* Melodies Unheard: Essays on
the Mysteries of Poetry *(2003).*

*Like "The Dover Bitch," which assumes a reader's familiarity with
Matthew Arnold's "Dover Beach" (page 778), much of Hecht's work glances at
earlier literature. The poem is dedicated to a critic and editor.*

The Dover Bitch   [1967]

A Criticism of Life

For Andrews Wanning*

So there stood Matthew Arnold and this girl
With the cliffs of England crumbling away behind them,
And he said to her, "Try to be true to me,
And I'll do the same for you, for things are bad
All over, etc., etc."   5
Well now, I knew this girl. It's true she had read
Sophocles in a fairly good translation
And caught that bitter allusion to the sea,
But all the time he was talking she had in mind
The notion of what his whiskers would feel like   10
On the back of her neck. She told me later on
That after a while she got to looking out
At the lights across the channel, and really felt sad,
Thinking of all the wine and enormous beds
And blandishments in French and the perfumes.   15
And then she got really angry. To have been brought
All the way down from London, and then be addressed
As sort of a mournful cosmic last resort
Is really tough on a girl, and she was pretty.
Anyway, she watched him pace the room   20
And finger his watch-chain and seem to sweat a bit,
And then she said one or two unprintable things.
But you mustn't judge her by that. What I mean to say is,
She's really all right. I still see her once in a while

***Andrews Wanning** (1913-1997), literary critic and professor of English at Bard College.

And she always treats me right. We have a drink   25
And I give her a good time, and perhaps it's a year
Before I see her again, but there she is,
Running to fat, but dependable as they come.
And sometimes I bring her a bottle of *Nuit d'Amour.*°

°**Nuit d'Amour** French for "night of love" and a brand of perfume.

ROBERT HERRICK

For a biographical note, see page 605.

Delight in Disorder   [1648]

A sweet disorder in the dress
Kindles in clothes a wantonness:
A lawn° about the shoulders thrown
Into a fine distraction:
An erring lace, which here and there   5
Enthralls the crimson stomacher:°
A cuff neglectful, and thereby
Ribbons to flow confusedly:
A winning wave, deserving note,
In the tempestuous petticoat: 10
A careless shoestring, in whose tie
I see a wild civility:
Do more bewitch me than when art
Is too precise in every part.

---

3 lawn scarf.   **6 stomacher** ornamental cloth.

GERARD MANLEY HOPKINS

*Gerard Manley Hopkins (1844–1889) was born near London and was edu-
cated at Oxford, where he studied the classics. A convert from Anglicanism to
Roman Catholicism, he was ordained a Jesuit priest in 1877. After serving as
a parish priest and teacher, he was appointed Professor of Greek at the
Catholic University in Dublin.*

*Hopkins published only a few poems during his lifetime, partly because
he believed that the pursuit of literary fame was incompatible with his voca-
tion as a priest, and partly because he was aware that his highly individual
style might puzzle readers.*

God's Grandeur   [1877]

The world is charged with the grandeur of God.
  It will flame out, like shining from shook foil;
  It gathers to a greatness, like the ooze of oil
Crushed. Why do men then now not reck his rod?

Generations have trod, have trod, have trod;   5
    And all is seared with trade; bleared, smeared with toil;
    And wears man's smudge and shares man's smell: the soil
Is bare now, nor can foot feel, being shod.

And for all this, nature is never spent;
    There lives the dearest freshness deep down things;   10
And though the last lights off the black West went
    Oh, morning, at the brown brink eastward, springs—
Because the Holy Ghost over the bent
    World broods with warm breast and with ah! bright wings.

Pied* Beauty   [1877]

Glory be to God for dappled things—
    For skies of couple-color as a brinded° cow;
        For rose-moles all in stipple upon trout that swim;
Fresh-firecoal chestnut-falls; finches' wings;
        Landscape plotted and pieced—fold, fallow, and plough;°   5
        And áll trádes, their gear and tackle and trim.°

All things counter, original, spare, strange;
    Whatever is fickle, freckled (who knows how?)
        With swift, slow; sweet, sour; adazzle, dim;
He fathers-forth whose beauty is past change: 10
                            Praise him.

---

*__Pied__ Variegated, particolored.   __2 brinded__ streaked.   __5 fold, fallow, and plough__ fields
used for pasture (sheep-fold), left fallow, or ploughed.   __6 trim__ equipment.

A. E. HOUSMAN

For a biographical note, see page 663.

To an Athlete Dying Young   [1896]

The time you won your town the race
We chaired you through the market-place;
Man and boy stood cheering by,
And home we brought you shoulder-high.   4

To-day, the road all runners come,
Shoulder-high we bring you home,
And set you at your threshold down,
Townsman of a stiller town.   8

Smart lad, to slip betimes away
From fields where glory does not stay
And early though the laurel grows
It withers quicker than the rose.   12

Eyes the shady night has shut
Cannot see the record cut,
And silence sounds no worse than cheers
After earth has stopped the ears: 16

Now you will not swell the rout
Of lads that wore their honors out,
Runners whom renown outran
And the name died before the man.   20

So set, before its echoes fade,
The fleet foot on the sill of shade,
And hold to the low lintel up
The still-defended challenge-cup.   24

And round that early-laurelled head
Will flock to gaze the strengthless dead,
And find unwithered on its curls
The garland briefer than a girl's.   30

When I Was One-and-Twenty   [1896]

When I was one-and-twenty
    I heard a wise man say,
"Give crowns and pounds and guineas
    But not your heart away;
Give pearls away and rubies   5
    But keep your fancy free."
But I was one-and-twenty,
    No use to talk to me.

When I was one-and-twenty
    I heard him say again,   10
"The heart out of the bosom
    Was never given in vain;
'Tis paid with sighs a plenty
    And sold for endless rue."
And I am two-and-twenty,   15
    And oh, 'tis true, 'tis true.

Loveliest of trees, the cherry now   [1896]

Loveliest of trees, the cherry now
Is hung with bloom along the bough,
And stands about the woodland ride
Wearing white for Eastertide.   4

Now, of my threescore years and ten,
Twenty will not come again,
And take from seventy springs a score,
It only leaves me fifty more.   8

And since to look at things in bloom
Fifty springs are little room,
About the woodlands I will go
To see the cherry hung with snow.   12

JAMES WELDON JOHNSON

*Born in Jacksonville, Florida, James Weldon Johnson (1871–1938) received a
bachelor's and a master's degree from Atlanta University. Johnson taught
school, served as a high school principal, and founded the* Daily American *(1895,
the first black daily in America). Later he became active in the NAACP, served
as consul to Venezuela and to Nicaragua, and taught creative writing at Fisk
University. Johnson published widely as a poet, novelist, and journalist, and he
edited books as well, including* The Book of American Negro Poetry *(1922).*
Johnson wrote dialect poems as well as poems in standard English.

To America   [1917]

How would you have us, as we are?
Or sinking 'neath the load we bear?
Our eyes fixed forward on a star?
Or gazing empty at despair?   4

Rising or falling? Men or things?
With dragging pace or footsteps fleet?
Strong, willing sinews in your wings?
Or tightening chains about your feet?   8

JOHN KEATS

For a biographical note, see page 559.

To Autumn   [1819]

I

Season of mists and mellow fruitfulness,
    Close bosom-friend of the maturing sun;
Conspiring with him how to load and bless
    With fruit the vines that round the thatch-eaves run;
To bend with apples the mossed cottage-trees,   5
    And fill all fruit with ripeness to the core;
        To swell the gourd, and plump the hazel shells
With a sweet kernel; to set budding more,
    And still more, later flowers for the bees,
    Until they think warm days will never cease,   10
        For summer has o'er-brimmed their clammy cells.

II

Who hath not seen thee oft amid thy store?
   Sometimes whoever seeks abroad may find
Thee sitting careless on a granary floor,
   Thy hair soft-lifted by the winnowing wind;   15
Or on a half-reaped furrow sound asleep,
   Drowsed with the fume of poppies, while thy hook
     Spares the next swath and all its twinéd flowers:
And sometime like a gleaner thou dost keep
   Steady thy laden head across a brook;   20
   Or by a cider-press, with patient look,
     Thou watchest the last oozings hours by hours.

III

Where are the songs of Spring? Ay, where are they?
   Think not of them, thou hast thy music too,—
While barréd clouds bloom the soft-dying day,   25
   And touch the stubble-plains with rosy hue;
Then in a wailful choir the small gnats mourn
   Among the river sallows, borne aloft
      Or sinking as the light wind lives or dies;
And full-grown lambs loud bleat from hilly bourn;   30
   Hedge-crickets sing; and now with treble soft
   The red-breast whistles from a garden-croft;
     And gathering swallows twitter in the skies.

X. J. KENNEDY

For a biographical note, see page 679.

   The following poem builds on "The Tyger" (page 786) by William Blake, a favorite poet of Allen Ginsberg. A New Yorker who established his fame in San Francisco, Ginsberg was noted for his declamatory poetry and his celebration of outsiders, especially protestors against the wars in Korea and Vietnam. He often chanted Blake's poems at his own poetry readings. In the following poem X. J. Kennedy pays homage to Ginsberg by adopting the form of one of Ginsberg's favorite poems. Kennedy alludes, in his poem, to Ginsberg's left-wing activities ("Taunter of the ultra right"), his view that his hearers should drop out of a corrupt and repressive society, his interest in Buddhist mantras (syllables laden with mystic power), his antiwar activity ("Mantra-minded flower child"), his homosexuality ("Queer," "Queen"), and his use of finger cymbals in some of his readings. *Om* (line 10) is a syllable that begins several mantras. Ginsberg often had his audience utter the sound.

For Allen Ginsberg   [1998]

Ginsberg, Ginsberg, burning bright,
Taunter of the ultra right,

What blink of the Buddha's eye
Chose the day for you to die?   4

Queer pied piper, howling wild,
Mantra-minded flower child,
Queen of Maytime, misrule's lord
Bawling, *Drop out! All aboard!*   8

Foe of fascist, bane of bomb,
Finger-cymbaled, chanting *Om,*
Proper poets' thorn in side,
Turner of a whole time's tide,   12

Who can fill your sloppy shoes?
What a catch for Death. We lose
Glee and sweetness, freaky light,
Ginsberg, Ginsberg, burning bright.   16

YUSEF KOMUNYAKAA

Yusef Komunyakaa was born in 1947 in Bogalusa, Louisiana. His name at birth was James Willie Brown Jr. but he later reclaimed the name Komunyakaa that his great-grandparents from Trinidad had given up. After graduating from high school he entered the army and served in Vietnam, where he was awarded the Bronze Star. On his return to the United States he earned a bachelor's degree at the University of Colorado, and then earned an MA at Colorado State University and an MFA in creative writing at the University of California, Irvine. The author of many books of poetry, he currently teaches at New York University. "Facing It" is the last poem in a book of poems about Vietnam, Dien Cai Dau *(1988). The title of the book is a slang term for "crazy."*

Facing It   [1988]

My black face fades,
hiding inside the black granite.
I said I wouldn't,
dammit: No tears.
I'm stone. I'm flesh.   5
My clouded reflection eyes me
like a bird of prey, the profile of night
slanted against morning. I turn
this way—the stone lets me go.
I turn that way—I'm inside   10
the Vietnam Veterans Memorial
again, depending on the light
to make a difference.
I go down the 58,022 names,
half-expecting to find   15
my own in letters like smoke.
I touch the name Andrew Johnson;

Vietnam Veterans Memorial, Washington, D.C.

I see the booby trap's white flash.
Names shimmer on a woman's blouse
but when she walks away   20
the names stay on the wall.
Brushstrokes flash, a red bird's
wings cutting across my stare.
The sky. A plane in the sky.
A white vet's image floats   25
closer to me, then his pale eyes
look through mine. I'm a window.
He's lost his right arm
inside the stone. In the black mirror
a woman's trying to erase names: 30
No, she's brushing a boy's hair.

ARCHIBALD MacLEISH

*Archibald MacLeish (1892-1982), born in Glencoe, Illinois, was educated at
Harvard and at Yale Law School. His early poetry, including "Ars Poetica," often
is condensed and allusive, though his later poems and his plays are readily
accessible. Under Franklin Delano Roosevelt, MacLeish served as Librarian of
Congress (1939-1944) and as assistant secretary of state (1944-1945). He
then taught at Harvard and at Amherst until he retired in 1967.*

Ars Poetica   [1926]

A poem should be palpable and mute
As a globed fruit,

Dumb
As old medallions to the thumb,

Silent as the sleeve-worn stone   5
Of casement ledges where the moss has grown—

A poem should be wordless
As the flight of birds.

   . . .

A poem should be motionless in time
As the moon climbs,   10

Leaving, as the moon releases
Twig by twig the night-entangled trees,

Leaving, as the moon behind the winter leaves,
Memory by memory the mind—

A poem should be motionless in time   15
As the moon climbs.

   . . .

A poem should be equal to:
Not true.

For all the history of grief
An empty doorway and a maple leaf.   20

For love
The leaning grasses and two lights above the sea—

A poem should not mean
But be.

CLAUDE McKAY

*Claude McKay (1889–1948), born in Jamaica, came to the United States
when he was twenty-three. McKay is known chiefly for his militant left-wing
writings—novels and essays as well as poems—but he wrote a wide range of
lyric poetry, and despite his radicalism he favored (like his friend Countee
Cullen) traditional poetic forms such as the sonnet.*

America   [1921]

Although she feeds me bread of bitterness,
And sinks into my throat her tiger's tooth,

Stealing my breath of life, I will confess
I love this cultured hell that tests my youth!
Her vigor flows like tides into my blood,   5
Giving me strength erect against her hate.
Her bigness sweeps my being like a flood.
Yet as a rebel fronts a king in state,
I stand within her walls with not a shred
Of terror, malice, not a word of jeer.   10
Darkly I gaze into the days ahead,
And see her might and granite wonders there,
Beneath the touch of Time's unerring hand,
Like priceless treasures sinking in the sand.

PAT MORA

For a biographical note, see page 26.

Illegal Alien   [1984]

Socorro, you free me
to sit in my yellow kitchen
waiting for a poem
while you scrub and iron.

Today you stand before me   5
holding cleanser and sponge
and say you can't sleep at night.
"My husband's fury is a fire.
His fist can burn.
We don't fight with words   10
on that side of the Rio Grande."

Your eyes fill. I want
to comfort you, but my arms
feel heavy, unaccustomed
to healing grown-up bodies.   15

I offer foolish questions
when I should hug you hard,
when I should dry your eyes, my sister,
sister because we are both women,
both married, both warmed   20
by Mexican blood.

It is not cool words you need
but soothing hands.
My plastic band-aid doesn't fit
your hurt.   25
I am the alien here.

Legal Alien   [1984]

Bi-lingual. Bi-cultural,
able to slip from "How's life?"
to *"Me'stan volviendo loca,"*°
able to sit in a paneled office
drafting memos in smooth English,   5
able to order in fluent Spanish
at a Mexican restaurant,
American but hyphenated,
viewed by Anglos as perhaps exotic,
perhaps inferior, definitely different,   10
viewed by Mexicans as alien,
(their eyes say, "You may speak
Spanish but you're not like me")
an American to Mexicans
a Mexican to Americans   15
a handy token
sliding back and forth
between the fringes of both worlds
by smiling
by masking the discomfort   20
of being pre-judged
Bi-laterally.

---

3 *Me'stan volviendo loca* They are driving me crazy.

SHARON OLDS

*Sharon Olds, born in San Francisco in 1942 and educated at Stanford
University and Columbia University, has published many volumes of poetry
and has received major awards. Olds held the position of New York State Poet
from 1998 to 2000, and currently teaches poetry workshops in the Graduate
Creative Writing Program at New York University.*

Rite of Passage   [1983]

As the guests arrive at my son's party
they gather in the living room—
short men, men in first grade
with smooth jaws and chins.
Hands in pockets, they stand around   5
jostling, jockeying for place, small fights
breaking out and calming. One says to another
How old are you? Six. I'm seven. So?
They eye each other, seeing themselves
tiny in the other's pupils. They clear their   10
throats a lot, a room of small bankers,

they fold their arms and frown. *I could beat you*
up, a seven says to a six,
the dark cake, round and heavy as a
turret, behind them on the table. My son,   15
freckles like specks of nutmeg on his cheeks,
chest narrow as the balsa keel of a
model boat, long hands
cool and thin as the day they guided him
out of me, speaks up as a host   20
for the sake of the group.
We could easily kill a two-year-old,
he says in his clear voice. The other
men agree, they clear their throats
like Generals, they relax and get down to   25
playing war, celebrating my son's life.

LINDA PASTAN

For a biographical note, see page 589.

Love Poem   [1988]

I want to write you
a love poem as headlong
as our creek
after thaw
when we stand   5
on its dangerous
banks and watch it carry
with it every twig
every dry leaf and branch
in its path   10
every scruple
when we see it
so swollen
with runoff
that even as we watch   15
we must grab
each other
and step back
we must grab each
other or   20
get our shoes
soaked we must
grab each other

SYLVIA PLATH

For a biographical note, see page 620.

Daddy

[1965]

You do not do, you do not do
Any more, black shoe
In which I have lived like a foot
For thirty years, poor and white,
Barely daring to breathe or Achoo.   5

Daddy, I have had to kill you.
You died before I had time—
Marble-heavy, a bag full of God,
Ghastly statue with one gray toe
Big as a Frisco seal   10

And a head in the freakish Atlantic
Where it pours bean green over blue
In the waters off beautiful Nauset.°
I used to pray to recover you.
Ach, du.°   15

In the German tongue, in the Polish town
Scraped flat by the roller
Of wars, wars, wars.
But the name of the town is common.
My Polack friend   20

Says there are a dozen or two.
So I never could tell where you
Put your foot, your root,
I never could talk to you.
The tongue stuck in my jaw.   25

It stuck in a barb wire snare.
Ich, ich, ich, ich,°
I could hardly speak.
I thought every German was you.
And the language obscene   30

An engine, an engine
Chuffing me off like a Jew.
A Jew to Dachau, Auschwitz, Belsen.°
I began to talk like a Jew.
I think I may well be a Jew.   35

The snows of the Tyrol,° the clear beer of Vienna
Are not very pure or true.
With my gypsy ancestress and my weird luck
And my Taroc pack and my Taroc° pack
I may be a bit of a Jew.   40

I have always been scared of *you,*
With your Luftwaffe,° your gobbledygoo.

---

13 Nauset town on the coast of Cape Cod, Massachusetts.   **15 Ach, du** O, you
(German).   **27 Ich, ich, ich, ich** I, I, I, I.   **33 Dachau . . . Belsen** concentration
camps.   **36 Tyrol** the Austrian Alps.   **39 Taroc** a variant of Tarot, fortune-telling cards.
42 Luftwaffe German air force.

And your neat moustache
And your Aryan eye, bright blue,
Panzer-man,° panzer-man, O You—   45

Not God but a swastika
So black no sky could squeak through.
Every woman adores a Fascist,
The boot in the face, the brute
Brute heart of a brute like you.   50

You stand at the blackboard, daddy,
In the picture I have of you,
A cleft in your chin instead of your foot
But no less a devil for that, no not
Any less the black man who   55

Bit my pretty red heart in two.
I was ten when they buried you.
At twenty I tried to die
And get back, back, back to you.
I thought even the bones would do.   60

But they pulled me out of the sack,
And they stuck me together with glue,
And then I knew what to do.
I made a model of you,
A man in black with a Meinkampf° look   65

And a love of the rack and the screw.
And I said I do, I do.
So daddy, I'm finally through.
The black telephone's off at the root,
The voices just can't worm through.   70

If I've killed one man, I've killed two—
The vampire who said he was you
And drank my blood for a year,
Seven years, if you want to know.
Daddy, you can lie back now.   75

There's a stake in your fat black heart
And the villagers never liked you.
They are dancing and stamping on you.
They always *knew* it was you.
Daddy, daddy, you bastard, I'm through.   80

---

45 Panzer-man member of a tank crew.   **65 Meinkampf** My Struggle (*Mein Kampf* is
the title of Hitler's autobiography).

EZRA POUND

*Ezra Pound (1885–1972), born in Hailey, Idaho, and raised in Philadelphia,
was one of the most influential American poets of the twentieth century. He
prepared to be a teacher of medieval and Renaissance Spanish, Italian, and*

French literature, but his career as an academician ended abruptly when he was fired from Wabash College for having a woman in his room overnight. Pound went to Venice, where he did odd jobs, and then to London, where he met T. S. Eliot and played a large role in editing Eliot's long poem, The Waste Land. *Among the other poets whom he assisted was Robert Frost, who was then living in England. In 1924 Pound settled in Italy. He espoused Mussolini's cause, was arrested by the American forces in 1945, and (having been declared insane and therefore not fit to be tried for treason) was confined in a mental institution in Washington, D.C. Released in 1958, he spent the remainder of his life in Italy.*

In a Station of the Metro*   [1916]

The apparition of these faces in the crowd;
Petals on a wet, black bough.

*****Metro** subway in Paris.

DUDLEY RANDALL

Born in Washington, D.C., Dudley Randall (1914–2000) graduated with a bachelor's degree from Wayne State University and with a master's degree in library science from the University of Michigan. He worked as a reference librarian for twenty years, and also served as poet in residence at the University of Detroit. In 1965 he founded the Broadside Press, widely recognized as influential far beyond its size, publishing excellent small books and single sheets with poems by African Americans.

The Melting Pot   [1968]

There is a magic melting pot
where any girl or man
can step in Czech or Greek or Scot,
step out American.   4

Johann and *Jan* and *Jean* and *Juan,*
Giovanni and *Ivan*
step in and then step out again
all freshly christened *John.*   8

Sam, watching, said, "Why, I was here
even before they came,"
and stepped in too, but was tossed out
before he passed the brim.   12

And every time Sam tried that pot,
they threw him out again.
"Keep out. This is our private pot
We don't want your black stain."   16

At last, thrown out a thousand times,
Sam said, "I don't give a damn.
Shove your old pot. You can like it or not,
but I'll be just what I am."   20

ADRIENNE RICH

For a biographical note, see page 641.

Living in Sin   [1955]

She had thought the studio would keep itself;
no dust upon the furniture of love.
Half heresy, to wish the taps less vocal,
the panes relieved of grime. A plate of pears,
a piano with a Persian shawl, a cat   5
stalking the picturesque amusing mouse
had risen at his urging.
Not that at five each separate stair would writhe
under the milkman's tramp; that morning light:
so coldly would delineate the scraps   10
of last night's cheese and three sepulchral bottles;
that on the kitchen shelf among the saucers
a pair of beetle-eyes would fix her own—
envoy from some black village in the moldings . . .
Meanwhile, he, with a yawn,   15
sounded a dozen notes upon the keyboard,
declared it out of tune, shrugged at the mirror,
rubbed at his beard, went out for cigarettes;
while she, jeered by the minor demons,
pulled back the sheets and made the bed and found   20
a towel to dust the table-top,
and let the coffee-pot boil over on the stove.
By evening she was back in love again,
though not so wholly but throughout the night
she woke sometimes to feel the daylight coming   25
like a relentless milkman up the stairs.

ANNE SEXTON

For a biographical note, see page 727.

Her Kind   [1960]

I have gone out, a possessed witch,
haunting the black air, braver at night;
dreaming evil, I have done my hitch

over the plain houses, light by light;
lonely thing, twelve-fingered, out of mind.   5
A woman like that is not a woman, quite.
I have been her kind.

I have found the warm caves in the woods,
filled them with skillets, carvings, shelves,
closets, silks, innumerable goods;   10
fixed the suppers for the worms and the elves:
whining, rearranging the disaligned.
A woman like that is misunderstood.
I have been her kind.

I have ridden in your cart, driver,   15
waved my nude arms at villages going by,
learning the last bright routes, survivor
where your flames still bite my thigh
and my ribs crack where your wheels wind.
A woman like that is not ashamed to die.   20
I have been her kind.

WILLIAM SHAKESPEARE

*William Shakespeare (1564–1616), born in Stratford-upon-Avon in England, is
chiefly known as a dramatic poet, but he also wrote nondramatic poetry. In
1609 a volume of 154 of his sonnets was published, apparently without his permission. Probably he chose to keep his sonnets unpublished not because he
thought that they were of little value, but because it was more prestigious to be
an amateur (unpublished) poet than a professional (published) poet. Although
the sonnets were published in 1609, they were probably written in the mid-
1590s, when there was a vogue for sonneteering. A contemporary writer in
1598 said that Shakespeare's "sugred Sonnets [circulate] among his private
friends." We print three other sonnets by Shakespeare on pages 631, 632, and 676.*

Sonnet 29

When, in disgrace with Fortune and men's eyes,
I all alone beweep my outcast state,
And trouble deaf heaven with my bootless° cries,
And look upon myself and curse my fate,
Wishing me like to one more rich in hope,   5
Featured like him, like him° with friends possessed,
Desiring this man's art, and that man's scope,
With what I most enjoy contented least;
Yet in these thoughts myself almost despising,
Haply° I think on thee, and then my state,   10

---

3 bootless useless.   **6 like him, like him** like a second man, like a third man.
10 Haply Perchance.

Like to the lark at break of day arising
From sullen earth, sings hymns at heaven's gate;
   For thy sweet love rememb'red such wealth brings,
   That then I scorn to change my state with kings.

Sonnet 116

Let me not to the marriage of true minds
Admit impediments; love is not love
Which alters when it alteration finds,
Or bends with the remover to remove.
O, no, it is an ever-fixèd mark°   5
That looks on tempests and is never shaken;
It is the star° to every wand'ring bark,
Whose worth's unknown, although his height be taken.
Love's not Time's fool,° though rosy lips and cheeks
Within his bending sickle's compass° come;   10
Love alters not with his° brief hours and weeks
But bears° it out even to the edge of doom.°
   If this be error and upon me proved,
   I never writ, nor no man ever loved.

---

5 mark guide to mariners.   **7 star** the North Star.   **9 fool** plaything.   **10 compass** range.   **11 his** Time's.   **12 bears** endures.   **doom** Judgment Day.

ALFRED, LORD TENNYSON

For a biographical note, see page 628.

Ulysses*   [1833]

It little profits that an idle king,
By this still hearth, among these barren crags,
Matched with an aged wife, I mete and dole
Unequal laws unto a savage race,
That hoard, and sleep, and feed, and know not me.   5
I cannot rest from travel; I will drink
Life to the lees. All times I have enjoyed
Greatly, have suffered greatly, both with those
That loved me, and alone; on shore, and when
Thro' scudding drifts the rainy Hyades   10
Vext the dim sea. I am become a name;
For always roaming with a hungry heart
Much have I seen and known,—cities of men

*****Ulysses** Odysseus, King of Ithaca, a leader of the Greeks in the Trojan War, famous for his ten years of journeying to remote places.

And manners, climates, councils, governments,
Myself not least, but honored of them all,—   15
And drunk delight of battle with my peers,
Far on the ringing plains of windy Troy.
I am a part of all that I have met;
Yet all experience is an arch wherethro'
Gleams that untravelled world whose margin fades   20
For ever and for ever when I move.
How dull it is to pause, to make an end,
To rust unburnished, not to shine in use!
As tho' to breathe were life! Life piled on life
Were all too little, and of one to me   25
Little remains; but every hour is saved
From that eternal silence, something more,
A bringer of new things; and vile it were
For some three suns to store and hoard myself,
And this gray spirit yearning in desire   30
To follow knowledge like a sinking star,
Beyond the utmost bound of human thought.

      This is my son, mine own Telemachus,
To whom I leave the scepter and the isle,—
Well-loved of me, discerning to fulfill   35
This labor, by slow prudence to make mild
A rugged people, and thro' soft degrees
Subdue them to the useful and the good.
Most blameless is he, centered in the sphere
Of common duties, decent not to fail   40
In offices of tenderness, and pay
Meet adoration to my household gods,
When I am gone. He works his work, I mine.

      There lies the port; the vessel puffs her sail;
There gloom the dark, broad seas. My mariners,   45
Souls that have toiled, and wrought, and thought with me,—
That ever with a frolic welcome took
The thunder and the sunshine, and opposed
Free hearts, free foreheads,—you and I are old;
Old age hath yet his honor and his toil.   50
Death closes all; but something ere the end,
Some work of noble note, may yet be done,
Not unbecoming men that strove with Gods.
The lights begin to twinkle from the rocks;
The long day wanes; the slow moon climbs; the deep   55
Moans round with many voices. Come, my friends.
'Tis not too late to seek a newer world.
Push off, and sitting well in order smite
The sounding furrows; for my purpose holds
To sail beyond the sunset, and the baths   60
Of all the western stars, until I die.
It may be that the gulfs will wash us down;
It may be we shall touch the Happy Isles,

And see the great Achilles, whom we knew.
Tho' much is taken, much abides; and tho'   65
We are not now that strength which in old days
Moved earth and heaven, that which we are, we are.
One equal temper of heroic hearts,
Made weak by time and fate, but strong in will
To strive, to seek, to find, and not to yield.   70

KITTY TSUI

*Born in Hong Kong in 1953, Kitty Tsui lived there and in England until 1969,
when she came to the United States. She is an actor, an artist, and a professional bodybuilder as well as a writer. Her publications include* Breathless:
Erotica *(1996).*

A Chinese Banquet   [1983]

for the one who was not invited

it was not a very formal affair but
all the women over twelve
wore long gowns and a corsage,
except for me.   4

it was not a very formal affair, just
the family getting together,
poa poa,°kuw fu° without *kuw mow°*
(her excuse this year is a headache).   8

aunts and uncles and cousins,
the grandson who is a dentist,
the one who drives a mercedes benz,
sitting down for shark's fin soup.   12

they talk about buying a house and
taking a two week vacation in beijing.
i suck on shrimp and squab,
dreaming of the cloudscape in your eyes.   16

my mother, her voice beaded with sarcasm:
you're twenty six and not getting younger.
it's about time you got a decent job.
she no longer asks when i'm getting married.   20

you're twenty six and not getting younger.
what are you doing with your life?
you've got to make a living.
why don't you study computer programming?   24

---

7 poa poa maternal grandmother.   **kuw fu** uncle.   **kuw mow** aunt.

she no longer asks when i'm getting married.
one day, wanting desperately to
bridge the boundaries that separate us,
wanting desperately to touch her,   28

tell her: mother, i'm gay,
mother i'm gay and so happy with her.
but she will not listen,
she shakes her head.   32

she sits across from me,
emotions invading her face.
her eyes are wet but
she will not let tears fall.   36

mother, i say,
you love a man.
i love a woman.
it is not what she wants to hear.   40

aunts and uncles and cousins,
very much a family affair.
but you are not invited,
being neither my husband nor my wife.   44

aunts and uncles and cousins
eating longevity noodles
fragrant with ham inquire:
sold that old car of yours yet?   48

i want to tell them: my back is healing,
i dream of dragons and water.
my home is in her arms,
our bedroom ceiling the wide open sky.   52

JOHN UPDIKE

For a biographical note, see page 191.

Ex-Basketball Player   [1958]

Pearl Avenue runs past the high-school lot,
Bends with the trolley tracks, and stops, cut off
Before it has a chance to go two blocks,
At Colonel McComsky Plaza. Berth's Garage
Is on the corner facing west, and there,   5
Most days, you'll find Flick Webb, who helps Berth out.

Flick stands tall among the idiot pumps—
Five on a side, the old bubble-head style,
Their rubber elbows hanging loose and low.
One's nostrils are two S's, and his eyes   10
An E and O. And one is squat, without
A head at all—more of a football type.

Once Flick played for the high-school team, the Wizards.
He was good: in fact, the best. In '46
He bucketed three hundred ninety points,   15
A county record still. The ball loved Flick.
I saw him rack up thirty-eight or forty
In one home game. His hands were like wild birds.

He never learned a trade, he just sells gas,
Checks oil, and changes flats. Once in a while,   20
As a gag, he dribbles an inner tube,
But most of us remember anyway.
His hands are fine and nervous on the lug wrench.
It makes no difference to the lug wrench, though.

Off work, he hangs around Mae's Luncheonette.   25
Grease-gray and kind of coiled, he plays pinball,
Smokes those thin cigars, nurses lemon phosphates.
Flick seldom says a word to Mae, just nods
Beyond her face toward bright applauding tiers
Of Necco Wafers, Nibs, and Juju Beads.   30

DEREK WALCOTT

Derek Walcott, born in 1930 on the Caribbean island of St. Lucia, was awarded the Nobel Prize in Literature in 1992. Although in the United States he is known chiefly as a poet, Walcott is also an important playwright and director of plays. Much of his work is concerned with his mixed heritage—a black writer from the Caribbean, whose language is English. Walcott retired from teaching poetry and drama in the Creative Writing Department at Boston University in 2007. In fall 2009, he began a three-year distinguished scholar in residence position at the University of Alberta, Canada.

A Far Cry from Africa   [1962]

A wind is ruffling the tawny pelt
Of Africa. Kikuyu,° quick as flies,
Batten upon the bloodstreams of the veldt.°
Corpses are scattered through a paradise.
Only the worm, colonel of carrion, cries: 5
"Waste no compassion on these separate dead!"
Statistics justify and scholars seize
The salients of colonial policy.
What is that to the white child hacked in bed?
To savages, expendable as Jews?   10

---

2 Kikuyu an African tribe who fought against British colonialists.   **3 veldt** grassland in southern Africa.

Threshed out by beaters, the long rushes break
In a white dust of ibises whose cries
Have wheeled since civilization's dawn
From the parched river or beast-teeming plain.
The violence of beast on beast is read   15
As natural law, but upright man
Seeks his divinity by inflicting pain.
Delirious as these worried beasts, his wars
Dance to the tightened carcass of a drum,
While he calls courage still that native dread   20
Of the white peace contracted by the dead.

Again brutish necessity wipes its hands
Upon the napkin of a dirty cause, again
A waste of our compassion, as with Spain,°
The gorilla wrestles with the superman.   25
I who am poisoned with the blood of both,
Where shall I turn, divided to the vein?
I who have cursed
The drunken officer of British rule, how choose
Between this Africa and the English tongue I love?   30
Betray them both, or give back what they give?
How can I face such slaughter and be cool?
How can I turn from Africa and live?

---

24 Spain a reference to the triumph of fascism in Spain after the Civil War of 1936–1939.

WALT WHITMAN

For a biographical note, see page 585.

A Sight in Camp in the Daybreak Gray and Dim [1865–1866]

A sight in camp in the daybreak gray and dim,
As from my tent I emerge so early sleepless,
As slow I walk in the cool fresh air the path near by the hospital tent,
Three forms I see on stretchers lying, brought out there untended lying,
Over each the blanket spread, ample brownish woolen blanket,   5
Gray and heavy blanket, folding, covering all.

Curious I halt and silent stand,
Then with light fingers I from the face of the nearest the first just lift
    the blanket;
Who are you elderly man so gaunt and grim, with well-gray'd hair,
    and flesh all sunken about the eyes?
Who are you my dear comrade?   10

Then to the second I step—and who are you my child and darling?
Who are you sweet boy with cheeks yet blooming?

Then to the third—a face nor child nor old, very calm, as of beautiful
   yellow-white ivory;
Young man I think I know you—I think this face is the face of the
   Christ himself,
Dead and divine and brother of all, and here again he lies.   15

WILLIAM CARLOS WILLIAMS

For a biographical note, see page 628.

Spring and All   [1923]

By the road to the contagious hospital
under the surge of the blue
mottled clouds driven from the
northeast—a cold wind. Beyond, the
waste of broad, muddy fields   5
brown with dried weeds, standing and fallen

patches of standing water
the scattering of tall trees

All along the road the reddish
purplish, forked, upstanding, twiggy   10
stuff of bushes and small trees
with dead, brown leaves under them
leafless vines—

Lifeless in appearance, sluggish
dazed spring approaches—   15

They enter the new world naked,
cold, uncertain of all
save that they enter. All about them
the cold, familiar wind—

Now the grass, tomorrow   20
the stiff curl of wildcarrot leaf

One by one objects are defined—
It quickens: clarity, outline of leaf

But now the stark dignity of
entrance—Still, the profound change   25
has come upon them: rooted, they
grip down and begin to awaken

WILLIAM WORDSWORTH

*William Wordsworth (1770–1850), the son of an attorney, grew up in the
Lake District of England. After graduating from Cambridge University in
1791, he spent a year in France, falling in love with a French girl, with whom*

he had a daughter. His enthusiasm for the French Revolution waned, and he returned alone to England, where, with the help of a legacy, he devoted his life to poetry. With his friend Samuel Taylor Coleridge, in 1798 he published anonymously a volume of poetry, Lyrical Ballads, *which changed the course of English poetry. In 1799 he and his sister Dorothy settled in Grasmere in the Lake District, where he married and was given the office of distributor of stamps. In 1843 he was appointed poet laureate.*

The World Is Too Much with Us   [1807]

The world is too much with us; late and soon,
Getting and spending, we lay waste our powers;
Little we see in Nature that is ours;
We have given our hearts away, a sordid boon!°
This Sea that bares her bosom to the moon,   5
The winds that will be howling at all hours,
And are up-gathered now like sleeping flowers,
For this, for everything, we are out of tune;
It moves us not.—Great God! I'd rather be
A Pagan suckled in a creed outworn;   10
So might I, standing on this pleasant lea,
Have glimpses that would make me less forlorn;
Have sight of Proteus° rising from the sea;
Or hear old Triton° blow his wreathèd horn.

---

4 boon gift. **13, 14 Proteus, Triton** sea gods.

I Wandered Lonely as a Cloud   [1807]

I wandered lonely as a cloud
That floats on high o'er vales and hills,
When all at once I saw a crowd,
A host, of golden daffodils,
Beside the lake, beneath the trees,   5
Fluttering and dancing in the breeze.

Continuous as the stars that shine
And twinkle on the milky way,
They stretched in never-ending line
Along the margin of a bay;   10
Ten thousand saw I at a glance,
Tossing their heads in sprightly dance.

The waves beside them danced, but they
Outdid the sparkling waves in glee;
A poet could not but be gay,   15
In such a jocund company;

I gazed—and gazed—but little thought
What wealth the show to me had brought:

For oft, when on my couch I lie
In vacant or in pensive mood,   20
They flash upon that inward eye
Which is the bliss of solitude;
And then my heart with pleasure fills,
And dances with the daffodils.

The Solitary Reaper   [1807]

Behold her, single in the field,
Yon solitary Highland lass!
Reaping and singing by herself;
Stop here, or gently pass!
Alone she cuts and binds the grain,   5
And sings a melancholy strain;
O listen! for the Vale profound
Is overflowing with the sound.

No Nightingale did ever chant
More welcome notes to weary bands   10
Of travelers in some shady haunt,
Among Arabian sands:
A voice so thrilling ne'er was heard
In spring-time from the Cuckoo-bird,
Breaking the silence of the seas   15
Among the farthest Hebrides.°

Will no one tell me what she sings?—
Perhaps the plaintive numbers° flow
For old, unhappy, far-off things,
And battles long ago: 20
Or is it some more humble lay,°
Familiar matter of to-day?
Some natural sorrow, loss, or pain,
That has been, and may be again?

Whate'er the theme, the Maiden sang   25
As if her song could have no ending;
I saw her singing at her work,
And o'er the sickle bending;—
I listened, motionless and still;
And, as I mounted up the hill,   30
The music in my heart I bore,
Long after it was heard no more.

---

16 Hebrides distant northern islands.   **18 plaintive numbers** mournful verses.
21 lay song.

JAMES WRIGHT

James Wright (1927–1980) was born in Martins Ferry, Ohio, which provided him with the locale for many of his poems. He is often thought of as a poet of the Midwest, but (as in the example that we give) his poems use this setting to explore more general themes. Wright was educated at Kenyon College in Ohio and at the University of Washington. He wrote many books of poetry and published many translations of European and Latin-American poetry. Wright's Collected Poems (1971) *was awarded the Pulitzer Prize;* Above the River: The Complete Poems *was published posthumously (1992).*

Lying in a Hammock at William Duffy's Farm in Pine Island, Minnesota   [1963]

Over my head, I see the bronze butterfly,
Asleep on the black trunk,
Blowing like a leaf in green shadow.
Down the ravine behind the empty house,
The cowbells follow one another   5
Into the distances of the afternoon.
To my right,
In a field of sunlight between two pines,
The droppings of last year's horses
Blaze up into golden stones.   10
I lean back, as the evening darkens and comes on.
A chicken hawk floats over, looking for home.
I have wasted my life.

MITSUYE YAMADA

Mitsuye Yamada, the daughter of Japanese immigrants to the United States, was born in Japan in 1923, during her mother's return visit to her native land. Yamada was raised in Seattle, but in 1942 she and her family were incarcerated and then relocated to an internment camp in Idaho. This was the result of Executive Order 9066, signed by President Franklin Roosevelt in February 1942. This order, in the aftermath of the Japanese attack on Pearl Harbor in December 1941, gave military authorities the right to remove any and all persons from "military areas." In 1954 Yamada became an American citizen. In addition to Camp Notes and Other Poems. *Yamada has written* Desert Run: Poems and Stories *(1988) and edited* Sowing TI Leaves: Writings by Multicultural Women *(1991).*

Note: From 1942 to 1945, before leaving an internment camp for eastern sections of the United States, Japanese Americans were expected to sign a statement known as "The Loyalty Oath."

The Question of Loyalty   [1976]

I met the deadline
for alien registration
once before
was numbered fingerprinted
and ordered not to travel   5
without permit.

But alien still they said I must
forswear allegiance to the emperor.

for me that was easy
I didn't even know him   10
but my mother who did cried out
    If I sign this
    What will I be?
    I am doubly loyal
    to my American children   15
    also to my own people.
    How can double mean nothing?
    I wish no one to lose this war
    Everyone does.
I was poor   20
at math.
I signed
my only ticket out

WILLIAM BUTLER YEATS

For a biographical note, see page 723.

In the seventh century BCE the ancient Greeks founded the city of Byzantium in Thrace, where Istanbul, Turkey, now stands. (Constantine, the first Christian ruler of the Roman empire, built a new city there in 330 CE. Named Con-
stantinople, the city served as the capital of the Roman empire until 1453, when
the Turks captured it. In 1930 the name was officially changed to Istanbul.) The
capital of the Roman Empire and the "holy city" of the Greek Orthodox Church,
Byzantium had two golden ages. The first, in its early centuries, continued the
traditions of the antique Greco-Roman world. The second, which is what Yeats
had in mind, extended from the mid-ninth to the mid-thirteenth century and
was a distinctive blend of classical, Christian, Slavic, and even Islamic culture.
This period is noted for mysticism, for the preservation of ancient learning, and
for exquisitely refined symbolic art. In short, Byzantium (as Yeats saw it) was
wise and passionless. In *A Vision,* his prose treatment of his complex mystical
system, Yeats says:

> I think that in early Byzantium, maybe never before or since
> in recorded history, religious, aesthetic and practical life were one,
> that architect and artificers—though not, it may be, poets, for lan-
> guage has been the instrument of controversy and must have grown

abstract—spoke to the multitude and the few alike. The painter, the mosaic worker, the worker in gold and silver, the illuminator of sacred books, were almost impersonal, almost perhaps without the consciousness of individual design, absorbed in their subject matter and that the vision of the whole people. They could copy out of old Gospel books those pictures that seemed as sacred as the text, and yet weave all into a vast design, the work of many that seemed the work of one, that made building, picture, pattern, metal-work of rail and lamp, seem but a single image.

Sailing to Byzantium

[1926]

I

That is no country for old men. The young
In one another's arms, birds in the trees
—Those dying generations—at their song,
The salmon-falls, the mackerel-crowded seas,
Fish, flesh, or fowl, commend all summer long   5
Whatever is begotten, born, and dies.
Caught in that sensual music all neglect
Monuments of unaging intellect.

II

An aged man is but a paltry thing,
A tattered coat upon a stick, unless   10
Soul clap its hands and sing, and louder sing
For every tatter in its mortal dress,
Nor is there singing school but studying
Monuments of its own magnificence;
And therefore I have sailed the seas and come   15
To the holy city of Byzantium.

III

O sages standing in God's holy fire
As in the gold mosaic of a wall,
Come from the holy fire, perne° in a gyre,
And be the singing-masters of my soul.   20
Consume my heart away; sick with desire
And fastened to a dying animal
It knows not what it is; and gather me
Into the artifice of eternity.

---

19 perne whirl down.

IV

Once out of nature I shall never take   25
My bodily form from any natural thing,
But such a form as Grecian goldsmiths make
Of hammered gold and gold enameling
To keep a drowsy Emperor awake;
Or set upon a golden bough to sing   30
To lords and ladies of Byzantium
Of what is past, or passing, or to come.

Drama

Drama usually tells an intense story by means of a fairly small number of characters. It can thus be contrasted both with the novel and with poetry. The novel tends to use a large number of characters and to cover a substantial period of time, thereby in some measure showing a picture of a society as well as of individuals; poetry, at the other extreme, tends to reveal the thoughts and emotions of a single individual. Drama usually gives us a heightened sense of life as we experience it daily—that is, of one character impinging on another, of actions having consequences, and of lives as comically or tragically interconnected. To quote Alfred Hitchcock, "Drama is life with the dull bits cut out."

Admittedly, some playwrights have used the stage as a platform for exploring ideas rather than as a way of showing intense representations of lives interacting, and Arthur Miller (1915–2005), shown here in his study, is among the playwrights who are sometimes said to be intellectuals. He indeed commented abundantly on the nature of society, both in essays and within the plays themselves (e.g., in *All My Sons* Chris Keller tells his mother, "There's a universe of people outside, and you're responsible to it"), but the fact remains that Miller is especially valued not for Big Ideas but because he gives us, through passionate characters, a sense that we are witnessing lives and human relationships in their most essential forms. Miller wished to make us think, but chiefly he makes us feel, and that is perhaps enough for a playwright to do. He cared deeply about social issues but one of the wisest things he said is not about any social issue but about the nature of drama itself: "The theater is above all else an instrument of passion."

Arthur Miller was born in New York, the son of Jewish immigrants from Austria. Miller went to the University of Michigan, where he first majored in journalism but then switched to English. As an undergraduate he won an award for playwrighting—one of the judges was Susan Glaspell, author of *Trifles* (see page 845)—and after graduation (1938) he returned to New York, where he wrote some radio plays and some unsuccessful stage plays. A novel, *Focus* (1945), was well received, and with *All My Sons* (1947), *Death of a Salesman* (1949), and *The Crucible* (1953), his reputation as a playwright was firmly established. His leftist views, however, caused difficulty: Subjected to questioning by the House Committee on Un-American Activities in the 1950s, he was convicted of contempt of Congress, but the conviction was overturned in 1958. Miller was widely regarded, in England and the rest of Europe as well as in the United States, as America's most important dramatist.

How to Read a Play

Thinking About the Language of Drama

The earlier parts of this book have dealt with fiction and poetry. A third chief literary type is drama, texts written to be performed.

A play is written to be seen and to be heard. We go to *see* a play in a theater (*theater* is derived from a Greek word meaning "to watch"), but in the theater we also *hear* it because we become an audience (*audience* is derived from a Latin word meaning "to hear"). Hamlet was speaking the ordinary language of his day when he said, "We'll hear a play tomorrow." When we read a play rather than see and hear it in a theater, we lose a good deal. We must see it in the mind's eye and hear it in the mind's ear.

When reading a play, it is not enough mentally to hear the lines. We must try to see the characters, costumed and moving within a specified setting, and we must try to hear not only their words but their tone, their joy or hypocrisy or tentativeness or aggression. Our job is much easier when we are in the theater and we have only to pay attention to the performers; as readers on our own, however, we must do what we can to perform the play in the theater of our minds.

If as a reader you develop the following principles into habits, you will get far more out of a play than if you read it as though it were a novel consisting only of dialogue.

1. *Pay attention to the **list of characters** and carefully read whatever descriptions the playwright has provided.* Early dramatists, such as Shakespeare, did not provide much in the way of description ("Othello, the Moor" or "Ariel, an airy spirit" is about as much as we find in Elizabethan texts), but later playwrights often are very forthcoming. Here, for instance, is Tennessee Williams introducing us to Amanda Wingfield in *The Glass Menagerie*. (We give only the beginning of his longish description.)

    Amanda Wingfield, the mother. A little woman of great but confused vitality clinging frantically to another time and place.

    And here is Susan Glaspell introducing us to all the characters in her one-act play, *Trifles:*

    . . . the Sheriff comes in, followed by the County Attorney and Hale. The Sheriff and Hale are men in middle life, the County Attorney is a young man; all are much bundled up and go at once to the stove. They are followed by the two women—the Sheriff's Wife, [Mrs. Peters] first; she is a slight wiry woman, a thin nervous face. Mrs. Hale is larger and would ordinarily be called more comfortable looking, but she is disturbed now and looks fearfully about as she enters. The women have come in slowly and stand close together near the door.

Glaspell's description of her characters is not nearly so explicit as Tennessee Williams's, but Glaspell does reveal much to a reader. What do we know about the men? They differ in age, they are bundled up, and they "go at once to the stove." What do we know about the women? Mrs. Peters is slight, and she has a "nervous face"; Mrs. Hale is "larger" but she too is "disturbed." The women enter "slowly," and they "stand close together near the door." In short, the men, who take over the warmest part of the room, are more confident than the women, who nervously huddle together near the door. It's a man's world.

2. *Pay attention to* **gestures** *and* **costumes** *that are specified in stage directions or are implied by the dialogue.* We have just seen how Glaspell distinguishes between the men and the women by what they do—the men take over the warm part of the room, the women stand insecurely near the door. Most dramatists from the late nineteenth century to the present have been fairly generous with their stage directions, but when we read the works of earlier dramatists we often have to deduce the gestures from the speeches. For instance, although the texts of Shakespeare's day have an occasional direction, such as "Enter Hamlet reading on a book," "Leaps in the grave," and "in scuffling, they change rapiers," such directions are rare. In reading Shakespeare, we must, again, see the action *in the mind's eye* (a phrase from *Hamlet,* by the way) Here, for instance, are Horatio's words (1.1.130–31) when he sees the Ghost:

> But soft, behold! Lo, where it comes again!
> I'll cross it, though it blast me. [*It spreads his arms.*] Stay, *illusion!*

As a footnote indicates, the "his" in the stage direction is the Ghost's; today we would say "its." There is no doubt about what the Ghost does, but what does Horatio do when he says "I'll cross it"? Conceivably "I'll cross it" means "I'll confront it; I'll stand in its path," and Horatio then walks up to the Ghost. Or perhaps the words mean "I'll make the sign of the cross, to protect myself from this creature from another world." If so, does Horatio make the sign of the cross with his hand, or does he perhaps hold up his sword, an object that by virtue of the sword guard at right angles to the blade is itself a cross? The words "Stay, *illusion*" similarly must be accompanied by a gesture; perhaps Horatio reaches out, to try to take hold of the Ghost.

Or consider the first reunion of Hamlet and Horatio, in the second scene (1.2.160–61) of the play:

> HORATIO. Hail to your lordship!
> HAMLET. I am glad to see you well.
>   Horatio!—or I do forget myself.

One cannot be positive, but it seems that the melancholy Hamlet, hearing a greeting ("Hail to your lordship"), at first replies with routine politeness ("I am glad to see you well") and, when an instant later he recognizes that this greeting comes from an old friend whom he has not seen for a while, he responds with an enthusiastic "Horatio!" and perhaps with an embrace.

In addition to thinking about gestures, don't forget the costumes that the characters wear. Costumes identify the characters as soldiers or kings or farmers or whatever, and changes of costume can be especially symbolic.

Costumes are always important, because they tell us something about the people who wear them. As even the fatuous Polonius knows, "the apparel oft proclaims the man." In *Hamlet,* the use of symbolic costume is evident; Hamlet is dressed in black (we hear of his "nighted color" and his "inky cloak"), a color that sets him apart from the courtiers, who presumably are dressed in colorful robes. Later in the play, when, having escaped from a sea journey that was supposed to end in his death, Hamlet is seen in the graveyard, perhaps he wears the "sea gown" that he mentions, and we feel that he is now a more energetic character, freed from his constricting suit of mourning.

3. *Keep in mind the **kind of theater** for which the play was written.* The plays in this book were written for various kinds of theaters. Sophocles, author of *Antigone* and *King Oedipus,* wrote for the ancient Greek theater, essentially a space where performers acted in front of an audience seated on a hillside. (See the photo on page 909.) This theater was open to the heavens, with a structure representing a palace or temple behind the actors, in itself a kind of image of a society governed by the laws of the state and the laws of the gods. Moreover, the chorus entered the playing space by marching down the side aisles, close to the audience, thus helping to unite the world of the audience and of the players. On the other hand, the audience in most modern theaters sits in a darkened area and looks through a proscenium arch at performers who move in a boxlike setting. The box set of the late nineteenth century and the twentieth century is, it often seems, an appropriate image of the confined lives of the unheroic characters of the play.

4. *If the playwright describes a location, try to **envision the set** clearly.* Glaspell, for instance, tells us a good deal about the set. We quote only the first part.

> The kitchen in the now abandoned farmhouse of John Wright, a gloomy kitchen, and left without having been put in order. . . .

These details about a gloomy and disordered kitchen may seem to be mere realism—after all, the play has to take place *somewhere*—but it turns out that the disorder and, for that matter, the gloominess are extremely important. You'll have to read the play to find out why.

Another example of a setting that provides important information is Arthur Miller's scene descriptions in *Death of a Salesman.* Again we quote only the beginning of one:

> Before us is the Salesman's house. We are aware of towering, angular shapes behind it, surrounding it on all sides. Only the blue light of the sky falls upon the house and forestage; the surrounding area shows an angry glow of orange.

If we read older drama, we find that playwrights do *not* give us much help, but by paying attention to the words we can to some degree visualize the locale. For instance, the first stage direction in *Hamlet* ("Enter Bernardo and Francisco, two sentinels"), along with the opening dialogue ("Who's there?"; "Nay, answer me. Stand and unfold yourself"), indicates that we are in some sort of public place where anyone may suddenly appear. Elizabethan plays were staged in daylight, and there was no way of darkening the stage, so if the scene is a night scene the playwright has to convey this information. In this instance, the audience understands that the meeting takes place at night because the characters can hear but cannot see each other; to make certain, however, a few lines later Shakespeare has Bernardo say, "'Tis now struck twelve. Get thee to bed, Francisco."

5. *Pay attention to whatever **sound effects** are specified in the play.* In *Hamlet* (1.2.125), when the king (called "Denmark" in the speech we quote) drinks, he does so to the rather vulgar accompaniment of a cannonade:

> No jocund health that Denmark drinks today
> But the great cannon to the clouds shall tell,
> And the King's rouse the heaven shall bruit again,
> Respeaking earthly thunder.

The point is made again several times, but these salutes to King Claudius are finally displaced by a military salute to Hamlet; "a peal of ordnance is shot off," we are told, when his body is carried off the stage at the end of the play. Thus, the last sound that we hear in *Hamlet* is a validation of Hamlet as a hero.

In *Death of a Salesman,* before the curtain goes up, "A melody is heard, played upon a flute. It is small and fine, telling of grass and trees and the horizon." Then the curtain rises, revealing the Salesman's house, with "towering, angular shapes behind it, surrounding it on all sides." Obviously the sound of the flute is meant to tell us of the world that the Salesman is shut off from.

A sound effect, however, need not be so evidently symbolic to be important in a play. In Glaspell's *Trifles,* almost at the very end of the play we hear the "sound of a knob turning in the other room." The sound has an electrifying effect on the audience, as it does on the two women on the stage, and it precedes a decisive action.

6. *Pay attention to what the characters say, and keep in mind that (like real people) **dramatic characters are not always to be trusted.*** An obvious case is Shakespeare's Iago, an utterly unscrupulous villain who knows that he is a liar. But a character may be self-deceived, or, to put it a bit differently, characters may say what they honestly think but may not know what they are talking about.

Plot and Character

Although **plot** is sometimes equated with the gist of the narrative—the story—it is sometimes reserved to denote the writer's *arrangement* of the happenings in the story. Thus, all plays about the assassination of Julius Caesar have pretty much the same story, but by beginning with a scene of workmen enjoying a holiday (and thereby introducing the motif of the fickleness of the mob), Shakespeare's play has a plot different from a play that omits such a scene.

Handbooks on drama often suggest that a plot (the arrangement of happenings) should have a **rising action,** a **climax,** and a **falling action.** This sort of plot can be diagrammed as a pyramid, the tension rising through complications, or **crises,** to a climax, at which point the fate of the **protagonist** (chief character) is firmly established; the climax is the apex, and the tension allegedly slackens as we witness the **dénouement** (unknotting). Shakespeare sometimes used a pyramidal structure, placing his climax neatly in the middle of what seems to us to be the third of five acts.* Roughly the first half of *Julius Caesar* shows Brutus rising, reaching his height in 3.1 with the death of Caesar; but later in this scene he gives Marc Antony permission to speak at Caesar's funeral and thus he sets in motion his own fall, which occupies the second half of the play. In *Macbeth* (3.4.137–39), the protagonist attains his height in 3.1 ("Thou hast it now: King"), but he soon perceives that he is going downhill:

> I am in blood
> Stepped in so far, that, should I wade no more,
> Returning were as tedious as go o'er.

Of course, no law demands such a structure, and a hunt for the pyramid usually causes the hunter to overlook all the crises but the middle one. William Butler Yeats once suggestively diagrammed a good plot not as a pyramid but as a line moving diagonally upward, punctuated by several crises. Perhaps it is sufficient to say that a good plot has its moments of tension, but the location of these will vary with the play. They are the product of **conflict,** but not all conflict produces tension; there is conflict but little tension in a ball game when the score is 10–0 in the ninth inning with two out and no one on base.

Regardless of how a plot is diagrammed, the **exposition** is that part that tells the audience what it has to know about the past, the **antecedent action.** When two gossiping servants tell each other that after a year away in Paris the young master is coming home tomorrow with a new wife, they are giving the audience the exposition by introducing characters and establishing relationships. The Elizabethans and the Greeks sometimes tossed out all pretense at dialogue and began with a **prologue,** like the one spoken by the Chorus at the outset of *Romeo and Juliet:*

> Two households, both alike in dignity
>   In fair Verona, where we lay our scene,
> From ancient grudge break to new mutiny,

---

*An **act** is a main division in a drama or opera. Act divisions probably stem from Roman theory and derive ultimately from the Greek practice of separating episodes in a play by choral interludes; but Greek (and probably Roman) plays were performed without interruption, for the choral interludes were part of the plays themselves. Elizabethan plays, too, may have been performed without breaks; the division of Elizabethan plays into five acts is usually the work of editors rather than of authors. Frequently an act division today (commonly indicated by lowering the curtain and turning up the houselights) denotes change in locale and lapse of time. A **scene** is a smaller unit, either (1) a division with no change of locale or abrupt shift of time, or (2) a division consisting of an actor or group of actors on the stage; according to the second definition, the departure or entrance of an actor changes the composition of the group and thus introduces a new scene. (In an entirely different sense, the scene is the locale where a work is set.)

Where civil blood makes civil hands unclean.
From forth the fatal loins of these two foes
A pair of star-crossed lovers take their life. . . .

And in Tennessee Williams's *The Glass Menagerie,* Tom's first speech is a sort of prologue. However, the exposition also may extend far into the play so that the audience keeps getting bits of information that both clarify the present and build suspense about the future. Occasionally the **soliloquy** (a speech given by a character alone on the stage, revealing his or her thoughts) or the **aside** (speech given in the presence of others but unheard by them) is used to do the job of putting the audience in possession of the essential facts. The soliloquy and the aside are not limited to exposition; they are used to reveal the private thoughts of characters who, like people in real life, do not always tell others what their inner thoughts are. The soliloquy is especially used for meditation, where we might say the character is interacting not with another character but with himself or herself.

Because a play is not simply words but words spoken with accompanying gestures by performers who are usually costumed and in a particular setting, it may be argued that to read a play (rather than to see and hear it) is to falsify it. Drama is not literature, some people hold, but theater. However, there are replies: a play can be literature as well as theater, and readers of a play can perhaps enact in the theater of their mind a more effective play than the one put on by imperfect actors. After all, as Shakespeare's Duke Theseus, in *A Midsummer Night's Dream* (5.1.205), says of actors, "The best in this kind are but shadows." In any case, we need not wait for actors to present a play; we can do much on our own.

A scene from The Theatre of a Two-Headed Calf's 2010 production of *Trifles,* directed by Brooke O'Harra and performed by Mike Mikos, Caitlin McDonough-Thayer, Becca Blackwell, Daniel Manley, and Laryssa Husiak.

SUSAN GLASPELL

Susan Glaspell (1882-1948) was born in Davenport, Iowa, and educated at Drake University in Des Moines. In 1903 she married George Cram Cook and, with Cook and other writers, actors, and artists, in 1915 founded the Provincetown Players in Massachusetts, a group that remained vital until 1929. Glaspell wrote Trifles *(1916) for the Provincetown Players, but she also wrote stories, novels, and a biography of her husband. In 1931 she won a Pulitzer Prize for* Alison's House, *a play about the family of a deceased poet who in some ways resembles Emily Dickinson.*

Trifles

[1916]

SCENE: *The kitchen in the now abandoned farmhouse of John Wright, a gloomy kitchen, and left without having been put in order—unwashed pans under the sink, a loaf of bread outside the breadbox, a dish towel on the table—other signs of incompleted work. At the rear the outer door opens, and the Sheriff comes in, followed by the County Attorney and Hale. The Sheriff and Hale are men in middle life, the County Attorney is a young man; all are much bundled up and go at once to the stove. They are followed by the two women—the Sheriff's Wife first; she is a slight wiry woman, a thin nervous face. Mrs. Hale is larger and would ordinarily be called more comfortable looking, but she is disturbed now and looks fearfully about as she enters. The women have come in slowly and stand close together near the door.*

COUNTY ATTORNEY (*rubbing his hands*). This feels good. Come up to the fire, ladies.

MRS. PETERS (*after taking a step forward*). I'm not—cold.

SHERIFF (*unbuttoning his overcoat and stepping away from the stove as if to the beginning of official business*). Now, Mr. Hale, before we move things about, you explain to Mr. Henderson just what you saw when you came here yesterday morning.

COUNTY ATTORNEY. By the way, has anything been moved? Are things just as you left them yesterday?

SHERIFF (*looking about*). It's just the same. When it dropped below zero last night, I thought I'd better send Frank out this morning to make a fire for us—no use getting pneumonia with a big case on; but I told him not to touch anything except the stove—and you know Frank.

COUNTY ATTORNEY. Somebody should have been left here yesterday.

SHERIFF. Oh—yesterday. When I had to send Frank to Morris Center for that man who went crazy—I want you to know I had my hands full yesterday. I knew you could get back from Omaha by today, and as long as I went over everything here myself—

COUNTY ATTORNEY. Well, Mr. Hale, tell just what happened when you came here yesterday morning.

HALE. Harry and I had started to town with a load of potatoes. We came along the road from my place; and as I got here, I said, "I'm going to see if I can't get John Wright to go in with me on a party telephone." I spoke to Wright about it once before, and he put me off, saying folks talked too much anyway, and all he asked was peace and quiet—I guess you know about how much he talked himself; but I thought maybe if I went to the house and talked about it before his wife, though I said to Harry that I didn't know as what his wife wanted made much difference to John—

COUNTY ATTORNEY. Let's talk about that later, Mr. Hale. I do want to talk about that, but tell now just what happened when you got to the house.

HALE. I didn't hear or see anything; I knocked at the door, and still it was all quiet inside. I knew they must be up, it was past eight o'clock. So I knocked again, and I thought I heard somebody say, "Come in." I wasn't sure, I'm not sure yet, but I opened the door—this door (*indicating the door by which the two women are still standing*), and there in that rocker—(*pointing to it*) sat Mrs. Wright. (*They all look at the rocker.*)

COUNTY ATTORNEY. What—was she doing?

HALE. She was rockin' back and forth. She had her apron in her hand and was kind of—pleating it.

COUNTY ATTORNEY. And how did she—look?

HALE. Well, she looked queer.

COUNTY ATTORNEY. How do you mean—queer?

HALE. Well, as if she didn't know what she was going to do next. And kind of done up.

COUNTY ATTORNEY. How did she seem to feel about your coming?

HALE. Why, I don't think she minded—one way or other. She didn't pay much attention. I said, "How do, Mrs. Wright, it's cold, ain't it?" And she said, "Is it?"—and went on kind of pleating at her apron. Well, I was surprised; she didn't ask me to come up to the stove, or to set down, but just sat there, not even looking at me, so I said, "I want to see John." And then she—laughed. I guess you would call it a laugh. I thought of Harry and the team outside, so I said a little sharp: "Can't I see John?" "No," she says, kind o' dull like. "Ain't he home?" says I. "Yes," says she, "he's home." "Then why can't I see him?" I asked her, out of patience. "'Cause he's dead," says she. "*Dead?*" says I. She just nodded her head, not getting a bit excited, but rockin' back and forth. "Why—where is he?" says I, not knowing what to say. She just pointed upstairs—like that (*himself pointing to the room above*). I got up, with the idea of going up there. I walked from there to here—then I says, "Why, what did he die of?" "He died of a rope around his neck," says she, and just went on pleatin' at her apron. Well, I went out and called Harry. I thought I might—need help. We went upstairs, and there he was lyin'—

COUNTY ATTORNEY. I think I'd rather have you go into that upstairs, where you can point it all out. Just go on now with the rest of the story.

HALE. Well, my first thought was to get that rope off. I looked . . . (*Stops, his face twitches.*) . . . but Harry, he went up to him, and he said, "No, he's dead all right, and we'd better not touch anything." So we went back downstairs. She was still sitting that same way. "Has anybody been notified?" I asked. "No," says she, unconcerned. "Who did this, Mrs. Wright?" said Harry. He said it business-like—and she stopped pleatin' of her apron. "I don't know," she says. "You don't *know?*" says Harry. "No," says she. "Weren't you sleepin' in the bed with him?" says Harry. "Yes," says she, "but I was on the inside." "Somebody slipped a rope round his neck and strangled him, and you didn't wake up?" says Harry. "I didn't wake up," she said after him. We must 'a looked as if we didn't see how that could be, for after a minute she said, "I sleep sound." Harry was going to ask her more questions, but I said maybe we ought to let her tell her story first to the coroner, or the sheriff, so Harry went fast as he could to Rivers' place, where there's a telephone.

COUNTY ATTORNEY. And what did Mrs. Wright do when she knew that you had gone for the coroner?

HALE. She moved from that chair to this over here . . . (*Pointing to a small chair in the corner.*) . . . and just sat there with her hands held together and looking down. I got a feeling that I ought to make some conversation, so I said I had come in to see if John wanted to put in a telephone, and at that she started to laugh, and then she stopped and looked at me—scared. (*The County Attorney, who has had his notebook out, makes a note.*) I dunno, maybe it wasn't scared. I wouldn't like to say it was. Soon Harry got back, and then Dr. Lloyd came, and you, Mr. Peters, and so I guess that's all I know that you don't.

COUNTY ATTORNEY (*looking around*). I guess we'll go upstairs first—and then out to the barn and around there. (*To the Sheriff.*) You're convinced that there was nothing important here—nothing that would point to any motive?

SHERIFF. Nothing here but kitchen things.

(*The County Attorney, after again looking around the kitchen, opens the door of a cupboard closet. He gets up on a chair and looks on a shelf. Pulls his hand away, sticky.*)

COUNTY ATTORNEY. Here's a nice mess.

(*The women draw nearer.*)

MRS. PETERS (*to the other woman*). Oh, her fruit; it did freeze. (*To the Lawyer.*) She worried about that when it turned so cold. She said the fire'd go out and her jars would break.

SHERIFF. Well, can you beat the women! Held for murder and worryin' about her preserves.

COUNTY ATTORNEY. I guess before we're through she may have something more serious than preserves to worry about.

HALE. Well, women are used to worrying over trifles.

(*The two women move a little closer together.*)

COUNTY ATTORNEY (*with the gallantry of a young politician*). And yet, for all their worries, what would we do without the ladies? (*The women do not unbend. He goes to the sink, takes a dipperful of water from the pail and, pouring it into a basin, washes his hands. Starts to wipe them on the roller towel, turns it for a cleaner place.*) Dirty towels! (*Kicks his foot against the pans under the sink.*) Not much of a housekeeper, would you say, ladies?

MRS. HALE (*stiffly*). There's a great deal of work to be done on a farm.

COUNTY ATTORNEY. To be sure. And yet . . . (*With a little bow to her.*) . . . I know there are some Dickson county farmhouses which do not have such roller towels. (*He gives it a pull to expose its full length again.*)

MRS. HALE. Those towels get dirty awful quick. Men's hands aren't always as clean as they might be.

COUNTY ATTORNEY. Ah, loyal to your sex, I see. But you and Mrs. Wright were neighbors. I suppose you were friends, too.

MRS. HALE (*shaking her head*). I've not seen much of her of late years. I've not been in this house—it's more than a year.

COUNTY ATTORNEY. And why was that? You didn't like her?

MRS. HALE. I liked her all well enough. Farmers' wives have their hands full, Mr. Henderson. And then—

COUNTY ATTORNEY. Yes—?

MRS. HALE (*looking about*). It never seemed a very cheerful place.

COUNTY ATTORNEY. No—it's not cheerful. I shouldn't say she had the home-making instinct.

MRS. HALE. Well, I don't know as Wright had, either.

COUNTY ATTORNEY. You mean that they didn't get on very well?

MRS. HALE. No, I don't mean anything. But I don't think a place'd be any cheerfuler for John Wright's being in it.

COUNTY ATTORNEY. I'd like to talk more of that a little later. I want to get the lay of things upstairs now. (*He goes to the left, where three steps lead to a stair door.*)

SHERIFF. I suppose anything Mrs. Peters does'll be all right. She was to take in some clothes for her, you know, and a few little things. We left in such a hurry yesterday.

COUNTY ATTORNEY. Yes, but I would like to see what you take, Mrs. Peters, and keep an eye out for anything that might be of use to us.

MRS. PETERS. Yes, Mr. Henderson.

(*The women listen to the men's steps on the stairs, then look about the kitchen.*)

MRS. HALE. I'd hate to have men coming into my kitchen, snooping around and criticizing. (*She arranges the pans under sink which the Lawyer had shoved out of place.*)

MRS. PETERS. Of course it's no more than their duty.

MRS. HALE. Duty's all right, but I guess that deputy sheriff that came out to make the fire might have got a little of this on. (*Gives the roller towel a pull.*) Wish I'd thought of that sooner. Seems mean to talk about her for not having things slicked up when she had to come away in such a hurry.

MRS. PETERS (*who has gone to a small table in the left rear corner of the room, and lifted one end of a towel that covers a pan*). She had bread set. (*Stands still.*)

MRS. HALE (*eyes fixed on a loaf of bread beside the breadbox, which is on a low shelf at the other side of the room. Moves slowly toward it*). She was going to put this in there. (*Picks up loaf, then abruptly drops it. In a manner of returning to familiar things.*) It's a shame about her fruit. I wonder if it's all gone. (*Gets up on the chair and looks.*) I think there's some here that's all right, Mrs. Peters. Yes—here; (*Holding it toward the window.*) this is cherries, too. (*Looking again.*) I declare I believe that's the only one. (*Gets down, bottle in her hand. Goes to the sink and wipes it off on the outside.*) She'll feel awful bad after all her hard work in the hot weather. I remember the afternoon I put up my cherries last summer. (*She puts the bottle on the big kitchen table, center of the room, front table. With a sigh, is about to sit down in the rocking chair. Before she is seated realizes what chair it is; with a slow look at it, steps back. The chair, which she has touched, rocks back and forth.*)

MRS. PETERS. Well, I must get those things from the front room closet. (*She goes to the door at the right, but after looking into the other room steps back.*) You coming with me, Mrs. Hale? You could help me carry them. (*They go into the other room; reappear, Mrs. Peters carrying a dress and skirt, Mrs. Hale following with a pair of shoes.*)

MRS. PETERS. My, it's cold in there. (*She puts the cloth on the big table, and hurries to the stove.*)

MRS. HALE (*examining the skirt*). Wright was close. I think maybe that's why she kept so much to herself. She didn't even belong to the Ladies' Aid. I suppose she felt she couldn't do her part, and then you don't enjoy things when you feel shabby. She used to wear pretty clothes and be lively, when she was Minnie Foster, one of the town girls singing in the choir. But that—oh, that was thirty years ago. This all you was to take in?

MRS. PETERS. She said she wanted an apron. Funny thing to want, for there isn't much to get you dirty in jail, goodness knows. But I suppose just to make her feel more natural. She said they was in the top drawer in this cupboard. Yes, here. And then her little shawl that always hung behind the door. (*Opens stair door and looks.*) Yes, here it is. (*Quickly shuts door leading upstairs.*)

MRS. HALE (*abruptly moving toward her*). Mrs. Peters?

MRS. PETERS. Yes, Mrs. Hale?

MRS. HALE. Do you think she did it?

MRS. PETERS (*in a frightened voice*). Oh, I don't know.

MRS. HALE. Well, I don't think she did. Asking for an apron and her little shawl. Worrying about her fruit.

MRS. PETERS (*starts to speak, glances up, where footsteps are heard in the room above. In a low voice*). Mr. Peters says it looks bad for her. Mr. Henderson is awful sarcastic in speech, and he'll make fun of her sayin' she didn't wake up.

MRS. HALE. Well, I guess John Wright didn't wake when they was slipping that rope under his neck.

MRS. PETERS. No, it's strange. It must have been done awful crafty and still. They say it was such a—funny way to kill a man, rigging it all up like that.

MRS. HALE. That's just what Mr. Hale said. There was a gun in the house. He says that's what he can't understand.

MRS. PETERS. Mr. Henderson said coming out that what was needed for the case was a motive; something to show anger, or—sudden feeling.

MRS. HALE (*who is standing by the table*). Well, I don't see any signs of anger around here. (*She puts her hand on the dish towel which lies on the table, stands looking down at the table, one half of which is clean, the other half messy*). It's wiped here. (*Makes a move as if to finish work, then turns and looks at loaf of bread outside the breadbox. Drops towel. In that voice of coming back to familiar things.*) Wonder how they are finding things upstairs? I hope she had it a little more red-up[1] there. You know, it seems kind of *sneaking*. Locking her up in town and then coming out here and trying to get her own house to turn against her!

---

[1] **red-up** readied-up, that is, neat, tidy, ready to be seen by visitors.

MRS. PETERS. But, Mrs. Hale, the law is the law.

MRS. HALE. I s'pose 'tis. (*Unbuttoning her coat.*) Better loosen up your things, Mrs. Peters. You won't feel them when you go out.

(*Mrs. Peters takes off her fur tippet, goes to hang it on hook at the back of room, stands looking at the under part of the small corner table.*)

MRS. PETERS. She was piecing a quilt. (*She brings the large sewing basket, and they look at the bright pieces.*)

MRS. HALE. It's log cabin pattern. Pretty, isn't it? I wonder if she was goin' to quilt or just knot it?

(*Footsteps have been heard coming down the stairs. The Sheriff enters, followed by Hale and the County Attorney.*)

SHERIFF. They wonder if she was going to quilt it or just knot it. (*The men laugh, the women look abashed.*)

COUNTY ATTORNEY (*rubbing his hands over the stove*). Frank's fire didn't do much up there, did it? Well, let's go out to the barn and get that cleared up.

(*The men go outside.*)

MRS. HALE (*resentfully*). I don't know as there's anything so strange, our takin' up our time with little things while we're waiting for them to get the evidence. (*She sits down at the big table, smoothing out a block with decision.*) I don't see as it's anything to laugh about.

MRS. PETERS (*apologetically*). Of course they've got awful important things on their minds. (*Pulls up a chair and joins Mrs. Hale at the table.*)

MRS. HALE (*examining another block*). Mrs. Peters, look at this one. Here, this is the one she was working on, and look at the sewing! All the rest of it has been so nice and even. And look at this! It's all over the place! Why, it looks as if she didn't know what she was about! (*After she has said this, they look at each other, then start to glance back at the door. After an instant Mrs. Hale has pulled at a knot and ripped the sewing.*)

MRS. PETERS. Oh, what are you doing, Mrs. Hale?

MRS. HALE (*mildly*). Just pulling out a stitch or two that's not sewed very good. (*Threading a needle.*) Bad sewing always made me fidgety.

MRS. PETERS (*nervously*). I don't think we ought to touch things.

MRS. HALE. I'll just finish up this end. (*Suddenly stopping and leaning forward.*) Mrs. Peters?

MRS. PETERS. Yes, Mrs. Hale?

MRS. HALE. What do you suppose she was so nervous about?

MRS. PETERS. Oh—I don't know. I don't know as she was nervous. I sometimes sew awful queer when I'm just tired. (*Mrs. Hale starts to say something, looks at Mrs. Peters, then goes on sewing.*) Well, I must get these things wrapped up. They may be through sooner than we think. (*Putting apron and other things together.*) I wonder where I can find a piece of paper, and string.

MRS. HALE. In that cupboard, maybe.

MRS. PETERS (*looking in cupboard*). Why, here's a birdcage. (*Holds it up.*) Did she have a bird, Mrs. Hale?

MRS. HALE. Why, I don't know whether she did or not—I've not been here for so long. There was a man around last year selling canaries cheap, but

I don't know as she took one; maybe she did. She used to sing real pretty herself.

MRS. PETERS (*glancing around*). Seems funny to think of a bird here. But she must have had one, or why should she have a cage? I wonder what happened to it?

MRS. HALE. I s'pose maybe the cat got it.

MRS. PETERS. No, she didn't have a cat. She's got that feeling some people have about cats—being afraid of them. My cat got in her room, and she was real upset and asked me to take it out.

MRS. HALE. My sister Bessie was like that. Queer, ain't it?

MRS. PETERS (*examining the cage*). Why, look at this door. It's broke. One hinge is pulled apart.

MRS. HALE (*looking, too*). Looks as if someone must have been rough with it.

MRS. PETERS. Why, yes. (*She brings the cage forward and puts it on the table.*)

MRS. HALE. I wish if they're going to find any evidence they'd be about it. I don't like this place.

MRS. PETERS. But I'm awful glad you came with me, Mrs. Hale. It would be lonesome for me sitting here alone.

MRS. HALE. It would, wouldn't it? (*Dropping her sewing.*) But I tell you what I do wish, Mrs. Peters. I wish I had come over sometimes when *she* was here. I—(*Looking around the room.*)—wish I had.

MRS. PETERS. But of course you were awful busy, Mrs. Hale—your house and your children.

MRS. HALE. I could've come. I stayed away because it weren't cheerful—and that's why I ought to have come. I—I've never liked this place. Maybe because it's down in a hollow, and you don't see the road. I dunno what it is, but it's a lonesome place and always was. I wish I had come over to see Minnie Foster sometimes. I can see now—(*Shakes her head.*)

MRS. PETERS. Well, you mustn't reproach yourself, Mrs. Hale. Somehow we just don't see how it is with other folks until—something comes up.

MRS. HALE. Not having children makes less work—but it makes a quiet house, and Wright out to work all day, and no company when he did come in. Did you know John Wright, Mrs. Peters?

MRS. PETERS. Not to know him; I've seen him in town. They say he was a good man.

MRS. HALE. Yes—good; he didn't drink, and kept his word as well as most, I guess, and paid his debts. But he was a hard man, Mrs. Peters. Just to pass the time of day with him. (*Shivers.*) Like a raw wind that gets to the bone. (*Pauses, her eye falling on the cage.*) I should think she would 'a wanted a bird. But what do you suppose went with it?

MRS. PETERS. I don't know, unless it got sick and died. (*She reaches over and swings the broken door, swings it again; both women watch it.*)

MRS. HALE. You weren't raised round here, were you? (*Mrs. Peters shakes her head.*) You didn't know—her?

MRS. PETERS. Not till they brought her yesterday.

MRS. HALE. She—come to think of it, she was kind of like a bird herself—real sweet and pretty, but kind of timid and—fluttery. How—she—did—change. (*Silence; then as if struck by a happy thought and relieved to get back to everyday things.*) Tell you what, Mrs. Peters, why don't you take the quilt in with you? It might take up her mind.

MRS. PETERS. Why, I think that's a real nice idea, Mrs. Hale. There couldn't possibly be any objection to it, could there? Now, just what would I take? I wonder if her patches are in here—and her things. (*They look in the sewing basket.*)

MRS. HALE. Here's some red. I expect this has got sewing things in it. (*Brings out a fancy box.*) What a pretty box. Looks like something somebody would give you. Maybe her scissors are in here. (*Opens box. Suddenly puts her hand to her nose.*) Why—(*Mrs. Peters bends nearer, then turns her face away.*) There's something wrapped up in this piece of silk.

MRS. PETERS. Why, this isn't her scissors.

MRS. HALE (*lifting the silk*). Oh, Mrs. Peters—it's—(*Mrs. Peters bends closer.*)

MRS. PETERS. It's the bird.

MRS. HALE (*jumping up*). But, Mrs. Peters—look at it. Its neck! Look at its neck! It's all—other side *to*.

MRS. PETERS. Somebody—wrung—its neck.

(*Their eyes meet. A look of growing comprehension of horror. Steps are heard outside. Mrs. Hale slips box under quilt pieces, and sinks into her chair. Enter Sheriff and County Attorney. Mrs. Peters rises.*)

COUNTY ATTORNEY (*as one turning from serious things to little pleasantries*). Well, ladies, have you decided whether she was going to quilt it or knot it?

MRS. PETERS. We think she was going to—knot it.

COUNTY ATTORNEY. Well, that's interesting, I'm sure. (*Seeing the birdcage.*) Has the bird flown?

MRS. HALE (*putting more quilt pieces over the box*). We think the—cat got it.

COUNTY ATTORNEY (*preoccupied*). Is there a cat?

(*Mrs. Hale glances in a quick covert way at Mrs. Peters.*)

MRS. PETERS. Well, not now. They're superstitious, you know. They leave.

COUNTY ATTORNEY (*to Sheriff Peters, continuing an interrupted conversation*). No sign at all of anyone having come from the outside. Their own rope. Now let's go up again and go over it piece by piece. (*They start upstairs.*) It would have to have been someone who knew just the—

(*Mrs. Peters sits down. The two women sit there not looking at one another, but as if peering into something and at the same time holding back. When they talk now, it is the manner of feeling their way over strange ground, as if afraid of what they are saying, but as if they cannot help saying it.*)

MRS. HALE. She liked the bird. She was going to bury it in that pretty box.

MRS. PETERS (*in a whisper*). When I was a girl—my kitten—there was a boy took a hatchet, and before my eyes—and before I could get there—(*Covers her face an instant.*) If they hadn't held me back, I would have—(*Catches herself, looks upstairs where steps are heard, falters weakly.*)—hurt him.

MRS. HALE (*with a slow look around her*). I wonder how it would seem never to have had any children around. (*Pause.*) No, Wright wouldn't like the bird—a thing that sang. She used to sing. He killed that, too.

MRS. PETERS (*moving uneasily*). We don't know who killed the bird.

MRS. HALE. I knew John Wright.

MRS. PETERS. It was an awful thing was done in this house that night, Mrs. Hale. Killing a man while he slept, slipping a rope around his neck that choked the life out of him.

MRS. HALE. His neck. Choked the life out of him.

(*Her hand goes out and rests on the birdcage.*)

MRS. PETERS (*with a rising voice*). We don't know who killed him. We don't *know.*

MRS. HALE (*her own feeling not interrupted*). If there'd been years and years of nothing, then a bird to sing to you, it would be awful—still, after the bird was still.

MRS. PETERS (*something within her speaking*). I know what stillness is. When we homesteaded in Dakota, and my first baby died—after he was two years old, and me with no other then—

MRS. HALE (*moving*). How soon do you suppose they'll be through, looking for evidence?

MRS. PETERS. I know what stillness is. (*Pulling herself back.*) The law has got to punish crime, Mrs. Hale.

MRS. HALE (*not as if answering that*). I wish you'd seen Minnie Foster when she wore a white dress with blue ribbons and stood up there in the choir and sang. (*A look around the room.*) Oh, I *wish* I'd come over here once in a while! That was a crime! That was a crime! Who's going to punish that?

MRS. PETERS (*looking upstairs*). We mustn't—take on.

MRS. HALE. I might have known she needed help! I know how things can be—for women. I tell you, it's queer, Mrs. Peters. We live close together and we live far apart. We all go through the same things—it's all just a different kind of the same thing. (*Brushes her eyes, noticing the bottle of fruit, reaches out for it.*) If I was you, I wouldn't tell her her fruit was gone. Tell her it *ain't.* Tell her it's all right. Take this in to prove it to her. She—she may never know whether it was broke or not.

MRS. PETERS (*takes the bottle, looks about for something to wrap it in; takes petticoat from the clothes brought from the other room, very nervously begins winding this around the bottle. In a false voice*). My, it's a good thing the men couldn't hear us. Wouldn't they just laugh! Getting all stirred up over a little thing like a—dead canary. As if that could have anything to do with—with—wouldn't they *laugh!*

(*The men are heard coming downstairs.*)

MRS. HALE (*under her breath*). Maybe they would—maybe they wouldn't.

COUNTY ATTORNEY. No, Peters, it's all perfectly clear except a reason for doing it. But you know juries when it comes to women. If there was some definite thing. Something to show—something to make a story about—a thing that would connect up with this strange way of doing it.

(*The women's eyes meet for an instant. Enter Hale from outer door.*)

HALE. Well, I've got the team around. Pretty cold out there.

COUNTY ATTORNEY. I'm going to stay here awhile by myself. (*To the Sheriff.*) You can send Frank out for me, can't you? I want to go over everything. I'm not satisfied that we can't do better.

SHERIFF. Do you want to see what Mrs. Peters is going to take in?

(*The Lawyer goes to the table, picks up the apron, laughs.*)

COUNTY ATTORNEY. Oh I guess they're not very dangerous things the ladies have picked up. (*Moves a few things about, disturbing the quilt pieces which cover the box. Steps back.*) No, Mrs. Peters doesn't need supervising. For that matter, a sheriff's wife is married to the law. Ever think of it that way, Mrs. Peters?

MRS. PETERS. Not—just that way.

SHERIFF (*chuckling*). Married to the law. (*Moves toward the other room.*) I just want you to come in here a minute, George. We ought to take a look at these windows.

COUNTY ATTORNEY (*scoffingly*). Oh, windows!

SHERIFF. We'll be right out, Mr. Hale.

(*Hale goes outside. The Sheriff follows the County Attorney into the other room. Then Mrs. Hale rises, hands tight together, looking intensely at Mrs. Peters, whose eyes take a slow turn, finally meeting Mrs. Hale's. A moment Mrs. Hale holds her, then her own eyes point the way to where the box is concealed. Suddenly Mrs. Peters throws back quilt pieces and tries to put the box in the bag she is wearing. It is too big. She opens box, starts to take the bird out, cannot touch it, goes to pieces, stands there helpless. Sound of a knob turning in the other room. Mrs. Hale snatches the box and puts it in the pocket of her big coat. Enter County Attorney and Sheriff.*)

COUNTY ATTORNEY (*facetiously*). Well, Henry, at least we found out that she was not going to quilt it. She was going to—what is it you call it, ladies?

MRS. HALE (*her hand against her pocket*). We call it—knot it, Mr. Henderson.

CURTAIN

YOUR TURN

The Play on the Page

1. How would you characterize Mr. Henderson, the county attorney?
2. In what way or ways are Mrs. Peters and Mrs. Hale different from each other?
3. On page 852, when Mrs. Peters tells of the boy who killed her cat, she says, "If they hadn't held me back, I would have—(*catches herself, looks upstairs where steps are heard, falters weakly.*)—hurt him." What do you think she was about to say before she faltered? Why do you suppose Glaspell included this speech about Mrs. Peters's girlhood?
4. We never see Mrs. Wright on stage. Nevertheless, by the end of *Trifles* we know a great deal about her. Explain both what we know about her—physical characteristics, habits, interests, personality, life before her marriage and after—and *how* we know these things.
5. The title of the play is ironic—the "trifles" are important. What other ironies do you find in the play. (On *irony,* see the Glossary, page 1473.)
6. Do you think the play is immoral? Explain.
7. Assume that the canary has been found, thereby revealing a possible motive, and that Minnie is indicted for murder. You are the defense attorney. In 500 words set forth your defense. (Take any position you

wish. For instance, you may want to argue that she committed justifiable homicide or that—on the basis of her behavior as reported by Mr. Hale—she is innocent by reason of insanity.)

8. Assume that the canary had been found and Minnie Wright convicted. Compose the speech you think she might have delivered before the sentence was given.

The Play on the Stage

9. Briefly describe the setting, indicating what it "says" and what atmosphere it evokes.

10. Several times the men "laugh" or "chuckle." In their contexts, what do these expressions of amusement convey?

11. At the bottom of page 853, *"The women's eyes meet for an instant."* What do you think this bit of action "says"? What do you understand by the exchange of glances?

TENNESSEE WILLIAMS

Tennessee Williams (1914–1983) was born Thomas Lanier Williams in Columbus, Mississippi. During his childhood his family moved to St. Louis, where his father had accepted a job as manager of a shoe company. Williams has written that neither he nor his sister Rose could adjust to the change from the South to the Midwest, but the children had already been deeply troubled. Nevertheless, at the age of sixteen he achieved some distinction as a writer when his prize-winning essay in a nationwide contest was published. After high school he attended the University of Missouri but flunked ROTC and was therefore withdrawn from school by his father. He worked in a shoe factory for a while, then attended Washington University, where he wrote several plays. He finally graduated from the University of Iowa with a major in playwrighting. After graduation he continued to write, supporting himself with odd jobs such as waiting on tables and running elevators. His first commercial success was The Glass Menagerie *(produced in Chicago in 1944, and in New York in 1945); among his other plays are* A Streetcar Named Desire *(1947),* Cat on a Hot Tin Roof *(1955), and* Suddenly Last Summer *(1958).*

The Glass Menagerie [1944]

nobody, not even the rain, has such small hands.

—e. e. cummings

LIST OF CHARACTERS

AMANDA WINGFIELD, *the mother. A little woman of great but confused vitality clinging frantically to another time and place. Her characterization must be carefully created, not copied from type. She is not paranoiac, but her life is paranoia. There is much to admire in Amanda, and as much to love and pity as there is to laugh at. Certainly she has endurance and a kind of heroism, and though her foolishness makes her unwittingly cruel at times, there is tenderness in her slight person.*

Left to right: Anthony Ross (Jim), Laurette Taylor (Amanda), Eddie Dowling (Tom), and Julie Hayden (Laura) in the 1945 original production of *The Glass Menagerie*, The Playhouse, New York.

LAURA WINGFIELD, *her daughter. Amanda, having failed to establish contact with reality, continues to live vitally in her illusions, but Laura's situation is even graver. A childhood illness has left her crippled, one leg slightly shorter than the other, and held in a brace. This defect need not be more than suggested on the stage. Stemming from this, Laura's separation increases till she is like a piece of her own glass collection, too exquisitely fragile to move from the shelf.*

TOM WINGFIELD, *her son. And the narrator of the play. A poet with a job in a warehouse. His nature is not remorseless, but to escape from a trap he has to act without pity.*

JIM O'CONNOR, *the gentleman caller. A nice, ordinary, young man.*

SCENE. *An alley in St. Louis.*

PART I. *Preparation for a Gentleman Caller.*

PART II. *The Gentleman Calls.*

TIME. *Now and the Past.*

Scene I

The Wingfield apartment is in the rear of the building, one of those vast hive-like conglomerations of cellular living-units that flower as warty growths in overcrowded urban centers of lower middle-class population and are symptomatic of the impulse of this largest and fundamentally

*enslaved section of American society to avoid fluidity and differentiation
and to exist and function as one interfused mass of automatism.*

*The apartment faces an alley and is entered by a fire-escape, a struc-
ture whose name is a touch of accidental poetic truth, for all of these
huge buildings are always burning with the slow and implacable fires of
human desperation. The fire-escape is included in the set—that is, the
landing of it and steps descending from it.*

*The scene is memory and is therefore nonrealistic. Memory takes a lot
of poetic license. It omits some details; others are exaggerated, according
to the emotional value of the articles it touches, for memory is seated predominantly in the heart. The interior is therefore rather dim and poetic.*

*At the rise of the curtain, the audience is faced with the dark, grim
rear wall of the Wingfield tenement. This building, which runs parallel to
the footlights, is flanked on both sides by dark, narrow alleys which run
into murky canyons of tangled clotheslines, garbage cans and the sinister
latticework of neighboring fire-escapes. It is up and down these side alleys
that exterior entrances and exits are made, during the play. At the end
of* TOM'S *opening commentary, the dark tenement wall slowly reveals
(by means of a transparency) the interior of the ground floor Wingfield
apartment.*

*Downstage is the living room, which also serves as a sleeping room
for* LAURA, *the sofa unfolding to make her bed. Upstage, center, and divided
by a wide arch or second proscenium with transparent faded portieres
(or second curtain), is the dining room. In an old-fashioned what-not in
the living room are seen scores of transparent glass animals. A blown-up
photograph of the father hangs on the wall of the living room, facing the
audience, to the left of the archway. It is the face of a very handsome
young man in a doughboy's First World War cap. He is gallantly smiling,
ineluctably smiling, as if to say, "I will be smiling forever."*

*The audience hears and sees the opening scene in the dining room
through both the transparent fourth wall of the building and the transparent gauze portieres of the dining-room arch. It is during this revealing
scene that the fourth wall slowly ascends, out of sight.*

*This transparent exterior wall is not brought down again until the
very end of the play, during* TOM'S *final speech.*

*The narrator is an undisguised convention of the play. He takes what-
ever license with dramatic convention as is convenient to his purposes.*

TOM *enters dressed as a merchant sailor from alley, stage left, and
strolls across the front of the stage to the fire-escape. There he stops and
lights a cigarette. He addresses the audience.*

TOM. Yes, I have tricks in my pocket, I have things up my sleeve. But I am the
opposite of a stage magician. He gives you illusion that has the appearance of truth. I give you truth in the pleasant disguise of illusion. To
begin with, I turn back time. I reverse it to that quaint period, the thir-
ties, when the huge middle class of America was matriculating in a
school for the blind. Their eyes had failed them, or they had failed their
eyes, and so they were having their fingers pressed forcibly down on
the fiery Braille alphabet of a dissolving economy. In Spain there was
revolution. Here there was only shouting and confusion. In Spain there
was Guernica. Here there were disturbances of labor, sometimes pretty

violent, in otherwise peaceful cities such as Chicago, Cleveland, Saint
Louis. . . . This is the social background of the play.

(*Music.*)

The play is memory. Being a memory play, it is dimly lighted, it is sentimental, it is not realistic. In memory everything seems to happen to music. That explains the fiddle in the wings. I am the narrator of the play,
and also a character in it. The other characters are my mother, Amanda,
my sister, Laura, and a gentleman caller who appears in the final scenes.
He is the most realistic character in the play, being an emissary from a
world of reality that we were somehow set apart from. But since I have
a poet's weakness for symbols, I am using this character also as a symbol; he is the long delayed but always expected something that we live
for. There is a fifth character in the play who doesn't appear except in
this larger-than-life photograph over the mantel. This is our father who
left us a long time ago. He was a telephone man who fell in love with
long distances; he gave up his job with the telephone company and
skipped the light fantastic out of town. . . . The last we heard of him was
a picture post-card from Mazatlan, on the Pacific coast of Mexico, containing a message of two words—"Hello—Goodbye!" and no address. I
think the rest of the play will explain itself. . . .

AMANDA's *voice becomes audible through the portieres.*

(*Legend on Screen: "Où Sont les Neiges?"*[1])

He divides the portieres and enters the upstage area.

AMANDA *and* LAURA *are seated at a drop-leaf table. Eating is indicated by
gestures without food or utensils.* AMANDA *faces the audience.* TOM *and*
LAURA *are seated in profile.*

The interior has lit up softly and through the scrim we see AMANDA
and LAURA *seated at the table in the upstage area.*

AMANDA (*calling*). Tom?
TOM. Yes, Mother.
AMANDA. We can't say grace until you come to the table!
TOM. Coming, Mother. (*He bows slightly and withdraws, reappearing a few
      moments later in his place at the table.*)
AMANDA (*to her son*). Honey, don't *push* with your *fingers.* If you have to
      push with something, the thing to push with is a crust of bread. And
      chew—chew! Animals have sections in their stomachs which enable
      them to digest food without mastication, but human beings are sup-
      posed to chew their food before they swallow it down. Eat food
      leisurely, son, and really enjoy it. A well-cooked meal has lots of delicate
      flavors that have to be held in the mouth for appreciation. So chew
      your food and give your salivary glands a chance to function!

TOM *deliberately lays his imaginary fork down and pushes his chair
back from the table.*

---

[1]**Où Sont les Neiges?** Refers to "Mais où sont les neiges d'antan?" by François Villon, a
fifteenth-century French poet. It is translated by D. G. Rossetti as "Where are the snows of
yesteryear?"

TOM. I haven't enjoyed one bite of this dinner because of your constant directions on how to eat it. It's you that makes me rush through meals with your hawk-like attention to every bite I take. Sickening—spoils my appetite—all this discussion of animals' secretion—salivary glands—mastication!

AMANDA (*lightly*). Temperament like a Metropolitan[2] star! (*He rises and crosses downstage.*) You're not excused from the table.

TOM. I am getting a cigarette.

AMANDA. You smoke too much.

LAURA *rises.*

LAURA. I'll bring in the blanc mange.

He remains standing with his cigarette by the portieres during the following.

AMANDA (*rising.*) No, sister, no, sister—you be the lady this time and I'll be the darky.

LAURA. I'm already up.

AMANDA. Resume your seat, little sister—I want you to stay fresh and pretty—for gentlemen callers!

LAURA. I'm not expecting any gentlemen callers.

AMANDA (*crossing out to kitchenette. Airily*). Sometimes they come when they are least expected! Why, I remember one Sunday afternoon in Blue Mountain—(*Enters kitchenette.*)

TOM. I know what's coming!

LAURA. Yes. But let her tell it.

TOM. Again?

LAURA. She loves to tell it.

AMANDA *returns with bowl of dessert.*

AMANDA. One Sunday afternoon in Blue Mountain—your mother received—*seventeen!*—gentlemen callers! Why, sometimes there weren't chairs enough to accommodate them all. We had to send the nigger over to bring in folding chairs from the parish house.

TOM (*remaining at portieres*). How did you entertain those gentlemen callers?

AMANDA. I understood the art of conversation!

TOM. I bet you could talk.

AMANDA. Girls in those days *knew* how to talk, I can tell you.

TOM. Yes?

(*Image:* AMANDA *as a Girl on a Porch Greeting Callers.*)

AMANDA. They knew how to entertain their gentlemen callers. It wasn't enough for a girl to be possessed of a pretty face and a graceful figure—although I wasn't slighted in either respect. She also needed to have a nimble wit and a tongue to meet all occasions.

TOM. What did you talk about?

---

[2]**Metropolitan** Refers to the Metropolitan Opera in New York City, founded in April 1880.

AMANDA. Things of importance going on in the world! Never anything coarse or common or vulgar. (*She addresses* TOM *as though he were seated in the vacant chair at the table though he remains by portieres. He plays this scene as though he held the book.*) My callers were gentlemen—all! Among my callers were some of the most prominent young planters of the Mississippi Delta—planters and sons of planters!

TOM *motions for music and a spot of light on* AMANDA.

Her eyes lift, her face glows, her voice becomes rich and elegiac.

(*Screen Legend:"Où Sont les Neiges?"*)

There was young Champ Laughlin who later became vice-president of the Delta Planters Bank. Hadley Stevenson who was drowned in Moon Lake and left his widow one hundred and fifty thousand in Government bonds. There were the Cutrere brothers, Wesley and Bates. Bates was one of my bright particular beaux! He got in a quarrel with that wild Wainright boy. They shot it out on the floor of Moon Lake Casino. Bates was shot through the stomach. Died in the ambulance on his way to Memphis. His widow was also well-provided for, came into eight or ten thousand acres, that's all. She married him on the rebound—never loved her—carried my picture on him the night he died! And there was that boy that every girl in Delta had set her cap for! That beautiful, brilliant young Fitzhugh boy from Green County!

TOM. What did he leave his widow?

AMANDA. He never married! Gracious, you talk as though all of my old admirers had turned up their toes to the daisies!

TOM. Isn't this the first you mentioned that still survives?

AMANDA. That Fitzhugh boy went North and made a fortune—came to be known as the Wolf of Wall Street! He had the Midas touch, whatever he touched turned to gold! And I could have been Mrs. Duncan J. Fitzhugh, mind you! But—I picked your *father!*

LAURA (*rising*). Mother, let me clear the table.

AMANDA. No dear, you go in front and study your typewriter chart. Or practice your shorthand a little. Stay fresh and pretty!—It's almost time for our gentlemen callers to start arriving. (*She flounces girlishly toward the kitchenette.*) How many do you suppose we're going to entertain this afternoon?

TOM *throws down the paper and jumps up with a groan.*

LAURA (*alone in the dining room*). I don't believe we're going to receive any, Mother.

AMANDA (*reappearing, airily*). What? No one—not one? You must be joking! (LAURA *nervously echoes her laugh. She slips in a fugitive manner through the half-open portieres and draws them gently behind her. A shaft of very clear light is thrown on her face against the faded tapestry of the curtains.*) (*Music: "The Glass Menagerie" Under Faintly.*) (*Lightly.*) Not one gentleman caller? It can't be true! There must be a flood, there must have been a tornado!

LAURA. It isn't a flood, it's not a tornado, Mother. I'm just not popular like you were in Blue Mountain. . . . (TOM *utters another groan.* LAURA *glances at him with a faint, apologetic smile. Her voice catching a little.*) Mother's afraid I'm going to be an old maid.

(The Scene Dims Out with "Glass Menagerie" Music.)

Scene II

"Laura, Haven't You Ever Liked Some Boy?"

On the dark stage the screen is lighted with the image of blue roses.

Gradually LAURA'S *figure becomes apparent and the screen goes out. The music subsides.*

LAURA *is seated in the delicate ivory chair at the small clawfoot table.*

She wears a dress of soft violet material for a kimono—her hair tied back from her forehead with a ribbon.

She is washing and polishing her collection of glass.

AMANDA *appears on the fire-escape steps. At the sound of her ascent,* LAURA *catches her breath, thrusts the bowl of ornaments away and seats herself stiffly before the diagram of the typewriter keyboard as though it held her spellbound. Something has happened to* AMANDA. *It is written in her face as she climbs to the landing: a look that is grim and hopeless and a little absurd.*

She has on one of those cheap or imitation velvety-looking cloth coats with imitation fur collar. Her hat is five or six years old, one of those dreadful cloche hats that were worn in the late twenties, and she is clasping an enormous black patent-leather pocketbook with nickel clasp and initials. This is her full-dress outfit, the one she usually wears to the D.A.R.[3]

Before entering she looks through the door.

She purses her lips, opens her eyes wide, rolls them upward and shakes her head.

Then she slowly lets herself in the door. Seeing her mother's expression LAURA *touches her lips with a nervous gesture.*

LAURA. Hello, Mother, I was—(*She makes a nervous gesture toward the chart on the wall.* AMANDA *leans against the shut door and stares at* LAURA *with a martyred look.*)

AMANDA. Deception? Deception? (*She slowly removes her hat and gloves, continuing the swift suffering stare. She lets the hat and gloves fall on the floor—a bit of acting.*)

LAURA (*shakily.*) How was the D.A.R. meeting? (AMANDA *slowly opens her purse and removes a dainty white handkerchief which she shakes out delicately and delicately touches to her lips and nostrils.*) Didn't you go to the D.A.R. meeting, Mother?

AMANDA (*faintly, almost inaudibly*). —No.—No. (*Then more forcibly.*) I did not have the strength—to go to the D.A.R. In fact, I did not have the courage! I wanted to find a hole in the ground and hide myself in it forever! (*She crosses slowly to the wall and removes the diagram of the typewriter keyboard. She holds it in front of her for a second, staring at it sweetly and sorrowfully—then bites her lips and tears it in two pieces.*)

LAURA (*faintly*). Why did you do that, Mother? (AMANDA *repeats the same procedure with the chart of the Gregg Alphabet.*) Why are you—

---

[3]**D.A.R.** The abbreviation for Daughters of the American Revolution, a charitable organization dedicated to patriotism, historic preservation, and education.

AMANDA. Why? Why? How old are you, Laura?

LAURA. Mother, you know my age.

AMANDA. I thought that you were an adult; it seems that I was mistaken. (*She crosses slowly to the sofa and sinks down and stares at* LAURA.)

LAURA. Please don't stare at me, Mother.

AMANDA *closes her eyes and lowers her head. Count ten.*

AMANDA. What are we going to do, what is going to become of us, what is the future?

Count ten.

LAURA. Has something happened, Mother? (AMANDA *draws a long breath and takes out the handkerchief again. Dabbing process.*) Mother, has— something happened?

AMANDA. I'll be all right in a minute. I'm just bewildered—(*count five*)—by life. . . .

LAURA. Mother, I wish that you would tell me what's happened.

AMANDA. As you know, I was supposed to be inducted into my office at the D.A.R. this afternoon. (*Image: A Swarm of Typewriters.*) But I stopped off at Rubicam's Business College to speak to your teachers about your having a cold and ask them what progress they thought you were making down there.

LAURA. Oh. . . .

AMANDA. I went to the typing instructor and introduced myself as your mother. She didn't know who you were. Wingfield, she said. We don't have any such student enrolled at the school! I assured her she did, that you had been going to classes since early in January. "I wonder," she said, "if you could be talking about that terribly shy little girl who dropped out of school after only a few days' attendance?" "No," I said, "Laura, my daughter, has been going to school every day for the past six weeks!" "Excuse me," she said. She took the attendance book out and there was your name, un- mistakably printed, and all the dates you were absent until they decided that you had dropped out of school. I still said, "No, there must have been some mistake! There must have been some mix-up in the records!" And she said, "No—I remember her perfectly now. Her hand shook so that she couldn't hit the right keys! The first time we gave a speed-test, she broke down completely—was sick at the stomach and almost had to be carried into the wash-room! After that morning she never showed up any more. We phoned the house but never got any answer"—while I was working at Famous and Barr, I suppose, demonstrating those—Oh! I felt so weak I could barely keep on my feet. I had to sit down while they got me a glass of water! Fifty dollars' tuition, all of our plans—my hopes and ambitions for you—just gone up the spout, just gone up the spout like that. (LAURA *draws a long breath and gets awkwardly to her feet. She crosses to the victrola and winds it up.*) What are you doing?

LAURA. Oh! (*She releases the handle and returns to her seat.*)

AMANDA. Laura, where have you been going when you've gone out pretend- ing that you were going to business college?

LAURA. I've just been going out walking.

AMANDA. That's not true.

LAURA. It is. I just went walking.

AMANDA. Walking? Walking? In winter? Deliberately courting pneumonia in
that light coat? Where did you walk to, Laura?

LAURA. It was the lesser of two evils, Mother. (*Image: Winter Scene in Park.*)
I couldn't go back up. I—threw up—on the floor!

AMANDA. From half past seven till after five every day you mean to tell me you
walked around in the park, because you wanted to make me think that
you were still going to Rubicam's Business College?

LAURA. It wasn't as bad as it sounds. I went inside places to get warmed up.

AMANDA. Inside where?

LAURA. I went in the art museum and the bird-houses at the Zoo. I visited the
penguins every day! Sometimes I did without lunch and went to the
movies. Lately I've been spending most of my afternoons in the Jewel-
box, that big glass house where they raise the tropical flowers.

AMANDA. You did all this to deceive me, just for the deception? (LAURA *looks
down.*) Why?

LAURA. Mother, when you're disappointed, you get that awful suffering look
on your face, like the picture of Jesus' mother in the museum!

AMANDA. Hush!

LAURA. I couldn't face it.

Pause. A whisper of strings.

(*Legend: "The Crust of Humility."*)

AMANDA (*hopelessly fingering the huge pocketbook*). So what are we going
to do the rest of our lives? Stay home and watch the parades go by?
Amuse ourselves with the glass menagerie, darling? Eternally play those
worn-out phonograph records your father left as a painful reminder of
him? We won't have a business career—we've given that up because it
gave us nervous indigestion! (*Laughs wearily.*) What is there left but de-
pendency all our lives? I know so well what becomes of unmarried
women who aren't prepared to occupy a position. I've seen such pitiful
cases in the South—barely tolerated spinsters living upon the grudging
patronage of sister's husband or brother's wife!—stuck away in some little mousetrap of a room—encouraged by one in-law to visit another—
little birdlike women without any nest—eating the crust of humility all
their life! Is that the future that we've mapped out for ourselves? I swear
it's the only alternative I can think of! It isn't a very pleasant alternative,
is it? Of course—some girls *do marry.* (LAURA *twists her hands nervously.*) Haven't you ever liked some boy?

LAURA. Yes. I liked one once. (*Rises.*) I came across his picture a while ago.

AMANDA (*with some interest*). He gave you his picture?

LAURA. No, it's in the year-book.

AMANDA (*disappointed*). Oh—a high-school boy.

(*Screen Image:* JIM *as a High-School Hero Bearing a Silver Cup.*)

LAURA. Yes. His name was Jim. (LAURA *lifts the heavy annual from the clawfoot table.*) Here he is in *The Pirates of Penzance.*

AMANDA (*absently*). The what?

LAURA. The operetta the senior class put on. He had a wonderful voice and
we sat across the aisle from each other Mondays, Wednesdays and Fridays in the Aud. Here he is with the silver cup for debating! See his grin?

AMANDA (*absently*). He must have had a jolly disposition.

LAURA. He used to call me—Blue Roses.

(*Image: Blue Roses.*)

AMANDA. Why did he call you such a name as that?

LAURA. When I had that attack of pleurosis—he asked me what was the matter when I came back. I said pleurosis—he thought that I said Blue Roses! So that's what he always called me after that. Whenever he saw me, he'd holler, "Hello, Blue Roses!" I didn't care for the girl that he went out with. Emily Meisenbach. Emily was the best-dressed girl at Soldan. She never struck me, though, as being sincere. . . . It says in the Personal Section— they're engaged. That's—six years ago! They must be married by now.

AMANDA. Girls that aren't cut out for business careers usually wind up married to some nice man. (*Gets up with a spark of revival.*) Sister, that's what you'll do!

LAURA *utters a startled, doubtful laugh. She reaches quickly for a piece of glass.*

LAURA. But, Mother—

AMANDA. Yes? (*Crossing to photograph.*)

LAURA (*in a tone of frightened apology*). I'm—crippled!

(*Image: Screen.*)

AMANDA. Nonsense! Laura, I've told you never, never to use that word. Why, you're not crippled, you just have a little defect—hardly noticeable, even! When people have some slight disadvantage like that, they cultivate other things to make up for it—develop charm—and vivacity— and—*charm!* That's all you have to do! (*She turns again to the photograph.*) One thing your father had *plenty* of—was *charm!*

TOM *motions to the fiddle in the wings.*

(*The Scene Fades Out with Music.*)

Scene III

(*Legend on the Screen: "After the Fiasco—"*)

TOM *speaks from the fire-escape landing.*

TOM. After the fiasco at Rubicam's Business College, the idea of getting a gentleman caller for Laura began to play a more important part in Mother's calculations. It became an obsession. Like some archetype of the universal unconscious, the image of the gentleman caller haunted our small apartment. . . . (*Image: Young Man at Door with Flowers.*) An evening at home rarely passed without some allusion to this image, this specter, this hope. . . . Even when he wasn't mentioned, his presence hung in Mother's preoccupied look and in my sister's frightened, apologetic manner—hung like a sentence passed upon the Wingfields! Mother was a woman of action as well as words. She began to take logical steps in the planned direction. Late that winter and in the early spring—realizing that extra money would be needed to properly feather the nest and plume the bird—she conducted a vigorous campaign on the telephone, roping in subscribers to one of those magazines for matrons called *The*

Home-maker's Companion, the type of journal that features the serial-
ized sublimations of ladies of letters who think in terms of delicate cup-
like breasts, slim, tapering waists, rich, creamy thighs, eyes like wood-
smoke in autumn, fingers that soothe and caress like strains of music,
bodies as powerful as Etruscan sculpture.

(Screen Image: Glamor Magazine Cover.)

AMANDA *enters with phone on long extension cord. She is spotted in
the dim stage.*

AMANDA. Ida Scott? This is Amanda Wingfield! We *missed* you at the D.A.R. last
Monday! I said to myself: She's probably suffering with that sinus condition! How is that sinus condition? Horrors! Heaven have mercy!—You're
a Christian martyr, yes, that's what you are, a Christian martyr! Well, I just
now happened to notice that your subscription to the *Companion's*
about to expire! Yes, it expires with the next issue, honey!—just when
that wonderful new serial by Bessie Mae Hopper is getting off to such an
exciting start. Oh, honey, it's something that you can't miss! You remember how *Gone With the Wind* took everybody by storm? You simply
couldn't go out if you hadn't read it. All everybody *talked* was Scarlett
O'Hara. Well, this is a book that critics already compare to *Gone With the
Wind.* It's the *Gone With the Wind* of the post–World War generation!—
What?—Burning?—Oh, honey, don't let them burn, go take a look in the
oven and I'll hold the wire! Heavens—I think she's hung up!

(Dim Out.)

*(Legend on Screen: "You Think I'm in Love with Continental
Shoemakers?")*

Before the stage is lighted, the violent voices of TOM *and* AMANDA *are
heard. They are quarreling behind the portieres. In front of them
stands* LAURA *with clenched hands and panicky expression.*

A clear pool of light on her figure throughout this scene.

TOM. What in Christ's name am I—
AMANDA *(shrilly).* Don't you use that—
TOM. Supposed to do!
AMANDA. Expression! Not in my—
TOM. Ohhh!
AMANDA. Presence! Have you gone out of your senses?
TOM. I have, that's true, *driven* out!
AMANDA. What is the matter with you, you—big—big—IDIOT!
TOM. Look—I've got *no thing,* no single thing—
AMANDA. Lower your voice!
TOM. In my life here that I can call my OWN! Everything is—
AMANDA. Stop that shouting!
TOM. Yesterday you confiscated my books! You had the nerve to—
AMANDA. I took that horrible novel back to the library—yes! That hideous
book by that insane Mr. Lawrence. (TOM *laughs wildly.*) I cannot control
the output of diseased minds or people who cater to them—(TOM
laughs still more wildly.) BUT I WON'T ALLOW SUCH FILTH BROUGHT INTO MY
HOUSE! No, no, no, no, no!

TOM. House, house! Who pays rent on it, who makes a slave of himself to—

AMANDA (*fairly screeching*). Don't you DARE to—

TOM. No, no, *I* musn't say things! *I've* got to just—

AMANDA. Let me tell you—

TOM. I don't want to hear any more! (*He tears the portieres open. The up-stage area is lit with a turgid smoky red glow.*)

AMANDA's *hair is in metal curlers and she wears a very old bathrobe, much too large for her slight figure, a relic of the faithless* MR. WINGFIELD.

An upright typewriter and a wild disarray of manuscripts are on the dropleaf table. The quarrel was probably precipitated by AMANDA's *interruption of his creative labor. A chair lying overthrown on the floor.*

Their gesticulating shadows are cast on the ceiling by the fiery glow.

AMANDA. You *will* hear more, you—

TOM. No, I won't hear more, I'm going out!

AMANDA. You come right back in—

TOM. Out, out, out! Because I'm—

AMANDA. Come back here, Tom Wingfield! I'm not through talking to you!

TOM. Oh, go—

LAURA (*desperately*). Tom!

AMANDA. You're going to listen, and no more insolence from you! I'm at the end of my patience! (*He comes back toward her.*)

TOM. What do you think I'm at? Aren't I supposed to have any patience to reach the end of, Mother? I know, I know. It seems unimportant to you, what I'm *doing*—what I *want* to do—having a little *difference* between them! You don't think that—

AMANDA. I think you've been doing things that you're ashamed of. That's why you act like this. I don't believe that you go every night to the movies. Nobody goes to the movies night after night. Nobody in their right minds goes to the movies as often as you pretend to. People don't go to the movies at nearly midnight, and movies don't let out at two A.M. Come in stumbling. Muttering to yourself like a maniac! You get three hours' sleep and then go to work. Oh, I can picture the way you're do-ing down there. Moping, doping, because you're in no condition.

TOM (*wildly*). No, I'm in no condition!

AMANDA. What right have you got to jeopardize your job? Jeopardize the se-curity of us all? How do you think we'd manage if you were—

TOM. Listen! You think I'm crazy *about the warehouse?* (*He bends fiercely toward her slight figure.*) You think I'm in love with the Continental Shoemakers? You think I want to spend fifty-five *years* down there in that—*celotex interior!* with—*fluorescent—tubes!* Look! I'd rather somebody picked up a crowbar and battered out my brains—than go back mornings! I go! Every time you come in yelling that God damn *"Rise and Shine!" "Rise and Shine!"* I say to myself "How *lucky dead* people are!" But I get up. I *go!* For sixty-five dollars a month I give up all that I dream of doing and being *ever!* And you say self—*self's* all I ever think of. Why, listen, if self is what I thought of, Mother, I'd be where he is—GONE! (*Pointing to father's picture.*) As far as the system of trans-portation reaches! (*He starts past her. She grabs his arm.*) Don't grab at me, Mother!

AMANDA. Where are you going?

TOM. I'm going to the *movies!*

AMANDA. I don't believe that lie!

TOM (*crouching toward her, overtowering her tiny figure. She backs away, gasping*). I'm going to opium dens! Yes, opium dens, dens of vice and criminals' hang-outs, Mother. I've joined the Hogan gang, I'm a hired assassin, I carry a tommy-gun in a violin case! I run a string of cat-houses in the Valley! They call me Killer, Killer Wingfield, I'm leading a double-life, a simple, honest warehouse worker by day, by night a dynamic *czar* of the *underworld, Mother.* I go to gambling casinos, I spin away fortunes on the roulette table! I wear a patch over one eye and a false mustache, sometimes I put on green whiskers. On those occasions they call me—*El Diablo!* Oh, I could tell you things to make you sleepless! My enemies plan to dynamite this place. They're going to blow us all sky-high some night! I'll be glad, very happy, and so will you! You'll go up, up on a broomstick, over Blue Mountain with seventeen gentlemen callers! You ugly—babbling old—*witch*. . . . (*He goes through a series of violent, clumsy movements, seizing his overcoat, lunging to the door, pulling it fiercely open. The women watch him, aghast. His arm catches in the sleeve of the coat as he struggles to pull it on. For a moment he is pinioned by the bulky garment. With an outraged groan he tears the coat off again, splitting the shoulders of it, and hurls it across the room. It strikes against the shelf of Laura's glass collection, there is a tinkle of shattering glass.* LAURA *cries out as if wounded.*)

(*Music Legend: "The Glass Menagerie."*)

LAURA (*shrilly*). My glass!—menagerie. . . . (*She covers her face and turns away.*)

But AMANDA *is still stunned and stupefied by the "ugly witch" so that she barely notices this occurrence. Now she recovers her speech.*

AMANDA (*in an awful voice*). I won't speak to you—until you apologize! (*She crosses through portieres and draws them together behind her.* TOM *is left with* LAURA. LAURA *clings weakly to the mantel with her face averted.* TOM *stares at her stupidly for a moment. Then he crosses to shelf. Drops awkwardly to his knees to collect the fallen glass, glancing at* LAURA *as if he would speak but couldn't.*)

"The Glass Menagerie" steals in as

(*The Scene Dims Out.*)

Scene IV

The interior is dark. Faint light in the alley.

A deep-voiced bell in a church is tolling the hour of five as the scene commences.

TOM *appears at the top of the alley. After each solemn boom of the bell in the tower, he shakes a little noise-maker or rattle as if to express the tiny spasm of man in contrast to the sustained power and dignity of the Almighty. This and the unsteadiness of his advance make it evident that he has been drinking.*

As he climbs the few steps to the fire-escape landing light steals up inside. LAURA *appears in night-dress, observing* TOM'S *empty bed in the front room.*

TOM *fishes in his pockets for the door-key, removing a motley assortment of articles in the search, including a perfect shower of movie-ticket stubs and an empty bottle. At last he finds the key, but just as he is about to insert it, it slips from his fingers. He strikes a match and crouches below the door.*

TOM (*bitterly*). One crack—and it falls through!

LAURA *opens the door.*

LAURA. Tom! Tom, what are you doing?

TOM. Looking for a door-key.

LAURA. Where have you been all this time?

TOM. I have been to the movies.

LAURA. All this time at the movies?

TOM. There was a very long program. There was a Garbo[4] picture and a Mickey Mouse and a travelogue and a newsreel and a preview of coming attractions. And there was an organ solo and a collection for the milk-fund—simultaneously—which ended up in a terrible fight between a fat lady and an usher!

LAURA (*innocently*). Did you have to stay through everything?

TOM. Of course! And, oh, I forgot! There was a big stage show! The headliner on this stage show was Malvolio the Magician. He performed wonderful tricks, many of them, such as pouring water back and forth between pitchers. First it turned to wine and then it turned to beer and then it turned to whiskey. I know it was whiskey it finally turned into because he needed somebody to come up out of the audience to help him, and I came up—both shows! It was Kentucky Straight Bourbon. A very generous fellow, he gave souvenirs. (*He pulls from his back pocket a shimmering rainbow-colored scarf.*) He gave me this. This is his magic scarf. You can have it, Laura. You wave it over a canary cage and you get a bowl of gold-fish. You wave it over the gold-fish bowl and they fly away canaries.... But the wonderfullest trick of all was the coffin trick. We nailed him into a coffin and he got out of the coffin without removing one nail. (*He has come inside.*) There is a trick that would come in handy for me—get me out of this 2 by 4 situation! (*Flops onto bed and starts removing shoes.*)

LAURA. Tom—Shhh!

TOM. What you shushing me for?

LAURA. You'll wake up Mother.

TOM. Goody, goody! Pay 'er back for all those "Rise an' Shines." (*Lies down, groaning.*) You know it don't take much intelligence to get yourself into a nailed-up coffin, Laura. But who in hell ever got himself out of one without removing one nail?

As if in answer, the father's grinning photograph lights up.

(*Scene Dims Out.*)

Immediately following: The church bell is heard striking six. At the sixth stroke the alarm clock goes off in AMANDA'S *room, and after a few*

---

[4]**Garbo** Greta Garbo (1905–1980), one of the greatest Hollywood film stars.

moments we hear her calling:"Rise and Shine! Rise and Shine! LAURA,
go tell your brother to rise and shine!"

TOM (*sitting up slowly*). I'll rise—but I won't shine.

The light increases.

AMANDA. Laura, tell your brother his coffee is ready.

LAURA *slips into front room.*

LAURA. Tom! It's nearly seven. Don't make Mother nervous. (*He stares at her
   stupidly. Beseechingly.*) Tom, speak to Mother this morning. Make up
   with her, apologize, speak to her!

TOM. She won't to me. It's her that started not speaking.

LAURA. If you just say you're sorry she'll start speaking.

TOM. Her not speaking—is that such a tragedy?

LAURA. Please—please!

AMANDA (*calling from kitchenette*). Laura, are you going to do what I asked
   you to do, or do I have to get dressed and go out myself?

LAURA. Going, going—soon as I get on my coat! (*She pulls on a shapeless felt
   hat with nervous, jerky movement, pleadingly glancing at* TOM.
   Rushes awkwardly for coat. The coat is one of AMANDA'S, *inaccurately
   made-over, the sleeves too short for* LAURA.) Butter and what else?

AMANDA (*entering upstage*). Just butter. Tell them to charge it.

LAURA. Mother, they make such faces when I do that.

AMANDA. Sticks and stones may break my bones, but the expression on Mr.
   Garfinkel's face won't harm us! Tell your brother his coffee is getting cold.

LAURA (*at door*). Do what I asked you, will you, will you, Tom?

He looks sullenly away.

AMANDA. Laura, go now or just don't go at all!

LAURA (*rushing out*). Going—going! (*A second later she cries out.* TOM
   springs up and crosses to the door. AMANDA *rushes anxiously in.* TOM
   opens the door.)

TOM. Laura?

LAURA. I'm all right. I slipped, but I'm all right.

AMANDA (*peering anxiously after her*). If anyone breaks a leg on those fire-
   escape steps, the landlord ought to be sued for every cent he possesses!
   (*She shuts door. Remembers she isn't speaking and returns to other
   room.*)

As TOM *enters listlessly for his coffee, she turns her back to him and
stands rigidly facing the window on the gloomy gray vault of the
areaway. Its light on her face with its aged but childish features is cruelly sharp, satirical as a Daumier print.*

(*Music Under: "Ave Maria."*)

TOM *glances sheepishly but sullenly at her averted figure and slumps
at the table. The coffee is scalding hot; he sips it and gasps and spits it
back in the cup. At his gasp,* AMANDA *catches her breath and half turns.
Then catches herself and turns back to window.*

TOM *blows on his coffee, glancing sidewise at his mother. She clears
her throat.* TOM *clears his. He starts to rise. Sinks back down again,
scratches his head, clears his throat again.* AMANDA *coughs.* TOM *raises*

his cup in both hands to blow on it, his eyes staring over the rim of it
at his mother for several moments. Then he slowly sets the cup down
and awkwardly and hesitantly rises from the chair.

TOM (*hoarsely*).   Mother. I—I apologize. Mother. (AMANDA *draws a quick, shud-*
dering breath. Her face works grotesquely. She breaks into childlike
tears.) I'm sorry for what I said, for everything that I said, I didn't mean it.

AMANDA (*sobbingly*).   My devotion has made me a witch and so I make myself hateful to my children!

TOM.   No you *don't.*

AMANDA.   I worry so much, don't sleep, it makes me nervous!

TOM (*gently*).   I understand that.

AMANDA.   I've had to put up a solitary battle all these years. But you're my
right-hand bower! Don't fall down, don't fail!

TOM (*gently*).   I try, Mother.

AMANDA (*with great enthusiasm*).   Try and you will SUCCEED! (*The notion*
makes her breathless.) Why, you—you're just *full* of natural endow-
ments! Both of my children—they're *unusual* children! Don't you think
I know it? I'm so—*proud!* Happy and—feel I've—so much to be thankful for but—Promise me one thing, son!

TOM.   What, Mother?

AMANDA.   Promise, son, you'll—never be a drunkard!

TOM (*turns to her grinning*).   I will never be a drunkard, Mother.

AMANDA.   That's what frightened me so, that you'd be drinking! Eat a bowl of
Purina!

TOM.   Just coffee, Mother.

AMANDA.   Shredded wheat biscuit?

TOM.   No. No, Mother, just coffee.

AMANDA.   You can't put in a day's work on an empty stomach. You've got ten
minutes—don't gulp! Drinking too-hot liquids makes cancer of the
stomach. . . . Put cream in.

TOM.   No, thank you.

AMANDA.   To cool it.

TOM.   No! No, thank you, I want it black.

AMANDA.   I know, but it's not good for you. We have to do all that we can to
build ourselves up. In these trying times we live in, all that we have to
cling to is—each other. . . . That's why it's so important to—Tom, I—I
sent out your sister so I could discuss something with you. If you hadn't
spoken I would have spoken to you. (*Sits down.*)

TOM (*gently*).   What is it, Mother, that you want to discuss?

AMANDA.   Laura!

TOM *puts his cup down slowly.*

(*Legend on Screen:* "LAURA.")

(*Music: "The Glass Menagerie."*)

TOM.   —Oh.—Laura . . .

AMANDA (*touching his sleeve*).   You know how Laura is. So quiet but—still
water runs deep! She notices things and I think she—broods about
them. (TOM *looks up.*) A few days ago I came in and she was crying.

TOM.   What about?

AMANDA.   You.

TOM. Me?

AMANDA. She has an idea that you're not happy here.

TOM. What gave her that idea?

AMANDA. What gives her any idea? However, you do act strangely. I—I'm not criticizing, understand *that!* I know your ambitions do not lie in the warehouse, that like everybody in the whole wide world—you've had to—make sacrifices, but—Tom—Tom—life's not easy, it calls for—Spartan endurance! There's so many things in my heart that I cannot describe to you! I've never told you but I—*loved* your father. . . .

TOM (*gently*). I know that, Mother.

AMANDA. And you—when I see you taking after his ways! Staying out late—and—well, you *had* been drinking the night you were in that—terrifying condition! Laura says that you hate the apartment and that you go out nights to get away from it! Is that true, Tom?

TOM. No. You say there's so much in your heart that you can't describe to me. That's true of me, too. There's so much in my heart that I can't describe to *you!* So let's respect each other's—

AMANDA. But, why—*why,* Tom—are you always so *restless?* Where do you go to, nights?

TOM. I—go to the movies.

AMANDA. Why do you go to the movies so much, Tom?

TOM. I go to the movies because—I like adventure. Adventure is something I don't have much of at work, so I go to the movies.

AMANDA. But, Tom, you go to the movies *entirely too much!*

TOM. I like a lot of adventure.

> AMANDA *looks baffled, then hurt. As the familiar inquisition resumes he becomes hard and impatient again.* AMANDA *slips back into her querulous attitude toward him.*

> (*Image on Screen: Sailing Vessel with Jolly Roger[5].*)

AMANDA. Most young men find adventure in their careers.

TOM. Then most young men are not employed in a warehouse.

AMANDA. The world is full of young men employed in warehouses and offices and factories.

TOM. Do all of them find adventure in their careers?

AMANDA. They do or they do without it! Not everybody has a craze for adventure.

TOM. Man is by instinct a lover, a hunter, a fighter, and none of those instincts are given much play at the warehouse!

AMANDA. Man is by instinct! Don't quote instinct to me! Instinct is something that people have got away from! It belongs to animals! Christian adults don't want it!

TOM. What do Christian adults want, then, Mother?

AMANDA. Superior things! Things of the mind and the spirit! Only animals have to satisfy instincts! Surely your aims are somewhat higher than theirs! Than monkeys—pigs—

TOM. I reckon they're not.

---

[5]**Jolly Roger** The name given to a flag flown to identify a ship's crew as pirates.

AMANDA. You're joking. However, that isn't what I wanted to discuss.

TOM (*rising*). I haven't much time.

AMANDA (*pushing his shoulders*). Sit down.

TOM. You want me to punch in red at the warehouse, Mother?

AMANDA. You have five minutes. I want to talk about Laura.

   (*Legend: "Plans and Provisions."*)

TOM. All right! What about Laura?

AMANDA. We have to be making plans and provisions for her. She's older than
   you, two years, and nothing has happened. She just drifts along doing
   nothing. It frightens me terribly how she just drifts along.

TOM. I guess she's the type that people call home girls.

AMANDA. There's no such type, and if there is, it's a pity! That is unless the
   home is hers, with a husband!

TOM. What?

AMANDA. Oh, I can see the handwriting on the wall as plain as I see the nose
   in the front of my face! It's terrifying! More and more you remind me of
   your father! He was out all hours without explanation—Then *left!*
   Goodbye! And me with the bag to hold. I saw that letter you got from
   the Merchant Marine. I know what you're dreaming of. I'm not standing
   here blindfolded. Very well, then. Then *do* it! But not till there's somebody to take your place.

TOM. What do you mean?

AMANDA. I mean that as soon as Laura has got somebody to take care of her,
   married, a home of her own, independent—why, then you'll be free to go
   wherever you please, on land, on sea, whichever way the wind blows! But
   until that time you've got to look out for your sister. I don't say me because I'm old and don't matter! I say for your sister because she's young
   and dependent. I put her in business college—a dismal failure! Frightened her so it made her sick to her stomach. I took her over to the Young
   People's League at the church. Another fiasco. She spoke to nobody, nobody spoke to her. Now all she does is fool with those pieces of glass and
   play those worn-out records. What kind of a life is that for a girl to lead!

TOM. What can I do about it?

AMANDA. Overcome selfishness! Self, self, self is all that you ever think of!
   (TOM *springs up and crosses to get his coat. It is ugly and bulky. He
   pulls on a cap with earmuffs.*) Where is your muffler? Put your wool
   muffler on! (*He snatches it angrily from the closet and tosses it
   around his neck and pulls both ends tight.*) Tom! I haven't said what I
   had in mind to ask you.

TOM. I'm too late to—

AMANDA (*catching his arms—very importunately. Then shyly*). Down at the
   warehouse, aren't there some—nice young men?

TOM. No!

AMANDA. There *must* be—*some.*

TOM. Mother—

        Gesture.

AMANDA. Find one that's clean-living—doesn't drink and—ask him out for
   sister!

TOM. What?

AMANDA. For *sister!* To *meet!* Get *acquainted!*

TOM (*stamping to door*). Oh, my *go-osh!*

AMANDA. Will you? (*He opens door. Imploringly.*) Will you? (*He starts down.*) Will you? *Will* you dear?

TOM (*calling back*). YES!

> AMANDA *closes the door hesitantly and with a troubled but faintly hopeful expression.*
>
> (*Screen Image: Glamor Magazine Cover.*)
>
> *Spot* AMANDA *at phone.*

AMANDA. Ella Cartwright? This is Amanda Wingfield! How are you honey? How is that kidney condition? (*Count five.*) Horrors! (*Count five.*) You're a Christian martyr, yes, honey, that's what you are, a Christian martyr! Well, I just happened to notice in my little red book that your subscription to the *Companion* has just run out! I knew that you wouldn't want to miss out on the wonderful serial starting in this new issue. It's by Bessie Mae Hopper, the first thing she's written since *Honeymoon for Three.* Wasn't that a strange and interesting story? Well, this one is even lovelier, I believe. It has a sophisticated society back-ground. It's all about the horsey set on Long Island!

> (*Fade Out.*)

Scene V

(*Legend on Screen: "Annunciation."*) *Fade with music.*

> *It is early dusk of a spring evening. Supper has just been finished at the Wingfield apartment.* AMANDA *and* LAURA *in light-colored dresses are re-moving dishes from the table, in the upstage area, which is shadowy, their movements formalized almost as a dance or ritual, their moving forms as pale and silent as moths.*
>
> TOM, *in white shirt and trousers, rises from the table and crosses to-ward the fire-escape.*

AMANDA (*as he passes her*). Son, will you do me a favor?

TOM. What?

AMANDA. Comb your hair! You look so pretty when your hair is combed! (TOM *slouches on sofa with evening paper. Enormous caption "Franco Triumphs."*) There is only one respect in which I would like you to em-ulate your father.

TOM. What respect is that?

AMANDA. The care he always took of his appearance. He never allowed him-self to look untidy. (*He throws down the paper and crosses to fire-escape.*) Where are you going?

TOM. I'm going out to smoke.

AMANDA. You smoke too much. A pack a day at fifteen cents a pack. How much would that amount to in a month? Thirty times fifteen is how much, Tom? Figure it out and you will be astounded at what you could save. Enough to give you a night-school course in accounting at Washing-ton U! Just think what a wonderful thing that would be for you, son!

> TOM *is unmoved by the thought.*

TOM. I'd rather smoke. (*He steps out on landing, letting the screen door slam.*)

AMANDA (*sharply*). I know! That's the tragedy of it. . . . (*Alone, she turns to look at her husband's picture.*)

(*Dance Music: "All the World Is Waiting for the Sunrise!"*)

TOM (*to the audience*). Across the alley from us was the Paradise Dance Hall. On evenings in spring the windows and doors were open and the music came outdoors. Sometimes the lights were turned out except for a large glass sphere that hung from the ceiling. It would turn slowly about and filter the dusk with delicate rainbow colors. Then the orchestra played a waltz or a tango, something that had a slow and sensuous rhythm. Couples would come outside, to the relative privacy of the alley. You could see them kissing behind ashpits and telephone poles. This was the compensation for lives that passed like mine, without any change or adventure. Adventure and change were imminent in this year. They were waiting around the corner for all these kids. Suspended in the mist over Berchtesgaden,[6] caught in the folds of Chamberlain's[7] umbrella—In Spain there was Guernica![8] But here there was only hot swing music and liquor, dance halls, bars, and movies, and sex that hung in the gloom like a chandelier and flooded the world with brief, deceptive rainbows. . . . All the world was waiting for bombardments!

AMANDA *turns from the picture and comes outside.*

AMANDA (*sighing*). A fire-escape landing's a poor excuse for a porch. (*She spreads a newspaper on a step and sits down, gracefully and demurely as if she were settling into a swing on a Mississippi veranda.*) What are you looking at?

TOM. The moon.

AMANDA. Is there a moon this evening?

TOM. It's rising over Garfinkel's Delicatessen.

AMANDA. So it is! A little silver slipper of a moon. Have you made a wish on it yet?

TOM. Um-hum.

AMANDA. What did you wish for?

TOM. That's a secret.

AMANDA. A secret, huh? Well, I won't tell mine either. I will be just as mysterious as you.

TOM. I bet I can guess what yours is.

AMANDA. Is my head so transparent?

TOM. You're not a sphinx.

AMANDA. No, I don't have secrets. I'll tell you what I wished for on the moon. Success and happiness for my precious children! I wish for that whenever there's a moon, and when there isn't a moon, I wish for it, too.

---

[6]**Berchtesgaden** A municipality in the German Bavarian Alps where Adolf Hitler had a residence.   [7]**Chamberlain** Arthur Neville Chamberlain (1869–1940), British politician who served as Prime Minister from 1937 to 1940, known in particular for his signing of the Munich Agreement in 1938, conceding the Sudetenland region of Czechoslovakia to Nazi Germany.   [8]**Guernica** A town in the Basque region of Spain, bombed by Nazi Germany in 1937 during the Spanish Civil War.

TOM. I thought perhaps you wished for a gentleman caller.

AMANDA. Why do you say that?

TOM. Don't you remember asking me to fetch one?

AMANDA. I remember suggesting that it would be nice for your sister if you brought some nice young man from the warehouse. I think I've made that suggestion more than once.

TOM. Yes, you have made it repeatedly.

AMANDA. Well?

TOM. We are going to have one.

AMANDA. *What?*

TOM. A gentleman caller!

(*The Annunciation Is Celebrated with Music.*)

AMANDA *rises.*

(*Image on Screen: Caller with Bouquet.*)

AMANDA. You mean you have asked some nice young man to come over?

TOM. Yep. I've asked him to dinner.

AMANDA. You really did?

TOM. I did!

AMANDA. You did, and did he—*accept?*

TOM. He did!

AMANDA. Well, well—well, well! That's—lovely!

TOM. I thought that you would be pleased.

AMANDA. It's definite, then?

TOM. Very definite.

AMANDA. Soon?

TOM. Very soon.

AMANDA. For heaven's sake, stop putting on and tell me some things, will you?

TOM. What things do you want me to tell you?

AMANDA. Naturally I would like to know when he's *coming!*

TOM. He's coming tomorrow.

AMANDA. *Tomorrow?*

TOM. Yep. Tomorrow.

AMANDA. But, Tom!

TOM. Yes, Mother?

AMANDA. Tomorrow gives me no time!

TOM. Time for what?

AMANDA. Preparations! Why didn't you phone me at once, as soon as you asked him, the minute that he accepted? Then, don't you see, I could have been getting ready!

TOM. You don't have to make any fuss.

AMANDA. Oh, Tom, Tom, Tom, of course I have to make a fuss! I want things nice, not sloppy! Not thrown together. I'll certainly have to do some fast thinking, won't I?

TOM. I don't see why you have to think at all.

AMANDA. You just don't know. We can't have a gentleman caller in a pigsty! All my wedding silver has to be polished, the monogrammed table linen ought to be laundered! The windows have to be washed and fresh curtains put up. And how about clothes? We have to *wear* something, don't we?

TOM. Mother, this boy is no one to make a fuss over!

AMANDA. Do you realize he's the first young man we've introduced to your sister? It's terrible, dreadful, disgraceful that poor little sister has never received a single gentleman caller! Tom, come inside! (*She opens the screen door.*)

TOM. What for?

AMANDA. I want to ask you some things.

TOM. If you're going to make such a fuss, I'll call it off, I'll tell him not to come.

AMANDA. You certainly won't do anything of the kind. Nothing offends people worse than broken engagements. It simply means I'll have to work like a Turk! We won't be brilliant, but we'll pass inspection. Come on inside. (TOM *follows, groaning.*) Sit down.

TOM. Any particular place you would like me to sit?

AMANDA. Thank heavens I've got that new sofa! I'm also making payments on a floor lamp I'll have sent out! And put the chintz covers on, they'll brighten things up! Of course I'd hoped to have these walls repapered. . . . What is the young man's name?

TOM. His name is O'Connor.

AMANDA. That, of course, means fish—tomorrow is Friday! I'll have that salmon loaf—with Durkee's dressing! What does he do? He works at the warehouse?

TOM. Of course! How else would I—

AMANDA. Tom, he—doesn't drink?

TOM. Why do you ask me that?

AMANDA. Your father *did!*

TOM. Don't get started on that!

AMANDA. He *does* drink, then?

TOM. Not that I know of!

AMANDA. Make sure, be certain! The last thing I want for my daughter's a boy who drinks!

TOM. Aren't you being a little premature? Mr. O'Connor has not yet appeared on the scene!

AMANDA. But will tomorrow. To meet your sister, and what do I know about his character? Nothing! Old maids are better off than wives of drunkards!

TOM. Oh, my God!

AMANDA. Be still!

TOM (*leaning forward to whisper*). Lots of fellows meet girls whom they don't marry!

AMANDA. Oh, talk sensibly, Tom—and don't be sarcastic! (*She has gotten a hairbrush.*)

TOM. What are you doing?

AMANDA. I'm brushing that cow-lick down! What is this young man's position at the warehouse?

TOM (*submitting grimly to the brush and the interrogation*). This young man's position is that of a shipping clerk, Mother.

AMANDA. Sounds to me like a fairly responsible job, the sort of a job *you* would be in if you just had more *get-up.* What is his salary? Have you got any idea?

TOM. I would judge it to be approximately eighty-five dollars a month.

AMANDA. Well—not princely, but—

TOM. Twenty more than I make.

AMANDA. Yes, how well I know! But for a family man, eighty-five dollars a month is not much more than you can just get by on. . . .

TOM. Yes, but Mr. O'Connor is not a family man.

AMANDA. He might be, mightn't he? Some time in the future?

TOM. I see. Plans and provisions.

AMANDA. You are the only man that I know of who ignores the fact that the future becomes the present, the present the past, and the past turns into everlasting regret if you don't plan for it!

TOM. I will think that over and see what I can make of it.

AMANDA. Don't be supercilious with your mother! Tell me some more about this—what do you call him?

TOM. James D. O'Connor. The D. is for Delaney.

AMANDA. Irish on *both* sides! *Gracious!* And doesn't drink?

TOM. Shall I call him up and ask him right this minute?

AMANDA. The only way to find out about those things is to make discreet inquiries at the proper moment. When I was a girl in Blue Mountain and it was suspected that a young man drank, the girl whose attentions he had been receiving, if any girl *was,* would sometimes speak to the minister of his church, or rather her father would if her father was living, and sort of feel him out on the young man's character. That is the way such things are discreetly handled to keep a young woman from making a tragic mistake!

TOM. Then how did you happen to make a tragic mistake?

AMANDA. That innocent look of your father's had everyone fooled! He *smiled*—the world was *enchanted!* No girl can do worse than put herself at the mercy of a handsome appearance! I hope that Mr. O'Connor is not too good-looking.

TOM. No, he's not too good-looking. He's covered with freckles and hasn't too much of a nose.

AMANDA. He's not right-down homely, though?

TOM. Not right-down homely. Just medium homely, I'd say.

AMANDA. Character's what to look for in a man.

TOM. That's what I've always said, Mother.

AMANDA. You've never said anything of the kind and I suspect you would never give it a thought.

TOM. Don't be suspicious of me.

AMANDA. At least I hope he's the type that's up and coming.

TOM. I think he really goes in for self-improvement.

AMANDA. What reason have you to think so?

TOM. He goes to night school.

AMANDA (*beaming*). Splendid! What does he do, I mean study?

TOM. Radio engineering and public speaking!

AMANDA. Then he has visions of being advanced in the world! Any young man who studies public speaking is aiming to have an executive job some day! And radio engineering? A thing for the future! Both of these facts are very illuminating. Those are the sort of things that a mother should know concerning any young man who comes to call on her daughter. Seriously or—not.

TOM. One little warning. He doesn't know about Laura. I didn't let on that we had dark ulterior motives. I just said, why don't you come have dinner with us? He said okay and that was the whole conversation.

AMANDA. I bet it was! You're eloquent as an oyster. However, he'll know about Laura when he gets here. When he sees how lovely and sweet and pretty she is, he'll thank his lucky stars he was asked to dinner.

TOM. Mother, you mustn't expect too much of Laura.

AMANDA. What do you mean?

TOM. Laura seems all those things to you and me because she's ours and we love her. We don't even notice she's crippled any more.

AMANDA. Don't say crippled! You know that I never allow that word to be used!

TOM. But face facts, Mother. She is and—that's not all—

AMANDA. What do you mean "not all"?

TOM. Laura is very different from other girls.

AMANDA. I think the difference is all to her advantage.

TOM. Not quite all—in the eyes of others—strangers—she's terribly shy and lives in a world of her own and those things make her seem a little peculiar to people outside the house.

AMANDA. Don't say peculiar.

TOM. Face the facts. She is.

(*The Dance-Hall Music Changes to a Tango that Has a Minor and Somewhat Ominous Tone.*)

AMANDA. In what way is she peculiar—may I ask?

TOM (*gently*). She lives in a world of her own—a world of—little glass ornaments, Mother. . . . (*Gets up.* AMANDA *remains holding brush, looking at him, troubled.*) She plays old phonograph records and—that's about all—(*He glances at himself in the mirror and crosses to door.*)

AMANDA (*sharply*). Where are you going?

TOM. I'm going to the movies. (*Out screen door.*)

AMANDA. Not to the movies, every night to the movies! (*Follows quickly to screen door.*) I don't believe you always go to the movies! (*He is gone.* AMANDA *looks worriedly after him for a moment. Then vitality and optimism return and she turns from the door. Crossing to portieres.*) Laura! Laura! (LAURA *answers from kitchenette.*)

LAURA. Yes, Mother.

AMANDA. Let those dishes go and come in front! (LAURA *appears with dish towel. Gaily.*) Laura, come here and make a wish on the moon!

LAURA (*entering*). Moon—moon?

AMANDA. A little silver slipper of a moon. Look over your left shoulder, Laura, and make a wish! (LAURA *looks faintly puzzled as if called out of sleep.* AMANDA *seizes her shoulders and turns her at an angle by the door.*) Now! Now, darling, *wish!*

LAURA. What shall I wish for, Mother?

AMANDA (*her voice trembling and her eyes suddenly filling with tears*). Happiness! Good Fortune!

The violin rises and the stage dims out.

Scene VI

(*Image: High School Hero.*)

TOM. And so the following evening I brought Jim home to dinner. I had known Jim slightly in high school. In high school Jim was a hero. He had tremendous Irish good nature and vitality with the scrubbed and polished look of white chinaware. He seemed to move in a continual spotlight. He was a star in basketball, captain of the debating club, president of the senior class and the glee club and he sang the male lead in the annual light operas. He was always running or bounding, never just walking. He seemed always at the point of defeating the law of gravity. He was shooting with such velocity through his adolescence that you would logically expect him to arrive at nothing short of the White House by the time he was thirty. But Jim apparently ran into more interference after his graduation from Soldan. His speed had definitely slowed. Six years after he left high school he was holding a job that wasn't much better than mine.

(*Image: Clerk.*)

He was the only one at the warehouse with whom I was on friendly terms. I was valuable to him as someone who could remember his former glory, who had seen him win basketball games and the silver cup in debating. He knew of my secret practice of retiring to a cabinet of the washroom to work on poems when business was slack in the warehouse. He called me Shakespeare. And while the other boys in the warehouse regarded me with suspicious hostility, Jim took a humorous attitude toward me. Gradually his attitude affected the others, their hostility wore off and they also began to smile at me as people smile at an oddly fashioned dog who trots across their path at some distance.

    I knew that Jim and Laura had known each other at Soldan, and I had heard Laura speak admiringly of his voice. I didn't know if Jim remembered her or not. In high school Laura had been as unobtrusive as Jim had been astonishing. If he did remember Laura, it was not as my sister, for when I asked him to dinner, he grinned and said, "You know, Shakespeare, I never thought of you as having folks!"

    He was about to discover that I did. . . .

(*Light up Stage.*)

(*Legend on Screen: "The Accent of a Coming Foot."*)

Friday evening. It is about five o'clock of a late spring evening which comes "scattering poems in the sky."

A delicate lemony light is in the Wingfield apartment.

AMANDA *has worked like a Turk in preparation for the gentleman caller. The results are astonishing. The new floor lamp with its rose-silk shade is in place, a colored paper lantern conceals the broken light fixture in the ceiling, new billowing white curtains are at the windows, chintz covers are on chairs and sofa, a pair of new sofa pillows make their initial appearance.*

Open boxes and tissue paper are scattered on the floor.

LAURA *stands in the middle with lifted arms while* AMANDA *crouches before her, adjusting the hem of the new dress, devout and ritualistic. The dress is colored and designed by memory. The arrangement of* LAURA'S *hair is changed; it is softer and more becoming. A fragile, unearthly prettiness has come out in* LAURA: *she is like a piece of translucent glass touched by light, given a momentary radiance, not actual, not lasting.*

AMANDA (*impatiently*). Why are you trembling?

LAURA. Mother, you've made me so nervous!

AMANDA. How have I made you nervous?

LAURA. By all this fuss! You make it seem so important!

AMANDA. I don't understand you, Laura. You couldn't be satisfied with just sitting home, and yet whenever I try to arrange something for you, you seem to resist it. (*She gets up.*) Now take a look at yourself. No, wait! Wait just a moment—I have an idea!

LAURA. What is it now?

AMANDA *produces two powder puffs which she wraps in handkerchiefs and stuffs in* LAURA'S *bosom.*

LAURA. Mother, what are you doing?

AMANDA. They call them "Gay Deceivers"!

LAURA. I won't wear them!

AMANDA. You will!

LAURA. Why should I?

AMANDA. Because, to be painfully honest, your chest is flat.

LAURA. You make it seem like we were setting a trap.

AMANDA. All pretty girls are a trap, a pretty trap, and men expect them to be. (*Legend: "A Pretty Trap."*) Now look at yourself, young lady. This is the prettiest you will ever be! I've got to fix myself now! You're going to be surprised by your mother's appearance! (*She crosses through portieres, humming gaily.*)

Laura moves slowly to the long mirror and stares solemnly at herself.

A wind blows the white curtains inward in a slow, graceful motion and with a faint, sorrowful sighing.

AMANDA (*off stage*). It isn't dark enough yet. (*She turns slowly before the mirror with a troubled look.*)

(*Legend on Screen: "This Is My Sister: Celebrate Her with Strings!" Music.*)

AMANDA (*laughing, off*). I'm going to show you something. I'm going to make a spectacular appearance!

LAURA. What is it, Mother?

AMANDA. Possess your soul in patience—you will see! Something I've resurrected from that old trunk! Styles haven't changed so terribly much after all. . . . (*She parts the portieres.*) Now just look at your mother! (*She wears a girlish frock of yellowed voile with a blue silk sash. She carries a bunch of jonquils—the legend of her youth is nearly revived. Feverishly.*) This is the dress in which I led the cotillion. Won the cakewalk twice at Sunset Hill, wore one spring to the Governor's ball in Jackson! See how I sashayed around the ballroom, Laura? (*She raises her skirt and does a mincing step around the room.*) I wore it on Sundays for my gentlemen callers! I had it on the day I met your father— I had malaria fever all that spring. The change of climate from East Tennessee to the Delta—weakened resistance—I had a little temperature all the time—not enough to be serious—just enough to make me restless and giddy! Invitations poured in—parties all over the Delta!—"stay in bed," said Mother, "you have fever!"—but I just wouldn't.—I took quinine but kept on going, going!—Evenings, dances!—Afternoons, long, long rides! Picnics—lovely!—So lovely, that country in May.—All lacy with dogwood, literally flooded with jonquils!—That was the spring I had the craze for jonquils. Jonquils became an absolute obsession. Mother said, "Honey, there's no more room for jonquils." And still I kept bringing in more jonquils. Whenever, wherever I saw them, I'd say, "Stop! Stop! I see jonquils!" I made the young men help me gather the jonquils! It was a joke, Amanda and her jonquils! Finally there were no more vases to hold them, every available space was filled with jonquils. No vases to hold them? All right, I'll hold them myself! And then I—(*She stops in front of the picture.*) (*Music.*) met your father! Malaria fever and jonquils and then—this—boy. . . . (*She switches on the rose-colored lamp.*) I hope they get here before it starts to rain. (*She crosses upstage and places the jonquils in bowl on table.*) I gave your brother a little extra change so he and Mr. O'Connor could take the service car home.

LAURA (*with altered look*). What did you say his name was?

AMANDA. O'Connor.

LAURA. What is his first name?

AMANDA. I don't remember. Oh, yes, I do. It was—Jim!

LAURA *sways slightly and catches hold of a chair.*

(*Legend on Screen: "Not Jim!"*)

LAURA (*faintly*). Not—Jim!

AMANDA. Yes, that was it, it was Jim! I've never known a Jim that wasn't nice!

(*Music: Ominous.*)

LAURA. Are you sure his name is Jim O'Connor?

AMANDA. Yes. Why?

LAURA. Is he the one that Tom used to know in high school?

AMANDA. He didn't say so. I think he just got to know him at the warehouse.

LAURA. There was a Jim O'Connor we both knew in high school—(*Then, with effort.*) If that is the one that Tom is bringing to dinner—you'll have to excuse me, I won't come to the table.

AMANDA. What sort of nonsense is this?

LAURA. You asked me once if I'd ever liked a boy. Don't you remember I showed you this boy's picture?

AMANDA. You mean the boy you showed me in the year-book?

LAURA. Yes, that boy.

AMANDA. Laura, Laura, were you in love with that boy?

LAURA. I don't know, Mother. All I know is I couldn't sit at the table if it was him!

AMANDA. It won't be him! It isn't the least bit likely. But whether it is or not, you will come to the table. You will not be excused.

LAURA. I'll have to be, Mother.

AMANDA. I don't intend to humor your silliness, Laura. I've had too much from you and your brother, both! So just sit down and compose yourself till they come. Tom has forgotten his key so you'll have to let them in, when they arrive.

LAURA (*panicky*). Oh, Mother—*you* answer the door!

AMANDA (*lightly*). I'll be in the kitchen—busy!

LAURA. Oh, Mother, please answer the door, don't make me do it!

AMANDA (*crossing into kitchenette*). I've got to fix the dressing for the salmon. Fuss, fuss—silliness!—over a gentleman caller!

Door swings shut. LAURA *is left alone.*

(*Legend: "Terror!"*)

She utters a low moan and turns off the lamp—sits stiffly on the edge of the sofa, knotting her fingers together.

(*Legend on Screen: "The Opening of a Door!"*)

TOM *and* JIM *appear on the fire-escape steps and climb to landing. Hearing their approach,* LAURA *rises with a panicky gesture. She retreats to the portieres.*

The doorbell. LAURA *catches her breath and touches her throat. Low drums.*

AMANDA (*calling*). Laura, sweetheart! The door!

LAURA *stares at it without moving.*

JIM. I think we just beat the rain.

TOM. Uh-huh. (*He rings again, nervously.* JIM *whistles and fishes for a cigarette.*)

AMANDA (*very, very gaily*). Laura, that is your brother and Mr. O'Connor! Will you let them in, darling?

LAURA *crosses toward kitchenette door.*

LAURA (*breathlessly*). Mother—you go to the door!

AMANDA *steps out of kitchenette and stares furiously at* LAURA. *She points imperiously at the door.*

LAURA. Please, please!

AMANDA (*in a fierce whisper*). What is the matter with you, you silly thing?

LAURA (*desperately*). Please, you answer it, *please!*

AMANDA. I told you I wasn't going to humor you, Laura. Why have you chosen this moment to lose your mind?

LAURA. Please, please, please, you go!

AMANDA. You'll have to go to the door because I can't!

LAURA (*despairingly*). I can't either!

AMANDA. Why?

LAURA. I'm sick!

AMANDA. I'm sick, too—of your nonsense! Why can't you and your brother be normal people? Fantastic whims and behavior! (TOM *gives a long ring.*) Preposterous goings on! Can you give me one reason—(*Calls out lyrically.*) COMING! JUST ONE SECOND!—why should you be afraid to open a door? Now you answer it, Laura!

LAURA. Oh, oh, oh. . . (*She returns through the portieres. Darts to the victrola and winds it frantically and turns it on.*)

AMANDA. Laura Wingfield, you march right to that door!

LAURA. Yes—yes, Mother!

A faraway, scratchy rendition of "dardanella" softens the air and gives her strength to move through it. She slips to the door and draws it cautiously open.

TOM *enters with caller,* JIM O'CONNOR.

TOM. Laura, this is Jim. Jim, this is my sister, Laura.

JIM (*stepping inside*). I didn't know that Shakespeare had a sister!

LAURA (*retreating stiff and trembling from the door*). How—how do you do?

JIM (*heartily extending his hand*). Okay!

LAURA *touches it hesitantly with hers.*

JIM. Your hand's *cold,* Laura!

LAURA. Yes, well—I've been playing the victrola. . . .

JIM. Must have been playing classical music on it! You ought to play a little hot swing music to warm you up!

LAURA. Excuse me—I haven't finished playing the victrola. . . .

She turns awkwardly and hurries into the front room. She pauses a second by the victrola. Then catches her breath and darts through the portieres like a frightened deer.

JIM (*grinning*). What was the matter?

TOM. Oh—with Laura? Laura is—terribly shy.

JIM. Shy, huh? It's unusual to meet a shy girl nowadays. I don't believe you ever mentioned you had a sister.

TOM. Well, now you know. I have one. Here is the *Post Dispatch.* You want a piece of it?

JIM. Uh-huh.

TOM. What piece? The comics?

JIM. Sports! (*Glances at it.*) Ole Dizzy Dean is on his bad behavior.

TOM (*disinterest*). Yeah? (*Lights cigarette and crosses back to fire-escape door.*)

JIM. Where are *you* going?

TOM. I'm going out on the terrace.

JIM (*goes after him*). You know, Shakespeare—I'm going to sell you a bill of goods!

TOM. What goods?

JIM. A course I'm taking.

TOM. Huh?

JIM. In public speaking! You and me, we're not the warehouse type.

TOM. Thanks—that's good news. But what has public speaking got to do with it?

JIM. It fits you for—executive positions!

TOM. Awww.

JIM. I tell you it's done a helluva lot for me.

(*Image: Executive at Desk.*)

TOM. In what respect?

JIM. In every! Ask yourself what is the difference between you an' me and men in the office down front? Brains?—No!—Ability?—No! Then what? Just one little thing—

TOM. What is that one little thing?

JIM. Primarily it amounts to—social poise! Being able to square up to people and hold your own on any social level!

AMANDA (*off stage*). Tom?

TOM. Yes, Mother?

AMANDA. Is that you and Mr. O'Connor?

TOM. Yes, Mother.

AMANDA. Well, you just make yourselves comfortable in there.

TOM. Yes, Mother.

AMANDA. Ask Mr. O'Connor if he would like to wash his hands.

JIM. Aw—no—no—thank you—I took care of that at the warehouse. Tom—

TOM. Yes?

JIM. Mr. Mendoza was speaking to me about you.

TOM. Favorably?

JIM. What do you think?

TOM. Well—

JIM. You're going to be out of a job if you don't wake up.

TOM. I am waking up—

JIM. You show no signs.

TOM. The signs are interior.

(*Image on Screen: The Sailing Vessel with Jolly Roger Again.*)

TOM. I'm planning to change. (*He leans over the rail speaking with quiet exhilaration. The incandescent marquees and signs of the first-run movie houses light his face from across the alley. He looks like a voyager.*) I'm right at the point of committing myself to a future that doesn't include the warehouse and Mr. Mendoza or even a night-school course in public speaking.

JIM. What are you gassing about?

TOM. I'm tired of the movies.

JIM. Movies!

TOM. Yes, movies! Look at them—(*a wave toward the marvels of Grand Avenue.*) All of those glamorous people—having adventures—hogging it all, gobbling the whole thing up! You know what happens? People go to the *movies* instead of *moving!* Hollywood characters are supposed to have all the adventures for everybody in America, while everybody in America sits in a dark room and watches them have them! Yes, until there's a war. That's when adventure becomes available to the masses! *Everyone's* dish, not only Gable's![9] Then the people in the dark room come out of the dark room to have some adventures themselves— Goody, goody—It's our turn now, to go to the South Sea Island—to make a safari—to be exotic, far-off—But I'm not patient. I don't want to wait till then. I'm tired of the *movies* and I am *about to move!*

JIM (*incredulously*). Move?

TOM. Yes.

JIM. When?

TOM. Soon!

---

[9]**Gable's** Clark Gable (1901–1960), American film star.

JIM. Where? Where?

(Theme Three: Music Seems to Answer the Question, while TOM *Thinks it Over. He Searches among his Pockets.)*

TOM. I'm starting to boil inside. I know I seem dreamy, but inside—well, I'm boiling! Whenever I pick up a shoe, I shudder a little thinking how short life is and what I am doing!—Whatever that means. I know it doesn't mean shoes—except as something to wear on a traveler's feet! *(Finds paper.)* Look—

JIM. What?

TOM. I'm a member.

JIM *(reading)*. The Union of Merchant Seamen.

TOM. I paid my dues this month, instead of the light bill.

JIM. You will regret it when they turn the lights off.

TOM. I won't be here.

JIM. How about your mother?

TOM. I'm like my father. The bastard son of a bastard! See how he grins? And he's been absent going on sixteen years!

JIM. You're just talking, you drip. How does your mother feel about it?

TOM. Shhh—Here comes Mother! Mother is not acquainted with my plans!

AMANDA *(enters portieres)*. Where are you all?

TOM. On the terrace, Mother.

They start inside. She advances to them. TOM *is distinctly shocked at her appearance. Even* JIM *blinks a little. He is making his first contact with girlish Southern vivacity and in spite of the night-school course in public speaking is somewhat thrown off the beam by the unexpected outlay of social charm.*

Certain responses are attempted by JIM *but are swept aside by* AMANDA's *gay laughter and chatter.* TOM *is embarrassed but after the first shock* JIM *reacts very warmly. Grins and chuckles, is altogether won over.*

(Image: AMANDA *as a Girl.)*

AMANDA *(coyly smiling, shaking her girlish ringlets)*. Well, well, well, so this is Mr. O'Connor. Introductions entirely unnecessary. I've heard so much about you from my boy. I finally said to him, Tom—good gracious!—why don't you bring this paragon to supper? I'd like to meet this nice young man at the warehouse!—Instead of just hearing him sing your praises so much! I don't know why my son is so standoffish—that's not Southern behavior! Let's sit down and—I think we could stand a little more air in here! Tom, leave the door open. I felt a nice fresh breeze a moment ago. Where has it gone? Mmm, so warm already! And not quite summer, even. We're going to burn up when summer really gets started. However, we're having—we're having a very light supper. I think light things are better fo' this time of year. The same as light clothes are. Light clothes an' light food are what warm weather calls fo'. You know our blood gets so thick during th' winter—it takes a while fo' us to *adjust* ou'selves!—when the season changes.... It's come so quick this year. I wasn't prepared. All of a sudden—heavens! Already summer!—I ran to the trunk an' pulled out this light dress—Terribly old! Historical almost! But feels so good—so good an' co-ol, y'know....

TOM. Mother—

AMANDA. Yes, honey?

TOM. How about—supper?

AMANDA. Honey, you go ask Sister if supper is ready! You know that Sister is
    in full charge of supper! Tell her you hungry boys are waiting for it. (*To
    JIM.*) Have you met Laura?

JIM. She—

AMANDA. Let you in? Oh, good, you've met already! It's rare for a girl as sweet
    an' pretty as Laura to be domestic! But Laura is, thank heavens, not only
    pretty but also very domestic. I'm not at all. I never was a bit. I never
    could make a thing but angel-food cake. Well, in the South we had so
    many servants. Gone, gone, gone. All vestiges of gracious living! Gone
    completely! I wasn't prepared for what the future brought me. All of my
    gentlemen callers were sons of planters and so of course I assumed that
    I would be married to one and raise my family on a large piece of land
    with plenty of servants. But man proposes—and woman accepts the
    proposal!—To vary that old, old saying a little bit—I married no planter!
    I married a man who worked for the telephone company!—that gal-
    lantly smiling gentleman over there! [*Points to the picture.*] A tele-
    phone man who—fell in love with long distance!—Now he travels and
    I don't even know where!—But what am I going on for about my—
    tribulations! Tell me yours—I hope you don't have any! Tom?

TOM (*returning*). Yes, Mother?

AMANDA. Is supper nearly ready?

TOM. It looks to me like supper is on the table.

AMANDA. Let me look—(*She rises prettily and looks through portieres.*) Oh,
    lovely—But where is Sister?

TOM. Laura is not feeling well and she says that she thinks she'd better not
    come to the table.

AMANDA. What?—Nonsense!—Laura? Oh, Laura!

LAURA (*off stage, faintly*). Yes, Mother.

AMANDA. You really must come to the table. We won't be seated until you
    come to the table! Come in, Mr. O'Connor. You sit over there and I'll—
    Laura? Laura Wingfield! You're keeping us waiting, honey! We can't say
    grace until you come to the table!

The back door is pushed weakly open and LAURA *comes in. She is obviously quite faint, her lips trembling, her eyes wide and staring. She
moves unsteadily toward the table.*

(*Legend: "Terror!"*)

*Outside a summer storm is coming abruptly. The white curtains bil-
low inward at the windows and there is a sorrowful murmur and
deep blue dusk.*

LAURA *suddenly stumbles—She catches a chair with a faint moan.*

TOM. Laura!

AMANDA. Laura! (*There is a clap of thunder.*) (*Legend: "Ah!"*) (*Despairingly.*)
    Why, Laura, you *are* sick, darling! Tom, help your sister into the living
    room, dear! Sit in the living room, Laura—rest on the sofa. Well! (*To the
    gentleman caller.*) Standing over the hot stove made her ill!—I told her

that it was just too warm this evening, but—(TOM *comes back in.* LAURA *is on the sofa.*) Is Laura all right now?

TOM. Yes.

AMANDA. What *is* that? Rain? A nice cool rain has come up! (*She gives the gentleman caller a frightened look.*) I think we may—have grace—now…(TOM *looks at her stupidly.*) Tom, honey—you say grace!

TOM. Oh…"For these and all thy mercies—" (*They bow their heads,* AMANDA *stealing a nervous glance at* JIM. *In the living room* LAURA, *stretched on the sofa, clenches her hand to her lips, to hold back a shuddering sob.*) God's Holy Name be praised—

(*The Scene Dims Out.*)

Scene VII

A Souvenir

Half an hour later. Dinner is just being finished in the upstage area which is concealed by the drawn portieres.

As the curtain rises LAURA *is still huddled upon the sofa, her feet drawn under her, her head resting on a pale blue pillow, her eyes wide and mysteriously watchful. The new floor lamp with its shade of rose-colored silk gives a soft, becoming light to her face, bringing out the fragile, unearthly prettiness which usually escapes attention. There is a steady murmur of rain, but it is slackening and stops soon after the scene begins; the air outside becomes pale and luminous as the moon breaks out.*

A moment after the curtain rises, the lights in both rooms flicker and go out.

JIM. Hey, there, Mr. Light Bulb!

AMANDA *laughs nervously.*

(*Legend: "Suspension of a Public Service."*)

AMANDA. Where was Moses when the lights went out? Ha-ha. Do you know the answer to that one, Mr. O'Connor?

JIM. No, Ma'am, what's the answer?

AMANDA. In the dark! (JIM *laughs appreciatively.*) Everybody sit still. I'll light the candles. Isn't it lucky we have them on the table? Where's a match? Which of you gentlemen can provide a match?

JIM. Here.

AMANDA. Thank you, sir.

JIM. Not at all, Ma'am!

AMANDA. I guess the fuse has burnt out. Mr. O'Connor, can you tell a burnt-out fuse? I know I can't and Tom is a total loss when it comes to mechanics. (*Sound: Getting Up: Voices Recede a Little to Kitchenette.*) Oh, be careful you don't bump into something. We don't want our gentleman caller to break his neck. Now wouldn't that be a fine howdy-do?

JIM. Ha-ha! Where is the fuse-box?

AMANDA. Right here next to the stove. Can you see anything?

JIM. Just a minute.

AMANDA. Isn't electricity a mysterious thing? Wasn't it Benjamin Franklin who tied a key to a kite? We live in such a mysterious universe, don't we? Some people say that science clears up all the mysteries for us. In my opinion it only creates more! Have you found it yet?

JIM. No, Ma'am. All these fuses look okay to me.

AMANDA. Tom!

TOM. Yes, Mother?

AMANDA. That light bill I gave you several days ago. The one I told you we got the notices about?

TOM. Oh.—Yeah.

(*Legend:"Ha!"*)

AMANDA. You didn't neglect to pay it by any chance?

TOM. Why, I—

AMANDA. Didn't! I might have known it!

JIM. Shakespeare probably wrote a poem on that light bill, Mrs. Wingfield.

AMANDA. I might have known better than to trust him with it! There's such a high price for negligence in this world!

JIM. Maybe the poem will win a ten-dollar prize.

AMANDA. We'll just have to spend the remainder of the evening in the nineteenth century, before Mr. Edison made the Mazda lamp!

JIM. Candlelight is my favorite kind of light.

AMANDA. That shows you're romantic! But that's no excuse for Tom. Well, we got through dinner. Very considerate of them to let us get through dinner before they plunged us into everlasting darkness, wasn't it, Mr. O'Connor?

JIM. Ha-ha!

AMANDA. Tom, as a penalty for your carelessness you can help me with the dishes.

JIM. Let me give you a hand.

AMANDA. Indeed you will not!

JIM. I ought to be good for something.

AMANDA. Good for something? (*Her tone is rhapsodic.*) You? Why, Mr. O'Connor, nobody, *nobody's* given me this much entertainment in years—as you have!

JIM. Aw, now, Mrs. Wingfield!

AMANDA. I'm not exaggerating, not one bit! But Sister is all by her lonesome. You go keep her company in the parlor! I'll give you this lovely old candelabrum that used to be on the altar at the church of the Heavenly Rest. It was melted a little out of shape when the church burnt down. Lightning struck it one spring. Gypsy Jones was holding a revival at the time and he intimated that the church was destroyed because the Episcopalians gave card parties.

JIM. Ha-ha.

AMANDA. And how about coaxing Sister to drink a little wine? I think it would be good for her! Can you carry both at once?

JIM. Sure. I'm Superman!

AMANDA. Now, Thomas, get into this apron!

The door of kitchenette swings closed on AMANDA's *gay laughter; the flickering light approaches the portieres.*

LAURA *sits up nervously as he enters. Her speech at first is low and breathless from the almost intolerable strain of being alone with a stranger.*

(*Legend: "I Don't Suppose You Remember Me at All!"*)

In her first speeches in this scene, before JIM's *warmth overcomes her paralyzing shyness,* LAURA's *voice is thin and breathless as though she has run up a steep flight of stairs.*

JIM's *attitude is gently humorous. In playing this scene it should be stressed that while the incident is apparently unimportant, it is to* LAURA *the climax of her secret life.*

JIM.   Hello, there, Laura.

LAURA (*faintly*).   Hello. (*She clears her throat.*)

JIM.   How are you feeling now? Better?

LAURA.   Yes. Yes, thank you.

JIM.   This is for you. A little dandelion wine. (*He extends it toward her with extravagant gallantry.*)

LAURA.   Thank you.

JIM.   Drink it—but don't get drunk! (*He laughs heartily.* LAURA *takes the glass uncertainly; laughs shyly.*) Where shall I set the candles?

LAURA.   Oh—oh, anywhere . . .

JIM.   How about here on the floor? Any objections?

LAURA.   No.

JIM.   I'll spread a newspaper under to catch the drippings. I like to sit on the floor. Mind if I do?

LAURA.   Oh, no.

JIM.   Give me a pillow?

LAURA.   What?

JIM.   A pillow!

LAURA.   Oh. . .(*Hands him one quickly.*)

JIM.   How about you? Don't you like to sit on the floor?

LAURA.   Oh—yes.

JIM.   Why don't you, then?

LAURA.   I—will.

JIM.   Take a pillow! (LAURA *does. Sits on the other side of the candelabrum.* JIM *crosses his legs and smiles engagingly at her.*) I can't hardly see you sitting way over there.

LAURA.   I can—see you.

JIM.   I know, but that's not fair, I'm in the limelight. (LAURA *moves her pillow closer.*) Good! Now I can see you! Comfortable?

LAURA.   Yes.

JIM.   So am I. Comfortable as a cow. Will you have some gum?

LAURA.   No, thank you.

JIM.   I think that I will indulge, with your permission. (*Musingly unwraps it and holds it up.*) Think of the fortune made by the guy that invented the first piece of chewing gum. Amazing, huh? The Wrigley Building is one of the sights of Chicago.—I saw it summer before last when I went up to the Century of Progress. Did you take in the Century of Progress?

LAURA.   No, I didn't.

JIM.   Well, it was quite a wonderful exposition. What impressed me most was the Hall of Science. Gives you an idea of what the future will be in America, even more wonderful than the present time is! (*Pause. Smiling at her.*) Your brother tells me you're shy. Is that right, Laura?

LAURA.   I—don't know.

JIM. I judge you to be an old-fashioned type of girl. Well, I think that's a pretty good type to be. Hope you don't think I'm being too personal—do you?

LAURA (*hastily, out of embarrassment*). I believe I *will* take a piece of gum, if you—don't mind. (*Clearing her throat.*) Mr. O'Connor, have you—kept up with your singing?

JIM. Singing? Me?

LAURA. Yes. I remember what a beautiful voice you had.

JIM. When did you hear me sing?

(*Voice Offstage in the Pause.*)

VOICE (*offstage*).

> O blow, ye winds, heigh-ho.
> A-roving I will go!
> I'm off to my love
> With a boxing glove—
> Ten thousand miles away!

JIM. You say you've heard me sing?

LAURA. Oh, yes! Yes, very often . . . I—don't suppose you remember me—at all?

JIM (*smiling doubtfully*). You know I have an idea I've seen you before. I had that idea soon as you opened the door. It seemed almost like I was about to remember your name. But the name that I started to call you—wasn't a name! And so I stopped myself before I said it.

LAURA. Wasn't it—Blue Roses?

JIM (*springs up, grinning*). Blue Roses! My gosh, yes—Blue Roses! That's what I had on my tongue when you opened the door! Isn't it funny what tricks your memory plays? I didn't connect you with the high school somehow or other. But that's where it was; it was high school. I didn't even know you were Shakespeare's sister! Gosh, I'm sorry.

LAURA. I didn't expect you to. You—barely knew me!

JIM. But we did have a speaking acquaintance, huh?

LAURA. Yes, we—spoke to each other.

JIM. When did you recognize me?

LAURA. Oh, right away!

JIM. Soon as I came in the door?

LAURA. When I heard your name I thought it was probably you. I knew that Tom used to know you a little in high school. So when you came in the door—Well, then I was—sure.

JIM. Why didn't you *say* something, then?

LAURA (*breathlessly*). I didn't know what to say, I was—too surprised!

JIM. For goodness' sakes! You know, this sure is funny!

LAURA. Yes! Yes, isn't it, though. . . .

JIM. Didn't we have a class in something together?

LAURA. Yes, we did.

JIM. What class was that?

LAURA. It was—singing—Chorus!

JIM. Aw!

LAURA. I sat across the aisle from you in the Aud.

JIM. Aw.

LAURA. Mondays, Wednesdays and Fridays.

JIM. Now I remember—you always came in late.

LAURA. Yes, it was so hard for me, getting upstairs. I had a brace on my leg—
it clumped so loud!

JIM. I never heard any clumping.

LAURA (*wincing at the recollection*). To me it sounded like—thunder!

JIM. Well, well, well. I never even noticed.

LAURA. And everybody was seated before I came in. I had to walk in front of
all those people. My seat was in the back row. I had to go clumping all
the way up the aisle with everyone watching!

JIM. You shouldn't have been self-conscious.

LAURA. I know, but I was. It was always such a relief when the singing
started.

JIM. Aw, yes, I've placed you now! I used to call you Blue Roses. How was it
that I got started calling you that?

LAURA. I was out of school a little while with pleurosis. When I came back
you asked me what was the matter. I said I had pleurosis—you thought
I said Blue Roses. That's what you always called me after that!

JIM. I hope you didn't mind.

LAURA. Oh, no—I liked it. You see, I wasn't acquainted with many—
people. . . .

JIM. As I remember you sort of stuck by yourself.

LAURA. I—I—never had much luck at—making friends.

JIM. I don't see why you wouldn't.

LAURA. Well, I—started out badly.

JIM. You mean being—

LAURA. Yes, it sort of—stood between me—

JIM. You shouldn't have let it!

LAURA. I know, but it did, and—

JIM. You were shy with people!

LAURA. I tried not to be but never could—

JIM. Overcome it?

LAURA. No, I—I never could!

JIM. I guess being shy is something you have to work out of kind of gradually.

LAURA (*sorrowfully*). Yes—I guess it—

JIM. Takes time!

LAURA. Yes—

JIM. People are not so dreadful when you know them. That's what you have
to remember! And everybody has problems, not just you, but practically
everybody has got some problems. You think of yourself as having the
only problems, as being the only one who is disappointed. But just look
around you and you will see lots of people as disappointed as you are.
For instance, I hoped when I was going to high school that I would be
further along at this time, six years after, than I am now—You remember that wonderful write-up I had in *The Torch?*

LAURA. Yes! (*She rises and crosses to table.*)

JIM. It said I was bound to succeed in anything I went into! (*Laura returns
with the annual.*) Holy Jeez! *The Torch!* (*He accepts it reverently. They
smile across it with mutual wonder.* LAURA *crouches beside him and they
begin to turn through it.* LAURA's *shyness is dissolving in his warmth.*)

LAURA. Here you are in *Pirates of Penzance!*

JIM (*wistfully*). I sang the baritone lead in that operetta.

LAURA (*rapidly*). So—*beautifully!*

JIM (*protesting*). Aw—

LAURA. Yes, yes—beautifully—beautifully!

JIM. You heard me?

LAURA. All three times!

JIM. No!

LAURA. Yes!

JIM. All three performances?

LAURA (*looking down*). Yes.

JIM. Why?

LAURA. I—wanted to ask you to—autograph my program.

JIM. Why didn't you ask me to?

LAURA. You were always surrounded by your own friends so much that I never had a chance to.

JIM. You should have just—

LAURA. Well, I—thought you might think I was—

JIM. Thought I might think you was—what?

LAURA. Oh—

JIM (*with reflective relish*). I was beleaguered by females in those days.

LAURA. You were terribly popular!

JIM. Yeah—

LAURA. You had such a—friendly way—

JIM. I was spoiled in high school.

LAURA. Everybody—liked you!

JIM. Including you?

LAURA. I—yes, I—I did, too—(*She gently closes the book in her lap.*)

JIM. Well, well, well!—Give me that program, Laura. (*She hands it to him. He signs it with a flourish.*) There you are—better late than never!

LAURA. Oh, I—what a—surprise!

JIM. My signature isn't worth very much right now. But some day—maybe—it will increase in value! Being disappointed is one thing and being discouraged is something else. I am disappointed but I'm not discouraged. I'm twenty-three years old. How old are you?

LAURA. I'll be twenty-four in June.

JIM. That's not old age!

LAURA. No, but—

JIM. You finished high school?

LAURA (*with difficulty*). I didn't go back.

JIM. You mean you dropped out?

LAURA. I made bad grades in my final examinations. (*She rises and replaces the book and the program. Her voice strained.*) How is—Emily Meisenbach getting along?

JIM. Oh, that kraut-head!

LAURA. Why do you call her that?

JIM. That's what she was.

LAURA. You're not still—going with her?

JIM. I never see her.

LAURA. It said in the Personal Section that you were—engaged!

JIM. I know, but I wasn't impressed by that—propaganda!

LAURA. It wasn't—the truth?

JIM. Only in Emily's optimistic opinion!

LAURA. Oh—

(*Legend: "What Have You Done since High School?"*)

JIM *lights a cigarette and leans indolently back on his elbows smiling at* LAURA *with a warmth and charm which light her inwardly with altar candles. She remains by the table and turns in her hands a piece of glass to cover her tumult.*

JIM (*after several reflective puffs on a cigarette*). What have you done since high school? (*She seems not to hear him.*) Huh? (LAURA *looks up.*) I said what have you done since high school, Laura?

LAURA. Nothing much.

JIM. You must have been doing something these six long years.

LAURA. Yes.

JIM. Well, then, such as what?

LAURA. I took a business course at business college—

JIM. How did that work out?

LAURA. Well, not very—well—I had to drop out, it gave me—indigestion—

JIM *laughs gently.*

JIM. What are you doing now?

LAURA. I don't do anything—much. Oh, please don't think I sit around doing nothing! My glass collection takes up a good deal of my time. Glass is something you have to take good care of.

JIM. What did you say—about glass?

LAURA. Collection I said—I have one—(*She clears her throat and turns away again, acutely shy.*)

JIM (*abruptly*). You know what I judge to be the trouble with you? Inferiority complex! Know what that is? That's what they call it when someone low-rates himself! I understand it because I had it, too. Although my case was not so aggravated as yours seems to be. I had it until I took up public speaking, developed my voice, and learned that I had an aptitude for science. Before that time I never thought of myself as being outstanding in any way whatsoever! Now I've never made a regular study of it, but I have a friend who says I can analyze people better than doctors that make a profession of it. I don't claim that to be necessarily true, but I can sure guess a person's psychology, Laura! (*Takes out his gum.*) Excuse me, Laura. I always take it out when the flavor is gone. I'll use this scrap of paper to wrap it in. I know how it is to get it stuck on a shoe. Yep— that's what I judge to be your principal trouble. A lack of confidence in yourself as a person. You don't have the proper amount of faith in yourself. I'm basing that fact on a number of your remarks and also on certain observations I've made. For instance that clumping you thought was so awful in high school. You say that you even dreaded to walk into class. You see what you did? You dropped out of school, you gave up an education because of a clump, which as far as I know was practically nonexistent! A little physical defect is what you have. Hardly noticeable even! Magnified thousands of times by imagination! You know what my strong advice to you is? Think of yourself as *superior* in some way!

LAURA. In what way would I think?

JIM. Why, man alive, Laura! Just look about you a little. What do you see? A
world full of common people! All of 'em born and all of 'em going to
die! Which of them has one-tenth of your good points! Or mine! Or anyone else's, as far as that goes—Gosh! Everybody excels in some one
thing. Some in many! (*Unconsciously glances at himself in the mirror.*)
All you've got to do is discover in *what!* Take me, for instance. (*He adjusts his tie at the mirror.*) My interest happens to lie in electrodynam-
ics. I'm taking a course in radio engineering at night school, Laura, on
top of a fairly responsible job at the warehouse. I'm taking that course
and studying public speaking.

LAURA. Ohhhh.

JIM. Because I believe in the future of television! (*Turning back to her.*) I wish
to be ready to go up right along with it. Therefore I'm planning to get in
on the ground floor. In fact, I've already made the right connections and
all that remains is for the industry itself to get under way! Full steam—
(*His eyes are starry.*) Knowledge—Zzzzzp! Money—Zzzzzp!—Power!
That's the cycle democracy is built on! (*His attitude is convincingly dynamic.* LAURA *stares at him, even her shyness eclipsed in her absolute
wonder. He suddenly grins.*) I guess you think I think a lot of myself!

LAURA. No—o-o-o, I—

JIM. Now how about you? Isn't there something you take more interest in
than anything else?

LAURA. Well, I do—as I said—have my—glass collection—

A peal of girlish laughter from the kitchen.

JIM. I'm not right sure I know what you're talking about. What kind of glass
is it?

LAURA. Little articles of it, they're ornaments mostly! Most of them are little
animals made out of glass, the tiniest little animals in the world. Mother
calls them a glass menagerie! Here's an example of one, if you'd like to
see it! This one is one of the oldest. It's nearly thirteen. (*He stretches
out his hand.*) (*Music: "The Glass Menagerie."*) Oh, be careful—if you
breathe, it breaks!

JIM. I'd better not take it. I'm pretty clumsy with things.

LAURA. Go on, I trust you with him! (*Places it in his palm.*) There now—
you're holding him gently! Hold him over the light, he loves the light!
You see how the light shines through him?

JIM. It sure does shine!

LAURA. I shouldn't be partial, but he is my favorite one.

JIM. What kind of a thing is this one supposed to be?

LAURA. Haven't you noticed the single horn on his forehead?

JIM. A unicorn, huh?

LAURA. Mmm-hmmm!

JIM. Unicorns, aren't they extinct in the modern world?

LAURA. I know!

JIM. Poor little fellow, he must feel sort of lonesome.

LAURA (*smiling*). Well, if he does he doesn't complain about it. He stays on a
shelf with some horses that don't have horns and all of them seem to
get along nicely together.

JIM. How do you know?

LAURA (*lightly*). I haven't heard any arguments among them!

JIM (*grinning*). No arguments, huh? Well, that's a pretty good sign! Where shall I set him?

LAURA. Put him on the table. They all like a change of scenery once in a while!

JIM (*stretching*). Well, well, well, well—Look how big my shadow is when I stretch!

LAURA. Oh, oh, yes—it stretches across the ceiling!

JIM (*crossing to door*). I think it's stopped raining. (*Opens fire-escape door.*) Where does the music come from?

LAURA. From the Paradise Dance Hall across the alley.

JIM. How about cutting the rug a little, Miss Wingfield?

LAURA. Oh, I—

JIM. Or is your program filled up? Let me have a look at it. (*Grasps imaginary card.*) Why, every dance is taken! I'll just have to scratch some out. (*Waltz Music: "La Golondrina."*) Ahhh, a waltz! (*He executes some sweeping turns by himself then holds his arms toward* LAURA.)

LAURA (*breathlessly*). I—can't dance!

JIM. There you go, that inferiority stuff!

LAURA. I've never danced in my life!

JIM. Come on, try!

LAURA. Oh, but I'd step on you!

JIM. I'm not made out of glass.

LAURA. How—how—how do we start?

JIM. Just leave it to me. You hold your arms out a little.

LAURA. Like this?

JIM. A little bit higher. Right. Now don't tighten up, that's the main thing about it—relax.

LAURA (*laughing breathlessly*). It's hard not to.

JIM. Okay.

LAURA. I'm afraid you can't budge me.

JIM. What do you bet I can't? (*He swings her into motion.*)

LAURA. Goodness, yes, you can!

JIM. Let yourself go, now, Laura, just let yourself go.

LAURA. I'm—

JIM. Come on!

LAURA. Trying!

JIM. Not so stiff—Easy does it!

LAURA. I know but I'm—

JIM. Loosen th' backbone! There now, that's a lot better.

LAURA. Am I?

JIM. Lots, lots better! (*He moves her about the room in a clumsy waltz.*)

LAURA. Oh, my!

JIM. Ha-ha!

LAURA. Oh, my goodness!

JIM. Ha-ha-ha! (*They suddenly bump into the table.* JIM *stops.*) What did we hit on?

LAURA. Table.

JIM. Did something fall off it? I think—

LAURA. Yes.

JIM. I hope that it wasn't the little glass horse with the horn!

LAURA. Yes.

JIM. Aw, aw, aw. Is it broken?

LAURA. Now it is just like all the other horses.

JIM. It's lost its—

LAURA. Horn! It doesn't matter. Maybe it's a blessing in disguise.

JIM. You'll never forgive me. I bet that that was your favorite piece of glass.

LAURA. I don't have favorites much. It's no tragedy, Freckles. Glass breaks so easily. No matter how careful you are. The traffic jars the shelves and things fall off them.

JIM. Still I'm awfully sorry that I was the cause.

LAURA (*smiling*). I'll just imagine he had an operation. The horn was removed to make him feel less—freakish! (*They both laugh.*) Now he will feel more at home with the other horses, the ones that don't have horns . . .

JIM. Ha-ha, that's very funny! (*Suddenly serious.*) I'm glad to see that you have a sense of humor. You know—you're—well—very different! Surprisingly different from anyone else I know! (*His voice becomes soft and hesitant with a genuine feeling.*) Do you mind me telling you that? (LAURA *is abashed beyond speech.*) You make me feel sort of—I don't know how to put it! I'm usually pretty good at expressing things, but—This is something that I don't know how to say! (LAURA *touches her throat and clears it—turns the broken unicorn in her hands.*) (*Even softer.*) Has anyone ever told you that you were pretty? (*Pause: Music.*) (LAURA *looks up slowly, with wonder, and shakes her head.*) Well, you are! In a very different way from anyone else. And all the nicer because of the difference, too. (*His voice becomes low and husky.* LAURA *turns away, nearly faint with the novelty of her emotions.*) I wish that you were my sister. I'd teach you to have some confidence in yourself. The different people are not like other people, but being different is nothing to be ashamed of. Because other people are not such wonderful people. They're one hundred times one thousand. You're one times one! They walk all over the earth. You just stay here. They're common as—weeds, but—you—well, you're *Blue Roses!*

(*Image on Screen: Blue Roses.*)

(*Music Changes.*)

LAURA. But blue is wrong for—roses . . .

JIM. It's right for you—You're—pretty!

LAURA. In what respect am I pretty?

JIM. In all respects—believe me! Your eyes—your hair—are pretty! Your hands are pretty! (*He catches hold of her hand.*) You think I'm making this up because I'm invited to dinner and have to be nice. Oh, I could do that! I could put on an act for you, Laura, and say lots of things without being very sincere. But this time I am. I'm talking to you sincerely. I happened to notice you had this inferiority complex that keeps you from feeling comfortable with people. Somebody needs to build your confidence up and make you proud instead of shy and turning away and—blushing—Somebody ought to—ought to—*kiss* you. Laura! (*His hand slips slowly up her arm to her shoulder.*) (*Music Swells Tumultuously.*) (*He suddenly turns her about and kisses her on the lips. When he releases her* LAURA *sinks on the sofa with a bright, dazed look.* JIM *backs away and fishes in his pocket for a cigarette.*) (*Legend on Screen: "Sou-venir."*) Stumble-john! (*He lights the cigarette, avoiding her look. There is a peal of girlish laughter from* AMANDA *in the kitchen.* LAURA *slowly raises and opens her hand. It still contains the little broken glass animal. She looks at it with a tender, bewildered expression.*) Stumble-john! I shouldn't have done that—That was way off the beam. You don't smoke, do you? (*She looks up, smiling, not hearing the question. He sits beside her a little gingerly. She looks at him speechlessly—waiting. He coughs decorously and moves a little farther aside as he considers the situation and senses her feelings, dimly, with perturbation. Gently.*) Would you—care for a—mint? (*She doesn't seem to hear him but her look grows brighter even.*) Peppermint—Life Saver? My pocket's a regular drug store—wherever I go . . . (*He pops a mint in his mouth. Then gulps and decides to make a clean breast of it. He speaks slowly and gingerly.*) Laura, you know, if I had a sister like you, I'd do the same thing as Tom. I'd bring out fellows—introduce her to them. The right type of boys—of a type to—appreciate her. Only—well—he made a mistake about me. Maybe I've got no call to be saying this. That may not have been the idea in having me over. But what if it was? There's nothing wrong about that. The only trouble is that in my case—I'm not in a situation to—do the right thing. I can't take down your number and say I'll phone. I can't call up next week and—ask for a date. I thought I had better explain the situation in case you misunderstood it and—hurt your feelings. . . . (*Pause. Slowly, very slowly,* LAURA'S *look changes, her eyes returning slowly from his to the ornament in her palm.*)

AMANDA *utters another gay laugh in the kitchen.*

LAURA (*faintly*). You—won't—call again?

JIM. No, Laura, I can't. (*He rises from the sofa.*) As I was just explaining, I've—got strings on me, Laura, I've—been going steady! I go out all the time with a girl named Betty. She's a home-girl like you, and Catholic, and Irish, and in a great many ways we—get along fine. I met her last summer on a moonlight boat trip up the river to Alton, on the *Majestic.* Well—right away from the start it was—love! (*Legend: Love!*) (LAURA *sways slightly forward and grips the arm of the sofa. He fails to notice, now enrapt in his own comfortable being.*) Being in love has made a new man of me! (*Leaning stiffly forward, clutching the arm of the sofa,* LAURA *struggles visibly with her storm. But* JIM *is oblivious, she is a long way off.*) The power of love is really pretty tremendous! Love is something that—changes the whole world, Laura! (*The storm abates a little and* LAURA *leans back. He notices her again.*) It happened that Betty's aunt took sick, she got a wire and had to go to Centralia. So Tom—when he asked me to dinner—I naturally just accepted the invitation, not knowing that you—that he—that I—(*He stops awkwardly.*) Huh—I'm a stumble-john! (*He flops back on the sofa. The holy candles in the altar of* LAURA'S *face have been snuffed out! There is a look of almost infinite desolation.* JIM *glances at her uneasily.*) I wish that you would—say something. (*She bites her lip which was trembling and then bravely smiles. She opens her hand again on the broken glass ornament. Then she gently takes his hand and raises it level with her own. She carefully places the unicorn in the palm of his hand, then pushes his fingers closed upon it.*) What are you—doing that for? You want me to have him?—Laura? (*She nods.*) What for?

LAURA. A—souvenir . . .

She rises unsteadily and crouches beside the victrola to wind it up.

(*Legend on Screen: "Things Have a Way of Turning Out So Badly."*)

(*Or Image: "Gentleman Caller Waving Good-Bye!—Gaily."*)

At this moment AMANDA *rushes brightly back in the front room. She bears a pitcher of fruit punch in an old-fashioned cut-glass pitcher and a plate of macaroons. The plate has a gold border and poppies painted on it.*

AMANDA. Well, well, well! Isn't the air delightful after the shower? I've made you children a little liquid refreshment. (*Turns gaily to the gentleman caller.*) Jim, do you know that song about lemonade?

> "Lemonade, lemonade
> Made in the shade and stirred with a spade—
> Good enough for any old maid!"

JIM (*uneasily*). Ha-ha! No—I never heard it.

AMANDA. Why, Laura! You look so serious!

JIM. We were having a serious conversation.

AMANDA. Good! Now you're better acquainted!

JIM (*uncertainly*). Ha-ha! Yes.

AMANDA. You modern young people are much more serious-minded than my generation. I was so gay as a girl!

JIM. You haven't changed, Mrs. Wingfield.

AMANDA. Tonight I'm rejuvenated! The gaiety of the occasion, Mr. O'Connor! (*She tosses her head with a peal of laughter. Spills lemonade.*) Oooo! I'm baptizing myself!

JIM. Here—let me—

AMANDA (*setting the pitcher down*). There now. I discovered we had some maraschino cherries. I dumped them in, juice and all!

JIM. You shouldn't have gone to that trouble, Mrs. Wingfield.

AMANDA. Trouble, trouble? Why it was loads of fun! Didn't you hear me cutting up in the kitchen? I bet your ears were burning! I told Tom how outdone with him I was for keeping you to himself so long a time! He should have brought you over much, much sooner! Well, now that you've found your way, I want you to be a very frequent caller! Not just occasional but all the time. Oh, we're going to have a lot of gay times together! I see them coming! Mmm, just breathe that air! So fresh, and the moon's so pretty! I'll skip back out—I know where my place is when young folks are having a—serious conversation!

JIM. Oh, don't go out, Mrs. Wingfield. The fact of the matter is I've got to be going.

AMANDA. Going, now? You're joking! Why, it's only the shank of the evening, Mr. O'Connor!

JIM. Well, you know how it is.

AMANDA. You mean you're a young workingman and have to keep workingmen's hours. We'll let you off early tonight. But only on the condition

that next time you stay later. What's the best night for you? Isn't Saturday night the best night for you workingmen?

JIM. I have a couple of time-clocks to punch, Mrs. Wingfield. One at morning,
another one at night!

AMANDA. My, but you *are* ambitious! You work at night, too?

JIM. No, Ma'am, not work but—Betty! (*He crosses deliberately to pick up his
hat. The band at the Paradise Dance Hall goes into a tender waltz.*)

AMANDA. Betty? Betty? Who's—Betty! (*There is an ominous cracking sound
in the sky.*)

JIM. Oh, just a girl. The girl I go steady with! (*He smiles charmingly. The sky
falls.*)

(*Legend: "The Sky Falls."*)

AMANDA (*a long-drawn exhalation*). Ohhhh...Is it a serious romance,
Mr. O'Connor?

JIM. We're going to be married the second Sunday in June.

AMANDA. Ohhhh—how nice! Tom didn't mention that you were engaged to
be married.

JIM. The cat's not out of the bag at the warehouse yet. You know how they
are. They call you Romeo and stuff like that. (*He stops at the oval mirror to put on his hat. He carefully shapes the brim and the crown to give
a discreetly dashing effect.*) It's been a wonderful evening, Mrs. Wingfield.
I guess this is what they mean by Southern hospitality.

AMANDA. It really wasn't anything at all.

JIM. I hope it don't seem like I'm rushing off. But I promised Betty I'd pick
her up at the Wabash depot, an' by the time I get my jalopy down there
her train'll be in. Some women are pretty upset if you keep 'em waiting.

AMANDA. Yes, I know—The tyranny of women! (*Extends her hand.*) Good-
bye, Mr. O'Connor. I wish you luck—and happiness—and success! All
three of them, and so does Laura!—Don't you, Laura?

LAURA. Yes!

JIM (*taking her hand*). Goodbye, Laura. I'm certainly going to treasure that
souvenir. And don't you forget the good advice I gave you. (*Raises his
voice to a cheery shout.*) So long, Shakespeare! Thanks again, ladies—
good night!

He grins and ducks jauntily out.

Still bravely grimacing, AMANDA *closes the door on the gentleman
caller. Then she turns back to the room with a puzzled expression. She
and* LAURA *don't dare to face each other.* LAURA *crouches beside the victrola to wind it.*

AMANDA (*faintly*). Things have a way of turning out so badly. I don't believe
that I would play the victrola. Well, well—well—Our gentleman caller
was engaged to be married! Tom!

TOM (*from back*). Yes, Mother?

AMANDA. Come in here a minute. I want to tell you something awfully funny.

TOM (*enters with macaroon and a glass of the lemonade*). Has the gentleman caller gotten away already?

AMANDA. The gentleman caller has made an early departure. What a wonderful joke you played on us!

TOM. How do you mean?

AMANDA. You didn't mention that he was engaged to be married.

TOM. Jim? Engaged?

AMANDA. That's what he just informed us.

TOM. I'll be jiggered! I didn't know about that.

AMANDA. That seems very peculiar.

TOM. What's peculiar about it?

AMANDA. Didn't you call him your best friend down at the warehouse?

TOM. He is, but how did I know?

AMANDA. It seems extremely peculiar that you wouldn't know your best friend was going to be married!

TOM. The warehouse is where I work, not where I know things about people!

AMANDA. You don't know things anywhere! You live in a dream; you manufacture illusions! (*He crosses to door.*) Where are you going?

TOM. I'm going to the movies.

AMANDA. That's right, now that you've had us make such fools of ourselves. The effort, the preparations, all the expense! The new floor lamp, the rug, the clothes for Laura! All for what? To entertain some other girl's fiancé! Go to the movies, go! Don't think about us, a mother deserted, an unmarried sister who's crippled and has no job! Don't let anything interfere with your selfish pleasure! Just go, go, go—to the movies!

TOM. All right, I will! The more you shout about my selfishness to me the quicker I'll go, and I won't go to the movies!

AMANDA. Go, then! Then go to the moon—you selfish dreamer!

TOM smashes his glass on the floor. He plunges out on the fire-escape, slamming the door. LAURA *screams—cut by door.*

Dance-hall music up. TOM *goes to the rail and grips it desperately, lifting his face in the chill white moonlight penetrating the narrow abyss of the alley.*

(*Legend on Screen: "And So Good-Bye . . ."*)

TOM'S *closing speech is timed with the interior pantomime. The interior scene is played as though viewed through sound-proof glass.* AMANDA *appears to be making a comforting speech to* LAURA *who is huddled upon the sofa. Now that we cannot hear the mother's speech, her silliness is gone and she has dignity and tragic beauty.* LAURA'S *dark hair hides her face until at the end of the speech she lifts it to smile at her mother.* AMANDA'S *gestures are slow and graceful, almost dancelike, as she comforts the daughter. At the end of her speech she glances a moment at the father's picture—then withdraws through the portieres. At close of* TOM'S *speech,* LAURA *blows out the candles, ending the play.*

TOM. I didn't go to the moon, I went much further—for time is the longest distance between two places—Not long after that I was fired for writing a poem on the lid of a shoe-box. I left Saint Louis. I descended the steps of this fire-escape for a last time and followed, from then on, in my

father's footsteps, attempting to find in motion what was lost in space—
I traveled around a great deal. The cities swept about me like dead
leaves, leaves that were brightly colored but torn away from the
branches. I would have stopped, but I was pursued by something. It always came upon me unawares, taking me altogether by surprise. Perhaps it was a familiar bit of music. Perhaps it was only a piece of transparent glass—Perhaps I am walking along a street at night, in some
strange city, before I have found companions. I pass the lighted window
of a shop where perfume is sold. The window is filled with pieces of
colored glass, tiny transparent bottles in delicate colors, like bits of a
shattered rainbow. Then all at once my sister touches my shoulder. I
turn around and look into her eyes . . . Oh, Laura, Laura, I tried to leave
you behind me, but I am more faithful than I intended to be! I reach for
a cigarette, I cross the street, I run into the movies or a bar, I buy a drink,
I speak to the nearest stranger—anything that can blow your candles
out! (LAURA *bends over the candles.*)—for nowadays the world is lit by
lightning! Blow out your candles, Laura—and so goodbye . . .

She blows the candles out.

(*The Scene Dissolves.*)

A Context for *The Glass Menagerie*

TENNESSEE WILLIAMS

Production Notes   [1944]

Being a "memory play," *The Glass Menagerie* can be presented with unusual
freedom of convention. Because of its considerably delicate or tenuous
material, atmospheric touches and subtleties of direction play a particularly
important part. Expressionism and all other unconventional techniques in
drama have only one valid aim, and that is a closer approach to truth. When
a play employs unconventional techniques, it is not, or certainly shouldn't
be, trying to escape its responsibility of dealing with reality, or interpreting
experience, but is actually or should be attempting to find a closer approach, a more penetrating and vivid expression of things as they are. The
straight realistic play with its genuine frigidaire and authentic ice cubes, its
characters that speak exactly as its audience speaks, corresponds to the academic landscape and has the same virtue of a photographic likeness. Everyone should know nowadays the unimportance of the photographic in art:
that truth, life, or reality is an organic thing which the poetic imagination can
represent or suggest, in essence, only through transformation, through changing into other forms than those which were merely present in appearance.

These remarks are not meant as comments only on this particular play.
They have to do with a conception of a new, plastic theater which must take
the place of the exhausted theater of realistic conventions if the theater is to
resume vitality as a part of our culture.

The Screen Device

There is *only one important difference between the original and acting version of the play* and that is the *omission* in the latter of the device which I tentatively included in my *original* script. This device was the use of a screen on which were projected magic-lantern slides bearing images or titles. I do not regret the omission of this device from the . . . Broadway production. The extraordinary power of Miss Taylor's[10] performance made it suitable to have the utmost simplicity in the physical production. But I think it may be interesting to some readers to see how this device was conceived. So I am putting it into the published manuscript. These images and legends, projected from behind, were cast on a section of wall between the front-room and dining-room areas, which should be indistinguishable from the rest when not in use.

The purpose of this will probably be apparent. It is to give accent to certain values in each scene. Each scene contains a particular point (or several) which is structurally the most important. In an episodic play, such as this, the basic structure or narrative line may be obscured from the audience; the effect may seem fragmentary rather than architectural. This may not be the fault of the play so much as a lack of attention in the audience. The legend or image upon the screen will strengthen the effect of what is merely allusion in the writing and allow the primary point to be made more simply and lightly than if the entire responsibility were on the spoken lines. Aside from this structural value, I think the screen will have a definite emotional appeal, less definable but just as important. An imaginative producer or director may invent many other uses for this device than those indicated in the present script. In fact the possibilities of the device seem much larger to me than the instance of this play can possibly utilize.

The Music

Another extra-literary accent in this play is provided by the use of music. A single recurring tune, "The Glass Menagerie," is used to give emotional emphasis to suitable passages. This tune is like circus music, not when you are on the grounds or in the immediate vicinity of the parade, but when you are at some distance and very likely thinking of something else. It seems under those circumstances to continue almost interminably and it weaves in and out of your preoccupied consciousness; then it is the lightest, most delicate music in the world and perhaps the saddest. It expresses the surface vivacity of life with the underlying strain of immutable and inexpressible sorrow. When you look at a piece of delicately spun glass you think of two things: how beautiful it is and how easily it can be broken. Both of those ideas should be woven into the recurring tune, which dips in and out of the play as if it were carried on a wind that changes. It serves as a thread of connection and allusion between the narrator with his separate point in time and space and the subject of his story. Between each episode it returns as reference to the emotion, nostalgia, which is the first condition of the play. It is

---

[10]**Miss Taylor** Laurette Taylor played the role of Amanda Wingfield in the first Broadway production, 1945–1946.

primarily Laura's music and therefore comes out most clearly when the play focuses upon her and the lovely fragility of glass which is her image.

The Lighting

The lighting in the play is not realistic. In keeping with the atmosphere of memory, the stage is dim. Shafts of light are focused on selected areas or actors, sometimes in contradistinction to what is the apparent center. For instance, in the quarrel scene between Tom and Amanda, in which Laura has no active part, the clearest pool of light is on her figure. This is also true of the supper scene. The light upon Laura should be distinct from the others, having a peculiar pristine clarity such as light used in early religious portraits of female saints or madonnas. A certain correspondence to light in religious paintings, such as El Greco's, where the figures are radiant in atmosphere that is relatively dusky, could be effectively used throughout the play. (It will also permit a more effective use of the screen.) A free, imaginative use of light can be of enormous value in giving a mobile, plastic quality to plays of a more or less static nature.

YOUR TURN

The Play on the Page

1. What does the victrola offer to Laura? Why is the typewriter a better symbol (for the purposes of the play) than, for example, a piano? After all, Laura could have been taking piano lessons.
2. What do you understand of Laura's glass menagerie? Why is it especially significant that the unicorn is Laura's favorite? How do you interpret the loss of the unicorn's horn? What is Laura saying to Jim in the gesture of giving him the unicorn?
3. Laura escapes to her glass menagerie. To what do Tom and Amanda escape? How complete do you think Tom's escape is at the end of the play?
4. Jim is described as "a nice, ordinary young man." To what extent can it be said that he, like the Wingfields, lives in a dream world? Tom says (speaking of the time of the play, 1939) that "The huge middle class was matriculating in a school for the blind." Does the play suggest that Jim, apparently a spokesperson for the American dream, is one of the pupils in this school?
5. There is an implication that had Jim not been going steady he might have rescued Laura, but Jim also seems to represent (for example, in his lines about money and power) the corrupt outside world that no longer values humanity. Is this a slip on Williams's part, or is it an interesting complexity?
6. How do you interpret the episode at the end when Laura blows out the candles? Is she blowing out illusions? her own life? both? Explain.
7. Some readers have seen great importance in the religious references in the play. To cite only a few examples: Scene 5 is called (on the screen) "Annunciation"; Amanda is associated with the music "Ave Maria"; Laura's candelabrum, from the altar of the Church of Heavenly Rest, was melted out of shape when the church burned down. Do you think these references add up to anything? If so, to what?

8. On page 900, Williams says, in a stage direction, *"Now that we cannot hear the mother's speech, her silliness is gone and she has dignity and tragic beauty."* Is Williams simply dragging in the word "tragic" because of its prestige, or is it legitimate? *Tragedy* is often distinguished from *pathos*: in tragedy, suffering is experienced by persons who act and are in some measure responsible for their suffering; in pathos, suffering is experienced by the passive and the innocent. For example, in a discussion of *The Suppliants,* a play by the ancient Greek dramatist Aeschylus, H. D. F. Kitto (in *Greek Tragedy: A Literary Study* (1939)) says, "The Suppliants are not only pathetic, as the victims of outrage, but also tragic, as the victims of their own misconceptions." Given this distinction, to what extent are Amanda and Laura tragic? pathetic? You might take into account the following quote from an interview with Williams, reprinted in *Conversations with Tennessee Williams,* ed. Albert J. Devlin (1986): "The mother's valor is the *core* of *The Glass Menagerie.* . . . She's confused, pathetic, even stupid, but everything has *got* to be all right. She fights to make it that way in the only way she knows how."

9. Before writing *The Glass Menagerie,* Williams wrote a short story with the same plot, "Portrait of a Girl in Glass" (later published in his *Collected Stories*). You may want to compare the two works, noticing especially the ways in which Williams has turned a story into a play.

The Play on the Stage

10. In what ways is the setting relevant to the issues raised in the play?

11. In his Production Notes (page 902) Williams called for the use of a "screen device." Over the years, some productions have incorporated it and some have not. If you were involved in producing *The Glass Menagerie,* would you use this device? Explain your reasons.

12. As director, would you want the actress playing Laura to limp? Give reasons for your decision, and provide additional comments on the ways in which you would ask an actress to portray the role.

13. List the various emotions that you find for Amanda in Scenes 2 and 3. If you were advising an actress playing this role, how would you suggest she convey these different feelings? Consider these questions: In what ways does she reveal her own sadnesses? Should her speeches to Tom be delivered differently from her speeches to Laura? When she looks at Laura's yearbook, should there be any physical contact between the two women? What effect would you wish to achieve at the close of Scene 3?

14. At the end of Scene 5, after an exasperated exchange between Tom and Amanda, Laura and her mother make a wish on the new moon. Three students can memorize this brief section and present it to the group. Then examine each speech, and discuss its emotion. Offer suggestions to the three actors—for instance, changes in emphasis, a slight difference in tone, a certain stance for the mother and daughter—and repeat the scene.

Tragedy

The Greek philosopher Aristotle defined "tragedy" as a dramatization of a serious happening—not necessarily one ending with the death of the protagonist—and his definition remains among the best. But many plays have been written since Aristotle defined tragedy. When we think of Shakespeare's tragedies, we cannot resist narrowing Aristotle's definition by adding something like "showing a struggle that rends the protagonist's whole being"; and when we think of the "problem plays" of the last hundred years—the serious treatments of such sociological problems as alcoholism and race prejudice—we might be inclined to exclude some of them by adding to the definition something about the need for universal appeal.

The question remains: Is there a single quality present in all works that we call tragedy and absent from works not called tragedy? If there is, no one has yet pointed it out to general satisfaction. But this failure does not mean that there is no such classification as "tragedy." We sense that tragedies resemble each other as members of the same family resemble each other: two children have the mother's coloring and eyes, a third child has the mother's coloring but the father's eyes, a fourth child has the mother's eyes but the father's coloring.

In the next few pages we will examine three comments on tragedy, none of which is entirely acceptable, but each of which seems to have some degree of truth, and each of which can help us detect resemblances and differences among tragedies. The first comment is by Cyril Tourneur, a tragic dramatist of the early seventeenth century:

When the bad bleed, then is the tragedy good.

We think of Macbeth ("usurper," "butcher"). Macbeth is much more than a usurper and butcher, but it is undeniable that he is an offender against the moral order. Whatever the merits of Tourneur's statement, however, if we think of *Romeo and Juliet* (to consider only one play), we realize its inadequacy. Tourneur so stresses the guilt of the protagonist that his or her suffering becomes mere retributive justice. But we cannot plausibly say, for example, that Romeo and Juliet deserved to die because they married without their parents' consent; it is much too simple to call them "bad." Romeo and Juliet are young, in love, nobler in spirit than their parents.

Tourneur's view is probably derived ultimately from an influential passage in Aristotle's *Poetics* in which Aristotle speaks of **hamartia,** sometimes literally translated as "missing the target," sometimes as "vice" or "flaw" or "weakness," but perhaps best translated as "mistake." Aristotle seems to imply that the hero is undone because of some mistake he or she commits, but this mistake need not be the result of a moral fault; it may be simply a miscalculation—for example, failure to foresee the consequences of a deed. Brutus makes a strategic mistake when he lets Marc Antony speak at Caesar's funeral, but we can hardly call it a vice.

Because Aristotle's *hamartia* includes mistakes of this sort, the common translation "tragic flaw" is erroneous. In many Greek tragedies the hero's *hamartia* is **hubris** (or **hybris**), usually translated as "overweening pride." The hero forgets that he or she is fallible, acts as though he or she has the power and wisdom of the gods, and is later humbled for this arrogance. But one can argue that this self-assertiveness is not a vice but a virtue, not a weakness but a strength; if the hero is destroyed for self-assertion, he or she is nevertheless greater than the surrounding people, just as the person who tries to stem a lynch mob is greater than the mob, although that person also may be lynched for his or her virtue. Or a hero may be undone by a high-mindedness that makes him or her vulnerable. Hamlet is vulnerable because he is, as his enemy says, "most generous and free from all contriving"; because Hamlet is high-minded, he will not suspect that the proposed fencing match is a murderous plot. Othello can be tricked into murdering Desdemona not simply because he is jealous but because he is (in the words of the villainous Iago) "of a free and open nature / That thinks men honest but seem so." Iago knows, too, that out of Desdemona's "goodness" he can "make the net / That shall enmesh them all."

Next, here is a statement more or less the reverse of Tourneur's, by a twentieth-century Russian critic, L. I. Timofeev:

> Tragedy in Soviet literature arouses a feeling of pride for the man who has accomplished a great deed for the people's happiness; it calls for continued struggle against the things which brought about the hero's death.

The distortions in Soviet criticism are often amusing: Hamlet is seen as an incipient Communist, undone by the decadent aristocracy; or Romeo and Juliet as young people of the future, undone by bourgeois parents. Soviet drama in the third quarter of the twentieth century so consistently showed the triumph of the worker that Western visitors to Russia commented on the absence of contemporary tragic plays. Still, there is much in the idea that the tragic hero accomplishes "a great deed," and perhaps we do resent "the things which brought about the hero's death." The stubbornness of the Montagues and Capulets, the fury of the mob that turns against Brutus, the crimes of Claudius in *Hamlet*—all these would seem to call for our indignation.

The third comment is by Arthur Miller:

> If it is true to say that in essence the tragic hero is intent upon claiming his whole due as a personality, and if this struggle must be total and without reservation, then it automatically demonstrates the indestructible will of man to achieve his humanity. . . . It is curious, although edifying, that the plays we revere, century after century, are the tragedies. In them, and in them alone, lies the belief—optimistic, if you will—in the perfectibility of man.

There is much in Miller's suggestions that the tragic hero makes a large and total claim and that the audience often senses triumph rather than despair in tragedies. We often feel that we have witnessed human greatness—that the hero, despite profound suffering, has lived according to his or her ideals. We may feel that we have achieved new insight into human greatness. But the perfectibility of man? Do we feel that *Julius Caesar* or *Macbeth* or *Hamlet* have to do with human perfectibility? Don't these plays suggest rather that people, whatever their nobility, have within them the seeds of their own destruction? Without overemphasizing the guilt of the protagonists, don't we feel that in part the plays dramatize the *im*perfectibility of human beings? In much tragedy, after all, the destruction comes from within, not from without:

> In tragic life, God wot,
> No villain need be! Passions spin the plot:
> We are betrayed by what is false within.
>
> —George Meredith

What we are talking about is **tragic irony,** the contrast between what is believed to be so and what is so, or between expectations and accomplishments.* Several examples from *Macbeth* illustrate something of the range of tragic irony within a single play. In the first act, King Duncan bestows on Macbeth the title of Thane of Cawdor. By his kindness Duncan seals his own doom, for Macbeth, having achieved this rank, will next want to achieve a higher one. In the third act, Macbeth, knowing that Banquo will soon be murdered, hypocritically urges Banquo to "fail not our feast." But Macbeth's hollow request is ironically fulfilled: the ghost of Banquo terrorizes Macbeth during the feast. The most pervasive irony of all, of course, is that Macbeth aims at happiness when he kills Duncan and takes the throne, but he wins only sorrow.

Aristotle's discussion of **peripeteia (reversal)** and **anagnorisis (recognition)** may be a way of getting at this sort of irony. He may simply have meant a reversal of fortune (for example, good luck ceases) and a recognition of who is who (for example, the pauper is really the prince), but more likely he meant profounder things. One can say that the reversal in *Macbeth* lies in the sorrow that Macbeth's increased power brings. The recognition comes when he realizes the consequences of his deeds:

> I have lived long enough: my way of life
> Is fall'n into the sere, the yellow leaf;
> And what which should accompany old age,
> As honor, love, obedience, troops of friends,
> I must not look to have; but, in their stead,
> Curses, not loud but deep, mouth-honor, breath
> Which the poor heart would fain deny, and dare not.

That our deeds often undo us, that we can aim at our good and produce our ruin, was not, of course, a discovery of the tragic dramatists. The archetype is the story of Adam and Eve: these two aimed at becoming like God, and as a consequence,

---

*Tragic irony is sometimes **dramatic irony** or **Sophoclean irony.** The terms are often applied to speeches or actions that the audience understands in a sense fuller than or different from the sense in which the dramatic characters understand them.

they brought upon themselves corruption, death, the loss of their earthly paradise. The Bible is filled with stories of tragic irony. A brief quotation from Ecclesiastes (10.8–9) can stand as an epitome of these stories:

> He that diggeth a pit shall fall into it; and whoso breaketh an hedge,
> a serpent shall bite him.
> Whoso removeth stones shall be hurt therewith; and he that
> cleaveth wood shall be endangered thereby.

"He that cleaveth wood shall be endangered thereby." Activity involves danger. To be inactive is, often, to be ignoble, but to be active is necessarily to imperil oneself. Perhaps we can attempt a summary of tragic figures: they act, and they suffer, usually as a consequence of their action. The question is not of the action's being particularly bad (Tourneur's view) or particularly good (Timofeev's view); the action is often both good and bad, a sign of courage and also of arrogance, a sign of greatness and also of limitations.

Finally, a brief consideration of the pleasure of tragedy: Why do we enjoy plays about suffering? Aristotle has some obscure comments on **catharsis (purgation)** that are often interpreted as saying that tragedy arouses in us both pity and fear and then purges us of these emotions. The idea, perhaps, is that just as we can (it is said) harmlessly discharge our aggressive impulses by witnessing a prizefight or by shouting at an umpire, so we can harmlessly discharge our impulses to pity and to fear by witnessing the dramatization of a person's destruction. The theater in this view is an outlet for emotions that elsewhere would be harmful. But, it must be repeated, Aristotle's comments on catharsis are obscure; perhaps, too, they are wrong.

Most later theories on the pleasure of tragedy are footnotes to Aristotle's words on catharsis. Some say that our pleasure is sadistic (we enjoy the sight of suffering); some, that our pleasure is masochistic (we enjoy lacerating ourselves); some, that it lies in sympathy (we enjoy extending pity and benevolence to the wretched); some, that it lies in self-congratulation (we are reminded, when we see suffering, of our own good fortune); some, that we take pleasure in tragedy because the tragic hero acts out our secret desires, and we rejoice in his or her aggression, expiating our guilt in his or her suffering; and so on.

But this is uncertain psychology, and it mostly neglects the distinction between real suffering and dramatized suffering. In the latter, surely, part of the pleasure is in the contemplation of an aesthetic object, an object that is unified and complete. The chaos of real life seems, for a few moments in drama, to be ordered: the protagonist's action, his or her subsequent suffering, and the total cosmos seem somehow related. Tragedy has no use for the passerby who is killed by a falling brick. The events (the person's walk, the brick's fall) have no meaningful relation. But suppose a person chooses to climb a mountain, and in making the ascent sets in motion an avalanche that destroys that person. Here we find (however simple the illustration) something closer to tragedy. We do not say that people should avoid mountains, or that mountain climbers deserve to die by avalanches. But we feel that the event is unified, as the accidental conjunction of brick and passerby is not.

Tragedy thus presents some sort of ordered action; tragic drama itself is orderly. As we see or read it, we feel it cannot be otherwise; word begets word, deed begets deed, and every moment is exquisitely appropriate. Whatever the relevance on sadism, masochism, sympathy, and the rest, the pleasure of tragedy surely comes in part from the artistic shaping of the material.

The theater at Epidaurus, located on the Peloponnesus east of Nauplia, Greece.

A Note on Greek Tragedy

Little or nothing is known for certain of the origin of Greek tragedy. The most common hypothesis holds that it developed from improvised speeches during choral dances honoring Dionysus, a Greek nature god associated with spring, fertility, and wine. Thespis (who perhaps never existed) is said to have introduced an actor into these choral performances in the sixth century BCE, Aeschylus (525–456 BCE), Greece's first great writer of tragedies, added the second actor, and Sophocles (496?–406 BCE) added the third actor and fixed the size of the chorus at fifteen. (Because the chorus leader often functioned as an additional actor, and because the actors sometimes doubled in their parts, a Greek tragedy could have more characters than might at first be thought.)

All the extant great Greek tragedy is of the fifth century BCE. It was performed at religious festivals in the winter and early spring, in large outdoor amphitheaters built on hillsides. Some of these theaters were enormous; the one at Epidaurus held about fifteen thousand people. The audience sat in tiers, looking down on the **orchestra** (a place for dancing), with the acting area behind it and the **skene** (the scene building) yet farther back. The scene building served as dressing room, background (suggesting a palace or temple), and place for occasional entrances and exits. Furthermore, this building helped to provide good acoustics, for speech travels well if there is a solid barrier behind the speakers and a hard, smooth surface in front of them, and if the audience sits in tiers. The wall of the scene building provided the barrier; the orchestra provided the surface in front of the actors; and the seats on the hillside fulfilled the third requirement. Moreover, the acoustics were somewhat improved by slightly elevating the actors above the orchestra, but it is not known exactly when this platform was first constructed in front of the scene building.

A tragedy commonly begins with a **prologos (prologue),** during which the exposition is given. Next comes the **párodos,** the chorus's ode of entrance, sung while the chorus marches into the theater through the side aisles and onto the orchestra. The **epeisodion (episode)** is the ensuing scene; it is followed by a **stasimon** (choral song, ode). Usually there are four or five *epeisodia*, alternating with *stasima*. Each of these choral odes has a **strophe** (lines presumably sung while the chorus dances in one direction) and an antistrophe (lines presumably sung while the chorus retraces its steps). Sometimes a third part, an **epode,** concludes an ode. (In addition to odes that are *stasima*, there can be odes within episodes; the fourth episode of *Antigonê* contains an ode complete with *epode*.) After the last part of the last ode comes the **exodos,** the epilogue or final scene.

The actors (all male) wore masks, and they seem to have chanted much of the play. Perhaps the total result of combining speech with music and dancing was a sort of music-drama roughly akin to opera with some spoken dialogue, such as Mozart's *The Magic Flute* (1791).

Two Plays by Sophocles

SOPHOCLES

One of the three great writers of tragedies in ancient Greece, Sophocles (496?–406 BCE) was born in Colonus, near Athens, into a well-to-do family. Well educated, he first won public acclaim as a tragic poet at the age of twenty-seven, in 468 BCE when he defeated Aeschylus in a competition for writing a tragic play. He is said to have written some 120 plays, but only seven tragedies are extant: among them are Oedipus the King, Antigone, *and* Oedipus at Colonus. *He died, much honored, in his ninetieth year, in Athens, where he had lived his entire life.*

Oedipus the King

Translated by Robert Fagles

CHARACTERS

OEDIPUS, *king of Thebes*
A PRIEST OF ZEUS

Laurence Olivier in *Oedipus Rex*.

CREON, *brother of Jocasta*
A CHORUS *of Theban citizens and their* LEADER
TIRESIAS, *a blind prophet*
JOCASTA, *the queen, wife of Oedipus*
A MESSENGER *from Corinth*
A SHEPHERD
A MESSENGER *from inside the palace*
ANTIGONE, ISMENE, *daughters of Oedipus and Jocasta*
GUARDS *and* ATTENDANTS
PRIESTS *of Thebes*

[**TIME AND SCENE:** *The royal house of Thebes. Double doors dominate the façade; a stone altar stands at the center of the stage.*

Many years have passed since OEDIPUS *solved the riddle of the Sphinx and ascended the throne of Thebes, and now a plague has struck the city. A procession of priests enters; suppliants, broken and despondent, they carry branches wound in wool and lay them on the altar.*

The doors open. GUARDS *assemble.* OEDIPUS *comes forward, majestic but for a telltale limp, and slowly views the condition of his people.*]

OEDIPUS. Oh my children, the new blood of ancient Thebes,
    why are you here? Huddling at my altar,
    praying before me, your branches wound in wool.°
    Our city reeks with the smoke of burning incense,
    rings with cries for the Healer° and wailing for the dead.   5

---

3 branches wound in wool Suppliants laid such offerings on the altar of Apollo, god of healing, until their request was granted. Notice that in line 161 Oedipus tells the suppliants to remove the branches, thus suggesting that he will heal them. **5 the Healer** Apollo.

I thought it wrong, my children, to hear the truth
from others, messengers. Here I am myself—
you all know me, the world knows my fame:
I am Oedipus.

[*Helping a* PRIEST *to his feet.*]

             Speak up, old man. Your years,
your dignity—you should speak for the others.   10
Why here and kneeling, what preys upon you so?
Some sudden fear? some strong desire?
You can trust me. I am ready to help,
I'll do anything. I would be blind to misery
not to pity my people kneeling at my feet.   15
PRIEST. Oh Oedipus, king of the land, our greatest power!
You see us before you now, men of all ages
clinging to your altars. Here are boys,
still too weak to fly from the nest,
and here the old, bowed down with the years,   20
the holy ones—a priest of Zeus° myself—and here
the picked, unmarried men, the young hope of Thebes.
And all the rest, your great family gathers now,
branches wreathed, massing in the squares,
kneeling before the two temples of queen Athena°   25
or the river-shrine where the embers glow and die
and Apollo sees the future in the ashes.°
                   Our city—
look around you, see with your own eyes—
our ship pitches wildly, cannot lift her head
from the depths, the red waves of death . . .   30
Thebes is dying. A blight on the fresh crops
and the rich pastures, cattle sicken and die,
and the women die in labor, children stillborn,
and the plague, the fiery god of fever hurls down
on the city, his lightning slashing through us—   35
raging plague in all its vengeance, devastating
the house of Cadmus!° And black Death luxuriates
in the raw, wailing miseries of Thebes.
Now we pray to you. You cannot equal the gods,
your children know that, bending at your altar.   40
But we do rate you first of men,
both in the common crises of our lives
and face-to-face encounters with the gods.
You freed us from the Sphinx,° you came to Thebes

---

21 Zeus chief deity on Mt. Olympus, and father of Apollo. **25 Athena** goddess of
wisdom and protector of cities.   **27 the ashes** Diviners foretold the future by examining
the ashes of burnt offerings.   **37 Cadmus** mythical founder of Thebes.   **44 the Sphinx**
a female monster (body of a lion, wings of a bird, face of a woman) who asked the riddle
"What goes on four legs in the morning, two at noon, and three in the evening?" and who
killed those who could not answer. When Oedipus responded correctly that man crawls
on all fours in infancy, walks upright in maturity, and uses a staff in old age, the Sphinx
destroyed herself.

and cut us loose from the bloody tribute° we had paid   45
that harsh, brutal singer. We taught you nothing,
no skill, no extra knowledge, still you triumphed.
A god was with you, so they say, and we believe it—
you lifted up our lives.
                          So now again,
Oedipus, king, we bend to you, your power—   50
we implore you, all of us on our knees:
find us strength, rescue! Perhaps you've heard
the voice of a god or something from other men,
Oedipus . . . what do you know?
The man of experience—you see it every day—   55
his plans will work in a crisis, his first of all.

Act now—we beg you, best of men, raise up our city!
Act, defend yourself, your former glory!
Your country calls you savior now
for your zeal, your action years ago.   60
Never let us remember of your reign:
you helped us stand, only to fall once more.
Oh raise up our city, set us on our feet.
The omens were good that day you brought us joy—
be the same man today!   65
Rule our land, you know you have the power,
but rule a land of the living, not a wasteland.
Ship and towered city are nothing, stripped of men
alive within it, living all as one.

OEDIPUS.   My children,
I pity you. I see—how could I fail to see   70
what longings bring you here? Well I know
you are sick to death, all of you,
but sick as you are, not one is sick as I.
Your pain strikes each of you alone, each
in the confines of himself, no other. But my spirit   75
grieves for the city, for myself and all of you.
I wasn't asleep, dreaming. You haven't wakened me—
I've wept through the nights, you must know that,
groping, laboring over many paths of thought.
After a painful search I found one cure: 80
I acted at once. I sent Creon,
my wife's own brother, to Delphi°—
Apollo the Prophet's oracle—to learn
what I might do or say to save our city.

Today's the day. When I count the days gone by   85
it torments me . . . what is he doing?
Strange, he's late, he's gone too long.
But once he returns, then, then I'll be a traitor
if I do not do all the god makes clear.

---

45 bloody tribute i.e., the young Thebans who had tried to solve the riddle and had
failed.   **82 Delphi** site of a shrine of Apollo.

PRIEST. Timely words. The men over there   90
  are signaling—Creon's just arriving.

OEDIPUS. [*Sighting* CREON, *then turning to the altar.*]
            Lord Apollo,
  let him come with a lucky word of rescue,
  shining like his eyes!

PRIEST. Welcome news, I think—he's crowned, look,
  and the laurel wreath is bright with berries.   95

OEDIPUS. We'll soon see. He's close enough to hear—

[*Enter* CREON *from the side; his face is shaded with a wreath.*]

  Creon, prince, my kinsman, what do you bring us?
  What message from the god?

CREON.   Good news.
  I tell you even the hardest things to bear,
  if they should turn out well, all would be well.   100

OEDIPUS. Of course, but what were the god's *words*? There's no hope
  and nothing to fear in what you've said so far.

CREON. If you want my report in the presence of these . . .

[*Pointing to the* PRIESTS *while drawing* OEDIPUS *toward the
palace.*]

  I'm ready now, or we might go inside.

OEDIPUS.   Speak out,
  speak to us all. I grieve for these, my people,   105
  far more than I fear for my own life.

CREON.   Very well,
  I will tell you what I heard from the god.
  Apollo commands us—he was quite clear—
  "Drive the corruption from the land,
  don't harbor it any longer, past all cure,   110
  don't nurse it in your soil—root it out!"

OEDIPUS. How can we cleanse ourselves—what rites?
  What's the source of the trouble?

CREON. Banish the man, or pay back blood with blood.
  Murder sets the plague-storm on the city.

OEDIPUS.   Whose murder?   115
  Whose fate does Apollo bring to light?

CREON.   Our leader,
  my lord, was once a man named Laius,
  before you came and put us straight on course.

OEDIPUS.   I know—
  or so I've heard. I never saw the man myself.

CREON. Well, he was killed, and Apollo commands us now—   120
  he could not be more clear,
  "Pay the killers back—whoever is responsible."

OEDIPUS. Where on earth are they? Where to find it now,
  the trail of the ancient guilt so hard to trace?

CREON. "Here in Thebes," he said.   125
  Whatever is sought for can be caught, you know,
  whatever is neglected slips away.

OEDIPUS.   But where,
    in the palace, the fields or foreign soil,
    where did Laius meet his bloody death?

CREON. He went to consult an oracle, Apollo said,   130
    and he set out and never came home again.

OEDIPUS. No messenger, no fellow-traveler saw what happened?
    Someone to cross-examine?

CREON.   No,
    they were all killed but one. He escaped,
    terrified, he could tell us nothing clearly,   135
    nothing of what he saw—just one thing.

OEDIPUS.   What's that?
    one thing could hold the key to it all,
    a small beginning give us grounds for hope.

CREON. He said thieves attacked them—a whole band,
    not single-handed, cut King Laius down.

OEDIPUS.   A thief, so daring,   140
    so wild, he'd kill a king? Impossible, unless conspirators paid
    him off in Thebes.

CREON. We suspected as much. But with Laius dead
    no leader appeared to help us in our troubles.

OEDIPUS. Trouble? Your *king* was murdered—royal blood!   145
    What stopped you from tracking down the killer
    then and there?

CREON.   The singing, riddling Sphinx.
    She . . . persuaded us to let the mystery go
    and concentrate on what lay at our feet.

OEDIPUS.   No,
    I'll start again—I'll bring it all to light myself!   150
    Apollo is right, and so are you, Creon,
    to turn our attention back to the murdered man.
    Now you have *me* to fight for you, you'll see:
    I am the land's avenger by all rights,
    and Apollo's champion too.   155
    But not to assist some distant kinsman, no,
    for my own sake I'll rid us of this corruption.
    Whoever killed the king may decide to kill me too,
    with the same violent hand—by avenging Laius
    I defend myself.

[*To the* PRIESTS.]

                Quickly, my children.   160
Up from the steps, take up your branches now.

[*To the* GUARDS.]

One of you summon the city here before us,
tell them I'll do everything. God help us,
we will see our triumph—or our fall.

[OEDIPUS *and* CREON *enter the palace, followed by the guards.*]

PRIEST. Rise, my sons. The kindness we came for   165
    Oedipus volunteers himself.

Apollo has sent his word, his oracle—
Come down, Apollo, save us, stop the plague.

[*The* PRIESTS *rise, remove their branches and exit to the side. Enter a* CHORUS, *the citizens of Thebes, who have not heard the news that* CREON *brings. They march around the altar, chanting.*]

CHORUS.   Zeus!
      Great welcome voice of Zeus,° what do you bring?
      What word from the gold vaults of Delphi   170
      comes to brilliant Thebes? Racked with terror—
            terror shakes my heart
      and I cry your wild cries, Apollo, Healer of Delos°
      I worship you in dread . . . what now, what is your price?
      some new sacrifice? some ancient rite from the past   175
      come round again each spring?—
            what will you bring to birth?
      Tell me, child of golden Hope
      warm voice that never dies!
      You are the first I call, daughter of Zeus   180
      deathless Athena—I call your sister Artemis,°
      heart of the market place enthroned in glory,
            guardian of our earth—
      I call Apollo, Archer astride the thunderheads of heaven—
      O triple shield against death, shine before me now!   185
      If ever, once in the past, you stopped some ruin
      launched against our walls
            you hurled the flame of pain
      far, far from Thebes—you gods
      come now, come down once more!
                                          No, no   190
      the miseries numberless, grief on grief, no end—
      too much to bear, we are all dying
      O my people . . .
            Thebes like a great army dying
      and there is no sword of thought to save us, no   195
      and the fruits of our famous earth, they will not ripen
      no and the women cannot scream their pangs to birth—
      screams for the Healer, children dead in the womb
            and life on life goes down
                  you can watch them go   200
            like seabirds winging west, outracing the day's fire
      down the horizon, irresistibly
            streaking on to the shores of Evening
                                          Death
      so many deaths, numberless deaths on deaths, no end—
      Thebes is dying, look, her children   205

---

169 welcome voice of Zeus Apollo, son of Zeus, spoke for Zeus.   **173 Delos** sacred island where Apollo was born.   **181 Artemis** a goddess, sister of Apollo.

stripped of pity . . .
   generations strewn on the ground
unburied, unwept, the dead spreading death
and the young wives and gray-haired mothers with them
cling to the altars, trailing in from all over the city—   210
Thebes, city of death, one long cortege
   and the suffering rises
      wails for mercy rise
   and the wild hymn for the Healer blazes out
clashing with our sobs our cries of mourning—   215
   O golden daughter of god,° send rescue
   radiant as the kindness in your eyes!

Drive him back!—the fever, the god of death
   that raging god of war
not armored in bronze, not shielded now, he burns me,   220
battle cries in the onslaught burning on—
O rout him from our borders!
Sail him, blast him out to the Sea-queen's chamber
   the black Atlantic gulfs
   or the northern harbor, death to all   225
where the Thracian surf comes crashing.
Now what the night spares he comes by day and kills—
the god of death.
                O lord of the stormcloud,
you who twirl the lightning, Zeus, Father,
thunder Death to nothing!   230

Apollo, lord of the light, I beg you—
   whip your longbow's golden cord
showering arrows on our enemies—shafts of power
champions strong before us rushing on!

Artemis, Huntress,   235
torches flaring over the eastern ridges—
ride Death down in pain!

God of the headdress gleaming gold, I cry to you—
your name and ours are one, Dionysus°—
   come with your face aflame with wine   240
      your raving women's cries
your army on the march! Come with the lightning
come with torches blazing, eyes ablaze with glory!
Burn that god of death that all gods hate!

[OEDIPUS *enters from the palace to address the* CHORUS, *as if addressing the entire city of Thebes.*]

OEDIPUS. You pray to the gods? Let me grant your prayers.   245
   Come, listen to me—do what the plague demands:
   you'll find relief and lift your head from the depths.

---

216 golden daughter of god Athena.   **239 Dionysus** god of wine and fertility. He was attended by the Maenads (the "raving women" of line 241).

I will speak out now as a stranger to the story,
a stranger to the crime. If I'd been present then,
there would have been no mystery, no long hunt   250
without a clue in hand. So now, counted
a native Theban years after the murder,
to all of Thebes I make this proclamation:
if any one of you knows who murdered Laius,
the son of Labdacus, I order him to reveal   255
the whole truth to me. Nothing to fear,
even if he must denounce himself,
let him speak up
and so escape the brunt of the charge—
he will suffer no unbearable punishment,   260
nothing worse than exile, totally unharmed.

[OEDIPUS *pauses, waiting for a reply.*]

                                                  Next,
if anyone knows the murderer is a stranger,
a man from alien soil, come, speak up.
I will give him a handsome reward, and lay up
gratitude in my heart for him besides.   265

[*Silence again, no reply.*]

But if you keep silent, if anyone panicking,
trying to shield himself or friend or kin,
rejects my offer, then hear what I will do.
I order you, every citizen of the state
where I hold throne and power: banish this man—   270
whoever he may be—never shelter him, never
speak a word to him, never make him partner
to your prayers, your victims burned to the gods.
Never let the holy water touch his hands
Drive him out, each of you, from every home.   275
He is the plague, the heart of our corruption,
as Apollo's oracle has just revealed to me.
So I honor my obligations:
I fight for the god and for the murdered man.

Now my curse on the murderer. Whoever he is,   280
a lone man unknown in his crime
or one among many, let that man drag out
his life in agony, step by painful step—
I curse myself as well . . . if by any chance
he proves to be an intimate of our house,   285
here at my hearth, with my full knowledge,
may the curse I just called down on him strike me!

These are your orders: perform them to the last.
I command you, for my sake, for Apollo's, for this country
blasted root and branch by the angry heavens.   290
Even if god had never urged you on to act,

how could you leave the crime uncleansed so long?
A man so noble—your king, brought down in blood—
you should have searched. But I am the king now,
I hold the throne that he held then, possess his bed   295
and a wife who shares our seed . . . why, our seed
might be the same, children born of the same mother
might have created blood-bonds between us
if his hope of offspring hadn't met disaster—
but fate swooped at his head and cut him short.   300
So I will fight for him as if he were my father,
stop at nothing, search the world
to lay my hands on the man who shed his blood,
the son of Labdacus descended of Polydorus,
Cadmus of old and Agenor, founder of the line: 305
their power and mine are one.
                                        Oh dear gods,
my curse on those who disobey these orders!
Let no crops grow out of the earth for them—
shrivel their women, kill their sons,
burn them to nothing in this plague   310
that hits us now, or something even worse.
But you, loyal men of Thebes who approve my actions,
may our champion, Justice, may all the gods
be with us, fight beside us to the end!

LEADER. In the grip of your curse, my king, I swear   315
    I'm not the murderer, I cannot point him out.
    As for the search, Apollo pressed it on us—
    he should name the killer.

OEDIPUS.   Quite right,
    but to force the gods to act against their will—
    no man has the power.

LEADER.   Then if I might mention   320
    the next best thing . . .

OEDIPUS.   The third best too—
    don't hold back, say it.

LEADER.   I still believe . . .
    Lord Tiresias° sees with the eyes of Lord Apollo.
    Anyone searching for the truth, my king,
    might learn it from the prophet, clear as day.   325

OEDIPUS. I've not been slow with that. On Creon's cue
    I sent the escorts, twice, within the hour.
    I'm surprised he isn't here.

LEADER.   We need him—
    without him we have nothing but old, useless rumors.

OEDIPUS. Which rumors? I'll search out every word.   330

LEADER. Laius was killed, they say, by certain travelers.

OEDIPUS. I know—but no one can find the murderer.

---

323 **Tiresias** a blind prophet.

LEADER. If the man has a trace of fear in him
　　　he won't stay silent long,
　　　not with your curses ringing in his ears.   335
OEDIPUS. He didn't flinch at murder,
　　　he'll never flinch at words.
　　　[*Enter* TIRESIAS, *the blind prophet, led by a boy with escorts in at-*
　　　tendance. He remains at a distance.]
LEADER. Here is the one who will convict him, look,
　　　they bring him on at last, the seer, the man of god.
　　　The truth lives inside him, him alone.
OEDIPUS.   O Tiresias,   340
　　　master of all the mysteries of our life,
　　　all you teach and all you dare not tell,
　　　signs in the heavens, signs that walk the earth!
　　　Blind as you are, you can feel all the more
　　　what sickness haunts our city. You, my lord,   345
　　　are the one shield, the one savior we can find.

　　　We asked Apollo—perhaps the messengers
　　　haven't told you—he sent his answer back:
　　　"Relief from the plague can only come one way.
　　　Uncover the murderers of Laius,   350
　　　put them to death or drive them into exile."
　　　So I beg you, grudge us nothing now, no voice,
　　　no message plucked from the birds, the embers
　　　or the other mantic ways within your grasp.
　　　Rescue yourself, your city, rescue me—   355
　　　rescue everything infected by the dead.
　　　We are in your hands. For a man to help others
　　　with all his gifts and native strength:
　　　that is the noblest work.
TIRESIAS.   How terrible—to see the truth
　　　when the truth is only pain to him who sees!   360
　　　I knew it well, but I put it from my mind,
　　　else I never would have come.
OEDIPUS. What's this? Why so grim, so dire?
TIRESIAS. Just send me home. You bear your burdens,
　　　I'll bear mine. It's better that way,   365
　　　please believe me.
OEDIPUS.   Strange response . . . unlawful,
　　　unfriendly too to the state that bred and reared you—
　　　you withhold the word of god.
TIRESIAS.   I fail to see
　　　that your own words are so well-timed.
　　　I'd rather not have the same thing said of me . . .   370
OEDIPUS. For the love of god, don't turn away,
　　　not if you know something. We beg you,
　　　all of us on our knees.
TIRESIAS.   None of you knows—
　　　and I will never reveal my dreadful secrets,
　　　not to say your own.   375

OEDIPUS. What? You know and you won't tell?
You're bent on betraying us, destroying Thebes?
TIRESIAS. I'd rather not cause pain for you or me.
So why this . . . useless interrogation?
You'll get nothing from me.
OEDIPUS.   Nothing! You,   380
you scum of the earth, you'd enrage a heart of stone!
You won't talk? Nothing moves you?
Out with it, once and for all!
TIRESIAS. You criticize my temper . . . unaware
of the one *you* live with, you revile me.   385
OEDIPUS. Who could restrain his anger hearing you?
What outrage—you spurn the city!
TIRESIAS. What will come will come.
Even if I shroud it all in silence.
OEDIPUS. What will come? You're bound to *tell* me that.   390
TIRESIAS. I'll say no more. Do as you like, build your anger
to whatever pitch you please, rage your worst—
OEDIPUS. Oh I'll let loose, I have such fury in me—
now I see it all. You helped hatch the plot,
you did the work, yes, short of killing him   395
with your own hands—and given eyes I'd say
you did the killing single-handed!
TIRESIAS.   Is that so!
I charge you, then, submit to that decree
you just laid down: from this day onward
speak to no one, not these citizens, not myself.   400
You are the curse, the corruption of the land!
OEDIPUS. You, shameless—
aren't you appalled to start up such a story?
You think you can get away with this?
TIRESIAS.   I have already.
The truth with all its power lives inside me.   405
OEDIPUS. Who primed you for this? Not your prophet's trade.
TIRESIAS. You did, you forced me, twisted it out of me.
OEDIPUS. What? Say it again—I'll understand it better.
TIRESIAS. Didn't you understand, just now?
Or are you tempting me to talk?   410
OEDIPUS. No, I can't say I grasped your meaning.
Out with it, again!
TIRESIAS. I say you are the murderer you hunt.
OEDIPUS. That obscenity, twice—by god, you'll pay.
TIRESIAS. Shall I say more, so you can really rage?   415
OEDIPUS. Much as you want. Your words are nothing—futile.
TIRESIAS. You cannot imagine . . . I tell you,
you and your loved ones live together in infamy,
you cannot see how far you've gone in guilt.
OEDIPUS. You think you can keep this up and never suffer?   420
TIRESIAS. Indeed, if the truth has any power.

OEDIPUS.   It does
    but not for you, old man. You've lost your power,
    stone-blind, stone-deaf—senses, eyes blind as stone!
TIRESIAS. I pity you, flinging at me the very insults
    each man here will fling at you so soon.
OEDIPUS.   Blind,   425
    lost in the night, endless night that cursed you!
    You can't hurt me or anyone else who sees the light—
    you can never touch me.
TIRESIAS.   True, it is not your fate
    to fall at my hands. Apollo is quite enough,
    and he will take some pains to work this out.   430
OEDIPUS. Creon! Is this conspiracy his or yours?
TIRESIAS. Creon is not your downfall, no, you are your own.
OEDIPUS.   O power—
    wealth and empire, skill outstripping skill
    in the heady rivalries of life,
    what envy lurks inside you! Just for this,   435
    the crown the city gave me—I never sought it,
    they laid it in my hands—for this alone, Creon,
    the soul of trust, my loyal friend from the start
    steals against me . . . so hungry to overthrow me
    he sets this wizard on me, this scheming quack,   440
    this fortune-teller peddling lies, eyes peeled
    for his own profit—seer blind in his craft!

    Come here, you pious fraud. Tell me,
    when did you ever prove yourself a prophet?
    When the Sphinx, that chanting Fury kept her deathwatch here,   445
    why silent then, not a word to set our people free?
    There was a riddle, not for some passer-by to solve—
    it cried out for a prophet. Where were you?
    Did you rise to the crisis? Not a word,
    you and your birds, your gods—nothing.   450
    No, but I came by, Oedipus the ignorant,
    I stopped the Sphinx! With no help from the birds,
    the flight of my own intelligence hit the mark.

    And this is the man you'd try to overthrow?
    You think you'll stand by Creon when he's king?   455
    You and the great mastermind—
    you'll pay in tears, I promise you, for this,
    this witch-hunt. If you didn't look so senile
    the lash would teach you what your scheming means!
LEADER. I would suggest his words were spoken in anger,   460
    Oedipus . . . yours too, and it isn't what we need.
    The best solution to the oracle, the riddle
    posed by god—we should look for that.
TIRESIAS. You are the king no doubt, but in one respect,
    at least, I am your equal: the right to reply.   465
    I claim that privilege too.
    I am not your slave. I serve Apollo.

I don't need Creon to speak for me in public.
                                         So,
you mock my blindness? Let me tell you this.
You with your precious eyes,   470
you're blind to the corruption of your life,
to the house you live in, those you live with—
who *are* your parents? Do you know? All unknowing
you are the scourge of your own flesh and blood,
the dead below the earth and the living here above,   475
and the double lash of your mother and your father's curse
will whip you from this land one day, their footfall
treading you down in terror, darkness shrouding
your eyes that now can see the light!
                             Soon, soon
you'll scream aloud—what haven won't reverberate?   480
What rock of Cithaeron° won't scream back in echo?
That day you learn the truth about your marriage,
the wedding-march that sang you into your halls,
the lusty voyage home to the fatal harbor!
And a crowd of other horrors you'd never dream   485
will level you with yourself and all your children.
There. Now smear us with insults—Creon, myself,
and every word I've said. No man will ever
be rooted from the earth as brutally as you.
OEDIPUS. Enough! Such filth from him? Insufferable—   490
    what, still alive? Get out—
    faster, back where you came from—vanish!
TIRESIAS. I would never have come if you hadn't called me here.
OEDIPUS. If I thought you would blurt out such absurdities,
    you'd have died waiting before I'd had you summoned.   495
TIRESIAS. Absurd, am I! To you, not to your parents:
    the ones who bore you found me sane enough.
OEDIPUS. Parents—who? Wait . . . who is my father?
TIRESIAS. This day will bring your birth and your destruction.
OEDIPUS. Riddles—all you can say are riddles, murk and darkness.   500
TIRESIAS. Ah, but aren't you the best man alive at solving riddles?
OEDIPUS. Mock me for that, go on, and you'll reveal my greatness.
TIRESIAS. Your great good fortune, true, it was your ruin.
OEDIPUS. Not if I saved the city—what do I care?
TIRESIAS. Well then, I'll be going.

[*To his attendant.*]

                                  Take me home, boy.   505
OEDIPUS. Yes, take him away. You're a nuisance here.
    Out of the way, the irritation's gone.

[*Turning his back on* TIRESIAS, *moving toward the palace.*]

---

481 **Cithaeron** mountains near Thebes, where Oedipus was abandoned as an infant.

TIRESIAS.   I will go,
  once I have said what I came here to say.
  I'll never shrink from the anger in your eyes—
  you can't destroy me. Listen to me closely: 510
  the man you've sought so long, proclaiming,
  cursing up and down, the murderer of Laius—
  he is here. A stranger,
  you may think, who lives among you,
  he soon will be revealed a native Theban   515
  but he will take no joy in the revelation.
  Blind who now has eyes, beggar who now is rich,
  he will grope his way toward a foreign soil,
  a stick tapping before him step by step.

[OEDIPUS *enters the palace.*]

  Revealed at last, brother and father both   520
  to the children he embraces; to his mother
  son and husband both—he sowed the loins
  his father sowed, he spilled his father's blood!

  Go in and reflect on that, solve that.
  And if you find I've lied   525
  from this day onward call the prophet blind.

[TIRESIAS *and the boy exit to the side.*]

CHORUS.   Who—
  who is the man the voice of god denounces
  resounding out of the rocky gorge of Delphi?
    The horror too dark to tell,
  whose ruthless bloody hands have done the work?   530
  His time has come to fly
    to outrace the stallions of the storm
      his feet a streak of speed—
  Cased in armor, Apollo son of the Father
  lunges on him, lightning-bolts afire!   535
  And the grim unerring Furies°
    closing for the kill.
        Look,
  the word of god has just come blazing
  flashing off Parnassus'° snowy heights!
    That man who left no trace—   540
  after him, hunt him down with all our strength!
  Now under bristling timber
    up through rocks and caves he stalks
      like the wild mountain bull—
  cut off from men, each step an agony, frenzied, racing blind   545
  but he cannot outrace the dread voices of Delphi
  ringing out of the heart of Earth,

---

536 Furies avenging deities.   **539 Parnassus** a mountain associated with Apollo.

the dark wings beating around him shrieking doom
   the doom that never dies, the terror—

The skilled prophet scans the birds and shatters me with terror!   550
I can't accept him, can't deny him, don't know what to say,
I'm lost, and the wings of dark foreboding beating—
I cannot see what's come, what's still to come . . .
and what could breed a blood feud between
   Laius' house and the son of Polybus?°   555
I know of nothing, not in the past and not now,
no charge to bring against our king, no cause
to attack his fame that rings throughout Thebes—
   not without proof—not for the ghost of Laius,
   not to avenge a murder gone without a trace.   560

Zeus and Apollo know, they know, the great masters
   of all the dark and depth of human life.
But whether a mere man can know the truth,
whether a seer can fathom more than I—
there is no test, no certain proof   565
   though matching skill for skill
a man can outstrip a rival. No, not till I see
these charges proved will I side with his accusers.
We saw him then, when the she-hawk° swept against him,
saw with our own eyes his skill, his brilliant triumph—   570
   there was the test—he was the joy of Thebes!
   Never will I convict my king, never in my heart.

[*Enter* CREON *from the side.*]

CREON. My fellow-citizens, I hear King Oedipus
levels terrible charges at me. I had to come.
I resent it deeply. If, in the present crisis   575
he thinks he suffers any abuse from me,
anything I've done or said that offers him
the slightest injury, why, I've no desire
to linger out this life, my reputation in ruins.
The damage I'd face from such an accusation   580
is nothing simple. No, there's nothing worse:
branded a traitor in the city, a traitor
to all of you and my good friends.

LEADER.   True,
but a slur might have been forced out of him,
by anger perhaps, not any firm conviction.   585

CREON. The charge was made in public, wasn't it?
I put the prophet up to spreading lies?

LEADER. Such things were said . . .
I don't know with what intent, if any.

CREON. Was his glance steady, his mind right   590
when the charge was brought against me?

---

555 son of Polybus Oedipus is mistakenly thought to be the son of Polybus, King of Corinth.   **569 the she-hawk** the Sphinx.

LEADER. I really couldn't say. I never look
         to judge the ones in power.

[*The doors open.* OEDIPUS *enters.*]

                            Wait,
    here's Oedipus now.
OEDIPUS.   You—here? You have the gall
    to show your face before the palace gates?   595
    You, plotting to kill me, kill the king—
    I see it all, the marauding thief himself
    scheming to steal my crown and power!
                            Tell me,
    in god's name, what did you take me for,
    coward or fool, when you spun out your plot?   600
    Your treachery—you think I'd never detect it
    creeping against me in the dark? Or sensing it,
    not defend myself? Aren't you the fool,
    you and your high adventure. Lacking numbers,
    powerful friends, out for the big game of empire—   605
    you need riches, armies to bring that quarry down!
CREON. Are you quite finished? It's your turn to listen
    for just as long as you've . . . instructed me.
    Hear me out, then judge me on the facts.
OEDIPUS. You've a wicked way with words, Creon,   610
    but I'll be slow to learn—from you.
    I find you a menace, a great burden to me.
CREON. Just one thing, hear me out in this.
OEDIPUS.   Just one thing,
    don't tell *me* you're not the enemy, the traitor.
CREON. Look, if you think crude, mindless stubbornness   615
    such a gift, you've lost your sense of balance.
OEDIPUS. If you think you can abuse a kinsman,
    then escape the penalty, you're insane.
CREON. Fair enough, I grant you. But this injury
    you say I've done you, what is it?   620
OEDIPUS. Did you induce me, yes or no,
    to send for that sanctimonious prophet?
CREON. I did. And I'd do the same again.
OEDIPUS. All right then, tell me, how long is it now
    since Laius . . .
CREON.   Laius—what did *he* do?
OEDIPUS.   Vanished,   625
    swept from sight, murdered in his tracks.
CREON. The count of the years would run you far back . . .
OEDIPUS. And that far back, was the prophet at his trade?
CREON. Skilled as he is today, and just as honored.
OEDIPUS. Did he ever refer to me then, at that time?
CREON.   No,   630
    never, at least, when I was in his presence.
OEDIPUS. But you did investigate the murder, didn't you?

CREON. We did our best, of course, discovered nothing.

OEDIPUS. But the great seer never accused me then—why not?

CREON. I don't know. And when I don't, *I* keep quiet.   635

OEDIPUS. You do know this, you'd tell it too—
    if you had a shred of decency.

CREON.   What?
    If I know, I won't hold back.

OEDIPUS.   Simply this:
    if the two of you had never put heads together,
    we would never have heard about *my* killing Laius.   640

CREON. If that's what he says . . . well, you know best.
    But now I have a right to learn from you
    as you just learned from me.

OEDIPUS.   Learn your fill,
    you never will convict me of the murder.

CREON. Tell me, you're married to my sister, aren't you?   645

OEDIPUS. A genuine discovery—there's no denying that.

CREON. And you rule the land with her, with equal power?

OEDIPUS. She receives from me whatever she desires.

CREON. And I am the third, all of us are equals?

OEDIPUS. Yes, and it's there you show your stripes—   650
    you betray a kinsman.

CREON.   Not at all.
Not if you see things calmly, rationally,
as I do. Look at it this way first:
who in his right mind would rather rule
and live in anxiety than sleep in peace?   655
Particularly if he enjoys the same authority.
Not I, I'm not the man to yearn for kingship,
not with a king's power in my hands. Who would?
Now, as it is, you offer me all I need,
not a fear in the world. But if I wore the crown . . .   660
there'd be many painful duties to perform,
hardly to my taste.

                How could kingship
please me more than influence, power
without a qualm? I'm not that deluded yet,
to reach for anything but privilege outright,   665
profit free and clear.
Now all men sing my praises, all salute me,
now all who request your favors curry mine.
I am their best hope: success rests in me.
Why give up that, I ask you, and borrow trouble?   670
A man of sense, someone who sees things clearly
would never resort to treason.
No, I've no lust for conspiracy in me,
nor could I ever suffer one who does.

Do you want proof? Go to Delphi yourself,   675
examine the oracle and see if I've reported

the message word-for-word. This too:
if you detect that I and the clairvoyant
have plotted anything in common, arrest me,
execute me. Not on the strength of one vote,   680
two in this case, mine as well as yours.
But don't convict me on sheer unverified surmise.
How wrong it is to take the good for bad,
purely at random, or take the bad for good.
But reject a friend, a kinsman? I would as soon   685
tear out the life within us, priceless life itself.
You'll learn this well, without fail, in time.
Time alone can bring the just man to light—
the criminal you can spot in one short day.

LEADER.   Good advice,
    my lord, for anyone who wants to avoid disaster.   690
    Those who jump to conclusions may go wrong.

OEDIPUS. When my enemy moves against me quickly,
    plots in secret, I move quickly too, I must,
    I plot and pay him back. Relax my guard a moment,
    waiting his next move—he wins his objective,   695
    I lose mine.

CREON.   What do you want?
    You want me banished?

OEDIPUS.   No, I want you dead.

CREON. Just to show how ugly a grudge can . . .

OEDIPUS.   So,
    still stubborn? you don't think I'm serious?

CREON. I think you're insane.

OEDIPUS.   Quite sane—in my behalf.   700

CREON. Not just as much in mine?

OEDIPUS.   You—my mortal enemy?

CREON. What if you're wholly wrong?

OEDIPUS.   No matter—I must rule.

CREON. Not if you rule unjustly.

OEDIPUS.   Hear him, Thebes, my city!

CREON. My city too, not yours alone!

LEADER. Please, my lords.

    [*Enter* JOCASTA *from the palace.*]

                                    Look, Jocasta's coming,   705
    and just in time too. With her help
    you must put this fighting of yours to rest.

JOCASTA. Have you no sense? Poor misguided men,
    such shouting—why this public outburst?
    Aren't you ashamed, with the land so sick,   710
    to stir up private quarrels?

    [*To* OEDIPUS.]

    Into the palace now. And Creon, you go home.
    Why make such a furor over nothing?

CREON. My sister, it's dreadful . . . Oedipus, your husband,
    he's bent on a choice of punishments for me,   715
    banishment from the fatherland or death.

OEDIPUS. Precisely. I caught him in the act, Jocasta,
    plotting, about to stab me in the back.

CREON. Never—curse me, let me die and be damned
    if I've done you any wrong you charge me with.   720

JOCASTA. Oh god, believe it, Oedipus,
    honor the solemn oath he swears to heaven.
    Do it for me, for the sake of all your people.

    [*The* CHORUS *begins to chant.*]

CHORUS. Believe it, be sensible
    give way, my king, I beg you!   725

OEDIPUS. What do you want from me, concessions?

CHORUS. Respect him—he's been no fool in the past
    and now he's strong with the oath he swears to god.

OEDIPUS. You know what you're asking?

CHORUS.   I do.

OEDIPUS.   Then out with it!

CHORUS. The man's your friend, your kin, he's under oath—   730
    don't cast him out, disgraced
    branded with guilt on the strength of hearsay only.

OEDIPUS. Know full well, if that is what you want
    you want me dead or banished from the land.

CHORUS.   Never—
    no, by the blazing Sun, first god of the heavens!   735
      Stripped of the gods, stripped of loved ones,
    let me die by inches if that ever crossed my mind.
    But the heart inside me sickens, dies as the land dies
    and now on top of the old griefs you pile this,
    your fury—both of you!

OEDIPUS.   Then let him go,   740
    even if it does lead to my ruin, my death
    or my disgrace, driven from Thebes for life.
    It's you, not him I pity—your words move me.
    He, wherever he goes, my hate goes with him.

CREON. Look at you, sullen in yielding, brutal in your rage—   745
    you'll go too far. It's perfect justice:
    natures like yours are hardest on themselves.

OEDIPUS. Then leave me alone—get out!

CREON.   I'm going.
    You're wrong, so wrong. These men know I'm right.

    [*Exit to the side. The* CHORUS *turns to* JOCASTA.]

CHORUS. Why do you hesitate, my lady   750
    why not help him in?

JOCASTA. Tell me what's happened first.

CHORUS. Loose, ignorant talk started dark suspicions
    and a sense of injustice cut deeply too.

JOCASTA. On both sides?

CHORUS.   Oh yes.

JOCASTA.   What did they say?   755

CHORUS. Enough, please, enough! The land's so racked already
        or so it seems to me . . .
        End the trouble here, just where they left it.

OEDIPUS. You see what comes of your good intentions now?
        And all because you tried to blunt my anger.

CHORUS.   My king,   760
        I've said it once, I'll say it time and again—
        I'd be insane, you know it,
        senseless, ever to turn my back on you.
        You who set our beloved land—storm-tossed, shattered—
        straight on course. Now again, good helmsman,   765
        steer us through the storm!

        [*The* CHORUS *draws away, leaving* OEDIPUS *and* JOCASTA *side by side.*]

JOCASTA.   For the love of god,
        Oedipus, tell me too, what is it?
        Why this rage? You're so unbending.

OEDIPUS. I will tell you. I respect you, Jocasta,
        much more than these . . .   770

        [*Glancing at the* CHORUS.]

        Creon's to blame, Creon schemes against me.

JOCASTA. Tell me clearly, how did the quarrel start?

OEDIPUS. He says I murdered Laius—I am guilty.

JOCASTA. How does he know? Some secret knowledge
        or simple hearsay?

OEDIPUS.   Oh, he sent his prophet in   775
        to do his dirty work. You know Creon,
        Creon keeps his own lips clean.

JOCASTA.   A prophet?
        Well then, free yourself of every charge!
        Listen to me and learn some peace of mind:
        no skill in the world,   780
        nothing human can penetrate the future.
        Here is proof, quick and to the point.

        An oracle came to Laius one fine day
        (I won't say from Apollo himself
        but his underlings, his priests) and it said   785
        that doom would strike him down at the hands of a son,
        our son, to be born of our own flesh and blood. But Laius,
        so the report goes at least, was killed by strangers,
        thieves, at a place where three roads meet . . . my son—
        he wasn't three days old and the boy's father   790
        fastened his ankles, had a henchman fling him away
        on a barren, trackless mountain.
                                    There, you see?
        Apollo brought neither thing to pass. My baby
        no more murdered his father than Laius suffered—
        his wildest fear—death at his own son's hands.   795

That's how the seers and all their revelations
mapped out the future. Brush them from your mind.
Whatever the god needs and seeks
he'll bring to light himself, with ease.

OEDIPUS.   Strange,
    hearing you just now . . . my mind wandered,   800
    my thoughts racing back and forth.

JOCASTA. What do you mean? Why so anxious, startled?

OEDIPUS. I thought I heard you say that Laius
    was cut down at a place where three roads meet.

JOCASTA. That was the story. It hasn't died out yet.   805

OEDIPUS. Where did this thing happen? Be precise.

JOCASTA. A place called Phocis, where two branching roads,
    one from Daulia, one from Delphi,
    come together—a crossroads.

OEDIPUS. When? How long ago?   810

JOCASTA. The heralds no sooner reported Laius dead
    than you appeared and they hailed you king of Thebes.

OEDIPUS. My god, my god—what have you planned to do to me?

JOCASTA. What, Oedipus? What haunts you so?

OEDIPUS.   Not yet.
    Laius—how did he look? Describe him.   815
    Had he reached his prime?

JOCASTA.   He was swarthy,
    and the gray had just begun to streak his temples,
    and his build . . . wasn't far from yours.

OEDIPUS.   Oh no no,
    I think I've just called down a dreadful curse
    upon myself—I simply didn't know!   820

JOCASTA. What are you saying? I shudder to look at you.

OEDIPUS. I have a terrible fear the blind seer can see.
    I'll know in a moment. One thing more—

JOCASTA.   Anything,
    afraid as I am—ask, I'll answer, all I can.

OEDIPUS. Did he go with a light or heavy escort,   825
    several men-at-arms, like a lord, a king?

JOCASTA. There were five in the party, a herald among them,
    and a single wagon carrying Laius.

OEDIPUS.   Ai—
    now I can see it all, clear as day.
    Who told you all this at the time, Jocasta?   830

JOCASTA. A servant who reached home, the lone survivor.

OEDIPUS. So, could he still be in the palace—even now?

JOCASTA. No indeed. Soon as he returned from the scene
    and saw you on the throne with Laius dead and gone,
    he knelt and clutched my hand, pleading with me   835
    to send him into the hinterlands, to pasture,
    far as possible, out of sight of Thebes.
    I sent him away. Slave though he was,
    he'd earned that favor—and much more.

OEDIPUS. Can we bring him back, quickly?   840

JOCASTA. Easily. Why do you want him so?

OEDIPUS.   I'm afraid,
    Jocasta, I have said too much already.
    That man—I've got to see him.

JOCASTA.   Then he'll come.
    But even I have a right, I'd like to think,
    to know what's torturing you, my lord.   845

OEDIPUS. And so you shall—I can hold nothing back from you,
    now I've reached this pitch of dark foreboding.
    Who means more to me than you? Tell me,
    whom would I turn toward but you
    as I go through all this?   850

    My father was Polybus, king of Corinth.
    My mother, a Dorian, Merope. And I was held
    the prince of the realm among the people there,
    till something struck me out of nowhere,
    something strange . . . worth remarking perhaps,   855
    hardly worth the anxiety I gave it.
    Some man at a banquet who had drunk too much
    shouted out—he was far gone, mind you—
    that I am not my father's son. Fighting words!
    I barely restrained myself that day   860
    but early the next I went to mother and father,
    questioned them closely, and they were enraged
    at the accusation and the fool who let it fly.
    So as for my parents I was satisfied,
    but still this thing kept gnawing at me,   865
    the slander spread—I had to make my move.

                                  And so,
    unknown to mother and father I set out for Delphi,
    and the god Apollo spurned me, sent me away,
    denied the facts I came for,
    but first he flashed before my eyes a future   870
    great with pain, terror, disaster—I can hear him cry,
    "You are fated to couple with your mother, you will bring
    a breed of children into the light no man can bear to see—
    you will kill your father, the one who gave you life!"
    I heard all that and ran. I abandoned Corinth,   875
    from that day on I gauged its landfall only
    by the stars, running, always running
    toward some place where I would never see
    the shame of all those oracles come true.
    And as I fled I reached that very spot   880
    where the great king, you say, met his death.
    Now, Jocasta, I will tell you all.
    Making my way toward this triple crossroad
    I began to see a herald, then a brace of colts
    drawing a wagon, and mounted on the bench . . . a man,   885
    just as you've described him, coming face-to-face,
    and the one in the lead and the old man himself

were about to thrust me off the road—brute force—
and the one shouldering me aside, the driver,
I strike him in anger!—and the old man, watching me   890
coming up along his wheels—he brings down
his prod, two prongs straight at my head!
I paid him back with interest!
Short work, by god—with one blow of the staff
in this right hand I knock him out of his high seat,   895
roll him out of the wagon, sprawling headlong—
I killed them all—every mother's son!
Oh, but if there is any blood-tie
between Laius and this stranger . . .
what man alive more miserable than I?   900
More hated by the gods? *I* am the man
no alien, no citizen welcomes to his house,
law forbids it—not a word to me in public,
driven out of every hearth and home.
And all these curses I—no one but I   905
brought down these piling curses on myself!
And you, his wife, I've touched your body with these,
the hands that killed your husband cover you with blood.

Wasn't I born for torment? Look me in the eyes!
I am abomination—heart and soul!   910
I must be exiled, and even in exile
never see my parents, never set foot
on native ground again. Else I am doomed
to couple with my mother and cut my father down . . .
Polybus who reared me, gave me life.

               But why, why?   915
Wouldn't a man of judgment say—and wouldn't he be right—
some savage power has brought this down upon my head?

Oh no, not that, you pure and awesome gods,
never let me see that day! Let me slip
from the world of men, vanish without a trace   920
before I see myself stained with such corruption,
stained to the heart.
LEADER. My lord, you fill our hearts with fear.
    But at least until you question the witness,
    do take hope.
OEDIPUS.   Exactly. He is my last hope—   925
    I am waiting for the shepherd. He is crucial.
JOCASTA. And once he appears, what then? Why so urgent?
OEDIPUS. I will tell you. If it turns out that his story
    matches yours, I've escaped the worst.
JOCASTA. What did I say? What struck you so?
OEDIPUS.   You said *thieves*—   930
    he told you a whole band of them murdered Laius.
    So, if he still holds to the same number,
    I cannot be the killer. One can't equal many.
    But if he refers to one man, one alone,

clearly the scales come down on me: 935
I am guilty.
JOCASTA.   Impossible. Trust me,
I told you precisely what he said,
and he can't retract it now;
the whole city heard it, not just I.
And even if he should vary his first report   940
by one man more or less, still, my lord,
he could never make the murder of Laius
truly fit the prophecy. Apollo was explicit:
my son was doomed to kill my husband . . . my son,
poor defenseless thing, he never had a chance   945
to kill his father. They destroyed him first.

So much for prophecy. It's neither here nor there.
From this day on, I wouldn't look right or left.
OEDIPUS. True, true. Still, that shepherd,
someone fetch him—now!   950
JOCASTA. I'll send at once. But do let's go inside.
I'd never displease you, least of all in this.

[OEDIPUS *and* JOCASTA *enter the palace.*]

CHORUS. Destiny guide me always
Destiny find me filled with reverence
    pure in word and deed.   955
Great laws tower above us, reared on high
born for the brilliant vault of heaven—
    Olympian Sky their only father,
nothing mortal, no man gave them birth,
their memory deathless, never lost in sleep: 960
within them lives a mighty god, the god does not grow old.

Pride breeds the tyrant
violent pride, gorging, crammed to bursting
    with all that is overripe and rich with ruin—
clawing up to the heights, headlong pride   965
crashes down the abyss—sheer doom!
    No footing helps, all foothold lost and gone.
But the healthy strife that makes the city strong—
I pray that god will never end that wrestling:
god, my champion, I will never let you go.   970

But if any man comes striding, high and mighty
    in all he says and does,
no fear of justice, no reverence
for the temples of the gods—
    let a rough doom tear him down,   975
repay his pride, breakneck, ruinous pride!
If he cannot reap his profits fairly
    cannot restrain himself from outrage—
mad, laying hands on the holy things untouchable!

    Can such a man, so desperate, still boast   980

he can save his life from the flashing bolts of god?
If all such violence goes with honor now
   why join the sacred dance?

Never again will I go reverent to Delphi,
   the inviolate heart of Earth   985
or Apollo's ancient oracle at Abae
or Olympia of the fires—
   unless these prophecies all come true
for all mankind to point toward in wonder.
King of kings, if you deserve your titles   990
Zeus, remember, never forget!
You and your deathless, everlasting reign.

   They are dying, the old oracles sent to Laius,
      now our masters strike them off the rolls.
         Nowhere Apollo's golden glory now—   995
            the gods, the gods go down.

[*Enter* JOCASTA *from the palace, carrying a suppliant's branch
wound in wool.*]

JOCASTA. Lords of the realm, it occurred to me,
   just now, to visit the temples of the gods,
   so I have my branch in my hand and incense too.

Oedipus is beside himself. Racked with anguish,   1000
no longer a man of sense, he won't admit
the latest prophecies are hollow as the old—
he's at the mercy of every passing voice
if the voice tells of terror.
I urge him gently, nothing seems to help,   1005
so I turn to you, Apollo, you are nearest.

[*Placing her branch on the altar, while an old herdsman enters
from the side, not the one just summoned by the King but an
unexpected* MESSENGER *from Corinth.*]

I come with prayers and offerings . . . I beg you,
cleanse us, set us free of defilement!
Look at us, passengers in the grip of fear,
watching the pilot of the vessel go to pieces.   1010
MESSENGER. [*Approaching* JOCASTA *and the* CHORUS.]
   Strangers, please, I wonder if you could lead us
   to the palace of the king . . . I think it's Oedipus.
   Better, the man himself—you know where he is?
LEADER. This is his palace, stranger. He's inside.
   But here is his queen, his wife and mother   1015
   of his children.
MESSENGER.   Blessings on you, noble queen,
   queen of Oedipus crowned with all your family—
   blessings on you always!
JOCASTA. And the same to you, stranger, you deserve it . . .
   such a greeting. But what have you come for?   1020
   Have you brought us news?

MESSENGER.   Wonderful news—
    for the house, my lady, for your husband too.
JOCASTA. Really, what? Who sent you?
MESSENGER.   Corinth.
    I'll give you the message in a moment.
    You'll be glad of it—how could you help it?—   1025
    though it costs a little sorrow in the bargain.
JOCASTA. What can it be, with such a double edge?
MESSENGER. The people there, they want to make your Oedipus
    king of Corinth, so they're saying now.
JOCASTA. Why? Isn't old Polybus still in power?   1030
MESSENGER. No more. Death has got him in the tomb.
JOCASTA. What are you saying? Polybus, dead?—dead?
MESSENGER.   If not,
    if I'm not telling the truth, strike me dead too.
JOCASTA. [*To a servant.*]
    Quickly, go to your master, tell him this!
    You prophecies of the gods, where are you now?   1035
    This is the man that Oedipus feared for years,
    he fled him, not to kill him—and now he's dead,
    quite by chance, a normal, natural death,
    not murdered by his son.
OEDIPUS. [*Emerging from the palace.*]
                  Dearest,
    what now? Why call me from the palace?   1040
JOCASTA. [*Bringing the* MESSENGER *closer.*]
    Listen to *him,* see for yourself what all
    those awful prophecies of god have come to.
OEDIPUS. And who is he? What can he have for me?
JOCASTA. He's from Corinth, he's come to tell you
    your father is no more—Polybus—he's dead!   1045
OEDIPUS. [*Wheeling on the* MESSENGER.]
    What? Let me have it from your lips.
MESSENGER.   Well,
    if that's what you want first, then here it is:
    make no mistake, Polybus is dead and gone.
OEDIPUS. How—murder? sickness?—what? what killed him?
MESSENGER. A light tip of the scales put old bones to rest.   1050
OEDIPUS. Sickness then—poor man, it wore him down.
MESSENGER.   That,
    and the long count of years he'd measured out.
OEDIPUS.   So!
    Jocasta, why, why look to the Prophet's hearth,
    the fires of the future? Why scan the birds
    that scream above our heads? They winged me on   1055
    to the murder of my father, did they? That was my doom?
    Well look, he's dead and buried, hidden under the earth,
    and here I am in Thebes, I never put hand to sword—
    unless some longing for me wasted him away,
    then in a sense you'd say I caused his death.   1060
    But now, all those prophecies I feared—Polybus

packs them off to sleep with him in hell!
They're nothing, worthless.

JOCASTA.   There.
Didn't I tell you from the start?

OEDIPUS. So you did. I was lost in fear.   1065

JOCASTA. No more, sweep it from your mind forever.

OEDIPUS. But my mother's bed, surely I must fear—

JOCASTA.   Fear?
What should a man fear? It's all chance,
chance rules our lives. Not a man on earth
can see a day ahead, groping through the dark.   1070
Better to live at random, best we can.
And as for this marriage with your mother—
have no fear. Many a man before you,
in his dreams, has shared his mother's bed.
Take such things for shadows, nothing at all—   1075
Live, Oedipus,
as if there's no tomorrow!

OEDIPUS.   Brave words,
and you'd persuade me if mother weren't alive.
But mother lives, so for all your reassurances
I live in fear, I must.

JOCASTA.   But your father's death,   1080
that, at least, is a great blessing, joy to the eyes!

OEDIPUS. Great, I know . . . but I fear her—she's still alive.

MESSENGER. Wait, who is this woman, makes you so afraid?

OEDIPUS. Merope, old man. The wife of Polybus.

MESSENGER. The queen? What's there to fear in her?   1085

OEDIPUS. A dreadful prophecy, stranger, sent by the gods.

MESSENGER. Tell me, could you? Unless it's forbidden
other ears to hear.

OEDIPUS.   Not at all.
Apollo told me once—it is my fate—
I must make love with my own mother,   1090
shed my father's blood with my own hands.
So for years I've given Corinth a wide berth,
and it's been my good fortune too. But still,
to see one's parents and look into their eyes
is the greatest joy I know.

MESSENGER.   You're afraid of that?   1095
That kept you out of Corinth?

OEDIPUS.   My *father*, old man—
so I wouldn't kill my father.

MESSENGER.   So that's it.
Well then, seeing I came with such good will, my king,
why don't I rid you of that old worry now?

OEDIPUS. What a rich reward you'd have for that!   1100

MESSENGER. What do you think I came for, majesty?
So you'd come home and I'd be better off.

OEDIPUS. Never, I will never go near my parents.

MESSENGER. My boy, it's clear, you don't know what you're doing.

OEDIPUS. What do you mean, old man? For god's sake, explain.   1105
MESSENGER. If you ran from *them,* always dodging home . . .
OEDIPUS. Always, terrified Apollo's oracle might come true—
MESSENGER. And you'd be covered with guilt, from both your parents.
OEDIPUS. That's right, old man, that fear is always with me.
MESSENGER. Don't you know? You've really nothing to fear.   1110
OEDIPUS. But why? If I'm their son—Merope, Polybus?
MESSENGER. Polybus was nothing to you, that's why, not in blood.
OEDIPUS. What are you saying—Polybus was not my father?
MESSENGER. No more than I am. He and I are equals.
OEDIPUS.   My father—
    how can my father equal nothing? You're nothing to me!   1115
MESSENGER. Neither was he, no more your father than I am.
OEDIPUS. Then why did he call me his son?
MESSENGER.   You were a gift,
    years ago—know for a fact he took you
    from my hands.
OEDIPUS.   No, from another's hands?
    Then how could he love me so? He loved me, deeply . . .   1120
MESSENGER. True, and his early years without a child
    made him love you all the more.
OEDIPUS.   And you, did you . . .
    buy me? find me by accident?
MESSENGER.   I stumbled on you,
    down the woody flanks of Mount Cithaeron.
OEDIPUS.   So close,
    what were you doing here, just passing through?   1125
MESSENGER. Watching over my flocks, grazing them on the slopes.
OEDIPUS. A herdsman, were you? A vagabond, scraping for wages?
MESSENGER. Your savior too, my son, in your worst hour.
OEDIPUS.   Oh—
    when you picked me up, was I in pain? What exactly?
MESSENGER. Your ankles . . . they tell the story. Look at them.   1130
OEDIPUS. Why remind me of that, that old affliction?
MESSENGER. Your ankles were pinned together. I set you free.
OEDIPUS. That dreadful mark—I've had it from the cradle.
MESSENGER. And you got your name° from that misfortune too,
    the name's still with you.
OEDIPUS.   Dear god, who did it?—   1135
    mother? father? Tell me.
MESSENGER.   I don't know.
    The one who gave you to me, he'd know more.
OEDIPUS. What? You took me from someone else?
    You didn't find me yourself?
MESSENGER.   No sir,
    another shepherd passed you on to me.   1140
OEDIPUS. Who? Do you know? Describe him.

1134 you got your name "Oedipus" means "swollen foot."

MESSENGER. He called himself a servant of . . .
    if I remember rightly—Laius.

[JOCASTA *turns sharply.*]

OEDIPUS. The king of the land who ruled here long ago?
MESSENGER. That's the one. That herdsman was *his* man.   1145
OEDIPUS. Is he still alive? Can I see him?
MESSENGER. They'd know best, the people of these parts.

[OEDIPUS *and the* MESSENGER *turn to the* CHORUS.]

OEDIPUS. Does anyone know that herdsman,
    the one he mentioned? Anyone seen him
    in the fields, in the city? Out with it!   1150
    The time has come to reveal this once for all.
LEADER. I think he's the very shepherd you wanted to see,
    a moment ago. But the queen, Jocasta,
    she's the one to say.
OEDIPUS.   Jocasta,
    you remember the man we just sent for?   1155
    Is *that* the one he means?
JOCASTA.   That man . . .
    why ask? Old shepherd, talk, empty nonsense,
    don't give it another thought, don't even think—
OEDIPUS. What—give up now, with a clue like this?
    Fail to solve the mystery of my birth?   1160
    Not for all the world!
JOCASTA.   Stop—in the name of god,
    if you love your own life, call off this search!
    My suffering is enough.
OEDIPUS.   Courage!
    Even if my mother turns out to be a slave,
    and I a slave, three generations back,   1165
    you would not seem common.
JOCASTA.   Oh no,
    listen to me, I beg you, don't do this.
OEDIPUS. Listen to you? No more. I must know it all,
    must see the truth at last.
JOCASTA.   No, please—
    for your sake—I want the best for you!   1170
OEDIPUS. Your best is more than I can bear.
JOCASTA.   You're doomed—
    may you never fathom who you are!
OEDIPUS. [*To a servant.*] Hurry, fetch me the herdsman, now!
    Leave her to glory in her royal birth.
JOCASTA. Aieeeeee—
                        man of agony—   1175
    that is the only name I have for you,
    that, no other—ever, ever, ever!

[*Flinging through the palace doors. A long, tense silence follows.*]

LEADER. Where's she gone, Oedipus?
    Rushing off, such wild grief . . .
    I'm afraid that from this silence   1180
    something monstrous may come bursting forth.

OEDIPUS. Let it burst! Whatever will, whatever must!
    I must know my birth, no matter how common
    it may be—I must see my origins face-to-face.
    She perhaps, she with her woman's pride   1185
    may well be mortified by my birth,
    but I, I count myself the son of Chance,
    the great goddess, giver of all good things—
    I'll never see myself disgraced. She is my mother!
    And the moons have marked me out, my blood-brothers,   1190
    one moon on the wane, the next moon great with power.
    That is my blood, my nature—I will never betray it,
    never fail to search and learn my birth!

CHORUS. Yes—if I am a true prophet
      if I can grasp the truth,   1195
      by the boundless skies of Olympus,
    at the full moon of tomorrow, Mount Cithaeron
    you will know how Oedipus glories in you—
    you, his birthplace, nurse, his mountain-mother!
    And we will sing you, dancing out your praise—   1200
    you lift our monarch's heart!
      Apollo, Apollo, god of the wild cry
        may our dancing please you!
                        Oedipus—
      son, dear child, who bore you?
    Who of the nymphs who seem to live forever   1205
    mated with Pan,° the mountain-striding Father?
    Who was your mother? who, some bride of Apollo
    the god who loves the pastures spreading toward the sun?
      Or was it Hermes, king of the lightning ridges?
    Or Dionysus, lord of frenzy, lord of the barren peaks—   1210
    did he seize you in his hands, dearest of all his lucky finds?—
    found by the nymphs, their warm eyes dancing, gift
    to the lord who loves them dancing out his joy!

[OEDIPUS *strains to see a figure coming from the distance. Attended by palace guards, an old* SHEPHERD *enters slowly, reluctant to approach the king.*]

OEDIPUS. I never met the man, my friends . . . still,
    if I had to guess, I'd say that's the shepherd,   1215
    the very one we've looked for all along.
    Brothers in old age, two of a kind,
    he and our guest here. At any rate
    the ones who bring him in are my own men,
    I recognize them.

1206 Pan god of shepherds (associated, like Hermes and Dionysus, with wilderness).

[*Turning to the* LEADER.]

                                 But you know more than I,   1220
you should, you've seen the man before.
LEADER. I know him, definitely. One of Laius' men,
    a trusty shepherd, if there ever was one.
OEDIPUS. You, I ask you first, stranger,
    you from Corinth—is this the one you mean?   1225
MESSENGER. You're looking at him. He's your man.
OEDIPUS. [*To the* SHEPHERD.]

    You, old man, come over here—
    look at me. Answer all my questions.
    Did you ever serve King Laius?
SHEPHERD.   So I did . . .
    a slave, not bought on the block though,   1230
    born and reared in the palace.
OEDIPUS. Your duties, your kind of work?
SHEPHERD. Herding the flocks, the better part of my life.
OEDIPUS. Where, mostly? Where did you do your grazing?
SHEPHERD.   Well,
    Cithaeron sometimes, or the foothills round about.   1235
OEDIPUS. This man—you know him? ever see him there?
SHEPHERD. [*Confused, glancing from the* MESSENGER *to the* KING.]

    Doing what?—what man do you mean?
OEDIPUS. [*Pointing to the* MESSENGER.]

    This one here—ever have dealings with him?
SHEPHERD. Not so I could say, but give me a chance,
    my memory's bad . . .   1240
MESSENGER. No wonder he doesn't know me, master.
    But let me refresh his memory for him.
    I'm sure he recalls old times we had
    on the slopes of Mount Cithaeron;
    he and I, grazing our flocks, he with two   1245
    and I with one—we both struck up together,
    three whole seasons, six months at a stretch
    from spring to the rising of Arcturus° in the fall,
    then with winter coming on I'd drive my herds
    to my own pens, and back he'd go with his   1250
    to Laius' folds.

[*To the* SHEPHERD.]

                        Now that's how it was,
    wasn't it—yes or no?
SHEPHERD.   Yes, I suppose . . .
    it's all so long ago.
MESSENGER.   Come, tell me,
    you gave me a child back then, a boy, remember?
    A little fellow to rear, my very own.   1255

1248 Arcturus a star whose rising signaled the end of summer.

SHEPHERD. What? Why rake up that again?
MESSENGER. Look, here he is, my fine old friend—
    the same man who was just a baby then.
SHEPHERD. Damn you, shut your mouth—quiet!
OEDIPUS. Don't lash out at him, old man—   1260
    you need lashing more than he does.
SHEPHERD.   Why,
    master, majesty—what have I done wrong?
OEDIPUS. You won't answer his question about the boy.
SHEPHERD. He's talking nonsense, wasting his breath.
OEDIPUS. So, you won't talk willingly—   1265
    then you'll talk with pain.

    [*The guards seize the* SHEPHERD.]

SHEPHERD. No, dear god, don't torture an old man!
OEDIPUS. Twist his arms back, quickly!
SHEPHERD.   God help us, why?—
    what more do you need to know?
OEDIPUS. Did you give him that child? He's asking.   1270
SHEPHERD. I did . . . I wish to god I'd died that day.
OEDIPUS. You've got your wish if you don't tell the truth.
SHEPHERD. The more I tell, the worse the death I'll die.
OEDIPUS. Our friend here wants to stretch things out, does he?

    [*Motioning to his men for torture.*]

SHEPHERD. No, no, I gave it to him—I just said so.   1275
OEDIPUS. Where did you get it? Your house? Someone else's?
SHEPHERD. It wasn't mine, no. I got it from . . . someone.
OEDIPUS. Which one of them?

    [*Looking at the citizens.*]

                            Whose house?
SHEPHERD.   No—
    god's sake, master, no more questions!
OEDIPUS. You're a dead man if I have to ask again.   1280
SHEPHERD. Then—the child came from the house. . . of Laius.
OEDIPUS. A slave? or born of his own blood?
SHEPHERD.   Oh no,
    I'm right at the edge, the horrible truth—I've got to say it!
OEDIPUS. And I'm at the edge of hearing horrors, yes, but I must hear!
SHEPHERD. All right! His son, they said it was—his son!   1285
    But the one inside, your wife,
    she'd tell it best.
OEDIPUS. My wife—
    she gave it to you?
SHEPHERD. Yes, yes, my king.   1290
OEDIPUS. Why, what for?
SHEPHERD. To kill it.
OEDIPUS. Her own child,
    how could she?

SHEPHERD. She was afraid—   1295
    frightening prophecies.
OEDIPUS. What?
SHEPHERD.   They said—
    he'd kill his parents.
OEDIPUS. But you gave him to this old man—why?
SHEPHERD. I pitied the little baby, master,   1300
    hoped he'd take him off to his own country,
    far away, but he saved him for this, his fate.
    If you are the man he says you are, believe me,
    you were born for pain.
OEDIPUS.   O god—
    all come true, all burst to light!   1305
    O light—now let me look my last on you!
    I stand revealed at last—
    cursed in my birth, cursed in marriage,
    cursed in the lives I cut down with these hands!

[*Rushing through the doors with a great cry. The Corinthian*
MESSENGER, *the* SHEPHERD *and attendants exit slowly to the side.*]

CHORUS. O the generations of men   1310
    the dying generations—adding the total
    of all your lives I find they come to nothing . . .
        does there exist, is there a man on earth
    who seizes more joy than just a dream, a vision?
    And the vision no sooner dawns than dies   1315
    blazing into oblivion.

    You are my great example, you, your life
    your destiny, Oedipus, man of misery—
    I count no man blest.
        You outranged all men!
    Bending your bow to the breaking-point   1320
    you captured priceless glory, O dear god,
    and the Sphinx came crashing down,
        the virgin, claws hooked
    like a bird of omen singing, shrieking death—
    like a fortress reared in the face of death   1325
    you rose and saved our land.

    From that day on we called you king
    we crowned you with honors, Oedipus, towering over all—
    mighty king of the seven gates of Thebes.

    But now to hear your story—is there a man more
        agonized?   1330
    More wed to pain and frenzy? Not a man on earth,
    the joy of your life ground down to nothing
    O Oedipus, name for the ages—
        one and the same wide harbor served you
        son and father both   1335

son and father came to rest in the same bridal chamber.
How, how could the furrows your father plowed
bear you, your agony, harrowing on
in silence O so long?
　　　　　　　But now for all your power
Time, all-seeing Time has dragged you to the light,   1340
judged your marriage monstrous from the start—
the son and the father tangling, both one—
O child of Laius, would to god
　　I'd never seen you, never never!
　　　Now I weep like a man who wails the dead   1345
and the dirge comes pouring forth with all my heart!
I tell you the truth, you gave me life
my breath leapt up in you
and now you bring down the night upon my eyes.

[*Enter a* MESSENGER *from the palace.*]

MESSENGER. Men of Thebes, always first in honor,   1350
　　what horrors you will hear, what you will see,
　　what a heavy weight of sorrow you will shoulder . . .
　　if you are true to your birth, if you still have
　　some feeling for the royal house of Thebes.
　　I tell you neither the waters of the Danube   1355
　　nor the Nile can wash this palace clean.
　　Such things it hides, it soon will bring to light—
　　terrible things, and none done blindly now,
　　all done with a will. The pains
　　we inflict upon ourselves hurt most of all.   1360
LEADER. God knows we have pains enough already.
　　What can you add to them?
MESSENGER. The queen is dead.
LEADER.   Poor lady—how?
MESSENGER. By her own hand. But you are spared the worst,
　　you never had to watch . . . I saw it all,   1365
　　and with all the memory that's in me
　　you will learn what that poor woman suffered.

Once she'd broken in through the gates,
dashing past us, frantic, whipped to fury,
ripping her hair out with both hands—   1370
straight to her rooms she rushed, flinging herself
across the bridal-bed, doors slamming behind her—
once inside, she wailed for Laius, dead so long,
remembering how she bore his child long ago,
the life that rose up to destroy him, leaving   1375
its mother to mother living creatures
with the very son she'd borne.
Oh how she wept, mourning the marriage-bed
where she let loose that double brood—monsters—
husband by her husband, children by her child.
　　　　　　　　　　And then—   1380

but how she died is more than I can say. Suddenly
Oedipus burst in, screaming, he stunned us so
we couldn't watch her agony to the end,
our eyes were fixed on him. Circling
like a maddened beast, stalking, here, there,   1385
crying out to us—
                            Give him a sword! His wife,
no wife, his mother, where can he find the mother earth
that cropped two crops at once, himself and all his children?
He was raging—one of the dark powers pointing the way,
none of us mortals crowding around him, no,   1390
with a great shattering cry—someone, something leading him on—
he hurled at the twin doors and bending the bolts back
out of their sockets, crashed through the chamber.
And there we saw the woman hanging by the neck,
cradled high in a woven noose, spinning,   1395
swinging back and forth. And when he saw her,
giving a low, wrenching sob that broke our hearts,
slipping the halter from her throat, he eased her down,
in a slow embrace he laid her down, poor thing . . .
then, what came next, what horror we beheld!   1400

He rips off her brooches, the long gold pins
holding her robes—and lifting them high,
looking straight up into the points,
he digs them down the sockets of his eyes, crying, "You,
you'll see no more the pain I suffered, all the pain I caused!   1405
Too long you looked on the ones you never should have seen,
blind to the ones you longed to see, to know! Blind
from this hour on! Blind in the darkness—blind!"
His voice like a dirge, rising, over and over
raising the pins, raking them down his eyes.   1410
And at each stroke blood spurts from the roots,
splashing his beard, a swirl of it, nerves and clots—
black hail of blood pulsing, gushing down.

These are the griefs that burst upon them both,
coupling man and woman. The joy they had so lately,   1415
the fortune of their old ancestral house
was deep joy indeed. Now, in this one day,
wailing, madness and doom, death, disgrace,
all the griefs in the world that you can name,
all are theirs forever.

LEADER.   Oh poor man, the misery—   1420
has he any rest from pain now?

[*A voice within, in torment.*]

MESSENGER.   He's shouting,
"Loose the bolts, someone, show me to all of Thebes!
My father's murderer, my mother's—"
No, I can't repeat it, it's unholy.
Now he'll tear himself from his native earth,   1425

not linger, curse the house with his own curse.
But he needs strength, and a guide to lead him on.
This is sickness more than he can bear.

[*The palace doors open.*]

                                                     Look,
he'll show you himself. The great doors are opening—
you are about to see a sight, a horror   1430
even his mortal enemy would pity.

[*Enter* OEDIPUS, *blinded, led by a boy. He stands at the palace steps,
as if surveying his people once again.*]

CHORUS.   O the terror—
    the suffering, for all the world to see,
    the worst terror that ever met my eyes.
    What madness swept over you? What god,
    what dark power leapt beyond all bounds,   1435
    beyond belief, to crush your wretched life?—
    godforsaken, cursed by the gods!
    I pity you but I can't bear to look.
    I've much to ask, so much to learn,
    so much fascinates my eyes,   1440
    but you . . . I shudder at the sight.
OEDIPUS.   Oh, Ohh—
    the agony! I am agony—
    where am I going? where on earth?
        where does all this agony hurl me?
    where's my voice?—   1445
        winging, swept away on a dark tide—
    My destiny, my dark power, what a leap you made!
CHORUS. To the depths of terror, too dark to hear, to see.
OEDIPUS. Dark, horror of darkness
    my darkness, drowning, swirling around me   1450
    crashing wave on wave—unspeakable, irresistible
      headwind, fatal harbor! Oh again,
    the misery, all at once, over and over
    the stabbing daggers, stab of memory
    raking me insane.
CHORUS.   No wonder you suffer   1455
    twice over, the pain of your wounds,
    the lasting grief of pain.
OEDIPUS.   Dear friend, still here?
    Standing by me, still with a care for me,
    the blind man? Such compassion,
    loyal to the last. Oh it's you,   1460
    I know you're here, dark as it is
    I'd know you anywhere, your voice—
    it's yours, clearly yours.
CHORUS.   Dreadful, what you've done . . .
    how could you bear it, gouging out your eyes?
    What superhuman power drove you on?   1465

OEDIPUS. Apollo, friends, Apollo—
    he ordained my agonies—these, my pains on pains!
      But the hand that struck my eyes was mine,
      mine alone—no one else—
        I did it all myself!   1470
    What good were eyes to me?
    Nothing I could see could bring me joy.
CHORUS. No, no, exactly as you say.
OEDIPUS.   What can I ever see?
      What love, what call of the heart
      can touch my ears with joy? Nothing, friends.   1475
        Take me away, far, far from Thebes,
        quickly, cast me away, my friends—
    this great murderous ruin, this man cursed to heaven,
      the man the deathless gods hate most of all!
CHORUS. Pitiful, you suffer so, you understand so much . . .   1480
    I wish you'd never known.
OEDIPUS.   Die, die—
    whoever he was that day in the wilds
  who cut my ankles free of the ruthless pins,
      he pulled me clear of death, he saved my life
      for this, this kindness—   1485
        Curse him, kill him!
    If I'd died then, I'd never have dragged myself,
    my loved ones through such hell.
CHORUS. Oh if only . . . would to god.
OEDIPUS.   I'd never have come to this,
    my father's murderer—never been branded   1490
  mother's husband, all men see me now! Now,
    loathed by the gods, son of the mother I defiled
    coupling in my father's bed, spawning lives in the loins
  that spawned my wretched life. What grief can crown this grief?
    It's mine alone, my destiny—I am Oedipus!   1495
CHORUS. How can I say you've chosen for the best?
    Better to die than be alive and blind.
OEDIPUS. What I did was best—don't lecture me,
    no more advice. I, with *my* eyes,
    how could I look my father in the eyes   1500
    when I go down to death? Or mother, so abused . . .
    I have done such things to the two of them,
    crimes too huge for hanging.
               Worse yet,
    the sight of my children, born as they were born,
    how could I long to look into their eyes?   1505
    No, not with these eyes of mine, never.
    Not this city either, her high towers,
    the sacred glittering images of her gods—
    I am misery! I, her best son, reared
    as no other son of Thebes was ever reared,   1510
    I've stripped myself, I gave the command myself.
    All men must cast away the great blasphemer,

the curse now brought to light by the gods,
the son of Laius—I, my father's son!

Now I've exposed my guilt, horrendous guilt,   1515
could I train a level glance on you, my countrymen?
Impossible! No, if I could just block off my ears,
the springs of hearing, I would stop at nothing—
I'd wall up my loathsome body like a prison,
blind to the sound of life, not just the sight: 1520
Oblivion—what a blessing . . .
for the mind to dwell a world away from pain.

O Cithaeron, why did you give me shelter?
Why didn't you take me, crush my life out on the spot?
I'd never have revealed my birth to all mankind.   1525

O Polybus, Corinth, the old house of my fathers,
so I believed—what a handsome prince you raised—
under the skin, what sickness to the core.
Look at me! Born of outrage, outrage to the core.
O triple roads—it all comes back, the secret,   1530
dark ravine, and the oaks closing in
where the three roads join . . .
You drank my father's blood, my own blood
spilled by my own hands—you still remember me?
What things you saw me do? Then I came here   1535
and did them all once more!
                                  Marriages! O marriage,
you gave me birth, and once you brought me into the world
you brought my sperm rising back, springing to light
fathers, brothers, sons—one murderous breed—
brides, wives, mothers. The blackest things   1540
a man can do, I have done them all!
                                  No more—
it's wrong to name what's wrong to do. Quickly,
for the love of god, hide me somewhere,
kill me, hurl me into the sea
where you can never look on me again.

[*Beckoning to the* CHORUS *as they shrink away.*]

                                  Closer,   1545
it's all right. Touch the man of grief.
Do. Don't be afraid. My troubles are mine
and I am the only man alive who can sustain them.

[*Enter* CREON *from the palace, attended by palace guards.*]

LEADER. Put your requests to Creon. Here he is,
just when we need him. He'll have a plan, he'll act.   1550
Now that he's the sole defense of the country
in your place.
OEDIPUS.   Oh no, what can I say to him?
How can I ever hope to win his trust?

I wronged him so, just now, in every way.
You must see that—I was so wrong, so wrong.   1555
CREON. I haven't come to mock you, Oedipus,
or to criticize your former failings.

[*Turning to the guards.*]

                        You there,
have you lost all respect for human feelings?
At least revere the Sun, the holy fire
that keeps us all alive. Never expose a thing   1560
of guilt and holy dread so great it appalls
the earth, the rain from heaven, the light of day!
Get him into the halls—quickly as you can.
Piety demands no less. Kindred alone
should see a kinsman's shame. This is obscene.   1565
OEDIPUS. Please, in god's name . . . you wipe my fears away,
coming so generously to me, the worst of men.
Do one thing more, for your sake, not mine.
CREON. What do you want? Why so insistent?
OEDIPUS. Drive me out of the land at once, far from sight,   1570
where I can never hear a human voice.
CREON. I'd have done that already, I promise you.
First I wanted the god to clarify my duties.
OEDIPUS. The god? His command was clear, every word:
death for the father-killer, the curse—   1575
he said destroy me!
CREON. So he did. Still, in such a crisis
it's better to ask precisely what to do.
OEDIPUS.   So miserable—
you'd consult the god about a man like me?
CREON. By all means. And this time, I assume,   1580
even you will obey the god's decrees.
OEDIPUS.   I will,
I will. And you, I command you—I beg you . . .
the woman inside, bury her as you see fit.
It's the only decent thing,
to give your own the last rites. As for me,   1585
never condemn the city of my fathers
to house my body, not while I'm alive, no,
let me live on the mountains, on Cithaeron,
my favorite haunt, I have made it famous.
Mother and father marked out that rock   1590
to be my everlasting tomb—buried alive.
Let me die there, where they tried to kill me.
Oh but this I know: no sickness can destroy me,
nothing can. I would never have been saved
from death—I have been saved   1595
for something great and terrible, something strange.
Well let my destiny come and take me on its way!
About my children, Creon, the boys at least,
don't burden yourself. They're men,

wherever they go, they'll find the means to live.   1600
But my two daughters, my poor helpless girls,
clustering at our table, never without me
hovering near them . . . whatever I touched,
they always had their share. Take care of them,
I beg you. Wait, better—permit me, would you?   1605
Just to touch them with my hands and take
our fill of tears. Please . . . my king.
Grant it, with all your noble heart.
If I could hold them, just once, I'd think
I had them with me, like the early days   1610
when I could see their eyes.

[ANTIGONE *and* ISMENE, *two small children, are led in from the*
palace by a nurse.]

                               What's that
O god! Do I really hear you sobbing?—
my two children. Creon, you've pitied me?
Sent me my darling girls, my own flesh and blood!
Am I right?

CREON.   Yes, it's my doing.   1615
I know the joy they gave you all these years,
the joy you must feel now.

OEDIPUS.   Bless you, Creon!
May god watch over you for this kindness,
better than he ever guarded me.
                              Children, where are you?

Here, come quickly—

[*Groping for* ANTIGONE *and* ISMENE, *who approach their father cau-*
tiously, then embrace him.]

                    Come to these hands of mine,   1620
your brother's hands, your own father's hands
that served his once bright eyes so well—
that made them blind. Seeing nothing, children,
knowing nothing, I became your father,
I fathered you in the soil that gave me life.   1625

How I weep for you—I cannot see you now . . .
just thinking of all your days to come, the bitterness,
the life that rough mankind will thrust upon you.
Where are the public gatherings you can join,
the banquets of the clans? Home you'll come,   1630
in tears, cut off from the sight of it all,
the brilliant rites unfinished.
And when you reach perfection, ripe for marriage,
who will he be, my dear ones? Risking all
to shoulder the curse that weighs down my parents,   1635
yes and you too—that wounds us all together.
What more misery could you want?
Your father killed his father, sowed his mother,

one, one and the selfsame womb sprang you—
he cropped the very roots of his existence.   1640

Such disgrace, and you must bear it all!
Who will marry you then? Not a man on earth.
Your doom is clear: you'll wither away to nothing,
single, without a child.

[*Turning to* CREON.]

                    Oh Creon,
you are the only father they have now . . .   1645
we who brought them into the world
are gone, both gone at a stroke—
Don't let them go begging, abandoned,
women without men. Your own flesh and blood!
Never bring them down to the level of my pains.   1650
Pity them. Look at them, so young, so vulnerable,
shorn of everything—you're their only hope.
Promise me, noble Creon, touch my hand!

[*Reaching toward* CREON, *who draws back.*]

You, little ones, if you were old enough
to understand, there is much I'd tell you.   1655
Now, as it is, I'd have you say a prayer.
Pray for life, my children,
live where you are free to grow and season.
Pray god you find a better life than mine,
the father who begot you.
CREON.   Enough.   1660
    You've wept enough. Into the palace now.
OEDIPUS. I must, but I find it very hard.
CREON. Time is the great healer, you will see.
OEDIPUS. I am going—you know on what condition?
CREON. Tell me. I'm listening.   1665
OEDIPUS. Drive me out of Thebes, in exile.
CREON. Not I. Only the gods can give you that.
OEDIPUS. Surely the gods hate me so much—
CREON. You'll get your wish at once.
OEDIPUS.   You consent?
CREON. I try to say what I mean; it's my habit.   1670
OEDIPUS. Then take me away. It's time.
CREON. Come along, let go of the children.
OEDIPUS.   No—
    don't take them away from me, not now! No no no!

[*Clutching his daughters as the guards wrench them loose and
take them through the palace doors.*]

CREON. Still the king, the master of all things?
    No more: here your power ends.   1675
    None of your power follows you through life.

[*Exit* OEDIPUS *and* CREON *to the palace. The* CHORUS *comes forward
to address the audience directly.*]

CHORUS. People of Thebes, my countrymen, look on Oedipus.
    He solved the famous riddle with his brilliance,
    he rose to power, a man beyond all power.
    Who could behold his greatness without envy?   1680
    Now what a black sea of terror has overwhelmed him.
    Now as we keep our watch and wait the final day,
    count no man happy till he dies, free of pain at last.

[*Exit in procession.*]

YOUR TURN

The Play on the Page

1. On the basis of lines 1–149, characterize Oedipus. Does he seem an effective leader? What additional traits are revealed in lines 205–491?
2. In your opinion, how fair is it to say that Oedipus is morally guilty? Does he argue that he is morally innocent because he did not intend to do immoral deeds? Can it be said that he is guilty of *hybris* but that *hybris* (see page 906) has nothing to do with his fall?
3. Oedipus says that he blinds himself in order not to look upon people he should not. What further reasons can be given? Why does he not (like Jocasta) commit suicide?
4. Does the play show the futility of human efforts to act intelligently?
5. In *Oedipus,* do you find the gods evil?
6. Are the choral odes lyrical interludes that serve to separate the scenes, or do they advance the dramatic action?
7. Matthew Arnold said that Sophocles saw life steadily and saw it whole. But in this play is Sophocles facing the facts of life? Or, on the contrary, is he avoiding what we think of as normal life, and presenting a series of unnatural and outrageous coincidences? In either case, do you think the play is relevant today?
8. Can you describe your emotions at the end of the play? Do they include pity for Oedipus? Pity for all human beings, including yourself? Fear that you might be punished for some unintended transgression? Awe, engendered by a perception of the interrelatedness of things? Relief that the story is only a story? Exhilaration? Explain your reaction.

The Play on the Stage

9. During your first consideration of the play, start with a reading of lines 1–149. Choose someone from the group to stand on a chair (Oedipus), two other readers to stand nearby (the Priest and Creon), and several others to kneel or lie on the floor (Theban citizens). After this rough enactment, ask the readers how they felt about their roles. Then discuss the ways a modern staging could create a powerful opening for the play. Some questions to consider: Do the Thebans ever touch Oedipus? Should the actor playing Oedipus make eye contact with anyone on the stage?

10. Originally the Greek chorus chanted and danced. What are your rec-
    ommendations for a director today? Choose a particular passage from
    the play to illustrate your ideas.
11. Imagine that you are directing a production of *Oedipus*. Propose a
    cast for the principal roles, using well-known actors or people from
    your own circle. Explain the reasons for your choices.
12. What might be gained or lost by performing the play in modern
    dress? Or is there some period other than ancient Greece—let's say
    the Victorian period—in which you think the play might be effectively
    set?
13. Alan MacVey, who directed a production at the University of Iowa,
    used classical costumes but afterward said that he wished he had
    used a conference table as the set and had costumed the royalty in
    "power suits." What is your response to this idea?

Antigone

Translated by Robert Fagles

CHARACTERS

ANTIGONE, *daughter of Oedipus and Jocasta*
ISMENE, *sister of Antigone*
A CHORUS, *of old Theban citizens and their* LEADER
CREON, *king of Thebes, uncle of Antigone and Ismene*
A SENTRY
HAEMON, *son of Creon and Eurydice*
TIRESIAS, *a blind prophet*
A MESSENGER
EURYDICE, *wife of Creon*
GUARDS, ATTENDANTS, and a BOY

[**TIME AND SCENE:** *The royal house of Thebes. It is still night, and the invading armies of Argos have just been driven from the city. Fighting on
opposite sides, the sons of* OEDIPUS, ETEOCLES *and* POLYNICES, *have killed each
other in combat. Their uncle,* CREON, *is now king of Thebes.*

Enter ANTIGONE, *slipping through the central doors of the palace. She motions to her sister,* ISMENE, *who follows her cautiously toward an altar at
the center of the stage.*]

ANTIGONE. My own flesh and blood—dear sister, dear Ismene,
    how many griefs our father Oedipus° handed down!
    Do you know one, I ask you, one grief

---

2 **Oedipus,** once King of Thebes, was the father of Antigone and Ismene, and of their
brothers Polynices and Eteocles. Oedipus unwittingly killed his father, Laius, and married
his own mother, Jocasta. When he learned what he had done, he blinded himself and left
Thebes. Eteocles and Polynices quarreled; Polynices was driven out but returned to assault
Thebes. In the battle, each brother killed the other, and Creon became king and ordered
that Polynices be left to rot unburied on the battlefield as a traitor.

Jane Lapotaire in *Antigone*, National Theater, London, 1984.

that Zeus° will not perfect for the two of us
while we still live and breathe! There's nothing,   5
no pain—our lives are pain—no private shame,
no public disgrace, nothing I haven't seen
in your griefs and mine. And now this:
an emergency decree, they say, the Commander
has just declared for all of Thebes.   10
What, haven't you heard? Don't you see?
The doom reserved for enemies
marches on the ones we love the most.
ISMENE. Not I, I haven't heard a word, Antigone.
Nothing of loved ones,   15
no joy or pain has come my way, not since
the two of us were robbed of our two brothers,
both gone in a day, a double blow—
not since the armies of Argos vanished,
just this very night. I know nothing more,   20
whether our luck's improved or ruin's still to come.
ANTIGONE. I thought so. That's why I brought you out here,
past the gates, so you could hear in private.
ISMENE. What's the matter? Trouble, clearly . . .
you sound so dark, so grim.   25
ANTIGONE. Why not? Our own brothers' burial!
Hasn't Creon graced one with all the rites,

---

4 Zeus highest of the deities on Mt. Olympus.

disgraced the other? Eteocles, they say,
has been given full military honors,
rightly so—Creon's laid him in the earth   30
and he goes with glory down among the dead.
But the body of Polynices, who died miserably—
why, a city-wide proclamation, rumor has it,
forbids anyone to bury him, even mourn him.
He's to be left unwept, unburied, a lovely treasure   35
for birds that scan the field and feast to their heart's content.

Such, I hear, is the martial law our good Creon
lays down for you and me—yes, me, I tell you—
and he's coming here to alert the uninformed
in no uncertain terms,   40
and he won't treat the matter lightly. Whoever
disobeys in the least will die, his doom is sealed:
stoning to death inside the city walls!

There you have it. You'll soon show what you are,
worth your breeding, Ismene, or a coward—   45
for all your royal blood.
ISMENE.   My poor sister, if things have come to this,
who am I to make or mend them, tell me,
what good am I to you?
ANTIGONE.   Decide.
Will you share the labor, share the work?   50
ISMENE.   What work, what's the risk? What do you mean?
ANTIGONE.   [*Raising her hands.*] Will you lift up his body with these
                                                          bare hands
and lower it with me?
ISMENE.   What? You'd bury him—
when a law forbids the city?
ANTIGONE.   Yes!
He is my brother and—deny it as you will—   55
your brother too.
No one will ever convict me for a traitor.
ISMENE.   So desperate, and Creon has expressly—
ANTIGONE.   No,
he has no right to keep me from my own.
ISMENE.   Oh my sister, think—   60
think how our own father died, hated,
his reputation in ruins, driven on
by the crimes he brought to light himself
to gouge out his eyes with his own hands—
then mother . . . his mother and wife, both in one,   65
mutilating her life in the twisted noose—
and last, our two brothers dead in a single day,
both shedding their own blood, poor suffering boys,
battling out their common destiny hand-to-hand.

Now look at the two of us, left so alone . . .   70
think what a death we'll die, the worst of all

if we violate the laws and override
the fixed decree of the throne, its power—
we must be sensible. Remember we are women,
we're not born to contend with men. Then too,   75
we're underlings, ruled by much stronger hands,
so we must submit in this, and things still worse.

I, for one, I'll beg the dead to forgive me—
I'm forced, I have no choice—I must obey
the ones who stand in power. Why rush to extremes?   80
It's madness, madness.
ANTIGONE.   I won't insist,
no, even if you should have a change of heart,
I'd never welcome you in the labor, not with me.
So, do as you like, whatever suits you best—
I'll bury him myself.   85
And even if I die in the act, that death will be a glory.
I'll lie with the one I love and loved by him—
an outrage sacred to the gods! I have longer
to please the dead than please the living here:
in the kingdom down below I'll lie forever.   90
Do as you like, dishonor the laws
the gods hold in honor.
ISMENE.   I'd do them no dishonor . . .
but defy the city? I have no strength for that.
ANTIGONE. You have your excuses. I am on my way,
I'll raise a mound for him, for my dear brother.   95
ISMENE. Oh Antigone, you're so rash—I'm so afraid for you!
ANTIGONE. Don't fear for me. Set your own life in order.
ISMENE. Then don't, at least, blurt this out to anyone.
Keep it a secret. I'll join you in that, I promise.
ANTIGONE. Dear god, shout it from the rooftops. I'll hate you 100
all the more for silence—tell the world!
ISMENE. So fiery—and it ought to chill your heart.
ANTIGONE. I know I please where I must please the most.
ISMENE. Yes, if you can, but you're in love with impossibility.
ANTIGONE. Very well then, once my strength gives out   105
I will be done at last.
ISMENE.   You're wrong from the start,
you're off on a hopeless quest.
ANTIGONE. If you say so, you will make me hate you,
and the hatred of the dead, by all rights,
will haunt you night and day.   110
But leave me to my own absurdity, leave me
to suffer this—dreadful thing. I'll suffer
nothing as great as death without glory.   [*Exit to the side.*]
ISMENE. Then go if you must, but rest assured,
wild, irrational as you are, my sister,   115
you are truly dear to the ones who love you.

[*Withdrawing to the palace. Enter a* CHORUS, *the old citizens of
Thebes, chanting as the sun begins to rise.*]

CHORUS. Glory!—great beam of sun, brightest of all
          that ever rose on the seven gates of Thebes,
                you burn through night at last!
                          Great eye of the golden day,   120
          mounting the Dirce's banks° you throw him back—
          the enemy out of Argos, the white shield, the man of bronze—
          he's flying headlong now
                          the bridle of fate stampeding him with pain!

                God and he had driven against our borders,   125
                launched by the warring claims of Polynices—
                like an eagle screaming, winging havoc
                over the land, wings of armor
                shielded white as snow,
                a huge army massing,   130
                crested helmets bristling for assault.

          He hovered above our roofs, his vast maw gaping
          closing down around our seven gates,
                his spears thirsting for the kill
                          but now he's gone, look,   135
          before he could glut his jaws with Theban blood
          or the god of fire put our crown of towers to the torch.
          He grappled the Dragon none can master—Thebes—
                the clang of our arms like thunder at his back!

                Zeus hates with a vengeance all bravado,   140
                the mighty boasts of men. He watched them
                coming on in a rising flood, the pride
                of their golden armor ringing shrill—
                and brandishing his lightning
                blasted the fighter just at the goal,   145
                rushing to shout his triumph from our walls.

          Down from the heights he crashed, pounding down on the earth!
          And a moment ago, blazing torch in hand—
                mad for attack, ecstatic
          he breathed his rage, the storm   150
                of his fury hurling at our heads!
          But now his high hopes have laid him low
          and down the enemy ranks the iron god of war
                deals his rewards, his stunning blows—Ares°
                rapture of battle, our right arm in the crisis.   155

                Seven captains marshaled at seven gates
                seven against their equals, gave
                their brazen trophies up to Zeus,
                god of the breaking rout of battle,
                all but two: those blood brothers,   160

---

121 the Dirce's banks banks of the River Dirce, near Thebes.   **154 Ares** god of war.

one father, one mother—matched in rage,
spears matched for the twin conquest—
clashed and won the common prize of death.

But now for Victory! Glorious in the morning,
joy in her eyes to meet our joy   165
    she is winging down to Thebes,
our fleets of chariots wheeling in her wake—
    Now let us win oblivion from the wars,
thronging the temples of the gods
in singing, dancing choirs through the night!   170
    Lord Dionysus,° god of the dance
    that shakes the land of Thebes, now lead the way!

[*Enter* CREON *from the palace, attended by his guard.*]

    But look, the king of the realm is coming,
    Creon, the new man for the new day,
    whatever the gods are sending now . . .   175
    what new plan will he launch?
    Why this, this special session?
    Why this sudden call to the old men
    summoned at one command?

CREON.   My countrymen,
the ship of state is safe. The gods who rocked her,   180
after a long, merciless pounding in the storm,
have righted her once more.

                              Out of the whole city
I have called you here alone. Well I know,
first, your undeviating respect
for the throne and royal power of King Laius.   185
Next, while Oedipus steered the land of Thebes,
and even after he died, your loyalty was unshakable,
you still stood by their children. Now then,
since the two sons are dead—two blows of fate
in the same day, cut down by each other's hands,   190
both killers, both brothers stained with blood—
as I am next in kin to the dead,
I now possess the throne and all its powers.

Of course you cannot know a man completely,
his character, his principles, sense of judgment,   195
not till he's shown his colors, ruling the people,
making laws. Experience, there's the test.
As I see it, whoever assumes the task,
the awesome task of setting the city's course,
and refuses to adopt the soundest policies   200
but fearing someone, keeps his lips locked tight,
he's utterly worthless. So I rate him now,
I always have. And whoever places a friend

---

171 Dionysus god of fertility and wine.

above the good of his own country, he is nothing:
I have no use for him. Zeus my witness,   205
Zeus who sees all things, always—
I could never stand by silent, watching destruction
march against our city, putting safety to rout,
nor could I ever make that man a friend of mine
who menaces our country. Remember this: 210
our country *is* our safety.
Only while she voyages true on course
can we establish friendships, truer than blood itself.
Such are my standards. They make our city great.
Closely akin to them I have proclaimed,   215
just now, the following decree to our people
concerning the two sons of Oedipus.
Eteocles, who died fighting for Thebes,
excelling all in arms: he shall be buried,
crowned with a hero's honors, the cups we pour   220
to soak the earth and reach the famous dead.

But as for his blood brother, Polynices,
who returned from exile, home to his father-city
and the gods of his race, consumed with one desire—
to burn them roof to roots—who thirsted to drink   225
his kinsmen's blood and sell the rest to slavery:
that man—a proclamation has forbidden the city
to dignify him with burial, mourn him at all.
No, he must be left unburied, his corpse
carrion for the birds and dogs to tear,   230
an obscenity for the citizens to behold!

These are my principles. Never at my hands
will the traitor be honored above the patriot.
But whoever proves his loyalty to the state:
I'll prize that man in death as well as life.   235
LEADER. If this is your pleasure, Creon, treating
  our city's enemy and our friend this way . . .
  The power is yours, I suppose, to enforce it
  with the laws, both for the dead and all of us,
  the living.
CREON.   Follow my orders closely then,   240
  be on your guard.
LEADER.   We're too old.
  Lay that burden on younger shoulders.
CREON.   No, no,
  I don't mean the body—I've posted guards already.
LEADER. What commands for us then? What other service?
CREON. See that you never side with those who break my orders.   245
LEADER. Never. Only a fool could be in love with death.
CREON. Death is the price—you're right. But all too often
  the mere hope of money has ruined many men.

[*A* SENTRY *enters from the side.*]

SENTRY.   My lord,
    I can't say I'm winded from running, or set out
    with any spring in my legs either—no sir,   250
    I was lost in thought, and it made me stop, often,
    dead in my tracks, wheeling, turning back,
    and all the time a voice inside me muttering,
    "Idiot, why? You're going straight to your death."
    Then muttering, "Stopped again, poor fool?   255
    If somebody gets the news to Creon first,
    what's to save your neck?"
                      And so,
    mulling it over, on I trudged, dragging my feet,
    you can make a short road take forever . . .
    but at last, look, common sense won out,   260
    I'm here, and I'm all yours,
    and even though I come empty-handed
    I'll tell my story just the same, because
    I've come with a good grip on one hope,
    what will come will come, whatever fate—   265
CREON. Come to the point!
    What's wrong—why so afraid?
SENTRY. First, myself, I've got to tell you,
    I didn't do it, didn't see who did—
    Be fair, don't take it out on me.   270
CREON. You're playing it safe, soldier,
    barricading yourself from any trouble.
    It's obvious, you've something strange to tell.
SENTRY. Dangerous too, and danger makes you delay
    for all you're worth.   275
CREON. Out with it—then dismiss!
SENTRY. All right, here it comes. The body—
    someone's just buried it, then run off . . .
    sprinkled some dry dust on the flesh,
    given it proper rites.
CREON.   What?   280
    What man alive would dare—
SENTRY.   I've no idea, I swear it.
    There was no mark of a spade, no pickaxe there,
    no earth turned up, the ground packed hard and dry,
    unbroken, no tracks, no wheelruts, nothing,
    the workman left no trace. Just at sunup   285
    the first watch of the day points it out—
    it was a wonder! We were stunned . . .
    a terrific burden too, for all of us, listen:
    you can't see the corpse, not that it's buried,
    really, just a light cover of road-dust on it,   290
    as if someone meant to lay the dead to rest
    and keep from getting cursed.
    Not a sign in sight that dogs or wild beasts
    had worried the body, even torn the skin.

But what came next! Rough talk flew thick and fast,   295
guard grilling guard—we'd have come to blows
at last, nothing to stop it; each man for himself
and each the culprit, no one caught red-handed,
all of us pleading ignorance, dodging the charges,
ready to take up red-hot iron in our fists,   300
go through fire, swear oaths to the gods—
"I didn't do it, I had no hand in it either,
not in the plotting, not in the work itself!"

Finally, after all this wrangling came to nothing,
one man spoke out and made us stare at the ground,   305
hanging our heads in fear. No way to counter him,
no way to take his advice and come through
safe and sound. Here's what he said:
"Look, we've got to report the facts to Creon,
we can't keep this hidden." Well, that won out,   310
and the lot fell on me, condemned me,
unlucky as ever, I got the prize. So here I am,
against my will and yours too, well I know—
no one wants the man who brings bad news.

LEADER.   My king,
ever since he began I've been debating in my mind,   315
could this possibly be the work of the gods?

CREON.   Stop—
before you make me choke with anger—the gods!
You, you're senile, must you be insane?
You say—why it's intolerable—say the gods
could have the slightest concern for that corpse?   320
Tell me, was it for meritorious service
they proceeded to bury him, prized him so? The hero
who came to burn their temples ringed with pillars,
their golden treasures—scorch their hallowed earth
and fling their laws to the winds.   325
Exactly when did you last see the gods
celebrating traitors? Inconceivable!

No, from the first there were certain citizens
who could hardly stand the spirit of my regime,
grumbling against me in the dark, heads together,   330
tossing wildly, never keeping their necks beneath
the yoke, loyally submitting to their king.
These are the instigators, I'm convinced—
they've perverted my own guard, bribed them
to do their work.
                          Money! Nothing worse   335
in our lives, so current, rampant, so corrupting.
Money—you demolish cities, root men from their homes,
you train and twist good minds and set them on
to the most atrocious schemes. No limit,
you make them adept at every kind of outrage,   340
every godless crime—money!

Everyone—

the whole crew bribed to commit this crime,
they've made one thing sure at least:
sooner or later they will pay the price.

[*Wheeling on the* SENTRY.]

You—

I swear to Zeus as I still believe in Zeus,   345
if you don't find the man who buried that corpse,
the very man, and produce him before my eyes,
simple death won't be enough for you,
not till we string you up alive
and wring the immortality out of you.   350
Then you can steal the rest of your days,
better informed about where to make a killing.
You'll have learned, at last, it doesn't pay
to itch for rewards from every hand that beckons.
Filthy profits wreck most men, you'll see—   355
they'll never save your life.

SENTRY.   Please,
    may I say a word or two, or just turn and go?

CREON. Can't you tell? Everything you say offends me.

SENTRY. Where does it hurt you, in the ears or in the heart?

CREON. And who are you to pinpoint my displeasure?   360

SENTRY. The culprit grates on your feelings,
    I just annoy your ears.

CREON.   Still talking?
    You talk too much! A born nuisance—

SENTRY.   Maybe so,
    but I never did this thing, so help me!

CREON.   Yes you did—
    what's more, you squandered your life for silver!   365

SENTRY. Oh it's terrible when the one who does the judging
    judges things all wrong.

CREON.   Well now,
    you just be clever about your judgments—
    if you fail to produce the criminals for me,
    you'll swear your dirty money brought you pain.   370

[*Turning sharply, reentering the palace.*]

SENTRY. I hope he's found. Best thing by far.
    But caught or not, that's in the lap of fortune;
    I'll never come back, you've seen the last of me.
    I'm saved, even now, and I never thought,
    I never hoped—   375
    dear gods, I owe you all my thanks!   [*Rushing out.*]

CHORUS.   Numberless wonders
    terrible wonders walk the world but none the match for man—
    that great wonder crossing the heaving gray sea,
        driven on by the blast of winter

on through breakers crashing left and right,   380
    holds his steady course
and the oldest of the gods he wears away—
the Earth, the immortal, the inexhaustible—
as his plows go back and forth, year in, year out
    with the breed of stallions turning up the furrows.   385

And the blithe, lightheaded race of birds he snares,
the tribes of savage beasts, the life that swarms the depths—
           with one fling of his nets
woven and coiled tight, he takes them all,
    man the skilled, the brilliant!   390
He conquers all, taming with his techniques
the prey that roams the cliffs and wild lairs,
training the stallion, clamping the yoke across
    his shaggy neck, and the tireless mountain bull.

And speech and thought, quick as the wind   395
and the mood and mind for law that rules the city—
    all these he has taught himself
and shelter from the arrows of the frost
when there's rough lodging under the cold clear sky
and the shafts of lashing rain—   400
        ready, resourceful man!
            Never without resources
never an impasse as he marches on the future—
only Death, from Death alone he will find no rescue
but from desperate plagues he has plotted his escapes.   405

Man the master, ingenious past all measure
past all dreams, the skills within his grasp—
    he forges on, now to destruction
now again to greatness. When he weaves in
the laws of the land, and the justice of the gods   410
that binds his oaths together
        he and his city rise high—
          but the city casts out
that man who weds himself to inhumanity
thanks to reckless daring. Never share my hearth   415
never think my thoughts, whoever does such things.

[*Enter* ANTIGONE *from the side, accompanied by the* SENTRY.]

    Here is a dark sign from the gods—
    what to make of this? I know her,
    how can I deny it? That young girl's Antigone!
    Wretched, child of a wretched father,   420
    Oedipus. Look, is it possible?
    They bring you in like a prisoner—
    why? did you break the king's laws?
    Did they take you in some act of mad defiance?
SENTRY. She's the one, she did it single-handed—   425
we caught her burying the body. Where's Creon?

[*Enter* CREON *from the palace.*]

LEADER. Back again, just in time when you need him.

CREON. In time for what? What is it?

SENTRY.   My king,
there's nothing you can swear you'll never do—
second thoughts make liars of us all.   430
I could have sworn I wouldn't hurry back
(what with your threats, the buffeting I just took),
but a stroke of luck beyond our wildest hopes,
what a joy, there's nothing like it. So,
back I've come, breaking my oath, who cares?   435
I'm bringing in our prisoner—this young girl—
we took her giving the dead the last rites.
But no casting lots this time, this is *my* luck,
my prize, no one else's.
                                Now, my lord,
here she is. Take her, question her,   440
cross-examine her to your heart's content.
But set me free, it's only right—
I'm rid of this dreadful business once for all.

CREON. Prisoner! Her? You took her—where, doing what?

SENTRY. Burying the man. That's the whole story.

CREON.   What?   445
You mean what you say, you're telling me the truth?

SENTRY. She's the one. With my own eyes I saw her
bury the body, just what you've forbidden.
There. Is that plain and clear?

CREON. What did you see? Did you catch her in the act?   450

SENTRY. Here's what happened. We went back to our post,
those threats of yours breathing down our necks—
we brushed the corpse clean of the dust that covered it,
stripped it bare . . . it was slimy, going soft,
and we took to high ground, backs to the wind   455
so the stink of him couldn't hit us;
jostling, baiting each other to keep awake,
shouting back and forth—no napping on the job,
not this time. And so the hours dragged by
until the sun stood dead above our heads,   460
a huge white ball in the noon sky, beating,
blazing down, and then it happened—
suddenly, a whirlwind!
Twisting a great dust-storm up from the earth,
a black plague of the heavens, filling the plain,   465
ripping the leaves off every tree in sight,
choking the air and sky. We squinted hard
and took our whipping from the gods.

And after the storm passed—it seemed endless—
there, we saw the girl!   470
And she cried out a sharp, piercing cry,
like a bird come back to an empty nest,
peering into its bed, and all the babies gone . . .

Just so, when she sees the corpse bare
she bursts into a long, shattering wail   475
and calls down withering curses on the heads
of all who did the work. And she scoops up dry dust,
handfuls, quickly, and lifting a fine bronze urn,
lifting it high and pouring, she crowns the dead
with three full libations.
                       Soon as we saw   480
we rushed her, closed on the kill like hunters,
and she, she didn't flinch. We interrogated her,
charging her with offenses past and present—
she stood up to it all, denied nothing. I tell you,
it made me ache and laugh in the same breath.   485
It's pure joy to escape the worst yourself,
it hurts a man to bring down his friends.
But all that, I'm afraid, means less to me
than my own skin. That's the way I'm made.

CREON. [*Wheeling on* ANTIGONE.]   You,
    with your eyes fixed on the ground—speak up.   490
    Do you deny you did this, yes or no?
ANTIGONE. I did it. I don't deny a thing.
CREON. [*To the* SENTRY.] You, get out, wherever you please—
    you're clear of a very heavy charge.

[*He leaves;* CREON *turns back to* ANTIGONE.]

    You, tell me briefly, no long speeches—   495
    were you aware a decree had forbidden this?
ANTIGONE. Well aware. How could I avoid it? It was public.
CREON. And still you had the gall to break this law?
ANTIGONE. Of course I did. It wasn't Zeus, not in the least,
    who made this proclamation—not to me.   500
    Nor did that Justice, dwelling with the gods
    beneath the earth, ordain such laws for men.
    Nor did I think your edict had such force
    that you, a mere mortal, could override the gods,
    the great unwritten, unshakable traditions.   505
    They are alive, not just today or yesterday:
    they live forever, from the first of time,
    and no one knows when they first saw the light.

    These laws—I was not about to break them,
    not out of fear of some man's wounded pride,   510
    and face the retribution of the gods.
    Die I must, I've known it all my life—
    how could I keep from knowing?—even without
    your death-sentence ringing in my ears.
    And if I am to die before my time   515
    I consider that a gain. Who on earth,
    alive in the midst of so much grief as I,
    could fail to find his death a rich reward?
    So for me, at least, to meet this doom of yours

is precious little pain. But if I had allowed   520
my own mother's son to rot, an unburied corpse—
that would have been an agony! This is nothing.
And if my present actions strike you as foolish,
let's just say I've been accused of folly
by a fool.

LEADER.   Like father like daughter,   525
passionate, wild . . .
she hasn't learned to bend before adversity.

CREON. No? Believe me, the stiffest stubborn wills
fall the hardest; the toughest iron,
tempered strong in the white-hot fire,   530
you'll see it crack and shatter first of all.
And I've known spirited horses you can break
with a light bit—proud, rebellious horses.
There's no room for pride, not in a slave
not with the lord and master standing by.   535

This girl was an old hand at insolence
when she overrode the edicts we made public.
But once she'd done it—the insolence,
twice over—to glory in it, laughing,
mocking us to our face with what she'd done.   540
I'm not the man, not now: she is the man
if this victory goes to her and she goes free.

Never! Sister's child or closer in blood
than all my family clustered at my altar
worshiping Guardian Zeus—she'll never escape,   545
she and her blood sister, the most barbaric death.
Yes, I accuse her sister of an equal part
in scheming this, this burial.

[*To his* ATTENDANTS.]

                         Bring her here!
I just saw her inside, hysterical, gone to pieces.
It never fails: the mind convicts itself   550
in advance, when scoundrels are up to no good,
plotting in the dark. Oh but I hate it more
when a traitor, caught red-handed,
tries to glorify his crimes.

ANTIGONE. Creon, what more do you want   555
than my arrest and execution?

CREON. Nothing. Then I have it all.

ANTIGONE. Then why delay? Your moralizing repels me,
every word you say—pray god it always will.
So naturally all I say repels you too.

                                        Enough.   560
Give me glory! What greater glory could I win
than to give my own brother decent burial?
These citizens here would all agree,

[*To the* CHORUS.]

they'd praise me too
if their lips weren't locked in fear.   565

[*Pointing to* CREON.]

Lucky tyrants—the perquisites of power!
Ruthless power to do and say whatever pleases *them*.
CREON. You alone, of all the people in Thebes,
    see things that way.
ANTIGONE.   They see it just that way
    but defer to you and keep their tongues in leash.   570
CREON. And you, aren't you ashamed to differ so from them?
    So disloyal!
ANTIGONE.   Not ashamed for a moment,
    not to honor my brother, my own flesh and blood.
CREON. Wasn't Eteocles a brother too—cut down, facing him?
ANTIGONE. Brother, yes, by the same mother, the same father.   575
CREON. Then how can you render his enemy such honors,
    such impieties in his eyes?
ANTIGONE. He'll never testify to that,
    Eteocles dead and buried.
CREON.   He will—
    if you honor the traitor just as much as him.   580
ANTIGONE. But it was his brother, not some slave that died—
CREON. Ravaging our country!—
    but Eteocles died fighting in our behalf.
ANTIGONE. No matter—Death longs for the same rites for all.
CREON. Never the same for the patriot and the traitor.   585
ANTIGONE. Who, Creon, who on earth can say the ones below
    don't find this pure and uncorrupt?
CREON. Never. Once an enemy, never a friend,
    not even after death.
ANTIGONE. I was born to join in love, not hate—   590
    that is my nature.
CREON.   Go down below and love,
    if love you must—love the dead! While I'm alive,
    no woman is going to lord it over me.

[*Enter* ISMENE *from the palace, under guard.*]

CHORUS.   Look,
    Ismene's coming, weeping a sister's tears,
    loving sister, under a cloud . . .   595
    her face is flushed, her cheeks streaming.
    Sorrow puts her lovely radiance in the dark.
CREON.   You—
    in my house, you viper, slinking undetected,
    sucking my life-blood! I never knew
    I was breeding twin disasters, the two of you   600
    rising up against my throne. Come, tell me,
    will you confess your part in the crime or not?
    Answer me. Swear to me.

ISMENE.   I did it, yes—
    if only she consents—I share the guilt,
    the consequences too.

ANTIGONE.   No,   605
    Justice will never suffer that—not you,
    you were unwilling. I never brought you in.

ISMENE. But now you face such dangers . . . I'm not ashamed
    to sail through trouble with you,
    make your troubles mine.

ANTIGONE.   Who did the work?   610
    Let the dead and the god of death bear witness!
    I've no love for a friend who loves in words alone.

ISMENE. Oh no, my sister, don't reject me, please,
    let me die beside you, consecrating
    the dead together.

ANTIGONE.   Never share my dying,   615
    don't lay claim to what you never touched.
    My death will be enough.

ISMENE. What do I care for life, cut off from you?

ANTIGONE. Ask Creon. Your concern is all for him.

ISMENE. Why abuse me so? It doesn't help you now.

ANTIGONE.   You're right—   620
    if I mock you, I get no pleasure from it,
    only pain.

ISMENE.   Tell me, dear one,
    what can I do to help you, even now?

ANTIGONE. Save yourself. I don't grudge you your survival.

ISMENE. Oh no, no, denied my portion in your death?   625

ANTIGONE. You chose to live, I chose to die.

ISMENE.   Not, at least,
    without every kind of caution I could voice.

ANTIGONE. Your wisdom appealed to one world—mine, another.

ISMENE. But look, we're both guilty, both condemned to death.

ANTIGONE. Courage! Live your life. I gave myself to death,   630
    long ago, so I might serve the dead.

CREON. They're both mad, I tell you, the two of them.
    One's just shown it, the other's been that way
    since she was born.

ISMENE.   True, my king,
    the sense we were born with cannot last forever . . .   635
    commit cruelty on a person long enough
    and the mind begins to go.

CREON.   Yours did,
    when you chose to commit your crimes with her.

ISMENE. How can I live alone, without her?

CREON.   Her?
    Don't even mention her—she no longer exists.   640

ISMENE. What? You'd kill your own son's bride?

CREON.   Absolutely:
    there are other fields for him to plow.

ISMENE.   Perhaps,
　but never as true, as close a bond as theirs.
CREON.　A worthless woman for my son? It repels me.
ISMENE.　Dearest Haemon, your father wrongs you so!   645
CREON.　Enough, enough—you and your talk of marriage!
ISMENE.　Creon—you're really going to rob your son of Antigone?
CREON.　Death will do it for me—break their marriage off.
LEADER.　So, it's settled then? Antigone must die?
CREON.　Settled, yes—we both know that.   650

　　[*To the* GUARDS.]

　Stop wasting time. Take them in.
　From now on they'll act like women.
　Tie them up, no more running loose;
　even the bravest will cut and run,
　once they see Death coming for their lives.   655

　　[*The* GUARDS *escort* ANTIGONE *and* ISMENE *into the palace.* CREON
　　remains while the old citizens form their chorus.]

CHORUS.　Blest, they are truly blest who all their lives
　have never tasted devastation. For others, once
　the gods have rocked a house to its foundations
　　　the ruin will never cease, cresting on and on
　from one generation on throughout the race—   660
　like a great mounting tide
　driven on by savage northern gales,
　　　surging over the dead black depths
　roiling up from the bottom dark heaves of sand
　and the headlands, taking the storm's onslaught full-force,   665
　roar, and the low moaning
　　　　　　　　　echoes on and on
　　　　　　　　　　　　and now
　as in ancient times I see the sorrows of the house,
　the living heirs of the old ancestral kings,
　piling on the sorrows of the dead
　　　and one generation cannot free the next—   670
　some god will bring them crashing down,
　the race finds no release.
　And now the light, the hope
　　　　　　springing up from the late last root
　in the house of Oedipus, that hope's cut down in turn   675
　by the long, bloody knife swung by the gods of death
　by a senseless word
　　　　　　　by fury at the heart.
　　　　　　　　　　　　Zeus,
　yours is the power, Zeus, what man on earth
　can override it, who can hold it back?
　Power that neither Sleep, the all-ensnaring   680
　　　no, nor the tireless months of heaven
　can ever overmaster—young through all time,
　mighty lord of power, you hold fast

the dazzling crystal mansions of Olympus.
And throughout the future, late and soon   685
as through the past, your law prevails:
no towering form of greatness
          enters into the lives of mortals
                    free and clear of ruin.
                                   True,
our dreams, our high hopes voyaging far and wide   690
bring sheer delight to many, to many others
     delusion, blithe, mindless lusts
and the fraud steals on one slowly . . . unaware
till he trips and puts his foot into the fire.
     He was a wise old man who coined   695
the famous saying: "Sooner or later
foul is fair, fair is foul
to the man the gods will ruin"—
     He goes his way for a moment only
                    free of blinding ruin.   700

[*Enter* HAEMON *from the palace.*]

Here's Haemon now, the last of all your sons.
Does he come in tears for his bride,
his doomed bride, Antigone—
bitter at being cheated of their marriage?
CREON. We'll soon know, better than seers could tell us. 705

[*Turning to* HAEMON.]

Son, you've heard the final verdict on your bride?
Are you coming now, raving against your father?
Or do you love me, no matter what I do?
HAEMON. Father, I'm your *son* . . . you in your wisdom
set my bearings for me—I obey you.   710
No marriage could ever mean more to me than you,
whatever good direction you may offer.
CREON.   Fine, Haemon.
That's how you ought to feel within your heart,
subordinate to your father's will in every way.
That's what a man prays for: to produce good sons—   715
households full of them, dutiful and attentive,
so they can pay his enemy back with interest
and match the respect their father shows his friend.
But the man who rears a brood of useless children,
what has he brought into the world, I ask you?   720
Nothing but trouble for himself, and mockery
from his enemies laughing in his face.
                                   Oh Haemon,
never lose your sense of judgment over a woman.
The warmth, the rush of pleasure, it all goes cold
in your arms, I warn you . . . a worthless woman   725
in your house, a misery in your bed.
What wound cuts deeper than a loved one

turned against you? Spit her out,
like a mortal enemy—let the girl go.
Let her find a husband down among the dead.   730

Imagine it: I caught her in naked rebellion,
the traitor, the only one in the whole city.
I'm not about to prove myself a liar,
not to my people, no, I'm going to kill her!
That's right—so let her cry for mercy, sing her hymns   735
to Zeus who defends all bonds of kindred blood.
Why, if I bring up my own kin to be rebels,
think what I'd suffer from the world at large.
Show me the man who rules his household well:
I'll show you someone fit to rule the state.   740
That good man, my son,
I have every confidence he and he alone
can give commands and take them too. Staunch
in the storm of spears he'll stand his ground,
a loyal, unflinching comrade at your side.   745

But whoever steps out of line, violates the laws
or presumes to hand out orders to his superiors,
he'll win no praise from me. But that man
the city places in authority, his orders
must be obeyed, large and small,   750
right and wrong.
                    Anarchy—
show me a greater crime in all the earth!
She, she destroys cities, rips up houses,
breaks the ranks of spearmen into headlong rout.
But the ones who last it out, the great mass of them   755
owe their lives to discipline. Therefore
we must defend the men who live by law,
never let some woman triumph over us.
Better to fall from power, if fall we must,
at the hands of a man—never be rated   760
inferior to a woman, never.

LEADER.   To us,
unless old age has robbed us of our wits,
you seem to say what you have to say with sense.

HAEMON. Father, only the gods endow a man with reason,
the finest of all their gifts, a treasure.   765
Far be it from me—I haven't the skill,
and certainly no desire, to tell you when,
if ever, you make a slip in speech . . . though
someone else might have a good suggestion.

Of course it's not for you,   770
in the normal run of things, to watch
whatever men say or do, or find to criticize.
The man in the street, you know, dreads your glance,
he'd never say anything displeasing to your face.

But it's for me to catch the murmurs in the dark,   775
the way the city mourns for this young girl.
"No woman," they say, "ever deserved death less,
and such a brutal death for such a glorious action.
She, with her own dear brother lying in his blood—
she couldn't bear to leave him dead, unburied,   780
food for the wild dogs or wheeling vultures.
Death? She deserves a glowing crown of gold!"
So they say, and the rumor spreads in secret,
darkly . . .
              I rejoice in your success, father—
nothing more precious to me in the world.   785
What medal of honor brighter to his children
than a father's growing glory? Or a child's
to his proud father? Now don't, please,
be quite so single-minded, self-involved,
or assume the world is wrong and you are right.   790
Whoever thinks that he alone possesses intelligence,
the gift of eloquence, he and no one else,
and character too . . . such men, I tell you,
spread them open—you will find them empty.
                                      No,
it's no disgrace for a man, even a wise man,   795
to learn many things and not to be too rigid.
You've seen trees by a raging winter torrent,
how many sway with the flood and salvage every twig,
but not the stubborn—they're ripped out, roots and all.
Bend or break. The same when a man is sailing: 800
haul your sheets too taut, never give an inch,
you'll capsize, go the rest of the voyage
keel up and the rowing-benches under.

Oh give way. Relax your anger—change!
I'm young, I know, but let me offer this: 805
it would be best by far, I admit,
if a man were born infallible, right by nature.
If not—and things don't often go that way,
it's best to learn from those with good advice.

LEADER. You'd do well, my lord, if he's speaking to the point,   810
    to learn from him.

    [*Turning to* HAEMON.]
                          and you, my boy, from him.
    You both are talking sense.
CREON.   So,
    men our age, we're to be lectured, are we?—
    schooled by a boy his age?
HAEMON. Only in what is right. But if I seem young,   815
    look less to my years and more to what I do.
CREON. Do? Is admiring rebels an achievement?
HAEMON. I'd never suggest that you admire treason.

CREON.   Oh?—
    isn't that just the sickness that's attacked her?
HAEMON. The whole city of Thebes denies it, to a man.   820
CREON. And is Thebes about to tell me how to rule?
HAEMON. Now, you see? Who's talking like a child?
CREON. Am I to rule this land for others—or myself?
HAEMON. It's no city at all, owned by one man alone.
CREON. What? The city *is* the king's—that's the law!   825
HAEMON. What a splendid king you'd make of a desert island—
    you and you alone.
CREON. [*To the* CHORUS.] This boy, I do believe,
    is fighting on her side, the woman's side.
HAEMON. If you are a woman, yes;
    my concern is all for you.   830
CREON. Why, you degenerate—bandying accusations,
    threatening me with justice, your own father!
HAEMON. I see my father offending justice—wrong.
CREON.   Wrong?
    To protect my royal rights?
HAEMON.   Protect your rights?
    When you trample down the honors of the gods?   835
CREON. You, you soul of corruption, rotten through—
    woman's accomplice!
HAEMON.   That may be,
    but you'll never find me accomplice to a criminal.
CREON. That's what *she* is,
    and every word you say is a blatant appeal for her—   840
HAEMON. And you, and me, and the gods beneath the earth.
CREON. You'll never marry her, not while she's alive.
HAEMON. Then she'll die . . . but her death will kill another.
CREON. What, brazen threats? You go too far!
HAEMON.   What threat?
    Combating your empty, mindless judgments with a word?   845
CREON. You'll suffer for your sermons, you and your empty wisdom!
HAEMON. If you weren't my father, I'd say you were insane.
CREON. Don't flatter me with Father—you woman's slave!
HAEMON. You really expect to fling abuse at me
    and not receive the same?
CREON.   Is that so!   850
    Now, by heaven, I promise you, you'll pay—
    taunting, insulting me! Bring her out,
    that hateful—she'll die now, here,
    in front of his eyes, beside her groom!
HAEMON. No, no, she will never die beside me—   855
    don't delude yourself. And you will never
    see me, never set eyes on my face again.
    Rage your heart out, rage with friends
    who can stand the sight of you.   [*Rushing out.*]
LEADER. Gone, my king, in a burst of anger.   860
    A temper young as his . . . hurt him once,
    he may do something violent.

CREON.   Let him do—
    dream up something desperate, past all human limit!
    Good riddance. Rest assured,
    he'll never save those two young girls from death.   865
LEADER. Both of them, you really intend to kill them both?
CREON. No, not her, the one whose hands are clean;
    you're quite right.
LEADER.   But Antigone—
    what sort of death do you have in mind for her?
CREON. I'll take her down some wild, desolate path   870
    never trod by men, and wall her up alive
    in a rocky vault, and set out short rations,
    just a gesture of piety
    to keep the entire city free of defilement.
    There let her pray to the one god she worships: 875
    Death—who knows?—may just reprieve her from death.
    Or she may learn at last, better late than never,
    what a waste of breath it is to worship Death.

    [*Exit to the palace.*]

CHORUS. Love, never conquered in battle
    Love the plunderer laying waste the rich!   880
    Love standing the night-watch
                    guarding a girl's soft cheek,
    you range the seas, the shepherds' steadings off in the wilds—
    not even the deathless gods can flee your onset,
    nothing human born for a day—   885
    whoever feels your grip is driven mad.
                                Love
    you wrench the minds of the righteous into outrage,
    swerve them to their ruin—you have ignited this,
    this kindred strife, father and son at war
                    and Love alone the victor—   890
    warm glance of the bride triumphant, burning with desire!
    Throned in power, side-by-side with the mighty laws!
    Irresistible Aphrodite,° never conquered—
    Love, you mock us for your sport.

    [ANTIGONE *is brought from the palace under guard.*]

            But now, even I'd rebel against the king,   895
            I'd break all bounds when I see this—
            I fill with tears, can't hold them back,
            not any more . . . I see Antigone make her way
            to the bridal vault where all are laid to rest.
ANTIGONE. Look at me, men of my fatherland,   900
            setting out on the last road
        looking into the last light of day
        the last I'll ever see . . .

_____

893 Aphrodite goddess of love.

the god of death who puts us all to bed
takes me down to the banks of Acheron° alive—   905
    denied my part in the wedding-songs,
no wedding-song in the dusk has crowned my marriage—
I go to wed the lord of the dark waters.
CHORUS. Not crowned with glory, crowned with a dirge,
    you leave for the deep pit of the dead.   910
No withering illness laid you low,
no strokes of the sword—a law to yourself,
alone, no mortal like you, ever, you go down
to the halls of Death alive and breathing.
ANTIGONE. But think of Niobe°—well I know her story—   915
    think what a living death she died,
Tantalus' daughter, stranger queen from the east:
there on the mountain heights, growing stone
binding as ivy, slowly walled her round
and the rains will never cease, the legends say   920
the snows will never leave her . . .
        wasting away, under her brows the tears
showering down her breasting ridge and slopes—
a rocky death like hers puts me to sleep.
CHORUS. But she was a god, born of gods,   925
and we are only mortals born to die.
And yet, of course, it's a great thing
for a dying girl to hear, just hear
she shares a destiny equal to the gods,
during life and later, once she's dead.
ANTIGONE.   O you mock me!   930
Why, in the name of all my fathers' gods
why can't you wait till I am gone—
    must you abuse me to my face?
O my city, all your fine rich sons!
And you, you springs of the Dirce,   935
holy grove of Thebes where the chariots gather,
    you at least, you'll bear me witness, look,
unmourned by friends and forced by such crude laws
I go to my rockbound prison, strange new tomb—
    always a stranger, O dear god,   940
    I have no home on earth and none below,
      not with the living, not with the breathless dead.
CHORUS. You went too far, the last limits of daring—
smashing against the high throne of Justice!
    Your life's in ruins, child—I wonder . . .   945
do you pay for your father's terrible ordeal?
ANTIGONE. There—at last you've touched it, the worst pain
the worst anguish! Raking up the grief for father
    three times over, for all the doom

---

905 Acheron river in the underworld.   **915 Niobe** a Theban queen whose pride in her children was punished by the gods, who turned her into stone.

that's struck us down, the brilliant house of Laius.   950
O mother, your marriage-bed
the coiling horrors, the coupling there—
    you with your own son, my father—doomstruck mother!
Such, such were my parents, and I their wretched child.
I go to them now, cursed, unwed, to share their home—   955
    I am a stranger! O dear brother, doomed
in your marriage—your marriage murders mine,
    your dying drags me down to death alive!

    [*Enter* CREON.]

CHORUS. Reverence asks some reverence in return—
    but attacks on power never go unchecked,   960
        not by the man who holds the reins of power.
    Your own blind will, your passion has destroyed you.
ANTIGONE. No one to weep for me, my friends,
    no wedding-song—they take me away
    in all my pain . . . the road lies open, waiting.   965
    Never again, the law forbids me to see
    the sacred eye of day. I am agony!
    No tears for the destiny that's mine,
    no loved one mourns my death.
CREON.   Can't you see?
    If a man could wail his own dirge *before* he dies,   970
    he'd never finish.

    [*To the* GUARDS.]

            Take her away, quickly!
Wall her up in the tomb, you have your orders.
Abandon her there, alone, and let her choose—
death or a buried life with a good roof for shelter.
As for myself, my hands are clean. This young girl—   975
dead or alive, she will be stripped of her rights,
her stranger's rights, here in the world above.
ANTIGONE. O tomb, my bridal-bed—my house, my prison
    cut in the hollow rock, my everlasting watch!
    I'll soon be there, soon embrace my own,   980
    the great growing family of our dead
    Persephone° has received among her ghosts.
                I,
    the last of them all, the most reviled by far,
    go down before my destined time's run out.
    But still I go, cherishing one good hope: 985
    my arrival may be dear to father,
    dear to you, my mother,
    dear to you, my loving brother, Eteocles—
    When you died I washed you with my hands,

---

982 Persephone queen of the underworld.

I dressed you all, I poured the cups   990
across your tombs. But now, Polynices,
because I laid your body out as well,
this, this is my reward. Nevertheless
I honored you—the decent will admit it—
well and wisely too.

                Never, I tell you,   995
if I had been the mother of children
or if my husband died, exposed and rotting—
I'd never have taken this ordeal upon myself,
never defied our people's will. What law,
you ask, do I satisfy with what I say?   1000
A husband dead, there might have been another.
A child by another too, if I had lost the first.
But mother and father both lost in the halls of Death,
no brother could ever spring to light again.

For this law alone I held you first in honor.   1005
For this, Creon, the king, judges me a criminal
guilty of dreadful outrage, my dear brother!
And now he leads me off, a captive in his hands,
with no part in the bridal-song, the bridal-bed,
denied all joy of marriage, raising children—   1010
deserted so by loved ones, struck by fate,
I descend alive to the caverns of the dead.
What law of the mighty gods have I transgressed?
Why look to the heavens any more, tormented as I am?
Whom to call, what comrades now? Just think,   1015
my reverence only brands me for irreverence!
Very well: if this is the pleasure of the gods,
once I suffer I will know that I was wrong.
But if these men are wrong, let them suffer
nothing worse than they mete out to me—   1020
these masters of injustice!

LEADER. Still the same rough winds, the wild passion
    raging through the girl.

CREON. [*To the* GUARDS.]   Take her away.
    You're wasting time—you'll pay for it too.

ANTIGONE. Oh god, the voice of death. It's come, it's here.   1025

CREON. True. Not a word of hope—your doom is sealed.

ANTIGONE. Land of Thebes, city of all my fathers—
    O you gods, the first gods of the race!
    They drag me away, now, no more delay.
    Look on me, you noble sons of Thebes—   1030
    the last of a great line of kings,
    I alone, see what I suffer now
    at the hands of what breed of men—
    all for reverence, my reverence for the gods!

[*She leaves under guard; the* CHORUS *gathers.*]

CHORUS.   Danaë,° Danaë—   1035
 even she endured a fate like yours,
  in all her lovely strength she traded
 the light of day for the bolted brazen vault—
 buried within her tomb, her bridal-chamber,
 wed to the yoke and broken.   1040
  But she was of glorious birth
     my child, my child
and treasured the seed of Zeus within her womb,
the cloudburst streaming gold!
  The power of fate is a wonder,   1045
  dark, terrible wonder—
  neither wealth nor armies
  towered walls nor ships
  black hulls lashed by the salt
  can save us from that force.   1050

The yoke tamed him too
 young Lycurgus° flaming in anger
king of Edonia, all for his mad taunts
Dionysus clamped him down, encased
in the chain-mail of rock   1055
 and there his rage
    his terrible flowering rage burst—
sobbing, dying away . . . at last that madman
came to know his god—
  the power he mocked, the power   1060
  he taunted in all his frenzy
  trying to stamp out
  the women strong with the god—
  the torch, the raving sacred cries—
  enraging the Muses° who adore the flute.   1065

And far north where the Black Rocks
 cut the sea in half
and murderous straits
split the coast of Thrace
 a forbidding city stands   1070
where once, hard by the walls
the savage Ares thrilled to watch
a king's new queen, a Fury rearing in rage
 against his two royal sons—
  her bloody hands, her dagger-shuttle   1075
stabbing out their eyes—cursed, blinding wounds—
their eyes blind sockets screaming for revenge!

1035 Danaë Danaë's father locked her in a cell because it had been predicted that she would bear a son who would kill him; Zeus entered the cell in the form of a shower of gold, and engendered Perseus.   **1052 Lycurgus** Lycurgus refused to worship Dionysus, and therefore Dionysus punished him.   **1065 Muses** nine goddesses of the arts and sciences.

They wailed in agony, cries echoing cries
     the princes doomed at birth . . .
and their mother doomed to chains,   1080
walled off in a tomb of stone—
     but she traced her own birth back
to a proud Athenian line and the high gods
and off in caverns half the world away,
born of the wild North Wind   1085
     she sprang on her father's gales,
          racing stallions up the leaping cliffs—
child of the heavens. But even on her the Fates
the gray everlasting Fates rode hard
my child, my child.

[*Enter* TIRESIAS, *the blind prophet, led by a* BOY.]

TIRESIAS.   Lords of Thebes,   1090
I and the boy have come together,
hand in hand. Two see with the eyes of one . . .
so the blind must go, with a guide to lead the way.
CREON. What is it, old Tiresias? What news now?
TIRESIAS. I will teach you. And you obey the seer.
CREON.   I will,   1095
I've never wavered from your advice before.
TIRESIAS. And so you kept the city straight on course.
CREON. I owe you a great deal, I swear to that.
TIRESIAS. Then reflect, my son: you are poised,
     once more, on the razor-edge of fate.   1100
CREON. What is it? I shudder to hear you.
TIRESIAS.   You will learn
when you listen to the warnings of my craft.
As I sat in the ancient seat of augury,
in the sanctuary where every bird I know
will hover at my hands—suddenly I heard it,   1105
a strange voice in the wingbeats, unintelligible,
barbaric, a mad scream! Talons flashing, ripping,
they were killing each other—that much I knew—
the murderous fury whirring in those wings
made that much clear!
               I was afraid,   1110
I turned quickly, tested the burnt-sacrifice,
ignited the altar at all points—but no fire,
the god in the fire never blazed.
Not from those offerings . . . over the embers
slid a heavy ooze from the long thighbones,   1115
smoking, sputtering out, and the bladder
puffed and burst—spraying gall into the air—
and the fat wrapping the bones slithered off
and left them glistening white. No fire!
The rites failed that might have blazed the future   1120
with a sign. So I learned from the boy here;
he is my guide, as I am guide to others.

And it's you—
your high resolve that sets this plague on Thebes.
The public altars and sacred hearths are fouled,
one and all, by the birds and dogs with carrion   1125
torn from the corpse, the doomstruck son of Oedipus!
And so the gods are deaf to our prayers, they spurn
the offerings in our hands, the flame of holy flesh.
No birds cry out an omen clear and true—
they're gorged with the murdered victim's blood and fat.   1130
Take these things to heart, my son, I warn you.
All men make mistakes, it is only human.
But once the wrong is done, a man
can turn his back on folly, misfortune too,
if he tries to make amends, however low he's fallen,   1135
and stops his bullnecked ways. Stubbornness
brands you for stupidity—pride is a crime.
No, yield to the dead!
Never stab the fighter when he's down.
Where's the glory, killing the dead twice over?   1140

I mean you well. I give you sound advice.
It's best to learn from a good adviser
when he speaks for your own good:
it's pure gain.

CREON.   Old man—all of you! So,
you shoot your arrows at my head like archers at the target—   1145
I even have *him* loosed on me, this fortune-teller.
Oh his ilk has tried to sell me short
and ship me off for years. Well,
drive your bargains, traffic—much as you like—
in the gold of India, silver-gold of Sardis.   1150
You'll never bury that body in the grave,
not even if Zeus's eagles rip the corpse
and wing their rotten pickings off to the throne of god!
Never, not even in fear of such defilement
will I tolerate his burial, that traitor.   1155
Well I know, we can't defile the gods—
no mortal has the power.
No,
reverend old Tiresias, all men fall,
it's only human, but the wisest fall obscenely
when they glorify obscene advice with rhetoric—   1160
all for their own gain.

TIRESIAS. Oh god, is there a man alive
who knows, who actually believes . . .

CREON.   What now?
What earth-shattering truth are you about to utter?

TIRESIAS. . . . just how much a sense of judgment, wisdom   1165
is the greatest gift we have?

CREON.   Just as much, I'd say,
as a twisted mind is the worst affliction going.

TIRESIAS. You are the one who's sick, Creon, sick to death.

CREON. I am in no mood to trade insults with a seer.

TIRESIAS. You have already, calling my prophecies a lie.

CREON.   Why not?   1170
You and the whole breed of seers are mad for money!

TIRESIAS. And the whole race of tyrants lusts to rake it in.

CREON. This slander of yours—
are you aware you're speaking to the king?

TIRESIAS. Well aware. Who helped you save the city?

CREON.   You—   1175
you have your skills, old seer, but you lust for injustice!

TIRESIAS. You will drive me to utter the dreadful secret in my heart.

CREON. Spit it out! Just don't speak it out for profit.

TIRESIAS. Profit? No, not a bit of profit, not for you.

CREON. Know full well, you'll never buy off my resolve.   1180

TIRESIAS. Then know this too, learn this by heart!
The chariot of the sun will not race through
so many circuits more, before you have surrendered
one born of your own loins, your own flesh and blood,
a corpse for corpses given in return, since you have thrust   1185
to the world below a child sprung from the world above,
ruthlessly lodged a living soul within the grave—
then you've robbed the gods below the earth,
keeping a dead body here in the bright air,
unburied, unsung, unhallowed by the rites.   1190

You, you have no business with the dead,
nor do the gods above—this is violence
you have forced upon the heavens.
And so the avengers, the dark destroyers late
but true to the mark, now lie in wait for you,   1195
the Furies sent by the gods and the god of death
to strike you down with the pains that you perfected!

There. Reflect on that, tell me I've been bribed.
The day comes soon, no long test of time, not now,
that wakes the wails for men and women in your halls.   1200
Great hatred rises against you—
cities in tumult, all whose mutilated sons
the dogs have graced with burial, or the wild beasts,
some wheeling crow that wings the ungodly stench of carrion
back to each city, each warrior's heart and home.   1205

These arrows for your heart! Since you've raked me
I loose them like an archer in my anger,
arrows deadly true. You'll never escape
their burning, searing force.

[*Motioning to his escort.*]

Come, boy, take me home.   1210
So he can vent his rage on younger men,
and learn to keep a gentler tongue in his head
and better sense than what he carries now.

[*Exit to the side.*]

LEADER. The old man's gone, my king—
  terrible prophecies. Well I know,   1215
  since the hair on his old head went gray,
  he's never lied to Thebes.
CREON. I know it myself—I'm shaken, torn.
  It's a dreadful thing to yield . . . but resist now?
  Lay my pride bare to the blows of ruin?   1220
  That's dreadful too.
LEADER.   But good advice,
  Creon, take it now, you must.
CREON. What should I do? Tell me . . . I'll obey.
LEADER. Go! Free the girl from the rocky vault
  and raise a mound for the body you exposed.   1225
CREON. That's your advice? You think I should give in?
LEADER. Yes, my king, quickly. Disasters sent by the gods
  cut short our follies in a flash.
CREON.   Oh it's hard,
  giving up the heart's desire . . . but I will do it—
  no more fighting a losing battle with necessity. 1230
LEADER. Do it now, go, don't leave it to others.
CREON. Now—I'm on my way! Come, each of you,
  take up axes, make for the high ground,
  over there, quickly! I and my better judgment
  have come round to this—I shackled her,   1235
  I'll set her free myself. I am afraid . . .
  it's best to keep the established laws
  to the very day we die.

[*Rushing out, followed by his entourage. The* CHORUS *clusters around the altar.*]

CHORUS. God of a hundred names!
        Great Dionysus—
    Son and glory of Semele! Pride of Thebes—   1240
  Child of Zeus whose thunder rocks the clouds—
  Lord of the famous lands of evening—
  King of the Mysteries!
       King of Eleusis, Demeter's plain°
  her breasting hills that welcome in the world—
  Great Dionysus!
      Bacchus,° living in Thebes   1245
  the mother-city of all your frenzied women—
          Bacchus
   living along the Ismenus'° rippling waters
  standing over the field sown with the Dragons' teeth!

1243 Demeter's plain Demeter, goddess of grain, was worshipped at Eleusis, near Athens. **1245 Bacchus** a name for Dionysus. **1247 Ismenus** a river near Thebes. The founders of Thebes sprang from a dragon's teeth sown by Cadmus (see line 1273) near the river.

You—we have seen you through the flaring smoky fires,
    your torches blazing over the twin peaks   1250
where nymphs of the hallowed cave climb onward
                fired with you, your sacred rage—
we have seen you at Castalia's running spring°
and down from the heights of Nysa° crowned with ivy
the greening shore rioting vines and grapes   1255
       down you come in your storm of wild women
ecstatic, mystic cries—
          Dionysus—
down to watch and ward the roads of Thebes!
First of all cities, Thebes you honor first
you and your mother, bride of the lightning—   1260
come, Dionysus! now your people lie
in the iron grip of plague,
come in your racing, healing stride
          down Parnassus'° slopes
or across the moaning straits.
          Lord of the dancing—   1265
dance, dance the constellations breathing fire!
Great master of the voices of the night!
Child of Zeus, God's offspring, come, come forth!
Lord, king, dance with your nymphs, swirling, raving
arm-in-arm in frenzy through the night   1270
they dance you, Iacchus°—
        Dance, Dionysus
giver of all good things!

[*Enter a* MESSENGER *from the side.*]

MESSENGER.   Neighbors,
friends of the house of Cadmus and the kings,
there's not a thing in this life of ours
I'd praise or blame as settled once for all.   1275
Fortune lifts and Fortune fells the lucky
and unlucky every day. No prophet on earth
can tell a man his fate. Take Creon:
there was a man to rouse your envy once,
as I see it. He saved the realm from enemies;   1280
taking power, he alone, the lord of the fatherland,
he set us true on course—flourished like a tree
with the noble line of sons he bred and reared . . .
and now it's lost, all gone.
          Believe me,
when a man has squandered his true joys,   1285
he's good as dead, I tell you, a living corpse.

1253 **Castalia's running spring** the sacred spring of Apollo's oracle at Delphi.
1254 **Nysa** a mountain where Dionysus was worshipped.   1264 **Parnassus** a mountain
sacred to Dionysus.   1271 **Iacchus** a lofty name for Dionysus.

Pile up riches in your house, as much as you like—
live like a king with a huge show of pomp,
but if real delight is missing from the lot,
I wouldn't give you a wisp of smoke for it,   1290
not compared with joy.

LEADER.   What now?
What new grief do you bring the house of kings?

MESSENGER. Dead, dead—and the living are guilty of their death!

LEADER. Who's the murderer? Who is dead? Tell us.

MESSENGER. Haemon's gone, his blood spilled by the very hand—   1295

LEADER. His father's or his own?

MESSENGER.   His own . . .
raging mad with his father for the death—

LEADER.   Oh great seer,
you saw it all, you brought your word to birth!

MESSENGER. Those are the facts. Deal with them as you will.

[*As he turns to go*, EURYDICE *enters from the palace.*]

LEADER. Look, Eurydice. Poor woman, Creon's wife,   1300
so close at hand. By chance perhaps,
unless she's heard the news about her son.

EURYDICE.   My countrymen,
all of you—I caught the sound of your words
as I was leaving to do my part,
to appeal to queen Athena° with my prayers.   1305
I was just loosing the bolts, opening the doors,
when a voice filled with sorrow, family sorrow,
struck my ears, and I fell back, terrified,
into the women's arms—everything went black.
Tell me the news, again, whatever it is . . .   1310
sorrow and I are hardly strangers;
I can bear the worst.

MESSENGER.   I—dear lady,
I'll speak as an eye-witness. I was there.
And I won't pass over one word of the truth.
Why should I try to soothe you with a story,   1315
only to prove a liar in a moment?
Truth is always best.

So,
I escorted your lord, I guided him
to the edge of the plain where the body lay,
Polynices, torn by the dogs and still unmourned.   1320
And saying a prayer to Hecate of the Crossroads,
Pluto° too, to hold their anger and be kind,
we washed the dead in a bath of holy water
and plucking some fresh branches, gathering . . .
what was left of him, we burned them all together   1325

1305 **Athena** goddess of wisdom.   1321–1322 **Hecate . . . Pluto** deities of the underworld.

and raised a high mound of native earth, and then
we turned and made for that rocky vault of hers,
the hollow, empty bed of the bride of Death.
And far off, one of us heard a voice,
a long wail rising, echoing   1330
out of that unhallowed wedding-chamber;
he ran to alert the master and Creon pressed on,
closer—the strange, inscrutable cry came sharper,
throbbing around him now, and he let loose
a cry of his own, enough to wrench the heart,   1335
"Oh god, am I the prophet now? going down
the darkest road I've ever gone? My son—
it's *his* dear voice, he greets me! Go, men,
closer, quickly! Go through the gap,
the rocks are dragged back—   1340
right to the tomb's very mouth—and look,
see if it's Haemon's voice I think I hear,
or the gods have robbed me of my senses."

The king was shattered. We took his orders,
went and searched, and there in the deepest,   1345
dark recesses of the tomb we found her . . .
hanged by the neck in a fine linen noose,
strangled in her veils—and the boy,
his arms flung around her waist,
clinging to her, wailing for his bride,   1350
dead and down below, for his father's crimes
and the bed of his marriage blighted by misfortune.
When Creon saw him, he gave a deep sob,
he ran in, shouting, crying out to him,
"Oh my child—what have you done? what seized you,   1355
what insanity? what disaster drove you mad?
Come out, my son! I beg you on my knees!"
But the boy gave him a wild burning glance,
spat in his face, not a word in reply,
he drew his sword—his father rushed out,   1360
running as Haemon lunged and missed!—
and then, doomed, desperate with himself,
suddenly leaning his full weight on the blade,
he buried it in his body, halfway to the hilt.
And still in his senses, pouring his arms around her,   1365
he embraced the girl and breathing hard,
released a quick rush of blood,
bright red on her cheek glistening white.
And there he lies, body enfolding body . . .
he has won his bride at last, poor boy,   1370
not here but in the houses of the dead.

Creon shows the world that of all the ills
afflicting men the worst is lack of judgment.

[EURYDICE *turns and reenters the palace.*]

LEADER. What do you make of that? The lady's gone,
   without a word, good or bad.

MESSENGER.   I'm alarmed too   1375
   but here's my hope—faced with her son's death,
   she finds it unbecoming to mourn in public.
   Inside, under her roof, she'll set her women
   to the task and wail the sorrow of the house.
   She's too discreet. She won't do something rash.   1380

LEADER. I'm not so sure. To me, at least,
   a long heavy silence promises danger,
   just as much as a lot of empty outcries.

MESSENGER. We'll see if she's holding something back,
   hiding some passion in her heart.   1385
   I'm going in. You may be right—who knows?
   Even too much silence has its dangers.

   [*Exit to the palace. Enter* CREON *from the side, escorted by attendants carrying* HAEMON's *body on a bier.*]

LEADER. The king himself! Coming toward us,
   look, holding the boy's head in his hands.
   Clear, damning proof, if it's right to say so—   1390
   proof of his own madness, no one else's,
   no, his own blind wrongs.

CREON.   Ohhh,
   so senseless, so insane . . . my crimes,
   my stubborn, deadly—
   Look at us, the killer, the killed,   1395
   father and son, the same blood—the misery!
   My plans, my mad fanatic heart,
   my son, cut off so young!
   Ai, dead, lost to the world,
   not through your stupidity, no, my own.

LEADER.   Too late,   1400
   too late, you see what justice means.

CREON.   Oh I've learned
   through blood and tears! Then, it was then,
   when the god came down and struck me—a great weight
   shattering, driving me down that wild savage path,
   ruining, trampling down my joy. Oh the agony,   1405
   the heartbreaking agonies of our lives.

   [*Enter the* MESSENGER *from the palace.*]

MESSENGER.   Master,
   what a hoard of grief you have, and you'll have more.
   The grief that lies to hand you've brought yourself—

   [*Pointing to* HAEMON's *body.*]

   the rest, in the house, you'll see it all too soon.

CREON. What now? What's worse than this?

MESSENGER.   The queen is dead.   1410
    The mother of this dead boy . . . mother to the end—
    poor thing, her wounds are fresh.
CREON.   No, no,
    harbor of Death, so choked, so hard to cleanse!—
    why me? why are you killing me?
    Herald of pain, more words, more grief?   1415
    I died once, you kill me again and again!
    What's the report, boy . . . some news for me?
    My wife dead? O dear god!
    Slaughter heaped on slaughter?

[*The doors open; the body of* EURYDICE *is brought out on her bier.*]

MESSENGER.   See for yourself:
    now they bring her body from the palace.
CREON.   Oh no,   1420
    another, a second loss to break the heart.
    What next, what fate still waits for me?
    I just held my son in my arms and now,
    look, a new corpse rising before my eyes—
        wretched, helpless mother—O my son!   1425
MESSENGER. She stabbed herself at the altar,
    then her eyes went dark, after she'd raised
    a cry for the noble fate of Megareus,° the hero
    killed in the first assault, then for Haemon,
    then with her dying breath she called down   1430
    torments on your head—you killed her sons.
CREON.   Oh the dread,
    I shudder with dread! Why not kill me too?—
    run me through with a good sharp sword?
    Oh god, the misery, anguish—
    I, I'm churning with it, going under.   1435
MESSENGER. Yes, and the dead, the woman lying there,
    piles the guilt of all their deaths on you.
CREON. How did she end her life, what bloody stroke?
MESSENGER. She drove home to the heart with her own hand,
    once she learned her son was dead . . . that agony.   1440
CREON. And the guilt is all mine—
    can never be fixed on another man,
    no escape for me. I killed you,
    I, god help me, I admit it all!

[*To his* ATTENDANTS.]

    Take me away, quickly, out of sight.   1445
    I don't even exist—I'm no one. Nothing.
LEADER. Good advice, if there's any good in suffering.
    Quickest is best when troubles block the way.

1428 **Megareus** son of Creon and Eurydice.

CREON.

[*Kneeling in prayer.*]

Come, let it come!—that best of fates for me
that brings the final day, best fate of all.   1450
Oh quickly, now—
so I never have to see another sunrise.
LEADER. That will come when it comes;
we must deal with all that lies before us.
The future rests with the ones who tend the future.   1455
CREON. That prayer—I poured my heart into that prayer!
LEADER. No more prayers now. For mortal men
there is no escape from the doom we must endure.
CREON. Take me away, I beg you, out of sight.
A rash, indiscriminate fool!   1460
I murdered you, my son, against my will—
you too, my wife . . .
                    Wailing wreck of a man,
whom to look to? where to lean for support?

[*Desperately turning from* HAEMON *to* EURYDICE *on their biers.*]

Whatever I touch goes wrong—once more
a crushing fate's come down upon my head.   1465

[*The* MESSENGER *and attendants lead* CREON *into the palace.*]

CHORUS. Wisdom is by far the greatest part of joy,
and reverence toward the gods must be safeguarded.
The mighty words of the proud are paid in full
with mighty blows of fate, and at long last
those blows will teach us wisdom.   1470

[*The old citizens exit to the side.*]

YOUR TURN

The Play on the Page

1. If you have read *Oedipus,* compare and contrast the Creon of *Antigone* with the Creon of *Oedipus.*
2. Although Sophocles called his play *Antigone,* many critics say that Creon is the real tragic hero, pointing out that Antigone is absent from the last third of the play. Evaluate this view.
3. In some Greek tragedies, fate plays a great role in bringing about the downfall of the tragic hero. Though there are references to the curse on the House of Oedipus in *Antigone,* do we feel that Antigone goes to her death as a result of the workings of fate? Do we feel that fate is responsible for Creon's fall? Are both Antigone and Creon the creators of their own tragedy?

4. Are the words *hamartia* and *hybris* (see pages 905–906) relevant to Antigone? To Creon?

5. Why does Creon, contrary to the Chorus's advice (lines 1224–1225), bury the body of Polynices before he releases Antigone? Does his action show a zeal for piety as short-sighted as his earlier zeal for law? Is his action plausible, in view of the facts that Tiresias has dwelt on the wrong done to Polynices and that Antigone has ritual food to sustain her? Or are we not to worry about Creon's motive?

6. A *foil* is a character who, by contrast, sets off or helps define another character. To what extent is Ismene a foil to Antigone? Is she entirely without courage?

7. What function does Eurydice serve? How deeply do we feel about her fate?

The Play on the Stage

8. Would you use masks for some (or all) of the characters? If so, would they be masks that fully cover the face, Greek-style, or some sort of half-masks? (A full mask enlarges the face, and conceivably the mouthpiece can amplify the voice, but only an exceptionally large theater might require such help. Perhaps half-masks are enough if the aim is chiefly to distance the actors from the audience and from daily reality, and to force the actors to develop resources other than facial gestures. One director, arguing in favor of half-masks, has said that actors who wear even a half-mask learn to act not with the eyes but with the neck.)

9. How would you costume the players? Would you dress them as the Greeks might have? Why? One argument sometimes used by those who hold that modern productions of Greek drama should use classical costumes is that Greek drama *ought* to be remote and ritualistic. Evaluate this view. What sort of modern dress might be effective?

10. If you were directing a college production of *Antigone,* how large a chorus would you use? (Sophocles is said to have used a chorus of fifteen.) Would you have the chorus recite (or chant) the odes in unison, or would you assign lines to single speakers? In Sophocles' day, the chorus danced. Would you use dance movements? If not, in what sorts of movements might they engage?

Hamlet, A Play by Shakespeare

This section contains (in addition to illustrations of the original texts of *Hamlet,* the Elizabethan theater, and modern productions) the following material:

1. A note on the Elizabethan theater
2. A note on the texts of *Hamlet* (with facsimiles of three versions of Hamlet's "to be or not to be")

A Note on the Elizabethan Theater

Shakespeare's theater, the Globe, which opened in 1599, was wooden, round or polygonal (the Chorus in *Henry V* calls it a "wooden O"). About eight hundred spectators could stand in the yard in front of—and perhaps along the two sides of—the stage that jutted from the rear wall, and another fifteen hundred or so spectators could sit in the three roofed galleries that ringed the stage.

That portion of the galleries that was above the rear of the stage was sometimes used by actors. For instance, in *The Tempest,* 3.3, a stage direction following line 17 mentions "Prospero on the top, invisible," that is, he is imagined to be invisible to the characters in the play.

Entry to the stage was normally gained by doors at the rear, but apparently on rare occasions use was made of a curtained alcove—or perhaps a booth— between the doors, which allowed characters to be "discovered" (revealed) as in the modern proscenium theater, which normally employs a curtain. Such "discovery" scenes are rare.

Although the theater as a whole was unroofed, the stage was protected by a roof, supported by two pillars. These could serve (by an act of imagination) as trees behind which actors might pretend to conceal themselves.

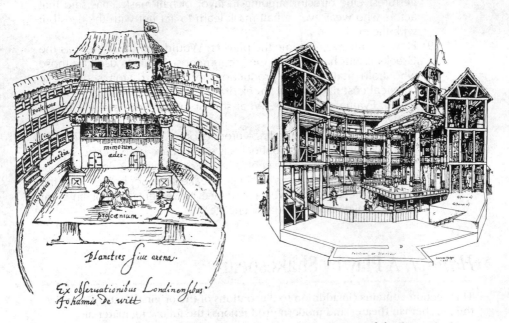

Left: Johannes de Witt, a Dutch visitor to London, made a drawing of the Swan Theater, a theater that must have been similar to the Globe in about the year 1596. The original drawing is lost; this is Arend van Buchel's copy of it. *Right:* C. Walter Hodges's drawing (1965) of an Elizabethan playhouse.

A performance was probably uninterrupted by intermissions or by long pauses for the changing of scenery; a group of characters leaves the stage, another enters, and if the locale has changed the new characters somehow tell us. (Modern editors customarily add indications of locales to help a reader, but it should be remembered that the action on the Elizabethan stage was continuous.)

WILLIAM SHAKESPEARE

William Shakespeare (1564–1616) was born in Stratford-upon-Avon, England, of middle-class parents. Little is known about his early years, but by 1590 he was acting and writing plays in London. By the end of the following decade he had worked in all three Elizabethan dramatic genres—tragedy, comedy, and history. Romeo and Juliet, *for example, was written about 1595, the year of* Richard II, *and in the following year he wrote* A Midsummer Night's Dream. Julius Caesar *(1599) probably preceded* As You Like It *by one year, and* Hamlet *probably followed* As You Like It *by less than a year. Among the plays that followed* Othello *(1603–1604) were* King Lear *(1605–1606),* Macbeth *(1605–1606), and several "romances"—plays that have happy endings but that seem more meditative and closer to tragedy than such comedies as* A Midsummer Night's Dream, As You Like It, *and* Twelfth Night.

A Note on the Texts of *Hamlet*

Shakespeare's *Hamlet* comes to us in three printed versions. The earliest, known as the First Quarto (Q1), was published in 1603. It is an illegitimate garbled version, perhaps derived from the memory of the actor who played Marcellus (this part is conspicuously more accurate than the rest of the play) in a short version of the play.

The second version (Q2), which appeared in 1604, is almost twice as long as Q1; all in all, it is the best text we have, doubtless published (as Q1 was not) with the permission of Shakespeare's theatrical company.

The third printed version, in the First Folio (the collected edition of Shakespeare's plays, published in 1623), is also legitimate, but it seems to be an acting version, for it lacks some two hundred lines of Q2. On the other hand, the Folio text includes some ninety lines not found in Q2.

Because Q2 is the longest version, giving us more of the play as Shakespeare conceived it than either of the other texts, it serves as the basic version for this text. Unfortunately, the printers of Q2 often worked carelessly: Words and phrases are omitted, there are plain misreadings of what must have been in Shakespeare's manuscript, and speeches are sometimes wrongly assigned. It is therefore necessary to turn to the First Folio for many readings. It has been found useful, also, to divide the play into acts and scenes; these divisions, not found in Q2 (and only a few are found in the Folio), are purely editorial additions, and they are therefore enclosed in square brackets.

We use the text edited by David Bevington.

The Tragedy of Hamlet

And so by continuance, and weakenesse of the braine
Into this frensie, which now posseffeth him:
And if this be not true, take this from this.

   King Thinke you t'is so?
   Cor. How? so my Lord, I would very faine know
That thing that I haue saide t'is so, positiuely,
And it hath fallen out otherwise.
Nay, if circumstances leade me on,
Ile finde it out, if it were hid
As deepe as the centre of the earth.

   King. how should wee trie this same?
   Cor. Mary my good lord thus,
The Princes walke is here in the galery,
There let *Ofelia*, walke vntill hee comes:
Your selfe and I will stand close in the study,
There shall you heare the effect of all his hart,
And if it proue any otherwise then loue,
Then let my censure faile an other time.

   King. see where hee comes poring vppon a booke.

          Enter Hamlet.

   Cor. Madame, will it please your grace
To leaue vs here?
   Que. With all my hart.   *exit.*
   Cor. And here *Ofelia*, reade you on this booke,
And walke aloofe, the King shal be vnseene.

   Ham. To be, or not to be, I there's the point,
To Die, to sleepe, is that all? I all:
No, to sleepe, to dreame, I mary there it goes,
For in that dreame of death, when wee awake,
And borne before an euerlasting Iudge,
From whence no passenger euer retur'nd,
The vndiscouered country, at whose sight
The happy smile, and the accursed damn'd.
But for this, the ioyfull hope of this,
Who'ld beare the scornes and flattery of the world,
Scorned by the right rich, the rich curssed of the poore?
                        The

Here and on the next page we print "To be or not to be," as given in the First Quarto (Q1, 1603). (On pages 994–95, we give the speech as it appears in the Second Quarto, and on page 996, the speech in the First Folio.)

Prince of Denmarke

The widow being oppreſſed the orphan wrong'd,
The taſte of hunger, or a tirants raigne,
And thouſand more calamities beſides,
To grunt and ſweate vnder this weary life,
When that he may his full *Quietus* make,
With a bare bodkin, who would this indure,
But for a hope of ſomething after death?
Which puſles the braine, and doth confound the ſence,
Which makes vs rather beare thoſe euilles we haue,
Than flie to others that we know not of.
I that, O this conſcience makes cowardes of vs all,
Lady in thy orizons, be all my ſinnes remembred.

Ofel. My Lord, I haue ſought opportunitie, which now
I haue, to redeliuer to your worthy handes, a ſmall remembrance, ſuch tokens which I haue receiued of you.

Ham. Are you faire?

Ofel. My Lord.

Ham. Are you honeſt?

Ofel. What meanes my Lord?

Ham. That if you be faire and honeſt,
Your beauty ſhould admit no diſcourſe to your honeſty.

Ofel. My Lord, can beauty haue better priuiledge than
with honeſty?

Ham. Yea mary may it; for Beauty may transforme,
Honeſty, from what ſhe was into a bawd:
Then Honeſty can transforme Beauty:
This was ſometimes a Paradox,
But now the time giues it ſcope.
I neuer gaue you nothing.

Ofel. My Lord, you know right well you did,
And with them ſuch earneſt vowes of loue,
As would haue moou'd the ſtonieſt breaſt aliue,
But now too true I finde,
Rich giftes waxe poore, when giuers grow vnkinde.

Ham. I neuer loued you.

Ofel. You made me beleeue you did.

E   *Ham.*

That show of such an exercise may cullour
Your lowlines; we are oft too blame in this,
Tis too much proou'd, that with deuotions visage
And pious action, we doe sugar ore
The deuill himselfe.

  King. O tis too true,
How smart a lash that speech doth giue my conscience.
The harlots cheeke beautied with plastring art,
Is not more ougly to the thing that helps it,
Then is my deede to my most painted word :
O heauy burthen.

Enter Hamlet.

  Pol. I heare him comming, with-draw my Lord.
  Ham. To be, or not to be, that is the question,
Whether tis nobler in the minde to suffer
The slings and arrowes of outragious fortune,
Or to take Armes against a sea of troubles,
And by opposing, end them; to die to sleepe
No more, and by a sleepe, to say we end
The hart-ake, and the thousand naturall shocks
That flesh is heire to; tis a consumation
Deuoutly to be wisht to die to sleepe,
To sleepe, perchance to dreame, I there's the rub,
For in that sleepe of death what dreames may come
When we haue shuffled off this mortall coyle
Must giue vs pause, there's the respect
That makes calamitie of so long life :
For who would beare the whips and scornes of time,
Th'oppressors wrong, the proude mans contumely,
The pangs of despiz'd loue, the lawes delay,
The insolence of office, and the spurnes
That patient merrit of th'vnworthy takes,
When he himselfe might his quietas make
With a bare bodkin; who would fardels beare,
To grunt and sweat vnder a wearie life,
But that the dread of something after death,
The vndiscouer'd country, from whose borne,

G 2

No

On this page and the next we print "To be or not to be," as given in the Second Quarto
(Q2, 1604).

The Tragedie of Hamlet

No trauiler returnes, puzzels the will,
And makes vs rather beare thofe ills we haue,
Then flie to others that we know not of,
Thus confcience dooes make cowards,
And thus the natiue hiew of refolution
Is fickled ore with the pale caft of thought,
And enterprifes of great pitch and moment,
With this regard theyr currents turne awry,
And loofe the name of action. Soft you now,
The faire *Ophelia*, Nimph in thy orizons
Be all my finnes remembred.

   Oph. Good my Lord,
How dooes your honour for this many a day?

   Ham. I humbly thanke you well.

   Oph. My Lord, I haue remembrances of yours
That I haue longed long to redeliuer,
I pray you now recciue them.

   Ham. No, not I, I neuer gaue you ought.

   Oph. My honor'd Lord, you know right well you did,
And with them words of fo fweet breath compofd
As made thefe things more rich, their perfume loft,
Take thefe againe, for to the noble mind
Rich gifts wax poore when giuers prooue vnkind,
There my Lord.

   Ham. Ha, ha, are you honeft.

   Oph. My Lord.

   Ham. Are you faire?

   Oph. What meanes your Lordfhip?

   Ham. That if you be honeft & faire, you fhould admit
no difcourfe to your beautie.

   Oph. Could beauty my Lord haue better comerfe
Then with honeftie?

   Ham. I truly, for the power of beautie will fooner transforme honeftie from what it is to a bawde, then the force of honeftie can tranf-
late beautie into his likenes, this was fometime a paradox, but now the
time giues it proofe, I did loue you once.

   Oph. Indeed my Lord you made me belieue fo.

   Ham. You fhould not haue beleeu'd me, for vertue cannot fo
euocutat our old ftock, but we fhall relifh of it, I loued you not.

The Tragedie of Hamlet.   265

With turbulent and dangerous Lunacy.

Rosin. He does confesse he feeles himselfe distracted,
But from what cause he will by no meanes speake.

Guil. Nor do we finde him forward to be sounded,
But with a crafty Madnesse keepes aloofe:
When we would bring him on to some Confession
Of his true state.

Qu. Did he receiue you well?

Rosin. Most like a Gentleman.

Guild. But with much forcing of his disposition.

Rosin. Niggard of question, but of our demands
Most free in his reply.

Qu. Did you assay him to any pastime?

Rosin. Madam, it so fell out, that certaine Players
We ore-wrought on the way: of these we told him,
And there did seeme in him a kinde of ioy
To heare of it: They are about the Court,
And (as I thinke) they haue already order
This night to play before him.

Pol. 'Tis most true:
And he beseech'd me to intreate your Maiesties
To heare, and see the matter.

King. With all my heart, and it doth much content me
To heare him so inclin'd. Good Gentlemen,
Giue him a further edge, and driue his purpose on
To these delights.

Rosin. We shall my Lord.   *Exeunt.*

King. Sweet *Gertrude* leaue vs too,
For we haue closely sent for *Hamlet* hither,
That he, as 'twere by accident, may there
Affront *Ophelia.* Her Father, and my selfe (lawful espials)
Will so bestow our selues, that seeing vnseene
We may of their encounter frankely iudge,
And gather by him, as he is behaued,
If t be th'affliction of his loue, or no.
That thus he suffers for.

Qu. I shall obey you,
And for your part *Ophelia,* I do wish
That your good Beauties be the happy cause
Of *Hamlets* wildenesse: so shall I hope your Vertues
Will bring him to his wonted way againe,
To both your Honors.

Ophe. Madam, I wish it may.

Pol. *Ophelia,* walke you heere. Gracious so please ye
We will bestow our selues: Reade on this booke,
That shew of such an exercise may colour
Your lonelinesse. We are oft too blame in this,
'Tis too much prou'd, that with Deuotions visage,
And pious Action, we do surge o're
The diuell himselfe.

King. Oh'tis true:
How smart a lash that speech doth giue my Conscience?
The Harlots Cheeke beautied with plaist'ring Art
Is not more vgly to the thing that helpes it,
Then is my deede, to my most painted word.
Oh heauie burthen!

Pol. I heare him comming, let's withdraw my Lord.
                                             Exeunt.

Enter Hamlet.

Ham. To be, or not to be, that is the Question:
Whether tis Nobler in the minde to suffer
The Slings and Arrowes of outragious Fortune,
Or to take Armes against a Sea of troubles,
And by opposing end them: to dye, to sleepe
No more; and by a sleepe, to say we end
The Heart-ake, and the thousand Naturall shockes

That Flesh is heyre too? 'Tis a consummation
Deuoutly to be wish'd. To dye to sleepe,
To sleepe, perchance to Dreame; I, there's the rub,
For in that sleepe of death, what dreames may come,
When we haue shuffiel'd off this mortall coile,
Must giue vs pawse. There's the respect
That makes Calamity of so long life:
For who would beare the Whips and Scornes of time,
The Oppressors wrong, the poore mans Contumely,
The pangs of dispriz'd Loue, the Lawes delay,
The insolence of Office, and the Spurnes
That patient merit of the vnworthy takes,
When he himselfe might his *Quietus* make
With a bare Bodkin? Who would these Fardles beare
To grunt and sweat vnder a weary life,
But that the dread of something after death,
The vndiscouered Countrey, from whose Borne
No Traueller returnes, Puzels the will,
And makes vs rather beare those illes we haue,
Then flye to others that we know not of.
Thus Conscience does make Cowards of vs all,
And thus the Natiue hew of Resolution
Is sicklied o're, with the pale cast of Thought,
And enterprizes of great pith and moment,
With this regard their Currants turne away,
And loose the name of Action. Soft you now,
The faire *Ophelia?* Nimph, in thy Orizons
Be all my sinnes remembred.

Ophe. Good my Lord,
How does your Honor for this many a day?

Ham. I humbly thanke you: well, well, well.

Ophe. My Lord, I haue Remembrances of yours,
That I haue longed long to re-deliuer.
I pray you now, receiue them.

Ham. No, no, I neuer gaue you ought.

Ophe. My honor'd Lord, I know right well you did,
And with them words of so sweet breath compos'd,
As made the things more rich, then perfume left:
Take these againe, for to the Noble minde
Rich gifts wax poore, when giuers proue vnkinde.
There my Lord.

Ham. Ha, ha: Are you honest?

Ophe. My Lord.

Ham. Are you faire?

Ophe. What meanes your Lordship?

Ham. That if you be honest and faire, your Honesty
sho uld admit no discourse to your Beautie.

Ophe. Could Beautie my Lord, haue better Comerce
then your Honestie?

Ham. I trulie: for the power of Beautie, will sooner
transforme Honestie from what it is, to a Bawd, then the
force of Honestie can translate Beautie into his likenesse.
This was sometime a Paradox, but now the time giues it
proofe. I did loue you once.

Ophe. Indeed my Lord, you made me beleeue so.

Ham. You should not haue beleeued me. For vertue
cannot so innoculate our old stocke, but we shall rellish
of it. I loued you not.

Ophe. I was the more deceiued.

Ham. Get thee to a Nunnerie. Why would'st thou
be a breeder of Sinners? I am my selfe indifferent honest,
but yet I could accuse me of such things, that it were better my Mother had not borne me. I am very prowd, re-
uengefull, Ambitious, with more offences at my becke,
then I haue thoughts to put them in imagination, to giue
them shape, or time to acte them in. What should such
                                             Fel-

"To be or not to be," as given in the First Folio (F1, 1623).

Portfolio: *Hamlet* on the Stage

We know that *Hamlet* was popular during Shakespeare's lifetime, but the earliest illustration (1709) showing a scene from the play was engraved more than a century after the play was written, so we know little about what *Hamlet* looked like on Shakespeare's stage. Still, we do have at least a little idea. We know, for instance, that at least in the first scene Hamlet wore black (he speaks of his "inky cloak"), and we know that when the Ghost first appears it is dressed in "the very armor he had on / When he the ambitious Norway combatted" (1.1.64–65). We know, too, that when the Ghost appears later, in the Queen's chamber (3.4), he does not wear armor, a sign that his mood is different.

We also have a few tantalizing glimpses of Elizabethan acting. Thus, in the dumb show (pantomime) preceding "The Murder of Gonzago" that the touring players in 3.2 produce for the court, we get this stage direction: "Enter a King and a Queen very lovingly: the Queen embracing him and he her." A little later, when the Queen in this dumb show finds that the King has been poisoned, she "makes passionate action," but then, when the poisoner woos her, "she seems harsh a while but in the end accepts love."

"The Murder of Gonzago" in *Hamlet* 3.3. Because this episode is a play-within-the-play, Shakespeare uses a distinctive form of verse (pairs of rhyming lines, eight syllables to a line) that sets it off from the language of the rest of the play (chiefly prose, or unrhymed lines of ten syllables). The language, too, is different, for it is conspicuously old-fashioned (the sun is called "Phoebus' cart"; the ocean is called "Neptune's salt wash"). In this modern-dress production done at Stratford, England, in 1975, Claudius wore a blue business suit and Fortinbras wore combat gear, but the characters in the play-within-the-play were masked, to emphasize their theatricality.

The "closet" scene in *Hamlet* 3.4. A line in the preceding scene specifically tells us that Hamlet is "going to his mother's closet." (In Elizabethan language, a "closet" is a private room, as opposed to a public room—for instance, a room in which a monarch might pray, or relax, as opposed to an audience chamber in which he or she would engage in official actions.) In the twentieth century, at least as early as John Gielgud's New York production in 1935, and probably in response to Freudian interpretations of the play, the Queen's "closet" has been fitted with a bed on which Hamlet and Gertrude tussle, and indeed the scene is often wrongly called "the bedroom scene." In this 1989 Royal Shakespeare Company production, with Mark Rylance as Hamlet, a ranting Hamlet (at the left) confronts Gertrude. The Ghost, unknown to Gertrude, sits on the bed, presumably seeking to protect her from Hamlet's assault. The setting was not realistic but expressionistic; that is, the curtains stirred and the lighting changed, not because a physical wind was blowing or the sources of illumination were changing, but to express the passions of the characters.

We know something, too, of the sound effects. Possibly the play begins with the bell tolling twelve (in 1.1 Bernardo says, "'Tis now struck twelve"), and certainly in the first scene we hear the crowing of a cock, which causes the Ghost to depart. Later we hear the sound of drums, trumpets, and cannon when Claudius drinks toasts, and the play ends with the sound of cannon, when Fortinbras orders the soldiers to pay tribute to the dead Hamlet.

What about costumes? In their own day, Elizabethan plays were staged chiefly in contemporary dress—doublet (close-fitting jacket) and hose (tights) for the men, gowns of various sorts for the women (whose roles were played by boy actors)—though for classical plays such as *Julius Caesar* some attempt was made in the direction of ancient costume, at least for the major characters. The seventeenth and eighteenth centuries, too, staged the plays in the costume of the day, which of course was not Elizabethan, but in much of the nineteenth century, and in the first third of the twentieth, a strong sense that the plays were "Elizabethan" caused producers to use Elizabethan costumes, although these costumes—contemporary when the plays were first performed—now had become historical costume, marking the plays as of an age remote from our own.

Kenneth Branagh as Hamlet meditates on death in the graveyard in 5.1. The 1993 production for the Royal Shakespeare Theatre used costumes suggesting the late nineteenth century.

In 1925 Barry Jackson staged a modern-dress production in London, in an effort to emphasize the play's contemporary relevance. Today, productions tend to be in modern dress in the sense that they avoid Elizabethan costume; but usually, in an effort to add some color to the stage as well as to add some (but not a great) sense of remoteness, they use costumes of the nineteenth century, which allow for splendid gowns and for military uniforms with sashes.

Hamlet, Prince of Denmark

[DRAMATIS PERSONAE
GHOST *of Hamlet, the former King of Denmark*
CLAUDIUS, *King of Denmark, the former King's brother*

The same scene (5.1) as in the previous photo shows Kevin Kline as Hamlet in the 1986 New York Shakespeare Festival production. Costumes are late nineteenth century. Horatio is played by an African American. Putting aside plays by black authors, and a very few plays by whites about blacks (such as Eugene O'Neill's *The Emperor Jones*), there are few roles in drama expressly written for blacks. Shakespeare offers only three: Othello, Aaron (a Moor in *Titus Adronicus*), and the Prince of Morroco (in *The Merchant of Venice*). The few black actors who played other Shakespearean roles, such as the great Ira Aldridge who in the nineteenth century was known for his King Lear, performed the roles in whiteface. Since the 1980s, however, directors have engaged in open casting, using blacks (and Asians) in any and all roles, and not requiring white makeup.

GERTRUDE, *Queen of Denmark, widow of the former King and now wife of Claudius*

HAMLET, *Prince of Denmark, son of the late King and of Gertrude*

POLONIUS, *councillor to the King*

LAERTES, *his son*

OPHELIA, *his daughter*

REYNALDO, *his servant*

HORATIO, *Hamlet's friend and fellow student*

VOLTIMAND,
CORNELIUS,
ROSENCRANTZ,
GUILDENSTERN } *members of the Danish court*
OSRIC,
A GENTLEMAN,
A LORD,

> BERNARDO,
> FRANCISCO,   } *officers and soldiers on watch*
> MARCELLUS,

FORTINBRAS, *Prince of Norway*
CAPTAIN *in his army*

Three or Four PLAYERS, *taking the roles of* PROLOGUE, PLAYER KING, PLAYER
    QUEEN, *and* LUCIANUS
Two MESSENGERS
FIRST SAILOR
Two CLOWNS, *a gravedigger and his companion*
PRIEST
FIRST AMBASSADOR *from England*

*Lords, Soldiers, Attendants, Guards, other Players, Followers of
Laertes, other Sailors, another Ambassador or Ambassadors from
England*

SCENE: *Denmark*]

    [1.1] *Enter* BERNARDO *and* FRANCISCO, *two sentinels [meeting].*

BERNARDO. Who's there?
FRANCISCO. Nay, answer me.° Stand and unfold yourself.°
BERNARDO. Long live the King!
FRANCISCO. Bernardo?
BERNARDO. He.   5
FRANCISCO. You come most carefully upon your hour.
BERNARDO. 'Tis now struck twelve. Get thee to bed, Francisco.
FRANCISCO. For this relief much thanks. 'Tis bitter cold,
    And I am sick at heart.
BERNARDO. Have you had quiet guard?   10
FRANCISCO. Not a mouse stirring.
BERNARDO. Well, good night.
    If you do meet Horatio and Marcellus,
    The rivals° of my watch, bid them make haste.

    Enter HORATIO *and* MARCELLUS.

FRANCISCO. I think I hear them.—Stand, ho! Who is there?   15
HORATIO. Friends to this ground.°
MARCELLUS. And liegemen to the Dane.°
FRANCISCO. Give° you good night.

1.1 Location: Elsinore castle. A guard platform. **2 me** (Francisco emphasizes that *he* is the sentry currently on watch.) **unfold yourself** reveal your identity. **14 rivals** partners. **16 ground** country, land. **17 liegemen to the Dane** men sworn to serve the Danish king. **18 Give** i.e., may God give.

MARCELLUS. O, farewell, honest soldier. Who hath relieved you?

FRANCISCO. Bernardo hath my place. Give you good night.   20

Exit FRANCISCO.

MARCELLUS. Holla! Bernardo!

BERNARDO. Say, what, is Horatio there?

HORATIO. A piece of him.

BERNARDO. Welcome, Horatio. Welcome, good Marcellus.

HORATIO. What, has this thing appeared again tonight?   25

BERNARDO. I have seen nothing.

MARCELLUS. Horatio says 'tis but our fantasy,°
    And will not let belief take hold of him
    Touching this dreaded sight twice seen of us.
    Therefore I have entreated him along°   30
    With us to watch° the minutes of this night,
    That if again this apparition come
    He may approve° our eyes and speak to it.

HORATIO. Tush, tush, 'twill not appear.

BERNARDO.   Sit down awhile,
    And let us once again assail your ears,   35
    That are so fortified against our story,
    What° we have two nights seen.

HORATIO.   Well, sit we down,
    And let us hear Bernardo speak of this.

BERNARDO. Last night of all,°
    When yond same star that's westward from the pole°   40
    Had made his° course t' illume° that part of heaven
    Where now it burns, Marcellus and myself,
    The bell then beating one—

    Enter GHOST.

MARCELLUS. Peace, break thee off! Look where it comes again!

BERNARDO. In the same figure like the King that's dead.   45

MARCELLUS. Thou art a scholar.° Speak to it, Horatio.

BERNARDO. Looks 'a° not like the King? Mark it, Horatio.

HORATIO. Most like. It harrows me with fear and wonder.

BERNARDO. It would be spoke to.°

MARCELLUS.   Speak to it, Horatio.

HORATIO. What art thou that usurp'st° this time of night,   50
    Together with that fair and warlike form
    In which the majesty of buried Denmark°
    Did sometime° march? By heaven, I charge thee, speak!

MARCELLUS. It is offended.

BERNARDO.   See, it stalks away.

---

27 **fantasy** imagination.   30 **along** to come along.   31 **watch** keep watch during.
33 **approve** corroborate.   37 **What** with what.   39 **Last . . . all** i.e., this *very* last
night. (Emphatic.)   40 **pole** polestar, north star.   41 **his** its.   **illume** illuminate.   46
scholar one learned enough to know how to question a ghost properly.   47 **'a** he.
49 **It . . . to** (It was commonly believed that a ghost could not speak until spoken
to.)   50 **usurp'st** wrongfully takes over.   52 **buried Denmark** the buried King of
Denmark.   53 **sometime** formerly.

HORATIO. Stay! Speak, speak! I charge thee, speak!   55

Exit GHOST.

MARCELLUS. 'Tis gone and will not answer.

BERNARDO. How now, Horatio? You tremble and look pale.
    Is not this something more than fantasy?
    What think you on 't?°

HORATIO. Before my God, I might not this believe   60
    Without the sensible° and true avouch°
    Of mine own eyes.

MARCELLUS.   Is it not like the King?

HORATIO. As thou art to thyself.
    Such was the very armor he had on
    When he the ambitious Norway° combated.   65
    So frowned he once when, in an angry parle,°
    He smote the sledded° Polacks° on the ice.
    'Tis strange.

MARCELLUS. Thus twice before, and jump° at this dead hour,
    With martial stalk° hath he gone by our watch.   70

HORATIO. In what particular thought to work° I know not,
    But in the gross and scope° of mine opinion
    This bodes some strange eruption to our state.

MARCELLUS. Good now,° sit down, and tell me, he that knows,
    Why this same strict and most observant watch   75
    So nightly toils° the subject° of the land,
    And why such daily cast° of brazen cannon
    And foreign mart° for implements of war,
    Why such impress° of shipwrights, whose sore task
    Does not divide the Sunday from the week.   80
    What might be toward,° that this sweaty haste
    Doth make the night joint-laborer with the day?
    Who is 't that can inform me?

HORATIO.   That can I;
    At least, the whisper goes so. Our last king,
    Whose image even but now appeared to us,   85
    Was, as you know, by Fortinbras of Norway,
    Thereto pricked on° by a most emulate° pride,°
    Dared to the combat; in which our valiant Hamlet—
    For so this side of our known world° esteemed him—
    Did slay this Fortinbras; who by a sealed° compact   90
    Well ratified by law and heraldry

---

59 on 't of it. **61 sensible** confirmed by the senses. **avouch** warrant, evidence.
65 Norway King of Norway. **66 parle** parley. **67 sledded** traveling on sleds. **Polacks**
Poles. **69 jump** exactly. **70 stalk** stride. **71 to work** i.e., to collect my thoughts and try
to understand this. **72 gross and scope** general drift. **74 Good now** (An expression
denoting entreaty or expostulation.) **76 toils** causes to toil. **subject** subjects. **77 cast**
casting. **78 mart** buying and selling. **79 impress** impressment, conscription. **81**
toward in preparation. **87 pricked on** incited. **emulate** emulous, ambitious. **Thereto**
. . . pride (Refers to old Fortinbras, not the Danish King.) **89 this . . . world** i.e., all
Europe, the Western world. **90 sealed** certified, confirmed.

Did forfeit, with his life, all those his lands
Which he stood seized° of, to the conqueror;
Against the° which a moiety competent°
Was gagèd° by our king, which had returned°   95
To the inheritance° of Fortinbras
Had he been vanquisher, as, by the same cov'nant°
And carriage of the article designed,°
His fell to Hamlet. Now, sir, young Fortinbras,
Of unimprovèd mettle° hot and full,   100
Hath in the skirts° of Norway here and there
Sharked up° a list° of lawless resolutes°
For food and diet° to some enterprise
That hath a stomach° in 't, which is no other—
As it doth well appear unto our state—   105
But to recover of us, by strong hand
And terms compulsatory, those foresaid lands
So by his father lost. And this, I take it,
Is the main motive of our preparations,
The source of this our watch, and the chief head°   110
Of this posthaste and rummage° in the land.
BERNARDO. I think it be no other but e'en so.
Well may it sort° that this portentous figure
Comes armèd through our watch so like the King
That was and is the question° of these wars.   115
HORATIO. A mote° it is to trouble the mind's eye.
In the most high and palmy° state of Rome,
A little ere the mightiest Julius fell,
The graves stood tenantless, and the sheeted° dead
Did squeak and gibber in the Roman streets;   120
As° stars with trains° of fire and dews of blood,
Disasters° in the sun; and the moist star°
Upon whose influence Neptune's° empire stands°
Was sick almost to doomsday° with eclipse.
And even the like precurse° of feared events,   125
As harbingers° preceding still° the fates

---

93 seized possessed.   **94 Against the** in return for.   **moiety competent** corresponding portion.   **95 gagèd** engaged, pledged.   **had returned** would have passed.   **96 in heritance** possession.   **97 cov'nant** i.e., the *sealed compact* of line 90.   **98 carriage . . . designed** carrying out of the article or clause drawn up to cover the point. **100 unimprovèd mettle** untried, undisciplined spirits.   **101 skirts** outlying regions, outskirts.   **102 Sharked up** gathered up, as a shark takes fish.   **list** i.e., troop.   **resolutes** desperadoes.   **103 For food and diet** i.e., they are to serve as *food,* or "means," *to some enterprise;* also they serve in return for the rations they get.   **104 stomach** (1) a spirit of daring (2) an appetite that is fed by the *lawless resolutes.*   **110 head** source. **111 rummage** bustle, commotion.   **113 sort** suit.   **115 question** focus of contention. **116 mote** speck of dust.   **117 palmy** flourishing.   **119 sheeted** shrouded.   **121 As** (This abrupt transition suggests that matter is possibly omitted between lines 120 and 121.) **trains** trails.   **122 Disasters** unfavorable signs or aspects.   **moist star** i.e., moon, governing tides.   **123 Neptune** god of the sea.   **stands** depends.   **124 sick . . . doomsday** (See Matthew 24.29 and Revelation 6.12.)   **125 precurse** heralding, foreshadowing. **126 harbingers** forerunners.   **still** continually.

And prologue to the omen° coming on,
Have heaven and earth together demonstrated
Unto our climatures° and countrymen.

Enter GHOST.

But soft,° behold! Lo, where it comes again!   130
I'll cross° it, though it blast° me. [*It spreads his° arms.*]
   Stay, *illusion!*
If thou hast any sound or use of voice,
Speak to me!
If there be any good thing to be done
That may to thee do ease and grace to me,   135
Speak to me!
If thou art privy to° thy country's fate,
Which happily,° foreknowing may avoid,
O, speak!
Or if thou hast uphoarded in thy life   140
Extorted treasure in the womb of earth,
For which, they say, you spirits oft walk in death,
Speak of it! [*The cock crows.*] Stay and speak!—Stop it, Marcellus.
MARCELLUS. Shall I strike at it with my partisan?°
HORATIO. Do, if it will not stand.   [*They strike at it.*]   145
BERNARDO. 'Tis here!
HORATIO. 'Tis here!   [*Exit* GHOST.]
MARCELLUS. 'Tis gone.
   We do it wrong, being so majestical,
To offer it the show of violence,   150
For it is as the air invulnerable,
And our vain blows malicious mockery.
BERNARDO. It was about to speak when the cock crew.
HORATIO. And then it started like a guilty thing
Upon a fearful summons. I have heard   155
The cock, that is the trumpet° to the morn,
Doth with his lofty and shrill-standing throat
Awake the god of day, and at his warning,
Whether in sea or fire, in earth or air,
Th' extravagant and erring° spirit hies°   160
To his confine; and of the truth herein
This present object made probation.°
MARCELLUS. It faded on the crowing of the cock.
Some say that ever 'gainst° that season comes
Wherein our Savior's birth is celebrated,   165
This bird of dawning singeth all night long,
And then, they say, no spirit dare stir abroad;

---

127 omen calamitous event. **129 climatures** regions. **130 soft** i.e., enough, break off.
131 cross stand in its path, confront. **blast** wither, strike with a curse. **s.d. his** its.
137 privy to in on the secret of. **138 happily** haply, perchance. **144 partisan** long-
handled spear. **156 trumpet** trumpeter. **160 extravagant and erring** wandering beyond bounds. (The words have similar meaning.) **160 hies** hastens. **162 probation**
proof. **164 'gainst** just before.

The nights are wholesome, then no planets strike,°
No fairy takes,° nor witch hath power to charm,
So hallowed and so gracious° is that time.   170
HORATIO. So have I heard and do in part believe it.
But, look, the morn in russet mantle clad
Walks o'er the dew of yon high eastward hill.
Break we our watch up, and by my advice
Let us impart what we have seen tonight   175
Unto young Hamlet; for upon my life,
This spirit, dumb to us, will speak to him.
Do you consent we shall acquaint him with it,
As needful in our loves, fitting our duty?
MARCELLUS. Let's do 't, I pray, and I this morning know   180
Where we shall find him most conveniently.

Exeunt.

[1.2] *Flourish. Enter* CLAUDIUS, *King of Denmark,* GERTRUDE *the*
       Queen, [the] *Council, as°* POLONIUS *and his son,* LAERTES, HAMLET
       cum aliis° [*including* VOLTIMAND *and* CORNELIUS].

KING. Though yet of Hamlet our° dear brother's death
The memory be green, and that it us befitted
To bear our hearts in grief and our whole kingdom
To be contracted in one brow of woe,
Yet so far hath discretion fought with nature   5
That we with wisest sorrow think on him
Together with remembrance of ourselves
Therefore our sometime° sister, now our queen,
Th' imperial jointress° to this warlike state,
Have we, as 'twere with a defeated joy—   10
With an auspicious and a dropping eye,°
With mirth in funeral and with dirge in marriage,
In equal scale weighing delight and dole°—
Taken to wife: nor have we herein barred
Your better wisdoms, which have freely gone   15
With this affair along. For all, our thanks.
Now follows that you know° young Fortinbras,
Holding a weak supposal° of our worth,
Or thinking by our late dear brother's death
Our state to be disjoint and out of frame,   20
Co-leaguèd with° this dream of his advantage,°
He hath not failed to pester us with message
Importing° the surrender of those lands

---

168 strike destroy by evil influence. **169 takes** bewitches. **170 gracious** full of
grace. **1.2. Location: The castle.   s.d. as** i.e., such as, including. **cum aliis** with others. **1 our** my. (The royal "we"; also in the following lines.) **8 sometime** former.
9 jointress woman possessing property with her husband. **11 With . . . eye** with one
eye smiling and the other weeping. **13 dole** grief. **17 that you know** what you know
already, that; or, that you be informed as follows. **18 weak supposal** low estimate.
21 Co-leaguèd with joined to, allied with. **dream . . . advantage** illusory hope of having the advantage. (His only ally is this hope.) **23 Importing** pertaining to.

Lost by his father, with all bonds° of law,
To our most valiant brother. So much for him.   25
Now for ourself and for this time of meeting.
Thus much the business is: we have here writ
To Norway, uncle of young Fortinbras—
Who, impotent° and bed-rid, scarcely hears
Of this his nephew's purpose—to suppress   30
His° further gait° herein, in that the levies,
The lists, and full proportions are all made
Out of his subject,° and we here dispatch
You, good Cornelius, and you, Voltimand,
For bearers of this greeting to old Norway,   35
Giving to you no further personal power
To business with the king more than the scope
Of these dilated° articles allow.   [*He gives a paper.*]
Farewell, and let your haste commend your duty.°
CORNELIUS, VOLTIMAND. In that, and all things, will we show our duty.   40
KING. We doubt it nothing.° Heartily farewell.

                    [*Exeunt* VOLTIMAND *and* CORNELIUS.]

And now, Laertes, what's the news with you?
You told us of some suit; what is 't, Laertes?
You cannot speak of reason to the Dane°
And lose your voice.° What wouldst thou beg, Laertes,   45
That shall not be my offer, not thy asking?
The head is not more native° to the heart,
The hand more instrumental° to the mouth,
Than is the throne of Denmark to thy father.
What wouldst thou have, Laertes?
LAERTES.   My dread lord,   50
Your leave and favor° to return to France,
From whence though willingly I came to Denmark
To show my duty in your coronation,
Yet now I must confess, that duty done,
My thoughts and wishes bend again toward France   55
And bow them to your gracious leave and pardon.°
KING. Have you your father's leave? What says Polonius?
POLONIUS. H'ath,° my lord, wrung from me my slow leave
By laborsome petition, and at last
Upon his will I sealed° my hard° consent.   60
I do beseech you, give him leave to go.

---

24 bonds contracts. **29 impotent** helpless. **31 His** i.e., Fortinbras's. **gait** proceeding. **31–33 in that . . . subject** since the levying of troops and supplies is drawn entirely from the King of Norway's own subjects. **38 dilated** set out at length. **39 let . . . duty** let your swift obeying of orders, rather than mere words, express your dutifulness. **41 nothing** not at all. **44 the Dane** the Danish king. **45 lose your voice** waste your speech. **47 native** closely connected, related. **48 instrumental** serviceable. **51 leave and favor** kind permission. **56 bow . . . pardon** entreatingly make a deep bow, asking your permission to depart. **58 H'ath** he has. **60 sealed** (as if sealing a legal document). **hard** reluctant.

KING. Take thy fair hour,° Laertes. Time be thine,
    And thy best graces spend it at thy will!°
    But now, my cousin° Hamlet, and my son—
HAMLET. A little more than kin, and less than kind.°   65
KING. How is it that the clouds still hang on you?
HAMLET. Not so, my lord. I am too much in the sun.°
QUEEN. Good Hamlet, cast thy nighted color° off,
    And let thine eye look like a friend on Denmark.°
    Do not forever with thy vailèd lids°   70
    Seek for thy noble father in the dust.
    Thou know'st 'tis common,° all that lives must die,
    Passing through nature to eternity.
HAMLET. Ay, madam, it is common.
QUEEN.   If it be,
    Why seems it so particular° with thee?   75
HAMLET. Seems, madam? Nay, it is. I know not "seems."
    'Tis not alone my inky cloak, good Mother,
    Nor customary° suits of solemn black,
    Nor windy suspiration° of forced breath,
    No, nor the fruitful° river in the eye,   80
    Nor the dejected havior° of the visage,
    Together with all forms, moods,° shapes of grief,
    That can denote me truly. These indeed seem,
    For they are actions that a man might play.
    But I have that within which passes show;   85
    These but the trappings and the suits of woe.
KING. 'Tis sweet and commendable in your nature, Hamlet,
    To give these mourning duties to your father.
    But you must know your father lost a father,
    That father lost, lost his, and the survivor bound   90
    In filial obligation for some term
    To do obsequious° sorrow. But to persever°
    In obstinate condolement° is a course
    Of impious stubbornness. 'Tis unmanly grief.
    It shows a will most incorrect to heaven,   95
    A heart unfortified,° a mind impatient,

---

62 Take thy fair hour enjoy your time of youth.   **63 And . . . will** and may your finest
qualities guide the way you choose to spend your time.   **64 cousin** any kin not of the immediate family.   **65 A little . . . kind** i.e., closer than an ordinary nephew (since I am
stepson), and yet more separated in natural feeling (with pun on *kind* meaning "affectionate" and "natural," "lawful"). This line is often read as an aside, but it need not be. The King
chooses perhaps not to respond to Hamlet's cryptic and bitter remark.   **67 the sun** i.e.,
the sunshine of the King's royal favor (with pun on *son*).   **68 nighted color** (1) mourning garments of black (2) dark melancholy.   **69 Denmark** the King of Denmark.
70 vailèd lids lowered eyes.   **72 common** of universal occurrence. (But Hamlet plays
on the sense of "vulgar" in line 74.)   **75 particular** personal.   **78 customary** (1) socially
conventional (2) habitual with me.   **79 suspiration** sighing.   **80 fruitful** abundant.
81 havior expression.   **82 moods** outward expression of feeling.   **92 obsequious**
suited to obsequies or funerals.   **persever** persevere.   **93 condolement** sorrowing.
96 unfortified i.e., against adversity.

An understanding simple° and unschooled.
For what we know must be and is as common
As any the most vulgar thing to sense,°
Why should we in our peevish opposition   100
Take it to heart? Fie, 'tis a fault to heaven,
A fault against the dead, a fault to nature,
To reason most absurd, whose common theme
Is death of fathers, and who still° hath cried,
From the first corpse° till he that died today,   105
"This must be so." We pray you, throw to earth
This unprevailing° woe and think of us
As of a father; for let the world take note,
You are the most immediate° to our throne,
And with no less nobility of love   110
Than that which dearest father bears his son
Do I impart toward° you. For° your intent
In going back to school° in Wittenberg,°
It is most retrograde° to our desire,
And we beseech you bend you° to remain   115
Here in the cheer and comfort of our eye,
Our chiefest courtier, cousin, and our son.
QUEEN. Let not thy mother lose her prayers, Hamlet.
   I pray thee, stay with us, go not to Wittenberg.
HAMLET. I shall in all my best° obey you, madam.   120
KING. Why 'tis a loving and a fair reply.
   Be as ourself in Denmark. Madam, come.
   This gentle and unforced accord of Hamlet
   Sits smiling to° my heart, in grace° whereof
   No jocund° health that Denmark drinks today   125
   But the great cannon to the clouds shall tell,
   And the King's rouse° the heaven shall bruit again,°
   Respeaking earthly thunder.° Come away.
                                  Flourish. Exeunt all but HAMLET.
HAMLET. O, that this too too sullied° flesh would melt,
   Thaw, and resolve itself into a dew!   130
   Or that the Everlasting had not fixed
   His canon° 'gainst self-slaughter! O God, God,
   How weary, stale, flat, and unprofitable
   Seem to me all the uses° of this world!

---

97 simple ignorant.   **99 As . . . sense** as the most ordinary experience.   **104 still** always.   **105 the first corpse** (Abel's).   **107 unprevailing** unavailing, useless.
109 most immediate next in succession.   **112 impart toward** i.e., bestow my affection on.   **For** as for.   **113 to school** i.e., to your studies.   **Wittenberg** famous German university founded in 1502.   **114 retrograde** contrary.   **115 bend you** incline yourself.
120 in all my best to the best of my ability.   **124 to** i.e., at.   **grace** thanksgiving.
125 jocund merry.   **127 rouse** drinking of a draft of liquor.   **bruit again** loudly echo.
128 thunder i.e., of trumpet and kettledrum, sounded when the King drinks; see 1.4.8–12.   **129 sullied** defiled. (The early quartos read *sallied;* the Folio, *solid.*)
132 canon law.   **134 all the uses** the whole routine.

Fie on 't, ah fie! 'Tis an unweeded garden   135
That grows to seed. Things rank and gross in nature
Possess it merely.° That it should come to this!
But two months dead—nay, not so much, not two.
So excellent a king, that was to° this
Hyperion° to a satyr,° so loving to my mother   140
That he might not beteem° the winds of heaven
Visit her face too roughly. Heaven and earth,
Must I remember? Why, she would hang on him
As if increase of appetite had grown
By what it fed on, and yet within a month—   145
Let me not think of 't; frailty, thy name is woman!—
A little month, or ere° those shoes were old
With which she followed my poor father's body,
Like Niobe;° all tears, why she, even she—
O God, a beast, that wants discourse of reason,°   150
Would have mourned longer—married with my uncle,
My father's brother, but no more like my father
Than I to Hercules. Within a month,
Ere yet the sale of most unrighteous tears
Had left the flushing in her gallèd° eyes,   155
She married. O, most wicked speed, to post°
With such dexterity to incestuous° sheets!
It is not, nor it cannot come to good.
But break, my heart, for I must hold my tongue.

Enter HORATIO, MARCELLUS *and* BERNARDO.

HORATIO. Hail to your lordship!
HAMLET.   I am glad to see you well.   160
    Horatio—or I do forget myself.
HORATIO. The same, my lord, and your poor servant ever.
HAMLET. Sir, my good friend; I'll change that name° with you.
    And what make you from° Wittenberg, Horatio?
    Marcellus.   165
MARCELLUS. My good lord.
HAMLET. I am very glad to see you. [*To* BERNARDO.] Good even, sir.—
    But what in faith make you from Wittenberg?
HORATIO. A truant disposition, good my lord.
HAMLET. I would not hear your enemy say so,   170

---

137 merely completely.   **139 to** in comparison to.   **140 Hyperion** Titan sun-god,
father of Helios.   **satyr** a lecherous creature of classical mythology, half-human but with
a goat's legs, tail, ears, and horns.   **141 beteem** allow.   **147 or ere** even before.   **149
Niobe** Tantalus' daughter, Queen of Thebes, who boasted that she had more sons and
daughters than Leto; for this, Apollo and Artemis, children of Leto, slew her fourteen
children. She was turned by Zeus into a stone that continually dropped tears.
150 wants . . . reason lacks the faculty of reason.   **155 gallèd** irritated, inflamed.   **156
post** hasten.   **157 incestuous** (In Shakespeare's day, the marriage of a man like Claudius
to his deceased brother's wife was considered incestuous.)   **163 change that name** i.e.,
give and receive reciprocally the name of "friend" (rather than talk of "servant").   **164
make you from** are you doing away from.

    Nor shall you do my ear that violence
    To make it truster of your own report
    Against yourself. I know you are no truant.
    But what is your affair in Elsinore?
    We'll teach you to drink deep ere you depart.   175
HORATIO. My lord, I came to see your father's funeral.
HAMLET. I prithee, do not mock me, fellow student;
    I think it was to see my mother's wedding.
HORATIO. Indeed, my lord, it followed hard° upon.
HAMLET. Thrift, thrift, Horatio! The funeral baked meats°   180
    Did coldly° furnish forth the marriage tables.
    Would I had met my dearest° foe in heaven
    Or ever° I had seen that day, Horatio.
    My father—Methinks I see my father.
HORATIO. Where, my lord?
HAMLET.   In my mind's eye, Horatio.   185
HORATIO. I saw him once. 'A° was a goodly king.
HAMLET. 'A was a man. Take him for all in all,
    I shall not look upon his like again.
HORATIO. My lord, I think I saw him yesternight.
HAMLET. Saw? Who?   190
HORATIO. My lord, the King your father.
HAMLET. The King my father?
HORATIO. Season your admiration° for a while
    With an attent° ear till I may deliver,
    Upon the witness of these gentlemen,   195
    This marvel to you.
HAMLET.   For God's love, let me hear!
HORATIO. Two nights together had these gentlemen,
    Marcellus and Bernardo, on their watch,
    In the dead waste° and middle of the night,
    Been thus encountered. A figure like your father,   200
    Armèd at point° exactly, cap-à-pie,°
    Appears before them, and with solemn march
    Goes slow and stately by them. Thrice he walked
    By their oppressed and fear-surprisèd eyes
    Within his truncheon's° length, whilst they, distilled°   205
    Almost to jelly with the act° of fear,
    Stand dumb and speak not to him. This to me
    In dreadful° secrecy impart they did,
    And I with them the third night kept the watch,
    Where, as they had delivered, both in time,   210
    Form of the thing, each word made true and good,
    The apparition comes. I knew your father;

---

179 hard close. **180 baked meats** meat pies. **181 coldly** i.e., as cold leftovers.
182 dearest closest (and therefore deadliest). **183 Or ever** before. **186 'A** he.
193 Season your admiration restrain your astonishment. **194 attent** attentive.
199 dead waste desolate stillness. **201 at point** correctly in every detail. **cap-à-pie**
from head to foot. **205 truncheon** officer's staff. **distilled** dissolved. **206 act**
action, operation. **208 dreadful** full of dread.

These hands are not more like.

HAMLET.   But where was this?

MARCELLUS. My lord, upon the platform where we watch.

HAMLET. Did you not speak to it?

HORATIO.   My lord, I did,   215
    But answer made it none. Yet once methought
    It lifted up its head and did address
    Itself to motion, like as it would speak;°
    But even then° the morning cock crew loud,
    And at the sound it shrunk in haste away   220
    And vanished from our sight.

HAMLET.   'Tis very strange.

HORATIO. As I do live, my honoured lord, 'tis true,
    And we did think it writ down in our duty
    To let you know of it.

HAMLET. Indeed, indeed, sirs. But this troubles me.   225
    Hold you the watch tonight?

ALL.   We do, my lord.

HAMLET. Armed, say you?

ALL. Armed, my lord.

HAMLET. From top to toe?

ALL. My lord, from head to foot.   230

HAMLET. Then saw you not his face?

HORATIO. O, yes, my lord, he wore his beaver° up.

HAMLET. What° looked he, frowningly?

HORATIO. A countenance more in sorrow than in anger.

HAMLET. Pale or red?   235

HORATIO. Nay, very pale.

HAMLET. And fixed his eyes upon you?

HORATIO. Most constantly.

HAMLET. I would I had been there.

HORATIO. It would have much amazed you.   240

HAMLET. Very like, very like. Stayed it long?

HORATIO. While one with moderate haste might tell° a hundred.

MARCELLUS, BERNARDO. Longer, longer.

HORATIO. Not when I saw't.

HAMLET. His beard was grizzled°—no?   245

HORATIO. It was, as I have seen it in his life,
    A sable silvered.°

HAMLET.   I will watch tonight.
    Perchance 'twill walk again.

HORATIO.   I warrant° it will.

HAMLET. If it assume my noble father's person,
    I'll speak to it though hell itself should gape   250
    And bid me hold my peace. I pray you all,

217–218 did . . . speak began to move as though it were about to speak.   **219 even
then** at that very instant.   **232 beaver** visor on the helmet.   **233 What** how.   **242 tell**
count.   **245 grizzled** gray.   **247 sable silvered** black mixed with white.   **248
warrant** assure you.

If you have hitherto concealed this sight,
Let it be tenable° in your silence still,
And whatsoever else shall hap tonight,
Give it an understanding but no tongue.   255
I will requite your loves. So, fare you well.
Upon the platform twixt eleven and twelve
I'll visit you.

ALL.   Our duty to your honor.

HAMLET. Your loves, as mine to you. Farewell.

                              Exeunt [*all but* HAMLET].

My father's spirit in arms! All is not well.   260
I doubt° some foul play. Would the night were come!
Till then sit still, my soul. Foul deeds will rise,
Though all the earth o'erwhelm them, to men's eyes.

                                                      Exit.

[1.3] *Enter* LAERTES *and* OPHELIA, *his sister.°*

LAERTES. My necessaries are embarked. Farewell.
And, sister, as the winds give benefit
And convoy is assistant,° do not sleep
But let me hear from you.

OPHELIA.   Do you doubt that?

LAERTES. For Hamlet, and the trifling of his favor,   5
Hold it a fashion and a toy in blood,°
A violet in the youth of primy° nature,
Forward,° not permanent, sweet, not lasting,
The perfume and suppliance° of a minute—
No more.

OPHELIA.   No more but so?

LAERTES.   Think it no more.   10
For nature crescent° does not grow alone
In thews° and bulk, but as this temple° waxes
The inward service of the mind and soul
Grows wide withal.° Perhaps he loves you now,
And now no soil° nor cautel° doth besmirch   15
The virtue of his will,° but you must fear,
His greatness weighed,° his will is not his own.
For he himself is subject to his birth.
He may not, as unvalued persons do,
Carve° for himself, for on his choice depends   20
The safety and health of this whole state,
And therefore must his choice be circumscribed

---

253 tenable held. **261 doubt** suspect. **1.3. Location: Polonius' chambers.**
3 convoy is assistant means of conveyance are available. **6 toy in blood** passing
amorous fancy. **7 primy** in its prime, springtime. **8 Forward** precocious. **9 sup-**
pliance supply, filler. **11 crescent** growing, waxing. **12 thews** bodily strength.
temple i.e., body. **14 Grows wide withal** grows along with it. **15 soil** blemish.
cautel deceit. **16 will** desire. **17 His greatness weighed** if you take into account
his high position. **20 Carve** i.e., choose.

Unto the voice and yielding° of that body
Whereof he is the head. Then if he says he loves you,
It fits your wisdom so far to believe it   25
As he in his particular act and place°
May give his saying deed, which is no further
Than the main voice° of Denmark goes withal.°
Then weigh what loss your honor may sustain
If with too credent° ear you list° his songs,   30
Or lose your heart, or your chaste treasure open
To his unmastered importunity.
Fear it, Ophelia, fear it, my dear sister,
And keep you in the rear of your affection,°
Out of the shot and danger of desire.   35
The chariest° maid is prodigal enough
If she unmask° her beauty to the moon.°
Virtue itself scapes not calumnious strokes.
The canker galls° the infants of the spring
Too oft before their buttons° be disclosed,°   40
And in the morn and liquid dew° of youth
Contagious blastments° are most imminent.
Be wary then; best safety lies in fear.
Youth to itself rebels,° though none else near.
OPHELIA. I shall the effect of this good lesson keep   45
As watchman to my heart. But, good my brother,
Do not, as some ungracious° pastors do,
Show me the steep and thorny way to heaven,
Whiles like a puffed° and reckless libertine
Himself the primrose path of dalliance treads,   50
And recks° not his own rede.°

Enter POLONIUS.

LAERTES.   O, fear me not.°
I stay too long. But here my father comes.
A double° blessing is a double grace;
Occasion smiles upon a second leave.°
POLONIUS. Yet here, Laertes? Aboard, aboard, for shame!   55
The wind sits in the shoulder of your sail,
And you are stayed for. There—my blessing with thee!

---

23 voice and yielding assent, approval.   **26 in . . . place** in his particular restricted circumstances.   **28 main voice** general assent.   **withal** along with.   **30 credent** credu-
lous.   **list** listen to.   **34 keep . . . affection** don't advance as far as your affection might
lead you. (A military metaphor.)   **36 chariest** most scrupulously modest.   **37 If she
unmask** if she does no more than show her beauty.   **moon** (Symbol of chastity.)
39 canker galls canker-worm destroys.   **40 buttons** buds.   **disclosed** opened.
41 liquid dew i.e., time when dew is fresh and bright.   **42 blastments** blights.
44 Youth . . . rebels youth is inherently rebellious.   **47 ungracious** ungodly.
49 puffed bloated, or swollen with pride.   **51 recks** heeds.   **rede** counsel.   **fear me
not** don't worry on my account.   **53 double** (Laertes has already bid his father good-
bye.)   **54 Occasion . . . leave** happy is the circumstance that provides a second leave-
taking. (The goddess Occasion, or Opportunity, smiles.)

And these few precepts in thy memory
Look° thou character.° Give thy thoughts no tongue,
Nor any unproportioned° thought his° act.   60
Be thou familiar,° but by no means vulgar.°
Those friends thou hast, and their adoption tried,°
Grapple them unto thy soul with hoops of steel,
But do not dull thy palm° with entertainment
Of each new-hatched, unfledged courage.° Beware   65
Of entrance to a quarrel, but being in,
Bear 't that° th' opposèd may beware of thee.
Give every man thy ear, but few thy voice;
Take each man's censure,° but reserve thy judgment.
Costly thy habit° as thy purse can buy,   70
But not expressed in fancy;° rich, not gaudy,
For the apparel oft proclaims the man,
And they in France of the best rank and station
Are of a most select and generous chief in that.°
Neither a borrower nor a lender be,   75
For loan oft loses both itself and friend,
And borrowing dulleth edge of husbandry.°
This above all: to thine own self be true,
And it must follow, as the night the day,
Thou canst not then be false to any man.   80
Farewell. My blessing season° this in thee!
LAERTES. Most humbly do I take my leave, my lord.
POLONIUS. The time invests° you. Go, your servants tend.°
LAERTES. Farewell, Ophelia, and remember well
    What I have said to you.   85
OPHELIA. 'Tis in my memory locked,
    And you yourself shall keep the key of it.
LAERTES. Farewell.

                                                        Exit LAERTES.

POLONIUS. What is 't, Ophelia, he hath said to you?
OPHELIA. So please you, something touching the Lord Hamlet.   90
POLONIUS. Marry,° well bethought.
    'Tis told me he hath very oft of late
    Given private time to you, and you yourself
    Have of your audience been most free and bounteous.
    If it be so—as so 'tis put on° me,   95
    And that in way of caution—I must tell you

---

59 **Look** be sure that. **character** inscribe. 60 **unproportioned** badly calculated, intemperate. **his** its. 61 **familiar** sociable. **vulgar** common. 62 **and their adoption tried** and also their suitability for adoption as friends having been tested. 64 **dull thy palm** i.e., shake hands so often as to make the gesture meaningless. 65 **courage** young man of spirit. 67 **Bear 't that** manage it so that. 69 **censure** opinion, judgment. 70 **habit** clothing. 71 **fancy** excessive ornament, decadent fashion. 74 **Are . . . that** are of a most refined and well-bred preeminence in choosing what to wear. 77 **husbandry** thrift. 81 **season** mature. 83 **invests** besieges, presses upon. **tend** attend, wait. 91 **Marry** i.e., by the Virgin Mary. (A mild oath.) 95 **put on** impressed on, told to.

You do not understand yourself so clearly
As it behooves° my daughter and your honor.
What is between you? Give me up the truth.

OPHELIA. He hath, my lord, of late made many tenders°   100
Of his affection to me.

POLONIUS. Affection? Pooh! You speak like a green girl,
Unsifted° in such perilous circumstance.
Do you believe his tenders, as you call them?

OPHELIA. I do not know, my lord, what I should think.   105

POLONIUS. Marry, I will teach you. Think yourself a baby
That you have ta'en these tenders for true pay
Which are not sterling.° Tender° yourself more dearly,
Or—not to crack the wind° of the poor phrase,
Running it thus—you'll tender me a fool.°   110

OPHELIA. My lord, he hath importuned me with love
In honorable fashion.

POLONIUS. Ay, fashion° you may call it. Go to,° go to.

OPHELIA. And hath given countenance° to his speech, my lord,
With almost all the holy vows of heaven.   115

POLONIUS. Ay, springes° to catch woodcocks.° I do know,
When the blood burns, how prodigal° the soul
Lends the tongue vows. These blazes, daughter,
Giving more light than heat, extinct in both
Even in their promise as it° is a-making,   120
You must not take for fire. From this time
Be something° scanter of your maiden presence.
Set your entreatments° at a higher rate
Than a command to parle.° For Lord Hamlet,
Believe so much in him° that he is young,   125
And with a larger tether may he walk
Than may be given you. In few,° Ophelia,
Do not believe his vows, for they are brokers,°
Not of that dye° which their investments° show,
But mere implorators° of unholy suits,   130
Breathing° like sanctified and pious bawds,
The better to beguile. This is for all:°

---

98 behooves befits. **100 tenders** offers. **103 Unsifted** i.e., untried. **108 sterling** legal currency. **Tender** hold, look after, offer. **109 crack the wind** i.e., run it until it is broken-winded. **110 tender me a fool** (1) show yourself to me as a fool (2) show me up as a fool (3) present me with a grandchild. (*Fool* was a term of endearment for a child.) **113 fashion** mere form, pretense. **Go to** (An expression of impatience.) **114 countenance** credit, confirmation. **116 springes** snares. **woodcocks** birds easily caught; here used to connote gullibility. **117 prodigal** prodigally. **120 it** i.e., the promise. **122 something** somewhat. **123 entreatments** negotiations for surrender. (A military term.) **124 parle** discuss terms with the enemy. (Polonius urges his daughter, in the metaphor of military language, not to meet with Hamlet and consider giving in to him merely because he requests an interview.) **125 so . . . him** this much concerning him. **127 In few** briefly. **128 brokers** go-betweens, procurers. **129 dye** color or sort. **investments** clothes. (The vows are not what they seem.) **130 mere implorators** out-and-out solicitors. **131 Breathing** speaking. **132 for all** once for all, in sum.

I would not, in plain terms, from this time forth
Have you so slander° any moment° leisure
As to give words or talk with the Lord Hamlet.   135
Look to 't, I charge you. Come your ways.°
OPHELIA. I shall obey, my lord.

                                        Exeunt.

     [1.4] *Enter* HAMLET, HORATIO, *and* MARCELLUS.

HAMLET. The air bites shrewdly,° it is very cold.
HORATIO. It is a nipping and eager° air.
HAMLET. What hour now?
HORATIO.   I think it lacks of° twelve.
MARCELLUS. No, it is struck.
HORATIO.   Indeed? I heard it not.
     It then draws near the season°   5
     Wherein the spirit held his wont° to walk.

          A flourish of trumpets, and two pieces° go off [*within*].

     What does this mean, my lord?
HAMLET. The King doth wake° tonight and takes his rouse,°
     Keeps wassail,° and the swaggering upspring° reels,°
     And as he drains his drafts of Rhenish° down,   10
     The kettledrum and trumpet thus bray out
     The triumph of his pledge.°
HORATIO.   It is a custom?
HAMLET. Ay, marry, is 't,
     But to my mind, though I am native here
     And to my manner° born, it is a custom   15
     More honored in the breach than the observance.°
     This heavy-headed revel east and west°
     Makes us traduced and taxed of° other nations.
     They clepe° us drunkards, and with swinish phrase°
     Soil our addition;° and indeed it takes   20
     From our achievements, though performed at height,°
     The pith and marrow of our attribute.°
     So, oft it chances in particular men,
     That for° some vicious mole of nature° in them,
     As in their birth—wherein they are not guilty,   25

---

134 slander abuse, misuse. **moment** moment's. **136 Come your ways** come along.
1.4. Location: The guard platform. 1 shrewdly keenly, sharply. **2 eager** biting.
3 lacks of is just short of. **5 season** time. **6 held his wont** was accustomed. **s.d.
pieces** i.e., of ordnance, cannon. **8 wake** stay awake and hold revel. **takes his
rouse** carouses. **9 wassail** carousal. **upspring** wild German dance. **reels** dances.
10 Rhenish Rhine wine. **12 The triumph . . . pledge** i.e., his feat in draining the wine
in a single draft. **15 manner** custom (of drinking). **16 More . . . observance** better
neglected than followed. **17 east and west** i.e., everywhere. **18 taxed of** censured by.
19 clepe call. **with swinish phrase** i.e., by calling us swine. **20 addition** reputation.
21 at height outstandingly. **22 The pith . . . attribute** the essence of the reputation
that others attribute to us. **24 for** on account of. **mole of nature** natural blemish in
one's constitution.

Since nature cannot choose his° origin—
By their o'ergrowth of some complexion,°
Oft breaking down the pales° and forts of reason,
Or by some habit that too much o'erleavens°
The form of plausive° manners, that these men,   30
Carrying, I say, the stamp of one defect,
Being nature's livery° or fortune's star,°
His virtues else,° be they as pure as grace,
As infinite as man may undergo,°
Shall in the general censure° take corruption   35
From that particular fault. The dram of evil
Doth all the noble substance often dout
To his own scandal.°

Enter GHOST.

HORATIO.   Look, my lord, it comes!
HAMLET. Angels and ministers of grace° defend us!
Be thou° a spirit of health° or goblin damned,   40
Bring° with thee airs from heaven or blasts from hell,
Be thy intents° wicked or charitable,
Thou com'st in such a questionable° shape
That I will speak to thee. I'll call thee Hamlet,
King, father, royal Dane. O, answer me!   45
Let me not burst in ignorance, but tell
Why thy canonized° bones, hearsèd° in death,
Have burst their cerements;° why the sepulcher
Wherein we saw thee quietly inurned°
Hath oped his ponderous and marble jaws   50
To cast thee up again. What may this mean,
That thou, dead corpse, again in complete steel,°
Revisits thus the glimpses of the moon,°
Making night hideous, and we fools of nature°
So horridly to shake our disposition°   55
With thoughts beyond the reaches of our souls?
Say, why is this? Wherefore? What should we do?

---

26 his its.   **27 their o'ergrowth . . . complexion** the excessive growth in individuals of some natural trait.   **28 pales** palings, fences (as of a fortification).   **29 o'erleavens** induces a change throughout (as yeast works in dough).   **30 plausive** pleasing.   **32 nature's livery** sign of one's servitude to nature.   **fortune's star** the destiny that chance brings.   **33 His virtues else** i.e., the other qualities of *these men* (line 30).   **34 may undergo** can sustain.   **35 general censure** general opinion that people have of him. **36–38 The dram . . . scandal** i.e., the small drop of evil blots out or works against the noble substance of the whole and brings it into disrepute. To *dout* is to blot out. (A famous crux.)   **39 ministers of grace** messengers of God.   **40 Be thou** whether you are.   **spirit of health** good angel.   **41 Bring** whether you bring.   **42 Be thy intents** whether your intentions are.   **43 questionable** inviting question.   **47 canonized** buried according to the canons of the church.   **hearsèd** coffined.   **48 cerements** grave clothes.   **49 inurned** entombed.   **52 complete steel** full armor. **53 glimpses of the moon** pale and uncertain moonlight.   **54 fools of nature** mere men, limited to natural knowledge and subject to nature.   **55 So . . . disposition** to distress our mental composure so violently.

[*The* GHOST] *beckons* [HAMLET].

HORATIO. It beckons you to go away with it,
As if it some impartment° did desire
To you alone.

MARCELLUS.   Look with what courteous action   60
It wafts you to a more removèd ground.
But do not go with it.

HORATIO.   No, by no means.

HAMLET. It will not speak. Then I will follow it.

HORATIO. Do not, my lord!

HAMLET.   Why, what should be the fear?
I do not set my life at a pin's fee,°   65
And for my soul, what can it do to that,
Being a thing immortal as itself?
It waves me forth again. I'll follow it.

HORATIO. What if it tempt you toward the flood,° my lord,
Or to the dreadful summit of the cliff   70
That beetles o'er° his° base into the sea,
And there assume some other horrible form
Which might deprive your sovereignty of reason°
And draw you into madness? Think of it.
The very place puts toys of desperation,°   75
Without more motive, into every brain
That looks so many fathoms to the sea
And hears it roar beneath.

HAMLET. It wafts me still.—Go on, I'll follow thee.

MARCELLUS. You shall not go, my lord.   [*They try to stop him.*]

HAMLET.   Hold off your hands!   80

HORATIO. Be ruled. You shall not go.

HAMLET.   My fate cries out,°
And makes each petty° artery° in this body
As hardy as the Nemean lion's° nerve.°
Still am I called. Unhand me, gentlemen.
By heaven, I'll make a ghost of him that lets° me!   85
I say, away!—Go on, I'll follow thee.

                    Exeunt GHOST *and* HAMLET.

HORATIO. He waxes desperate with imagination.

MARCELLUS. Let's follow. 'Tis not fit thus to obey him.

HORATIO. Have after.° To what issue° will this come?

MARCELLUS. Something is rotten in the state of Denmark.   90

HORATIO. Heaven will direct it.°

MARCELLUS.   Nay, let's follow him.

                    Exeunt.

---

59 impartment communication.   **65 fee** value.   **69 flood** sea.   **71 beetles o'er** overhangs threateningly (like bushy eyebrows).   **his** its.   **73 deprive . . . reason** take away the rule of reason over your mind.   **75 toys of desperation** fancies of desperate acts, i.e., suicide.   **81 My fate cries out** my destiny summons me.   **82 petty** weak.   **artery** (through which the vital spirits were thought to have been conveyed).   **83 Nemean lion** one of the monsters slain by Hercules in his twelve labors.   **nerve** sinew.   **85 lets** hinders.   **89 Have after** let's go after him.   **issue** outcome.   **91 it** i.e., the outcome.

[1.5] *Enter* GHOST *and* HAMLET.

HAMLET. Whither wilt thou lead me? Speak. I'll go no further.
GHOST. Mark me.
HAMLET.   I will.
GHOST.   My hour is almost come,
　　When I to sulfurous and tormenting flames
　　Must render up myself.
HAMLET.   Alas, poor ghost!
GHOST. Pity me not, but lend thy serious hearing   5
　　To what I shall unfold.
HAMLET. Speak. I am bound° to hear.
GHOST. So art thou to revenge, when thou shalt hear.
HAMLET. What?
GHOST. I am thy father's spirit,   10
　　Doomed for a certain term to walk the night,
　　And for the day confined to fast° in fires,
　　Till the foul crimes° done in my days of nature°
　　Are burnt and purged away. But that° I am forbid
　　To tell the secrets of my prison house,   15
　　I could a tale unfold whose lightest word
　　Would harrow up° thy soul, freeze thy young blood,
　　Make thy two eyes like stars start from their spheres,°
　　Thy knotted and combinèd locks° to part,
　　And each particular hair to stand on end   20
　　Like quills upon the fretful porcupine.
　　But this eternal blazon° must not be
　　To ears of flesh and blood. List, list, O, list!
　　If thou didst ever thy dear father love—
HAMLET. O God!   25
GHOST. Revenge his foul and most unnatural murder.
HAMLET. Murder?
GHOST. Murder most foul, as in the best° it is,
　　But this most foul, strange, and unnatural.
HAMLET. Haste me to know't, that I, with wings as swift   30
　　As meditation or the thoughts of love,
　　May sweep to my revenge.
GHOST.   I find thee apt;
　　And duller shouldst thou be° than the fat° weed
　　That roots itself in ease on Lethe° wharf,

1.5 Location: The battlements of the castle.   7 bound (1) ready (2) obligated by duty and fate. (The Ghost, in line 8, answers in the second sense.)   **12 fast** do penance by fasting.   **13 crimes** sins.   **of nature** as a mortal.   **14 But that** were it not that.   **17 harrow up** lacerate, tear.   **18 spheres** i.e., eye-sockets, here compared to the orbits or transparent revolving spheres in which, according to Ptolemaic astronomy, the heavenly bodies were fixed.   **19 knotted . . . locks** hair neatly arranged and confined.   **22 eternal blazon** revelation of the secrets of eternity.   **28 in the best** even at best.   **33 shouldst thou be** you would have to be.   **fat** torpid, lethargic.   **34 Lethe** the river of forgetfulness in Hades.

Wouldst thou not stir in this. Now, Hamlet, hear.   35
'Tis given out that, sleeping in my orchard,°
A serpent stung me. So the whole ear of Denmark
Is by a forgèd process° of my death
Rankly abused.° But know, thou noble youth,
The serpent that did sting thy father's life   40
Now wears his crown.

HAMLET. O, my prophetic soul! My uncle!

GHOST. Ay, that incestuous, that adulterate° beast,
With witchcraft of his wit, with traitorous gifts°—
O wicked wit and gifts, that have the power   45
So to seduce!—won to his shameful lust
The will of my most seeming-virtuous queen.
O Hamlet, what a falling off was there!
From me, whose love was of that dignity
That it went hand in hand even with the vow°   50
I made to her in marriage, and to decline
Upon a wretch whose natural gifts were poor
To° those of mine!
But virtue, as it° never will be moved,
Though lewdness court it in a shape of heaven,°   55
So lust, though to a radiant angel linked,
Will sate itself in a celestial bed°
And prey on garbage.
But soft, methinks I scent the morning air.
Brief let me be. Sleeping within my orchard,   60
My custom always of the afternoon,
Upon my secure° hour thy uncle stole,
With juice of cursèd hebona° in a vial,
And in the porches of my ears° did pour
The leprous distillment,° whose effect   65
Holds such an enmity with blood of man
That swift as quicksilver it courses through
The natural gates and alleys of the body,
And with a sudden vigor it doth posset°
And curd, like eager° droppings into milk,   70
The thin and wholesome blood. So did it mine,
And a most instant tetter° barked° about,

---

36 orchard garden. **38 forgèd process** falsified account. **39 abused** deceived.
43 adulterate adulterous. **44 gifts** (1) talents (2) presents. **50 even with the vow**
with the very vow. **53 To** compared to. **54 virtue, as it** as virtue. **55 shape of**
heaven heavenly form. **57 sate . . . bed** cease to find sexual pleasure in a virtuously
lawful marriage. **62 secure** confident, unsuspicious. **63 hebona** a poison. (The word
seems to be a form of *ebony,* though it is thought perhaps to be related to *henbane,*
a poison, or to *ebenus,* "yew.") **64 porches of my ears** ears as a porch or entrance of
the body. **65 leprous distillment** distillation causing leprosylike disfigurement.
69 posset coagulate, curdle. **70 eager** sour, acid. **72 tetter** eruption of scabs.
barked recovered with a rough covering, like bark on a tree.

Most lazar-like,° with vile and loathsome crust,
All my smooth body.
Thus was I, sleeping, by a brother's hand   75
Of life, of crown, of queen at once dispatched,°
Cut off even in the blossoms of my sin,
Unhouseled,° disappointed,° unaneled,°
No reckoning° made, but sent to my account
With all my imperfections on my head.   80
O, horrible! O, horrible, most horrible!
If thou hast nature° in thee, bear it not.
Let not the royal bed of Denmark be
A couch for luxury° and damnèd incest.
But, howsoever thou pursues this act,   85
Taint not thy mind nor let thy soul contrive
Against thy mother aught. Leave her to heaven
And to those thorns that in her bosom lodge,
To prick and sting her. Fare thee well at once.
The glowworm shows the matin° to be near,   90
And 'gins to pale his° uneffectual fire.
Adieu, adieu, adieu! Remember me.

                                                        [*Exit.*]
HAMLET. O all you host of heaven! O earth! What else?
     And shall I couple° hell? O, fie! Hold,° hold, my heart,
     And you, my sinews, grow not instant° old,   95
     But bear me stiffly up. Remember thee?
     Ay, thou poor ghost, whiles memory holds a seat
     In this distracted globe.° Remember thee?
     Yea, from the table° of my memory
     I'll wipe away all trivial fond° records,   100
     All saws° of books, all forms,° all pressures° past
     That youth and observations copied there,
     And thy commandment all alone shall live
     Within the book and volume of my brain,
     Unmixed with baser matter. Yes, by heaven!   105
     O most pernicious woman!
     O villain, villain, smiling, damnèd villain!
     My tables°—meet it is° I set it down
     That one may smile, and smile, and be a villain.
     At least I am sure it may be so in Denmark.   110
                                                      [*Writing.*]

---

73 lazar-like leperlike.   **76 dispatched** suddenly deprived.   **78 Unhouseled** without
having received the Sacrament.   **disappointed** unready (spiritually) for the last journey.
unaneled without having received extreme unction.   **79 reckoning** settling of accounts.   **82 nature** i.e., the promptings of a son.   **84 luxury** lechery.   **90 matin** morning.   **91 his** its.   **94 couple** add.   **Hold** hold together.   **95 instant** instantly.
98 globe (1) head (2) world.   **99 table** tablet, slate.   **100 fond** foolish.   **101 saws** wise
sayings.   **forms** shapes or images copied onto the slate; general ideas.   **pressures** impressions stamped.   **108 tables** writing tablets.   **meet it is** it is fitting.

So uncle, there you are.° Now to my word:
It is "Adieu, adieu! Remember me."
I have sworn't.

Enter HORATIO *and* MARCELLUS.

HORATIO. My lord, my lord!

MARCELLUS. Lord Hamlet!   115

HORATIO. Heavens secure him!°

HAMLET. So be it.

MARCELLUS. Hilo, ho, ho, my lord!

HAMLET. Hillo, ho, ho, boy! Come, bird, come.°

MARCELLUS. How is't, my noble lord?   120

HORATIO. What news, my lord?

HAMLET. O, wonderful!

HORATIO. Good my lord, tell it.

HAMLET. No, you will reveal it.

HORATIO. Not I, my lord, by heaven.   125

MARCELLUS. Nor I, my lord.

HAMLET. How say you, then, would heart of man once° think it?
     But you'll be secret?

HORATIO, MARCELLUS.   Ay, by heaven, my lord.

HAMLET. There's never a villain dwelling in all Denmark
     But he's an arrant° knave.   130

HORATIO. There needs no ghost, my lord, come from the grave
     To tell us this.

HAMLET.   Why, right, you are in the right.
     And so, without more circumstance° at all,
     I hold it fit that we shake hands and part,
     You as your business and desire shall point you—   135
     For every man hath business and desire,
     Such as it is—and for my own poor part,
     Look you, I'll go pray,

HORATIO. These are but wild and whirling words, my lord.

HAMLET. I am sorry they offend you, heartily;   140
     Yes, faith, heartily.

HORATIO.   There's no offense, my lord.

HAMLET. Yes, but Saint Patrick,° but there is, Horatio,
     And much offense° too. Touching this vision here,
     It is an honest ghost,° that let me tell you.
     For your desire to know what is between us,   145
     O'ermaster't as you may. And now, good friends,
     As you are friends, scholars, and soldiers,
     Give me one poor request.

---

111 there you are i.e., there, I've written that down against you.   **116 secure him** keep
him safe.   **119 Hilo . . . come** (A falconer's call to a hawk in air. Hamlet mocks the hal-
looing as though it were a part of hawking.)   **127 once** ever.   **130 arrant** thoroughgo-
ing.   **133 circumstance** ceremony, elaboration.   **142 Saint Patrick** (The keeper of
Purgatory and patron saint of all blunders and confusion.)   **143 offense** (Hamlet deliberately changes Horatio's "no offense taken" to "an offense against all decency.")   **144 an
honest ghost** i.e., a real ghost and not an evil spirit.

HORATIO. What is't, my lord? We will.

HAMLET. Never make known what you have seen tonight.   150

HORATIO, MARCELLUS. My lord, we will not.

HAMLET. Nay, but swear't.

HORATIO. In faith, my lord, not I.°

MARCELLUS. Nor I, my lord, in faith.

HAMLET. Upon my sword.°   [*He holds out his sword.*] 155

MARCELLUS. We have sworn, my lord, already.°

HAMLET. Indeed, upon my sword, indeed.

GHOST [*cries under the stage*]. Swear.

HAMLET. Ha, ha, boy, sayst thou so? Art thou there, truepenny°
    Come on, you hear this fellow in the cellarage.   160
    Consent to swear.

HORATIO.   Propose the oath, my lord.

HAMLET. Never to speak of this that you have seen,
    Swear by the sword.

GHOST [*beneath*]. Swear.   [*They swear.*°]

HAMLET. *Hic et ubique?*° Then we'll shift our ground.   165

                  [*He moves to another spot.*]

    Come hither, gentlemen,
    And lay your hands again upon my sword.
    Swear by my sword
    Never to speak of this that you have heard.

GHOST [*beneath*]. Swear by his sword.   [*They swear.*] 170

HAMLET. Well said, old mole. Canst work i' th' earth so fast?
    A worthy pioneer!°—Once more removed, good friends.

                  [*He moves again.*]

HORATIO. O day and night, but this is wondrous strange!

HAMLET. And henceforth as a stranger° give it welcome.
    There are more things in heaven and earth, Horatio,   175
    Than are dreamt of in your philosophy.°
    But come;
    Here, as before, never, so help you mercy,°
    How strange or odd soe'er I bear myself—
    As I perchance hereafter shall think meet   180
    To put an antic° disposition on—
    That you, at such times seeing me, never shall,
    With arms encumbered° thus, or this headshake,
    Or by pronouncing of some doubtful phrase

---

153 **In faith . . . I** i.e., I swear not to tell what I have seen. (Horatio is not refusing to swear.)   155 **sword** i.e., the hilt in the form of a cross.   156 **We . . . already** i.e., we swore in faith.   159 **truepenny** honest old fellow.   164 **s.d. They swear** (Seemingly they swear here, and at lines 170 and 190, as they lay their hands on Hamlet's sword. Triple oaths would have particular force; these three oaths deal with what they have seen, what they have heard, and what they promise about Hamlet's *antic disposition*.)   165 **Hic et ubique** here and everywhere. (Latin.)   172 **pioneer** foot soldier assigned to dig tunnels and excavations.   174 **as a stranger** i.e., needing your hospitality.   176 **your philosophy** this subject called "natural philosophy" or "science" that people talk about.   178 **so help you mercy** as you hope for God's mercy when you are judged.   181 **antic** fantastic.   183 **encumbered** folded.

As "Well, we know," or "We could, an if° we would,"   185
Or "If we list° to speak," or "There be, an if they might,"°
Or such ambiguous giving out,° to note°
That you know aught° of me—this do swear,
So grace and mercy at your most need help you.
GHOST [*beneath*]. Swear.   [*They swear.*]   190
HAMLET.   Rest, rest, perturbèd spirit! So, gentlemen,
With all my love I do commend me to you;°
And what so poor a man as Hamlet is
May do t' express his love and friending° to you,
God willing, shall not lack.° Let us go in together,   195
And still° your fingers on your lips, I pray.
The time° is out of joint. O cursèd spite°
That ever I was born to set it right!
                        [*They wait for him to leave first.*]
Nay, come, let's go together.°
                                                    Exeunt.

[2.1] *Enter old* POLONIUS *with his man* [REYNALDO].

POLONIUS.   Give him this money and these notes, Reynaldo.
                        [*He gives money and papers.*]
REYNALDO.   I will, my lord.
POLONIUS.   You shall do marvelous° wisely, good Reynaldo,
Before you visit him, to make inquire°
Of his behavior.
REYNALDO.   My lord, I did intend it.   5
POLONIUS.   Marry, well said, very well said. Look you, sir,
Inquire me first what Danskers° are in Paris,
And how, and who, what means,° and where they keep,°
What company, at what expense; and finding
By this encompassment° and drift° of question   10
That they do know my son, come you more nearer
Than your particular demands will touch it.°
Take you,° as 'twere, some distant knowledge of him,
As thus, "I know his father and his friends,
And in part him." Do you mark this, Reynaldo?   15
REYNALDO.   Ay, very well, my lord.
POLONIUS.   "And in part him, but," you may say, "not well.
But if 't be he I mean, he's very wild,

---

185 an if if.   **186 list** wished.   **There . . . might** i.e., there are people here (we, in fact)
who could tell news if we were at liberty to do so.   **187 giving out** intimation.   **note**
draw attention to the fact.   **188 aught** i.e., something secret.   **192 do . . . you** entrust
myself to you.   **194 friending** friendliness.   **195 lack** be lacking.   **196 still** always.
197 The time the state of affairs.   **spite** i.e., the spite of Fortune.   **199 let's go to-**
gether (Probably they wait for him to leave first, but he refuses this ceremoniousness.)
2.1 Location: Polonius's chambers.   **3 marvelous** marvelously.   **4 inquire** inquiry.
7 Danskers Danes.   **8 what means** what wealth (they have).   **keep** dwell.
10 encompassment roundabout talking.   **drift** gradual approach of course.   **11–12**
come . . . it you will find out more this way than by asking pointed questions (*particular*
demands).   **13 Take you** assume, pretend.

Addicted so and so," and there put on° him
What forgeries° you please—marry, none so rank°   20
As may dishonor him, take heed of that,
But, sir, such wanton,° wild, and usual slips
As are companions noted and most known
To youth and liberty.

REYNALDO.   As gaming, my lord.   25

POLONIUS.   Ay, or drinking, fencing, swearing,
Quarreling, drabbing°—you may go so far.

REYNALDO.   My lord, that would dishonor him.

POLONIUS.   Faith, no, as you may season° it in the charge.
You must not put another scandal on him   30
That he is open to incontinency°
That's not my meaning. But breathe his faults so quaintly°
That they may seem the taints of liberty,°
The flash and outbreak of a fiery mind,
A savageness in unreclaimèd blood,   35
Of general assault.°

REYNALDO.   But, my good lord—

POLONIUS.   Wherefore should you do this?

REYNALDO.   Ay, my lord, I would know that.

POLONIUS.   Marry, sir, here's my drift,   40
And I believe it is a fetch of warrant.°
You laying these slight sullies on my son,
As 'twere a thing a little soiled wi' the working,°
Mark you,
Your party in converse,° him you would sound,°   45
Having ever° seen in the prenominate crimes°
The youth you breathe° of guilty, be assured
He closes with you in this consequence:°
"Good sir," or so, or "friend," or "gentleman,"
According to the phrase or the addition°   50
Of man and country.

REYNALDO.   Very good, my lord.

POLONIUS.   And then, sir does 'a this—'a does—what was I about to say?
By the Mass, I was about to say something. Where did
I leave?

REYNALDO.   At "closes in the consequence."   55

POLONIUS.   At "closes in the consequence," ay, marry.
He closes thus: "I know the gentleman,
I saw him yesterday," or "th' other day,"

---

19 put on impute to.   **20 forgeries** invented tales.   **rank** gross.   **22 wanton** sportive,
unrestrained.   **27 drabbing** whoring.   **29 season** temper, soften.   **31 incontinency**
habitual sexual excess.   **32 quaintly** artfully, subtly.   **33 taints of liberty** faults result-
ing from free living.   **35–36 A savageness . . . assault** a wildness in untamed youth that
assails all indiscriminately.   **41 fetch of warrant** legitimate trick.   **43 soiled wi' the
working** soiled by handling while it is being made, i.e., by involvement in the ways of
the world.   **45 converse** conversion.   **sound** i.e., sound out.   **46 Having ever** if he
has ever.   **prenominate crimes** before-mentioned offenses.   **47 breathe** speak.
48 closes . . . consequence takes you into his confidence in some fashion, as follows.
50 addition title.

Or then, or then, with such or such, "and as you say,
There was 'a gaming," "there o'ertook in 's rouse,"°   60
There falling out° at tennis," or perchance
"I saw him enter such a house of sale,"
Videlicet° a brothel, or so forth. See you now,
Your bait of falsehood takes this carp° of truth;
And thus do we of wisdom and of reach,°   65
With windlasses° and with assays of bias,°
By indirections find directions° out.
So by my former lecture and advice
Shall you my son. You have° me, have you not?

REYNALDO. My lord, I have.

POLONIUS.   God b'wi'° ye; fare ye well.   70

REYNALDO. Good my lord.

POLONIUS. Observe his inclination in yourself.°

REYNALDO. I shall, my lord.

POLONIUS. And let him ply his music.

REYNALDO. Well, my lord.   75

POLONIUS. Farewell.

Exit REYNALDO.

Enter OPHELIA.

                        How now, Ophelia, what's the matter?

OPHELIA. O my lord, my lord, I have been so affrighted!

POLONIUS. With what, i' the name of God?

OPHELIA. My lord, as I was sewing in my closet,°
Lord Hamlet, with his doublet° all unbraced,°   80
No hat upon his head, his stockings fouled,
Ungartered, and down-gyvèd° to his ankle,
Pale as his shirt, his knees knocking each other,
And with a look so piteous in purport°
As if he had been loosèd out of hell   85
To speak of horrors—he comes before me.

POLONIUS. Mad for thy love?

OPHELIA.   My lord, I do not know,
But truly I do fear it.

POLONIUS.   What said he?

OPHELIA. He took me by the wrist and held me hard.
Then goes he to the length of all his arm,   90
And, with his other hand thus o'er his brow
He falls to such perusal of my face

---

60 o'ertook in 's rouse overcome by drink.   **61 falling out** quarreling.   **63 Videlicet**
namely.   **64 carp** a fish.   **65 reach** capacity, ability.   **66 windlasses** i.e., circuitous
paths. (Literally, circuits made to head off the game in hunting.)   **assays of bias** attempts
through indirection (like the curving path of the bowling ball, which is biased or
weighted to one side).   **67 directions** i.e., the way things really are.   **69 have** understand.   **70 b' wi'** be with.   **72 in yourself** in your own person (as well as by asking
questions).   **79 closet** private chamber.   **80 doublet** close-fitting jacket.   **unbraced**
unfastened.   **82 down-gyvèd** fallen to the ankles (like gyves or fetters).   **84 in purport**
in what it expressed.

As° 'a would draw it. Long stayed he so.
At last, a little shaking of mine arm
And thrice his head thus waving up and down,   95
He raised a sigh so piteous and profound
As it did seem to shatter all his bulk°
And end his being. That done, he lets me go,
And with his head over his shoulder turned
He seemed to find his way without his eyes,   100
For out o' doors he went without their helps,
And to the last bended their light on me.

POLONIUS. Come, go with me. I will go seek the King.
This is the very ecstasy° of love,
Whose violent property° fordoes° itself   105
And leads the will to desperate undertakings
As oft as any passion under heaven
That does afflict our natures. I am sorry.
What, have you given him any hard words of late?

OPHELIA. No, my good lord, but as you did command   110
I did repel his letters and denied
His access to me.

POLONIUS.   That hath made him mad.
I am sorry that with better heed and judgment
I had not quoted° him. I feared he did but trifle
And mean to wrack° thee. But beshrew my jealousy!°   115
By heaven, it is as proper to our age°
To cast beyond° ourselves in our opinions
As it is common for the younger sort
To lack discretion. Come, go we to the King.
This must be known,° which, being kept close,° might move   120
More grief to hide than hate to utter love.°
Come.

                                                          Exeunt.

[2.2] *Flourish. Enter* KING *and* QUEEN, ROSENCRANTZ,
        and GUILDENSTERN [*with others*].

KING. Welcome, dear Rosencrantz and Guildenstern.
Moreover that° we much did long to see you,
The need we have to use you did provoke
Our hasty sending. Something have you heard
Of Hamlet's transformation—so call it,   5
Sith nor° th' exterior nor the inward man
Resembles that° it was. What it should be,

---

93 As as if (also in line 97).   **97 bulk** body.   **104 ecstasy** madness.   **105 property** nature.   **fordoes** destroys.   **114 quoted** observed.   **115 wrack** ruin, seduce.   **beshrew**
my jealousy a plague upon my suspicious nature.   **116 proper . . . age** characteristic of
us (old) men.   **117 cast beyond** overshoot, miscalculate (a metaphor from hunting).   **120**
known made known (to the King).   **close** secret.   **120–121 might . . . love** i.e., might
cause more grief (because of what Hamlet might do) by hiding the knowledge of Hamlet's
strange behavior to Ophelia than unpleasantness by telling it.   **2.2. Location: The castle.**
2 Moreover that besides the fact that.   **6 Sith nor** since neither.   **7 that** what.

More than his father's death, that thus hath put him
So much from th' understanding of himself,
I cannot dream of. I entreat you both   10
That, being of so young days° brought up with him,
And sith so neighbored to° his youth and havior,°
That you vouchsafe your rest° here in our court
Some little time, so by your companies
To draw him on to pleasures, and to gather   15
So much as from occasion° you may glean,
Whether aught to us unknown afflicts him thus
That, opened,° lies within our remedy.

QUEEN. Good gentlemen, he hath much talked of you,
And sure I am two men there is not living   20
To whom he more adheres. If it will please you
To show us so much gentry° and good will
As to expend your time with us awhile
For the supply and profit of our hope,°
Your visitation shall receive such thanks   25
As fits a king's remembrance.°

ROSENCRANTZ.   Both Your Majesties
Might, by the sovereign power you have of° us,
Put your dread° pleasures more into command
Than to entreaty.

GUILDENSTERN.   But we both obey,
And here give up ourselves in the full bent°   30
To lay our service freely at your feet,
To be commanded.

KING. Thanks, Rosencrantz and gentle Guildenstern.

QUEEN. Thanks, Guildenstern and gentle Rosencrantz.
And I beseech you instantly to visit   35
My too much changèd son. Go, some of you,
And bring these gentlemen where Hamlet is.

GUILDENSTERN. Heavens make our presence and our practices°
Pleasant and helpful to him!

QUEEN.   Ay, amen!

Exeunt ROSENCRANTZ *and* GUILDENSTERN [*with some attendants*].

Enter POLONIUS.

POLONIUS. Th' ambassadors from Norway, my good lord,   40
Are joyfully returned.

KING. Thou still° hast been the father of good news.

POLONIUS. Have I, my lord? I assure my good liege
I hold° my duty, as° I hold my soul,

---

11 of . . . days from such early youth.   **12 And sith so neighbored to** and since you
are (or, and since that time you are) intimately acquainted with.   **havior** demeanor.
13 vouchsafe your rest please to stay.   **16 occasion** opportunity.   **18 opened** being
revealed.   **22 gentry** courtesy.   **24 supply . . . hope** aid and furtherance of what we
hope for.   **26 As fits . . . remembrance** as would be a fitting gift of a king who
rewards true service.   **27 of** over.   **28 dread** inspiring awe.   **30 in . . . bent** to the
utmost degree of our capacity (an archery metaphor).   **38 practices** doings.   **42 still**
always.   **44 hold** maintain.   **as** firmly as.

> Both to my God and to my gracious king;   45
> And I do think, or else this brain of mine
> Hunts not the trail of policy° so sure
> As it hath used to do, that I have found
> The very cause of Hamlet's lunacy.

KING. O, speak of that! That do I long to hear.   50
POLONIUS. Give first admittance to th' ambassadors.
> My news shall be the fruit° to that great feast.
KING. Thyself do grace° to them and bring them in.

[Exit POLONIUS.]

> He tells me, my dear Gertrude, he hath found
> The head and source of all your son's distemper.   55
QUEEN. I doubt° it is no other but the main,°
> His father's death and our o'erhasty marriage.

Enter Ambassadors VOLTIMAND *and* CORNELIUS, *with* POLONIUS.

KING. Well, we shall sift him.°—Welcome, my good friends!
> Say, Voltimand, what from our brother° Norway?
VOLTIMAND. Most fair return of greetings and desires.°   60
> Upon our first,° he sent out to suppress
> His nephew's levies, which to him appeared
> To be a preparation 'gainst the Polack,
> But, better looked into, he truly found
> It was against Your Highness. Whereat grieved   65
> That so his sickness, age, and impotence°
> Was falsely borne in hand,° sends out arrests°
> On Fortinbras, which he, in brief, obeys,
> Receives rebuke from Norway, and in fine°
> Makes vow before his uncle never more   70
> To give th' assay° of arms against Your Majesty.
> Whereon old Norway, overcome with joy,
> Gives him three thousand crowns in annual fee
> And his commission to employ those soldiers,
> So levied as before, against the Polack,   75
> With an entreaty, herein further shown,   [*giving a paper*]
> That it might please you to give quiet pass
> Through your dominions for this enterprise
> On such regards of safety and allowance°
> As therein are set down.
KING.   It likes° us well,   80
> And at more considered° time we'll read,
> Answer, and think upon this business.

---

47 **policy** sagacity.   52 **fruit** dessert.   53 **grace** honor (punning on *grace* said before a *feast*, line 52).   56 **doubt** fear, suspect.   **main** chief point, principal concern.   58 **sift him** question Polonius closely.   59 **brother** fellow king.   60 **desires** good wishes.   61 **Upon our first** at our first words on the business.   66 **impotence** helplessness.   67 **borne in hand** deluded, taken advantage of.   **arrests** orders to desist.   69 **in fine** in conclusion.   71 **give th' assay** make trial of strength, challenge.   78 **On . . . allowance** i.e., with such considerations for the safety of Denmark and permission for Fortinbras.   80 **likes** pleases.   81 **considered** suitable for deliberation.

Meantime we thank you for your well-took labor.
Go to your rest; at night we'll feast together.
Most welcome home!

Exeunt Ambassadors.

POLONIUS.   This business is well ended.   85
My liege, and madam, to expostulate°
What majesty should be, what duty is,
Why day is day, night night, and time is time,
Were nothing but to waste night, day, and time.
Therefore, since brevity is the soul of wit,°   90
And tediousness the limbs and outward flourishes,
I will be brief. Your noble son is mad.
Mad call I it, for, to define true madness.
What is't but to be nothing else but mad?
But let that go.
QUEEN.   More matter, with less art.   95
POLONIUS. Madam, I swear I use no art at all.
That he's mad 'tis true: 'tis true 'tis pity.
And pity 'tis 'tis true—a foolish figure,°
But farewell it, for I will use no art.
Mad let us grant him, then, and now remains   100
That we find out the cause of this defect,
Or rather say, the cause of this defect,
For this effect defective comes by cause.°
Thus it remains, and the remainder thus.
Perpend.°   105
I have a daughter—have while she is mine—
Who, in her duty and obedience, mark,
Hath given me this. Now gather and surmise.°
[*He reads the letter.*] "To the celestial and my soul's idol,
the most beautified Ophelia"—   110
That's an ill phrase, a vile phrase; "beautified" is a vile phrase. But
you shall hear. Thus: [*He reads.*]
"In her excellent white bosom,° these,° etc."
QUEEN. Came this from Hamlet to her?
POLONIUS. Good madam, stay° awhile, I will be faithful.°   [*He reads.*] 115
"Doubt thou the stars are fire,
   Doubt that the sun doth move,
Doubt° truth to be a liar,
   But never doubt I love.

O dear Ophelia, I am ill at these numbers.° I have not art to reckon° 120
my groans. But that I love thee best, O most best, believe it.

___

86 expostulate expound, inquire into. **90 wit** sense or judgment. **98 figure** figure of speech. **103 For . . . cause** i.e., for this defective behavior, this madness, has a cause. **105 Perpend** consider. **108 gather and surmise** draw your own conclusions. **113 In . . . bosom** (The letter is poetically addressed to her heart.) **these** i.e., the letter. **115 stay** wait. **faithful** i.e., in reading the letter accurately. **118 Doubt** suspect. **120 ill . . . numbers** unskilled at writing verses. **reckon** (1) count (2) number metrically, scan.

Adieu.
   Thine evermore, most dear lady, whilst this machine° is to him,
                             Hamlet."
This in obedience hath my daughter shown me,   125
And, more above,° hath his solicitings,
As they fell out° by° time, by means, and place,
All given to mine ear.°
KING.   But how hath she
Received his love?
POLONIUS.   What do you think of me?
KING. As of a man faithful and honorable.   130
POLONIUS. I would fain° prove so. But what might you think,
   When I had seen this hot love on the wing—
   As I perceived it, I must tell you that,
   Before my daughter told me—what might you,
   Or my dear Majesty your queen here, think,   135
   If I had played the desk or table book,°
   Or given my heart a winking,° mute and dumb,
   Or looked upon this love with idle sight?°
   What might you think? No, I went round° to work,
   And my young mistress thus I did bespeak:°   140
   "Lord Hamlet is a prince out of thy star;°
   This must not be." And then I prescripts° gave her,
   That she should lock herself from his resort,°
   Admit no messengers, receive no tokens.
   Which done, she took the fruits of my advice;   145
   And he, repellèd—a short tale to make—
   Fell into a sadness, then into a fast,
   Thence to a watch,° thence into a weakness,
   Thence to a lightness,° and by this declension°
   Into the madness wherein now he raves,   150
   And all we° mourn for.
POLONIUS. [to the QUEEN].   Do you think 'tis this?
QUEEN. It may be, very like.
POLONIUS. Hath there been such a time—I would fain know that—
   That I have positively said "'Tis so,"
   When it proved otherwise?
KING.   Not that I know.   155
POLONIUS. Take this from this,° if this be otherwise.

---

123 **machine** i.e., body.   126 **more above** moreover.   127 **fell out** occurred.   **by** according to.   128 **given . . . ear** i.e., told me about.   131 **fain** gladly.   136 **played . . .
table book** i.e., remained shut up, concealing the information.   137 **given . . . winking**
closed the eyes of my heart to this.   138 **with idle sight** complacently or incompre-
hendingly.   139 **round** roundly, plainly.   140 **bespeak** address.   141 **out of thy star**
above your sphere, position.   142 **prescripts** orders.   143 **his resort** his visits.
148 **watch** state of sleeplessness.   149 **lightness** lightheadedness.   **declension** decline, deterioration (with a pun on the grammatical sense).   151 **all we** all of us, or, into
everything that we.   156 **Take this from this** (The actor probably gestures, indicating
that he means his head from his shoulders, or his staff of office or chain from his hands or
neck, or something similar.)

If circumstances lead me, I will find
Where truth is hid, though it were hid indeed
Within the center.°

KING.   How may we try° it further?

POLONIUS. You know sometimes he walks for hours together   160
Here in the lobby.

QUEEN.   So he does indeed.

POLONIUS. At such a time I'll loose° my daughter to him.
Be you and I behind an arras° then.
Mark the encounter. If he love her not
And be not from his reason fall'n thereon,°   165
Let me be no assistant for a state,
But keep a farm and carters.°

KING.   We will try it.
    Enter HAMLET [*reading on a book*].

QUEEN. But look where sadly° the poor wretch comes reading.

POLONIUS. Away, I do beseech you both, away.
I'll board° him presently.° O, give me leave.°   170
                    Exeunt KING *and* QUEEN [*with attendants*].
How does my good Lord Hamlet?

HAMLET. Well, God-a-mercy.°

POLONIUS. Do you know me, my lord?

HAMLET. Excellent well. You are a fishmonger.°

POLONIUS. Not I, my lord.   175

HAMLET. Then I would you were so honest a man.

POLONIUS. Honest, my lord?

HAMLET. Ay, sir. To be honest, as this world goes, is to be one man
picked out of ten thousand.

POLONIUS. That's very true, my lord.   180

HAMLET. For if the sun breed maggots in a dead dog, being a good
kissing carrion°—Have you a daughter?

POLONIUS. I have, my lord.

HAMLET. Let her not walk i' the sun.° Conception° is a blessing, but as
your daughter may conceive, friend, look to 't.   185

POLONIUS [*aside*]. How say you by that? Still harping on my daughter. Yet
he knew me not at first; 'a° said I was a fishmonger. 'A is far gone.
And truly in my youth I suffered much extremity for love, very near
this. I'll speak to him again.—What do you read, my lord?

HAMLET. Words, words, words.   190

---

159 **center** middle point of the earth (which is also the center of the Ptolemaic universe).
try test, judge.   162 **loose** (as one might release an animal that is being mated).   163
arras hanging, tapestry.   165 **thereon** on that account.   167 **carters** wagon drivers.
168 **sadly** seriously.   170 **board** accost.   **presently** at once.   **give me leave** i.e., excuse me, leave me alone (said to those he hurries offstage, including the King and Queen).
172 **God a-mercy** God have mercy, i.e., thank you.   174 **fishmonger** fish merchant.
181–182 **a good kissing carrion** i.e., a good piece of flesh for kissing, or for the sun to
kiss.   184 **i' the sun** in public (with additional implication of the sunshine of princely
favors).   **Conception** (1) understanding (2) pregnancy.   187 **'a** he.

POLONIUS. What is the matter,° my lord?

HAMLET. Between who?

POLONIUS. I mean, the matter that you read, my lord.

HAMLET. Slanders, sir; for the satirical rogue says here that old men have
    gray beards, that their faces are wrinkled, their eyes purging° thick 195
    amber° and plum-tree gum, and that they have a plentiful lack of
    wit,° together with most weak hams. All which, sir, though I most
    powerfully and potently believe, yet I hold it not honesty° to have
    it thus set down, for yourself, sir, shall grow old° as I am, if like a
    crab you could go backward.   200

POLONIUS [aside]. Though this be madness, yet there is method in 't.—
    Will you walk out of the air,° my lord?

HAMLET. Into my grave.

POLONIUS. Indeed, that's out of the air. [Aside.]   How pregnant° some-
    times his replies are! A happiness° that often madness hits on,   205
    which reason and sanity could not so prosperously° be delivered
    of. I will leave him and suddenly° contrive the means of meeting
    between him and my daughter.—My honorable lord, I will most
    humbly take my leave of you.

HAMLET. You cannot, sir, take from me anything that I will more willingly 210
    part withal°—except my life, except my life, except my life.

    Enter GUILDENSTERN *and* ROSENCRANTZ.

POLONIUS. Fare you well, my lord.

HAMLET. These tedious old fools!°

POLONIUS. You go to seek the Lord Hamlet. There he is.

ROSENCRANTZ [to POLONIUS]. God save you, sir!   215

                                             [*Exit* POLONIUS.]

GUILDENSTERN. My honored lord!

ROSENCRANTZ. My most dear lord!

HAMLET. My excellent good friends! How dost thou, Guildenstern? Ah,
    Rosencrantz! Good lads, how do you both?

ROSENCRANTZ. As the indifferent° children of the earth.   220

GUILDENSTERN. Happy in that we are not overhappy.
    On Fortune's cap we are not the very button.

HAMLET. Nor the soles of her shoe?

ROSENCRANTZ. Neither, my lord.

HAMLET. Then you live about her waist, or in the middle of her favors?°   225

GUILDENSTERN. Faith, her privates we.°

HAMLET. In the secret parts of Fortune? O, most true, she is a strumpet.°
    What news?

---

191 matter substance. (But Hamlet plays on the sense of "basis for a dispute.")   **195 purging** discharging.   **196 amber** i.e., resin, like the resinous *plum-tree gum.*   **197 wit** understanding.   **198 honesty** decency, decorum.   **199 old** as old.   **202 out of the air** (The
open air was considered dangerous for sick people.)   **204 pregnant** quick-witted, full of
meaning.   **205 happiness** felicity of expression.   **206 prosperously** successfully.   **207
suddenly** immediately.   **211 withal** with.   **213 old fools** i.e., old men like Polonius.
220 indifferent ordinary, at neither extreme of fortune or misfortune.   **225 favors** i.e.,
sexual favors.   **226 her privates we** i.e., (1) we are sexually intimate with Fortune, the
fickle goddess who bestows her favors indiscriminately (2) we are her private citizens.
227 strumpet prostitute (a common epithet for indiscriminate Fortune; see line 452).

ROSENCRANTZ. None, my lord, but the world's grown honest.

HAMLET. Then is doomsday near. But your news is not true. Let me ques- 230
    tion more in particular. What have you, my good friends, deserved
    at the hands of Fortune that she sends you to prison hither?

GUILDENSTERN. Prison, my lord?

HAMLET. Denmark's a prison.

ROSENCRANTZ. Then is the world one.   235

HAMLET. A goodly one, in which there are many confines,° wards,° and
    dungeons, Denmark being one o' the worst.

ROSENCRANTZ. We think not so, my lord.

HAMLET. Why then 'tis none to you, for there is nothing either good or
    bad but thinking makes it so. To me it is a prison.   240

ROSENCRANTZ. Why then, your ambition makes it one. 'Tis too narrow
    for your mind.

HAMLET. O God, I could be bounded in a nutshell and count myself a
    king of infinite space, were it not that I have bad dreams.

GUILDENSTERN. Which dreams indeed are ambition, for the very substance 245
    of the ambitious° is merely the shadow of a dream.

HAMLET. A dream itself is but a shadow.

ROSENCRANTZ. Truly, and I hold ambition of so airy and light a quality
    that it is but a shadow's shadow.

HAMLET. Then are our beggars bodies,° and our monarchs and out   250
    stretched° heroes the beggars' shadows. Shall we to the court? For,
    by my fay,° I cannot reason.

ROSENCRANTZ, GUILDENSTERN. We'll wait upon° you.

HAMLET. No such matter. I will not sort° you with the rest of my ser-
    vants, for, to speak to you like an honest man, I am most dreadfully 255
    attended.° But, in the beaten way° of friendship, what make° you at
    Elsinore?

ROSENCRANTZ. To visit you, my lord, no other occasion.

HAMLET. Beggar that I am, I'm even poor in thanks; but I thank you, and
    sure, dear friends, my thanks are too dear a halfpenny.° Were you   260
    not sent for? Is it your own inclining? Is it a free° visitation? Come,
    come, deal justly with me. Come, come. Nay, speak.

GUILDENSTERN. What should we say, my lord?

HAMLET. Anything but to the purpose.° You were sent for, and there is a
    kind of confession in your looks which your modesties° have not 265
    craft enough to color.° I know the good King and Queen have sent
    for you.

---

236 confines places of confinement.   **wards** cells.   **245–246 the very . . . ambitious**
that seemingly very substantial thing that the ambitious pursue.   **250 bodies** i.e., solid
substances rather than shadows (since beggars are not ambitious).   **250–251 out
stretched** (1) far-reaching in their ambition (2) elongated as shadows.   **252 fay** faith.
253 wait upon accompany, attend (but Hamlet uses the phrase in the sense of providing
menial service).   **254 sort** class, categorize.   **255–256 dreadfully attended** waited
upon in slovenly fashion.   **256 beaten way** familiar path, tried-and-true course.   **make**
do.   **260 too dear a halfpenny** (1) too expensive at even a halfpenny, i.e., of little worth
(2) too expensive *by* a halfpenny in return for worthless kindness.   **261 free** voluntary.
264 Anything but to the purpose anything except a straightforward answer (said ironically).   **265 modesties** sense of shame.   **266 color** disguise.

ROSENCRANTZ. To what end, my lord?

HAMLET. That you must teach me. But let me conjure° you, by the rights
of our fellowship, by the consonancy of our youth,° by the obliga-   270
tion of our ever-preserved love, and by what more dear a better°
proposer could charge° you withal, be even° and direct with me
whether you were sent for or no.

ROSENCRANTZ [*aside to* GUILDENSTERN]. What say you?

HAMLET [*aside*]. Nay, then, I have an eye of° you.—If you love me, hold   275
not off.°

GUILDENSTERN. My lord, we were sent for.

HAMLET. I will tell you why; so shall my anticipation prevent your discovery,° and your secrecy to the King and Queen molt no feather,° I
have of late—but wherefore I know not—lost all my mirth, forgone   280
all custom of exercises; and indeed it goes so heavily with my disposition that this goodly frame, the earth, seems to me a sterile
promontory; this most excellent canopy, the air, look you, this
brave° o'erhanging firmament, this majestical roof fretted° with
golden fire, why, it appeareth nothing to me but a foul and pestilent   285
congregation° of vapors. What a piece of work° is a man! How noble
in reason, how infinite in faculties, in form and moving how express°
and admirable, in action how like an angel, in apprehension° how
like a god! The beauty of the world, the paragon of animals! And yet,
to me, what is this quintessence° of dust? Man delights not me—no,   290
nor woman neither, though by your smiling you seem to say so.

ROSENCRANTZ. My lord, there was no such stuff in my thoughts.

HAMLET. Why did you laugh, then, when I said man delights not me?

ROSENCRANTZ. To think, my lord, if you delight not in man, what Lenten
entertainment° the players shall receive from you. We coted° them   295
on the way, and higher are they coming to offer you service.

HAMLET. He that plays the king shall be welcome; His Majesty shall have
tribute° of° me. The adventurous knight shall use his foil and
target,° the lover shall not sigh gratis,° the humorous man° shall
end his part in peace,° the clown shall make those laugh whose   300
lungs are tickle o' the sear,° and the lady shall say her mind freely, or
the blank verse shall halt° for 't. What players are they?

---

269 conjure adjure, entreat.   **270 the consonancy of our youth** our closeness in our
younger days.   **271 better** more skillful.   **272 charge** urge.   **even** straight, honest.
275 of on.   **275–276 hold not off** don't hold back.   **278–279 so . . . discovery** in that
way my saying it first will spare you from revealing the truth.   **279 molt no feather** i.e.,
not diminish in the least.   **284 brave** splendid.   **fretted** adorned (with fretwork, as in a
vaulted ceiling).   **286 congregation** mass.   **piece of work** masterpiece.   **287
express** well-framed, exact, expressive.   **288 apprehension** power of comprehending.
290 quintessence the fifth essence of ancient philosophy, beyond earth, water, air, and
fire, supposed to be the substance of the heavenly bodies and to be latent in all things.
295–296 Lenten entertainment meager reception (appropriate to Lent).   **296 coted**
overtook and passed by.   **299 tribute** (1) applause (2) homage paid in money.   **of** from.
299–300 foil and target sword and shield.   **300 gratis** for nothing.   **humorous man**
eccentric character, dominated by one trait or "humor."   **301 in peace** i.e., with full license.   **302 tickle o' the sear** easy on the trigger, read to laugh easily
(a *sear* is part of a gunlock).   **303 halt** limp.

ROSENCRANTZ. Even those you were wont to take such delight in, the
tragedians° of the city.   305

HAMLET. How chances it they travel? Their residence,° both in reputation and profit, was better both ways.

ROSENCRANTZ. I think their inhibition° comes by the means of the late°
innovation.°

HAMLET. Do they hold the same estimation they did when I was in the   310
city? Are they so followed?

ROSENCRANTZ. No, indeed are they not.

HAMLET. How comes it? Do they grow rusty?

ROSENCRANTZ. Nay, their endeavor keeps° in the wonted° pace. But there
is, sir, an aerie° of children, little eyases,° that cry out on the top of   315
question° and are most tyrannically° clapped for 't. These are now
the fashion, and so berattle° the common stages°—so they call
them—that many wearing rapiers° are afraid of goose quills° and
dare scarce come thither.

HAMLET. What, are they children? Who maintains 'em? How are they   320
escoted?° Will they pursue the quality° no longer than they can
sing?° Will they not say afterwards, if they should grow themselves to
common° prayers—as it is most like,° if their means are no bet-
ter°—their writers do them wrong to make them exclaim against
their own succession?°   325

ROSENCRANTZ. Faith, there has been much to-do° on both sides, and the
nation holds it no sin to tar° them to controversy. There was for a
while no money bid for argument unless the poet and the player
went to cuffs in the question.°

HAMLET. Is 't possible?   330

GUILDENSTERN. O, there has been much throwing about of brains.

HAMLET. Do the boys carry it away?°

ROSENCRANTZ. Ay, that they do, my lord—Hercules and his load° too.°

---

305 tragedians actors.   **306 residence** remaining in their usual place, i.e., in the city.
308 inhibition formal prohibition (from acting plays in the city).   **late** recent.   **309
innovation** i.e., the new fashion in satirical plays performed by boy actors in the "private"
theaters; or possibly a political uprising; or the strict limitations set on the theaters in
London in 1600.   **314 keeps** continues.   **wonted** usual.   **315 aerie** nest.   **eyases**
young hawks.   **315–316 cry . . . question** speak shrilly, dominating the controversy (in
decrying the public theaters).   **316 tyrannically** outrageously.   **317 berattle** berate,
clamor against.   **common stages** public theaters.   **318 many wearing rapiers** i.e.,
many men of fashion, afraid to patronize the common players for fear of being satirized by
the poets writing for the boy actors.   **goose quills** i.e., pens of satirists.   **321 escoted**
maintained.   **321 quality** (acting) profession.   **321–322 no longer . . . sing** i.e., only
until their voices change.   **323 common** regular, adult.   **like** likely.   **323–324 if . . .
better** if they find no better way to support themselves.   **325 succession** i.e., future careers.   **326 to-do** ado.   **327 tar** set on (as dogs).   **327–329 There . . . question** i.e.,
for a while, no money was offered by the acting companies to playwrights for the plot to a
play unless the satirical poets who wrote for the boys and the adult actors came to blows
in the play itself.   **332 carry it away** i.e., win the day.   **333 Hercules . . . load**
(Thought to be an allusion to the sign of the Globe Theatre, which was Hercules bearing
the world on his shoulders.)   **313–333 How . . . load too** (The passage, omitted from
the early quartos, alludes to the so-called War of the Theaters, 1599–1602, the rivalry
between the children's companies and the adult actors.)

HAMLET. It is not very strange; for my uncle is King of Denmark, and
those that would make mouths° at him while my father lived give   335
twenty, forty, fifty, a hundred ducats° apiece for his picture in little.°
'Sblood,° there is something in this more than natural, if philoso-
phy° could find it out.

                                      A flourish [*of trumpets within*].

GUILDENSTERN. There are the players.

HAMLET. Gentlemen, you are welcome to Elsinore. Your hands, come   340
then. Th' appurtenance° of welcome is fashion and ceremony. Let
me comply° with you in this garb,° lest my extent° to the players,
which, I tell you, must show fairly outwards,° should more appear
like entertainment° than yours. You are welcome. But my uncle-
father and aunt-mother are deceived.   345

GUILDENSTERN. In what, my dear lord?

HAMLET. I am but mad north-north-west.° When the wind is southerly I
know a hawk from a handsaw.°

        Enter POLONIUS.

POLONIUS. Well be with you, gentlemen!

HAMLET. Hark you, Guildenstern, and you too; at each ear a hearer. That 350
great baby you see there is not yet out of his swaddling clouts.°

ROSENCRANTZ. Haply° he is the second time come to them, for they say
an old man is twice a child.

HAMLET. I will prophesy he comes to tell me of the players. Mark it.—
You say right, sir, o' Monday morning, 'twas then indeed.   355

POLONIUS. My lord, I have news to tell you.

HAMLET. My lord, I have news to tell you. When Roscius° was an actor in
Rome—

POLONIUS. The actors are come hither, my lord.

HAMLET. Buzz,° buzz!   360

POLONIUS. Upon my honor—

HAMLET. Then came each actor on his ass.

POLONIUS. The best actors in the world, either for tragedy, comedy, history, pastoral, pastoral-comical, historical-pastoral, tragical-historical,
tragical-comical-historical-pastoral, scene individable,° or poem   365

---

335 mouths faces.   **336 ducats** gold coins.   **in little** in miniature.   **337 'Sblood** by
God's (Christ's) blood.   **337–338 philosophy** i.e., scientific inquiry.   **341
appurtenance** proper accompaniment.   **342 comply** observe the formalities of courtesy.   **garb** i.e., manner.   **my extent** that which I extend, i.e., my polite behavior.
343 show fairly outwards show every evidence of cordiality.   **344 entertainment** a
(warm) reception.   **347 north-north-west** just off true north, only partly.   **348
hawk. . . handsaw** i.e., two very different things, though also perhaps meaning a mat-
tock (or *hack*) and a carpenter's cutting tool, respectively; also birds, with a play on
hernshaw, or heron.   **351 swaddling clouts** cloths in which to wrap a newborn baby.
352 Haply perhaps.   **357 Roscius** a famous Roman actor who died in 62 BCE   **360
Buzz** (An interjection used to denote stale news.)   **365 scene individable** a play observing the unity of place; or perhaps one that is unclassifiable, or performed without
intermission.

unlimited.° Seneca° cannot be too heavy, nor Plautus° too light. For
the law of writ and the liberty,° these° are the only men.

HAMLET. O Jephthah, judge of Israel,° what a treasure hadst thou!

POLONIUS. What a treasure had he, my lord?

HAMLET. Why,   370

"One fair daughter, and no more,
    The which he lovèd passing° well."

POLONIUS [*aside*]. Still on my daughter.

HAMLET. Am I not i' the right, old Jephthah?

POLONIUS. If you call me Jephthah, my lord, I have a daughter that I love   375
passing well.

HAMLET. Nay, that follows not.

POLONIUS. What follows then, my lord?

HAMLET. Why,

"As by lot,° God wot,"°   380
    and then, you know.
"It came to pass, as most like° it was"—
the first row° of the pious chanson° will show you more, for look
where my abridgement° comes.

Enter the PLAYERS.

You are welcome, masters; welcome, all. I am glad to see thee well.   385
Welcome, good friends. O, old friend! Why, thy face is valanced°
since I saw thee last. Com'st thou to beard° me in Denmark? What,
my young lady° and mistress! By 'r Lady,° your ladyship is nearer
to heaven than when I saw you last, by the altitude of a chopine.°
Pray God your voice, like a piece of uncurrent° gold, be not   390
cracked within the ring.° Masters, you are all welcome. We'll e'en to
't° like French falconers, fly at anything we see. We'll have a speech
straight.° Come, give us a taste of your quality.° Come, a passionate
speech.

FIRST PLAYER. What speech, my good lord?   395

HAMLET. I heard thee speak me a speech once, but it was never acted, or
if it was, not above once, for the play, I remember, pleased not the
million; 'twas caviar to the general.° But it was—as I received it, and

---

365–366 poem unlimited a play disregarding the unities of time and place; one that is
all-inclusive. **Seneca** writer of Latin tragedies. **Plautus** writer of Latin comedy. **367
law . . . liberty** dramatic composition both according to the rules and disregarding the
rules. **these** i.e., the actors. **368 Jephthah . . . Israel** (Jephthah had to sacrifice his
daughter; see Judges 11. Hamlet goes on to quote from a ballad on the theme.) **372
passing** surpassingly. **380 lot** chance. **wot** knows. **382 like** likely, probable. **383
row** stanza. **chanson** ballad, song. **384 my abridgement** something that cuts short
my conversation; also, a diversion. **386 valanced** fringed (with a beard). **387 beard**
confront, challenge (with obvious pun). **388 young lady** i.e., boy playing women's
parts. **By 'r Lady** by Our Lady. **389 chopine** thick-soled shoe of Italian fashion. **390
uncurrent** not passable as lawful coinage. **391 cracked . . . ring** i.e., changed from
adolescent to male voice, no longer suitable for women's roles. (Coins featured rings enclosing the sovereign's head; if the coin was cracked within this ring, it was unfit for currency). **391–392 e'en to 't** go at it. **393 straight** at once. **quality** professional skill.
398 caviar to the general caviar to the multitude, i.e., a choice dish too elegant for
coarse tastes.

others, whose judgments in such matters cried in the top of°
mine—an excellent play, well digested° in the scenes, set down   400
with as much modesty° as cunning.° I remember one said there
were no sallets° in the lines to make the matter savory, nor no matter in the phrase that might indict° the author of affectation, but
called it an honest method, as wholesome as sweet, and by very
much more handsome° than fine.° One speech in 't I chiefly loved: 405
'twas Aeneas' tale to Dido, and thereabout of it especially when he
speaks of Priam's slaughter.° If it live in your memory, begin at this
line: let me see, let me see—
    "The rugged Pyrrhus,° like th' Hyrcanian beast"°—
'Tis not so. It begins with Pyrrhus: 410
    "The rugged° Pyrrhus, he whose sable° arms,
    Black as his purpose, did the night resemble
    When he lay couchèd° in the ominous horse,°
    Hath now this dread and black complexion smeared
    With heraldry more dismal.° Head to foot   415
    Now is he total gules,° horridly tricked°
    With blood of fathers, mothers, daughters, sons,
    Baked and impasted° with the parching streets,°
    That lend a tyrannous° and a damnèd light
    To their lord's° murder. Roasted in wrath and fire,   420
    And thus o'ersized° with coaglate gore,
    With eyes like carbuncles,° the hellish Pyrrhus
    Old grandsire Priam seeks."
    So proceed you.
POLONIUS. 'Fore God, my lord, well spoken, with good accent and good   425
    discretion.
FIRST PLAYER. "Anon he finds him
    Striking too short at Greeks. His antique° sword,
    Rebellious to his arm, lies where it falls,
    Repugnant° to command. Unequal matched,   430
    Pyrrhus at Priam drives, in rage strikes wide,

---

399 cried in the top of i.e., spoke with greater authority than.   **400 digested**
arranged, ordered.   **401 modesty** moderation, restraint.   **cunning** skill.   **402 sallets**
i.e., something savory, spicy improprieties.   **403 indict** convict.   **405 handsome** well-
proportioned.   **fine** elaborately ornamented, showy.   **407 Priam's slaughter** the slay-
ing of the ruler of Troy, when the Greeks finally took the city.   **409 Pyrrhus** a Greek
hero in the Trojan War, also known as Neoptolemus, son of Achilles—another avenging
son.   **Hyrcanian beast** i.e., tiger. (On the death of Priam, see Virgil, *Aeneid,* 2.506 ff.;
compare the whole speech with Marlowe's *Dido Queen of Carthage,* 2.1.214 ff. On the
Hyrcanian tiger, see *Aeneid,* 4.366–367. Hyrcania is on the Caspian Sea.)   **411 rugged**
shaggy, savage.   **sable** black (for reasons of camouflage during the episode of the Trojan
horse).   **413 couchèd** concealed.   **ominous horse** fateful Trojan horse, by which the
Greeks gained access to Troy.   **415 dismal** ill-omened.   **416 total gules** entirely red (a
heraldic term).   **tricked** spotted and smeared (heraldic).   **418 impasted** crusted, like a
thick paste.   **with . . . streets** by the parching heat of the streets (because of the fires
everywhere).   **419 tyrannous** cruel.   **420 their lord's** i.e., Priam's.   **421 o'ersized**
covered as with size or glue.   **422 carbuncles** large fiery-red precious stones thought to
emit their own light.   **428 antique** ancient, long-used.   **430 Repugnant** disobedient,
resistant.

But with the whiff and wind of his fell° sword
Th' unnervèd° father falls. Then senseless Ilium,°
Seeming to feel this blow, with flaming top
Stoops to his° base, and with a hideous crash   435
Takes prisoner Pyrrhus' ear. For, lo! His sword,
Which was declining° on the milky° head
Of reverend Priam, seemed i' th' air to stick.
So as a painted° tyrant Pyrrhus stood,
And, like a neutral to his will and matter,°   440
Did nothing.
But as we often see against° some storm
A silence in the heavens, the rack° stand still,
The bold winds speechless, and the orb° below
As hush as death, anon the dreadful thunder   445
Doth rend the region,° so, after Pyrrhus' pause,
A rousèd vengeance sets him new a-work
And never did the Cyclops° hammers fall
On Mars's armor forged for proof eterne°
With less remorse° than Pyrrhus bleeding sword   450
Now falls on Priam.
Out, out, thou strumpet Fortune! All you gods
In general synod° take away her power!
Break all the spokes and fellies° from her wheel,
And bowl the round nave° down the hill of heaven°   455
As low as to the fiends!"
POLONIUS. This is too long.
HAMLET. It shall to the barber's with your beard.—Prithee, say on.
    He's for a jig° or a tale of bawdry, or he sleeps. Say on; come to
    Hecuba.°   460
FIRST PLAYER. "But who, ah woe! had° seen the moblèd° queen"—
HAMLET. "The moblèd queen?"
POLONIUS. That's good. "Moblèd queen" is good.
FIRST PLAYER. "Run barefoot up and down, threat'ning the flames°
    With bisson rheum,° a clout° upon that head   465
    Where late° the diadem stood, and, for a robe,
    About her lank and all o'erteemèd° loins
    A blanket, in the alarm of fear caught up—
    Who this had seen, with tongue in venom steeped,

---

432 fell cruel. **433 unnervèd** strengthless. **senseless Ilium** inanimate citadel of Troy. **435 his** its. **437 declining** descending. **milky** white-haired. **439 painted** i.e., painted in a picture. **440 like . . . matter** i.e., as though suspended between his intention and its fulfillment. **442 against** just before. **443 rack** mass of clouds. **444 orb** globe, earth. **446 region** sky. **448 Cyclops** giant armor makers in the smithy of Vulcan. **449 proof eterne** eternal resistance to assault. **450 remorse** pity. **453 synod** assembly. **454 fellies** pieces of wood forming the rim of a wheel. **455 nave** hub. **hill of heaven** Mount Olympus. **459 jig** comic song and dance often given at the end of a play. **460 Hecuba** wife of Priam. **461 who . . . had** anyone who had (also in line 469). **moblèd** muffled. **464 threat'ning the flames** i.e., weeping hard enough to dampen the flames. **465 bisson rheum** building tears. **clout** cloth. **466 late** lately. **467 all o'erteemèd** utterly worn out with bearing children.

'Gainst Fortune's state° would treason have pronounced.°   470
But if the gods themselves did see her then
When she saw Pyrrhus make malicious sport
In mincing with his sword her husband's limbs,
The instant burst of clamor that she made,
Unless things mortal move them not at all,   475
Would have made milch° the burning eyes of heaven,°
And passion° in the gods."

POLONIUS. Look whe'er° he has not turned his color and has tears in 's
    eyes. Prithee, no more.

HAMLET. 'Tis well; I'll have thee speak out the rest of this soon.—Good   480
    my lord, will you see the players well bestowed?° Do you hear, let
    them be well used, for they are the abstract° and brief chronicles of
    the time. After your death you were better have a bad epitaph than
    their ill report while you live.

POLONIUS. My lord, I will use them according to their desert.   485

HAMLET. God's bodikin,° man, much better. Use every man after his
    desert, and who shall scape whipping? Use them after° your own
    honor and dignity. The less they deserve, the more merit is in your
    bounty. Take them in.

POLONIUS. Come, sirs.   490

                                                            [Exit.]

HAMLET. Follow him, friends. We'll hear a play tomorrow. [As they start
    to leave, HAMLET detains the first PLAYER.] Dost thou hear me, old
    friend? Can you play The Murder of Gonzago?

FIRST PLAYER. Ay, my lord.

HAMLET. We'll ha 't° tomorrow night. You could, for a need, study° a   495
    speech of some dozen or sixteen lines which I would set down and
    insert in 't, could you not?

FIRST PLAYER. Ay, my lord.

HAMLET. Very well. Follow that lord, and look you mock him not.
    (Exeunt PLAYER.) My good friends, I'll leave you till night. You are   500
    welcome to Elsinore.

ROSENCRANTZ. Good my lord!

                              Exeunt [ROSENCRANTZ and GUILDENSTERN].

HAMLET. Ay, so goodbye to you.—Now I am alone.
    O, what a rogue and peasant slave am I!
    Is it not monstrous that this player here,   505
    But° in a fiction, in a dream of passion,
    Could force his soul so to his own conceit?°
    That from her working° all his visage wanned,°
    Tears in his eyes, distraction in his aspect,°

---

470 **state** rule, managing. **pronounced** proclaimed.   476 **milch** milky, moist with
tears.   **burning eyes of heaven** i.e., heavenly bodies.   477 **passion** overpowering
emotion.   478 **whe'er** whether.   481 **bestowed** lodged.   482 **abstract** summary account.   486 **God's bodikin** by God's (Christ's) little body, *bodykin* (not to be confused
with *bodkin,* "dagger").   487 **after** according to.   495 **ha 't** have it.   **study** memorize.
506 **But** merely.   507 **force . . . conceit** bring his innermost being so entirely into accord with his conception (of the role).   508 **from her working** as a result of, or in response to, his soul's activity.   **wanned** grew pale.   509 **aspect** look, glance.

A broken voice, and his whole function suiting   510
With forms to his conceit° And all for nothing!
For Hecuba!
What's Hecuba to him, or he to Hecuba,
That he should weep for her? What would he do
Had he the motive and the cue for passion   515
That I have? He would drown the stage with tears
And cleave the general ear° with horrid° speech,
Make mad the guilty and appall° the free,°
Confound the ignorant,° and amaze° indeed
The very faculties of eyes and ears. Yet I,   520
A dull and muddy-mettled° rascal, peak°
Like John-a-dreams,° unpregnant of° my cause,
And can say nothing—no, not for a king
Upon whose property° and most dear life
A damned defeat° was made. Am I a coward?   525
Who calls me villain? Breaks my pate° across?
Plucks off my beard and blows it in my face?
Tweaks me by the nose? Gives me the lie i' the throat°
As deep as to the lungs? Who does me this?
Ha, 'swounds,° I should take it; for it cannot be   530
But I am pigeon-livered° and lack gall
To make oppression bitter,° or ere this
I should ha' fatted all the region kites°
With this slave's offal.° Bloody, bawdy villain!
Remorseless,° treacherous, lecherous, kindless° villain!   535
O, vengeance!
Why, what an ass am I? This is most brave,°
That I, the son of a dear father murdered,
Prompted to my revenge by heaven and hell,
Must like a whore unpack my heart with words   540
And fall a-cursing, like a very drab,°
A scullion!° Fie upon 't, foh! About,° my brains!
Hum, I have heard
That guilty creatures sitting at a play
Have by the very cunning° of the scene°   545

510–511 his whole . . . conceit all his bodily powers responding with actions to suit his thought.   **517 the general ear** everyone's ear.   **horrid** horrible.   **518 appall** (literally, make pale.)   **free** innocent.   **519 Confound the ignorant** i.e., dumbfound those who know nothing of the crime that has been committed.   **amaze** stun.   **521 muddy-mettled** dull-spirited.   **peak** mope, pine.   **522 John-a-dreams** a sleepy, dreaming idler. **unpregnant of** not quickened by.   **524 property** i.e., the crown; also character, quality. **525 damned defeat** damnable act of destruction.   **526 pate** head.   **528 Gives . . . throat** calls me an out-and-out liar.   **530 'swounds** by his (Christ's) wounds.   **531 pigeon-livered** (The pigeon or dove was popularly supposed to be mild because it secreted no gall).   **532 bitter** i.e., bitter to me.   **533 region kites** kites (birds of prey) of the air.   **534 offal** entrails.   **535 Remorseless** pitiless.   **kindless** unnatural.   **537 brave** fine, admirable (said ironically).   **541 drab** whore.   **542 scullion** menial kitchen servant (apt to be foul-mouthed).   **About** about it, to work.   **545 cunning** art, skill. **scene** dramatic presentation.

Been struck so to the soul that presently°
They have proclaimed their malefactions;
For murder, though it have no tongue, will speak
With most miraculous organ. I'll have these players
Play something like the murder of my father   550
Before mine uncle. I'll observe his looks;
I'll tent° him to the quick.° If 'a do blench,°
I know my course. The spirit that I have seen
May be the devil, and the devil hath power
T' assume a pleasing shape; yea, and perhaps,   555
Out of my weakness and my melancholy,
As he is very potent with such spirits,°
Abuses° me to damn me. I'll have grounds
More relative° than this. The play's the thing
Wherein I'll catch the conscience of the King.   560

Exit.

[3.1] *Enter* KING, QUEEN, POLONIUS, OPHELIA, ROSENCRANTZ, GUILDEN-
STERN, *lords.*

KING. And can you by no drift of conference°
    Get from him why he puts on this confusion,
    Grating so harshly all his days of quiet
    With turbulent and dangerous lunacy?
ROSENCRANTZ. He does confess he feels himself distracted,   5
    But from what cause 'a will by no means speak.
GUILDENSTERN. Nor do we find him forward° to be sounded,°
    But with a crafty madness keeps aloof
    When we would bring him on to some confession
    Of his true state.
QUEEN.   Did he receive you well?   10
ROSENCRANTZ. Most like a gentleman.
GUILDENSTERN. But with much forcing of his disposition.°
ROSENCRANTZ. Niggard° of question,° but of our demands
    Most free in his reply.
QUEEN.   Did you assay° him
    To any pastime?   15
ROSENCRANTZ. Madam, it so fell out that certain players
    We o'erraught° on the way. Of these we told him,
    And there did seem in him a kind of joy
    To hear of it. They are here about the court,
    And, as I think, they have already order   20
    This night to play before him.

---

546 presently at once.   **552 tent** probe.   **the quick** the tender part of a wound,
the core.   **blench** quail, flinch.   **557 spirits** humors (of melancholy).   **558 Abuses**
deludes.   **559 relative** cogent, pertinent.   **3.1. Location: The castle.   1 drift of
conference** directing of conversation.   **7 forward** willing.   **sounded** questioned.
12 disposition inclination.   **13 Niggard** stingy.   **question** conversation.   **14 assay** try
to win.   **17 o'erraught** overtook.

POLONIUS.   'Tis most true,
And he beseeched me to entreat Your Majesties
To hear and see the matter.

KING. With all my heart, and it doth much content me
To hear him so inclined.   25
Good gentlemen, give him a further edge°
And drive his purpose into these delights.

ROSENCRANTZ. We shall, my lord.

Exeunt ROSENCRANTZ *and* GUILDENSTERN.

KING.   Sweet Gertrude, leave us too,
For we have closely° sent for Hamlet hither,
That he, as 'twere by accident, may here   30
Affront° Ophelia.
Her father and myself, lawful espials,°
Will so bestow ourselves that seeing, unseen,
We may of their encounter frankly judge,
And gather by him, as he is behaved,   35
If't be th' affliction of his love or no
That thus he suffers for.

QUEEN.   I shall obey you.
And for your part, Ophelia, I do wish
That your good beauties be the happy cause
Of Hamlet's wildness. So shall I hope your virtues   40
Will bring him to his wonted° way again,
To both your honors.

OPHELIA.   Madame, I wish it may.

[*Exit* QUEEN.]

POLONIUS. Ophelia, walk you here.—Gracious,° so please you,
We will bestow° ourselves. [*To* OPHELIA.] Read on this book,

[*giving her a book*]

That show of such an exercise° may color°   45
Your loneliness.° We are oft to blame in this—
'Tis too much proved°—that with devotion's visage
And pious action we do sugar o'er
The devil himself.

KING [*aside*]. O 'tis too true!   50
How smart a lash that speech doth give my conscience!
The harlot's check, beautied with plastering art,
Is not more ugly to° the thing° that helps it
Than is my deed to my most painted word.
O heavy burden!   55

POLONIUS. I hear him coming. Let's withdraw, my lord.

[*The* KING *and* POLONIUS *withdraw.*°]

---

26 edge incitement. **29 closely** privately. **31 Affront** confront, meet. **32 espials**
spies. **41 wonted** accustomed. **43 Gracious** Your Grace (i.e., the King). **44 bestow**
conceal. **45 exercise** religious exercise. (The book she reads is one of devotion.)
color give a plausible appearance to. **46 loneliness** being alone. **47 too much
proved** too often shown to be true, too often practiced. **53 to** compared to. **the
thing** i.e., the cosmetic. **56 s.d. withdraw** (The King and Polonius may retire behind an
arras. The stage directions specify that they "enter" again near the end of the scene.)

Enter HAMLET. [OPHELIA *pretends to read a book.*]

HAMLET. To be, or not to be, that is the question:
Whether 'tis nobler in the mind to suffer
The slings° and arrows of outrageous fortune,
Or to take arms against a sea of troubles   60
And by opposing end them. To die, to sleep—
No more—and by a sleep to say we end
The heartache and the thousand natural shocks
That flesh is heir to. 'Tis a consummation
Devoutly to be wished. To die, to sleep;   65
To sleep, perchance to dream. Ay, there's the rub,°
For in that sleep of death what dreams may come,
When we have shuffled° off this mortal coil,°
Must give us pause. There's the respect°
That makes calamity of so long life.°   70
For who would bear the whips and scorns of time,
Th' oppressor's wrong, the proud man's contumely,°
The pangs of disprized° love, the law's delay,
The insolence of office,° and the spurns°
That patient merit of th' unworthy takes,°   75
When he himself might his quietus° make
With a bare bodkin?° Who would fardels° bear,
To grunt and sweat under a weary life,
But that the dread of something after death,
The undiscovered country from whose bourn°   80
No traveler returns, puzzles the will,
And makes us rather bear those ills we have
Than fly to others that we know not of?
Thus conscience does make cowards of us all;
And thus the native hue° of resolution   85
Is sicklied o'er with the pale cast° of thought,
And enterprises of great pitch° and moment°
With this regard° their currents° turn awry
And lose the name of action.—Soft you° now,
The fair Ophelia. Nymph, in thy orisons°   90
Be all my sins remembered.
OPHELIA.   Good my lord,
How does your honor for this many a day?
HAMLET. I humbly thank you; well, well, well.

---

59 slings missiles.   **66 rub** (Literally, an obstacle in the game of bowls.)   **68 shuffled**
sloughed, cast.   **coil** turmoil.   **69 respect** consideration.   **70 of . . . life** so long-lived,
something we willingly endure for so long (also suggesting that long life is itself a calamity).
72 contumely insolent abuse.   **73 disprized** unvalued.   **74 office** officialdom.
spurns insults.   **75 of . . . takes** receives from unworthy persons.   **76 quietus** acqui-
tance; here, death.   **77 a bare bodkin** a mere dagger, unsheathed.   **fardels** burdens.
80 bourn frontier, boundary.   **85 native hue** natural color complexion.   **86 cast** tinge,
shade of color.   **87 pitch** height (as of a falcon's flight).   **moment** importance.
88 regard respect, consideration.   **currents** courses.   **89 Soft you** i.e., wait a minute,
gently.   **90 orisons** prayers.

OPHELIA. My lord, I have remembrances of yours,
   That I have longèd long to redeliver.   95
   I pray you, now receive them.   [*She offers tokens.*]
HAMLET. No, not I, I never gave you aught.
OPHELIA. My honored lord, you know right well you did,
   And with them words of so sweet breath composed
   As made the things more rich. Their perfume lost,   100
   Take these again, for to the noble mind
   Rich gifts wax poor when givers prove unkind.
   There, my lord.   [*She gives tokens.*]
HAMLET. Ha, ha! Are you honest?°
OPHELIA. My lord?   105
HAMLET. Are you fair?°
OPHELIA. What means your lordship?
HAMLET. That if you be honest and fair, your honesty° should admit no
   discourse° to your beauty.
OPHELIA. Could beauty, my lord, have better commerce° than with hon-   110
   esty?
HAMLET. Ay, truly, for the power of beauty will sooner transform honesty
   from what it is to a bawd than the force of honesty can translate
   beauty into his° likeness. This was sometime° a paradox,° but now
   the time° gives it proof. I did love you once.   115
OPHELIA. Indeed, my lord, you made me believe so.
HAMLET. You should not have believed me, for virtue cannot so inocu-
   late° our old stock but we shall relish of it.° I loved you not.
OPHELIA. I was the more deceived.
HAMLET. Get thee to a nunnery.° Why wouldst thou be a breeder of sin-   120
   ners? I am myself indifferent honest,° but yet I could accuse me of
   such things that it were better my mother had not borne me: I am
   very proud, revengeful, ambitious, with more offenses at my beck°
   than I have thoughts to put them in, imagination to give them
   shape, or time to act them in. What should such fellows as I do   125
   crawling between earth and heaven? We are arrant knaves all; believe none of us. Go thy ways to a nunnery. Where's your father?
OPHELIA. At home, my lord.
HAMLET. Let the doors be shut upon him, that he may play the fool
   nowhere but in's own house. Farewell.   130
OPHELIA. O, help him, you sweet heavens!
HAMLET. If thou dost marry, I'll give thee this plague for thy dowry: be
   thou as chaste as ice, as pure as snow, thou shalt not escape
   calumny. Get thee to a nunnery, farewell. Or, if thou wilt needs

---

104 honest (1) truthful (2) chaste.   **106 fair** (1) beautiful (2) just, honorable.   **108 your honesty** your chastity.   **109 discourse** to familiar dealings with.   **110 commerce** deal-ings, intercourse.   **114 his** its.   **sometime** formerly.   **a paradox** a view opposite to commonly held opinion.   **115 the time** the present age.   **117–118 inoculate** graft, be engrafted to.   **118 but . . . it** that we do not still have about us a taste of the old stock, i.e., retain our sinfulness.   **120 nunnery** convent (with possibly an awareness that the word was also used derisively to denote a brothel).   **121 indifferent honest** reasonably virtu-ous.   **123 beck** command.

marry, marry a fool, for wise men know well enough what mon-   135
sters° you° make of them. To a nunnery, go, and quickly too.
Farewell.

OPHELIA. Heavenly powers, restore him!

HAMLET. I have heard of your paintings too, well enough. God hath
given you one face, and you make yourselves another. You jig,° you   140
amble,° and you lisp, you nickname God's creatures,° and make
your wantonness your ignorance.° Go to, I'll no more on 't;° it hath
made me mad. I say we will have no more marriage. Those that are
married already—all but one—shall live. The rest shall keep as they
are. To a nunnery, go.   145

                                                              Exit.

OPHELIA. O, what a nobler mind is here o'erthrown!
    The courtier's, soldier's, scholar's, eye, tongue, sword,
    Th' expectancy° and rose° of the fair state,
    The glass of fashion and the mold of form,°
    Th' observed of all observers,° quite, quite down!   150
    And I, of ladies most deject and wretched,
    That sucked the honey of his music° vows,
    Now see that noble and most sovereign reason
    Like sweet bells jangled out of tune and harsh,
    That unmatched form and feature of blown° youth   155
    Blasted° with ecstasy.° O, woe is me,
    T' have seen what I have seen, see what I see!

    Enter KING *and* POLONIUS.

KING. Love? His affections° do not that way tend;
    Nor what he spake, though it lacked form a little,
    Was not like madness. There's something in his soul   160
    O'er which his melancholy sits on brood,°
    And I do doubt° the hatch and the disclose°
    Will be some danger, which for to prevent,
    I have in quick determination
    Thus set it down:° he shall with speed to England   165
    For the demand of° our neglected tribute.
    Haply the seas and countries different
    With variable objects° shall expel

135–136 monsters (An illusion to the horns of a cuckold.)   **you** i.e., you women.   **140
jig** dance.   **141 amble** move coyly.   **you nickname . . . creatures** i.e., you give
trendy names to things in place of their God-given names.   **141–142 make . . . ignorance** i.e., excuse your affectation on the grounds of pretended ignorance.   **on 't** of it.
148 expectancy hope.   **rose** ornament.   **149 The glass . . . form** the mirror of true
fashioning and the pattern of courtly behavior.   **150 Th' observed . . . observers** i.e.,
the center of attention and honor in the court.   **152 music** musical, sweetly uttered.
155 blown blooming.   **156 Blasted** withered.   **ecstasy** madness.   **158 affections**
emotions, feelings.   **161 sits on brood** sits like a bird on a nest, about to *hatch* mischief
(line 162).   **162 doubt** fear.   **disclose** disclosure, hatching.   **165 set it down** resolved.
166 For . . . of to demand.   **168 variable objects** various sights and surroundings to
divert him.

This something-settled matter in his heart,°
Whereon his brains still° beating puts him thus   170
From fashion of himself.° What think you on 't?
POLONIUS. It shall do well. But yet do I believe
The origin and commencement of his grief
Sprung from neglected love.—How now, Ophelia?
You need not tell us what Lord Hamlet said;   175
We heard it all.—My lord, do as you please,
But, if you hold it fit, after the play
Let his queen-mother° all alone entreat him
To show his grief. Let her be round° with him;
And I'll be placed, so please you, in the ear   180
Of all their conference. If she find him not,°
To England send him, or confine him where
Your wisdom best shall think.
KING.   It shall be so.
Madness in great ones must not unwatched to.

                                        Exeunt.

    [3.2] *Enter* HAMLET *and three of the* PLAYERS.

HAMLET. Speak the speech, I pray you, as I pronounced it to you, trip-
        pingly on the tongue. But if you mouth it, as many of our players°
        do, I had as lief° the town crier spoke my lines. Nor do not saw the
        air too much with your hand, thus, but use all gently; for in the very
        torrent, tempest, and, as I may say, whirlwind of your passion, you   5
        must acquire and beget a temperance that may give it smoothness.
        O, it offends me to the soul to hear a robustious° periwig-pated° fel-
        low tear a passion to tatters, to very rags, to split the ears of the
        groundlings,° who for the most part are capable of° nothing but in-
        explicable dumb shows° and noise. I would have such a fellow   10
        whipped for o'erdoing Termagant.° It out-Herods Herod.° Pray
        you, avoid it.
FIRST PLAYER. I warrant your honor.
HAMLET. Be not too tame neither, but let your own discretion be your tu-
        tor. Suit the action in the word, the word to the action, with this   15
        special observance, that you o'erstep not the modesty° of nature.
        For anything so o'erdone is from° the purpose of playing, whose

---

169 This something . . . heart the strange matter settled in his heart.   **170 still** continually.   **171 From . . . himself** out of his natural manner.   **178 queen-mother** queen
and mother.   **179 round** blunt.   **181 find him not** fails to discover what is troubling
him.   **3.2. Location: The castle.   2 our players** players nowadays.   **3 I had as lief** I
would just as soon.   **7 robustious** violent, boisterous.   **7 periwig-pated** wearing a wig.
9 groundlings spectators who paid least and stood in the yard of the theater.   **capable
of** able to understand.   **10 dumb shows** mimed performances, often used before Shakespeare's time to precede a play or each act.   **11 Termagant** a supposed deity of the Mo-
hammedans, not found in any English medieval play but elsewhere portrayed as violent
and blustering.   **Herod** Herod of Jewry. (A character in *The Slaughter of the Innocents*
and other cycle plays. The part was played with great noise and fury.)
16 modesty restraint, moderation.   **17 from** contrary to.

end, both at the first and now, was and is to hold as 't were the
mirror up to nature, to show virtue her feature, scorn° her own image, and the very age and body of the time° his° form and pres-   20
sure.° Now this overdone or come tardy off,° though it makes the
unskillful° laugh, cannot but make the judicious grieve, the censure of the which one° must in your allowance° o'erweigh a whole
theater of others. O, there be players that I have seen play, and
heard others praise, and that highly, not to speak it profanely,° that,   25
neither having th' accent of Christians° nor the gait of Christian,
pagan, nor man,° have so strutted and bellowed that I have thought
some of nature's journeymen° had made men and not made them
well, they imitated humanity so abominably.°

FIRST PLAYER. I hope we have reformed that indifferently° with us, sir.   30

HAMLET. O, reform it altogether. And let those that play your clowns
speak no more than is set down for them; for there be of them° that
will themselves laugh, to set on some quantity of barren° spectators to laugh too, though in the meantime some necessary question
of the play be then to be considered. That's villainous, and shows a   35
most pitiful ambition in the fool that uses it. Go make you
ready.

[Exeunt PLAYERS.]

Enter POLONIUS, GUILDENSTERN and ROSENCRANTZ.

How now, my lord, will the King hear this piece of work?

POLONIUS. And the Queen too, and that presently.°

HAMLET. Bid the players make haste.   40

[Exit POLONIUS.]

Will you two help to hasten them?

ROSENCRANTZ. Ay, my lord.

Exeunt they two.

HAMLET.   What ho, Horatio!

Enter HORATIO.

HORATIO. Here, sweet lord, at your service.

HAMLET. Horatio, thou art e'en as just a man
As e'er my conversation coped withal.°   45

HORATIO. O, my dear lord—

HAMLET.   Nay, do not think I flatter,

---

19 scorn i.e., something foolish and deserving of scorn.   **20 the very . . . time** i.e., the
present state of affairs.   **his** its.   **20–21 pressure** stamp, impressed character.   **21
come tardy off** inadequately done.   **21–22 the unskillful** those lacking in judgment.
22–23 the censure . . . one the judgment of even one of whom.   **23 your allowance**
your scale of values.   **25 not . . . profanely** (Hamlet anticipates his idea in lines 27–29
that some men were not made by God at all.)   **26 Christians** i.e., ordinary decent folk.
27 nor man i.e., nor any human being at all.   **28 journeymen** laborers who are not yet
masters in their trade.   **29 abominably** (Shakespeare's usual spelling, *abhominably*, suggests a literal though etymologically incorrect meaning, "removed from human nature.")
30 indifferently tolerably.   **32 of them** some among them.   **33 barren** i.e., of wit.
39 presently at once.   **45 my . . . withal** my dealings encountered.

For what advancement may I hope from thee
That no revenue hast but thy good spirits
To feed and clothe thee? Why should the poor be flattered?
No, let the candied° tongue lick absurd pomp,   50
And crook the pregnant° hinges of the knee
Where thrift° may follow fawning. Dost thou hear?
Since my dear soul was mistress of her choice
And could of men distinguish her election,°
Sh' hath sealed thee° for herself, for thou hast been   55
As one, in suffering all, that suffers nothing,
A man that Fortune's buffets and rewards
Hast ta'en with equal thanks; and blest are those
Whose blood° and judgment are so well commeddled°
That they are not a pipe for Fortune's finger   60
To sound what stop° she please. Give me that man
That is not passion's slave, and I will wear him
In my heart's core, ay, in my heart of heart,
As I do thee.—Something too much of this.—
There is a play tonight before the King.   65
One scene of it comes near the circumstance
Which I have told thee of my father's death.
I prithee, when thou seest that act afoot,
Even with the very comment of thy soul°
Observe my uncle. If his occulted° guilt   70
Do not itself unkennel° in one speech,
It is a damnèd° ghost that we have seen,
And my imaginations are as foul
As Vulcan't stithy.° Give him heedful note,
For I mine eyes will rivet to his face,   75
And after we will both our judgments join
In censure of his seeming.°
HORATIO.   Well, my lord.
If 'a steal aught° the whilst this play is playing
And scape detecting, I will pay the theft.

[*Flourish.*] *Enter trumpets and kettledrums,* KING, QUEEN, POLONIUS,
OPHELIA, [ROSENCRANTZ, GUILDENSTERN, *and other lords, with guards
carrying torches*].

HAMLET. They are coming to the play. I must be idle.°   80
   Get you a place.   [*The* KING, QUEEN, *and courtiers sit.*]
   KING. How fares our cousin° Hamlet?

---

50 candied sugared, flattering.   **51 pregnant** compliant.   **52 thrift** profit.   **54 could . . .
election** could make distinguishing choices among persons.   **55 sealed thee** (Literally, as
one would seal a legal document to mark possession.)   **59 blood** passion.   **commeddled**
commingled.   **61 stop** hole in a wind instrument for controlling the sound.   **69 very . . .
soul** your most penetrating observation and consideration.   **70 occulted** hidden.   **71
unkennel** (As one would say of a fox driven from its lair.)   **72 damnèd** in league with
Satan.   **74 stithy** smithy, place of stiths (anvils).   **77 censure of his seeming** judgment of
his appearance or behavior.   **78 If 'a steal aught** if he gets away with anything.   **80 idle**
(1) unoccupied (2) mad.   **82 cousin** i.e., close relative.

HAMLET. Excellent, i' faith, of the chameleon's dish:° I eat the air,
   promise-crammed. You cannot feed capons° so.

KING. I have nothing with° this answer, Hamlet. These words are not   85
   mine.°

HAMLET. No, nor mine now.° [*To* POLONIUS.] My lord, you played once i'
   th' university, you say?

POLONIUS. That did I, my lord, and was accounted a good actor.

HAMLET. What did you enact?   90

POLONIUS. I did enact Julius Caesar. I was killed i' the Capitol; Brutus
   killed me.

HAMLET. It was a brute° part° of him to kill so capital a calf° there.—Be
   the players ready?

ROSENCRANTZ. Ay, my lord. They stay upon° your patience.   95

QUEEN. Come hither, my dear Hamlet, sit by me.

HAMLET. No, good Mother, here's metal° more attractive.

POLONIUS [*to the King*]. O, ho, do you mark that?

HAMLET. Lady, shall I lie in your lap?

[Lying down at OPHELIA*'s feet.]*

OPHELIA. No, my lord.   100

HAMLET. I mean, my head upon your lap?

OPHELIA. Ay, my lord.

HAMLET. Do you think I meant country matters?°

OPHELIA. I think nothing, my lord.

HAMLET. That's a fair thought to lie between maids' legs.   105

OPHELIA. What is, my lord?

HAMLET. Nothing.°

OPHELIA. You are merry, my lord.

HAMLET. Who, I?

OPHELIA. Ay, my lord.   110

HAMLET. O God, your only jig maker.° What should a man do but be
   merry? For look you how cheerfully my mother looks, and my
   father died within's° two hours.

OPHELIA. Nay, 'tis twice two months, my lord.

---

83 chameleon's dish (Chameleons were supposed to feed on air. Hamlet deliberately
misinterprets the King's *fares* as "feeds." By his phrase *eat the air* he also plays on the
idea of feeding himself with the promise of succession, of being the *heir*.)   **84 capons**
roosters castrated and *crammed* with feed to make them succulent.   **85 have . . . with**
make nothing of, or gain nothing from.   **85–86 are not mine** do not respond to what I
asked.   **87 nor mine now** (Once spoken, words are proverbially no longer the
speaker's own—and hence should be uttered warily.)   **93 brute** (The Latin meaning of
brutus, "stupid," was often used punningly with the name Brutus.)   **part** (1) deed (2)
role.   **calf** fool.   **95 stay upon** await.   **97 metal** substance that is *attractive,* i.e., mag-
netic, but with suggestion also of *mettle,* "disposition."   **103 country matters** sexual intercourse (making a bawdy pun on the first syllable of *country*).   **107 Nothing** the figure zero or naught, suggesting the female sexual anatomy. (*Thing* not infrequently has a
bawdy connotation of male or female anatomy, and the reference here could be made.)
111 only jig maker very best composer of jigs, i.e., pointless merriment. (Hamlet replies
sardonically to Ophelia's observation that he is merry by saying, "If you're looking for
someone who is really merry, you've come to the right person.")   **113 within's** within
this (i.e., these).

HAMLET. So long? Nay then, let the devil wear black, for I'll have a suit of   115
sables.° O heavens! Die two months ago, and not forgotten yet?
Then there's hope a great man's memory may outlive his life half a
year. But, by 'r Lady, 'a must build churches, then, or else shall 'a suffer not thinking on,° with the hobbyhorse, whose epitaph is "For
O, for O, the hobbyhorse is forgot."°   120

The trumpets sound. Dumb show follows.

*Enter a King and a Queen [very lovingly]; the Queen embracing
him, and he her. [She kneels, and makes show of protestation
unto him.] He takes her up, and declines his head upon her
neck. He lies him down upon a bank of flowers. She, seeing him
asleep, leaves him. Anon comes in another man, takes off his
crown, kisses it, pours poison in the sleeper's ears, and leaves
him. The Queen returns, finds the King dead, makes passionate
action. The Poisoner with some three or four come in again,
seem to condole with her. The dead body is carried away. The
Poisoner woos the Queen with gifts; she seems harsh awhile, but
in the end accepts love.*

[*Exeunt* PLAYERS.]

OPHELIA. What means this, my lord?
HAMLET. Marry, this' miching mallico;° it means mischief.
OPHELIA. Belike° this show imports the argument° of the play.

Enter PROLOGUE.

HAMLET. We shall know by this fellow. The players cannot keep counsel;°
they'll tell all   125
OPHELIA. Will 'a tell us what this show meant?
HAMLET. Ay, or any show that you will show him. Be not you° ashamed to
show, he'll not shame to tell you what it means.
OPHELIA. You are naught,° you are naught. I'll mark the play.
PROLOGUE. For us and for our tragedy,   130
Here stooping° to your clemency,
We beg your hearing patiently.

[*Exit.*]

HAMLET. Is this a prologue, or the posy of a ring?°
OPHELIA. 'Tis brief, my lord.
HAMLET. As woman's love.   135

Enter [two PLAYERS *as]* King and Queen.

115–116 suit of sables garments trimmed with the fur of the sable and hence suited for
a wealthy person, not a mourner (but with a pun on *sable*, "black," ironically suggesting
mourning once again).   **118–119 suffer . . . on** undergone oblivion.   **119–120 For . . .
forgot** (Verse of a song occurring also in *Love's Labor Lost*, 3.1.27-28. The hobbyhorse
was a character made up to resemble a horse and rider, appearing in the morris dance and
such May-game sports. This song laments the disappearance of such customs under pressure from the Puritans.)   **122 this' miching mallico** this is sneaking mischief.   **123
Belike** probably.   **argument** plot.   **124 counsel** secret.   **127 Be not you** provided
you are not.   **129 naught** indecent. (Ophelia is reacting to Hamlet's pointed remarks
about not being ashamed to show all.)   **131 stooping** bowing.   **133 posy . . . ring**
brief motto in verse inscribed in a ring.

PLAYER KING.   Full thirty times hath Phoebus' cart° gone round
                 Neptune's salt wash° and Tellus'° orbèd ground,
                 And thirty dozen moons with borrowed° sheen
                 About the world have times twelve thirties been,
                 Since love our hearts and Hymen° did our hands   140
                 Unite commutual° in most sacred bands.°
PLAYER QUEEN.   So many journeys may the sun and moon
                 Make us again count o'er ere love be done!
                 But, woe is me, you are sick of late,
                 So far from cheer and from your former state,   145
                 That I distrust° you. Yet, though I distrust,
                 Discomfort° you, my lord, it is nothing° must.
                 For women's fear and love hold quantity;°
                 In neither aught, or in extremity.°
                 Now, what my love is, proof° hath made you know,   150
                 And as my love is sized,° my fear is so.
                 Where love is great, the littlest doubts are fear;
                 Where little fears grow great, great love grows there.
PLAYER KING.   Faith, I must leave thee, love, and shortly too;
                 My operant powers° their functions leave to do.°   155
                 And thou shalt live in this fair world behind,°
                 Honored, beloved; and haply one as kind
                 For husband shalt thou—
PLAYER QUEEN.   O, confound the rest!
                 Such love must needs be treason in my breast.
                 In second husband let me be accurst!   160
                 None° wed the second but who° killed the first.
HAMLET.   Wormwood,° wormwood.
PLAYER QUEEN.   The instances° that second marriage move°
                 Are base respects of thrift,° but none of love.
                 A second time I kill my husband dead   165
                 When second husband kisses me in bed.
PLAYER KING.   I do believe you think what now you speak,
                 But what we do determine oft we break.
                 Purpose is but the slave to memory,°
                 Of violent birth, but poor validity,°   170
                 Which° now, like fruit unripe, sticks on the tree,

---

136 Phoebus' cart the sun-god's chariot, making its yearly cycle.   **137 salt wash** the
sea.   **Tellus** goddess of the earth, of the *orbèd ground*.   **138 borrowed** i.e., reflected.
140 Hymen god of matrimony.   **141 commutual** mutually.   **bands** bonds.   **146 distrust** am anxious about.   **147 Discomfort** distress.   **nothing** not at all.   **148 hold
quantity** keep proportion with one another.   **149 In . . . extremity** i.e., women fear
and love either too little or too much, but the two, fear and love, are equal in either case.
150 proof experience.   **151 sized** in size.   **155 operant powers** vital functions.
leave to do cease to perform.   **156 behind** after I have gone.   **161 None** i.e., let no
woman.   **but who** except the one who.   **162 Wormwood** i.e., how bitter. (Literally, a
bitter-tasting plant.)   **163 instances** motives.   **move** motivate.   **164 base . . . thrift**
ignoble considerations of material prosperity.   **169 Purpose . . . memory** our good intentions are subject to forgetfulness.   **170 validity** strength, durability.   **171 Which** i.e.,
purpose.

But fall unshaken when they mellow be.
Most necessary 'tis that we forget
To pay ourselves what to ourselves is debt.°
What to ourselves in passion we propose,   175
The passion ending, doth the purpose lose.
The violence of either grief or joy
Their own enactures° with themselves destroy.
Where joy most revels, grief doth most lament;
Grief joys, joy grieves, on slender accident.°   180
This world is not for aye,° nor 'tis not strange
That even our loves should with our fortunes change;
For 'tis a question left us yet to prove,
Whether love lead fortune, or else fortune love.
The great man down,° you mark his favorite flies;   185
The poor advanced makes friends of enemies.°
And hitherto° doth love on fortune tend;°
For who not needs° shall never lack a friend,
And who in want° a hollow friend doth try°
Directly seasons him° his enemy.   190
But, orderly to end where I begun,
Our wills and fates do so contrary run°
That our devices still° are overthrown;
Our thoughts are ours, their ends° none of our own.
So think thou wilt no second husband wed,   195
But die thy thoughts when thy first lord is dead.
PLAYER QUEEN. Nor° earth to me give food, nor heaven light,
Sport and repose lock from me day and night,°
To desperation turn my trust and hope,
An anchor's cheer° in prison be my scope!°   200
Each opposite that blanks° the face of joy
Meet what I would have well and it destroy!°
Both here and hence° pursue me lasting strife
If, once a widow, ever I be wife!
HAMLET. If she should break it now!   205

173–174 Most . . . debt it's inevitable that in time we forget the obligations we have imposed on ourselves.   **178 enactures** fulfillments.   **179–180 Where . . . accident** the capacity for extreme joy and grief go together, and often one extreme is instantly changed into its opposite on the slightest provocation.   **181 aye** ever.   **185 down** fallen in fortune.   **186 The poor . . . enemies** when one of humble station is promoted, you see his enemies suddenly becoming his friends.   **187 hitherto** up to this point in the argument, or, to this extent.   **tend** attend.   **188 who not needs** he who is not in need (of wealth). **189 who in want** he who, being in need.   **try** test (his generosity).   **190 seasons him** ripens him into.   **192 Our . . . run** what we want and what we get go so contrarily. **193 devices still** intentions continually.   **194 ends** results.   **197 Nor** let neither.   **198 Sport . . . night** may day deny me its pastimes and night its repose.   **200 anchor's cheer** anchorite's or hermit's fare.   **my scope** the extent of my happiness.   **201 blanks** causes to blanch or grow pale.   **201–202 Each . . . destroy** may every adverse thing that causes the face of joy to turn pale meet and destroy everything that I desire to see prosper.   **203 hence** in the life hereafter.

PLAYER KING. 'Tis deeply sworn. Sweet, leave me here awhile; My spirits°
grow dull, and fain I would beguile. The tedious day with sleep.

PLAYER QUEEN.   Sleep rock thy brain,
And never come mischance between us twain!

                                [*He sleeps.*] *Exit* [PLAYER QUEEN].

HAMLET.   Madam, how like you this play?   210

QUEEN.   The lady doth protest too much,° methinks.

HAMLET.   O, but she'll keep her word.

KING.   Have you heard the argument?° Is there no offense in 't?

HAMLET.   No, no, they do but jest,° poison in jest. No offense° i' the
world.   215

KING.   What do you call the play?

HAMLET.   *The Mousetrap.* Marry, how? Tropically.° This play is the image
of a murder done in Vienna. Gonzago is the Duke's° name, his wife,
Baptista. You shall see anon. 'Tis a knavish piece of work, but what
of that? Your Majesty, and we that have free° souls, it touches us   220
not. Let the galled jade° wince, our withers° are unwrung.°

Enter LUCIANUS.

This is one Lucianus, nephew to the King.

OPHELIA.   You are as good as a chorus,° my lord.

HAMLET.   I could interpret° between you and your love, if I could see the
puppets dallying.°   225

OPHELIA.   You are keen,° my lord, you are keen.

HAMLET.   It would cost you a groaning to take off mine edge.

OPHELIA.   Still better, and worse.°

HAMLET.   So° you mis-take° your husbands. Begin, murder; leave thy
damnable faces and begin. Come, the croaking raven doth bellow   230
for revenge.

LUCIANUS.   Thoughts black, hands apt, drugs fit, and time agreeing,
Confederate season,° else° no creature seeing,°
Thou mixture rank, of midnight weeds collected,

---

206 spirits vital spirits.   **211 doth . . . much** makes too many promises and protesta-
tions.   **213 argument** plot.   **214 jest** make believe.   **213–214 offense . . . offense**
cause for objection . . . actual injury, crime.   **217 Tropically** figuratively. (The First
Quarto reading, *trapically,* suggests a pun on *trap* in *Mousetrap.*)   **218 Duke's** i.e.,
King's. (A slip that may be due to Shakespeare's possible source, the alleged murder of the
Duke of Urbino by Luigi Gonzaga in 1538.)   **220 free** guiltless.   **221 galled jade** horse
whose hide is rubbed by saddle or harness.   **withers** the part between the horse's shoulder blades.   **unwrung** not rubbed sore.   **223 chorus** (In many Elizabethan plays, the
forthcoming action was explained by an actor known as the "chorus"; at a puppet show,
the actor who spoke the dialogue was known as an "interpreter," as indicated by the lines
following.)   **224 interpret** (1) ventriloquize the dialogue, as in puppet show (2) act as
pander.   **225 puppets dallying** (With suggestion of sexual play, continued in *keen,* "sexually aroused," *groaning,* "moaning in pregnancy," and *edge,* "sexual desire" or "impetuosity.")   **226 keen** sharp, bitter.   **228 Still . . . worse** more keen, always *bettering* what
other people say with witty wordplay, but at the same time more offensive.   **229 So** even
thus (in marriage).   **mis-take** take falseheartedly and cheat on. (The marriage vows say
"for better, for worse.")   **233 Confederate season** the time and occasion conspiring (to
assist the murderer).   **else** otherwise.   **seeing** seeing me.

With Hecate's ban° thrice blasted, thrice infected,   235
Thy natural magic and dire property°
On wholesome life usurp immediately.

                [He pours the poison into the sleeper's ear.]

HAMLET. 'A poisons him i' the garden for his estate.° His° name's Gonzago. The story is extant, and written in very choice Italian.
You shall see anon how the murderer gets the love of Gonzago's   240
wife.

    [CLAUDIUS *rises.*]

OPHELIA. The King rises.
HAMLET. What, frighted with false fire?°
QUEEN. How fares my lord?
POLONIUS. Give o'er the play.   245
KING. Give me some light. Away!
POLONIUS. Lights, lights, lights!

              Exeunt all but HAMLET *and* HORATIO.

HAMLET. "Why, let the strucken deer go weep,
    The hart ungallèd° play.
  For some must watch,° while some must sleep;   250
    Thus runs the world away."°
Would not this,° sir, and a forest of feathers°—if the rest of my for-
  tunes turn Turk with° me—with two Provincial roses° on my
  razed° shoes, get me a fellowship in a cry° of players?°
HORATIO. Half a share.   255
HAMLET. A whole one, I.
  "For thou dost know, O Damon° dear,
    This realm dismantled° was
  Of Jove himself, and now reigns here
    A very, very—pajock."°   260
HORATIO. You might have rhymed.
HAMLET. O good Horatio, I'll take the ghost's word for a thousand
  pound. Didst perceive?
HORATIO. Very well, my lord.

---

235 Hecate's ban the curse of Hecate, the goddess of witchcraft.   **236 dire property**
baleful quality.   **238 estate** i.e., the kingship.   **His** i.e., the King's.   **243 false fire** the
blank discharge of a gun loaded with powder but no shot.   **248–251 Why . . . away**
(Probably from an old ballad, with allusion to the popular belief that a wounded deer
retires to weep and die; compare with *As You Like It,* 2.1.33–66.)   **249 ungallèd** unaf-
flicted.   **250 watch** remain awake.   **251 Thus . . . away** thus the world goes.
252 this i.e., the play.   **feathers** (Allusion to the plumes that Elizabethan actors
were fond of wearing.)   **253 turn Turk with** turn renegade against, go back on.   **Provincial
roses** rosettes of ribbon, named for roses grown in a part of France.   **254 razed** with ornamental slashing.   **cry** pack (of hounds).   **fellowship . . . players** partnership in a
theatrical company.   **257 Damon** the friend of Pythias, as Horatio is friend of Hamlet; or,
a traditional pastoral name.   **258 dismantled** stripped, divested.   **258–260 This realm
. . . pajock** i.e., Jove, representing divine authority and justice, has abandoned this realm
to its own devices, leaving in its stead only a peacock or vain pretender to virtue (though
the rhyme-word expected in place of *pajock* or "peacock" suggests that the realm is now
ruled over by an "ass").

HAMLET. Upon the talk of the poisoning?   265

HORATIO. I did very well note him.

Enter ROSENCRANTZ *and* GUILDENSTERN.

HAMLET. Aha! Come, some music! Come, the recorders.°
"For if the King like not the comedy,
Why then, belike, he likes it not, perdy."°
Come, some music.   270

GUILDENSTERN. Good my lord, vouchsafe me a word with you.

HAMLET. Sir, a whole history.

GUILDENSTERN. The King, sir—

HAMLET. Ay, sir, what of him?

GUILDENSTERN. Is in his retirement° marvelous distempered.°   275

HAMLET. With drink, sir?

GUILDENSTERN. No, my lord, with choler.°

HAMLET. Your wisdom should show itself more richer to signify this to
the doctor, for me to put him to his purgation° would perhaps
plunge him into more choler.   280

GUILDENSTERN. Good my lord, put your discourse into some frame° and
start° not so wildly from my affair.

HAMLET. I am tame, sir. Pronounce.

GUILDENSTERN. The Queen, your mother, in most great affliction of spirit,
hath sent me to you.   285

HAMLET. You are welcome.

GUILDENSTERN. Nay, good my lord, this courtesy is not of the right breed.°
If it shall please you to make me a wholesome answer, I will do
your mother's commandment; if not, your pardon° and my return
shall be the end of my business.   290

HAMLET. Sir, I cannot.

ROSENCRANTZ. What, my lord?

HAMLET. Make you a wholesome answer; my wit's diseased. But, sir, such
answer as I can make, you shall command, or rather, as you say,
my mother. Therefore no more, but to the matter. My mother, you 295
say—

ROSENCRANTZ. Then thus she says: your behavior hath struck her into
amazement and admiration.°

HAMLET. O wonderful son, that can so stonish a mother! But is there no
sequel at the heels of this mother's admiration? Impart.   300

ROSENCRANTZ. She desires to speak with you in her closet° ere you go to
bed.

---

267 recorders wind instruments of the flute kind. **269 perdy** (A corruption of the
French *par dieu,* "by God.") **275 retirement** withdrawal to his chambers.
distempered out of humor. (But Hamlet deliberately plays on the wider application to
any illness of mind or body, as in line 307, especially to drunkenness.) **277 choler** anger.
(But Hamlet takes the word in its more basic humoral sense of "bilious disorder.") **279
purgation** (Hamlet hints at something going beyond medical treatment to bloodletting
and the extraction of confession.) **281 frame** order. **282 start** shy or jump away (like
a horse; the opposite of *tame* in line 283). **287 breed** (1) kind (2) breeding, manners.
289 pardon permission to depart. **298 admiration** bewilderment. **301 closet** private chamber.

HAMLET. We shall obey, were she ten times our mother. Have you any
     further trade with us?

ROSENCRANTZ. My lord, you once did love me.   305

HAMLET. And so still, by these pickers and stealers.°

ROSENCRANTZ. Good my lord, what is your cause of distemper? You do
     surely bar the door upon your own liberty° if you deny° your griefs
     to your friend.

HAMLET. Sir, I lack advancement.   310

ROSENCRANTZ. How can that be, when you have the voice of the King
     himself for your succession in Denmark?

HAMLET. Ay, sir, but "While the grass grows"°—the proverb is some-
     thing° musty.

    Enter the PLAYERS° WITH RECORDERS.

O, the recorders. Let me see one. [*He takes a recorder.*]   315
     To withdraw° with you: why do you go about to recover the wind°
     of me, as if you would drive me into a toil?°

GUILDENSTERN. O, my lord, if my duty be too bold, my love is too un-
     mannerly.°

HAMLET. I do not well understand that.° Will you play upon this pipe? 320

GUILDENSTERN. My lord, I cannot.

HAMLET. I pray you.

GUILDENSTERN. Believe me, I cannot.

HAMLET. I do beseech you.

GUILDENSTERN. I know no touch of it, my lord.   325

HAMLET. It is as easy as lying. Govern these ventages° with your fingers
     and thumb, give it breath with your mouth, and it will discourse
     most eloquent music. Look you, these are the stops.

GUILDENSTERN. But these cannot I command to any utterance of har-
     mony. I have not the skill.   300

HAMLET. Why, look you now, how unworthy a thing you make of me!
     You would play upon me, you would seem to know my stops, you
     would pluck out the heart of my mystery, you would sound° me
     from my lowest note to the top of my compass,° and there is much
     music, excellent voice, in this little organ,° yet cannot you make it 335
     speak. 'Sblood, do you think I am easier to be played on than a
     pipe? Call me what instrument you will, though you can fret° me,
     you cannot play upon me.

---

306 pickers and stealers i.e., hands. (So called from the catechism, "to keep my hands
from picking and stealing.")   **308 liberty** i.e., being freed from *distemper,* line 307; but perhaps with a veiled threat as well.   **deny** refuse to share.   **313 While . . . grows** (The rest
of the proverb is "the silly horse starves"; Hamlet may not live long enough to succeed to the
kingdom.)   **313–314 something** somewhat.   **s.d. Players** actors.   **316 withdraw**
speak privately.   **recover the wind** get to the windward side (thus driving the game into
the *toil,* or "net").   **317 toil** snare.   **318–319 if . . . unmannerly** if I am using an unmannerly boldness, it is my love that occasions it.   **320 I . . . that** i.e., I don't understand how
genuine love can be unmannerly.   **326 ventages** finger-holes or *stops* (line 328) of the
recorder.   **333 sound** (1) fathom (2) produce sound in.   **334 compass** range (of voice).
335 organ musical instrument.   **337 fret** irritate (with a quibble on *fret,* meaning the
piece of wood, gut, or metal that regulates the fingering of an instrument).

Enter POLONIUS.

God bless you, sir!

POLONIUS. My lord, the Queen would speak with you, and presently.°   340

HAMLET. Do you see yonder cloud that's almost in shape of a camel?

POLONIUS. By the Mass and 'tis, like a camel indeed.

HAMLET. Methinks it is like a weasel.

POLONIUS. It is backed like a weasel.

HAMLET. Or like a whale.   345

POLONIUS. Very like a whale.

HAMLET. Then I will come to my mother by and by.° [*Aside.*] They fool
me° to the top of my bent.°—I will come by and by.

POLONIUS. I will say so.

[*Exit.*]

HAMLET. "By and by" is easily said. Leave me, friends.   350

[*Exeunt all but* HAMLET.]

'Tis now the very witching time° of night,
When churchyards yawn and hell itself breathes out
Contagion to his world. Now could I drink hot blood
And do such bitter business as the day
Would quake to look on. Soft, now to my mother.   355
O heart, lose not thy nature!° Let not ever
The soul of Nero° enter this firm bosom.
Let me be cruel, not unnatural;
I will speak daggers to her, but use none.
My tongue and soul in this be hypocrites: 360
How in my words soever° she be shent,°
To give them seals° never my soul consent!

Exit.

[3.3] *Enter* KING, ROSENCRANTZ, *and* GUILDENSTERN.

KING. I like him° not, nor stands it safe with us
To let his madness range. Therefore prepare you.
I your commission will forthwith dispatch,°
And he to England shall along with you.
The terms of our estate° may not endure   5
Hazard so near 's as doth hourly grow
Out of his brows.°

GUILDENSTERN.   We will ourselves provide.
Most holy and religious fear° it is
To keep those many bodies safe
That live and feed upon Your Majesty.   10

---

340 presently at once.   **347 by and by** quite soon.   **347–348 fool me** trifle with me,
humor my fooling.   **348 top of my bent** limit of my ability or endurance. (Literally, the
extent to which a bow may be bent.)   **351 witching time** time when spells are cast and
evil is abroad.   **356 nature** natural feeling.   **357 Nero** murderer of his mother, Agrip-
pina.   **361 How . . . soever** however much by my words.   **shent** rebuked.   **362 give
them seals** i.e., confirm them with deeds.   **3.3 Location: The castle.**   **1 him** i.e., his
behavior.   **3 dispatch** prepare, cause to be drawn up.   **5 terms of our estate** circumstances of my royal position.   **7 out of his brows** i.e., from his brain, in the form of plots
and threats.   **8 religious fear** sacred concern.

ROSENCRANTZ. The single and peculiar° life is bound
    With all the strength and armor of the mind
    To keep itself from noyance,° but much more
    That spirit upon whose weal depends and rests
    The lives of many. The cess° of majesty   15
    Dies not alone, but like a gulf° doth draw
    What's near it with it; or it is a massy° wheel
    Fixed on the summit of the highest mount,
    To whose huge spokes ten thousand lesser things
    Are mortised° and adjoined, which, when it falls,°   20
    Each small annexment, petty consequence,°
    Attends° the boisterous ruin. Never alone
    Did the King sigh, but with a general groan.
KING. Arm° you, I pray you, to this speedy voyage,
    For we will fetters put about this fear,   25
    Which now goes too free-footed.
ROSENCRANTZ.   We will haste us.

          Exeunt gentlemen [ROSENCRANTZ *and* GUILDENSTERN].

    Enter POLONIUS.

POLONIUS. My lord, he's going to his mother's closet.
    Behind the arras° I'll convey myself
    To hear the process.° I'll warrant she'll tax him home,°
    And, as you said—and wisely was it said—   30
    'Tis meet° that some more audience than a mother,
    Since nature makes them partial, should o'erhear
    The speech, of vantage.° Fare you well, my liege.
    I'll call upon you ere you go to bed
    And tell you what I know.
KING.   Thanks, dear my lord.   35

                          Exit [POLONIUS].

    O, my offense is rank! It smells to heaven.
    It hath the primal eldest curse° upon't,
    A brother's murder. Pray can I not,
    Though inclination be as sharp as will;°
    My stronger guilt defeats my strong intent,   40
    And like a man to double business bound°
    I stand in pause where I shall first begin,

---

11 single and peculiar individual and private.   **13 noyance** harm.   **15 cess** decease,
cessation.   **16 gulf** whirlpool.   **17 massy** massive.   **20 mortised** fastened (as with a
fitted joint).   **when it falls** i.e., when it descends, like the wheel of Fortune, bringing a
king down with it.   **21 Each . . . consequence** i.e., every hanger-on and unimportant
person or thing connected with the King.   **22 Attends** participates in.   **24 Arm** prepare.   **28 arras** screen of tapestry placed around the walls of household apartments. (On
the Elizabethan stage, the arras was presumably over a door or discovery space in the tiring-house facade.)   **29 process** proceedings.   **tax him home** reprove him severely.
31 meet fitting.   **33 of vantage** from an advantageous place, or, in addition.   **37 the
primal eldest curse** the curse of Cain, the first murderer; he killed his brother Abel.   **39
Though . . . will** though my desire is as strong as my determination.   **41 bound** (1) destined (2) obliged. (The King wants to repent and still enjoy what he has gained.)

And both neglect. What if this cursèd hand
Were thicker than itself with brother's blood,
Is there not rain enough in the sweet heavens   45
To wash it white as snow? Whereto serves mercy
But to confront the visage of offense?°
And what's in prayer but this twofold force,
To be forestallèd° ere we come to fall,
Or pardoned being down? Then I'll look up.   50
My fault is past. But O, what form of prayer
Can serve my turn? "Forgive me my foul murder"?
That cannot be, since I am still possessed
Of those effects for which I did the murder:
My crown, mine own ambition, and my Queen.   55
May one be pardoned and retain th' offense?°
In the corrupted currents° of this world
Offense's gilded hand° may shove by° justice,
And oft 'tis seen the wicked prize° itself
Buys out the law. But 'tis not so above.   60
There° is no shuffling,° there the action lies°
In his° true nature, and we ourselves compelled,
Even to the teeth and forehead° of our faults,
To give in° evidence. What then? What rests?°
Try what repentance can. What can it not?   65
Yet what can it, when one cannot repent?
O wretched state, O bosom black as death,
O limèd° soul, that, struggling to be free,
Are more engaged!° Help, angels! Make assay.°
Bow, stubborn knees, and heart with strings of steel,   70
Be soft as sinews of the newborn babe!
All may be well.

                                                          [He kneels.]

Enter HAMLET.

HAMLET. Now might I do it pat,° now 'a is a-praying;
    And now I'll do 't. [*He draws his sword.*] And so 'a goes to heaven,
    And so am I revenged. That would be scanned:°   75
    A villain kills my father, and for that,
    I, his sole son, do this same villain send
    To heaven.
    Why, this is hire and salary, not revenge.

46–47 Whereto . . . offense what function does mercy serve other than to meet sin face
to face? **49 forestallèd** prevented (from sinning). **56 th' offense** the thing for which
one offended. **57 currents** courses. **58 gilded hand** hand offering gold as a bribe.
shove by thrust aside. **59 wicked prize** prize won by wickedness. **61 There** i.e., in
heaven. **shuffling** escape by trickery. **the action lies** the accusation is made manifest
(a legal metaphor). **62 his** its. **63 to the teeth and forehead** face to face, concealing
nothing. **64 give in** provide. **rests** remains. **68 limèd** caught as with birdlime, a
sticky substance used to ensnare birds. **69 engaged** entangled. **assay** trial (said to
himself). **73 pat** opportunely. **75 would be scanned** needs to be looked into, or,
would be interpreted as follows.

'A took my father grossly, full of bread,°   80
With all his crimes broad blown,° as flush° as May;
And how his audit° stands who knows save° heaven?
But in our circumstance and course of thought°
'Tis heavy with him. And am I then revenged,
To take him in the purging of his soul,   85
When he is fit and seasoned° for his passage?
No!
Up, sword, and know thou a more horrid hent.°

                       [*He puts up his sword.*]

When he is drunk asleep, or in his rage,°
Or in th' incestuous pleasure of his bed,   90
At game,° a-swearing, or about some act
That has no relish° of salvation in 't—
Then trip him, that his heels may kick at heaven,
And that his soul may be as damned and black
As hell, whereto it goes. My mother stays.°   95
This physic° but prolongs thy sickly days.

                                         Exit.

KING. My words fly up, my thoughts remain below.
   Words without thoughts never to heaven go.

                                         Exit.

     [3.4] *Enter* [QUEEN] GERTRUDE *and* POLONIUS.

POLONIUS. 'A will come straight. Look you lay home° to him.
   Tell him his pranks have been too broad° to bear with,
   And that Your Grace hath screened and stood between
   Much heat° and him. I'll shroud° me even here.
   Pray you, be round° with him.   5
HAMLET [*within*]. Mother, Mother, Mother!
QUEEN. I'll warrant you, fear me not.
   Withdraw, I hear him coming.

                 [POLONIUS *hides behind the arras.*]

     Enter HAMLET.

HAMLET. Now, Mother, what's the matter?
QUEEN. Hamlet, thou hast thy father° much offended.   10
HAMLET. Mother, you have my father much offended.

---

80 grossly, full of bread i.e., enjoying his worldly pleasures rather than fasting. (See
Ezekiel 16.49.) **81 crimes broad blown** sins in full bloom. **flush** vigorous. **82
audit** account. **save** except for. **83 in . . . thought** as we see it from our mortal perspective. **86 seasoned** matured, readied. **88 know . . . hent** await to be grasped by
me on a more horrid occasion. **hent** act of seizing. **89 drunk . . . rage** dead drunk, or
in a fit of sexual passion. **91 game** gambling. **92 relish** trace, savor. **95 stays** awaits
(me). **96 physic** purging (by prayer), or, Hamlet's postponement of the killing. **3.4
Location: The Queen's private chamber. 1 lay home** thrust to the heart, reprove
him soundly. **2 broad** unrestrained. **4 Much heat** i.e., the King's anger. **shroud** conceal. (With ironic fitness to Polonius's imminent death. The word is only in the First
Quarto: the Second Quarto and the Folio read "silence.") **5 round** blunt. **10 thy father**
i.e., your stepfather, Claudius.

QUEEN. Come, come, you answer with an idle° tongue.

HAMLET. Go, go you question with a wicked tongue.

QUEEN. Why, how now, Hamlet?

HAMLET.   What's the matter now?

QUEEN. Have you forgot me?°

HAMLET.   No, by the rood,° not so: 15
    You are the Queen your husband's brother's wife,
    And—would it were not so!—you are my mother.

QUEEN. Nay, then, I'll set those to you that can speak.°

HAMLET. Come, come, and sit you down; you shall not budge.
    You go not till I set you up a glass   20
    Where you may see the inmost part of you.

QUEEN. What wilt thou do? Thou wilt not murder me?
    Help, ho!

POLONIUS [behind the arras]. What ho! Help!

HAMLET [drawing]. How now? A rat? Dead for a ducat,° dead!   25
               [He thrusts his rapier through the arras.]

POLONIUS [behind the arras]. O, I am slain!   [He falls and dies.]

QUEEN.   O me, what hast thou done?

HAMLET. Nay, I know not. Is it the King?

QUEEN. O, what a rash and bloody deed is this!

HAMLET. A bloody deed—almost as bad, good Mother,
    As kill a King, and marry with his brother.   30

QUEEN. As kill a King!

HAMLET.   Ay, lady, it was my word.
       [He parts the arras and discovers POLONIUS.]
    Thou wretched, rash, intruding fool, farewell!
    I took thee for thy better. Take thy fortune.
    Thou find'st to be too busy° is some danger.—
    Leave wringing of your hands. Peace, sit you down,   35
    And let me wring your heart, for so I shall,
    If it be made of penetrable stuff,
    If damnèd custom° have not brazed° it so
    That it be proof° and bulwark against sense.°

QUEEN. What have I done, that thou dar'st wag thy tongue   40
    In noise so rude against me?

HAMLET.   Such an act
    That blurs the grace and blush of modesty,
    Calls virtue hypocrite, takes off the rose
    From the fair forehead of an innocent love
    And sets a blister° there, makes marriage vows   45
    As false as dicers' oaths. O, such a deed
    As from the body of contraction° plucks
    The very soul, and sweet religion makes°

---

12 idle foolish. **15 forgot me** i.e., forgotten that I am your mother. **rood** cross of Christ. **18 speak** i.e., to someone so rude. **25 Dead for a ducat** i.e., I bet a ducat he's dead; or a ducat is his life's fee. **34 busy** nosey. **38 damnèd custom** habitual wickedness. **brazed** brazened, hardened. **39 proof** armor. **sense** feeling. **45 sets a blister** i.e., brands as a harlot. **47 contraction** the marriage contract. **48 sweet religion makes** i.e., makes marriage vows.

A rhapsody° of words. Heaven's face does glow
O'er this solidity and compound mass   50
With tristful visage, as against the doom,
Is thought-sick at the act.°

QUEEN.   Ay me, what act,
That roars so loud and thunders in the index?°

HAMLET [*showing her two likenesses*]. Look here upon this picture, and
  on this,
The counterfeit presentment° of two brothers.   55
See what a grace was seated on this brow:
Hyperion's° curls, the front° of Jove himself,
An eye like Mars° to threaten and command,
A station° like the herald Mercury°
New-lighted° on a heaven-kissing hill—   60
A combination and a form indeed
Where every god did seem to set his seal?°
To give the world assurance of a man.
This was your husband. Look you now what follows:
Here is your husband, like a mildewed ear,°   65
Blasting° his wholesome brother. Have you eyes?
Could you on this far mountain leave° to feed
And batten° on this moor?° Ha, have you eyes?
You cannot call it love, for at your age
The heyday° in the blood° is tame, it's humble,   70
And waits upon the judgment, and what judgment
Would step from this to this? Sense,° sure, you have,
Else could you not have motion, but sure that sense
Is apoplexed,° for madness would not err,°
Nor sense to ecstasy was ne'er so thralled,   75
But° it reserved some quantity of choice
To serve in such a difference.° What devil was 't
That thus hath cozened° you at hoodman-blind?°
Eyes without feeling, feeling without sight,

---

49 rhapsody senseless string. **49–52 Heaven's . . . act** heaven's face blushes at this solid world compounded of the various elements, with sorrowful face as though the day of doom were near, and is sick with horror at the deed (i.e., Gertrude's marriage). **53 index** table of contents, prelude or preface. **55 counterfeit presentment** portrayed representation. **57 Hyperion's** the sun god's. **front** brow. **58 Mars** god of war. **59 station** manner of standing. **Mercury** winged messenger of the gods. **60 New-lighted** newly alighted. **62 set his seal** i.e., affix his approval. **65 ear** i.e., of grain. **66 Blasting** blighting. **67 leave** cease. **68 batten** gorge. **moor** barren or marshy ground (suggesting also "dark-skinned"). **70 heyday** state of excitement. **blood** passion. **72 Sense** perception through the five senses (the functions of the middle or sensible soul). **74 apoplexed** paralyzed. (Hamlet goes on to explain that, without such a paralysis of will, mere madness would not so err, nor would the five senses so enthrall themselves to *ecstasy* or lunacy; even such deranged states of mind would be able to make the obvious choice between Hamlet Senior and Claudius.) **err** so err. **76 But** but that. **77 To . . . difference** to help in making a choice between two such men. **78 cozened** cheated. **hoodman-blind** blindman's bluff. (In this game, says Hamlet, the devil must have pushed Claudius toward Gertrude while she was blindfolded.)

Ears without hands or eyes, smelling sans° all,   80
Or but a sickly part of one true sense
Could not so mope.° O shame, where is thy blush?
Rebellious hell,
If thou canst mutine° in a matron's bones,
To flaming youth let virtue be as wax   85
And melt in her own fire.° Proclaim no shame
When the compulsive ardor gives the charge,
Since frost itself as actively doth burn,
And reason panders will.°

QUEEN. O Hamlet, speak no more!   90
Thou turn'st mine eyes into my very soul,
And there I see such black and grainèd° spots
As will not leave their tinct.°

HAMLET.   Nay, but to live
In the rank sweat of an enseamèd° bed,
Stewed° in corruption, honeying and making love   95
Over the nasty sty!

QUEEN. O, speak to me no more!
These words like daggers enter in my ears.
No more, sweet Hamlet!

HAMLET.   A murderer and a villain,
A slave that is not twentieth part the tithe°   100
Of your precedent lord,° a vice° of kings,
A cutpurse of the empire and the rule,
That from a shelf the precious diadem stole
And put it in his pocket!

QUEEN. No more!   105

Enter GHOST [*in his nightgown*].

HAMLET. A king of shreds and patches°—
Save me, and hover o'er me with your wings,
You heavenly guards! What would your gracious figure?

QUEEN. Alas, he's mad!

HAMLET. Do you not come your tardy son to chide,   110
That, lapsed° in time and passion, lets go by
Th' important° acting of your dread command?
O, say!

---

80 sans without.   **82 mope** be dazed, act aimlessly.   **84 mutine** incite mutiny.   **85–86
be as wax . . . fire** melt like a candle or stick of sealing wax held over the candle flame.
86–89 Proclaim . . . will call it no shameful business when the compelling ardor of
youth delivers the attack, i.e., commits lechery, since the *frost* of advanced age burns with
as active a fire of lust and reason perverts itself by fomenting lust rather than restraining it.
92 grainèd dyed in grain, indelible.   **93 leave their tinct** surrender their color.   **94
enseamèd** saturated in the grease and filth of passionate lovemaking.   **95 Stewed**
soaked, bathed (with a suggestion of "stew," brothel).   **100 tithe** tenth part.   **101
precedent lord** former husband.   **vice** buffoon. (A reference to the Vice of the morality
plays.)   **106 shreds and patches** i.e., motley, the traditional costume of the clown or
fool.   **111 lapsed** delaying.   **112 important** importunate, urgent.

GHOST. Do not forget. This visitation
    Is but to whet thy almost blunted purpose.   115
    But look, amazement° on thy mother sits.
    O, step between her and her fighting soul!
    Conceit° in weakest bodies strongest works.
    Speak to her, Hamlet.
HAMLET.   How is it with you, lady?
QUEEN. Alas, how is 't with you,   120
    That you do bend your eye on vacancy,
    And with th' incorporal° air do hold discourse?
    Forth at your eyes your spirits wildly peep,
    And, as the sleeping soldiers in th' alarm,°
    Your bedded° hair, like life in excrements,°   125
    Start up and stand on end. O gentle son,
    Upon the heat and flame of thy distemper°
    Sprinkle cool patience. Whereon do you look?
HAMLET. On him, on him! Look you how pale he glares!
    His form and cause conjoined,° preaching to stones,   130
    Would make them capable.°—Do not look upon me,
    Lest with this piteous action you convert
    My stern effects.° Then what I have to do
    Will want true color—tears perchance for blood.°
QUEEN. To whom do you speak this?   135
HAMLET. Do you see nothing there?
QUEEN. Nothing at all, yet all that is I see.
HAMLET. Nor did you nothing hear?
QUEEN. No, nothing but ourselves.
HAMLET. Why, look you there, look how it steals away!   140
    My father, in his habit° as° he lived!
    Look where he goes even now out at the portal!

                                  Exit GHOST.

QUEEN. This is the very° coinage of your brain.
    This bodiless creation ecstasy
    Is very cunning in.°   145
HAMLET. Ecstasy?
    My pulse as yours doth temperately keep time,
    And makes as healthful music. It is not madness
    That I have uttered. Bring me to the test,
    And I the matter will reword,° which madness   150

---

116 amazement distraction.   **118 Conceit** imagination.   **122 incorporal** immaterial.   **124 as . . . alarm** like soldiers called out of sleep by an alarm.   **125 bedded** laid flat.   **like life in excrements** i.e., as though hair, an outgrowth of the body, had a life of its own. (Hair was thought to be lifeless because it lacks sensation, and so its standing on end would be unnatural and ominous.)   **127 distemper** disorder.   **130 His . . . conjoined** his appearance joined to his cause for speaking.   **131 capable** receptive.   **132–133 convert . . . effects** divert me from my stern duty.   **134 want . . . blood** lack plausibility so that (with a play on the normal sense of *color*) I shall shed colorless tears instead of blood.   **141 habit** clothes. **as** as when.   **143 very** mere.   **144–145 This . . . in** madness is skillful in creating this kind of hallucination.   **150 reword** repeat word for word.

Would gambol° from. Mother, for love of grace,
Lay not that flattering unction° to your soul
That not your trespass but my madness speaks.
It will but skin° and film the ulcerous place,
Whiles rank corruption, mining° all within,   155
Infects unseen. Confess yourself to heaven,
Repeat what's past, avoid what is to come,
And do not spread the compost° on the weeds
To make them ranker. Forgive me this my virtue;°
For in the fatness° of these pursy° times   160
Virtue itself of vice must pardon beg,
Yea, curb° and woo for leave° to do him good.

QUEEN. O Hamlet, thou hast cleft my heart in twain.

HAMLET. O, throw away the worser part of it,
And live the purer with the other half.   165
Good night. But go not to my uncle's bed;
Assume a virtue, if you have it not.
That monster, custom, who all sense doth eat,°
Of habits devil,° is angel yet in this,
That to the use of actions fair and good   170
He likewise gives a frock or livery°
That aptly° is put on. Refrain tonight,
And that shall lend a kind of easiness
To the next abstinence; the next more easy;
For use° almost can change the stamp of nature,°   175
And either° . . . the devil, or throw him out
With wondrous potency. Once more, good night;
And when you are desirous to be blest,
I'll blessing beg of you.° For this same lord,

                                        [*Pointing to* POLONIUS.]

I do repent; but heaven hath pleased it so   180
To punish me with this, and this with me,
That I must be their scourge and minister.°
I will bestow° him, and will answer° well
The death I gave him. So again, good night.
I must be cruel only to be kind.   185

---

151 gambol skip away. **152 unction** ointment. **154 skin** grow a skin for. **155 mining** working under the surface. **158 compost** manure. **159 this my virtue** my virtuous talk in reproving you. **160 fatness** grossness. **pursy** flabby, out of shape. **162 curb** bow, bend the knee. **leave** permission. **168 who . . . eat** which consumes all proper or natural feeling, all sensibility. **169 Of habits devil** devil-like in prompting evil habits. **171 livery** an outer appearance, a customary garb (and hence a predisposition easily assumed in time of stress). **172 aptly** readily. **175 use** habit. **the stamp of nature** our inborn traits. **176 And either** (A defective line, usually emended by inserting the word *master* after *either*, following the Fourth Quarto and early editors.) **178–179 when . . . you** i.e., when you are ready to be penitent and seek God's blessing, I will ask your blessing as a dutiful son should. **182 their scourge and minister** i.e., agent of heavenly retribution. (By *scourge*, Hamlet also suggests that he himself will eventually suffer punishment in the process of fulfilling heaven's will.) **183 bestow** stow, dispose of. **answer** account or pay for.

This° bad begins, and worse remains behind.°
One word more, good lady.
QUEEN.   What shall I do?
HAMLET. Not this by no means that I bid you do:
Let the bloat° King tempt you again to bed,
Pinch wanton° on your cheek, call you his mouse,   190
And let him, for a pair of reechy° kisses,
Or paddling° in your neck with his damned fingers,
Make you to ravel all this matter out°
That I essentially am not in madness,
But mad in craft.° 'Twere good° you let him know,   195
For who that's but a Queen, fair, sober, wise,
Would from a paddock,° from a bat, a gib,°
Such dear concernings° hide? Who would do so?
No, in despite of sense and secrecy,°
Unpeg the basket° on the house's top,   200
Let the birds fly, and like the famous ape,°
To try conclusions,° in the basket creep
And break your own neck down.°
QUEEN. Be thou assured, if words be made of breath,
And breath of life, I have no life to breathe   205
What thou hast said to me.
HAMLET. I must to England. You know that?
QUEEN.   Alack,
I had forgot. 'Tis so concluded on.
HAMLET. There's letters sealed, and my two schoolfellows,
Whom I will trust as I will adders fanged,   210
They bear the mandate; they must sweep my way
And marshall me to knavery.° Let it work.°
For 'tis the sport to have the enginer°
Hoist with° his own petard,° and 't shall go hard
But I will° delve one yard below their mines°   215
And blow them at the moon. O, 'tis most sweet
When in one line° two crafts° directly meet.

---

186 This i.e., the killing of Polonius. **behind** to come. **189 bloat** bloated. **190
Pinch wanton** i.e., leave his love pinches on your cheeks, branding you as wanton. **191
reechy** dirty, filthy. **192 paddling** fingering amorously. **193 ravel . . . out** unravel,
disclose. **195 in craft** by cunning. **good** (Said sarcastically; also the following eight
lines.) **197 paddock** toad. **gib** tomcat. **198 dear concernings** important affairs.
199 sense and secrecy secrecy that common sense requires. **200 Unpeg the basket**
open the cage, i.e., let out the secret. **201 famous ape** (In a story now lost.) **202 try
conclusions** test the outcome (in which the ape apparently enters a cage from which
birds have been released and then tries to fly out of the cage as they have done, falling to
its death). **203 down** in the fall; utterly. **211–212 sweep . . . knavery** sweep a path
before me and conduct me to some *knavery* or treachery prepared for me. **212 work**
proceed. **213 enginer** maker of military contrivances. **214 Hoist with** blown up by.
petard an explosive used to blow in a door or make a breach. **214–215 't shall . . .
will** unless luck is against me, I will. **215 mines** tunnels used in warfare to undermine
the enemy's emplacements; Hamlet will countermine by going under their mines. **217
in one line** i.e., mines and countermines on a collision course, or the countermines directly below the mines. **crafts** acts of guile, plots.

This man shall set me packing.°
I'll lug the guts into the neighbor room.
Mother, good night indeed. This counselor   220
Is now most still, most secret, and most grave,
Who was in life a foolish prating knave.—
Come, sir, to draw toward an end° with you.—
Good night, Mother.

                              Exeunt [*separately,* HAMLET *dragging in* POLONIUS].

[4.1] *Enter* KING *and* QUEEN,° *with* ROSENCRANTZ *and* GUILDENSTERN.

KING. There's matter° in these sighs, these profound heaves.°
    You must translate: 'tis fit we understand them.
    Where is your son?
QUEEN. Bestow this place on us a little while.
                              [*Exeunt* ROSENCRANTZ *and* GUILDENSTERN.]
    Ah, mine own lord, what have I seen tonight!   5
KING. What, Gertrude? How does Hamlet?
QUEEN. Mad as the sea and wind when both contend
    Which is the mightier. In his lawless fit,
    Behind the arras hearing something stir,
    Whips out his rapier, cries, "A rat, a rat!"   10
    And in this brainish apprehension° kills
    The unseen good old man.
KING.   O heavy° deed!
    It had been so with us,° had we been there.
    His liberty is full of threats to all—
    To you yourself, to us, to everyone.   15
    Alas, how shall this bloody deed be answered?°
    It will be laid to us, whose providence°
    Should have kept short,° restrained, and out of haunt°
    This mad young man. But so much was our love,
    We would not understand what was most fit,   20
    But, like the owner of a foul disease,
    To keep it from divulging,° let it feed
    Even on the pith of life. Where is he gone?
QUEEN. To draw apart the body he hath killed,
    O'er whom his very madness, like some ore°   25

---

218 set me packing set me to making schemes, and set me to lugging (him), and, also,
send me off in a hurry.   **223 draw . . . end** finish up (with a pun on *draw,* "pull").   **4.1
Location: The castle.   s.d. Enter . . . Queen** (Some editors argue that Gertrude never
exits in 3.4 and that the scene is continuous here, as suggested in the Folio, but the Second
Quarto marks an entrance for her and at line 35 Claudius speaks of Gertrude's *closet* as
though it were elsewhere. A short time has elapsed, during which the King has become
aware of her highly wrought emotional state.)   **1 matter** significance.   **heaves** heavy
sighs.   **11 brainish apprehension** headstrong conception.   **12 heavy** grievous.   **13
us** i.e., me. (The royal "we"; also in line 15.)   **16 answered** explained.   **17 providence**
foresight.   **18 short** i.e., on a short tether.   **out of haunt** secluded.   **22 divulging** becoming evident.   **25 ore** vein of gold.

Among a mineral° of metals base,
Shows itself pure: 'a weeps for what is done.
KING. O Gertrude, come away!
The sun no sooner shall the mountains touch
But we will ship him hence, and this vile deed   30
We must with all our majesty and skill
Both countenance° and excuse.—Ho, Guildenstern!

Enter ROSENCRANTZ *and* GUILDENSTERN.

Friends both, go join you with some further aid.
Hamlet in madness hath Polonius slain,
And from his mother's closet hath he dragged him.   35
Go seek him out, speak fair, and bring the body
Into the chapel. I pray you, haste in this.
                    [Exeunt ROSENCRANTZ and GUILDENSTERN.]
Come, Gertrude, we'll call up our wisest friends
And let them know both what we mean to do
And what's untimely done°   40
Whose whisper o'er the world's diameter,°
As level° as the cannon to his blank,°
Transports his poisoned shot, may miss our name
And hit the woundless° air. O, come away!
My soul is full of discord and dismay.   45
                                              Exeunt.

[4.2] *Enter* HAMLET.

HAMLET. Safely stowed.
ROSENCRANTZ, GUILDENSTERN [*within*]. Hamlet! Lord Hamlet!
HAMLET. But soft, what noise? Who calls on Hamlet? O, here they come.

Enter ROSENCRANTZ *and* GUILDENSTERN.

ROSENCRANTZ. What have you done, my lord, with the dead body?
HAMLET. Compounded it with dust, whereto 'tis kin.   5
ROSENCRANTZ. Tell us where 'tis, that we may take it thence And bear it
    to the chapel.
HAMLET. Do not believe it.
ROSENCRANTZ. Believe what?
HAMLET. That I can keep your counsel and not mine own.° Besides, to   10
    be demanded of° a sponge, what replication° should be made by
    the son of a king?

---

26 mineral mine.   **32 countenance** put the best face on.   **40 And . . . done** (A defective line; conjectures as to the missing words include *So, haply, slander* [Capell and
others]; *For, haply, slander* [Theobald and others]; and *So envious slander* [Jenkins].)
41 diameter extent from side to side.   **42 As level** with as direct aim.   **his blank** its
target at point-blank range.   **44 woundless** invulnerable.   **4.2 Location: The castle.**
10 That . . . own i.e., that I can follow your advice (by telling where the body is) and
still keep my own secret.   **11 demanded of** questioned by.   **replication** reply.

ROSENCRANTZ. Take you me for a sponge, my lord?

HAMLET. Ay, sir, that soaks up the King's countenance,° his rewards, his
authorities.° But such officers do the King best service in the end.   15
He keeps them, like an ape, an apple, in the corner of his jaw, first
mouthed to be last swallowed. When he needs what you have
gleaned, it is but squeezing you, and, sponge, you shall be dry
again.

ROSENCRANTZ. I understand you not, my lord.   20

HAMLET. I am glad of it. A knavish speech sleeps in° a foolish ear.

ROSENCRANTZ. My lord, you must tell us where the body is and go with
us to the King.

HAMLET. The body is with the King, but the King is not with the body.°
The King is a thing—   25

GUILDENSTERN. A thing, my lord?

HAMLET. Of nothing.° Bring me to him. Hide fox, and all after!°

Exeunt [running].

[4.3] *Enter* KING, *and two or three.*

KING. I have sent to seek him, and to find the body.
How dangerous is it that this man goes loose!
Yet must not we put the strong law on him.
He's loved of° the distracted° multitude,
Who like not in their judgment, but their eyes,°   5
And where 'tis so, th' offender's scourge° is weighed,°
But never the offense. To bear all smooth and even,°
This sudden sending him away must seem
Deliberate pause.° Diseases desperate grown
By desperate appliance° are relieved,   10
Or not at all.

Enter ROSENCRANTZ, GUILDENSTERN, *and all the rest.*

How now, what hath befall'n?

ROSENCRANTZ. Where the dead body is bestowed, my lord,
We cannot get from him.

KING.   But where is he?

ROSENCRANTZ. Without, my lord; guarded, to know your pleasure.

---

14 countenance favor.   **15 authorities** delegated power, influence.   **21 sleeps in** has
no meaning to.   **24 The . . . body** (Perhaps alludes to the legal commonplace of "the
king's two bodies," which draw a distinction between the sacred office of kingship and
the particular mortal who possessed it at any given time. Hence, although Claudius's
body is necessarily a part of him, true kingship is not contained in it. Similarly, Claudius
will have Polonius's body when it is found, but there is no kingship in this business either.)   **27 Of nothing** (1) of no account (2) lacking the essence of kingship, as in lines
24–25 and note.   **Hide . . . after** (An old signal cry in the game of hide-and-seek, suggesting that Hamlet now runs away from them.)   **4.3 Location: The castle.   4 of** by.
distracted fickle, unstable.   **5 Who . . . eyes** who choose not by judgment but by appearance.   **6 scourge** punishment. (Literally, blow with a whip.)   **weighed** sympathetically considered.   **7 To . . . even** to manage the business in an unprovocative way.
9 Deliberate pause carefully considered action.   **10 appliance** remedies.

KING. Bring him before us.
ROSENCRANTZ.   Ho! Bring in the lord.   15

    They enter [with hamlet].

KING. Now, Hamlet, where's Polonius?
HAMLET. At supper.
KING. At supper? Where?
HAMLET. Not where he eats, but where 'a is eaten. A certain convocation
    of politic worms° are e'en° at him. Your worm° is your only   20
    emperor for diet.° We fat all creatures else to fat us, and we fat our-
    selves for maggots. Your fat king and your lean beggar is but vari-
    able service°—two dishes, but to one table. That's the end.
KING. Alas, alas!
HAMLET. A many may fish with the worm that hath eat° of a king, and eat   25
    of the fish that hath fed of that worm.
KING. What dost thou mean by this?
HAMLET. Nothing but to show you how a king may go a progress°
    through the guts of a beggar.
KING. Where is Polonius?   30
HAMLET. In heaven. Send thither to see. If your messenger find him not
    there, seek him i' th' other place yourself. But if indeed you find him
    not within this month, you shall nose him as you go up the stairs
    into the lobby.
KING [*to some attendants*]. Go seek him there.   35
HAMLET. 'A will stay till you come.

                            [*Exeunt attendants.*]

KING. Hamlet, this deed, for thine especial safety—
    Which we do tender,° as we dearly° grieve
    For that which thou hast done—must send thee hence
    With fiery quickness. Therefore prepare thyself.   40
    The bark° is ready, and the wind at help,
    Th' associates tend,° and everything is bent°
    For England.
HAMLET. For England!
KING. Ay, Hamlet.   45
HAMLET. Good.
KING. So is it, if thou knew'st our purposes.
HAMLET. I see a cherub° that sees them. But come, for England!
    Farewell, dear mother.
KING. Thy loving father, Hamlet.   50

---

20 politic worms crafty worms (suited to a master spy like Polonius).   **e'en** even now.
Your worm your average worm. (Compare *your fat king and your lean beggar* in line
22.)   **21 diet** food, eating (with a punning reference to the Diet of Worms, a famous
convocation held in 1521).   **22–23 variable service** different courses of a single meal.
25 eat eaten. (Pronounced *et*.)   **28 progress** royal journey of state.   **38 tender** regard,
hold dear.   **dearly** intensely.   **41 bark** sailing vessel.   **42 tend** wait.   **bent** in readiness.   **48 cherub** (Cherubim are angels of knowledge. Hamlet hints that both he and
heaven are onto Claudius's tricks.)

HAMLET. My mother. Father and mother is man and wife, man and wife
    is one flesh, and so, my mother. Come, for England!

                                                                         Exit.

KING. Follow him at foot;° tempt him with speed aboard.
    Delay it not. I'll have him hence tonight.
    Away! For everything is sealed and done   55
    That else leans on° th' affair. Pray you, make haste.
                                     [Exeunt all but the KING.*]*
    And, England,° if my love thou hold'st at aught°—
    As my great power thereof may give thee sense,°
    Since yet thy cicatrice° looks raw and red
    After the Danish sword, and thy free awe°   60
    Pays homage to us—thou mayst not coldly set°
    Our sovereign process,° which imports at full,°
    By letters congruing° to that effect,
    The present° death of Hamlet. Do it, England,
    For like the hectic° in my blood he rages,   65
    And thou must cure me. Till I know 'tis done,
    Howe'er my haps,° my joys were ne'er begun.
                                          Exit.

    [4.4] *Enter* FORTINBRAS *with his army over the stage.*

FORTINBRAS. Go, Captain, from me greet the Danish king.
    Tell him that by his license° Fortinbras
    Craves the conveyance of° a promised march
    Over his kingdom. You know the rendezvous.
    If that His Majesty would aught with us,   5
    We shall express our duty° in his eye;°
    And let him know so.
CAPTAIN. I will do 't, my lord.
FORTINBRAS. Go softly° on.
                            [Exeunt all but the CAPTAIN.*]*

    Enter HAMLET, ROSENCRANTZ, [GUILDENSTERN,] *etc.*

HAMLET. Good sir, whose powers° are these?   10
CAPTAIN. They are of Norway, sir.
HAMLET. How purposed, sir, I pray you?
CAPTAIN. Against some part of Poland.
HAMLET. Who commands them, sir?
CAPTAIN. The nephew to old Norway. Fortinbras.   15

---

53 at foot close behind, at heel.   **56 leans on** bears upon, is related to.   **57 England**
i.e., King of England.   **at aught** at any value.   **58 As . . . sense** for so my great power
may give you a just appreciation of the importance of valuing my love.   **59 cicatrice** scar.
60 free awe voluntary show of respect.   **61 coldly set** regard with indifference.
62 process command.   **imports at full** conveys specific directions for.   **63 congruing**
agreeing.   **64 present** immediate.   **65 hectic** persistent fever.   **67 haps** fortunes.
4.4 Location: The coast of Denmark.   2 license permission.   **3 the conveyance of**
escort during.   **6 duty** respect.   **eye** presence.   **9 softly** slowly, circumspectly.
10 powers forces.

HAMLET. Goes it against the main° of Poland, sir,
   Or for some frontier?
CAPTAIN. Truly to speak, and with no addition,°
   We go to gain a little patch of ground
   That hath in it no profit but the name.
   To pay° five ducats, five, I would not farm it;°   20
   Nor will it yield to Norway or the Pole
   A ranker° rate, should it be sold in fee.°
HAMLET. Why, then the Polack never will defend it.
CAPTAIN. Yes, it is already garrisoned.   25
HAMLET. Two thousand souls and twenty thousand ducats
   Will not debate the question of this straw.°
   This is th' impostume° of much wealth and peace,
   That inward breaks, and shows no cause without
   Why the man dies. I humbly thank you, sir.   30
CAPTAIN. God b' wi' you, sir.

                                          [*Exit.*]

ROSENCRANTZ.   Will 't please you go, my lord?
HAMLET. I'll be with you straight. Go a little before.

                          [*Exeunt all except* HAMLET.]
   How all occasions do inform against° me
   And spur my dull revenge! What is a man,
   If his chief good and market of° his time   35
   Be but to sleep and feed? A beast, no more.
   Sure he that made us with such large discourse,°
   Looking before and after,° gave us not
   That capability and godlike reason
   To fust° in us unused. Now, whether it be   40
   Bestial oblivion,° or some craven° scruple
   Of thinking too precisely° on th' event°—
   A thought which, quartered, hath but one part wisdom
   And ever three parts coward—I do not know
   Why yet I live to say "This thing's to do,"   45
   Sith° I have cause, and will, and strength, and means
   To do 't. Examples gross° as earth exhort me:
   Witness this army of such mass and charge,°
   Led by a delicate and tender° prince,
   Whose spirit with divine ambition puffed   50
   Makes mouths° at the invisible event,°

---

16 main main part   **18 addition** exaggeration.   **21 To pay** i.e., for a yearly rental of.
21 farm it take a lease of it.   **23 ranker** higher.   **in fee** fee simple, outright.   **27 debate . . . straw** settle this trifling matter.   **28 impostume** abscess.   **33 inform against** denounce, betray; take shape against.   **35 market of** profit of, compensation for.   **37 discourse** power of reasoning.   **38 Looking before and after** able to review past events and anticipate the future.   **40 fust** grow moldy.   **41 oblivion** forgetfulness.   **craven** cowardly.   **42 precisely** scrupulously.   **event** outcome.   **46 Sith** since.   **47 gross** obvious.   **48 charge** expense.   **49 delicate and tender** of fine and youthful qualities.   **51 Makes mouths** makes scornful faces   **invisible event** unforeseeable outcome.

Exposing what is moral and unsure
To all that fortune, death, and danger dare,°
Even for an eggshell. Rightly to be great
Is not to stir without great argument,   55
But greatly to find quarrel in a straw
When honor's at the stake.° How stand I, then,
That have a father killed, a mother stained,
Excitements of° my reason and my blood,
And let all sleep, while to my shame I see   60
The imminent death of twenty thousand men
That for a fantasy° and trick° of fame
Go to their graves like beds, fight for a plot°
Whereon the numbers cannot try the cause,°
Which is not tomb enough and continent°   65
To hide the slain? O, from this time forth
My thoughts be bloody or be nothing worth!

                                                                Exit.

[4.5]   *Enter* HORATIO, [QUEEN] GERTRUDE, *and a* GENTLEMAN.

QUEEN. I will not speak with her.
GENTLEMAN.   She is importunate,
    Indeed distract.° Her mood will needs be pitied.
QUEEN. What would she have?
GENTLEMAN. She speaks much of her father, says she hears
    There's tricks° i' the world, and hems,° and beats her heart,°   5
    Spurns enviously at straws,° speaks things in doubt°
    That carry but half sense. Her speech is nothing,
    Yet the unshapèd use° of it doth move
    The hearers to collection;° they yawn° at it,
    And botch° the words up fit to their own thoughts,   10
    Which,° as her winks and nods and gestures yield° them,
    Indeed would make one think there might be thought,°
    Though nothing sure, yet much unhappily.°
HORATIO. 'Twere good she were spoken with, for she may strew
    Dangerous conjectures in ill-breeding° minds.   15

---

53 dare could do (to him).   **54–57 Rightly . . . stake** true greatness does not normally
consist of rushing into action over some trivial provocation; however, when one's honor is
involved, even a trifling insult requires that one respond greatly (?).   **at the stake**
(A metaphor from gambling or bear-baiting.)   **59 Excitements of** promptings by.   **62**
fantasy fanciful caprice, illusion.   **trick** trifle, deceit.   **63 plot** plot of ground.   **64**
Whereon . . . cause on which there is insufficient room for the soldiers needed to engage
in a military contest.   **65 continent** receptacle; container.   **4.5 Location: The castle.**
2 distract distracted.   **5 tricks** deceptions.   **hems** makes "hmm" sounds.   **5 heart** i.e.,
breast.   **6 Spurns . . . straws** kicks spitefully, takes offense at trifles.   **in doubt** obscurely.   **8 unshapèd use** incoherent manner.   **9 collection** inference, a guess at some
sort of meaning.   **yawn** gape, wonder; grasp. (The Folio reading, *aim,* is possible.)   **10**
botch patch.   **11 Which** which words.   **yield** deliver, represent.   **12 thought** intended.
13 unhappily unpleasantly near the truth, shrewdly.   **15 ill-breeding** prone to suspect
the worst and to make mischief.

QUEEN. Let her come in.

                                                    [*Exit* GENTLEMAN]

[*Aside*.] To my sick soul, as sin's true nature is,
Each toy° seems prologue to some great amiss.°
So full of artless jealousy is guilt,
It spills itself in fearing to be spilt.°   20

    Enter OPHELIA° [*distracted*].

OPHELIA. Where is the beauteous majesty of Denmark?
QUEEN. How now, Ophelia?
OPHELIA [*she sings*].
    "How should I your true love know
      From another one?
    By his cockle hat° and staff,   25
      And his sandal shoon."°
QUEEN. Alas, sweet lady, what imports this song?
OPHELIA. Say you? Nay, pray you, mark.
    "He is dead and gone, lady,   [*Song.*]
      He is dead and gone;   30
    At his head a grass-green turf,
      At his heels a stone."
    O, ho!
QUEEN. Nay, but Ophelia—
OPHELIA. Pray you, mark.   [*Sings.*] 35
    "White his shroud as the mountain snow"—

    Enter KING.

QUEEN. Alas, look here, my lord.
OPHELIA.
    "Larded° with sweet flowers;   [*Song.*]
    Which bewept to the ground did not go
      With true-love showers."°   40
KING. How do you, pretty lady?
OPHELIA. Well, God 'ild° you! They say the owl° was a baker's daughter.
    Lord, we know what we are, but know not what we may be. God
    be at your table!
KING. Conceit° upon her father.   45
OPHELIA. Pray let's have no words of this; but when they ask you what it
    means, say you this:
    "Tomorrow is Saint Valentine's day,   [*Song.*]

---

18 toy trifle. **amiss** calamity. **19–20 So . . . split** guilt is so full of suspicion that it un-
skillfully betrays itself in fearing betrayal. **20 s.d. Enter Ophelia** (In the First Quarto,
Ophelia enters, "Playing on a lute, and her hair down, singing.") **25 cockle hat** hat with
cockle-shell stuck in it as a sign that the wearer had been a pilgrim to the shrine of Saint
James of Compostela in Spain. **26 shoon** shoes. **38 Larded** decorated. **40 showers**
i.e., tears. **42 God 'ild** God yield or reward. **owl** (Refers to a legend about a baker's
daughter who was turned into an owl for being ungenerous when Jesus begged a loaf of
bread.) **45 Conceit** brooding.

> All in the morning betime,°
> And I a maid at your window,   50
>   To be your Valentine.
> Then up he rose, and donned his clothes,
>   And dupped° the chamber door,
> Let in the maid, that out a maid
>   Never departed more."   55

KING. Pretty Ophelia—

OPHELIA. Indeed, la, without an oath, I'll make an end on 't: [*Sings.*]
> "By Gis° and by Saint Charity,
>   Alack, and fie for shame!
> Young men will do 't, if they come to 't;   60
>   By Cock,° they are to blame.
> Quoth she, 'Before you tumbled me.
>   You promised me to wed.'"

He answers:
> "'So would I ha' done, by yonder sun,   65
>   An° thou hadst not come to my bed.'"

KING. How long hath she been thus?

OPHELIA. I hope all will be well. We must be patient, but I cannot choose
but weep to think they would lay him i' the cold ground. My
brother shall know of it. And so I thank you for your good counsel. 70
Come, my coach! Good night, ladies, good night, sweet ladies, good
night, good night.

[*Exit.*]

KING [*to* HORATIO]. Follow her close. Give her good watch, I pray you.

[*Exit* HORATIO.]

> O, this is the poison of deep grief; it springs
> All from her father's death—and now behold!   75
> O Gertrude, Gertrude,
> When sorrows come, they come not single spies,°
> But in battalions. First, her father slain;
> Next, your son gone, and he most violent author
> Of his own just remove;° the people muddied,°   80
> Thick and unwholesome in their thoughts and whispers
> For good Polonius' death— and we have done but greenly,°
> In hugger-mugger° to inter him; poor Ophelia
> Divided from herself and her fair judgment.
> Without the which we are pictures or mere beasts;   85
> Last, and as much containing° as all these,
> Her brother is in secret come from France,
> Feeds on this wonder, keeps himself in clouds,°

---

49 betime early.   **53 dupped** did up, opened.   **58 Gis** Jesus.   **61 Cock** (A perversion
of "God" in oaths; here also with a quibble on the slang word for penis.)   **66 An** if.   **77**
spies scouts sent in advance of the main force.   **80 remove** removal.   **muddied** stirred
up, confused.   **82 greenly** in an inexperienced way, foolishly.   **83 hugger-mugger**
secret haste.   **86 as much containing** as full of serious matter.   **88 Feeds . . . clouds**
feeds his resentment or shocked grievance, holds himself inscrutable and aloof amid all
this rumor.

And wants° not buzzers° to infect his ear
With pestilent speeches of his father's death,   90
Wherein necessity,° of matter beggared,°
Will nothing stick our person to arraign
In ear and ear.° O my dear Gertrude, this,
Like to a murdering piece,° in many places
Gives me superfluous death.°   [*A noise within.*]   95

QUEEN. Alack, what noise is this?
KING. Attend!°
Where is my Switzers?° Let them guard the door.

Enter a MESSENGER.

What is the matter?
MESSENGER.   Save yourself, my lord!
The ocean, overpeering of his list,°   100
Eats not the flats° with more impetuous° haste
Than young Laertes, in a riotous head,°
O'erbears your officers. The rabble call him lord,
And, as° the world were now but to begin,
Antiquity forgot, custom not known,   105
The ratifiers and props of every word,°
They cry, "Choose we! Laertes shall be king!"
Caps,° hands, and tongues applaud it to the clouds,
"Laertes shall be king, Laertes king!"
QUEEN. How cheerfully on the false trail they cry!   110
                    [*A noise within.*]
O, this is counter,° you false Danish dogs!

Enter LAERTES *with others.*

KING. The doors are broke.
LAERTES. Where is this king?—Sirs, stand you all without.
ALL. No, let's come in.
LAERTES. I pray you, give me leave.   115
ALL. We will, we will.
LAERTES. I thank you. Keep the door. [*Exeunt followers.*] O thou vile
    king, Give me my father!
QUEEN [*restraining him*]. Calmly, good Laertes.

---

89 wants lacks. **buzzers** gossipers, informers. **91 necessity** i.e., the need to invent some plausible explanation. **of matter beggared** unprovided with facts. **92–93 Will . . . ear** will not hesitate to accuse my (royal) person in everybody's ears. **94 murdering piece** cannon loaded so as to scatter its shot. **95 Gives . . . death** kills me over and over. **97 Attend** i.e., guard me. **98 Switzers** Swiss guards, mercenaries. **100 over peering of his list** overflowing its shore, boundary. **101 flats** i.e., flatlands near shore. **impetuous** violent. (Perhaps also with the meaning of *impiteous* [*impitious*, Q2], "pitiless.") **102 head** insurrection. **104 as** as if. **106 The ratifiers . . . word** i.e., *antiquity* (or tradition) and *custom* ought to confirm (*ratify*) and underprop our every word or promise. **108 Caps** (The caps are thrown in the air.) **111 counter** (A hunting term, meaning to follow the trail in a direction opposite to that which the game has taken.)

LAERTES. That drop of blood that's calm proclaims me bastard,
　　　　　Cries cuckold to my father, brands the harlot   120
　　　　　Even here, between° the chaste unsmirchèd brow
　　　　　Of my true mother.
KING.　　　　　　　　　What is the cause, Laertes,
　　　　　That thy rebellion looks so giantlike?
　　　　　Let him go, Gertrude. Do not fear our° person.
　　　　　There's such divinity doth hedge° a king   125
　　　　　That treason can but peep to what it would,°
　　　　　Acts little of his will.° Tell me, Laertes,
　　　　　Why thou art thus incensed. Let him go, Gertrude.
　　　　　Speak, man.
LAERTES.　　　　　　　Where is my father?
KING.　　　　　　　　　　　　　　　Dead.
QUEEN. But not by him.
KING.　　　　　　　　　　　Let him demand his fill.   130
LAERTES. How came he dead? I'll not be juggled with.°
　　　　　To hell, allegiance! Vows, to the blackest devil!
　　　　　Conscience and grace, to the profoundest pit!
　　　　　I dare damnation. To this point I stand,°
　　　　　That both the worlds I give to negligence,°   135
　　　　　Let come what comes, only I'll be revenged
　　　　　Most throughly° for my father.
KING. Who shall stay you?
LAERTES. My will, not all the world's.°
　　　　　And for° my means, I'll husband them so well   140
　　　　　They shall go far with little.
KING.　　　　　　　　　Good Laertes,
　　　　　If you desire to know the certainty
　　　　　Of your dear father, is 't writ in your revenge
　　　　　That, swoopstake,° you will draw both friend and foe,
　　　　　Winner and loser?   145
LAERTES. None but his enemies.
KING. Will you know them, then?
LAERTES. To his good friends thus wide I'll ope my arms,
　　　　　And like the kind life-rendering pelican°
　　　　　Repast° them with my blood.

---

121 between in the middle of.　**124 fear our** fear for my.　**125 hedge** protect, as with a surrounding barrier.　**126 can . . . would** can only peep furtively, as through a barrier, at what it would intend.　**127 Acts . . . will** (but) performs little of what it intends.　**131 juggled with** cheated, deceived.　**134 To . . . stand** I am resolved in this.　**135 both . . . negligence** i.e., both this world and the next are of no consequence to me.　**137 throughly** thoroughly.　**139 My will . . . world's** I'll stop (*stay*) when my will is accomplished, not for anyone else's.　**140 for** as for.　**144 swoopstake** i.e., indiscriminately. (Literally, taking all stakes on the gambling table at once. *Draw* is also a gambling term, meaning "take from.")　**149 pelican** (Refers to the belief that the female pelican fed its young with its own blood.)　**150 Repast** feed.

KING.   Why, now you speak   150
   Like a good child and a true gentleman.
   That I am guiltless of your father's death,
   And am most sensibly° in grief for it,
   It shall as level° to your judgment 'pear
   As day does to your eye.   [*A noise within.*]   155
LAERTES. How now, what noise is that?

   Enter OPHELIA.

KING.   Let her come in.
LAERTES. O heat, dry up my brains! Tears seven times salt
   Burn out the sense and virtue° of mine eye!
   By heaven, thy madness shall be paid with weight°
   Till our scale turn the beam.° O rose of May!   160
   Dear maid, kind sister, sweet Ophelia!
   O heavens, is 't possible a young maid's wits
   Should be as mortal as an old man's life?
   Nature is fine in° love, and where 'tis fine
   It sends some precious instance° of itself   165
   After the thing it loves.°
OPHELIA.   [*Song.*]
   "They bore him barefaced on the bier,
      Hey non nonny, nonny, hey nonny,
      And in his grave rained many a tear—"
   Fare you well, my dove!   170
LAERTES. Hadst thou thy wits and didst persuade° revenge,
   It could not move thus.
OPHELIA. You must sing "A-down a-down," and you "call him a-down-a."°
   O, how the wheel° becomes it! It is the false steward° that stole his
   master's daughter.   175
LAERTES. This nothing's more than matter.°
OPHELIA. There's rosemary,° that's for remembrance; pray you, love,
   remember. And there is pansies;° that's for thoughts.
LAERTES. A document° in madness, thoughts and remembrance fitted.
OPHELIA. There's fennel° for you, and columbines.° There's rue° for   180
   you, and here's some for me; we may call it herb of grace o' Sundays.

---

153 sensibly feelingly.   **154 level** plain.   **158 virtue** faculty, power.   **159 paid with
weight** repaid, avenged equally or more.   **160 beam** crossbar of a balance.   **164 fine in**
refined by.   **165 instance** token.   **166 After . . . loves** i.e., into the grave, along with
Polonius.   **171 persuade** argue cogently for.   **173 You . . . a-down-a** (Ophelia assigns
the singing of refrains, like her own "Hey non nonny," to others present.)   **174 wheel**
spinning wheel as accompaniment to the song, or refrain.   **false steward** (The story is
unknown.)   **176 This . . . matter** this seeming nonsense is more eloquent than sane utterance.   **177 rosemary** (Used as a symbol of remembrance both at weddings and at funerals.)   **178 pansies** (Emblems of love and courtship; perhaps from French *pensées*,
"thoughts.")   **179 document** instruction, lesson.   **180 fennel** (Emblem of flattery.)
columbines (Emblems of unchastity or ingratitude.)   **rue** (Emblem of repentance—a
signification that is evident in its popular name, *herb of grace.*)

You must wear your rue with a difference.° There's a daisy.° I
would give you some violets,° but they withered all when my father died. They say 'a made a good end—
[*Sings.*] "For bonny sweet Robin is all my joy."   185
LAERTES. Thought° and affliction, passion,° hell itself,
     She turns to favor° and to prettiness.

OPHELIA.   [*Song.*]
          "And will 'a not come again?
          And will 'a not come again?
               No, no, he is dead.   190
               Go to thy deathbed,
          He never will come again.
          "His beard was as white as snow,
          All flaxen was his poll.°
               He is gone, he is gone,   195
               And we cast away moan.
          God ha' mercy on his soul!"

     And of all Christian souls, I pray God. God b' wi' you.

                         [*Exit, followed by* GERTRUDE.]

LAERTES. Do you see this, O God?
KING. Laertes, I must commune with your grief,   200
     Or you deny me right. Go but apart,
     Make choice of whom° your wisest friends you will,
     And they shall hear and judge twixt you and me.
     If by direct or by collateral hand°
     They find us touched,° we will our kingdom give,   205
     Our crown, our life, and all that we call ours
     To you in satisfaction; but if not,
     Be you content to lend your patience to us,
     And we shall jointly labor with your soul
     To give it due content.
LAERTES.   Let this be so.   210
     His means of death, his obscure funeral—
     No trophy,° sword, nor hatchment° o'er his bones,
     No noble rite, nor formal ostentation°—
     Cry to be heard, as 'twere from heaven to earth,
     That° I must call 't in question.°
KING.   So you shall,   215
     And where th' offense is, let the great ax fall.
     I pray you, go with me.
                                                      Exeunt.

---

182 with a difference (A device used in heraldry to distinguish one family from another
on the coat of arms, here suggesting that Ophelia and the others have different causes of
sorrow and repentance; perhaps with a play on *rue* in the sense of "ruth," "pity.") **daisy**
(Emblem of dissembling, faithlessness.)   **183 violets** (Emblems of faithfulness.)   **186
Thought** melancholy.   **passion** suffering.   **187 favor** grace, beauty.   **194 poll** head.
202 whom whichever of.   **204 collateral hand** indirect agency.   **205 us touched** me
implicated.   **212 trophy** memorial.   **hatchment** tablet displaying the armorial bearings
of a deceased person.   **213 ostentation** ceremony.   **215 That** so that.   **call 't in question** demand an explanation.

[4.6] *Enter* HORATIO *and others.*

HORATIO. What are they that would speak with me?
GENTLEMAN. Seafaring men, sir. They say they have letters for you.
HORATIO. Let them come in.

[Exit GENTLEMAN.]

I do not know from what part of the world
I should be greeted, if not from Lord Hamlet.   5

Enter Sailors.

FIRST SAILOR. God bless you, sir.
HORATIO. Let him bless thee too.
FIRST SAILOR. 'A shall, sir, an 't° please him. There's a letter for you, sir—
    it came from th' ambassador° that was bound for England—if your
    name be Horatio, as I am let to know it is. [*He gives a letter.*]   10
HORATIO [*reads*]. "Horatio, when thou shalt have overlooked° this, give
    these fellows some means° to the King; they have letters for him.
    Ere we were two days old at sea, a pirate of very warlike appoint-
    ment° gave us chase. Finding ourselves too slow of sail, we put on a
    compelled valor, and in the grapple I boarded them. On the instant   15
    they got clear of our ship, so I alone became their prisoner. They
    have dealt with me like thieves of mercy,° but they knew what
    they did: I am to do a good turn for them. Let the King have the let-
    ters I have sent, and repair° thou to me with as much speed as thou
    wouldest fly death. I have words to speak in thine ear will make   20
    thee dumb, yet are they much too light for the bore° of the matter.
    These good fellows will bring thee where I am. Rosencrantz and
    Guildenstern hold their course for England. Of them I have much
    to tell thee. Farewell.

He that thou knowest thine, Hamlet."   25
Come, I will give you way° for these your letters.
And do 't the speedier that you may direct me
To him from whom you brought them.

Exeunt.

[4.7] *Enter* KING *and* LAERTES.

KING. Now must your conscience my acquittance seal,°
    And you must put me in your heart for friend,
    Sith° you have heard, and with a knowing ear,
    That he which hath your noble father slain
    Pursued my life.
LAERTES.   It well appears. But tell me   5
    Why you proceeded not against these feats°
    So crimeful and so capital° in nature,

4.6 Location: The castle.   8 an 't if it.   **9 th' ambassador** (Evidently Hamlet. The
sailor is being circumspect.)   **11 overlooked** looked over.   **12 means** means of access.
13–14 appointment equipage.   **17 thieves of mercy** merciful thieves.   **19 repair**
come.   **21 bore** caliber, i.e., importance.   **26 way** means of access.   **4.7 Location: The
castle.   1 my acquittance seal** confirm or acknowledge my innocence.   **3 Sith** since.
6 feats acts.   **7 capital** punishable by death.

As by your safety, greatness, wisdom, all things else,
You mainly° were stirred up.
KING. O, for two special reasons,   10
Which may to you perhaps seem much unsinewed,°
But yet to me they're strong. The Queen his mother
Lives almost by his looks, and for myself—
My virtue or my plague, be it either which—
She is so conjunctive° to my life and soul   15
That, as the star moves not but in his° sphere,°
I could not but by her. The other motive
Why to a public count° I might not go
Is the great love the general gender° bear him,
Who, dipping all his faults in their affection,   20
Work° like the spring° that turneth wood to stone,
Convert his gyves° to graces, so that my arrows,
Too slightly timbered° for so loud° a wind,
Would have reverted° to my bow again
But not where I had aimed them.   25
LAERTES. And so have I a noble father lost,
A sister driven into desperate terms,°
Whose worth, if praises may go back° again,
Stood challenger on mount° of all the age
For her perfections. But my revenge will come.   30
KING. Break not your sleeps for that. You must not think
That we are made of stuff so flat and dull
That we can let our beard be shook with danger
And think it pastime. You shortly shall hear more.
I loved your father, and we love ourself;   35
And that, I hope, will teach you to imagine—

Enter a MESSENGER *with letters.*

How now? What news?
MESSENGER. Letters, my lord, from Hamlet:
This to Your Majesty, this to the Queen.

                                    [*He gives letters.*]

KING. From Hamlet? Who brought them?   40
MESSENGER. Sailors, my lord, they say. I saw them not.
They were given me by Claudio. He received them
Of him that brought them.

---

9 **mainly** greatly.   11 **unsinewed** weak.   15 **conjunctive** closely united. (An astronomical metaphor.)   16 **his** its.   **sphere** one of the hollow spheres in which, according to Ptolematic astronomy, the planets were supposed to move.   18 **count** account, reckoning, indictment.   19 **general gender** common people.   21 **Work** operate, act.   **spring** i.e., a spring with such a concentration of lime that it coats a piece of wood with limestone, in effect gilding and petrifying it.   22 **gyves** fetters (which, gilded by the people's praise, would look like badges of honor).   23 **slightly timbered** light.   **loud** (suggesting public outcry on Hamlet's behalf).   24 **reverted** returned.   27 **terms** state, condition.   28 **go back** i.e., recall what she was.   29 **on mount** set up on high.

KING.   Laertes, you shall hear them.—
     Leave us.

                              [*Exit* MESSENGER.]

     [*He reads.*] "High and mighty, you shall know I am set naked° on   45
     your kingdom. Tomorrow shall I beg leave to see your kingly eyes,
     when I shall, first asking your pardon,° thereunto recount the occa-
     sion of my sudden and more strange return.

                                         Hamlet."

     What should this mean? Are all the rest come back?
     Or is it some abuse,° and no such thing?°   50
LAERTES.   Know you the hand?
KING.   'Tis Hamlet's character.° "Naked!"
     And in a postscript here he says "alone."
     Can you devise° me?
LAERTES.   I am lost in it, my lord. But let him come.
     It warms the very sickness in my heart   55
     That I shall live and tell him to his teeth,
     "Thus didst thou."°
KING.   If it be so, Laertes—
     As how should it be so? How otherwise?°—
     Will you be ruled by me?
LAERTES.   Ay, my lord,
     So° you will not o'errule me to a peace.   60
KING.   To thine own peace. If he be now returned,
     As checking at° his voyage, and that° he means
     No more to undertake it, I will work him
     To an exploit, now ripe in my device,°
     Under the which he shall not choose but fall;   65
     And for his death no wind of blame shall breathe,
     But even his mother shall uncharge the practice°
     And call it an accident.
LAERTES.   My lord, I will be ruled,
     The rather if you could devise it so
     That I might be the organ.°
KING.   It falls right.   70
     You have been talked of since your travel much,
     And that in Hamlet's hearing, for a quality
     Wherein they say you shine. Your sum of parts°
     Did not together pluck such envy from him
     As did that one, and that, in my regard,   75
     Of the unworthiest siege.°

---

45 naked destitute, unarmed, without following.   **47 pardon** permission.   **50 abuse** deceit.   **no such thing** not what it appears.   **51 character** handwriting.   **53 devise** explain to.   **57 Thus didst thou** i.e., here's for what you did to my father.   **58 As . . . otherwise** how can this (Hamlet's return) be true? Yet how otherwise than true (since we have the evidence of his letter)?   **60 So** provided that.   **62 checking at** i.e., turning aside from (like a falcon leaving the quarry to fly at a chance bird).   **that** if.   **64 device** devising, invention.   **67 uncharge the practice** acquit the strategem of being a plot.   **70 organ** agent, instrument.   **73 Your . . . parts** i.e., all your other virtues.   **76 unworthiest siege** least important rank.

LAERTES. What part is that, my lord?
KING. A very ribbon in the cap of youth,
  Yet needful too, for youth no less becomes°
  The light and careless livery that it wears   80
  Than settled age his sables° and his weeds°
  Importing health and graveness.° Two months since
  Here was a gentleman of Normandy.
  I have seen myself, and served against, the French,
  And they can well° on horseback, but this gallant   85
  Had witchcraft in 't; he grew unto his seat,
  And to such wondrous doing brought his horse
  As had he been incorpsed and demi-natured°
  With the brave beast. So far he topped° my thought
  That I in forgery° of shapes and tricks   90
  Come short of what he did.
LAERTES.   A Norman was 't?
KING. A Norman.
LAERTES. Upon my life, Lamord.
KING.   The very same.
LAERTES. I know him well. He is the brooch° indeed
  And gem of all the nation.   95
KING. He made confession° of you,
  And gave you such a masterly report
  For art and exercise in your defense,°
  And for your rapier most especial,
  That he cried out 'twould be a sight indeed   100
  If one could match you. Th' escrimers° of their nation,
  He swore, had neither motion, guard, nor eye
  If you opposed them. Sir, this report of his
  Did Hamlet so envenom with his envy
  That he could nothing do but wish and beg   105
  Your sudden° coming o'er, to play° with you.
  Now, out of this—
LAERTES.   What out of this, my lord?
KING. Laertes, was your father dear to you?
  Or are you like the painting of a sorrow,
  A face without a heart?
LAERTES.   Why ask you this?   110
KING. Not that I think you did not love your father,
  But that I know love is begun by time,°

---

79 no less becomes is no less suited by. **81 his sables** its rich robes furred with sable.
weeds garments. **82 Importing . . . graveness** signifying a concern for health and dignified prosperity; also, giving an impression of comfortable prosperity. **85 can well** are
skilled. **88 As . . . demi-natured** as if he had been of one body and nearly of one nature
(like the centaur). **89 topped** surpassed. **90 forgery** imagining. **94 brooch** ornament. **96 confession** testimonial, admission of superiority. **98 For . . . defense** with
respect to your skill and practice with your weapon. **101 escrimers** fencers. **106
sudden** immediate. **play** fence. **112 begun by time** i.e., created by the right circumstance and hence subject to change.

And that I see, in passages of proof,°
Time qualifies° the spark and fire of it.
There lives within the very flame of love   115
A kind of wick or snuff° that will abate it,
And nothing is at a like goodness still,°
For goodness, growing to a pleurisy,°
Dies in his own too much.° That° we would do,
We should do when we would; for this "would" changes   120
And hath abatements° and delays as many
As there are tongues, are hands, are accidents,°
And then this "should" is like a spendthrift sigh,°
That hurts by easing.° But, to the quick o' th' ulcer:°
Hamlet comes back. What would you undertake   125
To show yourself in deed your father's son
More than in words?
LAERTES.   To cut his throat i' the church.
KING. No place, indeed, should murder sanctuarize;°
Revenge should have no bounds. But good Laertes,
Will you do this,° keep close within your chamber.   130
Hamlet returned shall know you are come home.
We'll put on those shall° praise your excellence
And set a double varnish on the fame
The Frenchman gave you, bring you in fine° together,
And wager on your heads. He, being remiss,°   135
Most generous,° and free from all contriving,
Will not peruse the foils, so that with ease,
Or with a little shuffling, you may choose
A sword unabated,° and in a pass of practice°
Requite him for your father.
LAERTES.   I will do 't.   140
And for that purpose I'll anoint my sword.
I bought an unction° of a mountebank°
So mortal that, but dip a knife in it,
Where it draws blood no cataplasm° so rare,
Collected from all simples° that have virtue°   145

---

113 **passages of proof** actual instances that prove it.   114 **qualifies** weakens, moderates.   116 **snuff** the charred part of a candlewick.   117 **nothing . . . still** nothing remains at a constant level of perfection.   118 **pleurisy** excess, plethora. (Literally, a chest inflammation.)   119 **in . . . much** of its own excess.   **That** that which.   121 **abatements** diminutions.   122 **As . . . accidents** as there are tongues to dissuade, hands to prevent, and chance events to intervene.   123 **spendthrift sigh** (An allusion to the belief that sighs draw blood from the heart.)   124 **hurts by easing** i.e., costs the heart blood and wastes precious opportunity even while it affords emotional relief.   124 **quick o' th' ulcer** i.e., heart of the matter.   128 **sanctuarize** protect from punishment. (Alludes to the right of sanctuary with which certain religious places were invested.)   130 **Will you do this** if you wish to do this.   132 **put on those shall** arrange for some to.   134 **in fine** finally.   135 **remiss** negligently unsuspicious.   136 **generous** nobleminded.   139 **unabated** not blunted, having no button.   **pass of practice** treacherous thrust.   142 **unction** ointment.   **mountebank** quack doctor.   144 **cataplasm** plaster or poultice.   145 **simples** herbs.   **virtue** potency.

Under the moon,° can save the thing from death
That is but scratched withal. I'll touch my point
With this contagion, that if I gall° him slightly,
It may be death.

KING.   Let's further think of this,
Weigh what convenience both of time and means   150
May fit us to our shape.° If this should fail,
And that our drift look through our bad performance,°
'Twere better not assayed. Therefore this project
Should have a back or second, that might hold
If this did blast in proof.° Soft, let me see   155
We'll make a solemn wager on your cunnings°—
I ha 't!
When in your motion you are hot and dry—
As° make your bouts more violent to that end—
And that he calls for drink, I'll have prepared him   160
A chalice for the nonce,° whereon but sipping,
If he by chance escape your venomed stuck,°
Our purpose may hold there. [*A cry within.*] But stay, what noise?

Enter QUEEN.

QUEEN. One woe doth tread upon another's heel,
So fast they follow. Your sister's drowned, Laertes.   165
LAERTES. Drowned! O, where?
QUEEN. There is a willow grows askant° the brook,
That shows his hoar leaves° in the glassy stream;
Therewith fantastic garlands did she make
Of crowflowers, nettles, daisies, and long purples,°   170
That liberal° shepherds give a grosser name,°
But our cold° maids do dead men's fingers call them.
There on the pendent° boughs her crownet° weeds
Clamb'ring to hang, an envious sliver° broke,
When down her weedy° trophies and herself   175
Fell in the weeping brook. Her clothes spread wide,
And mermaidlike awhile they bore her up,
Which time she chanted snatches of old lauds,°
As one incapable of° her own distress,

---

146 Under the moon i.e., anywhere (with reference perhaps to the belief that herbs
gathered at night had a special power).   **148 gall** graze, wound.   **151 shape** part we
propose to act.   **152 drift . . . performance** intention should be made visible by our
bungling.   **155 blast in proof** burst in the test (like a cannon).   **156 cunnings** respec-
tive skills.   **159 As** i.e., and you should.   **161 nonce** occasion.   **162 stuck** thrust. (From
stoccado, a fencing term.)   **167 askant** aslant.   **168 hoar leaves** white or gray under-
sides of the leaves.   **170 long purples** early purple orchids.   **171 liberal** free-spoken.
a grosser name (The testicle-resembling tubers of the orchid, which also in some cases
resemble *dead men's fingers,* have earned various slang names like "dogstones" and "cul-
lions.")   **172 cold** chaste.   **173 pendent** overhanging.   **crownet** made into a chaplet
or coronet.   **174 envious sliver** malicious branch.   **175 weedy** i.e., of plants.   **178**
lauds hymns.   **179 incapable of** lacking capacity to apprehend.

Or like a creature native and endued°   180
    Unto that element. But long it could not be
    Till that her garments, heavy with their drink,
    Pulled the poor wretch from her melodious lay
    To muddy death.
LAERTES.   Alas, then she is drowned?
QUEEN. Drowned, drowned.   185
LAERTES. Too much of water hast thou, poor Ophelia,
    And therefore I forbid my tears. But yet
    It is our trick;° nature her custom holds,
    Let shame say what it will. [*He weeps.*] When these are gone,
    The woman will be out.° Adieu, my lord.   190
    I have a speech of fire that fain would blaze,
    But that this folly douts° it.
                                                          Exit.
KING.   Let's follow, Gertrude.
    How much I had to do to calm his rage!
    Now fear I this will give it start again;
    Therefore let's follow.   195
                                                        Exeunt.

[5.1] *Enter two* CLOWNS° [*with spades and mattocks*].

FIRST CLOWN. Is she to be buried in Christian burial, when she willfully
    seeks her own salvation?°
SECOND CLOWN. I tell thee she is; therefore make her grave straight.° The
    crowner° hath sat on her,° and finds it° Christian burial.
FIRST CLOWN. How can that be, unless she drowned herself in her own   5
    defense?
SECOND CLOWN. Why, 'tis found so.°
FIRST CLOWN. It must be *se offendendo,*° it cannot be else. For here lies
    the point: if I drown myself wittingly, it argues an act, and an act
    hath three branches—it is to act, to do, and to perform. Argal,° she   10
    drowned herself wittingly.
SECOND CLOWN. Nay, but hear you, goodman° delver—
FIRST CLOWN. Give me leave. Here lies the water; good. Here stands the
    man; good. If the man go to this water and drown himself, it is, will
    he, nill he,° he goes, mark you that. But if the water come to him   15

---

180 **endued** adapted by nature.   188 **It is our trick** i.e., weeping is our natural way
(when sad).   189–190 **When . . . out** when my tears are all shed, the woman in me will
be expended, satisfied.   192 **douts** extinguishes. (The Second Quarto reads "drowns.")
5.1 Location: A churchyard. s.d. Clowns rustics.   2 **salvation** (A blunder for
"damnation," or perhaps a suggestion that Ophelia was taking her own shortcut to
heaven.)   3 **straight** straightway, immediately. (But with a pun on *strait,* "narrow.")
4 **crowner** coroner.   **sat on her** conducted an inquest on her case.   **finds it** gives his
official verdict that her means of death was consistent with.   7 **found so** determined so
in the coroner's verdict.   8 *se offendendo* (A comic mistake for *se defendendo,* a term
used in verdicts of justifiable homicide.)   10 **Argal** (Corruption of *ergo,* "therefore.")   12
goodman (An honorific title often used with the name of a profession or craft.)   14–15
will he, nill he whether he will or no, willy-nilly.

and drown him, he drowns not himself. Argal, he that is not guilty
of his own death shortens not his own life.

SECOND CLOWN. But is this law?

FIRST CLOWN. Ay, marry, is 't—crowner's quest° law.

SECOND CLOWN. Will you ha' the truth on 't? If this had not been a gentle-   20
woman, she should have been buried out o' Christian burial.

FIRST CLOWN. Why, there thou sayst.° And the more pity that great folk
should have countenance° in this world to drown or hang themselves, more than their even-Christian.° Come, my spade. There is
no ancient° gentlemen but gardeners, ditchers, and grave makers.   25
They hold up° Adam's profession.

SECOND CLOWN. Was he a gentleman?

FIRST CLOWN. 'A was the first that ever bore arms.°

SECOND CLOWN. Why, he had none.

FIRST CLOWN. What, art a heathen? How dost thou understand the Scrip-   30
ture? The Scripture says Adam digged. Could he dig without arms?°
I'll put another question to thee. If thou answerest me not to the
purpose, confess thyself°—

SECOND CLOWN. Go to.

FIRST CLOWN. What is he that builds stronger than either the mason, the   35
shipwright, or the carpenter?

SECOND CLOWN. The gallows maker, for that frame° outlives a thousand
tenants.

FIRST CLOWN. I like thy wit well, in good faith. The gallows does well.°
But how does it well? It does well to those that do ill. Now thou   40
dost ill to say the gallows is built stronger than the church. Argal,
the gallows may do well to thee. To 't again, come.

SECOND CLOWN. "Who builds stronger than a mason, a shipwright, or a
carpenter?"

FIRST CLOWN. Ay, tell me that, and unyoke.°   45

SECOND CLOWN. Marry, now I can tell.

FIRST CLOWN. To 't.

SECOND CLOWN. Mass,° I cannot tell.

Enter HAMLET *and* HORATIO [*at a distance*].

FIRST CLOWN. Cudgel thy brains no more about it, for your dull ass will
not mend his pace with beating; and when you are asked this   50
question next, say "a grave maker. The houses he makes lasts till
doomsday." Go get thee in and fetch me a stoup° of liquor.

[*Exit* SECOND CLOWN. FIRST CLOWN *digs.*]

---

19 **quest** inquest.   22 **there thou sayst** i.e., that's right.   23 **countenance** privilege.
24 **even-Christian** fellow Christians.   25 **ancient** going back to ancient times.   26
hold up maintain.   28 **bore arms** (To be entitled to bear a coat of arms would make
Adam a gentleman, but as one who bore a spade, our common ancestor was an ordinary
delver in the earth.)   31 **arms** i.e., the arms of the body.   33 **confess thyself** (The
saying continues, "and be hanged.")   37 **frame** (1) gallows (2) structure.   39 **does
well** (1) is an apt answer (2) does a good turn.   45 **unyoke** i.e., after this great effort,
you may unharness the team of your wits.   48 **Mass** by the Mass.   52 **stoup** two-quart
measure.

Song.

"In youth, when I did love, did love,°
    Methought it was very sweet,
To contract—O—the time for—a—my behove,°   55
    O, methought there—a—was nothing—a—meet."°

HAMLET. Has this fellow no feeling of his business, 'a° sings in grave-
    making?

HORATIO. Custom hath made it in him a property of easiness.°

HAMLET. 'Tis e'en so. The hand of little employment hath the daintier   60
    sense.°

FIRST CLOWN.   *Song.*

"But age with his stealing steps
    Hath clawed me in his clutch,
And hath shipped me into the land,°
    As if I had never been such."   65

                              [*He throws up a skull.*]

HAMLET. That skull had a tongue in it and could sing once. How the
    knave jowls° it to the ground, as if 'twere Cain's jawbone, that did
    the first murder! This might be the pate of a politician,° which this
    ass now o'erreaches,° one that would circumvent God, might it
    not?   70

HORATIO. It might, my lord.

HAMLET. Or of a courtier, which could say, "Good morrow, sweet lord!
    How dost thou, sweet lord?" This might be my Lord Such-a-one,
    that praised my Lord Such-a-one's horse when 'a meant to beg it,
    might it not?   75

HORATIO. Ay, my lord

HAMLET. Why e'en so, and now my lady Worm's, chapless,° and knocked
    about the mazard° with a sexton's spade. Here's fine revolution,°
    an° we had the trick to see° 't. Did these bones cost no more the
    breeding but to play° at loggets° with them? Mine ache to think   80
    on 't.

FIRST CLOWN.   *Song.*

"A pickax and a spade, a spade,
    For and° a shrouding sheet;

---

53 In . . . love (This and the two following stanzas, with nonsensical variations, are
from a poem attributed to Lord Vaux and printed in *Tottel's Miscellany,* 1557. The *O*
and *a* [for "ah"] seemingly are the grunts of the digger.)   **55 To contract . . . behove**
i.e., to shorten the time for my own advantage. (Perhaps he means to *prolong* it.)   **56
meet** suitable, i.e., more suitable.   **57 'a** that he.   **59 property of easiness** something he can do easily and indifferently.   **60–61 daintier sense** more delicate sense of
feeling.   **64 into the land** i.e., toward my grave (?). (But note the lack of rhyme in
steps, land.)   **67 jowls** dashes (with a pun on *jowl,* "jawbone").   **68 politician**
schemer, plotter.   **69 o'erreaches** circumvents, gets the better of (with a quibble on
the literal sense).   **77 chapless** having no lower jaw.   **78 mazard** i.e., head (literally,
a drinking vessel).   **78 revolution** turn of Fortune's wheel, change.   **79 an** if.   **trick
to see** knack of seeing.   **79–80 cost . . . play** involve so little expense and care in upbringing that we may play.   **80 loggets** a game in which pieces of hard wood shaped
like Indian clubs or bowling pins are thrown to lie as near as possible to a stake.   **83
For and** and moreover.

    O, a pit of clay for to be made
      For such a guest is meet."   85

                     [*He throws up another skull.*]

HAMLET. There's another. Why may not that be the skull of a lawyer?
    Where be his quiddities° now, his quillities,° his cases, his tenures,°
    and his tricks? Why does he suffer this mad knave now to knock
    him about the sconce° with a dirty shovel, and will not tell him of
    his action of battery?° Hum, this fellow might be in 's time a great   90
    buyer of land, with his statutes, his recognizances,° his fines, his
    double° vouchers,° his recoveries.° In this the fine of his fines and
    the recovery of recoveries, to have his fine pate full of fine dirt?°
    Will his vouchers vouch him no more of his purchases, and
    double ones too, than the length and breadth of a pair of inden-   95
    tures?° The very conveyances° of his lands will scarcely lie in this
    box,° and must th' inheritor° himself have no more, ha?
HORATIO. Not a jot more, my lord.
HAMLET. Is not parchment made of sheepskins?
HORATIO. Ay, my lord, and of calves' skins too.   100
HAMLET. They are sheep and calves, which seek out assurance in that.°
    I will speak to this fellow.—Whose grave's this, sirrah?°
FIRST CLOWN. Mine, sir.   [*Sings.*]
    "O, pit of clay for to be made
      For such a guest is meet."   105
HAMLET. I think it be thine, indeed, for thou liest in 't.
FIRST CLOWN. You lie out on 't, sir, and therefore 'tis not yours. For my
    part, I do not lie in 't, yet it is mine.
HAMLET. Thou dost lie in 't, to be in 't and say it is thine. 'Tis for the
    dead, not for the quick;° therefore thou liest   110
FIRST CLOWN. 'Tis a quick lie, sir; 'twill away again from me to you.
HAMLET. What man dost thou dig it for?
FIRST CLOWN. For no man, sir.
HAMLET. What woman, then?
FIRST CLOWN. For none, neither.   115
HAMLET. Who is to be buried in 't?
FIRST CLOWN. One that was a woman, sir, but, rest her soul, she's dead.

---

87 quiddities subtleties, quibbles (from Latin *quid,* "a thing"). **quillities** verbal niceties,
subtle distinctions (variation of *quiddities*). **tenures** the holding of a piece of property
or office, or the conditions or period of such holding. **89 sconce** head. **90 action of
battery** lawsuit about physical assault. **91 statutes, his recognizances** legal documents guaranteeing a debt by attaching land and property. **91–92 fines . . . recoveries**
ways of converting entailed estates into "fee simple" or freehold. **92 double** signed by
two signatories. **vouchers** guarantees of the legality of a title to real estate. **92–94
fine of his fines . . . fine pate . . . fine dirt** end of his legal maneuvers . . . elegant head
. . . minutely sifted dirt. **95–96 pair of indentures** legal documents drawn up in duplicate on a single sheet and then cut apart on a zigzag line so that each pair was uniquely
matched. (Hamlet may refer to two rows of teeth or dentures.) **96 conveyances** deeds.
97 box (1) deed box (2) coffin. ("Skull" has been suggested.) **inheritor** possessor,
owner. **101 assurance in that** safety in legal parchments. **102 sirrah** (A term of address to inferiors.) **110 quick** living.

HAMLET. How absolute° the knave is! We must speak by the card,° or
equivocation° will undo us. By the Lord, Horatio, this three years I
have took° note of it: the age is grown so picked° that the toe of   120
the peasant comes so near the heel of the courtier, he galls his
kibe.°—How long has thou been grave maker?

FIRST CLOWN. Of all the days i' the year, I came to 't that day that our last
king Hamlet overcame Fortinbras.

HAMLET. How long is that since?   125

FIRST CLOWN. Cannot you tell that? Every fool can tell that. It was that
very day that young Hamlet was born—he that is mad and sent into
England.

HAMLET. Ay, marry, why was he sent into England?

FIRST CLOWN. Why, because 'a was mad. 'A shall recover his wits there, or   130
if 'a do not, 'tis no great matter there.

HAMLET. Why?

FIRST CLOWN. 'Twill not be seen in him there. There the men are as mad
as he.

HAMLET. How came he mad?   135

FIRST CLOWN. Very strangely, they say.

HAMLET. How strangely?

FIRST CLOWN. Faith, e'en with losing his wits.

HAMLET. Upon what ground?°

FIRST CLOWN. Why, here in Denmark. I have been sexton here, man and   140
boy, thirty years.

HAMLET. How long will a man lie i' th' earth ere he rot?

FIRST CLOWN. Faith, if 'a be not rotten before 'a die—as we have many
pocky° corpses nowadays, that will scarce hold the laying in°—'a
will last you° some eight year or nine year. A tanner will last you   145
nine year.

HAMLET. Why he more than another?

FIRST CLOWN. Why, sir, his hide is so tanned with his trade that 'a will
keep out water a great while, and your water is a sore° decayer of
your whoreson° dead body. [*He picks up a skull.*] Here's a skull   150
now hath lien you° i' th' earth three-and-twenty years.

HAMLET. Whose was it?

FIRST CLOWN. A whoreson mad fellow's it was. Whose do you think it
was?

HAMLET. Nay, I know not.   155

FIRST CLOWN. A pestilence on him for a mad rogue! 'A poured a flagon of
Rhenish° on my head once. This same skull, sir, was, sir, Yorick's
skull, the King's jester.

---

118 absolute strict, precise. **by the card** i.e., with precision. (Literally, by the mariner's
compass-card, on which the points of the compass were marked.) **119 equivocation**
ambiguity in the use of terms. **120 took** taken. **picked** refined, fastidious. **121–122**
galls his kibe chafes the courtier's chilblain. **139 ground** cause. (But, in the next line,
the gravedigger takes the word in the sense of "land," "country.") **144 pocky** rotten, diseased (literally, with the pox, or syphilis). **hold the laying in** hold together long
enough to be interred. **145 last you** last. (*You* is used colloquially here and in the following lines.) **149 sore** i.e., terrible, great. **150 whoreson** i.e., vile, scurvy. **151 lien**
you lain. (See the note at line 145.) **157 Rhenish** Rhine wine.

HAMLET. **This?**

FIRST CLOWN. E'en that.   160

HAMLET. Let me see. [*He takes the skull.*] Alas, poor Yorick! I knew him,
    Horatio, a fellow of infinite jest, of most excellent fancy. He hath
    bore° me on his back a thousand times, and now how abhorred in
    my imagination it is! My gorge rises° at it. Here hung those lips that
    I have kissed I know not how oft. Where be your gibes now? Your   165
    gambols, your songs, your flashes of merriment that were wont° to
    set the table on a roar? Not one now, to mock your own grinning?°
    Quite chopfallen?° Now get you to my lady's chamber and tell her,
    let her paint an inch thick, to this favor° she must come. Make her
    laugh at that. Prithee, Horatio, tell me one thing.   170

HORATIO. What's that, my lord?

HAMLET. Dost thou think Alexander looked o' this fashion i' th' earth?

HORATIO. E'en so.

HAMLET. And smelt so? Pah!   [*He throws down the skull.*]

HORATIO. E'en so, my lord.   175

HAMLET. To what base uses we may return, Horatio! Why may not imagi-
    nation trace the noble dust of Alexander till 'a find it stopping a
    bunghole?°

HORATIO. 'Twere to consider too curiously° to consider so.

HAMLET. No, faith, not a jot, but to follow him thither with modesty°   180
    enough, and likelihood to lead it. As thus: Alexander died, Alexan-
    der was buried, Alexander returneth to dust, the dust is earth, of
    earth we make loam,° and why of that loam whereto he was con-
    verted might they not stop a beer barrel?
    Imperious° Caesar, dead and turned to clay   185
    Might stop a hole to keep the wind away.
    O, that that earth which kept the world in awe
    Should patch a wall t' expel the winter's flaw!°

Enter KING, QUEEN, LAERTES, *and the corpse* [*of* OPHELIA, *in proces-*
sion, with PRIEST, *lords, etc.*].

But soft,° but soft awhile! Here comes the King,
The Queen, the courtiers. Who is this they follow?   190
And with such maimèd° rites? This doth betoken
The corpse they follow did with desperate hand
Fordo° its own life. 'Twas of some estate.°
Couch we° awhile and mark.

[*He and* HORATIO *conceal themselves.* OPHELIA'S *body is taken to the*
grave.]

---

163 bore borne. **164 My gorge rises** i.e., I feel nauseated. **166 were wont** used.
167 mock your own grinning mock at the way your skull seems to be grinning (just as
you used to mock at yourself and those who grinned at you). **168 chopfallen** (1) lacking the lower jaw (2) dejected. **169 favor** aspect, appearance. **178 bunghole** hole for
filling or emptying a cask. **179 curiously** minutely. **180 modesty** plausible moderation. **183 loam** mortar consisting chiefly of moistened clay and straw. **185 Imperious**
imperial. **188 flaw** gust of wind. **189 soft** i.e., wait, be careful. **191 maimèd** mutilated, incomplete. **193 Fordo** destroy. **estate** rank. **194 Couch we** let's hide, lie low.

LAERTES. What ceremony else?   195

HAMLET [*to* HORATIO]. That is Laertes, a very noble youth. Mark.

LAERTES. What ceremony else?

PRIEST. Her obsequies have been as far enlarged
    As we have warranty.° Her death was doubtful,
    And but that great command o'ersways the order°   200
    She should in ground unsanctified been lodged°
    Till the last trumpet. For° charitable prayers,
    Shards,° flints, and pebbles should be thrown on her.
    Yet here she is allowed her virgin crants,°
    Her maiden strewments,° and the bringing home   205
    Of bell and burial.°

LAERTES. Must there no more be done?

PRIEST.   No more be done.
    We should profane the service of the dead
    To sing a requiem and such rest° to her
    As to peace-parted souls.°

LAERTES.   Lay her i' th' earth,   210
    And from her fair and unpolluted flesh
    May violets° spring! I tell thee, churlish priest,
    A ministering angel shall my sister be
    When thou liest howling.°

HAMLET [*to* HORATIO].   What, the fair Ophelia!

QUEEN [*scattering flowers*]. Sweets to the sweet! Farewell.   215
    I hoped thou shouldst have been my Hamlet's wife.
    I thought thy bride-bed to have decked, sweet maid,
    And not t' have strewed thy grave.

LAERTES.   O, treble woe
    Fall ten times treble on that cursèd head
    Whose wicked deed thy most ingenious sense°   220
    Deprived thee of! Hold off the earth awhile,
    Till I have caught her once more in mine arms.

[*He leaps into the grave and embraces* OPHELIA.]

    Now pile your dust upon the quick and dead,
    Till of this flat a mountain you have made
    T' o'ertop old Pelion or the skyish head   225
    Of blue Olympus.°

---

199 warranty i.e., ecclesiastical authority.   **200 great . . . order** orders from on high
overrule the prescribed procedures.   **201 She should . . . lodged** she should have
been buried in unsanctified ground.   **202 For** in place of.   **203 Shards** broken bits of
pottery.   **204 crants** garlands betokening maidenhood.   **205 strewments** flowers
strewn on a coffin.   **205–206 bringing . . . burial** laying the body to rest, to the sound
of the bell.   **209 such rest** i.e., to pray for such rest.   **210 peace-parted souls** those
who have died at peace with God.   **212 violets** (See 4.5.183 and note.)   **214 howling**
i.e., in hell.   **220 ingenious sense** a mind that is quick, alert, of fine qualities.
225–226 Pelion . . . Olympus sacred mountains in the north of Thessaly; see also *Ossa,*
below, at line 257.

HAMLET [*coming forward*]. What is he whose grief
    Bears such an emphasis,° whose phrase of sorrow
    Conjures the wandering stars° and makes them stand
    Like wonder-wounded° hearers? This is I,   230
    Hamlet the Dane.°
LAERTES [*grappling with him*°]. The devil take thy soul!
HAMLET. Thou pray'st not well.
    I prithee, take thy fingers from my throat,
    For though I am not splenitive° and rash,   235
    Yet have I in me something dangerous,
    Which let thy wisdom fear. Hold off thy hand.
KING. Pluck them asunder.
QUEEN. Hamlet, Hamlet!
ALL. Gentlemen!   240
HORATIO. Good my lord, be quiet.

      [HAMLET *and* LAERTES *are parted.*]

HAMLET. Why, I will fight with him upon this theme
    Until my eyelids will no longer wag.°
QUEEN. O my son, what theme?
HAMLET. I loved Ophelia. Forty thousand brothers   245
    Could not with all their quantity of love
    Make up my sum. What wilt thou do for her?
KING. O, he is mad, Laertes.
QUEEN. For love of God, forbear him.°
HAMLET. 'Swounds,° show me what thou'lt do.   250
    Woo't° weep? Woo't fight? Woo't fast? Woo't tear thyself?
    Woo't drink up° eisel?° Eat a crocodile?°
    I'll do 't. Dost come here to whine?
    To outface me with leaping in her grave?
    Be buried quick° with her, and so will I.   255
    And if thou prate of mountains, let them throw
    Millions of acres on us, till our ground,
    Singeing his pate° against the burning zone,°

---

227 emphasis i.e., rhetorical and florid emphasis. (*Phrase* has a similar rhetorical connotation.) **228 wandering stars** planets. **230 wonder-wounded** struck with amazement. **231 the Dane** (This title normally signifies the King; see 1.1.17 and note.) **s.d. grappling with him** The testimony of the First Quarto that *"Hamlet leaps in after Laertes"* and the "Elegy on Burbage" ("Oft have I seen him leap into the grave") seem to indicate one way in which this fight was staged; however, the difficulty of fitting two contenders and Ophelia's body into a confined space (probably the trapdoor) suggests to many editors the alternative, that Laertes jumps out of the grave to attack Hamlet. **235 splenitive** quick-tempered. **243 wag** move. (A fluttering eyelid is a conventional sign that life has not yet gone.) **249 forbear him** leave him alone. **250 'Swounds** by His (Christ's) wounds. **251 Woo't** wilt thou. **252 drink up** drink deeply. **eisel** vinegar. **crocodile** (Crocodiles were tough and dangerous, and were supposed to shed hypocritical tears.) **255 quick** alive. **258 his pate** its head, i.e., top. **burning zone** zone in the celestial sphere containing the sun's orbit, between the tropics of Cancer and Capricorn.

Make Ossa° like a wart! Nay, an° thou'lt mouth,°
I'll rant as well as thou.

QUEEN.   This is mere° madness,   260
And thus awhile the fit will work on him;
Anon, as patient as the female dove
When that her golden couplets° are disclosed,°
His silence will sit drooping.

HAMLET.   Hear you, sir,
What is the reason that you use me thus?   265
I loved you ever. But it is no matter.
Let Hercules himself do what he may,
The cat will mew, and dog will have his day.°

                                                Exit HAMLET.

KING. I pray thee, good Horatio, wait upon him.

                                         [*Exit* HORATIO.]

[*To* LAERTES.] Strengthen your patience in° our last night's speech;   270
We'll put the matter to the present push.°—
Good Gertrude, set some watch over your son.—
This grave shall have a living° monument.
An hour of quiet° shortly shall we see;
Till then, in patience our proceeding be.   275

                                                 Exeunt.

[5.2] *Enter* HAMLET *and* HORATIO.

HAMLET. So much for this, sir; now shall you see the other.°
You do remember all the circumstance?
HORATIO. Remember it, my lord!
HAMLET. Sir, in my heart there was a kind of fighting
That would not let me sleep. Methought I lay   5
Worse than the mutines° in the bilboes° Rashly,°
And praised be rashness for it—let us know°
Our indiscretion° sometimes serves us well
When our deep plots do pall,° and that should learn° us
There's a divinity that shapes our ends,   10
Rough-hew° them how we will—
HORATIO.   That is most certain.

---

259 Ossa another mountain in Thessaly. (In their war against the Olympian gods, the giants attempted to heap Ossa on Pelion to scale Olympus.) **an** if. **mouth** i.e., rant. **260 mere** utter. **263 golden couplets** two baby pigeons, covered with yellow down. **disclosed** hatched. **267–268 Let . . . day** i.e., (1) even Hercules couldn't stop Laertes's theatrical rant (2) I, too, will have my turn; i.e., despite any blustering attempts at interference, every person will sooner or later do what he or she must do. **270 in** i.e., by recalling. **271 present push** immediate test. **273 living** lasting. (For Laertes's private understanding, Claudius also hints that Hamlet's death will serve as such a monument.) **274 hour of quiet** time free of conflict. **5.2 Location: The castle. 1 see the other** hear the other news. **6 mutines** mutineers. **bilboes** shackles. **Rashly** on impulse (this adverb goes with lines 12 ff.). **7 know** acknowledge. **8 indiscretion** lack of foresight and judgment (not an indiscreet act). **9 pall** fail, falter, go stale. **learn** teach. **11 Rough-hew** shape roughly.

HAMLET. Up from my cabin,
    My sea-gown° scarfed° about me, in the dark
    Groped I to find out them,° had my desire,
    Fingered° their packet, and in fine° withdrew   15
    To mine own room again, making so bold,
    My fears forgetting manners, to unseal
    Their grand commission; where I found, Horatio—
    Ah, royal knavery!—an exact command,
    Larded° with many several° sorts of reasons   20
    Importing° Denmark's health and England's too,
    With, ho! such bugs° and goblins in my life,°
    That on the supervise,° no leisure bated,°
    No, not to stay° the grinding of the ax,
    My head should be struck off.
HORATIO.   Is't possible?   25
HAMLET [*giving a document*].
    Here's the commission. Read it at more leisure.
    But wilt thou hear now how I did proceed?
HORATIO. I beseech you.
HAMLET. Being thus benetted round with villainies—
    Ere I could make a prologue to my brains,   30
    They had begun the play°—I sat me down,
    Devised a new commission, wrote it fair.°
    I once did hold it, as our statists° do,
    A baseness° to write fair, and labored much
    How to forget that learning; but, sir, now   35
    It did me yeoman's° service. Wilt thou know
    Th' effect° of what I wrote?
HORATIO.   Ay, good my lord.
HAMLET. An earnest conjuration° from the King,
    As England was his faithful tributary,
    As love between them like the palm° might flourish,   40
    As peace should still° her wheaten garland° wear
    And stand a comma° 'tween their amities,
    And many suchlike "as"es° of great charge,°
    That on the view and knowing of these contents,
    Without debatement further more or less,   45

---

13 sea-gown seaman's coat. **scarfed** loosely wrapped. **14 them** i.e., Rosencrantz
and Guildenstern. **15 Fingered** pilfered, pinched. **in fine** finally, in conclusion.
20 Larded garnished **several** different. **21 Importing** relating to. **22 bugs** bug-
bears, hobgoblins. **in my life** i.e., to be feared if I were allowed to live. **23
supervise** reading. **leisure bated** delay allowed. **24 stay** await. **30–31 Ere . . .
play** before I could consciously turn my brain to the matter, it had started working on a
plan. **32 fair** in a clear hand. **33 statists** statesmen. **34 baseness** i.e., lower-class
trait. **36 yeoman's** i.e., substantial, faithful, loyal. **37 effect** purport. **38
conjuration** entreaty. **40 palm** (An image of health; see Psalm 92.12.) **41 still** always. **wheaten garland** (Symbolic of fruitful agriculture, of peace and plenty.) **42
comma** (Indicating continuity, link.) **43 "as"es** (1) the "whereases" of a formal document (2) asses. **charge** (1) import (2) burden (appropriate to asses).

   He should those bearers put to sudden death,
   Not shriving time° allowed.
HORATIO.   How was this sealed?
HAMLET. Why, even in that was heaven ordinant.°
   I had my father's signet° in my purse.
   Which was the model° of that Danish seal;   50
   Folded the writ° up in the form of th' other,
   Subscribed° it, gave 't th' impression,° placed it safely,
   The changeling° never known. Now, the next day
   Was our sea fight, and what to this was sequent°
   Thou knowest already.   55
HORATIO. So Guildenstern and Rosencrantz go to 't.
HAMLET. Why, man, they did make love to this employment.
   They are not near my conscience. Their defeat°
   Does by their own insinuation° grow.
   'Tis dangerous when the baser° nature comes   60
   Between the pass° and fell° incensèd points
   Of mightly opposites.°
HORATIO.   Why, what a king is this!
HAMLET. Does it not, think thee, stand me now upon°—
   He that hath killed my king and whored my mother,
   Popped in between th' election° and my hopes,   65
   Thrown out his angle° for my proper° life,
   And with such cozenage°—is 't not perfect conscience
   To quit° him with this arm? And is 't not to be damned
   To let this canker° of our nature come
   In° further evil?   70
HORATIO. It must be shortly known to him from England
   What is the issue of the business there.
HAMLET. It will be short. The interim is mine,
   And a man's life's no more than to say "one."°
   But I am very sorry, good Horatio,   75
   That to Laertes I forgot myself,
   For by the image of my cause I see
   The portraiture of his. I'll court his favors.
   But, sure, the bravery° of his grief did put me
   Into a tow'ring passion.

---

47 shriving time time for confession and absolution. **48 ordinant** directing.
49 signet small seal. **50 model** replica. **51 writ** writing. **52 Subscribed** signed
(with forged signature). **impression** i.e., with a wax seal. **53 changeling** i.e., substituted letter. (Literally, a fairy child substituted for a human one.) **54 was sequent** followed. **58 defeat** destruction. **59 insinuation** intrusive intervention, sticking their
noses in my business. **60 baser** of lower social station. **61 pass** thrust. **fell** fierce.
62 opposites antagonists. **63 stand me now upon** become incumbent on me now.
65 election (The Danish monarch was "elected" by a small number of high-ranking elec-
tors.) **66 angle** fishhook. **proper** very. **67 cozenage** trickery. **68 quit** requite,
pay back. **69 canker** ulcer. **69–70 come In** grow into. **74 a man's . . . "one"**
one's whole life occupies such a short time, only as long as it takes to count to 1.
79 bravery bravado.

HORATIO.   Peace, who comes here?   80

    Enter a Courtier [OSRIC].

OSRIC. Your lordship is right welcome back to Denmark.

HAMLET. I humbly thank you, sir. [*To* HORATIO.] Dost know this water fly?

HORATIO. No, my good lord.

HAMLET. Thy state is the more gracious, for 'tis a vice to know him. He   85
    hath much land, and fertile. Let a beast be lord of beasts, and his
    crib° shall stand at the King's mess.° 'Tis a chuff,° but, as I say, spa-
    cious in the possession of dirt.

OSRIC. Sweet lord, if your lordship were at leisure, I should impart a
    thing to you from His Majesty.   90

HAMLET. I will receive it, sir, with all diligence of spirit.
    Put your bonnet° to his° right use; 'tis for the head.

OSRIC. I thank your lordship, it is very hot.

HAMLET. No, believe me, 'tis very cold. The wind is northerly.

OSRIC. It is indifferent° cold, my lord, indeed.   95

HAMLET. But yet methinks it is very sultry and hot for my complexion.°

OSRIC. Exceedingly, my lord. It is very sultry, as 'twere—I cannot tell
    how. My lord, His Majesty bade me signify to you that 'a has laid a
    great wager on your head. Sir, this is the matter—

HAMLET. I beseech you, remember.   100

    [HAMLET *moves him to put on his hat.*]

OSRIC. Nay, good my lord; for my ease,° in good faith. Sir, here is newly
    come to court Laertes—believe me, an absolute° gentleman, full of
    most excellent differences,° of very soft society° and great show-
    ing.° Indeed, to speak feelingly° of him, he is the card° or calendar°
    of gentry,° for you shall find in him the continent of what part a   105
    gentleman would see.°

HAMLET. Sir, his definement° suffers no perdition° in you,° though I
    know to divide him inventorially° would dozy° th' arithmetic of
    memory, and yet but yaw° neither° in respect of° his quick sail. But,
    in the verity of extolment,° I take him to be a soul of great   110

---

87 crib manger.   **86–87 Let . . . mess** i.e., if a man, no matter how beastlike, is as rich in
livestock and possessions as Osric, he may eat at the King's table.   **87 chuff** boor, churl.
(The Second Quarto spelling, *chough,* is a variant spelling that also suggests the meaning
here of "chattering jackdaw.")   **92 bonnet** any kind of cap or hat. **his** its.
95 indifferent somewhat.   **96 complexion** temperament.   **101 for my ease** (A conventional reply declining the invitation to put his hat back on.)   **102 absolute** perfect.
103 differences special qualities.   **soft society** agreeable manners.   **103–104 great
showing** distinguished appearance.   **104 feelingly** with just perception.   **card** chart,
map.   **calendar** guide.   **105 gentry** good breeding.   **105–106 the continent . . . see**
one who contains in him all the qualities a gentleman would like to see (a *continent* is
that which contains).   **107 definement** definition. (Hamlet proceeds to mock Osric by
throwing his lofty diction back at him.)   **perdition** loss, diminution.   **you** your description.   **108 divide him inventorially** enumerate his graces.   **dozy** dizzy.   **109 yaw**
swing unsteadily off course (said of a ship).   **neither** for all that.   **in respect of** in comparison with.   **110 in . . . extolment** in true praise (of him).

article,° and his infusion° of such dearth and rareness° as, to make
true diction° of him, his semblable° is his mirror and who else
would trace° him his umbrage,° nothing more.

OSRIC. Your lordship speaks most infallibly of him.

HAMLET. The concernancy,° sir? Why do we wrap the gentleman in our   115
more rawer breath?°

OSRIC. Sir?

HORATIO. Is 't not possible to understand in another tongue?° You will
do 't,° sir, really.

HAMLET. What imports the nomination° of this gentleman?   120

OSRIC. Of Laertes?

HORATIO [*to* HAMLET]. His purse is empty already; all 's golden words are
spent.

HAMLET. Of him, sir.

OSRIC. I know you are not ignorant—   125

HAMLET. I would you did, sir. Yet in faith if you did, it would not much
approve° me. Well, sir?

OSRIC. You are not ignorant of what excellence Laertes is—

HAMLET. I dare not confess that, lest I should compare with him in excellence. But to know a man well were to know himself.°   130

OSRIC. I mean, sir, for° his weapon; but in the imputation laid on him by
them,° in his meed° he's unfellowed.°

HAMLET. What's his weapon?

OSRIC. Rapier and dagger.

HAMLET. That's two of his weapons—but well.°   135

OSRIC. The King, sir, hath wagered with him six Barbary horses, against
the which he° has impawned,° as I take it, six French rapiers and
poniards,° with their assigns,° as girdle, hangers,° and so.° Three of
the carriages,° in faith, are very dear to fancy,° very responsive° to
the hilts, most delicate° carriages, and of very liberal conceit.°   140

HAMLET. What call you the carriages?

110–111 of great article one with many articles in his inventory. **111 infusion**
essence, character infused into him by nature. **dearth and rareness** rarity. **111–112
make true diction** speak truly. **112 semblable** only true likeness. **112–113
who . . . trace** any other person who would wish to follow. **113 umbrage** shadow.
115 concernancy import, relevance. **116 rawer breath** unrefined speech that can
come short in praising him. **118 to understand . . . tongue** i.e., for you, Osric, to
understand when someone else speaks your language. (Horatio twits Osric for not being
able to understand the kind of flowery speech he himself uses, when Hamlet speaks in
such a vein. Alternatively, all this could be said to Hamlet.) **118–119 You will do 't** i.e.,
you can if you try, or, you may well have to try (to speak plainly). **120 nomination** naming. **127 approve** commend. **129–130 I dare . . . himself** I dare not boast of knowing Laertes's excellence lest I seem to imply a comparable excellence in myself. Certainly,
to know another person well, one must know oneself. **131 for** i.e., with. **131–132
imputation . . . them** reputation given him by others. **132 meed** merit. **unfellowed** unmatched. **135 but well** but never mind. **137 he** i.e., Laertes. **impawned**
staked, wagered. **138 poniards** daggers. **assigns** appurtenances. **hangers** straps on
the sword belt (*girdle*), from which the sword hung. **and so** and so on. **139 carriages**
(An affected way of saying *hangers;* literally, gun carriages.) **dear to fancy** delightful to
the fancy. **responsive** corresponding closely; matching or well adjusted. **140 delicate**
(i.e., in workmanship.) **liberal conceit** elaborate design.

HORATIO [*to* HAMLET]. I knew you must be edified by the margent° ere
    you had done.

OSRIC. The carriages, sir, are the hangers.

HAMLET. The phrase would be more germane to the matter if we could   145
    carry a cannon by our sides; I would it might be hangers till then.
    But, on: six Barbary horses against six French swords, their assigns,
    and three liberal-conceited carriages; that's the French bet against
    the Danish. Why is this impawned, as you call it?

OSRIC. The King, sir, hath laid,° sir, that in a dozen passes° between   150
    yourself and him, he shall not exceed you three hits. He hath laid
    on twelve for nine, and it would come to immediate trial, if your
    lordship would vouchsafe the answer.°

HAMLET. How if I answer no?

OSRIC. I mean, my lord, the opposition of your person in trial.   155

HAMLET. Sir, I will walk here in the hall. If it please His Majesty, it is the
    breathing time° of day with me. Let° the foils be brought, the gen-
    tleman willing, and the King hold his purpose. I will win for him
    and I can; if not, I will gain nothing but my shame and the odd hits.

OSRIC. Shall I deliver you° so?   160

HAMLET. To this effect, sir—after what flourish your nature will.

OSRIC. I commend° my duty to your lordship.

HAMLET. Yours, yours. [*Exit* OSRIC.] 'A does well to commend it himself;
    there are no tongues else for 's turn.°

HORATIO. This lapwing° runs away with the shell on his head.   165

HAMLET. 'A did comply with his dug° before a' sucked it. Thus has he—
    and many more of the same breed that I know the drossy° age
    dotes on—only got the tune° of the time and, out of an habit of en-
    counter,° a kind of yeasty° collection,° which carries them through
    and through the most fanned and winnowed opinions;° and do°   170
    but blow them to their trial, the bubbles are out.°

    Enter a LORD.

---

142 **margent** margin of a book, place for explanatory notes.   150 **laid** wagered.
passes bouts. (The odds of the betting are hard to explain. Possibly the King bets that
Hamlet will win at least five out of twelve, at which point Laertes raises the odds against
himself by betting he will win nine.)   153 **vouchsafe the answer** be so good as to accept the challenge. (Hamlet deliberately takes the phrase in its literal sense of replying.)
157 **breathing time** exercise period.   **Let** i.e., if.   160 **deliver you** report what you say.
162 **commend** commit to your favor. (A conventional salutation, but Hamlet wryly uses a
more literal meaning, "recommend," "praise," in line 163.)   164 **for 's turn** for his purposes, i.e., to do it for him.   165 **lapwing** (A proverbial type of youthful forwardness.
Also, a bird that draws intruders away from its nest and was thought to run about with its
head in the shell when newly hatched; a seeming reference to Osric's hat.)   166 **comply
. . . dug** observe ceremonious formality toward his nurse's or mother's teat.   167 **drossy**
laden with scum and impurities, frivolous.   168 **tune** temper, mood, manner of speech.
168–169 **an habit of encounter** a demeanor in conversing (with courtiers of his own
kind).   169 **yeasty** frothy.   **collection** i.e., of current phrases.   169–170 **carries . . .
opinions** sustains them right through the scrutiny of persons whose opinions are select
and refined. (Literally, like grain separated from its chaff. Osric is both the chaff and the
bubbly froth on the surface of the liquor that is soon blown away.)   170 **and do** yet do.
171 **blow . . . out** test them by merely blowing on them, and their bubbles burst.

LORD. My lord. His Majesty commended him to you by young Osric, who brings back to him that you attend him in the hall. He sends to know if your pleasure hold to play with Laertes, or that° you will take longer time.   175

HAMLET. I am constant to my purposes; they follow the King's pleasure. If his fitness speaks, mine is ready;° now or whensoever, provided I be so able as now.

LORD. The King and Queen and all are coming down.

HAMLET. In happy time.°   180

LORD. The Queen desires you to use some gentle entertainment° to Laertes before you fall to play.

HAMLET. She well instructs me.   [*Exit* LORD.]

HORATIO. You will lose, my lord.

HAMLET. I do not think so. Since he went into France, I have been in   185 continual practice; I shall win at the odds. But thou wouldst not think how ill all's here about my heart; but it is no matter.

HORATIO. Nay, good my lord—

HAMLET. It is but foolery, but it is such a kind of gaingiving° as would perhaps trouble a woman.   190

HORATIO. If your mind dislike anything, obey it. I will forestall their repair° hither and say you are not fit.

HAMLET. Not a whit, we defy augury. There is special providence in the fall of a sparrow. If it be now, 'tis not to come; if it be not to come, it will be now; if it be not now, yet it will come. The readiness is all.   195 Since no man of aught he leaves knows, what is 't to leave betimes? Let be.°

A table prepared. [*Enter*] *trumpets, drums, and officers with cushions;* KING, QUEEN, [OSRIC,] *and all the state; foils, daggers,* [*and wine borne in;*] *and* LAERTES.

KING. Come, Hamlet, come and take this hand from me.
[*The* KING *puts* LAERTES' *hand into* HAMLET'*s.*]

HAMLET [*to* LAERTES]. Give me your pardon, sir. I have done you wrong, But pardon 't as you are a gentleman.   200
This presence° knows,
And you must needs have heard, how I am punished°
With a sore distraction. What I have done
That might your nature, honor, and exception°
Roughly awake, I here proclaim was madness.   205
Was 't Hamlet wronged Laertes? Never Hamlet.
If Hamlet from himself be ta'en away,
And when he's not himself does wrong Laertes,

---

174 that if.   **177 If . . . ready** if he declares his readiness, my convenience waits on his. **180 In happy time** (A phrase of courtesy indicating that the time is convenient.)   **181 entertainment** greeting.   **189 gaingiving** misgiving.   **192 repair** coming.   **196–197 Since . . . Let be** Since no one has knowledge of what he is leaving behind, what does an early death matter after all? Enough; don't struggle against it.   **201 presence** royal assembly.   **202 punished** afflicted.   **204 exception** disapproval.

Then Hamlet does it not, Hamlet denies it.
Who does it, then? His madness. If 't be so,   210
Hamlet is of the faction° that is wronged;
His madness is poor Hamlet's enemy.
Sir, in this audience
Let my disclaiming from a purposed evil
Free me so far in your most generous thoughts   215
That I have° shot my arrow o'er the house
And hurt my brother.
LAERTES.   I am satisfied in nature,°
Whose motive° in this case should stir me most
To my revenge. But in my terms of honor
I stand aloof, and will no reconcilement   220
Till by some elder masters of known honor
I have a voice° and precedent of peace°
To keep my name ungored.° But till that time
I do receive our offered love like love,
And will not wrong it.
HAMLET.   I embrace it freely,   225
And will this brothers' wager frankly° play.—
Give us the foils. Come on.
LAERTES.   Come, one for me.
HAMLET. I'll be your foil,° Laertes. In mine ignorance
Your skill shall, like a star i' the darkest night.
Stick fiery off° indeed.
LAERTES.   You mock me, sir.   230
HAMLET. No, by this hand.
KING. Give them the foils, young Osric. Cousin Hamlet,
You know the wager?
HAMLET.   Very well, my lord.
Your Grace has laid the odds o'° the weaker side.
KING. I do not fear it; I have seen you both.   235
But since he is bettered,° we have therefore odds.
LAERTES. This is too heavy. Let me see another.
                              [*He exchanges his foil for another.*]
HAMLET. This likes me° well. These foils have all a length?
                              [*They prepare to play.*]
OSRIC. Ay, my good lord.
KING. Set me the stoups of wine upon that table.   240
If Hamlet give the first or second hit.
Or quit in answer of the third exchange,°

_____

211 **faction** party.   216 **That I have** as if I had.   217 **in nature** i.e., as to my personal
feelings.   218 **motive** prompting.   222 **voice** authoritative pronouncement.   **of peace**
for reconciliation.   223 **name ungored** reputation unwounded.   226 **frankly** without
ill feeling or the burden of rancor.   228 **foil** thin metal background which sets a jewel off
(with pun on the blunted rapier for fencing).   230 **Stick fiery off** stand out brilliantly.
234 **laid the odds o'** bet on, backed.   236 **is bettered** has improved; is the odds-on favorite. (Laertes' handicap is the "three hits" specified in line 151.)   238 **likes me** pleases
me.   242 **Or . . . exchange** i.e., or requites Laertes in the third bout for having won the
first two.

Let all the battlements their ordnance fire.
The King shall drink to Hamlet's better breath,°
And in the cup an union° shall he throw   245
Richer than that which four successive kings
In Denmark's crown have worn. Give me the cups,
And let the kettle° to the trumpet speak,
The trumpet to the cannoneer without,
The cannons to the heavens, the heaven to earth,   250
"Now the King drinks to Hamlet." Come, begin.

                                        Trumpets the while.
And you, the judges, bear a wary eye.

HAMLET. Come on, sir.

LAERTES. Come, my lord.   [*They play*. HAMLET *scores a hit.*]

HAMLET. One.   255

LAERTES. No.

HAMLET. Judgment.

OSRIC.   A hit, a very palpable hit.

                Drum, trumpets, and shot. Flourish. A piece goes off.

LAERTES. Well, again.

KING. Stay, give me drink. Hamlet, this pearl is thine.

[*He drinks, and throws a pearl in* HAMLET'S *cup.*]

Here's to thy health. Give him the cup.   260

HAMLET. I'll play this bout first. Set it by awhile.
Come. [*They play.*] Another hit; what say you?

LAERTES. A touch, a touch, I do confess 't.

KING. Our son shall win.

QUEEN.   He's fat° and scant of breath.
Here, Hamlet, take my napkin,° rub thy brows.   265
The Queen carouses° to thy fortune, Hamlet.

HAMLET. Good, madam!

KING. Gertrude, do not drink.

QUEEN. I will, my lord, I pray you pardon me.   [*She drinks.*]

KING [*aside*]. It is the poisoned cup. It is too late.   270

HAMLET. I dare not drink yet, madam; by and by.

QUEEN. Come, let me wipe thy face.

LAERTES [*to* KING]. My lord, I'll hit him now.

KING.   I do not think 't.

LAERTES [*aside*]. And yet it is almost against my conscience.

HAMLET. Come, for the third, Laertes. You do but dally.   275
I pray you, pass° with your best violence;
I am afeard you make a wanton of me.°

LAERTES. Say you so? Come on.   [*They play.*]

---

244 better breath improved vigor.   **245 union** pearl. (So called, according to Pliny's
Natural History, 9, because pearls are *unique*, never identical.)   **248 kettle** kettledrum.
264 fat not physically fit, out of training.   **265 napkin** handkerchief.   **266 carouses**
drinks a toast.   **276 pass** thrust.   **277 make . . . me** i.e., treat me like a spoiled child, trifle with me.

OSRIC. Nothing neither way.
LAERTES. Have at you now!

[LAERTES *wounds* HAMLET; *then, in scuffling, they change rapiers,*°
and HAMLET *wounds* LAERTES.]

KING.   Part them! They are incensed.   280
HAMLET. Nay, come, again.   [*The* QUEEN *falls.*]
OSRIC.   Look to the Queen there, ho!
HORATIO. They bleed on both sides. How is it, my lord?
OSRIC. How is 't, Laertes?
LAERTES. Why, as a woodcock° to mine own springe,° Osric;
    I am justly killed with mine own treachery.   285
HAMLET. How does the Queen?
KING.   She swoons to see them bleed.
QUEEN. No, no, the drink, the drink—O my dear Hamlet—
    The drink, the drink! I am poisoned.   [*She dies.*]
HAMLET. O villainy! Ho, let the door be locked!
    Treachery! Seek it out.   290

                                        [LAERTES *falls. Exit* OSRIC.]

LAERTES. It is here, Hamlet. Hamlet, thou art slain.
    No med'cine in the world can do thee good;
    In thee there is not half an hour's life.
    The treacherous instrument is in thy hand,
    Unbated° and envenomed. The foul practice°   295
    Hath turned itself on me. Lo, here I lie,
    Never to rise again. Thy mother's poisoned.
    I can no more. The King, the King's to blame.
HAMLET. The point envenomed too? Then, venom, to thy work.
                                            [*He stabs the* KING.]
ALL. Treason! Treason!   300
KING. O, yet defend me, friends! I am but hurt.
HAMLET [*forcing the* KING *to drink*].
    Here, thou incestuous, murderous, damnèd Dane,
    Drink off this potion. Is thy union° here?
    Follow my mother.   [*The* KING *dies.*]
LAERTES.   He is justly served.
    It is a poison tempered° by himself.   305
    Exchange forgiveness with me, noble Hamlet.
    Mine and my father's death come not upon thee,
    Nor thine on me!   [*He dies.*]
HAMLET. Heaven make thee free of it! I follow thee.
    I am dead, Horatio. Wretched Queen, adieu!   310

---

280 s.d. in scuffling, they change rapiers (This stage direction occurs in the Folio.
According to a widespread stage tradition, Hamlet receives a scratch, realizes that Laertes's
sword is unbated, and accordingly forces an exchange.)   **284 woodcock** a bird, a type of
stupidity or as a decoy.   **springe** trap, snare.   **295 Unbated** not blunted with a button.
practice plot.   **303 union** pearl. (See line 245; with grim puns on the word's other
meanings: marriage, shared death.)   **305 tempered** mixed.

You that look pale and tremble at this chance,°
That are but mutes° or audience to this act,
Had I but time—as this fell° sergeant,° Death,
Is strict° in his arrest°—O, I could tell you—
But let it be. Horatio, I am dead;   315
Thou livest. Report me and my cause aright
To the unsatisfied.
HORATIO.   Never believe it.
I am more an antique Roman° than a Dane.
Here's yet some liquor left.
[*He attempts to drink from the poisoned cup.* HAMLET *prevents him.*]
HAMLET.   As thou'rt a man,
Give me the cup! Let go! By heaven, I'll ha 't.   320
O God, Horatio, what a wounded name,
Things standing thus unknown, shall I leave behind me!
If thou didst ever hold me in thy heart,
Absent thee from felicity awhile,
And in this harsh world draw thy breath in pain   325
To tell my story.   *A march afar off* [*and a volley within*].
What warlike noise is this?

Enter OSRIC.

OSRIC. Young Fortinbras, with conquest come from Poland,
To th' ambassadors of England gives
This warlike volley.
HAMLET.   O, I die, Horatio!
The potent poison quite o'ercrows° my spirit.   330
I cannot live to hear the news from England,
But I do prophesy th' election lights
On Fortinbras. He has my dying voice.°
So tell him, with th' occurents° more and less
Which have solicited°—the rest is silence.   [*He dies.*] 335
HORATIO. Now cracks a noble heart. Good night, sweet prince,
And flights of angels sing thee to thy rest!

                                        [*March within.*]

Why does the drum come hither?

Enter FORTINBRAS, *with the* [*English*] *Ambassadors* [*with drum, colors, and attendants*].

FORTINBRAS. Where is this sight?

---

311 chance mischance.   **312 mutes** silent observers. (Literally, actors with nonspeaking parts.)   **313 fell** cruel.   **sergeant** sheriff's officer.   **314 strict** (1) severely just (2) unavoidable.   **314 arrest** (1) taking into custody (2) stopping my speech.   **318 Roman** (Suicide was an honorable choice for many Romans as an alternative to a dishonorable life.)   **330 o'ercrows** triumphs over (like the winner in a cockfight).   **333 voice** vote. **334 occurrents** events, incidents.   **335 solicited** moved, urged. (Hamlet doesn't finish saying what the events have prompted—presumably, his acts of vengeance, or his reporting of those events to Fortinbras.)

HORATIO.   What is it you would see?
    If aught of woe or wonder, cease your search.   340
FORTINBRAS. This quarry° cries on havoc.° O proud Death,
    What feast° is toward° in thine eternal cell,
    That thou so many princes at a shot
    So bloodily hast struck?
FIRST AMBASSADOR.   The sight is dismal,
    And our affirs from England come too late.   345
    The ears are senseless that should give us hearing,
    To tell him his commandment is fulfilled,
    That Rosencrantz and Guildenstern are dead.
    Where should we have our thanks?
HORATIO.   Not from his° mouth,
    Had it th' ability of life to thank you.   350
    He never gave commandment for their death.
    But since, so jump° upon this bloody question,°
    You from the Polack wars, and you from England,
    And here arrived, give orders that these bodies
    High on a stage° be placèd to the view,   355
    And let me speak to th' yet unknowing world
    How these things came about. So shall you hear
    Of carnal, bloody, and unnatural acts,
    Of accidental judgments,° casual° slaughters,
    Of deaths put on° by cunning and forced cause,°   360
    And, in this upshot, purposes mistook
    Fall'n on th' inventors' heads. All this can I
    Truly deliver.
FORTINBRAS.   Let us haste to hear it,
    And call the noblest to the audience.
    For me, with sorrow I embrace my fortune.   365
    I have some rights of memory° in this kingdom,
    Which now to claim my vantage° doth invite me.
HORATIO. Of that I shall have also cause to speak,
    And from his mouth whose voice will draw on more.°
    But let this same be presently° performed,   370
    Even while men's minds are wild, lest more mischance
    On° plots and errors happen.
FORTINBRAS.   Let four captains
    Bear Hamlet, like a soldier, to the stage,
    For he was likely, had he been put on,°

---

341 quarry heap of dead. **cries on havoc** proclaims a general slaughter. **342 feast**
i.e., Death feasting on those who have fallen. **toward** in preparation. **349 his** i.e.,
Claudius's. **352 jump** precisely, immediately. **question** dispute, affair. **355 stage**
platform. **359 judgments** retributions. **casual** occurring by chance. **360 put on** in-
stigated. **forced cause** contrivance. **366 of memory** traditional, remembered, unfor-
gotten. **367 vantage** favorable opportunity. **369 voice . . . more** vote will influence
still others. **370 presently** immediately. **372 On** on the basis of; on top of. **374 put
on** i.e., invested in royal office and so put to the test.

To have proved most royal; and for his passage,°   375
The soldiers' music and the rite of war
Speak° loudly for him.
Take up the bodies. Such a sight as this
Becomes the field,° but there shows much amiss.
Go bid the soldiers shoot.   380

                 Exeunt [marching, bearing off the dead bodies;
                        a peal of ordnance is shot off].

---

375 passage i.e., from life to death.   **377 Speak** (let them) speak.   **379 Becomes the field** suits the field of battle

---

YOUR TURN

Act 1

1. The first scene (like many other scenes in this play) is full of expressions of uncertainty. What are some of these uncertainties? The Ghost first appears at 1.1.42. Does his appearance surprise us, or have we been prepared for it? Or is there both preparation and surprise? Do the last four speeches of 1.1 help to introduce a note of hope? If so, how?

2. Does the King's opening speech in 1.2 reveal him to be an accomplished public speaker—or are lines 10–14 offensive? In his second speech (lines 41–49), what is the effect of naming Laertes four times? Claudius sometimes uses the royal pronouns ("we," "our"), sometimes the more intimate "I" and "my." Study his use of these in lines 1–4 and in 106–117. What do you think he is getting at?

3. Hamlet's first soliloquy (1.2.129–159) reveals that more than just his father's death distresses him. Be as specific as possible about the causes of Hamlet's anguish here. What traits does Hamlet reveal in his conversation with Horatio (1.2.160–258)?

4. What do you make of Polonius's advice to Laertes (1.3.55–81)? Is it sound? Sound advice, but here uttered by a fool? Ignoble advice? How would one follow the advice of line 78: "to thine own self be true"? In his words to Ophelia in 1.3.102–136, what does he reveal about himself?

5. Can 1.4.17–38 reasonably be taken as a speech on the "tragic flaw"? (On this idea, see page 906.) Or is the passage a much more limited discussion, a comment simply on Danish drinking habits?

6. Hamlet is convinced in 1.5.93–104 that the Ghost has told the truth, indeed, the only important truth. But do we detect in 105–112 a hint of a tone suggesting that Hamlet delights in hating villainy? If so, can it be said that later this delight grows, and that in some scenes (e.g., 3.3) we feel that Hamlet has almost become a diabolic revenger? Explain.

Act 2

1. Characterize Polonius on the basis of 2.1.1–76.
2. In light of what we have seen of Hamlet, is Ophelia's report of his strange behavior when he visits her understandable?
3. Why does 2.2.33–34 seem almost comic? How do these lines help us to form a view about Rosencrantz and Guildenstern?
4. Is "the hellish Pyrrhus" (2.2.422) Hamlet's version of Claudius? Or is he Hamlet, who soon will be responsible for the deaths of Polonius, Rosencrantz and Guildenstern, Claudius, Gertrude, Ophelia, and Laertes? Explain.
5. Is the First Player's speech (2.2.427ff.) an inflated speech? If so, why? To distinguish it from the poetry of the play itself? To characterize the bloody deeds that Hamlet cannot descend to?
6. In 2.2.504–542 Hamlet rebukes himself for not acting. Why has he not acted? Because he is a coward (line 531)? Because he has a conscience? Because no action can restore his father and his mother's purity? Because he doubts the Ghost? What reason(s) can you offer?

Act 3

1. What do you make of Hamlet's assertion to Ophelia: "I loved you not" (3.1.118)? Of his characterization of himself as full of "offenses" (3.1.121–127)? Why is Hamlet so harsh to Ophelia?
2. In 3.3.36–72 Claudius's conscience afflicts him. But is he repentant? What makes you say so?
3. Is Hamlet other than abhorrent in 3.3.73–96? Do we want him to kill Claudius at this moment, when Claudius (presumably with his back to Hamlet) is praying? Why?
4. The Ghost speaks of Hamlet's "almost blunted purpose" (3.4.115). Is the accusation fair? Explain.
5. How would you characterize the Hamlet who speaks in 3.4.209–224?

Act 4

1. Is Gertrude protecting Hamlet when she says he is mad (4.1.7), or does she believe that he is mad? If she believes he is mad, does it follow that she no longer feels ashamed and guilty? Explain.
2. Why should Hamlet hide Polonius's body (in 4.2)? Is he feigning madness? Is he on the edge of madness? Explain.
3. How can we explain Hamlet's willingness to go to England (4.3.52)?
4. Judging from 4.5, what has driven Ophelia mad? Is Laertes heroic, or somewhat foolish? Consider also the way Claudius treats him in 4.7.

Act 5

1. Would anything be lost if the gravediggers in 5.1 were omitted?
2. To what extent do we judge Hamlet severely for sending Rosencrantz and Guildenstern to their deaths, as he reports in 5.2? On the whole, do we think of Hamlet as an intriguer? What other intrigues has he engendered? How successful were they?

3. Does 5.2.193–197 show a paralysis of the will, or a wise recognition that more is needed than mere human scheming? Explain.

4. Does 5.2.280 suggest that Laertes takes advantage of a momentary pause and unfairly stabs Hamlet? Is the exchange of weapons accidental, or does Hamlet (as in Olivier's film version), realizing that he has been betrayed, deliberately get possession of Laertes's deadly weapon?

5. Fortinbras is often cut from the play. How much is lost by the cut? Explain.

6. Fortinbras gives Hamlet a soldier's funeral. Is this ridiculous? Can it fairly be said that, in a sense, Hamlet has been at war? Explain.

General Questions

1. Hamlet in 5.2.10–11 speaks of a "divinity that shapes our ends." To what extent does "divinity" (or Fate or mysterious Chance) play a role in the happenings?

2. How do Laertes, Fortinbras, and Horatio help to define Hamlet for us?

3. T. S. Eliot says in "Shakespeare and the Stoicism of Seneca" (1928) that Hamlet, having made a mess, "dies fairly well pleased with himself." Do you agree?

31

Comedy

Though etymology is not always helpful (after all, is it really illuminating to say that *tragedy* may come from a Greek word meaning "goat song"?), the etymology of *comedy* helps to reveal comedy's fundamental nature. **Comedy** (Greek: *komoidia*) is a revel-song; ancient Greek comedies are descended from fertility rituals that dramatized the joy of renewal, the joy of triumphing over obstacles, the joy of being (in a sense) reborn. Whereas the movement of tragedy is from prosperity to disaster, the movement of comedy is from some sort of minor disaster to prosperity.

To say, however, that comedy dramatizes the triumph over obstacles is to describe it as though it were melodrama, a play in which, after hairbreadth adventures, good prevails over evil, often in the form of the hero's unlikely last-minute rescue of the fair maiden from the clutches of the villain. What distinguishes comedy from melodrama is the pervasive high spirits of comedy. The joyous ending in comedy—usually a marriage—is in the spirit of what has gone before; the entire play, not only the end, is a celebration of fecundity.

The threats in the world of comedy are not taken very seriously; the parental tyranny that makes *Romeo and Juliet* and *Antigone* tragedies is, in comedy, laughable throughout. Parents may fret, fume, and lock doors, but in doing so they make themselves ridiculous, for love will find a way. Villains may threaten, but the audience never takes the threats seriously.

The marriage and renewal of society, so usual at the end of comedy, may be most improbable, but they do not therefore weaken the comedy. The stuff of comedy is, in part, improbability. In *A Midsummer Night's Dream*, Puck speaks for the spectator when he says:

And those things do best please me
That befall preposterously.

In tragedy, probability is important; in comedy, *im*probability is often desirable, for at least three reasons. First, comedy seeks to include as much as possible, to reveal the rich abundance of life. The motto of comedy (and the implication in the weddings with which it usually concludes) is, "The more the merrier." Second, the improbable is the surprising; surprise often evokes laughter, and laughter surely has a central place in comedy. Third, by getting the characters into improbable situations, the dramatist can show off the absurdity of their behavior. This point needs amplification.

Comedy often shows the absurdity of ideals. The miser, the puritan, the health faddist, and so on, are people of ideals, but their ideals are suffocating. The miser, for example, treats everything in terms of money; the miser's ideal causes him or her to renounce much of the abundance and joy of life. He or she is in love, but is unwilling to support a spouse; or he or she has a headache, but will not be so extravagant as to take an aspirin tablet. If a thief accosts the miser with "Your money or your life," the miser will prefer to give up life—and that is what in fact the miser has been doing all the while. Now, by putting this miser in a series of improbable situations, the dramatist can continue to demonstrate entertainingly the miser's absurdity.*

The comic protagonist's tenacious hold on his or her ideals is not very far from that of the tragic protagonist. In general, however, tragedy suggests the nobility of ideals; the tragic hero's ideals undo him or her, and they may be ideals about which we have serious reservations, but still we admire the nobility of these ideals. Romeo and Juliet will not put off their love for each other; Antigone will not yield to Creon, and Creon holds almost impossibly long to his stern position. But the comic protagonist who is always trying to keep his or her hands clean is funny; we laugh at this refusal to touch dirt with the rest of us, this refusal to enjoy the abundance life has to offer. The comic protagonist who is always talking about his or her beloved is funny; we laugh at the failure to see that the world is filled with people more attractive than the one with whom he or she is obsessed.

In short, the ideals for which the tragic protagonist loses the world seem important to us and gain, in large measure, our sympathy, but the ideals for which the comic protagonist loses the world seem trivial compared with the rich variety that life has to offer, and we laugh at their absurdity. The tragic figure makes a claim on our sympathy. The absurd comic figure continually sets up obstacles to our sympathetic interest; we feel detached from, superior to, and amused by comic figures. Something along these lines is behind William Butler Yeats's ("The Tragic Theatre," 1910) insistence that *character* is always present in comedy but not in tragedy. Though Yeats is eccentric in his notion that individual character is obliterated in tragedy, he interestingly gets at one of the important elements in comedy:

> When the tragic reverie is at its height . . . [we do not say,] "How well that man is realized. I should know him were I to meet him in the street," for it is always ourselves that we see upon the [tragic] stage. . . . Tragedy must always be a drowning and breaking of the dikes that separate man from man, and . . . it is upon these dikes comedy keeps house.

Most comic plays can be sorted into one of two types: romantic comedy and satiric comedy. **Romantic comedy** presents an ideal world, a golden world, a

---

*A character who is dominated by a single trait—avarice, jealousy, timidity, and so forth—is sometimes called a **humor character.** Medieval and Renaissance psychology held that an individual's personality depended on the mixture of four liquids (humors): blood (Latin: *sanguis*), choler, phlegm, and bile. An overabundance of one fluid produced a dominant trait, and even today "sanguine," "choleric," "phlegmatic," and "bilious" describe personalities.

Not all comedy, of course, depends on humor characters placed in situations that exhibit their absurdity. **High comedy** is largely verbal, depending on witty language; **farce,** at the other extreme, is dependent on inherently ludicrous situations—for example, a hobo is mistaken for a millionaire. Situation comedy, then, may use humor characters, but it need not do so.

world more delightful than our own; if there are difficulties in it, they are not briers but (to quote from Shakespeare's *As You Like It*) "burrs . . . thrown . . . in holiday foolery." It is the world of most of Shakespeare's comedies, a world of Illyria, of the Forest of Arden, of Belmont, of the moonlit Athens in *A Midsummer Night's Dream*. The chief figures are lovers; the course of their love is not smooth, but the outcome is never in doubt and the course is the more fun for being bumpy. Occasionally in this golden world there is a villain, but if so, the villain is a great bungler who never really does any harm; the world seems to be guided by a benevolent providence who prevents villains from seriously harming even themselves. In these plays, the world belongs to golden lads and lasses. When we laugh, we laugh not so much *at* them as *with* them.

If romantic comedy shows us a world with people more attractive than we find in our own, **satiric comedy** shows us a world with people less attractive. The satiric world seems dominated by morally inferior people—the decrepit wooer, the jealous spouse, the demanding parent. These unengaging figures go through their paces, revealing again and again their absurdity. The audience laughs *at* (rather than *with*) such figures, and writers justify this kind of comedy by claiming to reform society: antisocial members of the audience will see their grotesque images on the stage and will reform themselves when they leave the theater. But it is hard to believe that this theory is rooted in fact. Jonathan Swift was probably right when he said, "Satire is a sort of glass wherein beholders do generally discover everybody's face but their own."

Near the conclusion of a satiric comedy, the obstructing characters are dismissed, often perfunctorily, allowing for a happy ending—commonly the marriage of figures less colorful than the obstructionist(s). And so all-encompassing are the festivities at the end that even obstructionists are invited to join in the wedding feast. If they refuse to join, we may find them—yet again—laughable rather than sympathetic, though admittedly one may also feel lingering regret that this somewhat shabby world of ours cannot live up to the exalted (even if rigid and rather crazy) standards of the outsider who refuses to go along with the way of the world.

WILLIAM SHAKESPEARE

For a biographical note, see page 991.

*A Midsummer Night's Dream**

Edited by David Bevington

[DRAMATIS PERSONAE
THESEUS, *Duke of Athens*

---

* *A Midsummer Night's Dream* was first published in 1600 in a small book of a type called a quarto. A second quarto edition, printed in 1619 but based on the 1600 text, introduces a few corrections, but it also introduces many errors. The 1619 text in turn was the basis for the text in the first collected edition of Shakespeare's plays, the First Folio (1623). Bevington's edition is of course based on the text of 1600, but it includes a few corrections, and it modifies the punctuation in accordance with modern usage. Material added by the editor, such as amplifications in the *dramatis personae*, is enclosed within square brackets.

HIPPOLYTA, *Queen of the Amazons, betrothed to Theseus*
PHILOSTRATE, *Master of the Revels*
EGEUS, *father of Hermia*
HERMIA, *daughter of Egeus, in love with Lysander*
LYSANDER, *in love with Hermia*
DEMETRIUS, *in love with Hermia and favored by Egeus*
HELENA, *in love with Demetrius*

OBERON, *King of the Fairies*
TITANIA, *Queen of the Fairies*
PUCK, *or* ROBIN GOODFELLOW
PEASEBLOSSOM,
COBWEB,
MOTE, } *fairies attending Titania*
MUSTARDSEED,

Other FAIRIES *attending*

PETER QUINCE, *a carpenter,* PROLOGUE
NICK BOTTOM, *a weaver,* PYRAMUS
FRANCIS FLUTE, *a bellows mender,* THISBE
TOM SNOUT, *a tinker,* } *representing* WALL
SNUG, *a joiner,* LION
ROBIN STARVELING, *a tailor,* MOONSHINE

Lords and Attendants on Theseus and Hippolyta

SCENE: *Athens, and a wood near it*]

[1.1] *Enter* THESEUS, HIPPOLYTA, [*and* PHILOSTRATE,] *with others.*

THESEUS. Now, fair Hippolyta, our nuptial hour
  Draws on apace. Four happy days bring in
  Another moon; but, O, methinks, how slow
  This old moon wanes! She lingers° my desires,
  Like to a stepdame° or a dowager° 5
  Long withering out° a young man's revenue.
HIPPOLYTA. Four days will quickly steep themselves in night,
  Four nights will quickly dream away the time;
  And then the moon, like to a silver bow
  New bent in heaven, shall behold the night 10
  Of our solemnities.
THESEUS.   Go, Philostrate,
  Stir up the Athenian youth to merriments,
  Awake the pert and nimble spirit of mirth,
  Turn melancholy forth to funerals;
  The pale companion° is not for our pomp.°   [*Exit* PHILOSTRATE.] 15

1.1 Location: Athens, Theseus's court.   4 lingers postpones, delays the fulfillment of.
5 stepdame stepmother.   **dowager** i.e., a widow (whose right of inheritance from her
dead husband is eating into her son's estate).   **6 withering out** causing to dwindle.
15 companion fellow.   **pomp** ceremonial magnificence.

Hippolyta, I wooed thee with my sword°
And won thy love doing thee injuries;
But I will wed thee in another key,
With pomp, with triumph,° and with reveling.

Enter EGEUS *and his daughter* HERMIA, *and* LYSANDER, *and* DEMETRIUS.

EGEUS. Happy be Theseus, our renowned duke!   20
THESEUS. Thanks, good Egeus. What's the news with thee?
EGEUS. Full of vexation come I, with complaint
    Against my child, my daughter Hermia.
    Stand forth, Demetrius. My noble lord,
    This man hath my consent to marry her.   25
    Stand forth, Lysander. And, my gracious Duke,
    This man hath bewitched the bosom of my child.
    Thou, thou, Lysander, thou hast given her rhymes
    And interchanged love tokens with my child.
    Thou hast by moonlight at her window sung   30
    With feigning voice verses of feigning° love,
    And stol'n the impression of her fantasy°
    With bracelets of thy hair, rings, gauds,° conceits,°
    Knacks,° trifles, nosegays, sweetmeats—messengers
    Of strong prevailment in° unhardened youth.   35
    With cunning hast thou filched my daughter's heart,
    Turned her obedience, which is due to me,
    To stubborn harshness. And, my gracious Duke,
    Be it so° she will not here before Your Grace
    Consent to marry with Demetrius,   40
    I beg the ancient privilege of Athens:
    As she is mine, I may dispose of her,
    Which shall be either to this gentleman
    Or to her death, according to our law
    Immediately° provided in that case.   45
THESEUS. What say you, Hermia? Be advised, fair maid.
    To you your father should be as a god—
    One that composed your beauties, yea, and one
    To whom you are but as a form in wax
    By him imprinted, and within his power   50
    To leave° the figure or disfigure° it.
    Demetrius is a worthy gentleman.
HERMIA. So is Lysander.
THESEUS.   In himself he is;
    But in this kind,° wanting° your father's voice,°
    The other must be held the worthier.   55

---

16 with my sword i.e., in a military engagement against the Amazons, when Hippolyta was taken captive. **19 triumph** public festivity. **31 feigning** (1) counterfeiting (2) faining, desirous. **32 And . . . fantasy** and made her fall in love with you (imprinting your image on her imagination) by stealthy and dishonest means. **33 gauds** playthings. **conceits** fanciful trifles. **34 Knacks** knickknacks. **35 prevailment in** influence on. **39 Be it so** if. **45 Immediately** directly, with nothing intervening. **51 leave** i.e., leave unaltered. **disfigure** obliterate. **54 kind** respect. **wanting** lacking. **voice** approval.

HERMIA. I would my father looked but with my eyes.

THESEUS. Rather your eyes must with his judgment look.

HERMIA. I do entreat Your Grace to pardon me.
  I know not by what power I am made bold,
  Nor how it may concern° my modesty   60
  In such a presence here to plead my thoughts;
  But I beseech Your Grace that I may know
  The worst that may befall me in this case
  If I refuse to wed Demetrius.

THESEUS. Either to die the death or to abjure   65
  Forever the society of men.
  Therefore, fair Hermia, question your desires,
  Know of your youth, examine well your blood,°
  Whether, if you yield not to your father's choice,
  You can endure the livery° of a nun,   70
  For aye° to be in shady cloister mewed,°
  To live a barren sister all your life,
  Chanting faint hymns to the cold fruitless moon.
  Thrice blessèd they that master so their blood
  To undergo such maiden pilgrimage;   75
  But earthlier happy° is the rose distilled
  Than that which, withering on the virgin thorn,
  Grows, lives, and dies in single blessedness.

HERMIA. So will I grow, so live, so die, my lord,
  Ere I will yield my virgin patent° up   80
  Unto his lordship, whose unwishèd yoke
  My soul consents not to give sovereignty.

THESEUS. Take time to pause, and by the next new moon—
  The sealing day betwixt my love and me
  For everlasting bond of fellowship—   85
  Upon that day either prepare to die
  For disobedience to your father's will,
  Or° else to wed Demetrius, as he would,
  Or on Diana's altar to protest°
  For aye austerity and single life.   90

DEMETRIUS. Relent, sweet Hermia, and, Lysander, yield
  Thy crazèd° title to my certain right.

LYSANDER. You have her father's love, Demetrius;
  Let me have Hermia's. Do you marry him.

EGEUS. Scornful Lysander! True, he hath my love,   95
  And what is mine my love shall render him.
  And she is mine, and all my right of her
  I do estate unto° Demetrius.

LYSANDER. I am, my lord, as well derived° as he,
  As well possessed;° my love is more than his;   100

---

60 concern befit. **68 blood** passions. **70 livery** habit. **71 aye** ever. **mewed** shut
in (said of a hawk, poultry, etc.). **76 earthlier happy** happier as respects this world.
80 patent privilege. **88 Or** either. **89 protest** vow. **92 crazèd** cracked, unsound.
98 estate unto settle or bestow upon. **99 derived** descended, i.e., as well born.
100 possessed endowed with wealth.

My fortunes every way as fairly° ranked,
If not with vantage,° as Demetrius';
And, which is more than all these boasts can be,
I am beloved of beauteous Hermia.
Why should not I then prosecute my right?   105
Demetrius, I'll avouch it to his head,°
Made love to Nedar's daughter, Helena
And won her soul; and she, sweet lady, dotes,
Devoutly dotes, dotes in idolatry,
Upon this spotted° and inconstant man.   110

THESEUS. I must confess that I have heard so much,
And with Demetrius thought to have spoke thereof;
But, being overfull of self-affairs,°
My mind did lose it. But, Demetrius, come,
And come, Egeus, you shall go with me;   115
I have some private schooling° for you both.
For you, fair Hermia, look you arm° yourself
To fit your fancies° to your father's will;
Or else the law of Athens yields you up—
Which by no means we may extenuate°—   120
To death or to a vow of single life.
Come, my Hippolyta. What cheer, my love?
Demetrius and Egeus, go° along.
I must employ you in some business
Against° our nuptial and confer with you   125
Of something nearly that° concerns yourselves.

EGEUS. With duty and desire we follow you.
                    Exeunt [all but LYSANDER *and* HERMIA].

LYSANDER. How now, my love, why is your cheek so pale?
How chance the roses there do fade so fast?

HERMIA. Belike° for want of rain, which I could well   130
Beteem° them from the tempest of my eyes.

LYSANDER. Ay me! For aught that I could ever read,
Could ever hear by tale or history,
The course of true love never did run smooth
But either it was different in blood°—   135

HERMIA. O cross!° Too high to be enthralled to low.

LYSANDER. Or else misgrafted° in respect of years—

HERMIA. O spite! Too old to be engaged to young.

LYSANDER. Or else it stood upon the choice of friends°—

HERMIA. O hell, to choose love by another's eyes!   140

LYSANDER. Or if there were a sympathy° in choice,

---

101 fairly handsomely.   **102 vantage** superiority.   **106 head** i.e., face.   **110 spotted**
i.e., morally stained.   **113 self-affairs** my own concerns.   **116 schooling** admonition.
117 look you arm take care you prepare.   **118 fancies** likings, thoughts of love.   **120
extenuate** mitigate.   **123 go** i.e., come.   **125 Against** in preparation for.   **126 nearly
that** that closely.   **130 Belike** very likely.   **131 Beteem** grant, afford.   **135 blood**
hereditary station.   **136 cross** vexation.   **137 misgrafted** ill grafted, badly matched.
139 friends relatives.   **141 sympathy** agreement.

War, death, or sickness did lay siege to it,
Making it momentany° as a sound,
Swift as a shadow, short as any dream,
Brief as the lightning in the collied° night, 145
That in a spleen° unfolds° both heaven and earth,
And ere a man hath power to say "Behold!"
The jaws of darkness do devour it up.
So quick° bright things come to confusion.°

HERMIA. If then true lovers have been ever crossed,° 150
It stands as an edict in destiny.
Then let us teach our trial patience,°
Because it is a customary cross,
As due to love as thoughts and dreams and sighs,
Wishes and tears, poor fancy's° followers. 155

LYSANDER. A good persuasion.° Therefore, hear me, Hermia:
I have a widow aunt, a dowager
Of great revenue, and she hath no child.
From Athens is her house remote seven leagues;
And she respects° me as her only son. 160
There, gentle Hermia, may I marry thee,
And to that place the sharp Athenian law
Cannot pursue us. If thou lovest me, then,
Steal forth thy father's house tomorrow night;
And in the wood, a league without the town, 165
Where I did meet thee once with Helena
To do observance to a morn of May,°
There will I stay for thee.

HERMIA.   My good Lysander!
I swear to thee by Cupid's strongest bow,
By his best arrow° with the golden head, 170
By the simplicity° of Venus' doves,°
By that which knitteth souls and prospers loves,
And by that fire which burned the Carthage queen°
When the false Trojan° under sail was seen,
By all the vows that ever men have broke, 175
In number more than ever women spoke,
In that same place thou hast appointed me
Tomorrow truly will I meet with thee.

---

143 momentany lasting but a moment.   **145 collied** blackened (as with coal dust),
darkened.   **146 in a spleen** in a swift impulse, in a violent flash.   **unfolds** discloses.
149 quick quickly; or, perhaps, living, alive.   **confusion** ruin.   **150 ever crossed**
always thwarted.   **152 teach . . . patience** i.e., teach ourselves patience in this trial.
155 fancy's amorous passion's.   **156 persuasion** conviction.   **160 respects** regards.
167 do . . . May perform the ceremonies of May Day.   **170 best arrow** (Cupid's best
gold-pointed arrows were supposed to induce love; his blunt leaden arrows, aversion.)
171 simplicity innocence.   **doves** i.e., those that drew Venus's chariot.   **173, 174
Carthage queen, false Trojan** (Dido, Queen of Carthage, immolated herself on a funeral
pyre after having been deserted by the Trojan hero Aeneas.)

LYSANDER. Keep promise, love. Look, here comes Helena.

    Enter HELENA.

HERMIA. God speed, fair° Helena! Whither away?   180
HELENA. Call you me fair? That "fair" again unsay.
    Demetrius loves your fair.° O happy fair!°
    Your eyes are lodestars,° and your tongue's sweet air°
    More tunable° than lark to shepherd's ear
    When wheat is green, when hawthorn buds appear.   185
    Sickness is catching. O, were favor° so!
    Yours would I catch, fair Hermia, ere I go;
    My ear should catch your voice, my eye your eye,
    My tongue should catch your tongue's sweet melody.
    Were the world mine, Demetrius being bated,°   190
    The rest I'd give to be to you translated.°
    O, teach me how you look and with what art
    You sway the motion° of Demetrius' heart.
HERMIA. I frown upon him, yet he loves me still.
HELENA. O, that your frowns would teach my smiles such skill!   195
HERMIA. I give him curses, yet he gives me love.
HELENA. O, that my prayers could such affection° move!°
HERMIA. The more I hate, the more he follows me.
HELENA. The more I love, the more he hateth me.
HERMIA. His folly, Helena, is no fault of mine.   200
HELENA. None but your beauty. Would that fault were mine!
HERMIA. Take comfort. He no more shall see my face.
    Lysander and myself will fly this place.
    Before the time I did Lysander see
    Seemed Athens as a paradise to me.   205
    O, then, what graces in my love do dwell
    That he hath turned a heaven unto a hell!
LYSANDER. Helen, to you our minds we will unfold.
    Tomorrow night, when Phoebe° doth behold
    Her silver visage in the watery glass,°   210
    Decking with liquid pearl the bladed grass,
    A time that lovers' flights doth still° conceal,
    Through Athens' gates have we devised to steal.
HERMIA. And in the wood, where often you and I
    Upon faint° primrose beds were wont to lie,   215
    Emptying our bosoms of their counsel° sweet,
    There my Lysander and myself shall meet;
    And thence from Athens turn away our eyes,
    To seek new friends and stranger companies.
    Farewell, sweet playfellow. Pray thou for us,   220

---

180 fair fair-complexioned (generally regarded by the Elizabethans as more beautiful than dark-complexioned).   **182 your fair** your beauty (even though Hermia is dark-complexioned).   **happy fair** lucky fair one.   **183 lodestars** guiding stars.   **air** music.   **184 tunable** tuneful, melodious.   **186 favor** appearance, looks.   **190 bated** excepted.   **191 translated** transformed.   **193 motion** impulse.   **197 affection** passion.   **move** arouse.   **209 Phoebe** Diana, the moon.   **210 glass** mirror.   **212 still** always.   **215 faint** pale.   **216 counsel** secret thought.

And good luck grant thee thy Demetrius!
Keep word, Lysander. We must starve our sight
From lovers' food till morrow deep midnight.
LYSANDER.   I will, my Hermia.   *Exit* HERMIA.
                              Helena, adieu.
As you on him, Demetrius dote on you!   *Exit* LYSANDER.   225
HELENA.   How happy some o'er other some can be!°
Through Athens I am thought as fair as she.
But what of that? Demetrius thinks not so;
He will not know what all but he do know.
And as he errs, doting on Hermia's eyes,   230
So I, admiring of° his qualities.
Things base and vile, holding no quantity,°
Love can transpose to form and dignity.
Love looks not with the eyes, but with the mind,
And therefore is winged Cupid painted blind.   235
Nor hath Love's mind of any judgment taste;°
Wings, and no eyes, figure° unheedy haste.
And therefore is Love said to be a child,
Because in choice he is so oft beguiled.
As waggish° boys in game° themselves forswear,   240
So the boy Love is perjured everywhere.
For ere Demetrius looked on Hermia's eyne,°
He hailed down oaths that he was only mine;
And when this hail some heat from Hermia felt,
So he dissolved, and showers of oaths did melt.   245
I will go tell him of fair Hermia's flight.
Then to the wood will he tomorrow night
Pursue her; and for this intelligence°
If I have thanks, it is a dear expense.°
But herein mean I to enrich my pain,   250
To have his sight thither and back again.
                                                         Exit.

[1.2] *Enter* QUINCE *the carpenter, and* SNUG *the joiner, and* BOTTOM
       the weaver, and FLUTE *the bellows mender, and* SNOUT *the tin-*
       ker, and STARVELING *the tailor.*

QUINCE.   Is all our company here?
BOTTOM.   You were best to call them generally,° man by man, according
       to the scrip.°
QUINCE.   Here is the scroll of every man's name which is thought fit,
       through all Athens, to play in our interlude before the Duke and the   5
       Duchess on his wedding day at night.

---

226 o'er . . . can be can be in comparison to some others.   231 admiring of wondering at.   232 holding no quantity i.e., unsubstantial, unshapely.   236 Nor . . . taste i.e.,
nor has Love, which dwells in the fancy or imagination, any *taste* or least bit of judgment
or reason.   237 figure are a symbol of.   240 waggish playful, mischievous.   game
sport, jest.   242 eyne eyes. (Old form of plural.)   248 intelligence information.   249 a
dear expense i.e., a trouble worth taking, *dear* costly.   1.2 Location: Athens.   2
generally (Bottom's blunder for *individually.*)   3 scrip scrap (Bottom's error for *script*)

BOTTOM. First, good Peter Quince, say what the play treats on, then read
   the names of the actors, and so grow to° a point.

QUINCE. Marry,° our play is "The most lamentable comedy and most
   cruel death of Pyramus and Thisbe."   10

BOTTOM. A very good piece of work, I assure you, and a merry. Now,
   good Peter Quince, call forth your actors by the scroll. Masters,
   spread yourselves.

QUINCE. Answer as I call you. Nick Bottom,° the weaver.

BOTTOM. Ready. Name what part I am for, and proceed.   15

QUINCE. You, Nick Bottom, are set down for Pyramus.

BOTTOM. What is Pyramus? A lover or a tyrant?

QUINCE. A lover, that kills himself most gallant for love.

BOTTOM. That will ask some tears in the true performing of it. If I do it,
   let the audience look to their eyes. I will move storms; I will con-   20
   dole° in some measure. To the rest—yet my chief humor° is for a
   tyrant. I could play Ercles° rarely, or a part to tear a cat° in, to make
   all split.°
         "The raging rocks
         And shivering shocks   25
         Shall break the locks
            Of prison gates:
         And Phibbus' car°
         Shall shine from far
         And make and mar   30
            The foolish Fates."
   This was lofty! Now name the rest of the players. This is Ercles'
   vein, a tyrant's vein. A lover is more condoling.

QUINCE. Francis Flute, the bellows mender.

FLUTE. Here, Peter Quince.   35

QUINCE. Flute, you must take Thisbe on you.

FLUTE. What is Thisbe? A wandering knight?

QUINCE. It is the lady that Pyramus must love.

FLUTE. Nay, faith, let not me play a woman. I have a beard coming.

QUINCE. That's all one.° You shall play it in a mask, and you may speak as   40
   small° as you will.

BOTTOM. An° I may hide my face, let me play Thisbe too. I'll speak in a
   monstrous little voice, "Thisne, Thisne!" "Ah Pyramus, my lover dear!
   Thy Thisbe dear, and lady dear!"

QUINCE. No, no, you must play Pyramus, and, Flute, you Thisbe.   45

BOTTOM. Well, proceed.

QUINCE. Robin Starveling, the tailor.

STARVELING. Here, Peter Quince.

---

8 **grow** to come to.   9 **Marry** (A mild oath; originally the name of the Virgin Mary.)
14 **Bottom** (As a weaver's term, a *bottom* was an object around which thread was wound.)
20–21 **condole** lament, arouse pity.   21 **humor** inclination, whim.   22 **Ercles** Hercules.
(The tradition of ranting came from Seneca's *Hercules Furens*.)   **tear a cat** i.e., rant.
22–23 **make all split** i.e., cause a stir, bring the house down.   28 **Phibbus' car** Phoebus's
(the sun god) chariot.   40 **That's all one** it makes no difference.   41 **small** high-pitched.
42 **An** if (also at line 67).

QUINCE. Robin Starveling, you must play Thisbe's mother. Tom Snout, the
tinker.   50

SNOUT. Here, Peter Quince.

QUINCE. You, Pyramus' father; myself, Thisbe's father; Snug, the joiner,
you, the lion's part, and I hope here is a play fitted.

SNUG. Have you the lion's part written? Pray you, if it be, give it me, for
I am slow of study.   55

QUINCE. You may do it extempore, for it is nothing but roaring.

BOTTOM. Let me play the lion too. I will roar that I will do any man's
heart good to hear me. I will roar that I will make the Duke say, "Let
him roar again, let him roar again."

QUINCE. An you should do it too terribly, you would fright the Duchess   60
and the ladies, that they would shriek; and that were enough to
hang us all.

ALL. That would hang us, every mother's son.

BOTTOM. I grant you, friends, if you should fright the ladies out of their
wits, they would have no more discretion but to hang us; but I will   65
aggravate° my voice so that I will roar you° as gently as any sucking
dove;° I will roar you an 'twere any nightingale.

QUINCE. You can play no part but Pyramus; for Pyramus is a sweet-faced
man, a proper° man as one shall see in a summer's day, a most lovely
gentlemanlike man. Therefore you must needs play Pyramus.   70

BOTTOM. Well, I will undertake it. What beard were I best to play it in?

QUINCE. Why, what you will.

BOTTOM. I will discharge° it in either your° straw-color beard, your orange-
tawny beard, your purple-in-grain° beard, or your French-crown-color°
beard, your perfect yellow.   75

QUINCE. Some of your French crowns° have no hair at all, and then you
will play barefaced. But, masters, here are your parts. [*He distrib-
utes parts.*] And I am to entreat you, request you, and desire you to
con° them by tomorrow night; and meet me in the palace wood, a
mile without the town, by moonlight. There will we rehearse; for if   80
we meet in the city, we shall be dogged with company, and our
devices° known. In the meantime I will draw a bill° of properties,
such as our play wants. I pray you, fail me not.

BOTTOM. We will meet, and there we may rehearse most obscenely° and
courageously. Take pains, be perfect;° adieu.   85

QUINCE. At the Duke's oak we meet.

BOTTOM. Enough. Hold, or cut bowstrings.°

Exeunt.

---

66 aggravate (Bottom's blunder for *moderate.*) **roar you** i.e., roar for you.
66–67 sucking dove (Bottom conflates *sitting dove* and *sucking lamb,* two proverbial
images of innocence.) **69 proper** handsome. **73 discharge** perform. **your** i.e., you
know the kind I mean. **74 purple-in-grain** dyed a very deep red. (From *grain,* the
name applied to the dried insect used to make the dye.) **French-crown-color** i.e., color
of a French crown, a gold coin. **76 crowns** heads bald from syphilis, the "French disease." **79 con** learn by heart. **82 devices** plans. **bill** list. **84 obscenely** (An unintentionally funny blunder, whatever Bottom meant to say.) **85 perfect** i.e., letter-perfect
in memorizing your parts. **87 Hold . . . bowstrings** (An archer's expression not definitely explained, but probably meaning here "keep your promises, or give up the play.")

[2.1] *Enter a* FAIRY *at one door, and* ROBIN GOODFELLOW [PUCK] *at another.*

PUCK. How now, spirit, whither wander you?

FAIRY.
> Over hill, over dale,
>   Thorough° bush, thorough brier,
> Over park, over pale,°
>   Thorough flood, thorough fire,
> I do wander everywhere,   5
> Swifter than the moon's sphere;°
> And I serve the Fairy Queen,
> To dew her orbs° upon the green.
> The cowslips tall her pensioners° be.   10
> In their gold coats spots you see:
> Those be rubies, fairy favors;°
> In those freckles live their savors.°
> I must go seek some dewdrops here
> And hang a pearl in every cowslip's ear.   15
> Farewell, thou lob° of spirits: I'll be gone.
> Our Queen and all her elves come here anon.°

PUCK. The King doth keep his revels here tonight.
> Take heed the Queen come not within his sight.
> For Oberon is passing fell° and wrath,°   20
> Because that she as her attendant hath
> A lovely boy, stolen from an Indian king;
> She never had so sweet a changeling.°
> And jealous Oberon would have the child
> Knight of his train, to trace° the forests wild.   25
> But she perforce° withholds the lovèd boy,
> Crowns him with flowers, and makes him all her joy.
> And now they never meet in grove or green,
> By fountain° clear, or spangled starlight sheen,°
> But they do square,° that all their elves for fear   30
> Creep into acorn cups and hide them there.

FAIRY. Either I mistake your shape and making quite,
> Or else you are that shrewd° and knavish sprite°
> Called Robin Goodfellow. Are not you he
> That frights the maidens of the villagery,°   35
> Skim milk, and sometimes labor in the quern,°
> And bootless° make the breathless huswife° churn,

2.1 Location: A wood near Athens. 3 Thorough through. **4 pale** enclosure.
7 sphere orbit.   **9 orbs** circles, i.e., fairy rings (circular bands of grass, darker than the
surrounding area, caused by fungi enriching the soil). **10 pensioners** retainers, members of the royal bodyguard. **12 favors** love tokens. **13 savors** sweet smells. **16 lob**
country bumpkin. **17 anon** at once. **20 passing fell** exceedingly angry. **wrath**
wrathful. **23 changeling** child exchanged for another by the fairies. **25 trace** range
through. **26 perforce** forcibly. **29 fountain** spring. **starlight sheen** shining
starlight. **30 square** quarrel. **33 shrewd** mischievous. **sprite** spirit. **35 villagery**
village population. **36 quern** handmill. **37 bootless** in vain. **huswife** housewife.

And sometimes make the drink to bear no barm,°
Mislead night wanderers, laughing at their harm?
Those that "Hobgoblin" call you, and "Sweet Puck,"   40
You do their work, and they shall have good luck.
Are you not he?

PUCK.   Thou speakest aright;
I am that merry wanderer of the night.
I jest to Oberon and make him smile
When I a fat and bean-fed horse beguile,   45
Neighing in likeness of a filly foal;
And sometimes lurk I in a gossip's° bowl,
In very likeness of a roasted crab,°
And when she drinks, against her lips I bob
And on her withered dewlap° pour the ale.   50
The wisest aunt,° telling the saddest° tale,
Sometimes for three-foot stool mistaketh me;
Then slip I from her bum, down topples she,
And "Tailor"° cries, and falls into a cough;
And then the whole choir° hold their hips and laugh,   55
And waxen° in their mirth, and neeze,° and swear
A merrier hour was never wasted there.
But, room,° fairy! Here comes Oberon.

FAIRY.   And here my mistress. Would that he were gone!

Enter [OBERON] *the King of Fairies at one door, with his train; and*
[TITANIA] *the Queen at another, with hers.*

OBERON.   Ill met by moonlight, proud Titania.   60
TITANIA.   What, jealous Oberon? Fairies, skip hence.
I have forsworn his bed and company.
OBERON.   Tarry, rash wanton.° Am not I thy lord?
TITANIA.   Then I must be thy lady; but I know
When thou hast stolen away from Fairyland   65
And in the shape of Corin° sat all day,
Playing on pipes of corn° and versing love
To amorous Phillida.° Why art thou here
Come from the farthest step° of India
But that, forsooth, the bouncing Amazon,   70
Your buskined° mistress and your warrior love,
To Theseus must be wedded, and you come
To give their bed joy and prosperity.

---

38 barm yeast, head on the ale. **47 gossip's** old woman's. **48 crab** crabapple.
50 dewlap loose skin on neck. **51 aunt** old woman. **saddest** most serious. **54**
Tailor (possibly because she ends up sitting cross-legged on the floor, looking like a tailor.) **55 choir** company. **56 waxen** increase. **neeze** sneeze. **58 room** stand
aside, make room. **63 wanton** headstrong creature. **66, 68 Corin, Phillida** (Conventional names of pastoral lovers.) **67 corn** (Here, oat stalks.) **69 step** farthest limit
of travel, or, perhaps, *steep,* mountain range. **71 buskined** wearing half-boots called
buskins.

OBERON. How canst thou thus for shame, Titania,
    Glance at my credit with Hippolyta,°   75
    Knowing I know thy love to Theseus?
    Didst not thou lead him through the glimmering night
    From Perigenia,° whom he ravishèd?
    And make him with fair Aegles° break his faith,
    With Ariadne° and Antiopa?°   80
TITANIA. These are the forgeries of jealousy;
    And never, since the middle summer's spring,°
    Met we on hill, in dale, forest, or mead,
    By pavèd° fountain or by rushy° brook,
    Or in° the beachèd margent° of the sea,   85
    To dance our ringlets° to the whistling wind,
    But with thy brawls thou hast disturbed our sport.
    Therefore the winds, piping to us in vain,
    As in revenge, have sucked up from the sea
    Contagious° fogs; which, falling in the land,   90
    Hath every pelting° river made so proud
    That they have overborne their continents.°
    The ox hath therefore stretched his yoke in vain,
    The plowman lost his sweat, and the green corn°
    Hath rotted ere his youth attained a beard;   95
    The fold° stands empty in the drownèd field,
    And crows are fatted with the murrain° flock;
    The nine-men's-morris° is filled up with mud,
    And the quaint mazes° in the wanton° green
    For lack of tread are undistinguishable.   100
    The human mortals want° their winter° here;
    No night is now with hymn or carol blessed.
    Therefore° the moon, the governess of floods,
    Pale in her anger, washes all the air,

---

75 **Glance . . . Hippolyta** make insinuations about my favored relationship with Hippolyta.   78 **Perigenia** i.e., Perigouna, one of Theseus's conquests. (This and the following women are named in Thomas North's translation of Plutarch's "Life of Theseus.") 79 **Aegles** i.e., Aegle, for whom Theseus deserted Ariadne according to some accounts. 80 **Ariadne** the daughter of Minos, King of Crete, who helped Theseus to escape the labyrinth after killing the Minotaur; later she was abandoned by Theseus. **Antiopa** Queen of the Amazons and wife of Theseus; elsewhere identified with Hippolyta, but here thought of as a separate woman. 82 **middle summer's spring** beginning of midsummer. 84 **pavèd** with pebbled bottom. **rushy** bordered with rushes. 85 **in** on. **margent** edge, border. 86 **ringlets** dances in a ring (see *orbs* in line 9). 90 **Contagious** noxious. 91 **pelting** paltry. 92 **continents** banks that contain them. 94 **corn** grain of any kind. 96 **fold** pen for sheep or cattle. 97 **murrain** having died of the plague. 98 **nine-men's-morris** i.e., portion of the village green marked out in a square for a game played with nine pebbles or pegs. 99 **quaint mazes** i.e., intricate paths marked out on the village green to be followed rapidly on foot as a kind of contest. **wanton** luxuriant. 101 **want** lack. **winter** i.e., regular winter season; or, proper observances of winter, such as the *hymn or carol* in the next line (?). 103 **Therefore** i.e., as a result of our quarrel.

That rheumatic diseases° do abound.   105
And thorough this distemperature° we see
The seasons alter: hoary-headed frosts
Fall in the fresh lap of the crimson rose,
And on old Hiems'° thin and icy crown
An odorous chaplet of sweet summer buds   110
Is, as in mockery, set. The spring, the summer,
The childing° autumn, angry winter, change
Their wonted liveries,° and the mazèd° world
By their increase° now knows not which is which.
And this same progeny of evils comes   115
From our debate,° from our dissension;
We are their parents and original.°

OBERON.   Do you amend it, then; it lies in you.
Why should Titania cross her Oberon?
I do but beg a little changeling boy   120
To be my henchman.°

TITANIA.   Set your heart at rest.
The fairy land buys not the child of me.
His mother was a vot'ress of my order,
And in the spicèd Indian air by night
Full often hath she gossiped by my side   125
And sat with me on Neptune's yellow sands,
Marking th' embarkèd traders° on the flood,°
When we have laughed to see the sails conceive
And grow big-bellied with the wanton° wind;
Which she, with pretty and with swimming° gait,   130
Following—her womb then rich with my young squire—
Would imitate, and sail upon the land
To fetch me trifles, and return again
As from a voyage, rich with merchandise.
But she, being mortal, of that boy did die;   135
And for her sake do I rear up her boy,
And for her sake I will not part with him.

OBERON. How long within this wood intend you stay?

TITANIA. Perchance till after Theseus' wedding day.
If you will patiently dance in our round°   140
And see our moonlight revels, go with us;
If not, shun me, and I will spare° your haunts.

OBERON. Give me that boy and I will go with thee.

TITANIA. Not for thy fairy kingdom. Fairies, away!
We shall chide downright if I longer stay.   145

Exeunt [TITANIA *with her train*].

---

105 rheumatic diseases colds, flu, and other respiratory infections. **106
distemperature** disturbance in nature. **109 Hiems'** the winter god's. **112 childing**
fruitful, pregnant. **113 wonted liveries** usual apparel. **mazèd** bewildered. **114
their increase** their yield, what they produce. **116 debate** quarrel. **117 original** origin. **121 henchman** attendant, page. **127 traders** trading vessels. **flood** flood tide.
129 wanton sportive. **130 swimming** smooth, gliding. **140 round** circular dance.
142 spare shun.

OBERON. Well, go thy way. Thou shalt not from° this grove
    Till I torment thee for this injury.
    My gentle Puck, come hither. Thou rememb'rest
    Since° once I sat upon a promontory,
    And heard a mermaid on a dolphin's back   150
    Uttering such dulcet and harmonious breath°
    That the rude° sea grew civil at her song,
    And certain stars shot madly from their spheres
    To hear the sea-maid's music?
PUCK.   I remember.
OBERON. That very time I saw, but thou couldst not,   155
    Flying between the cold moon and the earth,
    Cupid all° armed. A certain aim he took
    At a fair vestal° thronèd by the west,
    And loosed° his love shaft smartly from his bow
    As° it should pierce a hundred thousand hearts;   160
    But I might° see young Cupid's fiery shaft
    Quenched in the chaste beams of the watery moon,
    And the imperial vot'ress passèd on
    In maiden meditation, fancy-free.°
    Yet marked I where the bolt° of Cupid fell: 165
    It fell upon a little western flower,
    Before milk-white, now purple with love's wound,
    And maidens call it "love-in-idleness."°
    Fetch me that flower; the herb I showed thee once.
    The juice of it on sleeping eyelids laid   170
    Will make or man or° woman madly dote
    Upon the next live creature that it sees.
    Fetch me this herb, and be thou here again
    Ere the leviathan° can swim a league.
PUCK. I'll put a girdle round about the earth   175
    In forty° minutes.   [*Exit.*]
OBERON.   Having once this juice,
    I'll watch Titania when she is asleep
    And drop the liquor of it in her eyes.
    The next thing then she waking looks upon,
    Be it on lion, bear, or wolf, or bull,   180
    On meddling monkey, or on busy ape,
    She shall pursue it with the soul of love.
    And ere I take this charm from off her sight,
    As I can take it with another herb,
    I'll make her render up her page to me.   185
    But who comes here? I am invisible,

---

146 from go from.   **149 Since** when.   **151 breath** voice, song.   **152 rude** rough.
157 all fully.   **158 vestal** vestal virgin. (Contains a complimentary allusion to Queen
Elizabeth as a votaress of Diana and probably refers to an actual entertainment in her
honor at Elvetham in 1591.)   **159 loosed** released.   **160 As** as if.   **161 might** could.
164 fancy-free free of love's spell.   **165 bolt** arrow.   **168 love-in-idleness** pansy,
heartsease.   **171 or . . . or** either . . . or.   **174 leviathan** sea monster, whale.
176 forty (Used indefinitely.)

And I will overhear their conference.

Enter DEMETRIUS, HELENA *following him.*

DEMETRIUS. I love thee not; therefore pursue me not.
Where is Lysander and fair Hermia?
The one I'll slay; the other slayeth me.   190
Thou toldst me they were stol'n unto this wood;
And here am I, and wode° within this wood,
Because I cannot meet my Hermia.
Hence, get thee gone, and follow me no more.

HELENA. You draw me, you hardhearted adamant!°   195
But yet you draw not iron, for my heart
Is true as steel. Leave° you your power to draw,
And I shall have no power to follow you.

DEMETRIUS. Do I entice you? Do I speak you fair?°
Or rather do I not in plainest truth   200
Tell you I do not nor I cannot love you?

HELENA. And even for that do I love you the more.
I am your spaniel; and, Demetrius,
The more you beat me, I will fawn on you.
Use me but as your spaniel, spurn me, strike me,   205
Neglect me, lose me; only give me leave,
Unworthy as I am, to follow you.
What worser place can I beg in your love—
And yet a place of high respect with me—
Than to be usèd as you use your dog?   210

DEMETRIUS. Tempt not too much the hatred of my spirit,
For I am sick when I do look on thee.

HELENA. And I am sick when I look not on you.

DEMETRIUS. You do impeach° your modesty too much
To leave the city and commit yourself   215
Into the hands of one that loves you not,
To trust the opportunity of night
And the ill counsel of a desert° place
With the rich worth of your virginity.

HELENA. Your virtue° is my privilege.° For that°   220
It is not night when I do see your face,
Therefore I think I am not in the night;
Nor doth this wood lack worlds of company,
For you, in my respect,° are all the world.
Then how can it be said I am alone   225
When all the world is here to look on me?

DEMETRIUS. I'll run from thee and hide me in the brakes,°
And leave thee to the mercy of wild beasts.

---

192 wode mad. (Pronounced "wood" and often spelled so.)   **195 adamant** lodestone, magnet (with pun on *hardhearted,* since adamant was also thought to be the hardest of all stones and was confused with the diamond).   **197 Leave** give up.   **199 fair** courteously.   **214 impeach** call into question.   **218 desert** deserted.   **220 virtue** goodness or power to attract.   **privilege** safeguard; warrant.   **For that** because.   **224 in my respect** as far as I am concerned.   **227 brakes** thickets.

HELENA. The wildest hath not such a heart as you.
         Run when you will, the story shall be changed: 230
         Apollo flies and Daphne holds the chase,°
         The dove pursues the griffin,° the mild hind°
         Makes speed to catch the tiger—bootless° speed,
         When cowardice pursues and valor flies!
DEMETRIUS. I will not stay° thy questions.° Let me go!   235
         Or if thou follow me, do not believe
         But I shall do thee mischief in the wood.
HELENA. Ay, in the temple, in the town, the field,
         You do me mischief. Fie, Demetrius!
         Your wrongs do set a scandal on my sex.°   240
         We cannot fight for love, as men may do;
         We should be wooed and were not made to woo.
                                              [Exit DEMETRIUS.]
         I'll follow thee and make a heaven of hell,
         To die upon° the hand I love so well.   [Exit.]
OBERON. Fare thee well, nymph. Ere he do leave this grove,   245
         Thou shalt fly him and he shall seek thy love.

         Enter PUCK.

         Hast thou the flower there? Welcome, wanderer.
PUCK. Ay, there it is.   [He offers the flower.]
OBERON.   I pray thee, give it me.
         I know a bank where the wild thyme blows,°
         Where oxlips° and the nodding violet grows,   250
         Quite overcanopied with luscious woodbine,°
         With sweet muskroses° and with eglantine.°
         There sleeps Titania sometimes of the night,
         Lulled in these flowers with dances and delight;
         And there the snake throws° her enameled skin,   255
         Weed° wide enough to wrap a fairy in.
         And with the juice of this I'll streak° her eyes
         And make her full of hateful fantasies.
         Take thou some of it, and seek through this grove.
                                              [He gives some love juice.]
         A sweet Athenian lady is in love   260
         With a disdainful youth. Anoint his eyes,
         But do it when the next thing he espies

---

231 Apollo . . . chase (In the ancient myth, Daphne fled from Apollo and was saved from rape by being transformed into a laurel tree; here it is the female who *holds the chase,* or pursues, instead of the male.)   **232 griffin** a fabulous monster with the head of an eagle and the body of a lion.   **hind** female deer.   **233 bootless** fruitless.   **235 stay** wait for. **questions** talk or argument.   **240 Your . . . sex** i.e., the wrongs that you do me cause me to act in a manner that disgraces my sex.   **244 upon** by.   **249 blows** blooms.   **250 oxlips** flowers resembling cowslip and primrose.   **251 woodbine** honeysuckle.   **252 muskroses** a kind of large, sweet-scented rose.   **eglantine** sweetbrier, another kind of rose.   **255 throws** sloughs off, sheds.   **256 Weed** garment.   **257 streak** anoint, touch gently.

May be the lady. Thou shalt know the man
By the Athenian garments he hath on.
Effect it with some care, that he may prove   265
More fond on° her than she upon her love;
And look thou meet me ere the first cock crow.
PUCK. Fear not, my lord, your servant shall do so.

Exeunt.

[2.2] *Enter* TITANIA, *Queen of Fairies, with her train.*

TITANIA. Come, now a roundel° and a fairy song;
    Then, for the third part of a minute, hence—
    Some to kill cankers° in the muskrose buds,
    Some war with reremice° for their leathern wings
    To make my small elves coats, and some keep back   5
    The clamorous owl, that nightly hoots and wonders
    At our quaint° spirits. Sing me now asleep.
    Then to your offices, and let me rest.

Fairies sing.

FIRST FAIRY.
            You spotted snakes with double° tongue,
                Thorny hedgehogs, be not seen;   10
            Newts° and blindworms, do no wrong,
                Come not near our Fairy Queen.
CHORUS.
                Philomel,° with melody
                Sing in our sweet lullaby;
            Lulla, lulla, lullaby, lulla, lulla, lullaby.   15
                Never harm
                Nor spell nor charm
            Come our lovely lady nigh.
            So good night, with lullaby.
FIRST FAIRY.
            Weaving spiders, come not here;   20
                Hence, you long-legged spinners, hence!
            Beetles black, approach not near;
                Worm nor snail, do no offense.
CHORUS.
                Philomel, with melody
                Sing in our sweet lullaby;   25
            Lulla, lulla, lullaby, lulla, lulla, lullaby.

---

266 fond on doting on.   **2.2 Location: The wood. 1 roundel** dance in a ring.
3 cankers cankerworms (i.e., caterpillars or grubs).   **4 reremice** bats.   **7 quaint** dainty.
9 double forked.   **11 Newts** water lizards (considered poisonous, as were *blindworms*—
small snakes with tiny eyes—and spiders).   **13 Philomel** the nightingale. (Philomela,
daughter of King Pandion, was transformed into a nightingale, according to Ovid's *Metamorphoses* 6, after she had been raped by her sister Procne's husband, Tereus.)

             Never harm
             Nor spell nor charm
             Come our lovely lady nigh.
             So good night, with lullaby.   30

                                          [TITANIA *sleeps.*]

SECOND FAIRY.
             Hence, away! Now all is well.
             One aloof stand sentinel.

                                          [*Exeunt* FAIRIES.]

Enter OBERON [*and squeezes the flower on* TITANIA'*s eyelids*].

OBERON.
             What thou seest when thou dost wake,
             Do it for thy true love take;
             Love and languish for his sake.   35
             Be it ounce,° or cat, or bear,
             Pard,° or boar with bristled hair,
             In thy eye that shall appear
             When thou wak'st, it is thy dear.
             Wake when some vile thing is near.   [*Exit.*]   40

Enter LYSANDER *and* HERMIA.

LYSANDER. Fair love, you faint with wandering in the wood;
           And to speak truth, I have forgot our way.
           We'll rest us, Hermia, if you think it good,
           And tarry for the comfort of the day.
HERMIA. Be it so, Lysander. Find you out a bed,   45
         For I upon this bank will rest my head.
LYSANDER. One turf shall serve as pillow for us both;
           One heart, one bed, two bosoms, and one troth.°
HERMIA. Nay, good Lysander, for my sake, my dear,
         Lie further off yet; do not lie so near.   50
LYSANDER. O, take the sense, sweet, of my innocence!°
           Love takes the meaning in love's conference.°
           I mean that my heart unto yours is knit
           So that but one heart we can make of it;
           Two bosoms interchainèd with an oath—   55
           So then two bosoms and a single troth.
           Then by your side no bed-room me deny,
           For lying so, Hermia, I do not lie.°
HERMIA. Lysander riddles very prettily.
         Now much beshrew° my manners and my pride   60
         If Hermia meant to say Lysander lied.
         But, gentle friend, for love and courtesy

---

36 ounce lynx. **37 Pard** leopard. **48 troth** faith, trothplight. **51 take . . . innocence** i.e., interpret my intention as innocent. **52 Love . . . conference** i.e., when
lovers confer, love teaches each lover to interpret the other's meaning lovingly. **58 lie**
tell a falsehood (with a riddling pun on *lie,* recline). **60 beshrew** curse. (But mildly
meant.)

Lie further off, in human° modesty;
Such separation as may well be said
Becomes a virtuous bachelor and a maid,   65
So far be distant; and good night, sweet friend.
Thy love ne'er alter till thy sweet life end!
LYSANDER. Amen, amen, to that fair prayer, say I,
And then end life when I end loyalty!
Here is my bed. Sleep give thee all his rest!   70
HERMIA. With half that wish the wisher's eyes be pressed!°
                  [*They sleep, separated by a short distance.*]

    Enter PUCK.

PUCK.
      Through the forest have I gone,
      But Athenian found I none
      On whose eyes I might approve°
      This flower's force in stirring love.   75
      Night and silence.—Who is here?
      Weeds of Athens he doth wear.
      This is he, my master said,
      Despisèd the Athenian maid;
      And here the maiden, sleeping sound,   80
      On the dank and dirty ground.
      Pretty soul, she durst not lie
      Near this lack-love, this kill-courtesy.
      Churl, upon thy eyes I throw
      All the power this charm doth owe.°   85

           [*He applies the love juice.*]

      When thou wak'st, let love forbid
      Sleep his seat on thy eyelid.
      So awake when I am gone,
      For I must now to Oberon.   *Exit.*

    Enter DEMETRIUS *and* HELENA, *running.*

HELENA. Stay, though thou kill me, sweet Demetrius!   90
DEMETRIUS. I charge thee, hence, and do not haunt me thus.
HELENA. O, wilt thou darkling° leave me? Do not so.
DEMETRIUS. Stay, on thy peril!° I alone will go.   [*Exit.*]
HELENA. O, I am out of breath in this fond° chase!
    The more my prayer, the lesser is my grace.°   95
    Happy is Hermia, wheresoe'er she lies,
    For she hath blessèd and attractive eyes.
    How came her eyes so bright? Not with salt tears;
    If so, my eyes are oftener washed than hers.

---

63 human courteous.   **71 With . . . pressed** i.e., may we share your wish, so that your
eyes too are *pressed*, closed, in sleep.   **74 approve** test.   **85 owe** own.   **92 darkling** in
the dark.   **93 on thy peril** i.e., on pain of danger to you if you don't obey me and stay.
94 fond doting.   **95 my grace** the favor I obtain.

No, no, I am as ugly as a bear;   100
For beasts that meet me run away for fear.
Therefore no marvel though Demetrius
Do, as a monster, fly my presence thus.°
What wicked and dissembling glass of mine
Made me compare° with Hermia's sphery eyne?°   105
But who is here? Lysander, on the ground?
Dead, or asleep? I see no blood, no wound.
Lysander, if you live, good sir, awake.

LYSANDER [*awaking*]. And run through fire I will for thy sweet sake.
Transparent° Helena! Nature shows art,   110
That through thy bosom makes me see thy heart.
Where is Demetrius? O, how fit a word
Is that vile name to perish on my sword!

HELENA. Do not say so, Lysander, say not so.
What though he love your Hermia? Lord, what though?   115
Yet Hermia still loves you. Then be content.

LYSANDER. Content with Hermia? No! I do repent
The tedious minutes I with her have spent.
Not Hermia but Helena I love.
Who will not change a raven for a dove?   120
The will of man is by his reason swayed,
And reason says you are the worthier maid.
Things growing are not ripe until their season;
So I, being young, till now ripe not° to reason.
And touching° now the point° of human skill,°   125
Reason becomes the marshal to my will
And leads me to your eyes, where I o'erlook°
Love's stories written in love's richest book.

HELENA. Wherefore° was I to this keen mockery born?
When at your hands did I deserve this scorn?   130
Is't not enough, is't not enough, young man,
That I did never, no, nor never can,
Deserve a sweet look from Demetrius' eye,
But you must flout my insufficiency?
Good troth,° you do me wrong, good sooth,° you do,   135
In such disdainful manner me to woo.
But fare you well. Perforce I must confess
I thought you lord of° more true gentleness.°
O, that a lady, of° one man refused,
Should of another therefore be abused!°   *Exit.*   140

LYSANDER. She sees not Hermia. Hermia, sleep thou there,
And never mayst thou come Lysander near!

102–103 no marvel . . . thus i.e., no wonder that Demetrius flies from me as from a
monster.   105 compare vie.   sphery eyne eyes as bright as stars in their spheres.
110 Transparent (1) radiant (2) able to be seen through.   124 ripe not (am) not
ripened.   125 touching reaching.   point summit.   skill judgment.   127 o'erlook
read.   129 Wherefore why.   135 Good troth, good sooth i.e., indeed, truly.
138 lord of i.e., possessor of.   gentleness courtesy.   139 of by.   140 abused ill
treated.

For as a surfeit of the sweetest things
The deepest loathing to the stomach brings,
Or as the heresies that men do leave   145
Are hated most of those they did deceive,°
So thou, my surfeit and my heresy,
Of all be hated, but the most of me!
And, all my powers, address° your love and might
To honor Helen and to be her knight!   *Exit.*   150
HERMIA [*awaking*]. Help me, Lysander, help me! Do thy best
To pluck this crawling serpent from my breast!
Ay me, for pity! What a dream was here!
Lysander, look how I do quake with fear.
Methought a serpent ate my heart away,   155
And you sat smiling at his cruel prey.°
Lysander! What, removed? Lysander! Lord!
What, out of hearing? Gone? No sound, no word?
Alack, where are you? Speak, an if° you hear;
Speak, of all loves!° I swoon almost with fear.   160
No? Then I well perceive you are not nigh.
Either death, or you, I'll find immediately.

                   Exit. [*The sleeping* TITANIA *remains.*]

[3.1] *Enter the clowns* [QUINCE, SNUG, BOTTOM, FLUTE, SNOUT, *and*
        STARVELING].

BOTTOM. Are we all met?
QUINCE. Pat, pat;° and here's a marvelous convenient place for our
    rehearsal. This green plot shall be our stage, this hawthorn brake°
    our tiring-house,° and we will do it in action as we will do it before
    the Duke.   5
BOTTOM. Peter Quince?
QUINCE. What sayest thou, bully° Bottom?
BOTTOM. There are things in this comedy of Pyramus and Thisbe that
    will never please. First, Pyramus must draw a sword to kill himself,
    which the ladies cannot abide. How answer you that?   10
SNOUT. By 'r lakin,° a parlous° fear.
STARVELING. I believe we must leave the killing out, when all is done.°
BOTTOM. Not a whit. I have a device to make all well. Write me° a pro-
    logue, and let the prologue seem to say we will do no harm with
    our swords, and that Pyramus is not killed indeed; and for the more 15
    better assurance, tell them that I, Pyramus, am not Pyramus but
    Bottom the weaver. This will put them out of fear.

145–146 **as . . . deceive** as renounced heresies are hated most by those persons who formerly were deceived by them.   **149 address** direct, apply.   **156 prey** act of preying.
159 an if if.   **160 of all loves** for all love's sake.   **3.1 Location: The action is continuous.**   **2 pat** on the dot, punctually.   **3 brake** thicket.   **4 tiring-house** attiring area,
hence backstage.   **7 bully** i.e., worthy, jolly, fine fellow.   **11 By 'r lakin** by our ladykin,
i.e., the Virgin Mary.   **parlous** alarming.   **12 when all is done** i.e., when all is said and
done.   **13 Write me** i.e., write at my suggestion. (*Me* is used colloquially.)

QUINCE. Well, we will have such a prologue, and it shall be written in
    eight and six.°

BOTTOM. No, make it two more; let it be written in eight and eight.   20

SNOUT. Will not the ladies be afeard of the lion?

STARVELING. I fear it, I promise you.

BOTTOM. Masters, you ought to consider with yourselves, to bring in—
    God shield us!—a lion among ladies° is a most dreadful thing. For
    there is not a more fearful° wildfowl than your lion living; and we   25
    ought to look to 't.

SNOUT. Therefore another prologue must tell he is not a lion.

BOTTOM. Nay, you must name his name, and half his face must be seen
    through the lion's neck, and he himself must speak through, saying
    thus, or to the same defect:° "Ladies"—or "Fair ladies—I would   30
    wish you"—or "I would request you"—or "I would entreat you—
    not to fear, not to tremble; my life for yours.° If you think I come
    hither as a lion, it were pity of my life.° No, I am no such thing: I am
    a man as other men are." And there indeed let him name his name
    and tell them plainly he is Snug the joiner.   35

QUINCE. Well, it shall be so. But there is two hard things: that is, to bring
    the moonlight into a chamber; for, you know, Pyramus and Thisbe
    meet by moonlight.

SNOUT. Doth the moon shine that night we play our play?

BOTTOM. A calendar, a calendar! Look in the almanac. Find out moonshine,   40
    find out moonshine.   [*They consult an almanac.*]

QUINCE. Yes, it doth shine that night.

BOTTOM. Why, then, may you leave a casement of the great chamber
    window, where we play, open, and the moon may shine in at the
    casement.   45

QUINCE. Ay; or else one must come in with a bush of thorns° and a
    lantern and say he comes to disfigure,° or to present,° the person of
    Moonshine. Then there is another thing: we must have a wall in
    the great chamber; for Pyramus and Thisbe, says the story, did talk
    through the chink of a wall.   50

SNOUT. You can never bring in a wall. What say you, Bottom?

BOTTOM. Some man or other must present Wall. And let him have some
    plaster, or some loam, or some roughcast° about him, to signify
    wall; or let him hold his fingers thus, and through that cranny
    shall Pyramus and Thisbe whisper.   55

---

19 eight and six alternate lines of eight and six syllables, a common ballad measure.   **24
lion among ladies** (A contemporary pamphlet tells how at the christening in 1594 of
Prince Henry, eldest son of King James VI of Scotland, later James I of England, a "black-
amoor" instead of a lion drew the triumphal chariot, since the lion's presence might have
"brought some fear to the nearest.")   **25 fearful** fear-inspiring.   **30 defect** (Bottom's
blunder for *effect*.)   **32 my life for yours** i.e., I pledge my life to make your lives safe.
33 it were . . . life my life would be endangered.   **46 bush of thorns** bundle of thorn-
bush faggots (part of the accoutrements of the man in the moon, according to the popular
notions of the time, along with his lantern and his dog).   **47 disfigure** (Quince's blunder
for *figure*.)   **present** represent.   **53 roughcast** a mixture of lime and gravel used to
plaster the outside of buildings.

QUINCE. If that may be, then all is well. Come, sit down, every mother's
son, and rehearse your parts. Pyramus, you begin. When you have
spoken your speech, enter into that brake, and so everyone according to his cue.

    Enter ROBIN [PUCK].

PUCK. What hempen homespuns° have we swaggering here   60
So near the cradle° of the Fairy Queen?
What, a play toward?° I'll be an auditor;
An actor too perhaps, if I see cause.
QUINCE. Speak, Pyramus. Thisbe, stand forth.
BOTTOM [*as* PYRAMUS].
    "Thisbe, the flowers of odious savors sweet—"   65
QUINCE. Odors, odors.
BOTTOM. "—Odors savors sweet;
    So hath thy breath, my dearest Thisbe dear.
    But hark, a voice! Stay thou but here awhile,
    And by and by I will to thee appear."   *Exit.*   70
PUCK. A stranger Pyramus than e'er played here.°   [*Exit.*]
FLUTE. Must I speak now?
QUINCE. Ay, marry, must you; for you must understand he goes but to see
a noise that he heard, and is to come again.
FLUTE [*as* THISBE]. "Most radiant Pyramus, most lily-white of hue,   75
Of color like the red rose on triumphant° brier,
Most brisky juvenal° and eke° most lovely Jew,°
    As true as truest horse, that yet would never tire.
I'll meet thee, Pyramus, at Ninny's tomb."
QUINCE. "Ninus'° tomb," man. Why, you must not speak that yet. That   80
you answer to Pyramus. You speak all your part° at once, cues and all.
Pyramus, enter. Your cue is past; it is "never tire."
FLUTE. O—"As true as truest horse, that yet would never tire."

    [*Enter* PUCK, *and* BOTTOM *as* PYRAMUS *with the ass head.*°]

BOTTOM. "If I were fair,° Thisbe, I were° only thine."
QUINCE. O, monstrous! O, strange! We are haunted. Pray, masters! Fly,   85
    masters! Help!
        [*Exeunt* QUINCE, SNUG, FLUTE, SNOUT, *and* STARVELING.]
PUCK. I'll follow you, I'll lead you about a round,°
    Through bog, through bush, through brake, through brier.

---

60 hempen homespuns i.e., rustics dressed in clothes woven of coarse, homespun fabric made from hemp.   **61 cradle** i.e., Titania's bower.   **62 toward** about to take place.
71 A stranger . . . here (Puck indicates that he has conceived of his plan to present a
"stranger" Pyramus than ever seen before, and so Puck exits to put his plan into effect.)
76 triumphant magnificent.   **77 brisky juvenal** lively youth.   **eke** also.   **Jew** (Probably an absurd repetition of the first syllable of *juvenal,* or Flute's error for *jewel.*)   **80
Ninus** mythical founder of Nineveh (whose wife, Semiramis, was supposed to have built
the walls of Babylon where the story of Pyramus and Thisbe takes place).   **81 part** (An
actor's *part* was a script consisting only of his speeches and their cues.)   **83 s.d. with
the ass head** (This stage direction, taken from the Folio, presumably refers to a standard
stage property.)   **84 fair** handsome.   **were** would be.   **87 about a round** roundabout.

Sometimes a horse I'll be, sometimes a hound,
  A hog, a headless bear, sometimes a fire;°   90
And neigh, and bark, and grunt, and roar, and burn,
Like horse, hound, hog, bear, fire, at every turn.   *Exit.*

BOTTOM. Why do they run away? This is a knavery of them to make me
  afeard.

    Enter SNOUT.

SNOUT. O Bottom, thou art changed! What do I see on thee?   95
BOTTOM. What do you see? You see an ass head of your own, do you?

                                                                [*Exit* SNOUT.]

    Enter QUINCE.

QUINCE. Bless thee, Bottom, bless thee! Thou art translated.°   *Exit.*
BOTTOM. I see their knavery. This is to make an ass of me, to fright me,
  if they could. But I will not stir from this place, do what they can.
  I will walk up and down here, and will sing, that they shall hear I am   100
  not afraid.   [*Sings.*]
      The ouzel cock° so black of hue,
        With orange-tawny bill,
      The throstle° with his note so true,
        The wren with little quill°—   105
TITANIA [*awaking*]. What angel wakes me from my flowery bed?
BOTTOM [*sings*].
      The finch, the sparrow, and the lark,
        The plainsong° cuckoo gray,
      Whose note full many a man doth mark,
        And dares not answer nay°—   110
  For, indeed, who would set his wit to so foolish a bird? Who would
  give a bird the lie,° though he cry "cuckoo" never so?°
TITANIA. I pray thee, gentle mortal, sing again.
  Mine ear is much enamored of thy note;
  So is mine eye enthrallèd to thy shape;   115
  And thy fair virtue's force° perforce doth move me
  On the first view to say, to swear, I love thee.
BOTTOM. Methinks, mistress, you should have little reason for that. And
  yet, to say the truth, reason and love keep little company together
  nowadays. The more the pity that some honest neighbors will not   120
  make them friends. Nay, I can gleek° upon occasion.
TITANIA. Thou art as wise as thou art beautiful.
BOTTOM. Not so, neither. But if I had wit enough to get out of this
  wood, I have enough to serve mine own turn.°

---

90 fire will-o'-the-wisp.   **97 translated** transformed.   **102 ouzel cock** male blackbird.
104 throstle song thrush.   **105 quill** (Literally, a reed pipe; hence, the bird's piping
song.)   **108 plainsong** singing a melody without variations.   **110 dares . . . nay** i.e.,
cannot deny that he is a cuckold.   **112 give . . . lie** call the bird a liar.   **never so** ever so
much.   **116 thy . . . force** the power of your beauty.   **121 gleek** scoff, jest.
124 serve . . . turn answer my purpose.

TITANIA. Out of this wood do not desire to go.   125
    Thou shalt remain here, whether thou wilt or no.
    I am a spirit of no common rate.°
    The summer still° doth tend upon my state,°
    And I do love thee. Therefore go with me.
    I'll give thee fairies to attend on thee   130
    And they shall fetch thee jewels from the deep,
    And sing while thou on pressèd flowers dost sleep.
    And I will purge thy mortal grossness° so
    That thou shalt like an airy spirit go.
    Peaseblossom, Cobweb, Mote,° and Mustardseed!   135

Enter four FAIRIES [PEASEBLOSSOM, COBWEB, MOTE, *and* MUSTARDSEED].

PEASEBLOSSOM. Ready.
COBWEB. And I.
MOTE.   And I.
MUSTARDSEED.   And I.
ALL.   Where shall we go?
TITANIA. Be kind and courteous to this gentleman.
    Hop in his walks and gambol in his eyes;°
    Feed him with apricots and dewberries,°   140
    With purple grapes, green figs, and mulberries;
    The honey bags steal from the humble-bees,
    And for night tapers crop their waxen thighs
    And light them at the fiery glowworms' eyes,
    To have my love to bed and to arise;   145
    And pluck the wings from painted butterflies
    To fan the moonbeams from his sleeping eyes.
    Nod to him, elves, and do him courtesies.
PEASEBLOSSOM. Hail, mortal!
COBWEB. Hail!   150
MOTE. Hail!
MUSTARDSEED. Hail!
BOTTOM. I cry Your Worships mercy, heartily. I beseech Your Worship's
    name.
COBWEB. Cobweb.   155
BOTTOM. I shall desire you of more acquaintance, good Master Cobweb.
    If I cut my finger, I shall make bold with you.°—Your name, honest
    gentleman?
PEASEBLOSSOM. Peaseblossom.
BOTTOM. I pray you, commend me to Mistress Squash,° your mother,   160
    and to Master Peascod,° your father. Good Master Peaseblossom, I

---

127 rate rank, value. **128 still** ever, always. **doth . . . state** waits upon me as a part of
my royal retinue. **133 mortal grossness** materiality (i.e., the corporeal nature of a mortal being). **135 Mote** i.e. speck. (The two words *moth* and *mote* were pronounced alike,
and both meanings may be present.) **139 in his eyes** in his sight (i.e., before him).
140 dewberries blackberries. **157 If . . . you** (Cobwebs were used to stanch bleeding.)
160 Squash unripe pea pod. **161 Peascod** ripe pea pod.

shall desire you of more acquaintance too.—Your name, I beseech
you, sir?

MUSTARDSEED. Mustardseed.

BOTTOM. Good Master Mustardseed I know your patience° well. That   165
same cowardly giantlike ox-beef hath devoured many a gentleman
of your house. I promise you, your kindred hath made my eyes
water° ere now. I desire you of more acquaintance, good Master
Mustardseed.

TITANIA. Come, wait upon him; lead him to my bower.   170
        The moon methinks looks with a watery eye;
And when she weeps,° weeps every little flower,
        Lamenting some enforcèd° chastity.
Tie up my lover's tongue,° bring him silently.

                                                    [*Exeunt.*]

[3.2] *Enter* [OBERON,] *King of Fairies.*

OBERON. I wonder if Titania be awaked;
        Then what it was that next came in her eye,
        Which she must dote on in extremity.

        [*Enter*] ROBIN GOODFELLOW [PUCK].

        Here comes my messenger. How now, mad spirit?
        What night-rule° now about this haunted° grove?   5

PUCK. My mistress with a monster is in love.
        Near to her close° and consecrated bower,
        While she was in her dull° and sleeping hour,
        A crew of patches,° rude mechanicals,°
        That work for bread upon Athenian stalls,°   10
        Were met together to rehearse a play
        Intended for great Theseus' nuptial day.
        The shallowest thick-skin of that barren sort,°
        Who Pyramus presented° in their sport,
        Forsook his scene° and entered in a brake.   15
        When I did him at this advantage take,
        An ass's noll° I fixèd on his head.
        Anon his Thisbe must be answered,
        And forth my mimic° comes. When they him spy,
        As wild geese that the creeping fowler° eye,   20
        Or russet-pated choughs,° many in sort,°

---

165 your patience what you have endured.   **168 water** (1) weep for sympathy (2)
smart, sting.   **172 she weeps** i.e., she causes dew.   **173 enforcèd** forced, violated; or,
possibly, constrained (since Titania at this moment is hardly concerned about chastity).
174 Tie . . . tongue (Presumably Bottom is braying like an ass.)   **3.2 Location: The
wood.   5 night-rule** diversion for the night.   **haunted** much frequented.   **7 close**
secret, private.   **8 dull** drowsy.   **9 patches** clowns, fools.   **rude mechanicals** ignorant
artisans.   **10 stalls** market booths.   **13 barren sort** stupid company or crew.   **14
presented** acted.   **15 scene** playing area.   **17 noll** noddle, head.   **19 mimic** burlesque
actor.   **20 fowler** hunter of game birds.   **21 russet-pated choughs** reddish brown or
gray-headed jackdaws.   **in sort** in a flock.

Rising and cawing at the gun's report,
Sever° themselves and madly sweep the sky,
So, at his sight, away his fellows fly;
And, at our stamp, here o'er and o'er one falls;   25
He "Murder!" cries and help from Athens calls.
Their sense thus weak, lost with their fears thus strong,
Made senseless things begin to do them wrong,
For briers and thorns at their apparel snatch;
Some, sleeves—some, hats; from yielders all things catch.°   30
I led them on in this distracted fear
And left sweet Pyramus translated there,
When in that moment, so it came to pass,
Titania waked and straightway loved an ass.

OBERON. This falls out better than I could devise.   35
But hast thou yet latched° the Athenian's eyes
With the love juice, as I did bid thee do?

PUCK. I took him sleeping—that is finished too—
And the Athenian woman by his side,
That, when he waked, of force° she must be eyed.   40

Enter DEMETRIUS *and* HERMIA.

OBERON. Stand close. This is the same Athenian.
PUCK. This is the woman, but not this the man.

                                              [*They stand aside.*]

DEMETRIUS. O, why rebuke you him that loves you so?
Lay breath so bitter on your bitter foe.

HERMIA. Now I but chide; but I should use thee worse,   45
For thou, I fear, hast given me cause to curse.
If thou hast slain Lysander in his sleep,
Being o'er shoes° in blood, plunge in the deep,
And kill me too.
The sun was not so true unto the day   50
As he to me. Would he have stolen away
From sleeping Hermia? I'll believe as soon
This whole° earth may be bored, and that the moon
May through the center creep, and so displease
Her brother's° noontide with th'Antipodes.°   55
It cannot be but thou hast murdered him;
So should a murderer look, so dead,° so grim.

DEMETRIUS. So should the murdered look, and so should I
Pierced through the heart with your stern cruelty.
Yet you, the murderer, look as bright, as clear,   60
As yonder Venus in her glimmering sphere.

─────────────

23 Sever i.e., scatter.   **30 from . . . catch** i.e., everything preys on those who yield to
fear.   **36 latched** fastened, snared.   **40 of force** perforce.   **48 o'er shoes** i.e., so far
gone.   **53 whole** solid.   **55 Her brother's** i.e., the sun's.   **th' Antipodes** the people
on the opposite side of the earth (where the moon is imagined bringing night to noontime).   **57 dead** deadly, or deathly pale.

HERMIA. What's this to° my Lysander? Where is he?
        Ah, good Demetrius, wilt thou give him me?
DEMETRIUS. I had rather give his carcass to my hounds.
HERMIA. Out, dog! Out, cur! Thou driv'st me past the bounds   65
        Of maiden's patience. Hast thou slain him, then?
        Henceforth be never numbered among men.
        O, once tell true, tell true, even for my sake:
        Durst thou have looked upon him being awake?
        And hast thou killed him sleeping? O brave touch!°   70
        Could not a worm,° an adder, do so much?
        An adder did it; for with doubler tongue
        Than thine, thou serpent, never adder stung.
DEMETRIUS. You spend your passion° on a misprised mood.°
        I am not guilty of Lysander's blood,   75
        Nor is he dead, for aught that I can tell.
HERMIA. I pray thee, tell me then that he is well.
DEMETRIUS. An if I could, what should I get therefor?
HERMIA. A privilege never to see me more.
        And from thy hated presence part I so.   80
        See me no more, whether he be dead or no.   *Exit.*
DEMETRIUS. There is no following her in this fierce vein.
        Here therefore for a while I will remain.
        So sorrow's heaviness doth heavier° grow
        For debt that bankrupt° sleep doth sorrow owe;   85
        Which now in some slight measure it will pay,
        If for his tender here I make some stay.°   *Lie[s] down [and sleeps].*
OBERON. What hast thou done? Thou hast mistaken quite
        And laid the love juice on some true love's sight.
        Of thy misprision° must perforce ensue   90
        Some true love turned, and not a false turned true.
PUCK. Then fate o'errules, that, one man holding troth,°
        A million fail, confounding oath on oath.°
OBERON. About the wood go swifter than the wind,
        And Helena of Athens look° thou find.   95
        All fancy-sick° she is and pale of cheer°
        With sighs of love, that cost the fresh blood° dear.
        By some illusion see thou bring her here.
        I'll charm his eyes against she do appear.°

---

62 to to do with.   **70 brave touch** noble exploit. (Said ironically.)   **71 worm** serpent.
74 passion violent feelings. **misprised mood** anger based on misconception.
84 heavier (1) harder to bear (2) more drowsy.   **85 bankrupt** (Demetrius is saying that
his sleepiness adds to the weariness caused by sorrow.)   **86–87 Which . . . stay** i.e., to a
small extent I will be able to "pay back" and hence find some relief from sorrow, if I pause
here awhile (*make some stay*) while sleep "tenders" or offers itself by way of paying the
debt owed to sorrow.   **90 misprision** mistake.   **92 troth** faith.   **93 confounding . . .
oath** i.e., invalidating one oath with another.   **95 look** i.e., be sure.   **96 fancy-sick**
lovesick. **cheer** face.   **97 sighs . . . blood** (An allusion to the physiological theory that
each sigh costs the heart a drop of blood.)   **99 against . . . appear** in anticipation of her
coming.

PUCK. I go. I go, look how I go,   100
    Swifter than arrow from the Tartar's bow.°   [*Exit.*]
OBERON [*applying love juice to Demetrius' eyes*].
    Flower of this purple dye,
    Hit with Cupid's archery,
    Sink in apple of his eye.
    When his love he doth espy,   105
    Let her shine as gloriously
    As the Venus of the sky.
    When thou wak'st, if she be by,
    Beg of her for remedy.

    Enter PUCK.

PUCK. Captain of our fairy band,   110
    Helena is here at hand,
    And the youth, mistook by me,
    Pleading for a lover's fee.°
    Shall we their fond pageant° see?
    Lord, what fools these mortals be!   115
OBERON. Stand aside. The noise they make
    Will cause Demetrius to awake.
PUCK. Then will two at once woo one;
    That must needs be sport alone.°
    And those things do best please me   120
    That befall preposterously.°

                                    [*They stand aside.*]

    Enter LYSANDER *and* HELENA.

LYSANDER. Why should you think that I should woo in scorn?
    Scorn and derision never come in tears.
    Look when° I vow, I weep; and vows so born,
    In their nativity all truth appears.°   125
    How can these things in me seem scorn to you,
    Bearing the badge° of faith to prove them true?
HELENA. You do advance° your cunning more and more.
    When truth kills truth,° O, devilish-holy fray!
    These vows are Hermia's. Will you give her o'er?   130
    Weigh oath with oath, and you will nothing weigh.
    Your vows to her and me, put in two scales,
    Will even weigh, and both as light as tales.°
LYSANDER. I had no judgment when to her I swore.
HELENA. Nor none, in my mind, now you give her o'er.   135
LYSANDER. Demetrius loves her, and he loves not you.

---

101 Tartar's bow (Tartars were famed for their skill with the bow.)   **113 fee** privilege, reward. **114 fond pageant** foolish exhibition. **119 alone** unequaled. **121 preposterously** out of the natural order.   **124 Look when** whenever.   **124–125 vows . . . appears** i.e., vows made by one who is weeping give evidence thereby of their sincerity.   **127 badge** identifying device such as that worn on servants' livery (here, his tears).   **128 advance** carry forward, display.   **129 truth kills truth** i.e., one of Lysander's vows must invalidate the other.   **133 tales** lies.

DEMETRIUS [*awaking*]. O Helen, goddess, nymph, perfect, divine!
    To what, my love, shall I compare thine eyne?
    Crystal is muddy. O, how ripe in show°
    Thy lips, those kissing cherries, tempting grow!   140
    That pure congealèd white, high Taurus'° snow,
    Fanned with the eastern wind, turns to a crow°
    When thou hold'st up thy hand. O, let me kiss
    This princess of pure white, this seal° of bliss!
HELENA. O spite! O hell! I see you all are bent   145
    To set against° me for your merriment.
    If you were civil and knew courtesy,
    You would not do me thus much injury.
    Can you not hate me, as I know you do,
    But you must join in souls to mock me too?   150
    If you were men, as men you are in show,
    You would not use a gentle lady so—
    To vow, and swear, and superpraise° my parts,°
    When I am sure you hate me with your hearts.
    You both are rivals, and love Hermia;   155
    And now both rivals, to mock Helena.
    A trim° exploit, a manly enterprise,
    To conjure tears up in a poor maid's eyes
    With your derision! None of noble sort°
    Would so offend a virgin and extort°   160
    A poor soul's patience, all to make you sport.
LYSANDER. You are unkind, Demetrius. Be not so;
    For you love Hermia; this you know I know.
    And here, with all good will, with all my heart,
    In Hermia's love I yield you up my part;   165
    And yours of Helena to me bequeath,
    Whom I do love and will do till my death.
HELENA. Never did mockers waste more idle breath.
DEMETRIUS. Lysander, keep thy Hermia; I will none.°
    If e'er I loved her, all that love is gone.   170
    My heart to her but as guest-wise sojourned,°
    And now to Helen is it home returned,
    There to remain.
LYSANDER.   Helen, it is not so.
DEMETRIUS. Disparage not the faith thou dost not know,
    Lest, to thy peril, thou aby° it dear.   175
    Look where thy love comes; yonder is thy dear.

    Enter HERMIA.

---

139 show appearance.   **141 Taurus** a lofty mountain range in Asia Minor.   **142 turns
to a crow** i.e., seems black by contrast.   **144 seal** pledge.   **146 set against** attack.
153 superpraise overpraise.   **parts** qualities.   **157 trim** pretty, fine (said ironically).
159 sort character, quality.   **160 extort** twist, torture.   **169 will none** i.e., want no part
of her.   **171 to . . . sojourned** only visited with her.   **175 aby** pay for.

HERMIA. Dark night, that from the eye his° function takes,
    The ear more quick of apprehension makes;
    Wherein it doth impair the seeing sense
    It pays the hearing double recompense.   180
    Thou art not by mine eye, Lysander, found;
    Mine ear, I thank it, brought me to thy sound.
    But why unkindly didst thou leave me so?
LYSANDER. Why should he stay whom love doth press to go?
HERMIA. What love could press Lysander from my side?   185
LYSANDER. Lysander's love, that would not let him bide—
    Fair Helena, who more engilds° the night
    Than all yon fiery oes° and eyes of light.
    Why seek'st thou me? Could not this make thee know,
    The hate I bear thee made me leave thee so?   190
HERMIA. You speak not as you think. It cannot be.
HELENA. Lo, she is one of this confederacy!
    Now I perceive they have conjoined all three
    To fashion this false sport in spite of me.°
    Injurious Hermia, most ungrateful maid!   195
    Have you conspired, have you with these contrived°
    To bait° me with this foul derision?
    Is all the counsel° that we two have shared,
    The sisters' vows, the hours that we have spent,
    When we have chid the hasty-footed time   200
    For parting us—O, is all forgot?
    All schooldays' friendship, childhood innocence?
    We, Hermia, like two artificial° gods,
    Have with our needles created both one flower,
    Both on one sampler, sitting on one cushion,   205
    Both warbling of one song, both in one key,
    As if our hands, our sides, voices, and minds
    Had been incorporate.° So we grew together
    Like to a double cherry, seeming parted
    But yet an union in partition,   210
    Two lovely° berries molded on one stem;
    So with two seeming bodies but one heart,
    Two of the first, like coats in heraldry,
    Due but to one and crowned with one crest.°
    And will you rend our ancient love asunder   215
    To join with men in scorning your poor friend?
    It is not friendly, tis not maidenly.
    Our sex, as well as I, may chide you for it,
    Though I alone do feel the injury.

---

177 his its.   **187 engilds** brightens with a golden light.   **188 oes** spangles (here, stars).
194 in spite of me to vex me.   **196 contrived** plotted.   **197 bait** torment, as one sets
on dogs to bait a bear.   **198 counsel** confidential talk.   **203 artificial** skilled in art or
creation.   **208 incorporate** of one body.   **211 lovely** loving.   **213–214 Two . . . crest**
i.e., we have two separate bodies, just as a coat of arms in heraldry can be represented
twice on a shield but surmounted by a single crest.

HERMIA. I am amazèd at your passionate words.   220
          I scorn you not. It seems that you scorn me.
HELENA. Have you not set Lysander, as in scorn,
          To follow me and praise my eyes and face?
          And made your other love, Demetrius,
          Who even but now did spurn me with his foot,   225
          To call me goddess, nymph, divine and rare,
          Precious, celestial? Wherefore speaks he this
          To her he hates? And wherefore doth Lysander
          Deny your love, so rich within his soul,
          And tender° me, forsooth, affection,   230
          But by your setting on, by your consent?
          What though I be not so in grace° as you,
          So hung upon with love, so fortunate,
          But miserable most, to love unloved?
          This you should pity rather than despise.   235
HERMIA. I understand not what you mean by this.
HELENA. Ay, do! Persever, counterfeit sad° looks,
          Make mouths° upon° me when I turn my back.
          Wink each at other, hold the sweet jest up.°
          This sport, well carried,° shall be chronicled.   240
          If you have any pity, grace, or manners,
          You would not make me such an argument.°
          But fare ye well. 'Tis partly my own fault,
          Which death, or absence, soon shall remedy.
LYSANDER. Stay, gentle Helena; hear my excuse,   245
          My love, my life, my soul, fair Helena!
HELENA. O excellent!
HERMIA [to LYSANDER]. Sweet, do not scorn her so.
DEMETRIUS. If she cannot entreat,° I can compel.
LYSANDER. Thou canst compel no more than she entreat.
          Thy threats have no more strength than her weak prayers.   250
          Helen, I love thee, by my life I do!
          I swear by that which I will lose for thee,
          To prove him false that says I love thee not.
DEMETRIUS. I say I love thee more than he can do.
LYSANDER. If thou say so, withdraw, and prove it too.   255
DEMETRIUS. Quick, come!
HERMIA.   Lysander, whereto tends all this?
LYSANDER. Away, you Ethiop!°
                    [He tries to break away from HERMIA.]
DEMETRIUS.   No, no; he'll
          Seem to break loose; take on as° you would follow,
          But yet come not. You are a tame man, go!

---

230 tender offer.   **232 grace** favor.   **237 sad** grave, serious.   **238 mouths** i.e., mows,
faces, grimaces.   **upon** at.   **239 hold . . . up** keep up the joke.   **240 carried** managed.
242 argument subject for a jest.   **248 entreat** i.e., succeed by entreaty.   **257 Ethiop**
(Referring to Hermia's relatively dark hair and complexion; see also *tawny Tartar* six lines
later.)   **258 take on as** act as if.

LYSANDER. Hang off,° thou cat, thou burr! Vile thing, let loose,   260
    Or I will shake thee from me like a serpent!
HERMIA. Why are you grown so rude? What change is this,
    Sweet love?
LYSANDER.   Thy love? Out, tawny Tartar, out!
    Out, loathèd med'cine!° O hated potion, hence!
HERMIA. Do you not jest?
HELENA.   Yes, sooth,° and so do you.   265
LYSANDER. Demetrius, I will keep my word with thee.
DEMETRIUS. I would I had your bond, for I perceive
    A weak bond° holds you. I'll not trust your word.
LYSANDER. What, should I hurt her, strike her, kill her dead?
    Although I hate her, I'll not harm her so.   270
HERMIA. What, can you do me greater harm than hate?
    Hate me? Wherefore? O me, what news,° my love?
    Am not I Hermia? Are not you Lysander?
    I am as fair now as I was erewhile.°
    Since night you loved me; yet since night you left me.   275
    Why, then you left me—O, the gods forbid!—
    In earnest, shall I say?
LYSANDER.   Ay, by my life!
    And never did desire to see thee more.
    Therefore be out of hope, of question, of doubt;
    Be certain, nothing truer. 'Tis no jest   280
    That I do hate thee and love Helena.
HERMIA [*to* HELENA]. O me! You juggler! You cankerblossom!°
    You thief of love! What, have you come by night
    And stol'n my love's heart from him?
HELENA.   Fine, i faith!
    Have you no modesty, no maiden shame,   285
    No touch of bashfulness? What, will you tear
    Impatient answers from my gentle tongue?
    Fie, fie! You counterfeit, you puppet,° you!
HERMIA. "Puppet"? Why, so!° Ay, that way goes the game.
    Now I perceive that she hath made compare   290
    Between our statures: she hath urged her height,
    And with her personage, her tall personage,
    Her height, forsooth, she hath prevailed with him.
    And are you grown so high in his esteem
    Because I am so dwarfish and so low?   295
    How low am I, thou painted maypole? Speak!
    How low am I? I am not yet so low
    But that my nails can reach unto thine eyes.
            [*She flails at* HELENA *but is restrained.*]

---

260 Hang off let go.   **264 med'cine** i.e., poison.   **265 sooth** truly.   **268 weak bond**
i.e., Hermia's arm (with a pun on *bond*, oath, in the previous line).   **272 what news**
what is the matter.   **274 erewhile** just now.   **282 cankerblossom** worm that destroys
the flower bud.   **288 puppet** (1) counterfeit (2) dwarfish woman (in reference to Hermia's
smaller stature).   **289 Why, so** i.e., Oh, so that's how it is.

HELENA. I pray you, though you mock me, gentlemen,
        Let her not hurt me. I was never curst;°   300
        I have no gift at all in shrewishness;
        I am a right° maid for my cowardice.
        Let her not strike me. You perhaps may think,
        Because she is something° lower than myself,
        That I can match her.
HERMIA.   Lower? Hark, again!   305
HELENA. Good Hermia, do not be so bitter with me.
        I evermore did love you, Hermia,
        Did ever keep your counsels, never wronged you;
        Save that, in love unto Demetrius,
        I told him of your stealth° unto this wood.   310
        He followed you; for love I followed him.
        But he hath chid me hence° and threatened me
        To strike me, spurn me, nay, to kill me too.
        And now, so° you will let me quiet go,
        To Athens will I bear my folly back   315
        And follow you no further. Let me go.
        You see how simple and how fond° I am.
HERMIA. Why, get you gone. Who is 't that hinders you?
HELENA. A foolish heart, that I leave here behind.
HERMIA. What, with Lysander?
HELENA.   With Demetrius.   320
LYSANDER. Be not afraid; she shall not harm thee, Helena.
DEMETRIUS. No, sir, she shall not, though you take her part.
HELENA. O, when she is angry, she is keen° and shrewd.°
        She was a vixen when she went to school,
        And though she be but little, she is fierce.   325
HERMIA. "Little" again? Nothing but "low" and "little"?
        Why will you suffer her to flout me thus?
        Let me come to her.
LYSANDER.   Get you gone, you dwarf!
        You minimus,° of hindering knotgrass° made!
        You bead, you acorn!
DEMETRIUS.   You are too officious   330
        In her behalf that scorns your services.
        Let her alone. Speak not of Helena;
        Take not her part. For, if thou dost intend°
        Never so little show of love to her,
        Thou shalt aby° it.
LYSANDER.   Now she holds me not;   335
        Now follow, if thou dar'st, to try whose right,
        Of thine or mine, is most in Helena.   [*Exit.*]

---

300 curst shrewish. **302 right** true. **304 something** somewhat. **310 stealth** stealing away. **312 chid me hence** driven me away with his scolding. **314 so** if only. **317
fond** foolish. **323 keen** fierce, cruel. **shrewd** shrewish. **329 minimus** diminutive
creature. **knotgrass** a weed, an infusion of which was thought to stunt the growth.
333 intend give sign of. **335 aby** pay for.

DEMETRIUS. Follow? Nay, I'll go with thee, cheek by jowl.°

                                                                     [Exit, following LYSANDER.*]*

HERMIA. You, mistress, all this coil° is 'long of° you.

    Nay, go not back.°

HELENA.   I will not trust you, I,   340

    Nor longer stay in your curst company.

    Your hands than mine are quicker for a fray;

    My legs are longer, though, to run away.   *[Exit.]*

HERMIA. I am amazed and know not what to say.   *Exit.*

    [OBERON *and* PUCK *come forward.*]

OBERON. This is thy negligence. Still thou mistak'st,   345

    Or else committ'st thy knaveries willfully.

PUCK. Believe me, king of shadows, I mistook.

    Did not you tell me I should know the man

    By the Athenian garments he had on?

    And so far blameless proves my enterprise   350

    That I have 'nointed an Athenian's eyes;

    And so far am I glad it so did sort,°

    As° this their jangling I esteem a sport.

OBERON. Thou seest these lovers seek a place to fight.

    Hie° therefore, Robin, overcast the night;   355

    The starry welkin° cover thou anon

    With drooping fog as black as Acheron,°

    And lead these testy rivals so astray

    As one come not within another's way.

    Like to Lysander sometimes frame thy tongue,   360

    Then stir Demetrius up with bitter wrong;°

    And sometimes rail thou like Demetrius.

    And from each other look thou lead them thus,

    Till o'er their brows death-counterfeiting sleep

    With leaden legs and batty° wings doth creep.   365

    Then crush this herb° into Lysander's eye,   *[Giving herb.]*

    Whose liquor hath this virtuous° property,

    To take from thence all error with his° might

    And make his eyeballs roll with wonted° sight.

    When they next wake, all this derision°   370

    Shall seem a dream and fruitless vision,

    And back to Athens shall the lovers wend

    With league whose date° till death shall never end.

    Whiles I in this affair do thee employ,

    I'll to my queen and beg her Indian boy;   375

---

338 cheek by jowl i.e., side by side. **339 coil** turmoil, dissension. **'long of** on account of. **340 go not back** i.e., don't retreat. (Hermia is again proposing a fight.) **352 sort** turn out. **353 As** that (also at line 359). **355 Hie** hasten. **356 welkin** sky. **357 Acheron** river of Hades (here representing Hades itself). **361 wrong** insults. **365 batty** batlike. **366 this herb** i.e., the antidote (mentioned in 2.1.184) to love-in-idleness. **367 virtuous** efficacious. **368 his** its. **369 wonted** accustomed. **370 derision** laughable business. **373 date** term of existence.

And then I will her charmèd eye release
From monster's view, and all things shall be peace.

PUCK. My fairy lord, this must be done with haste,
For night's swift dragons° cut the clouds full fast,
And yonder shines Aurora's harbinger,°   380
At whose approach, ghosts, wand'ring here and there,
Troop home to churchyards. Damnèd spirits all,
That in crossways and floods have burial,°
Already to their wormy beds are gone.
For fear lest day should look their shames upon,   385
They willfully themselves exile from light
And must for aye° consort with black-browed night.

OBERON. But we are spirits of another sort.
I with the Morning's love° have oft made sport,
And, like a forester,° the groves may tread   390
Even till the eastern gate, all fiery red,
Opening on Neptune with fair blessèd beams,
Turns into yellow gold his salt green streams.
But notwithstanding, haste, make no delay.
We may effect this business yet ere day.   [*Exit.*] 395

PUCK.
            Up and down, up and down,
            I will lead them up and down.
            I am feared in field and town.
            Goblin, lead them up and down.
Here comes one.   400

Enter LYSANDER.

LYSANDER. Where art thou, proud Demetrius? Speak thou now.
PUCK. [*mimicking* DEMETRIUS].
            Here, villain, drawn° and ready. Where art thou?
LYSANDER. I will be with thee straight.°
PUCK.   Follow me, then,
            To plainer° ground.
                    [LYSANDER *wanders about,° following the voice.*]

Enter DEMETRIUS.

DEMETRIUS.   Lysander! Speak again!
            Thou runaway, thou coward, art thou fled?   405
            Speak! In some bush? Where dost thou hide thy head?

---

379 dragons (Supposed by Shakespeare to be yoked to the car of the goddess of night.)
380 Aurora's harbinger the morning star, precursor of dawn. **383 crossways . . .
burial** (Those who had committed suicide were buried at crossways, with a stake driven
through them; those drowned, i.e., buried in floods or great waters, would be condemned
to wander disconsolate for want of burial rites.) **387 for aye** forever. **389 Morning's
love** Cephalus, a beautiful youth beloved by Aurora; or perhaps the goddess of the dawn
herself. **390 forester** keeper of a royal forest. **402 drawn** with drawn sword. **403
straight** immediately. **404 plainer** more open. **s.d. Lysander wanders about** (It is
not clearly necessary that Lysander exit at this point; neither exit nor reentrance is indicated in the early texts.)

PUCK [*mimicking* LYSANDER].
    Thou coward, art thou bragging to the stars,
    Telling the bushes that thou look'st for wars,
    And wilt not come? Come, recreant;° come, thou child,
    I'll whip thee with a rod. He is defiled   410
    That draws a sword on thee.
DEMETRIUS.   Yea, art thou there?
PUCK. Follow my voice. We'll try° no manhood here.

                                                 Exeunt.

    [LYSANDER *returns.*]

LYSANDER. He goes before me and still dares me on.
    When I come where he calls, then he is gone.
    The villain is much lighter-heeled than I.   415
    I followed fast, but faster he did fly,
    That fallen am I in dark uneven way,
    And here will rest me. [*He lies down.*] Come, thou gentle day!
    For if but once thou show me thy gray light,
    I'll find Demetrius and revenge this spite.   [*He sleeps.*] 420

    [*Enter*] ROBIN [PUCK] *and* DEMETRIUS.

PUCK. Ho, ho, ho! Coward, why com'st thou not?
DEMETRIUS. Abide° me, if thou dar'st; for well I wot°
    Thou runn'st before me, shifting every place,
    And dar'st not stand nor look me in the face.
    Where art thou now?
PUCK.   Come hither. I am here.   425
DEMETRIUS. Nay, then, thou mock'st me. Thou shalt buy° this dear,°
    If ever I thy face by daylight see.
    Now, go thy way. Faintness constraineth me
    To measure out my length on this cold bed.
    By day's approach look to be visited.   430
                             [*He lies down and sleeps.*]

    Enter HELENA.

HELENA. O weary night, O long and tedious night,
    Abate° thy hours! Shine comforts from the east,
    That I may back to Athens by daylight,
    From these that my poor company detest;
    And sleep, that sometimes shuts up sorrow's eye,   435
    Steal me awhile from mine own company.
                    [*She lies down and*] *sleep*[*s*].
PUCK. Yet but three? Come one more;
    Two of both kinds makes up four.
    Here she comes, curst° and sad.

---

409 **recreant** cowardly wretch.   **412 try** test.   **422 Abide** confront, face.   **wot** know.
426 buy aby, pay for.   **dear** dearly.   **432 Abate** lessen, shorten.   **439 curst** ill-tempered.

Cupid is a knavish lad,   440
Thus to make poor females mad.

[*Enter* HERMIA.]

HERMIA. Never so weary, never so in woe,
 Bedabbled with the dew and torn with briers
I can no further crawl, no further go;
 My legs can keep no pace with my desires.   445
Here will I rest me till the break of day.
Heavens shield Lysander, if they mean a fray!
        [*She lies down and sleeps.*]

PUCK.
   On the ground
   Sleep sound.
   I'll apply   450
   To your eye,
  Gentle lover, remedy.
     [*Squeezing the juice on* LYSANDER's *eyes.*]
   When thou wak'st,
   Thou tak'st
   True delight   455
   In the sight
  Of thy former lady's eye;
  And the country proverb known,
  That every man should take his own,
  In your waking shall be shown: 460
   Jack shall have Jill;°
   Naught shall go ill;
  The man shall have his mare again, and all shall be well.
     [*Exit. The four sleeping lovers remain.*]

  [4.1] *Enter* [TITANIA] *Queen of Fairies, and* [BOTTOM] *the clown,
  and* FAIRIES; *and* [OBERON,] *the King, behind them.*

TITANIA. Come, sit thee down upon this flowery bed,
 While I thy amiable° cheeks do coy,°
And stick muskroses in thy sleek smooth head,
 And kiss thy fair large ears, my gentle joy.
          [*They recline.*]

BOTTOM. Where's Peaseblossom?   5
PEASEBLOSSOM. Ready.
BOTTOM. Scratch my head, Peaseblossom. Where's Monsieur Cobweb?
COBWEB. Ready.
BOTTOM. Monsieur Cobweb, good monsieur, get you your weapons in
 your hand, and kill me a red-hipped humble-bee on the top of a   10
 thistle; and, good monsieur, bring me the honey bag. Do not fret

---

461 Jack shall have Jill (Proverbial for "boy gets girl.")   **4.1 Location: The action is continuous. The four lovers are still asleep onstage.   2 amiable** lovely.   **coy** caress.

yourself too much in the action, monsieur, and, good monsieur, have a care the honey bag break not; I would be loath to have you overflown with a honey bag, signor. [*Exit* COBWEB.] Where's Monsieur Mustardseed? 15

MUSTARDSEED. Ready.

BOTTOM. Give me your neaf,° Monsieur Mustardseed. Pray you, leave your courtesy,° good monsieur.

MUSTARDSEED. What's your will?

BOTTOM. Nothing, good monsieur, but to help Cavalery° Cobweb° to 20 scratch. I must to the barber's, monsieur, for methinks I am marvelous hairy about the face; and I am such a tender ass, if my hair do but tickle me, I must scratch.

TITANIA. What, wilt thou hear some music, my sweet love?

BOTTOM. I have a reasonable good ear in music. Let's have the tongs and 25 the bones.°

[Music: tongs, rural music.°]

TITANIA. Or say, sweet love, what thou desirest to eat.

BOTTOM. Truly, a peck of provender.° I could munch your good dry oats. Methinks I have a great desire to a bottle° of hay. Good hay, sweet hay, hath no fellow.° 30

TITANIA. I have a venturous fairy that shall seek
The squirrel's hoard, and fetch thee new nuts.

BOTTOM. I had rather have a handful or two of dried peas. But, I pray you, let none of your people stir° me. I have an exposition° of sleep come upon me. 35

TITANIA. Sleep thou, and I will wind thee in my arms.
Fairies, begone, and be all ways° away.

[Exeunt FAIRIES.]

So doth the woodbine the sweet honeysuckle
Gently entwist; the female ivy so
Enrings the barky fingers of the elm. 40
O, how I love thee! How I dote on thee!

[They sleep.]

Enter ROBIN GOODFELLOW [PUCK].

OBERON [*coming forward*].
Welcome, good Robin. Seest thou this sweet sight?
Her dotage now I do begin to pity.
For, meeting her of late behind the wood,

---

17 neaf fist. **17–18 leave your courtesy** i.e., stop bowing, or put on your hat. **20 Cavalery** cavalier. (Form of address for a gentleman.) **Cobweb** (Seemingly an error, since Cobweb has been sent to bring honey while Peaseblossom has been asked to scratch.) **25–26 tongs . . . bones** instruments for rustic music. (The tongs were played like a triangle, whereas the bones were held between the fingers and used as clappers.) **25–26 s.d. Music . . . music** (This stage direction is added from the Folio.) **28 peck of provender** one-quarter bushel of grain. **29 bottle** bundle. **30 fellow** equal. **34 stir** disturb. **exposition** (Bottom's word for *disposition*.) **37 all ways** in all directions.

Seeking sweet favors° for this hateful fool,   45
I did upbraid her and fall out with her.
For she his hairy temples then had rounded
With coronet of fresh and fragrant flowers;
And that same dew, which sometime° on the buds
Was wont to swell like round and orient pearls,°   50
Stood now within the pretty flowerets' eyes
Like tears that did their own disgrace bewail.
When I had at my pleasure taunted her,
And she in mild terms begged my patience,
I then did ask of her her changeling child,   55
Which straight she gave me, and her fairy sent
To bear him to my bower in Fairyland.
And, now I have the boy, I will undo
This hateful imperfection of her eyes.
And, gentle Puck, take this transformèd scalp   60
From off the head of this Athenian swain,
That he, awaking when the other° do,
May all to Athens back again repair,°
And think no more of this night's accidents
But as the fierce vexation of a dream.   65
But first I will release the Fairy Queen.

                    [*He squeezes a herb on her eyes.*]

  Be as thou wast wont to be;
  See as thou wast wont to see.
  Dian's bud° o'er Cupid's flower
  Hath such force and blessèd power.   70
Now, my Titania, wake you, my sweet queen.

TITANIA [*waking*]. My Oberon! What visions have I seen!
  Methought I was enamored of an ass.

OBERON. There lies your love.

TITANIA.   How came these things to pass?
  O, how mine eyes do loathe his visage now!   75

OBERON. Silence awhile. Robin, take off this head.
  Titania, music call, and strike more dead
  Than common sleep of all these five° the sense.

TITANIA. Music, ho! Music, such as charmeth° sleep!

                                                        [*Music.*]

PUCK [*removing the ass head*].
  Now, when thou wak'st, with thine own fool's eyes peep.   80

OBERON. Sound, music! Come, my queen, take hands with me,
  And rock the ground whereon these sleepers be.   [*They dance.*]
  Now thou and I are new in amity,

---

45 favors i.e., gifts of flowers.   **49 sometime** formerly.   **50 orient pearls** i.e., the most
beautiful of all pearls, those coming from the Orient.   **62 other** others.   **63 repair** return.   **69 Dian's bud** (Perhaps the flower of the *agnus castus* or chaste-tree, supposed
to preserve chastity; or perhaps referring simply to Oberon's herb by which he can undo
the effects of "Cupid's flower," the love-in-idleness of 2.1.166–168.)   **78 these five** i.e.,
the four lovers and Bottom.   **79 charmeth** brings about, as though by a charm.

And will tomorrow midnight solemnly°
Dance in Duke Theseus' house triumphantly,   85
And bless it to all fair prosperity.
There shall the pairs of faithful lovers be
Wedded, with Theseus, all in jollity.

PUCK.
    Fairy King, attend, and mark:
    I do hear the morning lark.   90

OBERON.
    Then, my queen, in silence sad,°
    Trip we after night's shade.
    We the globe can compass soon,
    Swifter than the wandering moon.

TITANIA.
    Come, my lord, and in our flight   95
    Tell me how it came this night
    That I sleeping here was found
    With these mortals on the ground.   *Exeunt.*

Wind horn [within].
Enter THESEUS *and all his train;* [HIPPOLYTA, EGEUS].

THESEUS. Go, one of you, find out the forester,
    For now our observation° is performed;   100
    And since we have the vaward° of the day,
    My love shall hear the music of my hounds.
    Uncouple° in the western valley, let them go.
    Dispatch, I say, and find the forester.   [*Exit an Attendant.*]
    We will, fair queen, up to the mountain's top   105
    And mark the musical confusion
    Of hounds and echo in conjunction.

HIPPOLYTA. I was with Hercules and Cadmus° once,
    When in a wood of Crete they bayed° the bear
    With hounds of Sparta.° Never did I hear   110
    Such gallant chiding;° for, besides the groves,
    The skies, the fountains, every region near
    Seemed all one mutual cry. I never heard
    So musical a discord, such sweet thunder.

THESEUS. My hounds are bred out of the Spartan kind,°   115
    So flewed,° so sanded;° and their heads are hung
    With ears that sweep away the morning dew;
    Crook-kneed, and dewlapped° like Thessalian bulls;
    Slow in pursuit, but matched in mouth like bells,

---

84 solemnly ceremoniously.   **91 sad** sober.   **100 observation** i.e., observance to a
morn of May (1.1.167).   **101 vaward** vanguard, i.e., earliest part.   **103 Uncouple** set
free for the hunt.   **108 Cadmus** mythical founder of Thebes (This story about him is unknown.)   **109 bayed** brought to bay.   **110 hounds of Sparta** (A breed famous in antiquity for their hunting skill.)   **111 chiding** i.e., yelping.   **115 kind** strain, breed.   **116 So
flewed** similarly having large hanging chaps or fleshy covering of the jaw.   **sanded** of
sandy color.   **118 dewlapped** having pendulous folds of skin under the neck.

Each under each.° A cry° more tunable°   120
Was never holloed to, nor cheered° with horn,
In Crete, in Sparta, nor in Thessaly.
Judge when you hear.   [*He sees the sleepers.*]
           But, soft! What nymphs are these?

EGEUS. My lord, this is my daughter here asleep,
And this Lysander; this Demetrius is,   125
This Helena, old Nedar's Helena.
I wonder of° their being here together.

THESEUS. No doubt they rose up early to observe
The rite of May, and hearing our intent,
Came here in grace of our solemnity.°   130
But speak, Egeus. Is not this the day
That Hermia should give answer of her choice?

EGEUS. It is, my lord.

THESEUS. Go, bid the huntsmen wake them with their horns.
                    [*Exit an Attendant.*]

Shout within. Wind horns. They all start up.

Good morrow, friends. Saint Valentine° is past.   135
Begin these woodbirds but to couple now?

LYSANDER. Pardon, my lord.   [*They kneel.*]

THESEUS.   I pray you all, stand up.
I know you two are rival enemies;
How comes this gentle concord in the world,
That hatred is so far from jealousy°   140
To sleep by hate and fear no enmity?

LYSANDER. My lord, I shall reply amazedly,
Half sleep, half waking; but as yet, I swear,
I cannot truly say how I came here.
But, as I think—for truly would I speak,   145
And now I do bethink me, so it is—
I came with Hermia hither. Our intent
Was to be gone from Athens, where° we might,
Without° the peril of the Athenian law—

EGEUS. Enough, enough, my lord; you have enough.   150
I beg the law, the law, upon his head.
They would have stol'n away; they would, Demetrius,
Thereby to have defeated° you and me,
You of your wife and me of my consent,
Of my consent that she should be your wife.   155

DEMETRIUS. My lord, fair Helen told me of their stealth,
Of this their purpose hither° to this wood,

119–120 matched . . . each i.e., harmoniously matched in their various cries like a set of
bells, from treble down to bass.   **120 cry** pack of hounds.   **tunable** well tuned, melodious.   **121 cheered** encouraged.   **127 wonder of** wonder at.   **130 in . . . solemnity** in
honor of our wedding.   **135 Saint Valentine** (Birds were supposed to choose their
mates on Saint Valentine's Day.)   **140 jealousy** suspicion.   **148 where** wherever; or, to
where.   **149 Without** outside of, beyond.   **153 defeated** defrauded.   **157 hither** in
coming hither.

And I in fury hither followed them,
Fair Helena in fancy following me.
But, my good lord, I wot not by what power—   160
But by some power it is—my love to Hermia,
Melted as the snow, seems to me now
As the remembrance of an idle gaud°
Which in my childhood I did dote upon;
And all the faith, the virtue of my heart,   165
The object and the pleasure of mine eye,
Is only Helena. To her, my lord,
Was I betrothed ere I saw Hermia,
But like a sickness did I loathe this food;
But, as in health, come to my natural taste,   170
Now I do wish it, love it, long for it,
And will for evermore be true to it.

THESEUS. Fair lovers, you are fortunately met.
Of this discourse we more will hear anon.
Egeus, I will overbear your will;   175
For in the temple, by and by, with us
These couples shall eternally be knit.
And, for° the morning now is something° worn,
Our purposed hunting shall be set aside.
Away with us to Athens. Three and three,   180
We'll hold a feast in great solemnity.
Come, Hippolyta.

          [*Exeunt* THESEUS, HIPPOLYTA, EGEUS, *and train.*]

DEMETRIUS. These things seem small and undistinguishable,
Like far-off mountains turnèd into clouds.

HERMIA. Methinks I see these things with parted° eye,   185
When everything seems double.

HELENA.   So methinks;
And I have found Demetrius like a jewel,
Mine own, and not mine own.°

DEMETRIUS.   Are you sure
That we are awake? It seems to me
That yet we sleep, we dream. Do not you think   190
The Duke was here, and bid us follow him?

HERMIA. Yea, and my father.

HELENA.   And Hippolyta.

LYSANDER. And he did bid us follow to the temple.

DEMETRIUS. Why, then, we are awake. Let's follow him,
And by the way let us recount our dreams.   [*Exeunt.*]   195

BOTTOM [*awaking*]. When my cue comes, call me, and I will answer.
My next is, "Most fair Pyramus." Heigh—ho! Peter Quince! Flute,
the bellows mender! Snout, the tinker! Starveling! God's° my life,

---

163 idle gaud worthless trinket. **178 for** since. **something** somewhat. **185 parted**
improperly focused. **187–188 like . . . mine own** i.e., like a jewel that one finds by
chance and therefore possesses but cannot certainly consider one's own property.
198 God's may God save.

stolen hence and left me asleep! I have had a most rare vision.
I have had a dream, past the wit of man to say what dream it was.   200
Man is but an ass if he go about° to expound this dream.
Methought I was—there is no man can tell what. Methought
I was—and methought I had—but man is but a patched° fool if he
will offer° to say what methought I had. The eye of man hath not
heard, the ear of man hath not seen, man's hand is not able to taste,   205
his tongue to conceive, nor his heart to report,° what my dream
was. I will get Peter Quince to write a ballad of this dream. It shall
be called "Bottom's Dream," because it hath no bottom; and I will
sing it in the latter end of a play, before the Duke. Peradventure, to
make it the more gracious, I shall sing it at her° death.   210

                                                          [*Exit.*]

[**4.2**] *Enter* QUINCE, FLUTE, [SNOUT, *and* STARVELING].

QUINCE. Have you sent to Bottom's house? Is he come home yet?
STARVELING. He cannot be heard of. Out of doubt he is transported.°
FLUTE. If he come not, then the play is marred. It goes not forward,
      doth it?
QUINCE. It is not possible. You have not a man in all Athens able to   5
      discharge° Pyramus but he.
FLUTE. No, he hath simply the best wit° of any handicraft man in Athens.
QUINCE. Yea, and the best person° too, and he is a very paramour for a
      sweet voice.
FLUTE. You must say "paragon." A paramour is, God bless us, a thing of   10
      naught.°

      Enter SNUG *the joiner.*

SNUG. Masters, the Duke is coming from the temple and there is two or
      three lords and ladies more married. If our sport had gone forward,
      we had all been made men.°
FLUTE. O sweet bully Bottom! Thus hath he lost sixpence a day during   15
      his life; he could not have scaped sixpence a day. An the Duke had
      not given him sixpence a day° for playing Pyramus, I'll be hanged.
      He would have deserved it. Sixpence a day in Pyramus, or nothing.

      Enter BOTTOM.

BOTTOM. Where are these lads? Where are these hearts?°
QUINCE. Bottom! O most courageous day! O most happy hour!   20
BOTTOM. Masters, I am to discourse wonders.° But ask me not what; for
      if I tell you, I am no true Athenian. I will tell you everything, right as
      it fell out.

---

201 go about attempt.   **203 patched** wearing motley, i.e., a dress of various colors.
204 offer venture.   **204–206 The eye . . . report** (Bottom garbles the terms of 1
Corinthians 2.9.   **210 her** Thisbe's (?).   **4.2 Location:** Athens.   **2 transported**
carried off by fairies; or, possibly, transformed.   **6 discharge** perform.   **7 wit** intellect.
8 person appearance.   **10–11 a . . . naught** a shameful thing.   **14 we . . . men** i.e., we
would have had our fortunes made.   **17 sixpence a day** i.e., as a royal pension.
19 hearts good fellows.   **21 am . . . wonders** have wonders to relate.

QUINCE. Let us hear, sweet Bottom.

BOTTOM. Not a word of° me. All that I will tell you is—that the Duke   25
hath dined. Get your apparel together, good strings° to your beards,
new ribbons to your pumps;° meet presently° at the palace; every
man look o'er his part; for the short and the long is, our play is
preferred.° In any case, let Thisbe have clean linen; and let not him
that plays the lion pare his nails, for they shall hang out for the lion's   30
claws. And, most dear actors, eat no onions nor garlic, for we are to
utter sweet breath; and I do not doubt but to hear them say it is a
sweet comedy. No more words. Away! Go, away!

[Exeunt.]

[5.1] *Enter* THESEUS, HIPPOLYTA, *and* PHILOSTRATE [*lords, and*
attendants].

HIPPOLYTA. 'Tis strange, my Theseus, that° these lovers speak of.

THESEUS. More strange than true. I never may° believe
These antique° fables nor these fairy toys.°
Lovers and madmen have such seething brains,
Such shaping fantasies,° that apprehend°   5
More than cool reason ever comprehends.°
The lunatic, the lover, and the poet
Are of imagination all compact.°
One sees more devils than vast hell can hold;
That is the madman. The lover, all as frantic,   10
Sees Helen's° beauty in a brow of Egypt.°
The poet's eye, in a fine frenzy rolling,
Doth glance from heaven to earth, from earth to heaven;
And as imagination bodies forth
The forms of things unknown, the poet's pen   15
Turns them to shapes and gives to airy nothing
A local habitation and a name.
Such tricks hath strong imagination
That, if it would but apprehend some joy,
It comprehends some bringer° of that joy;   20
Or in the night, imagining some fear,°
How easy is a bush supposed a bear!

HIPPOLYTA. But all the story of the night told over,
And all their minds transfigured so together,
More witnesseth than fancy's images°   25

---

25 of out of.   **26 strings** (to attach the beards).   **27 pumps** light shoes or slippers.
presently immediately.   **29 preferred** selected for consideration.   **5.1 Location:**
Athens. The palace of Theseus.   1 that that which.   **2 may** can.   **3 antique**
old-fashioned (punning too on *antic*, strange, grotesque).   **fairy toys** trifling stories
about fairies.   **5 fantasies** imaginations.   **apprehend** conceive, imagine.   **6**
comprehends understands.   **8 compact** formed, composed.   **11 Helen's** i.e., of Helen of Troy, pattern of beauty.   **brow of Egypt** i.e., face of a gypsy.   **20 bringer** i.e.,
source.   **21 fear** object of fear.   **25 More . . . images** testifies to something more substantial than mere imaginings.

And grows to something of great constancy;°
But, howsoever,° strange and admirable.°

Enter lovers: LYSANDER, DEMETRIUS, HERMIA, *and* HELENA.

THESEUS. Here come the lovers, full of joy and mirth.
Joy, gentle friends! Joy and fresh days of love
Accompany your hearts!
LYSANDER.   More than to us   30
Wait in your royal walks, your board, your bed!
THESEUS. Come now, what masques,° what dances shall we have
To wear away this long age of three hours
Between our after-supper and bedtime?
Where is our usual manager of mirth?   35
What revels are in hand? Is there no play
To ease the anguish of a torturing hour?
Call Philostrate.
PHILOSTRATE.   Here, mighty Theseus.
THESEUS. Say what abridgment° have you for this evening?
What masque? What music? How shall we beguile   40
The lazy time, if not with some delight?
PHILOSTRATE [*giving him a paper*].
There is a brief° how many sports are ripe.
Make choice of which Your Highness will see first.
THESEUS [*reads*]. "The battle with the Centaurs,° to be sung
By an Athenian eunuch to the harp"?   45
We'll none of that. That have I told my love,
In glory of my kinsman° Hercules.
[*reads.*] "The riot of the tipsy Bacchanals,
Tearing the Thracian singer in their rage"?°
That is an old device;° and it was played   50
When I from Thebes came last a conqueror.
[*reads.*] "The thrice three Muses mourning for the death
Of Learning, late deceased in beggary"?°
That is some satire, keen and critical,
Not sorting with° a nuptial ceremony.   55
[*reads.*] "A tedious brief scene of young Pyramus
And his love Thisbe; very tragical mirth"?
Merry and tragical? Tedious and brief?

---

26 **constancy** certainty.   27 **howsoever** in any case.   **admirable** a source of wonder.
32 **masques** courtly entertainments.   39 **abridgment** pastime (to abridge or shorten
the evening).   42 **brief** short written statement, summary.   44 **battle . . . Centaurs**
(Probably refers to the battle of the Centaurs and the Lapithae, when the Centaurs attempted to carry off Hippodamia, bride of Theseus's friend Pirothous.)   47 **kinsman**
(Plutarch's "Life of Theseus" states that Hercules and Theseus were near kinsmen. Theseus
is referring to a version of the battle of the Centaurs in which Hercules was said to be present.)   48–49 **The riot . . . rage** (This was the story of the death of Orpheus, as told in
Metamorphoses 9.)   50 **device** show, performance.   52–53 **The thrice . . . beggary**
(Possibly an allusion to Spenser's *Tears of the Muses,* 1591, though "satires" deploring the
neglect of learning and the creative arts were commonplace.)   55 **sorting with** befitting.

That is hot ice and wondrous strange° snow.
How shall we find the concord of this discord?   60
PHILOSTRATE. A play there is, my lord, some ten words long,
  Which is as brief as I have known a play;
  But by ten words, my lord, it is too long,
  Which makes it tedious. For in all the play
  There is not one word apt, one player fitted.   65
  And tragical, my noble lord, it is,
  For Pyramus therein doth kill himself.
  Which, when I saw rehearsed, I must confess,
  Made mine eyes water; but more merry tears
  The passion of loud laughter never shed.   70
THESEUS. What are they that do play it?
PHILOSTRATE. Hard-handed men that work in Athens here,
  Which never labored in their minds till now,
  And now have toiled° their unbreathed° memories
  With this same play, against° your nuptial.   75
THESEUS. And we will hear it.
PHILOSTRATE.   No, my noble lord,
  It is not for you. I have heard it over,
  And it is nothing, nothing in the world;
  Unless you can find sport in their intents,
  Extremely stretched° and conned° with cruel pain   80
  To do you service.
THESEUS.   I will hear that play;
  For never anything can be amiss
  When simpleness° and duty tender it.
  Go bring them in; and take your places, ladies.
                        [PHILOSTRATE *goes to summon the players.*]
HIPPOLYTA. I love not to see wretchedness o'ercharged,°   85
  And duty in his service° perishing.
THESEUS. Why, gentle sweet, you shall see no such thing.
HIPPOLYTA. He says they can do nothing in this kind.°
THESEUS. The kinder we, to give them thanks for nothing.
  Our sport shall be to take what they mistake;   90
  And what poor duty cannot do, noble respect°
  Takes it in might, not merit.°
  Where I have come, great clerks° have purposèd
  To greet me with premeditated welcomes;
  Where I have seen them shiver and look pale,   95
  Make periods in the midst of sentences,
  Throttle their practiced accent° in their fears,

---

59 strange (Sometimes emended to an adjective that would contrast with *snow,* just as
hot contrasts with *ice.*) **74 toiled** taxed. **unbreathed** unexercised. **75 against** in
preparation for. **80 stretched** strained. **conned** memorized. **83 simpleness** simplicity. **85 wretchedness o'ercharged** incompetence overburdened. **86 his service**
its attempt to serve. **88 kind** kind of thing. **91 respect** evaluation, consideration.
92 Takes . . . merit values it for the effort made rather than for the excellence achieved.
93 clerks learned men. **97 practiced accent** i.e., rehearsed speech; or, usual way of
speaking.

And in conclusion dumbly have broke off,
Not paying me a welcome. Trust me, sweet,
Out of this silence yet I picked a welcome;   100
And in the modesty of fearful duty
I read as much as from the rattling tongue
Of saucy and audacious eloquence.
Love, therefore, and tongue-tied simplicity
In least° speak most, to my capacity.°   105

[PHILOSTRATE *returns*.]

PHILOSTRATE. So please Your Grace, the Prologue° is addressed.°
THESEUS. Let him approach.   [*A flourish of trumpets.*]

Enter the Prologue [QUINCE].

PROLOGUE.
If we offend, it is with our good will.
    That you should think, we come not to offend,
But with good will. To show our simple skill,   110
    That is the true beginning of our end.
Consider then, we come but in despite.
    We do not come, as minding° to content you,
Our true intent is. All for your delight.
    We are not here. That you should here repent you,   115
The actors are at hand, and, by their show,
You shall know all that you are like to know.
THESEUS. This fellow doth not stand upon points.°
LYSANDER. He hath rid° his prologue like a rough° colt; he knows not
    the stop.° A good moral, my lord: it is not enough to speak, but to 120
    speak true.
HIPPOLYTA. Indeed he hath played on his prologue like a child on a
    recorder;° a sound, but not in government.°
THESEUS. His speech was like a tangled chain: nothing° impaired, but all
    disordered. Who is next?   125

Enter PYRAMUS [BOTTOM] *and* THISBE [FLUTE], *and* WALL [SNOUT], *and*
MOONSHINE [STARVELING], *and* LION [SNUG].

PROLOGUE.
Gentles, perchance you wonder at this show,
    But wonder on, till truth makes all things plain.
This man is Pyramus, if you would know;
    This beauteous lady Thisbe is certain.
This man with lime and roughcast doth present   130

---

105 least i.e., saying least. **to my capacity** in my judgment and understanding. **106
Prologue** speaker of the prologue. **addressed** ready. **113 minding** intending. **118
stand upon points** (1) heed niceties or small points (2) pay attention to punctuation in
his reading. (The humor of Quince's speech is in the blunders of its punctuation.) **119
rid** ridden. **rough** unbroken. **120 stop** (1) the stopping of a colt by reining it in (2)
punctuation mark. **123 recorder** a wind instrument like a flute or flageolet.
government control. **124 nothing** not at all.

Wall, that vile Wall which did these lovers sunder;
And through Wall's chink, poor souls, they are content
    To whisper. At the which let no man wonder.
This man, with lantern, dog, and bush of thorn,
    Presenteth Moonshine; for, if you will know,   135
By moonshine did these lovers think no scorn°
    To meet at Ninus' tomb, there, there to woo.
This grisly beast, which Lion hight° by name,
The trusty Thisbe coming first by night
Did scare away, or rather did affright;   140
And as she fled, her mantle she did fall,°
    Which Lion vile with bloody mouth did stain.
Anon comes Pyramus, sweet youth and tall,°
    And finds his trusty Thisbe's mantle slain;
Whereat, with blade, with bloody blameful blade,   145
    He bravely broached° his boiling bloody breast.
And Thisbe, tarrying in mulberry shade,
    His dagger drew, and died. For all the rest,
Let Lion, Moonshine, Wall, and lovers twain
At large° discourse while here they do remain.   150

                    Exeunt LION, THISBE, *and* MOONSHINE.

THESEUS. I wonder if the lion be to speak.
DEMETRIUS. No wonder, my lord. One lion may, when many asses do.
WALL. In this same interlude° it doth befall
    That I, one Snout by name, present a wall;
    And such a wall as I would have you think   155
    That had in it a crannied hole or chink,
    Through which the lovers, Pyramus and Thisbe,
    Did whisper often, very secretly.
    This loam, this roughcast, and this stone doth show
    That I am that same wall; the truth is so.   160
    And this the cranny is, right and sinister,°
    Through which the fearful lovers are to whisper.
THESEUS. Would you desire lime and hair to speak better?
DEMETRIUS. It is the wittiest partition° that ever I heard discourse, my lord.

    [PYRAMUS *comes forward.*]

THESEUS. Pyramus draws near the wall. Silence!   165
PYRAMUS.
    O grim-looked° night! O night with hue so black!
        O night, which ever art when day is not!
    O night, O night! Alack, alack, alack,
        I fear my Thisbe's promise is forgot.

---

136 **think no scorn** think it no disgraceful matter.   138 **hight** is called.   141 **fall** let
fall.   143 **tall** courageous.   146 **broached** stabbed.   150 **At large** in full, at length.
153 **interlude** play.   161 **right and sinister** i.e., the right side of it and the left; or, running from right to left, horizontally.   164 **partition** (1) wall (2) section of a learned trea-
tise or oration.   166 **grim-looked** grim-looking.

And thou, O wall, O sweet, O lovely wall,   170
    That stand'st between her father's ground and mine,
Thou wall, O wall, O sweet and lovely wall,
    Show me thy chink to blink through with mine eyne!
              [WALL *makes a chink with his fingers.*]
Thanks, courteous wall. Jove shield thee well for this.
    But what see I? No Thisbe do I see.   175
O wicked wall, through whom I see no bliss!
    Cursed by thy stones for thus deceiving me!

THESEUS. The wall, methinks, being sensible,° should curse *again*.

PYRAMUS. No, in truth, sir, he should not. "Deceiving me" is Thisbe's cue:
she is to enter now, and I am to spy her through the wall. You   180
shall see, it will fall pat° as I told you. Yonder she comes.

    Enter THISBE.

THISBE.
    O wall, full often hast thou heard my moans,
        For parting my fair Pyramus and me.
    My cherry lips have often kissed thy stones,
        Thy stones with lime and hair knit up in thee.   185

PYRAMUS.
    I see a voice. Now will I to the chink,
        To spy an° I can hear my Thisbe's face.
    Thisbe!

THISBE. My love! Thou art my love, I think.

PYRAMUS. Think what thou wilt, I am thy lover's grace,°   190
    And like Limander° am I trusty still.

THISBE. And I like Helen,° till the Fates me kill.

PYRAMUS. Not Shafalus to Procrus° was so true.

THISBE. As Shafalus to Procrus, I to you.

PYRAMUS. O, kiss me through the hole of this vile wall!   195

THISBE. I kiss the wall's hole, not your lips at all.

PYRAMUS. Wilt thou at Ninny's tomb meet me straightway?

THISBE. 'Tide° life, 'tide death, I come without delay.

              [*Exeunt* PYRAMUS *and* THISBE.]

WALL. Thus have I, Wall, my part dischargèd so;
    And, being done, thus Wall away doth go.   [*Exit.*]   200

THESEUS. Now is the mural down between the two neighbors.

DEMETRIUS. No remedy, my lord, when walls are so willful° to hear
    without warning.°

HIPPOLYTA. This is the silliest stuff that ever I heard.

THESEUS. The best in this kind° are but shadows;° and the worst are no   205
    worse, if imagination amend them.

---

178 sensible capable of feeling.   **181 pat** exactly.   **187 an** if.   **190 lover's grace** i.e.,
gracious lover.   **191, 192 Limander, Helen** (Blunders for *Leander* and *Hero.*)   **193
Shafalus, Procrus** (Blunders for *Cephalus* and *Procris,* also famous lovers.)   **198 'Tide**
betide, come.   **202 willful** willing.   **203 without warning** i.e., without warning the
parents. (Demetrius makes a joke on the proverb "Walls have ears.")   **205 in this kind** of
this sort.   **shadows** likenesses, representations.

HIPPOLYTA. It must be your imagination then, and not theirs.

THESEUS. If we imagine no worse of them than they of themselves, they
    may pass for excellent men. Here come two noble beasts in, a man
    and a lion.   210

Enter LION *and* MOONSHINE.

LION.
    You, ladies, you whose gentle hearts do fear
        The smallest monstrous mouse that creeps on floor,
    May now perchance both quake and tremble here,
        When lion rough in wildest rage doth roar.
    Then know that I, as Snug the joiner, am   215
    A lion fell,° nor else no lion's dam;
    For, if I should as lion come in strife
    Into this place, 'twere pity on my life.

THESEUS. A very gentle beast, and of a good conscience.

DEMETRIUS. The very best at a beast, my lord, that e'er I saw.   220

LYSANDER. This lion is a very fox for his valor.°

THESEUS. True; and a goose for his discretion.°

DEMETRIUS. Not so, my lord; for his valor cannot carry his discretion; and
    the fox carries the goose.

THESEUS. His discretion, I am sure, cannot carry his valor; for the goose 225
    carries not the fox. It is well. Leave it to his discretion, and let us
    listen to the moon.

MOON. This lanthorn° doth the hornèd moon present—

DEMETRIUS. He should have worn the horns on his head.°

THESEUS. He is no crescent, and his horns are invisible within the 230
    circumference.

MOON. This lanthorn doth the hornèd moon present;
    Myself the man i' the moon do seem to be.

THESEUS. This is the greatest error of all the rest. The man should be put
    into the lanthorn. How is it else the man i' the moon?   235

DEMETRIUS. He dares not come there for the° candle, for you see, it is
    already in snuff.°

HIPPOLYTA. I am aweary of this moon. Would he would change!

THESEUS. It appears, by his small light of discretion, that he is in the
    wane; but yet, in courtesy, in all reason, we must stay the time.   240

LYSANDER. Proceed, Moon.

MOON. All that I have to say is to tell you that the lanthorn is the moon,
    I the man i' the moon, this thornbush my thornbush, and this dog
    my dog.

---

216 lion fell fierce lion (with a play on the idea of "lion skin").   **221 is . . . valor** i.e., his
valor consists of craftiness and discretion.   **222 goose . . . discretion** i.e., as discreet as a
goose, that is, more foolish than discreet.   **228 lanthorn** (This original spelling,
lanthorn, may suggest a play on the *horn* of which lanterns were made, and also on a
cuckold's horns; but the spelling *lanthorn* is not used consistently for comic effect in this
play or elsewhere. At 5.1.134, for example, the word is *lantern* in the original.)   **229 on
his head** (As a sign of cuckoldry.)   **236 for the** because of the.   **237 in snuff** (1)
offended (2) in need of snuffing or trimming.

DEMETRIUS. Why, all these should be in the lanthorn, for all these are   245
    in the moon. But silence! Here comes Thisbe.

    Enter THISBE.

THISBE. This is old Ninny's tomb. Where is my love?
LION [*roaring*]. O!
DEMETRIUS. Well roared, Lion.

                  [THISBE *runs off, dropping her mantle.*]
THESEUS. Well run, Thisbe.   250
HIPPOLYTA. Well shone, Moon. Truly, the moon shines with a good grace.

                  [*The* LION *worries* THISBE's *mantle.*]
THESEUS. Well moused,° Lion.

    Enter PYRAMUS.   [*Exit* LION.]

DEMETRIUS. And then came Pyramus.
LYSANDER. And so the lion vanished.
PYRAMUS.
       Sweet Moon, I thank thee for thy sunny beams;   255
         I thank thee, Moon, for shining now so bright;
       For, by thy gracious, golden, glittering gleams,
         I trust to take of truest Thisbe sight.
           But stay, O spite!
           But mark, poor knight,   260
     What dreadful dole° is here?
           Eyes, do you see?
           How can it be?
         O dainty duck! O dear!
           Thy mantle good,   265
           What, stained with blood!
        Approach, ye Furies° fell!°
          O Fates,° come, come,
          Cut thread and thrum;°
         Quail,° crush, conclude, and quell!°   270
THESEUS. This passion, and the death of a dear friend, would go near to
    make a man look sad.°
HIPPOLYTA. Beshrew my heart, but I pity the man.
PYRAMUS. O, wherefore, Nature, didst thou lions frame?
       Since lion vile hath here deflowered my dear,   275
       Which is—no, no, which was—the fairest dame
       That lived, that loved, that liked, that looked with cheer.°
         Come, tears, confound,
         Out, sword, and wound

---

252 moused shaken, torn, bitten.   **261 dole** grievous event.   **267 Furies** avenging goddesses of Greek myth.   **fell** fierce.   **268 Fates** the three goddesses (Clotho, Lachesis,
Atropos) of Greek myth who drew and cut the thread of human life.   **269 thread and
thrum** the warp in weaving and the loose end of the warp.   **270 Quail** overpower.
quell kill, destroy.   **271–272 This . . . sad** i.e., if one had other reason to grieve, one
might be sad, but not from this absurd portrayal of passion.   **277 cheer** countenance.

     The pap° of Pyramus;   280
        Ay, that left pap,
        Where heart doth hop.   [*He stabs himself.*]
     Thus die I, thus, thus, thus.
        Now am I dead,
        Now am I fled;   285
     My soul is in the sky.
        Tongue, lose thy light;
        Moon, take thy flight.   [*Exit* MOONSHINE.]
     Now die, die, die, die, die.   [PYRAMUS *dies.*]

DEMETRIUS. No die, but an ace,° for him; for he is but one.°   290

LYSANDER. Less than an ace, man; for he is dead, he is nothing.

THESEUS. With the help of a surgeon he might yet recover, and yet
    prove an ass.°

HIPPOLYTA. How chance Moonshine is gone before Thisbe comes back
    and finds her lover?   295

THESEUS. She will find him by starlight.

    [*Enter* THISBE.]

     Here she comes, and her passion ends the play.

HIPPOLYTA. Methinks she should not use a long one for such a Pyramus.
    I hope she will be brief.

DEMETRIUS. A mote° will turn the balance, which Pyramus, which° Thisbe,   300
    is the better: he for a man, God warrant us; she for a woman, God
    bless us.

LYSANDER. She hath spied him already with those sweet eyes.

DEMETRIUS. And thus she means,° videlicet:°

THISBE.

     Asleep, my love?   305
     What, dead, my dove?
    O Pyramus, arise!
     Speak, speak. Quite dumb?
     Dead, dead? A tomb
    Must cover thy sweet eyes.   310
     These lily lips,
     This cherry nose,
    These yellow cowslip cheeks,
     Are gone, are gone!
     Lovers, make moan.   315
    His eyes were green as leeks.
     O Sisters Three,°
     Come, come to me,
    With hands as pale as milk;
     Lay them in gore,   320

---

280 pap breast.   **290 ace** the side of the die featuring the single pip, or spot. (The pun is
on *die* as a singular of *dice;* Bottom's performance is not worth a whole *die* but rather one
single face of it, one small portion.)   **one** (1) an individual person (2) unique.   **293 ass**
(With a pun on *ace.*)   **300 mote** small particle.   **which ... which** whether ... or.   **304
means** moans, laments.   **videlicet** to wit.   **317 Sisters Three** the Fates.

Since you have shore°
With shears his thread of silk.
Tongue, not a word.
Come, trusty sword,
Come, blade, my breast imbrue!°   [*Stabs herself.*]   325
And farewell, friends.
Thus Thisbe ends.
Adieu, adieu, adieu.   [*She dies.*]

THESEUS. Moonshine and Lion are left to bury the dead.

DEMETRIUS. Ay, and Wall too.   330

BOTTOM [*starting up, as* FLUTE *does also*]. No, I assure you, the wall is
down that parted their fathers. Will it please you to see the epilogue,
or to hear a Bergomask dance° between two of our company?
                                    [*The other players enter.*]

THESEUS. No epilogue, I pray you; for your play needs no excuse. Never
excuse; for when the players are all dead, there need none to be   335
blamed. Marry, if he that writ it had played Pyramus and hanged
himself in Thisbe's garter, it would have been a fine tragedy; and so
it is, truly, and very notably discharged. But, come, your Bergomask.
Let your epilogue alone.   [*A dance.*]
The iron tongue° of midnight hath told° twelve.   340
Lovers, to bed, 'tis almost fairy time.
I fear we shall outsleep the coming morn
As much as we this night have overwatched.°
This palpable-gross° play hath well beguiled
The heavy° gait of night. Sweet friends, to bed.   345
A fortnight hold we this solemnity,
In nightly revels and new jollity.   *Exeunt.*

Enter PUCK [*carrying a broom*].

PUCK.
Now the hungry lion roars,
    And the wolf behowls the moon;
Whilst the heavy° plowman snores,   350
    All with weary task fordone.°
Now the wasted brands° do glow,
    Whilst the screech owl, screeching loud
Puts the wretch that lies in woe
    In remembrance of a shroud.   355
Now it is the time of night
    That the graves, all gaping wide,
Every one lets forth his sprite,°
    In the church-way paths to glide.

---

321 **shore** shorn.   325 **imbrue** stain with blood.   333 **Bergomask dance** a rustic
dance named from Bergamo, a province in the state of Venice.   340 **iron tongue** i.e., of a
bell.   **told** counted, struck ("tolled").   343 **overwatched** stayed up too late.   344
palpable-gross gross, obviously crude.   345 **heavy** drowsy, dull.   350 **heavy** tired.
351 **fordone** exhausted.   352 **wasted brands** burned-out logs.   358 **Every . . . sprite**
every grave lets forth its ghost.

And we fairies, that do run   360
  By the triple Hecate's° team
From the presence of the sun,
  Following darkness like a dream,
Now are frolic.° Not a mouse
  Shall disturb this hallowed house.   365
I am sent with broom before,
To sweep the dust behind° the door.

Enter [OBERON *and* TITANIA,] *King and Queen of Fairies, with all their train.*

OBERON.

Through the house give glimmering light,
  By the dead and drowsy fire;
Every elf and fairy sprite   370
  Hop as light as bird from brier;
And this ditty, after me,
Sing, and dance it trippingly.

TITANIA.

First, rehearse your song by rote,
To each word a warbling note.   375
Hand in hand, with fairy grace,
Will we sing, and bless this place.

                                     [*Song and dance.*]

OBERON. Now, until the break of day,
Through this house each fairy stray.
To the best bride-bed will we,   380
Which by us shall blessèd be;
And the issue there create°
Ever shall be fortunate.
So shall all the couples three
Ever true in loving be;   385
And the blots of Nature's hand
Shall not in their issue stand;
Never mole, harelip, nor scar,
Nor mark prodigious,° such as are
Despisèd in nativity,   390
Shall upon their children be.
With this field dew consecrate°
Every fairy take his gait,°
And each several° chamber bless,
Through this palace, with sweet peace;   395
And the owner of it blest

---

361 triple Hecate's (Hecate ruled in three capacities: as Luna or Cynthia in heaven, as Diana on earth, and as Proserpina in hell.)   **364 frolic** merry.   **367 behind** from behind. (Robin Goodfellow was a household spirit who helped good housemaids and punished lazy ones.)   **382 create** created.   **389 prodigious** monstrous, unnatural.   **392 consecrate** consecrated.   **393 take his gait** go his way.   **394 several** separate.

Ever shall in safety rest.
Trip away; make no stay;
Meet me all by break of day.

                       Exeunt [OBERON, TITANIA, *and train*].

PUCK [*to the audience*]. If we shadows have offended,   400
Think but this, and all is mended,
That you have but slumbered here°
While these visions did appear.
And this weak and idle theme,
No more yielding but° a dream,   405
Gentles, do not reprehend.
If you pardon, we will mend.°
And, as I am an honest Puck,
If we have unearnèd luck
Now to scape the serpent's tongue,°   410
We will make amends ere long;
Else the Puck a liar call.
So, good night unto you all.
Give me your hands,° if we be friends,
And Robin shall restore amends.°   [*Exit.*] 415

---

402 That . . . here i.e., that it is a "midsummer night's dream." **405 No . . . but** yielding no more than. **407 mend** improve. **410 serpent's tongue** i.e., hissing. **414 Give . . . hands** applaud. **415 restore amends** give satisfaction in return.

YOUR TURN

Act 1

1. On the basis of the first scene, how would you characterize Theseus? Egeus? Hermia? Do you agree with some critics that Egeus is presented comically? (Support your view.)
2. What connections can you make between 1.2 and the first scene?

Act 2

1. Why do you suppose that in 2.1 Shakespeare included material about Theseus's past (lines 76–80)?
2. When the play is staged, audiences invariably laugh loudly at 2.2.109, when Lysander awakens and sees Helena. What's so funny about this?

Act 3

1. What assumptions does Bottom seem to make about the nature of drama? How do they compare with your own?
2. Puck himself has said that he is mischievous, but how mischievous is he? Why did he anoint the eyes of the wrong lover?

Act 4

1. Bottom is the only mortal who sees the fairies. What can we make of this? Or should we not try to make anything of it?

Act 5

1. What do you make of the debate between Theseus and Hippolyta (lines 1–27)? Which of the two seems to you to come closer to the truth? Explain.
2. Do you think it is cruel to laugh at the unintentional antics of the rustic performers? Why, or why not?
3. Puck is sometimes played by a woman. What advantages or disadvantages do you see to giving the part to a woman?

General Questions

1. Some critics speak of the play as a delightful fantasy that is engaging because it has so little connection with real life, but others find in it intimations of dark and dangerous elements in human beings. Where do you stand, and why?
2. Today Shakespeare's plays are sometimes done in modern dress or in costumes that reflect a particular time and place, such as the Wild West of the mid-nineteenth century or the South before the Civil War. How would you costume the play? What advantages might there be in your choice?

32

Students Writing About Plays

Perhaps more evidently than stories or poems, plays are writings that offer arguments. Characters, pitted against other characters, are likely to try to justify their behavior. At the end of *Othello,* for instance, the protagonist offers an account of his behavior—an account that some readers and spectators find convincing and emotionally satisfying, but that others find self-deluded and emotionally unsatisfying. Essays about plays often set forth highly controversial positions; for instance, "The women in Glaspell's *Trifles* are justified in concealing evidence of the murder" or, to take a more nuanced position, "Although viewers can scarcely approve of withholding evidence of murder, in Glaspell's *Trifles* viewers probably approve for three reasons: First, . . . , second, . . . , and third. . . ."

Assertions of a thesis will interest readers only when supported by evidence. In all probability you can find a thesis by examining your basic responses or by scanning the questions we give below, but almost certainly you will modify this thesis during the course of your reexamination of the play. Thinking skeptically about *your own* assertions is the heart of critical thinking, and critical thinking is at the heart of writing an effective argument. It is not, however, the *whole* of writing an argument. Once you have drafted your argument, and you are satisfied with the position that you have taken, you still need to make sure that you set forth this position effectively, in words that will engage your readers.

The following questions may help you to formulate ideas for an essay on a play.

Plot and Conflict

1. Does the exposition introduce elements that will be ironically fulfilled? During the exposition do you perceive things differently from the way the characters perceive them?
2. Are certain happenings or situations recurrent? If so, what significance do you attach to them?
3. If there is more than one plot, do the plots seem to you to be related? Is one plot clearly the main plot and another plot a subplot, a minor variation on the theme?
4. Do any scenes strike you as irrelevant?

5. Are certain scenes so strongly foreshadowed that you anticipated them? If so, did the happenings in these scenes merely fulfill your expectations, or did they also in some way surprise you?

6. What kinds of conflict are there? One character against another, one group against another, one part of a personality against another part in the same person?

7. How is the conflict resolved? By an unambiguous triumph of one side or by a triumph that is also in some degree a loss for the triumphant side? Do you find the resolution satisfying, unsettling, or what? Why?

Character

1. Is the character consistent and coherent? Is the character complex or, on the other hand, a simple representative of some human type?

2. How is the character defined? Consider what the character says and does and what others say about him or her and do to him or her. Also consider other characters who more or less resemble the character in question, for the similarities—and the differences—may be significant.

3. How trustworthy are the characters when they characterize themselves? When they characterize others?

4. Do characters change as the play goes on, or do we simply know them better at the end?

5. What do you make of the minor characters? Are they merely necessary to the plot, or are they foils to other characters? Or do they serve other functions?

6. If a character is tragic, does the tragedy seem to you to proceed from a moral flaw, from an intellectual error, from the malice of others, from sheer chance, or from some combination of these elements?

7. What are the character's goals? To what degree do you sympathize with them? If a character is comic, do you laugh *with* or *at* the character?

8. Do you think the characters are adequately motivated?

9. Is a given character so meditative that you feel he or she is engaged less in a dialogue with others than in a dialogue with the self? If so, do you feel that this character is in large degree a spokesperson for the author, commenting not only on the world of the play but also on the outside world?

Tragedy

1. What causes the tragedy? A flaw in the central character? A mistake (*not* the same thing as a flaw) made by this character? An outside force, such as another character or fate?

2. Is the tragic character defined partly by other characters, for instance, by characters who help us to sense what the character *might* have done, or who in some other way reveal the strengths or weaknesses of the protagonist?

3. Does a viewer know more than the tragic figure knows? More than most or all of the characters know?

4. Does the tragic character achieve any sort of wisdom at the end of the play?

5. To what degree do you sympathize with the tragic character?
6. Is the play depressing? If not, why not?

Comedy

1. Do the comic complications arise chiefly out of the personalities of the characters (for instance, pretentiousness or amorousness) or out of the situations (for instance, mistaken identity)?
2. What are the chief goals of the figures? Do we sympathize with these goals, or do we laugh at persons who pursue them? If we laugh, *why* do we laugh?
3. What are the personalities of those who oppose the central characters? Do we laugh at them, or do we sympathize with them?
4. What is funny about the play? Is the comedy high (including verbal comedy) or chiefly situational and physical?
5. Is the play predominantly genial, or is there a strong satiric tone?
6. Does the comedy have any potentially tragic elements in it? Might the plot be slightly rewritten so that it would become a tragedy?
7. What, if anything, do the characters learn by the end of the play?

Nonverbal Language

1. If the playwright does not provide full stage directions, try to imagine for at least one scene what gestures and tones might accompany each speech. (The first scene is usually a good one to try your hand at.)
2. What do you make of the setting? Does it help to reveal character? Do changes of scene strike you as symbolic? If so, symbolic of what?
3. Do certain costumes (dark suits, flowery shawls, stiff collars, etc.) or certain properties (books, pictures, toys, candlesticks, etc.) strike you as symbolic? If so, symbolic of what?

The Play in Performance

Often we can gain a special pleasure from, or insight into, a dramatic work when we actually see it produced onstage or made into a film. This gives us an opportunity to think about the choices that the director has made, and, even more, it may prompt us to imagine and ponder how we would direct the play for the theater or make a film version of it ourselves.

1. If you have seen the play in the theater or in a film version, what has been added? What has been omitted? Why?
2. In the case of a film, has the film medium been used to advantage—for example, in focusing attention through close-ups or reaction shots (shots showing not the speaker but a person reacting to the speaker)?
3. Do certain plays seem to be especially suited—maybe *only* suited—to the stage? Would they not work effectively as films? Is the reverse true: Are some plays best presented, and best understood, when they are done as films?

4. Critics have sometimes said about this or that play that it cannot really be staged successfully or presented well on film—that the best way to appreciate and understand it is as something to be *read,* like a poem or novel. Are there plays you have studied for which this observation appears to hold true? Which features of the work—its characters, settings, dialogue, central themes—might make it difficult to transfer the play from the page to the stage or to the movie screen?

5. Imagine that you are directing the play. What important decisions would you have to make about character, setting, and pacing of the action? Would you be inclined to omit certain scenes? To add new scenes that are not in the work itself? What kinds of advice would you give to the performers about their roles?

A Filmed Version of a Play

Although we might at first think that a film version of a play is pretty much the play caught on film, as soon as one realizes that movies use such techniques as close-ups and high and low angle shots (the action is seen from above or below), we realize that the filmed version of a play can be very different from the version on the stage, even though in both forms a story is told by means of actors. In Laurence Olivier's *Hamlet* (1948), dreamlike dissolves (the shot fades while a new shot appears to emerge from beneath it) suggest the prince's irresoluteness. Or consider the use of black-and-white versus color film; Olivier made Shakespeare's *Henry V* (1944) in color but *Hamlet* in black and white because, in Olivier's view, color conveyed a splendor appropriate to England's heroic history, whereas black-and-white seemed more suited to somber tragedy.

Filmmakers customarily "open out" plays, giving us scenes of skies, beaches, city streets, and so forth. In Olivier's *Hamlet* we get shots of the sea and the sky. The camera descends from a great height just before Hamlet delivers his first soliloquy, and when the Ghost leaves at 1.5.96 the camera soars into the air as though with the Ghost, and then, from above, the camera shows Hamlet fainting at the battlements. Even when the camera shows us scenes within the palace it in effect opens the play by panning and traveling through long empty corridors and over staircases, suggesting Hamlet's irresolute mind. (Kenneth Branagh's film version of *Hamlet* [1996], however, is very different.)

Getting Ready to Write

Writing an essay about a new film—one not yet available for study on DVD—presents difficulties not encountered in writing about stories, plays, or poems. Because we experience film in a darkened room, we cannot easily take notes, and because the film may be shown only once, we cannot always take another look at passages that puzzle us. But some brief notes can be taken even in the dark; it is best to amplify them as soon as light is available, while you still know what the scrawls mean. If you can see the film more than once, do so, and, of course, if the script has been published, study it. Draft your paper as soon as possible after your first viewing, and then see the film again. You can sometimes check hazy memories of certain scenes and techniques with fellow viewers. But even with multiple viewings and the aid of friends, it is almost impossible to get all of the details right; it is best for the writer to be humble and for the reader to be tolerant.

For a sample essay by a student, see the review of Kenneth Branagh's *Hamlet*, which begins on page 1186.

✔ CHECKLIST: *Writing About a Filmed Play*

Preliminaries

❑ Is the title of the film the same as the title of the play? If not, what is implied?

Dramatic Adaptations

❑ Does the film closely follow its original and neglect the potentialities of the camera? Or does it so revel in cinematic devices that it distorts the original?

❑ Does the film do violence to the theme of the original? Is the film better than its source? Are the additions or omissions due to the medium or to a crude or faulty interpretation of the original?

Plot and Character

❑ Can film deal as effectively with inner action—mental processes—as with external, physical action? In a given film, how is the inner action conveyed? Olivier uses voice-over for parts of Hamlet's soliloquies—that is, we hear Hamlet's voice but his lips do not move.

❑ Are shots and sequences adequately developed, or do they seem jerky? (A shot may be jerky by being extremely brief or at an odd angle; a sequence may be jerky by using discontinuous images or fast cuts. Sometimes, of course, jerkiness may be desirable.) If such cinematic techniques as wipes, dissolves, and slow motion are used, are they meaningful and effective?

❑ Are the characters believable?

❑ Are the actors appropriately cast?

Sound Track

❑ Does the sound track offer more than realistic dialogue? Is the music appropriate and functional? (Music may, among other things, imitate natural sounds, give a sense of locale or of ethnic group, suggest states of mind, provide ironic commentary, or—by repeated melodies—help establish connections.) Are volume, tempo, and pitch—whether of music or of such sounds as the wind blowing or cars moving—used to stimulate emotions?

Five Students Write About Plays

The college essays you write about plays will be similar in many respects to analytic essays about fiction. Unless you are writing a review of a performance, you probably will not try to write about all aspects of a play. Rather, you will choose one significant aspect as your topic. For instance, if you are writing about Tennessee Williams's *The Glass Menagerie,* you might compare the aspirations of Jim O'Connor and Tom Wingfield, or you might compare Tom's illusions with those of his sister, Laura, and his mother, Amanda. Or you might examine the symbolism, perhaps limiting your essay topic to the glass animals, perhaps extending it to include other symbols such as the fire escape, the lighting, and the Victrola. Similarly, if you are writing an analysis, you might decide to study the construction of one scene of a play or (if the play does not have a great many scenes) even the construction of the entire play.

The student essay that follows discusses the structure of *The Glass Menagerie*. It mentions various characters, but since its concern is with the arrangement of scenes, it does not examine any of the characters in detail. An essay might well be devoted to examining Williams's assertion that "There is much to admire in Amanda, and as much to love and pity as there is to laugh at," but an essay on the structure of the play is probably not the place to talk about Williams's characterization of Amanda.

A Student Essay on Plot: The Solid Structure of *The Glass Menagerie*

Preliminary Notes

After deciding to write on the structure of the play, with an eye toward seeing the overall pattern that the parts form, student Joel Shapiro reread *The Glass Menagerie* (page 855), jotted down some notes briefly summarizing each of the seven scenes, with an occasional comment, and then typed them. On rereading the typed notes, he added a few observations in handwriting.

1. begins with Tom talking to audience; ~~says he is a magician~~
   America, in 1930s
      "shouting and confusion"
   Father deserted
   Amanda nagging; ~~is she a bit cracked?~~
   Tom: bored, angry
   Laura: embarrassed, depressed

nagging

2. Laura: quit business school; sad, but Jim's name is mentioned, so, lighter tone introduced

out-and-out — 3. Tom and Amanda argue
battle   Tom almost destroys glass menagerie
   Rage: Can things get any worse?

4. T and A reconciled
      T to try to get a "gentleman caller"

reconciliation, 5. T tells A that Jim will visit
and false   things are looking up
hopes—then 6. Jim arrives; L terrified still, A thinks things can work
final collapse   out

7. Lights go out (foreshadowing dark ending?) Jim a jerk, clumsy; breaks unicorn, but L doesn't seem to mind. Maybe he is the right guy to draw her into normal world. Jim reveals he is engaged: "Desolation."
   Tom escapes into merchant marine, but can't escape memories. Speaks to audience. L. blows out candles (does this mean he forgets her? No, because he is remembering her right now. I don't get it, if the candles are supposed to be symbolic.)

These notes enabled Shapiro to prepare a rough draft, which he then submitted to some classmates for peer review.

Final Version of a Student Essay

Notice that the final version of the essay is *not* merely a summary (a brief retelling of the plot). Although it does indeed include summary, it is devoted to showing *how* the scenes are related.

Shapiro 1

Joel Shapiro
Professor Washington
English 1102
10 April 2010

Title is focused; it announces topic and thesis.

The Solid Structure of

The Glass Menagerie

In the "Production Notes" Tennessee Williams calls *The Glass Menagerie* a "memory play," a term that the narrator in the play also uses. Memories often consist of fragments of episodes that are so loosely connected that they seem chaotic, and therefore we might think that *The Glass Menagerie* will consist of very loosely related episodes. However, the play covers only one episode, and though it gives the illusion of random talk, it really has a firm structure and moves steadily toward a foregone conclusion.

Opening paragraph closes in on thesis.

Reasonable organization; the paragraph touches on the beginning and the end.

Tennessee Williams divides the play into seven scenes. The first scene begins with a sort of prologue, and the last scene concludes with a sort of epilogue that is related to the prologue. In the prologue Tom addresses the audience and comments on the 1930s as a time when America was "blind" and was a place of "shouting and confusion." Tom also mentions that our lives consist of expectations, and though he does not say that our expectations are unfulfilled, near the end of the prologue he quotes a postcard that his father wrote to the family he deserted: "Hello—Goodbye!" In the epilogue Tom tells us that he followed his "father's footsteps," deserting the family. And just before the epilogue, near the end of Scene VII, we see what can be considered another desertion: Jim explains to Tom's sister, Laura, that he is engaged

Brief but effective quotations.

Useful generalization based on earlier details.

and therefore cannot visit Laura again. Thus the end is closely related to the beginning, and the play is the steady development of the initial implications.

Chronological organization is reasonable. Opening topic sentence lets readers know where they are going.

The first three scenes show things going from bad to worse. Amanda is a nagging mother who finds her only relief in talking about the past to her crippled daughter, Laura, and her frustrated son, Tom. When she was young she was beautiful and was eagerly courted by rich young men, but now the family is poor and this harping on the past can only bore or infuriate Tom and embarrass or depress Laura, who have no happy past to look back to, who see no happy future, and who can only be upset by Amanda's insistence that they should behave as she behaved long ago. The second scene deepens the despair: Amanda learns that the

Brief plot summary supports thesis.

timorous Laura has not been attending a business school but has retreated in terror from this confrontation with the contemporary world. Laura's helplessness is made clear to the audience, and so is Amanda's lack of understanding. Near the end of the second scene, however, Jim's name is introduced; he is a boy Laura had a crush on in high school, and so the audience gets a glimpse of a happier Laura and a sense that possibly Laura's world is wider than the stifling tenement in which she and her mother and brother live. But in the third scene things get worse, when Tom and Amanda have so violent an argument that they are no longer on speaking terms. Tom is so angry with his mother that he almost by accident destroys his sister's treasured collection of glass animals, the fragile, lifeless world that is her refuge. The apartment is literally full of the "shouting and confusion" that Tom spoke of in his prologue.

Useful summary and transition.

The first three scenes have revealed a progressive worsening of relations; the next three scenes reveal a progressive improvement in relations. In Scene IV Tom and his mother are reconciled, and Tom reluctantly—apparently in an effort to make up with his mother— agrees to try to get a friend to come to dinner so that Laura will have "a gentleman caller." In Scene V Tom tells his mother that Jim will come to dinner on the next night, and Amanda brightens, because she sees a possibility of security for Laura at last. In Scene VI Jim arrives, and despite Laura's initial terror, there seems, at least in Amanda's mind, to be the possibility that things will go well.

The seventh scene, by far the longest, at first seems to be fulfilling Amanda's hopes. Despite the ominous fact that the lights go out because Tom has not paid the electric bill, Jim is at ease. He is an insensitive oaf, but that doesn't seem to bother Amanda, and almost miraculously he manages to draw Laura somewhat out of her sheltered world. Even when Jim in his clumsiness breaks the horn off Laura's treasured glass unicorn, she is not upset. In fact, she is almost relieved because the loss of the horn makes the animal less "freakish" and he "will feel more at home with the other horses." In a way, of course, the unicorn symbolizes the crippled Laura, who at least for the moment feels less freakish and isolated now that she is somewhat reunited with society through Jim. But this is a play about life in a blind and confused world, and though in a previous age the father escaped, there can be no escape now. Jim reveals that he is engaged, Laura relapses into "desolation," Amanda relapses into rage and bitterness, and Tom relapses into dreams of escape. In a limited sense Tom does escape. He leaves the family and joins the merchant marine, but his last speech or epilogue tells us that he cannot escape the memory of his sister: "Oh, Laura, Laura, I tried to leave you behind me, but I am more faithful than I intended to be!" And so the end of the last scene brings us back again to the beginning of the first scene: we are still in a world of "the blind" and of "confusion." But now at the end of the play the darkness is deeper, the characters are lost forever in their unhappiness as Laura "blows the candles out," the darkness being literal but also symbolic of their extinguished hopes.

The essayist is thinking and commenting, not merely summarizing the plot.

Work Cited

Williams, Tennessee. "The Glass Menagerie." *An Introduction to Literature.* Ed. Sylvan Barnet, William Burto, and William E. Cain. 16th ed. New York: Longman, 2011. 855–901. Print.

A Student Essay on Setting: What the Kitchen in *Trifles* Tells Us

One of our students, Margaret Hammer, wrote a short essay on setting in Susan Glaspell's *Trifles*. (The play begins on page 845.)

Margaret Hammer
Professor Cain
English 212
5 May 2010

What the Kitchen in *Trifles* Tells Us

Susan Glaspell's *Trifles* is a one-act play with only one setting. It cannot show us, therefore, a strong contrast such as we might see in the first two scenes of *Hamlet*, where at the start we encounter soldiers on guard during a cold night, and then, in the second scene, we are taken into the king's splendid court. Nevertheless, as we read *Trifles* we *do* become aware of a contrast: We see an untidy kitchen, with "dirty towels" (847), bread left unbaked, a cupboard closet with a "mess" of preserves (847), and a table "one half of which is clean, the other half messy" (849), but we hear about a pleasant woman who in happier days sang in the church choir, and who was an excellent quilter. The reader, or the spectator at the play, inevitably concludes that the gloomy and messy kitchen is *not* typical of the woman who worked in it. But what *is* it typical of?

In the first stage direction of the play Glaspell tells us what the spectator sees: "The kitchen in the now abandoned farmhouse of John Wright, a gloomy kitchen, and left without having been put in order . . ." (845). Later we hear that we are near Omaha (845), but nothing much is made of the particular part of the United States where the play is set. What much *is* made of is the fact that the kitchen is cold, that "it never seemed a very cheerful place" (848), and—here we get something crucial—that no "place'd be any cheerfuller for John Wright's being in it" (848). In short, the cold, cheerless, gloomy place is almost a symbol of the farmer, John Wright, and (perhaps surprisingly) the kitchen does not represent the woman who doubtless spent much of her time in it.

As the play progresses, we hear that the Wright house, "down
in a hollow," is "a lonesome place" (851), but the central fact—the
point repeatedly made in play—is how cold the kitchen is, and the
reader/viewer comes to identify the setting with John Wright himself, a
man who was "like a raw wind that gets to the bone" (851).

The mess in the kitchen provides Mrs. Hale and Mrs. Peters with
information as to what drove Mrs. Wright to murder her husband, but
the "gloomy" kitchen itself provides information about Mr. Wright, and
about the miserable life that he forced his wife to live.

Work Cited

Glaspell, Susan. "Trifles." *An Introduction to Literature*. Ed. Sylvan
Barnet, William Burto, and William E. Cain. 16th ed. New York:
Longman, 2011. 845–54. Print.

The Analysis Analyzed

We think Margaret Hammer has done a good job explaining the role of the setting in *Trifles*. What are some of the things that, in our view, make the essay
effective?

- The title is engaging and hints at the thesis (that the setting is important).
- The first paragraph makes a relevant comparison with another work that
  the student has studied. The comparison is not window-dressing; it makes
  the important point that a single setting can convey a good deal.
- The second paragraph focuses on the point that the kitchen is cold and
  cheerless—and that in these respects it is very like the farmer, John
  Wright, and *not* like the woman who worked there.
- The third paragraph pretty much makes the same point as the second,
  and in fact we would have combined the second and third paragraphs. If
  each of these paragraphs had been long—say, eight or ten sentences
  apiece—we might have kept them as two paragraphs, but given their relative brevity, we think a reader can take both at one gulp.
- The final paragraph briefly and emphatically restates the thesis.

A Student Essay on Character and Theme: Fairy Mischief and Morality in *A Midsummer Night's Dream*

A student, Carla Alonso, told us privately that when she began work on her paper, she was planning to write on the irrationality of the fairies in *A Midsummer Night's Dream* as a sort of mirror of the irrationality of the young lovers, but when she searched the play for supporting detail she found, to her surprise, that she had to revise her thesis.

Her earliest jottings—a sort of preliminary outline and guide to rereading the play—looked like this:

fairies--like lovers, irrational?
   Puck
      mischievous
   Titania and Oberon
      equally quarrelsome?
         quarrel disturbs human world
      Titania wants Indian boy
         isn't she right?
            if so, she's not irrational
      Oberon
         jealous
         cruel to Titania?
         unfaithful?
   Other fairies
      do they do anything?
      Ts different from O's?

In rereading the play and in jotting down notes, she came to see that the supernatural characters were not as malicious and irrational as she had thought, and so she changed the focus of her thesis.

Alonso 1

Carla Alonso
Professor Zee
English 1102
1 May 2010

Title is informative.

Fairy Mischief and Morality
in *A Midsummer Night's Dream*

Opening paragraph leads into the subject.

    If we read *A Midsummer Night's Dream* casually, or come away from a delightful performance, we may have the vague impression that the fairies are wild, mischievous, willful creatures who perhaps represent the irrational qualities of mankind. But in fact the text lends only a little support to this view. The irrationality of mankind is really represented chiefly by the human beings in the play—we are told in the first scene, for example, that Demetrius used to love Helena but now loves Hermia—and the fairies are largely responsible for the happy ending finally achieved.

It is, of course, easy to see why we may think of the fairies as wild and mischievous. Titania and Oberon have quarreled over a little Indian boy, and their quarrel has led to fogs, floods, and other disorders in nature. Moreover, Titania accuses Oberon of infidelity, and Oberon returns the charge:

> How canst thou thus for shame, Titania
> Glance at my credit with Hippolyta,
> Knowing I know thy love to Theseus?
>
> (2.1.74–76)

Short quotation provides evidence.

Titania rejects this countercharge, saying "These are the forgeries of jealousy" (2.1.81), but we are not convinced of her innocence. It would be easy to give additional examples of speeches in which the king and queen of fairyland present unflattering pictures of each other, but probably one of the strongest pieces of evidence of their alleged irrationality is the fact the Oberon causes Titania to fall in love with the asinine Bottom. We should not forget, however, that later Oberon will take pity on her: "Her dotage now I do begin to pity" (4.1.45).

Citation in parentheses reduces the number of footnotes.

In fact, it is largely through Oberon's sense of pity—this time for the quarreling young lovers in the forest—that the lovers finally are successfully paired off. And we should remember, too, before we claim that the fairies are consistently quarrelsome and mischievous, that at the very end of the play Oberon and Titania join in a song and dance blessing the newlyweds and promising healthy offspring. The fairies, though quarrelsome, are fundamentally benevolent spirits.

Her main point having been set forth, Alonso now turns to an apparent exception.

But what of Robin Goodfellow, the Puck of the play? Is he not mischievous? One of the fairies says Robin is a "shrewd and knavish sprite" (2.1.33) who frightens maids and plays tricks on housewives; Robin admits the charge, saying "Thou speakest aright" (2.1.42), and two lines later he says, "I jest to Oberon, and make him smile," and then

Alonso 3

he goes on to describe some of his practical jokes, including his fondness
for neighing to tease a horse and pulling a stool from under an old lady.

*Alonso
concedes a
point but then
goes on in the
rest of the
paragraph to
argue that the
main point
nevertheless
still holds.*

But this is not quite the whole story. The fact is, despite this speech,
that we do *not* see Robin engage in any mischievous pranks. After all, he
does not deliberately anoint the eyes of the wrong Athenian lover.
Oberon tells Robin that he will recognize the young man by his Athenian
clothing, and when Puck encounters a young man in Athenian clothing
he anoints the youth's eyes. The fault is really Oberon's, though of
course Oberon meant well when he instructed Robin:

> A sweet Athenian lady is in love
>
> With a disdainful youth. Anoint his eyes;
>
> But do it when the next thing he espies
>
> May be the lady.
>
> (2.1.260–63)

So Robin's error is innocent. He is speaking honestly when he
says, "Believe me, king of shadows, I mistook" (3.2.348). Of course he
does enjoy the confusion he mistakenly causes, but we can hardly blame

*Concluding
paragraph
summarizes,
but it does not
merely repeat
what has come
before; it offers
a few brief
new quota-
tions. The para-
graph ends by
setting the con-
clusion (fairies
are decent) in
a fresh context
(it's the mor-
tals who are
irrational)*

him severely for that. After all, we enjoy it, too.

The fairies, by their very nature, suggest a mysterious, irrational
world, but—even though, as we have just seen, Oberon is called the
"king of shadows"—they are not to be confused with "ghosts, wand'ring
here and there," "damned spirits" who "willfully themselves exile from
light / And must for aye consort with black-browed night" (3.2.382–88).
Oberon explicitly says, after this speech, "But we are spirits of another
sort," and his speech is filled with references not to darkness but to
light: "morning," "eastern gate," "blessed beams." The closer we
observe them in the play, then, the closer their behavior is to that of
normal, decent human beings. There is plenty of irrationality in the
play, but it is found for the most part in the human beings, not in the
fairies.

Alonso 4

Work Cited

Shakespeare, William. "A Midsummer Night's Dream." *An Introduction to Literature.* Ed. Sylvan Barnet, William Burto, and William E. Cain. 16th ed. New York: Longman, 2011. 1114–70. Print.

Notice that this first-rate essay

- Has a thesis, an argument.
- Develops the thesis effectively.

Also notice the following:

- The title gives the reader some idea of what is coming.
- The first paragraph clearly sets forth the thesis.
- The essay next takes up the evidence that might seem to contradict the thesis—Oberon and Titania, and Robin Goodfellow—and it shows that this evidence is not decisive.
- The essay continues to move the thesis forward, substantiating it, especially with well-chosen quotations.
- The last paragraph slightly restates the thesis in light of what the essay has demonstrated.

A Student Review of a Film Version of a Play: Branagh's Film of *Hamlet*

What follows is an undergraduate's review of Kenneth Branagh's film version of *Hamlet* (1996). In the margin we call attention to Will Saretta's rhetorical strategies.

Saretta 1

Will Saretta

Professor Diaz

English 2B

19 April 2010

Branagh's Film of *Hamlet*

The opening paragraph holds the reader's attention by (1) offering useful information and (2) strongly stating an evaluation.

Kenneth Branagh's *Hamlet* opened last night at the Harmor Auditorium and will be shown again on Wednesday and Thursday at 7:30 p.m. According to the clock the evening will be long—the film runs

Saretta 2

for four hours, and in addition there is one ten-minute intermission—but you will enjoy every minute of it.

The second paragraph begins with a near transition (its first sentence slightly modifies the last sentence of the preceding paragraph) and supports its point (about the film's weak spots) with specific evidence.

Well, almost every minute. Curiously, the film begins and ends relatively weakly, but most of what occurs between is good, and much of it is wonderful. The beginning is weak because it is too strong; Bernardo, the sentinel, offstage says "Who's there?" but before he gets a reply he crashes onto the screen and knocks Francisco down. The two soldiers grapple, swords flash in the darkness, and finally Francisco says, "Nay, answer me. Stand and unfold yourself." Presumably Branagh wanted to begin with a bang, but here, as often, more is less. A quieter, less physical opening in which Bernardo, coming on duty, hears a noise and demands that the maker of the noise identify himself, and Francisco, the sentinel on duty, rightly demands that the newcomer identify *himself*, would catch the uneasiness and the mystery that pervades the play much better than does Branagh's showy beginning.

The third paragraph uses a clear transition ("Similarly") and makes its points in an orderly fashion, using effective repetition ("Second," "Hamlet is not a play about," "or about," "Hamlet is not about," "It is about . . .")

Similarly, at the end of the film, we get too much. For one thing, shots of Fortinbras's army invading Elsinore alternate with shots of the duel between Hamlet and King Claudius's pawn, Laertes, and they merely distract us from what really counts in this scene, the duel itself, which will result in Hamlet's death but also in Hamlet's successful completion of his mission to avenge his father. Second, at the very end we get shots of Fortinbras's men pulling down a massive statue of Hamlet Senior, probably influenced by television and newspaper shots of statues of Lenin being pulled down when the Soviet Union was dissolved a few years before the film was made. This is ridiculous; *Hamlet* is not a play about the fall of Communism, or about the one form of tyranny replacing another. Shakespeare's *Hamlet* is not about the triumph of Fortinbras. It is about Hamlet's brave and ultimately successful efforts to do what is right, against overwhelming odds, and to offer us the consolation that in a world where death always triumphs there nevertheless is something that can be called nobility.

Having discussed the weaknesses, Saretta now turns to "what . . . is good about the film." Several points are made, in a reasonable sequence.

What, then, is good about the film? First, the film gives us the whole play, whereas almost all productions, whether on the stage or in the movie house, give us drastically abbreviated versions. Although less is often more, when it comes to the text of *Hamlet*, more is better, and we should be grateful to Branagh for letting us hear all of the lines. Second, it is very well performed, with only a few exceptions. Jack Lemmon as Marcellus is pretty bad, but fortunately the part is small. Other big-name actors in small parts—Charlton Heston as the Player King, Robin Williams as Osric, and Billy Crystal as the First Gravedigger—are admirable. But of course the success or failure of any production of *Hamlet* will depend chiefly on the actor who plays Hamlet, and to a considerable degree on the actors who play Claudius, Gertrude, Polonius, Ophelia, Laertes, and Horatio. There isn't space here to comment on all of these roles, but let it be said that Branagh's Prince Hamlet is indeed princely, a man who strikes us as having the ability to become a king, not a wimpy whining figure. When at the end Fortinbras says that if Hamlet had lived to become the king, he would "have proved most royal," we believe him. And his adversary, King Claudius, though morally despicable, is a man of great charm and great ability. The two men are indeed "mighty opposites," to use Hamlet's own words.

Although at first this paragraph may seem unconnected with the preceding paragraph, in fact it is firmly connected:"this sense of powerful forces" picks up the "mighty opposites" of the last sentence of the preceding paragraph.

Branagh's decision to set the play in the late nineteenth century rather than in the Elizabethan period of Shakespeare's day and rather than in our own day contributes to this sense of powerful forces at work. If the play were set in Shakespeare's day, the men would wear tights, and if it were set in our day they would wear suits or trousers and sports jackets and sweaters, but in the film all of the men wear military costumes (black for Hamlet, scarlet for Claudius, white for Laertes) and the women wear ball gowns of the Victorian period. Branagh gives us a world that is closer to our own than would Elizabethan costumes, but yet it is, visually at least, also distant enough to convey a sense of grandeur, which modern dress cannot suggest. Of course *Hamlet* can be done in modern dress, just as *Romeo and Juliet* was done, successfully, in the recent film staring Claire Danes and Leonardo DiCaprio, set in a world that seemed to be Miami Beach, but *Romeo and Juliet* is less concerned with heroism and grandeur than *Hamlet* is, so Branagh probably did well to avoid contemporary costumes.

Although Branagh is faithful to the text, in that he gives us the entire text, he knows that a good film cannot be made merely by

Saretta 4

The topic of this paragraph is Branagh's departures from the play, some of which are effective and some of which are not.

recording on film a stage production, and so he gives us handsome shots of landscape and of rich interiors—for instance, a great mirrored hall—that would be beyond the resources of any theatrical production. I have already said that at the end, when Fortinbras's army swarms over the countryside and then invades the castle we get material that is distracting, indeed irrelevant, but there are also a few other distractions. It is all very well to let us *see* the content of long narrative speeches (for instance, when the Player King talks of the fall of Troy and the death of King Priam and the lament of Queen Hecuba, Branagh shows us these things, with John Gielgud as Priam and Judi Dench as Hecuba performing in pantomime), but there surely is no need for us to see a naked Hamlet and a naked Ophelia in bed, when Polonius is warning Ophelia that Hamlet's talk of love cannot be trusted. Polonius's warning is not so long or so undramatic that we need to be entertained visually with an invention that finds not a word of support in the text. On the contrary, all of Ophelia's lines suggest that she would not be other than a dutiful young woman, obedient to the morals of the time and to her father's authority. Yet another of Branagh's unfortunate inventions is the prostitute who appears in Polonius's bedroom during Polonius's interview with Reynaldo. A final example of unnecessary spectacle is Hamlet's killing of Claudius: He hurls his rapier the length of the hall, impaling Claudius, and then like some 1930s movie star he swings on the chandelier and drops down on Claudius to finish him off.

Having offered some negative comments, Saretta reminds the reader that he thinks the film is very good.

But it is wrong to end this review by pointing out faults in Branagh's film of *Hamlet*. There is so much in this film that is exciting, so much that is moving, so much that is . . . well, so much that is *Hamlet* (which is to say that is a great experience), that the film must be recommended without reservation. Go to see it. The four hours will fly.

The "postscript" is tacked on, but reviews often have a relatively informal touch.

A postscript: It is good to see that Branagh uses color-blind casting. Volternard, Fortinbras's Captain, and the messenger who announces Laertes's return are all blacks—the messenger is a black woman—although of course medieval Denmark and Elizabethan England, and, for that matter, Victorian England, would not have routinely included blacks. These performers are effective, and it is appropriate that actors of color take their place in the world's greatest play.

Saretta 5

Work Cited

Hamlet. Dir. Kenneth Branagh. Perf. Kenneth Branagh, Derek Jacobi, and
Julie Christie. Columbia, 1996. Film.

A Student Essay on Using Sources:
The Women in *Death of a Salesman*

In Appendix B we discuss manuscript form and documentation (pages 1452–67).
Here we give a student's documented paper on Arthur Miller's *Death of a Salesman*. (The play begins on page 1199 of this book.) Ruth Katz had taken notes on
index cards, both from the play and from secondary sources, and she had
arranged and rearranged the notes as her topic and thesis became clearer to her.
We preface the final version of Katz's essay with the rough outline that she prepared before she wrote her first draft.

Linda

    realistic

    encourages Willy

    foolish? loving?   *Both? Not so foolish; Knows how to calm*

    prevented him from succeeding?   *him down*

    doesn't understand W's needs? or nothing else to
      do?

    quote some critics knocking Linda

    other women

5   the Woman

4   the two women in restaurant   *(Forsy the first, then Letta)*

3   Jenny

2   W's mother (compare with father?)

    check to see exactly what the play says about her

1   Howard's wife (and daughter?)   *(discuss this first)*

6   discuss Linda last

    titles?

    Linda Loman

    Women in Miller's *Salesman*

    Gender in . . .   *Male and Female in Death* . . .

    Men and Women: Arthur M's View
      Willy Loman's Women

Here is the final version of Katz's essay.

Ruth Katz
Professor Ling
English 102
10 April 2010

The Women in *Death of a Salesman*

Death of a Salesman is of course about a salesman, but it is
also about the American dream of success. Somewhere in between
the narrowest topic, the death of a salesman, and the largest topic, the
examination of American values, is Miller's picture of the American
family. This paper will chiefly study one member of the family,
Willy's wife, Linda Loman, but before examining Miller's depiction
of her, it will look at Miller's depiction of other women in the play
in order to make clear Linda's distinctive traits. We will see that
although her role in society is extremely limited, she is an admirable
figure, fulfilling the roles of wife and mother with remarkable
intelligence.

Linda is the only woman who is on stage much of the time, but
there are several other women in the play: "the Woman" (the unnamed
woman in Willy's hotel room), Miss Forsythe and her friend Letta (the
two women who join the brothers in the restaurant), Jenny (Charley's
secretary), the various women whom the brothers talk about, and the
voices of Howard's daughter and wife. We also hear a little about Willy's
mother.

We will look first at the least important (but not utterly
unimportant) of these, the voices of Howard's daughter and wife on the
wire recorder. Of Howard's seven-year-old daughter we know only that
she can whistle "Roll Out the Barrel" and that according to Howard she
"is crazy about me." The other woman in Howard's life is equally under
his thumb. Here is the dialogue that tells us about her—and her relation
to her husband.

> HOWARD'S VOICE. "Go on, say something." (*Pause.*) "Well,
>   you gonna talk?"
> HIS WIFE. "I can't think of anything."
> HOWARD'S VOICE. "Well, talk—it's turning."

HIS WIFE (*shyly, beaten*). "Hello." (*Silence.*) "Oh,
    Howard, I can't talk into this . . . "
HOWARD (*snapping the machine off*). That was my
    wife. (1235)

There is, in fact, a third woman in Howard's life, the maid. Howard says
that if he can't be at home when the Jack Benny program comes on, he
uses the wire recorder. He tells "the maid to turn the radio on when Jack
Benny comes on, and this automatically goes on with the radio . . ."
(1235). In short, the women in Howard's world exist to serve (and to
worship) him.

Another woman who seems to have existed only to serve men is
Willy Loman's mother. On one occasion, in speaking with Ben, Willy
remembers being on her lap, and Ben, on learning that his mother is
dead, utters a platitudinous description of her, "Fine specimen of a lady,
Mother" (1219), but that's as much as we learn of her. Willy is chiefly
interested in learning about his father, who left the family and went to
Alaska. Ben characterizes the father as "a very great and a very wild-
hearted man" (1220), but the fact that the father left his family and
apparently had no further communication with his wife and children
seems to mean nothing to Ben. Presumably the mother struggled alone
to bring up the boys, but her efforts are unmentioned. Curiously, some
writers defend the father's desertion of his family. Lois Gordon says,
"The first generation (Willy's father) has been forced, in order to make a
living, to break up the family" (278), but nothing in the play supports
this assertion that the father was "forced" to break up the family.

Willy, like Ben, assumes that men are heroic and women are
nothing except servants and sex machines. For instance, Willy says to
Ben, "Please tell about Dad. I want my boys to hear. I want them to
know the kind of stock they spring from" (1220). As Kay Stanton, a
feminist critic says, Willy's words imply "an Edenic birth myth," a world
"with all the Loman men springing directly from their father's side, with
no commingling with a female" (69).

Another woman who, like Howard's maid and Willy's mother,
apparently exists only to serve is Jenny, Charley's secretary. She is
courteous, and she is treated courteously by Charley and by Charley's

son, Bernard, but she has no identity other than that of a secretary. And, as a secretary—that is, as a nonentity in the eyes of at least some men—she can be addressed insensitively. Willy Loman makes off-color remarks to her:

> WILLY. . . . Jenny, Jenny, good to see you. How're ya?
> Workin'? Or still honest?
> JENNY. Fine. How've you been feeling?
> WILLY. Not much any more, Jenny. Ha, ha! (1241)

The first of these comments seems to suggest that a working woman is *not* honest—that is, is a prostitute or is engaged in some other sort of hanky-panky, as is the Woman who in exchange for silk stockings and sex sends Willy directly into the buyer's office. The second of Willy's jokes, with its remark about not feeling much, also refers to sex. In short, though readers or viewers of the play see Jenny as a thoroughly respectable woman, they see her not so much as an individual but as a person engaged in routine work and as a person to whom Willy can speak crudely.

It is a little harder to be certain about the characters of Miss Forsythe and Letta, the two women in the scene in Stanley's restaurant. For Happy, Miss Forsythe is "strudel," an object for a man to consume, and for Stanley she and her friend Letta are "chippies," that is, prostitutes. But is it clear that they are prostitutes? When Happy tells Miss Forsythe that he is in the business of selling, he makes a dirty joke, saying, "You don't happen to sell, do you?" (1246). She replies, "No, I don't sell," and if we take this seriously and if we believe her, we can say that she is respectable and is rightly putting Happy in his place. Further, her friend Letta says, "I gotta get up very early tomorrow. I got jury duty" (1253), which implies that she is a responsible citizen. Still, the girls do not seem especially thoughtful. When Biff introduces Willy to the girls, Letta says, "Isn't he cute? Sit down with us, Pop" (1253), and when Willy breaks down in the restaurant, Miss Forsythe says, "Say, I don't like that temper of his" (1254). Perhaps we can say this: It is going too far—on the basis of what we see—to agree with Stanley that the women are "chippies," or with Happy, who assumes that every woman is available for sex, but Miss Forsythe and Letta do not seem to be especially responsible or even interesting people. That is, as Miller presents them, they are of little substance, simply figures introduced into the play in order to show how badly Happy and Biff behave.

The most important woman in the play, other than Linda, is "the Woman," who for money or stockings and perhaps for pleasure has sex with Willy, and who will use her influence as a receptionist or secretary in the office to send Willy directly on to the buyer, without his having to wait at the desk. But even though the Woman gets something out of the relationship, she knows that she is being used. When Biff appears in the hotel room, she asks him, "Are you football or baseball?" Biff replies, "Football," and the Woman, "*angry, humiliated,*" says, "That's me too" (1256). We can admire her vigorous response, but, again, like the other women whom we have discussed, she is not really an impressive figure. We can say that, at best, in a society that assumes women are to be exploited by men, she holds her own.

So far, then—though we have not yet talked about Linda—the world of *Death of a Salesman* is not notable for its pictures of impressive women. True, most of the males in the play—Willy, Biff, Happy, Ben, and such lesser characters as Stanley and Howard—are themselves pretty sorry specimens, but Bernard and Charley are exceptionally decent and successful people, people who can well serve as role models. Can any female character in the play serve as a role model?

Linda has evoked strongly contrasting reactions from the critics. Some of them judge her very severely. For instance, Lois Gordon says that Linda "encourages Willy's dream, yet she will not let him leave her for the New Continent, the only realm where the dream can be fulfilled" (280). True, Linda urges Willy not to follow Ben's advice of going to Alaska, but surely the spectator of the play cannot believe that Willy is the sort of man who can follow in Ben's footsteps and violently make a fortune. And, in fact, Ben is so vile a person (as when he trips Biff, threatens Biff's eye with the point of his umbrella, and says, "Never fight fair with a stranger, boy" [1221]) that we would not want Willy to take Ben's advice.

A second example of a harsh view of Linda is Brian Parker's comment on "the essential stupidity of Linda's behavior. Surely it is both stupid and immoral to encourage the man you love in self-deceit and lies" (54). Parker also says that Linda's speech at the end, when she says she cannot understand why Willy killed himself, "is not only pathetic, it is also an explanation of the loneliness of Willy Loman which threw him into other women's arms" (54). Nothing in the play suggests that Linda was anything other than a highly supportive wife. If Willy turned to other women, surely it was not because Linda did not understand him. Finally, one last example of the Linda-bashing school of commentary: Guerin Bliquez speaks of "Linda's facility for prodding Willy to his doom" (383).

Very briefly, the arguments against Linda are that (1) she selfishly prevents Willy from going to Alaska, (2) she stupidly encourages him in his self-deceptions, and (3) she is materialistic, so that even at the end, in the Requiem, when she says she has made the last payment on the house, she is talking about money. But if we study the play we will see that all three of these charges are false. First, although Linda does indeed discourage Willy from taking Ben's advice and going to Alaska, she points out that there is no need for "everybody [to] conquer the world" and that Willy has "a beautiful job here" (1238), a job with excellent prospects. She may be mistaken in thinking that Willy has a good job—he may have misled her—but, given what seems to be the situation, her comment is entirely reasonable.

So far as the second charge goes, that she encourages him in self-deception, there are two answers. First, on some matters she does not know that Willy has lied to her, and so her encouragement is reasonable and right. Second, on other matters she does know that Willy is not telling the truth, but she rightly thinks it is best not to let him know that she knows, since such a revelation would crush what little self-respect remains in him. Consider, for example, this portion of dialogue, early in the play, when Willy, deeply agitated about his failure to drive and about Biff, has returned from what started out as a trip to Boston. Linda, trying to take his mind off his problems, urges him to go downstairs to the kitchen to try a new kind of cheese:

> LINDA. Go down, try it. And be quiet.
> WILLY (*turning to Linda, guiltily*). You're not worried about me, are you, sweetheart?
>
> . . . .

> LINDA. You've got too much on the ball to worry about.
>
> WILLY. You're my foundation and my support, Linda.
>
> LINDA. Just try to relax, dear. You make mountains out of
> molehills.
>
> WILLY. I won't fight with him any more. If he wants to go
> back to Texas, let him go.
>
> LINDA. He'll find his way. (1204–05)

Of course she does not really think he has a great deal on the ball, and she probably is not confident that Biff will "find his way," but surely she is doing the best thing possible—calming Willy, partly by using soothing words and partly by doing what she can to get Biff out of the house, since she knows that Biff and Willy can't live under the same roof.

The third charge, that she is materialistic, is ridiculous. She *has* to count the pennies because *someone* has to see that the bills are paid, and Willy is obviously unable to do so. Here is an example of her supposed preoccupation with money:

> LINDA. Well, there's nine-sixty for the washing machine. And
> for the vacuum cleaner there's three and a half due on the
> fifteenth. Then the roof, you got twenty-one dollars
> remaining.
>
> WILLY. It don't leak, does it?
>
> LINDA. No, they did a wonderful job. Then you owe Frank for
> the carburetor.
>
> WILLY. I'm not going to pay that man! That goddam Chevrolet,
> they ought to prohibit the manufacture of that car!
>
> LINDA. Well, you owe him three and a half. And odds
> and ends, comes to around a hundred and twenty dollars
> by the fifteenth. (1214)

It might be nice if Linda spent her time taking courses at an adult education center and thinking high thoughts, but it's obvious that *someone* in the Loman family (as in all families) has to keep track of the bills.

The worst that can be said of Linda is that she subscribes to three American ideas of the time—that the man is the breadwinner, that the

relationship between a father and his sons is far more important than
the relationship between a mother and her sons, and that a woman's
sole job is to care for the house and to produce sons for her husband.
She is the maidservant to her husband and to her sons, but in this she
is like the vast majority of women of her time, and she should not be
criticized for not being an innovator. Compared to her husband and her
sons, Linda (though of course not perfect) is a tower of common sense,
virtue, and strength. In fact, far from causing Willy's failure, she does
what she can to give him strength to face the facts, for instance when
she encourages him to talk to Howard about a job in New York: "Why
don't you go down to the place tomorrow and tell Howard you've simply
got to work in New York? You're too accommodating, dear" (1203).
Notice, too, her speech in which she agrees with Biff's decision that it
is best for Biff to leave for good: she goes to Willy and says, "I think
that's the best way, dear. 'Cause there's no use drawing it out, you'll
just never get along" (1261). Linda is not the most forceful person
alive, or the brightest, but she is decent and she sees more clearly than
do any of the other Lomans.

There is nothing in the play to suggest that Arthur Miller was a
feminist or was ahead of his time in his view of the role of women. On
the contrary, the play seems to give a pre-feminist view, with women
playing subordinate roles to men. The images of success of the best
sort—not of Ben's ruthless sort—are Charley and Bernard, two males.
Probably Miller, writing in the 1940s, could hardly conceive of a
successful woman other than as a wife or mother. Notice, by the way,
that Bernard—probably the most admirable male in the play—is not
only an important lawyer but the father of two sons, apparently a
sign of his complete success as a man. Still, Miller's picture of Linda
is by no means condescending. Linda may not be a genius, but she is
the brightest and the most realistic of the Lomans. Things turn out
badly, but not because of Linda. The viewer leaves the theater with
profound respect for her patience, her strength, her sense of decency,
and, yes, her intelligence and her competence in dealing with
incompetent men.

Katz 8

Works Cited

Bliquez, Guerin. "Linda's Role in *Death of a Salesman*." *Modern Drama* 10
    (1968): 383–86. Print.

Gordon, Lois. "*Death of a Salesman:* An Appreciation." *The Forties:*
    Fiction, Poetry, Drama. Ed. Warren French. Deland:
    Everett/Edwards, 1969. 273–83. Print.

Miller, Arthur. "Death of a Salesman." *An Introduction to Literature*. Ed.
    Sylvan Barnet, William Burto, and William E. Cain. 16th ed.
    New York: Longman, 2011. 1199–1267. Print.

Parker, Brian. "Point of View in Arthur Miller's *Death of a Salesman*."
    University of Toronto Quarterly 35 (1966): 144–47. Rpt. in
    Twentieth Century Interpretations of Death of a Salesman. Ed.
    Helene Wickham Koon. Englewood Cliffs: Prentice, 1983. 41–55.
    Print.

Stanton, Kay. "Women and the American Dream of *Death of a Salesman*."
    Feminist Readings of American Drama. Ed. Judith Schlueter.
    Rutherford: Fairleigh Dickinson UP, 1989. 67–102. Print.

33

A Casebook on
Death of a Salesman

This casebook, Arthur Miller's *Death of a Salesman*, also includes the following material:

> Arthur Miller, *Tragedy and the Common Man*
>
> Brooks Atkinson, *[Review of Premier Performance of]* Death of a Salesman
>
> Mary McCarthy, *On* Death of a Salesman
>
> Arthur Miller, *Remembering* Death of a Salesman
>
> Lorraine Hansberry, *Reflections on Willy Loman*
>
> John Lahr, *Hard Sell: A Black* Death of a Salesman

(We also call your attention to a documented essay by a student, "The Women in *Death of a Salesman*," included in Chapter 32, page 1191.)

ARTHUR MILLER

Arthur Miller (1915–2005) was born in New York. In 1938 he graduated from the University of Michigan, where he won prizes for drama. Six years later he had his first Broadway production, The Man Who Had All the Luck, *but the play was unlucky and closed after four days. By the time of his first commercial success,* All My Sons *(1947), he had already written several plays. In 1949 he won a Pulitzer Prize for* Death of a Salesman *and achieved an international reputation. Among his other works are an adaptation (1950) of Ibsen's* Enemy of the People *and a play about the Salem witch trials,* The Crucible *(1953), both containing political implications, and* The Misfits *(1961, a screenplay),* After the Fall *(1964), and* Incident at Vichy *(1965).*

Death of a Salesman

Certain Private Conversations in Two Acts and a Requiem   [1947]

LIST OF CHARACTERS

WILLY LOMAN

LINDA

BIFF

HAPPY

BERNARD

THE WOMAN

CHARLEY

UNCLE BEN

HOWARD WAGNER

JENNY

STANLEY

MISS FORSYTHE

LETTA

SCENE: *The action takes place in* WILLY LOMAN's *house and yard and in various places he visits in the New York and Boston of today.*

Act 1

SCENE: *A melody is heard, played upon a flute. It is small and fine, telling of grass and trees and the horizon. The curtain rises.*

Before us is the Salesman's house. We are aware of towering, angular shapes behind it, surrounding it on all sides. Only the blue light of the sky falls upon the house and forestage; the surrounding area shows an angry glow of orange. As more light appears, we see a solid vault of apartment houses around the small, fragile-seeming home. An air of the dream clings to the place, a dream rising out of reality. The kitchen at center seems actual enough, for there is a kitchen table with three chairs, and a refrigerator. But no other fixtures are seen. At the back of the kitchen there is a draped entrance, which leads to the living room. To the right of the kitchen, on a level raised two feet, is a bedroom furnished only with a brass bedstead and a straight chair. On a shelf over the bed a silver athletic trophy stands. A window opens onto the apartment house at the side.

Behind the kitchen, on a level raised six and a half feet, is the boys' bedroom, at present barely visible. Two beds are dimly seen, and at the back of the room a dormer window. (This bedroom is above the unseen living room.) At the left a stairway curves up to it from the kitchen.

The entire setting is wholly or, in some places, partially transparent. The roof-line of the house is one-dimensional; under and over it we see the apartment buildings. Before the house lies an apron, curving beyond the forestage into the orchestra. This forward area serves as the back yard as well as the locale of all WILLY's *imaginings and of his city scenes. Whenever the action is in the present the actors observe the imaginary wall-lines, entering the house only through its door at the left. But in the scenes of the past these boundaries are broken, and characters enter or leave a room by stepping "through" a wall onto the forestage.*

From the right, WILLY LOMAN, *the Salesman, enters, carrying two large sample cases. The flute plays on. He hears but is not aware of it. He is past sixty years of age, dressed quietly. Even as he crosses the stage to the doorway of the house, his exhaustion is apparent. He unlocks the door, comes into the kitchen, and thankfully lets his burden down, feeling the soreness of his palms. A word-sigh escapes his lips—it might be "Oh, boy, oh, boy." He closes the door, then carries his cases out into the living room, through the draped kitchen doorway.*

Lee J. Cobb as Willy Loman in the 1949 original Broadway production of *Death of a Salesman.*

Dustin Hoffman as Willy Loman, and John Malkovich as Biff, in the 1984 production.

LINDA, *his wife, has stirred in her bed at the right. She gets out and puts on a robe, listening. Most often jovial, she has developed an iron repression of her exceptions to* WILLY's *behavior—she more than loves him, she admires him, as though his mercurial nature, his temper, his massive dreams and little cruelties, served her only as sharp reminders of the turbulent longings within him, longings which she shares but lacks the temperament to utter and follow to their end.*

LINDA (*hearing* WILLY *outside the bedroom, calls with some trepidation*). Willy!

WILLY. It's all right. I came back.

LINDA. Why? What happened? (*Slight pause.*) Did something happen, Willy?

WILLY. No, nothing happened.

LINDA. You didn't smash the car, did you?

WILLY (*with casual irritation*). I said nothing happened. Didn't you hear me?

LINDA. Don't you feel well?

WILLY. I'm tired to the death. (*The flute has faded away. He sits on the bed beside her, a little numb.*) I couldn't make it. I just couldn't make it, Linda.

LINDA (*very carefully, delicately*). Where were you all day? You look terrible.

WILLY. I got as far as a little above Yonkers. I stopped for a cup of coffee. Maybe it was the coffee.

LINDA. What?

WILLY (*after a pause*). I suddenly couldn't drive any more. The car kept going off onto the shoulder, y'know?

LINDA (*helpfully*). Oh. Maybe it was the steering again. I don't think Angelo knows the Studebaker.

WILLY. No, it's me, it's me. Suddenly I realize I'm goin' sixty miles an hour and I don't remember the last five minutes. I'm—I can't seem to—keep my mind to it.

LINDA. Maybe it's your glasses. You never went for your new glasses.

WILLY. No, I see everything. I came back ten miles an hour. It took me nearly four hours from Yonkers.

LINDA (*resigned*). Well, you'll just have to take a rest, Willy, you can't continue this way.

WILLY. I just got back from Florida.

LINDA. But you didn't rest your mind. Your mind is overactive, and the mind is what counts, dear.

WILLY. I'll start out in the morning. Maybe I'll feel better in the morning. (*She is taking off his shoes.*) These goddam arch supports are killing me.

LINDA. Take an aspirin. Should I get you an aspirin? It'll soothe you.

WILLY (*with wonder*). I was driving along, you understand? And I was fine. I was even observing the scenery. You can imagine, me looking at scenery, on the road every week of my life. But it's so beautiful up there, Linda, the trees are so thick, and the sun is warm. I opened the windshield and just let the warm air bathe over me. And then all of a sudden I'm goin' off the road! I'm tellin' ya, I absolutely forgot I was driving. If I'd've gone the other way over the white line I might've killed somebody. So I went on again—and five minutes later I'm dreamin' again, and I nearly . . . (*He presses two fingers against his eyes.*) I have such thoughts, I have such strange thoughts.

LINDA. Willy, dear. Talk to them again. There's no reason why you can't work in New York.

WILLY. They don't need me in New York. I'm the New England man. I'm vital in New England.

LINDA. But you're sixty years old. They can't expect you to keep traveling every week.

WILLY. I'll have to send a wire to Portland. I'm supposed to see Brown and Morrison tomorrow morning at ten o'clock to show the line. God-dammit, I could sell them! (*He starts putting on his jacket.*)

LINDA (*taking the jacket from him*). Why don't you go down to the place tomorrow and tell Howard you've simply got to work in New York? You're too accommodating, dear.

WILLY. If old man Wagner was alive I'd a been in charge of New York now! That man was a prince, he was a masterful man. But that boy of his, that Howard, he don't appreciate. When I went north the first time, the Wagner Company didn't know where New England was!

LINDA. Why don't you tell those things to Howard, dear?

WILLY (*encouraged*). I will, I definitely will. Is there any cheese?

LINDA. I'll make you a sandwich.

WILLY. No, go to sleep. I'll take some milk. I'll be up right away. The boys in?

LINDA. They're sleeping. Happy took Biff on a date tonight.

WILLY (*interested*). That so?

LINDA. It was so nice to see them shaving together, one behind the other, in the bathroom. And going out together. You notice? The whole house smells of shaving lotion.

WILLY. Figure it out. Work a lifetime to pay off a house. You finally own it, and there's nobody to live in it.

LINDA. Well, dear, life is a casting off. It's always that way.

WILLY. No, no, some people—some people accomplish something. Did Biff say anything after I went this morning?

LINDA. You shouldn't have criticized him, Willy, especially after he just got off the train. You mustn't lose your temper with him.

WILLY. When the hell did I lose my temper? I simply asked him if he was making any money. Is that a criticism?

LINDA. But, dear, how could he make any money?

WILLY (*worried and angered*). There's such an undercurrent in him. He became a moody man. Did he apologize when I left this morning?

LINDA. He was crestfallen, Willy. You know how he admires you. I think if he finds himself, then you'll both be happier and not fight any more.

WILLY. How can he find himself on a farm? Is that a life? A farm hand? In the beginning, when he was young, I thought, well, a young man, it's good for him to tramp around, take a lot of different jobs. But it's more than ten years now and he has yet to make thirty-five dollars a week!

LINDA. He's finding himself, Willy.

WILLY. Not finding yourself at the age of thirty-four is a disgrace!

LINDA. Shh!

WILLY. The trouble is he's lazy, goddammit!

LINDA. Willy, please!

WILLY. Biff is a lazy bum!

LINDA. They're sleeping. Get something to eat. Go on down.

WILLY. Why did he come home? I would like to know what brought him home.

LINDA. I don't know. I think he's still lost, Willy. I think he's very lost.

WILLY. Biff Loman is lost. In the greatest country in the world a young man with such—personal attractiveness, gets lost. And such a hard worker. There's one thing about Biff—he's not lazy.

LINDA. Never.

WILLY (*with pity and resolve*). I'll see him in the morning; I'll have a nice talk with him. I'll get him a job selling. He could be big in no time. My God! Remember how they used to follow him around in high school? When he smiled at one of them their faces lit up. When he walked down the street . . . (*He loses himself in reminiscences.*)

LINDA (*trying to bring him out of it*). Willy, dear, I got a new kind of American-type cheese today. It's whipped.

WILLY. Why do you get American when I like Swiss?

LINDA. I just thought you'd like a change . . .

WILLY. I don't want a change! I want Swiss cheese. Why am I always being contradicted?

LINDA (*with a covering laugh*). I thought it would be a surprise.

WILLY. Why don't you open a window in here, for God's sake?

LINDA (*with infinite patience*). They're all open, dear.

WILLY. The way they boxed us in here. Bricks and windows, windows and bricks.

LINDA. We should've bought the land next door.

WILLY. The street is lined with cars. There's not a breath of fresh air in the neighborhood. The grass don't grow any more, you can't raise a carrot in the back yard. They should've had a law against apartment houses. Remember those two beautiful elm trees out there? When I and Biff hung the swing between them?

LINDA. Yeah, like being a million miles from the city.

WILLY. They should've arrested the builder for cutting those down. They massacred the neighborhood. (*Lost.*) More and more I think of those days, Linda. This time of year it was lilac and wisteria. And then the peonies would come out, and the daffodils. What fragrance in this room!

LINDA. Well, after all, people had to move somewhere.

WILLY. No, there's more people now.

LINDA. I don't think there's more people. I think . . .

WILLY. There's more people! That's what's ruining this country! Population is getting out of control. The competition is maddening! Smell the stink from that apartment house! And another one on the other side . . . How can they whip cheese?

> On WILLY's *last line,* BIFF *and* HAPPY *raise themselves up in their beds, listening.*

LINDA. Go down, try it. And be quiet.

WILLY (*turning to* LINDA, *guiltily*). You're not worried about me, are you, sweetheart?

BIFF. What's the matter?

HAPPY. Listen!

LINDA. You've got too much on the ball to worry about.

WILLY. You're my foundation and my support, Linda.

LINDA. Just try to relax, dear. You make mountains out of molehills.

WILLY. I won't fight with him any more. If he wants to go back to Texas, let him go.

LINDA. He'll find his way.

WILLY. Sure. Certain men just don't get started till later in life. Like Thomas Edison, I think. Or B. F. Goodrich. One of them was deaf. (*He starts for the bedroom doorway.*) I'll put my money on Biff.

LINDA. And Willy—if it's warm Sunday we'll drive in the country. And we'll open the windshield, and take lunch.

WILLY. No, the windshields don't open on the new cars.

LINDA. But you opened it today.

WILLY. Me? I didn't. (*He stops.*) Now isn't that peculiar! Isn't that a remarkable . . . (*He breaks off in amazement and fright as the flute is heard distantly.*)

LINDA. What, darling?

WILLY. That is the most remarkable thing.

LINDA. What, dear?

WILLY. I was thinking of the Chevvy. (*Slight pause.*) Nineteen twenty-eight . . . when I had that red Chevvy . . . (*Breaks off.*) That funny? I coulda sworn I was driving that Chevvy today.

LINDA. Well, that's nothing. Something must've reminded you.

WILLY. Remarkable. Ts. Remember those days? The way Biff used to simonize that car? The dealer refused to believe there was eighty thousand miles on it. (*He shakes his head.*) Heh! (*To Linda.*) Close your eyes, I'll be right up. (*He walks out of the bedroom.*)

HAPPY (*to* BIFF). Jesus, maybe he smashed up the car again!

LINDA (*calling after* WILLY). Be careful on the stairs, dear! The cheese is on the middle shelf. (*She turns, goes over to the bed, takes his jacket, and goes out of the bedroom.*)

Light has risen on the boys' room. Unseen, WILLY *is heard talking to himself; "Eighty thousand miles," and a little laugh.* BIFF *gets out of bed, comes downstage a bit, and stands attentively.* BIFF *is two years older than his brother* HAPPY, *well built, but in these days bears a worn air and seems less self-assured. He has succeeded less, and his dreams are stronger and less acceptable than* HAPPY's. HAPPY *is tall, powerfully made. Sexuality is like a visible color on him, or a scent that many women have discovered. He, like his brother, is lost, but in a different way, for he has never allowed himself to turn his face toward defeat and is thus more confused and hard-skinned, although seemingly more content.*

HAPPY (*getting out of bed*). He's going to get his license taken away if he keeps that up. I'm getting nervous about him, y'know, Biff?

BIFF. His eyes are going.

HAPPY. No, I've driven with him. He sees all right. He just doesn't keep his mind on it. I drove into the city with him last week. He stops at a green light and then it turns red and he goes. (*He laughs.*)

BIFF. Maybe he's color-blind.

HAPPY. Pop? Why he's got the finest eye for color in the business. You know that.

BIFF (*sitting down on his bed*). I'm going to sleep.

HAPPY. You're not still sour on Dad, are you, Biff?

BIFF. He's all right, I guess.

WILLY (*underneath them, in the living room*). Yes, sir, eighty thousand miles—eighty-two thousand!

BIFF. You smoking?

HAPPY (*holding out a pack of cigarettes*). Want one?

BIFF (*taking a cigarette*). I can never sleep when I smell it.

WILLY. What a simonizing job, heh!

HAPPY (*with deep sentiment*). Funny, Biff, y'know? Us sleeping in here again? The old beds. (*He pats his bed affectionately.*) All the talk that went across those beds, huh? Our whole lives.

BIFF. Yeah. Lotta dreams and plans.

HAPPY (*with a deep and masculine laugh*). About five hundred women would like to know what was said in this room. (*They share a soft laugh.*)

BIFF. Remember that big Betsy something—what the hell was her name—over on Bushwick Avenue?

HAPPY (*combing his hair*). With the collie dog!

BIFF. That's the one. I got you in there, remember?

HAPPY. Yeah, that was my first time—I think. Boy, there was a pig. (*They laugh, almost crudely.*) You taught me everything I know about women. Don't forget that.

BIFF. I bet you forgot how bashful you used to be. Especially with girls.

HAPPY. Oh, I still am, Biff.

BIFF. Oh, go on.

HAPPY. I just control it, that's all. I think I got less bashful and you got more so. What happened, Biff? Where's the old humor, the old confidence? (*He shakes* BIFF*'s knee.* BIFF *gets up and moves restlessly about the room.*) What's the matter?

BIFF. Why does Dad mock me all the time?

HAPPY. He's not mocking you, he . . .

BIFF. Everything I say there's a twist of mockery on his face. I can't get near him.

HAPPY. He just wants you to make good, that's all. I wanted to talk to you about Dad for a long time, Biff. Something's—happening to him. He—talks to himself.

BIFF. I noticed that this morning. But he always mumbled.

HAPPY. But not so noticeable. It got so embarrassing I sent him to Florida. And you know something? Most of the time he's talking to you.

BIFF. What's he say about me?

HAPPY. I can't make it out.

BIFF. What's he say about me?

HAPPY. I think the fact that you're not settled, that you're still kind of up in the air . . .

BIFF. There's one or two other things depressing him, Happy.

HAPPY. What do you mean?

BIFF. Never mind. Just don't lay it all to me.

HAPPY. But I think if you just got started—I mean—is there any future for you out there?

BIFF. I tell ya, Hap, I don't know what the future is. I don't know—what I'm supposed to want.

HAPPY. What do you mean?

BIFF. Well, I spent six or seven years after high school trying to work myself up. Shipping clerk, salesman, business of one kind or another. And it's a measly manner of existence. To get on that subway on the hot mornings in summer. To devote your whole life to keeping stock, or making phone calls, or selling or buying. To suffer fifty weeks of the year for the sake of a two-week vacation, when all you really desire is to be outdoors, with your shirt off. And always to have to get ahead of the next fella. And still—that's how you build a future.

HAPPY. Well, you really enjoy it on a farm? Are you content out there?

BIFF (*with rising agitation*). Hap, I've had twenty or thirty different kinds of jobs since I left home before the war, and it always turns out the same. I just realized it lately. In Nebraska when I herded cattle, and the Dakotas, and Arizona, and now in Texas. It's why I came home now, I guess, because I realized it. This farm I work on, it's spring there now, see? And they've got about fifteen new colts. There's nothing more inspiring or—beautiful than the sight of a mare and a new colt. And it's cool there now, see? Texas is cool now, and it's spring. And whenever spring comes to where I am, I suddenly get the feeling, my God, I'm not gettin' anywhere! What the hell am I doing, playing around with horses, twenty-eight dollars a week! I'm thirty-four years old, I oughta be makin' my future. That's when I come running home. And now, I get here, and I don't know what to do with myself. (*After a pause.*) I've always made a point of not wasting my life, and everytime I come back here I know that all I've done is to waste my life.

HAPPY. You're a poet, you know that, Biff? You're a—you're an idealist!

BIFF. No, I'm mixed up very bad. Maybe I oughta get married. Maybe I oughta get stuck into something. Maybe that's my trouble. I'm like a boy. I'm not married, I'm not in business, I just—I'm like a boy. Are you content, Hap? You're a success, aren't you? Are you content?

HAPPY. Hell, no!

BIFF. Why? You're making money, aren't you?

HAPPY (*moving about with energy, expressiveness*). All I can do now is wait for the merchandise manager to die. And suppose I get to be merchandise manager? He's a good friend of mine, and he just built a terrific estate on Long Island. And he lived there about two months and sold it, and now he's building another one. He can't enjoy it once it's finished. And I know that's just what I would do. I don't know what the hell I'm workin' for. Sometimes I sit in my apartment—all alone. And I think of the rent I'm paying. And it's crazy. But then, it's what I always wanted. My own apartment, a car, and plenty of women. And still, goddammit, I'm lonely.

BIFF (*with enthusiasm*). Listen, why don't you come out West with me?

HAPPY. You and I, heh?

BIFF. Sure, maybe we could buy a ranch. Raise cattle, use our muscles. Men built like we are should be working out in the open.

HAPPY (*avidly*). The Loman Brothers, heh?

BIFF (*with vast affection*). Sure, we'd be known all over the counties!

HAPPY (*enthralled*). That's what I dream about, Biff. Sometimes I want to just rip my clothes off in the middle of the store and outbox that goddam merchandise manager. I mean I can outbox, outrun, and outlift anybody in that store, and I have to take orders from those common, petty sons-of-bitches till I can't stand it any more.

BIFF.   I'm tellin' you, kid, if you were with me I'd be happy out there.

HAPPY *(enthused)*.   See, Biff, everybody around me is so false that I'm constantly lowering my ideals . . .

BIFF.   Baby, together we'd stand up for one another, we'd have someone to trust.

HAPPY.   If I were around you . . .

BIFF.   Hap, the trouble is we weren't brought up to grub for money. I don't know how to do it.

HAPPY.   Neither can I!

BIFF.   Then let's go!

HAPPY.   The only thing is—what can you make out there?

BIFF.   But look at your friend. Builds an estate and then hasn't the peace of mind to live in it.

HAPPY.   Yeah, but when he walks into the store the waves part in front of him. That's fifty-two thousand dollars a year coming through the revolving door, and I got more in my pinky finger than he's got in his head.

BIFF.   Yeah, but you just said . . .

HAPPY.   I gotta show some of those pompous, self-important executives over there that Hap Loman can make the grade. I want to walk into the store the way he walks in. Then I'll go with you, Biff. We'll be together yet, I swear. But take those two we had tonight. Now weren't they gorgeous creatures?

BIFF.   Yeah, yeah, most gorgeous I've had in years.

HAPPY.   I get that any time I want, Biff. Whenever I feel disgusted. The only trouble is, it gets like bowling or something. I just keep knockin' them over and it doesn't mean anything. You still run around a lot?

BIFF.   Naa. I'd like to find a girl—steady, somebody with substance.

HAPPY.   That's what I long for.

BIFF.   Go on! You'd never come home.

HAPPY.   I would! Somebody with character, with resistance! Like Mom, y'know? You're gonna call me a bastard when I tell you this. That girl Charlotte I was with tonight is engaged to be married in five weeks. *(He tries on his new hat.)*

BIFF.   No kiddin'!

HAPPY.   Sure, the guy's in line for the vice-presidency of the store. I don't know what gets into me, maybe I just have an over-developed sense of competition or something, but I went and ruined her, and furthermore I can't get rid of her. And he's the third executive I've done that to. Isn't that a crummy characteristic? And to top it all, I go to their weddings! *(Indignantly, but laughing.)* Like I'm not supposed to take bribes. Manufacturers offer me a hundred-dollar bill now and then to throw an order their way. You know how honest I am, but it's like this girl, see. I hate myself for it. Because I don't want the girl, and, still, I take it and— I love it!

BIFF.   Let's go to sleep.

HAPPY.   I guess we didn't settle anything, heh?

BIFF.   I just got one idea that I think I'm going to try.

HAPPY.   What's that?

BIFF.   Remember Bill Oliver?

HAPPY. Sure, Oliver is very big now. You want to work for him again?

BIFF. No, but when I quit he said something to me. He put his arm on my shoulder, and he said, "Biff, if you ever need anything, come to me."

HAPPY. I remember that. That sounds good.

BIFF. I think I'll go to see him. If I could get ten thousand or even seven or eight thousand dollars I could buy a beautiful ranch.

HAPPY. I bet he'd back you. 'Cause he thought highly of you, Biff. I mean, they all do. You're well liked, Biff. That's why I say to come back here, and we both have the apartment. And I'm tellin' you, Biff, any babe you want . . .

BIFF. No, with a ranch I could do the work I like and still be something. I just wonder though. I wonder if Oliver still thinks I stole that carton of basketballs.

HAPPY. Oh, he probably forgot that long ago. It's almost ten years. You're too sensitive. Anyway, he didn't really fire you.

BIFF. Well, I think he was going to. I think that's why I quit. I was never sure whether he knew or not. I know he thought the world of me, though. I was the only one he'd let lock up the place.

WILLY (*below*). You gonna wash the engine, Biff?

HAPPY. Shh!

BIFF looks at HAPPY, *who is gazing down, listening.* WILLY *is mumbling in the parlor.*

HAPPY. You hear that?

They listen. WILLY *laughs warmly.*

BIFF (*growing angry*). Doesn't he know Mom can hear that?

WILLY. Don't get your sweater dirty, Biff!

A look of pain crosses BIFF*'s face.*

HAPPY. Isn't that terrible? Don't leave again, will you? You'll find a job here. You gotta stick around. I don't know what to do about him, it's getting embarrassing.

WILLY. What a simonizing job!

BIFF. Mom's hearing that!

WILLY. No kiddin', Biff, you got a date? Wonderful!

HAPPY. Go on to sleep. But talk to him in the morning, will you?

BIFF (*reluctantly getting into bed*). With her in the house. Brother!

HAPPY (*getting into bed*). I wish you'd have a good talk with him.

The light on their room begins to fade.

BIFF (*to himself in bed*). That selfish, stupid . . .

HAPPY. Sh . . . Sleep, Biff.

Their light is out. Well before they have finished speaking, WILLY*'s form is dimly seen below in the darkened kitchen. He opens the refrigerator, searches in there, and takes out a bottle of milk. The apartment houses are fading out, and the entire house and surroundings become covered with leaves. Music insinuates itself as the leaves appear.*

WILLY. Just wanna be careful with those girls, Biff, that's all. Don't make any promises. No promises of any kind. Because a girl, y'know, they always believe what you tell 'em, and you're very young, Biff, you're too young to be talking seriously to girls.

Light rises on the kitchen. WILLY, *talking, shuts the refrigerator door and comes downstage to the kitchen table. He pours milk into a glass. He is totally immersed in himself, smiling faintly.*

WILLY. Too young entirely, Biff. You want to watch your schooling first. Then when you're all set, there'll be plenty of girls for a boy like you. (*He smiles broadly at a kitchen chair.*) That so? The girls pay for you? (*He laughs.*) Boy, you must really be makin' a hit.

WILLY *is gradually addressing—physically—a point offstage, speaking through the wall of the kitchen, and his voice has been rising in volume to that of a normal conversation.*

WILLY. I been wondering why you polish the car so careful. Ha! Don't leave the hubcaps, boys. Get the chamois to the hubcaps. Happy, use newspaper on the windows, it's the easiest thing. Show him how to do it, Biff! You see, Happy? Pad it up, use it like a pad. That's it, that's it, good work. You're doin' all right, Hap. (*He pauses, then nods in approbation for a few seconds, then looks upward.*) Biff, first thing we gotta do when we get time is clip that big branch over the house. Afraid it's gonna fall in a storm and hit the roof. Tell you what. We get a rope and sling her around, and then we climb up there with a couple of saws and take her down. Soon as you finish the car, boys, I wanna see ya. I got a surprise for you, boys.

BIFF (*offstage*). Whatta ya got, Dad?

WILLY. No, you finish first. Never leave a job till you're finished—remember that. (*Looking toward the "big trees."*) Biff, up in Albany I saw a beautiful hammock. I think I'll buy it next trip, and we'll hang it right between those two elms. Wouldn't that be something? Just swingin' there under those branches. Boy, that would be . . .

Young BIFF *and Young* HAPPY *appear from the direction* WILLY *was addressing.* HAPPY *carries rags and a pail of water.* BIFF, *wearing a sweater with a block "S," carries a football.*

BIFF (*pointing in the direction of the car offstage*). How's that, Pop, professional?

WILLY. Terrific. Terrific job, boys. Good work, Biff.

HAPPY. Where's the surprise, Pop?

WILLY. In the back seat of the car.

HAPPY. Boy! (*He runs off.*)

BIFF. What is it, Dad? Tell me, what'd you buy?

WILLY (*laughing, cuffs him*). Never mind, something I want you to have.

BIFF (*turns and starts off*). What is it, Hap?

HAPPY (*offstage*). It's a punching bag!

BIFF. Oh, Pop!

WILLY. It's got Gene Tunney's signature on it!

HAPPY *runs onstage with a punching bag.*

BIFF. Gee, how'd you know we wanted a punching bag?

WILLY. Well, it's the finest thing for the timing.

HAPPY (*lies down on his back and pedals with his feet*). I'm losing weight, you notice, Pop?

WILLY (*to* HAPPY). Jumping rope is good too.

BIFF. Did you see the new football I got?

WILLY (*examining the ball*). Where'd you get a new ball?

BIFF. The coach told me to practice my passing.

WILLY. That so? And he gave you the ball, heh?

BIFF. Well, I borrowed it from the locker room. (*He laughs confidentially.*)

WILLY (*laughing with him at the theft*). I want you to return that.

HAPPY. I told you he wouldn't like it!

BIFF (*angrily*). Well, I'm bringing it back!

WILLY (*stopping the incipient argument, to* HAPPY). Sure, he's gotta practice with a regulation ball, doesn't he? (*To* BIFF.) Coach'll probably congratulate you on your initiative!

BIFF. Oh, he keeps congratulating my initiative all the time, Pop.

WILLY. That's because he likes you. If somebody else took that ball there'd be an uproar. So what's the report, boys, what's the report?

BIFF. Where'd you go this time, Dad? Gee we were lonesome for you.

WILLY (*pleased, puts an arm around each boy and they come down to the apron*). Lonesome, heh?

BIFF. Missed you every minute.

WILLY. Don't say? Tell you a secret, boys. Don't breathe it to a soul. Someday I'll have my own business, and I'll never have to leave home any more.

HAPPY. Like Uncle Charley, heh?

WILLY. Bigger than Uncle Charley! Because Charley is not—liked. He's liked, but he's not—well liked.

BIFF. Where'd you go this time, Dad?

WILLY. Well, I got on the road, and I went north to Providence. Met the Mayor.

BIFF. The Mayor of Providence!

WILLY. He was sitting in the hotel lobby.

BIFF. What'd he say?

WILLY. He said, "Morning!" And I said, "Morning!" And I said, "You got a fine city here, Mayor." And then he had coffee with me. And then I went to Waterbury. Waterbury is a fine city. Big clock city, the famous Waterbury clock. Sold a nice bill there. And then Boston—Boston is the cradle of the Revolution. A fine city. And a couple of other towns in Mass., and on to Portland and Bangor and straight home!

BIFF. Gee, I'd love to go with you sometime, Dad.

WILLY. Soon as summer comes.

HAPPY. Promise?

WILLY. You and Hap and I, and I'll show you all the towns. America is full of beautiful towns and fine, upstanding people. And they know me, boys, they know me up and down New England. The finest people. And when I bring you fellas up, there'll be open sesame for all of us, 'cause one thing, boys: I have friends. I can park my car in any street in New England, and the cops protect it like their own. This summer, heh?

BIFF AND HAPPY (*together*). Yeah! You bet!

WILLY. We'll take our bathing suits.

HAPPY. We'll carry your bags, Pop!

WILLY. Oh, won't that be something! Me comin' into the Boston stores with you boys carryin' my bags. What a sensation!

BIFF *is prancing around, practicing passing the ball.*

WILLY. You nervous, Biff, about the game?

BIFF. Not if you're gonna be there.

WILLY. What do they say about you in school, now that they made you captain?

HAPPY. There's a crowd of girls behind him everytime the classes change.

BIFF (*taking* WILLY's *hand*). This Saturday, Pop, this Saturday—just for you, I'm going to break through for a touchdown.

HAPPY. You're supposed to pass.

BIFF. I'm takin' one play for Pop. You watch me, Pop, and when I take off my helmet, that means I'm breakin' out. Then you watch me crash through that line!

WILLY (*kisses* BIFF). Oh, wait'll I tell this in Boston!

BERNARD *enters in knickers. He is younger than* BIFF, *earnest and loyal, a worried boy.*

BERNARD. Biff, where are you? You're supposed to study with me today.

WILLY. Hey, looka Bernard. What're you lookin' so anemic about, Bernard?

BERNARD. He's gotta study, Uncle Willy. He's got Regents next week.

HAPPY (*tauntingly, spinning* BERNARD *around*). Let's box, Bernard!

BERNARD. Biff! (*He gets away from* HAPPY.) Listen, Biff, I heard Mr. Birnbaum say that if you don't start studyin' math he's gonna flunk you, and you won't graduate. I heard him!

WILLY. You better study with him, Biff. Go ahead now.

BERNARD. I heard him!

BIFF. Oh, Pop, you didn't see my sneakers! (*He holds up a foot for* WILLY *to look at.*)

WILLY. Hey, that's a beautiful job of printing!

BERNARD (*wiping his glasses*). Just because he printed University of Virginia on his sneakers doesn't mean they've got to graduate him, Uncle Willy!

WILLY (*angrily*). What're you talking about? With scholarships to three universities they're gonna flunk him?

BERNARD. But I heard Mr. Birnbaum say . . .

WILLY. Don't be a pest, Bernard! (*To his boys.*) What an anemic!

BERNARD. Okay, I'm waiting for you in my house, Biff.

BERNARD *goes off. The* LOMANS *laugh.*

WILLY. Bernard is not well liked, is he?

BIFF. He's liked, but he's not well liked.

HAPPY. That's right, Pop.

WILLY. That's just what I mean. Bernard can get the best marks in school, y'understand, but when he gets out in the business world, y'understand, you are going to be five times ahead of him. That's why I thank Almighty God you're both built like Adonises. Because the man who makes an appearance in the business world, the man who creates personal interest, is the man who gets ahead. Be liked and you will never want. You take me, for

instance. I never have to wait in line to see a buyer. "Willy Loman is
here!" That's all they have to know, and I go right through.

BIFF. Did you knock them dead, Pop?

WILLY. Knocked 'em cold in Providence, slaughtered 'em in Boston.

HAPPY (*on his back, pedaling again*). I'm losing weight, you notice, Pop?

LINDA *enters as of old, a ribbon in her hair, carrying a basket of
washing.*

LINDA (*with youthful energy*). Hello, dear!

WILLY. Sweetheart!

LINDA. How'd the Chevvy run?

WILLY. Chevrolet, Linda, is the greatest car ever built. (*To the boys.*) Since
when do you let your mother carry wash up the stairs?

BIFF. Grab hold there, boy!

HAPPY. Where to, Mom?

LINDA. Hang them up on the line. And you better go down to your friends,
Biff. The cellar is full of boys. They don't know what to do with
themselves.

BIFF. Ah, when Pop comes home they can wait!

WILLY (*laughs appreciatively*). You better go down and tell them what to
do, Biff.

BIFF. I think I'll have them sweep out the furnace room.

WILLY. Good work, Biff.

BIFF (*goes through wall-line of kitchen to doorway at back and calls
down*). Fellas! Everybody sweep out the furnace room! I'll be right
down!

VOICES. All right! Okay, Biff.

BIFF. George and Sam and Frank, come out back! We're hangin' up the wash!
Come on, Hap, on the double! (*He and* HAPPY *carry out the basket.*)

LINDA. The way they obey him!

WILLY. Well, that's training, the training. I'm tellin' you, I was sellin' thousands
and thousands, but I had to come home.

LINDA. Oh, the whole block'll be at that game. Did you sell anything?

WILLY. I did five hundred gross in Providence and seven hundred gross in
Boston.

LINDA. No! Wait a minute. I've got a pencil. (*She pulls pencil and paper out
of her apron pocket.*) That makes your commission . . . Two hundred—
my God! Two hundred and twelve dollars!

WILLY. Well, I didn't figure it yet, but . . .

LINDA. How much did you do?

WILLY. Well, I—I did—about a hundred and eighty gross in Providence. Well,
no—it came to—roughly two hundred gross on the whole trip.

LINDA (*without hesitation*). Two hundred gross. That's . . . (*She figures.*)

WILLY. The trouble was that three of the stores were half-closed for inventory in Boston. Otherwise I woulda broke records.

LINDA. Well, it makes seventy dollars and some pennies. That's very good.

WILLY. What do we owe?

LINDA. Well, on the first there's sixteen dollars on the refrigerator . . .

WILLY. Why sixteen?

LINDA. Well, the fan belt broke, so it was a dollar eighty.

WILLY. But it's brand new.

LINDA. Well, the man said that's the way it is. Till they work themselves in, y'know.

They move through the wall-line into the kitchen.

WILLY. I hope we didn't get stuck on that machine.

LINDA. They got the biggest ads of any of them!

WILLY. I know, it's a fine machine. What else?

LINDA. Well, there's nine-sixty for the washing machine. And for the vacuum cleaner there's three and a half due on the fifteenth. Then the roof, you got twenty-one dollars remaining.

WILLY. It don't leak, does it?

LINDA. No, they did a wonderful job. Then you owe Frank for the carburetor.

WILLY. I'm not going to pay that man! That goddam Chevrolet, they ought to prohibit the manufacture of that car!

LINDA. Well, you owe him three and a half. And odds and ends, comes to around a hundred and twenty dollars by the fifteenth.

WILLY. A hundred and twenty dollars! My God, if business don't pick up I don't know what I'm gonna do!

LINDA. Well, next week you'll do better.

WILLY. Oh, I'll knock 'em dead next week. I'll go to Hartford. I'm very well liked in Hartford. You know, the trouble is, Linda, people don't seem to take to me.

They move onto the forestage.

LINDA. Oh, don't be foolish.

WILLY. I know it when I walk in. They seem to laugh at me.

LINDA. Why? Why would they laugh at you? Don't talk that way, Willy.

WILLY *moves to the edge of the stage.* LINDA *goes into the kitchen and starts to darn stockings.*

WILLY. I don't know the reason for it, but they just pass me by. I'm not noticed.

LINDA. But you're doing wonderful, dear. You're making seventy to a hundred dollars a week.

WILLY. But I gotta be at it ten, twelve hours a day. Other men—I don't know—they do it easier. I don't know why—I can't stop myself—I talk too much. A man oughta come in with a few words. One thing about Charley. He's a man of few words, and they respect him.

LINDA. You don't talk too much, you're just lively.

WILLY *(smiling)*. Well, I figure, what the hell, life is short, a couple of jokes. *(To himself:)* I joke too much! *(The smile goes.)*

LINDA. Why? You're . . .

WILLY. I'm fat. I'm very—foolish to look at, Linda. I didn't tell you, but Christmas time I happened to be calling on F. H. Stewarts, and a salesman I know, as I was going in to see the buyer I heard him say something about—walrus. And I—I cracked him right across the face. I won't take that. I simply will not take that. But they do laugh at me. I know that.

LINDA. Darling . . .

WILLY. I gotta overcome it. I know I gotta overcome it. I'm not dressing to advantage, maybe.

LINDA. Willy, darling, you're the handsomest man in the world . . .

WILLY. Oh, no, Linda.

LINDA. To me you are. (*Slight pause.*) The handsomest.

From the darkness is heard the laughter of a woman. WILLY *doesn't turn to it, but it continues through* LINDA's *lines.*

LINDA. And the boys, Willy. Few men are idolized by their children the way you are.

Music is heard as behind a scrim, to the left of the house; THE WOMAN, *dimly seen, is dressing.*

WILLY (*with great feeling*). You're the best there is. Linda, you're a pal, you know that? On the road—on the road I want to grab you sometimes and just kiss the life outa you.

The laughter is loud now, and he moves into a brightening area at the left, where THE WOMAN *has come from behind the scrim and is standing, putting on her hat, looking into a "mirror" and laughing.*

WILLY. 'Cause I get so lonely—especially when business is bad and there's nobody to talk to. I get the feeling that I'll never sell anything again, that I won't make a living for you, or a business, a business for the boys. (*He talks through* THE WOMAN's *subsiding laughter;* THE WOMAN *primps at the "mirror."*) There's so much I want to make for . . .

THE WOMAN. Me? You didn't make me, Willy. I picked you.

WILLY (*pleased*). You picked me?

THE WOMAN (*who is quite proper-looking,* WILLY's *age*). I did. I've been sitting at that desk watching all the salesmen go by, day in, day out. But you've got such a sense of humor, and we do have such a good time together, don't we?

WILLY. Sure, sure. (*He takes her in his arms.*) Why do you have to go now?

THE WOMAN. It's two o'clock . . .

WILLY. No, come on in! (*He pulls her.*)

THE WOMAN. . . . . my sisters'll be scandalized. When'll you be back?

WILLY. Oh, two weeks about. Will you come up again?

THE WOMAN. Sure thing. You do make me laugh. It's good for me. (*She squeezes his arm, kisses him.*) And I think you're a wonderful man.

WILLY. You picked me, heh?

THE WOMAN. Sure. Because you're so sweet. And such a kidder.

WILLY. Well, I'll see you next time I'm in Boston.

THE WOMAN. I'll put you right through to the buyers.

WILLY (*slapping her bottom*). Right. Well, bottoms up!

THE WOMAN (*slaps him gently and laughs*). You just kill me, Willy. (*He suddenly grabs her and kisses her roughly.*) You kill me. And thanks for the stockings. I love a lot of stockings. Well, good night.

WILLY. Good night. And keep your pores open!

THE WOMAN. Oh, Willy!

THE WOMAN *bursts out laughing, and* LINDA's *laughter blends in.* THE WOMAN *disappears into the dark. Now the area at the kitchen table brightens.* LINDA *is sitting where she was at the kitchen table, but now is mending a pair of her silk stockings.*

LINDA. You are, Willy. The handsomest man. You've got no reason to feel that . . .

WILLY (*coming out of* THE WOMAN'*s dimming area and going over to* LINDA). I'll make it all up to you, Linda, I'll . . .

LINDA. There's nothing to make up, dear. You're doing fine, better than . . .

WILLY (*noticing her mending*). What's that?

LINDA. Just mending my stockings. They're so expensive . . .

WILLY (*angrily, taking them from her*). I won't have you mending stockings in this house! Now throw them out!

LINDA *puts the stockings in her pocket.*

BERNARD (*entering on the run*). Where is he? If he doesn't study!

WILLY (*moving to the forestage, with great agitation*). You'll give him the answers!

BERNARD. I do, but I can't on a Regents! That's a state exam! They're liable to arrest me!

WILLY. Where is he? I'll whip him, I'll whip him!

LINDA. And he'd better give back that football, Willy, it's not nice.

WILLY. Biff! Where is he? Why is he taking everything?

LINDA. He's too rough with the girls, Willy. All the mothers are afraid of him!

WILLY. I'll whip him!

BERNARD. He's driving the car without a license!

THE WOMAN'*s laugh is heard.*

WILLY. Shut up!

LINDA. All the mothers . . .

WILLY. Shut up!

BERNARD (*backing quietly away and out*). Mr. Birnbaum says he's stuck up.

WILLY. Get outa here!

BERNARD. If he doesn't buckle down he'll flunk math! (*He goes off.*)

LINDA. He's right, Willy, you've gotta . . .

WILLY (*exploding at her*). There's nothing the matter with him! You want him to be a worm like Bernard? He's got spirit, personality . . .

As he speaks, LINDA, *almost in tears, exits into the living room.* WILLY *is alone in the kitchen, wilting and staring. The leaves are gone. It is night again, and the apartment houses look down from behind.*

WILLY. Loaded with it. Loaded! What is he stealing? He's giving it back, isn't he? Why is he stealing? What did I tell him? I never in my life told him anything but decent things.

HAPPY *in pajamas has come down the stairs;* WILLY *suddenly becomes aware of* HAPPY'*s presence.*

HAPPY. Let's go now, come on.

WILLY (*sitting down at the kitchen table*). Huh! Why did she have to wax the floors herself? Everytime she waxes the floors she keels over. She knows that!

HAPPY. Shh! Take it easy. What brought you back tonight?

WILLY. I got an awful scare. Nearly hit a kid in Yonkers. God! Why didn't I go to Alaska with my brother Ben that time! Ben! That man was a genius, that man was success incarnate! What a mistake! He begged me to go.

HAPPY. Well, there's no use in . . .

WILLY. You guys! There was a man started with the clothes on his back and ended up with diamond mines!

HAPPY. Boy, someday I'd like to know how he did it.

WILLY. What's the mystery? The man knew what he wanted and went out and got it! Walked into a jungle, and comes out, the age of twenty-one, and he's rich! The world is an oyster, but you don't crack it open on a mattress!

HAPPY. Pop, I told you I'm gonna retire you for life.

WILLY. You'll retire me for life on seventy goddam dollars a week? And your women and your car and your apartment, and you'll retire me for life! Christ's sake, I couldn't get past Yonkers today! Where are you guys, where are you? The woods are burning! I can't drive a car!

CHARLEY has appeared in the doorway. He is a large man, slow of speech, laconic, immovable. In all he says, despite what he says, there is pity, and, now, trepidation. He has a robe over pajamas, slippers on his feet. He enters the kitchen.

CHARLEY. Everything all right?

HAPPY. Yeah, Charley, everything's . . .

WILLY. What's the matter?

CHARLEY. I heard some noise. I thought something happened. Can't we do something about the walls? You sneeze in here, and in my house hats blow off.

HAPPY. Let's go to bed, Dad. Come on.

CHARLEY signals to HAPPY to go.

WILLY. You go ahead, I'm not tired at the moment.

HAPPY (*to* WILLY). Take it easy, huh? (*He exits.*)

WILLY. What're you doin' up?

CHARLEY (*sitting down at the kitchen table opposite* WILLY). Couldn't sleep good. I had a heartburn.

WILLY. Well, you don't know how to eat.

CHARLEY. I eat with my mouth.

WILLY. No, you're ignorant. You gotta know about vitamins and things like that.

CHARLEY. Come on, let's shoot. Tire you out a little.

WILLY (*hesitantly*). All right. You got cards?

CHARLEY (*taking a deck from his pocket*). Yeah, I got them. Someplace. What is it with those vitamins?

WILLY (*dealing*). They build up your bones. Chemistry.

CHARLEY. Yeah, but there's no bones in a heartburn.

WILLY. What are you talkin' about? Do you know the first thing about it?

CHARLEY. Don't get insulted.

WILLY. Don't talk about something you don't know anything about.

They are playing. Pause.

CHARLEY. What're you doin' home?

WILLY. A little trouble with the car.

CHARLEY. Oh. (*Pause.*) I'd like to take a trip to California.

WILLY. Don't say.

CHARLEY. You want a job?

WILLY. I got a job, I told you that. (*After a slight pause.*) What the hell are you offering me a job for?

CHARLEY. Don't get insulted.

WILLY. Don't insult me.

CHARLEY. I don't see no sense in it. You don't have to go on this way.

WILLY. I got a good job. (*Slight pause.*) What do you keep comin' in here for?

CHARLEY. You want me to go?

WILLY (*after a pause, withering*). I can't understand it. He's going back to Texas again. What the hell is that?

CHARLEY. Let him go.

WILLY. I got nothin' to give him, Charley, I'm clean, I'm clean.

CHARLEY. He won't starve. None a them starve. Forget about him.

WILLY. Then what have I got to remember?

CHARLEY. You take it too hard. To hell with it. When a deposit bottle is broken you don't get your nickel back.

WILLY. That's easy enough for you to say.

CHARLEY. That ain't easy for me to say.

WILLY. Did you see the ceiling I put up in the living room?

CHARLEY. Yeah, that's a piece of work. To put up a ceiling is a mystery to me. How do you do it?

WILLY. What's the difference?

CHARLEY. Well, talk about it.

WILLY. You gonna put up a ceiling?

CHARLEY. How could I put up a ceiling?

WILLY. Then what the hell are you bothering me for?

CHARLEY. You're insulted again.

WILLY. A man who can't handle tools is not a man. You're disgusting.

CHARLEY. Don't call me disgusting, Willy.

> UNCLE BEN, *carrying a valise and an umbrella, enters the forestage from around the right corner of the house. He is a stolid man, in his sixties, with a mustache and an authoritative air. He is utterly certain of his destiny, and there is an aura of far places about him. He enters exactly as* WILLY *speaks.*

WILLY. I'm getting awfully tired, Ben.

> BEN'*s music is heard.* BEN *looks around at everything.*

CHARLEY. Good, keep playing; you'll sleep better. Did you call me Ben?

> BEN *looks at his watch.*

WILLY. That's funny. For a second there you reminded me of my brother Ben.

BEN. I only have a few minutes. (*He strolls, inspecting the place.* WILLY *and* CHARLEY *continue playing.*)

CHARLEY. You never heard from him again, heh? Since that time?

WILLY. Didn't Linda tell you? Couple of weeks ago we got a letter from his wife in Africa. He died.

CHARLEY. That so.

BEN (*chuckling*). So this is Brooklyn, eh?

CHARLEY. Maybe you're in for some of his money.

WILLY. Naa, he had seven sons. There's just one opportunity I had with that man . . .

BEN. I must make a train, William. There are several properties I'm looking at in Alaska.

WILLY. Sure, sure! If I'd gone with him to Alaska that time, everything would've been totally different.

CHARLEY. Go on, you'd froze to death up there.

WILLY. What're you talking about?

BEN. Opportunity is tremendous in Alaska, William. Surprised you're not up there.

WILLY. Sure, tremendous.

CHARLEY. Heh?

WILLY. There was the only man I ever met who knew the answers.

CHARLEY. Who?

BEN. How are you all?

WILLY (*taking a pot, smiling*). Fine, fine.

CHARLEY. Pretty sharp tonight.

BEN. Is Mother living with you?

WILLY. No, she died a long time ago.

CHARLEY. Who?

BEN. That's too bad. Fine specimen of a lady, Mother.

WILLY (*to* CHARLEY). Heh?

BEN. I'd hoped to see the old girl.

CHARLEY. Who died?

BEN. Heard anything from Father, have you?

WILLY (*unnerved*). What do you mean, who died?

CHARLEY (*taking a pot*). What're you talkin' about?

BEN (*looking at his watch*). William, it's half-past eight!

WILLY (*as though to dispel his confusion he angrily stops* CHARLEY'*s hand*). That's my build!

CHARLEY. I put the ace . . .

WILLY. If you don't know how to play the game I'm not gonna throw my money away on you!

CHARLEY (*rising*). It was my ace, for God's sake!

WILLY. I'm through, I'm through!

BEN. When did Mother die?

WILLY. Long ago. Since the beginning you never knew how to play cards.

CHARLEY (*picks up the cards and goes to the door*). All right! Next time I'll bring a deck with five aces.

WILLY. I don't play that kind of game!

CHARLEY (*turning to him*). You ought to be ashamed of yourself!

WILLY. Yeah?

CHARLEY. Yeah! (*He goes out.*)

WILLY (*slamming the door after him*). Ignoramus!

BEN (*as* WILLY *comes toward him through the wall-line of the kitchen*). So you're William.

WILLY (*shaking* BEN'*s hand*). Ben! I've been waiting for you so long! What's the answer? How did you do it?

BEN. Oh, there's a story in that.

LINDA *enters the forestage, as of old, carrying the wash basket.*

LINDA. Is this Ben?

BEN (*gallantly*). How do you do, my dear.

LINDA. Where've you been all these years? Willy's always wondered why you . . .

WILLY (*pulling* BEN *away from her impatiently*). Where is Dad? Didn't you follow him? How did you get started?

BEN. Well, I don't know how much you remember.

WILLY. Well, I was just a baby, of course, only three or four years old . . .

BEN. Three years and eleven months.

WILLY. What a memory, Ben!

BEN. I have many enterprises, William, and I have never kept books.

WILLY. I remember I was sitting under the wagon in—was it Nebraska?

BEN. It was South Dakota, and I gave you a bunch of wild flowers.

WILLY. I remember you walking away down some open road.

BEN (*laughing*). I was going to find Father in Alaska.

WILLY. Where is he?

BEN. At that age I had a very faulty view of geography, William. I discovered after a few days that I was heading due south, so instead of Alaska, I ended up in Africa.

LINDA. Africa!

WILLY. The Gold Coast!

BEN. Principally diamond mines.

LINDA. Diamond mines!

BEN. Yes, my dear. But I've only a few minutes . . .

WILLY. No! Boys! Boys! (*Young* BIFF *and* HAPPY *appear*.) Listen to this. This is your Uncle Ben, a great man! Tell my boys, Ben!

BEN. Why, boys, when I was seventeen I walked into the jungle, and when I was twenty-one I walked out. (*He laughs.*) And by God I was rich.

WILLY (*to the boys*). You see what I been talking about? The greatest things can happen!

BEN (*glancing at his watch*). I have an appointment in Ketchikan Tuesday week.

WILLY. No, Ben! Please tell about Dad. I want my boys to hear. I want them to know the kind of stock they spring from. All I remember is a man with a big beard, and I was in Mamma's lap, sitting around a fire, and some kind of high music.

BEN. His flute. He played the flute.

WILLY. Sure, the flute, that's right!

New music is heard, a high, rollicking tune.

BEN. Father was a very great and a very wild-hearted man. We would start in Boston, and he'd toss the whole family into the wagon, and then he'd drive the team right across the country; through Ohio, and Indiana, Michigan, Illinois, and all the Western states. And we'd stop in the towns and sell the flutes that he'd made on the way. Great inventor, Father. With one gadget he made more in a week than a man like you could make in a lifetime.

WILLY. That's just the way I'm bringing them up, Ben—rugged, well liked, all-around.

BEN. Yeah? (*To* BIFF.) Hit that, boy—hard as you can. (*He pounds his stomach.*)

BIFF. Oh, no, sir!

BEN (*taking boxing stance*). Come on, get to me! (*He laughs.*)

WILLY. Go to it. Biff! Go ahead, show him!

BIFF. Okay! (*He cocks his fists and starts in.*)

LINDA (*to* WILLY). Why must he fight, dear?

BEN (*sparring with* BIFF). Good boy! Good boy!

WILLY. How's that, Ben, heh?

HAPPY. Give him the left, Biff!

LINDA. Why are you fighting?

BEN. Good boy! (*Suddenly comes in, trips* BIFF, *and stands over him, the point of his umbrella poised over* BIFF's *eye.*)

LINDA. Look out, Biff!

BIFF. Gee!

BEN (*patting* BIFF's *knee*). Never fight fair with a stranger, boy. You'll never get out of the jungle that way. (*Taking* LINDA's *hand and bowing.*) It was an honor and a pleasure to meet you, Linda.

LINDA (*withdrawing her hand coldly, frightened*). Have a nice—trip.

BEN (*to* WILLY). And good luck with your—what do you do?

WILLY. Selling.

BEN. Yes. Well . . . (*He raises his hand in farewell to all.*)

WILLY. No, Ben, I don't want you to think . . . (*He takes* BEN's *arm to show him.*) It's Brooklyn, I know, but we hunt too.

BEN. Really, now.

WILLY. Oh, sure, there's snakes and rabbits and—that's why I moved out here. Why, Biff can fell any one of these trees in no time! Boys! Go right over to where they're building the apartment house and get some sand. We're gonna rebuild the entire front stoop right now! Watch this, Ben!

BIFF. Yes, sir! On the double, Hap!

HAPPY (*as he and* BIFF *run off*). I lost weight, Pop, you notice?

CHARLEY *enters in knickers, even before the boys are gone.*

CHARLEY. Listen, if they steal any more from that building the watchman'll put the cops on them!

LINDA (*to* WILLY). Don't let Biff . . .

BEN *laughs lustily.*

WILLY. You shoulda seen the lumber they brought home last week. At least a dozen six-by-tens worth all kinds a money.

CHARLEY. Listen, if that watchman . . .

WILLY. I gave them hell, understand. But I got a couple of fearless characters there.

CHARLEY. Willy, the jails are full of fearless characters.

BEN (*clapping* WILLY *on the back, with a laugh at* CHARLEY). And the stock exchange, friend!

WILLY (*joining in* BEN's *laughter*). Where are the rest of your pants?

CHARLEY. My wife bought them.

WILLY. Now all you need is a golf club and you can go upstairs and go to sleep. (*To* BEN.) Great athlete! Between him and his son Bernard they can't hammer a nail!

BERNARD (*rushing in*). The watchman's chasing Biff!

WILLY (*angrily*). Shut up! He's not stealing anything!

LINDA (*alarmed, hurrying off left*). Where is he? Biff, dear! (*She exits.*)

WILLY (*moving toward the left, away from* BEN). There's nothing wrong. What's the matter with you?

BEN. Nervy boy. Good!

WILLY (*laughing*). Oh, nerves of iron, that Biff!

CHARLEY. Don't know what it is. My New England man comes back and he's bleedin', they murdered him up there.

WILLY. It's contacts, Charley, I got important contacts!

CHARLEY (*sarcastically*). Glad to hear it, Willy. Come in later, we'll shoot a little casino. I'll take some of your Portland money. (*He laughs at* WILLY *and exits.*)

WILLY (*turning to* BEN). Business is bad, it's murderous. But not for me, of course.

BEN. I'll stop by on my way back to Africa.

WILLY (*longingly*). Can't you stay a few days? You're just what I need, Ben, because I—I have a fine position here, but I—well, Dad left when I was such a baby and I never had a chance to talk to him and I still feel—kind of temporary about myself.

BEN. I'll be late for my train.

They are at opposite ends of the stage.

WILLY. Ben, my boys—can't we talk? They'd go into the jaws of hell for me, see, but I . . .

BEN. William, you're being first-rate with your boys. Outstanding, manly chaps!

WILLY (*hanging on to his words*). Oh, Ben, that's good to hear! Because sometimes I'm afraid that I'm not teaching them the right kind of—Ben, how should I teach them?

BEN (*giving great weight to each word, and with a certain vicious audacity*). William, when I walked into the jungle, I was seventeen. When I walked out I was twenty-one. And, by God, I was rich! (*He goes off into darkness around the right corner of the house.*)

WILLY. . . . was rich! That's just the spirit I want to imbue them with! To walk into a jungle! I was right! I was right! I was right!

BEN *is gone, but* WILLY *is still speaking to him as* LINDA, *in nightgown and robe, enters the kitchen, glances around for* WILLY, *then goes to the door of the house, looks out and sees him. Comes down to his left. He looks at her.*

LINDA. Willy, dear? Willy?

WILLY. I was right!

LINDA. Did you have some cheese? (*He can't answer.*) It's very late, darling. Come to bed, heh?

WILLY (*looking straight up*). Gotta break your neck to see a star in this yard.

LINDA. You coming in?

WILLY. Whatever happened to that diamond watch fob? Remember? When Ben came from Africa that time? Didn't he give me a watch fob with a diamond in it?

LINDA. You pawned it, dear. Twelve, thirteen years ago. For Biff's radio correspondence course.

WILLY. Gee, that was a beautiful thing. I'll take a walk.

LINDA. But you're in your slippers.

WILLY (*starting to go around the house at the left*). I was right! I was! (*Half to* LINDA, *as he goes, shaking his head.*) What a man! There was a man worth talking to. I was right!

LINDA (*calling after* WILLY). But in your slippers, Willy!

> WILLY *is almost gone when* BIFF, *in his pajamas, comes down the stairs and enters the kitchen.*

BIFF. What is he doing out there?

LINDA. Sh!

BIFF. God Almighty, Mom, how long has he been doing this?

LINDA. Don't, he'll hear you.

BIFF. What the hell is the matter with him?

LINDA. It'll pass by morning.

BIFF. Shouldn't we do anything?

LINDA. Oh, my dear, you should do a lot of things, but there's nothing to do, so go to sleep.

> HAPPY *comes down the stairs and sits on the steps.*

HAPPY. I never heard him so loud, Mom.

LINDA. Well, come around more often; you'll hear him. (*She sits down at the table and mends the lining of* WILLY's *jacket.*)

BIFF. Why didn't you ever write me about this, Mom?

LINDA. How would I write to you? For over three months you had no address.

BIFF. I was on the move. But you know I thought of you all the time. You know that, don't you, pal?

LINDA. I know, dear, I know. But he likes to have a letter. Just to know that there's still a possibility for better things.

BIFF. He's not like this all the time, is he?

LINDA. It's when you come home he's always the worst.

BIFF. When I come home?

LINDA. When you write you're coming, he's all smiles, and talks about the future, and—he's just wonderful. And then the closer you seem to come, the more shaky he gets, and then, by the time you get here, he's arguing, and he seems angry at you. I think it's just that maybe he can't bring himself to—to open up to you. Why are you so hateful to each other? Why is that?

BIFF (*evasively*). I'm not hateful, Mom.

LINDA. But you no sooner come in the door than you're fighting!

BIFF. I don't know why. I mean to change. I'm tryin', Mom, you understand?

LINDA. Are you home to stay now?

BIFF. I don't know. I want to look around, see what's doin'.

LINDA. Biff, you can't look around all your life, can you?

BIFF. I just can't take hold, Mom. I can't take hold of some kind of a life.

LINDA. Biff, a man is not a bird, to come and go with the spring time.

BIFF. Your hair . . . (*He touches her hair.*) Your hair got so gray.

LINDA. Oh, it's been gray since you were in high school. I just stopped dyeing it, that's all.

BIFF. Dye it again, will ya? I don't want my pal looking old. (*He smiles.*)

LINDA. You're such a boy! You think you can go away for a year and ... You've got to get it into your head now that one day you'll knock on this door and there'll be strange people here ...

BIFF. What are you talking about? You're not even sixty, Mom.

LINDA. But what about your father?

BIFF (*lamely*). Well, I meant him too.

HAPPY. He admires Pop.

LINDA. Biff, dear, if you don't have any feeling for him, then you can't have any feeling for me.

BIFF. Sure I can, Mom.

LINDA. No. You can't just come to see me, because I love him. (*With a threat, but only a threat, of tears.*) He's the dearest man in the world to me, and I won't have anyone making him feel unwanted and low and blue. You've got to make up your mind now, darling, there's no leeway any more. Either he's your father and you pay him that respect, or else you're not to come here. I know he's not easy to get along with—nobody knows that better than me—but ...

WILLY (*from the left, with a laugh*). Hey, hey, Biffo!

BIFF (*starting to go out after* WILLY). What the hell is the matter with him? (HAPPY *stops him.*)

LINDA. Don't—don't go near him!

BIFF. Stop making excuses for him! He always, always wiped the floor with you. Never had an ounce of respect for you.

HAPPY. He's always had respect for ...

BIFF. What the hell do you know about it?

HAPPY (*surlily*). Just don't call him crazy!

BIFF. He's got no character—Charley wouldn't do this. Not in his own house—spewing out that vomit from his mind.

HAPPY. Charley never had to cope with what he's got to.

BIFF. People are worse off than Willy Loman. Believe me, I've seen them!

LINDA. Then make Charley your father, Biff. You can't do that, can you? I don't say he's a great man. Willy Loman never made a lot of money. His name was never in the paper. He's not the finest character that ever lived. But he's a human being, and a terrible thing is happening to him. So attention must be paid. He's not to be allowed to fall into his grave like an old dog. Attention, attention must be finally paid to such a person. You called him crazy ...

BIFF. I didn't mean ...

LINDA. No, a lot of people think he's lost his—balance. But you don't have to be very smart to know what his trouble is. The man is exhausted.

HAPPY. Sure!

LINDA. A small man can be just as exhausted as a great man. He works for a company thirty-six years this March, opens up unheard-of territories to their trademark, and now in his old age they take his salary away.

HAPPY (*indignantly*). I didn't know that, Mom.

LINDA. You never asked, my dear! Now that you get your spending money someplace else you don't trouble your mind with him.

HAPPY. But I gave you money last ...

LINDA. Christmas time, fifty dollars! To fix the hot water it cost ninety-seven fifty! For five weeks he's been on straight commission, like a beginner, an unknown!

BIFF. Those ungrateful bastards!

LINDA. Are they any worse than his sons? When he brought them business, when he was young, they were glad to see him. But now his old friends, the old buyers that loved him so and always found some order to hand him in a pinch—they're all dead, retired. He used to be able to make six, seven calls a day in Boston. Now he takes his valises out of the car and puts them back and takes them out again and he's exhausted. Instead of walking he talks now. He drives seven hundred miles, and when he gets there no one knows him any more, no one welcomes him. And what goes through a man's mind, driving seven hundred miles home without having earned a cent? Why shouldn't he talk to himself? Why? When he has to go to Charley and borrow fifty dollars a week and pretend to me that it's his pay? How long can that go on? How long? You see what I'm sitting here and waiting for? And you tell me he has no character? The man who never worked a day but for your benefit? When does he get the medal for that? Is this his reward—to turn around at the age of sixty-three and find his sons, who he loved better than his life, one a philandering bum . . .

HAPPY. Mom!

LINDA. That's all you are, my baby! (*To* BIFF.) And you! What happened to the love you had for him? You were such pals! How you used to talk to him on the phone every night! How lonely he was till he could come home to you!

BIFF. All right, Mom. I'll live here in my room, and I'll get a job. I'll keep away from him, that's all.

LINDA. No, Biff. You can't stay here and fight all the time.

BIFF. He threw me out of this house, remember that.

LINDA. Why did he do that? I never knew why.

BIFF. Because I know he's a fake and he doesn't like anybody around who knows!

LINDA. Why a fake? In what way? What do you mean?

BIFF. Just don't lay it all at my feet. It's between me and him—that's all I have to say. I'll chip in from now on. He'll settle for half my paycheck. He'll be all right. I'm going to bed. (*He starts for the stairs.*)

LINDA. He won't be all right.

BIFF (*turning on the stairs, furiously*). I hate this city and I'll stay here. Now what do you want?

LINDA. He's dying, Biff.

HAPPY *turns quickly to her, shocked.*

BIFF (*after a pause*). Why is he dying?

LINDA. He's been trying to kill himself.

BIFF (*with great horror*). How?

LINDA. I live from day to day.

BIFF. What're you talking about?

LINDA. Remember I wrote you that he smashed up the car again? In February?

BIFF. Well?

LINDA. The insurance inspector came. He said that they have evidence. That all these accidents in the last year—weren't—weren't—accidents.

HAPPY. How can they tell that? That's a lie.

LINDA. It seems there's a woman . . . (*She takes a breath as:*)

BIFF (*sharply but contained*). What woman?

LINDA (*simultaneously*).   . . . and this woman . . .

LINDA. What?

BIFF. Nothing. Go ahead.

LINDA. What did you say?

BIFF. Nothing. I just said what woman?

HAPPY. What about her?

LINDA. Well, it seems she was walking down the road and saw his car. She says that he wasn't driving fast at all, and that he didn't skid. She says he came to that little bridge, and then deliberately smashed into the railing, and it was only the shallowness of the water that saved him.

BIFF. Oh, no, he probably just fell asleep again.

LINDA. I don't think he fell asleep.

BIFF. Why not?

LINDA. Last month . . . (*With great difficulty.*) Oh, boys, it's so hard to say a thing like this! He's just a big stupid man to you, but I tell you there's more good in him than in many other people. (*She chokes, wipes her eyes.*) I was looking for a fuse. The lights blew out, and I went down the cellar. And behind the fuse box—it happened to fall out—was a length of rubber pipe—just short.

HAPPY. No kidding!

LINDA. There's a little attachment on the end of it. I knew right away. And sure enough, on the bottom of the water heater there's a new little nipple on the gas pipe.

HAPPY (*angrily*). That—jerk.

BIFF. Did you have it taken off?

LINDA. I'm—I'm ashamed to. How can I mention it to him? Every day I go down and take away that little rubber pipe. But, when he comes home, I put it back where it was. How can I insult him that way? I don't know what to do. I live from day to day, boys. I tell you, I know every thought in his mind. It sounds so old-fashioned and silly, but I tell you he put his whole life into you and you've turned your backs on him. (*She is bent over in the chair, weeping, her face in her hands.*) Biff, I swear to God! Biff, his life is in your hands!

HAPPY (*to* BIFF). How do you like that damned fool!

BIFF (*kissing her*). All right, pal, all right. It's all settled now. I've been remiss. I know that, Mom. But now I'll stay, and I swear to you, I'll apply myself. (*Kneeling in front of her, in a fever of self-reproach.*) It's just—you see, Mom, I don't fit in business. Not that I won't try. I'll try, and I'll make good.

HAPPY. Sure you will. The trouble with you in business was you never tried to please people.

BIFF. I know, I . . .

HAPPY. Like when you worked for Harrison's. Bob Harrison said you were tops, and then you go and do some damn fool thing like whistling whole songs in the elevator like a comedian.

BIFF (*against* HAPPY). So what? I like to whistle sometimes.

HAPPY. You don't raise a guy to a responsible job who whistles in the elevator!

LINDA. Well, don't argue about it now.

HAPPY. Like when you'd go off and swim in the middle of the day instead of taking the line around.

BIFF (*his resentment rising*). Well, don't you run off? You take off sometimes, don't you? On a nice summer day?

HAPPY. Yeah, but I cover myself!

LINDA. Boys!

HAPPY. If I'm going to take a fade the boss can call any number where I'm supposed to be and they'll swear to him that I just left. I'll tell you something that I hate to say, Biff, but in the business world some of them think you're crazy.

BIFF (*angered*). Screw the business world!

HAPPY. All right, screw it! Great, but cover yourself!

LINDA. Hap, Hap!

BIFF. I don't care what they think! They've laughed at Dad for years, and you know why? Because we don't belong in this nuthouse of a city! We should be mixing cement on some open plain or—or carpenters. A carpenter is allowed to whistle!

WILLY *walks in from the entrance of the house, at left.*

WILLY. Even your grandfather was better than a carpenter. (*Pause. They watch him.*) You never grew up. Bernard does not whistle in the elevator, I assure you.

BIFF (*as though to laugh* WILLY *out of it*). Yeah, but you do, Pop.

WILLY. I never in my life whistled in an elevator! And who in the business world thinks I'm crazy?

BIFF. I didn't mean it like that, Pop. Now don't make a whole thing out of it, will ya?

WILLY. Go back to the West! Be a carpenter, a cowboy, enjoy yourself!

LINDA. Willy, he was just saying . . .

WILLY. I heard what he said!

HAPPY (*trying to quiet* WILLY). Hey, Pop, come on now . . .

WILLY (*continuing over* HAPPY*'s line*). They laugh at me, heh? Go to Filene's, go to the Hub, go to Slattery's, Boston. Call out the name Willy Loman and see what happens! Big shot!

BIFF. All right, Pop.

WILLY. Big!

BIFF. All right!

WILLY. Why do you always insult me?

BIFF. I didn't say a word. (*To* LINDA.) Did I say a word?

LINDA. He didn't say anything, Willy.

WILLY (*going to the doorway of the living room*). All right, good night, good night.

LINDA. Willy, dear, he just decided . . .

WILLY (*to* BIFF). If you get tired hanging around tomorrow, paint the ceiling I put up in the living room.

BIFF. I'm leaving early tomorrow.

HAPPY. He's going to see Bill Oliver, Pop.

WILLY (*interestedly*). Oliver? For what?

BIFF (*with reserve, but trying; trying*). He always said he'd stake me. I'd like to go into business, so maybe I can take him up on it.

LINDA. Isn't that wonderful?

WILLY. Don't interrupt. What's wonderful about it? There's fifty men in the City of New York who'd stake him. (*To* BIFF.) Sporting goods?

BIFF. I guess so. I know something about it and ...

WILLY. He knows something about it! You know sporting goods better than Spalding, for God's sake! How much is he giving you?

BIFF. I don't know, I didn't even see him yet, but ...

WILLY. Then what're you talkin' about?

BIFF (*getting angry*). Well, all I said was I'm gonna see him, that's all!

WILLY (*turning away*). Ah, you're counting your chickens again.

BIFF (*starting left for the stairs*). Oh, Jesus, I'm going to sleep!

WILLY (*calling after him*). Don't curse in this house!

BIFF (*turning*). Since when did you get so clean?

HAPPY (*trying to stop them*). Wait a ...

WILLY. Don't use that language to me! I won't have it!

HAPPY (*grabbing* BIFF, *shouts*). Wait a minute! I got an idea. I got a feasible idea. Come here, Biff, let's talk this over now, let's talk some sense here. When I was down in Florida last time, I thought of a great idea to sell sporting goods. It just came back to me. You and I, Biff—we have a line, the Loman Line. We train a couple of weeks, and put on a couple of exhibitions, see?

WILLY. That's an idea!

HAPPY. Wait! We form two basketball teams, see? Two water-polo teams. We play each other. It's a million dollars' worth of publicity. Two brothers, see? The Loman Brothers. Displays in the Royal Palms—all the hotels. And banners over the ring and the basketball court: "Loman Brothers." Baby, we could sell sporting goods!

WILLY. That is a one-million-dollar idea!

LINDA. Marvelous!

BIFF. I'm in great shape as far as that's concerned.

HAPPY. And the beauty of it is, Biff, it wouldn't be like a business. We'd be out playin' ball again.

BIFF (*enthused*). Yeah, that's ...

WILLY. Million-dollar ...

HAPPY. And you wouldn't get fed up with it, Biff. It'd be the family again. There'd be the old honor, and comradeship, and if you wanted to go off for a swim or somethin'—well, you'd do it! Without some smart cooky gettin' up ahead of you!

WILLY. Lick the world! You guys together could absolutely lick the civilized world.

BIFF. I'll see Oliver tomorrow. Hap, if we could work that out ...

LINDA. Maybe things are beginning to ...

WILLY (*wildly enthused, to* LINDA). Stop interrupting! (*To* BIFF.) But don't wear sport jacket and slacks when you see Oliver.

BIFF. No, I'll ...

WILLY. A business suit, and talk as little as possible, and don't crack any jokes.

BIFF. He did like me. Always liked me.

LINDA. He loved you!

WILLY (*to* LINDA). Will you stop! (*To* BIFF.) Walk in very serious. You are not applying for a boy's job. Money is to pass. Be quiet, fine, and serious. Everybody likes a kidder, but nobody lends him money.

HAPPY. I'll try to get some myself, Biff. I'm sure I can.

WILLY. I see great things for you kids, I think your troubles are over. But remember, start big and you'll end big. Ask for fifteen. How much you
gonna ask for?

BIFF. Gee, I don't know ...

WILLY. And don't say "Gee." "Gee" is a boy's word. A man walking in for fifteen thousand dollars does not say "Gee!"

BIFF. Ten, I think, would be top though.

WILLY. Don't be so modest. You always started too low. Walk in with a big
laugh. Don't look worried. Start off with a couple of your good stories
to lighten things up. It's not what you say, it's how you say it—because
personality always wins the day.

LINDA. Oliver always thought the highest of him ...

WILLY. Will you let me talk?

BIFF. Don't yell at her, Pop, will ya?

WILLY (*angrily*). I was talking, wasn't I?

BIFF. I don't like you yelling at her all the time, and I'm tellin' you, that's all.

WILLY. What're you, takin' over this house?

LINDA. Willy ...

WILLY (*turning to her*). Don't take his side all the time, goddammit!

BIFF (*furiously*). Stop yelling at her!

WILLY (*suddenly pulling on his cheek, beaten down, guilt ridden*). Give my
best to Bill Oliver—he may remember me. (*He exits through the living
room doorway.*)

LINDA (*her voice subdued*). What'd you have to start that for? (BIFF *turns
away.*) You see how sweet he was as soon as you talked hopefully? (*She
goes over to* BIFF.) Come up and say good night to him. Don't let him go
to bed that way.

HAPPY. Come on, Biff, let's buck him up.

LINDA. Please, dear. Just say good night. It takes so little to make him happy.
Come. (*She goes through the living room doorway, calling upstairs
from within the living room.*) Your pajamas are hanging in the bathroom, Willy!

HAPPY (*looking toward where* LINDA *went out*). What a woman! They broke
the mold when they made her. You know that, Biff.

BIFF. He's off salary. My God, working on commission!

HAPPY. Well, let's face it: he's no hot-shot selling man. Except that sometimes,
you have to admit, he's a sweet personality.

BIFF (*deciding*). Lend me ten bucks, will ya? I want to buy some new ties.

HAPPY. I'll take you to a place I know. Beautiful stuff. Wear one of my striped
shirts tomorrow.

BIFF. She got gray. Mom got awful old. Gee, I'm gonna go in to Oliver tomorrow and knock him for a ...

HAPPY. Come on up. Tell that to Dad. Let's give him a whirl. Come on.

BIFF (*steamed up*). You know, with ten thousand bucks, boy!

HAPPY (*as they go into the living room*). That's the talk, Biff, that's the first
time I've heard the old confidence out of you! (*From within the living
room, fading off*) You're gonna live with me, kid, and any babe you
want just say the word ... (*The last lines are hardly heard. They are
mounting the stairs to their parents' bedroom.*)

LINDA (*entering her bedroom and addressing* WILLY, *who is in the bathroom. She is straightening the bed for him*). Can you do anything about the shower? It drips.

WILLY (*from the bathroom*). All of a sudden everything falls to pieces. Goddam plumbing, oughta be sued, those people. I hardly finished putting it in and the thing ... (*His words rumble off.*)

LINDA. I'm just wondering if Oliver will remember him. You think he might?

WILLY (*coming out of the bathroom in his pajamas*). Remember him? What's the matter with you, you crazy? If he'd've stayed with Oliver he'd be on top by now! Wait'll Oliver gets a look at him. You don't know the average caliber any more. The average young man today—(*he is getting into bed*)—is got a caliber of zero. Greatest thing in the world for him was to bum around.

BIFF *and* HAPPY *enter the bedroom. Slight pause.*

WILLY (*stops short, looking at* BIFF). Glad to hear it, boy.

HAPPY. He wanted to say good night to you, sport.

WILLY (*to* BIFF). Yeah. Knock him dead, boy. What'd you want to tell me?

BIFF. Just take it easy, Pop. Good night. (*He turns to go.*)

WILLY (*unable to resist*). And if anything falls off the desk while you're talking to him—like a package or something—don't you pick it up. They have office boys for that.

LINDA. I'll make a big breakfast ...

WILLY. Will you let me finish? (*To* BIFF.) Tell him you were in the business in the West. Not farm work.

BIFF. All right, Dad.

LINDA. I think everything ...

WILLY (*going right through her speech*). And don't undersell yourself. No less than fifteen thousand dollars.

BIFF (*unable to bear him*). Okay. Good night, Mom. (*He starts moving.*)

WILLY. Because you got a greatness in you, Biff, remember that. You got all kinds of greatness ... (*He lies back, exhausted.* BIFF *walks out.*)

LINDA (*calling after* BIFF). Sleep well, darling!

HAPPY. I'm gonna get married, Mom. I wanted to tell you.

LINDA. Go to sleep, dear.

HAPPY (*going*). I just wanted to tell you.

WILLY. Keep up the good work. (HAPPY *exits.*) God ... remember that Ebbets Field game? The championship of the city?

LINDA. Just rest. Should I sing to you?

WILLY. Yeah. Sing to me. (LINDA *hums a soft lullaby.*) When that team came out—he was the tallest, remember?

LINDA. Oh, yes. And in gold.

BIFF *enters the darkened kitchen, takes a cigarette, and leaves the house. He comes downstage into a golden pool of light. He smokes, staring at the night.*

WILLY. Like a young god. Hercules—something like that. And the sun, the sun all around him. Remember how he waved to me? Right up from the field, with the representatives of three colleges standing by? And the buyers I brought, and the cheers when he came out—Loman, Loman,

Loman! God Almighty, he'll be great yet. A star like that, magnificent, can
never really fade away!

The light on WILLY *is fading. The gas heater begins to glow through the
kitchen wall, near the stairs, a blue flame beneath red coils.*

LINDA (*timidly*). Willy dear, what has he got against you?
WILLY. I'm so tired. Don't talk any more.

BIFF *slowly returns to the kitchen. He stops, stares toward the heater.*

LINDA. Will you ask Howard to let you work in New York?
WILLY. First thing in the morning. Everything'll be all right.

BIFF *reaches behind the heater and draws out a length of rubber tubing. He is horrified and turns his head toward* WILLY's *room, still
dimly lit, from which the strains of* LINDA's *desperate but monotonous
humming rise.*

WILLY (*staring through the window into the moonlight*). Gee, look at the
moon moving between the buildings!

BIFF *wraps the tubing around his hand and quickly goes up the stairs.*

Act 2

SCENE: *Music is heard, gay and bright. The curtain rises as the music
fades away.* WILLY, *in shirt sleeves, is sitting at the kitchen table, sipping
coffee, his hat in his lap.* LINDA *is filling his cup when she can.*

WILLY. Wonderful coffee. Meal in itself.
LINDA. Can I make you some eggs?
WILLY. No. Take a breath.
LINDA. You look so rested, dear.
WILLY. I slept like a dead one. First time in months. Imagine, sleeping till ten
on a Tuesday morning. Boys left nice and early, heh?
LINDA. They were out of here by eight o'clock.
WILLY. Good work!
LINDA. It was so thrilling to see them leaving together. I can't get over the
shaving lotion in this house!
WILLY (*smiling*). Mmm . . .
LINDA. Biff was very changed this morning. His whole attitude seemed to be
hopeful. He couldn't wait to get downtown to see Oliver.
WILLY. He's heading for a change. There's no question, there simply are cer-
tain men that take longer to get—solidified. How did he dress?
LINDA. His blue suit. He's so handsome in that suit. He could be a—anything
in that suit!

WILLY *gets up from the table.* LINDA *holds his jacket for him.*

WILLY. There's no question, no question at all. Gee, on the way home tonight
I'd like to buy some seeds.
LINDA (*laughing*). That'd be wonderful. But not enough sun gets back there.
Nothing'll grow any more.
WILLY. You wait, kid, before it's all over we're gonna get a little place out in
the country, and I'll raise some vegetables, a couple of chickens . . .

LINDA. You'll do it yet, dear.

WILLY *walks out of his jacket.* LINDA *follows him.*

WILLY. And they'll get married, and come for a weekend. I'd build a little guest house. 'Cause I got so many fine tools, all I'd need would be a little lumber and some peace of mind.

LINDA (*joyfully*). I sewed the lining ...

WILLY. I could build two guest houses, so they'd both come. Did he decide how much he's going to ask Oliver for?

LINDA (*getting him into the jacket*). He didn't mention it, but I imagine ten or fifteen thousand. You going to talk to Howard today?

WILLY. Yeah. I'll put it to him straight and simple. He'll just have to take me off the road.

LINDA. And Willy, don't forget to ask for a little advance, because we've got the insurance premium. It's the grace period now.

WILLY. That's a hundred ...?

LINDA. A hundred and eight, sixty-eight. Because we're a little short again.

WILLY. Why are we short?

LINDA. Well, you had the motor job on the car ...

WILLY. That goddam Studebaker!

LINDA. And you got one more payment on the refrigerator ...

WILLY. But it just broke again!

LINDA. Well, it's old, dear.

WILLY. I told you we should've bought a well-advertised machine. Charley bought a General Electric and it's twenty years old and it's still good, that son-of-a-bitch.

LINDA. But, Willy ...

WILLY. Whoever heard of a Hastings refrigerator? Once in my life I would like to own something outright before it's broken! I'm always in a race with the junkyard! I just finished paying for the car and it's on its last legs. The refrigerator consumes belts like a goddam maniac. They time those things. They time them so when you finally paid for them, they're used up.

LINDA (*buttoning up his jacket as he unbuttons it*). All told, about two hundred dollars would carry us, dear. But that includes the last payment on the mortgage. After this payment, Willy, the house belongs to us.

WILLY. It's twenty-five years!

LINDA. Biff was nine years old when we bought it.

WILLY. Well, that's a great thing. To weather a twenty-five year mortgage is ...

LINDA. It's an accomplishment.

WILLY. All the cement, the lumber, the reconstruction I put in this house! There ain't a crack to be found in it any more.

LINDA. Well, it served its purpose.

WILLY. What purpose? Some stranger'll come along, move in, and that's that. If only Biff would take this house, and raise a family ... (*He starts to go.*) Good-by, I'm late.

LINDA (*suddenly remembering*). Oh, I forgot! You're supposed to meet them for dinner.

WILLY. Me?

LINDA. At Frank's Chop House on Forty-eighth near Sixth Avenue.

WILLY. Is that so! How about you?

LINDA. No, just the three of you. They're gonna blow you to a big meal!

WILLY. Don't say! Who thought of that?

LINDA. Biff came to me this morning, Willy, and he said, "Tell Dad, we want to blow him to a big meal." Be there six o'clock. You and your two boys are going to have dinner.

WILLY. Gee whiz! That's really somethin'. I'm gonna knock Howard for a loop, kid. I'll get an advance, and I'll come home with a New York job. Goddammit, now I'm gonna do it!

LINDA. Oh, that's the spirit, Willy!

WILLY. I will never get behind a wheel the rest of my life!

LINDA. It's changing, Willy, I can feel it changing!

WILLY. Beyond a question. G'by, I'm late. (*He starts to go again.*)

LINDA (*calling after him as she runs to the kitchen table for a handkerchief*). You got your glasses?

WILLY (*feels for them, then comes back in*). Yeah, yeah, got my glasses.

LINDA (*giving him the handkerchief*). And a handkerchief.

WILLY. Yeah, handkerchief.

LINDA. And your saccharine?

WILLY. Yeah, my saccharine.

LINDA. Be careful on the subway stairs.

She kisses him, and a silk stocking is seen hanging from her hand.
WILLY *notices it.*

WILLY. Will you stop mending stockings? At least while I'm in the house. It gets me nervous. I can't tell you. Please.

LINDA *hides the stocking in her hand as she follows* WILLY *across the forestage in front of the house.*

LINDA. Remember, Frank's Chop House.

WILLY (*passing the apron*). Maybe beets would grow out there.

LINDA (*laughing*). But you tried so many times.

WILLY. Yeah. Well, don't work hard today. (*He disappears around the right corner of the house.*)

LINDA. Be careful!

As WILLY *vanishes,* LINDA *waves to him. Suddenly the phone rings. She runs across the stage and into the kitchen and lifts it.*

LINDA. Hello? Oh, Biff! I'm so glad you called, I just . . . Yes, sure, I just told him. Yes, he'll be there for dinner at six o'clock, I didn't forget. Listen, I was just dying to tell you. You know that little rubber pipe I told you about? That he connected to the gas heater? I finally decided to go down the cellar this morning and take it away and destroy it. But it's gone! Imagine? He took it away himself, it isn't there! (*She listens.*) When? Oh, then you took it. Oh—nothing, it's just that I'd hoped he'd taken it away himself. Oh, I'm not worried, darling, because this morning he left in such high spirits, it was like the old days! I'm not afraid any more. Did Mr. Oliver see you? . . . Well, you wait there then. And make a nice impression on him, darling. Just don't perspire too much before you see him. And have a nice time with Dad. He may have big news too! . . . That's right, a New York job. And be sweet to him tonight, dear. Be loving to him. Because he's only a little boat looking for a harbor. (*She is trembling with sorrow and joy.*) Oh, that's wonderful, Biff, you'll save his life. Thanks, darling. Just put your arm around him when he comes into the restaurant. Give him a smile. That's the boy . . . Good-by, dear . . . . You got your comb? . . . That's fine. Good-by, Biff dear.

In the middle of her speech, HOWARD WAGNER, *thirty-six, wheels in a small typewriter table on which is a wire-recording machine and proceeds to plug it in. This is on the left forestage. Light slowly fades on* LINDA *as it rises on* HOWARD. HOWARD *is intent on threading the machine and only glances over his shoulder as* WILLY *appears.*

WILLY. Pst! Pst!

HOWARD. Hello, Willy, come in.

WILLY. Like to have a little talk with you, Howard.

HOWARD. Sorry to keep you waiting. I'll be with you in a minute.

WILLY. What's that, Howard?

HOWARD. Didn't you ever see one of these? Wire recorder.

WILLY. Oh. Can we talk a minute?

HOWARD. Records things. Just got delivery yesterday. Been driving me crazy, the most terrific machine I ever saw in my life. I was up all night with it.

WILLY. What do you do with it?

HOWARD. I bought it for dictation, but you can do anything with it. Listen to this. I had it home last night. Listen to what I picked up. The first one is my daughter. Get this. (*He flicks the switch and "Roll out the Barrel" is heard being whistled.*) Listen to that kid whistle.

WILLY. That is lifelike, isn't it?

HOWARD. Seven years old. Get that tone.

WILLY. Ts, ts. Like to ask a little favor if you . . .

The whistling breaks off, and the voice of HOWARD's *daughter is heard.*

HIS DAUGHTER. "Now you, Daddy."

HOWARD. She's crazy for me! (*Again the same song is whistled.*) That's me! Ha! (*He winks.*)

WILLY. You're very good!

The whistling breaks off again. The machine runs silent for a moment.

HOWARD. Sh! Get this now, this is my son.

HIS SON. "The capital of Alabama is Montgomery; the capital of Arizona is Phoenix; the capital of Arkansas is Little Rock; the capital of California is Sacramento . . ." (*and on, and on.*)

HOWARD (*holding up five fingers*). Five years old, Willy!

WILLY. He'll make an announcer some day!

HIS SON (*continuing*). "the capital . . ."

HOWARD. Get that—alphabetical order! (*The machine breaks off suddenly.*) Wait a minute. The maid kicked the plug out.

WILLY. It certainly is a . . .

HOWARD. Sh, for God's sake!

HIS SON. "It's nine o'clock, Bulova watch time. So I have to go to sleep."

WILLY. That really is . . .

HOWARD. Wait a minute! The next is my wife.

They wait.

HOWARD'S VOICE. "Go on, say something." (*Pause.*) "Well, you gonna talk?"

HIS WIFE. "I can't think of anything."

HOWARD'S VOICE. "Well, talk—it's turning."

HIS WIFE (*shyly, beaten*). "Hello." (*Silence.*) "Oh, Howard, I can't talk into this ..."

HOWARD (*snapping the machine off*). That was my wife.

WILLY. That is a wonderful machine. Can we ...

HOWARD. I tell you, Willy, I'm gonna take my camera, and my bandsaw, and all my hobbies, and out they go. This is the most fascinating relaxation I ever found.

WILLY. I think I'll get one myself.

HOWARD. Sure, they're only a hundred and a half. You can't do without it. Supposing you wanna hear Jack Benny, see? But you can't be at home at that hour. So you tell the maid to turn the radio on when Jack Benny comes on, and this automatically goes on with the radio ...

WILLY. And when you come home you ...

HOWARD. You can come home twelve o'clock, one o'clock, any time you like, and you get yourself a Coke and sit yourself down, throw the switch, and there's Jack Benny's program in the middle of the night!

WILLY. I'm definitely going to get one. Because lots of times I'm on the road, and I think to myself, what I must be missing on the radio!

HOWARD. Don't you have a radio in the car?

WILLY. Well, yeah, but who ever thinks of turning it on?

HOWARD. Say, aren't you supposed to be in Boston?

WILLY. That's what I want to talk to you about, Howard. You got a minute? (*He draws a chair in from the wing.*)

HOWARD. What happened? What're you doing here?

WILLY. Well ...

HOWARD. You didn't crack up again, did you?

WILLY. Oh, no. No ...

HOWARD. Geez, you had me worried there for a minute. What's the trouble?

WILLY. Well, tell you the truth, Howard. I've come to the decision that I'd rather not travel any more.

HOWARD. Not travel! Well, what'll you do?

WILLY. Remember, Christmas time, when you had the party here? You said you'd try to think of some spot for me here in town.

HOWARD. With us?

WILLY. Well, sure.

HOWARD. Oh, yeah, yeah. I remember. Well, I couldn't think of anything for you, Willy.

WILLY. I tell ya, Howard. The kids are all grown up, y'know. I don't need much any more. If I could take home—well, sixty-five dollars a week, I could swing it.

HOWARD. Yeah, but Willy, see I ...

WILLY. I tell ya why, Howard. Speaking frankly and between the two of us, y'know—I'm just a little tired.

HOWARD. Oh, I could understand that, Willy. But you're a road man, Willy, and we do a road business. We've only got a half-dozen salesmen on the floor here.

WILLY. God knows, Howard. I never asked a favor of any man. But I was with the firm when your father used to carry you in here in his arms.

HOWARD. I know that, Willy, but . . .

WILLY. Your father came to me the day you were born and asked me what I thought of the name Howard, may he rest in peace.

HOWARD. I appreciate that, Willy, but there just is no spot here for you. If I had a spot I'd slam you right in, but I just don't have a single solitary spot.

He looks for his lighter. WILLY *has picked it up and gives it to him. Pause.*

WILLY (*with increasing anger*). Howard, all I need to set my table is fifty dollars a week.

HOWARD. But where am I going to put you, kid?

WILLY. Look, it isn't a question of whether I can sell merchandise, is it?

HOWARD. No, but it's business, kid, and everybody's gotta pull his own weight.

WILLY (*desperately*). Just let me tell you a story, Howard . . .

HOWARD. 'Cause you gotta admit, business is business.

WILLY (*angrily*). Business is definitely business, but just listen for a minute. You don't understand this. When I was a boy—eighteen, nineteen—I was already on the road. And there was a question in my mind as to whether selling had a future for me. Because in those days I had a yearning to go to Alaska. See, there were three gold strikes in one month in Alaska, and I felt like going out. Just for the ride, you might say.

HOWARD (*barely interested*). Don't say.

WILLY. Oh, yeah, my father lived many years in Alaska. He was an adventurous man. We've got quite a little streak of self-reliance in our family. I thought I'd go out with my older brother and try to locate him, and maybe settle in the North with the old man. And I was almost decided to go, when I met a salesman in the Parker House. His name was Dave Singleman. And he was eighty-four years old, and he'd drummed merchandise in thirty-one states. And old Dave, he'd go up to his room, y'understand, put on his green velvet slippers—I'll never forget—and pick up his phone and call the buyers, and without ever leaving his room, at the age of eighty-four, he made his living. And when I saw that, I realized that selling was the greatest career a man could want. 'Cause what could be more satisfying than to be able to go, at the age of eighty-four, into twenty or thirty different cities, and pick up a phone, and be remembered and loved and helped by so many different people? Do you know? when he died—and by the way he died the death of a salesman, in his green velvet slippers in the smoker of the New York, New Haven and Hartford, going into Boston—when he died, hundreds of salesmen and buyers were at his funeral. Things were sad on a lotta trains for months after that. (*He stands up,* HOWARD *has not looked at him.*) In those days there was personality in it, Howard. There was respect, and comradeship, and gratitude in it. Today, it's all cut and dried, and there's no chance for bringing friendship to bear—or personality. You see what I mean? They don't know me any more.

HOWARD (*moving away, to the right*). That's just the thing, Willy.

WILLY. If I had forty dollars a week—that's all I'd need. Forty dollars, Howard.

HOWARD. Kid, I can't take blood from a stone, I . . .

WILLY (*desperation is on him now*). Howard, the year Al Smith was nomi-
nated, your father came to me and . . .

HOWARD (*starting to go off*). I've got to see some people, kid.

WILLY (*stopping him*). I'm talking about your father! There were promises
made across this desk! You mustn't tell me you've got people to see—I
put thirty-four years into this firm, Howard, and now I can't pay my insurance! You can't eat the orange and throw the peel away—a man is
not a piece of fruit! (*After a pause.*) Now pay attention. Your father—in
1928 I had a big year. I averaged a hundred and seventy dollars a week
in commissions.

HOWARD (*impatiently*). Now, Willy, you never averaged . . .

WILLY (*banging his hand on the desk*). I averaged a hundred and seventy
dollars a week in the year of 1928! And your father came to me—or
rather, I was in the office here—it was right over this desk—and he put
his hand on my shoulder . . .

HOWARD (*getting up*). You'll have to excuse me, Willy, I gotta see some people. Pull yourself together. (*Going out.*) I'll be back in a little while.

On HOWARD'*s exit, the light on his chair grows very bright and strange.*

WILLY. Pull myself together! What the hell did I say to him? My God, I was
yelling at him! How could I? (WILLY *breaks off, staring at the light,
which occupies the chair, animating it. He approaches this chair,
standing across the desk from it.*) Frank, Frank, don't you remember
what you told me that time? How you put your hand on my shoulder,
and Frank . . . (*He leans on the desk and as he speaks the dead man's
name he accidentally switches on the recorder, and instantly*)

HOWARD'S son. ". . . New York is Albany. The capital of Ohio is Cincinnati, the
capital of Rhode Island is . . ." (*The recitation continues.*)

WILLY (*leaping away with fright, shouting*). Ha! Howard! Howard! Howard!

HOWARD (*rushing in*). What happened?

WILLY (*pointing at the machine, which continues nasally, childishly, with
the capital cities*). Shut it off! Shut it off!

HOWARD (*pulling the plug out*). Look, Willy . . .

WILLY (*pressing his hands to his eyes*). I gotta get myself some coffee. I'll get
some coffee . . .

WILLY *starts to walk out.* HOWARD *stops him.*

HOWARD (*rolling up the cord*). Willy, look . . .

WILLY. I'll go to Boston.

HOWARD. Willy, you can't go to Boston for us.

WILLY. Why can't I go?

HOWARD. I don't want you to represent us. I've been meaning to tell you for a
long time now.

WILLY. Howard, are you firing me?

HOWARD. I think you need a good long rest, Willy.

WILLY. Howard . . .

HOWARD. And when you feel better, come back, and we'll see if we can work
something out.

WILLY. But I gotta earn money, Howard. I'm in no position to . . .

HOWARD. Where are your sons? Why don't your sons give you a hand?

WILLY. They're working on a very big deal.

HOWARD. This is no time for false pride, Willy. You go to your sons and you tell them that you're tired. You've got two great boys, haven't you?

WILLY. Oh, no question, no question, but in the meantime . . .

HOWARD. Then that's that, heh?

WILLY. All right, I'll go to Boston tomorrow.

HOWARD. No, no.

WILLY. I can't throw myself on my sons. I'm not a cripple!

HOWARD. Look, kid, I'm busy this morning.

WILLY (*grasping* HOWARD's *arm*). Howard, you've got to let me go to Boston!

HOWARD (*hard, keeping himself under control*). I've got a line of people to see this morning. Sit down, take five minutes, and pull yourself together, and then go home, will ya? I need the office, Willy. (*He starts to go, turns, remembering the recorder, starts to push off the table holding the recorder.*) Oh, yeah. Whenever you can this week, stop by and drop off the samples. You'll feel better, Willy, and then come back and we'll talk. Pull yourself together, kid, there's people outside.

HOWARD *exits, pushing the table off left.* WILLY *stares into space, exhausted. Now the music is heard—*BEN's *music—first distantly, then closer, closer. As* WILLY *speaks,* BEN *enters from the right. He carries valise and umbrella.*

WILLY. Oh, Ben, how did you do it? What is the answer? Did you wind up the Alaska deal already?

BEN. Doesn't take much time if you know what you're doing. Just a short business trip. Boarding ship in an hour. Wanted to say good-by.

WILLY. Ben, I've got to talk to you.

BEN (*glancing at his watch*). Haven't the time, William.

WILLY (*crossing the apron to* BEN). Ben, nothing's working out. I don't know what to do.

BEN. Now, look here, William. I've bought timberland in Alaska and I need a man to look after things for me.

WILLY. God, timberland! Me and my boys in those grand outdoors!

BEN. You've a new continent at your doorstep, William. Get out of these cities, they're full of talk and time payments and courts of law. Screw on your fists and you can fight for a fortune up there.

WILLY. Yes, yes! Linda, Linda!

LINDA *enters as of old, with the wash.*

LINDA. Oh, you're back?

BEN. I haven't much time.

WILLY. No, wait! Linda, he's got a proposition for me in Alaska.

LINDA. But you've got . . . (*To* BEN.) He's got a beautiful job here.

WILLY. But in Alaska, kid, I could . . .

LINDA. You're doing well enough, Willy!

BEN (*To* LINDA). Enough for what, my dear?

LINDA (*frightened of* BEN *and angry at him*). Don't say those things to him! Enough to be happy right here, right now. (*To* WILLY, *while* BEN *laughs.*) Why must everybody conquer the world? You're well liked, and the boys love you, and someday—(*To* BEN)—why, old man Wagner told him just the other day that if he keeps it up he'll be a member of the firm, didn't he, Willy?

WILLY. Sure, sure. I am building something with this firm, Ben, and if a man is building something he must be on the right track, mustn't he?

BEN. What are you building? Lay your hand on it. Where is it?

WILLY (*hesitantly*). That's true, Linda, there's nothing.

LINDA. Why? (*To* BEN.) There's a man eighty-four years old . . .

WILLY. That's right, Ben, that's right. When I look at that man I say, what is there to worry about?

BEN. Bah!

WILLY. It's true, Ben. All he has to do is go into any city, pick up the phone, and he's making his living and you know why?

BEN (*picking up his valise*). I've got to go.

WILLY (*holding* BEN *back*). Look at this boy!

BIFF, *in his high school sweater, enters carrying suitcase.* HAPPY *carries* BIFF's *shoulder guards, gold helmet, and football pants.*

WILLY. Without a penny to his name, three great universities are begging for him, and from there the sky's the limit, because it's not what you do, Ben. It's who you know and the smile on your face! It's contacts, Ben, contacts! The whole wealth of Alaska passes over the lunch table at the Commodore Hotel, and that's the wonder, the wonder of this country, that a man can end with diamonds here on the basis of being liked! (*He turns to* BIFF.) And that's why when you get out on that field today it's important. Because thousands of people will be rooting for you and loving you. (*To* BEN, *who has again begun to leave.*) And Ben! when he walks into a business office his name will sound out like a bell and all the doors will open to him! I've seen it, Ben, I've seen it a thousand times! You can't feel it with your hand like timber, but it's there!

BEN. Good-by, William.

WILLY. Ben, am I right? Don't you think I'm right? I value your advice.

BEN. There's a new continent at your doorstep, William. You could walk out rich. Rich! (*He is gone.*)

WILLY. We'll do it here, Ben! You hear me? We're gonna do it here!

Young BERNARD *rushes in. The gay music of the Boys is heard.*

BERNARD. Oh, gee, I was afraid you left already!

WILLY. Why? What time is it?

BERNARD. It's half-past one!

WILLY. Well, come on, everybody! Ebbets Field next stop! Where's the pennants? (*He rushes through the wall-line of the kitchen and out into the living room.*)

LINDA (*to* BIFF). Did you pack fresh underwear?

BIFF (*who has been limbering up*). I want to go!

BERNARD. Biff, I'm carrying your helmet, ain't I?

HAPPY. No, I'm carrying the helmet.

BERNARD. Oh, Biff, you promised me.

HAPPY. I'm carrying the helmet.

BERNARD. How am I going to get in the locker room?

LINDA. Let him carry the shoulder guards. (*She puts her coat and hat on in the kitchen.*)

BERNARD. Can I, Biff? 'Cause I told everybody I'm going to be in the locker room.

HAPPY. In Ebbets Field it's the clubhouse.

BERNARD. I meant the clubhouse. Biff!

HAPPY. Biff!

BIFF (*grandly, after a slight pause*). Let him carry the shoulder guards.

HAPPY (*as he gives* BERNARD *the shoulder guards*). Stay close to us now.

WILLY *rushes in with the pennants.*

WILLY (*handing them out*). Everybody wave when Biff comes out on the field. (HAPPY *and* BERNARD *run off.*) You set now, boy?

The music has died away.

BIFF. Ready to go, Pop. Every muscle is ready.

WILLY (*at the edge of the apron*). You realize what this means?

BIFF. That's right, Pop.

WILLY (*feeling* BIFF*'s muscles*). You're comin' home this afternoon captain of the All-Scholastic Championship Team of the City of New York.

BIFF. I got it, Pop. And remember, pal, when I take off my helmet, that touchdown is for you.

WILLY. Let's go! (*He is starting out, with his arm around* BIFF, *when* CHARLEY *enters, as of old, in knickers.*) I got no room for you, Charley.

CHARLEY. Room? For what?

WILLY. In the car.

CHARLEY. You goin' for a ride? I wanted to shoot some casino.

WILLY (*furiously*). Casino! (*Incredulously.*) Don't you realize what today is?

LINDA. Oh, he knows, Willy. He's just kidding you.

WILLY. That's nothing to kid about!

CHARLEY. No, Linda, what's goin' on?

LINDA. He's playing in Ebbets Field.

CHARLEY. Baseball in this weather?

WILLY. Don't talk to him. Come on, come on! (*He is pushing them out.*)

CHARLEY. Wait a minute, didn't you hear the news?

WILLY. What?

CHARLEY. Don't you listen to the radio? Ebbets Field just blew up.

WILLY. You go to hell! (CHARLEY *laughs. Pushing them out.*) Come on, come on! We're late.

CHARLEY (*as they go*). Knock a homer, Biff, knock a homer!

WILLY (*the last to leave, turning to* CHARLEY). I don't think that was funny, Charley. This is the greatest day of his life.

CHARLEY. Willy, when are you going to grow up?

WILLY. Yeah, heh? When this game is over, Charley, you'll be laughing out of the other side of your face. They'll be calling him another Red Grange. Twenty-five thousand a year.

CHARLEY (*kidding*). Is that so?

WILLY. Yeah, that's so.

CHARLEY. Well, then, I'm sorry, Willy. But tell me something.

WILLY. What?

CHARLEY. Who is Red Grange?

WILLY. Put up your hands. Goddam you, put up your hands!

CHARLEY, *chuckling, shakes his head and walks away, around the left corner of the stage.* WILLY *follows him. The music rises to a mocking frenzy.*

WILLY. Who the hell do you think you are, better than everybody else? You don't know everything, you big, ignorant, stupid . . . Put up your hands!

Light rises, on the right side of the forestage, on a small table in the reception room of CHARLEY's *office. Traffic sounds heard.* BERNARD, *now mature, sits whistling to himself. A pair of tennis rackets and an old overnight bag are on the floor beside him.*

WILLY (*offstage*). What are you walking away for? Don't walk away! If you're going to say something say it to my face! I know you laugh at me behind my back. You'll laugh out of the other side of your goddam face after this game. Touchdown! Touchdown! Eighty thousand people! Touchdown! Right between the goal posts.

(BERNARD *is a quiet, earnest, but self-assured young man.* WILLY's *voice is coming from right upstage now.* BERNARD *lowers his feet off the table and listens.* JENNY, *his father's secretary, enters.*)

JENNY (*distressed*). Say, Bernard, will you go out in the hall?

BERNARD. What is that noise? Who is it?

JENNY. Mr. Loman. He just got off the elevator.

BERNARD (*getting up*). Who's he arguing with?

JENNY. Nobody. There's nobody with him. I can't deal with him any more, and your father gets all upset every time he comes. I've got a lot of typing to do, and your father's waiting to sign it. Will you see him?

WILLY (*entering*). Touchdown! Touch—(*He sees* JENNY.) Jenny, Jenny, good to see you. How're ya? Workin'? Or still honest?

JENNY. Fine. How've you been feeling?

WILLY. Not much any more, Jenny. Ha, ha! (*He is surprised to see the rackets.*)

BERNARD. Hello, Uncle Willy.

WILLY (*almost shocked*). Bernard! Well, look who's here! (*He comes quickly, guiltily, to* BERNARD *and warmly shakes his hand.*)

BERNARD. How are you? Good to see you.

WILLY. What are you doing here?

BERNARD. Oh, just stopped by to see Pop. Get off my feet till my train leaves. I'm going to Washington in a few minutes.

WILLY. Is he in?

BERNARD. Yes, he's in his office with the accountant. Sit down.

WILLY (*sitting down*). What're you going to do in Washington?

BERNARD. Oh, just a case I've got there, Willy.

WILLY. That so? (*Indicating the rackets.*) You going to play tennis there?

BERNARD. I'm staying with a friend who's got a court.

WILLY. Don't say. His own tennis court. Must be fine people, I bet.

BERNARD. They are, very nice. Dad tells me Biff's in town.

WILLY (*with a big smile*). Yeah, Biff's in. Working on a very big deal, Bernard.

BERNARD. What's Biff doing?

WILLY. Well, he's been doing very big things in the West. But he decided to establish himself here. Very big. We're having dinner. Did I hear your wife had a boy?

BERNARD. That's right. Our second.

WILLY. Two boys! What do you know!

BERNARD. What kind of a deal has Biff got?

WILLY. Well, Bill Oliver—very big sporting-goods man—he wants Biff very badly. Called him in from the West. Long distance, carte blanche, special deliveries. Your friends have their own private tennis court?

BERNARD. You still with the old firm, Willy?

WILLY (*after a pause*). I'm—I'm overjoyed to see how you made the grade, Bernard, overjoyed. It's an encouraging thing to see a young man really—really . . . Looks very good for Biff—very . . . (*He breaks off, then.*) Bernard . . . (*He is so full of emotion, he breaks off again.*)

BERNARD. What is it, Willy?

WILLY (*small and alone*). What—what's the secret?

BERNARD. What secret?

WILLY. How—how did you? Why didn't he ever catch on?

BERNARD. I wouldn't know that, Willy.

WILLY (*confidentially, desperately*). You were his friend, his boyhood friend. There's something I don't understand about it. His life ended after that Ebbets Field game. From the age of seventeen nothing good ever happened to him.

BERNARD. He never trained himself for anything.

WILLY. But he did, he did. After high school he took so many correspondence courses. Radio mechanics; television; God knows what, and never made the slightest mark.

BERNARD (*taking off his glasses*). Willy, do you want to talk candidly?

WILLY (*rising, faces* BERNARD). I regard you as a very brilliant man, Bernard. I value your advice.

BERNARD. Oh, the hell with the advice, Willy. I couldn't advise you. There's just one thing I've always wanted to ask you. When he was supposed to graduate, and the math teacher flunked him . . .

WILLY. Oh, that son-of-a-bitch ruined his life.

BERNARD. Yeah, but, Willy, all he had to do was go to summer school and make up that subject.

WILLY. That's right, that's right.

BERNARD. Did you tell him not to go to summer school?

WILLY. Me? I begged him to go. I ordered him to go!

BERNARD. Then why wouldn't he go?

WILLY. Why? Why! Bernard, that question has been trailing me like a ghost for the last fifteen years. He flunked the subject, and laid down and died like a hammer hit him!

BERNARD. Take it easy, kid.

WILLY. Let me talk to you—I got nobody to talk to. Bernard, Bernard, was it my fault? Y'see? It keeps going around in my mind, maybe I did something to him. I got nothing to give him.

BERNARD. Don't take it so hard.

WILLY. Why did he lay down? What is the story there? You were his friend!

BERNARD. Willy, I remember, it was June, and our grades came out. And he'd flunked math.

WILLY. That son-of-a-bitch!

BERNARD. No, it wasn't right then. Biff just got very angry, I remember, and he was ready to enroll in summer school.

WILLY (*surprised*). He was?

BERNARD. He wasn't beaten by it at all. But then, Willy, he disappeared from the block for almost a month. And I got the idea that he'd gone up to New England to see you. Did he have a talk with you then?

WILLY *stares in silence.*

BERNARD. Willy?

WILLY (*with a strong edge of resentment in his voice*). Yeah, he came to Boston. What about it?

BERNARD. Well, just that when he came back—I'll never forget this, it always mystifies me. Because I'd thought so well of Biff, even though he'd always taken advantage of me. I loved him, Willy, y'know? And he came back after that month and took his sneakers—remember those sneakers with "University of Virginia" printed on them? He was so proud of those, wore them every day. And he took them down in the cellar, and burned them up in the furnace. We had a fist fight. It lasted at least half an hour. Just the two of us, punching each other down the cellar, and crying right through it. I've often thought of how strange it was that I knew he'd given up his life. What happened in Boston, Willy?

WILLY *looks at him as at an intruder.*

BERNARD. I just bring it up because you asked me.

WILLY (*angrily*). Nothing. What do you mean, "What happened?" What's that got to do with anything?

BERNARD. Well, don't get sore.

WILLY. What are you trying to do, blame it on me? If a boy lays down is that my fault?

BERNARD. Now, Willy, don't get ...

WILLY. Well, don't—don't talk to me that way! What does that mean, "What happened?"

CHARLEY *enters. He is in his vest, and he carries a bottle of bourbon.*

CHARLEY. Hey, you're going to miss that train. (*He waves the bottle.*)

BERNARD. Yeah, I'm going. (*He takes the bottle.*) Thanks, Pop. (*He picks up his rackets and bag.*) Good-by, Willy, and don't worry about it. You know, "If at first you don't succeed ... "

WILLY. Yes, I believe in that.

BERNARD. But sometimes, Willy, it's better for a man just to walk away.

WILLY. Walk away?

BERNARD. That's right.

WILLY. But if you can't walk away?

BERNARD (*after a slight pause*). I guess that's when it's tough. (*Extending his hand.*) Good-by, Willy.

WILLY (*shaking* BERNARD*'s hand*). Good-by, boy.

CHARLEY (*an arm on* BERNARD*'s shoulder*). How do you like this kid? Gonna argue a case in front of the Supreme Court.

BERNARD (*protesting*). Pop!

WILLY (*genuinely shocked, pained, and happy*). No! The Supreme Court!

BERNARD. I gotta run. 'By, Dad!

CHARLEY. Knock 'em dead, Bernard!

BERNARD *goes off.*

WILLY (*as* CHARLEY *takes out his wallet*). The Supreme Court! And he didn't even mention it!

CHARLEY (*counting out money on the desk*). He don't have to—he's gonna do it.

WILLY. And you never told him what to do, did you? You never took any interest in him.

CHARLEY. My salvation is that I never took any interest in anything. There's some money—fifty dollars. I got an accountant inside.

WILLY. Charley, look . . . (*with difficulty.*) I got my insurance to pay. If you can manage it—I need a hundred and ten dollars.

CHARLEY *doesn't reply for a moment; merely stops moving.*

WILLY. I'd draw it from my bank but Linda would know, and I . . .

CHARLEY. Sit down, Willy.

WILLY (*moving toward the chair*). I'm keeping an account of everything, remember. I'll pay every penny back. (*He sits.*)

CHARLEY. Now listen to me, Willy.

WILLY. I want you to know I appreciate . . .

CHARLEY (*sitting down on the table*). Willy, what're you doin'? What the hell is going on in your head?

WILLY. Why? I'm simply . . .

CHARLEY. I offered you a job. You make fifty dollars a week. And I won't send you on the road.

WILLY. I've got a job.

CHARLEY. Without pay? What kind of a job is a job without pay? (*He rises.*) Now, look, kid, enough is enough. I'm no genius but I know when I'm being insulted.

WILLY. Insulted!

CHARLEY. Why don't you want to work for me?

WILLY. What's the matter with you? I've got a job.

CHARLEY. Then what're you walkin' in here every week for?

WILLY (*getting up*). Well, if you don't want me to walk in here . . .

CHARLEY. I'm offering you a job.

WILLY. I don't want your goddam job!

CHARLEY. When the hell are you going to grow up?

WILLY (*furiously*). You big ignoramus, if you say that to me again I'll rap you one! I don't care how big you are! (*He's ready to fight.*)

Pause.

CHARLEY (*kindly, going to him*). How much do you need, Willy?

WILLY. Charley, I'm strapped. I'm strapped. I don't know what to do. I was just fired.

CHARLEY. Howard fired you?

WILLY. That snotnose. Imagine that? I named him. I named him Howard.

CHARLEY. Willy, when're you gonna realize that them things don't mean anything? You named him Howard, but you can't sell that. The only thing you got in this world is what you can sell. And the funny thing is that you're a salesman, and you don't know that.

WILLY. I've always tried to think otherwise, I guess. I always felt that if a man was impressive, and well liked, that nothing . . .

CHARLEY. Why must everybody like you? Who liked J. P. Morgan? Was he impressive? In a Turkish bath he'd look like a butcher. But with his pockets on he was very well liked. Now listen, Willy, I know you don't like me, and nobody can say I'm in love with you, but I'll give you a job because—just for the hell of it, put it that way. Now what do you say?

WILLY. I—I just can't work for you, Charley.

CHARLEY. What're you, jealous of me?

WILLY. I can't work for you, that's all, don't ask me why.

CHARLEY (*angered, takes out more bills*). You been jealous of me all your life, you damned fool! Here, pay your insurance. (*He puts the money in* WILLY's *hand.*)

WILLY. I'm keeping strict accounts.

CHARLEY. I've got some work to do. Take care of yourself. And pay your insurance.

WILLY (*moving to the right*). Funny, y'know? After all the highways, and the trains, and the appointments, and the years, you end up worth more dead than alive.

CHARLEY. Willy, nobody's worth nothin' dead. (*After a slight pause.*) Did you hear what I said?

WILLY *stands still, dreaming.*

CHARLEY. Willy!

WILLY. Apologize to Bernard for me when you see him. I didn't mean to argue with him. He's a fine boy. They're all fine boys, and they'll end up big—all of them. Someday they'll all play tennis together. Wish me luck, Charley. He saw Bill Oliver today.

CHARLEY. Good luck.

WILLY (*on the verge of tears*). Charley, you're the only friend I got. Isn't that a remarkable thing? (*He goes out.*)

CHARLEY. Jesus!

CHARLEY *stares after him a moment and follows. All light blacks out. Suddenly raucous music is heard, and a red glow rises behind the screen at right.* STANLEY, *a young waiter, appears, carrying a table, followed by* HAPPY, *who is carrying two chairs.*

STANLEY (*putting the table down*). That's all right, Mr. Loman, I can handle it myself. (*He turns and takes the chairs from* HAPPY *and places them at the table.*)

HAPPY (*glancing around*). Oh, this is better.

STANLEY. Sure, in the front there you're in the middle of all kinds of noise. Whenever you got a party, Mr. Loman, you just tell me and I'll put you back here. Y'know, there's a lotta people they don't like it private, because when they go out they like to see a lotta action around them because they're sick and tired to stay in the house by theirself. But I know you, you ain't from Hackensack. You know what I mean?

HAPPY (*sitting down*). So how's it coming, Stanley?

STANLEY. Ah, it's a dog life. I only wish during the war they'd a took me in the Army. I coulda been dead by now.

HAPPY. My brother's back, Stanley.

STANLEY. Oh, he come back, heh? From the Far West.

HAPPY. Yeah, big cattle man, my brother, so treat him right. And my father's coming too.

STANLEY. Oh, your father too!

HAPPY. You got a couple of nice lobsters?

STANLEY. Hundred percent, big.

HAPPY. I want them with the claws.

STANLEY. Don't worry, I don't give you no mice. (HAPPY *laughs.*) How about some wine? It'll put a head on the meal.

HAPPY. No. You remember, Stanley, that recipe I brought you from overseas? With the champagne in it?

STANLEY. Oh, yeah, sure. I still got it tacked up yet in the kitchen. But that'll have to cost a buck apiece anyways.

HAPPY. That's all right.

STANLEY. What'd you, hit a number or somethin'?

HAPPY. No, it's a little celebration. My brother is—I think he pulled off a big deal today. I think we're going into business together.

STANLEY. Great! That's the best for you. Because a family business, you know what I mean?—that's the best.

HAPPY. That's what I think.

STANLEY. 'Cause what's the difference? Somebody steals? It's in the family. Know what I mean? (*Sotto voce.*) Like this bartender here. The boss is goin' crazy what kinda leak he's got in the cash register. You put it in but it don't come out.

HAPPY (*raising his head*). Sh!

STANLEY. What?

HAPPY. You notice I wasn't lookin' right or left, was I?

STANLEY. No.

HAPPY. And my eyes are closed.

STANLEY. So what's the . . . ?

HAPPY. Strudel's comin'.

STANLEY (*catching on, looks around*). Ah, no, there's no . . .

> He breaks off as a furred, lavishly dressed GIRL enters and sits at the next table. Both follow her with their eyes.

STANLEY. Geez, how'd ya know?

HAPPY. I got radar or something. (*Staring directly at her profile.*) Oooooooo . . . Stanley.

STANLEY. I think that's for you, Mr. Loman.

HAPPY. Look at that mouth. Oh, God. And the binoculars.

STANLEY. Geez, you got a life, Mr. Loman.

HAPPY. Wait on her.

STANLEY (*going to the GIRL's table*). Would you like a menu, ma'am?

GIRL. I'm expecting someone, but I'd like a . . .

HAPPY. Why don't you bring her—excuse me, miss, do you mind? I sell champagne, and I'd like you to try my brand. Bring her a champagne, Stanley.

GIRL. That's awfully nice of you.

HAPPY. Don't mention it. It's all company money. (*He laughs.*)

GIRL. That's a charming product to be selling, isn't it?

HAPPY. Oh, gets to be like everything else. Selling is selling, y'know.

GIRL. I suppose.

HAPPY. You don't happen to sell, do you?

GIRL. No, I don't sell.

HAPPY. Would you object to a compliment from a stranger? You ought to be on a magazine cover.

GIRL (*looking at him a little archly*). I have been.

STANLEY *comes in with a glass of champagne.*

HAPPY. What'd I say before, Stanley? You see? She's a cover girl.

STANLEY. Oh, I could see, I could see.

HAPPY (*to the* GIRL). What magazine?

GIRL. Oh, a lot of them. (*She takes the drink.*) Thank you.

HAPPY. You know what they say in France, don't you? "Champagne is the drink of the complexion"—Hya, Biff!

BIFF *has entered and sits with* HAPPY.

BIFF. Hello, kid. Sorry I'm late.

HAPPY. I just got here. Uh, Miss . . . ?

GIRL. Forsythe.

HAPPY. Miss Forsythe, this is my brother.

BIFF. Is Dad here?

HAPPY. His name is Biff. You might've heard of him. Great football player.

GIRL. Really? What team?

HAPPY. Are you familiar with football?

GIRL. No, I'm afraid I'm not.

HAPPY. Biff is quarterback with the New York Giants.

GIRL. Well, that is nice, isn't it? (*She drinks.*)

HAPPY. Good health.

GIRL. I'm happy to meet you.

HAPPY. That's my name. Hap. It's really Harold, but at West Point they called me Happy.

GIRL (*now really impressed*). Oh, I see. How do you do? (*She turns her profile.*)

BIFF. Isn't Dad coming?

HAPPY. You want her?

BIFF. Oh, I could never make that.

HAPPY. I remember the time that idea would never come into your head. Where's the old confidence, Biff?

BIFF. I just saw Oliver . . .

HAPPY. Wait a minute. I've got to see that old confidence again. Do you want her? She's on call.

BIFF. Oh, no. (*He turns to look at the* GIRL.)

HAPPY. I'm telling you. Watch this. (*Turning to the* GIRL.) Honey? (*She turns to him.*) Are you busy?

GIRL. Well, I am . . . but I could make a phone call.

HAPPY. Do that, will you, honey? And see if you can get a friend. We'll be here for a while. Biff is one of the greatest football players in the country.

GIRL (*standing up*). Well, I'm certainly happy to meet you.

HAPPY. Come back soon.

GIRL. I'll try.

HAPPY. Don't try, honey, try hard.

The GIRL *exits.* STANLEY *follows, shaking his head in bewildered admiration.*

HAPPY. Isn't that a shame now? A beautiful girl like that? That's why I can't get married. There's not a good woman in a thousand. New York is loaded with them, kid!

BIFF. Hap, look …

HAPPY. I told you she was on call!

BIFF (*strangely unnerved*). Cut it out, will ya? I want to say something to you.

HAPPY. Did you see Oliver?

BIFF. I saw him all right. Now look, I want to tell Dad a couple of things and I want you to help me.

HAPPY. What? Is he going to back you?

BIFF. Are you crazy? You're out of your goddam head, you know that?

HAPPY. Why? What happened?

BIFF (*breathlessly*). I did a terrible thing today, Hap. It's been the strangest day I ever went through. I'm all numb, I swear.

HAPPY. You mean he wouldn't see you?

BIFF. Well, I waited six hours for him, see? All day. Kept sending my name in. Even tried to date his secretary so she'd get me to him, but no soap.

HAPPY. Because you're not showin' the old confidence, Biff. He remembered you, didn't he?

BIFF (*stopping* HAPPY *with a gesture*). Finally, about five o'clock, he comes out. Didn't remember who I was or anything. I felt like such an idiot, Hap.

HAPPY. Did you tell him my Florida idea?

BIFF. He walked away. I saw him for one minute. I got so mad I could've torn the walls down! How the hell did I ever get the idea I was a salesman there? I even believed myself that I'd been a salesman for him! And then he gave me one look and—I realized what a ridiculous lie my whole life has been! We've been talking in a dream for fifteen years. I was a shipping clerk.

HAPPY. What'd you do?

BIFF (*with great tension and wonder*). Well, he left, see. And the secretary went out. I was all alone in the waiting room. I don't know what came over me, Hap. The next thing I know I'm in his office—paneled walls, everything. I can't explain it. I—Hap. I took his fountain pen.

HAPPY. Geez, did he catch you?

BIFF. I ran out. I ran down all eleven flights. I ran and ran and ran.

HAPPY. That was an awful dumb—what'd you do that for?

BIFF (*agonized*). I don't know, I just—wanted to take something, I don't know. You gotta help me, Hap. I'm gonna tell Pop.

HAPPY. You crazy? What for?

BIFF. Hap, he's got to understand that I'm not the man somebody lends that kind of money to. He thinks I've been spiting him all these years and it's eating him up.

HAPPY. That's just it. You tell him something nice.

BIFF. I can't.

HAPPY. Say you got a lunch date with Oliver tomorrow.

BIFF. So what do I do tomorrow?

HAPPY. You leave the house tomorrow and come back at night and say Oliver is thinking it over. And he thinks it over for a couple of weeks, and gradually it fades away and nobody's the worse.

BIFF. But it'll go on forever!

HAPPY. Dad is never so happy as when he's looking forward to something!

WILLY *enters.*

HAPPY. Hello, scout!

WILLY. Gee, I haven't been here in years!

STANLEY *has followed* WILLY *in and sets a chair for him.* STANLEY *starts off but* HAPPY *stops him.*

HAPPY. Stanley!

STANLEY *stands by, waiting for an order.*

BIFF (*going to* WILLY *with guilt, as to an invalid*). Sit down, Pop. You want a drink?

WILLY. Sure, I don't mind.

BIFF. Let's get a load on.

WILLY. You look worried.

BIFF. N-no. (*To* STANLEY.) Scotch all around. Make it doubles.

STANLEY. Doubles, right. (*He goes.*)

WILLY. You had a couple already, didn't you?

BIFF. Just a couple, yeah.

WILLY. Well, what happened, boy? (*Nodding affirmatively, with a smile.*) Everything go all right?

BIFF (*takes a breath, then reaches out and grasps* WILLY*'s hand*). Pal . . . (*He is smiling bravely, and* WILLY *is smiling too.*) I had an experience today.

HAPPY. Terrific, Pop.

WILLY. That so? What happened?

BIFF (*high, slightly alcoholic, above the earth*). I'm going to tell you everything from first to last. It's been a strange day. (*Silence. He looks around, composes himself as best he can, but his breath keeps breaking the rhythm of his voice.*) I had to wait quite a while for him, and . . .

WILLY. Oliver?

BIFF. Yeah, Oliver. All day, as a matter of cold fact. And a lot of—instances— facts, Pop, facts about my life came back to me. Who was it, Pop? Who ever said I was a salesman with Oliver?

WILLY. Well, you were.

BIFF. No, Dad, I was a shipping clerk.

WILLY. But you were practically . . .

BIFF (*with determination*). Dad, I don't know who said it first, but I was never a salesman for Bill Oliver.

WILLY. What're you talking about?

BIFF. Let's hold on to the facts tonight, Pop. We're not going to get anywhere bullin' around. I was a shipping clerk.

WILLY (*angrily*). All right, now listen to me . . .

BIFF. Why don't you let me finish?

WILLY. I'm not interested in stories about the past or any crap of that kind because the woods are burning, boys, you understand? There's a big blaze going on all around. I was fired today.

BIFF (*shocked*). How could you be?

WILLY. I was fired, and I'm looking for a little good news to tell your mother, because the woman has waited and the woman has suffered. The gist of it is that I haven't got a story left in my head, Biff. So don't give me a lecture about facts and aspects. I am not interested. Now what've you got to say to me?

STANLEY *enters with three drinks. They wait until he leaves.*

WILLY. Did you see Oliver?

BIFF. Jesus, Dad!

WILLY. You mean you didn't go up there?

HAPPY. Sure he went up there.

BIFF. I did. I—saw him. How could they fire you?

WILLY (*on the edge of his chair*). What kind of a welcome did he give you?

BIFF. He won't even let you work on commission?

WILLY. I'm out! (*Driving.*) So tell me, he gave you a warm welcome?

HAPPY. Sure, Pop, sure!

BIFF (*driven*). Well, it was kind of . . .

WILLY. I was wondering if he'd remember you. (*To* HAPPY.) Imagine, man doesn't see him for ten, twelve years and gives him that kind of a welcome!

HAPPY. Damn right!

BIFF (*trying to return to the offensive*). Pop, look . . .

WILLY. You know why he remembered you, don't you? Because you impressed him in those days.

BIFF. Let's talk quietly and get this down to the facts, huh?

WILLY (*as though* BIFF *had been interrupting*). Well, what happened? It's great news, Biff. Did he take you into his office or'd you talk in the waiting room?

BIFF. Well, he came in, see, and . . .

WILLY (*with a big smile*). What'd he say? Betcha he threw his arm around you.

BIFF. Well, he kinda . . .

WILLY. He's a fine man. (*To* HAPPY.) Very hard man to see, y'know.

HAPPY (*agreeing*). Oh, I know.

WILLY (*to* BIFF). Is that where you had the drinks?

BIFF. Yeah, he gave me a couple of—no, no!

HAPPY (*cutting in*). He told him my Florida idea.

WILLY. Don't interrupt. (*To* BIFF.) How'd he react to the Florida idea?

BIFF. Dad, will you give me a minute to explain?

WILLY. I've been waiting for you to explain since I sat down here! What happened? He took you into his office and what?

BIFF. Well—I talked. And—and he listened, see.

WILLY. Famous for the way he listens, y'know. What was his answer?

BIFF. His answer was—(*He breaks off, suddenly angry.*) Dad, you're not letting me tell you what I want to tell you!

WILLY (*accusing, angered*). You didn't see him, did you?

BIFF. I did see him!

WILLY. What'd you insult him or something? You insulted him, didn't you?

BIFF. Listen, will you let me out of it, will you just let me out of it!

HAPPY. What the hell!

WILLY. Tell me what happened!

BIFF (*to* HAPPY). I can't talk to him!

A single trumpet note jars the ear. The light of green leaves stains the house, which holds the air of night and a dream. YOUNG BERNARD *enters and knocks on the door of the house.*

YOUNG BERNARD (*frantically*). Mrs. Loman, Mrs. Loman!

HAPPY. Tell him what happened!

BIFF (*to* HAPPY.) Shut up and leave me alone!

WILLY. No, no! You had to go and flunk math!

BIFF. What math? What're you talking about?

YOUNG BERNARD. Mrs. Loman, Mrs. Loman!

LINDA *appears in the house, as of old.*

WILLY (*wildly*). Math, math, math!

BIFF. Take it easy, Pop!

YOUNG BERNARD. Mrs. Loman!

WILLY (*furiously*). If you hadn't flunked you'd've been·set by now!

BIFF. Now, look, I'm gonna tell you what happened, and you're going to listen to me.

YOUNG BERNARD. Mrs. Loman!

BIFF. I waited six hours . . .

HAPPY. What the hell are you saying?

BIFF. I kept sending in my name but he wouldn't see me. So finally he . . . (*He continues unheard as light fades low on the restaurant.*)

YOUNG BERNARD. Biff flunked math!

LINDA. No!

YOUNG BERNARD. Birnbaum flunked him! They won't graduate him!

LINDA. But they have to. He's gotta go to the university. Where is he? Biff! Biff!

YOUNG BERNARD. No, he left. He went to Grand Central.

LINDA. Grand—You mean he went to Boston!

YOUNG BERNARD. Is Uncle Willy in Boston?

LINDA. Oh, maybe Willy can talk to the teacher. Oh, the poor, poor boy!

Light on house area snaps out.

BIFF (*at the table, now audible, holding up a gold fountain pen*). . . . so I'm washed up with Oliver, you understand? Are you listening to me?

WILLY (*at a loss*). Yeah, sure. If you hadn't flunked . . .

BIFF. Flunked what? What're you talking about?

WILLY. Don't blame everything on me! I didn't flunk math—you did! What pen?

HAPPY. That was awful dumb, Biff, a pen like that is worth—

WILLY (*seeing the pen for the first time*). You took Oliver's pen?

BIFF (*weakening*). Dad, I just explained it to you.

WILLY. You stole Bill Oliver's fountain pen!

BIFF. I didn't exactly steal it! That's just what I've been explaining to you!

HAPPY. He had it in his hand and just then Oliver walked in, so he got nervous and stuck it in his pocket!

WILLY. My God, Biff!

BIFF. I never intended to do it, Dad!

OPERATOR'S VOICE. Standish Arms, good evening!

WILLY (*shouting*). I'm not in my room!

BIFF (*frightened*). Dad, what's the matter? (*He and* HAPPY *stand up.*)

OPERATOR. Ringing Mr. Loman for you!

WILLY. I'm not there, stop it!

BIFF (*horrified, gets down on one knee before* WILLY). Dad, I'll make good, I'll make good. (WILLY *tries to get to his feet.* BIFF *holds him down.*) Sit down now.

WILLY. No, you're no good, you're no good for anything.

BIFF. I am, Dad, I'll find something else, you understand? Now don't worry about anything. (*He holds up* WILLY's *face.*) Talk to me, Dad.

OPERATOR. Mr. Loman does not answer. Shall I page him?

WILLY (*attempting to stand, as though to rush and silence the* OPERATOR). No, no, no!

HAPPY. He'll strike something, Pop.

WILLY. No, no . . .

BIFF (*desperately, standing over* WILLY). Pop, listen! Listen to me! I'm telling you something good. Oliver talked to his partner about the Florida idea. You listening? He—he talked to his partner, and he came to me . . . I'm going to be all right, you hear? Dad, listen to me, he said it was just a question of the amount!

WILLY. Then you . . . got it?

HAPPY. He's gonna be terrific, Pop!

WILLY (*trying to stand*). Then you got it, haven't you? You got it! You got it!

BIFF (*agonized, holds* WILLY *down*). No, no. Look, Pop. I'm supposed to have lunch with them tomorrow. I'm just telling you this so you'll know that I can still make an impression, Pop. And I'll make good somewhere, but I can't go tomorrow, see.

WILLY. Why not? You simply . . .

BIFF. But the pen, Pop!

WILLY. You give it to him and tell him it was an oversight!

HAPPY. Sure, have lunch tomorrow!

BIFF. I can't say that . . .

WILLY. You were doing a crossword puzzle and accidentally used his pen!

BIFF. Listen, kid, I took those balls years ago, now I walk in with his fountain pen? That clinches it, don't you see? I can't face him like that! I'll try elsewhere.

PAGE'S VOICE. Paging Mr. Loman!

WILLY. Don't you want to be anything?

BIFF. Pop, how can I go back?

WILLY. You don't want to be anything, is that what's behind it?

BIFF (*now angry at* WILLY *for not crediting his sympathy*). Don't take it that way! You think it was easy walking into that office after what I'd done to him? A team of horses couldn't have dragged me back to Bill Oliver!

WILLY. Then why'd you go?

BIFF. Why did I go? Why did I go! Look at you! Look at what's become of you!

Off left, THE WOMAN *laughs.*

WILLY. Biff, you're going to go to that lunch tomorrow, or . . .

BIFF. I can't go. I've got no appointment!

HAPPY. Biff, for . . . !

WILLY. Are you spiting me?

BIFF. Don't take it that way! Goddammit!

WILLY (*strikes* BIFF *and falters away from the table*). You rotten little louse! Are you spiting me?

THE WOMAN. Someone's at the door, Willy!

BIFF. I'm no good, can't you see what I am?

HAPPY (*separating them*). Hey, you're in a restaurant! Now cut it out, both of you! (*The girls enter.*) Hello, girls, sit down.

THE WOMAN *laughs, off left.*

MISS FORSYTHE. I guess we might as well. This is Letta.

THE WOMAN. Willy, are you going to wake up?

BIFF (*ignoring* WILLY). How're ya, miss, sit down. What do you drink?

MISS FORSYTHE. Letta might not be able to stay long.

LETTA. I gotta get up very early tomorrow. I got jury duty. I'm so excited! Were you fellows ever on a jury?

BIFF. No, but I been in front of them! (*The girls laugh.*) This is my father.

LETTA. Isn't he cute? Sit down with us, Pop.

HAPPY. Sit him down, Biff!

BIFF (*going to him*). Come on, slugger, drink us under the table. To hell with it! Come on, sit down, pal.

On BIFF's *last insistence,* WILLY *is about to sit.*

THE WOMAN (*now urgently*). Willy, are you going to answer the door!

THE WOMAN's *call pulls* WILLY *back. He starts right, befuddled.*

BIFF. Hey, where are you going?

WILLY. Open the door.

BIFF. The door?

WILLY. The washroom ... the door ... where's the door?

BIFF (*leading* WILLY *to the left*). Just go straight down.

WILLY *moves left.*

THE WOMAN. Willy, Willy, are you going to get up, get up, get up, get up?

WILLY *exits left.*

LETTA. I think it's sweet you bring your daddy along.

MISS FORSYTHE. Oh, he isn't really your father!

BIFF (*at left, turning to her resentfully*). Miss Forsythe, you've just seen a prince walk by. A fine, troubled prince. A hardworking, unappreciated prince. A pal, you understand? A good companion. Always for his boys.

LETTA. That's so sweet.

HAPPY. Well, girls, what's the program? We're wasting time. Come on, Biff. Gather round. Where would you like to go?

BIFF. Why don't you do something for him?

HAPPY. Me!

BIFF. Don't you give a damn for him, Hap?

HAPPY. What're you talking about? I'm the one who ...

BIFF. I sense it, you don't give a good goddam about him. (*He takes the rolled-up hose from his pocket and puts it on the table in front of* HAPPY.) Look what I found in the cellar, for Christ's sake. How can you bear to let it go on?

HAPPY. Me? Who goes away? Who runs off and . . .

BIFF. Yeah, but he doesn't mean anything to you. You could help him—I can't! Don't you understand what I'm talking about? He's going to kill himself, don't you know that?

HAPPY. Don't I know it! Me!

BIFF. Hap, help him! Jesus . . . help him . . . Help me, help me, I can't bear to look at his face! (*Ready to weep, he hurries out, up right.*)

HAPPY (*starting after him*). Where are you going?

MISS FORSYTHE. What's he so mad about?

HAPPY. Come on, girls, we'll catch up with him.

MISS FORSYTHE (*as* HAPPY *pushes her out*). Say, I don't like that temper of his!

HAPPY. He's just a little overstrung, he'll be all right!

WILLY (*off left, as* THE WOMAN *laughs*). Don't answer! Don't answer!

LETTA. Don't you want to tell your father . . .

HAPPY. No, that's not my father. He's just a guy. Come on, we'll catch Biff, and, honey, we're going to paint this town! Stanley, where's the check! Hey, Stanley!

They exit. STANLEY *looks toward left.*

STANLEY (*calling to* HAPPY *indignantly*). Mr. Loman! Mr. Loman!

STANLEY *picks up a chair and follows them off. Knocking is heard off left.* THE WOMAN *enters, laughing.* WILLY *follows her. She is in a black slip; he is buttoning his shirt. Raw, sensuous music accompanies their speech.*

WILLY. Will you stop laughing? Will you stop?

THE WOMAN. Aren't you going to answer the door? He'll wake the whole hotel.

WILLY. I'm not expecting anybody.

THE WOMAN. Whyn't you have another drink, honey, and stop being so damn self-centered?

WILLY. I'm so lonely.

THE WOMAN. You know you ruined me, Willy? From now on, whenever you come to the office, I'll see that you go right through to the buyers. No waiting at my desk anymore, Willy. You ruined me.

WILLY. That's nice of you to say that.

THE WOMAN. Gee, you are self-centered! Why so sad? You are the saddest, self-centeredest soul I ever did see-saw. (*She laughs. He kisses her.*) Come on inside, drummer boy. It's silly to be dressing in the middle of the night. (*As knocking is heard.*) Aren't you going to answer the door?

WILLY. They're knocking on the wrong door.

THE WOMAN. But I felt the knocking. And he heard us talking in here. Maybe the hotel's on fire!

WILLY (*his terror rising*). It's a mistake.

THE WOMAN. Then tell him to go away!

WILLY. There's nobody there.

THE WOMAN. It's getting on my nerves, Willy. There's somebody standing out there and it's getting on my nerves!

WILLY (*pushing her away from him*). All right, stay in the bathroom here, and don't come out. I think there's a law in Massachusetts about it, so don't come out. It may be that new room clerk. He looked very mean. So don't come out. It's a mistake, there's no fire.

The knocking is heard again. He takes a few steps away from her, and she vanishes into the wing. The light follows him, and now he is facing YOUNG BIFF, *who carries a suitcase.* BIFF *steps toward him. The music is gone.*

BIFF. Why didn't you answer?

WILLY. Biff! What are you doing in Boston?

BIFF. Why didn't you answer? I've been knocking for five minutes, I called you on the phone . . .

WILLY. I just heard you. I was in the bathroom and had the door shut. Did anything happen home?

BIFF. Dad—I let you down.

WILLY. What do you mean?

BIFF. Dad . . .

WILLY. Biffo, what's this about? (*Putting his arm around* BIFF.) Come on, let's go downstairs and get you a malted.

BIFF. Dad, I flunked math.

WILLY. Not for the term?

BIFF. The term. I haven't got enough credits to graduate.

WILLY. You mean to say Bernard wouldn't give you the answers?

BIFF. He did, he tried, but I only got a sixty-one.

WILLY. And they wouldn't give you four points?

BIFF. Birnbaum refused absolutely. I begged him, Pop, but he won't give me those points. You gotta talk to him before they close the school. Because if he saw the kind of man you are, and you just talked to him in your way, I'm sure he'd come through for me. The class came right before practice, see, and I didn't go enough. Would you talk to him? He'd like you, Pop. You know the way you could talk.

WILLY. You're on. We'll drive right back.

BIFF. Oh, Dad, good work! I'm sure he'll change it for you!

WILLY. Go downstairs and tell the clerk I'm checkin' out. Go right down.

BIFF. Yes, sir! See, the reason he hates me, Pop—one day he was late for class so I got up at the blackboard and imitated him. I crossed my eyes and talked with a lithp.

WILLY (*laughing*). You did? The kids like it?

BIFF. They nearly died laughing!

WILLY. Yeah? What'd you do?

BIFF. The thquare root of thixthy twee is . . . (WILLY *bursts out laughing;* BIFF *joins.*) And in the middle of it he walked in!

WILLY *laughs and* THE WOMAN *joins in offstage.*

WILLY (*without hesitation*). Hurry downstairs and . . .

BIFF. Somebody in there?

WILLY. No, that was next door.

THE WOMAN *laughs offstage.*

BIFF. Somebody got in your bathroom!

WILLY. No, it's the next room, there's a party . . .

THE WOMAN (*enters, laughing; she lisps this*). Can I come in? There's something in the bathtub, Willy, and it's moving!

WILLY *looks at* BIFF, *who is staring open-mouthed and horrified at* THE WOMAN.

WILLY. Ah—you better go back to your room. They must be finished painting by now. They're painting her room so I let her take a shower here. Go back, go back . . . (*He pushes her.*)

THE WOMAN (*resisting*). But I've got to get dressed, Willy, I can't . . .

WILLY. Get out of here! Go back, go back . . . (*Suddenly striving for the ordinary.*) This is Miss Francis, Biff, she's a buyer. They're painting her room. Go back, Miss Francis, go back . . .

THE WOMAN. But my clothes, I can't go out naked in the hall!

WILLY (*pushing her offstage*). Get outa here! Go back, go back!

(BIFF *slowly sits down on his suitcase as the argument continues offstage.*)

THE WOMAN. Where's my stockings? You promised me stockings, Willy!

WILLY. I have no stockings here!

THE WOMAN. You had two boxes of size nine sheers for me, and I want them!

WILLY. Here, for God's sake, will you get outa here!

THE WOMAN (*enters holding a box of stockings*). I just hope there's nobody in the hall. That's all I hope. (*To* BIFF.) Are you football or baseball?

BIFF. Football.

THE WOMAN (*angry, humiliated*). That's me too. G'night. (*She snatches her clothes from* WILLY, *and walks out.*)

WILLY (*after a pause*). Well, better get going. I want to get to the school first thing in the morning. Get my suits out of the closet. I'll get my valise. (BIFF *doesn't move.*) What's the matter! (BIFF *remains motionless, tears falling.*) She's a buyer. Buys for J. H. Simmons. She lives down the hall—they're painting. You don't imagine—(*He breaks off. After a pause.*) Now listen, pal, she's just a buyer. She sees merchandise in her room and they have to keep it looking just so . . . (*Pause. Assuming command.*) All right, get my suits. (BIFF *doesn't move.*) Now stop crying and do as I say. I gave you an order. Biff, I gave you an order! Is that what you do when I give you an order? How dare you cry! (*Putting his arm around* BIFF.) Now look, Biff, when you grow up you'll understand about these things. You mustn't—you mustn't overemphasize a thing like this. I'll see Birnbaum first thing in the morning.

BIFF. Never mind.

WILLY (*getting down beside* BIFF). Never mind! He's going to give you those points. I'll see to it.

BIFF. He wouldn't listen to you.

WILLY. He certainly will listen to me. You need those points for the U. of Virginia.

BIFF. I'm not going there.

WILLY. Heh? If I can't get him to change that mark you'll make it up in summer school. You've got all summer to . . .

BIFF (*his weeping breaking from him*). Dad . . .

WILLY (*infected by it*). Oh, my boy . . .

BIFF. Dad . . .

WILLY. She's nothing to me, Biff. I was lonely, I was terribly lonely.

BIFF. You—you gave her Mama's stockings! (*His tears break through and he rises to go.*)

WILLY (*grabbing for* BIFF). I gave you an order!

BIFF. Don't touch me, you—liar!

WILLY. Apologize for that!

BIFF. You fake! You phony little fake! You fake! (*Overcome, he turns quickly and weeping fully goes out with his suitcase.* WILLY *is left on the floor on his knees.*)

WILLY. I gave you an order! Biff, come back here or I'll beat you! Come back here! I'll whip you!

STANLEY *comes quickly in from the right and stands in front of* WILLY.

WILLY (*shouts at* STANLEY). I gave you an order . . .

STANLEY. Hey, let's pick it up, pick it up, Mr. Loman. (*He helps* WILLY *to his feet.*) Your boys left with the chippies. They said they'll see you home.

A second waiter watches some distance away.

WILLY. But we were supposed to have dinner together.

Music is heard, WILLY*'s theme.*

STANLEY. Can you make it?

WILLY. I'll—sure, I can make it. (*Suddenly concerned about his clothes.*) Do I—I look all right?

STANLEY. Sure, you look all right. (*He flicks a speck off* WILLY*'s lapel.*)

WILLY. Here—here's a dollar.

STANLEY. Oh, your son paid me. It's all right.

WILLY (*putting it in* STANLEY*'s hand*). No, take it. You're a good boy.

STANLEY. Oh, no, you don't have to . . .

WILLY. Here—here's some more, I don't need it any more. (*After a slight pause.*) Tell me—is there a seed store in the neighborhood?

STANLEY. Seeds? You mean like to plant?

As WILLY *turns,* STANLEY *slips the money back into his jacket pocket.*

WILLY. Yes. Carrots, peas . . .

STANLEY. Well, there's hardware stores on Sixth Avenue, but it may be too late now.

WILLY (*anxiously*). Oh, I'd better hurry. I've got to get some seeds. (*He starts off to the right.*) I've got to get some seeds, right away. Nothing's planted. I don't have a thing in the ground.

WILLY *hurries out as the light goes down.* STANLEY *moves over to the right after him, watches him off. The other waiter has been staring at* WILLY.

STANLEY (*to the waiter*). Well, whatta you looking at?

The waiter picks up the chairs and moves off right. STANLEY *takes the table and follows him. The light fades on this area. There is a long pause, the sound of the flute coming over. The light gradually rises on the kitchen, which is empty.* HAPPY *appears at the door of the house, followed by* BIFF. HAPPY *is carrying a large bunch of long-stemmed roses. He enters the kitchen, looks around for* LINDA. *Not seeing her, he turns to* BIFF, *who is just outside the house door, and makes a gesture with his hands, indicating "Not here, I guess." He looks into the living room and freezes. Inside,* LINDA, *unseen, is seated,* WILLY's *coat on her lap. She rises ominously and quietly and moves toward* HAPPY, *who backs up into the kitchen, afraid.*

HAPPY. Hey, what're you doing up? (LINDA *says nothing but moves toward him implacably.*) Where's Pop? (*He keeps backing to the right, and now* LINDA *is in full view in the doorway to the living room.*) Is he sleeping?

LINDA. Where were you?

HAPPY (*trying to laugh it off*). We met two girls, Mom, very fine types. Here, we brought you some flowers. (*Offering them to her.*) Put them in your room, Ma.

She knocks them to the floor at BIFF's *feet. He has now come inside and closed the door behind him. She stares at* BIFF, *silent.*

HAPPY. Now what'd you do that for? Mom, I want you to have some flowers . . .

LINDA (*cutting* HAPPY *off, violently to* BIFF). Don't you care whether he lives or dies?

HAPPY (*going to the stairs*). Come upstairs, Biff.

BIFF (*with a flare of disgust, to* HAPPY). Go away from me! (*To* LINDA.) What do you mean, lives or dies? Nobody's dying around here, pal.

LINDA. Get out of my sight! Get out of here!

BIFF. I wanna see the boss.

LINDA. You're not going near him!

BIFF. Where is he? (*He moves into the living room and* LINDA *follows.*)

LINDA (*shouting after* BIFF). You invite him for dinner. He looks forward to it all day—(BIFF *appears in his parents' bedroom, looks around, and exits*)—and then you desert him there. There's no stranger you'd do that to!

HAPPY. Why? He had a swell time with us. Listen, when I—(LINDA *comes back into the kitchen*)—desert him I hope I don't outlive the day!

LINDA. Get out of here!

HAPPY. Now look, Mom . . .

LINDA. Did you have to go to women tonight? You and your lousy rotten whores!

BIFF *re-enters the kitchen.*

HAPPY. Mom, all we did was follow Biff around trying to cheer him up! (*To* BIFF.) Boy, what a night you gave me!

LINDA. Get out of here, both of you, and don't come back! I don't want you tormenting him any more. Go on now, get your things together! (*To* BIFF.) You can sleep in his apartment. (*She starts to pick up the flowers and stops herself.*) Pick up this stuff, I'm not your maid any more. Pick it up, you bum, you!

HAPPY *turns his back to her in refusal.* BIFF *slowly moves over and gets down on his knees, picking up the flowers.*

LINDA. You're a pair of animals! Not one, not another living soul would have had the cruelty to walk out on that man in a restaurant!

BIFF (*not looking at her*). Is that what he said?

LINDA. He didn't have to say anything. He was so humiliated he nearly limped when he came in.

HAPPY. But, Mom, he had a great time with us ...

BIFF (*cutting him off violently*). Shut up!

Without another word, HAPPY *goes upstairs.*

LINDA. You! You didn't even go in to see if he was all right!

BIFF (*still on the floor in front of* LINDA, *the flowers in his hand; with self-loathing*). No. Didn't. Didn't do a damned thing. How do you like that, heh? Left him babbling in a toilet.

LINDA. You louse. You ...

BIFF. Now you hit it on the nose! (*He gets up, throws the flowers in the wastebasket.*) The scum of the earth, and you're looking at him!

LINDA. Get out of here!

BIFF. I gotta talk to the boss, Mom. Where is he?

LINDA. You're not going near him. Get out of this house!

BIFF (*with absolute assurance, determination*). No. We're gonna have an abrupt conversation, him and me.

LINDA. You're not talking to him.

Hammering is heard from outside the house, off right. BIFF *turns toward the noise.*

LINDA (*suddenly pleading*). Will you please leave him alone?

BIFF. What's he doing out there?

LINDA. He's planting the garden!

BIFF (*quietly*). Now? Oh, my God!

BIFF *moves outside,* LINDA *following. The light dies down on them and comes up on the center of the apron as* WILLY *walks into it. He is carrying a flashlight, a hoe, and a handful of seed packets. He raps the top of the hoe sharply to fix it firmly, and then moves to the left, measuring off the distance with his foot. He holds the flashlight to look at the seed packets, reading off the instructions. He is in the blue of night.*

WILLY. Carrots ... quarter-inch apart. Rows ... one-foot rows. (*He measures it off.*) One foot. (*He puts down a package and measures off.*) Beets. (*He puts down another package and measures again.*) Lettuce. (*He reads the package, puts it down.*) One foot—(*He breaks off as* BEN *appears at the right and moves slowly down to him.*) What a proposition, ts, ts. Terrific, terrific. 'Cause she's suffered, Ben, the woman has suffered. You understand me? A man can't go out the way he came in, Ben, a man has got to add up to something. You can't, you can't—(BEN *moves toward him as though to interrupt.*) You gotta consider now. Don't answer so quick. Remember, it's a guaranteed twenty-thousand-dollar proposition. Now look, Ben, I want you to go through the ins and outs of this thing with me. I've got nobody to talk to, Ben, and the woman has suffered, you hear me?

BEN (*standing still, considering*). What's the proposition?

WILLY. It's twenty thousand dollars on the barrelhead. Guaranteed, gilt-edged, you understand?

BEN. You don't want to make a fool of yourself. They might not honor the policy.

WILLY. How can they dare refuse? Didn't I work like a coolie to meet every premium on the nose? And now they don't pay off? Impossible!

BEN. It's called a cowardly thing, William.

WILLY. Why? Does it take more guts to stand here the rest of my life ringing up a zero?

BEN (*yielding*). That's a point, William. (*He moves, thinking, turns.*) And twenty thousand—that is something one can feel with the hand, it is there.

WILLY (*now assured, with rising power*). Oh, Ben, that's the whole beauty of it! I see it like a diamond, shining in the dark, hard and rough, that I can pick up and touch in my hand. Not like—like an appointment! This would not be another damned-fool appointment, Ben, and it changes all the aspects. Because he thinks I'm nothing, see, and so he spites me. But the funeral . . . (*Straightening up.*) Ben, that funeral will be massive! They'll come from Maine, Massachusetts, Vermont, New Hampshire! All the old-timers with the strange license plates—that boy will be thunderstruck, Ben, because he never realized—I am known! Rhode Island, New York, New Jersey—I am known, Ben, and he'll see it with his eyes once and for all. He'll see what I am, Ben! He's in for a shock, that boy!

BEN (*coming down to the edge of the garden*). He'll call you a coward.

WILLY (*suddenly fearful*). No, that would be terrible.

BEN. Yes. And a damned fool.

WILLY. No, no, he mustn't, I won't have that! (*He is broken and desperate.*)

BEN. He'll hate you, William.

The gay music of the Boys is heard.

WILLY. Oh, Ben, how do we get back to all the great times? Used to be so full of light, and comradeship, the sleigh-riding in winter, and the ruddiness on his cheeks. And always some kind of good news coming up, always something nice coming up ahead. And never even let me carry the valises in the house, and simonizing, simonizing that little red car! Why, why can't I give him something and not have him hate me?

BEN. Let me think about it. (*He glances at his watch.*) I still have a little time. Remarkable proposition, but you've got to be sure you're not making a fool of yourself.

BEN *drifts off upstage and goes out of sight.* BIFF *comes down from the left.*

WILLY (*suddenly conscious of* BIFF, *turns and looks up at him, then begins picking up the packages of seeds in confusion*). Where the hell is that seed? (*Indignantly.*) You can't see nothing out here! They boxed in the whole goddam neighborhood!

BIFF. There are people all around here. Don't you realize that?

WILLY. I'm busy. Don't bother me.

BIFF (*taking the hoe from* WILLY). I'm saying good-by to you, Pop. (WILLY *looks at him, silent, unable to move.*) I'm not coming back any more.

WILLY. You're not going to see Oliver tomorrow?

BIFF. I've got no appointment, Dad.

WILLY. He put his arm around you, and you've got no appointment?

BIFF. Pop, get this now, will you? Everytime I've left it's been a—fight that sent me out of here. Today I realized something about myself and I tried to explain it to you and I—I think I'm just not smart enough to make any sense out of it for you. To hell with whose fault it is or anything like that. (*He takes* WILLY's *arm.*) Let's just wrap it up, heh? Come on in, we'll tell Mom. (*He gently tries to pull* WILLY *to left.*)

WILLY (*frozen, immobile, with guilt in his voice*). No, I don't want to see her.

BIFF. Come on! (*He pulls again, and* WILLY *tries to pull away.*)

WILLY (*highly nervous*). No, no, I don't want to see her.

BIFF (*tries to look into* WILLY's *face, as if to find the answer there*). Why don't you want to see her?

WILLY (*more harshly now*). Don't bother me, will you?

BIFF. What do you mean, you don't want to see her? You don't want them calling you yellow, do you? This isn't your fault; it's me, I'm a bum. Now come inside! (WILLY *strains to get away.*) Did you hear what I said to you?

WILLY *pulls away and quickly goes by himself into the house.* BIFF *follows.*

LINDA (*to* WILLY). Did you plant, dear?

BIFF (*at the door; to* LINDA). All right, we had it out. I'm going and I'm not writing any more.

LINDA (*going to* WILLY *in the kitchen*). I think that's the best way, dear. 'Cause there's no use drawing it out, you'll just never get along.

WILLY *doesn't respond.*

BIFF. People ask where I am and what I'm doing, you don't know, and you don't care. That way it'll be off your mind and you can start brightening up again. All right? That clears it, doesn't it? (WILLY *is silent, and* BIFF *goes to him.*) You gonna wish me luck, scout? (*He extends his hand.*) What do you say?

LINDA. Shake his hand, Willy.

WILLY (*turning to her, seething with hurt*). There's no necessity—to mention the pen at all, y'know.

BIFF (*gently*). I've got no appointment, Dad.

WILLY (*erupting fiercely*). He put his arm around . . . ?

BIFF. Dad, you're never going to see what I am, so what's the use of arguing? If I strike oil I'll send you a check. Meantime forget I'm alive.

WILLY (*to* LINDA). Spite, see?

BIFF. Shake hands, Dad.

WILLY. Not my hand.

BIFF. I was hoping not to go this way.

WILLY. Well, this is the way you're going. Good-by.

BIFF *looks at him a moment, then turns sharply and goes to the stairs.*

WILLY (*stops him with*). May you rot in hell if you leave this house!

BIFF (*turning*). Exactly what is it that you want from me?

WILLY. I want you to know, on the train, in the mountains, in the valleys, wherever you go, that you cut down your life for spite!

BIFF. No, no.

WILLY. Spite, spite, is the word of your undoing! And when you're down and out, remember what did it. When you're rotting somewhere beside the railroad tracks, remember, and don't you dare blame it on me!

BIFF. I'm not blaming it on you!

WILLY. I won't take the rap for this, you hear?

HAPPY *comes down the stairs and stands on the bottom step, watching.*

BIFF. That's just what I'm telling you!

WILLY (*sinking into a chair at a table, with full accusation*). You're trying to put a knife in me—don't think I don't know what you're doing!

BIFF. All right, phony! Then let's lay it on the line. (*He whips the rubber tube out of his pocket and puts it on the table.*)

HAPPY. You crazy . . .

LINDA. Biff! (*She moves to grab the hose, but* BIFF *holds it down with his hand.*)

BIFF. Leave it there! Don't move it!

WILLY (*not looking at it*). What is that?

BIFF. You know goddam well what that is.

WILLY (*caged, wanting to escape*). I never saw that.

BIFF. You saw it. The mice didn't bring it into the cellar! What is this supposed to do, make a hero out of you? This supposed to make me sorry for you?

WILLY. Never heard of it.

BIFF. There'll be no pity for you, you hear it? No pity!

WILLY (*to* LINDA). You hear the spite!

BIFF. No, you're going to hear the truth—what you are and what I am!

LINDA. Stop it!

WILLY. Spite!

HAPPY (*coming down toward* BIFF). You cut it now!

BIFF (*to* HAPPY). The man don't know who we are! The man is gonna know! (*To* WILLY.) We never told the truth for ten minutes in this house!

HAPPY. We always told the truth!

BIFF (*turning on him*). You big blow, are you the assistant buyer? You're one of the two assistants to the assistant, aren't you?

HAPPY. Well, I'm practically . . .

BIFF. You're practically full of it! We all are! and I'm through with it. (*To* WILLY.) Now hear this, Willy, this is me.

WILLY. I know you!

BIFF. You know why I had no address for three months? I stole a suit in Kansas City and I was in jail. (*To* LINDA, *who is sobbing.*) Stop crying. I'm through with it.

LINDA *turns away from them, her hands covering her face.*

WILLY. I suppose that's my fault!

BIFF. I stole myself out of every good job since high school!

WILLY. And whose fault is that?

BIFF. And I never got anywhere because you blew me so full of hot air I could never stand taking orders from anybody! That's whose fault it is!

WILLY. I hear that!

LINDA. Don't, Biff!

BIFF. It's goddam time you heard that! I had to be boss big shot in two weeks, and I'm through with it!

WILLY. Then hang yourself! For spite, hang yourself!

BIFF. No! Nobody's hanging himself, Willy! I ran down eleven flights with a pen in my hand today. And suddenly I stopped, you hear me? And in the middle of that office building, do you hear this? I stopped in the middle of that building and I saw—the sky. I saw the things that I love in this world. The work and the food and time to sit and smoke. And I looked at the pen and said to myself, what the hell am I grabbing this for? Why am I trying to become what I don't want to be? What am I doing in an office, making a contemptuous, begging fool of myself, when all I want is out there, waiting for me the minute I say I know who I am! Why can't I say that, Willy? (*He tries to make* WILLY *face him, but* WILLY *pulls away and moves to the left.*)

WILLY (*with hatred, threateningly*). The door of your life is wide open!

BIFF. Pop! I'm a dime a dozen, and so are you!

WILLY (*turning on him now in an uncontrolled outburst*). I am not a dime a dozen! I am Willy Loman, and you are Biff Loman!

BIFF *starts for* WILLY, *but is blocked by* HAPPY. *In his fury,* BIFF *seems on the verge of attacking his father.*

BIFF. I am not a leader of men, Willy, and neither are you. You were never anything but a hard-working drummer who landed in the ash can like all the rest of them! I'm one dollar an hour, Willy! I tried seven states and couldn't raise it. A buck an hour! Do you gather my meaning? I'm not bringing home any prizes any more, and you're going to stop waiting for me to bring them home!

WILLY (*directly to* BIFF). You vengeful, spiteful mutt!

BIFF *breaks from* HAPPY. WILLY, *in fright, starts up the stairs.* BIFF *grabs him.*

BIFF (*at the peak of his fury*). Pop! I'm nothing! I'm nothing, Pop. Can't you understand that? There's no spite in it any more. I'm just what I am, that's all.

BIFF*'s fury has spent itself and he breaks down, sobbing, holding on to* WILLY, *who dumbly fumbles for* BIFF*'s face.*

WILLY (*astonished*). What're you doing? What're you doing? (*To* LINDA.) Why is he crying?

BIFF (*crying, broken*). Will you let me go, for Christ's sake? Will you take that phony dream and burn it before something happens? (*Struggling to contain himself he pulls away and moves to the stairs.*) I'll go in the morning. Put him—put him to bed. (*Exhausted,* BIFF *moves up the stairs to his room.*)

WILLY (*after a long pause, astonished, elevated*). Isn't that—isn't that remarkable? Biff—he likes me!

LINDA. He loves you, Willy!

HAPPY (*deeply moved*). Always did, Pop.

WILLY. Oh, Biff! (*Staring wildly.*) He cried! Cried to me. (*He is choking with his love, and now cries out his promise.*) That boy—that boy is going to be magnificent!

BEN *appears in the light just outside the kitchen.*

BEN.   Yes, outstanding, with twenty thousand behind him.

LINDA (*sensing the racing of his mind, fearfully, carefully.*) Now come to bed, Willy. It's all settled now.

WILLY (*finding it difficult not to rush out of the house*). Yes, we'll sleep. Come on. Go to sleep, Hap.

BEN.   And it does take a great kind of a man to crack the jungle.

In accents of dread, BEN's *idyllic music starts up.*

HAPPY (*his arm around* LINDA). I'm getting married, Pop, don't forget it. I'm changing everything. I'm gonna run that department before the year is up. You'll see, Mom. (*He kisses her.*)

BEN.   The jungle is dark but full of diamonds, Willy.

WILLY *turns, moves, listening to* BEN.

LINDA.   Be good. You're both good boys, just act that way, that's all.

HAPPY.   'Night, Pop. (*He goes upstairs.*)

LINDA (*to* WILLY).   Come, dear.

BEN (*with greater force*).   One must go in to fetch a diamond out.

WILLY (*to* LINDA, *as he moves slowly along the edge of the kitchen, toward the door*).   I just want to get settled down, Linda. Let me sit alone for a little.

LINDA (*almost uttering her fear*).   I want you upstairs.

WILLY (*taking her in his arms*).   In a few minutes, Linda. I couldn't sleep right now. Go on, you look awful tired. (*He kisses her.*)

BEN.   Not like an appointment at all. A diamond is rough and hard to the touch.

WILLY.   Go on now. I'll be right up.

LINDA.   I think this is the only way, Willy.

WILLY.   Sure, it's the best thing.

BEN.   Best thing!

WILLY.   The only way. Everything is gonna be—go on, kid, get to bed. You look so tired.

LINDA.   Come right up.

WILLY.   Two minutes.

LINDA *goes into the living room, then reappears in her bedroom.* WILLY *moves just outside the kitchen door.*

WILLY.   Loves me. (*Wonderingly.*) Always loved me. Isn't that a remarkable thing? Ben, he'll worship me for it!

BEN (*with promise*).   It's dark there, but full of diamonds.

WILLY.   Can you imagine that magnificence with twenty thousand dollars in his pocket?

LINDA (*calling from her room*).   Willy! Come up!

WILLY (*calling into the kitchen*).   Yes! Yes. Coming! It's very smart, you realize that, don't you, sweetheart? Even Ben sees it. I gotta go, baby. 'By! 'By! (*Going over to* BEN, *almost dancing.*) Imagine? When the mail comes he'll be ahead of Bernard again!

BEN.   A perfect proposition all around.

WILLY.   Did you see how he cried to me? Oh, if I could kiss him, Ben!

BEN.   Time, William, time!

WILLY. Oh, Ben, I always knew one way or another we were gonna make it, Biff and I.

BEN (*looking at his watch*). The boat. We'll be late. (*He moves slowly off into the darkness.*)

WILLY (*elegiacally, turning to the house*). Now when you kick off, boy, I want a seventy-yard boot, and get right down the field under the ball, and when you hit, hit low and hit hard, because it's important, boy. (*He swings around and faces the audience.*) There's all kinds of important people in the stands, and the first thing you know . . . (*Suddenly realizing he is alone.*) Ben! Ben, where do I . . . ? (*He makes a sudden movement of search.*) Ben, how do I . . . ?

LINDA (*calling*). Willy, you coming up?

WILLY (*uttering a gasp of fear, whirling about as if to quiet her*). Sh! (*He turns around as if to find his way; sounds, faces, voices, seem to be swarming in upon him and he flicks at them, crying.*) Sh! Sh! (*Suddenly music, faint and high, stops him. It rises in intensity, almost to an unbearable scream. He goes up and down on his toes, and rushes off around the house.*) Shhh!

LINDA. Willy?

There is no answer. LINDA *waits.* BIFF *gets up off his bed. He is still in his clothes.* HAPPY *sits up.* BIFF *stands listening.*

LINDA (*with real fear*). Willy, answer me! Willy!

There is the sound of a car starting and moving away at full speed.

LINDA. No!

BIFF (*rushing down the stairs*). Pop!

As the car speeds off the music crashes down in a frenzy of sound, which becomes the soft pulsation of a single cello string. BIFF *slowly returns to his bedroom. He and* HAPPY *gravely don their jackets.* LINDA *slowly walks out of her room. The music has developed into a dead march. The leaves of day are appearing over everything.* CHARLEY *and* BERNARD, *somberly dressed, appear and knock on the kitchen door.* BIFF *and* HAPPY *slowly descend the stairs to the kitchen as* CHARLEY *and* BERNARD *enter. All stop a moment when* LINDA, *in clothes of mourning, bearing a little bunch of roses, comes through the draped doorway into the kitchen. She goes to* CHARLEY *and takes his arm. Now all move toward the audience, through the wall-line of the kitchen. At the limit of the apron,* LINDA *lays down the flowers, kneels, and sits back on her heels. All stare down at the grave.*

Requiem

CHARLEY. It's getting dark, Linda.

LINDA *doesn't react. She stares at the grave.*

BIFF. How about it, Mom? Better get some rest, heh? They'll be closing the gate soon.

LINDA *makes no move. Pause.*

HAPPY (*deeply angered*). He had no right to do that. There was no necessity for it. We would've helped him.

CHARLEY (*grunting*). Hmmm.

BIFF. Come along, Mom.

LINDA. Why didn't anybody come?

CHARLEY. It was a very nice funeral.

LINDA. But where are all the people he knew? Maybe they blame him.

CHARLEY. Naa. It's a rough world, Linda. They wouldn't blame him.

LINDA. I can't understand it. At this time especially. First time in thirty-five years we were just about free and clear. He only needed a little salary. He was even finished with the dentist.

CHARLEY. No man only needs a little salary.

LINDA. I can't understand it.

BIFF. There were a lot of nice days. When he'd come home from a trip; or on Sundays, making the stoop; finishing the cellar; putting on the new porch; when he built the extra bathroom; and put up the garage. You know something, Charley, there's more of him in that front stoop than in all the sales he ever made.

CHARLEY. Yeah. He was a happy man with a batch of cement.

LINDA. He was so wonderful with his hands.

BIFF. He had the wrong dreams. All, all, wrong.

HAPPY (*almost ready to fight* BIFF). Don't say that!

BIFF. He never knew who he was.

CHARLEY (*stopping* HAPPY's *movement and reply; to* BIFF). Nobody dast blame this man. You don't understand: Willy was a salesman. And for a salesman, there is no rock bottom to the life. He don't put a bolt to a nut, he don't tell you the law or give you medicine. He's a man way out there in the blue, riding on a smile and a shoeshine. And when they start not smiling back—that's an earthquake. And then you get yourself a couple of spots on your hat, and you're finished. Nobody dast blame this man. A salesman is got to dream, boy. It comes with the territory.

BIFF. Charley, the man didn't know who he was.

HAPPY (*infuriated*). Don't say that!

BIFF. Why don't you come with me, Happy?

HAPPY. I'm not licked that easily. I'm staying right in this city, and I'm gonna beat this racket! (*He looks at* BIFF, *his chin set.*) The Loman Brothers!

BIFF. I know who I am, kid.

HAPPY. All right, boy. I'm gonna show you and everybody else that Willy Loman did not die in vain. He had a good dream. It's the only dream you can have—to come out number-one man. He fought it out here, and this is where I'm gonna win it for him.

BIFF (*with a hopeless glance at* HAPPY, *bends toward his mother*). Let's go, Mom.

LINDA. I'll be with you in a minute. Go on, Charley. (*He hesitates.*) I want to, just for a minute. I never had a chance to say good-by.

CHARLEY *moves away, followed by* HAPPY. BIFF *remains a slight distance up and left of* LINDA. *She sits there, summoning herself. The flute begins, not far away, playing behind her speech.*

LINDA. Forgive me, dear. I can't cry. I don't know what it is, but I can't cry. I don't understand it. Why did you ever do that? Help me, Willy, I can't cry. It seems to me that you're just on another trip. I keep expecting you. Willy, dear, I can't cry. Why did you do it? I search and search and I search, and I can't understand it, Willy. I made the last payment on the house today. Today, dear. And there'll be nobody home. (*A sob rises in her throat.*) We're free and clear. (*Sobbing mournfully, released.*) We're free. (BIFF *comes slowly toward her.*) We're free ... We're free ...

BIFF *lifts her to her feet and moves out up right with her in his arms.* LINDA *sobs quietly.* BERNARD *and* CHARLEY *come together and follow them, followed by* HAPPY. *Only the music of the flute is left on the darkening stage as over the house the hard towers of the apartment buildings rise into sharp focus and the curtain falls.*

YOUR TURN

The Play on the Page

1. Arthur Miller said in the *New York Times* (27 February 1949, Sec. II, p. 1) that tragedy shows man's struggle to secure "his sense of personal dignity" and that "his destruction in the attempt posits a wrong or an evil in his environment." Does this make sense when applied to some earlier tragedy (for example, *Oedipus Rex* or *Hamlet*), and does it apply convincingly to *Death of a Salesman*? Is this the tragedy of an individual's own making? Or is society at fault for corrupting and exploiting Willy? Or both?

2. Is Willy pathetic rather than tragic? If pathetic, does this imply that the play is less worthy than if he is tragic?

3. Do you feel that Miller is straining too hard to turn a play about a little man into a big, impressive play? For example, do the musical themes, the unrealistic setting, the appearances of Ben, and the speech at the grave seem out of keeping in a play about the death of a salesman?

4. We don't know what Willy sells, and we don't know whether or not the insurance will be paid after his death. Do you consider these uncertainties to be faults in the play?

5. Is Howard a villain?

6. Characterize Linda.

The Play on the Stage

7. It is sometimes said that in this realistic play that includes symbolic and expressionistic elements, Biff and Happy can be seen as two aspects of Willy. In this view, Biff more or less represents Willy's spiritual needs, and Happy represents his materialism and his sexuality. If you were directing the play, would you adopt this point of view? Whatever your interpretation, how would you costume the brothers?

8. Although Miller envisioned Willy as a small man (literally small), the role was first performed by Lee J. Cobb, a large man. If you were casting the play, what actor would you select? Why? Whom would you choose for Linda, Biff, Happy, Bernard, and Charley?

9. Select roughly thirty lines of dialogue, and discuss the movements (gestures and blocking) that as a director you would suggest to the performers.

Contexts for *Death of a Salesman*

ARTHUR MILLER

The following essay appeared in the New York Times *in 1949, while* Death of a
Salesman *was running on Broadway.*

Tragedy and the Common Man   [1949]

In this age few tragedies are written. It has often been held that the lack is
due to a paucity of heroes among us, or else that modern man has had the
blood drawn out of his organs of belief by the skepticism of science, and the
heroic attack on life cannot feed on an attitude of reserve and, circumspec-
tion. For one reason or another, we are often held to be below tragedy—or
tragedy above us. The inevitable conclusion is, of course, that the tragic mode
is archaic, fit only for the very highly placed, the kings or the kingly, and
where this admission is not made in so many words it is most often implied.

I believe that the common man is as apt a subject for tragedy in its highest sense as kings were. On the face of it this ought to be obvious in the light
of modern psychiatry, which bases its analysis upon classic formulations, such
as the Oedipus and Orestes complexes, for instance, which were enacted by
royal beings, but which apply to everyone in similar emotional situations.

More simply, when the question of tragedy in art is not at issue, we
never hesitate to attribute to the well-placed and the exalted the very same
mental processes as the lowly. And finally, if the exaltation of tragic action
were truly a property of the high-bred character alone, it is inconceivable
that the mass of mankind should cherish tragedy above all other forms, let
alone be capable of understanding it.

As a general rule, to which there may be exceptions unknown to me,
I think the tragic feeling is evoked in us when we are in the presence of a
character who is ready to lay down his life, if need be, to secure one thing—
his sense of personal dignity. From Orestes to Hamlet, Medea to Macbeth,
the underlying struggle is that of the individual attempting to gain his "rightful" position in his society.

Sometimes he is one who has been displaced from it, sometimes one
who seeks to attain it for the first time, but the fateful wound from which
the inevitable events spiral is the wound of indignity, and its dominant force
is indignation. Tragedy, then, is the consequence of a man's total compulsion
to evaluate himself justly.

In the sense of having been initiated by the hero himself, the tale always
reveals what has been called his "tragic flaw," a failing that is not peculiar to
grand or elevated characters. Nor is it necessarily a weakness. The flaw, or
crack in the character, is really nothing—and need be nothing, but his inherent unwillingness to remain passive in the face of what he conceives to be a
challenge to his dignity, his image of his rightful status. Only the passive, only
those who accept their lot without active retaliation, are "flawless." Most of
us are in that category.

But there are among us today, as there always have been, those who act against the scheme of things that degrades them, and in the process of action everything we have accepted out of fear or insensitivity or ignorance is shaken before us and examined, and from this total onslaught by an individual against the seemingly stable cosmos surrounding us—from this total examination of the "unchangeable" environment—comes the terror and the fear that is classically associated with tragedy.

More important, from this total questioning of what has previously been unquestioned, we learn. And such a process is not beyond the common man. In revolutions around the world, these past thirty years, he has demonstrated again and again this inner dynamic of all tragedy.

Insistence upon the rank of the tragic hero, or the so-called nobility of his character, is really but a clinging to the outward forms of tragedy. If rank or nobility of character was indispensable, then it would follow that the problems of those with rank were the particular problems of tragedy. But surely the right of one monarch to capture the domain from another no longer raises our passions, nor are our concepts of justice what they were to the mind of an Elizabethan king.

The quality in such plays that does shake us, however, derives from the underlying fear of being displaced, the disaster inherent in being torn away from our chosen image of what and who we are in this world. Among us today this fear is as strong, and perhaps stronger, than it ever was. In fact, it is the common man who knows this fear best.

Now, if it is true that tragedy is the consequence of a man's total compulsion to evaluate himself justly, his destruction in the attempt posits a wrong or an evil in his environment. And this is precisely the morality of tragedy and its lesson. The discovery of the moral law, which is what the enlightenment of tragedy consists of, is not the discovery of some abstract or metaphysical quantity.

The tragic right is a condition of life, a condition in which the human personality is able to flower and realize itself. The wrong is the condition which suppresses man, perverts the flowing out of his love and creative instinct. Tragedy enlightens—and it must, in that it points the heroic finger at the enemy of man's freedom. The thrust for freedom is the quality in tragedy which exalts. The revolutionary questioning of the stable environment is what terrifies. In no way is the common man debarred from such thoughts or such actions.

Seen in this light, our lack of tragedy may be partially accounted for by the turn which modern literature has taken toward the purely psychiatric view of life, or the purely sociological. If all our miseries, our indignities, are born and bred within our minds, then all action, let alone the heroic action, is obviously impossible.

And if society alone is responsible for the cramping of our lives, then the protagonist must needs be so pure and faultless as to force us to deny his validity as a character. From neither of these views can tragedy derive, simply because neither represents a balanced concept of life. Above all else, tragedy requires the finest appreciation by the writer of cause and effect.

No tragedy can therefore come about when its author fears to question absolutely everything, when he regards any institution, habit or custom as being either everlasting, immutable or inevitable. In the tragic view the need of man to wholly realize himself is the only fixed star, and whatever it is that hedges his nature and lowers it is ripe for attack and examination. Which is not to say that tragedy must preach revolution.

The Greeks could probe the very heavenly origin of their ways and return to confirm the rightness of laws. And Job could face God in anger, demanding his right and end in submission. But for a moment everything is in suspension, nothing is accepted, and in this stretching and tearing apart of the cosmos, in the very action of so doing, the character gains "size," the tragic stature which is spuriously attached to the royal or the highborn in our minds. The commonest of men may take on that stature to the extent of his willingness to throw all he has into the contest, the battle to secure his rightful place in his world.

There is a misconception of tragedy with which I have been struck in review after review, and in many conversations with writers and readers alike. It is the idea that tragedy is of necessity allied to pessimism. Even the dictionary says nothing more about the word than that it means a story with a sad or unhappy ending. This impression is so firmly fixed that I almost hesitate to claim that in truth tragedy implies more optimism in its author than does comedy, and that its final result ought to be the reinforcement of the onlooker's brightest opinions of the human animal.

For, if it is true to say that in essence the tragic hero is intent upon claiming his whole due as a personality, and if this struggle must be total and without reservation, then it automatically demonstrates the indestructible will of man to achieve his humanity.

The possibility of victory must be there in tragedy. Where pathos rules, where pathos is finally derived, a character has fought a battle he could not possibly have won. The pathetic is achieved when the protagonist is, by virtue of his witlessness, his insensitivity or the very air he gives off, incapable of grappling with a much superior force.

Pathos truly is the mode for the pessimist. But tragedy requires a nicer balance between what is possible and what is impossible. And it is curious, although edifying, that the plays we revere, century after century, are the tragedies. In them, and in them alone, lies the belief—optimistic, if you will—in the perfectibility of man.

It is time, I think, that we who are without kings, took up this bright thread of our history and followed it to the only place it can possibly lead in our time—the heart and spirit of the average man.

BROOKS ATKINSON

This review of the opening night of Death of a Salesman *appeared in* The New York Times *on Feb. 10, 1949.*

[Review of Premier Performance of] Death of a Salesman

Arthur Miller has written a superb drama. From every point of view "Death of a Salesman," which was acted at the Morosco[1] last evening, is rich and

---

[1] **the Morosco** the Morosco is a theater in New York City.

memorable drama. It is so simple in style and so inevitable in theme that it scarcely seems like a thing that has been written and acted. For Mr. Miller has looked with compassion into the hearts of some ordinary Americans and quietly transferred their hope and anguish to the theatre. Under Elia Kazan's masterly direction, Lee J. Cobb gives a heroic performance, and every member of the cast plays like a person inspired.

Two seasons ago Mr. Miller's "All My Sons" looked like the work of an honest and able playwright. In comparison with the new drama, that seems like a contrived play now. For "Death of a Salesman" has the flow and spontaneity of a suburban epic that may not be intended as poetry but becomes poetry in spite of itself because Mr. Miller has drawn it out of so many intangible sources.

It is the story of an aging salesman who has reached the end of his usefulness on the road. There has always been something unsubstantial about his work. But suddenly the unsubstantial aspects of it overwhelm him completely. When he was young, he looked dashing; he enjoyed the comradeship of other people—the humor, the kidding, the business.

In his early sixties he knows his business as well as he ever did. But the unsubstantial things have become decisive; the spring has gone from his step, the smile from his face and the heartiness from his personality. He is through. The phantom of his life has caught up with him. As literally as Mr. Miller can say it, dust returns to dust. Suddenly there is nothing.

This is only a little of what Mr. Miller is saying. For he conveys this elusive tragedy in terms of simple things—the loyalty and understanding of his wife, the careless selfishness of his two sons, the sympathetic devotion of a neighbor, the coldness of his former boss' son—the bills, the car, the tinkering around the house. And most of all: the illusions by which he has lived—opportunities missed, wrong formulas for success, fatal misconceptions about his place in the scheme of things.

Writing like a man who understands people, Mr. Miller has no moral precepts to offer and no solutions of the salesman's problems. He is full of pity, but he brings no piety to it. Chronicler of one frowsy corner of the American scene, he evokes a wraithlike tragedy out of it that spins through the many scenes of his play and gradually envelops the audience.

As theatre, "Death of a Salesman" is no less original than it is as literature. Jo Mielziner, always equal to an occasion, has designed a skeletonized set that captures the mood of the play and serves the actors brilliantly. Although Mr. Miller's text may be diffuse in form, Mr. Kazan has pulled it together into a deeply moving performance.

Mr. Cobb's tragic portrait of the defeated salesman is acting of the first rank. Although it is familiar and folksy in the details, it has something of the grand manner in the big size and the deep tone. Mildred Dunnock gives the performance of her career as the wife and mother—plain of speech but indomitable in spirit. The parts of the thoughtless sons are extremely well played by Arthur Kennedy and Cameron Mitchell, who are all youth, brag and bewilderment.

Other parts are well played by Howard Smith, Thomas Chalmers, Don Keefer, Alan Hewitt and Tom Pedi. If there were time, this report would gratefully include all the actors and fabricators of illusion. For they all realize that for once in their lives they are participating in a rare event in the theatre. Mr. Miller's elegy of a Brooklyn sidestreet is superb.

MARY McCARTHY

This excerpt is from McCarthy's Introduction to Sights and Spectacles: Theatre Chronicles, 1937–56.

American Realistic Drama*

The typical character of the so-called American realist school belongs to the urban lower middle class sociologically, but biologically he is a member of some indeterminate lower order of primates. This creature is housed in a living-room filled with installment-plan furniture, some of which will be broken before the play is over. The sound of breakage and the sound of heavy breathing will signify "theatre." As directed by Elia Kazan, the whip-cracking ringmaster of this school of brutes, the hero is found standing with clenched fists, stage left, yelling at some member of his family, stage right, until one of them breaks into hysterical weeping and collapses onto a chair by the stage-center table, his great head buried in his hands. The weeping character is confessing to being alcoholic, homosexual, a failure.

Nobody anywhere has ever behaved like these people. This fact, somehow, is supposed to make them more "typical." A disturbing aspect of *Death of a Salesman* was that Willy Loman seemed to be Jewish, to judge by his speech-cadences, but there was no mention of this on the stage. He could not be Jewish because he had to be "America." All the living-rooms, backyards, stoops, and fire-escapes of the American School claim to be "America," while containing no particular, individualized persons of the kind that are found in the plays of other nations and in novels. The absence of any specific information seems to guarantee profundity. Most of these plays are sadistic fantasies in realistic disguise.

That is what makes their popularity so puzzling. The public seems to be, literally, a glutton for punishment.

A joke used to be told about a man in the theatre lobby after *Death of a Salesman* confiding to his companion: "That damned New England territory never was any good." This man elicits my sympathy because he was turning over in his mind the single solid fact divulged by the playwright: that Willy Loman sold something in the New England area.

Still, *Death of a Salesman* is the only play of the new American School that can be said to touch home. What is the matter with Willy Loman? Why is he so unhappy? "America" is what is wrong with him, Arthur Miller would answer, and to some extent this is true. The conception of the salesman's installment-plan home as a house of shabby lies and competitive boasts, growing hollower and hollower as old age and penury hem it in, is close to our national life; it is in fact precisely a close-up of the "home" depicted in full color by advertisers in the national magazines, with Father, Mother, two fine Kids, and the Product. But the play is wholly conceptualized, like the ads to which it gives a bitter retort. Parents, children, and neighbors are cut-out figures, types, equally in both versions of the American dream. Ideally, according to this formula, the play would be a kind of grim satire, the negative

---

*The title is the editors'.

of the positive, keeping the same terms. *This is the way your pretty picture looks from the inside,* the playwright would be saying to the advertising men. Insofar as the play does this, it is arresting and moving in a sardonic way. The trouble is that it strives to be tragedy and becomes instead confused and hortatory.

"Attention must be paid," intones the shrill, singsong voice of the mother, ordering her sons to take notice of their father's plight. "Attention, attention, must finally be paid to such a person." She is really admonishing the audience that Willy is, as she says, "a human being." But that is just it; he is a capitalized Human Being without being anyone, a suffering animal who commands a helpless pity. The mother's voice raised in the age-old Jewish rhythms ("Attention must be paid," is not a normal English locution, nor is "finally" as it is used, nor is "such a person") seems to have drifted in from some other play that was about particular people. But Willy is only a type, demanding a statistical attention and generalized, impersonal condolence, like that of the editorial page. No one could write an editorial calling attention to the case of King Lear. Yet the problem is the same: an old man, failing powers, thankless children, and a grandiose dream of being "well liked" — i.e., of being shown the proofs of love—that ends in utter isolation, ignominy, and madness. Lear, however, has the gift of language, the human, individual accent that is not a class endowment, for his Fool has it too. Lear is not any king; he is Lear. Willy Loman in the stage direction is called the Salesman. Which is more universal?

ARTHUR MILLER

Remembering Death of a Salesman*

In 1987 Miller published an autobiography, *Timebends*. We reproduce relevant passages, with headings of our own.

On Getting the Play into Production

Willy had to be small, I thought, but we soon realized that Roman Bohnen and Ernest Truex and a few other very good actors seemed to lack the size of the character even if they fit the body. The script had been sent to Lee Cobb, an actor I remembered mainly as a mountainous hulk covered with a towel in a Turkish bath in an Irwin Shaw play, with the hilarious *oy vey* delivery of a forever persecuted businessman. Having flown himself across the country in his own two-engine airplane, he sat facing me in Bloomgarden's office and announced, "This is my part. Nobody else can play this part. I know this man." And he did indeed seem to be the man when a bit later in a coffee shop downstairs he looked up at the young waitress and smiled winsomely as though he had to win her loving embrace before she could be seduced into bringing him his turkey sandwich and coffee— ahead of all the other men's orders and only after bestowing on his unique slice of pickle her longing kiss.

• • •

---

*The title is the editors'.

The whole production was, I think, unusual for the openness with which every artist involved sought out his truths. It was all a daily, almost moment-to-moment testing of ideas. There was much about the play that had never been done before, and this gave an uncustomary excitement to our discussions about what would or would not be understood by an audience. The setting I had envisioned was three bare platforms and only the minimum necessary furniture for a kitchen and two bedrooms, with the Boston hotel room as well as Howard's office to be played in open space. Jo Mielziner took those platforms and designed an environment around them that was romantic and dreamlike yet at the same time lower-middle-class. His set, in a word, was an emblem of Willy's intense longing for the promises of the past, with which indeed the present state of his mind is always conflicting, and it was thus both a lyrical design and a dramatic one. The only notable mistake in his early concept was to put the gas hot-water heater in the middle of the kitchen, a symbol of menace that I thought obvious and Kazan finally eliminated as a hazard to his staging. But by balancing on the edges of the ordinary bounds of verisimilitude, Jo was stretching reality in parallel with the script, just as Kazan did by syncopating the speech rhythms of the actors. He made Mildred Dunnock deliver her long first-act speeches to the boys at double her normal speed, then he doubled that, and finally she—until recently a speech teacher—was standing there drumming out words as fast as her very capable tongue could manage. Gradually he slacked her off, but the drill straightened her spine, and her Linda filled up with outrage and protest rather than self-pity and mere perplexity. Similarly, to express the play's inner life, the speech rate in some scenes or sections was unnaturally speeded or slowed.

My one scary hour came with the climactic restaurant fight between Willy and the boys, when it all threatened to come apart. I had written a scene in which Biff resolves to tell Willy that the former boss from whom Biff had planned to borrow money to start a business has refused to so much as see him and does not even remember his working for the firm years ago. But on meeting his brother and father in the restaurant, he realizes that Willy's psychological stress will not permit the whole catastrophic truth to be told, and he begins to trim the bad news. From moment to moment the scene as originally written had so many shadings of veracity that Arthur Kennedy, a very intelligent citizen indeed, had trouble shifting from a truth to a half-truth to a fragment of truth and back to the whole truth, all of it expressed in quickly delivered, very short lines. The three actors, with Kazan standing beside them, must have repeated the scene through a whole working day, and it still wobbled. "I don't see how we can make it happen," Kazan said as we left the theatre that evening. "Maybe you ought to try simplifying it for them." I went home and worked through the night and brought in a new scene, which played much better and became the scene as finally performed.

The other changes were very small and a pleasure to make because they involved adding lines rather than cutting or rewriting. In Act I, Willy is alone in the kitchen muttering to himself, and as his memories overtake him the lighting brightens, the exterior of the house becomes covered with leaf shadows as of old, and in a moment the boys are calling to him in their youthful voices, entering the stage as they were in their teens. There was not sufficient time, however, for them to descend from their beds in the dark on the specially designed elevators and finish stripping out of their pajamas into sweaters and trousers and sneakers, so I had to add time to Willy's monologue. But that was easy since he loved talking to himself about his boys and his vision of them.

The moving in and out of the present had to be not simply indicative but a tactile transformation that the audience could feel as well as comprehend, and indeed come to dread as returning memory threatens to bring Willy closer to his end. Lighting was thus decisively important, and Mielziner, who also lit the show, with Eddie Kook by his side, once worked an entire afternoon lighting a chair.

Willy, in his boss's office, has exploded once too often, and Howard has gone out, leaving him alone. He turns to the office chair, which in the old days was occupied by Frank, Howard's father, who had promised Willy shares in the firm as a reward for all his good work, and as he does so the chair must become alive, quite as though his old boss were in it as he addresses him: "Frank, Frank, don't you remember what you told me? . . . " Rather than being lit, the chair subtly seemed to begin emanating light. But this was not merely an exercise in theatrical magic; it confirmed that we had moved inside Willy's system of loss, that we were seeing the world as he saw it even as we kept a critical distance and saw it for ourselves.

To set the chair off and make the light change work, all surrounding lights had to dim imperceptibly. That was when Eddie Kook, who had become so addicted to the work on this play that his office at his Century Lighting Company had all but ceased operations, turned to me and said, "You've been asking why we need so many lights. [We were using more than most musicals.] The reason is right there in front of you—it takes more lights to make it dark." With fewer lights each one would have to be dimmed more noticeably than if there were many, each only fractionally reduced in intensity to create the change without apparent source or contrivance.

On the Filmed Version of the Play

I had sold *Salesman* to Stanley Kramer, who made the film for Columbia. My sole participation was to complain that the screenplay had managed to chop off almost every climax of the play as though with a lawnmower, leaving a flatness that was baffling in view of the play's demonstrated capacity for stirring its audiences in the theatre. Stanley Roberts, the author of the screenplay, flew east to sit with me and bring me to reason, and I recall one response of his that may illuminate the problem.

In the first act, after Linda pleads with her sons to have compassion for their father, Biff relents and agrees to stay on in New York and look for a job, saying that he will simply keep out of Willy's way. But Linda rejects this as inadequate; he must give his father psychological support. To Biff this means relinquishing his opposition to Willy's ideas about how he should live his own life, and he explodes, "I hate this city and I'll stay here! Now what do you want?" To which Linda replies, "He's dying, Biff," and proceeds to describe Willy's preparations for suicide.

This small but important step toward the approaching climax was simply skipped over, and I was mystified. "But," Roberts explained, "how can he shout at his mother like that?"

This was only part of the trouble with the film and with Hollywood films in general, but it may have been related to the main and deeper difficulty:

Fredric March was directed to play Willy as a psycho, all but completely out of control, with next to no grip on reality. March had been our first choice for the stage role but had turned it down—although he persuaded himself in later years that he had not been offered it formally. He could certainly have been a wonder in the film, but as a psychotic, he was predictable in the extreme; more than that, the misconception melted the tension between a man and his society, drawing the teeth of the play's social contemporaneity, obliterating its very context. If he was nuts, he could hardly stand as a comment on anything. It was as though Lear had never had real political power but had merely imagined he was king.

On a Production in China, 1983

But some thirty-five years later, the Chinese reaction to my Beijing production of *Salesman* would confirm what had become more and more obvious over the decades in the play's hundreds of productions throughout the world: Willy was representative everywhere, in every kind of system, of ourselves in this time. The Chinese might disapprove of his lies and his self-deluding exaggerations as well as his immorality with women, but they certainly saw themselves in him. And it was not simply as a type but because of what he wanted. Which was, to excel, to win out over anonymity and meaninglessness, to love and be loved, and above all, perhaps, to *count*. When he roared out, "I am not a dime a dozen! *I am Willy Loman, and you are Biff Loman!*" it came as a nearly revolutionary declaration after what was now thirty-four years of leveling. (The play was the same age as the Chinese revolution.) I did not know in 1948 in Connecticut that I was sending a message of resurgent individualism to the China of 1983—especially when the revolution had signified, it seemed at the time, the long-awaited rule of reason and the historic ending of chaotic egocentricity and selfish aggrandizement. Ah, yes. I had not reckoned on a young Chinese student saying to a CBS interviewer in the theatre lobby, "We are moved by it because we also want to be number one, and to be rich and successful." What else is this but human unpredictability, which goes on escaping the nets of unfreedom?

LORRAINE HANSBERRY

"An Author's Reflections: Willy Loman, Walker Younger, and He Who Must Live"
first appeared in The Village Voice *on August 12, 1959.*

*Reflections on Willy Loman**

We knew who Willy Loman was instantaneously; we recognized his milieu. We also knew at once that he represented that curious paradox in what the *English* character in that *English* play could call, though dismally, "The American Age." Willy Loman was a product of a nation of great military strength, indescribable material wealth, and incredible mastery of the physical

---

*The title is the editors'.

realm, which nonetheless was unable, in 1949, to produce a *typical* hero who was capable of an affirmative view of life.

I believe it is a testament to Miller's brilliance that it is hardly a misstatement of the case, as some preferred to believe. Something has indeed gone wrong with at least part of the American dream, and Willy Loman is the victim of the detour. Willy had to be overwhelmed on the stage as, in fact, his prototypes are in everyday life. Coming out of his section of our great sprawling middle class, preoccupied with its own restlessness and displaying its obsession for the possession of trivia, Willy was indeed trapped. His predicament in a New World where there just aren't anymore forests to clear or virgin railroads to lay or native American empires to first steal and then build upon left him with nothing but some left-over values which had forgotten how to prize industriousness over cunning, usefulness over mere acquisition, and above all, humanism over "success." The potency of the great tale of a salesman's death was in our familiar recognition of his entrapment which, suicide or no, is *deathly.*

JOHN LAHR

"Hard Sell" appeared in The New Yorker *on May 25, 2009.*

Hard Sell: A Black Death of a Salesman

"To mount an all-black production of a 'Death of a Salesman' or any other play conceived for white actors as an investigation of the human condition through the specifics of white culture is to deny us our own humanity, our own history, and the need to make our own investigations from the cultural ground on which we stand as black Americans," August Wilson said in 1996. "It is an assault on our presence, and our difficult but honorable history in America; and it is an insult to our intelligence, our playwrights, and our many and varied contributions to the society and the world at large." At the Yale Repertory Theatre, in New Haven, where almost all of Wilson's plays were first produced, the director James Bundy has brought together a collection of first-rate black actors, including the commanding Charles S. Dutton (himself a graduate of the Yale School of Drama and an outstanding messenger of Wilson's work), to perform Arthur Miller's 1949 "Death of a Salesman." Wilson proves to have been prescient; the experiment doesn't work, for the same reason that staging an all-white production of one of his plays would be folly.

To replace the Jewish Willy Loman with an African-American is to change something elemental in the nature of the play's lament. Loman is driven crazy by America's obsession with winning. Although he has spent thirty-six years opening up the Northeastern territory for his company, he has little to show for it. Somehow, the Redeemer Nation has not redeemed him, or his beloved but stalled sons. Loman is a monument to envy and its hate-filled agitations—all pluck and no luck. His outraged bewilderment— "What's the mystery?," "What's the secret?," "What happened?"—is predicated on the notion that abundance is there for the taking. This sense of expectation and entitlement was simply not shared by African-Americans in

1949. "You were born into a society which spelled out with brutal clarity . . . that you were a worthless human being," James Baldwin wrote in 1962, in an open letter to his nephew. "You were not expected to aspire to excellence: you were expected to make peace with mediocrity." "Death of a Salesman" is a brilliant taxonomy of the spiritual atrophy of mid-twentieth-century white America. To remove from the play—through the novelty of casting—the issues of race, class, and history is not to challenge the imagination but to beggar it. "Death of a Salesman" is *about* alienation; it shouldn't be an exercise *in* it.

The confusion begins with Scott Dougan's set. Owning your own house, as the Lomans aspire to do, is part of the American Dream, which is why Miller's script calls for a "small, fragile-seeming home"; the fragility is emblematic of the family's precarious hold on life. Dougan, instead, gives us a painted scrim of three tiers of tenements surrounding the Yale Rep's wide proscenium stage. The Lomans, it would seem, live in a first-floor apartment in one of the tenements, in a space the size of an armory—which makes nonsense of the play's talk about being overheard.

Miller based Willy Loman in large part on his strong-willed, competitive uncle Manny Newman. Newman's "was a house without irony, trembling with resolutions and shouts of victories that had not yet taken place but surely would tomorrow," Miller recalled in his 1987 memoir "Timebends." Willy speaks with aphoristic authority; he is a walking Dale Carnegie course, all positive thinking. "Personality always wins," he tells his boys, the philandering Happy (Billy Eugene Jones) and his favorite, Biff (Ato Essandoh), a wanderer who "never made the slightest mark." The sound of Willy's buoyant endorsement of their futures— "Start big and you end big," "You guys together could absolutely lick the civilized world"—drowns out a deeper foreboding about his own. "I feel kind of temporary about myself," he says.

Willy has "his feet on the subway stairs and his head in the stars," Miller said. The distracted Loman is a figure of towering delusion. "It's all right. I came back": Willy's first words are a lie. Things are not all right, and as he enters, burdened as much by the weight of his deferred dreams as by his sample cases, he is back in body but not in mind. Blacking out, talking to himself, seeing visions, prone to sudden explosions of fury, he is a figure of both awe and awfulness, and, incidentally, a sensational reminder that collapse can be vigorous. Loman's grandiosity, which makes him alternately insolent and pathetic to the world at large, spackles over his disappointment with himself and his feckless sons. Willy inflates his sales figures, his commission, his accomplishment, and his sons' potential. "They'll all end up big—all of them," he tells his next-door neighbor and only friend, Charley (Stephen McKinley Henderson), whose own son, Bernard (Austin Durant), has grabbed the brass ring and become a successful lawyer. Even when Biff, at the eleventh hour, confronts Willy with the family's ordinariness, Willy will not accept it. "I am not a dime a dozen," he roars. "I am Willy Loman, and you are Biff Loman!"

Dutton, who is thickset and bald-headed, has a voice that comes at you straight and hard, like a four-seam fastball; at its greatest intensity, it can push you back in your seat. But there is more grief and gladness in Dutton than Miller's play can draw out. Here he is strongest not in rage but in regret. Of all the losses that Miller contrives to heap on Willy—salary, job, dignity, filial affection—the most heartbreaking is the loss of the ideal of himself as a good father. Loman goes to his death having never understood his sons, or his part in their undoing. He doesn't know who he is or what he feels; unfortunately, and perhaps inevitably, given the casting, this estrangement applies to most of the actors here as well, especially Kimberly Scott, whose Linda Loman is lost in the translation.

Seven Additional Plays

HENRIK IBSEN

*Henrik Ibsen (1828–1906) was born in Skien, Norway, of wealthy parents
who soon after his birth lost their money. Ibsen worked as a pharmacist's
apprentice, but at the age of twenty-two he had written his first play, a
promising melodrama entitled* Cataline. *He engaged in theater work first in
Norway and then in Denmark and Germany. By 1865 his plays had won
him a state pension that enabled him to settle in Rome. After writing romantic, historic, and poetic plays, he turned to realistic drama with* The
League of Youth *(1869). Among his major realistic "problem plays" are* A
Doll's House *(1879),* Ghosts *(1881), and* An Enemy of the People *(1882). In*
The Wild Duck *(1884) he moved toward a more symbolic tragic comedy,
and his last plays, written in the nineties, are more symbolic.* Hedda Gabler
*(1890) looks backward to the plays of the eighties rather than forward to
the plays of the nineties.*

A Doll's House
[1879]

Translated by R. Farquharson Sharp

CHARACTERS

TORVALD HELMER, *a lawyer and bank manager*
NORA, *his wife*
DOCTOR RANK
MRS. CHRISTINE LINDE
NILS KROGSTAD, *a lawyer and bank clerk*
IVAR, BOB, AND EMMY, *the Helmers' three young children*
ANNE, *their nurse*
HELEN, *a housemaid*
A PORTER

The action takes place in HELMER'S *apartment.*

Act 1

SCENE: *A room furnished comfortably and tastefully, but not extrava-
gantly. At the back, a door to the right leads to the entrance hall, another*

A Doll's House. In Act 3, Nora lights Dr. Rank's cigar while Torvald impatiently waits for him to leave.

to the left leads to Helmer's *study. Between the doors stands a piano. In the middle of the left-hand wall is a door, and beyond it a window. Near the window are a round table, armchairs and a small sofa. In the right-hand wall, at the farther end, another door; and on the same side, nearer the footlights, a stove, two easy chairs and a rocking-chair; between the stove and the door, a small table. Engravings on the walls; a cabinet with china and other small objects; a small book case with well-bound books. The floors are carpeted, and a fire burns in the stove. It is winter.*

A bell rings in the hall; shortly afterwards the door is heard to open. Enter NORA, *humming a tune and in high spirits. She is in outdoor dress and carries a number of parcels; these she lays on the table to the right. She leaves the outer door open after her, and through it is seen a* PORTER *who is carrying a Christmas Tree and a basket, which he gives to the* MAID *who has opened the door.*

NORA. Hide the Christmas Tree carefully, Helen. Be sure the children do not see it till this evening, when it is dressed. [*to the* PORTER, *taking out her purse.*] How much?

PORTER. Sixpence.

NORA. There is a shilling. No, keep the change. [*The* PORTER *thanks her, and goes out.* NORA *shuts the door. She is laughing to herself, as she takes off her hat and coat. She takes a packet of macaroons from her pocket and eats one or two; then goes cautiously to her husband's door and listens.*] Yes, he is in.

[*Still humming, she goes to the table on the right.*]

HELMER [*calls out from his room*]. Is that my little lark twittering out there?

NORA [*busy opening some of the parcels*]. Yes, it is!

HELMER. Is my little squirrel bustling about?

NORA. Yes!

HELMER. When did my squirrel come home?

NORA. Just now. [*puts the bag of macaroons into her pocket and wipes her mouth.*] Come in here, Torvald, and see what I have bought.

HELMER. Don't disturb me. [*A little later, he opens the door and looks into the room, pen in hand.*] Bought, did you say? All these things? Has my little spendthrift been wasting money again?

NORA. Yes, but, Torvald, this year we really can let ourselves go a little. This is the first Christmas that we have not needed to economise.

HELMER. Still, you know, we can't spend money recklessly.

NORA. Yes, Torvald, we may be a wee bit more reckless now, mayn't we? Just a tiny wee bit! You are going to have a big salary and earn lots and lots of money.

HELMER. Yes, after the New Year; but then it will be a whole quarter before the salary is due.

NORA. Pooh! we can borrow till then.

HELMER. Nora! [*goes up to her and takes her playfully by the ear.*] The same little featherhead! Suppose, now, that I borrowed fifty pounds today, and you spent it all in the Christmas week, and then on New Year's Eve a slate fell on my head and killed me, and—

NORA [*putting her hands over his mouth*]. Oh! don't say such horrid things.

HELMER. Still, suppose that happened—what then?

NORA. If that were to happen, I don't suppose I should care whether I owed money or not.

HELMER. Yes, but what about the people who had lent it?

NORA. They? Who would bother about them? I should not know who they were.

HELMER. That is like a woman! But seriously, Nora, you know what I think about that. No debt, no borrowing. There can be no freedom or beauty about a home life that depends on borrowing and debt. We two have kept bravely on the straight road so far, and we will go on the same way for the short time longer that there need be any struggle.

NORA [*moving towards the stove*]. As you please, Torvald.

HELMER [*following her*]. Come, come, my little skylark must not droop her wings. What is this! Is my little squirrel out of temper? [*taking out his purse.*] Nora, what do you think I have got here?

NORA [*turning around quickly*]. Money!

HELMER. There you are. [*gives her some money*] Do you think I don't know what a lot is wanted for housekeeping at Christmas-time?

NORA [*counting*]. Ten shillings—a pound—two pounds! Thank you, thank you, Torvald; that will keep me going for a long time.

HELMER. Indeed it must.

NORA. Yes, yes, it will. But come here and let me show you what I have bought. And all so cheap! Look, here is a new suit for Ivar, and a sword; and a horse and a trumpet for Bob; and a doll and dolly's bedstead for Emmy—they are very plain, but anyway she will soon break them in pieces. And here are dress-lengths and handkerchiefs for the maids; old Anne ought really to have something better.

HELMER. And what is in this parcel?

NORA [*crying out*]. No, no! you mustn't see that till this evening.

HELMER. Very well. But now tell me, you extravagant little person, what would you like for yourself?

NORA. For myself? Oh, I am sure I don't want anything.

HELMER. Yes, but you must. Tell me something reasonable that you would particularly like to have.

NORA. No, I really can't think of anything—unless, Torvald—

HELMER. Well?

NORA [*playing with his coat buttons, and without raising her eyes to his*]. If you really want to give me something, you might—you might—

HELMER. Well, out with it!

NORA [*speaking quickly*]. You might give me money, Torvald. Only just as much as you can afford; and then one of these days I will buy something with it.

HELMER. But, Nora—

NORA. Oh, do! dear Torvald; please, please do! Then I will wrap it up in beautiful gilt paper and hang it on the Christmas Tree. Wouldn't that be fun?

HELMER. What are little people called that are always wasting money?

NORA. Spendthrifts—I know. Let us do as you suggest, Torvald, and then I shall have time to think what I am most in want of. That is a very sensible plan, isn't it?

HELMER [*smiling*]. Indeed it is—that is to say, if you were really to save out of the money I give you, and then really buy something for yourself. But if you spend it all on the housekeeping and any number of unnecessary things, then I merely have to pay up again.

NORA. Oh but, Torvald—

HELMER. You can't deny it, my dear little Nora. [*puts his arm round her waist*] It's a sweet little spendthrift, but she uses up a deal of money. One would hardly believe how expensive such little persons are!

NORA. It's a shame to say that. I do really save all I can.

HELMER [*laughing*]. That's very true—all you can. But you can't save anything!

NORA [*smiling quietly and happily*]. You haven't any idea how many expenses we skylarks and squirrels have, Torvald.

HELMER. You are an odd little soul. Very like your father. You always find some new way of wheedling money out of me, and, as soon as you have got it, it seems to melt in your hands. You never know where it has gone. Still, one must take you as you are. It is in the blood; for indeed it is true that you can inherit these things, Nora.

NORA. Ah, I wish I had inherited many of papa's qualities.

HELMER. And I would not wish you to be anything but just what you are, my sweet little skylark. But, do you know, it strikes me that you are looking rather—what shall I say—rather uneasy today?

NORA. Do I?

HELMER. You do, really. Look straight at me.

NORA [*looks at him*]. Well?

HELMER [*wagging his finger at her*]. Hasn't Miss Sweet-Tooth been breaking rules in town today?

NORA. No; what makes you think that?

HELMER. Hasn't she paid a visit to the confectioner's?

NORA. No, I assure you, Torvald—

HELMER. Not been nibbling sweets?

NORA. No, certainly not.

HELMER. Not even taken a bite at a macaroon or two?

NORA. No, Torvald, I assure you really—

HELMER. There, there, of course I was only joking.

NORA [*going to the table on the right*]. I should not think of going against your wishes.

HELMER. No, I am sure of that! besides, you gave me your word—[*going up to her*] Keep your little Christmas secrets to yourself, my darling. They will all be revealed tonight when the Christmas Tree is lit, no doubt.

NORA. Did you remember to invite Doctor Rank?

HELMER. No. But there is no need; as a matter of course he will come to dinner with us. However, I will ask him when he comes in this morning. I have ordered some good wine. Nora, you can't think how I am looking forward to this evening.

NORA. So am I! And how the children will enjoy themselves, Torvald!

HELMER. It is splendid to feel that one has a perfectly safe appointment, and a big enough income. It's delightful to think of, isn't it?

NORA. It's wonderful!

HELMER. Do you remember last Christmas? For a full three weeks beforehand you shut yourself up every evening till long after midnight, making ornaments for the Christmas Tree and all the other fine things that were to be a surprise to us. It was the dullest three weeks I ever spent!

NORA. I didn't find it dull.

HELMER [*smiling*]. But there was precious little result, Nora.

NORA. Oh, you shouldn't tease me about that again. How could I help the cat's going in and tearing everything to pieces?

HELMER. Of course you couldn't, poor little girl. You had the best of intentions to please us all, and that's the main thing. But it is a good thing that our hard times are over.

NORA. Yes, it is really wonderful.

HELMER. This time I needn't sit here and be dull all alone, and you needn't ruin your dear eyes and your pretty little hands—

NORA [*clapping her hands*]. No, Torvald, I needn't any longer, need I! It's wonderfully lovely to hear you say so! [*taking his arm*] Now I will tell you how I have been thinking we ought to arrange things, Torvald. As soon as Christmas is over—[*A bell rings in the hall.*] There's the bell. [*She tidies the room a little.*] There's someone at the door. What a nuisance!

HELMER. If it is a caller, remember I am not at home.

MAID [*in the doorway*]. A lady to see you, ma'am—a stranger.

NORA. Ask her to come in.

MAID [*to* HELMER]. The doctor came at the same time, sir.

HELMER. Did he go straight into my room?

MAID. Yes sir.

[HELMER *goes into his room. The* MAID *ushers in* MRS. LINDE, *who is in travelling dress, and shuts the door.*]

MRS. LINDE [*in a dejected and timid voice*]. How do you do, Nora?

NORA [*doubtfully*]. How do you do—

MRS. LINDE. You don't recognise me, I suppose.

NORA. No, I don't know—yes, to be sure, I seem to—[*suddenly*] Yes! Christine! Is it really you?

MRS. LINDE. Yes, it is I.

NORA. Christine! To think of my not recognising you! And yet how could I—[*in a gentle voice*] How you have altered, Christine!

MRS. LINDE. Yes, I have indeed. In nine, ten long years—

NORA. Is it so long since we met? I suppose it is. The last eight years have been a happy time for me, I can tell you. And so now you have come into the town, and have taken this long journey in winter—that was plucky of you.

MRS. LINDE. I arrived by steamer this morning.

NORA. To have some fun at Christmas-time, of course. How delightful! We will have such fun together! But take off your things. You are not cold, I hope. [*helps her*] Now we will sit down by the stove, and be cosy. No, take this arm-chair; I will sit here in the rocking-chair. [*takes her hands*] Now you look like your old self again; it was only the first moment— You are a little paler, Christine, and perhaps a little thinner.

MRS. LINDE. And much, much older, Nora.

NORA. Perhaps a little older; very, very little; certainly not much. [*stops suddenly and speaks seriously*] What a thoughtless creature I am, chattering away like this. My poor, dear Christine, do forgive me.

MRS. LINDE. What do you mean, Nora?

NORA [*gently*]. Poor Christine, you are a widow.

MRS. LINDE. Yes; it is three years ago now.

NORA. Yes, I knew; I saw it in the papers. I assure you, Christine, I meant ever so often to write to you at the time, but I always put it off and something always prevented me.

MRS. LINDE. I quite understand, dear.

NORA. It was very bad of me, Christine. Poor thing, how you must have suffered. And he left you nothing?

MRS. LINDE. No.

NORA. And no children?

MRS. LINDE. No.

NORA. Nothing at all, then?

MRS. LINDE. Not even any sorrow or grief to live upon.

NORA [*looking incredulously at her*]. But, Christine, is that possible?

MRS. LINDE [*smiles sadly and strokes her hair*]. It sometimes happens, Nora.

NORA. So you are quite alone. How dreadfully sad that must be. I have three lovely children. You can't see them just now, for they are out with their nurse. But now you must tell me all about it.

MRS. LINDE. No, no; I want to hear you.

NORA. No, you must begin. I mustn't be selfish today; today I must only think of your affairs. But there is one thing I must tell you. Do you know we have just had a great piece of good luck?

MRS. LINDE. No, what is it?

NORA. Just fancy, my husband has been made manager of the Bank!

MRS. LINDE. Your husband? What good luck!

NORA. Yes, tremendous! A barrister's profession is such an uncertain thing, especially if he won't undertake unsavoury cases; and naturally Torvald has never been willing to do that, and I quite agree with him. You may imagine how pleased we are! He is to take up his work in the Bank at the New Year, and then he will have a big salary and lots of commissions. For the future we can live quite differently—we can do just as we like. I feel so relieved and so happy, Christine! It will be splendid to have heaps of money and not need to have any anxiety, won't it?

MRS. LINDE. Yes, anyhow I think it would be delightful to have what one needs.

NORA. No, not only what one needs, but heaps and heaps of money.

MRS. LINDE [*smiling*]. Nora, Nora haven't you learnt sense yet? In our schooldays you were a great spendthrift.

NORA [*laughing*]. Yes, that is what Torvald says now. [*wags her finger at her*] But "Nora, Nora" is not so silly as you think. We have not been in a position for me to waste money. We have both had to work.

MRS. LINDE. You too?

NORA. Yes; odds and ends, needlework, crochet-work, embroidery, and that kind of thing. [*dropping her voice*] And other things as well. You know Torvald left his office when we were married? There was no prospect of promotion there, and he had to try and earn more than before. But during the first year he overworked himself dreadfully. You see, he had to make money every way he could, and he worked early and late; but he couldn't stand it, and fell dreadfully ill, and the doctors said it was necessary for him to go south.

MRS. LINDE. You spent a whole year in Italy didn't you?

NORA. Yes. It was no easy matter to get away, I can tell you. It was just as Ivar was born; but naturally we had to go. It was a wonderfully beautiful journey, and it saved Torvald's life. But it cost a tremendous lot of money, Christine.

MRS. LINDE. So I should think.

NORA. It cost about two hundred and fifty pounds. That's a lot, isn't it?

MRS. LINDE. Yes, and in emergencies like that it is lucky to have the money.

NORA. I ought to tell you that we had it from papa.

MRS. LINDE. Oh, I see. It was just about that time that he died, wasn't it?

NORA. Yes; and, just think of it, I couldn't go and nurse him. I was expecting little Ivar's birth every day and I had my poor sick Torvald to look after. My dear, kind father—I never saw him again, Christine. That was the saddest time I have known since our marriage.

MRS. LINDE. I know how fond you were of him. And then you went off to Italy?

NORA. Yes; you see we had money then, and the doctors insisted on our going, so we started a month later.

MRS. LINDE. And your husband came back quite well?

NORA. As sound as a bell!

MRS. LINDE. But—the doctor?

NORA. What doctor?

MRS. LINDE. I thought your maid said the gentleman who arrived here just as I did was the doctor?

NORA. Yes, that was Doctor Rank, but he doesn't come here professionally. He is our greatest friend, and comes in at least once every day. No, Torvald has not had an hour's illness since then, and our children are strong and

healthy and so am I. [*jumps up and claps her hands*] Christine! Christine! it's good to be alive and happy!—But how horrid of me; I am talking of nothing but my own affairs. [*sits on a stool near her, and rests
her arms on her knees*] You mustn't be angry with me. Tell me, is it really true that you did not love your husband? Why did you marry him?

MRS. LINDE. My mother was alive then, and was bedridden and helpless, and I
had to provide for my two younger brothers; so I did not think I was justified in refusing his offer.

NORA. No, perhaps you were quite right. He was rich at that time, then?

MRS. LINDE. I believe he was quite well off. But his business was a precarious
one; and, when he died, it all went to pieces and there was nothing left.

NORA. And then?—

MRS. LINDE. Well, I had to turn my hand to anything I could find—first a small
shop, then a small school, and so on. The last three years have seemed
like one long working-day, with no rest. Now it is at an end, Nora. My
poor mother needs me no more, for she is gone; and the boys do not need
me either; they have got situations and can shift for themselves.

NORA. What a relief you must feel it—

MRS. LINDE. No, indeed; I only feel my life unspeakably empty. No one to live
for any more. [*gets up restlessly*] That was why I could not stand the life
in my little backwater any longer. I hope it may be easier here to find
something which will busy me and occupy my thoughts. If only I could
have the good luck to get some regular work—office work of some
kind—

NORA. But, Christine, that is so frightfully tiring, and you look tired out now.
You had far better go away to some watering-place.

MRS. LINDE [*walking to the window*]. I have no father to give me money for
a journey, Nora.

NORA [*rising*]. Oh, don't be angry with me.

MRS. LINDE [*going up to her*]. It is you that must not be angry with me, dear.
The worst of a position like mine is that it makes one so bitter. No one
to work for, and yet obliged to be always on the look-out for chances.
One must live, and so one becomes selfish. When you told me of the
happy turn your fortunes have taken—you will hardly believe it—I was
delighted not so much on your account as on my own.

NORA. How do you mean?—Oh, I understand. You mean that perhaps Torvald could get you something to do.

MRS. LINDE. Yes, that was what I was thinking of.

NORA. He must, Christine. Just leave it to me; I will broach the subject very
cleverly—I will think of something that will please him very much. It
will make me so happy to be of some use to you.

MRS. LINDE. How kind you are, Nora, to be so anxious to help me! It is doubly
kind in you, for you know so little of the burdens and troubles of life.

NORA. I—? I know so little of them?

MRS. LINDE [*smiling*]. My dear! Small household cares and that sort of
thing!—You are a child, Nora.

NORA [*tosses her head and crosses the stage*]. You ought not to be so superior.

MRS. LINDE. No?

NORA. You are just like the others. They all think that I am incapable of anything really serious—

MRS. LINDE. Come, come—

NORA. —that I have gone through nothing in this world of cares.

MRS. LINDE. But, my dear Nora, you have just told me all your troubles.

NORA. Pooh!—those were trifles. [*lowering her voice*] I have not told you the important thing.

MRS. LINDE. The important thing? What do you mean?

NORA. You look down upon me altogether, Christine—but you ought not to. You are proud, aren't you, of having worked so hard and so long for your mother?

MRS. LINDE. Indeed, I don't look down on any one. But it is true that I am both proud and glad to think that I was privileged to make the end of my mother's life almost free from care.

NORA. And you are proud to think of what you have done for your brothers.

MRS. LINDE. I think I have the right to be.

NORA. I think so, too. But now, listen to this; I too have something to be proud of and glad of.

MRS. LINDE. I have no doubt you have. But what do you refer to?

NORA. Speak low. Suppose Torvald were to hear! He mustn't on any account—no one in the world must know, Christine, except you.

MRS. LINDE. But what is it?

NORA. Come here [*pulls her down on the sofa beside her*] Now I will show you that I too have something to be proud and glad of. It was I who saved Torvald's life.

MRS. LINDE. "Saved"? How?

NORA. I told you about our trip to Italy. Torvald would never have recovered if he had not gone there—

MRS. LINDE. Yes, but your father gave you the necessary funds.

NORA [*smiling*]. Yes, that is what Torvald and all the others think, but—

MRS. LINDE. But—

NORA. Papa didn't give us a shilling. It was I who procured the money.

MRS. LINDE. You? All that large sum?

NORA. Two hundred and fifty pounds. What do you think of that?

MRS. LINDE. But, Nora, how could you possibly do it? Did you win a prize in the Lottery?

NORA [*contemptuously*]. In the Lottery? There would have been no credit in that.

MRS. LINDE. But where did you get it from, then?

NORA [*humming and smiling with an air of mystery*]. Hm, hm! Aha!

MRS. LINDE. Because you couldn't have borrowed it.

NORA. Couldn't I? Why not?

MRS. LINDE. No, a wife cannot borrow without her husband's consent.

NORA [*tossing her head*]. Oh, if it is a wife who has any head for business—a wife who has the wit to be a little bit clever—

MRS. LINDE. I don't understand it at all, Nora.

NORA. There is no need you should. I never said I had borrowed the money. I may have got it some other way. [*lies back on the sofa*] Perhaps I got it from some other admirer. When anyone is as attractive as I am—

MRS. LINDE. You are a mad creature.

NORA. Now, you know you're full of curiosity, Christine.

MRS. LINDE. Listen to me, Nora dear. Haven't you been a little bit imprudent?

NORA [*sits up straight*]. Is it imprudent to save your husband's life?

MRS. LINDE. It seems to me imprudent, without his knowledge, to—

NORA. But it was absolutely necessary that he should not know! My goodness, can't you understand that? It was necessary he should have no idea what a dangerous condition he was in. It was to me that the doctors came and said that his life was in danger, and that the only thing to save him was to live in the south. Do you suppose I didn't try, first of all, to get what I wanted as if it were for myself? I told him how much I should love to travel abroad like other young wives; I tried tears and entreaties with him; I told him that he ought to remember the condition I was in, and that he ought to be kind and indulgent to me; I even hinted that he might raise a loan. That nearly made him angry, Christine. He said I was thoughtless, and that it was his duty as my husband not to indulge me in my whims and caprices—as I believe he called them. Very well I thought, you must be saved—and that was how I came to devise a way out of the difficulty—

MRS. LINDE. And did your husband never get to know from your father that the money had not come from him?

NORA. No, never. Papa died just at that time. I had meant to let him into the secret and beg him never to reveal it. But he was so ill then—alas, there never was any need to tell him.

MRS. LINDE. And since then have you never told your secret to your husband?

NORA. Good Heavens, no! How could you think so? A man who has such strong opinions about these things! And besides, how painful and humiliating it would be for Torvald, with his manly independence, to know that he owed me anything! It would upset our mutual relations altogether; our beautiful happy home would no longer be what it is now.

MRS. LINDE. Do you mean never to tell him about it?

NORA [meditatively, and with a half smile]. Yes—some day, perhaps, after many years, when I am no longer as nice-looking as I am now. Don't laugh at me! I mean of course, when Torvald is no longer as devoted to me as he is now; when my dancing and dressing-up and reciting have palled on him; then it may be a good thing to have something in reserve—[breaking off] What nonsense! That time will never come. Now, what do you think of my great secret, Christine? Do you still think I am of no use? I can tell you, too, that this affair has caused me a lot of worry. It has been by no means easy for me to meet my engagements punctually. I may tell you that there is something that is called, in business, quarterly interest, and another thing called payment in instalments, and it is always so dreadfully difficult to manage them. I have had to save a little here and there, where I could, you understand. I have not been able to put aside much from my housekeeping money, for Torvald must have a good table. I couldn't let my children be shabbily dressed; I have felt obliged to use up all he gave me for them, the sweet little darlings!

MRS. LINDE. So it has all had to come out of your own necessaries of life, poor Nora?

NORA. Of course. Besides, I was the one responsible for it. Whenever Torvald has given me the money for new dresses and such things, I have never spent more than half of it; I have always bought the simplest and cheapest things. Thank Heaven, any clothes look well on me, and so Torvald has never noticed it. But it was often very hard on me, Christine—because it is delightful to be really well dressed, isn't it?

MRS. LINDE. Quite so.

NORA. Well, then I have found other ways of earning money. Last winter I
was lucky enough to get a lot of copying to do; so I locked myself up
and sat writing every evening until quite late at night. Many a time I was
desperately tired; but all the same it was a tremendous pleasure to sit
there working and earning money. It was like being a man.

MRS. LINDE. How much have you been able to pay off in that way?

NORA. I can't tell you exactly. You see, it is very difficult to keep an account
of a business matter of that kind. I only know that I have paid every
penny that I could scrape together. Many a time I was at my wit's end.
[smiles] Then I used to sit here and imagine that a rich old gentleman
had fallen in love with me—

MRS. LINDE. What! Who was it?

NORA. Be quiet!—that he had died; and that when his will was opened it
contained, written in big letters, the instruction "The lovely Mrs. Nora
Helmer is to have all I possess paid over to her at once in cash."

MRS. LINDE. But, my dear Nora—who could the man be?

NORA. Good gracious, can't you understand? There was no old gentleman at
all; it was only something that I used to sit here and imagine, when I
couldn't think of any way of procuring money. But it's all the same now;
the tiresome old person can stay where he is, as far as I am concerned; I
don't care about him or his will either, for I am free from care now.
[jumps up] My goodness, it's delightful to think of, Christine! Free from
care! To be able to be free from care, quite free from care; to be able to
play and romp with the children; to be able to keep the house beautifully and have everything just as Torvald likes it! And, think of it, soon the
spring will come and the big blue sky! Perhaps we shall be able to take a
little trip—perhaps I shall see the sea again! Oh, it's a wonderful thing to
be alive and be happy. [A bell is heard in the hall.]

MRS. LINDE [rising]. There is the bell; perhaps I had better go.

NORA. No, don't go; no one will come in here; it is sure to be for Torvald.

SERVANT [at the hall door]. Excuse me, ma'am—there is a gentleman to see
the master, and as the doctor is with him—

NORA. Who is it?

KROGSTAD [at the door]. It is I, Mrs. Helmer. [Mrs. Linde starts, trembles, and
turns to the window.]

NORA [takes a step towards him, and speaks in a strained, low voice].
You? What is it? What do you want to see my husband about?

KROGSTAD. Bank business—in a way. I have a small post in the Bank, and I
hear your husband is to be our chief now—

NORA. Then it is—

KROGSTAD. Nothing but dry business matters, Mrs. Helmer; absolutely nothing
else.

NORA. Be so good as to go into the study, then. [She bows indifferently to
him and shuts the door into the hall; then comes back and makes up
the fire in the stove.]

MRS. LINDE. Nora—who was that man?

NORA. A lawyer, of the name of Krogstad.

MRS. LINDE. Then it really was he.

NORA. Do you know the man?

MRS. LINDE. I used to—many years ago. At one time he was a solicitor's clerk
in our town.

NORA. Yes, he was.

MRS. LINDE. He is greatly altered.

NORA. He made a very unhappy marriage.

MRS. LINDE. He is a widower now, isn't he?

NORA. With several children. There now, it is burning up.

[*Shuts the door of the stove and moves the rocking-chair aside.*]

MRS. LINDE. They say he carries on various kinds of business.

NORA. Really! Perhaps he does; I don't know anything about it. But don't let us think of business; it is so tiresome.

DOCTOR RANK [*comes out of* HELMER'S *study. Before he shuts the door he calls to him.*]. No, my dear fellow, I won't disturb you; I would rather go in to your wife for a little while. [*shuts the door and sees* MRS. LINDE] I beg your pardon; I am afraid I am disturbing you too.

NORA. No, not at all. [*introducing him*] Doctor Rank, Mrs. Linde.

RANK. I have often heard Mrs. Linde's name mentioned here. I think I passed you on the stairs when I arrived, Mrs. Linde?

MRS. LINDE. Yes, I go up very slowly; I can't manage stairs well.

RANK. Ah! some slight internal weakness?

MRS. LINDE. No, the fact is I have been overworking myself.

RANK. Nothing more than that? Then I suppose you have come to town to amuse yourself with our entertainments?

MRS. LINDE. I have come to look for work.

RANK. Is that a good cure for overwork?

MRS. LINDE. One must live, Doctor Rank.

RANK. Yes, the general opinion seems to be that it is necessary.

NORA. Look here, Doctor Rank—you know you want to live.

RANK. Certainly. However wretched I may feel, I want to prolong the agony as long as possible. All my patients are like that. And so are those who are morally diseased; one of them, and a bad case too, is at this very moment with Helmer—

MRS. LINDE [*sadly*]. Ah!

NORA. Whom do you mean?

RANK. A lawyer of the name of Krogstad, a fellow you don't know at all. He suffers from a diseased moral character, Mrs. Helmer; but even he began talking of its being highly important that he should live.

NORA. Did he? What did he want to speak to Torvald about?

RANK. I have no idea; I only heard that it was something about the Bank.

NORA. I didn't know this—what's his name—Krogstad had anything to do with the Bank.

RANK. Yes, he has some sort of appointment there. [*to* MRS. LINDE] I don't know whether you find also in your part of the world that there are certain people who go zealously snuffing about to smell out moral corruption, and, as soon as they have found some, put the person concerned into some lucrative position where they can keep their eye on him. Healthy natures are left out in the cold.

MRS. LINDE. Still I think the sick are those who most need taking care of.

RANK [*shrugging his shoulders*]. Yes, there you are. That is the sentiment that is turning Society into a sickhouse.

[NORA, *who has been absorbed in her thoughts, breaks out into smothered laughter and claps her hands.*]

RANK. Why do you laugh at that? Have you any notion what Society really is?

NORA. What do I care about tiresome Society? I am laughing at something quite different, something extremely amusing. Tell me, Doctor Rank, are all the people who are employed in the Bank dependent on Torvald now?

RANK. Is that what you find so extremely amusing?

NORA [*smiling and humming*]. That's my affair! [*walking about the room*] It's perfectly glorious to think that we have—that Torvald has so much power over so many people. [*takes the packet from her pocket*] Doctor Rank, what do you say to a macaroon?

RANK. What, macaroons? I thought they were forbidden here.

NORA. Yes, but these are some Christine gave me.

MRS. LINDE. What! I?—

NORA. Oh, well, don't be alarmed! You couldn't know that Torvald had forbidden them. I must tell you that he is afraid they will spoil my teeth. But, bah!—once in a way—That's so, isn't it, Doctor Rank? By your leave? [*puts a macaroon into his mouth*] You must have one too, Christine. And I shall have one, just a little one—or at most two. [*walking about*] I am tremendously happy. There is just one thing in the world now that I should dearly love to do.

RANK. Well, what is that?

NORA. It's something I should dearly love to say, if Torvald could hear me.

RANK. Well, why can't you say it?

NORA. No, I daren't; it's so shocking.

MRS. LINDE. Shocking?

RANK. Well, I should not advise you to say it. Still, with us you might. What is it you would so much like to say if Torvald could hear you?

NORA. I should just love to say—Well, I'm damned!

RANK. Are you mad?

MRS. LINDE. Nora, dear—!

RANK. Say it, here he is!

NORA [*hiding the packet*]. Hush! Hush! Hush!

[HELMER *comes out of his room, with his coat over his arm and his hat in his hands.*]

NORA. Well, Torvald dear, have you got rid of him?

HELMER. Yes, he has just gone.

NORA. Let me introduce you—this is Christine, who has come to town.

HELMER. Christine—? Excuse me, but I don't know—

NORA. Mrs. Linde, dear; Christine Linde.

HELMER. Of course. A school friend of my wife's, I presume?

MRS. LINDE. Yes, we have known each other since then.

NORA. And just think, she has taken a long journey in order to see you.

HELMER. What do you mean?

MRS. LINDE. No, really, I—

NORA. Christine is tremendously clever at book-keeping, and she is frightfully anxious to work under some clever man, so as to perfect herself—

HELMER. Very sensible, Mrs. Linde.

NORA. And when she heard you had been appointed manager of the Bank—the news was telegraphed, you know—she travelled here as quick as she could. Torvald, I am sure you will be able to do something for Christine, for my sake, won't you?

HELMER. Well, it is not altogether impossible. I presume you are a widow, Mrs. Linde?

MRS. LINDE. Yes.

HELMER. And have had some experience of book-keeping?

MRS. LINDE. Yes, a fair amount.

HELMER. Ah! well, it's very likely I may be able to find something for you—

NORA [*clapping her hands*]. What did I tell you? What did I tell you?

HELMER. You have just come at a fortunate moment, Mrs. Linde.

MRS. LINDE. How am I to thank you?

HELMER. There is no need. [*puts on his coat*] But today you must excuse me—

RANK. Wait a minute; I will come with you.

[*Brings his fur coat from the hall and warms it at the fire.*]

NORA. Don't be long away, Torvald dear.

HELMER. About an hour, not more.

NORA. Are you going too, Christine?

MRS. LINDE [*putting on her cloak*]. Yes, I must go and look for a room.

HELMER. Oh, well then, we can walk down the street together.

NORA [*helping her*]. What a pity it is we are so short of space here I am afraid it is impossible for us—

MRS. LINDE. Please don't think of it! Good-bye, Nora dear, and many thanks.

NORA. Good-bye for the present. Of course you will come back this evening. And you too, Dr. Rank. What do you say? If you are well enough? Oh, you must be! Wrap yourself up well.

[*They go to the door all talking together. Children's voices are heard on the staircase.*]

NORA. There they are. There they are! [*She runs to open the door. The* NURSE *comes in with the children.*] Come in! Come in! [*stoops and kisses them*] Oh, you sweet blessings! Look at them, Christine! Aren't they darlings?

RANK. Don't let us stand here in the draught.

HELMER. Come along, Mrs. Linde; the place will only be bearable for a mother now!

[RANK, HELMER *and* MRS. LINDE *go downstairs. The* NURSE *comes forward with the children;* NORA *shuts the hall door.*]

NORA. How fresh and well you look! Such red cheeks!—like apples and roses. [*The children all talk at once while she speaks to them.*] Have you had great fun? That's splendid! What, you pulled both Emmy and Bob along on the sledge?—both at once?—that was good. You are a clever boy, Ivar. Let me take her for a little, Anne. My sweet little baby doll! [*takes the baby from the* MAID *and dances it up and down*] Yes, yes, mother will dance with Bob too. What! Have you been snowballing? I wish I had been there too! No, no, I will take their things off, Anne; please let me do it, it is such fun. Go in now, you look half frozen. There is some coffee for you on the stove.

[*The* NURSE *goes into the room on the left.* NORA *takes off the children's things and throws them about, while they all talk to her at once.*]

NORA. Really! Did a big dog run after you? But it didn't bite you? No, dogs don't bite nice little dolly children. You mustn't look at the parcels, Ivar. What are they? Ah, I daresay you would like to know. No, no—it's something nasty! Come, let us have a game! What shall we play at? Hide and Seek? Yes, we'll play Hide and Seek. Bob shall hide first. Must I hide? Very well, I'll hide first.

[*She and the children laugh and shout, and romp in and out of the room; at last* NORA *hides under the table, the children rush in and look for her, but do not see her; they hear her smothered laughter, run to the table, lift up the cloth and find her. Shouts of laughter. She crawls forward and pretends to frighten them. Fresh laughter. Meanwhile there has been a knock at the hall door, but none of them has noticed it. The door is half opened, and* KROGSTAD *appears. He waits a little; the game goes on.*]

KROGSTAD. Excuse me, Mrs. Helmer.

NORA [*with a stifled cry, turns round and gets up on to her knees*]. Ah! what do you want?

KROGSTAD. Excuse me, the outer door was ajar; I suppose someone forgot to shut it.

NORA [*rising*]. My husband is out, Mr. Krogstad.

KROGSTAD. I know that.

NORA. What do you want here, then?

KROGSTAD. A word with you.

NORA. With me?—[*to the children, gently*] Go in to nurse. What? No, the strange man won't do mother any harm. When he has gone we will have another game. [*She takes the children into the room on the left, and shuts the door after them.*] You want to speak to me?

KROGSTAD. Yes, I do.

NORA. Today? It is not the first of the month yet.

KROGSTAD. No, it is Christmas Eve, and it will depend on yourself what sort of a Christmas you will spend.

NORA. What do you want? Today it is absolutely impossible for me—

KROGSTAD. We won't talk about that till later on. This is something different. I presume you can give me a moment?

NORA. Yes—yes, I can—although—

KROGSTAD. Good. I was in Olsen's Restaurant and saw your husband going down the street—

NORA. Yes?

KROGSTAD. With a lady.

NORA. What then?

KROGSTAD. May I make so bold as to ask if it was a Mrs. Linde?

NORA. It was.

KROGSTAD. Just arrived in town?

NORA. Yes, to-day.

KROGSTAD. She is a great friend of yours, isn't she?

NORA. She is. But I don't see—

KROGSTAD. I knew her too, once upon a time.

NORA. I am aware of that.

KROGSTAD. Are you? So you know all about it; I thought as much. Then I can ask you, without beating about the bush—is Mrs. Linde to have an appointment in the Bank?

NORA. What right have you to question me, Mr. Krogstad?—You, one of my husband's subordinates! But since you ask, you shall know. Yes, Mrs. Linde *is* to have an appointment. And it was I who pleaded her cause, Mr. Krogstad, let me tell you that.

KROGSTAD. I was right in what I thought, then.

NORA [*walking up and down the stage*]. Sometimes one has a tiny little bit of influence, I should hope. Because one is a woman, it does not necessarily follow that—. When anyone is in a subordinate position, Mr. Krogstad, they should really be careful to avoid offending anyone who—who—

KROGSTAD. Who has influence?

NORA. Exactly.

KROGSTAD [*changing his tone*]. Mrs. Helmer, you will be so good as to use your influence on my behalf.

NORA. What? What do you mean?

KROGSTAD. You will be so kind as to see that I am allowed to keep my subordinate position in the Bank.

NORA. What do you mean by that? Who proposes to take your post away from you?

KROGSTAD. Oh, there is no necessity to keep up the pretence of ignorance. I can quite understand that your friend is not very anxious to expose herself to the chance of rubbing shoulders with me; and I quite understand, too, whom I have to thank for being turned out.

NORA. But I assure you—

KROGSTAD. Very likely; but, to come to the point, the time has come when I should advise you to use your influence to prevent that.

NORA. But, Mr. Krogstad, I *have* no influence.

KROGSTAD. Haven't you? I thought you said yourself just now—

NORA. Naturally I did not mean you to put that construction on it. I! What should make you think I have any influence of that kind with my husband?

KROGSTAD. Oh, I have known your husband from our student days. I don't suppose he is any more unassailable than other husbands.

NORA. If you speak slightingly of my husband, I shall turn you out of the house.

KROGSTAD. You are bold, Mrs. Helmer.

NORA. I am not afraid of you any longer. As soon as the New Year comes, I shall in a very short time be free of the whole thing.

KROGSTAD [*controlling himself*]. Listen to me, Mrs. Helmer. If necessary, I am prepared to fight for my small post in the Bank as if I were fighting for my life.

NORA. So it seems.

KROGSTAD. It is not only for the sake of the money; indeed, that weighs least with me in the matter. There is another reason—well, I may as well tell you. My position is this. I daresay you know, like everybody else, that once, many years ago, I was guilty of an indiscretion.

NORA. I think I have heard something of the kind.

KROGSTAD. The matter never came into court; but every way seemed to be closed to me after that. So I took to the business that you know of. I had to do something; and, honestly, I don't think I've been one of the worst. But now I must cut myself free from all that. My sons are growing up; for their sake I must try and win back as much respect as I can in the town. This post in the Bank was like the first step up for me—and now your husband is going to kick me downstairs again into the mud.

NORA. But you must believe me, Mr. Krogstad; it is not in my power to help you at all.

KROGSTAD. Then it is because you haven't the will; but I have means to compel you.

NORA. You don't mean that you will tell my husband that I owe you money?

KROGSTAD. Hm!—suppose I were to tell him?

NORA. It would be perfectly infamous of you. [*sobbing*] To think of his learning my secret, which has been my joy and pride, in such an ugly, clumsy way—that he should learn it from you! And it would put me in a horribly disagreeable position—

KROGSTAD. Only disagreeable?

NORA [*impetuously*]. Well, do it, then!—and it will be the worse for you. My husband will see for himself what a blackguard you are, and you certainly won't keep your post then.

KROGSTAD. I asked you if it was only a disagreeable scene at home that you were afraid of?

NORA. If my husband does get to know of it, of course he will at once pay you what is still owing, and we shall have nothing more to do with you.

KROGSTAD [*coming a step nearer*]. Listen to me, Mrs. Helmer. Either you have a very bad memory or you know very little of business. I shall be obliged to remind you of a few details.

NORA. What do you mean?

KROGSTAD. When your husband was ill, you came to me to borrow two hundred and fifty pounds.

NORA. I didn't know any one else to go to.

KROGSTAD. I promised to get you that amount—

NORA. Yes, and you did so.

KROGSTAD. I promised to get you that amount, on certain conditions. Your mind was so taken up with your husband's illness, and you were so anxious to get the money for your journey, that you seem to have paid no attention to the conditions of our bargain. Therefore it will not be amiss if I remind you of them. Now, I promised to get the money on the security of a bond which I drew up.

NORA. Yes, and which I signed.

KROGSTAD. Good. But below your signature there were a few lines constituting your father a surety for the money; those lines your father should have signed.

NORA. Should? He did sign them.

KROGSTAD. I had left the date blank; that is to say your father should himself have inserted the date on which he signed the paper. Do you remember that?

NORA. Yes, I think I remember—

KROGSTAD. Then I gave you the bond to send by post to your father. Is that not so?

NORA. Yes.

KROGSTAD. And you naturally did so at once, because five or six days afterwards you brought me the bond with your father's signature. And then I gave you the money.

NORA. Well, haven't I been paying it off regularly?

KROGSTAD. Fairly so, yes. But—to come back to the matter in hand—that must have been a very trying time for you, Mrs. Helmer?

NORA. It was, indeed.

KROGSTAD. Your father was very ill, wasn't he?

NORA. He was very near his end.

KROGSTAD. And died soon afterwards?

NORA. Yes.

KROGSTAD. Tell me, Mrs. Helmer, can you by any chance remember what day your father died?—on what day of the month, I mean.

NORA. Papa died on the 29th of September.

KROGSTAD. That is correct; I have ascertained it for myself. And, as that is so, there is a discrepancy [*taking a paper from his pocket*] which I cannot account for.

NORA. What discrepancy? I don't know—

KROGSTAD. The discrepancy consists, Mrs. Helmer, in the fact that your father signed this bond three days after his death.

NORA. What do you mean? I don't understand—

KROGSTAD. Your father died on the 29th of September. But, look here; your father has dated his signature the 2nd of October. It is a discrepancy, isn't it? [NORA *is silent.*] Can you explain it to me? [NORA *is still silent.*] It is a remarkable thing, too, that the words "2nd of October," as well as the year, are not written in your father's handwriting but in one that I think I know. Well, of course it can be explained; your father may have forgotten to date his signature, and someone else may have dated it haphazard before they knew of his death. There is no harm in that. It all depends on the signature of the name; and *that* is genuine, I suppose, Mrs. Helmer? It was your father himself who signed his name here?

NORA [*after a short pause, throws her head up and looks defiantly at him*]. No, it was not. It was I that wrote papa's name.

KROGSTAD. Are you aware that is a dangerous confession?

NORA. In what way? You shall have your money soon.

KROGSTAD. Let me ask you a question; why did you not send the paper to your father?

NORA. It was impossible; papa was so ill. If I had asked him for his signature, I should have had to tell him what the money was to be used for; and when he was so ill himself I couldn't tell him that my husband's life was in danger—it was impossible.

KROGSTAD. It would have been better for you if you had given up your trip abroad.

NORA. No, that was impossible. That trip was to save my husband's life; I couldn't give that up.

KROGSTAD. But did it never occur to you that you were committing a fraud on me?

NORA. I couldn't take that into account; I didn't trouble myself about you at all. I couldn't bear you, because you put so many heartless difficulties in my way, although you knew what a dangerous condition my husband was in.

KROGSTAD. Mrs. Helmer, you evidently do not realise clearly what it is that you have been guilty of. But I can assure you that my one false step, which lost me all my reputation, was nothing more or nothing worse than what you have done.

NORA. You? Do you ask me to believe that you were brave enough to run a risk to save your wife's life?

KROGSTAD. The law cares nothing about motives.

NORA. Then it must be a very foolish law.

KROGSTAD. Foolish or not, it is the law by which you will be judged, if I produce this paper in court.

NORA. I don't believe it. Is a daughter not to be allowed to spare her dying father anxiety and care? Is a wife not to be allowed to save her husband's life? I don't know much about law; but I am certain that there must be laws permitting such things as that. Have you no knowledge of such laws—you who are a lawyer? You must be a very poor lawyer, Mr. Krogstad.

KROGSTAD. Maybe. But matters of business—such business as you and I have had together—do you think I don't understand that? Very well. Do as you please. But let me tell you this—if I lose my position a second time, you shall lose yours with me.

[*He bows, and goes out through the hall.*]

NORA [*appears buried in thought for a short time, then tosses her head*]. Nonsense! Trying to frighten me like that!—I am not so silly as he thinks. [*begins to busy herself putting the children's things in order*] And yet—? No, it's impossible! I did it for love's sake.

THE CHILDREN [*in the doorway on the left*]. Mother, the stranger man has gone out through the gate.

NORA. Yes, dears, I know. But, don't tell anyone about the stranger man. Do you hear? Not even papa.

CHILDREN. No, mother; but will you come and play again?

NORA. No, no—not now.

CHILDREN. But, mother, you promised us.

NORA. Yes, but I can't now. Run away in; I have such a lot to do. Run away in, my sweet little darlings. [*She gets them into the room by degrees and shuts the door on them; then sits down on the sofa, takes up a piece of needlework and sews a few stitches, but soon stops.*] No! [*throws down the work, gets up, goes to the hall door and calls out*] Helen! bring the Tree in. [*goes to the table on the left, opens a drawer, and stops again*] No, no! it is quite impossible!

MAID [*coming in with the Tree*]. Where shall I put it, ma'am?

NORA. Here, in the middle of the floor.

MAID. Shall I get you anything else?

NORA. No, thank you. I have all I want.

[*Exit* MAID.]

NORA [*begins dressing the tree*]. A candle here—and flowers here—. The horrible man! It's all nonsense—there's nothing wrong. The Tree shall

be splendid! I will do everything I can think of to please you, Torvald!—
I will sing for you, dance for you— [HELMER *comes in with some papers
under his arm*] Oh! are you back already?

HELMER. Yes. Has anyone been here?

NORA. Here? No.

HELMER. That is strange. I saw Krogstad going out of the gate.

NORA. Did you? Oh yes, I forgot, Krogstad was here for a moment.

HELMER. Nora, I can see from your manner that he has been here begging
you to say a good word for him.

NORA. Yes.

HELMER. And you were to appear to do it of your own accord; you were to
conceal from me the fact of his having been here; didn't he beg that of
you too?

NORA. Yes, Torvald, but—

HELMER. Nora, Nora, and you would be a party to that sort of thing? To have
any talk with a man like that, and give him any sort of promise? And to
tell me a lie into the bargain?

NORA. A lie—?

HELMER. Didn't you tell me no one had been here? [*shakes his finger at
her*] My little song-bird must never do that again. A song-bird must
have a clean beak to chirp with—no false notes! [*puts his arm round
her waist*] That is so, isn't it? Yes, I am sure it is. [*lets her go*] We will
say no more about it. [*sits down by the stove*] How warm and snug it
is here!

[*Turns over his papers.*]

NORA [*after a short pause, during which she busies herself with the Christmas Tree*]. Torvald!

HELMER. Yes.

NORA. I am looking forward tremendously to the fancy dress ball at the
Stenborgs' the day after tomorrow.

HELMER. And I am tremendously curious to see what you are going to surprise me with.

NORA. It was very silly of me to want to do that.

HELMER. What do you mean?

NORA. I can't hit upon anything that will do; everything I think of seems so
silly and insignificant.

HELMER. Does my little Nora acknowledge that at last?

NORA [*standing behind his chair with her arms on the back of it*]. Are you
very busy, Torvald?

HELMER. Well—

NORA. What are all those papers?

HELMER. Bank business.

NORA. Already?

HELMER. I have got authority from the retiring manager to undertake the necessary changes in the staff and in the rearrangement of the work; and I must
make use of the Christmas week for that, so as to have everything in order
for the new year.

NORA. Then that was why this poor Krogstad—

HELMER. Hm!

NORA [*leans against the back of his chair and strokes his hair*]. If you hadn't been so busy I should have asked you a tremendously big favour, Torvald.

HELMER. What is that? Tell me.

NORA. There is no one has such good taste as you. And I do so want to look nice at the fancy-dress ball. Torvald, couldn't you take me in hand and decide what I shall go as, and what sort of a dress I shall wear?

HELMER. Aha! so my obstinate little woman is obliged to get someone to come to her rescue?

NORA. Yes, Torvald, I can't get along a bit without your help.

HELMER. Very well, I will think it over, we shall manage to hit upon something.

NORA. That is nice of you. [*Goes to the Christmas Tree. A short pause.*] How pretty the red flowers look—. But, tell me, was it really something very bad that this Krogstad was guilty of?

HELMER. He forged someone's name. Have you any idea what that means?

NORA. Isn't it possible that he was driven to do it by necessity?

HELMER. Yes; or, as in so many cases, by imprudence. I am not so heartless as to condemn a man altogether because of a single false step of that kind.

NORA. No you wouldn't, would you, Torvald?

HELMER. Many a man has been able to retrieve his character, if he has openly confessed his fault and taken his punishment.

NORA. Punishment—?

HELMER. But Krogstad did nothing of that sort; he got himself out of it by a cunning trick, and that is why he has gone under altogether.

NORA. But do you think it would—?

HELMER. Just think how a guilty man like that has to lie and play the hypocrite with everyone, how he has to wear a mask in the presence of those near and dear to him, even before his own wife and children. And about the children—that is the most terrible part of it all, Nora.

NORA. How?

HELMER. Because such an atmosphere of lies infects and poisons the whole life of a home. Each breath the children take in such a house is full of the germs of evil.

NORA [*coming nearer him*]. Are you sure of that?

HELMER. My dear, I have often seen it in the course of my life as a lawyer. Almost everyone who has gone to the bad early in life has had a deceitful mother.

NORA. Why do you only say—mother?

HELMER. It seems most commonly to be the mother's influence, though naturally a bad father's would have the same result. Every lawyer is familiar with the fact. This Krogstad, now, has been persistently poisoning his own children with lies and dissimulation; that is why I say he has lost all moral character. [*holds out his hands to her*] That is why my sweet little Nora must promise me not to plead his cause. Give me your hand on it. Come, come, what is this? Give me your hand. There now, that's settled. I assure you it would be quite impossible for me to work with him; I literally feel physically ill when I am in the company of such people.

NORA [*takes her hand out of his and goes to the opposite side of the Christmas Tree*]. How hot it is in here; and I have such a lot to do.

HELMER [*getting up and putting his papers in order*]. Yes, and I must try and read through some of these before dinner; and I must think about your costume, too. And it is just possible I may have something ready in gold paper to hang up on the Tree. [*Puts his hand on her head.*] My precious little singing-bird!

[*He goes into his room and shuts the door after him.*]

NORA [*after a pause, whispers*]. No, no—it isn't true. It's impossible; it must be impossible.

[*The* NURSE *opens the door on the left.*]

NURSE. The little ones are begging so hard to be allowed to come in to mamma.

NORA. No, no, no! Don't let them come in to me! You stay with them, Anne.

NURSE. Very well, ma'am.

[*Shuts the door.*]

NORA [*pale with terror*]. Deprave my little children? Poison my home? [*a short pause. Then she tosses her head.*] It's not true. It can't possibly be true.

Act 2

THE SAME SCENE. *The Christmas Tree is in the corner by the piano, stripped of its ornaments and with burnt-down candle-ends on its dishevelled branches.* NORA'S *cloak and hat are lying on the sofa. She is alone in the room, walking about uneasily. She stops by the sofa and takes up her cloak.*

NORA [*drops the cloak*]. Someone is coming now! [*goes to the door and listens*] No—it is no one. Of course, no one will come today, Christmas Day—nor tomorrow either. But, perhaps—[*opens the door and looks out*] No, nothing in the letter-box; it is quite empty. [*comes forward*] What rubbish! of course he can't be in earnest about it. Such a thing couldn't happen; it is impossible—I have three little children.

[*Enter the* NURSE *from the room on the left, carrying a big cardboard box.*]

NURSE. At last I have found the box with the fancy dress.

NORA. Thanks; put it on the table.

NURSE [*doing so*]. But it is very much in want of mending.

NORA. I should like to tear it into a hundred thousand pieces.

NURSE. What an idea! It can easily be put in order—just a little patience.

NORA. Yes, I will go and get Mrs. Linde to come and help me with it.

NURSE. What, out again? In this horrible weather? You will catch cold, ma'am, and make yourself ill.

NORA. Well, worse than that might happen. How are the children?

NURSE. The poor little souls are playing with their Christmas presents, but—

NORA. Do they ask much for me?

NURSE. You see, they are so accustomed to have their mamma with them.

NORA. Yes, but, nurse, I shall not be able to be so much with them now as I was before.

NURSE. Oh well, young children easily get accustomed to anything.

NORA. Do you think so? Do you think they would forget their mother if she went away altogether?

NURSE. Good heavens!—went away altogether?

NORA. Nurse, I want you to tell me something I have often wondered about—how could you have the heart to put your own child out among strangers?

NURSE. I was obliged to, if I wanted to be little Nora's nurse.

NORA. Yes, but how could you be willing to do it?

NURSE. What, when I was going to get such a good place by it? A poor girl who has got into trouble should be glad to. Besides, that wicked man didn't do a single thing for me.

NORA. But I suppose your daughter has quite forgotten you.

NURSE. No, indeed she hasn't. She wrote to me when she was confirmed, and when she was married.

NORA [*putting her arms round her neck*]. Dear old Anne, you were a good mother to me when I was little.

NURSE. Little Nora, poor dear, had no other mother but me.

NORA. And if my little ones had no other mother, I am sure you would—What nonsense I am talking! [*opens the box*] Go in to them. Now I must—. You will see tomorrow how charming I shall look.

NURSE. I am sure there will be no one at the ball so charming as you, ma'am.

[*Goes into the room on the left.*]

NORA [*begins to unpack the box, but soon pushes it away from her*]. If only I dared go out. If only no one would come. If only I could be sure nothing would happen here in the meantime. Stuff and nonsense! No one will come. Only I mustn't think about it. I will brush my muff. What, lovely gloves! Out of my thoughts, out of my thoughts! One, two, three, four, five, six—[*Screams.*] Ah! there is someone coming—

[*Makes a movement towards the door, but stands irresolute.*]

[*Enter* MRS. LINDE *from the hall, where she has taken off her cloak and hat.*]

NORA. Oh, it's you, Christine. There is no one else out there, is there? How good of you to come!

MRS. LINDE. I heard you were up asking for me.

NORA. Yes, I was passing by. As a matter of fact, it is something you could help me with. Let us sit down here on the sofa. Look here. Tomorrow evening there is to be a fancy-dress ball at the Stenborgs', who live about us; and Torvald wants me to go as a Neapolitan fisher-girl, and dance the Tarantella that I learnt at Capri.

MRS. LINDE. I see; you are going to keep up the character.

NORA. Yes, Torvald wants me to. Look, here is the dress; Torvald had it made for me there, but now it is all so torn, and I haven't any idea—

MRS. LINDE. We will easily put that right. It is only some of the trimming come unsewn here and there. Needle and thread? Now then, that's all we want.

NORA. It *is* nice of you.

MRS. LINDE [*sewing*]. So you are going to be dressed up tomorrow, Nora. I will tell you what—I shall come in for a moment and see you in your fine feathers. But I have completely forgotten to thank you for a delightful evening yesterday.

NORA [*gets up, and crosses the stages*]. Well I don't think yesterday was as pleasant as usual. You ought to have come to town a little earlier, Christine.

Certainly Torvald does understand how to make a house dainty and attractive.

MRS. LINDE. And so do you, it seems to me; you are not your father's daughter for nothing. But tell me, is Doctor Rank always as depressed as he was yesterday?

NORA. No; yesterday it was very noticeable. I must tell you that he suffers from a very dangerous disease. He has consumption of the spine, poor creature. His father was a horrible man who committed all sorts of excesses; and that is why his son was sickly from childhood, do you understand?

MRS. LINDE [*dropping her sewing*]. But, my dearest Nora, how do you know anything about such things?

NORA [*walking about*]. Pooh! When you have three children, you get visits now and then from—from married women, who know something of medical matters, and they talk about one thing and another.

MRS. LINDE [*goes on sewing. A short silence*]. Does Doctor Rank come here every day?

NORA. Every day regularly. He is Torvald's most intimate friend, and a great friend of mine too. He is just like one of the family.

MRS. LINDE. But tell me this—is he perfectly sincere? I mean, isn't he the kind of man that is very anxious to make himself agreeable?

NORA. Not in the least. What makes you think that?

MRS. LINDE. When you introduced him to me yesterday, he declared he had often heard my name mentioned in this house; but afterwards I noticed that your husband hadn't the slightest idea who I was. So how could Doctor Rank—?

NORA. That is quite right, Christine. Torvald is so absurdly fond of me that he wants me absolutely to himself, as he says. At first he used to seem almost jealous if I mentioned any of the dear folk at home, so naturally I gave up doing so. But I often talk about such things with Doctor Rank, because he likes hearing about them.

MRS. LINDE. Listen to me, Nora. You are still very like a child in many things, and I am older than you in many ways and have a little more experience. Let me tell you this—you ought to make an end of it with Doctor Rank.

NORA. What ought I to make an end of?

MRS. LINDE. Of two things, I think. Yesterday you talked some nonsense about a rich admirer who was to leave you money—

NORA. An admirer who doesn't exist, unfortunately! But what then?

MRS. LINDE. Is Doctor Rank a man of means?

NORA. Yes, he is.

MRS. LINDE. And has no one to provide for?

NORA. No, no one; but—

MRS. LINDE. And comes here every day?

NORA. Yes, I told you so.

MRS. LINDE. But how can this well-bred man be so tactless?

NORA. I don't understand you at all.

MRS. LINDE. Don't prevaricate, Nora. Do you suppose I don't guess who lent you the two hundred and fifty pounds?

NORA. Are you out of your senses? How can you think of such a thing! A friend of ours, who comes here every day! Do you realise what a horribly painful position that would be?

MRS. LINDE. Then it really isn't he?

NORA. No, certainly not. It would never have entered into my head for a moment. Besides, he had no money to lend then; he came into his money afterwards.

MRS. LINDE. Well, I think that was lucky for you, my dear Nora.

NORA. No, it would never have come into my head to ask Doctor Rank. Although I am quite sure that if I had asked him—

MRS. LINDE. But of course you won't.

NORA. Of course not. I have no reason to think it could possibly be necessary. But I am quite sure that if I told Doctor Rank—

MRS. LINDE. Behind your husband's back?

NORA. I *must* make an end of it with the other one, and that will be behind his back too. I *must* make an end of it with him.

MRS. LINDE. Yes, that is what I told you yesterday, but—

NORA [*walking up and down*]. A man can put a thing like that straight much easier than a woman—

MRS. LINDE. One's husband, yes.

NORA. Nonsense! [*standing still*] When you pay off a debt you get your bond back, don't you?

MRS. LINDE. Yes, as a matter of course.

NORA. And can tear it into a hundred thousand pieces, and burn it up—the nasty dirty paper!

MRS. LINDE [*looks hard at her, lays down her sewing and gets up slowly*]. Nora, you are concealing something from me.

NORA. Do I look as if I were?

MRS. LINDE. Something has happened to you since yesterday morning. Nora, what is it?

NORA [*going nearer to her*]. Christine! [*listens*] Hush! there's Torvald come home. Do you mind going in to the children for the present? Torvald can't bear to see dressmaking going on. Let Anne help you.

MRS. LINDE [*gathering some of the things together*]. Certainly—but I am not going away from here till we have had it out with one another.

[*She goes into the room on the left, as* HELMER *comes in from the hall.*]

NORA [*going up to* HELMER]. I have wanted you so much, Torvald dear.

HELMER. Was that the dressmaker?

NORA. No, it was Christine; she is helping me to put my dress in order. You will see I shall look quite smart.

HELMER. Wasn't that a happy thought of mine, now?

NORA. Splendid! But don't you think it is nice of me, too, to do as you wish?

HELMER. Nice?—because you do as your husband wishes? Well, well, you little rogue, I am sure you did not mean it in that way. But I am not going to disturb you; you will want to be trying on your dress, I expect.

NORA. I suppose you are going to work.

HELMER. Yes. [*shows her a bundle of papers*] Look at that. I have just been into the bank. [*Turns to go into his room.*]

NORA. Torvald.

HELMER. Yes.

NORA. If your little squirrel were to ask you for something very, very prettily—?

HELMER. What then?

NORA. Would you do it?

HELMER. I should like to hear what it is, first.

NORA. Your squirrel would run about and do all her tricks if you would be nice, and do what she wants.

HELMER. Speak plainly.

NORA. Your skylark would chirp about in every room, with her song rising and falling—

HELMER. Well, my skylark does that anyhow.

NORA. I would play the fairy and dance for you in the moonlight, Torvald.

HELMER. Nora—you surely don't mean that request you made of me this morning?

NORA [*going near him*]. Yes, Torvald, I beg you so earnestly—

HELMER. Have you really the courage to open up that question again?

NORA. Yes, dear, you *must* do as I ask; you *must* let Krogstad keep his post in the Bank.

HELMER. My dear Nora, it is his post that I have arranged Mrs. Linde shall have.

NORA. Yes, you have been awfully kind about that; but you could just as well dismiss some other clerk instead of Krogstad.

HELMER. This is simply incredible obstinacy! Because you chose to give him a thoughtless promise that you would speak for him, I am expected to—

NORA. That isn't the reason, Torvald. It is for your own sake. This fellow writes in the most scurrilous newspapers; you have told me so yourself. He can do you an unspeakable amount of harm. I am frightened to death of him—

HELMER. Ah, I understand; it is recollections of the past that scare you.

NORA. What do you mean?

HELMER. Naturally you are thinking of your father.

NORA. Yes—yes, of course. Just recall to your mind what these malicious creatures wrote in the papers about papa, and how horribly they slandered him. I believe they would have procured his dismissal if the Department had not sent you over to inquire into it, and if you had not been so kindly disposed and helpful to him.

HELMER. My little Nora, there is an important difference between your father and me. Your father's reputation as a public official was not above suspicion. Mine is, and I hope it will continue to be so, as long as I hold my office.

NORA. You never can tell what mischief these men may contrive. We ought to be so well off, so snug and happy here in our peaceful home, and have no cares—you and I and the children, Torvald! That is why I beg you so earnestly—

HELMER. And it is just by interceding for him that you make it impossible for me to keep him. It is already known at the Bank that I mean to dismiss Krogstad. Is it to get about now that the new manager has changed his mind at his wife's bidding—

NORA. And what if it did?

HELMER. Of course!—if only this obstinate little person can get her way! Do you suppose I am going to make myself ridiculous before my whole staff, to let people think that I am a man to be swayed by all sorts of outside influence? I should very soon feel the consequences of it, I can tell you! And besides, there is one thing that makes it quite impossible for me to have Krogstad in the Bank as long as I am manager.

NORA. Whatever is that?

HELMER. His moral failings I might perhaps have overlooked, if necessary—

NORA. Yes, you could—couldn't you?

HELMER. And I hear he is a good worker, too. But I knew him when we were boys. It was one of those rash friendships that so often prove an incubus in after life. I may as well tell you plainly, we were once on very intimate terms with one another. But this tactless fellow lays no restraint on himself when other people are present. On the contrary, he thinks it gives him the right to adopt a familiar tone with me, and every minute it is "I say, Helmer, old fellow!" and that sort of thing. I assure you it is extremely painful for me. He would make my position in the Bank intolerable.

NORA. Torvald, I don't believe you mean that.

HELMER. Don't you? Why not?

NORA. Because it is such a narrow-minded way of looking at things.

HELMER. What are you saying? Narrow-minded? Do you think I am narrow-minded?

NORA. No, just the opposite, dear—and it is exactly for that reason.

HELMER. It's the same thing. You say my point of view is narrow-minded, so I must be so too. Narrow-minded! Very well—I must put an end to this. [*Goes to the hall-door and calls.*] Helen!

NORA. What are you going to do?

HELMER [*looking among his papers*]. Settle it. [*Enter* MAID.] Look here; take this letter and go downstairs with it at once. Find a messenger and tell him to deliver it, and be quick. The address is on it, and here is the money.

MAID. Very well, sir.

[*Exits with the letter.*]

HELMER [*putting his papers together*]. Now then, little Miss Obstinate.

NORA [*breathlessly*]. Torvald—what was that letter?

HELMER. Krogstad's dismissal.

NORA. Call her back, Torvald! There is still time. Oh Torvald, call her back! Do it for my sake—for your own sake—for the children's sake! Do you hear me, Torvald? Call her back!! You don't know what that letter can bring upon us.

HELMER. It's too late.

NORA. Yes, it's too late.

HELMER. My dear Nora, I can forgive the anxiety you are in, although really it is an insult to me. It is, indeed. Isn't it an insult to think that I should be afraid of a starving quill-driver's vengeance? But I forgive you nevertheless, because it is such eloquent witness to your great love for me. [*takes her in his arms*] And that is as it should be, my own darling Nora. Come what will, you may be sure I shall have both courage and strength if they be needed. You will see I am man enough to take everything upon myself.

NORA [*in a horror-stricken voice*]. What do you mean by that?

HELMER. Everything, I say—

NORA [*recovering herself*]. You will never have to do that.

HELMER. That's right. Well, we will share it, Nora, as man and wife should. That is how it shall be. [*caressing her*] Are you content now? There! there!— not these frightened dove's eyes! The whole thing is only the wildest fancy!—Now, you must go and play through the Tarantella and practise with your tambourine. I shall go into the inner office and shut the door, and I shall hear nothing; you can make as much noise as you please. [*turns back at the door*] And when Rank comes, tell him where he will find me.

[*Nods to her, takes his papers and goes into his room, and shuts the door after him*]

NORA [*bewildered with anxiety, stands as if rooted to the spot, and whispers*]. He is capable of doing it. He will do it. He will do it in spite of everything.—No, not that! Never, never! Anything rather than that! Oh, for some help, some way out of it! [*The door-bell rings.*] Doctor Rank! Anything rather than that—anything, whatever it is!

[*She puts her hands over her face, pulls herself together, goes to the door and opens it.* RANK *is standing without, hanging up his coat. During the following dialogue it begins to grow dark.*]

NORA. Good-day, Doctor Rank. I knew your ring. But you mustn't go in to Torvald now; I think he is busy with something.

RANK. And you?

NORA [*brings him in and shuts the door after him*]. Oh, you know very well I always have time for you.

RANK. Thank you. I shall make use of as much of it as I can.

NORA. What do you mean by that? As much of it as you can?

RANK. Well, does that alarm you?

NORA. It was such a strange way of putting it. Is anything likely to happen?

RANK. Nothing but what I have long been prepared for. But I certainly didn't expect it to happen so soon.

NORA [*gripping him by the arm*]. What have you found out? Doctor Rank, you must tell me.

RANK [*sitting down by the stove*]. It is all up with me. And it can't be helped.

NORA [*with a sigh of relief*]. Is it about yourself?

RANK. Who else? It is no use lying to one's self. I am the most wretched of all my patients, Mrs. Helmer. Lately I have been taking stock of my internal economy. Bankrupt! Probably within a month I shall lie rotting in the churchyard.

NORA. What an ugly thing to say!

RANK. The thing itself is cursedly ugly, and the worst of it is that I shall have to face so much more that is ugly before that. I shall only make one more examination of myself; when I have done that, I shall know pretty certainly when it will be that the horrors of dissolution will begin. There is something I want to tell you. Helmer's refined nature gives him an unconquerable disgust at everything that is ugly; I won't have him in my sick-room.

NORA. Oh, but, Doctor Rank—

RANK. I won't have him there. Not on any account. I bar my door to him. As soon as I am quite certain that the worst has come, I shall send you my card with a black cross on it, and then you will know that the loathsome end has begun.

NORA. You are quite absurd today. And I wanted you so much to be in a really good humour.

RANK. With death stalking beside me?—To have to pay this penalty for another man's sin! Is there any justice in that? And in every single family, in one way or another, some such inexorable retribution is being exacted—

NORA [*putting her hands over her ears*]. Rubbish! Do talk of something cheerful.

RANK. Oh, it's a mere laughing matter, the whole thing. My poor innocent spine has to suffer for my father's youthful amusements.

NORA [*sitting at the table on the left*]. I suppose you mean that he was too partial to asparagus and pâté de foie gras, don't you.

RANK. Yes, and to truffles.

NORA. Truffles, yes. And oysters too, I suppose?

RANK. Oysters, of course, that goes without saying.

NORA. And heaps of port and champagne. It is sad that all these nice things should take their revenge on our bones.

RANK. Especially that they should revenge themselves on the unlucky bones of those who have not had the satisfaction of enjoying them.

NORA. Yes, that's the saddest part of it all.

RANK [*with a searching look at her*]. Hm!—

NORA [*after a short pause*]. Why did you smile?

RANK. No, it was you that laughed.

NORA. No, it was you that smiled, Doctor Rank!

RANK [*rising*]. You are a greater rascal than I thought.

NORA. I am in a silly mood today.

RANK. So it seems.

NORA [*putting her hands on his shoulders*]. Dear, dear Doctor Rank, death mustn't take you away from Torvald and me.

RANK. It is a loss you would easily recover from. Those who are gone are soon forgotten.

NORA [*looking at him anxiously*]. Do you believe that?

RANK. People form new ties, and then—

NORA. Who will form new ties?

RANK. Both you and Helmer, when I am gone. You yourself are already on the high road to it, I think. What did that Mrs. Linde want here last night?

NORA. Oho!—you don't mean to say you are jealous of poor Christine?

RANK. Yes, I am. She will be my successor in this house. When I am done for, this woman will—

NORA. Hush! don't speak so loud. She is in that room.

RANK. Today again. There, you see.

NORA. She has only come to sew my dress for me. Bless my soul, how unreasonable you are! [*sits down on the sofa*] Be nice now, Doctor Rank, and tomorrow you will see how beautifully I shall dance, and you can imagine I am doing it all for you—and for Torvald too, of course. [*takes various things out of the box*] Doctor Rank, come and sit down here, and I will show you something.

RANK [*sitting down*]. What is it?

NORA. Just look at those!

RANK. Silk stockings.

NORA. Flesh-coloured. Aren't they lovely? It is so dark here now, but tomorrow—. No, no, no! you must only look at the feet. Oh well, you may have leave to look at the legs too.

RANK. Hm!—

NORA. Why are you looking so critical? Don't you think they will fit me?

RANK. I have no means of forming an opinion about that.

NORA [*looks at him for a moment*]. For shame! [*hits him lightly on the ear with the stockings*] That's to punish you. [*folds them up again*]

RANK. And what other nice things am I to be allowed to see?

NORA. Not a single thing more, for being so naughty. [*She looks among the things, humming to herself.*]

RANK [*after a short silence*]. When I am sitting here, talking to you as intimately as this, I cannot imagine for a moment what would have become of me if I had never come into this house.

NORA [*smiling*]. I believe you do feel thoroughly at home with us.

RANK [*in a lower voice, looking straight in front of him*]. And to be obliged to leave it all—

NORA. Nonsense, you are not going to leave it.

RANK [*as before*]. And not be able to leave behind one the slightest token of one's gratitude, scarcely even a fleeting regret—nothing but an empty place which the first comer can fill as well as any other.

NORA. And if I asked you now for a—? No!

RANK. For what?

NORA. For a big proof of your friendship—

RANK. Yes, yes!

NORA. I mean a tremendously big favour—

RANK. Would you really make me so happy for once?

NORA. Ah, but you don't know what it is yet.

RANK. No—but tell me.

NORA. I really can't, Doctor Rank. It is something out of all reason; it means advice, and help, and a favour—

RANK. The bigger a thing it is the better. I can't conceive what it is you mean. Do tell me. Haven't I your confidence?

NORA. More than anyone else. I know you are my truest and best friend, and so I will tell you what it is. Well, Doctor Rank, it is something you must help me to prevent. You know how devotedly, how inexpressibly deeply Torvald loves me; he would never for a moment hesitate to give his life for me.

RANK [*leaning towards her*]. Nora—do you think he is the only one—?

NORA [*with a slight start*]. The only one—?

RANK. The only one who would gladly give his life for your sake.

NORA [*sadly*]. Is that it?

RANK. I was determined you should know it before I went away, and there will never be a better opportunity than this. Now you know it, Nora. And now you know, too, that you can trust me as you would trust no one else.

NORA [*rises, deliberately and quietly*]. Let me pass.

RANK [*makes room for her to pass him, but sits still*]. Nora!

NORA [*at the hall door*]. Helen, bring in the lamp. [*goes over to the stove*] Dear Doctor Rank, that was really horrid of you.

RANK. To have loved you as much as anyone else does? Was that horrid?

NORA. No, but to go and tell me so. There was really no need—

RANK. What do you mean? Did you know—? [MAID *enters with lamp, puts it down on the table, and goes out.*] Nora—Mrs. Helmer—tell me, had you any idea of this?

NORA. Oh, how do I know whether I had or whether I hadn't? I really can't tell you—To think you could be so clumsy, Doctor Rank! We were getting on so nicely.

RANK. Well, at all events you know now that you can command me, body and soul. So won't you speak out?

NORA [*looking at him*]. After what happened?

RANK. I beg you to let me know what it is.

NORA. I can't tell you anything now.

RANK. Yes, yes. You mustn't punish me in that way. Let me have permission to do for you whatever a man may do.

NORA. You can do nothing for me now. Besides, I really don't need any help at all. You will find that the whole thing is merely fancy on my part. It really is so—of course it is! [*Sits down in the rocking-chair, and looks at him with a smile*] You are a nice sort of man, Doctor Rank!—don't you feel ashamed of yourself, now the lamp has come?

RANK. Not a bit. But perhaps I had better go—for ever?

NORA. No, indeed, you shall not. Of course you must come here just as before. You know very well Torvald can't do without you.

RANK. Yes, but you?

NORA. Oh, I am always tremendously pleased when you come.

RANK. It is just that, that put me on the wrong track. You are a riddle to me. I have often thought that you would almost as soon be in my company as in Helmer's.

NORA. Yes—you see there are some people one loves best, and others whom one would almost always rather have as companions.

RANK. Yes, there is something in that.

NORA. When I was at home, of course I loved papa best. But I always thought it tremendous fun if I could steal down into the maid's room, because they never moralised at all, and talked to each other about such entertaining things.

RANK. I see—it is *their* place I have taken.

NORA [*jumping up and going to him*]. Oh, dear, nice Doctor Rank, I never meant that at all. But surely you can understand that being with Torvald is a little like being with papa—

[*Enter* MAID *from the hall*]

MAID. If you please, ma'am. [*whispers and hands her a card*]

NORA [*glancing at the card*]. Oh! [*puts it in her pocket*]

RANK. Is there anything wrong?

NORA. No, no, not in the least. It is only something—it is my new dress—

RANK. What? Your dress is lying there.

NORA. Oh, yes, that one; but this is another. I ordered it. Torvald mustn't know about it—

RANK. Oho! Then that was the great secret.

NORA. Of course. Just go in to him; he is sitting in the inner room. Keep him as long as—

RANK. Make your mind easy; I won't let him escape. [*goes into* HELMER'S *room*]

NORA [*to the* MAID]. And he is standing waiting in the kitchen?

MAID. Yes; he came up the back stairs.

NORA. But didn't you tell him no one was in?

MAID. Yes, but it was no good.

NORA. He won't go away?

MAID. No; he says he won't until he has seen you, ma'am.

NORA. Well, let him come in—but quietly. Helen, you mustn't say anything about it to anyone. It is a surprise for my husband.

MAID. Yes, ma'am, I quite understand.   [*Exit.*]

NORA. This dreadful thing is going to happen! It will happen in spite of me! No, no, no, it can't happen—it shan't happen!

[*She bolts the door of* HELMER'S *room. The* MAID *opens the hall door for* KROGSTAD *and shuts it after him. He is wearing a fur coat, high boots and a fur cap.*]

NORA [*advancing towards him*]. Speak low—my husband is at home.

KROGSTAD. No matter about that.

NORA. What do you want of me?

KROGSTAD. An explanation of something.

NORA. Make haste then. What is it?

KROGSTAD. You know, I suppose, that I have got my dismissal.

NORA. I couldn't prevent it, Mr. Krogstad. I fought as hard as I could on your side, but it was no good.

KROGSTAD. Does your husband love you so little, then? He knows that what I can expose you to, and yet he ventures—

NORA. How can you suppose that he has any knowledge of the sort?

KROGSTAD. I didn't suppose so at all. It would not be the least like our dear Torvald Helmer to show so much courage—

NORA. Mr. Krogstad, a little respect for my husband, please.

KROGSTAD. Certainly—all the respect he deserves. But since you have kept the matter so carefully to yourself, I make bold to suppose that you have a little clearer idea, than you had yesterday, of what it actually is that you have done?

NORA. More than you could ever teach me.

KROGSTAD. Yes, such a bad lawyer as I am.

NORA. What is it you want of me?

KROGSTAD. Only to see how you were, Mrs. Helmer. I have been thinking about you all day long. A mere cashier, a quill-driver, a—well, a man like me—even he has a little of what is called feeling, you know.

NORA. Show it, then; think of my little children.

KROGSTAD. Have you and your husband thought of mine? But never mind about that. I only wanted to tell you that you need not take this matter too seriously. In the first place there will be no accusation made on my part.

NORA. No, of course not; I was sure of that.

KROGSTAD. The whole thing can be arranged amicably; there is no reason why anyone should know anything about it. It will remain a secret between us three.

NORA. My husband must never get to know anything about it.

KROGSTAD. How will you be able to prevent it? Am I to understand that you can pay the balance that is owing?

NORA. No, not just at present.

KROGSTAD. Or perhaps that you have some expedient for raising the money soon?

NORA. No expedient that I mean to make use of.

KROGSTAD. Well, in any case, it would have been of no use to you now. If you
    stood there with ever so much money in your hand, I would never part
    with your bond.

NORA. Tell me what purpose you mean to put it to.

KROGSTAD. I shall only preserve it—keep it in my possession. No one who is
    not concerned in the matter shall have the slightest hint of it. So that if
    the thought of it has driven you to any desperate resolution—

NORA. It has.

KROGSTAD. If you had it in your mind to run away from your home—

NORA. I had.

KROGSTAD. Or even something worse—

NORA. How could you know that?

KROGSTAD. Give up the idea.

NORA. How did you know I had thought of *that?*

KROGSTAD. Most of us think of that at first. I did, too—but I hadn't the
    courage.

NORA [*faintly*]. No more had I.

KROGSTAD [*in a tone of relief*]. No, that's it, isn't it—you hadn't the courage
    either?

NORA. No, I haven't—I haven't.

KROGSTAD. Besides, it would have been a great piece of folly. Once the first
    storm at home is over—. I have a letter for your husband in my pocket.

NORA. Telling him everything?

KROGSTAD. In as lenient a manner as I possibly could.

NORA [*quickly*]. He mustn't get the letter. Tear it up. I will find some means
    of getting money.

KROGSTAD. Excuse me, Mrs. Helmer, but I think I told you just now—

NORA. I am not speaking of what I owe you. Tell me what sum you are asking
    my husband for, and I will get the money.

KROGSTAD. I am not asking your husband for a penny.

NORA. What do you want, then?

KROGSTAD. I will tell you. I want to rehabilitate myself, Mrs. Helmer; I want to
    get on; and in that your husband must help me. For the last year and a half
    I have not had a hand in anything dishonourable, and all that time I have
    been struggling in most restricted circumstances. I was content to work
    my way up step by step. Now I am turned out, and I am not going to be
    satisfied with merely being taken into favour again. I want to get on, I tell
    you. I want to get into the Bank again, in a higher position. Your husband
    must make a place for me—

NORA. That he will never do!

KROGSTAD. He will; I know him; he dare not protest. And as soon as I am in
    there again with him, then you will see! Within a year I shall be the man-
    ager's right hand. It will be Nils Krogstad and not Torvald Helmer who
    manages the Bank.

NORA. That's a thing you will never see!

KROGSTAD. Do you mean that you will—?

NORA. I have courage enough for it now.

KROGSTAD. Oh, you can't frighten me. A fine, spoilt lady like you—

NORA. You will see, you will see.

KROGSTAD. Under the ice, perhaps? Down into the cold, coal-black water?
    And then, in the spring, to float up to the surface, all horrible and un-
    recognisable, with your hair fallen out—

NORA. You can't frighten me.

KROGSTAD.   Nor you me. People don't do such things, Mrs. Helmer. Besides, what use would it be? I should have him completely in my power all the same.

NORA.   Afterwards? When I am no longer—

KROGSTAD.   Have you forgotten that it is I who have the keeping of your reputation? [NORA *stands speechlessly looking at him.*] Well, now, I have warned you. Do not do anything foolish. When Helmer has had my letter, I shall expect a message from him. And be sure you remember that it is your husband himself who has forced me into such ways as this again. I will never forgive him for that. Good-bye, Mrs. Helmer.

[*Exit through the hall*]

NORA [*goes to the hall door, opens it slightly and listens*].   He is going. He is not putting the letter in the box. Oh no, no! that's impossible! [*opens the door by degrees*] What is that? He is standing outside. He is not going downstairs. Is he hesitating? Can he—

[*A letter drops into the box; then* KROGSTAD'S *footsteps are heard, till they die away as he goes downstairs.* NORA *utters a stifled cry and runs across the room to the table by the sofa. A short pause.*]

NORA.   In the letter-box. [*steals across to the hall door*] There it lies—Torvald, Torvald, there is no hope for us now!

[MRS. LINDE *comes in from the room on the left, carrying the dress.*]

MRS. LINDE.   There, I can't see anything more to mend now. Would you like to try it on—?

NORA [*in a hoarse whisper*].   Christine, come here.

MRS. LINDE [*throwing the dress down on the sofa*].   What is the matter with you? You look so agitated!

NORA.   Come here. Do you see that letter? There, look—you can see it through the glass in the letter-box.

MRS. LINDE.   Yes, I see it.

NORA.   That letter is from Krogstad.

MRS. LINDE.   Nora—it was Krogstad who lent you the money!

NORA.   Yes, and now Torvald will know all about it.

MRS. LINDE.   Believe me, Nora, that's the best thing for both of you.

NORA.   You don't know all. I forged a name.

MRS. LINDE.   Good heavens—!

NORA.   I only want to say this to you, Christine—you must be my witness.

MRS. LINDE.   Your witness? What do you mean? What am I to—?

NORA.   If I should go out of my mind—and it might easily happen—

MRS. LINDE.   Nora!

NORA.   Or if anything else should happen to me—anything, for instance, that might prevent my being here—

MRS. LINDE.   Nora! Nora! you are quite out of your mind.

NORA.   And if it should happen that there were someone who wanted to take all the responsibility, all the blame, you understand—

MRS. LINDE.   Yes, yes—but how can you suppose—?

NORA.   Then you must be my witness, that it is not true, Christine. I am not out of my mind at all; I am in my right senses now, and I tell you no one else has known anything about it; I, and I alone, did the whole thing. Remember that.

MRS. LINDE. I will, indeed. But I don't understand all this.

NORA. How should you understand it? A wonderful thing is going to happen.

MRS. LINDE. A wonderful thing?

NORA. Yes, a wonderful thing!—But it is so terrible, Christine; it *mustn't* happen, not for all the world.

MRS. LINDE. I will go at once and see Krogstad.

NORA. Don't go to him; he will do you some harm.

MRS. LINDE. There was a time when he would gladly do anything for my sake.

NORA. He?

MRS. LINDE. Where does he live?

NORA. How should I know—? Yes [*feeling in her pocket*] here is his card. But the letter, the letter—!

HELMER [*calls from his room, knocking at the door*]. Nora!

NORA [*cries out anxiously*]. Oh, what's that? What do you want?

HELMER. Don't be so frightened. We are not coming in; you have locked the door. Are you trying on your dress?

NORA. Yes, that's it. I look so nice, Torvald.

MRS. LINDE [*who has read the card*]. I see he lives at the corner here.

NORA. Yes, but it's no use. It is hopeless. The letter is lying there in the box.

MRS. LINDE. And your husband keeps the key?

NORA. Yes, always.

MRS. LINDE. Krogstad must ask for his letter back unread, he must find some pretence—

NORA. But it is just at this time that Torvald generally—

MRS. LINDE. You must delay him. Go in to him in the meantime. I will come back as soon as I can.

[*She goes out hurriedly through the hall door.*]

NORA [*goes to* HELMER's *door, opens it and peeps in*]. Torvald!

HELMER [*from the inner room*]. Well? May I venture at last to come into my own room again? Come along, Rank, now you will see—[*halting in the doorway*] But what is this?

NORA. What is what, dear?

HELMER. Rank led me to expect a splendid transformation.

RANK [*in the doorway*]. I understood so, but evidently I was mistaken.

NORA. Yes, nobody is to have the chance of admiring me in my dress until tomorrow.

HELMER. But, my dear Nora, you look so worn out. Have you been practising too much?

NORA. No, I have not practised at all.

HELMER. But you will need to—

NORA. Yes, indeed I shall, Torvald. But I can't get on a bit without you to help me; I have absolutely forgotten the whole thing.

HELMER. Oh, we will soon work it up again.

NORA. Yes, help me, Torvald. Promise that you will! I am so nervous about it—all the people—. You must give yourself up to me entirely this evening. Not the tiniest bit of business—you mustn't even take a pen in your hand. Will you promise, Torvald dear?

HELMER. I promise. This evening I will be wholly and absolutely at your service, you helpless little mortal. Ah, by the way, first of all I will just—

[*Goes towards the hall door*]

NORA. What are you going to do there?

HELMER. Only see if any letters have come.

NORA. No, no! don't do that, Torvald!

HELMER. Why not?

NORA. Torvald, please don't. There is nothing there.

HELMER. Well, let me look. [*Turns to go to the letter-box.* NORA, *at the piano, plays the first bars of the Tarantella.* HELMER *stops in the doorway.*] Aha!

NORA. I can't dance tomorrow if I don't practise with you.

HELMER [*going up to her*]. Are you really so afraid of it, dear.

NORA. Yes, so dreadfully afraid of it. Let me practise at once; there is time now, before we go to dinner. Sit down and play for me, Torvald dear; criticise me, and correct me as you play.

HELMER. With great pleasure, if you wish me to.

[*Sits down at the piano.*]

NORA [*takes out of the box a tambourine and a long variegated shawl. She hastily drapes the shawl round her. Then she springs to the front of the stage and calls out.*]. Now play for me! I am going to dance!

[HELMER *plays and* NORA *dances.* RANK *stands by the piano behind* HELMER *and looks on.*]

HELMER [*as he plays*]. Slower, slower!

NORA. I can't do it any other way.

HELMER. Not so violently, Nora!

NORA. This is the way.

HELMER [*stops playing*]. No, no—that is not a bit right.

NORA [*laughing and swinging the tambourine*]. Didn't I tell you so?

RANK. Let me play for her.

HELMER [*getting up*]. Yes, do. I can correct her better then.

[RANK *sits down at the piano and plays.* NORA *dances more and more wildly.* HELMER *has taken up a position beside the stove, and during her dance gives her frequent instructions. She does not seem to hear him; her hair comes down and falls over her shoulders; she pays no attention to it, but goes on dancing. Enter* MRS. LINDE.]

MRS. LINDE [*standing as if spell-bound in the doorway*]. Oh!—

NORA [*as she dances*]. Such fun, Christine!

HELMER. My dear darling Nora, you are dancing as if your life depended on it.

NORA. So it does.

HELMER. Stop, Rank; this is sheer madness. Stop, I tell you! [RANK *stops playing, and* NORA *suddenly stands still.* HELMER *goes up to her.*] I could never have believed it. You have forgotten everything I taught you.

NORA [*throwing away the tambourine*]. There, you see.

HELMER. You will want a lot of coaching.

NORA. Yes, you see how much I need it. You must coach me up to the last minute. Promise me that, Torvald!

HELMER. You can depend on me.

NORA. You must not think of anything but me, either today or tomorrow; you mustn't open a single letter—not even open the letter-box—

HELMER. Ah, you are still afraid of that fellow—

NORA. Yes, indeed I am.

HELMER. Nora, I can tell from your looks that there is a letter from him lying there.

NORA. I don't know; I think there is; but you must not read anything of that kind now. Nothing horrid must come between us till this is all over.

RANK [*whispers to* HELMER]. You mustn't contradict her.

HELMER [*taking her in his arms*]. The child shall have her way. But tomorrow night, after you have danced—

NORA. Then you will be free.

[MAID *appears in the doorway to the right.*]

MAID. Dinner is served, ma'am.

NORA. We will have champagne, Helen.

MAID. Very good, ma'am.

[*Exit.*]

HELMER. Hullo!—are we going to have a banquet?

NORA. Yes, a champagne banquet till the small hours. [*calls out*] And a few macaroons, Helen—lots, just for once!

HELMER. Come, come, don't be so wild and nervous. Be my own little skylark, as you used.

NORA. Yes, dear, I will. But go in now and you too, Doctor Rank. Christine, you must help me to do up my hair.

RANK [*whispers to* HELMER *as they go out*]. I suppose there is nothing—she is not expecting anything?

HELMER. Far from it, my dear fellow; it is simply nothing more than this childish nervousness I was telling you of.

[*They go into the right-hand room.*]

NORA. Well!

MRS. LINDE. Gone out of town.

NORA. I could tell from your face.

MRS. LINDE. He is coming home tomorrow evening. I wrote a note for him.

NORA. You should have let it alone; you must prevent nothing. After all, it is splendid to be waiting for a wonderful thing to happen.

MRS. LINDE. What is it that you are waiting for?

NORA. Oh, you wouldn't understand. Go in to them, I will come in a moment. [MRS. LINDE *goes into the dining-room.* NORA *stands still for a little while, as if to compose herself. Then she looks at her watch.*] Five o'clock. Seven hours till midnight; and then four-and-twenty hours till the next midnight. Then the Tarantella will be over. Twenty-four and seven? Thirty-one hours to live.

HELMER [*from the doorway on the right*]. Where's my little skylark?

NORA [*going to him with her arms outstretched*]. Here she is!

Act 3

THE SAME SCENE. *The table has been placed in the middle of the stage, with chairs round it. A lamp is burning on the table. The door into the hall stands open. Dance music is heard in the room above.* MRS. LINDE *is sitting at the table idly turning over the leaves of a book; she tries to read, but does not seem able to collect her thoughts. Every now and then she listens intently for a sound at the outer door.*

MRS. LINDE [*looking at her watch*]. Not yet—and the time is nearly up. If only he does not—. [*listens again*] Ah, there he is. [*Goes into the hall and opens the outer door carefully. Light footsteps are heard on the stairs. She whispers.*] Come in. There is no one here.

KROGSTAD [*in the doorway*]. I found a note from you at home. What does this mean?

MRS. LINDE. It is absolutely necessary that I should have a talk with you.

KROGSTAD. Really? And is it absolutely necessary that it should be here?

MRS. LINDE. It is impossible where I live; there is no private entrance to my rooms. Come in; we are quite alone. The maid is asleep, and the Helmers are at the dance upstairs.

KROGSTAD [*coming into the room*]. Are the Helmers really at a dance to-night?

MRS. LINDE. Yes, why not?

KROGSTAD. Certainly—why not?

MRS. LINDE. Now, Nils, let us have a talk.

KROGSTAD. Can we two have anything to talk about?

MRS. LINDE. We have a great deal to talk about.

KROGSTAD. I shouldn't have thought so.

MRS. LINDE. No, you have never properly understood me.

KROGSTAD. Was there anything else to understand except what was obvious to all the world—a heartless woman jilts a man when a more lucrative chance turns up?

MRS. LINDE. Do you believe I am as absolutely heartless as all that? And do you believe that I did it with a light heart?

KROGSTAD. Didn't you?

MRS. LINDE. Nils, did you really think that?

KROGSTAD. If it were as you say, why did you write to me as you did at the time?

MRS. LINDE. I could do nothing else. As I had to break with you, it was my duty also to put an end to all that you felt for me.

KROGSTAD [*wringing his hands*]. So that was it, and all this—only for the sake of money!

MRS. LINDE. You must not forget that I had a helpless mother and two little brothers. We couldn't wait for you, Nils; your prospects seemed hope-less then.

KROGSTAD. That may be so, but you had no right to throw me over for any one else's sake.

MRS. LINDE. Indeed I don't know. Many a time did I ask myself if I had the right to do it.

KROGSTAD [*more gently*]. When I lost you, it was as if all the solid ground went from under my feet. Look at me now—I am a shipwrecked man clinging to a bit of wreckage.

MRS. LINDE. But help may be near.

KROGSTAD. It *was* near; but then you came and stood in my way.

MRS. LINDE. Unintentionally, Nils. It was only today that I learnt it was your place I was going to take in the Bank.

KROGSTAD. I believe you, if you say so. But now that you know it, are you not going to give it up to me?

MRS. LINDE. No, because that would not benefit you in the least.

KROGSTAD. Oh, benefit, benefit—I would have done it whether or no.

MRS. LINDE. I have learnt to act prudently. Life, and hard, bitter necessity have taught me that.

KROGSTAD. And life has taught me not to believe in fine speeches.

MRS. LINDE. Then life has taught you something very reasonable. But deeds you must believe in?

KROGSTAD. What do you mean by that?

MRS. LINDE. You said you were like a shipwrecked man clinging to some wreckage.

KROGSTAD. I had good reason to say so.

MRS. LINDE. Well, I am like a shipwrecked woman clinging to some wreckage—no one to mourn for, no one to care for.

KROGSTAD. It was your own choice.

MRS. LINDE. There was no other choice—then.

KROGSTAD. Well, what now?

MRS. LINDE. Nils, how would it be if we two shipwrecked people could join forces?

KROGSTAD. What are you saying?

MRS. LINDE. Two on the same piece of wreckage would stand a better chance than each on their own.

KROGSTAD. Christine!

MRS. LINDE. What do you suppose brought me to town?

KROGSTAD. Do you mean that you gave me a thought?

MRS. LINDE. I could not endure life without work. All my life, as long as I can remember, I have worked, and it has been my greatest and only pleasure. But now I am quite alone in the world—my life is so dreadfully empty and I feel so forsaken. There is not the least pleasure in working for one's self. Nils, give me someone and something to work for.

KROGSTAD. I don't trust that. It is nothing but a woman's overstrained sense of generosity that prompts you to make such an offer of yourself.

MRS. LINDE. Have you ever noticed anything of the sort in me?

KROGSTAD. Could you really do it? Tell me—do you know all about my past life?

MRS. LINDE. Yes.

KROGSTAD. And do you know what they think of me here?

MRS. LINDE. You seemed to me to imply that with me you might have been quite another man.

KROGSTAD. I am certain of it.

MRS. LINDE. Is it too late now?

KROGSTAD. Christine, are you saying this deliberately? Yes, I am sure you are. I see it in your face. Have you really the courage, then—?

MRS. LINDE. I want to be a mother to someone, and your children need a mother. We two need each other. Nils, I have faith in your real character—I can dare anything together with you.

KROGSTAD [*grasps her hands*]. Thanks, thanks, Christine! Now I shall find a way to clear myself in the eyes of the world. Ah, but I forgot—

MRS. LINDE [*listening*]. Hush! The Tarantella! Go, go!

KROGSTAD. Why? What is it?

MRS. LINDE. Do you hear them up there? When that is over, we may expect them back.

KROGSTAD. Yes, yes—I will go. But it is all no use. Of course you are not aware what steps I have taken in the matter of the Helmers.

MRS. LINDE. Yes. I know all about that.

KROGSTAD. And in spite of that have you the courage to—?

MRS. LINDE. I understand very well to what lengths a man like you might be driven by despair.

KROGSTAD. If I could only undo what I have done!

MRS. LINDE. You can. Your letter is lying in the letter-box now.

KROGSTAD. Are you sure of that?

MRS. LINDE. Quite sure, but—

KROGSTAD [*with a searching look at her*]. Is that what it all means?—that you want to save your friend at any cost? Tell me frankly. Is that it?

MRS. LINDE. Nils, a woman who has once sold herself for another's sake, doesn't do it a second time.

KROGSTAD. I will ask for my letter back.

MRS. LINDE. No, no.

KROGSTAD. Yes, of course I will. I will wait here till Helmer comes; I will tell him he must give me my letter back—that it only concerns my dismissal—that he is not to read it—

MRS. LINDE. No, Nils, you must not recall your letter.

KROGSTAD. But, tell me, wasn't it for that very purpose that you asked me to meet you here?

MRS. LINDE. In my first moment of fright, it was. But twenty-four hours have elapsed since then, and in that time I have witnessed incredible things in this house. Helmer must know all about it. This unhappy secret must be disclosed; they must have a complete understanding between them, which is impossible with all this concealment and falsehood going on.

KROGSTAD. Very well, if you will take the responsibility. But there is one thing I can do in any case, and I shall do it at once.

MRS. LINDE [*listening*]. You must be quick and go! The dance is over; we are not safe a moment longer.

KROGSTAD. I will wait for you below.

MRS. LINDE. Yes, do. You must see me back to my door.

KROGSTAD. I have never had such an amazing piece of good fortune in my life.

[*Goes out through the outer door. The door between the room and the hall remains open.*]

MRS. LINDE [*tidying up the room and laying her hat and cloak ready*]. What a difference! what a difference! Someone to work for and live for—a home to bring comfort into. That I will do, indeed. I wish they would be quick and come—[*listens*] Ah, there they are now. I must put on my things.

[*Takes up her hat and cloak.* HELMER'S *and* NORA'S *voices are heard outside; a key is turned, and* HELMER *brings* NORA *almost by force into the hall. She is in an Italian costume with a large black shawl round her; he is in evening dress and a black domino which is flying open.*]

NORA [*hanging back in the doorway, and struggling with him*]. No, no, no!—don't take me in. I want to go upstairs again; I don't want to leave so early.

HELMER. But, my dearest Nora—

NORA. Please, Torvald dear—please, *please*—only an hour more.

HELMER. Not a single minute, my sweet Nora. You know that was our agreement. Come along into the room; you are catching cold standing there.

[*He brings her gently into the room, in spite of her resistance.*]

MRS. LINDE. Good evening.

NORA. Christine!

HELMER. You here, so late, Mrs. Linde?

MRS. LINDE. Yes, you must excuse me; I was so anxious to see Nora in her dress.

NORA. Have you been sitting here waiting for me?

MRS. LINDE. Yes, unfortunately I came too late, you had already gone upstairs; and I thought I couldn't go away without having seen you.

HELMER [*taking off* NORA'*s shawl*]. Yes, take a good look at her. I think she is worth looking at. Isn't she charming, Mrs. Linde?

MRS. LINDE. Yes, indeed she is.

HELMER. Doesn't she look remarkably pretty? Everyone thought so at the dance. But she is terribly self-willed, this sweet little person. What are we to do with her? You will hardly believe that I had almost to bring her away by force.

NORA. Torvald, you will repent not having let me stay, even if it were only for half an hour.

HELMER. Listen to her, Mrs. Linde! She had danced her Tarantella, and it had been a tremendous success, as it deserved—although possibly the performance was a trifle too realistic—a little more so, I mean, than was strictly compatible with the limitations of art. But never mind about that! The chief thing is, she had made a success—she had made a tremendous success. Do you think I was going to let her remain there after that, and spoil the effect? No indeed! I took my charming little Capri maiden—my capricious little Capri maiden, I should say—on my arm; took one quick turn round the room; a curtsey on either side, and, as they say in novels, the beautiful apparition disappeared. An exit ought always to be effective, Mrs. Linde; but that is what I cannot make Nora understand. Pooh! this room is hot. [*throws his domino on a chair and opens the door of his room*] Hullo! it's all dark in here. Oh, of course—excuse me—.

[*He goes in and lights some candles.*]

NORA [*in a hurried and breathless whisper*]. Well?

MRS. LINDE [*in a low voice*]. I have had a talk with him.

NORA. Yes, and—

MRS. LINDE. Nora, you must tell your husband all about it.

NORA [*in an expressionless voice*]. I knew it.

MRS. LINDE. You have nothing to be afraid of as far as Krogstad is concerned; but you must tell him.

NORA. I won't tell him.

MRS. LINDE. Then the letter will.

NORA. Thank you, Christine. Now I know what I must do. Hush—!

HELMER [*coming in again*]. Well, Mrs. Linde, have you admired her?

MRS. LINDE. Yes, and now I will say good-night.

HELMER. What already? Is this yours, this knitting?

MRS. LINDE [*taking it*]. Yes, thank you, I had very nearly forgotten it.

HELMER. So you knit?

MRS. LINDE. Of course.

HELMER. Do you know, you ought to embroider.

MRS. LINDE. Really? Why?

HELMER. Yes, it's far more becoming. Let me show you. You hold the embroidery thus in your left hand, and use the needle with the right—like
this—with a long, easy sweep. Do you see?

MRS. LINDE. Yes, perhaps—

HELMER. But in the case of knitting—that can never be anything but ungrace-
ful; look here—the arms close together, the knitting-needles going up
and down—it has a sort of Chinese effect—. That was really excellent
champagne they gave us.

MRS. LINDE. Well,—good-night, Nora, and don't be self-willed any more.

HELMER. That's right, Mrs. Linde.

MRS. LINDE. Good-night, Mr. Helmer.

HELMER [*accompanying her to the door*]. Good-night, good-night. I hope you
will get home all right. I should be very happy to—but you haven't any
great distance to go. Good-night, good-night. [*She goes out; he shuts
the door after her, and comes in again.*] Ah!—at last we have got rid of
her. She is a frightful bore, that woman.

NORA. Aren't you very tired, Torvald?

HELMER. No, not in the least.

NORA. Nor sleepy?

HELMER. Not a bit. On the contrary, I feel extraordinarily lively. And you?—
you really look both tired and sleepy.

NORA. Yes, I am very tired. I want to go to sleep at once.

HELMER. There, you see it was quite right of me not to let you stay there any
longer.

NORA. Everything you do is quite right, Torvald.

HELMER [*kissing her on the forehead*]. Now my little skylark is speaking reasonably. Did you notice what good spirits Rank was in this evening?

NORA. Really? Was he? I didn't speak to him at all.

HELMER. And I very little, but I have not for a long time seen him in such
good form. [*looks for a while at her and then goes nearer to her*] It is
delightful to be at home by ourselves again, to be all alone with you—
you fascinating, charming little darling!

NORA. Don't look at me like that, Torvald.

HELMER. Why shouldn't I look at my dearest treasure?—at all the beauty that
is mine, all my very own?

NORA [*going to the other side of the table*]. You mustn't say things like that
to me tonight.

HELMER [*following her*]. You have still got the Tarantella in your blood, I see.
And it makes you more captivating than ever. Listen—the guests are beginning to go now. [*in a lower voice*] Nora—soon the whole house will
be quiet.

NORA. Yes, I hope so.

HELMER. Yes, my own darling Nora. Do you know, when I am out at a party
with you like this, why I speak so little to you, keep away from you, and
only send a stolen glance in your direction now and then?—do you
know why I do that? It is because I make believe to myself that we are

secretly in love, and you are my secretly promised bride, and that no one suspects there is anything between us.

NORA. Yes, yes—I know very well your thoughts are with me all the time.

HELMER. And when we are leaving, and I am putting the shawl over your beautiful young shoulders—on your lovely neck—then I imagine that you are my young bride and that we have just come from the wedding, and I am bringing you for the first time into our home—to be alone with you for the first time—quite alone with my shy little darling! All this evening I have longed for nothing but you. When I watched the seductive figures of the Tarantella, my blood was on fire; I could endure it no longer, and that was why I brought you down so early—

NORA. Go away, Torvald! You must let me go. I won't—

HELMER. What's that? You're joking, my little Nora! You won't—you won't? Am I not your husband—?

[*A knock is heard at the outer door.*]

NORA [*starting*]. Did you hear—?

HELMER [*going into the hall*]. Who is it?

RANK [*outside*]. It is I. May I come in for a moment?

HELMER [*in a fretful whisper*]. Oh, what does he want now? [*aloud*] Wait a minute! [*unlocks the door*] Come, that's kind of you not to pass by our door.

RANK. I thought I heard your voice, and felt as if I should like to look in. [*with a swift glance round*] Ah, yes!—these dear familiar rooms. You are very happy and cosy in here, you two.

HELMER. It seems to me that you looked after yourself pretty well upstairs too.

RANK. Excellently. Why shouldn't I? Why shouldn't one enjoy everything in this world?—at any rate as much as one can, and as long as one can. The wine was capital—

HELMER. Especially the champagne.

RANK. So you noticed that too? It is almost incredible how much I managed to put away!

NORA. Torvald drank a great deal of champagne tonight, too.

RANK. Did he?

NORA. Yes, and he is always in such good spirits afterwards.

RANK. Well, why should one not enjoy a merry evening after a well-spent day?

HELMER. Well spent? I am afraid I can't take credit for that.

RANK [*clapping him on the back*]. But I can, you know!

NORA. Doctor Rank, you must have been occupied with some scientific investigation today.

RANK. Exactly.

HELMER. Just listen!—little Nora talking about scientific investigations!

NORA. And may I congratulate you on the result?

RANK. Indeed you may.

NORA. Was it favourable, then?

RANK. The best possible, for both doctor and patient—certainty.

NORA [*quickly and searchingly*]. Certainty?

RANK. Absolute certainty. So wasn't I entitled to make a merry evening of it after
    that?

NORA. Yes, you certainly were, Doctor Rank.

HELMER. I think so too, so long as you don't have to pay for it in the morning.

RANK. Oh well, one can't have anything in this life without paying for it.

NORA. Doctor Rank—are you fond of fancy-dress balls?

RANK. Yes, if there is a fine lot of pretty costumes.

NORA. Tell me—what shall we two wear at the next?

HELMER. Little featherbrain!—are you thinking of the next already?

RANK. We two? Yes, I can tell you. You shall go as a good fairy—

HELMER. Yes, but what do you suggest as an appropriate costume for that?

RANK. Let your wife go dressed just as she is in everyday life.

HELMER. That was really very prettily turned. But can't you tell us what you
    will be?

RANK. Yes, my dear friend, I have quite made up my mind about that.

HELMER. Well?

RANK. At the next fancy dress ball I shall be invisible.

HELMER. That's a good joke!

RANK. There is a big black hat—have you never heard of hats that make you
    invisible? If you put one on, no one can see you.

HELMER [*suppressing a smile*]. Yes, you are quite right.

RANK. But I am clean forgetting what I came for. Helmer, give me a cigar—
    one of the dark Havanas.

HELMER. With the greatest pleasure [*offers him his case*].

RANK [*takes a cigar and cuts off the end*]. Thanks.

NORA [*striking a match*]. Let me give you a light.

RANK. Thank you. [*She holds the match for him to light his cigar.*] And now
    good-bye!

HELMER. Good-bye, good-bye, dear old man!

NORA. Sleep well, Doctor Rank.

RANK. Thank you for that wish.

NORA. Wish me the same.

RANK. You? Well, if you want me to sleep well! And thanks for the light.

[*He nods to them both and goes out.*]

HELMER [*in a subdued voice*]. He has drunk more than he ought.

NORA [*absently*]. Maybe. [HELMER *takes a bunch of keys out of his pocket
    and goes into the hall.*] Torvald! what are you going to do there?

HELMER. Empty the letter-box; it is quite full; there will be no room to put the
    newspaper in tomorrow morning.

NORA. Are you going to work tonight?

HELMER. You know quite well I'm not. What is this? Some one has been at the
    lock.

NORA. At the lock—?

HELMER. Yes, someone has. What can it mean? I should never have thought
    the maid—. Here is a broken hairpin. Nora, it is one of yours.

NORA [*quickly*]. Then it must have been the children—

HELMER. Then you must get them out of those ways. There, at last I have got
    it open. [*Takes out the contents of the letter-box, and calls to the
    kitchen.*] Helen!—Helen, put out the light over the front door. [*Goes

back into the room and shuts the door into the hall. He holds out his hand full of letters.] Look at that—look what a heap of them there are. [*turning them over*] What on earth is that?

NORA [*at the window*]. The letter—No! Torvald, no!

HELMER. Two cards—of Rank's.

NORA. Of Doctor Rank's?

HELMER [*looking at them*]. Doctor Rank. They were on the top. He must have put them in when he went out.

NORA. Is there anything written on them?

HELMER. There is a black cross over the name. Look there—what an uncomfortable idea! It looks as if he were announcing his own death.

NORA. It is just what he is doing.

HELMER. What? Do you know anything about it? Has he said anything to you?

NORA. Yes. He told me that when the cards came it would be his leave-taking from us. He means to shut himself up and die.

HELMER. My poor old friend. Certainly I knew we should not have him very long with us. But so soon! And so he hides himself away like a wounded animal.

NORA. If it has to happen, it is best it should be without a word—don't you think so, Torvald?

HELMER [*walking up and down*]. He had so grown into our lives. I can't think of him as having gone out of them. He, with his sufferings and his loneliness, was like a cloudy background to our sunlit happiness. Well, perhaps it is best so. For him, anyway. [*standing still*] And perhaps for us too, Nora. We two are thrown quite upon each other now. [*puts his arms round her*] My darling wife, I don't feel as if I could hold you tight enough. Do you know, Nora, I have often wished that you might be threatened by some great danger, so that I might risk my life's blood, and everything, for your sake.

NORA [*disengages herself, and says firmly and decidedly*]. Now you must read your letters, Torvald.

HELMER. No, no; not tonight. I want to be with you, my darling wife.

NORA. With the thought of your friend's death—

HELMER. You are right, it has affected us both. Something ugly has come between us—the thought of the horrors of death. We must try and rid our minds of that. Until then—we will each go to our own room.

NORA [*hanging on his neck*]. Good-night, Torvald—Good-night!

HELMER [*kissing her on the forehead*]. Good-night, my little singing-bird. Sleep sound, Nora. Now I will read my letters through.

[*He takes his letters and goes into his room, shutting the door after him.*]

NORA [*gropes distractedly about, seizes* HELMER'S *domino, throws it round her, while she says in quick, hoarse, spasmodic whispers*]. Never to see him again. Never! Never! [*puts her shawl over her head*] Never to see my children again either—never again. Never! Never!—Ah! the icy, black water—the unfathomable depths—If only it were over! He has got it now—now he is reading it. Good-by, Torvald and my children!

[*She is about to rush out through the hall, when* HELMER *opens his door hurriedly and stands with an open letter in his hand.*]

HELMER. Nora!

NORA. Ah!—

HELMER. What is this? Do you know what is in this letter?

NORA. Yes, I know. Let me go! Let me get out!

HELMER [*holding her back*]. Where are you going?

NORA [*trying to get free*]. You shan't save me, Torvald!

HELMER [*reeling*]. True? Is this true, that I read here? Horrible! No, no—it is impossible that it can be true.

NORA. It is true. I have loved you above everything else in the world.

HELMER. Oh, don't let us have any silly excuses.

NORA [*taking a step towards him*]. Torvald—!

HELMER. Miserable creature—what have you done?

NORA. Let me go. You shall not suffer for my sake. You shall not take it upon yourself.

HELMER. No tragedy airs, please. [*locks the hall door*] Here you shall stay and give me an explanation. Do you understand what you have done? Answer me? Do you understand what you have done?

NORA [*looks steadily at him and says with a growing look of coldness in her face*]. Yes, now I am beginning to understand thoroughly.

HELMER [*walking about the room*]. What a horrible awakening! All these eight years—she who was my joy and pride—a hypocrite, a liar—worse, worse—a criminal! The unutterable ugliness of it all! For shame! For shame! [NORA *is silent and looks steadily at him. He stops in front of her.*] I ought to have suspected that something of the sort would happen. I ought to have foreseen it. All your father's want of principle—be silent!—all your father's want of principle has come out in you. No religion, no morality, no sense of duty—. How I am punished for having winked at what he did! I did it for your sake, and this is how you repay me.

NORA. Yes, that's just it.

HELMER. Now you have destroyed all my happiness. You have ruined all my future. It is horrible to think of! I am in the power of an unscrupulous man; he can do what he likes with me, ask anything he likes of me, give me any orders he pleases—I dare not refuse. And I must sink to such miserable depths because of a thoughtless woman!

NORA. When I am out of the way, you will be free.

HELMER. No fine speeches, please. Your father had always plenty of those ready, too. What good would it be to me if you were out of the way, as you say? Not the slightest. He can make the affair known everywhere; and if he does, I may be falsely suspected of having been a party to your criminal action. Very likely people will think I was behind it all—that it was I who prompted you! And I have to thank you for all this—you whom I have cherished during the whole of our married life. Do you understand now what it is you have done for me?

NORA [*coldly and quietly*]. Yes.

HELMER. It is so incredible that I can't take it in. But we must come to some understanding. Take off that shawl. Take it off, I tell you. I must try and appease him some way or another. The matter must be hushed up at any cost. And as for you and me, it must appear as if everything between us were just as before—but naturally only in the eyes of the world. You will still remain in my house, that is a matter of course. But I shall not allow you to bring up the children; I dare not trust them to you. To think that I should be obliged to say so to one whom I have loved so dearly, and whom I still—. No, that is all over. From this moment happiness is not the question; all that concerns us is to save the remains, the fragments, the appearance—

[*A ring is heard at the front-door bell.*]

HELMER [*with a start*]. What is that? So late! Can the worst—? Can he—? Hide yourself, Nora. Say you are ill.

[NORA *stands motionless.* HELMER *goes and unlocks the hall door.*]

MAID [*half-dressed, comes to the door*]. A letter for the mistress.

HELMER. Give it to me. [*takes the letter, and shuts the door*] Yes, it is from him. You shall not have it; I will read it myself.

NORA. Yes, read it.

HELMER [*standing by the lamp*]. I scarcely have the courage to do it. It may mean ruin for both of us. No, I must know. [*tears open the letter, runs his eye over a few lines, looks at a paper enclosed and gives a shout of joy*] Nora! [*She looks at him questioningly.*] Nora!—No, I must read it once again—. Yes, it is true! I am saved! Nora, I am saved!

NORA. And I?

HELMER. You too, of course; we are both saved, both you and I. Look, he sends you your bond back. He says he regrets and repents—that a happy change in his life—never mind what he says! We are saved, Nora! No one can do anything to you. Oh, Nora, Nora!—no, first I must destroy these hateful things. Let me see—. [*takes a look at the bond*] No, no, I won't look at it. The whole thing shall be nothing but a bad dream to me. [*tears up the bond and both letters, throws them all into the stove, and watches them burn*] There—now it doesn't exist any longer. He says that since Christmas Eve you—. These must have been three dreadful days for you, Nora.

NORA. I have fought a hard fight these three days.

HELMER. And suffered agonies, and seen no way out but—. No, we won't call any of the horrors to mind. We will only shout with joy, and keep saying "It's all over! It's all over!" Listen to me, Nora. You don't seem to realise that it is all over. What is this?—such a cold, set face! My poor little Nora, I quite understand; you don't feel as if you could believe that I have forgiven you. But it is true, Nora, I swear it; I have forgiven you everything. I know that what you did, you did out of love for me.

NORA. That is true.

HELMER. You have loved me as a wife ought to love her husband. Only you had not sufficient knowledge to judge of the means you used. But do you suppose you are any the less dear to me, because you don't understand how to act on your own responsibility? No, no; only lean on me; I will advise you and direct you. I should not be a man if this womanly helplessness did not just give you a double attractiveness in my eyes. You must not think any more about the hard things I said in my first moment of consternation, when I thought everything was going to overwhelm me. I have forgiven you, Nora; I swear to you I have forgiven you.

NORA. Thank you for your forgiveness.

[*She goes out through the door to the right.*]

HELMER. No, don't go—. [*looks in*] What are you doing in there?

NORA [*from within*]. Taking off my fancy dress.

HELMER [*standing at the open door*]. Yes, do. Try and calm yourself, and make your mind easy again, my frightened little singing-bird. Be at rest, and feel secure; I have broad wings to shelter you under. [*walks up and down by the door*] How warm and cosy our home is, Nora. Here is shelter for you; here I will protect you like a hunted dove that I have saved from a hawk's claws. I will bring peace to your poor beating heart. It will come, little by little, Nora, believe me. Tomorrow morning you will look upon it all quite differently; soon everything will be just as it was before. Very soon you won't need me to assure you that I have forgiven you; you will yourself feel the certainty that I have done so. Can you suppose I should ever think of such a thing as repudiating you, or even reproaching you? You have no idea what a true man's heart is like, Nora. There is something so indescribably sweet and satisfying, to a man, in the knowledge that he has forgiven his wife—forgiven her freely, and with all his heart. It seems as if that had made her, as it were, doubly his own; he has given her a new life, so to speak; and she has in a way become both wife and child to him. So you shall be for me after this, my little scared, helpless darling. Have no anxiety about anything, Nora; only be frank and open with me, and I will serve as will and conscience both to you—. What is this? Not gone to bed? Have you changed your things?

NORA [*in everyday dress*]. Yes, Torvald, I have changed my things now.

HELMER. But what for?—so late as this.

NORA. I shall not sleep tonight.

HELMER. But, my dear Nora—

NORA [*looking at her watch*]. It is not so very late. Sit down here, Torvald. You and I have much to say to one another.

[*She sits down at one side of the table.*]

HELMER. Nora—what is this?—this cold, set face?

NORA. Sit down. It will take some time; I have a lot to talk over with you.

HELMER [*sits down at the opposite side of the table*]. You alarm me, Nora!—and I don't understand you.

NORA. No, that is just it. You don't understand me, and I have never understood you either—before tonight. No, you mustn't interrupt me. You must simply listen to what I say. Torvald, this is a settling of accounts.

HELMER. What do you mean by that?

NORA [*after a short silence*]. Isn't there one thing that strikes you as strange in our sitting here like this?

HELMER. What is that?

NORA. We have been married now eight years. Does it not occur to you that this is the first time we two, you and I, husband and wife, have had a serious conversation?

HELMER. What do you mean by serious?

NORA. In all these eight years—longer than that—from the very beginning of our acquaintance, we have never exchanged a word on any serious subject.

HELMER. Was it likely that I would be continually and for ever telling you about worries that you could not help me to bear?

NORA. I am not speaking about business matters. I say that we have never sat down in earnest together to try and get at the bottom of anything.

HELMER. But, dearest Nora, would it have been any good to you?

NORA. That is just it; you have never understood me. I have been greatly wronged, Torvald—first by papa and then by you.

HELMER. What! By us two—by us two, who have loved you better than anyone else in the world?

NORA [shaking her head]. You have never loved me. You have only thought it pleasant to be in love with me.

HELMER. Nora, what do I hear you saying?

NORA. It is perfectly true, Torvald. When I was at home with papa, he told me his opinion about everything, and so I had the same opinions; and if I differed from him I concealed the fact, because he would not have liked it. He called me his doll-child, and he played with me just as I used to play with my dolls. And when I came to live with you—

HELMER. What sort of an expression is that to use about our marriage?

NORA [undisturbed]. I mean that I was simply transferred from papa's hands into yours. You arranged everything according to your own taste, and so I got the same tastes as you—or else I pretended to, I am really not quite sure which—I think sometimes the one and sometimes the other. When I look back on it, it seems to me as if I had been living here like a poor woman—just from hand to mouth. I have existed merely to perform tricks for you, Torvald. But you would have it so. You and papa have committed a great sin against me. It is your fault that I have made nothing of my life.

HELMER. How unreasonable and how ungrateful you are, Nora! Have you not been happy here?

NORA. No, I have never been happy. I thought I was, but it has never really been so.

HELMER. Not—not happy!

NORA. No, only merry. And you have always been so kind to me. But our home has been nothing but a playroom. I have been your doll-wife, just as at home I was papa's doll-child; and here the children have been my dolls. I thought it great fun when you played with me, just as they thought it great fun when I played with them. That is what our marriage has been, Torvald.

HELMER. There is some truth in what you say—exaggerated and strained as your view of it is. But for the future it shall be different. Playtime shall be over, and lesson-time shall begin.

NORA. Whose lessons? Mine, or the children's?

HELMER. Both yours and the children's, my darling Nora.

NORA. Alas, Torvald, you are not the man to educate me into being a proper wife for you.

HELMER. And you can say that!

NORA. And I—how am I fitted to bring up the children?

HELMER. Nora!

NORA. Didn't you say so yourself a little while ago—that you dare not trust me to bring them up?

HELMER. In a moment of anger! Why do you pay any heed to that?

NORA. Indeed, you were perfectly right. I am not fit for the task. There is another task I must undertake first. I must try and educate myself—you are not the man to help me in that. I must do that for myself. And that is why I am going to leave you now.

HELMER [*springing up*]. What do you say?

NORA. I must stand quite alone, if I am to understand myself and everything about me. It is for that reason that I cannot remain with you any longer.

HELMER. Nora! Nora!

NORA. I am going away from here now, at once. I am sure Christine will take me in for the night—

HELMER. You are out of your mind! I won't allow it! I forbid you!

NORA. It is no use forbidding me anything any longer. I will take with me what belongs to myself. I will take nothing from you, either now or later.

HELMER. What sort of madness is this!

NORA. Tomorrow I shall go home—I mean, to my old home. It will be easiest for me to find something to do there.

HELMER. You blind, foolish woman!

NORA. I must try and get some sense, Torvald.

HELMER. To desert your home, your husband and your children! And you don't consider what people will say!

NORA. I cannot consider that at all. I only know that it is necessary for me.

HELMER. It's shocking. This is how you would neglect your most sacred duties.

NORA. What do you consider my most sacred duties?

HELMER. Do I need to tell you that? Are they not your duties to your husband and your children?

NORA. I have other duties just as sacred.

HELMER. That you have not. What duties could those be?

NORA. Duties to myself.

HELMER. Before all else, you are a wife and a mother.

NORA. I don't believe that any longer. I believe that before all else I am a reasonable human being, just as you are—or, at all events, that I must try and become one. I know quite well, Torvald, that most people would think you right, and that views of that kind are to be found in books; but I can no longer content myself with what most people say, or with what is found in books. I must think over things for myself and get to understand them.

HELMER. Can you not understand your place in your own home? Have you not a reliable guide in such matters as that?—have you no religion?

NORA. I am afraid, Torvald, I do not exactly know what religion is.

HELMER. What are you saying?

NORA. I know nothing but what the clergyman said when I went to be confirmed. He told us that religion was this, and that, and the other. When I am away from all this, and am alone, I will look into that matter too. I will see if what the clergyman said is true, or at all events if it is true for me.

HELMER. This is unheard of in a girl of your age! But if religion cannot lead you aright, let me try and awaken your conscience. I suppose you have some moral sense? Or—answer me—am I to think you have none?

NORA. I assure you, Torvald, that is not an easy question to answer. I really don't know. The thing perplexes me altogether. I only know that you and I look at it in quite a different light. I am learning, too, that the law is quite another thing from what I supposed; but I find it impossible to convince myself that the law is right. According to it a woman has no right to spare her old dying father, or to save her husband's life. I can't believe that.

HELMER. You talk like a child. You don't understand the conditions of the world in which you live.

NORA. No, I don't. But now I am going to try. I am going to see if I can make out who is right, the world or I.

HELMER. You are ill, Nora; you are delirious; I almost think you are out of your mind.

NORA. I have never felt my mind so clear and certain as tonight.

HELMER. And is it with a clear and certain mind that you forsake your husband and your children?

NORA. Yes, it is.

HELMER. Then there is only one possible explanation.

NORA. What is that?

HELMER. You do not love me any more.

NORA. No, that is just it.

HELMER. Nora!—and you can say that?

NORA. It gives me great pain, Torvald, for you have always been so kind to me, but I cannot help it. I do not love you any more.

HELMER [*regaining his composure*]. Is that a clear and certain conviction too?

NORA. Yes, absolutely clear and certain. That is the reason why I will not stay here any longer.

HELMER. And can you tell me what I have done to forfeit your love?

NORA. Yes, indeed I can. It was tonight, when the wonderful thing did not happen; then I saw you were not the man I had thought you.

HELMER. Explain yourself better—I don't understand you.

NORA. I have waited so patiently for eight years; for, goodness knows, I knew very well that wonderful things don't happen every day. Then this horrible misfortune came upon me; and then I felt quite certain that the wonderful thing was going to happen at last. When Krogstad's letter was lying out there, never for a moment did I imagine that you would consent to accept this man's conditions. I was so absolutely certain that you would say to him Publish the thing to the whole world. And when that was done—

HELMER. Yes, what then?—when I had exposed my wife to shame and disgrace?

NORA. When that was done, I was so absolutely certain, you would come forward and take everything upon yourself, and say I am the guilty one.

HELMER. Nora—!

NORA. You mean that I would never have accepted such a sacrifice on your part? No, of course not. But what would my assurances have been worth against yours? That was the wonderful thing which I hoped for and feared; and it was to prevent that, that I wanted to kill myself.

HELMER. I would gladly work night and day for you, Nora—bear sorrow and want for your sake. But no man would sacrifice his honour for the one he loves.

NORA. It is a thing hundreds of thousands of women have done.

HELMER. Oh, you think and talk like a heedless child.

NORA. Maybe. But you neither think nor talk like the man I could bind myself to. As soon as your fear was over—and it was not fear for what threatened me, but for what might happen to you—when the whole thing was past, as far as you were concerned it was exactly as if nothing at all had happened. Exactly as before, I was your little skylark, your doll, which you would in future treat with doubly gentle care, because it was so brittle and fragile. [*getting up*] Torvald—it was then it dawned upon me that for eight years I had been living here with a strange man, and had borne him three children—. Oh, I can't bear to think of it! I could tear myself into little bits!

HELMER [*sadly*]. I see, I see. An abyss has opened between us—there is no denying it. But, Nora, would it not be possible to fill it up?

NORA. As I am now, I am no wife for you.

HELMER. I have it in me to become a different man.

NORA. Perhaps—if your doll is taken away from you.

HELMER. But to part!—to part from you! No, no, Nora, I can't understand that idea.

NORA [*going out to the right*]. That makes it all the more certain that it must be done.

[*She comes back with her cloak and hat and a small bag which she puts on a chair by the table.*]

HELMER. Nora, Nora, not now! Wait till tomorrow.

NORA [*putting on her cloak*]. I cannot spend the night in a strange man's room.

HELMER. But can't we live here like brother and sister—?

NORA [*putting on her hat*]. You know very well that would not last long. [*puts the shawl round her*] Good-bye, Torvald. I won't see the little ones. I know they are in better hands than mine. As I am now, I can be of no use to them.

HELMER. But some day, Nora—some day?

NORA. How can I tell? I have no idea what is going to become of me.

HELMER. But you are my wife, whatever becomes of you.

NORA. Listen, Torvald. I have heard that when a wife deserts her husband's house, as I am doing now, he is legally freed from all obligations towards her. In any case I set you free from all your obligations. You are not to feel yourself bound in the slightest way, any more than I shall. There must be perfect freedom on both sides. See here is your ring back. Give me mine.

HELMER. That too?

NORA. That too.

HELMER. Here it is.

NORA. That's right. Now it is all over. I have put the keys here. The maids know all about everything in the house—better than I do. Tomorrow, after I have left her, Christine will come here and pack up my own things that I brought with me from home. I will have them sent after me.

HELMER. All over! All over!—Nora, shall you never think of me again?

NORA. I know I shall often think of you and the children and this house.

HELMER. May I write to you, Nora?

NORA. No—never. You must not do that.

HELMER. But at least let me send you—

NORA. Nothing—nothing—

HELMER. Let me help you if you are in want.

NORA. No. I can receive nothing from a stranger.

HELMER. Nora—can I never be anything more than a stranger to you?

NORA [*taking her bag*]. Ah, Torvald, the most wonderful thing of all would
   have to happen.

HELMER. Tell me what that would be!

NORA. Both you and I would have to be so changed that—. Oh, Torvald, I
   don't believe any longer in wonderful things happening.

HELMER. But I will believe in it. Tell me? So changed that—?

NORA. That our life together would be a real wedlock. Good-bye.

[*She goes out through the hall.*]

HELMER [*sinks down on a chair at the door and buries his face in his hands*]:
   Nora! Nora! [*looks round, and rises*] Empty. She is gone. [*A hope flashes
   across his mind.*] The most wonderful thing of all—?

[*The sound of a door slamming is heard from below.*]

YOUR TURN

1. Near the beginning of the play, how does Mrs. Linde's presence help to
   define Nora's character? How does Nora's response to Krogstad's entrance tell us something about Nora?

2. What does Dr. Rank contribute to the play? If he were eliminated, what
   would be lost?

3. In view of the fact that the last act several times seems to be moving toward a "happy ending" (e.g., Krogstad promises to recall his letter),
   what is wrong with the alternate ending (see page 1333) that Ibsen reluctantly provided for a German production?

4. Can it be argued that although at the end Nora goes out to achieve self-
   realization, her abandonment of her children—especially to Torvald's
   loathsome conventional morality—is a crime? (By the way, exactly why
   does Nora leave the children? She seems to imply, in some passages,
   that because she forged a signature she is unfit to bring them up. But
   do you agree with her?)

5. Michael Meyer, in his splendid biography *Henrik Ibsen,* says that the
   play is not so much about women's rights as about "the need of every
   individual to find out the kind of person he or she really is, and to
   strive to become that person." What evidence can you offer to support
   or refute this interpretation?

6. In *The Quintessence of Ibsenism* Bernard Shaw says that Ibsen, reacting against a common theatrical preference for strange situations, "saw
   that . . . the more familiar the situation, the more interesting the play.
   Shakespear[e] had put ourselves on the stage but not our situations.
   Our uncles seldom murder our fathers and . . . marry our mothers. . . .
   Ibsen . . . gives us not only ourselves, but ourselves in our own situations. The things that happen to his stage figures are things that happen
   to us. One consequence is that his plays are much more important to
   us than Shakespear[e]'s. Another is that they are capable both of hurting us cruelly and of filling us with excited hopes of escape from ideal-
   istic tyrannies, and with visions of intenser life in the future." How
   much of this do you believe? Focus on details in the play to explain
   your response.

Contexts for *A Doll's House*

HENRIK IBSEN

Notes for the Tragedy of Modern Times

The University Library, Oslo, has the following preliminary notes for A Doll's House.

Rome 19.10.78

There are two kinds of moral law, two kinds of conscience, one in man and a completely different one in woman. They do not understand each other; but in matters of practical living the woman is judged by man's law, as if she were not a woman but a man.

The wife in the play ends up quite bewildered and not knowing right from wrong; her natural instincts on the one side and her faith in authority on the other leave her completely confused.

A woman cannot be herself in contemporary society, it is an exclusively male society with laws drafted by men, and with counsel and judges who judge feminine conduct from the male point of view.

She has committed a crime, and she is proud of it; because she did it for love of her husband and to save his life. But the husband, with his conventional views of honour, stands on the side of the law and looks at the affair with male eyes.

Mental conflict. Depressed and confused by her faith in authority, she loses faith in her moral right and ability to bring up her children. Bitterness. A mother in contemporary society, just as certain insects go away and die when she has done her duty in the propagation of the race. Love of life, of home and husband and children and family. Now and then, woman-like, she shrugs off her thoughts. Sudden return of dread and terror. Everything must be borne alone. The catastrophe approaches, ineluctably, inevitably. Despair, resistance, defeat.

[*The following note was later added in the margin:*]

Krogstad has done some dishonest business, and thus made a bit of money; but his prosperity does not help him, he cannot recover his honour.

Adaptation of **A Doll's House** *for a German Production*

Because Norwegian works were not copyrighted in Germany, German theaters could stage and freely adapt Ibsen's works without his consent. When he heard that a German director was going to change the ending to a happy one, Ibsen decided that he had better do the adaptation himself, though he characterized it as "a barbaric outrage" against the play.

NORA. . . . . Where we could make a real marriage out of our lives together. Goodbye. (*Begins to go.*)

HELMER. Go then! (*Seizes her arm.*) But first you shall see your children for the last time!

NORA. Let me go! I will not see them! I cannot!

HELMER (*draws her over to the door, left*). You shall see them. (*Opens the door and says softly.*) Look, there they are asleep, peaceful and carefree. Tomorrow, when they wake up and call for their mother, they will be—motherless.

NORA (*trembling*). Motherless . . . !

HELMER. As you once were.

NORA. Motherless! (*Struggles with herself, lets her traveling-bag fall, and says.*) Oh, this is a sin against myself, but I cannot leave them. (*Half sinks down by the door.*)

HELMER (*joyfully, but softly*). Nora!

THE CURTAIN FALLS.

Speech at the Banquet of the Norwegian League for Women's Rights

A month after the official birthday celebrations were over, Ibsen and his wife were invited to a banquet in his honor given by the leading Norwegian feminist society.

Christiania, May 26, 1898

I am not a member of the Women's Rights League. Whatever I have written has been without any conscious thought of making propaganda. I have been more the poet and less the social philosopher than people generally seem inclined to believe. I thank you for the toast, but must disclaim the honor of having consciously worked for the women's rights movement. I am not even quite clear as to just what this women's rights movement really is. To me it has seemed a problem of mankind in general. And if you read my books carefully you will understand this. True enough, it is desirable to solve the woman problem, along with all the others; but that has not been the whole purpose. My task has been the *description of humanity*. To be sure, whenever such a description is felt to be reasonably true, the reader will read his own feelings and sentiments into the work of the poet. These are then attributed to the poet; but incorrectly so. Every reader remolds the work beautifully and neatly, each according to his own personality. Not only those who write but also those who read are poets. They are collaborators. They are often more poetical than the poet himself.

LUIS VALDEZ

Luis Valdez was born into a family of migrant farm workers in Delano, California, in 1940. After completing high school he entered San Jose State College on a scholarship. He wrote his first plays while still an undergraduate, and after receiving his degree (in English and drama) from San Jose in 1964 he joined the San Francisco Mime Troupe, a left-wing group that performed in parks and streets. Revolutionary in technique as well as in political content, the Mime Troupe rejected the traditional forms of drama and instead drew on the traditions of the circus and the carnival.

In 1965 Valdez returned to Delano, California, where Cesar Chavez had organized a strike of farm workers and a boycott against grape growers. It was here, under the wing of the United Farm Workers, that he established El Teatro Campesino (the Farm Workers' Theater), which at first specialized in doing short, improvised, satirical skits called actos. *When the* teatro *moved to Del Rey, California, it expanded its repertoire beyond farm issues, and it became part of a cultural center that gave workshops (in English and Spanish) in such subjects as history, drama, and politics.*

The actos, *performed by amateurs on college campuses and on flatbed trucks and at the edges of vineyards, were highly political. Making use of stereotypes (the boss, the scab), the* actos *sought to present not the individual thoughts of a gifted playwright but the social vision of ordinary people—the* pueblo—*though it was acknowledged that in an oppressive society the playwright might have to help guide the people to see their own best interests.*

Valdez moved from actos *to* mitos *(myths)—plays that drew on Aztec mythology, Mexican folklore, and Christianity—and then to* Zoot Suit, *a play that ran for many months in California and that became the first Mexican-American play to be produced on Broadway. More recently he wrote and directed a hit movie,* La Bamba, *and in 1991 received an award from the AT&T Foundation for his musical,* Bandido, *presented by El Teatro Campesino.*

Los Vendidos *was written in 1967, when Ronald Reagan was governor of California.*

Los Vendidos*

[1967]

LIST OF CHARACTERS

HONEST SANCHO
SECRETARY
FARM WORKER
JOHNNY
REVOLUCIONARIO
MEXICAN-AMERICAN

SCENE: HONEST SANCHO'*s Used Mexican Lot and Mexican Curio Shop. Three models are on display in* HONEST SANCHO'*s shop: to the right, there is a* REVOLUCIONARIO, *complete with sombrero,* carrilleras[1] *and carabina 30-30. At center, on the floor, there is the* FARM WORKER, *under a broad straw sombrero. At stage left is the* PACHUCO,[2] filero[3] *in hand.*

(HONEST SANCHO *is moving among his models, dusting them off and preparing for another day of business.*)

SANCHO. Bueno, bueno, mis monos, vamos a ver a quien vendemos ahora, ¿no?[4] (*To audience.*) ¡Quihubo! I'm Honest Sancho and this is my shop. Antes fui contratista pero ahora logré tener mi negocito.[5] All I need now is a customer. (*A bell rings offstage.*) Ay, a customer!

****Los Vendidos** the sellouts.   [1]**carrilleras** cartridge belts.   [2]**Pachuco** an urban tough guy.   [3]**filero** blade.   [4]**Bueno . . . no?** Well, well, darlings, let's see who we can sell now, O.K.?   [5]**Antes . . . negocito** I used to be a contractor, but now I've succeeded in having my little business.

Scene from TV adaptation, "El Teatro Campesino Special: *Los Vendidos*." KNBC, Los Angeles, 1972.

SECRETARY (*Entering*). Good morning, I'm Miss Jiménez from—
SANCHO. ¡Ah, una chicana! Welcome, welcome Señorita Jiménez.
SECRETARY (*Anglo pronunciation*). JIM-enez.
SANCHO. ¿Qué?
SECRETARY. My name is Miss JIM-enez. Don't you speak English? What's wrong with you?
SANCHO. Oh, nothing, Señorita JIM-enez. I'm here to help you.
SECRETARY. That's better. As I was starting to say, I'm a secretary from Governor Reagan's office, and we're looking for a Mexican type for the administration.
SANCHO. Well, you come to the right place, lady. This is Honest Sancho's Used Mexican lot, and we got all types here. Any particular type you want?
SECRETARY. Yes, we were looking for somebody suave—
SANCHO. Suave.
SECRETARY. Debonair.
SANCHO. De buen aire.
SECRETARY. Dark.
SANCHO. Prieto.
SECRETARY. But of course not too dark.
SANCHO. No muy prieto.
SECRETARY. Perhaps, beige.
SANCHO. Beige, just the tone. Así como cafecito con leche,[6] ¿no?

---

[6]**Así . . . leche** like coffee with milk.

SECRETARY. One more thing. He must be hard-working.

SANCHO. That could only be one model. Step right over here to the center of the shop, lady. (*They cross to the* FARM WORKER.) This is our standard farm worker model. As you can see, in the words of our beloved Senator George Murphy, he is "built close to the ground." Also take special notice of his four-ply Goodyear huaraches, made from the rain tire. This wide-brimmed sombrero is an extra added feature—keeps off the sun, rain, and dust.

SECRETARY. Yes, it does look durable.

SANCHO. And our farm worker model is friendly. Muy amable.[7] Watch. (*Snaps his fingers.*)

FARM WORKER (*Lifts up head*). Buenos días, señorita. (*His head drops.*)

SECRETARY. My, he's friendly.

SANCHO. Didn't I tell you? Loves his patrones! But his most attractive feature is that he's hard working. Let me show you. (*Snaps fingers.* FARM WORKER *stands.*)

FARM WORKER. ¡El jale![8] (*He begins to work.*)

SANCHO. As you can see, he is cutting grapes.

SECRETARY. Oh, I wouldn't know.

SANCHO. He also picks cotton. (*Snap.* FARM WORKER *begins to pick cotton.*)

SECRETARY. Versatile isn't he?

SANCHO. He also picks melons. (*Snap.* FARM WORKER *picks melons.*) That's his slow speed for late in the season. Here's his fast speed. (*Snap.* FARM WORKER *picks faster.*)

SECRETARY. ¡Chihuahua! . . . I mean, goodness, he sure is a hard worker.

SANCHO (*Pulls the* FARM WORKER *to his feet*). And that isn't the half of it. Do you see these little holes on his arms that appear to be pores? During those hot sluggish days in the field, when the vines or the branches get so entangled, it's almost impossible to move; these holes emit a certain grease that allow our model to slip and slide right through the crop with no trouble at all.

SECRETARY. Wonderful. But is he economical?

SANCHO. Economical? Señorita, you are looking at the Volkswagen of Mexicans. Pennies a day is all it takes. One plate of beans and tortillas will keep him going all day. That, and chile. Plenty of chile. Chile jalapeños, chile verde, chile colorado. But, of course, if you do give him chile (*Snap.* FARM WORKER *turns left face. Snap.* FARM WORKER *bends over.*) then you have to change his oil filter once a week.

SECRETARY. What about storage?

SANCHO. No problem. You know these new farm labor camps our Honorable Governor Reagan has built out by Parlier or Raisin City? They were designed with our model in mind. Five, six, seven, even ten in one of those shacks will give you no trouble at all. You can also put him in old barns, old cars, river banks. You can even leave him out in the field overnight with no worry!

SECRETARY. Remarkable.

SANCHO. And here's an added feature: Every year at the end of the season, this model goes back to Mexico and doesn't return, automatically, until next Spring.

SECRETARY. How about that. But tell me: does he speak English?

---

[7]**Muy amable** very friendly.   [8]**El jale** the job.

SANCHO. Another outstanding feature is that last year this model was programmed to go out on STRIKE! (*Snap.*)

FARM WORKER. ¡HUELGA! ¡HUELGA! Hermanos, sálganse de esos files.[9] (*Snap.*
He stops.)

SECRETARY. No! Oh no, we can't strike in the State Capitol.

SANCHO. Well, he also scabs. (*Snap.*)

FARM WORKER. Me vendo barato, ¿y qué?[10] (*Snap.*)

SECRETARY. That's much better, but you didn't answer my question. Does he
speak English?

SANCHO. Bueno . . . no, pero[11] he has other—

SECRETARY. No.

SANCHO. Other features.

SECRETARY. NO! He just won't do!

SANCHO. Okay, okay pues.[12] We have other models.

SECRETARY. I hope so. What we need is something a little more sophisticated.

SANCHO. Sophisti—¿qué?

SECRETARY. An urban model.

SANCHO. Ah, from the city! Step right back. Over here in this corner of the
shop is exactly what you're looking for. Introducing our new 1969
JOHNNY PACHUCO model! This is our fast-back model. Streamlined.
Built for speed, low-riding, city life. Take a look at some of these features. Mag shoes, dual exhausts, green chartreuse paint-job, dark-tint
windshield, a little poof on top. Let me just turn him on. (*Snap.* JOHNNY
walks to stage center with a pachuco bounce.)

SECRETARY. What was that?

SANCHO. That, señorita, was the Chicano shuffle.

SECRETARY. Okay, what does he do?

SANCHO. Anything and everything necessary for city life. For instance, survival: He knife fights. (*Snap.* JOHNNY *pulls out switchblade and swings*
at SECRETARY.)

(SECRETARY *screams.*)

SANCHO. He dances. (*Snap.*)

JOHNNY (*Singing*). "Angel Baby, my Angel Baby . . ." (*Snap.*)

SANCHO. And here's a feature no city model can be without. He gets arrested,
but not without resisting, of course. (*Snap.*)

JOHNNY. ¡En la madre, la placa![13] I didn't do it! I didn't do it! (JOHNNY *turns*
and stands up against an imaginary wall, legs spread out, arms be-
hind his back.)

SECRETARY. Oh no, we can't have arrests! We must maintain law and order.

SANCHO. But he's bilingual!

SECRETARY. Bilingual?

SANCHO. Simón que yes.[14] He speaks English! Johnny, give us some English.
(*Snap.*)

JOHNNY (*Comes downstage*). Fuck-you!

SECRETARY (*Gasps*). Oh! I've never been so insulted in my whole life!

SANCHO. Well, he learned it in your school.

SECRETARY. I don't care where he learned it.

SANCHO. But he's economical!

---

[9]**Huelga . . . files** Strike! Strike! Brothers, leave those rows.   [10]**Me . . . qué?** I come cheap.
So what?   [11]**Bueno . . . no, pero** Well, no, but.   [12]**pues** well   [13]**¡En . . . la placa!** Wow, the
cops!   [14]**Simón que yes** Yea, sure.

SECRETARY. Economical?

SANCHO. Nickels and dimes. You can keep Johnny running on hamburgers, Taco Bell tacos, Lucky Lager beer, Thunderbird wine, yesca—

SECRETARY. Yesca?

SANCHO. Mota.

SECRETARY. Mota?

SANCHO. Leños[15] . . . Marijuana. (*Snap;* JOHNNY *inhales on an imaginary joint.*)

SECRETARY. That's against the law!

JOHNNY (*Big smile, holding his breath*). Yeah.

SANCHO. He also sniffs glue. (*Snap.* JOHNNY *inhales glue, big smile.*)

JOHNNY. That's too much man, ése.[16]

SECRETARY. No, Mr. Sancho, I don't think this—

SANCHO. Wait a minute, he has other qualities I know you'll love. For example, an inferiority complex. (*Snap.*)

JOHNNY (*To* SANCHO). You think you're better than me, huh ése? (*Swings switchblade.*)

SANCHO. He can also be beaten and he bruises, cut him and he bleeds; kick him and he—(*He beats, bruises and kicks* PACHUCO.) would you like to try it?

SECRETARY. Oh, I couldn't.

SANCHO. Be my guest. He's a great scapegoat.

SECRETARY. No, really.

SANCHO. Please.

SECRETARY. Well, all right. Just once. (*She kicks* PACHUCO.) Oh, he's so soft.

SANCHO. Wasn't that good? Try again.

SECRETARY (*Kicks* PACHUCO). Oh, he's so wonderful! (*She kicks him again.*)

SANCHO. Okay, that's enough, lady. You ruin the merchandise. Yes, our Johnny Pachuco model can give you many hours of pleasure. Why, the L.A.P.D. just bought twenty of these to train their rookie cops on. And talk about maintenance. Señorita, you are looking at an entirely self-supporting machine. You're never going to find our Johnny Pachuco model on the relief rolls. No, sir, this model knows how to liberate.

SECRETARY. Liberate?

SANCHO. He steals. (*Snap.* JOHNNY *rushes the* SECRETARY *and steals her purse.*)

JOHNNY. ¡Dame esa bolsa, vieja![17] (*He grabs the purse and runs. Snap by* SANCHO. *He stops.*)

(SECRETARY *runs after* JOHNNY *and grabs purse away from him, kicking him as she goes.*)

SECRETARY. No, no, no! We can't have any *more* thieves in the State Administration. Put him back.

SANCHO. Okay, we still got other models. Come on, Johnny, we'll sell you to some old lady. (SANCHO *takes* JOHNNY *back to his place.*)

SECRETARY. Mr. Sancho, I don't think you quite understand what we need. What we need is something that will attract the women voters. Something more traditional, more romantic.

SANCHO. Ah, a lover. (*He smiles meaningfully.*) Step right over here, señorita. Introducing our standard Revolucionario and/or Early California Bandit type. As you can see he is well-built, sturdy, durable. This is the International Harvester of Mexicans.

---

[15]**Leños** joints (marijuana).   [16]**ése** fellow.   [17]**¡Dame . . . vieja!** Give me that bag, old lady!

SECRETARY. What does he do?

SANCHO. You name it, he does it. He rides horses, stays in the mountains, crosses deserts, plains, rivers, leads revolutions, follows revolutions, kills, can be killed, serves as a martyr, hero, movie star—did I say movie star? Did you ever see *Viva Zapata? Viva Villa? Villa Rides? Pancho Villa Returns? Pancho Villa Goes Back? Pancho Villa Meets Abbott and Costello*—

SECRETARY. I've never seen any of those.

SANCHO. Well, he was in all of them. Listen to this. (*Snap.*)

REVOLUCIONARIO (*Scream*). ¡VIVA VILLAAAAA!

SECRETARY. That's awfully loud.

SANCHO. He has a volume control. (*He adjusts volume. Snap.*)

REVOLUCIONARIO (*Mousey voice*). ¡Viva Villa!

SECRETARY. That's better.

SANCHO. And even if you didn't see him in the movies, perhaps you saw him on TV. He makes commercials. (*Snap.*)

REVOLUCIONARIO. Is there a Frito Bandito in your house?

SECRETARY. Oh yes, I've seen that one!

SANCHO. Another feature about this one is that he is economical. He runs on raw horsemeat and tequila!

SECRETARY. Isn't that rather savage?

SANCHO. Al contrario,[18] it makes him a lover. (*Snap.*)

REVOLUCIONARIO (*To* SECRETARY). ¡Ay, mamasota, cochota, ven pa'ca![19] (*He grabs* SECRETARY *and folds her back—Latin-Lover style.*)

SANCHO (*Snap.* REVOLUCIONARIO *goes back upright*). Now wasn't that nice?

SECRETARY. Well, it was rather nice.

SANCHO. And finally, there is one outstanding feature about this model I KNOW the ladies are going to love: He's a GENUINE antique! He was made in Mexico in 1910!

SECRETARY. Made in Mexico?

SANCHO. That's right. Once in Tijuana, twice in Guadalajara, three times in Cuernavaca.

SECRETARY. Mr. Sancho, I thought he was an American product.

SANCHO. No, but—

SECRETARY. No, I'm sorry. We can't buy anything but American-made products. He just won't do.

SANCHO. But he's an antique!

SECRETARY. I don't care. You still don't understand what we need. It's true we need Mexican models such as these, but it's more important that he be *American*.

SANCHO. American?

SECRETARY. That's right, and judging from what you've shown me, I don't think you have what we want. Well, my lunch hour's almost over. I better—

SANCHO. Wait a minute! Mexican but American?

SECRETARY. That's correct.

SANCHO. Mexican but . . . (*A sudden flash.*) AMERICAN! Yeah, I think we've got exactly what you want. He just came in today! Give me a minute. (*He exits. Talks from backstage.*) Here he is in the shop. Let me just get some papers off. There. Introducing our new 1970 Mexican-American! Ta-ra-ra-ra-ra-ra-RA-RAAA!

---

[18]**Al contrario** on the contrary.   [19]¡**Ay** . . . **pa'ca!** hot mama, get over here!

(SANCHO *brings out the* MEXICAN-AMERICAN *model, a clean-shaven middle-class type in a business suit, with glasses.*)

SECRETARY (*Impressed*). Where have you been hiding this one?

SANCHO. He just came in this morning. Ain't he a beauty? Feast your eyes on him! Sturdy US STEEL frame, streamlined, modern. As a matter of fact, he is built exactly like our Anglo models except that he comes in a variety of darker shades: naugahyde, leather, or leatherette.

SECRETARY. Naugahyde.

SANCHO. Well, we'll just write that down. Yes, señorita, this model represents the apex of American engineering! He is bilingual, college educated, ambitious! Say the word "acculturate" and he accelerates. He is intelligent, well-mannered, clean—did I say clean? (*Snap.* MEXICAN-AMERICAN *raises his arm.*) Smell.

SECRETARY (*Smells*). Old Sobaco, my favorite.

SANCHO (*Snap.* MEXICAN-AMERICAN *turns toward* SANCHO). Eric! (*To* SECRETARY.) We call him Eric García. (*To* ERIC.) I want you to meet Miss JIM-enez, Eric.

MEXICAN-AMERICAN. Miss JIM-enez, I am delighted to make your acquaintance. (*He kisses her hand.*)

SECRETARY. Oh, my, how charming!

SANCHO. Did you feel the suction? He has seven especially engineered suction cups right behind his lips. He's a charmer all right!

SECRETARY. How about boards? Does he function on boards?

SANCHO. You name them, he is on them. Parole boards, draft boards, school boards, taco quality control boards, surf boards, two-by-fours.

SECRETARY. Does he function in politics?

SANCHO. Señorita, you are looking at a political MACHINE. Have you ever heard of the OEO, EOC, COD, WAR ON POVERTY? That's our model! Not only that, he makes political speeches.

SECRETARY. May I hear one?

SANCHO. With pleasure. (*Snap.*) Eric, give us a speech.

MEXICAN-AMERICAN. Mr. Congressman, Mr. Chairman, members of the board, honored guests, ladies and gentlemen. (SANCHO *and* SECRETARY *applaud.*) Please, please. I come before you as a Mexican-American to tell you about the problems of the Mexican. The problems of the Mexican stem from one thing and one thing alone: He's stupid. He's uneducated. He needs to stay in school. He needs to be ambitious, forward-looking, harder-working. He needs to think American, American, American, AMERICAN, AMERICAN, AMERICAN. GOD BLESS AMERICA! GOD BLESS AMERICA! GOD BLESS AMERICA!! (*He goes out of control.*)

(SANCHO *snaps frantically and the* MEXICAN-AMERICAN *finally slumps forward, bending at the waist.*)

SECRETARY. Oh my, he's patriotic too!

SANCHO. Sí, señorita, he loves his country. Let me just make a little adjustment here. (*Stands* MEXICAN-AMERICAN *up.*)

SECRETARY. What about upkeep? Is he economical?

SANCHO. Well, no, I won't lie to you. The Mexican-American costs a little bit more, but you get what you pay for. He's worth every extra cent. You can keep him running on dry Martinis, Langendorf bread.

SECRETARY. Apple pie?

SANCHO. Only Mom's. Of course, he's also programmed to eat Mexican food on ceremonial functions, but I must warn you: an overdose of beans will plug up his exhaust.

SECRETARY. Fine! There's just one more question: HOW MUCH DO YOU WANT FOR HIM?

SANCHO. Well, I tell you what I'm gonna do. Today and today only, because you've been so sweet, I'm gonna let you steal this model from me! I'm gonna let you drive him off the lot for the simple price of—let's see taxes and license included—$15,000.

SECRETARY. Fifteen thousand DOLLARS? For a MEXICAN!

SANCHO. Mexican? What are you talking, lady? This is a Mexican-AMERICAN! We had to melt down two pachucos, a farm worker and three gabachos[20] to make this model! You want quality, but you gotta pay for it! This is no cheap run-about. He's got class!

SECRETARY. Okay, I'll take him.

SANCHO. You will?

SECRETARY. Here's your money.

SANCHO. You mind if I count it?

SECRETARY. Go right ahead.

SANCHO. Well, you'll get your pink slip in the mail. Oh, do you want me to wrap him up for you? We have a box in the back.

SECRETARY. No, thank you. The Governor is having a luncheon this afternoon, and we need a brown face in the crowd. How do I drive him?

SANCHO. Just snap your fingers. He'll do anything you want.

(SECRETARY *snaps.* MEXICAN-AMERICAN *steps forward.*)

MEXICAN-AMERICAN. RAZA QUERIDA, ¡VAMOS LEVANTANDO ARMAS PARA LIBERARNOS DE ESTOS DESGRACIADOS GABACHOS QUE NOS EXPLOTAN! VAMOS.[21]

SECRETARY. What did he say?

SANCHO. Something about lifting arms, killing white people, etc.

SECRETARY. But he's not supposed to say that!

SANCHO. Look, lady, don't blame me for bugs from the factory. He's your Mexican-American; you bought him, now drive him off the lot!

SECRETARY. But he's broken!

SANCHO. Try snapping another finger.

(SECRETARY *snaps.* MEXICAN-AMERICAN *comes to life again.*)

MEXICAN-AMERICAN. ¡ESTA GRAN HUMANIDAD HA DICHO BASTA! Y SE HA PUESTO EN MARCHA! ¡BASTA! ¡BASTA! ¡VIVA LA RAZA! ¡VIVA LA CAUSA! ¡VIVA LA HUELGA! ¡VIVAN LOS BROWN BERETS! ¡VIVAN LOS ESTUDIANTES![22] ¡CHICANO POWER!

(*The* MEXICAN-AMERICAN *turns toward the* SECRETARY, *who gasps and backs up. He keeps turning toward the* PACHUCO, FARM WORKER, *and* REVOLUCIONARIO, *snapping his fingers and turning each of them on, one by one.*)

---

[20]**gabachos** whites.   [21]**Raza . . . Vamos** Beloved Raza [persons of Mexican descent], let's take up arms to liberate ourselves from those damned whites who exploit us. Let's get going.   [22]**¡Esta . . . Estudiantes!** This great mass of humanity has said enough! And it has begun to march. Enough! Enough! Long live La Raza! Long live the Cause! Long live the strike! Long live the Brown Berets! Long live the students!

PACHUCO (*Snap. To* SECRETARY). I'm going to get you, baby! ¡Viva La Raza!

FARM WORKER (*Snap. To* SECRETARY). ¡Viva la huelga! ¡Viva la Huelga! ¡VIVA LA HUELGA!

REVOLUCIONARIO (*Snap. To* SECRETARY). ¡Viva la revolución! ¡VIVA LA REVOLUCIÓN!

(The three models join together and advance toward the SECRETARY *who backs up and runs out of the shop screaming.* SANCHO *is at the other end of the shop holding his money in his hand. All freeze. After a few seconds of silence, the* PACHUCO *moves and stretches, shaking his arms and loosening up. The* FARM WORKER *and* REVOLUCIONARIO *do the same.* SANCHO *stays where he is, frozen to his spot.)*

JOHNNY. Man, that was a long one, ése.[23] (*Others agree with him.*)

FARM WORKER. How did we do?

JOHNNY. Perty good, look at all that lana,[24] man! (*He goes over to* SANCHO *and removes the money from his hand.* SANCHO *stays where he is.*)

REVOLUCIONARIO. En la madre, look at all the money.

JOHNNY. We keep this up, we're going to be rich.

FARM WORKER. They think we're machines.

REVOLUCIONARIO. Burros.

JOHNNY. Puppets.

MEXICAN-AMERICAN. The only thing I don't like is—how come I always got to play the godamn Mexican-American?

JOHNNY. That's what you get for finishing high school.

FARM WORKER. How about our wages, ése?

JOHNNY. Here it comes right now. $3,000 for you, $3,000 for you, $3,000 for you, and $3,000 for me. The rest we put back into the business.

MEXICAN-AMERICAN. Too much, man. Heh, where you vatos[25] going tonight?

FARM WORKER. I'm going over to Concha's. There's a party.

JOHNNY. Wait a minute, vatos. What about our salesman? I think he needs an oil job.

REVOLUCIONARIO. Leave him to me.

(The PACHUCO, FARM WORKER, *and* MEXICAN-AMERICAN *exit, talking loudly about their plans for the night. The* REVOLUCIONARIO *goes over to* SANCHO, *removes his derby hat and cigar, lifts him up and throws him over his shoulder.* SANCHO *hangs loose, lifeless.)*

REVOLUCIONARIO (To audience). He's the best model we got! ¡Ajua![26]

(Exit.)

---

[23]**ése** man.   [24]**lana** money.   [25]**vatos** guys   [26]**¡Ajua!** Wow!

THE END

YOUR TURN

The Play on the Page

1. If you are an Anglo (shorthand for a Caucasian with traditional Northern European values), do you find the play deeply offensive? Why, or why not? If you are a Mexican American, do you find the play entertaining

or do you find parts of it offensive? What might Anglos enjoy in the play, and what might Mexican Americans find offensive?

2. What stereotypes of Mexican Americans are presented here? At the end of the play, what image of the Mexican American is presented? How does it compare with the stereotypes?

3. Putting aside the politics of the play (and your own politics), what do you think are the strengths of *Los Vendidos*? What do you think are the weaknesses?

4. The play was written in 1967. Putting aside a few specific references— for instance, to Governor Reagan—do you find it dated? If not, why not?

5. In his short essay "The Actos," Luis Valdez says that *actos* achieve the following: "Inspire the audience to social action. Illuminate specific points about social problems. Satirize the opposition. Show or hint at a solution. Express what people are feeling." How much of this do you think *Los Vendidos* does?

6. Many people assume that politics gets in the way of serious art. That is, they assume that artists ought to be concerned with issues that transcend politics. Does this point make any sense to you? Why or why not?

The Play on the Stage

7. In 1971 when *Los Vendidos* was produced by El Teatro de la Esperanza, the group altered the ending by having the men decide to use the money to build a community center. Evaluate this ending.

8. Jorge Huerta, who directed the 1971 El Teatro de la Esperanza production of *Los Vendidos*, suggests that it was a mistake for Jane Fonda to be cast as Miss Jimenes in the videotape of the play. "Something is lost," he says, "in the realization that this woman is not pretending to be white. . . ." Do you agree? Explain.

9. When the play was videotaped by KNBC in Los Angeles for broadcast in 1973, Valdez changed the ending. In the revised version we discover that a scientist (played by Valdez) masterminds the operation, placing Mexican American models wherever there are persons of Mexican descent. These models soon will become Chicanos (as opposed to persons with Anglo values) and will aid rather than work against their fellows. Evaluate this ending.

A Context for *Los Vendidos*

LUIS VALDEZ

The Actos   [1970]

Nothing represents the work of El Teatro Campesino (and other teatros Chicanos) better than the acto. In a sense, the acto is Chicano theatre, though we are now moving into a new, more mystical dramatic form we have begun to call the mito. The two forms are, in fact, cuates[1] that complement and balance each other as day goes into night, el sol la sombra, la vida la muerte, el pájaro la serpiente.[2] Our rejection of white western European (gabacho) proscenium theatre makes the birth of new Chicano forms necessary, thus, los actos y los mitos; one through the eyes of man, the other through the eyes of God.

The actos were born quite matter of factly in Delano. Nacieron hambrientos de la realidad. Anything and everything that pertained to the daily life, la vida cotidiana, of the huelguistas[3] became food for thought, material for actos. The reality of campesinos on strike had become dramatic (and theatrical as reflected by newspapers, TV newscasts, films, etc.), and so the actos merely reflected the reality. Huelguistas portrayed huelguistas, drawing their improvised dialogue from real words they exchanged with the esquiroles (scabs) in the fields every day.[4]

　　"Hermanos, compañeros, sálganse de esos files."
　　"Tenemos comida y trabajo para ustedes afuera de la huelga."
　　"Esquirol, ten vergüenza."
　　"Unidos venceremos."
　　"¡Sal de ahí barrigón!"

The first huelguista to portray an esquirol in the teatro did it to settle a score with a particularly stubborn scab he had talked with in the fields that day. Satire became a weapon that was soon aimed at known and despised contractors, growers and mayordomos. The effect of those early actos on the huelguistas de Delano packed into Filipino Hall was immediate, intense and cathartic. The actos rang true to the reality of the huelga.

Looking back at those early, crude, vital, beautiful, powerful actos of 1965, certain things have now become clear about the dramatic form we were just beginning to develop. There was, of course, no conscious deliberate plan to develop the acto as such. Even the name we gave our small presentations reflects the hard pressing expediency under which we worked from day to day. We could have called them "skits," but we lived and talked in San Joaquin Valley Spanish (with a strong Tejano influence), so we needed a name that made sense to the raza. Cuadros, pasquines, autos, entremeses[5] all seemed too highly intellectualized. We began to call them actos for lack of a better word, lack of time and lack of interest in trying to sound like classical Spanish scholars. De todos modos éramos raza, ¿quién se iba a fijar?[6]

The acto, however, developed its own structure through five years of experimentation. It evolved into a short dramatic form now used primarily by los teatros de Aztlán, but utilized to some extent by other non-Chicano guerrilla theatre companies throughout the U.S., including the San Francisco Mime Troupe and the Bread and Puppet Theatre. (Considerable creative crossfeeding has occurred on other levels, I might add, between the Mime Troupe, the Bread and Puppet, and the Campesino.) Each of these groups

---

[1]**cuates** twins.　[2]**el sol . . . serpiente** sun and shade, life and death, the bird and the serpent.　[3]**huelguistas** strikers.　[4]The following five lines of dialogue can be translated thus:　Brothers, friends, leave those rows. / We have food and work for you outside of the strike. / Scab, you ought to be ashamed. / United we will conquer. / Get out of here, fatso!　[5]**Cuadros . . . entremeses** various Spanish words for short plays.　[6]**De todos . . . fijar?** In all ways we are the Race (i.e., indigenous Americans mixed with European and African blood); who was going to pay attention?

may have their own definition of the acto, but the following are some of the guidelines we have established for ourselves over the years:

> Actos: Inspire the audience to social action. Illuminate specific points about social problems. Satirize the opposition. Show or hint at a solution. Express what people are feeling.

So what's new, right? Plays have been doing that for thousands of years. True, except that the major emphasis in the acto is the social vision, as opposed to the individual artist or playwright's vision. Actos are not written; they are created collectively, through improvisation by a group. The reality reflected in an acto is thus a social reality, whether it pertains to campesinos or to batos locos, not psychologically deranged self-projections, but rather, group archetypes. Don Sotaco, Don Coyote, Johnny Pachuco, Juan Raza, Jorge el Chingón, la Chicana, are all group archetypes that have appeared in actos.

The usefulness of the acto extended well beyond the huelga into the Chicano movement, because Chicanos in general want to identify themselves as a group. The teatro archetypes symbolize the desire for unity and group identity through Chicano heroes and heroines. One character can thus represent the entire Raza, and the Chicano audience will gladly respond to his triumphs or defeats. What to a non-Chicano audience may seem like oversimplification in an acto, is to the Chicano a true expression of his social state and therefore reality.

JANE MARTIN

Jane Martin has never given an interview and has never been photographed. The name presumably is the pseudonym of a writer who works with the Actors Theatre of Louisville, Kentucky. Rodeo *is one of a collection of monologues,* Talking With . . . , *first presented at the Actors Theatre during the 1981 Humana Festival of New American Plays. Jane Martin has also written full-length plays.*

Rodeo   [1981]

A young woman in her late twenties sits working on a piece of tack.* Beside her is a Lone Star beer in the can. As the lights come up we hear the last verse of a Tanya Tucker song or some other female country-western vocalist. She is wearing old worn jeans and boots plus a long-sleeved workshirt with the sleeves rolled up. She works until the song is over and then speaks.

BIG EIGHT.   Shoot—Rodeo's just goin' to hell in a handbasket. Rodeo used to be somethin'. I loved it. I did. Once Daddy an' a bunch of 'em was foolin' around with some old bronc over to our place and this ol' red nose named Cinch got bucked off and my Daddy hooted and said he had him a nine-year-old girl, namely me, wouldn't have no damn trouble cowboyin' that horse. Well, he put me on up there, stuck that ridin' rein in

---

***tack** harness for a horse, including the bridle and saddle.

Margo Martinale, in Jane Martin's *Rodeo,* at the Sixth Humana Festival of New American Plays (1982). Photograph by Sam Garst.

my hand, gimme a kiss, and said, "Now there's only one thing t' remember Honey Love, if ya fall off you jest don't come home." Well I stayed up. You gotta stay on a bronc eight seconds. Otherwise the ride don't count. So from that day on my daddy called me Big Eight. Heck! That's all the name I got anymore . . . Big Eight.

Used to be fer cowboys, the rodeo did. Do it in some open field, folks would pull their cars and pick-ups round it, sit on the hoods, some ranch hand'd bulldog him some rank steer and everybody'd wave their hats and call him by name. Ride us some buckin'stock, rope a few calves, git throwed off a bull, and then we'd jest git us to a bar and tell each other lies about how good we were.

Used to be a family thing. Wooly Billy Tilson and Tammy Lee had them five kids on the circuit. Three boys, two girls and Wooly and Tammy. Wasn't no two-beer rodeo in Oklahoma didn't have a Tilson entered. Used to call the oldest girl Tits. Tits Tilson. Never seen a girl that top-heavy could ride so well. Said she only fell off when the gravity got her. Cowboys used to say if she landed face down you could plant two young trees in the holes she'd leave. Ha! Tits Tilson.

Used to be people came to a rodeo had a horse of their own back home. Farm people, ranch people—lord, they *knew* what they were lookin' at. Knew a good ride from a bad ride, knew hard from easy. You broke some bones er spent the day eatin' dirt, at least ya got appreciated.

Now they bought the rodeo. Them. Coca-Cola, Pepsi Cola, Marlboro damn cigarettes. You know the ones I mean. Them. Hire some New York faggot t' sit on some ol' stuffed horse in front of a sagebrush photo n' smoke that junk. Hell, tobacco wasn't made to smoke, honey, it was made to chew. Lord wanted ya filled up with smoke he would've set ya on fire. Damn it gets me!

There's some guy in a banker's suit runs the rodeo now. Got him a pinky ring and a digital watch, honey. Told us we oughta have a watchamacallit, choriographus or somethin', some ol' ballbuster used to be with the Ice damn Capades. Wants us to ride around dressed up like Mickey Mouse, Pluto, crap like that. Told me I had to haul my butt through the barrel race done up like Minnie damn Mouse in a tu-tu. Huh uh, honey! Them people is so screwed-up they probably eat what they run over in the road.

Listen, they got the clowns wearin' Astronaut suits! I ain't lyin'. You know what a rodeo clown does! You go down, fall off whatever—the clown runs in front of the bull so's ya don't git stomped. Pinstripes, he got 'em in space suits tellin' jokes on a microphone. First horse see 'em, done up like the Star Wars went crazy. Best buckin' horse on the circuit, name of Piss 'N' Vinegar, took one look at them clowns, had him a heart attack and died. Cowboy was ridin' him got hisself squashed. Twelve hundred pounds of coronary arrest jes fell right through 'em. Blam! Vio con dios. Crowd thought that was funnier than the astronauts. I swear it won't be long before they're strappin' ice-skates on the ponies. Big crowds now. Ain't hardly no ranch people, no farm people, nobody I know. Buncha disco babies and dee-vorce lawyers—designer jeans and day-glo Stetsons. Hell, the whole bunch of 'em wears French perfume. Oh it smells like money now! Got it on the cable T and V—hey, you know what, when ya rodeo yer just bound to kick yerself up some dust—well now, seems like that fogs up the ol' TV camera, so they told us a while back that from now on we was gonna ride on some new stuff called Astro-dirt. Dust free. Artificial damn dirt, honey. Lord have mercy.

Banker Suit called me in the other day said "Lurlene . . ." "Hold it," I said. "Who's this Lurlene? Round here they call me Big Eight." "Well, Big Eight," he said, "my name's Wallace." "Well that's a real surprise t' me," I said, "cause aroun' here everybody jes calls you Dumb-ass." My, he laughed real big, slapped his big ol' desk, an' then he said I wasn't suitable for the rodeo no more. Said they was lookin' fer another type, somethin' a little more in the showgirl line, like the Dallas Cowgirls maybe. Said the ridin' and ropin' wasn't the thing no more. Talked on about floats, costumes, dancin' choreography. If I was a man I woulda pissed on his shoe. Said he'd give me a lifetime pass though. Said I could come to his rodeo any time I wanted.

Rodeo used to be people ridin' horses for the pleasure of people who rode horses—made you feel good about what you could do. Rodeo wasn't worth no money to nobody. Money didn't have nothing to do with it! Used to be seven Tilsons riding in the rodeo. Wouldn't none of 'em dress up like Donald damn Duck so they quit. That there's the law of gravity!

There's a bunch of assholes in this country sneak around until they see ya havin' fun and then they buy the fun and start in sellin' it. See, they figure if ya love it, they can sell it. Well you look out, honey! They want to make them a dollar out of what you love. Dress *you* up like Minnie Mouse. Sell your rodeo. Turn *yer* pleasure into Ice damn

Capades. You hear what I'm sayin'? You're jus' merchandise to them, sweetie. You're jus' merchandise to them.

BLACKOUT.

YOUR TURN

The Play on the Page

1. Try to recall your response to the title and the first paragraph or two of the play. Did Big Eight fit your view (perhaps a stereotypical view) of what a cowgirl might sound like?
2. Reread *Rodeo,* this time paying attention not only to what Big Eight says but also to your responses to her. By the end of the play has she become a somewhat more complicated figure than she seems to be after the first paragraph, or does she pretty much seem the same? Do you find that you become increasingly sympathetic? Increasingly unsympathetic? Or does your opinion not change?
3. If you have ever seen a rodeo, do you think Big Eight's characterization is on the mark? Or is she simply bitter because she has been fired?
4. If a local theater group were staging *Rodeo,* presumably with some other short plays, would you go to see it? Why, or why not?

The Play on the Stage

5. If you were directing a production of *Rodeo,* would you keep the actor seated, or would you have her get up, move around the stage, perhaps hang up one piece of tack and take down another? Why?
6. If you were directing *Rodeo,* would you tell Big Eight that her speech is essentially an interior monologue—a soliloquy—or would you tell her that she is speaking directly to the audience—i.e., that the audience is, collectively, a character in the play?
7. The play ends with a stage direction, "Blackout"; that is, the stage suddenly darkens. One director of a recent production, however, chose to end with a "fade out"; the illumination decreased slowly by means of dimmers (mechanical devices that regulate the intensity of a lighting unit). If you were directing a production, what sort of lighting would you use at the end? Why?

AUGUST WILSON

August Wilson (1945-2005) was born in Pittsburgh, the son of a black woman and a white man. After dropping out of school at the age of fifteen, Wilson took various odd jobs, such as stock clerk and short-order cook, in his spare time educating himself in the public library, chiefly by reading works by such black writers as Richard Wright, Ralph Ellison, Langston Hughes, and Amiri Baraka (LeRoi Jones). In 1978 the director of a black theater in St. Paul, Minnesota, who had known Wilson in Pittsburgh, invited him to write a play for the theater. Six months later Wilson moved to St. Paul, where he focused on his writing.

The winner of the Pulitzer Prize for drama in 1987, Wilson's Fences *was first presented as a staged reading in 1983 and was later performed in Chicago, Seattle, Rochester (New York), and New Haven (Connecticut) before reaching New York City in 1987. An earlier play,* Ma Rainey's Black Bottom, *was voted Best Play of the Year 1984–1985 by the New York Drama Critics' Circle. In 1981 when* Ma Rainey *was first read at the O'Neill Center in Waterford, Connecticut, Wilson met Lloyd Richards, an African American director with whom he continued to work closely.* The Piano Lesson, *directed by Richards, won Wilson a second Pulitzer Prize in 1990.*

Fences   [1987]

for Lloyd Richards,
who adds to whatever he touches

> *When the sins of our fathers visit us*
> *We do not have to play host.*
> *We can banish them with forgiveness*
> *As God, in His Largeness and Laws.*

—August Wilson

LIST OF CHARACTERS

TROY MAXSON
JIM BONO, *Troy's friend*
ROSE, *Troy's wife*
LYONS, *Troy's oldest son by previous marriage*
GABRIEL, *Troy's brother*
CORY, *Troy and Rose's son*
RAYNELL, *Troy's daughter*

SETTING: *The setting is the yard which fronts the only entrance to the Maxson household, an ancient two-story brick house set back off a small alley in a big-city neighborhood. The entrance to the house is gained by two or three steps leading to a wooden porch badly in need of paint.*

A relatively recent addition to the house and running its full width, the porch lacks congruence. It is a sturdy porch with a flat roof. One or two chairs of dubious value sit at one end where the kitchen window opens onto the porch. An old-fashioned icebox stands silent guard at the opposite end.

The yard is a small dirt yard, partially fenced, except for the last scene, with a wooden saw horse, a pile of lumber, and other fence-building equipment set off to the side. Opposite is a tree from which hangs a ball made of rags. A baseball bat leans against the tree. Two oil drums serve as garbage receptacles and sit near the house at right to complete the setting.

THE PLAY: *Near the turn of the century, the destitute of Europe sprang on the city with tenacious claws and an honest and solid dream. The city devoured them. They swelled its belly until it burst into a thousand furnaces and sewing machines, a thousand butcher shops and bakers' ovens, a thousand churches and hospitals and funeral parlors and money-lenders. The city grew. It nourished itself and offered each man a partnership limited only by his talent, his guile, and his willingness and*

Left to right: Frances Foster as Rose, Keith Amos as Cory, William Jay as Gabriel, and Gilbert Lewis as Troy, in the Seattle Repertory Theater production of *Fences*.

capacity for hard work. For the immigrants of Europe, a dream dared and won true.

The descendants of African slaves were offered no such welcome or participation. They came from places called the Carolinas and the Virginias, Georgia, Alabama, Mississippi, and Tennessee. They came strong, eager, searching. The city rejected them and they fled and settled along the river-banks and under bridges in shallow, ramshackle houses made of sticks and tarpaper. They collected rags and wood. They sold the use of their muscles and their bodies. They cleaned houses and washed clothes, they shined shoes, and in quiet desperation and vengeful pride, they stole, and lived in pursuit of their own dream. That they could breathe free, finally, and stand to meet life with the force of dignity and whatever eloquence the heart could call upon.

By 1957, the hard-won victories of the European immigrants had so-lidified the industrial might of America. War had been confronted and won with new energies that used loyalty and patriotism as its fuel. Life was rich, full, and flourishing. The Milwaukee Braves won the World Series, and the hot winds of change that would make the sixties a turbulent, racing, dangerous, and provocative decade had not yet begun to blow full.

Act 1

Scene 1

It is 1957. TROY *and* BONO *enter the yard, engaged in conversation.* TROY *is fifty-three years old, a large man with thick, heavy hands; it is this largeness that he strives to fill out and make an accommodation with. Together with his blackness, his largeness informs his sensibilities and the choices he has made in his life.*

Of the two men, BONO *is obviously the follower. His commitment to their friendship of thirty-odd years is rooted in his admiration of* TROY*'s honesty, capacity for hard work, and his strength, which* BONO *seeks to emulate.*

It is Friday night, payday, and the one night of the week the two men engage in a ritual of talk and drink. TROY *is usually the most talkative and at times he can be crude and almost vulgar, though he is capable of rising to profound heights of expression. The men carry lunch buckets and wear or carry burlap aprons and are dressed in clothes suitable to their jobs as garbage collectors.*

BONO. Troy, you ought to stop that lying!

TROY. I ain't lying! The nigger had a watermelon this big. (*He indicates with his hands.*) Talking about . . . "What watermelon, Mr. Rand?" I liked to fell out! "What watermelon, Mr. Rand?" . . . And it sitting there big as life.

BONO. What did Mr. Rand say?

TROY. Ain't said nothing. Figure if the nigger too dumb to know he carrying a watermelon, he wasn't gonna get much sense out of him. Trying to hide that great big old watermelon under his coat. Afraid to let the white man see him carry it home.

BONO. I'm like you . . . I ain't got no time for them kind of people.

TROY. Now what he look like getting mad cause he see the man from the union talking to Mr. Rand?

BONO. He come to me talking about . . . "Maxson gonna get us fired." I told him to get away from me with that. He walked away from me calling you a troublemaker. What Mr. Rand say?

TROY. Ain't said nothing. He told me to go down the Commissioner's office next Friday. They called me down there to see them.

BONO. Well, as long as you got your complaint filed, they can't fire you. That's what one of them white fellows tell me.

TROY. I ain't worried about them firing me. They gonna fire me 'cause I asked a question? That's all I did. I went to Mr. Rand and asked him, "Why? Why you got the white mens driving and the colored lifting?" Told him, "what's the matter, don't I count? You think only white fellows got sense enough to drive a truck. That ain't no paper job! Hell, anybody can drive a truck. How come you got all whites driving and the colored lifting?" He told me "take it to the union." Well, hell, that's what I done! Now they wanna come up with this pack of lies.

BONO. I told Brownie if the man come and ask him any questions . . . just tell the truth! It ain't nothing but something they done trumped up on you cause you filed a complaint on them.

TROY. Brownie don't understand nothing. All I want them to do is change the job description. Give everybody a chance to drive the truck. Brownie can't see that. He ain't got that much sense.

BONO. How you figure he be making out with that gal be up at Taylor's all the time . . . that Alberta gal?

TROY. Same as you and me. Getting just as much as we is. Which is to say nothing.

BONO. It is, huh? I figure you doing a little better than me . . . and I ain't saying what I'm doing.

TROY. Aw, nigger, look here . . . I know you. If you had got anywhere near that gal, twenty minutes later you be looking to tell somebody. And the first one you gonna tell . . . that you gonna want to brag to . . . is me.

BONO. I ain't saying that. I see where you be eyeing her.

TROY. I eye all the women. I don't miss nothing. Don't never let nobody tell you Troy Maxson don't eye the women.

BONO. You been doing more than eyeing her. You done bought her a drink or two.

TROY. Hell yeah, I bought her a drink! What that mean? I bought you one, too. What that mean cause I buy her a drink? I'm just being polite.

BONO. It's all right to buy her one drink. That's what you call being polite. But when you wanna be buying two or three . . . that's what you call eyeing her.

TROY. Look here, as long as you known me . . . you ever known me to chase after women?

BONO. Hell yeah! Long as I done known you. You forgetting I knew you when.

TROY. Naw, I'm talking about since I been married to Rose?

BONO. Oh, not since you been married to Rose. Now, that's the truth, there. I can say that.

TROY. All right then! Case closed.

BONO. I see you be walking up around Alberta's house. You supposed to be at Taylors' and you be walking up around there.

TROY. What you watching where I'm walking for? I ain't watching after you.

BONO. I seen you walking around there more than once.

TROY. Hell, you liable to see me walking anywhere! That don't mean nothing cause you see me walking around there.

BONO. Where she come from anyway? She just kinda showed up one day.

TROY. Tallahassee. You can look at her and tell she one of them Florida gals. They got some big healthy women down there. Grow them right up out the ground. Got a little bit of Indian in her. Most of them niggers down in Florida got some Indian in them.

BONO. I don't know about that Indian part. But she damn sure big and healthy. Woman wear some big stockings. Got them great big old legs and hips as wide as the Mississippi River.

TROY. Legs don't mean nothing. You don't do nothing but push them out of the way. But them hips cushion the ride!

BONO. Troy, you ain't got no sense.

TROY. It's the truth! Like you riding on Goodyears!

ROSE *enters from the house. She is ten years younger than* TROY, *her devotion to him stems from her recognition of the possibilities of her life without him: a succession of abusive men and their babies, a life of partying and running the streets, the Church, or aloneness with its attendant pain and frustration. She recognizes* TROY'*s spirit as a fine and illuminating one and she either ignores or forgives his faults, only some of which she recognizes. Though she doesn't drink, her presence is an integral part of the Friday night rituals. She alternates between the porch and the kitchen, where supper preparations are under way.*

ROSE. What you all out here getting into?

TROY. What you worried about what we getting into for? This is men talk, woman.

ROSE. What I care what you all talking about? Bono, you gonna stay for supper?

BONO. No, I thank you, Rose. But Lucille say she cooking up a pot of pigfeet.

TROY. Pigfeet! Hell, I'm going home with you! Might even stay the night if you got some pigfeet. You got something in there to top them pigfeet, Rose?

ROSE. I'm cooking up some chicken. I got some chicken and collard greens.

TROY. Well, go on back in the house and let me and Bono finish what we was talking about. This is men talk. I got some talk for you later. You know what kind of talk I mean. You go on and powder it up.

ROSE. Troy Maxson, don't you start that now!

TROY *(puts his arm around her).* Aw, woman . . . come here. Look here, Bono . . . when I met this woman . . . I got out that place, say, "Hitch up my pony, saddle up my mare . . . there's a woman out there for me somewhere. I looked here. Looked there. Saw Rose and latched on to her." I latched on to her and told her—I'm gonna tell you the truth—I told her, "Baby, I don't wanna marry, I just wanna be your man." Rose told me . . . tell him what you told me, Rose.

ROSE. I told him if he wasn't the marrying kind, then move out the way so the marrying kind could find me.

TROY. That's what she told me. "Nigger, you in my way. You blocking the view! Move out the way so I can find me a husband." I thought it over two or three days. Come back—

ROSE. Ain't no two or three days nothing. You was back the same night.

TROY. Come back, told her . . . "Okay, baby . . . but I'm gonna buy me a banty rooster and put him out there in the backyard . . . and when he see a stranger come, he'll flap his wings and crow . . . "Look here, Bono, I could watch the front door by myself . . . it was that back door I was worried about.

ROSE. Troy, you ought not talk like that. Troy ain't doing nothing but telling a lie.

TROY. Only thing is . . . when we first got married . . . forget the rooster . . . we ain't had no yard!

BONO. I hear you tell it. Me and Lucille was staying down there on Logan Street. Had two rooms with the outhouse in the back. I ain't mind the outhouse none. But when that goddamn wind blow through there in the winter . . . that's what I'm talking about! To this day I wonder why in the hell I ever stayed down there for six long years. But see, I didn't know I could do no better. I thought only white folks had inside toilets and things.

ROSE. There's a lot of people don't know they can do no better than they do-ing now. That's just something you got to learn. A lot of folks still shop at Bella's.

TROY. Ain't nothing wrong with shopping at Bella's. She got fresh food.

ROSE. I ain't said nothing about if she got fresh food. I'm talking about what she charge. She charge ten cents more than the A&P.

TROY. The A&P ain't never done nothing for me. I spends my money where I'm treated right. I go down to Bella, say, "I need a loaf of bread, I'll pay you Friday." She give it to me. What sense that make when I got money to go and spend it somewhere else and ignore the person who done right by me? That ain't in the Bible.

ROSE. We ain't talking about what's in the Bible. What sense it make to shop there when she overcharge?

TROY. You shop where you want to. I'll do my shopping where the people been good to me.

ROSE. Well, I don't think it's right for her to overcharge. That's all I was saying.

BONO. Look here . . . I got to get on. Lucille going be raising all kind of hell.

TROY. Where you going, nigger? We ain't finished this pint. Come here, finish this pint.

BONO. Well, hell, I am . . . if you ever turn the bottle loose.

TROY (*hands him the bottle*). The only thing I say about the A&P is I'm glad Cory got that job down there. Help him take care of his school clothes and things. Gabe done moved out and things getting tight around here. He got that job . . . He can start to look out for himself.

ROSE. Cory done went and got recruited by a college football team.

TROY. I told that boy about that football stuff. The white man ain't gonna let him get nowhere with that football. I told him when he first come to me with it. Now you come telling me he done went and got more tied up in it. He ought to go and get recruited in how to fix cars or some-thing where he can make a living.

ROSE. He ain't talking about making no living playing football. It's just some-thing the boys in school do. They gonna send a recruiter by to talk to you. He'll tell you he ain't talking about making no living playing foot-ball. It's a honor to be recruited.

TROY. It ain't gonna get him nowhere. Bono'll tell you that.

BONO. If he be like you in the sports . . . he's gonna be all right. Ain't but two men ever played baseball as good as you. That's Babe Ruth and Josh Gibson.[1] Them's the only two men ever hit more home runs than you.

TROY. What it ever get me? Ain't got a pot to piss in or a window to throw it out of.

ROSE. Times have changed since you was playing baseball, Troy. That was be-fore the war. Times have changed a lot since then.

TROY. How in hell they done changed?

ROSE. They got lots of colored boys playing ball now. Baseball and football.

BONO. You right about that, Rose. Times have changed, Troy. You just come along too early.

---

[1] **Josh Gibson** African American ballplayer (1911–1947), known as the Babe Ruth of the Negro Leagues.

TROY. There ought not never have been no time called too early! Now you take that fellow . . . what's that fellow they had playing right field for the Yankees back then? You know who I'm talking about, Bono. Used to play right field for the Yankees.

ROSE. Selkirk?

TROY. Selkirk! That's it! Man batting .269, understand? .269. What kind of sense that make? I was hitting .432 with thirty-seven home runs! Man batting .269 and playing right field for the Yankees! I saw Josh Gibson's daughter yesterday. She walking around with raggedy shoes on her feet. Now I bet you Selkirk's daughter ain't walking around with raggedy shoes on her feet! I bet you that!

ROSE. They got a lot of colored baseball players now. Jackie Robinson[2] was the first. Folks had to wait for Jackie Robinson.

TROY. I done seen a hundred niggers play baseball better than Jackie Robinson. Hell, I know some teams Jackie Robinson couldn't even make! What you talking about Jackie Robinson. Jackie Robinson wasn't nobody. I'm talking about if you could play ball then they ought to have let you play. Don't care what color you were. Come telling me I come along too early. If you could play . . . then they ought to have let you play.

TROY *takes a long drink from the bottle.*

ROSE. You gonna drink yourself to death. You don't need to be drinking like that.

TROY. Death ain't nothing. I done seen him. Done wrassled with him. You can't tell me nothing about death. Death ain't nothing but a fastball on the outside corner. And you know what I'll do to that! Lookee here, Bono . . . am I lying? You get one of them fastballs, about waist high, over the outside corner of the plate where you can get the meat of the bat on it . . . and good god! You can kiss it goodbye. Now, am I lying?

BONO. Naw, you telling the truth there. I seen you do it.

TROY. If I'm lying . . . that 450 feet worth of lying! (*Pause.*) That's all death is to me. A fastball on the outside corner.

ROSE. I don't know why you want to get on talking about death.

TROY. Ain't nothing wrong with talking about death. That's part of life. Everybody gonna die. You gonna die, I'm gonna die. Bono's gonna die. Hell, we all gonna die.

ROSE. But you ain't got to talk about it. I don't like to talk about it.

TROY. You the one brought it up. Me and Bono was talking about baseball . . . you tell me I'm gonna drink myself to death. Ain't that right, Bono? You know I don't drink this but one night out of the week. That's Friday night. I'm gonna drink just enough to where I can handle it. Then I cuts it loose. I leave it alone. So don't you worry about me drinking myself to death. 'Cause I ain't worried about Death. I done seen him. I done wrestled with him.

Look here, Bono . . . I looked up one day and Death was marching straight at me. Like Soldiers on Parade! The Army of Death was marching straight at me. The middle of July, 1941. It got real cold just like it be winter. It seem like Death himself reached out and touched me on the

---

[2]**Jackie Robinson** In 1947 Robinson (1919–1972) became the first African American to play baseball in the major leagues.

shoulder. He touch me just like I touch you. I got cold as ice and Death standing there grinning at me.

ROSE. Troy, why don't you hush that talk.

TROY. I say . . . what you want, Mr. Death? You be wanting me? You done brought your army to be getting me? I looked him dead in the eye. I wasn't fearing nothing. I was ready to tangle. Just like I'm ready to tangle now. The Bible say be ever vigilant. That's why I don't get but so drunk. I got to keep watch.

ROSE. Troy was right down there in Mercy Hospital. You remember he had pneumonia? Laying there with a fever talking plumb out of his head.

TROY. Death standing there staring at me . . . carrying that sickle in his hand. Finally he say, "You want bound over for another year?" See, just like that . . . "You want bound over for another year?" I told him, "Bound over hell! Let's settle this now!"

It seem like he kinda fell back when I said that, and all the cold went out of me. I reached down and grabbed that sickle and threw it just as far as I could throw it . . . and me and him commenced to wrestling.

We wrestled for three days and three nights. I can't say where I found the strength from. Everytime it seemed like he was gonna get the best of me, I'd reach way down deep inside myself and find the strength to do him one better.

ROSE. Everytime Troy tell that story he find different ways to tell it. Different things to make up about it.

TROY. I ain't making up nothing. I'm telling you the facts of what happened. I wrestled with Death for three days and three nights and I'm standing here to tell you about it. (*Pause.*) All right. At the end of the third night we done weakened each other to where we can't hardly move. Death stood up, throwed on his robe . . . had him a white robe with a hood on it. He throwed on that robe and went off to look for his sickle. Say, "I'll be back." Just like that. "I'll be back." I told him, say, "Yeah, but . . . you gonna have to find me!" I wasn't no fool. I wasn't going looking for him. Death ain't nothing to play with. And I know he's gonna get me. I know I got to join his army . . . his camp followers. But as long as I keep my strength and see him coming . . . as long as I keep up my vigilance . . . he's gonna have to fight to get me. I ain't going easy.

BONO. Well, look here, since you got to keep up your vigilance . . . let me have the bottle.

TROY. Aw hell, I shouldn't have told you that part. I should have left out that part.

ROSE. Troy be talking that stuff and half the time don't even know what he be talking about.

TROY. Bono know me better than that.

BONO. That's right. I know you. I know you got some Uncle Remus[3] in your blood. You got more stories than the devil got sinners.

TROY. Aw hell, I done seen him too! Done talked with the devil.

ROSE. Troy, don't nobody wanna be hearing all that stuff.

LYONS *enters the yard from the street. Thirty-four years old,* TROY's *son by a previous marriage, he sports a neatly trimmed goatee, sport*

---

[3]**Uncle Remus** narrator of traditional black tales in a book by Joel Chandler Harris.

coat, white shirt, tieless and buttoned at the collar. Though he fancies himself a musician, he is more caught up in the rituals and "idea" of being a musician than in the actual practice of the music. He has come to borrow money from TROY, *and while he knows he will be successful, he is uncertain as to what extent his lifestyle will be held up to scrutiny and ridicule.*

LYONS. Hey, Pop.

TROY. What you come "Hey, Popping" me for?

LYONS. How you doing, Rose? (*He kisses her.*) Mr. Bono. How you doing?

BONO. Hey, Lyons . . . how you been?

TROY. He must have been doing all right. I ain't seen him around here last week.

ROSE. Troy, leave your boy alone. He come by to see you and you wanna start all that nonsense.

TROY. I ain't bothering Lyons. (*Offers him the bottle.*) Here . . . get you a drink. We got an understanding. I know why he come by to see me and he know I know.

LYONS. Come on, Pop . . . I just stopped by to say hi . . . see how you was doing.

TROY. You ain't stopped by yesterday.

ROSE. You gonna stay for supper, Lyons? I got some chicken cooking in the oven.

LYONS. No, Rose . . . thanks. I was just in the neighborhood and thought I'd stop by for a minute.

TROY. You was in the neighborhood all right, nigger. You telling the truth there. You was in the neighborhood 'cause it's my payday.

LYONS. Well, hell, since you mentioned it . . . let me have ten dollars.

TROY. I'll be damned! I'll die and go to hell and play blackjack with the devil before I give you ten dollars.

BONO. That's what I wanna know about . . . that devil you done seen.

LYONS. What . . . Pop done seen the devil? You too much, Pops.

TROY. Yeah, I done seen him. Talked to him too!

ROSE. You ain't seen no devil. I done told you that man ain't had nothing to do with the devil. Anything you can't understand, you want to call it the devil.

TROY. Look here, Bono . . . I went down to see Hertzberger about some furniture. Got three rooms for two-ninety-eight. That what it say on the radio. "Three rooms . . . two-ninety-eight." Even made up a little song about it. Go down there . . . man tell me I can't get no credit. I'm working every day and can't get no credit. What to do? I got an empty house with some raggedy furniture in it. Cory ain't got no bed. He's sleeping on a pile of rags on the floor. Working every day and can't get no credit. Come back here—Rose'll tell you—madder than hell. Sit down . . . try to figure what I'm gonna do. Come a knock on the door. Ain't been living here but three days. Who know I'm here? Open the door . . . devil standing there bigger than life. White fellow . . . white fellow . . . got on good clothes and everything. Standing there with a clipboard in his hand. I ain't had to say nothing. First words come out of his mouth was . . . "I understand you need some furniture and can't get no credit." I liked to fell over. He say, "I'll give you all the credit you want, but you got to pay the interest on it." I told him, "Give me three rooms worth and charge whatever you want." Next day a truck pulled up here and two men unloaded them three rooms. Man what drove the truck give me a book. Say send ten dollars, first of every month to the address in the book and every thing will be all right. Say if I miss a payment the devil was coming back and it'll be hell to pay. That was fifteen years ago. To this day . . . the first of the month I send my ten dollars, Rose'll tell you.

ROSE. Troy lying.

TROY. I ain't never seen that man since. Now you tell me who else that could have been but the devil? I ain't sold my soul or nothing like that, you understand. Naw, I wouldn't have truck with the devil about nothing like that. I got my furniture and pays my ten dollars the first of the month just like clockwork.

BONO. How long you say you been paying this ten dollars a month?

TROY. Fifteen years!

BONO. Hell, ain't you finished paying for it yet? How much the man done charged you?

TROY. Ah hell, I done paid for it. I done paid for it ten times over! The fact is I'm scared to stop paying it.

ROSE. Troy lying. We got that furniture from Mr. Glickman. He ain't paying no ten dollars a month to nobody.

TROY. Aw hell, woman. Bono know I ain't that big a fool.

LYONS. I was just getting ready to say . . . I know where there's a bridge for sale.

TROY. Look here, I'll tell you this . . . it don't matter to me if he was the devil. It don't matter if the devil give credit. Somebody has got to give it.

ROSE. It ought to matter. You going around talking about having truck with the devil . . . God's the one you gonna have to answer to. He's the one gonna be at the Judgment.

LYONS. Yeah, well, look here, Pop . . . Let me have that ten dollars. I'll give it back to you. Bonnie got a job working at the hospital.

TROY. What I tell you, Bono? The only time I see this nigger is when he wants something. That's the only time I see him.

LYONS. Come on, Pop, Mr. Bono don't want to hear all that. Let me have the ten dollars. I told you Bonnie working.

TROY. What that mean to me? "Bonnie working." I don't care if she working. Go ask her for the ten dollars if she working. Talking about "Bonnie working." Why ain't you working?

LYONS. Aw, Pop, you know I can't find no decent job. Where am I gonna get a job at? You know I can't get no job.

TROY. I told you I know some people down there. I can get you on the rubbish if you want to work. I told you that the last time you came by here asking me for something.

LYONS. Naw, Pop . . . thanks. That ain't for me. I don't wanna be carrying nobody's rubbish. I don't wanna be punching nobody's time clock.

TROY. What's the matter, you too good to carry people's rubbish? Where you think that ten dollars you talking about come from? I'm just supposed to haul people's rubbish and give my money to you cause you too lazy to work. You too lazy to work and wanna know why you ain't got what I got.

ROSE. What hospital Bonnie working at? Mercy?

LYONS. She's down at Passavant working in the laundry.

TROY. I ain't got nothing as it is. I give you that ten dollars and I got to eat beans the rest of the week. Naw . . . you ain't getting no ten dollars here.

LYONS. You ain't got to be eating no beans. I don't know why you wanna say that.

TROY. I ain't got no extra money. Gabe done moved over to Miss Pearl's paying her the rent and things done got tight around here. I can't afford to be giving you every payday.

LYONS. I ain't asked you to give me nothing. I asked you to loan me ten dollars. I know you got ten dollars.

TROY. Yeah, I got it. You know why I got it? 'Cause I don't throw my money away out there in the streets. You living the fast life . . . wanna be a musician . . . running around in them clubs and things . . . then, you learn to take care of yourself. You ain't gonna find me going and asking nobody for nothing. I done spent too many years without.

LYONS. You and me is two different people, Pop.

TROY. I done learned my mistake and learned to do what's right by it. You still trying to get something for nothing. Life don't owe you nothing. You owe it to yourself. Ask Bono. He'll tell you I'm right.

LYONS. You got your way of dealing with the world . . . I got mine. The only thing that matters to me is the music.

TROY. Yeah, I can see that! It don't matter how you gonna eat . . . where your next dollar is coming from. You telling the truth there.

LYONS. I know I got to eat. But I got to live too. I need something that gonna help me to get out of the bed in the morning. Make me feel like I belong in the world. I don't bother nobody. I just stay with the music cause that's the only way I can find to live in the world. Otherwise there ain't no telling what I might do. Now I don't come criticizing you and how you live. I just come by to ask you for ten dollars. I don't wanna hear all that about how I live.

TROY. Boy, your mamma did a hell of a job raising you.

LYONS. You can't change me, Pop. I'm thirty-four years old. If you wanted to change me, you should have been there when I was growing up. I come by to see you . . . ask for ten dollars and you want to talk about how I was raised. You don't know nothing about how I was raised.

ROSE. Let the boy have ten dollars, Troy.

TROY (to LYONS). What the hell you looking at me for? I ain't got no ten dollars. You know what I do with my money. (To ROSE.) Give him ten dollars if you want him to have it.

ROSE. I will. Just as soon as you turn it loose.

TROY (handing ROSE the money). There it is. Seventy-six dollars and forty-two cents. You see this, Bono? Now, I ain't gonna get but six of that back.

ROSE. You ought to stop telling that lie. Here, Lyons. (She hands him the money.)

LYONS. Thanks, Rose. Look . . . I got to run . . . I'll see you later.

TROY. Wait a minute. You gonna say, "thanks, Rose" and ain't gonna look to see where she got that ten dollars from? See how they do me, Bono?

LYONS. I know she got it from you, Pop. Thanks. I'll give it back to you.

TROY. There he go telling another lie. Time I see that ten dollars . . . he'll be owing me thirty more.

LYONS. See you, Mr. Bono.

BONO. Take care, Lyons!

LYONS. Thanks, Pop. I'll see you again.

> LYONS *exits the yard.*

TROY. I don't know why he don't go and get him a decent job and take care of that woman he got.

BONO. He'll be all right, Troy. The boy is still young.

TROY. The *boy* is thirty-four years old.

ROSE. Let's not get off into all that.

BONO. Look here . . . I got to be going. I got to be getting on. Lucille gonna be waiting.

TROY (*puts his arm around* ROSE). See this woman, Bono? I love this woman. I love this woman so much it hurts. I love her so much . . . I done run out of ways of loving her. So I got to go back to basics. Don't you come by my house Monday morning talking about time to go to work . . . 'cause I'm still gonna be stroking!

ROSE. Troy! Stop it now!

BONO. I ain't paying him no mind, Rose. That ain't nothing but gin-talk. Go on, Troy. I'll see you Monday.

TROY. Don't you come by my house, nigger! I done told you what I'm gonna be doing.

> *The lights go down to black.*

Scene 2

The lights come up on ROSE *hanging up clothes. She hums and sings softly to herself. It is the following morning.*

ROSE (*sings*).
>> Jesus, be a fence all around me every day
>> Jesus, I want you to protect me as I travel on my way.
>> Jesus, be a fence all around me every day.

> TROY *enters from the house.*

>> Jesus, I want you to protect me
>> As I travel on my way.

(*To* TROY.) 'Morning. You ready for breakfast? I can fix it soon as I finish hanging up these clothes.

TROY. I got the coffee on. That'll be all right. I'll just drink some of that this morning.

ROSE. That 651 hit yesterday. That's the second time this month. Miss Pearl hit for a dollar . . . seem like those that need the least always get lucky. Poor folks can't get nothing.

TROY. Them numbers don't know nobody. I don't know why you fool with them. You and Lyons both.

ROSE. It's something to do.

TROY. You ain't doing nothing but throwing your money away.

ROSE. Troy, you know I don't play foolishly. I just play a nickel here and a nickel there.

TROY. That's two nickels you done thrown away.

ROSE. Now I hit sometimes . . . that makes up for it. It always comes in handy when I do hit. I don't hear you complaining then.

TROY. I ain't complaining now. I just say it's foolish. Trying to guess out of six hundred ways which way the number gonna come. If I had all the money niggers, these Negroes, throw away on numbers for one week— just one week—I'd be a rich man.

ROSE. Well, you wishing and calling it foolish ain't gonna stop folks from playing numbers. That's one thing for sure. Besides . . . some good things come from playing numbers. Look where Pope done bought him that restaurant off of numbers.

TROY. I can't stand niggers like that. Man ain't had two dimes to rub together. He walking around with his shoes all run over bumming money for cigarettes. All right. Got lucky there and hit the numbers . . .

ROSE. Troy, I know all about it.

TROY. Had good sense, I'll say that for him. He ain't throwed his money away. I seen niggers hit the numbers and go through two thousand dollars in four days. Man bought him that restaurant down there . . . fixed it up real nice . . . and then didn't want nobody to come in it! A Negro go in there and can't get no kind of service. I seen a white fellow come in there and order a bowl of stew. Pope picked all the meat out of the pot for him. Man ain't had nothing but a bowl of meat! Negro come behind him and ain't got nothing but the potatoes and carrots. Talking about what numbers do for people, you picked a wrong example. Ain't done nothing but make a worser fool out of him than he was before.

ROSE. Troy, you ought to stop worrying about what happened at work yesterday.

TROY. I ain't worried. Just told me to be down there at the Commissioner's office on Friday. Everybody think they gonna fire me. I ain't worried about them firing me. You ain't got to worry about that. (*Pause.*) Where's Cory? Cory in the house? (*Calls.*) Cory?

ROSE. He gone out.

TROY. Out, huh? He gone out 'cause he know I want him to help me with this fence. I know how he is. That boy scared of work.

GABRIEL *enters. He comes halfway down the alley and, hearing* TROY's *voice, stops.*

TROY (*continues*). He ain't done a lick of work in his life.

ROSE. He had to go to football practice. Coach wanted them to get in a little extra practice before the season start.

TROY. I got his practice . . . running out of here before he get his chores done.

ROSE. Troy, what is wrong with you this morning? Don't nothing set right with you. Go on back in there and go to bed . . . get up on the other side.

TROY. Why something got to be wrong with me? I ain't said nothing wrong with me.

ROSE. You got something to say about everything. First it's the numbers . . . then it's the way the man runs his restaurant . . . then you done got on Cory. What's it gonna be next? Take a look up there and see if the weather suits you . . . or is it gonna be how you gonna put up the fence with the clothes hanging in the yard?

TROY. You hit the nail on the head then.

ROSE. I know you like I know the back of my hand. Go on in there and get you some coffee . . . see if that straighten you up. 'Cause you ain't right this morning.

TROY starts into the house and sees GABRIEL. GABRIEL *starts singing. TROY's brother, he is seven years younger than* TROY. *Injured in World War II, he has a metal plate in his head. He carries an old trumpet tied around his waist and believes with every fiber of his being that he is the Archangel Gabriel. He carries a chipped basket with an assortment of discarded fruits and vegetables he has picked up in the strip district and which he attempts to sell.*

GABRIEL (*singing*).
       Yes, ma'am I got plums
       You ask me how I sell them
       Oh ten cents apiece
       Three for a quarter
       Come and buy now
       'Cause I'm here today
       And tomorrow I'll be gone

GABRIEL *enters.*

Hey, Rose!

ROSE. How you doing, Gabe?

GABRIEL. There's Troy . . . Hey, Troy!

TROY. Hey, Gabe.

Exit into kitchen.

ROSE (*to* GABRIEL). What you got there?

GABRIEL. You know what I got, Rose. I got fruits and vegetables.

ROSE (*looking in basket*). Where's all these plums you talking about?

GABRIEL. I ain't got no plums today, Rose. I was just singing that. Have some tomorrow. Put me in a big order for plums. Have enough plums tomorrow for St. Peter and everybody.

TROY reenters from kitchen, crosses to steps.

(*To* ROSE.) Troy's mad at me.

TROY. I ain't mad at you. What I got to be mad at you about? You ain't done nothing to me.

GABRIEL. I just moved over to Miss Pearl's to keep out from in your way. I ain't mean no harm by it.

TROY. Who said anything about that? I ain't said anything about that.

GABRIEL. You ain't mad at me, is you?

TROY. Naw . . . I ain't mad at you, Gabe. If I was mad at you I'd tell you about it.

GABRIEL. Got me two rooms. In the basement. Got my own door too. Wanna see my key? (*He holds up a key.*) That's my own key! My two rooms!

TROY. Well, that's good, Gabe. You got your own key . . . that's good.

ROSE. You hungry, Gabe? I was just fixing to cook Troy his breakfast.

GABRIEL. I'll take some biscuits. You got some biscuits? Did you know when I was in heaven . . . every morning me and St. Peter would sit down by

the gate and eat some big fat biscuits? Oh, yeah! We had us a good time.
We'd sit there and eat us them biscuits and then St. Peter would go off
to sleep and tell me to wake him up when it's time to open the gates for
the judgment.

ROSE. Well, come on . . . I'll make up a batch of biscuits.

ROSE *exits into the house.*

GABRIEL. Troy . . . St. Peter got your name in the book. I seen it. It say . . . Troy
Maxson. I say . . . I know him! He got the same name like what I got.
That's my brother!

TROY. How many times you gonna tell me that, Gabe?

GABRIEL. Ain't got my name in the book. Don't have to have my name. I done
died and went to heaven. He got your name though. One morning St. Peter
was looking at his book . . . marking it up for the judgment . . . and he
let me see your name. Got it in there under M. Got Rose's name . . . I
ain't seen it like I seen yours . . . but I know it's in there. He got a great
big book. Got everybody's name what was ever been born. That's what
he told me. But I seen your name. Seen it with my own eyes.

TROY. Go on in the house there. Rose going to fix you something to eat.

GABRIEL. Oh, I ain't hungry. I done had breakfast with Aunt Jemimah. She
come by and cooked me up a whole mess of flapjacks. Remember how
we used to eat them flapjacks?

TROY. Go on in the house and get you something to eat now.

GABRIEL. I got to sell my plums. I done sold some tomatoes. Got me two quarters. Wanna see? (*He shows* TROY *his quarters.*) I'm gonna save them
and buy me a new horn so St. Peter can hear me when it's time to open
the gates. (GABRIEL *stops suddenly. Listens.*) Hear that? That's the hellhounds. I got to chase them out of here. Go on get out of here! Get out!

GABRIEL *exits singing.*

Better get ready for the judgment
Better get ready for the judgment
My Lord is coming down

ROSE *enters from the house.*

TROY. He's gone off somewhere.

GABRIEL (*offstage*).
Better get ready for the judgment
Better get ready for the judgment morning
Better get ready for the judgment
My God is coming down

ROSE. He ain't eating right. Miss Pearl say she can't get him to eat nothing.

TROY. What you want me to do about it, Rose? I done did everything I can
for the man. I can't make him get well. Man got half his head blown
away . . . what you expect?

ROSE. Seem like something ought to be done to help him.

TROY. Man don't bother nobody. He just mixed up from that metal plate he
got in his head. Ain't no sense for him to go back into the hospital.

ROSE. Least he be eating right. They can help him take care of himself.

TROY. Don't nobody wanna be locked up, Rose. What you wanna lock him
up for? Man go over there and fight the war . . . messin' around with
them Japs, get half his head blown off . . . and they give him a lousy
three thousand dollars. And I had to swoop down on that.

ROSE. Is you fixing to go into that again?

TROY. That's the only way I got a roof over my head . . . 'cause of that metal
plate.

ROSE. Ain't no sense you blaming yourself for nothing. Gabe wasn't in no
condition to manage that money. You done what was right by him. Can't
nobody say you ain't done what was right by him. Look how long you
took care of him . . . till he wanted to have his own place and moved
over there with Miss Pearl.

TROY. That ain't what I'm saying, woman! I'm just stating the facts. If my
brother didn't have that metal plate in his head . . . I wouldn't have a
pot to piss in or a window to throw it out of. And I'm fifty-three years
old. Now see if you can understand that!

TROY gets up from the porch and starts to exit the yard.

ROSE. Where you going off to? You been running out of here every Saturday
for weeks. I thought you was gonna work on this fence?

TROY. I'm gonna walk down to Taylors'. Listen to the ball game. I'll be back
in a bit. I'll work on it when I get back.

He exits the yard. The lights go to black.

Scene 3

*The lights come up on the yard. It is four hours later. ROSE is taking down
the clothes from the line. CORY enters carrying his football equipment.*

ROSE. Your daddy like to had a fit with you running out of here this morning
without doing your chores.

CORY. I told you I had to go to practice.

ROSE. He say you were supposed to help him with this fence.

CORY. He been saying that the last four or five Saturdays, and then he don't
never do nothing, but go down to Taylors'. Did you tell him about the
recruiter?

ROSE. Yeah, I told him.

CORY. What he say?

ROSE. He ain't said nothing too much. You get in there and get started on
your chores before he gets back. Go on and scrub down them steps before he gets back here hollering and carrying on.

CORY. I'm hungry. What you got to eat, Mama?

ROSE. Go on and get started on your chores. I got some meat loaf in there. Go
on and make you a sandwich . . . and don't leave no mess in there.

*CORY exits into the house. ROSE continues to take down the clothes.
TROY enters the yard and sneaks up and grabs her from behind.*

Troy! Go on, now. You liked to scared me to death. What was the score
of the game? Lucille had me on the phone and I couldn't keep up with
it.

TROY. What I care about the game? Come here, woman. (*He tries to kiss her.*)

ROSE. I thought you went down Taylors' to listen to the game. Go on, Troy! You supposed to be putting up this fence.

TROY (*attempting to kiss her again*). I'll put it up when I finish with what is at hand.

ROSE. Go on, Troy. I ain't studying you.

TROY (*chasing after her*). I'm studying you . . . fixing to do my homework!

ROSE. Troy, you better leave me alone.

TROY. Where's Cory? That boy brought his butt home yet?

ROSE. He's in the house doing his chores.

TROY (*calling*). Cory! Get your butt out here, boy!

> ROSE *exits into the house with the laundry.* TROY *goes over to the pile of wood, picks up a board, and starts sawing.* CORY *enters from the house.*

TROY. You just now coming in here from leaving this morning?

CORY. Yeah, I had to go to football practice.

TROY. Yeah, what?

CORY. Yessir.

TROY. I ain't but two seconds off you noway. The garbage sitting in there overflowing . . . you ain't done none of your chores . . . and you come in here talking about "Yeah."

CORY. I was just getting ready to do my chores now, Pop . . .

TROY. Your first chore is to help me with this fence on Saturday. Everything else come after that. Now get that saw and cut them boards.

> CORY *takes the saw and begins cutting the boards.* TROY *continues working. There is a long pause.*

CORY. Hey, Pop . . . why don't you buy a TV?

TROY. What I want with a TV? What I want one of them for?

CORY. Everybody got one. Earl, Ba Bra . . . Jesse!

TROY. I ain't asked you who had one. I say what I want with one?

CORY. So you can watch it. They got lots of things on TV. Baseball games and everything. We could watch the World Series.

TROY. Yeah . . . and how much this TV cost?

CORY. I don't know. They got them on sale for around two hundred dollars.

TROY. Two hundred dollars, huh?

CORY. That ain't that much, Pop.

TROY. Naw, it's just two hundred dollars. See that roof you got over your head at night? Let me tell you something about that roof. It's been over ten years since that roof was last tarred. See now . . . the snow come this winter and sit up there on that roof like it is . . . and it's gonna seep inside. It's just gonna be a little bit . . . ain't gonna hardly notice it. Then the next thing you know, it's gonna be leaking all over the house. Then the wood rot from all that water and you gonna need a whole new roof. Now, how much you think it cost to get that roof tarred?

CORY. I don't know.

TROY. Two hundred and sixty-four dollars . . . cash money. While you thinking about a TV, I got to be thinking about the roof . . . and whatever else go wrong here. Now if you had two hundred dollars, what would you do . . . fix the roof or buy a TV?

CORY. I'd buy a TV. Then when the roof started to leak . . . when it needed fixing . . . I'd fix it.

TROY. Where you gonna get the money from? You done spent it for a TV. You gonna sit up and watch the water run all over your brand new TV.

CORY. Aw, Pop. You got money. I know you do.

TROY. Where I got it at, huh?

CORY. You got it in the bank.

TROY. You wanna see my bankbook? You wanna see that seventy-three dollars and twenty-two cents I got sitting up in there?

CORY. You ain't got to pay for it all at one time. You can put a down payment on it and carry it on home with you.

TROY. Not me. I ain't gonna owe nobody nothing if I can help it. Miss a payment and they come and snatch it right out of your house. Then what you got? Now, soon as I get two hundred dollars clear, then I'll buy a TV. Right now, as soon as I get two hundred and sixty-four dollars, I'm gonna have this roof tarred.

CORY. Aw . . . Pop!

TROY. You go on and get you two hundred dollars and buy one if ya want it. I got better things to do with my money.

CORY. I can't get no two hundred dollars. I ain't never seen two hundred dollars.

TROY. I'll tell you what . . . you get you a hundred dollars and I'll put the other hundred with it.

CORY. All right, I'm gonna show you.

TROY. You gonna show me how you can cut them boards right now.

CORY *begins to cut the boards. There is a long pause.*

CORY. The Pirates won today. That makes five in a row.

TROY. I ain't thinking about the Pirates. Got an all-white team. Got that boy . . . that Puerto Rican boy . . . Clemente. Don't even half-play him. That boy could be something if they give him a chance. Play him one day and sit him on the bench the next.

CORY. He gets a lot of chances to play.

TROY. I'm talking about playing regular. Playing every day so you can get your timing. That's what I'm talking about.

CORY. They got some white guys on the team that don't play every day. You can't play everybody at the same time.

TROY. If they got a white fellow sitting on the bench . . . you can bet your last dollar he can't play! The colored guy got to be twice as good before he get on the team. That's why I don't want you to get all tied up in them sports. Man on the team and what it get him? They got colored on the team and don't use them. Same as not having them. All them teams the same.

CORY. The Braves got Hank Aaron and Wes Covington. Hank Aaron hit two home runs today. That makes forty-three.

TROY. Hank Aaron ain't nobody. That what you supposed to do. That's how you supposed to play the game. Ain't nothing to it. It's just a matter of timing . . . getting the right follow-through. Hell, I can hit forty-three home runs right now!

CORY. Not off no major-league pitching, you couldn't.

TROY. We had better pitching in the Negro leagues. I hit seven home runs off of Satchel Paige.[4] You can't get no better than that!

CORY. Sandy Koufax. He's leading the league in strikeouts.

TROY. I ain't thinking of no Sandy Koufax.

CORY. You got Warren Spahn and Lew Burdette. I bet you couldn't hit no home runs off of Warren Spahn.

TROY. I'm through with it now. You go on and cut them boards. (*Pause.*) Your mama tell me you done got recruited by a college football team? Is that right?

CORY. Yeah. Coach Zellman say the recruiter gonna be coming by to talk to you. Get you to sign the permission papers.

TROY. I thought you supposed to be working down there at the A&P. Ain't you suppose to be working down there after school?

CORY. Mr. Stawicki say he gonna hold my job for me until after the football season. Say starting next week I can work weekends.

TROY. I thought we had an understanding about this football stuff? You suppose to keep up with your chores and hold that job down at the A&P. Ain't been around here all day on a Saturday. Ain't none of your chores done . . . and now you telling me you done quit your job.

CORY. I'm going to be working weekends.

TROY. You damn right you are! And ain't no need for nobody coming around here to talk to me about signing nothing.

CORY. Hey, Pop . . . you can't do that. He's coming all the way from North Carolina.

TROY. I don't care where he coming from. The white man ain't gonna let you get nowhere with that football noway. You go on and get your book-learning so you can work yourself up in that A&P or learn how to fix cars or build houses or something, get you a trade. That way you have something can't nobody take away from you. You go on and learn how to put your hands to some good use. Besides hauling people's garbage.

CORY. I get good grades, Pop. That's why the recruiter wants to talk with you. You got to keep up your grades to get recruited. This way I'll be going to college. I'll get a chance . . .

TROY. First you gonna get your butt down there to the A&P and get your job back.

CORY. Mr. Stawicki done already hired somebody else 'cause I told him I was playing football.

TROY. You a bigger fool than I thought . . . to let somebody take away your job so you can play some football. Where you gonna get your money to take out your girlfriend and whatnot? What kind of foolishness is that to let somebody take away your job?

CORY. I'm still gonna be working weekends.

TROY. Naw . . . naw. You getting your butt out of here and finding you another job.

CORY. Come on, Pop! I got to practice. I can't work after school and play football too. The team needs me. That's what Coach Zellman say . . .

TROY. I don't care what nobody else say. I'm the boss . . . you understand? I'm the boss around here. I do the only saying what counts.

---

[4]**Satchel Paige** (1906–1982) pitcher in the Negro leagues.

CORY. Come on, Pop!

TROY. I asked you . . . did you understand?

CORY. Yeah . . .

TROY. What?!

CORY. Yessir.

TROY. You go on down there to that A&P and see if you can get your job back. If you can't do both . . . then you quit the football team. You've got to take the crookeds with the straights.

CORY. Yessir. (*Pause.*) Can I ask you a question?

TROY. What the hell you wanna ask me? Mr. Stawicki the one you got the questions for.

CORY. How come you ain't never liked me?

TROY. Liked you? Who the hell say I got to like you? What law is there say I got to like you? Wanna stand up in my face and ask a damn foolass question like that. Talking about liking somebody. Come here, boy, when I talk to you.

CORY comes over to where TROY *is working. He stands slouched over and* TROY *shoves him on his shoulder.*

Straighten up, goddammit! I asked you a question . . . what law is there say I got to like you?

CORY. None.

TROY. Well, all right then! Don't you eat every day? (*Pause.*) Answer me when I talk to you! Don't you eat every day?

CORY. Yeah.

TROY. Nigger, as long as you in my house, you put that sir on the end of it when you talk to me.

CORY. Yes . . . sir.

TROY. You eat every day.

CORY. Yessir!

TROY. Got a roof over your head.

CORY. Yessir!

TROY. Got clothes on your back.

CORY. Yessir.

TROY. Why you think that is?

CORY. 'Cause of you.

TROY. Ah, hell I know it's cause of me . . . but why do you think that is?

CORY (*hesitant*). 'Cause you like me.

TROY. Like you? I go out of here every morning . . . bust my butt . . . putting up with them crackers every day . . . 'cause I like you? You are the biggest fool I ever saw. (*Pause.*) It's my job. It's my responsibility! You understand that? A man got to take care of his family. You live in my house . . . sleep you behind on my bedclothes . . . fill you belly up with my food . . . 'cause you my son. You my flesh and blood. Not 'cause I like you! 'Cause it's my duty to take care of you. I owe a responsibility to you! Let's get this straight right here . . . before it go along any further . . . I ain't got to like you. Mr. Rand don't give me my money come payday 'cause he likes me. He give me 'cause he owe me. I done give you everything I had to give you. I gave you your life! Me and your mama worked that out between us. And liking your black ass wasn't part of the bargain. Don't you try and go through life worrying about if somebody like you or not. You best be making sure they doing right by you. You understand what I'm saying, boy?

CORY. Yessir.

TROY. Then get the hell out of my face, and get on down to that A&P.

ROSE *has been standing behind the screen door for much of the scene. She enters as* CORY *exits.*

ROSE. Why don't you let the boy go ahead and play football, Troy? Ain't no harm in that. He's just trying to be like you with the sports.

TROY. I don't want him to be like me! I want him to move as far away from my life as he can get. You the only decent thing that ever happened to me. I wish him that. But I don't wish him a thing else from my life. I decided seventeen years ago that boy wasn't getting involved in no sports. Not after what they did to me in the sports.

ROSE. Troy, why don't you admit you was too old to play in the major leagues? For once . . . why don't you admit that?

TROY. What do you mean too old? Don't come telling me I was too old. I just wasn't the right color. Hell, I'm fifty-three years old and can do better than Selkirk's .269 right now!

ROSE. How's was you gonna play ball when you were over forty? Sometimes I can't get no sense out of you.

TROY. I got good sense, woman. I got sense enough not to let my boy get hurt over playing no sports. You been mothering that boy too much. Worried about if people like him.

ROSE. Everything that boy do . . . he do for you. He wants you to say "Good job, son." That's all.

TROY. Rose, I ain't got time for that. He's alive. He's healthy. He's got to make his own way. I made mine. Ain't nobody gonna hold his hand when he get out there in that world.

ROSE. Times have changed from when you was young, Troy. People change. The world's changing around you and you can't even see it.

TROY (*slow, methodical*). Woman . . . I do the best I can do. I come in here every Friday. I carry a sack of potatoes and a bucket of lard. You all line up at the door with your hands out. I give you the lint from my pockets. I give you my sweat and my blood. I ain't got no tears. I done spent them. We go upstairs in that room at night . . . and I fall down on you and try to blast a hole into forever. I get up Monday morning . . . find my lunch on the table. I go out. Make my way. Find my strength to carry me through to the next Friday. (*Pause.*) That's all I got, Rose. That's all I got to give. I can't give nothing else.

TROY *exits into the house. The lights go down to black.*

Scene 4

It is Friday. Two weeks later. CORY *starts out of the house with his football equipment. The phone rings.*

CORY (*calling*). I got it! (*He answers the phone and stands in the screen door talking.*) Hello? Hey, Jesse. Naw . . . I was just getting ready to leave now.

ROSE (*calling*). Cory!

CORY. I told you, man, them spikes is all tore up. You can use them if you want, but they ain't no good. Earl got some spikes.

ROSE (*calling*). Cory!

CORY (*calling to* ROSE). Mam? I'm talking to Jesse. (*Into phone.*) When she say that? (*Pause.*) Aw, you lying, man. I'm gonna tell her you said that.

ROSE (*calling*). Cory, don't you go nowhere!

CORY. I got to go to the game, Ma! (*Into the phone.*) Yeah, hey, look, I'll talk to you later. Yeah, I'll meet you over Earl's house. Later. Bye, Ma.

CORY *exits the house and starts out the yard.*

ROSE. Cory, where you going off to? You got that stuff all pulled out and thrown all over your room.

CORY (*in the yard*). I was looking for my spikes. Jesse wanted to borrow my spikes.

ROSE. Get up there and get that cleaned up before your daddy get back in here.

CORY. I got to go to the game! I'll clean it up when I get back.

CORY *exits.*

ROSE. That's all he need to do is see that room all messed up.

ROSE *exits into the house.* TROY *and* BONO *enter the yard.* TROY *is dressed in clothes other than his work clothes.*

BONO. He told him the same thing he told you. Take it to the union.

TROY. Brownie ain't got that much sense. Man wasn't thinking about nothing. He wait until I confront them on it . . . then he wanna come crying seniority. (*Calls.*) Hey, Rose!

BONO. I wish I could have seen Mr. Rand's face when he told you.

TROY. He couldn't get it out of his mouth! Liked to bit his tongue! When they called me down there to the Commissioner's office . . . he thought they was gonna fire me. Like everybody else.

BONO. I didn't think they was gonna fire you. I thought they was gonna put you on the warning paper.

TROY. Hey, Rose! (*To* BONO.) Yeah, Mr. Rand like to bit his tongue.

TROY *breaks the seal on the bottle, takes a drink, and hands it to* BONO.

BONO. I see you run right down to Taylors' and told that Alberta gal.

TROY (*calling*). Hey, Rose! (*To* BONO.) I told everybody. Hey, Rose! I went down there to cash my check.

ROSE (*entering from the house*). Hush all that hollering, man! I know you out here. What they say down there at the Commissioner's office?

TROY. You supposed to come when I call you, woman. Bono'll tell you that. (*To* BONO.) Don't Lucille come when you call her?

ROSE. Man, hush your mouth. I ain't no dog . . . talk about "come when you call me."

TROY (*puts his arm around* ROSE). You hear this, Bono? I had me an old dog used to get uppity like that. You say, "C'mere, Blue!" . . . and he just lay there and look at you. End up getting a stick and chasing him away trying to make him come.

ROSE. I ain't studying you and your dog. I remember you used to sing that old song.

TROY (*he sings*).

      Hear it ring! Hear it ring! I had a dog his name was Blue.

ROSE. Don't nobody wanna hear you sing that old song.

TROY (*sings*).

      You know Blue was mighty true.

ROSE. Used to have Cory running around here singing that song.

BONO. Hell, I remember that song myself.

TROY (*sings*).

      You know Blue was a good old dog.

      Blue treed a possum in a hollow log.

That was my daddy's song. My daddy made up that song.

ROSE. I don't care who made it up. Don't nobody wanna hear you sing it.

TROY (*makes a song like calling a dog*). Come here, woman.

ROSE. You come in here carrying on, I reckon they ain't fired you. What they say down there at the Commissioner's office?

TROY. Look here, Rose . . . Mr. Rand called me into his office today when I got back from talking to them people down there . . . it come from up top . . . he called me in and told me they was making me a driver.

ROSE. Troy, you kidding!

TROY. No I ain't. Ask Bono.

ROSE. Well, that's great, Troy. Now you don't have to hassle them people no more.

LYONS *enters from the street.*

TROY. Aw hell, I wasn't looking to see you today. I thought you was in jail. Got it all over the front page of the *Courier* about them raiding Sefus's place . . . where you be hanging out with all them thugs.

LYONS. Hey, Pop . . . that ain't got nothing to do with me. I don't go down there gambling. I go down there to sit in with the band. I ain't got nothing to do with the gambling part. They got some good music down there.

TROY. They got some rogues . . . is what they got.

LYONS. How you been, Mr. Bono? Hi, Rose.

BONO. I see where you playing down at the Crawford Grill tonight.

ROSE. How come you ain't brought Bonnie like I told you? You should have brought Bonnie with you, she ain't been over in a month of Sundays.

LYONS. I was just in the neighborhood . . . thought I'd stop by.

TROY. Here he come . . .

BONO. Your daddy got a promotion on the rubbish. He's gonna be the first colored driver. Ain't got to do nothing but sit up there and read the paper like them white fellows.

LYONS. Hey, Pop . . . if you knew how to read you'd be all right.

BONO. Naw . . . naw . . . you mean if the nigger knew how to drive he'd be all right. Been fighting with them people about driving and ain't even got a license. Mr. Rand know you ain't got no driver's license?

TROY. Driving ain't nothing. All you do is point the truck where you want it to go. Driving ain't nothing.

BONO. Do Mr. Rand know you ain't got no driver's license? That's what I'm talking about. I ain't asked if driving was easy. I asked if Mr. Rand know you ain't got no driver's license.

TROY. He ain't got to know. The man ain't got to know my business. Time he find out, I have two or three driver's licenses.

LYONS (*going into his pocket*). Say, look here, Pop . . .

TROY. I knew it was coming. Didn't I tell you, Bono? I know what kind of "Look here, Pop" that was. The nigger fixing to ask me for some money. It's Friday night. It's my payday. All them rogues down there on the avenue . . . the ones that ain't in jail . . . and Lyons is hopping in his shoes to get down there with them.

LYONS. See, Pop . . . if you give somebody else a chance to talk sometimes, you'd see that I was fixing to pay you back your ten dollars like I told you. Here . . . I told you I'd pay you when Bonnie got paid.

TROY. Naw . . . you go ahead and keep that ten dollars. Put it in the bank. The next time you feel like you wanna come by here and ask me for something . . . you go on down there and get that.

LYONS. Here's your ten dollars, Pop. I told you I don't want you to give me nothing. I just wanted to borrow ten dollars.

TROY. Naw . . . you go on and keep that for the next time you want to ask me.

LYONS. Come on, Pop . . . here go your ten dollars.

ROSE. Why don't you go on and let the boy pay you back, Troy?

LYONS. Here you go, Rose. If you don't take it I'm gonna have to hear about it for the next six months. (*He hands her the money.*)

ROSE. You can hand yours over here too, Troy.

TROY. You see this, Bono. You see how they do me.

BONO. Yeah, Lucille do me the same way.

> GABRIEL *is heard singing off stage. He enters.*

GABRIEL. Better get ready for the Judgment! Better get ready for . . . Hey! . . . Hey! . . . There's Troy's boy!

LYONS. How are you doing, Uncle Gabe?

GABRIEL. Lyons . . . The King of the Jungle! Rose . . . hey, Rose. Got a flower for you. (*He takes a rose from his pocket.*) Picked it myself. That's the same rose like you is!

ROSE. That's right nice of you, Gabe.

LYONS. What you been doing, Uncle Gabe?

GABRIEL. Oh, I been chasing hellhounds and waiting on the time to tell St. Peter to open the gates.

LYONS. You been chasing hellhounds, huh? Well . . . you doing the right thing, Uncle Gabe. Somebody got to chase them.

GABRIEL. Oh, yeah . . . I know it. The devil's strong. The devil ain't no pushover. Hellhounds snipping at everybody's heels. But I got my trumpet waiting on the judgment time.

LYONS. Waiting on the Battle of Armageddon, huh?

GABRIEL. Ain't gonna be too much of a battle when God get to waving that Judgment sword. But the people's gonna have a hell of a time trying to get into heaven if them gates ain't open.

LYONS (*putting his arm around* GABRIEL). You hear this, Pop. Uncle Gabe, you all right!

GABRIEL (*laughing with* LYONS). Lyons! King of the Jungle.

ROSE. You gonna stay for supper, Gabe? Want me to fix you a plate?

GABRIEL. I'll take a sandwich, Rose. Don't want no plate. Just wanna eat with
    my hands. I'll take a sandwich.

ROSE. How about you, Lyons? You staying? Got some short ribs cooking.

LYONS. Naw, I won't eat nothing till after we finished playing. (*Pause.*) You
    ought to come down and listen to me play, Pop.

TROY. I don't like that Chinese music. All that noise.

ROSE. Go on in the house and wash up, Gabe . . . I'll fix you a sandwich.

GABRIEL (*to* LYONS, *as he exits*). Troy's mad at me.

LYONS. What you mad at Uncle Gabe for, Pop?

ROSE. He thinks Troy's mad at him 'cause he moved over to Miss Pearl's.

TROY. I ain't mad at the man. He can live where he want to live at.

LYONS. What he move over there for? Miss Pearl don't like nobody.

ROSE. She don't mind him none. She treats him real nice. She just don't allow
    all that singing.

TROY. She don't mind that rent he be paying . . . that's what she don't mind.

ROSE. Troy, I ain't going through that with you no more. He's over there
    'cause he want to have his own place. He can come and go as he
    please.

TROY. Hell, he could come and go as he please here. I wasn't stopping him. I
    ain't put no rules on him.

ROSE. It ain't the same thing, Troy. And you know it.

GABRIEL *comes to the door.*

Now, that's the last I wanna hear about that. I don't wanna hear nothing
else about Gabe and Miss Pearl. And next week . . .

GABRIEL. I'm ready for my sandwich, Rose.

ROSE. And next week . . . when that recruiter come from that school . . . I
    want you to sign that paper and go on and let Cory play football. Then
    that'll be the last I have to hear about that.

TROY (*to* ROSE *as she exits into the house*). I ain't thinking about Cory
    nothing.

LYONS. What . . . Cory got recruited? What school he going to?

TROY. That boy walking around here smelling his piss . . . thinking he's
    grown. Thinking he's gonna do what he want, irrespective of what I say.
    Look here, Bono . . . I left the Commissioner's office and went down to
    the A&P . . . that boy ain't working down there. He lying to me. Telling
    me he got his job back . . . telling me he working weekends . . . telling
    me he working after school . . . Mr. Stawicki tell me he ain't working
    down there at all!

LYONS. Cory just growing up. He's just busting at the seams trying to fill out
    your shoes.

TROY. I don't care what he's doing. When he get to the point where he
    wanna disobey me . . . then it's time for him to move on. Bono'll tell you
    that. I bet he ain't never disobeyed his daddy without paying the
    consequences.

BONO. I ain't never had a chance. My daddy came on through . . . but I ain't
    never knew him to see him . . . or what he had on his mind or where he
    went. Just moving on through. Searching out the New Land. That's what
    the old folks used to call it. See a fellow moving around from place to

place . . . woman to woman . . . called it searching out the New Land. I can't say if he ever found it. I come along, didn't want no kids. Didn't know if I was gonna be in one place long enough to fix on them right as their daddy. I figured I was going searching too. As it turned out I been hooked up with Lucille near about as long as your daddy been with Rose. Going on sixteen years.

TROY. Sometimes I wish I hadn't known my daddy. He ain't cared nothing about no kids. A kid to him wasn't nothing. All he wanted was for you to learn how to walk so he could start you to working. When it come time for eating . . . he ate first. If there was anything left over, that's what you got. Man would sit down and eat two chickens and give you the wing.

LYONS. You ought to stop that, Pop. Everybody feed their kids. No matter how hard times is . . . everybody care about their kids. Make sure they have something to eat.

TROY. The only thing my daddy cared about was getting them bales of cotton in to Mr. Lubin. That's the only thing that mattered to him. Sometimes I used to wonder why he was living. Wonder why the devil hadn't come and got him. "Get them bales of cotton in to Mr. Lubin" and find out he owe him money . . .

LYONS. He should have just went on and left when he saw he couldn't get nowhere. That's what I would have done.

TROY. How he gonna leave with eleven kids? And where he gonna go? He ain't knew how to do nothing but farm. No, he was trapped and I think he knew it. But I'll say this for him . . . he felt a responsibility toward us. Maybe he ain't treated us the way I felt he should have . . . but without that responsibility he could have walked off and left us . . . made his own way.

BONO. A lot of them did. Back in those days what you talking about . . . they walk out their front door and just take on down one road or another and keep on walking.

LYONS. There you go! That's what I'm talking about.

BONO. Just keep on walking till you come to something else. Ain't you never heard of nobody having the walking blues? Well, that's what you call it when you just take off like that.

TROY. My daddy ain't had them walking blues! What you talking about? He stayed right there with his family. But he was just as evil as he could be. My mama couldn't stand him. Couldn't stand that evilness. She run off when I was about eight. She sneaked off one night after he had gone to sleep. Told me she was coming back for me. I ain't never seen her no more. All his women run off and left him. He wasn't good for nobody.

      When my turn come to head out, I was fourteen and got to sniffing around Joe Canewell's daughter. Had us an old mule we called Greyboy. My daddy sent me out to do some plowing and I tied up Greyboy and went to fooling around with Joe Canewell's daughter. We done found us a nice little spot, got real cozy with each other. She about thirteen and we done figured we was grown anyway . . . so we down there enjoying ourselves . . . ain't thinking about nothing. We didn't know Greyboy had got loose and wandered back to the house and my daddy was looking for me. We down there by the creek enjoying ourselves when my daddy come up on us. Surprised us. He had them leather straps off the mule and commenced to whupping me like there was no tomorrow. I jumped up, mad and embarrassed. I was scared of my daddy. When he commenced to whupping on me . . . quite naturally I run to get out of the way. (*Pause.*) Now I thought he was mad cause I ain't done my work. But I see where he was chasing me off so he could have the gal for himself. When I see what the matter of it was, I lost all fear of my daddy. Right there is where I become a man . . . at fourteen years of age. (*Pause.*) Now it was my turn to run him off. I picked up them same reins that he had used on me. I picked up them reins and commenced to whupping on him. The gal jumped up and run off . . . and when my daddy turned to face me, I could see why the devil had never come to get him . . . cause he was the devil himself. I don't know what happened. When I woke up, I was laying right there by the creek, and Blue . . . this old dog we had . . . was licking my face. I thought I was blind. I couldn't see nothing. Both my eyes were swollen shut. I laid there and cried. I didn't know what I was gonna do. The only thing I knew was the time had come for me to leave my daddy's house. And right there the world suddenly got big. And it was a long time before I could cut it down to where I could handle it.

Part of that cutting down was when I got to the place where I could feel him kicking in my blood and knew that the only thing that separated us was the matter of a few years.

GABRIEL *enters from the house with a sandwich.*

LYONS. What you got there, Uncle Gabe?

GABRIEL. Got me a ham sandwich. Rose gave me a ham sandwich.

TROY. I don't know what happened to him. I done lost touch with everybody except Gabriel. But I hope he's dead. I hope he found some peace.

LYONS. That's a heavy story, Pop. I didn't know you left home when you was fourteen.

TROY. And didn't know nothing. The only part of the world I knew was the forty-two acres of Mr. Lubin's land. That's all I knew about life.

LYONS. Fourteen's kinda young to be out on your own. (*Phone rings.*) I don't even think I was ready to be out on my own at fourteen. I don't know what I would have done.

TROY. I got up from the creek and walked on down to Mobile. I was through with farming. Figured I could do better in the city. So I walked the two hundred miles to Mobile.

LYONS. Wait a minute . . . you ain't walked no two hundred miles, Pop. Ain't nobody gonna walk no two hundred miles. You talking about some walking there.

BONO. That's the only way you got anywhere back in them days.

LYONS. Shhh. Damn if I wouldn't have hitched a ride with somebody!

TROY. Who you gonna hitch it with? They ain't had no cars and things like they got now. We talking about 1918.

ROSE (*entering*). What you all out here getting into?

TROY (*to* ROSE). I'm telling Lyons how good he got it. He don't know nothing about this I'm talking.

ROSE. Lyons, that was Bonnie on the phone. She say you supposed to pick her up.

LYONS. Yeah, okay, Rose.

TROY. I walked on down to Mobile and hitched up with some of them fellows that was heading this way. Got up here and found out . . . not only couldn't you get a job . . . you couldn't find no place to live. I thought I was in freedom. Shhh. Colored folks living down there on the riverbanks in whatever kind of shelter they could find for themselves. Right down there under the Brady Street Bridge. Living in shacks made of sticks and tarpaper. Messed around there and went from bad to worse. Started stealing. First it was food. Then I figured, hell, if I steal money I can buy me some food. Buy me some shoes too! One thing led to another. Met your mama. I was young and anxious to be a man. Met your mama and had you. What I do that for? Now I got to worry about feeding you and her. Got to steal three times as much. Went out one day looking for somebody to rob . . . that's what I was, a robber. I'll tell you the truth. I'm ashamed of it today. But it's the truth. Went to rob this fellow . . . pulled out my knife . . . and he pulled out a gun. Shot me in the chest. I felt just like somebody had taken a hot branding iron and laid it on me. When he shot me I jumped at him with my knife. They told me I killed him and they put me in the penitentiary and locked me up for fifteen years. That's where I met Bono. That's where I learned how to play baseball. Got out that place and your mama had taken you and went on to make life without me. Fifteen years was a long time for her to wait. But that fifteen years cured me of that robbing stuff. Rose'll tell you. She asked me when I met her if I had gotten all that foolishness out of my system. And I told her, "Baby, it's you and baseball all what count with me." You hear me, Bono? I meant it too. She say, "Which one comes first?" I told her, "Baby, ain't no doubt it's baseball . . . but you stick and get old with me and we'll both outlive this baseball." Am I right, Rose? And it's true.

ROSE. Man, hush your mouth. You ain't said no such thing. Talking about, "Baby you know you'll always be number one with me." That's what you was talking.

TROY. You hear that, Bono. That's why I love her.

BONO. Rose'll keep you straight. You get off the track, she'll straighten you up.

ROSE. Lyons, you better get on up and get Bonnie. She waiting on you.

LYONS (*gets up to go*). Hey, Pop, why don't you come on down to the Grill and hear me play?

TROY. I ain't going down there. I'm too old to be sitting around in them clubs.

BONO. You got to be good to play down at the Grill.

LYONS. Come on, Pop . . .

TROY. I got to get up in the morning.

LYONS. You ain't got to stay long.

TROY. Naw, I'm gonna get my supper and go on to bed.

LYONS. Well, I got to go. I'll see you again.

TROY. Don't you come around my house on my payday.

ROSE. Pick up the phone and let somebody know you coming. And bring Bonnie with you. You know I'm always glad to see her.

LYONS. Yeah, I'll do that, Rose. You take care now. See you, Pop. See you, Mr. Bono. See you, Uncle Gabe.

GABRIEL. Lyons! King of the Jungle!

LYONS *exits.*

TROY. Is supper ready, woman? Me and you got some business to take care of. I'm gonna tear it up too.

ROSE. Troy, I done told you now!

TROY (*puts his arm around* BONO). Aw hell, woman . . . this is Bono. Bono like family. I done known this nigger since . . . how long I done know you?

BONO. It's been a long time.

TROY. I done know this nigger since Skippy was a pup. Me and him done been through some times.

BONO. You sure right about that.

TROY. Hell, I done know him longer than I known you. And we still standing shoulder to shoulder. Hey, look here, Bono . . . a man can't ask for no more than that. (*Drinks to him.*) I love you, nigger.

BONO. Hell, I love you too . . . I got to get home see my woman. You got yours in hand. I got to get mine.

BONO *starts to exit as* CORY *enters the yard, dressed in his football uniform. He gives* TROY *a hard, uncompromising look.*

CORY. What you do that for, Pop?

He throws his helmet down in the direction of TROY.

ROSE. What's the matter? Cory . . . what's the matter?

CORY. Papa done went up to the school and told Coach Zellman I can't play football no more. Wouldn't even let me play the game. Told him to tell the recruiter not to come.

ROSE. Troy . . .

TROY. What you Troying me for. Yeah, I did it. And the boy know why I did it.

CORY. Why you wanna do that to me? That was the one chance I had.

ROSE. Ain't nothing wrong with Cory playing football, Troy.

TROY. The boy lied to me. I told the nigger if he wanna play football . . . to keep up his chores and hold down that job at the A&P. That was the conditions. Stopped down there to see Mr. Stawicki . . .

CORY. I can't work after school during the football season, Pop! I tried to tell you that Mr. Stawicki's holding my job for me. You don't never want to listen to nobody. And then you wanna go and do this to me!

TROY. I ain't done nothing to you. You done it to yourself.

CORY. Just cause you didn't have a chance! You just scared I'm gonna be better than you, that's all.

TROY. Come here.

ROSE. Troy . . .

CORY *reluctantly crosses over to* TROY.

TROY. All right! See. You done made a mistake.

CORY. I didn't even do nothing!

TROY. I'm gonna tell you what your mistake was. See . . . you swung at the
        ball and didn't hit it. That's strike one. See, you in the batter's box now.
        You swung and you missed. That's strike one. Don't you strike out!

Lights fade to black.

Act 2

Scene 1

The following morning. CORY *is at the tree hitting the ball with the
bat. He tries to mimic* TROY, *but his swing is awkward, less sure.* ROSE
enters from the house.

ROSE. Cory, I want you to help me with this cupboard.

CORY. I ain't quitting the team. I don't care what Poppa say.

ROSE. I'll talk to him when he gets back. He had to go see about your Uncle
        Gabe. The police done arrested him. Say he was disturbing the peace.
        He'll be back directly. Come on in here and help me clean out the top of
        this cupboard.

CORY *exits into the house.* ROSE *sees* TROY *and* BONO *coming down the
alley.*

Troy . . . what they say down there?

TROY. Ain't said nothing. I give them fifty dollars and they let him go. I'll talk
        to you about it. Where's Cory?

ROSE. He's in there helping me clean out these cupboards.

TROY. Tell him to get his butt out here.

TROY *and* BONO *go over to the pile of wood.* BONO *picks up the saw and
begins sawing.*

TROY *(to* BONO). All they want is the money. That makes six or seven times I
        done went down there and got him. See me coming they stick out their
        hands.

BONO. Yeah. I know what you mean. That's all they care about . . . that
        money. They don't care about what's right. (*Pause.*) Nigger, why you
        got to go and get some hard wood? You ain't doing nothing but building
        a little old fence. Get you some soft pine wood. That's all you need.

TROY. I know what I'm doing. This is outside wood. You put pine wood in-
        side the house. Pine wood is inside wood. This here is outside wood.
        Now you tell me where the fence is gonna be?

BONO. You don't need this wood. You can put it up with pine wood and it'll
        stand as long as you gonna be here looking at it.

TROY. How you know how long I'm gonna be here, nigger? Hell, I might just
        live forever. Live longer than old man Horsely.

BONO. That's what Magee used to say.

TROY. Magee's a damn fool. Now you tell me who you ever heard of gonna
        pull their own teeth with a pair of rusty pliers.

BONO. The old folks . . . my granddaddy used to pull his teeth with pliers.
        They ain't had no dentists for the colored folks back then.

TROY. Get clean pliers! You understand? Clean pliers! Sterilize them! Besides
        we ain't living back then. All Magee had to do was walk over to Doc
        Goldblum's.

BONO. I see where you and that Tallahassee gal . . . that Alberta . . . I see where you all done got tight.

TROY. What you mean "got tight"?

BONO. I see where you be laughing and joking with her all the time.

TROY. I laughs and jokes with all of them, Bono. You know me.

BONO. That ain't the kind of laughing and joking I'm talking about.

CORY *enters from the house.*

CORY. How you doing, Mr. Bono?

TROY. Cory? Get that saw from Bono and cut some wood. He talking about the wood's too hard to cut. Stand back there, Jim, and let that young boy show you how it's done.

BONO. He's sure welcome to it.

CORY *takes the saw and begins to cut the wood.*

Whew-e-e! Look at that. Big old strong boy. Look like Joe Louis. Hell, must be getting old the way I'm watching that boy whip through that wood.

CORY. I don't see why Mama want a fence around the yard noways.

TROY. Damn if I know either. What the hell she keeping out with it? She ain't got nothing nobody want.

BONO. Some people build fences to keep people out . . . and other people build fences to keep people in. Rose wants to hold on to you all. She loves you.

TROY. Hell, nigger, I don't need nobody to tell me my wife loves me. Cory . . . go on in the house and see if you can find that other saw.

CORY. Where's it at?

TROY. I said find it! Look for it till you find it!

CORY *exits into the house.*

What's that supposed to mean? Wanna keep us in?

BONO. Troy . . . I done known you seem like damn near my whole life. You and Rose both. I done know both of you all for a long time. I remember when you met Rose. When you was hitting them baseball out the park. A lot of them old gals was after you then. You had the pick of the litter. When you picked Rose, I was happy for you. That was the first time I knew you had any sense. I said . . . My man Troy knows what he's doing . . . I'm gonna follow this nigger . . . he might take me somewhere. I been following you too. I done learned a whole heap of things about life watching you. I done learned how to tell where the shit lies. How to tell it from the alfalfa. You done learned me a lot of things. You showed me how to not make the same mistakes . . . to take life as it comes along and keep putting one foot in front of the other. (*Pause.*) Rose a good woman, Troy.

TROY. Hell, nigger, I know she a good woman. I been married to her for eighteen years. What you got on your mind, Bono?

BONO. I just say she a good woman. Just like I say anything. I ain't got to have nothing on my mind.

TROY. You just gonna say she a good woman and leave it hanging out there like that? Why you telling me she a good woman?

BONO. She loves you, Troy. Rose loves you.

TROY. You saying I don't measure up. That's what you trying to say. I don't measure up cause I'm seeing this other gal. I know what you trying to say.

BONO. I know what Rose means to you, Troy. I'm just trying to say I don't want to see you mess up.

TROY. Yeah, I appreciate that, Bono. If you was messing around on Lucille I'd be telling you the same thing.

BONO. Well, that's all I got to say. I just say that because I love you both.

TROY. Hell, you know me . . . I wasn't out there looking for nothing. You can't find a better woman than Rose. I know that. But seems like this woman just stuck onto me where I can't shake her loose. I done wrestled with it, tried to throw her off me . . . but she just stuck on tighter. Now she's stuck on for good.

BONO. You's in control . . . that's what you tell me all the time. You responsible for what you do.

TROY. I ain't ducking the responsibility of it. As long as it sets right in my heart . . . then I'm okay. Cause that's all I listen to. It'll tell me right from wrong every time. And I ain't talking about doing Rose no bad turn. I love Rose. She done carried me a long ways and I love and respect her for that.

BONO. I know you do. That's why I don't want to see you hurt her. But what you gonna do when she find out? What you got then? If you try and juggle both of them . . . sooner or later you gonna drop one of them. That's common sense.

TROY. Yeah, I hear what you saying, Bono. I been trying to figure a way to work it out.

BONO. Work it out right, Troy. I don't want to be getting all up between you and Rose's business . . . but work it so it come out right.

TROY. Ah hell, I get all up between you and Lucille's business. When you gonna get that woman that refrigerator she been wanting? Don't tell me you ain't got no money now. I know who your banker is. Mellon don't need that money bad as Lucille want that refrigerator. I'll tell you that.

BONO. Tell you what I'll do . . . when you finish building this fence for Rose . . . I'll buy Lucille that refrigerator.

TROY. You done stuck your foot in your mouth now!

TROY *grabs up a board and begins to saw.* BONO *starts to walk out the yard.*

Hey, nigger . . . where you going?

BONO. I'm going home. I know you don't expect me to help you now. I'm protecting my money. I wanna see you put that fence up by yourself. That's what I want to see. You'll be here another six months without me.

TROY. Nigger, you ain't right.

BONO. When it comes to my money . . . I'm right as fireworks on the Fourth of July.

TROY. All right, we gonna see now. You better get out your bankbook.

BONO *exits, and* TROY *continues to work.* ROSE *enters from the house.*

ROSE. What they say down there? What's happening with Gabe?

TROY. I went down there and got him out. Cost me fifty dollars. Say he was disturbing the peace. Judge set up a hearing for him in three weeks. Say to show cause why he shouldn't be recommitted.

ROSE. What was he doing that cause them to arrest him?

TROY. Some kids was teasing him and he run them off home. Say he was howling and carrying on. Some folks seen him and called the police. That's all it was.

ROSE. Well, what's you say? What'd you tell the judge?

TROY. Told him I'd look after him. It didn't make no sense to recommit the man. He stuck out his big greasy palm and told me to give him fifty dollars and take him on home.

ROSE. Where's he at now? Where'd he go off to?

TROY. He's gone about his business. He don't need nobody to hold his hand.

ROSE. Well, I don't know. Seem like that would be the best place for him if they did put him into the hospital. I know what you're gonna say. But that's what I think would be best.

TROY. The man done had his life ruined fighting for what? And they wanna take and lock him up. Let him be free. He don't bother nobody.

ROSE. Well, everybody got their own way of looking at it I guess. Come on and get your lunch. I got a bowl of lima beans and some cornbread in the oven. Come and get something to eat. Ain't no sense you fretting over Gabe.

ROSE *turns to go into the house.*

TROY. Rose . . . got something to tell you.

ROSE. Well, come on . . . wait till I get this food on the table.

TROY. Rose!

She stops and turns around.

I don't know how to say this. (*Pause.*) I can't explain it none. It just sort of grows on you till it gets out of hand. It starts out like a little bush . . . and the next thing you know it's a whole forest.

ROSE. Troy . . . what is you talking about?

TROY. I'm talking, woman, let me talk. I'm trying to find a way to tell you . . . I'm gonna be a daddy. I'm gonna be somebody's daddy.

ROSE. Troy . . . you're not telling me this? You're gonna be . . . what?

TROY. Rose . . . now . . . see . . .

ROSE. You telling me you gonna be somebody's daddy? You telling your *wife* this?

GABRIEL *enters from the street. He carries a rose in his hand.*

GABRIEL. Hey, Troy! Hey, Rose!

ROSE. I have to wait eighteen years to hear something like this.

GABRIEL. Hey, Rose . . . I got a flower for you. (*He hands it to her.*) That's a rose. Same rose like you is.

ROSE. Thanks, Gabe.

GABRIEL. Troy, you ain't mad at me is you? Them bad mens come and put me away. You ain't mad at me is you?

TROY. Naw, Gabe, I ain't mad at you.

ROSE. Eighteen years and you wanna come with this.

GABRIEL (*takes a quarter out of his pocket*). See what I got? Got a brand new quarter.

TROY. Rose . . . it's just . . .

ROSE. Ain't nothing you can say, Troy. Ain't no way of explaining that.

GABRIEL. Fellow that give me this quarter had a whole mess of them. I'm gonna keep this quarter till it stop shining.

ROSE. Gabe, go on in the house there. I got some watermelon in the Frigidaire. Go on and get you a piece.

GABRIEL. Say, Rose . . . you know I was chasing hellhounds and them bad mens come and get me and take me away. Troy helped me. He come down there and told them they better let me go before he beat them up. Yeah, he did!

ROSE. You go on and get you a piece of watermelon, Gabe. Them bad mens is gone now.

GABRIEL. Okay, Rose . . . gonna get me some watermelon. The kind with the stripes on it.

GABRIEL *exits into the house.*

ROSE. Why, Troy? Why? After all these years to come dragging this in to me now. It don't make no sense at your age. I could have expected this ten or fifteen years ago, but not now.

TROY. Age ain't got nothing to do with it, Rose.

ROSE. I done tried to be everything a wife should be. Everything a wife could be. Been married eighteen years and I got to live to see the day you tell me you been seeing another woman and done fathered a child by her. And you know I ain't never wanted no half nothing in my family. My whole family is half. Everybody got different fathers and mothers . . . my two sisters and my brother. Can't hardly tell who's who. Can't never sit down and talk about Papa and Mama. It's your papa and your mama and my papa and my mama . . .

TROY. Rose . . . stop it now.

ROSE. I ain't never wanted that for none of my children. And now you wanna drag your behind in here and tell me something like this.

TROY. You ought to know. It's time for you to know.

ROSE. Well, I don't want to know, goddamn it!

TROY. I can't just make it go away. It's done now. I can't wish the circumstance of the thing away.

ROSE. And you don't want to either. Maybe you want to wish me and my boy away. Maybe that's what you want? Well, you can't wish us away. I've got eighteen years of my life invested in you. You ought to have stayed upstairs in my bed where you belong.

TROY. Rose . . . now listen to me . . . we can get a handle on this thing. We can talk this out . . . come to an understanding.

ROSE. All of a sudden it's "we." Where was "we" at when you was down there rolling around with some godforsaken woman? "We" should have come to an understanding before you started making a damn fool of yourself. You're a day late and a dollar short when it comes to an understanding with me.

TROY. It's just . . . She gives me a different idea . . . a different understanding about myself. I can step out of this house and get away from the pressures and problems . . . be a different man. I ain't got to wonder how I'm gonna pay the bills or get the roof fixed. I can just be a part of myself that I ain't never been.

ROSE. What I want to know . . . is do you plan to continue seeing her. That's all you can say to me.

TROY. I can sit up in her house and laugh. Do you understand what I'm saying. I can laugh out loud . . . and it feels good. It reaches all the way down to the bottom of my shoes. (*Pause.*) Rose, I can't give that up.

ROSE. Maybe you ought to go on and stay down there with her . . . if she's a better woman than me.

TROY. It ain't about nobody being a better woman or nothing. Rose, you ain't the blame. A man couldn't ask for no woman to be a better wife than you've been. I'm responsible for it. I done locked myself into a pattern trying to take care of you all that I forgot about myself.

ROSE. What the hell was I there for? That was my job, not somebody else's.

TROY. Rose, I done tried all my life to live decent . . . to live a clean . . . hard . . . useful life. I tried to be a good husband to you. In every way I knew how. Maybe I come into the world backwards, I don't know. But . . . you born with two strikes on you before you come to the plate. You got to guard it closely . . . always looking for the curve ball on the inside corner. You can't afford to let none get past you. You can't afford a call strike. If you going down . . . you going down swinging. Everything lined up against you. What you gonna do. I fooled them, Rose. I bunted. When I found you and Cory and a halfway decent job . . . I was safe. Couldn't nothing touch me. I wasn't gonna strike out no more. I wasn't going back to the penitentiary. I wasn't gonna lay in the streets with a bottle of wine. I was safe. I had me a family. A job. I wasn't gonna get that last strike. I was on first looking for one of them boys to knock me in. To get me home.

ROSE. You should have stayed in my bed, Troy.

TROY. Then when I saw that gal . . . she firmed up my backbone. And I got to thinking that if I tried . . . I just might be able to steal second. Do you understand after eighteen years I wanted to steal second.

ROSE. You should have held me tight. You should have grabbed me and held on.

TROY. I stood on first base for eighteen years and I thought . . . well, goddamn it . . . go on for it!

ROSE. We're not talking about baseball! We're talking about you going off to lay in bed with another woman . . . and then bring it home to me. That's what we're talking about. We ain't talking about no baseball.

TROY. Rose, you're not listening to me. I'm trying the best I can to explain it to you. It's not easy for me to admit that I been standing in the same place for eighteen years.

ROSE. I been standing with you! I been right here with you, Troy. I got a life too. I gave eighteen years of my life to stand in the same spot with you. Don't you think I ever wanted other things? Don't you think I had dreams and hopes? What about my life? What about me? Don't you think it ever crossed my mind to want to know other men? That I wanted to lay up somewhere and forget about my responsibilities? That I wanted someone to make me laugh so I could feel good? You not the only one who's got wants and needs. But I held on to you, Troy. I took all my feelings, my wants and needs, my dreams . . . and I buried them inside you. I planted a seed and watched and prayed over it. I planted myself inside you and waited to bloom. And it didn't take me no eighteen years to find out the soil was hard and rocky and it wasn't never gonna bloom.

But I held on to you, Troy. I held you tighter. You was my husband. I owed you everything I had. Every part of me I could find to give you. And upstairs in that room . . . with the darkness falling in on me . . . I gave everything I had to try and erase the doubt that you wasn't the finest man in the world. And wherever you was going . . . I wanted to be there with you. Cause you was my husband. Cause that's the only way I was gonna survive as your wife. You always talking about what you give . . . and what you don't have to give. But you take too. You take . . . and don't even know nobody's giving!

ROSE *turns to exit into the house;* TROY *grabs her arm.*

TROY. You say I take and don't give!
ROSE. Troy! You're hurting me!
TROY. You say I take and don't give!
ROSE. Troy . . . you're hurting my arm! Let go!
TROY. I done give you everything I got. Don't you tell that lie on me.
ROSE. Troy!
TROY. Don't you tell that lie on me!

CORY *enters from the house.*

CORY. Mama!
ROSE. Troy. You're hurting me.
TROY. Don't you tell me about no taking and giving.

CORY *comes up behind* TROY *and grabs him.* TROY, *surprised, is thrown off balance just as* CORY *throws a glancing blow that catches him on the chest and knocks him down.* TROY *is stunned, as is* CORY.

ROSE. Troy. Troy. No!

TROY *gets to his feet and starts at* CORY.

Troy . . . no. Please! Troy!

ROSE *pulls on* TROY *to hold him back.* TROY *stops himself.*

TROY (*to* CORY). All right. That's strike two. You stay away from around me, boy. Don't you strike out. You living with a full count. Don't you strike out.

TROY *exits out the yard as the lights go down.*

Scene 2

It is six months later, early afternoon. TROY *enters from the house and starts to exit the yard.* ROSE *enters from the house.*

ROSE. Troy, I want to talk to you.
TROY. All of a sudden, after all this time, you want to talk to me, huh? You ain't wanted to talk to me for months. You ain't wanted to talk to me last night. You ain't wanted no part of me then. What you wanna talk to me about now?
ROSE. Tomorrow's Friday.
TROY. I know what day tomorrow is. You think I don't know tomorrow's Friday? My whole life I ain't done nothing but look to see Friday coming and you got to tell me it's Friday.

ROSE. I want to know if you're coming home.

TROY. I always come home, Rose. You know that. There ain't never been a
     night I ain't come home.

ROSE. That ain't what I mean . . . and you know it. I want to know if you're
     coming straight home after work.

TROY. I figure I'd cash my check . . . hang out at Taylors' with the boys . . .
     maybe play a game of checkers . . .

ROSE. Troy, I can't live like this. I won't live like this. You livin' on borrowed
     time with me. It's been going on six months now you ain't been coming
     home.

TROY. I be here every night. Every night of the year. That's 365 days.

ROSE. I want you to come home tomorrow after work.

TROY. Rose . . . I don't mess up my pay. You know that now. I take my pay
     and I give it to you. I don't have no money but what you give me back. I
     just want to have a little time to myself . . . a little time to enjoy life.

ROSE. What about me? When's my time to enjoy life?

TROY. I don't know what to tell you, Rose. I'm doing the best I can.

ROSE. You ain't been home from work but time enough to change your
     clothes and run out . . . and you wanna call that the best you can do?

TROY. I'm going over to the hospital to see Alberta. She went into the hospi-
     tal this afternoon. Look like she might have the baby early. I won't be
     gone long.

ROSE. Well, you ought to know. They went over to Miss Pearl's and got Gabe
     today. She said you told them to go ahead and lock him up.

TROY. I ain't said no such thing. Whoever told you that is telling a lie. Pearl
     ain't doing nothing but telling a big fat lie.

ROSE. She ain't had to tell me. I read it on the papers.

TROY. I ain't told them nothing of the kind.

ROSE. I saw it right there on the papers.

TROY. What it say, huh?

ROSE. It said you told them to take him.

TROY. Then they screwed that up, just the way they screw up everything. I
     ain't worried about what they got on the paper.

ROSE. Say the government send part of his check to the hospital and the
     other part to you.

TROY. I ain't got nothing to do with that if that's the way it works. I ain't
     made up the rules about how it work.

ROSE. You did Gabe just like you did Cory. You wouldn't sign the paper for
     Cory . . . but you signed for Gabe. You signed that paper.

The telephone is heard ringing inside the house.

TROY. I told you I ain't signed nothing, woman! The only thing I signed was
     the release form. Hell, I can't read, I don't know what they had on that
     paper! I ain't signed nothing about sending Gabe away.

ROSE. I said send him to the hospital . . . you said let him be free . . . now you
     done went down there and signed him to the hospital for half his
     money. You went back on yourself, Troy. You gonna have to answer for
     that.

TROY. See now . . . you been over there talking to Miss Pearl. She done got
     mad cause she ain't getting Gabe's rent money. That's all it is. She's
     liable to say anything.

ROSE. Troy, I seen where you signed the paper.

TROY. You ain't seen nothing I signed. What she doing got papers on my brother anyway? Miss Pearl telling a big fat lie. And I'm gonna tell her about it too! You ain't seen nothing I signed. Say . . . you ain't seen nothing I signed.

ROSE *exits into the house to answer the telephone. Presently she returns.*

ROSE. Troy . . . that was the hospital. Alberta had the baby.

TROY. What she have? What is it?

ROSE. It's a girl.

TROY. I better get on down to the hospital to see her.

ROSE. Troy . . .

TROY. Rose . . . I got to go see her now. That's only right . . . what's the matter . . . the baby's all right, ain't it?

ROSE. Alberta died having the baby.

TROY. Died . . . you say she's dead? Alberta's dead?

ROSE. They said they done all they could. They couldn't do nothing for her.

TROY. The baby? How's the baby?

ROSE. They say it's healthy. I wonder who's gonna bury her.

TROY. She had family, Rose. She wasn't living in the world by herself.

ROSE. I know she wasn't living in the world by herself.

TROY. Next thing you gonna want to know if she had any insurance.

ROSE. Troy, you ain't got to talk like that.

TROY. That's the first thing that jumped out your mouth. "Who's gonna bury her?" Like I'm fixing to take on that task for myself.

ROSE. I am your wife. Don't push me away.

TROY. I ain't pushing nobody away. Just give me some space. That's all. Just give me some room to breathe.

ROSE *exits into the house.* TROY *walks about the yard.*

TROY (*with a quiet rage that threatens to consume him*). All right . . . Mr. Death. See now . . . I'm gonna tell you what I'm gonna do. I'm gonna take and build me a fence around this yard. See? I'm gonna build me a fence around what belongs to me. And then I want you to stay on the other side. See? You stay over there until you're ready for me. Then you come on. Bring your army. Bring your sickle. Bring your wrestling clothes. I ain't gonna fall down on my vigilance this time. You ain't gonna sneak up on me no more. When you ready for me . . . when the top of your list say Troy Maxson . . . that's when you come around here. You come up and knock on the front door. Ain't nobody else got nothing to do with this. This is between you and me. Man to man. You stay on the other side of that fence until you ready for me. Then you come up and knock on the front door. Anytime you want. I'll be ready for you.

The lights go down to black.

Scene 3

The lights come up on the porch. It is late evening three days later. ROSE *sits listening to the ball game waiting for* TROY. *The final out of the game is made and* ROSE *switches off the radio.* TROY *enters the yard carrying an infant wrapped in blankets. He stands back from the house and calls.*

ROSE *enters and stands on the porch. There is a long, awkward silence, the weight of which grows heavier with each passing second.*

TROY. Rose . . . I'm standing here with my daughter in my arms. She ain't but a wee bittie little old thing. She don't know nothing about grownups' business. She innocent . . . and she ain't got no mama.

ROSE. What you telling me for, Troy?

She turns and exits into the house.

TROY. Well . . . I guess we'll just sit out here on the porch.

He sits down on the porch. There is an awkward indelicateness about the way he handles the baby. His largeness engulfs and seems to swallow it. He speaks loud enough for ROSE *to hear.*

A man's got to do what's right for him. I ain't sorry for nothing I done. It felt right in my heart. (*To the baby.*) What you smiling at? Your daddy's a big man. Got these great big old hands. But sometimes he's scared. And right now your daddy's scared cause we sitting out here and ain't got no home. Oh, I been homeless before. I ain't had no little baby with me. But I been homeless. You just be out on the road by your lonesome and you see one of them trains coming and you just kinda go like this . . .

He sings as a lullaby.

> Please, Mr. Engineer let a man ride the line
> Please, Mr. Engineer let a man ride the line
> I ain't got no ticket please let me ride the blinds

ROSE *enters from the house.* TROY, *hearing her steps behind him, stands and faces her.*

She's my daughter, Rose. My own flesh and blood. I can't deny her no more than I can deny them boys. (*Pause.*) You and them boys is my family. You and them and this child is all I got in the world. So I guess what I'm saying is . . . I'd appreciate it if you'd help me take care of her.

ROSE. Okay, Troy . . . you're right. I'll take care of your baby for you . . . cause . . . like you say . . . she's innocent . . . and you can't visit the sins of the father upon the child. A motherless child has got a hard time. (*She takes the baby from him.*) From right now . . . this child got a mother. But you a womanless man.

ROSE *turns and exits into the house with the baby. Lights go down to black.*

Scene 4

It is two months later. LYONS *enters the street. He knocks on the door and calls.*

LYONS. Hey, Rose! (*Pause.*) Rose!

ROSE (*from inside the house*). Stop that yelling. You gonna wake up Raynell. I just got her to sleep.

LYONS. I just stopped by to pay Papa this twenty dollars I owe him. Where's Papa at?

ROSE. He should be here in a minute. I'm getting ready to go down to the church. Sit down and wait on him.

LYONS. I got to go pick up Bonnie over her mother's house.

ROSE. Well, sit it down there on the table. He'll get it.

LYONS (*enters the house and sets the money on the table*). Tell Papa I said thanks. I'll see you again.

ROSE. All right, Lyons. We'll see you.

> LYONS *starts to exit as* CORY *enters.*

CORY. Hey, Lyons.

LYONS. What's happening, Cory? Say man, I'm sorry I missed your graduation. You know I had a gig and couldn't get away. Otherwise, I would have been there, man. So what you doing?

CORY. I'm trying to find a job.

LYONS. Yeah I know how that go, man. It's rough out here. Jobs are scarce.

CORY. Yeah, I know.

LYONS. Look here, I got to run. Talk to Papa . . . he know some people. He'll be able to help get you a job. Talk to him . . . see what he say.

CORY. Yeah . . . all right, Lyons.

LYONS. You take care. I'll talk to you soon. We'll find some time to talk.

> LYONS *exits the yard.* CORY *wanders over to the tree, picks up the bat, and assumes a batting stance. He studies an imaginary pitcher and swings. Dissatisfied with the result, he tries again.* TROY *enters. They eye each other for a beat.* CORY *puts the bat down and exits the yard.* TROY *starts into the house as* ROSE *exits with* RAYNELL. *She is carrying a cake.*

TROY. I'm coming in and everybody's going out.

ROSE. I'm taking this cake down to the church for the bake sale. Lyons was by to see you. He stopped by to pay you your twenty dollars. It's laying in there on the table.

TROY (*going into his pocket*). Well . . . here go this money.

ROSE. Put it in there on the table, Troy. I'll get it.

TROY. What time you coming back?

ROSE. Ain't no use in you studying me. It don't matter what time I come back.

TROY. I just asked you a question, woman. What's the matter . . . can't I ask you a question?

ROSE. Troy, I don't want to go into it. Your dinner's in there on the stove. All you got to do is heat it up. And don't you be eating the rest of them cakes in there. I'm coming back for them. We having a bake sale at the church tomorrow.

> ROSE *exits the yard.* TROY *sits down on the steps, takes a pint bottle from his pocket, opens it, and drinks. He begins to sing.*

TROY.

> Hear it ring! Hear it ring!
> Had an old dog his name was Blue

> You know Blue was mighty true
> You know Blue as a good old dog
> Blue trees a possum in a hollow log
> You know from that he was a good old dog

BONO *enters the yard.*

BONO. Hey, Troy.

TROY. Hey, what's happening, Bono?

BONO. I just thought I'd stop by to see you.

TROY. What you stop by and see me for? You ain't stopped by in a month of Sundays. Hell, I must owe you money or something.

BONO. Since you got your promotion I can't keep up with you. Used to see you every day. Now I don't even know what route you working.

TROY. They keep switching me around. Got me out in Greentree now . . . hauling white folks' garbage.

BONO. Greentree, huh? You lucky, at least you ain't got to be lifting them barrels. Damn if they ain't getting heavier. I'm gonna put in my two years and call it quits.

TROY. I'm thinking about retiring myself.

BONO. You got it easy. You can drive for another five years.

TROY. It ain't the same, Bono. It ain't like working the back of the truck. Ain't got nobody to talk to . . . feel like you working by yourself. Naw, I'm thinking about retiring. How's Lucille?

BONO. She all right. Her arthritis get to acting up on her sometime. Saw Rose on my way in. She going down to the church, huh?

TROY. Yeah, she took up going down there. All them preachers looking for somebody to fatten their pockets. (*Pause.*) Got some gin here.

BONO. Naw, thanks. I just stopped by to say hello.

TROY. Hell, nigger . . . you can take a drink. I ain't never known you to say no to a drink. You ain't got to work tomorrow.

BONO. I just stopped by. I'm fixing to go over to Skinner's. We got us a domino game going over his house every Friday.

TROY. Nigger, you can't play no dominoes. I used to whup you four games out of five.

BONO. Well, that learned me. I'm getting better.

TROY. Yeah? Well, that's all right.

BONO. Look here . . . I got to be getting on. Stop by sometime, huh?

TROY. Yeah, I'll do that, Bono. Lucille told Rose you bought her a new refrigerator.

BONO. Yeah, Rose told Lucille you had finally built your fence . . . so I figured we'd call it even.

TROY. I knew you would.

BONO. Yeah . . . okay. I'll be talking to you.

TROY. Yeah, take care, Bono. Good to see you. I'm gonna stop over.

BONO. Yeah. Okay, Troy.

BONO *exits.* TROY *drinks from the bottle.*

TROY.

> Old Blue died and I dug his grave
> Let him down with a golden chain
> Every night when I hear old Blue bark

I know Blue treed a possum in Noah's Ark.
Hear it ring! Hear it ring!

CORY *enters the yard. They eye each other for a beat.* TROY *is sitting in the middle of the steps.* CORY *walks over.*

CORY. I got to get by.

TROY. Say what? What's you say?

CORY. You in my way. I got to get by.

TROY. You got to get by where? This is my house. Bought and paid for. In full. Took me fifteen years. And if you wanna go in my house and I'm sitting on the steps . . . you say excuse me. Like your mama taught you.

CORY. Come on, Pop . . . I got to get by.

CORY *starts to maneuver his way past* TROY. TROY *grabs his leg and shoves him back.*

TROY. You just gonna walk over top of me?

CORY. I live here too!

TROY (*advancing toward him*). You just gonna walk over top of me in my own house?

CORY. I ain't scared of you.

TROY. I ain't asked if you was scared of me. I asked you if you was fixing to walk over top of me in my own house? That's the question. You ain't gonna say excuse me? You just gonna walk over top of me?

CORY. If you wanna put it like that.

TROY. How else am I gonna put it?

CORY. I was walking by you to go into the house 'cause you sitting on the steps drunk, singing to yourself. You can put it like that.

TROY. Without saying excuse me???

CORY *doesn't respond.*

I asked you a question. Without saying excuse me???

CORY. I ain't got to say excuse me to you. You don't count around here no more.

TROY. Oh, I see . . . I don't count around here no more. You ain't got to say excuse me to your daddy. All of a sudden you done got so grown that your daddy don't count around here no more . . . Around here in his own house and yard that he done paid for with the sweat of his brow. You done got so grown to where you gonna take over. You gonna take over my house. Is that right? You gonna wear my pants. You gonna go in there and stretch out on my bed. You ain't got to say excuse me cause I don't count around here no more. Is that right?

CORY. That's right. You always talking this dumb stuff. Now, why don't you just get out my way?

TROY. I guess you got someplace to sleep and something to put in your belly. You got that, huh? You got that? That's what you need. You got that, huh?

CORY. You don't know what I got. You ain't got to worry about what I got.

TROY. You right! You one hundred percent right! I done spent the last seventeen years worrying about what you got. Now it's your turn, see? I'll tell you what to do. You grown . . . we done established that. You a man. Now, let's see you act like one. Turn your behind around and walk out this yard. And when you get out there in the alley . . . you can forget about this house. See? 'Cause this is my house. You go on and be a man and get your own house. You can forget about this. 'Cause this is mine. You go on and get yours 'cause I'm through with doing for you.

CORY. You talking about what you did for me . . . what'd you ever give me?

TROY. Them feet and bones! That pumping heart, nigger! I give you more than anybody else is ever gonna give you.

CORY. You ain't never gave me nothing! You ain't never done nothing but hold me back. Afraid I was gonna be better than you. All you ever did was try and make me scared of you. I used to tremble every time you called my name. Every time I heard your footsteps in the house. Wondering all the time . . . what's Papa gonna say if I do this? . . . What's he gonna say if I do that? . . . What's Papa gonna say if I turn on the radio? And Mama, too . . . she tries . . . but she's scared of you.

TROY. You leave your mama out of this. She ain't got nothing to do with this.

CORY. I don't know how she stand you . . . after what you did to her.

TROY. I told you to leave your mama out of this!

He advances toward CORY.

CORY. What you gonna do . . . give me a whupping? You can't whup me no more. You're too old. You just an old man.

TROY (*shoves him on his shoulder*). Nigger! That's what you are. You just another nigger on the street to me!

CORY. You crazy! You know that?

TROY. Go on now! You got the devil in you. Get on away from me!

CORY. You just a crazy old man . . . talking about I got the devil in me.

TROY. Yeah, I'm crazy! If you don't get on the other side of that yard . . . I'm gonna show you how crazy I am! Go on . . . get the hell out of my yard.

CORY. It ain't your yard. You took Uncle Gabe's money he got from the army to buy this house and then you put him out.

TROY (*advances on* CORY). Get your black ass out of my yard!

TROY'*s advance backs* CORY *up against the tree.* CORY *grabs up the bat.*

CORY. I ain't going nowhere! Come on . . . put me out! I ain't scared of you.

TROY. That's my bat!

CORY. Come on!

TROY. Put my bat down!

CORY. Come on, put me out.

CORY *swings at* TROY, *who backs across the yard.*

What's the matter? You so bad . . . put me out!

TROY *advances toward* CORY.

CORY (*backing up*). Come on! Come on!

TROY. You're gonna have to use it! You wanna draw that bat back on me . . . you're gonna have to use it.

CORY. Come on! . . . Come on!

CORY *swings the bat at* TROY *a second time. He misses.* TROY *continues to advance toward him.*

TROY. You're gonna have to kill me! You wanna draw that bat back on me. You're gonna have to kill me.

CORY, *backed up against the tree, can go no farther.* TROY *taunts him. He sticks out his head and offers him a target.*

Come on! Come on!

CORY *is unable to swing the bat.* TROY *grabs it.*

TROY. Then I'll show you.

CORY *and* TROY *struggle over the bat. The struggle is fierce and fully engaged.* TROY *ultimately is the stronger and takes the bat from* CORY *and stands over him ready to swing. He stops himself.*

Go on and get away from around my house.

CORY, *stung by his defeat, picks himself up, walks slowly out of the yard and up the alley.*

CORY. Tell Mama I'll be back for my things.

TROY. They'll be on the other side of that fence.

CORY *exits.*

TROY. I can't taste nothing. Helluljah! I can't taste nothing no more. (TROY *assumes a batting posture and begins to taunt Death, the fastball on the outside corner.*) Come on! It's between you and me now! Come on! Anytime you want! Come on! I be ready for you . . . but I ain't gonna be easy.

The lights go down on the scene.

Scene 5

The time is 1965. The lights come up in the yard. It is the morning of TROY's *funeral. A funeral plaque with a light hangs beside the door. There is a small garden plot off to the side. There is noise and activity in the house as* ROSE, LYONS, *and* BONO *have gathered. The door opens and* RAYNELL, *seven years old, enters dressed in a flannel nightgown. She crosses to the garden and pokes around with a stick.* ROSE *calls from the house.*

ROSE. Raynell!

RAYNELL. Mam?

ROSE. What you doing out there?

RAYNELL. Nothing.

ROSE *comes to the door.*

ROSE. Girl, get in here and get dressed. What you doing?

RAYNELL. Seeing if my garden growed.

ROSE. I told you it ain't gonna grow overnight. You got to wait.

RAYNELL. It don't look like it never gonna grow. Dag!

ROSE. I told you a watched pot never boils. Get in here and get dressed.

RAYNELL. This ain't even no pot, Mama.

ROSE. You just have to give it a chance. It'll grow. Now you come on and do what I told you. We got to be getting ready. This ain't no morning to be playing around. You hear me?

RAYNELL. Yes, mam.

ROSE *exits into the house.* RAYNELL *continues to poke at her garden with a stick.* CORY *enters. He is dressed in a Marine corporal's uniform, and carries a duffelbag. His posture is that of a military man, and his speech has a clipped sternness.*

CORY (*to* RAYNELL). Hi. (*Pause.*) I bet your name is Raynell.

RAYNELL. Uh huh.

CORY. Is your mama home?

RAYNELL *runs up on the porch and calls through the screen door.*

RAYNELL. Mama . . . there's some man out here. Mama?

ROSE *comes to the door.*

ROSE. Cory? Lord have mercy! Look here, you all!

ROSE *and* CORY *embrace in a tearful reunion as* BONO *and* LYONS *enter from the house dressed in funeral clothes.*

BONO. Aw, looka here . . .

ROSE. Done got all grown up!

CORY. Don't cry, Mama. What you crying about?

ROSE. I'm just so glad you made it.

CORY. Hey Lyons. How you doing, Mr. Bono?

LYONS *goes to embrace* CORY.

LYONS. Look at you, man. Look at you. Don't he look good, Rose. Got them Corporal stripes.

ROSE. What took you so long?

CORY. You know how the Marines are, Mama. They got to get all their paper-work straight before they let you do anything.

ROSE. Well, I'm sure glad you made it. They let Lyons come. Your Uncle Gabe's still in the hospital. They don't know if they gonna let him out or not. I just talked to them a little while ago.

LYONS. A Corporal in the United States Marines.

BONO. Your daddy knew you had it in you. He used to tell me all the time.

LYONS. Don't he look good, Mr. Bono?

BONO. Yeah, he remind me of Troy when I first met him. (*Pause.*) Say, Rose, Lucille's down at the church with the choir. I'm gonna go down and get the pallbearers lined up. I'll be back to get you all.

ROSE. Thanks, Jim.

CORY. See you, Mr. Bono.

LYONS (*with his arm around* RAYNELL). Cory . . . look at Raynell. Ain't she precious? She gonna break a whole lot of hearts.

ROSE. Raynell, come and say hello to your brother. This is your brother, Cory. You remember Cory.

RAYNELL. No, Mam.

CORY. She don't remember me, Mama.

ROSE. Well, we talk about you. She heard us talk about you. (*To* RAYNELL.) This is your brother, Cory. Come on and say hello.

RAYNELL. Hi.

CORY. Hi. So you're Raynell. Mama told me a lot about you.

ROSE. You all come on into the house and let me fix you some breakfast. Keep up your strength.

CORY. I ain't hungry, Mama.

LYONS. You can fix me something, Rose. I'll be in there in a minute.

ROSE. Cory, you sure you don't want nothing? I know they ain't feeding you right.

CORY. No, Mama . . . thanks. I don't feel like eating. I'll get something later.

ROSE. Raynell . . . get on upstairs and get that dress on like I told you.

ROSE *and* RAYNELL *exit into the house.*

LYONS. So . . . I hear you thinking about getting married.

CORY. Yeah, I done found the right one, Lyons. It's about time.

LYONS. Me and Bonnie been split up about four years now. About the time Papa retired. I guess she just got tired of all them changes I was putting her through. (*Pause.*) I always knew you was gonna make something out yourself. Your head was always in the right direction. So . . . you gonna stay in . . . make it a career . . . put in your twenty years?

CORY. I don't know. I got six already, I think that's enough.

LYONS. Stick with Uncle Sam and retire early. Ain't nothing out here. I guess Rose told you what happened with me. They got me down the workhouse. I thought I was being slick cashing other people's checks.

CORY. How much time you doing?

LYONS. They give me three years. I got that beat now. I ain't got but nine more months. It ain't so bad. You learn to deal with it like anything else. You got to take the crookeds with the straights. That's what Papa used to say. He used to say that when he struck out. I seen him strike out three times in a row . . . and the next time up he hit the ball over the grandstand. Right out there in Homestead Field. He wasn't satisfied hitting in the seats . . . he want to hit it over everything! After the game he had two hundred people standing around waiting to shake his hand. You got to take the crookeds with the straights. Yeah, Papa was something else.

CORY. You still playing?

LYONS. Cory . . . you know I'm gonna do that. There's some fellows down there we got us a band . . . we gonna try and stay together when we get out . . . but yeah, I'm still playing. It still helps me to get out of bed in the morning. As long as it do that I'm gonna be right there playing and trying to make some sense out of it.

ROSE (*calling*). Lyons, I got these eggs in the pan.

LYONS. Let me go on and get these eggs, man. Get ready to go bury Papa. (*Pause.*) How you doing? You doing all right?

CORY *nods.* LYONS *touches him on the shoulder and they share a moment of silent grief.* LYONS *exits into the house.* CORY *wanders about the yard.* RAYNELL *enters.*

RAYNELL. Hi.

CORY. Hi.

RAYNELL. Did you used to sleep in my room?

CORY. Yeah . . . that used to be my room.

RAYNELL. That's what Papa call it. "Cory's room." It got your football in the closet.

ROSE *comes to the door.*

ROSE. Raynell, get in there and get them good shoes on.

RAYNELL. Mama, can't I wear these? Them other one hurt my feet.

ROSE. Well, they just gonna have to hurt your feet for a while. You ain't said they hurt your feet when you went down to the store and got them.

RAYNELL. They didn't hurt then. My feet done got bigger.

ROSE. Don't you give me no backtalk now. You get in there and get them shoes on.

RAYNELL *exits into the house.*

Ain't too much changed. He still got that piece of rag tied to that tree. He was out here swinging that bat. I was just ready to go back in the house. He swung that bat and then he just fell over. Seem like he swung it and stood there with this grin on his face . . . and then he just fell over. They carried him on down to the hospital, but I knew there wasn't no need . . . why don't you come on in the house?

CORY. Mama . . . I got something to tell you. I don't know how to tell you this . . . but I've got to tell you . . . I'm not going to Papa's funeral.

ROSE. Boy, hush your mouth. That's your daddy you talking about. I don't want hear that kind of talk this morning. I done raised you to come to this? You standing there all healthy and grown talking about you ain't going to your daddy's funeral?

CORY. Mama . . . listen . . .

ROSE. I don't want to hear it, Cory. You just get that thought out of your head.

CORY. I can't drag Papa with me everywhere I go. I've got to say no to him. One time in my life I've got to say no.

ROSE. Don't nobody have to listen to nothing like that. I know you and your daddy ain't seen eye to eye, but I ain't got to listen to that kind of talk this morning. Whatever was between you and your daddy . . . the time has come to put it aside. Just take it and set it over there on the shelf and forget about it. Disrespecting your daddy ain't gonna make you a man, Cory. You got to find a way to come to that on your own. Not going to your daddy's funeral ain't gonna make you a man.

CORY. The whole time I was growing up . . . living in his house . . . Papa was like a shadow that followed you everywhere. It weighed on you and sunk into your flesh. It would wrap around you and lay there until you couldn't tell which one was you anymore. That shadow digging in your flesh. Trying to crawl in. Trying to live through you. Everywhere I looked, Troy Maxson was staring back at me . . . hiding under the bed . . . in the closet. I'm just saying I've got to find a way to get rid of that shadow, Mama.

ROSE. You just like him. You got him in you good.

CORY. Don't tell me that, Mama.

ROSE. You Troy Maxson all over again.

CORY. I don't want to be Troy Maxson. I want to be me.

ROSE. You can't be nobody but who you are, Cory. That shadow wasn't nothing but you growing into yourself. You either got to grow into it or cut it down to fit you. But that's all you got to make life with. That's all you got to measure yourself against that world out there. Your daddy wanted you to be everything he wasn't . . . and at the same time he tried to make you into everything he was. I don't know if he was right or wrong . . . but I do know he meant to do more good than he meant to do harm.

He wasn't always right. Sometimes when he touched he bruised. And sometimes when he took me in his arms he cut.

When I first met your daddy I thought . . . Here is a man I can lay down with and make a baby. That's the first thing I thought when I seen him. I was thirty years old and had done seen my share of men. But when he walked up to me and said, "I can dance a waltz that'll make you dizzy," I thought, Rose Lee, here is a man that you can open yourself up to and be filled to bursting. Here is a man that can fill all them empty spaces you been tipping around the edges of. One of them empty spaces was being somebody's mother.

I married your daddy and settled down to cooking his supper and keeping clean sheets on the bed. When your daddy walked through the house he was so big he filled it up. That was my first mistake. Not to make him leave some room for me. For my part in the matter. But at that time I wanted that. I wanted a house that I could sing in. And that's what your daddy gave me. I didn't know to keep up his strength I had to give up little pieces of mine. I did that. I took on his life as mine and mixed up the pieces so that you couldn't hardly tell which was which anymore. It was my choice. It was my life and I didn't have to live it like that. But that's what life offered me in the way of being a woman and I took it. I grabbed hold of it with both hands.

By the time Raynell came into the house, me and your daddy had done lost touch with one another. I didn't want to make my blessing off of nobody's misfortune . . . but I took on to Raynell like she was all them babies I had wanted and never had.

The phone rings.

Like I'd been blessed to relive a part of my life. And if the Lord see fit to keep up my strength . . . I'm gonna do her just like your daddy did you . . . I'm gonna give her the best of what's in me.

RAYNELL (*entering, still with her old shoes*). Mama . . . Reverend Tollivier on the phone.

ROSE *exits into the house.*

RAYNELL. Hi.
CORY. Hi.
RAYNELL. You in the Army or the Marines?
CORY. Marines.
RAYNELL. Papa said it was the Army. Did you know Blue?
CORY. Blue? Who's Blue?
RAYNELL. Papa's dog what he sing about all the time.
CORY (*singing*).

Hear it ring! Hear it ring!
I had a dog his name was Blue
You know Blue was mighty true
You know Blue was a good old dog
Blue treed a possum in a hollow log
You know from that he was a good old dog.
Hear it ring! Hear it ring!

RAYNELL *joins in singing.*

CORY AND RAYNELL.

> Blue treed a possum out on a limb
> Blue looked at me and I looked at him
> Grabbed that possum and put him in a sack
> Blue stayed there till I came back
> Old Blue's feets was big and round
> Never allowed a possum to touch the ground.
> Old Blue died and I dug his grave
> I dug his grave with a silver spade
> Let him down with a golden chain
> And every night I call his name
> Go on Blue, you good dog you
> Go on Blue, you good dog you.

RAYNELL.

> Blue laid down and died like a man
> Blue laid down and died . . .

BOTH.

> Blue laid down and died like a man
> Now he's treeing possums in the Promised Land
> I'm gonna tell you this to let you know
> Blue's gone where the good dogs go
> When I hear old Blue bark
> When I hear old Blue bark
> Blue treed a possum in Noah's Ark
> Blue treed a possum in Noah's Ark.

ROSE *comes to the screen door.*

ROSE.   Cory, we gonna be ready to go in a minute.

CORY (*to* RAYNELL). You go on in the house and change them shoes like Mama told you so we can go to Papa's funeral.

RAYNELL.   Okay, I'll be back.

RAYNELL *exits into the house.* CORY *gets up and crosses over to the tree.* ROSE *stands in the screen door watching him.* GABRIEL *enters from the alley.*

GABRIEL (*calling*). Hey, Rose!

ROSE.   Gabe?

GABRIEL.   I'm here, Rose. Hey, Rose, I'm here!

ROSE *enters from the house.*

ROSE.   Lord . . . Look here, Lyons!

LYONS.   See, I told you, Rose . . . I told you they'd let him come.

CORY.   How you doing, Uncle Gabe?

LYONS.   How you doing, Uncle Gabe?

GABRIEL.   Hey, Rose. It's time. It's time to tell St. Peter to open the gates. Troy, you ready? You ready, Troy. I'm gonna tell St. Peter to open the gates. You get ready now.

GABRIEL, *with great fanfare, braces himself to blow. The trumpet is without a mouthpiece. He puts the end of it into his mouth and blows with great force, like a man who has been waiting some twenty-odd years for this single moment. No sound comes out of the trumpet. He braces himself and blows again with the same result. A third time he blows. There is a weight of impossible description that falls away and leaves him bare and exposed to a frightful realization. It is a trauma that a sane and normal mind would be unable to withstand. He begins to dance. A slow, strange dance, eerie and life-giving. A dance of atavistic signature and ritual.* LYONS *attempts to embrace him.* GABRIEL *pushes* LYONS *away. He begins to howl in what is an attempt at song, or perhaps a song turning back into itself in an attempt at speech. He finishes his dance and the gates of heaven stand open as wide as God's closet.*

That's the way that go!

BLACKOUT

YOUR TURN

The Play on the Page

1. What do you think that Bono means when he says, early in Act 2, "Some people build fences to keep people out . . . and some people build fences to keep people in"? Why is the play called *Fences*? What has fenced Troy in? What is Troy fencing in? (Take account of Troy's last speech in Act 2, Scene 2, but do not limit your discussion to this speech.)

2. What do you think Troy's reasons are—conscious and unconscious— for not wanting Cory to play football at college?

3. Compare and contrast Cory and Lyons. Consider, too, in what ways they resemble Troy and in what ways they differ from him.

4. In what ways is Troy like his father, and in what ways unlike him?

5. What do you make out of the prominence given to the song about Blue?

6. There is a good deal of anger in the play, but there is also humor. Which passages do you find humorous, and why?

7. Characterize Rose Maxson.

The Play on the Stage

8. How would Wilson's remarks in the 1987 interview (see page 1400) help a director in staging *Fences*? For example, his assertion that every person (except Raynell) is institutionalized at the end of the play might suggest a certain tone or mood for a production.

9. In what ways is the role of Gabriel a challenge for an actor? What advice might you give to the other actors on stage during Gabriel's appearances?

10. Some scenes begin by specifying that "the lights come up." Others do not, presumably beginning with an illuminated stage. All scenes

except the last one end with the lights going down to blackness. Explain Wilson's use of lighting.

A Context for *Fences*

AUGUST WILSON

Talking About Fences

(Part of an interview conducted with David Savran on 13 March 1987.)

In reading Fences, *I came to view Troy more and more critically as the play progressed, sharing Rose's point of view. We see that Troy has been crippled by his father. That's being replayed in Troy's relationship with Cory. Do you think there's a way out of that cycle?*

Surely. First of all, we're all like our parents. The things we are taught early in life, how to respond to the world, our sense of morality—everything, we get from them. Now you can take that legacy and do with it anything you want to do. It's in your hands. Cory is Troy's son. How can he be Troy's son without sharing Troy's values? I was trying to get at why Troy made the choices he made, how they have influenced his values and how he attempts to pass those along to his son. Each generation gives the succeeding generation what they think they need. One question in the play is, "Are the tools we are given sufficient to compete in a world that is different from the one our parents knew?" I think they are—it's just that we have to do different things with the tools. That's all Troy has to give. Troy's flaw is that he does not recognize that the world was changing. That's because he spent fifteen years in a penitentiary.

As African-Americans, we should demand to participate in society as Africans. That's the way out of the vicious cycle of poverty and neglect that exists in 1987 in America, where you have a huge percentage of blacks living in the equivalent of South African townships, in housing projects. No one is inviting these people to participate in society. Look at the poverty levels—$8,500 for a family of four, if you have $8,501 you're not counted. Those statistics would go up enormously if we had an honest assessment of the cost of living in America. I don't know how anybody can support a family of four on $8,500. What I'm saying is that 85 or 90 percent of blacks in America are living in abject poverty and, for the most part, are crowded into what amount to concentration camps. The situation for blacks in America is worse than it was forty years ago. Some sociologists will tell you about the tremendous progress we've made. They didn't put me out when I walked in the door. And you can always point to someone who works on Wall Street, or is a doctor. But they don't count in the larger scheme of things.

Do you have any idea how these political changes could take place?

I'm not sure. I know that blacks must be allowed their cultural differences. I think the process of assimilation to white American society was a big mistake.

We don't want to be like you. Blacks living in housing projects are isolated from the society, for the most part—living as they choose, as Africans. Only they don't realize the value in what they're doing because they have accepted their victimization. They've marked themselves as victims. Once they recognize that, they can begin to move through society in a different manner, from a stronger position, and claim what is theirs.

A project of yours is to point up what happens when oppression is internalized.

Yes, transfer of aggression to the wrong target. I think it's interesting that the two roads open to blacks for "full participation" are entertainment and sports, *Ma Rainey* and *Fences,* and I didn't plan it that way. I don't think that they're the correct roads. I think Troy's right. Now with the benefit of historical perspective, I can say that the athletic scholarship was actually a way of exploiting. Now you've got two million kids who think they're going to play in the NBA. In the sixties the universities made a lot of money off of athletics. You had kids playing for free who, by and large, were not getting educated, were taking courses in basketweaving. Some of them could barely read.

Troy may be right about that issue, but it seems that he has passed on certain destructive traits in spite of himself. Take the hostility between father and son.

I think every generation says to the previous generation: you're in my way. I've got to get by. The father–son conflict is actually a normal generational conflict that happens all the time.

So it's a healthy and a good thing?

Oh, sure. Troy is seeing this boy walk around, smelling his piss. Two men cannot live in the same household. Troy would have been tremendously disappointed if Cory had not challenged him. Troy knows that this boy has to go out and do battle with that world: "So I had best prepare him because I know that's a harsh, cruel place out there. But that's going to be easy compared to what he's getting here. Ain't nobody gonna whip your ass like I'm gonna whip it." He has a tremendous love for the kid. But he's not going to say, "I love you," he's going to demonstrate it. He's carrying garbage for seventeen years just for the kid. The only world Troy knows is the one that he made. Cory's going to go on to find another one, he's going to arrive at the same place as Troy. I think one of the most important lines in the play is when Troy is talking about his father: "I got to the place where I could feel him kicking in my blood and knew that the only thing that separated us was the matter of a few years."

Hopefully, Cory will do things a bit differently with his son. For Troy, sports was not the way to go, the white man wouldn't let him get away with that. "Get you a job, with your hands, something that nobody can take away from you." The idea of school—he doesn't know what that is. That's for white folks. Very few blacks had paperwork jobs. But if you knew how to fix cars, you could always make some money. That's what Troy wants for Cory. There aren't many people who ever jumped up in Troy's face. So he's proud of the kid at the same time that he expresses a hurt that all men feel. You got to cut your kid loose at some point. There's that sense of loss and separation.

You find out how Troy left his father's house and you see how Cory leaves his house. I suspect with Cory it will repeat with some differences and maybe, after five or six generations, they'll find a different way to do it.

Where Cory ends up is very ambiguous, as a marine in 1965.

Yes. For the average black kid on the street, that was an alternative. You went into the army because you could learn how to do something. I can remember my parents talking about the son of some friends: "He's in the navy. He *did* something"—as opposed to standing on the street corner, shooting drugs, drinking wine, and robbing stores. Lyons says to Cory, "I always knew you were going to make something out of yourself." It really wounds me. He's a corporal in the marines. For blacks, that is a sense of accomplishment. Therein lies one of the tragedies of blacks in America. Cory says, "I don't know. I put in six years. That's enough." Anyone who goes into the army and makes a career out of it is a loser. They sit there and are nurtured by the army and they don't have to confront life. Then they get out of the army and find there's nothing to do. They didn't learn any skills. And if they did, they can't find a job. Four months later, they're shooting dope. In the sixties a whole bunch of blacks went over, fought and died in the Vietnam War. The survivors came back to the same street corners and found out nothing had changed. They still couldn't get a job.

At the end of *Fences* every person, with the exception of Raynell, is institutionalized. Rose is in a church. Lyons is in a penitentiary. Gabriel's in a mental hospital and Cory's in the marines. The only free person is the girl, Troy's daughter, the hope for the future. That was conscious on my part because in '57 that's what I saw. Blacks have relied on institutions which are really foreign—except for the black church, which has been our saving grace. I have some problems with it but I recognize it as a central social organization and sometimes an economic organization for the black community. I would like to see blacks develop their own institutions that respond to their needs.

SAMUEL BECKETT

Samuel Beckett (1906–1989) was born near Dublin, Ireland, in a middle-class Protestant home. Looking back on his childhood, he once remarked, "I had little talent for happiness." In 1928 he moved to Paris, and the city quickly won his heart. Shortly after he arrived, a mutual friend introduced him to James Joyce, to whom he became a disciple. A year later, he won his first literary prize for a poem entitled Whoroscope, *which dealt with the philosopher Descartes meditating on the subject of time and the transiency of life.*

After five years of wandering, Beckett finally settled in Paris in 1937. During World War II, he remained in Paris after it had become occupied by the Germans, but in 1942 he was forced to flee with his French-born wife to the unoccupied zone. In 1945, after Paris had been liberated from the Germans, he returned and began his most prolific period as a writer. His first real triumph came on 5 January 1953, when En attendant Godot *premiered in France. This play in which "nothing happens"—in fact, it has been said that "nothing happens twice"—became an instant success, running for 400 performances in Paris and as* Waiting for Godot *was soon given controversial, attention-getting productions in London and New York. His subsequent plays, of which* Krapp's Last Tape *(1958),* Happy Days *(1961), and* Play *(1963) are best known, became more and more minimalist as time went on. In 1969 Beckett was awarded the Nobel Prize for Literature.*

Krapp's Last Tape: A Play in One Act [1958]

A late evening in the future.

KRAPP'S *den.*

Front centre a small table, the two drawers of which open towards audience.

Sitting at the table, facing front, i.e. across from the drawers, a wearish[1] old man: KRAPP.

Rusty black narrow trousers too short for him. Rusty black sleeveless waistcoat, four capacious pockets. Heavy silver watch and chain. Grimy white shirt open at neck, no collar. Surprising pair of dirty white boots, size ten at least, very narrow and pointed.

White face. Purple nose. Disordered grey hair. Unshaven.

Very near-sighted (but unspectacled). Hard of hearing.

Cracked voice. Distinctive intonation.

Laborious walk.

On the table a tape-recorder with microphone and a number of cardboard boxes containing reels of recorded tapes.

Table and immediately adjacent area in strong white light. Rest of stage in darkness.

KRAPP *remains a moment motionless, heaves a great sigh, looks at his watch, fumbles in his pockets, takes out an envelope, puts it back, fumbles, takes out a small bunch of keys, raises it to his eyes, chooses a key, gets up and moves to front of table. He stoops, unlocks first drawer, peers into it, feels about inside it, takes out a reel of tape, peers at it, puts it back, locks drawer, unlocks second drawer, peers into it, feels about inside it, takes out a large banana, peers at it, locks drawer, puts keys back in his pocket. He turns, advances to edge of stage, halts, strokes banana, peels it, drops skin at his feet, puts end of banana in his mouth and remains motionless, staring vacuously before him. Finally he bites off the end, turns aside and begins pacing to and fro at edge of stage, in the light, i.e. not more than four or five paces either way, meditatively eating banana. He treads on skin, slips, nearly falls, recovers himself, stoops and peers at skin and finally pushes it, still stooping, with his foot over the edge of stage into pit. He resumes his pacing, finishes banana, returns to table, sits down, remains a moment motionless, heaves a great sigh, takes keys from his pockets, raises them to his eyes, chooses key, gets up and moves to front of table, unlocks second drawer, takes out a second large banana, peers at it, locks drawer, puts back keys in his pocket, turns, advances to edge of stage, halts, strokes banana, peels it, tosses skin into pit, puts end of banana in his mouth and remains motionless, staring vacuously before him. Finally he has an idea, puts banana in his waistcoat pocket, the end emerging, and goes with all the speed he can muster backstage into darkness. Ten seconds. Loud pop of cork. Fifteen seconds. He comes back*

---

[1]**wearish** wornout, withered.

into light carrying an old ledger and sits down at table. He lays ledger on table, wipes his mouth, wipes his hands on the front of his waistcoat, brings them smartly together and rubs them.

KRAPP (*briskly*). Ah! (*He bends over ledger, turns the pages, finds the entry he wants, reads.*) Box . . . thrree . . . spool . . . five. (*He raises his head and stares front. With relish.*) Spool! (*Pause.*) Spooool!. (*Happy smile. Pause. He bends over table, starts peering and poking at the boxes.*) Box . . . thrree . . . thrree . . . four . . . two . . . (*with surprise*) nine! good God! . . . seven . . . ah! the little rascal! (*He takes up box, peers at it.*) Box thrree. (*He lays it on table, opens it and peers at spools inside.*) Spool . . . (*he peers at ledger*) . . . five . . . (*he peers at spools*) . . . five . . . five . . . ah! the little scoundrel! (*He takes out a spool, peers at it.*) Spool five. (*He lays it on table, closes box three, puts it back with the other, takes up the spool.*) Box thrree, spool five. (*He bends over the machine, looks up. With relish.*) Spooool! (*Happy smile. He bends, loads spool on machine, rubs his hands.*) Ah! (*He peers at ledger, reads entry at foot of page.*) Mother at rest at last. . . Hm . . . The black ball . . . (*He raises his head, stares blankly front. Puzzled.*) Black ball?. . . (*He peers again at ledger, reads.*) The dark nurse . . . (*He raises his head, broods, peers again at ledger, reads.*) Slight improvement in bowel condition . . . Hm . . . Memorable . . . what? (*He peers closer.*) Equinox, memorable equinox. (*He raises his head, stares blankly front. Puzzled.*) Memorable equinox? . . . (*Pause. He shrugs his shoulders, peers again at ledger, reads.*) Farewell to—(*he turns the page*)—love.

He raises his head, broods, bends over machine, switches on and assumes listening posture, i.e. leaning forward, elbows on table, hand cupping ear towards machine, face front.

TAPE (*strong voice, rather pompous, clearly* KRAPP'S *at a much earlier time*). Thirty-nine today, sound as a—(*Settling himself more comfortably he knocks one of the boxes off the table, curses, switches off, sweeps boxes and ledger violently to the ground, winds tape back to beginning, switches on, resumes posture.*) Thirty-nine today, sound as a bell, apart from my old weakness, and intellectually I have now every reason to suspect at the . . . (*hesitates*) . . . crest of the wave—or thereabouts. Celebrated the awful occasion, as in recent years, quietly at the Winehouse. Not a soul. Sat before the fire with closed eyes, separating the grain from the husks. Jotted down a few notes, on the back of an envelope. Good to be back in my den, in my old rags. Have just eaten I regret to say three bananas and only with difficulty refrained from a fourth. Fatal things for a man with my condition. (*Vehemently.*) Cut 'em out! (*Pause.*) The new light above my table is a great improvement. With all this darkness round me I feel less alone. (*Pause.*) In a way. (*Pause.*) I love to get up and move about in it, then back here to . . . (*hesitates*) . . . me. (*Pause.*) Krapp.

Pause.

The grain, now what I wonder do I mean by that, I mean . . . (*hesitates*) . . . I suppose I mean those things worth having when all the dust has—when all *my* dust has settled. I close my eyes and try and imagine them.

Pause. KRAPP *closes his eyes briefly.*

Extraordinary silence this evening, I strain my ears and do not hear a sound. Old Miss McGlome always sings at this hour. But not tonight. Songs of her girlhood, she says. Hard to think of her as a girl. Wonderful woman though. Connaught, I fancy. (*Pause.*) Shall I sing when I am her age, if I ever am? No. (*Pause.*) Did I sing as a boy? No. (*Pause.*) Did I ever sing? No.

Pause.

Just been listening to an old year, passages at random. I did not check in the book, but it must be at least ten or twelve years ago. At that time I think I was still living on and off with Bianca in Kedar Street. Well out of that, Jesus yes! Hopeless business. (*Pause.*) Not much about her, apart from a tribute to her eyes. Very warm. I suddenly saw them again. (*Pause.*) Incomparable! (*Pause.*) Ah well . . . (*Pause.*) These old P.M.s are gruesome, but I often find them—(KRAPP *switches off, broods, switches on*)—a help before embarking on a new . . . (*hesitates*) . . . retrospect. Hard to believe I was ever that young whelp. The voice! Jesus! And the aspirations! (*Brief laugh in which* KRAPP *joins.*) And the resolutions! (*Brief laugh in which* KRAPP *joins.*) To drink less, in particular. (*Brief laugh of* KRAPP *alone.*) Statistics. Seventeen hundred hours, out of the preceding eight thousand odd, consumed on licensed premises alone. More than 20%, say 40% of his waking life. (*Pause.*) Plans for a less . . . (*hesitates*) . . . engrossing sexual life. Last illness of his father. Flagging pursuit of happiness. Unattainable laxation. Sneers at what he calls his youth and thanks to God that it's over. (*Pause.*) False ring there. (*Pause.*) Shadows of the opus . . . magnum. Closing with a—(*brief laugh*)—yelp to Providence. (*Prolonged laugh in which* KRAPP *joins.*) What remains of all that misery? A girl in a shabby green coat, on a railway-station platform? No?

Pause.

When I look—

(KRAPP *switches off, broods, looks at his watch, gets up, goes backstage into darkness. Ten seconds. Pop of cork. Ten seconds. Second cork. Ten seconds. Third cork. Ten seconds. Brief burst of quavering song.*)

KRAPP (*sings*). Now the day is over.
     Night is drawing nigh-igh,
     Shadows—

Fit of coughing. He comes back into light, sits down, wipes his mouth, switches on, resumes his listening posture.

TAPE —back on the year that is gone, with what I hope is perhaps a glint of the old eye to come, there is of course the house on the canal where mother lay a-dying, in the late autumn, after her long viduity (KRAPP *gives a start*), and the—(KRAPP *switches off, winds back tape a little, bends his ear closer to machine, switches on)*—a-dying, after her long viduity, and the—

KRAPP *switches off, raises his head, stares blankly before him. His lips move in the syllables of "viduity." No sound. He gets up, goes backstage into darkness, comes back with an enormous dictionary, lays it on table, sits down and looks up the word.*

KRAPP (*reading from dictionary*). State—or condition of being—or remaining—a widow—or widower. (*Looks up. Puzzled.*) Being—or remaining? . . . (*Pause. He peers again at dictionary. Reading.*) "Deep weeds of viduity" . . . Also of an animal, especially a bird . . . the vidua or weaver-bird . . . Black plumage of male . . . (*He looks up. With relish.*) The vidua-bird!

Pause. He closes dictionary, switches on, resumes listening posture.

TAPE —bench by the weir from where I could see her window. There I sat, in the biting wind, wishing she were gone. (*Pause.*) Hardly a soul, just a few regulars, nursemaids, infants, old men, dogs. I got to know them quite well—oh by appearance of course I mean! One dark young beauty I recollect particularly, all white and starch, incomparable bosom, with a big black hooded perambulator, most funereal thing. Whenever I looked in her direction she had her eyes on me. And yet when I was bold enough to speak to her—not having been introduced—she threatened to call a policeman. As if I had designs on her virtue! (*Laugh. Pause.*) The face she had! The eyes! Like . . . (*hesitates*) . . . chrysolite! (*Pause.*) Ah well . . . (*Pause.*) I was there when—(KRAPP *switches off, broods, switches on again*)—the blind went down, one of those dirty brown roller affairs, throwing a ball for a little white dog, as chance would have it. I happened to look up and there it was. All over and done with, at last. I sat on for a few moments with the ball in my hand and the dog yelping and pawing at me. (*Pause.*) Moments. Her moments, my moments. (*Pause.*) The dog's moments. (*Pause.*) In the end I held it out to him and he took it in his mouth, gently, gently. A small, old, black, hard, solid rubber ball. (*Pause.*) I shall feel it, in my hand, until my dying day. (*Pause.*) I might have kept it. (*Pause.*) But I gave it to the dog.

Pause.

    Ah well . . .

Pause.

    Spiritually a year of profound gloom and indigence until that memorable night in March, at the end of the jetty, in the howling wind, never to be forgotten, when suddenly I saw the whole thing. The vision, at last. This I fancy is what I have chiefly to record this evening, against the day when my work will be done and perhaps no place left in my memory, warm or cold, for the miracle that . . . (*hesitates*) . . . for the fire that set it alight. What I suddenly saw then was this, that the belief I had been going on all my life, namely—(KRAPP *switches off impatiently, winds tape forward, switches on again*)—great granite rocks the foam flying up in the light of the lighthouse and the wind-gauge spinning like a propellor, clear to me at last that the dark I have always struggled to keep under is in reality my most—(KRAPP *curses, switches off, winds tape forward, switches on again*)—unshatterable association until my dissolution of storm and night with the light of the understanding and the fire—(KRAPP curses *louder, switches off, winds tape forward, switches on again*)—my face in her breasts and my hand on her. We lay there without moving. But under us all moved, and moved us, gently, up and down, and from side to side.

Pause.

Past midnight. Never knew such silence. The earth might be uninhabited.

Pause.

Here I end—

KRAPP *switches off, winds tape back, switches on again.*

—upper lake, with the punt, bathed off the bank, then pushed out into the stream and drifted. She lay stretched out on the floorboards with her hands under her head and her eyes closed. Sun blazing down, bit of a breeze, water nice and lively. I noticed a scratch on her thigh and asked her how she came by it. Picking gooseberries, she said. I said again I thought it was hopeless and no good going on, and she agreed, without opening her eyes. (*Pause.*) I asked her to look at me and after a few moments—(*pause*)—after a few moments she did, but the eyes just slits, because of the glare. I bent over her to get them in the shadow and they opened. (*Pause. Low.*) Let me in. (*Pause.*) We drifted in among the flags and stuck. The way they went down, sighing, before the stem! (*Pause.*) I lay down across her with my face in her breasts and my hand on her. We lay there without moving. But under us all moved, and moved us, gently, up and down, and from side to side.

Pause.

Past midnight. Never knew—

KRAPP *switches off, broods. Finally he fumbles in his pockets, encounters the banana, takes it out, peers at it, puts it back, fumbles, brings out the envelope, fumbles, puts back envelope, looks at his watch, gets up and goes backstage into darkness. Ten seconds. Sound of bottle against glass, then brief siphon. Ten seconds. Bottle against glass alone. Ten seconds. He comes back a little unsteadily into light, goes to front of table, takes out keys, raises them to his eyes, chooses key, unlocks first drawer, peers into it, feels about inside, takes out reel, peers at it, locks drawer, puts keys back in his pocket, goes and sits down, takes reel off machine, lays it on dictionary, loads virgin reel on machine, takes envelope from his pocket, consults back of it, lays it on table, switches on, clears his throat and begins to record.*

KRAPP. Just been listening to that stupid bastard I took myself for thirty years ago, hard to believe I was ever as bad as that. Thank God that's all done with anyway. (*Pause.*) The eyes she had! (*Broods, realizes he is recording silence, switches off, broods. Finally.*) Everything there, everything, all the—(*Realizes this is not being recorded, switches on.*) Everything there, everything on this old muckball, all the light and dark and famine and feasting of. . . (*hesitates*) . . . the ages! (*In a shout.*) Yes! (*Pause.*) Let that go! Jesus! Take his mind off his homework! Jesus! (*Pause. Weary.*) Ah well, maybe he was right. (*Pause.*) Maybe he was right. (*Broods. Realizes. Switches off. Consults envelope.*) Pah! (*Crumples it and throws it away. Broods. Switches on.*) Nothing to say, not a squeak. What's a year now? The sour cud and the iron stool. (*Pause.*) Revelled in the word spool. (*With relish.*) Spooool! Happiest moment of the past half million. (*Pause.*) Seventeen copies sold, of which eleven at trade price to free circulating libraries beyond the seas. Getting known. (*Pause.*) One pound six and something, eight I have little doubt. (*Pause.*) Crawled out once or twice, before the summer was cold. Sat shivering in the park, drowned in dreams and burning to be gone. Not a soul. (*Pause.*) Last fancies. (*Vehemently.*) Keep 'em under? (*Pause.*) Scalded the eyes out of me reading *Effie* again, a page a day, with tears again. Effie . . . (*Pause.*) Could have been happy with her, up there on the Baltic, and the pines, and the dunes. (*Pause.*) Could I? (*Pause.*) And she? (*Pause.*) Pah! (*Pause.*) Fanny came in a couple of times. Bony old ghost of a whore. Couldn't do much, but I suppose better than a kick in the crutch. The last time wasn't so bad. How do you manage it, she said, at your age? I told her I'd been saving up for her all my life. (*Pause.*) Went to Vespers once, like when I was in short trousers. (*Pause. Sings.*)

> Now the day is over,
> Night is drawing nigh-igh,
> Shadows—(*coughing, then almost inaudible*)—of the evening
> Steal across the sky.

(*Gasping.*) Went to sleep and fell off the pew. (*Pause.*) Sometimes wondered in the night if a last effort mightn't —(*Pause.*) Ah finish your booze now and get to your bed. Go on with this drivel in the morning. Or leave it at that. (*Pause.*) Leave it at that. (*Pause.*) Lie propped up in the dark—and wander. Be again in the dingle on a Christmas Eve, gathering holly, the red-berried. (*Pause.*) Be again on Croghan on a Sunday morning, in the haze, with the bitch, stop and listen to the bells. (*Pause.*) And so on. (*Pause.*) Be again, be again. (*Pause.*) All that old misery. (*Pause.*) Once wasn't enough for you. (*Pause.*) Lie down across her.

Long pause. He suddenly bends over machine, switches off, wrenches off tape, throws it away, puts on the other, winds it forward to the passage he wants, switches on, listens staring front.

TAPE —gooseberries, she said. I said again I thought it was hopeless and no good going on, and she agreed, without opening her eyes. (*Pause.*) I asked her to look at me and after a few moments—(*pause*)—after a few moments she did, but the eyes just slits, because of the glare. I bent over her to get them in the shadow and they opened. (*Pause. Low.*) Let me in. (*Pause.*) We drifted in among the flags and stuck. The way they went down, sighing, before the stem! (*Pause.*) I lay down across her with my face in her breasts and my hand on her. We lay there without moving. But under us all moved, and moved us, gently, up and down, and from side to side.

Pause. KRAPP'S *lips move. No sound.*

Past midnight. Never knew such silence. The earth might be uninhabited.

Pause.

Here I end this reel. Box—(*pause*)—three, spool—(*pause*)—five. (*Pause.*) Perhaps my best years are gone. When there was a chance of happiness. But I wouldn't want them back. Not with the fire in me now. No, I wouldn't want them back.

KRAPP *motionless staring before him. The tape runs on in silence.*

CURTAIN

YOUR TURN

The Play on the Page

1. Why do you think Beckett makes Krapp so farcical a character, particularly at the outset?
2. Why do you think he gives him a quasi-obscene name?
3. How would you describe the character of Krapp as a younger man?
4. Discuss the themes of memory and desire as revealed in the play.

The Play on the Stage

5. How clownish should Krapp be played?
6. How would you handle the segments where he just listens to his recorded voice?
7. What mood would you (as director) try to establish in the play?
8. How much would you stress the play's humor?
9. The text calls only for a table, a chair, a tape recorder, a microphone, and a box of tapes. A film version with John Hurt, however, is set in a cramped private library packed with books, files, and papers. Do you approve the change? Why or why not?

DAVID IVES

David Ives, born in Chicago in 1950, was educated at Northwestern University and at the Yale Drama School. Sure Thing *was first presented in February 1988, directed by Jason Buzas, and later was publicly staged in 1988, and later was staged with six of his other one-act plays, grouped under the title* All in the Timing.

Sure Thing

[1988]

This play is for Jason Buzas

BETTY, *a woman in her late twenties, is reading at a café table. An empty chair is opposite her.* BILL, *same age, enters.*

BILL. Excuse me. Is this chair taken?
BETTY. Excuse me?

BILL. Is this taken?
BETTY. Yes it is.
BILL. Oh. Sorry.
BETTY. Sure thing.

> [*A bell rings softly.*]

BILL. Excuse me. Is this chair taken?
BETTY. Excuse me?
BILL. Is this taken?
BETTY. No, but I'm expecting somebody in a minute.
BILL. Oh. Thanks anyway.
BETTY. Sure thing.

> [*A bell rings softly.*]

BILL. Excuse me. Is this chair taken?
BETTY. No, but I'm expecting somebody very shortly.
BILL. Would you mind if I sit here till he or she or it comes?
BETTY [*glances at her watch*]. They do seem to be pretty late. . . .
BILL. You never know who you might be turning down.
BETTY. Sorry. Nice try, though.
BILL. Sure thing.

> [*Bell.*]

Is this seat taken?
BETTY. No it's not.
BILL. Would you mind if I sit here?
BETTY. Yes I would.
BILL. Oh.

> [*Bell.*]

Is this chair taken?
BETTY. No it's not.
BILL. Would you mind if I sit here?
BETTY. No. Go ahead.
BILL. Thanks. [*He sits. She continues reading.*] Everyplace else seems to be taken.
BETTY. Mm-hm.
BILL. Great place.
BETTY. Mm-hm.
BILL. What's the book?
BETTY. I just wanted to read in quiet, if you don't mind.
BILL. No. Sure thing.

> [*Bell.*]

BILL. Everyplace else seems to be taken.
BETTY. Mm-hm.
BILL. Great place for reading.
BETTY. Yes, I like it.
BILL. What's the book?
BETTY. *The Sound and the Fury.*
BILL. Oh. Hemingway.

[*Bell.*]

What's the book?

BETTY. *The Sound and the Fury.*

BILL. Oh. Faulkner.

BETTY. Have you read it?

BILL. Not . . . actually. I've sure read *about* it, though. It's supposed to be great.

BETTY. It is great.

BILL. I hear it's great. [*Small pause.*] Waiter?

[*Bell.*]

What's the book?

BETTY. *The Sound and the Fury.*

BILL. Oh. Faulkner.

BETTY. Have you read it?

BILL. I'm a Mets fan, myself.

[*Bell.*]

BETTY. Have you read it?

BILL. Yeah, I read it in college.

BETTY. Where was college?

BILL. I went to Oral Roberts University.

[*Bell.*]

BETTY. Where was college?

BILL. I was lying. I never really went to college. I just like to party.

[*Bell.*]

BETTY. Where was college?

BILL. Harvard.

BETTY. Do you like Faulkner?

BILL. I love Faulkner. I spent a whole winter reading him once.

BETTY. I've just started.

BILL. I was so excited after ten pages that I went out and bought everything else he wrote. One of the greatest reading experiences of my life. I mean, all that incredible psychological understanding. Page after page of gorgeous prose. His profound grasp of the mystery of time and human existence. The smells of the earth . . . What do you think?

BETTY. I think it's pretty boring.

[*Bell.*]

BILL. What's the book?

BETTY. *The Sound and the Fury.*

BILL. Oh! Faulkner!

BETTY. Do you like Faulkner?

BILL. I love Faulkner.

BETTY. He's incredible.

BILL. I spent a whole winter reading him once.

BETTY. I was so excited after ten pages that I went out and bought everything else he wrote.

BILL. All that incredible psychological understanding.

BETTY. And the prose is so gorgeous.

BILL. And the way he's grasped the mystery of time—

BETTY. —and human existence. I can't believe I've waited this long to read him.

BILL. You never know. You might not have liked him before.

BETTY. That's true.

BILL. You might not have been ready for him. You have to hit these things at the right moment or it's no good.

BETTY. That's happened to me.

BILL. It's all in the timing. [*Small pause.*] My name's Bill, by the way.

BETTY. I'm Betty.

BILL. Hi.

BETTY. Hi. [*Small pause.*]

BILL. Yes I thought reading Faulkner was . . . a great experience.

BETTY. Yes. [*Small pause.*]

BILL. *The Sound and the Fury* . . . [*Another small pause.*]

BETTY. Well. Onwards and upwards. [*She goes back to her book.*]

BILL. Waiter—?

[*Bell.*]

You have to hit these things at the right moment or it's no good.

BETTY. That's happened to me.

BILL. It's all in the timing. My name's Bill, by the way.

BETTY. I'm Betty.

BILL. Hi.

BETTY. Hi.

BILL. Do you come in here a lot?

BETTY. Actually I'm just in town for two days from Pakistan.

BILL. Oh. Pakistan.

[*Bell.*]

My name's Bill, by the way.

BETTY. I'm Betty.

BILL. Hi.

BETTY. Hi.

BILL. Do you come in here a lot?

BETTY. Every once in a while. Do you?

BILL. Not so much anymore. Not as much as I used to. Before my nervous breakdown.

[*Bell.*]

Do you come in here a lot?

BETTY. Why are you asking?

BILL. Just interested.

BETTY. Are you really interested, or do you just want to pick me up?

BILL. No, I'm really interested.

BETTY. Why would you be interested in whether I come in here a lot?

BILL. I'm just . . . getting acquainted.

BETTY. Maybe you're only interested for the sake of making small talk long enough to ask me back to your place to listen to some music, or because you've just rented this great tape for your VCR, or because you've got some terrific unknown Django Reinhardt record, only all you really want to do is fuck—which you won't do very well—after which you'll go into the bathroom and pee very loudly, then pad into the kitchen and get yourself a beer from the refrigerator without asking me whether I'd like anything, and then you'll proceed to lie back down beside me and confess that you've got a girlfriend named Stephanie who's away at medical school in Belgium for a year, and that you've been involved with her—*off and on*—in what you'll call a very "intricate" relationship, for the past *seven* YEARS. None of which *interests* me, mister!

BILL. Okay.

[*Bell.*]

Do you come in here a lot?

BETTY. Every other day, I think.

BILL. I come in here quite a lot and I don't remember seeing you.

BETTY. I guess we must be on different schedules.

BILL. Missed connections.

BETTY. Yes. Different time zones.

BILL. Amazing how you can live right next door to somebody in this town and never even know it.

BETTY. I know.

BILL. City life.

BETTY. It's crazy.

BILL. We probably pass each other in the street every day. Right in front of this place, probably.

BETTY. Yep.

BILL [*looks around*]. Well the waiters here sure seem to be in some different time zone. I can't seem to locate one anywhere. . . . Waiter! [*He looks back.*] So what do you—[*He sees that she's gone back to her book.*]

BETTY. I beg pardon?

BILL. Nothing. Sorry.

[*Bell.*]

BETTY. I guess we must be on different schedules.

BILL. Missed connections.

BETTY. Yes. Different time zones.

BILL. Amazing how you can live right next door to somebody in this town and never even know it.

BETTY. I know.

BILL. City life.

BETTY. It's crazy.

BILL. You weren't waiting for somebody when I came in, were you?

BETTY. Actually I was.

BILL. Oh. Boyfriend?

BETTY. Sort of.

BILL. What's a sort-of boyfriend?

BETTY. My husband.

BILL. Ah-ha.

[*Bell.*]

You weren't waiting for somebody when I came in, were you?

BETTY. Actually I was.

BILL. Oh. Boyfriend?

BETTY. Sort of.

BILL. What's a sort-of boyfriend?

BETTY. We were meeting here to break up.

BILL. Mm-hm . . .

[*Bell.*]

What's a sort-of boyfriend?

BETTY. My lover. Here she comes right now!

[*Bell.*]

BILL. You weren't waiting for somebody when I came in, were you?

BETTY. No, just reading.

BILL. Sort of a sad occupation for a Friday night, isn't it? Reading here, all by yourself?

BETTY. Do you think so?

BILL. Well sure. I mean, what's a good-looking woman like you doing out alone on a Friday night?

BETTY. Trying to keep away from lines like that.

BILL. No, listen—

[*Bell.*]

You weren't waiting for somebody when I came in, were you?

BETTY. No, just reading.

BILL. Sort of a sad occupation for a Friday night, isn't it? Reading here all by yourself?

BETTY. I guess it is, in a way.

BILL. What's a good-looking woman like you doing out alone on a Friday night anyway? No offense, but . . .

BETTY. I'm out alone on a Friday night for the first time in a very long time.

BILL. Oh.

BETTY. You see, I just recently ended a relationship.

BILL. Oh.

BETTY. Of rather long standing.

BILL. I'm sorry. [*Small pause.*] Well listen, since reading by yourself is such a sad occupation for a Friday night, would you like to go elsewhere?

BETTY. No . . .

BILL. Do something else?

BETTY. No thanks.

BILL. I was headed out to the movies in a while anyway.

BETTY. I don't think so.

BILL. Big chance to let Faulkner catch his breath. All those long sentences get him pretty tired.

BETTY. Thanks anyway.

BILL. Okay.

BETTY. I appreciate the invitation.

BILL. Sure thing.

[*Bell.*]

You weren't waiting for somebody when I came in, were you?

BETTY. No, just reading.

BILL. Sort of a sad occupation for a Friday night, isn't it? Reading here all by yourself?

BETTY. I guess I was trying to think of it as existentially romantic. You know— cappuccino, great literature, rainy night . . .

BILL. That only works in Paris. We *could* hop the late plane to Paris. Get on a Concorde. Find a café . . .

BETTY. I'm a little short on plane fare tonight.

BILL. Darn it, so am I.

BETTY. To tell you the truth, I was headed to the movies after I finished this section. Would you like to come along? Since you can't locate a waiter?

BILL. That's a very nice offer, but . . .

BETTY. Uh-huh. Girlfriend?

BILL. Two, actually. One of them's pregnant, and Stephanie—

[*Bell.*]

BETTY. Girlfriend?

BILL. No, I don't have a girlfriend. Not if you mean the castrating bitch I dumped last night.

[*Bell.*]

BETTY. Girlfriend?

BILL. Sort of. Sort of.

BETTY. What's a sort-of girlfriend?

BILL. My mother.

[*Bell.*]

I just ended a relationship, actually.

BETTY. Oh.

BILL. Of rather long standing.

BETTY. I'm sorry to hear it.

BILL. This is my first night out alone in a long time. I feel a little bit at sea, to tell you the truth.

BETTY. So you didn't stop to talk because you're a Moonie, or you have some weird political affiliation—?

BILL. Nope. Straight-down-the-ticket Republican.

[*Bell.*]

Straight-down-the-ticket Democrat.

[*Bell.*]

Can I tell you something about politics?

[*Bell.*]

I like to think of myself as a citizen of the universe.

[*Bell.*]

I'm unaffiliated.

BETTY. That's a relief. So am I.

BILL. I vote my beliefs.

BETTY. Labels are not important.

BILL. Labels are not important, exactly. Take me, for example. I mean, what does it matter if I had a two-point at—

[*Bell.*]

three-point at—

[*Bell.*]

four-point at college? Or if I did come from Pittsburgh—

[*Bell.*]

Cleveland—

[*Bell.*]

Westchester County?

BETTY. Sure.

BILL. I believe that a man is what he is.

[*Bell.*]

A person is what he is.

[*Bell.*]

A person is . . . what they are.

BETTY. I think so too.

BILL. So what if I admire Trotsky?

[*Bell.*]

So what if I once had a total-body liposuction?

[*Bell.*]

So what if I don't have a penis?

[*Bell.*]

So what if I spent a year in the Peace Corps? I was acting on my convictions.

BETTY. Sure.

BILL. You just can't hang a sign on a person.

BETTY. Absolutely. I'll bet you're a Scorpio.

[*Many bells ring.*]

Listen, I was headed to the movies after I finished this section. Would you like to come along?

BILL. That sounds like fun. What's playing?

BETTY. A couple of the really early Woody Allen movies.

BILL. Oh.

BETTY. You don't like Woody Allen?

BILL. Sure. I like Woody Allen.

BETTY. But you're not crazy about Woody Allen.

BILL. Those early ones kind of get on my nerves.

BETTY. Uh-huh.

[*Bell.*]

BILL. Y'know I was headed to the—

BETTY [*simultaneously*]. I was thinking about—

BILL. I'm sorry.

BETTY. No, go ahead.

BILL. I was going to say that I was headed to the movies in a little while, and . . .

BETTY. So was I.

BILL. The Woody Allen festival?

BETTY. Just up the street.

BILL. Do you like the early ones?

BETTY. I think anybody who doesn't ought to be run off the planet.

BILL. How many times have you seen *Bananas?*

BETTY. Eight times.

BILL. Twelve. So are you still interested? [*Long pause.*]

BETTY. Do you like Entenmann's crumb cake . . . ?

BILL. Last night I went out at two in the morning to get one. Did you have an Etch-a-Sketch as a child?

BETTY. Yes! And do you like Brussels sprouts? [*Pause.*]

BILL. No, I think they're disgusting.

BETTY. They *are* disgusting!

BILL. Do you still believe in marriage in spite of current sentiments against it?

BETTY. Yes.

BILL. And children?

BETTY. Three of them.

BILL. Two girls and a boy.

BETTY. Harvard, Vassar, and Brown.

BILL. And will you love me?

BETTY. Yes.

BILL. And cherish me forever?

BETTY. Yes.

BILL. Do you still want to go to the movies?

BETTY. Sure thing.

BILL AND BETTY [*together*]. *Waiter!*

BLACKOUT

YOUR TURN

1. Does the play have a plot? Does it follow the traditional formula of a beginning, a middle, and an end? (The conventional advice to playwrights is, "Get your guy up a tree, throw rocks at him, and get him down.") Is there an ending, a resolution, or do you think the play could go on and on? Please explain.

2. Ives's opening stage direction tells us that the play is set in a café, but no details are given. If you were staging the play, would you provide more than a table and two chairs? Some sort of atmosphere? Why, or why not?

3. Ives's text calls at the end for a blackout, that is, a sudden darkening of the stage. Do you think this ending is preferable to a gradual fading of the lights, or a gradual closing of the curtain? Or, for that matter, why shouldn't the two characters leave some money on the table and walk out together? In short, staying with Ives's dialogue, evaluate other possible endings and present an argument for which one you believe is most effective. Ask yourself, "What kind of evidence do I need to make my argument as convincing as possible?"

4. If someone were to say to you that the play shows the need for people to keep revising their personalities, to (so to speak) keep reinventing themselves if they wish to function efficiently in the world, what might you reply? What does it mean to say that someone is "reinventing" himself or herself? Is that a desirable thing to do?

5. If someone asked you, "What is the meaning of *Sure Thing*?" how would you reply? Is there one meaning, or more than one? What is your evidence? Please present your view, and the evidence for it, in the form of a good argument.

6. Imagine and write up a scene that Ives neglected to include in *Sure Thing*. How does your new scene change the play? In your view, does it make the play better?

7. Prepare an essay of 1–2 pages, which you might imagine being sent to Ives, in which you argue why his play would benefit from the addition of your new scene.

TERRENCE McNALLY

Terrence McNally, born in 1939 in St. Petersburg, Florida, grew up in Corpus Christi, Texas, and did his undergraduate work at Columbia University. "I'm a gay man who writes plays," he has said, and most of his work concerns gay people—or the responses of straight people to gay people.

We give the original script of Andre's Mother *(1988); McNally later amplified it for a 1990 television broadcast (running time is 58 minutes) that was awarded an Emmy.*

Andre's Mother   [1988]

CHARACTERS

CAL, a young man
ARTHUR, his father
PENNY, his sister
ANDRE'S MOTHER

TIME: *Now*
PLACE: *New York City, Central Park*

> *Four people—*CAL, ARTHUR, PENNY, *and* ANDRE'S MOTHER *—enter: They are nicely dressed and each carries a white helium-filled balloon on a string.*

> CAL. You know what's really terrible? I can't think of anything terrific to say. Good-bye. I love you. I'll miss you. And I'm supposed to be so great with words!

PENNY. What's that over there?

ARTHUR. Ask your brother.

CAL. It's a theatre. An outdoor theatre. They do plays there in the summer. Shakespeare's plays. [*To* ANDRE'S MOTHER.] God, how much he wanted to play Hamlet again. He would have gone to Timbuktu to have another go at that part. The summer he did it in Boston, he was so happy!

PENNY. Cal, I don't think she . . .! It's not the time. Later.

ARTHUR. Your son was a . . . the Jews have a word for it . . .

PENNY [*quietly appalled*]. Oh my God!

ARTHUR. Mensch, I believe it is, and I think I'm using it right. It means warm, solid, the real thing. Correct me if I'm wrong.

PENNY. Fine, Dad, fine. Just quit while you're ahead.

ARTHUR. I won't say he was like a son to me. Even my son isn't always like a son to me. I mean . . .! In my clumsy way, I'm trying to say how much I liked Andre. And how much he helped me to know my own boy. Cal was always two handsful but Andre and I could talk about anything under the sun. My wife was very fond of him, too.

PENNY. Cal, I don't understand about the balloons.

CAL. They represent the soul. When you let go, it means you're letting his soul ascend to Heaven. That you're willing to let go. Breaking the last earthly ties.

PENNY. Does the Pope know about this?

ARTHUR. Penny!

PENNY. Andre loved my sense of humor. Listen, you can hear him laughing. [*She lets go of her white balloon.*] So long, you glorious, wonderful, I-know-what-Cal-means-about-words . . . *man*! God forgive me for wishing you were straight every time I laid eyes on you. But if any man was going to have you, I'm glad it was my brother! Look how fast it went up. I bet that means something. Something terrific.

ARTHUR [*lets his balloon go*]. Good-bye. God speed.

PENNY. Cal?

CAL. I'm not ready yet.

PENNY. Okay. We'll be over there. Come on, Pop, you can buy your little girl a Good Humor.

ARTHUR. They still make Good Humor?

PENNY. Only now they're called Dove Bars and they cost twelve dollars.

[PENNY *takes* ARTHUR *off.* CAL *and* ANDRE'S MOTHER *stand with their balloons.*]

CAL. I wish I knew what you were thinking. I think it would help me. You know almost nothing about me and I only know what Andre told me about you. I'd always had it in my mind that one day we would be friends, you and me. But if you didn't know about Andre and me . . . If this hadn't happened, I wonder if he would have ever told you. When he was sick, if I asked him once I asked him a thousand times, tell her. She's your mother. She won't mind. But he was so afraid of hurting you and of your disapproval. I don't know which was worse. [*No response. He sighs.*] God, how many of us live in this city because we don't want to hurt our mothers and live in mortal terror of their disapproval. We lose ourselves here. Our lives aren't furtive, just our feelings toward people like you are! A city of fugitives from our parents' scorn or heartbreak. Sometimes he'd seem a little down and I'd say, "What's the matter, babe?" and this funny sweet, sad smile would cross his face and he'd say, "Just a little homesick, Cal, just a little bit." I always accused him of being a country boy just playing at being a hotshot, sophisticated New Yorker. [*He sighs.*]

It's bullshit. It's all bullshit. [*Still no response.*]

Do you remember the comic strip *Little Lulu?* Her mother had no name, she was so remote, so formidable to all the children. She was just Lulu's mother. "Hello, Lulu's Mother," Lulu's friends would say. She was almost anonymous in her remoteness. You remind me of her, Andre's Mother. Let me answer the questions you can't ask and then I'll leave you alone and you won't ever have to see me again. Andre died of AIDS. I don't know how he got it. I tested negative. He died bravely. You would have been proud of him. The only thing that frightened him was you. I'll have everything that was his sent to you. I'll pay for it. There isn't much. You should have come up the summer he played Hamlet. He was magnificent. Yes, I'm bitter. I'm bitter I've lost him. I'm bitter what's happening. I'm bitter even now, after all this, I can't reach you. I'm beginning to feel your disapproval and it's making me ill. [*He looks at his balloon.*] Sorry, old friend. I blew it. [*He lets go of the balloon.*]

Good night, sweet prince, and flights of angels sing thee to thy rest![1] [*Beat.*]

Goodbye, Andre's Mother.

[*He goes.* ANDRE'S MOTHER *stands alone holding her white balloon. Her lips tremble. She looks on the verge of breaking down. She is about to let go of the balloon when she pulls it down to her. She looks at it a while before she gently kisses it. She lets go of the balloon. She follows it with her eyes as it rises and rises. The lights are beginning to fade.* ANDRE'S MOTHER'S *eyes are still on the balloon. The lights fade.*]

---

[1]**Good night . . . rest!** Cal is quoting lines that Hamlet's friend Horatio speaks (5.2.336–37) at the moment of Hamlet's death.

YOUR TURN

1. Andre's Mother doesn't speak in the play, but we learn something about her through Cal's words, and something more through the description in the final stage direction. In a paragraph, characterize Andre's Mother.

2. Let's assume that you drafted this play, and now, on rereading it you decide that you want to give Andre's Mother one speech, and one speech only. Write the speech—it can go anywhere in the play that you think best—and then in a brief essay explain why you think the speech is effective.

3. Cal tells Penny that the balloons "represent the soul. When you let go, it means you're letting his soul ascend to Heaven." Is that exactly the way you see the balloons, or would see them if you attended a funeral where white balloons were distributed? Explain.

V

Critical Approaches

35

Critical Approaches: The Nature of Criticism

In everyday talk the most common meaning of **criticism** is something like "finding fault." And to be critical is to be censorious. But a critic can see excellences as well as faults. Because we turn to criticism with the hope that the critic has seen something we have missed, the most valuable criticism is not that which shakes its finger at faults, but that which calls our attention to interesting things going on in the work of art. Here is a statement by W. H. Auden (1907–1973), suggesting that criticism is most useful when it calls our attention to things worth attending to:

> What is the function of a critic? So far as I am concerned, he can do me one or more of the following services:
>
> 1. Introduce me to authors or works of which I was hitherto unaware.
> 2. Convince me that I have undervalued an author or a work because I had not read them carefully enough.
> 3. Show me relations between works of different ages and cultures which I could never have seen for myself because I do not know enough and never shall.
> 4. Give a "reading" of a work which increases my understanding of it.
> 5. Throw light upon the process of artistic "Making."
> 6. Throw light upon the relation of art to life, science, economics, ethics, religion, etc.
>
> —*The Dyer's Hand* (New York, 1963), 8–9

Auden does not neglect the delight we get from literature, but he extends (especially in his sixth point) the range of criticism to include topics beyond the literary work itself. Notice too the emphasis on observing, showing, and illuminating, which suggests that the function of critical writing is not very different from the most common view of the function of imaginative writing.

Whenever we talk about a work of literature or of art, or, for that matter, even about a so-so movie or television show, what we say depends in large measure on certain conscious or unconscious assumptions that we make: "I liked it; the characters were very believable" (here the assumption is that characters ought to be believable); "I didn't like it; there was too much violence" (here the

1422

assumption is that violence ought not to be shown, or if it is shown it should be made abhorrent); "I didn't like it; it was awfully slow" (here the assumption probably is that there ought to be a fair amount of physical action, perhaps even changes of scene, rather than characters just talking); "I didn't like it; I don't think topics of this sort ought to be discussed publicly" (here the assumption is a moral one, that it is indecent to present certain topics); "I liked it partly because it was refreshing to hear such frankness" (here again the assumption is moral, and more or less the reverse of the previous one).

In short, whether we realize it or not, we judge the work from a particular viewpoint—its realism, its morality, or whatever.

Professional critics, too, work from assumptions, but their assumptions are usually highly conscious, and the critics may define their assumptions at length. They regard themselves as, for instance, Freudians or Marxists or Queer Theorists. They read all texts through the lens of a particular theory, and their focus enables them to see things that otherwise might go unnoticed. It should be added, however, that if a lens or critical perspective or interpretive strategy helps us to see certain things, it also limits our vision. Many critics therefore regard their method not as an exclusive way of thinking but only as a useful tool.

What follows is a brief survey of the chief current approaches to literature. You may find, as you read these pages, that one or another approach sounds especially congenial, and therefore you may want to make use of it in your reading and writing. On the other hand, it's important to remember, first, that works of literature are highly varied, and, second, that we read them for various purposes—to kill time, to enjoy fanciful visions, to be amused, to explore alien ways of feeling, and to learn about ourselves. It may be best to try to respond to each text in the way that the text seems to require rather than to read all texts according to a single formula. You'll find that some works will lead you to want to think about them from several angles. A play by Shakespeare may stimulate you to read a book about the Elizabethan playhouse, and another that offers a Marxist interpretation of the English Renaissance, and still another that offers a feminist analysis of Shakespeare's plays. All of these approaches, and others, will help you to deepen your understanding of the literary works that you read.

Formalist (or New) Criticism

Formalist criticism emphasizes the work as an independent creation, a self-contained unit, something to be studied in itself, not as part of some larger context, such as the author's life or a historical period. This kind of study is called formalist criticism because the emphasis is on the *form* of the work, the relationships between the parts—the construction of the plot, the contrasts between characters, the functions of rhymes, the point of view, and so on.

Cleanth Brooks, perhaps America's most distinguished formalist critic, in an essay in the *Kenyon Review* (Winter 1951), reprinted in *The Modern Critical Spectrum,* edited by Gerald Jay Goldberg and Nancy Marmer Goldberg (1962), set forth what he called his "articles of faith":

That literary criticism is a description and an evaluation of its object.
That the primary concern of criticism is with the problem of unity—the
kind of whole which the literary work forms or fails to form, and the
relation of the various parts to each other in building up this whole.

That the formal relations in a work of literature may include, but cer-
tainly exceed, those of logic.
That in a successful work, form and content cannot be separated.
That form is meaning.

If you have read the earlier pages of this book you are already familiar with
most of these ideas, but in the next few pages we will look into some of them
in detail.

Formalist criticism is, in essence, *intrinsic* criticism, rather than extrinsic, for
(at least in theory) it concentrates on the work itself, independent of its writer
and the writer's background—that is, independent of biography, psychology, so-
ciology, and history. The discussions of Langston Hughes's "Harlem" (page 545)
and of Yeats's "The Balloon of the Mind" (page 82) are examples. The gist is that a
work of literature is complex, unified, and freestanding. In fact, of course, we usually bring outside knowledge to the work. For instance, a reader who is familiar
with, say, *Hamlet* can hardly study another tragedy by Shakespeare, let's say
Romeo and Juliet, without bringing to the second play some conception of
what Shakespearean tragedy is or can be. A reader of Alice Walker's *The Color
Purple* inevitably brings unforgettable outside material (perhaps the experience
of being an African American, or at least some knowledge of the history of
African Americans) to the literary work. It is very hard to talk only about *Hamlet*
or *The Color Purple* and not at the same time talk about, or at least have in mind,
aspects of human experience.

Formalist criticism begins with a personal response to the literary work, but
it goes on to try to account for the response by closely examining the work. It assumes that the author shaped the poem, play, or story so fully that the work
guides the reader's responses. The assumption that "meaning" is fully and completely presented within the text is not much in favor today, when many literary
critics argue that the active or subjective reader (or even what Judith Fetterley, a
feminist critic, has called "the resisting reader") and not the author of the text
makes the "meaning." Still, even if one grants that the reader is active, not passive
or coolly objective, one can hold with the formalists that the author is active too,
constructing a text that in some measure controls the reader's responses. During
the process of writing about our responses, we may find that our responses
change. A formalist critic would say that we see with increasing clarity what the
work is really like and what it really means. (Similarly, when authors write and revise a text, they may change their understanding of what they are doing. A story
that began as a lighthearted joke may turn into something far more serious than
the writer imagined at the start, but, at least for the formalist critic, the final work
contains a stable meaning that all competent readers can perceive.)

In practice, formalist criticism usually takes one of two forms, **explication**
(the unfolding of meaning, line by line or even word by word) or **analysis** (the
examination of the relations of parts). The essay on Yeats's "The Balloon of the
Mind" (page 82) is an explication, a setting forth of the implicit meanings of
the words. The essay on Kate Chopin's "The Story of an Hour" (page 74) is an
analysis.

To repeat: Formalist criticism assumes that a work of art is stable. An artist
constructs a coherent, comprehensible work, thus conveying to a reader an
emotion or an idea. T. S. Eliot said that the writer can't just pour out emotions
onto the page. Rather, Eliot said in an essay entitled "Hamlet and His Problems"
(1919), "The only way of expressing emotion in the form of art is by finding an

'objective correlative'; in other words, a set of objects, a situation, a chain of events which shall be the formula of the *particular* emotion."

With this in mind, consider Robert Frost's "The Span of Life":

The old dog barks backward without getting up.
I can remember when he was a pup.

The image of an old dog barking backward, and the speaker's memory—apparently triggered by the old dog's bark—of the dog as a pup, presumably is the "objective correlative" of Frost's emotion or idea; Frost is "expressing emotion" through this "formula." And all of us, as competent readers, can grasp pretty accurately what Frost expressed. Frost's emotion, idea, meaning, or whatever is "objectively" embodied in the text. Formalist critics try to explain how and why literary works—*these* words, in *this* order—constitute unique, complex structures that embody or set forth meanings.

Formalist criticism, also called the **New Criticism** (to distinguish it from the historical and biographical writing that in earlier decades had dominated literary study), began to achieve prominence in the late 1920s and was the dominant form from the late 1930s until about 1970, and even today it is widely considered the best way for a student to begin to study a work of literature. For one thing, formalist criticism empowers the student; that is, the student confronts the work immediately and is not told first to spend days or weeks or months, for instance, reading Freud and his followers in order to write a psychoanalytic essay or reading Marx and Marxists in order to write a Marxist essay, or doing research on "necessary historical background" in order to write a historical essay.

Deconstruction

Deconstruction, or deconstructive or poststructuralist criticism, can almost be characterized as the opposite of everything formalist criticism stands for. Deconstruction begins with the assumptions that the world is unknowable and that language is unstable, elusive, unfaithful. (Language is all of these things because meaning is largely generated by opposition: "Hot" means something in opposition to "cold," but a hot day may be 90 degrees whereas a hot oven is at least 400 degrees; and a "hot item" may be of any temperature.) Deconstructionists seek to show that a literary work (usually called "a text" or "a discourse") inevitably is self-contradictory. Unlike formalist critics—who hold that a competent author constructs a coherent work with a stable meaning, and that competent readers can perceive this meaning—deconstructionists (e.g., Barbara Johnson, in *The Critical Difference* [1980]) hold that a work has no coherent meaning at the center. Jonathan Culler, in *On Deconstruction* (1982), says that "to deconstruct a discourse is to show how it undermines the philosophy it asserts" (86). (Johnson and Culler provide accessible introductions, but the major document is Jacques Derrida's seminal, difficult work, *Of Grammatology* [1967, trans. 1976].) The text is only marks on paper, and therefore so far as a reader goes the author of a text is not the writer but the reader; texts are "indeterminate," "open," and "unstable."

Despite the emphasis on indeterminacy, one sometimes detects in deconstructionist interpretations a view associated with Marxism. This is the idea that authors are "socially constructed" from the "discourses of power" or "signifying practices" that surround them. Thus, although authors may think they are individuals with independent minds, their works usually reveal—unknown to the authors—the society's economic base. Deconstructionists "interrogate" a text, and they reveal what the authors were unaware of or had thought they had kept safely out of sight. That is, deconstructionists often find a rather specific meaning—though this meaning is one that might surprise the author.

Deconstruction is valuable insofar as—like the New Criticism—it encourages close, rigorous attention to the text. Furthermore, in its rejection of the claim that a work has a single stable meaning, deconstruction has had a positive influence on the study of literature. The problem with deconstruction, however, is that too often it is reductive, telling the same story about every text—that here, yet again, and again, we see how a text is incoherent and heterogeneous. There is, too, an irritating arrogance in some deconstructive criticism: "The author could not see how his/her text is fundamentally unstable and self-contradictory, but *I* can and now will interrogate the text and will issue my report." Readers, of course, should not prostrate themselves before texts, but there is something askew about an approach—however intense and detailed—that often leads readers to conclude that they know a good deal more than the benighted author.

Aware that their emphasis on the instability of language implies that their own texts are unstable or even incoherent, some deconstructionists seem to aim at entertaining rather than at edifying. They probably would claim that they do not deconstruct meaning in the sense of destroying it; rather, they might say, they exuberantly multiply meanings, and to this end they may use such devices as puns, irony, and allusions, somewhat as a poet might, and just as though (one often feels) they think they are as creative as the writers they are commenting on. Indeed, for many deconstructionists, the traditional conception of "literature" is merely an elitist "construct." All "texts" or "discourses" (novels, scientific papers, a Kewpie doll on the mantel, watching TV, suing in court, walking the dog, and all other signs that human beings make) are of a piece; all are unstable systems of signifying, all are fictions, all are "literature." If literature (in the usual sense) occupies a special place in deconstruction it is because literature delights in its playfulness, its fictiveness, whereas other discourses nominally reject playfulness and fictiveness.

Reader-Response Criticism

Probably all reading includes some sort of response—"This is terrific," "This is a bore," "I don't know what's going on here"—and probably almost all writing about literature begins with some such response, but specialists in literature disagree greatly about the role that response plays, or should play, in experiencing literature and in writing about it.

At one extreme are those who say that our response to a work of literature should be a purely aesthetic response—a response to a work of art—and not the response we would have to something comparable in real life. To take an obvious point: If in real life we heard someone plotting a murder, we would intervene, perhaps by calling the police or by attempting to warn the victim. But when we hear Macbeth and Lady Macbeth plot to kill King Duncan, we watch with deep *interest;* we hear their words with *pleasure,* and maybe we even look forward to seeing the murder and to seeing what the characters then will say and what will happen to the murderers.

When you think about it, the vast majority of the works of literature do not have a close, obvious resemblance to the reader's life. Most readers of *Macbeth* are not Scots, and no readers are Scottish kings or queens. (It's not just a matter of older literature; no readers of Toni Morrison's *Beloved* are nineteenth-century African Americans.) The connections readers make between themselves and the lives in most of the books they read are not, on the whole, connections based on ethnic or professional identities, but, rather, connections with states of consciousness—for instance, a young person's sense of isolation from the family, or a young person's sense of guilt for initial sexual experiences. Before we reject a work either because it seems too close to us ("I'm a man and I don't like the depiction of this man"), or on the other hand too far from our experience ("I'm not a woman, so how can I enjoy reading about these women?"), we probably should try to follow the advice of Virginia Woolf, who said, "Do not dictate to your author; try to become him." Nevertheless, some literary works of the past may today seem intolerable, at least in part. There are passages in Mark Twain's *The Adventures of Huckleberry Finn* that deeply upset us today. We should, however, try to reconstruct the cultural assumptions of the age in which the work was written. If we do so, we may find that if in some ways it reflected its age, in other ways it challenged that culture.

Still, some of our experiences, some of *what we are,* may make it virtually impossible for us to read a work sympathetically or "objectively," experiencing it only as a work of art and not as a part of life. Take so humble a form of literature as the joke. A few decades ago jokes about nagging wives and mothers-in-law were widely thought to be funny. Our fairly recent heightened awareness of sexism today makes those jokes unfunny. Twenty years ago the "meaning" of a joke about a nagging wife or about a mother-in-law was, in effect, "Here's a funny episode that shows what women typically are." Today the "meaning"—at least as the hearer conceives it—is "The unfunny story you have just told shows that you have stupid, stereotypical views of women." In short, the joke may "mean" one thing to the teller, and a very different thing to the hearer.

Reader-response criticism, then, says that the "meaning" of a work is not merely something put into the work by the writer; rather, the "meaning" is an interpretation created or constructed or produced by the reader as well as the writer. Stanley Fish, an exponent of reader-response theory, in *Is There a Text in This Class?* (1980), puts it this way: "Interpretation is not the art of construing but of constructing. Interpreters do not decode poems; they make them" (327).

Let's now try to relate these ideas more specifically to comments about literature. If "meaning" is the production or creation not simply of the writer but also of the perceiver, does it follow that there is no such thing as a "correct" interpretation of the meaning of a work of literature? Answers to this question differ. At one extreme, the reader is said to construct or reconstruct the text under the firm guidance of the author. That is, the author so powerfully shapes or constructs the text—encodes an idea—that the reader is virtually compelled to perceive or reconstruct or decode it the way the author wants it to be perceived. (We can call this view *the objective view,* since it essentially holds that readers look objectively at the work and see what the author put into it.) At the other extreme, the reader constructs the meaning according to his or her own personality—that is, according to the reader's psychological identity. (We can call this view *the subjective view,* since it essentially holds that readers inevitably project their feelings into what they perceive.) An extreme version of the subjective view holds that there is no such thing as literature; there are only texts, some of which some readers regard in a particularly elitist way.

Against the objective view one can argue thus: No author can fully control a reader's response to every detail of the text. No matter how carefully constructed the text is, it leaves something—indeed, a great deal—to the reader's imagination. For instance, when Macbeth says that life "is a tale/ Told by an idiot, full of sound and fury / Signifying nothing," are we getting a profound thought from Shakespeare or, on the contrary, are we getting a shallow thought from Macbeth, a man who does not see that his criminal deeds have been played out against a heaven that justly punishes his crimes? In short, the objective view neglects to take account of the fact that the author is not continually at our shoulder making sure that we interpret the work in a particular way.

It is probably true, as Flannery O'Connor says in *Mystery and Manners* (1969), that good writers select "every word, every detail, for a reason, every incident for a reason" (75), but there are always *gaps* or *indeterminacies,* to use the words of Wolfgang Iser, a reader-response critic. Readers always go beyond the text, drawing inferences, and evaluating the text in terms of their own experience. In the Hebrew Bible, for instance, in Genesis, the author tells us (Chapter 22) that God commanded Abraham to sacrifice his son Isaac, and then says that "Abraham rose up early in the morning" and prepared to fulfill the command. We are not explicitly told *why* Abraham "rose up early in the morning," or how he spent the intervening night, but some readers take "early in the morning" to signify (reasonably?) that Abraham has had a sleepless night. Others take it to signify (reasonably?) that Abraham is prompt in obeying God's command. Some readers fill the gap with both explanations, or with neither. Doubtless much depends on the reader, but there is no doubt that readers "naturalize"—make natural, according to their own ideas—what they read.

In an extreme form the subjective view denies that authors can make us perceive the meanings that they try to put into their works. This position suggests that every reader has a different idea of what a work means, an idea that reflects the reader's own ideas. Every reader, then, is Narcissus, who looked into a pool of water and thought he saw a beautiful youth but really saw only a reflection of himself. But does every reader see his or her individual image in each literary work? Of course not. Even *Hamlet,* a play that has generated an enormous range of interpretation, is universally seen as a tragedy, a play that deals with painful realities. If someone were to tell us that *Hamlet* is a comedy, and that the end, with a pile of corpses, is especially funny, we would not say, "Oh, well, we all see things in our own way." Rather, we would make our exit as quickly as possible.

Many people who subscribe to one version or another of a reader-response theory would agree that they are concerned not with all readers but with what they call *informed readers* or *competent readers.* Thus, informed or competent readers are familiar with the conventions of literature. They understand, for instance, that in a play such as *Hamlet* the characters usually speak in verse. Such readers, then, do not express amazement that Hamlet often speaks metrically, and that he sometimes uses rhyme. These readers understand that verse is the normal language for most of the characters in the play, and therefore such readers do not characterize Hamlet as a poet. Informed, competent readers, in short, know the rules of the game. There will still, of course, be plenty of room for differences of interpretation. Some people will find Hamlet not at all blameworthy;

others will find him somewhat blameworthy; and still others may find him highly blameworthy. In short, we can say that a writer works against a background that is *shared* by readers. As readers, we are familiar with various kinds of literature, and we read or see *Hamlet* as a particular kind of literary work, a tragedy, a play that evokes (in Shakespeare's words) "woe or wonder," sadness and astonishment. Knowing (to a large degree) how we ought to respond, our responses thus are not merely private.

Consider taking, as a guide to reading, a remark made by Mencius (372–289 BCE), the Chinese Confucian philosopher. Speaking of reading *The Book of Odes,* the oldest Chinese anthology, Mencius said that "a reader must let his thought go to meet the intention as he would a guest." We often cannot be sure about the author's intention (we do not know what Shakespeare intended to say in *Hamlet;* we have only the play itself), and even those relatively few authors who have explicitly stated their intentions may be untrustworthy for one reason or another. Yet there is something highly attractive in Mencius's suggestion that when we read we should—at least for a start—treat our author not with suspicion or hostility but with goodwill and with the expectation of pleasure.

What are the implications of reader-response theory for writing an essay on a work of literature? Even if we agree that we are talking only about competent readers, does this mean that *almost* anything goes in setting forth one's responses in an essay? Almost all advocates of any form of reader-response criticism agree on one thing: There are agreed-upon rules of *writing* if not of reading. This one point of agreement can be amplified to contain at least two aspects: (1) we all agree (more or less) as to what constitutes evidence, and (2) we all agree that a written response should be coherent. If you say that you find Hamlet to be less noble than his adversary, Claudius, you will be expected to provide evidence by pointing to specific passages, to specific things that Hamlet and Claudius say and do. And you will be expected to order the material into an effective, coherent sequence, so that the reader can move easily through your essay and will understand what you are getting at.

Archetypal (or Myth) Criticism

Carl G. Jung, the Swiss psychiatrist, in *Contributions to Analytical Psychology* (1928), postulates the existence of a "collective unconscious," an inheritance in our brains consisting of "countless typical experiences [such as birth, escape from danger, selection of a mate] of our ancestors." Few people today believe in an inherited "collective unconscious," but many people agree that certain repeated experiences, such as going to sleep and hours later awakening, or the perception of the setting and of the rising sun, or of the annual death and rebirth of vegetation, manifest themselves in dreams, myths, and literature—in these instances, as stories of apparent death and rebirth. This archetypal plot of death and rebirth is said to be evident in Coleridge's *The Rime of the Ancient Mariner,* for example. The ship suffers a deathlike calm and then is miraculously restored to motion, and, in a sort of parallel rebirth, the mariner moves from spiritual death to renewed perception of the holiness of life. Another archetypal plot is the quest, which usually involves the testing and initiation of a hero, and thus essentially represents the movement from innocence to experience. In addition to archetypal plots there are archetypal characters, since an archetype is any recurring unit. Among archetypal characters are the Scapegoat, the Hero (savior, deliverer), the Terrible Mother (witch, stepmother—even the wolf "grand-mother" in the tale of Little Red Riding Hood), and the Wise Old Man (father fig-ure, magician).

Because, the theory holds, both writer and reader share unconscious memo-ries, the tale an author tells (derived from the collective unconscious) may strangely move the reader, speaking to his or her collective unconscious. As Maud Bodkin puts it, in *Archetypal Patterns in Poetry* (1934), something within us "leaps in response to the effective presentation in poetry of an ancient theme" (4). But this emphasis on ancient (or repeated) themes has made archetypal criticism vulnerable to the charge that it is reductive. The critic looks for certain characters or patterns of action and values the work if the motifs are there, meanwhile overlooking what is unique, subtle, distinctive, and truly interesting about the work. That is, to put the matter crudely, a work is regarded as good if it is pretty much like other works, with the usual motifs and characters. A second weakness in some archetypal criticism is that in the search for the deepest mean-ing of a work the critic may crudely impose a pattern, seeing (for instance) The Quest in every walk down the street. But perhaps to say this is to beg the ques-tion; it is the critic's job to write so persuasively that the reader at least tenta-tively accepts the critic's view. For a wide-ranging study of one particular motif, see Barbara Fass Leavy's *In Search of the Swan Maiden* (1994), a discussion of the legend of a swan maiden who is forced to marry a mortal because he pos-sesses something of hers, usually a garment or an animal skin. Leavy analyzes sev-eral versions of the story, which she takes to be a representation not only of female rage against male repression but also a representation of male fear of fe-male betrayal. Leavy ends her book by examining this motif in Ibsen's *A Doll's House.* Her claim is that when Nora finds a lost object, the dance costume, she can flee from the tyrannical domestic world and thus she regains her freedom.

If archetypal criticism sometimes seems farfetched, it is nevertheless true that one of its strengths is that it invites us to use comparisons, and comparing is often an excellent way to see not only what a work shares with other works but what is distinctive in the work. The most successful practitioner of archetypal criticism was the late Northrop Frye (1912–1991), whose numerous books help readers to see fascinating connections between works. For Frye's explicit com-ments about archetypal criticism, as well as for examples of such criticism in ac-tion, see especially his *Anatomy of Criticism* (1957) and *The Educated Imagi-nation* (1964). On archetypes see also Chapter 16, "Archetypal Patterns," in Norman Friedman, *Form and Meaning in Fiction* (1975).

Historical Scholarship

Historical criticism studies a work within its historical context. Thus, a stu-dent of *Julius Caesar, Hamlet,* or *Macbeth*—plays in which ghosts appear—may try to find out about Elizabethan attitudes toward ghosts. We may find that the Elizabethans took ghosts more seriously than we do; on the other hand, we may find that ghosts were explained in various ways—for instance, sometimes as figments of the imagination and sometimes as shapes taken by the devil in order to mislead the virtuous. Similarly, a historical essay concerned with *Othello* may be devoted to Elizabethan attitudes toward Moors, or to Elizabethan ideas of love, or, for that matter, to Elizabethan ideas of a daughter's obligations toward her father's wishes concerning her suitor. The historical critic assumes (and one can hardly dispute the assumption) that writers, however individualistic, are shaped by the particular social contexts in which they live. One can put it this way: The goal of historical criticism is to understand how people in the past thought and felt. It assumes that such understanding can enrich our understanding of a particular work. The assumption is, however, disputable, since one may argue that the artist—let's say Shakespeare—may *not* have shared the age's view on this or that. All of the half-dozen or so Moors in Elizabethan plays other than *Othello* are villainous or foolish, but this evidence, one can argue, does not prove that *therefore* Othello is villainous or foolish.

Marxist Criticism

One form of historical criticism is **Marxist criticism,** named for Karl Marx (1818–1883). Actually, to say "one form" is misleading, since Marxist criticism today is varied, but essentially it sees history primarily as a struggle between socioeconomic classes, and it sees literature (and everything else) as the product of economic forces of the period.

For Marxists, economics is the "base" or "infrastructure"; on this base rests a "superstructure" of ideology (law, politics, philosophy, religion, and the arts, including literature), reflecting the interests of the dominant class. Thus, literature is a material product, produced—like bread or battleships—in order to be consumed in a given society. Like every other product, literature is the product of work, and it *does* work. A bourgeois society, for example, will produce literature that in one way or another celebrates bourgeois values, such as individualism. These works serve to assure the society that produces them that its values are solid, even universal. The enlightened Marxist writer or critic, on the other hand, exposes the fallacy of traditional values and replaces them with the truths found in Marxism. In the heyday of Marxism in the United States, during the depression of the 1930s, it was common for such Marxist critics as Granville Hicks to assert that the novel must show the class struggle.

Few critics of any sort would disagree that works of art in some measure reflect the age that produced them, but most contemporary Marxist critics go further. First, they assert—in a repudiation of what has been called "'vulgar' Marxist theory"—that the deepest historical meaning of a literary work is to be found in what it does *not* say, what its ideology does not permit it to express. Second, Marxists take seriously Marx's famous comment that "the philosophers have only *interpreted* the world in various ways; the point is to *change* it." The critic's job is to change the world, by revealing the economic basis of the arts. Not surprisingly, most Marxists are skeptical of such concepts as "genius" and "masterpiece." These concepts, they say, are part of the bourgeois myth that idealizes the individual and detaches it from its economic context. For an introduction to Marxist criticism, see Terry Eagleton, *Marxism and Literary Criticism* (1976).

The New Historicism

A recent school of scholarship, called the **New Historicism,** insists that there is no "history" in the sense of a narrative of indisputable past events. Rather, the New Historicism holds that there is only our version—our narrative, our representation—of the past. In this view, each age projects its own preconceptions on the past; historians may think they are revealing the past, but they are revealing only their own historical situation and their personal preferences. Thus, in the nineteenth century and in the twentieth almost up to 1992, Columbus was represented as the heroic benefactor of humankind who discovered the New World. But even while plans were being made to celebrate the five-hundredth anniversary of his first voyage across the Atlantic, voices were raised in protest: Columbus did not "discover" a New World; after all, the indigenous people knew where they were, and it was Columbus who was lost, since he thought he was in India. People who wrote history in, say, 1900, projected onto the past their current views (colonialism was a Good Thing), and people who in 1992 wrote history projected onto that same period a very different set of views (colonialism was a Bad Thing). Similarly, ancient Greece, once celebrated by historians as the source of democracy and rational thinking, is now more often regarded as a society that was built on slavery and on the oppression of women. And the Renaissance, once glorified as an age of enlightened thought, is now often seen as an age that tyrannized women, enslaved colonial people, and enslaved itself with its belief in witchcraft and astrology. Thinking about these changing views, one feels the truth of the witticism that the only thing more uncertain than the future is the past.

The New Historicism is especially associated with Stephen Greenblatt, who popularized the term in 1982 in the preface to a collection of essays published in the journal *Genre*. Greenblatt himself has said of the New Historicism that "it's no doctrine at all" (*Learning to Curse*, [1990]) but the term is nevertheless much used, and, as the preceding remarks have suggested, it is especially associated with power, most especially with revealing the tyrannical practices of a society that others have glorified. The New Historicism was in large measure shaped by the 1960s; the students who in the 1960s protested against the war in Vietnam by holding demonstrations, in the 1980s—they were now full professors—protested against Ronald Reagan by writing articles exposing Renaissance colonialism. Works of literature were used as a basis for a criticism of society. Academic writing of this sort was not dry, impartial, unimpassioned scholarship; rather, it connected the past with the present, and it offered value judgments. In Greenblatt's words,

> Writing that was not engaged, that withheld judgments, that failed to connect the present with the past seemed worthless. Such connection could be made either by analogy or causality; that is, a particular set of historical circumstances could be represented in such a way as to bring out homologies with aspects of the present or, alternatively, those circumstances could be analyzed as the generative forces that led to the modern condition. (*Learning to Curse* 167)

For a collection of fifteen essays exemplifying New Historicism, see *The New Historicism* (1994), edited by H. Aram Veeser.

Biographical Criticism

One kind of historical scholarship is the study of *biography,* which for our purposes includes not only biographies but also autobiographies, diaries, journals, letters, and so on. What experiences did (for example) Mark Twain undergo?

Are some of the apparently sensational aspects of *The Adventures of Huckleberry Finn* in fact close to events that Twain experienced? If so, is he a "realist"? If not, is he writing in the tradition of the "tall tale"?

The really good biographies not only tell us about the life of the author, but they enable us to return to the literary texts with a deeper understanding of how they came to be what they are. If you read Richard B. Sewall's biography of Emily Dickinson, you will find a wealth of material concerning her family and the world she moved in—for instance, the religious ideas that were part of her upbringing.

Biographical study may illuminate even the work of a living author. If you are writing about the poetry of Adrienne Rich, for example, you may want to consider what she has told us in many essays about her life, especially about her relations with her father and her husband.

Psychological (or Psychoanalytic) Criticism

One form that biographical study may take is **psychological** or **psychoanalytic criticism,** which usually examines the author and the author's writings in the framework of Freudian psychology. A central doctrine of Sigmund Freud (1856–1939) is the Oedipus complex, the view that all males (Freud seems not to have made his mind up about females) unconsciously wish to displace their fathers and to sleep with their mothers. According to Freud, hatred for the father and love of the mother, normally repressed, may appear disguised in dreams. Works of art, like dreams, are disguised versions of repressed wishes.

Consider the case of Edgar Allan Poe. An orphan before he was three years old, he was brought up in the family of John Allan, but he was never formally adopted. His relations with Allan were stormy, though he seems to have had better relations with Allan's wife and still better relations with an aunt, whose daughter he married. In the Freudian view, Poe's marriage to his cousin (the daughter of a mother figure) was a way of sleeping with his mother. According to psychoanalytic critics, if we move from Poe's life to his work, we see, it is alleged, this hatred for his father and love for his mother. Thus, the murderer in "The Cask of Amontillado" (page 509) is said to voice Poe's hostility toward his father, and the wine vault in which much of the story is set (an encompassing structure associated with fluids) is interpreted as symbolizing Poe's desire to return to his mother's womb. In Poe's other works, the longing for death is similarly taken to embody his desire to return to the womb.

Other psychoanalytic interpretations of Poe have been offered. Kenneth Silverman, author of a biography titled *Edgar Allan Poe* (1991) and the editor of a collection titled *New Essays on Poe's Major Tales* (1993), emphasizes the fact that Poe was orphaned before he was three, and was separated from his brother and his infant sister. In *New Essays* Silverman relates this circumstance to the "many instances of engulfment" that he finds in Poe's work. Images of engulfment, he points out, "are part of a still larger network of images having to do with biting, devouring, and similar oral mutilation." Why are they common in Poe? Here is Silverman's answer:

> Current psychoanalytic thinking about childhood bereavement explains the fantasy of being swallowed up as representing a desire,

> mixed with dread, to merge with the dead; the wish to devour repre-
> sents a primitive attempt at preserving loved ones, incorporating them
> so as not to lose them. (20)

Notice that psychoanalytic interpretations usually take us away from what the author consciously intended; they purport to tell us what the work reveals, whether or not the author was aware of this meaning. The "meaning" of the work is found not in the surface content of the work but in the author's psyche.

One additional example—and it is the most famous—of a psychoanalytic study of a work of literature may be useful. In *Hamlet and Oedipus* (1949) Ernest Jones, amplifying some comments by Freud, argued that Hamlet delays killing Claudius because Claudius (who has killed Hamlet's father and married Hamlet's mother) has done exactly what Hamlet himself wanted to do. For Hamlet to kill Claudius, then, would be to kill himself.

If this approach interests you, take a look at Norman N. Holland's *Psychoanalysis and Shakespeare* (1966), or Frederick Crews's study of Hawthorne, *The Sins of the Fathers* (1966). Crews finds in Hawthorne's work evidence of unresolved Oedipal conflicts, and he accounts for the appeal of the fictions thus: The stories "rest on fantasy, but on the shared fantasy of mankind, and this makes for a more penetrating fiction than would any illusionistic slice of life" (263). For applications to other authors, look at Simon O. Lesser's *Fiction and the Unconscious* (1957), or at an anthology of criticism, *Literature and Psychoanalysis* (1983), edited by Edith Kurzweil and William Phillips.

Psychological criticism can also turn from the author and the work to the reader, seeking to explain why we, as readers, respond in certain ways. Why, for example, is *Hamlet* so widely popular? A Freudian answer is that it is universal because it deals with a universal (Oedipal) impulse. One can, however, ask whether it appeals as strongly to women as to men (again, Freud was unsure about the Oedipus complex in women) and, if so, why it appeals to them. Or, more generally, one can ask if males and females read in the same way.

Gender (Feminist, and Lesbian and Gay) Criticism

This last question brings us to **gender criticism.** As we have seen, writing about literature usually seeks to answer questions. Historical scholarship, for instance, tries to answer such questions as, What did Shakespeare and his contemporaries believe about ghosts? or How did Victorian novelists and poets respond to Darwin's theory of evolution? Gender criticism, too, asks questions. It is especially concerned with two issues, one about reading and one about writing: Do men and women read in different ways, and Do they write in different ways?

Feminist criticism can be traced back to the work of Virginia Woolf (1882–1941), but chiefly it grew out of the women's movement of the 1960s. The women's movement at first tended to hold that women are pretty much the same as men and therefore should be treated equally, but much recent feminist criticism has emphasized and explored the differences between women and men. Because the experiences of the sexes are different, the argument goes, the values and sensibilities are different, and their responses to literature are different. Further, literature written by women is different from literature written by men. Works written by women are seen by some feminist critics as embodying the experiences of a minority culture—a group marginalized by the dominant male culture. (If you have read Charlotte Perkins Gilman's "The Yellow Wallpaper" or Susan Glaspell's *Trifles,* you'll recall that these literary works themselves are largely concerned about the differing ways in which men and women perceive the world.) Not all women are feminist critics, and not all feminist critics are women. Further, there are varieties of feminist criticism. For a good introduction see *The New Feminist Criticism: Essays on Women, Literature, and Theory* (1985), edited by Elaine Showalter. For the role of men in feminist criticism, see *Engendering Men* (1990), edited by Joseph A. Boone and Michael Cadden (1990). At this point it should also be said that some theorists, who hold that identity is socially constructed, strongly dispute the value of establishing "essentialist" categories such as *heterosexual, gay,* and *lesbian*—a point that we will consider in a moment.

Feminist critics rightly point out that men have established the conventions of literature and that men have established the canon—that is, the body of literature that is said to be worth reading. Speaking a bit broadly, in this patriarchal or male-dominated body of literature, men are valued for being strong and active, whereas women are expected to be weak and passive. Thus, in the world of fairy tales, the admirable male is the energetic hero (Jack, the Giant-Killer) but the admirable female is the passive Sleeping Beauty. Active women such as the wicked stepmother or—a disguised form of the same thing—the witch are generally villainous. (There are of course exceptions, such as Gretel, in "Hansel and Gretel.") A woman hearing or reading the story of Sleeping Beauty or of Little Red Riding Hood (rescued by the powerful woodcutter) or any other work in which women seem to be trivialized will respond differently from a man. For instance, a woman may be socially conditioned into admiring Sleeping Beauty, but only at great cost to her mental well-being. A more resistant female reader may recognize in herself no kinship with the beautiful, passive Sleeping Beauty and may respond to the story indignantly. Another way to put it is this: The male reader perceives a romantic story, but the resistant female reader perceives a story of oppression.

For discussions of the ways in which, it is argued, women *ought* to read, you may want to look at *Gender and Reading* (1986), edited by Elizabeth A. Flynn and Patrocinio Schweickart, and especially at Judith Fetterley's book *The Resisting Reader* (1978). Fetterley's point, briefly, is that women should resist the meanings (that is, the visions of how women ought to behave) that male authors—or female authors who have inherited patriarchal values—embed in their books. "To read the canon of what is currently considered classic American literature is perforce to identify as male," Fetterley says. "It insists on its universality in specifically male terms." Fetterley argues that a woman must read as a woman, "exorcising the male mind that has been implanted in women." In resisting the obvious meanings—for instance, the false claim that male values are universal values— women may discover more significant meanings. Fetterley argues that Faulkner's "A Rose for Emily"

> is a story not of a conflict between the South and the North or between the old order and the new; it is a story of the patriarchy North and South, new and old, and of the sexual conflict within it. As Faulkner himself has implied, it is a story of a woman victimized and betrayed by the system of sexual politics, who nevertheless has discovered, within the structures that victimize her, sources of power for herself. . . . "A

Rose for Emily" is the story of how to murder your gentleman caller and get away with it. (34–35)

Fetterley goes on to state that society made Emily a "lady"—society dehumanized her by elevating her. Emily's father, seeking to shape her life, stood in the doorway of their house and drove away her suitors. So far as he was concerned, Emily was a nonperson, a creature whose own wishes were not to be regarded; he alone would shape her future. Because society (beginning with her father) made her a "lady"—a creature so elevated that she is not taken seriously as a passionate human being—she is able to kill Homer Barron and not be suspected. Here is Fetterley speaking of the passage in which the townspeople crowd into her house when her death becomes known:

> When the would-be "suitors" finally get into her father's house, they discover the consequences of his oppression of her, for the violence contained in the rotted corpse of Homer Barron is the mirror image of the violence represented in the tableau, the back-flung front door flung back with a vengeance. (42)

Feminist criticism has been concerned not only with the depiction of women and men in a male-determined literary canon and with female responses to these images but also with yet another topic: women's writing. Women have had fewer opportunities than men to become writers of fiction, poetry, and drama—for one thing, they have been less well educated in the things that the male patriarchy valued—but even when they *have* managed to write, men sometimes have neglected their work simply because it had been written by a woman. Feminists have further argued that certain forms of writing have been especially the province of women—for instance, journals, diaries, and letters; and predictably, these forms have not been given adequate space in the traditional, male-oriented canon.

In 1972, in an essay titled "When We Dead Awaken: Writing as ReVision," the poet and essayist Adrienne Rich effectively summed up the matter:

> A radical critique of literature, feminist in its impulse, would take the work first of all as a clue to how we live, how we have been living, how we have been led to imagine ourselves, how our language has trapped as well as liberated us; and how we can begin to see—and therefore live—afresh. . . . We need to know the writing of the past and know it differently than we have ever known it; not to pass on a tradition but to break its hold over us.

Much feminist criticism concerned with women writers has emphasized connections between the writer's biography and her art. Suzanne Juhasz, in her introduction to *Feminist Critics Read Emily Dickinson* (1983), puts it this way:

> The central assumption of feminist criticism is that gender informs the nature of art, the nature of biography, and the relation between them. Dickinson is a woman poet, and this fact is integral to her identity. Feminist criticism's sensitivity to the components of female experience in general and to Dickinson's identity as a woman generates essential insights about her. . . . Attention to the relationship between biography and art is a requisite of feminist criticism. To disregard it further strengthens those divisions continually created by traditional criticism, so that nothing about the woman writer can be seen whole. (1–5)

Lesbian and gay criticism have their roots in feminist criticism; feminist criticism introduced many of the questions that these other, newer developments are now exploring.

In 1979, in a book entitled *On Lies, Secrets, and Silence,* Adrienne Rich reprinted a 1975 essay on Emily Dickinson, "Vesuvius at Home." In her new preface to the reprinted essay she said that a lesbian-feminist reading of Dickinson would not have to prove that Dickinson slept with another woman. Rather, lesbian-feminist criticism "will ask questions hitherto passed over; it will not search obsessively for heterosexual romance as the key to a woman artist's life and work" (157–158). Obviously such a statement is also relevant to a male artist's life and work. It should be mentioned, too, that Rich's comments on lesbian reading and lesbianism as an image of creativity have been much discussed. For a brief survey, see Marilyn R. Farwell, "Toward a Definition of the Lesbian Literary Imagination," *Signs* 14 (1988): 100–118.

Before turning to some of the questions that lesbian and gay critics address, it is necessary first to say that lesbian criticism and gay criticism are not—to use a word now current in much criticism—symmetrical, chiefly because lesbian and gay relationships themselves are not symmetrical. Straight society has traditionally been more tolerant of—or blinder to—lesbianism than to male homosexuality. Further, lesbian literary theory has tended to see its affinities more with feminist theory than with gay theory; the emphasis has been on gender (male/female) rather than on sexuality (homosexuality/bisexuality/heterosexuality). On the other hand, some gays and lesbians have been writing what is now being called **Queer Theory.**

Now for some of the questions that this criticism addresses: (1) Do lesbians and gays read in ways that differ from the ways straight people read? (2) Do they write in ways that differ from those of straight people? (Gregory Woods argues in *Lesbian and Gay Writing: An Anthology of Critical Essays* [1990], edited by Mark Lilly, that "modern gay poets . . . use . . . paradox, as weapon and shield, against a world in which heterosexuality is taken for granted as being exclusively natural and healthy" [176]. Another critic, Jeffrey Meyers, writing in *Journal of English and Germanic Philology* 88 [1989]: 126–29, in an unsympathetic review of a book on gay writers contrasts gay writers of the past with those of the present. According to Meyers, closeted homosexuals in the past, writing out of guilt and pain, produced a distinctive literature that is more interesting than the productions of today's uncloseted writers.) (3) How have straight writers portrayed lesbians and gays, and how have lesbian and gay writers portrayed straight women and men? (4) What strategies did lesbian and gay writers use to make their work acceptable to a general public in an age when lesbian and gay behavior was unmentionable?

Questions such as these have stimulated critical writing especially about bisexual and lesbian and gay authors (for instance, Virginia Woolf, Gertrude Stein, Elizabeth Bishop, Walt Whitman, Oscar Wilde, E. M. Forster, Hart Crane, Tennessee Williams), but they have also led to interesting writing on such a topic as Nathaniel Hawthorne's attitudes toward women. "An account of Hawthorne's misogyny that takes no account of his own and his culture's gender anxieties," Robert K. Martin says in Boone and Cadden's *Engendering Men,* "is necessarily inadequate" (122).

Shakespeare's work—and not only the sonnets, which praise a beautiful male friend—has stimulated a fair amount of gay criticism. Much of this criticism consists of "decoding" aspects of the plays. Seymour Kleinberg argues, in *Essays on Gay Literature* (1985), edited by Stuart Kellogg, that Antonio in *The Merchant of Venice,* whose melancholy is not made clear by Shakespeare, is melancholy because (again, this is according to Kleinberg) Antonio's lover, Bassanio, is deserting him, and because Antonio is ashamed of his own sexuality:

> Antonio is a virulently anti-Semitic homosexual and is melancholic to
> the point of despair because his lover, Bassanio, wishes to marry an immensely rich aristocratic beauty, to leave the diversions of the Rialto to
> return to his own class and to sexual conventionality. Antonio is also in
> despair because he despises himself for his homosexuality, which is romantic, obsessive, and exclusive, and fills him with sexual shame. (113)

Several earlier critics had suggested that Antonio is a homosexual, hopelessly pining for Bassanio, but Kleinberg goes further, and argues that Antonio and Bassanio are lovers, not just good friends, and that Antonio's hopeless and shameful (because socially unacceptable) passion for Bassanio becomes transformed into hatred for the Jew, Shylock. The play, according to Kleinberg, is partly about "a world where . . . sexual guilt is translated into ethnic hatred" (124).

Examination of matters of gender can help to illuminate literary works, but it should be added, too, that some—perhaps most—critics write also as activists, reporting their findings not only to help us to understand and to enjoy the works of (say) Whitman, but also to change society's view of sexuality. Thus, in *Disseminating Whitman* (1991), Michael Moon is impatient with earlier critical rhapsodies about Whitman's universalism. It used to be said that Whitman's celebration of the male body was a sexless celebration of brotherly love in a democracy, but the gist of Moon's view is that we must neither whitewash Whitman's poems with such high-minded talk, nor reject them as indecent; rather, we must see exactly what Whitman is saying about a kind of experience that society had shut its eyes to, and we must take Whitman's view seriously. Somewhat similarly, Gregory Woods in *Articulate Flesh* (1987) points out that until a few years ago discussions of Hart Crane regularly condemned his homosexuality, as is evident in L. S. Dembo's characterization of Crane (quoted by Woods) as "uneducated, alcoholic, homosexual, paranoic, suicidal" (140). Gay and lesbian writers do not adopt this sort of manner. But it should also be pointed out that today there are straight critics who study lesbian or gay authors and write about them insightfully and without hostility.

One assumption in much lesbian and gay critical writing is that although gender greatly influences the ways in which we read, reading is a skill that can be learned, and therefore straight people—aided by lesbian and gay critics—can learn to read, with pleasure and profit, lesbian and gay writers. This assumption of course also underlies much feminist criticism, which often assumes that men must stop ignoring books by women and must learn (with the help of feminist critics) how to read them, and, in fact, how to read—with newly opened eyes—the sexist writings of men of the past and present.

In addition to the titles mentioned earlier concerning gay and lesbian criticism, consult Eve Kosofsky Sedgwick, *Between Men: English Literature and Male Homosocial Desire* (1985) and an essay by Sedgwick, "Gender Criticism," in *Redrawing the Boundaries,* ed. Stephen Greenblatt and Giles Gunn (1992).

While many in the field of lesbian and gay criticism have turned their energies toward examining the effects that an author's—or a character's—sexual identity may have upon the text, others have begun to question, instead, the concept of sexual identity itself.* Drawing upon the work of the French social historian Michel Foucault, critics such as David Halperin (*One Hundred Years of Homosexuality and Other Essays on Greek Love,* [1990]) and Judith Butler (*Gender Trouble,* [1989]) explore how various categories of identity, such as "heterosexual" and "homosexual," represent ways of defining human beings that are distinct to particular cultures and historical periods. These critics, affiliated with what is known as the "social constructionist" school of thought, argue that the way a given society (modern American or ancient Greek) interprets sexuality will determine the particular categories within which individuals come to understand and to name their own desires. For such critics the goal of a lesbian or gay criticism is not to define the specificity of a lesbian or gay literature or mode of interpretation, but to show how the ideology (the normative understanding of a given culture) makes it seem natural to think about sexuality in terms of such identities as lesbian, gay, bisexual, or straight. By challenging the authority of those terms, or "denaturalizing" them, and by calling attention to moments in which literary (and nonliterary) representations make assumptions that reinforce the supposed inevitability of those distinctions, such critics attempt to redefine our understandings of the relations between sexuality and literature. They hope to make clear that sexuality is always, in a certain sense, "literary"; it is a representation of a fiction that society has constructed in order to make sense out of experience.

Because such critics have challenged the authority of the opposition between heterosexuality and homosexuality, and have read it as a historical construct rather than as a biological or psychological absolute, they have sometimes resisted the very terms *lesbian* and *gay.* Many now embrace what is called Queer Theory as an attempt to mark their resistance to the categories of identity they see our culture as imposing upon us.

Works written within this mode of criticism are often influenced by deconstructionist or psychoanalytic thought. They examine works by straight authors as frequently as they do works by writers who might be defined as lesbian or gay. Eve Kosofsky Sedgwick's reading of *Billy Budd* in her book *Epistemology of the Closet* (1990) provides a good example of this sort of criticism. Reading Claggart as "the homosexual" in the text of Melville's novella, Sedgwick is not interested in defining his difference from other characters. Instead, she shows how the novella sets up a large number of oppositions—such as public and private, sincerity and sentimentality, health and illness—all of which have a relationship to the way in which a distinct "gay" identity was being produced by American society at the end of the nineteenth century. Other critics whose work in this field may be useful for students of literature are D. A. Miller, *The Novel and the Police* (1988); Diana Fuss, *Essentially Speaking* (1989) and *Identification Papers* (1995); Judith Butler, *Bodies That Matter* (1990); and Lee Edelman, *Homographesis: Essays in Gay Literary and Cultural Theory* (1993).

• • •

This chapter began by making the obvious point that all readers, whether or not they consciously adopt a particular approach to literature, necessarily read through particular lenses. More precisely, a reader begins with a frame of interpretation—historical, psychological, sociological, or whatever—and from within the frame a reader selects one of the several competing methodologies.

---

*This paragraph and the next two are by Lee Edelman of Tufts University.

Critics often make great—even grandiose—claims for their approaches. For example, Frederic Jameson, a Marxist, begins *The Political Unconscious: Narrative as a Socially Symbolic Act* (1981) thus:

> This book will argue the priority of the political interpretation of literary texts. It conceives of the political perspective not as some supplemental method, not as an optional auxiliary to other interpretive methods current today—the psychoanalytic or the myth-critical, the stylistic, the ethical, the structural—but rather as the absolute horizon of all reading and all interpretation. (7)

Readers who are chiefly interested in politics may be willing to assume "the priority of the political interpretation . . . as the absolute horizon of all reading and all interpretation," but other readers may respectfully decline to accept this assumption.

In talking about a critical approach, it is sometimes said that readers decode a text by applying a grid to it; the grid enables them to see certain things clearly. Good; but what is sometimes forgotten is that (since there is no such thing as a free lunch) a lens or a grid—an angle of vision or interpretive frame and a methodology—also prevents a reader from seeing certain other things. This is to be expected. What is important, then, is to remember this fact, and thus not to deceive ourselves by thinking that our keen tools enable us to see the whole. A psychoanalytic reading of, say, *Hamlet,* may be helpful, but it does not reveal all that is in *Hamlet,* and it does not refute the perceptions of another approach, let's say a historical study. Each approach may illuminate aspects neglected by others.

It is too much to expect a reader to apply all useful methods (or even several) at once—that would be rather like looking through a telescope with one eye and through a microscope with the other—but it is not too much to expect readers to be aware of the limitations of their methods. If one reads much criticism, one finds two kinds of critics. There are, on the one hand, critics who methodically and mechanically peer through a lens or grid, and they find what one can easily predict they will find. On the other hand, there are critics who (despite what may be inevitable class and gender biases) are at least relatively open-minded in their approach—critics who, one might say, do not at the outset of their reading believe that their method assures them that (so to speak) they have got the text's number and that by means of this method they will expose the text for what it is. The philosopher Richard Rorty engagingly makes a distinction somewhat along these lines, in an essay he contributed to Umberto Eco's *Interpretation and Over-interpretation* (1992). There is a great difference, Rorty suggests,

> between knowing what you want to get out of a person or thing or text in advance and [on the other hand] hoping that the person or thing or text will help you want something different—that he or she or it will help you to change your purposes, and thus to change your life. This distinction, I think, helps us highlight the difference between methodical and inspired readings of texts. (106)

Rorty goes on to say he has seen an anthology of readings on Conrad's *Heart of Darkness,* containing a psychoanalytic reading, a reader-response reading, and so on. "None of the readers had, as far as I could see," Rorty says,

> been enraptured or destabilized by *Heart of Darkness.* I got no sense that the book had made a big difference to them, that they cared much about Kurtz or Marlow or the woman "with helmeted head and tawny

cheeks" whom Marlow sees on the bank of the river. These people, and that book, had no more changed these readers' purposes than the specimen under the microscope changes the purpose of the histologist. (107)

The kind of criticism that Rorty prefers he calls "unmethodical" criticism and "inspired" criticism. It is, for Rorty, the result of an "encounter" with some aspect of a work of art "which has made a difference to the critic's conception of who she is, what she is good for, what she wants to do with herself . . ." (107). This is not a matter of "respect" for the text, Rorty insists. Rather, he says, "love" and "hate" are better words, "For a great love or a great loathing is the sort of thing that changes us by changing our purposes, changing the uses to which we shall put people and things and texts we encounter later" (107).

Suggestions for Further Reading

Because a massive list of titles may prove discouraging rather than helpful, it seems advisable here to give a short list of basic titles. (Titles already mentioned in this chapter—which are good places to begin—are not repeated in the following list.)

A good sampling of contemporary criticism (sixty or so essays or chapters from books), representing all of the types discussed in this commentary except lesbian and gay criticism, can be found in *The Critical Tradition: Classic Texts and Contemporary Trends,* 3rd ed., Ed. David H. Richter (2006). See also Vincent B. Leitch et al., eds., *The Norton Anthology of Literary Theory and Criticism*, 2nd. ed. (2010).

For a readable introduction to various approaches, written for students who are beginning the study of literary theory, see Steven Lynn, *Texts and Contexts*, 5th ed. (2007). For a more advanced survey, that is, a work that assumes some familiarity with the material, see a short book by K. M. Newton, *Interpreting the Text: A Critical Introduction to the Theory and Practice of Literary Interpretation* (1990). A third survey, though considerably longer than the books by Lynn and Newton, is narrower because it confines itself to a study of critical writings about Shakespeare: Brian Vickers, *Appropriating Shakespeare: Contemporary Critical Quarrels* (1993), offers an astringent appraisal of deconstruction, New Historicism, psychoanalytic criticism, feminist criticism, and Marxist criticism. For a collection of essays on Shakespeare written from some of the viewpoints that Vickers deplores, see John Drakakis, ed., *Shakespearean Tragedy* (1992).

Sympathetic discussions (usually two or three pages long) of each approach, with fairly extensive bibliographic suggestions, are given in the appropriate articles in three encyclopedic works. Wendell V. Harris, *Dictionary of Concepts in Literary Criticism and Theory* (1992), devotes several pages to each concept (for instance, *author, context, evaluation, feminist literary criticism, narrative*) and gives a useful reading list for each entry. Fairly similar to Harris's book are Irene Makaryk, ed., *Encyclopedia of Contemporary Literary Theory: Approaches, Scholars, Terms* (1993), and Michael Groden, Martin Kreiswirth, and Imre Szeman, eds., *The Johns Hopkins Guide to Literary Theory and Criticism*, 2nd ed. (2005). *The Johns Hopkins Guide,* though it includes substantial entries on individual critics as well as on critical schools, is occasionally disappointing in the readability of some of its essays and especially in its coverage, since it does not include critical terms other than names of schools of criticism. Despite its title, then, it does not have entries for *theory* or for *criticism,* nor does it have entries for such words as *canon* and *evaluation.* Students thus should also consult an extremely valuable work with a misleading narrow title, *The New Princeton Encyclopedia of Poetry and Poetics,* edited by Alex Preminger and T. V. F. Brogan (1993). Although *The New Princeton Encyclopedia* does not include terms that are unique to, say, drama or fiction, it does include generous, lucid entries (with suggestions for further reading) on such terms as *allegory, criticism, canon, irony, sincerity, theory,* and *unity,* and the long entries on *poetics, poetry,* and *poetry, theories of,* are in many respects entries on *literature.*

For a collection of essays on the canon, see *Canons,* edited by Robert von Hallberg (1984); see also an essay by Robert Scholes, "Canonicity and Textuality," in *Introduction to Scholarship in Modern Languages and Literatures,* edited by Joseph Gibaldi, 2nd ed. (1992), 138–58. Gibaldi's collection includes essays on related topics—for instance, Literary Theory (by Jonathan Culler) and Cultural Studies (by David Bathrick). The third edition of this volume, edited by David G. Nicholls (2007), is also excellent.

Formalist Criticism (The New Criticism)

Cleanth Brooks, *The Well Wrought Urn: Studies in the Structure of Poetry* (1947), especially Chapters 1 and 11 ("The Language of Paradox" and "The Heresy of Paraphrase"); W. K. Wimsatt, *The Verbal Icon* (1954), especially "The Intentional Fallacy" and "The Affective Fallacy"; Murray Krieger, *The New Apologists for Poetry* (1956); and, for an accurate overview of a kind of criticism often misrepresented today, Chapters 9–12 in Volume 6 of René Wellek, *A History of Modern Criticism: 1750–1950* (1986). See also *The New Criticism and Contemporary Literary Theory: Connections and Continuities,* Ed. William J. Spurlin and Michael Fischer (1995).

Deconstruction

Christopher Norris, *Deconstruction: Theory and Practice,* rev. ed. (1991); Vincent B. Leitch, *Deconstructive Criticism: An Advanced Introduction and Survey* (1983); Christopher Norris, ed., *What Is Deconstruction?* (1988); Christopher Norris and Andrew Benjamin, *Deconstruction and the Interests of Theory* (1989). For a negative assessment, consult John M. Ellis, *Against Deconstruction* (1989). More generally, see *Deconstruction: A Reader,* Ed. Martin McQuillan (2001).

Reader-Response Criticism

Wolfgang Iser, *The Act of Reading: A Theory of Aesthetic Response* (1978); Wolfgang Iser, *Prospecting: From Reader Response to Literary Anthropology* (1993); Susan Suleiman and Inge Crossman, eds., *The Reader in the Text* (1980); Jane P. Tompkins, ed., *Reader-Response Criticism* (1980); Norman N. Holland, *The Dynamics of Literary Response* (1973, 1989); Steven Mailloux, *Interpretive Conventions: The Reader in the Study of American Fiction* (1982); Gerry Brenner, *Performative Criticism: Experiments in Reader Response* (2004).

Archetypal (or Myth) Criticism

G. Wilson Knight, *The Starlit Dome* (1941); Richard Chase, *Quest for Myth* (1949); Murray Krieger, ed., *Northrop Frye in Modern Criticism* (1966); Frank Lentricchia, *After the New Criticism* (1980). For a good survey of Frye's approach, see Robert D. Denham, *Northrop Frye and Critical Method* (1978). Also, *Rereading Frye: The Published and Unpublished Works,* Ed. David Boyd and Imre Salusinszky (1999).

Historical Criticism

For a brief survey of some historical criticism of the first half of the twentieth century, see René Wellek, *A History of Modern Criticism: 1750–1950,* Volume 6 (1986), Chapter 4 ("Academic Criticism"). See also E. M. W. Tillyard, *The Elizabethan World Picture* (1943), and Tillyard's *Shakespeare's History Plays* (1944), both of which relate Elizabethan literature to the beliefs of the age and are good examples of the historical approach. Also of interest is David Levin, *Forms of Uncertainty: Essays in Historical Criticism* (1992).

Marxist Criticism

Raymond Williams, *Marxism and Literature* (1977); Tony Bennett, *Formalism and Marxism* (1979); Lydia Sargent, ed., *Women and Revolution: A Discussion of the Unhappy Marriage of Marxism and Feminism* (1981); and for a brief survey of American Marxist writers of the 1930s and 1940s, see Chapter 5 of Volume 6 of René Wellek, *A History of Modern Criticism* (1986). Also helpful are Daniel Aaron, *Writers on the Left: Episodes in American Literary Communism* (1961; new ed., 1992); and Barbara Foley, *Radical Representations: Politics and Form in U.S. Proletarian Fiction, 1929–1941* (1993). Also stimulating are Terry Eagleton, *The Ideology of the Aesthetic* (1990) and *Marxist Shakespeares,* Ed. Jean E. Howard and Scott Cutler Shershow (2001).

New Historicism

Historicizing Theory, Ed. Peter C. Herman (2004); Stephen Greenblatt, *Renaissance Self-Fashioning from More to Shakespeare* (1980), especially the first chapter; Brook Thomas, *The New Historicism and Other Old-Fashioned Topics* (1991). Greenblatt's other influential books include *Shakespearean Negotiations: The Circulation of Social Energy in Renaissance England* (1988), and, with Catherine Gallagher, *Practicing New Historicism* (2000).

Biographical Criticism

Leon Edel, *Literary Biography* (1957); Estelle C. Jellinek, ed., *Women's Autobiography: Essays in Criticism* (1980); James Olney, *Metaphors of Self: The Meaning of Autobiography* (1981); and *Women, Autobiography, Theory: A Reader,* Ed. Sidonie Smith and Julia Watson. Important twentieth-century literary biographers are Richard Ellmann, *James Joyce* (1959, rev. ed., 1982); Juliet Barker, *The Brontës* (1994); Hermione Lee, *Virginia Woolf* (1997); Lyndall Gordon, *T. S. Eliot: An Imperfect Life* (1999); and Fred Kaplan, *The Singular Mark Twain: A Biography* (2003).

Psychological (or Psychoanalytic) Criticism

Edith Kurzweil and William Phillips, eds., *Literature and Psychoanalysis* (1983); Maurice Charney and Joseph Reppen, eds., *Psychoanalytic Approaches to Literature and Film* (1987); Madelon Sprengnether, *The Spectral Mother: Freud, Feminism, and Psychoanalysis* (1990); Frederick Crews, *Out of My System* (1975); and Graham Frankland, *Freud's Literary Culture* (2000).

Gender (Feminist, and Lesbian and Gay) Criticism

Gayle Greene and Coppèlia Kahn, eds., *Making a Difference: Feminist Literary Criticism* (1985), including an essay by Bonnie Zimmerman on lesbian criticism; Catherine Belsey and Jane Moore, eds., *The Feminist Reader: Essays in Gender and the Politics of Literary Criticism* (1989); Toril Moi, ed., *French Feminist Thought* (1987); Elizabeth A. Flynn and Patrocinio P. Schweikart, eds., *Gender and Reading: Essays on Readers, Texts, and Contexts* (1986); Barbara Christian, *Black Feminist Criticism: Perspectives on Black Women Writers* (1985); Shoshana Felman, *What Does a Woman Want? Reading and Sexual Difference* (1993); Robert Martin, *The Homosexual Tradition in American Poetry* (1979); Kathryn R. Kent, *Making Girls into Women: American Women's Writing and the Rise of Lesbian Identity* (2003); and Rita Felski, *Literature After Feminism* (2003). Henry Abelove et al., eds., *The Lesbian and Gay Studies Reader* (1993), has only a few essays concerning literature, but it has an extensive bibliography on the topic. See also *The Norton Anthology of Literature by Women: The Traditions in English,* Ed. Sandra M. Gilbert and Susan Gubar, 3rd ed. (2007); and *Feminist Literary Theory and Criticism: A Norton Reader,* Ed. Sandra M. Gilbert and Susan Gubar (2007).

Valuable reference works include *Encyclopedia of Feminist Literary Theory* (1997), Ed. Beth Kowaleski-Wallace; *The Gay & Lesbian Literary Companion,* Ed. Sharon Malinowski and Christa Brelin (1995); and *The Gay and Lesbian Literary Heritage: A Reader's Companion to the Writers and Their Works, from Antiquity to the Present,* Ed. Claude J. Summers (1995). See also Summers, *Gay Fictions: Wilde to Stonewall: Studies in a Male Homosexual Literary Tradition* (1990); *Novel Gazing: Queer Readings in Fiction,* Ed. Eve Kosofsky Sedgwick (1997); and Gregory Woods, *A History of Gay Literature: The Male Tradition* (1998). For further discussion of Queer Theory, see Annamarie Jagose, *Queer Theory: An Introduction* (1996); Alan Sinfield, *Cultural Politics—Queer Reading* (1994); *Feminism Meets Queer Theory* (1997), Ed. Elizabeth Weed and Naomi Schor; and *Queer Theory,* Ed. Iain Morland and Annabelle Willox (2005).

How Much Do You Know About Citing Sources? A Quiz with Answers*

Taking the quiz below will let you test yourself and will assist you in any discussion you have with your classmates about how to cite sources accurately and honestly.

QUIZ YOURSELF: HOW MUCH DO YOU KNOW ABOUT CITING SOURCES?

Section 1: Plagiarism and Academic Dishonesty

Which of the following examples describe violations of academic integrity? Check all the examples that are punishable under university rules.

_____ 1. You buy a term paper from a Web site and turn it in as your own work.

_____ 2. You ask a friend to write a paper for you.

_____ 3. You can't find the information you need, so you invent statistics, quotes, and sources that do not exist and cite these in your paper as if they were real.

_____ 4. Your professor requires you to use five sources, but you find one book written by one person that has all the information you need, so you cite that book as if it were information coming from other books and authors in order to make it look like you used five different sources.

_____ 5. Your history professor and your political science professor both assign a term paper. To save time, you write one paper that meets both requirements and hand it in to both professors.

---

*This quiz and the answers were written by Carmen Lowe, Director of the Tufts University Academic Resource Center. We are grateful to Ms. Lowe for permission to use her material.

_____ 6. You don't want to have too many quotes in your paper, so you do not put quotation marks around some sentences you copied from a source. You cite the source correctly at the end of the paragraph and in your bibliography.

_____ 7. You have copied a long passage from a book into your paper, and you changed some of the wording. You cite the source at the end of the passage and again in the bibliography.

_____ 8. While writing a long research paper, you come across an interesting hypothesis mentioned in a book, and you incorporate this hypothesis into your main argument. After you finish writing the paper, you can't remember where you initially found the hypothesis, so you don't bother to cite the source of your idea.

Section 2: Common Knowledge

Common knowledge is information that is widely known within a society or an intellectual community; therefore, if you include common knowledge in your paper, you do not need to cite where you found that information.

Answer *Yes* or *No* to the following questions:

_____ 1. In a high school class on American government, you learned about the checks-and-balances system of government which separates power into the judicial, executive, and legislative branches. Now, you are writing a paper for an introductory political science class and you mention the concept of checks-and-balances you learned in high school. Should you cite your old high school textbook?

_____ 2. In writing a paper about pop culture in the 1980s, you want to include the year that Reagan was shot but you cannot remember if it was 1980 or 1981, so you look up the correct date in an encyclopedia. Do you have to include that encyclopedia as a source for the date on which Reagan was shot?

_____ 3. You do most of your research online and find lots of interesting Web sites from which you quote several passages. After you write the first draft, you ask your older and more experienced roommate if he knows how to cite Web sites. He says that Web sites are in the public domain and constitute common knowledge, and therefore they do not need to be cited. Is this true?

_____ 4. In writing a research paper on astrophysics, you come across something called the Eridanus Effect several times. You have never heard of this effect nor discussed it in your class, but after reading about it in six different astrophysics journal articles, you have a pretty clear idea of what it is and its most common characteristics. Is the Eridanus Effect common knowledge within astrophysics?

_____ 5. Your older sister works for a nonprofit organization that runs adult literacy programs in factories and unemployment centers in several major cities. During winter break, she tells you about the success of one of the programs in St. Louis and the innovative curricula it has designed. Several weeks into spring semester, you remember your conversation as you are writing an economics term paper on empowerment zones and unemployment in the inner city. If you include a description of the program, do you need to cite a source, even if it is just your sister?

_____ 6. You are writing a paper on Shakespeare's *Hamlet*. Your textbook's introduction to the play mentions that Shakespeare was born in 1564 in Stratford-upon-Avon. You mention these facts in your paper's introduction. Do you need to cite the introduction to your textbook?

_____ 7. You are writing a paper on Shakespeare's *Hamlet*. A footnote in your textbook mentions that some literary historians now believe that Shakespeare himself played the ghost when the play was first performed. If you mention Shakespeare playing the ghost, do you need to cite this footnote in your textbook?

_____ 8. You are writing a paper on the assassination of Robert Kennedy. The three major biographies on him mention when he was killed and by whom. Do you have to cite all these biographies when you mention the date and murderer of RFK?

_____ 9. You are writing a paper on the assassination of Robert Kennedy. The most influential biography on him mentions a controversial conspiracy theory first put forward in the early 1970s by a journalist for the *Washington Post*. When you mention this conspiracy theory, should you cite the biography?

Section 3: Quoting, Paraphrasing, and Summarizing Texts

Read the following passage excerpted from an on-line edition of a foreign policy magazine. Determine whether any of the sample sentences that follow are improperly cited within the sentence or plagiarized.

> The illegal trade in drugs, arms, intellectual property, people, and money is booming. Like the war on terrorism, the fight to control these illicit markets pits governments against agile, stateless, and resourceful networks empowered by globalization. Governments will continue to lose these wars until they adopt new strategies to deal with a larger, unprecedented struggle that now shapes the world as much as confrontations between nation-states once did.
>
> —from Moisés Naím, "The Five Wars of Globalization."
> *Foreign Policy* Jan.-Feb. 2003: Web. 13 January 2003.

Read the following passages and mark **OK** if the passage is fine. If the passage is plagiarized, improperly paraphrased, or otherwise cited inadequately, mark it with **X**.

_____ 1. In his essay on "The Five Wars of Globalization," Moisés Naím argues that governments need to find new ways to handle the kinds of borderless illegal activity increasing under globalization.

_____ 2. In describing the "illegal trade in drugs, arms, intellectual property, people, and money" as "booming," Moisés Naím asserts that governments need to adopt new strategies to deal with this unprecedented struggle that now shapes the world (http://www.foreignpolicy.com).

_____ 3. Like the war on terror, the struggle to control illegal trade in drugs, arms, money, etc., pits governments against cunning, stateless, and enterprising networks empowered by globalization (Moises 2003).

_____ 4. Many experts believe that globalization is changing the face of foreign policy.

Read the following passage from a book on romance novels and soap operas, then read the citations of it that follow to determine whether any are plagiarized or improperly cited within the sentence.

> The complexity of women's responses to romances has not been sufficiently acknowledged. Instead of exploring the possibility that romances, while serving to keep women in their place, may at the same time be concerned with real female problems, analysts of women's romances have generally seen the fantasy embodied in romantic fiction either as evidence of female "masochism" or as a simple reflection of the dominant masculine ideology. For instance, Germaine Greer, referring to the idealized males of women's popular novels, says, "This is the hero that women have chosen for themselves. The traits invented for him have been invented by women cherishing the chains of their bondage."[9] But this places too much blame on women, and assumes a freedom of choice which is not often in evidence— not in their lives and therefore certainly not in their popular arts.
>
> —from Tania Modleski, *Loving with a Vengeance: Mass-Produced Fantasies for Women* (New York and London: Methuen, 1982), 37–38. Print.

Read the following passages and mark **OK** if the passage is fine as is. If the passage is plagiarized in part or whole or is otherwise cited improperly, mark it with **X**.

_____ 1. Tania Modleski claims that Germaine Greer oversimplifies why women read romance novels (38).

_____ 2. Modleski states that although romance novels may keep women in their place, they also address real female problems (37).

_____ 3. Feminist critics see the fantasy embodied in romance novels either as evidence of female "masochism" or as a simple reflection of male chauvinism (Modleski 37–38).

_____ 4. One feminist writer, Germaine Greer, says that the idealized male featured in women's popular romance novels "is the hero that women have chosen for themselves. The traits invented for him have been invented by women cherishing the chains of their bondage."(38).

_____ 5. Tania Modleski rejects the idea that the fantasies expressed in romance novels are merely a reflection of some innate masochism in women who, in the words of Germaine Greer, "cherish[...] the chains of their bondage" (37; Greer qtd. in Modleski, 38).

Section 4: Miscellaneous

_____ 1. **You read *Time* magazine every week and notice that the writers in the magazine never use footnotes or parenthetical citations. Why don't news-writers cite their sources?**

    a. Citing sources is only required of students, not professional writers.

b. Professional publications are free to decide if they will require foot-notes or citation of any kind.

c. By law, journalists are exempt from revealing their sources of infor-mation.

d. Newspapers and magazines have limited space on the page, so they cut off the citations or footnotes to make room for more copy.

_____ 2. **What is *not* the proper way to document a Web site in a bibliog-raphy?**

a. Naím, Moisés. (2003, Jan.-Feb.) The Five Wars of Globalization [Elec-tronic version]. *Foreign Policy.* Retrieved Jan. 15, 2003 from www.foreignpolicy.com/wwwboard/fivewars.html

b. Naím, Moisés. "The Five Wars of Globalization," *Foreign Policy* Jan.-Feb. 2003: Online Edition. <http://www.foreignpolicy.com>. Jan. 15, 2003.

c. [12]Naím, Moisés. (2003, Jan.-Feb.) The Five Wars of Globalization [Electronic version]. *Foreign Policy.* Retrieved Jan. 15, 2003 From www.foreignpolicy.com/wwwboard/fivewars.html

d. http://www.foreignpolicy.com/wwwboard/fivewars.html

e. Trick question: Web sites are in the public domain and do not need to be cited.

_____ 3. **Plagiarism is a violation of which of the following laws:**

a. Copyright.

b. Intellectual property.

c. Both (a) and (b) above.

d. None of the above; it is not a legal issue and is not punishable by law because it pertains only to students.

_____ 4. **If you use a quote found in a book of quotes or from an online compilation of quotes, such as Bartlett's, how do you cite the quote?**

a. You don't—quotes found in a collection of quotations (whether on-line or in a book) are considered well-known and in the public do-main. Just include the name of the person to whom the quote is at-tributed. You can also add the date if it seems relevant.

b. You should cite the original source of the quote followed by the bibliographic information from the quotation compilation, such as: Shakespeare, William. *A Midsummer Night's Dream.* Quoted in *Familiar Quotations: Being an Attempt to Trace to Their Sources Passages and Phrases in Common Use,* by John Bartlett (Boston: Little, Brown, 1886), 44.

c. You should find the original source and cite that.

d. All of the above: (a) is correct, and (b) and (c) are possible options if you want to be extra careful or if the quote is extremely important to your paper. Use your common sense in this situation.

Answer Key to Plagiarism Quiz

The Plagiarism Quiz works best when the answers are discussed in class or one-on-one with a student and professor.

Section 1: Plagiarism and Academic Dishonesty

All eight incidents are forms of plagiarism or academic dishonesty. Many students are confused about the last four incidents, so please discuss them with your instructor if you need clarification.

Section 2: Common Knowledge

1. No; the basic facts about the checks-and-balances system are common knowledge and do not need to be cited.
2. No; even if you cannot remember the exact date of the assassination attempt on Reagan, it is common knowledge because the date is undisputed and can be found in a variety of sources.
3. No; writing on the Web is protected by copyright and must be cited, even if no author is listed.
4. Yes; it's common knowledge if it appears *undocumented* in five or more sources.
5. Yes; such a small program would not be widely known, so you should cite your sister as a source if you mention it. If you describe the program in more detail, it would make sense to research documents or newspaper descriptions and cite these rather than Big Sis.
6. No; the date and location of Shakespeare's birth is not in dispute and can be found in many sources, so it is common knowledge even if you did not know it.
7. Hmmm. This is a tricky situation. Since *some,* but not all, literary historians believe Shakespeare himself played the ghost, this is probably common knowledge among Shakespeare experts. You, however, are not a Shakespeare expert, so it would be wise to cite the footnote just to be safe. So, the answer is, Yes—cite it!
8. No; undisputed dates are common knowledge.
9. Yes; conspiracy theories are controversial, and the details of such controversies need to be cited.

Section 3: Quoting, Paraphrasing, and Summarizing Texts

Illegal Trade Passage:

1. OK; an example of summary. The sentence gives the author and the title. (Remember, the bibliography would provide more publication information.)
2. X; two things are wrong: some of the language is too similar to the original, and the citation method is incorrect. Do not list the URL in your paper. The phrase "adopt new strategies to deal with this unprecedented struggle that now shapes the world" is too close to the source, in some places identical to it.
3. X; this paraphrase is too close to the original. The writer used a thesaurus to change key words, but the sentence structure is identical to the original. Plus, the author's last name (not first name) should appear in the parenthetical citation. (Also, using "etc" in the text is annoying!)
4. OK; This is common knowledge. The sentence is so general, it really has nothing to do with the passage from Moisés Naím, so there is no reason to cite him.

Romance Novel Passage:

1. OK; this summary is correct; the author's name appears in the sentence so it does not need to appear in the parenthetical citation.
2. X; although the source is documented properly, some of the language is too close to the source, especially the phrases "keep women in their place" and "real female problems." These phrases need to be put into quotation marks or rewritten.
3. X; most of this sentence is copied directly from the source; it needs to be rewritten or partially enclosed in quotes.
4. X; the quote is properly attributed to Greer, but the page number refers to Modleski's book. Also, there's no need to copy the footnote from the original.
5. OK; this example shows how to properly cite one writer quoted within the work of another. Also note how the ellipses and brackets indicate how the "-ing" part of "cherish" was deleted to make the quote flow better. The ellipses indicate that something was deleted; the brackets indicate that the ellipses were not in the original source.

Section 4: Miscellaneous

1. (c)
2. (d); (a) is an example of APA method of documenting Web sites; (b) is MLA; (c) is an APA footnote.
3. (c)
4. (d)

Remarks About Manuscript Form

Basic Manuscript Form

Much of what follows is nothing more than common sense.

- Use good quality **8½″ × 11″** paper. Print out a second copy, in case the instructor's copy goes astray. Make sure also to back up the file on an external hard drive or CD, or in your e-mail account.
- If you write on a computer, **double-space,** and print on one side of the page only; set the printer for professional or best quality.
- Use **one-inch margins** on all sides.
- Put your last name and then the **page number** (in arabic numerals), so that the number is flush with the right-hand margin and one-half inch from the top margin.
- On the first page, below the top margin and flush with the left-hand margin, put your **full name,** your **instructor's name,** the **course number** (including the section), and the **date,** one item per line, double-spaced.
- **Center the title** of your essay. Remember that the title is important—it gives readers their first glimpse of your essay. **Create your own title—** one that reflects your topic or thesis. For example, a paper on Charlotte Perkins Gilman's "The Yellow Wallpaper" should not be called "The Yellow Wallpaper" but might be called

  Disguised Tyranny in Gilman's "The Yellow Wallpaper"

  or

  How to Drive a Woman Mad

  These titles do at least a little in the way of rousing a reader's interest.
- **Capitalize the title thus:** Begin the first word of the title with a capital letter, and capitalize each subsequent word except articles (*a, an, the*), conjunctions (*and, but, if, when,* etc.), and prepositions (*in, on, with,* etc.):

A Word on Behalf of Love

Notice that you do *not* enclose your title within quotation marks, and you do *not* underline it—though if it includes the title of a poem or a story, *that* is enclosed within quotation marks, or if it includes the title of a novel or play, *that* is set in italics, thus:

Gilman's "The Yellow Wallpaper" and Medical Practice

and

Gender Stereotypes in *Hamlet*

- **After writing your title, double-space,** indent one-half inch and begin your first sentence.
- Unless your instructor tells you otherwise, **use a staple** to hold the pages together. (Do not use a stiff binder; it will only add to the bulk of the instructor's stack of papers.)
- Extensive revisions should have been made in your drafts, but minor **last-minute revisions** may be made—neatly—on the finished copy if your instructor permits. Proofreading may catch some typographical errors, and you may notice some small weaknesses.

Quotations and Quotation Marks

First, a word about the *point* of using quotations. Don't use quotations to pad the length of a paper. Rather, give quotations from the work you are discussing so that your readers will see the material being considered and (especially in a research paper) so that your readers will know what some of the chief interpretations are and what your responses to them are.

(*Note:* The next few paragraphs do *not* discuss how to include citations of sources, a topic taken up a little later in this appendix, under the heading "Documentation.")

The Golden Rule: If you quote, *comment on* the quotation. Let the reader know what you make of it and why you quote it.

Additional principles:

- **Identify the speaker or writer of the quotation** so that the reader is not left with a sense of uncertainty. Usually, in accordance with the principle of letting readers know where they are going, this identification precedes the quoted material, but occasionally it may follow the quotation, especially if it will provide something of a pleasant surprise. For instance, in a discussion of Flannery O'Connor's stories, you might quote a disparaging comment on one of the stories and then reveal that O'Connor herself was the speaker.
- If the quotation is part of your own sentence, **be sure to fit the quotation grammatically and logically into your sentence.**

  Incorrect: Holden Caulfield tells us very little about "what my lousy childhood was like."
  Correct: Holden Caulfield tells us very little about what his "lousy childhood was like."

- **Indicate any omissions or additions.** The quotation must be exact. Any material that you add—even one or two words—must be enclosed within square brackets, thus:

> Hawthorne tells us that "owing doubtless to the depth of the gloom at that particular spot [in the forest], neither the travellers nor their steeds were visible."

If you wish to omit material from within a quotation, indicate the ellipsis by three spaced periods. That is, at the point where you are omitting material, type a space, a period, a space, a period, a space, and a third period. If you are omitting material from the end of a sentence, the first period is not preceded by a space; it immediately follows the last letter of the last word and is then followed by a space, a period, a space, a period, a space, and a period to indicate the end of the sentence. The following example is based on a quotation from the sentences immediately above this one:

> The instructions say, "If you . . . omit material from within a quotation, [you must] indicate the ellipsis. . . . If you are omitting material from the end of a sentence, the first period is not preceded by a space; it . . . is then followed by a space, a period, a space, a period, a space, and a period to indicate the end. . . ."

Notice that although material preceded "If you," periods are not needed to indicate the omission because "If you" began a sentence in the original. Customarily, initial and terminal omissions are indicated only when they are part of the sentence you are quoting. Even such omissions need not be indicated when the quoted material is obviously incomplete—when, for instance, it is a word or phrase.

- **Distinguish between short and long quotations,** and treat each appropriately. **Short quotations** (usually defined as four or fewer lines of typed prose or three lines of poetry) are enclosed within quotation marks and run into the text (rather than being set off, without quotation marks), as in the following example:

> Hawthorne begins the story by telling us that "Young Goodman Brown came forth at sunset into the street at Salem village" (624), thus at the outset connecting the village with daylight. A few paragraphs later, when Hawthorne tells us that the road Brown takes was "darkened by all of the gloomiest trees of the forest" (624), he begins to associate the forest with darkness—and a very little later with evil.

If your short quotation is from a poem, be sure to follow the capitalization of the original, and use a slash mark (with a space before and after it) to indicate separate lines. Give the line numbers, if your source gives them, in parentheses, immediately after the closing quotation marks and before the closing punctuation, thus:

> In "Diving into the Wreck," Adrienne Rich's speaker says that she puts on "body-armor" (5). Obviously the journey is dangerous.

To set off a **long quotation** (more than four typed lines of prose or more than two lines of poetry), indent the entire quotation ten spaces or one inch from the left margin. Usually, a long quotation is introduced by a clause ending with a colon, as shown here:

> The following passage will make this point clear:

or

> The closest we come to hearing an editorial voice is a long passage in the middle of the story:

Or some such lead-in. After typing your lead-in, double-space, and then type the quotation, indented and double-spaced.

- **Place commas and periods inside the quotation marks.** If you are quoting some material within a sentence of your own, and you need to use a comma or a period, these marks of punctuation go *before* the closing quotation mark, as in the following example, in which the author uses a comma after "trouble" and a period after "disease."

> Chopin tells us in the first sentence that "Mrs. Mallard was afflicted with heart trouble," and in the last sentence the doctors say that Mrs. Mallard "died of heart disease."

Exception: If the quotation is immediately followed by material in parentheses or in square brackets, close the quotation, then give the parenthetic or bracketed material, and then—after closing the parenthesis or bracket—insert the comma or period.

> Chopin tells us in the first sentence that "Mrs. Mallard was afflicted with heart trouble" (22), and in the last sentence the doctors say that Mrs. Mallard "died of heart disease" (24).

- **Place semicolons, colons, and dashes outside the closing quotation marks.**
- **Place question marks and exclamation points** inside if they are part of the quotation, outside if they are your own.

    In the following passage from a student's essay, notice the difference in the position of the question marks. The first question mark is part of the quotation, so it is enclosed within the quotation marks. The second question mark, however, is the student's, so it comes after the closing quotation marks.

> The older man says to Goodman Brown, "Sayest thou so?" Doesn't a reader become uneasy when the man immediately adds, "We are but a little way in the forest yet"?

Quotation Marks or Italics?

Use quotation marks around titles of short stories and other short works—that is, titles of chapters in books, essays, and poems that might not be published by themselves. Use italics for titles of books, periodicals, collections of essays, plays, and long poems such as *The Rime of the Ancient Mariner.*

A Note on the Possessive

It is awkward to use the possessive case for titles of literary works and secondary sources. Rather than "*The Great Gatsby*'s final chapter," write instead "the final chapter of *The Great Gatsby.*" Not "*The Oxford Companion to American Literature*'s entry on Emerson," but, instead, "the entry on Emerson in *The Oxford Companion to American Literature.*"

Documentation: Internal Parenthetical Citations and a List of Works Cited (MLA Format)

Documentation tells your reader exactly what your sources are. Below we describe how to make internal parenthetical citations and the works cited list.

Internal Parenthetical Citations

On pages 1454–55 we distinguish between embedded quotations (which are short, are run right into your own sentence, and are enclosed in quotation marks) and quotations that are set off on the page and are not enclosed in quotation marks (for example, three or more lines of poetry, five or more lines of typed prose).

For an embedded quotation, put the page reference in parentheses immediately after the closing quotation marks *without* any intervening punctuation. Then, after the parenthesis that follows the number, insert the necessary punctuation (for instance, a comma or a period):

> Brent Staples says that he "learned to smother the rage" he felt at "often being
> taken for a criminal" (303).

The period comes *after* the parenthetical citation. In the next example *no* punctuation comes after the first citation—because none is needed—and a comma comes *after* (not before or within) the second citation, because a comma is needed in the sentence:

> This is ironic because almost at the start of the story, in the second
> paragraph, Richards with the best of motives "hastened" (23) to bring
> his sad message; if he had at the start been "too late" (24), Mallard
> would have arrived at home first.

For a quotation that is not embedded within the text but is set off (by being indented ten spaces), put the parenthetical citation on the last line of the quotation, one space *after* the period that ends the quoted sentence.
Four additional points:

- The abbreviations *p., pg.,* and *pp.* are *not* used in citing pages.
- If a story is very short, perhaps running for only a page or two, your instructor may tell you there is no need to keep citing the page reference for each quotation.

- If you are referring to a poem, your instructor may tell you to use parenthetical citations of line numbers rather than of page numbers.
- If you are referring to a play with numbered lines, your instructor may prefer that in your parenthetical citations you give act, scene, and line, rather than page numbers. Use arabic (not roman) numerals, separating the act from the scene, and the scene from the line, by periods. Here, then, is how a reference to Act 3, Scene 2, line 105 would be given:

> When Hamlet says to Ophelia, "That's a fair thought to lie between maids' legs
> (3.2.105), she does not understand that he is making a lewd comment.

Parenthetical Citations and List of Works Cited

Parenthetical citations are clarified by means of a list, headed "Works Cited," given at the end of the essay. In this list you give alphabetically (last name first) the authors and titles that you have quoted or referred to in the essay.

Briefly, the idea is that the reader of your paper encounters an author's name and a parenthetical citation of pages. By checking the author's name in works cited, the reader can find the passage in the book. Suppose you are writing about Kate Chopin's "The Story of an Hour." Let's assume that you have already mentioned the author and the title of the story—that is, you have let the reader know the subject of the essay—and now you introduce a quotation from the story in a sentence such as this. (Notice the parenthetical citation of page numbers immediately after the quotation.)

> True, Mrs. Mallard at first expresses grief when she hears the news, but soon
> (unknown to her friends) she finds joy in it. So, Richards's "sad message" (67),
> though sad in Richards's eyes, is in fact a happy message.

Turning to works cited, the reader, knowing the quoted words are by Chopin, looks for Chopin and finds the following:

> Chopin, Kate. "The Story of an Hour." *An Introduction to Literature*, Ed. Sylvan
>   Barnet, William Burto, and William E. Cain. 16th ed. New York: Longman,
>   2011. 67–68. Print.

Thus the essayist is informing the reader that the quoted words ("sad message") are to be found on page 67 of this anthology.

If you have not mentioned Chopin's name in some sort of lead-in, you will have to give her name within the parentheses so that the reader will know the author of the quoted words:

> What are we to make out of a story that ends by telling us that the leading
> character has died "of joy that kills" (Chopin 68)?

The closing quotation marks come immediately after the last word of the quotation; the citation and the final punctuation—in this case, the essayist's question mark—come *after* the closing quotation marks.

If you are comparing Chopin's story with Gilman's "The Yellow Wallpaper," in works cited you will give a similar entry for Gilman—her name, the title of the story, the book in which it is reprinted, and the page numbers that the story occupies.

If you are referring to several works reprinted within one volume, instead of listing each item fully, it is acceptable in works cited to list each item simply by giving the author's name, the title of the work, then a period, a space, and the name of the anthologist, followed by the page numbers that the selection spans. Thus a reference to Chopin's "The Story of an Hour" would be followed only by: Barnet 45–47. This form requires that the anthology itself be cited under the name of the first-listed editor, thus:

> Barnet, Sylvan, William Burto, and William E. Cain, eds. *An Introduction to Literature,* 16th ed. New York: Longman, 2011. Print.

If you are writing a research paper, you will use many sources. In the essay itself you will mention an author's name, quote or summarize from this author, and follow the quotation or summary with a parenthetical citation of the pages. In works cited you will give the full title, place of publication, and other bibliographic material.

Here are a few examples, all referring to an article by Joan Templeton, "The *Doll House* Backlash: Criticism, Feminism, and Ibsen." The article appeared in *PMLA* 104 (1989): 28–40, but this information is given only in works cited, not within the text of the student's essay.

If in the text of your essay you mention the author's name, the citation following a quotation (or a summary of a passage) is merely a page number in parentheses, followed by a period, thus:

> In 1989 Joan Templeton argued that many critics, unhappy with recognizing Ibsen as a feminist, sought "to render Nora inconsequential" (29).

Or:

> In 1989 Joan Templeton noted that many critics, unhappy with recognizing Ibsen as a feminist, have sought to make Nora trivial (29).

If you don't mention the name of the author in a lead-in, you will have to give the name within the parenthetical citation:

> Many critics, attempting to argue that Ibsen was not a feminist, have tried to make Nora trivial (Templeton 29).

Notice in all of these examples that the final period comes after the parenthetical citation. *Exception:* If the quotation is longer than four lines and is therefore set off by being indented ten spaces from the left margin, end the quotation with the appropriate punctuation (period, question mark, or exclamation mark), hit the space bar twice, and type (in parentheses) the page number. In this case, do not put a period after the citation.

Another point: If your list of works cited includes more than one work by an author, in your essay when you quote or refer to one or the other you'll have to identify *which* work you are drawing on. You can provide the title in a lead-in, thus:

> In "The *Doll House* Backlash: Criticism, Feminism, and Ibsen," Templeton says, "Nora's detractors have often been, from the first, her husband's defenders" (30).

Or you can provide the information in the parenthetic citation, giving a shortened version of the title. This usually consists of the first word, unless it is *A, An,* or *The,* in which case including the second word is usually enough. Certain titles may require still another word or two, as in this example:

> According to Templeton, "Nora's detractors have often been, from the first, her husband's defenders" (*"Doll House* Backlash" 30).

Forms of Citation in Works Cited

In looking over the following samples of entries in works cited, remember:

- The list of works cited appears at the end of the paper. It begins on a new page, and the page continues the numbering of the text.
- The list of works cited is arranged alphabetically by author (last name first).
- If a work is anonymous, list it under the first word of the title unless the first word is *A, An,* or *The,* in which case list it under the second word.
- If a work is by two authors, although the book is listed alphabetically under the first author's last name, the second author's name is given in the normal order, first name first.
- If you list two or more works by the same author, the author's name is not repeated but is represented by three hyphens followed by a period and a space.
- Each item begins flush left, but if an entry is longer than one line, subsequent lines in the entry are indented five spaces.

For details about almost every imaginable kind of citation, consult Joseph Gibaldi, *MLA Handbook for Writers of Research Papers,* 7th ed. (New York: Modern Language Association, 2009). We give here, however, information concerning the most common kinds of citations.

For citations of electronic sources, see pages 1464–67.

Here are samples of the kinds of citations you are most likely to include in your list of works cited.

A book by one author:

Douglas, Ann. *The Feminization of American Culture.* New York: Knopf, 1977. Print.

Notice that the author's last name is given first, but otherwise the name is given as on the title page. Do not substitute initials for names written out on the title page, but you may shorten the publisher's name—for example, from Little, Brown and Company to Little.

Take the title from the title page, not from the cover or the spine, but disregard unusual typography—for instance, the use of only capital letters or the use of & for *and.* Italicize the title and subtitle. The place of publication is indicated by the name of the city. If the title page lists several cities, give only the first. For print sources, use the word "Print" at the end of each entry.

A book by two or three authors:

Gilbert, Sandra, and Susan Gubar. *The Madwoman in the Attic: The Woman Writer and the Nineteenth-Century Literary Imagination.* New Haven: Yale UP, 1979. Print.

Notice that the book is listed under the last name of the first author (Gilbert) and that the second author's name is then given with first name (Susan) first. *If the book has more than three authors*, give the name of the first author only (last name first) and follow it with *et al.* (Latin for "and others").

A book by more than three authors:

Beidler, Peter G., et al. *A Reader's Companion to J. D. Salinger's* The Catcher in the Rye. Seattle: Coffeetown Press, 2009. Print.

A book in several volumes:

McQuade, Donald, et al. eds. *The Harper American Literature*. 2nd ed. 2 vols. New York: HarperCollins, 1994. Print.

Pope, Alexander. *The Correspondence of Alexander Pope*. 5 vols. Ed. George Sherburn. Oxford: Clarendon, 1955. Print.

The total number of volumes is given after the title, regardless of the number that you have used.

If you have used more than one volume, within your essay you will parenthetically indicate a reference to, for instance, page 30 of volume 3 thus: (3: 30). If you have used only one volume of a multivolume work—let's say you used only volume 2 of McQuade's anthology—in your entry in works cited write, after the period following the date, Vol. 2. In your parenthetical citation within the essay you will therefore cite only the page reference (without the volume number), since the reader will (on consulting works cited) understand that in this example the reference is in volume 2.

If, instead of using the volumes as a whole, you used only an independent work within one volume—say, an essay in volume 2—in works cited omit the abbreviation *Vol.* Instead, give an arabic 2 (indicating volume 2) followed by a colon, a space, and the page numbers that encompass the selection you used:

McPherson, James Alan. "Why I Like Country Music." *The Harper American Literature*. Ed. Donald McQuade, et al. 2nd ed. 2 vols. New York: Longman, 1994. 2: 2304–15. Print.

Notice that this entry for McPherson specifies not only that the book consists of two volumes, but also that only one selection ("Why I Like Country Music," occupying pages 2304–2315 in volume 2) was used. If you use this sort of citation in works cited, in the body of your essay a documentary reference to this work will be only to the page; the volume number will *not* be added.

A book with a separate title in a set of volumes:

Churchill, Winston. *The Age of Revolution*. Vol. 3 of *A History of the English-Speaking Peoples*. New York: Dodd, 1957. Print.

Jonson, Ben. *The Complete Masques*. Ed. Stephen Orgel. Vol. 4 of *The Yale Ben Jonson*. New Haven: Yale UP, 1969. Print.

A revised edition of a book:

Chaucer, Geoffrey. *The Riverside Chaucer*. Ed. Larry Benson. 3rd ed. Boston: Houghton, 1987. Print.

Ellmann, Richard. *James Joyce*. Rev. ed. New York: Oxford UP, 1982. Print.

A reprint, such as a paperback version of an older hardcover book:

> Rourke, Constance. *American Humor*. 1931. Garden City, New York: Doubleday,
> 1953. Print.

Notice that the entry cites the original date (1931) but indicates that the writer is using the Doubleday reprint of 1953.

An edited book other than an anthology:

> Keats, John. *The Letters of John Keats*. Ed. Hyder Edward Rollins. 2 vols.
> Cambridge, MA.: Harvard UP, 1958. Print.

An anthology: List an anthology under the editor's name.

> Barnet, Sylvan, William Burto, and William E. Cain, eds. *An Introduction to Liter-*
> *ature,* 16th ed. New York: Longman, 2011. Print.

A work in a volume of works by one author:

> Sontag, Susan. "The Aesthetics of Silence." In *Styles of Radical Will*. New York:
> Farrar, 1969. 3–34. Print.

This entry indicates that Sontag's essay, called "The Aesthetics of Silence," appears in a book of hers entitled *Styles of Radical Will.* Notice that the page numbers of the short work are cited (not page numbers that you may happen to refer to, but the page numbers of the entire piece).

A work in an anthology, that is, in a collection of works by several authors: Begin with the author and the title of the work you are citing, not with the name of the anthologist or the title of the anthology. The entry ends with the pages occupied by the selection you are citing:

> Ng, Fae Myenne. "A Red Sweater." *Charlie Chan Is Dead: An Anthology of Contem-*
> *porary Asian American Fiction*. Ed. Jessica Hagedorn. New York: Penguin,
> 1993. 358–68. Print.

Normally, you will give the title of the work you are citing (probably an essay, short story, or poem) in quotation marks. If you are referring to a book-length work (for instance, a novel or a full-length play), italicize it. If the work is translated, after the period that follows the title, write *Trans.* and give the name of the translator, followed by a period and the name of the anthology.

If the collection is a multivolume work and you are using only one volume, in works cited you will specify the volume, as in the example (page 1460) of McPherson's essay. Because the list of works cited specifies the volume, your parenthetical documentary reference within your essay will specify (as mentioned earlier) only the page numbers, not the volume. Thus, although McPherson's essay appears on pages 2304–2315 in the second volume of a two-volume work, a parenthetical citation will refer only to the page numbers because the citation in works cited specifies the volume.

Remember that the pages specified in the entry in your list of works cited are to the *entire selection*, not simply to pages you may happen to refer to within your paper.

If you are referring to a *reprint of a scholarly article*, give details of the original publication, as in the following example:

> Mack, Maynard. "The World of Hamlet." *Yale Review* 41 (1952): 502–23. Rpt. in
>   *Hamlet*. By William Shakespeare. Ed. Sylvan Barnet. New York: Penguin
>   Putnam, 1998. 265-87. Print.

Two or more works in an anthology: If you are referring to more than one work in an anthology in order to avoid repeating all the information about the anthology in each entry in works cited, under each author's name (in the appropriate alphabetical place) give the author and title of the work, then a period, a space, and the name of the anthologist, followed by the page numbers that the selection spans. Thus, a reference to Shakespeare's Hamlet would be followed only by

> Barnet 913–1016

rather than by a full citation of Barnet's anthology. This form requires that the anthology itself also be listed, under Barnet.

Two or more works by the same author: Notice that the works are given in alphabetical order (*Fables* precedes *Fools*) and that the author's name is not repeated but is represented by three hyphens followed by a period and a space. If the author is the translator or editor of a volume, the three hyphens are followed not by a period but by a comma, then a space, then the appropriate abbreviation (*Trans.* or *Ed.*), then the title:

> Frye, Northrop. *Fables of Identity: Studies in Poetic Mythology*. New York: Harcourt,
>   1963. Print.
> - - -. *Fools of Time: Studies in Shakespearean Tragedy*. Toronto: U of Toronto P,
>   1967. Print.

A translated book:

> Gogol, Nikolai. *Dead Souls*. Trans. Andrew McAndrew. New York: New American
>   Library, 1961. Print.

If you are discussing the translation itself, as opposed to the book, list the work under the translator's name. Then put a comma, a space, and "trans." After the period following "trans," skip a space, then give the title of the book, a period, a space, and then "By" and the author's name, first name first. Continue with information about the place of publication, publisher, and date, as in any entry for a book.

An introduction, foreword, or afterword, or other editorial apparatus:

> Fromm, Erich. Afterword. *1984*. By George Orwell. New York: New American
>   Library, 1961. Print.

Usually a book with an introduction or some such comparable material is listed under the name of the author of the book rather than the name of the author of the editorial material (see the entry for Pope on page 1460). But if you are referring to the editor's apparatus rather than to the work itself, use the form just given.

Words such as *preface, introduction, afterword,* and *conclusion* are capitalized in the entry but are neither enclosed within quotation marks nor underlined.

A book review: Here is an example of a review that does not have a title.

Vendler, Helen. Rev. of *Essays on Style.* Ed. Roger Fowler. *Essays in Criticism* 16

(1966): 457–63. Print.

If the review has a title, give the title after the period following the reviewer's name, before "Rev." If the review is unsigned, list it under the first word of the title, or the second word if the first word is *A, An,* or *The.* If an unsigned review has no title, begin the entry with "Rev. of" and alphabetize it under the title of the work being reviewed.

An encyclopedia: The first example is for a signed article, the second for an unsigned article.

Lang, Andrew. "Ballads." *Encyclopaedia Britannica.* 1910 ed. Print.

"Metaphor." *The New Encyclopaedia Britannica: Micropaedia.* 1974 ed. Print.

An article in a scholarly journal: Some journals are paginated consecutively; that is, the pagination of the second issue picks up where the first issue left off. Other journals begin each issue with a new page 1. The forms of the citations in works cited differ slightly.

The citation of a *journal that uses continuous pagination:*

Burbick, Joan. "Emily Dickinson and the Economics of Desire."

American Literature 58 (1986): 361–78. Print.

This article appeared in volume 58, which was published in 1986. (Notice that the volume number is followed by a space, then by the year in parentheses, and then by a colon, a space, and the page numbers of the entire article.) Although each volume consists of four issues, you do *not* specify the issue number when the journal is paginated continuously.

For a *journal that paginates each issue separately* (a quarterly journal will have four page 1's each year), give the issue number directly after the volume number and a period, with no spaces before or after the period:

Spillers, Hortense J. "Martin Luther King and the Style of the Black Sermon." *The*

Black Scholar 3.1 (1971): 14–27. Print.

An article in a weekly, biweekly, or monthly publication:

McCabe, Bernard. "Taking Dickens Seriously." *Commonweal* 14 May 1965: 24.

Print.

Notice that the volume number and the issue number are omitted for popular weeklies or monthlies such as *Time* and *Atlantic.*

An article in a newspaper: Because newspapers usually consist of several sections, a section number may precede the page number. The example indicates that an article begins on page 3 of section 2 and is continued on a later page:

Wu, Jim. "Authors Praise New Forms." *New York Times* 8 Mar. 1996, sec. 2: 3+.
Print.

You may also have occasion to cite something other than a printed source, for instance, a lecture. Here are the forms for the chief nonprint sources.

An interview:

Saretta, Howard. Personal interview. 3 Nov. 2008.

A lecture:

Heaney, Seamus. Tufts University, Medford. 15 Oct. 1998. Lecture.

A television or radio program:

60 Minutes. CBS. WCBS, New York. 30 Jan. 1994. Television.

A film or video recording:

Modern Times. Dir. Charles Chaplin. United Artists, 1936. Film.

A sound recording:

Frost, Robert. "The Road Not Taken." *Robert Frost Reads His Poetry*. Caedmon, TC
1060, 1956. LP.

A performance:

The Cherry Orchard. By Anton Chekhov. Dir. Ron Daniels. American Repertory
Theatre, Cambridge. 3 Feb. 1994. Performance.

Reminder: For the form of citations of electronic material, see the section that
follows.

Citing Sources on the World Wide Web

Many Web sites and pages are not prepared according to the style and form in
which you want to cite them. Sometimes the name of the author is unknown,
and other information may be missing or hard to find as well. Perhaps the main
point to remember is that a source on the WWW is as much a source as is a
book or article that you can track down and read in the library. If you have
made use of it, you must acknowledge that you have done so and include the
bibliographical information, as fully as you can, in your list of works cited for
the paper.

The Wellesley College Library offers a valuable site for searching the Web
and evaluating what you find there:

http://www.wellesley.edu/Library/Research/citation.html

✔ CHECKLIST: *Citing Sources on the Web*

Provide the following information:

❑ Author's name.
❑ Title of work in quotation marks or in italics if a longer work or book title.
❑ Title of Web site set in italics followed by a period.
❑ Publisher or sponsor of Web site followed by a comma. (Use *N.p.* if that information is not available.)
❑ Date of publication, followed by a period. (Use *n.d.* if that information is not available.)
❑ Publication medium—*Web*—followed by a period.
❑ Date of access—when you accessed the site.
❑ Include the URL only when your reader cannot locate the source without it.

A short work within a scholarly project:

> Whitman, Walt, "Crossing Brooklyn Ferry." *The Walt Whitman Archive*. Ed. Kenneth M. Price and Ed Folson. The Walt Whitman Archive. 16 Mar 1998. Web. 3 April 2008.

1. Author's name
2. Title of work in italics
3. Title of overall Web site in italics
4. Editors of Web site if available
5. Version or edition used
6. Publisher or sponsor of the site. If not available use *N.p.*
7. Date of publication
8. Medium of publication (*Web*)
9. Date of access

A personal or professional site:

> Winter, Mick *How to Talk New Age*. The Well. 6 Jan. 2004. Web. 6 April 2009.

An online book published independently:

> Smith, Adam. *The Wealth of Nations*. New York: Methuen. 1904. *Bibliomania*. Web. 3 Mar. 2008.

1. Author's name
2. Title of work in italics
3. Edition used
4. City of publication, publisher, and year of publication
5. Title of the database or Web site in italics
6. Medium of publication (*Web*)
7. Date of access (day, month, and year)

An online book within a scholarly project:

> Whitman, Walt. *Leaves of Grass*. Philadelphia: McKay, 1891–92. *The Walt Whitman Archive*. Ed. Kenneth M. Price and Ed Folson. The Walt Whitman Archive. 16 Mar 1998. Web. 3 April 2008.

An article in an online scholarly journal:

> Jackson, Francis L. "Mexican Freedom: The Ideal of the Indigenous State." *Animus* 2.3 (1997). N. pag. Web. 4 Apr. 2009.

1. Author's name
2. Title of article in quotation marks
3. Name of the publication in italics
4. Series number or name
5. Volume number
6. Issue number if available
7. Date of publication
8. Inclusive page numbers if available (use *N. pag.* if no pages are cited)
9. Medium of publication (*Web*)
10. Date of access (day, month, and year)

An unsigned article in a newspaper or on a newswire:

> "Drug Czar Wants to Sharpen Drug War." *TopNews* 6 Apr. 1998. N. pag. Web. 6 Apr. 2008.

An unsigned article in a newspaper or on a Web site:

> "Hiking: Richard W. DeKorte Park, Lyndhurst." *NorthJersey.com*. 2 July 2009. N. pag. Web. 10 July 2009.

An article in a magazine:

> Pitta, Julie. "Un-Wired?" *Forbes.com*. 20 April 1998. N. pag. Web. 6 April 2009.

A review:

> Beer, Francis A. Rev. of *Evolutionary Paradigms in the Social Sciences, Special Issue, International Studies Quarterly* 40, 3 (Sept. 1996). N. pag. *Journal of Memetics* 1 (1997). Web. 4 Jan. 2008.

An editorial or letter to the editor:

> "The Net Escape Censorship? Ha!" Editorial. *Wired*. 3.09. Web. 1 Apr. 2009.

A periodical source on CD-ROM or DVD-ROM:

> Ellis, Richard. "Whale Killing Begins Anew." *Audubon* [GAUD] 94.6 (1992): 20–22. *General Periodicals Ondisc-Magazine Express*. CD-ROM. UMI-Proquest. 1992.

1. Author's name
2. Publication information for analogous printed source (title and date)
3. Publication medium

4. Title of database
5. Name of vendor
6. Publication date of the database

A nonperiodical source on CD-ROM or DVD-ROM:

Clements, John. "War of 1812." *Chronology of the United States.* Dallas: Political
Research, Inc. 1997. CD-ROM.

1. Author's, editor's, compiler's, or translator's name (if given)
2. Title of the publication
3. Name of the editor, compiler, or translator (if relevant) of entire volume, if
   work appears in a collection
4. Edition, release, or version
5. Place of publication
6. Name of publisher
7. Date of publication
8. Medium of publication consulted
9. Supplementary information

E-mail:

Mendez, Michael R. "Re: Solar power." Message to Edgar V. Atamian. 11 Sept.
2009. E-mail.

Armstrong, David J. Message to the author. 30 Aug. 2009. E-mail.

AN ONLINE POSTING

For online postings or synchronous communications, try to cite a version stored
as a Web file, if one exists, as a courtesy to the reader. Label sources as needed
(e.g., *Online posting, Online defense of dissertation,* and so forth, with neither
underlining nor quotation marks). See the models that follow:

Listserv (electronic mailing lists):

Kosten, A. "Major update of the WWWVL Migration and Ethnic Relations." 7 Apr.
1998. Online posting. ERCOMER News. 7 May 1998.

Computer Software:

Gamma UniType for Windows 1.5. Vers. 1.1. San Diego: Gamma Productions, Inc.,
1997.

Glossary of Literary Terms

The terms briefly defined here are for the most part more fully defined earlier in the text. Hence many of the entries are followed by page references to the earlier discussions.

accent stress given to a syllable.

act a major division of a play.

action (1) the happenings in a narrative or drama, usually physical events (*B* marries *C*, *D* kills *E*), but also mental changes (*F* moves from innocence to experience); in short, the answer to the question, "What happens?" (2) less commonly, the theme or underlying idea of a work. (843)

allegory a work in which concrete elements (for instance, a pilgrim, a road, a splendid city) stand for abstractions (humanity, life, salvation), usually in an unambiguous, one-to-one relationship. The literal items (the pilgrim, and so on) thus convey a meaning, which is usually moral, religious, or political. To take a nonliterary example: The Statue of Liberty holds a torch (enlightenment, showing the rest of the world the way to freedom), and at her feet are broken chains (tyranny overcome). A caution: Not all of the details in an allegorical work are meant to be interpreted. For example, the hollowness of the Statue of Liberty does not stand for the insubstantiality or emptiness of liberty. (208)

alliteration repetition of consonant sounds, especially at the beginnings of words: *f*ree, *f*orm, *ph*antom. (668)

allusion an indirect reference; thus when Lincoln spoke of "a nation dedicated to the proposition that all men are created equal," he was making an allusion to the Declaration of Independence.

ambiguity multiplicity of meaning, often deliberate, that leaves the reader uncertain about the intended significance.

anagnorisis a recognition or discovery, especially in tragedy—for example, when the hero understands the reason for his or her fall. (907)

analysis an examination, which usually proceeds by separating the object of study into parts. (5, 52, 80)

anapest a metrical foot consisting of two unaccented syllables followed by an accented one. Example, showing three anapests: "As I came / to the edge / of the wood." (666)

anecdote a short narrative, usually reporting an amusing event in the life of an important person. (363)

antagonist a character or force that opposes (literally, "wrestles") the protagonist (the main character). Thus, in *Hamlet* the antagonist is King Claudius, the protagonist is Hamlet; in *Antigone*, the antagonist is Creon, the protagonist, Antigone.

antecedent action happenings (especially in a play) that occurred before the present action. (843)

apostrophe address to an absent figure or to a thing as if it were present and could listen. Example:"O rose, thou art sick!" (626)

approximate rhyme see *half-rhyme.*

archetype a theme, image, motif, or pattern that occurs so often in literary works it seems to be universal. Examples: a dark forest (for mental confusion), the sun (for illumination).

aside in the theater, words spoken by a character in the presence of other characters, but directed to the spectators (i.e., understood by the audience to be inaudible to the other characters). (844)

assonance repetition of similar vowel sounds in stressed syllables. Example: *light/bride.* (668)

atmosphere the emotional tone (for instance, joy or horror) in a work, most often established by the setting.

ballad a short narrative poem, especially one that is sung or recited, often in a stanza of four lines, with 8, 6, 8, 6 syllables, with the second and fourth lines rhyming. A **folk ballad** or **popular ballad** is a narrative song that has been transmitted orally by what used to be called "the folk"; a **literary ballad** is a conscious imitation (without music) of such a work, often with complex symbolism. (553–54)

blank verse unrhymed iambic pentameter, that is, unrhymed lines of ten syllables, with every second syllable stressed. (686–87)

cacophony an unpleasant combination of sounds.

caesura a strong pause within a line of verse. (667)

canon a term originally used to refer to those books accepted as Holy Scripture by the Christian Church. The term has come to be applied to literary works thought to have a special merit by a given culture—for instance, the body of literature traditionally taught in colleges and universities. Such works are sometimes called "classics" and their authors are "major authors." As conceived in the United States until recently, the canon consisted chiefly of works by dead white European and American males—partly, of course, because middle-class and upper-class white males were in fact the people who did most of the writing in the Western Hemisphere, but also because white males (for instance, college professors) were the people who chiefly established the canon. Not surprisingly the canon-makers valued (or valorized or "privileged") writings that revealed, asserted, or reinforced the canon-makers' own values. From about the 1960s feminists and Marxists and others argued that these works had been regarded as central not because they were inherently better than other works but because they reflected the interests of the dominant culture, and that other work, such as slave narratives and the diaries of women, had been "marginalized."

In fact, the literary canon has never been static (in contrast to the biblical canon, which has not changed for more than a thousand years), but it is true that certain authors, such as Homer, Chaucer, and Shakespeare have been permanent fixtures. Why? Partly because they do indeed support the values of those who in large measure control the high cultural purse strings, and perhaps partly because their works are rich enough to invite constant reinterpretation from age to age—that is, to allow each generation to find its needs and its values in them.

catastrophe the concluding action, especially in a tragedy.

catharsis Aristotle's term for the purgation or purification of the pity and terror supposedly experienced while witnessing a tragedy. (908)

character (1) a person in a literary work (Romeo); (2) the personality of such a figure (sentimental lover, or whatever). Characters (in the first sense) are sometimes classified as either "flat" (one-dimensional) or "round" (fully realized, complex).

characterization the presentation of a character, whether by direct description, by showing the character in action, or by the presentation of other characters who help to define each other. (128–33, 247)

cliché an expression that through overuse has ceased to be effective. Examples: *acid test; sigh of relief; the proud possessor.*

climax the culmination of a conflict; a turning point, often the point of greatest tension in a plot. (843)

comedy a literary work, especially a play, characterized by humor and by a happy ending. (1112–14)

comparison and contrast the process of noting similarities (comparison) and differences (contrast). But *comparison* is now often used for both activities. (84–85)

complication an entanglement in a narrative or dramatic work that causes a conflict. (226)

conflict a struggle between a character and some obstacle (for example, another character or fate) or between internal forces, such as divided loyalties. (843, 1172–73)

connotation the associations (suggestions, overtones) of a word or expression. Thus *seventy* and *three score and ten* both mean "one more than sixty-nine," but because *three score and ten* is a biblical expression, it has an association of holiness; see also *denotation.* (1470)

consistency building the process engaged in during the act of reading, of reevaluating the details that one has just read in order to make them consistent with the new information that the text is providing. See *gap.*

consonance the repetition of consonant sounds, especially in stressed syllables; also called *half-rhyme* or slant rhyme. Example: *arouse/doze.* (668)

convention a pattern (for instance, the 14-line poem, or sonnet) or motif (for instance, the bumbling police officer in detective fiction) or other device occurring so often that it is taken for granted. Thus it is a convention that actors in a performance of *Julius Caesar* are understood to be speaking Latin, though in fact they are speaking English. Similarly, the soliloquy (a character alone on the stage speaks his or her thoughts aloud) is a convention, for in real life sane people rarely talk aloud to themselves.

couplet a pair of lines of verse, usually rhyming. (674)

crisis the high point in a conflict that leads to the turning point. (843)

criticism the analysis or evaluation of a literary work. (1422–44)

cultural criticism criticism that sets literature in a social context, often of economics or politics or gender. Borrowing some of the methods of anthropology, cultural criticism usually extends the canon to include popular material—for instance, comic books and soap operas.

dactyl a metrical foot consisting of a stressed syllable followed by two unstressed syllables. Example: *underwear.* (666)

deconstruction a critical approach that assumes language is unstable and ambiguous and is therefore inherently contradictory. Because authors cannot control their language, texts reveal more than their authors are aware of. For instance, texts (like institutions such as the law, the churches, and the schools) are likely, when closely scrutinized, to reveal connections to a society's economic system, even though the authors may have believed they were outside of the system. (1425–26)

denotation the dictionary meaning of a word. Thus *soap opera* and *daytime serial* have the same denotation, but the connotations (associations, emotional overtones) of *soap opera* are less favorable. (627)

denouement the resolution or the outcome (literally, the "unknotting") of a plot. (112, 843)

deus ex machina literally, "a god out of a machine"; any unexpected and artificial way of resolving the plot—for example, by introducing a rich uncle, thought to be dead, who arrives on the scene and pays the debts that otherwise would overwhelm the young hero.

dialogue an exchange of words between characters; speech.

diction the choice of vocabulary and of sentence structure. For example, there is a difference in diction between "One never knows" and "You never can tell." (604-05, 691)

didactic pertaining to teaching; having a moral purpose.

dimeter a line of poetry containing two feet. (666)

discovery see *anagnorisis.*

drama (1) a play; (2) conflict or tension, as in "The story lacks drama."

dramatic irony see *irony.*

dramatic monologue a poem spoken entirely by one character but addressed to one or more other characters whose presence is strongly felt. (602)

effaced narrator a narrator who reports but who does not editorialize or enter into the minds of any of the characters in the story.

elegy a lyric poem, usually a meditation on a death. (570)

elision omission (usually of a vowel or unstressed syllable), as in *o'er* (for *over*) and in "Th' inevitable hour."

end rhyme identical sounds at the ends of lines of poetry. (668)

end-stopped line a line of poetry that ends with a pause (usually marked by a comma, semicolon, or period) because the grammatical structure and the sense reach (at least to some degree) completion. It is contrasted with a *run-on line.* (667)

English (or Shakespearean) sonnet a poem of 14 lines (three quatrains and a couplet), rhyming *ababcdcdefefgg.* (674)

enjambment a line of poetry in which the grammatical and logical sense run on, without pause, into the next line or lines. (667)

epic a long narrative, especially in verse, that usually records heroic material in an elevated style.

epigram a brief, witty poem or saying.

epigraph a quotation at the beginning of a work, just after the title, often giving a clue to the theme.

epiphany a "showing forth," as when an action reveals a character with particular clarity.

episode an incident or scene that has unity in itself but is also a part of a larger action.

epistle a letter, in prose or verse.

essay a work, usually in prose and usually fairly short, that purports to be true and that treats its subject tentatively. In most literary essays the reader's interest is as much in the speaker's personality as in any argument that is offered.

euphony literally, "good sound," a pleasant combination of sounds.

explication a line-by-line unfolding of the meaning of a text. (80-83, 692)

exposition a setting forth of information. In fiction and drama, introductory material introducing characters and the situation; in an essay, the presentation of information, as opposed to the telling of a story or the setting forth of an argument. (843)

eye rhyme words that look as though they rhyme but do not rhyme when pronounced. Example: *come/home.* (668)

fable a short story (often involving speaking animals) with an easily grasped moral. (129)

farce comedy based not on clever language or on subtleties of characters but on broadly humorous situations (for instance, a man trips and falls when he mistakenly enters the women's locker room).

feminine rhyme a rhyme of two or more syllables, with the stress falling on a syllable other than the last. Examples: *fatter/batter; tenderly/slenderly.* (668)

feminist criticism a critical approach especially concerned with analyzing the depiction of women in literature—the images that male authors present of female characters—and with the reappraisal of work by female authors. (1434-39)

fiction an imaginative work, usually a prose narrative (novel, short story), that reports incidents that did not in fact occur. The term may include all works that invent a world such as a lyric poem or a play.

figurative language, figures of speech words intended to be understood in a way that is other than literal. Thus *lemon* used literally refers to a citrus fruit, but used figuratively refers to a defective machine, especially a defective automobile. Other examples: "He's a beast." "She's a witch." "A sea of troubles." Literally, such expressions are nonsense, but writers use them to express meanings inexpressible in literal speech. Among the most common kinds of figures of speech are *apostrophe, metaphor,* and *simile* (see the discussions of these words in this glossary). (619–48)

flashback an interruption in a narrative that presents an earlier episode.

flat character a one-dimensional character (for instance, the figure who is only and always the jealous husband or the flirtatious wife) as opposed to a *round character*. (132) See *round character*.

fly-on-the-wall narrator a narrator who never editorializes and never enters a character's mind, reporting only what is said and done. (190)

foil a character who serves as a contrast with another character, especially a minor character who helps to set off a major character.

foot a metrical unit, consisting of two or three syllables, with a specified arrangement of the stressed syllable or syllables. Thus the iambic foot consists of an unstressed syllable followed by a stressed syllable. (665–66)

foreshadowing suggestions of what is to come.

formalist criticism analysis that assumes a work of art is a constructed object with a stable meaning that can be ascertained by studying the relationships between the elements of the work. Thus a poem is like a chair: a chair *can* of course be stood on, or used for firewood, but it was created with a specific purpose that was evident and remains evident to all viewers. (1423–25)

free verse poetry in lines of irregular length, usually unrhymed. (687)

gap a term from reader-response criticism, referring to a reader's perception that something is unstated in the text, requiring the reader to fill in the material—for instance, to draw a conclusion as to why a character behaves as she does. Filling in the gaps is related to *consistency building*. Different readers of course may fill the gaps differently, and readers may even differ as to whether a gap exists at a particular point in the text. See *consistency building*.

gay criticism see *gender criticism*.

gender criticism criticism concerned especially with alleged differences in the ways that males and females read and write, and with the representations of gender (straight, bisexual, gay, lesbian) in literature. (1434–39)

genre a kind or type, roughly analogous to the biological term *species*. The four chief literary genres are nonfiction, fiction, poetry, and drama; but these can be subdivided into further genres. Thus fiction obviously can be divided into the short story and the novel, and drama obviously can be divided into tragedy and comedy. But these can be still further divided—for instance, tragedy into heroic tragedy and bourgeois tragedy, comedy into romantic comedy and satirical comedy.

gesture a physical movement, especially in a play. (840)

haiku a Japanese form having three unrhymed lines of five, seven, and five syllables.

half-rhyme the repetition in accented syllables of the final consonant sound but without identity in the preceding vowel sound; words of similar but not identical sound. Also called near rhyme, slant rhyme, approximate rhyme, and off-rhyme. See also *consonance*. Examples: *light/bet; affirm/perform.* (668)

hamartia a flaw in a tragic hero, or an error made by the tragic hero. (905–06)

heptameter a metrical line of seven feet. (666)

hero, heroine the main character (not necessarily heroic or even admirable) in a work; cf. *protagonist.*

heroic couplet an end-stopped pair of rhyming lines of iambic pentameter. (674)

hexameter a metrical line of six feet. (666)

historical criticism the attempt to illuminate a literary work by placing it in its historical context. (1430–31)

hubris, hybris a Greek word, usually translated as "overweening pride," "arrogance," "excessive ambition," and often said to be characteristic of tragic figures. (1473)

humor character a character dominated by a single trait—the miser, the jealous husband, the flirtatious wife.

hymn a lyric on a lofty theme (from the Greek, "a song of praise"). (570)

hyperbole figurative language using overstatement, as in "He died a thousand deaths." (650)

iamb, iambic a poetic foot consisting of an unaccented syllable followed by an accented one. Example: *alone.* (1473)

image, imagery poetic language that appeals to the senses, especially sight ("deep blue sea") but also other senses ("tinkling bells," "perfumes of Arabia"). (632–48)

incremental repetition repetition with slight variations that advance a narrative, such as "She heard, . . . she rose, . . . she left."

indeterminacy a passage that careful readers agree is open to more than one interpretation. According to some poststructural critics, because language is unstable and because contexts can never be objectively viewed, all texts are indeterminate.

innocent eye a naive narrator in whose narration the reader sees more than the narrator sees. (188)

internal rhyme rhyme within a line. (668)

interpretation the assignment of meaning to a text.

intertextuality the influence of other works on a literary work—that is, its connections with a vast context of writings and indeed of all aspects of culture, and in part depending also on what the reader brings to the work. If an author writes (say) a short story, no matter how original she thinks she is, she inevitably brings to her own story a knowledge of other stories—for example, a conception of what a short story is; and speaking more generally, an idea of what a story (long or short, written or oral) is. In opposition to formalist critics, who see a literary work as an independent whole containing a fixed meaning, some contemporary critics emphasize the work's *intertextuality.* Because different readers bring different things, meaning is thus ever-changing. In this view, then, no text is self-sufficient, and no writer fully controls the meaning of the text. Because we are talking about connections of which the writer is unaware, and because "meaning" is in part the creation of the reader, the author is by no means an authority. Thus the critic should see a novel (for instance) in connection not only with other novels, past and present, but also in connection with other kinds of narratives, such as TV dramas and films, even though the author of the book lived before the age of film and TV.

invective abusive language, in literature often used for comic purposes.

irony a contrast of some sort. For instance, in *verbal irony* or *Socratic irony*, the contrast is between what is said and what is meant ("You're a great guy," meant bitterly). In **dramatic irony** or **Sophoclean irony**—also called **tragic irony**—the contrast is between what is intended and what is accomplished (Macbeth usurps the throne, thinking he will then be happy, but the action leads him to misery), or between what the audience knows (a murderer waits in the bedroom) and what a character says (the victim enters the bedroom, innocently saying, "I think I'll have a long sleep"). (649–59, 907)

Italian (or Petrarchan) sonnet a poem of 14 lines, consisting of an octave (rhyming *abbaabba*) and a sestet (usually *cdecde* or *cdccdc*). (674)

lesbian criticism see *gender criticism.*

litotes a form of understatement in which an affirmation is made by means of a negation; thus "He was not underweight," meaning "He was grossly over-weight."

lyric poem a short poem, often songlike, with the emphasis not on narrative but on the speaker's emotion or reverie. (569–91)

Marxist criticism the study of literature in the light of Karl Marx's view that economic forces, controlled by the dominant class, shape the literature (as well as the law, philosophy, religion, etc.) of a society. (1431, 1443)

masculine rhyme rhyme of one-syllable words (*lies/cries*) or, if more than one syllable, words ending with accented syllables (*behold/foretold*). (668)

mask a term used to designate the speaker of a poem, equivalent to *persona* or *voice.* (592–617)

meaning a word variously defined by critics as what the writer intended a work to say about the world and human experience, or as what the work says to the reader irrespective of the writer's intention. Both versions imply that a literary work is a nut to be cracked, with a kernel that is to be extracted. Because few critics today hold that meaning is clear and unchanging, the tendency now is to say that a critic offers "an interpretation" or "a reading" rather than a "statement of the meaning of a work." Many critics today would say that an alleged interpretation is really a creation of meaning.

melodrama a narrative, usually in dramatic form, involving threatening situations but ending happily. The characters are usually stock figures (virtuous heroine, villainous landlord).

metaphor a kind of figurative language equating one thing with another: "This novel is garbage" (a book is equated with discarded and probably inedible food), "a piercing cry" (a cry is equated with a spear or other sharp instrument). (621–22)

meter a pattern of stressed and unstressed syllables. (666–68)

metonymy a kind of figurative language in which a word or phrase stands not for itself but for something closely related to it: *saber rattling* means "militaristic talk or action." (622)

monologue a relatively long, uninterrupted speech by a character.

monometer a metrical line consisting of only one foot. (666)

montage in film, quick cutting; in fiction, quick shifts.

mood the atmosphere, usually created by descriptions of the settings and characters.

motif a recurrent theme within a work, or a theme common to many works.

motivation grounds for a character's action.

myth (1) a traditional story reflecting primitive beliefs, especially explaining the mysteries of the natural world (why it rains, or the origin of mountains); (2) a body of belief, not necessarily false, especially as set forth by a writer. Thus one may speak of Yeats and Alice Walker as myth-makers, referring to the visions of reality that they set forth in their works.

myth criticism the study of patterns that seem universal or archetypal. (1429–30)

narrative, narrator a narrative is a story (an anecdote, a novel); a narrator is one who tells a story (not the author, but the invented speaker of the story). On kinds of narrators, see *point of view.* (1429–30, 1442–43)

New Criticism a mid-twentieth-century movement (also called *formalist criticism*) that regarded a literary work as an independent, carefully constructed object; hence it made little or no use of the author's biography or of historical context, and it relied chiefly on explication. (1423–25)

New Historicism a school of criticism holding that the past cannot be known objectively. According to this view, because historians project their own "narrative"—their own invention or "construction"—on the happenings of the past, historical writings are not objective but are, at bottom, political statements. (1431–32)

novel a long work of prose fiction, especially one that is relatively realistic.

novella a work of prose fiction longer than a short story but shorter than a novel—say, about 40 to 80 pages.

objective point of view a point of view in which the narrator reports but does not editorialize or enter into the minds of any of the characters in the story. (190)

octameter a metrical line with eight feet. (668)

octave, octet an eight-line stanza, or the first eight lines of a sonnet, especially of an Italian sonnet. (674)

octosyllabic couplet a pair of rhyming lines, each line with four iambic feet.

ode a lyric exalting someone (for instance, a hero) or something (for instance, a season). (570)

off-rhyme see *half-rhyme.* (668)

omniscient narrator a speaker who knows the thoughts of all of the characters in the narrative. (189)

onomatopoeia words (or the use of words) that sound like what they mean. Examples: *buzz; whirr.* (668)

open form poetry whose form seems spontaneous rather than highly patterned.

overstatement exaggeration, to emphasize a point. (650)

oxymoron a compact paradox, as in *a mute cry; a pleasing pain; proud humility.*

parable a short narrative that is at least in part allegorical and that illustrates a moral or spiritual lesson. (37, 363)

paradox an apparent contradiction, as in Jesus's words "Whosoever will save his life shall lose it; but whosoever will lose his life for my sake, the same shall save it." (650)

paraphrase a restatement that sets forth an idea in diction other than that of the original. (24–25, 1447–48)

parody a humorous imitation of a literary work, especially of its style.

pathos pity, sadness.

pentameter a line of verse containing five feet. (666)

peripeteia a Greek word meaning a reversal in the action. (907)

persona literally, a mask; the "I" or speaker of a work, sometimes identified with the author but usually better regarded as the voice or mouthpiece created by the author. (592–617)

personification a kind of figurative language in which an inanimate object, animal, or other nonhuman is given human traits. Examples: *the creeping tide* (the tide is imagined as having feet); *the cruel sea* (the sea is imagined as having moral qualities). (624-25)

Petrarchan sonnet see *Italian sonnet.*

plot the episodes in a narrative or dramatic work—that is, what happens. (But even a lyric poem can be said to have a plot; for instance, the speaker's mood changes from anger to resignation.) Sometimes *plot* is defined as the author's particular arrangement (sequence) of these episodes, and *story* as the episodes in their chronological sequence. Until recently it was widely believed that a good plot had a logical structure: *A* caused *B* (*B* did not simply happen to follow *A*), but in the last few decades some critics have argued that such a concept merely represents the white male's view of experience. (109–12, 247, 265, 842–45, 1172–73)

poem an imaginative work in meter or in free verse, usually employing figurative language.

point of view the perspective from which a story is told—for example, by a major character or a minor character or a fly on the wall; see also *narrative, narrator, omniscient narrator.* (187–91)

postmodernism a term that came into prominence in the 1960s to distinguish the contemporary experimental writing of such authors as Samuel Beckett and Jorge Luis Borges from such early twentieth-century classics of modernism as James Joyce's *Ulysses* (1922) and T. S. Eliot's *The Waste Land* (1922). Although the classic modernists had been thought to be revolutionary in their day, after World War II they seemed to be conservative, and their works seemed remote from today's society with its new interests in such things as feminism, gay and lesbian rights, and pop culture. Postmodernist literature, though widely varied and not always clearly distinct from modernist literature, usually is more politically concerned, more playful—it is given to parody and pastiche—and more closely related to the art forms of popular culture than is modernist literature.

prologue an introductory statement, especially a monologue at the beginning of a play, summarizing the plot or introducing the characters. (843, 910)

prosody the principles of versification. (665)

protagonist the chief actor in any literary work. The term is usually preferable to *hero* and *heroine* because it can include characters—for example, villainous or weak ones—who are not aptly called heroes or heroines. (132, 843)

psychological criticism a form of analysis especially concerned both with the ways in which authors unconsciously leave traces of their inner lives in their works and with the ways in which readers respond, consciously and unconsciously, to works. (1433–34, 1443)

pyrrhic foot in poetry, a foot consisting of two unstressed syllables. (666)

quatrain a stanza of four lines. (674)

reader-response criticism criticism emphasizing the idea that various readers respond in various ways and therefore that readers as well as authors "create" meaning. (1426–29, 1442)

realism the presentation of plausible characters (usually middle class) in plausible (usually everyday) circumstances, as opposed, for example, to heroic characters engaged in improbable adventures. Realism in literature seeks to give the illusion of reality.

recognition see *anagnorisis*.

refrain a repeated phrase, line, or group of lines in a poem, especially in a ballad.

resolution the dénouement or untying of the complication of the plot. (364)

reversal a change in fortune, often an ironic twist. (907)

rhetorical question a question to which no answer is expected or to which only one answer is plausible. Example: "Do you think I am unaware of your goings-on?"

rhyme similarity or identity of accented sounds in corresponding positions, as, for example, at the ends of lines: *love/dove; tender/slender.* (668)

rhythm in poetry, a pattern of stressed and unstressed sounds; in prose, some sort of recurrence (for example, of a motif) at approximately identical intervals. (660–62)

rising action in a story or play, the events that lead up to the *climax.* (843)

rising meter a foot (for example, iambic or anapestic) ending with a stressed syllable.

romance narrative fiction, usually characterized by improbable adventures and love.

round character a many-sided character, one who does not always act predictably, as opposed to a one-dimensional, unchanging *flat character.* (132) See *flat character*.

run-on line a line of verse whose syntax and meaning require the reader to go on, without a pause, to the next line; an *enjambed* line. (667)

sarcasm crudely mocking or contemptuous language; heavy verbal irony. (650)

satire literature that entertainingly attacks folly or vice; amusingly abusive writing. (613, 1114)

scansion description of rhythm in poetry: metrical analysis. (667)

scene (1) a unit of a play, in which the setting is unchanged and the time continuous; (2) the setting (locale, and time of the action); (3) in fiction, a dramatic passage, as opposed to a passage of description or of summary.

selective omniscience a point of view in which the author enters the mind of one character and for the most part sees the other characters only from the outside. (189)

sentimentality excessive emotion, especially excessive pity, treated as appropriate rather than as disproportionate.

sestet a six-line stanza, or the last six lines of an Italian sonnet. (674)

sestina a poem with six stanzas of six lines each and a concluding stanza of three lines. The last word of each line in the first stanza appears as the last word of a line in each of the next five stanzas but in a different order. In the final (three-line) stanza, each line ends with one of these six words, and each line includes in the middle of the line one of the other three words. (683–85)

setting the time and place of a story, play, or poem (for instance, a Texas town in winter, about 1900). (133, 153–54, 266–67)

Shakespearean sonnet see *English sonnet*.

short story a fictional narrative, usually in prose, rarely longer than 30 pages and often much briefer.

simile a kind of figurative language explicitly making a comparison—for example, by using *as, like,* or a verb such as *seems.* (621)

soliloquy a speech in a play, in which a character alone on the stage speaks his or her thoughts aloud. (844)

sonnet a lyric poem of 14 lines; see *English sonnet, Italian sonnet.* (674–80)

speaker see *persona.* (592–617, 690)

spondee a metrical foot consisting of two stressed syllables. (666)

stage direction a playwright's indication to the actors or readers—for example, offering information about how an actor is to speak a line.

stanza a group of lines forming a unit that is repeated in a poem. (673–75)

stereotype a simplified conception, especially an oversimplification—for example, a stock character such as the heartless landlord, the kindly old teacher, the prostitute with a heart of gold. Such a character usually has only one personality trait, and this is boldly exaggerated.

stock epithet standardized descriptions, common in folk ballads, such as "golden hair," "milk-white steed." (554)

stream of consciousness the presentation of a character's unrestricted flow of thought, often with free associations, and often without punctuation. (189)

stress relative emphasis on one syllable as compared with another. (660, 663, 665–68)

structuralism a critical theory holding that a literary work consists of conventional elements that, taken together by a reader familiar with the conventions, give the work its meaning. Thus just as a spectator must know the rules of a game (e.g., three strikes and you're out) in order to enjoy the game, so a reader must know the rules of, say, a novel (coherent, realistic, adequately motivated characters, a plausible plot—for instance, *The Color Purple*) or of a satire (caricatures of contemptible figures in amusing situations that need not be at all plausible—for instance, *Gulliver's Travels*). Structuralists normally have no interest in the origins of a work (i.e., in the historical background, or in the author's biography), and no interest in the degree to which a work of art seems to correspond to reality. The interest normally is in the work as a self-sufficient construction.

structure the organization of a work, the relationship between the chief parts, and the large-scale pattern—for instance, a rising action or complication followed by a crisis and then a resolution.

style the manner of expression, evident not only in the choice of certain words (for instance, colloquial language) but also in the choice of certain kinds of sentence structure, characters, settings, and themes. (267)

subplot a sequence of events often paralleling or in some way resembling the main story.

summary a synopsis or condensation.

symbol a person, object, action, or situation that, charged with meaning, suggests another thing (for example, a dark forest may suggest confusion, or perhaps evil), though usually with less specificity and more ambiguity than an allegory. A symbol usually differs from a metaphor in that a symbol is expanded or repeated and works by accumulating associations. (208–11, 267, 638–48)

synecdoche a kind of figurative language in which the whole stands for a part (*the law,* for a police officer), or a part stands for the whole (*wheels,* for an automobile). (622)

tale a short narrative, usually less realistic and more romantic than a short story; a yarn.

tercet see *triplet.*

tetrameter a verse line of four feet. (666)

theme what a work is about; the underlying idea of a work; a conception of human experience suggested by the concrete details. Thus the theme of *Macbeth* is often said to be that "vaulting ambition o'erleaps itself." (210-11, 225-28, 248, 267, 273-74)

thesis the point or argument that a writer announces and develops. A thesis differs from a *topic* by making an assertion. "The fall of Oedipus" is a topic, but "Oedipus falls because he is impetuous" is a thesis, as is "Oedipus is impetuous, but his impetuosity has nothing to do with his fall." (72-73, 86, 225)

thesis sentence a sentence summarizing, as specifically as possible, the writer's chief point (argument and perhaps purpose). (73)

third-person narrator the teller of a story who does not participate in the happenings. (188-90)

tone the prevailing attitude (for instance, ironic, genial, objective) as perceived by the reader. Notice that a reader may feel that the tone of the persona of the work is genial while the tone of the author of the same work is ironic. (80-81, 592-617, 690)

topic a subject, such as "Hamlet's relation to Horatio." A topic becomes a *thesis* when a predicate is added to this subject, thus: "Hamlet's relation to Horatio helps to define Hamlet."

tragedy a serious play showing the protagonist moving from good fortune to bad and ending in death or a deathlike state. (905-08, 1173-74)

tragic flaw a supposed weakness (for example, arrogance) in the tragic protagonist. If the tragedy results from an intellectual error rather than from a moral weakness, it is better to speak of "a tragic error." (906)

tragicomedy a mixture of tragedy and comedy, usually a play with serious happenings that expose the characters to the threat of death but that ends happily.

transition a connection between one passage and the next. (87)

trimeter a verse line with three feet. (666)

triplet a group of three lines of verse, usually rhyming. (674)

trochee a metrical foot consisting of a stressed syllable followed by an unstressed syllable. Example: *garden.* (666)

understatement a figure of speech in which the speaker says less than what he or she means; an ironic minimizing, as in "You've done fairly well for yourself" said to the winner of a multimillion-dollar lottery. (649)

unity harmony and coherence of parts, absence of irrelevance.

unreliable narrator a narrator whose report a reader cannot accept at face value, perhaps because the narrator is naive or is too deeply implicated in the action to report it objectively. (188)

verbal irony see *irony.*

verse (1) a line of poetry; (2) a stanza of a poem.

verse paragraph a passage of blank verse that presents a unit of thought. (687)

vers libre *free verse,* unrhymed poetry. (687)

villanelle a poem with five stanzas of three lines rhyming *aba,* and a concluding stanza of four lines, rhyming *abaa.* The entire first line is repeated as the third line of the second and fourth stanzas; the entire third line is repeated as the third line of the third and fifth stanzas. These two lines form the final two lines of the last (four-line) stanza. (689)

voice see *persona, style,* and *tone.* (592-617)

Will Eisner: "Hamlet On a Rooftop" from *Comics and Sequential Art* by Will Eisner. Copyright ©1985 by Will Eisner. Copyright ©2008 by Will Eisner Studios, Inc. Used by permission of W. W. Norton & Company, Inc.

T. S. Eliot: "The Love Song of J. Alfred Prufrock" from T. S. Eliot: *The Complete Poems and Plays 1909-1950.* Copyright ©1917 by T. S. Eliot. Reprinted by permission of Faber and Faber Ltd.

Ralph Ellison: "Battle Royal," copyright 1948 by Ralph Ellison from *Invisible Man* by Ralph Ellison. Used by permission of Random House, Inc.

Louise Erdrich: "Dear John Wayne" from *Jacklight: Poems.* Copyright ©1984 by Louise Erdrich. Reprinted with permission of The Wylie Agency LLC.

Martín Espada: "Bully" from *Rebellion is the Circle of a Lover's Hands/Rebelión es el giro de manos del amante* by Martín Espada (Curbstone Press, 1990). Reprinted with permission of Curbstone Press. Distributed by Consortium. "Tony Went to the Bodega but He Didn't Buy Anything" from *Trumpets from the Islands of Their Eviction* by Martín Espada. Copyright ©1987. Reprinted by permission of Bilingual Press/Editorial Bilingüe, Arizona State University, Tempe, AZ.

William Faulkner: "A Rose for Emily" © 1930 and renewed 1958 by William Faulkner, "Barn Burning" © 1950 by Random House, Inc, renewed 1977 by Jill Faulkner Summers. Both pieces from *Collected Stories of William Faulkner* William Faulkner. Used by permission of Random House Inc. Excerpts (pages 47-48, 58-59, 87-88, 184-185, 199) from Faulkner in the University, edited by Frederick L. Gwynn and Joseph L. Blotner © 1995 by the Rector and visitors of the University of Virginia. Reprinted by permission of the University of Virginia Press. Facsimile of a manuscript page from "A Rose for Emily" MSS 6074 Special Collections, University of Virginia Library.

Lawrence Ferlinghetti: "Constantly Risking Absurdity" from *A Coney Island of the Mind,* copyright ©1958 by Lawrence Ferlinghetti. Reprinted by permission of New Directions Publishing Corp.

Carolyn Forché: "The Colonel" from *The Country Between Us.* Copyright ©1981 by Carolyn Forché. Originally appeared in Women's International Resource Exchange. Reprinted by permission of HarperCollins Publishers

Robert Frost: "The Silken Tent," "The Most of It," "Desert Places," "Come In," "Design," "The Aim Was Song," "The Need of Being Versed in Country Things," "Acquainted with the Night," and "Stopping by Woods on a Snowy Evening" from *The Poetry of Robert Frost* edited by Edward Connery Lathem. Copyright ©1923, 1928, 1969 by Henry Holt and Company, copyright ©1936, 1942, 1951, 1956 by Robert Frost, copyright ©1964, 1970 by Lesley Frost Ballantine. Reprinted by arrangement with Henry Holt and Company, LLC. "The Figure a Poem Makes" from *The Selected Prose of Robert Frost,* edited by Hyde Cox and Edward Connery Lathem. Copyright 1939, ©1967 by Henry Holt and Company. Reprinted by permission of Henry Holt and Company, LLC. Facsimile of "Stopping by Woods on a Snowy Evening" is reprinted by permission of the Jones Library, Inc., Amherst, Massachusetts. Manuscript text of "The Silken Tent" reprinted by permission of The Poetry Collection of the University Libraries, State University of New York at Buffalo.

Nation. Reprinted by permission of Harold Ober Associates, Incorporated. "On the Cultural Achievements of African Americans" in the James Weldon Johnson Collection, Langston Hughes Papers, Beinecke Rare Book and Manuscript Library, Yale University.

Henrik Ibsen: Adapted German ending to "A Doll's House" by Henrik Ibsen from pages 287–88 of *The Oxford Ibsen* Volume 5. Reprinted by permission of Oxford University Press.

Henrik Ibsen: "Speech at the Banquet of the Norwegian League for Women's Rights" from Ibsen: *Letters and Speeches* by Henrik Ibsen, translated and edited by Evert Sprinchorn. Copyright ©1964 renewed 1992 by Evert Sprinchorn. Reprinted by permission of Hill and Wang, a division of Farrar, Straus and Giroux LLC.

David Ives: "Sure Thing" from *All in the Timing: Fourteen Plays* by David Ives, copyright ©1989, 1990, 1992 by David Ives. Used by permission of Vintage Books, a division of Random House, Inc.

Shirley Jackson: "The Lottery" from *The Lottery* by Shirley Jackson. Copyright ©1948, 1949 by Shirley Jackson. Copyright renewed 1976, 1977 by Laurence Hyman, Barry Hyman, Mrs. Sarah Webster and Mrs. Joanne Schnurer. Reprinted by permission of Farrar, Straus and Giroux, LLC.

Gish Jen: "Who's Irish?" from *Who's Irish?* by Gish Jen, copyright ©1999 by Gish Jen. First published in *The New Yorker.* From the collection *Who's Irish?* By Gish Jen, published by Alfred A. Knopf in 1999. Reprinted by permission of the author.

Franz Kafka: "A Hunger Artist" from *Franz Kafka: The Complete Stories* by Franz Kafka, edited by Nahum N. Glatzer, copyright 1946, 1947, 1948, 1949, 1954, 1958, 1971 by Schocken Books. Used by permission of Schocken Books, a division of Random House, Inc.

X. J. Kennedy: "For Allen Ginsberg" from *The Lords of Misrule* by X. J. Kennedy. Copyright ©2002 by X. J. Kennedy. Reprinted with permission of The Johns Hopkins University Press. "Nothing in Heaven Functions as it Ought" from *In a Prominent Bar in Secaucus: New and Selected Poems, 1955-2007.* Copyright ©2007 by X. J. Kennedy. Reprinted with permission of The Johns Hopkins University Press.

Jesse Lee Kercheval: "Carpathia" by Jesse Lee Kercheval. Appeared in *Micro Fiction,* edited by Jerome Stern. Reprinted by permission of Jesse Lee Kercheval.

Jamaica Kincaid: "Girl" from *At the Bottom of the River* by Jamaica Kincaid. Copyright ©1983 by Jamaica Kincaid. Reprinted by permission of Farrar, Straus and Giroux, LLC.

Galway Kinnell: "Blackberry Eating" from *Three Books* by Galway Kinnell. Copyright ©1993 by Galway Kinnell. Reprinted by permission of Houghton Mifflin Harcourt Publishing Company. All rights reserved.

Yusef Komunyakaa: "Facing It" from *Dien Cai Dau* in *Pleasure Dome: New and Collected Poems.* ©2001 by Yusef Komunyakaa and reprinted by permission of Wesleyan University Press.

John Lahr: "Hard Sell" by John Lahr. Copyright ©2009 by John Lahr. Originally appeared in *The New Yorker* (May 25, 2009). Reprinted by permission of Georges Borchardt, Inc. on behalf of the author.

by John Updike. "Icarus" from *Americana and Other Poems* by John Updike, copyright ©2001 by John Updike. Used by permission of Alfred A. Knopf, a division of Random House, Inc.

Luis Valdez: "Los Vendidos" and "The Actos" from *Luis Valdez–Early Works: Actos, Bernabe and Pensamiento Serpentino*. (Houston: Arte Publico Press–University of Houston, 1990).

Helena Maria Viramontes: "The Moths" by Helena Maria Viramontes is reprinted with permission from the publisher of *The Moths and Other Stories* (Houston: Arte Public Press–University of Houston, 1995).

Derek Walcott: "A Far Cry from Africa" from *Collected Poems 1948–1984* by Derek Walcott. Copyright ©1986 by Derek Walcott. Reprinted by permission of Farrar, Straus and Giroux LLC.

Alice Walker: "Everyday Use" from *In Love & Trouble: Stories of Black Women*, copyright ©1973 by Alice Walker, reprinted by permission of Houghton Mifflin Harcourt, Inc.

Ron Wallace: "Worry" from *Quick Bright Things: Stories* by Ron Wallace. Copyright ©2000 by Ron Wallace. Published by Mid-List Press, Minneapolis, Minnesota. Used by permission.

Eudora Welty: "A Worn Path" from *A Curtain of Green and Other Stories,* copyright 1941 and renewed 1969 by Eudora Welty. Reprinted by permission of Houghton Mifflin Harcourt, Inc.

Walt Whitman: Manuscript pages of "I Saw in Louisiana a Live-Oak Growning" MSS 3829 Clifton Waller Barrett Library of American Literature, Special Collections, University of Virignia Library and "Once I Passed Through a Populous City" MSS 3829 Clifton Waller Barrett Library of American Literature, Special Collections, University of Virginia Library are reprinted by permission.

Tennessee Williams: "The Glass Menagerie" by Tennessee Williams, copyright 1945, renewed 1973 by The University of the South. Reprinted by permission of Georges Borchardt, Inc. for the Estate of Tennessee Williams.

William Carlos Williams: "The Use of Force" from *The Collected Stories of William Carlos Williams,* copyright ©1938 by William Carlos Williams. "The Great Figure," "Spring and All, Section I" "The Red Wheelbarrow" by William Carlos Williams from *The Collected Poems: Volume I, 1909–1939,* copyright ©1938 by New Directions Publishing Corp. "The Dance (In Brueghel's)" from *The Collected Poems: Volume II 1939–1962,* copyright ©1944 by William Carlos Williams. "The Artist" from *The Collected Poems: Volume II, 1939–1962,* copyright ©1954 by William Carlos Williams. All reprinted by permission of New Directions Publishing Corp.

August Wilson: "Fences" by August Wilson, copyright ©1986 by August Wilson. Used by permission of Dutton Signet, a division of Penguin Group (USA) Inc. Excerpt ("Talking About Fences") from pages 299–301 of *In Their Own Words* by David Savran. Copyright 1988 by David Savran. Published by Theatre Communications Group. Used by permission of Theatre Communications Group.

Tobias Wolff: "Hunters in the Snow" from *In the Garden of the North American Martyrs* by Tobias Wolff. Copyright ©1981 by Tobias Wolff. Reprinted by permission of HarperCollins Publishers. "Say Yes" from *Back in*

1, Robert Capa © 2001 by Cornell Capa / Magnum Photos; **26,** Arte Publico Press / University of Houston; **40,** Hulton Archives / Getty Images; **43,** Sigrid Estrada; **91,** Courtesy of Jose Arams; **97,** Alfred Eriss / Time & Life Pictures / Getty Images; **99,** Bettmann / Corbis; **125T,** Mark Eifert / Michigan State University Museum; **125B,** Tom McCarthy / PhotoEdit; **141,** Jerry Bauer; **164,** Bettmann / Corbis; **177,** Gordon Parks / Magnum Ulf Andersen; **191,** Bettmann / Corbis; **305,** AP / Wide World Photos; **308,** Manuscript page of "A Good Man Is Hard to Find" © by permission of the Mary Flannery O'Connor Charitable Trust, via Harold Matson Company, Inc.; **338,** Ulf Andersen / Getty Images; **366,** Ulf Andersen / Getty Images; **421, 423, 426, 427,** "A Rose for Emily" MSS 6077 Special Collections, University of Virginia Library; **460,** Nancy Crampton; **465,** Marion Etlinger; **539,** Bettmann / Corbis; **559,** Thomas Clarkson, 1808 / from The History of the Rise, Boston Athenaeum; **583,** Dorothy Alexander; **634, 635,** "I Saw in Louisiana a Live-Oak Growing" MSS 3829 Clifton Waller Barrett Library of American Literature, Special Collections, University of Virginia Library; **640,** Getty Images; **720,** "Once I Passed Through a Populous City" MSS 3829 Clifton Waller Barrett Library of American Literature, Special Collections, University of Virginia Library; **722,** "Out of Our Hands" reprinted by permission of Cathy Song; **723,** Hulton Deutsch Collection / Corbis; **736,** By permission of Amherst College / Amherst College and Special Archives; **740,** "I heard a Fly Buzz–when I died," facsimile manuscript version reprinted by permission of the Trustees of Amherst College; **744, 745,** "I felt a funeral, in my Brain," facsimile manuscript version by permission of the Houghton Library, Harvard University. MS Am 1118.3(53c) © The President and Fellows of Harvard College; **750,** By permission of Jones Library Inc., Amherst, MA; **iii, 755,** Manuscript text of "Stopping by Woods on a Snowy Evening" reprinted by permission of the Jones Library, Inc., Amherst, Massachusetts; **758,** Manuscript text of "The Silken Tent" reprinted by permission of The Poetry Collection of the University Libraries, State University of New York at Buffalo; **761,** Bettmann / Corbis; **788,** Bettmann / Corbis; **832,** AP / Wide World Photos; **837,** Inge Morath / Magnum Photos; **844,** By The Theatre of a Two-Headed Calf, in association with the Ontological-Hysteric Incubator in New York City; **856,** Billy Rose Collection / New York Public Library / Performing Arts, Astor, Lennox, and Tilden Collections; **909,** Frederick Ayer / Photo Researchers; **911,** John Vickers / London; **954,** Donald Cooper / Photostage; **990,** Arend van Buchel's copy of Hodges' drawing / Reproduced courtesy of the Trustees, British Museum Library; **997,** Joe Cock's Studio Collection / Shakespeare Birthplace Trust; **998,** Joe Cock's Studio Collection / Shakespeare Birthplace Trust; **1000,** Martha Swope; **1199,** Inge Morath / Magnum Photos; **1201T,** Harry Ransom Humanities Research Center / University of Texas at Austin; **1201B,** Inge Morath / Magnum Photos; **1281,** Harvard Theater Collection, Harvard University; **1336,** KNBC Los Angeles, 1972; **1347,** Sam Garst / Actor's Theatre, Lexington, KY; **1351,** Chris Benion / Theatre Pix, IL.

1499